W9-BIO-695

The Compression Guide notations
found in the Chapter Planning Guides
were included by error and will be removed.

ANNOTATED TEACHER'S EDITION

MODERN CHEMISTRY

Turn to page T16 to See
What's New for this Edition!

Build Student Success
with Tutor CD-ROMs!
See page T20.

Keep Up-to-Date with
Chemistry Web Resources!
See page T21.

Make Organizing Resources
a Breeze with the New
One-Stop Planner CD-ROM!
See pages T22–T24.

HOLT, RINEHART AND WINSTON

A Harcourt Classroom Education Company

Austin · New York · Orlando · Atlanta · San Francisco · Boston · Dallas · Toronto · London

Authors

RAYMOND E. DAVIS, PH.D.
Distinguished Teaching Professor

Department of Chemistry and Biochemistry
The University of Texas at Austin
Austin, TX

H. CLARK METCALFE
*Former Chemistry Teacher
and Science Department Chair*

Wilkinsburg, PA

JOHN E. WILLIAMS
*Former Chemistry Teacher
and Science Department Chair*

Indianapolis, IN

JOSEPH F. CASTKA
Former Adjunct Associate Professor

C. S. Post College
Long Island, NY

Contributing Writers

Seth Madej
Associate Producer

Pulse of the Planet radio series
Jim Metzner Productions, Inc.
Yorktown Heights, NY

Jim Metzner
Executive Producer

Pulse of the Planet radio series
Yorktown Heights, NY

Jay A. Young, Ph.D.
Chemical Safety Consultant

Silver Spring, MD

Cover: Portion of the periodic table superimposed on a
photomicrograph of crystals of the amino-acid dimer cystine.
Photo by © Mel Pollinger/Fran Heyl Associates, NYC

Printed in the United States of America

ISBN 0-03-056538-3   1 2 3 4 5 6 7   048   05   04   03   02   01   00

Contents in Brief

TEACHER'S INTRODUCTION

Reviewers	4T	Holt ChemFile Laboratory Program	30T
Acknowledgments	5T	Lesson Structure	32T
What's New in this Edition	16T	Review, Practice, and Assessment	34T
Program Resources	18T	Special Features	36T
Media Resources	20T	Elements Handbook	37T
One-Stop Planner CD-ROM	22T	Teacher's Edition Format	38T
Graphing Calculator Integration	25T	National Science Education Standards	40T
Building Problem-Solving Skills	26T	Safety in the Chemistry Lab	43T
Laboratory Instruction	28T	Master Materials List for the In-Text Labs	50T

UNIT 1 *Introduction to Chemistry and Matter* — 2
 1 Matter and Change — 4
 2 Measurements and Calculations — 28

UNIT 2 *Organization of Matter* — 62
 3 Atoms: The Building Blocks of Matter — 64
 4 Arrangement of Electrons in Atoms — 90
 5 The Periodic Law — 122
 6 Chemical Bonding — 160

UNIT 3 *Language of Chemistry* — 200
 7 Chemical Formulas and Chemical Compounds — 202
 8 Chemical Equations and Reactions — 240
 9 Stoichiometry — 274

UNIT 4 *Phases of Matter* — 300
 10 Physical Characteristics of Gases — 302
 11 Molecular Composition of Gases — 332
 12 Liquids and Solids — 362

UNIT 5 *Solutions and Their Behavior* — 392
 13 Solutions — 394
 14 Ions in Aqueous Solutions and Colligative Properties — 424
 15 Acids and Bases — 452
 16 Acid-Base Titration and pH — 480

UNIT 6 *Chemical Reactions* — 508
 17 Reaction Energy and Reaction Kinetics — 510
 18 Chemical Equilibrium — 552
 19 Oxidation-Reduction Reactions — 590

UNIT 7 *Organic and Nuclear Chemistry* — 622
 20 Carbon and Hydrocarbons — 624
 21 Other Organic Compounds — 662
 22 Nuclear Chemistry — 700

Elements Handbook — 726

Laboratory Program — 784

Appendices — 894

George F. Atkinson, Ph.D.
Professor of Chemistry
Department of Chemistry
University of Waterloo
Waterloo, Ontario, Canada

G. Lynn Carlson, Ph.D.
Department of Chemistry
University of Wisconsin–Parkside
Kenosha, WI

Doris I. Lewis, Ph.D.
Professor of Chemistry
Suffolk University
Boston, MA

Daniel B. Murphy, Ph.D.
Professor Emeritus of Chemistry
Department of Chemistry
Herbert H. Lehman College
The City University of New York
Bronx, NY

R. Thomas Myers, Ph.D.
Professor Emeritus of Chemistry
Kent State University
Kent, OH

Keith B. Oldham, Ph.D.
Professor of Chemistry
Trent University
Peterborough, Ontario, Canada

Charles Scaife, Ph.D.
Professor of Chemistry
Union College
Schenectady, NY

David C. Taylor, Ph.D.
Professor of Chemistry
Department of Chemistry
Slippery Rock University
Slippery Rock, PA

Richard S. Treptow, Ph.D.
Professor of Chemistry
Department of Chemistry and Physics
Chicago State University
Chicago, IL

Martin VanDyke, Ph.D.
Consultant
Chem-Safe Environmental Services
Denver, CO

Laverne Weidler, Ph.D.
Professor of Chemistry
Science and Engineering
Black Hawk College
Kewanee, IL

Charles M. Wynn, Sr., Ph.D.
Professor of Chemistry
Department of Physical Sciences
Eastern Connecticut State University
Willimantic, CT

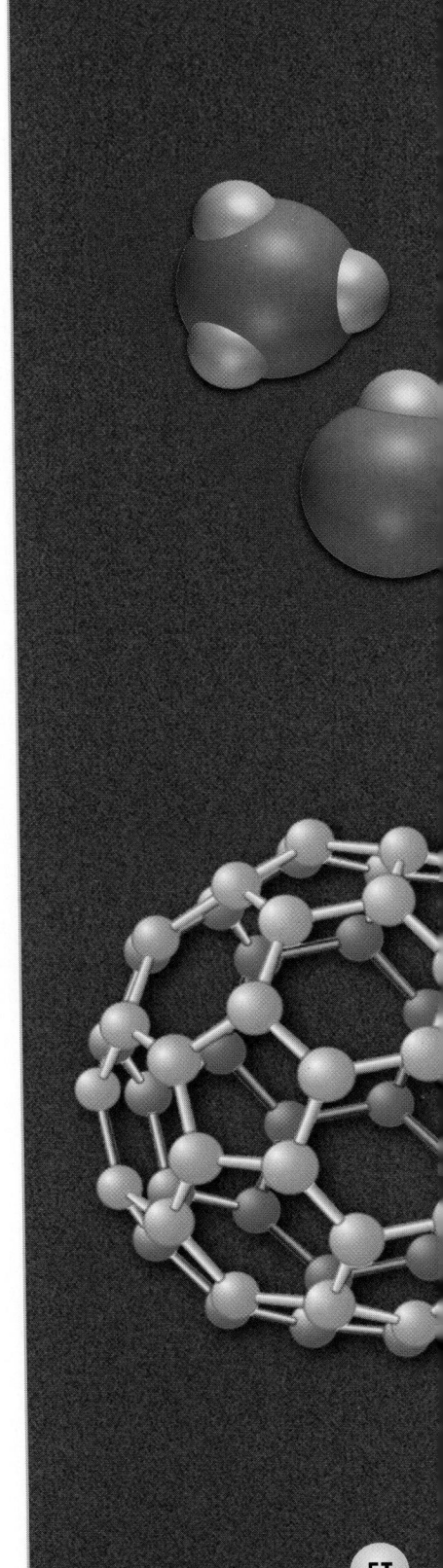

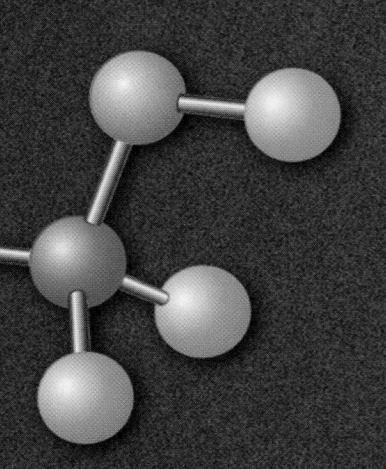

Contents

 internet**connect**

This textbook contains the following on-line resources to help you make the most of your science experience.

Visit **go.hrw.com** for extra help and study aids matched to your textbook. Just type in the keyword HC2 HOME.

 *SCI*LINKS NSTA

Visit **www.scilinks.org** to find resources specific to topics in your textbook. Keywords appear through-out your book to take you further.

Smithsonian Institution® Internet Connections

Visit **www.si.edu/hrw** for specifically chosen on-line materials from one of our nation's premier science museums.

 CNN**fyi**.com

Visit **www.cnnfyi.com** for late-breaking news and current events stories selected just for you.

UNIT 1 *Introduction to Chemistry and Matter* 2

CHAPTER 1
Matter and Change

CHAPTER 1 PLANNING GUIDE 4A

1-1 Chemistry Is a Physical Science 5
1-2 Matter and Its Properties 10
1-3 Elements 20

GREAT DISCOVERIES
Modern Alchemy 8

RESEARCH NOTES
Secrets of the Cremona Violins 19

CHAPTER 2
Measurements and Calculations

CHAPTER 2 PLANNING GUIDE 28A

2-1 Scientific Method 29
2-2 Units of Measurement 33
2-3 Using Scientific Measurements 44

CHEMICAL COMMENTARY
Chemistry's Holy Grail 32

QUICK LAB
Density of Pennies 39

RESEARCH NOTES
Roadside Pollution Detector 43

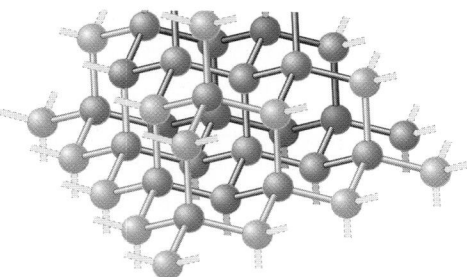

CHAPTER 3

Atoms: The Building Blocks of Matter

CHAPTER 3 PLANNING GUIDE	**64A**
3-1 The Atom: From Philosophical Idea to Scientific Theory	65
3-2 The Structure of the Atom	70
3-3 Counting Atoms	75
CHEMICAL COMMENTARY Travels with C	68
QUICK LAB Constructing a Model	69

CHAPTER 4

Arrangement of Electrons in Atoms

CHAPTER 4 PLANNING GUIDE	**90A**
4-1 The Development of a New Atomic Model	91
4-2 The Quantum Model of the Atom	98
4-3 Electron Configurations	105
QUICK LAB The Wave Nature of Light: Interference	100
GREAT DISCOVERIES The Noble Decade	108

CHAPTER 5

The Periodic Law

CHAPTER 5 PLANNING GUIDE	**122A**
5-1 History of the Periodic Table	123
5-2 Electron Configuration and the Periodic Table	128
5-3 Electron Configuration and Periodic Properties	140
QUICK LAB Designing Your Own Periodic Table	127
CHEMICAL COMMENTARY The Wild Kingdom	135

CHAPTER 6

Chemical Bonding

CHAPTER 6 PLANNING GUIDE	**160A**
6-1 Introduction to Chemical Bonding	161
6-2 Covalent Bonding and Molecular Compounds	164
6-3 Ionic Bonding and Ionic Compounds	176
6-4 Metallic Bonding	181
6-5 Molecular Geometry	183
RESEARCH NOTES Ultrasonic Toxic-Waste Destroyer	166

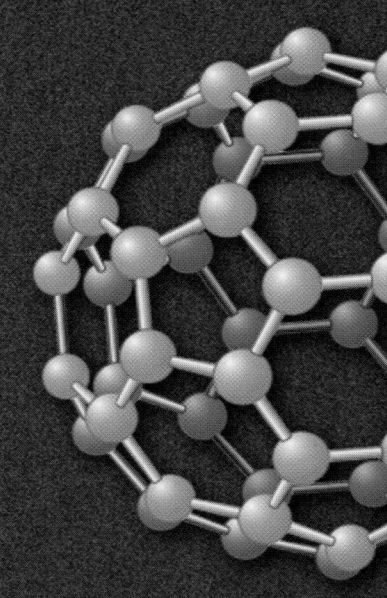

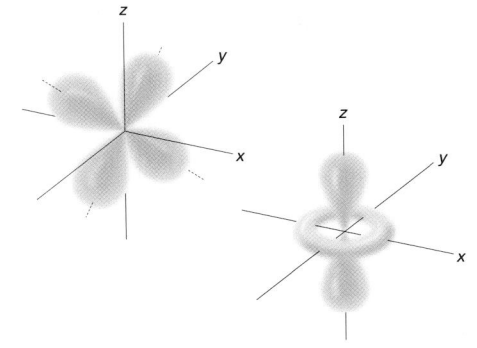

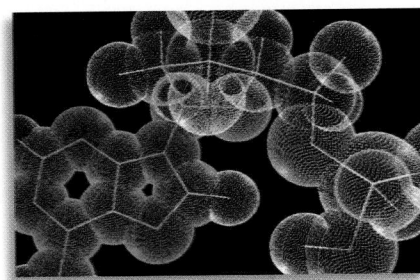

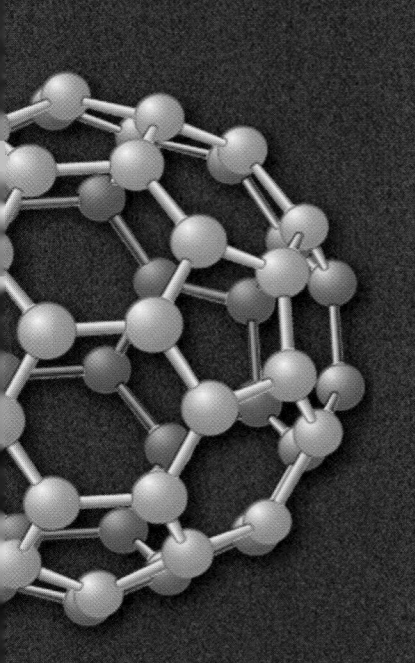

CHAPTER 8

Chemical Equations and Reactions

CHAPTER 8 PLANNING GUIDE	240A
8-1 Describing Chemical Reactions	241
8-2 Types of Chemical Reactions	256
8-3 Activity Series of the Elements	265

CHEMICAL COMMENTARY
A Chemical Mystery — 255

QUICK LAB
Balancing Equations Using Models — 264

RESEARCH NOTES
Acid Water—A Hidden Menace — 268

CHAPTER 7

Chemical Formulas and Chemical Compounds

CHAPTER 7 PLANNING GUIDE	202A
7-1 Chemical Names and Formulas	203
7-2 Oxidation Numbers	216
7-3 Using Chemical Formulas	221
7-4 Determining Chemical Formulas	229

CHEMICAL COMMENTARY
Chemistry and Art — 220

CHAPTER 9

Stoichiometry

CHAPTER 9 PLANNING GUIDE	274A
9-1 Introduction to Stoichiometry	275
9-2 Ideal Stoichiometric Calculations	280
9-3 Limiting Reactants and Percent Yield	288

GREAT DISCOVERIES
The Case of Combustion — 278

QUICK LAB
Limiting Reactants in a Recipe — 292

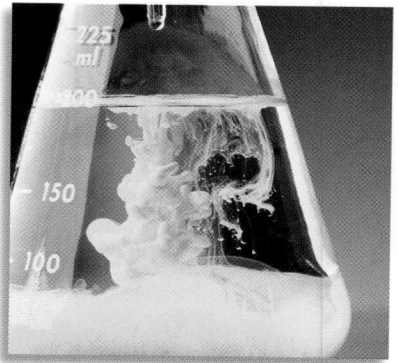

CHAPTER 11

Molecular Composition of Gases

CHAPTER 11 PLANNING GUIDE	332A
11-1 Volume-Mass Relationships of Gases	333
11-2 The Ideal Gas Law	340
11-3 Stoichiometry of Gases	347
11-4 Effusion and Diffusion	351

GREAT DISCOVERIES Chemistry's First Law	338
QUICK LAB Diffusion	353

CHAPTER 10

Physical Characteristics of Gases

CHAPTER 10 PLANNING GUIDE	302A
10-1 The Kinetic-Molecular Theory of Matter	303
10-2 Pressure	308
10-3 The Gas Laws	313

RESEARCH NOTES Carbon Monoxide Catalyst— Stopping the Silent Killer	307

CHAPTER 12

Liquids and Solids

CHAPTER 12 PLANNING GUIDE	362A
12-1 Liquids	363
12-2 Solids	367
12-3 Changes of State	372
12-4 Water	384

RESEARCH NOTES Phase-Change Materials	383

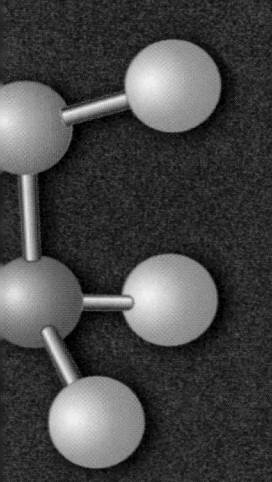

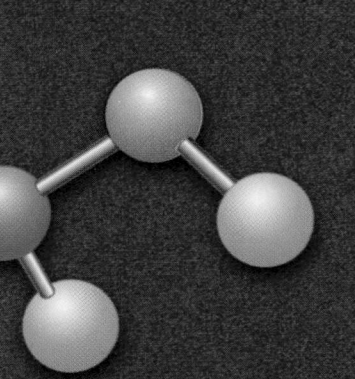

CHAPTER 15

Acids and Bases

CHAPTER 15 PLANNING GUIDE	452A
15-1 Properties of Acids and Bases	453
15-2 Acid-Base Theories	464
15-3 Acid-Base Reactions	469

QUICK LAB	
Household Acids and Bases	458
CHEMICAL COMMENTARY	
Logic in the Laboratory	463

CHAPTER 13

Solutions

CHAPTER 13 PLANNING GUIDE	394A
13-1 Types of Mixtures	395
13-2 The Solution Process	401
13-3 Concentration of Solutions	412

QUICK LAB	
Observing Solutions, Suspensions, and Colloids	399
RESEARCH NOTES	
Artificial Blood	411

CHAPTER 16

Acid-Base Titration and pH

CHAPTER 16 PLANNING GUIDE	480A
16-1 Aqueous Solutions and the Concept of pH	481
16-2 Determining pH and Titrations	493

RESEARCH NOTES	
Liming Streams	492
QUICK LAB	
Testing the pH of Rainwater	496

CHAPTER 14

Ions in Aqueous Solutions and Colligative Properties

CHAPTER 14 PLANNING GUIDE	424A
14-1 Compounds in Aqueous Solutions	425
14-2 Colligative Properties of Solutions	436

| GREAT DISCOVERIES | |
| The Riddle of Electrolysis | 434 |

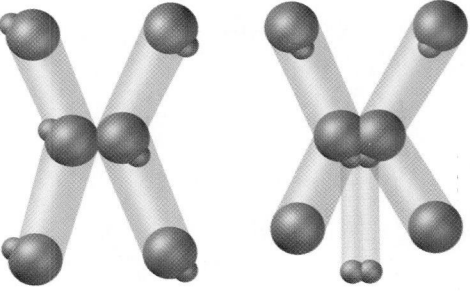

CHAPTER 17

Reaction Energy and Reaction Kinetics

CHAPTER 17 PLANNING GUIDE		510A
17-1	Thermochemistry	511
17-2	Driving Force of Reactions	526
17-3	The Reaction Process	531
17-4	Reaction Rate	538

RESEARCH NOTES
Self-Heating Meals — 525

QUICK LAB
Factors Influencing Reaction Rate — 545

CHAPTER 18

Chemical Equilibrium

CHAPTER 18 PLANNING GUIDE		552A
18-1	The Nature of Chemical Equilibrium	553
18-2	Shifting Equilibrium	562
18-3	Equilibria of Acids, Bases, and Salts	569
18-4	Solubility Equilibrium	577

GREAT DISCOVERIES
Fixing the Nitrogen Problem — 560

CHAPTER 19

Oxidation-Reduction Reactions

CHAPTER 19 PLANNING GUIDE		590A
19-1	Oxidation and Reduction	591
19-2	Balancing Redox Equations	597
19-3	Oxidizing and Reducing Agents	602
19-4	Electrochemistry	606

RESEARCH NOTES
Skunk-Spray Remedy — 596

QUICK LAB
Redox Reactions — 604

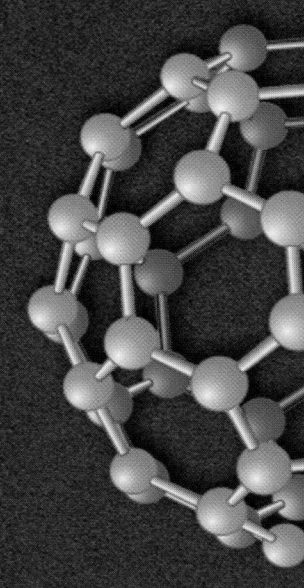

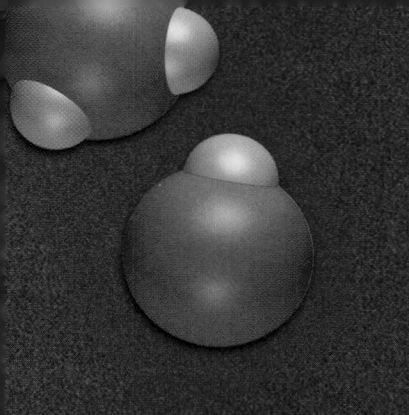

CHAPTER 20

Carbon and Hydrocarbons

CHAPTER 20 PLANNING GUIDE	624A
20-1 Abundance and Importance of Carbon	625
20-2 Organic Compounds	629
20-3 Saturated Hydrocarbons	634
20-4 Unsaturated Hydrocarbons	647
RESEARCH NOTES Synthetic Diamonds	646

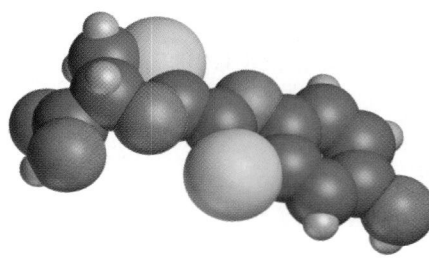

CHAPTER 22

Nuclear Chemistry

CHAPTER 22 PLANNING GUIDE	700A
22-1 The Nucleus	701
22-2 Radioactive Decay	705
22-3 Nuclear Radiation	713
22-4 Nuclear Fission and Nuclear Fusion	717
GREAT DISCOVERIES An Unexpected Finding	720

CHAPTER 21

Other Organic Compounds

CHAPTER 21 PLANNING GUIDE	662A
21-1 Functional Groups and Classes of Organic Compounds	663
21-2 More Classes of Organic Compounds	672
21-3 Organic Reactions	682
21-4 Polymers	685
GREAT DISCOVERIES Unraveling the Mystery of DNA	680
RESEARCH NOTES High-Barrier Plastics	692

| GROUP 1 | ALKALI METALS | 728 |

APPLICATION: *Technology*
Sodium Vapor Lighting — 730

APPLICATION: *Health*
Electrolyte Balance in the Body — 731

| GROUP 2 | ALKALINE EARTH METALS | 734 |

APPLICATION: *Technology*
Fireworks — 736

APPLICATION: *Health*
Calcium: An Essential
Mineral in the Diet — 738

Magnesium: An Essential
Mineral in the Diet — 738

| GROUPS 3–12 | TRANSITION METALS | 740 |

APPLICATION: *Geology*
Gemstones and Color — 743

APPLICATION: *Technology*
Alloys — 744

APPLICATION: *The Environment*
Mercury Poisoning — 747

APPLICATION: *Health*
Elements in the Body — 748
Role of Iron — 749

| GROUP 13 | BORON FAMILY | 750 |

APPLICATION: *Technology*
Aluminum — 752
Aluminum Alloys — 753

| GROUP 14 | CARBON FAMILY | 754 |

APPLICATION: *Chemical Industry*
Carbon and the Reduction
of Iron Ore — 756
Carbon Dioxide — 757
Carbon Monoxide — 757

APPLICATION: *Biochemistry*
Carbon Dioxide and Respiration — 758
Macromolecules — 761

APPLICATION: *The Environment*
Carbon Monoxide Poisoning — 760

APPLICATION: *Chemical Industry*
Silicon and Silicates — 767
Silicones — 767

APPLICATION: *Technology*
Semiconductors — 768

| GROUP 15 | NITROGEN FAMILY | 770 |

APPLICATION: *Biology*
Plants and Nitrogen — 772

APPLICATION: *Chemical Industry*
Fertilizers — 773

| GROUP 16 | OXYGEN FAMILY | 774 |

APPLICATION: *Chemical Industry*
Oxides — 776

APPLICATION: *The Environment*
Ozone — 778

APPLICATION: *Chemical Industry*
Sulfuric Acid — 779

| GROUP 17 | HALOGEN FAMILY | 780 |

APPLICATION: *The Environment*
Chlorine in Water Treatment — 782
Fluoride and Tooth Decay — 783

Laboratory Experiments

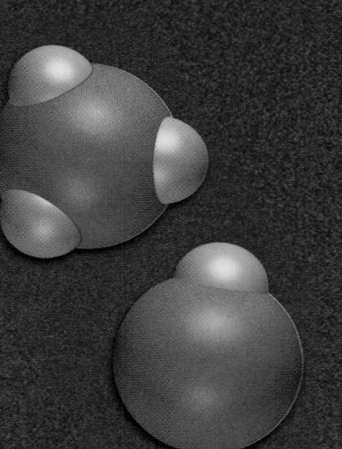

Safety in the Chemistry Laboratory   786

Pre-Lab	Extraction and Filtration	790
1-1	Mixture Separation	792
1-2	Water Purification	794
3-1	Conservation of Mass	798
4-1	Flame Tests	801
Pre-Lab	Gravimetric Analysis	804
7-1	Separation of Salts by Fractional Crystallization	806
7-2	Naming Ionic Compounds	810
7-3	Determining the Empirical Formula of Magnesium Oxide	813
9-1	Mass and Mole Relationships in a Chemical Reaction	816
9-2	Stoichiometry and Gravimetric Analysis	819
12-1	"Wet" Dry Ice	822
12-2	Measuring the Triple Point Pressure of CO_2	824
Pre-Lab	Paper Chromatography	828
13-1	Separation of Pen Inks by Paper Chromatography	830
13-2	Colorimetry and Molarity	834
14-1	Testing Water	838
Pre-Lab	Volumetric Analysis	842
16-1	How Much Calcium Carbonate Is in an Eggshell?	844
16-2	Investigating Overwrite Marking Pens	848
16-3	Is It an Acid or a Base?	851
16-4	Percentage of Acetic Acid in Vinegar	
Pre-Lab	Calorimetry	858
17-1	Measuring the Specific Heats of Metals	860
17-2	Calorimetry and Hess's Law	864
17-3	Rate of a Chemical Reaction	868
18-1	Equilibrium Expression	871
18-2	Measuring K_a for Acetic Acid	875
19-1	Blueprint Paper	878
19-2	Reduction of Manganese in Permanganate Ion	881
21-1	Acid Catalyzed Iodination of Acetone	884
21-2	Casein Glue	888
21-3	Polymers and Toy Balls	891

Reference Section

Appendix A: Reference Tables 894

Appendix B: Study Skills for Chemistry . . . 904

Appendix C: Graphing Calculators Technology 919

Appendix D: Problem Bank 921

Glossary 956

Index 966

Features

RESEARCH NOTES

Chapter 1 Secrets of the Cremona Violins 19

Chapter 2 Roadside Pollution Detector 43

Chapter 6 Ultrasonic Toxic-Waste Destroyer 166

Chapter 8 Acid Water—A Hidden Menace 268

Chapter 10 Carbon Monoxide Catalyst— Stopping the Silent Killer 307

Chapter 12 Phase-Change Materials 383

Chapter 13 Artificial Blood 411

Chapter 16 Liming Streams 492

Chapter 17 Self-Heating Meals 525

Chapter 19 Skunk-Spray Remedy 596

Chapter 20 Synthetic Diamonds 646

Chapter 21 High-Barrier Plastics 692

CHEMICAL COMMENTARY

Chapter 2 Chemistry's Holy Grail 32

Chapter 3 Travels with C 68

Chapter 5 The Wild Kingdom 135

Chapter 7 Chemistry and Art 220

Chapter 8 A Chemical Mystery 255

Chapter 15 Logic in the Laboratory 463

GREAT DISCOVERIES

Chapter 1 Modern Alchemy 8

Chapter 4 The Noble Decade 108

Chapter 9 The Case of Combustion 278

Chapter 11 Chemistry's First Law 338

Chapter 14 The Riddle of Electrolysis 434

Chapter 18 Fixing the Nitrogen Problem 560

Chapter 21 Unraveling the Mystery of DNA 680

Chapter 22 An Unexpected Finding 720

QUICK LABS

Chapter 2 Density of Pennies 39

Chapter 3 Constructing a Model 69

Chapter 4 The Wave Nature of Light: Interference 100

Chapter 5 Designing Your Own Periodic Table 127

Chapter 8 Balancing Equations Using Models 264

Chapter 9 Limiting Reactants in a Recipe 292

Chapter 11 Diffusion 353

Chapter 13 Observing Solutions, Suspensions, and Colloids 399

Chapter 15 Household Acids and Bases 458

Chapter 16 Testing the pH of Rainwater 496

Chapter 17 Factors Influencing Reaction Rate 545

Chapter 19 Redox Reactions 604

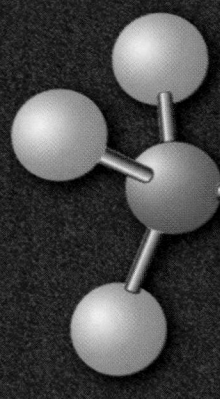

What's New and Different

*Since its first publication in 1918, **Modern Chemistry** has set the high standards by which all other chemistry texts are measured.*

STUDENT TEXT

Core Chapters

- The thorough coverage you've come to expect is still found in a new streamlined table of contents. A more efficient writing style helps you get through the core content faster.

- Expanded *Chapter Reviews* include more questions, problems, and activities.

- **NEW** • **Graphing Calculator Technology** Practice integrated throughout the text, from end-of-chapter problems to CBL™ technology in the lab experiments. Extra help is given in Appendix C. *(See page 25T.)*

- **NEW** • **Study Skills** An expanded Appendix B discusses the reading strategies and study skills that students need for success in the classroom and on standardized tests.

Laboratory Program

- A revision of the laboratory program gives you more experiment options, right in the text. *(See page 28T.)*

- *Pre-laboratory Procedures* emphasize the development of solid laboratory techniques before students do an actual experiment.

Descriptive Chemistry

- *Elements Handbook* gives you relevant applications to reinforce or extend the material in the core chapters. *(See page 37T.)*

Special Features

- **Chemical Commentary** gives students a broader perspective on chemistry with excerpts taken from books and articles.

- **Great Discoveries** gives students historical insights about major discoveries in chemistry.

- **Research Notes** shows students the wide variety of problems being researched to find solutions and expand our knowledge.

INTERNET RESOURCES

 Visit **go.hrw.com** for extra help and study aids matched to *Modern Chemistry (See page 21T.)*

 Visit **www.scilinks.org** for Web resources specific to the topics in *Modern Chemistry's* chapters. Codes for access are given at point of use. *(See page 21T.)*

 Smithsonian Institution®
Internet Connections
Visit **www.si.edu/hrw** for material specially chosen on-line materials from the Smithsonian Institution. *(See page 21T.)*

CNNfyi.com
Visit **www.cnnfyi.com** for late-breaking news and current events stories selected just for you. *(See page 21T.)*

for this Edition

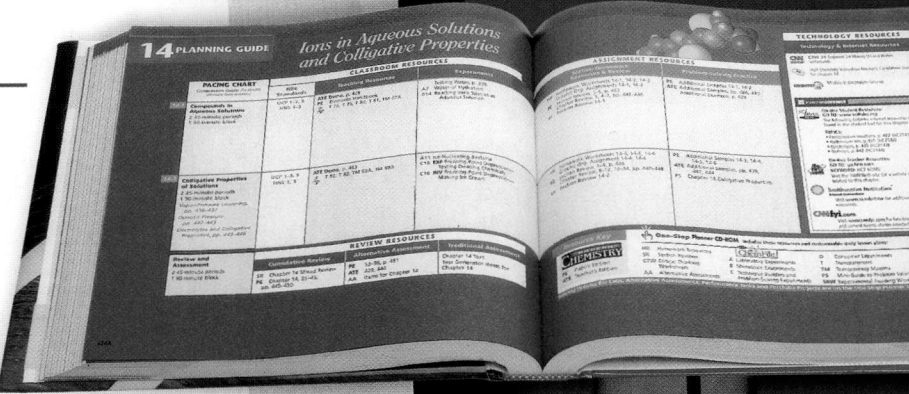

TEACHER'S EDITION

- Extended margin format for this edition gives you the teaching support you need where you need it.
- Planning Charts help you organize all the supplements listed below into your instructional plan.
- 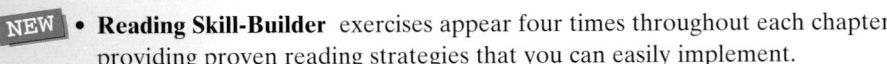**NEW** **Reading Skill-Builder** exercises appear four times throughout each chapter, providing proven reading strategies that you can easily implement.

SUPPLEMENTS

Technology

- Technology components that enhance your instructional effectiveness

  NEW **Holt ChemFile Interactive Tutor CD-ROM** for individualized student review and reinforcement of key concepts and problem-solving techniques *(See page 20T.)*

  Holt Chemistry Videodiscs for large group instruction *(See page 20T.)*

Modern Chemistry

- **NEW** **One-Stop-Planner CD-ROM** One easy-to-carry CD-ROM quickly shows you all available program resources, linked to editable lesson plans, including additional resources not available in print, such as daily homework assignments and a powerful test generator! *(See page 22T.)*

- Chapter Tests and Section Reviews workbook with more emphasis on higher order thinking.

ChemFile

- Laboratory manuals *(See page 30T.)*

  A Laboratory Experiments

  B Microscale Experiments

  C Technique Builders and Problem-Solving Experiments

  NEW **D** Consumer Experiments

- Mini-Guide to Problem Solving *(See page 27T.)*

- Teaching Transparencies

- Test Generator with more questions and improved software capabilities.

Modern Chemistry Resources

To review and assess core content

Assessment Resources

Modern Chemistry Section Reviews

Modern Chemistry Chapter Tests

Technology Resources

Holt Chemistry Videodiscs

Holt Chemistry Videodiscs Teacher's Correlation Guide for Modern Chemistry

CNN Presents Science in the News: Chemistry Connections

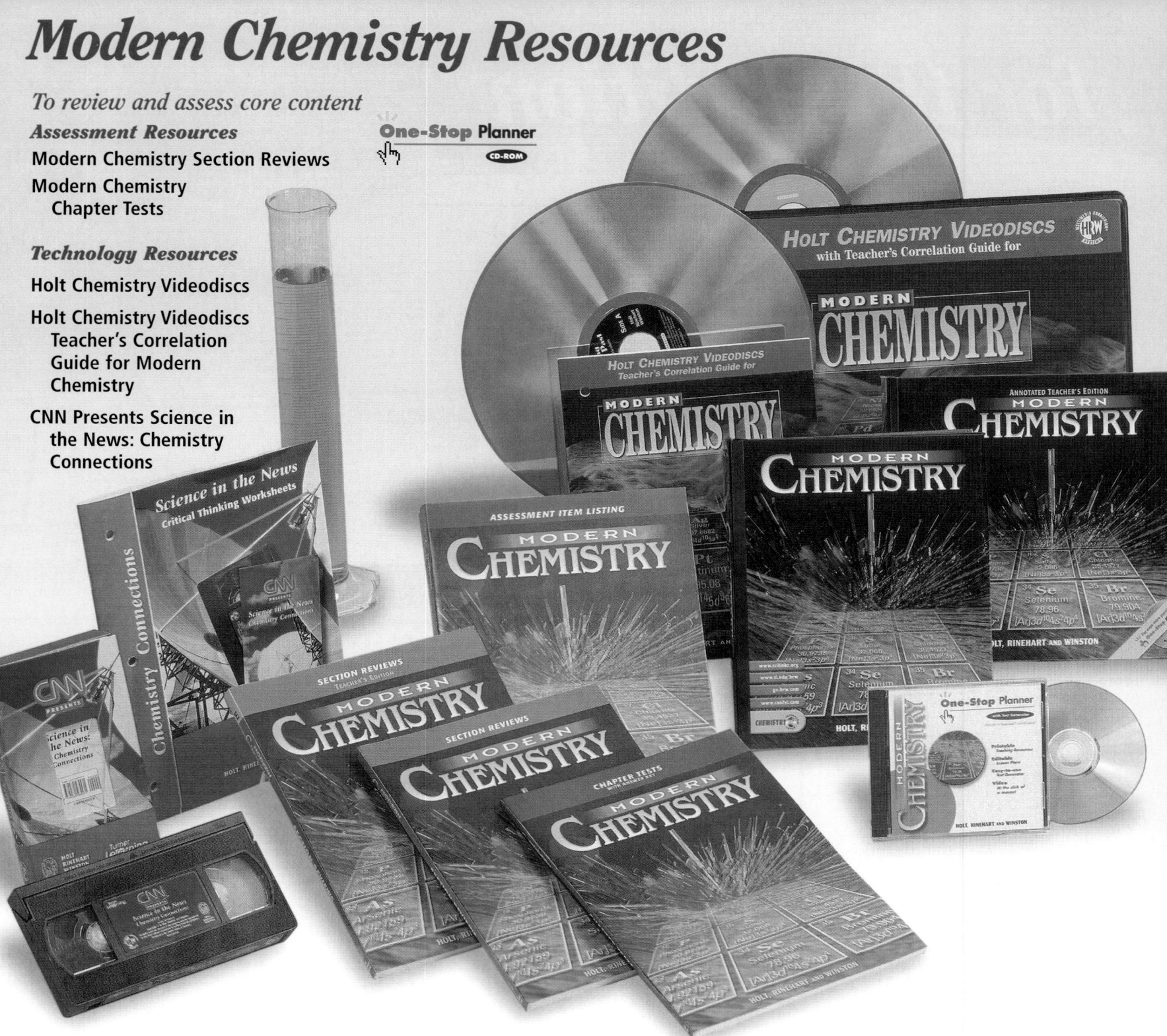

HOLT ChemFile RESOURCES

To customize and enhance your course

Reinforcement

ChemFile: **Mini-Guide to Problem Solving**
ChemFile: **Interactive Tutor**

Classroom Instruction and Management

ChemFile A: **Laboratory Experiments**

ChemFile B: **Microscale Experiments**

ChemFile C: **Technique Builders and Problem-Solving Experiments**

ChemFile D: **Consumer Experiments**

ChemFile **Teaching Transparencies**

ChemFile **Transparency Directory**

Media and Internet Resources

Integrating chemistry concepts with interactive problem-solving practice.

This CD-ROM provides an interactive environment which brings the particle world of chemistry to life in a "virtual laboratory." It models the motion and interaction that occurs in chemical systems.

Modules are divided into the following lesson types:

- **Topic tutorials**
- **Topic practice**
- **Problem-solving tutorials**
- **Problem-solving practice**

The tutor guides students every step of the way by providing encouragement for correct choices and gently pointing out errors or misunderstandings resulting from incorrect choices.

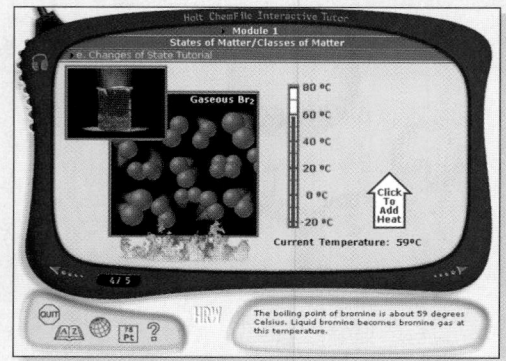

Modules include:

States of Matter/Classes of Matter	Equations and Stoichiometry
Models of the Atom	Gas Laws
Periodic Properties	Equilibrium
Chemical Bonding	Strong and Weakly Ionized Species, pH, and Titrations
	Thermochemistry
	Electrochemical Cells

HOLT CHEMISTRY VIDEODISCS

Two videodiscs contains hundreds of still-frame images, video clips, animation sequences, molecular rotations, and question screens. The *Holt Chemistry Videodiscs Teacher's Correlation Guide for Modern Chemistry* provides barcodes organized by text chapter.

Modern Chemistry and the Internet

TOPIC: Chemical reactions
GO TO: www.scilinks.org
*sci*LINKS **CODE:** HC2081

Instant access to Web content selected specifically for *Modern Chemistry*

- All *sci*LINKS® topics shown in icons throughout the text are managed and monitored by staff from the National Science Teachers Association.

- Sites are selected by teachers for appropriate content and grade level to match your text.

- Sites are continuously added to and deleted from the system.

- Students don't end up at dead ends, dark sites, or sites under construction.

- *sci*LINKS® offers sites from all over the world, giving a global view of the dynamic nature of science communication.

Web materials from the Smithsonian Institution

The Smithsonian Institution maintains special Web sites for use with Holt Physics. Visit **www.si.edu/hrw** for a complete list of these resources. You can find interactive exhibits, classroom activities, interviews with scientists, and a variety of application and extension topics.

Smithsonian Institution®
Internet Connections

Downloadable resources for *Modern Chemistry* from Holt, Rinehart and Winston

Visit **go.hrw.com** to stay up-to-date as additional resources are developed for *Modern Chemistry*. Look for content updates to keep you current, additional articles, activities, teaching suggestions, lab tips, and other resources.

> Includes link to web-based homework grading system containing thousands of *Modern Chemistry* practice problems with randomized values. Saves you time by customizing student assignments and grading work for you!

Web and video resources from CNN demonstrate the relevance of chemistry

Visit **www.cnnfyi.com** for late-breaking and archived news and current-events stories selected just for you. Content is updated frequently, and a special teacher's section provides detailed lesson plans that show you how to integrate news reports from CNN and other resources from the Web site into your classroom.

The *CNN Presents Science in the News: Chemistry Connections* includes more than 30 short video clips that show the newsworthy nature of chemistry. They make great warm-up activities to start lessons. A Teacher's Guide and Critical Thinking Worksheets for the student reinforce the chemistry in each story.

Video News Features include:

Alloy Technology	Mixing Oil and Water: Surfactants
Atom Lasers	Radioisotopes in Medicine
Change of State: Icebergs	Science Controversy: Salt in the Diet

One-Stop Planner

CD-ROM

ONE EASY-TO-CARRY CD-ROM

Saves you time by making lesson planning and managing resources as easy as point-and-click.

TEACHER MANAGEMENT SYSTEM

Printable Teaching Resources

- All program resources are integrated into the suggested lesson plans. **You'll know exactly how to organize and when to use all the resources!**

- Within the lesson plan, hyperlinks take you to full previews of worksheets, labes, and other resources. **One CD-ROM is all you need to carry when planning lessons, whether at home or school!**

- You can print the previews you choose directly from the CD-ROM and photocopy them for classroom use. **No more fumbling with stacks of booklets and lists of page numbers when making photocopies for your classroom!**

- You also get additional resources not found in printed format, such as Homework Resources, including graphic organizer items. **Reinforce key chapter content on a daily basis!**

Easy-to-Use Test Generator

- **Test Generator** can be used to create customized tests from a bank of over 2000 items, with each item correlated to the Section Objectives from the textbook. **Provides a great foundation that you can build on with your own test questions!**

Editable Lesson Plans

- Lesson plans are arranged to show both Traditional and Block Schedules. **You can hit the ground running, whatever your situation!**

- Suggested lesson plans are available as PDF files and as editable word processing documents. **Easily customize them to match your calendar and your district's requirements!**

- Resources can also be viewed by category, such as labs or worksheets. **Preview what's coming up later in the year quickly and efficiently!**

One-Stop Planner

You can drop the *One-Stop Planner CD-ROM* into your computer and start, without consulting long software manuals!

The entire package is designed to be simple to navigate. Just identify the chapter and section you're covering, and click! Easy-to-understand menus put you just one more click away from any resource you might need, including the lesson plans shown here.

Name _____ Class _____ Date_____

Chapter 13: Solutions

Section 13-1: Types of Mixtures
This lesson may be edited by selecting one of the forms listed above.

Pacing

Regular Schedule:	**with lab(s):** 4 days	**without lab(s):** 2 days
Block Schedule:	**with lab(s):** 2 days	**without lab(s):** 1 day

Objectives
1. Distinguish between heterogeneous and homogeneous mixtures.
2. List three different solute-solvent combinations.
3. Compare the properties of suspensions, colloids, and solutions.
4. Distinguish between electrolytes and nonelectrolytes.

Standards Covered

National Science Education Standards
UCP 1: Systems, order, and organization

UCP 2: Evidence, models, and explanation

Block 1
Focus *5 minutes*
_____**Lesson Starter:** ATE p. 395. Students examine mixtures that consist of different sized particles.

Teach *30 minutes*
_____ChemFile Transparency 64: *Particle Model for a Solution.* Examine the solution process microscopically.

Lab *30 minutes*
_____**Quick Lab:** p. 399, *Observing Solutions, Suspensions, and Colloids.* Students observe and classify different mixtures based on their properties.

Extend *10 minutes*
_____**CNN Chemistry Connections:** Segment 24, *Mixing Oil and Water: Surfactants.* Students review types of mixtures and explain the action of soaps and detergents.

Close *10 minutes*
_____**Alternative Assessment:** ATE p. 395. Have students construct a concept map involving terms relating to mixtures.

Homework
_____**Homework Worksheet:** Assign 13–2.

_____**Section Review:** p. 400. Assign items 2–3.

_____**Chapter Review:** p. 420. Assign items 1–2.

_____**Critical Thinking Worksheet 24:** *Mixing Oil and Water: Surfactants.* Students think critically about topics investigated in **CNN Chemistry Connections,** Segment 24.

Other Resource Options
_____**Section Reviews Workbook:** *Section 13-1.* Students review key concepts in the section. (*30 minutes*)

Pacing suggestions consider block and traditional schedules.

Titles that appear in blue are linked to the actual resource. Click to view any resource or to print any worksheet.

Make your own custom lesson plan by selecting materials listed in the Other Resource Options section.

One-Stop Planner *Resources*

CUTTING-EDGE CONTENTS INCLUDE:

Lesson Plans for regular and block scheduling include correlations to National Science Education Standards.

Daily Homework assignments feature graphic organizers.

Chapter Tests assess mastery of content objectives in a variety of formats.

Student Worksheets provide opportunities for students to practice skills and apply what they've learned.

Transparencies are included within a directory that provides teaching tips and questions for class discussion.

Laboratory experiments with detailed teacher's notes and disposal instructions help you create the best hands-on learning environment.

Lab safety information helps ensure the safety of you, your students, and the environment.

Test Generator and Assessment Item Listing allows you to assess the content you have emphasized.

Options for Portfolio Assessments to expand your assessment to demonstrate how student's abilities have evolved during the year.

Scoring Rubrics ensure fairness in scoring portfolio items and lab activities as alternative assessments.

Direct Internet Launch connects you to related Web sites.

Graphing Calculator Integration

Never before has it been so easy to integrate the latest that graphing-calculator technology has to offer!

LABORATORY EXPERIMENTS AND THE CBL™

Just visit **go.hrw.com** for links to FREE Calculator-Based Laboratory™ (CBL) programs from Vernier Software and Technology. *(See page 29T and page 919.)*

CHAPTER REVIEW TECHNOLOGY & LEARNING EXERCISES

With new Flash™ Technology for the TI-82 Plus and TI-83 graphing calculators, visit **go.hrw.com** to download ready-to-use applications onto your computer, and move them to your graphing calculator. Detailed instructions are given in the all-new Appendix C *(see page 919)*.

Instructions in the textbook challenge students to use these applications, which include both programs and datasets, to explore and understand functions, extrapolate and interpret data, evaluate solutions, and formulate hypotheses.

Ready-to-use applications:

- feature expanded datasets with more points, allowing for more reasoning and analysis

- give students more time for higher-order thinking about the meaning of graphs

- require less time keystroking

- eliminate the frustration of keystroking mistakes rendering a program inoperable

For users of calculators without Flash™ Technology, such as the TI-82 and TI-83, keystroking guides are available on the One-Stop Planner CD-ROM. These guides provide an alternative exercise for the graphing calculator and show all of the keystroking and programming in detail.

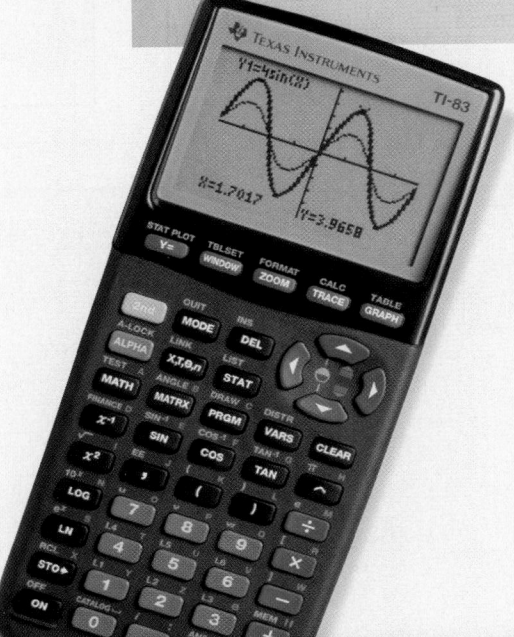

Building Problem-Solving Skills

Students must acquire the ability to analyze a problem, make a plan for reaching a solution, apply the mathematical models needed, and verify the reasonableness of an answer.

CHAPTER EXAMPLES AND PRACTICE

Sample Problems **develop problem analysis and plan-of-attack skills**

Additional Sample Problems **provide more problems like the Sample Problem to review with students for reinforcement**

SECTION 9-3

ADDITIONAL SAMPLE PROBLEM

9-8 Huge quantities of sulfur dioxide are produced from zinc sulfide by means of the following reaction.

$$2ZnS(s) + 3O_2(g) \longrightarrow 2ZnO(s) + 2SO_2(g)$$

If the typical yield is 86.78%, how much SO_2 should be expected if 4897 g of ZnS are used?

Ans. 2794 g

Problem-Solving Practice HOLT ChemFile

Chapter 10 of the Mini-Guide to Problem Solving (also found on the One-Stop Planner CD-ROM) includes more worked-out samples and additional practice problems involving percent yield.

SECTION REVIEW

limiting reactant.
CS_2 remains.
CO_2, 0.667 mol SO_2
he limiting reactant.
Mg remains
$OH)_2$, 0.673 g H_2
he limiting reactant.

Section Review **provides further practice with concepts presented in that section**

SAMPLE PROBLEM 9-6

Silicon dioxide (quartz) is usually quite unreactive but reacts readily with hydrogen fluoride according to the following equation.

$$SiO_2(s) + 4HF(g) \longrightarrow SiF_4(g) + 2H_2O(l)$$

If 2.0 mol of HF are exposed to 4.5 mol of SiO_2, which is the limiting reactant?

SOLUTION

1 ANALYZE **Given:** amount of HF = 2.0 mol
amount of SiO_2 = 4.5 mol
Unknown: limiting reactant

2 PLAN The given amount of either reactant is used to calculate the required amount of the other reactant. The calculated amount is then compared with the amount actually available, and the limiting reactant can be identified. We will choose to calculate the moles of SiO_2 required by the given amount of HF.

$$\text{mol HF} \times \frac{\text{mol } SiO_2}{\text{mol HF}} = \text{mol } SiO_2 \text{ required}$$

3 COMPUTE
$$2.0 \text{ mol HF} \times \frac{1 \text{ mol } SiO_2}{4 \text{ mol HF}} = 0.50 \text{ mol } SiO_2 \text{ required}$$

Under ideal conditions, the 2.0 mol of HF will require 0.50 mol of SiO_2 for complete reaction. Because the amount of SiO_2 available (4.5 mol) is more than the amount required (0.50 mol), the limiting reactant is HF.

4 EVALUATE The calculated amount of SiO_2 is correctly given to two significant figures. Because each mole of SiO_2 requires 4 mol of HF, it is reasonable that HF is the limiting reactant because the molar amount of HF available is less than half that of SiO_2.

PRACTICE 1. Some rocket engines use a mixture of hydrazine, N_2H_4, and hydrogen peroxide, H_2O_2, as the propellant. The reaction is given by the following equation.

$$N_2H_4(l) + 2H_2O_2(l) \longrightarrow N_2(g) + 4H_2O(g)$$

Answer

a. Which is the limiting reactant in this reaction when 0.750 mol of N_2H_4 is mixed with 0.500 mol of H_2O_2?   1. a. H_2O_2

b. How much of the excess reactant, in moles, remains unchanged?   b. 0.500 mol N_2H_4

c. How much of each product, in moles, is formed?   c. 0.250 mol N_2, 1.00 mol H_2O

2. If 20.5 g of chlorine is reacted with 20.5 g of sodium, which reactant is in excess? How do you know?   2. Sodium is in excess because only 0.578 mol Na is needed.

STOICHIOMETRY **289**

SECTION 9-3

✔ Teaching Tip

Whenever the amounts of two reactants are given, students should know that they must solve a limiting reactant problem.

ADDITIONAL SAMPLE PROBLEMS

9-6 Methanol, CH_3OH, is the simplest of the alcohols. It is synthesized by the reaction of hydrogen and carbon monoxide.

$$CO(g) + 2H_2(g) \longrightarrow CH_3OH$$

a. If 500 mol of CO and 750 mol of H_2 are present, which is the limiting reactant?
b. How many moles of the excess reactant remain unchanged?
c. How many moles of CH_3OH are formed?

Ans. **a.** H_2
b. 125 mol CO **c.** 375 mol CH_3OH

9-6 Zinc citrate, $Zn_3(C_6H_5O_7)_2$, is an ingredient in toothpaste. It is synthesized by the reaction of zinc carbonate with citric acid.

$$3ZnCO_3(s) + 2C_6H_8O_7(aq) \longrightarrow Zn_3(C_6H_5O_7)_2(aq) + 3H_2O(l) + CO_2(g)$$

a. If there is 1 mol of $ZnCO_3$ and 1 mol of $C_6H_8O_7$, which is the limiting reactant?
b. If there is 6 mol of $ZnCO_3$ and 10 mol of $C_6H_8O_7$, which is the reactant in excess?
c. How many moles of $Zn_3(C_6H_5O_7)_2$ would be produced under the condition described in **(b)**?

Ans. **a.** $ZnCO_3$
b. $C_6H_8O_7$ **c.** 2 mol $Zn_3(C_6H_5O_7)_2$

289

3 COMPUTE Use the

36.8 g·C

4 EVALUATE The answ
The units
(one-half

PRACTICE 1. Metl
pres

If 75
yield

2. Alu
tion
56.6

A

SECTION REVIEW

1. Carbon disulfide burns in oxygen to yield carbon dioxide and sulfur dioxide according to the following chemical equation.

$$CS_2(l) + 3O_2(g) \longrightarrow CO_2(g) + 2SO_2(g)$$

a. If 1.00 mol of CS_2 is combined with 1.00 mol of O_2, identify the limiting reactant.
b. How many moles of excess reactant remain?
c. How many moles of each product are formed?

2. Metallic magnesium reacts with steam to produce magnesium hydroxide and hydrogen gas.
a. If 16.2 g of Mg are heated with 12.0 g of H_2O, what is the limiting reactant?
b. How many moles of excess reactant are left?
c. How many grams of each product are formed?

3. a. What is the limiting reactant when 19.9 g of CuO are exposed to 2.02 g of H_2 according to the following equation?

$$CuO(s) + H_2(g) \longrightarrow Cu(s) + H_2O(g)$$

b. How many grams of Cu are produced?

4. Quicklime, CaO, can be prepared by roasting limestone, $CaCO_3$, according to the following reaction.

$$CaCO_3(s) \xrightarrow{\Delta} CaO(s) + CO_2(g)$$

When 2.00×10^3 g of $CaCO_3$ are heated, the actual yield of CaO is 1.05×10^3 g. What is the percent yield?

294

294 CHAPTER 9

Practice Problems **provide an immediate review of skills developed in the Sample Problems**

F.Y.I.

Answers are provided for all Section Reviews and Chapter Reviews in the extended margins

CHAPTER REVIEW PROBLEMS

Mixed Review provides a thorough review of quantitative concepts prior to the Chapter Test.

REVIEWING CONCEPTS

1. a. What is the Tyndall effect?
   b. Identify one example of this effect. (13-1)
2. Given an unknown mixture consisting of two or more substances, explain one technique that could be used to determine whether that mixture is a true solution, a colloid, or a suspension. (13-1)
3. a. What is solution equilibrium?
   b. What factors determine the point at which a given solute-solvent combination reaches equilibrium? (13-2)
4. a. What is a saturated solution?
   b. What visible evidence indicates that a solution is saturated?
   c. What is an unsaturated solution? (13-2)
5. a. What is meant by the solubility of a substance?

b. KNO₃ at 60°C
c. NaCl at 30°C (13-2)

9. Based on Figure 13-15, at what temperature would each of the following solubility levels be observed?
   a. 40 g KCl in 100 g H₂O
   b. 100 g NaNO₃ in 100 g H₂O
   c. 50 g KNO₃ in 100 g H₂O (13-2)
10. The heat of solution for AgNO₃ is +22.8 kJ/mol.
    a. Write the equation that represents the dissolution of AgNO₃ in water.
    b. Is the dissolution process endothermic or exothermic? Is the crystallization process endothermic or exothermic?
    c. As AgNO₃ dissolves, what change occurs in the temperature of the solution?
    d. When the system is at equilibrium, how do the rates of dissolution and crystallization compare?
    e. If the solution is then heated, how will the rates of dissolution and crystallization be affected? Why?
    f. How will the increased temperature affect the amount of solute that can be dissolved?
    g. If the solution is allowed to reach equilibrium and is then cooled, how will the system be affected? (13-2)
11. Under what circumstances might we prefer to express solution concentrations in terms of
    a. molarity?
    b. molality? (13-3)
12. What opposing forces are at equilibrium in the sodium chloride system shown in Figure 13-7? (13-2)

PROBLEMS

Solubility
13. Plot a solubility graph for AgNO₃ from the following data, with grams of solute (by increments of 50) per 100 grams of H₂O on the vertical axis and with temperature in °C on the horizontal axis.

Many Problems are correlated to Sample Problems within the chapter to help students with homework assignments.

APPENDIX D
PROBLEM BANK

Problem Bank

Conversions, Section 2-2
Converting Simple SI Units
1. State the following measured quantities in the units indicated.
   a. 5.2 cm of magnesium ribbon in millimeters
   b. 0.049 kg of sulfur in grams
   c. 1.60 mL of ethanol in microliters
   d. 0.0025 g of vitamin A in micrograms
   e. 0.020 kg of tin in milligrams
   f. 3 kL of saline solution in liters
2. State the following measured quantities in the units indicated.
   a. 150 mg of aspirin in grams
   b. 2500 mL of hydrochloric acid in liters
   c. 0.5 g of sodium in kilograms
   d. 55 L of carbon dioxide gas in kiloliters
   e. 35 mm in centimeters
   f. 8740 m in kilometers
   g. 209 nm in millimeters
   h. 500 000 μg in kilograms
3. The greatest distance between Earth and the sun during Earth's revolution is 152 million kilometers. What is this distance in megameters?
4. How many milliliters of water will it take to fill a 2 L bottle that already contains 1.87 L of water?
5. A piece of copper wire is 150 cm long. How long is the wire in millimeters? How many 50 mm segments of wire can be cut from the length?
6. The ladle at an iron foundry can hold 8500 kg of molten iron; 646 metric tons of iron are needed to make rails. How many ladlefuls of iron will it take to make 646 metric tons of iron? (1 metric ton = 1000 kg)

Converting Derived SI Units
7. State the following measured quantities in the units indicated.
   a. 310 000 cm³ of concrete in cubic meters
   b. 6.5 m² of steel sheet in square centimeters
   c. 0.035 m³ of chlorine gas in cubic centimeters
   d. 0.49 cm² of copper in square millimeters
   e. 1200 dm³ of acetic acid solution in cubic meters
   f. 87.5 mm³ of actinium in cubic centimeters
   g. 250 000 cm² of polyethylene sheet in square meters

8. How many palisade cells from plant leaves would fit in a volume of 1.0 cm³ of cells if the average volume of a palisade cell is 0.0147 mm³?

Mixed Review
9. Convert each of the following quantities to the required unit.
   a. 12.75 Mm to kilometers
   b. 277 cm to meters
   c. 30 560 m² to hectares (1 ha = 10 000 m²)
   d. 81.9 cm² to square meters
   e. 300 000 km to megameters
10. Convert each of the following quantities to the required unit.
    a. 0.62 km to meters
    b. 3857 g to milligrams
    c. 0.0036 mL to microliters
    d. 0.342 metric tons to kg (1 metric ton = 1000 kg)
    e. 68.71 kL to liters
11. Convert each of the following quantities to the required unit.
    a. 856 mg to kilograms
    b. 1 210 000 μg to kilograms
    c. 6598 μL to cubic centimeters (1 mL = 1 cm³)
    d. 80 600 nm to millimeters
    e. 10.74 cm³ to liters
12. Convert each of the following quantities to the required unit.
    a. 7.93 L to cubic centimeters
    b. 0.0059 km to centimeters
    c. 4.19 L to cubic decimeters
    d. 7.48 m² to square centimeters
    e. 0.197 m³ to liters
13. An automobile uses 0.05 mL of oil for each kilometer it is driven. How much oil in liters is consumed if the automobile is driven 20 000 km?
14. How many microliters are there in a volume of 370 mm³ of cobra venom?
15. A baker uses 1.5 tsp of vanilla extract in each cake. How much vanilla extract in liters should the baker order to make 800 cakes? (1 tsp = 5 mL)
16. A person drinks eight glasses of water each day, and each glass contains 300 mL. How many liters of water will that person consume in a year? What is the mass of this volume of water in kilograms? (Assume one year has 365 days and the density of water is 1.00 kg/L.)
17. At the equator Earth rotates with a velocity of about 465 m/s.

MIXED REVIEW

28. Na₂SO₄ is dissolved in water to make 450 mL of a 0.250 M solution.
    a. What is the molar mass of Na₂SO₄?
    b. How many moles of Na₂SO₄ are needed?
29. Citric acid is one component of some soft drinks. Suppose that a 2 L solution is made from 150 mg of citric acid, C₆H₈O₇.
    a. What is the molar mass of citric acid?
    b. What products are produced once the soft drink is opened?
    c. Would increasing the concentration of citric acid decrease the bubbling?
    d. What is the molarity of citric acid in the solution?
30. Suppose you wanted to know how many grams of KCl would be left if 350 mL of a 6.0 M KCl solution were evaporated to dryness.
    a. What is the molar mass of KCl?
    b. How would heating the solution affect the mass of KCl remaining?
    c. How many grams of KCl would remain?
31. Sodium metal reacts violently with water to form NaOH and release hydrogen gas. Suppose that 10.0 g of Na react completely with 1.00 L of water, and the final volume of the system is 1 L.
    a. What is the molar mass of NaOH?
    b. Write a balanced equation for the reaction.
    c. What is the molarity of the NaOH solution formed by the reaction?
32. In cars, ethylene glycol, C₂H₆O₂, is used as a coolant and antifreeze. A mechanic fills a radiator with 6.5 kg of ethylene glycol and 1.5 kg of water.
    a. What is the molar mass of ethylene glycol?
    b. What is the molality of the water in the solution?

CRITICAL THINKING

33. **Predicting Outcomes** You have been investigating the nature of suspensions, colloids, and solutions and have collected the following observational data on four unknown samples. From the data, infer whether each sample is a solution, suspension, or colloid.

DATA TABLE 1 — SAMPLES

Sample	Color	Clarity (clear or cloudy)	Settle out	Tyndall effect
1	green	clear	no	no
2	blue	cloudy	yes	no
3	colorless	clear	no	no
4	white	clear	no	yes

DATA TABLE 2 — FILTRATE OF SAMPLES

Sample	Color	Clarity (clear or cloudy)	On filter paper	Tyndall effect
1	green	clear	nothing	no
2	blue	cloudy	gray solid	yes
3	colorless	cloudy	none	yes
4	white	clear	white solid	no

Based on your inferences in Data Table 1, you decide to conduct one more test of the particles. You filter the samples and then reexamine the filtrate. You obtain the data found in Data Table 2. Infer the classifications based on the data in Table 2.

TECHNOLOGY & LEARNING

34. **Graphing Calculator** Predicting Solubility from Tabular Data

The graphing calculator can run a program that estimates data such as solubility at a given temperature. Given solubility measurements for KCl, you will use the data to predict its solubility at 50°C. Begin by creating a table of data. Then the program will carry out an extrapolation. The last step will involve solubility predictions.

Go to Appendix C. If you are using a TI 83 Plus, you can download the program and data and run the application as directed. If you are using another calculator, your teacher will provide you with keystrokes and data sets to use. Remember that after creating your lists, you will need to name the program and check the display, as explained in Appendix C. You will then be ready to run the program. After you have graphed the data, answer these questions.

Problems are categorized by concept and correlated by section in the chapter Planning Guides so it is easy for you to make homework assignments.

Even more practice problems are provided in Appendix D the Problem Bank. You'll never run out of problems to assign!

Technology and Learning exercises integrate graphing calculator technology into the classroom, providing opportunities for data analysis and interpretation.

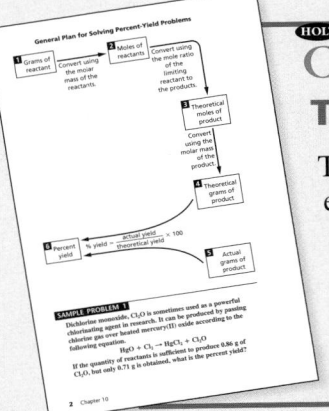

HOLT
ChemFile MINI-GUIDE
TO PROBLEM SOLVING

This paperback reference is a must for students who need extra help, reteaching, and extra practice. The guide moves students through the same quantitative concepts as the text, but at a much slower pace. More-descriptive detail along with visual algorithms give the Sample Problems in this book a more-structured approach. Each chapter closes with a large bank of practice problems.

F.Y.I.

To assist students using calculators with Flash technology, use the programming information in Appendix C to download programs and datasets from the Web. For students using calculators without Flash, you will find all the keystroking information on the *One-Stop Planner CD-ROM*.

Laboratory Instruction

The newly expanded lab program provides a mix of classic experiments, microscale experiments, and real-world scenarios—all developed with safety in mind

IN-TEXT LABORATORY PROGRAM

QUICK LAB

These simple, quick activities can be done at home or in the classroom. Each Quick Lab closes with a set of Discussion questions that direct students to formulate conclusions from their observations.

PRE-LABORATORY PROCEDURE

Calorimetry

Calorimetry, the measurement of heat transfer, allows chemists to determine thermal constants, such as the specific heat of metals and the heat of solution.

When two substances at different temperatures touch one another, heat flows from the warmer substance to the cooler substance until the two substances are at the same temperature. The amount of heat transferred is measured in joules. (One joule equals 4.184 calories.)

A device used to measure heat transfer is a calorimeter. Calorimeters vary in construction depending on the purpose and the accuracy of the heat measurement required. No calorimeter is a perfect insulator; some heat is always lost to the surroundings. Therefore, every calorimeter must be calibrated to obtain its calorimeter constant.

GENERAL SAFETY

Always wear safety goggles and a lab apron to protect your eyes and clothing. If you get a chemical in your eyes, immediately flush the chemical out at the eyewash station while calling to your teacher. Know the location of the emergency lab shower and eyewash station and the procedure for using them.

Turn off hot plates and other heat sources when not in use. Do not touch a hot plate after it has just been turned off; it is probably hotter than you think. Use tongs when handling heated containers. Never hold or touch containers with your hands while heating them.

The general setup for a calorimeter made from plastic foam cups is shown in Figure A. The steps for constructing this setup follow.

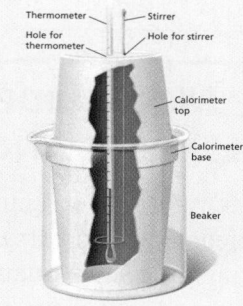

Thermometer — Stirrer
Hole for thermometer — Hole for stirrer
Calorimeter top
Calorimeter base
Beaker

FIGURE A Position the hole for the stirrer so that the thermometer is in the center of the wire ring.

CONSTRUCTING THE CALOR...

1. Trim the lip of one plastic foam... that cup as the top of your calor... other cup will be used as the ba...

2. Use the pointed end of a pencil... make a hole in the center of the... top. The hole should be large en... a thermometer. Make a hole for... As you can see in Figure A, this... be positioned so that the wire s... raised and lowered without inte... the thermometer.

3. Place the calorimeter in a beake... from tipping over.

CALIBRATING A PLASTIC FO... CUP CALORIMETER

1. Measure 50 mL of distilled wat... cylinder. Pour it into the calori... and record the temperature of t... polystyrene cup.

2. Pour another 50 mL of distilled water into a beaker. Set the beaker on a hot plate, and warm the water to about 60°C, as shown in Figure B. Measure and record the temperature of the water.

3. Immediately pour the warm water into the cup, as shown in Figure C. Cover the cup, and move

60°C

FIGURE B Heat the distilled water to approximately 60°C.

---

temperature attained (usually after about 30 s).

5. Empty the calorimeter.

6. The derivation of the equation to find the calorimeter constant starts with the following relationship.

Heat lost by the warm water = Heat gained by the cool water + Heat gained by the calorimeter

$$q_{warm\ H_2O} = q_{cool\ H_2O} + q_{calorimeter}$$

The heat lost by the warm water is calculated by

$$q_{warm\ H_2O} = mass_{warm\ H_2O} \times 4.184\ J/g \cdot °C \times \Delta t$$

The heat gained by the calorimeter system equals the heat lost by the warm water. You can use the following equation to calculate the calorimeter constant C' for your calorimeter.

$$q_{calorimeter} = q_{warm\ H_2O}$$
$$= (mass_{cool\ H_2O})\ (4.184\ J/g \cdot °C)\ (\Delta t_{cool\ H_2O}) + C'(\Delta t_{cool\ H_2O})$$

Substitute the data from your calibration and solve for C'.

Quick LAB

Wear Safety Goggles and an Apron.

Household Acids and Bases

Materials

- dishwashing liquid, dish-washer detergent, laundry detergent, laundry stain remover, fabric softener, and bleach
- fresh red cabbage
- hot plate
- beaker, 500 mL or larger
- beakers, 50 mL
- mayonnaise, baking powder, baking soda, white vinegar, cider vinegar, lemon juice, soft drinks, mineral water, and milk
- spatula
- tap water
- tongs

Question

Which of the household substances are acids, and which are bases?

Procedure

Record all your results in a data table.

1. To make an acid-base indicator, extract juice from red cabbage. First, cut up some red cabbage and place it in a large beaker. Add enough water so that the beaker is half full. Then bring the mixture to a boil. Let it cool, and pour off the cabbage juice. Save the solution.

2. Assemble foods, beverages, and cleaning products to be tested.

3. If the substance being tested is a liquid, pour about 5 mL into a small beaker. If it is a solid, place a small amount into a beaker, and moisten it with about 5 mL of water.

4. Add a drop or two of the red cabbage juice to the solution being tested, and note the color. The solution will turn red if it is acidic and green if it is basic.

Red cabbage can be made into an acid-base indicator.

Discussion

1. Are the cleaning products acids, bases, or neither?

2. What are acid/base characteristics of foods and beverages?

3. Did you find consumer warning labels on basic or acidic products?

3. *Dilute aqueous solutions of bases feel slippery.* You encounter this property of aqueous bases whenever you wash with soap.

4. *Bases react with acids to produce salts and water.* The properties of an acid disappear with the addition of an equivalent amount of a base. It could also be said that "neutralization" of the base occurs when these two substances react to produce salts and water.

5. *Bases conduct electric current.* Like acids, bases form ions in aqueous solutions and are thus electrolytes.

internetconnect

sciLINKS.
NSTA
TOPIC: Household acids and bases
GO TO: www.scilinks.org
sciLINKS CODE: HC2153

458   *CHAPTER 15*

PRE-LABORATORY PROCEDURES

Important techniques are described in detail in these handy reference sections. They can be used as a pre-lab to help students understand a process before working on an actual experiment.

The 28 experiments in the program are a blend of classic, micro, and new experiments. Labs that utilize a technique covered in the Pre-Laboratory Procedures are referenced back to those pages. Micro-labs are also clearly labeled. Safety is emphasized in all experiments.

Background sets the stage for the experiment.

Preparation helps students organize their materials before they start to work with equipment. Students prepare their notebooks for recording data.

Conclusions helps students through their calculations and focuses their attention on improving their techniques and procedures.

Analysis and Interpretation helps students analyze and evaluate their data and procedure to prepare them for the Conclusions phase of the lab.

Extensions gives students opportunities to explore the topic of the experiment further.

F.Y.I.

CBL™ Technology by Vernier Software and Technology enables students to collect their own real-world data and download it directly to their calculator or computer.

EXPERIMENT 16-1

PRE-LAB · PAGE 842
VOLUMETRIC ANALYSIS

MICRO-LAB

How Much Calcium Carbonate Is in an Eggshell?

OBJECTIVES

- *Determine* the amount of calcium carbonate present in an eggshell.
- *Relate* experimental titration measurements to a balanced chemical equation.
- *Infer* a conclusion from experimental data.
- *Apply* reaction-stoichiometry concepts.

MATERIALS

- 1.00 M HCl
- 1.00 M NaOH
- 10 mL graduated cylinder
- 50 mL micro solution bottle, or small Erlenmeyer flask
- 100 mL beaker
- balance
- dessicator (optional)
- drying oven
- eggshell
- forceps
- mortar and pestle
- phenolphthalein solution
- thin-stemmed pipets or medicine droppers, 3
- weighing paper

BACKGROUND

The calcium carbonate content of eggshells can be easily determined by means of an acid/base back-titration, using some of the techniques and calculations described in Chapter 16. In this back-titration, a carefully measured excess of a strong acid will react with the calcium carbonate. The resulting solution will be titrated with a strong base to determine how much acid remains unreacted. From this measurement, the amount of acid that reacted with the eggshell and the amount of calcium carbonate it reacted with can be determined. Phenolphthalein will be used as an indicator to signal the endpoint of the titration.

SAFETY

Always wear safety goggles and a lab apron to protect your eyes and clothing. If you get a chemical in your eyes, immediately flush the chemical out at the eyewash station while calling to your teacher. Know the location of the emergency lab shower

The oven used in this experiment is hot; use tongs to remove beakers from the oven because heated glassware does not always look hot.

Call your teacher in the event of an acid or base spill. Acid or base spills should be cleaned up promptly, according to your teacher's instructions.

PREPARATION

1. Remove the white and the yolk from an egg as shown in Figure A and dispose of them according to your teacher's directions. Wash the shell with distilled water and carefully peel all the membranes from the inside of the shell. Place *all* of the shell in a premassed beaker and dry the shell in the drying oven at 110°C for about 15 min. Continue with Preparation steps 2–5 while the eggshell is drying.

2. Make data and calculations tables like the ones below in your lab notebook.

3. Put exactly 5.0 mL of water in the 10.0 mL graduated cylinder. Record this volume in the data table in your lab notebook. Fill the first thin-stemmed pipet with water. This pipet should be labeled *acid.* **Do not use this pipet for the base solution.** Holding the pipet vertically, add 20 drops of water to the cylinder. **For the best results, keep the sizes of the drops as even as possible throughout this investigation.** Recor

FIGURE A

4. Without emptying the graduated cylinder, add an additional 20 drops from the pipet as before, and record the new volume for Trial 2. Repeat this procedure once more for Trial 3.

5. Repeat Preparation steps 3 and 4 for the second thin-stemmed pipet. Label this pipet *base.* **Do**

EXPERIMENT 16-1

FIGURE B
Use a mortar and pestle to grind the eggshell

7. Remove the eggshell and beaker from the oven. Cool them in a dessicator. Record the mass of the entire eggshell in the second table. Place half of the shell into the clean mortar and grind it to a very fine powder as shown in Figure B. This will save time when you are dissolving the eggshell. (If time permits, dry the powder again and cool it in the dessicator.)

PROCEDURE

1. Measure the mass of a piece of weighing paper. Transfer about 0.1 g of ground eggshell to a piece of weighing paper, and measure the eggshell's mass as accurately as possible. Record the mass in the second data table. Place this eggshell sample into a clean 50 mL micro solution bottle (or Erlenmeyer flask).

2. Fill the acid pipet with 1.00 M HCl acid solution, and then empty the pipet into an extra 100 mL beaker. Label the beaker *waste.* Fill the base pipet with the 1.00 M NaOH base solution, and then empty the pipet into the waste beaker.

3. Fill the acid pipet once more with 1.00 M HCl. Holding the acid pipet vertically, add exactly 150 drops of 1.00 M HCl to the bottle or flask [containing] the reaction [mixture as in] Figure C. [Note] the reaction [inside] of the flask [Using a phenol]phthalein

Acid pipet
Ground eggshell
FIGURE C

4. Fill the base pipet with the 1.00 M NaOH. Slowly add NaOH from the base pipet into the bottle or flask containing the eggshell reaction mixture, as shown in Figure D, until a faint pink color persists in the mixture, even after it is swirled gently. **Be sure to add the base drop by drop, and be certain the drops end up in the reaction mixture and not on the walls of the bottle or flask. Keep careful count of the number of drops used.** Record the number of drops of base used in the second data table.

CLEANUP AND DISPOSAL

5. Clean all apparatus and your lab station. Return the equipment to its proper place. Dispose of chemicals and solutions in the containers designated by your teacher. Do not pour any chemicals down the drain or in the trash unless your teacher directs you to do so. Wash your hands thoroughly before you leave the lab and after all work is finished.

ANALYSIS AND INTERPRETATION

1. **Organizing Ideas:** The calcium carbonate in the eggshell sample undergoes a double-replacement

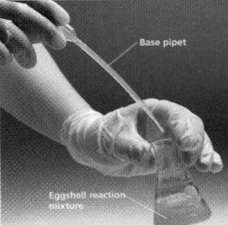
Base pipet
Eggshell reaction mixture
FIGURE D

reaction with the hydrochloric acid in Procedure step 3. Write a balanced chemical equation for this reaction. (Hint: The gas observed was carbon dioxide.)

2. **Organizing Ideas:** Write the balanced chemical equation for the acid/base neutralization of the excess unreacted HCl with the NaOH.

3. **Organizing Data:** Make the necessary calculations from the first data table to find the volume of each drop in milliliters. Using this mL/drop ratio, convert the number of drops of each solution in the second data table to volume in mL of each solution used.

4. **Organizing Data:** Using the relationship between the molarity and volume of acid and the molarity and volume of base needed to neutralize it, calculate the volume of the HCl solution that was neutralized by the NaOH, and record it in your table. (Hint: This relationship was discussed in Section 16-2.)

5. **Analyzing Results:** If the volume of HCl originally added is known and the volume of excess acid is determined by the titration, then the difference will be the amount of HCl that reacted

with the $CaCO_3$. Calculate the volume and the number of moles of HCl that reacted with the $CaCO_3$ and record both in your table.

CONCLUSIONS

1. **Organizing Data:** Use the stoichiometry of the reaction in Analysis and Interpretation item 1 to calculate the number of moles of calcium carbonate that reacted with the HCl, and record this number in your table.

2. **Organizing Data:** Use the periodic table to calculate the molar mass of calcium carbonate. In your data table, record the mass of calcium carbonate present in your eggshell sample by using the number of moles of $CaCO_3$ you calculated in Conclusions item 1.

3. **Organizing Data:** Using your answer to Conclusions item 2, calculate the percentage of calcium carbonate in your eggshell sample, and record it in your table.

4. **Evaluating Methods:** The percentage of calcium carbonate in a normal eggshell ranges from 95% to 99%. Calculate the percent error for your measurement of the $CaCO_3$ content, using 97% $CaCO_3$ as the accepted value.

EXTENSIONS

1. **Inferring Conclusions:** Calculate an estimate of the mass of $CaCO_3$ present in the entire [eggshell] based on your results for the sample of [eggshell] (Hint: Apply the percent composition of [the] sample to the mass of the entire eggshell.)

2. **Designing Experiments:** What possible [sources] of error can you identify in this proce[dure]? If you can think of ways to eliminate th[em] ask your teacher to approve your sugg[estion] and run the procedure again.

HOW MUCH CALCIUM CAR[BONATE IS IN AN EGGSHELL?] 845

A — LABORATORY EXPERIMENTS

These classic experiments provide students with the data collection opportunities to reinforce concepts covered in the text.

A1 Laboratory Procedures
A2 Accuracy and Precision in Measurements
A3 Reactivity of Halide Ions
A4 Test for Iron(II) and Iron(III)
A5 Evidence for Chemical Change
A6 Calcium and Its Compounds
A7 Water of Hydration

A8 Boyle's Law
A9 Molar Volume of Gas
A10 Molar Heat of Fusion of Ice
A11 Ice-Nucleating Bacteria
A12 Hydronium Ion Concentration and pH
A13 Titration with an Acid and a Base
A14 Energy and Entropy
A15 Heat of Crystallization
A16 Temperature of a Bunsen Burner Flame
A17 Heat of Solution
A18 Heat of Combustion

A19 The Solubility Product Constant of Sodium Chloride
A20 Buffering Capacity
A21 Oxidation-Reduction Reactions
A22 Cathodic Protection: Factors Affecting the Corrosion of Iron
A23 Carbon
A24 Oil-Degrading Microbes
A25 Polymers
A26 Radioactivity
A27 Detecting Radioactivity

B — MICROSCALE EXPERIMENTS

You now have more low-cost options for some of your favorite experiments. Micro-labs will require some specialized equipment, but pose less danger, less waste, less breakage, and they involve shorter experiment times. Because the use of reagents is limited, they do require more precise techniques.

B1 Laboratory Procedures
B2 Accuracy and Precision: Calibrating a Pipet
B3 Relative Solubility of Transition Elements
B4 Periodicity of Properties of Oxides
B5 Reactivity of Halide Ions

B6 Chemical Bonds
B7 Conductivity as an Indicator of Bond Type
B8 Test for Iron(II) and Iron(III)
B9 Colored Precipitates
B10 Simple Qualitative Analysis
B11 Generating and Collecting O_2
B12 Generating and Collecting H_2
B13 Testing Reaction Combinations of H_2 and O_2
B14 Reacting Ionic Species in Aqueous Solution
B15 Hydronium Ion Concentration, pH
B16 Titration of an Acid with a Base

B17 Percentage of Acetic Acid in Vinegar
B18 Clock Reactions
B19 Equilibrium
B20 Oxidation-Reduction Reactions
B22 Cathodic Protection: Factors that Affect the Corrosion of Iron
B22 Determination of Vitamin C in Fruit Juices

Rice Vinegar   Red Wine Vinegar   Cider Vinegar

C | TECHNIQUE BUILDERS AND PROBLEM-SOLVING EXPERIMENTS

Explorations have a standard format to build the fundamental skills for a procedure or technique. **Investigations** require students to apply a procedure or technique from an Exploration to solve a problem. These experiments emphasize scientific inquiry and give your students the opportunity to solve analytical problems.

C1 **Exploration:** Conservation of Mass

C2 **Exploration:** Separation of Mixtures
    Investigation: Separation of Mixtures—Tanker Truck Spill

C3 **Investigation:** Covalent and Ionic Bonding—Ceramics Fixative

C4 **Exploration:** Viscosity of Liquids
    Investigation: Viscosity—New Lubricants

C5 **Exploration:** Chemical Reactions and Solid Fuel

C6 **Exploration:** Specific Heat Capacity
    Investigation: Specific Heat Capacity—Terrorist Investigation

C7 **Exploration:** Constructing a Heating/Cooling Curve
    Investigation: Constructing a Cooling Curve—Melting Oils for Soap Production

C8 **Exploration:** Heat of Fusion

C9 **Exploration:** Heat of Solution

C10 **Exploration:** Gas Pressure-Volume Relationship
    Investigation: Gas Temperature-Volume Relationship—Balloon Flight

C11 **Exploration:** Masses of Equal Volumes of Gases

C12 **Exploration:** Paper Chromatography
    Investigation: Paper Chromatography—Forensic Investigation

C13 **Exploration:** Testing for Dissolved Oxygen

C14 **Exploration:** Solubility of Ammonia

C15 **Exploration:** Solubility Product Constant
    Investigation: Solubility Product Constant—Algae Blooms

C16 **Exploration:** Freezing-Point Depression—Testing De-icing Chemicals
    Investigation: Freezing-Point Depression—Making Ice Cream

C17 **Investigation:** Measuring pH—Home Test Kit

C18 **Investigation:** Measuring pH—Acid Precipitation Testing

C19 **Investigation:** Acid-Base Titration—Vinegar Tampering Investigation

C20 **Exploration:** Catalysts Investigation: Catalysts—Peroxide Disposal

C21 **Exploration:** Electroplating for Corrosion Protection

C22 **Exploration:** Voltaic Cells
    Investigation: Voltaic Cells—Designing Batteries

D | CONSUMER EXPERIMENTS

Students apply concepts from the text when performing these experiments, which use materials generally found around the home.

D1 How Sweet It Is!

D2 What's So Special About Bottled Drinking Water?

D3 A Close Look at Toothpaste

D4 Matter and Change: Pizza Mixture

D5 A Close Look at Aspirin

D6 Cloth of Many Colors

D7 All Fats Are Not Equal!

D8 Polymers as Straws

D9 The Slime Challenge

D10 Counting Calories

D11 Factors Affecting CO_2 Production in Yeast

D12 Solutions: Rock Formation

D13 A Close Look at Soaps and Detergents

D14 Acids and Bases: Lemon Cheese

D15 How Effective Is an Antacid?

D16 Titration of Aspirin

D17 Household Indicators

D18 Shampoo Chemistry

D19 Rust Race

D20 Measuring the Iron Content of Cereals

D21 Curdling the Bio-Tech Way

D22 Electric Charge

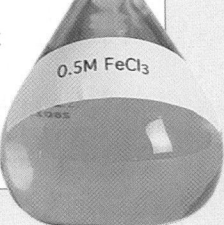

0.5M $FeCl_3$

Lesson Structure

Objectives define the concept coverage for each section. Students know what they are expected to learn and how that learning will be assessed.

CHAPTER 10

Physical Characteristics of Gases

The density of a gas decreases as its temperature increases.

The Kinetic-Molecular Theory of Matter

SECTION 10-1

In Chapter 1, you read that matter exists on Earth in the forms of solids, liquids, and gases. Although it is not usually possible to observe individual particles directly, scientists have studied large groups of these particles as they occur in solids, liquids, and gases.

In the late nineteenth century, scientists developed the kinetic-molecular theory of matter to account for the behavior of the atoms and molecules that make up matter. *The* **kinetic-molecular theory** *is based on the idea that particles of matter are always in motion.* The theory can be used to explain the properties of solids, liquids, and gases in terms of the energy of particles and the forces that act between them. In this section, you will study the theory as it applies to gas molecules. In that form, it is called the kinetic-molecular theory of gases.

The Kinetic-Molecular Theory of Gases

The kinetic-molecular theory can help you understand the behavior of gas molecules and the physical properties of gases. The theory provides a model of what is called an ideal gas. *An* **ideal gas** *is an imaginary gas that perfectly fits all the assumptions of the kinetic-molecular theory.*

The kinetic-molecular theory of gases is based on the following five assumptions:

1. *Gases consist of large numbers of tiny particles that are far apart relative to their size.* These particles, usually molecules or atoms, typically occupy a volume about 1000 times greater than the volume occupied by particles in the liquid or solid state. Thus, molecules of gases are much farther apart than those of liquids or solids. Most of the volume occupied by a gas is empty space. This accounts for the lower density of gases compared with that of liquids and solids. It also explains the fact that gases are easily compressed.

2. *Collisions between gas particles and between particles and container walls are elastic collisions. An* **elastic collision** *is one in which there is no net loss of kinetic energy.* Kinetic energy is transferred between two particles during collisions. However, the total kinetic energy of the two particles remains the same as long as temperature is constant.

OBJECTIVES

- State the kinetic-molecular theory of matter, and describe how it explains certain properties of matter.

- List the five assumptions of the kinetic-molecular theory of gases. Define the terms *ideal gas* and *real gas.*

- Describe each of the following characteristic properties of gases: expansion, density, fluidity, compressibility, diffusion, and effusion.

- Describe the conditions under which a real gas deviates from "ideal" behavior.

CHEMISTRY TUTOR INTERACTIVE

Module 1: States of Matter/Classes of Matter

internet connect

*sci*LINKS
NSTA

TOPIC: Gases
GO TO: www.scilinks.org
*sci*LINKS **CODE:** HC2101

---

barometer. The average atmospheric pressure at sea level at 0°C is 760 mm Hg.

Pressures are often measured in units of atmospheres. *One* **atmosphere of pressure** *(atm) is defined as being exactly equivalent to 760 mm Hg.*

In SI, pressure is expressed in derived units called pascals. The unit is named for Blaise Pascal, a French mathematician and philosopher who studied pressure during the seventeenth century. *One* **pascal** *(Pa) is defined as the pressure exerted by a force of one newton (1 N) acting on an area of one square meter.*

In many cases, it is more convenient to express pressure in kilopascals (kPa). The standard atmosphere (1 atm) is equal to $1.013\ 25 \times 10^5$ Pa, or 101.325 kPa. The pressure units used in this book are summarized in Table 10-1.

FIGURE 10-7 Torricelli discovered that the pressure of the atmosphere supports a column of mercury about 760 mm above the surface of the mercury in the dish.

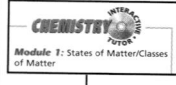

TABLE 10-1 *Units of Pressure*		
Unit	Symbol	Definition/relationship
pascal	Pa	SI pressure unit $1\ \text{Pa} = \frac{1\ \text{N}}{\text{m}^2}$
millimeter of mercury	mm Hg	pressure that supports a 1 mm mercury column in a barometer
torr	torr	1 torr = 1 mm Hg
atmosphere	atm	average atmospheric pressure at sea level and 0°C 1 atm = 760 mm Hg = 760 torr = $1.013\ 25 \times 10^5$ Pa = 101.325 kPa

Vacuum

Pressure of oxygen gas in mm Hg

Oxygen gas molecules exert a force

Oxygen molecules

Mercury

FIGURE 10-8 In the manometer above, the pressure of the oxygen gas in the flask pushes on the mercury column. The difference in the height of the mercury in the two arms of the U-tube indicates the oxygen gas pressure.

Section objectives define the instructional flow for each lesson.

Authoritative, straight-forward, and readable explanations are used to present key concepts.

ChemFile Interactive Tutor CD-ROM references direct students to the applicable modules and sections in this complete tutorial

***sci*LINKS ®** codes enable students to access recommended on-line resources for specific content.

Chemistry **vocabulary** is highlighted with boldfaced type and defined in context.

Tables are used extensively to visually organize data and provide quantitative support for fundamental relationships.

Detailed and accurate **macro- and mini-illustrations** help students understand and apply the concepts discussed in the accompanying text.

Topic-focused headings provide an easily referenced outline of the chapter content.

Chapter Summaries provide a complete overview of the concepts and vocabulary of the chapter.

Vocabulary terms labeled with page references where the terms are first introduced.

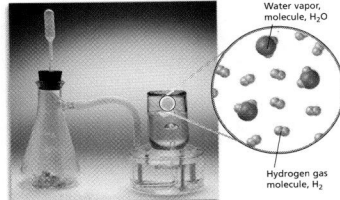

FIGURE 10-15
Hydrogen can be collected by water displacement by reacting zinc with sulfuric acid. The hydrogen gas produced displaces the water in the gas collecting bottle. It now contains some water vapor.

Water vapor, molecule, H_2O

Hydrogen gas molecule, H_2

Gases Collected by Water Displacement

Gases produced in the laboratory are often collected over water, as shown in Figure 10-15. The gas produced by the reaction displaces the water, which is more dense, in the collection bottle. You can apply Dalton's law of partial pressures in calculating the pressures of gases collected in this way. A gas collected by water displacement is not pure but is always mixed with water vapor. That is because water molecules at the liquid surface evaporate and mix with the gas molecules. Water vapor, like other gases, exerts a pressure, known as *water-vapor pressure*.

Suppose you wished to determine the total pressure of the gas and water vapor inside a collection bottle. You would raise the bottle until the water levels inside and outside the bottle were the same. At that point, the total pressure inside the bottle would be the same as the atmospheric pressure, P_{atm}. According to Dalton's law of partial pressures, the following is true.

$$P_{atm} = P_{gas} + P_{H_2O}$$

Suppose you then needed to calculate the partial pressure of the dry gas collected. You would read the atmospheric pressure, P_{atm}, from a barometer in the laboratory. To make the calculation, subtract the vapor pressure of the water at the given temperature from the total pressure. The vapor pressure of water varies with temperature. You need to look up the value of P_{H_2O} at the temperature of the experiment in a standard reference table like that in Table A-8 of this book.

SAMPLE PROBLEM 10-6

Oxygen gas from the decomposition of potassium chlorate, $KClO_3$, was collected by water displacement. The barometric pressure and the temperature during the experiment were 731.0 torr and 20.0°C, respectively. What was the partial pressure of the oxygen collected?

SOLUTION

1 ANALYZE

Given: $P_T = P_{atm} = 731.0$ torr
$P_{H_2O} = 17.5$ torr (vapor pressure of water at 20.0°C, from Table A-8)
$P_{atm} = P_{O_2} + P_{H_2O}$
Unknown: P_{O_2} in torr

2 PLAN

The partial pressure of the collected oxygen is found by subtracting the partial pressure of water vapor from the atmospheric pressure, according to Dalton's law of partial pressures.

$$P_{O_2} = P_{atm} - P_{H_2O}$$

3 COMPUTE

Substituting values for P_{atm} and P_{H_2O} gives P_{O_2}.

$$P_{O_2} = 731.0 \text{ torr} - 17.5 \text{ torr} = 713.5 \text{ torr}$$

4 EVALUATE

As expected, the oxygen partial pressure is less than atmospheric pressure. It is also much larger than the partial pressure of water vapor at this temperature. The answer has the appropriate number of significant figures. It is reasonably close to an estimated value of 713, calculated as 730 − 17.

PRACTICE

1. Some hydrogen gas is collected over water at 20.0°C. The levels of water inside and outside the gas-collection bottle are the same. The partial pressure of hydrogen is 742.5 torr. What is the barometric pressure at the time the gas is collected?
   Answer 760.0 torr

2. Helium gas is collected over water at 25°C. What is the partial pressure of the helium, given that the barometric pressure is 750.0 mm Hg?
   Answer 726.2 mm Hg

SECTION REVIEW

1. State Boyle's law, Charles's law, and the combined gas law in mathematical terms.

2. A sample of helium gas has a volume of 200.0 mL at 0.960 atm. What pressure, in atm, is needed to reduce the volume at constant temperature to 50.0 mL?

3. A certain quantity of gas has a volume of 0.750 L at 298 K. At what temperature, in degrees Celsius, would this quantity of gas be reduced to 0.500 L, assuming constant pressure?

4. An aerosol can contains gases under a pressure of 4.50 atm at 20.0°C. If the can is left on a hot, sandy beach, the pressure of the gases increases to 4.80 atm. What is the Celsius temperature on the beach?

5. Discuss the significance of the absolute-zero temperature.

6. A certain mass of oxygen was collected over water when potassium chlorate was decomposed by heating. The volume of the oxygen sample collected was 720. mL at 25.0°C and a barometric pressure of 755 torr. What would the volume of the oxygen be at STP? (Hint: First calculate the partial pressure of the oxygen, using Appendix Table A-8. Then use the combined gas law.)

Section Review measures mastery of the Section Objectives.

CHAPTER 10 REVIEW

CHAPTER SUMMARY

10-1
- The kinetic-molecular theory of matter can be used to explain the properties of gases, liquids, and solids.
- The kinetic-molecular theory of gases describes a model of an ideal gas. The behavior of most gases is close to ideal except at very high pressures and low temperatures.
- Gases consist of large numbers of tiny, fast-moving particles that are far apart relative to their size. The average kinetic energy of the particles depends on the temperature of the gas.
- Gases exhibit expansion, fluidity, low density, compressibility, diffusion, and effusion.

Vocabulary
diffusion (305)   elastic collision (303)   ideal gas (303)   real gas (306)
effusion (306)   fluids (305)   kinetic-molecular theory (303)

10-2
- Conditions of standard temperature and pressure (STP) allow comparison of volumes of different gases.
- Pressure, volume, temperature, and number of molecules are the four measurable quantities needed to fully describe a gas.
- The gas molecules that make up the atmosphere exert pressure against Earth's surface, varying with weather conditions and elevation.
- A barometer measures the pressure of the atmosphere. The pressure of a gas in a closed container can be measured by a manometer.

Vocabulary
atmosphere of pressure (311)   millimeters of mercury (311)   pascal (311)   standard temperature and pressure (312)
barometer (310)   newton (309)   pressure (308) torr (311)

10-3
- Boyle's law shows the inverse relationship between the volume and the pressure of a gas.
  $$PV = k$$
- Charles's law illustrates the direct relationship between the volume of a gas and its temperature in kelvins.
  $$V = kT$$
- Gay-Lussac's law represents the direct relationship between the pressure of a gas and its temperature in kelvins.
  $$P = kT$$
- The combined gas law, as its name implies, combines the previous relationships into the following mathematical expression.
  $$\frac{PV}{T} = k$$
- A gas exerts pressure on the walls of its container. In a mixture of unreacting gases, the total pressure equals the sum of the partial pressures of each gas.

Vocabulary
absolute zero (317)   Charles's law (317)   Dalton's law of partial pressures (322)   Gay-Lussac's law (319)
Boyle's law (314)   combined gas law (321) gas laws (313)   partial pressure (322)

CHAPTER 10 REVIEW

REVIEWING CONCEPTS

1. What idea is the kinetic-molecular theory based on? (10-1)
2. What is an ideal gas? (10-1)
3. State the five basic assumptions of the kinetic-molecular theory. (10-1)
4. How do gases compare with liquids and solids in terms of the distance between their molecules? (10-1)
5. What is an elastic collision? (10-1)
6. a. Write and label the equation that relates the average kinetic energy and speed of gas particles.
   b. What is the relationship between the temperature, speed, and kinetic energy of gas molecules? (10-1)
7. a. What is diffusion?
   b. What factors affect the rate of diffusion of one gas through another?
   c. What is the relationship between the mass of a gas particle and the rate at which it diffuses through another gas?
   d. What is effusion? (10-1)
8. a. Why does a gas in a closed container exert pressure?
   b. What is the relationship between the area a force is applied to and the resulting pressure? (10-2)
9. a. What is atmospheric pressure?
   b. Why does the atmosphere exert pressure?
   c. What is the value of atmospheric pressure at sea level, in newtons per square centimeter? (10-2)
10. a. Why does a column of mercury in a tube that is inverted in a dish of mercury have a height of about 760 mm at sea level?
    b. What height would be maintained by a column of water inverted in a dish of water at sea level?
    c. What accounts for the difference in the heights of the mercury and water columns? (10-2)
11. a. Identify three units used to express pressure.
    b. Convert one atmosphere to torr.
    c. What is a pascal?
    d. What is the SI equivalent of one standard atmosphere of pressure? (10-2)
12. a. At constant pressure, how does temperature relate to the volume of a given quantity of gas?
    b. How does this explain the danger of throwing an aerosol can into a fire? (10-3)
13. a. What is the Celsius equivalent of absolute zero?
    b. What is the significance of this temperature?
    c. What is the relationship between Kelvin temperature and the average kinetic energy of gas molecules? (10-3)
14. a. Explain what is meant by the partial pressure of each gas within a mixture of gases.
    b. How do the partial pressures of gases in a mixture affect each other? (10-3)

PROBLEMS

Pressure and Temperature Conversions

15. If the atmosphere can support a column of mercury 760 mm high at sea level, what height (in mm) of each of the following could be supported, given the relative density values cited?
    a. water, whose density is approximately 1/14 that of mercury
    b. a hypothetical liquid with a density 1.40 times that of mercury

16. Convert each of the following into a pressure reading expressed in torr. (Hint: See Sample Problem 10-1.)
    a. 1.25 atm
    b. 2.48×10^{-3} atm
    c. 4.75×10^4 atm
    d. 7.60×10^6 atm

17. Convert each of the following into the unit specified.
    a. 125 mm Hg into atm
    b. 3.20 atm into Pa
    c. 5.38 kPa into torr

18. Convert each of the following Celsius temperatures to Kelvin temperatures.
    a. 0.°C
    b. 27°C
    c. −50.°C
    d. −273°C

19. Convert each of the following Kelvin temperatures to Celsius temperatures.
    a. 273 K
    b. 350. K
    c. 100. K
    d. 20. K

Each chapter closes with a substantial **review section** containing both questions and problems ranging from simple to complex.

Review, Practice, and Assessment

Summaries **highlight key concepts and vocabulary in each section.**

Reviewing Concepts **items are keyed to sections so they are easy for you to assign and for students to look back and review.**

Research & Writing **gives students options for projects and extra-credit work.**

Critical Thinking **questions will challenge students to use higher-order thinking skills in applying their knowledge.**

Problems and Mixed Review **provide the practice needed in developing problem-solving skills.**

Alternative Assessment **gives options for evaluating concept mastery using methods other than objective tests.**

Technology & Learning **develops data analysis skills with the graphing calculator. (See page 25T.)**

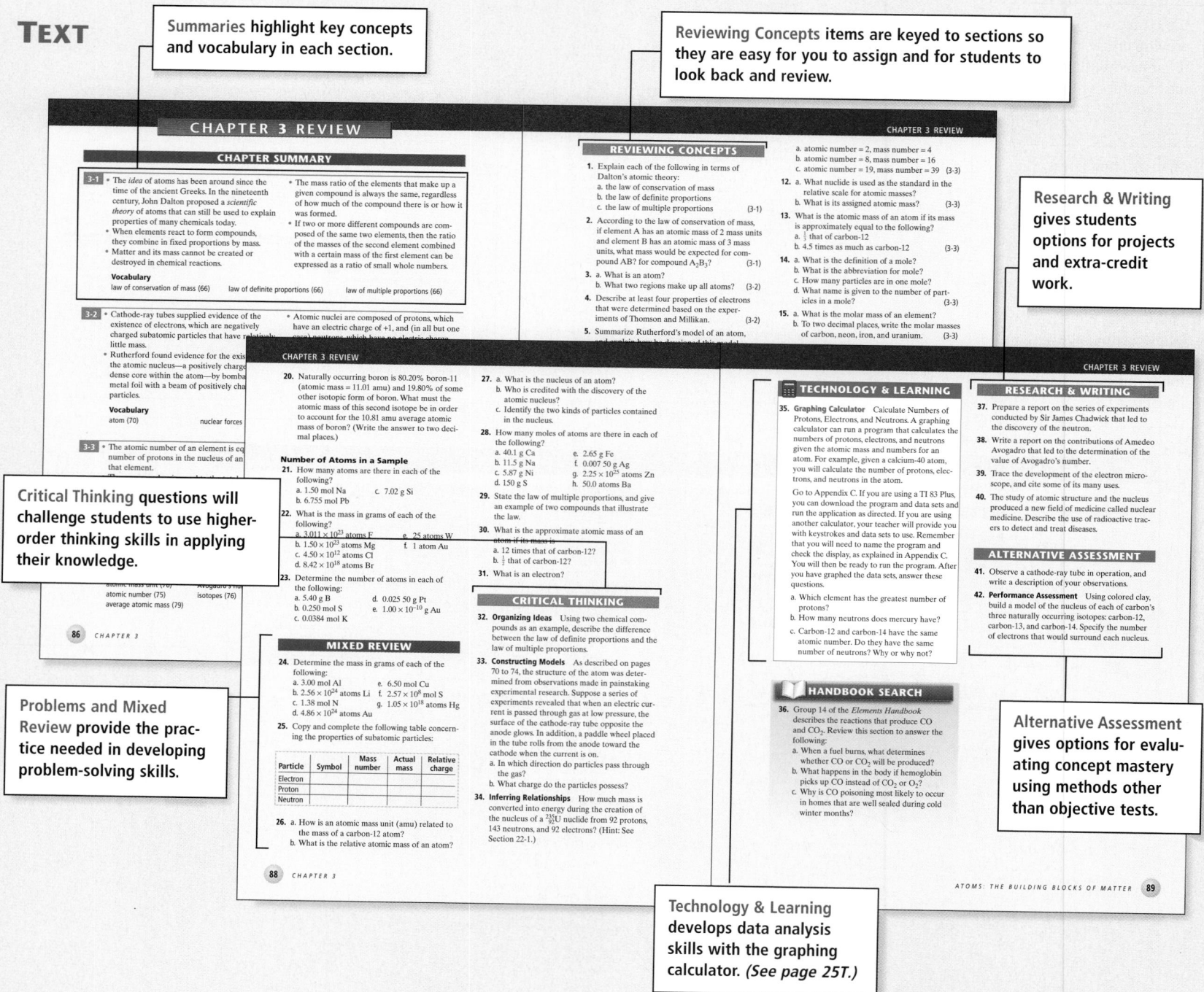

CHAPTER 3 REVIEW

CHAPTER SUMMARY

3-1 • The *idea* of atoms has been around since the time of the ancient Greeks. In the nineteenth century, John Dalton proposed a *scientific theory* of atoms that can still be used to explain properties of many chemicals today.
• When elements react to form compounds, they combine in fixed proportions by mass.
• Matter and its mass cannot be created or destroyed in chemical reactions.

• The mass ratio of the elements that make up a given compound is always the same, regardless of how much of the compound there is or how it was formed.
• If two or more different compounds are composed of the same two elements, then the ratio of the masses of the second element combined with a certain mass of the first element can be expressed as a ratio of small whole numbers.

Vocabulary
law of conservation of mass (66)   law of definite proportions (66)   law of multiple proportions (66)

3-2 • Cathode-ray tubes supplied evidence of the existence of electrons, which are negatively charged subatomic particles that have relatively little mass.
• Rutherford found evidence for the existence of the atomic nucleus—a positively charged dense core within the atom—by bombarding metal foil with a beam of positively charged particles.

• Atomic nuclei are composed of protons, which have an electric charge of +1, and (in all but one case) neutrons, which have no electric charge.

Vocabulary
atom (70)   nuclear forces

3-3 • The atomic number of an element is equal to the number of protons in the nucleus of an atom of that element.

atomic mass unit (76)   Avogadro's number
atomic number (75)   isotopes (76)
average atomic mass (79)

86 CHAPTER 3

REVIEWING CONCEPTS

1. Explain each of the following in terms of Dalton's atomic theory:
   a. the law of conservation of mass
   b. the law of definite proportions
   c. the law of multiple proportions   (3-1)
2. According to the law of conservation of mass, if element A has an atomic mass of 2 mass units and element B has an atomic mass of 3 mass units, what mass would be expected for compound AB? for compound A_2B_3?   (3-1)
3. a. What is an atom?
   b. What two regions make up all atoms?   (3-2)
4. Describe at least four properties of electrons that were determined based on the experiments of Thomson and Millikan.   (3-2)
5. Summarize Rutherford's model of an atom, and explain how he developed this model.

a. atomic number = 2, mass number = 4
b. atomic number = 8, mass number = 16
c. atomic number = 19, mass number = 39   (3-3)
12. a. What nuclide is used as the standard in the relative scale for atomic masses?
    b. What is its assigned atomic mass?   (3-3)
13. What is the atomic mass of an atom if its mass is approximately equal to the following?
    a. $\frac{1}{3}$ that of carbon-12
    b. 4.5 times as much as carbon-12   (3-3)
14. a. What is the definition of a mole?
    b. What is the abbreviation for mole?
    c. How many particles are in one mole?
    d. What name is given to the number of particles in a mole?   (3-3)
15. a. What is the molar mass of an element?
    b. To two decimal places, write the molar masses of carbon, neon, iron, and uranium.   (3-3)

CHAPTER 3 REVIEW

20. Naturally occurring boron is 80.20% boron-11 (atomic mass = 11.01 amu) and 19.80% of some other isotopic form of boron. What must the atomic mass of this second isotope be in order to account for the 10.81 amu average atomic mass of boron? (Write the answer to two decimal places.)

Number of Atoms in a Sample

21. How many atoms are there in each of the following?
    a. 1.50 mol Na   c. 7.02 g Si
    b. 6.755 mol Pb
22. What is the mass in grams of each of the following?
    a. 3.011×10^{23} atoms F   e. 25 atoms W
    b. 1.50×10^{23} atoms Mg   f. 1 atom Au
    c. 4.50×10^{12} atoms Cl
    d. 8.42×10^{18} atoms Br
23. Determine the number of atoms in each of the following:
    a. 5.40 g B   d. 0.025 50 g Pt
    b. 0.250 mol S   e. 1.00×10^{-10} g Au
    c. 0.0384 mol K

MIXED REVIEW

24. Determine the mass in grams of each of the following:
    a. 3.00 mol Al   e. 6.50 mol Cu
    b. 2.56×10^{24} atoms Li f. 2.57×10^8 mol S
    c. 1.38 mol N   g. 1.05×10^{18} atoms Hg
    d. 4.86×10^{24} atoms Au
25. Copy and complete the following table concerning the properties of subatomic particles:

Particle	Symbol	Mass number	Actual mass	Relative charge
Electron				
Proton				
Neutron				

26. a. How is an atomic mass unit (amu) related to the mass of a carbon-12 atom?
    b. What is the relative atomic mass of an atom?

27. a. What is the nucleus of an atom?
    b. Who is credited with the discovery of the atomic nucleus?
    c. Identify the two kinds of particles contained in the nucleus.
28. How many moles of atoms are there in each of the following?
    a. 40.1 g Ca   e. 2.65 g Fe
    b. 11.5 g Na   f. 0.007 50 g Ag
    c. 5.87 g Ni   g. 2.25×10^{25} atoms Zn
    d. 150 g S   h. 50.0 atoms Ba
29. State the law of multiple proportions, and give an example of two compounds that illustrate the law.
30. What is the approximate atomic mass of an atom if its mass is
    a. 12 times that of carbon-12?
    b. $\frac{1}{2}$ that of carbon-12?
31. What is an electron?

CRITICAL THINKING

32. **Organizing Ideas** Using two chemical compounds as an example, describe the difference between the law of definite proportions and the law of multiple proportions.
33. **Constructing Models** As described on pages 70 to 74, the structure of the atom was determined from observations made in painstaking experimental research. Suppose a series of experiments revealed that when an electric current is passed through gas at low pressure, the surface of the cathode-ray tube opposite the anode glows. In addition, a paddle wheel placed in the tube rolls from the anode toward the cathode when the current is on.
    a. In which direction do particles pass through the gas?
    b. What charge do the particles possess?
34. **Inferring Relationships** How much mass is converted into energy during the creation of the nucleus of a $^{235}_{92}U$ nuclide from 92 protons, 143 neutrons, and 92 electrons? (Hint: See Section 22-1.)

TECHNOLOGY & LEARNING

35. **Graphing Calculator** Calculate Numbers of Protons, Electrons, and Neutrons. A graphing calculator can run a program that calculates the numbers of protons, electrons, and neutrons given the atomic mass and numbers for an atom. For example, given a calcium-40 atom, you will calculate the number of protons, electrons, and neutrons in the atom.

    Go to Appendix C. If you are using a TI 83 Plus, you can download the program and data sets and run the application as directed. If you are using another calculator, your teacher will provide you with keystrokes and data sets to use. Remember that you will need to name the program and check the display, as explained in Appendix C. You will then be ready to run the program. After you have graphed the data sets, answer these questions.
    a. Which element has the greatest number of protons?
    b. How many neutrons does mercury have?
    c. Carbon-12 and carbon-14 have the same atomic number. Do they have the same number of neutrons? Why or why not?

HANDBOOK SEARCH

36. Group 14 of the *Elements Handbook* describes the reactions that produce CO and CO_2. Review this section to answer the following:
    a. When a fuel burns, what determines whether CO or CO_2 will be produced?
    b. What happens in the body if hemoglobin picks up CO instead of CO_2 or O_2?
    c. Why is CO poisoning most likely to occur in homes that are well sealed during cold winter months?

RESEARCH & WRITING

37. Prepare a report on the series of experiments conducted by Sir James Chadwick that led to the discovery of the neutron.
38. Write a report on the contributions of Amedeo Avogadro that led to the determination of the value of Avogadro's number.
39. Trace the development of the electron microscope, and cite some of its many uses.
40. The study of atomic structure and the nucleus produced a new field of medicine called nuclear medicine. Describe the use of radioactive tracers to detect and treat diseases.

ALTERNATIVE ASSESSMENT

41. Observe a cathode-ray tube in operation, and write a description of your observations.
42. **Performance Assessment** Using colored clay, build a model of the nucleus of each of carbon's three naturally occurring isotopes: carbon-12, carbon-13, and carbon-14. Specify the number of electrons that would surround each nucleus.

88 CHAPTER 3

ATOMS: THE BUILDING BLOCKS OF MATTER **89**

SUPPLEMENTS

Section Reviews blackline master worksheets provide additional review and practice with text concepts, and an answer key in color.

Chapter Tests thoroughly cover text objectives using a variety of item types including multiple choice, short answer, and problem.

Worksheets available on the **One-Stop** Planner **CD-ROM**

Daily homework assignments feature graphic organizers, standardized test-prep, vocabulary, and skills practice.

PORTFOLIO ASSESSMENT

Modern Chemistry and HOLT ChemFile *contain a variety of materials that can be used to build portfolios.*

STUDENTS CAN MAKE SELECTIONS FROM THE FOLLOWING AREAS:

Content One concept map from the chapter. See the rubric Evaluating Concept Maps* for evaluation criteria.

Outside Reading One or more Supplemental Reading Guides*.

Writing A research paper related to material covered in a chapter.
See the Science Research Paper* worksheets and Internet Activities.*

Performance Assessment One lab report for an in-text lab or a student-designed investigation from the **Chem**File Technique Builders and Problem-Solving Experiments manual (see page 31T).

TEACHERS CAN MAKE SELECTIONS FROM THE FOLLOWING AREAS:

Formal Assessment A chapter exam from the Chapter Tests booklet or test constructed using the **Chem**File Test Generator with Exam View® Software.

Informal Assessment The Informal Assessment Direct Observation Checklist* can be used during a laboratory or other cooperative learning experience.

Performance Assessment A student-designed investigation from the **Chem**File Technique Builders and Problem-Solving Experiments manual or a performance assessment item from the Alternative Assessment section of the chapter review.

*Denotes material found on the *One-Stop Planner CD-ROM*. See page 22T for a complete description of this product. For more background on portfolio assessment, see the scoring Rubrics and Checklist on the *One-Stop Planner CD-ROM*.

Special Features

A feature program gives you more opportunities to show students the value of chemical knowledge in everyday life.

CHEMICAL COMMENTARY

A Chemical Mystery

From "The Chemical Adventures of Sherlock Holmes: The Hound of Henry Armitage" by Thomas G. Waddell and Thomas R. Rybolt in *The Journal of Chemical Education*

"**I** knew it," the old man snapped. "He was poisoned, wasn't he? . . ."

. . . But Holmes was not listening. He had picked up the dog's bowl, now empty, and was vigorously sniffing, not unlike the hound itself, at the crusted remains of the last meal . . .

An hour later I was in my chair at 221B Baker Street. Holmes was in his laboratory and I could hear him humming. In the background was the usual clanking and clanking of laboratory equipment . . . Suddenly, Holmes called to me.

"Watson, come here. I need you." . . . He calmly scribbled an equation on a slip of paper and handed it to me. "If you can balance this equation, Watson, you solve this mystery." I looked at the page as best I could and saw the following equation with the formula of a reactant clearly missing.

$C_6H_5NH_2 + 3KOH + \underline{\quad} \longrightarrow$

$C_6H_5NC + 3KCl + 3H_2O$

Holmes paced back and forth with his hands clasped behind his back. "One part aniline, three parts potassium hydroxide, and one unknown poison yields one part phenylisocyanide, three parts potassium chloride, and three parts water. The missing reactant is

identified by balancing the equation with respect to all the atoms involved. The product phenyliso-

equation confirms it!"

"I can do it, Holmes. I remember that much chemistry. Let me see . . . the missing reactant must have chlorine . . . 3 units to balance Cl in the product!"

"Very good, Watson. Go on with it."

"It gets more complex, now, but look, there is one extra carbon atom in the products! Is CCl_3 the compound?"

Chemical Commentary

Articles and excerpts from contemporary science writers give students a broader perspective of chemistry.

RESEARCH NOTES

Skunk-Spray Remedy

So that pretty black cat with the white stripe down its back wasn't a cat after all? Well, hold off on dumping Fido into a tomato-juice bath. Chemistry has a much better way of conquering skunk spray.

Paul Krebaum, the inventor of a new deskunking formula, says that while working as a materials engineer, he constantly had to deal with the less-than-pleasant smell of the hydrogen sulfide gas that was released from one of his experiments. Mr. Krebaum was losing popularity with his neighbors, and venting off the gas only partially solved the problem. A better solution, he decided, would be to find a way to eliminate the smell entirely.

Mr. Krebaum rifled through his old chemistry books and found that hydrogen peroxide could oxidize these sulfur-containing compounds to much less smelly components. And by decreasing the chemical's volatility, the reaction prevents the gas from reaching our noses quite so easily. He immediately whipped up a hydrogen peroxide mixture, and it worked like a charm.

The reaction by which the hydrogen sulfide was destroyed, producing sulfate compounds that do not have the unpleasant odor, can be seen in the following equation.

$2NaOH + 4H_2O_2 + H_2S \longrightarrow$
$Na_2SO_4 + 6H_2O$

Skunk spray gets its odor from chemicals called mercaptans.

"The receptors that are in your nose are sensitive to sulfur in its low oxidation state," says Mr. Krebaum. "However, they are not sensitive to sulfur in its high oxidation state."

Some time later, a friend of Mr. Krebaum's complained to him that a skunk had sprayed his pet. Because the odor in a skunk's spray also comes from compounds containing sulfur in a low oxidation state, Mr. Krebaum thought his solution might also work on this age-old problem. He mixed up a milder version to try out on the pet: 1 quart 3% hydrogen peroxide solution, 1/4 cup baking soda, and 1 teaspoon liquid soap. His friend tried it out, and the result was one wet and unhappy—but much less smelly—pet.

Mr. Krebaum says that the hydrogen peroxide in the remedy actually oxidizes the compounds, while the baking soda reduces the acidity of the mixture and the soap helps to wash out the greasy skunk spray. The reaction that occurs can be seen in the following equation, which represents all the sulfur-containing compounds in skunk spray.

$RSH + 3H_2O_2 \longrightarrow$

The pet should be thoroughly washed, taking care to keep the mixture away from its eyes. After a few minutes—long enough for the solution to occur—it should be washed away with water and the odor will disappear.

There's just one catch in mixing up this spray: Although Mr. Krebaum's solution does not become explosive, negative side effects . . . with one warning: Do not mix it before using . . . because the mixture breaks down . . . the reaction requires that the formula should not be . . . sealed container because the pressure and . . . the top. For this reason the inventor of "Krebaum's Skunk Remedy" . . . not be applied to the . . . shelves any time soon.

Research Notes

Students go "behind the scenes" in reading about the current research that could solve some very practical problems. Many of these features focus on chemical solutions to environmental problems.

GREAT DISCOVERIES

The Case of Combustion

HISTORICAL PERSPECTIVE

People throughout history have transformed substances by burning them in the air. Yet at the dawn of the scientific revolution, very little was known about the process of combustion. In attempting to explain this common phenomenon, chemists of the eighteenth century developed one of the first universally accepted theories in their field. But, as one man would show, scientific theories do not always stand the test of time.

Changing Attitudes

Shunning the ancient Greek approach of logical argument based on untested premises, investigators of the seventeenth century began to understand the laws of nature by observing, measuring, and performing experiments on the world around them. However, this scientific method was incorporated into chemistry slowly. Though early chemists experimented extensively, most disregarded the importance of measurement, an oversight that set chemistry on the wrong path for nearly a century.

A Flawed Theory

By 1700, combustion was assumed to be the decomposition of a material into simpler substances. People saw burning substances emitting heat, smoke, and light. To account for it, a theory was proposed that combustion depended on the emission of a substance called phlogiston, which appeared as a combination of heat and light while the material was burning but which couldn't be detected beforehand.

Antoine-Laurent Lavoisier and his wife, Marie-Anne Pierrette Lavoisier, who assisted him. One of her important roles was to translate the papers of important scientists for her husband.

The Metropolitan Museum of Art, Purchase, Mr. and Mrs. Charles Wrightsman Gift, in honor of Everett Fahy, 1977. (1977.10) Copyright © 1989 By The Metropolitan Museum of Art.

The phlogiston theory was used to explain many chemical observations of the day. For example, a lit candle under a glass jar burned until the surrounding air became saturated with phlogiston, at which time the flame died because the air

inside could not absorb more phlogiston.

A New Phase of Study

By the 1770s, the phlogiston theory had gained universal acceptance. At that time, chemists also began to experiment with air, which was generally believed to be an element.

In 1772, when Daniel Rutherford found that a mouse kept in a closed container soon died, he explained the results based on the phlogiston theory. Like a burning candle, the mouse emitted phlogiston; when the air could hold no more phlogiston, the mouse died. Thus, Rutherford figured he had obtained "phlogisticated air."

A couple of years later, Joseph Priestley found that when he heated mercury in air, he obtained a reddish powder, which he assumed to be mercury devoid of phlogiston. But when he decided to heat the powder, he recorded an unexpected result:

I endeavored to extract air from [the powder by heating it]; and I presently found that

Great Discoveries

Students step back in history as they read interesting accounts of important chemical discoveries and the thoughts and ideas of the scientists who made those discoveries.

F.Y.I.

Make outside readings an integral part of your program using the Supplemental Reading Guides on the *One-Stop Planner CD-ROM*. (See page 22T for more information.)

ELEMENTS HANDBOOK

The chemistry of representative elements is covered in a reference that is both easy to follow and interesting to read.

Common Reactions show some of the characteristic reactions for the elements in that group.

Characteristics are listed for each group covered, so students can compare and contrast properties.

GROUP 1
ALKALI METALS

CHARACTERISTICS

- do not occur in nature as elements
- are reactive metals obtained by reducing the 1+ ions in their natural compounds
- are stored under kerosene or other hydrocarbon solvent because they react with water vapor or oxygen in air
- consist of atoms with one electron in the outermost energy level
- form colorless ions, each with a 1+ charge
- form ionic compounds
- form water-soluble bases
- are strong reducing agents
- consist of atoms that have low ionization energies
- are good conductors of electricity and heat
- are ductile, malleable, and soft enough to be cut with a knife
- have a silvery luster, low density, and low melting point

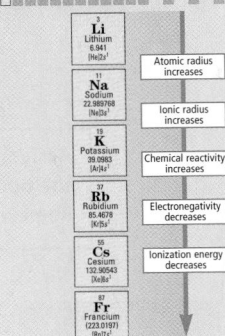

3 **Li** Lithium 6.941 [He]2s¹	Atomic radius increases
11 **Na** Sodium 22.989768 [Ne]3s¹	Ionic radius increases
19 **K** Potassium 39.0983 [Ar]4s¹	Chemical reactivity increases
37 **Rb** Rubidium 85.4678 [Kr]5s¹	Electronegativity decreases
55 **Cs** Cesium 132.90543 [Xe]6s¹	Ionization energy decreases
87 **Fr** Francium (223.0197) [Rn]7s¹	

...s name from the word ...solated in 1807 from the ...stic soda, NaOH. Sodium ... be cut with a knife. It is ...ts with oxygen, which ... to lose its luster.

Potassium was first isolated in 1807 from the electrolysis of caustic potash, KOH.

COMMON REACTIONS

With Water and Acids to Form Bases and Hydrogen Gas
Example: $2Na(s) + 2H_2O(l) \longrightarrow 2NaOH(aq) + H_2(g)$
Li, K, Rb, and Cs also follow this pattern.
Example: $2Na(s) + 2HCl(aq) \longrightarrow 2NaCl(aq) + H_2(g)$
Li, K, Rb, and Cs also follow this pattern.

With Halogens to Form Salts
Example: $2Na(s) + F_2(g) \longrightarrow 2NaF(s)$
Li, K, Rb, and Cs also follow this pattern in reacting with $F_2, Cl_2, Br_2,$ and I_2.

With Oxygen to Form Oxides, Peroxides, or Superoxides
Lithium forms an oxide.
$4Li(s) + O_2(g) \longrightarrow 2Li_2O(s)$
Sodium forms a peroxide.
$2Na(s) + O_2(g) \longrightarrow Na_2O_2(s)$
Alkali metals with higher molecular masses can form superoxides.
$K(s) + O_2(g) \longrightarrow KO_2(s)$
Rb and Cs also follow this pattern.

Alkali-Metal Oxides with Water to Form Bases
Oxides of Na, K, Rb, and Cs can be prepared indirectly. These basic anhydrides form hydroxides in water.
Example: $K_2O(s) + H_2O(l) \longrightarrow 2KOH(aq)$
Li, Na, Rb, and Cs also follow this pattern.

A small piece of potassium dropped into water will react explosively, releasing H₂ to form a strongly basic hydroxide solution. The heat of the reaction ignites the hydrogen gas that is produced.

Sodium reacts vigorously with chlorine to produce NaCl. Most salts of Group 1 metals are white crystalline compounds.

ANALYTICAL TEST

Alkali metals are easily detected by flame tests because each metal imparts a characteristic color to a flame.
  When sodium and potassium are both present in a sample, the yellow color of the sodium masks the violet color of the potassium. The violet color can be seen only when the combined sodium-potassium flame is viewed through a cobalt-blue glass. The glass blocks the yellow flame of sodium and makes it possible to see the violet flame of potassium.

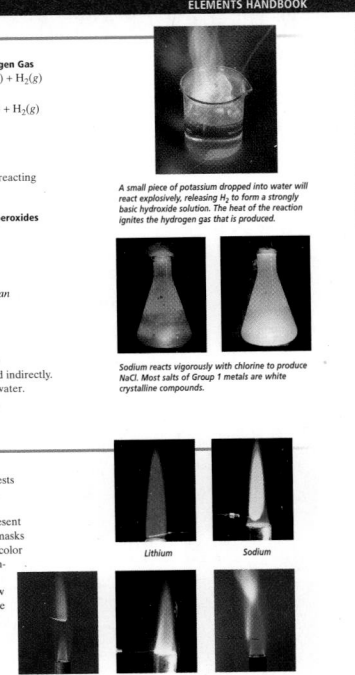

Lithium   Sodium

Potassium   Rubidium   Cesium

Analytical Test describes tests or the qualitative analysis reactions used to denote the presence of a particular element in a sample.

APPLICATION *Health*

Calcium: An Essential Mineral in the Diet
Calcium is the most abundant mineral in the body. It is the mineral that makes up a good portion of the teeth and the bone mass of the body. A small percentage of calcium in the body is used in the reactions by which cells communicate and in the regulation of certain body processes. Calcium is so important to normal body functioning that if the calcium level of the blood falls far below normal, hormones signal the release of calcium from bone and signal the gastrointestinal tract to absorb more calcium during the digestion process.
  A prolonged diet that is low in calcium is linked to a disease characterized by a decrease in bone mass, a condition called osteoporosis. Reduced bone mass results in brittle bones that fracture easily. Osteoporosis generally occurs later in life and is more prevalent in females. However, because you achieve peak bone mass during the late teens or early twenties, it is critical that your diet meet the recommended requirements to increase your peak bone mass. The recommended dietary intake for calcium is 1000 mg per day. Maintaining that level in the diet along with regular exercise through adulthood are thought to reduce the rate of bone loss later in life. Excess calcium in the diet (consuming more than 2500 mg daily) can interfere with the absorption of other minerals.

Dairy products are generally good sources of calcium.

Magnesium: An Essential Mineral in the Diet
Though magnesium has several functio... one of the more important functions i... absorption of calcium by cells. Magnes... dium and potassium, is involved in the... of nerve impulses. Like calcium, magn... component of bone.
  A major source of magnesium in th... plants. Magnesium is the central atom... plant pigment chlorophyll. The structu... phyll in plants is somewhat similar to t... of heme—the oxygen-carrying molecu... (See page 758 for the heme structure.)

Applications highlight relevant uses of the elements. Students see how chemistry influences other areas of study. Applications are presented for the following categories:
- Biochemistry
- Biology
- Chemical Industry
- The Environment
- Geology
- Health
- Technology

TABLE 2A   Good Sources of Calcium in the Diet

Food	Serving size	Calcium present (mg)
Broccoli	6.3 oz	82
Cheddar cheese	1 oz	204
Cheese pizza, frozen	pizza for one	375
Milk, low-fat 1%	8 oz	300
Tofu, regular	4 oz	130
Vegetable pizza, frozen	pizza for one	500
Yogurt, low-fat	8 oz	415
Yogurt, plain whole milk	8 oz	274

F.Y.I.

📖 HANDBOOK SEARCH

Handbook Search in the Chapter Reviews prompts students to look up information in the Elements Handbook to extend the chapter content.

HANDBOOK 📖 CONNECTION

Handbook Connections in the Teacher's Edition highlights the links between chapter material and handbook applications.

Modern Chemistry Teacher's Edition

CHAPTER INTERLEAVES

The chapter Planning Guide is your master plan for integrating all the resources available into your weekly lesson planning.

Technology Resources clearly highlights all of the options for Internet resources, video discs, video tapes, and the ChemFile *Interactive* Tutor CD-ROM.

Classroom Resources correlates all of the materials you would use during class lecture and discussion.

Assignment Resources lists the options you have for homework assignments.

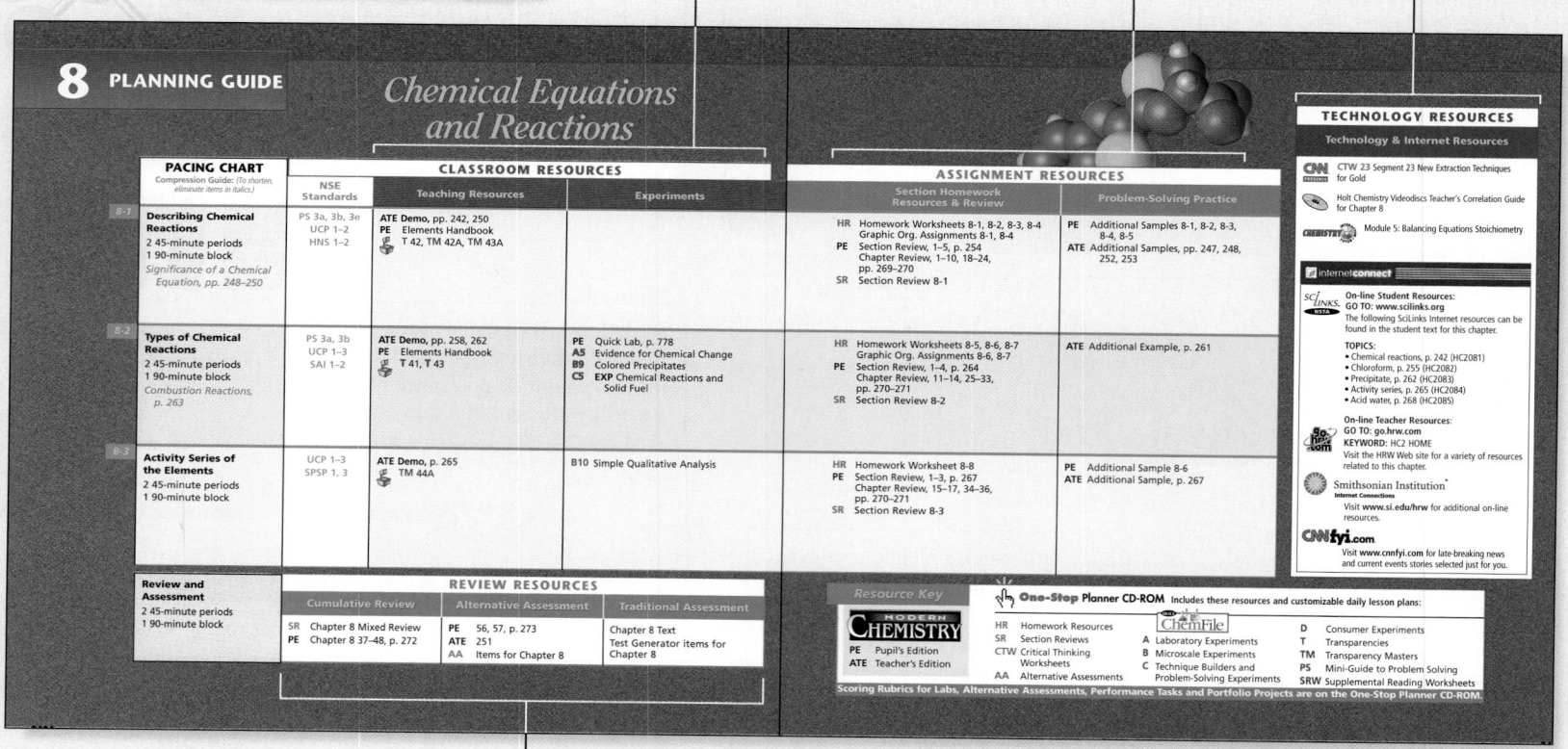

8 PLANNING GUIDE

Chemical Equations and Reactions

CLASSROOM RESOURCES

PACING CHART	NSE Standards	Teaching Resources	Experiments
8-1 **Describing Chemical Reactions** 2 45-minute periods 1 90-minute block *Significance of a Chemical Equation, pp. 248–250*	PS 3a, 3b, 3e UCP 1–2 HNS 1–2	**ATE** Demo, pp. 242, 250 **PE** Elements Handbook T 42, TM 42A, TM 43A	
8-2 **Types of Chemical Reactions** 2 45-minute periods 1 90-minute block *Combustion Reactions, p. 263*	PS 3a, 3b UCP 1–3 SAI 1–2	**ATE** Demo, pp. 258, 262 **PE** Elements Handbook T 41, T 43	**PE** Quick Lab, p. 778 **A5** Evidence for Chemical Change **B9** Colored Precipitates **C5** **EXP** Chemical Reactions and Solid Fuel
8-3 **Activity Series of the Elements** 2 45-minute periods 1 90-minute block	UCP 1–3 SPSP 1, 3	**ATE** Demo, p. 265 TM 44A	**B10** Simple Qualitative Analysis

ASSIGNMENT RESOURCES

Section Homework Resources & Review	Problem-Solving Practice
HR Homework Worksheets 8-1, 8-2, 8-3, 8-4 Graphic Org. Assignments 8-1, 8-4 **PE** Section Review, 1–5, p. 254 Chapter Review, 1–10, 18–24, pp. 269–270 **SR** Section Review 8-1	**PE** Additional Samples 8-1, 8-2, 8-3, 8-4, 8-5 **ATE** Additional Samples, pp. 247, 248, 252, 253
HR Homework Worksheets 8-5, 8-6, 8-7 Graphic Org. Assignments 8-6, 8-7 **PE** Section Review, 1–4, p. 264 Chapter Review, 11–14, 25–33, pp. 270–271 **SR** Section Review 8-2	**ATE** Additional Example, p. 261
HR Homework Worksheet 8-8 **PE** Section Review, 1–3, p. 267 Chapter Review, 15–17, 34–36, pp. 270–271 **SR** Section Review 8-3	**PE** Additional Sample 8-6 **ATE** Additional Sample, p. 267

REVIEW RESOURCES

Review and Assessment	Cumulative Review	Alternative Assessment	Traditional Assessment
2 45-minute periods 1 90-minute block	**SR** Chapter 8 Mixed Review **PE** Chapter 8 37–48, p. 272	**PE** 56, 57, p. 273 **ATE** 251 **AA** Items for Chapter 8	Chapter 8 Text Test Generator items for Chapter 8

TECHNOLOGY RESOURCES

Technology & Internet Resources

CNN CTW 23 Segment 23 New Extraction Techniques for Gold

Holt Chemistry Videodiscs Teacher's Correlation Guide for Chapter 8

CHEMISTRY Module 5: Balancing Equations Stoichiometry

internetconnect

SCILINKS **On-line Student Resources:**
GO TO: www.scilinks.org
The following SciLinks Internet resources can be found in the student text for this chapter.
TOPICS:
• Chemical reactions, p. 242 (HC2081)
• Chloroform, p. 255 (HC2082)
• Precipitate, p. 262 (HC2083)
• Activity series, p. 265 (HC2084)
• Acid water, p. 268 (HC2085)

On-line Teacher Resources:
GO TO: go.hrw.com
KEYWORD: HC2 HOME
Visit the HRW Web site for a variety of resources related to this chapter.

Smithsonian Institution
Internet Connections
Visit www.si.edu/hrw for additional on-line resources.

CNNfyi.com
Visit www.cnnfyi.com for late-breaking news and current events stories selected just for you.

Resource Key

MODERN CHEMISTRY
PE Pupil's Edition
ATE Teacher's Edition

One-Stop Planner CD-ROM Includes these resources and customizable daily lesson plans:

HR Homework Resources	**D** Consumer Experiments
SR Section Reviews	**T** Transparencies
CTW Critical Thinking Worksheets	**TM** Transparency Masters
AA Alternative Assessments	**PS** Mini-Guide to Problem Solving
	SRW Supplemental Reading Worksheets

ChemFile
A Laboratory Experiments
B Microscale Experiments
C Technique Builders and Problem-Solving Experiments

Scoring Rubrics for Labs, Alternative Assessments, Performance Tasks and Portfolio Projects are on the One-Stop Planner CD-ROM.

Review Resources reminds you of material to help your students prepare and help you assess what they've learned.

The extended margins provide the daily instructional strategies that help you use your class time more effectively.

Chapter Overview gives a brief synopsis of the chapter.

Lesson Starter provides a quick and easy strategy for introducing the lesson.

Visual Strategy gives you ideas on how to make more effective use of the text illustrations in your instruction.

Common Misconception highlights a common error in students' thinking and suggests a way to overcome the problem.

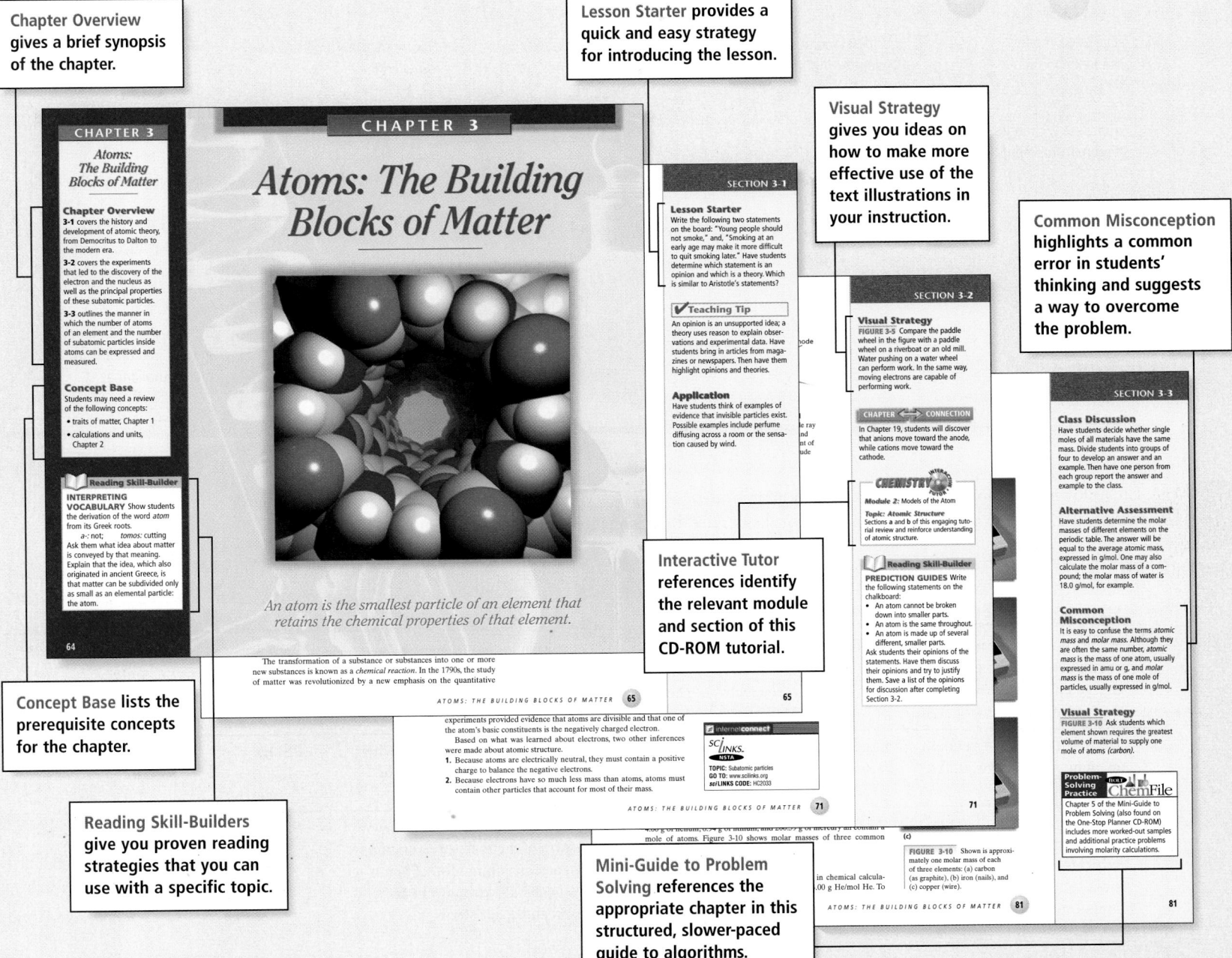

CHAPTER 3

Atoms: The Building Blocks of Matter

An atom is the smallest particle of an element that retains the chemical properties of that element.

Concept Base lists the prerequisite concepts for the chapter.

Reading Skill-Builders give you proven reading strategies that you can use with a specific topic.

Interactive Tutor references identify the relevant module and section of this CD-ROM tutorial.

Mini-Guide to Problem Solving references the appropriate chapter in this structured, slower-paced guide to algorithms.

National Science Education Standards Correlation

Unifying concepts and processes	Science as inquiry	Science and technology	History and nature of science	Science in personal and social perspectives
Systems, order, and organization **UCP 1**	Abilities necessary to do scientific inquiry **SAI 1**	Abilities of technological design **ST 1**	Science as a human endeavor **HNS 1**	Personal and community health **SPSP 1**
Evidence, models, and explanation **UCP 2**	Understandings about scientific inquiry **SAI 2**	Understandings about science and technology **ST 2**	Nature of scientific knowledge **HNS 2**	Population growth **SPSP 2**
Constancy, change, and measurement **UCP 3**			Historical perspectives **HNS 3**	Natural resources **SPSP 3**
Evolution and equilibrium **UCP 4**				Environmental quality **SPSP 4**
Form and function **UCP 5**				Natural and human-induced hazards **SPSP 5**
				Science and technology in local, national, and global challenges **SPSP 6**

The following list shows the chapter correlation of *Modern Chemistry* with the National Science Education Standards (grades 9–12) for Physical Science content. For further detail, see the interleaf pages between each chapter.

Physical Science Content Standards	Code	Chapter Correlation
Structure of Atoms		
Matter is made of minute particles called atoms, and atoms are composed of even smaller components. These components have measurable properties, such as mass and electrical charge. Each atom has a positively charged nucleus surrounded by negatively charged electrons. The electric force between the nucleus and electrons holds the atom together.	**PS 1a**	Chapter 1 Chapter 3
The atom's nucleus is composed of protons and neutrons, which are much more massive than electrons. When an element has atoms that differ in the number of neutrons, these atoms are called different isotopes of the element.	**PS 1b**	Chapter 3 Chapter 22
The nuclear forces that hold the nucleus of an atom together, at nuclear distances, are usually stronger than the electric forces that would make it fly apart. Nuclear reactions convert a fraction of the mass of interacting particles into energy, and they can release much greater amounts of energy than atomic interactions. Fission is the splitting of a large nucleus into smaller pieces. Fusion is the joining of two nuclei at extremely high temperature and pressure, and is the process responsible for the energy of the sun and other stars.	**PS 1c**	Chapter 3 Chapter 22

	Code	Chapter Correlation
Radioactive isotopes are unstable and undergo spontaneous nuclear reactions, emitting particles and/or wave-like radiation. The decay of any one nucleus cannot be predicted, but a large group of identical nuclei decay at a predictable rate. This predictability can be used to estimate the age of materials that contain radioactive isotopes.	PS 1d	Chapter 22

Structure and Properties of Matter

	Code	Chapter Correlation
Atoms interact with one another by transferring or sharing electrons that are furthest from the nucleus. These outer electrons govern the chemical properties of the element.	PS 2a	Chapter 5 Chapter 6
An element is composed of a single type of atom. When elements are listed in order according to the number of protons (called the atomic number), repeating patterns of physical and chemical properties identify families of elements with similar properties. This "Periodic Table" is a consequence of the repeating pattern of outermost electrons and their permitted energies.	PS 2b	Chapter 1 Chapter 3 Chapter 5
Bonds between atoms are created when electrons are paired up by being transferred or shared. A substance composed of a single kind of atom is called an element. The atoms may be bonded together into molecules or crystalline solids. A compound is formed when two or more kinds of atoms bind together chemically.	PS 2c	Chapter 5 Chapter 6 Chapter 19 Chapter 20 Chapter 21
The physical properties of compounds reflect the nature of the interactions among its molecules. These interactions are determined by the structure of the molecule, including the constituent atoms and the distances and angles between them.	PS 2d	Chapter 6 Chapter 12
Solids, liquids, and gases differ in the distances and angles between molecules or atoms and therefore the energy that binds them together. In solids the structure is nearly rigid; in liquids molecules or atoms move around each other but do not move apart; and in gases molecules or atoms move almost independently of each other and are mostly far apart.	PS 2e	Chapter 1 Chapter 10 Chapter 12 Chapter 13
Carbon atoms can bond to one another in chains, rings, and branching networks to form a variety of structures, including synthetic polymers, oils, and the large molecules essential to life.	PS 2f	Chapter 6 Chapter 20 Chapter 21

Chemical Reactions

	Code	Chapter Correlation
Chemical reactions occur all around us, for example in health care, cooking, cosmetics, and automobiles. Complex chemical reactions involving carbon-based molecules take place constantly in every cell in our bodies.	PS 3a	Chapter 8
Chemical reactions may release or consume energy. Some reactions such as the burning of fossil fuels release large amounts of energy by losing heat and by emitting light. Light can initiate many chemical reactions such as photosynthesis and the evolution of urban smog.	PS 3b	Chapter 1 Chapter 8 Chapter 17 Chapter 19
A large number of important reactions involve the transfer of either electrons (oxidation/reduction reactions) or hydrogen ions (acid/base reactions) between reacting ions, molecules, or atoms. In other reactions, chemical bonds are broken by heat or light to form very reactive radicals with electrons ready to form new bonds. Radical reactions control many processes such as the presence of ozone and greenhouse gases in the atmosphere, burning and processing of fossil fuels, the formation of polymers, and explosions.	PS 3c	Chapter 6 Chapter 16 Chapter 18 Chapter 19
Chemical reactions can take place in time periods ranging from the few femtoseconds (10–15 seconds) required for an atom to move a fraction of a chemical bond distance to geologic time scales of billions of years. Reaction rates depend on how often the reacting atoms and molecules encounter one another, on the temperature, and on the properties—including shape—of the reacting species.	PS 3d	Chapter 17
Catalysts, such as metal surfaces, accelerate chemical reactions. Chemical reactions in living systems are catalyzed by protein molecules called enzymes.	PS 3e	Chapter 8 Chapter 17

Physical Science Content Standards	Code	Chapter Correlation
Motions and Forces	**PS 4**	Chapter 4
Conservation of Energy and the Increase in Disorder		
The total energy of the universe is constant. Energy can be transferred by collisions in chemical and nuclear reactions, by light waves and other radiations, and in many other ways. However, it can never be destroyed. As these transfers occur, the matter involved becomes steadily less ordered.	**PS 5a**	
All energy can be considered to be either kinetic energy, which is the energy of motion; potential energy, which depends on relative position; or energy contained by a field, such as electromagnetic waves.	**PS 5b**	
Heat consists of random motion and the vibrations of atoms, molecules, and ions. The higher the temperature, the greater the atomic or molecular motion.	**PS 5c**	Chapter 10 Chapter 11 Chapter 12 Chapter 17
Everything tends to become less organized and less orderly over time. Thus, in all energy transfers, the overall effect is that the energy is spread out uniformly. Examples are the transfer of energy from hotter to cooler objects by conduction, radiation, or convection and the warming of our surroundings when we burn fuels.	**PS 5d**	Chapter 17
Interactions of Energy and Matter		
Waves, including sound and seismic waves, waves on water, and light waves, have energy and can transfer energy when they interact with matter.	**PS 6a**	Chapter 4
Electromagnetic waves result when a charged object is accelerated or decelerated. Electromagnetic waves include radio waves (the longest wavelength), microwaves, infrared radiation (radiant heat), visible light, ultraviolet radiation, x-rays, and gamma rays. The energy of electromagnetic waves is carried in packets whose magnitude is inversely proportional to the wavelength.	**PS 6b**	Chapter 4
Each kind of atom or molecule can gain or lose energy only in particular discrete amounts and thus can absorb and emit light only at wavelengths corresponding to these amounts. These wavelengths can be used to identify the substance.	**PS 6c**	Chapter 4
In some materials, such as metals, electrons flow easily, whereas in insulating materials such as glass they can hardly flow at all. Semiconducting materials have intermediate behavior. At low temperatures some materials become superconductors and offer no resistance to the flow of electrons.	**PS 6d**	Chapter 19

Safety in the Chemistry Lab

The direct cause of most lab accidents is doing something that is unsafe or disregarding a known safety principle. The fundamental cause of every accident is not recognizing the importance of a precaution that could have prevented the accident. ("I didn't know that paying attention to the label was that important.")

The following is a list of several possible unrecognized causes of accidents and suggestions for accident prevention. Of course, the list is not complete; no such list can be. Use it to help you identify some of the hazards in your laboratory. Once the potential causes of accidents are identified, you can then begin to work on their elimination.

Some causes of accidents can be eliminated by considering alternatives.

1. Some classic experiments can be altered to use small-scale or micro-scale amounts and techniques. Some of your favorite labs should be dropped due to the known hazards.
2. Some procedures that are unsafe for students can be performed by the teacher as demonstrations.
3. Many dangerous but popular chemical demonstrations are available on videotape.

Your guiding philosophy should be that there is nothing that can be learned from a lab that justifies someone getting hurt.

Accidents waiting to happen	Precautions for prevention
Attitudes about safety	
• There is an attitude that precautions are optional if you are pressed for time.	• Practice zero-tolerance for unsafe conditions and practices. There is nothing that can be accomplished in your lab that is worth the risk of a serious accident.
• There is no assessment of students' knowledge and attitudes regarding safety.	• Conduct frequent safety quizzes. Students with perfect scores should be the only ones allowed to work in the lab.
• Neither you nor your supervisors have established a comprehensive safety plan.	• Include regular safety inspections and detailed recordkeeping in your safety plan.
• The recommendations of the most recent safety inspection or audit have not been incorporated into the safety program.	• Implement improvements to the safety plan immediately. Such improvements can protect you, your life, and your liability, but only if you implement them.
• The most recent safety inspection or audit was conducted more than six months ago.	• Conduct regular in-house safety and health inspections with an emphasis on improvement rather than placing blame.
• You feel that things are safe enough already because you know that you and the other teachers will not do anything unsafe.	• Judge your safety considerations by whether they make the laboratory safe for everyone, including students, cleaning and building staff, and emergency workers.
Fires and other emergencies	
• Fire and other emergency drills are infrequent, and no records or measurements are made of the results of the drills.	• Always carry out critical reviews of fire and other emergency drills. Don't wait until an emergency to find the flaws in your procedures.
• You haven't thought much about what you would do during the middle of a lab exercise if the building had to be evacuated. You don't know how long it would take to secure the lab and any hazardous chemicals.	• Have actions preplanned in case of an emergency (e.g., establish what devices should be turned off, which escape route to use, where to meet personnel outside the building, who is designated to count people at that meeting place, who is authorized to reenter).

Safety in the Chemistry Lab CONTINUED

Accidents waiting to happen	Precautions for prevention
• Students are unsure what to do when the fire alarm or another alarm sounds.	• Inform everyone in the lab about any alarms and what to do if they sound.
• There are items stored in hallways along escape routes. Fire doors are propped open for ventilation.	• Keep escape routes clear. Do not prop open fire doors or block them for any reason.
• You know your escape route but no alternatives.	• Always plan alternative escape routes in case of unforeseen problems.
• The emergency phone numbers are kept at the main switchboard only.	• Post current emergency phone numbers next to all phones.
• Fire extinguishers are placed at "dead ends" so they will not be in the way along escape routes.	• Place fire extinguishers near escape routes so that they will be of use to those escaping.
• You have no idea how many fire extinguishers there are or when they were last charged. You've never used an extinguisher, and neither have the other teachers.	• Regularly maintain fire extinguishers and train supervisory personnel in the proper use of extinguishers by having them extinguish real fires.
• Students believe that if a fire breaks out they should run for the nearest fire extinguisher and use it to put out the fire as quickly as possible.	• Instruct students (who should not use fire extinguishers because they have not been trained in their use) that in case of a fire they should call a teacher (who should be trained).
• You don't know who in the building has had CPR or first-aid training.	• Get trained in CPR or first aid by your local chapter of the American Red Cross. Be sure to take frequent refresher courses. Post lists of trained staff.

Accident investigations

• The investigation conducted after a serious accident was superficial; it did not identify any previously unrecognized cause or causes and did not result in the implementation of safer procedures.	• Record all details of the accident, even those that may seem insignificant, to allow meaningful retrospective studies of accidents.
• Accidents are investigated so that the person causing the accident can be identified and disciplined.	• Analyze accidents to prevent reoccurrence and not for any other reason.

Facilities and equipment

• Eyewash fountains are present, but no one knows anything about their specifications.	• Ensure that eyewash fountains and safety showers meet the requirements of the ANSI standard (Z358.1).
• Eyewash fountains are checked and cleaned once at the beginning of each school year.	• Flush eyewash fountains for 5 min every month to remove any bacteria or other organisms from pipes.
• No records are kept of routine checks and maintenance on the safety showers and eyewash fountains.	• Test safety showers (measure flow in gallons per minute) and eyewash fountains every six months and keep records of the test results.
• If the fan can be turned on, the fume hood is presumed to work well enough to keep everyone in the room safe.	• Ensure that laboratory ventilation and fume hood performance and use conform to the requirements of the ANSI standard (Z358.1).

Accidents waiting to happen	Precautions for prevention
• Chronic contamination of breathing air is dealt with by keeping windows propped open at all times.	• Engage an industrial hygienist to conduct the appropriate measurements when contamination of breathing air is suspected. Keep records of any such measurements.
• Spills are handled on a case-by-case basis with whatever materials happen to be on hand.	• Have the appropriate equipment and materials available for spill control; replace them before their expiration dates.
• Labs are opened in the morning and locked after school is out.	• Lock all laboratory rooms whenever a teacher is not present.
• Compressed gas cylinders are carried by hand and set up in a corner of the laboratory.	• Secure all compressed gas cylinders when in use, and transport them secured on a hand truck.
• Equipment with moving parts is used without any precautions.	• All moving belts and pulleys should have safety guards.

Safety Wear

• Instead of goggles, you prefer to wear safety glasses with hard plastic lenses. You do not use a face shield when preparing solutions from concentrated acids.	• Wear eye protection in the laboratory at all times; use safety goggles, ANSI Type G or H. When circumstances require, wear face, neck, and ear protection also (face shield, ANSI Type N). For details, see the ANSI standard (Z87.1)
• Students or teachers who wear contact lenses use regular lab goggles.	• Require ANSI Type K cupped goggles for students or teachers who wear contact lenses.
• Gloves are reused to save money. They are discarded only after they begin to fall apart.	• Check gloves routinely for pin holes, tears, or rips. Because gloves cannot resist penetration by a chemical after being handled for long periods of time, replace them before that time period expires.
• You wear old clothes in the lab instead of a laboratory coat or apron so that spills won't be a problem.	• Wear a laboratory coat or apron to protect skin and clothing from chemicals.
• You assume that your lab coat or apron offers the appropriate protection.	• Wear a long-sleeved shirt or blouse and slacks that extend to the ankles under the lab coat or apron.
• You leave your hair down when you work in the laboratory.	• Tie back or tuck in loose clothing (e.g., sleeves, full-cut blouses, neckties, etc.), long hair, and dangling jewelry.
• You allow students to wear sandals in the laboratory.	• Do not allow any footwear in the lab that does not cover feet completely; including open-toed shoes.
• Observers are allowed into the lab but told to stay away from the lab benches.	• Keep a spare set of protective equipment on hand for visitors.

Work habits

• New lab procedures are used with students without a pre-lab session or demonstration.	• Analyze new lab procedures in advance to pinpoint potential hazards.
• You work alone during your preparation period to organize the day's labs.	• Never work alone in a science laboratory or storage area.

Safety in the Chemistry Lab CONTINUED

Accidents waiting to happen	Precautions for prevention
• Honor students do independent study alone in the laboratory.	• Never allow students to occupy a science laboratory unless a teacher is present.
• Although students do not eat or drink in the lab, you sometimes drink a soda or coffee in the storage area.	• Never eat, drink, smoke, or chew gum or tobacco in a science laboratory or storage area.
• You keep your lunch stored in the laboratory refrigerator because it's closer than the teacher's lounge.	• Do not store food or beverages in the laboratory environment.
• After work, you're in a hurry to get home, so you don't wash your hands.	• Always wash hands after work in a science laboratory and after spill cleanups.
• Sometimes you leave the room while a hot water bath is warming up.	• Never leave any heat sources (such as gas burners, hot plates, heating mantles, sand baths, etc.) unattended.
• The storeroom is too crowded, so you decide to keep some equipment on the lab benches.	• Do not store reagents or equipment on lab benches, and keep lab shelves organized. Never place reactive chemicals (in bottles, beakers, flasks, wash bottles, etc.) near the edges of a lab bench.
• The windows are opened whenever volatile substances are used.	• Use a fume hood when working with volatile substances.
• When you work in the fume hood, you put your head inside so you can see what you are doing.	• Never lean into the fume hood.
• Reagents are kept in the fume hood because you lack appropriate storage areas.	• Do not use the fume hood as a storage area.
• Students who have finished their lab work take off their goggles when they begin writing up their results.	• Make sure protection is used not only by the lab worker but also by anyone working nearby.
• You pipette by mouth because you know how to do it properly.	• Never pipette by mouth.
• No extra precautions are taken when handling liquid nitrogen.	• Tape all Dewar flasks.

Purchasing and using chemicals

• You prepare your solutions from concentrated stock to save money.	• Reduce risks by ordering diluted instead of concentrated substances.
• You purchase plenty of chemicals to be sure that you won't run out.	• Purchase chemicals in class-size quantities, if at all possible.
• You purchase chemicals in large quantities to save money.	• Do not purchase or have on hand more than one year's supply of each chemical.
• Each year you have some excess chemicals, but you reorder more so that you don't run out.	• Dispose of or use up any chemicals leftover at the end of one year before the next year is over.
• When chemicals arrive, you unpack them and place them in your storage room.	• Label all chemicals accurately with the date of receipt, and write the initials of the person responsible for unpacking that chemical on the label.

Accidents waiting to happen	Precautions for prevention
• You don't generally read labels on chemicals when preparing solutions for a lab.	• Never open a reagent package until the label has been read and completely understood.
• You don't read labels on chemicals you have been using for years because you already know all there is to know about them already.	• Read each label to be sure it states the hazards and describes the precautions and first aid procedures (when appropriate) that apply to the contents in case someone else has to deal with the chemical in an emergency.
• You never read the Material Safety Data Sheets (MSDSs) that come with your chemicals.	• Always read the Material Safety Data Sheet (MSDS) for a chemical before using it. Follow the precautions described in that Material Safety Data Sheet.
• You throw away the MSDS after you read them because they clutter your storage area.	• File and organize MSDSs for all chemicals where they can be found easily in case of an emergency.
• You put a copy of the warnings from the concentrated acid label on a bottle of the diluted acid.	• Label the diluted acids and bases with the hazards, precautions, and first aid procedures that apply specifically to them.
• Large reagent bottles of flammable chemicals are kept on the open shelves of the laboratory for days at a time.	• Store no more than one day's supply of flammable liquids or solids on the open shelves of the laboratory. At the end of the day, store any such unused chemical in a flammable-liquid storage cabinet.
• Bottles of chemicals are kept on shelves in the lab. The main stockroom contains chemicals that haven't been used for years.	• Do not leave bottles of chemicals unused on shelves in the lab for more than one week or unused in the main stockroom for more than one year.
• No extra precautions are taken when flammable liquids are dispensed from their containers.	• When transferring flammable liquids from bulk containers, ground the container, and before transferring to a smaller metal container, ground both containers.

Chemical Storage

• Students are told to put their broken glass and solid chemical wastes in the trash can.	• Have separate containers for trash, for broken glass, and for different categories of hazardous chemical wastes.
• Students obtain their chemicals and equipment from stockrooms or storage areas.	• Lock all storage spaces; only permit teachers to enter.
• You haven't updated your chemical inventory in years.	• Keep an accurate and up-to-date inventory of chemicals on hand.
• You're not sure which chemicals are incompatible.	• Use MSDSs to determine which chemicals are incompatible.
• You keep mutually reactive chemicals stored by hazard class, but flammable liquids and solids are stored on the shelves of the storage area.	• Keep incompatible classes of mutually reactive chemicals (e.g., acids and bases, oxidizers and reducers, nitric acid and glacial acetic acid) separate from each other in the storage area. Store bulk quantities of flammable liquids and solids in a flammable materials storage cabinet or in a separate room specifically designed and designated to be used for such storage only.
• Corrosives are kept above eye level, out of reach from anyone who is not authorized to be in the storeroom.	• Always store corrosive chemicals on shelves below eye level.

Accidents waiting to happen	Precautions for prevention
• Chemicals are kept on the floor of the stockroom on the days that they will be used so that they are easy to find.	• Never store chemicals or other materials on floors or in the aisles of the laboratory or storeroom, even for a few minutes.
• Chemicals are stored on laboratory shelves because the storage room is too crowded.	• Return chemicals on the laboratory shelves to storage as soon as they are no longer needed.
• Stacked boxes are used instead of shelves.	• Equip chemical storage shelves with lips; never use stacked boxes in lieu of shelves.
• A second-hand refrigerator is used for lab storage.	• Use only an "explosion-proof" refrigerator for lab storage.
• Chemicals are stored without consideration of possible emergencies (fire, earthquake, flood, etc.), which could compound the hazards.	• Store chemicals that are incompatible with common fire-fighting media like water (such as alkali metals) or carbon dioxide (such as alkali and alkaline-earth metals) under conditions that eliminate the possibility of a reaction with water or carbon dioxide if it is necessary to fight a fire in the storage area.
• Batteries are stored with no extra precautions.	• Cover both terminals of dry cells and rechargeable batteries with insulating tape when storing them.

Disposal of Chemicals

Although all chemicals can potentially cause harm to a great or lesser degree, only a relatively small percentage of waste chemicals is classified as hazardous by EPA regulations. The EPA regulations are derived from two acts (as amended) passed by the Congress of the United States: RCRA (Resource Conservation and Recovery Act) and CERCLA (Comprehensive Environmental Response, Compensation, and Liability Act).

In addition, some states have enacted legislation governing the disposal of hazardous wastes that differs to some extent from the federal legislation. The disposal procedures described in this book have been designed to comply with the federal legislation as described in the EPA regulations.

• In most cases these disposal procedures will probably comply with your state's disposal requirements. However, to be sure of this, check with your state's environmental agency. If a particular disposal procedure does not comply with your state requirements, ask that office to assist you in devising a procedure that is in compliance.

The following general practices are recommended in addition to the procedures identified above.

• Except when otherwise specified in the disposal procedures, neutralize acidic and basic wastes with 1.0 M sodium hydroxide, NaOH, or 1.0 M sulfuric acid, H_2SO_4, which you add slowly while stirring.

• In dealing with a waste-disposal contractor, prepare a complete list of the chemicals you want to dispose of.

• Classify each of the chemicals on your disposal list as a hazardous or nonhazardous waste chemical. Check with your local environmental agency office for the details of such classification.

• Unlabeled bottles are a special problem. They must be identified to the extent that they can be classified as a hazardous or nonhazardous waste. Some landfills will analyze an unknown waste for a fee. It must be labeled as a sample and shipped to the landfill in a separate package with instructions to analyze the contents sufficiently to allow proper disposal.

Electrical Safety

The following safety precautions to avoid electric shocks must be followed any time electrical equipment is present in the lab.

- Each electrical socket in the laboratory must be a three-hole socket and must be protected with a GFI (ground-fault interrupter) type circuit.

- Check the polarity of all circuits with a polarity tester from an electronics supply store before use. Repair any incorrectly wired sockets.

- Use only electrical equipment equipped with a three-wire cord and three-prong plug.

- Be sure all electrical equipment is turned off before it is plugged into a socket. Turn off electrical equipment before it is unplugged.

- Wiring hookups should be made or altered only when the apparatus is disconnected from the power source and the power switch is turned off.

- Do not let electric cords dangle from work stations; dangling cords are a tripping and shock hazard.

- Do not use electrical equipment with frayed or twisted cords.

- The area under and around electrical equipment should be dry; cords should not lie in puddles of spilled liquid.

- Hands should be dry when using electrical equipment.

- Do not use electrical equipment powered by 110–115 V alternating current for "conductivity" demonstrations or for any other use in which bare wires are exposed, even if the current is connected to a lower voltage AC or DC connection.

- Use dry cells or Ni-Cad rechargeable batteries as direct current sources. Do not use automobile storage batteries or AC to DC converters; these two sources of DC current can present serious shock hazards.

Eyewash Fountain

Do you know how to operate an eyewash fountain?

Make sure you know exactly how to use an eyewash fountain—it could save someone's eyesight. Be certain to instruct anyone working in the lab in the proper use of the eyewash fountain, as outlined below.

- If your eyes are exposed to chemicals, walk immediately to an eyewash fountain, preferably within 15 s of exposure.

- Immediately start flushing your eyes; continue for at least 15 min while someone else calls a doctor.

- Keep your eyes wide open; with your fingers, lift your upper and lower lids away from the eyeball so that the flowing water washes across it.

- Move your eyes continuously up, down, left, right, across, and around. This will help the flowing water get inside the eyeball socket and wash out any chemicals.

Prepared by Jay A. Young, Consultant, Chemical Health and Safety, Silver Spring, MD

References

1. Budavari, Susan, ed. *The Merck Index.* 12th ed. Rahway, NJ: Merck and Co., 1996. Use this reference for reliable general information about a chemical instead of using a less reliable chemical dictionary or one of the many books with the words "Dangerous Properties" as part of the title.

2. Council Committee of Chemical Safety. *Safety in Academic Chemistry Laboratories.* 5th ed., Washington, DC: American Chemical Society, 1995. This is the authority if you wish a brief treatment. Single copies are free. For a more extensive treatment, see Young, below.

3. "Fire Protection for Laboratories Using Chemicals" (also known as "NFPA-45") Current edition. National Fire Protection Association. Batterymarch Park, Quincy, MA This is the national safety code for laboratory fire protection and prevention.

4. Gerlovich, J. A., et al. *School Science Safety.* Batavia, IL: Flinn Scientific, Inc., 1984. This is a practical guide in two volumes for teachers.

5. Pipitone, D. A., and D. Hedberg. "Safe Chemical Storage." *Journal of Chemical Education.* Vol. 59 (1982), A159. A discussion on the proper storage of chemicals. Also see Pipitone, D. A. *Safe Storage of Laboratory Chemicals.* 2nd ed. New York: Wiley-Interscience, 1991 and the current edition of the *Flinn Scientific Catalog,* Flinn Scientific, Inc., Batavia, IL.

6. "Practice for Occupational and Educational Eye and Face Protection, Z87.1," "Emergency Eyewash and Shower Equipment, Z358.1," "American National Standard for Laboratory Ventilation, Z9.5." Current editions. American National Standards Institute. New York. These standards are recognized worldwide as reliable. Safety goggles and face shields that meet Z87.1 requirements are marked Z87.

7. Reese, K. M. *Health and Safety Guidelines for Chemistry Teachers.* Washington, DC: American Chemical Society, 1980. This source contains several useful tips on enhancing safety in your laboratory.

8. *Standard First Aid and Personal Safety,* American Red Cross. Your local Red Cross chapter probably gives a short course in first aid. This book summarizes the content of that course.

9. Young, Jay A. "Risk Assessment and Hazard Evaluation for Undergraduate Laboratory Experiments," *Journal of Chemical Education,* 59 (1982), A265. This provides some suggestions on teaching your students how to practice safety in the lab.

10. Young, Jay A., ed. *Improving Safety in the Chemical Laboratory: A Practical Guide.* 2nd ed. New York: Wiley-Interscience, 1991. The details of this topic are fully discussed.

Master Materials List for In-Text Labs

Chemicals

This listing shows the amounts needed for 15 lab groups to perform all of the Quick Labs (Q) and Experiments. Solution preparations are found in the Teacher's Edition margin for that lab and on the *One-Stop Planner* CD-ROM. Catalog numbers are given for ordering from Sargent-Welch, 1-800-727-4368.

Chemical	Amount Needed	Experiment	Cat. No.	Pack. Quant.
Acetic acid solution, 5%	12.2 L	Q17, 3-1, 9-1, 16-4, 21-2, 21-3	WLC3016	
Acetic acid, glacial	2.3 mL	9-1, 18-2	WLC3016E	
Acetone	40 mL	21-1	WLC3028E	500 mL
Alizarin red	1.0 g	16-2	WLC3066P	10 G
Aniline blue	1.0 g	16-2		
Brilliant green	1.0 g	16-2		
Bromcresol green	1.0 g	16-2	WLC3310C	100 mL
Bromcresol purple	1.0 g	16-2	WLC3313E	500 mL
Bromophenol blue	1.0 g	16-2	WLC3317N	5 G
Calcium carbonate	105 g	16-3	WLC3409R	100 g
Calcium chloride	55 g	4-1	WLC3421R	100 g
Calcium sulfate	0.1 g	14-1	WLC3457T	500 g
Copper(II) chloride	5 g	Q19, 7-2	WLC3634Q	25 g
Crystal violet	1.0 g	16-2	WLC3616K	1 g
Dry ice	150 g	12-1, 12-2	Local Supply	
Ethanol (denatured)	250 mL	7-2, 16-1, 16-2, 16-3, 16-4	WLC3061E	500 mL
Ethanol solution, 50%	50 mL	21-3		
Hydrochloric acid, concentrated	350 mL	1-2, 4-1, 13-2, 16-1, 16-2, 16-4, 17-2, 18-2, 21-1	WLC3895E	500 mL
Hydrogen peroxide, 3%	150 mL	Q19	WLC3922E	500 mL
Iodine, crystal	0.4 g	16-3, 21-1	WLC3958Q	25 g
Iron(III) ammonium citrate (10% solution)	100 g	19-1	WLC3757R	100 g
Iron(III) chloride, hexahydrate	0.65 kg	7-2, 13-2, 14-1, 16-3	WLC3763T	500 g
Iron(III) nitrate, nonahydrate	82.0 g	18-1	WLC3772R	100 g
Iron(II) sulfate, heptahydrate	350 mL	19-2		
Isopropanol	425 mL	13-1, 16-2	WLC3991E	500 mL
Lactic acid, 85%, lab grade	2.2 mL	18-2	WLC4000C	100 mL
Latex, liquid	155 mL	21-3	WLC4009E	500 mL
Lithium sulfate, hydrate	65 g	4-1		
Manganese(IV) oxide	15 g	Q19	WLC4150R	100 g
Methyl orange	4.00 g	16-3	WLC4219Q	25 g
Methyl red	1.0 g	16-2		
Nitric acid, concentrated	38 mL	18-1	WLC4306E	500 mL
Phenolphthalein	4.00 g	7-2, 16-1, 16-2, 16-3, 16-4	WLC4381Q	25 g
Potassium ferricyanide	100 g	19-1	WLC4444R	100 g
Potassium iodate	1.07 g	17-3	WLC4471Q	25 g
Potassium nitrate	320 g	7-1	WLC4486T	500 g
Potassium permanganate	3.16 g	19-2	WLC4504R	100 g
Potassium sulfate	87 g	4-1	WLC4516R	100 g

Chemical	Amount Needed	Experiment	Cat. No.	Pack. Quant.
Potassium thiocyanate	0.194 g	18-1	WLC4522R	100 g
Rock salt	300 g	7-1	WLC4545V	2.5 kg
Silver nitrate	0.43 g	14-1	WLC4579N	5 G
Sodium bicarbonate	65 g	9-1, 21-2	WLC4609T	500 g
Sodium carbonate	53.0 g	9-2	WLC4630T	500 g
Sodium chloride	175 g	4-1, 7-1	WLC4642T	500 g
Sodium chloride crystals	45 g	4-1	WLC4535T	500 g
Sodium hydroxide pellets	60 g	7-1, 16-3, 16-4, 17-2	WLC4678T	500 g
Sodium oxalate	1.68 g	14-1	WLC4720R	100 g
Sodium pyrosulfate	0.05 g	17-3	WLC4727T	500 g
Sodium silicate solution	185 mL	21-3	WLC4729E	500 mL
Sodium sulfate	71 g	4-1	WLC4735R	100 g
Sodium tetraborate, decahydrate	30 g	Q13	WLC4621T	500 g
Sodium thiocyanate	1.01 g	14-1	WLC4741T	500 g
Starch (water-soluble)	1.0 g	Q13, 17-3, 21-1	WLC4768R	100 g
Strontium chloride, hexahydrate	220 g	4-1, 9-2	WLC4786T	500 g
Strontium nitrate	2.64 g	14-1	WLC4789R	100 g
Sucrose	180 g	Q13	WLC4798T	500 g
Sulfuric acid, concentrated	60 mL	17-3	WLC4825E	500 mL
Thymolphthalein	1.0 g	16-2	WLC4882N	5 g

Equipment

This list shows the equipment and laboratory apparatus needed for 15 lab groups to perform all of the Quick Labs (Q) and Experiments. In some cases, students can work through the Experiments faster if there is more glassware available so they do not need to stop and wash glassware during the procedures.

Equipment	Amount Needed	Experiment	Cat. No.	Pack. Quant.
Aspirator	15	7-1, 9-2	WLS33585	
Balance, centigram	15	Q2, Q13, 7-1, 9-1, 17-2	WLS3448	
Balance, triple beam	15	Q3, 3-1, 9-2, 16-1, 16-4, 17-1	WLS3455	
Beaker tongs	15	9-1, 9-2, 17-1	WLS82105	
Beaker, 100 mL	45	16-1, 16-4	WLS4678-HH	12
Beaker, 150 mL	60	7-1	WLS4678-JJ	12
Beaker, 250 mL	45	Q19, 4-1, 9-2, 13-2, 16-4, 19-2, 21-2	WLS4678-KK	12
Beaker, 400 mL	30	Q13, 17-1, 19-2	WLS4678-LL	12
Beaker, 50 mL	60	Q15	WLS4678-GG	12
Beaker, 600 mL	15	Q15	WLS4678-MM	6
Bottle, 50 mL	15	16-1	WLS8625-B	
Büchner funnel	15	7-1, 9-2	WLS35555-C	
Bunsen burner	15	Q17, 4-1, 7-1, 7-3, 9-1, 17-1	WLS11705	
Bunsen burner lighter	15	Q17, 4-1, 7-1, 7-3, 9-1, 17-1	WLS13110-10	
Bunsen burner tubing	15	Q17, 4-1, 7-1, 7-3, 9-1, 17-1	WLS13121-A	
Buret clamp, double	15	16-4, 19-2	WL4727D	
Burets, 50 mL	30	16-4, 19-2	WLS10627-C	
Chromatography paper, 12 cm circular	60	13-1, 16-2		
Clay triangle	15	7-3	WLS82415-B	10
Clock with second hand	1	Q11, 17-3, 21-1	WLS19790	
Cobalt glass plate	15	14-1	WLS69945-B	12

Equipment	Amount Needed	Experiment	Cat. No.	Pack. Quant.
Conductivity tester, LED	15	14-1, 16-3, 18-2	WL7990-01	
Crucible and lid (ceramic)	15	7-3	WLS23687-E	
Crucible tongs	15	4-1, 7-3	WLS82115	
Cuvette wipes, lint-free	80	13-2, 18-1	WLS19812-A	280
Cuvettes	30	13-2, 18-1	WLS75348-36	100
Dessicator (optional)	15	16-1	WLS25137-A	
Distilled water		Throughout	Local supply	
Drying oven	15	9-2, 16-1	WLS64077-A	
Erlenmeyer flask, 125 mL	60	16-1, 16-4, 19-2	WLS34107-DD	12
Erlenmeyer flask, 250 mL	15	21-2	WLS34107-FF	12
Evaporating dish	15	9-1	WLS25505-C	
Eye dropper	15	7-3, 9-1	WLS69695	12
Filter flask, with sidearm	15	7-1	WLS34365-D	6
Fine tipped droppers (pipets)	170	7-2, 12-2, 14-1, 17-3	WLS69684-35	500
Flame test wire (nichrome)	75 cm	4-1	WLS85125-C	17 m
Forceps	15	1-1, 12-1, 12-2, 16-1, 17-2	WLS35155-20	
Freezer	1	14-1		
Funnels	15	1-1, 7-1, 9-2, 14-1, 21-2	WLS35308-C	
Glass plate (7 × 15 cm)	15	4-1	WLS69945-C	
Glass stirring rod	15	Q13, 7-1, 9-2, 13-2, 17-1, 17-2, 18-1, 19-1, 21-2	WLS40097-B	100
Gloves	15 pair	16-2	WLS40305-05F	Pair
Graduated cylinder, 10 mL	15	Q11, 7-3, 13-2, 16-1, 18-1, 21-3	WLS24667-BB	12
Graduated cylinder, 100 mL	15	Q2, 3-1, 7-1, 9-1, 9-2, 17-1, 17-2, 19-2, 21-2, 21-3	WLS24667-EE	12
Graduated cylinder, 25 mL	30	19-1	WLS24667-CC	12
Hot plate	15	Q13, 7-1, 9-1, 17-1, 21-2	WLS41002	
Litmus paper		16-2, 16-3	WLS6523	100
Magnets	15	1-1	CP32950-10	Pair
Medicine dropper	60	16-1, 21-2	WLS69695	12
Meterstick	15	21-3	WLS44685	
Metric ruler, transparent (0.1 cm)	15	Q3, Q16, 12-2, 13-1	WLS44625-10	12
Microfunnels, long-stemmed	30	1-2	WLS35335-C	12
Micropipet	45	17-3	WLS69684-40B	500
Microplunger	15	3-1	WLS69684-30A	500
Micropressure gauge	15	12-2	Local supply	
Mortar and pestle	15	16-1	WLS62250-50B WLS62251-B	
Petri dish and lid (100 × 15 mm)	15	1-1, 13-1, 16-2, 19-1	WLS26028-25	20
Pipe-stem triangle	15	9-2	WLS82415-B	
Pipet, graduated	60	1-2, 3-1, 12-1, 12-2	WLS69684-40B	
Pipet, jumbo	15	1-2	WLS69684-40B	
Pipet, thin-stemmed	400	1-2, 12-2, 16-1, 16-3, 18-2, 21-1	WLS60684-33	
Pliers	15	12-1, 12-2	WLS70180	
Pneumatic trough	15	7-1	WLS82580	
Portable pH meter	15	Q16, 16-3	WLS30018-01	
Ring	15	7-1, 9-1, 9-2, 17-1	WLS73045-B	

Equipment	Amount Needed	Experiment	Cat. No.	Pack. Quant.
Ring stand	15	7-1, 7-3, 9-1, 9-2, 16-4, 17-1, 19-2	WLS78306-A	
Rubber policeman	15	7-1, 9-2	WLS73215-A	12
Rubber stopper (for test tubes)	15	1-1	WLS73305-C	64
Rubber stopper (one-hole)	15	7-1	WLS73315-C	69
Scissors	15	Q4, Q19, 12-1, 12-2, 13-1, 16-2, 17-1	WLS74367-C	
Separatory bulb	15	1-2	Local supply	
Spatulas	15	Q15, 7-1, 9-1, 9-2, 17-2	WLS75289-A	
Spectrophotometer	1	13-2, 18-1	WLS75410-K	
Stopwatch	15	17-3, 21-1	WLA5615	
Strainer	15	1-2	Local supply	
Test paper, pH, narrow range, 7–10 pH	1 roll	Q16	WLS6520-D	
Test tube (13 × 100 mm)	105	1-1, 1-2, 13-2, 18-1	WLS79515-C	72
Test tube (large, 20 × 150 mm)	15	Q19, 17-1	WLS79515-H	72
Test tube (small, 12 × 75 mm)	360	Q17, 16-3	WLS79515-B	72
Test tube clamp	15	Q19, 17-1	WLS19555	
Test tube rack	15	Q13, 1-1, 1-2, 13-2, 18-1	WLS79065	
Thermometer (−20 to 110°C)	15	7-1, 14-1, 17-1, 17-2, 17-3, 21-2	WLS80008-E	
Tongs	15	Q15, Q17, 17-1, 19-1	WLS82120	
Vacuum tubing for filter flask	15	7-1	WLS73575-F	10 ft
Volumetric flask, 1 L	3-5	For general solution preparation	WLS34810-L	6
Volumetric flask, 250 mL	15	13-2, 21-2	WLS34810-J	6
Wash basins	2	1-2	Local supply	
Wash bottle, 500 mL	15	9-2, 16-4, 19-2	WLS9486-07C	6
Watch glass	15	Q11, 9-1, 17-2	WLS83605-D	
Weighing paper	15	16-1	WLS65223-10A	1000
24-well microplate and lid	15	14-1, 16-3, 18-2, 21-1	WLS70014-80A	
8-well plate	30	4-1, 7-2, 17-3		
Wire gauze with ceramic center	15	7-1, 9-1, 17-1	WLS85335-B	
Wire hooks	15	3	Local supply	
Wire stirrer	15	17-1	Local supply	
Wooden splints	45	Q19, 1-1, 1-2, 21-2	WLS75943	500
Zinc strip, 0.03″	15	Q17	WLC4969T	500 g

Safety Equipment	Amount Required	Cat. No.	Pack. Quant.	Used in Unit
Face shield	1	WLS40414-04		Teacher use only
Impermeable gloves	1 pair	WLS40305-05F		Teacher use only
Lab apron, rubberized, 42 × 27″	30	WLS955-B		All
Safety goggles	30	WLS40380-03B		All

Miscellaneous Materials

This list shows the miscellaneous materials needed for 15 lab groups to perform all of the Quick Labs (Q) and Experiments. Some items in this list are reusable.

Miscellaneous Equipment	Amount Required	Experiment
Aluminum foil	1 roll	Q4, Q19, 1-1
Ammonia, household	150 mL	Q11
Baking soda	255 g	Q9, 3-1, 21-2
Ball point pens, black (4 kinds)	15 sets	13-1
Boiling chips	60 g	17-1
Cabbage, red, fresh	1 head	Q15
Cellophane	1 roll	1-1
Charcoal, activated	60 g	1-2
Chocolate chips	20 cups	Q9
Clay	75 g	Q13
Coffee can covered with sock & objects inside	15	Q3
Coffee grounds, sifted	1/4 tsp	1-2
Cookie sheet	15	Q9
Cooking oil	0.75 L	Q13
Copper foil strip	45 cm	Q17
Corrugated cardboard, 20 × 30 cm	30	Q4, 19-1
Cotton balls	15	1-1
Dark colored water	30 mL	12-2
Dishwashing liquid, dishwasher detergent, laundry detergent, laundry stain remover, fabric softener and bleach	15 mL or 15 g test samples	Q15
Egg	15	Q9
Eggshells	15	16-1
Filter paper	200	1-1, 7-1, 9-2, 13-1, 14-1
Filter paper wicks	30	13-1
Fine-tipped permanent markers	15	Q4, Q13, 1-2
Flashlight	15	Q4, Q13, 1-2
Flour	22.5 cups	Q9
Food coloring, red	1 bottle	Q13
Garlic powder, sifted	1/4 tsp	1-2
Gelatin, plain	45 g	Q13
Glass beads	75 g	17-1
Gumdrops, large and small, 4 colors	Bag	Q8
Hook-insert cap for bottle	15	3-1
Hot-glue gun	15	12-2
Ice	22.5 L	7-1
Index cards	15 packs	Q5
Iron filings	180 g	1-1, 16-3

Miscellaneous Equipment	Amount Required	Experiment
Local river or lake water	15 mL	14-1
Magnesium ribbon	450 cm	Q17, 7-3
Manila folders	15	Q4
Margarine	20 sticks	Q9
Marker, fine-tipped, permanent	15	12-2
Markers, color change (overwrite)	15 sets	16-2
Marking pencil	15	7-2
Matches, safety	1 box	Q17
Mayonnaise, baking soda, white vinegar, cider vinegar, lemon juice, soft drinks, mineral water and milk	15 mL or 15 g test samples	Q15
Measuring spoons and cups	15 sets	Q9
Metal samples, 75 g	30	17-1
Milk, nonfat	18.75 L	21-2
Mineral oil	15 mL	1-2
Mixing bowl	15	Q9
Mixing spoon	15	Q9
Oven	1	Q9
Overhead projector	1	14-1
Paper	45 sheets	21-2
Paper ash		Q17
Paper clips	25	Q17, 1-1
Paper cups, 5 oz	30	21-3
Paper towels	5 rolls	1-1, 9-2, 14-1, 18-2, 21-2, 21-3
Pencils	15	13-1, 16-2
Pennies, dated after 1982	600	Q2
Pennies, dated before 1982	600	Q2
Perfume or cologne	1 bottle	Q11
Plastic bags, resealable	15	3-1
Plastic bucket	15	21-3
Plastic cups, foam	60	17-1, 17-2
Plastic cups, transparent	60	3-1, 12-1, 12-2
Plastic forks	10	1-1
Plastic soda bottle, 2 L	15	3-1
Plastic spoons	25	1-1, 1-2
Plastic straws	10	1-1
Plastic tray	15	1-2
Plastic tub	15	21-3
Poppy seeds	75 g	1-1
Rainwater		Q16
Salt	75 g	Q9, 1-1
Sand	75 g	1-1
Sand paper	15 sheets	Q17
Scissors	15	Q4
Spring water, bottled	15 mL	14-1

Miscellaneous Equipment	Amount Required	Experiment
Stapler and staples	15	13-1, 16-2
Steel wool	15 pads	Q17
Sugar cubes	30	Q17
Sugar, brown	8 cups	Q9
Sugar, white	8 cups	Q9
Tap water	15 mL	14-1
Tape (masking)	Roll	Q4
Tape (transparent)	Roll	1-1, 13-1, 16-2
Tape dispenser	15	1-1, 13-1, 16-2
Thread	Roll	12-2

Miscellaneous Equipment	Amount Required	Experiment
Thumb tacks	60	Q4, 19-1
Tissue paper	1 pkg	1-1, 1-2
Toothpicks	150	Q8, 7-2, 16-3, 21-1
Vanilla extract	15 tsp	Q9
Water		Q2, Q13, Q15
White paper (1 sheet)	45	14-1, 16-1, 21-1
White paper, 8 × 15 cm	15	19-1
White poster board	15	Q4
Wooden stick	15	21-3

UNIT 1

Introduction to Chemistry and Matter

CHAPTERS

1   **Matter and Change**

2   **Measurements and Calculations**

WILLIAM H. HALVERSON, ON THE DIFFERENCE BETWEEN SCIENCE AND THE GADGETS OF SCIENCE

It is a grave mistake to think of science as having to do primarily with test tubes, microscopes, cyclotrons, and the like. One should not confuse the gadgets of science with science itself. "Science" is simply the collective name for the totality of human efforts to achieve a systematic understanding of the physical universe through disciplined inquiry. The purpose of the gadgets is merely to assist in these efforts.

(From *A Concise Introduction to Philosophy*)

Matter and Change

PACING CHART Compression Guide: (To shorten, eliminate items in italics)	CLASSROOM RESOURCES		
	NSE Standards	Teaching Resources	Experiments
1-1 **Chemistry Is a Physical Science** 1 45-minute period *Branches of Chemistry, pp. 6–7*	UCP 1, 5 SAI 2 ST 2 HNS 1, 2 SPSP 5	PE Elements Handbook	A1 Laboratory Procedures B1 Laboratory Procedures
1-2 **Matter and Its Properties** 1 45-minute period	PS 1a, 2b, 2e, 3b UCP 1, 2, 5 HNS 3	**ATE** Demo, p. 12 **ATE** Demo, p. 15 T 1, T 2, T 3, T 4, T 5, TM 1A, TM 2A	Extraction and Filtration, p. 790 Mixture Separation, p. 792 Water Purification, p. 794 C2 **EXP** Separation of Mixtures C2 **INV** Separation of Mixtures—Tanker Truck Spill
1-3 **Elements** 1 45-minute period	PS 2b UCP 1	PE Elements Handbook T 6	

Review and Assessment 1 45-minute period	REVIEW RESOURCES		
	Cumulative Review	Alternative Assessment	Traditional Assessment
	SR Chapter 1 Mixed Review	PE p. 27 **ATE** p. 13 AA Items for Chapter 1	Chapter 1 Text Test Generator Items for Chapter 1

ASSIGNMENT RESOURCES

Section Homework Resources & Review	Problem-Solving Practice
HR Homework Worksheet 1-1 Graphic Org. Assignment 1-1 **PE** Section Review, 1–3, p. 7 Chapter Review, 1–4, 16, 22, 27 **SR** Section Review 1-1	
HR Homework Worksheet 1-2, 1-3, 1-4, 1-5 **PE** Section Review, 1–4, p. 18 Chapter Review, 5–13, 17, 19, 24, 25, 28 **SR** Section Review 1-2	
HR Homework Worksheet 1-6, 1-7 **PE** Section Review, 1–4, p. 24 Chapter Review, 14, 15, 18, 20, 21, 23, 26, 29 **SR** Section Review 1-3	

TECHNOLOGY RESOURCES

Technology & Internet Resources

 CTW 1   Segment 1 Chemical Industry Report
CTW 3   Segment 3 Chemicals in the Home
CTW 10 Segment 10 Paint and Mercury Poisoning
CTW 12 Segment 12 Alloy Technology
CTW 27 Segment 27 Synthetic Soil

 Holt Chemistry Videodiscs Teacher's Correlation Guide for Chapter 1

internet connect

 On-line Student Resources:
www.scilinks.org
The following SciLinks Internet resources can be found in the student text for this chapter.

TOPICS:
• Alchemy, p. 8 (HC2011)
• Physical/chemical changes, p. 12 (HC2012)
• Periodic table, p. 20 (HC2013)
• Element names, p. 22 (HC2014)

On-line Teacher Resources:
GO TO: go.hrw.com
KEYWORD: HC2 HOME
Visit the HRW Web site for a variety of resources related to this chapter.

 Smithsonian Institution
Internet Connections
Visit **www.si.edu/hrw** for additional on-line resources.

 CNNfyi.com
Visit **www.cnnfyi.com** for late-breaking news and current events stories selected just for you.

Resource Key

PE Pupil's Edition
ATE Teacher's Edition

One-Stop Planner CD-ROM Includes these resources and customizable daily lesson plans:

HR Homework Resources
SR Section Reviews
CTW Critical Thinking Worksheets
AA Alternative Assessments

ChemFile
A Laboratory Experiments
B Microscale Experiments
C Technique Builders and Problem-Solving Experiments

D Consumer Experiments
T Transparencies
TM Transparency Masters
PS Mini-Guide to Problem Solving
SRW Supplemental Reading Worksheets

Scoring Rubrics for Labs, Alternative Assessments, Performance Tasks and Portfolio Projects are on the One-Stop Planner CD-ROM.

Matter and Change

Chapter Overview

1-1 defines the field of chemistry and distinguishes between different branches of chemistry.

1-2 defines matter and contrasts major physical and chemical changes that matter can undergo. This section also outlines the basic form of a chemical equation and describes how matter is classified.

1-3 introduces the periodic table as a classification scheme for the elements with descriptions of metals, nonmetals, and metalloids.

Concept Base

This text assumes that students have some prior background in the physical sciences. Therefore, terms such as *atom, element, compound, proton,* and *electron* should be familiar to them.

 Reading Skill-Builder

K/W/L Students probably have preconceptions about chemistry. Have them list what they know about chemistry. Then have them list what they want to know about it. After they have completed Section 1-1, have them look at their lists and write down what they have learned about chemistry. Also, have them write down any new questions that they may have after reading the section.

Matter and Change

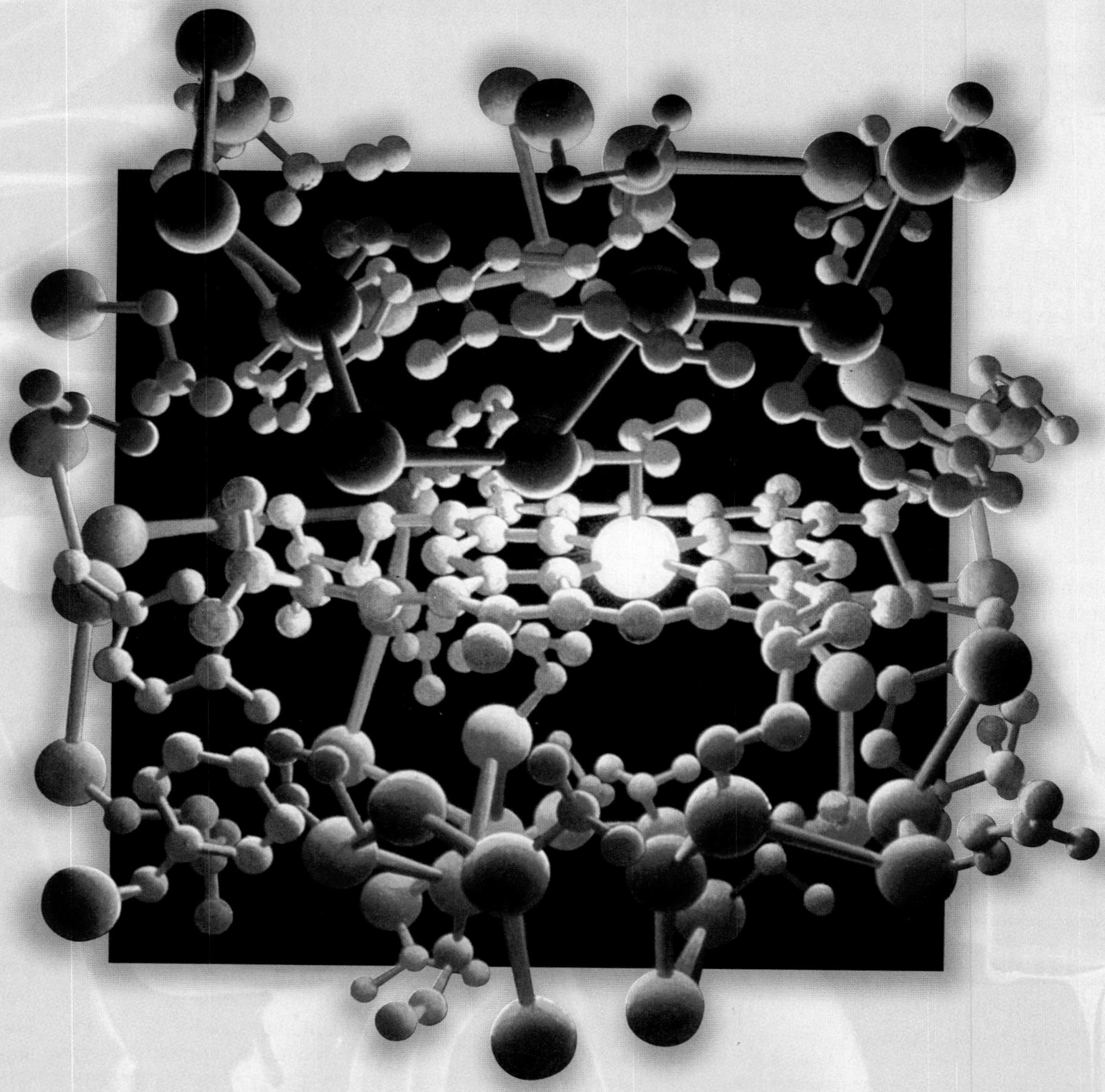

Chemistry is central to all of the sciences.

Chemistry Is a Physical Science

OBJECTIVES

- Define *chemistry*.

- List examples of the branches of chemistry.

- Compare and contrast basic research, applied research, and technological development.

The natural sciences were once divided into two broad categories: the biological sciences and the physical sciences. Living things are the main focus of the biological sciences. The physical sciences focus mainly on nonliving things. However, because we now know that both living and nonliving matter have a chemical structure, chemistry is central to all the sciences, and there are no longer distinct divisions between the biological and physical sciences.

Chemistry *is the study of the composition, structure, and properties of matter and the changes it undergoes.* Chemistry deals with questions such as, What is that material made of? What is its makeup and internal arrangement? How does it behave and change when heated, cooled, or mixed with other materials and why does this behavior occur? Chemists answer these kinds of questions in their daily work.

Instruments are routinely used in chemistry to extend our ability to observe and make measurements. Instruments make it possible, for example, to look at microstructures—things too tiny to be seen with the unaided eye. The scanning electron microscope reveals tiny structures by beaming particles called electrons at materials. When the electrons hit a material, they scatter and produce a pattern that shows the material's microstructure. Invisible rays called X rays can also be used to

FIGURE 1-1 A balance (a) is an instrument used to measure the mass of materials. A sample of DNA placed in a scanning electron microscope produces an image (b) showing the contours of the DNA's surface.

Lesson Starter
Have students consider all of the objects in their classroom that are related to the study of chemistry. Bring different materials, such as plastics, fabrics, fertilizer, clothes, cooking oil, motor oil, nail polish, nail polish remover, aspirin, and vitamins, to class to help initiate discussion. Have students consider their daily activities. How many of these activities have something to do with chemistry?

Visual Strategy
FIGURE 1-1 Use this figure to remind students that there are limits to the ability of our senses to make measurements. Instruments extend our senses and allow us to make quantitative measurements. Try to get students to recognize the benefits of making observations that include measurements.

(a)

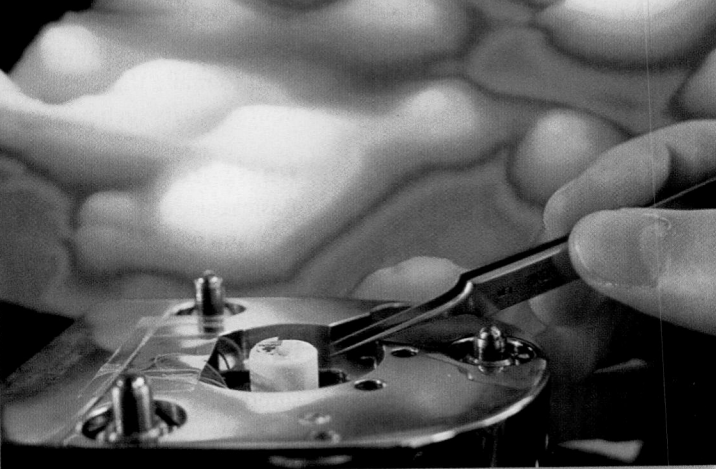

(b)

MATTER AND CHANGE **5**

5

- Students should know that there are no clear-cut divisions that separate one kind of chemist from another. Just as doctors specialize in a certain type of medicine, chemists too have more specialized fields of study, but these fields often overlap.

- Have students bring in articles from news magazines and other periodicals showing chemistry in action. Photography magazines are one good source. Students are often surprised at the number of industries that rely in some way on basic chemical knowledge.

Common Misconception

Students often think of chemicals as artificial, or unnatural. You want them to understand that all matter—living and nonliving, natural or artificial—has a chemical basis. Ask students to try naming anything that they think is not made of at least one chemical.

"look at" microstructures. The patterns that appear, called X-ray diffraction patterns, can be analyzed to reveal the arrangement of atoms, molecules, or other particles that make up the material. By learning about microstructures, chemists can explain the behavior of macrostructures—the visible things all around you.

Branches of Chemistry

Chemistry includes many different branches of study and research. The following are six main areas, or branches, of study. But like the biological and physical sciences, these branches often overlap.

1. *Organic chemistry*—the study of most carbon-containing compounds
2. *Inorganic chemistry*—the study of all substances not classified as organic, mainly those compounds that do not contain carbon
3. *Physical chemistry*—the study of the properties and changes of matter and their relation to energy
4. *Analytical chemistry*—the identification of the components and composition of materials
5. *Biochemistry*—the study of substances and processes occurring in living things
6. *Theoretical chemistry*—the use of mathematics and computers to understand the principles behind observed chemical behavior and to design and predict the properties of new compounds

In all areas of chemistry, scientists work with chemicals. *A **chemical** is any substance that has a definite composition.* For example, consider the material called sucrose, or cane sugar. It has a definite composition in terms of the atoms that compose it. It is produced by certain plants in the chemical process of photosynthesis. Sucrose is a chemical. Carbon dioxide, water, and countless other substances are chemicals as well.

Knowing the properties of chemicals allows chemists to find suitable uses for them. For example, researchers have synthesized new substances, such as artificial sweeteners and synthetic fibers. The reactions used to make these chemicals are carried out on a large scale to make new products such as sweeteners and fabrics available for consumers.

Basic Research

Basic research is carried out for the sake of increasing knowledge, such as how and why a specific reaction occurs and what the properties of a substance are. Chance discoveries can be the result of basic research. The properties of Teflon, for example, were first discovered by accident. A researcher named Roy Plunkett was puzzled by the fact that a gas cylinder used for an experiment appeared to be empty even though the measured mass of the cylinder clearly indicated there was something inside. Plunkett cut the cylinder open and found a white solid. Through basic research, Plunkett's research team determined the nonstick properties, chemical structure, and chemical composition of the new material.

Applied Research

Applied research is generally carried out to solve a problem. For example, when refrigerants escape into the upper atmosphere, they damage the ozone layer, which helps block harmful ultraviolet rays from reaching the surface of Earth. In response to concerns that this atmospheric damage could pose potential health problems, chemists have developed new refrigerants. In applied research, the researchers are driven not by simple curiosity or a desire to know but by a desire to solve a specific problem.

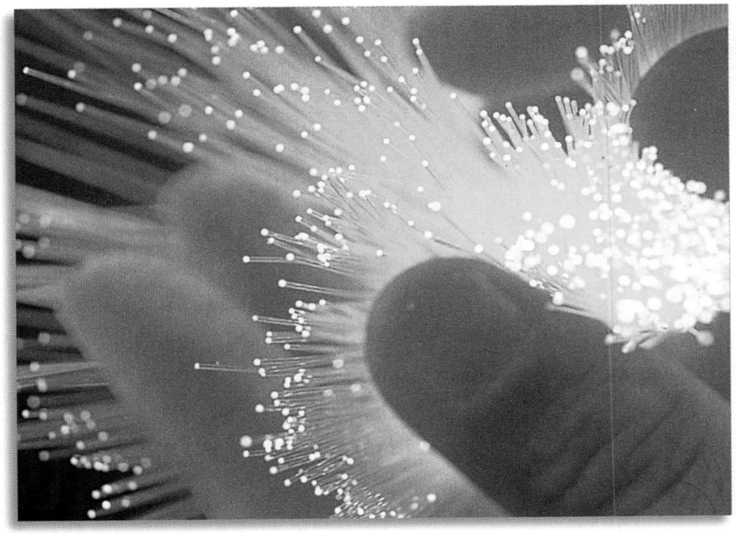

FIGURE 1-2 The chemical structure of the material in an optical fiber gives it the property of total internal reflection. This property, which allows these fibers to carry light, was discovered through basic and applied research. The use of this property to build telecommunications networks by sending data on light pulses is the technological development of fiber optics.

Technological Development

Technological development typically involves the production and use of products that improve our quality of life. Examples include computers, catalytic converters for cars, and biodegradable materials.

Technological applications often lag far behind the basic discoveries that are eventually used in the technologies. For example, nonstick cookware, a technological application, was developed well after the accidental discovery of Teflon. When it was later discovered that the Teflon coating on cookware often peeled off, a new problem had to be solved. Using applied research, scientists were then able to improve the bond between the Teflon and the metal surface of the cookware so that it did not peel.

Basic research, applied research, and technological development often overlap. Discoveries made in basic research may trigger ideas for applications that can result in new technologies. For example, knowledge of crystals and the behavior of light was gained from basic research, and this knowledge was used to develop lasers. It was then discovered that pulses of light from lasers can be sent through optical fibers. Today, information, such as telephone messages and cable television signals, can now be carried quickly over long distances using fiber optics.

SECTION REVIEW

1. Define *chemistry.*
2. Name the six branches of study in chemistry.
3. Compare and contrast basic research, applied research, and technological development.

Class Discussion

Survey students to find out if anyone has a friend or relative who works in the field of chemistry. Invite these people to speak to the class and describe their work. Encourage students to bring questions to class regarding the level of chemistry preparation the speaker needed to work in his or her field. Assign students the task of collecting items for a "Chemistry Careers" bulletin board. Award extra credit to students who find information on chemistry careers that are not within the traditional "scientist" role.

Common Misconception

Students often think that science and technology are the same. Science includes knowledge in its major disciplines, such as biology, chemistry, and physics. Technology is the application of that knowledge for practical purposes.

SECTION REVIEW

1. Chemistry is the study of the composition, structure, and properties of matter and the changes matter undergoes.

2. organic, inorganic, physical, analytical, biochemistry, theoretical chemistry

3. Basic research is conducted for the sake of knowledge only and not to meet practical goals. Applied research is conducted to meet goals defined by specific needs. Technology employs existing knowledge to make life easier or more convenient.

Class Discussion

Ask students if they have ever made a prediction that later turned out to be true. Imagine the hopes of alchemists to be able to change matter from one substance to another. Scientists can now turn metals into gold, but it's too expensive to make gold this way.

Have students construct a time line of the ideas about matter that are represented in this feature, or perhaps use this as a topic of discussion. Ask students if any of the discoveries in this feature were accidental. Were the discoverers always aware of what they discovered?

GREAT DISCOVERIES

Modern Alchemy

HISTORICAL PERSPECTIVE

Until a hundred years ago, chemists were still debating the validity of John Dalton's atomic theory. Few, however, challenged the notion that the elements were unchangeable. Near the beginning of the twentieth century, the discovery of some new elements and the strange radiation they emitted established the connection between atoms and the elements while resurrecting an ancient notion long discarded by science.

Before Chemistry

Until the chemical revolution of the seventeenth and eighteenth centuries, most theories about matter were based on the ideas of the ancient Greek philosopher Aristotle. He postulated that all matter consisted of four elements: earth, water, air, and fire. In turn, each of these elements exhibited two of four fundamental properties: moistness, dryness, coldness, and hotness. By altering these basic properties, Aristotle claimed, the elements could be transformed, or transmuted, into one another.

The practical pursuit of transmutation became known as alchemy, and for more than 1,500 years investigators searched in vain for alchemical methods that would transform common metals such as mercury and lead into precious gold. Then, in the seventeenth

The interior of an alchemist's laboratory is depicted by artist Eugene Isabey.

century, chemists began to question Aristotle's assumptions. They defined an element as a material that can't be broken down into simpler substances, and with no evidence to support the possibility of transmutation of the modern elements, alchemy fell into ill repute.

Strange Rays

In 1896, French scientist Henri Becquerel discovered that the element uranium gave off a strange, invisible radiation. The report of these "uranic rays" caught the

attention of a young chemist by the name of Marie Curie.

Working with her husband, Pierre, Marie began to test various substances for radioactivity. Analyzing a mineral composite called pitchblende, a known source of uranium, she was startled to find that the composite's level of radioactivity was greater than that of a similar amount of pure uranium. This meant that another radioactive material besides uranium was present in the pitchblende.

After months of tedious work, Marie had isolated two new radioactive elements, which she

internet**connect**

SC*L*INKS.
NSTA

TOPIC: Alchemy
GO TO: www.scilinks.org
*sci***LINKS CODE:** HC2011

named polonium and radium, from pitchblende. Curie later won the Nobel Prize for her discovery, but at the time, she was troubled by the seemingly constant energy source of the radioactive process that had led her to the new elements. As she wrote in 1900:

The emission of the uranic rays is very constant . . . The uranium shows no appreciable change of state, no visible chemical transformation, it remains, in appearance at least, the same as ever, the source of the energy it discharges remains undetectable. . . .

The Revival of Transmutation

While Marie Curie was making her momentous discoveries, other scientists were establishing that the chemical elements were actually different types of atoms. The connection between this emerging theory of matter and radioactivity was made by the famous scientist Ernest Rutherford.

In 1902, Rutherford and his assistant, Frederick Soddy, reported that the radioactivity of a sealed sample of thorium (a known element determined to be radioactive by the Curies) had actually *increased* over time. This increase was accompanied by the simultaneous evolution of a radioactive gas. The two investigators began to question whether radioactive elements were as stable as elements were supposed to be. After further studies, Rutherford and Soddy presented their shocking explanation:

The cause and nature of radioactivity is at once an atomic phenomenon and the accompaniment of a chemical change in which new kinds of matter are produced. The two considerations force us to the conclusion that radioactivity is a manifestation of subatomic chemical change.

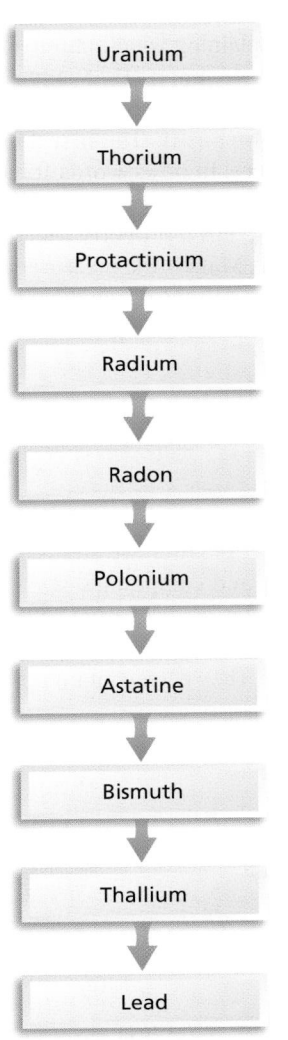

A simplified decay diagram for uranium

Rutherford and Soddy's "subatomic chemical change" was nothing less than transmutation. Nature had turned out to be an alchemist!

The New Alchemy Explained

Rutherford later showed that the spontaneous transmutation, or decay, of radioactive atoms involves the emission of nuclear particles or high-energy waves known as gamma rays, or both. The atom's nucleus is consequently reconfigured, changing the atom into that of another element.

Thus, the source of energy in Marie Curie's uranium sample came from within the radioactive atoms. And although it seemed as if the energy output was constant, the sources of the radiation were continually changing as one radioactive element decayed into another.

Years later, it would be shown that the transmutation of certain elements could be deliberately initiated by bombarding nuclei with accelerated subatomic particles. But the goal of modern alchemy is no longer gold, as Soddy remarked in 1917:

If man ever achieves this control over Nature, it is quite certain that the last thing he would want to do would be to turn lead or mercury into gold—for the sake of gold. The energy that would be liberated, if the control of these sub-atomic processes were possible . . . would far exceed in importance and value the gold.

SECTION 1-2

Lesson Starter

Determine the mass of a deflated balloon. Then blow up the balloon, tie it, and find its new mass. Because the balloon increases in mass, the matter in the balloon must have mass. Point out to students that matter does not need to be visible to us and that it may be made of particles that we cannot see.

✔ Teaching Tip

Ask students to consider the following questions: Which is heavier, a pound of lead or a pound of feathers? What does a pound represent? What happens to the matter of an astronaut who is weightless?

Divide the class into small groups to design a tool that could be used to weigh something aboard the space shuttle. Use the Internet to find out how NASA really does it.

Visual Strategy

FIGURE 1-3 Be sure students understand that the models used throughout this book are *representations* of atoms, elements, and compounds.

Have students compare the models shown. Point out that chemists have different ways of representing the structures of substances. The diamond model is a ball-and-stick representation. Sucrose is shown as a space-fill model. Students will see both types throughout this book.

Explain that sucrose has fixed proportions of the elements that make it up. Carbon consists of all of the same kind of atoms. In this case, the element shown is a solid, so the model reflects the extended array of a crystal. Be sure students understand that elements such as sulfur, phosphorus, and oxygen consist of molecules that have a fixed number of atoms per molecule.

Matter and Its Properties

OBJECTIVES

● Distinguish between the physical properties and chemical properties of matter.

● Classify changes of matter as physical or chemical.

● Explain the gas, liquid, and solid states in terms of particles.

● Distinguish between a mixture and a pure substance.

Look around you. You can see a variety of objects—books, desks, chairs, and perhaps trees or buildings outside. All those things are made up of matter, but exactly what is matter? What characteristics, or properties, make matter what it is? In this section, you will learn the answers to these questions.

Explaining what matter is involves finding properties that all matter has in common. That may seem difficult, given that matter takes so many different forms. For the moment, just consider one example of matter—a rock. The first thing you might notice is that the rock takes up space. In other words, it has *volume*. Volume is the amount of three-dimensional space an object occupies. All matter has volume. All matter also has a property called mass. **Mass** *is a measure of the amount of matter*. Mass is the measurement you make using a balance. **Matter** can thus be defined as *anything that has mass and takes up space*. These two properties are the general properties of all matter.

Basic Building Blocks of Matter

You know that matter comes in many forms. The fundamental building blocks of matter are atoms and molecules. These particles make up elements and compounds. *An* **atom** *is the smallest unit of an element that maintains the properties of that element. An* **element** *is a pure substance made of only one kind of atom.* Carbon, hydrogen, and oxygen are elements. They each contain only one kind of atom.

Carbon atom

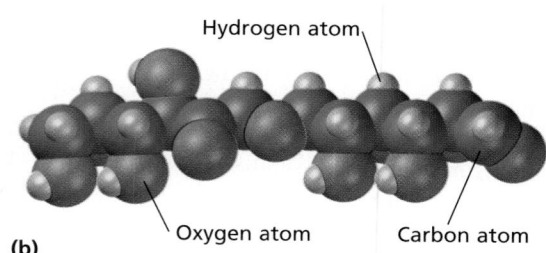

Hydrogen atom

Oxygen atom   Carbon atom

(b)

(a)

FIGURE 1-3 Both elements and compounds are made of atoms, as shown in these models of (a) diamond and (b) sucrose (table sugar).

10

A **compound** *is a substance that is made from the atoms of two or more elements that are chemically bonded.* Many compounds consist of molecules. Water is an example of a compound. It is made of two elements, hydrogen and oxygen. The atoms of hydrogen and oxygen are chemically bonded to form a water molecule. You will learn more about the particles that make up compounds when you study chemical bonding in Chapter 6. For now, you can think of a *molecule* as the smallest unit of an element or compound that retains all of the properties of that element or compound.

Properties and Changes in Matter

Every substance, whether it is an element or a compound, has characteristic properties. Chemists use properties to distinguish between substances and to separate them. Most chemical investigations are related to or depend on the properties of substances.

A property may be a characteristic that defines an entire group of substances. That property can be used to classify an unknown substance as a member of that group. For example, one large group of elements is the metals. The distinguishing property of metals is that they conduct electricity well. Therefore, if an unknown element is tested and found to conduct electricity well, it is a metal.

Properties can help reveal the identity of an unknown substance. However, conclusive identification usually cannot be made based on only one property. Comparisons of several properties can be used together to establish the identity of an unknown. Properties are either intensive or extensive. **Extensive properties** *depend on the amount of matter that is present.* Such properties include volume, mass, and the amount of energy in a substance. In contrast, **intensive properties** *do not depend on the amount of matter present.* Such properties include the melting point, boiling point, density, and ability to conduct electricity and heat. These properties are the same for a given substance regardless of how much of the substance is present. Properties can also be grouped into two general types: physical properties and chemical properties.

Physical Properties and Physical Changes

A **physical property** *is a characteristic that can be observed or measured without changing the identity of the substance.* Physical properties describe the substance itself, rather than describing how it can change into other substances. Examples of physical properties are melting point and boiling point. Those points are, respectively, the temperature at which a substance melts from solid to liquid and the temperature at which it boils from liquid to gas. For example, water melts from ice to liquid at 0°C (273 K or 32°F). Liquid water boils to vapor at 100°C (373 K or 212°F).

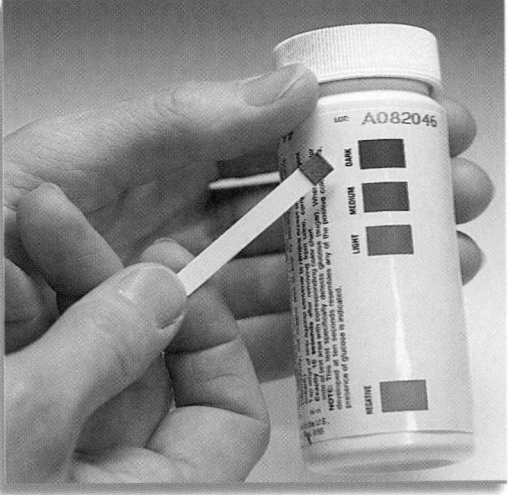

FIGURE 1-4 Because it possesses certain chemical properties, a test strip containing Benedict's solution is used to test for the presence of sugar in urine. The test strip is dipped into the sample. The test strip is then matched to a color scale to determine the sugar level in the urine.

✔ **Teaching Tip**

The particles that make up compounds will be further discussed in Chapter 6. Students may be confused regarding the use of the term *molecule* because all compounds are not made of molecules. It is not necessary to get into the details now.

DEMONSTRATIONS

• Have students look at water and glycerin. They look the same, but they feel different. Tell students that a difference in properties may not be immediately obvious, so we use instruments to measure differences that we may not be able to see. Have students speculate about whether the two liquids are different *substances*.

• Show students the difference in electrical conductivity between distilled water and salt water. This demonstration shows students that differences in properties are not always obvious without using an instrument to measure properties.

Reading Skill-Builder

DISCUSSION Have students read about physical and chemical properties and changes. Then have them choose items in the classroom and classify the properties of each item, giving justification for each classification.

✔ Teaching Tip

Present different properties to students and have them determine whether they are *intensive* or *extensive* properties. Density, conductivity, and melting and boiling points are examples of intensive properties. Heat absorbed, volume, and mass are extensive properties. Compare the two types of properties by heating 100 mL and 400 mL of water. Both will boil at the same temperature (intensive) but the 400 mL sample will absorb more heat (extensive) and will therefore take longer to reach the boiling point. Ask students to predict which beaker will reach room temperature first.

✔ Teaching Tip

Along with the three common states of matter, there are several more. The ultradense matter in a neutron star is unlike a solid, a liquid, or a gas. Another form of matter, the Bose-Einstein condensate, can be created at low temperatures, when a collection of atoms all occupy the same quantum state.

DEMONSTRATION

You can easily model the amount of energy a substance can have by putting marbles in a cup or beaker. The intensity with which you shake the beaker represents the energy of the particles and is demonstrated by how much the marbles move. With very little shaking, the marbles merely vibrate in their positions, like the particles of a solid. With moderate shaking, the marbles move relative to one another but stay inside the container (as in a liquid). With vigorous shaking, the marbles have enough energy to escape the container (as with a gas).

internet**connect**

SC*LINKS*
NSTA

TOPIC: Physical/chemical changes
GO TO: www.scilinks.org
*sci***LINKS CODE:** HC2012

FIGURE 1-5 Water boils at 100°C no matter how much water is in the container. Boiling point is an intensive property.

A change in a substance that does not involve a change in the identity of the substance is called a **physical change.** Examples of physical changes include grinding, cutting, melting, and boiling a material. These types of changes do not change the identity of the substance present.

Melting and boiling are part of an important class of physical changes called changes of state. As the name suggests, *a **change of state** is a physical change of a substance from one state to another.* The three common states of matter are solid, liquid, and gas.

Matter in the **solid** *state has definite volume and definite shape.* For example, a piece of quartz or coal keeps its size and its shape, regardless of the container it is in. Solids have this characteristic because the particles in them are packed together in relatively fixed positions. The particles are held close together by strong attractive forces between them, and only vibrate about fixed points.

Matter in the **liquid** *state has a definite volume but an indefinite shape;* a liquid assumes the shape of its container. For example, a given quantity of liquid water takes up a definite amount of space, but the water takes the shape of its container. Liquids have this characteristic because the particles in them are close together but can move past one another. The particles in a liquid move more rapidly than those in a solid. This causes them to overcome temporarily the attractive forces between them, allowing the liquid to flow.

Matter in the **gas** *state has neither definite volume nor definite shape.* For example, a given quantity of helium expands to fill any size container and takes the shape of the container. All gases have this characteristic because they are composed of particles that move very rapidly and are at great distances from one another compared with the particles of liquids and solids.

At these great distances, the attractive forces between gas particles are much weaker than those in liquids and solids.

An important fourth state of matter is **plasma.** Plasma is a *high-temperature physical state of matter in which atoms lose their electrons* (which you may know about from your earlier work in general science). Plasma is found in a fluorescent bulb.

Melting, the change from solid to liquid, is an example of a change of state. Boiling is a change of state from liquid to gas. Freezing, the opposite of melting, is the change from a liquid to a solid. A change of state does not affect the identity of the substance. For example, when ice melts to liquid water or when liquid water boils to form water vapor, the same substance, water, is still present, as shown in Figure 1-6. The water has simply changed state, but it has not turned into a different compound. Only the distances and interactions between the particles that make up water have changed.

Chemical Properties and Chemical Changes

Physical properties can be observed without changing the identity of the substance, but properties of the second type—chemical properties—cannot. *A **chemical property** relates to a substance's ability to undergo changes that transform it into different substances.* Chemical properties are easiest to see when substances react to form new substances.

Solid

Gas

Liquid

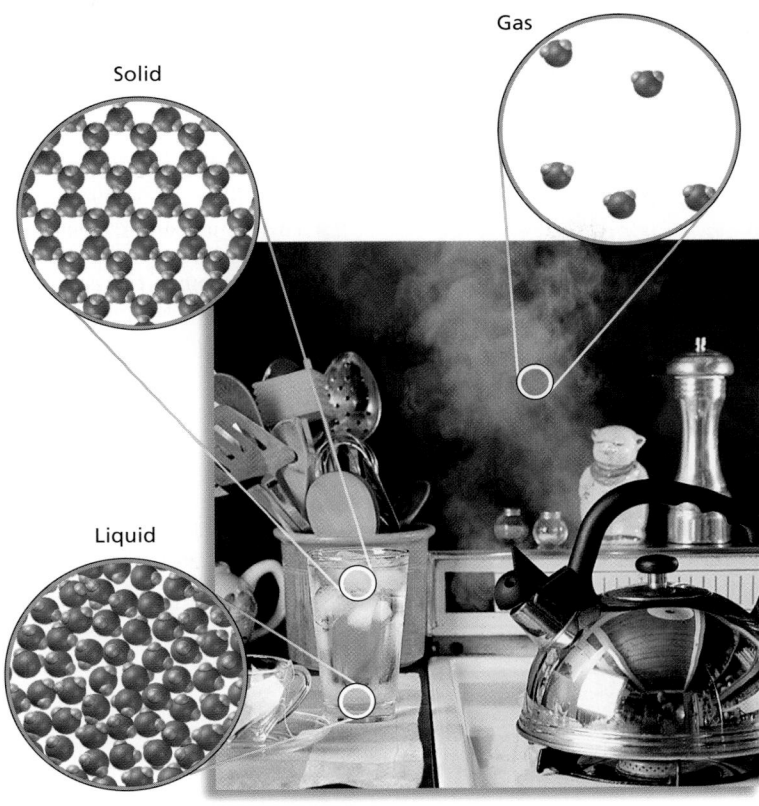

FIGURE 1-6 Models for water in three states. The molecules are close together in the solid and liquid states but far apart in the gas state. The molecules in the solid state are relatively fixed in position, but those in the liquid and gas states can flow around each other.

For example, the ability of charcoal (carbon) to burn in air is a chemical property. When charcoal burns, it combines with oxygen in air to become a new substance, carbon dioxide gas. After the chemical change, the original substances, carbon and oxygen, are no longer present. A different substance with different properties has been formed. Other examples of chemical properties include the ability of iron to rust by combining with oxygen in air and the ability of silver to tarnish by combining with sulfur.

A change in which one or more substances are converted into different substances is called a **chemical change** *or* **chemical reaction.** *The substances that react in a chemical change are called the* **reactants.** *The substances that are formed by the chemical change are called the* **products.** In the case of burning charcoal, carbon and oxygen are the reactants in a combustion, or burning, reaction. Carbon dioxide is the product. The chemical change can be described as follows:

Carbon plus oxygen yields (or forms) carbon dioxide.

Arrows and plus signs can be substituted for the words *yields* and *plus,* respectively:

carbon + oxygen ⟶ carbon dioxide

Make students aware that *all* physical and chemical changes involve some transfer of energy. The body uses energy from the chemical reactions that break down food. Weather involves a transfer of energy to evaporate or condense water in the atmosphere. Therefore, the study of matter also involves the study of energy.

Visual Strategy

FIGURE 1-7 This figure gives students the opportunity to see descriptions of the physical and chemical properties of substances found in the chemical literature.

Have students identify aspects in this figure that signify a chemical change. Ask students to verify that the substances produced have properties different from those of the reactant.

✔ Teaching Tip

This may be a good time to review with students the use of material safety data sheets (MSDS), the *Merck Index*, the *CRC Handbook of Chemistry and Physics, Lange's Handbook of Chemistry,* or other reference materials you may have available in the laboratory. It is important that students take responsibility for knowing the hazards of chemicals in the classroom.

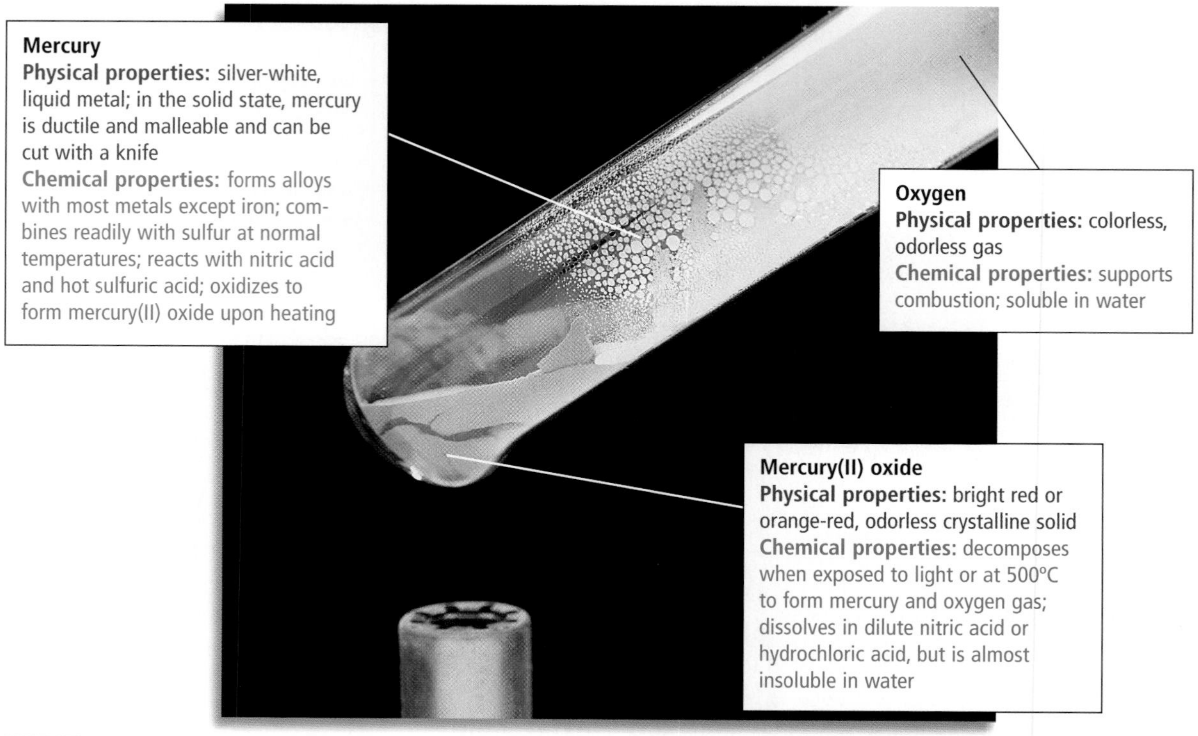

Mercury
Physical properties: silver-white, liquid metal; in the solid state, mercury is ductile and malleable and can be cut with a knife
Chemical properties: forms alloys with most metals except iron; combines readily with sulfur at normal temperatures; reacts with nitric acid and hot sulfuric acid; oxidizes to form mercury(II) oxide upon heating

Oxygen
Physical properties: colorless, odorless gas
Chemical properties: supports combustion; soluble in water

Mercury(II) oxide
Physical properties: bright red or orange-red, odorless crystalline solid
Chemical properties: decomposes when exposed to light or at 500°C to form mercury and oxygen gas; dissolves in dilute nitric acid or hydrochloric acid, but is almost insoluble in water

FIGURE 1-7 When mercury(II) oxide is heated, it decomposes to form oxygen gas and mercury (which can be seen on the side of the test tube). Decomposition is a chemical change that can be observed by comparing the properties of mercury(II) oxide, mercury, and oxygen.

The decomposition of the mercury compound shown in Figure 1-7 can be expressed as follows:

$$\text{mercury(II) oxide} \longrightarrow \text{mercury} + \text{oxygen}$$

Chemical changes and reactions, such as combustion and decomposition, form products whose properties differ greatly from those of the reactants. However, chemical changes do not affect the total amount of matter present before and after a reaction. The amount of matter, and therefore the total mass, remains the same.

Energy and Changes in Matter

When physical or chemical changes occur, energy is always involved. The energy can take several different forms, such as heat or light. Sometimes heat provides enough energy to cause a physical change, as in the melting of ice, and sometimes heat provides enough energy to cause a chemical change, as in the decomposition of water vapor to form oxygen gas and hydrogen gas. But the boundary between physical and chemical changes isn't always so clear. For example, while most chemists would consider the dissolving of sucrose in water to be a physical change, many chemists would consider the dissolving of table salt in water to be a chemical change. As you learn more about the structure of matter, you will better understand why the boundaries between chemical and physical changes can be confusing.

Although energy can be absorbed or released in a change, it is not destroyed or created. It simply assumes a different form. This is the law of conservation of energy. Accounting for all the energy present before and after a change is not a simple process. But scientists who have done such experimentation are confident that the total amount of energy remains the same.

Classification of Matter

The variety of forms in which matter exists is enormous. However, all matter can be classified into one of two groups: pure substances or mixtures. A pure substance can be an element or compound. The composition of a pure substance is the same throughout and does not vary from sample to sample. Mixtures, in contrast, contain more than one substance. They can vary in composition and properties from sample to sample and sometimes from one part of a sample to another part of the same sample. All matter, whether it is a pure substance or a mixture, can be classified in terms of uniformity of composition and properties of a given sample. Figure 1-8 illustrates the overall classification of matter into elements, compounds, and mixtures.

Mixtures

You deal with mixtures every day. Nearly every object around you, including most things you eat and drink and even the air you breathe, is a mixture. *A **mixture** is a blend of two or more kinds of matter, each*

FIGURE 1-8 This classification scheme for matter shows the relationships among mixtures, compounds, and elements.

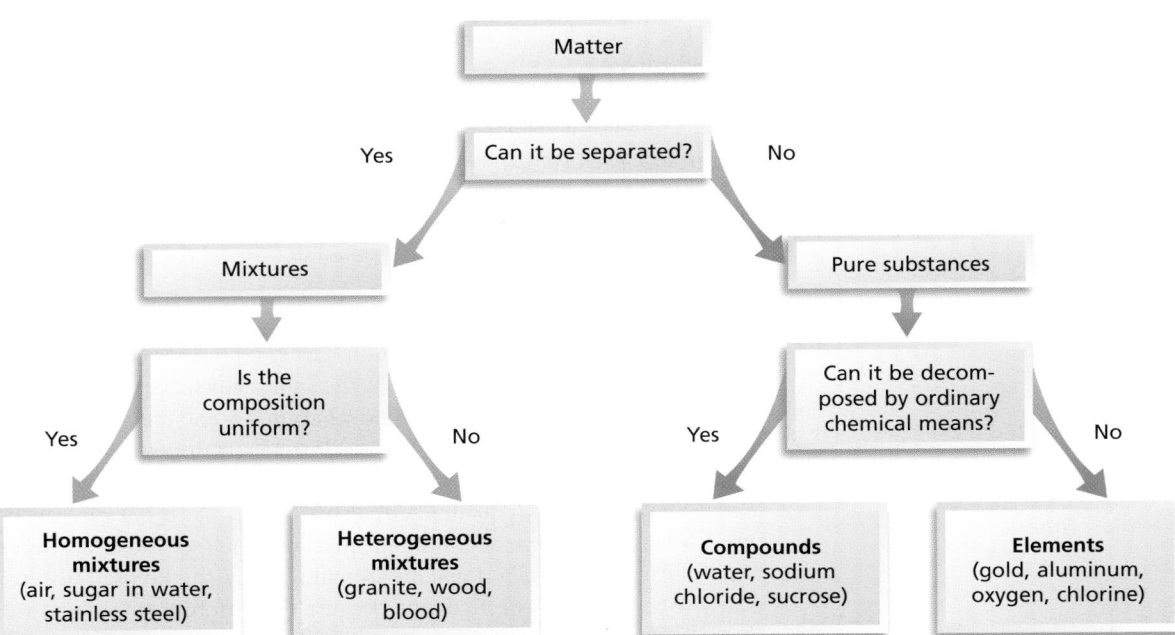

(a)

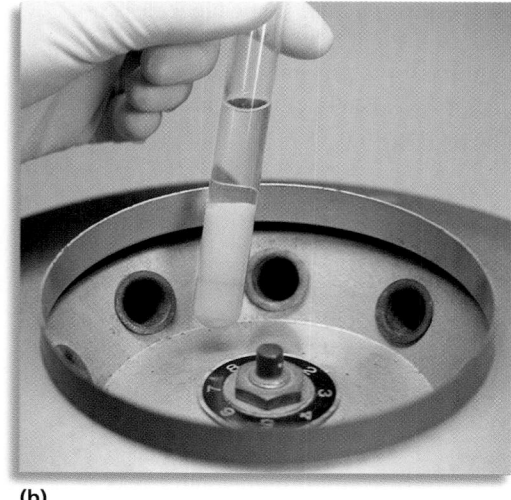

(b)

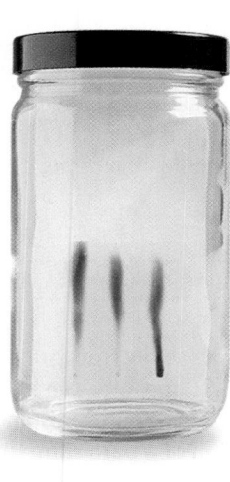

(c)

FIGURE 1-9 (a) Barium chromate can be separated from the solution in the beaker using filtration. (b) A centrifuge can be used to separate certain solid components. The centrifuge spins rapidly, which pushes the solids to the bottom of the test tube. (c) The components of an ink can be separated using paper chromatography.

of which retains its own identity and properties. The parts, or components, of a mixture are simply mixed together physically and can usually be separated. As a result, the properties of a mixture are a combination of the properties of its components. Because mixtures can contain various amounts of different substances, a mixture's composition must be specified. This is often done in terms of percentage by mass or by volume. For example, a mixture might be 5% sodium chloride and 95% water by mass.

Some mixtures are *uniform in composition;* that is, they are said to be **homogeneous.** They have the same proportion of components throughout. *Homogeneous mixtures are also called* **solutions.** A salt-water solution is an example of such a mixture. Other mixtures are *not uniform throughout;* that is, they are **heterogeneous.** For example, in a mixture of clay and water, heavier clay particles concentrate near the bottom of the container.

Some mixtures can be separated by filtration or vaporized to separate the different components. Filtration can be used to separate a mixture of solid barium chromate from the other substances, as shown in the beaker in Figure 1-9(a). The yellow barium compound is trapped by the filter paper, but the solution passes through. If the solid in a liquid-solid mixture settles to the bottom of the container, the liquid can be carefully poured off (decanted). A centrifuge (Figure 1-9(b)) can be used to separate some solid-liquid mixtures, such as those in blood. Another technique, called paper chromatography, can be used to separate mixtures of dyes or pigments because the different substances will move at different rates on the paper (Figure 1-9(c)).

Pure Substances

In contrast to a mixture, a pure substance is homogenous as a single entity. *A* **pure substance** *has a fixed composition and differs from a mixture in the following ways:*

1. *Every sample of a given pure substance has exactly the same characteristic properties.* All samples of a pure substance have the same characteristic physical and chemical properties. These properties are so specific that they can be used to identify the substance. In contrast, the properties of a mixture depend on the relative amounts of the mixture's components.

2. *Every sample of a given pure substance has exactly the same composition.* Unlike mixtures, all samples of a pure substance have the same makeup. For example, pure water is always 11.2% hydrogen and 88.8% oxygen by mass.

Pure substances are either compounds or elements. A compound can be decomposed, or broken down, into two or more simpler compounds or elements by a chemical change. Water is a compound made of hydrogen and oxygen chemically bonded to form a single substance. Water can be broken down into hydrogen and oxygen through a chemical reaction called electrolysis, as shown in Figure 1-10(a).

Sucrose is made of carbon, hydrogen, and oxygen. Sucrose breaks down to form the other substances shown in Figure 1-10(b). Under intense heating, sucrose breaks down to produce carbon and water.

Visual Strategy

FIGURE 1-10 Two very different reactions are shown, but they are both decomposition reactions. Ask students how they know if a chemical reaction has taken place in each photograph. Students should recognize that gases are produced during the electrolysis of water, while there is a color change in the oxidation of sugar.

Point out to students that hydrogen gas differs chemically from oxygen gas even though they look the same. Use this illustration to reinforce the definitions of *atoms*, *molecules*, and *compounds*. Students should also note that two states of matter are represented in the electrolysis experiment.

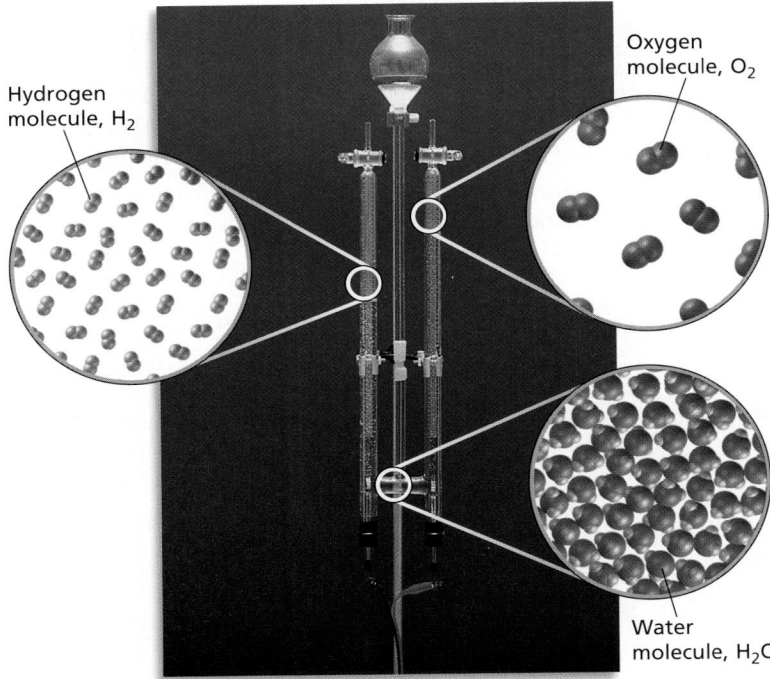

Hydrogen molecule, H_2

Oxygen molecule, O_2

Water molecule, H_2O

(a)

FIGURE 1-10 (a) Passing an electric current through water causes the compound to break down into the elements hydrogen and oxygen, which differ in composition from water. (b) When sucrose is heated, it caramelizes. When it is heated to a high temperature, it breaks down completely into carbon and water.

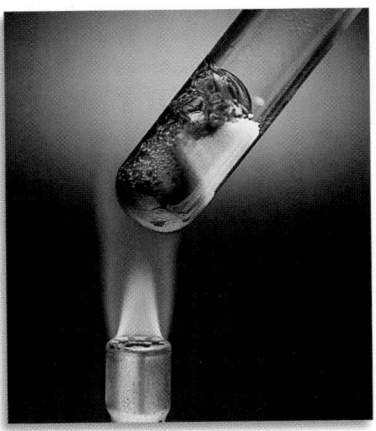

(b)

SECTION REVIEW

1. a. Physical properties can be observed without changing the identity of the substance; chemical properties are observed by changing the substance into different substances. **b.** physical: color, size, boiling point, etc.; chemical: burning of coal, rusting of iron, etc.

2. a. physical
b. physical
c. chemical

3. You can compare the sample with the characteristic properties of solids, liquids, and gases. If the sample has a fixed shape, it is a solid. If its volume changes to fill the volume of different containers, then it is a gas. If neither condition applies, the sample is a liquid.

4. Mixtures contain two or more substances blended together and generally can be separated. Pure substances have a fixed composition.

TABLE 1-1 *Some Grades of Chemical Purity*
Primary standard reagents
ACS (American Chemical Society–specified reagents)
USP (United States Pharmacopoeia standards)
CP (chemically pure; purer than technical grade)
NF (National Formulary specifications)
FCC (Food Chemical Code specifications)
Technical (industrial chemicals)

Increasing purity (vertical label)

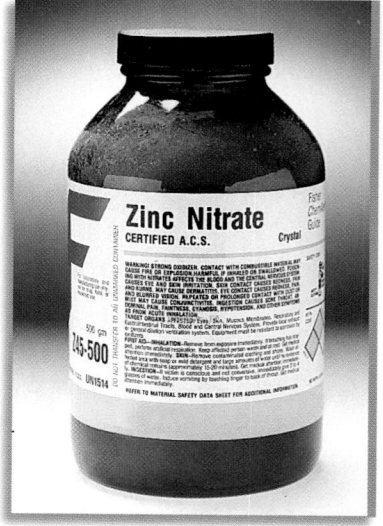

$Zn(NO_3)_2 \bullet 6H_2O$ F.W. 297.47

Certificate of Actual Lot Analysis

Acidity (as HNO_3)	0.008%
Alkalies and Earths	0.02%
Chloride (Cl)	0.005%
Insoluble Matter	0.001%
Iron (Fe)	0.0002%
Lead (Pb)	0.001%
Phosphate (PO_4)	0.0002%
Sulfate (SO_4)	0.002%

Store separately from and avoid contact with combustible materials. Keep container closed and in a cool, dry place. Avoid contact with skin, eyes and clothing.

LOT NO. 917356

FL-02-0588   CAS 10196-18-6

FIGURE 1-11   The labeling on a reagent bottle lists the grade of the reagent and the percentages of impurities for that grade. What grade is this chemical?

Laboratory Chemicals and Purity

The chemicals in laboratories are generally treated as if they are pure. However, all chemicals have some impurities. Chemical grades of purity are listed in Table 1-1. The purity ranking of the grades can vary when agencies differ in their standards. For some chemicals, the USP grade may specify higher purity than the CP grade. For other chemicals, the opposite may be true. However, the primary standard reagent grade is always purer than the technical grade for the same chemical. Chemists need to be aware of the kinds of impurities in a reagent because these impurities could affect the results of a reaction. For example, the chemical label shown in Figure 1-11 shows the impurities for that grade. The chemical manufacturer must ensure that the standards set for that reagent by the American Chemical Society are met.

SECTION REVIEW

1. a. What is the main difference between physical properties and chemical properties?
b. Give an example of each.

2. Classify each of the following as either a physical change or a chemical change.
a. tearing a sheet of paper
b. melting a piece of wax
c. burning a log

3. You are given a sample of matter to examine. How do you decide whether the sample is a solid, liquid, or gas?

4. Contrast mixtures with pure substances.

RESEARCH NOTES

Secrets of the Cremona Violins

What are the most beautiful sounding of all violins? Most professionals will pick the instruments created in Cremona, Italy, following the Renaissance. At that time, Antonio Stradivari, the Guarneri family, and other designers created instruments of extraordinary sound that have yet to be matched. The craftsmen were notoriously secretive about their techniques, but, based on 20 years of research, Dr. Joseph Nagyvary, a professor of biochemistry at Texas A&M University, thinks he has discovered the key to the violins' sound hidden in the chemistry of their materials.

According to Dr. Nagyvary, Stradivarius instruments are nearly free of the shrill, high-pitched noises produced by modern violins. Generally, violin makers attribute this to the design of the instrument, but Dr. Nagyvary traces it to a different source. In Stradivari's day, wood for the violins was transported by floating it down a river from the mountains to Venice, where it was stored in sea water. Dr. Nagyvary first theorized that the soaking process could have removed ingredients from the wood that made it inherently noisy. His experiments revealed that microbes and minerals also permeated the wood, making their own contribution to the mellow musical sound.

Dr. Nagyvary and his violin

Dr. Nagyvary found other clues to the sound of the violins in the work of Renaissance alchemists. Aside from trying to turn lead into gold, alchemists made many useful experiments, including investigating different chemical means of preserving wood in musical instruments. Attempting to duplicate their techniques and to reproduce the effects of sea water, Dr. Nagyvary soaks all his wood in a "secret" solution. One of his favorite ingredients is a cherry-and-plum puree, which contains an enzyme called pectinase. The pectinase softens the wood, making it resonate more freely.

"The other key factor in a violin's sound," says Dr. Nagyvary, "is the finish, which is the filler and the varnish covering the instrument. Most modern finishes are made from rubbery materials, which limit the vibrations of the wood." Modern analysis has revealed that the Cremona finish was different: it was a brittle mineral microcomposite of a very sophisticated nature. According to historical accounts, all violin makers, including Stradivari, procured their varnishes from the local drugstore chemist, and they didn't even know what they were using! Dr. Nagyvary thinks this unknown and unsung drugstore chemist could have been the major factor behind the masterpieces for which violin makers like Stradivari received exclusive credit. By now, Dr. Nagyvary and his co-workers have identified most of the key ingredients of the Cremona finish.

Many new violins made from the treated wood and replicated finish have been made, and their sound has been analyzed by modern signal analyzers. These violins have been favorably compared with authentic Stradivari violins.

A number of expert violinists have praised the sound of Dr. Nagyvary's instruments, but some violin makers remain skeptical of the chemist's claims. They insist that it takes many years to reveal just how good a violin is. In the meantime, most everyone agrees that the art and science of violin making are still epitomized by the instruments of Cremona.

RESEARCH NOTES

Class Discussion
This story is a good example of how chemistry plays a fundamental role in other areas of study. Dr. Nagyvary's study of biochemistry and interest in music led him to investigate the origin and nature of the famous Stradivarius sound.

Students may be surprised to learn that modern technology has not been able to duplicate the effect created by the violin makers of Cremona.

This story is also a good example of the concept of reverse engineering. Reverse engineering is an attempt to duplicate a product already in existence.

Lesson Starter

This might be a good time to make copies of the blackline-master periodic table for each student for use during class and tests. Use these periodic tables or the large table in the room to get students to practice locating particular elements on the table.

TABLE STRATEGY

Table 1-2 Have students use the *CRC Handbook of Chemistry and Physics* to find the language of origin (or meaning) for each of the older names listed in the table.

Stibium—German
Cuprum—Latin
Aurum—Latin
Ferrum—Latin
Plumbum—Latin
Hydrargyrum—Latin
Kalium—Latin
Argentum—Latin
Natrium—Latin
Stannum—Latin
Wolfram—German

✔ Teaching Tip

Have students memorize the names and symbols of the first 30 elements. Quiz them on sets of 10 each week for three weeks. This exercise will help students prepare for writing formulas and balancing equations later in the text. They will also learn names of other common elements with frequent use throughout the course.

📖 Reading Skill-Builder

BRAINSTORMING Review with students the definition of *element*. Have them brainstorm a list of substances that they think are elements. Have them use Section 1-3 to confirm whether each of the substances on their list is an element and to devise a classification system for elements.

OBJECTIVES

- Use a periodic table to name elements, given their symbols.

- Use a periodic table to write the symbols of elements, given their names.

- Describe the arrangement of the periodic table.

- List the characteristics that distinguish metals, nonmetals, and metalloids.

internet connect

SCI LINKS
NSTA

TOPIC: Periodic table
GO TO: www.scilinks.org
***sci*LINKS CODE:** HC2013

Elements

As you have read, elements are pure substances that cannot be decomposed by chemical changes. The elements serve as the building blocks of matter. Each element has characteristic properties. The elements are organized into groups based on similar chemical properties. This organization of elements is the *periodic table*, which is shown in Figure 1-12 on the next page.

Introduction to the Periodic Table

Each small square of the periodic table shows the name of one element and the letter symbol for the element. For example, the first square, at the upper left, represents element 1, hydrogen, which has the atomic symbol H.

As you look through the table, you will see many familiar elements, including iron, sodium, neon, silver, copper, aluminum, sulfur, and lead. You can often relate the symbols to the English names of the elements. Though some symbols are derived from the element's older name, which was often in Latin, wolfram comes from the German name for tungsten. Table 1-2 lists some of those elements.

TABLE 1-2 *Elements with Symbols Based on Older Names*		
Modern name	**Symbol**	**Older name**
Antimony	Sb	stibium
Copper	Cu	cuprum
Gold	Au	aurum
Iron	Fe	ferrum
Lead	Pb	plumbum
Mercury	Hg	hydrargyrum
Potassium	K	kalium
Silver	Ag	argentum
Sodium	Na	natrium
Tin	Sn	stannum
Tungsten	W	wolfram

Periodic Table

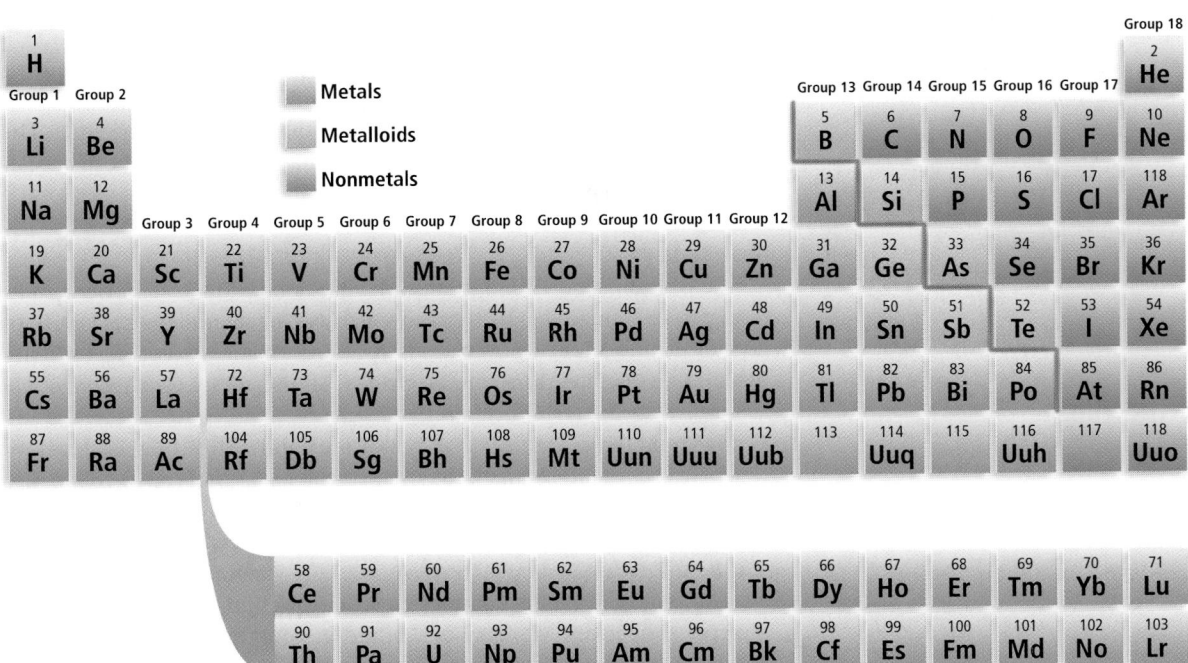

FIGURE 1-12 The periodic table of elements. The names of the elements can be found on Table A-6 in the appendix, pages 896–897.

The vertical columns of the periodic table are called **groups,** or **families.** Notice that they are numbered from 1 to 18 from left to right. Each group contains elements with similar chemical properties. For example, the elements in Group 2 are beryllium, magnesium, calcium, strontium, barium, and radium. All of these elements are reactive metals with similar abilities to bond to other kinds of atoms. The two major categories of elements are metals and nonmetals. Metalloids have properties intermediate between those of metals and nonmetals.

The horizontal rows of elements in the periodic table are called **periods.** Physical and chemical properties change somewhat regularly across a period. Elements that are close to each other in the same period tend to be more similar than elements that are farther apart. For example, in Period 2, the elements lithium and beryllium, in Groups 1 and 2, respectively, are somewhat similar in properties. However, their properties are very different from the properties of fluorine, the Period-2 element in Group 17.

The two sets of elements placed below the periodic table make up what are called the lanthanide series and the actinide series. These metallic elements fit into the table just after elements 57 and 89. They are placed below the table to keep the table from being too wide.

There is a section in the back of this book called the *Elements Handbook,* pages 726–783, which covers some representative elements in greater detail. You will use information from the handbook to complete the questions in the Handbook Search sections in the chapter reviews.

✔ Teaching Tip

Assign each student a different element to research, or have an "element of the day," where a particular element, its properties, and its position on the periodic table are highlighted.

Visual Strategy

FIGURE 1-12 The periodic table will be formally introduced in Chapter 5. This table is included here to give students a context for the discussion of elements.

Be sure students recognize the difference between the vertical columns (groups, or families) and the horizontal rows (periods) on the periodic table. Point out that the members of the same group have very similar chemical properties. Tell students that the elements at the base of the table are placed there for convenience. Placing them in the correct sequence makes the table very wide.

Use the periodic table to point out that there are many more metals than there are nonmetals. Summarize the differences between the properties of metals and those of nonmetals.

go.hrw.com
Visit the HRW Web site to see the most recent version of the periodic table.

FIGURE 1-13 Use this figure to show how the properties of metals often determine how they are used, and explain that this is an example of the link between science and technology. Have students brainstorm about other uses of metals that depend on their physical or chemical properties.

Common Misconception

Students often think that all "metals" are the same. Because they are familiar with rusting as a corrosive property of iron, they may think that all metals rust. Make sure they understand that the definition and characteristics of metals are based on their functional properties and not just their appearance.

internet connect

SC/LINKS
NSTA

TOPIC: Element names
GO TO: www.scilinks.org
*sci*LINKS CODE: HC2014

Types of Elements

The periodic table is broadly divided into two main sections: metals and nonmetals. As you can see in Figure 1-12, the metals are at the left and in the center of the table. The nonmetals are toward the right. The elements along the dividing line show characteristics of both metals and nonmetals.

Metals

Some of the properties of metals may be familiar to you. For example, you can recognize metals by their shininess, or metallic luster. Perhaps the most important characteristic property of metals is the ease with which they conduct heat and electricity. Thus, *a* **metal** *is an element that is a good conductor of heat and electricity.*

At room temperature, most metals are solids. Most metals also have the property of *malleability,* that is, they can be hammered or rolled into thin sheets. Metals also tend to be *ductile,* which means that they can be drawn into a fine wire. Metals behave this way because they have high *tensile strength,* the ability to resist breaking when pulled.

Although all metals conduct electricity well, metals also have very diverse properties. Mercury is a liquid at room temperature, whereas tungsten has the highest melting point of any element. The metals in Group 1 are so soft that they can be cut with a knife, yet others, like chromium, are very hard. Some metals, such as manganese and bismuth, are very brittle, yet others, such as iron and copper, are very malleable and ductile. Most metals have a silvery or grayish white *luster.* Two exceptions are gold and copper, which are yellow and reddish brown, respectively. Figure 1-13 shows examples of metals.

FIGURE 1-13 (a) Gold has a low reactivity, which is why it may be found in nature in relatively pure form. (b) Copper is used in wiring because it is ductile and is an excellent conductor of electricity. (c) Aluminum is malleable. It can be rolled into foil that is used for wrapping food.

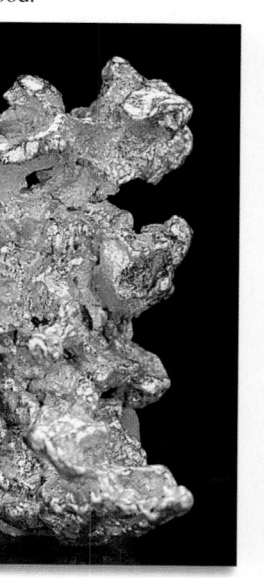

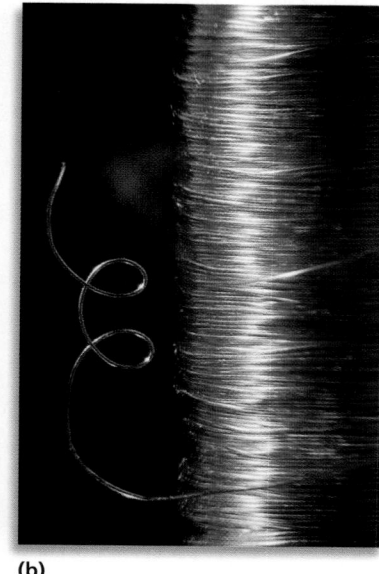

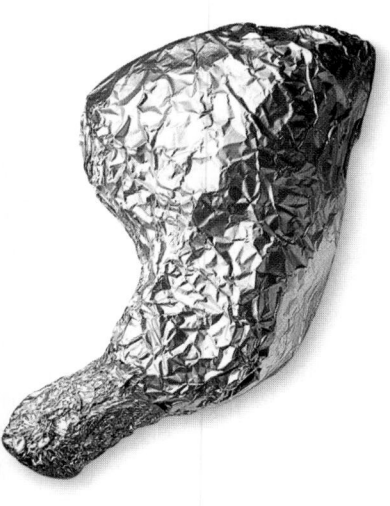

(a)

(b)

(c)

(a)   (b)   (c)   (d)

HANDBOOK CONNECTION

The properties of the elements are discussed in greater detail in the *Elements Handbook,* pages 726–783. Students can look over the transition-metal section to find out more about copper. Group 15 covers phosphorus, and Group 14 includes a section on the properties of semiconductors.

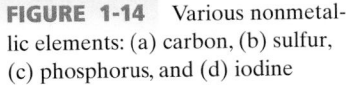

FIGURE 1-14 Various nonmetallic elements: (a) carbon, (b) sulfur, (c) phosphorus, and (d) iodine

Copper: A Representative Metal

Copper has a characteristic reddish color and a metallic luster. It is found naturally in minerals such as chalcopyrite and malachite. Pure copper melts at 1083°C and boils at 2567°C. It can be readily drawn into fine wire, pressed into thin sheets, and formed into tubing. Copper conducts electricity with little loss of energy.

Copper remains unchanged in pure, dry air at room temperature. When heated, it reacts with oxygen in air. It also reacts with sulfur and the elements in Group 17 of the periodic table. The green coating on a piece of weathered copper comes from the reaction of copper with oxygen, carbon dioxide, and sulfur compounds. Copper is an essential mineral in the human diet.

Nonmetals

Many nonmetals are gases at room temperature. These include nitrogen, oxygen, fluorine, and chlorine. One nonmetal, bromine, is a liquid. The solid nonmetals include carbon, phosphorus, selenium, sulfur, and iodine. These solids tend to be brittle rather than malleable and ductile. Some nonmetals are illustrated in Figure 1-14.

Low conductivity can be used to define nonmetals. *A **nonmetal** is an element that is a poor conductor of heat and electricity.* If you look at Figure 1-12, you will see that there are fewer nonmetals than metals.

Phosphorus: A Representative Nonmetal

Phosphorus is one of five solid nonmetals. Pure phosphorus is known in two common forms. Red phosphorus is a dark red powder that melts at 597°C. White phosphorus is a waxy solid that melts at 44°C. Because it ignites in air, white phosphorus is stored underwater.

Phosphorus is too reactive to exist in pure form in nature. It is present in huge quantities in phosphate rock, where it is combined with oxygen and calcium. All living things contain phosphorus.

Metalloids

A stair-step line separates the metals from the nonmetals on the periodic table. Several of the elements in the vicinity of this line are often

FIGURE 1-15 Selenium is a nonmetal, though it looks metallic.

FIGURE 1-16 The noble gases helium, neon, argon, krypton, and xenon are all used to make lighted signs of various colors.

referred to as metalloids. *A* **metalloid** *is an element that has some characteristics of metals and some characteristics of nonmetals.* All metalloids are solids at room temperature. They tend to be less malleable than metals but not as brittle as nonmetals. Some metalloids, such as antimony, have a somewhat metallic luster.

Metalloids tend to be semiconductors of electricity. That is, their ability to conduct electricity is intermediate between that of metals and that of nonmetals. Metalloids are used in the semiconducting materials found in desktop computers, hand-held calculators, digital watches, televisions, and radios.

Noble Gases

The elements in Group 18 of the periodic table are the noble gases. These elements are generally unreactive. In fact, prior to 1962 no noble gas compounds had been identified. That year, the first noble gas compound, xenon tetrafluoride, was prepared. Their low reactivity sets noble gases apart from the other families of elements. Group-18 elements are gases at room temperature. Neon, argon, krypton, and xenon are all used in lighting. Helium is used in party balloons and weather balloons because it is less dense than air.

SECTION REVIEW

1. oxygen, sulfur, copper, silver

2. Fe, N, Ca, Hg

3. Elements in a group have similar chemical properties.

4. Metals tend to be shiny, malleable, ductile, and good conductors of heat and electricity. Nonmetals tend to be brittle and poor conductors of heat and electricity. Metalloids tend to be intermediate in properties between metals and nonmetals and are therefore semiconductors of electricity.

SECTION REVIEW

1. Use the periodic table on the inside back cover to write the names for the elements that have the following symbols: O, S, Cu, Ag.

2. Use the periodic table to write the symbols for the following elements: iron, nitrogen, calcium, mercury.

3. Which elements are most likely to undergo the same kinds of reactions, those in a group or those in a period?

4. Describe the main differences between metals, nonmetals, and metalloids.

CHAPTER **1** REVIEW

CHAPTER SUMMARY

1-1
- Chemistry is the study of the composition, structure, and properties of matter and its changes.
- Chemistry is classified as physical science. Six areas of study in chemistry are organic chemistry, inorganic chemistry, physical chemistry, analytical chemistry, biochemistry, and theoretical chemistry.
- A chemical is any substance that has a definite composition or is used or produced in a chemical process.
- Basic research is carried out for the sake of increasing knowledge. Applied research is carried out to solve practical problems. Technological development involves the use of existing knowledge to make life easier or more convenient.

Vocabulary

chemical (6) chemistry (5)

1-2
- All matter has mass and takes up space. Mass is one measure of the amount of matter.
- An element is composed of one kind of atom. Compounds are made from two or more elements. Any pure compound has fixed proportions of elements.
- All substances have characteristic properties that enable chemists to tell the substances apart and to separate them.
- The physical properties of a substance can be observed or measured without changing the identity of the substance. Physical changes do not involve changes in identity.
- The three major states of matter are solid, liquid, and gas. The particles in these states differ in proximity to one another and ease of flow. Changes of state, such as melting and boiling, are physical changes.
- Chemical properties refer to a substance's ability to undergo changes that alter its composition and identity. Chemical changes, or chemical reactions, involve changes in identity.
- Energy changes accompany physical and chemical changes. Energy may be released or absorbed, but it is neither created nor destroyed.
- Matter can be classified into mixtures and pure substances. Pure substances differ from mixtures in that they have a definite composition that does not vary. Solutions are homogeneous mixtures.

Vocabulary

atom (10)	compound (11)	liquid (12)	physical property (12)
change of state (12)	element (10)	mass (10)	product (13)
chemical change (13)	extensive property (11)	matter (10)	pure substance (17)
chemical property (12)	gas (12)	mixture (15)	reactant (13)
chemical reaction (13)	intensive property (11)	physical change (12)	solid (12)

1-3
- Each element has a unique symbol. The periodic table shows the elements organized by their chemical properties. Columns on the table represent groups or families of elements with similar chemical properties. Properties vary across the rows, or periods.
- The elements can be classified as metals, nonmetals, metalloids, and noble gases. These classes occupy different areas of the periodic table. Metals tend to be shiny, malleable, ductile, and good conductors. Nonmetals tend to be brittle and poor conductors. Metalloids are intermediate in properties between metals and nonmetals, and they tend to be semiconductors of electricity. The noble gases are generally unreactive elements.

Vocabulary

family (21)	metal (22)	nonmetal (23)
group (21)	metalloid (24)	period (21)

REVIEW ANSWERS

1. the study of the composition, structure, and properties of substances and their changes

2. organic

3. a substance that has a definite composition

4. Basic research is carried out to increase knowledge; for example, how and why a reaction occurs. Applied research is practical problem solving; for example, developing new compounds useful as refrigerants. Technological development involves using existing knowledge to improve quality of life; for example, using optical fibers for communications networks.

5. **a.** a measure of an amount of matter
   b. a measure of an amount of space

6. The proportions of elements in a pure substance are fixed.

7. **a.** A property is any characteristic of a substance or material.
   b. useful for classifing unknown materials as members of known groups or subgroups of substances, or to identify substances directly

8. Extensive properties depend on the amount of matter that is present. Intensive properties do not.

9. **a.** a property that can be observed or measured without changing the identity of the substance
   b. Examples include color, odor, length, size, and melting point.

10. **a.** a property that describes the ability of a substance to undergo changes that alter its identity
    b. Examples include the ability of coal to burn and of iron to rust.

11. Physical change does not involve a change in a substance's identity; chemical change converts one substance into other substances.

12. a. A solid state has definite volume and definite shape, whereas a liquid has a definite volume but takes the shape of its container. **b.** A gas has neither definite volume nor definite shape. **c.** Liquids and gases take the shape of the container. **d.** A plasma is a high temperature physical state of matter in which atoms lose their electrons.

13. a change of a substance from one state of matter to another

14. Elements with similar properties are placed in the same vertical columns. Properties vary from left to right along the rows.

15. Metals (at left and center of table) are good conductors of heat and electricity. Nonmetals (at right of table) tend to be poor conductors. Metalloids (on the zig-zag line of the table) are intermediate in properties and are semiconductors. Noble gases (at extreme right) are generally unreactive.

16. a. physical   **c.** biochemical
b. organic   **d.** analytical

17. Reactants are potassium and oxygen; products are potassium hydroxide and hydrogen

18. X is probably a nonmetal on the right side of the table. Z is a metal on the left side of the table.

19. a. physical, because the wood remains wood
b. chemical, because the milk changes composition, as signified by the change in flavor
c. physical, because the butter remains butter

20. a. potassium, metal
b. silver, metal
c. silicon, metalloid
d. sodium, metal
e. mercury, metal
f. helium, noble gas

21. may be malleable, ductile, and a good conductor of electricity

REVIEWING CONCEPTS

1. What is chemistry?   (1-1)

2. What branch of chemistry is most concerned with the study of carbon compounds.   (1-1)

3. What is meant by the word *chemical*, as used by scientists?   (1-1)

4. Briefly describe the differences between basic research, applied research, and technological development. Provide an example of each. (1-1)

5. a. What is mass?
b. What is volume?   (1-2)

6. How does the composition of a pure compound differ from that of a mixture?   (1-2)

7. a. Define *property*.
b. How are properties useful in classifying materials?   (1-2)

8. What is the difference between extensive properties and intensive properties?   (1-2)

9. a. Define *physical property*.
b. List two examples of physical properties. (1-2)

10. a. Define *chemical property*.
b. List two examples of chemical properties. (1-2)

11. Distinguish between a *physical change* and a *chemical change*.   (1-2)

12. a. How does a solid differ from a liquid?
b. How does a liquid differ from a gas?
c. How is a liquid similar to a gas?
d. What is a plasma?   (1-2)

13. What is meant by a change in state?   (1-2)

14. What is the significance of the vertical columns of the periodic table? What is the significance of the horizontal rows?   (1-3)

15. Compare the physical properties of metals, nonmetals, metalloids, and noble gases and describe where in the periodic table each of these kinds of elements is located.   (1-3)

16. In which of the six branches of chemistry would a scientist be working if he or she were doing the following: (1-1)
a. investigating energy relationships for various reactions

b. comparing properties of alcohols with those of sugars
c. studying reactions that occur during the digestion of food
d. carrying out tests to identify unknown substances

17. Identify the reactants and products in the following reaction: (1-2)
potassium + water ⟶
                              potassium hydroxide + hydrogen

18. Suppose element X is a poor conductor of electricity and breaks when hit with a hammer. Element Z is a good conductor of electricity and heat. In what area of the periodic table does each element most likely belong?   (1-3)

19. Identify each of the following as either a physical change or a chemical change. Explain your answers.   (1-2)
a. A piece of wood is sawed in half.
b. Milk turns sour.
c. Melted butter solidifies in the refrigerator.

20. Use the periodic table to write the names of the elements that have the following symbols, and identify each as a metal, nonmetal, metalloid, or noble gas.   (1-3)
a. K   c. Si   e. Hg
b. Ag   d. Na   f. He

21. An unknown element is shiny and is found to be a good conductor of electricity. What other properties would you predict for it?   (1-3)

22. Identify each of the following as an example of either basic research, applied research, or technological development: (1-1)
a. A new type of refrigerant is developed that is less damaging to the environment.
b. A new element is synthesized in a particle accelerator.
c. A computer chip is redesigned to increase the speed of the computer.

23. Use the periodic table to identify the group numbers and period numbers of the following elements: (1-3)
a. carbon, C   c. chromium, Cr
b. argon, Ar   d. barium, Ba

24. a. Suppose different parts of a sample material have different compositions. What can you conclude about the material?　(1-2)

　b. Suppose different parts of a sample have the same composition. What can you conclude about the material? Explain your answer. (1-2)

TECHNOLOGY & LEARNING

25. Graphing Calculator　Graphing Tabular Data

The graphing calculator can run a program that graphs ordered pairs of data, such as temperature versus time. In this problem you will learn how to create a table of data. Then you will learn how to use the program to plot the data.

Go to Appendix C. If you are using a TI 83 Plus, you can download the program and data sets and run the application as directed. If you are using another calculator, your teacher will provide you with keystrokes and data sets to use. Remember that after creating the lists, you will need to name the program and check the display, as explained in Appendix C. You will then be ready to run the program. After you have graphed the data sets, answer these questions.

　a. Approximately what would the temperature be at the 16-minute interval?

　b. Between which two intervals did the temperature increase the most: between 6 and 7 minutes, between 5 and 6 minutes, or between 8 and 9 minutes?

　c. If the graph extended to 20 minutes, what would you expect the temperature to be?

HANDBOOK SEARCH

26. Review the information on trace elements in the *Elements Handbook* in the back of this text.

　a. What are the functions of trace elements in the body?

　b. What transition metal plays an important role in oxygen transport throughout the body?

　c. What two Group 1 elements are part of the electrolyte balance in the body?

RESEARCH & WRITING

27. Research any current technological product of your choosing. Find out about its manufacture and uses. Also find out about the basic research and applied research that made its development possible.

ALTERNATIVE ASSESSMENT

28. Make a list of all the changes that you see around you involving matter during a one-hour period. Note whether each change seems to be a physical change or a chemical change. Give reasons for your answers.

29. Make a concept map using at least 15 terms from the vocabulary lists. An introduction to concept mapping is found in Appendix B of this book.

22. a. applied research
　b. basic research
　c. applied research

23. a. Group 14, Period 2
　b. 18, 3　　**c.** 6, 4　　**d.** 2, 6

24. a. It must be a mixture.
　b. Some mixtures and all elements and compounds fit the description.

25. a. Accept range from 48.4° to 48.6° C.
　b. Between 5 and 6 minutes.
　c. Accept range from 52° to 54° C.

26. a. Trace elements are minerals that are essential for normal body function.
　b. iron　　**c.** sodium, potassium

27. Reports will vary. You can use the scoring rubric on the *One-Stop Planner CD-ROM* to set criteria for evaluating student reports.

28. Students should be able to correctly categorize most of the changes on the basis of whether new substances are being formed (chemical changes) or are not being formed (physical changes).

29. See the criteria for evaluating student concept maps on the One-Stop Planner CD-ROM.

Measurements and Calculations

PACING CHART **Compression Guide:** *(To shorten, eliminate items in italics.)*	CLASSROOM RESOURCES		
	NSE Standards	Teaching Resources	Experiments
2-1 **Scientific Method** 2 45-minute periods 1 90-minute block *Observing and Collecting Data, p. 29* *Testing Hypotheses, p. 30* *Theorizing, p. 31*	UCP 1–3 SAI 1, 2 ST 1 HNS 1–3	**ATE Demo,** p. 29 T 7	**PE** Conservation of Mass, p. 798 **C1** **EXP** Conservation of Mass
2-2 **Units of Measurement** 2 45-minute periods 1 90-minute block *Derived SI Units, pp. 36–38* *Conversion Factors, pp. 40–42*	UCP 1, 3, 5 SAI 1–2 ST 1 HNS 1 SPSP 2, 5	**ATE Demo,** pp. 35, 37 T 8, TM 3A, TM 4A, TM 5A, TM 6A	**PE** Quick Lab, p. 39
2-3 **Using Scientific Measurements** 2 45-minute periods 1 90-minute block *Direct Proportions, pp. 55–56* *Inverse Proportions, pp. 56–57*	UCP 1, 2, 3, 5 HNS 2	**ATE Demo,** p. 51 T 9, T 10, T 11, TM 7A, TM 8A, TM 9A, TM 10A	**A2** Accuracy and Precision in Measurement **B2** Accuracy and Precision: Calibrating a Pipet

Review and Assessment 2 45-minute periods 1 90-minute block	REVIEW RESOURCES		
	Cumulative Review	Alternative Assessment	Traditional Assessment
	SR Chapter 2 Mixed Review **PE** Chapter 2 47–51, pp. 60–61	**PE** 57, 58, p. 61 **ATE** 35, 41, 48 **AA** Items for Chapter 2	Chapter 2 Text Test Generator items for Chapter 2

ASSIGNMENT RESOURCES

Section Homework Resources & Review	Problem-Solving Practice
HR Homework Worksheet 2-1 Graphic Org. Assignment 2-1 **PE** Section Review, 2–1, p. 31 Chapter Review, 1–3, p. 59 **SR** Section Review 2-1	
HR Homework Worksheets 2-2, 2-4 Graphic Org. Assignment 2-2 **PE** Section Review, 3–4, p. 42 Chapter Review, 15, 30–32, p. 59 **SR** Section Review 2-2	**PE** Additional Samples 2-1, 2-2 **PS** Chapter 1 Conversions
HR Homework Worksheets 2-5, 2-8 Graphic Org. Assignment 2-7 **PE** Section Review, 1–4, 7, p. 57 Chapter Review, 16–22, 33–40, p. 59 **SR** Section Review 2-3	**PE** Additional Samples 2-3, 2-4, 2-5, 2-6 **ATE** Additional Samples, pp. 45, 47, 50, 54 **PS** Chapter 2 Significant Figures Chapter 3 Scientific Notation Chapter 4 Four Steps for Solving Quantitative Problems

TECHNOLOGY RESOURCES

Technology & Internet Resources

 CTW 20 Segment 20 Chemical Industry Report

 Holt Chemistry Videodiscs Teacher's Correlation Guide for Chapter 2

internet connect

 On-line Student Resources:
GO TO: www.scilinks.org
The following SciLinks Internet resources can be found in the student text for this chapter.

TOPICS:
• Scientific methods, p. 29 (HC2021)
• SI units, p. 34 (HC2022)
• Detecting air pollution, p. 43 (HC2023)
• Significant figures, p. 46 (HC2024)

 On-line Teacher Resources:
GO TO: go.hrw.com
KEYWORD: HC2 HOME
Visit the HRW Web site for a variety of resources related to this chapter.

 Smithsonian Institution®
Internet Connections
Visit **www.si.edu/hrw** for additional on-line resources.

CNNfyi.com
Visit **www.cnnfyi.com** for late-breaking news and current events stories selected just for you.

Resource Key

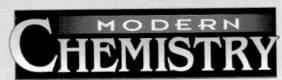

PE Pupil's Edition
ATE Teacher's Edition

One-Stop Planner CD-ROM Includes these resources and customizable daily lesson plans:

HR Homework Resources	**ChemFile**	**D** Consumer Experiments	
SR Section Reviews	**A** Laboratory Experiments	**T** Transparencies	
CTW Critical Thinking Worksheets	**B** Microscale Experiments	**TM** Transparency Masters	
AA Alternative Assessments	**C** Technique Builders and Problem-Solving Experiments	**PS** Mini-Guide to Problem Solving **SRW** Supplemental Reading Worksheets	

Scoring Rubrics for Labs, Alternative Assessments, Performance Tasks and Portfolio Projects are on the One-Stop Planner CD-ROM.

Measurements and Calculations

Chapter Overview

2-1 covers the scientific method and its component activities, such as observing, collecting data, formulating and testing hypotheses, and theorizing.

2-2 presents SI units of measurement, the concepts of mass and density, and the use of conversion factors.

2-3 describes accuracy and precision, percent error, the use of significant figures and scientific notation, and steps to use in solving problems.

Concept Base

Students may need a review of the following concepts:

• the nature of mass and matter, Chapter 1

 Reading Skill-Builder

DISCUSSION It is important for students to understand that science is a process, not just a set of facts. Explain that information about the world around us is always changing. Lead students in a discussion that explores the idea that science always starts with a question. Ask students what they do when they have questions and discuss their responses. Be sure students understand that every time they search for an answer to a question about the world, they are doing science.

Measurements and Calculations

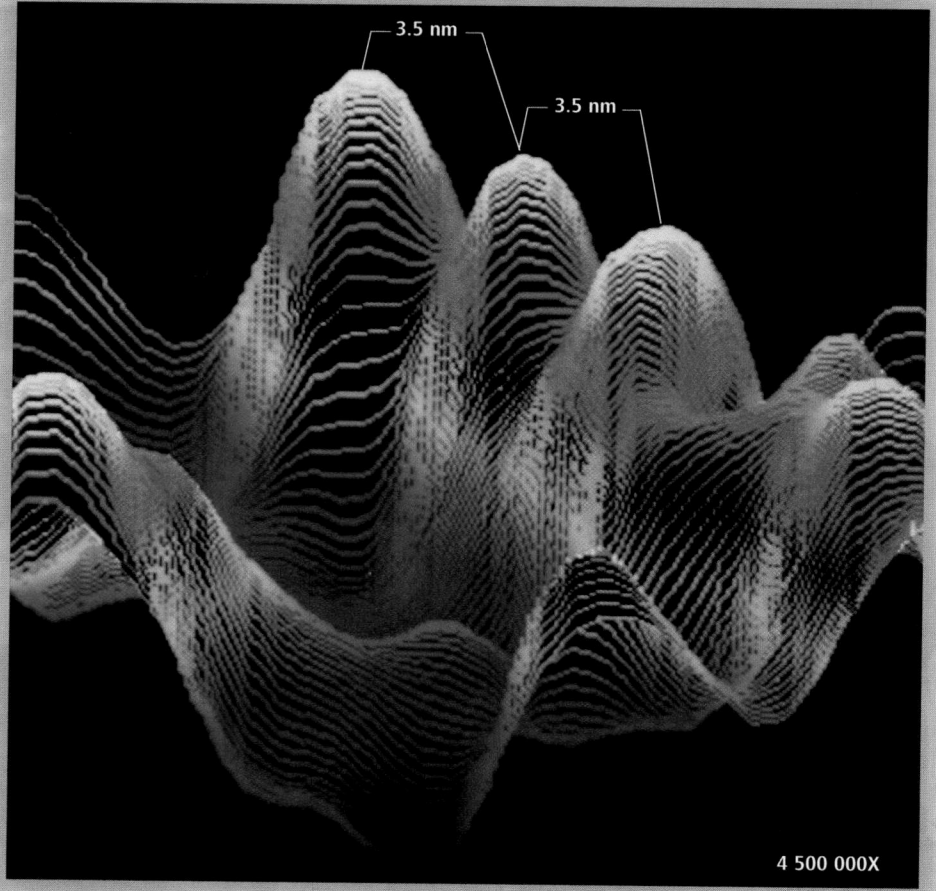

3.5 nm

3.5 nm

4 500 000X

Measurements provide quantitative information.

Scientific Method

S ometimes progress in science comes about through accidental discoveries. However, most scientific advances result from carefully planned investigations. The process researchers use to carry out their investigations is often called the scientific method. *The* **scientific method** *is a logical approach to solving problems by observing and collecting data, formulating hypotheses, testing hypotheses, and formulating theories that are supported by data.*

Observing and Collecting Data

Observing is the use of the senses to obtain information. Observation often involves making measurements and collecting data. The data may be descriptive (qualitative) or numerical (quantitative) in nature. Numerical information, such as the fact that a sample of copper ore has a mass of 25.7 grams, is *quantitative*. Non-numerical information, such as the fact that the sky is blue, is *qualitative*.

Experimenting involves carrying out a procedure under controlled conditions to make observations and collect data. To learn more about matter, chemists study systems. *A* **system** *is a specific portion of matter in a given region of space that has been selected for study during an experiment or observation.* When you observe a reaction in a test tube, the test tube and its contents form a system.

OBJECTIVES

- Describe the purpose of the scientific method.

- Distinguish between qualitative and quantitative observations.

- Describe the differences between hypotheses, theories, and models.

internet connect

SCiLINKS
NSTA

TOPIC: Scientific methods
GO TO: www.scilinks.org
*sci*LINKS CODE: HC2021

FIGURE 2-1 These students are designing an experiment to determine how to get the largest volume of popped corn from a fixed number of kernels. They think that the volume is likely to increase as the moisture in the kernels increases. Their experiment will involve soaking some kernels in water and observing whether the volume of the popped corn is greater than that of corn popped from kernels that have not been soaked.

Visual Strategy
FIGURE 2-2 Have students decide whether the hypothesis proposed in the caption is valid, based on the results in the graph.

Ask students to predict how the data might look for a 75% phosphorus plot. Ask them to draw a conclusion from the data shown regarding the best percentage of phosphorus to use on these plants. *(Using 25% gives about the same results as using 50%. Using 25% would be more economical.)*

Class Discussion
Discuss generalizations that play a role in everyday life. For example, ask students what they observe each time they drop a heavy object. Ask how repeated observations have led them to the generalization that objects fall. Have students propose other real-life examples of forming and applying generalizations.

FIGURE 2-2 A graph of data can show relationships between two variables. In this case the graph shows data collected during an experiment to determine the effect of phosphorus fertilizer compounds on plant growth. The following is one possible hypothesis: *If* phosphorus stimulates corn-plant growth, *then* corn plants treated with a soluble phosphorus compound should grow faster, under the same conditions, than corn plants that are not treated.

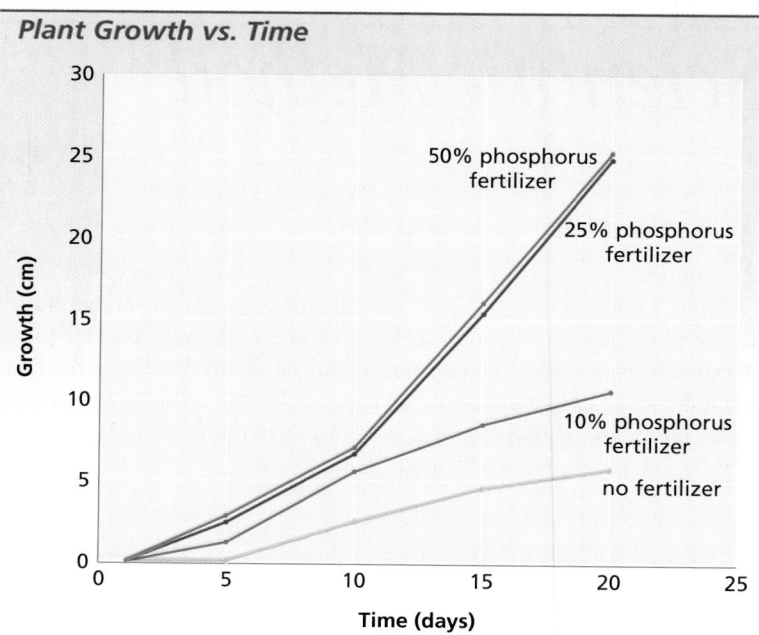

Formulating Hypotheses

As scientists examine and compare the data from their own experiments, they attempt to find relationships and patterns—in other words, they make generalizations based on the data. Generalizations are statements that apply to a range of information. To make generalizations, data are sometimes organized in tables and analyzed using statistics or other mathematical techniques, often with the aid of graphs and a computer.

Scientists use generalizations about the data to formulate a **hypothesis,** *or testable statement.* The hypothesis serves as a basis for making predictions and for carrying out further experiments. Hypotheses are often drafted as "if-then" statements. The "then" part of the hypothesis is a prediction that is the basis for testing by experiment. Figure 2-2 shows data collected to test a hypothesis.

Testing Hypotheses

Testing a hypothesis requires experimentation that provides data to support or refute a hypothesis or theory. Do the data in Figure 2-2 support the hypothesis? If testing reveals that the predictions were not correct, the generalizations on which the predictions were based must be discarded or modified. One of the most difficult, yet most important, aspects of science is rejecting a hypothesis that is not supported by data.

STAGES IN THE SCIENTIFIC METHOD

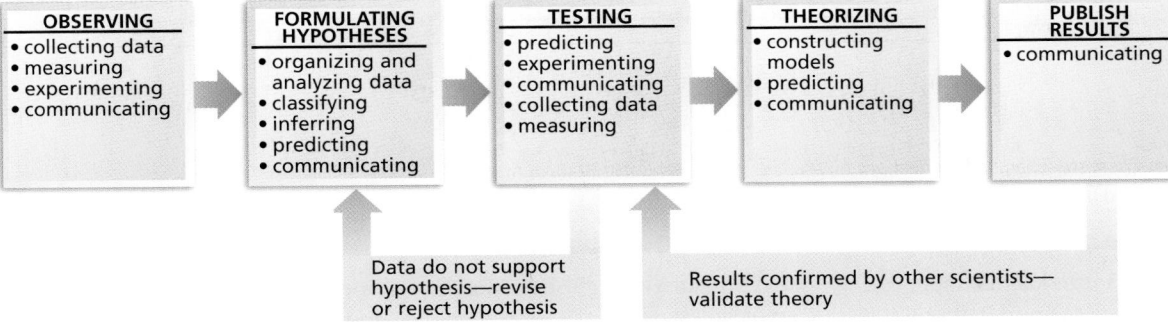

FIGURE 2-3 The scientific method is not a stepwise process. Scientists may repeat steps many times before there is sufficient evidence to formulate a theory. You can see that each stage represents a number of different activities.

Theorizing

When the data from experiments show that the predictions of the hypothesis are successful, scientists typically try to explain the phenomena they are studying by constructing a model. *A **model** in science is more than a physical object; it is often an explanation of how phenomena occur and how data or events are related.* Models may be visual, verbal, or mathematical. One of the most important models in chemistry is the atomic model of matter, which states that matter is composed of tiny particles called atoms.

If a model successfully explains many phenomena, it may become part of a theory. The atomic model is a part of the atomic theory, which you will study in Chapter 3. *A **theory** is a broad generalization that explains a body of facts or phenomena.* Theories are considered successful if they can predict the results of many new experiments. Examples of the important theories you will study in chemistry are kinetic-molecular theory and collision theory. Figure 2-3 shows where theory fits in the scheme of the scientific method.

SECTION REVIEW

1. What is the scientific method?

2. Which of the following are quantitative?
   a. the liquid floats on water
   b. the metal is malleable
   c. the liquid has a temperature of 55.6°C

3. How do hypotheses and theories differ?

4. How are models related to theories and hypotheses?

5. What are the components of the system in the graduated cylinder shown on page 38?

CHAPTER ⟷ CONNECTION

The kinetic-molecular theory is discussed in Chapter 10.

SECTION REVIEW

1. a logical approach to solving problems by observing and collecting data, formulating hypotheses, testing hypotheses, and formulating theories supported by data

2. c

3. A hypothesis is a testable statement that serves as a basis for making predictions and for carrying out further experiments. A theory is a broad generalization that explains a body of facts or phenomena.

4. A useful model is usually proposed after a hypothesis is shown to be correct. A model that successfully explains many phenomena may become part of a theory.

5. water, copper shot, and mercury

CHEMICAL COMMENTARY

Background

Chemistry Imagined, Reflections on Science, first published in 1993, was a collaboration between Nobel Prize winner Roald Hoffmann and artist Vivian Torrence.

In the book, Hoffmann used different literary devices, such as poetry, to emphasize the importance of chemistry in our everyday lives. Torrence drew on Hoffmann's literary views to illustrate the chemist's perception of the world. The result is a book that captures the essence of how chemists think about and visualize the world on the atomic scale.

The book gives students a broader perspective of the nature of chemistry than can be presented in a textbook. Students interested in the arts might gain a new appreciation for their chemistry course.

Reading for Meaning

Hoffmann's description of chemistry as an intermediate science focuses on chemical activities involving the synthesis, or building, of new molecules.

Chemistry's Holy Grail

From *Chemistry Imagined, Reflections on Science,* written by Roald Hoffmann and illustrated by Vivian Torrence

In other fields the important questions seem to be breathtakingly simple: How does the brain work? Let's land a manned space craft on Mars . . . What is the "cure" for cancer? The outsider romanticizes, to be sure. But what about chemistry, where is the Holy Grail of the molecular science? . . .

To search for the Holy Grail, 150 of King Arthur's knights committed their hearts and resources. Translated to modern times, a like group effort demands some gigantic, or at least intricately expensive, machinery. Big science, in other words: a supercollider to search the innards, a space telescope to probe the outer fringes, a genome project to map human heredity. None of these is typical of chemistry, where from the beginning small groupings of people, working with relatively cheap cookware, have transformed a wondrous variety of matter.

Chemistry is an intermediate science. Its universe is defined not by reduction to a few elementary particles, or even to the hundred or so elements, but by a reaching out to the infinities of molecules that can be synthesized. A registry of new molecules contains over ten million man-made entries. A small fraction of these is of natural origin, though millions are waiting to be analyzed. And millions more are lost in species that our ecologi-

cal pressure extinguishes. Most molecules are man- and woman-made. The beauty I would claim for chemistry is that of richness and complexity, the realm of the possible. There is no end to the range of structure and function that molecules exhibit. . . .

Roald Hoffmann

There is no Holy Grail in chemistry. Yes, we would like to have a magic machine that separates the most awful mixture, purifies every component to 99.4% purity (or better if we pay more) and determines the precise arrangement of atoms in space in each molecule. Yes, we'd like to know in complete detail the resistance of a molecule to every twist, bend, stretch, rock, and roll. And, yes, we certainly must espy the secret, rapid motions molecules undergo in their most

intimate transformations. And, most of all, most fundamental to the science of transformations, we desire control—ways to synthesize to order, in a short time, using cheap materials, in one pot, any molecule in the world.

The secret of the Holy Grail is that it is to be found not in the consummation but in the search. Imagine every woman rejuvenated, every man saved, all ills, physical and mental, cured, all humanity perfect, and, of course, at peace. What a dull world! . . .

If the grand desires of chemistry were achieved—to know what one has, how things happen on the molecular scale, how to create molecules with absolute control—chemistry would simply vanish. To come to terms with complexity and the never-ending search, to find joy and beauty in the plain thing, the small step— that is the grail.

Reading for Meaning
What does Hoffmann mean when he says that chemistry is an intermediate science?

Read Further
Hoffmann states that, most of all, chemists desire ways to control chemical reactions. Research three ways that chemists control reactions, and write a paragraph describing each.

Units of Measurement

Measurements are quantitative information. A measurement is more than just a number, even in everyday life. Suppose a chef were to write a recipe listing quantities such as 1 salt, 3 sugar, and 2 flour. The cooks could not use the recipe without more information. They would need to know whether the number 3 represented teaspoons, tablespoons, cups, ounces, grams, or some other unit for sugar.

Measurements *represent* quantities. A **quantity** *is something that has magnitude, size, or amount.* A quantity is not the same as a measurement. For example, the quantity represented by a teaspoon is volume. The teaspoon is a unit of measurement, while volume is a quantity. A teaspoon is a measurement standard in this country. Units of measurement compare what is to be measured with a previously defined size. Nearly every measurement is a number plus a unit. The choice of unit depends on the quantity being measured.

Many centuries ago, people sometimes marked off distances in the number of foot lengths it took to cover the distance. But this system was unsatisfactory because the number of foot lengths used to express a distance varied with the size of the measurer's foot. Once there was agreement on a standard for foot length, confusion as to the real length was eliminated. It no longer mattered who made the measurement, as long as the standard measuring unit was correctly applied.

SI Measurement

Scientists all over the world have agreed on a single measurement system called *Le Système International d'Unités*, abbreviated **SI.** This system was adopted in 1960 by the General Conference on Weights and Measures. SI has seven base units, and most other units are derived from these seven. Some non-SI units are still commonly used by chemists and are also used in this book.

SI units are defined in terms of standards of measurement. The standards are objects or natural phenomena that are of constant value, easy to preserve and reproduce, and practical in size. International organizations monitor the defining process. In the United States, the National Institute of Standards and Technology plays the main role in maintaining standards and setting style conventions. For example, numbers are written in a form that is agreed upon internationally. The number seventy-five thousand is written 75 000, not 75,000, because the comma is used in other countries to represent a decimal point.

OBJECTIVES

- Distinguish between a quantity, a unit, and a measurement standard.

- Name SI units for length, mass, time, volume, and density.

- Distinguish between mass and weight.

- Perform density calculations.

- Transform a statement of equality to a conversion factor.

Lesson Starter
Ask students whether they would be breaking the speed limit in a 40 mi/h zone if they were traveling at 60 km/h. Lead students to conclude that mi/h and km/h measure the same quantity using different units.

✔ Teaching Tip

It is important to emphasize the difference between a *quantity* and a *unit* and how each is represented. The Sample Problems throughout the text show both at various stages in the development of the solution to the problem. If students don't have a firm grasp of the difference, they will get confused.

Did You Know?
The metric system—the forerunner of SI—was first used in France in the late 18th century, around the time of the French Revolution. The revolutionaries embraced the system and wanted to standardize the number of days per month as 30, which is divisible by 10. There was even a movement to increase the number of days per week from seven to ten.

Reading Skill-Builder

BRAINSTORMING Write the words *qualitative* and *quantitative* on the board. Review the difference between qualitative (descriptive) and quantitative (numerical) data as described in Section 2-1. Have students brainstorm to come up with examples of each type of data. Invite two volunteers to write down students' contributions in a list under each word. Have students revise and/or add to their lists as they read Section 2-2.

Table 2-1 Discuss each SI base unit, making sure students understand what each column and row in the table represents. The first five units will be the most important in their study of chemistry.

Draw attention to the following possible source of confusion for students. The letter *m* is used in three ways—in roman (plain) type, m, as the abbreviation for *meter* and *milli-*, and italicized, *m,* as the quantity symbol for *mass.*

✔ Teaching Tip

Negative exponents represent inverses of numbers, not negative values. For example, 10^{-3} indicates $1/10^3$, 1/1000, or 0.001.

TABLE 2-1 *SI Base Units*

Quantity	Quantity symbol	Unit name	Unit abbreviation	Defined standard
Length	l	meter	m	the length of the path traveled by light in a vacuum during a time interval of 1/299 792 458 of a second
Mass	m	kilogram	kg	the unit of mass equal to the mass of the international prototype of the kilogram
Time	t	second	s	the duration of 9 192 631 770 periods of the radiation corresponding to the transition between the two hyperfine levels of the ground state of the cesium-133 atom
Temperature	T	kelvin	K	the fraction 1/273.16 of the thermodynamic temperature of the triple point of water
Amount of substance	n	mole	mol	the amount of substance of a system which contains as many elementary entities as there are atoms in 0.012 kilogram of carbon-12
Electric current	I	ampere	A	the constant current which, if maintained in two straight parallel conductors of infinite length, of negligible circular cross section, and placed 1 meter apart in vacuum, would produce between these conductors a force equal to 2×10^{-7} newton per meter of length
Luminous intensity	I_v	candela	cd	the luminous intensity, in a given direction, of a source that emits monochromatic radiation of frequency 540×10^{12} hertz and that has a radiant intensity in that direction of 1/683 watt per steradian

internet connect

SC*i*LINKS.
NSTA

TOPIC: SI units
GO TO: www.scilinks.org
***sci*LINKS CODE:** HC2022

SI Base Units

The seven SI base units and their standard abbreviated symbols are listed in Table 2-1. All the other SI units can be derived from the fundamental units.

Prefixes added to the names of SI base units are used to represent quantities that are larger or smaller than the base units. Table 2-2 lists SI prefixes using units of length as examples. For example, the prefix *centi-*, abbreviated c, represents an exponential factor of 10^{-2}, which equals 1/100. Thus, 1 centimeter, 1 cm, equals 0.01 m, or 1/100 of a meter.

Mass

As you learned in Chapter 1, mass is a measure of the quantity of matter. The SI standard unit for mass is the kilogram. The standard for mass defined in Table 2-1 is used to calibrate balances all over the world.

TABLE 2-2 *SI Prefixes*

Prefix	Unit abbreviation	Exponential factor	Meaning	Example
tera	T	10^{12}	1 000 000 000 000	1 terameter (Tm) $= 1 \times 10^{12}$ m
giga	G	10^{9}	1 000 000 000	1 gigometer (Gm) $= 1 \times 10^{9}$ m
mega	M	10^{6}	1 000 000	1 megameter (Mm) $= 1 \times 10^{6}$ m
kilo	k	10^{3}	1000	1 kilometer (km) $= 1000$ m
hecto	h	10^{2}	100	1 hectometer (hm) $= 100$ m
deka	da	10^{1}	10	1 decameter (dam) $= 10$ m
		10^{0}	**1**	**1 meter (m)**
deci	d	10^{-1}	1/10	1 decimeter (dm) $= 0.1$ m
centi	c	10^{-2}	1/100	1 centimeter (cm) $= 0.01$ m
milli	m	10^{-3}	1/1000	1 millimeter (mm) $= 0.001$ m
micro	μ	10^{-6}	1/1 000 000	1 micrometer (μm) $= 1 \times 10^{-6}$ m
nano	n	10^{-9}	1/1 000 000 000	1 nanometer (nm) $= 1 \times 10^{-9}$ m
pico	p	10^{-12}	1/1 000 000 000 000	1 picometer (pm) $= 1 \times 10^{-12}$ m
femto	f	10^{-15}	1/1 000 000 000 000 000	1 femtometer (fm) $= 1 \times 10^{-15}$ m
atto	a	10^{-18}	1/1 000 000 000 000 000 000	1 attometer (am) $= 1 \times 10^{-18}$ m

The mass of a typical textbook is about 1 kg. The gram, g, which is 1/1000 of a kilogram, is more useful for measuring masses of small objects, such as flasks and beakers. For even smaller objects, such as tiny quantities of chemicals, the milligram, mg, is often used. One milligram is 1/1000 of a gram, or 1/1 000 000 of a kilogram.

Mass is often confused with weight because people often express the weight of an object in grams. Mass is determined by comparing the mass of an object with a set of standard masses that are part of the balance. **Weight** *is a measure of the gravitational pull on matter.* Unlike weight, mass does not depend on such an attraction. Mass is measured on instruments such as a balance, and weight is typically measured on a spring scale. Taking weight measurements involves reading the amount that an object pulls down on a spring. As the force of Earth's gravity on an object increases, the object's weight increases. The weight of an object on the moon is about one-sixth of its weight on Earth.

Length

The SI standard unit for length is the meter. A distance of 1 m is about the width of an average doorway. To express longer distances, the kilometer, km, is used. One kilometer equals 1000 m. Road signs in the United States sometimes show distances in kilometers as well as miles. The kilometer is the unit used to express highway distances in most other countries of the world. To express shorter distances, the centimeter

Alternative Assessment
Provide groups of students with several common objects or photos of common objects. Have each student use Table 2-1 and Table 2-2 to determine the best unit for measuring the length of each object, and have each explain why that unit was chosen. Have the group come to a consensus for each object. Repeat the activity for units of mass. To help students visualize the base units, have a 1 kg mass and a meterstick available.

DEMONSTRATION
Use a triple-beam balance to determine the mass in grams of a fishing weight or some other small object. Then use a spring scale to determine the weight in newtons of the same object. Ask students what determined the result in each case. (The mass measurement is a comparison of the mass of the object and the masses built into the balance. The weight measurement is determined by the force of gravity on the object.) Ask students what would happen if the same experiment were repeated on a satellite hundreds of miles above Earth. They should conclude that the mass would not change but the weight would.

 Reading Skill-Builder

VOCABULARY BUILDING
Students are probably familiar with many of the prefixes listed in Table 2-2. Write each prefix on the board as a column heading. Have students list as many different measurement words as they can that begin with each of the prefixes. Help students identify similarities and differences among terms based on these prefixes.

FIGURE 2-4 The meter is the SI unit of length, but the centimeter is often used to measure smaller distances. What is the width in cm of the rectangular piece of aluminum foil shown?

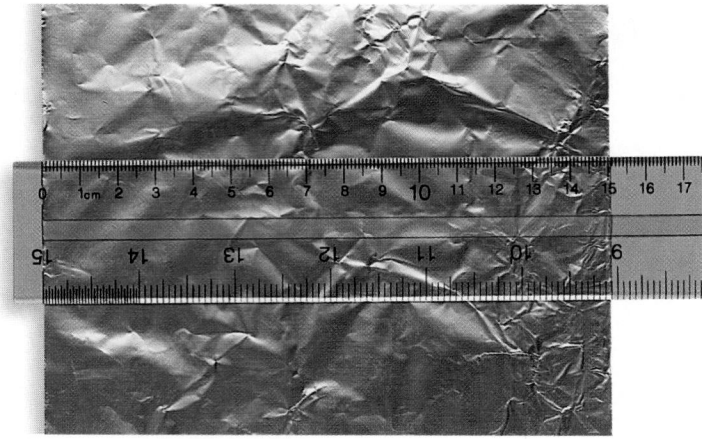

is often used. From Table 2-2, you can see that one centimeter equals 1/100 of a meter. The width of this book is just over 20 cm.

Derived SI Units

Many SI units are combinations of the quantities shown in Table 2-1. *Combinations of SI base units form* **derived units.** Some derived units are shown in Table 2-3.

Derived units are produced by multiplying or dividing standard units. For example, area, a derived unit, is length times width. If both length and width are expressed in meters, the area unit equals meters times meters, or square meters, abbreviated m^2. The last column of

TABLE 2-3 *Derived SI Units*

Quantity	Quantity symbol	Unit	Unit abbreviation	Derivation
Area	A	square meter	m^2	length × width
Volume	V	cubic meter	m^3	length × width × height
Density	D	kilograms per cubic meter	$\frac{kg}{m^3}$	$\frac{mass}{volume}$
Molar mass	M	kilograms per mole	$\frac{kg}{mol}$	$\frac{mass}{amount\ of\ substance}$
Concentration	c	moles per liter	M	$\frac{amount\ of\ substance}{volume}$
Molar volume	V_m	cubic meters per mole	$\frac{m^3}{mol}$	$\frac{volume}{amount\ of\ substance}$
Energy	E	joule	J	force × length

Table 2-3 shows the combination of fundamental units used to obtain derived units.

Some combination units are given their own names. For example, pressure expressed in base units is the following.

$$kg/m \cdot s^2$$

The name *pascal*, Pa, is given to this combination. You will learn more about pressure in Chapter 10. Prefixes can also be added to express derived units. Area can be expressed in cm^2, square centimeters, or mm^2, square millimeters.

Volume

Volume *is the amount of space occupied by an object.* The derived SI unit of volume is cubic meters, m^3. One cubic meter is equal to the volume of a cube whose edges are 1 m long. Such a large unit is inconvenient for expressing the volume of materials in a chemistry laboratory. Instead, a smaller unit, the cubic centimeter, cm^3, is often used. There are 100 centimeters in a meter, so a cubic meter contains 1 000 000 cm^3.

$$1 \; m^3 \times \frac{100 \; cm}{1 \; m} \times \frac{100 \; cm}{1 \; m} \times \frac{100 \; cm}{1 \; m} = 1 \; 000 \; 000 \; cm^3$$

When chemists measure the volumes of liquids and gases, they often use a non-SI unit called the liter. The liter is equivalent to one cubic decimeter. Thus, a liter, L, is also equivalent to 1000 cm^3. Another non-SI unit, the milliliter, mL, is used for smaller volumes. There are 1000 mL in 1 L. Because there are also 1000 cm^3 in a liter, the two units—milliliter and cubic centimeter—are interchangeable.

FIGURE 2-5 The speed that registers on a speedometer represents distance traveled per hour and is expressed in the derived units kilometers per hour or miles per hour.

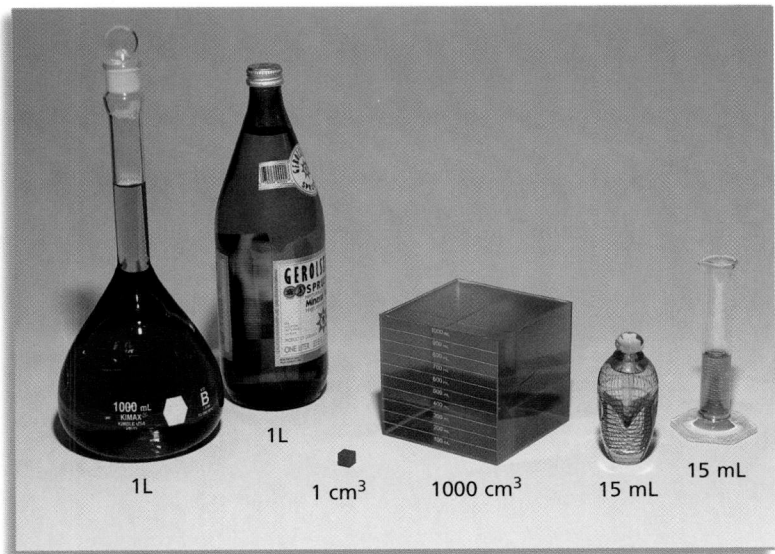

1L   1 cm^3 1000 cm^3 15 mL   15 mL

FIGURE 2-6 The relationships between various volumes are shown here. One liter contains 1000 mL of liquid, and 1 mL is equivalent to 1 cm^3. A small perfume bottle contains about 15 mL of liquid. The volumetric flask and graduated cylinder are used for measuring liquid volumes in the lab.

Common Misconception

Draw models of cubes on the board or display some three-dimensional models of cubes to help students with spatial relationships. Students often make errors in comparing related cubic units. For example, students know that there are 1000 mm in 1 m. They may then incorrectly assume that there are 1000 mm^3 (10^3 mm^3) in 1 m^3 instead of the 10^9 mm^3 that are actually present (10^3 mm × 10^3 mm × 10^3 mm = 10^9 mm^3). Draw a model for this cube so students can see why a cube with lengths of 1000 mm per side has a volume of 1×10^9 mm^3. The numerical value as well as the unit must be cubed.

✔ Teaching Tip

The conversion factor $\frac{100^3 \; cm^3}{1 \; m^3}$ is simply the cube of the conversion factor $\frac{100 \; cm}{1 \; m}$. This is a good opportunity to point out to students that a conversion factor raised to any power is still a valid conversion factor.

DEMONSTRATION

Fill a large beaker or graduated cylinder nearly full with cold club soda or seltzer. Add about a dozen raisins. The raisins will rise to the surface, where they appear to "dance." The raisins will then sink, only to rise again, and they will repeat the pattern over and over. Have students attempt to explain what is occurring. *(Raisins are more dense than soda water, so raisins sink. However, gas bubbles are less dense than soda water, and they rise. When these bubbles attach to a raisin, the raisin-bubbles system is less dense than the soda water, and the raisin rises. At the surface, the bubbles escape, and the more-dense raisin falls until more bubbles attach to it.)*

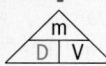

FIGURE 2-7 Density is the ratio of mass to volume. Both water and copper shot float on mercury because mercury is more dense.

Density

An object made of cork feels lighter than a lead object of the same size. What you are actually comparing in such cases is how massive objects are compared with their size. This property is called density. **Density** *is the ratio of mass to volume, or mass divided by volume.* Mathematically, the relationship for density can be written in the following way.

$$density = \frac{mass}{volume} \text{ or } D = \frac{m}{V}$$

The quantity m is mass, V is volume, and D is density.

The SI unit for density is derived from the base units for mass and volume—the kilogram and the cubic meter, respectively—and can be expressed as kilograms per cubic meter, kg/m^3. This unit is inconveniently large for the density measurements you will make in the laboratory. You will often see density expressed in grams per cubic centimeter, g/cm^3, or grams per milliliter, g/mL. The densities of gases are generally reported either in kilograms per cubic meter, kg/m^3, or in grams per liter, g/L.

Density is a characteristic physical property of a substance. It does not depend on the size of the sample because as the sample's mass increases, its volume increases proportionately, and the ratio of mass to volume is constant. Therefore, density can be used as one property to help identify a substance. Table 2-4 shows the densities of some common materials. As you can see, cork has a density of only 0.24 g/cm^3, which is less than the density of liquid water. Because cork is less dense than water, it floats on water. Lead, on the other hand, has a density of 11.35 g/cm^3. The density of lead is greater than that of water, so lead sinks in water.

Note that Table 2-4 specifies the temperatures at which the densities were measured. That is because density varies with temperature. Most objects expand as temperature increases, thereby increasing in volume. Because density is mass divided by volume, density usually decreases with increasing temperature.

TABLE 2-4 *Densities of Some Familiar Materials*

Solids	Density at 20°C (g/cm³)	Liquids	Density at 20°C (g/mL)
cork	0.24*	gasoline	0.67*
butter	0.86	ethyl alcohol	0.791
ice	0.92†	kerosene	0.82
sucrose	1.59	turpentine	0.87
bone	1.85*	water	0.998
diamond	3.26*	sea water	1.025**
copper	8.92	milk	1.031*
lead	11.35	mercury	13.6

† measured at 0°C
* typical density

** measured at 15°C

Wear Safety Goggles and an Apron.

Density of Pennies

Materials

- balance
- 100 mL graduated cylinder
- 40 pennies dated before 1982
- 40 pennies dated after 1982
- water

Procedure

1. Using the balance, determine the mass of the 40 pennies minted prior to 1982. Repeat this measurement two more times. Average the results of the three trials to determine the average mass of the pennies.

2. Repeat step 1 with the 40 pennies minted after 1982.

3. Pour about 50 mL of water into the 100 mL graduated cylinder. Record the exact volume of the water. Add the 40 pennies minted before 1982. Record the volume of the water and pennies. Repeat this process two more times. Determine the volume of the pennies for each trial. Average the results of those trials to determine the average volume of the pennies.

4. Repeat step 3 with the 40 pennies minted after 1982.

5. Review your data for any large differences between trials that could increase the error of your results. Repeat those measurements.

6. Use the average volume and average mass to calculate the average density for each group of pennies.

7. Compare the average calculated densities with the density of the copper listed in Table 2-4.

Discussion

1. Why is it best to use the results of three trials rather than a single trial for determining the density?

2. How did the densities of the two groups of pennies compare? How do you account for any difference?

3. Use the results of this investigation to formulate a hypothesis about the composition of the two groups of pennies. How could you test your hypothesis?

SAMPLE PROBLEM 2-1

A sample of aluminum metal has a mass of 8.4 g. The volume of the sample is 3.1 cm³. Calculate the density of aluminum.

SOLUTION

Given: mass (m) = 8.4 g
volume (V) = 3.1 cm³
Unknown: density (D)

$$density = \frac{mass}{volume} = \frac{8.4\ g}{3.1\ cm^3} = 2.7\ g/cm^3$$

SAMPLE PROBLEMS

2-1 What is the density of a sample of ore that has a mass of 74.0 g and occupies 20.3 cm^3?

Ans. 3.65 g/cm^3

2-1 Find the volume of a sample of wood that has a mass of 95.1 g and a density of 0.857 g/cm^3.

Ans. 111 cm^3

NOTE: Students should not have to deal with significant figures in calculations until page 50.

Application

Carbon dioxide can be used to put out a fire because it is more dense than oxygen and thus sinks, blocking out oxygen from the fire.

Class Discussion

Ask students to name examples of how conversion factors can be used in everyday life. An example would be using a vehicle's mileage conversion factor (number of miles/gallon) to estimate how much gasoline it would take for a trip of a certain length.

✔ Teaching Tip

Help students understand that an equality statement is the basis for most conversion factors. Refer to Table 2-2 and have students write three equalities based on the table. Then have students express those equalities as ratios. For example, 1 kg = 1 × 10^3 g.

$$\frac{1 \times 10^3 \text{ g}}{\text{kg}} \quad \text{or} \quad \frac{1 \text{ kg}}{1 \times 10^3 \text{ g}}$$

PRACTICE

1. What is the density of a block of marble that occupies 310 cm^3 and has a mass of 853 g?

   Answer
   2.75 g/cm^3

2. Diamond has a density of 3.26 g/cm^3. What is the mass of a diamond that has a volume of 0.350 cm^3?

   Answer
   1.14 g

3. What is the volume of a sample of liquid mercury that has a mass of 76.2 g, given that the density of mercury is 13.6 g/mL?

   Answer
   5.60 mL

Conversion Factors

A **conversion factor** *is a ratio derived from the equality between two different units that can be used to convert from one unit to the other.* For example, suppose you want to know how many quarters there are in a certain number of dollars. To figure out the answer, you need to know how quarters and dollars are related. There are four quarters per dollar and one dollar for every four quarters. Those facts can be expressed as ratios in three conversion factors.

$$\frac{4 \text{ quarters}}{1 \text{ dollar}} = 1 \qquad \frac{1 \text{ dollar}}{4 \text{ quarters}} = 1 \qquad \frac{0.25 \text{ dollar}}{1 \text{ quarter}} = 1$$

Notice that each conversion factor equals 1. That is because the two quantities divided in any conversion factor are equivalent to each other—as in this case, where 4 quarters equal 1 dollar. Because conversion factors are equal to 1, they can be multiplied by other factors in equations without changing the validity of the equations. When you want to use a conversion factor to change a unit in a problem, you can set up the problem in the following way.

$$\text{quantity sought} = \text{quantity given} \times \text{conversion factor}$$

For example, to determine the number of quarters in 12 dollars, you would carry out the unit conversion that allows you to change from dollars to quarters.

$$\text{number of quarters} = 12 \text{ dollars} \times \text{conversion factor}$$

Next you would have to decide which conversion factor gives you an answer in the desired unit. In this case, you have dollars and you want quarters. To obtain quarters, you must divide the quantity by dollars. Therefore, the conversion factor in this case must have dollars in the denominator. That factor is 4 quarters/1 dollar. Thus, you would set up the calculation as follows.

$$? \text{ quarters} = 12 \text{ dollars} \times \text{conversion factor}$$

$$= 12 \text{ dollars} \times \frac{4 \text{ quarters}}{1 \text{ dollar}} = 48 \text{ quarters}$$

Notice that the dollars have divided out, leaving an answer in the desired unit—quarters.

Suppose you had guessed wrong and used 1 dollar/4 quarters when choosing which of the two conversion factors to use. You would have an answer with entirely inappropriate units.

$$? \text{ quarters} = 12 \text{ dollars} \times \frac{1 \text{ dollar}}{4 \text{ quarters}} = \frac{3 \text{ dollars}^2}{\text{quarter}}$$

You will work many problems in this book. It is always best to begin with an idea of the units you will need in your final answer. When working through the Sample Problems, keep track of the units needed for the unknown quantity. Check your final answer against what you've written as the unknown quantity.

Deriving Conversion Factors

You can derive conversion factors if you know the relationship between the unit you have and the unit you want. For example, from the fact that *deci-* means "1/10," you know that there is 1/10 of a meter per decimeter and that each meter must have 10 decimeters. Thus, from the equality

$$1 \text{ m} = 10 \text{ dm}$$

you can write the following conversion factors relating meters and decimeters.

$$\frac{1 \text{ m}}{10 \text{ dm}} \text{ and } \frac{0.1 \text{ m}}{\text{dm}^*} \text{ and } \frac{10 \text{ dm}}{\text{m}}$$

The following sample problem illustrates an example of deriving conversion factors to make a unit conversion.

SAMPLE PROBLEM 2-2

Express a mass of 5.712 grams in milligrams and in kilograms.

SOLUTION

Given: 5.712 g
Unknown: mass in mg and kg

The expression that relates grams to milligrams is

$$1 \text{ g} = 1000 \text{ mg}$$

The possible conversion factors that can be written from this expression are

$$\frac{1000 \text{ mg}}{\text{g}} \text{ and } \frac{1 \text{ g}}{1000 \text{ mg}}$$

*In this book, when there is no digit shown in the denominator, you can assume the value is 1.

Alternative Assessment

Give students a calendar, and ask them what conversion factors would be used to convert days to months, months to weeks, and so on. You could also use an egg carton and ask about conversions involving the unit *dozen,* or show a picture of shoes in a closet and ask about conversions involving the unit *pair.* Ask students to think of other examples of such conversion factors.

ADDITIONAL SAMPLE PROBLEMS

2-2 Express a time period of exactly 1.00 day in terms of seconds. Have students begin by writing out all of the equalities needed to solve this problem.

Ans. 1 day = 24 hours
1 hour = 60 minutes
1 minute = 60 seconds
86 400 s

2-2 How many centigrams are there in 6.25 kg?

Ans. 625 000 cg

Problem-Solving Practice HOLT ChemFile

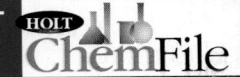

Chapter 1 of the Mini-Guide to Problem Solving (also found on the One-Stop Planner CD-ROM) includes more worked-out samples and additional practice problems for converting measures.

To derive an answer in mg, you'll need to multiply 5.712 g by 1000 mg/g.

$$5.712 \, \cancel{g} \times \frac{1000 \text{ mg}}{\cancel{g}} = 5712 \text{ mg}$$

This answer makes sense because milligrams is a smaller unit than grams and, therefore, there should be more of them.

The kilogram problem is solved similarly.

$$1 \text{ kg} = 1000 \text{ g}$$

Conversion factors representing this expression are

$$\frac{1 \text{ kg}}{1000 \text{ g}} \quad \text{and} \quad \frac{1000 \text{ g}}{\text{kg}}$$

To derive an answer in kg, you'll need to multiply 5.712 g by 1 kg/1000 g.

$$5.712 \, \cancel{g} \times \frac{1 \text{ kg}}{1000 \, \cancel{g}} = 0.005712 \text{ kg}$$

The answer makes sense because kilograms is a larger unit than grams and, therefore, there should be fewer of them.

PRACTICE

1. Express a length of 16.45 m in centimeters and in kilometers.

   Answer
   1645 cm, 0.01645 km

2. Express a mass of 0.014 mg in grams.

   Answer
   0.000 014 g

SECTION REVIEW

1. There needs to be agreement on meaning and size of units. Standards for units must be unchanging to avoid confusion and ambiguity.

2. **a.** density
   b. time
   c. energy
   d. mass
   e. volume
   f. time
   g. area
   h. volume
   i. mass
   j. volume

3. **a.** 0.0105 kg
   b. 1570 m
   c. 0.000 003 54 g
   d. 3 500 000 μmol
   e. 1200 mL
   f. 0.000 358 m³
   g. 548.6 cm³

4. **a.** 1 m³/1 000 000 cm³ and 1 000 000 cm³/m³
   b. 1 in./2.54 cm and 2.54 cm/in.
   c. 1 μg/0.000 001 g and 0.000 001 g/μg
   d. 1 Mm/1 000 000 m and 1 000 000 m/Mm

5. **a.** 1.71 g/cm³
   b. 4.53 cm³

SECTION REVIEW

1. Why are standards needed for measured quantities?

2. Label each of the following measurements by the quantity each represents. For instance, a measurement of 10.6 kg/m³ represents density.
   a. 5.0 g/mL   f. 325 ms
   b. 37 s   g. 500 m²
   c. 47 J   h. 30.23 mL
   d. 39.56 g   i. 2.7 mg
   e. 25.3 cm³   j. 0.005 L

3. Complete the following conversions.
   a. 10.5 g = _____ kg
   b. 1.57 km = _____ m
   c. 3.54 μg = _____ g
   d. 3.5 mol = _____ μmol

   e. 1.2 L = _____ mL
   f. 358 cm³ = _____ m³
   g. 548.6 mL = _____ cm³

4. Write conversion factors to represent the following equalities.
   a. 1 m³ = 1 000 000 cm³
   b. 1 in. = 2.54 cm
   c. 1 μg = 0.000 001 g
   d. 1 Mm = 1 000 000 m

5. a. What is the density of an 84.7 g sample of an unknown substance if the sample occupies 49.6 cm³?
   b. What volume would be occupied by 7.75 g of this same substance?

RESEARCH NOTES

Roadside Pollution Detector

Dr. Donald Stedman, a chemist at the University of Denver, has developed a device that monitors exhaust emissions on highways.

The pollution detector sits on the side of a highway and shines a beam of infrared light across the road. After the beam passes through a car's exhaust fumes, it strikes a rotating mirror on the other side of the highway, which reflects the light onto four different sensors. These sensors detect changes in the infrared beam, and then each sensor uses that information to make different measurements. One detector gauges the amount of carbon dioxide in the exhaust. The second calculates the amount of carbon monoxide. A third sensor measures the amount of hydrocarbons, which contribute to the production of smog. To ensure accurate measurements, the fourth sensor measures a reference beam.

A car driving down the highway will break the infrared beam, which signals the detector to store the measurement of the air directly in front of the vehicle. Then an

A carbon monoxide rating of higher than 4.5% gets a poor rating on the display.

exhaust reading is taken after the car passes for half a second to ensure that the beam measures data from the middle of the exhaust fumes. At the same instant, a video camera captures an image of the automobile.

Stedman put the detector into action on a highway exit ramp in Denver. The device gives every car that drives by an emissions rating and automatically displays the rating on a nearby billboard. If less than 1.3% of the car's exhaust is carbon monoxide, it earns a "good" rating. A rating of less than 4.5% carbon monoxide receives a "fair" rating. A rating higher than 4.5% is a "poor" rating. Stedman has found that the billboard not only informs people

that their cars are polluters but also motivates the drivers to get their cars fixed.

Stedman has determined that only a small percentage of cars are responsible for automobile pollution. In fact, half of all the pollution from automobiles is created by about 10% of the cars on the road.

Stedman adds that the drivers will share the economic benefits of cleaning up their act. "If you have a gross-polluting car," he says, "you will save the amount of money that the repair might cost you in your fuel economy in a couple of years because you get a tremendous 10 to 15% fuel-economy improvement by fixing a gross-polluting car."

TOPIC: Detecting air pollution
GO TO: www.scilinks.org
*sci*LINKS CODE: HC2023

Lesson Starter

Students are often able to understand precision if they think of measurement instruments. Distribute some science-equipment catalogs among the students, and have them look at the specifications for electronic balances. They can see how measuring instruments vary in precision. Ask students to discuss using a beaker to measure volume versus using a graduated cylinder. Which is more precise?

Visual Strategy

FIGURE 2-8 Help students analyze the four dartboard situations. Use the illustration to compare and contrast various situations in terms of precision and accuracy. An additional example might be a pitcher's throws during a baseball game. Have students relate pitching results that have varying degrees of precision and accuracy.

Reading Skill-Builder

PAIRED SUMMARIZING

Pair students together and have them silently read the section on Accuracy and Precision. Choose one of the pair to be the "reteller" and the other to be the "listener." First, have the reteller summarize the selection for the listener, who does not interrupt until the reteller has finished, or if there is a portion of the summary that requires clarification. Let the reteller consult the text during his or her summary. Next, have the listener state any inaccuracies or omissions. Finally, have the students work together to refine the summary. Students then alternate roles as they read the sections on Significant Figures, Scientific Notation, and Using Sample Problems. Use students' summaries to generate a summary for the class.

OBJECTIVES

- Distinguish between accuracy and precision.

- Determine the number of significant figures in measurements.

- Perform mathematical operations involving significant figures.

- Convert measurements into scientific notation.

- Distinguish between inversely and directly proportional relationships.

FIGURE 2-8 The sizes and locations of the areas covered by thrown darts illustrate the difference between precision and accuracy.

Using Scientific Measurements

If you have ever measured something several times, you know that the results can vary. In science, for a reported measurement to be useful, there must be some indication of its reliability or uncertainty.

Accuracy and Precision

The terms *accuracy* and *precision* mean the same thing to most people. However, in science their meanings are quite distinct. **Accuracy** *refers to the closeness of measurements to the correct or accepted value of the quantity measured*. **Precision** *refers to the closeness of a set of measurements of the same quantity made in the same way*. Thus, measured values that are accurate are close to the accepted value. Measured values that are precise are close to one another but not necessarily close to the accepted value.

Figure 2-8 should help you visualize the difference between precision and accuracy. A set of darts thrown separately at a dartboard may land in various positions, relative to the bull's-eye and to one another. The

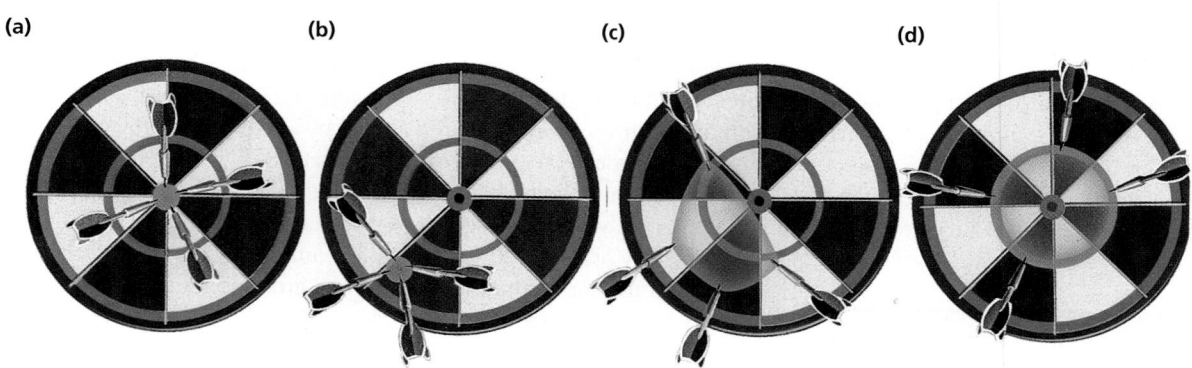

(a) Darts within small area
= High precision

Area covered on bull's-eye
= High accuracy

(b) Darts within small area
= High precision

Area far from bull's-eye
= Low accuracy

(c) Darts within large area
= Low precision

Area far from bull's-eye
= Low accuracy

(d) Darts within large area
= Low precision

Area centered around bull's-eye
= High accuracy (on average)

closer the darts land to the bull's-eye, the more accurately they were thrown. The closer they land to one another, the more precisely they were thrown. Thus, the set of results shown in Figure 2-8(a) is both accurate and precise because the darts are close to the bull's-eye and close to each other. In Figure 2-8(b), the set of results is inaccurate but precise because the darts are far from the bull's-eye but close to each other. In Figure 2-8(c), the set of results is both inaccurate and imprecise because the darts are far from the bull's-eye and far from each other. Notice also that the darts are not evenly distributed around the bull's-eye, so the set, even considered on average, is inaccurate. In Figure 2-8(d), the set on average is accurate compared with the third case, but it is imprecise. That is because the darts are distributed evenly around the bull's-eye but are far from each other.

Percent Error

The accuracy of an individual value or of an average experimental value can be compared quantitatively with the correct or accepted value by calculating the percent error. **Percent error** *is calculated by subtracting the experimental value from the accepted value, dividing the difference by the accepted value, and then multiplying by 100.*

$$Percent\ error = \frac{Value_{accepted} - Value_{experimental}}{Value_{accepted}} \times 100$$

Percent error has a positive value if the accepted value is greater than the experimental value. It has a negative value if the accepted value is less than the experimental value. The following sample problem illustrates the concept of percent error.

SAMPLE PROBLEM 2-3

A student measures the mass and volume of a substance and calculates its density as 1.40 g/mL. The correct, or accepted, value of the density is 1.36 g/mL. What is the percent error of the student's measurement?

SOLUTION

$$Percent\ error = \frac{Value_{accepted} - Value_{experimental}}{Value_{accepted}} \times 100$$

$$= \frac{1.36\ \text{g/mL} - 1.40\ \text{g/mL}}{1.36\ \text{g/mL}} \times 100 = -2.9\%$$

PRACTICE

1. What is the percent error for a mass measurement of 17.7 g, given that the correct value is 21.2 g?

   Answer
   17%

2. A volume is measured experimentally as 4.26 mL. What is the percent error, given that the correct value is 4.15 mL?

   Answer
   −2.7%

Common Misconception

The term *precision* is often misunderstood as meaning the same thing as *accuracy*. Make sure students understand what precision is, and take time to reinforce the concept throughout the course.

ADDITIONAL SAMPLE PROBLEMS

2-3 Calculate the percent error in a length measurement of 4.25 cm if the correct value is 4.08 cm.

Ans. −4.2%

2-3 The actual density of a certain material is 7.44 g/cm³. A student measures the density of the same material as 7.30 g/cm³. What is the percent error of the measurement?

Ans. 1.9%

Class Discussion

Have students consider examples of precision and accuracy. For example, assume two technicians independently measure the density of a new substance. Technician A records values of 2.000, 1.999, and 2.001 g/mL. Technician B records values of 2.5, 2.9, and 2.7 g/mL. The correct value is found to be 2.701 g/mL. Students should be able to explain that A's results are more precise because they are closer together and B's results are more accurate because they are closer to the correct value.

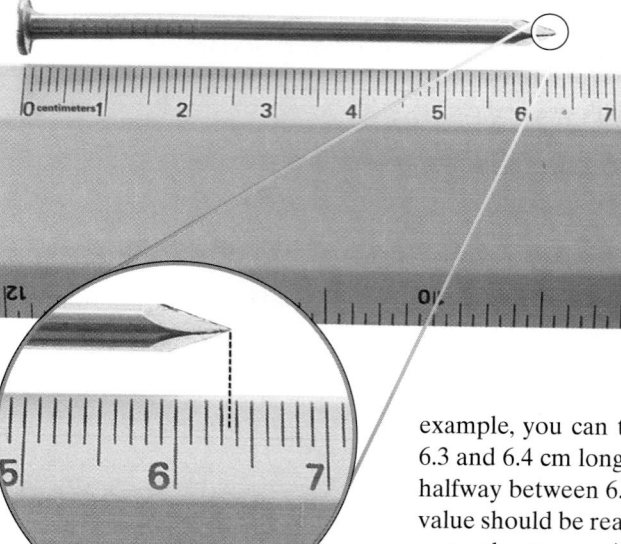

FIGURE 2-9 What value should be recorded for the length of this nail?

Error in Measurement

Some error or uncertainty always exists in any measurement. The skill of the measurer places limits on the reliability of results. The conditions of measurement also affect the outcome. The measuring instruments themselves place limitations on precision. Some balances can be read more precisely than others. The same is true of rulers, graduated cylinders, and other measuring devices.

When you use a properly calibrated measuring device, you can be almost certain of a particular number of digits in a reading. For example, you can tell that the nail in Figure 2-9 is definitely between 6.3 and 6.4 cm long. Looking more closely, you can see that the value is halfway between 6.3 and 6.4 cm. However, it is hard to tell whether the value should be read as 6.35 cm or 6.36 cm. The hundredths place is thus somewhat uncertain. Simply leaving it out would be misleading because you do have *some* indication of the value's likely range. Therefore, you would estimate the value to the final questionable digit, perhaps reporting the length of the nail as 6.36 cm. You might include a plus-or-minus value to express the range, for example, 6.36 cm ± 0.01 cm.

Significant Figures

In science, measured values are reported in terms of significant figures. **Significant figures** *in a measurement consist of all the digits known with certainty plus one final digit, which is somewhat uncertain or is estimated.* For example, in the reported nail length of 6.36 cm discussed above, the last digit, 6, is uncertain. All the digits, including the uncertain one, are significant, however. All contain information and are included in the reported value. Thus, the term *significant* does not mean *certain*. In any correctly reported measured value, the final digit is significant but not certain. Insignificant digits are never reported. As a chemistry student, you will need to use and recognize significant figures when you work with measured quantities and report your results, and when you evaluate measurements reported by others.

Determining the Number of Significant Figures

When you look at a measured quantity, you need to determine which digits are significant. That process is very easy if the number has no zeros because all the digits shown are significant. For example, if you see a number reported as 3.95, all three digits are significant. The significance of zeros in a number depends on their location, however. You need to learn and follow several rules involving zeros. After you have studied the rules in Table 2-5, use them to express the answers in the sample problem that follows.

TABLE 2-5 *Rules for Determining Significant Zeros*

Rule	Examples
1. Zeros appearing between nonzero digits are significant.	a. 40.7 L has three significant figures. b. 87 009 km has five significant figures.
2. Zeros appearing in front of all nonzero digits are not significant.	a. 0.095 897 m has five significant figures. b. 0.0009 kg has one significant figure.
3. Zeros at the end of a number and to the right of a decimal point are significant.	a. 85.00 g has four significant figures. b. 9.000 000 000 mm has 10 significant figures.
4. Zeros at the end of a number but to the left of a decimal point may or may not be significant. If a zero has not been measured or estimated but is just a placeholder, it is not significant. A decimal point placed after zeros indicates that they are significant.	a. 2000 m may contain from one to four significant figures, depending on how many zeros are placeholders. **For measurements given in this text, assume that 2000 m has one significant figure.** b. 2000. m contains four significant figures, indicated by the presence of the decimal point.

TABLE STRATEGY

Table 2-5 After going over each of the rules and examples listed in the table, have students determine the number of significant figures in other values containing zeros. Have them state the rule used in each case. For example, 0.0023 has two significant figures (rule 2), 70 000. has five (rule 4), and 6.200 has four (rule 3).

ADDITIONAL SAMPLE PROBLEMS

2-4 How many significant figures are there in the measured value 91.0020 m?

Ans. 6

2-4 Express the value of "exactly 15 centimeters" to three significant figures.

Ans. 15.0 cm

2-4 What is the number of significant figures in 0.092010 kg? Which rules did you apply?

Ans. 5; rules 1, 2, and 3

SAMPLE PROBLEM 2-4

How many significant figures are in each of the following measurements?
a. 28.6 g
b. 3440. cm
c. 910 m
d. 0.046 04 L
e. 0.006 700 0 kg

SOLUTION Determine the number of significant figures in each measurement using the rules listed in Table 2-5.

a. 28.6 g
There are no zeros, so all three digits are significant.

b. 3440. cm
By rule 4, the zero is significant because it is immediately followed by a decimal point; there are 4 significant figures.

c. 910 m
By rule 4, the zero is not significant; there are 2 significant figures.

d. 0.046 04 L
By rule 2, the first two zeros are not significant; by rule 1, the third zero is significant; there are 4 significant figures.

e. 0.006 700 0 kg
By rule 2, the first three zeros are not significant; by rule 3, the last three zeros are significant; there are 5 significant figures.

Common Misconception

Students typically have difficulty in rounding numbers that are exactly halfway between two numbers. Use examples to show that these numbers are rounded to the nearest even number. Students may also be confused in rounding numbers that contain a 5 but to which the odd/even rule does not apply. For example, the number 1.651 rounded to two digits is 1.7, not 1.6; the fact that 6 is even is irrelevant, given that the number is closer to 1.7 than it is to 1.6.

PRACTICE	

1. Determine the number of significant figures in each of the following.
   a. 804.05 g
   b. 0.014 403 0 km
   c. 1002 m
   d. 400 mL
   e. 30 000. cm
   f. 0.000 625 000 kg

2. Suppose the value "seven thousand centimeters" is reported to you. How should the number be expressed if it is intended to contain the following?
   a. 1 significant figure
   b. 4 significant figures
   c. 6 significant figures

Answer
1. a. 5
   b. 6
   c. 4
   d. 1
   e. 5
   f. 6

2. a. 7000 cm
   b. 7000. cm
   c. 7000.00 cm

Rounding

When you perform calculations involving measurements, you need to know how to handle significant figures. This is especially true when you are using a calculator to carry out mathematical operations. The answers given on a calculator can be derived results with more digits than are justified by the measurements.

Suppose you used a calculator to divide a measured value of 154 g by a measured value of 327 mL. Each of these values has three significant figures. The calculator would show a numerical answer of 0.470948012. The answer contains digits not justified by the measurements used to calculate it. Such an answer has to be rounded off to make its degree of certainty match that in the original measurements. The answer should be 0.471 g/mL.

The rules for rounding are shown in Table 2-6. The extent of rounding required in a given case depends on whether the numbers are being added, subtracted, multiplied, or divided.

TABLE 2-6 *Rules for Rounding Numbers*

If the digit following the last digit to be retained is:	then the last digit should:	Example (rounded to three significant figures)
greater than 5	be increased by 1	42.68 g ⟶ 42.7 g
less than 5	stay the same	17.32 m ⟶ 17.3 m
5, followed by nonzero digit(s)	be increased by 1	2.7851 cm ⟶ 2.79 cm
5, not followed by nonzero digit(s), and preceded by an odd digit	be increased by 1	4.635 kg ⟶ 4.64 kg (because 3 is odd)
5, not followed by nonzero digit(s), and the preceding significant digit is even	stay the same	78.65 mL ⟶ 78.6 mL (because 6 is even)

Addition or Subtraction with Significant Figures

Consider two mass measurements, 25.1 g and 2.03 g. The first measurement, 25.1 g, has one digit to the right of the decimal point, in the tenths place. There is no information on possible values for the hundredths place. That place is simply blank and cannot be assumed to be zero. The other measurement, 2.03 g, has two digits to the right of the decimal point. It provides information up to and including the hundredths place.

Suppose you were asked to add the two measurements. Simply carrying out the addition would result in an answer of 25.1 g + 2.03 g = 27.13 g. That answer suggests there is certainty all the way to the hundredths place. However, that result is not justified because the hundredths place in 25.1 g is completely unknown. The answer must be adjusted to reflect the uncertainty in the numbers added.

When adding or subtracting decimals, the answer must have the same number of digits to the right of the decimal point as there are in the measurement having the fewest digits to the right of the decimal point. When working with whole numbers, the answer should be rounded so that the final digit is in the same place as the leftmost uncertain digit. Comparing the two values 25.1 g and 2.03 g, the measurement with the fewest digits to the right of the decimal point is 25.1 g. It has only one such digit. Following the rule, the answer must be rounded so that it has no more than one digit to the right of the decimal point. It should therefore be rounded to 27.1 g.

Multiplication and Division with Significant Figures

Suppose you calculated the density of an object that has a mass of 3.05 g and a volume of 8.47 mL. The following division on a calculator will give a value of 0.360094451.

$$density = \frac{mass}{volume} = \frac{3.05 \text{ g}}{8.47 \text{ mL}} = 0.360094451 \text{ g/mL}$$

The answer must be rounded to the correct number of significant figures. The values of mass and volume used to obtain the answer have only three significant figures each. The degree of certainty in the calculated result is not justified. *For multiplication or division, the answer can have no more significant figures than are in the measurement with the fewest number of significant figures.* In the calculation just described, the answer, 0.360094451 g/mL, would be rounded to three significant figures to match the significant figures in 8.47 mL and 3.05 g. The answer would thus be 0.360 g/mL.

SAMPLE PROBLEM 2-5

Carry out the following calculations. Express each answer to the correct number of significant figures.
a. 5.44 m − 2.6103 m
b. 2.4 g/mL × 15.82 mL

2-5 Find the volume of a cube that is 3.23 cm on each edge.

Ans. 33.7 cm^3

2-5 What is the sum of 67.14 kg and 8.2 kg?

Ans. 75.3 kg

2-5 Calculate the density of a 17.982 g object that occupies 4.13 cm^3.

Ans. 4.35 g/cm^3

Class Discussion

An example of a simple conversion factor that is not exact is the conversion of time from days to years. Because the year is defined by one revolution of Earth around the sun, it is not an exact value. We generally use 365 days for a year, but it is more like 365.25 days per year at a low level of precision.

SOLUTION Carry out each mathematical operation. Follow the rules in Table 2-5 and Table 2-6 for determining significant figures and for rounding.

a. The answer is rounded to 2.83 m (for subtraction there should be two digits to the right of the decimal point, to match 5.44 m).

b. The answer is rounded to 38 g (for multiplication there should be two significant figures in the answer, to match 2.4 g/mL).

PRACTICE

1. What is the sum of 2.099 g and 0.05681 g?

   Answer
   2.156 g

2. Calculate the quantity 87.3 cm − 1.655 cm.

   Answer
   85.6 cm

3. Calculate the area of a crystal surface that measures 1.34 μm by 0.7488 μm. (Hint: Recall that *area = length × width* and is measured in square units.)

   Answer
   1.00 μm^2

4. Polycarbonate plastic has a density of 1.2 g/cm^3. A photo frame is constructed from two 3.0 mm sheets of polycarbonate. Each sheet measures 28 cm by 22 cm. What is the mass of the photo frame?

   Answer
   440 g

Conversion Factors and Significant Figures

Earlier in this chapter, you learned how conversion factors are used to change one unit to another. Such conversion factors are typically exact. That is, there is no uncertainty in them. For example, there are exactly 100 cm in a meter. If you were to use the conversion factor 100 cm/m to change meters to centimeters, the 100 would not limit the degree of certainty in the answer. Thus, 4.608 m could be converted to centimeters as follows.

$$4.608 \text{ m} \times \frac{100 \text{ cm}}{\text{m}} = 460.8 \text{ cm}$$

The answer still has four significant figures. Because the conversion factor is considered exact, the answer would not be rounded. Most exact conversion factors are defined, rather than measured, quantities. Counted numbers also produce conversion factors of unlimited precision. For example, if you counted that there are 10 test tubes for every student, that would produce an exact conversion factor of 10 test tubes/ student. There is no uncertainty in that factor.

Scientific Notation

In **scientific notation,** *numbers are written in the form* M × 10^n, *where the factor* M *is a number greater than or equal to 1 but less than 10 and* n *is a whole number. For example, to write the quantity 65 000 km in* scientific notation and show the first two digits as significant, you would write the following.

$$6.5 \times 10^4 \text{ km}$$

Writing the M factor as 6.5 shows that there are exactly two significant figures. If, instead, you intended the first three digits in 65 000 to be significant, you would write 6.50×10^4 km. When numbers are written in scientific notation, only the significant figures are shown.

Suppose you are expressing a very small quantity, such as the length of a flu virus. In ordinary notation this length could be 0.000 12 mm. That length can be expressed in scientific notation as follows.

$$0.000\ 12 \text{ mm} = 1.2 \times 10^{-4} \text{ mm}$$

move the decimal point four places to the
right and multiply the number by 10^{-4}

1. Determine M by moving the decimal point in the original number to the left or the right so that only one nonzero digit remains to the left of the decimal point.
2. Determine n by counting the number of places that you moved the decimal point. If you moved it to the left, n is positive. If you moved it to the right, n is negative.

Mathematical Operations Using Scientific Notation

1. *Addition and subtraction* These operations can be performed only if the values have the same exponent (n factor). If they do not, adjustments must be made to the values so that the exponents are equal. Once the exponents are equal, the M factors can be added or subtracted. The exponent of the answer can remain the same, or it may then require adjustment if the M factor of the answer has more than one digit to the left of the decimal point. Consider the example of the addition of 4.2×10^4 kg and 7.9×10^3 kg.

We can make both exponents either 3 or 4. The following solutions are possible.

$$\begin{array}{r} 4.2\ \times 10^4 \text{ kg} \\ +0.79 \times 10^4 \text{ kg} \\ \hline 4.99 \times 10^4 \text{ kg rounded to } 5.0 \times 10^4 \text{ kg} \end{array}$$

or

$$\begin{array}{r} 7.9\ \times 10^3 \text{ kg} \\ +42\ \ \ \times 10^3 \text{ kg} \\ \hline 49.9\ \times 10^3 \text{ kg} = 4.99 \times 10^4 \text{ kg rounded to } 5.0 \times 10^4 \text{ kg} \end{array}$$

Note that the units remain kg throughout.

DEMONSTRATION
Volume and Significant Figures

Measure the length, width, and thickness in centimeters of a small, regular rectangular prism or cube (such as a die) that will not float in water. Record each value to two decimal places. Multiply the three values to obtain the volume. Do not round the value obtained. Then submerge the object in a measured amount of water in a graduated cylinder. Read the new volume in the cylinder. Subtract the final volume measurement from the initial measurement to obtain the volume of the object. The actual value will not match the unrounded result of the original calculation. Point out that there cannot be a net gain in significant information simply as a result of calculation. A calculation result cannot be more precise than the numbers used to generate it.

FIGURE 2-10 Emphasize that the number displayed on the calculator is expressed in scientific notation. If possible, use a calculator designed for use on an overhead projector to demonstrate the technique of working with numbers in scientific notation. Be sure students who have calculators that use different keystrokes know how to work with scientific notation on their particular calculators.

✔ Teaching Tip

The *most common* error that students make in entering numbers in scientific notation follows. For instance, to enter 5.44×10^7, many students enter 5.44, then press ×, then press 10, then press EE, then press 7. Of course, this gives 5.44×10^8. Students need to be warned that the EE button already *includes* the "× 10". Another common error is pressing the "−" (for subtract) button when they are trying to change the sign of a quantity, especially to get a negative exponent, as in 3.4×10^{-3}. Space does not permit comprehensive instruction here on how to use every make of calculator, but these are errors that are common to nearly all brands.

Problem-Solving Practice — HOLT ChemFile

Chapter 4 of the Mini-Guide to Problem Solving (also found on the One-Stop Planner CD-ROM) includes more worked-out samples and additional practice problems for solving quantitative problems by using the 4-step process.

FIGURE 2-10 When you use a scientific calculator to work problems in scientific notation, don't forget to express the value on the display to the correct number of significant figures and show the units when you write the final answer.

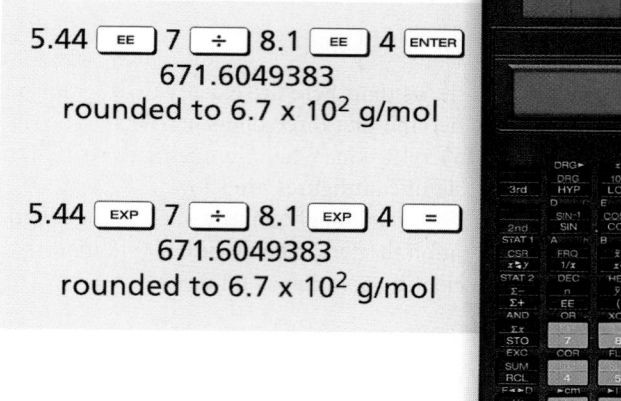

$$5.44 \;\boxed{\text{EE}}\; 7 \;\boxed{\div}\; 8.1 \;\boxed{\text{EE}}\; 4 \;\boxed{\text{ENTER}}$$
671.6049383
rounded to 6.7×10^2 g/mol

$$5.44 \;\boxed{\text{EXP}}\; 7 \;\boxed{\div}\; 8.1 \;\boxed{\text{EXP}}\; 4 \;\boxed{=}$$
671.6049383
rounded to 6.7×10^2 g/mol

2. *Multiplication* The M factors are multiplied, and the exponents are added algebraically.

Consider the multiplication of 5.23×10^6 μm by 7.1×10^{-2} μm.

$$(5.23 \times 10^6 \text{ μm})(7.1 \times 10^{-2} \text{ μm}) = (5.23 \times 7.1)(10^6 \times 10^{-2})$$
$$= 37.133 \times 10^4 \text{ μm}^2 \text{ (adjust to two significant digits)}$$
$$= 3.7 \times 10^5 \text{ μm}^2$$

Note that when length measurements are multiplied, the result is area. The unit is now μm².

3. *Division* The M factors are divided, and the exponent of the denominator is subtracted from that of the numerator. The calculator keystrokes for this problem are shown in Figure 2-10.

$$\frac{5.44 \times 10^7 \text{ g}}{8.1 \times 10^4 \text{ mol}} = \frac{5.44}{8.1} \times 10^{7-4} \text{ g/mol}$$

$$= 0.6716049383 \times 10^3 \text{ (adjust to two significant figures)}$$
$$= 6.7 \times 10^2 \text{ g/mol}$$

Note that the unit for the answer is the ratio of grams to moles.

Using Sample Problems

Learning to analyze and solve such problems requires practice and a logical approach. In this section, you will review a process that can help you analyze problems effectively. Most Sample Problems in this book are organized by four basic steps to guide your thinking in how to work out the solution to a problem.

Analyze

The first step in solving a quantitative word problem is to read the problem carefully at least twice and to analyze the information in it. Note any important descriptive terms that clarify or add meaning to the problem. Identify and list the data given in the problem. Also identify the unknown—the quantity you are asked to find.

Plan

The second step is to develop a plan for solving the problem. The plan should show how the information given is to be used to find the unknown. In the process, reread the problem to make sure you have gathered all the necessary information. It is often helpful to draw a picture that represents the problem. For example, if you were asked to determine the volume of a crystal given its dimensions, you could draw a representation of the crystal and label the dimensions. This drawing would help you visualize the problem.

Decide which conversion factors, mathematical formulas, or chemical principles you will need to solve the problem. Your plan might suggest a single calculation or a series of them involving different conversion factors. Once you understand how you need to proceed, you may wish to sketch out the route you will take, using arrows to point the way from one stage of the solution to the next. Sometimes you will need data that are not actually part of the problem statement. For instance, you'll often use data from the periodic table.

Compute

The third step involves substituting the data and necessary conversion factors into the plan you have developed. At this stage you calculate the answer, cancel units, and round the result to the correct number of significant figures. It is very important to have a plan worked out in step 2 before you start using the calculator. All too often, students start multiplying or dividing values given in the problem before they really understand what they need to do to get an answer.

Evaluate

Examine your answer to determine whether it is reasonable. Use the following methods, when appropriate, to carry out the evaluation.

1. Check to see that the units are correct. If they are not, look over the setup. Are the conversion factors correct?
2. Make an estimate of the expected answer. Use simpler, rounded numbers to do so. Compare the estimate with your actual result. The two should be similar.
3. Check the order of magnitude in your answer. Does it seem reasonable compared with the values given in the problem? If you calculated the density of vegetable oil and got a value of 54.9 g/mL, you would know that something is wrong. Oil floats on water; therefore, its density is less than water, so the value obtained should be less than 1.0 g/mL.
4. Be sure that the answer given for any problem is expressed using the correct number of significant figures.

SECTION 2-3

Alternative Assessment

Ask students to explain each step involved in problem solving. Then have students work at the chalkboard, perhaps in competing teams, to solve practice problems according to the analyze, plan, compute, and evaluate sequence of steps. Have the students constructively critique one another's solution strategies and setups.

ADDITIONAL

SAMPLE PROBLEMS

2-6 Calculate the density of a liquid, given that 41.4 mL of it has a mass of 58.24 g.

Ans. 1.41 g/mL

2-6 How many kilometers are there in 6.2×10^7 cm?

Ans. 6.2×10^2 km

2-6 How many hours are there in exactly 3 weeks?

Ans. 504 hours

Look over the following quantitative Sample Problems. Notice how the four-step approach is used in each, and then apply the approach yourself in solving the practice problems that follow.

SAMPLE PROBLEM 2-6

Calculate the volume of a sample of aluminum that has a mass of 3.057 kg. The density of aluminum is 2.70 g/cm³.

SOLUTION

1 ANALYZE

Given: mass = 3.057 g, density = 2.70 g/cm³
Unknown: volume of aluminum

2 PLAN

The density unit in the problem is g/cm³, and the mass given in the problem is expressed in kg. Therefore, in addition to using the density equation, you will need a conversion factor representing the relationship between grams and kilograms.

$$1000 \text{ g} = 1 \text{ kg}$$

Also, rearrange the density equation to solve for volume.

$$density = \frac{mass}{volume} \quad \text{or} \quad D = \frac{m}{V}$$

$$V = \frac{m}{D}$$

3 COMPUTE

$$V = \frac{3.057 \text{ kg}}{2.70 \text{ g/cm}^3} \times \frac{1000 \text{ g}}{\text{kg}} = 1132.222 \ldots \text{cm}^3 \text{ (calculator answer)}$$

The answer should be rounded to three significant figures.

$$V = 1.13 \times 10^3 \text{ cm}^3$$

4 EVALUATE

The unit of volume, cm³, is correct. An order-of-magnitude estimate would put the answer at over 1000 cm³.

$$\frac{3}{2} \times 1000$$

The correct number of significant digits is three, to match the number of significant figures in 2.70 g/cm³.

PRACTICE

1. What is the volume of a sample of helium that has a mass of 1.73×10^{-3} g, given that the density is 0.178 47 g/L?

   Answer
   9.69 mL

2. What is the density of a piece of metal that has a mass of 6.25×10^5 g and is 92.5 cm × 47.3 cm × 85.4 cm?

   Answer
   1.67 g/cm³

3. How many millimeters are there in 5.12×10^5 kilometers?

   Answer
   5.12×10^{11} mm

4. A clock gains 0.020 second per minute. How many seconds will the clock gain in exactly six months, assuming exactly 30 days per month?

   Answer
   5.2×10^3 s

Direct Proportions

Two quantities are **directly proportional** *to each other if dividing one by the other gives a constant value.* For example, if the masses and volumes of different samples of aluminum are measured, the masses and volumes will be directly proportional to each other. As the masses of the samples increase, their volumes increase at the same rate, as you can see from the data in Table 2-7. Doubling the mass doubles the volume. Halving the mass halves the volume.

When two variables, x and y, are directly proportional to each other, the relationship can be expressed as $y \propto x$, which is read as "y is *proportional* to x." The general equation for a directly proportional relationship between the two variables can also be written as follows.

$$\frac{y}{x} = k$$

The value of k is a constant called the proportionality constant. Written in this form, the equation expresses an important fact about direct proportion: the ratio between the variables remains constant. Note that using the mass and volume values in Table 2-7 gives a mass-volume ratio that is constant (neglecting measurement error). The equation can be rearranged into the following form.

$$y = kx$$

The equation $y = kx$ may look familiar to you. It is the equation for a special case of a straight line. If two variables related in this way are graphed versus one another, a straight line, or linear plot that passes through the origin (0,0), results. The data for aluminum from Table 2-7 are graphed in Figure 2-11. The mass and volume of a pure substance are directly proportional to each other. Consider mass to be y and volume to be x. The constant ratio, k, for the two variables is density. The slope of the line reflects the constant density, or mass-volume ratio, of

Visual Strategy
FIGURE 2-11 Have each student choose a mass of aluminum that is not listed in Table 2-7 but lies on the line shown on the graph. Have the students use the graph to find the corresponding volume. Students should then be able to calculate the density of aluminum for their chosen samples and compare these values with those in Table 2-7.

Common Misconception
Students may make the common error of thinking that all linear plots represent direct proportions. Point out that only straight lines that pass through the point (0,0) represent direct proportions. You can illustrate that fact by drawing a linear graph that does not pass through the origin and then showing that the ratio for the two variables does not remain constant.

FIGURE 2-11 The graph of mass versus volume shows a relationship of direct proportion. Notice that the line is extrapolated to pass through the origin.

TABLE 2-7	Mass-Volume Data for Aluminum at 20°C	
Mass (g)	Volume (cm³)	$\frac{m}{V}$ (g/cm³)
54.4	20.1	2.70
65.7	24.15	2.72
83.5	30.9	2.70
97.2	35.8	2.71
105.7	39.1	2.70

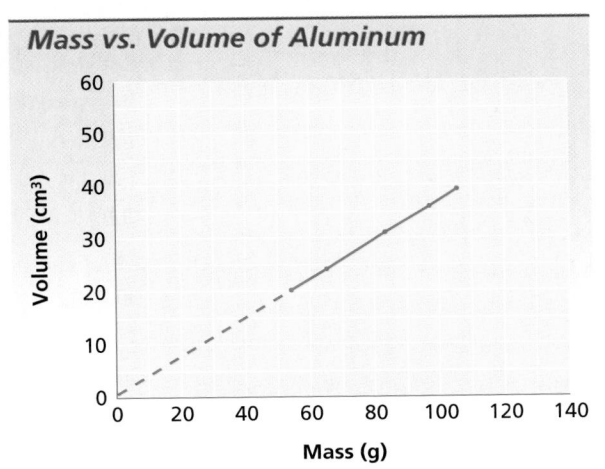

Mass vs. Volume of Aluminum

TABLE STRATEGY

Table 2-8 Use the table to show that the products of the two variables—pressure and volume—remain essentially equal, which is the criterion for an inverse relationship. Have students attempt to plot the values before they look at Figure 2-12 on page 57, which displays the correct plot.

CHAPTER ⟷ CONNECTION

The inversely proportional relationship between gas pressure and volume, $P \times V = k$, is called Boyle's law. It will be covered in Chapter 10.

aluminum, which is 2.70 g/cm^3 at 20°C. Notice also that the plotted line passes through the origin. All directly proportional relationships produce linear graphs that pass through the origin.

Inverse Proportions

Two quantities are **inversely proportional** *to each other if their product is constant.* An example of an inversely proportional relationship is that between speed of travel and the time required to cover a fixed distance. The greater the speed, the less time that is needed to go a certain fixed distance. Doubling the speed cuts the required time in half. Halving the speed doubles the required time.

When two variables, x and y, are inversely proportional to each other, the relationship can be expressed as follows.

$$y \propto \frac{1}{x}$$

This is read "y is *proportional* to 1 divided by x." The general equation for an inversely proportional relationship between the two variables can be written in the following form.

$$xy = k$$

In the equation, k is the proportionality constant. If x increases, y must decrease to keep the product constant.

A graph of variables that are inversely proportional produces a curve called a hyperbola. Such a graph is illustrated in Figure 2-12. When the temperature of the gas is kept constant, the volume (V) of the gas sample decreases as the pressure (P) increases. Look at the data shown in Table 2-8. Note that $P \times V$ gives a reasonably constant value. The graph of this data is shown in Figure 2-12.

TABLE 2-8 *Pressure-Volume Data for Nitrogen at Constant Temperature*		
Pressure (kPa)	**Volume (cm³)**	**$P \times V$**
100	500	50 000
150	333	49 500
200	250	50 000
250	200	50 000
300	166	49 800
350	143	50 500
400	125	50 000
450	110	49 500

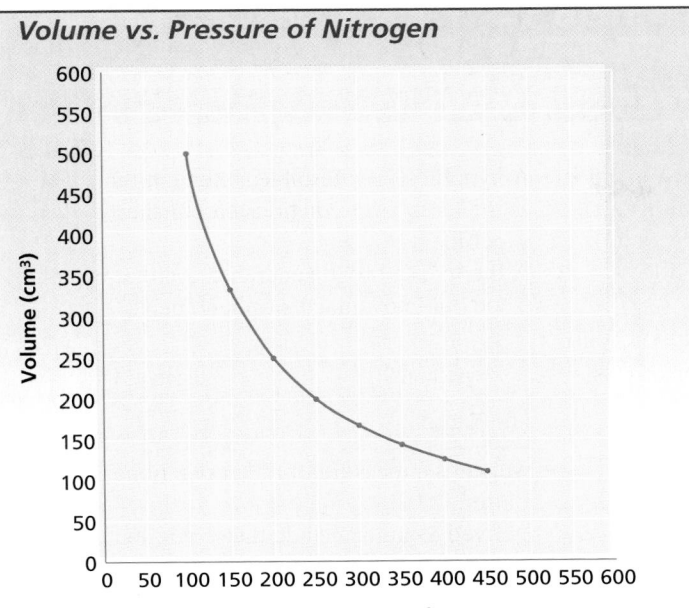

Volume vs. Pressure of Nitrogen

FIGURE 2-12 The graph of pressure versus volume shows an inversely proportional relationship. Note the difference between the shape of this graph and that of the graph in Figure 2-11.

SECTION REVIEW

1. The density of copper is listed as 8.94 g/cm³. Two students each make three density determinations of samples of the substance. Student A's results are 7.3 g/mL, 9.4 g/mL, and 8.3 g/mL. Student B's results are 8.4 g/cm³, 8.8 g/cm³, and 8.0 g/cm³. Compare the two sets of results in terms of precision and accuracy.

2. How many significant figures are there in each of the following measured values?
   a. 6.002 cm
   b. 0.0020 m
   c. 10.0500 g
   d. 7000 kg
   e. 7000. kg

3. Round 2.6765 to two significant figures.

4. Carry out the following calculations.
   a. 52.13 g + 1.7502 g
   b. 12 m × 6.41 m
   c. $\dfrac{16.25 \text{ g}}{5.1442 \text{ mL}}$

5. Perform the following operations. Express each answer in scientific notation.

   a. $(1.54 \times 10^{-2} \text{ g}) + (2.86 \times 10^{-1} \text{ g})$
   b. $(7.023 \times 10^{9} \text{ g}) - (6.62 \times 10^{7} \text{ g})$
   c. $(8.99 \times 10^{-4} \text{ m}) \times (3.57 \times 10^{4} \text{ m})$
   d. $\dfrac{2.17 \times 10^{-3} \text{ g}}{5.022 \times 10^{4} \text{ mL}}$

6. Write the following numbers in scientific notation.
   a. 560 000
   b. 33 400
   c. 0.000 4120

7. A student measures the mass of a beaker filled with corn oil. The mass reading averages 215.6 g. The mass of the beaker is 110.4 g.
   a. What is the mass of the corn oil?
   b. What is the density of the corn oil if its volume is 114 cm³?

8. Calculate the mass of a sample of gold that occupies 5.0×10^{-3} cm³. The density of gold is 19.3 g/cm³.

9. What is the difference between a graph representing data that are directly proportional and a graph of data that are inversely proportional?

SECTION REVIEW

1. B's results are more precise and more accurate.

2. a. 4
   b. 2
   c. 6
   d. 1
   e. 4

3. 2.7

4. a. 53.88 g
   b. 77 m²
   c. 3.159 g/mL

5. a. 3.01×10^{-1} g
   b. 6.957×10^{9} g
   c. 3.21×10^{1} m²
   d. 4.32×10^{-8} g/mL

6. a. 5.6×10^{5}
   b. 3.34×10^{4}
   c. 4.120×10^{-4}

7. a. 105.2 g
   b. 0.923 g/cm³

8. 9.6×10^{-2} g/cm³

9. directly proportional: straight line that passes through origin; inversely proportional: hyperbola

REVIEW ANSWERS

1. Quantitative information is numerical; qualitative information is non-numerical.

2. a testable statement that serves as a basis for making predictions and carrying out further experiments

3. **a.** a visual, verbal, or mathematical explanation of how phenomena occur and data are related
   b. A model, if it is successful, may become part of a theory. A theory is much broader than a model.

4. to have universal agreement and avoid confusion

5. A quantity is something that has magnitude, size, or amount (e.g., volume, mass). A unit compares what is to be measured with a previously defined size (e.g., meter, gram).

6. meter, length; kilogram, mass; second, time; kelvin, temperature; mole, amount of substance; ampere, electric current; candela, luminous intensity

7. **a.** 1000 or 10^3

   b. $\frac{1}{100}$ or 10^{-2}

   c. 1 000 000 or 10^6

   d. $\frac{1}{1\,000\,000}$ or 10^{-6}

   e. $\frac{1}{1000}$ or 10^{-3}

8. **a.** meter
   b. millimeter or centimeter
   c. kilometer
   d. micrometer

9. **a.** kilogram   **c.** gram
   b. gram

10. Fundamental units must be unvarying, but day length depends on Earth's rotation rate, which is not constant.

CHAPTER SUMMARY

2-1
- The scientific method is a logical approach to solving problems that lend themselves to investigation.
- The processes of observing, generalizing, theorizing, and testing are aspects of the scientific method.
- A hypothesis is a testable statement that serves as the basis for predictions and further experiments.
- A theory is a broad generalization that explains a body of known facts or phenomena.

Vocabulary

hypothesis (30)	scientific method (29)
model (31)	

system (29)	theory (31)

2-2
- The result of nearly every measurement is a number and a unit.
- The SI system of measurement is used in science. It has seven base units: the meter (length), kilogram (mass), second (time), kelvin (temperature), mole (quantity of substance), ampere (electric current), and candela (luminous intensity).
- Weight is a measure of the gravitational pull on matter.
- Derived SI units include the square meter (area) and the cubic meter (volume).
- Density is the ratio of mass to volume.
- Conversion factors are used to convert from one unit to another.

Vocabulary

conversion factor (40)	derived unit (36)
density (38)	quantity (33)

SI (33)	weight (35)
volume (37)	

2-3
- Accuracy refers to the closeness of a measurement to the correct or accepted value. Precision refers to the closeness of values for a set of measurements.
- The measurement average is the sum of a group of measurements divided by the total number of measurements.
- Percent error is the difference between the accepted and the experimental value, divided by the accepted value, then multiplied by 100.
- The significant figures in a number consist of all digits known with certainty plus one final digit, which is uncertain or estimated. A set of logical rules must be followed to determine the number of significant figures in numbers containing zeros.
- After addition or subtraction, the answer should be rounded so that it has no more digits to the right of the decimal point than there are in the measurement with the smallest number of digits
- to the right of the decimal point. After multiplication or division, the answer should be rounded so that it has no more significant figures than there are in the measurement with the fewest number of significant figures.
- Exact conversion factors are completely certain and do not limit the number of digits in a calculation.
- A number written in scientific notation is of the form $M \times 10^n$, where M is greater than or equal to 1 but less than 10 and n is an integer.
- Two quantities are directly proportional to each other if dividing one by the other gives a constant value. The graphs of variables related in this way are straight lines that pass through the origin.
- Two quantities are inversely proportional to each other if their product has a constant value. The graphs of variables related in this way are hyperbolas.

Vocabulary

accuracy (44)	indirectly proportional (55)
directly proportional (56)	percent error (45)

precision (44)	significant figures (46)
scientific notation (50)	

REVIEWING CONCEPTS

1. How does quantitative information differ from qualitative information? (2-1)

2. What is a hypothesis? (2-1)

3. a. What is a model in the scientific sense?
   b. How does a model differ from a theory? (2-1)

4. Why is it important for a measurement system to have an international standard? (2-2)

5. How does a quantity differ from a unit? Use two examples to explain the difference. (2-2)

6. List the seven SI base units and the quantities they represent. (2-2)

7. What is the numerical equivalent of each of the following SI prefixes?
   a. kilo-   d. micro-
   b. centi-   e. milli-
   c. mega-   (2-2)

8. Identify the SI unit that would be most appropriate for expressing the length of the following.
   a. width of a gymnasium
   b. length of a finger
   c. distance between your town and the closest border of the next state
   d. length of a bacterial cell (2-2)

9. Identify the SI unit that would be most appropriate for measuring the mass of each of the following objects.
   a. table
   b. coin
   c. a 250 mL beaker (2-2)

10. Explain why the second is not defined by the length of the day. (2-2)

11. a. What is a derived unit?
    b. What is the SI derived unit for area? (2-2)

12. a. List two SI derived units for volume.
    b. List two non-SI units for volume, and explain how they relate to the cubic centimeter. (2-2)

13. a. Why are the units used to express the densities of gases different from those used to express the densities of solids or liquids?
    b. Name two units for density.
    c. Why is the temperature at which a density is measured usually specified? (2-2)

14. a. Which of the solids listed in Table 2-4 will float on water?
    b. Which of the liquids will sink in milk?

15. a. Define *conversion factor*.
    b. Explain how conversion factors are used. (2-2)

16. Contrast accuracy and precision. (2-3)

17. a. Write the equation that is used to calculate percent error.
    b. Under what condition will percent error be negative? (2-3)

18. How is the average for a set of values calculated?

19. What is meant by a mass measurement expressed in this form: 4.6 g ± 0.2 g?

20. Suppose a graduated cylinder were not correctly calibrated. How would this affect the results of a measurement? How would it affect the results of a calculation using this measurement?

21. Round each of the following measurements to the number of significant figures indicated.
    a. 67.029 g to three significant figures
    b. 0.15 L to one significant figure
    c. 52.8005 mg to five significant figures
    d. 3.174 97 mol to three significant figures (2-3)

22. State the rules governing the number of significant figures that result from each of the following operations.
    a. addition and subtraction
    b. multiplication and division (2-3)

23. What is the general form for writing numbers in scientific notation? (2-3)

24. a. State the general equation for quantities that are directly proportional.
    b. For two directly proportional quantities, what happens to one variable when the other increases? (2-3)

25. a. State the general equation for quantities that are inversely proportional.
    b. For two inversely proportional quantities, what happens to one variable when the other increases? (2-3)

26. Arrange in proper order the following four basic steps in working out the solution to a problem: compute, plan, evaluate, analyze. (2-3)

11. a. a unit that can be obtained from combinations of fundamental units
    b. the square meter (m^2)

12. a. cubic meter, cubic centimeter
    b. liter (= 1000 cm^3), milliliter (= 1 cm^3)

13. a. Smaller units are used because gases are less dense.
    b. g/cm^3, g/L
    c. Temperature affects volume.

14. a. cork, butter, ice   b. mercury

15. a. a ratio derived from the equality between different units and that can be used to convert from one unit to another
    b. The unit to be changed is multiplied by a conversion factor that has the desired unit in the numerator and the unit to be canceled in the denominator.

16. Accuracy refers to the closeness of measurements to the correct or accepted value. Precision refers to the closeness of a set of measurements to one another.

17. a. % error = $\frac{Value_{accepted} - Value_{experimental}}{Value_{accepted}} \times 100$
    b. if the experimental value is higher than the accepted value

18. by adding the values and dividing by the number of values

19. between 4.4 and 4.8 g

20. It would introduce error in the measurement and any subsequent calculations.

21. a. 67.0 g   c. 52.800 mg
    b. 0.2 L   d. 3.17 mol

22. a. The answer must have the same number of digits to the right of the decimal point as there are in the measurement with the fewest digits to the right of the decimal point.
    b. The answer can have no more significant figures than are in the

measurement with the fewest number of significant figures.

23. $M \times 10^n$, where M is greater than or equal to 1 but less than 10 and n is a whole number

24. **a.** $y/x = k$, or $y = kx$
    b. It also increases.

25. **a.** $xy = k$ **b.** It decreases.

26. analyze, plan, compute, evaluate

27. 7.5 m^3

28. 1.55 g/mL

29. 3.70×10^2 g

30. 0.547 mL

31. 8.82×10^{-4} g

32. 6.03×10^2 mL

33. **a.** 37.0 cm^3 **b.** 3.33 cm

34. **a.** 9.225×10^{-2} km
    b. 9.225×10^3 cm

35. 1.5%

36. 19%

37. −2%

38. **a.** four   **c.** six
    b. one   **d.** three

39. 6.411 g

40. 1.1 cm

41. 2.79 m^2

42. 29.74 g/mL

43. **a.** 6.730×10^{-4}
    b. $5.000\ 00 \times 10^4$
    c. 3.010×10^{-6}

44. **a.** 0.007 050 g
    b. 40 000 500 mg
    c. 23 500. mL

45. $8.57 \times 10^8 \text{ m}^2$

46. $2.22 \times 10^{-3} \text{ cm}^3$

47. rewritten numbers:
    1.006×10^2 kg, 9.64×10^1 kg;
    final answer: 4.2 kg

48. $1.4 \times 10^6 \text{ m}^3$

49. 1.43 g/cm^3

50. 9.47×10^{-4} g; 9.47×10^{-7} kg

51. 13.5%

52. Li $= 1.47 \times 10^7 \text{ pm}^3$
    Na $= 2.70 \times 10^7 \text{ pm}^3$

PROBLEMS

Volume and Density

27. What is the volume, in cubic meters, of a rectangular solid that is 0.25 m long, 6.1 m wide, and 4.9 m high?

28. Find the density of a material, given that a 5.03 g sample occupies 3.24 mL. (Hint: See Sample Problem 2-1.)

29. What is the mass of a sample of material that has a volume of 55.1 cm^3 and a density of 6.72 g/cm^3?

30. A sample of a substance that has a density of 0.824 g/mL has a mass of 0.451 g. Calculate the volume of the sample.

Conversion Factors

31. How many grams are there in 882 μg? (Hint: See Sample Problem 2-2.)

32. Calculate the number of mL in 0.603 L.

33. The density of gold is 19.3 g/cm^3.
    a. What is the volume, in cm^3, of a sample of gold with mass 0.715 kg?
    b. If this sample of gold is a cube, how long is each edge in cm?

34. a. Find the number of km in 92.25 m.
    b. Convert the answer in km to cm.

Percent Error

35. A student measures the mass of a sample as 9.67 g. Calculate the percent error, given that the correct mass is 9.82 g. (Hint: See Sample Problem 2-3.)

36. A handbook gives the density of calcium as 1.54 g/cm^3. What is the percent error of a density calculation of 1.25 g/cm^3 based on lab measurements?

37. What is the percent error of a length measurement of 0.229 cm if the correct value is 0.225 cm?

Significant Figures

38. How many significant figures are there in each of the following measurements? (Hint: See Sample Problem 2-4.)
    a. 0.4004 mL
    b. 6000 g

c. 1.000 30 km
d. 400. mm

39. Calculate the sum of 6.078 g and 0.3329 g.

40. Subtract 7.11 cm from 8.2 cm. (Hint: See Sample Problem 2-5.)

41. What is the product of 0.8102 m and 3.44 m?

42. Divide 94.20 g by 3.167 22 mL.

Scientific Notation

43. Write the following numbers in scientific notation.
    a. 0.000 673 0
    b. 50 000.0
    c. 0.000 003 010

44. The following numbers are in scientific notation. Write them in ordinary notation.
    a. 7.050×10^{-3} g
    b. $4.000\ 05 \times 10^7$ mg
    c. $2.350\ 0 \times 10^4$ mL

45. Perform the following operation. Express the answer in scientific notation and with the correct number of significant figures.
$$\frac{6.124\ 33 \times 10^6 \text{ m}^3}{7.15 \times 10^{-3} \text{ m}}$$

46. A sample of a certain material has a mass of 2.03×10^{-3} g. Calculate the volume of the sample, given that the density is $9.133 \times 10^{-1} \text{ g/cm}^3$. Use the four-step method in solving the problem. (Hint: See Sample Problem 2-6.)

MIXED REVIEW

47. A man finds that he has a mass of 100.6 kg. He goes on a diet, and several months later he finds that he has a mass of 96.4 kg. Express each number in scientific notation, and calculate the number of kilograms the man has lost by dieting.

48. A large office building is 1.07×10^2 m long, 31 m wide, and 4.25×10^2 m high. What is its volume?

49. An object is found to have a mass of 57.6 g. Find the object's density, given that its volume is 40.25 cm^3.

50. A student measures the mass of some sucrose as 0.947 mg. Convert that quantity to grams and to kilograms.

51. A student calculates the density of iron as 6.80 g/cm^3 using lab data for mass and volume. A handbook reveals that the correct value is 7.86 g/cm^3. What is the percent error?

 HANDBOOK SEARCH

52. Find the table of properties for Group 1 elements in the *Elements Handbook*, pages 726–783. Calculate the volume of a single atom of each element listed in the table using the equation for the volume of a sphere.

$$\frac{4}{3}\pi r^3$$

53. Use the radius of a sodium atom from the *Elements Handbook* to calculate the number of sodium atoms in a row 5.00 cm long. Assume that each sodium atom touches its two neighbors.

54. a. A block of sodium with measurements 3.00 cm × 5.00 cm × 5.00 cm has a measured mass of 75.5 g. Calculate the density of sodium.
   b. Compare your calculated density with the value in the properties table for Group 1 elements. Calculate the percent error for your density determination.

RESEARCH & WRITING

55. Find out how the metric system, which was once a standard for measurement, differs from SI. Why was it necessary to change to SI?

56. Find out what ISO 9000 standards are. How do they affect industry on an international level?

ALTERNATIVE ASSESSMENT

57. Performance Obtain three metal samples from your teacher. Determine the mass and volume of each sample. Calculate the density of each metal from your measurement data. (Hint:

Consider using the water displacement technique to measure the volume of your samples.)

58. Using the data from the Nutrition Facts label below, answer the following.
   a. Use the data given on the label for grams of fat and Calories from fat to construct a conversion factor with the units Calories per gram.
   b. Calculate the mass in kilograms of 20 servings of the food.
   c. Calculate the mass of protein in micrograms for one serving of the food.
   d. What is the correct number of significant figures for the answer in item a? Why?

Nutrition Facts

Serving Size ¾ cup (30g)
Servings Per Container About 14

Amount Per Serving	Corn Crunch	with ½ cup skim milk
Calories	120	160
Calories from Fat	15	20

	% Daily Value**	
Total Fat 2g*	**3**%	**3**%
Saturated Fat 0g	**0**%	**0**%
Cholesterol 0mg	**0**%	**1**%
Sodium 160mg	**7**%	**9**%
Potassium 65mg	**2**%	**8**%
Total Carbohydrate 25g	**8**%	**10**%
Dietary Fiber 3g		
Sugars 3g		
Other Carbohydrate 11g		
Protein 2g		

*Amount in Cereal. A serving of cereal plus skim milk provides 2g fat, less 5mg cholesterol, 220mg sodium, 270mg potassium, 31g carbohydrate (19g sugars) and 6g protein.

**Percent Daily Values are based on a 2,000 calorie diet. Your daily values may be higher or lower depending on your calorie needs:

	Calories	2,000	2,500
Total Fat	Less than	65g	80g
Sat Fat	Less than	20g	25g
Cholesterol	Less than	300mg	300mg
Sodium	Less than	2,400mg	2,400mg
Potassium		3,500mg	3,500mg
Total Carbohydrate		300g	375g
Dietary Fiber		25g	30g

K = 5.23 × 10^7 pm^3
Rb = 6.39 × 10^7 pm^3
Cs = 7.80 × 10^7 pm^3
Fr = 8.24 × 10^7 pm^3

53. 4.90 × 10^{12} atoms

54. a. 1.01 g/cm^3 **b.** 3%

55. SI is the modern, more-simplified form of the metric system that has seven base units as its foundation. The older metric system was based on standards for length, time, capacity (volume), and mass. Use of SI in the United States allows a greater marketability for this country's goods and services throughout the world.

56. ISO, International Standards Organization in Geneva, Switzerland, promotes international uniformity of standards in technical fields.

57. Density data for some metals are found in Appendix A. The following metals are suggested for this activity: Zn, Fe, W, Mg, Cr, and Pb.

58. a. 2 g fat : 15 Calories
        1 g : 7.5 Cal
            8 Cal/g
   b. 0.6 kg
   c. 2 × 10^5 μg
   d. one; the value 2 g limits the number of significant figures for these data.

UNIT
2

Organization of Matter

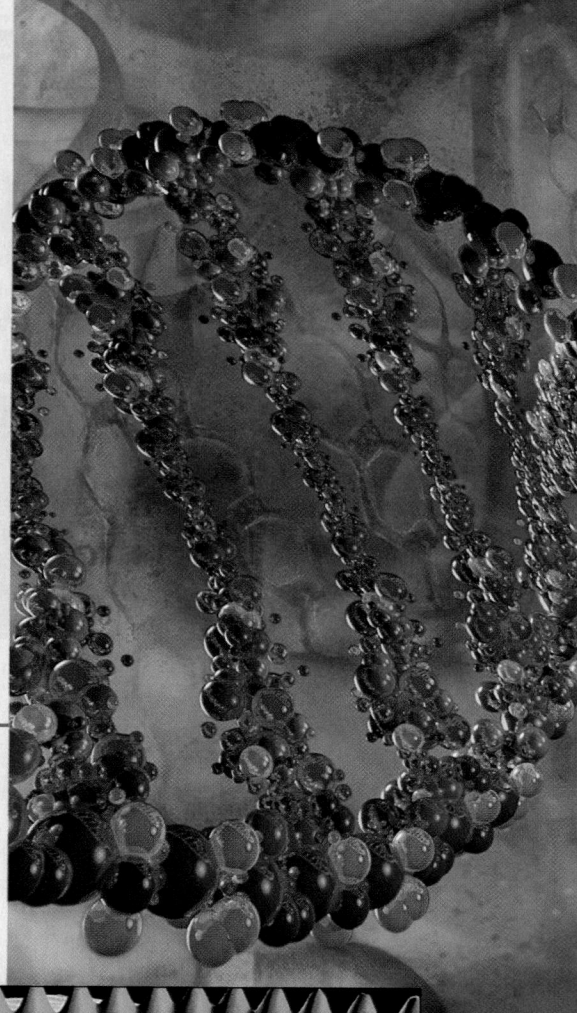

CHAPTERS

3   **Atoms: The Building Blocks of Matter**

4   **Arrangement of Electrons in Atoms**

5   **The Periodic Law**

6   **Chemical Bonding**

Our knowledge of the atoms in a given molecule, of how they are connected to each other, and even of the molecule's three-dimensional shape, is largely indirect. We use various instruments, perturbing the molecules (often by light) and measure their responses.

The ingenious way analytical chemistry knows without seeing is an incredible achievement of this century.

(From Scientific American's *Triumph of Discovery*)

Atoms: The Building Blocks of Matter

PACING CHART	CLASSROOM RESOURCES		
Compression Guide: *(To shorten, eliminate items in italics.)*	NSE Standards	Teaching Resources	Experiments
3-1 **The Atom: From Philosophical Idea to Scientific Theory** 2 45-minute periods 1 90-minute block	PS 1a, 2b UCP 2, 4 SAI 1–2 HNS 1–3	T 12, T 13	**PE** Quick Lab, p. 69 **PE** Conservation of Mass, p. 798 **C1** **EXP** Conservation of Mass
3-2 **The Structure of the Atom** 2 45-minute periods 1 90-minute block *The Sizes of Atoms, p. 74* *Average Atomic Masses of Elements, pp. 79–80*	PS 1a, 1b, 1c UCP 1–2 SAI 2 HNS 1–3	**ATE** Demo, p. 70 T 14, T 15	
3-3 **Counting Atoms** 2 45-minute periods 1 90-minute block	PS 1b UCP 1–3 SAI 2	T 16, TM 12A	

Review and Assessment	REVIEW RESOURCES		
2 45-minute periods 1 90-minute block	Cumulative Review	Alternative Assessment	Traditional Assessment
	SR Chapter 3 Mixed Review **PE** Chapter 3 24–31, p. 88	**PE** 41, 42, p. 89 **ATE** 73, 80, 81 **AA** Items for Chapter 3	Chapter 3 Text Test Generator items for Chapter 3

ASSIGNMENT RESOURCES

Section Homework Resources & Review	Problem-Solving Practice
HR Homework Worksheets 3-1, 3-2 Graphic Org. Assignments 3-1, 3-2 **PE** Section Review, 1–3, p. 69 Chapter Review, 1–2, p. 87 **SR** Section Review 3-1	
HR Homework Worksheets 3-3, 3-4 Graphic Org. Assignments 3-3, 3-4 **PE** Section Review, 1–5, p. 74 Chapter Review, 3–6, p. 87 **SR** Section Review 3-2	
HR Homework Worksheets 3-5, 3-6, 3-7 **PE** Section Review, 1, 4–7, p. 85 Chapter Review, 7–18, 21–23, p. 87 **SR** Section Review 3-3	**PE** Additional Samples 3-1, 3-2, 3-3, 3-4, 3-5 **ATE** Additional Samples, pp. 78, 82, 83, 84 **PS** Chapter 5 Mole Concept

TECHNOLOGY RESOURCES

Technology & Internet Resources

 CTW **8** Segment 8 The Top Quark
CTW **13** Segment 13 Atom Builders

 Holt Chemistry Videodiscs Teacher's Correlation Guide for Chapter 3

 Module 2: Atomic Structure

internet connect

 On-line Student Resources:
GO TO: www.scilinks.org
The following SciLinks Internet resources can be found in the student text for this chapter.

TOPICS:
• Atomic theory, p. 66 (HC2031)
• Carbon, p. 67 (HC2032)
• Subatomic particles, p. 71 (HC2033)
• Isotopes, p. 77 (HC2034)

 On-line Teacher Resources:
GO TO: go.hrw.com
KEYWORD: HC2 HOME
Visit the HRW Web site for a variety of resources related to this chapter.

 Smithsonian Institution
Internet Connections
Visit **www.si.edu/hrw** for additional on-line resources.

CNNfyi.com
Visit **www.cnnfyi.com** for late-breaking news and current events stories selected just for you.

Resource Key	One-Stop Planner CD-ROM Includes these resources and customizable daily lesson plans:			
 **PE** Pupil's Edition **ATE** Teacher's Edition	**HR** Homework Resources **SR** Section Reviews **CTW** Critical Thinking Worksheets **AA** Alternative Assessments	**ChemFile** **A** Laboratory Experiments **B** Microscale Experiments **C** Technique Builders and Problem-Solving Experiments	**D** Consumer Experiments **T** Transparencies **TM** Transparency Masters **PS** Mini-Guide to Problem Solving **SRW** Supplemental Reading Worksheets	

Scoring Rubrics for Labs, Alternative Assessments, Performance Tasks and Portfolio Projects are on the One-Stop Planner CD-ROM.

Chapter 3

*Atoms:
The Building
Blocks of Matter*

Chapter Overview

3-1 covers the history and development of atomic theory, from Democritus to Dalton to the modern era.

3-2 covers the experiments that led to the discovery of the electron and the nucleus as well as the principal properties of these subatomic particles.

3-3 outlines the manner in which the number of atoms of an element and the number of subatomic particles inside atoms can be expressed and measured.

Concept Base

Students may need a review of the following concepts:

• traits of matter, Chapter 1

• calculations and units, Chapter 2

 Reading Skill-Builder

INTERPRETING VOCABULARY Show students the derivation of the word *atom* from its Greek roots.

a-: not; *tomos:* cutting
Ask them what idea about matter is conveyed by that meaning. Explain that the idea, which also originated in ancient Greece, is that matter can be subdivided only as small as an elemental particle: the atom.

Atoms: The Building Blocks of Matter

An atom is the smallest particle of an element that retains the chemical properties of that element.

The Atom: From Philosophical Idea to Scientific Theory

When you crush a lump of sugar, you can see that it is made up of many smaller particles of sugar. You may grind these particles into a very fine powder, but each tiny piece is still sugar. Now suppose you dissolve the sugar in water. The tiny particles seem to disappear completely. Even if you look at the sugar-water solution through a powerful microscope, you cannot see any sugar particles. Yet if you were to taste the solution, you'd know that the sugar is still there. Observations like these led early philosophers to ponder the fundamental nature of matter. Is it continuous and infinitely divisible, or is it divisible only until a basic, invisible particle that cannot be divided further is reached?

The particle theory of matter was supported as early as 400 B.C. by certain Greek thinkers, such as Democritus. He called nature's basic particle an *atom*, based on the Greek word meaning "indivisible." Aristotle was part of the generation that succeeded Democritus. His ideas had a lasting impact on Western civilization, and he did not believe in atoms. He thought that all matter was continuous, and his opinion was accepted for nearly 2000 years. Neither the view of Aristotle nor that of Democritus was supported by experimental evidence, so each remained speculation until the eighteenth century. Then scientists began to gather evidence favoring the atomic theory of matter.

Foundations of Atomic Theory

Virtually all chemists in the late 1700s accepted the modern definition of an element as a substance that cannot be further broken down by ordinary chemical means. It was also clear that elements combine to form compounds that have different physical and chemical properties than those of the elements that form them. There was great controversy, however, as to whether elements always combine in the same ratio when forming a particular compound.

The transformation of a substance or substances into one or more new substances is known as a *chemical reaction*. In the 1790s, the study of matter was revolutionized by a new emphasis on the quantitative

SECTION 3-1

OBJECTIVES

- Explain the law of conservation of mass, the law of definite proportions, and the law of multiple proportions.

- Summarize the five essential points of Dalton's atomic theory.

- Explain the relationship between Dalton's atomic theory and the law of conservation of mass, the law of definite proportions, and the law of multiple proportions.

Lesson Starter

Write the following two statements on the board: "Young people should not smoke," and, "Smoking at an early age may make it more difficult to quit smoking later." Have students determine which statement is an opinion and which is a theory. Which is similar to Aristotle's statements?

✔ Teaching Tip

An opinion is an unsupported idea; a theory uses reason to explain observations and experimental data. Have students bring in articles from magazines or newspapers. Then have them highlight opinions and theories.

Application

Have students think of examples of evidence that invisible particles exist. Possible examples include perfume diffusing across a room or the sensation caused by wind.

Visual Strategy

FIGURE 3-1 Stress that no matter how few sodium chloride crystals one inspects, the mass percentage of sodium and chloride remains unchanged. This is an example of the law of definite proportions.

CHAPTER ⟷ CONNECTION

Students will use the law of conservation of mass to balance chemical equations in Chapter 8.

FIGURE 3-1 Each of the salt crystals shown here contains exactly 39.34% sodium and 60.66% chlorine by mass.

TOPIC: Atomic theory
GO TO: www.scilinks.org
*sci***LINKS CODE:** HC2031

analysis of chemical reactions. Aided by improved balances, investigators began to accurately measure the masses of the elements and compounds they were studying. This lead to the discovery of several basic laws. One of these laws was the **law of conservation of mass,** *which states that mass is neither destroyed nor created during ordinary chemical reactions or physical changes.* This discovery was soon followed by the assertion that, regardless of where or how a pure chemical compound is prepared, it is composed of a fixed proportion of elements. For example, sodium chloride, also known as ordinary table salt, *always* consists of 39.34% by mass of the element sodium, Na, and 60.66% by mass of the element chlorine, Cl. *The fact that a chemical compound contains the same elements in exactly the same proportions by mass regardless of the size of the sample or source of the compound is known as the* **law of definite proportions.**

It was also known that two elements sometimes combine to form more than one compound. For example, the elements carbon and oxygen form two compounds, carbon dioxide and carbon monoxide. Consider samples of each of these compounds, each containing 1.0 g of carbon. In carbon dioxide, 2.66 g of oxygen combine with 1.0 g of carbon. In carbon monoxide, 1.33 g of oxygen combine with 1.0 g of carbon. The ratio of the masses of oxygen in these two compounds is exactly 2.66 to 1.33, or 2 to 1. This illustrates the **law of multiple proportions:** *If two or more different compounds are composed of the same two elements, then the ratio of the masses of the second element combined with a certain mass of the first element is always a ratio of small whole numbers.*

Dalton's Atomic Theory

In 1808, an English schoolteacher named John Dalton proposed an explanation for the law of conservation of mass, the law of definite proportions, and the law of multiple proportions. He reasoned that elements were composed of atoms and that only whole numbers of atoms can combine to form compounds. His theory can be summed up by the following statements.

1. All matter is composed of extremely small particles called atoms.
2. Atoms of a given element are identical in size, mass, and other properties; atoms of different elements differ in size, mass, and other properties.
3. Atoms cannot be subdivided, created, or destroyed.
4. Atoms of different elements combine in simple whole-number ratios to form chemical compounds.
5. In chemical reactions, atoms are combined, separated, or rearranged.

According to Dalton's atomic theory, the law of conservation of mass is explained by the fact that chemical reactions involve merely the combination, separation, or rearrangement of atoms and that during these processes atoms are not subdivided, created, or destroyed. This

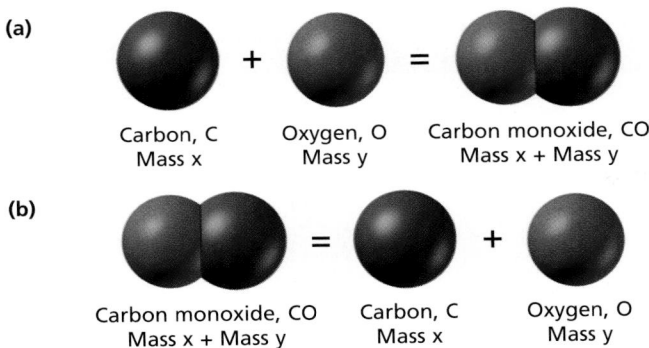

(a)

Carbon, C
Mass x

Oxygen, O
Mass y

Carbon monoxide, CO
Mass x + Mass y

(b)

Carbon monoxide, CO
Mass x + Mass y

Carbon, C
Mass x

Oxygen, O
Mass y

FIGURE 3-2 (a) An atom of carbon, C, and an atom of oxygen, O, can combine chemically to form a molecule of carbon monoxide, CO. The mass of the CO molecule is equal to the mass of the C atom plus the mass of the O atom. (b) The reverse holds true in a reaction in which a CO molecule is broken down into its elements.

idea is illustrated in Figure 3-2 for the formation of carbon monoxide from carbon and oxygen.

The law of definite proportions, on the other hand, results from the fact that a given chemical compound is always composed of the same combination of atoms (see Figure 3-3). As for the law of multiple proportions, in the case of the carbon oxides, the 2-to-1 ratio of oxygen masses results because carbon dioxide always contains twice as many atoms of oxygen (per atom of carbon) as does carbon monoxide. This can also be seen in Figure 3-3.

(a)

Carbon, C   Oxygen, O   Carbon monoxide, CO

(b)

Carbon, C   Oxygen, O   Oxygen, O   Carbon dioxide, CO_2

FIGURE 3-3 (a) CO molecules are always composed of one C atom and one O atom. (b) CO_2 molecules are always composed of one C atom and two O atoms. Note that a molecule of carbon dioxide contains twice as many oxygen atoms as does a molecule of carbon monoxide.

Modern Atomic Theory

By relating atoms to the measurable property of mass, Dalton turned Democritus's *idea* into a *scientific theory* that could be tested by experiment. But not all aspects of Dalton's atomic theory have proven to be correct. For example, today we know that atoms are divisible into even smaller particles (although the law of conservation of mass still holds true for chemical reactions). And, as you will see in Section 3-3, we know that a given element can have atoms with different masses. Atomic theory has not been discarded, however. Instead, it has been modified to explain the new observations. The important concepts that (1) all matter is composed of atoms and that (2) atoms of any one element differ in properties from atoms of another element remain unchanged.

Visual Strategy

FIGURE 3-2 Point out to students that the number of oxygen atoms and the number of carbon atoms are the same before and after each reaction shown. This is an illustration of the law of conservation of mass.

FIGURE 3-3 The mass of a molecule of carbon dioxide is greater than the mass of a molecule of carbon monoxide by the mass of one oxygen atom. This is an illustration of the law of multiple proportions. Have students draw analogies from the world around them. The mass of pennies in a jar is divisible by the mass of a single penny, for example.

Figures 3-2 and 3-3 also illustrate the law of definite proportions. (Each type of molecule is always composed of the same ratio of atoms.)

✔**Teaching Tip**

The ability of scientists to divide atoms into protons, neutrons, and electrons and to then further divide neutrons into quarks and gluons is an example of how atoms are no longer thought of as indivisible. Scientists also now know that atoms of a given element do not necessarily have the same mass. In nature, each element consists of various *isotopes*, atoms with the same number of protons but a different number of neutrons.

internet**connect**

$SC_{\overset{\cdot}{L}INKS}$

NSTA

TOPIC: Carbon
GO TO: www.scilinks.org
*sci***LINKS CODE:** HC2032

Class Discussion

Have students offer their own ideas about how this story demonstrates the law of conservation of mass. *(Following the mass of carbon from one form to another demonstrates how the carbon is neither created nor destroyed but simply combined with different elements.)*

Reading for Meaning

The carbon atom was first part of a molecule of calcium carbonate, $CaCO_3$. In the furnace it became part of a molecule of carbon dioxide, CO_2. Finally, it was incorporated in a molecule of glucose, $C_6H_{12}O_6$, in the plant's leaf.

Read Further

As part of a CO_2 molecule, the carbon atom is unlikely to have been taken into the bird's bloodstream because carbon dioxide is a (waste) product of a bird's oxidative processes, as opposed to oxygen, which is a critical reactant that is taken into the bloodstream.

CHAPTER ⟷ CONNECTION

After students have studied Chapter 19, have them return to this feature to determine whether carbon is being oxidized or reduced in each reaction.

CHEMICAL COMMENTARY

Travels with C

From "Travels with C" by Primo Levi in *Creation to Chaos*

It was to carbon, the element of life, that my first literary dream was turned—and now I want to tell the story of a single atom of carbon.

My fictional character lies, for hundreds of millions of years, bound to three atoms of oxygen and one of calcium, in the form of limestone. (It already has behind it a very long cosmic history, but that we shall ignore.) Time does not exist for it, or exists only in the form of sluggish daily or seasonal variations in temperature. Its existence, whose monotony cannot be conceived of without horror, is an alternation of hots and colds.

The limestone ledge of which the atom forms a part lies within reach of man and his pickax. At any moment—which I, as narrator, decide out of pure caprice to be the year of 1840—a blow of the pickax detached the limestone and sent it on its way to the lime furnace, where it was plunged into the world of things that change. The atom of carbon was roasted until it separated from the limestone's calcium, which remained, so to speak, with its feet on the ground and went on to meet a less brilliant destiny. Still clinging firmly to two of its three companions, our fictional character issued from the chimney and rode the path of the air. Its story, which once was immobile, now took wing.

Accompanied by two oxygen atoms (red), the carbon atom (green) took to the air.

The atom was caught by the wind, flung down onto the earth, lifted ten kilometers high. It was breathed in by a falcon, but did not penetrate the bird's rich blood and was exhaled. It dissolved three times in the sea, once in the water of a cascading torrent, and again was expelled. It traveled with the wind for eight years—now high, now low, on the sea and among the clouds, over forests, deserts and limitless expanses of ice. Finally, it stumbled into capture and the organic adventure.

The year was 1848. The atom of carbon, accompanied by its two satellites of oxygen, which maintained it in a gaseous state, was borne by the wind along a row of vines. It had the good fortune to brush against a leaf, penetrate it, and be nailed there by a ray of the sun. On entering the leaf, it collided with other innumerable molecules of nitrogen and oxygen. It adhered to a large and complicated molecule that activated it, and simultaneously it received the decisive message

from the sky, in the flashing form of a packet of solar light: in an instant, like an insect caught by a spider, the carbon atom was separated from its oxygen, combined with hydrogen, and finally inserted in a chain of life. All this happened swiftly, in silence, at the temperature and pressure of the atmosphere.

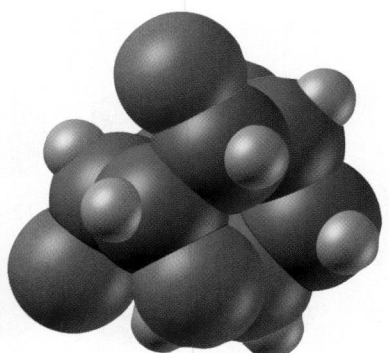

Once inside the leaf, the carbon atom joined other carbon atoms (green), as well as hydrogen (blue) and oxygen (red) atoms, to form this molecule essential to life.

Reading for Meaning

Name the various compounds that the carbon atom was a component of during the course of Levi's story.

Read Further

As a component of one particular compound, Levi's carbon atom is breathed in and exhaled by a falcon. Why was it unlikely for the carbon atom to have been taken into the bird's bloodstream?

 **Quick LAB**

Wear Safety Goggles and an Apron.

Constructing a Model

Materials

- can covered by a sock sealed with tape
- one or more objects that fit in the container
- metric ruler
- balance

Question

How can you construct a model of an unknown object by (1) making inferences about an object that is in a closed container and (2) touching the object without seeing it?

Procedure

1. Your teacher will provide you with a can that is covered by a sock sealed with tape. Without unsealing the container, try to determine the number of objects inside the can as well as the mass, shape, size, composition, and texture of each. To do this, you may carefully tilt or shake the can.

Record your observations in a data table.

2. Remove the tape from the top of the sock. Do *not* look inside the can. Put one hand through the opening, and make the same observations as in step 1 by handling the objects. To make more-accurate estimations, practice estimating the sizes and masses of some known objects outside the can. Then compare your estimates of these objects with actual measurements using a metric ruler and a balance.

Discussion

1. Scientists often use more than one method to gather data. How was this illustrated in the investigation?

2. Of the observations you made, which were qualitative and which were quantitative?

3. Using the data you gathered, draw a model of the unknown object(s) and write a brief summary of your conclusions.

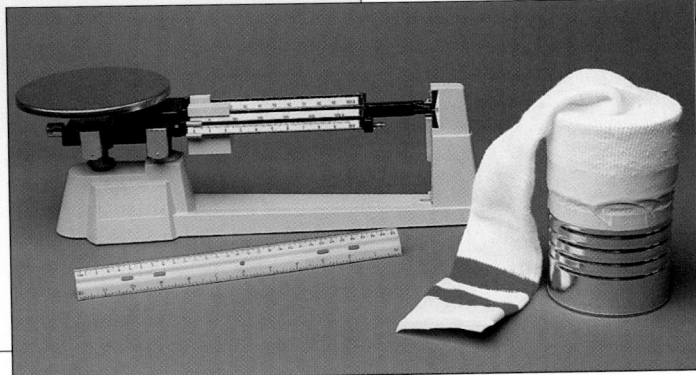

SECTION REVIEW

1. Describe the major contributions of each of the following to the modern theory of the atom:
a. Democritus
b. John Dalton

2. List the five essential points of Dalton's atomic theory.

3. What chemical laws can be explained on the basis of Dalton's theory?

SECTION 3-2

Lesson Starter

Show students two different shapes made from identical pieces of a commercially available construction set. Demonstrate how even though the two shapes look different, the characteristics of the various parts that compose them are the same. The same is true with the atom. Though atoms of different elements display different properties, isolated subatomic particles have the same properties, regardless of their source. As technology improved, scientists learned to isolate portions of atoms that display similar properties. The cathode-ray tube is an example of technology that led to the isolation of a subatomic particle, the electron.

Did You Know?

In a television tube, a cathode ray constantly undergoes deflections that result from the varying magnetic field within the tube. The ray strikes a coated screen, where a luminescent image is created.

DEMONSTRATION

Bring in an oscilloscope or an old computer monitor. Show how the image on the screen seems to be distorted by a magnetic field, which alters the path of electrons as they approach the screen.

Visual Strategy

FIGURE 3-4 Alert students to the difference between the flow of electrons, or the cathode ray, and the flow of electric current. The figure depicts a cathode ray, created by electrons, flowing from the negatively charged cathode to the positively charged anode. Electric current flows from the anode to the cathode.

OBJECTIVES

- Summarize the observed properties of cathode rays that led to the discovery of the electron.

- Summarize the experiment carried out by Rutherford and his co-workers that led to the discovery of the nucleus.

- List the properties of protons, neutrons, and electrons.

- Define *atom.*

The Structure of the Atom

Although John Dalton thought atoms were indivisible, investigators in the late 1800s proved otherwise. As scientific advances allowed a deeper exploration of matter, it became clear that atoms are actually composed of several basic types of smaller particles and that the number and arrangement of these particles within an atom determine that atom's chemical properties. Today we define an **atom** *as the smallest particle of an element that retains the chemical properties of that element.*

All atoms consist of two regions. The *nucleus* is a very small region located near the center of an atom. In every atom the nucleus contains at least one positively charged particle called a *proton* and usually one or more neutral particles called *neutrons.* Surrounding the nucleus is a region occupied by negatively charged particles called *electrons.* This region is very large compared with the size of the nucleus. Protons, neutrons, and electrons are often referred to as *subatomic particles.*

Discovery of the Electron

The first discovery of a subatomic particle resulted from investigations into the relationship between electricity and matter. In the late 1800s, many experiments were performed in which electric current was passed through various gases at low pressures. (Gases at atmospheric pressure don't conduct electricity well.) These experiments were carried out in glass tubes like the one shown in Figure 3-4. Such tubes are known as *cathode-ray tubes.*

Cathode Rays and Electrons

Investigators noticed that when current was passed through a cathode-ray tube, the surface of the tube directly opposite the cathode glowed. They hypothesized that the glow was caused by a stream of particles, which they called a cathode ray. The ray traveled from the cathode to the anode when current was passed through the tube. Experiments devised to test

FIGURE 3-4 A simple cathode-ray tube. Particles pass through the tube from the *cathode,* the metal disk connected to the negative terminal of the voltage source, to the *anode,* the metal disk connected to the positive terminal.

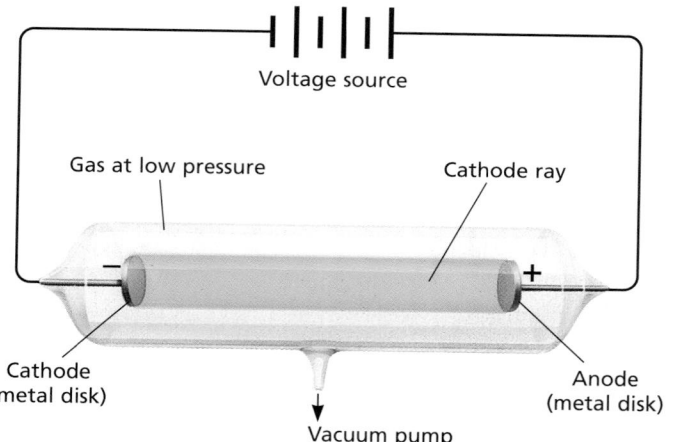

Voltage source

Gas at low pressure

Cathode ray

Cathode (metal disk)

Anode (metal disk)

Vacuum pump

this hypothesis revealed the following observations.

1. An object placed between the cathode and the opposite end of the tube cast a shadow on the glass.

2. A paddle wheel placed on rails between the electrodes rolled along the rails from the cathode toward the anode (see Figure 3-5).

These facts supported the existence of a cathode ray. Furthermore, the paddle-wheel experiment showed that a cathode ray had sufficient mass to set the wheel in motion.

Additional experiments provided more information.

3. Cathode rays were deflected by a magnetic field in the same manner as a wire carrying electric current, which was known to have a negative charge.

4. The rays were deflected away from a negatively charged object.

These observations led to the hypothesis that the particles that compose cathode rays are negatively charged. This hypothesis was strongly supported by a series of experiments carried out in 1897 by the English physicist Joseph John Thomson. In one investigation, he was able to measure the ratio of the charge of cathode-ray particles to their mass. He found that this ratio was always the same, regardless of the metal used to make the cathode or the nature of the gas inside the cathode-ray tube. Thomson concluded that all cathode rays are composed of identical negatively charged particles, which were later named electrons.

Charge and Mass of the Electron

Thomson's experiment revealed that the electron has a very large charge for its tiny mass. In 1909, experiments conducted by the American physicist Robert A. Millikan showed that the mass of the electron is in fact about one two-thousandth the mass of the simplest type of hydrogen atom, which is the smallest atom known. More-accurate experiments conducted since then indicate that the electron has a mass of 9.109×10^{-31} kg, or 1/1837 the mass of the simplest type of hydrogen atom.

Millikan's experiments also confirmed that the electron carries a negative electric charge. And because cathode rays have identical properties regardless of the element used to produce them, it was concluded that electrons are present in atoms of all elements. Thus, cathode-ray experiments provided evidence that atoms are divisible and that one of the atom's basic constituents is the negatively charged electron.

Based on what was learned about electrons, two other inferences were made about atomic structure.

1. Because atoms are electrically neutral, they must contain a positive charge to balance the negative electrons.

2. Because electrons have so much less mass than atoms, atoms must contain other particles that account for most of their mass.

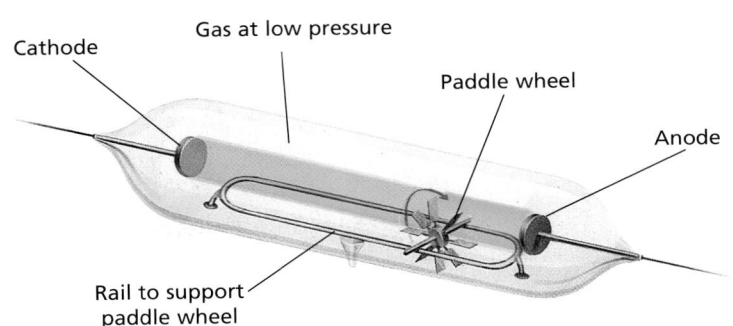

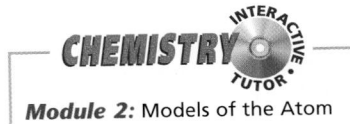

FIGURE 3-5 A paddle wheel placed in the path of the cathode ray moves away from the cathode and toward the anode. The movement of the wheel led scientists to conclude that cathode rays have mass.

CHEMISTRY INTERACTIVE TUTOR

Module 2: Models of the Atom

TOPIC: Subatomic particles
GO TO: www.scilinks.org
***sci*LINKS CODE:** HC2033

Visual Strategy

FIGURE 3-5 Compare the paddle wheel in the figure with a paddle wheel on a riverboat or an old mill. Water pushing on a water wheel can perform work. In the same way, moving electrons are capable of performing work.

CHAPTER ⬅➡ CONNECTION

In Chapter 19, students will discover that anions move toward the anode, while cations move toward the cathode.

CHEMISTRY INTERACTIVE TUTOR

Module 2: Models of the Atom

Topic: Atomic Structure
Sections **a** and **b** of this engaging tutorial review and reinforce understanding of atomic structure.

📖 Reading Skill-Builder

PREDICTION GUIDES Write the following statements on the chalkboard:

- An atom cannot be broken down into smaller parts.
- An atom is the same throughout.
- An atom is made up of several different, smaller parts.

Ask students their opinions of the statements. Have them discuss their opinions and try to justify them. Save a list of the opinions for discussion after completing Section 3-2.

Visual Strategy

FIGURE 3-6 Have students explain what is happening in the figure. Students should realize that Figure 3-6(a) shows merely the setup of the Rutherford foil experiment and that Figure 3-6(b) shows the results.

✔ Teaching Tip

If an atom were the size of a large football stadium, the nucleus would be about the size of a marble. This model suggests that the atom is mostly empty space. Ask students to consider how many alpha particles penetrated the gold atoms in the Rutherford experiment compared with the number that were redirected.

Discovery of the Atomic Nucleus

More detail of the atom's structure was provided in 1911 by New Zealander Ernest Rutherford and his associates Hans Geiger and Ernest Marsden. The scientists bombarded a thin, gold foil with fast-moving *alpha particles,* which are positively charged particles with about four times the mass of a hydrogen atom. Geiger and Marsden assumed that mass and charge were uniformly distributed throughout the atoms of the gold foil. So they expected the alpha particles to pass through with only a slight deflection. And for the vast majority of the particles, this was the case. However, when the scientists checked for the possibility of wide-angle deflections, they were shocked to find that roughly 1 in 8000 of the alpha particles had actually been redirected back toward the source (see Figure 3-6). As Rutherford later exclaimed, it was "as if you had fired a 15-inch [artillery] shell at a piece of tissue paper and it came back and hit you."

After thinking about the startling result for two years, Rutherford finally came up with an explanation. He reasoned that the rebounded alpha particles must have experienced some powerful force within the atom. And he figured that the source of this force must occupy a very small amount of space because so few of the total number of alpha particles had been affected by it. He concluded that the force must be caused by a very densely packed bundle of matter with a positive electric charge. Rutherford called this positive bundle of matter the nucleus (see Figure 3-7).

Rutherford had discovered that the volume of a nucleus was very small compared with the total volume of an atom. In fact, if the nucleus were the size of a marble, then the size of the atom would be about the size of a football field. But where were the electrons? Although he had no supporting evidence, Rutherford suggested that the electrons surrounded the positively charged nucleus like planets around the sun. He could not explain, however, what kept the electrons in motion around the nucleus.

FIGURE 3-6 (a) Geiger and Marsden bombarded a thin piece of gold foil with a narrow beam of alpha particles. (b) Some of the particles were redirected by the gold foil back toward their source.

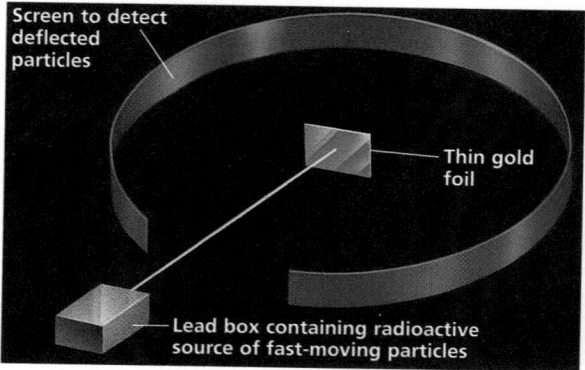

(a)

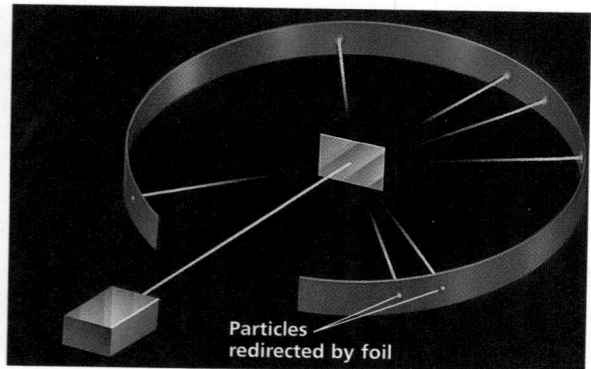

(b)

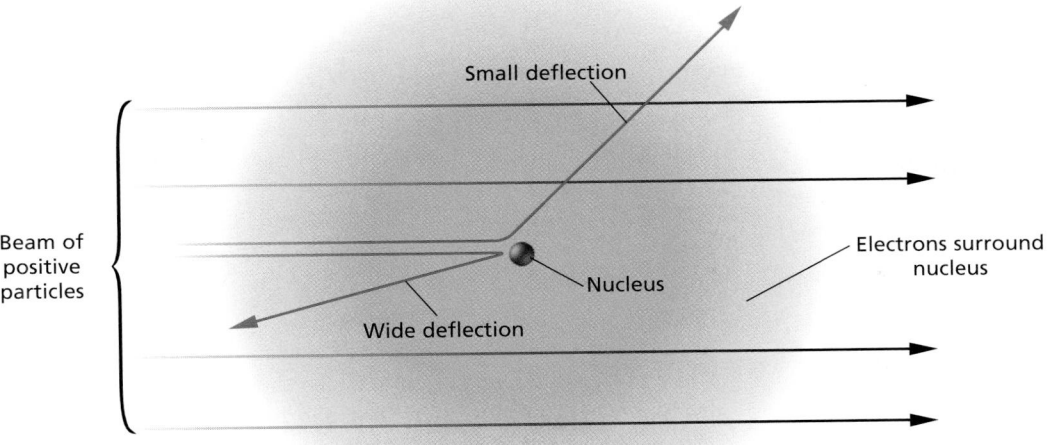

Small deflection

Beam of
positive
particles

Nucleus

Wide deflection

Electrons surround
nucleus

FIGURE 3-7 Rutherford reasoned that each atom in the gold foil contained a small, dense, positively charged nucleus surrounded by electrons. A small number of the alpha particles directed toward the foil were deflected by the tiny nucleus (red arrows). Most of the particles passed through undisturbed (black arrows).

Composition of the Atomic Nucleus

Except for the nucleus of the simplest type of hydrogen atom (discussed in the next section), all atomic nuclei are made of two kinds of particles, protons and neutrons. A proton has a positive charge equal in magnitude to the negative charge of an electron. Atoms are electrically neutral because they contain equal numbers of protons and electrons. A neutron is electrically neutral.

The simplest hydrogen atom consists of a single-proton nucleus with a single electron moving about it. A proton has a mass of 1.673×10^{-27} kg, which is 1836 times greater than the mass of an electron and 1836/1837, or virtually all, of the mass of the simplest hydrogen atom. All atoms besides the simplest hydrogen atom also contain neutrons. The mass of a neutron is 1.675×10^{-27} kg—slightly larger than that of a proton.

The nuclei of atoms of different elements differ in the number of protons they contain and therefore in the amount of positive charge they possess. Thus, the number of protons in an atom's nucleus determines that atom's identity. Physicists have identified other subatomic particles, but particles other than electrons, protons, and neutrons have little effect on the chemical properties of matter. Table 3-1 on page 74 summarizes the properties of electrons, protons, and neutrons.

Forces in the Nucleus

Generally, particles that have the same electric charge repel one another. Therefore, we would expect a nucleus with more than one proton to be unstable. However, when two protons are extremely close to each other, there is a strong attraction between them. In fact, more than 100

SECTION REVIEW

1. a. the smallest particle of an element that retains the chemical properties of that element
b. a negatively charged subatomic particle located outside the nucleus
c. the positively charged, dense central portion of an atom that contains nearly all the atom's mass but takes up a very small fraction of its volume
d. the subatomic particle of the nucleus that has a positive charge equal in magnitude to the negative charge of the electron
e. the electrically neutral subatomic particle found in atomic nuclei

2. a. concluded that electrons were found in all atoms
b. confirmed the negative charge of the electron and suggested a possible mass
c. determined that most of the mass of an atom is found in the nucleus and that the nucleus occupies very little space within an atom

3. Electrons surround the nucleus and have a negative charge and small mass relative to protons and neutrons. Most of an atom's mass is in its nucleus, which is near the center and is composed of protons and neutrons. Protons have a positive charge; neutrons have no charge.

4. because charges will flow through gases only at very low pressures

5. a. positive; connected to the positive terminal of the voltage source
b. negative; connected to the negative terminal of the voltage source

Reading Skill-Builder

PREDICTION GUIDES Have students revisit their opinions from the beginning of the section. Have them discuss whether their opinions have changed or remain the same. Have them cite passages in the text that account for their decisions.

TABLE 3-1 *Properties of Subatomic Particles*

Particle	Symbols	Relative electric charge	Mass number	Relative mass (amu*)	Actual mass (kg)
Electron	$e^-, {}_{-1}^{0}e$	-1	0	0.000 5486	9.109×10^{-31}
Proton	$p^+, {}_{1}^{1}\text{H}$	$+1$	1	1.007 276	1.673×10^{-27}
Neutron	$n^\circ, {}_{0}^{1}n$	0	1	1.008 665	1.675×10^{-27}

*1 amu (atomic mass unit) = $1.660\ 540 \times 10^{-27}$ kg (see page 78)

protons can exist close together in a nucleus. A similar attraction exists when neutrons are very close to each other, or when protons and neutrons are very close together. *These short-range proton-neutron, proton-proton, and neutron-neutron forces hold the nuclear particles together and are referred to as* **nuclear forces.**

The Sizes of Atoms

It is convenient to think of the region occupied by the electrons as an electron cloud—a cloud of negative charge. The radius of an atom is the distance from the center of the nucleus to the outer portion of this electron cloud. Because atomic radii are so small, they are expressed using a unit that is more convenient for the sizes of atoms. This unit is the picometer. The abbreviation for the picometer is pm (1 pm = 10^{-12} m = 10^{-10} cm). To get an idea of how small a picometer is, consider that 1 cm is the same fractional part of 10^3 km (about 600 mi) as 100 pm is of 1 cm. Atomic radii range from about 40 to 270 pm. By contrast, the nuclei of atoms have much smaller radii, about 0.001 pm. Nuclei also have incredibly high densities, about 2×10^8 metric tons/cm^3.

SECTION REVIEW

1. Define each of the following:
   a. atom   c. nucleus   e. neutron
   b. electron   d. proton

2. Describe one conclusion made by each of the following scientists that led to the development of the current atomic theory:
   a. Thomson   c. Rutherford
   b. Millikan

3. Compare and contrast the three types of subatomic particles in terms of location in the atom, mass, and relative charge.

4. Why is the cathode-ray tube in Figure 3-4 connected to a vacuum pump?

5. Label the charge on the following in a cathode-ray tube. State the reasons for your answers.
   a. anode   b. cathode

Counting Atoms

OBJECTIVES

- Explain what isotopes are.

- Define *atomic number* and *mass number,* and describe how they apply to isotopes.

- Given the identity of a nuclide, determine its number of protons, neutrons, and electrons.

- Define *mole* in terms of Avogadro's number, and define *molar mass.*

- Solve problems involving mass in grams, amount in moles, and number of atoms of an element.

Consider neon, Ne, the gas used in many illuminated signs. Neon is a minor component of the atmosphere. In fact, dry air contains only about 0.002% neon. And yet there are about 5×10^{17} atoms of neon present in each breath you inhale. In most experiments, atoms are much too small to be measured individually. Chemists can analyze atoms quantitatively, however, by knowing fundamental properties of the atoms of each element. In this section you will be introduced to some of the basic properties of atoms. You will then discover how to use this information to count the number of atoms of an element in a sample with a known mass. You will also become familiar with the *mole,* a special unit used by chemists to express amounts of particles, such as atoms and molecules.

Atomic Number

All atoms are composed of the same basic particles. Yet all atoms are not the same. Atoms of different elements have different numbers of protons. Atoms of the same element all have the same number of protons. *The* **atomic number** *(Z) of an element is the number of protons in the nucleus of each atom of that element.*

Turn to the inside back cover of this textbook. In the periodic table shown, an element's atomic number is indicated above its symbol. Notice that the elements are placed in order of increasing atomic number. At the top left of the table is hydrogen, H, which has atomic number 1. Atoms of the element hydrogen have one proton in the nucleus. Next in order is helium, He, which has two protons in each nucleus. Lithium, Li, has three protons; beryllium, Be, has four protons; and so on.

The atomic number identifies an element. If you want to know which element has atomic number 47, for example, look at the periodic table. You can see that it is silver, Ag. All silver atoms contain 47 protons in their nuclei. Because atoms are neutral, we know from the atomic number that all silver atoms must also contain 47 electrons.

Isotopes

The simplest atoms are those of hydrogen. All hydrogen atoms contain only one proton. However, like many naturally occurring elements, hydrogen atoms can contain different numbers of neutrons.

3

Li

Lithium

6.941

[He]$2s^1$

FIGURE 3-8 The atomic number in this periodic-table entry reveals that an atom of lithium has three protons in its nucleus.

Lesson Starter
Have students consider a familiar example of a weighted average. For instance, if a student's semester grade depends 60% on exam scores and 40% on laboratory explorations, then the student's exam scores count more heavily toward his or her final grade. Hand out sample exam scores and laboratory scores, and have students determine the weighted average of the two. In this section, students will learn that the atomic mass of an element is a weighted average of the masses of the naturally occurring isotopes of that element.

Common Misconception
Make it clear to students that the identity of the atom is determined by the number of protons, not the number of electrons or neutrons. The number of electrons and the number of neutrons can each vary and the atom will still be of the same element. But if the number of protons changes, then the atom becomes an atom of a different element.

Visual Strategy
FIGURE 3-8 Have students identify the atomic number, atomic mass, and chemical symbol for different elements on the classroom's periodic table. Have them deduce the number of electrons from the atomic number for neutral atoms.

Visual Strategy

FIGURE 3-9 Note that the only difference between the hydrogen isotopes is the number of neutrons that they contain.

TABLE STRATEGY

Table 3-2 How are hydrogen's isotopes different from one another? *(They have different numbers of neutrons.)* How does this information alter Dalton's atomic theory? *(Atoms of a single element do not always have the same mass, as Dalton suggested.)* Hydrogen is the only element whose isotopes have names. Isotopes of other elements are identified by their mass number.

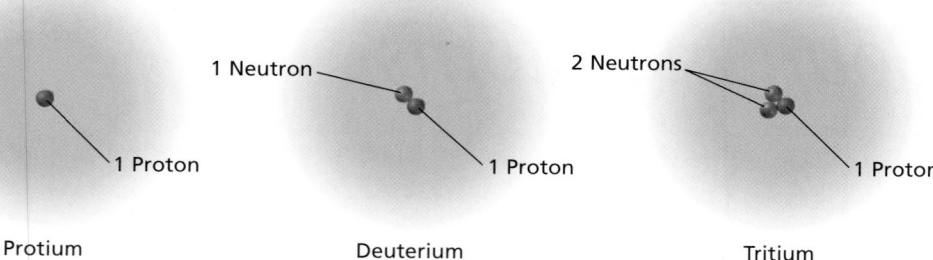

Protium   Deuterium   Tritium

FIGURE 3-9 The nuclei of different isotopes of the same element have the same number of protons but different numbers of neutrons. This is illustrated above by the three isotopes of hydrogen.

Three types of hydrogen atoms are known. The most common type of hydrogen is sometimes called *protium*. It accounts for 99.985% of the hydrogen atoms found on Earth. The nucleus of a protium atom consists of one proton only, and it has one electron moving about it. There are two other known forms of hydrogen. One is called *deuterium*, which accounts for 0.015% of Earth's hydrogen atoms. Each deuterium atom has a nucleus containing one proton and one neutron. The third form of hydrogen is known as *tritium*, which is radioactive. It exists in very small amounts in nature, but it can be prepared artificially. Each tritium atom contains one proton, two neutrons, and one electron.

Protium, deuterium, and tritium are isotopes of hydrogen. **Isotopes** *are atoms of the same element that have different masses.* The isotopes of a particular element all have the same number of protons and electrons but different numbers of neutrons. In all three isotopes of hydrogen, the positive charge of the single proton is balanced by the negative charge of the electron. Most of the elements consist of mixtures of isotopes. Tin has 10 stable isotopes, for example, the most of any element.

Mass Number

Identifying an isotope requires knowing both the name or atomic number of the element and the mass of the isotope. *The* **mass number** *is the total number of protons and neutrons in the nucleus of an isotope.* The three isotopes of hydrogen described earlier have mass numbers 1, 2, and 3, as shown in Table 3-2.

TABLE 3-2 *Mass Numbers of Hydrogen Isotopes*		
Atomic number (number of protons)	**Number of neutrons**	**Mass number**
Protium	1	0	$1 + 0 = 1$
Deuterium	1	1	$1 + 1 = 2$
Tritium	1	2	$1 + 2 = 3$

Designating Isotopes

The isotopes of hydrogen are unusual in that they have distinct names. Isotopes are usually identified by specifying their mass number. There are two methods for specifying isotopes. In the first method, the mass number is written with a hyphen after the name of the element. Tritium, for example, is written as hydrogen-3. We will refer to this method as *hyphen notation*. The uranium isotope used as fuel for nuclear power plants has a mass number of 235 and is therefore known as uranium-235. The second method shows the composition of a nucleus as the isotope's *nuclear symbol*. For example, uranium-235 is written as $^{235}_{92}U$. The superscript indicates the mass number and the subscript indicates the atomic number. The number of neutrons is found by subtracting the atomic number from the mass number.

mass number − atomic number = number of neutrons

235 (protons + neutrons) − 92 protons = 143 neutrons

Thus, a uranium-235 nucleus contains 92 protons and 143 neutrons.

Table 3-3 gives the names, symbols, and compositions of the isotopes of hydrogen and helium. **Nuclide** *is a general term for any isotope of any element.* We could say that Table 3-3 lists the compositions of five different nuclides.

internet**connect**

SC*L*INKS.
NSTA

TOPIC: Isotopes
GO TO: www.scilinks.org
*sci*LINKS CODE: HC2034

TABLE STRATEGY

Table 3-3 Draw students' attention to the meaning of the two numbers associated with an isotope's nuclear symbol. The number on the bottom is the number of protons (the atomic number). For a neutral atom, the number of protons equals the number of electrons. The number on the top is the sum of the protons and the neutrons (the mass number). Have students determine the number of protons, neutrons, and electrons for some other elements.

TABLE 3-3 *Isotopes of Hydrogen and Helium*

Isotope	Nuclear symbol	Number of protons	Number of electrons	Number of neutrons
Hydrogen-1 (protium)	$^{1}_{1}H$	1	1	0
Hydrogen-2 (deuterium)	$^{2}_{1}H$	1	1	1
Hydrogen-3 (tritium)	$^{3}_{1}H$	1	1	2
Helium-3	$^{3}_{2}He$	2	2	1
Helium-4	$^{4}_{2}He$	2	2	2

SAMPLE PROBLEM 3-1

How many protons, electrons, and neutrons are there in an atom of chlorine-37?

SOLUTION

1 ANALYZE

Given: name and mass number of chlorine-37
Unknown: numbers of protons, electrons, and neutrons

2 PLAN

atomic number = number of protons = number of electrons
mass number = number of neutrons + number of protons

3-1 How many protons, electrons, and neutrons are in an atom of carbon-13?

Ans. 6 protons, 6 electrons, 7 neutrons

3-1 Write the nuclear symbol for oxygen-16.

Ans. $^{16}_{8}O$

3-1 Write the hyphen notation for the element whose atoms contain 7 electrons and 9 neutrons.

Ans. nitrogen-16

✔Teaching Tip

You may wish to point out that 1 amu is equal to $1.660\ 540 \times 10^{-27}$ kg or $1.660\ 540 \times 10^{-24}$ g.

---

3 COMPUTE

The mass number of chlorine-37 is 37. Consulting the periodic table reveals that chlorine's atomic number is 17. The number of neutrons can be found by subtracting the atomic number from the mass number.

$$\text{mass number of chlorine-37} - \text{atomic number of chlorine} = \\ \text{number of neutrons in chlorine-37}$$

$$\text{mass number} - \text{atomic number} = 37 \text{ (protons plus neutrons)} - 17 \text{ protons}$$
$$= 20 \text{ neutrons}$$

An atom of chlorine-37 contains 17 electrons, 17 protons, and 20 neutrons.

4 EVALUATE

The number of protons in a neutral atom equals the number of electrons. And the sum of the protons and neutrons equals the given mass number.

PRACTICE

1. How many protons, electrons, and neutrons are in an atom of bromine-80?

   Answer
   35 protons, 35 electrons, 45 neutrons

2. Write the nuclear symbol for carbon-13.

   Answer
   $^{13}_{6}C$

3. Write the hyphen notation for the element that contains 15 electrons and 15 neutrons.

   Answer
   phosphorus-30

Relative Atomic Masses

Masses of atoms expressed in grams are very small. As we shall see, an atom of oxygen-16, for example, has a mass of 2.657×10^{-23} g. For most chemical calculations it is more convenient to use *relative* atomic masses. As you read in Chapter 2, scientists use standards of measurement that are constant and are the same everywhere. In order to set up a relative scale of atomic mass, one atom has been arbitrarily chosen as the standard and assigned a relative mass value. The masses of all other atoms are expressed in relation to this defined standard.

The standard used by scientists to govern units of atomic mass is the carbon-12 nuclide. It has been arbitrarily assigned a mass of exactly 12 atomic mass units, or 12 amu. *One* **atomic mass unit,** *or 1 amu, is exactly 1/12 the mass of a carbon-12 atom.* The atomic mass of any nuclide is determined by comparing it with the mass of the carbon-12 atom. The hydrogen-1 atom has an atomic mass of *about* 1/12 that of the carbon-12 atom, or about 1 amu. The precise value of the atomic mass of a hydrogen-1 atom is 1.007 825 amu. An oxygen-16 atom has about 16/12 (or 4/3) the mass of a carbon-12 atom. Careful measurements show the atomic mass of oxygen-16 to be 15.994 915 amu. The mass of a magnesium-24 atom is found to be slightly less than twice that of a carbon-12 atom. Its atomic mass is 23.985 042 amu.

Some additional examples of the atomic masses of the naturally occurring isotopes of several elements are given in Table 3-4 on page 80. Isotopes of an element may occur naturally, or they may be made in the laboratory *(artificial isotopes). Although isotopes have different masses, they do not differ significantly in their chemical behavior.*

The masses of subatomic particles can also be expressed on the atomic mass scale (see Table 3-1). The mass of the electron is 0.000 5486 amu, that of the proton is 1.007 276 amu, and that of the neutron is 1.008 665 amu. Note that the proton and neutron masses are close to but not equal to 1 amu. You have learned that the mass number is the total number of protons and neutrons in the nucleus of an atom. You can now see that the mass number and relative atomic mass of a given nuclide are quite close to each other. They are not identical because the proton and neutron masses deviate slightly from 1 amu and the atomic masses include electrons. Also, as you will read in Chapter 22, a small amount of mass is changed to energy in the creation of a nucleus from protons and neutrons.

Average Atomic Masses of Elements

Most elements occur naturally as mixtures of isotopes, as indicated in Table 3-4. The percentage of each isotope in the naturally occurring element on Earth is nearly always the same, no matter where the element is found. The percentage at which each of an element's isotopes occurs in nature is taken into account when calculating the element's average atomic mass. **Average atomic mass** *is the weighted average of the atomic masses of the naturally occurring isotopes of an element.*

The following is a simple example of how to calculate a *weighted average.* Suppose you have a box containing two sizes of marbles. If 25% of the marbles have masses of 2.00 g each and 75% have masses of 3.00 g each, how is the weighted average calculated? You could count the marbles, calculate the total mass of the mixture, and divide by the total number of marbles. If you had 100 marbles, the calculations would be as follows.

$$25 \text{ marbles} \times 2.00 \text{ g} = 50 \text{ g}$$
$$75 \text{ marbles} \times 3.00 \text{ g} = 225 \text{ g}$$

Adding these masses gives the total mass of the marbles.

$$50 \text{ g} + 225 \text{ g} = 275 \text{ g}$$

Dividing the total mass by 100 gives an average marble mass of 2.75 g.

A simpler method is to multiply the mass of each marble by the decimal fraction representing its percentage in the mixture. Then add the products.

$$25\% = 0.25 \qquad 75\% = 0.75$$
$$(2.00 \text{ g} \times 0.25) + (3.00 \text{ g} \times 0.75) = 2.75 \text{ g}$$

Common Misconception

Many students think that protons and neutrons have the same mass in all elements. In fact, the masses of a proton and a neutron listed on this page are only the masses of single protons and neutrons. These subatomic particles actually have slightly different masses in different elements.

CHAPTER ⟷ CONNECTION

Chapter 22 outlines how the difference between the mass of an atom and the sum of the masses of the same number of individual protons, neutrons, and electrons is converted into the energy that holds the atom together. This energy is called *nuclear binding energy.* This is why the actual mass of an isotope is slightly different from its mass number.

TABLE STRATEGY

Table 3-4 Point out to students that the average atomic mass of an element is often closest to the atomic mass of the most abundant isotope.

Alternative Assessment

Follow the example on this page to confirm the average atomic mass of hydrogen, carbon, oxygen, copper, and uranium using the percentage abundances and isotope masses listed in the table on this page.

 Reading Skill-Builder

SEQUENCING After reading the text on pp. 80–82 to them-selves, ask students to discuss the relationships illustrated in Figure 3-11. Have them work in pairs to write in their own words the steps they would follow to change from one expression to the other. Ask for volunteers to list the steps on the board.

TABLE 3-4 *Atomic Masses and Abundances of Several Naturally Occurring Isotopes*

Isotope	Mass number	Percentage natural abundance	Atomic mass (amu)	Average atomic mass of element (amu)
Hydrogen-1	1	99.985	1.007 825	
Hydrogen-2	2	0.015	2.014 102	1.007 94
Carbon-12	12	98.90	12 (by definition)	
Carbon-13	13	1.10	13.003 355	12.0111
Carbon-14	14	trace	14.003 242	
Oxygen-16	16	99.762	15.994 915	
Oxygen-17	17	0.038	16.999 131	15.9994
Oxygen-18	18	0.200	17.999 160	
Copper-63	63	69.17	62.929 599	
Copper-65	65	30.83	64.927 793	63.546
Cesium-133	133	100	132.905 429	132.905
Uranium-234	234	0.005	234.040 947	
Uranium-235	235	0.720	235.043 924	238.029
Uranium-238	238	99.275	238.050 784	

Calculating Average Atomic Mass

The average atomic mass of an element depends on both the mass and the relative abundance of each of the element's isotopes. For example, naturally occurring copper consists of 69.17% copper-63, which has an atomic mass of 62.929 598 amu, and 30.83% copper-65, which has an atomic mass of 64.927 793 amu. The average atomic mass of copper can be calculated by multiplying the atomic mass of each isotope by its relative abundance (expressed in decimal form) and adding the results.

$$0.6917 \times 62.929\ 599\ \text{amu} + 0.3083 \times 64.927\ 793\ \text{amu} = 63.55\ \text{amu}$$

The calculated average atomic mass of naturally occurring copper is 63.55 amu.

The average atomic mass is included for the elements listed in Table 3-4. As illustrated in the table, most atomic masses are known to four or more significant figures. *In this book, an element's atomic mass is usually rounded to two decimal places before it is used in a calculation.*

Relating Mass to Numbers of Atoms

The relative atomic mass scale makes it possible to know how many atoms of an element are present in a sample of the element with a measurable mass. Three very important concepts—the mole, Avogadro's number, and molar mass—provide the basis for relating masses in grams to numbers of atoms.

The Mole

The mole is the SI unit for amount of substance. *A **mole** (abbreviated mol) is the amount of a substance that contains as many particles as there are atoms in exactly 12 g of carbon-12.* The mole is a counting unit, just like a dozen is. We don't usually order 12 or 24 ears of corn; we order one dozen or two dozen. Similarly, a chemist may want 1 mol of carbon, or 2 mol of iron, or 2.567 mol of calcium. In the sections that follow, you will see how the mole relates to masses of atoms and compounds.

Avogadro's Number

The number of particles in a mole has been experimentally determined in a number of ways. The best modern value is $6.022\,1367 \times 10^{23}$. This means that exactly 12 g of carbon-12 contains $6.022\,1367 \times 10^{23}$ carbon-12 atoms. The number of particles in a mole is known as Avogadro's number, named for the nineteenth-century Italian scientist Amedeo Avogadro, whose ideas were crucial in explaining the relationship between mass and numbers of atoms. ***Avogadro's number**—$6.022\,1367 \times 10^{23}$—is the number of particles in exactly one mole of a pure substance.* For most purposes, Avogadro's number is rounded to 6.022×10^{23}.

To get a sense of how large Avogadro's number is, consider the following: If every person living on Earth (5 billion people) worked to count the atoms in one mole of an element, and if each person counted continuously at a rate of one atom per second, it would take about 4 million years for all the atoms to be counted.

Molar Mass

An alternative definition of *mole* is the amount of a substance that contains Avogadro's number of particles. Can you figure out the approximate mass of one mole of helium atoms? You know that a mole of carbon-12 atoms has a mass of exactly 12 g and that a carbon-12 atom has an atomic mass of 12 amu. The atomic mass of a helium atom is 4.00 amu, which is about one-third the mass of a carbon-12 atom. It follows that a mole of helium atoms will have about one-third the mass of a mole of carbon-12 atoms. Thus, one mole of helium has a mass of about 4.00 g.

*The mass of one mole of a pure substance is called the **molar mass** of that substance.* Molar mass is usually written in units of g/mol. The molar mass of an element is numerically equal to the atomic mass of the element in atomic mass units (which can be found in the periodic table). For example, the molar mass of lithium, Li, is 6.94 g/mol, while the molar mass of mercury, Hg, is 200.59 g/mol (rounding each value to two decimal places).

A molar mass of an element contains one mole of atoms. For example, 4.00 g of helium, 6.94 g of lithium, and 200.59 g of mercury all contain a mole of atoms. Figure 3-10 shows molar masses of three common elements.

Gram/Mole Conversions

Chemists use molar mass as a conversion factor in chemical calculations. For example, the molar mass of helium is 4.00 g He/mol He. To

(a)

(b)

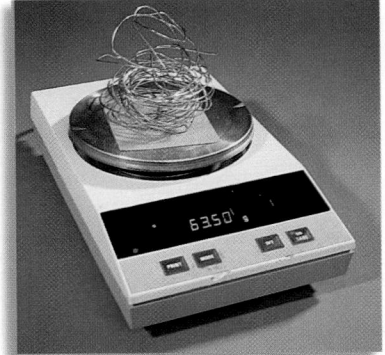
(c)

FIGURE 3-10 Shown is approximately one molar mass of each of three elements: (a) carbon (as graphite), (b) iron (nails), and (c) copper (wire).

Visual Strategy
FIGURE 3-11 Ask students how they would convert from mass in grams to amount in moles *(divide by molar mass);* from amount in moles to mass in grams *(multiply by molar mass);* and from amount in moles to number of particles *(multiply by Avogadro's number).*

ADDITIONAL

SAMPLE
PROBLEMS

3-2 What is the mass in grams of 3.6 mol of the element carbon, C?

Ans. 43 g

3-2 What is the mass in grams of 0.733 mol of the element chlorine, Cl?

Ans. 26.0 g

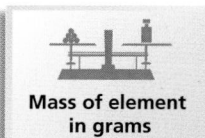 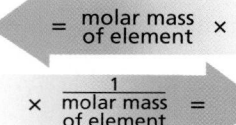 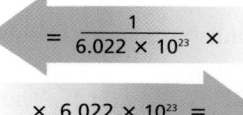 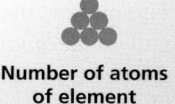

FIGURE 3-11 The diagram shows the relationship between mass in grams, amount in moles, and number of atoms of an element in a sample.

find how many grams of helium there are in two moles of helium, multiply by the molar mass.

$$2.00 \text{ mol He} \times \frac{4.00 \text{ g He}}{\text{mol He}} = 8.00 \text{ g He}$$

Figure 3-11 shows how to use molar mass, moles, and Avogadro's number to relate mass in grams, amount in moles, and number of atoms of an element.

SAMPLE PROBLEM 3-2

What is the mass in grams of 3.50 mol of the element copper, Cu?

SOLUTION

1 *ANALYZE*   **Given:** 3.50 mol Cu
Unknown: mass of Cu in grams

2 *PLAN*   amount of Cu in moles $\longrightarrow$ mass of Cu in grams

According to Figure 3-11, the mass of an element in grams can be calculated by multiplying the amount of the element in moles by the element's molar mass.

$$\text{moles Cu} \times \frac{\text{grams Cu}}{\text{moles Cu}} = \text{grams Cu}$$

3 *COMPUTE*   The molar mass of copper from the periodic table is rounded to 63.55 g/mol.

$$3.50 \text{ mol Cu} \times \frac{63.55 \text{ g Cu}}{\text{mol Cu}} = 222 \text{ g Cu}$$

4 *EVALUATE*   Because the amount of copper in moles was given to three significant figures, the answer was rounded to three significant figures. The size of the answer is reasonable because it is somewhat more than 3.5 times 60.

PRACTICE

1. What is the mass in grams of 2.25 mol of the element iron, Fe?

Answer
126 g Fe

2. What is the mass in grams of 0.375 mol of the element potassium, K?

Answer
14.7 g K

3. What is the mass in grams of 0.0135 mol of the element sodium, Na?

Answer
0.310 g Na

4. What is the mass in grams of 16.3 mol of the element nickel, Ni?

Answer
957 g Ni

ADDITIONAL
SAMPLE
PROBLEMS

3-3 How many moles of copper, Cu, are in 3.22 g of copper?

Ans. 0.0507 mol

3-3 How many moles of lithium, Li, are in 2.72×10^{-4} g of lithium?

Ans. 3.92×10^{-5} mol

SAMPLE PROBLEM 3-3

A chemist produced 11.9 g of aluminum, Al. How many moles of aluminum were produced?

SOLUTION

1 ANALYZE

Given: 11.9 g Al
Unknown: amount of Al in moles

2 PLAN

$$\text{mass of Al in grams} \longrightarrow \text{amount of Al in moles}$$

As shown in Figure 3-11, amount in moles can be obtained by *dividing* mass in grams by molar mass, which is mathematically the same as *multiplying* mass in grams by the *reciprocal* of molar mass.

$$\text{grams Al} \times \frac{\text{moles Al}}{\text{grams Al}} = \text{moles Al}$$

3 COMPUTE

The molar mass of aluminum from the periodic table is rounded to 26.98 g/mol.

$$11.9 \text{ g Al} \times \frac{\text{mol Al}}{26.98 \text{ g Al}} = 0.441 \text{ mol Al}$$

4 EVALUATE

The answer is correctly given to three significant figures. The answer is reasonable because 11.9 g is somewhat less than half of 26.98 g.

PRACTICE

1. How many moles of calcium, Ca, are in 5.00 g of calcium?

Answer
0.125 mol Ca

2. How many moles of gold, Au, are in 3.60×10^{-10} g of gold?

Answer
1.83×10^{-12} mol Au

3-4 How many moles of carbon, C, are in 2.25×10^{22} atoms of carbon?

Ans. 0.0374 mol

3-4 How many moles of oxygen, O, are in 2,000,000 atoms of oxygen?

Ans. 3.321×10^{-18} mol

3-5 How many atoms of sodium, Na, are in 3.80 mol of sodium?

Ans. 2.29×10^{24} atoms

3-5 What is the mass in grams of 5.0×10^9 atoms of neon, Ne?

Ans. 1.7×10^{-13} g

3-5 How many atoms of carbon, C, are in 0.020 g of carbon?

Ans. 1.0×10^{21} atoms

3-5 What mass of silver, Ag, contains the same number of atoms as 10.0 g of boron, B?

Ans. 99.8 g

Conversions with Avogadro's Number

Figure 3-11 shows that Avogadro's number can be used to find the number of atoms of an element from the amount in moles or to find the amount of an element in moles from the number of atoms. While these types of problems are less common in chemistry than converting between amount in moles and mass in grams, they are useful in demonstrating the meaning of Avogadro's number. Note that in these calculations, Avogadro's number is expressed in units of atoms per mole.

SAMPLE PROBLEM 3-4

How many moles of silver, Ag, are in 3.01×10^{23} atoms of silver?

SOLUTION

1 ANALYZE

Given: 3.01×10^{23} atoms of Ag
Unknown: amount of Ag in moles

2 PLAN

$$\text{number of atoms of Ag} \longrightarrow \text{amount of Ag in moles}$$

From Figure 3-11, we know that number of atoms is converted to amount in moles by dividing by Avogadro's number. This is equivalent to multiplying numbers of atoms by the reciprocal of Avogrado's number.

$$\text{Ag atoms} \times \frac{\text{moles Ag}}{\text{Avogadro's number of Ag atoms}} = \text{moles Ag}$$

3 COMPUTE

$$3.01 \times 10^{23} \text{ Ag atoms} \times \frac{\text{mol Ag}}{6.022 \times 10^{23} \text{ Ag atoms}} = 0.500 \text{ mol Ag}$$

4 EVALUATE The answer is correct—units cancel correctly and the number of atoms is exactly one-half of Avogadro's number.

PRACTICE

1. How many moles of lead, Pb, are in 1.50×10^{12} atoms of lead?

   Answer
   2.49×10^{-12} mol Pb

2. How many moles of tin, Sn, are in 2500 atoms of tin?

   Answer
   4.2×10^{-21} mol Sn

3. How many atoms of aluminum, Al, are in 2.75 mol of aluminum?

   Answer
   1.66×10^{24} atoms Al

SAMPLE PROBLEM 3-5

What is the mass in grams of 1.20×10^8 atoms of copper, Cu?

SOLUTION

1 ANALYZE

Given: 1.20×10^8 atoms of Cu
Unknown: mass of Cu in grams

2 PLAN

number of atoms of Cu $\longrightarrow$ amount of Cu in moles $\longrightarrow$ mass of Cu in grams

As indicated in Figure 3-11, the given number of atoms must first be converted to amount in moles by dividing by Avogadro's number. Amount in moles is then multiplied by molar mass to yield mass in grams.

$$\text{Cu atoms} \times \frac{\text{moles Cu}}{\text{Avogadro's number of Cu atoms}} \times \frac{\text{grams Cu}}{\text{moles Cu}} = \text{grams Cu}$$

3 COMPUTE

The molar mass of copper from the periodic table is rounded to 63.55 g/mol.

$$1.20 \times 10^8 \text{ Cu atoms} \times \frac{1 \text{ mol Cu}}{6.022 \times 10^{23} \text{ Cu atoms}} \times \frac{63.55 \text{ g Cu}}{\text{mol Cu}} = 1.27 \times 10^{-14} \text{ g Cu}$$

4 EVALUATE

Units cancel correctly to give the answer in grams. The size of the answer is reasonable—10^8 has been divided by about 10^{24} and multiplied by about 10^2.

PRACTICE

1. What is the mass in grams of 7.5×10^{15} atoms of nickel, Ni?

   Answer
   7.3×10^{-7} g Ni

2. How many atoms of sulfur, S, are in 4.00 g of sulfur?

   Answer
   7.51×10^{-22} atoms S

3. What mass of gold, Au, contains the same number of atoms as 9.0 g of aluminum, Al?

   Answer
   66 g Au

SECTION REVIEW

1. Define each of the following:
   a. atomic number
   b. mass number
   c. relative atomic mass
   d. average atomic mass
   e. mole
   f. Avogadro's number
   g. molar mass
   h. isotope

2. Determine the number of protons, electrons, and neutrons in each of the following isotopes:
   a. sodium-23
   b. calcium-40
   c. $^{64}_{29}$Cu
   d. $^{108}_{47}$Ag

3. Write the nuclear symbol and hyphen notation for each of the following isotopes:
   a. mass number of 28 and atomic number of 14
   b. 26 protons and 30 neutrons
   c. 56 electrons and 82 neutrons

4. To two decimal places, what is the relative atomic mass and the molar mass of the element potassium, K?

5. Determine the mass in grams of the following:
   a. 2.00 mol N
   b. 3.01×10^{23} atoms Cl

6. Determine the amount in moles of the following:
   a. 12.15 g Mg
   b. 1.50×10^{23} atoms F

7. Determine the number of atoms in the following:
   a. 2.50 mol Zn
   b. 1.50 g C

SECTION REVIEW

1. a. the number of protons in the nucleus of an atom of that element
   b. the total number of protons and neutrons in a nucleus
   c. the mass of an atom given in atomic mass units
   d. the weighted average of the masses of the naturally occurring isotopes of an element
   e. the amount of a substance that contains a number of particles equal to the number of atoms in exactly 12 g of carbon-12
   f. the number of particles in exactly one mole of a pure substance
   g. the mass of one mole of a pure substance, usually given in units of g/mol
   h. an atom that has the same number of protons as another atom but a different number of neutrons

2. a. 11 protons, 11 electrons, 12 neutrons
   b. 20 protons, 20 electrons, 20 neutrons
   c. 29 protons, 29 electrons, 35 neutrons
   d. 47 protons, 47 electrons, 61 neutrons

3. a. $^{28}_{14}$Si, silicon-28
   b. $^{56}_{26}$Fe, iron-56
   c. $^{138}_{56}$Ba, barium-138

4. 39.10 amu, 39.10 g/mol

5. a. 28.0 g N
   b. 17.8 g Cl

6. a. 0.5000 mol Mg
   b. 0.249 mol F

7. a. 1.50×10^{24} atoms Zn
   b. 7.52×10^{22} atoms C

REVIEW ANSWERS

1. a. Because all chemical reactions involve the rearrangement of atoms, mass is neither created nor destroyed in such changes.
b. Atoms of each element have their own characteristic mass, so compounds consisting of these atoms always have the same composition by mass.
c. Only whole atoms combine in chemical compounds, so different compounds between the same two elements must result from the combination of different whole numbers of atoms.

2. 5 mass units; 13 mass units

3. a. the smallest particle of an element that retains the chemical properties of that element
b. the nucleus and the surrounding electrons

4. An electron is negatively charged, has a mass approximately 1/2000 that of a hydrogen atom, has a fixed charge-to-mass ratio, and is present in atoms of all elements.

5. His model had most of the mass in the nucleus. He bombarded gold atoms with positively charged particles; most went through the atom, but some bounced back.

6. the atomic number

7. a. atoms of an element that contain the same number of protons but a different number of neutrons
b. They have the same number of protons and electrons.
c. They have different numbers of neutrons.

8.

Isotope	Protons	Electrons	Neutrons
Si-28	14	14	14
Si-29	14	14	15
Si-30	14	14	16

9. a. its number of protons
b. the total number of protons and neutrons in an isotope
c. atomic = 1, mass = 2

CHAPTER SUMMARY

3-1
- The *idea* of atoms has been around since the time of the ancient Greeks. In the nineteenth century, John Dalton proposed a *scientific theory* of atoms that can still be used to explain properties of many chemicals today.
- When elements react to form compounds, they combine in fixed proportions by mass.
- Matter and its mass cannot be created or destroyed in chemical reactions.
- The mass ratio of the elements that make up a given compound is always the same, regardless of how much of the compound there is or how it was formed.
- If two or more different compounds are composed of the same two elements, then the ratio of the masses of the second element combined with a certain mass of the first element can be expressed as a ratio of small whole numbers.

Vocabulary

law of conservation of mass (66)   law of definite proportions (66)   law of multiple proportions (66)

3-2
- Cathode-ray tubes supplied evidence of the existence of electrons, which are negatively charged subatomic particles that have relatively little mass.
- Rutherford found evidence for the existence of the atomic nucleus—a positively charged, very dense core within the atom—by bombarding metal foil with a beam of positively charged particles.
- Atomic nuclei are composed of protons, which have an electric charge of +1, and (in all but one case) neutrons, which have no electric charge.
- Isotopes of an element differ in the number of neutrons in their nuclei.
- Atomic nuclei have radii of about 0.001 pm (pm = picometers; 1 pm = 10^{-12} m), while atoms have radii of about 40–270 pm.

Vocabulary

atom (70)   nuclear forces (74)

3-3
- The atomic number of an element is equal to the number of protons in the nucleus of an atom of that element.
- The mass number is equal to the total number of protons and neutrons in the nucleus of an atom of that element.
- The relative atomic mass unit (amu) is based on the carbon-12 atom and is a convenient unit for measuring the mass of atoms. It equals $1.660\,540 \times 10^{-24}$ g.
- The average atomic mass of an element is found by calculating the weighted average of the atomic masses of the naturally occurring isotopes of the element.
- Avogadro's number is equal to approximately $6.022\,137 \times 10^{23}$. It is equal to the number of atoms in exactly 12 g of carbon-12. A sample that contains a number of particles equal to Avogadro's number contains a mole of those particles.
- The molar mass of an element is the mass of one mole of atoms of that element.

Vocabulary

atomic mass unit (78)   Avogadro's number (81)   mass number (76)   mole (81)
atomic number (75)   isotopes (76)   molar mass (81)   nuclide (77)
average atomic mass (79)

REVIEWING CONCEPTS

1. Explain each of the following in terms of Dalton's atomic theory:
   a. the law of conservation of mass
   b. the law of definite proportions
   c. the law of multiple proportions   (3-1)

2. According to the law of conservation of mass, if element A has an atomic mass of 2 mass units and element B has an atomic mass of 3 mass units, what mass would be expected for compound AB? for compound A_2B_3?   (3-1)

3. a. What is an atom?
   b. What two regions make up all atoms?   (3-2)

4. Describe at least four properties of electrons that were determined based on the experiments of Thomson and Millikan.   (3-2)

5. Summarize Rutherford's model of an atom, and explain how he developed this model based on the results of his famous gold-foil experiment.   (3-2)

6. What one number identifies an element?   (3-2)

7. a. What are isotopes?
   b. How are the isotopes of a particular element alike?
   c. How are they different?   (3-3)

8. Copy and complete the following table concerning the three isotopes of silicon, Si. (Hint: See Sample Problem 3-1.)   (3-3)

Isotope	Number of protons	Number of electrons	Number of neutrons
Si-28			
Si-29			
Si-30			

9. a. What is the atomic number of an element?
   b. What is the mass number of an isotope?
   c. In the nuclear symbol for deuterium, $_1^2H$, identify the atomic number and the mass number.   (3-3)

10. What is a nuclide?   (3-3)

11. Use the periodic table and the information that follows to write the hyphen notation for each isotope described.

   a. atomic number = 2, mass number = 4
   b. atomic number = 8, mass number = 16
   c. atomic number = 19, mass number = 39   (3-3)

12. a. What nuclide is used as the standard in the relative scale for atomic masses?
    b. What is its assigned atomic mass?   (3-3)

13. What is the atomic mass of an atom if its mass is approximately equal to the following?
    a. $\frac{1}{3}$ that of carbon-12
    b. 4.5 times as much as carbon-12   (3-3)

14. a. What is the definition of a mole?
    b. What is the abbreviation for mole?
    c. How many particles are in one mole?
    d. What name is given to the number of particles in a mole?   (3-3)

15. a. What is the molar mass of an element?
    b. To two decimal places, write the molar masses of carbon, neon, iron, and uranium.   (3-3)

16. Suppose you have a sample of an element.
    a. How is the mass in grams of the element converted to amount in moles?
    b. How is the mass in grams of the element converted to number of atoms?   (3-3)

PROBLEMS

The Mole and Molar Mass

17. What is the mass in grams of each of the following? (Hint: See Sample Problems 3-2 and 3-5.)
    a. 1.00 mol Li
    b. 1.00 mol Al
    c. 1.00 molar mass Ca
    d. 1.00 molar mass Fe
    e. 6.022×10^{23} atoms C
    f. 6.022×10^{23} atoms Ag

18. How many moles of atoms are there in each of the following? (Hint: See Sample Problems 3-3 and 3-4.)
    a. 6.022×10^{23} atoms Ne
    b. 3.011×10^{23} atoms Mg
    c. 3.25×10^5 g Pb
    d. 4.50×10^{-12} g O

Relative Atomic Mass

19. Three isotopes of argon occur in nature—$_{18}^{36}Ar$, $_{18}^{38}Ar$, and $_{18}^{40}Ar$. Calculate the average atomic mass of argon to two decimal places, given the following relative atomic masses and abundances of each of the isotopes: argon-36 (35.97 amu; 0.337%), argon-38 (37.96 amu; 0.063%), and argon-40 (39.96 amu; 99.600%).

10. any isotope of any element
11. a. helium-4   c. potassium-39
    b. oxygen-16
12. a. carbon-12   b. exactly 12 amu
13. a. 4 amu   b. 54 amu
14. a. the number of particles equal to the number of atoms in exactly 12 g of carbon-12
    b. mol
    c. 6.022×10^{23}
    d. Avogadro's number
15. a. the mass of one mole of atoms
    b. 12.01 g/mol, 20.18 g/mol, 55.85 g/mol, 238.03 g/mol
16. a. divide by molar mass
    b. divide by molar mass, then multiply by Avogadro's number
17. a. 6.94 g   d. 55.8 g
    b. 27.0 g   e. 12.01 g
    c. 40.1 g   f. 107.9 g
18. a. 1.000 mol   c. 1.57×10^3 mol
    b. 0.5000 mol d. 2.81×10^{-13} mol
19. 39.95 amu
20. 10.01 amu
21. a. 9.03×10^{23} atoms
    b. 4.068×10^{24} atoms
    c. 1.50×10^{23} atoms
22. a. 9.500 g   d. 1.12×10^{-3} g
    b. 6.05 g   e. 7.6×10^{-21} g
    c. 2.65×10^{-10} g f. 3×10^{-22} g
23. a. 3.01×10^{23} atoms
    b. 1.51×10^{23} atoms
    c. 2.31×10^{22} atoms
    d. 7.871×10^{19} atoms
    e. 3.06×10^{11} atoms
24. a. 80.9 g   e. 413 g
    b. 29.5 g   f. 8.25×10^9 g
    c. 19.3 g   g. 3.50×10^{-4} g
    d. 1590 g

25.

Particle	Symbol	Mass no.
Electron	$_{-1}^0e$, e^-	0
Proton	$_1^1H$, p^+	1
Neutron	$_0^1n$, n^0	1

Actual mass	Relative charge
9.109×10^{-31} kg	−1
1.673×10^{-27} kg	+1
1.675×10^{-27} kg	0

26. a. 1 amu = 1/12 of the mass of one carbon-12 atom
b. the mass of an atom as it compares with the mass of a carbon-12 atom

27. a. central portion of the atom containing most of the mass
b. Ernest Rutherford
c. protons and neutrons

28. a. 1.00 mol   **e.** 0.0474 mol
b. 0.500 mol   **f.** 6.96×10^{-5} mol
c. 0.100 mol   **g.** 37.4 mol
d. 4.7 mol   **h.** 8.30×10^{-23} mol

29. If two or more compounds are composed of the same two elements, then the ratio of the masses of the second element combined with a certain mass of the first element is always a ratio of small whole numbers. CO and CO_2 are examples.

30. a. 144 amu   **b.** 6 amu

31. a small, negatively charged particle of small mass that moves around the nucleus

32. Using carbon and oxygen: The law of definite proportions states that any amount of CO will contain a constant percentage by mass of C and O. The law of multiple proportions accounts for the difference between the mass of a CO molecule and a CO_2 molecule, which is the mass of one oxygen atom.

33. a. from the anode to the cathode
b. positive

34. 1.9 g/mol

35. a. fermium-257
b. 121
c. No. The atomic masses are different, and the number of neutrons can be found by subtracting the atomic number from the mass. Carbon-12: $12 - 6 = 6$. Carbon-14: $14 - 6 = 8$

36. a. amount of O_2 present
b. CO poisoning

20. Naturally occurring boron is 80.20% boron-11 (atomic mass = 11.01 amu) and 19.80% of some other isotopic form of boron. What must the atomic mass of this second isotope be in order to account for the 10.81 amu average atomic mass of boron? (Write the answer to two decimal places.)

Number of Atoms in a Sample

21. How many atoms are there in each of the following?
a. 1.50 mol Na   c. 7.02 g Si
b. 6.755 mol Pb

22. What is the mass in grams of each of the following?
a. 3.011×10^{23} atoms F   e. 25 atoms W
b. 1.50×10^{23} atoms Mg   f. 1 atom Au
c. 4.50×10^{12} atoms Cl
d. 8.42×10^{18} atoms Br

23. Determine the number of atoms in each of the following:
a. 5.40 g B   d. 0.025 50 g Pt
b. 0.250 mol S   e. 1.00×10^{-10} g Au
c. 0.0384 mol K

MIXED REVIEW

24. Determine the mass in grams of each of the following:
a. 3.00 mol Al   e. 6.50 mol Cu
b. 2.56×10^{24} atoms Li   f. 2.57×10^8 mol S
c. 1.38 mol N   g. 1.05×10^{18} atoms Hg
d. 4.86×10^{24} atoms Au

25. Copy and complete the following table concerning the properties of subatomic particles:

Particle	Symbol	Mass number	Actual mass	Relative charge
Electron				
Proton				
Neutron				

26. a. How is an atomic mass unit (amu) related to the mass of a carbon-12 atom?
b. What is the relative atomic mass of an atom?

27. a. What is the nucleus of an atom?
b. Who is credited with the discovery of the atomic nucleus?
c. Identify the two kinds of particles contained in the nucleus.

28. How many moles of atoms are there in each of the following?
a. 40.1 g Ca   e. 2.65 g Fe
b. 11.5 g Na   f. 0.007 50 g Ag
c. 5.87 g Ni   g. 2.25×10^{25} atoms Zn
d. 150 g S   h. 50.0 atoms Ba

29. State the law of multiple proportions, and give an example of two compounds that illustrate the law.

30. What is the approximate atomic mass of an atom if its mass is
a. 12 times that of carbon-12?
b. $\frac{1}{2}$ that of carbon-12?

31. What is an electron?

CRITICAL THINKING

32. Organizing Ideas   Using two chemical compounds as an example, describe the difference between the law of definite proportions and the law of multiple proportions.

33. Constructing Models   As described on pages 70 to 74, the structure of the atom was determined from observations made in painstaking experimental research. Suppose a series of experiments revealed that when an electric current is passed through gas at low pressure, the surface of the cathode-ray tube opposite the anode glows. In addition, a paddle wheel placed in the tube rolls from the anode toward the cathode when the current is on.
a. In which direction do particles pass through the gas?
b. What charge do the particles possess?

34. Inferring Relationships   How much mass is converted into energy during the creation of the nucleus of a $^{235}_{92}U$ nuclide from 92 protons, 143 neutrons, and 92 electrons? (Hint: See Section 22-1.)

TECHNOLOGY & LEARNING

35. Graphing Calculator   Calculate Numbers of Protons, Electrons, and Neutrons. A graphing calculator can run a program that calculates the numbers of protons, electrons, and neutrons given the atomic mass and numbers for an atom. For example, given a calcium-40 atom, you will calculate the number of protons, electrons, and neutrons in the atom.

Go to Appendix C. If you are using a TI 83 Plus, you can download the program and data sets and run the application as directed. If you are using another calculator, your teacher will provide you with keystrokes and data sets to use. Remember that you will need to name the program and check the display, as explained in Appendix C. You will then be ready to run the program. After you have graphed the data sets, answer these questions.

a. Which element has the greatest number of protons?

b. How many neutrons does mercury have?

c. Carbon-12 and carbon-14 have the same atomic number. Do they have the same number of neutrons? Why or why not?

 HANDBOOK SEARCH

36. Group 14 of the *Elements Handbook* describes the reactions that produce CO and CO_2. Review this section to answer the following:
a. When a fuel burns, what determines whether CO or CO_2 will be produced?
b. What happens in the body if hemoglobin picks up CO instead of CO_2 or O_2?
c. Why is CO poisoning most likely to occur in homes that are well sealed during cold winter months?

RESEARCH & WRITING

37. Prepare a report on the series of experiments conducted by Sir James Chadwick that led to the discovery of the neutron.

38. Write a report on the contributions of Amedeo Avogadro that led to the determination of the value of Avogadro's number.

39. Trace the development of the electron microscope, and cite some of its many uses.

40. The study of atomic structure and the nucleus produced a new field of medicine called nuclear medicine. Describe the use of radioactive tracers to detect and treat diseases.

ALTERNATIVE ASSESSMENT

41. Observe a cathode-ray tube in operation, and write a description of your observations.

42. Performance Assessment   Using colored clay, build a model of the nucleus of each of carbon's three naturally occurring isotopes: carbon-12, carbon-13, and carbon-14. Specify the number of electrons that would surround each nucleus.

c. CO produced by a heating system cannot be adequately ventilated.

Refer to the *One-Stop Planner CD-ROM* for appropriate scoring rubrics for items 37–40. Look for these points in each report:

37. Chadwick bombarded beryllium-9 with alpha particles to obtain carbon-12 and a single neutron.

38. Avogadro's work with gases

39. the wave nature of electrons; quantum theory; it is an essential tool in the study of science

40. Report should mention elements and compounds commonly used in nuclear medicine.

41. Answers will vary.

42. 12 in each isotope

Arrangement of Electrons in Atoms

PACING CHART Compression Guide: (To shorten, eliminate items in italics.)	NSE Standards	CLASSROOM RESOURCES	
		Teaching Resources	Experiments

4-1 **The Development of a New Atomic Model** 2 45-minute periods 1 90-minute block *Properties of Light, pp. 91–93* *The Hydrogen-Atom Line-Emission Spectrum, pp. 94–95* *Bohr Model of the Hydrogen Atom, pp. 96–97*	PS 6a–6c UCP 1–2 SAI 1–2 HNS 1–3	**PE** Elements Handbook **ATE Demo,** pp. 92, 94 T 17, T 18, T 19, T 20, T 21	**PE** Flame Tests, p. 801
4-2 **The Quantum Model of the Atom** 2 45-minute periods 1 90-minute block *The Heisenberg Uncertainty Principle, p. 99* *The Schrödinger Wave Equation, p. 99*	PS4e UCP 1–2 SAI 1–2 HNS 3	T 22	**PE** Quick Lab, p. 100
4-3 **Electron Configurations** 2 45-minute periods 1 90-minute block *Rules Governing Electron Configurations, pp. 105–106* *Representing Electron Configurations, pp. 106–107*	UCP 1–3 UCP 5 SAI 2 HNS 1–3	T 23, TM 13A, TM 14A, TM 15A, TM 16A, TM 17A	

Review and Assessment 2 45-minute periods 1 90-minute block	REVIEW RESOURCES		
	Cumulative Review	Alternative Assessment	Traditional Assessment
	SR Chapter 4 Mixed Review **PE** Chapter 4 39–48, p. 120	**PE** 55, p. 121 **ATE** 96, 101, 109 **AA** Items for Chapter 4	Chapter 4 Text Test Generator Items for Chapter 4

ASSIGNMENT RESOURCES

Section Homework Resources & Review	Problem-Solving Practice
HR Homework Worksheets 4-1, 4-2 Graphic Org. Assignment 4-1 **PE** Section Review, 1–5, p. 97 Chapter Review, 1–9, 31–35, p. 118 **SR** Section Review 4-1	
HR Homework Worksheets 4-3, 4-4 Graphic Org. Assignment 4-4 **PE** Section Review, 1–3, p. 104 Chapter Review, 10–17, p. 118 **SR** Section Review 4-2	
HR Homework Worksheets 4-5, 4-6, 4-7, 4-8 Graphic Org. Assignments 4-7, 4-8 **PE** Section Review, 1–5, p. 116 Chapter Review, 19–30, 37–38, p. 118 **SR** Section Review 4-3	**PE** Additional Samples 4-1, 4-2, 4-3 **ATE** Additional Samples, pp. 107, 114, 116 Additional Examples, p. 113

TECHNOLOGY RESOURCES

Technology & Internet Resources

 CTW 9 Segment 9 Atom Lasers

 Holt Chemistry Videodiscs Teacher's Correlation Guide for Chapter 4

 Module 2: Electronic Structure

internet connect

 On-line Student Resources:
GO TO: www.scilinks.org
The following SciLinks Internet resources can be found in the student text for this chapter.

TOPICS:
• Electromagnetic spectrum, p. 91 (HC2041)
• Photoelectric effect, p. 93 (HC2042)
• William Ramsay, p. 108 (HC2043)

On-line Teacher Resources:
GO TO: go.hrw.com
KEYWORD: HC2 HOME
Visit the HRW Web site for a variety of resources related to this chapter.

 Smithsonian Institution®
Internet Connections
Visit www.si.edu/hrw for additional on-line resources.

 CNNfyi.com
Visit www.cnnfyi.com for late-breaking news and current events stories selected just for you.

Resource Key

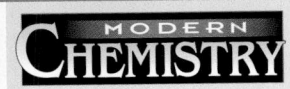
PE Pupil's Edition
ATE Teacher's Edition

One-Stop Planner CD-ROM Includes these resources and customizable daily lesson plans:

HR Homework Resources		**D** Consumer Experiments
SR Section Reviews	**A** Laboratory Experiments	**T** Transparencies
CTW Critical Thinking Worksheets	**B** Microscale Experiments	**TM** Transparency Masters
AA Alternative Assessments	**C** Technique Builders and Problem-Solving Experiments	**PS** Mini-Guide to Problem Solving
		SRW Supplemental Reading Worksheets

Scoring Rubrics for Labs, Alternative Assessments, Performance Tasks and Portfolio Projects are on the One-Stop Planner CD-ROM.

Arrangement of Electrons in Atoms

Chapter Overview

4-1 describes the principles of electromagnetic radiation and the development of the Bohr model of the atom.

4-2 describes the location of electrons around the nucleus from a wave-mechanical, or quantum, perspective using quantum numbers.

4-3 discusses the rules used to determine the electron configurations of the elements and introduces electron-configuration notations.

Concept Base

Students may need a review of the following concepts:

- inverse proportions, Chapter 2
- the mass of electrons, Chapter 3

 Reading Skill-Builder

K/W/L Write the words *light* and *electron* on the board. Have students list what they know or think they know about how these terms are related. Then have them list what they want to know. After they have read Section 4-1, have them look at their lists and write down what they have learned about light and electrons. Also have them write down any new questions that they have after reading the section.

Arrangement of Electrons in Atoms

The emission of light is fundamentally related to the behavior of electrons.

The Development of a New Atomic Model

OBJECTIVES

- Explain the mathematical relationship among the speed, wavelength, and frequency of electromagnetic radiation.

- Discuss the dual wave-particle nature of light.

- Discuss the significance of the photoelectric effect and the line-emission spectrum of hydrogen to the development of the atomic model.

- Describe the Bohr model of the hydrogen atom.

Lesson Starter
Have students look at the colors on a computer screen. Although the colors look continuous, close inspection reveals that they are actually made of separate colored dots that our eyes perceive as one color. The study of electrons demonstrates that electromagnetic energy comes in bundles divisible by a quantity called Planck's constant. The value of Planck's constant is so small, however, that electromagnetic energy seems to vary continuously, just like the colors on a computer screen.

Common Misconception
Show students a slide or picture of the planets. Explain that even though many people think that the organization of electrons in an atom is similar to the organization of the planets in a solar system, the two situations are quite different. Planets occur at one point in space, moving through elliptical *orbits*. The *orbitals* that describe the locations of atomic electrons vary in shape, and the electrons move so quickly over such a small distance that they seem to occupy the entire space at once. And electrons can exist only at certain, specific distances from the nucleus. A planet or satellite may take an orbit of any radius.

Reading Skill-Builder

BRAINSTORMING Have students brainstorm a list of different types of waves. Invite students to speculate about how the different types of waves are similar and how they are different.

The Rutherford model of the atom was an improvement over previous models, but it was incomplete. It did not explain where the atom's negatively charged electrons are located in the space surrounding its positively charged nucleus. After all, it was well known that oppositely charged particles attract each other. So what prevented the negative electrons from being drawn into the positive nucleus?

In the early twentieth century, a new atomic model evolved as a result of investigations into the absorption and emission of light by matter. The studies revealed an intimate relationship between light and an atom's electrons. This new understanding led directly to a revolutionary view of the nature of energy, matter, and atomic structure.

Properties of Light

Before 1900, scientists thought light behaved solely as a wave. This belief changed when it was later discovered that light also has particle-like characteristics. Still, many of light's properties can be described in terms of waves. A quick review of these wavelike properties will help you understand the basic theory of light as it existed at the beginning of the twentieth century.

The Wave Description of Light

Visible light is a kind of **electromagnetic radiation,** *which is a form of energy that exhibits wavelike behavior as it travels through space.* Other kinds of electromagnetic radiation include X rays, ultraviolet and infrared light, microwaves, and radio waves. *Together, all the forms of electromagnetic radiation form the* **electromagnetic spectrum.** The electromagnetic spectrum is represented in Figure 4-1 on page 92. All forms of electromagnetic radiation move at a constant speed of about 3.0×10^8 meters per second (m/s) through a vacuum and at slightly slower speeds through matter. Because air is mostly space, the value of 3.0×10^8 m/s is also light's approximate speed through air.

The significant feature of wave motion is its repetitive nature, which can be characterized by the measurable properties of wavelength and frequency. **Wavelength** (λ) *is the distance between corresponding points on adjacent waves.* Depending on the particular form of electromagnetic radiation, the unit for wavelength is the meter, centimeter, or nanome-

internet connect

SC*i*LINKS.
NSTA

TOPIC: Electromagnetic spectrum
GO TO: www.scilinks.org
*sci*LINKS CODE: HC2041

FIGURE 4-2 In each water wave, the wavelength is shown as the distance between the crest of one wave and the crest of the next. However, students should realize that wavelength is the distance between *any* two corresponding points on adjacent waves. Frequency refers to how often the waves pass any point. Have students imagine that they are watching waves at the beach. If the waves begin to break more frequently on the beach, then the frequency of the waves could be increasing or the distance between the waves could be decreasing.

DEMONSTRATION

Have two students hold a coiled spring along the floor or a tabletop. Have one of the students begin moving the spring back and forth so that a wave pattern forms. How does the wavelength change when the student moves the spring back and forth with greater frequency? *(The wavelength decreases.)*

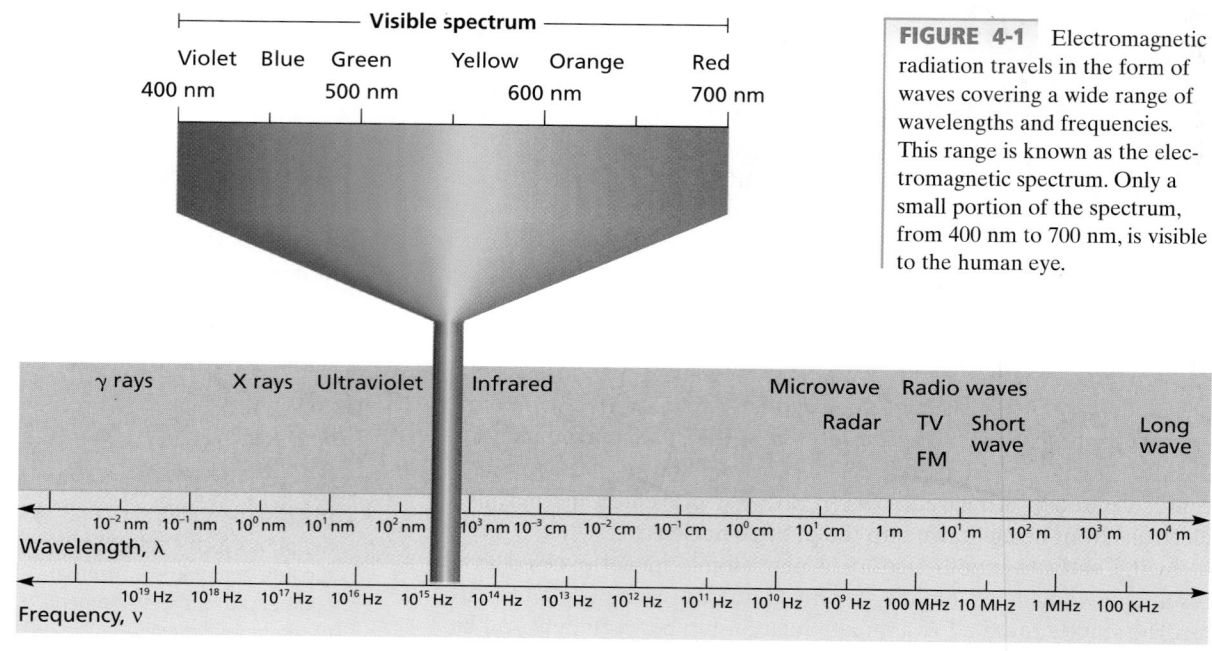

FIGURE 4-1 Electromagnetic radiation travels in the form of waves covering a wide range of wavelengths and frequencies. This range is known as the electromagnetic spectrum. Only a small portion of the spectrum, from 400 nm to 700 nm, is visible to the human eye.

ter $(1 \text{ nm} = 1 \times 10^{-9} \text{ m})$, as shown in Figure 4-1. **Frequency** (ν) *is defined as the number of waves that pass a given point in a specific time, usually one second.* Frequency is expressed in waves/second. One wave/second is called a hertz (Hz), named for Heinrich Hertz, who was a pioneer in the study of electromagnetic radiation. Figure 4-2 illustrates the properties of wavelength and frequency for a familiar kind of wave, a wave on the surface of water. The wavelength in Figure 4-2(a) has a longer wavelength and a lower frequency than the wave in Figure 4-2(b).

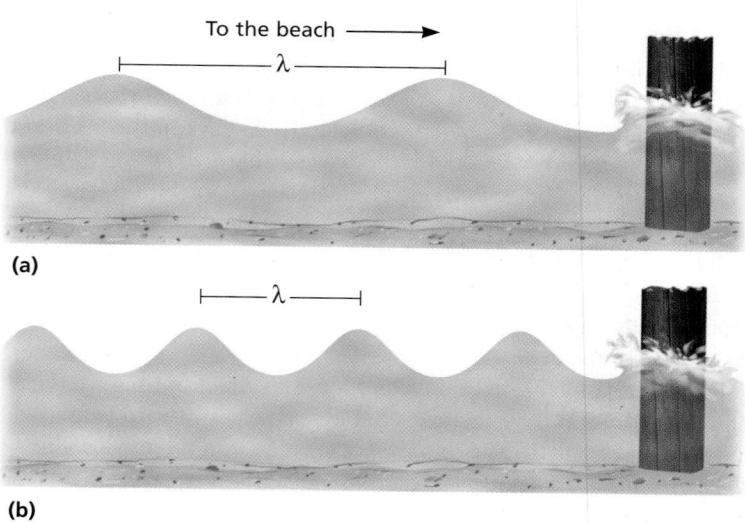

FIGURE 4-2 The distance between any two corresponding points on one of these water waves, such as from crest to crest, is the wave's wavelength, λ. We can measure the wave's frequency, ν, by observing how often the water level rises and falls at a given point, such as at the post.

Frequency and wavelength are mathematically related to each other. For electromagnetic radiation, this relationship is written as follows.

$$c = \lambda \nu$$

In the equation, c is the speed of light, λ is the wavelength of the electromagnetic wave, and ν is the frequency of the electromagnetic wave. Because c is the same for all electromagnetic radiation, the product $\lambda \nu$ is a constant. Consequently, we know that λ is inversely proportional to ν. In other words, as the wavelength of light decreases, its frequency increases, and vice versa.

The Photoelectric Effect

In the early 1900s, scientists conducted two experiments involving interactions of light and matter that could not be explained by the wave theory of light. One experiment involved a phenomenon known as the photoelectric effect. *The* **photoelectric effect** *refers to the emission of electrons from a metal when light shines on the metal*, as illustrated in Figure 4-3.

The mystery of the photoelectric effect involved the frequency of the light striking the metal. For a given metal, no electrons were emitted if the light's frequency was below a certain minimum—regardless of how long the light was shone. Light was known to be a form of energy, capable of knocking loose an electron from a metal. But the wave theory of light predicted that light of any frequency could supply enough energy to eject an electron. Scientists couldn't explain why the light had to be of a minimum frequency in order for the photoelectric effect to occur.

The Particle Description of Light

The explanation of the photoelectric effect dates back to 1900, when German physicist Max Planck was studying the emission of light by hot objects. He proposed that a hot object does not emit electromagnetic energy continuously, as would be expected if the energy emitted were in the form of waves. Instead, Planck suggested that the object emits energy in small, specific amounts called quanta. *A* **quantum** *is the minimum quantity of energy that can be lost or gained by an atom.* Planck proposed the following relationship between a quantum of energy and the frequency of radiation.

$$E = h\nu$$

In the equation, E is the energy, in joules, of a quantum of radiation, ν is the frequency of the radiation emitted, and h is a fundamental physical constant now known as Planck's constant; $h = 6.626 \times 10^{-34}$ J·s.

In 1905, Albert Einstein expanded on Planck's theory by introducing the radical idea that electromagnetic radiation has a dual wave-particle nature. While light exhibits many wavelike particles, it can also be

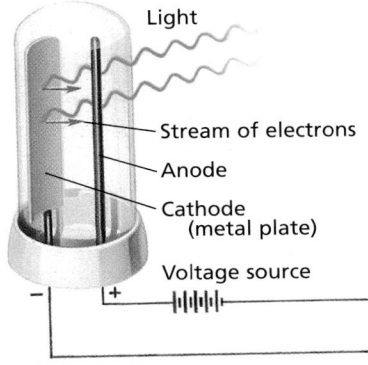

FIGURE 4-3 The photoelectric effect: electromagnetic radiation strikes the surface of the metal, ejecting electrons from the metal and creating an electric current.

Light — Stream of electrons — Anode — Cathode (metal plate) — Voltage source

Analogy
The photoelectric effect is like a coin-operated soft-drink machine that works only when a single coin of sufficient value is inserted. If a combination of smaller coins is inserted, nothing happens, even if the combination adds up to the value of the single coin. An electron remains bound to a metal unless a single photon with the required minimum energy hits the electron.

Application
The photoelectric effect allows electrons to flow through a conducting material when light of high enough frequency hits the material's surface. This phenomenon is utilized in light meters and photovoltaic cells.

internet**connect**

SC*LINKS*
NSTA

TOPIC: Photoelectric effect
GO TO: www.scilinks.org
*sci*LINKS **CODE:** HC2042

thought of as a stream of particles. Each particle of light carries a quantum of energy. Einstein called these particles photons. *A* **photon** *is a particle of electromagnetic radiation having zero mass and carrying a quantum of energy.* The energy of a particular photon depends on the frequency of the radiation.

$$E_{photon} = h\nu$$

Einstein explained the photoelectric effect by proposing that electromagnetic radiation is absorbed by matter only in whole numbers of photons. In order for an electron to be ejected from a metal surface, the electron must be struck by a single photon possessing at least the minimum energy required to knock the electron loose. According to the equation $E_{photon} = h\nu$, this minimum energy corresponds to a minimum frequency. If a photon's frequency is below the minimum, then the electron remains bound to the metal surface. Electrons in different metals are bound more or less tightly, so different metals require different minimum frequencies to exhibit the photoelectric effect.

The Hydrogen-Atom Line-Emission Spectrum

When current is passed through a gas at low pressure, the potential energy of some of the gas atoms increases. *The lowest energy state of an atom is its* **ground state.** *A state in which an atom has a higher potential energy than it has in its ground state is an* **excited state.** When an excited atom returns to its ground state, it gives off the energy it gained in the form of electromagnetic radiation. The production of colored light in neon signs, as shown in Figure 4-4, is a familiar example of this process.

When investigators passed electric current through a vacuum tube containing hydrogen gas at low pressure, they observed the emission of a characteristic pinkish glow. *When a narrow beam of the emitted light was shined through a prism, it was separated into a series of specific frequencies (and therefore specific wavelengths, $\lambda = c/\nu$) of visible light.* The bands of light were part of what is known as hydrogen's **line-emission spectrum.** The production of hydrogen's line-emission spectrum is illustrated in Figure 4-5. Additional series of lines were discovered in the ultraviolet and infrared regions of hydrogen's line-emission spectrum. The wavelengths of some of the spectral series are shown in Figure 4-6. They are known as the Lyman, Balmer, and Paschen series, after their discoverers.

Classical theory predicted that the hydrogen atoms would be excited by whatever amount of energy was added to them. Scientists had thus expected to observe *the emission of a continuous range of frequencies of electromagnetic radiation,* that is, a **continuous spectrum.** Why had the hydrogen atoms given off only specific frequencies of light? Attempts to explain this observation led to an entirely new theory of the atom called *quantum theory.*

FIGURE 4-4 Excited neon atoms emit light when falling back to the ground state or to a lower-energy excited state.

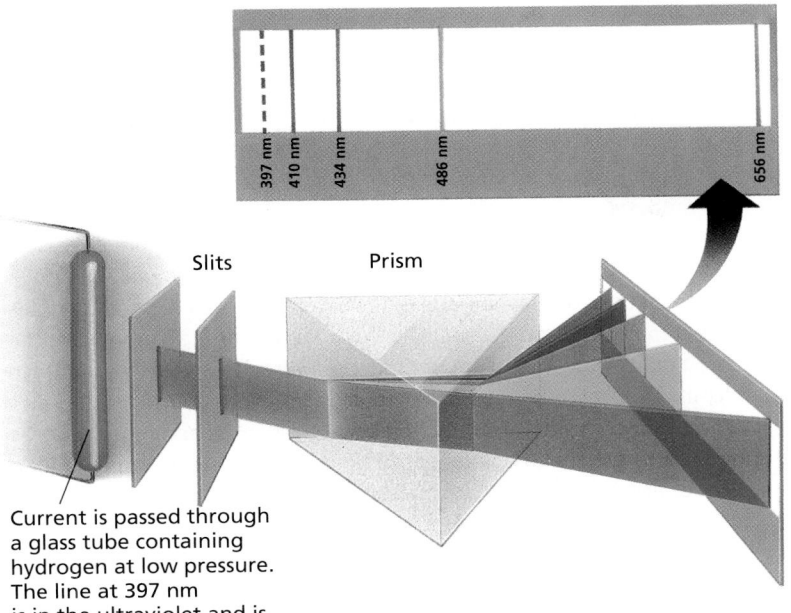

FIGURE 4-5 Excited hydrogen atoms emit a pinkish glow. When the visible portion of the emitted light is passed through a prism, it is separated into specific wavelengths that are part of hydrogen's line-emission spectrum. The line at 397 nm is in the ultraviolet and is not visible to the human eye.

Slits

Prism

Current is passed through a glass tube containing hydrogen at low pressure. The line at 397 nm is in the ultraviolet and is not visible to the human eye.

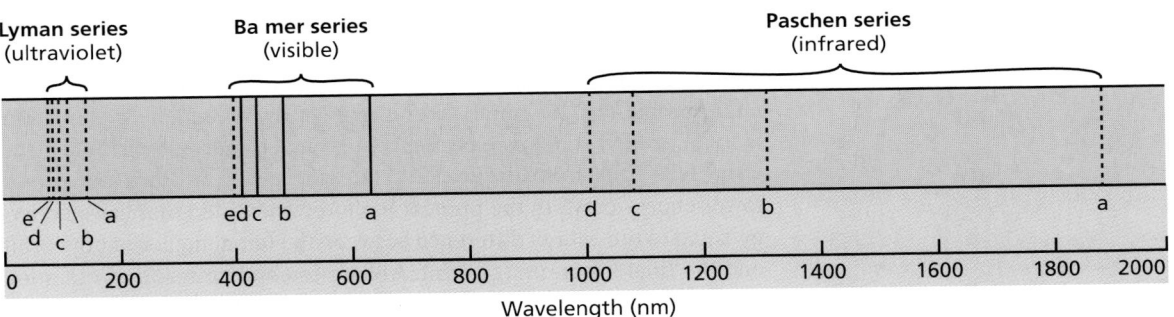

Lyman series (ultraviolet)

Ba mer series (visible)

Paschen series (infrared)

Wavelength (nm)

FIGURE 4-6 A series of specific wavelengths of emitted light makes up hydrogen's line-emission spectrum. The letters below the lines label hydrogen's various energy-level transitions. Niels Bohr's model of the hydrogen atom provided an explanation for these transitions.

Whenever an excited hydrogen atom falls back from an excited state to its ground state or to a lower-energy excited state, it emits a photon of radiation. The energy of this photon ($E_{photon} = h\nu$) is equal to the difference in energy between the atom's initial state and its final state, as illustrated in Figure 4-7. The fact that hydrogen atoms emit only specific frequencies of light indicated that the energy differences between the atoms' energy states were fixed. This suggested that the electron of a hydrogen atom exists only in very specific energy states.

In the late nineteenth century, a mathematical relationship that related the various wavelengths of hydrogen's line-emission spectrum was discovered. The challenge facing scientists was to provide a model of the hydrogen atom that accounted for this relationship.

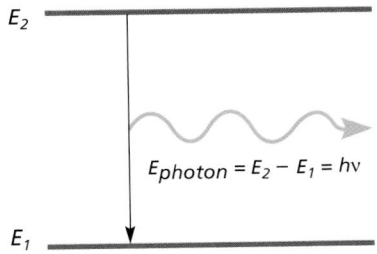

E_2

$E_{photon} = E_2 - E_1 = h\nu$

E_1

FIGURE 4-7 When an excited atom with energy E_2 falls back to energy E_1, it releases a photon that has energy $E_2 - E_1 = E_{photon} = h\nu$.

Analogy

When considering the energy of an electron around a nucleus, students can imagine connecting a ball to a string and swinging it in circles. As the ball is swung with greater energy, the radius from the vertical position increases. Likewise, the distance of an electron from the nucleus increases with increasing electron energy.

✔Teaching Tip

Bohr used classical Newtonian mechanics to study the angular momentum and radius of the electron around the nucleus. In the next section, students will see how *quantum mechanics* allows a more complete description of atomic structure.

Alternative Assessment

This section continues the discussion of atomic structure from Chapter 3. Have students revise their chronology of modern atomic theory to include Bohr and give reasons why he should be included.

Bohr Model of the Hydrogen Atom

The puzzle of the hydrogen-atom spectrum was solved in 1913 by the Danish physicist Niels Bohr. He proposed a model of the hydrogen atom that linked the atom's electron with photon emission. According to the model, the electron can circle the nucleus only in allowed paths, or *orbits*. When the electron is in one of these orbits, the atom has a definite, fixed energy. The electron, and therefore the hydrogen atom, is in its lowest energy state when it is in the orbit closest to the nucleus. This orbit is separated from the nucleus by a large empty space where the electron cannot exist. The energy of the electron is higher when it is in orbits that are successively farther from the nucleus.

The electron orbits or atomic energy levels in Bohr's model can be compared to the rungs of a ladder. When you are standing on a ladder, your feet are on one rung or another. The amount of potential energy that you possess corresponds to standing on the first rung, the second rung, and so forth. Your energy cannot correspond to standing between two rungs because you cannot stand in midair. In the same way, an electron can be in one orbit or another, but not in between.

How does Bohr's model of the hydrogen atom explain the observed spectral lines? While in an orbit, the electron can neither gain nor lose energy. It can, however, move to a higher energy orbit by gaining an amount of energy equal to the difference in energy between the higher-energy orbit and the initial lower-energy orbit. When a hydrogen atom is in an excited state, its electron is in a higher-energy orbit. When the atom falls back from the excited state, the electron drops down to a lower-energy orbit. In the process, a photon is emitted that has an energy equal to the energy difference between the initial higher-energy orbit and the final lower-energy orbit. Absorption and emission of radiation according to the Bohr model of the hydrogen atom are illustrated in Figure 4-8. The energy of each emitted photon corresponds to a particular frequency of emitted radiation, $E_{photon} = h\nu$.

Based on the wavelengths of hydrogen's line-emission spectrum, Bohr calculated the energies that an electron would have in the allowed energy levels for the hydrogen atom. He then used these values to show

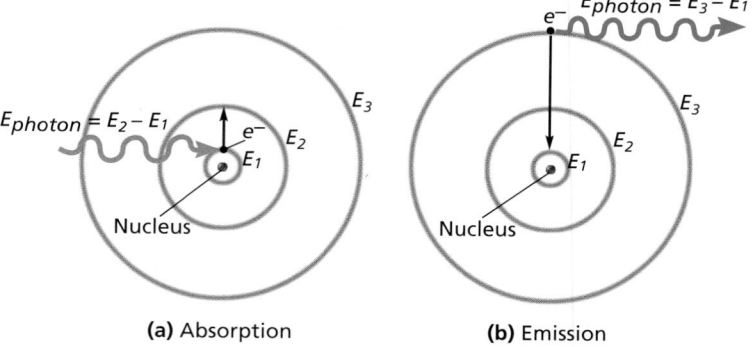

FIGURE 4-8 (a) Absorption and (b) emission of a photon by a hydrogen atom according to Bohr's model. The frequencies of light that can be absorbed and emitted are restricted because the electron can only be in orbits corresponding to the energies E_1, E_2, E_3, and so forth.

(a) Absorption   **(b) Emission**

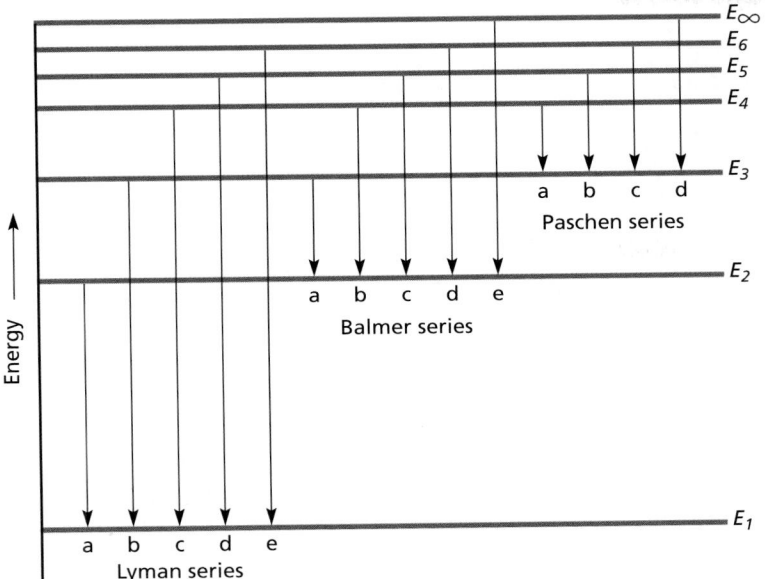

E_∞
E_6
E_5
E_4

E_3

a b c d
Paschen series

a b c d e $\quad E_2$
Balmer series

Energy →

E_1

a b c d e
Lyman series

FIGURE 4-9 This electron energy-level diagram for hydrogen shows the energy transitions for the Lyman, Balmer, and Paschen spectral series. Bohr's model of the atom accounted mathematically for the energy of each of the transitions shown.

mathematically how the various spectral series of hydrogen were produced. The Lyman spectral series, for example, was shown to be the result of electrons dropping from various higher-energy levels to the ground-state energy level.

Bohr's calculated values agreed with the experimentally observed values for the lines in each series. The origins of several of the series of lines in hydrogen's line-emission spectrum are shown in Figure 4-9.

The success of Bohr's model of the hydrogen atom in explaining observed spectral lines led many scientists to conclude that a similar model could be applied to all atoms. It was soon recognized, however, that Bohr's approach did not explain the spectra of atoms with more than one electron. Nor did Bohr's theory explain the chemical behavior of atoms.

SECTION REVIEW

1. What was the major shortcoming of Rutherford's model of the atom?

2. Write and label the equation that relates the speed, wavelength, and frequency of electromagnetic radiation.

3. Define the following:
   a. electromagnetic radiation   b. wavelength
   c. frequency   d. quantum   e. photon

4. What is meant by the dual wave-particle nature of light?

5. Describe the Bohr model of the hydrogen atom.

1. It did not explain how negative electrons fill the space surrounding a positive nucleus.

2. $c = \lambda \nu$; c = speed, λ = wavelength, ν = frequency

3. **a.** a form of energy that exhibits wavelike behavior as it travels through space
   b. the distance between corresponding points on adjacent waves
   c. the number of waves that pass a given point in a specified amount of time, usually 1 s
   d. a finite quantity of energy gained or lost by an atom
   e. a quantum of light

4. Depending on the experiment devised to observe it, the behavior of light can be described in terms of waves or in terms of particles.

5. The Bohr model depicts a hydrogen nucleus with a single electron circling the nucleus at a specific radius in a path called an orbit. The electron exists in one of only a finite number of allowed orbits.

SECTION 4-2

The Quantum Model of the Atom

OBJECTIVES

- Discuss Louis de Broglie's role in the development of the quantum model of the atom.

- Compare and contrast the Bohr model and the quantum model of the atom.

- Explain how the Heisenberg uncertainty principle and the Schrödinger wave equation led to the idea of atomic orbitals.

- List the four quantum numbers, and describe their significance.

- Relate the number of sublevels corresponding to each of an atom's main energy levels, the number of orbitals per sublevel, and the number of orbitals per main energy level.

To the scientists of the early twentieth century, Bohr's model of the hydrogen atom contradicted common sense. Why did hydrogen's electron exist around the nucleus only in certain allowed orbits with definite energies? Why couldn't the electron exist in a limitless number of orbits with slightly different energies? To explain why atomic energy states are quantized, scientists had to change the way they viewed the nature of the electron.

Electrons as Waves

The investigations into the photoelectric effect and hydrogen atomic emission revealed that light could behave as both a wave and a particle. Could electrons have a dual wave-particle nature as well? In 1924, the French scientist Louis de Broglie asked himself this very question. And the answer that he proposed led to a revolution in our basic understanding of matter.

De Broglie pointed out that in many ways the behavior of Bohr's quantized electron orbits was similar to the known behavior of waves. For example, scientists at the time knew that any wave confined to a space can have only certain frequencies. De Broglie suggested that electrons be considered waves confined to the space around an atomic nucleus. It followed that the electron waves could exist only at specific frequencies. And according to the relationship $E = h\nu$, these frequencies corresponded to specific energies—the quantized energies of Bohr's orbits.

Other aspects of de Broglie's hypothesis that electrons have wavelike properties were soon confirmed by experiments. Investigators demonstrated that electrons, like light waves, can be bent, or diffracted. *Diffraction* refers to the bending of a wave as it passes by the edge of an object, such as the edge of an atom in a crystal. Diffraction experiments and other investigations also showed that electron beams, like waves, can interfere with each other. *Interference* occurs when waves overlap (see the Quick Lab on page 100). This overlapping results in a reduction of energy in some areas and an increase of energy in others. The effects of diffraction and interference can be seen in Figure 4-10.

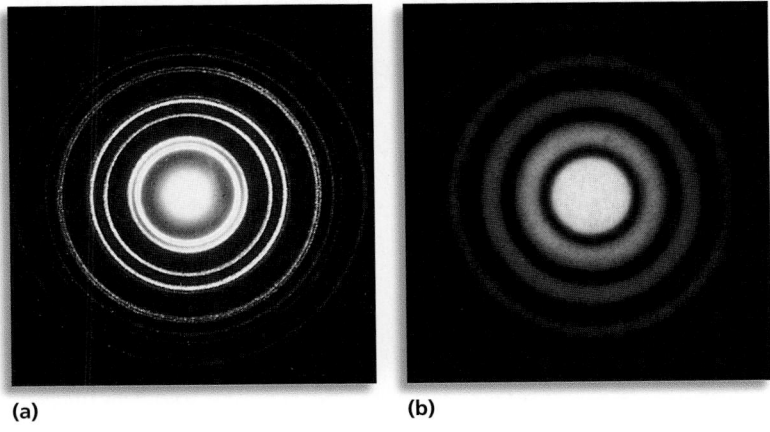

(a)   **(b)**

FIGURE 4-10 Diffraction patterns produced by (a) a beam of electrons passed through a crystal and (b) a beam of visible light passed through a tiny aperture. Each pattern shows the results of bent waves that have interfered with each other. The bright areas correspond to areas of increased energy, while the dark areas correspond to areas of decreased energy.

Visual Strategy

FIGURE 4-10 Diffraction and interference are two traits common to all waves. For example, water waves coming from two nearby sources will create diffraction and interference patterns. This could be demonstrated using a wave table if one is available.

✔ **Teaching Tip**

Understanding modern quantum mechanics can be very difficult for new chemistry students. One way to make the process simpler is to use entertaining stories that contain rich analogies. George Gamov's *Mr. Tompkins in Paperback* contains several vignettes that clarify atomic theory in an entertaining manner.

The Heisenberg Uncertainty Principle

The idea of electrons having a dual wave-particle nature troubled scientists. If electrons are both particles and waves, then where are they in the atom? To answer this question, it is important to consider a proposal first made in 1927 by the German theoretical physicist Werner Heisenberg.

Heisenberg's idea involved the detection of electrons. Electrons are detected by their interaction with photons. Because photons have about the same energy as electrons, any attempt to locate a specific electron with a photon knocks the electron off its course. As a result, there is always a basic uncertainty in trying to locate an electron (or any other particle). *The* **Heisenberg uncertainty principle** *states that it is impossible to determine simultaneously both the position and velocity of an electron or any other particle.* Although it was difficult for scientists to accept this fact at the time, it has proven to be one of the fundamental principles of our present understanding of light and matter.

The Schrödinger Wave Equation

In 1926, the Austrian physicist Erwin Schrödinger used the hypothesis that electrons have a dual wave-particle nature to develop an equation that treated electrons in atoms as waves. Unlike Bohr's theory, which assumed quantization as a fact, quantization of electron energies was a natural outcome of Schrödinger's equation. Only waves of specific energies, and therefore frequencies, provided solutions to the equation. Together with the Heisenberg uncertainty principle, the Schrödinger wave equation laid the foundation for modern quantum theory. **Quantum theory** *describes mathematically the wave properties of electrons and other very small particles.*

QUICK LAB

Both light and electrons exhibit wave-like properties during experiments that test for wave properties. Interference is one property of waves. This activity duplicates a historic experiment that tested both light and electrons for interference.

Discussion

1. Most students should observe light and dark rings around the edge of the hole illuminated on the screen. These light and dark patterns are a result of interference.

2. Light has wavelike properties.

Analogy

Ask students to imagine the propeller of an airplane. They can be certain of its position as long as it has no kinetic energy, that is, as long as it is not moving. But as the propeller begins to move, it seems to take a different shape—that of a disk—and its position at any one instant is extremely uncertain. Electrons are much smaller and move much more quickly, creating even greater uncertainty. Like the propeller taking the shape of a disk, the electron is no longer considered to be at a single point in space, but rather it is thought of as a *cloud*. Schrödinger established the different possible cloud shapes that electrons could occupy. These shapes are summarized using quantum numbers.

Quick LAB

Wear Safety Goggles and an Apron.

The Wave Nature of Light: Interference

Materials

- scissors
- manila folders
- thumbtack
- masking tape
- aluminum foil
- white poster board or cardboard
- flashlight

Question

Does light show the wave property of interference when a beam of light is projected through a pinhole onto a screen?

Procedure

Record all your observations.

1. To make the pinhole screen, cut a 20 cm × 20 cm square from a manila folder. In the center of the square, cut a 2 cm square hole.

Cut a 7 cm × 7 cm square of aluminum foil. Using a thumbtack, make a pinhole in the center of the foil square. Tape the aluminum foil over the 2 cm square hole, making sure the pinhole is centered as shown in the diagram.

2. Use white poster board to make a projection screen 35 cm × 35 cm.

3. In a dark room, center the light beam from a flashlight on the pinhole. Hold the flashlight about 1 cm from the pinhole. The pinhole screen should be about 50 cm from the projection screen, as shown in the diagram. Adjust the distance to form a sharp image on the projection screen.

1cm

Image

50 cm

Discussion

1. Did you observe interference patterns on the screen?

2. As a result of your observations, what do you conclude about the nature of light?

Solutions to the Schrödinger wave equation are known as wave functions. Based on the Heisenberg uncertainty principle, the early developers of quantum theory determined that wave functions give only the *probability* of finding an electron at a given place around the nucleus. Thus, electrons do not travel around the nucleus in neat orbits, as Bohr had postulated. Instead, they exist in certain regions called orbitals. *An* **orbital** *is a three-dimensional region around the nucleus that indicates the probable location of an electron.*

Figure 4-11 illustrates two ways of picturing one type of atomic orbital. As you will see later in this section, atomic orbitals have different shapes and sizes.

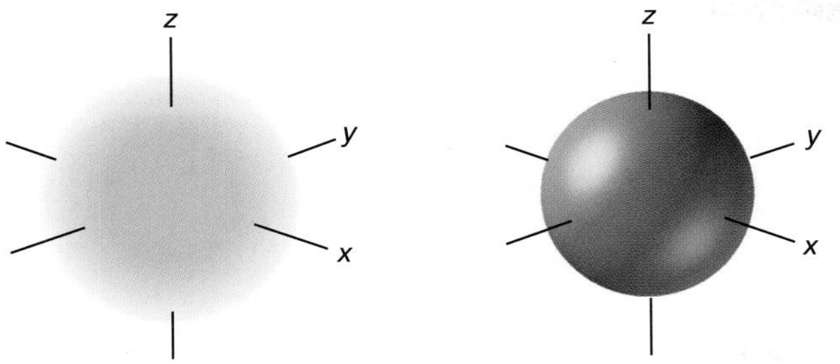
z
y
x
z
y
x

(a) (b)

FIGURE 4-11 Two ways of showing a simple atomic orbital are presented. In (a) the probability of finding the electron is proportional to the density of the cloud. Shown in (b) is a surface within which the electron can be found a certain percentage of the time, in this case 90%.

Atomic Orbitals and Quantum Numbers

In the Bohr atomic model, electrons of increasing energy occupy orbits farther and farther from the nucleus. According to the Schrödinger equation, electrons in atomic orbitals also have quantized energies. An electron's energy level is not the only characteristic of an orbital that is indicated by solving the Schrödinger equation.

In order to completely describe orbitals, scientists use quantum numbers. **Quantum numbers** *specify the properties of atomic orbitals and the properties of electrons in orbitals.* The first three quantum numbers result from solutions to the Schrödinger equation. They indicate the main energy level, the shape, and the orientation of an orbital. The fourth, the spin quantum number, describes a fundamental state of the electron that occupies the orbital. As you read the following descriptions of the quantum numbers, refer to the appropriate columns in Table 4-2 on page 104.

Principal Quantum Number

The **principal quantum number,** *symbolized by n, indicates the main energy level occupied by the electron.* Values of n are positive integers only—1, 2, 3, and so on. As n increases, the electron's energy and its average distance from the nucleus increase (see Figure 4-12). For example, an electron for which $n = 1$ occupies the first, or lowest, main energy level and is located closest to the nucleus. As you will see, more than one electron can have the same n value. These electrons are sometimes said to be in the same electron *shell.* The total number of orbitals that exist in a given shell, or main energy level, is equal to n^2.

Angular Momentum Quantum Number

Except at the first main energy level, orbitals of different shapes—known as *sublevels*—exist for a given value of n. *The* **angular momentum quantum number,** *symbolized by l, indicates the shape of the orbital.* For a specific main energy level, the number of orbital shapes possible is equal to n. The values of l allowed are zero and all positive integers less

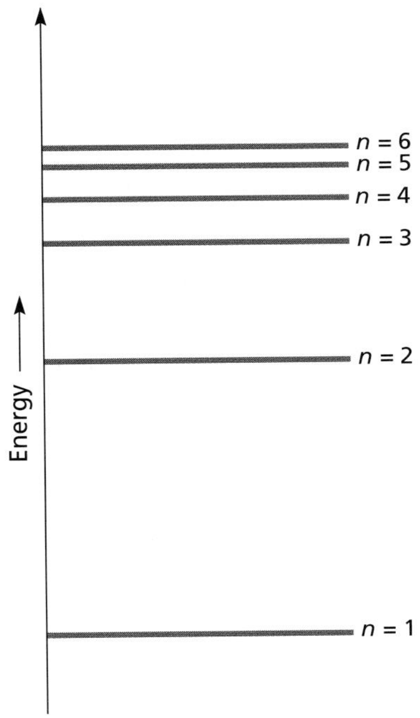
n = 6
n = 5
n = 4
n = 3
n = 2
n = 1
Energy

FIGURE 4-12 The main energy levels of an atom are represented by the principal quantum number, n.

Visual Strategy

FIGURE 4-11 Remind students that these images represent densities in three dimensions.

FIGURE 4-12 Each n value, or energy level, is one possible location for electrons around the nucleus. Emphasize that electrons cannot have energies corresponding to anything but values of n. The principal quantum number, n, also indicates the general distance of an electron to the nucleus. Electrons farther from the nucleus have greater energies and thus greater values of n.

Common Misconception

Although the word *orbital* is used to describe the location of electrons, electrons do not actually occur in planetlike orbits. In the quantum model, orbitals are actually electron clouds, or most likely locations for electrons. Students often cling to the Bohr model, which suggested that an orbiting electron moves at a specific radius, like a planet does. Help students move away from the Bohr model toward the quantum model.

Alternative Assessment

At this point, students can complete their chronology of the building of modern atomic theory. Suggest that they put a new chronology on a concept map that also contains the experiments or ideas used to make each step: isolating different subatomic particles, locating each particle, discovering the nature of electrons, and so on.

Table 4-1 Emphasize that the values of *l* and the letters *s, p, d,* and *f* are synonymous for the names of differently shaped orbitals. Be sure students are aware of the general orbital shapes, which are shown in Figure 4-13.

 Teaching Tip

Distinguish between the concepts of *sublevel* and *orbital.* An orbital is a single allowed location for atomic electrons. It is specified by definite values of *n, m,* and *l,* and it is capable of holding, at most, two electrons of opposite spin, according to the Pauli exclusion principle. A sublevel includes *all* the similarly shaped orbitals in a particular main energy level. In other words, for a given value of *n,* a sublevel consists of all orbitals with the same value of *l.*

Answers to In-Text Questions

• The *p* sublevel in the third main energy level is designated 3*p*.

• There are two other sublevels in the third main energy level, 3*s* and 3*d*.

Reading Skill-Builder

READING HINT Explain the different quantum numbers. Then have students form pairs and use the following figures to explain what the different quantum numbers indicate. Have them use Figure 4-12 to explain the principal quantum number, *n;* Figure 4-13 to explain the angular momentum number, *l;* and Figures 4-14 and 4-15 to explain the magnetic quantum number, *m.*

l	Letter
0	*s*
1	*p*
2	*d*
3	*f*

TABLE 4-1 *Orbital Letter Designations According to Values of l*

than or equal to $n - 1$. For example, orbitals for which $n = 2$ can have one of two shapes corresponding to $l = 0$ and $l = 1$. Depending on its value of l, an orbital is assigned a letter, as shown in Table 4-1.

As shown in Figure 4-13, *s* orbitals are spherical, *p* orbitals have dumbbell shapes, and *d* orbitals are more complex. (The *f* orbital shapes are too complex to discuss here.) In the first energy level, $n = 1$, there is only one sublevel possible—an *s* orbital. As mentioned, the second energy level, $n = 2$, has two sublevels—the *s* and *p* orbitals. The third energy level, $n = 3$, has three sublevels—the *s, p,* and *d* orbitals. The fourth energy level, $n = 4$, has four sublevels—the *s, p, d,* and *f* orbitals. In an *n*th main energy level, there are *n* sublevels.

Each atomic orbital is designated by the principal quantum number followed by the letter of the sublevel. For example, the 1*s* sublevel is the *s* orbital in the first main energy level, while the 2*p* sublevel is the set of *p* orbitals in the second main energy level. On the other hand, a 4*d* orbital is part of the *d* sublevel in the fourth main energy level. How would you designate the *p* sublevel in the third main energy level? How many other sublevels are in the same main energy level with this one?

Magnetic Quantum Number

Atomic orbitals can have the same shape but different orientations around the nucleus. *The* **magnetic quantum number,** *symbolized by m, indicates the orientation of an orbital around the nucleus.* Here we describe the orbital orientations that correspond to various values of *m.* Because an *s* orbital is spherical and is centered around the nucleus, it has only one possible orientation. This orientation corresponds to a

FIGURE 4-13 The orbitals *s, p,* and *d* have different shapes. Each of the orbitals shown occupies a different region of space around the nucleus.

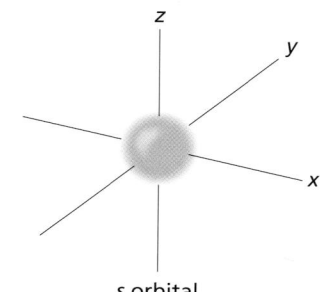

s orbital

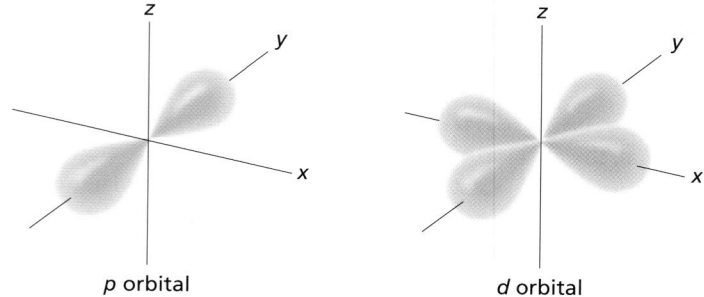

p orbital

d orbital

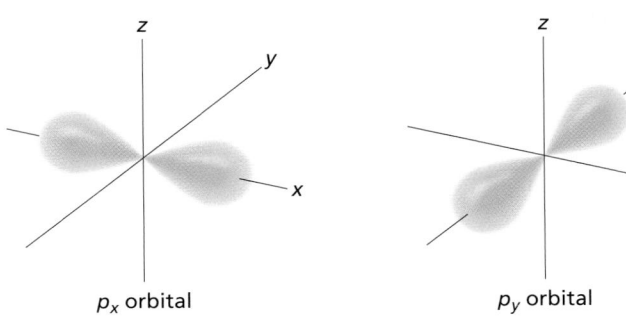

| p_x orbital | p_y orbital | p_z orbital |

FIGURE 4-14 The subscripts *x*, *y*, and *z* indicate the three different orientations of *p* orbitals. The intersection of the *x*, *y*, and *z* axes indicates the location of the center of the nucleus.

magnetic quantum number of $m = 0$. There is therefore only one *s* orbital in each *s* sublevel. As shown in Figure 4-14, the lobes of a *p* orbital can extend along the *x*, *y*, or *z* axis of a three-dimensional coordinate system. There are therefore three *p* orbitals in each *p* sublevel, which are designated as p_x, p_y, and p_z orbitals. The three *p* orbitals occupy different regions of space and correspond, in no particular order, to values of $m = -1$, $m = 0$, and $m = +1$.

There are five different *d* orbitals in each *d* sublevel (see Figure 4-15). The five different orientations, including one with a different shape, correspond to values of $m = -2$, $m = -1$, $m = 0$, $m = +1$, and $m = +2$. There are seven different *f* orbitals in each *f* sublevel.

Visual Strategy
FIGURE 4-14 Use three rulers at right angles to help students visualize the three-dimensional nature of the *x*, *y*, *z* coordinate system.

Teaching Strategy
The number of different possible values for the magnetic quantum number determines the number of orbitals in a particular sublevel. For example, when $l = 1$, m can equal −1, 0, or 1. These three possible values for m indicate that there are three different orbitals (each oriented differently around the nucleus) in the sublevel corresponding to $l = 1$. These three orbitals are known as *p* orbitals. More specifically, they are the p_x, p_y, and p_z orbitals, as shown in Figure 4-14.

TABLE STRATEGY

(page 104)

Table 4-2 Have students use the table to determine the number of electrons each sublevel can hold and the number of electrons that may be contained in a given main energy level.

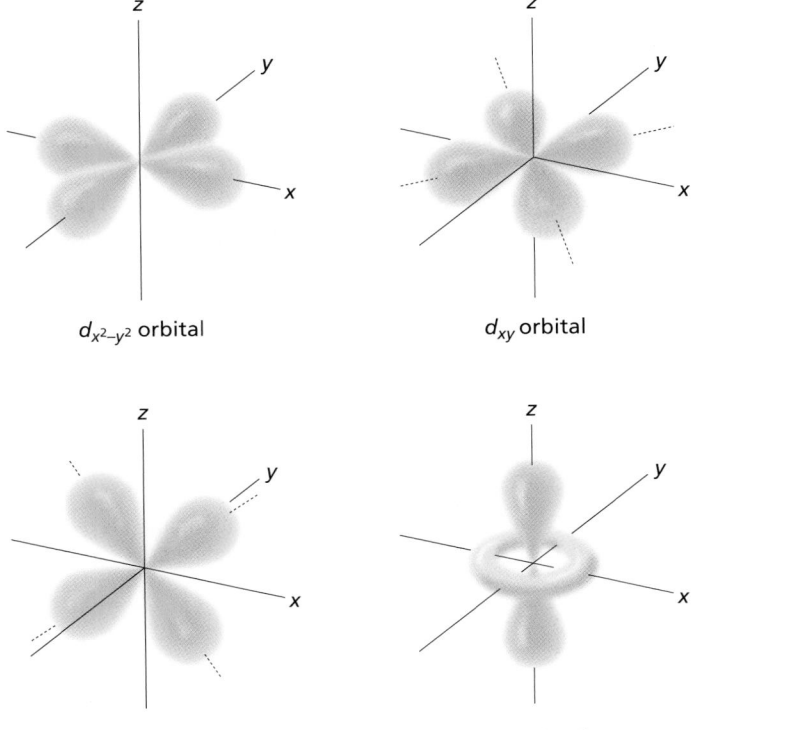

| $d_{x^2-y^2}$ orbital | d_{xy} orbital | d_{yz} orbital |

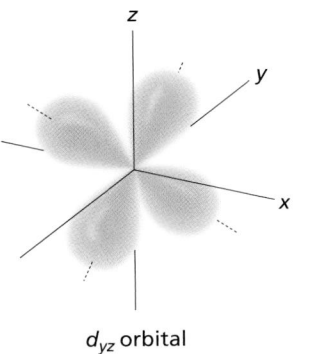

| d_{xz} orbital | d_{z^2} orbital |

FIGURE 4-15 The five different orientations of the *d* orbitals. Four have the same shape but different orientations. The fifth has a different shape and a different orientation than the others. Each orbital occupies a different region of space.

Answer to In-Text Question

There are 9 orbitals in the third main energy level: $3s$, $3p_x$, $3p_y$, $3p_z$, $3d_{x^2-y^2}$, $3d_{xy}$, $3d_{yz}$, $3d_{xz}$, and $3d_{z^2}$.

Teaching Strategy

Hold two bar magnets parallel to each other. If *north* on both magnets faces the same direction, the magnets will repel one another. If *north* on one magnet faces the opposite direction as *north* on the other magnet, then the magnets will attract each other. The magnets represent the magnetic fields around two spinning electrons. For the two electrons to coexist in the same orbital, the magnetic attraction from their opposite spins is needed to overcome their electrical repulsion.

SECTION REVIEW

1. a. quantized levels of increasing energy, specified by the quantum number *n,* at which atomic orbitals can exist
b. numbers used to specify the energy, location, shape, and orientation of atomic orbitals, as well as the spins of electrons in these orbitals
2. a. principal, *n;* orbital, *l;* magnetic, *m;* and spin ($+\frac{1}{2}$ or $-\frac{1}{2}$)
b. the distance of an orbital to the nucleus, the energy, shape, and orientation of the orbital, and the spin of the electrons in the orbital

3. The principal quantum number, *n,* describes the energy of the orbital as well as the orbital's distance to the nucleus. The angular momentum quantum number, *l,* signifies the shape of the orbital. The magnetic quantum number, *m,* indicates the orientation of an orbital. The spin quantum number indicates which of an electron's two fundamental states within an orbital an electron is in.

TABLE 4-2 *Quantum Number Relationships in Atomic Structure*

Principal quantum number: main energy level (*n*)	Sublevels in main energy level (*n* sublevels)	Number of orbitals per sublevel	Number of orbitals per main energy level (n^2)	Number of electrons per sublevel	Number of electrons per main energy level ($2n^2$)
1	*s*	1	1	2	2
2	*s*	1	4	2	8
	p	3		6	
3	*s*	1	9	2	18
	p	3		6	
	d	5		10	
4	*s*	1	16	2	32
	p	3		6	
	d	5		10	
	f	7		14	

As you can see in Table 4-2, the total number of orbitals at a main energy level increases with the value of *n*. In fact, the number of orbitals at each main energy level equals the square of the principal quantum number, n^2. What is the total number of orbitals in the third energy level? Specify each of the sublevels using the three quantum numbers you've learned so far.

Spin Quantum Number

Like Earth, an electron in an orbital can be thought of as spinning on an internal axis. It spins in one of two possible directions, or states. As it spins, it creates a magnetic field. To account for the magnetic properties of the electron, theoreticians of the early twentieth century created the spin quantum number. *The* **spin quantum number** *has only two possible values—($+\frac{1}{2}$, $-\frac{1}{2}$)—which indicate the two fundamental spin states of an electron in an orbital.* A single orbital can hold a maximum of two electrons, which must have opposite spins.

SECTION REVIEW

1. Define the following:
a. main energy levels
b. quantum numbers

2. a. List the four quantum numbers.
b. What general information about atomic orbitals is provided by the quantum numbers?

3. Describe briefly what specific information is given by each of the four quantum numbers.

Electron Configurations

SECTION 4-3

OBJECTIVES

- List the total number of electrons needed to fully occupy each main energy level.

- State the Aufbau principle, the Pauli exclusion principle, and Hund's rule.

- Describe the electron configurations for the atoms of any element using orbital notation, electron-configuration notation, and, when appropriate, noble-gas notation.

The quantum model of the atom improves on the Bohr model because it describes the arrangements of electrons in atoms other than hydrogen. *The arrangement of electrons in an atom is known as the atom's* **electron configuration.** Because atoms of different elements have different numbers of electrons, a distinct electron configuration exists for the atoms of each element. Like all systems in nature, electrons in atoms tend to assume arrangements that have the lowest possible energies. The lowest-energy arrangement of the electrons for each element is called the element's *ground-state electron configuration.* A few simple rules, combined with the quantum number relationships discussed in Section 4-2, allow us to determine these ground-state electron configurations.

Rules Governing Electron Configurations

To build up electron configurations for the ground state of any particular atom, first the energy levels of the orbitals are determined. Then electrons are added to the orbitals one by one according to three basic rules. (Remember that real atoms are not built up by adding protons and electrons one at a time.)

The first rule shows the order in which electrons occupy orbitals. According to the **Aufbau principle,** *an electron occupies the lowest-energy orbital that can receive it.* Figure 4-16 shows the atomic orbitals in order of increasing energy. The orbital with the lowest energy is the 1s orbital. In a ground-state hydrogen atom, the electron is in this orbital. The 2s orbital is the next highest in energy, then the 2p orbitals. Beginning with the third main energy level, $n = 3$, the energies of the sublevels in different main energy levels begin to overlap.

Note in the figure, for example, that the 4s sublevel is lower in energy than the 3d sublevel. Therefore, the 4s orbital is filled before any electrons enter the 3d orbitals. (Less energy is required for two electrons to pair up in the 4s orbital than for a single electron to

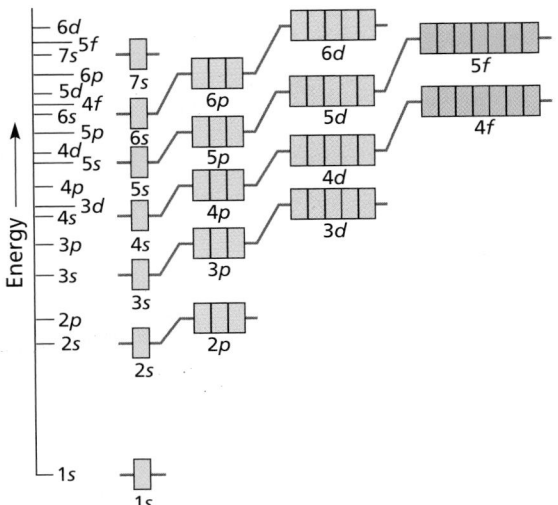

FIGURE 4-16 The order of increasing energy for atomic sublevels is shown on the vertical axis. Each individual box represents an orbital.

Analogy
Hund's rule can be compared to the way students would arrange themselves on a school bus after a muddy game of soccer. Each student will try to have his or her own seat until all the seats are filled. Only then will students begin to double up. In a like manner, each orbital in a sublevel will hold one electron until all of the sublevel's orbitals are half-filled. Only then will orbitals begin accepting second, higher-energy electrons.

Answers to In-Text Questions
- The 4p orbitals will begin to fill after the 3d orbitals are fully occupied.
- The maximum number of unpaired electrons in a d sublevel is five.

✔ Teaching Tip
Emphasize the relationship between orbital diagrams and electron configurations. Write an orbital diagram on the board and show how the number of arrows corresponds to the superscripts in an electron configuration. When students begin to feel comfortable with electron configurations, organize a friendly competition between different groups. Have students from each group go to the board, then give them an element. The first group member who puts the correct electron configuration on the board earns a point for his or her group.

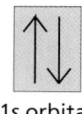

1s orbital

FIGURE 4-17 According to the Pauli exclusion principle, an orbital can hold two electrons of opposite spin. In this electron configuration of a helium atom, each arrow represents one of the atom's two electrons. The direction of the arrow indicates the electron's spin.

FIGURE 4-18 The figure shows how (a) two, (b) three, and (c) four electrons fill the p sublevel of a given main energy level according to Hund's rule.

occupy a 3d orbital.) Once the 3d orbitals are fully occupied, which sublevel will be occupied next?

The second rule reflects the importance of the spin quantum number. According to the **Pauli exclusion principle,** *no two electrons in the same atom can have the same set of four quantum numbers.* The principal, angular momentum, and magnetic quantum numbers specify the energy, shape, and orientation of an orbital. The two values of the spin quantum number allow two electrons of opposite spins to occupy the orbital (see Figure 4-17).

The third rule requires placing as many unpaired electrons as possible in separate orbitals in the same sublevel. In this way, electron-electron repulsion is minimized so that the electron arrangements have the lowest energy possible. According to **Hund's rule,** *orbitals of equal energy are each occupied by one electron before any orbital is occupied by a second electron, and all electrons in singly occupied orbitals must have the same spin.* Applying this rule shows, for example, that one electron will enter each of the three p orbitals in a main energy level before a second electron enters any of them. This is illustrated in Figure 4-18. What is the maximum number of unpaired electrons in a d sublevel?

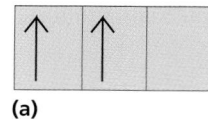 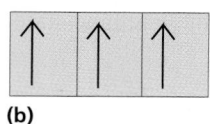 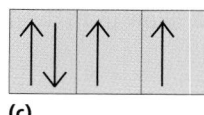

(a) (b) (c)

Representing Electron Configurations

Three methods, or notations, are used to indicate electron configurations. Two of these notations will be discussed in the next two sections for the first-period elements, hydrogen and helium. The third notation applies mostly to elements of the third period and higher. It will be discussed in the section on third-period elements.

In a ground-state hydrogen atom, the single electron is in the lowest-energy orbital, the 1s orbital. The electron can be in either one of its two spin states. Helium has two electrons, which are paired in the 1s orbital.

Orbital Notation
In orbital notation, an unoccupied orbital is represented by a line, ____ , with the orbital's name written underneath the line. An orbital containing one electron is represented as ↑ . An orbital containing two electrons is represented as ↑↓ , showing the electrons paired and with opposite spins. The lines are labeled with the principal quantum number

and sublevel letter. For example, the orbital notations for hydrogen and helium are written as follows.

$$H \frac{\uparrow}{1s} \qquad He \frac{\uparrow\downarrow}{1s}$$

Electron-Configuration Notation

Electron-configuration notation eliminates the lines and arrows of orbital notation. Instead, the number of electrons in a sublevel is shown by adding a superscript to the sublevel designation. The hydrogen configuration is represented by $1s^1$. The superscript indicates that one electron is present in hydrogen's $1s$ orbital. The helium configuration is represented by $1s^2$. Here the superscript indicates that there are two electrons in helium's $1s$ orbital.

CHEMISTRY INTERACTIVE TUTOR

Module 2: Models of the Atom

ADDITIONAL SAMPLE PROBLEMS

4-1 The electron configuration of carbon is $1s^2 2s^2 2p^2$. How many electrons are present in carbon? What is the atomic number of carbon?

Ans. 6, 6

4-1 Write the electron configuration of the element sulfur, which has an atomic number of 16.

Ans. $1s^2 2s^2 2p^6 3s^2 3p^4$

CHEMISTRY INTERACTIVE TUTOR

Module 2: Models of the Atom

Topic: Electron Structure
Section c of this engaging tutorial reviews and reinforces understanding of electron structure.

SAMPLE PROBLEM 4-1

The electron configuration of boron is $1s^2 2s^2 2p^1$. **How many electrons are present in an atom of boron? What is the atomic number for boron? Write the orbital notation for boron.**

SOLUTION

The number of electrons in a boron atom is equal to the sum of the superscripts in its electron-configuration notation: $2 + 2 + 1 = 5$ electrons. The number of protons equals the number of electrons in a neutral atom. So we know that boron has 5 protons and thus has an atomic number of 5. To write the orbital notation, first draw the lines representing orbitals.

$$\overline{}_{1s} \quad \overline{}_{2s} \quad \overline{}_{2p_x} \, \overline{}_{2p_y} \, \overline{}_{2p_z}$$

Next, add arrows showing the electron locations. The first two electrons occupy $n = 1$ energy level and fill the $1s$ orbital.

$$\frac{\uparrow\downarrow}{1s} \quad \overline{}_{2s} \quad \overline{}_{2p_x} \, \overline{}_{2p_y} \, \overline{}_{2p_z}$$

The next three electrons occupy the $n = 2$ main energy level. According to the Aufbau principle, two of these occupy the lower-energy $2s$ orbital. The third occupies a higher-energy p orbital.

$$\frac{\uparrow\downarrow}{1s} \quad \frac{\uparrow\downarrow}{2s} \quad \frac{\uparrow}{2p_x} \, \overline{}_{2p_y} \, \overline{}_{2p_z}$$

PRACTICE

1. The electron configuration of nitrogen is $1s^2 2s^2 2p^3$. How many electrons are present in a nitrogen atom? What is the atomic number of nitrogen? Write the orbital notation for nitrogen.

Answer

$7, 7, \dfrac{\uparrow\downarrow}{1s} \quad \dfrac{\uparrow\downarrow}{2s} \quad \dfrac{\uparrow}{2p_x} \, \dfrac{\uparrow}{2p_y} \, \dfrac{\uparrow}{2p_z}$

2. The electron configuration of fluorine is $1s^2 2s^2 2p^5$. What is the atomic number of fluorine? How many of its p orbitals are filled? How many unpaired electrons does a fluorine atom contain?

Answer

9, 2, 1

GREAT DISCOVERIES

Class Discussion

This feature outlines the progression of scientific activity that uncovered a whole new group in the periodic table, the noble gases. Ask students if there are other examples—even outside the scientific world—where several discoveries are made after a single person had a new insight. *(Examples within the scientific world may include the discoveries of the lanthanides and actinides or of the subatomic particles.)* Discuss the importance of using scientific literature to report findings in this process of discovery. For example, Watson and Crick had a special insight about the structure of DNA, using the laboratory results of other researchers. Sharing information is important because different people have different talents. One investigator may be diligent in the laboratory and obtain clear results. Another may be better suited to reflect on the meaning of the results.

The Noble Decade

HISTORICAL PERSPECTIVE

By the late nineteenth century, the science of chemistry had begun to be organized. The first international congress of chemistry, in 1860, established the field's first standards. And Dmitri Mendeleev's periodic table of elements gave chemists across the globe a systematic understanding of matter's building blocks. But many important findings were yet to come, including the discovery of a family of rare, unreactive gases that were unlike any substances known at the time.

Cross-Disciplinary Correspondence

In 1888, the British physicist Lord Rayleigh encountered a small but significant discrepancy in the results of one of his experiments. In an effort to redetermine the atomic mass of nitrogen, he measured the densities of several samples of nitrogen gas. Each sample had been prepared by a different method. The samples that had been isolated from chemical reactions all exhibited similar densities. But they were about one-tenth of a percent lighter than the nitrogen isolated from air, which at the time was believed to be a mixture of nitrogen, oxygen, water vapor, and carbon dioxide.

Rayleigh was at a loss to explain his discovery. Finally, in 1892, he published a letter in *Nature* magazine appealing to his colleagues for an explanation. A month later he received a reply from a Scottish chemist named William Ramsay. Ramsay related that he too had been stumped by the density difference between chemical and atmospheric nitrogen. Rayleigh decided

---

SEPTEMBER 29, 1892   *NATURE*

LETTERS TO THE EDITOR.

[*The Editor does not hold himself responsible for opinions expressed by his correspondents. Neither can he undertake to return, or to correspond with the writers of, rejected manuscripts intended for this or any other part of NATURE. No notice is taken of anonymous communications.*]

Density of Nitrogen.

I AM much puzzled by some recent results as to the density of *nitrogen*, and shall be obliged if any of your chemical readers can offer suggestions as to the cause. According to two methods of preparation I obtain quite distinct values. The relative difference, amounting to about $\frac{1}{1000}$ part, is small in itself; but it lies entirely outside the errors of experiment, and can only be attributed to a variation in the character of the gas...

Is it possible that the difference is independent of impurity, the nitrogen itself being to some extent in a different (dissociated) state?...

                                        RAYLEIGH.

Terling Place, Witham, September 24.

An excerpt of Lord Rayleigh's letter as originally published in Nature *magazine in 1892*

to report his findings to the Royal Society of Chemistry, adding:

Until the questions arising out of these observations are thoroughly cleared up, the above number [density] for nitrogen must be received with a certain reserve.

A Chemist's Approach

With Rayleigh's permission, Ramsay attempted to remove all the known components from a sample of air and analyze what, if anything, remained. First he heated

magnesium in the air to remove all of the nitrogen in the form of magnesium nitride. Then he removed the oxygen, water vapor, and carbon dioxide factions. What remained was a minuscule portion of a mysterious gas.

Ramsay tried to cause the gas to react with chemically active substances, such as hydrogen, sodium, and caustic soda, but the gas remained unaltered. He decided to name this new atmospheric component argon (Greek for "inert" or "idle"):

---

internet connect

SC*i*LINKS.
NSTA

TOPIC: William Ramsay
GO TO: www.scilinks.org
*sci*LINKS CODE: HC2043

In 1893, Scottish chemist William Ramsay isolated a previously unknown component of the atmosphere.

The gas deserves the name "argon," for it is a most astonishingly indifferent body. . . .

Periodic Problems

Rayleigh and Ramsay were sure that they had discovered a new element. But this created a problem. Their calculations indicated that argon had an atomic mass of about 40. However, there was no space in the periodic table as it appeared in 1894 for such an element. The elements with atomic masses closest to that of argon were chlorine and potassium. Unfortunately, the chemical properties of the families of each of these elements were completely dissimilar to those of the strange gas.

Ramsay contemplated argon's lack of reactivity. He knew that Mendeleev had created the periodic table on the basis of valence, or the number of atomic partners an element bonds with in forming a compound. As Ramsay could not cause argon to form any compounds, he assigned it a valence of zero. And because the valence of the elements in the families of

both chlorine and potassium was one, perhaps argon fit in between them. In May 1894, Ramsay wrote to Rayleigh:

Has it occurred to you that there is room for gaseous elements at the end of the first column of the periodic table?. . .Such elements should have the density 20 or thereabouts, and 0.8 pc [percent] (1/120th about) of the nitrogen of the air could so raise the density of nitrogen that it would stand to pure [chemical] nitrogen in the ratio of 230:231.

Ramsay's insight that argon merited a new spot in the periodic table, between the chlorine family and the potassium family, was correct. And, as he would soon confirm, his newly discovered gas was indeed one of a previously unknown family of elements.

New Neighbors

In 1895, Ramsay isolated a light, inert gas from a mineral called cleveite. Physical analysis revealed that the gas was the same as one that had been identified in the sun in 1868—helium. Helium was the second zero-valent element found on Earth, and its discovery made chemists aware that the periodic table had been missing a whole column of elements.

Over the next three years, Ramsay and his assistant, Morris Travers, identified three more inert gases present in the atmosphere: neon (Greek for "new"), krypton ("hidden"), and xenon ("stranger"). Finally in 1900, German chemist Friedrich Ernst Dorn discovered radon, the last of the new family of elements known today as the noble gases. For his discovery, Ramsay received the Nobel Prize in 1904.

Groups / Periods	III b	IV b	V b	VI b	VII b	VIII b	I b	II b	III a	IV a	V a	VI a	VII a	0 a	I a	II a
1															H	He
2															Li	Be
3									B	C	N	O	F	Ne	Na	Mg
4									Al	Si	P	S	Cl	Ar	K	Ca
5	Sc	Ti	V	Cr	Mn	Fe Co Ni	Cu	Zn	Ga	Ge	As	Se	Br	Kr	Rb	Sr
6	Y	Zr	Nb	Mo	Tc	Ru Rh Pd	Ag	Cd	In	Sn	Sb	Te	I	Xe	Cs	Ba
7	La	Hf	Ta	W	Re	Os Ir Pt	Au	Hg	Tl	Pb	Bi	Po	At	Rn	Fr	Ra
8	Ac															

Transition elements · Main-group elements

One version of the periodic table as it appeared after the discovery of the noble gases. The placement of the Group 1 and 2 elements at the far right of the table shows clearly how the noble gases fit in between the chlorine family and the potassium family of elements. The "0" above the noble-gas family indicates the zero valency of the gases.

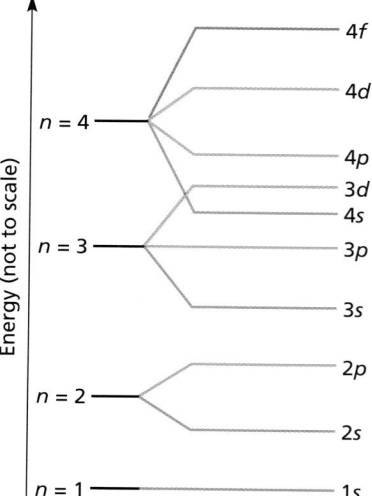

FIGURE 4-19 The direction of the arrow indicates the order in which atomic orbitals are filled according to the Aufbau principle.

Elements of the Second Period

In the first-period elements, hydrogen and helium, electrons occupy the first main energy level. The ground-state configurations in Table 4-3 illustrate how the Aufbau principle, the Pauli exclusion principle, and Hund's rule are applied to atoms of elements in the second period. Figure 4-19 shows the first four main energy levels in order of increasing energy for applying the Aufbau principle.

According to the Aufbau principle, after the $1s$ orbital is filled, the next electron occupies the s sublevel in the second main energy level. Thus, lithium, Li, has a configuration of $1s^2 2s^1$. The electron occupying the $2s$ level of a lithium atom is in the atom's highest, or outermost, occupied level. *The* **highest occupied level** *is the electron-containing main energy level with the highest principal quantum number.* The two electrons in the $1s$ sublevel of lithium are no longer in the outermost main energy level. They have become **inner-shell electrons,** *which are electrons that are not in the highest occupied energy level.*

The fourth electron in an atom of beryllium, Be, must complete the pair in the $2s$ sublevel because this sublevel is of lower energy than the $2p$ sublevel. With the $2s$ sublevel filled, the $2p$ sublevel, which has three vacant orbitals of equal energy, can be occupied. Hund's rule applies here, as is shown in the orbital notations in Table 4-3. One of the three p orbitals is occupied by a single electron in an atom of boron, B. Two of the three p orbitals are occupied by unpaired electrons in an atom of carbon, C. And all three p orbitals are occupied by unpaired electrons in an atom of nitrogen, N.

According to the Aufbau principle, the next electron must pair with another electron in one of the $2p$ orbitals rather than enter the third main energy level. The Pauli exclusion principle allows the electron to pair with

TABLE 4-3	*Electron Configurations of Atoms of Second-Period Elements Showing Two Notations*					
			Orbital notation			**Electron-configuration notation**
Name	**Symbol**	**1s**	**2s**	**2p**		
Lithium	Li	↑↓	↑	—	—	—	$1s^2 2s^1$
Beryllium	Be	↑↓	↑↓	—	—	—	$1s^2 2s^2$
Boron	B	↑↓	↑↓	↑	—	—	$1s^2 2s^2 2p^1$
Carbon	C	↑↓	↑↓	↑	↑	—	$1s^2 2s^2 2p^2$
Nitrogen	N	↑↓	↑↓	↑	↑	↑	$1s^2 2s^2 2p^3$
Oxygen	O	↑↓	↑↓	↑↓	↑	↑	$1s^2 2s^2 2p^4$
Fluorine	F	↑↓	↑↓	↑↓	↑↓	↑	$1s^2 2s^2 2p^5$
Neon	Ne	↑↓	↑↓	↑↓	↑↓	↑↓	$1s^2 2s^2 2p^6$

one of the electrons occupying the $2p$ orbitals as long as the spins of the paired electrons are opposite. Thus, atoms of oxygen, O, have the configuration $1s^2 2s^2 2p^4$. Oxygen's orbital notation is shown in Table 4-3.

Two $2p$ orbitals are filled in fluorine, F, and all three are filled in neon, Ne. Atoms such as those of neon, which have the s and p sublevels of their highest occupied level filled with eight electrons, are said to have an *octet* of electrons. Examine the periodic table inside the back cover of the text. Notice that neon is the last element in the second period.

Elements of the Third Period

After the outer octet is filled in neon, the next electron enters the s sublevel in the $n = 3$ main energy level. Thus, atoms of sodium, Na, have the configuration $1s^2 2s^2 2p^6 3s^1$. Compare the configuration of a sodium atom with that of an atom of neon in Table 4-3. Notice that the first 10 electrons in a sodium atom have the same configuration as a neon atom, $1s^2 2s^2 2p^6$. In fact, the first 10 electrons in an atom of each of the third-period elements have the same configuration as neon. This similarity allows us to use a shorthand notation for the electron configurations of the third-period elements.

Noble-Gas Notation

Neon is a member of the Group 18 elements. *The Group 18 elements (helium, neon, argon, krypton, xenon, and radon) are called the* **noble gases.** To simplify sodium's notation, the symbol for neon, enclosed in square brackets, is used to represent the complete neon configuration: $[\text{Ne}] = 1s^2 2s^2 2p^6$. This allows us to write sodium's electron configuration as $[\text{Ne}]3s^1$, which is called sodium's *noble-gas notation*. Table 4-4 shows the noble-gas notation of the electron configuration of each of the third-period elements.

Name	Symbol	Atomic number	1s	2s	2p	3s	3p	Noble-gas notation
Sodium	Na	11	2	2	6	1		$[\text{Ne}]3s^1$
Magnesium	Mg	12	2	2	6	2		$[\text{Ne}]3s^2$
Aluminum	Al	13	2	2	6	2	1	$[\text{Ne}]3s^2 3p^1$
Silicon	Si	14	2	2	6	2	2	$[\text{Ne}]3s^2 3p^2$
Phosphorus	P	15	2	2	6	2	3	$[\text{Ne}]3s^2 3p^3$
Sulfur	S	16	2	2	6	2	4	$[\text{Ne}]3s^2 3p^4$
Chlorine	Cl	17	2	2	6	2	5	$[\text{Ne}]3s^2 3p^5$
Argon	Ar	18	2	2	6	2	6	$[\text{Ne}]3s^2 3p^6$

TABLE 4-4 *Electron Configurations of Atoms of Third-Period Elements*

Number of electrons in sublevels

The last element in the third period is argon, Ar, which is a noble gas. As in neon, the highest-occupied energy level of argon has an octet of electrons, $[Ne]3s^23p^6$. In fact, each noble gas other than He has an electron octet in its highest energy level. *A **noble-gas configuration** is an outer main energy level fully occupied, in most cases, by eight electrons.*

Elements of the Fourth Period

The electron configurations of atoms in the fourth-period elements are shown in Table 4-5. The period begins by filling the 4*s* orbital, the empty orbital of lowest energy. Thus, the first element in the fourth period is potassium, K, which has the electron configuration $[Ar]4s^1$. The next element is calcium, Ca, which has the electron configuration $[Ar]4s^2$.

With the 4*s* sublevel filled, the 4*p* and 3*d* sublevels are the next available vacant orbitals. Figure 4-19 on page 110 shows that the 3*d* sublevel

TABLE 4-5 *Electron Configuration of Atoms of Elements in the Fourth Period*

Name	Symbol	Atomic number	3s	3p	3d	4s	4p	Noble-gas notation
Potassium	K	19	2	6		1		*$[Ar]4s^1$
Calcium	Ca	20	2	6		2		$[Ar]4s^2$
Scandium	Sc	21	2	6	1	2		$[Ar]3d^14s^2$
Titanium	Ti	22	2	6	2	2		$[Ar]3d^24s^2$
Vanadium	V	23	2	6	3	2		$[Ar]3d^34s^2$
Chromium	Cr	24	2	6	5	1		$[Ar]3d^54s^1$
Manganese	Mn	25	2	6	5	2		$[Ar]3d^54s^2$
Iron	Fe	26	2	6	6	2		$[Ar]3d^64s^2$
Cobalt	Co	27	2	6	7	2		$[Ar]3d^74s^2$
Nickel	Ni	28	2	6	8	2		$[Ar]3d^84s^2$
Copper	Cu	29	2	6	10	1		$[Ar]3d^{10}4s^1$
Zinc	Zn	30	2	6	10	2		$[Ar]3d^{10}4s^2$
Gallium	Ga	31	2	6	10	2	1	$[Ar]3d^{10}4s^24p^1$
Germanium	Ge	32	2	6	10	2	2	$[Ar]3d^{10}4s^24p^2$
Arsenic	As	33	2	6	10	2	3	$[Ar]3d^{10}4s^24p^3$
Selenium	Se	34	2	6	10	2	4	$[Ar]3d^{10}4s^24p^4$
Bromine	Br	35	2	6	10	2	5	$[Ar]3d^{10}4s^24p^5$
Krypton	Kr	36	2	6	10	2	6	$[Ar]3d^{10}4s^24p^6$

*$[Ar] = 1s^22s^22p^63s^23p^6$

is lower in energy than the $4p$ sublevel. Therefore, the five $3d$ orbitals are next to be filled. A total of 10 electrons can occupy the $3d$ orbitals. These are filled successively in the 10 elements from scandium (atomic number 21) to zinc (atomic number 30).

Scandium, Sc, has the electron configuration $[Ar]3d^14s^2$. Titanium, Ti, has the configuration $[Ar]3d^24s^2$. And vanadium, V, has the configuration $[Ar]3d^34s^2$. Up to this point, three electrons with the same spin have been added to three separate d orbitals, as required by Hund's rule.

Surprisingly, chromium, Cr, has the electron configuration $[Ar]3d^54s^1$. Not only did the added electron go into the fourth $3d$ orbital, but an electron also moved from the $4s$ orbital into the fifth $3d$ orbital, leaving the $4s$ orbital with a single electron. Chromium's electron configuration is contrary to what is expected according to the Aufbau principle. However, in reality the $[Ar]3d^54s^1$ configuration is of lower energy than a $[Ar]3d^44s^2$ configuration. For chromium, having six outer orbitals with unpaired electrons is a more stable arrangement than having four unpaired electrons in the $3d$ orbitals and forcing two electrons to pair up in the $4s$ orbital. On the other hand, for tungsten, W, which is in the same group as chromium, having four electrons in the $5d$ orbitals and two electrons paired in the $6s$ orbital is the most stable arrrangement. Unfortunately, there is no simple explanation for such deviations from the ideal order given in Figure 4-19.

Manganese, Mn, has the electron configuration $[Ar]3d^54s^2$. The added electron goes to the $4s$ orbital, completely filling this orbital while leaving the $3d$ orbitals still half-filled. Beginning with the next element, electrons continue to pair in the d orbitals. Thus, iron, Fe, has the configuration $[Ar]3d^64s^2$; cobalt, Co, has the configuration $[Ar]3d^74s^2$; and nickel, Ni, has the configuration $[Ar]3d^84s^2$. Next is copper, Cu, in which an electron moves from the $4s$ orbital to pair with the electron in the fifth $3d$ orbital. The result is an electron configuration of $[Ar]3d^{10}4s^1$—the lowest-energy configuration for Cu.

In atoms of zinc, Zn, the $4s$ sublevel is filled to give the electron configuration $[Ar]3d^{10}4s^2$. In atoms of the next six elements, electrons add one by one to the three $4p$ orbitals. According to Hund's rule, one electron is added to each of the three $4p$ orbitals before electrons are paired in any $4p$ orbital.

Elements of the Fifth Period

In the 18 elements of the fifth period, sublevels fill in a similar manner as in elements of the fourth period. However, they start at the $5s$ orbital instead of the $4s$. Successive electrons are added first to the $5s$ orbital, then to the $4d$ orbitals, and finally to the $5p$ orbitals. This can be seen in Table 4-6 on page 114. There are occasional deviations from the predicted configurations here also. The deviations differ from those for fourth-period elements, but in each case the preferred configuration has the lowest possible energy.

Additional Example Problems

1. Identify the element whose atoms have two electrons in the p sublevel of their second main energy level. What is the total number of electrons in the second main energy level of an atom of this element? Name the element in the third period that has the same number of electrons in its outermost main energy level as the element described in the first part of the problem.

Ans. carbon; 4; silicon

2. Identify the element whose atoms have five electrons in the p sublevel of their third main energy level. What is the total number of electrons in the third main energy level of an atom of this element? Name the element in the fourth period that has the same number of electrons in its outermost main energy level as the element described in the first part of the problem.

Ans. chlorine; 7; bromine

3. Which element does the noble-gas notation $[Ne]3s^1$ represent the electron configuration of? How many inner-shell electrons do its atoms contain?

Ans. sodium; 10

4. Write the noble-gas notation for aluminum. How many outer-shell electrons does an atom of aluminum contain? How many unpaired electrons does an atom of aluminum contain?

Ans. $[Ne]3s^23p^1$; 3; 1

4-2 a. Write both the complete electron-configuration notation and the noble-gas notation for titanium, Ti.
b. How many electron-containing orbitals are in an atom of titanium? How many of these orbitals are filled? How many unpaired electrons are there in an atom of titanium?

Ans.
a. $1s^2 2s^2 2p^6 3s^2 3p^6 3d^2 4s^2$, $[Ar]3d^2 4s^2$
b. 12 (one 1s orbital, one 2s orbital, three 2p orbitals, one 3s orbital, three 3p orbitals, one 4s orbital, and two 3d orbitals); 10; 2

TABLE 4-6 Electron Configurations of Atoms of Elements in the Fifth Period

Name	Symbol	Atomic number	4s	4p	4d	5s	5p	Noble-gas notation
Rubidium	Rb	37	2	6		1		*$[Kr]5s^1$
Strontium	Sr	38	2	6		2		$[Kr]5s^2$
Yttrium	Y	39	2	6	1	2		$[Kr]4d^1 5s^2$
Zirconium	Zr	40	2	6	2	2		$[Kr]4d^2 5s^2$
Niobium	Nb	41	2	6	4	1		$[Kr]4d^4 5s^1$
Molybdenum	Mo	42	2	6	5	1		$[Kr]4d^5 5s^1$
Technetium	Tc	43	2	6	6	1		$[Kr]4d^5 5s^1$
Ruthenium	Ru	44	2	6	7	1		$[Kr]4d^7 5s^1$
Rhodium	Rh	45	2	6	8	1		$[Kr]4d^8 5s^1$
Palladium	Pd	46	2	6	10			$[Kr]4d^{10}$
Silver	Ag	47	2	6	10	1		$[Kr]4d^{10} 5s^1$
Cadmium	Cd	48	2	6	10	2		$[Kr]4d^{10} 5s^2$
Indium	In	49	2	6	10	2	1	$[Kr]4d^{10} 5s^2 5p^1$
Tin	Sn	50	2	6	10	2	2	$[Kr]4d^{10} 5s^2 5p^2$
Antimony	Sb	51	2	6	10	2	3	$[Kr]4d^{10} 5s^2 5p^3$
Tellurium	Te	52	2	6	10	2	4	$[Kr]4d^{10} 5s^2 5p^4$
Iodine	I	53	2	6	10	2	5	$[Kr]4d^{10} 5s^2 5p^5$
Xenon	Xe	54	2	6	10	2	6	$[Kr]4d^{10} 5s^2 5p^6$

*$[Kr] = 1s^2 2s^2 2p^6 3s^2 3p^6 3d^{10} 4s^2 4p^6$

SAMPLE PROBLEM 4-2

a. Write both the complete electron-configuration notation and the noble-gas notation for iron, Fe.

b. How many electron-containing orbitals are in an atom of iron? How many of these orbitals are completely filled? How many unpaired electrons are there in an atom of iron? In which sublevel are the unpaired electrons located?

SOLUTION

a. The complete electron-configuration notation of iron is $1s^2 2s^2 2p^6 3s^2 3p^6 3d^6 4s^2$. The periodic table inside the back cover of the text reveals that $1s^2 2s^2 2p^6 3s^2 3p^6$ is the electron configuration of the noble gas argon, Ar. Therefore, as shown in Table 4-5 on page 112, iron's noble-gas notation is $[Ar]3d^6 4s^2$.

b. An iron atom has 15 orbitals that contain electrons. They consist of one 1s orbital, one 2s orbital, three 2p orbitals, one 3s orbital, three 3p orbitals, five 3d orbitals, and one 4s orbital. Eleven of these orbitals are filled. The notation $3d^6$ represents $3d$ ↑↓ ↑ ↑ ↑ ↑, so there are four unpaired electrons. They are located in the 3d sublevel.

PRACTICE

1. a. Write both the complete electron-configuration notation and the noble-gas notation for iodine, I. How many inner-shell electrons does an iodine atom contain?

   b. How many electron-containing orbitals are in an atom of iodine? How many of these orbitals are filled? How many unpaired electrons are there in an atom of iodine?

2. a. Write the noble-gas notation for tin, Sn. How many unpaired electrons are there in an atom of tin?

   b. How many electron-containing d orbitals are there in an atom of tin? Name the element in the fourth period whose atoms have the same number of highest-energy-level electrons as tin.

3. a. Without consulting the periodic table or a table in this chapter, write the complete electron configuration for the element with atomic number 25.

   b. Identify the element described in item 3a.

Answer

1. a. $1s^2 2s^2 2p^6 3s^2 3p^6 3d^{10} 4s^2 4p^6 4d^{10} 5s^2 5p^5$,

   $[Kr]4d^{10}5s^2 5p^5$,

   46

   b. 27, 26, 1

2. a. $[Kr]4d^{10}5s^2 5p^2$, 2

   b. 10, germanium

3. a. $1s^2 2s^2 2p^6 3s^2 3p^6 3d^5 4s^2$

   b. manganese

Elements of the Sixth and Seventh Periods

The sixth period consists of 32 elements. It is much longer than the periods that precede it in the periodic table. To build up electron configurations for elements of this period, electrons are added first to the $6s$ orbital in cesium, Cs, and barium, Ba. Then, in lanthanum, La, an electron is added to the $5d$ orbital.

With the next element, cerium, Ce, the $4f$ orbitals begin to fill, giving cerium atoms a configuration of $[Xe]4f^1 5d^1 6s^2$. In the next 13 elements, the $4f$ orbitals are filled. Next the $5d$ orbitals are filled and the period is completed by filling the $6p$ orbitals. Because the $4f$ and the $5d$ orbitals are very close in energy, numerous deviations from the simple rules occur as these orbitals are filled. The electron configurations of the sixth-period elements can be found in the periodic table inside the back cover of the text.

The seventh period is incomplete and consists largely of synthetic elements, which will be discussed in Chapter 22.

4-3 a. How many inner-shell electrons does an atom of silicon, Si, contain?
b. How many electron-containing orbitals are in an atom of silicon? How many of these orbitals are filled? How many unpaired electrons are there in an atom of silicon?
c. How many electron-containing p orbitals are there in an atom of silicon? Name the element in the fourth period whose atoms have the same number of highest-energy-level electrons as atoms of silicon.

Ans.
a. 10   **b.** 8, 6, 2   **c.** 5; germanium

SAMPLE PROBLEM 4-3

a. Write both the complete electron-configuration notation and the noble-gas notation for a rubidium atom.

b. Identify the elements in the second, third, and fourth periods that have the same number of highest-energy-level electrons as rubidium.

SOLUTION

a. $1s^2 2s^2 2p^6 3s^2 3p^6 3d^{10} 4s^2 4p^6 5s^1$, $[Kr]5s^1$

b. Rubidium has one electron in its highest energy level (the fifth). The elements with the same outermost configuration are, in the second period, lithium, Li; in the third period, sodium, Na; and in the fourth period, potassium, K.

PRACTICE

1. a. Write both the complete electron-configuration notation and the noble-gas notation for a barium atom.

   b. Identify the elements in the second, third, fourth, and fifth periods that have the same number of highest-energy-level electrons as barium.

2. a. Write the noble-gas notation for a gold atom.

   b. Identify the elements in the sixth period that have one unpaired electron in their 6s sublevel.

Answer
1. a. $1s^2 2s^2 2p^6 3s^2 3p^6 3d^{10} 4s^2 4p^6 4d^{10} 5s^2 5p^6 6s^2$,
   $[Xe]6s^2$

   b. Be, Mg, Ca, Sr

2. a. $[Xe]4f^{14}5d^{10}6s^1$

   b. Au, Cs, Pt

SECTION REVIEW

Answers to Section 4-3 Review are found on page 121A.

SECTION REVIEW

1. a. What is an atom's electron configuration?
   b. What three principles guide the electron configuration of an atom?

2. What three methods are used to represent the arrangement of electrons in atoms?

3. What is an octet of electrons? Which elements contain an octet of electrons?

4. Write the complete electron-configuration notation, the noble-gas notation, and the orbital notation for the following elements:
   a. carbon   b. neon   c. sulfur

5. Identify the elements having the following electron configurations:
   a. $1s^2 2s^2 2p^6 3s^2 3p^3$
   b. $[Ar]4s^1$
   c. contains four electrons in its third and outer main energy level
   d. contains one paired and three unpaired electrons in its fourth and outer main energy level

CHAPTER SUMMARY

4-1
- In the early twentieth century, light was determined to have a dual wave-particle nature.
- Quantum theory was developed to explain such observations as the photoelectric effect and the line-emission spectrum of hydrogen.
- Quantum theory states that electrons can exist in atoms only at specific energy levels.
- When an electron moves from one main energy level to a main energy level of lower energy,

a photon is emitted. The photon's energy equals the energy difference between the two levels.
- An electron in an atom can move from one main energy level to a higher main energy level only by absorbing an amount of energy exactly equal to the difference between the two levels.

Vocabulary

continuous spectrum (94)

electromagnetic radiation (91)

electromagnetic spectrum (91)

excited state (94)

frequency (92)

ground state (94)

line-emission spectrum (94)

photoelectric effect (93)

photon (94)

quantum (93)

wavelength (91)

4-2
- In the early twentieth century, electrons were determined to have a dual wave-particle nature.
- The Heisenberg uncertainty principle states that it is impossible to determine simultaneously both the position and velocity of an electron or any other particle.
- Quantization of electron energies is a natural outcome of the Schrödinger wave equation, which treats an atom's electrons as waves surrounding the nucleus.

- An orbital is a three-dimensional region around the nucleus that shows the region of probable electron locations.
- The four quantum numbers that describe the properties of electrons in atomic orbitals are the principal quantum number, the angular momentum quantum number, the magnetic quantum number, and the spin quantum number.

Vocabulary

angular momentum quantum number (101)

Heisenberg uncertainty principle (99)

magnetic quantum number (102)

orbital (100)

principal quantum number (101)

quantum numbers (101)

quantum theory (99)

spin quantum number (104)

4-3
- Electrons occupy atomic orbitals in the ground state of an atom according to the Aufbau principle, the Pauli exclusion principle, and Hund's rule.
- Electron configurations can be depicted using different types of notation. In this book, three types of notation are used: orbital notation,

electron-configuration notation, and noble-gas notation.
- Electron configurations of some atoms, such as chromium, do not strictly follow the Aufbau principle, but the ground-state configuration that results is the configuration with the minimum possible energy.

Vocabulary

Aufbau principle (105)

electron configuration (105)

highest occupied level (110)

Hund's rule (106)

inner-shell electrons (110)

noble gases (111)

noble-gas configuration (112)

Pauli exclusion principle (106)

REVIEW ANSWERS

1. **a.** Examples include gamma rays, X rays, ultraviolet light, visible light, infrared light, microwaves, and radio waves.
   b. 3.0×10^8 m/s
   c. $c = \lambda\nu$, where λ is the wavelength of the light, ν is the frequency, and c is the velocity

2. Light's wavelike properties include the measurable characteristics of frequency and wavelength, as well as the ability to interfere and diffract. Light exhibits particle-like properties when it is absorbed and emitted by matter in phenomena such as the photoelectric effect, emission of light by hot objects, and the line-emission spectra of elements.

3. Frequency ranges from approximately 5×10^{14} to 1×10^{15} Hz. Wavelength ranges from 400 to 700 nm.

4. red, orange, yellow, green, blue, violet

5. The wave theory could not explain the photoelectric effect or hydrogen's line-emission spectrum.

6. **a.** $c = \lambda\nu$, where λ is the wavelength, ν is the frequency, and c is the velocity
   b. $E = h\nu$, where E is energy, h is Planck's constant, and ν is the frequency
   c. $E = hc/\lambda$

7. **a.** wave theory
   b. particle theory
   c. particle theory

8. The ground state of an atom is the atom's lowest energy state. An excited state of an atom is any energy state that is higher in energy than the atom's ground state.

9. According to Bohr, a line-emission spectrum is produced when an electron drops from a

REVIEWING CONCEPTS

1. **a.** List five examples of electromagnetic radiation.
   b. What is the speed of all forms of electromagnetic radiation in a vacuum?
   c. Relate the frequency and wavelength of any form of electromagnetic radiation. (4-1)

2. Prepare a two-column table. List the properties of light that can best be explained by the wave theory in one column. List those best explained by the particle theory in the second column. You may want to consult a physics textbook for reference. (4-1)

3. What are the frequency and wavelength ranges of visible light? (4-1)

4. List the colors of light in the visible spectrum in order of increasing frequency. (4-1)

5. In the early twentieth century, what two experiments involving light and matter could not be explained by the wave theory of light? (4-1)

6. **a.** How are the wavelength and frequency of electromagnetic radiation related?
   b. How are the energy and frequency of electromagnetic radiation related?
   c. How are the energy and wavelength of electromagnetic radiation related? (4-1)

7. Which theory of light, the wave or particle theory, best explains the following phenomena?
   a. the interference of light
   b. the photoelectric effect
   c. the emission of electromagnetic radiation by an excited atom (4-1)

8. Distinguish between the ground state and an excited state of an atom. (4-1)

9. According to the Bohr model of the hydrogen atom, how is hydrogen's emission spectrum produced? (4-1)

10. Describe two major shortcomings of the Bohr model of the atom. (4-2)

11. **a.** What is the principal quantum number?
    b. How is it symbolized?
    c. What are shells?
    d. How does n relate to the number of orbitals

per main energy level and the number of electrons allowed per main energy level? (4-2)

12. **a.** What information is given by the angular momentum quantum number?
    b. What are sublevels, or subshells? (4-2)

13. For each of the following values of n, indicate the numbers and types of sublevels possible for that main energy level. (Hint: See Table 4-2.)
    a. $n = 1$
    b. $n = 2$
    c. $n = 3$
    d. $n = 4$
    e. $n = 7$ (number only) (4-2)

14. **a.** What information is given by the magnetic quantum number?
    b. How many orbital orientations are possible in each of the s, p, d, and f sublevels?
    c. Explain and illustrate the notation for distinguishing among the different p orbitals in a sublevel. (4-2)

15. **a.** What is the relationship between n and the total number of orbitals in a main energy level?
    b. How many total orbitals are contained in the third main energy level? in the fifth? (4-2)

16. **a.** What information is given by the spin quantum number?
    b. What are the possible values for this quantum number? (4-2)

17. How many electrons could be contained in the following main energy levels with n equal to:
    a. 1
    b. 3
    c. 4
    d. 6
    e. 7 (4-2)

18. **a.** In your own words, state the Aufbau principle.
    b. Explain the meaning of this principle in terms of an atom with many electrons. (4-3)

19. **a.** In your own words, state Hund's rule.
    b. What is the basis for this rule? (4-3)

20. **a.** In your own words, state the Pauli exclusion principle.
    b. What is the significance of the spin quantum number?

c. Compare the values of the spin quantum number for two electrons in the same orbital. (4-3)

21. a. What is meant by the highest occupied energy level in an atom?
    b. What are inner-shell electrons? (4-3)

22. Determine the highest occupied energy level in the following elements:
    a. He
    b. Be
    c. Al
    d. Ca
    e. Sn (4-3)

23. Write the orbital notation for the following elements. (Hint: See Sample Problem 4-1.)
    a. P
    b. B
    c. Na
    d. C (4-3)

24. Write the electron-configuration notation for an unidentified element that contains the following number of electrons:
    a. 3
    b. 6
    c. 8
    d. 13 (4-3)

25. Given that the electron configuration for oxygen is $1s^2 2s^2 2p^4$, answer the following questions:
    a. How many electrons are in each atom?
    b. What is the atomic number of this element?
    c. Write the orbital notation for oxygen's electron configuration.
    d. How many unpaired electrons does oxygen have?
    e. What is the highest occupied energy level?
    f. How many inner-shell electrons does the atom contain?
    g. In which orbital(s) are these inner-shell electrons located? (4-3)

26. a. What are the noble gases?
    b. What is a noble-gas configuration?
    c. How does noble-gas notation simplify writing an atom's electron configuration? (4-3)

27. Write the noble-gas notation for the electron configuration of each of the elements that

follow. (Hint: See Sample Problem 4-2.)
    a. Cl
    b. Ca
    c. Se (4-3)

28. a. What information is given by the noble-gas notation [Ne]$3s^2$?
    b. What element does this represent? (4-3)

29. Write both the complete electron-configuration notation and the noble-gas notation for each of the following elements. (Hint: See Sample Problem 4-3.)
    a. Na
    b. Sr
    c. P (4-3)

30. Identify each of the following atoms on the basis of its electron configuration:
    a. $1s^2 2s^2 2p^1$
    b. $1s^2 2s^2 2p^5$
    c. [Ne]$3s^2$
    d. [Ne]$3s^2 3p^2$
    e. [Ne]$3s^2 3p^5$
    f. [Ar]$4s^1$
    g. [Ar]$3d^6 4s^2$ (4-3)

PROBLEMS

Photons and Electromagnetic Radiation

31. Determine the frequency of light with a wavelength of 4.257×10^{-7} cm.

32. Determine the energy in joules of a photon whose frequency is 3.55×10^{17} Hz.

33. Using the two equations $E = h\nu$ and $c = \lambda\nu$, derive an equation expressing E in terms of h, c, and λ.

34. How long would it take a radio wave with a frequency of 7.25×10^5 Hz to travel from Mars to Earth if the distance between the two planets is approximately 8.00×10^7 km?

35. Cobalt-60 ($^{60}_{27}$Co) is an artificial radioisotope that is produced in a nuclear reactor for use as a gamma-ray source in the treatment of certain types of cancer. If the wavelength of the gamma radiation from a cobalt-60 source is 1.00×10^{-3} nm, calculate the energy of a photon of this radiation.

higher-energy orbit to one with lower energy, emitting a photon whose energy is equal to the difference in energy between the two levels.

10. The Bohr model was valid only for a single-electron atom and it did not explain the chemical nature of atoms.

11. a. the number used to specify the main energy level of an atom
    b. by the letter n
    c. all the orbitals within the same main energy level
    d. The number of orbitals per main energy level is equal to n^2. The number of electrons allowed per main energy level is equal to $2n^2$.

12. a. The angular momentum quantum number indicates an orbital's shape.
    b. A sublevel, or subshell, consists of the orbitals within a given main energy level that share the same value of l. For example, an atom's 3d subshell consists of five d orbitals.

13. a. 1; s
    b. 2; s and p
    c. 3; s, p, and d
    d. 4; s, p, d, and f
    e. 7

14. a. the orientation of an orbital about the nucleus
    b. 1, 3, 5, and 7, respectively
    c. Subscripts are used to indicate the various orbital orientations possible in terms of an x, y, z, three-dimensional coordinate system centered on the nucleus. For example, p_x refers to a p orbital along the x axis, p_y indicates a p orbital along the y axis, and p_z indicates a p orbital along the z axis.

15. a. The total number of possible orbitals in each main energy level is equal to n^2.

b. There are nine orbitals in the third energy level and 25 orbitals in the fifth energy level.

16. a. The spin quantum number indicates which of the two fundamental spin states an electron is in in an orbital.
b. +1/2 and –1/2.

17. a. 2
b. 18
c. 32
d. Theoretically, $n = 6$ can contain 72 electrons.
e. Theoretically, $n = 7$ can contain 98 electrons.

18. a. An electron occupies the lowest-energy orbital that can receive it.
b. In a multi-electron atom, the lowest-energy orbital is filled first. Electrons are then added to the orbital with the next lowest energy, and so on, until all of the electrons in the atom have been placed in orbitals.

19. a. Orbitals of equal energy are each occupied by one electron before any orbital is occupied by a second electron.
b. By placing as many single electrons as possible in separate orbitals in the same energy level, electron-electron repulsion is minimized and favorable lower-energy arrangements result.

20. a. No two electrons in the same atom can have the same four quantum numbers.
b. The two different values of the spin quantum number permit two electrons of opposite spins to occupy the same orbital.
c. One electron would have a spin quantum number of +1/2, the other would have a spin quantum number of –1/2.

Orbitals and Electron Configuration

36. List the order in which orbitals generally fill, from the $1s$ to the $7p$ orbital.

37. Write the noble-gas notation for the electron configurations of each of the following elements:
a. As
b. Pb
c. Lr
d. Hg
e. Sn
f. Xe
g. La

38. How do the electron configurations of chromium and copper contradict the Aufbau principle?

MIXED REVIEW

39. a. Which has a longer wavelength, green or yellow light?
b. Which has a higher frequency, an X ray or a microwave?
c. Which travels at a greater speed, ultraviolet or infrared light?

40. Write both the complete electron-configuration and noble-gas notation for each of the following:
a. Ar   b. Br   c. Al

41. Given the speed of light as 3.0×10^8 m/s, calculate the wavelength of the electromagnetic radiation whose frequency is 7.500×10^{12} Hz.

42. a. What is the electromagnetic spectrum?
b. What units are used to express wavelength?
c. What unit is used to express frequencies of electromagnetic waves?

43. Given that the electron configuration for phosphorus is $1s^2 2s^2 2p^6 3s^2 3p^3$, answer the following questions:
a. How many electrons are in each atom?
b. What is the atomic number of this element?
c. Write its orbital notation.
d. How many unpaired electrons does an atom of phosphorus have?
e. What is its highest occupied energy level?
f. How many inner-shell electrons does the atom contain?
g. In which orbital(s) are these inner-shell electrons located?

44. What is the frequency of a radio wave with an energy of 1.55×10^{-24} J/photon?

45. Write the noble-gas notation for the electron configurations of each of the following elements:
a. Hf
b. Sc
c. Fe
d. At
e. Ac
f. Zn

46. Describe the major similarities and differences between Schrödinger's model of the atom and the model proposed by Bohr.

47. When sodium is heated, a yellow spectral line whose energy is 3.37×10^{-19} J/photon is produced.
a. What is the frequency of this light?
b. What is its wavelength?

48. a. What is an orbital?
b. Describe an orbital in terms of an electron cloud.

CRITICAL THINKING

49. Inferring Relationships In the emission spectrum of hydrogen shown in Figure 4-5 on page 95, each colored line is produced by the emission of photons with specific energies. Substances also produce absorption spectra when electromagnetic radiation passes through them. Certain wavelengths are absorbed. Using the diagram below, predict what the wavelengths of the absorption lines will be when white light (all the colors of the visible spectrum) is passed through hydrogen gas.

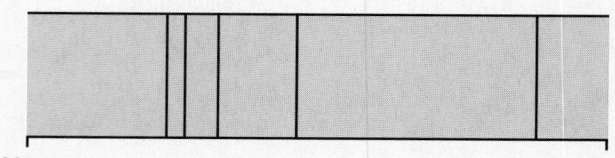

300 nm   700 nm
Hydrogen absorption spectrum

50. Applying Models When discussing the photoelectric effect, the minimum energy needed to remove an electron from the metal is called the *work function* and is a characteristic of the metal. For example, chromium, Cr, will emit electrons when the wavelength of the radiation is 284 nm or less. Calculate the work function for chromium. (Hint: You will need to use the two equations that describe the relationships among wavelength, frequency, speed of light, and Planck's constant.)

TECHNOLOGY & LEARNING

51. Graphing Calculator Calculating Quantum Number Relationships

The graphing calculator can run a program that calculates relationships in atomic structure given the quantum number. Given the principal quantum number 3, you will calculate the number of orbitals, orbital shapes, and electrons. The program will then be used to make the calculations.

Go to Appendix C. If you are using a TI 83 Plus, you can download the program and data and run the application as directed. If you are using another calculator, your teacher will provide you with keystrokes and data sets to use. Remember that you will need to name the program and check the display, as explained in Appendix C. You will then be ready to run the program. After you have graphed the data, answer these questions.

a. How many oribitals are there given the principle quantum number 12?

b. For the primary quantum number 3, how many possible combinations have a cloverleaf orbital shape (or orbital shape = 0)?

c. Name the total number of electrons for the principle quantum number 4.

HANDBOOK SEARCH

52. Sections 1 and 2 of the *Elements Handbook* (pages 728–739) contain information on an analytical test and a technological application for Group 1 and 2 elements that are based on the emission of light from atoms. Review these sections to answer the following:

a. What analytical technique utilizes the emission of light from excited atoms?

b. What elements in Groups 1 and 2 can be identified by this technique?

c. What types of compounds are used to provide color in fireworks?

d. What wavelengths within the visible spectrum would most likely contain emission lines for barium?

RESEARCH & WRITING

53. Neon signs do not always contain neon gas. The various colored lights produced by the signs are due to the emission of a variety of low-pressure gases in different tubes. Research other kinds of gases used in neon signs and list the colors that they emit.

54. Prepare a report about the photoelectric effect and cite some of its practical uses. Explain the basic operation of each device or technique mentioned.

ALTERNATIVE ASSESSMENT

55. Performance Assessment A spectroscope is a device used to produce and analyze spectra. Construct a simple spectroscope and determine the absorption spectra of several elemental gases. (Your teacher will provide you with the elemental samples.)

21. a. The highest occupied energy level in an atom is the electron-containing main energy level with the highest principal quantum number.
b. Inner-shell electrons are electrons that are not in the highest occupied energy level.

22. a. first main energy level ($n = 1$)
b. second main energy level ($n = 2$)
c. third main energy level ($n = 3$)
d. fourth main energy level ($n = 4$)
e. fifth main energy level ($n = 5$)

23. a.

$\uparrow\downarrow$	$\uparrow\downarrow$	$\uparrow\downarrow$	$\uparrow\downarrow$	$\uparrow\downarrow$
$1s$	$2s$	$2p_x$	$2p_y$	$2p_z$

$\uparrow\downarrow$	$\uparrow$	$\uparrow$	$\uparrow$
$3s$	$3p_x$	$3p_y$	$3p_z$

b.

$\uparrow\downarrow$	$\uparrow\downarrow$	$\uparrow$		
$1s$	$2s$	$2p_x$	$2p_y$	$2p_z$

c.

$\uparrow\downarrow$	$\uparrow\downarrow$	$\uparrow\downarrow$	$\uparrow\downarrow$	$\uparrow\downarrow$
$1s$	$2s$	$2p_x$	$2p_y$	$2p_z$

$\uparrow$
$3s$

d.

$\uparrow\downarrow$	$\uparrow\downarrow$	$\uparrow\downarrow$	$\uparrow$	$\uparrow$
$1s$	$2s$	$2p_x$	$2p_y$	$2p_z$

24. a. $1s^2 2s^1$
b. $1s^2 2s^2 2p^2$
c. $1s^2 2s^2 2p^4$
d. $1s^2 2s^2 2p^6 3s^2 3p^1$

25. a. 8
b. 8
c.

$\uparrow\downarrow$	$\uparrow\downarrow$	$\uparrow\downarrow$	$\uparrow$	$\uparrow$
$1s$	$2s$	$2p_x$	$2p_y$	$2p_z$

d. 2
e. second main energy level ($n = 2$)
f. 2
g. the $1s$ orbital

26. a. The noble gases are the Group 18 elements: helium, neon, argon, krypton, xenon, and radon.
b. A noble-gas configuration refers to an outer main energy level fully occupied by eight electrons.

SECTION REVIEW

Answers to Section 4-3 Review on page 116

1. a. a description of the arrangement of an atom's electrons

b. the Aufbau principle, Hund's rule, and the Pauli exclusion principle

2. orbital notation, electron-configuration notation, and noble-gas notation

3. An octet of electrons corresponds to filled s and p orbitals in an atom's highest main energy level. Noble gases (except helium, which has a filled outermost $1s$ orbital) contain octets.

4. a. $1s^2 2s^2 2p^2$,

[He]$2s^2 2p^2$,

$$\underline{\uparrow\downarrow}_{1s} \quad \underline{\uparrow\downarrow}_{1s} \quad \underline{\uparrow}_{2p_x} \, \underline{\uparrow}_{2p_y} \, \underline{}_{2p_z}$$

b. $1s^2 2s^2 2p^6$,

[He]$2s^2 2p^6$,

$$\underline{\uparrow\downarrow}_{1s} \quad \underline{\uparrow\downarrow}_{2s} \quad \underline{\uparrow\downarrow}_{2p_x} \, \underline{\uparrow\downarrow}_{2p_y} \, \underline{\uparrow\downarrow}_{2p_z}$$

c. $1s^2 2s^2 2p^6 3s^2 3p^4$,

[Ne]$3s^2 3p^4$,

$$\underline{\uparrow\downarrow}_{1s} \quad \underline{\uparrow\downarrow}_{2s} \quad \underline{\uparrow\downarrow}_{2p_x} \, \underline{\uparrow\downarrow}_{2p_y} \, \underline{\uparrow\downarrow}_{2p_z}$$

$$\underline{\uparrow\downarrow}_{3s} \quad \underline{\uparrow\downarrow}_{3p_x} \, \underline{\uparrow}_{3p_y} \, \underline{\uparrow}_{3p_z}$$

5. a. P
b. K
c. Si
d. As

REVIEW ANSWERS

Continued from page 121

c. It allows one to abbreviate large portions of the configuration.

27. a. [Ne]$3s^2 3p^5$

b. [Ar]$4s^2$

c. [Ar]$3d^{10} 4s^2 4p^4$

28. a. The notation indicates that in addition to all the electrons that would be contained by neon (10), the atom has two electrons in its $3s$ orbital.

b. magnesium

29. a. $1s^2 2s^2 2p^6 3s^1$,
[Ne]$3s^1$

b. $1s^2 2s^2 2p^6 3s^2 3p^6 3d^{10} 4s^2 4p^6 5s^2$,
[Kr]$5s^2$

c. $1s^2 2s^2 2p^6 3s^2 3p^3$,
[Ne]$3s^2 3p^3$

30. a. boron
b. fluorine
c. magnesium
d. silicon
e. chlorine
f. potassium
g. iron

31. 7.0×10^{16} Hz

32. 2.35×10^{-16} J

33. $E = hc/\lambda$

34. 2.67×10^2 s

35. 1.99×10^{-13} J

36. $1s, 2s, 2p, 3s, 3p, 4s, 3d, 4p, 5s, 4d, 5p, 6s, 4f, 5d, 6p, 7s, 5f, 6d, 7p$

37. a. [Ar]$3d^{10} 4s^2 4p^3$
b. [Xe]$4f^{14} 5d^{10} 6s^2 6p^2$
c. [Rn]$5f^{14} 6d^1 7s^2$
d. [Xe]$4f^{14} 5d^{10} 6s^2$
e. [Kr]$4d^{10} 5s^2 5p^2$
f. [Kr]$4d^{10} 5s^2 5p^6$
g. [Xe] $5d^1 6s^2$

38. Electrons occupy the higher-energy $3d$ sublevel before filling the lower-energy $4s$ orbital. These unusual configurations result because they are the electron arrangements of minimum energy.

39. a. yellow light
b. an X ray
c. Both travel at the same speed in a vacuum, the speed of light.

40. a. $1s^2 2s^2 2p^6 3s^2 3p^6$,
[Ne]$3s^2 3p^6$
b. $1s^2 2s^2 2p^6 3s^2 3p^6 3d^{10} 4s^2 4p^5$,
[Ar]$3d^{10} 4s^2 4p^5$
c. $1s^2 2s^2 2p^6 3s^2 3p^1$,
[Ne]$3s^2 3p^1$

41. 4.0×10^{-5} m (4.0×10^4 nm)

42. a. all the forms of electromagnetic radiation arranged according to increasing wavelength or frequency

b. Shorter wavelengths are measured in nanometers, whereas longer wavelengths are measured in centimeters or meters.

c. hertz, Hz; one Hz equals one wave/second

43. a. 15

b. 15

c.

$\uparrow\downarrow$	$\uparrow\downarrow$	$\uparrow\downarrow$	$\uparrow\downarrow$	$\uparrow\downarrow$
$1s$	$2s$	$2p_x$	$2p_y$	$2p_z$

$\uparrow\downarrow$	$\uparrow$	$\uparrow$	$\uparrow$
$3s$	$3p_x$	$3p_y$	$3p_z$

d. 3

e. the third main energy level ($n = 3$)

f. 10

g. the $1s$, $2s$, and $2p$ orbitals

44. 2.34×10^9 Hz

45. a. $[Xe]4f^{14}5d^26s^2$

b. $[Ar]3d^14s^2$

c. $[Ar]3d^64s^2$

d. $[Xe]4f^{14}5d^{10}6s^26p^5$

e. $[Rn]6d^17s^2$

f. $[Ar]3d^{10}4s^2$

46. Bohr's model worked only for the hydrogen atom, whereas Schrödinger's mathematical model applies to all atoms. The essential difference between the two models involves the issue of certainty. Bohr described definite orbits occupied by electron particles, whereas Schrödinger treated electrons as waves having a certain probability of being found at various distances from the nucleus in orbitals. The two models are similar in that both associate the energy of an electron with its location relative to the nucleus. Also, the most probable location of an electron in hydrogen according to Schrödinger is at a distance from the nucleus exactly equal to that of Bohr's lowest energy orbit.

47. a. 5.09×10^{14} Hz

b. 5.9×10^{-7} m (590 nm)

48. a. An orbital is a three-dimensional region about the nucleus in which there is a high probability that a particular electron is located.

b. Orbitals are like clouds showing the region of probable electron locations. The sizes and shapes of electron clouds depend on the energies of the electrons that occupy them.

49. 656 nm, 486 nm, 434 nm, 410 nm, and 397 nm. Students should realize that these are the same frequencies of hydrogen's line-emission spectrum. Electronic transitions occur at the same frequencies whether an electron is absorbing energy and being excited or losing energy and emitting a photon.

50. 7.0×10^{-19} J

51. a. 144

b. 5

c. 32

52. a. flame tests

b. lithium, sodium, potassium, rubidium, cesium, calcium, strontium, and barium

c. chloride salts

d. those near 500 nm

53. Answers will vary, depending on which gases students choose. One of the most common gases used or mixed with the red glow of neon is sodium, which appears yellow.

54. Be sure students focus on the movement of electrons that results from photons striking the surface of metal. Photovoltaic solar cells may be one device mentioned in which the moving electrons create an electrical current. Many other answers are possible.

55. The spectroscope can be constructed with a long tube of black paper covered on one end with a slit, over which a diffraction grating is attached.

PACING CHART Compression Guide: *(To shorten, eliminate items in italics.)*	CLASSROOM RESOURCES		
	NSE Standards	Teaching Resources	Experiments
5-1 **History of the Periodic Table** 2 45-minute periods 1 90-minute block *Mendeleev and Chemical Periodicity, pp. 123–125*	PS 2b UCP 1–2, 5 SAI 1–2 HNS 1, 3	T 24, TM 18A, TM 19A	PE Quick Lab, p. 127
5-2 **Electron Configuration and the Periodic Table** 2 45-minute periods 1 90-minute block	PS 2b UCP 1–3, 5	PE Elements Handbook ATE **Demo,** p. 132 T 25, TM 20A	
5-3 **Electron Configuration and Periodic Properties** 2 45-minute periods 1 90-minute block *Atomic Radii, pp. 140–142* *Ionic Radii, pp. 149–150* *Periodic Properties of the d- and f-Block Elements, pp. 153–154*	PS 2a–2c UCP 1–3, 5	PE Elements Handbook T 26, T 27, T 28, T 29, TM 21A, TM 22A, TM 23A, TM 24A, TM 25A	A3 Reactivity of Halide Ions B3 Relative Solubility of Transition Elements B4 Periodicity of Properties of Oxides B5 Reactivity of Halide Ions

Review and Assessment 2 45-minute periods 1 90-minute block	REVIEW RESOURCES		
	Cumulative Review	Alternative Assessment	Traditional Assessment
	SR Chapter 5 Mixed Review PE Chapter 5 39–49, pp. 157–158	PE 59, 60, p. 159 ATE 129, 153 AA Items for Chapter 5	Chapter 5 Text Test Generator Items for Chapter 5

ASSIGNMENT RESOURCES

Section Homework Resources & Review	Problem-Solving Practice
HR Homework Worksheets 5-1, 5-2 Graphic Org. Assignment 5-2 **PE** Section Review, 1, 3, p. 127 Chapter Review, 1–3, p. 155 **SR** Section Review 5-1	
HR Homework Worksheets 5-3, 5-4, 5-5, 5-6 Graphic Org. Assignments 5-3, 5-5, 5-6 **PE** Section Review, 1–5, p. 139 Chapter Review, 4–16, 27–31, pp. 155–157 **SR** Section Review 5-2	**PE** Additional Samples 5-1, 5-2, 5-3, 5-4 **ATE** Additional Samples, pp. 133, 136, 138, 139
HR Homework Worksheets 5-7, 5-8, 5-9, 5-10 Graphic Org. Assignments 5-9, 5-10 **PE** Section Review, 1–3, p. 154 Chapter Review, 17–26, 32–34, 35–38, pp. 156–157 **SR** Section Review 5-3	**PE** Additional Samples 5-5, 5-6, 5-7 **ATE** Additional Samples, pp. 142, 146, 152

Resource Key

PE Pupil's Edition
ATE Teacher's Edition

One-Stop Planner CD-ROM Includes these resources and customizable daily lesson plans:

HR Homework Resources
SR Section Reviews
CTW Critical Thinking Worksheets
AA Alternative Assessments

ChemFile
A Laboratory Experiments
B Microscale Experiments
C Technique Builders and Problem-Solving Experiments

D Consumer Experiments
T Transparencies
TM Transparency Masters
PS Mini-Guide to Problem Solving
SRW Supplemental Reading Worksheets

Scoring Rubrics for Labs, Alternative Assessments, Performance Tasks and Portfolio Projects are on the One-Stop Planner CD-ROM.

CHAPTER 5

The Periodic Law

Chapter Overview

5-1 covers the work of Mendeleev and other chemists in developing the periodic table and explains how the periodic law is used to predict elements' physical and chemical properties.

5-2 explains the relationship between electron configuration and the arrangement of elements in groups, blocks, and periods of the periodic table, as well as the elements' general properties.

5-3 further explores the relationship between the periodic law and electron configuration, including trends in the properties of electron affinity, electronegativity, ionization energy, atomic radii, and ionic radii.

Concept Base

Students may need a review of the following concepts:

• structure of the atom, atomic number, Chapter 3

• quantum numbers and atomic orbitals, Chapter 4

• electron configurations, Chapter 4

The Periodic Law

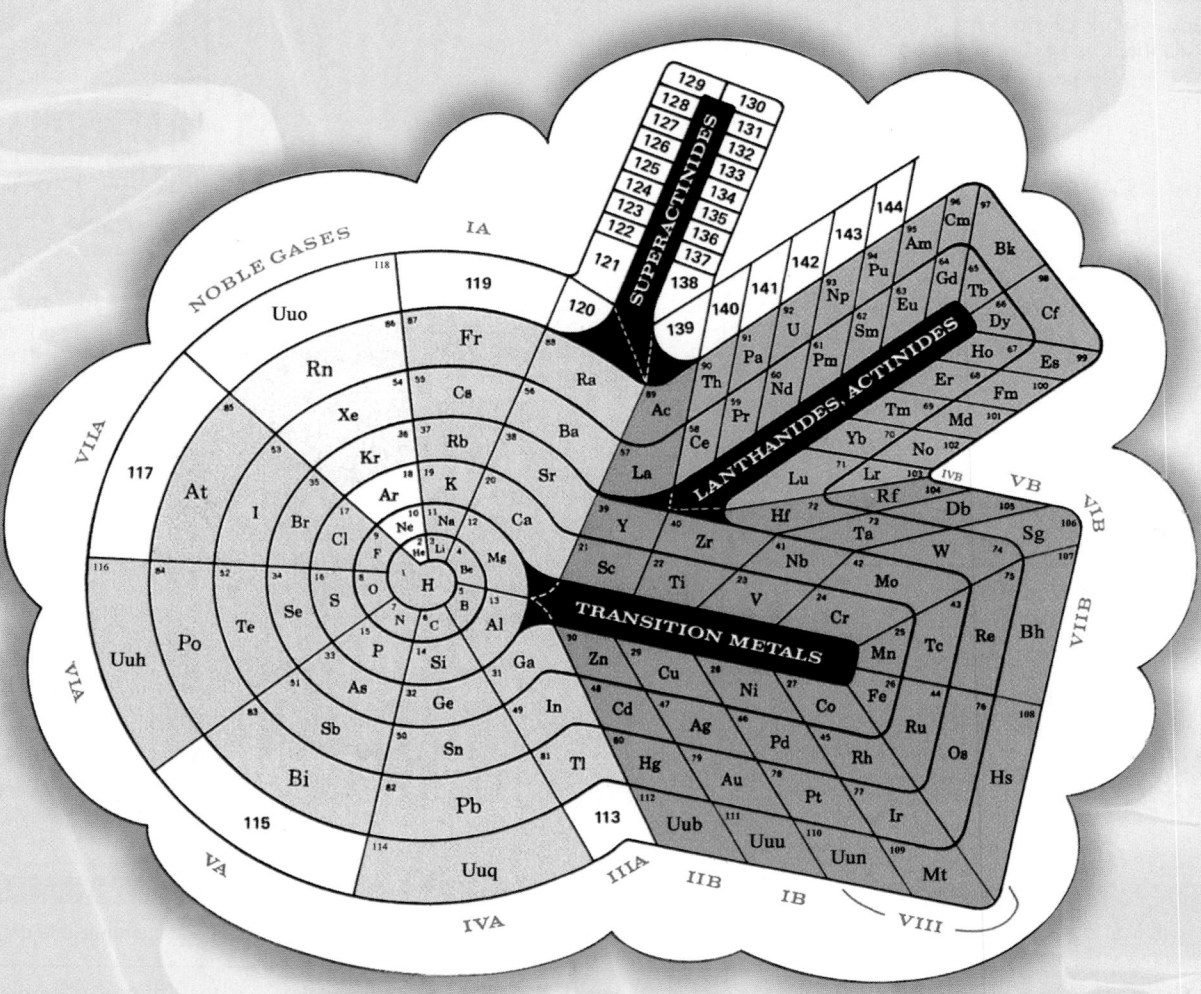

The physical and chemical properties of the elements are periodic functions of their atomic numbers.

History of the Periodic Table

OBJECTIVES

- Explain the roles of Mendeleev and Moseley in the development of the periodic table.

- Describe the modern periodic table.

- Explain how the periodic law can be used to predict the physical and chemical properties of elements.

- Describe how the elements belonging to a group of the periodic table are interrelated in terms of atomic number.

Imagine the confusion among chemists during the middle of the nineteenth century. By 1860, more than 60 elements had been discovered. Chemists had to learn the properties of these elements as well as those of the many compounds that they formed—a difficult task. And to make matters worse, there was no method for accurately determining an element's atomic mass or the number of atoms of an element in a particular chemical compound. Different chemists used different atomic masses for the same elements, resulting in different compositions being proposed for the same compounds. This made it nearly impossible for one chemist to understand the results of another.

In September 1860, a group of chemists assembled at the First International Congress of Chemists in Karlsruhe, Germany, to settle the issue of atomic mass as well as some other matters that were making communication difficult. At the Congress, Italian chemist Stanislao Cannizzaro presented a convincing method for accurately measuring the relative masses of atoms. Cannizzaro's method enabled chemists to agree on standard values for atomic mass and initiated a search for relationships between atomic mass and other properties of the elements.

Mendeleev and Chemical Periodicity

When the Russian chemist Dmitri Mendeleev heard about the new atomic masses discussed at Karlsruhe, he decided to include the new values in a chemistry textbook that he was writing. In the book, Mendeleev hoped to organize the elements according to their properties. He went about this much as you might organize information for a research paper. He placed the name of each known element on a card, together with the atomic mass of the element and a list of its observed physical and chemical properties. He then arranged the cards according to various properties and looked for trends or patterns.

Mendeleev noticed that when the elements were arranged in order of increasing atomic mass, certain similarities in their chemical properties appeared at regular intervals. Such a repeating pattern is referred to as *periodic*. The second hand of a watch, for example, passes over any given mark at periodic, 60-second intervals. The circular waves created by a drop of water hitting a water surface are also periodic.

internet connect

SC*LINKS*
NSTA

TOPIC: Periodic table
GO TO: www.scilinks.org
*sci*LINKS **CODE:** HC2051

FIGURE 5-1 The regularly spaced water waves represent a simple periodic pattern.

Lesson Starter

Place a transparency of the periodic table on an overhead projector or refer students to a periodic table displayed in your classroom. Ask students to share what they've learned previously about the periodic table. List their responses on the board to start a discussion of the periodic table.

Common Misconception

Explain to students that something does not need to vary uniformly in order to vary periodically. For example, although the spaces between the water waves shown in Figure 5-1 are not equal, the waves spread in a periodic manner: as each wave spreads outward, it follows the same pattern as that of the preceding wave.

Reading Skill-Builder

BRAINSTORMING To help students understand the meaning of the periodic law, write the word *periodic* on the board. Ask students to brainstorm examples of phenomena that occur periodically, such as the phases of the moon, or other examples of periodic functions, such as sine curves and magazine publications. Discuss the different examples and tell students to keep these in mind as you point out the arrangement of elements in the periodic table.

Visual Strategy

FIGURE 5-2 The illustration shows a representation of Mendeleev's original periodic table of the elements. Ask students to compare this arrangement with that of the modern periodic table. *(In Mendeleev's table, the periods are arranged vertically and the groups are arranged horizontally, which is the opposite of the modern periodic table's arrangement.)* Ask students how Mendeleev arranged the elements on the table *(in order of increasing atomic mass).* Point out that part of Mendeleev's fame came from his ability to predict the properties of the missing elements Sc, Ga, and Ge.

✔Teaching Tip

To emphasize that the modern periodic table arranges elements according to increasing atomic numbers rather than atomic masses, have students examine the atomic numbers on the periodic table to see if any are out of numerical sequence. Then have them do the same with atomic masses. They will find that Ar and K, Co and Ni, and Te and I are reversed in terms of atomic mass but that all elements are in order in terms of atomic numbers.

Did You Know?

Surprisingly, Mendeleev never won a Nobel Prize; the monumental importance of his work was not recognized during his lifetime. In 1906, the year before his death, he was nominated for the Nobel Prize in chemistry but lost by one vote to Henri Moissan, who discovered fluorine.

FIGURE 5-2 In his first published periodic table, Mendeleev arranged the elements in vertical periods according to relative atomic mass. The atomic mass for each element is indicated by the number following the element's symbol. The unknown elements indicated by question marks at estimated atomic masses 45, 68, and 70 were later identified as scandium, Sc, gallium, Ga, and germanium, Ge.

но въ ней, мнѣ кажется, уже ясно выражается примѣнимость выставллемаго мною начала ко всей совокупности элементовъ, пай которыхъ извѣстенъ съ достовѣрностію. На этотъ разъ я и желалъ преимущественно найдти общую систему элементовъ. Вотъ этотъ опытъ:

			Ti=50	Zr=90	?=180.
			V=51	Nb=94	Ta=182.
			Cr=52	Mo=96	W=186.
			Mn=55	Rh=104,4	Pt=197,4
			Fe=56	Ru=104,4	Ir=198.
			Ni=Co=59	Pl=106,6	Os=199.
H=1			Cu=63,4	Ag=108	Hg=200.
	Be=9,4	Mg=24	Zn=65,2	Cd=112	
	B=11	Al=27,4	?=68	Ur=116	Au=197?
	C=12	Si=28	?=70	Su=118	
	N=14	P=31	As=75	Sb=122	Bi=210
	O=16	S=32	Se=79,4	Te=128?	
	F=19	Cl=35,5	Br=80	I=127	
Li=7	Na=23	K=39	Rb=85,4	Cs=133	Tl=204
		Ca=40	Sr=87,6	Ba=137	Pb=207.
		?=45	Ce=92		
		?Er=56	La=94		
		?Yt=60	Di=95		
		?In=75,6	Th=118?		

а потому приходится въ разныхъ рядахъ имѣть различное измѣненіе разностей, чего нѣтъ въ главныхъ числахъ предлагаемой таблицы. Или же придется предполагать при составленіи системы очень много недостающихъ членовъ. То и другое мало выгодно. Мнѣ кажется притомъ, наиболѣе естественнымъ составить

Mendeleev created a table in which elements with similar properties were grouped together—a periodic table of the elements. His first periodic table, shown in Figure 5-2, was published in 1869. Note that Mendeleev placed iodine, I (atomic mass 127), after tellurium, Te (atomic mass 128). Although this contradicted the pattern of listing the elements in order of increasing atomic mass, it allowed Mendeleev to place tellurium in a group of elements with which it shares similar properties. Reading horizontally across Mendeleev's table, this group includes oxygen, O, sulfur, S, and selenium, Se. Iodine could also, then, be placed in the group it resembles chemically, which includes fluorine, F, chlorine, Cl, and bromine, Br.

Mendeleev's procedure left several empty spaces in his periodic table (see Figure 5-2). In 1871, the Russian chemist boldly predicted the existence and properties of the elements that would fill three of the spaces. By 1886, all three elements had been discovered. Today these elements are known as scandium, Sc, gallium, Ga, and germanium, Ge. Their properties are strikingly similar to those predicted by Mendeleev.

The success of Mendeleev's predictions persuaded most chemists to accept his periodic table and earned him credit as the discoverer of the periodic law. Two questions remained, however. (1) Why could most of the elements be arranged in the order of increasing atomic mass but a few could not? (2) What was the reason for chemical periodicity?

Moseley and the Periodic Law

The first question was not answered until more than 40 years after Mendeleev's first periodic table was published. In 1911, the English scientist Henry Moseley, who was working with Ernest Rutherford, examined the spectra of 38 different metals. When analyzing his data, Moseley discovered a previously unrecognized pattern. The elements in the periodic table fit into patterns better when they were arranged in increasing order according to nuclear charge, or the number of protons in the nucleus. Moseley's work led to both the modern definition of atomic number and the recognition that atomic number, not atomic mass, is the basis for the organization of the periodic table.

Moseley's discovery was consistent with Mendeleev's ordering of the periodic table by properties rather than strictly by atomic mass. For example, according to Moseley, tellurium, with an atomic number of 52, belongs before iodine, which has an atomic number of 53. Today, Mendeleev's principle of chemical periodicity is correctly stated in what is known as the **periodic law:** *The physical and chemical properties of the elements are periodic functions of their atomic numbers.* In other words, when the elements are arranged in order of increasing atomic number, elements with similar properties appear at regular intervals.

The Modern Periodic Table

The periodic table has undergone extensive change since Mendeleev's time (see Figure 5-6 on pages 130–131). Chemists have discovered new elements and, in more recent years, synthesized new ones in the laboratory. Each of the more than 40 new elements, however, can be placed in a group of other elements with similar properties. *The* **periodic table** *is an arrangement of the elements in order of their atomic numbers so that elements with similar properties fall in the same column, or group.*

The Noble Gases

Perhaps the most significant addition to the periodic table came with the discovery of the noble gases. In 1894, English physicist John William Strutt (Lord Rayleigh) and Scottish chemist Sir William Ramsay discovered argon, Ar, a gas in the atmosphere that had previously escaped notice because of its total lack of chemical reactivity. Back in 1868,

internet connect

SCI**LINKS**
NSTA

TOPIC: Noble gases
GO TO: www.scilinks.org
*sci***LINKS CODE:** HC2052

FIGURE 5-3 The noble gases, also known as the Group 18 elements, are all rather unreactive. As you will read, the reason for this low reactivity also accounts for the special place occupied by the noble gases in the periodic table.

Did You Know?
Remind students that scientists are constantly looking for order in the universe. Early chemists searched for ways to organize the elements before the establishment of the periodic table, but no one was able to discern the relationship between them.

German chemist Julius Lothar Meyer arranged the elements by their atomic volume and produced findings similar to those of Mendeleev. Meyer published his findings in 1870, one year after Mendeleev published his.

Visual Strategy

FIGURE 5-3 Ask students to explain the meaning of *unreactive.* Explain that materials referred to as reactive (or active) undergo chemical reactions easily or quickly. Materials of low reactivity undergo few chemical changes, and when they do react, they do so with difficulty (and often only after the addition of energy). The noble gases are either unreactive (helium, neon, argon) or have very low reactivity (xenon, krypton, radon).

Reading Skill-Builder

READING HINT Have students place bookmarks in their texts to mark the periodic table on pp. 130–131. Encourage students to familiarize themselves with the information listed in the table and to make frequent reference to these pages as they read the rest of the chapter.

- Helium was discovered in 1868 by Pierre Janssen as he was studying a solar eclipse. However, helium was not accepted as an element until William Ramsay discovered that it also exists on Earth. Ramsay's discovery of helium as well as most of the other noble gases is examined in the Great Discoveries feature on pages 108–109.

- Radon is the heaviest noble gas. Its isotopes are radioactive, making radon the only gas that is radioactive at normal temperatures and pressures.

Application

The noble gases are used in making lighted signs and displays. Neon is a colorless, odorless, tasteless gas. But it emits red light when its electrons are excited, such as with the application of a high voltage. True neon signs are red. Other colors in signs are obtained by using other gases.

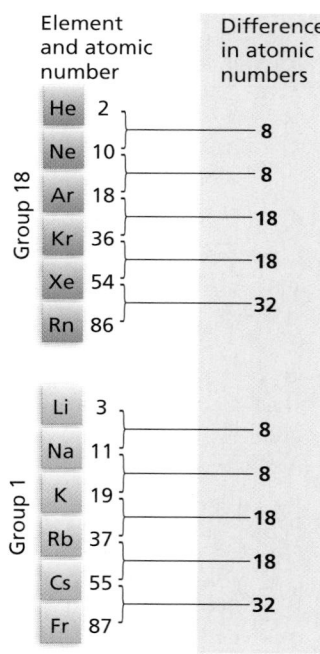

FIGURE 5-4 In each of Groups 1 and 18, the differences between the atomic numbers of successive elements are 8, 8, 18, 18, and 32, respectively. Groups 2 and 13–17 follow a similar pattern.

another noble gas, helium, He, had been discovered as a component of the sun, based on the emission spectrum of sunlight. In 1895, Ramsay showed that helium also exists on Earth.

In order to fit argon and helium into the periodic table, Ramsay proposed a new group. He placed this group between the groups now known as Group 17 (the fluorine family) and Group 1 (the lithium family). In 1898, Ramsay discovered two more noble gases to place in his new group, krypton, Kr, and xenon, Xe. The final noble gas, radon, Rn, was discovered in 1900 by the German scientist Friedrich Ernst Dorn.

The Lanthanides

The next step in the development of the periodic table was completed in the early 1900s. It was then that the puzzling chemistry of the lanthanides was finally understood. *The* **lanthanides** *are the 14 elements with atomic numbers from 58 (cerium, Ce) to 71 (lutetium, Lu).* Because these elements are so similar in chemical and physical properties, the process of separating and identifying them was a tedious task that required the effort of many chemists.

The Actinides

Another major step in the development of the periodic table was the discovery of the actinides. *The* **actinides** *are the 14 elements with atomic numbers from 90 (thorium, Th) to 103 (lawrencium, Lr).* The lanthanides and actinides belong in Periods 6 and 7, respectively, of the periodic table, between the elements of Groups 3 and 4. To save space, the lanthanides and actinides are usually set off below the main portion of the periodic table, as shown in Figure 5-6 on pages 130–131.

Periodicity

Periodicity with respect to atomic number can be observed in any group of elements in the periodic table. Consider the noble gases of Group 18. The first noble gas is helium, He. It has an atomic number of 2. The elements following helium in atomic number have completely different properties until the next noble gas, neon, Ne, which has an atomic number of 10, is reached. The remaining noble gases in order of increasing atomic number are argon (Ar, atomic number 18), krypton (Kr, atomic number 36), xenon (Xe, atomic number 54), and radon (Rn, atomic number 86). The differences in atomic number between successive noble gases are shown in Figure 5-4. Also shown in Figure 5-4 are atomic-number differences between the elements of Group 1, which are all solid, silvery metals. As you can see, the differences in atomic number between the Group 1 metals follow the same pattern as the differences in atomic number between the noble gases.

Starting with the first member of Groups 13–17, a similar periodic pattern is repeated. The atomic number of each successive element is 8, 18, 18, and 32 higher than the atomic number of the element above it. In Section 5-2, you will see that the second mystery presented by Mendeleev's periodic table—the reason for periodicity—is explained by the arrangement of the electrons around the nucleus.

Designing Your Own Periodic Table

Materials
• index cards

Question
Can you design your own periodic table using information similar to that available to Mendeleev? as you think Mendeleev might have done.

Procedure
1. Write down the information available for each element on separate index cards. The following information is appropriate: a letter of the alphabet (A, B, C, etc.) to identify each element; atomic mass; state; density; melting point; boiling point; and any other readily observable physical properties. Do not write the name of the element on the index card, but keep a separate list indicating the letters you have assigned to each element.

2. Organize the cards for the elements in a logical pattern

Discussion
1. Keeping in mind that the information you have is similar to that available to Mendeleev in 1869, answer the following questions.
   a. Why are atomic masses given instead of atomic numbers?
   b. Can you identify each element by name?

2. How many groups of elements, or families, are in your periodic table? How many periods, or series, are in the table?

3. Predict the characteristics of any missing elements. When you have finished, check your work using your separate list of elements and a periodic table.

(index cards shown:)
Element B
average atomic mass = 24.6 amu
Element A
average atomic mass = 201.9 amu
density = 2.7 g/cm³
m.p. = 660.4°C
b.p. = 2467°C
Element C
Element D
average atomic mass = 123 amu
g/cm³
Element E

QUICK LAB
In this activity, students will follow Mendeleev's strategy for designing a periodic table by formulating their own table. Assign letters or numbers to all or some of the elements. Then write down chemical and physical characteristics of each element and have students organize the "unknown" elements according to their properties. Students may organize their elements in a manner similar to the modern periodic table or they may develop less orthodox styles.

Discussion
1. a. Atomic numbers were not discovered until about 45 years later.

2. Answers will vary, depending on the number of elements assigned.

3. Answers will vary.

SECTION REVIEW

1. a. Who is credited with developing a method that led to the determination of standard relative atomic masses?
   b. Who discovered the periodic law?
   c. Who established atomic numbers as the basis for organizing the periodic table?

2. State the periodic law.

3. Name three sets of elements added to the periodic table after Mendeleev's time.

4. How do the atomic numbers of the elements within each of Groups 1, 2, and 13–18 of the periodic table vary? (Refer to Figure 5-4 as a guide.)

SECTION REVIEW

1. a. Cannizzaro
   b. Mendeleev
   c. Moseley

2. The physical and chemical properties of the elements are periodic functions of their atomic numbers.

3. the noble gases, the lanthanides, and the actinides

4. The atomic numbers of successive elements in Groups 1, 2, and 18 differ by 8, 8, 18, 18, and 32, respectively. The atomic numbers of successive elements in Groups 13–17 differ by 8, 18, 18, and 32, respectively.

Lesson Starter

Ask students to name as many properties shared by elements of the same group in the periodic table as possible. Keep track of the characteristics by listing them on the board. For example, a good starting point would be to note the antiseptic characteristics of the halogens Cl, Br, and I. Then ask students to describe what they already know about an element by looking at its position in the periodic table. List students' responses on the board and have them identify any noticeable trends.

TABLE STRATEGY

Table 5-1 Review with students the rules from Chapter 4 governing electron configurations. The Aufbau principle states that an electron occupies the lowest energy orbital that can receive it. For example, the 4*s* sublevel is lower in energy than the 3*d* sublevel. Therefore, the 4*s* sublevel will fill before any electrons enter the 3*d* orbitals. Once the 3*d* orbitals are fully occupied, the 4*p* sublevel will start to fill.

✔ Teaching Tip

You may want to introduce dot notation here and then review it in Chapter 6. If you do so, emphasize that dot notation is normally used only for the *s*-block (Groups 1 and 2) and *p*-block (Groups 13–18) elements. Explain that dot notation for Groups 3–12 would usually not be useful.

OBJECTIVES

- Describe the relationship between electrons in sublevels and the length of each period of the periodic table.

- Locate and name the four blocks of the periodic table. Explain the reasons for these names.

- Discuss the relationship between group configurations and group numbers.

- Describe the locations in the periodic table and the general properties of the alkali metals, the alkaline-earth metals, the halogens, and the noble gases.

Electron Configuration and the Periodic Table

The Group 18 elements of the periodic table (the noble gases) undergo few chemical reactions. This stability results from the gases' special electron configurations. Helium's highest occupied level, the 1*s* orbital, is completely filled with electrons. And the highest occupied levels of the other noble gases contain stable octets. Generally the electron configuration of an atom's highest occupied energy level governs the atom's chemical properties.

Periods and Blocks of the Periodic Table

While the elements are arranged vertically in the periodic table in groups that share similar chemical properties, they are also organized horizontally in rows, or *periods*. (As shown in Figure 5-6, there are a total of seven periods of elements in the modern periodic table.) As can be seen in Table 5-1, the length of each period is determined by the number of electrons that can occupy the sublevels being filled in that period.

TABLE 5-1 *Relationship Between Period Length and Sublevels Being Filled in the Periodic Table*		
Period number	**Number of elements in period**	**Sublevels in order of filling**
1	2	1*s*
2	8	2*s* 2*p*
3	8	3*s* 3*p*
4	18	4*s* 3*d* 4*p*
5	18	5*s* 4*d* 5*p*
6	32	6*s* 4*f* 5*d* 6*p*
7	32	7*s* 5*f* 6*d*, etc.

In the first period, the 1s sublevel is being filled. The 1s sublevel can hold a total of two electrons. Therefore, the first period consists of two elements—hydrogen and helium. In the second period, the 2s sublevel, which can hold two electrons, and the 2p sublevel, which can hold six electrons, are being filled. Consequently, the second period totals eight elements. Similarly, filling of the 3s and 3p sublevels accounts for the eight elements of the third period. Filling 3d and 4d sublevels in addition to the s and p sublevels adds 10 elements to both the fourth and fifth periods. Therefore, each of these periods totals 18 elements. Filling 4f sublevels in addition to s, p, and d sublevels adds 14 elements to the sixth period, which totals 32 elements. And as new elements are created, the 29 known elements in Period 7 could, in theory, be extended to 32.

The period of an element can be determined from the element's electron configuration. For example, arsenic, As, has the electron configuration $[Ar]3d^{10}4s^24p^3$. The 4 in $4p^3$ indicates that arsenic's highest occupied energy level is the fourth energy level. Arsenic is therefore in the fourth period in the periodic table. The period and electron configuration for each element can be found in the periodic table on pages 130–131.

Based on the electron configurations of the elements, the periodic table can be divided into four blocks, the s, p, d, and f blocks. This division is illustrated in Figure 5-5. The name of each block is determined by whether an s, p, d, or f sublevel is being filled in successive elements of that block.

FIGURE 5-5 Based on the electron configurations of the elements, the periodic table can be subdivided into four sublevel blocks.

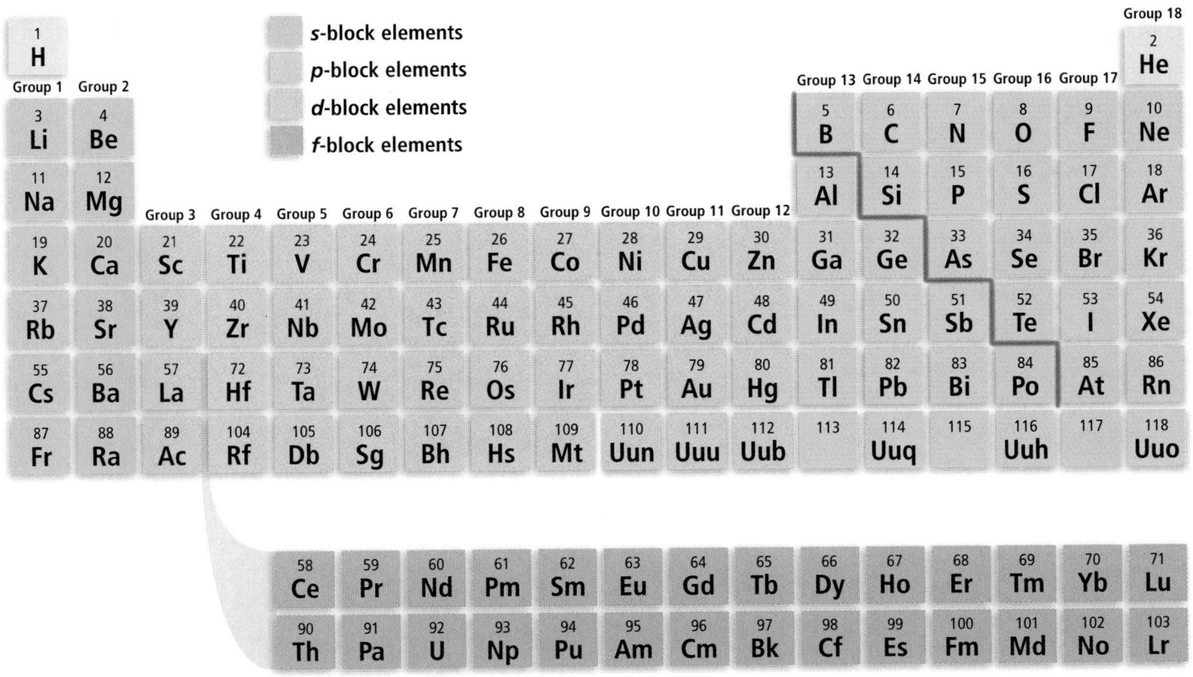

Class Discussion
Have students write electron configurations for magnesium, calcium, fluorine, and chlorine. Then have them check their answers by looking up the configurations in the periodic table on pages 130–131. Ask students to compare properties of the four elements and discuss their observations. (*Magnesium and calcium each have two valence electrons, and they share similar chemical properties. Fluorine and chlorine, with s^2p^5 outer-shell configurations, also have similar properties.*) Ask students to choose other elements from the same group and to make observations about their chemical properties based on electron configurations.

Alternative Assessment
Divide the class into groups of three or four, and assign each group one chemical family. Select from Groups 1, 2, 13, 14, 15, 16, 17, or 18. Have students use the text, the *CRC Handbook*, and other references to determine six properties of their chemical family. Each group should write their findings on the board in order to compile a class list of properties of all the families of the periodic table.

Sublevel Blocks of the Periodic Table

s-block elements
p-block elements
d-block elements
f-block elements

THE PERIODIC LAW **129**

129

Explain that not all periodic tables have the information in each block organized in the same way. Some tables have the atomic number in a corner, and some have it under the element's name.

Application

To help students connect the symbols of the elements with the elements they represent, have them locate examples of metals, metalloids, non-metals, and noble gases in the periodic table. Then show them samples or pictures of several elements, or ask them to bring in their own pictures from magazines. Ask students to form generalizations about the properties shared by groups of elements.

Visual Strategy

FIGURE 5-6 Discuss with students all of the information available from the periodic table, including atomic number, symbol, name, atomic mass, group, electron configuration, and whether the element is a metal, non-metal, metalloid, or noble gas. Also point out the positions of the actinide and lanthanide series. Explain that these elements are found at the base of the table for convenience, to keep the table from being too wide. Ask students to sketch how large the periodic table would need to be to accommodate these elements in place. Point out that often the periodic table is shown with only the atomic number, element symbol, and atomic mass in each box.

Periodic Table of the Elements

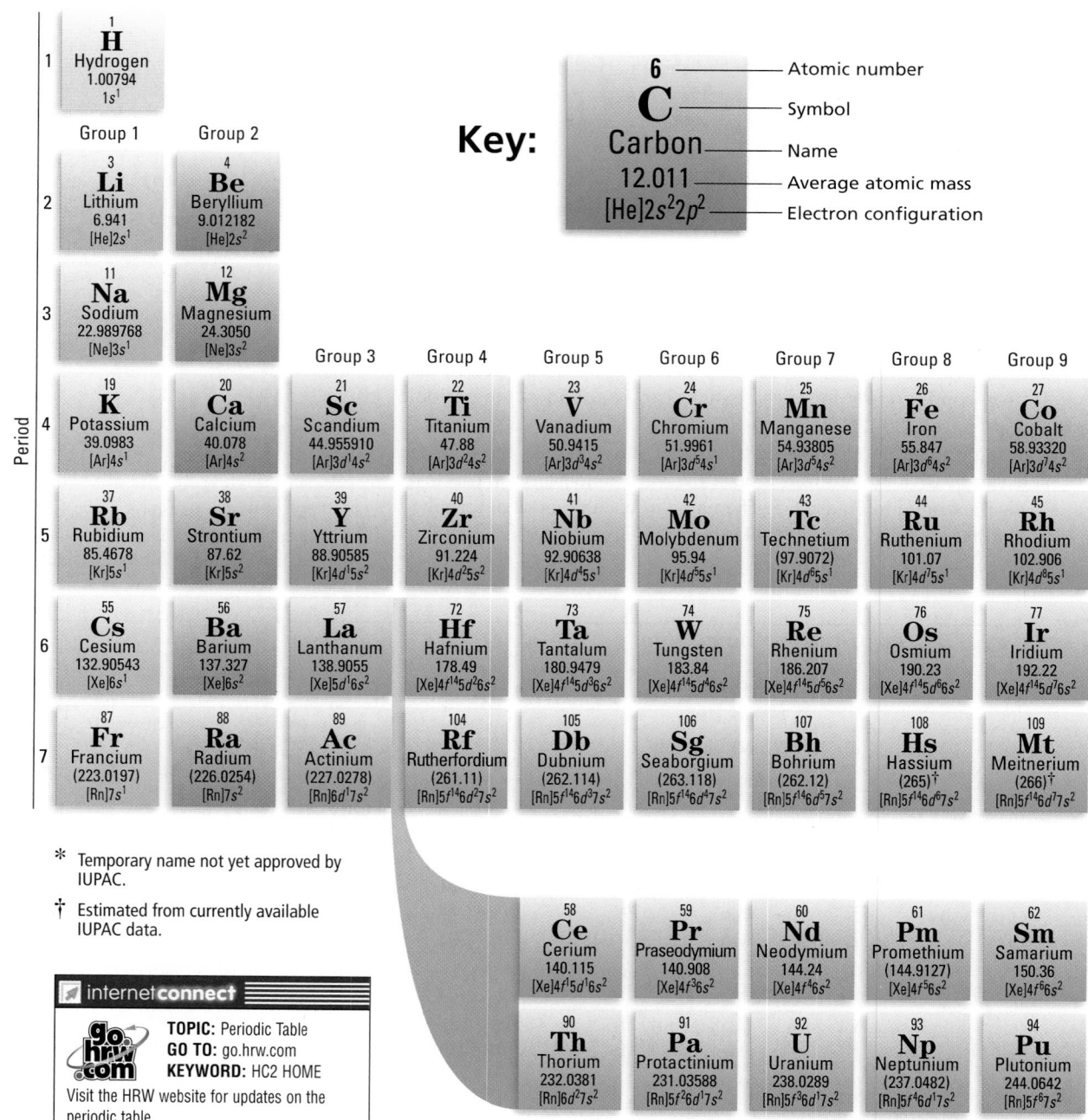

Key:

- 6 — Atomic number
- C — Symbol
- Carbon — Name
- 12.011 — Average atomic mass
- $[He]2s^2 2p^2$ — Electron configuration

* Temporary name not yet approved by IUPAC.

† Estimated from currently available IUPAC data.

FIGURE 5-6 In the common periodic table, the elements are arranged in vertical groups and in horizontal periods.

Metals

- Alkali metals
- Alkaline earth metals
- Transition metals
- Other metals

Metalloids
- Semiconductors

Nonmetals
- Halogens
- Other nonmetals
- Noble gases

HANDBOOK CONNECTION

Properties and uses of Group 1 and 2 elements are further discussed in the *Elements Handbook* (pages 728–739).

Group 18

2
He
Helium
4.002602
$1s^2$

1

Group 13 | Group 14 | Group 15 | Group 16 | Group 17

5	6	7	8	9	10
B	**C**	**N**	**O**	**F**	**Ne**
Boron	Carbon	Nitrogen	Oxygen	Fluorine	Neon
10.811	12.011	14.00674	15.9994	18.9984032	20.1797
$[He]2s^2 2p^1$	$[He]2s^2 2p^2$	$[He]2s^2 2p^3$	$[He]2s^2 2p^4$	$[He]2s^2 2p^5$	$[He]2s^2 2p^6$

2

13	14	15	16	17	18
Al	**Si**	**P**	**S**	**Cl**	**Ar**
Aluminum	Silicon	Phosphorus	Sulfur	Chlorine	Argon
26.981539	28.0855	30.9738	32.066	35.4527	39.948
$[Ne]3s^2 3p^1$	$[Ne]3s^2 3p^2$	$[Ne]3s^2 3p^3$	$[Ne]3s^2 3p^4$	$[Ne]3s^2 3p^5$	$[Ne]3s^2 3p^6$

3

Group 10 | Group 11 | Group 12

28	29	30	31	32	33	34	35	36
Ni	**Cu**	**Zn**	**Ga**	**Ge**	**As**	**Se**	**Br**	**Kr**
Nickel	Copper	Zinc	Gallium	Germanium	Arsenic	Selenium	Bromine	Krypton
58.6934	63.546	65.39	69.723	72.61	74.92159	78.96	79.904	83.80
$[Ar]3d^8 4s^2$	$[Ar]3d^{10}4s^1$	$[Ar]3d^{10}4s^2$	$[Ar]3d^{10}4s^2 4p^1$	$[Ar]3d^{10}4s^2 4p^2$	$[Ar]3d^{10}4s^2 4p^3$	$[Ar]3d^{10}4s^2 4p^4$	$[Ar]3d^{10}4s^2 4p^5$	$[Ar]3d^{10}4s^2 4p^6$

4

46	47	48	49	50	51	52	53	54
Pd	**Ag**	**Cd**	**In**	**Sn**	**Sb**	**Te**	**I**	**Xe**
Palladium	Silver	Cadmium	Indium	Tin	Antimony	Tellurium	Iodine	Xenon
106.42	107.8682	112.411	114.818	118.710	121.757	127.60	126.904	131.29
$[Kr]4d^{10}5s^0$	$[Kr]4d^{10}5s^1$	$[Kr]4d^{10}5s^2$	$[Kr]4d^{10}5s^2 5p^1$	$[Kr]4d^{10}5s^2 5p^2$	$[Kr]4d^{10}5s^2 5p^3$	$[Kr]4d^{10}5s^2 5p^4$	$[Kr]4d^{10}5s^2 5p^5$	$[Kr]4d^{10}5s^2 5p^6$

5

78	79	80	81	82	83	84	85	86
Pt	**Au**	**Hg**	**Tl**	**Pb**	**Bi**	**Po**	**At**	**Rn**
Platinum	Gold	Mercury	Thallium	Lead	Bismuth	Polonium	Astatine	Radon
195.08	196.96654	200.59	204.3833	207.2	208.98037	(208.9824)	(209.9871)	(222.0176)
$[Xe]4f^{14}5d^9 6s^1$	$[Xe]4f^{14}5d^{10}6s^1$	$[Xe]4f^{14}5d^{10}6s^2$	$[Xe]4f^{14}5d^{10}6s^2 6p^1$	$[Xe]4f^{14}5d^{10}6s^2 6p^2$	$[Xe]4f^{14}5d^{10}6s^2 6p^3$	$[Xe]4f^{14}5d^{10}6s^2 6p^4$	$[Xe]4f^{14}5d^{10}6s^2 6p^5$	$[Xe]4f^{14}5d^{10}6s^2 6p^6$

6

110	111	112	113	114	115	116	117	118
Uun*	**Uuu***	**Uub***		**Uuq***		**Uuh***		**Uuo***
Ununnilium	Unununium	Ununbium		Ununquadium		Ununhexium		Ununoctium
(269)†	(272)†	(277)†		(285)†		(289)†		(293)†
$[Rn]5f^{14}6d^9 7s^1$	$[Rn]5f^{14}6d^{10}7s^1$	$[Rn]5f^{14}6d^{10}7s^2$		$[Rn]5f^{14}6d^{10}7s^2 7p^2$		$[Rn]5f^{14}6d^{10}7s^2 7p^4$		$[Rn]5f^{14}6d^{10}7s^2 7p^6$

7

Period

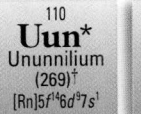

63	64	65	66	67	68	69	70	71
Eu	**Gd**	**Tb**	**Dy**	**Ho**	**Er**	**Tm**	**Yb**	**Lu**
Europium	Gadolinium	Terbium	Dysprosium	Holmium	Erbium	Thulium	Ytterbium	Lutetium
151.966	157.25	158.92534	162.50	164.930	167.26	168.93421	173.04	174.967
$[Xe]4f^7 6s^2$	$[Xe]4f^7 5d^1 6s^2$	$[Xe]4f^9 6s^2$	$[Xe]4f^{10}6s^2$	$[Xe]4f^{11}6s^2$	$[Xe]4f^{12}6s^2$	$[Xe]4f^{13}6s^2$	$[Xe]4f^{14}6s^2$	$[Xe]4f^{14}5d^1 6s^2$

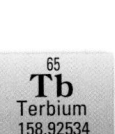
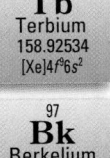

95	96	97	98	99	100	101	102	103
Am	**Cm**	**Bk**	**Cf**	**Es**	**Fm**	**Md**	**No**	**Lr**
Americium	Curium	Berkelium	Californium	Einsteinium	Fermium	Mendelevium	Nobelium	Lawrencium
(243.0614)	(247.0703)	(247.0703)	(251.0796)	(252.083)	(257.0951)	(258.10)	(259.1009)	(262.11)
$[Rn]5f^7 7s^2$	$[Rn]5f^7 6d^1 7s^2$	$[Rn]5f^9 7s^2$	$[Rn]5f^{10}7s^2$	$[Rn]5f^{11}7s^2$	$[Rn]5f^{12}7s^2$	$[Rn]5f^{13}7s^2$	$[Rn]5f^{14}7s^2$	$[Rn]5f^{14}6d^1 7s^2$

The atomic masses listed in this table reflect the precision of current measurements. (Values listed in parentheses are those of the element's most stable or most common isotope.) In calculations throughout the text, however, atomic masses have been rounded to two places to the right of the decimal.

Comparing Reactivities of Alkaline-Earth Metals

Place 10 mL of water into each of two test tubes. Add two drops of phenolphthalein to each tube. To one test tube, add a 5 cm piece of freshly sandpapered magnesium ribbon rolled into a coil. To a second test tube, add a piece of calcium about the size of half a pea. The magnesium will react very slowly, forming hydrogen gas bubbles and turning the water-phenolphthalein solution light pink. The calcium is more reactive. It will fizz and turn the water-phenolphthalein solution dark pink. The equations for these reactions are as follows:

$$Mg + 2H_2O \longrightarrow Mg(OH)_2 + H_2$$
$$Ca + 2H_2O \longrightarrow Ca(OH)_2 + H_2$$

Safety: Wear goggles and lab coat at all times.

Disposal: Combine all liquids, neutralize with 1 M HCl to a pH between 5 and 9, and pour down the drain. Solid hydroxides may be dried and put in the trash. DO NOT put Ca metal in the trash; react any that is left over with water, and then neutralize and pour down the drain.

Class Discussion

Compare the reactivity of the alkali metals with that of the alkaline-earth metals. *(The alkali metals also react with water to form hydrogen and are even more reactive than the alkaline-earth metals.)*

Did You Know?

Hydrogen and helium are the simplest and most abundant elements. Hydrogen makes up 76% of the mass of the universe, and helium makes up 23%.

(a)

(b)

FIGURE 5-7 (a) Like other alkali metals, potassium reacts so strongly with water that (b) it must be stored in kerosene or oil to prevent it from reacting with moisture in the air.

FIGURE 5-8 Calcium, an alkaline-earth metal, is too reactive to be found in nature in its pure state (a). Instead, it exists in compounds, such as in the minerals that make up marble (b).

The s-Block Elements: Groups 1 and 2

The elements of the *s* block are chemically reactive *metals*. The Group 1 metals are more reactive than those of Group 2. The outermost energy level in an atom of each Group 1 element contains a single *s* electron. For example, the configurations of lithium and sodium are $[He]2s^1$ and $[Ne]3s^1$, respectively. As you will learn in Section 5-3, the ease with which the single electron is lost helps to make the Group 1 metals extremely reactive. Using *n* for the number of the highest occupied energy level, the outer, or group, configurations of the Group 1 and 2 elements are written ns^1 and ns^2, respectively. For example, the configuration of Na is $[Ne]3s^1$, so the group configuration is written ns^1, where $n = 3$.

The elements of Group 1 of the periodic table (lithium, sodium, potassium, rubidium, cesium, and francium) are known as the **alkali metals.** In their pure state, all of the alkali metals have a silvery appearance and are soft enough to cut with a knife. However, because they are so reactive, alkali metals are not found in nature as free elements. They combine vigorously with most nonmetals. And they react strongly with water to produce hydrogen gas and aqueous solutions of substances known as alkalis. Because of their extreme reactivity with air or moisture, alkali metals are usually stored in kerosene. Proceeding down the column, the elements of Group 1 melt at successively lower temperatures.

The elements of Group 2 of the periodic table (beryllium, magnesium, calcium, strontium, barium, and radium) are called the **alkaline-earth metals.** Atoms of alkaline-earth metals contain a pair of electrons in their outermost *s* sublevel. Consequently, the group configuration for Group 2 is ns^2. The Group 2 metals are harder, denser, and stronger than the alkali metals. They also have higher melting points. Although they are less reactive than the alkali metals, the alkaline-earth metals are also too reactive to be found in nature as free elements.

Hydrogen and Helium

Before discussing the other blocks of the periodic table, let's consider two special cases in the classification of the elements—hydrogen and helium. Hydrogen has an electron configuration of $1s^1$, but despite the ns^1 configuration, it does not share the same properties as the elements

(a)   **(b)**

of Group 1. Although it is located above the Group 1 elements in many periodic tables, hydrogen is a unique element, with properties that do not closely resemble those of any group.

Like the Group 2 elements, helium has an ns^2 group configuration. Yet it is part of Group 18. Because its highest occupied energy level is filled by two electrons, helium possesses special chemical stability, exhibiting the unreactive nature of a Group 18 element. By contrast, the Group 2 metals have no special stability; their highest occupied energy levels are not filled because each metal has an empty available p sublevel.

internet connect

SCi LINKS.

NSTA

TOPIC: Alkali metals
GO TO: www.scilinks.org
*sci*LINKS CODE: HC2053

TOPIC: Alkaline-earth metals
GO TO: www.scilinks.org
*sci*LINKS CODE: HC2054

SAMPLE PROBLEM 5-1

a. **Without looking at the periodic table, give the group, period, and block in which the element with the electron configuration [Xe]$6s^2$ is located.**

b. **Without looking at the periodic table, write the electron configuration for the Group 1 element in the third period. Is this element likely to be more active or less active than the element described in (a)?**

SOLUTION

a. The element is in Group 2, as indicated by the group configuration of ns^2. It is in the sixth period, as indicated by the highest principal quantum number in its configuration, 6. The element is in the s block.

b. In a third-period element, the highest occupied energy level is the third main energy level, $n = 3$. The $1s$, $2s$, and $2p$ sublevels are completely filled (see Table 5-1). A Group 1 element has a group configuration of ns^1, which indicates a single electron in its highest s sublevel. Therefore, this element has the following configuration.

$$1s^2 2s^2 2p^6 3s^1 \quad \text{or} \quad [\text{Ne}]3s^1$$

Because it is in Group 1 (the alkali metals), this element is likely to be more reactive than the element described in (a), which is in Group 2 (the alkaline-earth metals).

PRACTICE

1. Without looking at the periodic table, give the group, period, and block in which the element with the electron configuration [Kr]$5s^1$ is located.

2. a. Without looking at the periodic table, write the group configuration for the Group 2 elements.

   b. Without looking at the periodic table, write the complete electron configuration for the Group 2 element in the fourth period.

   c. Refer to Figure 5-6 to identify the element described in (b). Then write the element's noble-gas notation.

   d. How does the reactivity of the element in (b) compare with the reactivity of the element in Group 1 of the same period?

Answer
1. Group 1, fifth period, s block

2. a. ns^2

   b. $1s^2 2s^2 2p^6 3s^2 3p^6 4s^2$

   c. Ca, [Ar]$4s^2$

   d. The element is in Group 2, so it is probably less reactive than the Group 1 element of the same period.

ADDITIONAL SAMPLE PROBLEMS

5-1 Without looking at the periodic table, give the group, period, and block in which the element with the electron configuration [Rn]$7s^1$ is located.

Ans. Group 1, seventh period, s block

5-1 a. Without looking at the periodic table, give the group, period, and block in which the element with the electron configuration [He]$2s^2$ is located.

b. How does the reactivity of the element described in (a) compare with the reactivity of the element with the electron configuration [He]$2s^1$?

Ans. **a.** Group 2, second period, s block

b. Both elements are in the same period, but the element described in (a) is in Group 2 and the element described in (b) is in Group 1. Therefore, the element in (b) is probably more reactive.

✓ **Teaching Tip**

The n in a group notation is also equal to the period number.

Properties and uses of transition metals are further discussed in the *Elements Handbook* (pages 740–749).

Visual Strategy

FIGURE 5-10 The transition elements fill *s* and *p* orbitals with electrons at the same time, which leads to the variety of oxidation states that are characteristic of transition metals. The series of 10 groups exists as a transition from the highly reactive metals to the less reactive metals.

Application

Jewelry is made from alloys of gold, silver, and platinum because of the softness of these metals in their pure state. Sterling silver is an alloy containing 7.5% copper.

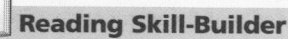
Reading Skill-Builder

SUMMARIZING As students read each passage about a group of elements, have them make connections to what they learned in Chapter 4 about quantum numbers and electron configurations. Ask for volunteers to summarize each passage for the class, including how to solve problems. Then have the class, as listeners, ask for clarification of parts of the summary. All students may consult the text during the clarification process.

FIGURE 5-9 The diagram shows the electron configuration of scandium, Sc, the Group 3 element of the third period. In general, the $(n-1)d$ sublevel in Groups 3–12 is occupied by electrons after the ns sublevel is filled.

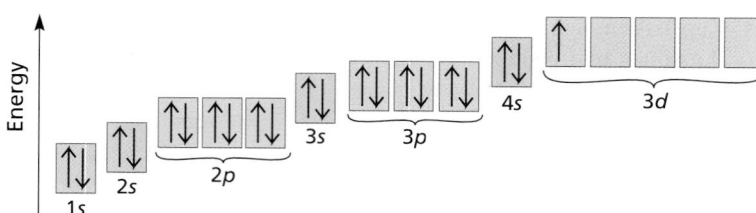

The *d*-Block Elements: Groups 3–12

For energy level n, there are n possible sublevels, so the d sublevel first appears when $n = 3$. This $3d$ sublevel is slightly higher in energy than the $4s$ sublevel, so these are filled in the order $4s3d$ (see Figure 5-9). This order of filling is also seen for higher values of n. Each d sublevel consists of five orbitals with a maximum of two electrons each, or up to 10 electrons possible in each d sublevel. In addition to the two ns electrons of Group 2, atoms of the Group 3 elements each have one electron in the d sublevel of the $(n-1)$ energy level. The group configuration for Group 3 is therefore $(n-1)d^1ns^2$. Atoms of the Group 12 elements have 10 electrons in the d sublevel plus two electrons in the ns sublevel. The group configuration for Group 12 is $(n-1)d^{10}ns^2$.

As you read in Chapter 4, some deviations from orderly d sublevel filling occur in Groups 4–11. As a result, elements in these d-block groups, unlike those in s-block and p-block groups, do not necessarily have identical outer electron configurations. For example, in Group 10, nickel, Ni, has the electron configuration $[Ar]3d^84s^2$. Palladium, Pd, has the configuration $[Kr]4d^{10}5s^0$. And platinum, Pt, has the configuration $[Xe]4f^{14}5d^96s^1$. Notice, however, that in each case the sum of the outer s and d electrons is equal to the group number.

The d-block elements are metals with typical metallic properties and are often referred to as **transition elements.** They are good conductors of electricity and have a high luster. They are typically less reactive than the alkali metals and the alkaline-earth metals. Some are so unreactive that they do not easily form compounds, existing in nature as free elements. Palladium, platinum, and gold are among the least reactive of all the elements. Some d-block elements are shown in Figure 5-10.

FIGURE 5-10 Mercury, tungsten, and vanadium are transition elements. Locate them in the d block of the periodic table on page 129.

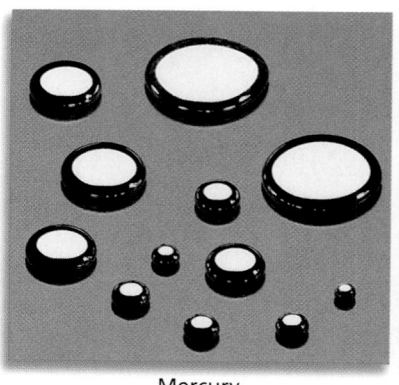
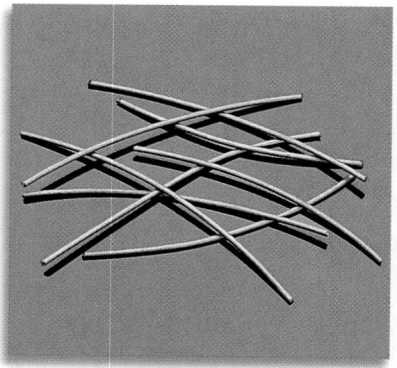

| Mercury | Tungsten | Vanadium |

CHEMICAL COMMENTARY

The Wild Kingdom

From *The Periodic Kingdom: A Journey Into the World of the Chemical Elements* by P. W. Atkins

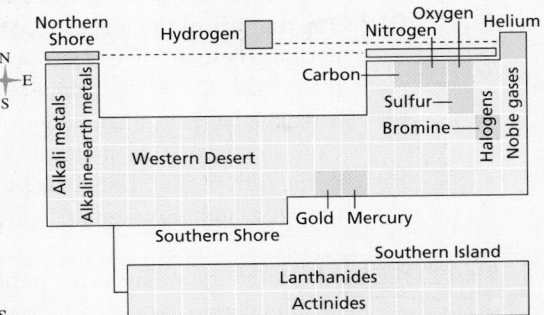

The general layout of the Periodic Kingdom.

Welcome to the Periodic Kingdom. This is a land of the imagination, but it is closer to reality than it appears to be. This is the kingdom of the chemical elements, the substances from which everything tangible is made. It is not an extensive country, for it consists of only a hundred or so regions . . . yet it accounts for everything material in our actual world. From the hundred elements that are at the center of our story, all planets, rocks, vegetation, and animals are made. These elements are the basis of the air, the oceans, and the Earth itself. We stand on the elements, we eat the elements, we *are* the elements. Because our brains are made up of elements, even our opinions are, in a sense, properties of the elements and hence inhabitants of the kingdom.

Even from . . . far above the country, we can see broad features of the landscape. There are the glittering, lustrous regions made up of metals and lying together in what we shall call the Western Desert. This desert is broadly uniform, but there is a subtlety of shades, indicating a variety of characteristics. Here and there are gentle splashes of color, such as the familiar glint of gold and the blush of copper. How remarkable it is that these desert lands make up so much

of the kingdom . . . yet the kingdom supplies such luxuriance in the real world!

Generally speaking, the Western Desert was explored and exploited from east to west; that is, technology and industry made use of them in that order. Copper displaced stone to give us the Bronze Age. Then, as the explorers pressed westward, applying ever more vigorous means of discovery, they encountered iron and used it to fabricate more effective weaponry . . . The strongest states enjoyed freedom from constant aggression, and this gave them time for scholarship; thus in due course explorers were able to penetrate into more distant western regions of the desert.

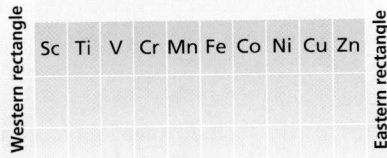

The Isthmus

Deep in the Western Desert, in an isthmuslike zone running from zinc on the east to scandium on the west, they finally stumbled upon titanium, a remarkable prize indeed. Titanium has exactly the properties that a society bent on high technology needs if it is to

take to the skies: this is a metal that is tough and resistant to corrosion, yet light, and it is typical of its part of the Western Desert. Titanium and its neighbors vanadium and molybdenum, in alliance with iron, form the durable steels that enable us to chop through stone and build on a massive scale. It is a remarkable feature of the Periodic Kingdom that the Isthmus . . . has provided so many of the workhorses of our society, and that its members so readily form alliances with one another.

Reading for Meaning

What does Atkins mean when he says that metals of the Isthmus form "alliances" with one another? What does this imply about these elements?

Read Further

Atkins remarks that titanium has properties that are well-suited for a high-tech society. Find out how we obtain titanium, and list five ways that it is used in our society.

Class Disscussion

Ask students to explain the statement "we eat the elements, we *are* the elements." Have them brainstorm to form a list of the elements found in the human body.

Did You Know?

The elements oxygen, carbon, hydrogen, and nitrogen make up 96% of the human body mass. Calcium and phosphorus make up 3%; sodium, potassium, chloride, and magnesium make up 0.7%. The trace elements include iron, cobalt, copper, zinc, iron, selenium, and fluorine. All of these elements are essential for life.

Reading for Meaning

The alliances refer to intimate mixtures of transition metals, such as that of iron with chromium, nickel, or vanadium to create alloyed steel. Other examples of alloys include bronze, brass, and pewter.

Read Further

Titanium is obtained from its natural ore via metallurgy by a process in which titanium cations are reduced to elemental titanium. Titanium is strong, has a low mass and a low density, and resists corrosion. Some of its applications include uses in high-performance jet engines and missiles. Also, because it doesn't react with living tissue, it is used to make surgical pins.

ADDITIONAL SAMPLE PROBLEM

5-2 Without looking at the periodic table, identify the period, block, and group in which the element with the electron configuration $[Ar]3d^{10}4s^1$ is located. Then consult the periodic table to identify this element and the other elements in its group.

Ans. fourth period, *d* block, Group 11; Cu; other elements: Ag, Au

✔ Teaching Tip

- Remind students that Groups 13–16 are known by the top member of each group, i.e., the boron family, carbon family, nitrogen family, and oxygen family.

- Although they are not specifically indicated by the definition given, hydrogen and helium are also considered main-group elements.

- Point out that the main-group elements have traditionally also been called the *representative elements*.

HANDBOOK CONNECTION

Properties and uses of elements in Groups 13–17 are further discussed in the *Elements Handbook* (pages 750–783).

An element has the electron configuration $[Kr]4d^55s^1$. Without looking at the periodic table, identify the period, block, and group in which this element is located. Then consult the periodic table to identify this element and the others in its group.

SOLUTION The number of the highest occupied energy level is five, so the element is in the fifth period. There are five electrons in the *d* sublevel. This means that the *d* sublevel is incompletely filled because it can hold 10 electrons. Therefore, the element is in the *d* block. For *d*-block elements, the number of electrons in the *ns* sublevel (1) plus the number of electrons in the $(n-1)d$ sublevel (5) equals the group number, 6. This is the Group 6 element in the fifth period. The element is molybdenum. The others in Group 6 are chromium, tungsten, and seaborgium.

PRACTICE

1. Without looking at the periodic table, identify the period, block, and group in which the element with the electron configuration $[Ar]3d^84s^2$ is located.

   Answer
   1. fourth period, *d* block, Group 10

2. a. Without looking at the periodic table, write the outer electron configuration for the Group 12 element in the fifth period.

   2. a. $4d^{10}5s^2$

   b. Refer to the periodic table to identify the element described in (a) and to write the element's noble-gas notation.

   b. Cd, $[Kr]4d^{10}5s^2$

The *p*-Block Elements: Groups 13–18

The *p*-block elements consist of all the elements of Groups 13–18 except helium. Electrons add to a *p* sublevel only after the *s* sublevel in the same energy level is filled. Therefore, atoms of all *p*-block elements contain two electrons in the *ns* sublevel. *The p-block elements together with the s-block elements are called the* **main-group elements.** For Group 13 elements, the added electron enters the *np* sublevel, giving a group configuration of ns^2np^1. Atoms of Group 14 elements contain two electrons in the *p* sublevel, giving ns^2np^2 for the group configuration. This pattern continues in Groups 15–18. In Group 18, the stable noble-gas configuration of ns^2np^6 is reached. The relationships among group numbers and electron configurations for all the groups are summarized in Table 5-2.

For atoms of *p*-block elements, the total number of electrons in the highest occupied level is equal to the group number minus 10. For example, bromine is in Group 17. It has $17 - 10 = 7$ electrons in its highest energy level. Because atoms of *p*-block elements contain two electrons in the *ns* sublevel, we know that bromine has five electrons in its outer *p* sublevel. The electron configuration of bromine is $[Ar]3d^{10}4s^24p^5$.

The properties of elements of the *p* block vary greatly. At its right-hand end, the *p* block includes all of the *nonmetals* except hydrogen and helium. All six of the *metalloids* (boron, silicon, germanium, arsenic,

TABLE 5-2 *Relationships Among Group Numbers, Blocks, and Electron Configurations*

Group number	Group configuration	Block	Comments
1, 2	$ns^{1,2}$	s	One or two electrons in ns sublevel
3–12	$(n-1)d^{1-10}ns^{0-2}$	d	Sum of electrons in ns and $(n-1)d$ levels equals group number
13–18	ns^2np^{1-6}	p	Number of electrons in np sublevel equals group number minus 12

antimony, and tellurium) are also in the *p* block. At the left-hand side and bottom of the block, there are eight *p*-block metals. The locations of the nonmetals, metalloids, and metals in the *p* block are shown with distinctive colors in Figure 5-6 and in the periodic table printed on the inside back cover of this textbook.

The elements of Group 17 (fluorine, chlorine, bromine, iodine, and astatine) are known as the **halogens.** The halogens are the most reactive nonmetals. They react vigorously with most metals to form examples of the type of compound known as salts. As you will see later, the reactivity of the halogens is based on the presence of seven electrons in their outer energy levels—one electron short of the stable noble-gas configuration. Fluorine and chlorine are gases at room temperature, bromine is a reddish liquid, and iodine is a dark purple solid. Astatine is a synthetic element prepared in only very small quantities. Most of its properties are estimated, although it is known to be a solid.

The metalloids, or semiconducting elements, fall on both sides of a line separating nonmetals and metals in the *p* block. They are mostly brittle solids with some properties of metals and some of nonmetals. The metalloid elements have electrical conductivity intermediate between that of metals, which are good conductors, and nonmetals, which are nonconductors.

The metals of the *p* block are generally harder and denser than the *s*-block alkaline-earth metals, but softer and less dense than the *d*-block metals. With the exception of bismuth, these metals are sufficiently reactive to be found in nature only in the form of compounds. Once obtained as free metals, however, they are stable in the presence of air.

internet**connect**

SCI*LINKS*

NSTA

TOPIC: Halogens
GO TO: www.scilinks.org
*sci***LINKS CODE:** HC2055

FIGURE 5-11 Fluorine, chlorine, bromine, and iodine are members of Group 17 of the periodic table, also known as the halogens. Locate the halogens in the *p* block of the periodic table on page 129.

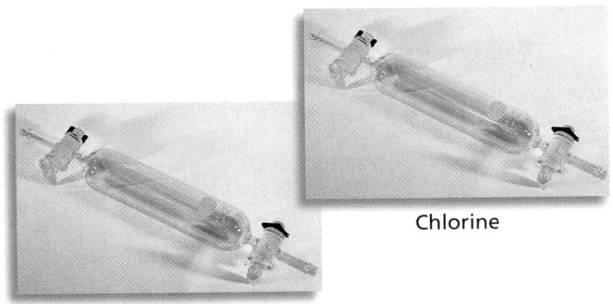

Chlorine

Fluorine

Bromine

Iodine

Table 5-2 Point out that in atoms of the *p*-block elements, the number of outer *s* and *p* electrons is equal to the last digit in the group number. Point out also that *n* represents the principal quantum number for the outermost occupied energy level. The superscripts given in this table represent the possible ranges.

✔ **Teaching Tip**

Students are generally surprised by the metallic appearance of metalloids. Emphasize that despite their similar appearances, metals are good conductors of electricity, while metalloids are semiconductors.

HANDBOOK **CONNECTION**

The chemistry of semiconductors is further discussed with Group 14 in the *Elements Handbook* (pages 754–769).

Application

Many students will recognize the term *halogen* from halogen light bulbs in cars and flashlights. Others may recognize the term *halite,* which is derived from halogen. Halite is the name given to sodium chloride found in nature.

5-3 Without referring to the periodic table, write the outer electron configuration for the Group 16 element in the third period. Then name the element and characterize it as a metal, nonmetal, or metalloid.

Ans. $3s^23p^4$; S, nonmetal

5-3 Without looking at the periodic table, identify the period, block, and group of the element with the electron configuration $[Kr]4d^{10}5s^25p^3$. Then name the element and characterize it as a metal, nonmetal, or metalloid.

Ans. fifth period, *p* block, Group 15; Sb, metalloid

Did You Know?
All members of the lanthanide series have an oxidation state of +3 in their compounds and share similar chemical properties.

CHAPTER ⟷ CONNECTION

Radioactivity and the synthesis of new elements by nuclear reactions are discussed in Chapter 22.

SAMPLE PROBLEM 5-3

Without looking at the periodic table, write the outer electron configuration for the Group 14 element in the second period. Then name the element, and identify it as a metal, non-metal, or metalloid.

SOLUTION The group number is higher than 12, so the element is in the *p* block. The total number of electrons in the highest occupied *s* and *p* sublevels is therefore equal to the group number minus ten, $14 - 10 = 4$. With two electrons in the *s* sublevel, two electrons must also be present in the 2*p* sublevel, giving an outer electron configuration of $2s^22p^2$. The element is carbon, C, which is a nonmetal.

PRACTICE

1. a. Without looking at the periodic table, write the outer electron configuration for the Group 17 element in the third period.

   b. Name the element described in (a), and identify it as a metal, nonmetal, or metalloid.

2. a. Without looking at the periodic table, identify the period, block, and group of an element with the electron configuration $[Ar]3d^{10}4s^24p^3$.

   b. Name the element described in (a), and identify it as a metal, nonmetal, or metalloid.

Answer
1. a. $3s^23p^5$

   b. chlorine, nonmetal

2. a. fourth period, *p* block, Group 15

   b. arsenic, metalloid

The *f*-Block Elements: Lanthanides and Actinides
In the periodic table, the *f*-block elements are wedged between Groups 3 and 4 in the sixth and seventh periods. Their position reflects the fact that they involve the filling of the 4*f* sublevel. With seven 4*f* orbitals to be filled with two electrons each, there are a total of 14 *f*-block elements between lanthanum, La, and hafnium, Hf, in the sixth period. The lanthanides are shiny metals similar in reactivity to the Group 2 alkaline-earth metals.

There are also 14 *f*-block elements, the actinides, between actinium, Ac, and element 104, Unq, in the seventh period. In these elements the 5*f* sublevel is being filled with 14 electrons. The actinides are all radioactive. The first four actinides (thorium, Th, through neptunium, Np) have been found naturally on Earth. The remaining actinides are known only as laboratory-made elements.

SAMPLE PROBLEM 5-4

The electron configurations of atoms of four elements are written at the top of page 139. For each element, name the block and group in the periodic table in which it is located. Then name the element by consulting the periodic table on pages 130–131. Identify each

element as a metal, nonmetal, or metalloid. Finally, describe it as likely to be of high reactivity or of low reactivity.

a. $[Xe]4f^{14}5d^9 6s^1$
b. $[Ne]3s^2 3p^5$
c. $[Ne]3s^2 3p^6$
d. $[Xe]4f^6 6s^2$

SOLUTION

a. The 4*f* sublevel is filled with 14 electrons. The 5*d* sublevel is partially filled with nine electrons. Therefore, this is a *d*-block element. The element is the transition metal platinum, Pt, which is in Group 10 and has a low reactivity.

b. The incompletely filled *p* sublevel shows this to be a *p*-block element. With a total of seven electrons in the *ns* and *np* sublevels, this is a Group 17 element, a halogen. The element is chlorine, Cl, and is highly reactive.

c. This element has a noble-gas configuration and thus is in Group 18 in the *p* block. The element is argon, Ar, an unreactive nonmetal and a noble gas.

d. The incomplete 4*f* sublevel shows that it is an *f*-block element and a lanthanide. Group numbers are not assigned to the *f* block. The element is samarium, Sm. The lanthanides are all reactive metals.

PRACTICE

1. For each of the following, identify the block, period, group, group name (where appropriate), element name, element type (metal, nonmetal, or metalloid), and relative reactivity (high or low):

a. $[He]2s^2 2p^5$
b. $[Ar]3d^{10}4s^1$
c. $[Kr]5s^1$

Answer
1. a. *p* block, second period, Group 17, halogens, fluorine, nonmetal, high reactivity
b. *d* block, fourth period, Group 11, transition elements, copper, metal, low reactivity
c. *s* block, fifth period, Group 1, alkali metals, rubidium, metal, high reactivity

SECTION REVIEW

1. Into what four blocks can the periodic table be divided to illustrate the relationship between the elements' electron configurations and their placement in the periodic table?
2. What name is given to each of the following groups of elements on the periodic table:
a. Group 1 c. Groups 3–12 e. Group 18
b. Group 2 d. Group 17
3. What are the relationships between group configuration and group number for elements in the *s*, *p*, and *d* blocks?
4. Without looking at the periodic table, write the outer electron configuration for the Group 15 element in the fourth period.
5. Without looking at the periodic table, identify the period, block, and group of the element with the electron configuration $[Ar]3d^7 4s^2$.

ADDITIONAL SAMPLE PROBLEM

5-4 For each of the following electron configurations, locate the corresponding element in the periodic table by determining its block, period, and group. Then use the periodic table to name the element and predict whether it is likely to be of high or low reactivity.

a. $[He]2s^2 2p^3$
b. $[Xe]4f^{14}5d^{10}6s^1$
c. $[Rn]7s^1$
d. $[Ar]3d^{10}4s^2 4p^5$

Ans. **a.** *p* block, second period, Group 15; nitrogen, low reactivity
b. *d* block, sixth period, Group 11; gold, low reactivity
c. *s* block, seventh period, Group 1; francium, high reactivity
d. *p* block, fourth period, Group 17; bromine, high reactivity

SECTION REVIEW

1. *s, p, d,* and *f* blocks
2. a. alkali metals
b. alkaline-earth metals
c. transition metals
d. halogens
e. noble gases
3. See Table 5-2, on page 137.
4. $3d^{10}4s^2 4p^3$
5. fourth period, *d* block, Group 9

Electron Configuration and Periodic Properties

So far, you have learned that the elements are arranged in the periodic table according to their atomic number and that there is a rough correlation between the arrangement of the elements and their electron configurations. In this section, the relationship between the periodic law and electron configurations will be further explored.

Atomic Radii

Ideally, the size of an atom is defined by the edge of its orbital. However, this boundary is fuzzy and varies under different conditions. Therefore, to estimate the size of an atom, the conditions under which the atom exists must be specified. One way to express an atom's radius is to measure the distance between the nuclei of two identical atoms that are chemically bonded together, then divide this distance by two. As illustrated in Figure 5-12, **atomic radius** *may be defined as one-half the distance between the nuclei of identical atoms that are bonded together.*

Period Trends

Figure 5-13 gives the atomic radii of the elements and Figure 5-14 presents this information graphically. Note that there is a gradual decrease in atomic radii across the second period from lithium, Li, to neon, Ne.

FIGURE 5-12 One method of determining atomic radius is to measure the distance between the nuclei of two identical atoms that are bonded together in an element or compound, then divide this distance by two. The atomic radius of a chlorine atom, for example, is 99 picometers (pm).

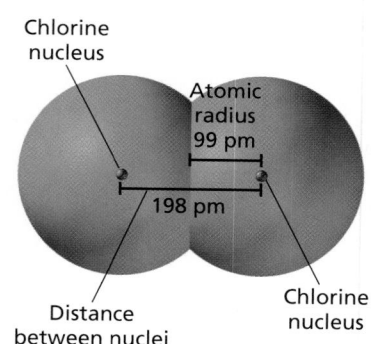

Chlorine nucleus

Atomic radius 99 pm

198 pm

Distance between nuclei

Chlorine nucleus

Periodic Table of Atomic Radii (pm)

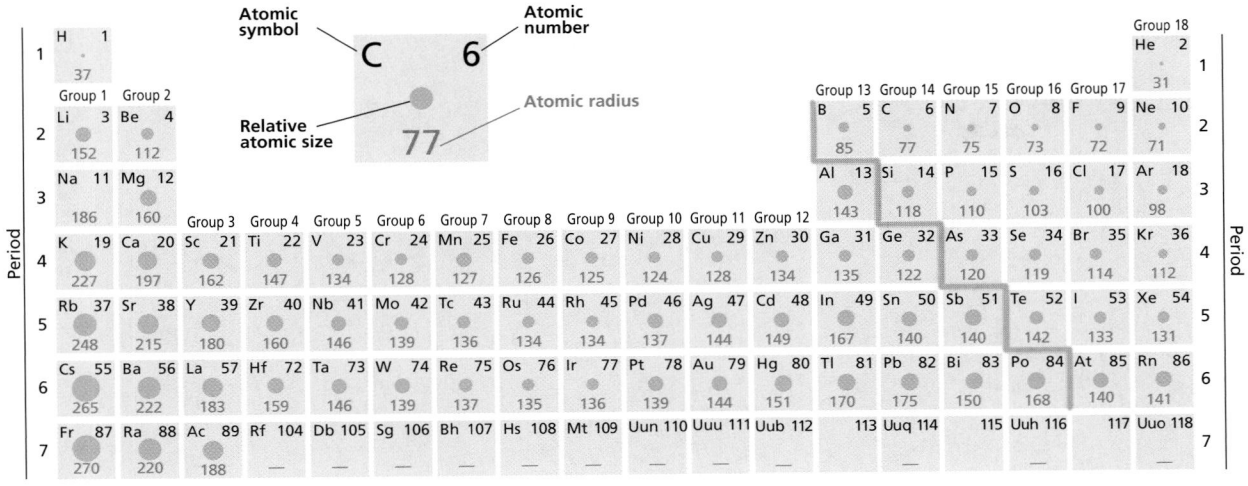

HANDBOOK   CONNECTION

Summaries of group trends for Groups 1–17 can be found in the *Elements Handbook* (pages 726–783).

CHEMISTRY INTERACTIVE TUTOR

Module 3: Periodic Properties

Topic: Atomic Radii
Sections **a, b, c,** and **d** of this engaging tutorial review and reinforce understanding of atomic radii.

FIGURE 5-13 Atomic radii decrease from left to right across a period and increase down a group.

The trend to smaller atoms across a period is caused by the increasing positive charge of the nucleus. As electrons add to *s* and *p* sublevels in the same main energy level, they are gradually pulled closer to the more highly charged nucleus. This increased pull results in a decrease in atomic radii. The attraction of the nucleus is somewhat offset by repulsion among the increased number of electrons in the same outer energy level. As a result, the difference in radii between neighboring atoms in each period grows smaller, as shown in Figure 5-13.

Group Trends
Examine the atomic radii of the Group 1 elements in Figure 5-13. Notice that the radii of the elements increase as you read down the group. As electrons occupy sublevels in successively higher main energy levels located farther from the nucleus, the sizes of the atoms increase. *In general, the atomic radii of the main-group elements increase down a group.*

Now examine the radii of the Group 13 elements. Although gallium, Ga, follows aluminum, Al, it has a slightly smaller atomic radius than does aluminum. This is because gallium, unlike aluminum, is preceded in its period by the 10 *d*-block elements. The expected increase in gallium's radius caused by the filling of the fourth main-energy level is outweighed by a shrinking of the electron cloud caused by a nuclear charge that is considerably higher than that of aluminum.

CHEMISTRY INTERACTIVE TUTOR

Module 3: Periodic Properties

ADDITIONAL

SAMPLE PROBLEMS

5-5 Which of the elements Li, Rb, K, and Na has the smallest atomic radius and which has the largest?

Ans. Li, Rb

5-5 Which of the elements O, Se, S, and Po has the smallest atomic radius and which has the largest?

Ans. O, Po

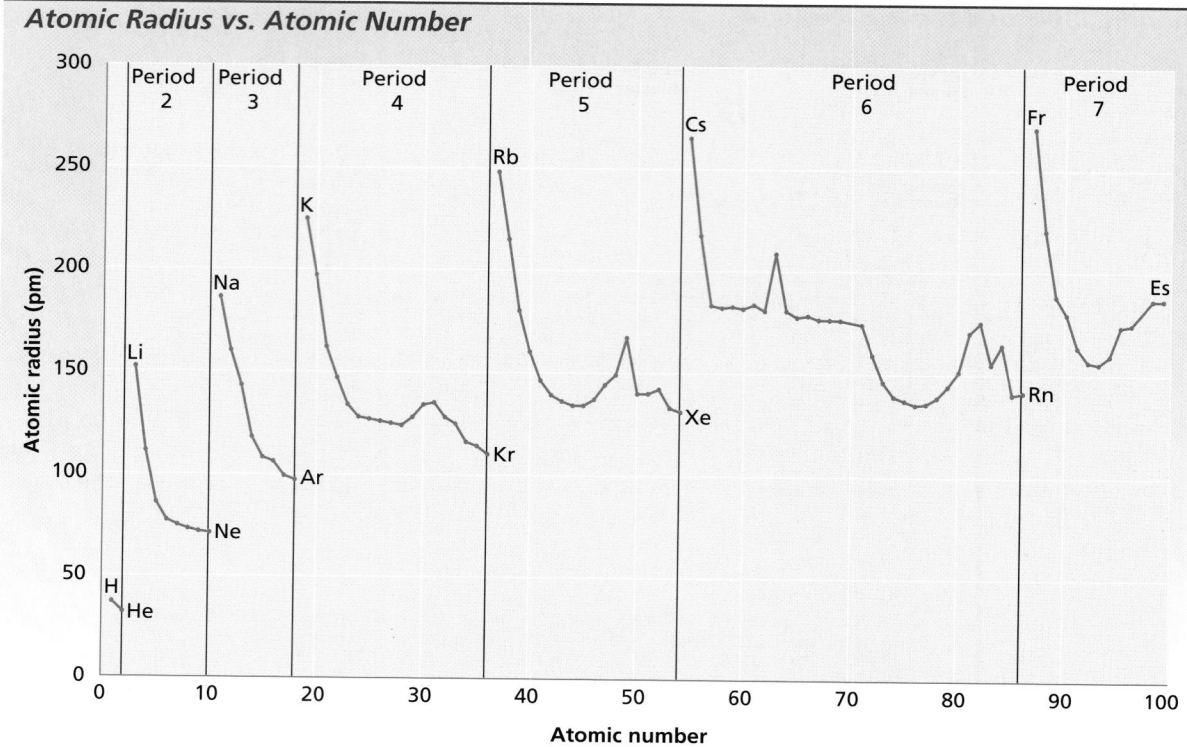

Atomic Radius vs. Atomic Number

FIGURE 5-14 The plot of atomic radius versus atomic number shows period and group trends.

SAMPLE PROBLEM 5-5

a. **Of the elements magnesium, Mg, chlorine, Cl, sodium, Na, and phosphorus, P, which has the largest atomic radius? Explain your answer in terms of trends in the periodic table.**

b. **Of the elements calcium, Ca, beryllium, Be, barium, Ba, and strontium, Sr, which has the largest atomic radius? Explain your answer in terms of trends in the periodic table.**

SOLUTION

a. All of the elements are in the third period. Of the four, sodium has the lowest atomic number and is the first element in the period. Therefore, sodium has the largest atomic radius because atomic radii decrease across a period.

b. All of the elements are in Group 2. Of the four, barium has the highest atomic number and is farthest down the group. Therefore, barium has the largest atomic radius because atomic radii increase down a group.

PRACTICE

1. Of the elements Li, O, C, and F, identify the one with the largest atomic radius and the one with the smallest atomic radius.

   Answer
   Li, F

2. Of the elements Br, At, F, I, and Cl, identify the one with the smallest atomic radius and the one with the largest atomic radius.

   Answer
   F, At

Ionization Energy

An electron can be removed from an atom if enough energy is supplied. Using A as a symbol for an atom of any element, the process can be expressed as follows.

$$A + \text{energy} \rightarrow A^{+} + e^{-}$$

The A^{+} represents an ion of element A with a single positive charge, referred to as a 1+ ion. *An* **ion** *is an atom or group of bonded atoms that has a positive or negative charge.* Sodium, for example, forms an Na^{+} ion. *Any process that results in the formation of an ion is referred to as* **ionization.**

To compare the ease with which atoms of different elements give up electrons, chemists compare ionization energies. *The energy required to remove one electron from a neutral atom of an element is the* **ionization energy, *IE*** *(or first ionization energy, IE_1).* To avoid the influence of nearby atoms, measurements of ionization energies are made on isolated atoms in the gas phase. Figure 5-15 gives the first ionization energies for the elements in kilojoules per mole (kJ/mol). Figure 5-16 presents this information graphically.

FIGURE 5-15 In general, first ionization energies increase across a period and decrease down a group.

Periodic Table of Ionization Energies (kJ/mol)

Key: 6 (Atomic number), C (Symbol), 1086 (First ionization energy)

Period	Group 1	Group 2	Group 3	Group 4	Group 5	Group 6	Group 7	Group 8	Group 9	Group 10	Group 11	Group 12	Group 13	Group 14	Group 15	Group 16	Group 17	Group 18
1	1 H 1312																	2 He 2372
2	3 Li 520	4 Be 900											5 B 801	6 C 1086	7 N 1402	8 O 1314	9 F 1681	10 Ne 2081
3	11 Na 496	12 Mg 738											13 Al 578	14 Si 787	15 P 1012	16 S 1000	17 Cl 1251	118 Ar 1521
4	19 K 419	20 Ca 590	21 Sc 633	22 Ti 659	23 V 651	24 Cr 653	25 Mn 717	26 Fe 762	27 Co 760	28 Ni 737	29 Cu 746	30 Zn 906	31 Ga 579	32 Ge 762	33 As 947	34 Se 941	35 Br 1140	36 Kr 1351
5	37 Rb 403	38 Sr 550	39 Y 600	40 Zr 640	41 Nb 652	42 Mo 684	43 Tc 702	44 Ru 710	45 Rh 720	46 Pd 804	47 Ag 731	48 Cd 868	49 In 558	50 Sn 709	51 Sb 834	52 Te 869	53 I 1008	54 Xe 1170
6	55 Cs 376	56 Ba 503	57 La 538	72 Hf 659	73 Ta 761	74 W 770	75 Re 760	76 Os 839	77 Ir 878	78 Pt 868	79 Au 890	80 Hg 1007	81 Tl 589	82 Pb 716	83 Bi 703	84 Po 812	85 At —	86 Rn 1038
7	87 Fr —	88 Ra 509	89 Ac 490	104 Rf —	105 Db —	106 Sg —	107 Bh —	108 Hs —	109 Mt —	110 Uun —	111 Uuu —	112 Uub —	113	114 Uuq —	115	116 Uuh —	117	118 Uuo —

Series														
Lanthanide series	58 Ce 534	59 Pr 527	60 Nd 533	61 Pm 536	62 Sm 545	63 Eu 547	64 Gd 592	65 Tb 566	66 Dy 573	67 Ho 581	68 Er 589	69 Tm 597	70 Yb 603	71 Lu 523
Actinide series	90 Th 587	91 Pa 570	92 U 598	93 Np 600	94 Pu 585	95 Am 578	96 Cm 581	97 Bk 601	98 Cf 608	99 Es 619	100 Fm 627	101 Md 635	102 No 642	103 Lr —

Common Misconception

Make sure students understand that ionization energy concerns only the *loss* of electrons. Students may be confused by the way in which electron loss is represented ($A + \text{energy} \longrightarrow A^{+} + e^{-}$) because the electron appears to be added on the right side of the equation—especially because ions can have positive and negative charges.

Also, many students mistakenly think atoms should become more negative (like on a number line) as they lose electrons. List the number of protons and electrons for some atoms and their accompanying ions. Show how the charges add to give a neutral or charged particle.

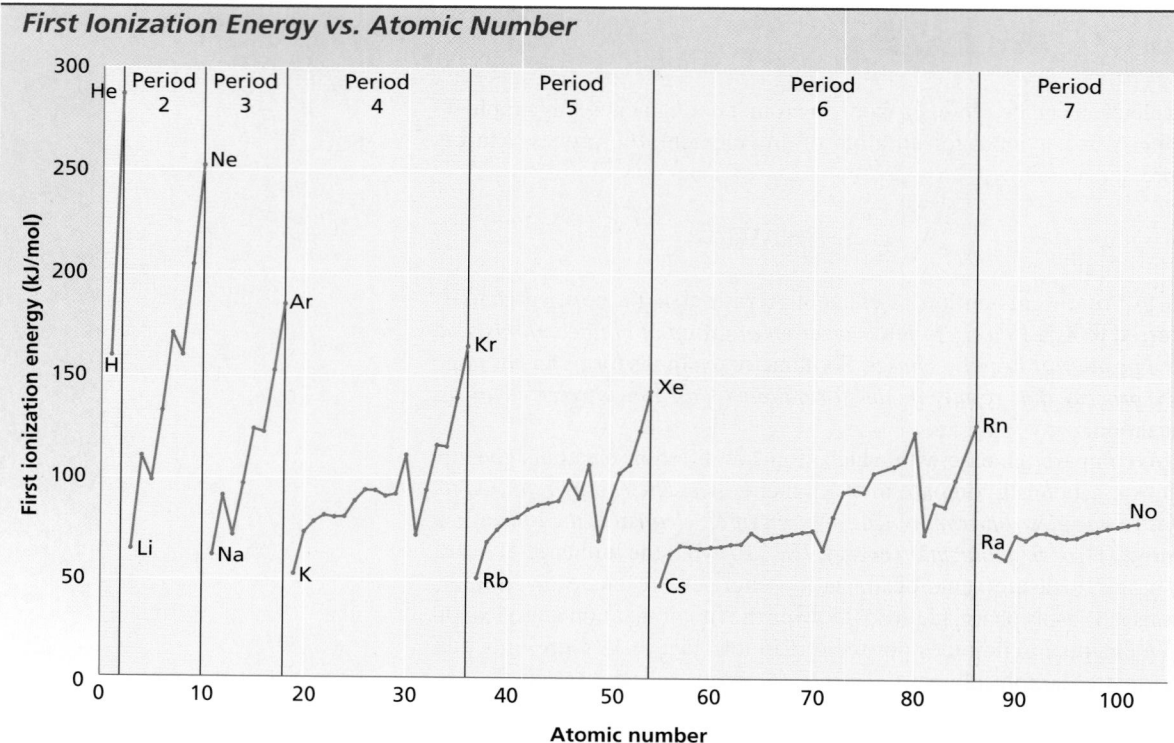

First Ionization Energy vs. Atomic Number

FIGURE 5-16 Plot of first ionization energy, IE_1, versus atomic number. As atomic number increases, both the period and the group trends become less pronounced.

Period Trends

In Figures 5-15 and 5-16, examine the ionization energies for the first and last elements in each period. You can see that the Group 1 metals have the lowest first ionization energies in their respective periods. Therefore, they lose electrons most easily. This ease of electron loss is a major reason for the high reactivity of the Group 1 (alkali) metals. The Group 18 elements, the noble gases, have the highest ionization energies. They do not lose electrons easily. The low reactivity of the noble gases is partly based on this difficulty of electron removal.

In general, ionization energies of the main-group elements increase across each period. This increase is caused by increasing nuclear charge. A higher charge more strongly attracts electrons in the same energy level. Increasing nuclear charge is responsible for both increasing ionization energy and decreasing radii across the periods. Note that, in general, nonmetals have higher ionization energies than metals do. In each period, the element of Group 1 has the lowest ionization energy and the element of Group 18 has the highest ionization energy.

Group Trends

Among the main-group elements, ionization energies generally decrease down the groups. Electrons removed from atoms of each succeeding element in a group are in higher energy levels, farther from the nucleus. Therefore, they are removed more easily. Also, as atomic number increases going down a group, more electrons lie between the nucleus and the electrons in the highest occupied energy levels. This partially shields the outer electrons from the effect of the nuclear charge. Together, these influences overcome the attraction of the electrons to the increasing nuclear charge.

Removing Electrons from Positive Ions

With sufficient energy, electrons can be removed from positive ions as well as from neutral atoms. The energies for removal of additional electrons from an atom are referred to as *the second ionization energy* (IE_2), *third ionization energy* (IE_3), and so on.

Table 5-3 shows the first five ionization energies for the elements of the first, second, and third periods. You can see that the second ionization energy is always higher than the first, the third is always higher than the second, and so on. This is because as electrons are removed in successive ionizations, fewer electrons remain within the atom to shield the attractive force of the nucleus. *Thus, each successive electron removed from an ion feels an increasingly stronger effective nuclear charge (the nuclear charge minus the electron shielding).*

The first ionization energies in Table 5-3 show that removing a single electron from an atom of a Group 18 element is more difficult than removing an electron from atoms of other elements in the same period. This special stability of the noble-gas configuration also applies to ions that have noble-gas configurations. Notice in Table 5-3 the large increases between the first and second ionization energies of lithium, Li, and between the second and third ionization energies of beryllium, Be. Even larger increases in ionization energy exist between the third and

TABLE 5-3 *Ionization Energies (in kJ/mol) for Elements of Periods 1–3*

	Period 1		Period 2							
	H	He	Li	Be	B	C	N	O	F	Ne
IE_1	1312	2372	520	900	801	1086	1402	1314	1681	2081
IE_2		5250	7298	1757	2427	2353	2856	3388	3374	3952
IE_3			11 815	14 849	3660	4621	4578	5300	6050	6122
IE_4				21 007	25 026	6223	7475	7469	8408	9370
IE_5					32 827	37 830	9445	10 990	11 023	12 178
	Period 3									
			Na	Mg	Al	Si	P	S	Cl	Ar
IE_1			496	738	578	787	1012	1000	1251	1521
IE_2			4562	1451	1817	1577	1903	2251	2297	2666
IE_3			6912	7733	2745	3232	2912	3361	3822	3931
IE_4			9544	10 540	11 578	4356	4957	4564	5158	5771
IE_5			13 353	13 628	14 831	16 091	6274	7013	6540	7238

5-6 In each of the following pairs of elements, choose the element that has the higher first ionization energy.

a. Ca and Ba
b. Ca and Br
c. Ca and K
d. Ca and Mg

Ans. **a.** Ca **b.** Br **c.** Ca **d.** Mg

5-6 State in words the general trends in ionization energies down a group and across a period of the periodic table.

Ans. In general, ionization energies increase across a period and decrease down a group.

fourth ionization energies of boron, B, and between the fourth and fifth ionization energies of carbon, C. In each case, the jump in ionization energy occurs when an ion assumes a noble-gas configuration. For example, the removal of one electron from a lithium atom ($[He]2s^1$) leaves the helium noble-gas configuration. The removal of four electrons from a carbon atom ($[He]2s^22p^2$) also leaves the helium configuration. A bigger table would show that this trend continues across the entire periodic system.

SAMPLE PROBLEM 5-6

Consider two main-group elements A and B. Element A has a first ionization energy of 419 kJ/mol. Element B has a first ionization energy of 1000 kJ/mol. For each element, decide if it is more likely to be in the s block or p block. Which element is more likely to form a positive ion?

SOLUTION

Element A has a very low ionization energy, meaning that atoms of A lose electrons easily. Therefore, element A is most likely to be a metal of the s block because ionization energies increase across the periods. Element B has a very high ionization energy, meaning that atoms of B lose electrons with difficulty. We would expect element B to lie at the end of a period in the p block. Element A is more likely to form a positive ion because it has a much lower ionization energy than does element B.

PRACTICE

1. Consider the four hypothetical main-group elements Q, R, T, and X with the outer electron configurations indicated below. Then answer the questions that follow.

Q: $3s^23p^5$ R: $3s^1$ T: $4d^{10}5s^25p^5$ X: $4d^{10}5s^25p^1$

a. Identify the block location of each hypothetical main-group element.

b. Which of these elements are in the same period? Which are in the same group?

c. Which element would you expect to have the highest first ionization energy? Which would have the lowest first ionization energy?

d. Which element would you expect to have the highest second ionization energy?

e. Which of the elements is most likely to form a 1+ ion?

Answer

1. a. Q is in the p block, R is in the s block, T is in the p block, and X is in the p block.

b. Q and R, and X and T are in the same period. Q and T are in the same group.

c. Q would have the highest ionization energy, and R would have the lowest.

d. R

e. R

Electron Affinity

Neutral atoms can also acquire electrons. *The energy change that occurs when an electron is acquired by a neutral atom is called the atom's* **electron affinity.** Most atoms release energy when they acquire an electron.

$$A + e^- \longrightarrow A^- + \text{energy}$$

In this book, the quantity of energy released is represented by a negative number. On the other hand, some atoms must be "forced" to gain an electron by the addition of energy.

$$A + e^- + \text{energy} \longrightarrow A^-$$

The quantity of energy absorbed is represented by a positive number. An ion produced in this way will be unstable and will lose the added electron spontaneously.

Figure 5-17 shows the electron affinity in kilojoules per mole for the elements. Figure 5-18 presents these data graphically.

Period Trends

Among the elements of each period, the halogens (Group 17) gain electrons most readily. This is indicated in Figure 5-17 by the large negative values of halogens' electron affinities. The ease with which halogen atoms gain electrons is a major reason for the high reactivities of the Group 17 elements. In general, as electrons add to the same p sublevel of atoms with increasing nuclear charge, electron affinities become more negative across each period within the p block. An exception to this trend occurs between Groups 14 and 15. Compare the electron affinities of carbon ($[He]2s^22p^2$) and nitrogen ($[He]2s^22p^3$). Adding an electron to a carbon atom gives a half-filled p sublevel. This occurs much more easily

Module 3: Periodic Properties

FIGURE 5-17 The values listed in parentheses in this periodic table of electron affinities are approximate. Electron affinity is estimated to be −50 kJ/mol for each of the lanthanides and 0 kJ/mol for each of the actinides.

Periodic Table of Electron Affinities (kJ/mol)

Group 1	Group 2											Group 13	Group 14	Group 15	Group 16	Group 17	Group 18
1 **H** −75.4																	2 **He** (0)
3 **Li** −61.8	4 **Be** (0)											5 **B** −27.7	6 **C** −126.3	7 **N** (0)	8 **O** −146.1	9 **F** −339.9	10 **Ne** (0)
11 **Na** −54.8	12 **Mg** (0)	Group 3	Group 4	Group 5	Group 6	Group 7	Group 8	Group 9	Group 10	Group 11	Group 12	13 **Al** −44.1	14 **Si** −138.5	15 **P** −74.6	16 **S** −207.7	17 **Cl** −361.7	18 **Ar** (0)
19 **K** −50.1	20 **Ca** (0)	21 **Sc** −18.8	22 **Ti** −7.9	23 **V** −52.5	24 **Cr** −66.6	25 **Mn** (0)	26 **Fe** −16.3	27 **Co** −66.1	28 **Ni** −115.6	29 **Cu** −122.8	30 **Zn** (0)	31 **Ga** −30	32 **Ge** −135	33 **As** −81	34 **Se** −202.1	35 **Br** −336.5	36 **Kr** (0)
37 **Rb** −48.6	38 **Sr** (0)	39 **Y** −30.7	40 **Zr** −42.6	41 **Nb** −89.3	42 **Mo** −74.6	43 **Tc** −55	44 **Ru** −105	45 **Rh** −113.7	46 **Pd** −55.7	47 **Ag** −130.2	48 **Cd** (0)	49 **In** −30	50 **Sn** −120	51 **Sb** −107	52 **Te** −197.1	53 **I** −305.9	54 **Xe** (0)
55 **Cs** −47.2	56 **Ba** (0)	57 **La** −50	72 **Hf** (0)	73 **Ta** −32.2	74 **W** −81.5	75 **Re** −15	76 **Os** −110	77 **Ir** −156.5	78 **Pt** −212.8	79 **Au** −230.9	80 **Hg** (0)	81 **Tl** −20	82 **Pb** −36	83 **Bi** −94.6	84 **Po** −190	85 **At** −280	86 **Rn** (0)
87 **Fr** −47.0	88 **Ra** (0)	89 **Ac** —	104 **Rf** —	105 **Db** —	106 **Sg** —	107 **Bh** —	108 **Hs** —	109 **Mt** —	110 **Uun** —	111 **Uuu** —	112 **Uub** —	113	114 **Uuq** —	115	116 **Uuh** —	117	118 **Uuo** —

Atomic number

6

C

−126.3

Symbol

Electron affinity

✔ Teaching Tip

To help students understand positive and negative electron affinities, use the analogy of buying and selling. Those atoms that really need another electron to complete an octet (for example, Cl) will pay a lot for it (or expend a large amount of energy). Atoms that don't need another electron but that have space in their orbital (such as Na) would only pay a small amount. Atoms that already have a small amount of stability in their filled *s* sublevel (such as Mg) and those with total stability (such as Ne) would expect to be paid to take on another electron.

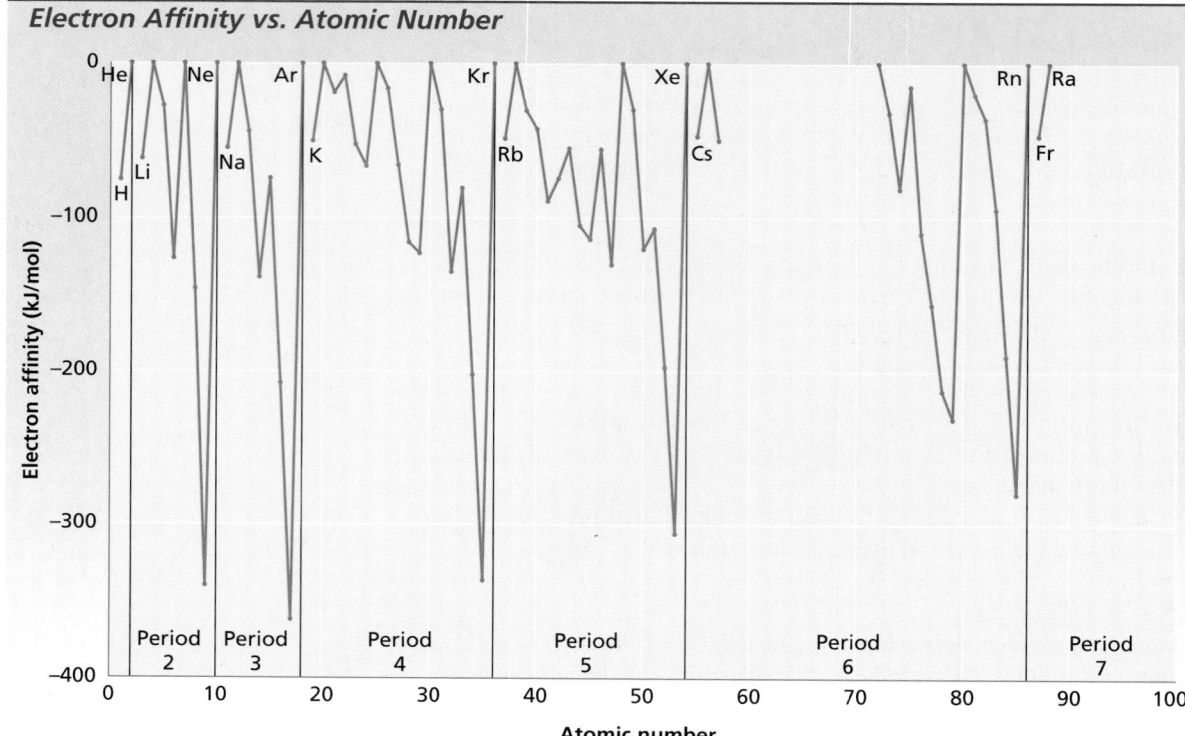

Electron Affinity vs. Atomic Number

FIGURE 5-18 The plot of electron affinity versus atomic number shows that most atoms release energy when they acquire an electron, as indicated by negative values.

than forcing an electron to pair with another electron in an orbital of the already half-filled *p* sublevel of a nitrogen atom.

Group Trends

Trends for electron affinities within groups are not as regular as trends for ionization energies. As a general rule, electrons add with greater difficulty down a group. This pattern is a result of two competing factors. The first is a slight increase in effective nuclear charge down a group, which increases electron affinities. The second is an increase in atomic radius down a group, which decreases electron affinities. In general, the size effect predominates. But there are exceptions, especially among the heavy transition metals, which tend to be the same size or even decrease in radius down a group.

Adding Electrons to Negative Ions

For an isolated ion in the gas phase, it is always more difficult to add a second electron to an already negatively charged ion. Therefore, second electron affinities are all positive. Certain *p*-block nonmetals tend to form negative ions that have noble gas configurations. The halogens do so by adding one electron. For example, chlorine has the configuration $[Ne]3s^23p^5$. An atom of chlorine achieves the configuration of the noble gas argon by adding an electron to form the ion Cl^- ($[Ne]3s^23p^6$). Adding another electron is so difficult that Cl^{2-} never occurs. Atoms of

Group 16 elements are present in many compounds as 2– ions. For example, oxygen ([He]$2s^2 2p^4$) achieves the configuration of the noble gas neon by adding two electrons to form the ion O^{2-}([He]$2s^2 2p^6$). Nitrogen achieves a neon configuration by adding three electrons to form the ion N^{3-}.

Ionic Radii

Module 3: Periodic Properties

Figure 5-19 shows the radii of some of the most common ions of the elements. Positive and negative ions have specific names.

A positive ion is known as a **cation.** The formation of a cation by the loss of one or more electrons always leads to a decrease in atomic radius because the removal of the highest-energy-level electrons results in a smaller electron cloud. Also, the remaining electrons are drawn closer to the nucleus by its unbalanced positive charge.

A negative ion is known as an **anion.** The formation of an anion by the addition of one or more electrons always leads to an increase in atomic radius. This is because the total positive charge of the nucleus remains unchanged when an electron is added to an atom or an ion. So the electrons are not drawn to the nucleus as strongly as they were before the addition of the extra electron. The electron cloud also spreads out because of greater repulsion between the increased number of electrons.

Period Trends

Within each period of the periodic table, the metals at the left tend to form cations and the nonmetals at the upper right tend to form anions. Cationic radii decrease across a period because the electron cloud shrinks due to the increasing nuclear charge acting on the electrons in

FIGURE 5-19 The ionic radii of the ions most common in chemical compounds are shown. Cations are smaller and anions are larger than the atoms from which they are formed.

Module 3: Periodic Properties

Topic: Ionic Radii
Sections **e, f, g,** and **h** of this engaging tutorial review and reinforce understanding of ionic radii.

Periodic Table of Ionic Radii (pm)

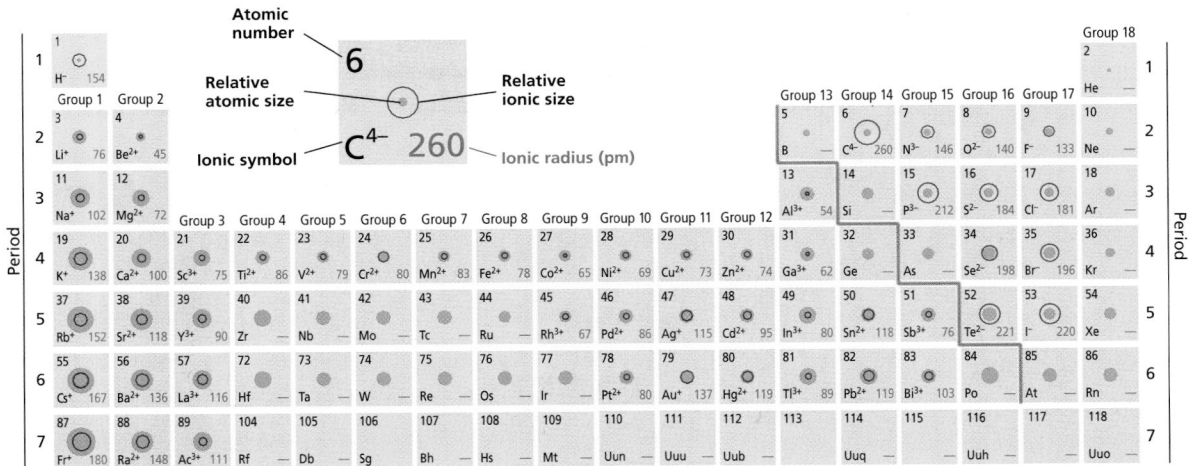

CHAPTER ⟷ **CONNECTION**

Students will learn more about valence electrons and bond formation in Chapter 6.

✔ Teaching Tip

To help students identify valence electrons in electron configurations, have them underline the largest Arabic numeral as often as it occurs and then add the superscripts together. For example, the electron configuration for Cl would have two underlined terms: $1s^2 2s^2 2p^6 \underline{3s^2} \underline{3p^5}$. The number of valence electrons is $2 + 5$, or 7. Calcium's electron configuration has 1 underlined term: $1s^2 2s^2 2p^6 3s^2 3p^6 \underline{4s^2}$. There are two valence electrons.

TABLE STRATEGY

Table 5-4 As students study the table, have them focus on the reactivity or stability of the elements in relation to the elements' positions in the periodic table. Ask why elements in the same group tend to react similarly. *(They have the same valence electron configuration.)* Also, point out to students that for an element in the *s*-block or the *p*-block (Group 1, 2, or 13–18), the number of valence electrons is equal to the sum of the superscripts in the element's group configuration.

the same main energy level. Starting with Group 15, in which atoms assume stable noble-gas configurations by gaining three electrons, anions are more common than cations. Anionic radii decrease across each period for the elements in Groups 15–18. The reasons for this trend are the same as the reasons that cationic radii decrease from left to right across a period.

Group Trends

As they are in atoms, the outer electrons in both cations and anions are in higher energy levels as one reads down a group. Therefore, just as there is a gradual increase of atomic radii down a group, there is also a gradual increase of ionic radii.

Valence Electrons

Chemical compounds form because electrons are lost, gained, or shared between atoms. The electrons that interact in this manner are those in the highest energy levels. These are the electrons most subject to the influence of nearby atoms or ions. *The electrons available to be lost, gained, or shared in the formation of chemical compounds are referred to as* **valence electrons.** Valence electrons are often located in incompletely filled main-energy levels. For example, the electron lost from the $3s$ sublevel of Na to form Na^+ is a valence electron.

For main-group elements, the valence electrons are the electrons in the outermost s and p sublevels. The inner electrons are in filled energy levels and are held too tightly by the nucleus to be involved in compound formation. The Group 1 and Group 2 elements have one and two valence electrons, respectively, as shown in Table 5-4. The elements of Groups 13–18 have a number of valence electrons equal to the group number minus 10. In some cases, both the s and p sublevel valence electrons of the p-block elements are involved in compound formation. In other cases, only the electrons from the p sublevel are involved.

TABLE 5-4	*Valence Electrons in Main-Group Elements*	
Group number	**Group configuration**	**Number of valence electrons**
1	ns^1	1
2	ns^2	2
13	$ns^2 p^1$	3
14	$ns^2 p^2$	4
15	$ns^2 p^3$	5
16	$ns^2 p^4$	6
17	$ns^2 p^5$	7
18	$ns^2 p^6$	8

Electronegativity

Valence electrons hold atoms together in chemical compounds. In many compounds, the negative charge of the valence electrons is concentrated closer to one atom than to another. This uneven concentration of charge has a significant effect on the chemical properties of a compound. It is therefore useful to have a measure of how strongly one atom attracts the electrons of another atom within a compound.

Linus Pauling, one of America's most famous chemists, devised a scale of numerical values reflecting the tendency of an atom to attract electrons. **Electronegativity** *is a measure of the ability of an atom in a chemical compound to attract electrons.* The most electronegative element, fluorine, is arbitrarily assigned an electronegativity value of four. Values for the other elements are then calculated in relation to this value.

Period Trends

As shown in Figure 5–20, electronegativities tend to increase across each period, although there are exceptions. The alkali and alkaline-earth metals are the least electronegative elements. In compounds, their atoms have a low attraction for electrons. Nitrogen, oxygen, and the halogens are the most electronegative elements. Their atoms attract electrons strongly in compounds. *Electronegativities tend to either decrease down a group or*

FIGURE 5-20 Shown are the electronegativities of the elements according to the Pauling scale. The most-electronegative elements are located in the upper right of the *p* block. The least-electronegative elements are located in the lower left of the *s* block.

Periodic Table of Electronegativities

Key: 6 — Atomic number; C — Symbol; 2.5 — Electronegativity

Period	Group 1	Group 2	Group 3	Group 4	Group 5	Group 6	Group 7	Group 8	Group 9	Group 10	Group 11	Group 12	Group 13	Group 14	Group 15	Group 16	Group 17	Group 18
1	1 H 2.1																	2 He —
2	3 Li 1.0	4 Be 1.5											5 B 2.0	6 C 2.5	7 N 3.0	8 O 3.5	9 F 4.0	10 Ne —
3	11 Na 0.9	12 Mg 1.2											13 Al 1.5	14 Si 1.8	15 P 2.1	16 S 2.5	17 Cl 3.0	118 Ar —
4	19 K 0.8	20 Ca 1.0	21 Sc 1.3	22 Ti 1.5	23 V 1.6	24 Cr 1.6	25 Mn 1.5	26 Fe 1.8	27 Co 1.8	28 Ni 1.8	29 Cu 1.9	30 Zn 1.6	31 Ga 1.6	32 Ge 1.8	33 As 2.0	34 Se 2.4	35 Br 2.8	36 Kr 3.0
5	37 Rb 0.8	38 Sr 1.0	39 Y 1.2	40 Zr 1.4	41 Nb 1.6	42 Mo 1.8	43 Tc 1.9	44 Ru 2.2	45 Rh 2.2	46 Pd 2.2	47 Ag 1.9	48 Cd 1.7	49 In 1.7	50 Sn 1.8	51 Sb 1.9	52 Te 2.1	53 I 2.5	54 Xe 2.6
6	55 Cs 0.7	56 Ba 0.9	57 La 1.1	72 Hf 1.3	73 Ta 1.5	74 W 1.7	75 Re 1.9	76 Os 2.2	77 Ir 2.2	78 Pt 2.2	79 Au 2.4	80 Hg 1.9	81 Tl 1.8	82 Pb 1.8	83 Bi 1.9	84 Po 2.0	85 At 2.2	86 Rn 2.4
7	87 Fr 0.7	88 Ra 0.9	89 Ac 1.1	104 Rf —	105 Db —	106 Sg —	107 Bh —	108 Hs —	109 Mt —	110 Uun —	111 Uuu —	112 Uub —	113	114 Uuq —	115	116 Uuh —	117	118 Uuo —

Lanthanide series													
58 Ce 1.1	59 Pr 1.1	60 Nd 1.1	61 Pm 1.1	62 Sm 1.2	63 Eu 1.1	64 Gd 1.2	65 Tb 1.1	66 Dy 1.2	67 Ho 1.2	68 Er 1.2	69 Tm 1.3	70 Yb 1.1	71 Lu 1.3

Actinide series													
90 Th 1.3	91 Pa 1.5	92 U 1.4	93 Np 1.4	94 Pu 1.3	95 Am 1.3	96 Cm 1.3	97 Bk 1.3	98 Cf 1.3	99 Es 1.3	100 Fm 1.3	101 Md 1.3	102 No 1.3	103 Lr —

✔ Teaching Tip

Note that electronegativity is a property of atoms in compounds and thus differs from ionization energy and electron affinity, which are properties of isolated atoms.

Did You Know?

- In general, metals are less electronegative than nonmetals.
- Electronegativity can also be related to the size of the atom. The smaller the atom in a family, the greater its electronegativity. A small atom has a stronger force of attraction for its own electrons and for other atoms' electrons.

Visual Strategy

FIGURE 5-20 Have students compare Figure 5-20 with Figure 5-17. What general trends do they observe? *(Electronegativity follows the same periodic trend as electron affinity: values generally decrease or remain about the same down a group and, with some exceptions, increase across a period.)*

5-7 Explain why elements with high electron affinities are also the most electronegative.

Ans. Electron affinity and electronegativity measure an atom's ability to attract electrons—both its own (electron affinity) and those of other atoms (electronegativity).

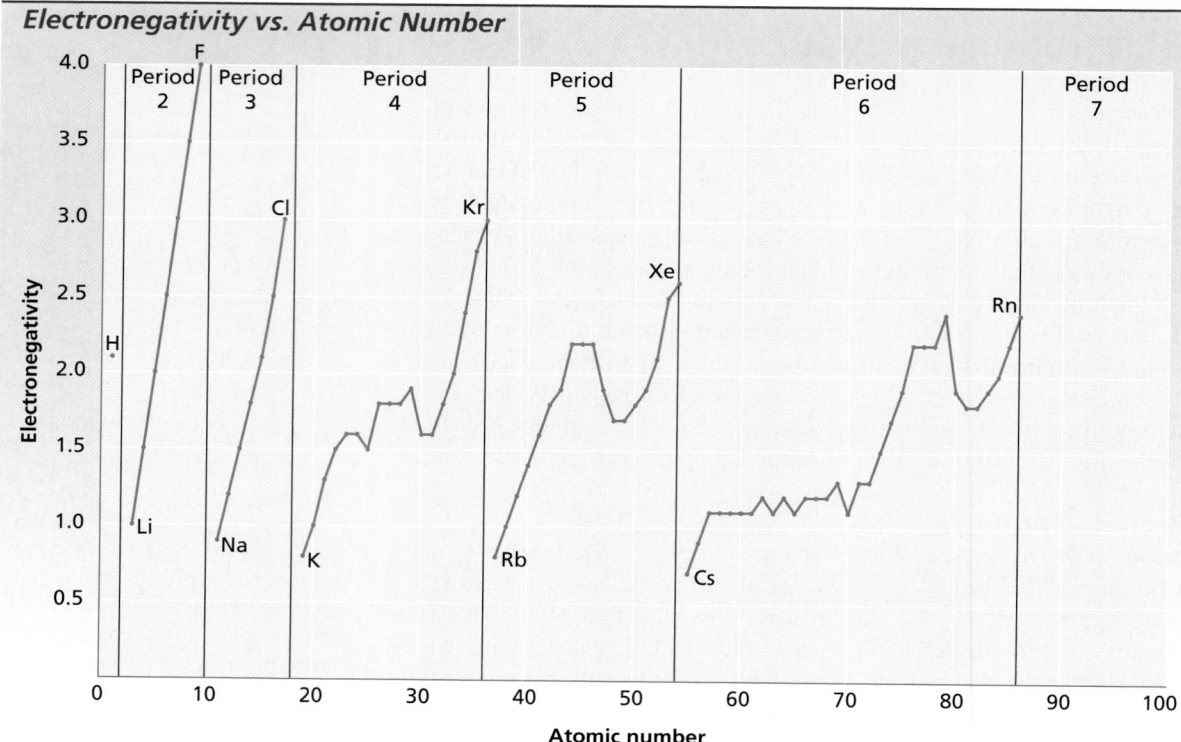

Electronegativity vs. Atomic Number

FIGURE 5-21 The plot shows electronegativity versus atomic number for Periods 1–6.

remain about the same. The noble gases are unusual in that some of them do not form compounds and therefore cannot be assigned electronegativities. When a noble gas does form a compound, its electronegativity is rather high, similar to the values for the halogens. The combination of the period and group trends in electronegativity results in the highest values belonging to the elements in the upper right of the periodic table. The lowest values belong to the elements in the lower left of the table. These trends are shown graphically in Figure 5-21.

SAMPLE PROBLEM 5-7

Among the elements gallium, Ga, bromine, Br, and calcium, Ca, which has the highest electronegativity? Explain why in terms of periodic trends.

SOLUTION

The elements are all in the fourth period. Bromine has the highest atomic number and is farthest to the right in the period. Therefore, it should have the highest electronegativity because electronegativity increases across the periods.

PRACTICE

1. Consider the five hypothetical main-group elements E, G, J, L, and M with the outer electron configurations shown at the top of page 153.

$$E = 2s^2 2p^5 \quad G = 4d^{10} 5s^2 5p^5 \quad J = 2s^2 2p^2$$
$$L = 5d^{10} 6s^2 6p^5 \quad M = 2s^2 2p^4$$

a. Identify the block location for each element. Then determine which elements are in the same period and which are in the same group.

b. Which element would you expect to have the highest electron affinity? Which would you expect to form a 1– ion? Which should have the highest electronegativity?

c. Compare the ionic radius of the typical ion formed by the element G with the radius of its neutral atom.

d. Which element(s) contains seven valence electrons?

Answer

1. a. All are in the *p* block. E, J, and M are in the same period, and E, G, and L are in the same group.

b. E should have the highest electron affinity; E, G, and L are most likely to form 1– ions; E should have the highest electronegativity.

c. The ionic radius would be larger.

d. E, G, and L

Periodic Properties of the *d-* and *f-*Block Elements

The properties of the *d*-block elements (which are all metals) vary less and with less regularity than those of the main-group elements. This trend is indicated by the curves in Figures 5-14 and 5-16, which flatten where the *d*-block elements fall in the middle of Periods 4–6.

Recall that atoms of the *d*-block elements contain from zero to two electrons in the *s* orbital of their highest occupied energy level and one to ten electrons in the *d* sublevel of the next-lower energy level. Therefore, electrons in both the *ns* sublevel and the $(n - 1)d$ sublevel are available to interact with their surroundings. As a result, electrons in the incompletely filled *d* sublevels are responsible for many characteristic properties of the *d*-block elements.

Atomic Radii

The atomic radii of the *d*-block elements generally decrease across the periods. However, this decrease is less than that for the main-group elements because the electrons added to the $(n - 1)d$ sublevel shield the outer electrons from the nucleus. Also, note in Figure 5-14 that the radii dip to a low and then increase slightly across each of the four periods that contain *d*-block elements. As the number of electrons in the *d* sublevel increases, the radii increase because of repulsion among the electrons.

In the sixth period, the *f*-block elements fall between lanthanum (Group 3) and hafnium (Group 4). Because of the increase in atomic number that occurs from lanthanum to hafnium, the atomic radius of hafnium is actually slightly less than that of zirconium, Zr, the element immediately above it. The radii of elements following hafnium in the sixth period vary with increasing atomic number in the usual manner.

Ionization Energy

As they do for the main-group elements, ionization energies of the d-block and f-block elements generally increase across the periods. In contrast to the decrease down the main groups, however, the first ionization energies of the d-block elements generally increase down each group. This is because the electrons available for ionization in the outer s sublevels are less shielded from the increasing nuclear charge by electrons in the incomplete $(n-1)d$ sublevels.

Ion Formation and Ionic Radii

The order in which electrons are removed from all atoms of the d-block and f-block elements is *exactly the reverse of the order given by the electron-configuration notation.* In other words, electrons in the highest occupied sublevel are always removed first. For the d-block elements, this means that although newly added electrons occupy the d sublevels, the first electrons to be removed are those in the outermost s sublevels. For example, iron, Fe, has the electron configuration $[Ar]3d^64s^2$. It loses a 4s electron first to form Fe^+ ($[Ar]3d^64s^1$). Fe^+ can then lose the second 4s electron to form Fe^{2+} ($[Ar]3d^6$). Fe^{2+} can then lose a 3d electron to form Fe^{3+} ($[Ar]3d^5$).

Most d-block elements commonly form 2+ ions in compounds. Some, such as iron and chromium, also commonly form 3+ ions. The Group 3 elements form only ions with a 3+ charge. Copper forms 1+ and 2+ ions, and silver usually forms only 1+ ions. As expected, the cations have smaller radii than the atoms do. Comparing 2+ ions across the periods shows a decrease in size that parallels the decrease in atomic radii.

Electronegativity

The d-block elements all have electronegativities between 1.1 and 2.54. Only the active metals of Groups 1 and 2 have lower electronegativities. The d-block elements also follow the general trend for electronegativity values to increase as radii decrease, and vice versa. The f-block elements all have similar electronegativities, which range from 1.1 to 1.5.

SECTION REVIEW

1. State the general period and group trends among main-group elements with respect to each of the following properties:

   a. atomic radii   d. ionic radii
   b. first ionization energy   e. electronegativity
   c. electron affinity

2. Among the main-group elements, what is the relationship between group number and the number of valence electrons among group members?

3. a. In general, how do the periodic properties of the d-block elements compare with those of the main-group elements?
   b. Explain the comparisons made in (a).

CHAPTER 5 REVIEW

CHAPTER SUMMARY

5-1
- The periodic law states that the physical and chemical properties of the elements are periodic functions of their atomic numbers.
- The periodic table is an arrangement of the elements in order of their atomic numbers so that elements with similar properties fall in the same column.
- The columns in the periodic table are referred to as groups.

Vocabulary

actinide (126)	lanthanide (126)	periodic law (125)	periodic table (125)

5-2
- The rows in the periodic table are called periods.
- Many chemical properties of the elements can be explained by the configurations of the elements' outermost electrons.
- The noble gases exhibit unique chemical stability because their highest occupied levels have an octet of electrons, ns^2np^6 (with the exception of helium, whose stability arises from its highest occupied level being completely filled with two electrons, $1s^2$).
- Based on the electron configurations of the elements, the periodic table can be divided into four blocks: the s block, the p block, the d block, and the f block.

Vocabulary

alkali metals (132)	halogens (137)	main-group elements (136) transition elements (134)
alkaline-earth metals (132)		

5-3
- The groups and periods of the periodic table display general trends in the following properties of the elements: electron affinity, electronegativity, ionization energy, atomic radius, and ionic radius.
- The electrons in an atom that are available to be lost, gained, or shared in the formation of chemical compounds are referred to as valence electrons.
- In determining the electron configuration of an ion, the order in which electrons are removed from the atom is the reverse of the order given by the atom's electron-configuration notation.

Vocabulary

anion (149)	electron affinity (147)	ion (143) ionization energy (143)
atomic radius (140)	electronegativity (151)	ionization (143) valence electrons (150)
cation (149)		

REVIEWING CONCEPTS

1. Describe the contributions made by the following scientists to the development of the periodic table:
   a. Stanislao Cannizzaro
   b. Dmitri Mendeleev
   c. Henry Moseley   (5-1)

2. State the periodic law.   (5-1)

3. How is the periodic law demonstrated within the groups of the periodic table?   (5-1)

4. a. How do the electron configurations within the same group of elements compare?
   b. Why are the noble gases relatively unreactive?   (5-2)

5. What determines the length of each period in the periodic table?   (5-2)

6. What is the relationship between the electron configuration of an element and the period in which that element appears in the periodic table?   (5-2)

REVIEW ANSWERS

1. a. Cannizzaro developed a standard method for measuring atomic masses, which allowed chemists to search for periodic trends among elements.
b. Mendeleev organized the elements according to increasing atomic mass and noticed that similar properties appeared periodically.
c. Moseley discovered that nuclear charge (i.e., atomic number), not atomic mass, should be the basis for organizing the periodic table.

2. The physical and chemical properties of the elements are periodic functions of their atomic numbers.

3. Groups of elements exhibit similar chemical and physical properties and behavior.

4. a. Generally the configurations of the outermost electron shells of elements within the same group are the same. There are a number of exceptions to this rule, however, among the transition elements.
b. Their outer shells are completely filled.

5. The length of a period is determined by the total number of electrons that can fill the outer sublevels of the elements of that period.

6. An element's period corresponds to its highest occupied main energy level.

7. a. the type of sublevel being filled in successive elements of that block
b. *s* block: Groups 1 and 2; *p* block: Groups 13–18 (except for He); *d* block: Groups 3–12 (except for the *f*-block elements); *f* block: those elements of the sixth and seventh periods between Groups 3 and 4

7. a. What information is provided by the specific block location of an element?
b. Identify, by number, the groups located within each of the four block areas. (5-2)

8. a. Which elements are designated as the alkali metals?
b. List four of their characteristic properties. (5-2)

9. a. Which elements are designated as the alkaline-earth metals?
b. How do their characteristic properties compare with those of the alkali metals? (5-2)

10. a. Write the usual group configuration notation for each *d*-block group.
b. How do the group numbers of those groups relate to the number of outer *s* and *d* electrons? (5-2)

11. What name is sometimes used to refer to the entire set of *d*-block elements? (5-2)

12. a. What types of elements make up the *p* block?
b. How do the properties of the *p*-block metals compare with those of the metals in the *s* and *d* blocks? (5-2)

13. a. Which elements are designated as the halogens?
b. List three of their characteristic properties. (5-2)

14. a. Which elements are metalloids?
b. Describe their characteristic properties. (5-2)

15. Which elements make up the *f* block in the periodic table? (5-2)

16. a. What are the main-group elements?
b. What trends can be observed across the various periods within the main-group elements? (5-2)

17. a. What is meant by atomic radius?
b. What trend is observed among the atomic radii of main-group elements across a period?
c. How can this trend be explained? (5-3)

18. a. What trend is observed among the atomic radii of main-group elements down a group?
b. How can this trend be explained? (5-3)

19. Define each of the following terms:
a. ion

b. ionization
c. first ionization energy
d. second ionization energy (5-3)

20. a. How do the first ionization energies of main-group elements vary across a period and down a group?
b. Explain the basis for each trend. (5-3)

21. a. What is electron affinity?
b. What signs are associated with electron affinity values, and what is the significance of each sign? (5-3)

22. a. Distinguish between a cation and an anion.
b. How does the size of each compare with the size of the neutral atom from which it is formed? (5-3)

23. a. What are valence electrons?
b. Where are such electrons located? (5-3)

24. For each of the following groups, indicate whether electrons are more likely to be lost or gained in compound formation and give the number of such electrons typically involved:
a. Group 1   d. Group 16
b. Group 2   e. Group 17
c. Group 13   f. Group 18 (5-3)

25. a. What is electronegativity?
b. Why is fluorine special in terms of electronegativity? (5-3)

26. Identify the most- and least-electronegative groups of elements in the periodic table. (5-3)

PROBLEMS

Electron Configuration and Periodic Properties

27. Write the noble-gas notation for the electron configuration of each of the following elements, and indicate the period in which each belongs:
a. Li   c. Cu   e. Sn
b. O   d. Br

28. Without looking at the periodic table, identify the period, block, and group in which the elements with the following electron configurations are located. (Hint: See Sample Problem 5-1.)
a. $[Ne]3s^23p^4$
b. $[Kr]4d^{10}5s^25p^2$
c. $[Xe]4f^{14}5d^{10}6s^26p^5$

29. Based on the information given below, give the group, period, block, and identity of each element described. (Hint: See Sample Problem 5-2.)
a. $[He]2s^2$
b. $[Ne]3s^1$
c. $[Kr]5s^2$
d. $[Ar]4s^2$
e. $[Ar]3d^54s^1$

30. Without looking at the periodic table, write the expected outer electron configuration for each of the following elements. (Hint: See Sample Problem 5-3.)
a. Group 7, fourth period
b. Group 3, fifth period
c. Group 12, sixth period

31. Identify the block, period, group, group name (where appropriate), element name, element type, and relative reactivity for the elements with the following electron configurations. (Hint: See Sample Problem 5-4.)
a. $[Ne]3s^23p^1$
b. $[Ar]3d^{10}4s^24p^6$
c. $[Kr]4d^{10}5s^1$
d. $[Xe]4f^15d^16s^2$

Atomic Radius, Ionization, Electron Affinity, and Electronegativity

32. Of cesium, Cs, hafnium, Hf, and gold, Au, which element has the smallest atomic radius? Explain your answer in terms of trends in the periodic table. (Hint: see Sample Problem 5-5.)

33. a. Distinguish between the first, second, and third ionization energies of an atom.
b. How do the values of successive ionization energies compare?
c. Why does this occur?

34. Without looking at the electron affinity table, arrange the following elements in order of *decreasing* electron affinities: C, O, Li, Na, Rb, and F.

35. a. Without looking at the ionization energy table, arrange the following elements in order of decreasing first ionization energies: Li, O, C, K, Ne, and F.
b. Which of the elements listed in (a) would you expect to have the highest second ionization energy? Why?

36. a. Which of the following cations is least likely to form: Sr^{2+}, Al^{3+}, K^{2+}?
b. Which of the following anions is least likely to form: I^-, Cl^-, O^{2-}?

37. Which element is the most electronegative among C, N, O, Br, and S? Which group does it belong to? (Hint: See Sample Problem 5-7.)

38. The two ions K^+ and Ca^{2+} each have 18 electrons surrounding the nucleus. Which would you expect to have the smaller radius? Why?

MIXED REVIEW

39. Without looking at the periodic table, identify the period, block, and group in which each of the following elements is located:
a. $[Rn]7s^1$
b. $[Ar]3d^24s^2$
c. $[Kr]4d^{10}5s^1$
d. $[Xe]4f^{14}5d^96s^1$

40. a. Which elements are designated as the noble gases?
b. What is the most significant property of these elements?

41. Which of the following does not have a noble-gas configuration: Na^+, Rb^+, O^{2-}, Br^-, Ca^+, Al^{3+}, S^{2-}?

42. a. How many groups are in the periodic table?
b. How many periods are in the periodic table?
c. Which two blocks of the periodic table make up the main-group elements?

43. Write the noble-gas notation for the electron configuration of each of the following elements, and indicate the period and group in which each belongs:
a. Mg
b. P
c. Sc
d. Y

44. Use the periodic table to describe the chemical properties of the following elements:
a. fluorine, F
b. xenon, Xe
c. sodium, Na
d. gold, Au

8. a. the Group 1 elements
b. The Group 1 elements are extremely reactive. They react vigorously with water, they are silvery in appearance, and each is soft enough to be cut with a knife.

9. a. the Group 2 elements
b. The Group 2 elements are harder, denser, and stronger than the Group 1 elements. They also have higher melting points. Group 2 elements are less reactive than Group 1 elements.

10. a. Group 3: $(n-1)d^1ns^2$
Group 4: $(n-1)d^2ns^2$
Group 5: $(n-1)d^3ns^2$
Group 6: $(n-1)d^5ns^1$
Group 7: $(n-1)d^5ns^2$
Group 8: $(n-1)d^6ns^2$
Group 9: $(n-1)d^7ns^2$
Group 10: $(n-1)d^8ns^2$
Group 11: $(n-1)d^{10}ns^1$
Group 12: $(n-1)d^{10}ns^2$

b. The group number equals the sum of the outer s and d electrons.

11. the transition elements

12. a. The p block consists of nonmetals at the right, metalloids in the middle, and metals at the left.
b. The p-block metals are generally harder and more dense than the s-block metals but softer and less dense than the d-block metals.

13. a. the Group 17 elements
b. The halogens are the most-reactive nonmetals; they react vigorously with most metals to form salts. They are also the most-electronegative elements.

14. a. B, Si, Ge, As, Sb, Te
b. The metalloids are mostly brittle solids with electrical conductivities intermediate between those of metals (good conductors) and nonmetals (non-conductors).

15. the lanthanides and the actinides

16. a. the elements of the *s* and *p* blocks (plus hydrogen and helium)
b. decrease in atomic size, increase in ionization energy, increase in electron affinity, decrease in cationic size, decrease in anionic size, increase in electronegativity

17. a. one half the distance between the nuclei of two bonded identical atoms
b. They decrease.
c. As electrons are added to *s* and *p* sublevels in the same main energy level, the increasing positive charge of the nucleus pulls electrons closer to the nucleus, resulting in decreasing atomic radii.

18. a. They generally increase.
b. Down a group, the outer electrons of each element occupy comparable sublevels in successively higher main energy levels farther from the nucleus.

19. a. a charged atom or a charged group of bonded atoms
b. any process that results in the formation of an ion
c. the energy required to remove one electron from a neutral atom of an element
d. the energy required to remove an electron from a 1+ ion

20. a. They increase across a period and decrease down a group.
b. Across a period, the increasing nuclear charge more strongly attracts electrons in the same energy level and makes them more difficult to remove. Down a group, the electrons to be removed from each successive element are in increasingly higher energy levels farther from the nucleus and are thus more easily removed.

45. Identify which trends in the diagrams below describe atomic radius, ionization energy, electron affinity, and electronegativity.

Increases

a.

Increases

b.

Increases

c.

46. For each element listed below, determine the charge of the ion most likely to be formed and the identity of the noble gas whose electron configuration is thus achieved.
a. Li   e. Mg   i. Br
b. Rb   f. Al   j. Ba
c. O   g. P
d. F   h. S

47. Describe some differences between the *s*-block metals and the *d*-block metals.

48. Why do the halogens readily form 1– ions?

49. The electron configuration of argon differs from those of chlorine and potassium by one electron each. Compare the reactivity of these three elements.

CRITICAL THINKING

As a member on the newly inhabited space station Alpha, you are given the task of organizing information on newly discovered elements as it comes in from the laboratory. To date, five elements have been discovered and have been assigned names and symbols from the Greek alphabet. An analysis of the new elements has yielded the following data:

Element name	Atomic no.	Atomic mass	Properties
Epsilon ε	23	47.33	nonmetal, very reactive, produces a salt when combined with a metal, gaseous state
Beta β	13	27.01	metal, very reactive, soft solid, low melting point
Gamma γ	12	25.35	nonmetal, gaseous element, extremely unreactive
Delta Δ	4	7.98	nonmetal, very abundant, forms compounds with most other elements
Lambda Λ	9	16.17	metal, solid state, good conductor, high luster, hard and dense

50. Applying Models Using the data on the five new elements, create a periodic table based on their properties.

51. Predicting Outcomes Using your newly created periodic table, predict the atomic number of an element with an atomic mass of 11.29 that has nonmetallic properties and is very reactive.

52. Predicting Outcomes Predict the atomic number of an element having an atomic mass of 15.02 that exhibits metallic properties but is softer than lambda and harder than beta.

53. Analyzing Information Analyze your periodic table for periodic trends, and describe the trends that you identify.

TECHNOLOGY & LEARNING

54. Graphing Calculator Graphing Atomic Radius vs. Atomic Number

The graphing calculator can run a program that graphs data such as atomic radius versus atomic number. Graphing the data within the different periods will allow you to discover trends. Begin by creating a table of data. Then use the program to plot the data.

Go to Appendix C. If you are using a TI 83 Plus, you can download the program and data sets and run the application as directed. If you are using another calculator, your teacher will provide you with keystrokes and data sets to use. Remember that after creating the lists, you will need to name the program and check the display, as explained in Appendix C. You will then be ready to run the program. After you have graphed the data, answer these questions.

a. Would you expect any atomic number to have an atomic radius of 20? Why or why not?

b. A relationship is considered a function if it can pass a vertical line test. That is, if a vertical line can be drawn anywhere on the graph and only pass through one point, the relationship is a function. Do either of these sets of data represent a function? If so, which one(s)?

c. How would you describe the graphical relationship between the atomic numbers and atomic radii?

HANDBOOK SEARCH

55. Review the boiling point and melting point data in Tables 1A through 8A of the *Elements Handbook* (page 731). Make a list of the elements that exist as liquids or gases at the boiling point of water, 100°C.

56. Because transition metals have vacant *d* orbitals, they form a greater variety of colored compounds than do the metals of Groups 1 and 2. Review the section of the *Elements Handbook* on transition metals (pages 740–749) and answer the following:

a. What colors are exhibited by chromium in its common oxidation states?

b. What gems contain chromium impurities?

c. What colors are often associated with the following metal ions: copper, cadmium, cobalt, zinc, and nickel?

d. What transition elements are considered noble metals? What are the characteristics of a noble metal?

RESEARCH & WRITING

57. Prepare a report tracing the evolution of the current periodic table since 1900. Cite the chemists involved and their major contributions.

58. Write a report describing the contributions of Glenn Seaborg toward the discovery of many of the actinide elements.

ALTERNATIVE ASSESSMENT

59. Your teacher will give you an index card that identifies the electronegativity, ionization energy, and electron affinity of an element. Identify the element by analyzing these properties in relation to periodic trends.

60. Construct your own periodic table or obtain a poster that shows related objects, such as fruits or vegetables, in periodic arrangement. Describe the organization of the table and the trends it illustrates. Use this table to make predictions about your subject matter.

21. a. the energy taken in or given off when an electron is added to an atom
b. Electron affinity values are either negative or positive. A negative sign indicates that energy is given off; a positive sign indicates that energy is taken in.

22. a. A cation is a positive ion, and an anion is a negative ion.
b. Cations are always smaller than the atoms from which they are formed; anions are always larger.

23. a. Valence electrons are atomic electrons available to be lost, gained, or shared in the formation of chemical compounds.
b. Valence electrons are located in an atom's outermost energy level.

24. a. lost, 1
b. lost, 2
c. lost, 3
d. gained, 2
e. gained, 1
f. neither lost nor gained, 0

25. a. Electronegativity is the ability of an atom in a chemical compound to attract electrons from other atoms.
b. Fluorine is the most electronegative element and is arbitrarily assigned an electronegativity of 4.0. The values for all other elements are assigned in relation to this value.

26. Group 17, Group 1

27. a. [He]$2s^1$, second period
b. [He]$2s^22p^4$, second period
c. [Ar]$3d^{10}4s^1$, fourth period
d. [Ar]$3d^{10}4s^24p^5$, fourth period
e. [Kr]$4d^{10}5s^25p^2$, fifth period

28. a. third period, *p* block, Group 16
b. fifth period, *p* block, Group 14
c. sixth period, *p* block, Group 17

29. a. Group 2, second period, *s* block, Be

Continued from page 159

b. Group 1, third period, s block, Na
c. Group 2, fifth period, s block, Sr
d. Group 2, fourth period, s block, Ca
e. Group 6, fourth period, d block, Cr

30. a. $3d^54s^2$
b. $4d^15s^2$
c. $4f^{14}5d^{10}6s^2$

31. a. p block, third period, Group 13, Al, metal, high reactivity
b. p block, fourth period, Group 18, noble gases, Kr, nonmetal, low reactivity
c. d block, fifth period, Group 11, Ag, metal, low reactivity
d. f block, sixth period, between Groups 3 and 4, Ce, metal, high reactivity

32. gold—atomic radii decrease across a period and gold is farthest to the right in the sixth period, in which all three elements are found

33. a. First ionization energy is the energy required to remove one electron from an atom, which is neutral. Second ionization energy is the energy required to remove an electron from a 1+ ion. Third ionization energy is the energy required to remove an electron from a 2+ ion.
b. Each successive ionization energy is larger than the preceding one.
c. Each successive electron must be removed from a particle with a greater positive charge.

34. In order of decreasing electron affinities, the elements are F, O, C, Li, Na, and Rb.

35. a. Ne, F, O, C, Li, K
b. Li and K would have the highest second ionization energies because in both cases the second electron must come from a completely filled noble-gas electron configuration. Of the two, Li would have the higher second ionization energy because the Li^+ ion is smaller than the K^+ ion.

36. a. K^{2+}
b. O^{2-}

37. O; Group 16

38. Ca^{2+}; because of the greater attraction its 20 protons exert on the 18 electrons

39. a. seventh period, s block, Group 1
b. fourth period, d block, Group 4
c. fifth period, d block, Group 11

d. sixth period, d block, Group 10

40. a. the Group 18 elements
b. They are very unreactive.

41. Ca^+

42. a. 18
b. 7
c. the s and p blocks

43. a. [Ne]$3s^2$, third period, Group 2
b. [Ne]$3s^23p^3$, third period, Group 15
c. [Ar]$3d^14s^2$, fourth period, Group 3
d. [Kr]$4d^15s^2$, fifth period, Group 3

44. a. a highly reactive nonmetal in Group 17, Period 2; it needs one electron to achieve a noble-gas configuration, which explains its high electron affinity; it has a high ionization energy, and thus the formation of positive ions is not likely; fluorine is the most-electronegative element
b. a nonmetal of low reactivity in Group 18, Period 5; it has a filled outer energy level, so there is little tendency to lose, gain, or share electrons; it has the highest ionization energy of the elements in the fifth period
c. a highly reactive metal in Group 1, Period 3; it has a low first ionization energy because losing an electron to form Na^+ gives it a noble-gas configuration; it has a low electron affinity and a low electronegativity
d. a metal of fairly low reactivity in Group 11, Period 6; its ionization energy is relatively low, so it forms positive ions

45. ionization energy, electron affinity, electronegativity: diagram a; atomic radius: diagram b

46. a. 1+, He
b. 1+, Kr
c. 2−, Ne
d. 1−, Ne
e. 2+, Ne
f. 3+, Ne
g. 3−, Ar
h. 2−, Ar
i. 1−, Kr
j. 2+, Xe

47. The d-block metals are harder, denser, and less reactive, and, except for mercury, they have higher melting points than s-block metals.

48. In doing so they achieve a noble-gas configuration.

49. Chlorine and potassium are reactive elements, whereas argon is unreactive. Chlorine readily gains

one electron to achieve the configuration of argon, and potassium readily loses one electron to achieve the argon configuration.

50.

		4 Δ		
	9 Λ			12 γ
13 β				
			23 ε	

51. 5

52. 8

53. From left to right, the elements are organized according to their atomic numbers. Elements are organized into families or columns according to their properties. The elements also exhibit increasingly nonmetallic behavior from left to right across the table. And their physical states suggest that melting points and boiling points also increase from left to right.

54. a. No. The graph seems to be approaching a limit of approximately 65–70.

b. Neither

c. As the atomic number increases, the atomic radius decreases.

55. Hg is liquid at −38.8°C.
N as N_2 is a gas at −195.8°C.
P is a liquid at 44.1°C.
O as O_2 is a gas at −182.962°C.
F as F_2 is a gas at −188.14°C.
Cl as Cl_2 is a gas at −34.6°C.
Br as Br_2 is a gas at 58.78°C.

56. a. Cr^{3+}, violet or green; Cr^{6+}, yellow or orange
b. rubies
c. copper, blue; cadmium, yellow; cobalt, pink; zinc, white; nickel, green
d. gold, silver, platinum, palladium, iridium, rhodium, ruthenium, osmium; they have low reactivity

57. Possible responses include Friedrich Dorn's discovery of radon in 1900, Moseley's determination of the nuclear charge (i.e., atomic number) of each element by 1913, the discovery of the lanthanides by 1913, the synthesis in 1940 of the first element beyond uranium in the periodic table (neptunium) by Philip Abelson and Edwin McMillan, the creation of plutonium in 1941 by Seaborg, and the synthesis of element 109 in Germany in 1982.

58. Reports should mention Seaborg's various roles in the syntheses of curium (element 96) in 1944, californium (element 98) in 1950, mendelevium (element 101) in 1955, and nobelium (element 102) in 1958.

Chemical Bonding

PACING CHART Compression Guide: *(To shorten, eliminate items in italics.)*	NSE Standards	CLASSROOM RESOURCES		
		Teaching Resources		Experiments
6-1 Introduction to Chemical Bonding 2 45-minute periods 1 90-minute block	PS 2a, 2c, 3c UCP 1–2	 T 30, T 31		
6-2 Covalent Bonding and Molecular Compounds 2 45-minute periods 1 90-minute block *The Octet Rule, pp. 168–169*	PS 2a, 2c UCP 1–2 SPSP 1, 2, 5	T 32		
6-3 Ionic Bonding and Ionic Compounds 2 45-minute periods 1 90-minute block	PS 2a, 2c UCP 1–2	T 33, TM 26A		C3 **INV** Covalent and Ionic Bonding— Ceramics Fixative BC Chemical Bonds
6-4 Metallic Bonding 2 45-minute periods 1 90-minute block *The Metallic-Bond Model, pp. 181–182*	PS 2c, 2d UCP 1–2	**PE** Elements Handbook T 34		B7 Conductivity as an Indicator of Bond Type
6-5 Molecular Geometry 2 45-minute periods 1 90-minute block *Hybridization, pp. 187–189*	PS 2d, 2f UCP 1–2, 5 SAI 2	T 35, T 36, T 37, T 38, TM 27A		

Review and Assessment 2 45-minute periods 1 90-minute block	REVIEW RESOURCES		
	Cumulative Review	Alternative Assessment	Traditional Assessment
	SR Chapter 6 Mixed Review PE Chapter 6 50–67, pp. 197–198	PE 74, 75, p. 199 ATE 166 AA Items for Chapter 6	Chapter 6 Text Test Generator Items for Chapter 6

ASSIGNMENT RESOURCES

Section Homework Resources & Review	Problem-Solving Practice
HR Homework Worksheet 6-1 Graphic Org. Assignment 6-1 **PE** Section Review, 1–4, p. 163 Chapter Review, 1–5, 33–34, pp. 195–196 **SR** Section Review 6-1	**PE** Additional Samples 6-1 **ATE** Additional Samples, p. 163
HR Homework Worksheets 6-2, 6-3, 6-4, 6-5 Graphic Org. Assignment 6-2 **PE** Section Review, 1–4, p. 175 Chapter Review, 6–14, 35, 37–39, 41, pp. 195–196 **SR** Section Review 6-2	**PE** Additional Samples 6-2, 6-3, 6-4 **ATE** Additional Samples, pp. 170, 171, 174
HR Homework Worksheets 6-6, 6-7 Graphic Org. Assignment 6-3 **PE** Section Review, 1–4, p. 180 Chapter Review, 15–19, 36, 42, pp. 195–196 **SR** Section Review 6-3	
HR Homework Worksheet 6-8 Graphic Org. Assignment 6-4 **PE** Section Review, 1–3, p. 182 Chapter Review, 20–22, p. 196 **SR** Section Review 6-4	
HR Homework Worksheets 6-9, 6-10, 6-11, 6-12 Graphic Org. Assignment 6-5 **PE** Section Review, 5, p. 193 Chapter Review, 27–32, 45–47, pp 196–197 **SR** Section Review 6-5	**PE** Additional Samples 6-5, 6-6 **ATE** Additional Samples, pp. 185, 187

TECHNOLOGY RESOURCES

Technology & Internet Resources

 CTW 11 Segment 11 Superconductivity

 Holt Chemistry Videodiscs Teacher's Correlation Guide for Chapter 6

 Module 4: Covalent Bonding, Ionic Bonding, Molecular Geometry

internet connect

On-line Student Resources:
GO TO: www.scilinks.org
The following SciLinks Internet resources can be found in the student text for this chapter.

TOPICS:
• Covalent bonding, p. 162 (HC2061)
• Ultrasound, p. 166 (HC2062)
• Ionic bonding, p. 177 (HC2063)
• Metallic bonding, p. 181 (HC2064)
• VSEPR theory, p. 185 (HC2065)
• Hydrogen bonding, p. 192 (HC2066)

On-line Teacher Resources:
 GO TO: go.hrw.com
KEYWORD: HC2 HOME
Visit the HRW Web site for a variety of resources related to this chapter.

Smithsonian Institution®
Internet Connections
Visit www.si.edu/hrw for additional on-line resources.

.com
Visit www.cnnfyi.com for late-breaking news and current events stories selected just for you.

Resource Key	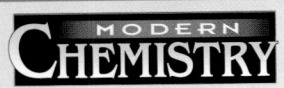 **One-Stop Planner CD-ROM** Includes these resources and customizable daily lesson plans:				
MODERN CHEMISTRY **PE** Pupil's Edition **ATE** Teacher's Edition	**HR** Homework Resources **SR** Section Reviews **CTW** Critical Thinking Worksheets **AA** Alternative Assessments	**ChemFile** **A** Laboratory Experiments **B** Microscale Experiments **C** Technique Builders and Problem-Solving Experiments		**D** Consumer Experiments **T** Transparencies **TM** Transparency Masters **PS** Mini-Guide to Problem Solving **SRW** Supplemental Reading Worksheets	

Scoring Rubrics for Labs, Alternative Assessments, Performance Tasks and Portfolio Projects are on the One-Stop Planner CD-ROM.

Chapter Overview

6-1 defines chemical bonding and uses electronegativity values to contrast polar-covalent, nonpolar-covalent, and ionic bonding.

6-2 covers the characteristics of covalent bonding, including the relationship between bond length and bond strength and the use of Lewis structures.

6-3 covers the characteristics of ionic bonding.

6-4 covers the characteristics of metallic bonding and the resulting properties of metals.

6-5 covers theories of molecular geometry, including VSEPR theory and hybridization theory. It also covers how intermolecular attraction is affected by molecular geometry.

Concept Base

Students may need a review of the following concepts:

- boiling points, Chapter 1
- arrangement of electrons around atoms, including electron configurations and orbital notation, Chapter 4
- ion formation and electronegativity, Chapter 5

Chemical Bonding

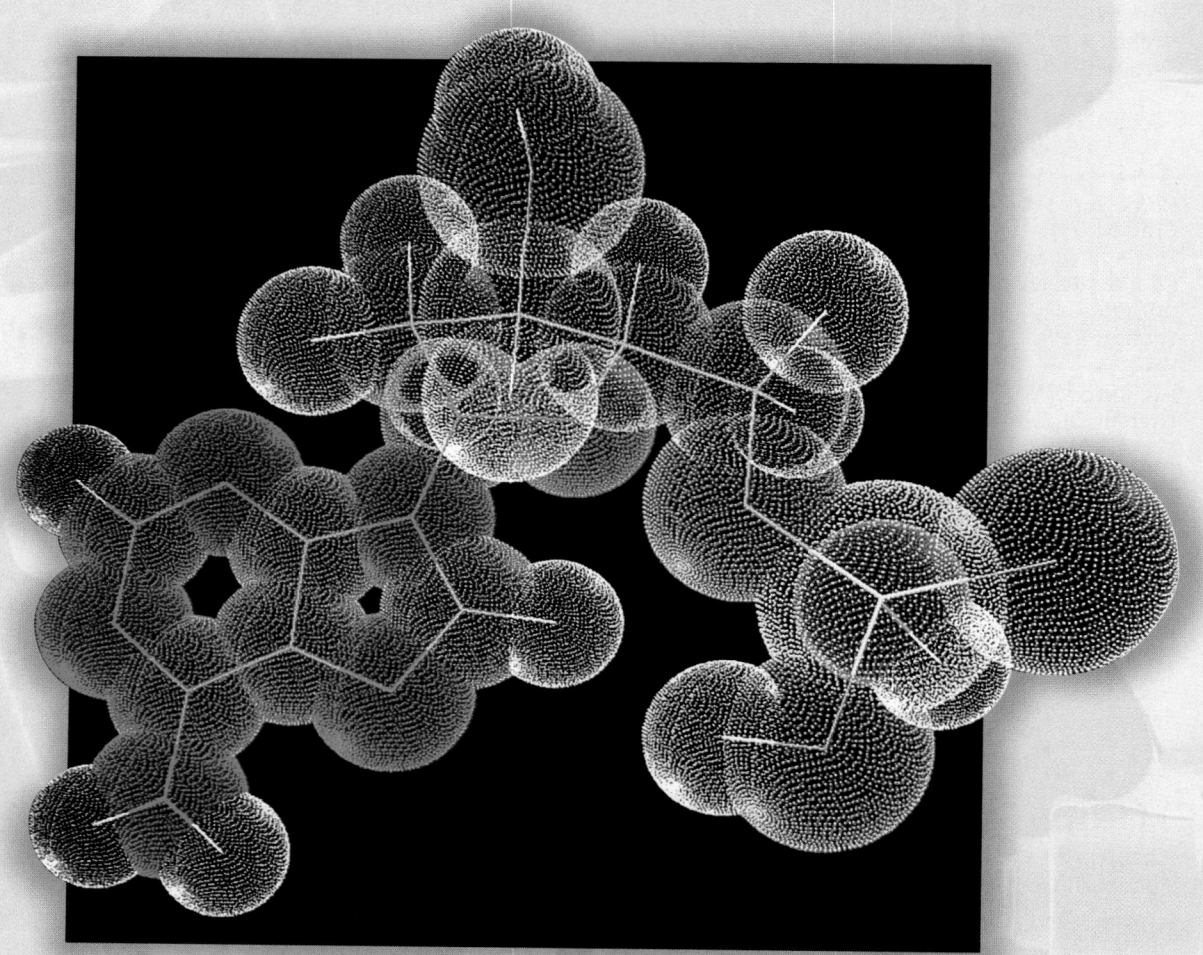

In nature, most atoms are joined to other atoms by chemical bonds.

Introduction to Chemical Bonding

A toms seldom exist as independent particles in nature. The oxygen you breathe, the water that makes up most of your body, and nearly all other substances are made up of combinations of atoms that are held together by chemical bonds. *A **chemical bond** is a mutual electrical attraction between the nuclei and valence electrons of different atoms that binds the atoms together.*

Why are most atoms chemically bonded to each other? As independent particles, they are at relatively high potential energy. Nature, however, favors arrangements in which potential energy is minimized. This means that most atoms are less stable existing by themselves than when they are combined. By bonding with each other, atoms decrease in potential energy, thereby creating more stable arrangements of matter.

Types of Chemical Bonding

When atoms bond, their valence electrons are redistributed in ways that make the atoms more stable. The way in which the electrons are redistributed determines the type of bonding. In Chapter 5, you read that main-group metals tend to lose electrons to form positive ions, or cations, and nonmetals tend to gain electrons to form negative ions, or anions. *Chemical bonding that results from the electrical attraction between large numbers of cations and anions is called **ionic bonding.*** In purely ionic bonding, atoms completely give up electrons to other atoms, as illustrated in Figure 6-1 on page 162. In contrast to atoms joined by ionic bonding, atoms joined by covalent bonding share electrons. **Covalent bonding** *results from the sharing of electron pairs between two atoms* (see Figure 6-1). In a purely covalent bond, the shared electrons are "owned" equally by the two bonded atoms.

Ionic or Covalent?

Bonding between atoms of different elements is rarely purely ionic or purely covalent. It usually falls somewhere between these two extremes, depending on how strongly the atoms of each element attract electrons. Recall that electronegativity is a measure of an atom's ability to attract electrons. The degree to which bonding between atoms of two elements

OBJECTIVES

- Define *chemical bond.*

- Explain why most atoms form chemical bonds.

- Describe ionic and covalent bonding.

- Explain why most chemical bonding is neither purely ionic nor purely covalent.

- Classify bonding type according to electronegativity differences.

Module 4: Chemical Bonding

Visual Strategy

FIGURE 6-1 Have students recognize the fundamental difference between ionic and covalent bonding. In ionic bonding, large numbers of oppositely charged ions come together because of electrical attraction. (Be sure students identify the cations and the anions.) In covalent bonding, two atoms join by sharing one or more of their valence electrons. The shared electrons are simultaneously attracted to both atomic nuclei.

Some students will notice the changes in sizes for atoms A and B and ions A and B. Have them recall what they learned about atomic radii and ionic radii in Chapter 5.

FIGURE 6-2 Remind students that the ability of atoms to attract electrons—as expressed by electronegativity values—ultimately determines whether bonding is ionic or covalent. The illustration is a model for a continuum used to *predict* the bonding in various substances. As a model it holds true for a great many substances but not all. Be sure that students are aware that the model is not a physical law that describes the bonding behavior of all substances.

Common Misconception

Electronegativity difference is only a general guide for determining bonding type. For example, the electronegativity difference between boron and fluorine is 2.0. Yet scientists know through experimentation that boron trifluoride, BF_3, is a covalently bonded compound.

FIGURE 6-1 In ionic bonding, many atoms transfer electrons. The resulting positive and negative ions combine due to mutual electrical attraction. In covalent bonding, atoms share electron pairs to form independent molecules.

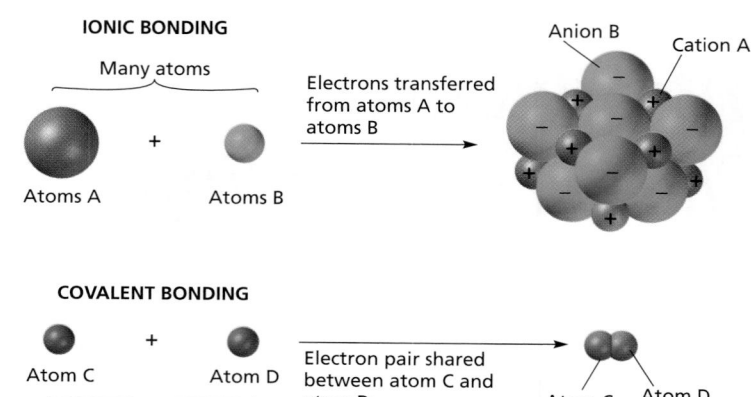

IONIC BONDING

COVALENT BONDING

---

internet connect

SCLINKS

NSTA

TOPIC: Covalent bonding
GO TO: www.scilinks.org
sciLINKS CODE: HC2061

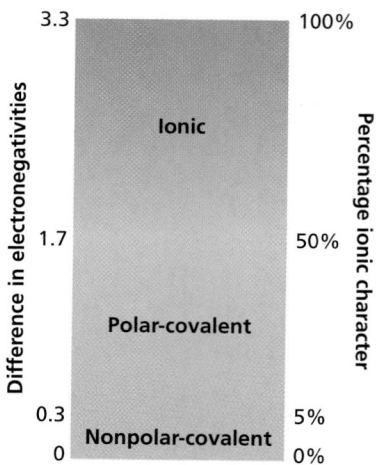

FIGURE 6-2 Differences in electronegativities reflect the character of bonding between elements. The electronegativity of the less-electronegative element is subtracted from that of the more-electronegative element. The greater the electronegativity difference, the more ionic is the bonding.

is ionic or covalent can be estimated by calculating the difference in the elements' electronegativities (see Figure 6-2). For example, the electronegativity difference between fluorine, F, and cesium, Cs, is $4.0 - 0.7 = 3.3$. (See Figure 5-20 on page 151 for a periodic table of electronegativity values.) So, according to Figure 6-2, cesium-fluorine bonding is ionic. The valence electrons are close to the highly electronegative fluorine atoms, causing the atoms to resemble anions, and far from the barely electronegative cesium atoms, which resemble cations.

Bonding between atoms with an electronegativity difference of 1.7 or less has an ionic character of 50% or less and is classified as covalent. Bonding between two atoms of the same element is completely covalent. Hydrogen, for example, exists in nature not as isolated atoms, but as pairs of atoms held together by covalent bonds. The hydrogen-hydrogen bond has 0% ionic character. It is a **nonpolar-covalent bond,** *a covalent bond in which the bonding electrons are shared equally by the bonded atoms, resulting in a balanced distribution of electrical charge.* Bonds having 0 to 5% ionic character, corresponding to electronegativity differences of roughly 0 to 0.3, are generally considered nonpolar-covalent bonds. In bonds with significantly different electronegativities, the electrons are more strongly attracted by the more-electronegative atom. *Such bonds are* **polar,** *meaning that they have an uneven distribution of charge.* Covalent bonds having 5 to 50% ionic character, corresponding to electronegativity differences of 0.3 to 1.7, are classified as polar. *A* **polar-covalent bond** *is a covalent bond in which the bonded atoms have an unequal attraction for the shared electrons.*

Nonpolar- and polar-covalent bonds are compared in Figure 6-3, which illustrates the electron density distribution in hydrogen-hydrogen and hydrogen-chlorine bonds. The electronegativity difference between chlorine and hydrogen is $3.0 - 2.1 = 0.9$, indicating a polar-covalent bond. The electrons in this bond are closer to the more-electronegative chlorine atom than to the hydrogen atom, as indicated in Figure 6-3(b). Consequently, the chlorine end of the bond has a partial negative charge, indicated by the symbol $\delta-$. The hydrogen end of the bond then has an equal partial positive charge, $\delta+$.

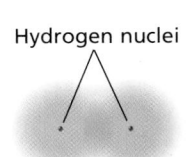

Hydrogen nuclei

Hydrogen nucleus

Chlorine nucleus

δ^+ δ^-

(a) Nonpolar-covalent bond   **(b)** Polar-covalent bond

FIGURE 6-3 Comparison of the electron density in (a) a nonpolar, hydrogen-hydrogen bond and (b) a polar, hydrogen-chlorine bond. Because chlorine is more electronegative than hydrogen, the electron density in the hydrogen-chlorine bond is greater around the chlorine atom.

ADDITIONAL
SAMPLE
PROBLEM

6-1 *Additional Sample Problem is found on page 199A.*

SAMPLE PROBLEM 6-1

Use electronegativity differences and Figure 6-2 to classify bonding between sulfur, S, and the following elements: hydrogen, H; cesium, Cs; and chlorine, Cl. In each pair, which atom will be more negative?

SOLUTION   From Figure 5-20 on page 151, we know that the electronegativity of sulfur is 2.5. The electronegativities of hydrogen, cesium, and chlorine are 2.1, 0.7, and 3.0, respectively. In each pair, the atom with the larger electronegativity will be the more-negative atom.

Bonding between sulfur and	Electronegativity difference	Bond type	More-negative atom
hydrogen	$2.5 - 2.1 = 0.4$	polar-covalent	sulfur
cesium	$2.5 - 0.7 = 1.8$	ionic	sulfur
chlorine	$3.0 - 2.5 = 0.5$	polar-covalent	chlorine

PRACTICE   Use electronegativity differences and Figure 6-2 to classify bonding between chlorine, Cl, and the following elements: calcium, Ca; oxygen, O; and bromine, Br. Indicate the more-negative atom in each pair.

Answer

Bonding between chlorine and	Electronegativity difference	Bond type	More-negative atom
calcium	$3.0 - 1.0 = 2.0$	ionic	chlorine
oxygen	$3.5 - 3.0 = 0.5$	polar-covalent	oxygen
bromine	$3.0 - 2.8 = 0.2$	nonpolar-covalent	chlorine

SECTION REVIEW

1. What is the main distinction between ionic and covalent bonding?

2. How is electronegativity used in determining the ionic or covalent character of the bonding between two elements?

3. What type of bonding would be expected between the following atoms?

   a. H and F
   b. Cu and S
   c. I and Br

4. List the three pairs of atoms referred to in the previous question in order of increasing ionic character of the bonding between them.

SECTION REVIEW

1. Ionic bonding involves the electrical attraction between large numbers of anions and cations. Covalent bonding involves the sharing of electron pairs between two atoms.

2. A large difference in electronegativity between two atoms in a bond will result in ionic bonding. A small difference in electronegativity between two atoms will result in covalent bonding.

3. **a.** ionic
   b. ionic
   c. polar-covalent

4. I and Br, Cu and S, F and H

Lesson Starter

Have students consider what happens if a soccer ball is rolled toward a ditch. The ball rolls down the near slope of the ditch, passes the bottom of the ditch, and rolls part of the way up the opposite slope of the ditch. It then rolls back down, passes the bottom, and rolls part of the way up the near side of the ditch. The ball continues moving in this pattern, each time rolling to a lesser height, until it eventually comes to rest in the bottom of the ditch. At this point, the ball's potential energy is at a minimum. The formation of a covalent bond between two atoms is like the ball in the ditch. The atoms alternately attract and repel each other until they reach a distance (or bond length) at which their potential energy is minimized.

Visual Strategy

FIGURE 6-4 Have students carefully examine the atoms involved in these molecules. Point out that all the atoms are nonmetals and that the oxygen and carbon atoms can each form more than one bond. The ability of atoms to form more than one covalent bond allows the formation of extremely large molecules.

Did You Know?

Molecules range in size from 62 to more than 23,000 pm.

OBJECTIVES

- Define *molecule* and *molecular formula.*

- Explain the relationships between potential energy, distance between approaching atoms, bond length, and bond energy.

- State the octet rule.

- List the six basic steps used in writing Lewis structures.

- Explain how to determine Lewis structures for molecules containing single bonds, multiple bonds, or both.

- Explain why scientists use resonance structures to represent some molecules.

Covalent Bonding and Molecular Compounds

Many chemical compounds, including most of the chemicals that are in living things and are produced by living things, are composed of molecules. *A* **molecule** *is a neutral group of atoms that are held together by covalent bonds.* A single molecule of a chemical compound is an individual unit capable of existing on its own. It may consist of two or more atoms of the same element, as in oxygen, or of two or more different atoms, as in water or sugar (see Figure 6-4 below). *A chemical compound whose simplest units are molecules is called a* **molecular compound.**

The composition of a compound is given by its chemical formula. *A* **chemical formula** *indicates the relative numbers of atoms of each kind in a chemical compound by using atomic symbols and numerical subscripts.* The chemical formula of a molecular compound is referred to as a molecular formula. *A* **molecular formula** *shows the types and numbers of atoms combined in a single molecule of a molecular compound.* The molecular formula for water, for example, is H_2O, which reflects the fact that a single water molecule consists of one oxygen atom joined by separate covalent bonds to two hydrogen atoms. A molecule of oxygen, O_2, is an example of a diatomic molecule. *A* **diatomic molecule** *is a molecule containing only two atoms.*

(a) Water molecule, H_2O

(b) Oxygen molecule, O_2

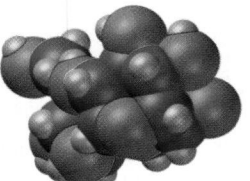

(c) Sucrose molecule, $C_{12}H_{22}O_{11}$

FIGURE 6-4 The models for (a) water, (b) oxygen, and (c) sucrose, or table sugar, represent a few examples of the many molecular compounds in and around us. Atoms within molecules may form one or more covalent bonds.

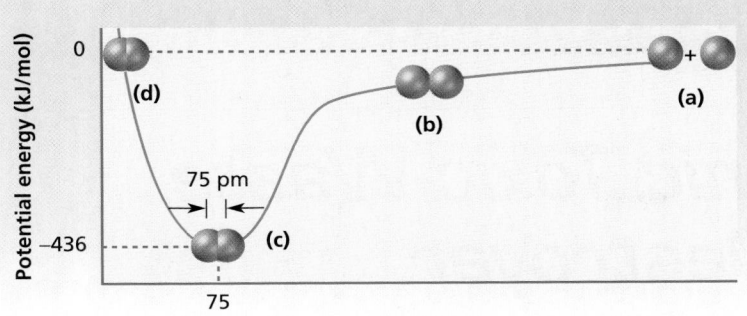

Distance between hydrogen nuclei (pm)

FIGURE 6-5 Potential energy changes during the formation of a hydrogen-hydrogen bond. (a) The separated hydrogen atoms do not affect each other. (b) Potential energy decreases as the atoms are drawn together by attractive forces. (c) Potential energy is at a minimum when attractive forces are balanced by repulsive forces. (d) Potential energy increases when repulsion between like charges outweighs attraction between opposite charges.

Visual Strategy

FIGURE 6-5 Ask students why the potential energy of the atoms increases as the atoms get very close to or far from each other. Have students consider the attraction between the electrons and the nuclei, as well as the repulsion between the two nuclei and between the two electrons.

Reading Skill-Builder

INTERPRETING GRAPHIC SOURCES OF INFORMATION Have students read the selections on the Formation of a Covalent Bond and Characteristics of a Covalent bond silently. Lead a discussion about the features of the graph in Figure 6-5 that correspond to the changes in potential energy described in the text. You may wish to highlight these features on an overhead transparency as you discuss them. Have students make notes on their own copies of the graph.

Formation of a Covalent Bond

As you read in Section 6-1, nature favors chemical bonding because most atoms are at lower potential energy when bonded to other atoms than they are at as independent particles. In the case of covalent bond formation, this idea is illustrated by a simple example, the formation of a hydrogen-hydrogen bond.

Picture two isolated hydrogen atoms separated by a distance large enough to prevent them from influencing each other. At this distance, the overall potential energy of the atoms is arbitrarily set at zero, as shown in part (a) of Figure 6-5.

Now consider what happens if the hydrogen atoms approach each other. Each atom has a nucleus containing a single positively charged proton. The nucleus of each atom is surrounded by a negatively charged electron in a spherical $1s$ orbital. As the atoms near each other, their charged particles begin to interact. As shown in Figure 6-6, the approaching nuclei and electrons are *attracted* to each other, which corresponds to a *decrease* in the total potential energy of the atoms. At the same time, the two nuclei *repel* each other and the two electrons *repel* each other, which results in an *increase* in potential energy.

The relative strength of attraction and repulsion between the charged particles depends on the distance separating the atoms. When the atoms first "see" each other, the electron-proton attraction is stronger than the electron-electron and proton-proton repulsions. Thus, the atoms are drawn to each other and their potential energy is lowered, as shown in part (b) of Figure 6-5.

The attractive force continues to dominate and the total potential energy continues to decrease until, eventually, a distance is reached at which the repulsion between the like charges equals the attraction of the opposite charges. This is shown in part (c) of Figure 6-5. At this point, which is represented by the bottom of the valley in the curve, potential energy is at a minimum and a stable hydrogen molecule forms. A closer approach of the atoms, shown in part (d) of Figure 6-5, results in a sharp rise in potential energy as repulsion becomes increasingly greater than attraction.

Both nuclei repel each other, as do both electron clouds.

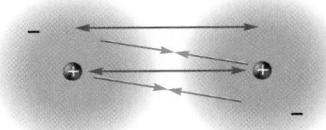

The nucleus of one atom attracts the electron cloud of the other atom, and vice versa.

FIGURE 6-6 The arrows indicate the attractive and repulsive forces between the electrons (shown as electron clouds) and nuclei of two hydrogen atoms. Attraction between particles corresponds to a decrease in potential energy of the atoms, while repulsion corresponds to an increase.

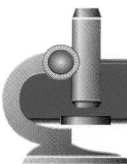

RESEARCH NOTES

Class Discussion
Have students assess the benefits and drawbacks of Professor Hoffmann's device. One possible benefit includes reducing the amount of toxic wastes in the environment. Two possible drawbacks are that this method requires considerable energy, and it would not remove all toxins from waste.

Alternative Assessment
Have students research the existing methods used to dispose of toxic wastes in your region.

Ultrasonic Toxic-Waste Destroyer

Paints, pesticides, solvents, and sulfides—these are just a few components of the 600 million tons of toxic waste that flow out of America's factories every year. Much of this waste ends up in ground water, contaminating our streams and drinking water.

Eliminating hazardous waste is a constant challenge. Unfortunately, today's disposal methods often damage the environment as much as they help it. Incinerators burning certain waste, for example, produce dioxins, one of the most dangerous class of toxins known to man.

Finding new methods to destroy toxic waste is a puzzle. Michael Hoffmann, a professor of environmental chemistry at the California Institute of Technology, thinks that part of the solution lies in sound-wave technology.

According to Hoffmann, the key to eliminating certain chemical wastes from polluted water is a phenomenon called cavitation. Cavitation occurs when the pressure in water is made to fluctuate from slightly above to slightly below normal, causing bubbles. The bubbles are unstable and collapse, creating tiny areas of extremely high pressure and heat. The pressure inside a collapsing bubble can be 1000 times greater than normal, and the temperature reaches about

5000°C—just a bit cooler than the surface of the sun. These conditions are harsh enough to combust most toxic-waste compounds in the water, breaking them down into harmless components.

Professor Hoffmann has employed a device that uses ultrasound—sound waves at frequencies just above the range of human hearing—to create cavitation in polluted water. Composed of two panels that generate ultrasound at different frequencies, the toxic-waste destroyer is simple in design and in concept. As water flows between the panels, the ultrasonic waves generated by one panel form cavitation bubbles. An instant later, the ultrasound produced by the other panel collapses the bubbles. The intense pressure and heat generated break down the complex toxic compounds into simple, innocuous substances such as carbon dioxide, chloride ions, and hydrogen ions.

"With ultrasound," says Hoffmann, "we can harness frequencies . . . of about 16 kilohertz up to 1 megahertz, and different . . . compounds are destroyed more readily at one frequency versus another . . . applying a particular frequency range, we can destroy a very broad range of chemical compounds."

The device destroys simple toxins in a few minutes and other toxins in several hours. Some compounds must be broken down into intermediate chemicals first and then treated again to destroy them completely. To be sure the waste is totally removed, scientists use sophisticated tracking methods to trace what happens to every single molecule of the toxin.

The ultrasound toxic-waste destroyer treats about 10% of all types of waste, eliminating both organic and inorganic compounds, such as hydrogen cyanide, TNT, and many pesticides. While the device cannot destroy complex mixtures of compounds, such as those found in raw sewage, it does have many advantages over current technologies. Aside from having no harmful environmental side effects, ultrasonic waste destruction is much cheaper and simpler than the process of combustion. By using the destroyer preventively, manufacturers can pretreat their waste products before they dump them in the sewer, thus stopping a problem before it starts.

---

internet connect

SCiLINKS

NSTA

TOPIC: Ultrasound
GO TO: www.scilinks.org
*sci*LINKS **CODE:** HC2062

Characteristics of the Covalent Bond

In Figure 6-5 on page 165, the bottom of the valley in the curve represents the balance between attraction and repulsion in a stable covalent bond. At this point, the electrons of each hydrogen atom of the hydrogen molecule are shared between the nuclei. As shown below in Figure 6-7, the molecule's electrons can be pictured as occupying overlapping orbitals, moving about freely in either orbital.

The bonded atoms vibrate a bit, but as long as their potential energy remains close to the minimum, they are covalently bonded to each other. *The distance between two bonded atoms at their minimum potential energy, that is, the average distance between two bonded atoms, is the* **bond length.** The bond length of a hydrogen-hydrogen bond is 75 pm.

In forming a covalent bond, the hydrogen atoms need to release energy as they change from isolated individual atoms to parts of a molecule. The amount of energy released equals the difference between the potential energy at the zero level (separated atoms) and that at the bottom of the valley (bonded atoms) in Figure 6-5. The same amount of energy must be added to separate the bonded atoms. **Bond energy** *is the energy required to break a chemical bond and form neutral isolated atoms.* Scientists usually report bond energies in kilojoules per mole (kJ/mol), which indicates the energy required to break one mole of bonds in isolated molecules. For example, 436 kJ of energy is needed to break the hydrogen-hydrogen bonds in one mole of hydrogen molecules and form two moles of separated hydrogen atoms.

The energy relationships described here for the formation of a hydrogen-hydrogen bond apply generally to all covalent bonds. However, bond lengths and bond energies vary with the types of atoms that have combined. Even the energy of a bond between the same two types of atoms varies somewhat, depending on what other bonds the atoms have formed. These facts should be considered in examining the data in Table 6-1 on page 168. The first three columns in the table list bonds, bond lengths, and bond energies of atoms in specific diatomic molecules. The last three columns give average values of specified bonds in many different compounds.

Visual Strategy

FIGURE 6-7 The electron of an isolated hydrogen atom exists mostly within a predictable radius of the nucleus. Have students describe how the location of the electrons differs in a hydrogen molecule. *(The electrons spend more time in between the hydrogen nuclei, resulting in an increased electron density there.)*

Did You Know?

A microwave oven works by bathing food with radiation that has a frequency of about 3 GHz. This radiation vibrates the bonds of water molecules, creating heat and thereby cooking the food.

✔ Teaching Tip

Be sure that students understand that longer bonds tend to be weaker. Bond strength is reflected by the amount of energy needed to break a bond, or the bond energy.

CHAPTER ⟷ CONNECTION

Students may want to review electron configurations and orbital notation, discussed in Chapter 4.

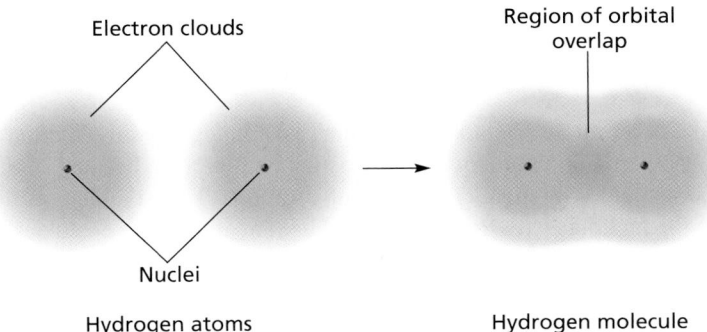

Electron clouds

Region of orbital overlap

Nuclei

Hydrogen atoms

Hydrogen molecule

FIGURE 6-7 The orbitals of the hydrogen atoms in a hydrogen molecule overlap, allowing each electron to feel the attraction of both nuclei. The result is an increase in electron density between the nuclei.

Table 6-1 Students can see a clear relationship between bond length and bond strength by plotting a graph with bond length on the *x*-axis and bond energy on the *y*-axis. Even without the graph, they may see that the bond length decreases as the strength of the bond—as represented by bond energy—increases.

Also, students should understand that the bonds, bond lengths, and bond energies in the first three columns of the table correspond to specific diatomic molecules. The bond lengths and bond energies listed in the fifth and sixth columns, on the other hand, are average values for the bonds specified in the fourth column. The bonds listed in the fourth column exist in many different molecules, and their lengths and energies vary from molecule to molecule.

TABLE 6-1 *Bond Lengths and Bond Energies for Selected Covalent Bonds*

Bond	Bond length (pm)	Bond energy (kJ/mol)	Bond	Bond length (pm)	Bond energy (kJ/mol)
H–H	74	436	C–C	154	346
F–F	141	159	C–N	147	305
Cl–Cl	199	243	C–O	143	358
Br–Br	228	193	C–H	109	418
I–I	267	151	C–Cl	177	327
H–F	92	569	C–Br	194	285
H–Cl	127	432	N–N	145	163
H–Br	141	366	N–H	101	386
H–I	161	299	O–H	96	459

All individual hydrogen atoms contain a single, unpaired electron in a $1s$ atomic orbital. When two hydrogen atoms form a molecule, they share electrons in a covalent bond. As illustrated in Figure 6-8, sharing electrons allows each atom in the hydrogen molecule to experience the effect of the stable electron configuration of helium, $1s^2$. This tendency for atoms to achieve noble-gas configurations through covalent bonding extends beyond the simple case of a hydrogen molecule.

FIGURE 6-8 By sharing electrons in overlapping orbitals, each hydrogen atom in a hydrogen molecule experiences the effect of a stable $1s^2$ configuration.

Bonding electron pair in overlapping orbitals

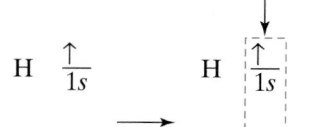

Hydrogen atoms   Hydrogen molecule

The Octet Rule

Unlike other atoms, the noble-gas atoms exist independently in nature. They possess a minimum of energy existing on their own because of the special stability of their electron configurations. This stability results from the fact that, with the exception of helium and its two electrons in a completely filled outer shell, the noble-gas atoms' outer *s* and *p* orbitals are completely filled by a total of eight electrons. Other main-group atoms can effectively fill their outermost *s* and *p* orbitals with electrons by sharing electrons through covalent bonding. Such bond formation follows the **octet rule:** *Chemical compounds tend to form so that each atom, by gaining, losing, or sharing electrons, has an octet of electrons in its highest occupied energy level.*

Let's examine how the bonding in a fluorine molecule illustrates the octet rule. An independent fluorine atom has seven electrons in its highest energy level ($[He]2s^22p^5$). Like hydrogen atoms, fluorine atoms bond covalently with each other to form diatomic molecules, F_2. When two fluorine atoms bond, each atom shares one of its valence electrons with its partner. The shared electron pair effectively fills each atom's outermost energy level with an octet of electrons, as illustrated in Figure 6-9(a). Figure 6-9(b) shows another example of the octet rule, in which the chlorine atom in a molecule of hydrogen chloride, HCl, achieves an outermost octet by sharing an electron pair with an atom of hydrogen.

FIGURE 6-9 (a) By sharing valence electrons in overlapping orbitals, each atom in a fluorine molecule feels the effect of neon's stable configuration, $[He]2s^22p^6$. (b) In a hydrogen chloride molecule, the hydrogen atom effectively fills its $1s$ orbital with two electrons, while the chlorine atom experiences the stability of an outermost octet of electrons.

CHAPTER ⟷ CONNECTION

Boron trifluoride, BF_3, mentioned on this page as an exception to the octet rule, will easily attract an atom or molecule that has an unbonded pair of electrons, such as ammonia, NH_3. This kind of reaction yields a product that is more stable because an octet is formed around boron. The ability of BF_3 to attract a pair of electrons makes it a *Lewis acid,* which is described in further detail in Chapter 15. The namesake for this type of acid, Gilbert Lewis, also proposed the octet rule and the electron-dot symbols—called Lewis structures—introduced on the next page.

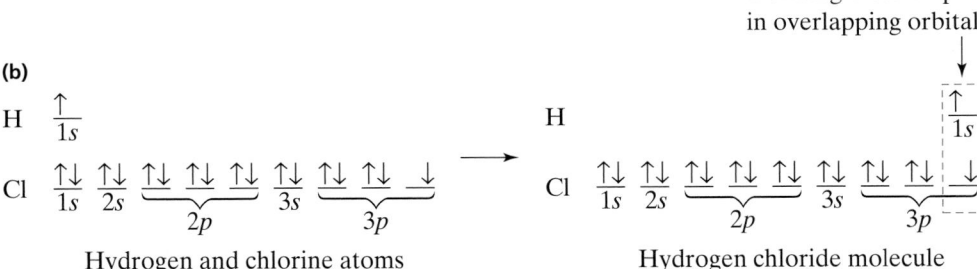

(a)

Fluorine atoms   Fluorine molecule

Bonding electron pair in overlapping orbitals

(b)

Hydrogen and chlorine atoms   Hydrogen chloride molecule

Bonding electron pair in overlapping orbitals

Exceptions to the Octet Rule

Most main-group elements tend to form covalent bonds according to the octet rule. However, there are exceptions. As you have seen, hydrogen forms bonds in which it is surrounded by only two electrons. Boron, B, has just three valence electrons ($[He]2s^22p^1$). Because electron pairs are shared in covalent bonds, boron tends to form bonds in which it is surrounded by six electrons. In boron trifluoride, BF_3, for example, the boron atom is surrounded by its own three valence electrons plus one from each of the three fluorine atoms bonded to it. Other elements can be surrounded by *more* than eight electrons when they combine with the highly electronegative elements fluorine, oxygen, and chlorine. In these cases of *expanded valence,* bonding involves electrons in *d* orbitals as well as in *s* and *p* orbitals.

6-2 Write the electron-dot notation for the following elements:
a. phosphorus
b. silicon
c. sulfur
d. chlorine
e. xenon

Ans.
a. $\cdot\overset{\cdot}{P}:$

b. $\cdot\overset{\cdot}{Si}\cdot$

c. $:\overset{\cdot}{S}:$

d. $:\overset{\cdot}{Cl}:$

e. $:\overset{\cdot\cdot}{Xe}:$

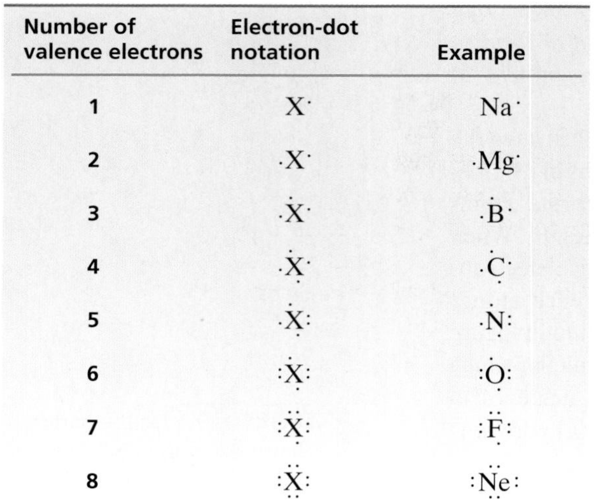

Number of valence electrons	Electron-dot notation	Example
1	X·	Na·
2	·X·	·Mg·
3	·X̣·	·Ḅ·
4	·X̣·	·Ċ·
5	·X̣:	·N̈:
6	:X̣:	:Ö:
7	:X̣:	:F̈:
8	:X̣:	:N̈e:

FIGURE 6-10 To write an element's electron-dot notation, determine the element's number of valence electrons. Then place a corresponding number of dots around the element's symbol, as shown.

Electron-Dot Notation

Covalent bond formation usually involves only the electrons in an atom's outermost energy levels, or the atom's valence electrons. To keep track of these electrons, it is helpful to use electron-dot notation. **Electron-dot notation** *is an electron-configuration notation in which only the valence electrons of an atom of a particular element are shown, indicated by dots placed around the element's symbol.* The inner-shell electrons are not shown. For example, the electron-dot notation for a fluorine atom (electron configuration $[He]2s^2p^5$) may be written as follows.

$$:\overset{\cdot\cdot}{F}:$$

In general, an element's number of valence electrons can be determined by adding the superscripts of the element's noble-gas notation. In this book, the electron-dot notations for elements with 1–8 valence electrons are written as shown in Figure 6-10.

SAMPLE PROBLEM 6-2

a. Write the electron-dot notation for hydrogen.
b. Write the electron-dot notation for nitrogen.

SOLUTION a. A hydrogen atom has only one occupied energy level, the $n = 1$ level, which contains a single electron. Therefore, the electron-dot notation for hydrogen is written as follows.

$$H\cdot$$

b. The group notation for nitrogen's family of elements is ns^2np^3, which indicates that nitrogen has five valence electrons. Therefore, the electron-dot notation for nitrogen is written as follows.

$$\cdot\overset{\cdot}{N}:$$

Lewis Structures

Electron-dot notation can also be used to represent molecules. For example, a hydrogen molecule, H_2, is represented by combining the notations of two individual hydrogen atoms, as follows.

$$H:H$$

The pair of dots represents the shared electron pair of the hydrogen-hydrogen covalent bond. For a molecule of fluorine, F_2, the electron-dot notations of two fluorine atoms are combined.

$$:\ddot{F}:\ddot{F}:$$

Here also the pair of dots between the two symbols represents the shared pair of a covalent bond. In addition, each fluorine atom is surrounded by three pairs of electrons that are not shared in bonds. *An* **unshared pair,** *also called a* **lone pair,** *is a pair of electrons that is not involved in bonding and that belongs exclusively to one atom.*

The pair of dots representing a shared pair of electrons in a covalent bond is often replaced by a long dash. According to this convention, hydrogen and fluorine molecules are represented as follows.

$$H-H \quad :\ddot{F}-\ddot{F}:$$

These representations are all **Lewis structures,** *formulas in which atomic symbols represent nuclei and inner-shell electrons, dot-pairs or dashes between two atomic symbols represent electron pairs in covalent bonds, and dots adjacent to only one atomic symbol represent unshared electrons.* It is common to write Lewis structures that show only the electrons that are shared, using dashes to represent the bonds. *A* **structural formula** *indicates the kind, number, arrangement, and bonds but not the unshared pairs of the atoms in a molecule.* For example, $F-F$ and $H-Cl$ are structural formulas.

The Lewis structures (and therefore the structural formulas) for many molecules can be drawn if one knows the composition of the molecule and which atoms are bonded to each other. The following sample problem illustrates the basic steps for writing Lewis structures. The molecule described in this problem contains bonds with single shared electron pairs. A single covalent bond, or a **single bond,** *is a covalent bond produced by the sharing of one pair of electrons between two atoms.*

SECTION 6-2

CHAPTER ⟷ CONNECTION

Structural formulas can be used to discern the difference between two *isomers*—compounds with the same formula but a different arrangement of atoms. Isomers are discussed in Chapter 20.

ADDITIONAL SAMPLE PROBLEM

6-3 *Additional Sample Problem is found on page 199A.*

✔ **Teaching Tip**

Some students might derive Lewis structures more easily by representing the valence electrons from each atom in the molecule or ion with a different symbol. Emphasize, however, that this is only an intermediate representation, and that the other symbols should then be converted to dots. For example,

$$H\!:\!H \quad \text{or} \quad H\!:\!H$$

$$:\ddot{F} {\times\!\!\times} \ddot{F} {\times\!\!\times} \quad \text{or} \quad :\ddot{F}:\ddot{F}:$$

SAMPLE PROBLEM 6-3

Draw the Lewis structure of iodomethane, CH_3I.

SOLUTION

1. *Determine the type and number of atoms in the molecule.*
   The formula shows one carbon atom, one iodine atom, and three hydrogen atoms.

2. *Write the electron-dot notation for each type of atom in the molecule.*
   Carbon is from Group 14 and has four valence electrons. Iodine is from Group 17 and has seven valence electrons. Hydrogen has one valence electron.

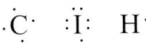

CHAPTER ⟷ CONNECTION

The geometries of hydrocarbon double and triple bonds are discussed in Chapter 20.

3. *Determine the total number of valence electrons in the atoms to be combined.*

$$
\begin{array}{lll}
\text{C} & 1 \times 4e^- = & 4e^- \\
\text{I} & 1 \times 7e^- = & 7e^- \\
\text{H} & 3 \times 1e^- = & \underline{3e^-} \\
& & 14e^-
\end{array}
$$

4. *Arrange the atoms to form a skeleton structure for the molecule. If carbon is present, it is the central atom. Otherwise, the least-electronegative atom is central (except for hydrogen, which is never central). Then connect the atoms by electron-pair bonds.*

$$
\begin{array}{c}
\text{H} \\
\text{H} : \ddot{\text{C}} : \text{I} \\
\text{H}
\end{array}
$$

5. *Add unshared pairs of electrons so that each hydrogen atom shares a pair of electrons and each other nonmetal is surrounded by eight electrons.*

$$
\begin{array}{c}
\text{H} \\
\text{H} : \ddot{\text{C}} : \ddot{\text{I}} : \\
\text{H}
\end{array}
\quad \text{or} \quad
\begin{array}{c}
\text{H} \\
| \\
\text{H} - \text{C} - \ddot{\text{I}} : \\
| \\
\text{H}
\end{array}
$$

6. *Count the electrons in the structure to be sure that the number of valence electrons used equals the number available.*

   There are eight electrons in the four covalent bonds and six electrons in the three unshared pairs, giving the correct total of 14 valence electrons.

PRACTICE

1. Draw the Lewis structure of ammonia, NH_3.

   Answer

   $$
   \begin{array}{c}
   \text{H} : \ddot{\text{N}} : \text{H} \quad \text{or} \quad \text{H} - \ddot{\text{N}} - \text{H} \\
   \text{H} \qquad\qquad\qquad \text{H}
   \end{array}
   $$

2. Draw the Lewis structure for hydrogen sulfide, H_2S.

   Answer

   $$
   \text{H} : \ddot{\ddot{\text{S}}} : \text{H} \quad \text{or} \quad \text{H} - \ddot{\ddot{\text{S}}} - \text{H}
   $$

Multiple Covalent Bonds

Atoms of some elements, especially carbon, nitrogen, and oxygen, can share more than one electron pair. A double covalent bond, or simply a **double bond,** *is a covalent bond produced by the sharing of two pairs of electrons between two atoms.* A double bond is shown either by two side-by-side pairs of dots or by two parallel dashes. All four electrons in a double bond "belong" to both atoms. In ethene, C_2H_4, for example, two electron pairs are simultaneously shared by two carbon atoms.

$$
\begin{array}{cc}
\text{H} \qquad \text{H} \\
\diagdown \quad \diagup \\
\text{C} :: \text{C} \qquad \text{or} \\
\diagup \quad \diagdown \\
\text{H} \qquad \text{H}
\end{array}
\qquad
\begin{array}{cc}
\text{H} \qquad \text{H} \\
\diagdown \quad \diagup \\
\text{C} = \text{C} \\
\diagup \quad \diagdown \\
\text{H} \qquad \text{H}
\end{array}
$$

A triple covalent bond, or simply a **triple bond,** *is a covalent bond produced by the sharing of three pairs of electrons between two atoms.* For example, elemental nitrogen, N_2, like hydrogen and the halogens, normally exists as diatomic molecules. In this case, however, each nitrogen atom, which has five valence electrons, acquires three electrons to complete an octet by sharing three pairs of electrons with its partner. This is illustrated in the Lewis structure and the formula structure for N_2, as shown below.

:N⋮⋮N: or N≡N

Figure 6-11 represents nitrogen's triple bond through orbital notation. Like the single bonds in hydrogen and halogen molecules, the triple bond in nitrogen molecules is nonpolar.

Carbon forms a number of compounds containing triple bonds. For example, the compound ethyne, C_2H_2, contains a carbon-carbon triple bond.

H:C⋮⋮C:H or H−C≡C−H

Double and triple bonds are referred to as **multiple bonds,** or multiple covalent bonds. Double bonds in general have higher bond energies and are shorter than single bonds. Triple bonds are even stronger and shorter. Table 6-2 compares average bond lengths and bond energies for some single, double, and triple bonds.

In writing Lewis structures for molecules that contain carbon, nitrogen, or oxygen, one must remember that multiple bonds between pairs of these atoms are possible. (A hydrogen atom, on the other hand, has only one electron and therefore always forms a single covalent bond.) The need for a multiple bond becomes obvious if there are not enough valence electrons to complete octets by adding unshared pairs. Sample Problem 6-4 on page 174 illustrates how to deal with this situation.

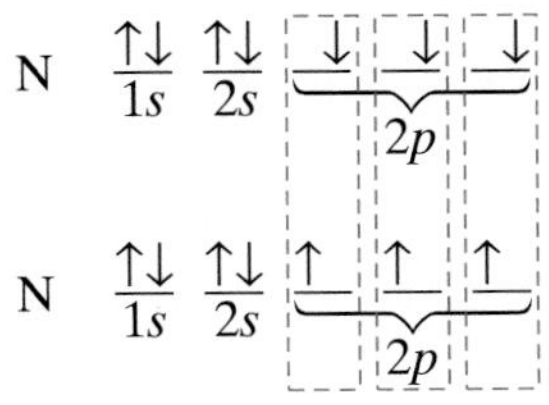

Nitrogen molecule

FIGURE 6-11 In a molecule of nitrogen, N_2, each nitrogen atom is surrounded by six shared electrons plus one unshared pair of electrons. Thus, each nitrogen atom follows the octet rule in forming a triple covalent bond.

TABLE 6-2 ***Bond Lengths and Bond Energies for Single and Multiple Covalent Bonds***

Bond	Bond length (pm)	Bond energy (kJ/mol)	Bond	Bond length (pm)	Bond energy (kJ/mol)
C−C	154	346	C−O	143	358
C=C	134	612	C=O	120	732
C≡C	120	835	C≡O	113	1072
C−N	147	305	N−N	145	163
C=N	132	615	N=N	125	418
C≡N	116	887	N≡N	110	945

TABLE STRATEGY

Table 6-2 Once again, have students observe the relationship between bond length and bond energy. In general, stronger bonds (those with higher bond energies) are shorter bonds.

✔Teaching Tip

The C=O bond energy in carbon dioxide is an exception, having a value of 799 kJ/mol.

6-4 *Additional Sample Problem is found on page 199A.*

Did You Know?

Formaldehyde, the molecule mentioned in Sample Problem 6-4, is believed to cause cancer. Because of its bacterial-killing characteristic, it was at one time used to preserve animals in biology labs. Now, however, safer chemicals are used.

SAMPLE PROBLEM 6-4

Draw the Lewis structure for methanal, CH₂O, which is also known as formaldehyde.

SOLUTION

1. *Determine the number of atoms of each element present in the molecule.*
   The formula shows one carbon atom, two hydrogen atoms, and one oxygen atom.

2. *Write the electron-dot notation for each type of atom.*
   Carbon from Group 14 has four valence electrons. Oxygen, which is in Group 16, has six valence electrons. Hydrogen has only one electron.

   $$\cdot \dot{C} \cdot \quad : \dot{O} : \quad H \cdot$$

3. *Determine the total number of valence electrons in the atoms to be combined.*

   $$
   \begin{array}{lll}
   C & 1 \times 4e^- = & 4e^- \\
   O & 1 \times 6e^- = & 6e^- \\
   2H & 2 \times 1e^- = & \underline{2e^-} \\
   & & 12e^-
   \end{array}
   $$

4. *Arrange the atoms to form a skeleton structure for the molecule, and connect the atoms by electron-pair bonds.*

   $$
   \begin{array}{c}
   H \\
   H:\ddot{C}:O
   \end{array}
   $$

5. *Add unshared pairs of electrons so that each hydrogen atom shares a pair of electrons and each other nonmetal is surrounded by eight electrons.*

   $$
   \begin{array}{c}
   H \\
   H:\ddot{C}:\ddot{O}:
   \end{array}
   $$

6a. *Count the electrons in the Lewis structure to be sure that the number of valence electrons used equals the number available.*
   The structure above has six electrons in covalent bonds and eight electrons in four lone pairs, for a total of 14 electrons. The structure has two valence electrons too many.

6b. *If too many electrons have been used, subtract one or more lone pairs until the total number of valence electrons is correct. Then move one or more lone electron pairs to existing bonds between non-hydrogen atoms until the outer shells of all atoms are completely filled.*
   Subtract the lone pair of electrons from the carbon atom. Then move one lone pair of electrons from the oxygen to the bond between carbon and oxygen to form a double bond.

   $$
   H:\ddot{C}::\ddot{O} \quad \text{or} \quad
   \begin{array}{c}
   H \\
   | \\
   H{-}C{=}\ddot{O}
   \end{array}
   $$

   There are eight electrons in covalent bonds and four electrons in lone pairs, for a total of 12 valence electrons.

PRACTICE

1. Draw the Lewis structure for carbon dioxide, CO₂.

   Answer
   $$\ddot{O}{=}C{=}\ddot{O}$$

2. Draw the Lewis structure for hydrogen cyanide, which contains one hydrogen atom, one carbon atom, and one nitrogen atom.

   Answer
   $$H{-}C{\equiv}N:$$

Resonance Structures

Some molecules and ions cannot be represented adequately by a single Lewis structure. One such molecule is ozone, O_3, which can be represented by either of the following Lewis structures.

$$\ddot{O}=\ddot{O}-\ddot{\ddot{O}}: \quad or \quad :\ddot{\ddot{O}}-\ddot{O}=\ddot{O}$$

Notice that each structure indicates that the ozone molecule has two types of O—O bonds, one single and one double. Chemists once speculated that ozone split its time existing as one of these two structures, constantly alternating, or "resonating," from one to the other. Experiments, however, revealed that the oxygen-oxygen bonds in ozone are identical. Therefore, scientists now say that ozone has a single structure that is the average of these two structures. Together the structures are referred to as *resonance structures* or *resonance hybrids*. **Resonance** *refers to bonding in molecules or ions that cannot be correctly represented by a single Lewis structure.* To indicate resonance, a double-headed arrow is placed between a molecule's resonance structures.

$$\ddot{O}=\ddot{O}-\ddot{\ddot{O}}: \longleftrightarrow :\ddot{\ddot{O}}-\ddot{O}=\ddot{O}$$

Covalent-Network Bonding

All the covalent compounds that you have read about to this point are molecular. They consist of many identical molecules bound together by forces acting between the molecules. (You will read more about intermolecular forces in Section 6-5.) There are many covalently bonded compounds that do not contain individual molecules, but instead can be pictured as continuous, three-dimensional networks of bonded atoms. You will read more about covalently bonded networks in Chapter 11.

SECTION REVIEW

1. Define the following:
   a. bond length   b. bond energy

2. State the octet rule.

3. How many pairs of electrons are shared in the following types of covalent bonds?
   a. a single bond
   b. a double bond
   c. a triple bond

4. Draw the Lewis structures for the following molecules:
   a. IBr
   b. CH_3Br
   c. C_2HCl
   d. $SiCl_4$
   e. F_2O

Teaching Tip

Lewis structures assume that electrons are found only between the two atoms in a bond. However, sometimes electrons are *delocalized,* which means that they are distributed over three or more atoms. In such cases, Lewis structures do not clearly model the location of the electrons in the bond unless resonance structures are used.

Did You Know?

Diamond, the hardest material known, is actually made of carbon atoms that are bonded together with single bonds. A diamond crystal is an example of a covalent network.

SECTION REVIEW

1. a. the distance at which two covalently bonded atoms minimize their potential energy
b. the energy required to break a chemical bond and form neutral atoms in the gas phase

2. Chemical compounds tend to form so that each atom gains, loses, or shares electrons until an octet of electrons exists in its highest energy level.

3. a. one
b. two
c. three

4. a. $:\ddot{I}:\ddot{Br}:$

b.
$\quad H$
$H:\ddot{C}:\ddot{Br}:$
$\quad H$

c. $H:C::C:\ddot{Cl}:$

d.
$\quad :\ddot{Cl}:$
$:\ddot{Cl}:Si:\ddot{Cl}:$
$\quad :\ddot{Cl}:$

e. $:\ddot{F}:\ddot{O}:\ddot{F}:$

Ionic Bonding and Ionic Compounds

Lesson Starter

Use plastic, interlocking building blocks to demonstrate the difference between ionic and covalent bonding. Assemble a number of blocks so that all sides of the object created are flush. This is a model of a molecule—the atoms are bonded to create an individual unit capable of existing on its own. Assemble a number of blocks so that pieces of the various blocks are jutting out of the sides of the object created. This represents a small portion of the ionic arrangement within an ionic compound. The pieces of blocks jutting out represent cations and anions, which attract more ions (more blocks) to create a large array of packed ions. The result is a huge aggregate of ions that have minimized their potential energy through electrical attraction (as opposed to electron sharing).

Common Misconception

Remind students that the chemical formulas for ionic compounds represent the simplest formula of the compound, as opposed to the formulas for molecules, which represent a discrete group of separate molecules.

OBJECTIVES

- Compare and contrast a chemical formula for a molecular compound with one for an ionic compound.

- Discuss the arrangements of ions in crystals.

- Define *lattice energy* and explain its significance.

- List and compare the distinctive properties of ionic and molecular compounds.

- Write the Lewis structure for a polyatomic ion given the identity of the atoms combined and other appropriate information.

Most of the rocks and minerals that make up Earth's crust consist of positive and negative ions held together by ionic bonding. A familiar example of an ionically bonded compound is sodium chloride, or common table salt, which is found in nature as rock salt. A sodium ion, Na^+, has a charge of 1+. A chloride ion, Cl^-, has a charge of 1−. In sodium chloride, these ions combine in a one-to-one ratio—Na^+Cl^-—so that each positive charge is balanced by a negative charge. Because chemists are aware of this balance of charge, the chemical formula for sodium chloride is usually written simply as NaCl.

An **ionic compound** *is composed of positive and negative ions that are combined so that the numbers of positive and negative charges are equal.* Most ionic compounds exist as crystalline solids (see Figure 6-12). A crystal of any ionic compound is a three-dimensional network of positive and negative ions mutually attracted to one another. As a result, in contrast to a molecular compound, an ionic compound is not composed of independent, neutral units that can be isolated and examined. The chemical formula of an ionic compound merely represents the simplest ratio of the compound's combined ions that gives electrical neutrality.

The chemical formula of an ionic compound shows the ratio of the ions present in a sample of any size. *A* **formula unit** *is the simplest collection of atoms from which an ionic compound's formula can be established.* For example, one formula unit of sodium chloride, NaCl, is one sodium cation plus one chloride anion. (In naming anions, the *-ine* ending of the element's name is replaced with *-ide*. You'll read more about naming compounds in Chapter 7.)

The ratio of ions in a formula unit depends on the charges of the ions combined. For example, to achieve electrical neutrality in the ionic compound calcium fluoride, two fluoride anions, F^-, each with a charge of 1−, must balance the 2+ charge of each calcium cation, Ca^{2+}. Therefore, the formula of calcium fluoride is CaF_2.

FIGURE 6-12 Like most ionic compounds, sodium chloride is a crystalline solid.

Formation of Ionic Compounds

Electron-dot notation can be used to demonstrate the changes that take place in ionic bonding. Ionic compounds do not ordinarily form by the combination of isolated ions, but consider for a moment a sodium atom and a chlorine atom approaching each other. The two atoms are neutral and have one and seven valence electrons, respectively.

Na·

Sodium atom

:C̈l:

Chlorine atom

We have already seen that atoms of sodium and the other alkali metals readily lose one electron to form cations. And we have seen that atoms of chlorine and the other halogens readily gain one electron to form anions. The combination of sodium and chlorine atoms to produce one formula unit of sodium chloride can thus be represented as follows.

Na·   +   :C̈l: ⟶   Na⁺   +   :C̈l:⁻

Sodium atom   Chlorine atom   Sodium cation   Chloride anion

The transfer of an electron from the sodium atom to the chlorine atom transforms each atom into an ion with a noble-gas configuration. In the combination of calcium with fluorine, two fluorine atoms are needed to accept the two valence electrons given up by one calcium atom.

·Ca·   +   :F̈:   +   :F̈:   ⟶   Ca²⁺   +   :F̈:⁻   +   :F̈:⁻

Calcium atom   Fluorine atoms   Calcium cation   Fluoride anions

Characteristics of Ionic Bonding

Recall that nature favors arrangements in which potential energy is minimized. In an ionic crystal, ions minimize their potential energy by combining in an orderly arrangement known as a *crystal lattice* (see Figure 6-13). The attractive forces at work within an ionic crystal include those between oppositely charged ions and those between the nuclei and electrons of adjacent ions. The repulsive forces include those between like-charged ions and those between electrons of adjacent ions. The distances between ions and their arrangement in a crystal represent a balance among all these forces. Sodium chloride's crystal structure is shown in Figure 6-14 below.

internet**connect**

SC*LINKS*

NSTA

TOPIC: Ionic bonding
GO TO: www.scilinks.org
*sci*LINKS CODE: HC2063

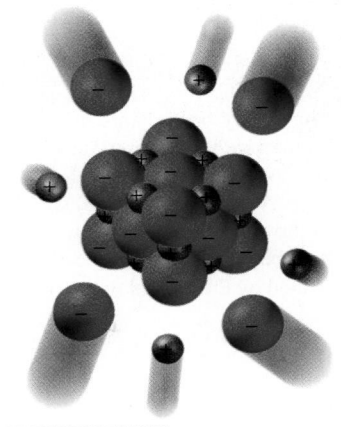

FIGURE 6-13 The ions in an ionic compound lower their potential energy by forming an orderly, three-dimensional array in which the positive and negative charges are balanced. The electrical forces of attraction between oppositely charged ions extend over long distances, causing a large decrease in potential energy.

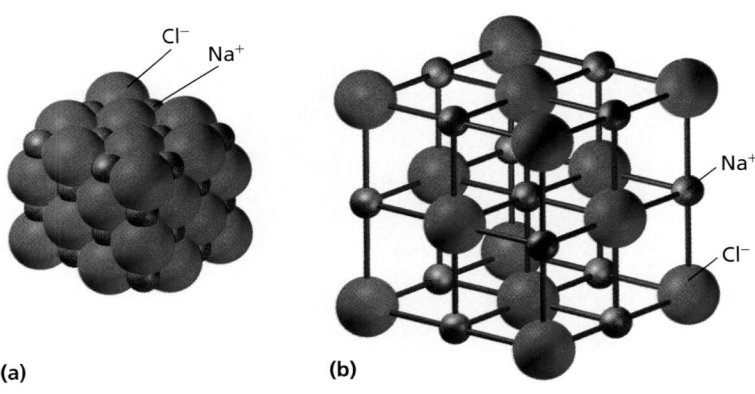

Cl⁻
Na⁺

Na⁺

Cl⁻

(a)   (b)

FIGURE 6-14 Two models of the crystal structure of sodium chloride are shown. (a) To illustrate the ions' actual arrangement, the sodium and chloride ions are shown with their electron clouds just touching. (b) In an expanded view, the distances between ions have been exaggerated in order to clarify the positioning of the ions in the structure.

Visual Strategy

FIGURE 6-15 Have students look at the portion of sodium chloride's crystal arrangement from the perspective of the chloride ion, which is surrounded by six sodium ions. Then have them consider the perspective of a sodium ion, which is surrounded by six chloride ions. Ask students to deduce the ratio of sodium ions to chloride ions in sodium chloride *(one-to-one)*.

✔ **Teaching Tip**

Students are often confused about the difference in signs of bond energies (Table 6-2) and lattice energies (Table 6-3). The lattice energy describes the energies associated with the *formation* of bonds, whereas the bond energy describes the energies associated with the *breaking* of bonds. In any case, the bonded atoms are *more stable* than the separate ones. The larger the *magnitude* of the lattice energy or the bond energy, the more stable the bonding.

FIGURE 6-15 The figure shows the ions that most closely surround a chloride anion and a sodium cation within the crystal structure of NaCl. The structure is composed such that (a) six Na$^+$ ions surround each Cl$^-$ ion. At the same time, (b) six Cl$^-$ ions surround each Na$^+$ ion (which cannot be seen but whose location is indicated by the dashed outline).

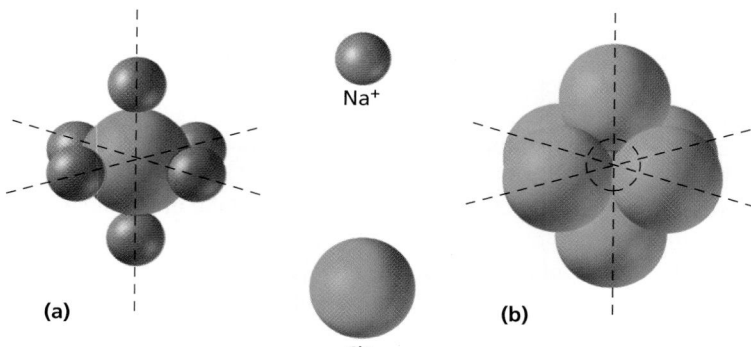

(a)   (b)

Na$^+$

Cl$^-$

Figure 6-15 shows the crystal structure of sodium chloride in greater detail. Within the arrangement, each sodium cation is surrounded by six chloride anions. At the same time, each chloride anion is surrounded by six sodium cations. Attraction between the adjacent oppositely charged ions is much stronger than repulsion by other ions of the same charge, which are farther away.

The three-dimensional arrangements of ions and the strengths of attraction between them vary with the sizes and charges of the ions and the numbers of ions of different charges. For example, in calcium fluoride, there are two anions for each cation. Each calcium cation is surrounded by eight fluoride anions. At the same time, each fluoride ion is surrounded by four calcium cations, as shown in Figure 6-16.

To compare bond strengths in ionic compounds, chemists compare the amounts of energy released when separated ions in a gas come together to form a crystalline solid. **Lattice energy** *is the energy released when one mole of an ionic crystalline compound is formed from gaseous ions.* Lattice energy values for a few common ionic compounds are shown in Table 6-3. The negative energy values indicate that energy is *released* when the crystals are formed.

Calcium ion, Ca^{2+}

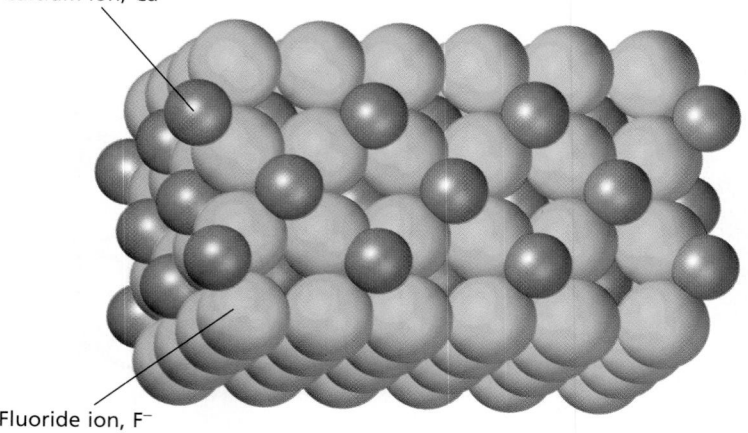

FIGURE 6-16 In the crystal structure of calcium fluoride, CaF$_2$, each calcium cation is surrounded by eight fluoride anions and each fluoride ion is surrounded by four calcium cations. This is the closest possible packing of the ions in which the positive and negative charges are balanced.

Fluoride ion, F$^-$

A Comparison of Ionic and Molecular Compounds

The force that holds ions together in ionic compounds is a very strong overall attraction between positive and negative charges. In a molecular compound, the covalent bonds of the atoms making up each molecule are also strong. But the forces of attraction *between* molecules are much weaker than the forces of ionic bonding. This difference in the strength of attraction between the basic units of molecular and ionic compounds gives rise to different properties in the two types of compounds.

The melting point, boiling point, and hardness of a compound depend on how strongly its basic units are attracted to each other. Because the forces of attraction between individual molecules are not very strong, many molecular compounds melt at low temperatures. In fact, many molecular compounds are already completely gaseous at room temperature. In contrast, the ions in ionic compounds are held together by strong attractive forces, so ionic compounds generally have higher melting and boiling points than do molecular compounds. Further, they do not vaporize at room temperature as many molecular compounds do.

Ionic compounds are hard but brittle. Why? In an ionic crystal, even a slight shift of one row of ions relative to another causes a large buildup of repulsive forces, as shown in Figure 6-17. These forces make it difficult for one layer to move relative to another, causing ionic compounds to be hard. If one layer is moved, however, the repulsive forces make the layers part completely, causing ionic compounds to be brittle.

In the solid state, the ions cannot move, so the compounds are not electrical conductors. In the molten state, ionic compounds are electrical conductors because the ions can move freely to carry electrical current. Many ionic compounds can dissolve in water. When they dissolve, their ions separate from each other and become surrounded by water molecules. These ions are free to move through the solution, so such solutions are electrical conductors. Other ionic compounds do not dissolve in water, however, because the attraction of the water molecules cannot overcome the attractions between the ions.

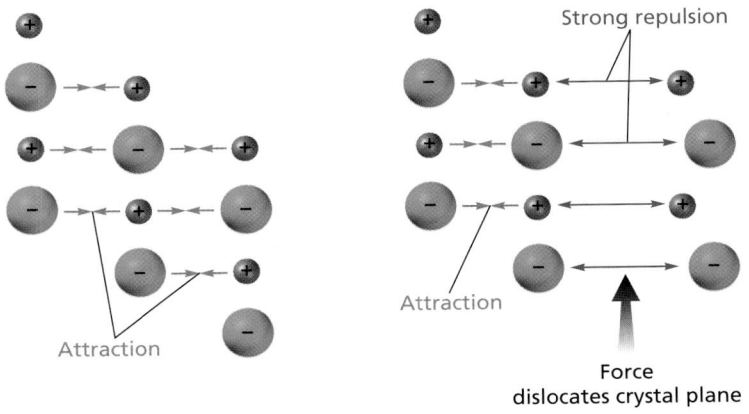

(a)

Attraction

(b)

Strong repulsion

Attraction

Force
dislocates crystal plane

FIGURE 6-17 (a) The attraction between positive and negative ions in a crystalline ionic compound causes layers of ions to resist motion. (b) When struck with sufficient force, the layers shift so that ions of the same charge approach each other, causing repulsion. As a result, the crystal shatters along the planes.

Compound	Lattice energy (kJ/mol)
NaCl	−787.5
NaBr	−751.4
CaF₂	−2634.7
CaO	−3385
LiCl	−861.3
LiF	−1032
MgO	−3760
KCl	−715

TABLE 6-3 *Lattice Energies of Some Common Ionic Compounds*

 Teaching Tip

Lattice energies are listed as negative values to indicate that energy is given off when the gaseous ions come together to form the ionic crystal.

TABLE STRATEGY

Table 6-3 The lattice energy must be overcome in order for an ionic compound to dissolve in water. Have students form a hypothesis about which two ionic compounds listed in the table are the least soluble in water (*MgO and CaO*).

Reading Skill-Builder

COMPARING AND CONTRASTING Have students use the selection A Comparison of Ionic and Molecular Compounds as a starting point for a chart comparing and contrasting covalent and ionic bonding. Have students reread Sections 6-1, 6-2, and 6-3 to help them complete their charts. Suggest that they incorporate the boldfaced terms in these sections as well as any other relevant information.

Common Misconception

Many students forget that although polyatomic ions are involved in ionic bonding, the ions themselves are held together by covalent bonding. For example, the ammonium ion is held together by covalent bonding, but ammonium ions and chloride ions are held together by ionic bonding in the compound ammonium chloride. We call ammonium chloride an ionic compound.

SECTION REVIEW

1. Two possible examples are sodium chloride, NaCl, and magnesium chloride, $MgCl_2$.

2. a. $Li^{\cdot} + :\ddot{C}l: \longrightarrow$

$\qquad Li^+ + :\ddot{C}l:^- \;(LiCl)$

b. $\cdot Ca \cdot + :\ddot{I}: + :\ddot{I}: \longrightarrow$

$\qquad Ca^{2+} + :\ddot{I}:^- + :\ddot{I}:^- \;(CaI_2)$

3. Ionic compounds consist of positive and negative ions bound together by electrical attraction. Molecular compounds are groups of atoms held together by covalent bonding, or the sharing of electrons.

4. Compound B is probably a molecular substance; compound A is probably ionic. The intermolecular attractions that hold molecules together are weaker than ionic attraction, resulting in lower melting and boiling points in molecular substances.

Polyatomic Ions

Certain atoms bond covalently with each other to form a group of atoms that has both molecular and ionic characteristics. *A charged group of covalently bonded atoms is known as a* **polyatomic ion.** Polyatomic ions combine with ions of opposite charge to form ionic compounds. The charge of a polyatomic ion results from an excess of electrons (negative charge) or a shortage of electrons (positive charge). For example, an ammonium ion, a common positively charged polyatomic ion, contains one nitrogen atom and four hydrogen atoms and has a single positive charge. Its formula is NH_4^+, sometimes written as $[NH_4]^+$ to show that the group of atoms *as a whole* has a charge of 1+. The seven protons in the nitrogen atom plus the four protons in the four hydrogen atoms give the ammonium ion a total positive charge of 11+. An independent nitrogen atom has seven electrons, and four independent hydrogen atoms have a total of four electrons. When these atoms combine to form an ammonium ion, one of their electrons is lost, giving the polyatomic ion a total negative charge of 10−.

Lewis structures for the ammonium ion and some common negative polyatomic ions—the nitrate, sulfate, and phosphate ions—are shown below. To find the Lewis structure for a polyatomic ion, follow the steps of Sample Problem 6-4 on page 174, with the following exception. If the ion is negatively charged, add to the total number of valence electrons a number of e^- corresponding to the ion's negative charge. If the ion is positively charged, subtract from the total number of valence electrons a number of e^- corresponding to the ion's positive charge.

Ammonium ion   Nitrate ion   Sulfate ion   Phosphate ion

SECTION REVIEW

1. Give two examples of an ionic compound.

2. Use electron-dot notation to demonstrate the formation of ionic compounds involving the following:
   a. Li and Cl
   b. Ca and I

3. Distinguish between ionic and molecular compounds in terms of the basic units that each is composed of.

4. Compound B has lower melting and boiling points than compound A. At the same temperature, compound B vaporizes faster and to a greater extent than compound A. If one of these compounds is ionic and the other is molecular, which would you expect to be molecular? ionic? Explain the reasoning behind your choices.

Metallic Bonding

Chemical bonding is different in metals than it is in ionic, molecular, or covalent-network compounds. This difference is reflected in the unique properties of metals. They are excellent electrical conductors in the solid state—much better conductors than even molten ionic compounds. This property is due to the highly mobile valence electrons of the atoms that make up a metal. Such mobility is not possible in molecular compounds, in which valence electrons are localized in electron-pair bonds between neutral atoms. Nor is it possible in solid ionic compounds, in which electrons are bound to individual ions that are held in place in crystal structures.

The Metallic-Bond Model

The highest energy levels of most metal atoms are occupied by very few electrons. In *s*-block metals, for example, one or two valence electrons occupy the outermost orbital, whereas all three outermost *p* orbitals, which can hold a total of six electrons, are vacant. In addition to completely vacant outer *p* orbitals, *d*-block metals also possess many vacant *d* orbitals in the energy level just below their highest energy level.

   Within a metal, the vacant orbitals in the atoms' outer energy levels overlap. This overlapping of orbitals allows the outer electrons of the atoms to roam freely throughout the entire metal. The electrons are *delocalized*, which means that they do not belong to any one atom but move freely about the metal's network of empty atomic orbitals. These mobile electrons form a *sea of electrons* around the metal atoms, which are packed together in a crystal lattice (see Figure 6-18). *The chemical bonding that results from the attraction between metal atoms and the surrounding sea of electrons is called* **metallic bonding.**

Metallic Properties

The freedom of electrons to move in a network of metal atoms accounts for the high electrical and thermal conductivity characteristic of all metals. In addition, because they contain many orbitals separated by extremely small energy differences, metals can absorb a wide range of light frequencies. This absorption of light results in the excitation of the metal atoms' electrons to higher energy levels. The electrons immediately fall back down to lower levels, emitting energy in the form of light. This de-excitation is responsible for the shiny appearance of metal surfaces.

OBJECTIVES

- Describe the electron-sea model of metallic bonding, and explain why metals are good electrical conductors.

- Explain why metal surfaces are shiny.

- Explain why metals are malleable and ductile but ionic-crystalline compounds are not.

internetconnect

SCILINKS
NSTA

TOPIC: Metallic bonding
GO TO: www.scilinks.org
*sci*LINKS CODE: HC2064

FIGURE 6-18 The model shows a portion of the crystal structure of solid sodium. The atoms are arranged so that each sodium atom is surrounded by eight other sodium atoms. The atoms are relatively fixed in position, while the electrons are free to move throughout the crystal, forming an electron sea.

Lesson Starter

Place a sample of sodium chloride or magnesium chloride and a sample of mossy zinc on the table top. Hit both with a hammer. (Use eye protection, and make sure that students are at a sufficient distance from the samples to avoid the possibility of salt fragments getting in their eyes. You may want to put the salt in a plastic bag before you hit it.) The salt is brittle and shatters. The zinc will just flatten because it is malleable. The malleability of metal is a property that results from metallic bonding.

CHAPTER ◄——► **CONNECTION**

The luster of metals is caused by the emission of photons when excited electrons return to the ground state. This principle was discussed in Chapter 4.

✔ **Teaching Tip**

Because electrons are delocalized and mobile, they can move from the region around one nucleus to the region around another. This allows for the conductivity of heat and electricity.

HANDBOOK  **CONNECTION**

The band theory of conductivity is presented with Group 14 of the *Elements Handbook* (pages 754–769).

Analogy

Metallically bonded atoms are like large objects embedded in the material used for packing boxes, which represents the electron sea. In the same way that the objects can move freely relative to each other within the packing material, the nuclei of metals can move freely relative to one another in the electron "packing material"; malleability and ductility result.

SECTION REVIEW

1. Metallic bonding is generally viewed as the result of the mutual sharing of many electrons by many atoms. Each atom contributes its valence electrons to a region surrounding the atoms. These electrons are then free to move about the mostly vacant outer orbitals of all the metal atoms. The mobile electrons are often referred to as an *electron sea*.

2. In general, the higher the heat of vaporization, the stronger the metallic bonding.

3. Metallic bonding is not directional but rather uniform throughout the solid. One group of atoms can slide past another group of atoms amid the electron sea without breaking any attractions. Ionic crystals are held together by strong electrical attraction between oppositely charged ions. Moving one plane of ions relative to another requires breaking this attraction.

FIGURE 6-19 Unlike ionic crystalline compounds, most metals are malleable. This property allows iron, for example, to be shaped into useful tools.

Most metals are also easy to form into desired shapes. Two important properties related to this characteristic are malleability and ductility. **Malleability** *is the ability of a substance to be hammered or beaten into thin sheets.* **Ductility** *is the ability of a substance to be drawn, pulled, or extruded through a small opening to produce a wire.* The malleability and ductility of metals are possible because metallic bonding is the same in all directions throughout the solid. One plane of atoms in a metal can slide past another without encountering any resistance or breaking any bonds. By contrast, recall from Section 6-3 that shifting the layers of an ionic crystal causes the bonds to break and the crystal to shatter.

Metallic Bond Strength

Metallic bond strength varies with the nuclear charge of the metal atoms and the number of electrons in the metal's electron sea. Both of these factors are reflected in a metal's *heat of vaporization.* When a metal is vaporized, the bonded atoms in the normal (usually solid) state are converted to individual metal atoms in the gaseous state. The amount of heat required to vaporize the metal is a measure of the strength of the bonds that hold the metal together. Some heats of vaporization for metals are given in Table 6-4.

TABLE 6-4 *Heats of Vaporization of Some Metals (kJ/mol)*		
Period	**Element**	
Second	Li 147	Be 297	
Third	Na 97	Mg 128	Al 294
Fourth	K 77	Ca 155	Sc 333
Fifth	Rb 76	Sr 137	Y 365
Sixth	Cs 64	Ba 140	La 402

SECTION REVIEW

1. Describe the electron-sea model of metallic bonding.

2. What is the relationship between metallic bond strength and heat of vaporization?

3. Explain why most metals are malleable and ductile but ionic crystals are not.

Molecular Geometry

The properties of molecules depend not only on the bonding of atoms but also on molecular geometry—the three-dimensional arrangement of a molecule's atoms in space. The polarity of each bond, along with the geometry of the molecule, determines **molecular polarity,** *or the uneven distribution of molecular charge.* As you will read, molecular polarity strongly influences the forces that act *between* molecules in liquids and solids.

A chemical formula reveals little information about a molecule's geometry. After performing many tests designed to reveal the shapes of various molecules, chemists developed two different, equally successful theories to explain certain aspects of their findings. One theory accounts for molecular bond angles. The other is used to describe the orbitals that contain the valence electrons of a molecule's atoms.

VSEPR Theory

As shown in Figure 6-20, diatomic molecules, like those of hydrogen, H_2, and hydrogen chloride, HCl, must be linear because they consist of only two atoms. To predict the geometries of more-complicated molecules, one must consider the locations of all electron pairs surrounding the bonded atoms. This is the basis of VSEPR theory.

The abbreviation VSEPR stands for "valence-shell, electron-pair repulsion," referring to the repulsion between pairs of valence electrons of the atoms in a molecule. **VSEPR theory** *states that repulsion between the sets of valence-level electrons surrounding an atom causes these sets to be oriented as far apart as possible.* How does the assumption that electrons in molecules repel each other account for molecular shapes? For now let us consider only molecules with no unshared valence electron pairs on the central atom.

Let's examine the simple molecule BeF_2. Recall that beryllium does not follow the octet rule. The beryllium atom forms a covalent bond with each fluorine atom. It is surrounded by only the two electron pairs that it shares with the fluorine atoms.

$$:\ddot{F}:Be:\ddot{F}:$$

According to VSEPR, the shared pairs are oriented as far away from each other as possible. As shown in Figure 6-21(a) on page 184, the distance between electron pairs is maximized if the bonds to fluorine are

OBJECTIVES

- Explain VSEPR theory.

- Predict the shapes of molecules or polyatomic ions using VSEPR theory.

- Explain how the shapes of molecules are accounted for by hybridization theory.

- Describe dipole-dipole forces, hydrogen bonding, induced dipoles, and London dispersion forces.

- Explain what determines molecular polarity.

(a) Hydrogen, H_2

(b) Hydrogen chloride, HCl

FIGURE 6-20 Ball-and-stick models illustrate the linearity of diatomic molecules. (a) A hydrogen molecule is represented by two identical balls (the hydrogen atoms) joined by a solid bar (the covalent bond). (b) A hydrogen chloride molecule is composed of dissimilar atoms, but it is still linear.

VSEPR theory describes *where* covalently bonded atoms are relative to one another; hybridization theory describes *how* the atoms are bonded.

Visual Strategy

FIGURE 6-20 Students should realize that in the ball-and-stick representations in this textbook, all atoms are drawn the same size. Relative atomic and ionic sizes are shown only in space-filling models.

Visual Strategy

FIGURE 6-21 Give students four matches and a protractor to duplicate the models shown. Have them arrange two of the matches so that the matches touch each other and the match heads are as far apart as possible. Then have them measure the angle between the match heads. Repeat using three and four matches.

✔ **Teaching Tip**

The central atom of a molecule or polyatomic ion usually is the one with the lowest electronegativity. The more electronegative atoms are generally around the outside of a molecule or polyatomic ion, so they share electrons with fewer other atoms. Note, however, that H is never a central atom, because it can bond to only one other atom.

✔ **Teaching Tip**

Exceptions of the type shown in Sample Problem 6-5 (the central atom has *fewer* than eight electrons) are common for Group 2 and Group 3 elements. Group 2 elements in covalent compounds commonly have only four valence electrons (two bonds); BeF_2 in Figure 6-21(b) is an example of such an exception. Group 3 elements in covalent compounds commonly have only six valence electrons (three bonds); $AlCl_3$ is an example of such an exception.

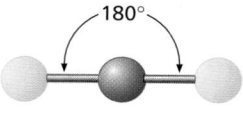

(a) Beryllium fluoride, BeF_2

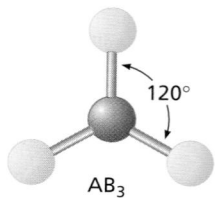

(b) Boron trifluoride, BF_3

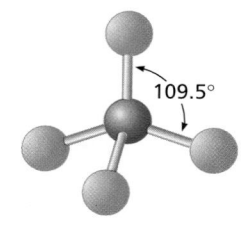

(c) Methane, CH_4

FIGURE 6-21 Ball-and-stick models show the shapes of (a) AB_2, (b) AB_3, and (c) AB_4 molecules according to VSEPR.

on opposite sides of the beryllium atom, 180° apart. Thus, all three atoms lie on a straight line. The molecule is linear.

If we represent the central atom in a molecule by the letter *A* and we represent the atoms bonded to the central atom by the letter *B*, then according to VSEPR, BeF_2 is an example of an AB_2 molecule, which is linear. Can you determine what an AB_3 molecule looks like? The three A—B bonds stay farthest apart by pointing to the corners of an equilateral triangle, giving 120° angles between the bonds. This trigonal-planar geometry is shown in Figure 6-21(b) for the AB_3 molecule boron trifluoride, BF_3.

Unlike AB_2 and AB_3 molecules, the central atoms in AB_4 molecules follow the octet rule by sharing four electron pairs with B atoms. The distance between electron pairs is maximized if each A—B bond points to one of four corners of a tetrahedron. This geometry is shown in Figure 6-21(c) for the AB_4 molecule methane, CH_4. The same figure shows that in a tetrahedral molecule, each of the bond angles formed by the A atom and any two of the B atoms is equal to 109.5°.

The shapes of various molecules are summarized in Table 6-5 on page 186. B can represent a single type of atom, a group of identical atoms, or a group of different atoms on the same molecule. The shape of the molecule will still be based on the forms given in the table. However, different sizes of B groups distort the bond angles, making some bond angles larger or smaller than those given in the table.

SAMPLE PROBLEM 6-5

Use VSEPR theory to predict the molecular geometry of aluminum trichloride, $AlCl_3$.

SOLUTION First write the Lewis structure for $AlCl_3$. Aluminum is in Group 13 and has three valence electrons.

$$\cdot \dot{A}l \cdot$$

Chlorine is in Group 17 and has seven valence electrons.

$$:\ddot{\underset{..}{C}l}:$$

The total number of available valence electrons is therefore $24e^-$ ($3e^-$ from aluminum and $21e^-$ from chlorine). The following Lewis structure uses all $24e^-$.

$$:\overset{..}{\underset{..}{C}l}:$$
$$:\overset{..}{\underset{..}{C}l}:\dot{A}l:\overset{..}{\underset{..}{C}l}:$$

This molecule is an exception to the octet rule because in this case Al forms only three bonds. Aluminum trichloride is an AB_3 type of molecule. Therefore, according to VSEPR theory, it should have trigonal-planar geometry.

PRACTICE

1. Use VSEPR theory to predict the molecular geometry of the following molecules:
   a. HI   c. AlBr$_3$
   b. CBr$_4$ d. CH$_2$Cl$_2$

Answer
a. linear
b. tetrahedral
c. trigonal-planar
d. tetrahedral

VSEPR and Unshared Electron Pairs

Ammonia, NH$_3$, and water, H$_2$O, are examples of molecules in which the central atom has both shared and unshared electron pairs (see Table 6-5 for their Lewis structures). How does VSEPR theory account for the geometries of these molecules?

The Lewis structure of ammonia shows that in addition to the three electron pairs it shares with the three hydrogen atoms, the central nitrogen atom has one unshared pair of electrons.

$$H\!:\!\ddot{N}\!:\!H$$
$$\overset{\cdot\cdot}{\underset{H}{|}}$$

VSEPR theory postulates that the lone pair occupies space around the nitrogen atom just as the bonding pairs do. Thus, as in an AB$_4$ molecule, the electron pairs maximize their separation by assuming the four corners of a tetrahedron. Lone pairs do occupy space, but our description of the observed shape of a molecule refers to the *positions of atoms only*. Consequently, as shown in Figure 6-22(a), the molecular geometry of an ammonia molecule is that of a pyramid with a triangular base. The general VSEPR formula for molecules such as ammonia is AB$_3$E, where E represents the unshared electron pair.

A water molecule has two unshared electron pairs. It is an AB$_2$E$_2$ molecule. Here, the oxygen atom is at the center of a tetrahedron, with two corners occupied by hydrogen atoms and two by the unshared pairs (Figure 6-22(b)). Again, VSEPR theory states that the lone pairs occupy space around the central atom but that the actual shape of the molecule is determined by the positions of the atoms only. In the case of water, this results in a "bent," or angular, molecule.

internet**connect**

SC/LINKS

NSTA

TOPIC: VSEPR theory
GO TO: www.scilinks.org
*sci*LINKS **CODE:** HC2065

FIGURE 6-22 The locations of bonds and unshared electrons are shown for molecules of (a) ammonia and (b) water. Although unshared electrons occupy space around the central atoms, the shapes of the molecules depend only on the position of the molecules' atoms, as clearly shown by the ball-and-stick models.

ADDITIONAL SAMPLE PROBLEM

6-5 Use VSEPR theory to predict the molecular geometry of the following molecules:
a. CCl$_4$
b. HCN
c. SiBr$_4$

Ans.
a. tetrahedral
b. linear
c. tetrahedral

Visual Strategy

FIGURE 6-22 Inform students that a pair of unshared electrons will take up at least as much space as a pair of electrons in a bond. As a result, pairs of unshared electrons play a significant role in determining the geometry of a molecule, despite the fact that only atoms are taken into account when we visualize the shape of a molecule.

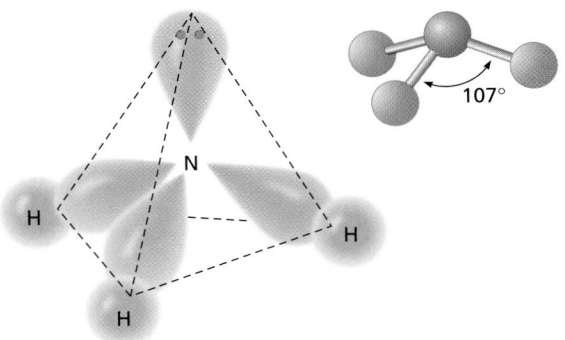

(a) Ammonia, NH$_3$

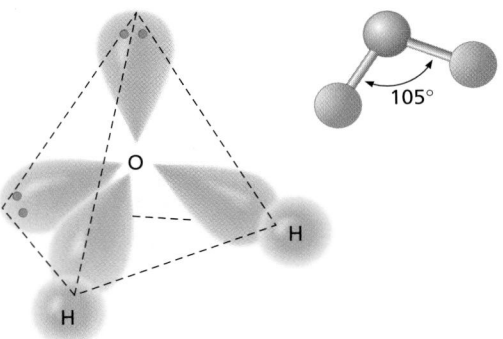

(b) Water, H$_2$O

You may return to the use of matches to illustrate the molecular shapes in this table. Once students can visualize how the electron pairs repel one another, the three-dimensional geometry is more straightforward.

✔ Teaching Tip

It might be useful to point out that AB_2E structures are similar to AB_3 structures, but with an unshared electron pair in place of one of the bonds. Similarly, AB_3E and AB_2E_2 structures are similar to AB_4 structures, but with one and two unshared electron pairs, respectively, in place of bonds. This will help students to recognize the hybridizations later in the chapter. sp^2 for AB_3 and AB_2E; sp^3 for AB_4, AB_3E, and AB_2E_2.

In Figure 6-22(b), note that the bond angles in ammonia and water are somewhat less than the 109.5° bond angles of a perfectly tetrahedral molecule. These angles are smaller because the unshared electron pairs repel electrons more strongly than do bonding electron pairs.

Table 6-5 also includes an example of an AB_2E type molecule. This type of molecule results when a central atom forms two bonds and retains one unshared electron pair.

Finally, in VSEPR theory, double and triple bonds are treated in the same way as single bonds. And polyatomic ions are treated similarly to molecules. (Remember to consider *all* of the electron pairs present in any ion or molecule.) Thus, Lewis structures and Table 6-5 can be used together to predict the shapes of polyatomic ions as well as molecules with double or triple bonds.

TABLE 6-5 *VSEPR and Molecular Geometry*

Molecular shape		Atoms bonded to central atom	Lone pairs of electrons	Type of molecule	Formula example	Lewis structure
Linear		2	0	AB_2	BeF_2	$:\!\ddot{F}\!-\!Be\!-\!\ddot{F}\!:$
Bent or angular		2	1	AB_2E	$SnCl_2$	Sn, :Cl Cl:
Trigonal-planar		3	0	AB_3	BF_3	F F B F
Tetrahedral		4	0	AB_4	CH_4	H, H–C–H, H
Trigonal-pyramidal		3	1	AB_3E	NH_3	N H H H
Bent or angular		2	2	AB_2E_2	H_2O	O H H
Trigonal-bipyramidal		5	0	AB_5	PCl_5	Cl Cl, Cl–P, Cl Cl
Octahedral		6	0	AB_6	SF_6	F F F, S, F F F

SAMPLE PROBLEM 6-6

a. Use VSEPR theory to predict the shape of a molecule of carbon dioxide, CO_2.

b. Use VSEPR theory to predict the shape of a chlorate ion, ClO_3^-.

SOLUTION

a. The Lewis structure of carbon dioxide shows two carbon-oxygen double bonds and no unshared electron pairs on the carbon atom. To simplify the molecule's Lewis structure, we represent the covalent bonds with lines instead of dots.

$$\ddot{O}=C=\ddot{O}$$

This is an AB_2 molecule, which is linear.

b. The Lewis structure of a chlorate ion shows three oxygen atoms and an unshared pair of electrons surrounding a central chlorine atom. Again, lines are used to represent the covalent bonds.

$$\left[\begin{array}{c} \overset{\displaystyle Cl}{\underset{\displaystyle \ddot{O} \; \ddot{O} \; \ddot{O}}{|}} \end{array} \right]^{-}$$

The chlorate ion is an AB_3E type. It has trigonal-pyramidal geometry, with the three oxygen atoms at the base of the pyramid and the chlorine atom at the top.

PRACTICE

1. Use VSEPR theory to predict the molecular geometries of the molecules whose Lewis structures are given below.

a. $:\ddot{F}-\ddot{S}-\ddot{F}:$

b. $:\ddot{Cl}-\overset{\displaystyle |}{\underset{\displaystyle :\ddot{Cl}:}{P}}-\ddot{Cl}:$

Answer
a. bent or angular
b. trigonal-pyramidal

Hybridization

VSEPR theory is useful for explaining the shapes of molecules. However, it does not reveal the relationship between a molecule's geometry and the orbitals occupied by its bonding electrons. To explain how the orbitals of an atom become rearranged when the atom forms covalent bonds, a different model is used. This model is called **hybridization,** *which is the mixing of two or more atomic orbitals of similar energies on the same atom to produce new orbitals of equal energies.*

Methane, CH_4, provides a good example of how hybridization is used to explain the geometry of molecular orbitals. The orbital notation for a carbon atom shows that it has four valence electrons, two in the $2s$ orbital and two in $2p$ orbitals.

$$C \quad \underset{1s}{\uparrow\downarrow} \quad \underset{2s}{\uparrow\downarrow} \quad \underset{\underbrace{}_{2p}}{\uparrow \quad \uparrow \quad \underline{}}$$

CHAPTER ⟷ CONNECTION

Be sure students are familiar with orbital notation, which was introduced in Chapter 4.

Common Misconception

The labeling of hybrid orbitals is different from that used for electron configurations. The superscripts in hybrid orbitals refer to the number of orbitals of that particular type that are involved in the orbital blending. The superscripts in electron configurations refer to the number of electrons in that type of orbital.

We know from experiments that a methane molecule has tetrahedral geometry. How does carbon form four equivalent, tetrahedrally arranged covalent bonds by orbital overlap with four other atoms?

Two of carbon's valence electrons occupy the $2s$ orbital, and two occupy the $2p$ orbitals. Recall that the $2s$ orbital and the $2p$ orbitals have different shapes. To achieve four equivalent bonds, carbon's $2s$ and three $2p$ orbitals *hybridize* to form four new, identical orbitals called sp^3 orbitals. The superscript 3 indicates that three p orbitals were included in the hybridization; the superscript 1 on the s is understood. The sp^3 orbitals all have the same energy, which is greater than that of the $2s$ orbital but less than that of the $2p$ orbitals, as shown in Figure 6-23.

FIGURE 6-23 The sp^3 hybridization of carbon's outer orbitals combines one s and three p orbitals to form four sp^3 hybrid orbitals. Whenever hybridization occurs, the resulting hybrid orbitals are at an energy level between the levels of the orbitals that have combined.

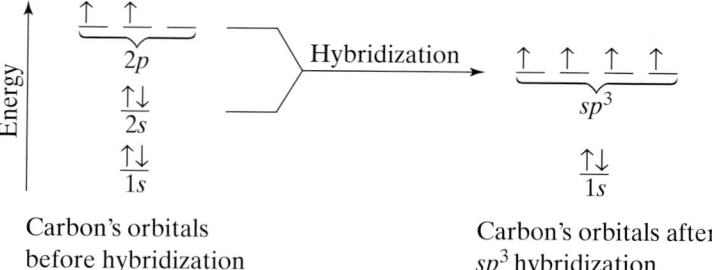

Carbon's orbitals before hybridization

Carbon's orbitals after sp^3 hybridization

Hybrid orbitals *are orbitals of equal energy produced by the combination of two or more orbitals on the same atom.* The number of hybrid orbitals produced equals the number of orbitals that have combined. Bonding with carbon sp^3 orbitals is illustrated in Figure 6-24(a) for a molecule of methane.

Hybridization also explains the bonding and geometry of many molecules formed by Group 15 and 16 elements. The sp^3 hybridization of a nitrogen atom ([He]$2s^2 2p^3$) yields four hybrid orbitals—one orbital containing a pair of electrons and three orbitals that each contain an unpaired electron. Each unpaired electron is capable of forming a single bond, as shown for ammonia in Figure 6-24(b). Similarly, two of the four sp^3 hybrid orbitals on an oxygen atom ([He]$2s^2 2p^4$) are occupied by two electron pairs and two are occupied by unpaired electrons. Each unpaired electron can form a single bond, as shown for water in Figure 6-24(c).

FIGURE 6-24 Bonds formed by the overlap of the $1s$ orbitals of hydrogen atoms and the sp^3 orbitals of (a) carbon, (b) nitrogen, and (c) oxygen. For the sake of clarity, only the hybrid orbitals of the central atoms are shown.

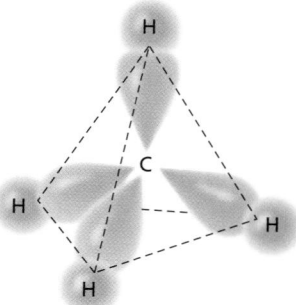

(a) Methane, CH_4

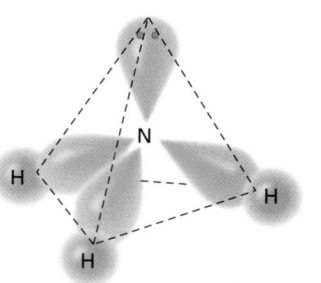

(b) Ammonia, NH_3

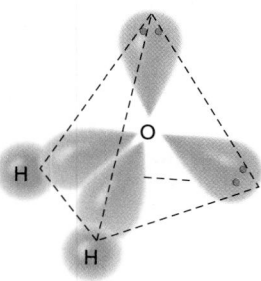

(c) Water, H_2O

TABLE 6-6 *Geometry of Hybrid Orbitals*			
Atomic orbitals	Type of hybridization	Number of hybrid orbitals	Geometry
s, p	sp	2	 180° Linear
s, p, p	sp²	3	120° Trigonal-planar
s, p, p, p	sp³	4	109.5° Tetrahedral

The linear geometry of molecules such as beryllium fluoride, BeF_2, (see Table 6-5 on page 186) is made possible by hybridization involving the *s* orbital and one available empty *p* orbital to yield *sp* hybrid orbitals. The trigonal-planar geometry of molecules such as boron fluoride, BF_3, is made possible by hybridization involving the *s* orbital, one singly occupied *p* orbital, and one empty *p* orbital to yield *sp²* hybrid orbitals. The geometries of *sp*, *sp²*, and *sp³* hybrid orbitals are summarized in Table 6-6.

Intermolecular Forces

As a liquid is heated, the kinetic energy of its particles increases. At the boiling point, the energy is sufficient to overcome the force of attraction between the liquid's particles. The particles pull away from each other and enter the gas phase. Boiling point is therefore a good measure of the force of attraction between particles of a liquid. The higher the boiling point, the stronger the forces between particles.

The forces of attraction between molecules are known as **intermolecular forces.** Intermolecular forces vary in strength but are generally weaker than bonds that join atoms in molecules, ions in ionic compounds, or metal atoms in solid metals. Compare the boiling points of the metals and ionic compounds in Table 6-7 on page 190 with those of the molecular substances listed. Note that the values for ionic compounds and metals are much higher than those for molecular substances.

Module 4: Chemical Bonding

Module 4: Chemical Bonding

Topic: Molecular Geometry
Sections **e**, **f**, **g**, and **h** of this engaging tutorial review and reinforce understanding of ionic molecular geometry.

Remind students that boiling point is a measure of the force of attraction between molecules in covalent compounds, between ions in ionic compounds, and between atoms in metals.

TABLE STRATEGY

Table 6-7 Have students use the boiling points on this table to assess the relative strengths of the forces of attraction at work in molecular, ionic, and metallic substances.

Common Misconception

Some might infer from the table on this page that covalent bonding involves the weakest force of attraction. In fact, covalent bonding involves the strongest force of attraction—as evidenced by the fact that boiling a diamond is more difficult than boiling any metal. The attraction that must be overcome to boil a molecular compound is the *intermolecular attraction,* not covalent bonding.

TABLE 6-7 *Boiling Points and Bonding Types*

Bonding type	Substance	bp (1 atm, °C)
Nonpolar-covalent (molecular)	H_2	−253
	O_2	−183
	Cl_2	−34
	Br_2	59
	CH_4	−164
	CCl_4	77
	C_6H_6	80
Polar-covalent (molecular)	PH_3	−88
	NH_3	−33
	H_2S	−61
	H_2O	100
	HF	20
	HCl	−85
	ICl	97
Ionic	NaCl	1413
	MgF_2	2239
Metallic	Cu	2567
	Fe	2750
	W	5660

Molecular Polarity and Dipole-Dipole Forces

The strongest intermolecular forces exist between polar molecules. Polar molecules act as tiny dipoles because of their uneven charge distribution. *A* **dipole** *is created by equal but opposite charges that are separated by a short distance.* The direction of a dipole is from the dipole's positive pole to its negative pole. A dipole is represented by an arrow with a head pointing toward the negative pole and a crossed tail situated at the positive pole. The dipole created by a hydrogen chloride molecule, which has its negative end at the more electronegative chlorine atom, is indicated as follows.

$$\xrightarrow{}$$
$$H-Cl$$

The negative region in one polar molecule attracts the positive region in adjacent molecules, and so on throughout a liquid or solid. *The forces of attraction between polar molecules are known as* **dipole-dipole forces.** These forces are short-range forces, acting only between nearby molecules. The effect of dipole-dipole forces is reflected, for example, by the significant difference between the boiling points of bromine fluoride, Br−F, and fluorine, F−F. The boiling point of polar bromine fluoride is −20°C, whereas that of nonpolar fluorine is only −188°C. The dipole-dipole forces responsible for the relatively high boiling point of BrF are illustrated schematically in Figure 6-25.

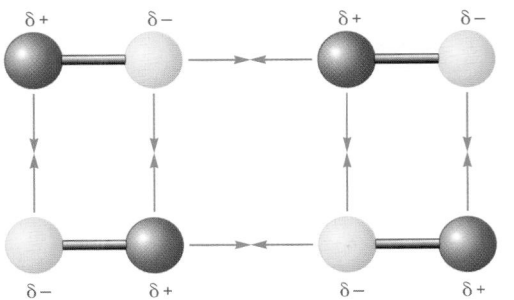

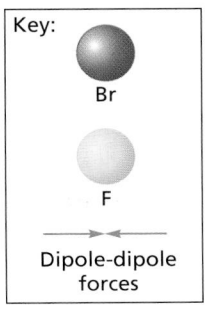

Key:

Br

F

Dipole-dipole
forces

FIGURE 6-25 Ball-and-stick models illustrate the dipole-dipole forces between molecules of bromine fluoride, BrF. In each molecule, the highly electronegative fluorine atom has a partial negative charge, leaving each bromine atom with a partial positive charge. Consequently, the negative and positive ends of neighboring molecules attract each other.

Visual Strategy

FIGURE 6-26 Emphasize to students that a large difference in electronegativities between the atoms in a molecule does not necessarily mean that the molecule will be polar. Dipoles within a molecule can cancel each other out, resulting in a nonpolar molecule, as in carbon tetrachloride. Polarity is a result of both the existence of polar covalent bonds and the nature of the molecule's geometry.

The polarity of diatomic molecules such as BrF is determined by just one bond. For molecules containing more than two atoms, molecular polarity depends on both the polarity and the orientation of each bond. A molecule of water, for example, has two hydrogen-oxygen bonds in which the more-electronegative oxygen atom is the negative pole of each bond. Because the molecule is bent, the polarities of these two bonds combine to make the molecule highly polar, as shown in Figure 6-26. An ammonia molecule is also highly polar because the dipoles of the three nitrogen-hydrogen bonds are additive, combining to create a net molecular dipole. In some molecules, individual bond dipoles cancel one another, causing the resulting molecular polarity to be zero. Carbon dioxide and carbon tetrachloride are molecules of this type.

A polar molecule can *induce* a dipole in a nonpolar molecule by temporarily attracting its electrons. The result is a short-range intermolecular force that is somewhat weaker than the dipole-dipole force. The force of an induced dipole accounts for the solubility of nonpolar O_2 in water. The positive pole of a water molecule attracts the outer electrons

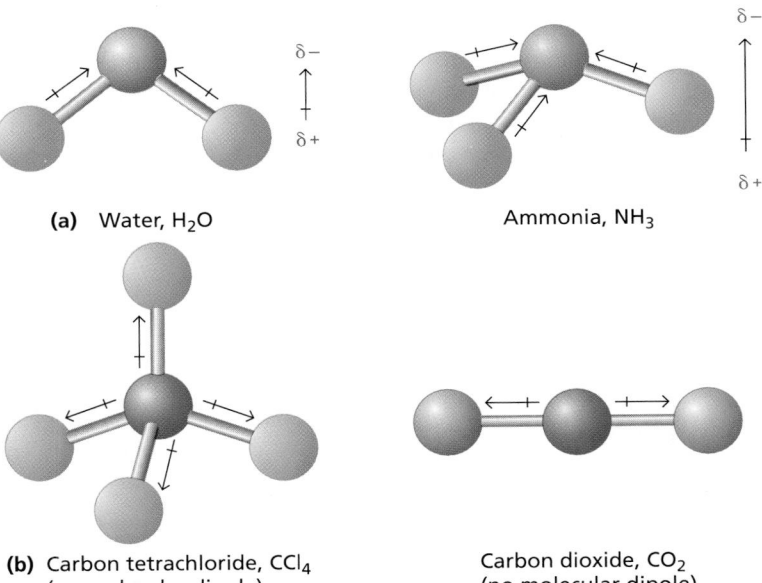

(a) Water, H_2O

Ammonia, NH_3

(b) Carbon tetrachloride, CCl_4
(no molecular dipole)

Carbon dioxide, CO_2
(no molecular dipole)

FIGURE 6-26 (a) The bond polarities in a water or an ammonia molecule are additive, causing the molecule as a whole to be polar. (b) In molecules of carbon tetrachloride and carbon dioxide, the bond polarities extend equally and symmetrically in different directions, canceling each other's effect and causing each molecule as a whole to be nonpolar.

Common Misconception

Many students think of hydrogen bonding as a separate type of inter-molecular force. In fact, it is a particularly strong dipole-dipole force.

Did You Know?

Hydrogen bonds are responsible for holding DNA in its helical shape.

Answer to In-Text Question

H_2S boils at a much lower temperature than does H_2O. This is explained by the fact that sulfur is not nearly as electronegative as oxygen, so hydrogen bonding between H_2S molecules is much weaker than it is between H_2O molecules.

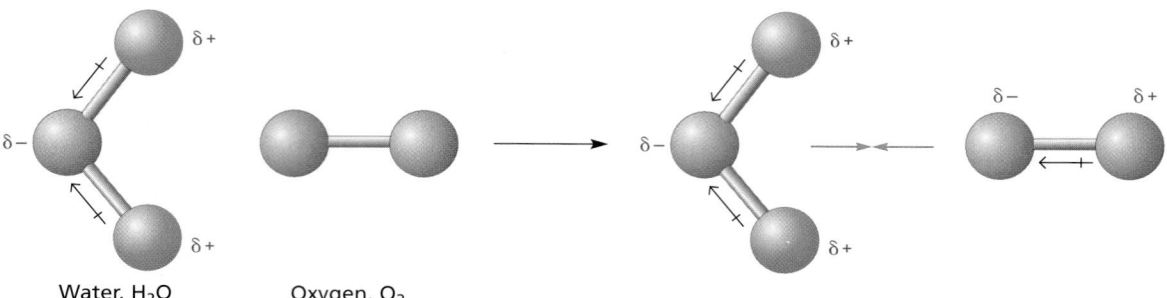

Water, H_2O Oxygen, O_2

FIGURE 6-27 Dipole-induced dipole interaction. The positive pole of a water molecule causes a temporary change in the electron distribution of an oxygen molecule. The negative pole induced in the oxygen molecule is then attracted to the positive pole of the water molecule.

internet connect

SCiLINKS

NSTA

TOPIC: Hydrogen bonding
GO TO: www.scilinks.org
*sci***LINKS CODE:** HC2066

of an adjacent oxygen molecule. The oxygen molecule, then, has an induced negative pole on the side toward the water molecule and an induced positive pole on the opposite side. The result is an attraction to the water molecule, as shown in Figure 6-27.

Hydrogen Bonding

Some hydrogen-containing compounds, such as hydrogen fluoride (HF), water (H_2O), and ammonia (NH_3), have unusually high boiling points. This is explained by the presence of a particularly strong type of dipole-dipole force. In compounds containing H–F, H–O, or H–N bonds, the large electronegativity differences between hydrogen atoms and fluorine, oxygen, or nitrogen atoms make the bonds connecting them highly polar. This gives the hydrogen atom a positive charge that is almost half as large as that of a proton. Moreover, the small size of the hydrogen atom allows the atom to come very close to an unshared pair of electrons on an adjacent molecule. *The intermolecular force in which a hydrogen atom that is bonded to a highly electronegative atom is attracted to an unshared pair of electrons of an electronegative atom in a nearby molecule is known as* **hydrogen bonding.**

Hydrogen bonds are usually represented by dotted lines connecting the hydrogen-bonded hydrogen to the unshared electron pair of the electronegative atom to which it is attracted, as illustrated for water in Figure 6-28. The effect of hydrogen bonding can be seen by comparing the boiling points in Table 6-7 on page 190. Look at phosphine, PH_3, compared with hydrogen-bonded ammonia, NH_3. How does hydrogen sulfide, H_2S, compare with strongly hydrogen-bonded water, H_2O?

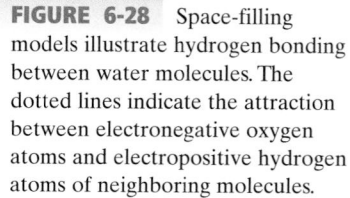

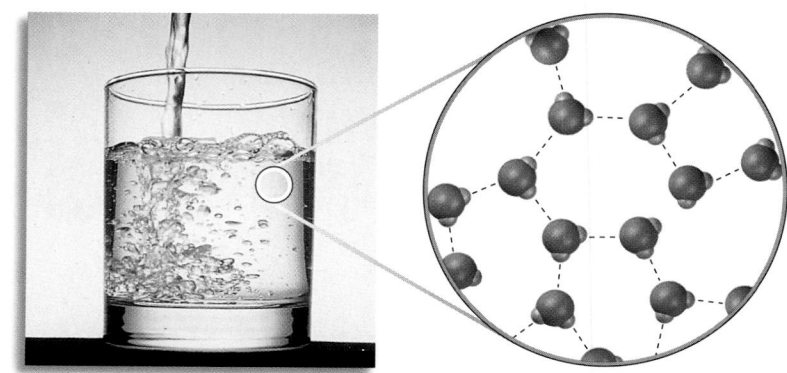

FIGURE 6-28 Space-filling models illustrate hydrogen bonding between water molecules. The dotted lines indicate the attraction between electronegative oxygen atoms and electropositive hydrogen atoms of neighboring molecules.

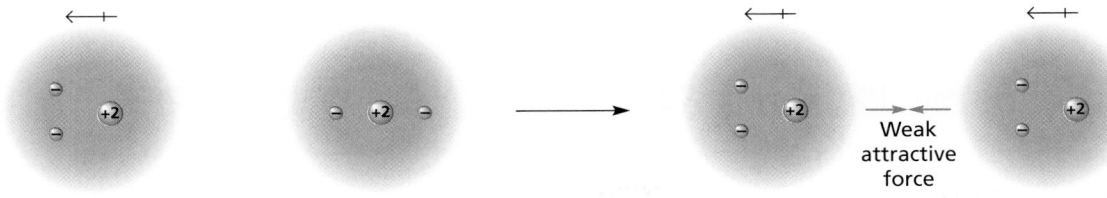

Momentary dipole
in one helium atom

Weak
attractive
force

Dipole induced in
neighboring atom

London Dispersion Forces

Even noble-gas atoms and molecules that are nonpolar experience a weak intermolecular attraction. In any atom or molecule—polar or nonpolar—the electrons are in continuous motion. As a result, at any instant the electron distribution may be slightly uneven. The momentary, uneven charge creates a positive pole in one part of the atom or molecule and a negative pole in another. This temporary dipole can then induce a dipole in an adjacent atom or molecule. The two are held together for an instant by the weak attraction between the temporary dipoles, as illustrated in Figure 6-29. *The intermolecular attractions resulting from the constant motion of electrons and the creation of instantaneous dipoles are called* **London dispersion forces,** after Fritz London, who first proposed their existence in 1930.

London forces act between all atoms and molecules. But they are the *only* intermolecular forces acting among noble-gas atoms and nonpolar molecules. This fact is reflected in the low boiling points of the noble gases and nonpolar molecular compounds listed in Table 6-7 on page 190. Because London forces are dependent on the motion of electrons, their strength increases with the number of electrons in the interacting atoms or molecules. In other words, London forces increase with increasing atomic or molar mass. This trend can be seen by comparing the boiling points of the gases helium, He, and argon, Ar; hydrogen, H_2, and oxygen, O_2; and chlorine, Cl_2, and bromine, Br_2.

FIGURE 6-29 When an instantaneous, temporary dipole develops in a helium atom, it induces a dipole in a neighboring atom.

Common Misconception

Some students might think that a molecule experiences either dipole-dipole forces or London dispersion forces with another molecule. In fact, *all* molecules experience London dispersion forces. In polar molecules, London dispersion forces are insignificant relative to dipole-dipole forces.

SECTION REVIEW

1. VSEPR theory and hybridization theory

2. **a.** :Ö:S::Ö:
      bent or angular

   b.   :Ï:
         :Ï:C:Ï:
            :Ï:
      tetrahedral

   c.   :Ċl:
         :Ċl:B:Ċl:
      trigonal-planar

3. Factors include the number of bonds formed by each atom in the molecule, the number of lone pairs of electrons on the atoms, the sizes of the various types of atoms, and the hybridization of some of the atoms' orbitals.

4. One *s* orbital and three *p* orbitals have combined to form four bonding orbitals of equal energy.

5. Hydrogen bonding is responsible for water's high boiling point. In general, boiling point is a measure of the amount of energy required to overcome intermolecular attractions. Hydrogen bonding, a particularly strong dipole-dipole force, causes a powerful attraction between water molecules, which results in a high boiling point.

SECTION REVIEW

1. What two theories can be used to predict molecular geometry?

2. Draw the Lewis structure, and use the VSEPR theory to predict the molecular geometry of the following molecules:
   a. SO_2 b. Cl_4 c. BCl_3

3. What are some factors that affect the geometry of a molecule?

4. Explain what is meant by sp^3 hybridization.

5. What type of intermolecular force contributes to the high boiling point of water? Explain.

REVIEW ANSWERS

1. A chemical bond is a link between atoms resulting from the mutual attraction of their nuclei and electrons.

2. The three major types of chemical bonding are ionic, covalent, and metallic. In *ionic bonding,* large numbers of oppositely charged ions join because of mutual electrical attraction. In *covalent bonding,* atoms join by sharing electron pairs. In *metallic bonding,* atoms join through an attraction to a sea of valence electrons.

3. In general, the greater the electronegativity difference between two atoms is, the more ionic the bond between them is.

4. a. *Polar* refers to bonds that have an uneven distribution of charge.
b. In a polar-covalent bond there is an unequal attraction for the electron pair, resulting in one of the bonded atoms possessing a partial negative charge and the other atom possessing a partial positive charge. In a nonpolar-covalent bond the electron pair is shared equally by the bonded atoms.

5. In general, atoms will form a chemical bond if their potential energy is lowered in doing so.

6. A molecule is a neutral group of two or more atoms—usually nonmetals—held together by covalent bonds.

7. a. The distance at which potential energy is at a minimum; bond length is the point at which there is a balance between attraction and repulsion between atoms in a covalent bond.
b. In general, higher bond energies correspond to shorter bond lengths.

CHAPTER SUMMARY

6-1
- Most atoms are chemically bonded to other atoms.
- The three major types of chemical bonding are ionic, covalent, and metallic.
- In general, atoms of metals bond ionically with atoms of nonmetals, atoms of metals bond metallically with each other, and atoms of nonmetals bond covalently with each other.

Vocabulary

chemical bond (161)	ionic bonding (161)	polar (162)	polar-covalent bond (162)
covalent bonding (161)	nonpolar-covalent bond (162)		

6-2
- Atoms in molecules are joined by covalent bonds.
- The bond length between two atoms in a molecule is the distance at which the potential energy of the bonded atoms is minimized.
- The octet rule states that many chemical compounds tend to form bonds so that each atom, by gaining, losing, or sharing electrons, shares or has eight electrons in its highest occupied energy level.
- A single bond is a covalent bond in which a pair of electrons is shared between two atoms. Covalent bonds in which more than one pair of electrons is shared are called multiple bonds.
- Bonding within many molecules and ions can be indicated by a Lewis structure. Molecules or ions that cannot be correctly represented by a single Lewis structure are represented by resonance structures.

Vocabulary

bond energy (167)	electron-dot notation (170)	molecular formula (164)	single bond (171)
bond length (167)		molecule (164)	structural formula (171)
chemical formula (164)	Lewis structures (171)	multiple bond (173)	triple bond (173)
diatomic molecule (164)	lone pair (171)	octet rule (169)	unshared pair (171)
double bond (172)	molecular compound (164)	resonance (175)	

6-3
- An ionic compound is a three-dimensional network of positive and negative ions mutually attracted to one another.
- Because of the strong attraction between positive and negative ions, ionic compounds tend to be harder and more brittle and to have higher boiling points than materials containing only covalently bonded atoms.
- Polyatomic ions are charged groups of atoms held together by covalent bonds.

Vocabulary

formula unit (176)	ionic compound (176)	lattice energy (178)
		polyatomic ion (180)

6-4
- Metallic bonding is a type of chemical bonding that results from the attraction between metal atoms and a surrounding sea of mobile electrons.
- The electron sea formed in metallic bonding gives metals their properties of high electrical and thermal conductivity, malleability, ductility, and luster.

Vocabulary

ductility (182)	malleability (182)	metallic bonding (181)

CHAPTER SUMMARY (continued)

6-5
- VSEPR theory is used to predict the shapes of molecules based on the fact that electron pairs strongly repel each other and tend to be oriented as far apart as possible.
- Hybridization theory is used to predict the shapes of molecules based on the fact that orbitals within an atom can mix to form orbitals of equal energy.
- Intermolecular forces, such as dipole-dipole forces and London dispersion forces, exist between certain types of molecules. Hydrogen bonding is a special case of dipole-dipole forces.

Vocabulary

dipole (190)	hybridization (187)
dipole-dipole forces (190)	hydrogen bonding (192)
hybrid orbitals (188)	

intermolecular forces (189)	molecular polarity (183)
London dispersion forces (193)	VSEPR theory (183)

REVIEWING CONCEPTS

1. What is a chemical bond? (6-1)

2. Identify and define the three major types of chemical bonding. (6-1)

3. What is the relationship between electronegativity and the ionic character of a chemical bond? (6-1)

4. a. What is the meaning of the term *polar*, as applied to chemical bonding?
   b. Distinguish between polar-covalent and nonpolar-covalent bonds. (6-1)

5. In general, what determines whether atoms will form chemical bonds? (6-1)

6. What is a molecule? (6-2)

7. a. What determines bond length?
   b. In general, how are bond energies and bond lengths related? (6-2)

8. Describe the general location of the electrons in a covalent bond. (6-2)

9. As applied to covalent bonding, what is meant by an unshared or lone pair of electrons? (6-2)

10. Describe the octet rule in terms of noble-gas configurations and potential energy. (6-2)

11. Determine the number of valence electrons in an atom of each of the following elements:
    a. H   b. F
    c. Mg   d. O
    e. Al   f. N
    g. C   (6-2)

12. When drawing Lewis structures, which atom is usually the central atom? (6-2)

13. Distinguish between single, double, and triple covalent bonds by defining each and providing an illustration of each type. (6-2)

14. In writing Lewis structures, how is the need for multiple bonds generally determined? (6-2)

15. a. What is an ionic compound?
    b. In what form do most ionic compounds occur? (6-3)

16. a. What is a formula unit?
    b. What are the components of one formula unit of CaF_2? (6-3)

17. a. What is lattice energy?
    b. In general, what is the relationship between lattice energy and the strength of ionic bonding? (6-3)

18. a. In general, how do ionic and molecular compounds compare in terms of melting points, boiling points, and ease of vaporization?
    b. What accounts for the observed differences in the properties of ionic and molecular compounds?
    c. Cite three physical properties of ionic compounds. (6-3)

19. a. What is a polyatomic ion?
    b. Give two examples of polyatomic ions.

8. The electrons in a covalent bond occupy overlapping orbitals; each electron is free to occupy either of the orbitals, but both are more likely to be in the space between the nuclei of the bonded atoms.

9. a pair of electrons that is not involved in bonding but instead belongs exclusively to one atom

10. A noble-gas configuration corresponds to a set of outer s and p orbitals that is completely filled with a total of eight electrons. These eight outer electrons are referred to as an octet. Atoms that possess a noble-gas configuration are very stable because the potential energy of their electrons is relatively low. The octet rule states that elements will gain or lose electrons to form a noble-gas configuration.

11. a. 1   d. 6   g. 4
    b. 7   e. 3
    c. 2   f. 5

12. The least-electronegative atom is usually the central atom (except for hydrogen, which is never central). If carbon is present, however, it is usually the central atom, regardless of what other atoms are in the molecule.

13. A single bond involves one pair of electrons, as in the bond between hydrogen and oxygen in water, H_2O. A double bond involves two electron pairs, as in the bond between the carbon and oxygen atoms in a molecule of carbon dioxide, CO_2. A triple bond involves three electron pairs, as in the bond between carbon and nitrogen in hydrogen cyanide, HCN.

14. A multiple bond is needed when there are not enough valence electrons to complete octets by adding unshared pairs.

15. a. An ionic compound is composed of cations and anions such that the total positive and negative charges are equal.
b. Most ionic compounds occur naturally as crystalline solids.

16. a. the simplest collection of atoms from which an ionic compound's formula can be established
b. one calcium ion, Ca^{2+}, and two fluorine ions, F^-

17. a. the energy released when one mole of an ionic compound is formed from gaseous ions
b. The greater the lattice energy, the stronger the ionic bonding.

18. a. Ionic compounds have higher melting and boiling points than molecular compounds do, and they do not vaporize at room temperature.
b. The differences in the properties of ionic and molecular compounds are generally a result of differences in how strongly the compound's basic units are held together.
c. hardness, brittleness, electrical conductivity in the molten state

19. a. a charged group of covalently bonded atoms
b. Some common examples of polyatomic anions include the nitrate ion, NO_3^-, the ammonium ion, NH_4^+, the sulfate ion, SO_4^{2-}, and the phosphate ion, PO_4^{3-}.
c. Polyatomic ions combine with ions of opposite charge to form ionic compounds.

20. a. Metals are better conductors of heat than ionic or molecular compounds. In the solid state, metals are more easily deformed and are better electrical conductors than solid ionic or molecular compounds. Unlike ionic and molecular compounds, metals are also shiny in appearance.

c. In what form do such ions often occur in nature? (6-3)

20. a. How do the properties of metals differ from those of both ionic and molecular compounds?
b. What specific property of metals accounts for their unusual electrical conductivity? (6-4)

21. What properties of metals contribute to their tendency to form metallic bonds? (6-4)

22. a. What is metallic bonding?
b. How can the strength of metallic bonding be measured? (6-4)

23. a. How is the VSEPR theory used to classify molecules?
b. What molecular geometry would be expected for F_2 and HF? (6-5)

24. According to the VSEPR theory, what molecular geometries are associated with the following types of molecules?
a. AB_2
b. AB_3
c. AB_4
d. AB_5
e. AB_6 (6-5)

25. Describe the role of each of the following in predicting molecular geometries:
a. unshared electron pairs
b. double bonds (6-5)

26. a. What are hybrid orbitals?
b. What determines the number of hybrid orbitals produced by an atom? (6-5)

27. a. What are intermolecular forces?
b. In general, how do these forces compare in strength with those in ionic and metallic bonding?
c. Where are the strongest intermolecular forces found? (6-5)

28. What is the relationship between electronegativity and the polarity of a chemical bond? (6-5)

29. a. What are dipole-dipole forces?
b. What determines the polarity of a molecule? (6-5)

30. a. What is meant by an induced dipole?
b. What is the everyday importance of this type of intermolecular force? (6-5)

31. a. What is hydrogen bonding?
b. What accounts for its extraordinary strength? (6-5)

32. What are London dispersion forces? (6-5)

PROBLEMS

Chemical Bond Character

33. Determine the electronegativity difference, the probable bond type, and the more-electronegative atom with respect to bonds formed between the following pairs of atoms. (Hint: See Sample Problem 6-1.)
a. H and I
b. S and O
c. K and Br
d. Si and Cl
e. H and F
f. Se and S
g. C and H

34. List the bonding pairs described in item 33 in order of increasing covalent character.

35. Use orbital notation to illustrate the bonding in each of the following molecules:
a. chlorine, Cl_2
b. oxygen, O_2
c. hydrogen fluoride, HF

36. The lattice energy of sodium chloride, NaCl, is -787.5 kJ/mol. The lattice energy of potassium chloride, KCl, is -715 kJ/mol. In which compound is the bonding between ions stronger? Why?

Electron-Dot Notation and Lewis Structures

37. Use electron-dot notation to illustrate the number of valence electrons present in one atom of each of the following elements. (Hint: See Sample Problem 6-2.)
a. Li
b. Ca
c. Cl
d. O

e. C
f. P
g. Al
h. S

38. Use electron-dot structures to demonstrate the formation of ionic compounds involving the following elements:
a. Na and S
b. Ca and O
c. Al and S

39. Draw Lewis structures for each of the following molecules. (Hint: See Sample Problem 6-4.)
a. contains one C and four F atoms
b. contains two H and one Se atom
c. contains one N and three I atoms
d. contains one Si and four Br atoms
e. contains one C, one Cl, and three H atoms

40. Determine the type of hybrid orbitals formed by the boron atom in a molecule of boron fluoride, BF_3. (Hint: See Sample Problems 6-5 and 6-6.)

41. Draw Lewis structures for each of the following molecules. Show resonance structures, if they exist.
a. O_2
b. N_2
c. CO
d. SO_2

42. Draw Lewis structures for each of the following polyatomic ions. Show resonance structures, if they exist.
a. OH^-
b. $H_3C_2O_2^-$
c. BrO_3^-

VSEPR Theory and Molecular Geometry

43. According to the VSEPR theory, what molecular geometries are associated with the following types of molecules?
a. AB_3E
b. AB_2E_2
c. AB_2E

44. Use hybridization to explain the bonding in methane, CH_4.

45. For each of the following polar molecules, indicate the direction of the resulting dipole:

a. H—F
b. H—Cl
c. H—Br
d. H—I

46. Determine whether each of the following bonds would be polar or nonpolar:
a. H—H
b. H—O
c. H—F
d. Br—Br
e. H—Cl
f. H—N

47. On the basis of individual bond polarity and orientation, determine whether each of the following molecules would be polar or nonpolar:
a. H_2O
b. I_2
c. CF_4
d. NH_3
e. CO_2

48. Draw a Lewis structure for each of the following molecules, and then use the VSEPR theory to predict the molecular geometry of each:
a. SCl_2
b. PI_3
c. Cl_2O
d. NH_2Cl
e. $SiCl_3Br$
f. ONCl

49. Draw a Lewis structure for each of the following polyatomic ions, and then use VSEPR theory to determine the geometry of each:
a. NO_3^-
b. NH_4^+
c. SO_4^{2-}
d. ClO_2^-

MIXED REVIEW

50. Arrange the following pairs from strongest to weakest attraction:
a. polar molecule and polar molecule
b. nonpolar molecule and nonpolar molecule
c. polar molecule and ion
d. ion and ion

b. Metals are good electrical conductors because of the presence of highly mobile electrons within the bonding networks of their atoms.

21. Most contain sparsely populated outermost orbitals, they have low ionization energies, and they have low electronegativities.

22. a. Metallic bonding results from the attraction between metal atoms and a sea of surrounding electrons.
b. A metal's heat of vaporization is a measure of the strength of the metal's bonding.

23. a. According to VSEPR theory, the shapes of molecules are classified based on the number of bonding electron pairs and lone pairs that surround a molecule's central atom.
b. Both molecules are linear.

24. a. linear
b. trigonal-planar
c. tetrahedral
d. trigonal-bipyramidal
e. octahedral

25. a. Unshared electron pairs occupy space as bonded electrons do, but they are not part of the visualized molecular geometry.
b. Double (and triple) bonds are treated the same as single bonds.

26. a. Hybrid orbitals are identically shaped orbitals of equal energy that are produced by the mixing of two or more atomic orbitals of similar, but not identical, energies on the same atom.
b. The number of hybrid orbitals produced is always equal to the number of orbitals that have combined.

27. a. Intermolecular forces are the forces of attraction between molecules.
b. Intermolecular forces are weaker than the forces involved

in ionic and metallic bonding.
c. The strongest intermolecular forces occur between polar molecules.

28. The more-electronegative atom in a covalent bond draws electrons toward it, creating a polar bond.

29. a. Dipole-dipole forces are the forces of attraction between polar molecules.
b. The overall polarity of a molecule is determined by the polarity of the molecule's individual bonds as well as the orientation of the bonds with respect to one another.

30. a. An induced dipole is an instantaneous dipole that is produced in a nonpolar molecule when the molecule's electrons are momentarily attracted by a polar molecule.
b. Induced dipoles account for the solubility of nonpolar compounds, such as oxygen, in polar compounds, such as water.

31. a. Hydrogen bonding is a particularly strong dipole-dipole force that occurs among molecules containing hydrogen atoms and and highly electronegative atoms, such as those of N,O, Cl, and F.
b. Because of the great electronegativity difference between H and F, N, O, or Cl, an atom of hydrogen has a positive charge approaching that of a proton. This, coupled with the small size of the hydrogen atom, results in a very strong dipole-dipole attraction.

32. London dispersion forces are intermolecular forces resulting from the creation of instantaneous dipoles.

33. *See page 199A.*

34. K and Br, H and F, Si and Cl, S and O, H and I/Cand H, Se and S

35. *See page 199A.*

51. Determine the geometry of the following molecules:
  a. CCl_4
  b. $BeCl_2$
  c. PH_3

52. What types of atoms tend to form the following types of bonding?
  a. ionic
  b. covalent
  c. metallic

53. What happens to the energy level and stability of two bonded atoms when they are separated and become individual atoms?

54. Draw the three resonance structures for sulfur trioxide, SO_3.

55. a. How do ionic and covalent bonding differ?
  b. How does an ionic compound differ from a molecular compound?
  c. How does an ionic compound differ from a metal?

56. Write the electron-dot notation for each of the following elements:
  a. He   d. P
  b. Cl   e. B
  c. O

57. Write the structural formula for methanol, CH_3OH.

58. How many K^+ and S^{2-} ions would be in one formula unit of the ionic compound formed by these ions?

59. Explain metallic bonding in terms of the sparsely populated outermost orbitals of metal atoms.

60. Explain the role of molecular geometry in determining molecular polarity.

61. How does the energy level of a hybrid orbital compare with the energy levels of the orbitals it was formed from?

62. Aluminum's heat of vaporization is 284 kJ/mol. Beryllium's heat of vaporization is 224 kJ/mol. In which element is the bonding stronger between atoms?

63. Determine the electronegativity difference, the probable bonding type, and the more-

electronegative atom for each of the following pairs of atoms:
  a. Zn and O   c.   S and Cl
  b. Br and I

64. Draw the Lewis structure for each of the following molecules:
  a. PCl_3 c. CH_3NH_2
  b. CCl_2F_2

65. Write the Lewis structure for $BeCl_2$. (Hint: Beryllium atoms do not follow the octet rule.)

66. Draw a Lewis structure for each of the following polyatomic ions and determine their geometries:
  a. NO_2^- c. NH_4^+
  b. NO_3^-

67. Why are most atoms chemically bonded to other atoms in nature?

CRITICAL THINKING

68. Inferring Relationships The length of a bond varies depending on the type of bond formed. Predict and compare the lengths of the carbon-carbon bonds in the following molecules. Explain your answer. (Hint: See Table 6-2.)

C_2H_6 C_2H_4 C_2H_2

TECHNOLOGY & LEARNING

69. Graphing Calculator Classify Bonding Type According to Difference in Electronegativity

The graphing calculator can run a program that classifies bonding between atoms according to the difference between the atoms' electronegativities. Use this program to determine the electronegativity difference between the bonded atoms and to classify bonding type.

Go to Appendix C. If you are using a TI 83 Plus, you can download the program and data sets and run the application as directed. If you are using another calculator, your teacher will provide you with the keystrokes and data sets to use. Remember that you will need to name the program and check the display, as explained in Appendix C. You will then be ready to run the program. After you have graphed the data, answer these questions.

a. Which element pair(s) has/have a pure covalent bond?

b. What type of bond does the pair H, O have?

c. What type of bond does the pair Ca, O have?

HANDBOOK SEARCH

70. Figure 6-18 on page 181 shows a model for a body-centered cubic crystal. Review the Properties tables for all of the metals in the *Elements Handbook* (pages 728–749). What metals exist in body-centered cubic structures?

71. Group 14 of the *Elements Handbook* (pages 754–769) contains a discussion of the band theory of metals. How does this model explain the electrical conductivity of metals?

RESEARCH & WRITING

72. Prepare a report on the work of Linus Pauling.
a. Discuss his work on the nature of the chemical bond.

b. Linus Pauling was an advocate of the use of vitamin C as a preventative for colds. Evaluate Pauling's claims. Determine if there is any scientific evidence that indicates whether vitamin C helps prevent colds.

73. Covalently bonded solids, such as silicon, an element used in computer components, are harder than pure metals. Research theories that explain the hardness of covalently bonded solids and their usefulness in the computer industry. Present your findings to the class.

ALTERNATIVE ASSESSMENT

74. Devise a set of criteria that will allow you to classify the following substances as ionic or non-ionic: $CaCO_3$, Cu, H_2O, NaBr, and C (graphite). Show your criteria to your instructor.

75. Performance Assessment Identify 10 common substances in and around your home, and indicate whether you would expect these substances to contain ionic, covalent, or metallic bonds.

36. Bonding is stronger between the ions in sodium chloride because its lattice energy is greater (more negative). Greater lattice energy indicates stronger ionic bonding.

37. a. Li· **d.** :Ö: **g.** ·Àl·

   b. ·Ca· **e.** ·Ċ· **h.** :Ṡ:

   c. :Ċl: **f.** ·Ṗ:

38. *See page 199A.*

39. *See page 199A.*

40. sp^2 hybrid orbitals

41. *See page 199A.*

42. *See page 199A.*

43. a. trigonal-pyramidal
   b. bent or angular
   c. bent or angular

44. The carbon atom contains four valence electrons, two in the $2s$ and two in the $2p$ orbitals. Hybridization of the $2s$ orbital and the three $2p$ orbitals creates four sp^3 hybrid orbitals, each of which can bond with a hydrogen atom to form four covalent bonds.

45. The direction of the dipole is toward
   a. F   **c.** Br
   b. Cl   **d.** I

46. a. nonpolar   **d.** nonpolar
   b. polar   **e.** polar
   c. polar   **f.** polar

47. a. polar   **d.** polar
   b. nonpolar   **e.** nonpolar
   c. nonpolar

48. *See page 199A.*

49. *See page 199B.*

50. d, c, a, b

51. a. tetrahedral
   b. linear
   c. trigonal-pyramidal

52–75. *See page 199B.*

ADDITIONAL SAMPLE PROBLEMS

Additional Sample Problem from page 163

6-1 Ask students to complete the following chart:

Elements bonded	Electro-negativity difference	Bond type	More-negative atom
a. C and H	0.4		
b. C and S	0.0		
c. O and H	1.4		
d. Na and Cl	2.1		
e. Cs and S	1.8		

Ans.

a. polar-covalent; C
b. nonpolar-covalent; same electronegativity
c. polar-covalent; O
d. ionic; Cl
e. ionic; S

Additional Sample Problem from page 171

6-3 Draw the Lewis structure for each of the following compounds:

a. H_2O
b. CH_4
c. CH_4O
d. HCl

Ans.

a. H:Ö:H

b.
H
H:C:H
H

c.
H
H:C:Ö:H
H

d. H:Cl:

Additional Sample Problem from page 174

6-4 Determine the Lewis structure for each of the following molecules:

a. O_2
b. C_2H_4
c. C_2H_2

Ans.

a. Ö::Ö

b.
H H
C::C
H H

c. H:C::C:H

REVIEW ANSWERS

Answers from page 198

33.

Elements bonded	Electro-negativity difference	Bond type	More-negative atom
a. H and I	0.4	polar-covalent	I
b. S and O	1.0	polar-covalent	O
c. K and Br	2.0	ionic	Br
d. Si and Cl	1.2	polar-covalent	Cl
e. H and F	1.9	ionic	F
f. Se and S	0.1	nonpolar-covalent	S
g. C and H	0.4	polar-covalent	C

35.

a. Cl

b. O

c. F

Answers from page 199

38.

a. $Na\cdot + Na\cdot + :\overset{..}{\underset{..}{S}}: \longrightarrow Na^+ + Na^+ + :\overset{..}{\underset{..}{S}}:^{2-}$ (Na₂S)

b. $\cdot Ca\cdot + :\overset{..}{O}: \longrightarrow Ca^{2+} + :\overset{..}{\underset{..}{O}}:^{2-}$ (CaO)

c. $\cdot\overset{.}{Al}\cdot + \cdot\overset{.}{Al}\cdot + :\overset{..}{S}: + :\overset{..}{S}: + :\overset{..}{S}: \longrightarrow$

$Al^{3+} + Al^{3+} + :\overset{..}{\underset{..}{S}}:^{2-} + :\overset{..}{\underset{..}{S}}:^{2-} + :\overset{..}{\underset{..}{S}}:^{2-}$ (Al₂S₃)

39. a.
:F:
:F:C:F:
:F:

d.
:Br:
:Br:Si:Br:
:Br:

b. H:Se:H

e.
H
H:C:Cl:
H

c.
:I:N:I:
:I:

41. a. :Ö::Ö:

c. :C::O:

b. :N:::N:

d. :Ö:S::Ö: ⟷ :Ö::S:Ö:

42. a. [:Ö:H]⁻

c. [:Ö:Br:Ö:]⁻ with :Ö: below

b.
[H:C:C::Ö with H:Ö: below]⁻ ⟷ [H:C:C:Ö: with H:Ö: below]⁻

48. a. :Cl:S:Cl:
bent or angular

b. :I:P:I: with :I: below
trigonal-pyramidal

c. :Cl:Ö:Cl:
bent or angular

d. H:N:H with :Cl: below
trigonal-pyramidal

e.
:Cl:
:Cl:Si:Cl:
:Br:
tetrahedral

f. $\overset{..}{\underset{..}{O}}::N:\overset{..}{\underset{..}{Cl}}:$

bent or angular

49. a. $\left[:\overset{..}{O}:N::\overset{..}{O}:\right]^{-}$ ... $:\overset{..}{\underset{..}{O}}:$

trigonal-planar

c. $\left[\begin{array}{c} :\overset{..}{O}: \\ :\overset{..}{O}:S:\overset{..}{O}: \\ :\overset{..}{O}: \end{array}\right]^{2-}$

tetrahedral

b. $\left[\begin{array}{c} H \\ H:\overset{..}{N}:H \\ H \end{array}\right]^{+}$

tetrahedral

d. $\left[:\overset{..}{O}:\overset{..}{Cl}:\overset{..}{O}:\right]^{-}$

bent or angular

52. a. metals and nonmetals
b. nonmetals only
c. metals only

53. The energies of the atoms increase and the atoms become less stable.

54.
$:\overset{..}{O}:$ ... $\overset{..}{O}:$ ... $:\overset{..}{O}:$
$S \longleftrightarrow S \longleftrightarrow S$
$:\overset{..}{O}: :\overset{..}{O}:$ ... $:\overset{..}{O}: :\overset{..}{O}:$ ... $:\overset{..}{O}: :\overset{..}{O}:$

55. a. In ionic bonding, valence electrons of the atoms of the less-electronegative element are donated entirely to the atoms of the more-electronegative element. In covalent bonding, valence electrons are shared between the bonded atoms.
b. A molecular compound consists of individual units capable of existing on their own. An ionic compound consists of an arrangement of a large number of ions. There is no discrete, independent particle in an ionic compound.
c. An ionic compound is held together by electrical attraction between ions. A metal is held together by the sharing by atoms of a sea of mobile valence electrons.

56. a. $\cdot He \cdot$ ... **c.** $:\overset{..}{O}:$ ... **e.** $\cdot \overset{.}{B} \cdot$

b. $:\overset{..}{Cl}:$ ... **d.** $\cdot \overset{.}{P}:$

57.
$$\begin{array}{c} H \\ | \\ H-C-O-H \\ | \\ H \end{array}$$

58. two potassium cations, K^+, and one sulfide anion, S^{2-}

59. Vacant orbitals in the outer energy levels of the metal's atoms overlap and are occupied by electrons from adjacent atoms.

60. Although a particular bond in a molecule may be polar, it is the arrangement of all the polar bonds in space—or molecular geometry—that determines whether a molecule is polar.

61. It lies between the energy levels of the orbitals from which it was made.

62. aluminum

63.

Elements bonded	Electro-negativity difference	Bond type	More-negative atom
a. Zn and O	1.9	ionic	O
b. Br and I	0.3	nonpolar-covalent	Br
c. S and Cl	0.5	polar-covalent	Cl

64. a. $:\overset{..}{Cl}:\overset{..}{P}:\overset{..}{Cl}:$
$:\overset{..}{Cl}:$

b. $:\overset{..}{Cl}:$
$:\overset{..}{F}:\overset{..}{C}:\overset{..}{Cl}:$
$:\overset{..}{F}:$

c. H
$H:\overset{..}{C}:\overset{..}{N}:H$
$H\ H$

65. $:\overset{..}{Cl}:Be:\overset{..}{Cl}:$

66. a. $\left[:\overset{..}{O}::N:\overset{..}{O}:\right]^{-}$

bent or angular

b. $\left[\begin{array}{c} :\overset{..}{O}: \\ :\overset{..}{O}:N::\overset{..}{O}: \end{array}\right]^{-}$

trigonal-planar

c. $\left[\begin{array}{c} H \\ H:\overset{..}{N}:H \\ H \end{array}\right]^{+}$

tetrahedral

67. Most atoms are bonded to other atoms in nature because bonding lowers their potential energy.

68. The carbon-carbon triple bond in C_2H_2 is the strongest of the bonds. Therefore, it is the shortest because stronger bonds are shorter bonds. The carbon-carbon single bond in C_2H_6 is the weakest of the bonds, so it is the longest. From Table 6-2, students should surmise that the lengths of the single, double, and triple carbon-carbon bonds are about 154 pm, 134 pm, and 120 pm, respectively.

69. a. C, C and O, O
b. polar covalent
c. ionic

70. Lithium, sodium, potassium, rubidium, cesium, barium, and radium are listed as bcc.

71. The electrons in metals require very little energy to enter the conduction band, which is a set of overlapping orbitals. Thus, electrons can move freely through a metal with a small applied voltage.

Refer to the *One-Stop Planner CD-ROM* for appropriate scoring rubrics for items 72 and 73. Look for these points in each report:

72. a. Students should mention Dr. Pauling's role in establishing the electronegativity scale and in discovering the hydrogen bond. For this work, Dr. Pauling received a Nobel Prize.
b. Some scientists criticize Pauling for being an advocate of something as trendy as vitamin supplements. Be sure students examine real scientific data, rather than political responses, to make their decision.

73. Students should discuss some properties of metalloids.

74. Students might use either physical or chemical properties to distinguish between these substances. Ionic substances will be solid at room temperature, eliminating water. They will not conduct electricity, eliminating Cu. And they will be composed of more than one type of atom, eliminating C. Ionic solids are brittle and have high melting points.

75. Students' answers will vary greatly. Some possible responses include plastics (*covalent*), paper (*covalent*), wood (*covalent*), dishes (*ionic or covalent*), pots (*metallic*), and cloth (*covalent*).

Photo Descriptions
Center: organic structural formula

Lower left: reaction of iron wool with chlorine gas

Lower right: citrus fruits and a citric acid space-filling model

UNIT 3

Language of Chemistry

CHAPTERS

7   **Chemical Formulas and Chemical Compounds**

8   **Chemical Equations and Reactions**

9   **Stoichiometry**

The hearing of lectures, and the reading of books, will never benefit him who attends to nothing else; for Chemistry can only be studied to advantage practically. One experiment, well-conducted, and carefully observed by the student, from first to last, will afford more knowledge than the mere perusal of a whole volume. It may be added to this, that chemical operations are, in general, the most interesting that could possibly be devised—Reader! what is more requisite to induce you to MAKE EXPERIMENTS?

(From *The Norton History of Chemistry*)

Chemical Formulas and Chemical Compounds

PACING CHART

Compression Guide: *(To shorten, eliminate items in italics.)*

CLASSROOM RESOURCES

	NSE Standards	Teaching Resources	Experiments
7-1 **Chemical Names and Formulas** 2 45-minute periods 1 90-minute block *Covalent-Network Compounds, p. 214*	UCP 1–2	**PE** Elements Handbook TM 39A, TM 40A	Gravimetric Analysis, p. 804 Naming Ionic Compounds, p. 810
7-2 **Oxidation Numbers** 2 45-minute periods 1 90-minute block *Assigning Oxidation Numbers, pp. 216–218*	UCP 1–2 ST 1 SPSP 3, 5	**ATE Demo,** p. 217 TM 41A	Separation of Salts by Fractional Crystallization, p. 806 **A4** Test for Iron(II) and Iron(III) **B8** Test for Iron(II) and Iron(III)
7-3 **Using Chemical Formulas** 2 45-minute periods 1 90-minute block *Molar Mass as a Coversion Factor, pp. 224–226*	UCP 1–3	T 39, T 40	
7-4 **Determining Chemical Formulas** 2 45-minute periods 1 90-minute block *Calculation of Empirical Formulas, pp. 229–231* *Calculation of Molecular Formulas, pp. 232–233*	UCP 1–3		Determining the Empirical Formula of MgO, p. 813

REVIEW RESOURCES

Review and Assessment 2 45-minute periods 1 90-minute block	Cumulative Review	Alternative Assessment	Traditional Assessment
	SR Chapter 7 Mixed Review **PE** Chapter 7 40–50, pp. 237–238	**PE** 60, 61, p. 239 **ATE** 212 **AA** Items for Chapter 7	Chapter 7 Text Test Generator items for Chapter 7

ASSIGNMENT RESOURCES

Section Homework Resources & Review	Problem-Solving Practice
HR Homework Worksheets 7-1, 7-2, 7-3, 7-4 Graphic Org. Assignments 7-2, 7-3 **PE** Section Review, 1–4, p. 215 Chapter Review, 1–14, 23–25, pp. 235–236 **SR** Section Review 7-1	**PE** Additional Samples 7-1, 7-2, 7-3, 7-4 **ATE** Additional Samples, pp. 207, 209, 211, 213
HR Homework Worksheets 7-5, 7-6 Graphic Org. Assignment 7-5 **PE** Section Review, 1–2, p. 219 Chapter Review, 15–18, 27–28, p. 235 **SR** Section Review 7-2	**PE** Additional Samples 7-5 **ATE** Additional Samples, p. 218
HR Homework Worksheets 7-7, 7-8, 7-9 Graphic Org. Assignment 7-8 **PE** Section Review, 1–5, p. 228 Chapter Review, 19–20, 29–34, pp. 235–236 **SR** Section Review 7-3	**PE** Additional Samples 7-6, 7-7, 7-8, 7-9, 7-10, 7-11 **ATE** Additional Samples, pp. 222, 223, 224, 225, 227, 228
HR Homework Worksheets 7-10, 7-11 Graphic Org. Assignment 7-11 **PE** Section Review, 1–5, p. 233 Chapter Review, 21–22, 35–37, pp. 236–237 **SR** Section Review 7-4	**PE** Additional Samples 7-12, 7-13, 7-14 **ATE** Additional Samples, pp. 230, 231, 233

TECHNOLOGY RESOURCES

Technology & Internet Resources

 CTW 14 Segment 14 Harvesting Salt

 Holt Chemistry Videodiscs Teacher's Correlation Guide for Chapter 7

internet connect

 On-line Student Resources:
GO TO: www.scilinks.org
The following SciLinks Internet resources can be found in the student text for this chapter.

TOPICS:
• Chemical formulas, p. 203 (HC2071)
• Acids, p. 214 (HC2072)
• Photochemical reaction, p. 221 (HC2073)

 On-line Teacher Resources:
GO TO: go.hrw.com
KEYWORD: HC2 HOME
Visit the HRW Web site for a variety of resources related to this chapter.

Smithsonian Institution®
Internet Connections
Visit www.si.edu/hrw for additional on-line resources.

 CNNfyi.com
Visit www.cnnfyi.com for late-breaking news and current events stories selected just for you.

Resource Key	One-Stop Planner CD-ROM Includes these resources and customizable daily lesson plans:		
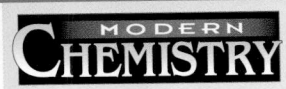 **PE** Pupil's Edition **ATE** Teacher's Edition	**HR** Homework Resources **SR** Section Reviews **CTW** Critical Thinking Worksheets **AA** Alternative Assessments	**ChemFile** **A** Laboratory Experiments **B** Microscale Experiments **C** Technique Builders and Problem-Solving Experiments	**D** Consumer Experiments **T** Transparencies **TM** Transparency Masters **PS** Mini-Guide to Problem Solving **SRW** Supplemental Reading Worksheets

Scoring Rubrics for Labs, Alternative Assessments, Performance Tasks and Portfolio Projects are on the One-Stop Planner CD-ROM.

Chemical Formulas and Chemical Compounds

Chapter Overview

7-1 describes the naming of binary ionic and molecular compounds.

7-2 describes how oxidation numbers are assigned and the Stock system of naming compounds.

7-3 describes how to calculate formula masses, molar masses, and percentage compositions.

7-4 describes how to determine chemical formulas from percentage compositions and empirical data.

Concept Base

Students may need a review of the following concepts:

- laws of multiple and definite proportions, Chapter 3
- conversions between mass in grams and amount in moles, Chapter 3
- electronegativity, Chapter 5
- bonding in polyatomic ions, Chapter 6

Reading Skill-Builder

BRAINSTORMING Have students list and think about as many uses of the term *compound* as they can. Lists might include compound sentences, chemical compounds, or compound interest rates. Students should recognize that *compound* involves more than one thing.

Chemical Formulas and Chemical Compounds

Chemists use chemical names and formulas to describe the atomic composition of compounds.

Chemical Names and Formulas

The total number of natural and synthetic chemical compounds runs in the millions. For some of these substances, certain common names remain in everyday use. For example, calcium carbonate is better known as limestone, and sodium chloride is usually referred to simply as table salt. And everyone recognizes dihydrogen monoxide by its popular name, water.

Unfortunately, common names usually give no information about chemical composition. To describe the atomic makeup of compounds, chemists use systematic methods for naming compounds and for writing chemical formulas. In this chapter, you will be introduced to some of the rules used to identify simple chemical compounds.

Significance of a Chemical Formula

Recall that a chemical formula indicates the relative number of atoms of each kind in a chemical compound. For a molecular compound, the chemical formula reveals the number of atoms of each element contained in a single molecule of the compound, as shown below for the hydrocarbon octane. (*Hydrocarbons* are molecular compounds composed solely of carbon and hydrogen.)

$$C_8H_{18}$$

Subscript indicates that there are 8 carbon atoms in a molecule of octane.   Subscript indicates that there are 18 hydrogen atoms in a molecule of octane.

Unlike a molecular compound, an ionic compound consists of a lattice of positive and negative ions held together by mutual attraction. The chemical formula for an ionic compound represents one formula unit—the simplest ratio of the compound's positive ions (cations) and its negative ions (anions). The chemical formula for aluminum sulfate, an ionic compound consisting of aluminum cations and polyatomic sulfate anions, is written as shown on page 204.

OBJECTIVES

- Explain the significance of a chemical formula.

- Determine the formula of an ionic compound formed between two given ions.

- Name an ionic compound given its formula.

- Using prefixes, name a binary molecular compound from its formula.

- Write the formula of a binary molecular compound given its name.

internetconnect

SCi*LINKS*
NSTA

TOPIC: Chemical formulas
GO TO: www.scilinks.org
*sci*LINKS CODE: HC2071

Lesson Starter

Write the formula for a binary molecular compound, such as carbon tetrachloride, CCl_4, and the formula for a binary ionic compound, such as magnesium chloride, $MgCl_2$, on the chalkboard. Have students guess the name of each compound based on its formula. Ask what kind of information they can discern from the formulas. Then ask them to guess which of the compounds represented is molecular and which is ionic. Explain that chemical formulas form the basis of the language of chemistry and reveal much information about the substances they represent.

CHAPTER ⟷ CONNECTION

Students will learn about hydrocarbons in detail in Chapter 20.

✔Teaching Tip

The subscripts in the chemical formula for a compound reveal the ratio of atoms that make up the compound.

Common Misconception

Students often misinterpret subscripts that appear after a closing parenthesis in chemical formulas as applying only to the immediately preceding atom. Point out that such subscripts multiply the subscripts of all the atoms within the preceding parentheses. Give students adequate practice in interpreting formulas that contain such subscripts.

Teaching Tip

This text uses the common convention of writing ion charges with the number preceding the sign, $n+$ and $n-$; this is done to distinguish ion charges from oxidation numbers, introduced later in this chapter, which are written as $+n$ and $-n$.

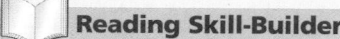Reading Skill-Builder

SUMMARIZING Have students read about how to name and write formulas for ionic and covalent compounds in Sections 7-1 and 7-2. After reading each topic, have volunteers summarize each process for the rest of the class. Have students ask for clarification of anything they do not understand once each summary is completed.

Naming cations

K^+

Potassium cation

Mg^{2+}

Magnesium cation

$$Al_2(SO_4)_3$$

Subscript 2 refers to 2 aluminum atoms.

Subscript 4 refers to 4 oxygen atoms in sulfate ion.

Subscript 3 refers to everything inside parentheses giving 3 sulfate ions, with a total of 3 sulfur atoms and 12 oxygen atoms.

Note how the parentheses are used. They surround the polyatomic anion to identify it as a unit. The subscript 3 refers to the entire unit. Notice also that there is no subscript written next to the symbol for sulfur. When there is no subscript written next to an atom's symbol, the value of the subscript is understood to be 1.

Monatomic Ions

By gaining or losing electrons, many main-group elements form ions with noble-gas configurations. For example, Group 1 metals lose one electron to give 1+ cations, such as Na^+. Group 2 metals lose two electrons to give 2+ cations, such as Mg^{2+}. *Ions formed from a single atom are known as* **monatomic ions.** The nonmetals of Groups 15, 16, and 17 gain electrons to form anions. For example, in ionic compounds nitrogen forms the 3– anion, N^{3-}. The three added electrons plus the five outermost electrons in nitrogen atoms give a completed outermost octet. Similarly, the Group 16 elements oxygen and sulfur form 2– anions, and the Group 17 halogens form 1– anions.

Not all main-group elements readily form ions, however. Rather than gain or lose electrons, atoms of carbon and silicon form covalent bonds in which they share electrons with other atoms. Other elements tend to form ions that do not have noble-gas configurations. For instance, it is difficult for the Group 14 metals tin and lead to lose four electrons to achieve a noble-gas configuration. Instead, they tend to lose the two electrons in their outer p orbitals but retain the two electrons in their outer s orbitals to form 2+ cations. (Tin and lead can also form molecular compounds in which all four valence electrons are involved in covalent bonding.)

Elements from the d-block form 2+, 3+, or, in a few cases, 1+ or 4+ cations. Many d-block elements form two ions of different charges. For example, copper forms 1+ cations and 2+ cations. Iron and chromium, on the other hand, each form 2+ cations as well as 3+ cations. And vanadium and lead form 2+, 3+, and 4+ cations.

Naming Monatomic Ions

Monatomic cations are identified simply by the element's name, as illustrated by the examples at left. Naming monatomic anions is slightly more

ions. The name of the cation is given first, followed by the name of the anion. For most simple ionic compounds, the ratio of the ions is not indicated in the compound's name because it is understood based on the relative charges of the compound's ions. The naming of a simple binary ionic compound is illustrated below.

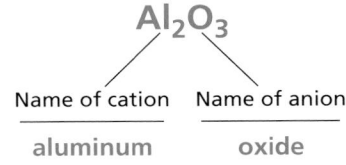

$$Al_2O_3$$

Name of cation   Name of anion

aluminum   oxide

ADDITIONAL SAMPLE PROBLEMS

7-1 Write the formula for the binary ionic compound formed between each of the following pairs of elements:
a. magnesium and iodine
b. potassium and sulfur
c. aluminum and chlorine
d. zinc and bromine
e. cesium and sulfur
f. strontium and oxygen
g. calcium and nitrogen

Ans. **a.** MgI_2
b. K_2S
c. $AlCl_3$
d. $ZnBr_2$
e. Cs_2S
f. SrO
g. Ca_3N_2

7-1 Name the following binary ionic compounds:
a. BaF_2 **e.** K_3N
b. CaO **f.** NaI
c. AgF **g.** $AlBr_3$
d. CdO

Ans. **a.** barium fluoride
b. calcium oxide
c. silver fluoride
d. cadmium oxide
e. potassium nitride
f. sodium iodide
g. aluminum bromide

SAMPLE PROBLEM 7-1

Write the formulas for the binary ionic compounds formed between the following elements:
a. zinc and iodine   **b. zinc and sulfur**

SOLUTION *Write the symbols for the ions side by side. Write the cation first.*
a. Zn^{2+} I^-
b. Zn^{2+} S^{2-}

Cross over the charges to give subscripts.
a. Zn_1^{2+} I_2^-
b. Zn_2^{2+} S_2^{2-}

Check the subscripts and divide them by their largest common factor to give the smallest possible whole-number ratio of ions. Then write the formula.

a. The subscripts are mathematically correct because they give equal total charges of $1 \times 2+ = 2+$ and $2 \times 1- = 2-$. The largest common factor of the subscripts is 1. The smallest possible whole-number ratio of ions in the compound is therefore 1:2. *The subscript 1 is not written*, so the formula is ZnI_2.

b. The subscripts are mathematically correct because they give equal total charges of $2 \times 2+ = 4+$ and $2 \times 2- = 4-$. The largest common factor of the subscripts is 2. The smallest whole-number ratio of ions in the compound is therefore 1:1. The correct formula is ZnS.

PRACTICE

1. Write formulas for the binary ionic compounds formed between the following elements:
   a. potassium and iodine   d. aluminum and sulfur
   b. magnesium and chlorine   e. aluminum and nitrogen
   c. sodium and sulfur

Answer
1. a. KI d. Al_2S_3
   b. $MgCl_2$ e. AlN
   c. Na_2S

2. Name the binary ionic compounds indicated by the following formulas:
   a. $AgCl$ e. BaO
   b. ZnO f. $CaCl_2$
   c. $CaBr_2$
   d. SrF_2

2. a. silver chloride
   b. zinc oxide
   c. calcium bromide
   d. strontium fluoride
   e. barium oxide
   f. calcium chloride

The Stock System of Nomenclature

Some elements, such as iron, form two or more cations with different charges. To distinguish the ions formed by such elements, the Stock system of nomenclature is used. This system uses a Roman numeral to indicate an ion's charge. The numeral is enclosed in parentheses and placed *immediately* after the metal name.

$$Fe^{2+} \qquad\qquad Fe^{3+}$$
$$\text{iron(II)} \qquad\qquad \text{iron(III)}$$

Names of metals that commonly form only one cation *do not* include a Roman numeral.

$$Na^+ \qquad\qquad Ba^{2+} \qquad\qquad Al^{3+}$$
$$\text{sodium} \qquad\qquad \text{barium} \qquad\qquad \text{aluminum}$$

There is no element that commonly forms more than one monatomic anion.

Naming a binary ionic compound according to the Stock system is illustrated below.

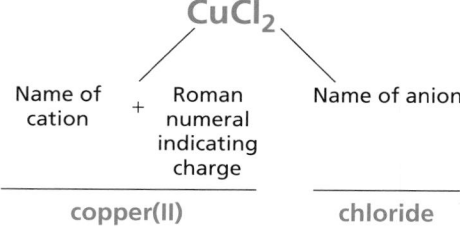

FIGURE 7-1 Different cations of the same metal form different compounds even when they combine with the same anion. Compare (a) lead(IV) oxide, PbO_2, with (b) lead(II) oxide, PbO.

SAMPLE PROBLEM 7-2

Write the formula and give the name for the compound formed by the ions Cr^{3+} and F^-.

SOLUTION *Write the symbols for the ions side by side. Write the cation first.*

$$Cr^{3+} \quad F^-$$

Cross over the charges to give subscripts.

$$Cr^{3+}_1 \quad F^-_3$$

Check the subscripts and write the formula.
The subscripts are correct because they give charges of $1 \times 3+ = 3+$ and $3 \times 1- = 3-$. The largest common factor of the subscripts is 1, so the smallest whole-number ratio of the ions is 1:3. The formula is therefore CrF_3. As Table 7-1 on page 205 shows, chromium forms more than one ion. Therefore, the name of the 3+ chromium ion must be followed by a Roman numeral indicating its charge. The compound's name is chromium(III) fluoride.

PRACTICE

1. Write the formula and give the name for the compounds formed between the following ions:
   a. Cu^{2+} and Br^-
   b. Fe^{2+} and O^{2-}
   c. Pb^{2+} and Cl^-
   d. Hg^{2+} and S^{2-}
   e. Sn^{2+} and F^-
   f. Fe^{3+} and O^{2-}

2. Give the names for the following compounds:
   a. CuO
   b. CoF_3
   c. SnI_4
   d. FeS

Answer
1. a. $CuBr_2$, copper(II) bromide
   b. FeO, iron(II) oxide
   c. $PbCl_2$, lead(II) chloride
   d. HgS, mercury(II) sulfide
   e. SnF_2, tin(II) fluoride
   f. Fe_2O_3, iron(III) oxide

2. a. copper(II) oxide
   b. cobalt(III) fluoride
   c. tin(IV) iodide
   d. iron(II) sulfide

ADDITIONAL SAMPLE PROBLEMS

7-2 Write the formula and give the name for the compound formed between each of the following pairs of ions:
a. Cu^+ and O^{2-}
b. Fe^{3+} and S^{2-}
c. Cu^{2+} and Cl^-
d. Sn^{2+} and Cl^-
e. Hg^{2+} and O^{2-}
f. Sn^{4+} and S^{2-}
g. V^{2+} and F^-
h. V^{3+} and Br^-

Ans. a. Cu_2O, copper(I) oxide
b. Fe_2S_3, iron(III) sulfide
c. $CuCl_2$, copper(II) chloride
d. $SnCl_2$, tin(II) chloride
e. HgO, mercury(II) oxide
f. SnS_2, tin(IV) sulfide
g. VF_2, vanadium(II) fluoride
h. VBr_3, vanadium(III) bromide

7-2 Give the names for the following compounds:
a. CoI_2
b. HgI_2
c. PbS_2
d. $CuBr_2$

Ans. a. cobalt(II) iodide
b. mercury(II) iodide
c. lead(IV) sulfide
d. copper(II) bromide

Compounds Containing Polyatomic Ions

Table 7-2 on page 210 lists some common polyatomic ions. All but the ammonium ion are negatively charged and most are **oxyanions**—*polyatomic ions that contain oxygen.* In several cases, two different oxyanions are formed by the same two elements. Nitrogen and oxygen, for example, are combined in both NO_3^- and NO_2^-. When naming compounds containing such oxyanions, the most common ion is given the ending -*ate*. The ion with one less oxygen atom is given the ending -*ite*.

$$NO_2^- \qquad\qquad NO_3^-$$
$$\text{nitrite} \qquad\qquad \text{nitrate}$$

Sometimes two elements form more than two different oxyanions. In this case, an anion with one less oxygen than the -*ite* anion is given the

Table 7-2 Point out that the atoms composing polyatomic ions are held together by covalent bonds. These ions can therefore be modeled with Lewis dot structures. Have students construct such structures for various polyatomic ions in the table.

Application

Hypochlorites are often used in laundry bleaches and in swimming pool disinfectants. The hypochlorite ion reacts with water to produce hypochlorous acid, HClO, which, like elemental chlorine, is effective in killing bacteria.

TABLE 7-2 *Some Polyatomic Ions*

1+		2+			
ammonium	NH_4^+	dimercury*	Hg_2^{2+}		

1−		2−		3−	
acetate	CH_3COO^-	carbonate	CO_3^{2-}	phosphate	PO_4^{3-}
bromate	BrO_3^-	chromate	CrO_4^{2-}	arsenate	AsO_4^{3-}
chlorate	ClO_3^-	dichromate	$Cr_2O_7^{2-}$		
chlorite	ClO_2^-	hydrogen phosphate	HPO_4^{2-}		
cyanide	CN^-	oxalate	$C_2O_4^{2-}$		
dihydrogen phosphate	$H_2PO_4^-$	peroxide	O_2^{2-}		
hydrogen carbonate (bicarbonate)	HCO_3^-	sulfate	SO_4^{2-}		
hydrogen sulfate	HSO_4^-	sulfite	SO_3^{2-}		
hydroxide	OH^-				
hypochlorite	ClO^-				
nitrate	NO_3^-				
nitrite	NO_2^-				
perchlorate	ClO_4^-				
permanganate	MnO_4^-				

*The mercury(I) cation exists as two Hg^+ ions joined together by a covalent bond and is written as Hg_2^{2+}.

prefix *hypo-*. An anion with one more oxygen than the *-ate* anion is given the prefix *per-*. This nomenclature is illustrated by the four oxyanions formed between chlorine and oxygen.

ClO^-	ClO_2^-	ClO_3^-	ClO_4^-
hypochlorite	chlorite	chlorate	perchlorate

Compounds containing polyatomic ions are named in the same manner as binary ionic compounds. The name of the cation is given first, followed by the name of the anion. For example, the two compounds formed with silver by the nitrate and nitrite anions are named silver nitrate, $AgNO_3$, and silver nitrite, $AgNO_2$, respectively. When more than one polyatomic ion is present in a compound, the formula for the entire ion is surrounded by parentheses. This is illustrated on page 204 for aluminum sulfate, $Al_2(SO_4)_3$. The formula indicates that an aluminum sulfate formula unit has 2 aluminum cations and 3 sulfate anions.

SAMPLE PROBLEM 7-3

Write the formula for tin(IV) sulfate.

SOLUTION *Write the symbols for the ions side by side. Write the cation first.*

$$Sn^{4+} \quad SO_4^{2-}$$

Cross over the charges to give subscripts. Add parentheses around the polyatomic ion if necessary.

$$Sn_2^{4+} \quad (SO_4)_4^{2-}$$

Check the subscripts and write the formula.
The total positive charge is $2 \times 4+ = 8+$. The total negative charge is $4 \times 2- = 8-$. The charges are equal. The largest common factor of the subscripts is 2, so the smallest whole-number ratio of ions in the compound is 1:2. The correct formula is therefore $Sn(SO_4)_2$.

PRACTICE

1. Write formulas for the following ionic compounds: *Answer*
   a. sodium iodide   e. copper(II) sulfate   1. a. NaI   e. $CuSO_4$
   b. calcium chloride   f. sodium carbonate   b. $CaCl_2$ f. Na_2CO_3
   c. potassium sulfide   g. calcium nitrite   c. K_2S g. $Ca(NO_2)_2$
   d. lithium nitrate   h. potassium perchlorate   d. $LiNO_3$ h. $KClO_4$

2. Give the names for the following compounds: 2. a. silver oxide
   a. Ag_2O b. calcium hydroxide
   b. $Ca(OH)_2$ c. potassium chlorate
   c. $KClO_3$ d. ammonium hydroxide
   d. NH_4OH e. iron(II) chromate
   e. $FeCrO_4$ f. potassium hypochlorite
   f. $KClO$

Naming Binary Molecular Compounds

Unlike ionic compounds, molecular compounds are composed of individual covalently bonded units, or molecules. Chemists use two nomenclature systems to name binary molecules. The newer system is the Stock system for naming molecular compounds, which requires an understanding of oxidation numbers. This system will be discussed in Section 7-2.

The old system of naming molecular compounds is based on the use of prefixes. For example, the molecular compound CCl_4 is named carbon *tetra*chloride. The prefix *tetra-* indicates that four chloride atoms are present in a single molecule of the compound. The two oxides of carbon, CO and CO_2, are named carbon *mon*oxide and carbon *di*oxide, respectively.

ADDITIONAL SAMPLE PROBLEMS

7-3 Write formulas for the following ionic compounds:
a. copper(II) nitrate
b. potassium iodide
c. sodium hydroxide
d. ammonium acetate
e. calcium carbonate
f. potassium permanganate
g. sodium sulfate
h. iron(III) nitrate

Ans. a. $Cu(NO_3)_2$
b. KI
c. NaOH
d. NH_4CH_3COO
e. $CaCO_3$
f. $KMnO_4$
g. Na_2SO_4
h. $Fe(NO_3)_3$

7-3 Give the names of the following compounds:
a. Ag_2S
b. $NaMnO_4$
c. $Ba(OH)_2$
d. NH_4NO_3
e. $Fe(ClO)_2$
f. $Ca(NO_3)_2$
g. K_2SO_3
h. $NaCH_3COO$

Ans. a. silver sulfide
b. sodium permanganate
c. barium hydroxide
d. ammonium nitrate
e. iron(II) hypochlorite
f. calcium nitrate
g. potassium sulfite
h. sodium acetate

TABLE 7-3 Numerical Prefixes	
Number	Prefix
1	mono-
2	di-
3	tri-
4	tetra-
5	penta-
6	hexa-
7	hepta-
8	octa-
9	nona-
10	deca-

In these names the prefix *mon-* indicates one oxygen atom and the prefix *di-* indicates two oxygen atoms. The prefixes used to specify the number of atoms, or sometimes the number of *groups* of atoms, in a molecule are listed in Table 7-3.

The rules for the prefix system of nomenclature of binary molecular compounds are as follows.

1. The less-electronegative element is given first. It is given a prefix only if it contributes more than one atom to a molecule of the compound.

2. The second element is named by combining (a) a prefix indicating the number of atoms contributed by the element, (b) the root of the name of the second element, and (c) the ending *-ide*. With few exceptions, the ending *-ide* indicates that a compound contains only two elements.

3. The *o* or *a* at the end of a prefix is usually dropped when the word following the prefix begins with another vowel, e.g., monoxide or pentoxide.

The prefix system is illustrated below.

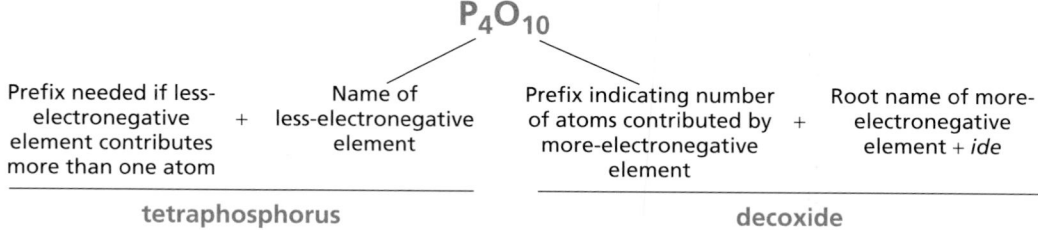

$$P_4O_{10}$$

Prefix needed if less-electronegative element contributes more than one atom	+	Name of less-electronegative element	Prefix indicating number of atoms contributed by more-electronegative element	+	Root name of more-electronegative element + *ide*

tetraphosphorus · decoxide

Because the less-electronegative element is written first, oxygen and the halogens are usually given second, as in carbon tetrachloride and the carbon oxides. In general, the order of nonmetals in binary compound names and formulas is C, P, N, H, S, I, Br, Cl, O, F.

TABLE 7-4 Binary Compounds of Nitrogen and Oxygen

Formula	Prefix-system name
N_2O	dinitrogen monoxide
NO	nitrogen monoxide
NO_2	nitrogen dioxide
N_2O_3	dinitrogen trioxide
N_2O_4	dinitrogen tetroxide
N_2O_5	dinitrogen pentoxide

The prefix system is illustrated further in Table 7-4, which lists the names of the six oxides of nitrogen. Note the application of rule 1, for example, in the name *nitrogen dioxide* for NO_2. No prefix is needed with *nitrogen* because only one atom of nitrogen, the less-electronegative element, is present in a molecule of NO_2. On the other hand, the prefix *di-* in *dioxide* is needed according to rule 2 to indicate the presence of two atoms of the more-electronegative element, oxygen. Take a moment to review the prefixes in the other names in Table 7-4.

SAMPLE PROBLEM 7-4

a. Give the name for As_2O_5.
b. Write the formula for oxygen difluoride.

SOLUTION

a. A molecule of the compound contains two arsenic atoms, so the first word in the name is "*di*arsenic." The five oxygen atoms are indicated by adding the prefix *pent-* to the word "oxide." The complete name is diarsenic pentoxide.

b. The first symbol in the formula is that for oxygen. Oxygen is first in the name because it is less electronegative than fluorine. Since there is no prefix, there must be only one oxygen atom. The prefix *di-* in *difluoride* shows that there are two fluorine atoms in the molecule. The formula is OF_2.

PRACTICE

1. Name the following binary molecular compounds:
a. SO_3
b. ICl_3
c. PBr_5

2. Write formulas for the following compounds:
a. carbon tetraiodide
b. phosphorus trichloride
c. dinitrogen trioxide

Answer
1. a. sulfur trioxide
b. iodine trichloride
c. phosphorus pentabromide
2. a. CI_4
b. PCl_3
c. N_2O_3

Teaching Tip

It is common practice to omit the prefix *mono-* when naming the second element of a binary molecular compound. For example, nitrogen monoxide, NO, is frequently referred to as nitrogen oxide. One exception to this practice is carbon monoxide, in which the prefix is never omitted.

ADDITIONAL SAMPLE PROBLEMS

7-4 Name the following binary molecular compounds:
a. PF_5
b. XeF_4
c. CCl_4

Ans. **a.** phosphorus pentafluoride
b. xenon tetrafluoride
c. carbon tetrachloride

7-4 Write formulas for the following compounds:
a. carbon dioxide
b. dinitrogen pentoxide
c. sulfur hexafluoride

Ans. **a.** CO_2
b. N_2O_5
c. SF_6

- Covalent-network compounds will be discussed in more detail in Chapter 12.

- The ability of a substance to donate a proton, or H⁺, makes it an acid under the Brønsted-Lowry definition. The definition of a Brønsted-Lowry acid as well as other definitions of acids and bases will be discussed in Chapter 15.

TABLE STRATEGY

Table 7-5 Ask students to identify what is similar about the formulas of all the acids shown in the table. *(All contain the symbol for hydrogen.)* Point out that most common acidic substances contain hydrogen. Ask students to familiarize themselves with the formulas of a few of the most common acids, such as hydrochloric acid, sulfuric acid, nitric acid, phosphoric acid, carbonic acid, and acetic acid.

✔ Teaching Tip

In diluting concentrated acids, it is important never to add water to acid because the water, being less dense, tends to remain on top, where it becomes hot and may boil and spatter.

---

internet connect

*SCi*LINKS

NSTA

TOPIC: Acids
GO TO: www.scilinks.org
*sci*LINKS CODE: HC2072

Covalent-Network Compounds

As you read in Chapter 6, some covalent compounds do not consist of individual molecules. Instead, each atom is joined to all its neighbors in a covalently bonded, three-dimensional network. There are no distinct units in these compounds, just as there are no such units in ionic compounds. The subscripts in a formula for a covalent-network compound indicate the smallest whole-number ratio of the atoms in the compound. Naming such compounds is similar to naming molecular compounds. Some common examples are given below.

SiC	SiO_2	Si_3N_4
silicon carbide	silicon dioxide	trisilicon tetranitride

Acids and Salts

An *acid* is a distinct type of molecular compound about which you will read much more in Chapter 15. Most acids used in the laboratory can be classified as either binary acids or oxyacids. *Binary acids* are acids that consist of two elements, usually hydrogen and one of the halogens—fluorine, chlorine, bromine, iodine. *Oxyacids* are acids that contain hydrogen, oxygen, and a third element (usually a nonmetal).

Acids were first recognized as a specific class of compounds based on their properties in solutions of water. Consequently, in chemical nomenclature, the term *acid* usually refers to a solution in water of one of these special compounds rather than to the compound itself. For example, *hydrochloric acid* refers to a water solution of the molecular compound hydrogen chloride, HCl. Some common binary and oxyacids are listed in Table 7-5.

Many polyatomic ions are produced by the loss of hydrogen ions from oxyacids. A few examples of the relationship between oxyacids and oxyanions are shown below.

sulfuric acid	H_2SO_4	sulfate	SO_4^{2-}
nitric acid	HNO_3	nitrate	NO_3^-
phosphoric acid	H_3PO_4	phosphate	PO_4^{3-}

TABLE 7-5 *Common Binary Acids and Oxyacids*

HF	hydrofluoric acid	HNO_2	nitrous acid	HClO	hypochlorous acid
HCl	hydrochloric acid	HNO_3	nitric acid	$HClO_2$	chlorous acid
HBr	hydrobromic acid	H_2SO_3	sulfurous acid	$HClO_3$	chloric acid
HI	hydriodic acid	H_2SO_4	sulfuric acid	$HClO_4$	perchloric acid
H_3PO_4	phosphoric acid	CH_3COOH	acetic acid	H_2CO_3	carbonic acid

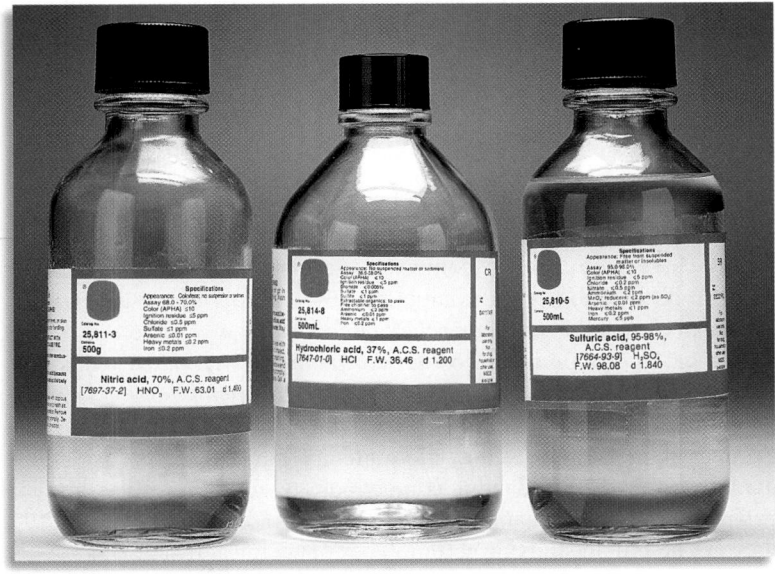

FIGURE 7-2 Some common laboratory acids. Acids should always be handled with care and according to instructions. They can burn the skin, and they burn holes in clothing.

Visual Strategy
FIGURE 7-2 Review the formulas for each of the three acids pictured. Point out that all of these acids are extremely corrosive and potentially dangerous. Ask students to discuss laboratory safety principles they should use in working with such acids.

CHAPTER ◀▶ CONNECTION

Table 15-2, in Chapter 15, lists the name and formula of many oxyacids and oxyanions. Point out to students that the names of *hypo____ous*, *____ous*, *____ic*, and *per____ic* acids (and the names of their anions) follow a progression of an increasing number of oxygen atoms on the central atom.

An ionic compound composed of a cation and the anion from an acid is often referred to as a **salt.** Table salt, NaCl, contains the anion from hydrochloric acid. Calcium sulfate, $CaSO_4$, is a salt containing an anion from sulfuric acid. Some salts contain anions in which one or more hydrogen atoms from the acid are retained. Such anions are named by adding the word *hydrogen* or the prefix *bi-* to the anion name. The best known such anion comes from carbonic acid, H_2CO_3.

$$HCO_3^-$$
hydrogen carbonate ion
bicarbonate ion

SECTION REVIEW

1. What is the significance of a chemical formula?

2. Write formulas for the compounds formed between the following:
   a. aluminum and bromine
   b. sodium and oxygen
   c. magnesium and iodine
   d. Pb^{2+} and O^{2-}
   e. Sn^{2+} and I^-
   f. Fe^{3+} and S^{2-}
   g. Cu^{2+} and NO_3^-
   h. NH_4^+ and SO_4^{2-}

3. Name the following compounds using the Stock system:
   a. NaI   c. CaO   e. CuBr
   b. MgS   d. K_2S f. $FeCl_2$

4. Write formulas for each of the following compounds:
   a. barium sulfide   g. disulfur dichloride
   b. sodium hydroxide   h. carbon diselenide
   c. lead(II) nitrate   i. acetic acid
   d. potassium permanganate   j. chloric acid
   e. iron(II) sulfate   k. sulfurous acid
   f. diphosphorus trioxide   l. phosphoric acid

SECTION REVIEW

1. It indicates the types and numbers of atoms or ions present in a formula unit or molecule of a compound.

2. a. $AlBr_3$
   b. Na_2O
   c. MgI_2
   d. PbO
   e. SnI_2
   f. Fe_2S_3
   g. $Cu(NO_3)_2$
   h. $(NH_4)_2SO_4$

3. a. sodium iodide
   b. magnesium sulfide
   c. calcium oxide
   d. potassium sulfide
   e. copper(I) bromide
   f. iron(II) chloride

4. a. BaS
   b. NaOH
   c. $Pb(NO_3)_2$
   d. $KMnO_4$
   e. $FeSO_4$
   f. P_2O_3
   g. S_2Cl_2
   h. CSe_2
   i. CH_3COOH
   j. $HClO_3$
   k. H_2SO_3
   l. H_3PO_4

Lesson Starter

Remind students that it is possible to determine the charge of an ion in an ionic compound given the charges of the other ions present in the compound. For example, ask students to determine the charge on the bromide ion in the compound NaBr given that Na^+ has a 1+ charge. *(The total charge is 0, so Br^- must have a charge of 1– in order to balance the 1+ charge of Na^+.)* Explain that, in similar fashion, numbers called oxidation numbers can be assigned to atoms in order to keep track of electron distributions in molecular as well as ionic compounds. Point out that the system is based on electronegativity, which was covered in Chapter 5. Explain that in this section, students will learn how to use oxidation numbers in compounds and polyatomic ions.

Common Misconception

Students often confuse oxidation numbers with charges. Point out that charges are physically real characteristics but that oxidation numbers are simply artificial "bookkeeping" devices to keep track of overall electron distribution and are not actual physical characteristics of atoms.

CHAPTER ⟷ CONNECTION

As students will learn in Chapter 8, most elements do not exist in their natural state as bonded molecules. They are thus represented in equations simply by their chemical symbols. Exceptions include those elements, such as O_2, that exist in nature as diatomic molecules, and the elements sulfur and phosphorus, which exist as covalently bonded units best described by the formulas S_8 and P_4, respectively.

SECTION 7-2

OBJECTIVES

- List the rules for assigning oxidation numbers.

- Give the oxidation number for each element in the formula of a chemical compound.

- Name binary molecular compounds using oxidation numbers and the Stock system.

Oxidation Numbers

The charges on the ions composing an ionic compound reflect the electron distribution of the compound. *In order to indicate the general distribution of electrons among the bonded atoms in a molecular compound or a polyatomic ion,* **oxidation numbers,** *also called* **oxidation states,** *are assigned to the atoms composing the compound or ion.* Unlike ionic charges, oxidation numbers do not have an exact physical meaning. In fact, in some cases they are quite arbitrary. However, oxidation numbers are useful in naming compounds, in writing formulas, and in balancing chemical equations. And, as will be discussed in Chapter 19, they are helpful in studying certain types of chemical reactions.

Assigning Oxidation Numbers

As a general rule in assigning oxidation numbers, shared electrons are assumed to belong to the more-electronegative atom in each bond. More specific rules for determining oxidation numbers are provided by the following guidelines.

1. The atoms in a pure element have an oxidation number of zero. For example, the atoms in pure sodium, Na, oxygen, O_2, phosphorus, P_4, and sulfur, S_8, all have oxidation numbers of zero.
2. The more-electronegative element in a binary molecular compound is assigned the number equal to the negative charge it would have as an anion. The less-electronegative atom is assigned the number equal to the positive charge it would have as a cation.
3. Fluorine has an oxidation number of –1 in all of its compounds because it is the most electronegative element.
4. Oxygen has an oxidation number of –2 in almost all compounds. Exceptions include when it is in peroxides, such as H_2O_2, in which its oxidation number is –1, and when it is in compounds with halogens, such as OF_2, in which its oxidation number is +2.
5. Hydrogen has an oxidation number of +1 in all compounds containing elements that are more-electronegative than it; it has an oxidation number of –1 in compounds with metals.
6. The algebraic sum of the oxidation numbers of all atoms in a neutral compound is equal to zero.
7. The algebraic sum of the oxidation numbers of all atoms in a polyatomic ion is equal to the charge of the ion.
8. Although rules 1 through 7 apply to covalently bonded atoms, oxidation numbers can also be assigned to atoms in ionic compounds.

A monatomic ion has an oxidation number equal to the charge of the ion. For example, the ions Na^+, Ca^{2+}, and Cl^- have oxidation numbers of +1, +2, and −1, respectively.

Let's examine the assignment of oxidation numbers to the atoms in two molecular compounds, hydrogen fluoride, HF, and water, H_2O. In HF the bond is polar, with a partial negative charge on the fluorine atom and a partial positive charge on the hydrogen atom. If HF were an ionic compound in which an electron was fully transferred to the fluorine atom, H would have a 1+ charge and F would have a 1− charge. Thus, the oxidation numbers of H and F in hydrogen fluoride are +1 and −1, respectively. In a water molecule, the oxygen atom is more electronegative than the hydrogen atoms. If H_2O were an ionic compound, the oxygen atom would have a charge of 2− and the hydrogen atoms would each have a charge of 1+. The oxidation numbers of H and O in water are therefore +1 and −2, respectively.

Because the sum of the oxidation numbers of the atoms in a compound must satisfy rule 6 or 7 of the guidelines on page 216, it is often possible to assign oxidation numbers when they are not known. This is illustrated in Sample Problem 7-5.

SAMPLE PROBLEM 7-5

Assign oxidation numbers to each atom in the following compounds or ions:

a. UF_6

b. H_2SO_4

c. ClO_3^-

SOLUTION

a. Start by placing known oxidation numbers above the appropriate elements. From the guidelines, we know that fluorine always has an oxidation number of −1.

$$\overset{-1}{U}F_6$$

Multiply known oxidation numbers by the appropriate number of atoms and place the totals underneath the corresponding elements. There are six fluorine atoms, $6 \times -1 = -6$.

$$\overset{-1}{U}F_6 \atop {-6}$$

The compound UF_6 is molecular. According to the guidelines, the sum of the oxidation numbers must equal zero. The total of positive oxidation numbers is therefore +6.

$$\overset{-1}{U}F_6 \atop {+6 \quad -6}$$

Divide the total calculated oxidation number by the appropriate number of atoms. There is only one uranium atom in the molecule, so it must have an oxidation number of +6.

DEMONSTRATION
Oxidation States

In advance, prepare a 0.0004 M $KMnO_4$ solution by dissolving 0.06 g of solute in 1 L of water. Also prepare a 0.1 M $NaHSO_3$ solution by dissolving 1.0 g of solute in 100 mL water. You will also need 1 M solutions of HCl and NaOH.

   Place 20 mL of the $KMnO_4$ solution in each of four 50 mL beakers. Place the beakers on an overhead projector. Point out that all the beakers contain Mn^{7+} (violet). For a control, add nothing to the first beaker. To the second, add 48 drops of the HCl solution and 8 drops of the $NaHSO_3$ solution. The pale pink color is the result of production of Mn^{2+}. To the third beaker, add 4 drops of the $NaHSO_3$ solution. An orange color, characteristic of Mn^{4+} (in MnO_2), should result. To the fourth beaker, add 64 drops of NaOH solution and 1 drop of $NaHSO_3$ solution. The green color of Mn^{6+} (in MnO_4^{2-}) should result. Too little $NaHSO_3$ will produce a blue color and too much will produce orange, so you may need to make slight adjustments in the amount added.

Safety: The solutions will stain the skin. Wear gloves, an apron, and goggles.

Disposal: Combine all solutions, adjust the pH to 8 to 10, and pour down the drain.

7-5 Assign oxidation numbers to each atom in the following compounds or ions:

a. $KClO_4$

b. SO_3^{2-}

c. NF_3

d. CO_2

e. NO_3^-

f. NH_4Cl

Ans. **a.** +1, +7, −2

b. +4, −2

c. +3, −1

d. +4, −2

e. +5, −2

f. −3, +1, −1

$$\overset{+6\ -1}{UF_6}$$
$$\underset{+6\ -6}{}$$

b. Oxygen and sulfur are each more electronegative than hydrogen, so hydrogen has an oxidation number of +1. Oxygen is not combined with a halogen, nor is H_2SO_4 a peroxide. Therefore, the oxidation number of oxygen is −2. Place these known oxidation numbers above the appropriate symbols. Place the total of the oxidation numbers underneath.

$$\overset{+1\quad -2}{H_2SO_4}$$
$$\underset{+2\quad -8}{}$$

The sum of the oxidation numbers must equal zero, and there is only one sulfur atom in each molecule of H_2SO_4. Each sulfur atom therefore must have an oxidation number of $(+2) + (-8) = +6$.

c. To assign oxidation numbers to the elements in ClO_3^-, proceed as in parts (a) and (b). Remember, however, that the total of the oxidation numbers should equal the overall charge of the anion, 1−. The oxidation number of a single oxygen atom in the ion is −2. The total oxidation number due to the three oxygen atoms is −6. For the chlorate ion to have a 1− charge, chlorine must be assigned an oxidation number of +5.

$$\overset{+5\ -2}{ClO_3^-}$$
$$\underset{+5\ -6}{}$$

PRACTICE

1. Assign oxidation numbers to each atom in the following compounds or ions:

a. HCl   e. HNO_3 h. $HClO_3$

b. CF_4 f. KH   i. N_2O_5

c. PCl_3 g. P_4O_{10} j. $GeCl_2$

d. SO_2

Answer

a. +1, −1   e. +1, +5, −2   h. +1, +5, −2

b. +4, −1   f. +1, −1   i. +5, −2

c. +3, −1   g. +5, −2   j. +2, −1

d. +4, −2

Using Oxidation Numbers for Formulas and Names

As shown in Table 7-6, many nonmetals can have more than one oxidation number. (A more extensive list of oxidation numbers is given in Appendix Table A-15.) These numbers can sometimes be used in the same manner as ionic charges to determine formulas. Suppose, for example, you want to know the formula of a binary compound formed between sulfur and oxygen. From the common +4 and +6 oxidation states of sulfur, you could expect that sulfur might form SO_2 or SO_3. Both are known compounds. Of course, a formula must represent facts. Oxidation numbers alone cannot be used to predict the existence of a compound.

TABLE 7-6 Common Oxidation Numbers of Some Nonmetals That Have Variable Oxidation States*

Group 14	carbon	−4, +2, +4
Group 15	nitrogen	−3, +3, +5
	phosphorus	−3, +3, +5
Group 16	sulfur	−2, +4, +6
Group 17	chlorine	−1, +1, +3, +5, +7
	bromine	−1, +1, +3, +5, +7
	iodine	−1, +1, +3, +5, +7

*In addition to the values shown, atoms of each element in its pure state are assigned an oxidation number of zero.

In Section 7-1 we introduced the use of Roman numerals to denote ionic charges in the Stock system of naming ionic compounds. The Stock system is actually based on oxidation numbers, and it can be used as an alternative to the prefix system for naming binary molecular compounds. In the prefix system, for example, SO_2 and SO_3 are named sulfur dioxide and sulfur trioxide, respectively. Their names according to the Stock system are sulfur(IV) oxide and sulfur(VI) oxide. The international body that governs nomenclature has endorsed the Stock system, which is more practical for complicated compounds. Prefix-based names and Stock-system names are still used interchangeably for many simple compounds, however. A few additional examples of names in both systems are given below.

	Prefix system	Stock system
PCl_3	phosphorus trichloride	phosphorus(III) chloride
PCl_5	phosphorus pentachloride	phosphorus(V) chloride
N_2O	dinitrogen monoxide	nitrogen(I) oxide
NO	nitrogen monoxide	nitrogen(II) oxide
PbO_2	lead dioxide	lead(IV) oxide
Mo_2O_3	dimolybdenum trioxide	molybdenum(III) oxide

SECTION REVIEW

1. Assign oxidation numbers to each atom in the following compounds or ions:
   a. HF
   b. Cl_4
   c. H_2O
   d. PI_3
   e. CS_2
   f. Na_2O_2
   g. H_2CO_3
   h. NO_2^-
   i. SO_4^{2-}
   j. ClO_2^-
   k. IO_3^-

2. Name each of the following binary molecular compounds according to the Stock system:
   a. Cl_4
   b. SO_3
   c. As_2S_3
   d. NCl_3

✔ Teaching Tip

In practical chemistry, the use of the prefix system is still much more common than that of the Stock system in naming binary molecular compounds.

Class Discussion

Have students compare the Stock system with the older prefix system of naming binary molecular compounds. Students should discuss the advantages of each system. For example, they might point out the convenience of using easily recognizable prefixes, such as *mono-, di-,* and *tri-,* in the prefix system and the more informative and less ambiguous nature of the Roman numerals used in the Stock system. Encourage students to offer and discuss their own ideas for naming such compounds.

SECTION REVIEW

1. a. +1, −1
   b. +4, −1
   c. +1, −2
   d. +3, −1
   e. +4, −2
   f. +1, −1
   g. +1, +4, −2
   h. +3, −2
   i. +6, −2
   j. +3, −2
   k. +5, −2

2. a. carbon(IV) iodide
   b. sulfur(VI) oxide
   c. arsenic(III) sulfide
   d. nitrogen(III) chloride

CHEMICAL COMMENTARY

Understanding the chemistry of materials used in works of art and the methods of preserving these materials is essential in art preservation.

Application

Traditionally, paper is made from materials that, over time, react with moisture in the air to form acids, which destroy the paper. For art involving paper and documents that need to be preserved, paper that is neutral or slightly basic is used.

Reading for Meaning

Acrylic plastics are composed of polymers.

Read Further

Answers may include that sunlight activates a compound in the paper that reacts with oxygen in the air. The new substance that is formed reflects yellow light, so the exposed paper appears yellow.

Class Discussion

Ask students to name some other photochemical reactions. Point out that materials that undergo such reactions are often packaged in dark or opaque containers.

CHEMICAL COMMENTARY

Chemistry and Art

From "Chemistry and the Plastic and Graphic Arts" by Jonathan E. Ericson in *The Central Science, Essays on the Uses of Chemistry*

The preservation of art is dependent on the control of the environment of the piece. Modern museums are air conditioned, maintaining their temperature between 68°–72°F and a 50–65% relative humidity. These controls provide the conditions under which most works of art are stable. Occasionally, the relative humidity will have to be increased or decreased depending on the stability of an individual piece. Here, art conservation has borrowed techniques from physical chemistry to determine proper conditions experimentally.

In many museums, the temperature and relative humidity of the surroundings are recorded on the same graph by a hygrothermograph, as shown here.

The lighting of a work of art is also a critical part of its environment. Fluorescent light and sunlight contain a lot of ultraviolet. The exposure of art to this light can cause it to fade tremendously. Papers, textiles, and organic dyes are the most sensitive to ultraviolet fading. Here, the polymer research chemist has developed special acrylic plastics like Plexiglas® UF-3, a Rohm and Haas product, which filters out the ultraviolet light.

The relative humidity, temperature and lighting are rather easy to control in a large museum. However, the agents of attack which deteriorate the appearance of the art piece are now not always so easily identified. For paintings, the accumulation of dirt and grime, dis-coloring of the protective varnish layer, or the tension and distortion of canvas or wood supports are destructive to the piece and distorting to us when viewing it. In the past, when cleaning a painting, people either used stronger cleaning methods like sandpaper, or, if smart, gave up. Modern chemistry has developed ways and means of using whole families of safer cleaning agents like acetone, alcohol and other organic solvents. After careful examination and evaluation, the painting conservator can remove the old varnish, reline or bond a new supporting canvas with natural wax resin or synthetic resin, spray on an isolating layer of synthetic resin, paint in pigment losses, and seal the painting with a final protective layer. All these steps use products which have been developed in the chemical laboratory.

Finally, the agents of attack are not always so subtle. Sometimes works of art fall and break, or are torn, cut, or burned. For each case and for each object, a particular conservation method is used. Almost always, the products used or the treatment itself are direct contributions of a chemist. Without chemistry, art conservation, as we know it, would be very primitive, indeed.

Reading for Meaning

What kind of molecules are acrylic plastics composed of?

Read Further

When light interacts with paper, it can cause a *photochemical reaction*. Research photochemical reactions, and explain why a newspaper left in the sunlight for a long period of time turns yellow.

Using Chemical Formulas

As you have seen, a chemical formula indicates the elements as well as the relative number of atoms or ions of each element present in a compound. Chemical formulas also allow chemists to calculate a number of characteristic values for a given compound. In this section, you will learn how to use chemical formulas to calculate the *formula mass,* the *molar mass,* and the *percentage composition* by mass of a compound.

Formula Masses

In Chapter 3 we saw that hydrogen atoms have an average atomic mass of 1.007 94 amu and that oxygen atoms have an average atomic mass of 15.9994 amu. Like individual atoms, a molecule, a formula unit, or an ion has a characteristic average mass. For example, we know from the chemical formula H_2O that a single water molecule is composed of exactly two hydrogen atoms and one oxygen atom. The mass of a water molecule is found by summing the masses of the three atoms in the molecule. (In the calculation, the average atomic masses have been rounded to two decimal places.)

$$\text{average atomic mass of H: 1.01 amu}$$
$$\text{average atomic mass of O: 16.00 amu}$$

$$2 \text{ H atoms} \times \frac{1.01 \text{ amu}}{\text{H atom}} = 2.02 \text{ amu}$$

$$1 \text{ O atom} \times \frac{16.00 \text{ amu}}{\text{O atom}} = 16.00 \text{ amu}$$

$$\text{average mass of } H_2O \text{ molecule} = 18.02 \text{ amu}$$

The mass of a water molecule can be correctly referred to as a *molecular mass.* The mass of one NaCl formula unit, on the other hand, is not a molecular mass because NaCl is an ionic compound. The mass of *any* unit represented by a chemical formula, whether the unit is a molecule, a formula unit, or an ion, is known as the formula mass. *The* **formula mass** *of any molecule, formula unit, or ion is the sum of the average atomic masses of all the atoms represented in its formula.*

SECTION 7-3

OBJECTIVES

- Calculate the formula mass or molar mass of any given compound.

- Use molar mass to convert between mass in grams and amount in moles of a chemical compound.

- Calculate the number of molecules, formula units, or ions in a given molar amount of a chemical compound.

- Calculate the percentage composition of a given chemical compound.

internet connect

*SCI*LINKS
NSTA

TOPIC: Photochemical reaction
GO TO: www.scilinks.org
*sci*LINKS CODE: HC2073

Lesson Starter
Write a common chemical formula, such as that of water, on the chalkboard. Then hold up or pass around a model of a water molecule. Have students identify the number of atoms of hydrogen and oxygen in one water molecule. Ask students how they think they might calculate the mass of a water molecule, given the atomic masses of hydrogen and oxygen. Explain that in this section, they will learn how to carry out these and other calculations for any compound.

Common Misconception
Students often mistakenly think that the subscripts in a compound's formula reveal a mass ratio. Point out that the subscripts actually reveal an atom ratio and a mole ratio. A mass ratio can be obtained by converting amounts in moles to masses in grams.

 Teaching Tip

Atomic masses are rounded to two decimal places for all calculations in this book.

Reading Skill-Builder

SEQUENCING When students have completed Section 7-3, divide the class into groups and have each group choose one of the calculations described in this section (Formula Masses, Molar Masses, Percentage Composition). Ask each group to create a visual graphic showing the steps involved in their calculation process and present it as a summary to the class.

7-6 Find the formula mass of each of the following:
a. Na_2SO_3
b. $HClO_3$
c. MnO_4^-
d. C_2H_6O

Ans. **a.** 126.05 amu
b. 84.46 amu
c. 118.94 amu
d. 46.08 amu

Problem-Solving Practice  ChemFile

Chapter 5 of the Mini-Guide to Problem Solving (also found on the One-Stop Planner CD-ROM) includes more worked-out samples and additional practice problems relating mass, amount, and number of particles.

The procedure illustrated for calculating the formula mass of a water molecule can be used to calculate the mass of any unit represented by a chemical formula. In each of the problems that follow, the atomic masses from the periodic table on pages 130–131 have been rounded to two decimal places.

SAMPLE PROBLEM 7-6

Find the formula mass of potassium chlorate, $KClO_3$.

SOLUTION The mass of a formula unit of $KClO_3$ is found by summing the masses of one K atom, one Cl atom, and three O atoms. The required atomic masses can be found in the periodic table on pages 130–131. In the calculation, each atomic mass has been rounded to two decimal places.

$$1 \text{ K atom} \times \frac{39.10 \text{ amu}}{\text{K atom}} = 39.10 \text{ amu}$$

$$1 \text{ Cl atom} \times \frac{35.45 \text{ amu}}{\text{Cl atom}} = 35.45 \text{ amu}$$

$$3 \text{ O atoms} \times \frac{16.00 \text{ amu}}{\text{O atom}} = 48.00 \text{ amu}$$

$$\text{formula mass of } KClO_3 = 122.55 \text{ amu}$$

PRACTICE 1. Find the formula mass of each of the following:
 a. H_2SO_4
 b. $Ca(NO_3)_2$
 c. PO_4^{3-}
 d. $MgCl_2$

Answer
a. 98.08 amu
b. 164.10 amu
c. 94.97 amu
d. 95.21 amu

Molar Masses

In Chapter 3 you learned that the molar mass of a substance is equal to the mass in grams of one mole, or approximately 6.022×10^{23} particles, of the substance. For example, the molar mass of pure calcium, Ca, is 40.08 g/mol because one mole of calcium atoms has a mass of 40.08 g.

The molar mass of a compound is calculated by summing the masses of the elements present in a mole of the molecules or formula units that make up the compound. For example, one mole of water molecules contains exactly two moles of H atoms and one mole of O atoms. Rounded to two decimal places, a mole of hydrogen atoms has a mass of 1.01 g, and a mole of oxygen atoms has a mass of 16.00 g. The molar mass of water is calculated as follows.

$$2 \text{ mol H} \times \frac{1.01 \text{ g H}}{\text{mol H}} = 2.02 \text{ g H}$$

$$1 \text{ mol O} \times \frac{16.00 \text{ g O}}{\text{mol O}} = 16.00 \text{ g O}$$

molar mass of H_2O = 18.02 g/mol

Figure 7-3 shows a mole of water as well as a mole of several other substances.

You may have noticed that *a compound's molar mass is numerically equal to its formula mass*. For instance, in Sample Problem 7-6 the formula mass of $KClO_3$ was found to be 122.55 amu. Therefore, because molar mass is numerically equal to formula mass, we know that the molar mass of $KClO_3$ is 122.55 g/mol.

FIGURE 7-3 Every compound has a characteristic molar mass. Shown here are one mole each of nitrogen (in balloon), water (in graduated cylinder), cadmium sulfide, CdS (yellow substance), and sodium chloride, NaCl (white substance).

SAMPLE PROBLEM 7-7

What is the molar mass of barium nitrate, $Ba(NO_3)_2$?

SOLUTION One mole of barium nitrate contains exactly one mole of Ba^{2+} ions and two moles of NO_3^- ions. The two moles of NO_3^- ions contain two moles of N atoms and six moles of O atoms. Therefore, the molar mass of $Ba(NO_3)_2$ is calculated as follows.

$$1 \text{ mol Ba} \times \frac{137.33 \text{ g Ba}}{\text{mol Ba}} = 137.33 \text{ g Ba}$$

$$2 \text{ mol N} \times \frac{14.01 \text{ g N}}{\text{mol N}} = 28.02 \text{ g N}$$

$$6 \text{ mol O} \times \frac{16.00 \text{ g O}}{\text{mol O}} = 96.00 \text{ g O}$$

molar mass of $Ba(NO_3)_2$ = 261.35 g/mol

PRACTICE

1. How many moles of atoms of each element are there in one mole of the following compounds?
   a. Al_2S_3
   b. $NaNO_3$
   c. $Ba(OH)_2$

2. Find the molar mass of each of the compounds listed in item 1.

Answer
1. a. 2 mol Al, 3 mol S
   b. 1 mol Na, 1 mol N, 3 mol O
   c. 1 mol Ba, 2 mol O, 2 mol H

2. a. 150.17 g/mol
   b. 85.00 g/mol
   c. 171.35 g/mol

Visual Strategy
FIGURE 7-4 Have students formulate different general types of questions that can be answered by means of the relationships illustrated. For example, they might formulate questions such as: "How many moles of a substance are found in a given mass of the substance?" or "What is the mass in grams of a given number of moles of a substance?" Then have them use the diagram to explain how the question can be answered.

✔ Teaching Tip

Remind students that the subscripts in a compound's chemical formula reveal a molar ratio of the elements composing the compound. The subscript next to a particular element therefore indicates how many moles of atoms of the element there are in a mole of the compound.

ADDITIONAL
SAMPLE
PROBLEMS

7-8 What is the mass in grams of 3.04 mol of ammonia vapor, NH_3?

Ans. 51.8 g

7-8 Calculate the mass of 0.257 mol of calcium nitrate, $Ca(NO_3)_2$.

Ans. 42.2 g

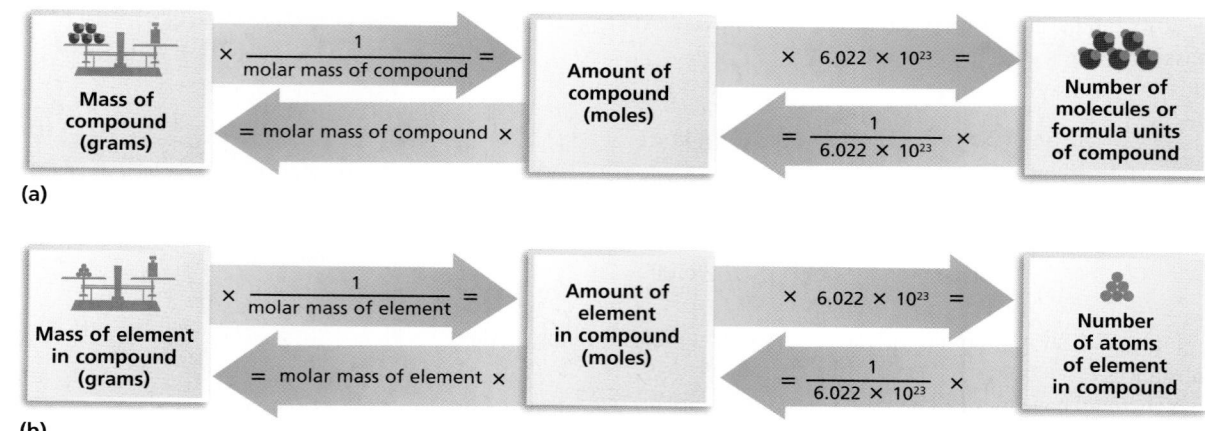

(a)

(b)

FIGURE 7-4 (a) The diagram shows the relationships between mass in grams, amount in moles, and number of molecules or atoms for a given compound. (b) Similar relationships exist for an element within a compound.

Molar Mass as a Conversion Factor

The molar mass of a compound can be used as a conversion factor to relate an amount in moles to a mass in grams for a given substance. Recall that molar mass usually has the units of grams per mole. To convert a known amount of a compound in moles to a mass in grams, multiply the amount in moles by the molar mass.

amount in moles × molar mass (g/mol) = mass in grams

Conversions of this type for elements and compounds are summarized above in Figure 7-4.

SAMPLE PROBLEM 7-8

What is the mass in grams of 2.50 mol of oxygen gas?

SOLUTION

1 *ANALYZE*   **Given:** 2.50 mol O_2
Unknown: mass of O_2 in grams

2 *PLAN*   moles $O_2 \longrightarrow$ grams O_2
To convert amount of O_2 in moles to mass of O_2 in grams, multiply by the molar mass of O_2.

amount of O_2 (mol) × molar mass of O_2 (g/mol) = mass of O_2 (g)

3 **COMPUTE**   First the molar mass of O_2 must be calculated.

$$2 \text{ mol O} \times \frac{16.00 \text{ g O}}{\text{mol O}} = 32.00 \text{ g (mass of one mole of } O_2)$$

The molar mass of O_2 is therefore 32.00 g/mol. Now do the calculation shown in step 2.

$$2.50 \text{ mol } O_2 \times \frac{32.00 \text{ g } O_2}{\text{mol } O_2} = 80.0 \text{ g } O_2$$

4 **EVALUATE**   The answer is correctly given to three significant figures and is close to an estimated value of 75 g (2.50 mol × 30 g/mol).

To convert a known mass of a compound in grams to an amount in moles, the mass must be divided by the molar mass. Or you can invert the molar mass and multiply so that units are easily canceled.

$$\text{mass in grams} \times \frac{1}{\text{molar mass (g/mol)}} = \text{amount in moles}$$

SAMPLE PROBLEM 7-9

Ibuprofen, $C_{13}H_{18}O_2$, is the active ingredient in many nonprescription pain relievers. Its molar mass is 206.29 g/mol.
a. If the tablets in a bottle contain a total of 33 g of ibuprofen, how many moles of ibuprofen are in the bottle?
b. How many molecules of ibuprofen are in the bottle?
c. What is the total mass in grams of carbon in 33 g of ibuprofen?

SOLUTION

1 **ANALYZE**   **Given:** 33 g of $C_{13}H_{18}O_2$, molar mass 206.29 g/mol
Unknown: **a.** moles $C_{13}H_{18}O_2$
b. molecules $C_{13}H_{18}O_2$
c. total mass of C

2 **PLAN**   **a.** grams ⟶ moles
To convert mass of ibuprofen in grams to amount of ibuprofen in moles, multiply by the inverted molar mass of $C_{13}H_{18}O_2$.

$$\text{g } C_{13}H_{18}O_2 \times \frac{1 \text{ mol } C_{13}H_{18}O_2}{206.29 \text{ g } C_{13}H_{18}O_2} = \text{mol } C_{13}H_{18}O_2$$

b. moles ⟶ molecules
To find the number of molecules of ibuprofen, multiply amount of $C_{13}H_{18}O_2$ in moles by Avogadro's number.

$$\text{mol } C_{13}H_{18}O_2 \times \frac{6.022 \times 10^{23} \text{ molecules}}{\text{mol}} = \text{molecules } C_{13}H_{18}O_2$$

Application

The percentage composition of any pure substance is always constant, whatever the source or sample size. Therefore, percentage composition is an identifying characteristic of any substance. For that reason, percentage composition is used by investigators in many different fields—from analytical chemistry to criminal forensics—to determine the identity of unknown materials.

Problem-Solving Practice HOLT ChemFile

Chapter 6 of the Mini-Guide to Problem Solving (also found on the One-Stop Planner CD-ROM) includes more worked-out samples and additional practice problems involving percentage composition.

c. moles $C_{13}H_{18}O_2 \longrightarrow$ moles C $\longrightarrow$ grams C

To find the mass of carbon present in the ibuprofen, the two conversion factors needed are the amount of carbon in moles per mole of $C_{13}H_{18}O_2$ and the molar mass of carbon.

$$\text{mol } C_{13}H_{18}O_2 \times \frac{13 \text{ mol C}}{\text{mol } C_{13}H_{18}O_2} \times \frac{12.01 \text{ g C}}{\text{mol C}} = \text{g C}$$

3 COMPUTE

a. $33 \text{ g } C_{13}H_{18}O_2 \times \dfrac{1 \text{ mol } C_{13}H_{18}O_2}{206.29 \text{ g } C_{13}H_{18}O_2} = 0.16 \text{ mol } C_{13}H_{18}O_2$

b. $0.16 \text{ mol } C_{13}H_{18}O_2 \times \dfrac{6.022 \times 10^{23} \text{ molecules}}{\text{mol}} = 9.6 \times 10^{22} \text{ molecules } C_{13}H_{18}O_2$

c. $0.16 \text{ mol } C_{13}H_{18}O_2 \times \dfrac{13 \text{ mol C}}{\text{mol } C_{13}H_{18}O_2} \times \dfrac{12.01 \text{ g C}}{\text{mol C}} = 25 \text{ g C}$

The bottle contains 0.16 mol of ibuprofen, which is 9.6×10^{22} molecules of ibuprofen. The sample of ibuprofen contains 25 g of carbon.

4 EVALUATE Checking each step shows that the arithmetic is correct, significant figures have been used correctly, and units have canceled as desired.

PRACTICE

1. How many moles of compound are there in the following?
a. 6.60 g $(NH_4)_2SO_4$
b. 4.5 kg $Ca(OH)_2$

Answer
1. a. 0.0500 mol
   b. 61 mol

2. How many molecules are there in the following?
a. 25.0 g H_2SO_4
b. 125 g of sugar, $C_{12}H_{22}O_{11}$

2. a. 1.53×10^{23} molecules
   b. 2.20×10^{23} molecules

3. What is the mass in grams of 6.25 mol of copper(II) nitrate?

3. 1170 g

Percentage Composition

It is often useful to know the percentage by mass of a particular element in a chemical compound. For example, suppose the compound potassium chlorate, $KClO_3$, were to be used as a source of oxygen. It would be helpful to know the percentage of oxygen in the compound. To find the mass percentage of an element in a compound, one can divide the mass of the element in a sample of the compound by the total mass of the sample, then multiply this value by 100.

$$\frac{\text{mass of element in sample of compound}}{\text{mass of sample of compound}} \times 100 = \frac{\% \text{ element in}}{\text{compound}}$$

The mass percentage of an element in a compound is the same regardless of the sample's size. Therefore, a simpler way to calculate the percentage of an element in a compound is to determine how many grams of the element are present in one mole of the compound. Then divide this value by the molar mass of the compound and multiply by 100.

$$\frac{\text{mass of element in 1 mol of compound}}{\text{molar mass of compound}} \times 100 = \frac{\% \text{ element in}}{\text{compound}}$$

The percentage by mass of each element in a compound is known as the **percentage composition** *of the compound.*

ADDITIONAL SAMPLE PROBLEMS

7-10 Calculate the percentage composition of sodium nitrate, $NaNO_3$.
Ans. 27.05% Na, 16.48% N, 56.47% O

7-10 Calculate the percentage composition of silver sulfate, Ag_2SO_4.
Ans. 69.19% Ag, 10.29% S, 20.53% O

SAMPLE PROBLEM 7-10

Find the percentage composition of copper(I) sulfide, Cu_2S.

SOLUTION

1 ANALYZE
Given: formula, Cu_2S
Unknown: percentage composition of Cu_2S

2 PLAN
formula $\longrightarrow$ molar mass $\longrightarrow$ mass percentage of each element

The molar mass of the compound must be found. Then the mass of each element present in one mole of the compound is used to calculate the mass percentage of each element.

3 COMPUTE

$$2 \text{ mol Cu} \times \frac{63.55 \text{ g Cu}}{\text{mol Cu}} = 127.1 \text{ g Cu}$$

$$1 \text{ mol S} \times \frac{32.07 \text{ g S}}{\text{mol S}} = 32.07 \text{ g S}$$

$$\text{molar mass of } Cu_2S = 159.2 \text{ g}$$

$$\frac{127.1 \text{ g Cu}}{159.2 \text{ g } Cu_2S} \times 100 = 79.84\% \text{ Cu}$$

$$\frac{32.07 \text{ g S}}{159.2 \text{ g } Cu_2S} \times 100 = 20.14\% \text{ S}$$

4 EVALUATE
A good check is to see if the results add up to about 100%. (Because of rounding, the total may not always be exactly 100%.)

SAMPLE PROBLEM 7-11

As some salts crystallize from a water solution, they bind water molecules in their crystal structure. Sodium carbonate forms such a *hydrate,* in which 10 water molecules are present for every formula unit of sodium carbonate. Find the mass percentage of water in sodium carbonate decahydrate, $Na_2CO_3 \cdot 10H_2O$, which has a molar mass of 286.14 g/mol.

ADDITIONAL
SAMPLE
PROBLEMS

7-11 What is the mass percentage of water in the hydrate $CuSO_4 \cdot 5H_2O$?

Ans. 36.08%

7-11 Zinc chloride, $ZnCl_2$, is 52.02% chlorine by mass.
a. What mass of chlorine is contained in 80.3 g of $ZnCl_2$?
b. How many moles of Cl is this?

Ans. **a.** 41.8 g
b. 1.18 mol

SOLUTION

1 ANALYZE

Given: chemical formula, $Na_2CO_3 \cdot 10H_2O$
molar mass of $Na_2CO_3 \cdot 10H_2O$
Unknown: mass percentage of H_2O

2 PLAN

chemical formula $\longrightarrow$ mass H_2O per mole of $Na_2CO_3 \cdot 10H_2O$ $\longrightarrow$ % water

The mass of water per mole of sodium carbonate decahydrate must first be found. This value is then divided by the mass of one mole of $Na_2CO_3 \cdot 10H_2O$.

3 COMPUTE

One mole of $Na_2CO_3 \cdot 10H_2O$ contains 10 mol of H_2O. Recall from page 223 that the molar mass of H_2O is 18.02 g/mol. The mass of 10 mol of H_2O is calculated as follows.

$$10 \text{ mol } H_2O \times \frac{18.02 \text{ g } H_2O}{\text{mol } H_2O} = 180.2 \text{ g } H_2O$$

mass of H_2O per mole of $Na_2CO_3 \cdot 10H_2O$ = 180.2 g

The molar mass of $Na_2CO_3 \cdot 10H_2O$ is 286.14 g/mol, so we know that 1 mol of the hydrate has a mass of 286.14g. The mass percentage of 10 mol of H_2O in 1 mol of $Na_2CO_3 \cdot 10H_2O$ can now be calculated.

$$\text{mass percentage of } H_2O \text{ in } Na_2CO_3 \cdot 10H_2O = \frac{180.2 \text{ g } H_2O}{286.14 \text{ g } Na_2CO_3 \cdot 10H_2O} \times 100 = 62.98\% \ H_2O$$

4 EVALUATE

Checking shows that the arithmetic is correct and that units cancel as desired.

PRACTICE

1. Find the percentage compositions of the following:
   a. $PbCl_2$ b. $Ba(NO_3)_2$

2. Find the mass percentage of water in $ZnSO_4 \cdot 7H_2O$.

3. Magnesium hydroxide is 54.87% oxygen by mass. How many grams of oxygen are in 175 g of the compound? How many moles of oxygen is this?

Answer
1. a. 74.51% Pb, 25.49% Cl
   b. 52.546% Ba, 10.72% N, 36.73% O
2. 43.86% H_2O
3. 96.0 g O; 6.00 mol O

SECTION REVIEW

1. formula mass = 96.11 amu; molar mass = 96.11 g/mol

2. 2 mol N, 8 mol H, 1 mol C, 3 mol O

3. 1.30×10^3 g

4. 3.97 mol

5. 3.342×10^{20} molecules

6. 29.15% N, 8.407% H, 12.50% C, 49.94% O

SECTION REVIEW

1. Determine both the formula mass and molar mass of ammonium carbonate, $(NH_4)_2CO_3$.

2. How many moles of atoms of each element are there in one mole of $(NH_4)_2CO_3$?

3. What is the mass in grams of 3.25 mol $Fe_2(SO_4)_3$?

4. How many moles of molecules are there in 250 g of hydrogen nitrate, HNO_3?

5. How many molecules of aspirin, $C_9H_8O_4$, are there in a 100.0 mg tablet of aspirin?

6. Calculate the percentage composition of $(NH_4)_2CO_3$.

Determining Chemical Formulas

W hen a new substance is synthesized or is discovered, it is analyzed quantitatively to reveal its percentage composition. From this data, the empirical formula is then determined. *An* **empirical formula** *consists of the symbols for the elements combined in a compound, with subscripts showing the smallest whole-number mole ratio of the different atoms in the compound.* For an ionic compound, the formula unit is usually the compound's empirical formula. For a molecular compound, however, the empirical formula does not necessarily indicate the actual numbers of atoms present in each molecule. For example, the empirical formula of the gas diborane is BH_3, but the molecular formula is B_2H_6. In this case, the number of atoms given by the molecular formula corresponds to the empirical ratio multiplied by two.

Calculation of Empirical Formulas

To determine a compound's empirical formula from its percentage composition, begin by converting percentage composition to a mass composition. Assume that you have a 100.0 g sample of the compound. Then calculate the amount of each element in the sample. For example, the percentage composition of diborane is 78.1% B and 21.9% H. Therefore, 100.0 g of diborane contains 78.1 g of B and 21.9 g of H.

Next, the mass composition of each element is converted to a composition in moles by dividing by the appropriate molar mass.

$$78.1 \text{ g B} \times \frac{1 \text{ mol B}}{10.81 \text{ g B}} = 7.22 \text{ mol B}$$

$$21.9 \text{ g H} \times \frac{1 \text{ mol H}}{1.01 \text{ g H}} = 21.7 \text{ mol H}$$

These values give a mole ratio of 7.22 mol B to 21.7 mol H. However, this is not a ratio of smallest whole numbers. To find such a ratio, divide each number of moles by the smallest number in the existing ratio.

$$\frac{7.22 \text{ mol B}}{7.22} : \frac{21.7 \text{ mol H}}{7.22} = 1 \text{ mol B}:3.01 \text{ mol H}$$

OBJECTIVES

- Define *empirical formula*, and explain how the term applies to ionic and molecular compounds.

- Determine an empirical formula from either a percentage or a mass composition.

- Explain the relationship between the empirical formula and the molecular formula of a given compound.

- Determine a molecular formula from an empirical formula.

Lesson Starter
Show the students models of molecules in which the numbers of the various types of atoms differ but the ratios are the same, for example, NO_2 and N_2O_4. Have them compare and contrast the molecules, and lead them to the conclusion that the ratios are equal but the numbers of atoms differ. This will help prepare the class for the concept of empirical formula.

Reading Skill-Builder

VOCABULARY BUILDING
Have students look up the meaning of the word *empirical* in the dictionary. Have them use the definition to explain where information is obtained about an empirical formula. Their explanations should reflect that empirical formulas are determined from experimental data.

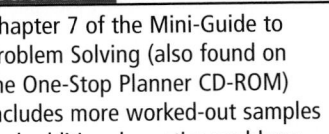

Problem-Solving Practice

Chapter 7 of the Mini-Guide to Problem Solving (also found on the One-Stop Planner CD-ROM) includes more worked-out samples and additional practice problems involving empirical formulas.

7-12 A compound is analyzed and found to contain 36.70% potassium, 33.27% chlorine, and 30.03% oxygen. What is the empirical formula of the compound?

Ans. $KClO_2$

7-12 Determine the empirical formula of the compound that contains 17.15% carbon, 1.44% hydrogen, and 81.41% fluorine.

Ans. CHF_3

Because of rounding or experimental error, a compound's mole ratio sometimes consists of numbers close to whole numbers instead of exact whole numbers. In this case, the differences from whole numbers may be ignored and the nearest whole number taken. Thus, diborane contains atoms in the ratio 1 B:3 H. The compound's empirical formula is BH_3.

Sometimes mass composition is known instead of percentage composition. To determine the empirical formula in this case, convert mass composition to composition in moles. Then calculate the smallest whole-number mole ratio of atoms. This process is shown in Sample Problem 7-13.

SAMPLE PROBLEM 7-12

Quantitative analysis shows that a compound contains 32.38% sodium, 22.65% sulfur, and 44.99% oxygen. Find the empirical formula of this compound.

SOLUTION

1 ANALYZE

Given: percentage composition: 32.38% Na, 22.65% S, and 44.99% O
Unknown: empirical formula

2 PLAN

percentage composition $\longrightarrow$ mass composition $\longrightarrow$ composition in moles $\longrightarrow$ smallest whole-number mole ratio of atoms

3 COMPUTE

Mass composition (mass of each element in 100.0 g sample): 32.38 g Na, 22.65 g S, 44.99 g O

Composition in moles: $32.38 \text{ g Na} \times \dfrac{1 \text{ mol Na}}{22.99 \text{ g Na}} = 1.408 \text{ mol Na}$

$22.65 \text{ g S} \times \dfrac{1 \text{ mol S}}{32.07 \text{ g S}} = 0.7063 \text{ mol S}$

$44.99 \text{ g O} \times \dfrac{1 \text{ mol O}}{16.00 \text{ g O}} = 2.812 \text{ mol O}$

Smallest whole-number mole ratio of atoms:
The compound contains atoms in the ratio 1.408 mol Na:0.7063 mol S:2.812 mol O. To find the smallest whole-number mole ratio, divide each value by the smallest number in the ratio.

$$\frac{1.408 \text{ mol Na}}{0.7063} : \frac{0.7063 \text{ mol S}}{0.7063} : \frac{2.812 \text{ mol O}}{0.7063} = 1.993 \text{ mol Na:1 mol S:3.981 mol O}$$

Rounding each number in the ratio to the nearest whole number yields a mole ratio of 2 mol Na:1 mol S:4 mol O. The empirical formula of the compound is Na_2SO_4.

4 EVALUATE

Calculating the percentage composition of the compound based on the empirical formula determined in the problem reveals a percentage composition of 32.37% Na, 22.58% S, and 45.05% O. These values agree reasonably well with the given percentage composition.

SAMPLE PROBLEM 7-13

Analysis of a 10.150 g sample of a compound known to contain only phosphorus and oxygen indicates a phosphorus content of 4.433 g. What is the empirical formula of this compound?

SOLUTION

1 ANALYZE

Given: sample mass = 10.150 g
phosphorus mass = 4.433 g
Unknown: empirical formula

2 PLAN

Mass composition $\longrightarrow$ composition in moles $\longrightarrow$ smallest whole-number ratio of atoms

3 COMPUTE

The mass of oxygen is found by subtracting the phosphorus mass from the sample mass.

$$\text{sample mass} - \text{phosphorus mass} = 10.150 \text{ g} - 4.433 \text{ g} = 5.717 \text{ g}$$

Mass composition: 4.433 g P, 5.717 g O

Composition in moles:

$$4.433 \text{ g P} \times \frac{1 \text{ mol P}}{30.97 \text{ g P}} = 0.1431 \text{ mol P}$$

$$5.717 \text{ g O} \times \frac{1 \text{ mol O}}{16.00 \text{ g O}} = 0.3573 \text{ mol O}$$

Smallest whole-number mole ratio of atoms:

$$\frac{0.1431 \text{ mol P}}{0.1431} : \frac{0.3573 \text{ mol O}}{0.1431}$$

$$1 \text{ mol P} : 2.497 \text{ mol O}$$

The number of O atoms is not close to a whole number. But if we multiply each number in the ratio by 2, then the number of O atoms becomes 4.994 mol, which is close to 5 mol. The simplest whole-number mole ratio of P atoms to O atoms is 2:5. The compound's empirical formula is P_2O_5.

4 EVALUATE

The arithmetic is correct, significant figures have been used correctly, and units cancel as desired. The formula is reasonable because +5 is a common oxidation state of phosphorus.

PRACTICE

1. A compound is found to contain 63.52% iron and 36.48% sulfur. Find its empirical formula.

   Answer
   FeS

2. Find the empirical formula of a compound found to contain 26.56% potassium, 35.41% chromium, and the remainder oxygen.

   Answer
   $K_2Cr_2O_7$

3. Analysis of 20.0 g of a compound containing only calcium and bromine indicates that 4.00 g of calcium are present. What is the empirical formula of the compound formed?

   Answer
   $CaBr_2$

ADDITIONAL SAMPLE PROBLEMS

7-13 A 60.00 g sample of tetraethyllead, a gasoline additive, is found to contain 38.43 g lead, 17.83 g carbon, and 3.74 g hydrogen. Find its empirical formula.

Ans. PbC_8H_{20}

7-13 A 170.00 g sample of an unidentified compound contains 29.84 g sodium, 67.49 g chromium, and 72.67 g oxygen. What is the compound's empirical formula?

Ans. $Na_2Cr_2O_7$

✔ Teaching Tip

Point out to students that the decimals 0.33, 0.67, 0.25, 0.75, and 0.20 are equivalent (to two decimal places) to the fractions $\frac{1}{3}, \frac{2}{3}, \frac{1}{4}, \frac{3}{4}$, and $\frac{1}{5}$, and that a number ending in one of these decimals is converted to a whole number when it is multiplied by the denominator of the corresponding fraction. Remind students that they must multiply each number in the mole ratio by the same factor in order to avoid changing the mole ratio.

232

Teaching Tip

The subscripts in an empirical formula can be obtained by dividing all the subscripts of the corresponding molecular formula by the same whole number.

CHAPTER ⟷ CONNECTION

Carbon forms a great many compounds that have the same empirical formula but different molecular formulas. The methods of writing correct molecular formulas for organic compounds, given their names, is covered in Chapters 20 and 21.

Calculation of Molecular Formulas

Remember that the *empirical formula* contains the smallest possible whole numbers that describe the atomic ratio. The *molecular formula* is the actual formula of a molecular compound. An empirical formula may or may not be a correct molecular formula. For example, diborane's empirical formula is BH_3. Any multiple of BH_3, such as B_2H_6, B_3H_9, B_4H_{12}, and so on, represents the same ratio of B atoms to H atoms. The molecular compounds ethene, C_2H_4, and cyclopropane, C_3H_6, also share an identical atomic ratio (2 H:1 C), yet they are very different substances. How is the correct formula of a molecular compound found from an empirical formula?

The relationship between a compound's empirical formula and its molecular formula can be written as follows.

$$x(\text{empirical formula}) = \text{molecular formula}$$

The number represented by x is a whole-number multiple indicating the factor by which the subscripts in the empirical formula must be multiplied to obtain the molecular formula. (The value of x is sometimes 1.) The formula masses have a similar relationship.

$$x(\text{empirical formula mass}) = \text{molecular formula mass}$$

To determine the molecular formula of a compound, you must know the compound's formula mass. For example, experimentation shows the formula mass of diborane to be 27.67 amu. The formula mass for the empirical formula, BH_3, is 13.84 amu. Dividing the experimental formula mass by the empirical formula mass gives the value of x for diborane.

$$x = \frac{27.67 \text{ amu}}{13.84 \text{ amu}} = 2.000$$

The molecular formula of diborane is therefore B_2H_6.

$$(BH_3)_2 = B_2H_6$$

Recall that a compound's molecular formula mass is numerically equal to its molar mass, so a compound's molecular formula can also be found given the compound's empirical formula and its molar mass.

SAMPLE PROBLEM 7-14

In Sample Problem 7-13, the empirical formula of a compound of phosphorus and oxygen was found to be P_2O_5. Experimentation shows that the molar mass of this compound is 283.89 g/mol. What is the compound's molecular formula?

SOLUTION

1   ANALYZE   **Given:** empirical formula
Unknown: molecular formula

2 PLAN

$$x(\text{empirical formula}) = \text{molecular formula}$$

$$x = \frac{\text{molecular formula mass}}{\text{empirical formula mass}}$$

3 COMPUTE Molecular formula mass is numerically equal to molar mass. Thus, changing the g/mol unit of the compound's molar mass to amu yields the compound's molecular formula mass.

$$\text{molecular molar mass} = 283.89 \text{ g/mol}$$
$$\text{molecular formula mass} = 283.89 \text{ amu}$$

The empirical formula mass is found by adding the masses of each of the atoms indicated in the empirical formula.

$$\text{mass of phosphorus atom} = 30.97 \text{ amu}$$
$$\text{mass of oxygen atom} = 16.00 \text{ amu}$$
$$\text{empirical formula mass of } P_2O_5 = 2 \times 30.97 \text{ amu} + 5 \times 16.00 \text{ amu} = 141.94 \text{ amu}$$

Dividing the experimental formula mass by the empirical formula mass gives the value of x. The formula mass is numerically equal to the molar mass.

$$x = \frac{283.89 \text{ amu}}{141.94 \text{ amu}} = 2.0001$$

The compound's molecular formula is therefore P_4O_{10}.

$$2 \times (P_2O_5) = P_4O_{10}$$

4 EVALUATE Checking the arithmetic shows that it is correct.

PRACTICE

1. Determine the molecular formula of the compound with an empirical formula of CH and a formula mass of 78.110 amu.

   Answer
   C_6H_6

2. A sample of a compound with a formula mass of 34.00 amu is found to consist of 0.44 g H and 6.92 g O. Find its molecular formula.

   Answer
   H_2O_2

SECTION REVIEW

1. A compound is found to contain 36.48% Na, 25.41% S, and 38.11% O. Find its empirical formula.

2. Find the empirical formula of a compound that contains 53.70% iron and 46.30% sulfur.

3. Analysis of a compound indicates that it contains 1.04 g K, 0.70 g Cr, and 0.86 g O. Find its empirical formula.

4. If 4.04 g of N combine with 11.46 g O to produce a compound with a formula mass of 108.0 amu, what is the molecular formula of this compound?

5. The molar mass of a compound is 92 g/mol. Analysis of a sample of the compound indicates that it contains 0.606 g N and 1.390 g O. Find its molecular formula.

REVIEW ANSWERS

1. **a.** ions formed from a single atom
   b. Examples include Na^+, Mg^{2+}, and Cl^-.

2. The nitrate ion has one more oxygen atom than the nitrite ion (NO_3^- versus NO_2^-).

3. **a.** K^+ **d.** Cl^-
   b. Ca^{2+} **e.** Ba^{2+}
   c. S^{2-} **f.** Br^-

4. **a.** Na^+, 1+   **d.** N^{3-}, 3−
   b. Al^{3+}, 3+   **e.** Fe^{2+}, 2+
   c. Cl^-, 1−   **f.** Fe^{3+}, 3+

5. **a.** potassium ion (or potassium cation)
   b. magnesium ion (or magnesium cation)
   c. aluminum ion (or aluminum cation)
   d. chloride ion (or chloride anion)
   e. oxide ion (or oxide anion)
   f. calcium ion (or calcium cation)

6. **a.** NaI   **d.** BaF_2
   b. CaS   **e.** Li_2O
   c. $ZnCl_2$

7. **a.** potassium chloride
   b. calcium bromide
   c. lithium oxide
   d. magnesium chloride

8. **a.** CrF_2, chromium(II) fluoride
   b. NiO, nickel(II) oxide
   c. Fe_2O_3, iron(III) oxide

9. The less-electronegative element is written first.

10. **a.** carbon dioxide
    b. carbon tetrachloride
    c. phosphorus pentachloride
    d. selenium hexafluoride
    e. diarsenic pentoxide

11. **a.** CBr_4 **c.** P_4O_{10}
    b. SiO_2 **d.** As_2S_3

12. Binary acids, such as HCl and HBr, contain only two elements, usually hydrogen and a halogen. Oxyacids, such as H_2SO_4 and

CHAPTER SUMMARY

7-1 • A positive monatomic ion is identified simply by the name of the appropriate element. A negative monatomic ion is named by dropping parts of the ending of the element's name and adding *-ide* to the root.
• The charge of each ion in an ionic compound may be used to determine the simplest chemical formula for the compound.
• Compounds composed of two different elements are known as binary compounds.

• Binary ionic compounds are named by combining the names of the positive and negative ions. Compounds containing polyatomic ions are named in the same manner.
• The old system of naming binary molecular compounds uses prefixes. The new system, known as the Stock system, uses oxidation numbers.

Vocabulary

binary compounds (206)   nomenclature (206)   oxyanions (209)   salt (215)
monatomic ions (204)

7-2 • Oxidation numbers, or oxidation states, are assigned to atoms in compounds according to a set of specific rules. Oxidation numbers are useful in naming compounds, in writing formulas, and in balancing chemical equations.
• Compounds containing elements that have more than one oxidation state are named using the Stock system of nomenclature.
• Stock-system names and prefix-system names

are used interchangeably for many molecular compounds.
• In many molecular compounds, oxidation numbers of each element in the compound may be used to determine the compound's simplest chemical formula.
• By knowing oxidation numbers, we can name compounds without knowing whether they are ionic or molecular.

Vocabulary

oxidation numbers (216)   oxidation states (216)

7-3 • Formula mass, molar mass, and percentage composition can be calculated from the chemical formula for a compound.
• The percentage composition of a compound is the percentage by mass of each element in the compound.

• Molar mass can be used as a conversion factor between an amount in moles and a mass in grams of a given compound or element.

Vocabulary

formula mass (221)   percentage composition (227)

7-4 • An empirical formula shows the simplest whole-number ratio of atoms in a given compound.
• Each molecule of a molecular compound contains a whole-number multiple of the atoms in the empirical formula. In some cases this whole-number multiple is equal to 1.

• Empirical formulas indicate how many atoms of each element are combined in the simplest unit of a chemical compound.
• A molecular formula can be found from the empirical formula if the molar mass is measured.

Vocabulary

empirical formula (229)

REVIEWING CONCEPTS

1. a. What are monatomic ions?
   b. Give three examples of monatomic ions. (7-1)

2. What is the difference between the nitrite ion and the nitrate ion? (7-1)

3. Using only the periodic table, write the symbol of the ion most typically formed by each of the following elements:
   a. K
   b. Ca
   c. S
   d. Cl
   e. Ba
   f. Br (7-1)

4. Write the formulas and indicate the charges for each of the following ions:
   a. sodium ion
   b. aluminum ion
   c. chloride ion
   d. nitride ion
   e. iron(II) ion
   f. iron(III) ion (7-1)

5. Name each of the following monatomic ions:
   a. K^+ d. Cl^-
   b. Mg^{2+} e. O^{2-}
   c. Al^{3+} f. Ca^{2+} (7-1)

6. Write formulas for the binary ionic compounds formed between the following elements. (Hint: See Sample Problem 7-1.)
   a. sodium and iodine
   b. calcium and sulfur
   c. zinc and chlorine
   d. barium and fluorine
   e. lithium and oxygen (7-1)

7. Give the name of each of the following binary ionic compounds. (Hint: See Sample Problem 7-2.)
   a. KCl   c. Li_2O
   b. $CaBr_2$ d. $MgCl_2$ (7-1)

8. Write the formulas and give the names of the compounds formed by the following ions:
   a. Cr^{2+} and F^-
   b. Ni^{2+} and O^{2-}
   c. Fe^{3+} and O^{2-} (7-1)

9. In naming and writing formulas for binary molecular compounds, what determines the order in which the component elements are written? (7-1)

10. Name the following binary molecular compounds according to the prefix system. (Hint: See Sample Problem 7-4.)
    a. CO_2 d. SeF_6
    b. CCl_4 e. As_2O_5
    c. PCl_5 (7-1)

11. Write formulas for each of the following binary molecular compounds. (Hint: See Sample Problem 7-4.)
    a. carbon tetrabromide
    b. silicon dioxide
    c. tetraphosphorus decoxide
    d. diarsenic trisulfide (7-1)

12. Distinguish between binary acids and oxyacids, and give two examples of each. (7-1)

13. a. What is a salt?
    b. Give two examples of salts. (7-1)

14. Name each of the following acids:
    a. HF   d. H_2SO_4
    b. HBr   e. H_3PO_4
    c. HNO_3 (7-1)

15. Give the molecular formula of each of the following acids:
    a. sulfurous acid
    b. chloric acid
    c. hydrochloric acid
    d. hypochlorous acid
    e. perchloric acid
    f. carbonic acid
    g. acetic acid (7-3)

16. Name each of the following ions according to the Stock system:
    a. Fe^{2+} d. Pb^{4+}
    b. Fe^{3+} e. Sn^{2+}
    c. Pb^{2+} f. Sn^{4+} (7-2)

17. Name each of the binary molecular compounds in item 11 using the Stock system. (7-2)

18. Write formulas for each of the following compounds:
    a. phosphorus(III) iodide
    b. sulfur(II) chloride
    c. carbon(IV) sulfide
    d. nitrogen(V) oxide (7-2)

HNO_3, contain hydrogen, oxygen, and a third element.

13. a. an ionic compound composed of a cation and the anion from an acid
    b. Examples include NaCl and $MgSO_4$.

14. a. hydrofluoric acid
    b. hydrobromic acid
    c. nitric acid
    d. sulfuric acid
    e. phosphoric acid

15. a. H_2SO_3 e. $HClO_4$
    b. $HClO_3$ f. H_2CO_3
    c. HCl   g. CH_3COOH
    d. HClO

16. a. iron(II) ion   d. lead(IV) ion
    b. iron(III) ion   e. tin(II) ion
    c. lead(II) ion   f. tin(IV) ion

17. a. carbon(IV) bromide
    b. silicon(IV) oxide
    c. phosphorus(V) oxide
    d. arsenic(III) sulfide

18. a. PI_3 c. CS_2
    b. SCl_2 d. N_2O_5

19. a. numbers assigned to bonded atoms in molecular compounds or polyatomic ions to indicate the general distribution of electrons
    b. They aid in naming compounds, writing formulas, balancing chemical equations, and studying chemical reactions.

20. a. the sum of the average atomic masses of all the atoms represented in the formula of a molecule, formula unit, or ion
    b. amu

21. the mass in grams of 1 mol of the basic particles of a compound; it is numerically equal to formula mass

22. percentage composition, mass composition, and composition by moles

23. x(empirical formula) = molecular formula, where x is a multiple of the subscripts in the molecular formula

24. a. NH_4^+, 1+
 b. CH_3COO^-, 1−
 c. OH^-, 1−
 d. CO_3^{2-}, 2−
 e. SO_4^{2-}, 2−
 f. PO_4^{3-}, 3−
 g. Cu^{2+}, 2+
 h. Sn^{2+}, 2+
 i. Fe^{3+}, 3+
 j. Cu^+, 1+
 k. Hg_2^{2+}, 2+
 l. Hg^{2+}, 2+

25. a. ammonium ion
 b. chlorate ion
 c. hydroxide ion
 d. sulfate ion
 e. nitrate ion
 f. carbonate ion
 g. phosphate ion
 h. acetate ion
 i. hydrogen carbonate ion (or bicarbonate ion)
 j. chromate ion

26. a. NaF   **e.** $AlBr_3$
 b. CaO   **f.** Li_3N
 c. K_2S **g.** FeO
 d. $MgCl_2$

27. a. sodium chloride
 b. potassium fluoride
 c. calcium sulfide
 d. cobalt(II) nitrate
 e. iron(III) phosphate
 f. mercury(I) sulfate
 g. mercury(II) phosphate

28. a. +1, −1   **d.** +1, −1
 b. +3, −1   **e.** +5, −2
 c. +4, −2   **f.** +1, +5, −2

29. a. +5, −2   **d.** +6, −2
 b. +7, −2   **e.** +4, −2
 c. +5, −2

30. a. 180.18 amu
 b. 158.18 amu
 c. 18.05 amu
 d. 83.45 amu

31. a. 1 mol K^+, 1 mol NO_3^-;
 1 mol N, 3 mol O
 b. 2 mol Na^+, 1 mol SO_4^{2-};
 1 mol S, 4 mol O

19. a. What are oxidation numbers?
 b. What useful functions do oxidation numbers serve?   (7-2)

20. a. Define *formula mass.*
 b. In what unit is formula mass expressed? (7-3)

21. What is meant by the molar mass of a compound?   (7-3)

22. What three types of information are needed in order to find an empirical formula from percentage composition data?   (7-4)

23. What is the relationship between the empirical formula and the molecular formula of a compound?   (7-4)

PROBLEMS

Nomenclature and Chemical Formulas

24. Write the formula and charge for each of the following ions:
 a. ammonium ion
 b. acetate ion
 c. hydroxide ion
 d. carbonate ion
 e. sulfate ion
 f. phosphate ion
 g. copper(II) ion
 h. tin(II) ion
 i. iron(III) ion
 j. copper(I) ion
 k. mercury(I) ion
 l. mercury(II) ion

25. Name each of the following ions:
 a. NH_4^+ f. CO_3^{2-}
 b. ClO_3^- g. PO_4^{3-}
 c. OH^- h. CH_3COO^-
 d. SO_4^{2-} i. HCO_3^-
 e. NO_3^- j. CrO_4^{2-}

26. Write formulas for each of the following compounds:
 a. sodium fluoride
 b. calcium oxide
 c. potassium sulfide
 d. magnesium chloride
 e. aluminum bromide
 f. lithium nitride
 g. iron(II) oxide

Oxidation Number and Stock System

27. Name each of the following ionic compounds using the Stock system:
 a. NaCl
 b. KF
 c. CaS
 d. $Co(NO_3)_2$
 e. $FePO_4$
 f. Hg_2SO_4
 g. $Hg_3(PO_4)_2$

28. Assign oxidation numbers to each atom in the following compounds. (Hint: See Sample Problem 7-5.)
 a. HI
 b. PBr_3
 c. GeS_2
 d. KH
 e. As_2O_5
 f. H_3PO_4

29. Assign oxidation numbers to each atom in the following ions. (Hint: See Sample Problem 7-5.)
 a. NO_3^-
 b. ClO_4^-
 c. PO_4^{3-}
 d. $Cr_2O_7^{2-}$
 e. CO_3^{2-}

Mole Relationships and Percentage Composition

30. Determine the formula mass of each of the following compounds or ions. (Hint: See Sample Problem 7-6.)
 a. glucose, $C_6H_{12}O_6$
 b. calcium acetate, $Ca(CH_3COO)_2$
 c. the ammonium ion, NH_4^+
 d. the chlorate ion, ClO_3^-

31. Determine the number of moles of each type of monatomic or polyatomic ion in one mole of the following compounds. For each polyatomic ion, determine the number of moles of each atom present in one mole of the ion.
 a. KNO_3
 b. Na_2SO_4
 c. $Ca(OH)_2$
 d. $(NH_4)_2SO_3$
 e. $Ca_3(PO_4)_2$
 f. $Al_2(CrO_4)_3$

32. Determine the molar mass of each compound listed in item 30. (Hint: See Sample Problem 7-7.)

33. Determine the number of moles of compound in each of the following samples. (Hint: See Sample Problem 7-9.)
a. 4.50 g H_2O
b. 471.6 g $Ba(OH)_2$
c. 129.68 g $Fe_3(PO_4)_2$

34. Determine the percentage composition of each of the following compounds. (Hint: See Sample Problem 7-10.)
a. NaCl
b. $AgNO_3$
c. $Mg(OH)_2$

35. Determine the percentage by mass of water in the hydrate $CuSO_4 \cdot 5H_2O$. (Hint: See Sample Problem 7-11.)

36. Determine the empirical formula of a compound containing 63.50% silver, 8.25% nitrogen, and the remainder oxygen. (Hint: See Sample Problem 7-12.)

37. Determine the empirical formula of a compound found to contain 52.11% carbon, 13.14% hydrogen, and 34.75% oxygen.

38. What is the molecular formula of the molecule that has an empirical formula of CH_2O and a molar mass of 120.12 g/mol?

39. A compound with a formula mass of 42.08 amu is found to be 85.64% carbon and 14.36% hydrogen by mass. Find its molecular formula.

MIXED REVIEW

40. Chemical analysis of citric acid shows that it contains 37.51% C, 4.20% H, and 58.29% O. What is its empirical formula?

41. Name each of the following compounds using the Stock system:
a. LiBr
b. $Sn(NO_3)_2$
c. $FeCl_2$
d. MgO
e. KOH
f. Fe_2O_3
g. $AgNO_3$
h. $Fe(OH)_2$
i. CrF_2

42. What is the mass in grams of each of the following samples?
a. 1.000 mol NaCl
b. 2.000 mol H_2O
c. 3.500 mol $Ca(OH)_2$
d. 0.625 mol $Ba(NO_3)_2$

43. Determine the formula mass and molar mass of each of the following compounds:
a. XeF_4
b. $C_{12}H_{24}O_6$
c. Hg_2I_2
d. CuCN

44. Write the chemical formulas for the following compounds:
a. aluminum fluoride
b. magnesium oxide
c. vanadium(V) oxide
d. cobalt(II) sulfide
e. strontium bromide
f. sulfur trioxide

45. How many atoms of each element are contained in a single formula unit of iron(III) formate, $Fe(CHO_2)_3 \cdot H_2O$? What percentage by mass of the compound is water?

46. Name each of the following acids, and assign oxidation numbers to the atoms in each:
a. HNO_2 c. H_2CO_3
b. H_2SO_3 d. HI

47. Determine the percentage composition of the following compounds:
a. NaClO
b. H_2SO_3
c. C_2H_5COOH
d. $BeCl_2$

48. Name each of the following binary compounds:
a. MgI_2 e. SO_2
b. NaF   f. PBr_3
c. CS_2 g. $CaCl_2$
d. N_2O_4 h. AgI

49. Assign oxidation numbers to each atom in the following molecules and ions:
a. CO_2 e. H_2O_2
b. NH_4^+ f. P_4O_{10}
c. MnO_4^- g. OF_2
d. $S_2O_3^{2-}$

c. 1 mol Ca^{2+}, 2 mol OH^-;
1 mol O, 1 mol H
d. 2 mol NH_4^+, 1 mol SO_3^{2-};
1 mol N, 4 mol H, 1 mol S, 3 mol O
e. 3 mol Ca^{2+}, 2 mol PO_4^{3-};
1 mol P, 4 mol O
f. 2 mol Al^{3+}, 3 mol CrO_4^{2-};
1 mol Cr, 4 mol O

32. a. 101.11 g/mol
b. 142.05 g/mol
c. 74.10 g/mol
d. 116.17 g/mol
e. 310.18 g/mol
f. 401.96 g/mol

33. a. 0.250 mol   **c.** 0.36275 mol
b. 2.752 mol

34. a. 39.34% Na, 60.66% Cl
b. 63.50% Ag, 8.25% N, 28.26% O
c. 41.67% Mg, 54.87% O, 3.46% H

35. 36.08%

36. $AgNO_3$

37. C_2H_6O

38. $C_4H_8O_4$

39. C_3H_8

40. $C_6H_8O_7$

41. a. lithium bromide
b. tin(II) nitrate
c. iron(II) chloride
d. magnesium oxide
e. potassium hydroxide
f. iron(III) oxide
g. silver nitrate
h. iron(II) hydroxide
i. chromium(II) fluoride

42. a. 58.44 g   **c.** 259.4 g
b. 36.04 g   **d.** 163 g

43. a. 207.29 amu, 207.29 g/mol
b. 264.36 amu, 264.36 g/mol
c. 654.98 amu, 654.98 g/mol
d. 89.57 amu, 89.57 g/mol

44. a. AlF_3 **d.** CoS
b. MgO   **e.** $SrBr_2$
c. V_2O_5 **f.** SO_3

45. 1 Fe, 3 C, 5 H, 7 O; 8.62%

46. a. nitrous acid; +1, +3, −2
   b. sulfurous acid; +1, +4, −2
   c. carbonic acid; +1, +4, −2
   d. hydriodic acid; +1, −1

47. a. 30.88% Na, 47.62% Cl, 21.49% O
   b. 2.46% H, 39.07% S, 58.47% O
   c. 48.63% C, 8.18% H, 43.19% O
   d. 11.28% Be, 88.72% Cl

48. a. magnesium iodide
   b. sodium fluoride
   c. carbon disulfide
   d. dinitrogen tetroxide
   e. sulfur dioxide
   f. phosphorus tribromide
   g. calcium chloride
   h. silver iodide

49. a. +4, −2   **e.** +1, −1
   b. −3, +1   **f.** +5, −2
   c. +7, −2   **g.** +2, −1
   d. +2, −2

50. $C_5H_{10}O_5NNa$

51. The formula is SO_3, so there are 1 sulfur and 3 oxygen atoms in the molecule. The oxidation numbers are +6 and −2, respectively.

52. mass of nickel = 1.05 g
   mass of nickel oxide = 1.34 g
   mass of oxygen = 0.29 g
   empirical formula: NiO

53. a. 233.21 g
   b. 278.11 g
   c. 80.04 g

54. a. KO_2, RbO_2, CsO_2
   b. 1+
   c. 2− in oxides, 1− in peroxides, 1− for the two oxygen atoms together in superoxides

55. a. MgO, BeO, CaO
   b. SrO_2, BaO_2
   c. Mg_3N_2, Be_3N_2, Ca_3N_2
   d. −1

56. a. Cd = +2, Zn = +2, Pb = +2
   b. Fe = +3, Mn = +7, Co = +2
   c. Cu = +2

57. a. N_2O_3, N_2O_5, As_2O_5, Sb_2O_5, Bi_2O_5

50. A 175.0 g sample of a compound contains 56.15 g C, 9.43 g H, 74.81 g O, 13.11 g N, and 21.49 g Na. What is its empirical formula?

CRITICAL THINKING

51. Analyzing Information   Sulfur trioxide is produced in the atmosphere through a reaction of sulfur dioxide and oxygen. Sulfur dioxide is a primary air pollutant. List all of the chemical information you can by analyzing the formula for sulfur trioxide.

52. Analyzing Data   In the laboratory, a sample of pure nickel was placed in a clean, dry, weighed crucible. The crucible was heated so that the nickel would react with the oxygen in the air. After the reaction appeared complete, the crucible was allowed to cool and the mass was determined. The crucible was reheated and allowed to cool. Its mass was then determined again to be certain that the reaction was complete. The following data were collected:

Mass of crucible	= 30.02 g
Mass of nickel and crucible	= 31.07 g
Mass of nickel oxide and crucible	= 31.36 g

Determine the following information based on the data given above:

Mass of nickel	=
Mass of nickel oxide	=
Mass of oxygen	=

Based on your calculations, what is the empirical formula for the nickel oxide?

▦ TECHNOLOGY & LEARNING

53. Graphing Calculator   Calculate the Molar Mass of a Compound

The graphing calculator can run a program that calculates the molar mass of a compound given the chemical formula for the compound. This program will prompt for the number of elements in the formula, the number of atoms of each element in the formula, and the atomic

mass of each element in the formula. It then can be used to find the molar masses of various compounds.

Go to Appendix C. If you are using a TI 83 Plus, you can download the program and data and run the application as directed. If you are using another calculator, your teacher will provide you with keystrokes and data sets to use. Remember that you will need to name the program and check the display, as explained in Appendix C. You will then be ready to run the program. After you have graphed the data, answer these questions.

Note: All answers are written with 2 significant digits beyond the decimal point.

a. What is the molar mass of $BaTiO_3$?
b. What is the molar mass of $PbCl_2$?
c. What is the molar mass of NH_4NO_3?

📖 HANDBOOK SEARCH

54. Review the common reactions of Group 1 metals in the *Elements Handbook* and answer the following:
   a. Some of the Group 1 metals react with oxygen to form superoxides. Write the formulas for these compounds.
   b. What is the charge on each cation for the formulas you wrote in (a)?
   c. How does the charge on the anion vary for oxides, peroxides, and superoxides?

55. Review the common reactions of Group 2 metals in the *Elements Handbook* and answer the following:
   a. Some of the Group 2 metals react with oxygen to form oxides. Write the formulas for these compounds.
   b. Some of the Group 2 metals react with oxygen to form peroxides. Write the formulas for these compounds.
   c. Some of the Group 2 metals react with nitrogen to form nitrides. Write the formulas for these compounds.

d. Most Group 2 elements form hydrides. What is hydrogen's oxidation state in these compounds?

56. Review the analytical tests for transition metals in the *Elements Handbook* and answer the following:
   a. Determine the oxidation state of each metal in the precipitates shown for cadmium, zinc, and lead.
   b. Determine the oxidation state of each metal in the complex ions shown for iron, manganese, and cobalt.
   c. The copper compound shown is called a coordination compound. The ammonia shown in the formula exists as molecules with no charge. Determine copper's oxidation state in this compound.

57. Review the common reactions of Group 15 elements in the *Elements Handbook* and answer the following:
   a. Write formulas for each of the oxides listed for the Group 15 elements.
   b. Determine nitrogen's oxidation state in the oxides listed in (a).

RESEARCH & WRITING

58. **Nomenclature** Biologists who name newly discovered organisms use a system that is structured very much like the one used by chemists in naming compounds. The system used by biologists is called the Linnaeus system, after its creator, Carolus Linnaeus. Research this system in a biology textbook, and then note similarities and differences between the Linnaeus system and chemical nomenclature.

59. **Common Chemicals** Find out the systematic chemical name and write the chemical formula for each of the following common compounds:
   a. baking soda
   b. milk of magnesia
   c. Epsom salts
   d. limestone
   e. lye
   f. wood alcohol

ALTERNATIVE ASSESSMENT

60. **Performance Assessment** Your teacher will supply you with a note card with one of the following formulas on it: $NaCH_3COO \cdot 3H_2O$, $MgCl_2 \cdot 6H_2O$, $LiC_2H_3O_2 \cdot 2H_2O$, or $MgSO_4 \cdot 7H_2O$. Design an experiment to determine the percentage of water by mass in the hydrated salt assigned to you. Be sure to explain what steps you will take to ensure that the salt is completely dry. If your teacher approves your design, obtain the salt and perform the experiment. What percentage of water does the salt contain?

61. Both ammonia, NH_3, and ammonium nitrate, NH_4NO_3, are used in fertilizers as a source of nitrogen. Which compound has the higher percentage of nitrogen? Research the physical properties of both compounds, and find out how each is manufactured and used. Explain why each compound has its own particular application. (Consider factors such as the cost of raw ingredients, the ease of manufacture, shipping costs, and so forth.)

b. for N_2O_3, N = +3; for N_2O_5, N = +5

58. Answers will vary.

59. a. sodium bicarbonate, $NaHCO_3$
   b. magnesium hydroxide, $Mg(OH)_2$
   c. magnesium sulfate septa-hydrate, $MgSO_4 \cdot 7H_2O$
   d. calcium carbonate, $CaCO_3$
   e. sodium hydroxide, NaOH
   f. methanol, CH_3OH

60. Answers will vary.

61. Answers will vary.

Chemical Equations and Reactions

PACING CHART	CLASSROOM RESOURCES		
Compression Guide: *(To shorten, eliminate items in italics.)*	**NSE Standards**	**Teaching Resources**	**Experiments**
8-1 Describing Chemical Reactions 2 45-minute periods 1 90-minute block *Significance of a Chemical Equation, pp. 248–250*	PS 3a, 3b, 3e UCP 1–2 HNS 1–2	**ATE Demo,** pp. 242, 250 **PE** Elements Handbook T 42, **TM 42A, TM 43A**	
8-2 Types of Chemical Reactions 2 45-minute periods 1 90-minute block *Combustion Reactions, p. 263*	PS 3a, 3b UCP 1–3 SAI 1–2	**ATE Demo,** pp. 258, 262 **PE** Elements Handbook **T 41, T 43**	**PE** Quick Lab, p. 778 **A5** Evidence for Chemical Change **B9** Colored Precipitates **C5 EXP** Chemical Reactions and Solid Fuel
8-3 Activity Series of the Elements 2 45-minute periods 1 90-minute block	UCP 1–3 SPSP 1, 3	**ATE Demo,** p. 265 **TM 44A**	**B10** Simple Qualitative Analysis

Review and Assessment	REVIEW RESOURCES		
2 45-minute periods 1 90-minute block	**Cumulative Review**	**Alternative Assessment**	**Traditional Assessment**
	SR Chapter 8 Mixed Review **PE** Chapter 8 37–48, p. 272	**PE** 56, 57, p. 273 **ATE** 251 **AA** Items for Chapter 8	Chapter 8 Text Test Generator items for Chapter 8

ASSIGNMENT RESOURCES

Section Homework Resources & Review	Problem-Solving Practice
HR Homework Worksheets 8-1, 8-2, 8-3, 8-4 Graphic Org. Assignments 8-1, 8-4 **PE** Section Review, 1–5, p. 254 Chapter Review, 1–10, 18–24, pp. 269–270 **SR** Section Review 8-1	**PE** Additional Samples 8-1, 8-2, 8-3, 8-4, 8-5 **ATE** Additional Samples, pp. 247, 248, 252, 253
HR Homework Worksheets 8-5, 8-6, 8-7 Graphic Org. Assignments 8-6, 8-7 **PE** Section Review, 1–4, p. 264 Chapter Review, 11–14, 25–33, pp. 270–271 **SR** Section Review 8-2	**ATE** Additional Example, p. 261
HR Homework Worksheet 8-8 **PE** Section Review, 1–3, p. 267 Chapter Review, 15–17, 34–36, pp. 270–271 **SR** Section Review 8-3	**PE** Additional Sample 8-6 **ATE** Additional Sample, p. 267

TECHNOLOGY RESOURCES

Technology & Internet Resources

 CTW 23 Segment 23 New Extraction Techniques for Gold

 Holt Chemistry Videodiscs Teacher's Correlation Guide for Chapter 8

 Module 5: Balancing Equations Stoichiometry

internet connect

 On-line Student Resources:
GO TO: www.scilinks.org
The following SciLinks Internet resources can be found in the student text for this chapter.

TOPICS:
• Chemical reactions, p. 242 (HC2081)
• Chloroform, p. 255 (HC2082)
• Precipitate, p. 262 (HC2083)
• Activity series, p. 265 (HC2084)
• Acid water, p. 268 (HC2085)

 On-line Teacher Resources:
GO TO: go.hrw.com
KEYWORD: HC2 HOME
Visit the HRW Web site for a variety of resources related to this chapter.

 Smithsonian Institution*
Internet Connections
Visit **www.si.edu/hrw** for additional on-line resources.

Visit **www.cnnfyi.com** for late-breaking news and current events stories selected just for you.

Resource Key

PE Pupil's Edition
ATE Teacher's Edition

One-Stop Planner CD-ROM Includes these resources and customizable daily lesson plans:

HR	Homework Resources	**A** Laboratory Experiments	**D**	Consumer Experiments
SR	Section Reviews	**B** Microscale Experiments	**T**	Transparencies
CTW	Critical Thinking Worksheets	**C** Technique Builders and Problem-Solving Experiments	**TM**	Transparency Masters
AA	Alternative Assessments		**PS**	Mini-Guide to Problem Solving
			SRW	Supplemental Reading Worksheets

Scoring Rubrics for Labs, Alternative Assessments, Performance Tasks and Portfolio Projects are on the One-Stop Planner CD-ROM.

Chemical Equations and Reactions

Chapter Overview

8-1 covers the writing and balancing of chemical equations and lists the information contained in an equation.

8-2 describes five basic types of chemical reactions: synthesis, decomposition, single-replacement, double-replacement, and combustion.

8-3 presents activity series for metals and the halogens and explains how they are used in writing chemical equations.

Concept Base

Students may need a review of the following concepts:

- energy in chemical reactions, Chapter 1

- conservation of mass, Chapter 3

- writing chemical formulas, Chapter 7

 Reading Skill-Builder

PREDICTION GUIDES Write the following assertions on the chalkboard:

- In a chemical reaction, atoms change identity.
- A change of color indicates a chemical reaction.
- All chemical reactions give off energy.

Ask students their opinions of each statement, then have them discuss these opinions in small groups. Keep a list of the opinions for discussion at the end of Section 8-2.

240

Chemical Equations and Reactions

The evolution of light and heat is an indication that a chemical reaction is taking place.

Describing Chemical Reactions

A *chemical reaction* is the process by which one or more substances are changed into one or more different substances. In any chemical reaction, the original substances are known as the *reactants* and the resulting substances are known as the *products*. According to the law of conservation of mass, the total mass of reactants must equal the total mass of products for any given chemical reaction.

Chemical reactions are described by chemical equations. *A* **chemical equation** *represents, with symbols and formulas, the identities and relative amounts of the reactants and products in a chemical reaction.* For example, the following chemical equation shows that the reactant ammonium dichromate yields the products nitrogen, chromium(III) oxide, and water.

$$(NH_4)_2Cr_2O_7(s) \longrightarrow N_2(g) + Cr_2O_3(s) + 4H_2O(g)$$

This strongly exothermic reaction is shown in Figure 8-1.

OBJECTIVES

- List three observations that suggest that a chemical reaction has taken place.

- List three requirements for a correctly written chemical equation.

- Write a word equation and a formula equation for a given chemical reaction.

- Balance a formula equation by inspection.

Lesson Starter

Show students a sample of ammonium dichromate, $(NH_4)_2Cr_2O_7$, and then refer them to Figure 8-1. The photograph provides evidence that an exothermic chemical reaction is occurring. Encourage students to think about how they would convey to other scientists what is occurring in the photograph. Explain that a chemical equation is a shorthand way of communicating this information. A chemical equation packs a great deal of information into relatively few symbols.

Class Discussion

Encourage students to think of chemical changes that they have observed in their everyday experience: hydrocarbons (gasoline, fuel oil) are oxidized, iron rusts, food spoils, leaves change color in fall, deposits form in pipes. Follow the discussion with the Demonstration on page 242, in which evidence of chemical change is observed.

Indications of a Chemical Reaction

To know for certain that a chemical reaction has taken place requires evidence that one or more substances have undergone a change in identity. Absolute proof of such a change can be provided only by chemical analysis of the products. However, certain easily observed changes usually indicate that a chemical reaction has occurred.

1. *Evolution of heat and light.* A change in matter that releases energy as both heat and light is strong evidence that a chemical reaction has taken place. For example, you can see in Figure 8-1 that the decomposition of ammonium dichromate is accompanied by the evolution of much heat and light. And you can see evidence that a chemical reaction occurs between natural gas and oxygen if you burn gas for cooking in your house. Some reactions release only heat or only light. But the evolution of heat or light by itself is not necessarily a sign of chemical change because many physical changes also release either heat or light.

FIGURE 8-1 The decomposition of ammonium dichromate proceeds rapidly, releasing energy in the form of light and heat.

Evidence of a Chemical Reaction

Place a small piece of mossy zinc in a Petri dish containing 0.1 M HCl. Observe. When the reaction is complete, have students list the evidence of chemical change. *(Bubbles of H_2 form and the Zn disappears or decreases in size.)*

Safety: Wear safety goggles and a lab apron.

Disposal: Treat the contents in the Petri dish with an excess of 1 M NaOH in order to precipitate the Zn as $Zn(OH)_2$. Filter the products. Then wrap the precipitate in paper and put it in the trash. Neutralize the filtrate with 1 M concentrated acid and pour down the drain.

FIGURE 8-2 (a) The reaction of vinegar and baking soda is evidenced by the production of bubbles of carbon dioxide gas. (b) When water solutions of ammonium sulfide and cadmium nitrate are combined, the yellow precipitate cadmium sulfide forms.

(a)

(b)

internet connect

SCLINKS

NSTA

TOPIC: Chemical reactions
GO TO: www.scilinks.org
*sci*LINKS CODE: HC2081

2. *Production of a gas.* The evolution of gas bubbles when two substances are mixed is often evidence of a chemical reaction. For example, bubbles of carbon dioxide gas form immediately when baking soda is mixed with vinegar, in the vigorous reaction that is shown in Figure 8-2(a).
3. *Formation of a precipitate.* Many chemical reactions take place between substances that are dissolved in liquids. If a solid appears after two solutions are mixed, a reaction has likely occurred. *A solid that is produced as a result of a chemical reaction in solution and that separates from the solution is known as a* **precipitate.** A precipitate-forming reaction is shown in Figure 8-2(b).
4. *Color change.* A change in color is often an indication of a chemical reaction.

Characteristics of Chemical Equations

A properly written chemical equation can summarize any chemical change. The following requirements will aid you in writing and reading chemical equations correctly.

1. *The equation must represent known facts.* All reactants and products must be identified, either through chemical analysis in the laboratory or from sources that give the results of experiments.
2. *The equation must contain the correct formulas for the reactants and products.* Remember what you learned in Chapter 7 about symbols and formulas. Knowledge of the common oxidation states of the elements and of methods of writing formulas will enable you to supply formulas for reactants and products if they are not available. Recall that the elements listed in Table 8-1 exist primarily as diatomic molecules, such as H_2 and O_2. Each of these elements is represented in an equation by its molecular formula. Other elements in the elemental state are usually represented simply by their atomic symbols. For example, iron is represented as Fe and carbon is represented as C. The symbols are not given any subscripts because the elements do not

TABLE 8-1   *Elements That Normally Exist as Diatomic Molecules*

Element	Symbol	Molecular formula	Physical state at room temperature
Hydrogen	H	H_2	gas
Nitrogen	N	N_2	gas
Oxygen	O	O_2	gas
Fluorine	F	F_2	gas
Chlorine	Cl	Cl_2	gas
Bromine	Br	Br_2	liquid
Iodine	I	I_2	solid

form definite molecular structures. Two exceptions to this rule are sulfur, which is usually written S_8, and phosphorus, which is usually written P_4. In these cases, the formulas reflect each element's unique atomic arrangement in its natural state.

3. *The law of conservation of mass must be satisfied.* Atoms are neither created nor destroyed in ordinary chemical reactions. Therefore, the same number of atoms of each element must appear on each side of a correct chemical equation. To equalize numbers of atoms, coefficients are added where necessary. *A **coefficient** is a small whole number that appears in front of a formula in a chemical equation.* Placing a coefficient in front of a formula specifies the relative number of moles of the substance; if no coefficient is written, the coefficient is assumed to be 1. For example, the coefficient 4 in the equation on page 241 indicates that 4 mol of water are produced for each mole of nitrogen and chromium(III) oxide that is produced.

Word and Formula Equations

The first step in writing a chemical equation is to identify the facts to be represented. It is often helpful to write a **word equation,** *an equation in which the reactants and products in a chemical reaction are represented by words.* A word equation has only qualitative (descriptive) meaning. It does not give the whole story because it does not give the quantities of reactants used or products formed.

Consider the reaction of methane, the principal component of natural gas, with oxygen. When methane burns in air, it combines with oxygen to produce carbon dioxide and water vapor. In the reaction, methane and oxygen are the reactants, and carbon dioxide and water are the products. The word equation for the reaction of methane and oxygen is written as follows.

$$\text{methane} + \text{oxygen} \longrightarrow \text{carbon dioxide} + \text{water}$$

The arrow, $\longrightarrow$, is read as *react to yield* or *yield* (also *produce* or *form*). So the equation above is read, "methane and oxygen react to yield

carbon dioxide and water," or simply, "methane and oxygen yield carbon dioxide and water."

The next step in writing a correct chemical equation is to replace the names of the reactants and products with appropriate symbols and formulas. Methane is a molecular compound composed of one carbon atom and four hydrogen atoms. Its chemical formula is CH_4. Recall that oxygen exists in nature as diatomic molecules; it is therefore represented as O_2. The correct formulas for carbon dioxide and water are CO_2 and H_2O, respectively.

A **formula equation** *represents the reactants and products of a chemical reaction by their symbols or formulas.* The formula equation for the reaction of methane and oxygen is written as follows.

$$CH_4(g) + O_2(g) \longrightarrow CO_2(g) + H_2O(g) \text{ (not balanced)}$$

The *g* in parentheses after each formula indicates that the corresponding substance is in the gaseous state. Like a word equation, a formula equation is a qualitative statement. It gives no information about the amounts of reactants or products.

A formula equation meets two of the three requirements for a correct chemical equation. It represents the facts and shows the correct symbols and formulas for the reactants and products. To complete the process of writing a correct equation, the law of conservation of mass must be taken into account. The relative amounts of reactants and products represented in the equation must be adjusted so that the numbers and types of atoms are the same on both sides of the equation. This process is called *balancing an equation* and is carried out by inserting coefficients. Once it is balanced, a formula equation is a correctly written chemical equation.

Look again at the formula equation for the reaction of methane and oxygen.

$$CH_4(g) + O_2(g) \longrightarrow CO_2(g) + H_2O(g) \text{ (not balanced)}$$

CHEMISTRY INTERACTIVE TUTOR

Module 5: Equations and Stoichiometry

To balance the equation, begin by counting atoms of elements that are combined with atoms of other elements and that appear only once on each side of the equation. In this case, we could begin by counting either carbon or hydrogen atoms. Usually, the elements hydrogen and oxygen are balanced only after balancing all other elements in an equation. (You will read more about the rules of balancing equations later in the chapter.) Thus, we begin by counting carbon atoms.

Inspecting the formula equation reveals that there is one carbon atom on each side of the arrow. Therefore, carbon is already balanced in the equation. Counting hydrogen atoms reveals that there are four hydrogen atoms in the reactants but only two in the products. Two additional hydrogen atoms are needed on the right side of the equation. They can be added by placing the coefficient 2 in front of the chemical formula H_2O.

$$CH_4(g) + O_2(g) \longrightarrow CO_2(g) + 2H_2O(g) \text{ (partially balanced)}$$

A coefficient multiplies the number of atoms of each element indicated in a chemical formula. Thus, $2H_2O$ represents *four* H atoms and *two* O atoms. To add two more hydrogen atoms to the right side of the equation, one may be tempted to change the subscript in the formula of water so that H_2O becomes H_4O. However, this would be a mistake because changing the subscripts of a chemical formula changes the *identity* of the compound. H_4O is not a product in the combustion of methane. In fact, there is no such compound. One must use only coefficients to change the relative number of atoms in a chemical equation because coefficients change the numbers of atoms without changing the identities of the reactants or products.

Now consider the number of oxygen atoms. There are four oxygen atoms on the right side of the arrow in the partially balanced equation. Yet there are only two oxygen atoms on the left side of the arrow. One can increase the number of oxygen atoms on the left side to four by placing the coefficient 2 in front of the molecular formula for oxygen. This results in a correct chemical equation, or *balanced formula equation*, for the burning of methane in oxygen.

$$CH_4(g) + 2O_2(g) \longrightarrow CO_2(g) + 2H_2O(g)$$

This reaction is further illustrated in Figure 8-3.

Additional Symbols Used in Chemical Equations

Table 8-2 on page 246 summarizes the symbols commonly used in chemical equations. Sometimes a gaseous product is indicated by an arrow pointing upward, ↑, instead of (g), as shown in the table. A downward arrow, ↓, is often used to show the formation of a precipitate during a reaction in solution.

The conditions under which a reaction takes place are often indicated by placing information above or below the reaction arrow. The word *heat*,

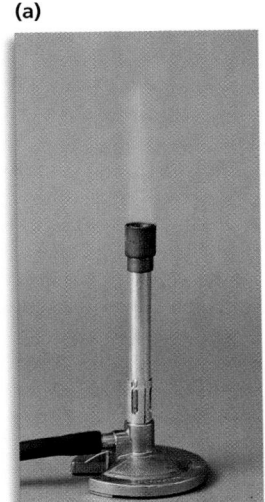

(a)

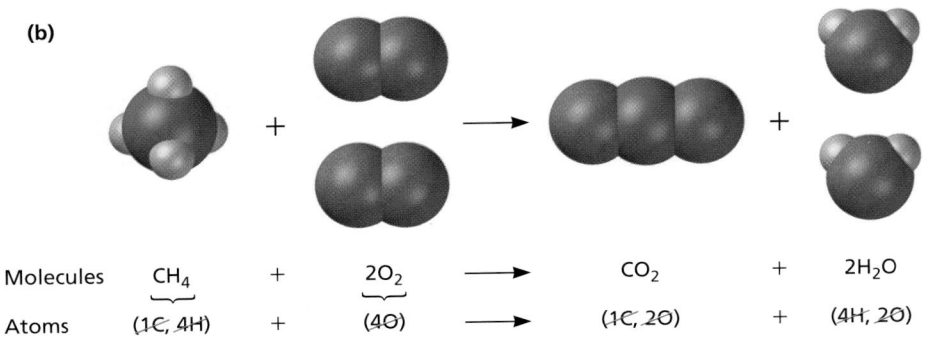

(b)

Molecules	CH_4	+	$2O_2$		CO_2	+	$2H_2O$
Atoms	(1C, 4H)	+	(4O)		(1C, 2O)	+	(4H, 2O)

FIGURE 8-3 (a) In a Bunsen burner, methane combines with oxygen in the air to form carbon dioxide and water vapor. (b) The reaction is represented by both a molecular model and a balanced equation. Each shows that the number of atoms of each element in the reactants equals the number of atoms of each element in the products.

Table 8-2 Point out to students that the table summarizes the symbols needed to incorporate the maximum amount of information into a chemical equation. Encourage students to refer to it often until they know its contents. Emphasize that the last five symbols represent conditions that are often necessary to make a reaction occur.

CHAPTER ⟷ CONNECTION

In Chapter 18, students will learn that reversible reactions result in chemical equilibrium, a dynamic state in which the forward and reverse reactions occur at the same rate.

✔ **Teaching Tip**

Although a catalyst speeds up a reaction, it does not appear as a reactant in the equation because it can be recovered unchanged after the reaction.

TABLE 8-2 *Symbols Used in Chemical Equations*

Symbol	Explanation
$\longrightarrow$	"Yields"; indicates result of reaction
$\rightleftharpoons$	Used in place of a single arrow to indicate a reversible reaction
(s)	A reactant or product in the solid state; also used to indicate a precipitate
$\downarrow$	Alternative to (s), but used only to indicate a precipitate
(l)	A reactant or product in the liquid state
(aq)	A reactant or product in an aqueous solution (dissolved in water)
(g)	A reactant or product in the gaseous state
$\uparrow$	Alternative to (g), but used only to indicate a gaseous product
$\xrightarrow{\Delta}$ or $\xrightarrow{\text{heat}}$	Reactants are heated
$\xrightarrow{2\text{ atm}}$	Pressure at which reaction is carried out, in this case 2 atm
$\xrightarrow{\text{pressure}}$	Pressure at which reaction is carried out exceeds normal atmospheric pressure
$\xrightarrow{0°\text{C}}$	Temperature at which reaction is carried out, in this case 0°C
$\xrightarrow{\text{MnO}_2}$	Formula of catalyst, in this case manganese dioxide, used to alter the rate of the reaction

symbolized by a Greek capital delta, Δ, indicates that the reactants must be heated. The specific temperature at which a reaction occurs may also be written over the arrow. For some reactions, it is important to specify the pressure at which the reaction occurs or to specify that the pressure must be above normal. Many reactions are speeded up and can take place at lower temperatures in the presence of a *catalyst*. A catalyst is a substance that changes the rate of a chemical reaction but can be recovered unchanged. To show that a catalyst is present, the formula for the catalyst or the word *catalyst* is written over the reaction arrow.

In many reactions, as soon as the products begin to form, they immediately begin to react with each other and re-form the reactants. In other words, the reverse reaction also occurs. The reverse reaction may occur to a greater or lesser degree than the original reaction, depending on the specific reaction and the conditions. *A* **reversible reaction** *is a chemical reaction in which the products re-form the original* reactants. The reversibility of a reaction is indicated by writing two arrows pointing in opposite directions. For example, the reversible reaction between iron and water vapor is written as follows.

$$3Fe(s) + 4H_2O(g) \rightleftharpoons Fe_3O_4(s) + 4H_2(g)$$

With an understanding of all the symbols and formulas used, it is possible to translate a chemical equation into a sentence. Consider the following equation.

$$2HgO(s) \xrightarrow{\Delta} 2Hg(l) + O_2(g)$$

Translated into a sentence, this equation reads, "When heated, solid mercury(II) oxide yields liquid mercury and gaseous oxygen."

It is also possible to write a chemical equation from a sentence describing a reaction. Consider the sentence, "Under pressure and in the presence of a platinum catalyst, gaseous ethene and hydrogen form gaseous ethane." This sentence can be translated into the following equation.

$$C_2H_4(g) + H_2(g) \xrightarrow[\text{Pt}]{\text{pressure}} C_2H_6(g)$$

Throughout this chapter we will often include the symbols for physical states (s, l, g, and aq) in balanced formula equations. You should be able to interpret these symbols when they are used and to supply them when the necessary information is available.

SAMPLE PROBLEM 8-1

Write word and formula equations for the chemical reaction that occurs when solid sodium oxide is added to water at room temperature and forms sodium hydroxide (dissolved in the water). Include symbols for physical states in the formula equation. Then balance the formula equation to give a balanced chemical equation.

SOLUTION   The word equation must show the reactants, sodium oxide and water, to the left of the arrow. The product, sodium hydroxide, must appear to the right of the arrow.

$$\text{sodium oxide} + \text{water} \longrightarrow \text{sodium hydroxide}$$

The word equation is converted to a formula equation by replacing the name of each compound with the appropriate chemical formula. To do this requires knowing that sodium has an oxidation state of +1, that oxygen usually has an oxidation state of −2, and that a hydroxide ion has a charge of 1−.

$$\text{Na}_2\text{O} + \text{H}_2\text{O} \longrightarrow \text{NaOH} \quad (\text{not balanced})$$

Adding symbols for the physical states of the reactants and products and the coefficient 2 in front of NaOH produces a balanced chemical equation.

$$\text{Na}_2\text{O}(s) + \text{H}_2\text{O}(l) \longrightarrow 2\text{NaOH}(aq)$$

ADDITIONAL SAMPLE PROBLEM

8-1 Write word and balanced chemical equations for each of the following chemical reactions. Include symbols for physical states when indicated.
a. Hydrogen peroxide in an aqueous solution decomposes to produce oxygen and water.
b. Solid copper metal reacts with aqueous silver nitrate to produce solid silver metal and aqueous copper nitrate.
c. Solid zinc metal reacts with aqueous copper sulfate to produce solid copper metal and aqueous zinc sulfate.

Ans. **a.** hydrogen peroxide $\longrightarrow$ oxygen + water;

$$2H_2O_2(aq) \longrightarrow O_2(g) + 2H_2O(l)$$

b. copper + silver nitrate $\longrightarrow$ silver + copper nitrate;

$$Cu(s) + 2AgNO_3(aq) \longrightarrow 2Ag(s) + Cu(NO_3)_2(aq)$$

c. zinc + copper sulfate $\longrightarrow$ copper + zinc sulfate;

$$Zn(s) + CuSO_4(aq) \longrightarrow Cu(s) + ZnSO_4(aq)$$

8-2 Translate the following equations into sentences:

a. $2ZnO(s) + C(s) \longrightarrow$
$$2Zn(s) + CO_2(g)$$

b. $Na_2O(s) + 2CO_2(g) + H_2O(g) \longrightarrow$
$$2NaHCO_3(s)$$

Ans. **a.** Solid zinc oxide and solid carbon react to produce solid zinc metal and carbon dioxide gas.
b. Solid sodium oxide reacts with carbon dioxide gas and water vapor to produce solid sodium hydrogen carbonate.

CHAPTER ⟷ CONNECTION

In Chapter 9, students will use the balanced equation as the basis for stoichiometric calculations.

SAMPLE PROBLEM 8-2

Translate the following chemical equation into a sentence:

$$PbCl_2(aq) + Na_2CrO_4(aq) \longrightarrow PbCrO_4(s) + 2NaCl(aq)$$

SOLUTION Each reactant is an ionic compound and is named according to the rules for such compounds. Both reactants are in aqueous solution. One product is a precipitate and the other remains in solution. The equation is translated as follows: Aqueous solutions of lead(II) chloride and sodium chromate react to produce a precipitate of lead(II) chromate plus sodium chloride in aqueous solution.

PRACTICE

1. Write word and balanced chemical equations for the following reactions. Include symbols for physical states when indicated.
   a. Solid calcium reacts with solid sulfur to produce solid calcium sulfide.
   b. Hydrogen gas reacts with fluorine gas to produce hydrogen fluoride gas. (Hint: See Table 8-1.)
   c. Solid aluminum metal reacts with aqueous zinc chloride to produce solid zinc metal and aqueous aluminum chloride.

2. Translate the following chemical equations into sentences:
   a. $CS_2(l) + 3O_2(g) \longrightarrow CO_2(g) + 2SO_2(g)$

   b. $NaCl(aq) + AgNO_3(aq) \longrightarrow$
   $$NaNO_3(aq) + AgCl(s)$$

Answer
1. a. calcium + sulfur $\longrightarrow$ calcium sulfide;
   $$8Ca(s) + S_8(s) \longrightarrow 8CaS(s)$$

   b. hydrogen + fluorine $\longrightarrow$
   $$\text{hydrogen fluoride;}$$
   $$H_2(g) + F_2(g) \longrightarrow 2HF(g)$$

   c. aluminum + zinc chloride $\longrightarrow$
   $$\text{zinc + aluminum chloride;}$$
   $$2Al(s) + 3ZnCl_2(aq) \longrightarrow$$
   $$3Zn(s) + 2AlCl_3(aq)$$

2. a. Liquid carbon disulfide reacts with oxygen gas to produce carbon dioxide gas and sulfur dioxide gas.

   b. Aqueous solutions of sodium chloride and silver nitrate react to produce aqueous sodium nitrate and a precipitate of silver chloride.

Significance of a Chemical Equation

Chemical equations are very useful in doing quantitative chemical work. The arrow in a balanced chemical equation is like an equal sign. And the chemical equation as a whole is similar to an algebraic equation in that it expresses an equality. Let's examine some of the quantitative information revealed by a chemical equation.

1. *The coefficients of a chemical reaction indicate relative, not absolute, amounts of reactants and products.* A chemical equation usually shows the smallest numbers of atoms, molecules, or ions that will satisfy the law of conservation of mass in a given chemical reaction.

Consider the equation for the formation of hydrogen chloride from hydrogen and chlorine.

$$H_2(g) + Cl_2(g) \longrightarrow 2HCl(g)$$

The equation indicates that 1 molecule of hydrogen reacts with 1 molecule of chlorine to produce 2 molecules of hydrogen chloride, giving the following molecular ratio of reactants and products.

1 molecule H_2 : 1 molecule Cl_2 : 2 molecules HCl

This ratio shows the smallest possible relative amounts of the reaction's reactants and products. To obtain larger relative amounts, we simply multiply each coefficient by the same number. Thus, 20 molecules of hydrogen would react with 20 molecules of chlorine to yield 40 molecules of hydrogen chloride. The reaction can also be considered in terms of amounts in moles: 1 mol of hydrogen molecules reacts with 1 mol of chlorine molecules to yield 2 mol of hydrogen chloride molecules.

2. *The relative masses of the reactants and products of a chemical reaction can be determined from the reaction's coefficients.* Recall from Figure 7-4 on page 224 that an amount of an element or compound in moles can be converted to a mass in grams by multiplying by the appropriate molar mass. We know that 1 mol of hydrogen reacts with 1 mol of chlorine to yield 2 mol of hydrogen chloride. The relative masses of the reactants and products are calculated as follows.

$$\text{1 mol } H_2 \times \frac{2.02 \text{ g } H_2}{\text{mol } H_2} = 2.02 \text{ g } H_2$$

$$\text{1 mol } Cl_2 \times \frac{70.90 \text{ g } Cl_2}{\text{mol } Cl_2} = 70.90 \text{ g } Cl_2$$

$$\text{2 mol HCl} \times \frac{36.46 \text{ g HCl}}{\text{mol HCl}} = 72.92 \text{ g HCl}$$

The chemical equation shows that 2.02 g of hydrogen will react with 70.90 g of chlorine to yield 72.92 g of hydrogen chloride.

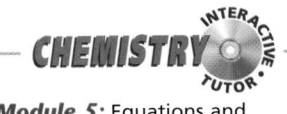

Module 5: Equations and Stoichiometry

FIGURE 8-4 This representation of the reaction of hydrogen and chlorine to yield hydrogen chloride shows several ways to interpret the quantitative information of a chemical reaction.

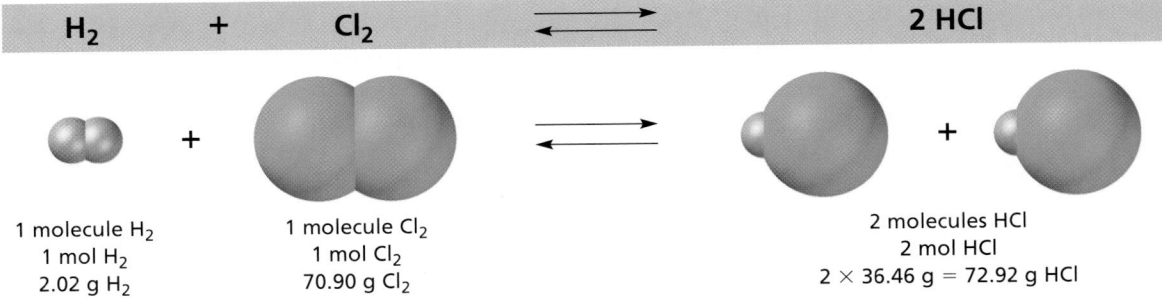

$$H_2 \quad + \quad Cl_2 \quad \rightleftharpoons \quad 2 \text{ HCl}$$

1 molecule H_2	1 molecule Cl_2	2 molecules HCl
1 mol H_2	1 mol Cl_2	2 mol HCl
2.02 g H_2	70.90 g Cl_2	2×36.46 g $= 72.92$ g HCl

✔Teaching Tip

Mass ratios are derived by multiplying mole ratios by the molar mass of each substance.

CHEMISTRY INTERACTIVE TUTOR

Module 5: Equations and Stoichiometry

Topic: Stoichiometry
Sections **d, e, f, g,** and **h** of this engaging tutorial review and reinforce understanding of stoichiometry.

Problem-Solving Practice HOLT ChemFile

Chapter 8 of the Mini-Guide to Problem Solving (also found on the One-Stop Planner CD-ROM) includes more worked-out samples and additional practice problems involving stoichiometry.

FIGURE 8-5 Although students have not yet learned that equal volumes of gases under the same conditions of temperature and pressure contain the same number of molecules, they are likely to understand intuitively that the 2:1 ratio of volumes of H_2 to O_2 shown in the photograph confirms the ratio found in the balanced equation.

DEMONSTRATION
Electrolysis of Water

Put 300 mL of 0.01 M aqueous Na_2SO_4 in a 500 mL beaker. Add 1 mL of bromothymol blue and stir. Fill two small test tubes with the colored solution from the beaker, and carefully invert the test tubes into the solution. Do not introduce any air bubbles into the test tubes. Immerse a 9 V battery into the solution and position it upright in the center of the beaker. Put the open mouth of each test tube over one terminal of the battery.

Students will observe that twice as much H_2 as O_2 is produced. Relate this observation to the balanced chemical equation. (Note: the solution at the anode—where O_2 is produced—turns yellow because of the presence of H_3O^+ ions; the solution at the cathode turns blue because of the presence of OH^- ions.)

Safety: Wear safety goggles and a lab apron.

Disposal: Pour the liquid down the drain. Dry the battery, put tape over the terminals, and save it for reuse.

Reading Skill-Builder

READING HINT As students read through the remainder of this section, have them use the balanced and unbalanced chemical equations on pp. 252–254 to help them understand the difference between the two.

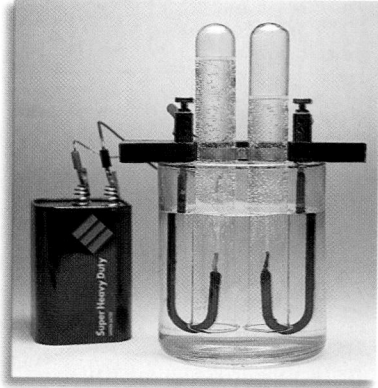

FIGURE 8-5 When an electric current is passed through water that has been made slightly conductive, the water molecules break down to yield hydrogen (in tube at right) and oxygen (in tube at left). Bubbles of each gas are evidence of the reaction. Note that twice as much hydrogen as oxygen is produced.

3. *The reverse reaction for a chemical equation has the same relative amounts of substances as the forward reaction.* Because a chemical equation is like an algebraic equation, the equality can be read in either direction. Reading the hydrogen chloride formation equation on page 249 from right to left, we can see that 2 molecules of hydrogen chloride break down to form 1 molecule of hydrogen plus 1 molecule of chlorine. Similarly, 2 mol (72.92 g) of hydrogen chloride yield 1 mol (2.02 g) of hydrogen and 1 mol (70.90 g) of chlorine.

We have seen that a chemical equation provides useful quantitative information about a chemical reaction. However, there is also important information that is *not* provided by a chemical equation. For instance, an equation gives no indication of whether a reaction will actually occur. A chemical equation can be written for a reaction that may not even take place. Some guidelines about the types of simple reactions that can be expected to occur are given in Sections 8-2 and 8-3. And later chapters provide additional guidelines for other types of reactions. In all these guidelines, it is important to remember that experimentation forms the basis for confirming that a particular chemical reaction will occur.

In addition, chemical equations give no information about the speed at which reactions occur or about how the bonding between atoms or ions changes during the reaction. These aspects of chemical reactions are discussed in Chapter 17.

Balancing Chemical Equations

Most of the equations in the remainder of this chapter can be balanced by inspection. The following procedure demonstrates how to master balancing equations by inspection using a step-by-step approach. The equation for the decomposition of water (see Figure 8-5) will be used as an example.

1. *Identify the names of the reactants and the products, and write a word equation.* The word equation for the reaction shown in Figure 8-5 is written as follows.

$$\text{water} \longrightarrow \text{hydrogen} + \text{oxygen}$$

2. *Write a formula equation by substituting correct formulas for the names of the reactants and the products.* We know that the formula for water is H_2O. And recall that both hydrogen and oxygen exist as diatomic molecules. Therefore, their correct formulas are H_2 and O_2, respectively.

$$H_2O(l) \longrightarrow H_2(g) + O_2(g) \text{ (not balanced)}$$

3. *Balance the formula equation according to the law of conservation of mass.* This last step is done by trial and error. Coefficients are changed and the numbers of atoms are counted on both sides of the equation. When the numbers of each type of atom are the same for both the products and the reactants, the equation is balanced. The trial-and-error method of balancing equations is made easier by the use of the following guidelines.

- Balance the different types of atoms one at a time.
- First balance the atoms of elements that are combined and that appear only once on each side of the equation.
- Balance polyatomic ions that appear on both sides of the equation as single units.
- Balance H atoms and O atoms after atoms of all other elements have been balanced.

The formula equation in our example shows that there are two oxygen atoms on the right and only one on the left. To balance oxygen atoms, the number of H_2O molecules must be increased. Placing the coefficient 2 before H_2O gives the necessary two oxygen atoms on the left.

$$2H_2O(l) \longrightarrow H_2(g) + O_2(g) \quad \text{(partially balanced)}$$

The coefficient 2 in front of H_2O has upset the balance of hydrogen atoms. Placing the coefficient 2 in front of hydrogen, H_2, on the right, gives an equal number of hydrogen atoms (4) on both sides of the equation.

$$2H_2O(l) \longrightarrow 2H_2(g) + O_2(g)$$

4. *Count atoms to be sure that the equation is balanced.* Make sure that equal numbers of atoms of each element appear on both sides of the arrow.

$$2H_2O(l) \longrightarrow 2H_2(g) + O_2(g)$$
$$(4H + 2O) = (4H) + (2O)$$

Occasionally at this point, the coefficients do not represent the smallest possible whole-number ratio of reactants and products. When this happens, the coefficients should be divided by their greatest common factor in order to obtain the smallest possible whole-number coefficients.

Balancing chemical equations by inspection becomes easier as you gain experience. Learn to avoid the most common mistakes: (1) writing incorrect chemical formulas for reactants or products and (2) trying to balance an equation by changing subscripts. Remember that subscripts cannot be added, deleted, or changed. Eventually, you will probably be able to skip writing the word equation and each separate step. However, *do not* leave out the final step of counting atoms to be sure the equation is balanced.

Alternative Assessment
Have students use Figure 8-4 on page 249 as a model for making a chart for the formation of NH_3 from H_2 and N_2. Have them draw representations of the molecules of reactants and product, and then have them calculate the number of molecules and moles of each reactant and product. Ask them to show that mass is conserved.

8-3 Write word, formula, and balanced chemical equations for each of the following reactions:
a. Solid calcium metal reacts with water to form aqueous calcium hydroxide and hydrogen gas.
b. Nitrogen dioxide gas reacts with water to form aqueous nitric acid and nitrogen monoxide gas.
c. Solid potassium chlorate decomposes to form solid potassium chloride and oxygen gas.

Ans. **a.** calcium + water $\longrightarrow$
    calcium hydroxide + hydrogen;
$Ca(s) + H_2O(l) \longrightarrow$
    $Ca(OH)_2(aq) + H_2(g)$;
$Ca(s) + 2H_2O(l) \longrightarrow$
    $Ca(OH)_2(aq) + H_2(g)$
b. nitrogen dioxide + water $\longrightarrow$
    nitric acid + nitrogen monoxide;
$NO_2(g) + H_2O(l) \longrightarrow$
    $HNO_3(aq) + NO(g)$;
$3NO_2(g) + H_2O(l) \longrightarrow$
    $2HNO_3(aq) + NO(g)$
c. potassium chlorate $\longrightarrow$
    potassium chloride + oxygen;
$KClO_3(s) \longrightarrow KCl(s) + O_2(g)$;
$2KClO_3(s) \longrightarrow 2KCl(s) + 3O_2(g)$

SAMPLE PROBLEM 8-3

The reaction of zinc with aqueous hydrochloric acid produces a solution of zinc chloride and hydrogen gas. This reaction is shown at right in Figure 8-6. Write a balanced chemical equation for the reaction.

FIGURE 8-6 Solid zinc reacts with hydrochloric acid to form aqueous zinc chloride and hydrogen gas.

SOLUTION

1 ANALYZE   *Write the word equation.*

$$zinc + hydrochloric\ acid \longrightarrow zinc\ chloride + hydrogen$$

2 PLAN   *Write the formula equation.*

$$Zn(s) + HCl(aq) \longrightarrow ZnCl_2(aq) + H_2(g)\ \ (not\ balanced)$$

3 COMPUTE   *Adjust the coefficients.* Note that chlorine and hydrogen each appear only once on each side of the equation. We balance chlorine first because it is combined on both sides of the equation. Also, recall from the guidelines on page 251 that hydrogen and oxygen are balanced only after all other elements in the reaction are balanced. To balance chlorine, we place the coefficient 2 before HCl. Two molecules of hydrogen chloride also yield the required two hydrogen atoms on the right. Finally, note that there is one zinc atom on each side in the formula equation. Therefore, no further coefficients are needed.

$$Zn(s) + 2HCl(aq) \longrightarrow ZnCl_2(aq) + H_2(g)$$

4 EVALUATE   *Count atoms to check balance.*

$$Zn(s) + 2HCl(aq) \longrightarrow ZnCl_2(aq) + H_2(g)$$
$$(1Zn) + (2H + 2\cancel{Cl}) = (1\cancel{Zn} + 2\cancel{Cl}) + (2\cancel{H})$$

The equation is balanced.

PRACTICE

1. Write word, formula, and balanced chemical equations for each of the following reactions:

a. Magnesium and hydrochloric acid react to produce magnesium chloride and hydrogen.

b. Aqueous nitric acid reacts with solid magnesium hydroxide to produce aqueous magnesium nitrate and water.

Answer

1. a. Word: magnesium + hydrochloric acid $\longrightarrow$
        magnesium chloride + hydrogen
    Formula: $Mg + HCl \longrightarrow MgCl_2 + H_2$
    Balanced: $Mg + 2HCl \longrightarrow MgCl_2 + H_2$

   b. Word: nitric acid + magnesium hydroxide
        $\longrightarrow$ magnesium nitrate + water
    Formula: $HNO_3(aq) + Mg(OH)_2(s) \longrightarrow$
        $Mg(NO_3)_2(aq) + H_2O(l)$
    Balanced: $2HNO_3(aq) + Mg(OH)_2(s) \longrightarrow$
        $Mg(NO_3)_2(aq) + 2H_2O(l)$

SAMPLE PROBLEM 8-4

Solid aluminum carbide, Al_4C_3, reacts with water to produce methane gas and solid aluminum hydroxide. Write a balanced chemical equation for this reaction.

SOLUTION The reactants are aluminum carbide and water. The products are methane and aluminum hydroxide. The formula equation is written as follows.

$$Al_4C_3(s) + H_2O(l) \longrightarrow CH_4(g) + Al(OH)_3(s) \quad \text{(not balanced)}$$

Begin balancing the formula equation by counting either aluminum atoms or carbon atoms. (Remember that hydrogen and oxygen atoms are balanced last.) There are four Al atoms on the left. To balance Al atoms, place the coefficient 4 before $Al(OH)_3$ on the right.

$$Al_4C_3(s) + H_2O(l) \longrightarrow CH_4(g) + 4Al(OH)_3(s) \quad \text{(partially balanced)}$$

Now balance the carbon atoms. With three C atoms on the left, the coefficient 3 must be placed before CH_4 on the right.

$$Al_4C_3(s) + H_2O(l) \longrightarrow 3CH_4(g) + 4Al(OH)_3(s) \quad \text{(partially balanced)}$$

Balance oxygen atoms next because oxygen, unlike hydrogen, appears only once on each side of the equation. There is one O atom on the left and 12 O atoms in the four $Al(OH)_3$ formula units on the right. Placing the coefficient 12 before H_2O balances the O atoms.

$$Al_4C_3(s) + 12H_2O(l) \longrightarrow 3CH_4(g) + 4Al(OH)_3(s)$$

This leaves the hydrogen atoms to be balanced. There are 24 H atoms on the left. On the right, there are 12 H atoms in the methane molecules and 12 in the aluminum hydroxide formula units, totaling 24 H atoms. The H atoms are balanced.

$$Al_4C_3(s) \;+\; 12H_2O(l) \;\longrightarrow\; 3CH_4(g) \;+\; 4Al(OH)_3(s)$$
$$(4\cancel{Al} + 3\cancel{C}) + (24\cancel{H} + \cancel{12O}) \;=\; (3\cancel{C} + \cancel{12H}) + (4\cancel{Al} + \cancel{12H} + \cancel{12O})$$

The equation is balanced.

SAMPLE PROBLEM 8-5

Aluminum sulfate and calcium hydroxide are used in a water-purification process. When added to water, they dissolve and react to produce two insoluble products, aluminum hydroxide and calcium sulfate. These products settle out, taking suspended solid impurities with them. Write a balanced chemical equation for the reaction.

SOLUTION Each of the reactants and products is an ionic compound. Recall from Chapter 7 that the formulas of ionic compounds are determined by the charges of the ions composing each compound. The formula reaction is thus written as follows.

$$Al_2(SO_4)_3 + Ca(OH)_2 \longrightarrow Al(OH)_3 + CaSO_4 \quad \text{(not balanced)}$$

ADDITIONAL SAMPLE PROBLEMS

8-4 Write balanced chemical equations for each of the following reactions:
a. When aqueous solutions of sulfuric acid and barium chloride are mixed, barium sulfate precipitates from an aqueous solution of hydrochloric acid.
b. Aluminum sulfate, an ingredient in antiperspirants, is made by the reaction of solid aluminum oxide with aqueous sulfuric acid. In addition to aqueous aluminum sulfate, water is also produced.

Ans. **a.** $H_2SO_4(aq) + BaCl_2(aq) \longrightarrow$
$2HCl(aq) + BaSO_4(s)$
b. $Al_2O_3(s) + 3H_2SO_4(aq) \longrightarrow$
$Al_2(SO_4)_3(aq) + 3H_2O(l)$

8-5 Write balanced chemical equations for each of the following reactions:
a. The white paste that lifeguards rub on their noses to prevent sunburn contains the active ingredient zinc oxide. Zinc oxide is made by reacting solid zinc sulfide with oxygen gas. Sulfur dioxide gas is also produced.
b. One of the most important uses of sulfuric acid is in the production of phosphoric acid for use in the making of fertilizers. Solid calcium phosphate is reacted with aqueous sulfuric acid to form phosphoric acid and solid calcium sulfate.

Ans. **a.** $2ZnS(s) + 3O_2(g) \longrightarrow$
$2ZnO(s) + 2SO_2(g)$
b. $Ca_3(PO_4)_2(s) + 3H_2SO_4(aq) \longrightarrow$
$2H_3PO_4(aq) + 3CaSO_4(s)$

CHEMICAL EQUATIONS AND REACTIONS **253**

SECTION REVIEW

1. A word equation is qualitative; it uses words to represent the reactants and products in a chemical reaction. A formula equation is also qualitative; it uses chemical symbols or formulas, but it does not reveal the ratios of the reactants and products. A chemical equation is a balanced formula equation.

2. sulfuric acid + sodium hydroxide $\longrightarrow$ sodium sulfate + water;
$H_2SO_4(aq) + NaOH(aq) \longrightarrow$
$Na_2SO_4(aq) + H_2O(l)$

3. a. Solid potassium metal reacts with (liquid) water to form aqueous potassium hydroxide and hydrogen gas.
b. Solid iron metal reacts with chlorine gas to produce solid iron(III) chloride.

4. hydrogen sulfide + oxygen $\longrightarrow$ sulfur dioxide + water vapor;
$H_2S(g) + O_2(g) \longrightarrow SO_2(g) + H_2O(g)$;
$2H_2S(g) + 3O_2(g) \longrightarrow$
$2SO_2(g) + 2H_2O(g)$

5. a. $2NH_4Cl + Ca(OH)_2 \longrightarrow$
$CaCl_2 + 2NH_3 + 2H_2O$
b. $2C_6H_{14} + 19O_2 \longrightarrow$
$12CO_2 + 14H_2O$

There is one Ca atom on each side of the equation, so the calcium atoms are already balanced. There are two Al atoms on the left and one Al atom on the right. Placing the coefficient 2 in front of $Al(OH)_3$ produces the same number of Al atoms on each side of the equation.

$$Al_2(SO_4)_3 + Ca(OH)_2 \longrightarrow 2Al(OH)_3 + CaSO_4 \text{ (partially balanced)}$$

Next, checking SO_4^{2-} ions shows that there are three SO_4^{2-} ions on the left side of the equation and only one on the right side. Placing the coefficient 3 before $CaSO_4$ gives an equal number of SO_4^{2-} ions on each side.

$$Al_2(SO_4)_3 + Ca(OH)_2 \longrightarrow 2Al(OH)_3 + 3CaSO_4 \text{ (partially balanced)}$$

There are now three Ca atoms on the right, however. By placing the coefficient 3 in front of $Ca(OH)_2$, we once again have an equal number of Ca atoms on each side. This last step also gives six OH^- ions on both sides of the equation.

$$Al_2(SO_4)_3(aq) + 3Ca(OH)_2(aq) \longrightarrow 2Al(OH)_3(s) + 3CaSO_4(s)$$
$$(2Al + 3SO_4^{2-}) + (3Ca + 6OH^-) = (2Al + 6OH^-) + (3Ca + 3SO_4^{2-})$$

The equation is balanced.

PRACTICE

1. Write balanced chemical equations for each of the following reactions:

a. Solid sodium combines with chlorine gas to produce solid sodium chloride.

b. When solid copper reacts with aqueous silver nitrate, the products are aqueous copper(II) nitrate and solid silver.

c. In a blast furnace, the reaction between solid iron(III) oxide and carbon monoxide gas produces solid iron and carbon dioxide gas.

Answer
1. a. $2Na(s) + Cl_2(g) \longrightarrow$
$2NaCl(s)$

b. $Cu(s) + 2AgNO_3(aq) \longrightarrow$
$Cu(NO_3)_2(aq) + 2Ag(s)$

c. $Fe_2O_3(s) + 3CO(g) \longrightarrow$
$2Fe(s) + 3CO_2(g)$

SECTION REVIEW

1. Describe the differences between word equations, formula equations, and chemical equations.

2. Write word and formula equations for the reaction in which aqueous solutions of sulfuric acid and sodium hydroxide react to form aqueous sodium sulfate and water.

3. Translate the following chemical equations into sentences:
a. $2K(s) + 2H_2O(l) \longrightarrow 2KOH(aq) + H_2(g)$
b. $2Fe(s) + 3Cl_2(g) \longrightarrow 2FeCl_3(s)$

4. Write the word, formula, and chemical equations for the reaction between hydrogen sulfide gas and oxygen gas that produces sulfur dioxide gas and water vapor.

5. Write the chemical equation for each of the following reactions:
a. ammonium chloride + calcium hydroxide $\longrightarrow$ calcium chloride + ammonia + water
b. hexane, C_6H_{14}, + oxygen $\longrightarrow$ carbon dioxide + water

CHEMICAL COMMENTARY

A Chemical Mystery

From "The Chemical Adventures of Sherlock Holmes: The Hound of Henry Armitage"
by Thomas G. Waddell and Thomas R. Rybolt in *The Journal of Chemical Education*

"**I** knew it," the old man snapped. "He was poisoned, wasn't he? . . ."

. . . But Holmes was not listening. He had picked up the dog's bowl, now empty, and was vigorously sniffing, not unlike the hound itself, at the crusted remains of the last meal . . .

An hour later I was in my chair at 221B Baker Street. Holmes was in his laboratory and I could hear him humming. In the background was the usual clattering and clanking of laboratory equipment . . . Suddenly, Holmes called to me.

"Watson, come here. I need you." . . . He calmly scribbled an equation on a slip of paper and handed it to me. "If you can balance this equation, Watson, you can solve this mystery." I looked at the page as best I could and saw the following equation with the formula of a reactant clearly missing.

$$C_6H_5NH_2 + 3KOH + \underline{} \Rightarrow$$
$$C_6H_5NC + 3KCl + 3H_2O$$

Holmes paced back and forth with his hands clasped behind his back. "One part aniline, three parts potassium hydroxide, and one part unknown poison yields one part phenylisocyanide, three parts potassium chloride, and three parts water. The missing reactant can be identified by balancing the equation with respect to all the atoms involved. The product phenylisocyanide . . . is derived by this reaction from that missing chemical which was the poison deliberately placed in the hound's food."

"I can follow you part of the way," I submitted. "You undoubtedly detected a foreign substance in the dog food due to a characteristic aroma."

"Correct, Watson," Holmes replied. "And as a chemist I knew immediately that the poison was *volatile* . . . We observed the compound to be a liquid at room temperature, immiscible with water, and having a density greater than 1.00 g/mL! The unpleasant sweetness of it was also very helpful. The possibilities were quite limited at that point, Watson . . .

I formed a working hypothesis and performed a known chemical test for such a poisonous liquid meeting all these criteria. Did you balance the equation, Watson? The equation confirms it!"

"I can do it, Holmes. I remember that much chemistry. Let me see . . . the missing reactant must have chlorine . . . 3 units to balance Cl in the product!"

"Very good, Watson. Go on with it."

"It gets more complex, now, but look, there is one extra carbon atom in the products! Is CCl_3 the compound?"

"Carbon makes *four* bonds, Watson, not three," said Holmes with a frown.

"I have it! $CHCl_3$ balances the equation! That's *chloroform*, Holmes! Of course. It all is consistent."

Reading for Meaning

Can you infer the meaning of the word *volatile* from the story? Write down your definition. Then compare your definition with one from a chemical or technical dictionary.

internet**connect**

sci**LINKS**
NSTA

TOPIC: Chloroform
GO TO: www.scilinks.org
*sci***LINKS CODE:** HC2082

CHEMICAL COMMENTARY

The use of chemical analysis is commonplace in police investigations. In this excerpt, the balancing of a basic chemical equation proves vital in determining the culprit of the fictional account of the poisoning of a dog. Students may be interested to know that in the story the perpetrator is ultimately identified as a young man who was able to obtain the toxic chloroform from his father's dry-cleaning business.

Reading for Meaning
Volatile, as it applies to chemistry, refers to a substance that vaporizes readily at relatively low temperatures.

Lesson Starter

Start off with the message that so many chemical reactions can occur or are occurring that it would be impossible to predict their products if it was not possible to place many of them into categories. Then begin with an introductory discussion of synthesis reactions as the first category to be studied.

Class Discussion

Describe synthesis reactions, and then ask students to name examples of such reactions. Students may mention the formation of rust from iron and oxygen, the formation of aluminum oxide from aluminum metal exposed to oxygen in the air, or the formation of water when hydrogen and oxygen gases are ignited. Emphasize that in synthesis reactions, elements or compounds combine to form a new compound.

✔ Teaching Tip

A reaction with more than one reactant and only one product is a synthesis reaction. Be careful to specify that there must be more than one reactant; a rearrangement reaction, which has only one reactant and one product, is neither a synthesis reaction nor a decomposition reaction. (It is not suggested that you introduce rearrangements here.)

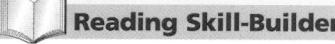

Reading Skill-Builder

READING ORGANIZER Have students read the section and then organize what they have learned in a concept map. Concept maps should start with *Reaction Types.* They should list each type of reaction, describe it, and provide examples.

OBJECTIVES

- Define and give general equations for *synthesis, decomposition, single-replacement,* and *double-replacement* reactions.

- Classify a reaction as synthesis, decomposition, single-replacement, double-replacement, or combustion.

- List three types of synthesis reactions and six types of decomposition reactions.

- List four types of single-replacement reactions and three types of double-replacement reactions.

- Predict the products of simple reactions given the reactants.

Types of Chemical Reactions

Thousands of known chemical reactions occur in living systems, in industrial processes, and in chemical laboratories. Often it is necessary to predict the products formed in one of these reactions. Memorizing the equations for so many chemical reactions would be a difficult task. It is therefore more useful and realistic to classify reactions according to various similarities and regularities. This general information about reaction types can then be used to predict the products of specific reactions.

There are several different ways to classify chemical reactions, and none are entirely satisfactory. The classification scheme described in this section provides an introduction to five basic types of reactions: synthesis, decomposition, single-replacement, double-replacement, and combustion. In later chapters you will be introduced to categories that are useful in classifying other types of chemical reactions.

Synthesis Reactions

In a **synthesis reaction,** *also known as a* **composition reaction,** *two or more substances combine to form a new compound.* This type of reaction is represented by the following general equation.

$$A + X \longrightarrow AX$$

A and X can be elements or compounds. AX is a compound. The following examples illustrate several kinds of synthesis reactions.

Reactions of Elements with Oxygen and Sulfur

One simple type of synthesis reaction is the combination of an element with oxygen to produce an *oxide* of the element. Almost all metals react with oxygen to form oxides. For example, when a thin strip of magnesium metal is placed in an open flame, it burns with bright white light. When the metal strip is completely burned, only a fine white powder of magnesium oxide is left. This chemical reaction, shown in Figure 8-7, is represented by the following equation.

$$2Mg(s) + O_2(g) \longrightarrow 2MgO(s)$$

The other Group 2 elements react in a similar manner, forming oxides with the formula MO, where M represents the metal. The Group 1 metals form oxides with the formula M_2O, for example, Li_2O. The Group 1 and Group 2 elements react similarly with sulfur, forming *sulfides* with the formulas M_2S and MS, respectively. Examples of these types of synthesis reactions are shown below.

$$16Rb(s) + S_8(s) \longrightarrow 8Rb_2S(s)$$
$$8Ba(s) + S_8(s) \longrightarrow 8BaS(s)$$

Some metals, such as iron, combine with oxygen to produce two different oxides.

$$2Fe(s) + O_2(g) \longrightarrow 2FeO(s)$$
$$4Fe(s) + 3O_2(g) \longrightarrow 2Fe_2O_3(s)$$

In the product of the first reaction, iron is in an oxidation state of +2. In the product of the second reaction, iron is in an oxidation state of +3. The particular oxide formed depends on the conditions surrounding the reactants. Both oxides are shown below in Figure 8-8.

Nonmetals also undergo synthesis reactions with oxygen to form oxides. Sulfur, for example, reacts with oxygen to form sulfur dioxide. And when carbon is burned in air, carbon dioxide is produced.

$$S_8(s) + 8O_2(g) \longrightarrow 8SO_2(g)$$
$$C(s) + O_2(g) \longrightarrow CO_2(g)$$

In a limited supply of oxygen, carbon monoxide is formed.

$$2C(s) + O_2(g) \longrightarrow 2CO(g)$$

Hydrogen reacts with oxygen to form hydrogen oxide, better known as water.

$$2H_2(g) + O_2(g) \longrightarrow 2H_2O(g)$$

(a)

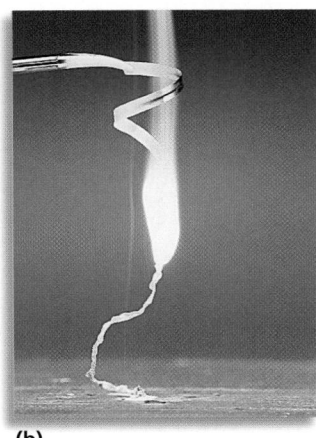
(b)

FIGURE 8-7 Magnesium, Mg, pictured in (a), undergoes a synthesis reaction with oxygen, O_2, in the air to produce magnesium oxide, MgO, as shown in (b).

(a)   (b)

FIGURE 8-8 Iron, Fe, and oxygen, O_2, combine to form two different oxides: (a) iron(II) oxide, FeO, and (b) iron(III) oxide, Fe_2O_3.

Visual Strategy
FIGURE 8-7 In synthesis reactions, the reactants and the products are usually quite different in appearance and in properties. Here, shiny, silver-colored magnesium metal and gaseous oxygen react to form the white ionic solid magnesium oxide.

✔ **Teaching Tip**

Students are probably familiar with the characteristic appearance of many metallic elements. With the exceptions of copper and gold, most metals are silver in color. But students may not be as familiar with the appearance of compounds synthesized from metals, many of them ionic salts. Acquaint students with the section of a handbook that provides physical and chemical properties of inorganic compounds.

258

DEMONSTRATION

Synthesis of a Base from a Metal Oxide

Add a few drops of phenolphthalein solution to 25 mL of water in a 50 mL beaker, and place the beaker on an overhead projector. Add approximately 0.005 g of calcium oxide. After students have noted that the phenolphthalein has turned pink, indicating the presence of OH$^-$ ions, ask them to interpret the results and write the equation for the synthesis. ($CaO + H_2O \longrightarrow Ca(OH)_2$)

Safety: Wear safety goggles and a lab apron.

Disposal: Pour the solution down the drain.

Reactions of Metals with Halogens

Most metals react with the Group 17 elements, the halogens, to form either ionic or covalent compounds. For example, Group 1 metals react with halogens to form ionic compounds with the formula MX, where M is the metal and X is the halogen. Examples of this type of synthesis reaction include the reactions of sodium with chlorine and potassium with iodine.

$$2Na(s) + Cl_2(g) \longrightarrow 2NaCl(s)$$
$$2K(s) + I_2(g) \longrightarrow 2KI(s)$$

Group 2 metals react with the halogens to form ionic compounds with the formula MX$_2$.

$$Mg(s) + F_2(g) \longrightarrow MgF_2(s)$$
$$Sr(s) + Br_2(l) \longrightarrow SrBr_2(s)$$

The halogens undergo synthesis reactions with many different metals. Fluorine in particular is so reactive that it combines with almost all metals. For example, fluorine reacts with sodium to produce sodium fluoride. Similarly, it reacts with cobalt to form cobalt(III) fluoride and with uranium to form uranium(VI) fluoride.

$$2Na(s) + F_2(g) \longrightarrow 2NaF(s)$$
$$2Co(s) + 3F_2(g) \longrightarrow 2CoF_3(s)$$
$$U(s) + 3F_2(g) \longrightarrow UF_6(g)$$

Sodium fluoride, NaF, is added to municipal water supplies in trace amounts to provide fluoride ions, which help to prevent tooth decay in the people who drink the water. Cobalt(III) fluoride, CoF_3, is a strong fluorinating agent. And natural uranium is converted to uranium(VI) fluoride, UF_6, as the first step in the production of uranium for use in nuclear power plants.

Synthesis Reactions with Oxides

Active metals are highly reactive metals. Oxides of active metals react with water to produce metal hydroxides. For example, calcium oxide reacts with water to form calcium hydroxide, an ingredient in some stomach antacids.

$$CaO(s) + H_2O(l) \longrightarrow Ca(OH)_2(s)$$

Calcium oxide, CaO, also known as lime or quicklime, is manufactured in large quantities. The addition of water to lime to produce $Ca(OH)_2$, which is also known as slaked lime, is a crucial step in the setting of cement.

Many oxides of nonmetals in the upper right portion of the periodic table react with water to produce oxyacids. For example, sulfur dioxide, SO_2, reacts with water to produce sulfurous acid.

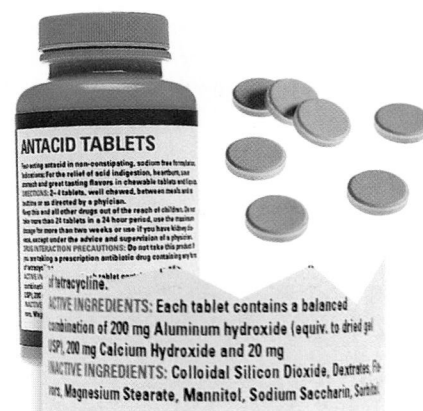

FIGURE 8-9 Calcium hydroxide, a base, can be used to *neutralize* hydrochloric acid in your stomach. You will read more about acids, bases, and neutralization in Chapter 15.

$$SO_2(g) + H_2O(l) \longrightarrow H_2SO_3(aq)$$

In air polluted with SO_2, sulfurous acid further reacts with oxygen to form sulfuric acid, one of the main ingredients in *acid rain.*

$$2H_2SO_3(aq) + O_2(g) \longrightarrow 2H_2SO_4(aq)$$

Certain metal oxides and nonmetal oxides react with each other in synthesis reactions to form salts. For example, calcium sulfite is formed by the reaction of calcium oxide and sulfur dioxide.

$$CaO(s) + SO_2(g) \longrightarrow CaSO_3(s)$$

Decomposition Reactions

In a **decomposition reaction,** *a single compound undergoes a reaction that produces two or more simpler substances.* Decomposition reactions are the opposite of synthesis reactions and are represented by the following general equation.

$$AX \longrightarrow A + X$$

AX is a compound. A and X can be elements or compounds.

Most decomposition reactions take place only when energy in the form of electricity or heat is added. Examples of several types of decomposition reactions are given in the following sections.

Decomposition of Binary Compounds

The simplest kind of decomposition reaction is the decomposition of a binary compound into its elements. We have already examined one example of a decomposition reaction. Figure 8-5 on page 250 shows that passing an electric current through water will decompose the water into its constituent elements, hydrogen and oxygen.

$$2H_2O(l) \xrightarrow{\text{electricity}} 2H_2(g) + O_2(g)$$

The decomposition of a substance by an electric current is called **electrolysis.**

Oxides of the less-active metals, which are located in the lower center of the periodic table, decompose into their elements when heated. Joseph Priestley discovered oxygen through such a decomposition reaction in 1774, when he heated mercury(II) oxide to produce mercury and oxygen.

$$2HgO(s) \xrightarrow{\Delta} 2Hg(l) + O_2(g)$$

This reaction is shown in Figure 8-10 on page 260.

Class Discussion

If you performed the demonstration on page 250, remind students of what they observed. Have them write the equation for the reaction, and be sure they recognize it as a decomposition reaction. Ask students if there is any relationship between this decomposition reaction and the reaction for the synthesis of water.

✔ **Teaching Tip**

A reaction with only one reactant and more than one product is a decomposition reaction. See the comment in the Teaching Tip on page 256.

FIGURE 8-10 When mercury(II) oxide (the red-orange substance in the bottom of the test tube) is heated, it decomposes into oxygen and metallic mercury, which can be seen as droplets on the inside wall of the test tube.

Decomposition of Metal Carbonates

When a metal carbonate is heated, it breaks down to produce a metal oxide and carbon dioxide gas. For example, calcium carbonate decomposes to produce calcium oxide and carbon dioxide.

$$CaCO_3(s) \xrightarrow{\Delta} CaO(s) + CO_2(g)$$

Decomposition of Metal Hydroxides

All metal hydroxides except those containing Group 1 metals decompose when heated to yield metal oxides and water. For example, calcium hydroxide decomposes to produce calcium oxide and water.

$$Ca(OH)_2(s) \xrightarrow{\Delta} CaO(s) + H_2O(g)$$

Decomposition of Metal Chlorates

When a metal chlorate is heated, it decomposes to produce a metal chloride and oxygen. For example, potassium chlorate, $KClO_3$, decomposes in the presence of the catalyst $MnO_2(s)$ to produce potassium chloride and oxygen.

$$2KClO_3(s) \xrightarrow[MnO_2(s)]{\Delta} 2KCl(s) + 3O_2(g)$$

Decomposition of Acids

Certain acids decompose into nonmetal oxides and water. Carbonic acid is unstable and decomposes readily at room temperature to produce carbon dioxide and water.

$$H_2CO_3(aq) \longrightarrow CO_2(g) + H_2O(l)$$

When heated, sulfuric acid decomposes into sulfur trioxide and water.

$$H_2SO_4(aq) \xrightarrow{\Delta} SO_3(g) + H_2O(l)$$

Sulfurous acid, H_2SO_3, decomposes similarly.

Single-Replacement Reactions

In a **single-replacement reaction,** *also known as a* **displacement reaction,** *one element replaces a similar element in a compound.* Many single-replacement reactions take place in aqueous solution. The amount of energy involved in this type of reaction is usually smaller than the amount involved in synthesis or decomposition reactions. Single-replacement reactions can be represented by the following general equations.

$$A + BX \longrightarrow AX + B$$

or

$$Y + BX \longrightarrow BY + X$$

A, B, X, and Y are elements. AX, BX, and BY are compounds.

Replacement of a Metal in a Compound by Another Metal

Aluminum is more active than lead. When solid aluminum is placed in aqueous lead(II) nitrate, $Pb(NO_3)_2(aq)$, the aluminum replaces the lead. Solid lead and aqueous aluminum nitrate are formed.

$$2Al(s) + 3Pb(NO_3)_2(aq) \longrightarrow 3Pb(s) + 2Al(NO_3)_3(aq)$$

Replacement of Hydrogen in Water by a Metal

The most-active metals, such as those in Group 1, react vigorously with water to produce metal hydroxides and hydrogen. For example, sodium reacts with water to form sodium hydroxide and hydrogen gas.

$$2Na(s) + 2H_2O(l) \longrightarrow 2NaOH(aq) + H_2(g)$$

Less-active metals, such as iron, react with steam to form a metal oxide and hydrogen gas.

$$3Fe(s) + 4H_2O(g) \longrightarrow Fe_3O_4(s) + 4H_2(g)$$

Replacement of Hydrogen in an Acid by a Metal

The more-active metals react with certain acidic solutions, such as hydrochloric acid and dilute sulfuric acid, replacing the hydrogen in the acid. The reaction products are a metal compound (a salt) and hydrogen gas. For example, when solid magnesium reacts with hydrochloric acid, as shown in Figure 8-11, the reaction products are hydrogen gas and aqueous magnesium chloride.

$$Mg(s) + 2HCl(aq) \longrightarrow H_2(g) + MgCl_2(aq)$$

Replacement of Halogens

In another type of single-replacement reaction, one halogen replaces another halogen in a compound. Fluorine is the most-active halogen. As

FIGURE 8-11 In this single-replacement reaction, the hydrogen in hydrochloric acid, HCl, is replaced by magnesium, Mg.

Additional Example Problem

1. Write a balanced chemical equation for the heated decomposition of sulfurous acid.

Ans. $H_2SO_3(aq) \xrightarrow{\Delta} SO_2(g) + H_2O(l)$

Reading Skill-Builder

PREDICTION GUIDES Review the opinions listed at the beginning of Section 8-1. Ask students whether their opinions are the same or have changed. Have them cite passages in the text that account for any changes.

DEMONSTRATION

Double-Replacement Reactions

Produce five products of different colors by mixing 0.1 M aqueous solutions of $SrCl_2$, Na_2SO_4, $CuSO_4$, NH_3, $MnCl_2$, Na_2CO_3, $FeCl_3$, and KSCN, and a saturated solution of NaCl. Mix 5 mL of the respective solutions according to the following scheme. If mixture number 3 does not turn green, add more NaCl solution.

Mixture
1. $SrCl_2$ and Na_2SO_4
2. $CuSO_4$ and NH_3
3. $CuSO_4$ and NaCl
4. $MnCl_2$ and Na_2CO_3
5. $FeCl_3$ and KSCN

Results	Color
1. $SrSO_4$ precipitate	white
2. ammoniacal copper hydroxide	blue
3. chloro-copper complex	green
4. $MnCO_3$ precipitate	pink
5. $[Fe(SCN)]^{2+}$ complex ion	red

Have students write equations for the double-replacement reactions that occur in mixtures 1 and 4.

Safety: Wear safety goggles and a lab apron.

Disposal: Combine mixtures 1 and 4, and filter the result. Dry the solid and put it into the trash. Pour the filtrate down the drain. Combine mixtures 2, 3, and 5, and add sufficient 1 M H_2SO_4 to dissolve all copper-containing precipitates. Scour six 6d iron nails with steel wool until they are shiny. Immerse the nails in the solution. Let the nails remain immersed until all Cu has precipitated (overnight). Remove the nails and filter the solution. Heat the nails

such, it can replace any of the other halogens in their compounds. Each halogen is less active than the one above it in the periodic table. Therefore, in Group 17 each element can replace any element below it, but not any element above it. For example, while chlorine can replace bromine in potassium bromide, it cannot replace fluorine in potassium fluoride. The reaction of chlorine with potassium bromide produces bromine and potassium chloride, whereas the combination of fluorine and sodium chloride produces sodium fluoride and solid chlorine.

$$Cl_2(g) + 2KBr(aq) \longrightarrow 2KCl(aq) + Br_2(l)$$
$$F_2(g) + 2NaCl(aq) \longrightarrow 2NaF(aq) + Cl_2(s)$$
$$Br_2(l) + KCl(aq) \longrightarrow \text{no reaction}$$

internet connect

SCI LINKS NSTA

TOPIC: Precipitate
GO TO: www.scilinks.org
***sci*LINKS CODE:** HC2083

Double-Replacement Reactions

In **double-replacement reactions,** *the ions of two compounds exchange places in an aqueous solution to form two new compounds.* One of the compounds formed is usually a precipitate, an insoluble gas that bubbles out of the solution, or a molecular compound, usually water. The other compound is often soluble and remains dissolved in solution. A double-replacement reaction is represented by the following general equation.

$$AX + BY \longrightarrow AY + BX$$

A, X, B, and Y in the reactants represent ions. AY and BX represent ionic or molecular compounds.

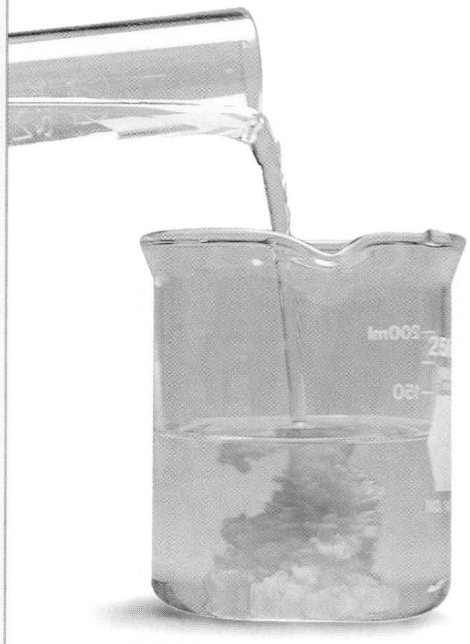

FIGURE 8-12 The double-replacement reaction between aqueous lead(II) nitrate, $Pb(NO_3)_2(aq)$, and aqueous potassium iodide, $KI(aq)$, yields the precipitate lead(II) iodide, $PbI_2(s)$.

Formation of a Precipitate

The formation of a precipitate occurs when the cations of one reactant combine with the anions of another reactant to form an insoluble or slightly soluble compound. For example, when an aqueous solution of potassium iodide is added to an aqueous solution of lead(II) nitrate, the yellow precipitate lead(II) iodide forms. This is shown in Figure 8-12.

$$2KI(aq) + Pb(NO_3)_2(aq) \longrightarrow PbI_2(s) + 2KNO_3(aq)$$

The precipitate forms as a result of the very strong attractive forces between the Pb^{2+} cations and the I^- anions. The other product is the water-soluble salt potassium nitrate, KNO_3. The potassium and nitrate ions do not take part in the reaction. They remain in solution as aqueous ions. The guidelines that help identify which ions form a precipitate and which ions remain in solution are developed in Chapter 14.

Formation of a Gas

In some double-replacement reactions, one of the products is an insoluble gas that bubbles out of the mixture. For example, iron(II) sulfide reacts with hydrochloric acid to form hydrogen sulfide gas and iron(II) chloride.

$$FeS(s) + 2HCl(aq) \longrightarrow H_2S(g) + FeCl_2(aq)$$

Formation of Water

In some double-replacement reactions, a very stable molecular compound, such as water, is one of the products. For example, hydrochloric acid reacts with an aqueous solution of sodium hydroxide to yield aqueous sodium chloride and water.

$$HCl(aq) + NaOH(aq) \longrightarrow NaCl(aq) + H_2O(l)$$

Combustion Reactions

In a **combustion reaction,** *a substance combines with oxygen, releasing a large amount of energy in the form of light and heat.* The combustion of hydrogen is shown below in Figure 8-13. The reaction's product is water vapor.

$$2H_2(g) + O_2(g) \longrightarrow 2H_2O(g)$$

The burning of natural gas, propane, gasoline, and wood are also examples of combustion reactions. For example, the burning of propane, C_3H_8, results in the production of carbon dioxide and water vapor.

$$C_3H_8(g) + 5O_2(g) \longrightarrow 3CO_2(g) + 4H_2O(g)$$

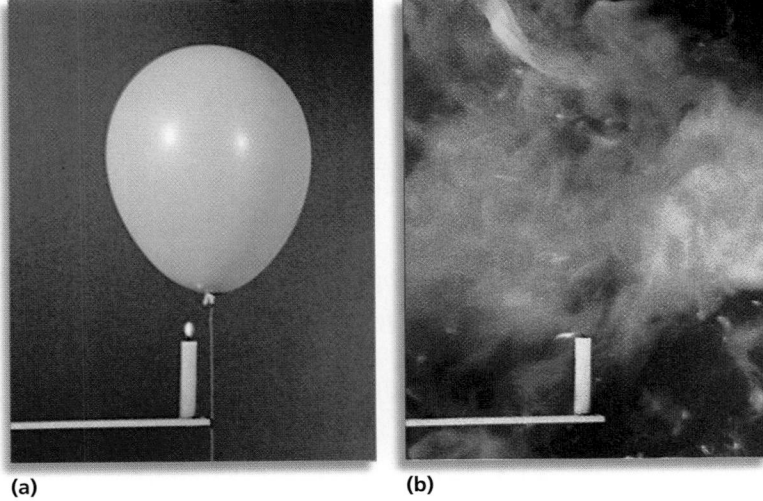

(a)

(b)

FIGURE 8-13 (a) The candle supplies heat to the hydrogen and oxygen in the balloon, triggering the explosive combustion reaction shown in (b).

and any precipitate from the filtration sufficiently to convert the copper precipitate and the copper on the nails to CuO. Cool and put the CuO and the nails in the trash. Treat the filtrate with sufficient 1 M NaOH to bring the pH to 8 to 10. Heat to boiling, let cool, and filter. Dry the precipitate and put into the trash. Pour the filtrate down the drain.

QUICK LAB

(page 264)
Models provide visual insights into the five types of reactions introduced in this chapter. Students can count model atoms as they balance equations. To avoid confusion, have students write down a key of the colors of the gumdrops representing each kind of atom. Do not be concerned with molecular geometry at this time.

Safety: Make sure that students do not eat any of the gumdrops.

Answers
1. Group A: **a.** $H_2 + Cl_2 \longrightarrow 2HCl$
b. $2Mg + O_2 \longrightarrow 2MgO$
Group B: **a.** $H_2CO_3 \longrightarrow CO_2 + H_2O$
b. $2KClO_3 \longrightarrow 2KCl + 3O_2$
Group C: **a.** $Ca + 2H_2O \longrightarrow$
$Ca(OH)_2 + H_2$
b. $2KI + Br_2 \longrightarrow 2KBr + I_2$
Group D: **a.** $AgNO_3 + NaCl \longrightarrow$
$AgCl + NaNO_3$
b. $FeS + 2HCl \longrightarrow FeCl_2 + H_2S$
Group E: **a.** $CH_4 + 2O_2 \longrightarrow$
$CO_2 + 2H_2O$
b. $2CO + O_2 \longrightarrow 2CO_2$

2. Group A: $Ba(OH)_2$
Group B: $H_2 + O_2$
Group C: $H_2 + ZnCl_2$
Group D: $K_2SO_4 + H_2O$
Group E: $CO_2 + H_2O$

3. Group A: $BaO + H_2O \longrightarrow Ba(OH)_2$
Group B: $2H_2O \longrightarrow 2H_2 + O_2$
Group C: $Zn + 2HCl \longrightarrow ZnCl_2 + H_2$
Group D: $H_2SO_4 + 2KOH \longrightarrow$
$K_2SO_4 + 2H_2O$
Group E: $C_3H_8 + 5O_2 \longrightarrow$
$3CO_2 + 4H_2O$

4. Group A: synthesis
Group B: decomposition
Group C: single-replacement
Group D: double-replacement
Group E: combustion

SECTION REVIEW

1. synthesis, decomposition, single-replacement, double-replacement, combustion

2. a. synthesis
b. single-replacement
c. decomposition
d. combustion
e. decomposition
f. synthesis
g. double-replacement

3. a. $2Li + O \longrightarrow Li_2O$
b. $Mg(ClO_3)_2 \longrightarrow MgCl_2 + 3O_2$
c. $2Na + 2H_2O \longrightarrow 2NaOH + H_2$
d. $2HNO_3 + Ca(OH)_2 \longrightarrow$
$Ca(NO_3)_2 + 2H_2O$
e. $C_5H_{12} + 8O_2 \longrightarrow 5CO_2 + 6H_2O$

4. a. $Br_2 + 2KI \longrightarrow 2KBr + I_2$;
single-replacement
b. $Zn + 2HCl \longrightarrow ZnCl_2 + H_2$;
single-replacement
c. $Ca(s) + Cl_2(g) \longrightarrow CaCl_2(s)$;
synthesis
d. $2NaClO_3 \xrightarrow{\Delta} 2NaCl + 3O_2$;
decomposition
e. $2C_7H_{14} + 21O_2 \longrightarrow$
$14CO_2 + 14H_2O$;
combustion
f. $CuCl_2 + Na_2S \longrightarrow 2NaCl + CuS$;
double-replacement

 ## Quick LAB

Balancing Equations Using Models

Wear Safety Goggles and an Apron.

Materials

- large and small gumdrops in at least four different colors
- toothpicks

Question

How can molecular models and formula-unit ionic models be used to balance chemical equations and classify chemical reactions?

Procedure

Examine the partial equations in Groups A–E. Using different-colored gumdrops to represent atoms of different elements, make models of the reactions by connecting the appropriate "atoms" with toothpicks. Use your models to (1) balance equations (a) and (b) in each group, (2) determine the products for reaction (c) in each group, and (3) complete and balance each equation (c). Finally, (4) classify each group of reactions by type.

Group A
a. $H_2 + Cl_2 \longrightarrow HCl$
b. $Mg + O_2 \longrightarrow MgO$
c. $BaO + H_2O \longrightarrow$ _____

Group B
a. $H_2CO_3 \longrightarrow CO_2 + H_2O$
b. $KClO_3 \longrightarrow KCl + O_2$
c. $H_2O \xrightarrow{electricity}$ _____

Group C
a. $Ca + H_2O \longrightarrow Ca(OH)_2 + H_2$
b. $KI + Br_2 \longrightarrow KBr + I_2$
c. $Zn + HCl \longrightarrow$ _____

Group D
a. $AgNO_3 + NaCl \longrightarrow$
$AgCl + NaNO_3$
b. $FeS + HCl \longrightarrow FeCl_2 + H_2S$
c. $H_2SO_4 + KOH \longrightarrow$ _____

Group E
a. $CH_4 + O_2 \longrightarrow CO_2 + H_2O$
b. $CO + O_2 \longrightarrow CO_2$
c. $C_3H_8 + O_2 \longrightarrow$ _____

SECTION REVIEW

1. List five types of chemical reactions.

2. Classify each of the following reactions as synthesis, decomposition, single-replacement, double-replacement, or combustion:
a. $N_2(g) + 3H_2(g) \longrightarrow 2NH_3(g)$
b. $2Li(s) + 2H_2O(l) \longrightarrow 2LiOH(aq) + H_2(g)$
c. $2NaNO_3(s) \longrightarrow 2NaNO_2(s) + O_2(g)$
d. $2C_6H_{14}(l) + 19O_2(g) \longrightarrow 12CO_2(g) + 14H_2O(l)$
e. $NH_4Cl(s) \longrightarrow NH_3(g) + HCl(g)$
f. $BaO(s) + H_2O(l) \longrightarrow Ba(OH)_2(aq)$
g. $AgNO_3(aq) + NaCl(aq) \longrightarrow AgCl(s) + NaNO_3(aq)$

3. For each of the following reactions, identify the missing reactant(s) or products(s) and then balance the resulting equation. Note that each empty slot may require one or more substances.

a. synthesis: _____ $\longrightarrow Li_2O$
b. decomposition: $Mg(ClO_3)_2 \longrightarrow$ _____
c. single-replacement: $Na + H_2O \longrightarrow$ _____
d. double-replacement:
$HNO_3 + Ca(OH)_2 \longrightarrow$ _____
e. combustion: $C_5H_{12} + O_2 \longrightarrow$ _____

4. For each of the following reactions, write the missing product(s) and then balance the resulting equation. Identify each reaction by type.
a. $Br_2 + KI \longrightarrow$ _____
b. $Zn + HCl \longrightarrow$ _____
c. $Ca + Cl_2 \longrightarrow$ _____
d. $NaClO_3 \xrightarrow{\Delta}$ _____
e. $C_7H_{14} + O_2 \longrightarrow$ _____
f. $CuCl_2 + Na_2S \longrightarrow$ _____

Activity Series of the Elements

OBJECTIVES

• Explain the significance of an activity series.

• Use an activity series to predict whether a given reaction will occur and what the products will be.

The ability of an element to react is referred to as the element's *activity*. The more readily an element reacts with other substances, the greater its activity is. *An* **activity series** *is a list of elements organized according to the ease with which the elements undergo certain chemical reactions.* For metals, greater activity means a greater ease of *loss* of electrons, to form positive ions. For nonmetals, greater activity means a greater ease of *gain* of electrons, to form negative ions.

The order in which the elements are listed is usually determined by single-replacement reactions. The most-active element, placed at the top in the series, can replace each of the elements below it from a compound in a single-replacement reaction. An element farther down can replace any element below it but not any above it. For example, in the discussion of single-replacement reactions in Section 8-2, it was noted that each halogen will react to replace any halogen listed below it in the periodic table. Therefore, an activity series for the Group 17 elements lists them in the same order, from top to bottom, as they appear in the periodic table. This is shown in Table 8-3 on page 266.

As mentioned in Section 8-1, the fact that a chemical equation can be written does not necessarily mean that the reaction it represents will actually take place. Activity series are used to help predict whether certain chemical reactions will occur. For example, according to the activity series for metals in Table 8-3, aluminum replaces zinc. Therefore, we could predict that the following reaction does occur.

$$2Al(s) + 3ZnCl_2(aq) \longrightarrow 3Zn(s) + 2AlCl_3(aq)$$

Cobalt, however, cannot replace sodium. Therefore, we write the following.

$$Co(s) + 2NaCl(aq) \longrightarrow \text{no reaction}$$

It is important to remember that like many other aids used to predict the products of chemical reactions, activity series are based on experiment. The information that they contain is used as a general guide for predicting reaction outcomes. For example, the activity series reflects the fact that some metals (potassium, for example) react vigorously with water and acids, replacing hydrogen to form new compounds. Other metals, such as iron or zinc, replace hydrogen in acids such as hydrochloric acid but react with water only when the water is hot

internet**connect**

SC*i*LINKS™

NSTA

TOPIC: Activity series
GO TO: www.scilinks.org
*sci*LINKS CODE: HC2084

Lesson Starter
Perform the following demonstration of an activity series.

DEMONSTRATION
Activity Series of Metals

Label four 50 mL beakers for each of the five metal ions Al^{3+}, Zn^{2+}, Fe^{3+}, Cu^{2+}, and H^+. Arrange the 20 beakers in five rows, one row for each solution. Add 15 mL of 0.1 M aqueous solutions of $Al(NO_3)_3$, $Zn(NO_3)_2$, $Fe(NO_3)_3$, $Cu(NO_3)_2$, and HCl to the appropriate four beakers. To the $Al(NO_3)_3$ solutions, add 0.5 g pieces of Al, Zn, Fe, and Cu. Do the same for the other four solutions so that each metal is immersed in every solution.

Make tables for each set of four beakers with space for recording observations after 3 min, 30 min, and one day. Count the number of reactions for each metal. Count the number of reactions for each metal ion. Have students use this information to develop an activity series.

Safety: Wear safety goggles and a lab apron.

Disposal: Rinse off remaining metal pieces and save for reuse or put into the trash. Combine the rinses with the solutions and any solid formed. Add 1 M aqueous NaOH to bring the pH to approximately 10. Filter. Heat the precipitate sufficiently to convert any $Cu(OH)_2$ to CuO. Cool and put in the trash. Treat the filtrate with sufficient 1 M acid to bring the pH to between 6 and 8. Pour the neutralized filtrate down the drain.

Table 8-3 The table can be used to verify the results of the demonstration on page 265. Encourage students to refer to the table until they become familiar with its contents. Point out that the activity series of the halogens is separate from the activity series of the metals.

CHAPTER ⟷ CONNECTION

In Chapter 19, students will relate the activity series to standard reduction potentials.

✔ **Teaching Tip**

Relate the order of activities of the halogens (all in Group 17) to their positions in the periodic table. The activities of the halogens decrease going down the group. To help students remember which direction is which in the activity series of the metals, remind them that the elements near the top include the very reactive metals at the left-hand end of the periodic table, whereas Ag, Pt, and Au, the metals at the bottom, are so unreactive that they are used for jewelry.

enough to become steam. Nickel, on the other hand, will replace hydrogen in acids but will not react with steam at all. And gold will not react with acid or water, either as a liquid or as steam. Such experimental observations are the basis for the activity series shown in Table 8-3.

TABLE 8-3 Activity Series of the Elements

Activity of metals		Activity of halogen nonmetals
Li	React with cold H_2O and acids, replacing hydrogen. React with oxygen, forming oxides.	F_2
Rb		Cl_2
K		Br_2
Ba		I_2
Sr		
Ca		
Na		
Mg	React with steam (but not cold water) and acids, replacing hydrogen. React with oxygen, forming oxides.	
Al		
Mn		
Zn		
Cr		
Fe		
Cd		
Co	Do not react with water. React with acids, replacing hydrogen. React with oxygen, forming oxides.	
Ni		
Sn		
Pb		
H_2	React with oxygen, forming oxides.	
Sb		
Bi		
Cu		
Hg		
Ag	Fairly unreactive, forming oxides only indirectly.	
Pt		
Au		

Using the activity series shown in Table 8-3, explain whether each of the possible reactions listed below will occur. For those reactions that will occur, predict what the products will be.

a. $Zn(s) + H_2O(l) \xrightarrow{50°C}$ _____

b. $Sn(s) + O_2(g) \longrightarrow$ _____

c. $Cd(s) + Pb(NO_3)_2(aq) \longrightarrow$ _____

d. $Cu(s) + HCl(aq) \longrightarrow$ _____

SOLUTION

a. This is a reaction between a metal and water at 50°C. Zinc reacts with water only when it is hot enough to be steam. Therefore, no reaction will occur.

b. Any metal more active than silver will react with oxygen to form an oxide. Tin is above silver in the activity series. Therefore, a reaction will occur, and the product will be a tin oxide, either SnO or SnO_2.

c. An element will replace any element below it in the activity series from a compound in aqueous solution. Cadmium is above lead, and therefore a reaction will occur to produce lead, Pb, and cadmium nitrate, $Cd(NO_3)_2$.

d. Any metal more active than hydrogen will replace hydrogen from an acid. Copper is not above hydrogen in the series. Therefore, no reaction will occur.

PRACTICE

1. Using the activity series shown in Table 8-3, predict whether each of the possible reactions listed below will occur. For the reactions that will occur, write the products and balance the equation.

a. $Cr(s) + H_2O(l) \longrightarrow$ _____

b. $Pt(s) + O_2(g) \longrightarrow$ _____

c. $Cd(s) + 2HBr(aq) \longrightarrow$ _____

d. $Mg(s) + steam \longrightarrow$ _____

Answer

1. a. no

b. no

c. yes;
$$2Cd(s) + 2HBr(aq) \longrightarrow$$
$$2CdBr(aq) + H_2(g)$$

d. yes;
$$Mg(s) + 2H_2O(g) \longrightarrow$$
$$Mg(OH)_2(aq) + H_2(g)$$

2. Identify the element that replaces hydrogen from acids but cannot replace tin from its compounds.

2. Pb

3. According to Table 8-3, what is the most-active transition metal?

3. Mn

SECTION REVIEW

1. How is the activity series useful in predicting chemical behavior?

2. Based on the activity series, predict whether each of the following possible reactions listed will occur:
   a. $Ni(s) + H_2O(l) \longrightarrow$ _____
   b. $Br_2(l) + KI(aq) \longrightarrow$ _____
   c. $Au(s) + HCl(aq) \longrightarrow$ _____
   d. $Cd(s) + HCl(aq) \longrightarrow$ _____
   e. $Mg(s) + Co(NO_3)_2(aq) \longrightarrow$ _____

3. For each of the reactions in item 2 that will occur, write the products and balance the equation.

ADDITIONAL SAMPLE PROBLEMS

8-6 Using the activity series in Table 8-3, predict whether each of the possible reactions listed below will occur. For reactions that will occur, write the products and balance the equation.
a. $MgCl_2(aq) + Zn(s) \longrightarrow$
b. $Al(s) + H_2O(g) \longrightarrow$
c. $Cd(s) + O_2(g) \longrightarrow$
d. $I_2(s) + KF(g) \longrightarrow$

Ans. **a.** no
b. yes; $2Al(s) + 3H_2O(g) \longrightarrow$
$$Al_2O_3(s) + 3H_2(g)$$
c. yes; $2Cd(s) + O_2(g) \longrightarrow 2CdO(s)$
d. no

8-6 a. Identify the halogen that will not replace any other halogen in a compound.
b. Identify the halide ion that will not be replaced by any of the other halogens.

Ans. **a.** I_2
b. F^-

SECTION REVIEW

1. It helps predict whether a chemical reaction will occur and what the product(s) of the reaction will be.

2. **a.** no
b. yes
c. no
d. yes
e. yes

3. **b.** $Br_2(l) + 2KI(aq) \longrightarrow$
$$2KBr(aq) + I_2(s)$$
d. $Cd(s) + 2HCl(aq) \longrightarrow$
$$CdCl_2(aq) + H_2(g)$$
e. $Mg(s) + Co(NO_3)_2(aq) \longrightarrow$
$$Mg(NO_3)_2(aq) + Co(s)$$

RESEARCH NOTES

Acid Water—A Hidden Menace

When purchasing a home with its own well, it is common practice to have the water in the well tested. Usually, the purpose of the tests is to indicate the presence of disease-causing microorganisms. Rarely is the water's acidity measured.

Many people are unaware of their water's pH value (see Chapter 16) until they are confronted with such phenomena as a blue ring materializing around a porcelain sink drain, a water heater suddenly giving out, or tropical fish that keep dying. Each of these events could be traced to acidic water, which can also be a cause of lead poisoning.

The possibility of lead poisoning from home water supplies has gone largely unreported. Many older homes still have lead pipes in their plumbing, while most modern homes use copper piping. All pipe joints, however, are sealed with lead solder. Highly acidic water can leach out both the lead from the solder joints and copper from the pipes themselves, which turns the sink drain blue. In addition, people who are in the habit of filling their kettles

in the morning without letting the tap run awhile first could be adding a number of unwanted chemicals to their tea or coffee.

Lead poisoning is of particular concern in young children. The absorption rate of lead in the intestinal tract of a child is much higher than that of an adult, and lead poisoning can permanently impair a child's rapidly growing nervous system. The good news is that lead poisoning and other effects of acidic water in the home can be easily prevented. Here's what you can do about it:

1. Monitor the pH of your water on a regular basis, especially if you have well water. This can easily be done with pH test kits (see photograph) that are sold in hardware or pet stores—many tropical fish are intolerant of water with a pH that is either too high (basic) or too low (acidic). The pH of most municipal water supplies should already be regulated, but it doesn't hurt to check.

2. In the morning, let your water tap run for about half a minute before you fill your kettle or drink the water. If the water is acidic, the first flush of water will have the

highest concentration of lead and copper ions.

3. Installing an alkali-injection pump is a low-cost, low-maintenance solution that can save your plumbing and lessen the risk of lead poisoning from your own water supply. The pump injects a small amount of an alkali (usually potassium carbonate or sodium carbonate) in your water-holding tank each time you activate your well's pump. This effectively neutralizes the acidity of your water. The reaction below shows the neutralizing effect of potassium carbonate on well water that has been made acidic by acid rain.

$$K_2CO_3(aq) + H_2SO_4(aq) \longrightarrow$$
$$K_2SO_4(aq) + CO_2(g) + H_2O(l)$$

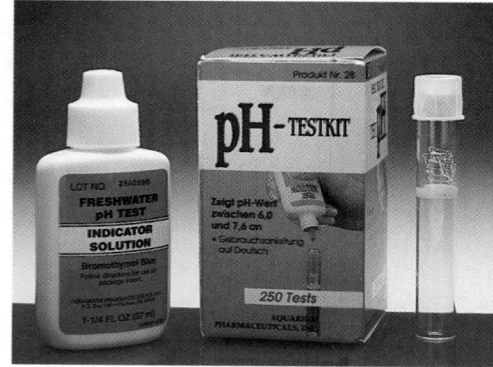

The pH of your home's water supply can be easily monitored using a test kit like the one shown here.

CHAPTER SUMMARY

8-1
- Five observations that suggest a chemical reaction is taking place are the evolution of heat or light, the production of gas, a change in color, and the formation of a precipitate.

Vocabulary

chemical equation (241) formula equation (244) reversible reaction (246) word equation (243)
coefficient (243) precipitate (242)

- A balanced chemical equation represents, with symbols and formulas, the identities and relative amounts of reactants and products in a chemical reaction.

8-2
- Synthesis reactions are represented by the general equation A + X $\longrightarrow$ AX.
- Decomposition reactions are represented by the general equation AX $\longrightarrow$ A + X.
- Single-replacement reactions are represented by

the general equations A + BX $\longrightarrow$ AX + B and Y + BX $\longrightarrow$ BY + X.
- Double-replacement reactions are represented by the general equation AX + BY $\longrightarrow$ AY + BX.

Vocabulary

combustion reaction (263) displacement reaction (261) electrolysis (259) synthesis reaction (256)
composition reaction (256) single-replacement reaction (261)
decomposition reaction (259) double-replacement reaction (262)

8-3
- Activity series list the elements in order of their chemical reactivity and are useful in predicting whether a chemical reaction will occur.
- Chemists determine activity series through experiments.

Vocabulary

activity series (265)

REVIEWING CONCEPTS

1. List five observations that indicate that a chemical reaction may be taking place. (8-1)

2. List the three requirements for a correctly written chemical equation. (8-1)

3. a. What is meant by the term *coefficient* in relation to a chemical equation?
   b. How does the presence of a coefficient affect the number of atoms of each type in the formula that it precedes? (8-1)

4. Give an example of a word equation, a formula equation, and a chemical equation. (8-1)

5. What quantitative information is revealed by a chemical equation? (8-1)

6. What limitations are associated with the use of both word and formula equations? (8-1)

7. Define each of the following:
   a. aqueous solution
   b. catalyst
   c. reversible reaction (8-1)

8. Write formulas for each of the following compounds:
   a. potassium hydroxide
   b. calcium nitrate
   c. sodium carbonate
   d. carbon tetrachloride
   e. magnesium bromide
   f. sulfur dioxide
   g. ammonium sulfate (8-1)

REVIEW ANSWERS

1. the evolution of energy, the production of a gas, the formation of a precipitate, a color change

2. A correctly written chemical equation must represent the known facts, contain the correct formulas for the reactants and products, and satisfy the law of conservation of mass.

3. **a.** It is a number that appears in front of a formula in a chemical equation.
   b. The number of atoms of each type in the formula is multiplied by the coefficient.

4. methane + oxygen $\longrightarrow$ carbon dioxide + water;
   $CH_4(g) + O_2(g) \longrightarrow$
   $CO_2(g) + H_2O(g)$;
   $CH_4(g) + 2O_2(g) \longrightarrow$
   $CO_2(g) + 2H_2O(g)$

5. A chemical equation provides the number of molecules, moles, and atoms of each element or compound composing the reactants and products as well as the mole ratios of the reactants to each other and to the products.

6. Word and formula equations have only qualitative meaning; they do not express the relative quantities of a reaction's reactants or products.

7. **a.** a solution in water
   b. a substance that accelerates a chemical reaction but can be recovered unchanged
   c. a chemical reaction in which the products re-form the original reactants

8. **a.** KOH **e.** $MgBr_2$
   b. $Ca(NO_3)_2$ **f.** SO_2
   c. Na_2CO_3 **g.** $(NH_4)_2SO_4$
   d. CCl_4

9. (1) balance different types of atoms one at a time; (2) balance

types of atoms that appear only
once on each side of the equation first; (3) balance as single
units any polyatomic ions that
appear on both sides of the
equation; (4) balance H atoms
and O atoms last

10. a. 6N
  b. 4H, 2O
  c. 4H, 4N, 12O
  d. 2Ca, 4O, 4H
  e. 3Ba, 6Cl, 18O
  f. 5Fe, 10N, 30O
  g. 12Mg, 8P, 32O
  h. 4N, 16H, 2S, 8O
  i. 12Al, 18Se, 72O
  j. 12C, 32H

11. (1) In a *synthesis reaction,*
two or more substances com-
bine to form a new substance:
$A + X \longrightarrow AX$.
(2) In a *decomposition reaction,*
a single compound undergoes a
reaction that produces two or
more simpler substances:
$AX \longrightarrow A + X$.
(3) In a *single-replacement reaction,* one element replaces
another element in a compound:
$A + BX \longrightarrow AX + B$ or
$Y + BX \longrightarrow BY + X$.
(4) In a *double-replacement
reaction,* the ions of two compounds exchange places in an
aqueous solution to form two
new compounds:
$AX + BY \longrightarrow BX + AY$.
(5) In a *combustion reaction,*
a substance combines with oxygen, releasing a large amount
of energy in the form of light
and heat, for example:
$C_3H_8(g) + 5O_2(g) \longrightarrow$
$3CO_2(g) + 4H_2O(g)$.

12. by the addition of energy in
the form of electricity or heat

13. the decomposition of a substance by an electric current

9. What four guidelines are useful in balancing
an equation? (8-1)

10. How many atoms of each type are represented
in each of the following?
  a. $3N_2$
  b. $2H_2O$
  c. $4HNO_3$
  d. $2Ca(OH)_2$
  e. $3Ba(ClO_3)_2$
  f. $5Fe(NO_3)_2$
  g. $4Mg_3(PO_4)_2$
  h. $2(NH_4)_2SO_4$
  i. $6Al_2(SeO_4)_3$
  j. $4C_3H_8$ (8-1)

11. Define and give general equations for the five
basic types of chemical reactions introduced
in Chapter 8. (8-2)

12. How are most decomposition reactions
initiated? (8-2)

13. What is electrolysis? (8-2)

14. a. In what environment do many single-
replacement reactions commonly occur?
  b. In general, how do single-replacement
reactions compare with synthesis and
decomposition reactions in terms of the
amount of energy involved? (8-2)

15. a. What is meant by the *activity* of an element?
  b. How does this description differ for metals
and nonmetals? (8-3)

16. a. What is an activity series of elements?
  b. What is the basis for the ordering of the
elements in the activity series? (8-3)

17. a. What is the chemical principle upon which
the activity series of metals is based?
  b. What is the significance of the distance
between two metals in the activity series? (8-3)

PROBLEMS

Chemical Equations

18. Write the chemical equation that relates to each
of the following word equations. Include symbols for physical states in the equation. (Hint:
See Sample Problem 8-1.)
  a. solid zinc sulfide + oxygen gas $\longrightarrow$
            solid zinc oxide + sulfur dioxide gas

  b. hydrochloric acid + aqueous magnesium
hydroxide $\longrightarrow$ aqueous magnesium chloride
                             + water
  c. nitric acid + aqueous calcium hydroxide $\longrightarrow$
             aqueous calcium nitrate + water

19. Translate each of the following chemical equations into a sentence. (Hint: See Sample
Problem 8-2.)
  a. $2ZnS(s) + 3O_2(g) \longrightarrow 2ZnO(s) + 2SO_2(g)$
  b. $CaH_2(s) + 2H_2O(l) \longrightarrow$
                   $Ca(OH)_2(aq) + 2H_2(g)$
  c. $AgNO_3(aq) + KI(aq) \longrightarrow AgI(s) + KNO_3(aq)$

20. Balance each of the following:
  a. $H_2 + Cl_2 \longrightarrow HCl$
  b. $Al + Fe_2O_3 \longrightarrow Al_2O_3 + Fe$
  c. $Pb(CH_3COO)_2 + H_2S \longrightarrow PbS + CH_3COOH$

21. The following equations are incorrect in some
way. Identify and correct each error, and then
balance each equation.
  a. $Li + O_2 \longrightarrow LiO_2$
  b. $H_2 + Cl_2 \longrightarrow H_2Cl_2$
  c. $MgCO_3 \longrightarrow MgO_2 + CO_2$
  d. $NaI + Cl_2 \longrightarrow NaCl + I$

22. Write chemical equations for each of the
following sentences:
  a. Aluminum reacts with oxygen to produce
aluminum oxide.
  b. Phosphoric acid, H_3PO_4, is produced through
the reaction between tetraphosphorus decoxide and water.
  c. Iron(III) oxide reacts with carbon monoxide
to produce iron and carbon dioxide.

23. Carbon tetrachloride is used as an intermediate
chemical in the manufacture of other chemicals.
It is prepared in liquid form by reacting chlorine gas with methane gas. Hydrogen chloride
gas is also formed in this reaction. Write the
balanced chemical equation for the production
of carbon tetrachloride. (Hint: See Sample
Problems 8-3 and 8-4.)

24. For each of the following synthesis reactions,
identify the missing reactant(s) or product(s),
and then balance the resulting equation:
  a. $Mg + \underline{\hspace{1cm}} \longrightarrow MgO$
  b. $\underline{\hspace{1cm}} + O_2 \longrightarrow Fe_2O_3$
  c. $Li + Cl_2 \longrightarrow \underline{\hspace{1cm}}$
  d. $Ca + \underline{\hspace{1cm}} \longrightarrow CaI_2$

Types of Chemical Reactions

25. Complete the following synthesis reactions by writing both word and chemical equations for each:
   a. sodium + oxygen $\longrightarrow$ _____
   b. magnesium + fluorine $\longrightarrow$ _____

26. Complete and balance the equation for each of the following decomposition reactions:
   a. $HgO \xrightarrow{\Delta}$
   b. $H_2O(l) \xrightarrow{\text{electricity}}$
   c. $Ag_2O \xrightarrow{\Delta}$
   d. $CuCl_2 \xrightarrow{\text{electricity}}$

27. Complete and balance the equations for each of the following single-replacement reactions:
   a. $Zn + Pb(NO_3)_2 \longrightarrow$ _____
   b. $Al + Hg(CH_3COO)_2 \longrightarrow$ _____
   c. $Al + NiSO_4 \longrightarrow$ _____
   d. $Na + H_2O \longrightarrow$ _____

28. Complete and balance the equations for the following double-replacement reactions:
   a. $AgNO_3(aq) + NaCl(aq) \longrightarrow$ _____
   b. $Mg(NO_3)_2(aq) + KOH(aq) \longrightarrow$ _____
   c. $LiOH(aq) + Fe(NO_3)_3(aq) \longrightarrow$ _____

29. Complete and balance the equation for each of the following combustion reactions:
   a. $CH_4 + O_2 \longrightarrow$ _____
   b. $C_3H_6 + O_2 \longrightarrow$ _____
   c. $C_5H_{12} + O_2 \longrightarrow$ _____

30. Write and balance each of the following equations, and then identify each by type:
   a. hydrogen + iodine $\longrightarrow$ hydrogen iodide
   b. lithium + hydrochloric acid $\longrightarrow$ lithium chloride + hydrogen
   c. sodium carbonate $\longrightarrow$ sodium oxide + carbon dioxide
   d. mercury(II) oxide $\longrightarrow$ mercury + oxygen
   e. magnesium hydroxide $\longrightarrow$ magnesium oxide + water

31. Identify the compound that could undergo decomposition to produce the following products, and then balance the final equation:
   a. magnesium oxide and water
   b. lead(II) oxide and water
   c. lithium chloride and oxygen
   d. barium chloride and oxygen

   e. nickel chloride and oxygen

32. In each of the following combustion reactions, identify the missing reactant(s), product(s), or both, and then balance the resulting equation:
   a. $C_3H_8 +$ _____ $\longrightarrow$ _____ $+ H_2O$
   b. _____ $+ 8O_2 \longrightarrow 5CO_2 + 6H_2O$
   c. $C_2H_5OH +$ _____ $\longrightarrow$ _____ $+$ _____

33. Complete and balance each of the following reactions observed to occur, and then identify each by type:
   a. zinc + sulfur $\longrightarrow$ _____
   b. calcium + sodium nitrate $\longrightarrow$ _____
   c. silver nitrate + potassium iodide $\longrightarrow$ _____
   d. sodium iodide $\xrightarrow{\Delta}$ _____
   e. toluene, C_7H_8 + oxygen $\longrightarrow$ _____
   f. nonane, C_9H_{20} + oxygen $\longrightarrow$ _____

Activity Series

34. Based on the activity series of metals and halogens, which element within each pair is more likely to replace the other in a compound?
   a. K and Na
   b. Al and Ni
   c. Bi and Cr
   d. Cl and F
   e. Au and Ag
   f. Cl and I
   g. Fe and Sr
   h. I and F

35. Using the activity series in Table 8-3 on page 266, predict whether each of the possible reactions listed below will occur. For the reactions that will occur, write the products and balance the equation.
   a. $Ni(s) + CuCl_2(aq) \longrightarrow$ _____
   b. $Zn(s) + Pb(NO_3)_2(aq) \longrightarrow$ _____
   c. $Cl_2(g) + KI(aq) \longrightarrow$ _____
   d. $Cu(s) + FeSO_4(aq) \longrightarrow$ _____
   e. $Ba(s) + H_2O(l) \longrightarrow$ _____

36. Use the activity series to predict whether each of the following synthesis reactions will occur, and write the chemical equations for those predicted to occur:
   a. $Ca(s) + O_2(g) \longrightarrow$ _____
   b. $Ni(s) + O_2(g) \longrightarrow$ _____
   c. $Au(s) + O_2(g) \longrightarrow$ _____

14. a. aqueous solutions
   b. They generally involve less energy than do synthesis or decomposition reactions.

15. a. the element's ability to react
   b. For metals, the activity describes the element's ability to lose electrons. For nonmetals, it describes the ability to gain electrons.

16. a. a set of elements listed according to the ease with which they undergo certain chemical reactions
   b. Elements are usually listed in order of their tendency to undergo single-replacement reactions. An element in such a series can replace any element listed below it.

17 a. The activity series of metals is based on the ease with which metal atoms lose electrons to form ions in aqueous solution; the higher a metal is in the series, the more easily its atoms lose electrons, and thus the greater the reactivity of that metal.
   b. The greater the distance, the more likely it is that one metal will replace the other in a reaction.

18. a. $2ZnS(s) + 3O_2(g) \longrightarrow 2ZnO(s) + 2SO_2(g)$
   b. $2HCl(aq) + Mg(OH)_2(aq) \longrightarrow MgCl_2(aq) + 2H_2O(l)$
   c. $2HNO_3(aq) + Ca(OH)_2(aq) \longrightarrow Ca(NO_3)_2(aq) + 2H_2O(l)$

19. a. Solid zinc sulfide reacts with oxygen gas to form solid zinc oxide and sulfur dioxide gas.
   b. When solid calcium hydride is added to water, aqueous calcium hydroxide and hydrogen gas are formed.
   c. Aqueous silver nitrate mixed with aqueous potassium iodide produces a precipitate of silver iodide and aqueous potassium nitrate.

20. a. $H_2 + Cl_2 \longrightarrow 2HCl$
  b. $2Al + Fe_2O_3 \longrightarrow$
                 $Al_2O_3 + 2Fe$
  c. $Pb(CH_3COO)_2 + H_2S \longrightarrow$
                 $PbS + 2CH_3COOH$

21. a. LiO_2 is an incorrect formula;
    $4Li + O_2 \longrightarrow 2Li_2O$
  b. H_2Cl_2 is an incorrect formula;
    $H_2 + Cl_2 \longrightarrow 2HCl$
  c. MgO_2 is an incorrect formula, and the equation as written is not balanced;
    $MgCO_3 \longrightarrow MgO + CO_2$
  d. I is an incorrect formula for iodine, and the equation is not balanced;
    $2NaI + Cl_2 \longrightarrow 2NaCl + I_2$

22. a. $4Al + 3O_2 \longrightarrow 2Al_2O_3$
  b. $P_4O_{10} + 6H_2O \longrightarrow 4H_3PO_4$
  c. $Fe_2O_3 + 3CO \longrightarrow$
              $2Fe + 3CO_2$

23. $CH_4(g) + 4Cl_2(g) \longrightarrow$
              $CCl_4(l) + 4HCl(g)$

24. a. $2Mg + O_2 \longrightarrow 2MgO$
  b. $4Fe + 3O_2 \longrightarrow 2Fe_2O_3$
  c. $2Li + Cl_2 \longrightarrow 2LiCl$
  d. $Ca + I_2 \longrightarrow CaI_2$

25. a. Sodium and oxygen react to form sodium oxide;
    $4Na + O_2 \longrightarrow 2Na_2O$
  b. Magnesium and fluorine combine to form magnesium fluoride;
    $Mg + F_2 \longrightarrow MgF_2$

26. a. $2HgO \xrightarrow{\Delta} 2Hg + O_2$
  b. $2H_2O(l) \xrightarrow{electricity} 2H_2(g) + O_2(g)$
  c. $2Ag_2O \xrightarrow{\Delta} 4Ag + O_2$
  d. $CuCl_2 \xrightarrow{electricity} Cu + Cl_2$

27. a. $Zn + Pb(NO_3)_2 \longrightarrow$
              $Pb + Zn(NO_3)_2$
  b. $2Al + 3Hg(CH_3COO)_2 \longrightarrow$
              $3Hg + 2Al(CH_3COO)_3$
  c. $2Al + 3NiSO_4 \longrightarrow$
              $3Ni + Al_2(SO_4)_3$
  d. $2Na + 2H_2O \longrightarrow$
              $2NaOH + H_2$

MIXED REVIEW

37. Ammonia reacts with oxygen to yield nitrogen and water.

$$4NH_3(g) + 3O_2(g) \longrightarrow 2N_2(g) + 6H_2O(l)$$

Given this chemical equation, as well as the number of moles of the reactant or product indicated below, determine the number of moles of all remaining reactants and products.
  a. 3.0 mol O_2
  b. 8.0 mol NH_3
  c. 1.0 mol N_2
  d. 0.40 mol H_2O

38. Complete the following synthesis reactions by writing both the word and chemical equation for each:
  a. potassium + chlorine $\longrightarrow$ _____
  b. hydrogen + iodine $\longrightarrow$ _____
  c. magnesium + oxygen $\longrightarrow$ _____

39. Use the activity series to predict which metal, Sn, Mn, or Pt, would be the best choice as a container for an acid.

40. Aqueous sodium hydroxide is produced commercially by the electrolysis of aqueous sodium chloride. Hydrogen and chlorine gases are also produced. Write the balanced chemical equation for the production of sodium hydroxide. Include the physical states of the reactants and products.

41. Balance each of the following:
  a. $Ca(OH)_2 + (NH_4)_2SO_4 \longrightarrow$
              $CaSO_4 + NH_3 + H_2O$
  b. $C_2H_6 + O_2 \longrightarrow CO_2 + H_2O$
  c. $Cu_2S + O_2 \longrightarrow Cu_2O + SO_2$
  d. $Al + H_2SO_4 \longrightarrow Al_2(SO_4)_3 + H_2$

42. Use the activity series to predict whether each of the following reactions will occur, and write the balanced chemical equations for those predicted to occur:
  a. $Al(s) + O_2(g) \longrightarrow$ _____
  b. $Pb(s) + ZnCl_2(s) \longrightarrow$ _____
  c. $Rb(s) + Zn(NO_3)_2(aq) \longrightarrow$ _____

43. Complete and balance the equations for the following reactions, and identify the type of reaction each represents:
  a. $(NH_4)_2S(aq) + ZnCl_2(aq) \longrightarrow$ _____ $+ ZnS(s)$

  b. $Al(s) + Pb(NO_3)_2(aq) \longrightarrow$ _____
  c. $Ba(s) + H_2O(l) \longrightarrow$ _____
  d. $Cl_2(g) + KBr(aq) \longrightarrow$
  e. $NH_3(g) + O_2(g) \xrightarrow{Pt} NO(g) + H_2O(l)$
  f. $H_2O(l) \longrightarrow H_2(g) + O_2(g)$

44. Write and balance each of the following equations, and then identify each by type:
  a. copper + chlorine $\longrightarrow$ copper(II) chloride
  b. calcium chlorate $\longrightarrow$
              calcium chloride + oxygen
  c. lithium + water $\longrightarrow$
              lithium hydroxide + hydrogen
  d. lead(II) carbonate $\longrightarrow$
              lead(II) oxide + carbon dioxide

45. How many moles of HCl can be made from 6.15 mol of H_2 and an excess of Cl_2?

46. What product is missing in the following equation?

$$MgO + 2HCl \longrightarrow MgCl_2 + \underline{\hphantom{xxxx}}$$

47. Balance the following equations:
  a. $Pb(NO_3)_2(aq) + NaOH(aq) \longrightarrow$
              $Pb(OH)_2(s) + NaNO_3(aq)$
  b. $C_{12}H_{22}O_{11}(l) + O_2(g) \longrightarrow CO_2(g) + H_2O(l)$
  c. $Al(OH)_3(s) + H_2SO_4(aq) \longrightarrow$
              $Al_2(SO_4)_3(aq) + H_2O(l)$

48. Translate the following word equations into balanced chemical equations:
  a. silver nitrate + potassium iodide $\longrightarrow$
              silver iodide + potassium nitrate
  b. nitrogen dioxide + water $\longrightarrow$
              nitric acid + nitrogen monoxide
  c. silicon tetrachloride + water $\longrightarrow$
              silicon dioxide + hydrochloric acid

CRITICAL THINKING

49. Inferring Relationships Activity series are prepared by comparing single-displacement reactions between metals. Based on observations, the metals can be ranked by their ability to react. However, reactivity can be explained by the ease with which atoms of metals lose electrons. Using information from the activity series, identify the locations in the periodic table of the most-reactive metals and the least-reactive metals. Based on your knowledge of electron configurations and periodic trends, infer possible explanations for their reactivity and position in the periodic table.

50. Analyzing Results Formulate an activity series for the hypothetical elements A, J, Q, and Z using the reaction information provided.

$$A + ZX \longrightarrow AX + Z$$
$$J + ZX \longrightarrow \text{no reaction}$$
$$Q + AX \longrightarrow QX + A$$

 HANDBOOK SEARCH

51. Find the common-reactions section for Group 1 metals in the *Elements Handbook*. Use this information to answer the following:
   a. Write a balanced chemical equation for the formation of rubidium hydroxide from rubidum oxide.
   b. Write a balanced chemical equation for the formation of cesium iodide.
   c. Classify the reactions you wrote in (a) and (b).
   d. Write word equations for the reactions you wrote in (a) and (b).

52. Find the common-reactions section for Group 13 in the *Elements Handbook*. Use this information to answer the following:
   a. Write a balanced chemical equation for the formation of gallium bromide prepared from hydrobromic acid.
   b. Write a balanced chemical equation for the formation of gallium oxide.
   c. Classify the reactions you wrote in (a) and (b).
   d. Write word equations for the reactions you wrote in (a) and (b).

53. Find the common-reactions section for Group 16 in the *Elements Handbook*. Use this information to answer the following:
   a. Write a balanced chemical equation for the formation of selenium trioxide.
   b. Write a balanced chemical equation for the formation of tellurium iodide.

   c. Classify the reactions you wrote in (a) and (b).
   d. Write word equations for the reactions you wrote in (a) and (b).

RESEARCH & WRITING

54. Trace the evolution of municipal water fluoridation. What advantages and disadvantages are associated with this practice?

55. Research how a soda-acid fire extinguisher works, and write the chemical equation for the reaction. Check your house and other structures for different types of fire extinguishers, and ask your local fire department to verify the effectiveness of each type of extinguisher.

ALTERNATIVE ASSESSMENT

56. Performance Assessment For one day, record situations that show evidence of a chemical change. Identify the reactants and the products, and determine whether there is proof of a chemical reaction. Classify each of the chemical reactions according to the common reaction types discussed in the chapter.

57. Design a set of experiments that will enable you to create an activity series for the elements composing the following metals and solutions:
   a. aluminum and aluminum chloride
   b. chromium and chromium(III) chloride
   c. iron and iron(II) chloride
   d. magnesium and magnesium chloride

28. a. $AgNO_3(aq) + NaCl(aq) \longrightarrow$
$$NaNO_3(aq) + AgCl(s)$$
b. $Mg(NO_3)_2(aq) + 2KOH(aq)$
$$\longrightarrow Mg(OH)_2(s) + 2KNO_3(aq)$$
c. $3LiOH(aq) + Fe(NO_3)_3(aq)$
$$\longrightarrow Fe(OH)_3(s) + 3LiNO_3(aq)$$

29. a. $CH_4 + 2O_2 \longrightarrow CO_2 + 2H_2O$
b. $2C_3H_6 + 9O_2 \longrightarrow$
$$6CO_2 + 6H_2O$$
c. $C_5H_{12} + 8O_2 \longrightarrow$
$$5CO_2 + 6H_2O$$

30. a. $H_2 + I_2 \longrightarrow 2HI$; synthesis
b. $2Li + 2HCl \longrightarrow 2LiCl + H_2$;
single-replacement
c. $Na_2CO_3 \longrightarrow Na_2O + CO_2$;
decomposition
d. $2HgO \longrightarrow 2Hg + O_2$;
decomposition
e. $Mg(OH)_2 \longrightarrow MgO + H_2O$;
decomposition

31. a. magnesium hydroxide;
$Mg(OH)_2 \longrightarrow MgO + H_2O$
b. lead(II) hydroxide;
$Pb(OH)_2 \longrightarrow PbO + H_2O$
c. lithium chlorate;
$2LiClO_3 \longrightarrow 2LiCl + 3O_2$
d. barium chlorate;
$Ba(ClO_3)_2 \longrightarrow BaCl_2 + 3O_2$
e. nickel chlorate;
$Ni(ClO_3)_2 \longrightarrow NiCl_2 + 3O_2$

32. a. oxygen, carbon dioxide;
$C_3H_8 + 5O_2 \longrightarrow 3CO_2 + 4H_2O$
b. pentane;
$C_5H_{12} + 8O_2 \longrightarrow$
$$5CO_2 + 6H_2O$$
c. oxygen, carbon dioxide, water;
$C_2H_5OH + 3O_2 \longrightarrow$
$$2CO_2 + 3H_2O$$

33. a. $Zn + S \longrightarrow ZnS$; synthesis
b. $Ca + 2NaNO_3 \longrightarrow$
$$Ca(NO_3)_2 + 2Na;$$
single-replacement
c. $AgNO_3 + KI \longrightarrow AgI + KNO_3$;
double-replacement
d. $2NaI \xrightarrow{\Delta} 2Na + I_2$;
decomposition
e. $C_7H_8 + 9O_2 \longrightarrow$
$$7CO_2 + 4H_2O;$$
combustion

Continued from page 273

f. $C_9H_{20} + 14O_2 \longrightarrow 9CO_2 + 10H_2O$; combustion

34. a. K

   b. Al

   c. Cr

   d. F

   e. Ag

   f. Cl

   g. Sr

   h. F

35. a. $Ni(s) + CuCl_2(aq) \longrightarrow NiCl_2(aq) + Cu(s)$

   b. $Zn(s) + Pb(NO_3)_2(aq) \longrightarrow Zn(NO_3)_2(aq) + Pb(s)$

   c. $Cl_2(g) + 2KI(aq) \longrightarrow 2KCl(aq) + I_2(s)$

   d. no reaction

   e. $Ba(s) + 2H_2O(l) \longrightarrow H_2(g) + Ba(OH)_2(s)$

36. a. $2Ca(s) + O_2(g) \longrightarrow 2CaO(s)$

   b. $2Ni(s) + O_2(g) \longrightarrow 2NiO(s)$

   c. no reaction

37. a. 4.0 mol NH_3, 2.0 mol N_2, 6.0 mol H_2O

   b. 6.0 mol O_2, 4.0 mol N_2, 12.0 mol H_2O

   c. 2.0 mol NH_3, 1.5 mol O_2, 3.0 mol H_2O

   d. 0.27 mol NH_3, 0.20 mol O_2, 0.13 mol N_2

38. a. Potassium and chlorine react to form potassium chloride; $2K + Cl_2 \longrightarrow 2KCl$

   b. Hydrogen and iodine react to produce hydrogen iodide; $H_2 + I_2 \longrightarrow 2HI$

   c. Magnesium and oxygen react to produce magnesium oxide; $2Mg + O_2 \longrightarrow 2MgO$

39. Pt

40. $2NaCl(aq) + 2H_2O(l) \xrightarrow{\text{electricity}} 2NaOH(aq) + H_2(g) + Cl_2(g)$

41. a. $Ca(OH)_2 + (NH_4)_2SO_4 \longrightarrow CaSO_4 + 2NH_3 + 2H_2O$

   b. $2C_2H_6 + 7O_2 \longrightarrow 4CO_2 + 6H_2O$

   c. $2Cu_2S + 3O_2 \longrightarrow 2Cu_2O + 2SO_2$

   d. $2Al + 3H_2SO_4 \longrightarrow Al_2(SO_4)_3 + 3H_2$

42. a. $4Al(s) + 3O_2(g) \longrightarrow 2Al_2O_3(s)$

   b. no reaction

   c. $2Rb(s) + Zn(NO_3)_2(aq) \longrightarrow 2RbNO_3(aq) + Zn(s)$

43. a. $(NH_4)_2S(aq) + ZnCl_2(aq) \longrightarrow 2NH_4Cl(aq) + ZnS(s)$; double-replacement

   b. $2Al(s) + 3Pb(NO_3)_2(aq) \longrightarrow 3Pb(s) + 2Al(NO_3)_3(aq)$; single-replacement

   c. $Ba(s) + 2H_2O(l) \longrightarrow Ba(OH)_2(s) + H_2(g)$; single-replacement

   d. $Cl_2(g) + 2KBr(aq) \longrightarrow 2KCl(aq) + Br_2(l)$; single-replacement

   e. $4NH_3(g) + 5O_2(g) \xrightarrow{\text{Pt}} 4NO(g) + 6H_2O(l)$; combustion

   f. $2H_2O(l) \longrightarrow 2H_2(g) + O_2(g)$; decomposition

44. a. $Cu(s) + Cl_2(g) \longrightarrow CuCl_2(s)$; synthesis

   b. $Ca(ClO_3)_2(s) \longrightarrow CaCl_2(s) + 3O_2(g)$; decomposition

   c. $2Li(s) + 2H_2O(l) \longrightarrow 2LiOH(aq) + H_2(g)$; single-replacement

   d. $PbCO_3(s) \longrightarrow PbO(s) + CO_2(g)$; decomposition

45. 12.3 mol HCl

46. H_2O

47. a. $Pb(NO_3)_2(aq) + 2NaOH(aq) \longrightarrow Pb(OH)_2(s) + 2NaNO_3(aq)$

   b. $C_{12}H_{22}O_{11}(l) + 12O_2(g) \longrightarrow 12CO_2(g) + 11H_2O(l)$

   c. $2Al(OH)_3(s) + 3H_2SO_4(aq) \longrightarrow Al_2(SO_4)_3(aq) + 6H_2O(l)$

48. a. $AgNO_3 + KI \longrightarrow AgI + KNO_3$

   b. $3NO_2 + H_2O \longrightarrow 2HNO_3 + NO$

   c. $SiCl_4 + 2H_2O \longrightarrow SiO_2 + 4HCl$

49. The most-reactive metals are on the left side of the periodic table in Groups 1 and 2. These metals have 1 (Group 1) or 2 (Group 2) electrons in their outer energy level. The energy needed to lose these electrons and achieve a stable configuration is much less than the energy needed to gain electrons. The least-reactive metals are in the lower right of the transition metal block. The d sublevel of the fifth energy level is more than half full in these metals. They are much more stable than metals on the left side of the periodic table.

50. Q is most reactive, followed by A, then Z, then J, which is the least reactive.

51. a. $Rb_2O(s) + H_2O(l) \longrightarrow 2RbOH(aq)$
b. $2Cs(s) + I_2(s) \longrightarrow 2CsI(s)$
c. Both are synthesis reactions.
d. Solid rubidium oxide reacts with water to yield an aqueous solution of rubidium hydroxide. Solid cesium reacts with solid iodine to yield solid cesium iodide.

52. a. $2Ga(s) + 6HBr(aq) \longrightarrow 2GaBr_3(aq) + 3H_2(g)$
b. $4Ga(s) + 3O_2(g) \longrightarrow 2Ga_2O_3(s)$
c. The first reaction is a single replacement; the second reaction is a synthesis reaction.
d. Solid gallium reacts with hydrobromic acid to yield aqueous gallium bromide and hydrogen gas. Solid gallium reacts with oxygen gas to yield solid gallium oxide.

53. a. $2Se(s) + 3O_2(g) \longrightarrow 2SeO_3(s)$
b. $Te(s) + I_2(g) \longrightarrow TeI_2(s)$
You may wish to point out to students that the reaction would occur at a temperature at which iodine is a gas.
c. Both reactions are synthesis reactions.
d. Solid selenium reacts with oxygen gas to yield solid selenium oxide. Solid tellurium reacts with gaseous iodine to yield solid tellurium iodide.

Refer to the *One-Stop Planner CD-ROM* for appropriate scoring rubrics for items 54 and 55. Look for these points in each report:

54. Students may discover that tin(II) fluoride and sodium fluoride harden tooth enamel when the fluoride ion participates in a double-replacement reaction with the principle constituent of tooth enamel, hydroxyapatite, $Ca_5(PO_4)_3OH$.
$$Ca_5(PO_4)_3OH(aq) + NaF(aq) \longrightarrow$$
$$Ca_5(PO_4)_3F(s) + NaOH(aq)$$
Fluoroapatite is harder, stronger, and more resistant to bacterial attack than hydroxyapatite.

55. The soda-acid fire extinguisher has been generally replaced by extinguishers consisting of tanks of liquid CO_2. However, students can write the soda-acid equation:
$$H_2SO_4 + 2NaHCO_3 \longrightarrow 2CO_2 + Na_2SO_4 + 2H_2O.$$

56. Students may see evidence of chemical changes that are too complex to incorporate into a simple equation. Ask them to include the evidence. Students could summarize their findings on a chart.

57. Students' procedures should lead reasonably to a definite order of activity. They should include data tables. If the procedures are sound and safe, allow them to test them in the lab.

273B

Stoichiometry

PACING CHART

Compression Guide: *(To shorten, eliminate items in italics.)*

CLASSROOM RESOURCES

	NSE Standards	Teaching Resources	Experiments
9-1 **Introduction to Stoichiometry** 2 45-minute periods 1 90-minute block *Reaction-Stoichiometry Problems, pp. 275–277*	UCP 1–3 SPSP 1–3	**ATE Demo**, p. 276 T 44, T 45, T 46, T 47	
9-2 **Ideal Stoichiometric Calculations** 2 45-minute periods 1 90-minute block *Conversion of Quantities in Moles, pp. 280–282* *Conversions of Amounts in Moles to Mass, pp. 282–284* *Conversions of Mass to Amounts in Moles, pp. 284–286*	UCP 1–3		Mass and Mole Relationships in a Chemical Reaction, p. 816
9-3 **Limiting Reactants and Percent Yield** 2 45-minute periods 1 90-minute block *Percent Yield, pp. 293–294*	UCP 1–3 SAI 1–2	**ATE Demo**, p. 288	Quick Lab, p. 292 Stoichiometry and Gravimetric Analysis, p. 819

REVIEW RESOURCES

Review and Assessment 2 45-minute periods 1 90-minute block	Cumulative Review	Alternative Assessment	Traditional Assessment
	SR Chapter 9 Mixed Review **PE** Chapter 9 31–36, pp. 297–298	**PE** 46, 47, p. 299 **ATE** 286 **AA** Items for Chapter 9	Chapter 9 Text Test Generator items for Chapter 9

ASSIGNMENT RESOURCES

Section Homework Resources & Review	Problem-Solving Practice
HR Homework Worksheet 9-1 **PE** Section Review, 1–3, p. 277 Chapter Review, 1–2, p. 296 **SR** Section Review 9-1	
HR Homework Worksheets 9-2, 9-3, 9-4 Graphic Org. Assignment 9-3 **PE** Section Review, 1–5, p. 287 Chapter Review, 3, 9–21, p. 296 **SR** Section Review 9-2	**PE** Additional Samples 9-1, 9-2, 9-3, 9-4, 9-5 **ATE** Additional Samples, pp. 281, 283, 285, 287
HR Homework Worksheets 9-5, 9-6 Graphic Org. Assignment 9-6 **PE** Section Review, 1–4, p. 294 Chapter Review, 5–8, 22–30, pp. 295–297 **SR** Section Review 9-3	**PE** Additional Samples 9-6, 9-7, 9-8 **ATE** Additional Samples, pp. 289, 290, 294 **PS** Chapter 9 Limiting Reactants Chapter 10 Percent Yield

TECHNOLOGY RESOURCES

Technology & Internet Resources

 CTW 4 Segment 4 Student Superconductors

 Holt Chemistry Videodiscs Teacher's Correlation Guide for Chapter 9

 Module 5: Stoichiometry, Limiting Reactants

internet connect

 On-line Student Resources:
GO TO: www.scilinks.org
The following SciLinks Internet resources can be found in the student text for this chapter.

TOPICS:
• Lavoisier, p. 279 (HC2091)

On-line Teacher Resources:
GO TO: go.hrw.com
KEYWORD: HC2 HOME
Visit the HRW Web site for a variety of resources related to this chapter.

 Smithsonian Institution®
Internet Connections
Visit **www.si.edu/hrw** for additional on-line resources.

CNNfyi.com
Visit **www.cnnfyi.com** for late-breaking news and current events stories selected just for you.

Resource Key

PE Pupil's Edition
ATE Teacher's Edition

⚡ One-Stop Planner CD-ROM Includes these resources and customizable daily lesson plans:

HR Homework Resources	**ChemFile**	**D** Consumer Experiments
SR Section Reviews	**A** Laboratory Experiments	**T** Transparencies
CTW Critical Thinking Worksheets	**B** Microscale Experiments	**TM** Transparency Masters
AA Alternative Assessments	**C** Technique Builders and Problem-Solving Experiments	**PS** Mini-Guide to Problem Solving
		SRW Supplemental Reading Worksheets

Scoring Rubrics for Labs, Alternative Assessments, Performance Tasks and Portfolio Projects are on the One-Stop Planner CD-ROM.

Stoichiometry

Chapter Overview

9-1 defines mole ratio and introduces molar mass as a conversion factor in solving stoichiometry problems.

9-2 demonstrates solutions to problems involving conversions from moles of *given* to moles of *unknown*, from moles to mass, from mass to moles, and from mass to mass.

9-3 explains the concepts of limiting reactant and percent yield and provides strategies for solving problems based on these concepts.

Concept Base

Students may need a review of the following concepts:

• coefficients in a chemical reaction, Chapter 8

• molar mass, Chapter 7

• composition-stoichiometry problems, Chapters 3 and 7

 Reading Skill-Builder

BRAINSTORMING Write the words *reactants* and *products* on the board. Then direct students' attention to the statement on p. 274. Have them brainstorm a list of measurements a chemist might want to make in relation to reactants and products, such as mass, amount of substance in moles, and so on. Discuss the difference between the measurements studied in Chapter 3 (mass relationships of elements in compounds) and those related to reactants and products in a chemical reaction.

Stoichiometry

Stoichiometry *comes from the Greek words* stoicheion, *meaning "element," and* metron, *meaning "measure."*

Introduction to Stoichiometry

Much of our knowledge of chemistry is based on the careful quantitative analysis of substances involved in chemical reactions. **Composition stoichiometry** (which you studied in Chapter 3) *deals with the mass relationships of elements in compounds.* **Reaction stoichiometry** *involves the mass relationships between reactants and products in a chemical reaction.* Reaction stoichiometry is the subject of this chapter and it is based on chemical equations and the law of conservation of matter. All reaction-stoichiometry calculations start with a balanced chemical equation. This equation gives the relative numbers of moles of reactants and products.

Reaction-Stoichiometry Problems

The reaction-stoichiometry problems in this chapter can be classified according to the information *given* in the problem and the information you are expected to find, the *unknown.* The *given* and the *unknown* may both be reactants, they may both be products, or one may be a reactant and the other a product. The masses are generally expressed in grams, but you will encounter both large-scale and microscale problems with other mass units, such as kg or mg. Stoichiometric problems are solved by using ratios from the balanced equation to convert the given quantity using the methods described here.

Problem Type 1: *Given* **and** *unknown* **quantities are amounts in moles.**
When you are given the amount of a substance in moles and asked to calculate the amount in moles of another substance in the chemical reaction, the general plan is

amount of
given substance (in mol) $\longrightarrow$ amount of
unknown substance (in mol)

Problem Type 2: *Given* **is an amount in moles and the** *unknown* **is a mass that is often expressed in grams.**
When you are given the amount in moles of one substance and asked to calculate the mass of another substance in the chemical reaction, the general plan is

amount of   amount of   mass of
given substance $\longrightarrow$ *unknown* substance $\longrightarrow$ *unknown* substance
(in mol)   (in mol)   (in g)

OBJECTIVES

- Define *stoichiometry.*

- Describe the importance of the *mole ratio* in stoichiometric calculations.

- Write a mole ratio relating two substances in a chemical equation.

Module 5: Equations and Stoichiometry

Lesson Starter
Write on the chalkboard the equation for the reaction of Mg with HCl.

$$Mg(s) + 2HCl(aq) \longrightarrow MgCl_2(aq) + H_2(g)$$

Use it to help students realize that if they know the amount of one substance in a reaction, they can determine the amounts of all the other substances. Ask how many moles of H_2 are obtained from 2 mol of HCl. Ask how many moles of Mg will react with 2 mol of HCl. Double the moles of HCl, and ask about the moles of $MgCl_2$ and H_2 that would result. Finally, ask students how they might convert moles of these substances to masses.

✔ **Teaching Tip**

Emphasize that solving a stoichiometry problem depends on the balanced chemical equation, which provides the ratio of moles of each reactant and product to all other reactants and products.

Problem-Solving Practice  HOLT ChemFile

Chapter 8 of the Mini-Guide to Problem Solving (also found on the One-Stop Planner CD-ROM) includes more worked-out samples and additional practice problems involving stoichiometry.

Module 5: Equations and Stoichiometry

Topic: Stoichiometry
Sections **d, e, f, g,** and **h** of this engaging tutorial review and reinforce understanding of stoichiometry.

Use the reaction of Na_2CO_3 with HCl to trace mass relationships in a reaction and set the stage for the concepts of limiting reagent and percent yield.

$$Na_2CO_3(s) + 2HCl(aq) \longrightarrow$$
$$2NaCl(aq) + H_2O(l) + CO_2(g)$$

1. Determine the mass of a Pyrex evaporating dish to the thousandth of a gram, and record the mass.

2. Add 1 g of anhydrous Na_2CO_3, and record the mass of the dish and salt.

3. Add 1 M HCl dropwise until the bubbling stops. Then add a little more HCl to make sure the reaction has gone to completion.

4. In a fume hood place the evaporating dish on a piece of wire gauze on a ring stand. Boil the liquid to dryness (heat gently at first).

5. Record the mass of the dish and dried NaCl.

6. Have students use molar mass as a conversion factor to find the moles of Na_2CO_3 and NaCl.

7. Save the results for use in Section 9-3.

Safety: Wear safety goggles and a lab apron. Students should stand back 10 feet.

Disposal: Wrap the NaCl in newspaper, and put it in the trash.

Problem Type 3: *Given* is a mass in grams and the *unknown* is an amount in moles.

When you are given the mass of one substance and asked to calculate the amount in moles of another substance in the chemical reaction, the general plan is

mass of   amount of   amount of
given substance $\longrightarrow$ *given* substance $\longrightarrow$ *unknown* substance
(in g)   (in mol)   (in mol)

Problem Type 4: *Given* is a mass in grams and the *unknown* is a mass in grams.

When you are given the mass of one substance and asked to calculate the mass of another substance in the chemical reaction, the general plan is

mass of   amount of   amount of   mass of
given substance $\longrightarrow$ *given* substance $\longrightarrow$ *unknown* substance $\longrightarrow$ *unknown* substance
(in g)   (in mol)   (in mol)   (in g)

Mole Ratio

Solving any reaction-stoichiometry problem requires the use of a mole ratio to convert from moles or grams of one substance in a reaction to moles or grams of another substance. *A* **mole ratio** *is a conversion factor that relates the amounts in moles of any two substances involved in a chemical reaction.* This information is obtained directly from the balanced chemical equation. Consider, for example, the chemical equation for the electrolysis of aluminum oxide to produce aluminum and oxygen.

$$2Al_2O_3(l) \longrightarrow 4Al(s) + 3O_2(g)$$

Recall from Chapter 8 that the coefficients in a chemical equation satisfy the law of conservation of matter and represent the relative amounts in moles of reactants and products. Therefore, 2 mol of aluminum oxide decompose to produce 4 mol of aluminum and 3 mol of oxygen gas. These relationships can be expressed in the following mole ratios.

$$\frac{2 \text{ mol } Al_2O_3}{4 \text{ mol } Al} \quad \text{or} \quad \frac{4 \text{ mol } Al}{2 \text{ mol } Al_2O_3}$$

$$\frac{2 \text{ mol } Al_2O_3}{3 \text{ mol } O_2} \quad \text{or} \quad \frac{3 \text{ mol } O_2}{2 \text{ mol } Al_2O_3}$$

$$\frac{4 \text{ mol } Al}{3 \text{ mol } O_2} \quad \text{or} \quad \frac{3 \text{ mol } O_2}{4 \text{ mol } Al}$$

For the decomposition of aluminum oxide, the appropriate mole ratio would be used as a conversion factor to convert a given amount in moles of one substance to the corresponding amount in moles of another substance. To determine the amount in moles of aluminum that can be produced from 13.0 mol of aluminum oxide, the mole ratio needed is that of Al to Al_2O_3.

$$13.0 \; \text{mol Al}_2\text{O}_3 \times \frac{4 \; \text{mol Al}}{2 \; \text{mol Al}_2\text{O}_3} = 26.0 \; \text{mol Al}$$

Mole ratios are exact, so they do not limit the number of significant figures in a calculation. The number of significant figures in the answer is therefore determined only by the number of significant figures of any measured quantities in a particular problem.

Molar Mass

Recall from Chapter 7 that the molar mass is the mass, in grams, of one mole of a substance. The molar mass is the conversion factor that relates the mass of a substance to the amount in moles of that substance. To solve reaction-stoichiometry problems, you will need to determine molar masses using the periodic table.

Returning to the previous example, the decomposition of aluminum oxide, the rounded masses from the periodic table are the following.

$$Al_2O_3 = 101.96 \; \text{g/mol} \qquad O_2 = 32.00 \; \text{g/mol} \qquad Al = 26.98 \; \text{g/mol}$$

These molar masses can be expressed by the following conversion factors.

$$\frac{101.96 \; \text{g Al}_2\text{O}_3}{\text{mol Al}_2\text{O}_3} \quad \text{or} \quad \frac{1 \; \text{mol Al}_2\text{O}_3}{101.96 \; \text{g Al}_2\text{O}_3}$$

$$\frac{26.98 \; \text{g Al}}{\text{mol Al}} \quad \text{or} \quad \frac{1 \; \text{mol Al}}{26.98 \; \text{g Al}}$$

$$\frac{32.00 \; \text{g O}_2}{\text{mol O}_2} \quad \text{or} \quad \frac{1 \; \text{mol O}_2}{32.00 \; \text{g O}_2}$$

To find the number of grams of aluminum equivalent to 26.0 mol of aluminum, the calculation would be as follows.

$$26.0 \; \text{mol Al} \times \frac{26.98 \; \text{g Al}}{\text{mol Al}} = 701 \; \text{g Al}$$

SECTION REVIEW

1. What is stoichiometry?

2. How is a mole ratio from a reaction used in stoichiometric problems?

3. For each of the following chemical equations, write all possible mole ratios.
   a. $2HgO(s) \longrightarrow 2Hg(l) + O_2(g)$
   b. $4NH_3(g) + 6NO(g) \longrightarrow 5N_2(g) + 6H_2O(l)$
   c. $2Al(s) + 3H_2SO_4(aq) \longrightarrow Al_2(SO_4)_3(aq) + 3H_2(g)$

SECTION REVIEW

1. the branch of chemistry that deals with the mass relationships of elements in compounds and the mass relationships between reactants and products in a chemical reaction

2. Mole ratio is used to convert moles of one substance to moles of another substance.

3. a. $\dfrac{2 \; \text{mol HgO}}{2 \; \text{mol Hg}}$, $\dfrac{2 \; \text{mol HgO}}{1 \; \text{mol O}_2}$,

$\dfrac{2 \; \text{mol Hg}}{2 \; \text{mol HgO}}$, $\dfrac{2 \; \text{mol Hg}}{1 \; \text{mol O}_2}$,

$\dfrac{1 \; \text{mol O}_2}{2 \; \text{mol HgO}}$, $\dfrac{1 \; \text{mol O}_2}{2 \; \text{mol Hg}}$

b.
$\dfrac{4 \; \text{mol NH}_3}{6 \; \text{mol NO}}$, $\dfrac{4 \; \text{mol NH}_3}{5 \; \text{mol N}_2}$, $\dfrac{4 \; \text{mol NH}_3}{6 \; \text{mol H}_2\text{O}}$

$\dfrac{6 \; \text{mol NO}}{4 \; \text{mol NH}_3}$, $\dfrac{6 \; \text{mol NO}}{5 \; \text{mol N}_2}$, $\dfrac{6 \; \text{mol NO}}{6 \; \text{mol H}_2\text{O}}$

$\dfrac{5 \; \text{mol N}_2}{6 \; \text{mol H}_2\text{O}}$, $\dfrac{5 \; \text{mol N}_2}{6 \; \text{mol NO}}$, $\dfrac{5 \; \text{mol N}_2}{4 \; \text{mol NH}_3}$

$\dfrac{6 \; \text{mol H}_2\text{O}}{5 \; \text{mol N}_2}$, $\dfrac{6 \; \text{mol H}_2\text{O}}{6 \; \text{mol NO}}$, $\dfrac{6 \; \text{mol H}_2\text{O}}{4 \; \text{mol NH}_3}$

c. $\dfrac{2 \; \text{mol Al}}{3 \; \text{mol H}_2\text{SO}_4}$, $\dfrac{2 \; \text{mol Al}}{1 \; \text{mol Al}_2(\text{SO}_4)_3}$,

$\dfrac{2 \; \text{mol Al}}{3 \; \text{mol H}_2}$, $\dfrac{3 \; \text{mol H}_2\text{SO}_4}{2 \; \text{mol Al}}$,

$\dfrac{3 \; \text{mol H}_2\text{SO}_4}{1 \; \text{mol Al}_2(\text{SO}_4)_3}$, $\dfrac{3 \; \text{mol H}_2\text{SO}_4}{3 \; \text{mol H}_2}$,

$\dfrac{1 \; \text{mol Al}_2(\text{SO}_4)_3}{2 \; \text{mol Al}}$, $\dfrac{1 \; \text{mol Al}_2(\text{SO}_4)_3}{3 \; \text{mol H}_2\text{SO}_4}$,

$\dfrac{1 \; \text{mol Al}_2(\text{SO}_4)_3}{3 \; \text{mol H}_2}$, $\dfrac{3 \; \text{mol H}_2}{1 \; \text{mol Al}_2(\text{SO}_4)_3}$,

$\dfrac{3 \; \text{mol H}_2}{3 \; \text{mol H}_2\text{SO}_4}$, $\dfrac{3 \; \text{mol H}_2}{2 \; \text{mol Al}}$

GREAT DISCOVERIES

Teaching Strategy
Ask students to try to forget everything they know about combustion. Tell them that all they know about burning is what they can observe qualitatively. Then have them read *The Case of Combustion*, and prepare to discuss it. Some suggested topics follow. See Discussion Points on page 279 for brief summaries of the topics.

Class Discussion
This Historical Perspective provides a number of topics for discussion.

1. A theory is useful as long as it can help explain new scientific evidence. Have students describe how the phlogiston theory was at first supported by new findings but later abandoned in favor of a new theory.

2. Have students describe what Rutherford named *phlogisticated air* and what Priestley called *dephlogisticated air.*

3. Discuss the results of the experiment that Daniel Rutherford performed in 1772 in terms of what is known today.

4. Lavoisier burned a known mass of tin in a closed container. When he opened the container and air rushed in, he observed that the tin increased in mass. Discuss how this finding was critical in destroying the phlogiston theory.

5. Do you suppose that the new theory proposed by Lavoisier was immediately adopted by other scientists? Why or why not?

GREAT DISCOVERIES

The Case of Combustion

HISTORICAL PERSPECTIVE

People throughout history have transformed substances by burning them in the air. Yet at the dawn of the scientific revolution, very little was known about the process of combustion. In attempting to explain this common phenomenon, chemists of the eighteenth century developed one of the first universally accepted theories in their field. But, as one man would show, scientific theories do not always stand the test of time.

Changing Attitudes
Shunning the ancient Greek approach of logical argument based on untested premises, investigators of the seventeenth century began to understand the laws of nature by observing, measuring, and performing experiments on the world around them. However, this scientific method was incorporated into chemistry slowly. Though early chemists experimented extensively, most disregarded the importance of measurement, an oversight that set chemistry on the wrong path for nearly a century.

A Flawed Theory
By 1700, combustion was assumed to be the decomposition of a material into simpler substances. People saw burning substances emitting heat, smoke, and light. To account for it, a theory was proposed that combustion depended on the emission of a substance called phlogiston, which appeared as a combination of heat and light while the material was burning but which couldn't be detected beforehand.

Antoine-Laurent Lavoisier and his wife, Marie-Anne Pierrette Lavoisier, who assisted him. One of her important roles was to translate the papers of important scientists for her husband.

The Metropolitan Museum of Art, Purchase, Mr. and Mrs. Charles Wrightsman Gift, in honor of Everett Fahy, 1977. (1977.10) Copyright © 1989 By The Metropolitan Museum of Art.

The phlogiston theory was used to explain many chemical observations of the day. For example, a lit candle under a glass jar burned until the surrounding air became saturated with phlogiston, at which time the flame died because the air inside could not absorb more phlogiston.

A New Phase of Study
By the 1770s, the phlogiston theory had gained universal acceptance. At that time, chemists also began to experiment with air, which was generally believed to be an element.

In 1772, when Daniel Rutherford found that a mouse kept in a closed container soon died, he explained the results based on the phlogiston theory. Like a burning candle, the mouse emitted phlogiston; when the air could hold no more phlogiston, the mouse died. Thus, Rutherford figured he had obtained "phlogisticated air."

A couple of years later, Joseph Priestley found that when he heated mercury in air, he obtained a reddish powder, which he assumed to be mercury devoid of phlogiston. But when he decided to heat the powder, he recorded an unexpected result:

I endeavored to extract air from [the powder by heating it]; and I presently found that

... air was expelled from it readily. Having got about three or four times as much as the bulk of my materials, I admitted water to it, and found that water was not imbibed by it. But what surprised me more ... was, that a candle in this air burned ... remarkably ...

Following the phlogiston theory, he believed this gas that supports combustion to be "dephlogisticated air."

Nice Try, But . . .

Antoine Laurent Lavoisier was a meticulous scientist. He realized that Rutherford and Priestley had carefully observed and described their experiments but had not weighed anything. Unlike his colleagues, Lavoisier knew the importance of using a balance:

... making experiments ... is founded on this principle ... always suppose an exact equality or equation between the principles [masses] of the body examined and those of the products of its analysis.

Applying this rule, which would become known as the law of conservation of mass, Lavoisier endeavored to explain the results of Rutherford and Priestley.

He put some tin in a closed vessel and weighed the entire system. He then burned the tin. When he opened the vessel, air rushed into it, as if something had been *removed* from the air during combustion. He then weighed the burnt metal and observed a weight increase relative to the original tin. Curiously, this increase equaled the weight of the air that had rushed into the vessel. To Lavoisier, this did not support the idea of phlogiston escaping the burning material. Instead, it indicated that during combustion a portion of air was depleted.

After obtaining similar results using a variety of substances, Lavoisier concluded that air was not an element at all but a mixture composed principally of two gases, Priestley's "dephlogisticated air" (which Lavoisier renamed oxygen) and Rutherford's "phlogisticated air" (which was mostly nitrogen, with traces of other nonflammable atmospheric gases). When a substance burned, it chemically combined with oxygen, resulting in a product Lavoisier named an "oxide." Lavoisier's theory of combustion persists today. He used the name *oxygen* because he thought that all acids contained oxygen. *Oxygen* means "acid former."

The Father of Chemistry

By emphasizing the importance of quantitative analysis, Lavoisier helped establish chemistry as a science. His work on combustion laid to rest the theories of phlogiston and that air is an element. He also explained why hydrogen burned in oxygen to form water, or hydrogen oxide. He later published one of the first chemistry textbooks, which established a common naming system of compounds and elements and helped unify chemistry worldwide, earning him the reputation as the father of chemistry.

internet connect

SC*LINKS*

NSTA

TOPIC: Lavoisier
GO TO: www.scilinks.org
*sci*LINKS **CODE:** HC2091

TABLE OF SIMPLE SUBSTANCES.

Simple fubftances belonging to all the kingdoms of nature, which may be confidered as the elements of bodies.

New Names.				Correfpondent old Names.
Light	-	-	-	Light.
Caloric	-	-	-	{ Heat. } { Principle or element of heat. } { Fire. Igneous fluid. } { Matter of fire and of heat. }
Oxygen	-	-	-	{ Dephlogifticated air. } { Empyreal air. } { Vital air, or } { Bafe of vital air. }
Azote	-	-	-	{ Phlogifticated air or gas. } { Mephitis, or its bafe. }
Hydrogen	-	-	-	{ Inflammable air or gas, } { or the bafe of inflammable air. }

Lavoisier's concept of simple substances as published in his book Elements of Chemistry *in 1789.*

1. The phlogiston theory explained combustion and respiration. It was expanded by Priestley to include dephlogisticated air when he could not explain his experimental results. The quantitative experiments of Lavoisier showed that another interpretation of the evidence was more likely.

2. Phlogisticated air is air from which oxygen has been removed. Dephlogisticated air is oxygen.

3. The mouse used up all the oxygen and added CO_2 to the container.

4. According to the phlogiston theory, a substance loses phlogiston to the air when it burns. The gain in the mass of the tin and the presence of a partial vacuum are opposed to these expectations.

5. A well-established theory is not easily abandoned. It's natural for scientists to hang on to a theory until the accumulating evidence against it is overwhelming.

6. Some students may notice the Old English or French character used in the table for the letter s.

Lesson Starter

Use this demonstration to relate moles of an acid to moles of base in a neutralization reaction.

1. Set up two burets, one containing 25–50 mL of 0.1 M NaOH and the other containing 25–50 mL of 0.1 M HCl. Read and record the initial volumes of both solutions.

2. Allow about 20 mL of acid to flow from the HCl buret into a 125 mL Erlenmeyer flask, and add a few drops of phenolphthalein to the flask.

3. Add NaOH solution from the buret to the HCl flask while swirling. Continue to add base until the presence of the red color of phenolphthalein indicates that the neutralization reaction is complete.

4. Read and record the volumes of both HCl and NaOH.

5. Compare the volumes of the two solutions. Tell students that this procedure allows investigators to determine the number of moles of acid in a solution if the number of moles of base in solution are known. Similarly, if the number of moles of acid in solution are known, the unknown number of moles of base in a solution can be determined.

6. Given that both solutions are of the same concentrations, ask students to write an equation for the reaction of HCl and NaOH. Have them write the mole ratio of HCl to NaOH.

Safety: Wear safety goggles and a lab apron. Students should remain back at least 10 feet.

Disposal: Combine all liquids, adjust the pH to between 5 and 9, and pour down the drain.

OBJECTIVES

- Calculate the amount in moles of a reactant or product from the amount in moles of a different reactant or product.

- Calculate the mass of a reactant or product from the amount in moles of a different reactant or product.

- Calculate the amount in moles of a reactant or product from the mass of a different reactant or product.

- Calculate the mass of a reactant or product from the mass of a different reactant or product.

Ideal Stoichiometric Calculations

The chemical equation plays a very important part in all stoichiometric calculations because the mole ratio is obtained directly from it. Solving any reaction-stoichiometry problem must begin with a balanced equation.

Chemical equations help us make predictions about chemical reactions without having to run the reactions in the laboratory. The reaction-stoichiometry calculations described in this chapter are theoretical. They tell us the amounts of reactants and products for a given chemical reaction under *ideal conditions*, in which all reactants are completely converted into products. However, ideal conditions are rarely met in the laboratory or in industry. Yet, theoretical stoichiometric calculations serve the very important function of showing the maximum amount of product that could be obtained before a reaction is run in the laboratory.

Solving stoichiometric problems requires practice. These problems are extensions of the composition-stoichiometry problems you solved in Chapters 3 and 7. Practice by working the sample problems in the rest of this chapter. Using a logical, systematic approach will help you successfully solve these problems.

Conversions of Quantities in Moles

In these stoichiometric problems, you are asked to calculate the amount in moles of one substance that will react with or be produced from the given amount in moles of another substance. The plan for a simple mole conversion problem is

$$\text{amount of } given \text{ substance (in mol)} \longrightarrow \text{amount of } unknown \text{ substance (in mol)}$$

This plan requires one conversion factor—the stoichiometric mole ratio of the *unknown* substance to the *given* substance from the balanced equation. To solve this type of problem, simply multiply the *known* quantity by the appropriate conversion factor.

$$given \text{ quantity} \times \text{conversion factor} = unknown \text{ quantity}$$

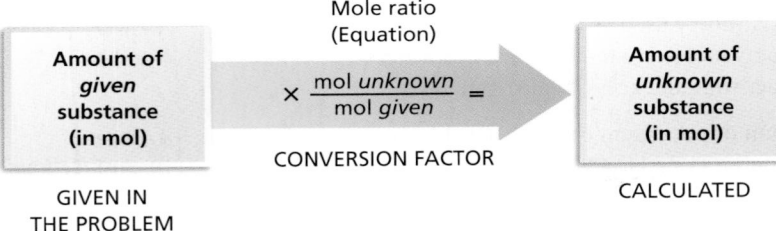

Mole ratio
(Equation)

Amount of *given* substance (in mol) $\times \dfrac{\text{mol } unknown}{\text{mol } given} =$ Amount of *unknown* substance (in mol)

CONVERSION FACTOR

GIVEN IN THE PROBLEM   CALCULATED

FIGURE 9-1 This is a solution plan for problems in which the given and unknown quantities are expressed in moles.

SAMPLE PROBLEM 9-1

In a spacecraft, the carbon dioxide exhaled by astronauts can be removed by its reaction with lithium hydroxide, LiOH, according to the following chemical equation.

$$CO_2(g) + 2LiOH(s) \longrightarrow Li_2CO_3(s) + H_2O(l)$$

How many moles of lithium hydroxide are required to react with 20 mol of CO_2, the average amount exhaled by a person each day?

SOLUTION

1 ANALYZE

Given: amount of CO_2 = 20 mol
Unknown: amount of LiOH in moles

2 PLAN

amount of CO_2 (in mol) $\longrightarrow$ amount of LiOH (in mol)

This problem requires one conversion factor—the mole ratio of LiOH to CO_2. The mole ratio is obtained from the balanced chemical equation. Because you are given moles of CO_2, select a mole ratio that will give you mol LiOH in your final answer. The correct ratio is the following.

$$\frac{\text{mol LiOH}}{\text{mol } CO_2}$$

This ratio gives the units mol LiOH in the answer.

$$\text{mol } CO_2 \times \overset{\text{mol ratio}}{\frac{\text{mol LiOH}}{\text{mol } CO_2}} = \text{mol LiOH}$$

3 COMPUTE

Substitute the values in the equation in step 2, and compute the answer.

$$20 \;\cancel{\text{mol } CO_2} \times \frac{2 \text{ mol LiOH}}{1 \;\cancel{\text{mol } CO_2}} = 40 \text{ mol LiOH}$$

4 EVALUATE

The answer is rounded correctly to one significant figure to match that in the factor 20 mol CO_2, and the units cancel to leave mol LiOH, which is the unknown. The equation shows that twice the amount in moles of LiOH react with CO_2. Therefore, the answer should be greater than 20.

Visual Strategy

FIGURE 9-1 This diagram is the first in a series students can use as visual models when comparing the solution steps for the different problem types. Your teaching models may vary, but it is important that students see how similar these problem types are.

✔ Teaching Tip

Do not underestimate the difficulties students may have in understanding a problem statement. Focus on analyzing problem statements as an important problem-solving technique. You may find it helpful to have students write down what is *given* and what is *unknown* before they begin a problem.

ADDITIONAL
SAMPLE
PROBLEMS

9-1 The elements lithium and oxygen react explosively to form lithium oxide, Li_2O. How many moles of lithium oxide will form if 2 mol of lithium react?

Ans. 1 mol Li_2O

9-1 The disinfectant hydrogen peroxide, H_2O_2, decomposes to form water and oxygen gas. How many moles of O_2 will result from the decomposition of 5 mol of hydrogen peroxide?

Ans. 2.5 mol O_2

 **Reading Skill-Builder**

SUMMARIZING Have students read pp. 280–287. Ask students to condense and summarize Section 9-2 under the heading "Solving Four Types of Stoichiometric Problems." Have students use Figures 9-1–9-4 to help them summarize.

PRACTICE

1. Ammonia, NH_3, is widely used as a fertilizer and in many household cleaners. How many moles of ammonia are produced when 6 mol of hydrogen gas react with an excess of nitrogen gas?

   Answer
   4 mol NH_3

2. The decomposition of potassium chlorate, $KClO_3$, is used as a source of oxygen in the laboratory. How many moles of potassium chlorate are needed to produce 15 mol of oxygen?

   Answer
   10. mol $KClO_3$

Conversions of Amounts in Moles to Mass

In these stoichiometric calculations, you are asked to calculate the mass (usually in grams) of a substance that will react with or be produced from a given amount in moles of a second substance. The plan for these mole to gram conversions is

amount of   amount of

given substance $\longrightarrow$ *unknown* substance $\longrightarrow$ *unknown* substance

(in mol)   (in mol)   (in g)

This plan requires two conversion factors—the mole ratio of the *unknown* substance to the *given* substance and the molar mass of the *unknown* substance for the mass conversion. To solve this kind of problem, you simply multiply the known quantity, which is the amount in moles, by the appropriate conversion factors.

FIGURE 9-2 This is a solution plan for problems in which the given quantity is expressed in moles and the unknown quantity is expressed in grams.

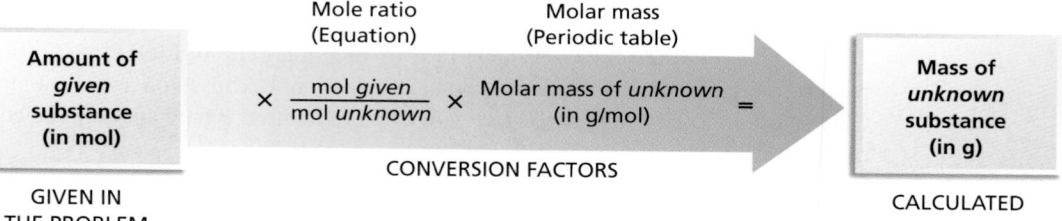

SAMPLE PROBLEM 9-2

In photosynthesis, plants use energy from the sun to produce glucose, $C_6H_{12}O_6$, and oxygen from the reaction of carbon dioxide and water. What mass, in grams, of glucose is produced when 3.00 mol of water react with carbon dioxide?

SOLUTION

1 ANALYZE   **Given:** amount of H_2O = 3.00 mol
                      Unknown: mass of $C_6H_{12}O_6$ produced (in g)

2 PLAN You must start with a balanced equation.

$$6CO_2(g) + 6H_2O(l) \longrightarrow C_6H_{12}O_6(s) + 6O_2(g)$$

Given the amount in mol of H_2O, you need to get the mass of $C_6H_{12}O_6$ in grams. Two conversion factors are needed—the mole ratio of $C_6H_{12}O_6$ to H_2O and the molar mass of $C_6H_{12}O_6$.

$$\text{mol } H_2O \times \underbrace{\frac{\text{mol } C_6H_{12}O_6}{\text{mol } H_2O}}_{\text{mol ratio}} \times \underbrace{\frac{\text{g } C_6H_{12}O_6}{\text{mol } C_6H_{12}O_6}}_{\text{molar mass}} = \text{g } C_6H_{12}O_6$$

3 COMPUTE Use the periodic table to compute the molar mass of $C_6H_{12}O_6$.
$$C_6H_{12}O_6 = 180.18 \text{ g/mol}$$

$$3.00 \text{ mol } H_2O \times \frac{1 \text{ mol } C_6H_{12}O_6}{6 \text{ mol } H_2O} \times \frac{180.18 \text{ g } C_6H_{12}O_6}{1 \text{ mol } C_6H_{12}O_6} = 90.1 \text{ g } C_6H_{12}O_6$$

4 EVALUATE The answer is correctly rounded to three significant figures, to match those in 3.00 mol H_2O. The units cancel in the problem, leaving g $C_6H_{12}O_6$ as the units for the answer, which matches the unknown. The answer is reasonable because it is one-half of 180.

SAMPLE PROBLEM 9-3

What mass of carbon dioxide, in grams, is needed to react with 3.00 mol of H_2O in the photosynthetic reaction described in Sample Problem 9-2?

SOLUTION

1 ANALYZE **Given:** amount of H_2O = 3.00 mol
Unknown: mass of CO_2 in grams

2 PLAN The chemical equation from Sample Problem 9-2 is

$$6CO_2(g) + 6H_2O(l) \longrightarrow C_6H_{12}O_6(s) + 6O_2(g).$$

Two conversion factors are needed—the mole ratio of CO_2 to H_2O and the molar mass of CO_2.

$$\text{mol } H_2O \times \underbrace{\frac{\text{mol } CO_2}{\text{mol } H_2O}}_{\text{mol ratio}} \times \underbrace{\frac{\text{g } CO_2}{\text{mol } CO_2}}_{\text{molar mass}} = \text{g } CO_2$$

3 COMPUTE Use the periodic table to compute the molar mass of CO_2.
$$CO_2 = 44.01 \text{ g/mol}$$

$$3.00 \text{ mol } H_2O \times \frac{6 \text{ mol } CO_2}{6 \text{ mol } H_2O} \times \frac{44.01 \text{ g } CO_2}{\text{mol } CO_2} = 132 \text{ g } CO_2$$

4 EVALUATE The answer is rounded correctly to three significant figures to match those in 3.00 mol H_2O. The units cancel to leave g CO_2, which is the unknown. The answer is close to an estimate of 120, which is 3×40.

9-2 When sodium azide is activated in an automobile airbag, nitrogen gas and sodium are produced according to the equation:
$$2NaN_3(s) \longrightarrow 2Na(s) + 3N_2(g).$$
If 0.500 mol of NaN_3 react, what mass in grams of nitrogen would result?

Ans. 21.0 g Na

9-2 Carborundum, SiC, is a hard substance made by combining silicon dioxide with coke (C) as follows:
$$SiO_2(s) + 3C(s) \longrightarrow SiC(s) + 2CO(g).$$
What mass in grams of SiC is formed from the complete reaction of 2.00 mol of carbon?

Ans. 26.7 g SiC

9-3 Zinc metal can be obtained from zinc oxide, ZnO, by reacting the oxide with the element carbon. The products of the reaction are Zn and CO_2. What mass in grams of zinc oxide is needed to react completely with 5.00 mol of carbon?

Ans. 814 g ZnO

9-3 Coal can be converted to methane gas by a process called coal gasification. The equation for the reaction is the following:
$$2C(s) + 2H_2O(l) \longrightarrow CH_4(g) + CO_2(g).$$
What mass in grams of carbon is required to react with water to form 1.00 mol CH_4?

Ans. 24.0 g C

9-3 Sulfur dioxide, SO_2, is an unwelcome result of burning soft coal in power plants. Some of the SO_2 ends up as sulfuric acid in acid precipitation. The net reaction is as follows.
$$2SO_2(g) + O_2(g) + 2H_2O(l) \longrightarrow 2H_2SO_4(l)$$
What mass in grams of SO_2 is needed to react with 1200. g of O_2?

Ans. 4805 g

284

Visual Strategy

FIGURE 9-3 Have students set up a generic calculation scheme in which they show the units of each term and cancel them to produce the result in moles.

Common Misconception

Some students use their calculators inefficiently when they have numbers that are multiplied in the denominator of fractions. For example, a student might calculate the problem

$$\frac{62 \times 70}{15 \times 35}$$

by dividing the product of the numerator by the product of the denominator. This requires that the products be written down. Show students that if the number is in the numerator, it is multiplied, and if it is in the denominator, it is divided. The problem then becomes a single process of pressing the keys: 62 × 70 divided by 15 divided by 35 =

✔ Teaching Tip

The text labels the factor used to convert from grams to moles as the inverted molar mass.

✔ Teaching Tip

If the mass of the *given* substance is known in grams, then the molar mass of the given substance must be known.

PRACTICE

1. When magnesium burns in air, it combines with oxygen to form magnesium oxide according to the following equation.

$$2Mg(s) + O_2(g) \longrightarrow 2MgO(s)$$

What mass in grams of magnesium oxide is produced from 2.00 mol of magnesium?

Answer
80.6 g MgO

2. What mass in grams of oxygen combines with 2.00 mol of magnesium in this same reaction?

Answer
32.0 g O_2

3. What mass of glucose can be produced from a photosynthesis reaction that occurs using 10 mol CO_2?

$$6CO_2(g) + 6H_2O(l) \longrightarrow C_6H_{12}O_6(aq) + 6O_2(g)$$

Answer
300 g $C_6H_{12}O_6$

Conversions of Mass to Amounts in Moles

In these stoichiometric calculations, you are asked to calculate the amount in moles of one substance that will react with or be produced from a given mass of another substance. In this type of problem you are starting with a mass (probably in grams) of some substance. The plan for this conversion is

$$\begin{array}{ccc} \text{mass of} & \text{amount of} & \text{amount of} \\ given \text{ substance} \longrightarrow & given \text{ substance} \longrightarrow & unknown \text{ substance} \\ \text{(in g)} & \text{(in mol)} & \text{(in mol)} \end{array}$$

This route also requires two additional pieces of data: the molar mass of the *given* substance and the mole ratio. The molar mass is determined using masses from the periodic table. To convert the mass of a substance to moles we are using a factor which we will call the inverted molar mass. It is simply one over the molar mass. To solve this type of problem, simply multiply or divide the known quantity by the appropriate conversion factors as follows.

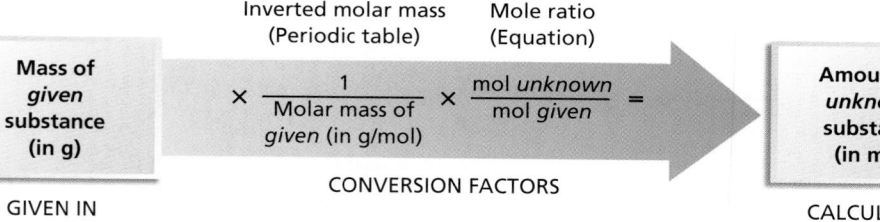

CONVERSION FACTORS

GIVEN IN THE PROBLEM   CALCULATED

FIGURE 9-3 This is a solution plan for problems in which the given quantity is expressed in grams and the unknown quantity is expressed in moles.

SAMPLE PROBLEM 9-4

The first step in the industrial manufacture of nitric acid is the catalytic oxidation of ammonia.

$$NH_3(g) + O_2(g) \longrightarrow NO(g) + H_2O(g) \quad \text{(unbalanced)}$$

The reaction is run using 824 g of NH_3 and excess oxygen.
a. How many moles of NO are formed?
b. How many moles of H_2O are formed?

SOLUTION

1 ANALYZE

Given: mass of $NH_3 = 824$ g
Unknown: a. amount of NO produced (in mol)
   b. amount of H_2O produced (in mol)

2 PLAN

First, write the balanced chemical equation.

$$4NH_3(g) + 5O_2(g) \longrightarrow 4NO(g) + 6H_2O(g)$$

Two conversion factors are needed to solve part (a)—the molar mass of NH_3 and the mole ratio of NO to NH_3. Part (b) starts with the same conversion factor as part (a), but then the mole ratio of H_2O to NH_3 is used to convert to the amount in moles of H_2O. The first conversion factor in each part is the inverted molar mass of NH_3.

$$\text{a. g } NH_3 \times \underbrace{\frac{1 \text{ mol } NH_3}{\text{g } NH_3}}_{\text{inverted molar mass}} \times \underbrace{\frac{\text{mol NO}}{\text{mol } NH_3}}_{\text{mol ratio}} = \text{mol NO}$$

$$\text{b. g } NH_3 \times \underbrace{\frac{1 \text{ mol } NH_3}{\text{g } NH_3}}_{\text{inverted molar mass}} \times \underbrace{\frac{\text{mol } H_2O}{\text{mol } NH_3}}_{\text{mol ratio}} = \text{mol } H_2O$$

3 COMPUTE

Use the periodic table to compute the molar mass of NH_3.
$$NH_3 = 17.04 \text{ g/mol}$$

$$\text{a. } 824 \text{ g } NH_3 \times \frac{1 \text{ mol } NH_3}{17.04 \text{ g } NH_3} \times \frac{4 \text{ mol NO}}{4 \text{ mol } NH_3} = 48.4 \text{ mol NO}$$

$$\text{b. } 824 \text{ g } NH_3 \times \frac{1 \text{ mol } NH_3}{17.04 \text{ g } NH_3} \times \frac{6 \text{ mol } H_2O}{4 \text{ mol } NH_3} = 72.6 \text{ mol } H_2O$$

4 EVALUATE

The answers are correctly given to three significant figures. The units cancel in the two problems to leave mol NO and mol H_2O, respectively, which are the unknowns.

PRACTICE

Oxygen was discovered by Joseph Priestley in 1774 when he heated mercury(II) oxide to decompose it to form its constituent elements.

1. How many moles of mercury(II) oxide, HgO, are needed to produce 125 g of oxygen, O_2?

Answer
7.81 mol HgO

2. How many moles of mercury are produced?

Answer
7.81 mol Hg

STOICHIOMETRY **285**

9-4 Chlorine gas can be produced commercially by passing an electric current through a concentrated solution of sodium chloride (brine). The unbalanced equation is as follows:

$$2NaCl(aq) + 2H_2O(l) \longrightarrow$$
$$2NaOH(aq) + Cl_2(g) + H_2(g)$$

a. If the brine contains 250 g of NaCl, how many moles of Cl_2 can be produced?
b. How many moles of H_2 can be produced?

Ans. **a.** 2.14 mol Cl_2
b. 2.14 mol H_2

9-4 The compound $PtCl_2(NH_3)_2$ is effective as a treatment for some cancers. It is synthesized by the reaction shown in the following equation.

$$K_2PtCl_4(aq) + 2NH_3(aq) \longrightarrow$$
$$2KCl(aq) + PtCl_2(NH_3)_2(aq)$$

a. How many moles of K_2PtCl_4 must react in order to produce 30.0 g of $PtCl_2(NH_3)_2$?

b. How many moles of NH_3 are needed to produce 30.0 g of $PtCl_2(NH_3)_2$?

Ans. **a.** 0.100 mol K_2PtCl_4
b. 0.200 mol NH_3

The sum of the masses on the reactant side of an equation must equal the sum of the masses on the product side. Encourage students to use this fact as a verification strategy to determine if a problem is correctly solved.

Visual Strategy

FIGURE 9-4 Again have students verify the process by means of a unit analysis, and encourage them to return to this figure and Figures 9-2 and 9-3 whenever they are in doubt about how to proceed with a problem.

Alternative Assessment

Ask students to determine the mass in grams of sodium to add to 50. g of fluorine to make sodium fluoride, the salt that is added to drinking water to help stop tooth decay. Students should work without calculators (estimate answers) and proceed according to the methods described in the sample problems. Provide these values as molar masses: Na = 23 g/mol, F = 19 g/mol.

Expected solution:

$$2Na + F_2 \longrightarrow 2NaF$$

$$50.\ g\ F_2 \times \frac{1\ mol\ F_2}{38\ g\ F_2} \times \frac{2\ mol\ Na}{1\ mol\ F_2} \times$$

$$\frac{23\ g\ Na}{1\ mol\ Na} = 61\ g\ Na$$

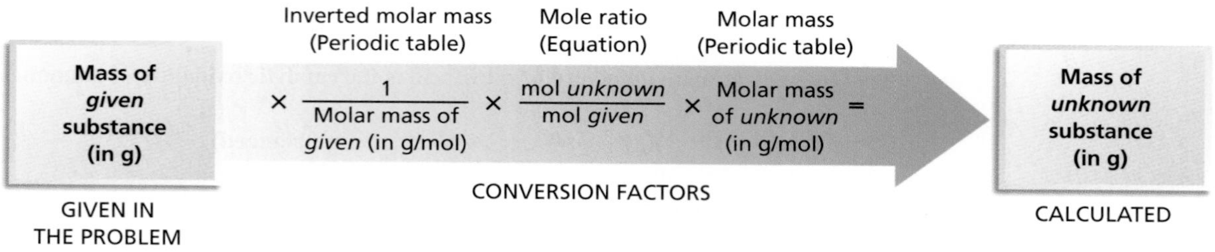

Inverted molar mass (Periodic table) Mole ratio (Equation) Molar mass (Periodic table)

$$\boxed{\begin{array}{c}\text{Mass of}\\ \textit{given}\\ \text{substance}\\ \text{(in g)}\end{array}} \times \frac{1}{\begin{array}{c}\text{Molar mass of}\\ \textit{given}\ \text{(in g/mol)}\end{array}} \times \frac{\text{mol}\ \textit{unknown}}{\text{mol}\ \textit{given}} \times \begin{array}{c}\text{Molar mass}\\ \text{of}\ \textit{unknown}\\ \text{(in g/mol)}\end{array} = \boxed{\begin{array}{c}\text{Mass of}\\ \textit{unknown}\\ \text{substance}\\ \text{(in g)}\end{array}}$$

GIVEN IN THE PROBLEM CONVERSION FACTORS CALCULATED

FIGURE 9-4 This is a solution plan for problems in which the given quantity is expressed in grams and the unknown quantity is also expressed in grams.

Mass-Mass Calculations

Mass-mass calculations are more practical than other mole calculations you have studied. You can never measure moles directly. You are generally required to calculate the amount in moles of a substance from its mass, which you can measure in the lab. Mass-mass problems can be viewed as the combination of the other types of problems. The plan for solving mass-mass problems is

$$\begin{array}{cccc}\text{mass of} & \text{amount of} & \text{amount of} & \text{mass of}\\ \textit{given}\ \text{substance} \longrightarrow & \textit{given}\ \text{substance} \longrightarrow & \textit{unknown}\ \text{substance} \longrightarrow & \textit{unknown}\ \text{substance}\\ \text{(in g)} & \text{(in mol)} & \text{(in mol)} & \text{(in g)}\end{array}$$

Three additional pieces of data are needed to solve mass-mass problems: the molar mass of the *given* substance, the mole ratio, and the molar mass of the *unknown* substance.

SAMPLE PROBLEM 9-5

Tin(II) fluoride, SnF$_2$, is used in some toothpastes. It is made by the reaction of tin with hydrogen fluoride according to the following equation.

$$Sn(s) + 2HF(g) \longrightarrow SnF_2(s) + H_2(g)$$

How many grams of SnF$_2$ are produced from the reaction of 30.00 g of HF with Sn?

SOLUTION

1 ANALYZE **Given:** amount of HF = 30.00 g
Unknown: mass of SnF$_2$ produced in grams

2 PLAN The conversion factors needed are the molar masses of HF and SnF$_2$ and the mole ratio of SnF$_2$ to HF.

inverted molar mass mol ratio molar mass

$$g\ HF \times \frac{1\ mol\ HF}{g\ HF} \times \frac{mol\ SnF_2}{mol\ HF} \times \frac{g\ SnF_2}{mol\ SnF_2} = g\ SnF_2$$

3 COMPUTE Use the periodic table to compute the molar masses of HF and SnF_2.

$$HF = 20.01 \text{ g/mol}$$
$$SnF_2 = 156.71 \text{ g/mol}$$

$$30.00 \text{ g HF} \times \frac{1 \text{ mol HF}}{20.01 \text{ g HF}} \times \frac{1 \text{ mol } SnF_2}{2 \text{ mol HF}} \times \frac{156.71 \text{ g } SnF_2}{1 \text{ mol } SnF_2} = 117.5 \text{ g } SnF_2$$

4 EVALUATE The answer is correctly rounded to four significant figures. The units cancel to leave g SnF_2, which matches the unknown. The answer is close to an estimated value of 120.

PRACTICE

1. Laughing gas (nitrous oxide, N_2O) is sometimes used as an anesthetic in dentistry. It is produced when ammonium nitrate is decomposed according to the following reaction.

$$NH_4NO_3(s) \longrightarrow N_2O(g) + 2H_2O(l)$$

a. How many grams of NH_4NO_3 are required to produce 33.0 g of N_2O?

b. How many grams of water are produced in this reaction?

2. When copper metal is added to silver nitrate in solution, silver metal and copper(II) nitrate are produced. What mass of silver is produced from 100. g of Cu?

3. What mass of aluminum is produced by the decomposition of 5.0 kg of Al_2O_3?

Answer

1. a. 60.0 g NH_4NO_3

b. 27.0 g H_2O

2. 339 g

3. 2.6 kg

SECTION REVIEW

1. Balance the following equation. Then, based on the amount in moles of each reactant or product given, determine the corresponding amount in moles of each of the other reactants and products involved in the reaction.

$$NH_3 + O_2 \longrightarrow N_2 + H_2O$$

a. 4 mol NH_3
b. 4 mol N_2
c. 4.5 mol O_2

2. One reaction that produces hydrogen gas can be represented by the following unbalanced chemical equation.

$$Mg(s) + HCl(aq) \longrightarrow MgCl_2(aq) + H_2(g)$$

a. What mass of HCl is consumed by the reaction of 2.50 mol of magnesium?
b. What mass of each product is produced in part (a)?

3. Acetylene gas (C_2H_2) is produced as a result of the following reaction.

$$CaC_2(s) + 2H_2O(l) \longrightarrow C_2H_2(g) + Ca(OH)_2(aq)$$

a. If 32.0 g of CaC_2 are consumed in this reaction, how many moles of H_2O are needed?
b. How many moles of each product would be formed?

4. When sodium chloride reacts with silver nitrate, silver chloride precipitates. What mass of AgCl is produced from 75.0 g of $AgNO_3$?

5. Acetylene gas, C_2H_2, used in welding, produces an extremely hot flame when it burns in pure oxygen according to the following reaction.

$$2C_2H_2(g) + 5O_2(g) \longrightarrow 4CO_2(g) + 2H_2O(g)$$

How many grams of each product are produced when 2.50×10^4 g of C_2H_2 burns completely?

ADDITIONAL SAMPLE PROBLEMS

9-5 Sodium peroxide reacts vigorously with water to produce sodium hydroxide and oxygen. The unbalanced equation is the following:

$$Na_2O_2(s) + H_2O(l) \longrightarrow NaOH(aq) + O_2(g)$$

a. What mass in grams of O_2 is produced when 50.0 g of Na_2O_2 react?
b. What mass in grams of water is needed to react completely with the Na_2O_2?

Ans. **a.** 30.7 g O_2
b. 11.5 g H_2O

9-5 Milk of magnesia, a suspension of $Mg(OH)_2$ in water, reacts with stomach acid, HCl, in a neutralization reaction.

$$Mg(OH)_2(s) + 2HCl(aq) \longrightarrow 2H_2O(l) + MgCl_2(aq)$$

a. What mass in grams of $MgCl_2$ will be produced if 3.00 g of $Mg(OH)_2$ reacts?
b. What mass in grams of HCl is required to completely react with 3.00 g of $MgCl_2$?

Ans. **a.** 4.90. g $MgCl_2$
b. 3.75 g HCl

SECTION REVIEW

1. $4NH_3 + 3O_2 \longrightarrow 2N_2 + 6H_2O$
a. 3 mol O_2, 2 mol N_2, 6 mol H_2O
b. 8 mol NH_3, 6 mol O_2, 12 mol H_2O
c. 6.0 mol NH_3, 3.0 mol N_2, 9.0 mol H_2O

2. a. 182 g HCl
b. 238 g $MgCl_2$, 5.05 g H_2

3. a. 0.998 mol H_2O
b. 0.499 mol C_2H_2, 0.499 mol $Ca(OH)_2$

4. 63.3 g AgCl

5. 8.47×10^4 g CO_2, 1.73×10^4 g H_2O

Limiting Reactants and Percent Yield

OBJECTIVES

- Describe a method for determining which of two reactants is a limiting reactant.

- Calculate the amount in moles or mass in grams of a product, given the amounts in moles or masses in grams of two reactants, one of which is in excess.

- Distinguish between theoretical yield, actual yield, and percent yield.

- Calculate percent yield, given the actual yield and quantity of a reactant.

In the laboratory, a reaction is rarely carried out with exactly the required amounts of each of the reactants. In most cases, one or more reactants is present in excess; that is, there is more than the exact amount required to react.

Once one of the reactants is used up, no more product can be formed. The substance that is completely used up first in a reaction is called the limiting reactant. *The* **limiting reactant** *is the reactant that limits the amounts of the other reactants that can combine and the amount of product that can form in a chemical reaction. The substance that is not used up completely in a reaction is sometimes called the* **excess reactant.** A limiting reactant may also be referred to as a limiting reagent.

The concept of the limiting reactant is analogous to the relationship between the number of people who want to take a certain airplane flight and the number of seats available in the airplane. If 400 people want to travel on the flight and only 350 seats are available, then only 350 people can go on the flight. The number of seats on the airplane limits the number of people who can travel. There are 50 people in excess.

The same reasoning can be applied to chemical reactions. Consider the reaction between carbon and oxygen to form carbon dioxide.

$$C(s) + O_2(g) \longrightarrow CO_2(g)$$

According to the equation, one mole of carbon reacts with one mole of oxygen to form one mole of carbon dioxide. Suppose you could mix 5 mol of C with 10 mol of O_2 and allow the reaction to take place. Figure 9-5 shows that there is more oxygen than is needed to react with the carbon. Carbon is the limiting reactant in this situation, and it limits the amount of CO_2 that is formed. Oxygen is the excess reactant, and 5 mol of O_2 will be left over at the end of the reaction.

FIGURE 9-5 If you think of a mole as a multiple of molecules and atoms, you can see why the amount of O_2 is in excess.

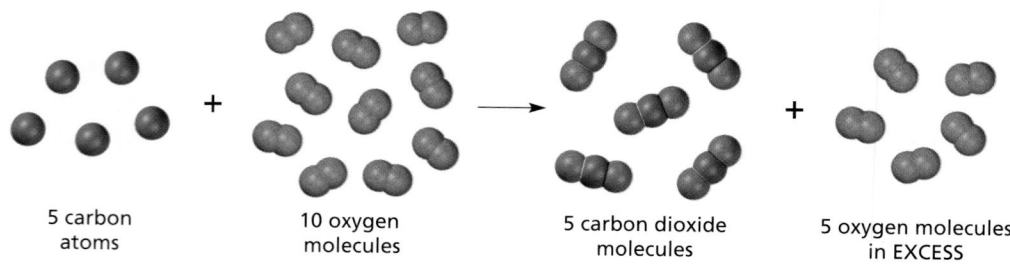

| 5 carbon atoms | 10 oxygen molecules | 5 carbon dioxide molecules | 5 oxygen molecules in EXCESS |

SAMPLE PROBLEM 9-6

Silicon dioxide (quartz) is usually quite unreactive but reacts readily with hydrogen fluoride according to the following equation.

$$SiO_2(s) + 4HF(g) \longrightarrow SiF_4(g) + 2H_2O(l)$$

If 2.0 mol of HF are exposed to 4.5 mol of SiO_2, which is the limiting reactant?

SOLUTION

1 ANALYZE

Given: amount of HF = 2.0 mol
amount of SiO_2 = 4.5 mol
Unknown: limiting reactant

2 PLAN

The given amount of either reactant is used to calculate the required amount of the other reactant. The calculated amount is then compared with the amount actually available, and the limiting reactant can be identified. We will choose to calculate the moles of SiO_2 required by the given amount of HF.

$$\text{mol HF} \times \frac{\text{mol } SiO_2}{\text{mol HF}} = \text{mol } SiO_2 \text{ required}$$

3 COMPUTE

$$2.0 \text{ mol HF} \times \frac{1 \text{ mol } SiO_2}{4 \text{ mol HF}} = 0.50 \text{ mol } SiO_2 \text{ required}$$

Under ideal conditions, the 2.0 mol of HF will require 0.50 mol of SiO_2 for complete reaction. Because the amount of SiO_2 available (4.5 mol) is more than the amount required (0.50 mol), the limiting reactant is HF.

4 EVALUATE

The calculated amount of SiO_2 is correctly given to two significant figures. Because each mole of SiO_2 requires 4 mol of HF, it is reasonable that HF is the limiting reactant because the molar amount of HF available is less than half that of SiO_2.

PRACTICE

1. Some rocket engines use a mixture of hydrazine, N_2H_4, and hydrogen peroxide, H_2O_2, as the propellant. The reaction is given by the following equation.

$$N_2H_4(l) + 2H_2O_2(l) \longrightarrow N_2(g) + 4H_2O(g)$$

a. Which is the limiting reactant in this reaction when 0.750 mol of N_2H_4 is mixed with 0.500 mol of H_2O_2?

b. How much of the excess reactant, in moles, remains unchanged?

c. How much of each product, in moles, is formed?

2. If 20.5 g of chlorine is reacted with 20.5 g of sodium, which reactant is in excess? How do you know?

Answer
1. a. H_2O_2

b. 0.500 mol N_2H_4

c. 0.250 mol N_2, 1.00 mol H_2O

2. Sodium is in excess because only 0.578 mol Na is needed.

Teaching Tip

In part c of Sample Problem 9-7, emphasize that the balanced chemical equation cannot be used to calculate the amounts of substances that do *not* react, only the amounts that *do* react. The amount of the excess reactant left over must be determined as the difference between the amount originally present and the amount that reacts.

ADDITIONAL
SAMPLE
PROBLEMS

9-7 Aspirin, $C_9H_8O_4$, is synthesized by the reaction of salicylic acid, $C_7H_6O_3$, with acetic anhydride, $C_4H_6O_3$.

$$2C_7H_6O_3 + C_4H_6O_3 \longrightarrow$$
$$2C_9H_8O_4 + H_2O$$

a. When 20.0 g of $C_7H_6O_3$ and 20.0 g of $C_4H_6O_3$ react, which is the limiting reagent? How many moles of the excess reactant are used when the reaction is complete?
b. What mass in grams of aspirin is formed?

Ans. **a.** $C_7H_6O_3$, 0.0724 mol
b. 26.1 g

9-7 The unbalanced equation for the reaction of calcium phosphate with sulfuric acid is as follows:

$$Ca_3(PO_4)_2(s) + H_2SO_4(aq) \longrightarrow$$
$$CaSO_4(s) + H_3PO_4(aq)$$

If 250 g of $Ca_3(PO_4)_2$ react with 3 mol of H_2SO_4, will 3 mol of $CaSO_4$ be formed? Explain your answer by identifying the limiting reactant and calculating the number of moles and the mass in grams of $CaSO_4$ that could be obtained.

Ans. No, $Ca_3(PO_4)_2$ is the limiting reactant. Therefore, the reaction produces 2.42 mol or 329 g of $CaSO_4$.

The black oxide of iron, Fe_3O_4, occurs in nature as the mineral magnetite. This substance can also be made in the laboratory by the reaction between red-hot iron and steam according to the following equation.

$$3Fe(s) + 4H_2O(g) \longrightarrow Fe_3O_4(s) + 4H_2(g)$$

a. When 36.0 g of H_2O is mixed with 167 g of Fe, which is the limiting reactant?
b. What mass in grams of black iron oxide is produced?
c. What mass in grams of excess reactant remains when the reaction is completed?

SOLUTION

1 *ANALYZE*

Given: mass of H_2O = 36.0 g
mass of Fe = 167 g
Unknown: limiting reactant
mass of Fe_3O_4, in grams
mass of excess reactant remaining

2 *PLAN*

a. First convert both given masses in grams to amounts in moles. Choose one reactant and calculate the needed amount of the other to determine which is the limiting reactant. We have chosen Fe. The mole ratio from the balanced equation is 3 mol Fe for every 4 mol H_2O.

inverted molar mass

$$\text{g Fe} \times \frac{1 \text{ mol Fe}}{\text{g Fe}} = \text{mol Fe available}$$

inverted molar mass

$$\text{g } H_2O \times \frac{1 \text{ mol } H_2O}{\text{g } H_2O} = \text{mol } H_2O \text{ available}$$

mol ratio

$$\text{mol Fe} \times \frac{\text{mol } H_2O}{\text{mol Fe}} = \text{mol } H_2O \text{ required}$$

b. To find the maximum amount of Fe_3O_4 that can be produced, the given amount in moles of the limiting reactant must be used in a simple stoichiometric problem.

mol ratio   molar mass

$$\text{limiting reactant (in mol)} \times \frac{\text{mol } Fe_3O_4}{\text{mol limiting reactant}} \times \frac{\text{g } Fe_3O_4}{\text{mol } Fe_3O_4} = \text{g } Fe_3O_4 \text{ produced}$$

c. To find the amount of excess reactant remaining, the amount of the excess reactant that is consumed must first be determined. The given amount in moles of the limiting reactant must be used in a simple stoichiometric problem.

$$\begin{array}{l}\text{limiting reactant} \\ \text{(in mol)}\end{array} \times \frac{\text{mol excess reactant}}{\text{mol limiting reactant}} \times \frac{\text{g excess reactant}}{\text{mol excess reactant}} = \begin{array}{l}\text{g excess reactant} \\ \text{consumed}\end{array}$$

The amount of excess reactant remaining can then be found by subtracting the amount consumed from the amount originally present.

original g excess reactant − g excess reactant consumed = g excess reactant remaining

3 COMPUTE Use the periodic table to determine the molar masses of H_2O, Fe, and Fe_3O_4.

$H_2O = 18.02$ g/mol
$Fe = 55.85$ g/mol
$Fe_3O_4 = 231.55$ g/mol

$$36.0 \text{ g } H_2O \times \frac{1 \text{ mol } H_2O}{18.02 \text{ g } H_2O} = 2.00 \text{ mol } H_2O$$

$$167 \text{ g Fe} \times \frac{1 \text{ mol Fe}}{55.85 \text{ g Fe}} = 2.99 \text{ mol Fe}$$

$$2.99 \text{ mol Fe} \times \frac{4 \text{ mol } H_2O}{3 \text{ mol Fe}} = 3.99 \text{ mol } H_2O \text{ required}$$

a. The required 3.99 mol of H_2O is more than the 2.00 mol of H_2O available, so H_2O is the limiting reactant.

b. $2.00 \text{ mol } H_2O \times \dfrac{1 \text{ mol } Fe_3O_4}{4 \text{ mol } H_2O} \times \dfrac{231.55 \text{ g } Fe_3O_4}{\text{mol } Fe_3O_4} = 116 \text{ g } Fe_3O_4$

c. $2.00 \text{ mol } H_2O \times \dfrac{3 \text{ mol Fe}}{4 \text{ mol } H_2O} \times \dfrac{55.85 \text{ g Fe}}{\text{mol Fe}} = 83.8 \text{ g Fe consumed}$

167 g Fe originally present − 83.8 g Fe consumed = 83.2 g Fe remaining

4 EVALUATE Three significant digits are carried through each calculation. The result of the final subtraction is rounded to match the significance of the least accurately known number, that is, the units digit for the original mass of Fe. The mass of Fe_3O_4 is close to an estimated answer of 115, which is one-half of 230. The amount of the limiting reactant, H_2O, is about one-half the amount needed to use all of the Fe, so about one-half the Fe remains unreacted.

PRACTICE

1. Zinc and sulfur react to form zinc sulfide according to the following equation.

$$8Zn(s) + S_8(s) \longrightarrow 8ZnS(s)$$

a. If 2.00 mol of Zn are heated with 1.00 mol of S_8, identify the limiting reactant.

b. How many moles of excess reactant remain?

c. How many moles of the product are formed?

2. Carbon reacts with steam, H_2O, at high temperatures to produce hydrogen and carbon monoxide.

a. If 2.40 mol of carbon are exposed to 3.10 mol of steam, identify the limiting reactant.

b. How many moles of each product are formed?

c. What mass of each product is formed?

CHEMISTRY
Module 5: Equations and Stoichiometry

Answer
1. a. Zn

   b. 0.75 mol S_8 remains

   c. 2.00 mol ZnS

2. a. carbon

   b. 2.40 mol H_2 and 2.40 mol CO

   c. 4.85 g H_2 and 67.2 g CO

✔Teaching Tip

Fe_3O_4 actually contains iron in both the +2 and +3 oxidation states. Its actual formula can be written as $Fe(II)Fe(III)_2O_4$.

Problem-Solving Practice HOLT **ChemFile**

Chapter 9 of the Mini-Guide to Problem Solving (also found on the One-Stop Planner CD-ROM) includes more worked-out samples and additional practice problems involving limiting reactants.

CHEMISTRY

Module 5: Equations and Stoichiometry

Topic: Limiting Reactants
Sections **i** and **j** of this engaging tutorial review and reinforce understanding of limiting reactants.

Note: This activity should *not* be done in the chemistry lab. It can be done at home or in a home economics room at school.

Background

Students soon realize that putting together the ingredients for a batch of cookies is analogous to measuring known masses of reactants for a chemical reaction. The yield from the recipe is 24 cookies. To increase the yield, the ingredients may be increased proportionally. Just as the number of cookies that can be produced is limited by the amounts of the ingredients available to use, the amount of product that can be obtained from a chemical reaction is limited by the amount of each reactant available to react.

Discussion Answers

1. a. 1 dozen eggs: 188 cookies
24 tsp. of vanilla: 576 cookies
82 tsp. of salt: 3936 cookies
84 tsp. of baking soda: 4032 cookies
3 cups of chocolate chips: 54 cookies
11 cups of sugar: 528 cookies
4 cups of brown sugar: 192 cookies
4 sticks of margarine: 72 cookies
b. chocolate chips and margarine
c. 54 cookies

Wear oven mitts when handling heated items.

Materials

- 1/2 cup sugar
- 1/2 cup brown sugar
- 1 1/3 stick margarine (at room temperature)
- 1 egg
- 1/2 tsp. of salt
- 1 tsp. vanilla
- 1/2 tsp. baking soda
- 1 1/2 cup flour
- 1 1/3 cup chocolate chips
- mixing bowl
- mixing spoon
- measuring spoons and cups
- cookie sheet
- oven preheated to 350°F

Procedure

1. In the mixing bowl, combine the sugars and margarine together until smooth. (An electric mixer will make this process go much faster.)

2. Add the egg, salt, and vanilla. Mix well.

3. Stir in the baking soda, flour, and chocolate chips. Chill the dough for an hour in the refrigerator for best results.

4. Divide the dough into 24 small balls about 3 cm in diameter. Place the balls on an ungreased cookie sheet.

5. Bake at 350°F for about 10 minutes, or until the cookies are light brown.

Yield: 24 cookies

Discussion

1. Suppose you are given the following amounts of ingredients:
1 dozen eggs
24 tsp. of vanilla

1 lb. (82 tsp.) of salt
1 lb. (84 tsp.) of baking soda
3 cups of chocolate chips
5 lb. (11 cups) of sugar
2 lb. (4 cups) of brown sugar
1 lb. (4 sticks) of margarine

a. For each ingredient, calculate how many cookies could be prepared if all of that ingredient were consumed. (For example, the recipe shows that using 1 egg—with the right amounts of the other ingredients—yields 24 cookies. How many cookies can you make if the recipe is increased proportionately for 12 eggs?)

b. To determine the limiting reactant for the new ingredients list, identify which ingredients will result in the fewest number of cookies.

c. What is the maximum number of cookies that can be produced from the new amounts of ingredients?

Percent Yield

The amounts of products calculated in the stoichiometric problems in this chapter so far represent theoretical yields. *The **theoretical yield** is the maximum amount of product that can be produced from a given amount of reactant.* In most chemical reactions, the amount of product obtained is less than the theoretical yield. There are many reasons for this. Some of the reactant may be used in competing side reactions that reduce the amount of the desired product. Also, once a product is formed, it often is usually collected in impure form, and some of the product is often lost during the purification process. *The measured amount of a product obtained from a reaction is called the **actual yield** of that product.*

Chemists are usually interested in the efficiency of a reaction. The efficiency is expressed by comparing the actual and theoretical yields. *The **percent yield** is the ratio of the actual yield to the theoretical yield, multiplied by 100.*

$$\text{percent yield} = \frac{\text{actual yield}}{\text{theoretical yield}} \times 100$$

SAMPLE PROBLEM 9-8

Chlorobenzene, C_6H_5Cl, is used in the production of many important chemicals, such as aspirin, dyes, and disinfectants. One industrial method of preparing chlorobenzene is to react benzene, C_6H_6, with chlorine, as represented by the following equation.

$$C_6H_6(l) + Cl_2(g) \longrightarrow C_6H_5Cl(s) + HCl(g)$$

When 36.8 g of C_6H_6 react with an excess of Cl_2, the actual yield of C_6H_5Cl is 38.8 g. What is the percent yield of C_6H_5Cl?

SOLUTION

1 ANALYZE

Given: mass of C_6H_6 = 36.8 g
mass of Cl_2 = excess
actual yield of C_6H_5Cl = 38.8 g
Unknown: percent yield of C_6H_5Cl

2 PLAN

First do a mass-mass calculation to find the theoretical yield of C_6H_5Cl.

$$\text{g } C_6H_6 \times \underbrace{\frac{\text{mol } C_6H_6}{\text{g } C_6H_6}}_{\text{inverted molar mass}} \times \underbrace{\frac{\text{mol } C_6H_5Cl}{\text{mol } C_6H_6}}_{\text{mol ratio}} \times \underbrace{\frac{\text{g } C_6H_5Cl}{\text{mol } C_6H_5Cl}}_{\text{molar mass}} = \text{g } C_6H_5Cl \text{ (theoretical yield)}$$

Then the percent yield can be found.

$$\text{percent yield } C_6H_5Cl = \frac{\text{actual yield}}{\text{theoretical yield}} \times 100$$

Teaching Tip

A chemical reaction system is not as simple as the balanced equation implies. Competing side reactions may interfere with the production of the desired product.

Common Misconception

Students often think all reactions go to completion. In Chapter 18, they will learn that reversible reactions and equilibrium systems limit the masses of products in chemical reactions. Reintroduce the concept of percent yield at that time.

Class Discussion

Discuss the results of the demonstration on page 276 in terms of percent yield. The theoretical yield for a 2.000 g sample of sodium carbonate is calculated as follows.

$$2.000 \text{ g } Na_2CO_3 \times \frac{1 \text{ mol } Na_2CO_3}{106.01 \text{ g } Na_2CO_3}$$

$$\frac{2 \text{ mol } NaCl}{1 \text{ mol } Na_2CO_3} \times \frac{58.45 \text{ g } NaCl}{1 \text{ mol } NaCl}$$

$$= 2.205 \text{ g } NaCl$$

The actual yield is typically 2.100 g. Therefore,

$$\% \text{ yield} = \frac{2.100 \text{ g}}{2.205 \text{ g}} \times 100 = 95.24\%$$

 Reading Skill-Builder

DISCUSSION Discuss with students the difference between *theoretical yield* and *actual yield*. Have them speculate as to what factors might cause the actual yield to be less than the theoretical yield.

9-8 Huge quantities of sulfur dioxide are produced from zinc sulfide by means of the following reaction.

$2ZnS(s) + 3O_2(g) \longrightarrow$
$\qquad 2ZnO(s) + 2SO_2(g)$

If the typical yield is 86.78%, how much SO_2 should be expected if 4897 g of ZnS are used?

Ans. 2794 g

Problem-
Solving
Practice

Chapter 10 of the Mini-Guide to Problem Solving (also found on the One-Stop Planner CD-ROM) includes more worked-out samples and additional practice problems involving percent yield.

SECTION REVIEW

1. a. O_2 is the limiting reactant.
b. 0.667 mol CS_2 remains.
c. 0.333 mol CO_2, 0.667 mol SO_2

2. a. H_2O is the limiting reactant.
b. 0.333 mol Mg remains
c. 19.4 g $Mg(OH)_2$, 0.673 g H_2

3. a. CuO is the limiting reactant.
b. 15.9 g Cu

4. 93.7%

---

3 COMPUTE   Use the periodic table to determine the molar masses of C_6H_6 and C_6H_5Cl.
$$C_6H_6 = 78.12 \text{ g/mol}$$
$$C_6H_5Cl = 112.56 \text{ g/mol}$$

$$36.8 \text{ g } C_6H_6 \times \frac{1 \text{ mol } C_6H_6}{78.12 \text{ g } C_6H_6} \times \frac{1 \text{ mol } C_6H_5Cl}{1 \text{ mol } C_6H_6} \times \frac{112.56 \text{ g } C_6H_5Cl}{\text{mol } C_6H_5Cl} = 53.0 \text{ g } C_6H_5Cl$$
$$\text{(theoretical yield)}$$

$$\text{percent yield} = \frac{38.8 \text{ g}}{53.0 \text{ g}} \times 100 = 73.2\%$$

4 EVALUATE   The answer is correctly rounded to three significant figures to match those in 36.8 g C_6H_6. The units have canceled correctly. The theoretical yield is close to an estimated value of 50 g, (one-half of 100 g). The percent yield is close to an estimated value of 80%, (40/50 × 100).

PRACTICE

1. Methanol can be produced through the reaction of CO and H_2 in the presence of a catalyst.

$$CO(g) + 2H_2(g) \xrightarrow{\text{catalyst}} CH_3OH(l)$$

If 75.0 g of CO reacts to produce 68.4 g CH_3OH, what is the percent yield of CH_3OH?

Answer
79.8%

2. Aluminum reacts with excess copper(II) sulfate according to the reaction given below. If 1.85 g of Al react and the percent yield of Cu is 56.6%, what mass of Cu is produced?

$$Al(s) + CuSO_4(aq) \longrightarrow Al_2(SO_4)_3(aq) + Cu(s) \text{ (unbalanced)}$$

Answer
3.70 g

SECTION REVIEW

1. Carbon disulfide burns in oxygen to yield carbon dioxide and sulfur dioxide according to the following chemical equation.

$$CS_2(l) + 3O_2(g) \longrightarrow CO_2(g) + 2SO_2(g)$$

a. If 1.00 mol of CS_2 is combined with 1.00 mol of O_2, identify the limiting reactant.
b. How many moles of excess reactant remain?
c. How many moles of each product are formed?

2. Metallic magnesium reacts with steam to produce magnesium hydroxide and hydrogen gas.
a. If 16.2 g of Mg are heated with 12.0 g of H_2O, what is the limiting reactant?
b. How many moles of the excess reactant are left?
c. How many grams of each product are formed?

3. a. What is the limiting reactant when 19.9 g of CuO are exposed to 2.02 g of H_2 according to the following equation?

$$CuO(s) + H_2(g) \longrightarrow Cu(s) + H_2O(g)$$

b. How many grams of Cu are produced?

4. Quicklime, CaO, can be prepared by roasting limestone, $CaCO_3$, according to the following reaction.

$$CaCO_3(s) \xrightarrow{\Delta} CaO(s) + CO_2(g).$$

When 2.00×10^3 g of $CaCO_3$ are heated, the actual yield of CaO is 1.05×10^3 g. What is the percent yield?

CHAPTER SUMMARY

9-1
• Reaction stoichiometry involves the mass relationships between reactants and products in a chemical reaction.
• A *mole ratio* is the conversion factor that relates the amount in moles of any two substances in a chemical reaction. The mole ratio is derived from the balanced equation.

• Amount of a substance is expressed in moles, and mass of a substance is expressed using mass units such as grams, kilograms, and milligrams.
• Mass and amount of substance are quantities, whereas moles and grams are units.
• A balanced chemical equation is necessary to solve any stoichiometric problem.

Vocabulary
composition stoichiometry (275)   mole ratio (276)   reaction stoichiometry (275)

9-2
• In an ideal stoichiometric calculation, the mass or the amount of any reactant or product can be calculated if the balanced chemical equation and

the mass or amount of any other reactant or product are known.

9-3
• In actual reactions, the reactants are usually combined in proportions different from the precise proportions required for complete reaction.
• The limiting reactant controls the maximum possible amount of product formed.
• Given certain quantities of reactants, the quantity of the product is always less than the maximum

possible. Percent yield shows the relationship between the theoretical yield and actual yield for the product of a reaction.

$$\text{percent yield} = \frac{\text{actual yield}}{\text{theoretical yield}} \times 100$$

Vocabulary
actual yield (293)   limiting reactant (288)   percent yield (293)   theoretical yield (293)
excess reactant (288)

REVIEWING CONCEPTS

1. a. Explain the concept of *mole ratio* as used in reaction-stoichiometry problems.
b. What is the source of this value? (9-1)

2. For each of the following chemical equations, write all possible mole ratios:
a. $2Ca + O_2 \longrightarrow 2CaO$
b. $Mg + 2HF \longrightarrow MgF_2 + H_2$ (9-1)

3. a. What is molar mass?
b. What is its role in reaction stoichiometry? (9-2)

4. Distinguish between ideal and real stoichiometric calculations. (9-3)

5. Distinguish between the limiting reactant and the excess reactant in a chemical reaction. (9-3)

6. a. Distinguish between the theoretical and actual yields in stoichiometric calculations.
b. How do the values of the theoretical and actual yields generally compare? (9-3)

7. What is the percent yield of a reaction? (9-3)

8. Why are actual yields generally less than those calculated theoretically? (9-3)

REVIEW ANSWERS

1. a. A mole ratio is a conversion factor that relates the number of moles of any two substances involved in a chemical reaction.
b. Mole ratios are obtained from the chemical equation.

2. a. $\dfrac{2 \text{ mol Ca}}{1 \text{ mol } O_2}, \dfrac{2 \text{ mol Ca}}{2 \text{ mol CaO}}$

$\dfrac{1 \text{ mol } O_2}{2 \text{ mol Ca}}, \dfrac{1 \text{ mol } O_2}{2 \text{ mol CaO}}$

$\dfrac{2 \text{ mol CaO}}{2 \text{ mol Ca}}, \dfrac{2 \text{ mol CaO}}{1 \text{ mol } O_2}$

b.
$\dfrac{1 \text{ mol Mg}}{2 \text{ mol HF}}, \dfrac{1 \text{ mol Mg}}{1 \text{ mol } MgF_2}, \dfrac{1 \text{ mol Mg}}{1 \text{ mol } H_2}$

$\dfrac{2 \text{ mol HF}}{1 \text{ mol Mg}}, \dfrac{2 \text{ mol HF}}{1 \text{ mol } MgF_2}, \dfrac{2 \text{ mol HF}}{1 \text{ mol } H_2}$

$\dfrac{1 \text{ mol } MgF_2}{1 \text{ mol Mg}}, \dfrac{1 \text{ mol } MgF_2}{2 \text{ mol HF}}, \dfrac{1 \text{ mol } MgF_2}{1 \text{ mol } H_2}$

$\dfrac{1 \text{ mol } H_2}{1 \text{ mol Mg}}, \dfrac{1 \text{ mol } H_2}{2 \text{ mol HF}}, \dfrac{1 \text{ mol } H_2}{1 \text{ mol } MgF_2}$

3. a. the mass in grams of one mole of a substance
b. the conversion factor that relates the mass of a substance to the number of moles of that substance

4. Ideal stoichiometry calculations do not account for factors that can affect the relative amounts of reactants needed or products produced in chemical reactions; they deal with the amounts of reactants or products under ideal conditions. Real stoichiometry calculations account for actual conditions.

5. The limiting reactant is the reactant that controls the amount of product formed in a chemical reaction. The excess reactant is the substance that is not used up completely in a reaction.

6. a. The theoretical yield is the maximum amount of product that can be produced from a given amount of reactant. The actual yield is the measured amount obtained.
b. actual yields are less

7. The percent yield is the ratio of the actual yield to the theoretical yield multiplied by 100.

8. because reactions sometimes do not go to completion; impure reactants produce less product than expected; competing side reactions may consume some of the reactants; some of the product may be lost when it is purified

9.

$$\frac{105.99 \text{ g Na}_2\text{CO}_3}{1 \text{ mol Na}_2\text{CO}_3} , \frac{1 \text{ mol Na}_2\text{CO}_3}{105.99 \text{ g Na}_2\text{CO}_3}$$

$$\frac{74.10 \text{ g Ca(OH)}_2}{1 \text{ mol Ca(OH)}_2} , \frac{1 \text{ mol Ca(OH)}_2}{74.10 \text{ g Ca(OH)}_2}$$

$$\frac{40.00 \text{ g NaOH}}{1 \text{ mol NaOH}} , \frac{1 \text{ mol NaOH}}{40.00 \text{ g NaOH}}$$

$$\frac{100.09 \text{ g CaCO}_3}{1 \text{ mol CaCO}_3} , \frac{1 \text{ mol CaCO}_3}{100.09 \text{ g NaOH}}$$

10. a. 5.0 mol H_2 **b.** 2.5 mol O_2

11. a. 15.8 mol O_2
b. 9.00 mol CO_2, 13.5 mol H_2O

12. 575 g Na, 886 g Cl_2

13. a. 75.1 mol CO
b. 50.1 mol Fe, 75.1 mol CO_2

14. 8.742×10^4 g CO, 1.261×10^4 g H_2

15. a. 1.10×10^3 g NO_2
b. 720. g NO

16. a. 42.04 mol NaOH
b. 21.02 mol Na_2CO_3, 21.02 mol H_2O

17. a. 463 g NaBr   **b.** 845 g AgBr

18. a. 3.058 mol $NaHCO_3$
b. 3.058 mol CO_2, 1.530 mol Na_2SO_4, 3.058 mol H_2O

PROBLEMS

General Stoichiometry

Do not assume that equations without listed coefficients are balanced.

9. Given the chemical equation $Na_2CO_3(aq) + Ca(OH)_2(s) \longrightarrow 2NaOH(aq) + CaCO_3(s)$, determine to two decimal places the molar masses of all substances involved, and then write them as conversion factors.

10. Hydrogen and oxygen react under a specific set of conditions to produce water according to the following: $2H_2(g) + O_2(g) \longrightarrow 2H_2O(g)$.
a. How many moles of hydrogen would be required to produce 5.0 mol of water?
b. How many moles of oxygen would be required? (Hint: See Sample Problem 9-1.)

11. a. If 4.50 mol of ethane, C_2H_6, undergo combustion according to the unbalanced equation $C_2H_6 + O_2 \longrightarrow CO_2 + H_2O$, how many moles of oxygen are required?
b. How many moles of each product are formed?

12. Sodium chloride is produced from its elements through a synthesis reaction. What mass of each reactant would be required to produce 25.0 mol of sodium chloride?

13. Iron is generally produced from iron ore through the following reaction in a blast furnace: $Fe_2O_3(s) + CO(g) \longrightarrow Fe(s) + CO_2(g)$.
a. If 4.00 kg of Fe_2O_3 are available to react, how many moles of CO are needed?
b. How many moles of each product are formed?

14. Methanol, CH_3OH, is an important industrial compound that is produced from the following reaction: $CO(g) + H_2(g) \longrightarrow CH_3OH(g)$. What mass of each reactant would be needed to produce 100.0 kg of methanol? (Hint: See Sample Problem 9-5.)

15. Nitrogen combines with oxygen in the atmosphere during lightning flashes to form nitrogen monoxide, NO, which then reacts further with O_2 to produce nitrogen dioxide, NO_2.
a. What mass of NO_2 is formed when NO reacts with 384 g of O_2?
b. How many grams of NO are required to react with this amount of O_2?

16. As early as 1938, the use of NaOH was suggested as a means of removing CO_2 from the cabin of a spacecraft according to the following reaction: $NaOH + CO_2 \longrightarrow Na_2CO_3 + H_2O$.
a. If the average human body discharges 925.0 g of CO_2 per day, how many moles of NaOH are needed each day for each person in the spacecraft?
b. How many moles of each product are formed?

17. The double-replacement reaction between silver nitrate and sodium bromide produces silver bromide, a component of photographic film.
a. If 4.50 mol of silver nitrate reacts, what mass of sodium bromide is required?
b. What mass of silver bromide is formed?

18. In a soda-acid fire extinguisher, concentrated sulfuric acid reacts with sodium hydrogen carbonate to produce carbon dioxide, sodium sulfate, and water.
a. How many moles of sodium hydrogen carbonate would be needed to react with 150.0 g of sulfuric acid?
b. How many moles of each product would be formed?

19. Sulfuric acid reacts with sodium hydroxide according to the following:

$$H_2SO_4 + NaOH \longrightarrow Na_2SO_4 + H_2O.$$

a. Balance the equation for this reaction.
b. What mass of H_2SO_4 would be required to react with 0.75 mol of NaOH?
c. What mass of each product is formed by this reaction? (Hint: See Sample Problem 9-2.)

20. Copper reacts with silver nitrate through single replacement.
a. If 2.25 g of silver are produced from the reaction, how many moles of copper(II) nitrate are also produced?
b. How many moles of each reactant are required in this reaction? (Hint: See Sample Problem 9-4.)

21. Aspirin, $C_9H_8O_4$, is produced through the following reaction of salicylic acid, $C_7H_6O_3$, and acetic anhydride, $C_4H_6O_3$: $C_7H_6O_3(s) + C_4H_6O_3(l) \longrightarrow C_9H_8O_4(s) + HC_2H_3O_2(l)$.
a. What mass of aspirin (in kg) could be produced from 75.0 mol of salicylic acid?

b. What mass of acetic anhydride (in kg) would be required?

c. At 20°C, how many liters of acetic acid, $HC_2H_3O_2$, would be formed? The density of $HC_2H_3O_2$ is 1.05 g/cm^3.

Limiting Reactant

22. Given the reactant amounts specified in each chemical equation, determine the limiting reactant in each case:

a. HCl + $NaOH$ $\longrightarrow$ $NaCl + H_2O$
   2.0 mol   2.5 mol

b. Zn + $2HCl$ $\longrightarrow$ $ZnCl_2 + H_2$
   2.5 mol   6.0 mol

c. $2Fe(OH)_3 + 3H_2SO_4 \longrightarrow Fe_2(SO_4)_3 + 6H_2O$
   4.0 mol   6.5 mol

(Hint: See Sample Problem 9-6.)

23. For each reaction specified in Problem 22, determine the amount in moles of excess reactant that remains. (Hint: See Sample Problem 9-7.)

24. For each reaction specified in Problem 22, calculate the amount in moles of each product formed.

25. a. If 2.50 mol of copper and 5.50 mol of silver nitrate are available to react by single replacement, identify the limiting reactant.

b. Determine the amount in moles of excess reactant remaining.

c. Determine the amount in moles of each product formed.

d. Determine the mass of each product formed.

26. Sulfuric acid reacts with aluminum hydroxide by double replacement.

a. If 30.0 g of sulfuric acid react with 25.0 g of aluminum hydroxide, identify the limiting reactant.

b. Determine the mass of excess reactant remaining.

c. Determine the mass of each product formed. Assume 100% yield.

27. The energy used to power one of the Apollo lunar missions was supplied by the following overall reaction: $2N_2H_4 + (CH_3)_2N_2H_2 + 3N_2O_4$ $\longrightarrow 6N_2 + 2CO_2 + 8H_2O$. For the phase of the mission when the lunar module ascended from the surface of the moon, a total of 1200. kg of

N_2H_4 were available to react with 1000. kg of $(CH_3)_2N_2H_2$ and 4500. kg of N_2O_4.

a. For this portion of the flight, which of the allocated components was used up first?

b. How much water, in kilograms, was put into the lunar atmosphere through this reaction?

Percent Yield

28. Calculate the indicated quantity for each of the various chemical reactions given:

a. theoretical yield = 20.0 g, actual yield = 15.0 g, percent yield = ?

b. theoretical yield = 1.0 g, percent yield = 90.0%, actual yield = ?

c. theoretical yield = 5.00 g, actual yield = 4.75 g, percent yield = ?

d. theoretical yield = 3.45 g, percent yield = 48.0%, actual yield = ?

29. The percentage yield for the reaction

$PCl_3 + Cl_2 \longrightarrow PCl_5$

is 83.2%. What mass of PCl_5 is expected from the reaction of 73.7 g of PCl_3 with excess chlorine?

30. The Ostwald Process for producing nitric acid from ammonia consists of the following steps:

$4NH_3(g) + 5O_2(g) \longrightarrow 4NO(g) + 6H_2O(g)$
$2NO(g) + O_2(g) \longrightarrow 2NO_2(g)$
$3NO_2(g) + H_2O(g) \longrightarrow 2HNO_3(aq) + NO(g)$

If the yield in each step is 94.0%, how many grams of nitric acid can be produced from 5.00 kg of ammonia?

MIXED REVIEW

31. Magnesium is obtained from sea water. $Ca(OH)_2$ is added to sea water to precipitate $Mg(OH)_2$. The precipitate is filtered and reacted with HCl to produce $MgCl_2$. The $MgCl_2$ is electrolyzed to produce Mg and Cl_2. If 185.0 g of magnesium are recovered from 1000. g of $MgCl_2$, what is the percent yield for this reaction?

32. Phosphate baking powder is a mixture of starch, sodium hydrogen carbonate, and calcium dihydrogen phosphate. When mixed with water, phosphate baking powder releases carbon dioxide gas, causing a dough or batter to bubble and rise.

19. a. $H_2SO_4 + 2NaOH \longrightarrow$
       $Na_2SO_4 + 2H_2O$
   b. 37 g H_2SO_4
   c. 53 g Na_2SO_4, 14 g H_2O

20. a. 0.0104 mol $Cu(NO_3)_2$
   b. 0.0104 mol Cu, 0.0209 mol $AgNO_3$

21. a. 13.5 kg $C_9H_8O_4$
   b. 7.66 kg $C_4H_6O_3$
   c. 4.29 L $HC_2H_3O_2$

22. a. HCl is the limiting reactant.
   b. Zn is the limiting reactant.
   c. $Fe(OH)_3$ is the limiting reactant.

23. a. 0.5 mol excess NaOH
   b. 1.0 mol excess HCl
   c. 0.5 mol excess H_2SO_4

24. a. 2.0 mol NaCl, 2.0 mol H_2O
   b. 2.5 mol $ZnCl_2$, 2.5 mol H_2
   c. 2.0 mol $Fe_2(SO_4)_3$, 12 mol H_2O

25. a. Cu is the limiting reactant.
   b. 0.50 mol $AgNO_3$
   c. 2.50 mol $Cu(NO_3)_2$, 5.00 mol Ag
   d. 460. g $Cu(NO_3)_2$, 539. g Ag

26. a. H_2SO_4 is the limiting reactant
   b. 9.09 g excess $Al(OH)_3$
   c. 34.9 g $Al_2(SO_4)_3$, 11.0 g H_2O

27. a. N_2O_4 was used up first.
   b. 2.350×10^3 kg H_2O

28. a. 75.0%   c. 95.0%
   b. 0.90 g   d. 1.66 g

29. 93.2 g PCl_5

30. 1.02×10^4 g HNO_3

31. 72.48%

32. 10.7 g baking powder

33. 710. g CH_4

34. 1740. g CH_4

35. 3.13 L water vapor

36. 3.23 g Au

37. The chemical equation shows the theoretical yield of product to be expected under ideal conditions. Because it is rare for a reaction to meet ideal conditions, the

actual yield is usually less than that predicted by the equation.

38. To ensure that all magnesium is converted to MgO, the reaction should be carried out using pure oxygen, not air, because Mg could react with N_2 in air to form Mg_3N_2. The pure oxygen should be in excess. Any leftover O_2 should be recycled for use with a new charge of Mg.

39. A percent yield greater than 100% is not possible because the actual yield can never be greater than the theoretical yield, the yield predicted by the chemical equation. If the calculated percent yield is greater than 100%, it may be because the product is not dry or it contains impurities, for example, some unreacted reactant or the product of a competing reaction.

40. A smoldering campfire is not getting enough oxygen to produce the products of complete combustion, CO_2 and H_2O. Blowing on the smoldering fire may increase the amount of oxygen to the stoichiometric amount and cause the fire to burn completely.

41. a. 61.2%
b. 58.7%
c. 54.7 g, 55.0 g

42. a. 2.62×10^2 kg C
b. 4.00×10^3 kg Fe_3C

43. a. 56.6 g
b. Because the reaction occurs on the surface of the metal, 30 g of Al will not react completely, thereby reducing the yield.

44. a. 168.8 g
b. 323.4 g
c. 99.9 g

45. Refer to the *One-Stop Planner CD-ROM* for appropriate scoring rubrics. Be sure that students

$$2NaHCO_3(aq) + Ca(H_2PO_4)_2(aq) \longrightarrow$$
$$2Na_2HPO_4(aq) + CaHPO_4(aq) + 2CO_2(g) +$$
$$2H_2O(l)$$

If 0.750 L of CO_2 is needed for a cake and each kilogram of baking powder contains 168 g of $NaHCO_3$, how many grams of baking powder must be used to generate this amount of CO_2? The density of CO_2 at baking temperature is about 1.20 g/L.

33. Coal gasification is a process that converts coal into methane gas. If this reaction has a percent yield of 85.0%, how much methane can be obtained from 1250 g of carbon?

$$2C(s) + 2H_2O(l) \longrightarrow CH_4(g) + CO_2(g)$$

34. If the percent yield for the coal gasification process is increased to 95%, how much methane can be obtained from 2750 g of carbon?

35. Builders and dentists must store plaster of Paris, $CaSO_4 \cdot \frac{1}{2}H_2O$, in airtight containers to prevent it from absorbing water vapor from the air and changing to gypsum, $CaSO_4 \cdot 2H_2O$. How many liters of water evolve when 5.00 L of gypsum are heated at 110°C to produce plaster of Paris? At 110°C, the density of $CaSO_4 \cdot 2H_2O$ is 2.32 g/mL, and the density of water vapor is 0.581 g/mL.

36. Gold can be recovered from sea water by reacting the water with zinc, which is refined from zinc oxide. The zinc displaces the gold in the water. What mass of gold can be recovered if 2.00 g of ZnO and an excess of sea water are available?

$$2ZnO(s) + C(s) \longrightarrow 2Zn(s) + CO_2(g)$$
$$2Au^{3+}(aq) + 3Zn(s) \longrightarrow 3Zn^{2+}(aq) + 2Au(s)$$

CRITICAL THINKING

37. Relating Ideas The chemical equation is a good source of information concerning a reaction. Explain the relationship that exists between the actual yield of a reaction product and the chemical equation of the product.

38. Analyzing Results Very seldom are chemists able to achieve a 100% yield of a product from a chemical reaction. However, the yield of a

reaction is usually important because of the expense involved in producing less product. For example, when magnesium metal is heated in a crucible at high temperatures, the product magnesium oxide, MgO, is formed. Based on your analysis of the reaction, describe some of the actions you would take to increase your percent yield. The reaction is as follows:

$$2 Mg(s) + O_2(g) \longrightarrow 2MgO(s)$$

39. Analyzing Results In the lab, you run an experiment that appears to have a percent yield of 115%. Propose reasons for this result. Can an actual yield ever exceed a theoretical yield? Explain your answer.

40. Relating Ideas Explain the stoichiometry of blowing air on a smoldering campfire to keep the coals burning.

▦ TECHNOLOGY & LEARNING

41. Graphing Calculator Calculating Percent Yield of a Chemical Reaction

The graphing calculator can run a program that calculates the percent yield of a chemical reaction when you enter the actual yield and the theoretical yield. Using an example in which the actual yield is 38.8 g and the theoretical yield is 53.2 g, you will calculate the percent yield. First, the program will carry out the calculation. Then it will be used to make other calculations.

Go to Appendix C. If you are using a TI 83 Plus, you can download the program and data and run the application as directed. If you are using another calculator, your teacher will provide you with keystrokes and data sets to use. Remember that you will need to name the program and check the display, as explained in Appendix C. You will then be ready to run the program. After you have graphed the data, answer these questions.

Note: all answers are written with three significant figures.

a. What is the percent yield when the actual yield is 27.3 g and the theoretical yield is 44.6 g?

b. What is the percent yield when the actual yield is 5.4 g and the theoretical yield is 9.2 g?

c. What actual yield/theoretical yield pair produced the largest percent yield?

HANDBOOK SEARCH

42. The steel-making process described in the Transition Metal section of the *Elements Handbook* shows the equation for the formation of iron carbide. Use this equation to answer the following.

a. If 3.65×10^3 kg of iron is used in a steelmaking process, what is the minimum mass of carbon needed to react with all of the iron?

b. What is the theoretical mass of iron carbide formed?

43. The reaction of aluminum with oxygen to produce a protective coating for the metal's surface is described in the discussion of aluminum in Group 13 of the *Elements Handbook*. Use this equation to answer the following.

a. What mass of aluminum oxide would theoretically be formed if a 30.0 g piece of aluminum foil reacted with excess oxygen?

b. Why would you expect the actual yield from this reaction to be far less than the mass you calculated in item (a)?

44. The reactions of oxide compounds to produce carbonates, phosphates, and sulfates are described in the section on oxides in Group 16 of the *Elements Handbook*. Use those equations to answer the following.

a. What mass of CO_2 is needed to react with 154.6 g of MgO?

b. What mass of magnesium carbonate is produced?

c. 45.7 g of P_4O_{10} is reacted with an excess of calcium oxide. What mass of calcium phosphate is produced?

RESEARCH & WRITING

45. Research the history of the Haber process for the production of ammonia. What was the significance of this process in history? How is this process related to the discussion of reaction yields in this chapter?

ALTERNATIVE ASSESSMENT

46. Performance Just as reactants combine in certain proportions to form a product, colors can be combined to create other colors. Artists do this all the time to find just the right color for their paintings. Using poster paint, determine the proportions of primary pigments used to create the following colors. Your proportions should be such that anyone could mix the color perfectly. (Hint: Don't forget to record the amount of the primary pigment and water used when you mix them.)

47. Performance Write two of your own sample problems that are descriptions of how to solve a mass-mass problem. Assume that your sample problems will be used by other students to learn how to solve mass-mass problems.

include information about Germany's need for nitrogen compounds for the manufacture of explosives prior to World War I. A reasonable yield of ammonia could be obtained only by careful adjusting of conditions of temperature and pressure.

46. As students begin to experimentally mix pigments, warn them to keep track of how much of each pigment they are using. For each color they mix, have them develop a quasi equation with coefficients indicating the proportions of water and primary pigments used in compounding the color.

47. Allow students to chose any two chemical reactions they know or find in the text. The completed sample problems should include a statement of the problem and the four elements of the solution as developed in Sample Problem 9-5.

UNIT 4

Phases of Matter

CHAPTERS

10 **Physical Characteristics of Gases**

11 **Molecular Composition of Gases**

12 **Liquids and Solids**

ALBERT EINSTEIN, ON THE NECESSITY OF HUMAN CURIOSITY FOR THE FURTHERING OF SCIENTIFIC PURSUITS

The important thing is not to stop questioning. Curiosity has its own reasons for existing. One cannot help but be in awe when he contemplates the mysteries of eternity, of life, of the marvelous structure of reality. It is enough if one tries to comprehend a little of this mystery every day. Never lose a holy curiosity.

(Albert Einstein)

Physical Characteristics of Gases

PACING CHART	CLASSROOM RESOURCES		
Compression Guide: (To shorten, eliminate items in italics.)	NSE Standards	Teaching Resources	Experiments
10-1 **The Kinetic-Molecular Theory of Matter** 2 45-minute periods 1 90-minute block *Deviations of Real Gases from Ideal Behavior, p. 306*	PS 2e, 5c UCP 1–2 ST 1 HNS 1 SPSP 1, 5	**PE** Elements Handbook T 56	
10-2 **Pressure** 2 45-minute periods 1 90-minute block	PS 2e UCP 2–3	**ATE Demo,** pp. 308, 310 **PE** Elements Handbook T 48, T 49, TM 48A	
10-3 **The Gas Laws** 2 45-minute periods 1 90-minute block *The Combined Gas Law, pp. 321–322* *Dalton's Law of Partial Pressures, pp. 322–325*	PS 5c UCP 1–3	**ATE Demo,** pp. 316, 324 **PE** Elements Handbook T 50, T 51, TM 49A, TM 50A, TM 51A, TM 52A	A8 Boyle's Law B11 Generating and Collecting O_2 B12 Generating and Collecting H_2 B13 Testing Reaction Combinations of H_2 and O_2 C10 **EXP** Gas Pressure-Volume Relationship C10 **INV** Temperature-Volume Relationship—Balloon Flight

Review and Assessment	REVIEW RESOURCES		
2 45-minute periods 1 90-minute block	Cumulative Review	Alternative Assessment	Traditional Assessment
	SR Chapter 10 Mixed Review **PE** Chapter 10 46–51, p. 329	**PE** 65, p. 331 **ATE** 308, 309 **AA** Items for Chapter 10	Chapter 10 Text Test Generator items for Chapter 10

ASSIGNMENT RESOURCES

Section Homework Resources & Review	Problem-Solving Practice
HR Homework Worksheets 10-1, 10-2 PE Section Review, 1–4, p. 306 Chapter Review, 1–7, p. 327 SR Section Review 10-1	

HR Homework Worksheets 10-3, 10-4
      Graphic Org. Assignment 10-3
PE Section Review, 1–4, p. 312
      Chapter Review, 8–11, 15–19,
          p. 327
SR Section Review 10-2
	PE Additional Sample 10-1
	ATE Additional Sample, p. 312

HR Homework Worksheets 10-5, 10-6, 10-7,
          10-8
      Graphic Org. Assignment 10-6
PE Section Review, 1–6, p. 325
      Chapter Review, 12–14, 20–43,
          pp. 327–328
SR Section Review 10-3
	PE Additional Samples 10-2, 10-3, 10-4,
	          10-5, 10-6
	ATE Additional Samples, pp. 315, 319, 320,
	          322, 325
	      Additional Example, p. 323
	PS Chapter 11 Gas Laws

TECHNOLOGY RESOURCES

Technology & Internet Resources

 CTW 10 Segment 10 Ozone-eater Radiator

 Holt Chemistry Videodiscs Teacher's Correlation Guide for Chapter 10

 Module 1: States of Matter/Classes of Matter
Module 6: Gas Laws

internet connect

 On-line Student Resources:
GO TO: www.scilinks.org
The following SciLinks Internet resources can be found in the student text for this chapter.

TOPICS:
• Gases, p. 303 (HC2101)
• Diffusion/effusion, p. 305 (HC2102)
• Carbon monoxide, p. 307 (HC2103)
• Gas laws, p. 314 (HC2104)

On-line Teacher Resources:
GO TO: go.hrw.com
KEYWORD: HC2 HOME
Visit the HRW Web site for a variety of resources related to this chapter.

Smithsonian Institution®
Internet Connections
Visit **www.si.edu/hrw** for additional on-line resources.

 CNNfyi.com.
Visit **www.cnnfyi.com** for late-breaking news and current events stories selected just for you.

Resource Key

PE Pupil's Edition
ATE Teacher's Edition

✋ **One-Stop Planner CD-ROM** Includes these resources and customizable daily lesson plans:

HR Homework Resources			D Consumer Experiments	
SR Section Reviews	ChemFile		T Transparencies	
CTW Critical Thinking Worksheets	A Laboratory Experiments		TM Transparency Masters	
	B Microscale Experiments		PS Mini-Guide to Problem Solving	
AA Alternative Assessments	C Technique Builders and Problem-Solving Experiments		SRW Supplemental Reading Worksheets	

Scoring Rubrics for Labs, Alternative Assessments, Performance Tasks and Portfolio Projects are on the One-Stop Planner CD-ROM.

CHAPTER 10

*Physical
Characteristics
of Gases*

Chapter Overview

10-1 introduces the kinetic-molecular theory of matter and explains how the theory accounts for certain physical properties of ideal gases, which differ from real gases.

10-2 defines pressure and standard pressure in terms of force, explains how pressure is measured, and defines and converts units of pressure.

10-3 presents gas laws that express simple mathematical relationships between the pressure, temperature, volume, and quantity of gases.

Concept Base

Students may need a review of the following concepts:

• states and physical properties of matter, Chapter 1

• density and SI units of pressure, Chapter 2

 Reading Skill-Builder

K/W/L Write the word *gases* on the board. Have students list what they know or think they know about the physical properties of gases, such as density and temperature, and how gases behave. Then have them list what they want to know. After reading the sections in this chapter, students should determine whether their questions have been answered, noting any unanswered questions as well as new questions they may have.

Physical Characteristics of Gases

The density of a gas decreases as its temperature increases.

The Kinetic-Molecular Theory of Matter

I n Chapter 1, you read that matter exists on Earth in the forms of solids, liquids, and gases. Although it is not usually possible to observe individual particles directly, scientists have studied large groups of these particles as they occur in solids, liquids, and gases.

In the late nineteenth century, scientists developed the kinetic-molecular theory of matter to account for the behavior of the atoms and molecules that make up matter. *The **kinetic-molecular theory** is based on the idea that particles of matter are always in motion.* The theory can be used to explain the properties of solids, liquids, and gases in terms of the energy of particles and the forces that act between them. In this section, you will study the theory as it applies to gas molecules. In that form, it is called the kinetic-molecular theory of gases.

The Kinetic-Molecular Theory of Gases

The kinetic-molecular theory can help you understand the behavior of gas molecules and the physical properties of gases. The theory provides a model of what is called an ideal gas. *An **ideal gas** is an imaginary gas that perfectly fits all the assumptions of the kinetic-molecular theory.*

The kinetic-molecular theory of gases is based on the following five assumptions:

1. *Gases consist of large numbers of tiny particles that are far apart relative to their size.* These particles, usually molecules or atoms, typically occupy a volume about 1000 times greater than the volume occupied by particles in the liquid or solid state. Thus, molecules of gases are much farther apart than those of liquids or solids. Most of the volume occupied by a gas is empty space. This accounts for the lower density of gases compared with that of liquids and solids. It also explains the fact that gases are easily compressed.
2. *Collisions between gas particles and between particles and container walls are elastic collisions.* An **elastic collision** is one in which there is no net loss of kinetic energy. Kinetic energy is transferred between two particles during collisions. However, the total kinetic energy of the two particles remains the same as long as temperature is constant.

OBJECTIVES

- State the kinetic-molecular theory of matter, and describe how it explains certain properties of matter.

- List the five assumptions of the kinetic-molecular theory of gases. Define the terms *ideal gas* and *real gas*.

- Describe each of the following characteristic properties of gases: expansion, density, fluidity, compressibility, diffusion, and effusion.

- Describe the conditions under which a real gas deviates from "ideal" behavior.

Module 1: States of Matter/Classes of Matter

---

internetconnect

SC*i*LINKS

NSTA

TOPIC: Gases
GO TO: www.scilinks.org
*sci*LINKS CODE: HC2101

Lesson Starter
Open a bottle of strong-smelling perfume or dilute ammonia solution in the middle of the classroom. Ask students to raise their hand when they first detect the odor of the vapor. Ask them to try to explain this event in terms of the motion of molecules.

Safety: Be sure no one breathes the fumes directly from or close to the bottle.

Class Discussion
You may choose to begin this chapter by discussing the fundamental physical properties of gases covered on pages 304 through 306, then introduce the kinetic-molecular theory of gases.

To clarify the differences between an ideal gas and a real gas, discuss other instances in which real and ideal situations exist. For example, an ideal car might be completely energy-efficient, but a real car loses energy through friction and unburned fuel. Ideal situations are important models, but ideal situations rarely, if ever, exist in real life.

Module 1: States of Matter/Classes of Matter

Topic: Gases
Section c of this engaging tutorial reviews and reinforces understanding of gases.

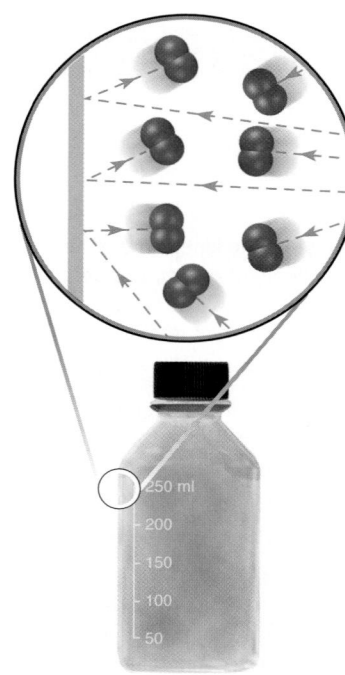

FIGURE 10-1 Gas particles travel in a straight-line motion until they collide with each other or the walls of their container.

3. *Gas particles are in continuous, rapid, random motion. They therefore possess kinetic energy, which is energy of motion.* Gas particles move in all directions, as shown in Figure 10-1. The kinetic energy of the particles overcomes the attractive forces between them, except near the temperature at which the gas condenses and becomes a liquid.

4. *There are no forces of attraction or repulsion between gas particles.* You can think of ideal gas molecules as behaving like small billiard balls. When they collide, they do not stick together but immediately bounce apart.

5. *The average kinetic energy of gas particles depends on the temperature of the gas.* The kinetic energy of any moving object, including a particle, is given by the following equation.

$$KE = \frac{1}{2}mv^2$$

In the equation, m is the mass of the particle and v is its speed. Because all the particles of a specific gas have the same mass, their kinetic energies depend only on their speeds. The average speeds and kinetic energies of gas particles increase with an increase in temperature and decrease with a decrease in temperature.

All gases at the same temperature have the same average kinetic energy. Therefore, at the same temperature, lighter gas particles, such as hydrogen molecules, have higher average speeds than do heavier gas particles, such as oxygen molecules.

The Kinetic-Molecular Theory and the Nature of Gases

The kinetic-molecular theory applies only to ideal gases. Although ideal gases do not actually exist, many gases behave nearly ideally if pressure is not very high or temperature is not very low. In the following sections, you will see how the kinetic-molecular theory accounts for the physical properties of gases.

Expansion

Gases do not have a definite shape or a definite volume. They completely fill any container in which they are enclosed, and they take its shape. A gas transferred from a one-liter vessel to a two-liter vessel will quickly expand to fill the entire two-liter volume. The kinetic-molecular theory explains these facts. According to the theory, gas particles move rapidly in all directions (assumption 3) without significant attraction or repulsion between them (assumption 4).

Fluidity

Because the attractive forces between gas particles are insignificant (assumption 4), gas particles glide easily past one another. This ability to flow causes gases to behave similarly to liquids. *Because liquids and gases flow, they are both referred to as* **fluids.**

Low Density

The density of a substance in the gaseous state is about 1/1000 the density of the same substance in the liquid or solid state. That is because the particles are so much farther apart in the gaseous state (assumption 1).

Compressibility

During compression, the gas particles, which are initially very far apart (assumption 1), are crowded closer together. The volume of a given sample of a gas can be greatly decreased. Steel cylinders containing gases under pressure are widely used in industry. When they are full, such cylinders may contain 100 times as many particles of gas as would be contained in nonpressurized containers of the same size.

Diffusion and Effusion

Gases spread out and mix with one another, even without being stirred. If the stopper is removed from a container of ammonia in a room, ammonia gas will mix uniformly with the air and spread throughout the room. The random and continuous motion of the ammonia molecules (assumption 3) carries them throughout the available space. *Such spontaneous mixing of the particles of two substances caused by their random motion is called* **diffusion.**

The rate of diffusion of one gas through another depends on three properties of the gas particles: their speeds, their diameters, and the attractive forces between them. In Figure 10-2, hydrogen gas diffuses rapidly into other gases at the same temperature because its molecules are lighter and move faster than the molecules of the other gases.

CHAPTER ⟷ CONNECTION

Diffusion and effusion as they relate to Graham's law are covered again in Chapter 11.

internet**connect**

SC/*INKS*

NSTA

TOPIC: Diffusion/effusion
GO TO: www.scilinks.org
sciLINKS **CODE:** HC2102

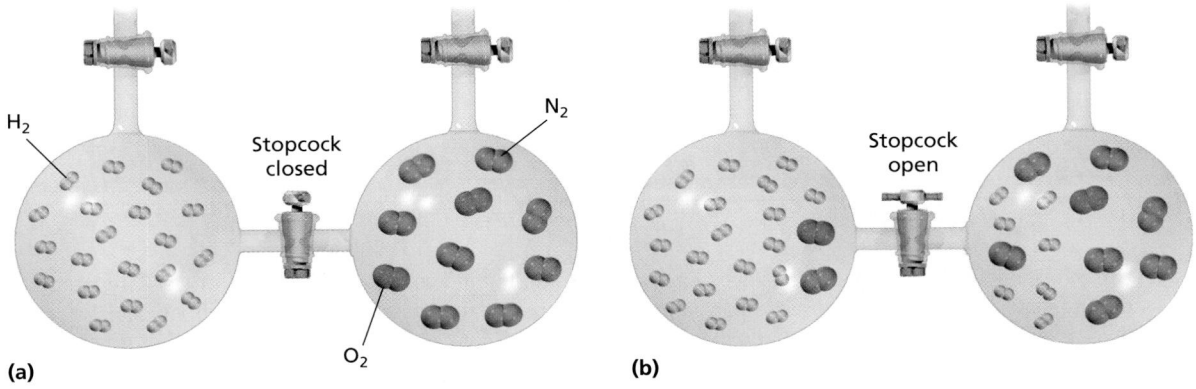

(a)   (b)

H₂   Stopcock closed   N₂   Stopcock open

O₂

FIGURE 10-2 When hydrogen gas in a flask is allowed to mix with air at the same pressure in another flask, the low-mass molecules of hydrogen diffuse rapidly into the flask with the air. The heavier molecules of nitrogen and oxygen in the air diffuse more slowly into the flask with the hydrogen.

SECTION REVIEW

1. Expansion: gas particles move rapidly in all directions without significant attraction or repulsion between them. Fluidity: attractive forces between gas particles are insignificant. Low density and compressibility: gas particles are farther apart than they are in any other state. Diffusion: gas particles are in continuous and random motion.

2. Under high temperature and low pressure, real gases approach ideal gas behavior.

3. Gas particles occupy space. Gas particles exert attractive forces on each other.

4. H_2O, NH_3, and HCl because they are the most polar.

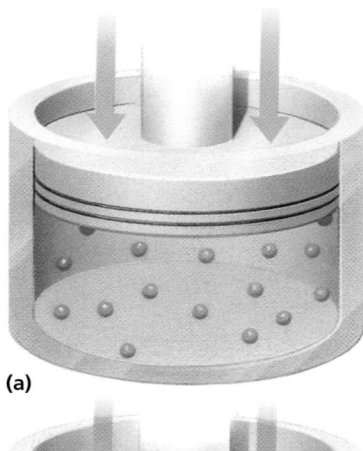

(a)

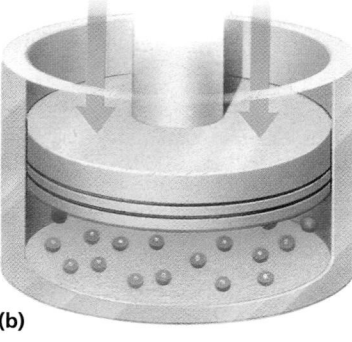

(b)

FIGURE 10-3 (a) Gas molecules in a car engine cylinder expand to fill the cylinder. (b) As pressure is exerted on them, the gas molecules move closer together, reducing their volume.

Diffusion is a process by which particles of a gas spread out spontaneously and mix with other gases. In contrast, **effusion** *is a process by which gas particles pass through a tiny opening.* The rates of effusion of different gases are directly proportional to the velocities of their particles. Because of this proportionality, molecules of low mass effuse faster than molecules of high mass.

Deviations of Real Gases from Ideal Behavior

When their particles are far enough apart and have enough kinetic energy, most gases behave ideally. However, all real gases deviate to some degree from ideal-gas behavior. *A* **real gas** *is a gas that does not behave completely according to the assumptions of the kinetic-molecular theory.* In 1873, Johannes van der Waals accounted for this deviation from ideal behavior by pointing out that particles of real gases occupy space and exert attractive forces on each other. At very high pressures and low temperatures, the deviation may be considerable. Under such conditions, the particles will be closer together and their kinetic energy will be insufficient to completely overcome the attractive forces. These conditions are illustrated in Figure 10-3.

The kinetic-molecular theory is more likely to hold true for gases whose particles have little attraction for each other. The noble gases, such as helium, He, and neon, Ne, show essentially ideal gas behavior over a wide range of temperatures and pressures. The particles of these gases are monatomic and thus nonpolar. The particles of gases, such as nitrogen, N_2, and hydrogen, H_2, are nonpolar diatomic molecules. The behavior of these gases most closely approximates that of the ideal gas under certain conditions. The more polar a gas's molecules are, the greater the attractive forces between them and the more the gas will deviate from ideal gas behavior. For example, highly polar gases, such as ammonia, NH_3, and water vapor, deviate from ideal behavior to a larger degree than nonpolar gases.

SECTION REVIEW

1. Use the kinetic-molecular theory to explain each of the following properties of gases: expansion, fluidity, low density, compressibility, and diffusion.

2. Describe the conditions under which a real gas is most likely to behave ideally.

3. State the two factors that van der Waals proposed to explain why real gases deviate from ideal behavior.

4. Which of the following gases would you expect to deviate significantly from ideal behavior: He, O_2, H_2, H_2O, N_2, HCl, or NH_3?

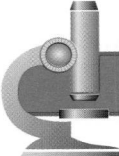

RESEARCH NOTES

Carbon Monoxide Catalyst—Stopping the Silent Killer

Colorless, odorless, and deadly—carbon monoxide, "the silent killer," causes the deaths of hundreds of Americans every year. When fuel does not burn completely in a combustion process, carbon monoxide is produced. Often this occurs in a malfunctioning heater, furnace, or fireplace. When the carbon monoxide is inhaled, it bonds to the hemoglobin in the blood, leaving the body oxygen starved. Before people realize a combustion device is malfunctioning, it's often too late.

$$O_2Hb + CO \longrightarrow COHb + O_2$$

Carbon monoxide, CO, has almost 200 times the affinity to bind with the hemoglobin, Hb, in the blood as oxygen. This means if the body has a choice, it will bind to carbon monoxide over oxygen. If enough carbon monoxide is present in the blood, it can be fatal.

Carbon monoxide poisoning can be prevented by installing filters that absorb the gas. After a time, however, filters become saturated, and then carbon monoxide can pass freely into the air. The best way to prevent carbon monoxide poisoning is not just to filter out the gas, but to eliminate it completely.

The solution came to research chemists at NASA who were working on a problem with a space-based laser. In order to operate properly, NASA's space-based carbon dioxide laser needed to be fed a continuous supply of CO_2. This was necessary because as a byproduct of its operation, the laser degraded some of the CO_2 into carbon monoxide and oxygen. To address this problem, NASA scientists developed a catalyst made of tin oxide and platinum that oxidized the waste carbon monoxide back into carbon dioxide. The NASA scientists then realized that this catalyst had the potential to be used in many applications here on Earth, including removing carbon monoxide from houses and other buildings.

Typically, a malfunctioning heater circulates the carbon monoxide it produces through its air intake system back into a dwelling space. By installing the catalyst in the air intake, any carbon monoxide would be eliminated by oxidation to non-toxic carbon dioxide before it reentered the room.

"The form of our catalyst is a very thin coating on some sort of a support, or substrate as we call it," says NASA chemist David Schryer. "And that support, or

substrate, can be any one of a number of things. The great thing about a catalyst is that the only thing that matters about it is its surface. So a catalyst can be incredibly thin and still be very effective."

The idea of using catalysts to oxidize gases is not a new one. Catalytic converters in cars oxidize carbon monoxide and unburned hydrocarbons to minimize pollution. Many substances are oxidized into new materials for manufacturing purposes. But both of these types of catalytic reactions occur at very high temperatures. NASA's catalyst is special, because it's able to eliminate carbon monoxide at room temperature. Also, it has the ability to oxidize formaldehyde, a noxious chemical often found in building materials, curtains, and carpets.

According to David Schryer, low-temperature catalysts constitute a whole new class of catalysts with abundant applications for the future.

TOPIC: Carbon monoxide
GO TO: www.scilinks.org
***sci*LINKS CODE:** HC2103

RESEARCH NOTES

Common Misconception
Students may think that all effects of carbon monoxide are undesirable. The gas has some important useful applications. It is used to reduce metallic ores to pure metals. It is also an important component of several industrial fuels.

Application
Pollution-control devices like the one described here have been partially responsible for a 28 percent reduction in carbon monoxide levels in urban areas of the United States between 1984 and 1992. Still, many urban areas have carbon monoxide levels that exceed the minimum standards established by the United States Environmental Protection Agency.

HANDBOOK **CONNECTION**

More-detailed information on CO poisoning can be found in Group 14 of the *Elements Handbook*.

SECTION 10-2

Pressure

OBJECTIVES

- Define *pressure* and relate it to force.

- Describe how pressure is measured.

- Convert units of pressure.

- State the standard conditions of temperature and pressure.

Suppose you have a one-liter bottle of air. How much air do you actually have? The expression *a liter of air* means little unless the conditions at which the volume is measured are known. A liter of air can be compressed to a few milliliters. It can also be allowed to expand to fill an auditorium.

To describe a gas fully, you need to state four measurable quantities: volume, temperature, number of molecules, and pressure. You already know what is meant by volume, temperature, and number of molecules. In this section, you will learn about pressure and its measurement. Then, in Section 10-3, you will examine the mathematical relationships between volume, temperature, number of gas molecules, and pressure.

Pressure and Force

If you blow air into a rubber balloon, the balloon will increase in size. The volume increase is caused by the collisions of molecules of air with the inside walls of the balloon. The collisions cause an outward push, or force, against the inside walls. **Pressure** *(P) is defined as the force per unit area on a surface.* The equation defining pressure follows.

FIGURE 10-4 The pressure the ballet dancer exerts against the floor depends on the area of contact. The smaller the area of contact, the greater the pressure.

Force = 500 N

(a) Area of contact = 325 cm²
Pressure = $\dfrac{\text{force}}{\text{area}}$
$= \dfrac{500 \text{ N}}{325 \text{ cm}^2} = 1.5 \text{ N/cm}^2$

Force = 500 N

(b) Area of contact = 13 cm²
Pressure = $\dfrac{\text{force}}{\text{area}}$
$= \dfrac{500 \text{ N}}{13 \text{ cm}^2} = 38.5 \text{ N/cm}^2$

Force = 500 N

(c) Area of contact = 6.5 cm²
Pressure = $\dfrac{\text{force}}{\text{area}}$
$= \dfrac{500 \text{ N}}{6.5 \text{ cm}^2} = 77 \text{ N/cm}^2$

$$pressure = \frac{force}{area}$$

The SI unit for force is the **newton,** abbreviated N. *It is the force that will increase the speed of a one kilogram mass by one meter per second each second it is applied.* At Earth's surface, each kilogram of mass exerts 9.8 N of force, due to gravity. Consider a ballet dancer with a mass of 51 kg, as shown in Figure 10-4. A mass of 51 kg exerts a force of 500 N (51×9.8) on Earth's surface. No matter how the dancer stands, she exerts that much force against the floor. However, the pressure she exerts against the floor depends on the area of contact. When she rests her weight on the soles of both feet, as shown in Figure 10-4(a), the area of contact with the floor is about 325 cm^2. The pressure, or force per unit area, when she stands in this manner is 500 $N/325$ cm^2. That equals roughly 1.5 N/cm^2. When she stands on her toes, as in Figure 10-4(b), the total area of contact with the floor is only 13 cm^2. The pressure exerted is then equal to 500 $N/13$ cm^2—roughly 38.5 N/cm^2. And when she stands on one toe, as in Figure 10-4(c), the pressure she exerts is twice that, or about 77 N/cm^2. Thus, the same force applied to a smaller area results in a greater pressure.

Gas molecules exert pressure on any surface with which they collide. The pressure exerted by a gas depends on volume, temperature, and the number of molecules present.

The atmosphere—the blanket of air surrounding Earth—exerts pressure. Figure 10-5 shows that atmospheric pressure at sea level is about equal to the weight of a 1.03 kg mass per square centimeter of surface, or 10.1 N/cm^2. The pressure of the atmosphere can be thought of as caused by the weight of the gases that compose the atmosphere. The atmosphere contains about 78% nitrogen, 21% oxygen, and 1% other gases, including

Module 6: Gas Laws

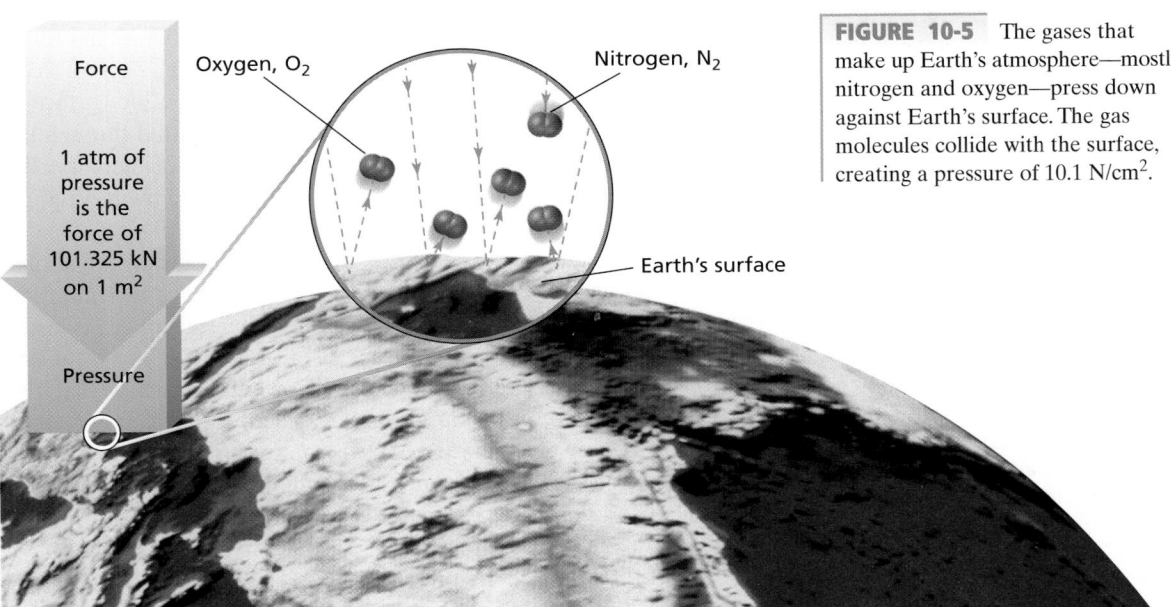

Force

1 atm of pressure is the force of 101.325 kN on 1 m^2

Pressure

Oxygen, O_2

Nitrogen, N_2

Earth's surface

FIGURE 10-5 The gases that make up Earth's atmosphere—mostly nitrogen and oxygen—press down against Earth's surface. The gas molecules collide with the surface, creating a pressure of 10.1 N/cm^2.

Visual Strategy

FIGURE 10-5 Ask students to explain why airplanes that fly at high altitudes must have pressurized cabins.

Alternative Assessment

The following chart shows changes in air pressure in relation to altitude above Earth's surface. Have students graph these data, then discuss the relationship shown between altitude and atmospheric pressure.

Altitude (km)	Percent of sea-level pressure
0	100
5.6	50
16.2	10
31.2	1
48.1	0.1
65.1	0.01
79.2	0.001

Did You Know?

The average number of collisions per second experienced by an air molecule near sea level is about 7×10^9; at an altitude of 600 km, it experiences an average of about one collision per minute.

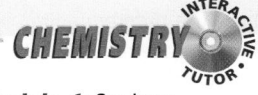

Module 6: Gas Laws

Topic: Gases
Section **a** of this engaging tutorial reviews and reinforces understanding of gases.

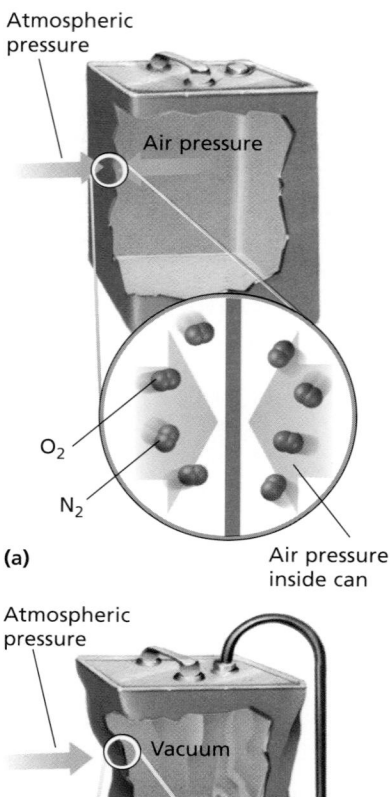

Atmospheric pressure

Air pressure

O_2

N_2

(a)

Air pressure inside can

Atmospheric pressure

Vacuum

To vacuum pump

O_2

N_2

(b)

Vacuum inside can

FIGURE 10-6 (a) The "empty" can has the mixture of gases in air inside that push outward and balance the atmospheric pressure that pushes inward. (b) When the air inside the can is removed by a vacuum pump, there is insufficient force to balance the atmospheric pressure. As a result, the can collapses.

argon and carbon dioxide. Atmospheric pressure is the sum of the individual pressures of the various gases in the atmosphere.

To understand the concept of gas pressure and its magnitude, consider the model of an "empty" can shown in Figure 10-6(a). The can does contain a small amount of air. The atmosphere exerts a pressure of 10.1 N/cm^2 against the outside of the can. If the can measures $15 \, cm \times 10 \, cm \times 28 \, cm$, it has a total area of 1700 cm^2. The resulting inward force on the can is greater than 1.0 metric ton of weight. The air inside the can pushes outward and balances the atmosphere's inward-pushing force. If a vacuum pump is used to remove the air from the can, as shown in Figure 10-6(b), the balancing outward force is removed. As a result, the unbalanced force due to atmospheric pressure immediately crushes the can.

Measuring Pressure

A **barometer** *is a device used to measure atmospheric pressure.* The first type of barometer, illustrated in Figure 10-7, was introduced by Evangelista Torricelli during the early 1600s. Torricelli wondered why water pumps could raise water to a maximum height of only about 34 feet. He thought that the height must depend somehow on the weight of water compared with the weight of air. He reasoned that liquid mercury, which is about 14 times as dense as water, could be raised only 1/14 as high as water. To test this idea, Torricelli sealed a long glass tube at one end and filled it with mercury. Holding the open end with his thumb, he inverted the tube into a dish of mercury without allowing any air to enter the tube. When he removed his thumb, the mercury column in the tube dropped to a height of about 30 in. (760 mm) above the surface of the mercury in the dish. He repeated the experiment with tubes of different diameters and lengths longer than 760 mm. In every case, the mercury dropped to a height of about 760 mm.

The space above the mercury in such a tube is nearly a vacuum. The mercury in the tube pushes downward because of gravitational force. The column of mercury in the tube is stopped from falling beyond a certain point because the atmosphere exerts a pressure on the surface of the mercury outside the tube. This pressure is transmitted through the fluid mercury and is exerted upward on the column of mercury. The mercury in the tube falls only until the pressure exerted by its weight is equal to the pressure exerted by the atmosphere.

The exact height of the mercury in the tube depends on the atmospheric pressure, or force per unit area. The pressure is measured directly in terms of the height of the mercury column supported in the barometer tube.

From experiments like Torricelli's, it is known that at sea level at 0°C, the average pressure of the atmosphere can support a 760 mm column of mercury. At any given place on Earth, the specific atmospheric pressure depends on the elevation and the weather conditions at the time. If the atmospheric pressure is greater than the average at sea level, the height of the mercury column in a barometer will be greater than 760 mm. If the atmospheric pressure is less, the height of the mercury column will be less than 760 mm.

All gases, not only those in the atmosphere, exert pressure. A device called a manometer can be used to measure the pressure of an enclosed gas sample, as shown in Figure 10-8. The difference in the height of mercury in the two arms of the U-tube is a measure of the oxygen gas pressure in the container.

Units of Pressure

A number of different units are used to measure pressure. Because atmospheric pressure is often measured by a mercury barometer, pressure can be expressed in terms of the height of a mercury column. *Thus, a common unit of pressure is* **millimeters of mercury,** *symbolized mm Hg. A pressure of 1 mm Hg is now called 1* **torr** *in honor of Torricelli for his invention of the barometer.* The average atmospheric pressure at sea level at 0°C is 760 mm Hg.

Pressures are often measured in units of atmospheres. *One* **atmosphere of pressure** *(atm) is defined as being exactly equivalent to 760 mm Hg.*

In SI, pressure is expressed in derived units called pascals. The unit is named for Blaise Pascal, a French mathematician and philosopher who studied pressure during the seventeenth century. *One* **pascal** *(Pa) is defined as the pressure exerted by a force of one newton (1 N) acting on an area of one square meter.*

In many cases, it is more convenient to express pressure in kilopascals (kPa). The standard atmosphere (1 atm) is equal to $1.013\,25 \times 10^5$ Pa, or 101.325 kPa. The pressure units used in this book are summarized in Table 10-1.

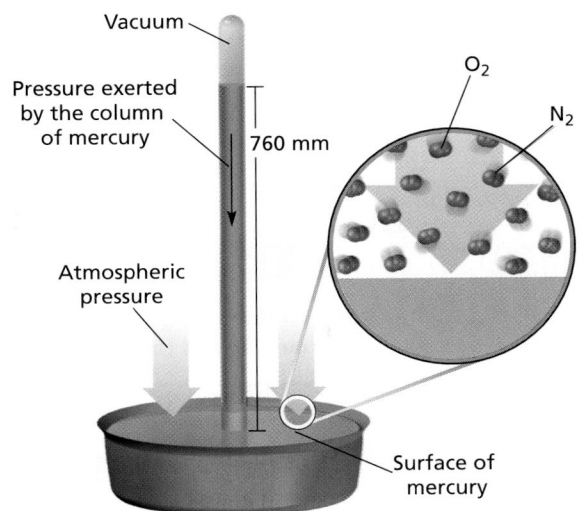

FIGURE 10-7 Torricelli discovered that the pressure of the atmosphere supports a column of mercury about 760 mm above the surface of the mercury in the dish.

TABLE 10-1 *Units of Pressure*		
Unit	**Symbol**	**Definition/relationship**
pascal	Pa	SI pressure unit $1\text{ Pa} = \dfrac{1\text{ N}}{\text{m}^2}$
millimeter of mercury	mm Hg	pressure that supports a 1 mm mercury column in a barometer
torr	torr	1 torr = 1 mm Hg
atmosphere	atm	average atmospheric pressure at sea level and 0°C 1 atm = 760 mm Hg = 760 torr = $1.013\,25 \times 10^5$ Pa = 101.325 kPa

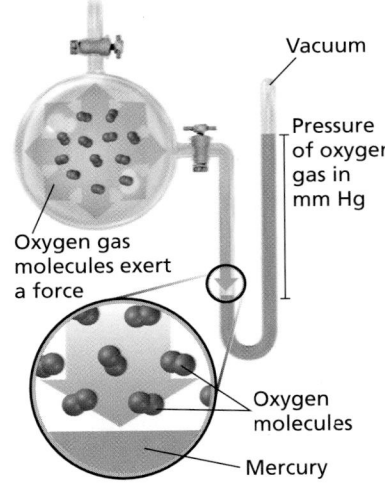

FIGURE 10-8 In the manometer above, the pressure of the oxygen gas in the flask pushes on the mercury column. The difference in the height of the mercury in the two arms of the U-tube indicates the oxygen gas pressure.

✔ **Teaching Tip**

Do not confuse STP (0°C and 1 atm) with the thermodynamic standard-state conditions (25°C and 1 atm), which will be used in Chapter 17.

ADDITIONAL SAMPLE PROBLEM

10-1 A weather report gives a current atmospheric pressure reading of 745.8 mm Hg. Express this reading in the following units:
a. atmospheres
b. torrs
c. kilopascals

Ans: **a.** 0.9813 atm
b. 745.8 torr
c. 99.43 kPa

SECTION REVIEW

1. Pressure is force per unit area.

2. Pressure is measured in Pa, kPa, mm Hg, atm, or torr.

3. 0°C and 1 atm pressure

4. **a.** 1.4999 atm
b. 0.600 atm
c. 1.20 atm

Standard Temperature and Pressure

To compare volumes of gases, it is necessary to know the temperature and pressure at which the volumes are measured. *For purposes of comparison, scientists have agreed on standard conditions of exactly 1 atm pressure and 0°C. These conditions are called* **standard temperature and pressure** *and are commonly abbreviated STP.*

SAMPLE PROBLEM 10-1

The average atmospheric pressure in Denver, Colorado, is 0.830 atm. Express this pressure **(a) in mm Hg and (b) in kPa.**

SOLUTION

1 ANALYZE

Given: P of atmosphere = 0.830 atm

760 mm Hg = 1 atm (definition);   101.325 kPa = 1 atm (definition)

Unknown: **a.** P of atmosphere in mm Hg;   **b.** P of atmosphere in kPa

2 PLAN

a. atm $\longrightarrow$ mm Hg; $atm \times \dfrac{mm\ Hg}{atm} = mm\ Hg$

b. atm $\longrightarrow$ kPa; $atm \times \dfrac{kPa}{atm} = kPa$

3 COMPUTE

a. $0.830\ atm \times \dfrac{760\ mm\ Hg}{atm} = 631\ mm\ Hg$

b. $0.830\ atm \times \dfrac{101.325\ kPa}{atm} = 84.1\ kPa$

4 EVALUATE

Units have canceled to give the desired units, and answers are properly expressed to the correct number of significant figures. The known pressure is roughly 80% of atmospheric pressure. The results are therefore reasonable because each is roughly 80% of the pressure as expressed in the new units.

PRACTICE

1. Convert a pressure of 1.75 atm to kPa and to mm Hg.

   Answer
   177 kPa, 1330 mm Hg

2. Convert a pressure of 570. torr to atmospheres and to kPa.

   Answer
   0.750 atm, 76.0 kPa

SECTION REVIEW

1. Define *pressure.*

2. What units are used to express pressure measurements?

3. What are standard conditions for gas measurements?

4. Convert the following pressures to pressures in standard atmospheres:
   a. 151.98 kPa   **c.** 912 mm Hg
   b. 456 torr

The Gas Laws

Scientists have been studying physical properties of gases for hundreds of years. In 1662, Robert Boyle discovered that gas pressure and volume are related mathematically. The observations of Boyle and others led to the development of the gas laws. *The **gas laws** are simple mathematical relationships between the volume, temperature, pressure, and amount of a gas.*

Boyle's Law: Pressure-Volume Relationship

Robert Boyle discovered that doubling the pressure on a sample of gas at constant temperature reduces its volume by one-half. Tripling the gas pressure reduces its volume to one-third of the original. Reducing the pressure on a gas by one-half allows the volume of the gas to double. As one variable increases, the other decreases. Figure 10-9 shows that as the volume of gas in the syringe decreases, the pressure of the gas increases.

You can use the kinetic-molecular theory to understand why this pressure-volume relationship holds. The pressure of a gas is caused by

Lower pressure

Higher pressure

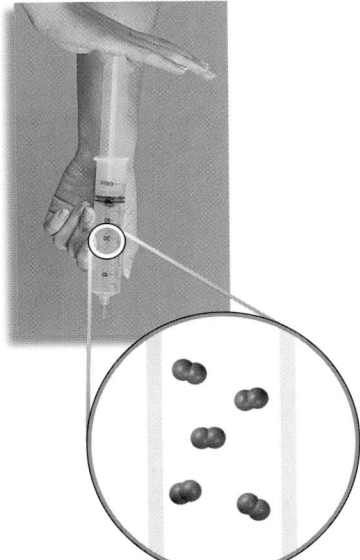 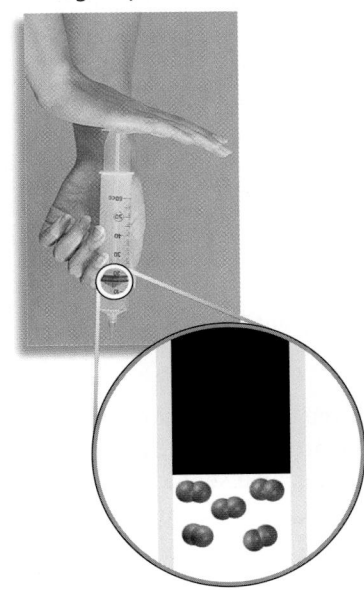

OBJECTIVES

- Use the kinetic-molecular theory to explain the relationships between gas volume, temperature, and pressure.

- Use Boyle's law to calculate volume-pressure changes at constant temperature.

- Use Charles's law to calculate volume-temperature changes at constant pressure.

- Use Gay-Lussac's law to calculate pressure-temperature changes at constant volume.

- Use the combined gas law to calculate volume-temperature-pressure changes.

- Use Dalton's law of partial pressures to calculate partial pressures and total pressures.

FIGURE 10-9 The volume of gas in the syringe shown in the photo is reduced when the plunger is pushed down. The gas pressure increases as the volume is reduced because the molecules collide more frequently with the walls of the container in a smaller volume.

Lesson Starter
Place a marshmallow under a bell jar. Tell students that the marshmallow is mostly air. Use a vacuum pump to reduce the pressure in the bell jar. Students will observe that the marshmallow increases in size as the pressure in the bell jar decreases. Help students infer that the volume and pressure of a gas are related.

Common Misconception
Students often are unclear about whether gas law references to *pressure* refer to pressure exerted *by* the gas or pressure exerted *on* the gas. Point out that in most cases the two quantities are the same. In Figure 10-9, for example, the pressure exerted by the syringe on the gas is matched by the pressure exerted by the gas on the syringe.

Did You Know?
Robert Boyle was the first person to collect a gas for study and analysis and to determine that a gas is compressible. This discovery led Boyle to conclude that a gas must be composed of separate particles separated by empty space.

Reading Skill-Builder

IDENTIFYING CAUSE AND EFFECT As students read Section 10-3, have them look for reading signal words and phrases, such as "causes," "as a result," "if . . . then," and "depends on," that indicate a cause-and-effect relationship among temperature, pressure, and volume of gases. Have student pairs write cause-and-effect statements to summarize the relationships shown in the graphs and expressed mathematically in this section. Later, students can use these statements as study notes.

TABLE 10-2	Volume-Pressure Data for a Gas Sample (at Constant Mass and Temperature)	
Volume (mL)	**Pressure (atm)**	$P \times V$
1200	0.5	600
600	1.0	600
300	2.0	600
200	3.0	600
150	4.0	600
120	5.0	600
100	6.0	600

moving molecules hitting the container walls. Suppose the volume of a container is decreased but the same number of gas molecules is present at the same temperature. There will be more molecules per unit volume. The number of collisions with a given unit of wall area will increase as a result. Therefore, pressure will also increase.

Table 10-2 shows pressure and volume data for a constant mass of gas at constant temperature. Plotting the values of volume versus pressure gives a curve like that in Figure 10-10. The general volume-pressure relationship that is illustrated is called Boyle's law. **Boyle's law** *states that the volume of a fixed mass of gas varies inversely with the pressure at constant temperature.*

Mathematically, Boyle's law is expressed as follows.

$$V = k \frac{1}{P} \quad \text{or} \quad PV = k$$

The value of k is constant for a given sample of gas and depends only on the mass of gas and the temperature. (Note that for the data in Table 10-2, $k = 600$ mL·atm.) If the pressure of a given gas sample at constant temperature changes, the volume will change. However, the quantity *pressure times volume* will remain equal to the same value of k.

Boyle's law can be used to compare changing conditions for a gas. Using P_1 and V_1 to stand for initial conditions and P_2 and V_2 to stand for new conditions results in the following equations.

$$P_1 V_1 = k \qquad P_2 V_2 = k$$

Two quantities that are equal to the same thing are equal to each other.

$$P_1 V_1 = P_2 V_2$$

Given three of the four values P_1, V_1, P_2, and V_2, you can use this equation to calculate the fourth value for a system at constant temperature. For example, suppose that 1.0 L of gas is initially at 1.0 atm pressure ($V_1 = 1.0$ L, $P_1 = 1.0$ atm). The gas is allowed to expand fivefold at constant temperature to 5.0 L ($V_2 = 5.0$ L). You can then calculate the new pressure, P_2, by rearranging the equation as follows.

Volume vs. Pressure for a Gas at Constant Temperature

Volume (mL)

1200
900
600
300
0

0 1 2 3 4 5 6

Pressure (atm)

FIGURE 10-10 This graph shows that there is an inverse relationship between volume and pressure. As the pressure drops by half, the volume doubles.

$$P_2 = \frac{P_1 V_1}{V_2}$$

$$P_2 = \frac{(1.0 \text{ atm})(1.0 \text{ L})}{5.0 \text{ L}} = 0.20 \text{ atm}$$

The pressure has decreased to one-fifth the original pressure, while the volume increased fivefold.

ADDITIONAL SAMPLE PROBLEMS

10-2 The piston of an internal combustion engine compresses 450. mL of gas. The final pressure is 15 times greater than the initial pressure. What is the final volume of the gas, assuming constant temperature? (Treat "15 times" as a pure number, with unlimited significant figures.)

Ans. 30.0 mL

10-2 A helium-filled balloon contains 125 mL of gas at a pressure of 0.974 atm. What volume will the gas occupy at standard pressure?

Ans. 122 mL

10-2 A weather balloon with a volume of 1.375 L is released from Earth's surface at sea level. What volume will the balloon occupy at an altitude of 20.0 km, where the air pressure is 10.0 kPa?

Ans. 13.9 L

SAMPLE PROBLEM 10-2

A sample of oxygen gas has a volume of 150. mL when its pressure is 0.947 atm. What will the volume of the gas be at a pressure of 0.987 atm if the temperature remains constant?

SOLUTION

1 ANALYZE

Given: V_1 of O_2 = 150. mL
P_1 of O_2 = 0.947 atm; P_2 of O_2 = 0.987 atm
Unknown: V_2 of O_2 in mL

2 PLAN

$$P_1, V_1, P_2 \longrightarrow V_2$$

Rearrange the equation for Boyle's law ($P_1 V_1 = P_2 V_2$) to obtain V_2.

$$V_2 = \frac{P_1 V_1}{P_2}$$

3 COMPUTE

Substitute values for P_1, V_1, and P_2 to obtain the new volume, V_2.

$$V_2 = \frac{P_1 V_1}{P_2} = \frac{(0.947 \text{ atm})(150. \text{ mL } O_2)}{0.987 \text{ atm}} = 144 \text{ mL } O_2$$

4 EVALUATE

When the pressure is increased slightly at constant temperature, the volume decreases slightly, as expected. Units cancel to give milliliters, a volume unit.

PRACTICE

1. A balloon filled with helium gas has a volume of 500 mL at a pressure of 1 atm. The balloon is released and reaches an altitude of 6.5 km, where the pressure is 0.5 atm. Assuming that the temperature has remained the same, what volume does the gas occupy at this height?

   Answer
   1000 mL He

2. A gas has a pressure of 1.26 atm and occupies a volume of 7.40 L. If the gas is compressed to a volume of 2.93 L, what will its pressure be, assuming constant temperature?

   Answer
   3.18 atm

3. Divers know that the pressure exerted by the water increases about 100 kPa with every 10.2 m of depth. This means that at 10.2 m below the surface, the pressure is 201 kPa; at 20.4 m, the pressure is 301 kPa; and so forth. Given that the volume of a balloon is 3.5 L at STP and that the temperature of the water remains the same, what is the volume 51 m below the water's surface?

   Answer
   0.59 L

Blow up three balloons of identical size to the same extent. Place one of the balloons in a freezer and one in a warm place. Keep the third balloon at room temperature. After 30 min, place the three balloons side by side. Ask students to describe changes that have taken place.

The demonstration can be made quantitative by finding the volume of each balloon by water displacement. The volume measurements must be made quickly after the balloons are removed from the freezer and the warm place.

Measure the temperature of all three locations. Use these temperatures to calculate the theoretical changes in volume of the balloons. Compare those results with the volumes actually determined by experimentation.

Class Discussion

Discuss why kelvins must be used when measuring temperature for gas law calculations. Even though 1°C is the same size as 1 K, Celsius degrees may have negative values. Kelvin is the most widely used scale that uses only positive numbers to indicate temperature. Point out how the use of negative temperature values in gas law calculations leads to negative gas volume answers, an impossible condition.

Module 6: Gas Laws

Topic: Gases–Temperature and Volume
Section **b** of this engaging tutorial reviews and reinforces understanding of temperature and volume of gases.

Module 6: Gas Laws

FIGURE 10-11 As air-filled balloons are exposed to liquid nitrogen, they shrink greatly in volume. When they are removed from the liquid nitrogen and the air inside them is warmed to room temperature, the balloons expand to their original volume.

Charles's Law: Volume-Temperature Relationship

Balloonists, such as those in the photo at the beginning of this chapter, are making use of a physical property of gases: if pressure is constant, gases expand when heated. When the temperature increases, the volume of a fixed number of gas molecules must increase if the pressure is to stay constant. At the higher temperature, the gas molecules move faster. They collide with the walls of the container more frequently and with more force. The increased pressure causes the volume of a flexible container to increase; then the molecules must travel farther before reaching the walls. The rate of collisions against each unit of wall area decreases. This lower collision frequency offsets the greater collision force at the higher temperature. The pressure thus stays constant.

The quantitative relationship between volume and temperature was discovered by the French scientist Jacques Charles in 1787. Charles's experiments showed that all gases expand to the same extent when heated through the same temperature interval. Charles found that the volume changes by 1/273 of the original volume for each Celsius degree, at constant pressure and an initial temperature of 0°C. For example, raising the temperature to 1°C causes the gas volume to increase by 1/273 of the volume it had at 0°C. A 10°C temperature increase causes the volume to expand by 10/273 of the original volume at 0°C. If the temperature is increased by 273°C, the volume increases by 273/273 of the original, that is, the volume doubles.

The same regularity of volume change occurs if a gas is cooled at constant pressure, as the balloons in Figure 10-11 show. At 0°C, a 1°C decrease in temperature decreases the original volume by 1/273. At this rate of volume decrease, a gas cooled from 0°C to –273°C would be decreased by 273/273. In other words, it would have zero volume, which

TABLE 10-3 *Volume-Temperature Data for a Gas Sample (at Constant Mass and Pressure)*	
Temperature (°C)	Volume (mL)
273	1092
100	746
10	566
1	548
0	546
−1	544
−73	400
−173	200
−223	100

is not actually possible. In fact, real gases cannot be cooled to −273°C. Before they reach that temperature, intermolecular forces exceed the kinetic energy of the molecules, and the gases condense to form liquids or solids.

The data in Table 10-3 illustrate the temperature-volume relationship at constant pressure for a gas sample with a volume of 546 mL at 0°C. When the gas is warmed by 1°C, it expands by 1/273 its original volume. In this case, each 1°C temperature change from 0°C causes a volume change of 2 mL, or 1/273 of 546 mL. Raising the temperature to 100°C from 0°C increases the volume by 200 mL, or 100/273 of 546 mL.

Note that in Table 10-3, the volume does not increase in direct proportion to the Celsius temperature. For example, notice what happens when the temperature is increased tenfold from 10°C to 100°C. The volume does not increase tenfold but increases only from 566 mL to 746 mL.

The Kelvin temperature scale is a scale that starts at a temperature corresponding to −273.15°C. That temperature is the lowest one possible. *The temperature −273.15°C is referred to as* **absolute zero** *and is given a value of zero in the Kelvin scale.* This fact gives the following relationship between the two temperature scales.

$$K = 273.15 + °C$$

For calculations in this book, 273.15 is rounded off to 273.

The average kinetic energy of gas molecules is more closely related to the Kelvin temperature. Gas volume and Kelvin temperature are directly proportional to each other. For example, quadrupling the Kelvin temperature causes the volume of a gas to quadruple, and reducing the Kelvin temperature by half causes the volume of a gas to decrease by half.

The relationship between Kelvin temperature and gas volume is known as Charles's law. **Charles's law** *states that the volume of a fixed mass of gas at constant pressure varies directly with the Kelvin temperature.*

TABLE 10-4	Volume-Temperature Data for a Gas Sample (at Constant Mass and Pressure)		
Volume (mL)		Kelvin temperature (K)	V/T or k (mL/K)
1092		546	2
746		373	2
566		283	2
548		274	2
546		273	2
544		272	2
400		200	2
100		50	2

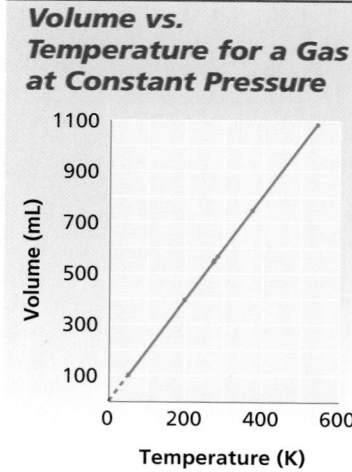

Volume vs. Temperature for a Gas at Constant Pressure

FIGURE 10-12 This graph shows the plot of the volume versus the Kelvin temperature data from Table 10-4. It gives a straight line that, when extended, indicates the volume will become 0 at –273°C. Such a plot is characteristic of directly proportional variables.

Figure 10-12 illustrates the relationship between gas volume and Kelvin temperature by plotting the data from Table 10-4. Charles's law may be expressed as follows.

$$V = kT \quad \text{or} \quad \frac{V}{T} = k$$

The value of T is the Kelvin temperature, and k is a constant. The value of k depends only on the quantity of gas and the pressure. The ratio V/T for any set of volume-temperature values always equals the same k. The form of Charles's law that can be applied directly to most volume-temperature problems involving gases is as follows.

$$\frac{V_1}{T_1} = \frac{V_2}{T_2}$$

V_1 and T_1 represent initial conditions. V_2 and T_2 represent a new set of conditions. When three of the four values V_1, T_1, V_2, and T_2 are known, this equation can be used to calculate the fourth value.

SAMPLE PROBLEM 10-3

A sample of neon gas occupies a volume of 752 mL at 25°C. What volume will the gas occupy at 50°C if the pressure remains constant?

SOLUTION

1 ANALYZE

Given: V_1 of Ne = 752 mL

T_1 of Ne = 25°C + 273 = 298 K; T_2 of Ne = 50°C + 273 = 323 K

Note that Celsius temperatures have been converted to kelvins. This is a *very important* step for working the problems in this chapter.

Unknown: V_2 of Ne in mL

2 PLAN Because the gas remains at constant pressure, an increase in temperature will cause an increase in volume. To obtain V_2, rearrange the equation for Charles's law.

$$V_2 = \frac{V_1 T_2}{T_1}$$

3 COMPUTE Substitute values for V_1, T_1, and T_2 to obtain the new volume, V_2.

$$V_2 = \frac{V_1 T_2}{T_1} = \frac{(752 \text{ mL Ne})(323 \text{ K})}{298 \text{ K}} = 815 \text{ mL Ne}$$

4 EVALUATE As expected, the volume of the gas increases as the temperature increases. Units cancel to yield milliliters, as desired. The answer contains the appropriate number of significant figures. It is also reasonably close to an estimated value of 812, calculated as $(750 \times 325)/300$.

PRACTICE	
1. A helium-filled balloon has a volume of 2.75 L at 20.°C. The volume of the balloon decreases to 2.46 L after it is placed outside on a cold day. What is the outside temperature in K? in °C?	*Answer* 262 K, or −11°C
2. A gas at 65°C occupies 4.22 L. At what Celsius temperature will the volume be 3.87 L, assuming the same pressure?	*Answer* 37°C

Gay-Lussac's Law: Pressure-Temperature Relationship

You have just learned about the quantitative relationship between volume and temperature at constant pressure. What would you predict about the relationship between pressure and temperature at constant volume? You have seen that pressure is the result of collisions of molecules with container walls. The energy and frequency of collisions depend on the average kinetic energy of molecules, which depends on temperature. For a fixed quantity of gas at constant volume, the pressure should be directly proportional to the Kelvin temperature, which depends directly on average kinetic energy.

That prediction turns out to be correct. For every kelvin of temperature change, the pressure of a confined gas changes by 1/273 of the pressure at 0°C. Joseph Gay-Lussac is given credit for recognizing this in 1802. The data plotted in Figure 10-13 illustrate **Gay-Lussac's law:** *The pressure of a fixed mass of gas at constant volume varies directly with the Kelvin temperature.* Mathematically, Gay-Lussac's law is expressed as follows.

$$P = kT \quad \text{or} \quad \frac{P}{T} = k$$

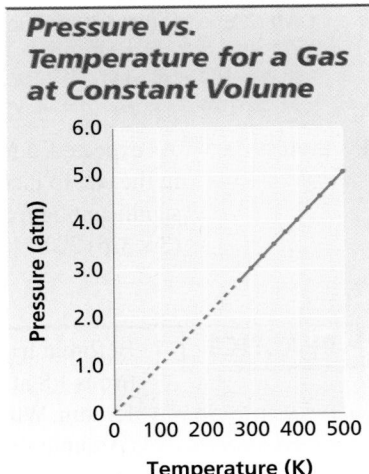

Pressure vs. Temperature for a Gas at Constant Volume

FIGURE 10-13 This graph shows that gas pressure varies directly with Kelvin temperature at constant volume.

The value of T is the temperature in kelvins, and k is a constant that depends on the quantity of gas and the volume. For a given mass of gas at constant volume, the ratio P/T is the same for any set of pressure-temperature values. Unknown values can be found using this form of Gay-Lussac's law.

$$\frac{P_1}{T_1} = \frac{P_2}{T_2}$$

When values are known for three of the four quantities, the fourth value can be calculated.

10-4 An empty aerosol-spray can at room temperature (20.°C) is thrown into an incinerator where the temperature reaches 500.°C. If the gas inside the empty container was initially at a pressure of 1.0 atm, what pressure did it reach inside the incinerator? Assume the gas was at constant volume and the can did not explode.

Ans. 2.6 atm

10-4 The temperature within an automobile tire at the beginning of a long trip is 25°C. At the conclusion of the trip, the tire has a pressure of 1.80 atm. What is the final Celsius temperature within the tire if its original pressure was 1.75 atm?

Ans. 33.5°C

10-4 A sample of gas in a closed container at a temperature of 100.°C and a pressure of 3.0 atm is heated to 300.°C. What pressure does the gas exert at the higher temperature?

Ans. 4.6 atm

SAMPLE PROBLEM 10-4

The gas in an aerosol can is at a pressure of 3.00 atm at 25°C. Directions on the can warn the user not to keep the can in a place where the temperature exceeds 52°C. What would the gas pressure in the can be at 52°C?

SOLUTION

1 ANALYZE

Given: P_1 of gas = 3.00 atm

T_1 of gas = 25°C + 273 = 298 K; T_2 of gas = 52°C + 273 = 325 K

Unknown: P_2 of gas in atm

2 PLAN

Because the gaseous contents remain at the constant volume of the can, an increase in temperature will cause an increase in pressure. Rearrange Gay-Lussac's law to obtain P_2.

$$P_2 = \frac{P_1 T_2}{T_1}$$

3 COMPUTE

Substitute values for P_1, T_2, and T_1 to obtain the new pressure, P_2.

$$P_2 = \frac{(3.00 \text{ atm})(325 \text{ K})}{298 \text{ K}} = 3.27 \text{ atm}$$

4 EVALUATE

As expected, a temperature increase at constant volume causes the pressure of the contents in the can to increase. Units cancel correctly. The answer contains the proper number of significant figures. It also is reasonably close to an estimated value of 3.25, calculated as $(3 \times 325)/300$.

PRACTICE

1. Before a trip from New York to Boston, the pressure in an automobile tire is 1.8 atm at 20.°C. At the end of the trip, the pressure gauge reads 1.9 atm. What is the new Celsius temperature of the air inside the tire? (Assume tires with constant volume.)

   Answer 36°C

2. At 120.°C, the pressure of a sample of nitrogen is 1.07 atm. What will the pressure be at 205°C, assuming constant volume?

   Answer 1.30 atm

3. A sample of helium gas has a pressure of 1.20 atm at 22°C. At what Celsius temperature will the helium reach a pressure of 2.00 atm?

   Answer 219°C

The Combined Gas Law

A gas sample often undergoes changes in temperature, pressure, and volume all at the same time. When this happens, three variables must be dealt with at once. Boyle's law, Charles's law, and Gay-Lussac's law can be combined into a single expression that is useful in such situations. *The **combined gas law** expresses the relationship between pressure, volume, and temperature of a fixed amount of gas.* The combined gas law can be expressed as follows.

$$\frac{PV}{T} = k$$

In the equation, k is constant and depends on the amount of gas. The combined gas law can also be written as follows.

$$\frac{P_1 V_1}{T_1} = \frac{P_2 V_2}{T_2}$$

The subscripts in the equation above indicate two different sets of conditions, and T represents Kelvin temperature. From this expression, any value can be calculated if the other five are known. Note that each of the individual gas laws can be obtained from the combined gas law when the proper variable is constant. Thus, when temperature is constant, T can be canceled out of both sides of the general equation because it represents the same value ($T_1 = T_2$). This leaves Boyle's law.

$$P_1 V_1 = P_2 V_2$$

If the pressure is held constant, P will cancel out of both sides of the general equation, since $P_1 = P_2$. Charles's law is obtained.

$$\frac{V_1}{T_1} = \frac{V_2}{T_2}$$

Keeping the volume constant means V can be canceled out of both sides of the general equation because $V_1 = V_2$. This gives Gay-Lussac's law.

$$\frac{P_1}{T_1} = \frac{P_2}{T_2}$$

✔ Teaching Tip

The combined gas law can appear overwhelming to students who have difficulty with math skills. To be certain that students possess the algebraic skills necessary to solve for any one of the six variables expressed in the equation, write the combined gas law on the chalkboard. Have students solve for each variable in terms of the other variables.

CHAPTER ⟷ CONNECTION

The relationships shown in Boyle's law, Charles's law, and Gay-Lussac's law are mentioned as they relate to the ideal gas law in Chapter 11. Changes of state as a result of changes in temperature and pressure are discussed in Chapter 12.

SAMPLE PROBLEM 10-5

A helium-filled balloon has a volume of 50.0 L at 25°C and 1.08 atm. What volume will it have at 0.855 atm and 10.°C?

SOLUTION

1 **ANALYZE**   **Given:** V_1 of He = 50.0 L
T_1 of He = 25°C + 273 = 298 K; T_2 of He = 10°C + 273 = 283 K
P_1 of He = 1.08 atm; P_2 of He = 0.855 atm
Unknown: V_2 of He in L

10-5 The volume of a gas at 27.0°C and 0.200 atm is 80.0 mL. What volume will the same gas sample occupy at standard conditions?

Ans. 14.6 mL

10-5 A gas occupying 75 mL at standard conditions is heated to 17°C while the pressure is reduced to 0.97 atm. What is the new volume occupied by the gas?

Ans. 82 mL

10-5 What pressure is required to reduce 60.0 mL of a gas at standard conditions to 10.0 mL at a temperature of 25.0°C?

Ans. 6.55 atm

Did You Know?

Air is rich in oxygen and poor in carbon dioxide. By contrast, cellular fluids are relatively rich in carbon dioxide and poor in oxygen. Therefore, the partial pressures of oxygen and carbon dioxide vary in the lungs; in veins, arteries, and capillaries; and in cells.

Reading Skill-Builder

PAIRED READING Have pairs of students read the section on Dalton's Law of Partial Pressures silently and make notes on the portions of the text they do not understand. Have them discuss the passages that they found difficult. If one student is unable to clarify the passage for his or her partner, have the pair pose a question for the class or teacher.

---

2 PLAN Because the gas changes in both temperature and pressure, the combined gas law is needed. Rearrange the combined gas law to solve for the final volume, V_2.

$$\frac{P_1 V_1}{T_1} = \frac{P_2 V_2}{T_2} \longrightarrow V_2 = \frac{P_1 V_1 T_2}{P_2 T_1}$$

3 COMPUTE Substitute the known values into the equation to obtain a value for V_2.

$$V_2 = \frac{(1.08 \text{ atm})(50.0 \text{ L He})(283 \text{ K})}{(0.855 \text{ atm})(298 \text{ K})} = 60.0 \text{ L He}$$

4 EVALUATE Here the pressure decreases much more than the temperature decreases. As expected, the net result of the two changes gives an increase in the volume, from 50.0 L to 60.0 L. Units cancel appropriately. The answer is correctly expressed to three significant figures. It is also reasonably close to an estimated value of 50, calculated as $(50 \times 300)/300$.

PRACTICE

1. The volume of a gas is 27.5 mL at 22.0°C and 0.974 atm. What will the volume be at 15.0°C and 0.993 atm?

   Answer
   26.3 mL

2. A 700. mL gas sample at STP is compressed to a volume of 200. mL, and the temperature is increased to 30.0°C. What is the new pressure of the gas in Pa?

   Answer
   3.94×10^5 Pa, or 394 kPa

Dalton's Law of Partial Pressures

John Dalton, the English chemist who proposed the atomic theory, also studied gas mixtures. He found that *in the absence of a chemical reaction*, the pressure of a gas mixture is the sum of the individual pressures of each gas alone. Figure 10-14 shows a 1.0 L container filled with oxygen gas at a pressure of 0.12 atm at 0°C. In another 1.0 L container, an equal number of molecules of nitrogen gas exert a pressure of 0.12 atm at 0°C. The gas samples are then combined in a 1.0 L container. (At 0°C, oxygen gas and nitrogen gas are unreactive.) The total pressure of the mixture is found to be 0.24 atm at 0°C. The pressure that each gas exerts in the mixture is independent of that exerted by other gases present. *The pressure of each gas in a mixture is called the* **partial pressure** *of that gas.* **Dalton's law of partial pressures** *states that the total pressure of a mixture of gases is equal to the sum of the partial pressures of the component gases.* The law is true regardless of the number of different gases that are present. Dalton's law may be expressed as follows.

$$P_T = P_1 + P_2 + P_3 + \ldots$$

P_T is the total pressure of the mixture. $P_1, P_2, P_3, \ldots$ are the partial pressures of component gases 1, 2, 3, and so on.

You can understand Dalton's law in terms of the kinetic-molecular theory. The rapidly moving particles of each gas in a mixture have an equal chance to collide with the container walls. Therefore, each gas exerts a pressure independent of that exerted by the other gases present. The total pressure is the result of the total number of collisions per unit of wall area in a given time. (Note that because gas particles move independently, the other gas laws, as well as Dalton's law, can be applied to unreacting gas mixtures.)

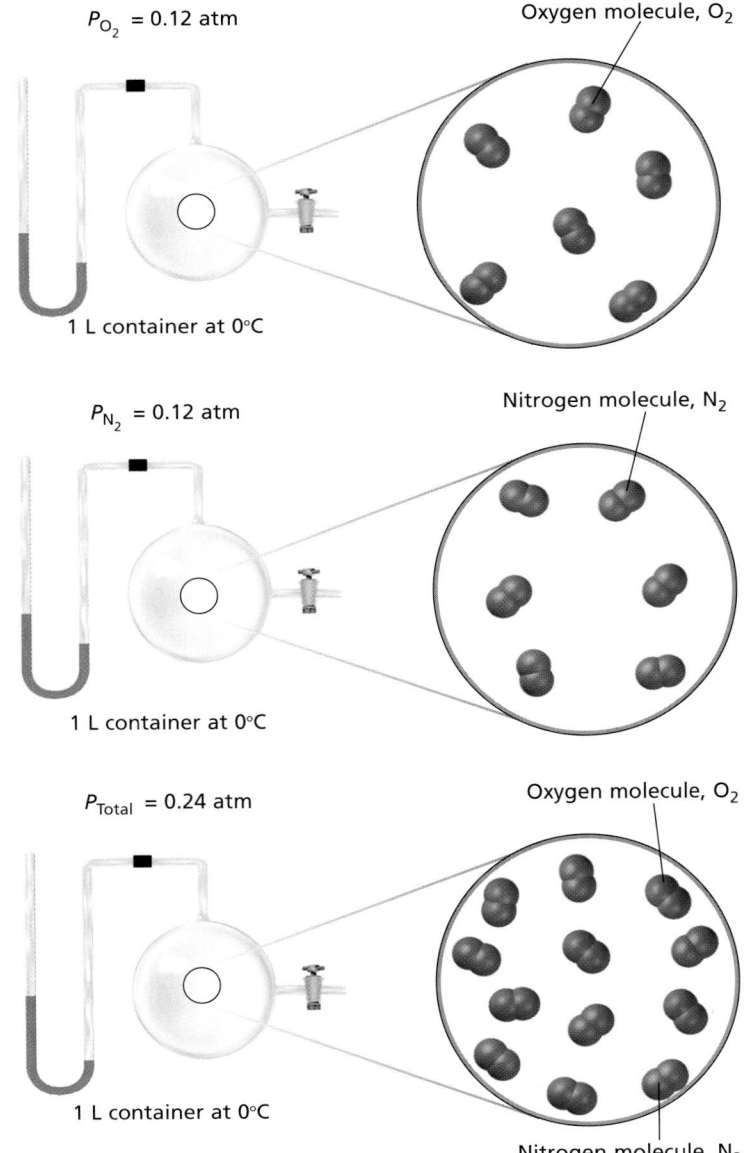

$P_{O_2} = 0.12$ atm

Oxygen molecule, O_2

1 L container at 0°C

$P_{N_2} = 0.12$ atm

Nitrogen molecule, N_2

1 L container at 0°C

$P_{Total} = 0.24$ atm

Oxygen molecule, O_2

1 L container at 0°C

Nitrogen molecule, N_2

FIGURE 10-14 Samples of oxygen gas and nitrogen gas are mixed. The total pressure of the mixture is the sum of the pressures of the gases.

Visual Strategy

FIGURE 10-14 Point out that equal amounts of gas at the same temperature and volume have equal pressure.

Application

Dalton's law of partial pressures has important applications for people who work at high altitudes, such as mountain climbers and pilots. For example, at an altitude of about 10 000 m (higher than Mount Everest), air pressure is about one-third of an atmosphere. The partial pressure of oxygen at this altitude is 0.3 atm × 0.21 (percent of O_2 in air) × 760 mm Hg, or less than 50 mm Hg. By comparison, the partial pressure of oxygen in human alveolar blood needs to be about 100 mm Hg. Thus, respiration cannot occur normally at this altitude, and an outside source of oxygen is needed in order to survive.

Additional Example Problem

1. Calculate the partial pressure in millimeters of mercury exerted by the four main gases in air at 760 mm Hg: nitrogen, oxygen, argon, and carbon dioxide. Their abundance by volume is 78.08%, 20.95%, 0.934%, and 0.035%, respectively.

Ans. N_2: 593.4 mm Hg
O_2: 159.2 mm Hg
Ar: 7.10 mm Hg
CO_2: 0.27 mm Hg

324

DEMONSTRATION

Amount of Oxygen in Air

Wet the inside of a test tube, and add iron filings until the tube is about one-tenth full. Gently shake the tube to disperse the filings onto the wet tube walls. Place a finger over the test tube mouth, invert the tube, and place it in a 250 mL beaker of water so that the mouth is 1 cm below the water's surface. Clamp the tube in place. As the iron filings are oxidized, oxygen will be removed from the air. By the next day, the water level will have risen about one-fifth of the tube length, an amount equal to the volume occupied by the oxygen.

Safety: Wear safety goggles during setup.

Disposal: Throw rusty iron into the trash.

Class Discussion

Ask students what kinds of gases could not be collected by water displacement *(gases that are soluble in or that react with water)*. Discuss other methods by which such gases can be collected.

HANDBOOK CONNECTION

The effect of gas pressures in a mixture is further discussed using the exchange of O_2 and CO_2 in the blood as an example. See Group 14 of the *Elements Handbook*.

FIGURE 10-15

Hydrogen can be collected by water displacement by reacting zinc with sulfuric acid. The hydrogen gas produced displaces the water in the gas collecting bottle. It now contains some water vapor.

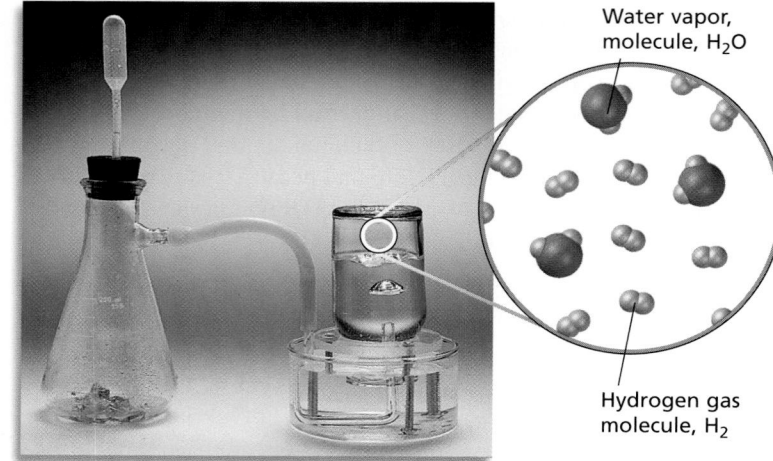

Water vapor, molecule, H_2O

Hydrogen gas molecule, H_2

Gases Collected by Water Displacement

Gases produced in the laboratory are often collected over water, as shown in Figure 10-15. The gas produced by the reaction displaces the water, which is more dense, in the collection bottle. You can apply Dalton's law of partial pressures in calculating the pressures of gases collected in this way. A gas collected by water displacement is not pure but is always mixed with water vapor. That is because water molecules at the liquid surface evaporate and mix with the gas molecules. Water vapor, like other gases, exerts a pressure, known as *water-vapor pressure*.

Suppose you wished to determine the total pressure of the gas and water vapor inside a collection bottle. You would raise the bottle until the water levels inside and outside the bottle were the same. At that point, the total pressure inside the bottle would be the same as the atmospheric pressure, P_{atm}. According to Dalton's law of partial pressures, the following is true.

$$P_{atm} = P_{gas} + P_{H_2O}$$

Suppose you then needed to calculate the partial pressure of the dry gas collected. You would read the atmospheric pressure, P_{atm}, from a barometer in the laboratory. To make the calculation, subtract the vapor pressure of the water at the given temperature from the total pressure. The vapor pressure of water varies with temperature. You need to look up the value of P_{H_2O} at the temperature of the experiment in a standard reference table like that in Table A-8 of this book.

SAMPLE PROBLEM 10-6

Oxygen gas from the decomposition of potassium chlorate, $KClO_3$, was collected by water displacement. The barometric pressure and the temperature during the experiment were 731.0 torr and 20.0°C, respectively. What was the partial pressure of the oxygen collected?

SOLUTION

1 ANALYZE

Given: $P_T = P_{atm} = 731.0$ torr

$P_{H_2O} = 17.5$ torr (vapor pressure of water at 20.0°C, from Table A-8)

$P_{atm} = P_{O_2} + P_{H_2O}$

Unknown: P_{O_2} in torr

2 PLAN

The partial pressure of the collected oxygen is found by subtracting the partial pressure of water vapor from the atmospheric pressure, according to Dalton's law of partial pressures.

$$P_{O_2} = P_{atm} - P_{H_2O}$$

3 COMPUTE

Substituting values for P_{atm} and P_{H_2O} gives P_{O_2}.

$$P_{O_2} = 731.0 \text{ torr} - 17.5 \text{ torr} = 713.5 \text{ torr}$$

4 EVALUATE

As expected, the oxygen partial pressure is less than atmospheric pressure. It is also much larger than the partial pressure of water vapor at this temperature. The answer has the appropriate number of significant figures. It is reasonably close to an estimated value of 713, calculated as 730 − 17.

PRACTICE

1. Some hydrogen gas is collected over water at 20.0°C. The levels of water inside and outside the gas-collection bottle are the same. The partial pressure of hydrogen is 742.5 torr. What is the barometric pressure at the time the gas is collected?

   Answer
   760.0 torr

2. Helium gas is collected over water at 25°C. What is the partial pressure of the helium, given that the barometric pressure is 750.0 mm Hg?

   Answer
   726.2 mm Hg

SECTION REVIEW

1. State Boyle's law, Charles's law, and the combined gas law in mathematical terms.

2. A sample of helium gas has a volume of 200.0 mL at 0.960 atm. What pressure, in atm, is needed to reduce the volume at constant temperature to 50.0 mL?

3. A certain quantity of gas has a volume of 0.750 L at 298 K. At what temperature, in degrees Celsius, would this quantity of gas be reduced to 0.500 L, assuming constant pressure?

4. An aerosol can contains gases under a pressure of 4.50 atm at 20.0°C. If the can is left on a hot,

sandy beach, the pressure of the gases increases to 4.80 atm. What is the Celsius temperature on the beach?

5. Discuss the significance of the absolute-zero temperature.

6. A certain mass of oxygen was collected over water when potassium chlorate was decomposed by heating. The volume of the oxygen sample collected was 720. mL at 25.0°C and a barometric pressure of 755 torr. What would the volume of the oxygen be at STP? (Hint: First calculate the partial pressure of the oxygen, using Appendix Table A-8. Then use the combined gas law.)

REVIEW ANSWERS

1. Particles of matter are always in motion.

2. An ideal gas is a theoretical gas that fits perfectly all the assumptions of the kinetic theory.

3. Gases consist of large numbers of tiny particles that are far apart in comparison to their size. The particles of a gas are in constant rapid motion. All collisions between gas particles and between particles and container walls are elastic collisions. There are no forces of attraction or repulsion between gas particles. The average kinetic energy of gas particles depends on the temperature of the gas.

4. The molecules of gases are much farther apart.

5. A collision is an elastic collision if no net kinetic energy is lost.

6. **a.** $KE = \frac{1}{2}mv^2$, where m is the mass of the particle and v is its speed.
   b. The average speed and kinetic energy of gas molecules increase with an increase in temperature and decrease with a decrease in temperature.

7. **a.** the spontaneous mixing of the particles of two substances due to their random motion
   b. the speeds, diameters, and attractive forces of the gas particles
   c. In general, the more massive the gas particle is, the lower is its speed and the more slowly it diffuses through another gas.
   d. the process by which gas particles under pressure pass through a tiny opening

8. **a.** Its moving molecules hit the container walls.

CHAPTER SUMMARY

10-1
- The kinetic-molecular theory of matter can be used to explain the properties of gases, liquids, and solids.
- The kinetic-molecular theory of gases describes a model of an ideal gas. The behavior of most gases is close to ideal except at very high pressures and low temperatures.
- Gases consist of large numbers of tiny, fast-moving particles that are far apart relative to their size. The average kinetic energy of the particles depends on the temperature of the gas.
- Gases exhibit expansion, fluidity, low density, compressibility, diffusion, and effusion.

Vocabulary

diffusion (305)	elastic collision (303)	ideal gas (303)	real gas (306)
effusion (306)	fluids (305)	kinetic-molecular theory (303)	

10-2
- Conditions of standard temperature and pressure (STP) allow comparison of volumes of different gases.
- Pressure, volume, temperature, and number of molecules are the four measureable quantities needed to fully describe a gas.
- The gas molecules that make up the atmosphere exert pressure against Earth's surface, varying with weather conditions and elevation.
- A barometer measures the pressure of the atmosphere. The pressure of a gas in a closed container can be measured by a manometer.

Vocabulary

atmosphere of pressure (311)	millimeters of mercury (311)	pascal (311)	standard temperature and pressure (312)
barometer (310)	newton (309)	pressure (308)	torr (311)

10-3
- Boyle's law shows the inverse relationship between the volume and the pressure of a gas.
$$PV = k$$
- Charles's law illustrates the direct relationship between the volume of a gas and its temperature in kelvins.
$$V = kT$$
- Gay-Lussac's law represents the direct relationship between the pressure of a gas and its temperature in kelvins.
$$P = kT$$
- The combined gas law, as its name implies, combines the previous relationships into the following mathematical expression.
$$\frac{PV}{T} = k$$
- A gas exerts pressure on the walls of its container. In a mixture of unreacting gases, the total pressure equals the sum of the partial pressures of each gas.

Vocabulary

absolute zero (317)	Charles's law (317)	Dalton's law of partial pressures (322)	Gay-Lussac's law (319)
Boyle's law (314)	combined gas law (321)	gas laws (313)	partial pressure (322)

REVIEWING CONCEPTS

1. What idea is the kinetic-molecular theory based on? (10-1)
2. What is an ideal gas? (10-1)
3. State the five basic assumptions of the kinetic-molecular theory. (10-1)
4. How do gases compare with liquids and solids in terms of the distance between their molecules? (10-1)
5. What is an elastic collision? (10-1)
6. a. Write and label the equation that relates the average kinetic energy and speed of gas particles.
   b. What is the relationship between the temperature, speed, and kinetic energy of gas molecules? (10-1)
7. a. What is diffusion?
   b. What factors affect the rate of diffusion of one gas through another?
   c. What is the relationship between the mass of a gas particle and the rate at which it diffuses through another gas?
   d. What is effusion? (10-1)
8. a. Why does a gas in a closed container exert pressure?
   b. What is the relationship between the area a force is applied to and the resulting pressure? (10-2)
9. a. What is atmospheric pressure?
   b. Why does the atmosphere exert pressure?
   c. What is the value of atmospheric pressure at sea level, in newtons per square centimeter? (10-2)
10. a. Why does a column of mercury in a tube that is inverted in a dish of mercury have a height of about 760 mm at sea level?
    b. What height would be maintained by a column of water inverted in a dish of water at sea level?
    c. What accounts for the difference in the heights of the mercury and water columns? (10-2)
11. a. Identify three units used to express pressure.
    b. Convert one atmosphere to torr.
    c. What is a pascal?
    d. What is the SI equivalent of one standard atmosphere of pressure? (10-2)

12. a. At constant pressure, how does temperature relate to the volume of a given quantity of gas?
    b. How does this explain the danger of throwing an aerosol can into a fire? (10-3)
13. a. What is the Celsius equivalent of absolute zero?
    b. What is the significance of this temperature?
    c. What is the relationship between Kelvin temperature and the average kinetic energy of gas molecules? (10-3)
14. a. Explain what is meant by the partial pressure of each gas within a mixture of gases.
    b. How do the partial pressures of gases in a mixture affect each other? (10-3)

PROBLEMS

Pressure and Temperature Conversions

15. If the atmosphere can support a column of mercury 760 mm high at sea level, what height (in mm) of each of the following could be supported, given the relative density values cited?
    a. water, whose density is approximately 1/14 that of mercury
    b. a hypothetical liquid with a density 1.40 times that of mercury

16. Convert each of the following into a pressure reading expressed in torr. (Hint: See Sample Problem 10-1.)
    a. 1.25 atm   c. 4.75×10^4 atm
    b. 2.48×10^{-3} atm   d. 7.60×10^6 atm

17. Convert each of the following into the unit specified.
    a. 125 mm Hg into atm
    b. 3.20 atm into Pa
    c. 5.38 kPa into torr

18. Convert each of the following Celsius temperatures to Kelvin temperatures.
    a. 0.°C   c. −50.°C
    b. 27°C   d. −273°C

19. Convert each of the following Kelvin temperatures to Celsius temperatures.
    a. 273 K   c. 100. K
    b. 350. K   d. 20. K

b. The same force applied to a smaller area results in a greater pressure.

9. a. the sum of the individual pressures of all the gases in the atmosphere
   b. The force of gravity acting on gases in the atmosphere results in their having weight, which presses on areas it contacts.
   c. 10.1 N/cm²

10. a. The pressure exerted by the mercury in the tube equals that exerted by the atmosphere, which, at sea level, is equal to the force exerted by a column of mercury approximately 760 mm in height.
    b. about 34 ft
    c. Mercury is 14 times as dense as water, so it exerts 14 times more pressure than does a comparable column of water.

11. a. millimeters of mercury (mm Hg), torrs (torr), atmospheres (atm), and pascals (Pa)
    b. 1 atm = 760 torr
    c. the pressure exerted by a force of one newton (N) acting on an area of 1 m²; 1 Pa = 1N/m²
    d. 1.01325×10^5 Pa, or 101.325 kPa

12. a. As temperature increases, volume increases; as temperature decreases, volume decreases.
    b. As the temperature of the gas inside the container increases, the volume of the gas may increase to such an extent that the container may explode.

13. a. −273.15°C
    b. It is the lowest temperature possible.
    c. The average kinetic energy of gas molecules is directly proportional to the Kelvin temperature.

14. a. It is the pressure each gas exerts in the mixture of gases.

b. They are independent of one another.

15. a. 11 000 mm
b. 543 mm

16. a. 950. torr
b. 1.88 torr
c. 3.61×10^7 torr
d. 5.78×10^9 torr

17. a. 0.164 atm
b. 3.24×10^5 Pa
c. 40.4 torr

18. a. 273 K
b. 300 K
c. 223 K
d. 0 K

19. a. 0°C
b. 77°C
c. −173°C
d. −253°C

20. a. 100. mL
b. 280 mL
c. 1.4 mm Hg

21. 142 mL

22. 38.8 kPa

23. a. 225.0 mL
b. 1800. mL

24. 6.05×10^5 mL

25. a. 93.3 mL
b. 588 K or 315°C
c. 29.9 mL

26. 121 K or −152°C

27. 406 mL

28. 0.360 atm

29. 540. K or 267°C

30. 127°C

31. 3.41 L

32. 485 torr

33. 260. K or −13°C

34. 2.01 atm

35. −16°C

36. 243 L

37. −43°C

38. 9.98 m³

Boyle's Law

20. Use Boyle's law to solve for the missing value in each of the following. (Hint: See Sample Problem 10-2.)
 a. $P_1 = 350.$ torr, $V_1 = 200.$ mL, $P_2 = 700.$ torr, $V_2 = ?$
 b. $P_1 = 0.75$ atm, $V_2 = 435$ mL, $P_2 = 0.48$ atm, $V_1 = ?$
 c. $V_1 = 2.4 \times 10^5$ L, $P_2 = 180$ mm Hg, $V_2 = 1.8 \times 10^3$ L, $P_1 = ?$

21. The pressure exerted on a 240. mL sample of hydrogen gas at constant temperature is increased from 0.428 atm to 0.724 atm. What will the final volume of the sample be?

22. A flask containing 155 cm³ of hydrogen was collected under a pressure of 22.5 kPa. What pressure would have been required for the volume of the gas to have been 90.0 cm³, assuming the same temperature?

23. A gas has a volume of 450.0 mL. If the temperature is held constant, what volume would the gas occupy if the pressure were
 a. doubled? (Hint: Express P_2 in terms of P_1.)
 b. reduced to one-fourth of its original value?

24. A sample of oxygen that occupies 1.00×10^6 mL at 575 mm Hg is subjected to a pressure of 1.25 atm. What will the final volume of the sample be if the temperature is held constant?

Charles's Law

25. Use Charles's law to solve for the missing value in each of the following. (Hint: See Sample Problem 10-3.)
 a. $V_1 = 80.0$ mL, $T_1 = 27°C$, $T_2 = 77°C$, $V_2 = ?$
 b. $V_1 = 125$ L, $V_2 = 85.0$ L, $T_2 = 127°C$, $T_1 = ?$
 c. $T_1 = -33°C$, $V_2 = 54.0$ mL, $T_2 = 160.°C$, $V_1 = ?$

26. A sample of air has a volume of 140.0 mL at 67°C. At what temperature will its volume be 50.0 mL at constant pressure?

27. At standard temperature, a gas has a volume of 275 mL. The temperature is then increased to 130.°C, and the pressure is held constant. What is the new volume?

Gay-Lussac's Law

28. A sample of hydrogen at 47°C exerts a pressure of 0.329 atm. The gas is heated to 77°C at constant volume. What will its new pressure be? (Hint: See Sample Problem 10-4.)

29. To what temperature must a sample of nitrogen at 27°C and 0.625 atm be taken so that its pressure becomes 1.125 atm at constant volume?

30. The pressure on a gas at −73°C is doubled, but its volume is held constant. What will the final temperature be in degrees Celsius?

Combined Gas Law

31. A sample of gas at 47°C and 1.03 atm occupies a volume of 2.20 L. What volume would this gas occupy at 107°C and 0.789 atm? (Hint: See Sample Problem 10-5.)

32. A 350. mL air sample collected at 35°C has a pressure of 550. torr. What pressure will the air exert if it is allowed to expand to 425 mL at 57°C?

33. A gas has a volume of 1.75 L at −23°C and 150. kPa. At what temperature would the gas occupy 1.30 L at 210. kPa?

34. A sample of oxygen at 40.°C occupies 820. mL. If this sample later occupies 1250 mL at 60.°C and 1.40 atm, what was its original pressure?

35. A gas at 7.75×10^4 Pa and 17°C occupies a volume of 850. cm³. At what temperature, in degrees Celsius, would the gas occupy 720. cm³ at 8.10×10^4 Pa?

36. A meteorological balloon contains 250. L of He at 22°C and 740. mm Hg. If the volume of the balloon can vary according to external conditions, what volume would it occupy at an altitude at which the temperature is −52°C and the pressure is 0.750 atm?

37. The balloon in the previous problem will burst if its volume reaches 400. L. Given the initial conditions specified in that problem, at what temperature, in degrees Celsius, will the balloon burst if its pressure at that bursting point is 0.475 atm?

38. The normal respiratory rate for a human being is 15.0 breaths per minute. The average volume of air for each breath is 505 cm³ at 20.°C and 9.95×10^4 Pa. What is the volume of air at STP that an individual breathes in one day? Give your answer in cubic meters.

Dalton's Law of Partial Pressures

39. Three of the primary components of air are carbon dioxide, nitrogen, and oxygen. In a sample containing a mixture of only these gases at exactly one atmosphere pressure, the partial pressures of carbon dioxide and nitrogen are given as $P_{CO_2} = 0.285$ torr and $P_{N_2} = 593.525$ torr. What is the partial pressure of oxygen? (Hint: See Sample Problem 10-6.)

40. Determine the partial pressure of oxygen collected by water displacement if the water temperature is 20.0°C and the total pressure of the gases in the collection bottle is 730.0 torr.

41. A sample of gas is collected over water at a temperature of 35.0°C when the barometric pressure reading is 742.0 torr. What is the partial pressure of the dry gas?

42. A sample of oxygen is collected in a 175 mL container over water at 15°C, and the barometer reads 752.0 torr. What volume would the dry gas occupy at 770.0 torr and 15°C?

43. Suppose that 120. mL of argon is collected over water at 25°C and 780.0 torr. Compute the volume of the dry argon at STP.

MIXED REVIEW

44. A mixture of three gases, A, B, and C, is at a total pressure of 6.11 atm. The partial pressure of gas A is 1.68 atm; that of gas B is 3.89 atm. What is the partial pressure of gas C?

45. A child receives a balloon filled with 2.30 L of helium from a vendor at an amusement park. The temperature outside is 311 K. What will the volume of the balloon be when the child brings it home to an air-conditioned house at 295 K? Assume that the pressure stays the same.

46. A sample of argon gas occupies a volume of 295 mL at 36°C. What volume will the gas occupy at 55°C, assuming constant pressure?

47. A sample of carbon dioxide gas occupies 638 mL at 0.893 atm and 12°C. What will the pressure be at a volume of 881 mL and a temperature of 18°C?

48. At 84°C, a gas in a container exerts a pressure of 0.503 atm. Assuming the size of the container has not changed, at what Celsius temperature would the pressure be 1.20 atm?

49. A weather balloon at Earth's surface has a volume of 4.00 L at 304 K and 755 mm Hg. If the balloon is released and the volume reaches 4.08 L at 728 mm Hg, what is the temperature?

50. A gas has a pressure of 4.62 atm when its volume is 2.33 L. What will the pressure be when the volume is changed to 1.03 L, assuming constant temperature? Express the final pressure in torr.

51. At a deep-sea station 200. m below the surface of the Pacific Ocean, workers live in a highly pressurized environment. How many liters of gas at STP must be compressed on the surface to fill the underwater environment with 2.00×10^7 L of gas at 20.0 atm? Assume that temperature remains constant.

CRITICAL THINKING

52. **Applying Models**
    a. Why do we say the graph in Figure 10-10 illustrates an inverse relationship?
    b. Why does the data plotted in Figure 10-12 show a direct relationship?

53. **Relating Ideas**   Explain how different gases in a mixture can have the same average kinetic energy value, even though the masses of their individual particles differ.

54. **Inferring Conclusions**   If all gases behaved as ideal gases under all conditions of temperature and pressure, there would be no solid or liquid forms of these substances. Explain.

55. **Relating Ideas**   Pressure is defined as force per unit area. Yet Torricelli found that the diameter of the barometer dish and the surface area of contact between the mercury in the tube and in the dish did not affect the height of mercury

39. 166.190 torr
40. 712.5 torr
41. 699.8 torr
42. 168 mL
43. 109 mL
44. 0.54 atm
45. 2.18 L
46. 313 mL
47. 0.660 atm
48. 579°C
49. 299 K
50. 7940 torr
51. 4.00×10^8 L

52. **a.** An increase in one variable is accompanied by a corresponding decrease in the other variable.
    b. An increase in one variable is accompanied by a corresponding increase in the second variable.

53. At the same temperature, the molecules of higher mass have a slower average velocity, and kinetic energy depends on both mass and velocity.

54. If all gases behaved ideally, the individual gas particles would never exert the attractive forces on one another that are needed to form liquids or solids.

55. Both the pressure exerted by the column of mercury in the tube and the pressure exerted by the atmosphere on the surface of mercury in the dish can be thought of as acting on the imaginary surface of the mercury in the tube that is level with the surface of the mercury in the dish outside the tube. Because both forces are acting on the same surface, the size of the surface is not a factor in determining the eventual pressures.

56. 820 mm Hg

57. a. The temperature for B is greater.
b. The average kinetic energy is greater for B.
c. The average molecular velocity is greater for B.
d. There is not enough information to tell.
e. There is not enough information to tell.

58. a. 1.20 atm
b. 27.27 mL
c. 53.33 mL

59. nitrogen, oxygen, fluorine, and chlorine

60. nitrogen, oxygen, ethylene, ammonia, propylene, and chlorine

61. a. 135 g/cm^3; the density of Hg is higher than most other transition metals.
b. Mercury vapor is highly toxic and can be absorbed through the skin, respiratory system, and digestive tract. Absorption of mercury is cumulative. It damages the kidney, heart, and brain. Some students may go on to describe the link between mercury and mental illness.
c. Methylmercury; if methylmercury enters the food chain in a water ecosystem, its concentration increases for each consumer in the food chain.
d. Symptoms include numbness, tunnel vision, garbled speech, bleeding and inflammation of the gums, muscle spasms, anemia, and emotional disorders.

Refer to the *One-Stop Planner* CD-ROM for appropriate scoring rubrics for items 62 through 64.

---

that was supported. Explain this seemingly inconsistent observation in view of the relationship between pressure and surface areas.

56. Interpreting Graphics   Examine Boyle's J-tube apparatus shown here. The tube is open to the atmosphere at the top. The other end is closed and contains a gas with a volume labeled V_{gas}. If $h = 60$ mm Hg, what is the pressure exerted by the enclosed gas?

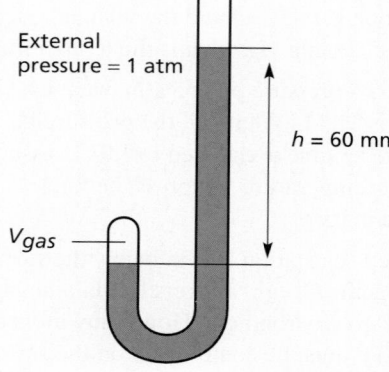

External pressure = 1 atm

$h = 60$ mm

V_{gas}

57. Velocity distribution curves are shown in the following graph for the same gas under two different conditions, A and B. Compare the behavior of the gas under conditions A and B in relation to each of the following:
a. temperature
b. average kinetic energy
c. average molecular velocity
d. gas volume
e. gas pressure

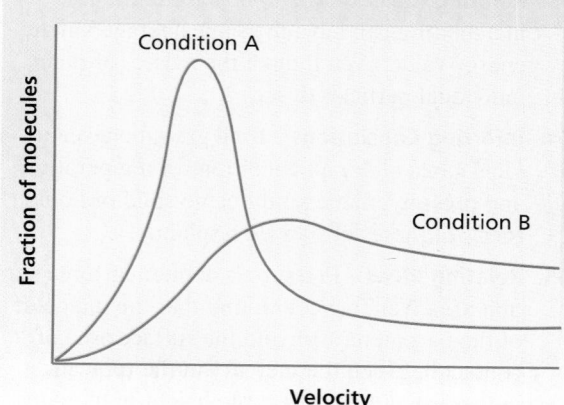

Condition A

Condition B

Fraction of molecules

Velocity

---

58. Graphing Calculator   Deriving the Boyle's Law Equation

The graphing calculator can run a program that derives the equation for a curve, given data such as volume vs. pressure. Begin by creating a table of data. Then the program will plot the data.

Go to Appendix C. If you are using a TI 83 Plus, you can download the program and data and run the application as directed. If you are using another calculator, your teacher will provide you with keystrokes and data sets to use. Remember that you will need to name the program and check the display, as explained in Appendix C. You will then be ready to run the program. After you have graphed the data, answer these questions.

Note: Answers are written with two significant figures.

a. What is the pressure if the measured volume is 500 mL?
b. What is the volume if the measured pressure is 22 atm?
c. What is the volume if the measured pressure is 7.5 atm?

HANDBOOK SEARCH

59. Review the melting point data in the properties tables for each group of the *Elements Handbook*. What elements on the periodic table exist as gases at room temperature?

60. Review the listing found in the *Elements Handbook* of the top 10 chemicals produced in the United States. Which of the top 10 chemicals are gases?

61. Though mercury is an ideal liquid to use in barometers, it is highly toxic. Review the transition metals section of the *Elements Handbook*, and answer the following questions:
a. What is the density of mercury? How does the density of Hg compare with that of other transition metals?

b. In what ways is mercury toxic?

c. What mercury compound is becoming more common as a pollutant in lakes and streams? Why is this pollutant so dangerous to fresh-water ecosystems?

d. What are the symptoms of mercury poisoning?

RESEARCH & WRITING

62. Prepare a report on the development of the modern submarine. Include a discussion of the technology that enables the submarine to withstand the tremendous pressures at great ocean depths. Also report on the equipment used to ensure a sufficient supply of oxygen for submarine crew members.

63. Design and conduct a meteorological study to examine the interrelationships among baromet-ric pressure, temperature, humidity, and other weather variables. Prepare a report explaining your results.

64. Conduct library research on attempts made to approach absolute zero and on the interesting properties that materials exhibit near that temperature. Write a report on your findings.

ALTERNATIVE ASSESSMENT

65. The air pressure of car tires should be checked regularly for safety reasons and to prevent uneven tire wear. Find out the units of measure-ment on a typical tire gauge, and determine how gauge pressure relates to atmospheric pressure.

Molecular Composition of Gases

PACING CHART Compression Guide: *(To shorten, eliminate items in italics.)*	CLASSROOM RESOURCES		
	NSE Standards	Teaching Resources	Experiments
11-1 Volume–Mass Relationships of Gases 2 45-minute periods 1 90-minute block *Measuring and Comparing the Volumes of Reacting Gases, p. 333*	UCP 1–3 SAI 2 HNS 1–3	T 52	A9 Molar Volume of Gas C11 **EXP** Masses of Equal Volumes of Gases
11-2 The Ideal Gas Law 2 45-minute periods 1 90-minute block *Derivation of the Ideal Gas Law, p. 341* *The Ideal Gas Constant, p. 342*	PS 5c UCP 1–3	**ATE Demo,** p. 345 T 53, TM 53A	
11-3 Stoichiometry of Gases 2 45-minute periods 1 90-minute block *Volume-Mass and Mass-Volume Calculations, pp. 348–350*	UCP 1–3		
11-4 Effusion and Diffusion 2 45-minute periods 1 90-minute block *Graham's Law of Effusion, pp. 351–353* *Applications of Graham's Law, pp. 353–355*	UCP 1–3 SAI 1–2 HNS 1, 3	T 54	Quick Lab, p. 353

Review and Assessment 2 45-minute periods 1 90-minute block	REVIEW RESOURCES		
	Cumulative Review	Alternative Assessment	Traditional Assessment
	SR Chapter 11 Mixed Review PE Chapter 11 43–51, pp. 359–360	PE 65, 66, p. 361 ATE 335, 346, 350, 361 AA Items for Chapter 11	Chapter 11 Text Test Generator items for Chapter 11

ASSIGNMENT RESOURCES

Section Homework Resources & Review	Problem-Solving Practice
HR Homework Worksheets 11-1, 11-2 Graphic Org. Assignment 11-1 **PE** Section Review, 1–5, p. 337 Chapter Review, 1–4, 9–15, p. 357 **SR** Section Review 11-1	**PE** Additional Samples 11-1, 11-2 **ATE** Additional Samples, pp. 336, 337 Additional Examples, p. 335
HR Homework Worksheets 11-3, 11-4 Graphic Org. Assignment 11-4 **PE** Section Review, 1–5, p. 346 Chapter Review, 5–6, 16–22, p. 357 **SR** Section Review 11-2	**PE** Additional Samples 11-3, 11-4, 11-5, 11-6 **ATE** Additional Samples, pp. 343–346 **PS** Chapter 12 Ideal Gas Law
HR Homework Worksheets 11-5, 11-6 **PE** Section Review, 1–4, p. 350 Chapter Review, 7, 23–38, p. 358 **SR** Section Review 11-3	**PE** Additional Samples 11-7, 11-8, 11-9 **ATE** Additional Samples, pp. 348, 349, 350 **PS** Chapter 13 Stoichiometry of Gases
HR Homework Worksheets 11-7, 11-8 Graphic Org. Assignments 11-7, 11-8 **PE** Section Review, 1–5, p. 355 Chapter Review, 8, 39–42, p. 359 **SR** Section Review 11-4	**PE** Additional Sample, 11-10 **ATE** Additional Sample, p. 355 Additional Examples, p. 352

TECHNOLOGY RESOURCES

Technology & Internet Resources

 CTW 21 Segment 21 Global Warming

 Holt Chemistry Videodiscs Teacher's Correlation Guide for Chapter 11

 Module 5: Equations and Stoichiometry

internet connect

On-line Student Resources:
GO TO: www.scilinks.org
The following SciLinks Internet resources can be found in the student text for this chapter.

TOPICS:
• Avogadro's Law, p. 333 (HC2111)
• Torricelli, p. 338 (HC2112)
• Robert Boyle, p. 338 (HC2113)
• Thomas Graham, p. 352 (HC2114)

On-line Teacher Resources:
GO TO: go.hrw.com
KEYWORD: HC2 HOME
Visit the HRW Web site for a variety of resources related to this chapter.

 Smithsonian Institution®
Internet Connections
Visit www.si.edu/hrw for additional on-line resources.

CNNfyi.com
Visit www.cnnfyi.com for late-breaking news and current events stories selected just for you.

CHAPTER 11

Molecular Composition of Gases

Chapter Overview

11-1 develops the relationships between the volume, mass, and number of particles of a gas. Avogadro's law leads to the concept of molar volume of a gas.

11-2 uses the concepts from Section 11-1 to derive the ideal gas law, which is put to practical use in calculations.

11-3 shows students how to use the relationship between the volume and moles of a gas to carry out stoichiometric calculations from chemical reactions.

11-4 demonstrates the relationship between the mass of gas particles and their rate of effusion.

Concept Base

Students may need a review of the following concepts:

- scientific notation and significant figures, Chapter 2

- writing and balancing chemical equations, Chapter 8

- stoichiometric calculations, Chapter 9

- the relationship between temperature and particle motion, Chapter 10

Molecular Composition of Gases

The study of gases led to the formulation of the laws and principles that are the foundations of modern chemistry.

Volume-Mass Relationships of Gases

In this section, you will study the relationships between the volumes of gases that react with each other. You will also learn how volume, density, and molar mass are related.

Measuring and Comparing the Volumes of Reacting Gases

In the early 1800s, French chemist Joseph Gay-Lussac studied gas volume relationships involving a chemical reaction between hydrogen and oxygen. He observed that 2 L of hydrogen can react with 1 L of oxygen to form 2 L of water vapor at constant temperature and pressure.

$$\text{hydrogen gas} + \text{oxygen gas} \longrightarrow \text{water vapor}$$

2 L	1 L	2 L
2 volumes	1 volume	2 volumes

In other words, this reaction shows a simple and definite 2:1:2 relationship between the volumes of the reactants and the product. Two volumes of hydrogen react with 1 volume of oxygen to produce 2 volumes of water vapor. The 2:1:2 relationship for this reaction applies to any proportions for volume—for example, 2 mL, 1 mL, and 2 mL; 600 L, 300 L, and 600 L; or 400 cm³, 200 cm³, and 400 cm³.

Gay-Lussac also noticed simple and definite proportions by volume in other reactions of gases, such as in the reaction between hydrogen gas and chlorine gas.

$$\text{hydrogen gas} + \text{chlorine gas} \longrightarrow \text{hydrogen chloride gas}$$

1 L	1 L	2 L
1 volume	1 volume	2 volumes

In 1808, Gay-Lussac summarized the results of his experiments in a statement known today as **Gay-Lussac's law of combining volumes of gases.** The law states that *at constant temperature and pressure, the volumes of gaseous reactants and products can be expressed as ratios of small whole numbers.* This simple observation, combined with the insight of Avogadro, provided more understanding of how gases react and combine with each other.

OBJECTIVES

- State the law of combining volumes.

- State Avogadro's law and explain its significance.

- Define *standard molar volume of a gas,* and use it to calculate gas masses and volumes.

- Use standard molar volume to calculate the molar mass of a gas.

Lesson Starter

Have students write balanced chemical equations for the two reactions described on this page. Ask them to compare the balanced equation with the expressions on the page. They should notice that the balancing coefficients are the same as the volume in liters of the gases in each reaction.

Did You Know?

When Gay-Lussac made his discovery involving volume relationships in chemical reactions, chemists had not accepted the atomic theory, nor did they know the correct composition of substances. Therefore, they could not have written chemical equations. Work such as that of Gay-Lussac and Avogadro made it possible to write chemical equations as we do today.

Reading Skill-Builder

READING HINT As students read through the section, have them use Figures 11-1, 11-2, and 11-3 to help them understand the relationships among volume, mass, number of moles, and number of molecules in a gas sample.

internet **connect**

SC*I* **LINKS**
NSTA

TOPIC: Avogadro's law
GO TO: www.scilinks.org
*sci*LINKS CODE: HC2111

334

FIGURE 11-1 Ask students to compare the masses of the balloons, which contain the same number of particles. Establish that the masses of equal volumes are in the same ratio as the molecular mass of each substance. This knowledge is important later in the section.

Common Misconception

Students may think that because the molecules shown in the figures are drawn large, the volume of gas depends on the volume of the molecules. Remind students that in reality gas molecules are very far apart at ordinary temperatures and pressures and that the sizes of the molecules themselves are inconsequential when compared to the total volume of the gas.

✔ Teaching Tip

You may want to remind students of the common diatomic elements: H_2, N_2, O_2, F_2, Cl_2, Br_2, and I_2.

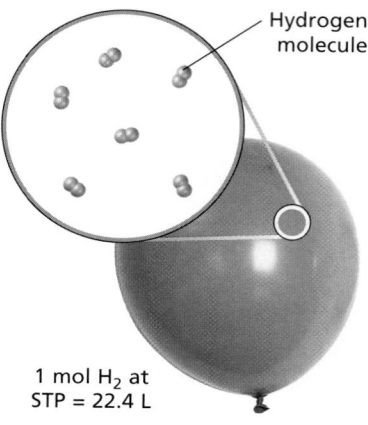

Hydrogen molecule

1 mol H_2 at STP = 22.4 L

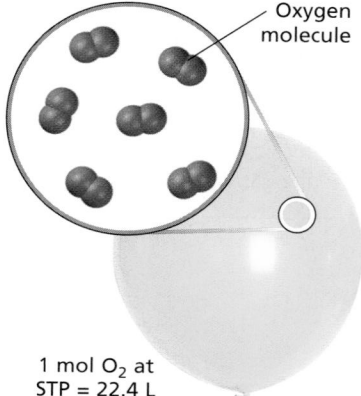

Oxygen molecule

1 mol O_2 at STP = 22.4 L

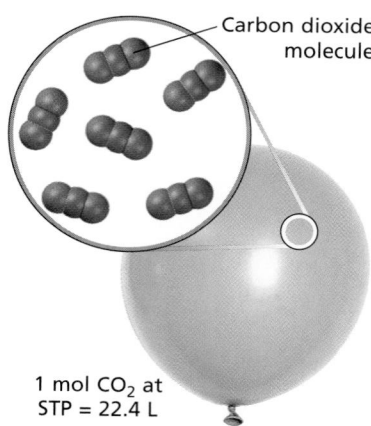

Carbon dioxide molecule

1 mol CO_2 at STP = 22.4 L

FIGURE 11-1 At the same temperature and pressure, balloons of equal volume have equal numbers of molecules, regardless of which gas they contain.

Avogadro's Law

Recall an important point of Dalton's atomic theory: atoms are indivisible. Dalton also thought that the particles of gaseous elements exist in the form of isolated single atoms. He believed that one atom of one element always combines with one atom of another element to form a single particle of the product. Accounting for some of the volume relationships observed by Gay-Lussac presented a problem for Dalton's theory. For example, in reactions such as the formation of water vapor, mentioned on the preceding page, it would seem that the oxygen involved would have to divide into two parts.

In 1811, Avogadro found a way to explain Gay-Lussac's simple ratios of combining volumes without violating Dalton's idea of indivisible atoms. He did this by rejecting Dalton's idea that reactant elements are always in monatomic form when they combine to form products. He reasoned that these molecules could contain more than one atom. Avogadro also put forth an idea known today as **Avogadro's law.** The law states that *equal volumes of gases at the same temperature and pressure contain equal numbers of molecules.* Figure 11-1 illustrates Avogadro's law. It follows that at the same temperature and pressure, the volume of any given gas varies directly with the number of molecules.

Consider the reaction of hydrogen and chlorine to produce hydrogen chloride, illustrated in Figure 11-2. According to Avogadro's law, equal volumes of hydrogen and chlorine contain the same number of molecules. Avogadro accepted Dalton's idea that atoms of hydrogen and chlorine are indivisible. However, he rejected Dalton's belief that these elements are monatomic. He concluded that the hydrogen and chlorine components must each consist of two or more atoms joined together. The simplest assumption was that hydrogen and chlorine molecules are composed of two atoms each. That assumption leads to the following balanced equation for the reaction of hydrogen with chlorine.

$$H_2(g) \quad + \quad Cl_2(g) \quad \longrightarrow \quad 2HCl(g)$$

| 1 volume | 1 volume | 2 volumes |
| 1 molecule | 1 molecule | 2 molecules |

The simplest hypothetical formula for hydrogen chloride, HCl, indicates that the molecule contains one hydrogen atom and one chlorine atom. Given the ratios of the combined volumes, the simplest formulas for hydrogen and chlorine must be H_2 and Cl_2, respectively.

Avogadro's reasoning applied equally well to the combining volumes for the reaction of hydrogen and oxygen to form water vapor. The simplest hypothetical formula for oxygen indicated two oxygen atoms, which turns out to be correct. The simplest possible molecule of water indicated two hydrogen atoms and one oxygen atom per molecule, which is also correct. Experiments eventually showed that all elements that are gases near room temperature, except the noble gases, normally exist as diatomic molecules.

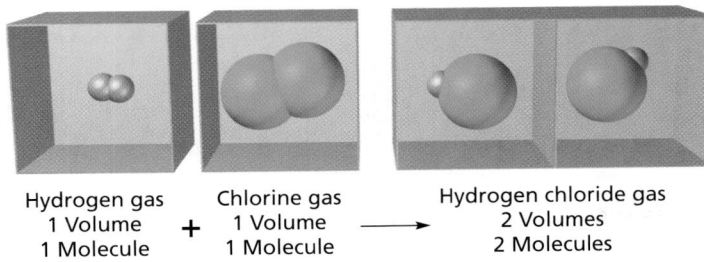

Hydrogen gas   Chlorine gas   Hydrogen chloride gas
1 Volume   + 1 Volume   ⟶   2 Volumes
1 Molecule   1 Molecule   2 Molecules

Avogadro's law also indicates that gas volume is directly proportional to the amount of gas, at a given temperature and pressure. Note the equation for this relationship.

$$V = kn$$

Here, n is the amount of gas, in moles, and k is a constant. As shown below, the coefficients in a chemical reaction involving gases indicate the relative numbers of molecules, the relative numbers of moles, and the relative volumes.

$$2H_2(g) \quad + \quad O_2(g) \quad \longrightarrow \quad 2H_2O(g)$$

2 molecules	1 molecule	2 molecules
2 mol	1 mol	2 mol
2 volumes	1 volume	2 volumes

Molar Volume of Gases

Recall that one mole of a molecular substance contains a number of molecules equal to Avogadro's constant (6.022×10^{23}). One mole of oxygen, O_2, contains 6.022×10^{23} diatomic oxygen molecules and has a mass of 31.9988 g. One mole of hydrogen contains the same number of diatomic hydrogen molecules but has a mass of only 2.015 88 g. One mole of helium, a monatomic gas, contains the same number of helium atoms and has a mass of 4.002 602 g.

According to Avogadro's law, one mole of any gas will occupy the same volume as one mole of any other gas at the same temperature and pressure, despite mass differences. *The volume occupied by one mole of a gas at STP is known as the* **standard molar volume of a gas.** *It has been found to be 22.414 10 L.* For calculations in this book, we use 22.4 L as the standard molar volume.

Knowing the volume of a gas, you can use 1 mol/22.4 L as a conversion factor to find the number of moles, and therefore the mass, of a given volume of a given gas at STP. You can also use the molar volume of a gas to find the volume, at STP, of a known number of moles or a known mass of a gas. These types of problems can also be solved using the ideal gas law, as you will see in Section 11-2.

Visual Strategy

FIGURE 11-2 Ask students to draw a representation of the reaction of hydrogen and oxygen in the same style as Figure 11-2. Use both diagrams to help students understand that if equal volumes of gases under the same conditions contain the same number of molecules, then the reverse is also true—equal numbers of molecules will occupy the same volume under the same conditions. Thus, it is possible to represent "one volume" with a single molecule.

Additional Example Problems

1. Ozone, O_3, can be formed from diatomic oxygen by the following reaction.

$$3O_2(g) \longrightarrow 2O_3(g)$$

Both gases are measured at the same temperature and pressure.

a. How many molecules of ozone are formed from the reaction of 24 oxygen molecules?

b. How many moles of oxygen are required to produce 24 moles of ozone?

c. How many liters of ozone are formed from 12 L of oxygen?

Ans. **a.** 16 molecules O_3
b. 36 mol O_2
c. 8 L O_3

2. How many liters of chlorine at STP will react with 35 L O_2 at STP? Use the following reaction.

$$2Cl_2(g) + 7O_2(g) \longrightarrow 2Cl_2O_7(l)$$

Ans. 10 L Cl_2

Alternative Assessment

Challenge students to find or construct containers having a volume of 22.4 L. (*A cubic box 22.4 L in volume would measure* $(22\ 400\ cm^3)^{1/3}$, *about 28.2 cm, or 11.1 in., on a side.*)

FIGURE 11-3 One-mole quantities of two different gases each occupy 22.4 L at STP and have equal numbers of molecules. However, their masses are different.

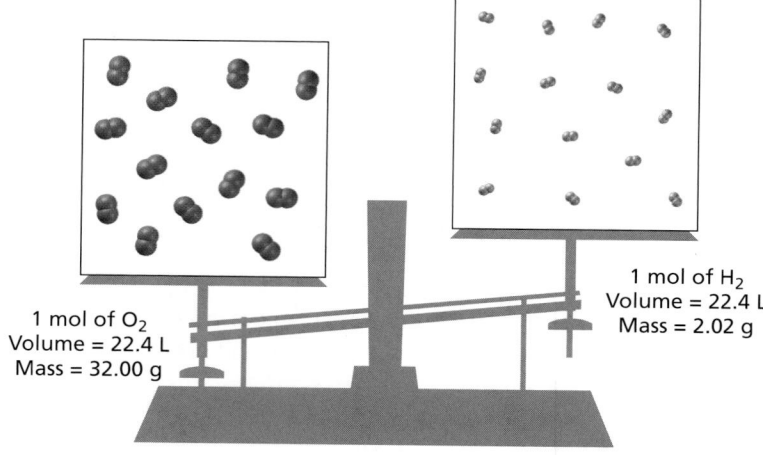

1 mol of O_2
Volume = 22.4 L
Mass = 32.00 g

1 mol of H_2
Volume = 22.4 L
Mass = 2.02 g

Figure 11-3 shows that 22.4 L of each gas contains the same number of molecules, but the mass of this volume is different for different gases. The mass of each is equal to the molar mass of the gas—the mass of one mole of molecules.

SAMPLE PROBLEM 11-1

A chemical reaction produces 0.0680 mol of oxygen gas. What volume in liters is occupied by this gas sample at STP?

SOLUTION

1 ANALYZE

Given: molar mass of O_2 = 0.0680 mol
Unknown: volume of O_2 in liters at STP

2 PLAN

$$\text{moles of } O_2 \longrightarrow \text{liters of } O_2 \text{ at STP}$$

The standard molar volume can be used to find the volume of a known molar amount of a gas at STP.

$$\text{mol} \times \frac{22.4 \text{ L}}{\text{mol}} = \text{volume of } O_2 \text{ in L}$$

3 COMPUTE

$$0.0680 \text{ mol } O_2 \times \frac{22.4 \text{ L}}{\text{mol}} = 1.52 \text{ L } O_2$$

4 EVALUATE

The answer is close to an estimated value of 1.4, computed as 0.07×20. Units have canceled to yield liters. The calculated result is correctly expressed to three significant figures.

PRACTICE

1. At STP, what is the volume of 7.08 mol of nitrogen gas?

Answer
159 L N_2

2. A sample of hydrogen gas occupies 14.1 L at STP. How many moles of the gas are present?

Answer
0.629 mol H_2

3. At STP, a sample of neon gas occupies 550. cm³. How many moles of neon gas does this represent?

Answer
0.0246 mol Ne

SAMPLE PROBLEM 11-2

A chemical reaction produced 98.0 mL of sulfur dioxide gas, SO_2, at STP. What was the mass (in grams) of the gas produced?

SOLUTION

1 ANALYZE

Given: volume of SO_2 at STP = 98.0 mL
Unknown: mass of SO_2 in grams

2 PLAN

$$\text{liters of } SO_2 \text{ at STP} \longrightarrow \text{moles of } SO_2 \longrightarrow \text{grams of } SO_2$$

$$mL \times \frac{1 \text{ L}}{1000 \text{ mL}} \times \frac{1 \text{ mol } SO_2}{22.4 \text{ L}} \times \frac{\text{g } SO_2}{\text{mol } SO_2} = \text{g } SO_2$$

3 COMPUTE

$$98.0 \text{ mL} \times \frac{1 \text{ L}}{1000 \text{ mL}} \times \frac{1 \text{ mol } SO_2}{22.4 \text{ L}} \times \frac{64.07 \text{ g } SO_2}{\text{mol } SO_2} = 0.280 \text{ g } SO_2$$

4 EVALUATE

The result is correctly expressed to three significant figures. Units cancel correctly to give the answer in grams. The known volume is roughly 1/200 of the molar volume (22 400 mL/200 = 112 mL). The answer is reasonable: the mass should also be roughly 1/200 of the molar mass (64 g/200 = 0.32 g).

PRACTICE

1. What is the mass of 1.33×10^4 mL of oxygen gas at STP?

Answer
19.0 g O_2

2. What is the volume of 77.0 g of nitrogen dioxide gas at STP?

Answer
37.5 L NO_2

3. At STP, 3 L of chlorine is produced during a chemical reaction. What is the mass of this gas?

Answer
9 g Cl_2

SECTION REVIEW

1. Explain Gay-Lussac's law of combining volumes.

2. State Avogadro's law and explain its significance.

3. Define *molar volume*.

4. How many moles of oxygen gas are there in 135 L of oxygen at STP?

5. What volume (in mL) at STP will be occupied by 0.0035 mol of methane, CH_4?

ADDITIONAL SAMPLE PROBLEM

11-2 Suppose you need 4.22 g of chlorine gas, Cl_2. What volume at STP would you need to use?

Ans. 1.33 L

Alternative Assessment
Ask students to draw a representation of the following gas reaction in a way similar to Figure 11-2.

$$N_2(g) + 3F_2(g) \longrightarrow 2NF_3(g)$$

Have students interpret the equation in terms of the number of molecules, number of moles, volume of gases at STP, and masses of each substance.

SECTION REVIEW

1. At constant temperature and pressure, the volumes of gaseous reactants and products can be expressed as ratios of small whole numbers.

2. Equal volumes of gases at the same temperature and pressure contain equal numbers of molecules. This law led to the realization that elements that are gases at around room temperature must consist of molecules having more than one atom. This was contrary to the ideas of Dalton, who assumed that all elements consisted of single atoms.

3. Molar volume is the volume occupied by a mole of gas at STP, 22.4 L.

4. 6.03 mol

5. 78 mL

GREAT DISCOVERIES

Chemistry's First Law

HISTORICAL PERSPECTIVE

The notion that nature abhors a vacuum was proposed by the Greek philosopher Aristotle, and his word went unchallenged for nearly 2000 years. Then in the mid-1600s, a new breed of thinkers known as experimental philosophers—later to be called scientists—began testing the long-held assumption that space must contain matter. These investigations represent some of the earliest experiments with gases, and they led to the discovery of the first empirical principle of chemistry, Boyle's law.

Overturning an Ancient Assumption

The first scientist to demonstrate the existence of a vacuum was Evangelista Torricelli. In 1643, he showed that when a glass tube 3 ft long and about an inch in diameter was sealed at one end, filled with mercury, and inverted in a container full of mercury, the mercury in the tube fell to a height of about 30 in. above the level of mercury in the container. Although some thinkers remained skeptical, it was generally accepted that the space between the mercury and the sealed end of the tube was indeed a vacuum.

Torricelli then turned his attention to how the mercury in the glass tube of his apparatus was supported. The known observation that liquids exerted a pressure on objects immersed in them inspired him to hypothesize that a "sea of air" surrounded Earth. He further hypothesized that the air exerted pressure on the mercury in the container and thus supported the mercury in the column.

Evangelista Torricelli invented the mercury barometer.

Support for the New Theory

Although the idea of an atmosphere that has weight and exerts a pressure on the objects within it seems obvious today, it was a radical theory at the time.

To test the effects of the atmosphere, one of the period's great scientists, Robert Boyle, had his talented assistant, Robert Hooke, create a piece of equipment that would revolutionize the study of air. The apparatus was an improved version of a pump designed by the famous German experimenter Otto von Guericke; the pump had a large receptacle in which a partial vacuum could be created.

Boyle placed Torricelli's setup, known today as a barometer, in the receptacle of the pump and observed the mercury column as he reduced the pressure around it. He noted that the height of the mercury decreased as the pressure surrounding the mercury in the container was lowered, strongly supporting Torricelli's atmospheric theory.

Using Hooke's pump, Boyle performed additional studies that verified the idea that air exerted pressure and had weight. His

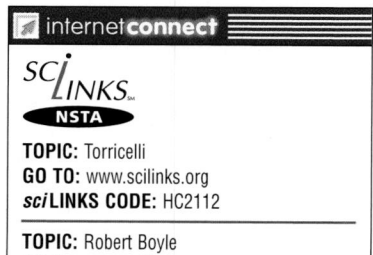

internet connect

SCLINKS
NSTA

TOPIC: Torricelli
GO TO: www.scilinks.org
sciLINKS CODE: HC2112

TOPIC: Robert Boyle
GO TO: www.scilinks.org
sciLINKS CODE: HC2113

experiments also led him to the important conclusion that air was elastic, that is, it could expand and contract. It was during an investigation into air's elasticity that Boyle discovered the fundamental law that bears his name.

An Ingenious Experiment

In response to a criticism of his findings, Boyle performed an experiment to show that air could be compressed to a pressure greater than that of the atmosphere. First he prepared a glass J tube with the short end sealed off and the long end left open. Then he poured mercury into the tube, making sure that the levels in each end were the same and letting air travel freely between the ends, to ensure that each column was at atmospheric pressure.

Boyle then poured more mercury into the long end of the tube until it was about 30 in. above the level of mercury in the short end, making the trapped air exposed to about twice as much atmospheric pressure. He observed that the volume of the trapped air was halved. He continued to add mercury until the total pressure on the trapped air was about four times that of the atmosphere.

We can measure the difference between the atmospheric pressure on a mountaintop and the atmospheric pressure at sea level thanks to the work of Torricelli and Boyle.

Noting that the air had been compressed to about one-quarter of its original value, Boyle discovered the inverse relationship between air's pressure and its volume:

> *It is evident, that as common air, when reduced to half its wonted extent [volume], obtained near about twice as forcible a spring [pressure] as it had before; so this thus comprest air being further thrust into half this narrow room, obtained thereby a spring about . . . four times as strong as that of common air.*

A Long-Standing Contribution

Boyle went on to show that the relationship between air pressure and volume, $P \propto 1/V$ (at constant temperature), held not only when the gas was compressed but also when it was allowed to expand. It would be up to future investigators to show that the law was a principle applying to gases in general. Together with the findings of other researchers, such as Jacques Charles, Joseph Gay-Lussac, and Amadeo Avogadro, Boyle's discovery led chemists to the famous ideal gas law, $PV = nRT$, which serves as a starting point in the study of chemistry today.

Application

Boyle's law can be used to explain how a plunger opens a clogged drain. As the plunger is pushed down, the volume of air in the plunger becomes less, and the pressure increases. Increased pressure is transferred throughout any water in the drain, and this pressure is applied to the clog.

Class Discussion

Have students compare and contrast Boyle's work with tubes and mercury to their drinking a beverage through a straw.

SECTION 11-2

The Ideal Gas Law

Lesson Starter

Ask students what steps they would use, given their knowledge at this point, to determine the volume at 25°C and 0.968 atm of 1.65 kg of methane, CH_4, compressed in a tank at 4.24 atm. Students should not actually work out the solution but should merely list the steps, starting with the mass of CH_4 given.

The steps are:
a. Convert the mass in kilograms to 1650 g.
b. Determine moles of CH_4 by dividing the mass by the molar mass of CH_4.
c. Convert moles CH_4 to volume at STP by multiplying moles CH_4 by 22.4 L/mol.
d. Apply Boyle's law to correct the volume at STP to 0.968 atm.
e. Apply Charles's law to correct the volume resulting from the previous step to 25°C (298 K). The result is 2.60×10^3 L. Ask students if they believe this to be a tedious process. Point out that this problem can be solved more quickly using the ideal gas law.

Problem-Solving Practice

Chapter 12 of the Mini-Guide to Problem Solving (also found on the One-Stop Planner CD-ROM) includes more worked-out samples and additional practice problems involving the ideal gas law.

OBJECTIVES

- State the ideal gas law.

- Derive the ideal gas constant and discuss its units.

- Using the ideal gas law, calculate pressure, volume, temperature, or amount of gas when the other three quantities are known.

- Using the ideal gas law, calculate the molar mass or density of a gas.

- Reduce the ideal gas law to Boyle's law, Charles's law, and Avogadro's law. Describe the conditions under which each applies.

In Section 10-3, you learned about three quantities—pressure, volume, and temperature—needed to describe a gas sample. A gas sample can be further characterized using a fourth quantity—the number of moles. The number of molecules or moles present will always affect at least one of the other three quantities. The collision rate of molecules per unit area of container wall depends on the number of molecules present. If the number of molecules is increased for a sample at constant volume and temperature, the collision rate increases. Therefore, the pressure increases, as shown by the model in Figure 11-4(a). Consider what would happen if the pressure and temperature were kept constant while the number of molecules increased. According to Avogadro's law, the volume would increase. As Figure 11-4(b) shows, an increase in volume keeps the pressure constant at constant temperature. Increasing the volume keeps the collision rate per unit of wall area constant.

You can see that gas pressure, volume, temperature, and the number of moles are all interrelated. There is a mathematical relationship that describes the behavior of a gas sample for any combination of these conditions. *The **ideal gas law** is the mathematical relationship among pressure, volume, temperature, and the number of moles of a gas.* It is the equation of state for an ideal gas, because the state of a gas can be defined by its pressure, volume, temperature, and number of moles.

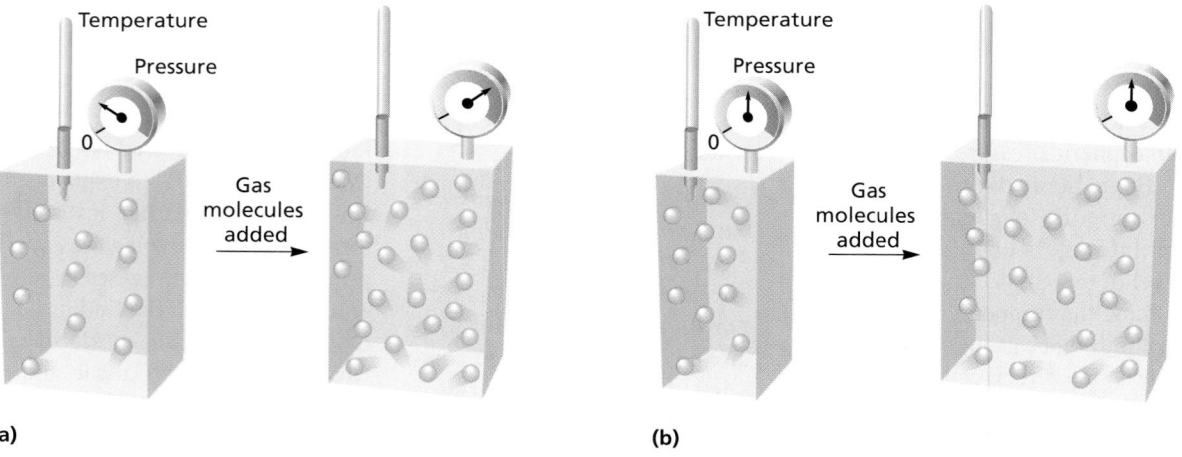

(a)   (b)

FIGURE 11-4   (a) When volume and temperature are constant, gas pressure increases as the number of molecules increases. (b) When pressure and temperature are constant, gas volume increases as the number of molecules increases.

Derivation of the Ideal Gas Law

The general equation that can be used to calculate unknown information about gas samples can be derived by combining Boyle's law and Charles's law with a statement that follows logically from Avogadro's law. First, consider each of those laws and the principle again.

Boyle's law: At constant temperature, the volume of a given mass of gas is inversely proportional to the pressure.

$$V \propto \frac{1}{P}$$

Charles's law: At constant pressure, the volume of a given mass of gas is directly proportional to the Kelvin temperature.

$$V \propto T$$

Avogadro's law implies that at constant pressure and temperature, the volume of a given mass of a gas is directly proportional to the number of moles.

$$V \propto n$$

A quantity—in this case, volume—that is proportional to each of several quantities is also proportional to their product. Therefore, combining the three relationships above gives the following.

$$V \propto \frac{1}{P} \times T \times n$$

Mathematically, you can change a proportionality to an equality by introducing a constant. In this case, the symbol R is used for the constant.

$$V = R \times \frac{1}{P} \times T \times n$$

R represents the value that the quantity PV/nT approaches for any gas whose behavior approaches that of an ideal gas. The equation for the ideal gas law is derived as follows.

$$V = \frac{nRT}{P} \text{ or } PV = nRT$$

This equation states that the volume of a gas varies directly with the number of moles (or molecules) of a gas and its Kelvin temperature. The volume also varies inversely with the pressure. Under ordinary conditions, most gases exhibit behavior that is nearly ideal. The equation can then be applied with reasonable accuracy.

The ideal gas law reduces to Boyle's law, Charles's law, Gay-Lussac's law, or Avogadro's law when the appropriate variables are held constant. For example, if n and T are constant, the product nRT is constant because R is also constant. In this case, the ideal gas law reduces to $PV = $ a constant, which is Boyle's law.

✔ Teaching Tip

The ideal gas law is not a magic expression. It is a combination of all the gas laws students have learned so far. The gas constant combines all of the proportionality constants of the individual relationships (Boyle's law, Charles's law, Avogadro's law) into a single value.

Class Discussion

Ask students to discuss whether there is such a thing as a mole of air. Remind them that air is not a substance but a mixture. A mole of air can be defined as an Avogadro's number of particles of the mixture of gases that make up air. Ask students if it would be possible to determine the volume of a mole of air, and have them explain their conclusions. A mole of air occupies 22.4 L at STP, just as any pure gas would. All of the components of air behave as ideal gases at ordinary temperatures and pressures; therefore, the mixture would also behave as an ideal gas.

✔ Teaching Tip

Remind students that they can convert a proportionality

$$y \propto x$$

to an equality by multiplying by a constant:

$$y = kx$$

Table 11-1 Have students compare the values of *R* shown in the table to reinforce the idea that the value 0.0821 L•atm/(mol•K) can be used only with measurements that match these units. Measurements with different units must be converted, or another value of *R* must be used.

Did You Know?

Although students will continue to use 22.4 L as standard molar volume at STP, true molar volume varies according to how much a gas deviates from the ideal. The following list shows values for specific gases.

H_2	22.42 L
He	22.42 L
N_2	22.40 L

To three significant figures, these values still round off to 22.4 L. Other common gases deviate further from the ideal because of interactions among the molecules. Note the following molar volumes.

CO_2	22.26 L
NH_3	22.08 L
Cl_2	22.06 L

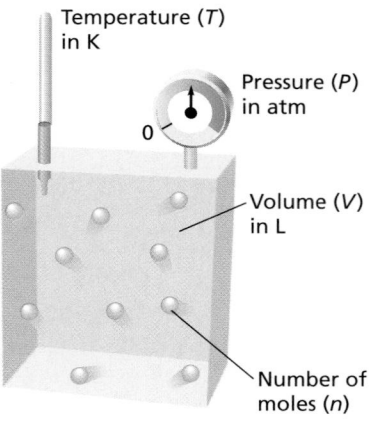

Temperature (*T*) in K

Pressure (*P*) in atm

Volume (*V*) in L

Number of moles (*n*)

Gas constant (*R*) = 0.0821 $\dfrac{\text{L} \cdot \text{atm}}{\text{mol} \cdot \text{K}}$

PV = nRT

FIGURE 11-5   The ideal gas law relates the pressure, volume, number of moles, and temperature of an ideal gas. Note the value of the gas constant, *R*, when the other quantities are in the units shown.

The Ideal Gas Constant

In the equation representing the ideal gas law, *the constant R is known as the* **ideal gas constant.** Its value depends on the units chosen for pressure, volume, and temperature. Figure 11-5 shows that measured values of *P, V, T,* and *n* for a gas at near-ideal conditions can be used to calculate *R*. Recall from Section 11-1 that the volume of one mole of an ideal gas at STP (1 atm and 273.15 K) is 22.414 10 L. Substituting these values and solving the ideal gas law equation for *R* gives the following.

$$R = \frac{PV}{nT} = \frac{(1\ \text{atm})(22.414\ 10\ \text{L})}{(1\ \text{mol})(273.15\ \text{K})} = 0.082\ 057\ 84\ \frac{\text{L} \cdot \text{atm}}{\text{mol} \cdot \text{K}}$$

This calculated value of *R* is usually rounded to 0.0821 L•atm/(mol•K). Use this value in ideal gas law calculations when the volume is in liters, the pressure is in atmospheres, and the temperature is in kelvins. See Table 11-1 for the value of *R* when other units for *n, P, V,* and *T* are used.

Finding *P, V, T,* or *n* from the Ideal Gas Law

The ideal gas law can be applied to determine the existing conditions of a gas sample when three of the four variables, *P, V, T,* and *n,* are known. It can also be used to calculate the molar mass or density of a gas sample.

Be sure to match the units of the known quantities and the units of *R*. In this book, you will be using *R* = 0.0821 L•atm/(mol•K). Your first step in solving any ideal gas law problem should be to check the known values to be sure you are working with the correct units. If necessary, you must convert volumes to liters, pressures to atmospheres, temperatures to kelvins, and masses to numbers of moles before using the ideal gas law.

TABLE 11-1   *Numerical Values of the Gas Constant, R*

Unit of *R*	Numerical value of *R*	Unit of *P*	Unit of *V*	Unit of *T*	Unit of *n*
$\dfrac{\text{L} \cdot \text{mm Hg}}{\text{mol} \cdot \text{K}}$	62.4	mm Hg	L	K	mol
$\dfrac{\text{L} \cdot \text{atm}}{\text{mol} \cdot \text{K}}$	0.0821	atm	L	K	mol
$\dfrac{\text{J}}{\text{mol} \cdot \text{K}}$	8.314*	Pa	m^3	K	mol
$\dfrac{\text{L} \cdot \text{kPa}}{\text{mol} \cdot \text{K}}$	8.314	kPa	L	K	mol

Note: 1 L•atm = 101.325 J; 1 J = 1 Pa•m^3
* SI units

SAMPLE PROBLEM 11-3

What is the pressure in atmospheres exerted by a 0.500 mol sample of nitrogen gas in a 10.0 L container at 298 K?

SOLUTION

1 ANALYZE

Given: V of N_2 = 10.0 L
n of N_2 = 0.500 mol
T of N_2 = 298 K
Unknown: P of N_2 in atm

2 PLAN

$$n, V, T \longrightarrow P$$

The gas sample undergoes no change in conditions. Therefore, the ideal gas law can be rearranged and used to find the pressure as follows.

$$P = \frac{nRT}{V}$$

3 COMPUTE

$$P = \frac{(0.500 \text{ mol})\left(\dfrac{0.0821 \text{ L} \cdot \text{atm}}{\text{mol} \cdot \text{K}}\right)(298 \text{ K})}{10.0 \text{ L}} = 1.22 \text{ atm}$$

4 EVALUATE

All units cancel correctly to give the result in atmospheres. The answer is properly limited to three significant figures. It is also close to an estimated value of 1.5, computed as $(0.5 \times 0.1 \times 300)/10$.

PRACTICE

1. What pressure, in atmospheres, is exerted by 0.325 mol of hydrogen gas in a 4.08 L container at 35°C?

   Answer
   2.01 atm

2. A gas sample occupies 8.77 L at 20°C. What is the pressure, in atmospheres, given that there are 1.45 mol of gas in the sample?

   Answer
   3.98 atm

SAMPLE PROBLEM 11-4

What is the volume, in liters, of 0.250 mol of oxygen gas at 20.0°C and 0.974 atm pressure?

SOLUTION

1 ANALYZE

Given: P of O_2 = 0.974 atm
n of O_2 = 0.250 mol
To use the value 0.0821 L·atm/(mol·K) for R, the temperature (°C) must be converted to kelvins.
T of O_2 = 20.0°C + 273.2 = 293.2 K
Unknown: V of O_2 in L

11-4 A reaction yields 0.008 56 mol of O_2 gas. What volume in mL will the gas occupy if it is collected at 43°C and 0.926 atm pressure?

Ans. 240. mL

11-4 A researcher collects 9.09×10^{-3} mol of an unknown gas by water displacement at a temperature of 16°C and 0.873 atm pressure (after the partial pressure of water vapor has been subtracted). What volume of gas in mL does the researcher have?

Ans. 247 mL

2 PLAN

$$P, n, T \longrightarrow V$$

The ideal gas law can be rearranged to solve for V for this sample, which undergoes no change in conditions.

$$V = \frac{nRT}{P}$$

3 COMPUTE

$$V = \frac{(0.250 \text{ mol } O_2)\left(\dfrac{0.0821 \text{ L} \cdot \text{atm}}{\text{mol} \cdot \text{K}}\right)(293.2 \text{ K})}{0.974 \text{ atm}} = 6.17 \text{ L } O_2$$

4 EVALUATE Units cancel to give liters, as desired. The answer is correctly limited to three significant figures. It is also close to an estimated value of 6, calculated as $0.2 \times 0.1 \times 300$.

PRACTICE

1. A sample that contains 4.38 mol of a gas at 250 K has a pressure of 0.857 atm. What is the volume?

   Answer
   105 L

2. How many liters are occupied by 0.909 mol of nitrogen at 125°C and 0.901 atm pressure?

   Answer
   33.0 L N_2

SAMPLE PROBLEM 11-5

What mass of chlorine gas, Cl_2, in grams, is contained in a 10.0 L tank at 27°C and 3.50 atm of pressure?

SOLUTION

1 ANALYZE **Given:** P of Cl_2 = 3.50 atm
V of Cl_2 = 10.0 L
T of Cl_2 = 27°C + 273 = 300. K
Unknown: mass of Cl_2 in g

2 PLAN The ideal gas law can be rearranged to solve for n after temperature is converted to kelvins.

$$n = \frac{PV}{RT}$$

The number of moles is then converted to grams.

$$m \text{ (in g)} = n \times \frac{\text{g}}{\text{mol}}$$

3 COMPUTE

$$n = \frac{(3.50 \text{ atm})(10.0 \text{ L } Cl_2)}{\left(\dfrac{0.0821 \text{ L} \cdot \text{atm}}{\text{mol} \cdot \text{K}}\right)(300. \text{ K})} = 1.42 \text{ mol } Cl_2$$

$$\text{mass of } Cl_2 = 1.42 \text{ mol} \times \frac{70.90 \text{ g } Cl_2}{\text{mol}} = 101 \text{ g } Cl_2$$

4 EVALUATE Units cancel to leave the desired unit. The result is correctly given to three significant figures. The answer is close to the estimated value.

PRACTICE	

1. How many grams of carbon dioxide gas are there in a 45.1 L container at 34°C and 1.04 atm? *Answer* 81.9 g CO_2

2. What is the mass, in grams, of oxygen gas in a 12.5 L container at 45°C and 7.22 atm? *Answer* 111 g O_2

3. A sample of carbon dioxide with a mass of 0.30 g was placed in a 250 mL container at 400. K. What is the pressure exerted by the gas? *Answer* 0.90 atm

Finding Molar Mass or Density from the Ideal Gas Law

Suppose that the pressure, volume, temperature, and mass are known for a gas sample. You can calculate the number of moles (n) in the sample, using the ideal gas law. Then you can calculate the molar mass (grams per mole) by dividing the known mass by the number of moles.

An equation showing the relationship between density, pressure, temperature, and molar mass can be derived from the ideal gas law. The number of moles (n) is equal to mass (m) divided by molar mass (M). Substituting m/M for n into $PV = nRT$ gives the following.

$$PV = \frac{mRT}{M} \text{ or } M = \frac{mRT}{PV}$$

Density (D) is mass (m) per unit volume (V). Writing this definition in the form of an equation gives $D = m/V$. You can see that m/V appears in the right-hand equation above. Introducing density into that equation gives the following.

$$M = \frac{mRT}{PV} = \frac{DRT}{P}$$

Solving for density gives this equation.

$$D = \frac{MP}{RT}$$

You can see that the density of a gas varies directly with molar mass and pressure and inversely with Kelvin temperature.

SAMPLE PROBLEM 11-6

At 28°C and 0.974 atm, 1.00 L of gas has a mass of 5.16 g. What is the molar mass of this gas?

SOLUTION

1 ANALYZE

Given: P of gas = 0.974 atm
V of gas = 1.00 L
T of gas = 28°C + 273 = 301 K
m of gas = 5.16 g

11-6 A chemist determines the mass of a sample of gas to be 3.17 g. Its volume is 942 mL at a temperature of 14°C and a pressure of 1.09 atm. What is the molar mass of the gas?

Ans. 72.7 g/mol

11-6 The density of dry air at sea level (1 atm) is 1.225 g/L at 15°C. What is the average molar mass of the air?

Ans. 29.0 g/mol

Alternative Assessment

Ask students to explain why different gases have different densities under the same conditions, considering that equal volumes contain the same number of molecules. They should be able to relate varying densities to varying masses of the molecules.

Unknown: M of gas in g/mol

2 PLAN

$$P, V, T, m \longrightarrow M$$

You can use the rearranged ideal gas law provided earlier in this section to find the answer.

$$M = \frac{mRT}{PV}$$

3 COMPUTE

$$M = \frac{(5.16 \text{ g})\left(\dfrac{0.0821 \text{ L} \cdot \text{atm}}{\text{mol} \cdot \text{K}}\right)(301 \text{ K})}{(0.974 \text{ atm})(1.00 \text{ L})} = 131 \text{ g/mol}$$

4 EVALUATE Units cancel as needed. The answer is correctly given to three significant figures. It is also close to an estimated value of 150, calculated as $(5 \times 0.1 \times 300)/1$.

PRACTICE

1. What is the molar mass of a gas if 0.427 g of the gas occupies a volume of 125 mL at 20.0°C and 0.980 atm? — *Answer* 83.8 g/mol

2. What is the density of a sample of ammonia gas, NH_3, if the pressure is 0.928 atm and the temperature is 63.0°C? — *Answer* 0.572 g/L NH_3

3. The density of a gas was found to be 2.0 g/L at 1.50 atm and 27°C. What is the molar mass of the gas? — *Answer* 33 g/mol

4. What is the density of argon gas, Ar, at a pressure of 551 torr and a temperature of 25°C? — *Answer* 1.18 g/L Ar

SECTION REVIEW

1. a. hold n and T constant, leaving $PV = k$

b. hold P and n constant, leaving $V = kT$

c. hold V and n constant, leaving $P = kT$

d. hold P and T constant, leaving $V = kn$

2. 0.256 L

3. The units of P, V, T, and n must be the same as those used in R in order for units to cancel. The units would be L·Pa/(K·mol).

4. 32.0 g/mol

5. molar mass and density

SECTION REVIEW

1. How does the ideal gas law reduce to the following:
   a. Boyle's law
   b. Charles's law
   c. Gay-Lussac's law
   d. Avogadro's law

2. What is the volume, in liters, of 0.100 g of $C_2H_2F_4$ vapor at 0.0928 atm and 22.3°C?

3. Why must the units P, V, T, and n match up to those of the ideal gas constant in solving problems? What would be the units for R if P is in pascals, T is in kelvins, V is in liters, and n is in moles?

4. What is the molar mass of a 1.25 g sample of gas that occupies a volume of 1.00 L at a pressure of 0.961 atm and a temperature of 27.0°C?

5. Name two quantities besides pressure, mass, volume, and number of moles that can be calculated using the ideal gas law.

Stoichiometry of Gases

OBJECTIVES

- Explain how Gay-Lussac's law and Avogadro's law apply to the volumes of gases in chemical reactions.

- Use a chemical equation to specify volume ratios for gaseous reactants or products, or both.

- Use volume ratios and the gas laws to calculate volumes, masses, or molar amounts of gaseous reactants or products.

You can apply the discoveries of Gay-Lussac and Avogadro to calculate the stoichiometry of reactions involving gases. For gaseous reactants or products, the coefficients in chemical equations not only indicate molar amounts and mole ratios but also reveal volume ratios. For example, consider the reaction of carbon monoxide with oxygen to give carbon dioxide.

$$2CO(g) \;+\; O_2(g) \longrightarrow 2CO_2(g)$$

2 molecules	1 molecule	2 molecules
2 mol	1 mol	2 mol
2 volumes	1 volume	2 volumes

The possible volume ratios can be expressed in the following ways.

a. $\dfrac{2 \text{ volumes CO}}{1 \text{ volume O}_2}$ or $\dfrac{1 \text{ volume O}_2}{2 \text{ volumes CO}}$

b. $\dfrac{2 \text{ volumes CO}}{2 \text{ volumes CO}_2}$ or $\dfrac{2 \text{ volumes CO}_2}{2 \text{ volumes CO}}$ **c.** $\dfrac{1 \text{ volume O}_2}{2 \text{ volumes CO}_2}$ or $\dfrac{2 \text{ volumes CO}_2}{1 \text{ volume O}_2}$

Volumes can be compared in this way only if all are measured at the same temperature and pressure.

Volume-Volume Calculations

Suppose the volume of a gas involved in a reaction is known and you need to find the volume of another gaseous reactant or product, assuming both reactant and product exist under the same conditions. Use volume ratios like those given above in exactly the same way you would use mole ratios.

SAMPLE PROBLEM 11-7

Propane, C_3H_8, is a gas that is sometimes used as a fuel for cooking and heating. The complete combustion of propane occurs according to the following equation.

$$C_3H_8(g) + 5O_2(g) \longrightarrow 3CO_2(g) + 4H_2O(g)$$

Lesson Starter
Write the following equation on the chalkboard.

$$2HCl(aq) + Na_2SO_3(s) \longrightarrow$$
$$2NaCl(aq) + SO_2(g) + H_2O(l)$$

Ask students to compare this equation with the one on this page and determine whether the stated relationships involving molecules, moles, and volumes would also hold for this reaction. Use this comparison to reinforce the idea that the relationship between volumes is true only when the *gases* involved in a reaction are being considered.

Reading Skill-Builder

PAIRED SUMMARIZING
Assign pairs of students to read pp. 347–350. One member of the pair should concentrate on summarizing how to solve problems involving volume-volume calculations. The other member of the pair should do the same for volume-mass and mass-volume calculations.

Problem-Solving Practice — HOLT ChemFile

Chapter 13 of the Mini-Guide to Problem Solving (also found on the One-Stop Planner CD-ROM) includes more worked-out samples and additional practice problems involving stoichiometry of gases.

ADDITIONAL
SAMPLE
PROBLEMS

11-7 Xenon gas reacts with fluorine gas to produce the compound xenon hexafluoride, XeF_6. Write the balanced equation for this reaction. If a researcher needs 3.14 L of XeF_6 for an experiment, what volumes of xenon and fluorine should be reacted? Assume all volumes are measured under the same conditions of temperature and pressure.

Ans. $Xe(g) + 3F_2(g) \longrightarrow XeF_6(g)$
3.14 L of Xe and 9.42 L of F_2

11-7 Nitric acid can be produced by the reaction of gaseous nitrogen dioxide with water.

$3NO_2(g) + H_2O(l) \longrightarrow$
$\qquad\qquad 2HNO_3(l) + NO(g)$

If 708 L of NO_2 gas react with water, what volume of NO gas will be produced? Assume the gases are measured under the same conditions.

Ans. 236 L

Common Misconception

Students may believe that volume-volume calculations are possible only if all reactants and products are gases. Consider using the example problem above to demonstrate that volume-volume ratio calculations are applicable only if the given substance and the unknown substance are both gases, although other states of matter may be involved.

Module 5: Equations and Stoichiometry

Topic: Stoichiometry
Sections **d, e, f, g,** and **h** of this engaging tutorial review and reinforce understanding of stoichiometry.

(a) What will be the volume, in liters, of oxygen required for the complete combustion of 0.350 L of propane? (b) What will be the volume of carbon dioxide produced in the reaction? Assume that all volume measurements are made at the same temperature and pressure.

SOLUTION

1 ANALYZE

Given: balanced chemical equation
V of propane = 0.350 L
Unknown: a. V of O_2 in L; **b.** V of CO_2 in L

2 PLAN

a. V of $C_3H_8 \longrightarrow V$ of O_2; **b.** V of $C_3H_8 \longrightarrow V$ of CO_2

All volumes are to be compared at the same temperature and pressure. Therefore, volume ratios can be used like mole ratios to find the unknowns.

3 COMPUTE

a. $0.350 \text{ L } C_3H_8 \times \dfrac{5 \text{ L } O_2}{1 \text{ L } C_3H_8} = 1.75 \text{ L } O_2$

b. $0.350 \text{ L } C_3H_8 \times \dfrac{3 \text{ L } CO_2}{1 \text{ L } C_3H_8} = 1.05 \text{ L } CO_2$

4 EVALUATE

Each result is correctly given to three significant figures. The answers are reasonably close to estimated values of 2, calculated as 0.4×5, and 1.2, calculated as 0.4×3, respectively.

PRACTICE

1. Assuming all volume measurements are made at the same temperature and pressure, what volume of hydrogen gas is needed to react completely with 4.55 L of oxygen gas to produce water vapor?

   Answer
   9.10 L H_2

2. What volume of oxygen gas is needed to react completely with 0.626 L of carbon monoxide gas, CO, to form gaseous carbon dioxide? Assume all volume measurements are made at the same temperature and pressure.

   Answer
   0.313 L O_2

Module 5: Equations and Stoichiometry

Volume-Mass and Mass-Volume Calculations

Stoichiometric calculations may involve both masses and gas volumes. Sometimes the volume of a reactant or product is given and the mass of a second gaseous substance is unknown. In other cases, a mass amount may be known and a volume may be the unknown. The calculations require routes such as the following.

gas volume A $\longrightarrow$ moles A $\longrightarrow$ moles B $\longrightarrow$ mass B

or

mass A $\longrightarrow$ moles A $\longrightarrow$ moles B $\longrightarrow$ gas volume B

To find the unknown in cases like these, you must know the conditions under which both the known and unknown gas volumes have been measured. The ideal gas law is useful for calculating values at standard and nonstandard conditions.

SAMPLE PROBLEM 11-8

Calcium carbonate, $CaCO_3$, also known as limestone, can be heated to produce calcium oxide (lime), an industrial chemical with a wide variety of uses. The balanced equation for the reaction follows.

$$CaCO_3(s) \xrightarrow{\Delta} CaO(s) + CO_2(g)$$

How many grams of calcium carbonate must be decomposed to produce 5.00 L of carbon dioxide gas at STP?

SOLUTION

1 ANALYZE
Given: balanced chemical equation
desired volume of CO_2 produced at STP = 5.00 L
Unknown: mass of $CaCO_3$ in grams

2 PLAN
The known volume is given at STP. This tells us the pressure and temperature. The ideal gas law can be used to find the moles of CO_2. The mole ratios from the balanced equation can then be used to calculate the moles of $CaCO_3$ needed. (Note that volume ratios do not apply here because calcium carbonate is a solid.)

3 COMPUTE

$$n = \frac{PV}{RT} = \frac{(1 \text{ atm})(5.00 \text{ L } CO_2)}{\left(\dfrac{0.0821 \text{ L} \cdot \text{atm}}{\text{mol} \cdot \text{K}} \right)(273 \text{ K})} = 0.223 \text{ mol } CO_2$$

$$0.223 \text{ mol } CO_2 \times \frac{1 \text{ mol } CaCO_3}{1 \text{ mol } CO_2} \times \frac{100.09 \text{ g } CaCO_3}{1 \text{ mol } CaCO_3} = 22.3 \text{ g } CaCO_3$$

4 EVALUATE
Units all cancel correctly. The answer is properly given to three significant figures. It is close to an estimated value of 20, computed as $(0.2 \times 100)/25$.

PRACTICE

1. What mass of sulfur must be used to produce 12.61 L of gaseous sulfur dioxide at STP according to the following equation?

$$S_8(s) + 8O_2(g) \longrightarrow 8SO_2(g)$$

Answer
18.0 g S_8

2. How many grams of water can be produced from the complete reaction of 3.44 L of oxygen gas, at STP, with hydrogen gas?

Answer
5.53 g H_2O

SAMPLE PROBLEM 11-9

Tungsten, W, a metal used in light-bulb filaments, is produced industrially by the reaction of tungsten oxide with hydrogen.

$$WO_3(s) + 3H_2(g) \longrightarrow W(s) + 3H_2O(l)$$

How many liters of hydrogen gas at 35°C and 0.980 atm are needed to react completely with 875 g of tungsten oxide?

ADDITIONAL SAMPLE PROBLEM

11-8 Aluminum granules are a component of some drain cleaners because they react with sodium hydroxide to release both heat and gas bubbles, which help clear the drain clog. The reaction is

$$2NaOH(aq) + 2Al(s) + 6H_2O(l) \longrightarrow$$
$$2NaAl(OH)_4(aq) + 3H_2(g)$$

What mass of aluminum would be needed to produce 4.00 L of hydrogen gas at STP?

Ans. 3.21 g

Application

Rocket propulsion systems and some explosives employ reactions that suddenly produce a large volume of hot gas from a small volume of reactants. For example, the explosive substance nitroglycerin undergoes the following decomposition reaction when detonated.

$$4C_3H_5(ONO_2)_3(l) \longrightarrow 12CO_2(g) +$$
$$10H_2O(g) + 6N_2(g) + O_2(g) + \text{energy}$$

Four moles of liquid nitroglycerin occupies a volume of 570 mL, or 0.57 L. All of the gases given off by the decomposition of this amount would have a volume of 650 L at STP. The energy produced by this reaction heats the product gases and the surrounding air, causing the gases to expand to a much greater volume.

1 ANALYZE

Given: balanced chemical equation
reactant mass of WO_3 = 875 g
P of H_2 = 0.980 atm
T of H_2 = 35°C + 273 = 308 K
Unknown: V of H_2 in L at known nonstandard conditions

2 PLAN

Moles of H_2 are found by converting the mass of WO_3 to moles and then using the mole ratio. The ideal gas law is used to find the volume from the calculated number of moles of H_2.

3 COMPUTE

$$875 \text{ g } WO_3 \times \frac{1 \text{ mol } WO_3}{231.84 \text{ g } WO_3} \times \frac{3 \text{ mol } H_2}{1 \text{ mol } WO_3} = 11.3 \text{ mol } H_2$$

$$V = \frac{nRT}{P} = \frac{(11.3 \text{ mol } H_2)\left(\dfrac{0.0821 \text{ L} \cdot \text{atm}}{\text{mol} \cdot \text{K}}\right)(308 \text{ K})}{0.980 \text{ atm}} = 292 \text{ L } H_2$$

4 EVALUATE

Unit cancellations are correct, as is the use of three significant figures for each result. The answer is reasonably close to an estimated value of 330, computed as $(11 \times 0.1 \times 300)/1$.

11-9 Air bags in cars are inflated by the sudden decomposition of sodium azide, NaN_3, by the following reaction.

$2NaN_3(s) \longrightarrow 3N_2(g) + 2Na(s)$

What volume of N_2 gas, measured at 1.30 atm and 87°C, would be produced by the reaction of 70.0 g of NaN_3?

Ans. 36.7 L

Alternative Assessment

Ask students to write descriptive statements explaining how changes in *P, T,* and *n* each affect the volume of a gas sample. Students should explain why each effect occurs.

CHAPTER ⟷ CONNECTION

Many reactions involving gases do not go to completion but reach an equilibrium state. Students will learn about equilibrium reactions in Chapter 18.

SECTION REVIEW

1. 100. L

2. 2.24 L

3. 0.821 g

4. 9.28 L

PRACTICE

1. What volume of chlorine gas at 38°C and 1.63 atm is needed to react completely with 10.4 g of sodium to form NaCl?

   Answer
   3.54 L Cl_2

2. How many liters of gaseous carbon monoxide at 27°C and 0.247 atm can be produced from the burning of 65.5 g of carbon according to the following equation?

   $$2C(s) + O_2(g) \longrightarrow 2CO(g)$$

   Answer
   544 L CO

SECTION REVIEW

1. How many liters of ammonia gas can be formed from the reaction of 150. L of hydrogen gas? Assume that there is complete reaction of hydrogen with excess nitrogen gas and that all measurements are made at the same temperature and pressure.

2. How many liters of H_2 gas at STP can be produced by the reaction of 4.60 g of Na and excess water, according to the following equation?

   $$2Na(s) + 2H_2O(l) \longrightarrow H_2(g) + 2NaOH(aq)$$

3. How many grams of Na are needed to react with H_2O to liberate 4.00×10^2 mL of H_2 gas at STP?

4. What volume of oxygen gas in liters can be collected at 0.987 atm pressure and 25.0°C when 30.6 g of $KClO_3$ decompose by heating, according to the following equation?

   $$2KClO_3(s) \xrightarrow[MnO_2]{\Delta} 2KCl(s) + 3O_2(g)$$

Effusion and Diffusion

The constant motion of gas molecules causes them to spread out to fill any container in which they are placed. As you learned in Chapter 10, the gradual mixing of two gases due to their spontaneous, random motion is known as *diffusion*, illustrated in Figure 11-6. *Effusion* is the process whereby the molecules of a gas confined in a container randomly pass through a tiny opening in the container. In this section, you will learn how effusion can be used to estimate the molar mass of a gas.

Graham's Law of Effusion

The rates of effusion and diffusion depend on the relative velocities of gas molecules. The velocity of a gas varies inversely with its mass. Lighter molecules move faster than heavier molecules at the same temperature.

Recall that the average kinetic energy of the molecules in any gas depends only on the temperature and equals $\frac{1}{2}mv^2$. For two different gases, A and B, at the same temperature, the following relationship is true.

$$\frac{1}{2}M_A v_A^2 = \frac{1}{2}M_B v_B^2$$

OBJECTIVES

- State Graham's law of effusion.

- Determine the relative rates of effusion of two gases of known molar masses.

- State the relationship between the molecular velocities of two gases and their molar masses.

Lesson Starter
FIGURE 11-6 Ask students to assume that the perfume bottle stands open in a room where the air is perfectly still. Ask them to speculate on what will happen as time passes.

✔ **Teaching Tip**

If students have difficulty understanding the relationship in the last paragraph, the following might help:

$$(KE)_A = \frac{1}{2}m_A v_A^2$$
$$(KE)_B = \frac{1}{2}m_B v_B^2$$

At the same temperature,

$$(KE)_A = (KE)_B$$

so

$$\frac{1}{2}m_A v_A^2 = \frac{1}{2}m_B v_B^2$$

The value of m_A (the mass of an individual molecule of gas A) is proportional to M_A (the molar mass of gas A), so

$$\frac{1}{2}M_A v_A^2 = \frac{1}{2}M_B v_B^2$$

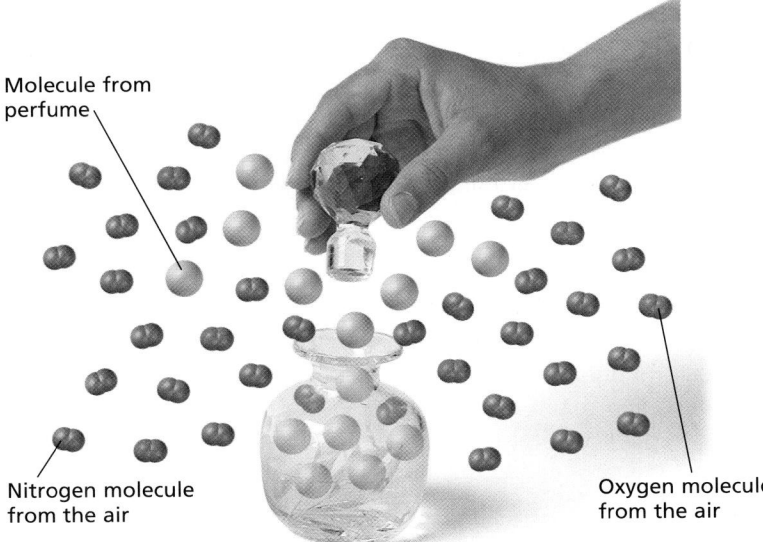

Molecule from perfume

Nitrogen molecule from the air

Oxygen molecule from the air

FIGURE 11-6 When a bottle of perfume is opened, some of its molecules diffuse into the air and mix with the molecules in the air. At the same time, molecules from the air, such as nitrogen and oxygen, diffuse into the bottle and mix with the gaseous scent molecules.

Reading Skill-Builder

VOCABULARY BUILDING
Write the words *diffusion* and *effusion* on the board. Point out that both words come from the same Latin root word—*fundere*, meaning "to pour." Explain that before the letter *f*, the prefix *dis-* (meaning "apart") becomes *dif-* and the prefix *ex-* (meaning "out") becomes *ef-*. Students may notice that both words describe a "pouring out" of molecules. Refer students to Figures 11-6 and 11-7 to clarify the difference between the terms.

Additional Example Problems

1. At 25°C, the average velocity of oxygen molecules is 420 m/s. What is the average velocity of helium atoms at the same temperature?

Ans. 1200 m/s

2. At a certain temperature, hydrogen molecules move at an average velocity of 1.84×10^3 m/s. Estimate the molar mass of a gas whose molecules have an average velocity of 312 m/s.

Ans. 70 g/mol

FIGURE 11-7 If you can smell the onions even when the bag is tightly sealed, molecules from the onions may be effusing through a small hole in the bag.

M_A and M_B represent the molar masses of gases A and B, and v_A and v_B represent their molecular velocities. Multiplying the equation by 2 gives the following.

$$M_A v_A^2 = M_B v_B^2$$

Suppose you wanted to compare the velocities of the two gases. You would first rearrange the equation above to give the velocities as a ratio.

$$\frac{v_A^2}{v_B^2} = \frac{M_B}{M_A}$$

The square root of each side of the equation is then taken.

$$\frac{v_A}{v_B} = \frac{\sqrt{M_B}}{\sqrt{M_A}}$$

This equation shows that the molecular velocities of two different gases are inversely proportional to the square roots of their molar masses. Because the rates of effusion are directly proportional to molecular velocities, the equation can be written as follows.

$$\frac{\text{rate of effusion of A}}{\text{rate of effusion of B}} = \frac{\sqrt{M_B}}{\sqrt{M_A}}$$

In the mid-1800s, the Scottish chemist Thomas Graham studied the effusion and diffusion of gases. Figure 11-7 illustrates the process of effusion. Compare this with the diffusion process. The equation derived above is a mathematical statement of some of Graham's discoveries. It describes the rates of effusion. **Graham's law of effusion** *states that the rates of effusion of gases at the same temperature and pressure are inversely proportional to the square roots of their molar masses.*

internetconnect

SC*i*LINKS.
NSTA

TOPIC: Thomas Graham
GO TO: www.scilinks.org
*sci*LINKS CODE: HC2114

Quick LAB

Wear Safety Goggles and an Apron.

Diffusion

Materials

- household ammonia
- perfume or cologne
- two 250 mL beakers
- Two watch glasses
- 10 mL graduated cylinder
- clock or watch with second hand

Question

Do different gases diffuse at different rates?

Procedure

Record all of your results in a data table.

1. Outdoors or in a room separate from the one in which you will carry out the rest of the investigation, pour approximately 10 mL of the household ammonia into one of the 250 mL beakers, and cover it with a watch glass. Pour roughly the same amount of perfume or cologne into the second beaker. Cover it with a watch glass also.

2. Take the two samples you just prepared into a large, draft-free room. Place the samples about 12 to 15 feet apart and at the same height. Position someone as the observer midway between the two beakers. Remove both watch-glass covers at the same time.

3. Note whether the observer smells the ammonia or the perfume first. Record how long this takes. Also, record how long it takes the vapor of the other substance to reach them. Air the room after you have finished.

Discussion

1. What do the times that the two vapors took to reach the observer show about the two gases?

2. What factors other than molecular mass (which determines diffusion rate) could affect how quickly the observer smells each vapor?

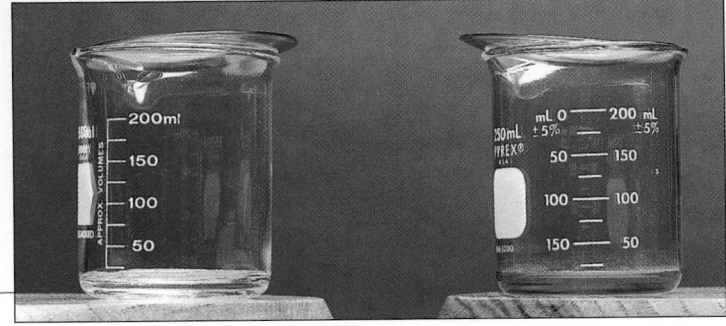

QUICK LAB

Students should make a data table to record their results.

Students should record the following:

- the identity of the two materials
- the location of each material relative to the observer
- the distance from each sample to the observer
- the time in seconds until the observer detects each material

(*If the air is quite still, the observer will detect the ammonia first.*)

Safety: Ammonia vapors are very irritating to human tissue. Be sure students do not breathe concentrated vapors. Before performing this activity, survey students to determine whether any of them have asthma or allergies to perfumes.

Disposal: Combine all liquids, dilute tenfold with water, and pour down the drain.

Discussion

1. Ammonia molecules diffuse more rapidly than do perfume-scent molecules.

2. concentration, vapor pressure, and the sensitivity of the observer to the two odors

Applications of Graham's Law

Graham's experiments dealt with the densities of gases. The density of a gas varies directly with its molar mass. Therefore, the square roots of the molar masses in the equation on page 352 can be replaced by the square roots of the gas densities, giving the following relationship.

$$\frac{\text{rate of effusion of A}}{\text{rate of effusion of B}} = \frac{\sqrt{M_B}}{\sqrt{M_A}} = \frac{\sqrt{\text{density}_B}}{\sqrt{\text{density}_A}}$$

Application

When bombarded with neutrons, the U-235 nucleus breaks down and releases energy and more neutrons, which go on to bombard other U-235 nuclei. This chain reaction, when controlled, can be used to generate heat to make steam to turn electric generators. The low content of U-235 (0.72%) in natural uranium is not enough to sustain a chain reaction, so the concentration must be increased. Uranium reacts with fluorine to form uranium hexafluoride, UF_6, which is easily vaporized to a gas. The UF_6 molecules containing U-235 are lighter than those with U-238 and effuse slightly faster. After many successive effusions, collections, and recompressions, more-concentrated U-235 is obtained. It can be used to make reactor fuel rods that will sustain a chain reaction.

In the experiment shown in Figure 11-8, ammonia gas, NH_3, and hydrogen chloride gas, HCl, diffuse toward each other from opposite ends of a glass tube. A white ring forms at the point where the two gases meet and combine chemically. The white ring is solid ammonium chloride, NH_4Cl. Notice that it forms closer to the HCl end of the tube than to the NH_3 end. The NH_3 has diffused faster than the HCl.

If the two gases had equal vapor pressures (resulting in equal concentrations), this result could be attributed completely to differences in molar mass. The lighter NH_3 molecules (molar mass 17.04 g) diffuse faster than the heavier HCl molecules (molar mass 36.46 g). However, diffusion rates depend on both molar mass and concentration.

The diffusion of the two gases in the tube takes longer than would be predicted from the known velocities of NH_3 and HCl. This is because the experiment does not take place in a vacuum. The oxygen and nitrogen molecules present in the air collide with the diffusing ammonia and hydrogen chloride molecules, slowing them down. To describe all these random collisions taking place in this system would be very complicated. This is why we use these equations to represent the *relative* rates of effusion based on the *relative* velocities of the molecules.

Graham's law also provides a method for determining molar masses. The rates of effusion of gases of known and unknown molar mass can be compared at the same temperature and pressure. The unknown molar mass can then be calculated using Graham's law. One application of Graham's law was used in order to separate the heavier $^{238}_{92}U$ isotope from the lighter $^{235}_{92}U$ isotope. The uranium was converted to a gaseous compound and passed through porous membranes, where the isotopes diffused at different rates due to their different densities and were thereby separated.

FIGURE 11-8 Cotton plugs moistened with solutions of ammonia and hydrogen chloride were placed at opposite ends of the glass tube several minutes before this photograph was taken. Why does the white ring of ammonium chloride form closer to the right end than the left end?

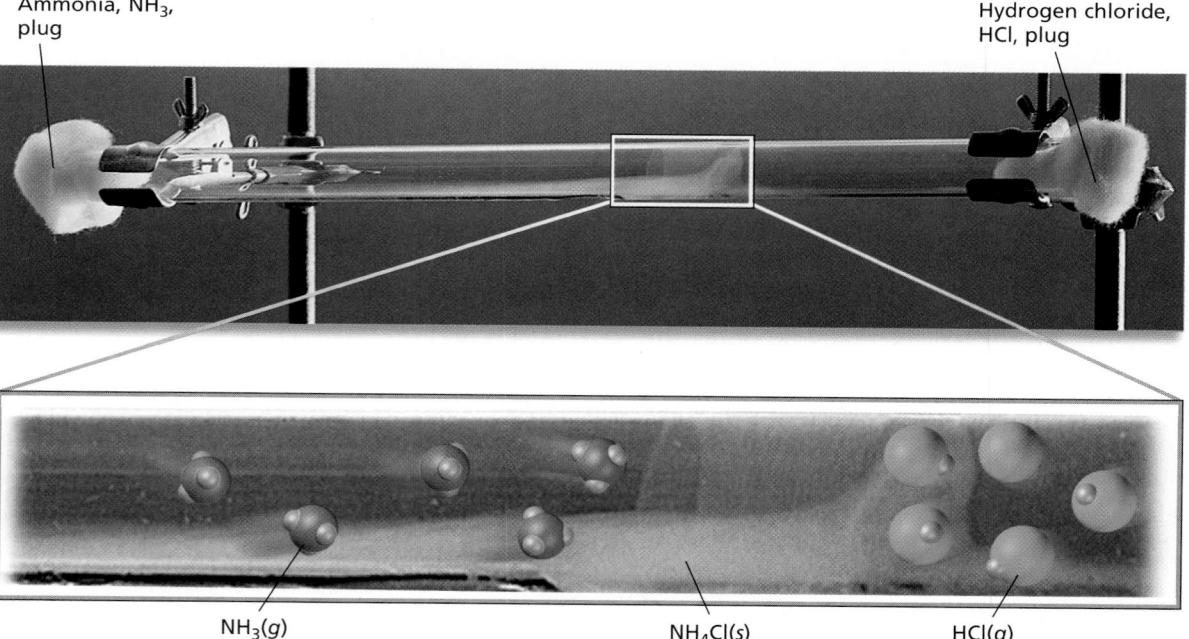

Ammonia, NH_3, plug

Hydrogen chloride, HCl, plug

$NH_3(g)$ $NH_4Cl(s)$ $HCl(g)$

SAMPLE PROBLEM 11-10

Compare the rates of effusion of hydrogen and oxygen at the same temperature and pressure.

SOLUTION

1 ANALYZE

Given: identities of two gases, H_2 and O_2
Unknown: relative rates of effusion

2 PLAN

$$\text{molar mass ratio} \longrightarrow \text{ratio of rates of effusion}$$

The ratio of the rates of effusion of two gases at the same temperature and pressure can be found from Graham's law.

$$\frac{\text{rate of effusion of A}}{\text{rate of effusion of B}} = \frac{\sqrt{M_B}}{\sqrt{M_A}}$$

3 COMPUTE

$$\frac{\text{rate of effusion of H}_2}{\text{rate of effusion of O}_2} = \frac{\sqrt{M_{O_2}}}{\sqrt{M_{H_2}}} = \frac{\sqrt{32.00 \text{ g/mol}}}{\sqrt{2.02 \text{ g/mol}}} = \sqrt{\frac{32.00 \text{ g/mol}}{2.02 \text{ g/mol}}} = 3.98$$

Hydrogen effuses 3.98 times faster than oxygen.

4 EVALUATE

The result is correctly reported to three significant figures. It is also approximately equivalent to an estimated value of 4, calculated as $\sqrt{32} / \sqrt{2}$.

PRACTICE

1. A sample of hydrogen effuses through a porous container about 9 times faster than an unknown gas. Estimate the molar mass of the unknown gas.

   Answer
   160 g/mol

2. Compare the rate of effusion of carbon dioxide with that of hydrogen chloride at the same temperature and pressure.

   Answer
   CO_2 will effuse about 0.9 times as fast as HCl.

3. If a molecule of neon gas travels at an average of 400 m/s at a given temperature, estimate the average speed of a molecule of butane gas, C_4H_{10}, at the same temperature.

   Answer
   about 235 m/s

SECTION REVIEW

1. Compare diffusion with effusion.

2. Estimate the molar mass of a gas that effuses at 1.6 times the effusion rate of carbon dioxide.

3. List the following gases in order of increasing average molecular velocity at 25°C: H_2O, He, HCl, BrF, and NO_2.

REVIEW ANSWERS

1. a. It applies only to gases measured under the same temperature and pressure.
b. The volume varies directly with the number of molecules.

2. a. If temperature and pressure remain constant, the volume varies directly with the number of moles present.
b. $V = kn$, where V is volume, n is the number of moles, and k is a proportionality constant

3. At STP, 22.4 L of any gas contains one mole of molecules. The mass of 22.4 L of gas is therefore equal to the molar mass of that gas.

4. Density is mass per unit volume. The volume of a gas, and therefore its density, varies according to its temperature and pressure. Densities of different gases can be compared only at the same temperature and pressure.

5. a. $PV = nRT$
b. It relates pressure, volume, temperature, and number of moles of any gas under any set of conditions at which the gas behaves as an ideal gas.

6. a. when three of the four variables P, V, T, and n are known
b. The units of volume, temperature, and pressure must match those of the gas constant used.

7. a. As long as temperature and pressure are the same, the volume ratios will be the same as the mole ratios.
b. Volume ratios are valid only when the volumes of all gases being compared are measured under the same temperature and pressure. Volume ratios also apply only to gases.

CHAPTER SUMMARY

11-1 • Gay-Lussac's law of combining volumes of gases states that the volumes of reacting gases and their products at the same temperature and pressure can be expressed as ratios of small whole numbers.
• Avogadro's law states that equal volumes of gases at the same temperature and pressure contain equal numbers of molecules. At constant temperature and pressure, gas volume is thus directly proportional to the number of moles.

• Gay-Lussac's law and Avogadro's law can be used to show that molecules of the reactive elemental gases are diatomic.
• The volume occupied by one mole of an ideal gas at STP is called the standard molar volume. The standard molar volume of an ideal gas is 22.414 10 L at standard temperature and pressure.

Vocabulary
Avogadro's law (334)   Gay-Lussac's law of combining volumes of gases (333)   standard molar volume of a gas (335)

11-2 • Charles's law, Boyle's law, and Avogadro's law can be combined to create the ideal gas law. The ideal gas law is stated mathematically as follows.
$$PV = nRT$$
• The value and units of the ideal gas constant depend on the units of the variables used in the ideal gas law.

• The ideal gas law can be used to calculate gas pressure, volume, temperature, or number of moles when three of these four variables are known and the gas sample does not undergo a change in conditions.
• The ideal gas law can also be used to calculate the density or molar mass of a gas sample.

Vocabulary
ideal gas constant (342)   ideal gas law (340)

11-3 • Given a balanced equation and the volume of a reacting gas, the volume of another gaseous product or reactant can be calculated using their volume ratios, as long as reactants and products exist under the same conditions.
• Given the volume of a reactant or product gas, the mass of a second reactant or product can be

calculated using the ideal gas law and mole-to-mass conversion factors.
• If the mass of a substance is known, the ideal gas law and the proper mass-to-mole conversion factors can be used to calculate the volume of a gas.

11-4 • Graham's law of effusion states that the relative rates of effusion of gases at the same temperature and pressure are inversely proportional to the square roots of their molar masses.
• Graham's law reflects the fact that less massive molecules effuse faster than do more massive ones.

• Graham's law can be used to compare the rates of effusion of gases at the same temperature and pressure.
• Given the relative rates of effusion of two gases and the identity of one of them, Graham's law can be used to estimate the molar mass of the other.

Vocabulary
Graham's law of effusion (352)

REVIEWING CONCEPTS

1. a. What restrictions are there on the use of Gay-Lussac's law of combining volumes?
   b. At the same temperature and pressure, what is the relationship between the volume of a gas and the number of molecules present? (11-1)

2. According to Avogadro,
   a. what is the relationship between gas volume and number of moles at constant temperature and pressure?
   b. what is the mathematical expression denoting this relationship? (11-1)

3. What is the relationship between the number of molecules and the mass of 22.4 L of different gases at STP? (11-1)

4. Why must the temperature and pressure be specified when stating gas density values? (11-1)

5. a. Write the equation for the ideal gas law.
   b. What relationship is expressed in the ideal gas law? (11-2)

6. a. In what situation does the ideal gas law apply?
   b. Why do you have to pay particular attention to units when using this law? (11-2)

7. a. In a balanced chemical equation, what is the relationship between the molar ratios and the volume ratios of gaseous reactants and products?
   b. What restriction applies to the use of the volume ratios in solving stoichiometry problems? (11-3)

8. a. Distinguish between diffusion and effusion.
   b. At a given temperature, what factor determines the rates at which different molecules undergo these processes? (11-4)

PROBLEMS

Molar Volume and Gas Density

9. Suppose a 5.00 L sample of O_2 at a given temperature and pressure contains 1.08×10^{23} molecules. How many molecules would be contained in each of the following at the same temperature and pressure?
   a. 5.00 L H_2
   b. 5.00 L CO_2
   c. 10.00 L NH_3

10. How many molecules are contained in each of the following?
   a. 1.00 mol O_2
   b. 2.50 mol He
   c. 0.0650 mol NH_3
   d. 11.5 g NO_2

11. Find the mass of each of the following.
   a. 2.25 mol Cl_2
   b. 3.01×10^{23} molecules H_2S
   c. 25.0 molecules SO_2

12. What is the volume, in liters, of each of the following at STP? (Hint: See Sample Problem 11-1.)
   a. 1.00 mol O_2
   b. 3.50 mol F_2
   c. 0.0400 mol CO_2
   d. 1.20×10^{-6} mol He

13. How many moles are contained in each of the following at STP?
   a. 22.4 L N_2
   b. 5.60 L Cl_2
   c. 0.125 L Ne
   d. 70.0 mL NH_3

14. Find the mass, in grams, of each of the following at STP. (Hint: See Sample Problem 11-2.)
   a. 11.2 L H_2
   b. 2.80 L CO_2
   c. 15.0 mL SO_2
   d. 3.40 cm^3 F_2

15. Find the volume, in liters, of each of the following at STP.
   a. 8.00 g O_2
   b. 3.50 g CO
   c. 0.0170 g H_2S
   d. 2.25×10^5 kg NH_3

Ideal Gas Law

16. Calculate the pressure, in atmospheres, exerted by each of the following. (Hint: See Sample Problem 11-3.)
   a. 2.50 L of HF containing 1.35 mol at 320. K
   b. 4.75 L of NO_2 containing 0.86 mol at 300. K
   c. 7.50×10^2 mL of CO_2 containing 2.15 mol at 57°C

8. a. Diffusion occurs when two gases mix by random molecular motion. Effusion occurs when a gas passes through a small opening.
   b. At the same temperature, heavier molecules have a lower average velocity than lighter molecules. Thus, heavier molecules diffuse and effuse more slowly than lighter molecules. The rate varies inversely with the square root of the molecular mass.

9. a. 1.08×10^{23} molecules H_2
   b. 1.08×10^{23} molecules CO_2
   c. 2.16×10^{23} molecules NH_3

10. a. 6.022×10^{23} molecules O_2
   b. 1.51×10^{24} molecules He
   c. 3.91×10^{22} molecules NH_3
   d. 1.51×10^{23} molecules NO_2

11. a. 160. g Cl_2
   b. 17.0 g H_2S
   c. 2.66×10^{-21} g SO_2

12. a. 22.4 L O_2
   b. 78.4 L F_2
   c. 0.896 L CO_2
   d. 2.69×10^{-5} L He

13. a. 1.00 mol N_2
   b. 0.250 mol Cl_2
   c. 5.58×10^{-3} mol Ne
   d. 3.12×10^{-3} mol NH_3

14. a. 1.01 g H_2
   b. 5.50 g CO_2
   c. 0.0429 g SO_2
   d. 5.77×10^{-3} g F_2

15. a. 5.60 L O_2
   b. 2.80 L CO
   c. 0.0112 L H_2S
   d. 2.96×10^8 L NH_3

16. a. 14.2 atm
   b. 4.5 atm
   c. 77.7 atm

17. a. 39.4 L H_2
   b. 14.9 L NH_3
   c. 3.81 L O_2

18. a. 0.0646 mol
   b. 0.030 mol
   c. 0.0377 mol

19. a. 15.3 g O_2
  b. 2.23 g NH_3
  c. 0.364 g SO_2

20. a. 11.7 g/mol
  b. 13.5 g/mol
  c. 11.5 g/mol

21. 30.9 g/mol

22. $2.26 \times 10^7 °C$

23. a. 0.50 L O_2
  b. 1.0 L CO_2

24. a. 37.5 L C_2H_2
  b. 37.5 L H_2O
  c. 93.8 L O_2

25. 0.150 L CO_2, 0.300 L SO_2

26. a. 0.250 mol H_2
  b. 0.250 mol Cu
  c. 15.9 g Cu

27. a. 2.4 g $Fe(OH)_3$
  b. 1.8 g Fe_2O_3

28. 29.0 L CO_2, 58.0 L H_2O vapor

29. a. 1.50×10^3 L air
  b. 200. L CO_2, 225 L H_2O vapor

30. 193 L NH_3

31. 358 L

32. 1.18×10^8 L SO_2, 2.35×10^8 L H_2S

33. 1.26×10^3 mL C_2H_2

34. a. 1.00 mol O_2, 2.00 mol MgO
  b. 0.500 mol O_2, 1.00 mol MgO
  c. 0.0625 mol O_2, 0.125 mol MgO

35. a. 0.379 mol I_2
  b. 0.758 mol KI
  c. 126 g KI

36. 4.41 g $FeSO_4$

37. a. CO is in excess
  b. 38 mL CO
  c. 412 mL CH_3OH

38. a. 0.500 mol Al
  b. 0.750 mol H_2
  c. 16.8 L H_2

39. a. rate H_2/rate N_2 = 3.72
  b. rate F_2/rate Cl_2 = 1.37

40. velocity H_2/velocity Ne = 3.16

41. 0.0400 m/s

17. Calculate the volume, in liters, occupied by each of the following. (Hint: See Sample Problem 11-4.)
  a. 2.00 mol of H_2 at 300. K and 1.25 atm
  b. 0.425 mol of NH_3 at 37°C and 0.724 atm
  c. 4.00 g of O_2 at 57°C and 0.888 atm

18. Determine the number of moles of gas contained in each of the following.
  a. 1.25 L at 250. K and 1.06 atm
  b. 0.80 L at 27°C and 0.925 atm
  c. 7.50×10^2 mL at –50.°C and 0.921 atm

19. Find the mass of each of the following. (Hint: See Sample Problem 11-5.)
  a. 5.60 L of O_2 at 1.75 atm and 250. K
  b. 3.50 L of NH_3 at 0.921 atm and 27°C
  c. 125 mL of SO_2 at 0.822 atm and –53°C

20. Find the molar mass of each gas measured at the specified conditions. (Hint: See Sample Problem 11-6.)
  a. 0.650 g occupying 1.12 L at 280. K and 1.14 atm
  b. 1.05 g occupying 2.35 L at 37°C and 0.840 atm
  c. 0.432 g occupying 7.50×10^2 mL at –23°C and 1.03 atm

21. If the density of an unknown gas is 3.20 g/L at –18°C and 2.17 atm, what is the molar mass of this gas?

22. One method of estimating the temperature of the center of the sun is based on the assumption that the center consists of gases that have an average molar mass of 2.00 g/mol. If the density of the center of the sun is 1.40 g/cm^3 at a pressure of 1.30×10^9 atm, calculate the temperature in degrees Celsius.

Gas Stoichiometry

23. Carbon monoxide reacts with oxygen to produce carbon dioxide. If 1.0 L of carbon monoxide reacts with oxygen,
  a. how many liters of oxygen are required? (Hint: See Sample Problem 11-7.)
  b. how many liters of carbon dioxide are produced?

24. Acetylene gas, C_2H_2, undergoes combustion to produce carbon dioxide and water vapor. If 75.0 L of CO_2 are produced,
  a. how many liters of C_2H_2 are required?
  b. what volume of H_2O vapor is produced?

  c. what volume of O_2 is required?

25. If liquid carbon disulfide reacts with 4.50×10^2 mL of oxygen to produce the gases carbon dioxide and sulfur dioxide, what volume of each product is produced?

26. Assume that 5.60 L of H_2 at STP react with CuO according to the following equation:
  $CuO(s) + H_2(g) \longrightarrow Cu(s) + H_2O(g)$
  Make sure the equation is balanced before beginning your calculations.
  a. How many moles of H_2 react? (Hint: See Sample Problem 11-8.)
  b. How many moles of Cu are produced?
  c. How many grams of Cu are produced?

27. Solid iron(III) hydroxide decomposes to produce iron(III) oxide and water vapor. If 0.75 L of water vapor is produced at STP,
  a. how many grams of iron(III) hydroxide were used?
  b. how many grams of iron(III) oxide are produced?

28. If 29.0 L of methane, CH_4, undergoes complete combustion at 0.961 atm and 20°C, how many liters of each product are formed?

29. If air is 20.9% oxygen by volume,
  a. how many liters of air are needed for complete combustion of 25.0 L of octane vapor, C_8H_{18}?
  b. what volume of each product is produced?

30. A modified Haber process for making ammonia is conducted at 550.°C and 2.50×10^2 atm. If 10.0 kg of nitrogen (the limiting reactant) is used and the process goes to completion, what volume of ammonia is produced?

31. When liquid nitroglycerin, $C_3H_5(NO_3)_3$, explodes, the products are carbon dioxide, nitrogen, oxygen, and water vapor. If 5.00×10^2 g of nitroglycerin explode at STP, what is the total volume, at STP, for all gases produced?

32. The principal source of sulfur on Earth is deposits of free sulfur occurring mainly in volcanically active regions. The sulfur was initially formed by the reaction between the two volcanic vapors SO_2 and H_2S to form $H_2O(l)$ and $S_8(s)$. What volume of each gas, at 0.961 atm and 22°C, was needed to form a sulfur deposit of 4.50×10^5 kg on the slopes of a volcano in Hawaii?

33. A 3.25 g sample of solid calcium carbide, CaC_2, reacted with water to produce acetylene gas, C_2H_2, and aqueous calcium hydroxide. If the acetylene was collected over water at 17°C and 0.974 atm, how many milliliters of acetylene were produced?

34. Balance the following chemical equation.
$$Mg(s) + O_2(g) \longrightarrow MgO(s)$$
Then, based on the quantity of reactant or product given, determine the corresponding quantities of the specified reactants or products, assuming that the system is at STP.
a. 22.4 L O_2 = ___ mol O_2 ⟶ ___ mol MgO
b. 11.2 L O_2 = ___ mol O_2 ⟶ ___ mol MgO
c. 1.40 L O_2 = ___ mol O_2 ⟶ ___ mol MgO

35. Assume that 8.50 L of I_2 are produced using the following reaction that takes place at STP:
$$KI(aq) + Cl_2(g) \longrightarrow KCl(aq) + I_2(g)$$
Balance the equation before beginning your calculations.
a. How many moles of I_2 are produced?
b. How many moles of KI were used?
c. How many grams of KI were used?

36. Suppose that 6.50×10^2 mL of hydrogen gas are produced through a replacement reaction involving solid iron and sulfuric acid, H_2SO_4, at STP. How many grams of iron(II) sulfate are also produced?

37. Methanol, CH_3OH, is made by causing carbon monoxide and hydrogen gases to react at high temperature and pressure. If 4.50×10^2 mL of CO and 825 mL of H_2 are mixed,
a. which reactant is present in excess?
b. how much of that reactant remains after the reaction?
c. what volume of CH_3OH is produced, assuming the same pressure?

38. Assume that 13.5 g of Al react with HCl according to the following equation, at STP:
$$Al(s) + HCl(aq) \longrightarrow AlCl_3(aq) + H_2(g)$$
Remember to balance the equation first.
a. How many moles of Al react?
b. How many moles of H_2 are produced?
c. How many liters of H_2 at STP are produced? (Hint: See Sample Problem 11-9.)

Effusion and Diffusion

39. Quantitatively compare the rates of effusion for the following pairs of gases at the same temperature and pressure.
a. hydrogen and nitrogen (Hint: See Sample Problem 11-10.)
b. fluorine and chlorine

40. What is the ratio of the average velocity of hydrogen molecules to that of neon atoms at the same temperature and pressure?

41. At a certain temperature and pressure, chlorine molecules have an average velocity of 0.0380 m/s. What is the average velocity of sulfur dioxide molecules under the same conditions?

42. A sample of helium effuses through a porous container 6.50 times faster than does unknown gas X. What is the molar mass of the unknown gas?

MIXED REVIEW

43. An unknown gas effuses at 0.850 times the effusion rate of nitrogen dioxide, NO_2. Estimate the molar mass of the unknown gas.

44. Use the ideal gas law, $PV = nRT$, to derive Boyle's law and Charles's law.

45. A container holds 265 mL of chlorine gas, Cl_2. Assuming that the gas sample is at STP, what is its mass?

46. Suppose that 3.11 mol of carbon dioxide is at a pressure of 0.820 atm and a temperature of 39°C. What is the volume of the sample, in liters?

47. Compare the rates of diffusion of carbon monoxide, CO, and sulfur trioxide, SO_3.

48. A gas sample that has a mass of 0.993 g occupies 0.570 L. Given that the temperature is 281 K and the pressure is 1.44 atm, what is the molar mass of the gas?

49. The density of a gas is 3.07 g/L at STP. Calculate the gas's molar mass.

50. How many moles of helium gas would it take to fill a gas balloon with a volume of 1000. cm^3 when the temperature is 32°C and the atmospheric pressure is 752 mm Hg?

42. 169 g/mol

43. 64 g/mol

44. *Boyle's law:* temperature and moles of gas remain constant. $P_2V_2 = nRT$, and therefore $P_1V_1 = nRT = P_2V_2$, or $P_1V_1 = P_2V_2$. *Charles's law:* Likewise, at constant pressure and moles, $V_1/T_1 = nR/P = V_2/T_2$, and thus $V_1/T_1 = V_2/T_2$.

45. 0.839 g

46. 97.2 L

47. CO diffuses approximately 1.7 times as fast as SO_3.

48. 27.9 g/mol

49. 68.8 g/mol

50. 0.0395 mol He

51. 3.67 L, 45.2 g/mol

52. a. The combined gas law applies when a sample of gas changes from one set of *P*, *V*, and *T* conditions to another. It assumes that the molar quantity of gas does not change.
b. The ideal gas law applies to any situation in which you must determine *P*, *V*, *T*, or *n*, given any three of the four variables.

53.
$$\frac{\text{rate of effusion}_A}{\text{rate of effusion}_B} = \frac{\sqrt{M_B}}{\sqrt{M_A}} = \frac{\sqrt{\text{density}_B}}{\sqrt{\text{density}_A}}$$

54. According to Avogadro's law, equal volumes of gases under the same conditions of pressure and temperature contain equal numbers of molecules. It follows that the volume of a gas is proportional to the number of molecules present under the same conditions of *P* and *T*, $V \propto n$, or $V = kn$. Gay-Lussac did not know of moles and molecules, but he observed that at constant *T* and *P*, volumes of gaseous reactants and products can be expressed in small, whole-number ratios.

Today, we know the exact composition of most common substances. Therefore, we can write balanced chemical equations for a reaction by using a set of whole numbers as balancing coefficients to represent the relative numbers of molecules involved in the reaction. In a reaction, a ratio between the number of molecules of two components, 1 and 2, can be represented as a ratio of the balancing coefficients—simple whole numbers. If these components are gases under the same conditions, we know that volumes are proportional to the number of molecules. Therefore, the volumes will be in simple whole-number ratios, just as the number of molecules are.

55. One approach would be to electrolyze several different samples of water and observe that the ratio volume H_2/volume O_2 = 2/1 in all cases. Then this ratio could be compared with the ratio of the numbers of molecules shown in the balanced chemical equation $2H_2O \longrightarrow 2H_2 + O_2$.

56. a. No. If the gases were at the same temperature and pressure, all of the boxes would contain the same number of molecules.
b. gas C
c. gas C
d. The molecular mass of gas A is less than that of gas C because it takes more molecules of A in the same space to equal the density of C.

57. a. 4.00043 atm
b. 8.08050 atm
c. 300° K

51. A gas sample is collected at 16°C and 0.982 atm. If the sample has a mass of 7.40 g and a volume of 3.96 L, find the volume of the gas at STP and the molar mass.

CRITICAL THINKING

52. Evaluating Methods In solving a problem, what types of conditions involving temperature, pressure, volume, or number of moles would allow you to use
a. the combined gas law?
b. the ideal gas law?

53. Relating Ideas Write expressions relating the rates of effusion, molar masses, and densities of two different gases, A and B.

54. Evaluating Ideas Gay-Lussac's law of combining volumes holds true for relative volumes at any proportionate size. Use Avogadro's law to explain why this proportionality exists.

55. Designing Experiments Design an experiment to prove that the proportionality described in item 54 exists.

56. Interpreting Concepts The diagrams that follow represent equal volumes of four different gases.

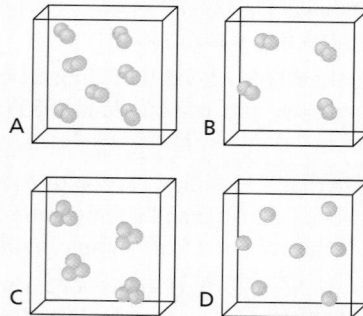

Use the diagrams to answer the following questions:
a. Are these gases at the same temperature and pressure? How do you know?
b. If the molar mass of gas B is 38 g/mol and that of gas C is 46 g/mol, which gas sample is more dense?
c. To make the densities of gas samples B and C equal, which gas should expand in volume?
d. If the densities of gas samples A and C are equal, what is the relationship between their molecular masses?

TECHNOLOGY & LEARNING

57. Graphing Calculator Calculating Pressure Using the Ideal Gas Law

The graphing calculator can run a program that calculates the pressure in atmospheres, given the number of moles of a gas (n), volume (V), and temperature (T). Given a 0.50 mol gas sample with a volume of 10. L at 298 K, you can calculate the pressure according to the ideal gas law. Begin by using the program to carry out the calculation. Next, use it to make calculations.

Go to Appendix C. If you are using a TI 83 Plus, you can download the program and data and run the application as directed. If you are using another calculator, your teacher will provide you with keystrokes and data sets to use. Remember that you will need to name the program and check the display, as explained in Appendix C. You will then be ready to run the program. After you have graphed the data, answer these questions.

Note: Answers are written with five significant figures.

a. What is the pressure for a gas with a mass of 1.3 mol, volume of 8.0 L, and temperature of 293 K?
b. What is the pressure for a gas with a mass of 2.7 mol, volume of 8.5 L, and temperature of 310 K?
c. A gas with a mass of 0.75 mol and a volume of 6.0 L is measured at two different temperatures: 300 K and 275 K. At which temperature is the pressure greater?

HANDBOOK SEARCH

58. Most elements from Groups 1, 2, and 13 will react with water, acids, or bases to produce hydrogen gas. Review the common reactions information in the *Elements Handbook* and answer the following:
a. Write the equation for the reaction of barium with water.

b. Write the equation for the reaction between cesium and hydrochloric acid.

c. Write the equation for the reaction of gallium with hydrofluoric acid.

d. What mass of barium would be needed to react with excess water to produce 10.1 L of H_2 at STP?

e. What masses of cesium and hydrochloric acid would be required to produce 10.1 L of H_2 at STP?

59. Group 1 metals react with oxygen to produce oxides, peroxides, or superoxides. Review the equations for these common reactions in the *Elements Handbook* and answer the following:

a. How do oxides, peroxides, and superoxides differ?

b. What mass of product will be formed from a reaction of 5.00 L of oxygen with excess sodium? The reaction occurs at 27°C and 1 atm.

60. Most metals react with chlorine from Group 17 to produce salts. Review these common reactions in the *Elements Handbook* and answer the following:

a. Write the equation for the reaction of iron and chlorine gas.

b. What mass of iron salt is produced if an excess of iron reacts with 450. mL of chlorine gas at 27°C and 1 atm?

RESEARCH & WRITING

61. How do scuba divers use the laws and principles that describe the behavior of gases to their advantage? What precautions do they take to prevent the bends?

62. Explain the processes involved in the liquefaction of gases. What substances that are gases under normal room conditions are typically used in the liquid form? Why?

63. Research the relationship between explosives and the establishment of Nobel Prizes. Prepare a report that describes your findings.

64. Write a summary describing how Gay-Lussac's work on combining volumes relates to Avogadro's study of gases. Explain how certain conclusions about gases followed logically from consideration of the work of both scientists.

ALTERNATIVE ASSESSMENT

65. During a typical day, record every instance in which you encounter the diffusion or effusion of gases (for example, smelling perfume).

66. **Performance** Qualitatively compare the molecular masses of various gases by noting how long it takes you to smell them from a fixed distance. Work only with materials that are not dangerous, such as flavor extracts, fruit peels, and onions.

58. a. $Ba(s) + 2H_2O(l) \longrightarrow Ba(OH)_2 (aq) + H_2(g)$
b. $2Cs(s) + 2HCl(aq) \longrightarrow 2CsCl(aq) + H_2(g)$
c. $2Ga(s) + 6HF(aq) \longrightarrow 2GaF_3(aq) + 3H_2(g)$
d. 61.6 g Ba
e. 120 g Cs, 32.8 g HCl

59. a. The charge on oxygen in oxides is −2, in peroxides it is −1, and in super oxides it is −1/2, or written as O_2^-.
b. 0.2 g Na_2O_2

60. a. $2Fe(s) + 3Cl_2(g) \longrightarrow 2FeCl_3(s)$
b. 0.02 g $FeCl_3$

Liquids and Solids

PACING CHART Compression Guide: *(To shorten, eliminate items in italics.)*	CLASSROOM RESOURCES		
	NSE Standards	Teaching Resources	Experiments
12-1 Liquids 2 45-minute periods 1 90-minute block	PS 2e UCP 1–2	**ATE Demo,** p. 365 T 55	
12-2 Solids 2 45-minute periods 1 90-minute block	PS 2e UCP 1–2	**PE** Elements Handbook T 57, T 58	
12-3 Changes of State 2 45-minute periods 1 90-minute block *Equilibrium Vapor Pressure of a Liquid, pp. 376–378* *Phase Diagrams, pp. 381–382*	PS 2d, 5c UCP 1–4 HNS 1, 3 SPSP 5	**ATE Demo,** p. 380 T 59, T 60, T 62, T 63, **TM 54A,** **TM 55A**	"Wet" Dry Ice, p. 822 Measuring the Triple-Point Pressure of CO_2, p. 824 **A10** Molar Heat of Fusion of Ice **A15** Heat of Crystallization **C8 EXP** Heat of Fusion
12-4 Water 2 45-minute periods 1 90-minute block	PS 2d UCP 1–3	T 61	

Review and Assessment 2 45-minute periods 1 90-minute block	REVIEW RESOURCES		
	Cumulative Review	Alternative Assessment	Traditional Assessment
	SR Chapter 12 Mixed Review **PE** Chapter 12 27–37, pp. 389–390	**PE** 53, 54, p. 391 **ATE** 366, 369, 379, 385 **AA** Items for Chapter 12	Chapter 12 Text Test Generator items for Chapter 12

ASSIGNMENT RESOURCES

Section Homework Resources & Review	Problem-Solving Practice
HR Homework Worksheet 12-1 Graphic Org. Assignment 12-1 **PE** Section Review, 1–5, p. 366 Chapter Review, 1–3, p. 388 **SR** Section Review 12-1	
HR Homework Worksheet 12-2 Graphic Org. Assignment 12-2 **PE** Section Review, 1–4, p. 371 Chapter Review, 4–7, p. 388 **SR** Section Review 12-2	
HR Homework Worksheets 12-3, 12-4, 12-5, 12-6 Graphic Org. Assignment 12-4, 12-6 **PE** Section Review, 1–8, p. 382 Chapter Review, 8–15, 18–22, pp. 388–389 **SR** Section Review 12-3	
HR Homework Worksheet 12-7 **PE** Section Review, 1–4, p. 386 Chapter Review, 16–17, 23–25, pp. 388–389 **SR** Section Review 12-4	**PE** Additional Samples 12-1 **ATE** Additional Samples, p. 386

TECHNOLOGY RESOURCES

Technology & Internet Resources

 CTW 19 Segment 19 Change of State: Icebergs
CTW 21 Segment 21 Global Warming

 Holt Chemistry Videodiscs Teacher's Correlation Guide for Chapter 12

 **CHEMISTRY** Module 1: Liquid, Solid, Changes of State
Module 7: Equilibrium, Shifting Equilibrium

internet connect

 **SciLINKS** **On-line Student Resources:**
www.scilinks.org
The following SciLinks Internet resources can be found in the student text for this chapter.

TOPICS:
• Properties of liquids, p. 363 (HC2121)
• Crystalline solids, p. 370 (HC2122)
• Factors affecting equilibrium, p. 372 (HC2123)
• Volatile/nonvolatile liquids, p. 377 (HC2124)

On-line Teacher Resources:
 GO TO: go.hrw.com
KEYWORD: HC2 HOME
Visit the HRW Web site for a variety of resources related to this chapter.

 Smithsonian Institution®
Internet Connections
Visit **www.si.edu/hrw** for additional on-line resources.

CNNfyi.com
Visit **www.cnnfyi.com** for late-breaking news and current events stories selected just for you.

 **One-Stop Planner CD-ROM** Includes these resources and customizable daily lesson plans:

Resource Key

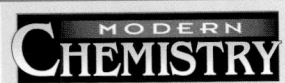 MODERN **CHEMISTRY**

PE Pupil's Edition
ATE Teacher's Edition

HR	Homework Resources	**ChemFile**	**D**	Consumer Experiments
SR	Section Reviews	**A** Laboratory Experiments	**T**	Transparencies
CTW	Critical Thinking Worksheets	**B** Microscale Experiments	**TM**	Transparency Masters
AA	Alternative Assessments	**C** Technique Builders and Problem-Solving Experiments	**PS**	Mini-Guide to Problem Solving
			SRW	Supplemental Reading Worksheets

Scoring Rubrics for Labs, Alternative Assessments, Performance Tasks and Portfolio Projects are on the One-Stop Planner CD-ROM.

CHAPTER **12**

Liquids and Solids

Chapter Overview

12-1 uses the kinetic-molecular theory to describe properties of liquids and explain changes of state involving liquids.

12-2 describes the properties of solids, contrasts them with liquid properties, and explains them on the basis of the kinetic-molecular theory.

12-3 covers changes of state and the factors that determine them. It introduces the concept of equilibrium in terms of changes of state.

12-4 covers the structure, physical properties, and changes of state of water.

Concept Base

Students may need a review of the following concepts:

- the properties of matter, Chapter 1
- density, Chapter 2
- covalent and ionic bonding, Chapter 6
- kinetic-molecular theory, Chapter 10

Liquids and Solids

Courtesy of the artist and Galerie Lelong, New York

The total three-dimensional arrangement of particles of a crystal is its crystal structure.

Liquids

The water in the waves crashing on a beach and the molten lava rushing down the sides of a volcano are examples of matter in the liquid state. When you think of Earth's oceans, lakes, and rivers and the many liquids you use every day, it is hard to believe that liquids are the *least* common state of matter in the universe. Liquids are less common than solids, gases, and plasmas because a substance in the liquid state can exist only within a relatively narrow range of temperatures and pressures.

In this section, you will examine the properties of the liquid state. You will also compare them with those of the solid state and the gas state. These properties will be discussed in terms of the kinetic-molecular theory.

Properties of Liquids and the Kinetic-Molecular Theory

A liquid can be described as a form of matter that has a definite volume and takes the shape of its container. The properties of liquids can be understood by applying the kinetic-molecular theory, considering the motion and arrangement of molecules and the attractive forces between them.

As in a gas, particles in a liquid are in constant motion. However, the particles in a liquid are closer together and lower in kinetic energy than those in a gas. Therefore, the attractive forces between particles in a liquid are more effective than those between particles in a gas. This attraction between liquid particles is caused by the intermolecular forces discussed in Chapter 6: dipole-dipole forces, London dispersion forces, and hydrogen bonding.

Liquids are more ordered than gases because of the stronger intermolecular forces and the lower mobility of the liquid particles. According to the kinetic-molecular theory of liquids, the particles are not bound together in fixed positions. Instead, they move about constantly. This particle mobility explains why liquids and gases are referred to as fluids. *A* **fluid** *is a substance that can flow and therefore take the shape of its container.* Most liquids naturally flow downhill because of gravity. However, some liquids can flow in other directions as well. For example, liquid helium near absolute zero has the unusual property of being able to flow uphill.

OBJECTIVES

- Describe the motion of particles in liquids and the properties of liquids according to the kinetic-molecular theory.

- Discuss the process by which liquids can change into a gas. Define *vaporization*.

- Discuss the process by which liquids can change into a solid. Define *freezing*.

CHEMISTRY TUTOR

Module 1: States of Matter/Classes of Matter

internet connect

SC/LINKS
NSTA

TOPIC: Properties of liquids
GO TO: www.scilinks.org
*sci*LINKS CODE: HC2121

Lesson Starter
Show students a closed, colorless container of soft drink. Ask them how they are able to tell that it is filled with a liquid. Lead them to the idea that liquids have definite volume but take the shape of their container. Contrast these properties with those of gases, which have neither fixed shape nor fixed volume.

Common Misconception
Students often think the terms *liquid* and *fluid* are synonymous. Point out that gases are also fluids because they have the ability to flow.

 **Reading Skill-Builder**

L.I.N.K. Write the words *liquid* and *solid* on the board. Have students brainstorm all the words, phrases, and ideas that they associate with liquids and solids. Have a volunteer write students' contributions on the board. Lead students in a discussion about the listed terms, and use them as a starting point for developing a list of physical properties of liquids and solids. At the end of the discussion have students make notes of everything they remember. Then have students look over their notes to see what they know about liquids and solids based on experience.

CHEMISTRY TUTOR

Module 1: States of Matter/Classes of Matter

Topic: Liquid
Section **b** of this engaging tutorial reviews and reinforces understanding of liquids.

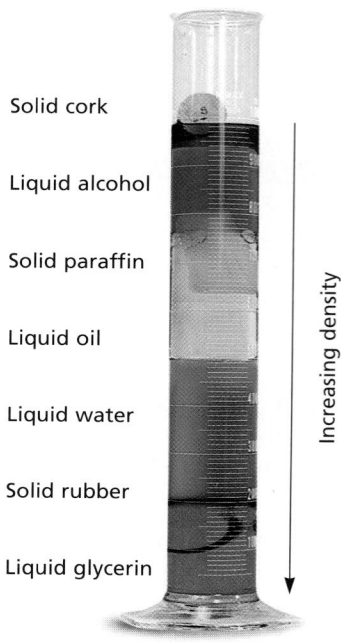

Solid cork

Liquid alcohol

Solid paraffin

Liquid oil

Liquid water

Solid rubber

Liquid glycerin

Increasing density

FIGURE 12-1 Solids and liquids of different densities are shown. The densest materials are at the bottom. The least dense are at the top. (Dyes have been added to the liquids to make the layers more visible.)

FIGURE 12-2 Like gases, the two liquids in this beaker diffuse over time. The green liquid food coloring from the drop will eventually form a uniform solution with the water.

Relatively High Density

At normal atmospheric pressure, most substances are thousands of times denser as liquids than as gases. This higher density is a result of the close arrangement of liquid particles. Most substances are only slightly less dense (about 10%) as liquids than as solids, however. Water is one of the few substances that becomes less dense when it solidifies, as will be discussed further in Section 12-4.

At the same temperature and pressure, different liquids can differ greatly in density. Figure 12-1 shows some liquids and solids with different densities. The densities differ to such an extent that the liquids form layers.

Relative Incompressibility

When liquid water at 20°C is compressed by a pressure of 1000 atm, its volume decreases by only 4%. Such behavior is typical of all liquids and is similar to the behavior of solids. In contrast, a gas under a pressure of 1000 atm would have only about 1/1000 of its volume at normal atmospheric pressure. Liquids are much less compressible than gases because liquid particles are more closely packed together. In addition, liquids can transmit pressure equally in all directions.

Ability to Diffuse

As described in Chapter 10, gases diffuse and mix with other gas particles. Liquids also diffuse and mix with other liquids, as shown in Figure 12-2. Any liquid gradually diffuses throughout any other liquid in which it can dissolve. As in gases, diffusion in liquids occurs because of the constant, random motion of particles. Yet diffusion is much slower in liquids than in gases because liquid particles are closer together. Also, the attractive forces between the particles of a liquid slow their movement. As the temperature of a liquid is increased, diffusion occurs more rapidly. That is because the average kinetic energy, and therefore the average speed of the particles, is increased.

Water molecule

Dye molecule

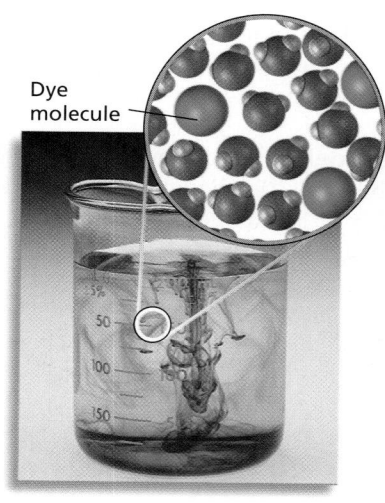

Surface Tension

A property common to all liquids, **surface tension,** *is a force that tends to pull adjacent parts of a liquid's surface together, thereby decreasing surface area to the smallest possible size.* Surface tension results from the attractive forces between particles of a liquid. The higher the force of attraction, the higher the surface tension. Water has a higher surface tension than most liquids. This is due to the hydrogen bonds water molecules can form with each other. The molecules at the surface of the water are a special case. They can form hydrogen bonds with the other water molecules beneath them and beside them, but not with the molecules in the air above them. As a result, the surface water molecules are drawn together and toward the body of the liquid, creating a high surface tension. Surface tension causes liquid droplets to take on a spherical shape because a sphere has the smallest possible surface area for a given volume. An example of this phenomenon is shown in Figure 12-3.

Capillary action, *the attraction of the surface of a liquid to the surface of a solid,* is a property closely related to surface tension. A liquid will rise quite high in a very narrow tube if a strong attraction exists between the liquid molecules and the molecules that make up the surface of the tube. This attraction tends to pull the liquid molecules upward along the surface against the pull of gravity. This process continues until the weight of the liquid balances the gravitational force. Capillary action can occur between water molecules and paper fibers, as shown in Figure 12-4. Capillary action is at least partly responsible for the transportation of water from the roots of a plant to its leaves. The same process is responsible for the concave liquid surface, called a *meniscus,* that forms in a test tube or graduated cylinder.

Evaporation and Boiling

The process by which a liquid or solid changes to a gas is **vaporization.** Evaporation is a form of vaporization. **Evaporation** *is the process by which particles escape from the surface of a nonboiling liquid and enter the gas state.*

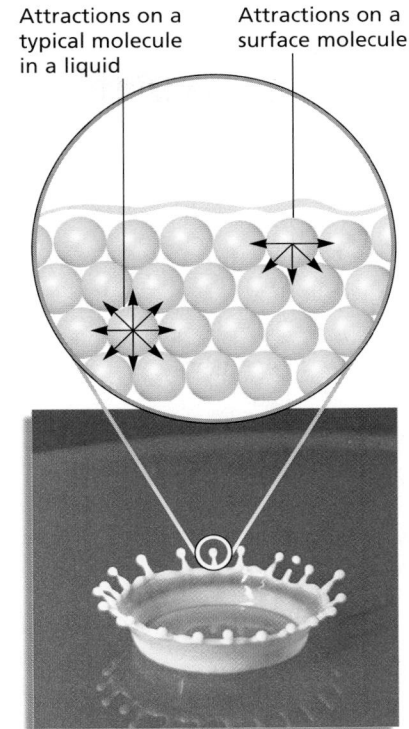

Attractions on a typical molecule in a liquid

Attractions on a surface molecule

FIGURE 12-3 As a result of surface tension, liquids form roughly spherical drops. The net attractive forces between the particles pull the molecules on the surface inward and closer together than those farther down in the liquid, minimizing the surface area.

(a)   (b)

FIGURE 12-4 The attraction between polar water molecules and polar cellulose molecules in paper fibers causes the water to move up in the paper. The water-soluble ink placed near the bottom of the paper in (a) rises up the paper along with the water, as seen in (b). As the ink moves up the paper, it is separated into its various components, producing the different bands of color. This separation occurs because the water and the paper attract the molecules of the ink components differently. These phenomena are used in the separation process of paper chromatography seen here.

Alternative Assessment

Have students draw a simple outline or concept map that illustrates the relationships between evaporation, boiling, and vaporization, and have them include examples. The outlines or concept maps should show vaporization as the top entry, with evaporation and boiling listed as types of vaporization.

SECTION REVIEW

1. Liquid particles are held close together by intermolecular forces, but they are in constant motion because of their kinetic energy.

2. Liquids have definite volume, take the shape of their container, can flow, have relatively high density, are relatively incompressible, can diffuse, and have surface tension.

3. a. Intermolecular forces hold particles close together.
b. Liquid particles are in constant motion.
c. Some particles have enough kinetic energy to escape into the gas state.

4. If the liquid is attracted to the glass, it is pulled upward into the test tube creating a concave surface. This effect is called capillary action, and the surface is called a meniscus. (If the liquid is not attracted to the glass, it is pushed downward in the test tube, and the surface becomes convex.)

5. Vaporization is any change to the gas state. Evaporation is a type of vaporization in which particles from the surface of a nonboiling liquid escape into the gas state.

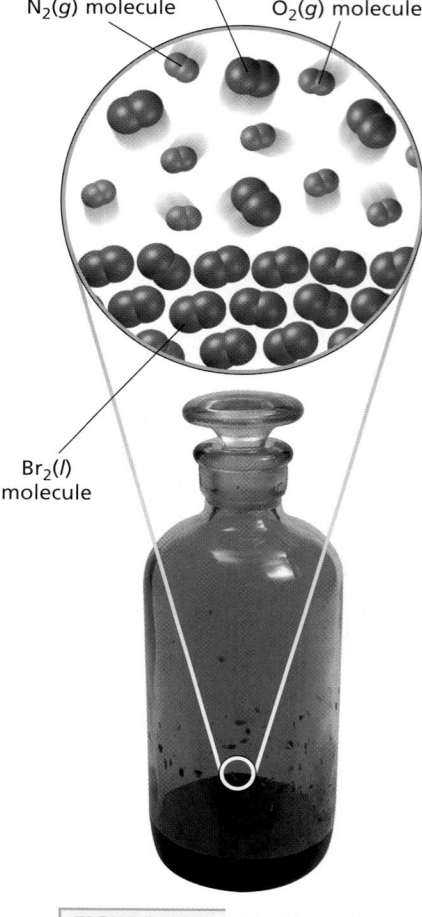

Evaporated $Br_2(g)$ molecule diffusing into air

$N_2(g)$ molecule $O_2(g)$ molecule

$Br_2(l)$ molecule

FIGURE 12-5 Liquid bromine, Br_2, evaporates near room temperature. The resulting brownish red gas diffuses into the air above the surface of the liquid.

A small amount of liquid bromine was added to the bottle shown in Figure 12-5. Within a few minutes, the air above the liquid bromine turned brownish-red. That is because some bromine molecules escaped from the surface of the liquid. They have changed into the gas state, becoming bromine vapor, which mixed with the air. A similar phenomenon occurs if you apply perfume to your wrist. Within seconds, you become aware of the perfume's fragrance. Scent molecules evaporate from your skin and diffuse through the air, to be detected by your nose.

Evaporation occurs because the particles of a liquid have different kinetic energies. Particles with higher-than-average energies move faster. Some surface particles with higher-than-average energies can overcome the intermolecular forces that bind them to the liquid. They can then escape into the gas state.

Evaporation is a crucial process in nature. Evaporation removes fresh water from the surface of the ocean, leaving behind a higher concentration of salts. In subtropical areas, evaporation occurs at a higher rate, causing the surface water to be saltier. All water that falls to Earth in the form of rain and snow previously evaporated from oceans, lakes, and rivers. Evaporation of perspiration plays an important role in keeping you cool. Perspiration, which is mostly water, cools you by absorbing body heat when it evaporates. Heat energy is absorbed from the skin, causing the cooling effect.

Boiling is the change of a liquid to bubbles of vapor that appear throughout the liquid. Boiling differs from evaporation, as you will see in Section 12-3.

Formation of Solids

When a liquid is cooled, the average energy of its particles decreases. If the energy is low enough, attractive forces pull the particles into an even more orderly arrangement. The substance then becomes a solid. *The physical change of a liquid to a solid by removal of heat is called* **freezing** *or solidification.* Perhaps the best-known example of freezing is the change of liquid water to solid water, or ice, at 0°C. Another familiar example is the solidification of paraffin at room temperature. All liquids freeze, although not necessarily at temperatures you normally encounter. Ethanol, for example, freezes near −115°C.

SECTION REVIEW

1. Describe the liquid state according to the kinetic-molecular theory.

2. List the properties of liquids.

3. How does the kinetic-molecular theory explain the following properties of liquids? (a) their relatively high density, (b) their ability to diffuse, and (c) their ability to evaporate

4. Explain why liquids in a test tube form a meniscus.

5. Compare vaporization and evaporation.

Solids

"Solid as a rock" is a common expression that suggests something that is hard or unyielding and that has a definite shape and volume. In this section, you will examine the properties of solids and compare them with those of liquids and gases. As with the other states of matter, the properties of solids are explained in terms of the kinetic-molecular theory.

Properties of Solids and the Kinetic-Molecular Theory

The particles of a solid are more closely packed than those of a liquid or gas. Intermolecular forces between particles are therefore much more effective in solids. Dipole-dipole attractions, London dispersion forces, and hydrogen bonding exert stronger effects in solids than in the corresponding liquids or gases. These forces tend to hold the particles of a solid in relatively fixed positions, with only vibrational movement around fixed points. Because the motions of the particles are restricted in this way, solids are more ordered than liquids and are much more ordered than gases. The importance of order and disorder in physical and chemical changes will be discussed in Chapter 17. Compare the physical appearance and molecular arrangement of the element in Figure 12-6 in solid, liquid, and gas form.

OBJECTIVES

- Describe the motion of particles in solids and the properties of solids according to the kinetic-molecular theory.

- Distinguish between the two types of solids.

- Describe the different types of crystal symmetry. Define *crystal structure* and *unit cell*.

CHEMISTRY INTERACTIVE TUTOR

Module 1: States of Matter/Classes of Matter

FIGURE 12-6   Particles of sodium metal in three different states are shown. Sodium exists in a gaseous state in a sodium-vapor lamp.

Lesson Starter
Mix up a small amount of plaster of Paris according to directions. Pour the mixture onto a piece of cardboard, and allow it to harden. Ask students to compare the mixture before it hardens to the product after it hardens. Student observations should include differences in the plaster of Paris as a fluid and the plaster of Paris as a solid.

Visual Strategy
FIGURE 12-6 Have students compare the movement of particles shown to the movement of people at a crowded football or soccer game. The people in the stands have very limited movement, like the particles in the solid. The people walking in front of the stands are somewhat limited but have more freedom of movement than those in the stands, like the particles in a liquid. While playing, the players on the field are similar to particles in a gas; they have more kinetic energy, and few limitations are placed on their locations.

CHEMISTRY INTERACTIVE TUTOR

Module 1: States of Matter/Classes of Matter

Topic: Solid
Section **a** of this engaging tutorial reviews and reinforces understanding of solids.

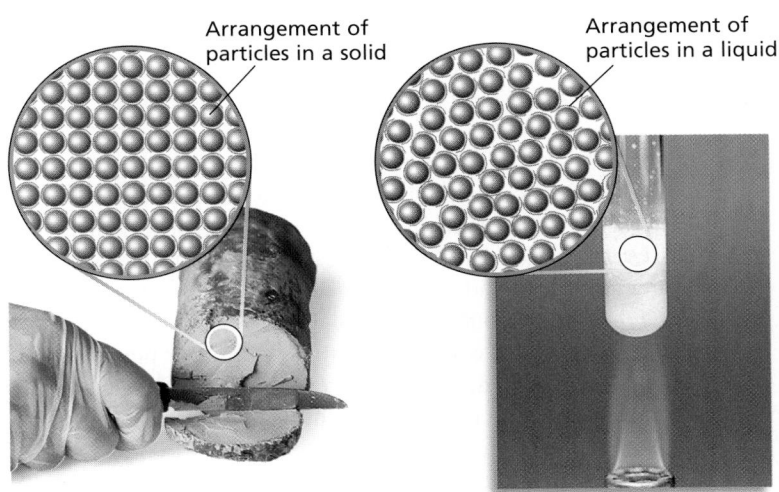

Arrangement of particles in a solid

Arrangement of particles in a liquid

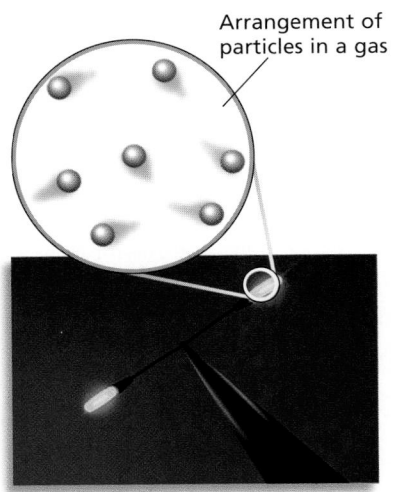

Arrangement of particles in a gas

(a)

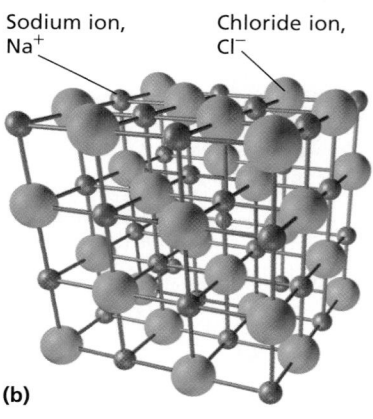

Sodium ion, Na$^+$ Chloride ion, Cl$^-$

(b)

FIGURE 12-7 (a) This is a scanning electron micrograph (SEM) of a sodium chloride crystal. A sodium chloride crystal can be represented by its crystal structure (b), which is made up of individual unit cells represented regularly in three dimensions. Here, one unit cell is outlined in red.

There are two types of solids: crystalline solids and amorphous solids. *Most solids are* **crystalline solids**—*they consist of crystals. A* **crystal** *is a substance in which the particles are arranged in an orderly, geometric, repeating pattern.* Noncrystalline solids, including glass and plastics, are called amorphous solids. *An* **amorphous solid** *is one in which the particles are arranged randomly.* The two types of solids will be discussed in more detail later in this section.

Definite Shape and Volume
Unlike liquids and gases, solids can maintain a definite shape without a container. In addition, crystalline solids are geometrically regular. Even the fragments of a shattered crystalline solid have distinct geometric shapes that reflect their internal structure. Amorphous solids maintain a definite shape, but they do not have the distinct geometric shapes of crystalline solids. For example, glass can be molded into any shape. If it is shattered, glass fragments can have a wide variety of irregular shapes.

The volume of a solid changes only slightly with a change in temperature or pressure. Solids have definite volume because their particles are packed closely together. There is very little empty space into which the particles can be compressed. Crystalline solids generally do not flow because their particles are held in relatively fixed positions.

Definite Melting Point
Melting *is the physical change of a solid to a liquid by the addition of heat. The temperature at which a solid becomes a liquid is its* **melting point.** At this temperature, the kinetic energies of the particles within the solid overcome the attractive forces holding them together. The particles can then break out of their positions in crystalline solids, which have definite melting points. In contrast, amorphous solids, such as glass and plastics, have no definite melting point. They have the ability to flow over a range of temperatures. Therefore, amorphous solids are sometimes classified as **supercooled liquids,** *which are substances that retain certain liquid properties even at temperatures at which they appear to be solid.* These properties exist because the particles in amorphous solids are arranged randomly, much like the particles in a liquid. Unlike the particles in a true liquid, however, the particles in amorphous solids are not constantly changing their positions.

High Density and Incompressibility
In general, substances are most dense in the solid state. Solids tend to be slightly denser than liquids and much denser than gases. The higher density results from the fact that the particles of a solid are more closely packed than those of a liquid or a gas. Solid hydrogen is the least dense solid; it has a density of about 1/320 of the densest element, osmium, Os.

Solids are generally less compressible than liquids. For practical purposes, solids can be considered incompressible. Some solids, such as wood and cork, may *seem* compressible, but they are not. They contain pores that are filled with air. When subjected to intense pressure, the pores are compressed, not the wood or cork itself.

Fluorite
Cubic

Chalcopyrite
Tetragonal

Emerald
Hexagonal

Calcite
Trigonal

Aragonite
Orthorhombic

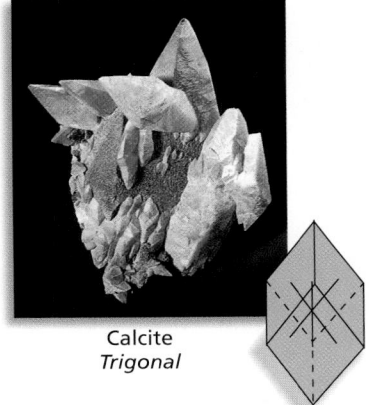

Azurite
Monoclinic

Low Rate of Diffusion

If a zinc plate and a copper plate are clamped together for a long time, a few atoms of each metal will diffuse into the other. This observation shows that diffusion does occur in solids. The rate of diffusion is millions of times slower in solids than in liquids, however.

Crystalline Solids

Crystalline solids exist either as single crystals or as groups of crystals fused together. *The total three-dimensional arrangement of particles of a crystal is called a* **crystal structure.** The arrangement of particles in the crystal can be represented by a coordinate system called a lattice. *The smallest portion of a crystal lattice that shows the three-dimensional pattern of the entire lattice is called a* **unit cell.** Each crystal lattice contains many unit cells packed together. Figure 12-7 shows the relationship between a crystal lattice and its unit cell. A crystal and its unit cells can have any one of seven types of symmetry. This fact enables scientists to classify crystals by their shape. Diagrams and examples of each type of crystal symmetry are shown in Figure 12-8.

Binding Forces in Crystals

Crystal structures can also be described in terms of the types of particles in them and the types of chemical bonding between the particles.

Rhodonite
Triclinic

FIGURE 12-8 Shown are the seven basic crystalline systems and representative minerals of each.

CHAPTER ⟺ CONNECTION

Elemental carbon and carbon compounds will be covered extensively in Chapter 20.

TABLE STRATEGY

Table 12-1 Point out that general trends in melting point can be determined but that ranges overlap.

Did You Know?

Glasslike materials can be made from combinations of metals. The alloys take on amorphous forms when they are melted, formed into thin films, and cooled rapidly. The "metallic glasses" are strong, flexible, and resistant to corrosion.

Reading Skill-Builder

INTERPRETING VOCABULARY Ask students what they think of when they hear the term *network*. They may mention television networks or networked computers. Elicit from students that a network takes many individual parts and joins them as a unit. Covalent network crystals form giant molecules, or *macromolecules*.

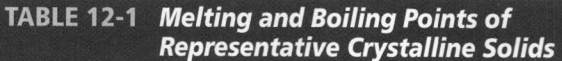

internet connect

SC*LINKS*
NSTA

TOPIC: Crystalline solids
GO TO: www.scilinks.org
*sci*LINKS CODE: HC2122

TABLE 12-1 *Melting and Boiling Points of Representative Crystalline Solids*

Type of substance	Formula	Melting point (°C)	Boiling point at 1 atm (°C)
Ionic	NaCl	801	1413
	MgF_2	1266	2239
Covalent network	$(SiO_2)_x$	1610	2230
	C_x (diamond)	3500	3930
Metallic	Hg	−39	357
	Cu	1083	2567
	Fe	1535	2750
	W	3410	5660
Covalent molecular (nonpolar)	H_2	−259	−253
	O_2	−218	−183
	CH_4	−182	−164
	CCl_4	−23	77
	C_6H_6	6	80
Covalent molecular (polar)	NH_3	−78	−33
	H_2O	0.	100.

According to this method of classification, there are four types of crystals. These types are listed in Table 12-1. Refer to this table as you read the following discussion.

1. *Ionic crystals.* As discussed in Chapter 6, the ionic crystal structure consists of positive and negative ions arranged in a regular pattern. The ions can be monatomic or polyatomic. Generally, ionic crystals form when Group-1 or Group-2 metals combine with Group-16 or Group-17 nonmetals or nonmetallic polyatomic ions. The strong binding forces between the positive and negative ions in the crystal structure give the ionic crystals certain properties. For example, these crystals are hard and brittle, have high melting points, and are good insulators.

2. *Covalent network crystals.* In covalent network crystals, the sites contain single atoms. Each atom is covalently bonded to its nearest neighboring atoms. The covalent bonding extends throughout a network that includes a very large number of atoms. Three-dimensional covalent network solids include diamond, C_x, quartz, $(SiO_2)_x$—shown in Figure 12-9—silicon carbide, $(SiC)_x$, and many oxides of transition metals. Such solids are essentially giant molecules. The subscript x in these formulas indicates that the component within the parentheses extends indefinitely. The network solids are nearly always very hard and brittle. They have rather high melting points and are usually nonconductors or semiconductors.

3. *Metallic crystals.* As discussed in Chapter 6, the metallic crystal structure consists of metal atoms surrounded by a sea of valence electrons. The electrons are donated by the metal atoms and belong to

the crystal as a whole. The freedom of the outer-structure electrons to move throughout the crystal explains the high electric conductivity of metals. As you can see from Table 12-1, the melting points of different metallic crystals vary greatly.

4. *Covalent molecular crystals.* The crystal structure of a covalent molecular substance consists of covalently bonded molecules held together by intermolecular forces. If the molecules are nonpolar—for example, hydrogen, H_2, methane, CH_4, and benzene, C_6H_6—then there are only weak London dispersion forces between molecules. In a polar covalent molecular crystal—for example, water, H_2O, and ammonia, NH_3—molecules are held together by dispersion forces, by somewhat stronger dipole-dipole forces, and sometimes by even stronger hydrogen bonding. The forces that hold polar or nonpolar molecules together in the structure are much weaker than the covalent chemical bonds between the atoms within each molecule. Covalent molecular crystals thus have low melting points. They are easily vaporized, are relatively soft, and are good insulators. Ice crystals, the most familiar molecular crystals, are discussed in Section 12-4.

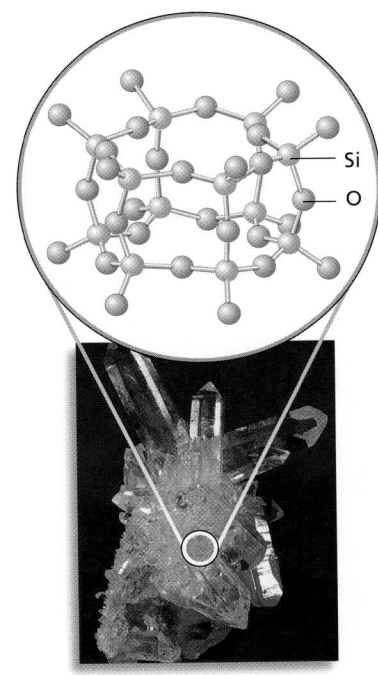

FIGURE 12-9 Covalent network crystals include three-dimensional network solids, such as this quartz, $(SiO_2)_x$, shown here with its three-dimensional atomic structure.

Amorphous Solids

The word *amorphous* comes from the Greek for "without shape." Unlike crystals, amorphous solids do not have a regular, natural shape.

Amorphous solids tend to hold their shape for a long time. However, some amorphous solids do flow, although usually very slowly. Some samples of very old window glass are thicker at the bottom than at the top suggesting that the glass has flowed downward over the years. Glasses make up a distinctive group of amorphous solids. They are made by cooling certain molten materials in such a way that they do not crystallize but remain amorphous.

There are hundreds of types of plastic and glass, all of which have thousands of important applications. Glass is used for everything from fiberglass automobile bodies to optical fibers that use light to transmit telephone conversations.

SECTION REVIEW

1. Describe the solid state according to the kinetic-molecular theory.

2. What is the difference between an amorphous solid and a crystalline solid?

3. Account for each of the following properties of solids: (a) the definite volume, (b) the relatively high density of solids, (c) the extremely low rate of diffusion.

4. Compare and contrast the four types of crystals.

SECTION REVIEW

1. Solids consist of closely packed particles held together by intermolecular forces; these particles are able to move back and forth about fixed positions.

2. The particles in an amorphous solid are arranged randomly. Those in a crystalline solid are in an orderly, geometric, repeating pattern.

3. **a.** Particles are packed closely together.
b. Particles are packed closely together.
c. Particles are in relatively fixed positions and are unable to flow.

4. Ionic crystals have a regular arrangement of charged particles, melt at a high temperature, are brittle, and are good insulators. Covalent network crystals have a large number of atoms covalently bonded to one another, melt at a high temperature, and tend to be nonconductors or semiconductors. Metallic crystals have metal atoms surrounded by a sea of valence electrons and are good conductors. Covalent molecular crystals have covalently bonded molecules held together by intermolecular forces, have low melting points, and are good insulators.

SECTION 12-3

Lesson Starter

Break a golf-ball-sized piece of dry ice into small pieces. Use tongs and a funnel to put the chips inside a deflated balloon. Tie the opening shut. As the dry ice sublimes the balloon will inflate. Ask students to try to explain what is happening.

Safety: Do not touch the dry ice.

TABLE STRATEGY

Table 12-2 Have students list additional examples of each change of state listed in the table.

Reading Skill-Builder

READING ORGANIZER As students read this section, have them create a concept map that shows what happens during changes of state. Concept maps should include terms such as evaporation, condensation, boiling point, freezing point, sublimation, deposition, as well as indicating where energy is absorbed or released. Have students compare their concept maps to Figure 12-15 on p. 382 and make revisions as needed.

Module 1: States of Matter/Classes of Matter

Topic: Changes of State
Sections **e**, **f**, and **g** of this engaging tutorial review and reinforce understanding of state.

Module 7: Equilibrium

Topic: Equilibrium
Section **a** of this engaging tutorial reviews and reinforces understanding of equilibrium.

OBJECTIVES

- Explain the relationship between equilibrium and changes of state.

- Predict changes in equilibrium using Le Châtelier's principle.

- Explain what is meant by equilibrium vapor pressure.

- Describe the processes of boiling, freezing, melting, and sublimation.

- Interpret phase diagrams.

Module 1: States of Matter/Classes of Matter
Module 7: Equilibrium

internet**connect**

SCILINKS.
NSTA

TOPIC: Factors affecting equilibrium
GO TO: www.scilinks.org
sciLINKS CODE: HC2123

Changes of State

Matter on Earth can exist in any of these states—gas, liquid, or solid—and can change from one state to another. Table 12-2 lists the possible changes of state. In this section, you will examine these changes of state and the factors that determine them.

Equilibrium

Equilibrium *is a dynamic condition in which two opposing changes occur at equal rates in a closed system.* In a closed system, matter cannot enter or leave, but energy can. Both matter and energy can escape or enter an open system. For example, sunlight, heat from a burner, or cooling by ice can cause energy to enter or leave a system.

For an analogy of equilibrium, think of a public swimming pool on a summer day. In the morning, more people enter the pool than leave to go home. The pool gets more and more crowded. This system is not in equilibrium. Later in the day, the number of people entering and leaving will be the same. While the total number of people in the pool stays the same for a long time, individuals are constantly coming and going. The system is in equilibrium.

Equilibrium is a very important chemical concept. Here you will learn about it in relation to changes of state. In Chapter 18, you will study equilibrium in terms of chemical reactions.

Equilibrium and Changes of State

Consider the evaporation of water in a closed container in which there is initially a vacuum over the liquid, as illustrated in Figure 12-10.

TABLE 12-2 Possible Changes of State

Change of state	Process	Example
Solid $\longrightarrow$ liquid	melting	ice $\longrightarrow$ water
Solid $\longrightarrow$ gas	sublimation	dry ice $\longrightarrow$ CO_2 gas
Liquid $\longrightarrow$ solid	freezing	water $\longrightarrow$ ice
Liquid $\longrightarrow$ gas	vaporization	liquid bromine $\longrightarrow$ bromine vapor
Gas $\longrightarrow$ liquid	condensation	water vapor $\longrightarrow$ water
Gas $\longrightarrow$ solid	deposition	water vapor $\longrightarrow$ ice

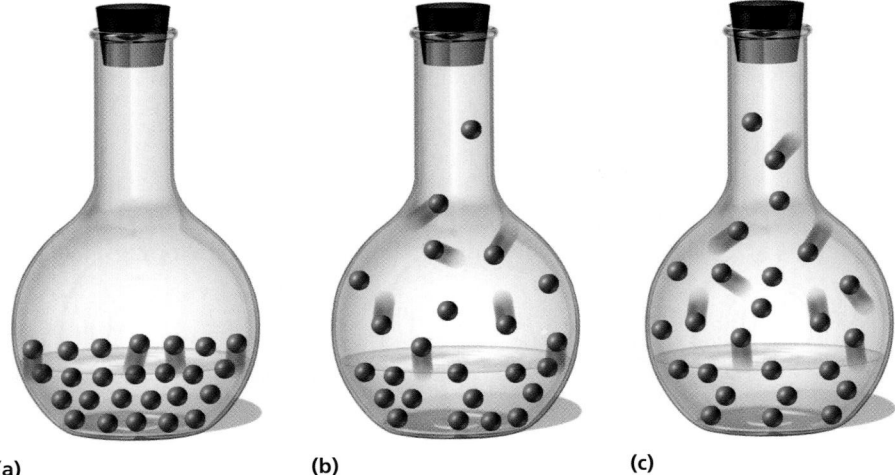

(a)   (b)   (c)

FIGURE 12-10 A liquid-vapor equilibrium develops in a closed system. (a) At first there is only liquid present, but molecules are beginning to evaporate. (b) Evaporation continues at a constant rate. Some vapor molecules are beginning to condense to liquid. (c) Equilibrium has been reached between the rate of condensation and the rate of evaporation.

Assume that the contents of the container maintain the same temperature as the surroundings, approximately 25°C. The water and the container are the system. Initially, there is a single phase inside this system—the liquid phase. *A **phase** is any part of a system that has uniform composition and properties.*

If the energy of a water molecule at the upper surface of the liquid is high enough, the molecule can overcome the attraction of neighboring molecules, leave the liquid phase, and evaporate. Water molecules that have entered the vapor phase behave as typical gas molecules. Some of these vapor molecules move down toward the liquid surface and condense. That is, they reenter the liquid phase. **Condensation** *is the process by which a gas changes to a liquid.*

If the temperature and surface area of the liquid remain constant, the rate at which its molecules enter the vapor phase remains constant. The rate at which the water molecules pass from the vapor phase to the liquid phase depends on the concentration of molecules in the vapor phase. The concentration of vapor molecules, and therefore the rate of condensation, is initially zero, as shown in Figure 12-10(a). As time passes and evaporation continues, the concentration of vapor molecules increases. This increase in concentration results in an increase in the condensation rate. However, the rate of condensation is still lower than the rate of evaporation, as shown in Figure 12-10(b). Eventually, the concentration of vapor increases to the point at which the rate of condensation becomes equal to the rate of evaporation, as shown in Figure 12-10(c). In other words, equilibrium is reached and the amounts of liquid and of vapor now remain constant.

Common Misconception

Because of the unchanging numbers of particles involved in an equilibrium, students often think that equilibrium is static, or involves no changes. Point out and periodically remind them that equilibrium is a dynamic condition in which two opposing processes continue to occur.

CHAPTER ⟷ CONNECTION

Chemical equilibrium will be discussed in Chapter 18.

CHAPTER ⟷ **CONNECTION**

The energy involved in physical and chemical changes will be discussed in Chapter 17.

Class Discussion

Ask students to give examples of Le Châtelier's principle that result from stress caused by changes in concentration, pressure, or temperature.

CHEMISTRY *INTERACTIVE TUTOR*

Module 7: Equilibrium

Topic: Shifting Equilibrium
Sections **b**, **c**, and **d** of this engaging tutorial review and reinforce understanding of shifting equilibrium.

CHEMISTRY *INTERACTIVE TUTOR*

Module 7: Equilibrium

An Equilibrium Equation

Whenever a liquid changes to a vapor, it absorbs heat energy from its surroundings. Evaporation can therefore be represented by the following equation.

$$\text{liquid} + \text{heat energy} \longrightarrow \text{vapor}$$

Whenever a vapor condenses, it gives off heat energy to its surroundings. Condensation can therefore be represented by the following equation.

$$\text{vapor} \longrightarrow \text{liquid} + \text{heat energy}$$

The liquid-vapor equilibrium can be represented by the following equation.

$$\text{liquid} + \text{heat energy} \rightleftharpoons \text{vapor}$$

The "double-yields" sign in the equation above represents a reversible reaction. It means that the reaction can proceed in either direction. The forward reaction is represented when the equation is read from left to right (liquid + heat energy $\longrightarrow$ vapor). The reverse reaction is represented when the equation is read from right to left (vapor $\longrightarrow$ liquid + heat energy).

Le Châtelier's Principle

A system will remain at equilibrium until something occurs to change this condition. It is important to understand the factors that can be used to control the equilibrium of a system. In 1888, the French chemist Henri Louis Le Châtelier developed a principle that enables us to predict how a change in conditions will affect a system at equilibrium. **Le Châtelier's principle** can be stated as follows: *When a system at equilibrium is disturbed by application of a stress, it attains a new equilibrium position that minimizes the stress.* A stress is typically a change in concentration, pressure, or temperature.

Equilibrium and Temperature

You can use Le Châtelier's principle to predict how the liquid-vapor equilibrium changes when a stress is applied in the closed container of liquid discussed earlier. For example, suppose the temperature of the system is increased from 25°C to 50°C. The equilibrium of the system can be represented by the following reversible reaction.

$$\text{liquid} + \text{heat energy} \rightleftharpoons \text{vapor}$$

According to Le Châtelier's principle, the system will respond to an increase in temperature. In this case, the forward reaction is endothermic; that is, it absorbs heat energy. The forward reaction is favored to counteract a rise in temperature and to minimize the stress applied to it (in this case, the change in temperature). The forward reaction proceeds at a higher rate than the reverse reaction until a new equilibrium is reached. At 50°C, the concentration of vapor is higher than it was at 25°C. However, at equilibrium, the reverse reaction, condensation, also occurs at a higher rate than it did at the lower temperature.

Suppose, on the other hand, that the temperature of the system in equilibrium at 25°C is lowered to 5°C. According to Le Châtelier's principle, the system will adjust to counteract the temperature decrease. Now the reverse reaction is favored because it is exothermic; that is, it releases heat energy. Equilibrium is shifted to the left and reestablished at 5°C. The vapor concentration is now lower than it originally was at 25°C.

Equilibrium and Concentration

Suppose the mass and temperature of this equilibrium system remain the same, but the volume suddenly increases. What happens to the equilibrium? Initially, the concentration of molecules in the vapor phase decreases because the same number of vapor-phase molecules now occupies a larger volume. Because the concentration of vapor molecules decreases, fewer vapor molecules strike the liquid surface per second and return to the liquid phase. Therefore, the rate of condensation decreases. The rate of evaporation, however, has remained the same and is therefore higher now than the rate of condensation. As a result, an additional net evaporation of liquid occurs. When a new equilibrium is finally reestablished, the concentration of molecules in the vapor phase is the same as in the lower-volume system. Because there was a net movement of molecules from the liquid phase to the vapor phase, the number of liquid molecules has decreased. The equilibrium has therefore shifted to the right. Table 12-3 summarizes the effects on the equilibrium of this liquid-vapor system caused by certain changes.

TABLE STRATEGY

Table 12-3 Write the general equation on the chalkboard, and have students account for each of the given shifts in the equilibrium.

Common Misconception

Students often think that Le Châtelier's principle applies to all stresses placed on equilibrium systems and that resulting shifts completely counteract the imposed changes. Point out that systems will shift their equilibrium in response to a stress only when doing so will bring about counteraction. Any counteraction produced will only partially counteract the imposed stress.

TABLE 12-3 *Shifts in the Equilibrium for the Reaction* Liquid + Heat Energy ⇌ Vapor	
Change	**Shift**
Addition of liquid	right
Removal of liquid	left
Addition of vapor	left
Removal of vapor	right
Decrease in container volume	left
Increase in container volume	right
Decrease in temperature	left
Increase in temperature	right

Visual Strategy

FIGURE 12-11 Ask students to explain what is meant by "evacuating" the flask and why it is important that the flask be evacuated and the system be closed.

Application

Airtight containers, such as cans and screw-top bottles and jars, prevent net evaporation of water from juices and water-packed foods. The containers allow the systems to reach equilibrium vapor pressure so that condensation rate equals evaporation rate.

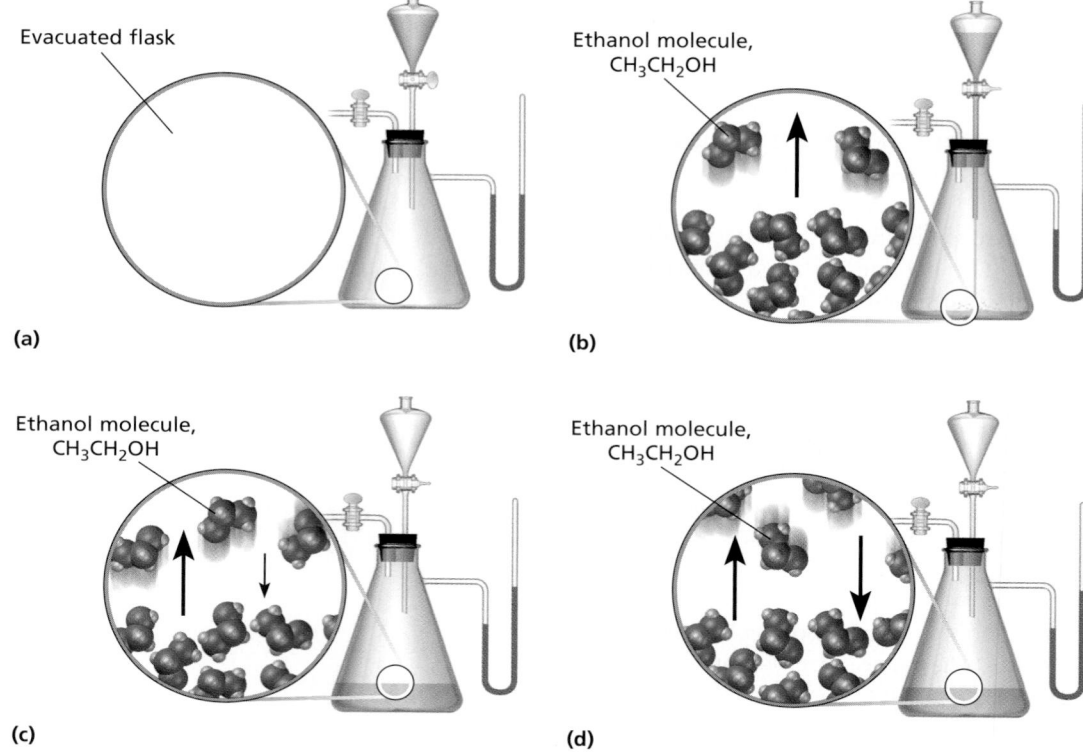

(a)   Evacuated flask

(b)   Ethanol molecule, CH_3CH_2OH

(c)   Ethanol molecule, CH_3CH_2OH

(d)   Ethanol molecule, CH_3CH_2OH

FIGURE 12-11 (a) The vapor pressure of ethanol, CH_3CH_2OH, can be measured by dispensing liquid ethanol into an evacuated flask that is part of a closed system. (b) Ethanol molecules leave the liquid surface to form vapor. (c) Molecules continue to vaporize and condense until equilibrium is reached. (d) At equilibrium, the pressure exerted by the vapor is recorded by noting the mercury levels in the side arm.

Equilibrium Vapor Pressure of a Liquid

Vapor molecules in equilibrium with a liquid in a closed system exert a pressure proportional to the vapor concentration. *The pressure exerted by a vapor in equilibrium with its corresponding liquid at a given temperature is called the* **equilibrium vapor pressure** *of the liquid.* Figure 12-11 shows the apparatus and method used to measure the equilibrium vapor pressure of a liquid.

Figure 12-12 is a graph of the equilibrium vapor pressures of water, diethyl ether, and ethanol. The curve shows that at any given temperature, vapor in equilibrium with liquid exerts a specific vapor pressure. The equilibrium vapor pressure of the liquid increases as temperature increases (although not in direct proportion).

Equilibrium Vapor Pressure and the Kinetic-Molecular Theory

The increase in equilibrium vapor pressure with increasing temperature can be explained in terms of the kinetic-molecular theory for the liquid and gaseous states. Increasing the temperature of a liquid

Vapor Pressures of Diethyl Ether, Ethanol, and Water at Various Temperatures

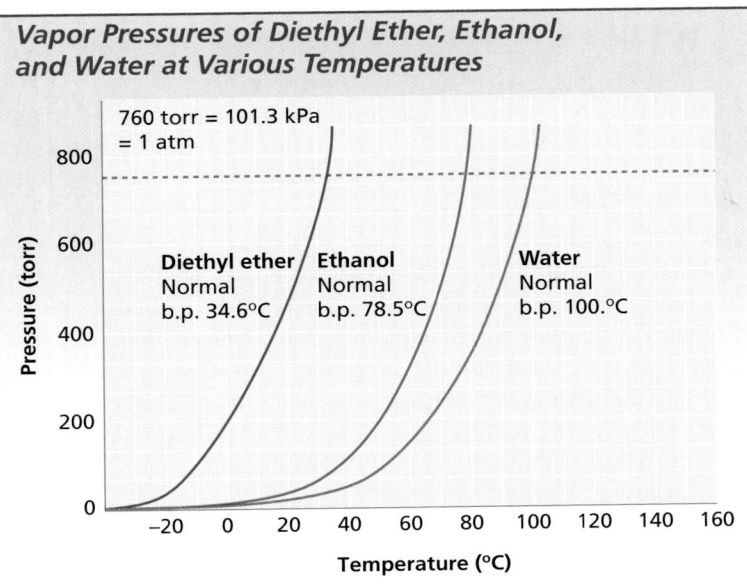

FIGURE 12-12 The vapor pressure of liquids increases as their temperature increases. A liquid boils when its vapor pressure equals the pressure of the atmosphere.

increases its average kinetic energy. That, in turn, increases the number of molecules that have enough energy to escape from the liquid phase into the vapor phase. The resulting increased evaporation rate increases the concentration of molecules in the vapor phase, which in turn increases the equilibrium vapor pressure. The liquid-vapor equilibrium is thus disturbed. However, the increase in concentration of vapor molecules then increases the rate at which molecules condense to liquid. Equilibrium is soon reestablished, but at a higher equilibrium vapor pressure.

Volatile and Nonvolatile Liquids

Because all liquids have characteristic forces of attraction between their particles, every liquid has a specific equilibrium vapor pressure at a given temperature. The stronger these attractive forces are, the smaller is the percentage of liquid particles that can evaporate at any given temperature. A low percentage of evaporation results in a low equilibrium vapor pressure. **Volatile liquids,** *which are liquids that evaporate readily,* have relatively weak forces of attraction between particles. Ether is a typical volatile liquid. Nonvolatile liquids, which evaporate slowly, have relatively strong attractive forces between particles. Molten ionic compounds are examples of nonvolatile liquids.

It is important not to confuse the equilibrium vapor pressure of a liquid with the pressure of a vapor not in equilibrium with its corresponding liquid. The equilibrium vapor pressure of a liquid depends only on temperature. The pressure of a vapor not in equilibrium with the corresponding liquid follows the gas laws, like any other gas. Its pressure is inversely proportional to its volume at constant temperature, according to Boyle's law.

internet connect

SCi LINKS

NSTA

TOPIC: Volatile/nonvolatile liquids
GO TO: www.scilinks.org
sci **LINKS CODE:** HC2124

Visual Strategy

FIGURE 12-12 Have students read off the vapor pressures for the substances on the graph at various temperatures. Point out that all three of the liquids boil when their vapor pressure equals the prevailing atmospheric pressure. The normal boiling point of each is the temperature at which vapor pressure equals 760 torr, which is standard atmospheric pressure.

Application

Perfumes are generally complex mixtures of fragrance oils dissolved in alcohol. The oils typically differ in volatility, which is why a perfume applied to the skin changes in scent as the oils evaporate at different rates. Fixative oils are often added to perfume to slow down and equalize the effective evaporation rates.

DEMONSTRATION

Pour a small volume of an alcohol into a beaker, and pour a small volume of water into a second beaker. Dip one finger into each beaker simultaneously, and rub the fingers on a chalkboard. The alcohol will evaporate much more quickly than the water. Have students explain this observation in terms of attractive forces, and relate this property to predicted vapor pressure.

Common Misconception

Students often assume that boiling indicates that a large amount of heat has been added to the liquid. Point out that the lowering of the boiling point that comes with a reduction in atmospheric pressure also reduces the amount of heat necessary for boiling to occur. For example, water under near-vacuum conditions can boil at 25°C, but that water would not be able to cook an egg because cooking depends on the amount of heat added, not on whether the liquid is boiling.

Boiling

Equilibrium vapor pressures can be used to explain and define the concept of boiling, which you read about in Section 12-1. **Boiling** *is the conversion of a liquid to a vapor within the liquid as well as at its surface. It occurs when the equilibrium vapor pressure of the liquid equals the atmospheric pressure.*

If the temperature of the liquid is increased, the equilibrium vapor pressure also increases. Finally, the boiling point is reached. *The **boiling point** of a liquid is the temperature at which the equilibrium vapor pressure of the liquid equals the atmospheric pressure.* The lower the atmospheric pressure is, the lower the boiling point is. Therefore, at high elevations, where atmospheric pressures are lower than at sea level, a cooking liquid boils at a lower temperature and foods take longer to cook.

At the boiling point, all of the heat absorbed goes to evaporate the liquid, and the temperature remains constant as long as the pressure does not change. If the pressure above the liquid being heated is increased, the temperature of the liquid will rise until the vapor pressure equals the new pressure and the liquid boils once again. This is the principle behind the operation of a pressure cooker. The cooker is sealed so that steam pressure builds up over the surface of the boiling water inside. The pressure increases the boiling temperature of the water, resulting in shorter cooking times. Conversely, a device called a vacuum evaporator causes boiling at lower-than-normal temperatures. Vacuum evaporators are used to remove water from milk and sugar solutions. Under reduced pressure, the water boils away at a temperature low enough to avoid scorching the milk or sugar. This process is used to prepare evaporated milk and sweetened condensed milk.

At normal atmospheric pressure (1 atm, 760. torr, or 101.3 kPa), the boiling point of water is exactly 100.°C. This temperature is known as the *normal* boiling point of water. The normal boiling points of water and other liquids are shown in Figure 12-12. Note that the normal boiling point of each liquid is the temperature at which the liquid's equilibrium vapor pressure equals 760 torr.

Energy and Boiling

As you know from experience, heat must be added continuously in order to keep a liquid boiling. A pot of boiling water stops boiling almost immediately after it is removed from the stove. Suppose you were to carefully measure the temperature of a boiling liquid and its vapor. You might be surprised to find that they are at the same constant temperature. The temperature, or average kinetic energy of the particles, at the boiling point remains constant despite the continuous addition of heat. Where does the added heat energy go? It is used to overcome the attractive forces between molecules of the liquid during the liquid-to-gas change. The energy is stored in the vapor as potential energy.

Energy Distribution of Molecules in a Liquid at Different Temperatures

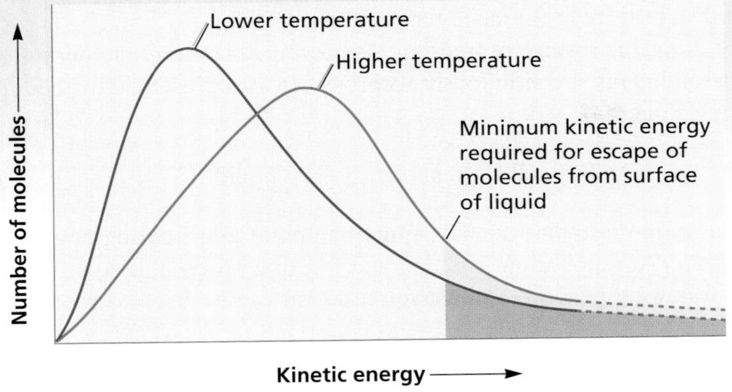

FIGURE 12-13 The number of molecules in a liquid with various kinetic energies is represented at two different temperatures. Notice the shaded area, which shows the minimum amount of kinetic energy required for evaporation to take place.

Application
Heat is given off during freezing of a liquid. This fact is used to protect developing citrus fruits during a frost. Water is sprayed onto the trees, and as the water freezes, it gives off heat that is absorbed by the fruit, protecting it from freezing.

Class Discussion
Ask students to explain how it is possible for boiling water and the steam produced to be at the same temperature, even though heat is absorbed during the boiling process. Students should point out the significance of potential energy and the fact that temperature reflects kinetic energy only.

Alternative Assessment
Have students interpret changes of state and heat energy for equilibrium situations, and then have them write equations relating those changes. For example, ask them to write an equation for the equilibrium between a liquid and its vapor, including a heat term. (The equation would show the liquid plus a heat term on one side of a double arrow, and the vapor on the other side.)

Molar Heat of Vaporization

The amount of heat energy needed to vaporize one mole of liquid at its boiling point is called the liquid's **molar heat of vaporization.** The magnitude of the molar heat of vaporization is a measure of the attraction between particles of the liquid. The stronger this attraction is, the more energy that is required to overcome it, which results in a higher molar heat of vaporization. Each liquid has a characteristic molar heat of vaporization. Compared with other liquids, water has an unusually high molar heat of vaporization due to the extensive hydrogen bonding in liquid water. This property makes water a very effective cooling agent. When water evaporates from your skin, the escaping molecules carry a great deal of heat away with them. Figure 12-13 shows the distribution of the kinetic energies of molecules in a liquid at two different temperatures. You can see that at the higher temperature a greater portion of the molecules have the kinetic energy required to escape from the liquid surface and become vapor.

Freezing and Melting

As you learned in Section 12-1, the physical change of a liquid to a solid is called freezing. Freezing involves a loss of heat energy by the liquid and can be represented by the following reaction.

$$\text{liquid} \longrightarrow \text{solid} + \text{heat energy}$$

In the case of a pure crystalline substance, this change occurs at constant temperature. *The normal* **freezing point** *is the temperature at which the solid and liquid are in equilibrium at 1 atm (760. torr, or 101.3 kPa) pressure.* At the freezing point, particles of the liquid and the solid have the same average kinetic energy. Therefore, the energy loss during freezing is

DEMONSTRATION

Changes of State in Ice and Liquid Water

Half fill a 250 mL beaker with an ice-and-water mixture. Place the beaker on a hot plate. Stirring with a glass rod, measure and record the ice-water temperature initially and at roughly 1-minute intervals throughout the melting process. Continue to do so for the pure liquid water that results and then for the boiling water that is produced. Have students plot the temperature data on the vertical axis versus the time data on the horizontal axis. Then have them interpret the results. *(The temperature will remain at 0°C throughout the melting period. Then the liquid will increase in temperature to 100°C at boiling and will remain at that temperature as long as liquid water still remains. The absorbed heat energy is converted to potential energy to provide the heats of fusion and vaporization during the changes of state.)*

Safety: Be careful using heat sources and working with the hot water.

a loss of potential energy that was present in the liquid. At the same time energy decreases, there is a significant increase in particle order because the solid state of a substance is much more ordered than the liquid state, even at the same temperature.

Melting, the reverse of freezing, also occurs at constant temperature. As a solid melts, it continuously absorbs heat, as represented by the following equation.

$$\text{solid} + \text{heat energy} \longrightarrow \text{liquid}$$

For pure crystalline solids, the melting point and freezing point are the same. At equilibrium, melting and freezing proceed at equal rates. The following general equilibrium equation can be used to represent these states.

$$\text{solid} + \text{heat energy} \rightleftharpoons \text{liquid}$$

At normal atmospheric pressure, the temperature of a system containing ice and liquid water will remain at 0.°C as long as both ice and water are present. That temperature will persist no matter what the surrounding temperature. As predicted by Le Châtelier's principle, adding heat to such a system shifts the equilibrium to the right. That shift increases the proportion of liquid water and decreases that of ice. Only after all the ice has melted will the addition of heat increase the temperature of the system.

Molar Heat of Fusion

The amount of heat energy required to melt one mole of solid at its melting point is its **molar heat of fusion.** The heat absorbed increases the potential energy of the solid as its particles are pulled apart, overcoming the attractive forces holding them together. At the same time, there is a significant decrease in particle order as the substance makes the transformation from solid to liquid. Similar to the molar heat of vaporization, the magnitude of the molar heat of fusion depends on the attraction between the solid particles.

Sublimation and Deposition

At sufficiently low temperature and pressure conditions, a liquid cannot exist. Under such conditions, a solid substance exists in equilibrium with its vapor instead of its liquid, as represented by the following equation.

$$\text{solid} + \text{heat energy} \rightleftharpoons \text{vapor}$$

The change of state from a solid directly to a gas is known as **sublimation.** The reverse process is called **deposition,** *the change of state from a gas directly to a solid.* Among the common substances that sublime at ordinary temperatures are dry ice (solid CO_2) and iodine. Ordinary ice sublimes slowly at temperatures lower than its melting point (0.°C). This explains how a thin layer of snow can eventually disappear, even if the temperature remains below 0.°C. Sublimation occurs in frost-free refrigerators when the temperature in the freezer compartment is periodically raised to cause any ice that has formed to sublime. A blower then removes the water vapor that has formed. The formation of frost on a cold surface is a familiar example of deposition.

Phase Diagrams

A **phase diagram** *is a graph of pressure versus temperature that shows the conditions under which the phases of a substance exist.* A phase diagram also reveals how the states of a system change with changing temperature or pressure.

Figure 12-14 shows the phase diagram for water over a range of temperatures and pressures. Note the three curves, AB, AC, and AD. Curve AB indicates the temperature and pressure conditions at which ice and water vapor can coexist at equilibrium. Curve AC indicates the temperature and pressure conditions at which liquid water and water vapor coexist at equilibrium. Similarly, curve AD indicates the temperature and pressure conditions at which ice and liquid water coexist at equilibrium. Because ice is less dense than liquid water, an increase in pressure lowers the melting point. (Most substances have a positive slope for this curve.) Point A is the triple point of water. *The* **triple point** *of a substance indicates the temperature and pressure conditions at which the solid, liquid, and vapor of the substance can coexist at equilibrium.* Point C is the critical point of water. *The* **critical point** *of a substance indicates the critical temperature and critical pressure. The* **critical temperature** *(t_c) is the temperature above which the substance cannot exist in the liquid state.* The critical temperature of water is 373.99°C. Above this temperature, water cannot be liquefied, no matter how much pressure is

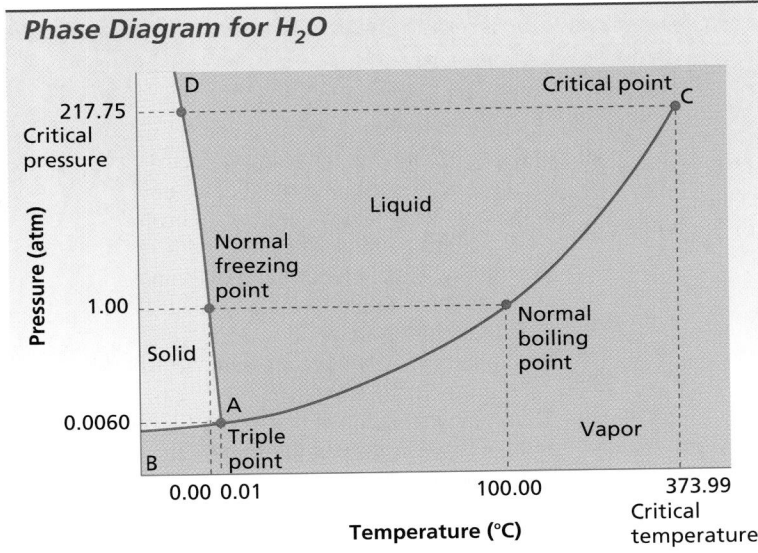

Phase Diagram for H₂O

Visual Strategy
FIGURE 12-14 After students understand what information is on the phase diagram and are able to interpret the diagram, give them several sets of temperature and pressure values and have them find the state in which water exists under each set of conditions. Another strategy would be to give them either a temperature or a pressure and ask them to find the other (pressure or temperature) at which a certain phase change occurs, if it occurs at all.

Application
The sublimation of ice into water vapor accounts for the fact that wet clothing hung outside on a clothesline eventually dries, even if the temperature is below freezing.

 Reading Skill-Builder

DISCUSSION Have students read the section on Phase Diagrams silently. Lead a discussion of the important features of the diagram that are mentioned in the text. Highlight these features on an overhead transparency as you discuss them. Have students make notes on their own copies of a phase diagram.

FIGURE 12-14 This phase diagram shows the relationships between the physical states of water and its pressure and temperature.

SECTION REVIEW

1. a dynamic condition in which two opposing changes occur at equal rates in a closed system

2. When a system at equilibrium is disturbed by application of a stress, it attains a new equilibrium position that minimizes the stress.

3. During a temperature increase, the system shifts toward formation of more vapor, absorbing energy and counteracting the temperature increase. During a temperature decrease, the system shifts toward formation of more liquid, releasing heat energy and counteracting the effect of the temperature decrease.

4. frost forming on a cold surface

5. pressure exerted by a vapor in equilibrium with its corresponding liquid at a given temperature

6. the temperature at which equilibrium vapor pressure equals atmospheric pressure

7. triple point: temperature and pressure conditions under which ice, liquid water, and water vapor all exist together at equilibrium; critical point: temperature above which water cannot exist in the liquid state and the lowest pressure at which water can exist as a liquid at that temperature

8. a. melt to a liquid, then boil, then heat up as a vapor
b. condense to a liquid, then continue to cool as a liquid
c. at pressures less than roughly 0.006 atm
d. within 1.00 atm and 217.75 atm

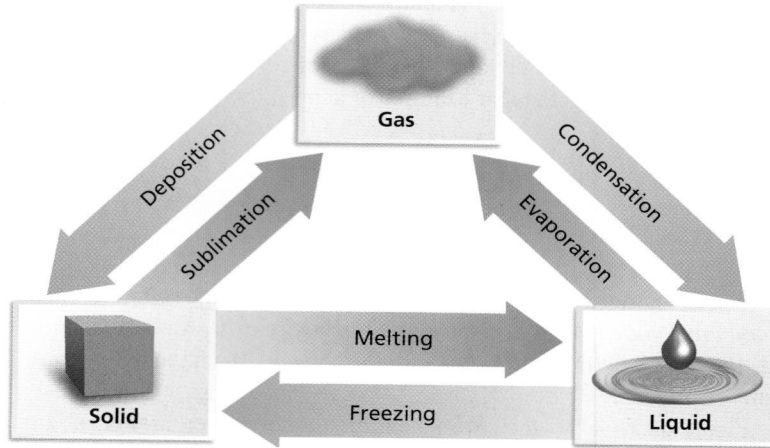

FIGURE 12-15 Solids, liquids, and gases can undergo various changes of state. The changes shown in green are exothermic, and those shown in blue are endothermic.

applied. *The* **critical pressure** *(P_c) is the lowest pressure at which the substance can exist as a liquid at the critical temperature. The critical pressure of water is 217.75 atm.*

The phase diagram in Figure 12-14 indicates the normal boiling point and the normal freezing point of water. It also shows how boiling point and freezing point change with pressure. As shown by the slope of line AD, ice melts at a higher temperature with decreasing pressure. Below the triple point, the temperature of sublimation decreases with decreasing pressure. Foods are freeze-dried by freezing the food and then lowering the pressure to cause the ice in the food to sublime rather than melt. Figure 12-15 summarizes the changes of state of solids, liquids, and gases.

SECTION REVIEW

1. What is equilibrium?

2. State Le Châtelier's principle.

3. What happens when a liquid-vapor system at equilibrium experiences an increase in temperature? What happens when it experiences a decrease in temperature?

4. What would be an example of deposition?

5. What is the equilibrium vapor pressure of a liquid?

6. What is the boiling point of a liquid?

7. In the phase diagram for water, what is meant by the triple point and the critical point?

8. Refer to the phase diagram for water on page 381 to answer the following questions.
   a. Describe all the phase changes a sample of solid water would undergo when heated to its critical temperature at a pressure of 1.00 atm.
   b. Describe all the phase changes a sample of water vapor would undergo when cooled to 5°C at a pressure of 1.00 atm.
   c. At approximately what pressure will water be a vapor at 0°C?
   d. Within what range of pressures will water be a liquid at temperatures above its normal boiling point?

RESEARCH NOTES

Phase-Change Materials

✔ **Teaching Tip**

In order to be useful as energy-saving construction materials, phase-change materials must have melting points near room temperature at normal atmospheric pressure.

Class Discussion
Ask the class what problems might arise while doing anything that breaks the surface of paraffin-containing wallboard, such as installing electrical outlets. Ask students to explain how they think the wallboard might be designed to minimize such problems.

The real estate ad of tomorrow could read like this: "Just listed! Perfect starter home! Two bedrooms, 2 1/2 baths, walk-in closets, heats and cools itself with minimal electricity or other power." Ival Salyer, a senior research scientist at the University of Dayton Research Institute, says that homes like these may soon be commonplace. Phase-change technology will help control indoor temperature with walls that melt or freeze a bit as the weather changes.

When any material goes through a change in its physical form or state, it releases or absorbs heat. Salyer has designed walls that work on this principle. The wallboards are filled with a type of paraffin that melts or freezes above or below 75°F. When the temperature outside rises above 75°F, the paraffin melts and absorbs the heat inside the house. The opposite happens when the outdoor temperature drops. This change of state keeps the temperature of a house comfortably constant while using little power other than the heat of the sun.

By heating the material with electricity overnight, heat could be stored by changing the paraffin in the walls to a liquid state. When the heat is discontinued, the walls would freeze, radiating heat into the house and keeping it warm all day. Shifting the heating and cooling loads to off-peak nighttime

Changes of state are physical changes that can be exothermic or endothermic, depending on the direction of energy flow between an object and its surroundings.

hours is of strong interest to utility companies, which offer off-peak discounts to encourage the use of surplus nighttime power.

According to Salyer, because state change is an inherent property of matter, the walls heat and cool automatically, with no need for monitoring by people and no degradation from wear.

Another recent discovery that can dramatically reduce building, heating, and cooling costs is the use of molded inserts of phase-change materials in the hollow spaces of hollow-core concrete blocks. In the outside walls of buildings, this phase-change material can store warmth from the winter sun for heating and the coolness of a summer night for cooling.

Salyer foresees this technology being used in dozens of other

applications. Phase-change material is already being marketed as a food warmer; after being microwaved for a few minutes, a pillow-like pad can release heat for hours. The same idea is being adapted for use with bowls and plates to keep food warm. Winter weather might not feel quite so harsh with phase-change material lining coats, hats, and gloves. Phase-change flowerpots could keep plants warm, and the asphalt of highway bridges and liners for car batteries could be protected from freezing with the use of phase-change materials. Phase-change uniforms for firefighters and soldiers could keep them comfortably cool, and the material could be used as a protective, heat-resistant coating around airplane flight-data recorders and cockpit voice recorders.

SECTION **12-4**

Water

Lesson Starter

Show students a model of a water molecule. Ask them to think about how the molecule's structure would affect the properties of water. Remind them to think in terms of hydrogen bonding.

Common Misconception

Students sometimes think that any bond involving hydrogen is a hydrogen bond. Remind them that intramolecular bonds, such as the bond that exists between a hydrogen atom and an oxygen atom within a water molecule, are covalent bonds. True hydrogen bonds are intermolecular attractions between a hydrogen atom on one molecule and a highly electronegative atom on another molecule.

CHAPTER ⟷ CONNECTION

Refer back to Section 6-3 to remind students that the lone pairs on the electronegative oxygen atom are concentrations of negative charge, while the less electronegative hydrogen atoms are relatively positive. This accounts for the attractions between water molecules in liquid water and in ice, as shown in Figures 12-16 and 12-17, respectively.

OBJECTIVES

- Describe the structure of a water molecule.

- Discuss the physical properties of water. Explain how they are determined by the structure of water.

- Calculate the amount of heat energy absorbed or released when a quantity of water changes state.

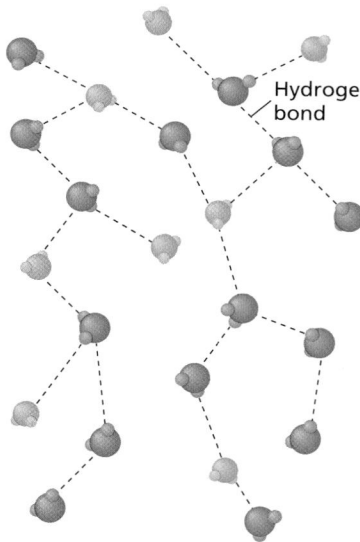

Liquid water

FIGURE 12-16 The structure of liquid water shows that within the water molecule, oxygen and hydrogen are covalently bonded to each other, while the molecules are held together in groups by hydrogen bonds.

Water is a familiar substance in all three physical states: solid, liquid, and gas. On Earth, water is by far the most abundant liquid. Oceans, rivers, and lakes cover about 75% of Earth's surface. Significant quantities of water are also frozen in glaciers. Water is an essential component of all organisms; 70% to 90% of the mass of living things is water. The chemical reactions of most life processes take place in water, and water is frequently a reactant or product in such reactions. In order to better understand the importance of water, let us take a closer look at its structure and its properties.

Structure of Water

As discussed in Chapter 6, water molecules consist of two atoms of hydrogen and one atom of oxygen united by polar-covalent bonds. Research shows that a water molecule is bent. The structure can be represented as follows.

$$H \overset{\ddot{O}}{\diagdown_{105°}} H$$

The angle between the two hydrogen-oxygen bonds is about 105°. This is close to the angle expected for sp^3 hybridization of the oxygen-atom orbitals.

The molecules in solid or liquid water are linked by hydrogen bonding. The number of linked molecules decreases with increasing temperature because increases in kinetic energy make hydrogen bond formation difficult. Nevertheless, there are usually from four to eight molecules per group in liquid water, as shown in Figure 12-16. If it were not for these molecular groups, water would be a gas at room temperature. Nonpolar molecules, such as methane, CH_4, that are similar in size and mass to water molecules, do not undergo hydrogen bonding. Such substances are gases at room temperature.

Ice consists of water molecules in the hexagonal arrangement shown in Figure 12-17. The empty spaces between molecules in this pattern account for the relatively low density of ice. As ice is heated, the increased energy of the molecules causes them to move and vibrate more vigorously. When the melting point is reached, the energy of the molecules is so great that the rigid open structure of the ice crystals breaks down, and ice turns into liquid water.

Figures 12-16 and 12-17 also show that the hydrogen bonds between molecules of liquid water at 0.°C are fewer and more disordered than those between molecules of ice at the same temperature. Because the rigid open structure of ice has broken down, water molecules can crowd closer together. Thus, liquid water is denser than ice.

As the liquid water is warmed from 0.°C, the water molecules crowd still closer together. Water molecules are as tightly packed as possible at 3.98°C. At temperatures above 3.98°C, the increasing kinetic energy of the water molecules causes them to overcome molecular attractions. The molecules move farther apart as the temperature continues to rise. As the temperature approaches the boiling point, groups of liquid water molecules absorb enough energy to break up into separate molecules. Because of hydrogen bonding between water molecules, a high kinetic energy is needed, causing water's boiling point to be relatively high (100.°C) compared to other liquids that have similar molar masses.

Physical Properties of Water

At room temperature, pure liquid water is transparent, odorless, tasteless, and almost colorless. Any observable odor or taste is caused by impurities such as dissolved minerals, liquids, or gases.

As shown by its phase diagram in Figure 12-14 on page 381, water freezes at a pressure of 1 atm (101.3 kPa) and melts at 0.°C. The molar heat of fusion of ice is 6.009 kJ/mol. That value is relatively large compared with the molar heats of fusion of other solids. As you have read, water has the unusual property of expanding in volume as it freezes because its molecules form an open rigid structure. As a result, ice at 0.°C has a density of only about 0.917 g/cm^3, compared with a density of 0.999 84 g/cm^3 for liquid water at 0.°C.

This lower density explains why ice floats in liquid water. The insulating effect of floating ice is particularly important in the case of large bodies of water. If ice were more dense than liquid water, it would sink to the bottom of lakes and ponds, where it would be less likely to melt completely. The water of such bodies of water in temperate climates would eventually freeze solid, killing nearly all the living things in it.

Under a pressure of 1 atm (101.3 kPa), water boils at 100.°C. At this temperature, water's molar heat of vaporization is 40.79 kJ/mol. Both the boiling point and the molar heat of vaporization of water are quite high compared with those of nonpolar substances of comparable molecular mass, such as methane. The values are high because of the strong hydrogen bonding that must be overcome for boiling to occur. The high molar heat of vaporization makes water useful for household steam-heating systems. The steam (vaporized water) stores a great deal of heat. When the steam condenses in radiators, great quantities of heat are released.

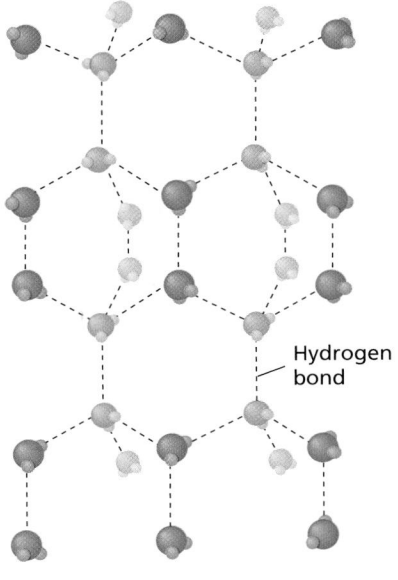

Hydrogen bond

Ice

FIGURE 12-17 Ice contains the same types of bonding as liquid water. However, the structure of the hydrogen bonding is much more rigid and open than it is in liquid water.

12-1 Find the mass of liquid water required to absorb 5.23×10^4 kJ of heat energy on boiling.

Ans. 2.31×10^4 g

12-1 How much heat energy is absorbed when 16.3 g of ice melts?

Ans. 5.44 kJ

12-1 Calculate the quantity of heat energy released when 783 g of steam condenses.

Ans. 1.77×10^3 kJ

SECTION REVIEW

1. Because of the bent (angular) shape of the molecule, the large electronegativity difference between oxygen and hydrogen atoms results in overall polarity of the molecule.

2. The structure allows for hydrogen bonding, resulting in the formation of molecular groups that produce a high heat of fusion, boiling point, and heat of vaporization.

3. There are intermolecular hydrogen bonds in both. The liquid usually has 4 to 8 molecules per group. In the solid, all the molecules are arranged in a hexagonal structure.

4. Ice floats because it is less dense than liquid water. Due to its low density, ice forms only on the surface of lakes. The solid top layer insulates the liquid water beneath it, preventing a total freeze, which would kill most living things in the lake.

SAMPLE PROBLEM 12-1

How much heat energy is absorbed when 47.0 g of ice melts at STP? How much heat energy is absorbed when this same mass of liquid water boils?

SOLUTION

1 ANALYZE

Given: mass of $H_2O(s) = 47.0$ g
mass of $H_2O(l) = 47.0$ g
molar heat of fusion of ice = 6.009 kJ/mol (given on page 385)
molar heat of vaporization = 40.79 kJ/mol (given on page 385)

Unknown: heat energy absorbed when ice melts
heat energy absorbed when liquid water boils

2 PLAN

First, convert the mass of water in grams to moles.

$$g\ H_2O \times \frac{1\ \text{mol}\ H_2O}{g\ H_2O} = \text{mol}\ H_2O$$

Then, use the molar heat of fusion of a solid to calculate the amount of heat absorbed when the solid melts. Multiply the number of moles by the amount of energy needed to melt one mole of ice at its melting point (the molar heat of fusion of ice). Using the same method, calculate the amount of heat absorbed when water boils by using the molar heat of vaporization.

amount of substance (mol) $\times$ molar heat of fusion or vaporization (kJ/mol) = heat energy (kJ)

3 COMPUTE

$$47.0\ g\ H_2O \times \frac{1\ \text{mol}\ H_2O}{18.02\ g\ H_2O} = 2.61\ \text{mol}\ H_2O$$

$2.61\ \text{mol} \times 6.009\ \text{kJ/mol} = 15.7$ kJ (on melting)
$2.61\ \text{mol} \times 40.79\ \text{kJ/mol} = 106$ kJ (on vaporizing or boiling)

4 EVALUATE

Units have canceled correctly. The answers have the proper number of significant digits and are reasonably close to estimated values of 18 (3×6) and 120 (3×40), respectively.

PRACTICE

1. What quantity of heat energy is released when 506 g of liquid water freezes?

   Answer
   169 kJ

2. What mass of steam is required to release 4.97×10^5 kJ of heat energy on condensation?

   Answer
   2.19×10^5 g

SECTION REVIEW

1. Why is a water molecule polar?

2. How is the structure of water responsible for some of water's unique characteristics?

3. Describe the arrangement of molecules in liquid water and in ice.

4. Why does ice float? Why is this phenomenon important?

CHAPTER SUMMARY

12-1
- The particles of a liquid are closer together and more ordered than those of a gas and less ordered than those of a solid.
- Liquids have a definite volume and a fairly high density, and they are relatively incompressible. Like gases, liquids can flow and are thus considered to be fluids. Liquids can dissolve other substances.
- Liquids have the ability to diffuse. They exhibit surface tension, and they can evaporate or boil. A liquid is said to freeze when it becomes a solid.

Vocabulary

capillary action (365)	fluid (363)	surface tension (365)	vaporization (365)
evaporation (365)	freezing (366)		

12-2
- The particles of a solid are not nearly so free to move about as are those of a liquid or a gas. They can only vibrate about definite, fixed positions.
- Solids have a definite shape and may be crystalline or amorphous. They have a definite volume and are generally nonfluid. Additional characteristics of solids are high density, incompressibility, extremely low rates of diffusion, and definite melting points (for crystals).
- A crystal structure is the total three-dimensional array of points that describes the arrangement of the particles of a crystal. A crystal can be classified into one of seven crystalline systems on the basis of the three-dimensional shape of its unit cell. A crystal can also be described as one of four types, based on the kind of particles it contains and the type of chemical bonding between its particles.
- Amorphous solids do not have a regular shape. Instead, they take on whatever shape is imposed on them.

Vocabulary

amorphous solids (368)	crystal structure (369)	melting (368)	supercooled liquids (368)
crystal (368)	crystalline solids (368)	melting point (368)	unit cell (369)

12-3
- A liquid in a closed system will gradually reach a liquid-vapor equilibrium as the rate at which molecules condense equals the rate at which they evaporate.
- When two opposing changes occur at equal rates in the same closed system, the system is said to be in dynamic equilibrium. Le Châtelier's principle states that if any factor determining an equilibrium is changed, the system will adjust itself in a way that tends to minimize that change.
- The pressure exerted by a vapor in equilibrium with its corresponding liquid at a given temperature is the liquid's equilibrium vapor pressure. A liquid boils when the equilibrium vapor pressure of the liquid is equal to the atmospheric pressure. The amount of heat energy required to vaporize one mole of liquid at its boiling point is called the molar heat of vaporization.
- Freezing involves a loss of energy, in the form of heat, by a liquid. Melting is the physical change of a solid to a liquid by the addition of heat. The amount of heat required to melt one mole of solid at its melting point is its molar heat of fusion.

Vocabulary

boiling (378)	critical temperature (381)	freezing point (379)	phase (373)
boiling point (378)	deposition (380)	Le Châtelier's principle (374)	phase diagram (381)
condensation (373)	equilibrium (372)		sublimation (380)
critical point (381)	equilibrium vapor pressure (376)	molar heat of fusion (380)	triple point (381)
critical pressure (382)		molar heat of vaporization (379)	volatile liquids (377)

REVIEW ANSWERS

1. a substance that flows and conforms to the shape of its container

2. a force that tends to pull adjacent parts of a liquid's surface together, decreasing surface area

3. Water that falls to Earth evaporates from oceans and lakes. Evaporating perspiration cools the body.

4. maintain a definite shape, because of relatively fixed arrangement of particles; have definite volume, because of close packing; are nonfluid, because of relatively fixed positions; have definite melting points, because of kinetic energies needed to overcome attractive forces; have high densities, because of close packing; are incompressible, because of close packing; have a low rate of diffusion, because of low mobility of particles

5. **a.** rubber, glass, plastics, synthetic fibers
   b. It softens to become a thick, sticky liquid over a range of temperatures, and it can flow.
   c. windows, drinking glasses

6. crystal structure: total three-dimensional arrangement of particles of a crystal; lattice: coordinate system of particles; unit cell: smallest portion of the crystal lattice that shows the pattern

7. **a.** ionic: ionically bonded positive and negative ions in a regular pattern; covalent network: single atoms covalently bonded to nearest neighbors in extensive pattern; metallic: positive metal cations surrounded by negative valence electrons that belong to the crystal as a whole and are attracted to the cations; covalent molecular: covalently bonded molecules held together by London dispersion forces, dipole-dipole forces, or hydrogen bonding

b. ionic: hard, brittle, high-melting, good insulators; covalent network: hard, brittle, high-melting, usually nonconducting or semiconducting; metallic: good conductors, varying melting points; covalent molecular: low-melting, soft, easily vaporized, good insulators

8. a. 40 torr   **c.** 300 torr
    b. 350 torr   **d.** 375 torr

9. a. change of state directly from solid to gas
    b. dry ice, iodine

10. the temperature at which solid and liquid are in equilibrium at 1 atm pressure

11. Increasing temperature increases a liquid's average kinetic energy, thus increasing the number of molecules that have enough energy to escape as vapor.

12. the stronger the attractive forces, the lower the percentage of particles that can escape to the vapor phase and the lower the equilibrium vapor pressure

13. a. the higher the atmospheric pressure, the higher the boiling point; the liquid must be heated to a higher temperature to allow the equilibrium vapor pressure to equal atmospheric pressure
    b. equal and constant
    c. Energy from the heat source is used to overcome attractive forces and is stored as potential energy rather than increasing kinetic energy.

14. the greater the attraction, the greater the energy required to overcome it, and the higher the molar heat of vaporization

15. the greater the attraction, the greater the energy required to overcome it, and the higher the molar heat of fusion

16. two atoms of H join to the same O atom by polar covalent bonds at an angle of about 105°

CHAPTER SUMMARY continued

12-4 • Water is a polar-covalent compound. A water molecule has a bent shape and a partial negative charge near its oxygen atom and a partial positive charge near each hydrogen atom.
• The structure and the types of bonds water is able to form are responsible for its relatively high melting point, molar heat of fusion, boiling point, and molar heat of vaporization.
• The structure and bonding of water also explain why water expands upon freezing and why ice is able to float in liquid water.

REVIEWING CONCEPTS

1. What is a fluid?   (12-1)

2. What is surface tension?   (12-1)

3. Give two reasons why evaporation is a crucial process in nature.   (12-1)

4. List seven properties of solids, and explain each in terms of the kinetic-molecular theory of solids.   (12-2)

5. a. List four common examples of amorphous solids.
    b. Why is glass sometimes classified as a supercooled liquid?
    c. Name some uses of glass.   (12-2)

6. Distinguish between a crystal structure, a lattice, and a unit cell.   (12-2)

7. a. List and describe the four types of crystals in terms of the nature of their component particles and the type of bonding between them.
    b. What physical properties are associated with each type of crystal?   (12-2)

8. Using Figure 12-12, estimate the approximate equilibrium vapor pressure of each of the following at the specified temperature.
    a. water at 40°C
    b. water at 80°C
    c. diethyl ether at 20°C
    d. ethanol at 60°C   (12-3)

9. a. What is sublimation?
    b. Give two examples of common substances that sublime at ordinary temperatures. (12-3)

10. What is meant by the normal freezing point of a substance?   (12-3)

11. Explain why the vapor pressure of a liquid increases with increasing temperature.   (12-3)

12. Explain how the attractive forces between the particles in a liquid and the equilibrium vapor pressure of that liquid are related.   (12-3)

13. a. Explain the relationship between atmospheric pressure and the actual boiling point of a liquid.
    b. During continual boiling at this pressure, what is the relationship between the temperature of the liquid and that of its vapor?
    c. How can this phenomenon be explained? (12-3)

14. Explain the relationship between the magnitude of the molar heat of vaporization of a liquid and the strength of attraction between the particles of that liquid.   (12-3)

15. Explain the relationship between the molar heat of fusion of a solid and the strength of attraction between its particles.   (12-3)

16. Describe the structure of a water molecule.   (12-4)

17. List at least eight physical properties of water.   (12-4)

PROBLEMS

Molar Heat

18. a. The molar heat of vaporization for water is 40.79 kJ/mol. Express this heat of vaporization in joules per gram.
    b. The molar heat of fusion for water is 6.009 kJ/mol. Express this heat of fusion in joules per gram.

19. The standard molar heat of vaporization for water is 40.79 kJ/mol. How much energy would be required to vaporize each of the following?
    a. 5.00 mol H_2O
    b. 45.0 g H_2O
    c. 8.45×10^{10} molecules H_2O

20. The molar heat of fusion for water is 6.009 kJ/mol. How much energy would be required to melt each of the following?
   a. 12.75 mol ice   b. 6.48×10^5 kg ice

21. Calculate the molar heat of vaporization of a substance given that 0.433 mol of the substance absorbs 36.5 kJ of energy when it is vaporized.

22. Given that a substance has a molar mass of 259.0 g/mol and 71.8 g of the substance absorbs 4.307 kJ when it melts,
   a. calculate the number of moles in the 71.8 g sample.
   b. calculate the molar heat of fusion.

23. a. Calculate the number of moles in a liquid sample of a substance that has a molar heat of fusion of 3.811 kJ/mol, given that the sample releases 83.2 kJ when it freezes.
   b. Calculate the molar mass of this substance if the mass of the sample is 5519 g.

Water

24. Which contains more molecules of water; 5.00 cm³ of ice at 0°C or 5.00 cm³ of liquid water at 0.°C? How many more? What is the ratio of the numbers of molecules in these two samples?

25. Which contains more molecules of water; 5.00 cm³ of liquid water at 0.°C or 5.00 cm³ of water vapor at STP? How many more? What is the ratio of the numbers of molecules in these two samples?

26. a. What volume and mass of steam at 100.°C and 1.00 atm would, during condensation, release the same amount of heat as 100. cm³ of liquid water during freezing?
   b. What do you note, qualitatively, about the relative volumes and masses of steam and liquid water required to release the same amount of heat? (Hint: See Sample Problem 12-1.)

MIXED REVIEW

27. Find the molar heat of vaporization for a substance, given that 3.21 mol of the substance absorbs 28.4 kJ of energy when it changes from a liquid to a gas.

28. Water's molar heat of fusion is 6.009 kJ/mol. Calculate the amount of energy required to melt 7.95×10^5 g of ice.

29. A certain substance has a molar heat of vaporization of 31.6 kJ/mol. How much of the substance is in a sample that requires 57.0 kJ to vaporize?

30. Given that water has a molar heat of vaporization of 40.79 kJ/mol, how many grams of water could be vaporized by 0.545 kJ?

31. Calculate the amount of energy released by the freezing of 13.3 g of a liquid substance, given that the substance has a molar mass of 82.9 g/mol and a molar heat of fusion of 4.60 kJ/mol.

32. What volume and mass of steam at 100.°C and 760. torr would release the same amount of heat during condensation as 65.5 cm³ of liquid water would release during freezing?

33. A substance has a molar heat of fusion of 3.43 kJ/mol. Calculate the molar mass of the substance, given that a 64.2 g sample of it absorbs 2.77 kJ on melting.

34. The following liquid-vapor system is at equilibrium at a given temperature in a closed system.

$$\text{liquid} + \text{heat energy} \rightleftharpoons \text{vapor}$$

Suppose the temperature is increased and equilibrium is established at the higher temperature. How does the final value of each of the following compare with its initial value? (In each case, answer either higher, lower, or the same.)
   a. the rate of evaporation
   b. the rate of condensation
   c. the final concentration of vapor molecules
   d. the final number of liquid molecules

35. Decide whether the temperature of a liquid-vapor equilibrium system should be increased or decreased to make each of the following changes in the system.
   a. an increased final rate of evaporation
   b. an increased final concentration of vapor
   c. an increased final rate of condensation
   d. an increased final number of liquid molecules.

36. Given a sample of water at any point on curve AB in Figure 12-14, what effect would each of the following changes have on that sample?
   a. adding heat energy at constant pressure
   b. decreasing the volume at constant temperature
   c. removing heat energy at constant pressure
   d. increasing the volume at constant temperature

17. at room temperature, a transparent, tasteless, odorless, nearly colorless liquid; freezing point, 0°C at 1 atm; molar heat of fusion, 6.008 kJ/mol; expands during freezing; maximum density at about 4°C; boiling point at 1 atm, 100°C; molar heat of vaporization, 40.79 kJ/mol

18. a. 2265 J/g   b. 334 J/g

19. a. 204 kJ   c. 5.72×10^{-12} kJ
    b. 102 kJ

20. a. 76.61 kJ   b. 2.16×10^8 kJ

21. 84.3 kJ/mol

22. a. 0.277 mol   b. 15.5 kJ/mol

23. a. 21.8 mol   b. 253 g/mol

24. liquid water; 1.4×10^{22} more molecules; ratio is 1.09:1.00

25. liquid water; 1.67×10^{23} more molecules; ratio is approximately 1000:1

26. a. 25.0 L, 14.7 g
    b. A larger volume but a smaller mass of steam is required.

27. 8.85 kJ/mol

28. 2.65×10^5 kJ

29. 1.80 mol

30. 0.241 g

31. 0.738 kJ

32. 16.4 L, 9.63 g

33. 79.5 g/mol

34. a. higher   c. higher
    b. higher   d. lower

35. a. increased   c. increased
    b. increased   d. decreased

36. a. More solid would sublime.
    b. More vapor would deposit.
    c. More vapor would deposit.
    d. More solid would vaporize.

37. At 6 atm and −100.°C, CO_2 is a solid and remains so until about −60°C, when it melts. At about −45°C, the liquid boils.

38. The body is cooled by evaporation (which absorbs energy) of water-based perspiration from the skin. On a humid day, water collects on

the skin faster than it can evaporate because of the high rate of condensation (which releases energy) of atmospheric water.

39. The energy being removed is a loss of potential energy resulting from attracting particles moving closer together, and not a loss of kinetic energy that would be reflected in the temperature.

40. Adding heat to an ice-water system pushes the equilibrium to the right. Removing heat shifts it to the left. If both ice and liquid are present, adding or removing heat is reflected in the phase change, which involves potential energy, and not in kinetic energy.

41. When a substance melts, its intermolecular attractions are overcome just enough to allow the molecules to move past one another, while remaining close together. For the substance to vaporize, the intermolecular attractions must be completely overcome to allow the molecules to separate to get into the gas phase, which requires much more energy.

42. Decrease the pressure because the system would try to reduce the imposed stress by the liquid taking a less dense form, increasing its volume by becoming a solid. The diagram shows that a movement into the solid region of the graph would occur at the lower pressure.

43. a. It changes from solid directly to gas (sublimes).
b. Yes. Liquid exists only at pressures higher than the triple point pressure (the dashed line). This pressure is about 5 atm.

44. Methane is nonpolar and does not undergo hydrogen bonding. Water is polar and undergoes extensive hydrogen bonding. Higher temperatures are required

37. Using the phase diagram for CO_2, describe all the phase changes that would occur when CO_2 is heated from −100°C to −10°C at a constant pressure of 6 atm.

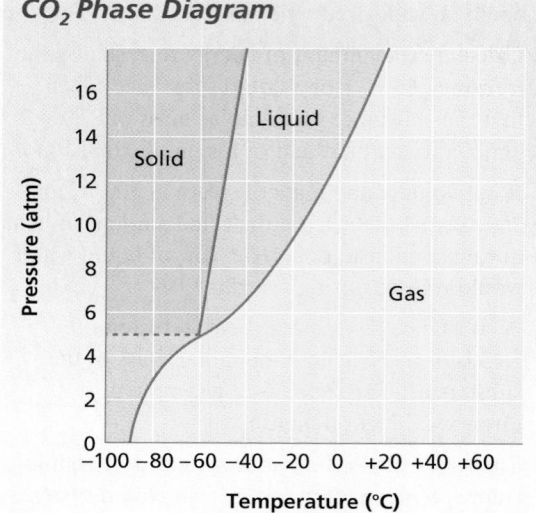

CO₂ Phase Diagram

CRITICAL THINKING

38. Applying Ideas Explain the role of humidity of the air in determining relative comfort on a hot day.

39. Interpreting Concepts During the freezing of a substance, energy is being removed from that substance. Yet the temperature of the liquid-solid system remains constant. Explain this phenomenon.

40. Applying Models At normal atmospheric pressure, the temperature of an ice-water system remains at 0°C as long as both ice and liquid water are present, regardless of the surrounding temperature. Explain this in terms of Le Châtelier's principle.

41. Describe the forces that must be overcome to explain why the heat of vaporization of a substance is always greater than its heat of fusion.

42. Predicting Outcomes Given a sample of water at any point on curve AD in Figure 12-14, how could more of the liquid water in that sample be converted into a solid without changing the temperature? Explain your reasoning.

43. Interpreting Diagrams Refer to the phase diagram in question 37.
a. Explain what happens when solid CO_2 ("dry ice") warms up to room temperature at normal atmospheric pressure.
b. Is there a pressure below which liquid CO_2 cannot exist? Estimate that pressure from the graph.

44. Interpreting Concepts Methane, CH_4, which is similar to water in molecular size and mass, is a gas at room temperature. However, water is a liquid at that temperature. Explain why.

45. Three simple unit cells found in metals are shown below. The dimensions of each unit cell can be described mathematically using the following information.

s = **length of the edge**
r = **atomic radius**

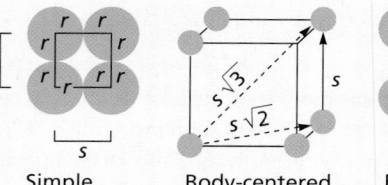

Simple cubic   Body-centered cubic   Face-centered cubic

Which of the following relationships applies to the simple cubic cell?
a. $2r = s$ c. $r = s$
b. $8r = 2s$ d. $2s = r$

46. Which of the following relationships applies to the face-centered cubic cell?
a. $2s = 4r$ c. $4r = s\sqrt{2}$
b. $2r = s$ d. $3r = s$

TECHNOLOGY & LEARNING

47. Graphing Calculator Calculating Vapor Pressure Using a Table

The graphing calculator can run a program that calculates a table for the vapor pressure in atmospheres at different temperatures (K) given the number of moles of a gas and its volume (V). Given a 0.50 mol gas sample with a volume of 10 L, you can calculate the pressure at 290 K, using a table. Use this program to create the table. Next, use the table to perform the calculations.

Go to Appendix C. If you are using a TI 83 Plus, you can download the program and data and run the application as directed. If you are using another calculator, your teacher will provide you with keystrokes and data sets to use. Remember that you will need to name the program and check the display, as explained in Appendix C. You will then be ready to run the program. After you have graphed the data, answer these questions.

Note: All answers show five significant digits.

a. What is the pressure for a gas with a mass of 1.3 mol, volume of 8.0 L, and temperature of 320° K?
b. What is the pressure for a gas with a mass of 1.5 mol, volume of 10.0 L, and temperature of 340° K?
c. Two gases are measures at 300° K. One has a mass of 1.3 mol and has a volume of 7.5 L, and the other has a mass of 0.5 mol and a volume of 10.0 L. Which gas has the lesser pressure?

HANDBOOK SEARCH

48. The *Elements Handbook* contains a table of properties for each group that includes information on the crystal structures of the elements. Most metals crystallize in one of three lattice arrangements: body-centered cubic, face-centered cubic, or hexagonal close-packed. Figure 12-7 shows a model of the face-centered cubic lattice for sodium chloride. Use this figure and the information in the *Elements Handbook* to answer the following.
    a. What elements in Group 2 have the same lattice structure as sodium chloride?

b. How would the model of an element in a face-centered cubic lattice differ from the compound shown in Figure 12-7?
c. The body-centered cubic lattice is the least-efficient packing structure of the metals. What elements in Groups 1 and 2 show this arrangement?

RESEARCH & WRITING

49. Ceramics are formed from silicates found in the soil. Artists use them to create pottery, but engineers and scientists have created ceramics with superconductive properties. Investigate the growing field of superconductive ceramics.

50. Liquid crystals are substances that possess the combined properties of both liquids and crystals. Write a report on these substances and the various uses we are finding for them.

51. Consult reference materials at the library, and prepare a report on the process of freeze-drying, describing its history and applications.

52. Prepare a report about the adjustments that must be made when cooking and baking at high elevations. Collect instructions for high-elevation adjustments from packages of prepared food mixes. Explain why changes must be made in recipes that will be prepared at high elevations. Check your library for cookbooks containing information about food preparation at high elevations.

ALTERNATIVE ASSESSMENT

53. Compile separate lists of crystalline and amorphous solids found in your home. Compare your lists with those of your classmates.

54. Design an experiment to grow crystals of various safe, common household materials. Record the conditions under which each type of crystal is best grown.

to overcome the resultant attractive forces and vaporize water.

45. a
46. c
47. a. 4.26712 atm
    b. 4.18506 atm
    c. the gas with a mass of 0.5 mol and volume of 6.0 L
48. a. calcium and strontium
    b. The model would show all atoms to be of the same size.
    c. Group 1: Li, Na, K, Rb, Cs; Group 2: Ba, Ra

Refer to the *One-Stop Planner CD-ROM* for appropriate scoring rubrics for items 49 through 52.

Photo Descriptions

Center: some aquatic life in the ocean solution of a coral reef

Lower left: hydrangea flower color affected by soil acidity

Lower right: sulfuric acid space-filling model with solutions colored by indicators

UNIT 5

Solutions and Their Behavior

CHAPTERS

13 Solutions

14 Ions in Aqueous Solutions and Colligative Properties

15 Acids and Bases

16 Acid–Base Titration and pH

Perfection is rare in the science of chemistry. Our scientific theories do not spring full-armed from the brow of the creator. They are subject to slow and gradual growth, and we must candidly admit that the ionic theory in its growth has reached the 'awkward age'. Instead, however, of judging it according to the standard of perfection, let us simply ask what it has accomplished, and what it may accomplish in scientific service.

(From *The Norton History of Chemistry*)

PACING CHART Compression Guide: *(To shorten, eliminate items in italics.)*	CLASSROOM RESOURCES		
	NSE Standards	Teaching Resources	Experiments
13-1 Types of Mixtures 2 45-minute periods 1 90-minute block	UCP 1–2, 5 SAI 1–2	**PE** Elements Handbook **ATE Demo,** p. 396 T 64, T 65, T 66, T 67, TM 64A, TM 65A	Quick Lab, p. 399 Chromatography, p. 828 Pen Ink Separation, p. 830 **C2 EXP** Separation of Mixtures **C2 INV** Separation of Mixtures— Tanker Truck Spill
13-2 The Solution Process 2 45-minute periods 1 90-minute block *Solute–Solvent Interactions, pp. 404–409*	PS 2e UCP 1–2, 5 SPSP 1, 5	**ATE Demo,** pp. 402, 404 T 68, T 69, T 70, T 71, T 72, T 73, T 74	**A17** Heat of Solution **C12 EXP** Paper Chromatography **C12 INV** Paper Chromatography— Forensic Investigation **C13 EXP** Testing for Dissolved O_2 **C14 EXP** Solubility of Ammonia
13-3 Concentration of Solutions 2 45-minute periods 1 90-minute block	UCP 1–3, 5	T 75, T 76, T 77, TM 66A	Colorimetry and Molarity, p. 834 **C9 EXP** Heat of Solution

Review and Assessment 2 45-minute periods 1 90-minute block	REVIEW RESOURCES		
	Cumulative Review	Alternative Assessment	Traditional Assessment
	SR Chapter 13 Mixed Review **PE** Chapter 13 28–32, p. 422	**PE** 38, 39, p. 423 **ATE** 395, 406, 413, 417 **AA** Items for Chapter 13	Chapter 13 Text Test Generator items for Chapter 13

ASSIGNMENT RESOURCES

Section Homework Resources & Review	Problem-Solving Practice
HR Homework Worksheets 13-1, 13-2 Graphic Org. Assignments 13-1, 13-2 **PE** Section Review, 1–5, p. 400 Chapter Review, 1–2, p. 420 **SR** Section Review 13-1	
HR Homework Worksheets 13-3, 13-4, 13-5 Graphic Org. Assignment 13-4 **PE** Section Review, 1–5, p. 410 Chapter Review, 3–10, 12–14, p. 420–421 **SR** Section Review 13-2	
HR Homework Worksheets 13-6, 13-7 Graphic Org. Assignment 13-7 **PE** Section Review, 1–2, p. 418 Chapter Review, 15–32, pp. 421–422 **SR** Section Review 13-3	**PE** Additional Samples 13-1, 13-2, 13-5 **ATE** Additional Samples, pp. 414, 415, 418 **PS** Chapter 14 Concentration of Solutions **PS** Chapter 15 Dilutions

TECHNOLOGY RESOURCES

Technology & Internet Resources

 CTW 14 Segment 14 Harvesting Salt
CTW 24 Segment 24 Mixing Oil and Water
CTW 25 Segment 25 Multivitamins

 Holt Chemistry Videodiscs Teacher's Correlation Guide
for Chapter 13

 Module 1: Solutions
Module 8: Solutions and Electrolytes

internetconnect

 On-line Student Resources:
GO TO: www.scilinks.org
The following SciLinks Internet resources can be
found in the student text for this chapter.

TOPICS:
• Solutions, p. 397 (HC2131)
• Colloids, p. 397 (HC2132)
• Electrolytes/nonelectrolytes, p. 399 (HC2133)
• Perfluorcarbons, p. 411 (HC2134)

 On-line Teacher Resources:
GO TO: go.hrw.com
KEYWORD: HC2 HOME
Visit the HRW Web site for a variety of resources
related to this chapter.

Smithsonian Institution®
Internet Connections
Visit www.si.edu/hrw for additional on-line
resources.

 CNNfyi.com
Visit www.cnnfyi.com for late-breaking news
and current events stories selected just for you.

Resource Key   **One-Stop Planner CD-ROM** Includes these resources and customizable daily lesson plans:

PE Pupil's Edition
ATE Teacher's Edition

HR Homework Resources
SR Section Reviews
CTW Critical Thinking
Worksheets
AA Alternative Assessments

ChemFile
A Laboratory Experiments
B Microscale Experiments
C Technique Builders and
Problem-Solving Experiments

D Consumer Experiments
T Transparencies
TM Transparency Masters
PS Mini-Guide to Problem Solving
SRW Supplemental Reading Worksheets

Scoring Rubrics for Labs, Alternative Assessments, Performance Tasks and Portfolio Projects are on the One-Stop Planner CD-ROM.

Solutions

Chapter Overview

13-1 outlines characteristics that distinguish solutions from suspensions and colloids.

13-2 covers the physical and chemical factors that affect solubility.

13-3 presents concentration expressed as molarity and molality with calculations.

Concept Base

Students may need a review of the following concepts:

- properties and types of mixtures, Chapter 2
- electronegativity, Chapter 4
- molecular polarity and inter-molecular forces, Chapter 6
- mass and mole relationships, Chapter 9

 Reading Skill-Builder

BRAINSTORMING Discuss with students the definition of *solution*. Have them brainstorm a list of common solutions. Then have them use Section 13-1 and other resources to confirm or deny the items on their lists, giving reasons why the listed item is or is not a solution. Students may be familiar with many water-based solutions, but may be surprised to learn that air, a mixture of gases, and brass, a mixture of solids, are also solutions.

Solutions

Solutions are homogeneous mixtures of two or more substances in a single phase.

Types of Mixtures

It is easy to determine that some materials are mixtures because you can see their component parts. For example, soil is a mixture of various substances, including small rocks and decomposed animal and plant matter. You can see this by picking up some soil in your hand and looking at it closely. Milk, on the other hand, does not appear to be a mixture, but in fact it is. Milk is composed principally of fats, proteins, milk sugar, and water. If you look at milk under a microscope, it will look something like Figure 13-1(a). You can see round lipid droplets that measure from 1 to 10 µm in diameter. Irregularly shaped protein (casein) particles that are about 0.2 µm wide can also be seen. Both milk and soil are examples of heterogeneous mixtures because their composition is not uniform.

Salt (sodium chloride) and water form a homogeneous mixture. The sodium and chloride ions are interspersed among the water molecules, and the mixture appears uniform throughout. A model for a homogeneous mixture like salt water is shown in Figure 13-1(b).

Solutions

Suppose a sugar cube is dropped into a glass of water. You know from experience that the sugar will dissolve. Sugar is described as "soluble in water." *By* **soluble** *we mean capable of being dissolved.*

What happens as sugar dissolves? The lump gradually disappears as sugar molecules leave the surface of their crystals and mix with water molecules. Eventually all the sugar molecules become uniformly distributed among the water molecules, as indicated by the equally sweet taste of any part of the mixture. All visible traces of the solid sugar are

OBJECTIVES

- Distinguish between heterogeneous and homogeneous mixtures.

- List three different solute-solvent combinations.

- Compare the properties of suspensions, colloids, and solutions.

- Distinguish between electrolytes and nonelectrolytes.

CHEMISTRY TUTOR

Module 1: States of Matter/Classes of Matter

FIGURE 13-1 (a) Milk consists of visible particles in a nonuniform arrangement. (b) Salt water is an example of a homogeneous mixture. Ions and water molecules are in a uniform arrangement.

(a) Heterogeneous mixture—milk

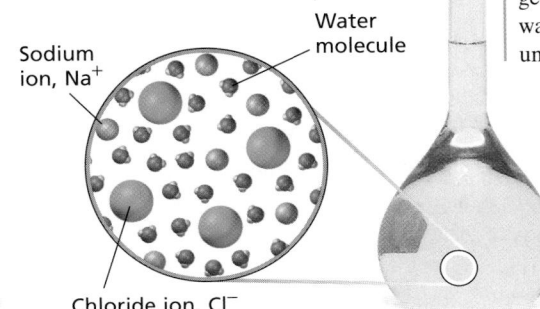

Water molecule

Sodium ion, Na⁺

Chloride ion, Cl⁻

(b) Homogeneous mixture—saltwater solution

(a)

(b)

FIGURE 13-2 The solute in a solution can be a solid, liquid, or gas. (a) The ethanol-water solution is made from a liquid solute in a liquid solvent. (b) The copper(II) chloride–water solution is made from a solid solute in a liquid solvent. Note that the composition of each solution is uniform.

gone. Such a mixture is called a solution. *A* **solution** *is a homogeneous mixture of two or more substances in a single phase.* In a solution, atoms, molecules, or ions are thoroughly mixed, resulting in a mixture that has the same composition and properties throughout.

Components of Solutions

In the simplest type of solution, such as a sugar-water solution, the particles of one substance are randomly mixed with the particles of another substance. *The dissolving medium in a solution is called the* **solvent,** *and the substance dissolved in a solution is called the* **solute.** The solute is generally designated as that component of a solution that is of lesser quantity. In the ethanol-water solution shown in Figure 13-2, ethanol is the solute and water is the solvent. Occasionally, these terms have little meaning. For example, in a 50%-50% solution of ethanol and water, it would be difficult, and in fact unnecessary, to say which is the solvent and which is the solute.

In a solution, the dissolved solute particles are so small that they cannot be seen. They remain mixed with the solvent indefinitely, so long as the existing conditions remain unchanged. If the solutions in Figure 13-2 are poured through filter paper, both the solute and the solvent will pass through the paper. The solute-particle dimensions are those of atoms, molecules, and ions—which range from about 0.01 to 1 nm in diameter.

Types of Solutions

Solutions may exist as gases, liquids, or solids. Some possible solute-solvent combinations of gases, liquids, and solids in solutions are summarized in Table 13-1. In each example, one component is designated as the solvent and one as the solute.

Many alloys, such as brass (made from zinc and copper) and sterling silver (made from silver and copper), are solid solutions in which the atoms of two of more metals are uniformly mixed. By properly choosing the proportions of each metal in the alloy, many desirable properties

TABLE 13-1 *Some Solute-Solvent Combinations for Solutions*		
Solute state	**Solvent state**	**Example**
Gas	gas	oxygen in nitrogen
Gas	liquid	carbon dioxide in water
Liquid	gas	water in air
Liquid	liquid	alcohol in water
Liquid	solid	mercury in silver and tin (dental amalgam)
Solid	liquid	sugar in water
Solid	solid	copper in nickel (Monel™ alloy)

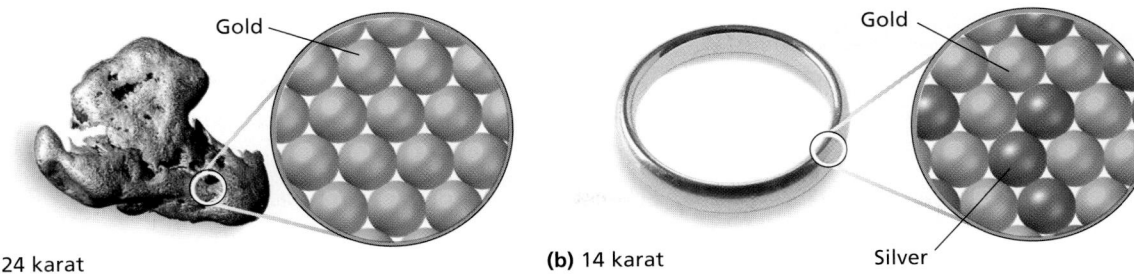

(a) 24 karat **(b)** 14 karat

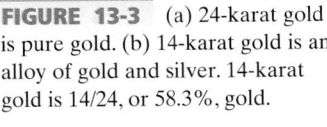

Silver

FIGURE 13-3 (a) 24-karat gold is pure gold. (b) 14-karat gold is an alloy of gold and silver. 14-karat gold is 14/24, or 58.3%, gold.

can be obtained. For example, alloys can have higher strength and greater resistance to corrosion than the pure metals. Pure gold (24K), for instance, is too soft to use in jewelry. Alloying it with silver greatly increases its strength and hardness while retaining its appearance and corrosion resistance. Figure 13-3 shows a model for comparing pure gold with a gold alloy.

Suspensions

If the particles in a solvent are so large that they settle out unless the mixture is constantly stirred or agitated, the mixture is called a **suspension.** Think of a jar of muddy water. If left undisturbed, particles of soil collect on the bottom of the jar. The soil particles are much larger and denser than water molecules. Gravity pulls them to the bottom of the container. Particles over 1000 nm in diameter—1000 times as large as atoms, molecules, or ions—form suspensions. The particles in suspension can be separated from the heterogeneous mixtures by passing the mixture through a filter.

Colloids

Particles that are intermediate in size between those in solutions and suspensions form mixtures known as colloidal dispersions, or simply **colloids.** Particles between 1 nm and 1000 nm in diameter may form colloids. After large soil particles settle out of muddy water, the water is often still cloudy because colloidal particles remain dispersed in the water. If the cloudy mixture is poured through a filter, the colloidal particles will pass through, and the mixture will remain cloudy. The particles in a colloid are small enough to be suspended throughout the solvent by the constant movement of the surrounding molecules. The colloidal particles make up the *dispersed phase,* and water is the *dispersing medium.* Examples of the various types of colloids are given in Table 13-2. Note that some familiar terms, such as *emulsion* and *foam,* refer to specific types of colloids. For example, mayonnaise is an emulsion

internet**connect**

SC**LINKS**
NSTA

TOPIC: Solutions
GO TO: www.scilinks.org
*sci***LINKS CODE:** HC2131

TOPIC: Colloids
GO TO: www.scilinks.org
*sci***LINKS CODE:** HC2132

TABLE STRATEGY

Table 13-1 Have students identify specific, common examples of each type of solution. For example, fish depend on oxygen gas dissolved in water.

Common Misconception

Many students think solvents must be liquids. Use Table 13-1 to remind them that many solutions do not involve a liquid solvent. A common example is metal alloy, which is a solution of two metals. The metal in the greatest abundance is the solvent, and the other metals in the alloy are the solutes.

Application

Lecithin is a common emulsifying agent. Emulsions are mixtures that consist of colloidal-sized particles. The emulsifying agent causes the solutes and solvent to form a colloidal-type mixture. Lecithin is used in margarine, mayonnaise, chocolate, candy, baked goods, salad dressing, printing inks, soaps, and cosmetics.

HANDBOOK   CONNECTION

Alloys are discussed in greater detail in the *Elements Handbook.*

Did You Know?

Thomas Graham, an English chemist, began the study of colloids in 1861. Because the first colloids were gelatin or glue, he used the Greek word *kolla,* meaning "glue," as the root for the name.

TABLE STRATEGY

Table 13-2 Have students think of common examples of different types of colloids. For example, shaving cream is a foam.

Table 13-3 Be sure students notice that a major distinguishing characteristic of solutions, colloids, and suspensions is the size of their solute particles. Ask students to predict whether the components of a solution are separated with filter paper or a centrifuge.

✔ Teaching Tip

Smog is a combination of a solid aerosol and a liquid aerosol, that is, both solid and liquid dispersed in gas.

TABLE 13-2 *Classes of Colloids*

Class of colloid	Phases	Example
Sol	solid dispersed in liquid	paints, mud
Gel	solid network extending throughout liquid	gelatin
Liquid emulsion	liquid dispersed in a liquid	milk, mayonnaise
Foam	gas dispersed in liquid	shaving cream, whipped cream
Solid aerosol	solid dispersed in gas	smoke, airborne particulate matter, auto exhaust
Liquid aerosol	liquid dispersed in gas	fog, mist, clouds, aerosol spray
Solid emulsion	liquid dispersed in solid	cheese, butter

of oil droplets in water; the egg yolk in it acts as an emulsifying agent, which helps to keep the oil droplets dispersed.

Tyndall Effect

Many colloids appear homogeneous because the individual particles cannot be seen. The particles are, however, large enough to scatter light. You have probably noticed that a headlight beam is visible on a foggy night. This effect, known as the Tyndall effect, occurs when light is scattered by colloidal particles dispersed in a transparent medium. The Tyndall effect is a property that can be used to distinguish between a solution and a colloid, as demonstrated in Figure 13-4.

The distinctive properties of solutions, colloids, and suspensions are summarized in Table 13-3. The individual particles of a colloid can be detected under a microscope if a bright light is cast on the specimen at a right angle. The particles, which appear as tiny specks of light, are seen to move rapidly in a random motion. This motion is due to collisions of rapidly moving molecules and is called Brownian motion, after its discoverer, Robert Brown.

FIGURE 13-4 A beam of light distinguishes a colloid from a solution. The particles in a colloid will scatter light, making the beam visible. The mixture of gelatin and water in the jar on the right is a colloid. The mixture of water and sodium chloride in the jar on the left is a true solution.

TABLE 13-3 *Properties of Solutions, Colloids, and Suspensions*

Solutions	Colloids	Suspensions
Homogeneous	Heterogeneous	Heterogeneous
Particle size: 0.01–1 nm; can be atoms, ions, molecules	Particle size: 1–1000 nm, dispersed; can be aggregates or large molecules	Particle size: over 1000 nm, suspended; can be large particles or aggregates
Do not separate on standing	Do not separate on standing	Particles settle out
Cannot be separated by filtration	Cannot be separated by filtration	Can be separated by filtration
Do not scatter light	Scatter light (Tyndall effect)	May scatter light, but are not transparent

Observing Solutions, Suspensions, and Colloids

Wear Safety Goggles and an Apron.

Materials

- balance
- 7 beakers, 400 mL
- clay
- cooking oil
- flashlight
- gelatin, plain
- hot plate (to boil H₂O)
- red food coloring
- sodium borate
  (Na₂B₄O₇•10H₂O)
- soluble starch
- stirring rod
- sucrose
- test-tube rack
- water

Procedure

1. Prepare seven mixtures, each containing 250 mL of water and one of the following substances.
  a. 12 g of sucrose
  b. 3 g of soluble starch
  c. 5 g of clay
  d. 2 mL of food coloring
  e. 2 g of sodium borate
  f. 50 mL of cooking oil
  g. 3 g of gelatin

Making the gelatin mixture: Soften the gelatin in 65 mL of cold water, and then add 185 mL of boiling water.

2. Observe the seven mixtures and their characteristics. Record the appearance of each mixture after stirring.

3. Transfer to individual test tubes 10 mL of each mixture that does not separate after stirring. Shine a flashlight on each mixture in a dark room. Make note of the mixtures in which the path of the light beam is visible.

Discussion

1. Using your observations, classify each mixture as a solution, suspension, or colloid.

2. What characteristics did you use to classify each mixture?

Solutes: Electrolytes vs. Nonelectrolytes

Substances that dissolve in water are classified according to whether they yield molecules or ions in solution. When an ionic compound dissolves, the positive and negative ions separate from each other and are surrounded by water molecules. These solute ions are free to move, making it possible for an electric current to pass through the solution. *A substance that dissolves in water to give a solution that conducts electric current is called an* **electrolyte.** Sodium chloride, NaCl, is an electrolyte, as is any soluble ionic compound. Certain highly polar molecular compounds, such as hydrogen chloride, HCl, are also electrolytes because HCl molecules form the ions H_3O^+ and Cl^- when dissolved in water.

By contrast, a solution containing neutral solute molecules does not conduct electric current because it does not contain mobile charged

Module 8: Strong and Weakly Ionized Species, pH, and Titrations

internet connect

SCi LINKS
NSTA

TOPIC: Electrolytes/nonelectrolytes
GO TO: www.scilinks.org
sci **LINKS CODE:** HC2133

Module 8: Strong and Weakly Ionized Species, pH, and Titrations

Topic: Solutions and Electrolytes
Sections **a, b,** and **c** of this engaging tutorial review and reinforce understanding of solutions and electrolytes.

Visual Strategy

FIGURE 13-5 As students inspect the figure on this page, ask them why aqueous solutions with electrolyte solutes conduct electricity and solutions with nonelectrolyte solutes do not.

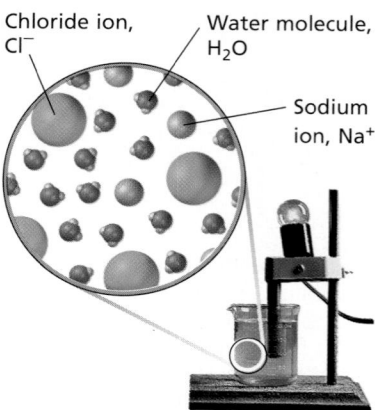

(a) Salt solution— electrolyte solute

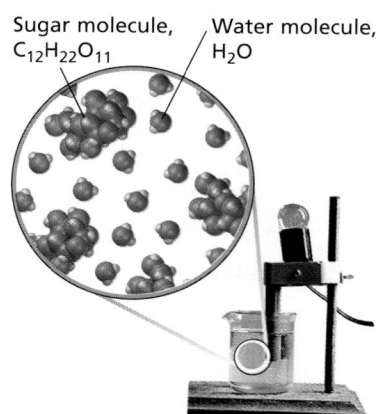

(b) Sugar solution— nonelectrolyte solute

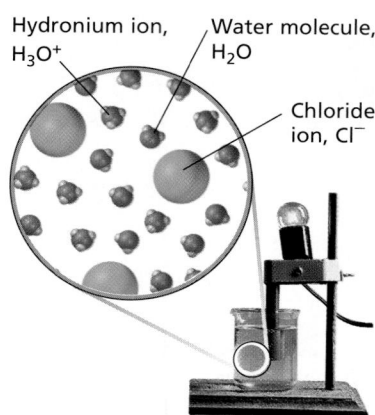

(c) Hydrochloric acid solution— electrolyte solute

FIGURE 13-5 (a) Sodium chloride dissolves in water to produce a salt solution that conducts electric current. NaCl is an electrolyte. (b) Sucrose dissolves in water to produce a sugar solution that does not conduct electricity. Sucrose is a nonelectrolyte. (c) Hydrogen chloride dissolves in water to produce a solution that conducts current. HCl is an electrolyte.

particles. *A substance that dissolves in water to give a solution that does not conduct an electric current is called a* **nonelectrolyte.** Sugar is a nonelectrolyte. Figure 13-5 shows an apparatus for testing the conductivity of solutions. The electrodes are conductors that are attached to a power supply and that make electric contact with the test solution. For a current to pass through the light-bulb filament, the test solution must provide a conducting path between the two electrodes. A nonconducting solution is like an open switch between the electrodes, and there is no current in the circuit.

The light bulb glows brightly if a solution that is a good conductor is tested. Such solutions contain solutes that are electrolytes. For a moderately conductive solution, however, the light bulb is dim. If a solution is a poor conductor, the light bulb does not glow at all. Such solutions contain solutes that are nonelectrolytes. You will learn more about the strengths and behavior of electrolytes in Chapter 14.

SECTION REVIEW

1. a. heterogeneous
b. homogeneous

2. a. Electrolytes. **b.** A saltwater solution conducts electricity because mobile ions can move a charge from one point in the solution to another. **c.** A sugar solution will not conduct electricity because there are no charged particles in the solution.

3. Student drawings should look similar to Figure 13-5(a) showing ions dispersed in a solvent. The solid NaCl should look like Figure 6-14(a). The ions are not free to move.

4. Sand in water can settle or be filtered out, proving that it is not a solution. Dissolved sugar cannot be removed from water through settling or filtration; the water must be evaporated.

5.

	solvent	solute
a.	gold	silver
b.	air	water
c.	water	carbon dioxide
d.	water	tea

SECTION REVIEW

1. Classify the following as either a heterogeneous or homogeneous mixture, and explain your answers.
   a. orange juice   b. tap water

2. a. What are substances called whose water solutions conduct electricity? b. Why does a saltwater solution conduct electricity? c. Why does a sugar-water solution not conduct electricity?

3. Make a drawing of the particles in an NaCl solution to show why this solution conducts electricity. Make a drawing of the particles in an NaCl crystal to show why pure salt does not conduct.

4. Describe one way to prove that a mixture of sugar and water is a solution and that a mixture of sand and water is not a solution.

5. Label the solute and solvent in each of the following:
   a. 14-karat gold
   b. water vapor in air
   c. carbonated, or sparkling, water
   d. hot tea

The Solution Process

Factors Affecting the Rate of Dissolution

If you have ever tried to dissolve sugar in iced tea, you know that temperature has something to do with how quickly a solute dissolves. What other factors affect how quickly you can dissolve sugar in iced tea?

Increasing the Surface Area of the Solute

Sugar dissolves as sugar molecules leave the crystal surface and mix with water molecules. The same is true for any solid solute in a liquid solvent: molecules or ions of the solute are attracted by the solvent.

Because the dissolution process occurs at the surface of the solute, it can be speeded up if the surface area of the solute is increased. Crushing sugar that is in cubes or large crystals increases the surface area. In general, the more finely divided a substance is, the greater the surface area per unit mass and the more quickly it dissolves. Figure 13-6 shows a model of solutions that are made from the same solute but have a different amount of surface area exposed to the solvent.

Agitating a Solution

Very close to the surface of a solute, the concentration of dissolved solute is high. Stirring or shaking helps to disperse the solute particles

Small surface area exposed to solvent—slow rate

Large surface area exposed to solvent—faster rate

Solvent particle
Solute

$CuSO_4 \cdot 5H_2O$ large crystals

$CuSO_4 \cdot 5H_2O$ powdered
Increased surface area

OBJECTIVES

- List and explain three factors that affect the rate at which a solid solute dissolves in a liquid solvent.

- Explain solution equilibrium, and distinguish among saturated, unsaturated, and supersaturated solutions.

- Explain the meaning of "like dissolves like" in terms of polar and nonpolar substances.

- List the three interactions that contribute to the heat of solution, and explain what causes dissolution to be exothermic or endothermic.

- Compare the effects of temperature and pressure on solubility.

FIGURE 13-6 The rate at which a solid solute dissolves can be increased by increasing the surface area. A powdered solute has a greater surface area exposed to solvent particles and therefore dissolves faster than a solute in large crystals.

Lesson Starter

Obtain three pieces of iron(II) chloride of equal mass and shape, and three different beakers containing water. Add the $FeCl_2$ to one beaker, and mix the contents using a magnetic stirrer while introducing this lesson. Pulverize the $FeCl_2$ and let it sit in the second beaker. Add the last crystal to the third beaker and allow it to stand still. Use the results of this demonstration to introduce the principles of this section.

Reading Skill-Builder

PREDICTION GUIDES Write the following statements on the chalkboard:
- The rate at which any substance dissolves varies with temperature.
- The solubility of any substance varies with temperature.
- The solubility of any substance varies with pressure.

Ask students for their opinions of each statement. Then have them discuss their opinions, giving reasons based on knowledge and/or experience. Keep a list of the opinions for discussion at the end of the section.

and bring fresh solvent into contact with the solute surface. Thus, the effect of stirring is similar to that of crushing a solid—contact between the solvent and the solute surface is increased.

Heating a Solvent

You have probably noticed that sugar and many other materials dissolve more quickly in warm water than in cold water. As the temperature of the solvent increases, solvent molecules move faster, and their average kinetic energy increases. Therefore, at higher temperatures, collisions between the solvent molecules and the solute are more frequent and are of higher energy than at lower temperatures. This helps to separate solute molecules from one another and to disperse them among the solvent molecules.

Solubility

If you add spoonful after spoonful of sugar to tea, eventually no more sugar will dissolve. For every combination of solvent with a solid solute at a given temperature, there is a limit to the amount of solute that can be dissolved. The point at which this limit is reached for any solute-solvent combination is difficult to predict precisely and depends on the nature of the solute, the nature of the solvent, and the temperature.

The following model describes why there is a limit. When solid sugar is first dropped into the water, sugar molecules leave the solid surface and move about at random in the solvent. Some of these dissolved molecules may collide with the crystal and remain there (recrystallize). As more of the solid dissolves and the concentration of dissolved molecules increases, these collisions become more frequent. Eventually, molecules are returning to the crystal at the same rate at which they are going into solution, and a dynamic equilibrium is established between dissolution and crystallization, as represented by the model in Figure 13-7.

Solution equilibrium *is the physical state in which the opposing processes of dissolution and crystallization of a solute occur at equal rates.*

FIGURE 13-7 A saturated solution in a closed system is at equilibrium. The solute is recrystallizing at the same rate that it is dissolving, even though it appears that there is no activity in the system.

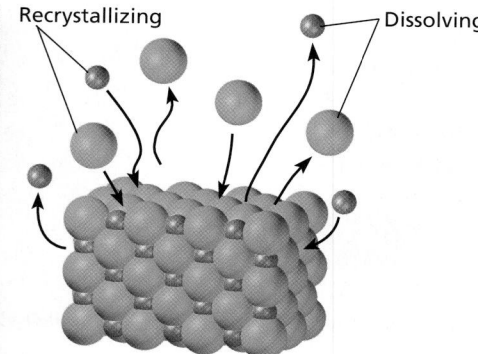

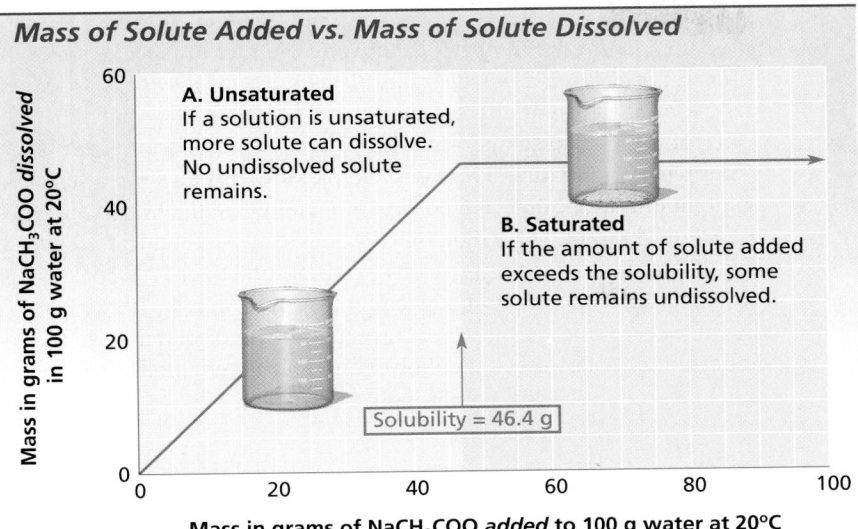

Mass of Solute Added vs. Mass of Solute Dissolved

A. Unsaturated
If a solution is unsaturated, more solute can dissolve. No undissolved solute remains.

B. Saturated
If the amount of solute added exceeds the solubility, some solute remains undissolved.

Solubility = 46.4 g

(y-axis) Mass in grams of $NaCH_3COO$ dissolved in 100 g water at 20°C

(x-axis) Mass in grams of $NaCH_3COO$ *added* to 100 g water at 20°C

FIGURE 13-8 The graph shows the range of solute masses that will produce an unsaturated solution. Once the saturation point is exceeded, the system will contain undissolved solute.

Saturated vs. Unsaturated Solutions

A solution that contains the maximum amount of dissolved solute is described as a **saturated solution.** How can you tell that the NaCl solution pictured in Figure 13-8 is saturated? If more sodium chloride is added to the solution, it falls to the bottom and does not dissolve because an equilibrium has been established between molecules leaving and entering the solid phase. If more water is added to the saturated solution, then more sodium chloride will dissolve in it. At 20°C, 35.9 g of NaCl is the maximum amount that will dissolve in 100. g of water. *A solution that contains less solute than a saturated solution under the existing conditions is an* **unsaturated solution.**

Supersaturated Solutions

When a saturated solution of a solute whose solubility increases with temperature is cooled, the excess solute usually comes out of solution, leaving the solution saturated at the lower temperature. But sometimes, if the solution is left to cool undisturbed, the excess solute does not separate and a supersaturated solution is produced. *A* **supersaturated solution** *is a solution that contains more dissolved solute than a saturated solution contains under the same conditions.* A supersaturated solution may remain unchanged for a long time if it is not disturbed, but once crystals begin to form, the process continues until equilibrium is reestablished at the lower temperature. An example of a supersaturated solution is one prepared from a saturated solution of sodium thiosulfate, $Na_2S_2O_3$, or sodium acetate, $NaCH_3COO$. Solute is added to hot water until the solution is saturated, and the hot solution is filtered. The filtrate is left to stand undisturbed as it cools. Dropping a small crystal of the solute into the supersaturated solution ("seeding") or disturbing the solution causes a rapid formation of crystals by the excess solute.

Visual Strategy

FIGURE 13-8 Students should notice that solutions can be unsaturated over a range of solute masses. However, once the saturation point is reached, excess solute remains undissolved unless the temperature of the system changes.

✔ Teaching Tip

Point out that the formula for sodium acetate is written several ways.

$$NaC_2H_3O_2$$
$$CH_3COONa$$
$$NaCH_3COO$$

DEMONSTRATION

The seeding of a supersaturated solution is a very effective demonstration. Test tubes containing a supersaturated solution of sodium thiosulfate, $Na_2S_2O_3$, can be reused year after year. Several hours before performing the demonstration, heat the test tube until the solute is all dissolved. Then allow the solution to stand undisturbed until it has cooled to room temperature before seeding the supersaturated solution with a small crystal of $Na_2S_2O_3$. It is suggested that you prepare and store several test tubes, as the solution occasionally crystallizes when it is cooled. It might be necessary occasionally to filter the warm solution to remove dust particles that can initiate crystallization.

Solubility Values

*The **solubility*** *of a substance is the amount of that substance required to form a saturated solution with a specific amount of solvent at a specified temperature.* The solubility of sugar, for example, is 204 g per 100. g of water at 20.°C. The temperature must be specified because solubility varies with temperature. For gases, the pressure must also be specified. Solubilities must be determined experimentally, and they vary widely, as illustrated in Table 13-4. Solubility values can be found in chemical handbooks and are usually given as grams of solute per 100. g of solvent or per 100. mL of solvent at a given temperature.

The rate at which a solid dissolves is unrelated to solubility. The maximum amount of solute that dissolves and reaches equilibrium is always the same under the same conditions.

Solute-Solvent Interactions

Lithium chloride is highly soluble in water, but gasoline is not. On the other hand, gasoline mixes readily with benzene, C_6H_6, but lithium chloride does not. Why are there such differences in solubility?

"Like dissolves like" is a rough but useful rule for predicting whether one substance will dissolve in another. What makes substances similar depends on the type of bonding, the polarity or nonpolarity of molecules, and the intermolecular forces between the solute and solvent.

TABLE 13-4 *Solubility of Solutes as a Function of Temperature (in g solute/100. g H_2O)*

Substance	Temperature (°C)					
	0	20	40	60	80	100
$AgNO_3$	122	216	311	440	585	733
$Ba(OH)_2$	1.67	3.89	8.22	20.94	101.4	—
$C_{12}H_{22}O_{11}$	179	204	238	287	362	487
$Ca(OH)_2$	0.189	0.173	0.141	0.121	—	0.07
$Ce_2(SO_4)_3$	20.8	10.1	—	3.87	—	—
KCl	28.0	34.2	40.1	45.8	51.3	56.3
KI	128	144	162	176	192	206
KNO_3	13.9	31.6	61.3	106	167	245
LiCl	69.2	83.5	89.8	98.4	112	128
Li_2CO_3	1.54	1.33	1.17	1.01	0.85	0.72
NaCl	35.7	35.9	36.4	37.1	38.0	39.2
$NaNO_3$	73	87.6	102	122	148	180
CO_2 (gas at SP)	0.335	0.169	0.0973	0.058	—	—
O_2 (gas at SP)	0.00694	0.00537	0.00308	0.00227	0.00138	0.00

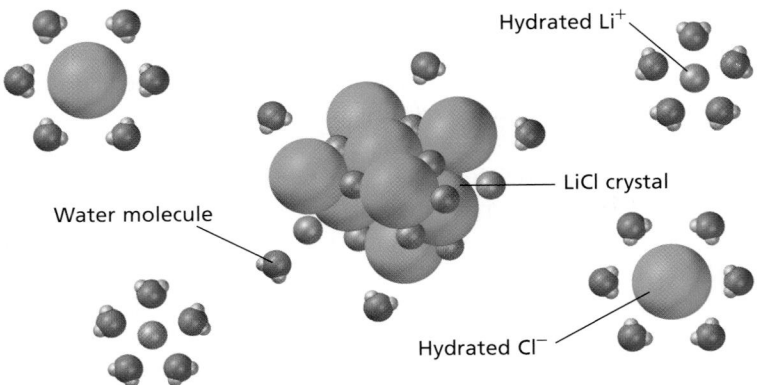

Hydrated Li⁺

LiCl crystal

Water molecule

Hydrated Cl⁻

FIGURE 13-9 When LiCl dissolves, the ions are hydrated. The attraction between ions and water molecules is strong enough that each ion in solution is surrounded by water molecules.

CHAPTER ⬌ CONNECTION

The forces that hold a solute to a solvent vary depending on the material. When some metals dissolve in other metals, they form metallic bonds. Ions and polar molecules are linked to water with dipole-dipole attractions. Nonpolar molecules are linked to nonpolar solvents with London dispersion forces. These forces and attractions are further described in Chapter 6.

Dissolving Ionic Compounds in Aqueous Solution

The polarity of water molecules plays an important role in the formation of solutions of ionic compounds in water. The charged ends of water molecules attract the ions in the ionic compounds and surround them to keep them separated from the other ions in the solution. Suppose we drop a few crystals of lithium chloride into a beaker of water. At the crystal surfaces, water molecules come into contact with Li^+ and Cl^- ions. The positive ends of the water molecules are attracted to Cl^- ions, while the negative ends are attracted to Li^+ ions. The attraction between water molecules and the ions is strong enough to draw the ions away from the crystal surface and into solution, as illustrated in Figure 13-9. *This solution process with water as the solvent is referred to as* **hydration.** The ions are said to be *hydrated*. As hydrated ions diffuse into the solution, other ions are exposed and are drawn away from the crystal surface by the solvent. The entire crystal gradually dissolves, and hydrated ions become uniformly distributed in the solution.

When crystallized from aqueous solutions, some ionic substances form crystals that incorporate water molecules. These crystalline compounds, known as *hydrates*, retain specific ratios of water molecules and are represented by formulas such as $CuSO_4 \cdot 5H_2O$. Heating the crystals of a hydrate can drive off the water of hydration and leave the anhydrous salt. When a crystalline hydrate dissolves in water, the water of hydration returns to the solvent. The behavior of a solute in its hydrated form is no different from the behavior of the anhydrous form. Dissolving either form results in a system containing hydrated ions and water.

Nonpolar Solvents

Ionic compounds are generally not soluble in nonpolar solvents such as carbon tetrachloride, CCl_4, and toluene, $C_6H_5CH_3$. The nonpolar solvent molecules do not attract the ions of the crystal strongly enough to overcome the forces holding the crystal together.

Would you expect lithium chloride to dissolve in toluene? No, LiCl is not soluble in toluene. LiCl and $C_6H_5CH_3$ differ widely in bonding, polarity, and intermolecular forces.

Visual Strategy

FIGURE 13-9 Students should notice that the orientation of the water molecules changes depending on which ion they surround. Ask students what kind of forces are represented in this model *(dipole-dipole interactions)*.

FIGURE 13-10 Have students decide whether the water in hydrates is a solute or a solvent. Point out that four water molecules are part of the octahedral complex held in place by shared pairs from H_2O in coordinate covalent bonds. The fifth water molecule is attracted to the octahedral complex by dipole interactions. Two sulfate ions are shown even though each is also bound to another copper ion in the extended array for this crystal.

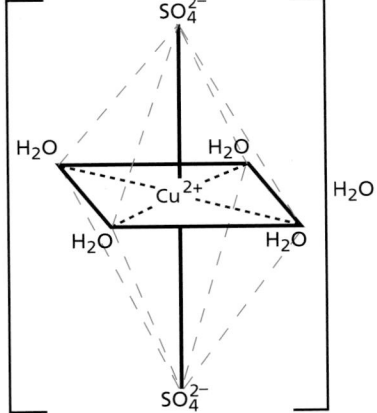

FIGURE 13-10 Hydrated copper(II) sulfate has water trapped in the crystal structure. Heating releases the water and produces the anhydrous form of the substance, which has the formula $CuSO_4$.

406

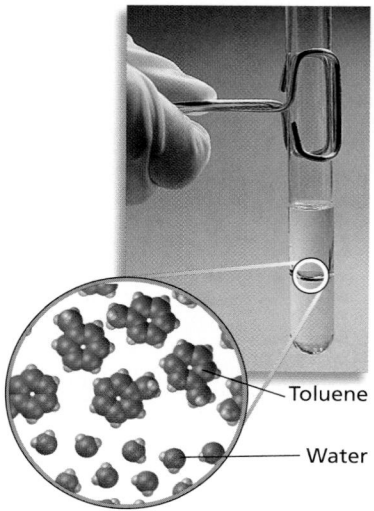

Insoluble and immiscible

FIGURE 13-11 Toluene and water are immiscible. The components of this system exist in two distinct phases.

— Toluene

— Water

Liquid Solutes and Solvents

When you shake a bottle of salad dressing, oil droplets become dispersed in the water. As soon as you stop shaking the bottle, the strong attraction between the water molecules squeezes out the oil droplets, forming separate layers. *Liquid solutes and solvents that are not soluble in each other are* **immiscible.** Toluene and water, shown in Figure 13-11, are another example of immiscible substances.

Nonpolar substances, such as fats, oils, and greases, are generally quite soluble in nonpolar liquids, such as carbon tetrachloride, toluene, and gasoline. The only attractions between the nonpolar molecules are relatively weak London forces. The intermolecular forces existing in the solution are therefore very similar to those in pure substances. Thus, the molecules can mix freely with one another.

Liquids that dissolve freely in one another in any proportion are said to be completely **miscible.** Benzene and carbon tetrachloride are completely miscible. The nonpolar molecules of these substances exert no strong forces of attraction or repulsion, and the molecules mix freely. Ethanol and water, shown in Figure 13-12, also mix freely, but for a different reason. The $-OH$ group on an ethanol molecule is somewhat polar. This group can form hydrogen bonds with water as well as with other ethanol molecules. The intermolecular forces in the mixture are so similar to those in the pure liquids that the liquids are mutually soluble in all proportions.

$$H-\overset{\displaystyle H}{\underset{\displaystyle H}{C}}-\overset{\displaystyle H}{\underset{\displaystyle H}{C}}-OH$$

Gasoline contains mainly nonpolar hydrocarbons and is also an excellent solvent for fats, oils, and greases. The major intermolecular forces acting between the nonpolar molecules are relatively weak London forces.

Ethanol is intermediate in polarity between water and carbon tetrachloride. It is not as good a solvent for polar or ionic substances as water is. Sodium chloride is only slightly soluble in ethanol. On the other hand, ethanol is a better solvent than water is for less-polar substances because the molecule has a nonpolar region.

FIGURE 13-12 (a) Water and ethanol are miscible. The components of this system exist in a single phase with a uniform arrangement. (b) Hydrogen bonding between the solute and solvent enhances the solubility of ethanol in water.

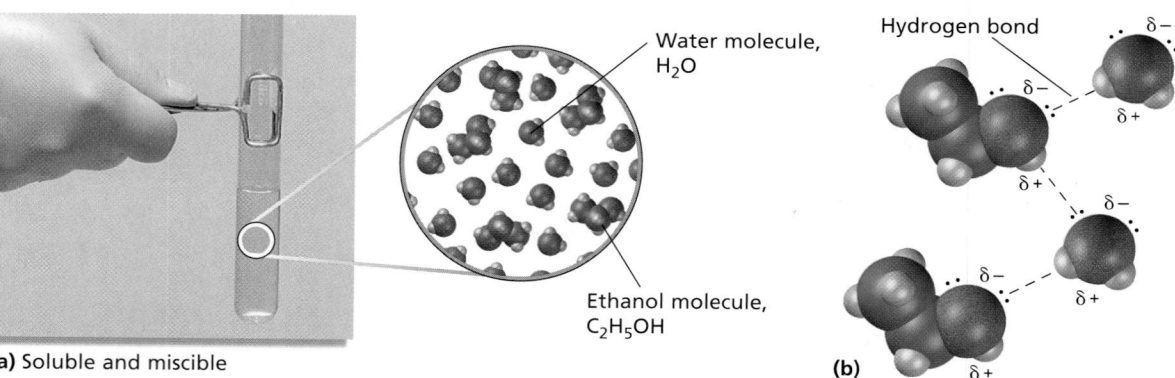

(a) Soluble and miscible

Water molecule, H_2O

Ethanol molecule, C_2H_5OH

Hydrogen bond

$\delta-$ $\delta+$ $\delta-$ $\delta+$

(b)

Effects of Pressure on Solubility

Changes in pressure have very little effect on the solubilities of liquids or solids in liquid solvents. However, increases in pressure increase gas solubilities in liquids.

When a gas is in contact with the surface of a liquid, gas molecules can enter the liquid. As the amount of dissolved gas increases, some molecules begin to escape and reenter the gas phase. An equilibrium is eventually established between the rates at which gas molecules enter and leave the liquid phase. As long as this equilibrium is undisturbed, the solubility of the gas in the liquid is unchanged at a given pressure.

$$gas + solvent \rightleftharpoons solution$$

Increasing the pressure of the solute gas above the solution puts stress on the equilibrium. Molecules collide with the liquid surface more often. The increase in pressure is partially offset by an increase in the rate of gas molecules entering the solution. In turn, the increase in the amount of dissolved gas causes an increase in the rate at which molecules escape from the liquid surface and become vapor. Eventually, equilibrium is restored at a higher gas solubility. As expected from Le Châtelier's principle, an increase in gas pressure causes the equilibrium to shift so that fewer molecules are in the gas phase.

Henry's Law

The solubility of a gas in a liquid is directly proportional to the partial pressure of that gas on the surface of the liquid. This is a statement of **Henry's law,** named after the English chemist William Henry. Henry's law applies to gas-liquid solutions at constant temperature.

Recall that when a mixture of ideal gases is confined in a constant volume at a constant temperature, each gas exerts the same pressure it would exert if it occupied the space alone. Assuming that the gases do not react in any way, each gas dissolves to the extent it would dissolve if no other gases were present.

In carbonated beverages, the solubility of CO_2 is increased by increasing the pressure. At the bottling plant, carbon dioxide gas is forced into the solution of flavored water at a pressure of 5–10 atm. The gas-in-liquid solution is then sealed in bottles or cans. When the cap is removed, the pressure is reduced to 1 atm, and some of the carbon dioxide escapes as gas bubbles. *The rapid escape of a gas from a liquid in which it is dissolved is known as* **effervescence** *and is shown in Figure 13-13.*

FIGURE 13-13 (a) There are no gas bubbles in the unopened bottle of soda because the pressure of CO_2 applied during bottling keeps the carbon dioxide gas dissolved in the liquid. (b) When the cap on the bottle is removed, the pressure of CO_2 on the liquid is reduced, and CO_2 can escape from the liquid. The soda effervesces when the bottle is opened and the pressure is reduced.

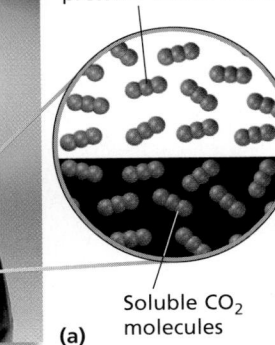

CO_2 under high pressure above solvent

Soluble CO_2 molecules

(a)

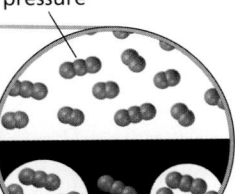

Air at atmospheric pressure

Soluble CO_2 molecules

CO_2 gas bubble

(b)

Application

When scuba divers remain underwater at high pressures for a long period of time, more nitrogen dissolves in their blood, as described by Henry's law. This can lead to a state called nitrogen narcosis, which causes sleepiness and poor judgment that can lead to serious accidents and death.

Divers use oxygen in pressurized tanks to increase their oxygen absorption. At high partial pressures, the oxygen concentration can actually become toxic.

To prevent nitrogen narcosis and oxygen toxicity, divers use a mixture of helium with less than 20% oxygen. Henry's law also provides an explanation for "the bends." After being underwater for a long time, a diver will have more gases dissolved in the blood. The diver must pause during the ascent to allow the dissolved gas to come out of solution slowly and to be exhaled. If the ascent is too fast, the gas can come out of solution while flowing through blood vessels and block essential blood vessels, causing extreme pain, paralysis, or even death.

Visual Strategy

FIGURE 13-13 Have students squeeze an unopened 2 L bottle of soda the next time they have a chance. They will find that the plastic bottle seems firm. This is due to the pressure of the liquid-gas system pushing out on the bottle. When opened, the bottle seems "softer" due to the drop in pressure. The decreased pressure also allows some of the dissolved gas to come out of solution.

FIGURES 13-14 and 13-15 Have students interpret the data in both graphs. SO_2 is more soluble at 30°C. Ask students how the solubility of different substances is affected by an increase in temperature. Have them identify the saturation point on each graph for any given temperature.

Application

Sodium nitrite and sodium nitrate are used as preservatives in meat to prevent bacterial growth. However, large doses can be unhealthy. Have students explain why meat that is boiled contains fewer nitrates and nitrites.

✔**Teaching Tip**

Hot sodas tend to "fizz" more than cold ones. Have students explain this tendency in terms of solubility and temperature. (Gases are less soluble in liquid at high temperature, so they escape more readily when the pressure is released.)

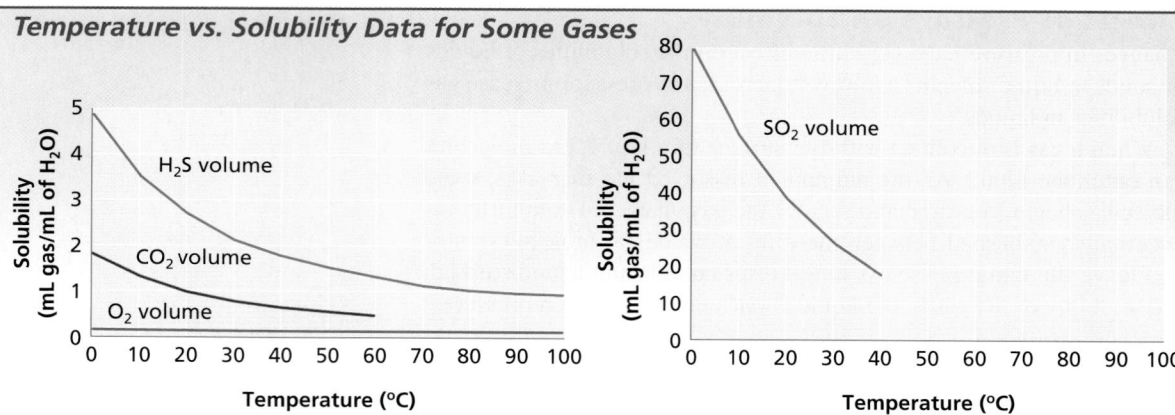

Temperature vs. Solubility Data for Some Gases

FIGURE 13-14 The solubility of gases in water decreases with increasing temperature. Which gas has the greater solubility at 30°C—CO_2 or SO_2?

Effects of Temperature on Solubility

First let's consider gas solubility. Increasing the temperature usually decreases gas solubility. As the temperature increases, the average kinetic energy of the molecules in solution increases. A greater number of solute molecules are able to escape from the attraction of solvent molecules and return to the gas phase. At higher temperatures, therefore, equilibrium is reached with fewer gas molecules in solution and gases are generally less soluble, as shown in Figure 13-14.

The effect of temperature on the solubility of solids in liquids is more difficult to predict. Often, increasing the temperature increases the solubility of solids. However, an equivalent temperature increase can

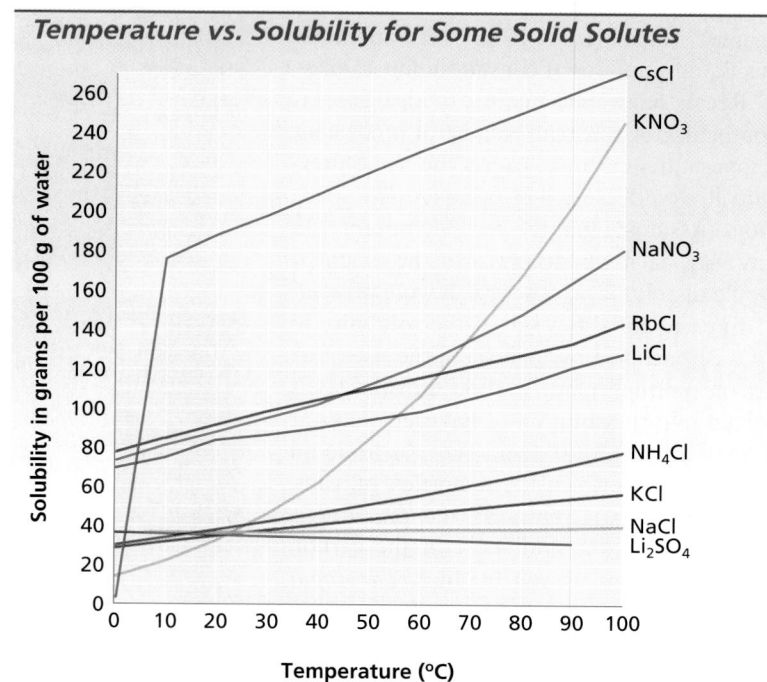

Temperature vs. Solubility for Some Solid Solutes

FIGURE 13-15 Solubility curves for various solid solutes generally show increasing solubility with increases in temperature. From the graph, you can see that the solubility of $NaNO_3$ is affected more by temperature than is NaCl.

result in a large increase in solubility in one case and only a slight increase in another.

In Table 13-4 and Figure 13-15, compare the effect of temperature on the solubilities of potassium nitrate, KNO_3, and sodium chloride, $NaCl$. About 14 g of potassium nitrate will dissolve in 100. g of water at 0.°C. The solubility of potassium nitrate increases by more than 150 g KNO_3 per 100. g H_2O when the temperature is raised to 80.°C. Under similar circumstances, the solubility of sodium chloride increases by only about 2 g $NaCl$ per 100. g H_2O. In some cases, solubility of a solid *decreases* with an increase in temperature. For example, between 0.°C and 60.°C the solubility of cerium sulfate, $Ce_2(SO_4)_3$, decreases by about 17 g.

Heats of Solution

The formation of a solution is accompanied by an energy change. If you dissolve some potassium iodide, KI, in water, you will find that the outside of the container feels cold to the touch. But if you dissolve some lithium chloride, LiCl, in the same way, the outside of the container feels hot. The formation of a solid-liquid solution can apparently either absorb heat (KI in water) or release heat (LiCl in water).

During the formation of a solution, solvent and solute particles experience changes in the forces attracting them to other particles. Before dissolving begins, solvent molecules are held together by intermolecular forces (solvent-solvent attraction). In the solute, molecules are held together by intermolecular forces (solute-solute attraction). Energy is required to separate solute molecules and solvent molecules from their neighbors. *A solute particle that is surrounded by solvent molecules,* as shown by the model in Figure 13-9, *is said to be* **solvated.**

Solution formation can be pictured as the result of the three interactions summarized in Figure 13-16.

FIGURE 13-16 The graph shows the changes in the heat content that occur during the formation of a solution. How would the graph differ for a system with an endothermic heat of solution?

SECTION 13-2

Application
Hot packs and cold packs depend on exothermic and endothermic heats of solution, respectively. Bring in a cold pack to demonstrate.

✔ Teaching Tip
The heat of solution for ionic compounds can be found by subtracting the heat of hydration from the lattice energy. The lattice energy represents the energy required to break the solute-solute attraction. The heat of hydration represents both the solvent-solvent attraction being broken and the solvent-solute attraction being formed. In Chapter 17, students will learn how to use Hess's law to prove this.

📖 Reading Skill-Builder
PREDICTION GUIDES Review the list of opinions developed at the beginning of this section. Ask students whether their opinions have changed or are the same. Have students cite passages in the text that account for the change or reinforcement of their opinions.

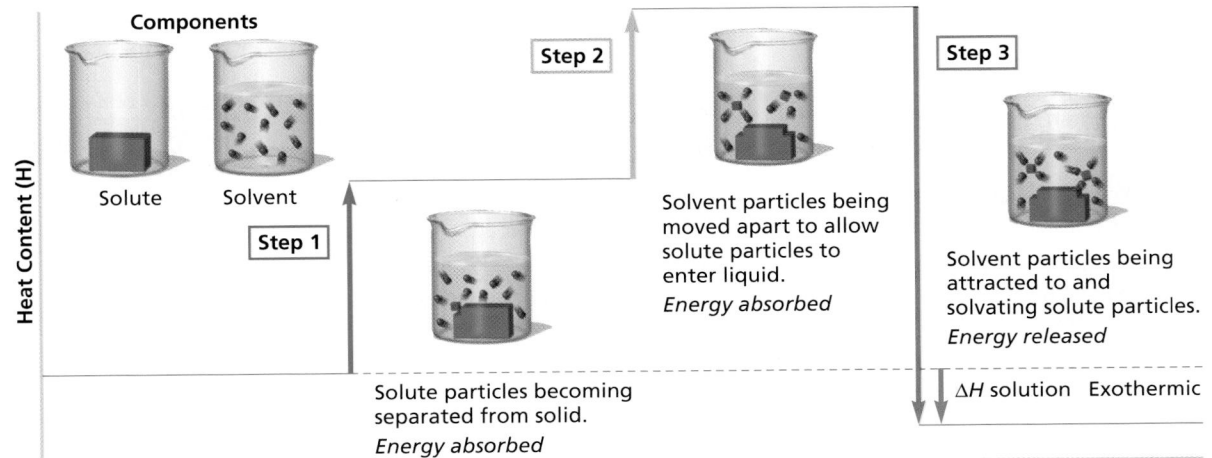

Components

Solute   Solvent

Step 1

Step 2

Solvent particles being moved apart to allow solute particles to enter liquid.
Energy absorbed

Step 3

Solvent particles being attracted to and solvating solute particles.
Energy released

Heat Content (H)

Solute particles becoming separated from solid.
Energy absorbed

ΔH solution   Exothermic

Table 13-5 Ask students whether dissolving $AgNO_3$ in water would increase or decrease the temperature of the system *(decrease; dissolving $AgNO_3$ is endothermic).*

Ask students which substance listed in the table would have the strongest solute bonds *($KClO_3$).* Ask students which substance would have the weakest solute bonds *(HI).*

SECTION REVIEW

1. The particles in hot tea move faster than in iced tea. Therefore, there are more collisions between the tea and sugar molecules at the surface of the sugar grains, and sugar molecules leave the surface of the grains faster in hot tea than in cold tea.

2. a. Continually add sugar to hot water until undissolved grains remain at the bottom of the container. This is a saturated solution of sugar and water. **b.** Filter the hot solution to remove any seed crystals. Set the saturated solution aside until it cools to room temperature. Once it cools, it will be supersaturated.

3. Ethanol and water are each polar molecules. The negatively charged region of the ethanol molecules is attracted to the positively charged region of the water molecules, and vice versa. Carbon tetrachloride is nonpolar and will not form a strong enough attraction to water molecules to dissolve.

4. Intermolecular attraction brings the solvent and solute molecules together. Energy is released in this process.

5. The warm bottle will effervesce more because less gas will be dissolved in the warmer bottle of soda.

TABLE 13-5 *Heats of Solution (kJ/mol solute at 25°C)*

Substance	Heat of solution	Substance	Heat of solution
$AgNO_3(s)$	+22.59	$KOH(s)$	−57.61
$CH_3COOH(l)$	−1.51	$LiCl(s)$	−37.03
$HCl(g)$	−74.84	$MgSO_4(s)$	+15.9
$HI(g)$	−81.67	$NaCl(s)$	+3.88
$KCl(s)$	+17.22	$NaNO_3(s)$	+20.50
$KClO_3(s)$	+41.38	$NaOH(s)$	−44.51
$KI(s)$	+20.33	$NH_3(g)$	−30.50
$KNO_3(s)$	+34.89	$NH_4Cl(s)$	+14.78
		$NH_4NO_3(s)$	+25.69

The net amount of heat energy absorbed or released when a specific amount of solute dissolves in a solvent is the **heat of solution.** From the model in Figure 13-16, you can see that the heat of solution is negative (heat is released) when the sum of attractions from Steps 1 and 2 is less than Step 3. The heat of solution is positive (heat is absorbed) when the sum of attractions from Steps 1 and 2 is greater than Step 3.

You know that heating decreases the solubility of a gas, so dissolution of gases is exothermic. How do the values for the heats of solution in Table 13-5 support this idea of exothermic solution processes for gaseous solutes?

In the gaseous state, molecules are so far apart that there are virtually no intermolecular forces of attraction between them. Therefore, the solute-solute interaction has little effect on the heat of a solution of a gas. Energy is released when a gas dissolves in a liquid because attraction between solute gas and solvent molecules outweighs the energy needed to separate solvent molecules.

SECTION REVIEW

1. Why would you expect a packet of sugar to dissolve faster in hot tea than in iced tea?

2. a. Explain how you would prepare a saturated solution of sugar in water. b. How would you then make it a supersaturated solution?

3. Explain why ethanol will dissolve in water and carbon tetrachloride will not.

4. When a solute molecule is solvated, is heat released or absorbed?

5. If a warm bottle of soda and a cold bottle of soda are opened, which will effervesce more and why?

RESEARCH NOTES

Artificial Blood

Background

This article is an example of how molecules are researched or developed with specific properties to fulfill specific needs.

Point out that Dr. Keipert uses a surfactant as a "bridge molecule" to enable the oily perfluorocarbons to "mix" with the polar saltwater solution.

Discussion

Have students find out more about the different functions performed by blood. How many of these functions are performed by Dr. Keipert's new blood?

A patient lies bleeding on a stretcher. The doctor leans over to check the patient's wounds and barks an order to a nearby nurse: "Get him a unit of artificial blood, stat!" According to Dr. Peter Keipert, Program Director of Oxygen Carriers Development at Alliance Pharmaceutical Corp., this scenario may soon be commonplace thanks to a synthetic solution that can perform one of the main functions of human blood—transporting oxygen.

The hemoglobin inside red blood cells collects oxygen in our lungs, transports the oxygen to all the tissues of the body, and then takes carbon dioxide back to the lungs. Dr. Keipert's blood substitute accomplishes the same task, but it uses oily chemicals called perfluorocarbons instead of hemoglobin to transport the oxygen. The perfluorocarbons are carried in a water-based saline solution, but because oil and water do not mix, a bonding chemical called a surfactant is added to hold the mixture together. The perfluorocarbons are sheared into tiny

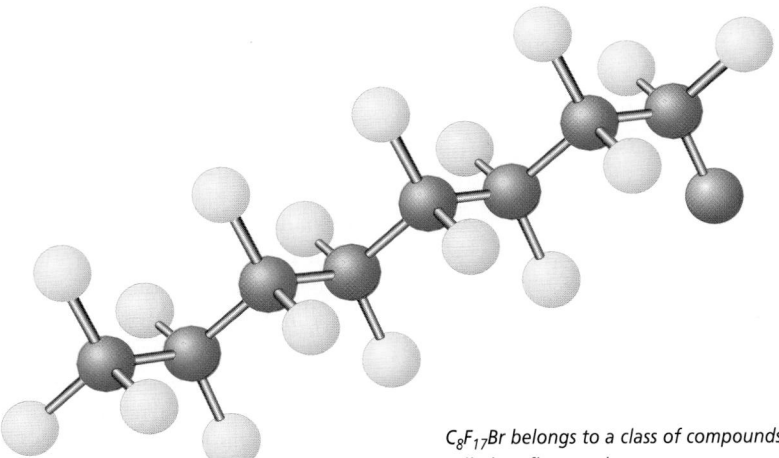

$C_8F_{17}Br$ belongs to a class of compounds called perfluorocarbons.

droplets and then coated with the bonding molecules. One end of these molecules attaches to the perfluorocarbon, and the other end attaches to the water, creating a milky solution. The process is similar to shaking a bottle of salad dressing to form a creamy mixture of the oily portion and the liquid portion. The blood-substitute solution, called Oxygent™, is administered to a patient in the same way regular blood is. The perfluorocarbons are eventually exhaled through the lungs.

Dr. Keipert is quick to point out that Oxygent is not a true artificial blood. The solution only functions to carry gases to and from tissues; it cannot clot or perform any of the immune-system functions that blood does. Still, the substitute has several advantages

over real blood. Oxygent has a shelf life of more than a year. Oxygent also eliminates many of the risks associated with blood transfusions. Because the substitute can dissolve larger amounts of oxygen than real blood can, smaller amounts of the solution are needed.

Oxygent is currently being tested in surgical patients.

"Once this product is approved and has been demonstrated to be safe and effective in elective surgery, I think you will see its use spread into the emergency critical-care arena," says Dr. Keipert. "A patient who has lost a lot of blood and who is currently being resuscitated with normal fluids like saline solutions would be given Oxygent as an additional oxygen-delivery agent in the emergency room."

internet connect

SC*LINKS*
NSTA

TOPIC: Perfluorocarbons
GO TO: www.scilinks.org
***sci*LINKS CODE:** HC2134

Lesson Starter

Fill four different test tubes with varying concentrations of potassium permanganate. Students can see how the color of the solution varies with the concentration. Tell students that permanganate ions in solution absorb light in the visible range. Light reflected in the purple and red range makes the solution appear purple. The greater the concentration, the more purple the solution appears. Tell students that color alone is a qualitative measure of concentration. Light absorbency by colored solutions can be used to make a quantitative determination of concentration.

Experiment 13-2 of the text explores colorimetry. Use this discussion to introduce molarity, another quantitative measure of concentration.

Common Misconception

Most students have a vague notion that the terms *weak acid* and *dilute acid* mean the same thing. In fact, a *dilute* acid means any acid with a low concentration. A *weak* acid has nothing to do with concentration, but describes the nature of the acid molecule and its ability to donate protons. Therefore, it is possible to have a *dilute* solution of *strong* acid or a *concentrated* solution of *weak* acid.

Problem-Solving Practice HOLT ChemFile

Chapters 14 and 15 of the Mini-Guide to Problem Solving (also found on the One-Stop Planner CD-ROM) include more worked-out samples and additional practice problems involving solutions and dilutions.

OBJECTIVES

- Given the mass of solute and volume of solvent, calculate the concentration of a solution.

- Given the concentration of a solution, determine the amount of solute in a given amount of solution.

- Given the concentration of a solution, determine the amount of solution that contains a given amount of solute.

Concentration of Solutions

*T*he **concentration** *of a solution is a measure of the amount of solute in a given amount of solvent or solution.* Some medications are solutions of drugs—a one-teaspoon dose at the correct concentration might cure the patient, while the same dose in the wrong concentration might kill the patient.

In this section, we introduce two different ways of expressing the concentrations of solutions: molarity and molality.

Sometimes solutions are referred to as "dilute" or "concentrated," but these are not very definite terms. "Dilute" just means that there is a relatively small amount of solute in a solvent. "Concentrated," on the other hand, means that there is a relatively large amount of solute in a solvent. Note that these terms are unrelated to the degree to which a solution is saturated. A saturated solution of a substance that is not very soluble might be very dilute.

Molarity

Molarity *is the number of moles of solute in one liter of solution.* To find the molarity of a solution, you must know the molar mass of the solute. For example, a "one-molar" solution of sodium hydroxide, NaOH, contains one mole of NaOH in every liter of solution. The symbol for molarity is M, and the concentration of a one-molar solution of sodium hydroxide is written as 1 M NaOH.

One mole of NaOH has a mass of 40.0 g. If this quantity of NaOH is dissolved in enough water to make exactly 1.00 L of solution, the solution is a 1 M solution. If 20.0 g of NaOH, which is 0.500 mol, is dissolved in enough water to make 1.00 L of solution, a 0.500 M NaOH solution is produced. This relationship between molarity, moles, and volume may be expressed in the following ways.

$$\text{molarity (M)} = \frac{\text{amount of solute (mol)}}{\text{volume of solution (L)}}$$

$$= \frac{0.500 \text{ mol NaOH}}{1.00 \text{ L}}$$

$$= 0.500 \text{ M NaOH}$$

If twice the molar mass of NaOH, 80.0 g, is dissolved in enough water to make 1 L of solution, a 2 M solution is produced. The molarity of any solution can be calculated by dividing the number of moles of solute by the number of liters of solution.

Note that a 1 M solution is *not* made by adding 1 mol of solute to 1 L of *solvent*. In such a case, the final total volume of the solution would not be 1 L. Instead, 1 mol of solute is first dissolved in less than 1 L of solvent. Then the resulting solution is carefully diluted with more solvent to bring the *total volume* to 1 L, as shown in Figure 13-17. The following sample problem will show you how molarity is often used.

FIGURE 13-17 The preparation of a 0.5000 M solution of $CuSO_4 \cdot 5H_2O$ starts with calculating the mass of solute needed.

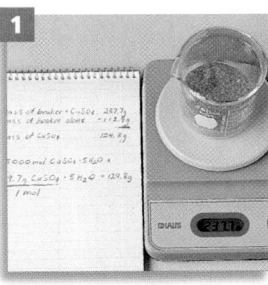

Start by calculating the mass of $CuSO_4 \cdot 5H_2O$ needed. Making a liter of this solution requires 0.5000 mol of solute. Convert the moles to mass by multiplying by the molar mass of $CuSO_4 \cdot 5H_2O$. This mass is calculated to be 124.8 g.

Add some solvent to the solute to dissolve it, then pour it into a 1.0 L volumetric flask.

Rinse the weighing beaker with more solvent to remove all the solute, and pour the rinse into the flask. Add water until the volume of the solution nears the neck of the flask.

Put the stopper in the flask, and swirl the solution thoroughly.

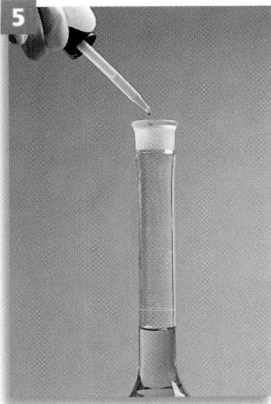

Carefully fill the flask to the 1.0 L mark with water.

Restopper the flask and invert it at least 10 times to ensure complete mixing.

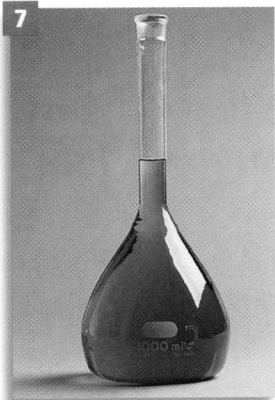

The resulting solution has 0.5000 mol of solute dissolved in 1.000 L of solution, which is a 0.5000 M concentration.

13-1 a. What is the molarity of a 2.0 L solution that is made from 14.6 g of NaCl?

b. What is the molarity of a HCl solution that contains 10.0 g of HCl in 250 mL of solution?

c. How many moles of NaCl are in 1.25 L of 0.330 M NaCl?

d. How many moles of HCl exist in 500. mL of 0.50 M solution of HCl?

Ans. **a.** 0.12 M
b. 1.1 M
c. 0.413 mol
d. 0.25 mol

SAMPLE PROBLEM 13-1

You have 3.50 L of solution that contains 90.0 g of sodium chloride, NaCl. What is the molarity of that solution?

SOLUTION

1 *ANALYZE*   **Given:** solute mass = 90.0 g NaCl
solution volume = 3.50 L
Unknown: molarity of NaCl solution

2 *PLAN*   Molarity is the number of moles of solute per liter of solution. The solute is described in the problem by mass, not the amount in moles. You need one conversion (grams to moles of solute) using the inverted molar mass of NaCl to arrive at your answer.

$$\text{grams of solute} \longrightarrow \text{number of moles of solute} \longrightarrow \text{molarity}$$

$$\text{g NaCl} \times \frac{1 \text{ mol NaCl}}{\text{g NaCl}} = \text{mol NaCl}$$

$$\frac{\text{amount of solute (mol)}}{V \text{ solution (L)}} = \text{molarity of solution (M)}$$

3 *COMPUTE*   You will need the molar mass of NaCl.
NaCl = 58.44 g/mol

$$90.0 \text{ g NaCl} \times \frac{1 \text{ mol NaCl}}{58.44 \text{ g NaCl}} = 1.54 \text{ mol NaCl}$$

$$\frac{1.54 \text{ mol NaCl}}{3.50 \text{ L of solution}} = 0.440 \text{ M NaCl}$$

4 *EVALUATE*   Because each factor involved is limited to three significant digits, the answer should have three significant digits, which it does. The units cancel correctly to give the desired moles of solute per liter of solution, which is molarity.

SAMPLE PROBLEM 13-2

You have 0.8 L of a 0.5 M HCl solution. How many moles of HCl does this solution contain?

SOLUTION

1 *ANALYZE*   **Given:** volume of solution = 0.8 L
concentration of solution = 0.5 M HCl
Unknown: moles of HCl in a given volume

2 *PLAN*   The molarity indicates the moles of solute that are in one liter of solution. Given the volume of the solution, the number of moles of solute can then be found.

$$\text{concentration (mol of HCl/L of solution)} \times \text{volume (L of solution)} = \text{mol of HCl}$$

3 COMPUTE

$$\frac{0.5 \text{ mol HCl}}{1.0 \text{ L of solution}} \times 0.8 \text{ L of solution} = 0.4 \text{ mol HCl}$$

4 EVALUATE The answer is correctly given to one significant digit. The units cancel correctly to give the desired unit, mol. There should be less than 0.5 mol HCl, because less than 1 L of solution was used.

SAMPLE PROBLEM 13-3

To produce 40.0 g of silver chromate, you will need at least 23.4 g of potassium chromate in solution as a reactant. All you have on hand in the stock room is 5 L of a 6.0 M K$_2$CrO$_4$ solution. What volume of the solution is needed to give you the 23.4 g K$_2$CrO$_4$ needed for the reaction?

SOLUTION

1 ANALYZE **Given:** volume of solution = 5 L
concentration of solution = 6.0 M K$_2$CrO$_4$
mass of solute = 23.4 g K$_2$CrO$_4$
mass of product = 40.0 g Ag$_2$CrO$_4$
Unknown: volume of K$_2$CrO$_4$ solution in L

2 PLAN The molarity indicates the moles of solute that are in 1 L of solution. Given the mass of solute needed, the amount in moles of solute can then be found. Use the molarity and the amount in moles of K$_2$CrO$_4$ to determine the volume of K$_2$CrO$_4$ that will provide 23.4 g.

grams of solute $\longrightarrow$ moles solute
moles solute and molarity $\longrightarrow$ liters of solution needed

3 COMPUTE To get the moles of solute, you'll need to calculate the molar mass of K$_2$CrO$_4$.

$$1 \text{ mol K}_2\text{CrO}_4 = 194.2 \text{ g K}_2\text{CrO}_4$$

$$23.4 \text{ g K}_2\text{CrO}_4 = \frac{1.0 \text{ mol K}_2\text{CrO}_4}{194.2 \text{ g K}_2\text{CrO}_4} = 0.120 \text{ mol K}_2\text{CrO}_4$$

$$6.0 \text{ M K}_2\text{CrO}_4 = \frac{0.120 \text{ mol K}_2\text{CrO}_4}{x \text{ L K}_2\text{CrO}_4 \text{ soln}}$$

$$x = 0.020 \text{ L K}_2\text{CrO}_4 \text{ soln}$$

4 EVALUATE The answer is correctly given to two significant digits. The units cancel correctly to give the desired unit, liters of solution.

ADDITIONAL SAMPLE PROBLEM

13-2 a. What is the molarity of a solution composed of 6.25 g of HCl in 0.300 L of solution?

b. How many moles of KI are present in 0.250 L of a 2.30 M solution?

c. What volume of a 0.500 M solution of HBr is needed for a reaction that requires 32.5 g of HBr?

Ans. **a.** 0.571 M
b. 0.575 mol
c. 0.803 L

PRACTICE

1. What is the molarity of a solution composed of 5.85 g of potassium iodide, KI, dissolved in enough water to make 0.125 L of solution?
Answer
0.282 M KI

2. How many moles of H$_2$SO$_4$ are present in 0.500 L of a 0.150 M H$_2$SO$_4$ solution?
Answer
0.0750 mol

3. What volume of 3.00 M NaCl is needed for a reaction that requires 146.3 g of NaCl?
Answer
0.834 L

Molality

Molality *is the concentration of a solution expressed in moles of solute per kilogram of solvent.* A solution that contains 1 mol of solute, sodium hydroxide, NaOH, for example, dissolved in exactly 1 kg of solvent is a "one-molal" solution. The symbol for molality is *m,* and the concentration of this solution is written as 1 *m* NaOH.

One mole of NaOH has a molar mass of 40.0 g, so 40.0 g of NaOH dissolved in 1 kg of water results in a one-molal NaOH solution. If 20.0 g of NaOH, which is 0.500 mol of NaOH, is dissolved in exactly 1 kg of water, the concentration of the solution is 0.500 *m* NaOH.

$$\text{molality} = \frac{\text{moles solute}}{\text{mass of solvent (kg)}}$$

$$\frac{0.500 \text{ mol NaOH}}{1 \text{ kg } H_2O} = 0.500 \ m \text{ NaOH}$$

If 80.0 g of sodium hydroxide, which is 2 mol, is dissolved in 1 kg of water, a 2.00 *m* solution of NaOH is produced. The molality of any solution can be found by dividing the number of moles of solute by the mass in kilograms of the solvent in which it is dissolved. Note that if the amount of solvent is expressed in grams, the mass of solvent must be converted to kilograms by multiplying by the following conversion factor.

$$1 \text{ kg}/1000 \text{ g}$$

Figure 13-18 shows how a 0.5000 *m* solution of $CuSO_4 \cdot 5H_2O$ is prepared, in contrast with the 0.5000 M solution in Figure 13-17.

FIGURE 13-18 The preparation of a 0.5000 *m* solution of $CuSO_4 \cdot 5H_2O$ also starts with the calculation of the mass of solute needed.

Calculate the mass of $CuSO_4 \cdot 5H_2O$ needed. To make this solution, each kilogram of solvent (1000 g) will require 0.5000 mol of $CuSO_4 \cdot 5H_2O$. This mass is calculated to be 124.8 g.

Add exactly 1 kg of solvent to the solute in the beaker. Because the solvent is water, 1 kg will equal 1000 mL.

Mix thoroughly.

The resulting solution has 0.5000 mol of solute dissolved in 1 kg of solvent.

Concentrations are expressed as molalities when studying properties of solutions related to vapor pressure and temperature changes. Molality is used because it does not change with changes in temperature. Below is a comparison of the equations for molarity and molality.

$$\text{molarity, M} = \frac{\text{amount of A (mol)}}{\text{volume of solution (L)}}$$

$$\text{molality, } m = \frac{\text{amount of A (mol)}}{\text{mass of solvent (kg)}}$$

SAMPLE PROBLEM 13-4

A solution was prepared by dissolving 17.1 g of sucrose (table sugar, $C_{12}H_{22}O_{11}$) in 125 g of water. Find the molal concentration of this solution.

SOLUTION

1 ANALYZE

Given: solute mass = 17.1 g $C_{12}H_{22}O_{11}$
solvent mass = 125 g H_2O
Unknown: molal concentration

2 PLAN

To find molality, you need moles of solute and kilograms of solvent. The given grams of sucrose must be converted to moles. The mass in grams of solvent must be converted to kilograms.

$$\text{mol } C_{12}H_{22}O_{11} = \frac{\text{g } C_{12}H_{22}O_{11}}{\text{molar mass } C_{12}H_{22}O_{11}}$$

$$\text{kg } H_2O = \text{g } H_2O \times \frac{1 \text{ kg}}{1000 \text{ g}}$$

$$\text{molality } C_{12}H_{22}O_{11} = \frac{\text{mol } C_{12}H_{22}O_{11}}{\text{kg } H_2O}$$

3 COMPUTE

Use the periodic table to compute the molar mass of $C_{12}H_{22}O_{11}$.
$C_{12}H_{22}O_{11}$ = 342.34 g/mol

$$17.1 \text{ g } C_{12}H_{22}O_{11} \times \frac{1 \text{ mol } C_{12}H_{22}O_{11}}{342.34 \text{ g } C_{12}H_{22}O_{11}} = 0.0500 \text{ mol } C_{12}H_{22}O_{11}$$

$$\frac{125 \text{ g } H_2O}{1000 \text{ g/kg}} = 0.125 \text{ kg } H_2O$$

$$\frac{0.0500 \text{ mol } C_{12}H_{22}O_{11}}{0.125 \text{ kg } H_2O} = 0.400 \text{ } m \text{ } C_{12}H_{22}O_{11}$$

4 EVALUATE

The answer is correctly given to three significant digits. The unit mol solute/kg solvent is correct for molality.

CHAPTER ⟷ CONNECTION

The application of molality to colligative properties will be covered in Chapter 14.

Alternative Assessment

Have students construct a concept map that includes the following terms: miscible, immiscible, soluble, insoluble, saturated, unsaturated, concentration, molarity, molality, dilute, concentrated.

Reading Skill-Builder

SEQUENCING/PATTERN PUZZLES On a sheet of paper, have student pairs list the steps for solving molarity and molality problems, one step per line without numbering the steps. Encourage students to write the steps in their own words, dividing longer steps into two or three shorter steps if necessary.

When students have finished, have them cut their sheets of paper into strips with only one step per strip. Direct students to shuffle the strips so they are out of order. Have students trade strips with their partners and place the strips in the proper sequence. Students can confirm the order of the process by checking with the text or their class notes.

13-3 a. What is the molality of a solution composed of 13.0 g NaCl dissolved in 500. g of water?

b. How many grams of NaCl are needed to prepare a 1.0 *m* solution using 250 g of solute?

c. What volume of 0.245 *m* NaCl contains 1.0 mol of this salt?

Ans. **a.** 0.445 *m*
b. 15 g
c. 4.1 L

SECTION REVIEW

1. molarity

2. The solution is 0.01 M.

SAMPLE PROBLEM 13-5

A solution of iodine, I_2, in carbon tetrachloride, CCl_4, is used when iodine is needed for certain chemical tests. How much iodine must be added to prepare a 0.480 *m* solution of iodine in CCl_4 if 100.0 g of CCl_4 is used?

SOLUTION

1 ANALYZE   **Given:** molality of solution = 0.480 *m* I_2
mass of solvent = 100.0 g CCl_4
Unknown: mass of solute

2 PLAN   Your first step should be to convert the grams of solvent to kilograms. The molality gives you the moles of solute, which can be converted to the grams of solute using the molar mass of I_2.

3 COMPUTE   Use the periodic table to compute the molar mass of I_2.
I_2 = 253.8 g/mol

$$100.0 \text{ g } CCl_4 \times \frac{1 \text{ kg}}{1000 \text{ g } CCl_4} = 0.100 \text{ kg } CCl_4$$

$$0.480 \ m = \frac{x \text{ mol } I_2}{0.1 \text{ kg } H_2O} = 0.0480 \text{ mol } I_2$$

$$0.0480 \text{ mol } I_2 \times \frac{253.8 \text{ g } I_2}{\text{mol } I_2} = 12.2 \text{ g } I_2$$

4 EVALUATE   The answer has three significant digits and the units for mass of I_2.

PRACTICE

1. What is the molality of a solution composed of 255 g of acetone, $(CH_3)_2CO$, dissolved in 200. g of water?
Answer
22 *m* acetone

2. What quantity, in grams, of methanol, CH_3OH, is required to prepare a 0.244 *m* solution in 400. g of water?
Answer
3.12 g CH_3OH

3. How many grams of $AgNO_3$ are needed to prepare a 0.125 *m* solution in 250. mL of water?
Answer
5.31 g $AgNO_3$

4. What is the molality of a solution containing 18.2 g HCl and 250. g of water?
Answer
1.99 *m*

SECTION REVIEW

1. What quantity represents the ratio of the number of moles of solute for a given volume of solution?

2. Five grams of sugar, $C_{12}H_{22}O_{11}$, are dissolved in water to make 1 L of solution. What is the concentration of this solution expressed as a molarity?

CHAPTER SUMMARY

13-1
- Solutions are homogeneous mixtures.
- Mixtures are classified as solutions, suspensions, or colloids, depending on the size of the solute particles in the mixture.
- The dissolved substance is the solute. Solutions that have water as a solvent are aqueous solutions.
- Solutions can consist of solutes and solvents that are solids, liquids, or gases.

- Suspensions settle out upon standing. Colloids do not settle out, and they scatter light that is shined through them.
- Most ionic solutes and some molecular solutes form aqueous solutions that conduct an electric current. These solutes are called electrolytes.
- Nonelectrolytes are solutes that dissolve in water to form solutions that do not conduct.

Vocabulary

colloid (397)	nonelectrolyte (400)	solute (396)	solvent (396)
electrolyte (399)	soluble (395)	solution (396)	suspension (397)

13-2
- A solute dissolves at a rate that depends on the surface area of the solute, how vigorously the solution is mixed, and the temperature of the solvent.
- The solubility of a substance indicates how much of that substance will dissolve in a specified amount of solvent under certain conditions.
- The solubility of a substance depends on the temperature.

- The solubility of gases in liquids increases with increases in pressure.
- The solubility of gases in liquids decreases with increases in temperature.
- The overall energy change per mole during solution formation is called the heat of solution.

Vocabulary

effervescence (407)	immiscible (406)	solubility (404)	supersaturated solution (403)
heat of solution (410)	miscible (406)	solvated (409)	
Henry's law (407)	saturated solution (403)	solution equilibrium (402)	unsaturated solution (403)
hydration (405)			

13-3
- Two useful expressions of concentration are molarity and molality.
- The molar concentration of a solution represents the ratio of moles of solute to liters of solution.

- The molal concentration of a solution represents the ratio of moles of solute to kilograms of solvent.

Vocabulary

concentration (412)	molality (416)	molarity (412)

REVIEW ANSWERS

1. **a.** The Tyndall effect is the scattering of light by colloidal particles dispersed in a transparent medium.
   b. The visibility of a headlight beam on a foggy night is an example of this effect.

2. Shine a beam of light through the mixture. If it is a solution, no light scattering will be observed. If it is a colloid, the light will be scattered. A suspension will settle out.

3. **a.** Solution equilibrium is the state in which the opposing processes of the dissolution and crystallization of a solute occur at equal rates.
   b. The factors that determine the equilibrium point are the nature of the solute, the nature of the solvent, and the temperature. In the case of a gaseous solution, pressure is also a factor.

4. **a.** A saturated solution is one that contains the maximum possible amount of dissolved solute at solution equilibrium under the existing conditions.
   b. A residual quantity of undissolved solute remains in contact with a saturated solution.
   c. An unsaturated solution contains less solute than does a saturated solution under the existing conditions.

5. **a.** The solubility of a substance is the amount of that substance that is dissolved at solution equilibrium in a specific amount of solvent at a specified temperature.
   b. Temperature and pressure (for gases) must be specified.

6. a. The rule of thumb for predicting solubility is "like dissolves like."
b. In general, the rule means that polar substances dissolve in polar solvents, and nonpolar substances dissolve in nonpolar solvents.

7. a. The solubility of a gas in a liquid is directly proportional to its pressure above the liquid.
b. This is a statement of Henry's law.
c. If the pressure above the gas increases, the amount of gas that can dissolve will increase.
d. The cold soda will effervesce more than the partially frozen soda. The gas is less soluble in the warmer solvent.

8. a. about 84 g per 100 g solvent
b. about 105 g per 100 g solvent
c. about 36 g per 100 g solvent

9. a. 25°C
b. 40°C
c. 32°C

10. a. $AgNO_3(s) + \xrightarrow{H_2O} AgNO_3(aq)$ + 22.8 kJ/mol solution
b. The dissolution process is endothermic; crystallization is exothermic.
c. The temperature drops as silver nitrate dissolves.
d. At equilibrium, the rates of dissolution and crystallization are equal.
e. The rate of dissolution will initially increase at a faster pace than the rate of crystallization because the dissolution process is endothermic and will serve to reduce the stress placed on the system.
f. The amount will increase if additional solute is available.
g. The rate of crystallization will increase to relieve the stress, and the solubility of the solute will then decrease.

REVIEWING CONCEPTS

1. a. What is the Tyndall effect?
b. Identify one example of this effect. (13-1)

2. Given an unknown mixture consisting of two or more substances, explain one technique that could be used to determine whether that mixture is a true solution, a colloid, or a suspension. (13-1)

3. a. What is solution equilibrium?
b. What factors determine the point at which a given solute-solvent combination reaches equilibrium? (13-2)

4. a. What is a saturated solution?
b. What visible evidence indicates that a solution is saturated?
c. What is an unsaturated solution? (13-2)

5. a. What is meant by the solubility of a substance?
b. What condition(s) must be specified when expressing the solubility of a substance? (13-2)

6. a. What rule of thumb is useful for predicting whether one substance will dissolve in another?
b. Describe what the rule means in terms of various combinations of polar and nonpolar solutes and solvents. (13-2)

7. a. How does pressure affect the solubility of a gas in a liquid?
b. What law is a statement of this relationship? (13-1)
c. If the pressure of a gas above a liquid is increased, what happens to the amount of the gas that will dissolve in the liquid, if all other conditions remain constant?
d. Two bottles of soda are opened. One is a cold bottle and the other is partially frozen. Which system will show more effervescence and why? (13-2)

8. Based on Figure 13-15, determine the solubility of each of the following in grams of solute per 100. g H_2O.
a. $NaNO_3$ at 10°C

b. KNO_3 at 60°C
c. NaCl at 50°C (13-2)

9. Based on Figure 13-15, at what temperature would each of the following solubility levels be observed?
a. 40 g KCl in 100 g H_2O
b. 100 g $NaNO_3$ in 100 g H_2O
c. 50 g KNO_3 in 100 g H_2O (13-2)

10. The heat of solution for $AgNO_3$ is +22.8 kJ/mol.
a. Write the equation that represents the dissolution of $AgNO_3$ in water.
b. Is the dissolution process endothermic or exothermic? Is the crystallization process endothermic or exothermic?
c. As $AgNO_3$ dissolves, what change occurs in the temperature of the solution?
d. When the system is at equilibrium, how do the rates of dissolution and crystallization compare?
e. If the solution is then heated, how will the rates of dissolution and crystallization be affected? Why?
f. How will the increased temperature affect the amount of solute that can be dissolved?
g. If the solution is allowed to reach equilibrium and is then cooled, how will the system be affected? (13-2)

11. Under what circumstances might we prefer to express solution concentrations in terms of
a. molarity?
b. molality? (13-3)

12. What opposing forces are at equilibrium in the sodium chloride system shown in Figure 13-7? (13-2)

PROBLEMS

Solubility

13. Plot a solubility graph for $AgNO_3$ from the following data, with grams of solute (by increments of 50) per 100 grams of H_2O on the vertical axis and with temperature in °C on the horizontal axis.

Grams solute per 100 g H_2O	Temperature (°C)
122	0
216	30
311	40
440	60
585	80
733	100

a. How does the solubility of $AgNO_3$ vary with the temperature of the water?

b. Estimate the solubility of $AgNO_3$ at 35°C, 55°C, and 75°C.

c. At what temperature would the solubility of $AgNO_3$ be 275 g per 100 g of H_2O?

d. If 100 g of $AgNO_3$ were added to 100 g of H_2O at 10°C, would the resulting solution be saturated or unsaturated? What would occur if 325 g of $AgNO_3$ were added to 100 g of H_2O at 35°C?

14. If a saturated solution of KNO_3 in 100. g of H_2O at 60°C is cooled to 20°C, approximately how many grams of the solute will precipitate out of the solution? (Use Table 13-4.)

Molarity

15. a. Suppose you wanted to dissolve 40.0 g NaOH in enough H_2O to make 6.00 L of solution.
(1) What is step 1 in solving the problem?
(2) What is the molar mass of NaOH?
(3) What is the molarity of this solution?

b. What is the molarity of a solution of 14.0 g NH_4Br in enough H_2O to make 150 mL of solution?

16. a. Suppose you wanted to produce 1.00 L of a 3.50 M solution of H_2SO_4.
(1) What is the solute?
(2) What is the solvent?
(3) How many grams of solute are needed to make this solution?

b. How many grams of solute are needed to make 2.50 L of a 1.75 M solution of $Ba(NO_3)_2$?

17. How many moles of NaOH are contained in 65.0 mL of a 2.20 M solution of NaOH in H_2O? (Hint: See Sample Problem 13-2.)

18. A solution is made by dissolving 26.42 g of $(NH_4)_2SO_4$ in enough H_2O to make 50.00 mL of solution.

a. What is the molar mass of $(NH_4)_2SO_4$?
b. What are the products of the solution?
c. What is the molarity of this solution?

19. Suppose you wanted to find out how many milliliters of 1.0 M $AgNO_3$ are needed to provide 168.88 g of pure $AgNO_3$.
a. What is step 1 in solving the problem?
b. What is the molar mass of $AgNO_3$?
c. How many milliliters of solution are needed?

20. a. Balance the equation:
$$H_3PO_4 + Ca(OH)_2 \longrightarrow Ca_3(PO_4)_2 + H_2O$$
b. What mass of each product results if 750 mL of 6.00 M H_3PO_4 reacts according to the equation?

21. How many milliliters of 18.0 M H_2SO_4 are required to react with 250. mL of 2.50 M $Al(OH)_3$ if the products are aluminum sulfate and water?

22. 75.0 g of an $AgNO_3$ solution reacts with enough Cu to produce 0.250 g of Ag by single replacement. What is the molarity of the initial $AgNO_3$ solution if $Cu(NO_3)_2$ is the other product?

Molality

23. a. Suppose you wanted to dissolve 294.3 g H_2SO_4 in 1.000 kg H_2O.
(1) What is the solute?
(2) What is the solvent?
(3) What is the molality of this solution?

b. What is the molality of a solution of 63.0 g HNO_3 in 0.250 kg H_2O?

24. Determine the number of grams of solute needed to make each of the following molal solutions:
a. a 4.50 *m* solution of H_2SO_4 in 1.00 kg H_2O
b. a 1.00 *m* solution of HNO_3 in 2.00 kg H_2O

25. A solution is prepared by dissolving 17.1 g of sucrose, $C_{12}H_{22}O_{11}$, in 275 g of H_2O.
a. What is the molar mass of sucrose?
b. What is the molality of that solution?

26. How many kilograms of H_2O must be added to 75.5 g of $Ca(NO_3)_2$ to form a 0.500 *m* solution?

27. A solution made from ethanol, C_2H_5OH, and water is 1.75 *m*. How many grams of C_2H_5OH are contained per 250. g of water?

11. a. Molality would be used when it is important to know the molar mass of solute in a given volume of solution.
b. Molality is preferred when it is important to know the relative numbers of solute and solvent particles.

12. dissolution and recrystallization

13. Graphs should accurately match data shown. A good range for the *y*-axis is 0 to 800 g. The *x*-axis range should be 0 to 100°C.
a. Solubility increases with increasing temperature.
b. at 35°C, 250 g per 100 g solvent; at 55°C, 380 g per 100 g solvent; at 75°C, 540 g per 100 g solvent
c. This solubility would be observed at about 35°C.
d. The solution would be unsaturated; the solution would be saturated.

14. 68.4 g

15. a. (1) Determine the molar mass of NaOH.
(2) 40 g
(3) 0.167 M
b. 0.953 M NH_4Br

16. a. (1) H_2SO_4 **b.** 1140 g
(2) H_2O
(3) 343 g

17. 0.143 mol NaOH

18. a. 132 g
b. $NH_4OH + H_2SO_4$
c. 3.998 M

19. a. Determine the molar mass of $AgNO_3$.
b. 168.88 g
c. 1000 mL

20. a. $2H_3PO_4 + 3Ca(OH)_2 \longrightarrow$ $Ca_3(PO_4)_2 + 6H_2O$
b. 698 g calcium phosphate; 243 g water

21. 52.1 mL

22. 0.0309 M

23. a. (1) H_2SO_4 **b.** 4.00 *m*
(2) H_2O
(3) 3.000 *m*

24. a. 441 g   **b.** 126 g

25. a. 342 g   **b.** 0.182 m

26. 0.920 kg

27. 20.2 g

28. a. 142 g
b. 0.11 mol

29. a. 192 g
b. H_2O and CO_2
c. no
d. 3.9×10^{-4} M

30. a. 74.6 g
b. not at all
c. 160 g

31. a. 40 g
b. $2Na + 2H_2O \longrightarrow$
$2NaOH + H_2\uparrow$
c. 0.435 M

32. a. 62 g
b. 13 m

33.

DATA TABLE 1
sample 1 = solution
sample 2 = suspension
sample 3 = colloid
sample 4 = colloid

DATA TABLE 2
sample 1 = solution
sample 2 = colloid
sample 3 = colloid
sample 4 = suspension

34. a. 20°C
b. 65°C
c. 66.8 g/100 g SatdSoln

35. a. It is lightweight and strong, resists corrosion, and has good conductivity properties.
b. copper and tin
c. copper and zinc
d. any alloy of iron with less than 2.5% carbon
e. pure iron, carbon, and cementite—an iron ore

36. a. 500 ppm
b. 2.5 times the limit

MIXED REVIEW

28. Na_2SO_4 is dissolved in water to make 450 mL of a 0.250 M solution.
 a. What is the molar mass of Na_2SO_4?
 b. How many moles of Na_2SO_4 are needed?

29. Citric acid is one component of some soft drinks. Suppose that a 2 L solution is made from 150 mg of citric acid, $C_6H_8O_7$.
 a. What is the molar mass of citric acid?
 b. What products are produced once the soft drink is opened?
 c. Would increasing the concentration of citric acid decrease the bubbling?
 d. What is the molarity of citric acid in the solution?

30. Suppose you wanted to know how many grams of KCl would be left if 350 mL of a 6.0 M KCl solution were evaporated to dryness.
 a. What is the molar mass of KCl?
 b. How would heating the solution affect the mass of KCl remaining?
 c. How many grams of KCl would remain?

31. Sodium metal reacts violently with water to form NaOH and release hydrogen gas. Suppose that 10.0 g of Na react completely with 1.00 L of water, and the final volume of the system is 1 L.
 a. What is the molar mass of NaOH?
 b. Write a balanced equation for the reaction.
 c. What is the molarity of the NaOH solution formed by the reaction?

32. In cars, ethylene glycol, $C_2H_6O_2$, is used as a coolant and antifreeze. A mechanic fills a radiator with 6.5 kg of ethylene glycol and 1.5 kg of water.
 a. What is the molar mass of ethylene glycol?
 b. What is the molality of the water in the solution?

CRITICAL THINKING

33. Predicting Outcomes   You have been investigating the nature of suspensions, colloids, and solutions and have collected the following observational data on four unknown samples. From the data, infer whether each sample is a solution, suspension, or colloid.

DATA TABLE 1 — SAMPLES				
Sample	Color	Clarity (clear or cloudy)	Settle out	Tyndall effect
1	green	clear	no	no
2	blue	cloudy	yes	no
3	colorless	clear	no	yes
4	white	clear	no	yes

DATA TABLE 2 — FILTRATE OF SAMPLES				
Sample	Color	Clarity (clear or cloudy)	On filter paper	Tyndall effect
1	green	clear	nothing	no
2	blue	cloudy	gray solid	yes
3	colorless	cloudy	none	yes
4	white	clear	white solid	no

Based on your inferences in Data Table 1, you decide to conduct one more test of the particles. You filter the samples and then reexamine the filtrate. You obtain the data found in Data Table 2. Infer the classifications based on the data in Table 2.

TECHNOLOGY & LEARNING

34. Graphing Calculator   Predicting Solubility from Tabular Data

The graphing calculator can run a program that estimates data such as solubility at a given temperature. Given solubility measurements for KCl, you will use the data to predict its solubility at 50°C. Begin by creating a table of data. Then the program will carry out an extrapolation. The last step will involve solubility predictions.

Go to Appendix C. If you are using a TI 83 Plus, you can download the program and data and run the application as directed. If you are using another calculator, your teacher will provide you with keystrokes and data sets to use. Remember that after creating your lists, you will need to name the program and check the display, as explained in Appendix C. You will then be ready to run the program. After you have graphed the data, answer these questions.

a. At what temperature would you expect the solubility to be 48.9 g/100 g SatdSoln?

b. At what temperature would you expect the solubility to be 59 g/100 g SatdSoln?

c. At what solubility would you expect the temperature to be 100° C?

 HANDBOOK SEARCH

35. Review the information on alloys in the *Elements Handbook*.

a. Why is aluminum such an important component of alloys?

b. What metals make up bronze?

c. What metals make up brass?

d. What is steel?

e. What is the composition of the mixture called cast iron?

36. Table 5B of the *Elements Handbook* contains carbon monoxide concentration data expressed as parts per million (ppm). The OSHA (Occupational Safety and Health Administration) limit for worker exposure to CO is 200 ppm for an eight-hour period.

a. At what concentration do harmful effects occur in less than one hour?

b. By what factor does the concentration in item (b) exceed the maximum limit set by OSHA?

RESEARCH & WRITING

37. Find out about the chemistry of emulsifying agents. How do these substances affect the dissolution of immiscible substances such as oil and water? As part of your research on this topic, find out why eggs are an emulsifying agent for baking mixtures.

ALTERNATIVE ASSESSMENT

38. Make a comparison of the electrolyte concentration in various brands of sports drinks. Using the labeling information for sugar, calculate the molarity of sugar in each product or brand. Construct a poster to show the results of your analysis of the product labels.

39. Write a set of instructions on how to prepare a solution that is 1 M $CuSO_4$ using $CuSO_4 \cdot 5H_2O$ as the solute. How do the instructions differ if the solute is anhydrous $CuSO_4$? Your instructions should include a list of all materials needed.

37. Students will discover that emulsifying agents contain a polar center and a nonpolar center to the molecule.

38. Usually the information regarding sugar will be given in units of grams per amount of drink. Have students convert the mass of sugar to moles of sugar, which will result in the units of mole per liter, or molarity.

39. At some point, students will need to convert from mass of solute to moles of solute. The number of grams in one mole of copper sulfate pentahydrate is 90 g more than the molar mass of copper sulfate anhydrous.

Ions in Aqueous Solutions and Colligative Properties

PACING CHART

Compression Guide: *(To shorten, eliminate items in italics.)*

CLASSROOM RESOURCES

	NSE Standards	Teaching Resources	Experiments
14-1 **Compounds in Aqueous Solutions** 2 45-minute periods 1 90-minute block	UCP 1–2, 5 HNS 1–3	**ATE Demo,** p. 428 **PE** Elements Handbook T 78, T 79, T 80, T 81, TM 67A	Testing Water, p. 838 **A7** Water of Hydration **B14** Reacting Ionic Species in Aqueous Solution
14-2 **Colligative Properties of Solutions** 2 45-minute periods 1 90-minute block *Vapor-Pressure Lowering, pp. 436–437* *Osmotic Pressure, pp. 442–443* *Electrolytes and Colligative Properties, pp. 443–446*	UCP 1–3, 5 HNS 1, 3	**ATE Demo,** p. 443 T 82, T 83, TM 68A, TM 69A	**A11** Ice-Nucleating Bacteria **C16 EXP** Freezing-Point Depression— Testing De-Icing Chemicals **C16 INV** Freezing-Point Depression— Making Ice Cream

Review and Assessment

2 45-minute periods
1 90-minute block

REVIEW RESOURCES

Cumulative Review	Alternative Assessment	Traditional Assessment
SR Chapter 14 Mixed Review **PE** Chapter 14, 35–45, pp. 449–450	**PE** 53–56, p. 451 **ATE** 429, 444 **AA** Items for Chapter 14	Chapter 14 Text Test Generator items for Chapter 14

ASSIGNMENT RESOURCES

Section Homework Resources & Review	Problem-Solving Practice

HR Homework Worksheets 14-1, 14-2, 14-3
    Graphic Org. Assignments 14-1, 14-3
PE Section Review, 1–5, p. 433
    Chapter Review, 1, 4–7, pp. 447–448
SR Section Review 14-1
	PE Additional Samples 14-1, 14-2
	ATE Additional Samples, pp. 426, 430
	    Additional Example, p. 429

HR Homework Worksheets 14-4, 14-5, 14-6
    Graphic Org. Assignment 14-4, 14-6
PE Section Review, 1–4, p. 446
    Chapter Review, 8–12, 19–34, pp. 448–449
SR Section Review 14-2
	PE Additional Samples 14-3, 14-4,
	      14-5, 14-6
	ATE Additional Samples, pp. 439,
	      441, 444
	PS Chapter 16 Colligative Properties

TECHNOLOGY RESOURCES

Technology & Internet Resources

 CTW 24 Segment 24 Mixing Oil and Water: Surfactants

 Holt Chemistry Videodiscs Teacher's Correlation Guide for Chapter 14

 Module 8: Electrolyte Tutorial

internetconnect

 On-line Student Resources:
GO TO: www.scilinks.org
The following SciLinks Internet resources can be found in the student text for this chapter.

TOPICS:
• Precipitation reactions, p. 427 (HC2141)
• Hydronium ion, p. 431 (HC2142)
• Electrolysis, p. 435 (HC2143)
• Osmosis, p. 442 (HC2144)

 On-line Teacher Resources:
GO TO: go.hrw.com
KEYWORD: HC2 HOME
Visit the HRW Web site for a variety of resources related to this chapter.

 Smithsonian Institution®
Internet Connections
Visit **www.si.edu/hrw** for additional on-line resources.

CNNfyi.com
Visit **www.cnnfyi.com** for late-breaking news and current events stories selected just for you.

Resource Key

PE Pupil's Edition
ATE Teacher's Edition

☝  **One-Stop Planner CD-ROM** Includes these resources and customizable daily lesson plans:

HR Homework Resources	**A** Laboratory Experiments	**D** Consumer Experiments
SR Section Reviews	**B** Microscale Experiments	**T** Transparencies
CTW Critical Thinking Worksheets	**C** Technique Builders and Problem-Solving Experiments	**TM** Transparency Masters
AA Alternative Assessments		**PS** Mini-Guide to Problem Solving
		SRW Supplemental Reading Worksheets

Scoring Rubrics for Labs, Alternative Assessments, Performance Tasks and Portfolio Projects are on the One-Stop Planner CD-ROM.

CHAPTER 14

Ions in Aqueous Solutions and Colligative Properties

Chapter Overview
14-1 describes the dissociation of ionic compounds and the ionization of some molecular compounds when they dissolve in water, distinguishes between strong and weak electrolytes, shows how precipitation reactions occur, and describes methods of writing ionic equations for precipitation reactions.

14-2 describes, both descriptively and mathematically, boiling-point elevation and freezing-point depression. The mechanism of osmosis and the cause of osmotic pressure are described.

Concept Base
Students may need a review of the following concepts:

• bonding and structure in both ionic and covalent compounds, Chapter 6

• writing and interpreting chemical formulas, Chapter 7

• the process of dissolution, Chapter 13

 Reading Skill-Builder

BRAINSTORMING Write the word *precipitation* on the board. Ask students to list words or phrases that relate to precipitation. Have them use their list, the chapter overview, and objectives for Section 14-1 to devise a hypothesis about the chemical definition of precipitation.

Ions in Aqueous Solutions and Colligative Properties

These formations were made by the precipitation of ionic compounds from an aqueous solution.

Compounds in Aqueous Solutions

OBJECTIVES

- Write equations for the dissolution of soluble ionic compounds in water.

- Predict whether a precipitate will form when solutions of soluble ionic compounds are combined, and write net ionic equations for precipitation reactions.

- Compare dissociation of ionic compounds with ionization of molecular compounds.

- Draw the structure of the hydronium ion, and explain why it is used to represent the hydrogen ion in solution.

- Distinguish between strong electrolytes and weak electrolytes.

Lesson Starter

Display a colored crystalline salt, such as $CuSO_4 \cdot 5H_2O$, in its solid form alongside a large beaker or flask containing an aqueous solution of the same salt. Ask students to compare the composition and arrangement of particles in the crystals with those in the solution.

✔**Teaching Tip**

When ionic compounds dissolve in water, their ions are hydrated by water molecules as they dissociate, or separate from one another.

📖 **Reading Skill-Builder**

DISCUSSION Have students read pp. 425–433. When students complete the reading, lead a discussion that addresses these questions:
- How can you predict whether a certain compound will form a precipitate when dissolved in water?
- How do you write a net ionic equation?
- How is dissociation different from ionization?
- What compounds are strong electrolytes? Why?

A s you have learned, solid compounds can be ionic or molecular. In an ionic solid, a crystal structure is made up of charged particles held together by ionic attractions. In a molecular solid, molecules are composed of covalently bonded atoms held together by intermolecular forces. When they dissolve in water, ionic compounds and molecular compounds behave differently.

Dissociation

When a compound that is made of ions dissolves in water, the ions separate from one another, as shown in Figure 14-1. *This separation of ions that occurs when an ionic compound dissolves is called* **dissociation.** For example, dissociation of sodium chloride and calcium chloride in water can be represented by the following equations. (As usual, (*s*) indicates a solid species and (*aq*) indicates a species in an aqueous solution. Note that the equation is balanced for charge as well as for atoms.)

$$NaCl(s) \xrightarrow{H_2O} Na^+(aq) + Cl^-(aq)$$

$$CaCl_2(s) \xrightarrow{H_2O} Ca^{2+}(aq) + 2Cl^-(aq)$$

Notice the number of ions produced per formula unit in the equations above. One formula unit of sodium chloride gives two ions in solution, whereas one formula unit of calcium chloride gives three ions in solution.

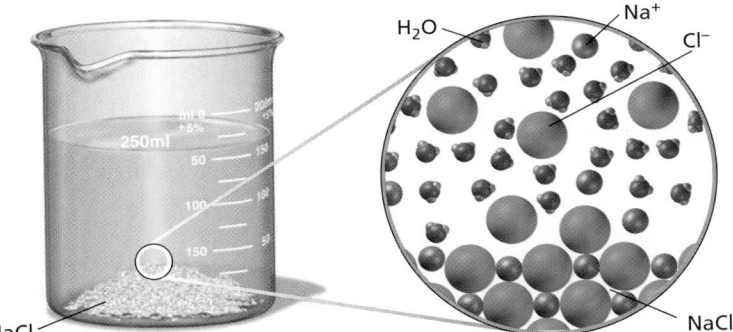

FIGURE 14-1 When NaCl dissolves in water, the ions separate as they leave the crystal.

ADDITIONAL

SAMPLE

PROBLEMS

14-1 Write the equation for the dissolution of magnesium chlorate in water. How many moles of ions are produced for every 1 mol of magnesium chlorate dissolved?

Ans.

$Mg(ClO_3)_2(s) \xrightarrow{H_2O}$
$\qquad Mg^{2+}(aq) + 2ClO_3^-(aq);$

3 mol

14-1 Write the equation for the dissolution of NH_4NO_3 in water. If 3.5 mol of NH_4NO_3 are dissolved, how many moles of each type of ion are produced? How many total moles of ions are produced?

Ans.

$NH_4NO_3(s) \xrightarrow{H_2O}$
$\qquad NH_4^+(aq) + NO_3^-(aq);$

3.5 mol of each ion, 7.0 mol total ions

14-1 An aqueous solution is analyzed and found to contain potassium ions and sulfite ions. Write the equation for the dissolution of the salt that produced this solution. If the solution contains 0.50 mol of potassium ions, how many moles of sulfite ions are present?

Ans.

$K_2SO_3(s) \xrightarrow{H_2O} 2K^+(aq) + SO_3^{2-}(aq);$

0.25 mol SO_3^{2-}

Assuming 100% dissociation, a solution that contains 1 mol of sodium chloride contains 1 mol of Na^+ ions and 1 mol of Cl^- ions. In this book, you can assume 100% dissociation for all ionic compounds. The dissociation of NaCl can be represented as follows.

$$NaCl(s) \xrightarrow{H_2O} Na^+(aq) + Cl^-(aq)$$
$$\quad 1 \text{ mol} \qquad\qquad 1 \text{ mol} \quad\; 1 \text{ mol}$$

A solution that contains 1 mol of calcium chloride contains 1 mol of Ca^{2+} ions and 2 mol of Cl^- ions—a total of 3 mol of ions.

$$CaCl_2(s) \xrightarrow{H_2O} Ca^{2+}(aq) + 2Cl^-(aq)$$
$$\quad 1 \text{ mol} \qquad\qquad 1 \text{ mol} \quad\;\; 2 \text{ mol}$$

SAMPLE PROBLEM 14-1

Write the equation for the dissolution of aluminum sulfate, $Al_2(SO_4)_3$, in water. How many moles of aluminum ions and sulfate ions are produced by dissolving 1 mol of aluminum sulfate? What is the total number of moles of ions produced by dissolving 1 mol of aluminum sulfate?

SOLUTION

1 ANALYZE

Given: amount of solute = 1 mol $Al_2(SO_4)_3$
solvent identity = water

Unknown: **a.** moles of aluminum ions and sulfate ions
b. total number of moles of solute ions produced

2 PLAN

The coefficients in the balanced dissociation equation will reveal the mole relationships, so you can use the equation to determine the number of moles of solute ions produced.

$$Al_2(SO_4)_3(s) \xrightarrow{H_2O} 2Al^{3+}(aq) + 3SO_4^{2-}(aq)$$

3 COMPUTE

a. 1 mol $Al_2(SO_4)_3 \rightarrow 2$ mol $Al^{3+} + 3$ mol SO_4^{2-}
b. 2 mol $Al^{3+} + 3$ mol $SO_4^{2-} = 5$ mol of solute ions

4 EVALUATE

The equation is correctly balanced. Because one formula unit of $Al_2(SO_4)_3$ produces 5 ions, 1 mol of $Al_2(SO_4)_3$ produces 5 mol of ions.

PRACTICE

1. Write the equation for the dissolution of each of the following in water, and then determine the number of moles of each ion produced as well as the total number of moles of ions produced.
   a. 1 mol ammonium chloride
   b. 1 mol sodium sulfide
   c. 0.5 mol barium nitrate

Answer
a. $NH_4Cl(s) \xrightarrow{H_2O} NH_4^+(aq) + Cl^-(aq);$
   1 mol NH_4^+, 1 mol Cl^-, 2 mol ions

b. $Na_2S(s) \xrightarrow{H_2O} 2Na^+(aq) + S^{2-}(aq);$
   2 mol Na^+, 1 mol S^{2-}, 3 mol ions

c. $Ba(NO_3)_2(s) \xrightarrow{H_2O} Ba^{2+}(aq) + 2NO_3^-(aq);$
   0.5 mol Ba^{2+}, 1 mol NO_3^-, 1.5 mol ions

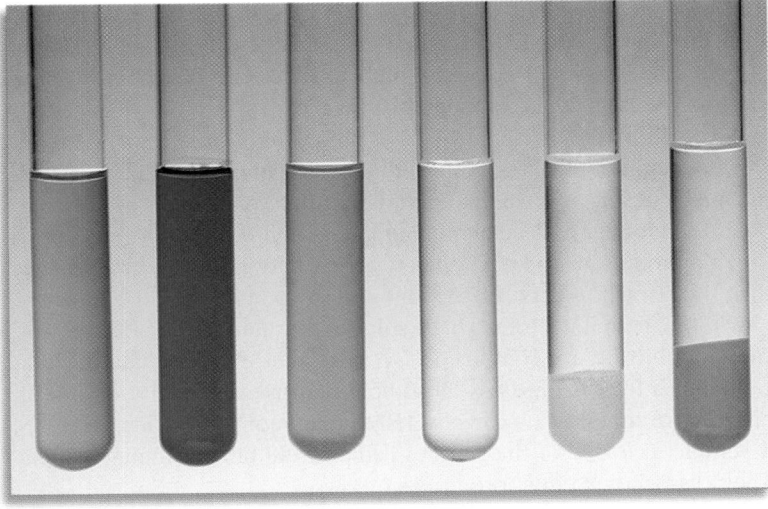

FIGURE 14-2 Ionic compounds can be soluble or insoluble in water. $NiCl_2$, $KMnO_4$, $CuSO_4$, and $Pb(NO_3)_2$ are soluble in water. AgCl and CdS are insoluble in water.

Precipitation Reactions

Although no compound is completely insoluble, compounds of very low solubility can be considered insoluble for most practical purposes. Some examples of ionic compounds that are soluble and insoluble in water are shown in Figure 14-2. It is difficult to write solubility rules that cover all possible conditions. However, we can write some general guidelines to help predict whether a compound made of a certain combination of ions is soluble. These general solubility guidelines are given in Table 14-1.

By looking at the table you can tell that most sodium compounds are soluble. Sodium carbonate, Na_2CO_3, is soluble because it contains sodium. Its dissociation equation is as follows.

$$Na_2CO_3(s) \xrightarrow{H_2O} 2Na^+(aq) + CO_3^{2-}(aq)$$

internetconnect

SCi**LINKS**

NSTA

TOPIC: Precipitation reactions
GO TO: www.scilinks.org
*sci***LINKS CODE:** HC2141

TABLE 14-1 *General Solubility Guidelines*

1. Most sodium, potassium, and ammonium compounds are soluble in water.

2. Most nitrates, acetates, and chlorates are soluble.

3. Most chlorides are soluble, except those of silver, mercury(I), and lead. Lead(II) chloride is soluble in hot water.

4. Most sulfates are soluble, except those of barium, strontium, and lead.

5. Most carbonates, phosphates, and silicates are insoluble, except those of sodium, potassium, and ammonium.

6. Most sulfides are insoluble, except those of calcium, strontium, sodium, potassium, and ammonium.

Visual Strategy
FIGURE 14-2 Have students find the guidelines in Table 14-1 that apply to the compounds in this figure.

Common Misconception
Until now, most of the ionic compounds that students have studied have been highly soluble in water. Students therefore may have the impression that high solubility in water is a characteristic of ionic compounds. Use Figure 14-2 and Table 14-1 to dispel that perception.

TABLE STRATEGY

Table 14-1 Emphasize that no ionic compound is entirely insoluble in water. Some ionic compounds are just considered insoluble because their solubility is less than 0.1g/100 g water. Also, students will learn later in this chapter that no matter how insoluble an ionic compound may be, it is still an electrolyte because the amount that *does* dissolve in water completely dissociates. This is why most tap water, which contains ions from the dissociation of "insoluble" carbonates or phosphates of magnesium and calcium, conducts electricity.

CHAPTER ⟺ CONNECTION

Chapter 18 discusses solubility in terms of solubility equilibrium. Solutions of ionic compounds that are considered insoluble reach saturation at extremely low concentrations.

Is calcium phosphate, $Ca_3(PO_4)_2$, soluble or insoluble? According to Table 14-1, most phosphates are insoluble. Calcium phosphate is not one of the exceptions listed, so it is insoluble. Dissociation equations cannot be written for insoluble compounds.

The information in Table 14-1 is also useful in predicting what will happen if solutions of two different soluble compounds are mixed. If the mixing results in a combination of ions that forms an insoluble compound, a double-replacement reaction and precipitation will occur. Precipitation occurs because the attraction between the ions is greater than the attraction between the ions and surrounding water molecules.

Will a precipitate form when solutions of ammonium sulfide and cadmium nitrate are combined? By using the table, you can tell that cadmium nitrate, $Cd(NO_3)_2$, is soluble because it is a nitrate and all nitrates are soluble. You can also tell that ammonium sulfide, $(NH_4)_2S$, is soluble. It is one of the sulfides listed in the table as being soluble. Their dissociation equations are as follows.

$$(NH_4)_2S(s) \xrightarrow{H_2O} 2NH_4^+(aq) + S^{2-}(aq)$$

$$Cd(NO_3)_2(s) \xrightarrow{H_2O} Cd^{2+}(aq) + 2NO_3^-(aq)$$

FIGURE 14-3 Ammonium sulfide is a soluble compound that dissociates in water to form NH_4^+ and S^{2-} ions. Cadmium nitrate is a soluble compound that dissociates in water to form NO_3^- and Cd^{2+} ions. Precipitation of cadmium sulfide occurs when the two solutions are mixed.

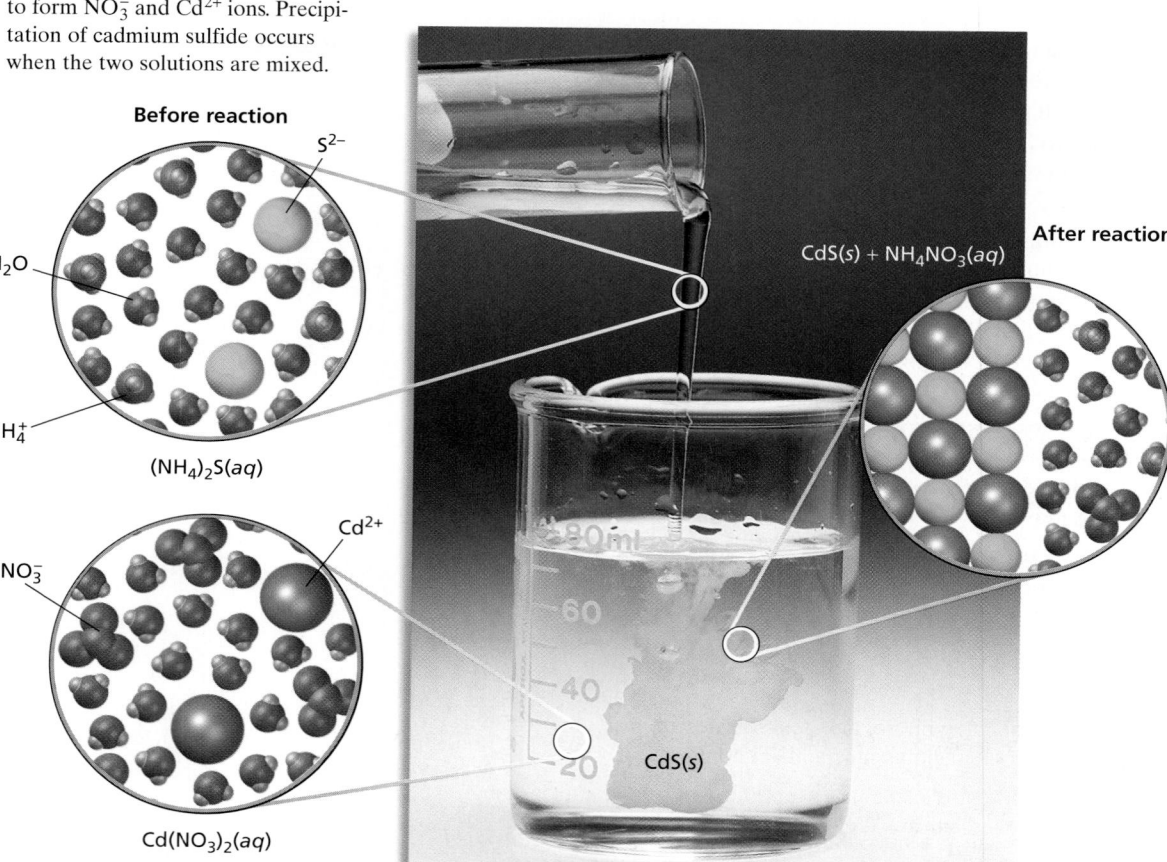

The two possible products of a double-replacement reaction between $(NH_4)_2S$ and $Cd(NO_3)_2$ are ammonium nitrate, NH_4NO_3, and cadmium sulfide, CdS. (The question marks indicate that the states are unknown.)

$$(NH_4)_2S(aq) + Cd(NO_3)_2(aq) \longrightarrow NH_4NO_3(?) + CdS(?)$$

To decide whether a precipitate can form, you must know the solubilities of these two compounds. Consulting Table 14-1, you can see that NH_4NO_3 is soluble in water. However, CdS is insoluble. You can therefore predict that when solutions of ammonium sulfide and cadmium nitrate are combined, ammonium nitrate will not precipitate and cadmium sulfide will. As illustrated in Figure 14-3, crystals of CdS form when the solutions are mixed. In the following equation, the designations (aq) and (s) show that ammonium nitrate remains in solution and cadmium sulfide precipitates.

$$(NH_4)_2S(aq) + Cd(NO_3)_2(aq) \longrightarrow NH_4NO_3(aq) + CdS(s)$$

Net Ionic Equations

Reactions of ions in aqueous solution are usually represented by net ionic equations rather than formula equations. *A **net ionic equation** includes only those compounds and ions that undergo a chemical change in a reaction in an aqueous solution.* To write a net ionic equation, you first convert the chemical equation into an overall ionic equation. All soluble ionic compounds are shown as dissociated ions in solution. The precipitates are shown as solids. The precipitation of cadmium sulfide described previously can be shown by the following overall ionic equation.

$$Cd^{2+}(aq) + 2NO_3^-(aq) + 2NH_4^+(aq) + S^{2-}(aq) \longrightarrow$$
$$CdS(s) + 2NO_3^-(aq) + 2NH_4^+(aq)$$

Notice that the ammonium ion, NH_4^+, and the nitrate ion, NO_3^-, appear on both sides of this equation. Therefore, they have not undergone any chemical change and are still present in their original form. *Ions that do not take part in a chemical reaction and are found in solution both before and after the reaction are **spectator ions.***

To convert an ionic equation into a net ionic equation, the spectator ions are canceled on both sides of the equation. Eliminating the NH_4^+ and NO_3^- ions from the overall ionic equation above gives the following net ionic equation.

$$Cd^{2+}(aq) + S^{2-}(aq) \longrightarrow CdS(s)$$

This net ionic equation applies not only to the reaction between $(NH_4)_2S$ and $Cd(NO_3)_2$ but also to *any* reaction in which a precipitate of cadmium sulfide forms when the ions are combined in solution. For example, it is also the net ionic equation for the precipitation of CdS when $CdSO_4$ and H_2S react.

Additional Example Problem

1. Have students reduce the full ionic equation they wrote for the demonstration on page 428 to its net form by eliminating spectator ions.

Ans.

$$Sr^{2+}(aq) + SO_4^{2-}(aq) \longrightarrow SrSO_4(s)$$

Common Misconception

Students sometimes view balancing ionic equations and writing net ionic equations as strictly mathematical operations because they have more experience with mathematical equations than with chemical equations. Encourage students to recognize the physical reality of ions as reactive particles that form new substances.

Alternative Assessment

Have students manipulate physical models of ionic reactions. Have them eliminate spectator ions and isolate the ions that combine. Ask the class to develop a verbal description of what is taking place in each ionic reaction.

ADDITIONAL
SAMPLE
PROBLEMS

14-2 A solution of strontium chloride is added to a solution of potassium sulfate. Write the net ionic equation for any reaction that takes place.

Ans.
$Sr^{2+}(aq) + SO_4^{2-}(aq) \longrightarrow SrSO_4(s)$

14-2 A solution of sodium sulfide is combined with a solution of iron(II) nitrate. Write the net ionic equation for any reaction that occurs.

Ans. $Fe^{2+}(aq) + S^{2-}(aq) \longrightarrow FeS(s)$

14-2 A solution of aluminum and chloride ions is added to a solution of silver and nitrate ions, and they react completely. Write the net ionic equation for the reaction. Write the formula for the substance that would form if the remaining solution were evaporated to dryness.

Ans. $Ag^+(aq) + Cl^-(aq) \longrightarrow AgCl(s)$;
$Al(NO_3)_3(s)$

✔ **Teaching Tip**

Point out that the reactions in Practice problems (1) and (3) have the same net ionic equation.

SAMPLE PROBLEM 14-2

Identify the precipitate that forms when aqueous solutions of zinc nitrate and ammonium sulfide are combined. Write the equation for the possible double-replacement reaction. Then write the formula equation, overall ionic equation, and net ionic equation for the reaction.

SOLUTION

1 *ANALYZE*

Given: identity of reactants: zinc nitrate and ammonium sulfide
reaction medium: aqueous solution

Unknown: a. equation for the possible double-replacement reaction **b.** identity of the precipitate **c.** formula equation **d.** overall ionic equation **e.** net ionic equation

2 *PLAN*

Write the possible double-replacement reaction between $Zn(NO_3)_2$ and $(NH_4)_2S$. Use Table 14-1 to determine if any of the products are insoluble and will precipitate. Write a formula equation and an overall ionic equation, then cancel the spectator ions to produce a net ionic equation.

3 *COMPUTE*

a. The equation for the possible double-replacement reaction is as follows.

$$Zn(NO_3)_2(aq) + (NH_4)_2S(aq) \longrightarrow ZnS(?) + 2NH_4NO_3(?)$$

b. Table 14-1 reveals that zinc sulfide is not a soluble sulfide and is therefore a precipitate. Ammonium nitrate is soluble according to the table.

c. The formula equation is as follows.

$$Zn(NO_3)_2(aq) + (NH_4)_2S(aq) \longrightarrow ZnS(s) + 2NH_4NO_3(aq)$$

d. The overall ionic equation is as follows.

$$Zn^{2+}(aq) + 2NO_3^-(aq) + 2NH_4^+(aq) + S^{2-}(aq) \longrightarrow ZnS(s) + 2NH_4^+(aq) + 2NO_3^-(aq)$$

e. The ammonium and nitrate ions appear on both sides of the equation as spectator ions. The net ionic equation is as follows.

$$Zn^{2+}(aq) + S^{2-}(aq) \longrightarrow ZnS(s)$$

PRACTICE

1. Will a precipitate form if solutions of potassium sulfate and barium nitrate are combined? If so, write the net ionic equation for the reaction.

   Answer
   Yes;
   $Ba^{2+}(aq) + SO_4^{2-}(aq) \longrightarrow BaSO_4(s)$

2. Will a precipitate form if solutions of potassium nitrate and magnesium sulfate are combined? If so, write the net ionic equation for the reaction.

   Answer
   No

3. Will a precipitate form if solutions of barium chloride and sodium sulfate are combined? If so, identify the spectator ions and write the net ionic equation.

   Answer
   Yes; Na^+ and Cl^-;
   $Ba^{2+}(aq) + SO_4^{2-}(aq) \longrightarrow BaSO_4(s)$

4. Write the net ionic equation for the precipitation of nickel(II) sulfide.

   Answer
   $Ni^{2+}(aq) + S^{2-}(aq) \longrightarrow NiS(s)$

Ionization

Some molecular compounds can also form ions in solution. Usually such compounds are polar. *Ions are formed from solute molecules by the action of the solvent in a process called* **ionization.** The more general meaning of this term is the creation of ions where there were none. Note that *ionization* is different from *dissociation*. When an ionic compound dissolves, the ions that were already present separate from one another. When a molecular compound dissolves and ionizes in a polar solvent, ions are formed where none existed in the undissolved compound. Like all ions in aqueous solution, the ions formed by such a molecular solute are hydrated. The heat released during the hydration of the ions provides the energy needed to break the covalent bonds.

In general, the extent to which a solute ionizes in solution depends on the strength of the bonds within the molecules of the solute and the strength of attraction between the solute and solvent molecules. If the strength of a bond within the solute molecule is weaker than the attractive forces of the solvent molecules, then the covalent bond of the solute breaks and the molecule is separated into ions. Hydrogen chloride, HCl, is a molecular compound that ionizes in aqueous solution. It contains a highly polar bond. The attraction between a polar HCl molecule and the polar water molecules is strong enough to break the HCl bond, forming hydrogen ions and chloride ions.

$$HCl \xrightarrow{H_2O} H^+(aq) + Cl^-(aq)$$

The Hydronium Ion

The H^+ ion attracts other molecules or ions so strongly that it does not normally exist alone. The ionization of hydrogen chloride in water is better described as a chemical reaction in which a proton is transferred directly from HCl to a water molecule, where it becomes covalently bonded to oxygen and forms H_3O^+.

$$H_2O(l) + HCl(g) \longrightarrow H_3O^+(aq) + Cl^-(aq)$$

This process is represented in Figure 14-4. *The H_3O^+ ion is known as the* **hydronium ion.**

The hydration of the H^+ ion to form the hydronium ion is a highly exothermic reaction. The energy released makes a large contribution to the energy needed to ionize a molecular solute. Many molecular compounds that ionize in an aqueous solution contain hydrogen and form H_3O^+.

internet**connect**

SC*LINKS*

NSTA

TOPIC: Hydronium ion
GO TO: www.scilinks.org
*sci*LINKS CODE: HC2142

FIGURE 14-4 When hydrogen chloride gas dissolves in water, it ionizes to form an H^+ ion and a Cl^- ion. The H^+ ion immediately bonds to a water molecule, forming a hydronium ion. The aqueous solution of hydrogen chloride is called hydrochloric acid.

FIGURE 14-5 Have students look back to the solubility guidelines in Table 14-1 to name another compound that is insoluble but, like AgCl, is considered to be a strong electrolyte. Possible responses might include mercury(I) chloride or barium sulfate. Use this apparent contradiction to again reinforce the idea that even if a compound is nearly insoluble, the part that does dissolve is dissociated.

✔ Teaching Tip

An ionic compound is nearly always a strong electrolyte. Only molecular compounds that ionize in water solution are electrolytes; some molecular compounds are nonelectrolytes.

CHAPTER ⟷ CONNECTION

A saturated solution involves a dynamic equilibrium between an undissolved substance and ions or molecules in solution. "Insoluble" substances reach an equilibrium at extremely low concentrations of solute. Students will learn more about this phenomenon when they study solution equilibria in Chapter 18.

CHEMISTRY INTERACTIVE TUTOR

Module 8: Strong and Weakly Ionized Species, pH, and Titrations

Topic: Electrolyte Tutorial
Section **c** of this engaging tutorial reviews and reinforces understanding of electrolytes.

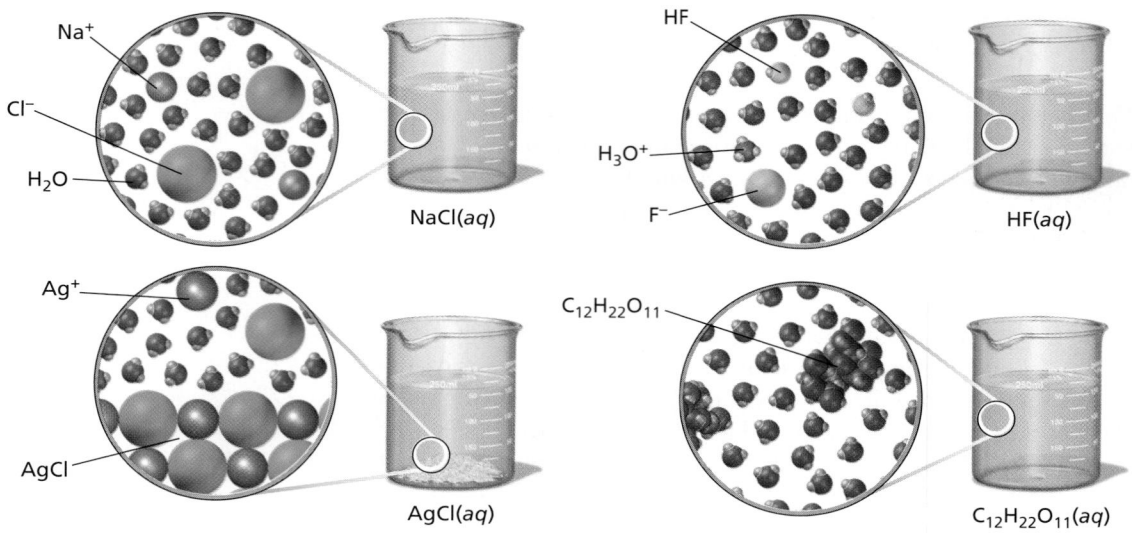

FIGURE 14-5 Strong electrolytes, such as NaCl and AgCl, yield only ions when they dissolve in aqueous solution. Weak electrolytes, such as HF, exist as both ions and unionized molecules in aqueous solution. Nonelectrolytes, such as sucrose, $C_{12}H_{22}O_{11}$, do not form any ions in aqueous solution.

CHEMISTRY INTERACTIVE TUTOR

Module 8: Strong and Weakly Ionized Species, pH, and Titrations

Strong and Weak Electrolytes

As discussed in Chapter 13, substances that yield ions and conduct an electric current in solution are electrolytes. Substances that do not yield ions and do not conduct an electric current in solution are nonelectrolytes. Hydrogen chloride is one of a series of compounds composed of hydrogen and the members of Group 17 (known as the halogens). The hydrogen halides are all molecular compounds with single polar-covalent bonds. All are gases, all are very soluble in water, and all are electrolytes. Hydrogen chloride, hydrogen bromide, and hydrogen iodide strongly conduct an electric current in an aqueous solution. However, hydrogen fluoride only weakly conducts an electric current at the same concentration. The strength with which substances conduct an electric current is related to their ability to form ions in solution, as shown in Figure 14-5.

Strong Electrolytes

Hydrogen chloride, hydrogen bromide, and hydrogen iodide are 100% ionized in dilute aqueous solution. *Any compound of which all or almost all of the dissolved compound exists as ions in an aqueous solution is a* **strong electrolyte.** Hydrogen chloride, hydrogen bromide, and hydrogen iodide are all acids in aqueous solution. These acids, several other acids, and all ionic compounds are strong electrolytes.

The distinguishing feature of strong electrolytes is that, to whatever extent they dissolve in water, they yield only ions. For example, an ionic compound may be highly soluble in water and dissociate into ions in solution, such as NaCl. Other ionic compounds may not dissolve much, but the amount that does dissolve exists solely as hydrated ions in solution. Silver chloride, AgCl, is almost insoluble, with a solubility of only

0.000 089 g/100. g of water. However, it is considered a strong electrolyte because the small amount that does dissolve exists as dissociated ions.

Weak Electrolytes

An aqueous solution of some molecular compounds contains not only dissolved ions but also some dissolved molecules that are not ionized. Hydrogen fluoride, HF, dissolves in water to give an acid solution known as hydrofluoric acid. However, the hydrogen-fluorine bond is much stronger than the bonds between hydrogen and the other halogens. When hydrogen fluoride dissolves, some molecules ionize. But the reverse reaction—the transfer of H^+ ions back to F^- ions to form hydrogen fluoride molecules—also takes place.

$$HF(aq) + H_2O(l) \rightleftharpoons H_3O^+(aq) + F^-(aq)$$

Thus, the concentration of dissolved unionized HF molecules remains high and the concentration of H_3O^+ and F^- ions remains low.

Hydrogen fluoride is an example of a *weak electrolyte*. A **weak electrolyte** *is a compound of which a relatively small amount of the dissolved compound exists as ions in an aqueous solution.* This is in contrast to a nonelectrolyte, of which none of the dissolved compound exists as ions. Another example of a weak electrolyte is acetic acid, CH_3COOH. Only a small percentage of the acetic acid molecules ionize in aqueous solution.

$$CH_3COOH(aq) + H_2O(l) \rightleftharpoons CH_3COO^-(aq) + H_3O^+(aq)$$

The description of an electrolyte as strong or weak must not be confused with the description of a solution as concentrated or dilute. Strong and weak electrolytes differ in the *degree of ionization or dissociation*. Concentrated and dilute solutions differ in the *amount of solute dissolved* in a given quantity of a solvent. Hydrochloric acid is always a strong electrolyte. This is true even in a solution that is 0.000 01 M—a very dilute solution. By contrast, acetic acid is always considered a weak electrolyte, even in a 10 M solution—a fairly concentrated solution.

SECTION REVIEW

1. Write the equation for the dissolution of $Sr(NO_3)_2$ in water. How many moles of strontium ions and nitrate ions are produced by dissolving 0.5 mol of strontium nitrate?

2. Will a precipitate form if solutions of magnesium acetate and strontium chloride are combined?

3. What determines whether a molecular compound will be ionized in a polar solvent?

4. How is a hydronium ion formed when a compound like HCl dissolves in water? What is its net charge?

5. Explain why HCl is a strong electrolyte and HF is a weak electrolyte.

SECTION REVIEW

1. $Sr(NO_3)_2(s) \xrightarrow{H_2O}$
$Sr^{2+}(aq) + 2NO_3^-(aq)$;
0.5 mol of Sr^{2+} ions and 1 mol of NO_3^- ions

2. No. The salts that could potentially form, magnesium chloride and strontium acetate, are soluble.

3. If the attraction of polar solvent molecules is greater than a covalent bond in the solute, the molecule will break into ions.

4. A hydronium ion is formed by the hydration of a proton resulting from the ionization of a molecule. Its charge is 1+.

5. HCl is essentially 100% ionized in water solution, whereas HF is only slightly ionized because its H-F covalent bond is strong.

GREAT DISCOVERIES

GREAT DISCOVERIES

Application

Many common products are made using electrolysis. Examples include aluminum items, such as keys, measuring spoons, and lipstick tubes, that have thin layers of another metal attached to the surface of the aluminum by a process known as anodizing. Other common examples include gold- and silver-plated jewelry.

The Riddle of Electrolysis

HISTORICAL PERSPECTIVE

When Michael Faraday performed his electrochemical experiments, little was known about the relationship between matter and electricity. Chemists were still debating the existence of atoms, and the discovery of the electron was more than 50 years away. Combining his talents in electrical and chemical investigation, Faraday pointed researchers to the intimate connection between chemical reactions and electricity while setting the stage for the development of a new branch of chemistry.

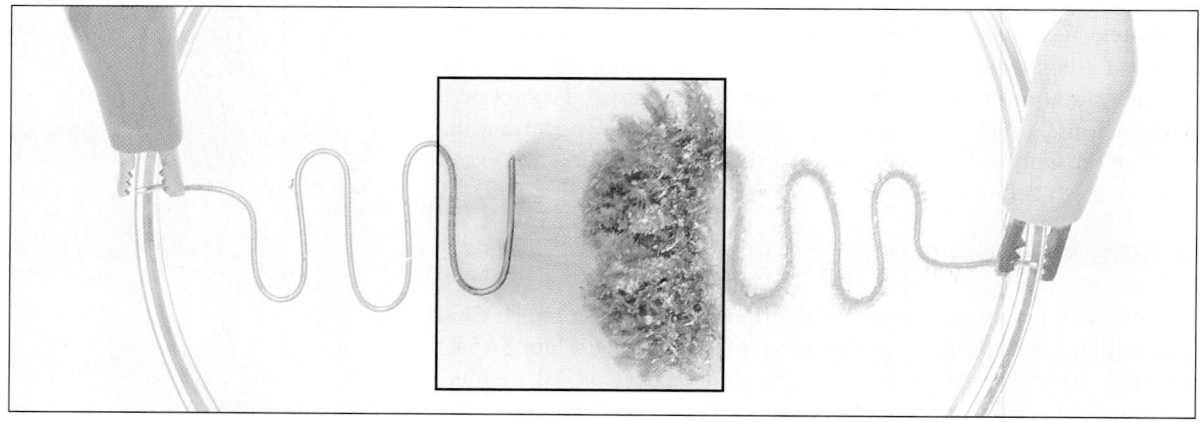

Chlorine being produced by electrolysis.

Electrifying Experiments

In 1800, the Italian physicist Alessandro Volta introduced his "voltaic pile," better known as the battery. The stack of alternating zinc and silver disks provided scientists with a source of electric current for the first time, and, in the words of the famous English chemist Humphry Davy, it acted as "an alarm-bell to experimenters in every part of Europe."

That same year, chemists discovered a new phenomenon using Volta's device. They immersed the two poles of a battery at different locations in a container of water. As current flowed, the water decomposed into its elemental components, with hydrogen evolving at the positive pole of the battery and oxygen evolving at the negative pole. Similar experiments using solutions of certain solids dissolved in water resulted in the decomposition of the solids, with the two products of their breakdown also evolving at opposite poles of the battery. This electrochemical decomposition was later named electrolysis.

The Roots of Electrolytic Theory

The discovery of electrolysis led two pioneering chemists to ponder the connection between chemical forces and electricity. One of them was Davy:

Is not what has been called chemical affinity merely the union . . . of particles in naturally opposite states? And are not chemical attractions of particles and electrical attractions of masses owing to one property and governed by one simple law?

The Swedish chemist Jöns Jacob Berzelius took Davy's idea a step further. He postulated that matter consisted of combinations of "electropositive" and "electronegative" substances, classifying the parts by the pole at which they accumulated during electrolysis.

These ideas inspired two early electrolytic theories, each of which ultimately proved incorrect but which contributed to our present understanding of the phenomenon. The "contact theory" proposed that electrolytic current was due merely to the contact of the battery's metals with the electrolytic solution. The "chemical theory," on the other hand, attributed the flow of current to undefined changes in the solution's components.

Faraday Provides a Spark

Although Michael Faraday is best remembered for his work in electromagnetism, he began his career as Humphry Davy's laboratory assistant at the Royal Institution, in London, and went on to be the professor of chemistry there for over 30 years. In the 1830s, Faraday devised several ingenious experiments to determine whether the flow of current in an electrolytic

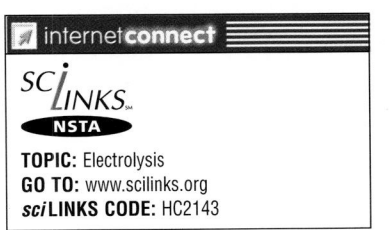

internetconnect

SC*LINKS*
NSTA

TOPIC: Electrolysis
GO TO: www.scilinks.org
*sci*LINKS CODE: HC2143

solution is dependent solely on the contact of the battery's poles with the solution. In a typical setup, one of the poles was separated from the solution and electricity was permitted to enter it by way of a spark. In all cases, Faraday observed current to flow in the electrolytic cell despite one or both of the poles not being in direct contact with the electrolytic solution. In 1833 he wrote the following:

I conceive the effects [of electrolysis] to arise from forces which are internal, *relative to the matter under decomposition, and not* external, *as they might be considered, if directly dependent on the poles. I suppose that the effects are due to a modification, by the electric current, of the chemical affinity of the particles through or by which the current is passing.*

Although the battery's poles were, in fact, later shown to play a part in the flow of the current, Faraday had established the active role of the electrolytic solution in electrolysis. And in realizing that electricity affected the chemical nature of the solution, he anticipated the ideas of oxidation and reduction—despite the fact that the concepts of electrons and ions were half a century away.

Faraday's Legacy

Faraday continued to study the role of the electrolytic solution, or *electrolyte,* as he named it, in electrolysis. (He also coined most

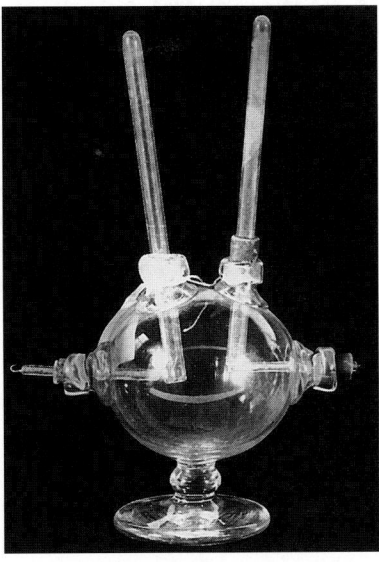

Instrument used by Michael Faraday in his studies of electrolysis.

of the other modern terms of electrolysis, for example, *electrode, ion, anode, cathode, anion,* and *cation.*) These investigations culminated in the discovery of his basic laws of electrolysis.

Still valid today, these principles not only put electrolysis on a quantitative footing, leading to our current understanding of the phenomenon, but also bolstered the atomic theory, which was still seriously contested by many chemists at the time. And perhaps most important, Faraday's experiments inspired his successors to further clarify the chemical nature of solutions. This ultimately led to Svante Arrhenius's theory of electrolytic dissociation and the evolution of a new division in the chemical field, known today as physical chemistry.

Class Discussion

Ask students to explain why electrolysis might be used to coat a sheet of iron with another metal, such as zinc. Students should be able to infer that other metals might protect iron from substances in the air that might cause it to rust. Zinc electroplated onto iron objects produces materials that are galvanized. Try to find a piece of galvanized steel so students can view its appearance.

✔ Teaching Tip

Electrolysis can be defined as the use of an electric current to bring about a chemical change.

Lesson Starter

Demonstrate that NaCl lowers the freezing point of water. At the beginning of class, fill two containers with the same amount of ice. Add a large handful of rock salt to one of the containers, and mix the solution. During class, observe the containers and note the rate at which the ice melts in both containers. Ask students to explain why the ice mixed with NaCl melts faster.

Visual Strategy

FIGURE 14-6 Before students read the caption, have them interpret the graph to tell how the solution curve differs from the normal curve of pure water and how the boiling and freezing points have changed. Then have them check their conclusions against the caption information.

Problem-Solving Practice

HOLT ChemFile

Chapter 16 of the Mini-Guide to Problem Solving (also found on the One-Stop Planner CD-ROM) includes more worked-out samples and additional practice problems involving colligative properties.

OBJECTIVES

- List four colligative properties, and explain why they are classified as colligative properties.

- Calculate freezing-point depression, boiling-point elevation, and solution molality of nonelectrolytic solutions.

- Calculate the expected changes in freezing point and boiling point of an electrolytic solution.

- Discuss causes of the differences between expected and experimentally observed colligative properties of electrolytic solutions.

Colligative Properties of Solutions

The presence of solutes affects the properties of the solutions. Some of these properties are not dependent on the nature of the dissolved substance but only on how many dissolved particles are present. *Properties that depend on the concentration of solute particles but not on their identity are called* **colligative properties.** In calculations involving some colligative properties, the concentration is given in terms of molality, *m*.

Vapor-Pressure Lowering

The boiling point and freezing point of a solution differ from those of the pure solvent. The graph in Figure 14-6 shows that a nonvolatile solute raises the boiling point and lowers the freezing point. *A* **nonvolatile substance** *is one that has little tendency to become a gas under existing conditions.*

FIGURE 14-6 Vapor pressure as a function of temperature is shown for a pure solvent, a solution of that solvent, and a nonvolatile solute. The vapor pressure of the solution is lower than the vapor pressure of the pure solvent. (This can be seen by noting the decrease in pressure between the pure solvent and the solution at the temperature that is the boiling point of the pure solvent.) The solute thus reduces the freezing point and elevates the boiling point.

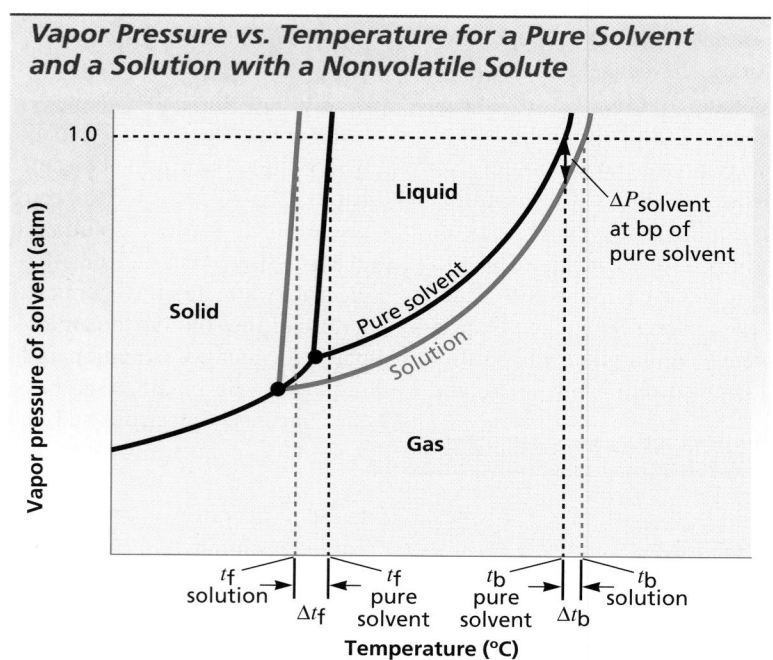

Vapor Pressure vs. Temperature for a Pure Solvent and a Solution with a Nonvolatile Solute

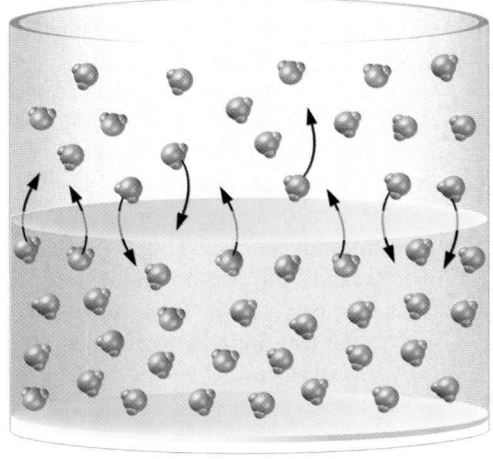
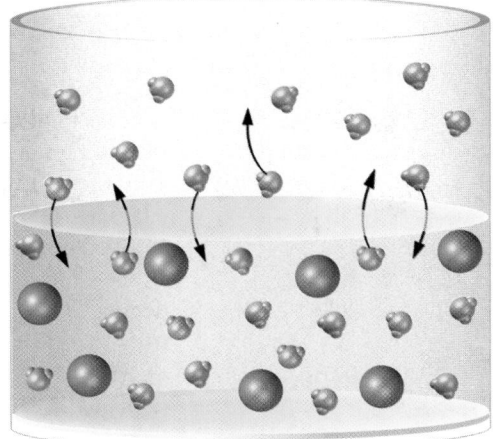

Pure water

Aqueous solution of nonvolatile solute

 Used to represent $C_{12}H_{22}O_{11}$, sucrose

 Used to represent H_2O, water

Reading Skill-Builder

READING ORGANIZER
Students can use two-column notes to help them distinguish between main ideas and details. Have students label a blank sheet of notebook paper with the title "Colligative Properties." Then have them divide their papers into two columns. In the left-hand column, have them write the four colligative properties discussed in Section 14-2 (vapor-pressure lowering, freezing-point depression, boiling-point elevation, and osmotic pressure). In the right-hand column, direct students to write the definition, an example, and other details for each property.

FIGURE 14-7 The vapor pressure of water over pure water is greater than the vapor pressure of water over an aqueous solution containing a nonvolatile solute, such as sucrose.

To understand why a nonvolatile solute changes the boiling point and freezing point, you must consider equilibrium vapor pressure, which was discussed in Chapter 12. Vapor pressure is the pressure caused by molecules that have escaped from the liquid phase to the gaseous phase. Experiments show that the vapor pressure of a solvent containing a nonvolatile solute is lower than the vapor pressure of the pure solvent at the same temperature, as shown in Figure 14-7. Notice the liquid-vapor boundaries. Vapor pressure can be thought of as a measure of the tendency of molecules to escape from a liquid. Addition of sucrose, a nonvolatile solute, lowers the concentration of water molecules at the surface of the liquid. This lowers the tendency of water molecules to leave the solution and enter the vapor phase. Thus, the vapor pressure of the solution is lower than the vapor pressure of pure water.

Nonelectrolyte solutions of the same molality have the same concentration of particles. Dilute solutions of the same solvent and equal molality of any nonelectrolyte solute lower vapor pressure equally. For example, a 1 m aqueous solution of the nonelectrolyte glucose, $C_6H_{12}O_6$, lowers the vapor pressure of water 5.5×10^{-4} atm at 25°C. A 1 m solution of sucrose, $C_{12}H_{22}O_{11}$, another nonelectrolyte, also lowers the vapor pressure 5.5×10^{-4} atm. Because vapor-pressure lowering depends on the concentration of a nonelectrolyte solute and is independent of solute identity, it is a colligative property.

Refer to the graph in Figure 14-6. Because the vapor pressure has been lowered, the solution remains liquid over a larger temperature range. This lowers the freezing point and raises the boiling point. It follows that changes in boiling point and freezing point also depend on the concentration of solute and are therefore colligative properties.

TABLE STRATEGY

Table 14-2 Ask students which solvents have the greatest freezing-point-depression constants. Point out that the table emphasizes that freezing-point depression is entirely a function of the solvent and has nothing to do with the nonvolatile, nonelectrolyte solute used (at dilute concentrations and under ordinary conditions of temperature and pressure). Solutes are not mentioned on this table.

Freezing-Point Depression

The freezing point of a 1-molal solution of any nonelectrolyte solute in water is found by experiment to be 1.86°C lower than the freezing point of water. That is, when 1 mol of a nonelectrolyte solute is dissolved in 1 kg of water, the freezing point of the solution is −1.86°C instead of 0.00°C. When 2 mol of a nonelectrolyte solute is dissolved in 1 kg of water, the freezing point of the solution is −3.72°C. This is 2 × −1.86°C. In fact, for any concentration of a nonelectrolyte solute in water, the decrease in freezing point can be determined by using the value of −1.86°C/m. This value, called the **molal freezing-point constant (K_f),** *is the freezing-point depression of the solvent in a 1-molal solution of a nonvolatile, nonelectrolyte solute.*

Each solvent has its own characteristic molal freezing-point constant. The values of K_f for some common solvents are given in Table 14-2. These values are most accurate for dilute solutions at 1 atmosphere of pressure. Some variations are introduced in the value of K_f at other pressures and with more-concentrated solutions. The table also shows the values of a related quantity called K_b, which you will study next.

As stated earlier, the freezing point of a solution containing 1 mol of a nonelectrolyte solute in water is 1.86°C lower than the normal freezing point of water. *The **freezing-point depression,** Δt_f, is the difference between the freezing points of the pure solvent and a solution of a non-electrolyte in that solvent, and it is directly proportional to the molal concentration of the solution.* As shown by the previous example, if the molal concentration is doubled, the freezing-point depression is doubled. Freezing-point depression can be calculated by the following equation.

$$\Delta t_f = K_f m$$

K_f is expressed as °C/m, m is expressed in mol solute/kg solvent (molality), and Δt_f is expressed in °C. Sample Problems 14-3 and 14-4 show how this relationship can be used to determine the freezing-point depression and molal concentration of a solution.

TABLE 14-2 *Molal Freezing-Point and Boiling-Point Constants*

Solvent	Normal f.p. (°C)	Molal f.p. constant, K_f (°C/m)	Normal b.p. (°C)	Molal b.p. constant, K_b (°C/m)
Acetic acid	16.6	−3.90	117.9	3.07
Camphor	178.8	−39.7	207.4	5.61
Ether	−116.3	−1.79	34.6	2.02
Naphthalene	80.2	−6.94	217.7	5.80
Phenol	40.9	−7.40	181.8	3.60
Water	0.00	−1.86	100.0	0.51

SAMPLE PROBLEM 14-3

What is the freezing-point depression of water in a solution of 17.1 g of sucrose, $C_{12}H_{22}O_{11}$, and 200. g of water? What is the actual freezing point of the solution?

SOLUTION

1 ANALYZE **Given:** solute mass and chemical formula = 17.1 g $C_{12}H_{22}O_{11}$
solvent mass and identity = 200.0 g water
Unknown: **a.** freezing-point depression
b. freezing point of the solution

2 PLAN Find the molal freezing-point constant, K_f, for water in Table 14-2. To use the equation for freezing-point depression, $\Delta t_f = K_f m$, you need to determine the molality of the solution.

$$\text{mass of solute (g)} \times \frac{1 \text{ mol solute}}{\text{molar mass of solute (g)}} = \text{amount of solute (mol)}$$

$$\frac{\text{amount of solute (mol)}}{\text{mass of solvent (g)}} \times \frac{1000 \text{ g water}}{1 \text{ kg water}} = \text{molality}$$

$$\Delta t_f = K_f m$$
$$\text{f.p. solution} = \text{f.p. solvent} + \Delta t_f$$

3 COMPUTE $17.1 \text{ g } C_{12}H_{22}O_{11} \times \dfrac{1 \text{ mol } C_{12}H_{22}O_{11}}{342.34 \text{ g } C_{12}H_{22}O_{11}} = 0.0500 \text{ mol } C_{12}H_{22}O_{11}$

$$\frac{0.0500 \text{ mol } C_{12}H_{22}O_{11}}{200. \text{ g water}} \times \frac{1000 \text{ g water}}{\text{kg water}} = \frac{0.250 \text{ mol } C_{12}H_{22}O_{11}}{\text{kg water}} = 0.250 \text{ } m$$

a. $\Delta t_f = 0.250 \text{ } m \times (-1.86°C/m) = -0.465°C$
b. f.p. solution $= 0.000°C + (-0.465°C) = -0.465°C$

SAMPLE PROBLEM 14-4

A water solution containing an unknown quantity of a nonelectrolyte solute is found to have a freezing point of $-0.23°C$. What is the molal concentration of the solution?

SOLUTION

1 ANALYZE **Given:** freezing point of solution $= -0.23°C$
Unknown: molality of the solution

2 PLAN Water is the solvent, so you will need the value of K_f, the molal-freezing-point constant for water, from Table 14-2. The Δt_f for this solution is the difference between the f.p. of water and the f.p. of the solution. Use the equation for freezing-point depression to calculate molality.

$$\Delta t_f = \text{f.p. of solution} - \text{f.p. of pure solvent}$$
$$\Delta t_f = K_f m \qquad \text{Solve for molality, } m.$$

$$m = \frac{\Delta t_f}{K_f}$$

14-3 Determine the freezing point of a water solution of fructose, $C_6H_{12}O_6$, made by dissolving 58.0 g of fructose in 185 g of water.

Ans. $-3.24°C$

14-3 Calculate the molality of a solution of 39.2 g of urea, H_2NCONH_2, in 485 g of pure acetic acid. Determine the freezing point of this solution.

Ans. 1.35 m; 11.3°C

14-4 Determine the molal concentration of a solution of ethylene glycol, $HOCH_2CH_2OH$, if the solution's freezing point is $-6.40°C$. What mass of ethylene glycol would you dissolve in 500. g of water to prepare such a solution?

Ans. 3.44 m; 107 g ethylene glycol

Application

A common antifreeze is a solution of ethylene glycol, $HOCH_2CH_2OH$, a relatively nonvolatile liquid substance, combined with dissolved dyes and corrosion inhibitors. This solution is also a coolant because it provides not only a lower freezing point but also a higher boiling point as compared with plain water. Car manufacturers recommend that people leave the coolant mixture in the engine year-round. A typical coolant mixture is 50% water and 50% ethylene glycol by volume. This mixture contains 1.116 kg of ethylene glycol per 1.000 kg of water, which is a 17.98 m solution. (Ethylene glycol has a density of 1.1135 g/mL at 20°C, compared with water's 0.998 g/mL at 20°C.) The theoretical boiling point of this solution is 109.2°C, or 229.6°F. (The theoretical freezing point of this solution is −33.4°C, or −28.1°F.)

3 COMPUTE

$$\Delta t_f = -0.23°C - 0.00°C = -0.23°C$$

$$m = \frac{-0.23°C}{-1.86°C/m} = 0.12 \ m$$

4 EVALUATE As shown by the unit cancellation, the answer gives the molality, as desired. The answer is properly limited to two significant digits.

PRACTICE

1. A solution consists of 10.3 g of the nonelectrolyte glucose, $C_6H_{12}O_6$, dissolved in 250. g of water. What is the freezing-point depression of the solution?

   Answer
   −0.426°C

2. In a laboratory experiment, the freezing point of an aqueous solution of glucose is found to be −0.325°C. What is the molal concentration of this solution?

   Answer
   0.175 m

3. If 0.500 mol of a nonelectrolyte solute are dissolved in 500.0 g of ether, what is the freezing point of the solution?

   Answer
   −118.1°C

4. The freezing point of an aqueous solution that contains a non-electrolyte is −9.0°C.
   a. What is the freezing-point depression of the solution?
   b. What is the molal concentration of the solution?

   Answer
   a. −9.0°C
   b. 4.8 m

Boiling-Point Elevation

As you learned in Chapter 12, the boiling point of a liquid is the temperature at which the vapor pressure of the liquid is equal to the prevailing atmospheric pressure. Therefore, a change in the vapor pressure of the liquid will cause a corresponding change in the boiling point. As stated earlier, the vapor pressure of a solution containing a nonvolatile solute is lower than the vapor pressure of the pure solvent. This means that more heat will be required to raise the vapor pressure of the solution to equal the atmospheric pressure. Thus, the boiling point of a solution is higher than the boiling point of the pure solvent.

The **molal boiling-point constant** (K_b) *is the boiling-point elevation of the solvent in a 1-molal solution of a nonvolatile, nonelectrolyte solute.* The boiling-point elevation of a 1-molal solution of any nonelectrolyte solute in water has been found by experiment to be 0.51°C. Thus, the molal boiling-point constant for water is 0.51°C/m.

For different solvents, the boiling-point elevations of 1-molal solutions have different values. Some other values for K_b are included in Table 14-2. Like the freezing-point constants, these values are most accurate for dilute solutions.

The **boiling-point elevation,** Δt_b, *is the difference between the boiling points of the pure solvent and a nonelectrolyte solution of that solvent,* and it is directly proportional to the molal concentration of the solution. Boiling-point elevation can be calculated by the following equation.

$$\Delta t_b = K_b m$$

When Δt_b is expressed in $°C/m$ and m is expressed in mol of solute/kg of solvent, Δt_b is the boiling-point elevation in $°C$.

ADDITIONAL SAMPLE PROBLEMS

14-5 What is the boiling point of a solution of 25.0 g of 2-butoxyethanol (butyl cellosolve), $HOCH_2CH_2OC_4H_9$, in 68.7 g of ether?

Ans. 40.8°C

14-5 What mass of glycerol, $CH_2OHCHOHCH_2OH$, must be dissolved in 1.00×10^3 g of water in order to have a boiling point of 104.5°C at standard pressure?

Ans. 810 g

SAMPLE PROBLEM 14-5

What is the boiling-point elevation of a solution made from 20.0 g of a nonelectrolyte solute and 400.0 g of water? The molar mass of the solute is 62.0 g.

SOLUTION

1 ANALYZE

Given: solute mass = 20.0 g
solute molar mass = 62.0 g
solvent mass and identity = 400.0 g of water
Unknown: boiling-point elevation

2 PLAN

Find the molal boiling-point constant, K_b, for water in Table 14-2. To use the equation for boiling-point elevation, $\Delta t_b = K_b m$, you need to determine the molality of the solution.

$$\text{mass of solute (g)} \times \frac{1 \text{ mol solute}}{\text{molar mass of solute (g)}} = \text{amount of solute (mol)}$$

$$\frac{\text{amount of solute (mol)}}{\text{mass of solvent (g)}} \times \frac{1000 \text{ g water}}{1 \text{ kg water}} = \text{molality}$$

$$\Delta t_b = K_b m$$

3 COMPUTE

$$20.0 \text{ g of solute} \times \frac{1 \text{ mol solute}}{62.0 \text{ g of solute}} = 0.323 \text{ mol of solute}$$

$$\frac{0.323 \text{ mol of solute}}{400.0 \text{ g water}} \times \frac{1000 \text{ g water}}{1 \text{ kg water}} = 0.808 \frac{\text{mol solute}}{\text{kg water}} = 0.808 \text{ } m$$

$$\Delta t_b = 0.51°C/m \times 0.808 \text{ } m = 0.41°C$$

PRACTICE

1. A solution contains 50.0 g of sucrose, $C_{12}H_{22}O_{11}$, a nonelectrolyte, dissolved in 500.0 g of water. What is the boiling-point elevation?

   Answer
   0.15°C

2. A solution contains 450.0 g of sucrose, $C_{12}H_{22}O_{11}$, a nonelectrolyte, dissolved in 250 g of water. What is the boiling point of the solution?

   Answer
   102.7°C

3. If the boiling point elevation of an aqueous solution containing a nonvolatile electrolyte is 1.02°C, what is the molality of the solution?

   Answer
   2.0 m

4. The boiling point of an aqueous solution containing a nonvolatile electrolyte is 100.75°C.
   a. What is the boiling-point elevation?
   b. What is the molality of the solution?

   Answer
   a. 0.75°C
   b. 1.5 m

FIGURE 14-8 Make sure the students understand that osmosis stops because the column of water in (b) is now high enough to exert a pressure equal to the osmotic pressure. Point out that if a piston were used to apply pressure to the solution side of the tube in (a), osmosis would stop when the piston applied a pressure equal to the osmotic pressure. If the piston were used to apply a pressure greater than the osmotic pressure, reverse osmosis would occur and the height of the pure water side would rise.

Application

Reverse osmosis is a process often used to get drinking water from sea water. A pressure greater than the osmotic pressure of sea water is applied to sea water on one side of a semipermeable membrane. This forces pure water through the semipermeable membrane.

Classroom Discussion

Ask students to explain osmosis using a mental model based on a theoretical model of how semipermeable membranes work. From a molecule's viewpoint, a membrane is like a wire fence or a net—little structural material and lots of openings. Water molecules are able to pass through these openings freely. Large solute molecules cannot get through the holes but are able to block the passage of many water molecules. Meanwhile, water molecules from the other side are still passing through freely.

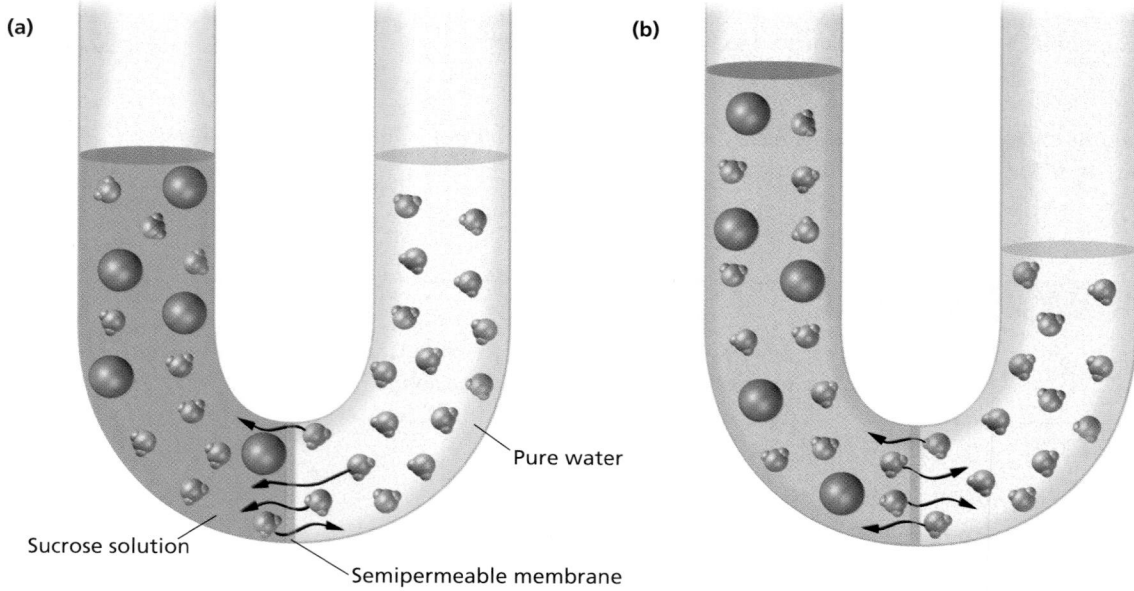

(a) (b)

Pure water

Sucrose solution

Semipermeable membrane

● Used to represent $C_{12}H_{22}O_{11}$, sucrose

🌀 Used to represent H_2O, water

FIGURE 14-8 (a) When pure water and an aqueous sucrose solution are separated by a semipermeable membrane, the net movement of water molecules through the membrane is from the pure water side into the aqueous solution. (b) The level of the solution rises until pressure exerted by the height of the solution equals the osmotic pressure, at which point no net movement of water molecules occurs.

🖥 internet**connect**

SC*L*INKS™

◀ **NSTA** ▶

TOPIC: Osmosis
GO TO: www.scilinks.org
*sci*LINKS CODE: HC2144

Osmotic Pressure

Figure 14-8 illustrates another colligative property. In the figure, an aqueous sucrose solution is separated from pure water by a semipermeable membrane. **Semipermeable membranes** *allow the movement of some particles while blocking the movement of others.* The level of the sucrose solution will rise until a certain height is reached. What causes the level of the solution to rise?

The semipermeable membrane allows water molecules, but not sucrose molecules, to pass through. The sucrose molecules on the solution side allow fewer water molecules to strike the membrane than strike on the pure water side in the same amount of time. Thus, the rate at which water molecules leave the pure water side is greater than the rate at which they leave the solution. This causes the level of the solution to rise. The level rises until the pressure exerted by the height of the solution is large enough to force water molecules back through the membrane from the solution at a rate equal to that at which they enter from the pure water side.

The movement of solvent through a semipermeable membrane from the side of lower solute concentration to the side of higher solute concentration is **osmosis.** Osmosis occurs whenever two solutions of different concentrations are separated by a semipermeable membrane. **Osmotic pressure** *is the external pressure that must be applied to stop osmosis.* In the example given above, osmosis caused the level of the solution to rise until the height of the solution provided the pressure necessary to stop osmosis. Because osmotic pressure is dependent on the concentration of solute particles and not on the type of solute particles, it is a colligative property. The greater the concentration of a solution, the greater the osmotic pressure of the solution.

Regulation of osmosis is vital to the life of a cell because cell membranes are semipermeable. Cells lose water and shrink when placed in a solution of higher concentration. They gain water and swell when placed in a solution of lower concentration. In vertebrates, cells are protected from swelling and shrinking by blood and lymph that surround the cells. Blood and lymph are equal in concentration to the concentration inside the cell.

Electrolytes and Colligative Properties

Early investigators were puzzled by experiments in which certain substances depressed the freezing point or elevated the boiling point of a solvent more than expected. For example, a 0.1 m solution of sodium chloride, NaCl, lowers the freezing point of the solvent nearly twice as much as a 0.1 m solution of sucrose. A 0.1 m solution of calcium chloride, $CaCl_2$, lowers the freezing point of the solvent nearly three times as much as a 0.1 m solution of sucrose. The effect on boiling points is similar.

To understand why this is so, contrast the behavior of sucrose with that of sodium chloride in aqueous solutions. Each sucrose molecule dissolves to produce only one particle in solution. So 1 mol of sucrose dissolves to produce only 1 mol of particles in solution. Sugar is a nonelectrolyte. NaCl, however, is a strong electrolyte. Each mole of NaCl dissolves to produce 2 mol of particles in solution: 1 mol of sodium ions and 1 mol of chloride ions. Figure 14-9 compares the production of particles in solution for three different solutes. As you can see, electrolytes produce more than 1 mol of solute particles for each mole of compound dissolved.

FIGURE 14-9 Compare the number of particles produced per formula unit for these three solutes. Colligative properties depend on the total concentration of particles.

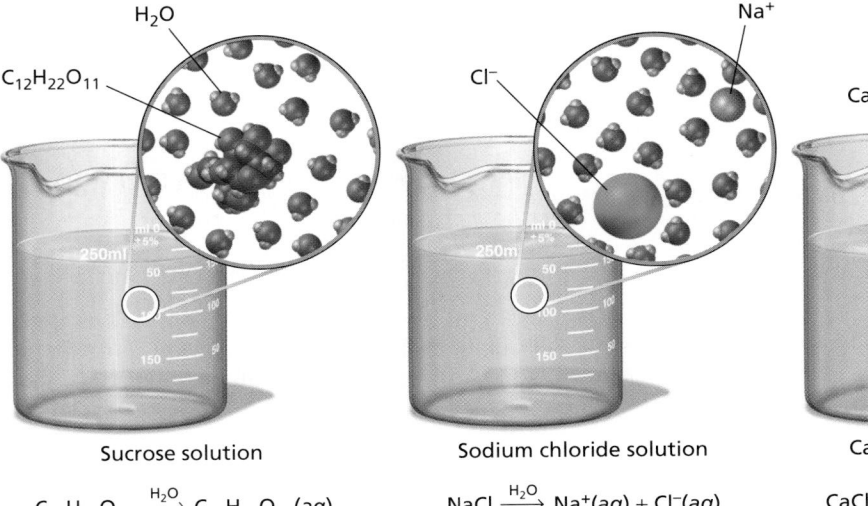
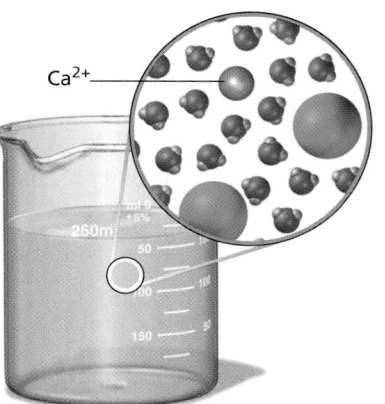

Sucrose solution

$C_{12}H_{22}O_{11} \xrightarrow{H_2O} C_{12}H_{22}O_{11}(aq)$

Sodium chloride solution

$NaCl \xrightarrow{H_2O} Na^+(aq) + Cl^-(aq)$

Calcium chloride solution

$CaCl_2 \xrightarrow{H_2O} Ca^{2+}(aq) + 2Cl^-(aq)$

14-6 What is the expected boiling point of a 1.70 *m* solution of sodium sulfate in water?

Ans. 102.6°C

14-6 A water solution contains 42.9 g of calcium nitrate dissolved in 500. g of water. Calculate the freezing point of the solution.

Ans. −2.92°C

Alternative Assessment

Have students do an experiment to determine the concentration of salt required to prevent 500 mL of an aqueous solution from freezing when placed in their home freezer overnight. (A 0.9 *m* NaCl solution has a freezing point of approximately −3°C, or 27°F. A 1.9 *m* NaCl solution has a freezing point of approximately −6.5°C, or 20°F.) Make sure the students use a plastic container large enough to allow for ice expansion if their solution does freeze.

Calculated Values for Electrolyte Solutions

Remember that colligative properties depend on the total concentration of solute particles regardless of their identity. So electrolytes cause changes in colligative properties proportional to the total molality in terms of all dissolved particles instead of formula units. For the same molal concentrations of sucrose and sodium chloride, you would expect the effect on colligative properties to be twice as large for sodium chloride as for sucrose. What about barium nitrate, $Ba(NO_3)_2$? Each mole of barium nitrate yields 3 mol of ions in solution.

$$Ba(NO_3)_2(s) \longrightarrow Ba^{2+}(aq) + 2NO_3^-(aq)$$

You would expect a $Ba(NO_3)_2$ solution of a given molality to lower the freezing point of its solvent three times as much as a nonelectrolytic solution of the same molality.

SAMPLE PROBLEM 14-6

What is the expected change in the freezing point of water in a solution of 62.5 g of barium nitrate, $Ba(NO_3)_2$, in 1.00 kg of water?

SOLUTION

1 **ANALYZE**

Given: solute mass and formula = 62.5 g $Ba(NO_3)_2$
solvent mass and identity = 1.00 kg water
$\Delta t_f = K_f m$

Unknown: expected freezing-point depression

2 **PLAN**

The molality can be calculated by converting the solute mass to moles and then dividing by the number of kilograms of solvent. That molality is in terms of formula units of $Ba(NO_3)_2$ and must be converted to molality in terms of dissociated ions in solution. It must be multiplied by the number of moles of ions produced per mole of formula unit. This adjusted molality can then be used to calculate the freezing-point depression.

$$\frac{\text{mass of solute (g)}}{\text{mass of solvent (kg)}} \times \frac{1 \text{ mol solute}}{\text{molar mass of solute (g)}} = \text{molality of solution} \left(\frac{\text{mol}}{\text{kg}} \right)$$

$$\text{molality of solution} \left(\frac{\text{mol}}{\text{kg}} \right) \times \text{molality conversion} \left(\frac{\text{mol ions}}{\text{mol}} \right) \times K_f \left(\frac{°C \cdot \text{kg H}_2O}{\text{mol ions}} \right)$$

$$= \text{expected freezing-point depression (°C)}$$

This problem is similar to Sample Problem 14-5, except that the solute is ionic rather than a nonionizing molecular solute. The number of particles in solution will therefore equal the number of ions of the solute.

3 **COMPUTE**

$$\frac{62.5 \text{ g } Ba(NO_3)_2}{1.00 \text{ kg H}_2O} \times \frac{\text{mol } Ba(NO_3)_2}{261.35 \text{ g } Ba(NO_3)_2} = \frac{0.239 \text{ mol } Ba(NO_3)_2}{\text{kg H}_2O}$$

$$Ba(NO_3)_2(s) \longrightarrow Ba^{2+}(aq) + 2NO_3^-(aq)$$

Each formula unit of barium nitrate yields three ions in solution.

$$\frac{0.239 \text{ mol } Ba(NO_3)_2}{\text{kg } H_2O} \times \frac{3 \text{ mol ions}}{\text{mol } Ba(NO_3)_2} \times \frac{-1.86°C \cdot \text{kg } H_2O}{\text{mol ions}} = -1.33°C$$

4   EVALUATE   The units cancel properly to give the desired answer in °C. The answer is correctly given to three significant digits. The mass of the solute is approximately one-fourth its molar mass and would give 0.75 mol of ions in the 1 kg of solvent, so the estimated answer of $0.75 \times -1.86°C = -1.4°C$ supports our computation.

PRACTICE

1. What is the expected freezing-point depression for a solution that contains 2.0 mol of magnesium sulfate dissolved in 1.0 kg of water?

   Answer
   −7.4°C

2. What is the expected boiling-point elevation of water for a solution that contains 150 g of sodium chloride dissolved in 1.0 kg of water?

   Answer
   2.7°C

3. The freezing point of an aqueous sodium chloride solution is −20.0°C. What is the molality of the solution?

   Answer
   5.4 *m* NaCl

Actual Values for Electrolyte Solutions

It is important to remember that the values just calculated are only *expected* values. As stated earlier, a 0.1 *m* solution of sodium chloride lowers the freezing point *nearly* twice as much as a 0.1 *m* solution of sucrose. The actual values of the colligative properties for all strong electrolytes are *almost* what would be expected based on the number of particles they produce in solution. Some specific examples are given in Table 14-3. The freezing-point depression of a compound that produces two ions per formula unit is almost twice that of a nonelectrolytic solution. The freezing-point depression of a compound that produces three ions per formula unit is almost three times that of a nonelectrolytic solution.

TABLE 14-3   *Molal Freezing-Point Depressions for Aqueous Solutions of Ionic Solutes*

Solute	Concentration (*m*)	Δt_f, observed (°C)	Δt_f, nonelectrolyte solution (°C)	$\dfrac{\Delta t_f, \text{ observed}}{\Delta t_f, \text{ nonelectrolyte solution}}$
KCl	0.1	−0.345	−0.186	1.85
	0.01	−0.0361	−0.0186	1.94
	0.001	−0.00366	−0.00186	1.97
MgSO$_4$	0.1	−0.225	−0.186	1.21
	0.01	−0.0285	−0.0186	1.53
	0.001	−0.00338	−0.00186	1.82
BaCl$_2$	0.1	−0.470	−0.186	2.53
	0.01	−0.0503	−0.0186	2.70
	0.001	−0.00530	−0.00186	2.84

Common Misconception

Students may think that adding salt to cooking water raises the boiling point and causes food to cook faster. As a practical example, a cook might add about 30 g (about $1\frac{1}{2}$ tbsp) of NaCl to 5 L of water to cook pasta. This 5 L solution contains 1.0 mol of ions, so its ion concentration is 0.2 m. At best, such a solution would have a boiling point about 0.1°C higher than that of pure water, hardly enough to make a difference in cooking time. Raising the boiling point from 100°C to 102°C would require almost 600 g (1.3 lb) of salt in 5 L of water.

SECTION REVIEW

1. a. freezing-point depression
b. freezing-point depression

2. −3.9°C/m; acetic acid

3. the more-concentrated solution

4. a. −0.744°C
b. No. At this concentration, clustering of ions will cause the freezing-point depression to be less than expected.

FIGURE 14-10 The salts applied to icy roads are electrolytes. They lower the freezing point of water and melt the ice.

Look at the values given for KCl solutions in Table 14-3. The freezing-point depression of a 0.1 m KCl solution is only 1.85 times greater than that of a nonelectrolyte solution. However, as the concentration decreases, the freezing-point depression comes closer to the value that is twice that of a nonelectrolytic solution.

The differences between the expected and calculated values are caused by the attractive forces that exist between dissociated ions in aqueous solution. The attraction between the hydrated ions in the solution is small compared with those in the crystalline solid. However, forces of attraction do interfere with the movements of the aqueous ions. The more concentrated a solution is, the closer together the ions are, and the greater the attraction between ions is. Only in very dilute solutions is the average distance between the ions large enough and the attraction between ions small enough for the solute ions to move about almost completely freely.

Peter Debye and Erich Hückel introduced a theory in 1923 to account for this attraction between ions in dilute aqueous solutions. According to this theory, the attraction between dissociated ions of ionic solids in dilute aqueous solutions is caused by an ionic atmosphere that surrounds each ion. This means that each ion is, on average, surrounded by more ions of opposite charge than of like charge. This clustering effect hinders the movements of solute ions. A cluster of hydrated ions can act as a single unit rather than as individual ions. Thus, the effective total concentration is less than expected, based on the number of ions known to be present.

Ions of higher charge attract other ions very strongly. They therefore cluster more and have lower effective concentrations than ions with smaller charge. For example, ions formed by $MgSO_4$ have charges of 2+ and 2−. Ions formed by KCl have charges of 1+ and 1−. Note in Table 14-3 that $MgSO_4$ in a solution does not depress the freezing point as much as the same concentration of KCl.

SECTION REVIEW

1. What colligative properties are displayed by each of the following situations?
   a. Antifreeze is added to a car's cooling system to prevent freezing when the air temperature is below 0°C.
   b. Ice melts on sidewalks after salt has been spread on them.

2. Two moles of a nonelectrolytic solute are dissolved in 1 kg of an unknown solvent. The solution freezes at 7.8°C *below* its normal freezing point. What is the molal freezing-point constant of the unknown solvent? What is your prediction for the identity of the solvent?

3. If two solutions of equal amounts in a U-tube are separated by a semipermeable membrane, will the level of the more-concentrated solution or the less-concentrated solution rise?

4. a. Calculate the expected freezing-point depression of a 0.2 m KNO_3 solution.
   b. Will the value you calculated match the actual freezing-point depression for this solution? Why or why not?

CHAPTER **14** REVIEW

CHAPTER SUMMARY

14-1
- The separation of ions that occurs when an ionic solid dissolves is called dissociation.
- When two different ionic solutions are mixed, a precipitate may form if ions from the two solutions react to form an insoluble compound.
- A net ionic equation for a reaction in aqueous solution includes only compounds and ions that change chemically in the reaction. Spectator ions are ions that do not take part in such a reaction.

- Formation of ions from solute molecules is called ionization. A molecular compound may ionize in a water solution if the attraction of the polar water molecules is strong enough to break the polar-covalent bonds of the solute molecules.
- An H_3O^+ ion is called a hydronium ion.
- All, or almost all, of a dissolved strong electrolyte exists as ions in an aqueous solution, whereas a relatively small amount of a dissolved weak electrolyte exists as ions in an aqueous solution.

Vocabulary

dissociation (425)	ionization (431)	spectator ions (429)	weak electrolyte (433)
hydronium ion (431)	net ionic equation (429)	strong electrolyte (432)	

14-2
- Colligative properties of solutions depend only on the total number of solute particles present. Boiling-point elevation, freezing-point depression, vapor-pressure lowering, and osmotic pressure are all colligative properties.
- The molal boiling-point and freezing-point constants are used to calculate boiling-point elevations and freezing-point depressions of solvents containing nonvolatile solutes.

- Electrolytes have a greater effect on the freezing and boiling points of solvents than do nonelectrolytes.
- Except in very dilute solutions, the values of colligative properties of electrolytic solutions are less than expected because of the attraction between ions in solution.

Vocabulary

boiling-point elevation, Δt_b (440)	molal boiling-point constant, K_b (440)	nonvolatile substance (436)	osmotic pressure (442)
colligative properties (436)	molal freezing-point constant, K_f (438)	osmosis (442)	semipermeable membranes (442)
freezing-point depression, Δt_f (438)			

REVIEWING CONCEPTS

1. How many moles of ions are contained in 1 L of a 1 M solution of KCl? of $Mg(NO_3)_2$? (14-1)

2. Use Table 14-1 to predict whether each of the following compounds is considered soluble or insoluble:
   a. KCl
   b. $NaNO_3$
   c. AgCl
   d. $BaSO_4$
   e. $Ca_3(PO_4)_2$
   f. $Pb(ClO_3)_2$
   g. $(NH_4)_2S$
   h. $PbCl_2$ (in cold water)
   i. FeS
   j. $Al_2(SO_4)_3$ (14-1)

3. What is a net ionic equation? (14-1)

4. a. What is ionization?
   b. Distinguish between ionization and dissociation. (14-1)

REVIEW ANSWERS

1. 2 mol; 3 mol

2.
a. soluble	**f.** soluble
b. soluble	**g.** soluble
c. insoluble	**h.** insoluble
d. insoluble	**i.** insoluble
e. insoluble	**j.** soluble

3. an equation that includes only those compounds and ions that are involved in a chemical change in aqueous solution

4. **a.** the formation of ions from solute molecules by the action of the solvent
   b. In dissociation, ions of an ionic compound separate from each other. In ionization, ions form where none existed in the undissolved compound.

5. **a.** A strong electrolyte exists almost entirely as ions in dilute aqueous solution, to whatever extent the solute dissolves in water. A weak electrolyte dissolves in water but ionizes only to a slight extent.
   b. Answers may include: hydrogen chloride and aluminum chloride are strong electrolytes; hydrogen fluoride and acetic acid are weak electrolytes.

6. the extent to which a compound forms ions when dissolved

7. *Strong* and *weak* refer to the extent to which the solute is dissociated or ionized. *Dilute* and *concentrated* refer to the quantity of solute dissolved in a given quantity of solvent.

8. **a.** lowers the vapor pressure
   b. lowers the freezing point
   c. raises the boiling point
   d. increases the osmotic pressure across the membrane

9.

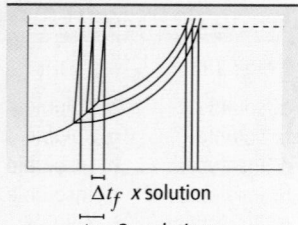

$\overleftrightarrow{\Delta t_f}$ x solution

$\overleftrightarrow{\Delta t_f}$ 2x solution

Δt_f for 2x amount of solute is twice that for x amount of solute.

10. a. Water from the less-concentrated solution passes through the membrane by osmosis into the more-concentrated solution.
b. when the added pressure resulting from the height of the solution equals the osmotic pressure
c. There is no net movement.

11. a. A nonvolatile electrolyte will lower the freezing point or raise the boiling point more than a nonelectrolyte at the same concentration.
b. One mole of a nonelectrolyte produces 1 mol of particles in solution. A mole of a nonvolatile electrolyte produces more than 1 mol of ions in solution.

12. The difference is caused by attractive forces between ions in solution.

13. a. $KI(s) \xrightarrow{H_2O} K^+(aq) + I^-(aq)$

b. $NaNO_3(s) \xrightarrow{H_2O}$ $Na^+(aq) + NO_3^-(aq)$

c. $MgCl_2(s) \xrightarrow{H_2O}$ $Mg^{2+}(aq) + 2Cl^-(aq)$

d. $Na_2SO_4(s) \xrightarrow{H_2O}$ $2Na^+(aq) + SO_4^{2-}(aq)$

14. a. 1 mol K^+, 1 mol I^-; 2 mol ions
b. 1 mol Na^+, 1 mol NO_3^-; 2 mol ions
c. 1 mol Mg^{2+}, 2 mol Cl^-; 3 mol ions
d. 2 mol Na^+, 1 mol SO_4^{2-}; 3 mol ions

5. a. Define and distinguish between strong electrolytes and weak electrolytes.
b. Give two examples of each type.   (14-1)

6. What determines the strength with which a solute acts as an electrolyte?   (14-1)

7. Distinguish between the use of the terms *strong* and *weak* and the use of the terms *dilute* and *concentrated* when used to describe electrolyte solutions.   (14-1)

8. How does the presence of a nonvolatile solute affect each of the following properties of the solvent into which the solute is dissolved?
a. vapor pressure
b. freezing point
c. boiling point
d. osmotic pressure   (14-2)

9. Using Figure 14-6 as a guide, make a sketch of a vapor pressure-versus-temperature curve that shows the comparison of pure water, a solution with x amount of solute, and a solution with 2x the amount of solute. What is the relationship between Δt_f for the x curve and Δt_f for the 2x curve?   (14-2)

10. a. Why does the level of the more-concentrated solution rise when two solutions of different concentrations are separated by a semipermeable membrane?
b. When does the level of the solution stop rising?
c. When the level stops rising, what is the net movement of water molecules across the membrane?   (14-2)

11. a. Compare the effects of nonvolatile electrolytes with the effects of nonvolatile nonelectrolytes on the freezing and boiling points of solvents in which they are dissolved.
b. Why are such differences observed?   (14-2)

12. Why does the actual freezing-point depression of an electrolytic solution differ from the freezing-point depression calculated on the basis of the concentration of particles?   (14-2)

Dissociation

13. Write the equation for the dissolution of each of the following ionic compounds in water. (Hint: See Sample Problem 14-1.)
a. KI
b. $NaNO_3$
c. $MgCl_2$
d. Na_2SO_4

14. For the compounds listed in the previous problem, determine the number of moles of each ion produced as well as the total number of moles of ions produced when 1 mol of each compound dissolves in water.

15. Write the equation for the dissolution of each of the following in water, and then indicate the total number of moles of solute ions formed.
a. 0.50 mol strontium nitrate
b. 0.50 mol sodium phosphate

Precipitation Reactions

16. Using Table 14-1, write the balanced chemical equation, write the overall ionic equation, identify the spectator ions and possible precipitates, and write the net ionic equation for each of the following reactions. (Hint: See Sample Problem 14-2.)
a. mercury(II) chloride (*aq*) + potassium sulfide (*aq*) $\longrightarrow$
b. sodium carbonate (*aq*) + calcium chloride (*aq*) $\longrightarrow$
c. copper(II) chloride (*aq*) + ammonium phosphate (*aq*) $\longrightarrow$

17. Identify the spectator ions in the reaction between KCl and $AgNO_3$ in an aqueous solution.

18. Copper(II) chloride and lead(II) nitrate react in aqueous solutions by double replacement. Write the balanced chemical equation, the overall ionic equation, and the net ionic equation for this reaction. If 13.45 g of copper(II) chloride react, what is the maximum amount of precipitate that could be formed?

Freezing-Point Depression of Nonelectrolytes

19. Determine the freezing-point depression of H_2O in each of the following solutions. (Hint: See Sample Problem 14-3.)
  a. 1.50 *m* solution of $C_{12}H_{22}O_{11}$ (sucrose) in H_2O
  b. 171 g of $C_{12}H_{22}O_{11}$ in 1.00 kg H_2O
  c. 77.0 g of $C_{12}H_{22}O_{11}$ in 400. g H_2O

20. Determine the molality of each solution of an unknown nonelectrolyte in water, given the following freezing-point depressions. (Hint: See Sample Problem 14-4.)
  a. −0.930°C
  b. −3.72°C
  c. −8.37°C

21. A solution contains 20.0 g of $C_6H_{12}O_6$ (glucose) in 250. g of water.
  a. What is the freezing-point depression of the solvent?
  b. What is the freezing point of the solution?

22. How many grams of antifreeze, $C_2H_4(OH)_2$, would be required per 500. g of water to prevent the water from freezing at a temperature of −20.0°C?

23. Pure benzene, C_6H_6, freezes at 5.45°C. A solution containing 7.24 g of $C_2Cl_4H_2$ in 115 g of benzene (specific gravity = 0.879) freezes at 3.55°C. Based on these data, what is the molal freezing-point constant for benzene?

24. If 1.500 g of a solute having a molar mass of 125.0 g were dissolved in 35.00 g of camphor, what would be the resulting freezing point of the solution?

Boiling-Point Elevation of Nonelectrolytes

25. Determine the boiling-point elevation of H_2O in each of the following solutions. (Hint: See Sample Problem 14-5.)
  a. 2.5 *m* solution of $C_6H_{12}O_6$ (glucose) in H_2O
  b. 3.20 g $C_6H_{12}O_6$ in 1.00 kg H_2O
  c. 20.0 g $C_{12}H_{22}O_{11}$ (sucrose) in 500. g H_2O

26. Determine the molality of each water solution given the following boiling points:
  a. 100.25°C
  b. 101.53°C
  c. 102.805°C

Colligative Properties of Electrolytes

27. Given 1.00 *m* aqueous solutions of each of the following electrolytic substances, what is the expected change in the freezing point of the solvent? (Hint: See Sample Problem 14-6.)
  a. KI
  b. $CaCl_2$
  c. $Ba(NO_3)_2$

28. What is the expected change in the freezing point of water for an aqueous solution that is 0.015 *m* $AlCl_3$?

29. What is the expected freezing point of a solution containing 85.0 g of NaCl dissolved in 450. g of water?

30. Determine the expected boiling point of a solution made by dissolving 25.0 g of barium chloride in 0.150 kg of water.

31. The change in the boiling point of water for an aqueous solution of potassium iodide is 0.65°C. Determine the apparent molal concentration of potassium iodide.

32. The freezing point of an aqueous solution of barium nitrate is −2.65°C. Determine the apparent molal concentration of barium nitrate.

33. Calculate the expected freezing point of a solution containing 1.00 kg of H_2O and 0.250 mol of NaCl.

34. Experimental data for a 1.00 *m* MgI_2 aqueous solution indicate an actual change in the freezing point of water of −4.78°C. Determine the expected change in the freezing point of water. Suggest a possible reason for discrepancies between the experimental and the expected values.

MIXED REVIEW

35. Given 0.01 *m* aqueous solutions of each of the following, arrange the solutions in order of increasing change in the freezing point of the solution.
  a. NaI
  b. $CaCl_2$
  c. K_3PO_4
  d. $C_6H_{12}O_6$ (glucose)

15. a. $Sr(NO_3)_2(s) \xrightarrow{H_2O}$
  $Sr^{2+}(aq) + 2NO_3^-(aq)$
  1.50 mol ions
  b. $Na_3PO_4(s) \xrightarrow{H_2O}$
  $3Na^+(aq) + PO_4^{3-}(aq)$
  2.00 mol ions

16. a. $HgCl_2(aq) + K_2S(aq) \longrightarrow$
  $HgS(s) + 2KCl(aq)$

  $Hg^{2+}(aq) + 2Cl^-(aq) + 2K^+(aq) + S^{2-}(aq) \longrightarrow HgS(s) + 2K^+(aq) + 2Cl^-(aq)$

  spectator ions: Cl^- and K^+
  precipitate: HgS
  $Hg^{2+}(aq) + S^{2-}(aq) \longrightarrow HgS(s)$

  b. $Na_2CO_3(aq) + CaCl_2(aq) \longrightarrow$
  $2NaCl(aq) + CaCO_3(s)$

  $2Na^+(aq) + CO_3^{2-}(aq) + Ca^{2+}(aq) + 2Cl^-(aq) \longrightarrow CaCO_3(s) + 2Na^+(aq) + 2Cl^-(aq)$

  spectator ions: Na^+ and Cl^-
  precipitate: $CaCO_3$

  $Ca^{2+}(aq) + CO_3^{2-}(aq) \longrightarrow CaCO_3(s)$

  c. $3CuCl_2(aq) + 2(NH_4)_3PO_4(aq) \longrightarrow Cu_3(PO_4)_2(s) + 6NH_4Cl(aq)$

  $3Cu^{2+}(aq) + 6Cl^-(aq) + 6NH_4^+(aq) + 2PO_4^{3-}(aq) \longrightarrow Cu_3(PO_4)_2(s) + 6NH_4^+(aq) + 6Cl^-(aq)$

  spectator ions: NH_4^+ and Cl^-
  precipitate: $Cu_3(PO_4)_2$

  $3Cu^{2+}(aq) + 2PO_4^{3-}(aq) \longrightarrow Cu_3(PO_4)_2(s)$

17. K^+ and NO_3^-

18. $CuCl_2(aq) + Pb(NO_3)_2(aq) \longrightarrow Cu(NO_3)_2(aq) + PbCl_2(s)$

  $Cu^{2+}(aq) + 2Cl^-(aq) + Pb^{2+}(aq) + 2NO_3^-(aq) \longrightarrow Cu^{2+}(aq) + 2NO_3^-(aq) + PbCl_2(s)$

  $Pb^{2+}(aq) + 2Cl^-(aq) \longrightarrow PbCl_2(s)$

  27.81 g $PbCl_2$

19. a. −2.79°C   **c.** −1.05°C
  b. −0.93°C

20. a. 0.500 *m*   **c.** 4.50 *m*
  b. 2.00 *m*

21. a. −0.826°C
  b. −0.826°C

22. 334 g $C_2H_4(OH)_2$

23. −5.07°C/m

24. 165.2°C

25. a. 1.3°C   **c.** 0.060°C
  b. 0.0091°C

26. a. 0.49 m solute   **c.** 5.5 m solute
  b. 3.0 m solute

27. a. −3.72°C   **c.** −5.58°C
  b. −5.58°C

28. −0.11°C

29. −12.0°C

30. 101.2°C

31. 0.64 m KI

32. 0.475 m $Ba(NO_3)_2$

33. −0.930°C

34. −5.58°C; the ions do not move freely because of forces of attraction between them

35. d, a, b, c

36. 0.435 m $CaCl_2$

37. a. $Ca(NO_3)_2(aq) + 2NaCl(aq)$
     $\longrightarrow CaCl_2(aq) + 2NaNO_3(aq)$

  b. No precipitate forms.

38. $HBr(g) + H_2O(l) \longrightarrow$
         $H_3O^+(aq) + Br^-(aq)$

39. a. $K_2S(s) \xrightarrow{H_2O} 2K^+(aq) + S^{2-}(aq)$
   0.825 mol solute ions

  b. $Al_2(SO_4)_3(s) \xrightarrow{H_2O}$
         $2Al^{3+}(aq) + 3SO_4^{2-}(aq)$
   0.75 mol solute ions

40. 0.39°C

41. $HNO_2(aq) + H_2O(l) \rightleftharpoons$
         $H_3O^+(aq) + NO_2^-(aq)$

   $HNO_3(aq) + H_2O(l) \longrightarrow$
         $H_3O^+(aq) + NO_3^-(aq)$

42. 101.8°C

43. $Na_2CO_3(s) \xrightarrow{H_2O}$
         $2Na^+(aq) + CO_3^{2-}(aq)$

   0.40 mol Na^+; 0.20 mol CO_3^{2-};
   0.60 mol solute ions

36. What is the molal concentration of an aqueous calcium chloride solution that freezes at −2.43°C?

37. a. Write the balanced formula equation that shows the possible products of a double replacement reaction between calcium nitrate and sodium chloride.

  b. Using Table 14-1, determine if there is a precipitate.

38. Write a balanced equation to show what occurs when hydrogen bromide dissolves and reacts with water. Include a hydronium ion in the equation.

39. Write the equation for the dissolution of each of the following in water, and then indicate the total number of moles of solute ions formed.
  a. 0.275 mol potassium sulfide
  b. 0.15 mol aluminum sulfate

40. Calculate the expected change in the boiling point of water in a solution made up of 131.2 g of silver nitrate, $AgNO_3$, in 2.00 kg of water.

41. Nitrous acid, HNO_2, is a weak electrolyte. Nitric acid, HNO_3, is a strong electrolyte. Write equations to represent the ionization of each in water. Include the hydronium ion, and show the appropriate kind of arrow in each case.

42. Find the boiling point of an aqueous solution containing a nonelectrolyte that freezes at −6.51°C.

43. Write a balanced equation for the dissolution of sodium carbonate, Na_2CO_3, in water. Find the number of moles of each ion produced when 0.20 mol of sodium carbonate dissolves. Then find the total number of moles of ions.

44. Given the reaction below and the information in Table 14-1, write the net ionic equation for the reaction.

   potassium phosphate (aq) + lead (II) nitrate (aq)

45. Find the expected freezing point of a water solution that contains 268 g of aluminum nitrate, $Al(NO_3)_3$, in 8.50 kg of water.

CRITICAL THINKING

46. Applying Models
  a. You are conducting a freezing-point determination in the laboratory using an aqueous solution of KNO_3. The observed freezing point of the solution is −1.15°C. Using a pure water sample, you recorded the freezing point of the pure solvent on the same thermometer as 0.25°C. Determine the molal concentration of KNO_3. Assume that there are no forces of attraction between ions.

  b. You are not satisfied with the result in part (a) because you suspect that you should not ignore the effect of ion interaction. You take a 10.00 mL sample of the solution. After carefully evaporating the water from the solution, you obtain a mass of 0.415 g KNO_3. Determine the actual molal concentration of KNO_3 and the percentage difference between the predicted concentration and the actual concentration of KNO_3. Assume that the solution's density is 1.00 g/mL.

47. Analyzing Information The observed freezing-point depression for electrolyte solutions is sometimes less than the calculated value. Why does this occur? Is the difference greater for concentrated solutions or dilute solutions?

48. Analyzing Information The osmotic pressure of a dilute solution can be calculated as follows.

   $\pi = MRT$
   π = osmotic pressure
   M = concentration in moles per liter
   R = ideal gas constant
   T = absolute temperature of the solution

   How does the osmotic-pressure equation compare with the ideal gas law?

HANDBOOK SEARCH

49. Common reactions for Group 13 elements are found in the *Elements Handbook*. Review this material and answer the following.

a. Write net ionic equations for each of the example reactions shown on page 751.

b. Which reactions did not change when written in net ionic form? Why?

50. Common reactions for Group 14 elements are found in the *Elements Handbook*. Review this material and answer the following.

a. Write net ionic equations for each of the example reactions shown on page 755.

b. Which reactions did not change when written in net ionic form? Why?

RESEARCH & WRITING

51. Find out how much salt a large northern city, such as New York City or Chicago, uses on its streets in a typical winter. What environmental problems result from this use of salt? What substitutes for salt are being used to melt ice and snow?

52. Research the role of electrolytes and electrolytic solutions in your body. Find out how electrolytes work in the functioning of nerves and muscles. What are some of the health problems that can arise from an imbalance of electrolytes in body fluids?

ALTERNATIVE ASSESSMENT

53. Performance Determine the freezing point of four different mixtures of water and ethylene glycol (use commercial antifreeze). What mixture shows the lowest freezing point?

54. Performance Find the optimum mixture of salt and ice for reducing the temperature of the chilling bath for an ice-cream freezer. Use your data to write a set of instructions on how to prepare the chilling bath for making ice cream.

55. Performance Using a low-voltage dry cell, assemble a conductivity apparatus. Secure several unknown aqueous solutions of equal molality from your instructor, and use the apparatus to distinguish the electrolytes from the non-electrolytes. Among those identified as electrolytes, rank their relative strengths as conductors from good to poor.

56. Performance Using equal volumes of the unknown solutions from the preceding activity, explain how you could use the freezing-point depression concept to distinguish the electrolytes from the nonelectrolytes. Explain how you could determine the number of ions contained per molecule among the solutes identified as electrolytes. Design and conduct an experiment to test your theories.

44. $3Pb^{2+}(aq) + 2PO_4^{3-}(aq) \longrightarrow$
$Pb_3(PO_4)_2(s)$

45. $-1.10°C$

46. a. $0.376\ m$
b. $0.410\ m;\ 91.7\%$

47. There are attractive forces between ions. The attractive forces are greater for concentrated solutions.

48. In the equation $\pi = MRT$, the variable M stands for molarity, which is expressed as a concentration in moles/L. So M = number of moles per unit volume = n/V. Substituting n/V into the equation gives

$$\pi = \frac{nRT}{V}$$

or $\pi V = nRT$, which is identical to the ideal gas law except for π, which represents osmotic pressure.

49. a. $2Al(s) + 2OH^-(aq) + 2H_2O(l)$
$\longrightarrow 2AlO_2^-(aq) + 3H_2(g)$

$2Al(s) + 6H^+(aq) \longrightarrow$
$2Al^{3+}(aq) + 3H_2(g)$

$Al(s) + 4H^+(aq) + NO_3^-(aq) \longrightarrow$
$Al^{3+}(aq) + NO(g) + 2H_2O(l)$

$2Al(s) + 3Cl_2(g) \longrightarrow 2AlCl_3(s)$

$4Al(s) + 3O_2(g) \longrightarrow 2Al_2O_3(s)$

b. formation of the halide and oxide; because there are no spectator ions

50. a. $Sn(s) + O_2(g) \longrightarrow SnO_2(s)$

$Sn(s) + 2H^+(aq) \longrightarrow$
$Sn^{2+}(aq) + H_2(g)$

$Sn(s) + 2Cl_2(g) \longrightarrow SnCl_4(s)$

b. formation of the halide and oxide; because there are no spectator ions

Acids and Bases

PACING CHART Compression Guide: *(To shorten, eliminate items in italics.)*	CLASSROOM RESOURCES		
	NSE Standards	Teaching Resources	Experiments
15-1 **Properties of Acids and Bases** 2 45-minute periods 1 90-minute block *Arrhenius Acids and Bases, pp. 459–462*	UCP 1–2, 4–5 SAI 1–2 HNS 1, 3	**ATE Demo,** pp. 454, 460 **PE** Elements Handbook **TM 70A, TM 71A**	Quick Lab, p. 458
15-2 **Acid-Base Theories** 2 45-minute periods 1 90-minute block *Monoprotic and Polyprotic Acids, pp. 465–466*	UCP 1–2, 4–5 HNS 1, 3	**PE** Elements Handbook **T 84, T 85, TM 72A**	
15-3 **Acid-Base Reactions** 2 45-minute periods 1 90-minute block *Acid Rain, p. 475*	UCP 1–2, 5 HNS 1, 3	**PE** Elements Handbook **T 86, TM 73A**	

Review and Assessment 2 45-minute periods 1 90-minute block	REVIEW RESOURCES		
	Cumulative Review	Alternative Assessment	Traditional Assessment
	SR Chapter 15 Mixed Review PE Chapter 15 34–37, pp. 478–479	PE 44–45, p. 479 ATE 474–475 AA Items for Chapter 15	Chapter 15 Text Test Generator items for Chapter 15

ASSIGNMENT RESOURCES

Section Homework Resources & Review	Problem-Solving Practice

HR Homework Worksheets 15-1, 15-2, 15-3,
     15-4
     Graphic Org. Assignments 15-1, 15-3
PE Section Review, 1–4, p. 462
     Chapter Review, 1–3, 17–25, 30, p. 477
SR Section Review 15-1
	ATE Additional Examples, p. 455

HR Homework Worksheets 15-5, 15-6
     Graphic Org. Assignments 15-5, 15-6
PE Section Review, 1–3, p. 468
     Chapter Review, 8–15, p. 477
SR Section Review 15-2	

HR Homework Worksheets 15-7, 15-8, 15-9
     Graphic Org. Assignment 15-9
PE Section Review, 1–2, p. 475
     Chapter Review, 16, 26–29, 31–32, p. 477
SR Section Review 15-3	

TECHNOLOGY RESOURCES

Technology & Internet Resources

 CTW 7 Segment 7 Science Controversy:
Salt in the Diet
CTW 26 Segment 26 Acids in the Environment

 Holt Chemistry Videodiscs Teacher's Correlation Guide
for Chapter 15

 Module 8: Brønsted Acid/Base Tutorial

 internet**connect**

On-line Student Resources:
GO TO: www.scilinks.org
The following SciLinks Internet resources can be
found in the student text for this chapter.

TOPICS:
• Acids, p. 456 (HC2151)
• Bases, p. 457 (HC2152)
• Household acids and bases, p. 458 (HC2153)
• Salt, p. 474 (HC2154)

On-line Teacher Resources:
GO TO: go.hrw.com
KEYWORD: HC2 HOME
Visit the HRW Web site for a variety of resources
related to this chapter.

 Smithsonian Institution®
Internet Connections
Visit **www.si.edu/hrw** for additional on-line
resources.

 CNN**fyi**.com
Visit **www.cnnfyi.com** for late-breaking news
and current events stories selected just for you.

CHAPTER 15

Acids and Bases

Chapter Overview

15-1 describes acids and bases, defines Arrhenius acids and bases, introduces acid-base nomenclature, and characterizes strong and weak acids and bases.

15-2 describes two more acid-base theories: the Brønsted-Lowry and Lewis theories.

15-3 explains acid-base reactions in aqueous solutions.

Concept Base

Students may need a review of the following concepts:

- chemical bonding, Chapter 6
- writing chemical formulas, Chapter 7
- writing and balancing chemical equations and the activity series, Chapter 8
- properties of solutions, Chapter 13
- ions in aqueous solution, Chapter 14

 Reading Skill-Builder

BRAINSTORMING Write the words *acids* and *bases* on the board. Ask students to brainstorm examples of each and write them under the corresponding words. Have them use Section 15-1 and other resources to confirm or deny whether each of the substances is an acid or a base. Then elicit properties that the substances have in common. Use students' responses as a basis for developing properties of acids and bases.

Acids and Bases

Acids and bases change the color of compounds called indicators.

Properties of Acids and Bases

How many foods can you think of that are sour? Chances are that almost all the foods you thought of, like those in Figure 15-1(a), owe their sour taste to an acid. Sour milk contains *lactic acid*. Vinegar, which can be produced by fermenting juices, contains *acetic acid*. *Phosphoric acid* gives a tart flavor to many carbonated beverages. Most fruits contain some kind of acid. Lemons, oranges, grapefruits, and other citrus fruits contain *citric acid*. Apples contain *malic acid*, and grape juice contains *tartaric acid*.

Many substances known as bases are commonly found in household products, such as those in Figure 15-1(b). Household ammonia is an ammonia-water solution that is useful for all types of general cleaning. Sodium hydroxide, NaOH, known by the common name *lye*, is present in some commercial drain and oven cleaners. Milk of magnesia is a suspension in water of magnesium hydroxide, $Mg(OH)_2$, which is not very water-soluble. It is used as an antacid to relieve discomfort caused by excess hydrochloric acid in the stomach. Aluminum hydroxide, $Al(OH)_3$, and sodium hydrogen carbonate, $NaHCO_3$, are also bases commonly found in antacids.

SECTION 15-1

OBJECTIVES

- List five general properties of aqueous acids and bases.

- Name common binary acids and oxyacids, given their chemical formulas.

- List five acids commonly used in industry and the laboratory, and give two properties of each.

- Define *acid* and *base* according to Arrhenius's theory of ionization.

- Explain the differences between strong and weak acids and bases.

Lesson Starter
Before class, pour 200 mL of water into each of two 400 mL beakers. Add a few drops of ammonia solution to the water in one beaker and a few drops of hydrochloric acid to the water in the other beaker. Stir each. At the beginning of class, test the contents of each beaker with pH paper. Help students conclude that although the contents look the same, the solutions in the two beakers have different properties. Save the solutions for the Demonstration on page 454.

Visual Strategy
FIGURE 15-1 Ask students how they can find out the names of some of the acids that are present in a packaged beverage, such as a soft drink or a fruit drink. See how many names of acids they can recognize on the labels of various commercial drink products. Point out that not all acids present may be listed separately. For example, orange juice contains citric and ascorbic acids, but these names are not listed.

Benzoic acid, C_6H_5COOH
Sorbic acid, C_5H_7COOH
Phosphoric acid, H_3PO_4
Carbonic acid, H_2CO_3

Citric acid, $C_6H_8O_7$
Ascorbic acid, $C_6H_8O_6$

(a)

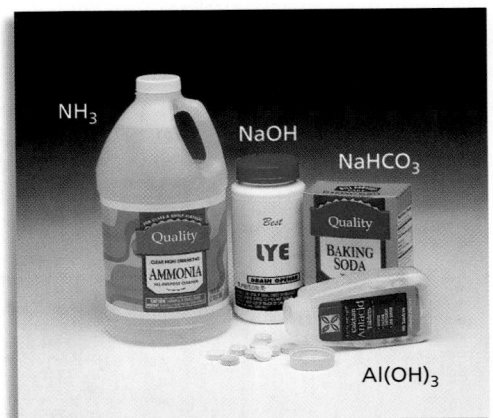

NH_3
NaOH
$NaHCO_3$
$Al(OH)_3$

(b)

FIGURE 15-1 (a) Fruits and fruit juices contain acids such as citric acid and ascorbic acid. Carbonated beverages contain benzoic acid, phosphoric acid, and carbonic acid. (b) Many household cleaners contain bases such as ammonia and sodium hydroxide.

Visual Strategy

FIGURE 15-2 Introduce an acid-base indicator as a substance that is one color in an acid and a different color in a base. Demonstrate the effect shown in the figure with vinegar and other acids and bases. Use a variety of indicators to show that various indicators have different colors in acids and bases.

DEMONSTRATION
Color Change of Phenolphthalein

Tell students what solutions are in the Lesson Starter. Add a drop of phenolphthalein solution to each. Students will note that the indicator turns pink in the ammonia solution (base) and remains colorless in the acidic solution. If students have trouble seeing the difference in color, hold the beakers in front of sheets of white paper.

Safety: Wear goggles and a lab apron.

Disposal: Solutions may be further diluted and poured down the drain.

Class Discussion

Ask students to predict which metals will react with acids and which metals will not react with acids, based on their position in the activity series.

FIGURE 15-2 A strip of pH paper dipped into vinegar turns red, showing that vinegar is an acid.

Acids

Acids were first recognized as a distinct class of compounds because of the common properties of their aqueous solutions. These properties are listed below.

1. *Aqueous solutions of acids have a sour taste.* Taste, however, should NEVER be used as a test to evaluate any chemical substance. Many acids, especially in concentrated solutions, are corrosive; that is, they destroy body tissue and clothing. Many are also poisons.

2. *Acids change the color of acid-base indicators.* When pH paper is used as an indicator, the paper turns certain colors in acidic solution. This reaction is demonstrated in Figure 15-2.

3. *Some acids react with active metals to release hydrogen gas, H_2.* Recall that metals can be ordered in terms of an activity series. Metals above hydrogen in the series undergo single-replacement reactions with certain acids. Hydrogen gas is formed as a product, as shown by the reaction of barium with sulfuric acid.

$$Ba(s) + H_2SO_4(aq) \longrightarrow BaSO_4(aq) + H_2(g)$$

4. *Acids react with bases to produce salts and water.* When chemically equivalent amounts of acids and bases react, the three properties just described disappear because the acid is "neutralized." The reaction products are water and an ionic compound called a *salt*.

5. *Some acids conduct electric current.* Acids that form many ions in aqueous solution are electrolytes.

Acid Nomenclature

A **binary acid** *is an acid that contains only two different elements: hydrogen and one of the more electronegative elements.* Many common inorganic acids are binary acids. The hydrogen halides—HF, HCl, HBr, and HI—are all binary acids.

The procedure used to name binary acids is illustrated by the examples given in Table 15-1. In pure form, each acid listed in the table is a gas. Aqueous solutions of these compounds are known by the acid names. From the table you can see that naming binary compounds can be summarized as follows.

TABLE 15-1 *Names of Binary Acids*	
Formula	**Acid name**
HF	hydrofluoric acid
HCl	hydrochloric acid
HBr	hydrobromic acid
HI	hydriodic acid
H_2S	hydrosulfuric acid

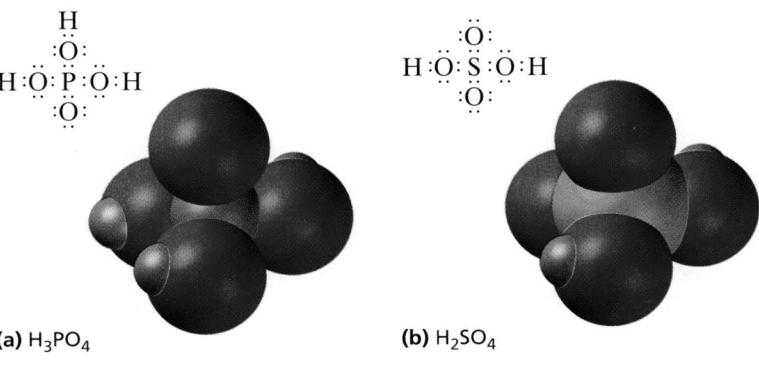

FIGURE 15-3 Structures of (a) phosphoric acid and (b) sulfuric acid

(a) H_3PO_4

(b) H_2SO_4

Binary Acid Nomenclature

1. The name of a binary acid begins with the prefix *hydro-*.
2. The root of the name of the second element follows this prefix.
3. The name then ends with the suffix *-ic.*

An **oxyacid** *is an acid that is a compound of hydrogen, oxygen, and a third element, usually a nonmetal.* Nitric acid, HNO_3, is an oxyacid. The structures of two other oxyacids are shown in Figure 15-3. Oxyacids are one class of ternary acids, which are acids that contain three different elements. Usually, the elements in an oxyacid formula are written as one or more hydrogen atoms followed by a polyatomic anion. The name of an oxyacid is based on this anion. Some common oxyacids and their anions are given in Table 15-2.

TABLE 15-2 *Names of Common Oxyacids and Oxyanions*

Formula	Acid name	Anion
CH_3COOH	acetic acid	CH_3COO^-, acetate
H_2CO_3	carbonic acid	CO_3^{2-}, carbonate
HIO_3	iodic acid	IO_3^-, iodate
$HClO$	hypochlorous acid	ClO^-, hypochlorite
$HClO_2$	chlorous acid	ClO_2^-, chlorite
$HClO_3$	chloric acid	ClO_3^-, chlorate
$HClO_4$	perchloric acid	ClO_4^-, perchlorate
HNO_2	nitrous acid	NO_2^-, nitrite
HNO_3	nitric acid	NO_3^-, nitrate
H_3PO_3	phosphorous acid	PO_3^{3-}, phosphite
H_3PO_4	phosphoric acid	PO_4^{3-}, phosphate
H_2SO_3	sulfurous acid	SO_3^{2-}, sulfite
H_2SO_4	sulfuric acid	SO_4^{2-}, sulfate

456

internet connect

SCILINKS

NSTA

TOPIC: Acids
GO TO: www.scilinks.org
*sci***LINKS CODE:** HC2151

Some Common Industrial Acids

The properties of acids make them important chemicals both in the laboratory and in industry. Sulfuric acid, nitric acid, phosphoric acid, hydrochloric acid, and acetic acid are all common industrial acids.

Sulfuric Acid

Sulfuric acid is the most commonly produced industrial chemical in the world. More than 47 million tons of it are made each year in the United States alone. Sulfuric acid is used in large quantities in petroleum refining and metallurgy as well as in the manufacture of fertilizer. It is also essential to a vast number of industrial processes, including the production of metals, paper, paint, dyes, detergents, and many chemical raw materials. Sulfuric acid is the acid used in automobile batteries.

Because it attracts water, concentrated sulfuric acid is an effective dehydration (water-removing) agent. It can be used to remove water from gases with which it does not react. Sugar and certain other organic compounds are also dehydrated by sulfuric acid. Skin contains organic compounds that are attacked by concentrated sulfuric acid, which can cause serious burns.

Nitric Acid

Pure nitric acid is a volatile, unstable liquid rarely used in industry or laboratories. Dissolving the acid in water provides stability. Nitric acid stains proteins yellow. The feather in Figure 15-4 was stained by nitric acid. The acid has a suffocating odor, stains skin, and can cause serious burns. It is used in making explosives, many of which are nitrogen-containing compounds. It is also used to make rubber, plastics, dyes, and

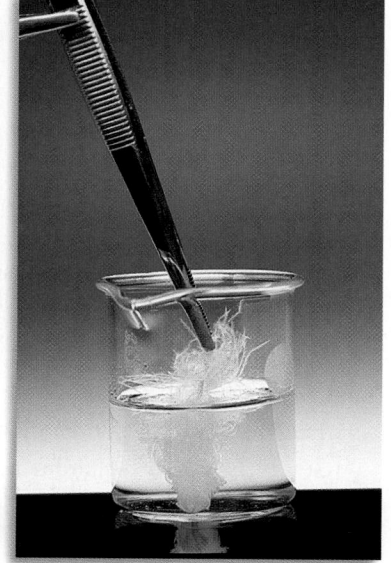

FIGURE 15-4 Concentrated nitric acid stains a feather yellow.

pharmaceuticals. Initially, nitric acid solutions are colorless; however, upon standing, they gradually become yellow because of slight decomposition to brown nitrogen dioxide gas.

Phosphoric Acid

Phosphorus, along with nitrogen and potassium, is an essential element for plants and animals. The bulk of phosphoric acid produced each year is used directly for manufacturing fertilizers and animal feed. Dilute phosphoric acid has a pleasant but sour taste and is not toxic. It is used as a flavoring agent in beverages and as a cleaning agent for dairy equipment. Phosphoric acid is also important in the manufacture of detergents and ceramics.

Hydrochloric Acid

The stomach produces HCl to aid in digestion. Industrially, hydrochloric acid is important for "pickling" iron and steel. Pickling is the immersion of metals in acid solutions to remove surface impurities. This acid is also used in industry as a general cleaning agent, in food processing, in the activation of oil wells, in the recovery of magnesium from sea water, and in the production of other chemicals.

A dilute solution of hydrochloric acid, commonly referred to as muriatic acid, may be found in hardware stores. It is used to maintain the correct acidity in swimming pools and for general cleaning of masonry.

Acetic Acid

Concentrated acetic acid is a clear, colorless, pungent-smelling liquid known as glacial acetic acid. This name derives from the fact that pure acetic acid has a freezing point of only 17°C. It can form crystals in a cold room. The fermentation of certain plants produces vinegars containing acetic acid. White vinegar contains 4–8% acetic acid.

Acetic acid is important industrially in synthesizing chemicals used in the manufacture of plastics. It is a raw material in the production of food supplements—for example, lysine, an essential amino acid. Acetic acid is also used as a fungicide.

Bases

How do bases differ from acids? You can answer this question by comparing the following properties of bases with those of acids.

1. *Aqueous solutions of bases taste bitter.* You may have noticed this fact if you have ever gotten soap, a basic substance, in your mouth. As with acids, taste should NEVER be used to test a substance to see if it is a base. Many bases are caustic; they attack the skin and tissues, causing severe burns.
2. *Bases change the color of acid-base indicators.* As Figure 15-5 shows, an indicator will be a different color in a basic solution than it would be in an acidic solution.

---

internet**connect**

SC*i*LINKS

NSTA

TOPIC: Bases
GO TO: www.scilinks.org
*sci*LINKS CODE: HC2152

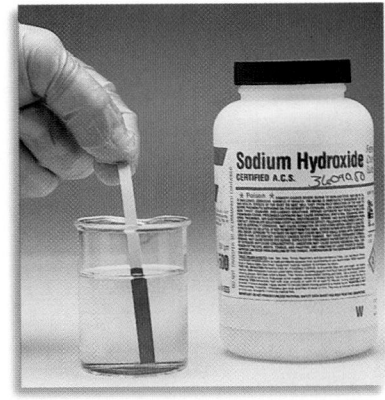

FIGURE 15-5 pH paper turns blue in the presence of this solution of sodium hydroxide.

QUICK LAB

Products containing acids and bases are commonly found in the kitchen at home. Occasionally these products consist of an acid or a base that is simply mixed with water, such as vinegar or household ammonia. In most cases, the acid or base is a part of a more complex mixture, such as soft drinks or dishwashing liquid.

Safety: Wear goggles and a lab apron. Avoid skin contact with the items to be tested. Caution students never to taste any materials in the lab. Turn off hot plate when not in use. Use tongs when handling hot glassware. Never hold or touch glassware with your hands while heating it or while it is cooling.

Disposal: Place all solids in the trash. Pour all liquids down the drain.

Discussion

1. Most cleaning products tend to be basic or neutral.

2. Acidic food products taste tart or sour. Basic food products taste bitter. Of the food products listed, only baking soda is basic.

3. Consumer warning labels about the acidity or basicity of food products will probably not be found. Most cleaning products have warning labels; a caustic warning indicates a strongly basic substance that can cause burns.

Quick LAB

Household Acids and Bases

Wear Safety Goggles and an Apron.

Materials

- dishwashing liquid, dishwasher detergent, laundry detergent, laundry stain remover, fabric softener, and bleach
- fresh red cabbage
- hot plate
- beaker, 500 mL or larger
- beakers, 50 mL
- mayonnaise, baking powder, baking soda, white vinegar, cider vinegar, lemon juice, soft drinks, mineral water, and milk
- spatula
- tap water
- tongs

Question

Which of the household substances are acids, and which are bases?

Procedure

Record all your results in a data table.

1. To make an acid-base indicator, extract juice from red cabbage. First, cut up some red cabbage and place it in a large beaker. Add enough water so that the beaker is half full. Then bring the mixture to a boil. Let it cool, and pour off the cabbage juice. Save the solution.

2. Assemble foods, beverages, and cleaning products to be tested.

3. If the substance being tested is a liquid, pour about 5 mL into a small beaker. If it is a solid, place a small amount into a beaker, and moisten it with about 5 mL of water.

4. Add a drop or two of the red cabbage juice to the solution being tested, and note the color. The solution will turn red if it is acidic and green if it is basic.

Red cabbage can be made into an acid-base indicator.

Discussion

1. Are the cleaning products acids, bases, or neither?

2. What are acid/base characteristics of foods and beverages?

3. Did you find consumer warning labels on basic or acidic products?

internet connect

SCILINKS
NSTA

TOPIC: Household acids and bases
GO TO: www.scilinks.org
sciLINKS CODE: HC2153

3. *Dilute aqueous solutions of bases feel slippery.* You encounter this property of aqueous bases whenever you wash with soap.

4. *Bases react with acids to produce salts and water.* The properties of an acid disappear with the addition of an equivalent amount of a base. It could also be said that "neutralization" of the base occurs when these two substances react to produce salts and water.

5. *Bases conduct electric current.* Like acids, bases form ions in aqueous solutions and are thus electrolytes.

Arrhenius Acids and Bases

Svante Arrhenius, a Swedish chemist who lived from 1859 to 1927, understood that aqueous solutions of acids and bases conducted electric current. Arrhenius therefore theorized that acids and bases must produce ions in solution. *An **Arrhenius acid** is a chemical compound that increases the concentration of hydrogen ions, H^+, in aqueous solution.* In other words, an acid will ionize in solution, increasing the number of hydrogen ions present. *An **Arrhenius base** is a substance that increases the concentration of hydroxide ions, OH^-, in aqueous solution.* Some bases are ionic hydroxides. These bases dissociate in solution to release hydroxide ions into the solution. Other bases are substances that react with water to remove a hydrogen ion, leaving hydroxide ions in the solution.

Aqueous Solutions of Acids

The acids described by Arrhenius are molecular compounds with ionizable hydrogen atoms. Their water solutions are known as *aqueous acids*. All pure aqueous acids are electrolytes.

Acid molecules are sufficiently polar so that one or more hydrogen ions are attracted by water molecules. Negatively charged anions are left behind. As explained in Chapter 14, the hydrogen ion in aqueous solution is best represented as H_3O^+, the hydronium ion. The ionization of an HNO_3 molecule is shown by the following equation. Figure 15-6 shows how the hydrogen atoms combine with water to form a hydronium ion when nitric acid is diluted.

$$HNO_3(l) + H_2O(l) \longrightarrow H_3O^+(aq) + NO_3^-(aq)$$

Similarly, ionization of a hydrogen chloride molecule in hydrochloric acid can be represented in the following way.

$$HCl(g) + H_2O(l) \longrightarrow H_3O^+(aq) + Cl^-(aq)$$

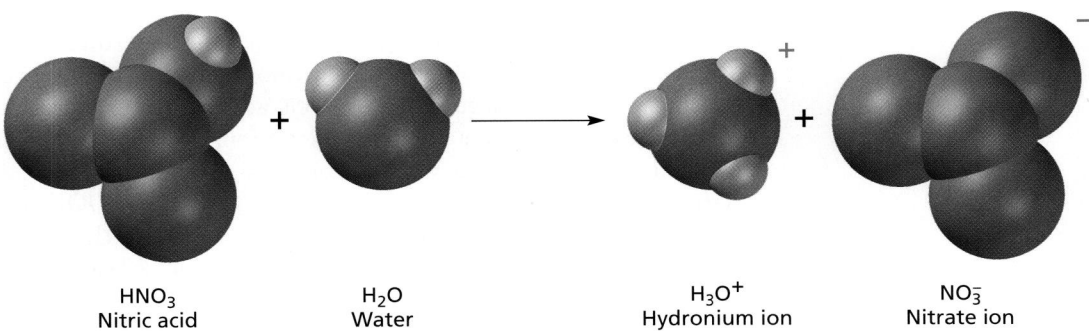

| HNO$_3$ | H$_2$O | H$_3$O$^+$ | NO$_3^-$ |
| Nitric acid | Water | Hydronium ion | Nitrate ion |

FIGURE 15-6   Arrhenius's observations form the basis of a definition of acids. Arrhenius acids, such as the nitric acid shown here, produce hydronium ions in aqueous solution.

Class Discussion
To indicate the role of polarity in the ionization of acids, ask students why a nonpolar molecule, such as methane, CH_4, is so much less likely to ionize than is hydrogen chloride, HCl.

Visual Strategy
FIGURE 15-6 Have students demonstrate an understanding of the proton-transfer reaction by using electron-dot formulas to explain how a proton bonds with a water molecule to yield a hydronium ion.

TABLE STRATEGY

TABLE 15-3 Ask students to explain why double arrows are used in the weak-acid equations.

CHAPTER ⬌ CONNECTION

Equilibrium systems, such as those involving weak acids and bases, will be covered in Chapter 18.

DEMONSTRATION
Strength and Conductivity
To make sure that students understand the relationship between acid and base strength and electrical conductivity, test a variety of solutions with a battery-powered conductivity set. For the solutions, use the same concentrations of strong and weak acids and strong and weak bases. Have students note the conductivity of each solution tested and, from that information, infer the strength of the acid or base tested.

Safety: Wear goggles and a lab apron. Avoid skin contact with the solutions to be tested. Use a conductivity set with leads long enough that students can read the results without getting close to the solutions.

Disposal: Combine liquids, adjust the pH to a range from 5 to 9, and pour the solution down the drain.

TABLE 15-3 *Common Aqueous Acids*

Strong acids	Weak acids	
$H_2SO_4 + H_2O \longrightarrow H_3O^+ + HSO_4^-$	$HSO_4^- + H_2O$	$\rightleftarrows H_3O^+ + SO_4^{2-}$
$HClO_4 + H_2O \longrightarrow H_3O^+ + ClO_4^-$	$H_3PO_4 + H_2O$	$\rightleftarrows H_3O^+ + H_2PO_4^-$
$HCl + H_2O \longrightarrow H_3O^+ + Cl^-$	$HF + H_2O$	$\rightleftarrows H_3O^+ + F^-$
$HNO_3 + H_2O \longrightarrow H_3O^+ + NO_3^-$	$CH_3COOH + H_2O \rightleftarrows H_3O^+ + CH_3COO^-$	
$HBr + H_2O \longrightarrow H_3O^+ + Br^-$	$H_2CO_3 + H_2O$	$\rightleftarrows H_3O^+ + HCO_3^-$
$HI + H_2O \longrightarrow H_3O^+ + I^-$	$H_2S + H_2O$	$\rightleftarrows H_3O^+ + HS^-$
	$HCN + H_2O$	$\rightleftarrows H_3O^+ + CN^-$
	$HCO_3^- + H_2O$	$\rightleftarrows H_3O^+ + CO_3^{2-}$

Strength of Acids
A **strong acid** *is one that ionizes completely in aqueous solution.* A strong acid is a strong electrolyte. Perchloric acid, $HClO_4$, hydrochloric acid, HCl, and nitric acid, HNO_3, are examples of strong acids. The strength of an acid depends on the polarity of the bond between hydrogen and the element to which it is bonded and the ease with which that bond can be broken. Acid strength increases with increasing polarity and decreasing bond energy.

Acids that are weak electrolytes are known as **weak acids.** The aqueous solution of a weak acid contains hydronium ions, anions, and dissolved acid molecules. Hydrocyanic acid is an example of a weak electrolyte. In aqueous solution, both the ionization of HCN and the reverse reaction occur simultaneously. Although hydronium and cyanide ions are present in solution, the reverse reaction is favored. Most of the solution is composed of hydrogen cyanide and water.

$$HCN(aq) + H_2O(l) \rightleftarrows H_3O^+(aq) + CN^-(aq)$$

Common aqueous acids are listed in Table 15-3. Each strong acid is assumed to ionize completely to give up one hydrogen ion. Notice that the number of hydrogen atoms in the formula does not affect acid strength. Molecules with multiple hydrogen atoms may not readily give up each hydrogen. The fact that phosphoric acid has three hydrogen atoms per molecule does not mean that it is a strong acid. None of these ionize completely in solution, so phosphoric acid is weak.

Organic acids, which contain the acidic carboxyl group —COOH, are generally weak acids. For example, acetic acid, CH_3COOH, ionizes slightly in water to give hydronium ions and acetate ions, CH_3COO^-.

$$CH_3COOH(aq) + H_2O(l) \rightleftarrows H_3O^+(aq) + CH_3COO^-(aq)$$

A molecule of acetic acid contains four hydrogen atoms. However, only one of the hydrogen atoms is ionizable. The hydrogen atom in the carboxyl group in acetic acid is the one that is "acidic" and forms the hydronium ion. This acidic hydrogen can be seen in the structural diagram in Figure 15-7.

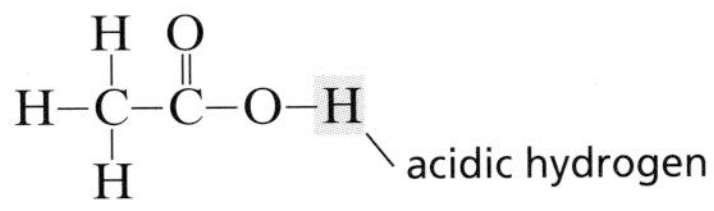

Aqueous Solutions of Bases

Most bases are ionic compounds containing metal cations and the hydroxide anion, OH^-. Because these bases are ionic, they dissociate to some extent when placed in solution. *When a base completely dissociates in water to yield aqueous OH^- ions, the solution is referred to as* **alkaline.** Sodium hydroxide, NaOH, is a common laboratory base. It is water-soluble and dissociates as shown by the equation below.

$$NaOH(s) \xrightarrow{H_2O} Na^+(aq) + OH^-(aq)$$

You will remember from Chapter 5 that sodium is one of the alkali metals. This group gets its name from the fact that the hydroxides of Li, Na, K, Rb, and Cs all form alkaline solutions.

Not all bases are ionic compounds. A base commonly used in household cleaners is ammonia, NH_3, which is molecular. Ammonia is a base because it produces hydroxide ions when it reacts with water molecules, as shown in the equation below.

$$NH_3(g) + H_2O(l) \rightleftharpoons NH_4^+(aq) + OH^-(aq)$$

Strength of Bases

As with acids, the strength of a base also depends on the extent to which the base dissociates, or adds hydroxide ions to the solution. For example, potassium hydroxide, KOH, is a strong base because it completely dissociates into its ions in dilute aqueous solutions.

$$KOH(s) \xrightarrow{H_2O} K^+(aq) + OH^-(aq)$$

Strong bases are strong electrolytes, just as strong acids are strong electrolytes. Table 15-4 lists some strong bases.

FIGURE 15-7 Acetic acid contains four hydrogen atoms, but only one of them is "acidic" or forms the hydronium ion in solution.

TABLE 15-4 *Common Aqueous Bases*

Strong bases	Weak bases
$Ca(OH)_2 \longrightarrow Ca^{2+} + 2OH^-$	$NH_3 + H_2O \rightleftharpoons NH_4^+ + OH^-$
$Sr(OH)_2 \longrightarrow Sr^{2+} + 2OH^-$	$C_6H_5NH_2 + H_2O \rightleftharpoons C_6H_5NH_3^+ + OH^-$
$Ba(OH)_2 \longrightarrow Ba^{2+} + 2OH^-$	
$NaOH \longrightarrow Na^+ + OH^-$	
$KOH \longrightarrow K^+ + OH^-$	
$RbOH \longrightarrow Rb^+ + OH^-$	
$CsOH \longrightarrow Cs^+ + OH^-$	

Visual Strategy

FIGURE 15-7 Discuss the reason why only one hydrogen in the acetic acid molecule is easily ionized. Contrast acetic acid with phosphoric acid. There are four hydrogen atoms in acetic acid, only one of which is ionizable. There are three hydrogen atoms in phosphoric acid, all of which are ionizable.

SECTION REVIEW

1. a. sour taste; react with metals to give off H$_2$; change color of indicator; react with bases to produce salts and water; are electrolytes
b. vinegar, many soft drinks, sour milk, fruits and fruit juices, muriatic acid

2. a. hypobromous acid
b. bromic acid

3. a. bitter taste; slippery feel; change color of indicator; react with acids to produce salts and water; are electrolytes
b. household ammonia, milk of magnesia, antacids, lye

4. a. Strong acids ionize completely in aqueous solution
b. No; materials other than acids can ionize in aqueous solution.

FIGURE 15-8 The hydroxides of most *d*-block metals are nearly insoluble in water, as is shown by the gelatinous precipitate, copper(II) hydroxide, Cu(OH)$_2$, in the beaker on the right.

Chloride ion, Cl$^-$

Water molecule, H$_2$O

NaOH(*aq*)

Sodium ion, Na$^+$

Copper(II) ion, Cu^{2+}

Cu(OH)$_2$(*s*)

$$Cu^{2+}(aq) + 2OH^-(aq) \longrightarrow Cu(OH)_2(s)$$

Bases that are not very soluble do not produce a large number of hydroxide ions when added to water. Some metal hydroxides, such as Cu(OH)$_2$, are not very soluble in water, as seen in Figure 15-8. They cannot produce strongly alkaline solutions. The alkalinity of aqueous solutions depends on the concentration of OH$^-$ ions in solution. It is unrelated to the number of hydroxide ions in the undissolved compound.

Now consider ammonia, which is highly soluble but is a weak electrolyte. The concentration of OH$^-$ ions in an ammonia solution is relatively low. Ammonia is therefore a *weak base*. Many organic compounds that contain nitrogen atoms are also weak bases. For example, aniline, a substance used to make dyes, is a weak base.

$$C_6H_5NH_2(aq) + H_2O(l) \rightleftharpoons C_6H_5NH_3^+(aq) + OH^-(aq)$$

SECTION REVIEW

1. a. What are five general properties of aqueous acids?
   b. Name some common substances that have one or more of these properties.

2. Name the following acids: a. HBrO b. HBrO$_3$.

3. a. What are five general properties of aqueous bases?
   b. Name some common substances that have one or more of these properties.

4. a. Why are strong acids also strong electrolytes?
   b. Is every strong electrolyte also a strong acid?

CHEMICAL COMMENTARY

Logic in the Laboratory

From "Acid and Water: A Socratic Dialogue," by David Todd, in *The Journal of Chemical Education*.

Tutor: . . . tell me, how does one set about diluting an acid with water?

Student: The rule is: pour the acid into the water.

Tutor: Why so? . . .

Student: I believe much heat is given off if you do it the wrong way, and the mixture can boil up in your face.

Tutor: Indeed, that is so . . . But is there not heat also developed if you pour the acid into the water?

Student: (thoughtfully) I suppose so. But then I can only assume since there is a rule, that the heat developed is a lot less if you do it that way.

Tutor: Let us reason together. Have you ever heard of Hess's Law?

Student: . . . Doesn't it have something to do with A going to B and the heat change involved?

Tutor: Very good . . . Now suppose I start with 100 g of water in one container at 25°C, and 100 g of concentrated sulfuric acid at 25°C in another container. We can call these two items your A . . . Now let us assume that the two have been mixed—regardless of the mode of mixing—do we not obtain a diluted acid that is 100 g of acid and 100 g of water, and we can call this B?

Student: (cautiously) Well— almost. But . . . concentrated sulfuric acid is 96% by weight H_2SO_4

and 4% water. This means that B is 96 g of pure sulfuric acid and 104 g of water.

Tutor: . . . Oh, excellent! You have had good teachers . . . But the main point is that B has the same composition regardless of the route by which it is obtained. Agreed?

Student: That most assuredly must be so.

Tutor: Now let us return to Hess's Law. It states that the heat change involved in going from A to B is the same regardless of the path taken.

Student: . . . Yes—I remember it now. You mean this law says that the same heat is evolved (or absorbed) if I pour the acid into the water, or vice versa?

Tutor: Yes, indeed.

Student: (now bewildered) You mean that the rule is nonsense, and therefore useless?

Tutor: Oh no, not at all! . . .

Student: . . . Hmm. Then in that case there must be some other factor involved.

Tutor: Indeed there is . . . May I drop a hint? . . . Which is the more dense—concentrated sulfuric acid or water?

Student: The acid . . .

Tutor: Good. Now if I put water on the acid, does it float or sink?

Student: Of course it will stay on the top.

Tutor: Right. And it will begin to mix . . .

Always dilute by pouring acid into water.

Student: I get it—it reacts on the surface, generates a lot of heat, and some of the diluted acid can boil up in my face.

Tutor: Exactly. And if I pour the acid into . . .

Student: (interrupting) Yes, yes— of course. The acid falls down through the water generating the heat in the entire body of the liquid—not just on the surface. So it won't form steam and boil up in my face . . . now I see the reason for the rule.

Reading for Meaning

In your own words, sum up the reason behind the rule for diluting acid with water.

Read Further

Hydrofluoric acid is a fairly weak acid. It does not burn the skin the way sulfuric acid and other strong acids do. Find an explanation of why this acid can greatly damage body tissue when it comes into contact with the skin.

SECTION 15-2

Lesson Starter

Show students an action photo of a person, and ask each student to list three terms that describe that person. Make a master list of the terms. Point out that although the person has been described in many different ways—appearance, apparent vocation, attitude—he or she is still the same person. Point out that acids and bases also can be described differently based on the circumstances.

Common Misconception

Have students examine the equations on this page. They may have difficulty recognizing how the positive charges on the hydronium and ammonium ions are distributed. Point out that brackets are used with both ions to show that the charge is distributed over the whole ion and is not localized on any one hydrogen atom.

Module 8: Strong and Weakly Ionized Species, pH, and Titrations

Topic: Brønsted Acids/Bases Tutorial
Section **d** of this engaging tutorial reviews and reinforces understanding of Brønsted acids and bases.

OBJECTIVES

- Define and recognize *Brønsted-Lowry acids* and *bases.*

- Define a *Lewis acid* and a *Lewis base.*

- Name compounds that are acids under the Lewis definition but are not acids under the Brønsted-Lowry definition.

Module 8: Strong and Weakly Ionized Species, pH, and Titrations

Acid-Base Theories

For most uses, scientists found the Arrhenius definition of acids and bases to be adequate. However, as scientists further investigated acid-base behavior, they found that some substances acted as acids or bases when they were not in a water solution. Because the Arrhenius definition requires that the substances be aqueous, the definitions of acids and bases had to be revised.

Brønsted-Lowry Acids and Bases

In 1923, the Danish chemist J. N. Brønsted and the English chemist T. M. Lowry independently expanded the Arrhenius acid definition. *A* **Brønsted-Lowry acid** *is a molecule or ion that is a proton donor.* Because H^+ is a proton, all acids as defined by Arrhenius donate protons to water and are Brønsted-Lowry acids as well. Substances other than molecules, such as certain ions, can also donate protons. Such substances are not Arrhenius acids but are included in the category of Brønsted-Lowry acids.

Hydrogen chloride acts as a Brønsted-Lowry acid when it is dissolved in ammonia. It transfers protons to the solvent much as it does in water.

$$HCl + NH_3 \longrightarrow NH_4^+ + Cl^-$$

A proton is transferred from the hydrogen chloride molecule, HCl, to the ammonia molecule, NH_3. The ammonium ion, NH_4^+, is formed. Electron-dot formulas show the similarity of this reaction to the reaction of HCl with water.

$$H\!:\!\ddot{C}l\!: \; + \; H\!:\!\ddot{O}\!: \longrightarrow \left[H\!:\!\ddot{O}\!:\!H \right]^+ + \; :\!\ddot{C}l\!:^-$$
$$\qquad\qquad\quad\; H \qquad\qquad\;\; H$$

$$H\!:\!\ddot{C}l\!: \; + \; H\!:\!\ddot{N}\!:\!H \longrightarrow \left[\begin{array}{c} H \\ H\!:\!\ddot{N}\!:\!H \\ H \end{array} \right]^+ + \; :\!\ddot{C}l\!:^-$$

In both reactions, hydrogen chloride is a Brønsted-Lowry acid.

Water can also act as a Brønsted-Lowry acid. Consider, for example, the following reaction, in which the water molecule donates a proton to the ammonia molecule.

$$H_2O(l) + NH_3(g) \rightleftharpoons NH_4^+(aq) + OH^-(aq)$$

$$H\!:\!\ddot{O}\!: \; + \; H\!:\!\ddot{N}\!:\!H \rightleftharpoons \left[\begin{array}{c} H \\ H\!:\!\ddot{N}\!:\!H \\ H \end{array} \right]^+ + \left[:\!\ddot{O}\!: \right]^-$$
$$\quad H \qquad\quad\; H \qquad\qquad\qquad\qquad\qquad H$$

FIGURE 15-9 Hydrogen chloride gas escapes from a hydrochloric acid solution and combines with ammonia gas that has escaped from an aqueous ammonia solution. The resulting cloud is solid ammonium chloride.

A **Brønsted-Lowry base** *is a molecule or ion that is a proton acceptor.* In the reaction between hydrochloric acid and ammonia, ammonia accepts a proton from the hydrochloric acid. It is a Brønsted-Lowry base. The Arrhenius hydroxide bases, such as NaOH, are not, strictly speaking, Brønsted-Lowry bases. That is because as compounds they are not proton acceptors. The OH^- ion produced in solution is the Brønsted-Lowry base. It is the species that can accept a proton.

In a **Brønsted-Lowry acid-base reaction,** *protons are transferred from one reactant (the acid) to another (the base).* Figure 15-9 shows the reaction between the Brønsted-Lowry acid HCl and the Brønsted-Lowry base NH_3.

Monoprotic and Polyprotic Acids

An acid that can donate only one proton (hydrogen ion) per molecule is known as a **monoprotic acid.** Perchloric acid, $HClO_4$, hydrochloric acid, HCl, and nitric acid, HNO_3, are all monoprotic. The following equation shows how a molecule of the monoprotic acid HCl donates a proton to a water molecule. HCl is completely ionized; it has no more hydrogen atoms to lose.

$$HCl(g) + H_2O(l) \longrightarrow H_3O^+(aq) + Cl^-(aq)$$

A **polyprotic acid** *is an acid that can donate more than one proton per molecule.* Sulfuric acid, H_2SO_4, and phosphoric acid, H_3PO_4, are examples of polyprotic acids. The ionization of a polyprotic acid occurs in stages. The acid loses its hydrogen atoms one at a time. Sulfuric acid

Visual Strategy

FIGURE 15-9 Ask students to explain why the Arrhenius definition of acids and bases cannot be used to explain the chemical reaction shown in the figure.

Common Misconception

Students may not understand that the status of bases according to the Arrhenius and Brønsted-Lowry definitions is different from the status of acids. Because they are molecular, most Arrhenius acids are also Brønsted-Lowry acids. Because they are ionic and the compound as a whole does not accept a proton, most Arrhenius bases are *not* Brønsted-Lowry bases. Make sure that students understand the logic behind this difference.

Class Discussion

Clarify the relationships among the terms *monoprotic, polyprotic, binary,* and *ternary.* For example, ask whether all binary acids are also monoprotic, or have students give examples of polyprotic acids that are also binary.

Reading Skill-Builder

VOCABULARY BUILDING
Explain that the suffix *-protic* is related to the word *proton.* Have students use their knowledge of the prefixes *mono-, bi-, tri-,* and *poly-* to develop definitions for the terms monoprotic acid, biprotic acid, triprotic acid, and polyprotic acid.

FIGURE 15-10 Have students predict the relative numbers of H_3O^+, HSO_4^-, and SO_4^{2-} ions in the space-fill models at the right of the figure.

Common Misconception

It is not unusual for an equation such as the following to be written for a polyprotic acid.

$$H_3PO_4 + 3H_2O \longrightarrow 3H_3O^+ + PO_4^{3-}$$

Such a representation may lead students to think that the phosphoric acid molecule loses all three protons at the same time. Ask students why this assumption is incorrect.

ionizes in two stages. In its first ionization, sulfuric acid is a strong acid. It is completely converted to hydrogen sulfate ions, HSO_4^-.

$$H_2SO_4(l) + H_2O(l) \longrightarrow H_3O^+(aq) + HSO_4^-(aq)$$

The hydrogen sulfate ion is itself a weak acid. It establishes the following equilibrium in solution.

$$HSO_4^-(aq) + H_2O(l) \rightleftharpoons H_3O^+(aq) + SO_4^{2-}(aq)$$

All stages of ionization of a polyprotic acid occur in the same solution. Sulfuric acid solutions therefore contain H_3O^+, HSO_4^-, and SO_4^{2-} ions.

Sulfuric acid is the type of polyprotic acid that *can donate two protons per molecule, and it is therefore known as a* **diprotic acid.** Ionizations of a monoprotic acid and a diprotic acid are shown in Figure 15-10.

Phosphoric acid is the type of polyprotic acid known as a **triprotic acid**—*an acid able to donate three protons per molecule.* The equations for these reactions are shown below.

$$H_3PO_4(aq) + H_2O(l) \rightleftharpoons H_3O^+(aq) + H_2PO_4^-(aq)$$
$$H_2PO_4^-(aq) + H_2O(l) \rightleftharpoons H_3O^+(aq) + HPO_4^{2-}(aq)$$
$$HPO_4^{2-}(aq) + H_2O(l) \rightleftharpoons H_3O^+(aq) + PO_4^{3-}(aq)$$

FIGURE 15-10 Hydrochloric acid, HCl, is a strong monoprotic acid. A dilute HCl solution contains hydronium ions and chloride ions. Sulfuric acid, H_2SO_4, is a strong diprotic acid. A dilute H_2SO_4 solution contains hydrogen sulfate ions from the first ionization, sulfate ions from the second ionization, and hydronium ions from both ionizations.

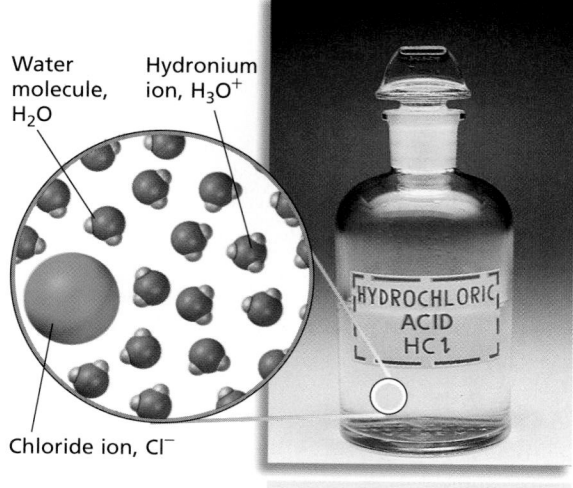
Water molecule, H_2O
Hydronium ion, H_3O^+
Chloride ion, Cl^-

$$HCl + H_2O \longrightarrow H_3O^+ + Cl^-$$

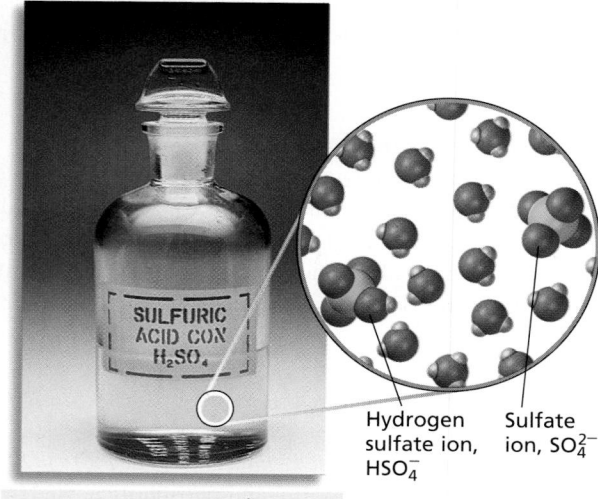
Hydrogen sulfate ion, HSO_4^-
Sulfate ion, SO_4^{2-}

$$H_2SO_4 + H_2O \longrightarrow H_3O^+ + HSO_4^-$$
$$HSO_4^- + H_2O \rightleftharpoons H_3O^+ + SO_4^{2-}$$

A solution of phosphoric acid contains H_3O^+, H_3PO_4, $H_2PO_4^-$, HPO_4^{2-}, and PO_4^{3-}. As with most polyprotic acids, the concentration of ions formed in the first ionization is the greatest. There are lesser concentrations of the respective ions from each succeeding ionization. Phosphoric acid is a weak acid in each step of its ionization.

Lewis Acids and Bases

The Arrhenius and Brønsted-Lowry definitions describe most acids and bases. Both definitions assume that the acid contains or produces hydrogen ions. A third acid classification, based on bonding and structure, includes, as acids, substances that do not contain hydrogen at all. This definition of acids was introduced in 1923 by G. N. Lewis, the American chemist whose name was given to electron-dot structures. Lewis's definition emphasizes the role of electron pairs in acid-base reactions. *A **Lewis acid** is an atom, ion, or molecule that accepts an electron pair to form a covalent bond.*

The Lewis definition is the broadest of the three acid definitions you have read about so far. It applies to any species that can accept an electron pair to form a covalent bond with another species. A bare proton (hydrogen ion) is a Lewis acid in reactions in which it forms a covalent bond, as shown below.

$$H^+(aq) + :NH_3(aq) \longrightarrow [H-NH_3]^+(aq) \text{ or } [NH_4]^+(aq)$$

The formula for a Lewis acid need not include hydrogen. Even a silver ion can be a Lewis acid, accepting electron pairs from ammonia to form covalent bonds.

$$Ag^+(aq) + 2:NH_3(aq) \longrightarrow [H_3N-Ag-NH_3]^+(aq) \text{ or } [Ag(NH_3)_2]^+$$

Any compound in which the central atom has three valence electrons and forms three covalent bonds can react as a Lewis acid. It does so by accepting a pair of electrons to form a fourth covalent bond, completing an electron octet. Boron trifluoride, for example, is an excellent Lewis acid. It forms a fourth covalent bond with many molecules and ions. Its reaction with a fluoride ion is shown below.

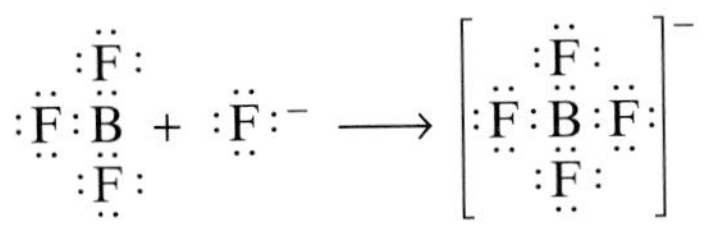

$$BF_3(aq) + F^-(aq) \longrightarrow BF_4^-(aq)$$

✔ Teaching Tip

Students sometimes think that the number of H atoms in the formula is an indication of whether the acid is strong or weak. Emphasize that this is not the case. Work with students to identify a weak diprotic acid, a strong diprotic acid, a strong monoprotic acid, and a weak monoprotic acid.

TABLE 15-5 *Acid-Base Systems*		
Type	**Acid**	**Base**
Arrhenius	H^+ or H_3O^+ producer	OH^- producer
Brønsted-Lowry	proton (H^+) donor	proton (H^+) acceptor
Lewis	electron-pair acceptor	electron-pair donor

The Lewis definition of acids can apply to species in any phase. For example, boron trifluoride is a Lewis acid in the gas-phase combination with ammonia.

$$:\ddot{F}: \quad H \qquad\qquad :\ddot{F}:H$$
$$:\ddot{F}:\ddot{B} + :\ddot{N}:H \longrightarrow :\ddot{F}:\ddot{B}:\ddot{N}:H$$
$$:\ddot{F}: \quad H \qquad\qquad :\ddot{F}:H$$

A **Lewis base** *is an atom, ion, or molecule that donates an electron pair to form a covalent bond.* An anion is a Lewis base in a reaction in which it forms a covalent bond by donating an electron pair. In the example of boron trifluoride reacting with the fluoride anion, F^- donates an electron pair to boron trifluoride. F^- acts as a Lewis base.

$$BF_3(aq) + :\ddot{F}:^- (aq) \longrightarrow BF_4^-(aq)$$

A **Lewis acid-base reaction** *is the formation of one or more covalent bonds between an electron-pair donor and an electron-pair acceptor.*

Note that although the three acid-base definitions differ, many compounds may be categorized as acids or bases according to all three descriptions. For example, ammonia is an Arrhenius base because OH^- ions are created when ammonia is in solution, it is a Brønsted-Lowry base because it accepts a proton in an acid-base reaction, and it is a Lewis base in all reactions in which it donates its lone pair to form a covalent bond. A comparison of the three acid-base definitions is given in Table 15-5.

SECTION REVIEW

1. proton donors/acidic: H_2CO_3 and H_3O^+; proton acceptors/basic: HCO_3^- and H_2O

2. a. NaOH = Arrhenius base; OH^- = Brønsted-Lowry and Lewis base

b. H_2O and F^- = Brønsted-Lowry and Lewis bases

c. NH_3 = Arrhenius, Brønsted-Lowry, and Lewis base

SECTION REVIEW

1. Label each reactant and each product in the reaction below as a proton donor or a proton acceptor and as acidic or basic.
$$H_2CO_3 + H_2O \rightleftharpoons HCO_3^- + H_3O^+$$

2. Consider the following three reactions. Identify the Arrhenius bases, Brønsted-Lowry bases, and Lewis bases in these reactions. Explain your answers.
a. $NaOH(s) \longrightarrow Na^+(aq) + OH^-(aq)$
b. $HF(aq) + H_2O(l) \longrightarrow F^-(aq) + H_3O^+(aq)$
c. $H^+(aq) + NH_3(aq) \longrightarrow NH_4^+(aq)$

Acid-Base Reactions

OBJECTIVES

- Describe a conjugate acid, a conjugate base, and an amphoteric compound.

- Explain the process of neutralization.

- Explain how acid rain damages marble structures.

Lesson Starter

Ask students for their ideas about the meaning of the word *neutralization.* How is it used in everyday life, and how is it likely to apply to acids and bases?

✔ **Teaching Tip**

The terms *conjugate acid* and *conjugate base* are typically reserved for products of a reaction. The terms *acid* and *base* are generally reserved for reactants. If the reaction is reversible, the conjugate acid and base can be on either the left or right side of the double arrow.

In the previous section, you learned about three acid-base theories: Arrhenius, Brønsted-Lowry, and Lewis. The Brønsted-Lowry theory is especially useful for describing acid-base reactions that take place in aqueous solutions. This section will use the Brønsted-Lowry description to explore reactions between acids and bases.

Conjugate Acids and Bases

The Brønsted-Lowry definitions of acids and bases provide a basis for studying proton-transfer reactions. Suppose that a Brønsted-Lowry acid gives up a proton; the remaining ion or molecule can re-accept that proton and can act as a base. Such a base is known as a conjugate base. Thus, *the species that remains after a Brønsted-Lowry acid has given up a proton is the* **conjugate base** *of that acid.* For example, the fluoride ion is the conjugate base of hydrogen fluoride.

$$HF(aq) + H_2O(l) \rightleftharpoons F^-(aq) + H_3O^+(aq)$$
$$\text{acid} \qquad\qquad\qquad \text{conjugate base}$$

In this reaction, the water molecule is a Brønsted-Lowry base. It accepts a proton to form H_3O^+, which is an acid. The hydronium ion is the conjugate acid of water. *The species that is formed when a Brønsted-Lowry base gains a proton is the* **conjugate acid** *of that base.*

$$HF(aq) + H_2O(l) \rightleftharpoons F^-(aq) + H_3O^+(aq)$$
$$\text{base} \qquad\qquad\qquad \text{conjugate acid}$$

In general, Brønsted-Lowry acid-base reactions are equilibrium systems meaning that both the forward and reverse reactions occur. They involve two acid-base pairs, known as conjugate acid-base pairs.

$$HF(aq) + H_2O(l) \rightleftharpoons F^-(aq) + H_3O^+(aq)$$
$$\text{acid}_1 \quad \text{base}_2 \qquad \text{base}_1 \quad \text{acid}_2$$

The subscripts designate the two conjugate acid-base pairs: (1) HF and F^- and (2) H_3O^+ and H_2O. In every conjugate acid-base pair, the acid has one more proton than its conjugate base.

Strength of Conjugate Acids and Bases

The extent of the reaction between a Brønsted-Lowry acid and base depends on the relative strengths of the acids and bases involved. Consider the following example. Hydrochloric is a strong acid. It gives up protons readily. It follows that the Cl^- ion has little tendency to attract and retain a proton. Consequently, the Cl^- ion is an extremely weak base.

$$HCl(g) + H_2O(l) \longrightarrow H_3O^+(aq) + Cl^-(aq)$$
$$\text{strong acid}\quad\text{base}\qquad\qquad\text{acid}\qquad\text{weak base}$$

This observation leads to an important conclusion: *the stronger an acid is, the weaker its conjugate base; the stronger a base is, the weaker its conjugate acid.*

This concept allows strengths of different acids and bases to be compared to predict the outcome of a reaction. As an example, consider the reaction of perchloric acid, $HClO_4$, and water.

$$HClO_4(aq) + H_2O(l) \longrightarrow H_3O^+(aq) + ClO_4^-(aq)$$
$$\text{stronger acid}\quad\text{stronger base}\qquad\text{weaker acid}\quad\text{weaker base}$$

The hydronium ion is too weak an acid to compete successfully with perchloric acid in donating a proton; $HClO_4$ is the stronger acid. In this reaction, the perchlorate ion, ClO_4^-, and H_2O are both bases. Because $HClO_4$ is a very strong acid, ClO_4^- is an extremely weak base. Therefore, H_2O competes more strongly than ClO_4^- to acquire a proton. The reaction proceeds such that the stronger acid reacts with the stronger base to produce the weaker acid and base.

Now consider a comparable reaction between water and acetic acid.

$$CH_3COOH(aq) + H_2O(l) \longleftarrow H_3O^+(aq) + CH_3COO^-(aq)$$
$$\text{weaker acid}\quad\text{weaker base}\qquad\text{stronger acid}\quad\text{stronger base}$$

The H_3O^+ ion concentration in this solution is much lower than it was in the $HClO_4$ solution because acetic acid is a weak acid. The CH_3COOH molecule does not compete successfully with the H_3O^+ ion in donating protons to a base. The acetate ion, CH_3COO^-, is a stronger base than H_2O. Therefore, the H_2O molecule does not compete successfully with the CH_3COO^- ion in accepting a proton. The H_3O^+ ion is the stronger acid, and the CH_3COO^- ion is the stronger base. Thus, the reaction to the left is more favorable.

Note that in the reactions for both perchloric acid and acetic acid, the favored direction is toward the weaker acid and the weaker base. This observation leads to a second important general conclusion: *proton-transfer reactions favor the production of the weaker acid and the weaker base.* For a reaction to approach completion, the reactants must be much stronger as an acid and as a base than the products.

By comparing many different acids and bases, a table of relative strengths, such as Table 15-6, can be assembled. Note that a very strong acid, such as $HClO_4$, has a very weak conjugate base, ClO_4^-. The strongest base listed in the table, the hydride ion, H^-, has the weakest

TABLE 15-6 Relative Strengths of Acids and Bases

	Conjugate acid	Formula	Conjugate base	Formula	
	chloric acid	$HClO_3$	chlorate ion	ClO_3^-	
	hydrobromic acid	HBr	bromide ion	Br^-	
	hydrochloric acid	HCl	chloride ion	Cl^-	
	hydriodic acid	HI	iodide ion	I^-	
	nitric acid	HNO_3	nitrate ion	NO_3^-	
	perchloric acid	$HClO_4$	perchlorate ion	ClO_4^-	
	sulfuric acid	H_2SO_4	hydrogen sulfate ion	HSO_4^-	
	hydronium ion	H_3O^+	water	H_2O	
	chlorous acid	$HClO_2$	chlorite ion	ClO_2^-	
	hydrogen sulfate ion	HSO_4^-	sulfate ion	SO_4^{2-}	
	phosphoric acid	H_3PO_4	dihydrogen phosphate ion	$H_2PO_4^-$	
	hydrofluoric acid	HF	fluoride ion	F^-	
	acetic acid	CH_3COOH	acetate ion	CH_3COO^-	
	carbonic acid	H_2CO_3	hydrogen carbonate ion	HCO_3^-	
	hydrosulfuric acid	H_2S	hydrosulfide ion	HS^-	
	dihydrogen phosphate ion	$H_2PO_4^-$	hydrogen phosphate ion	HPO_4^{2-}	
	hypochlorous acid	$HClO$	hypochlorite ion	ClO^-	
	ammonium ion	NH_4^+	ammonia	NH_3	
	hydrogen carbonate ion	HCO_3^-	carbonate ion	CO_3^{2-}	
	hydrogen phosphate ion	HPO_4^{2-}	phosphate ion	PO_4^{3-}	
	water	H_2O	hydroxide ion	OH^-	
	ammonia	NH_3	amide ion	NH_2^-	
	hydrogen	H_2	hydride ion	H^-	

Strong acids ← (left bracket top rows) · *Increasing acid strength* ↑ (left) · *Very weak bases* (right, top rows) · *Increasing base strength* ↓ (right)

conjugate acid, H_2. A violent proton-transfer reaction could result from bringing together a very strong acid and a very strong base in certain proportions because the reaction has almost no tendency to go in the reverse direction. Such a reaction would give off a great deal of heat and would be dangerous. In fact, even the reaction between hydride ions and water—a much weaker acid than perchloric acid—is quite vigorous. The reaction is illustrated in Figure 15-11.

Amphoteric Compounds

You have probably noticed that water can be either an acid or a base. *Any species that can react as either an acid or a base is described as* **amphoteric.** For example, consider the first ionization of sulfuric acid, in which water acts as a base.

FIGURE 15-11 Because H⁻ is an extremely strong base, calcium hydride, CaH₂, reacts vigorously with water to produce hydrogen gas. The hydride ion accepts a proton from water, which acts as an acid in this reaction.

$$H^-(aq) + H_2O(l) \longrightarrow OH^-(aq) + H_2(g)$$

$$H_2SO_4(aq) + H_2O(l) \longrightarrow H_3O^+(aq) + HSO_4^-(aq)$$
$$\text{acid} \qquad\quad \text{base} \qquad\qquad \text{acid} \qquad\quad \text{base}$$

However, water acts as an acid in the following reaction.

$$NH_3(g) + H_2O(l) \rightleftharpoons NH_4^+(aq) + OH^-(aq)$$
$$\text{base} \qquad\quad \text{acid} \qquad\qquad \text{acid} \qquad\quad \text{base}$$

Thus, water can act as either an acid or a base and is amphoteric. Such a substance acts as either an acid or a base, depending on the strength of the acid or base with which they are reacting. For example, if water reacts with a compound that is a stronger acid than itself, water acts as a base. If water reacts with a weaker acid, water acts as an acid.

FIGURE 15-12 Each oxyacid of chlorine contains one chlorine atom and one hydrogen atom. They differ in the number of oxygen atoms they contain. The effect of the changing O—H bond polarity can be seen in the increasing acid strength from hypochlorous acid to perchloric acid.

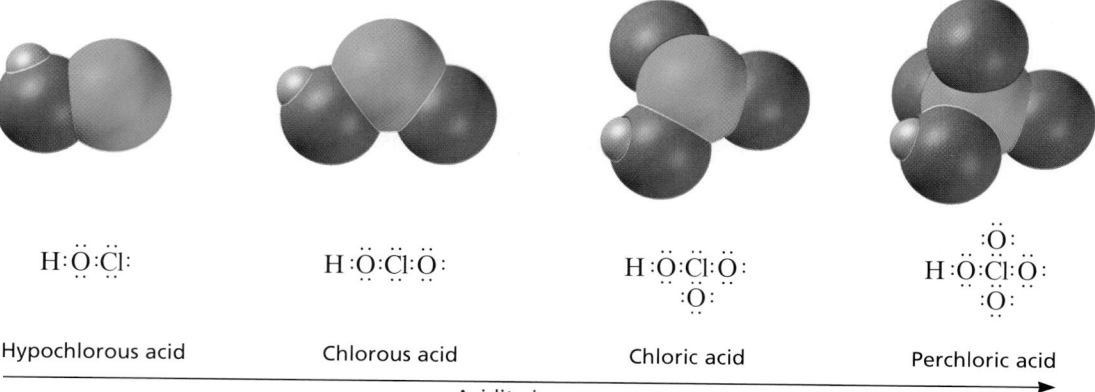

Hypochlorous acid   Chlorous acid   Chloric acid   Perchloric acid

Acidity increases

–OH in a Molecule

Molecular compounds containing –OH groups can be acidic or amphoteric. The covalently bonded –OH group in an acid is referred to as a *hydroxyl group*. For the compound to be acidic, a water molecule must be able to attract a hydrogen atom from a hydroxyl group. This occurs more easily when the O–H bond is very polar. Any feature of a molecule that increases the polarity of the O–H bond increases the acidity of a molecular compound. The small, more-electronegative atoms of nonmetals at the upper right in the periodic table form compounds with acidic hydroxyl groups. All oxyacids are molecular electrolytes that contain one or more of these O–H bonds. Such compounds include chloric and perchloric acids.

Figure 15-12 shows the electron-dot formulas of the four oxyacids of chlorine. Notice that all of the oxygen atoms are bonded to the chlorine atom. Each hydrogen atom is bonded to an oxygen atom. Aqueous solutions of these molecules are acids because the O–H bonds are broken as the hydrogen is attracted away by water molecules.

The behavior of a compound is affected by the number of oxygen atoms bonded to the atom connected to the – OH group. The larger the number of such oxygen atoms is, the more acidic the compound is likely to be. The electronegative oxygen atoms draw electron density away from the O–H bond and make it more polar. For example, chromium forms three different compounds containing – OH groups, as shown below.

basic	*amphoteric*	*acidic*
$Cr(OH)_2$	$Cr(OH)_3$	H_2CrO_4
chromium(II)	chromium(III)	chromic acid
hydroxide	hydroxide	

Notice that as the number of oxygen atoms increases, so does the acidity of the compound.

Consider also the compounds shown in Figure 15-13. In acetic acid, but not in ethanol, a second oxygen atom is bonded to the carbon atom connected to the –OH group. That explains why acetic acid is acidic but ethanol is not, even though the same elements form each compound.

Neutralization Reactions

There are many common examples of acidic compounds reacting with basic compounds, each neutralizing the other. Sodium bicarbonate, $NaHCO_3$, and tartaric acid, $C_4H_6O_6$, are two components in baking powder. When allowed to react in solution, the two compounds produce carbon dioxide. The escaping carbon dioxide causes foods, such as biscuits, to rise. An antacid soothes an overly acidic stomach by neutralizing the stomach acid.

Class Discussion
Ask students to write the net ionic equation for the reaction between HCl and NaOH. Ask them to explain what the net ionic equation tells about the specific acid and specific base used in a neutralization reaction.

CHAPTER ⟷ CONNECTION

Organic acids, also known as carboxylic acids, will be discussed in Chapter 21.

Visual Strategy
FIGURE 15-13 Draw the structure of formic acid, and ask students to predict whether it would be more or less acidic than acetic acid.

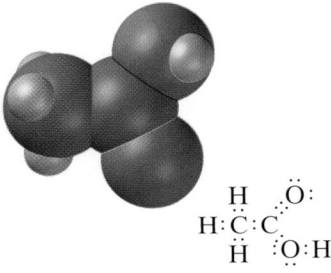

(a) CH_3COOH
Acetic acid

(b) C_2H_5OH
Ethanol

FIGURE 15-13 (a) Acetic acid is acidic. The second oxygen atom on the carbon draws electron density away from the –OH group, making the O–H bond more polar. (b) Ethanol is essentially neutral. It has no second oxygen atom, so ethanol is less polar than acetic acid, and is a much weaker acid.

internet**connect**

SCI*LINKS*

NSTA

TOPIC: Salt
GO TO: www.scilinks.org
*sci*LINKS CODE: HC2154

Strong Acid-Strong Base Neutralization

An acid-base reaction occurs in aqueous solution between hydrochloric acid, a strong acid that completely dissociates to produce H_3O^+, and sodium hydroxide, a strong base that completely dissociates to produce OH^-. The formula equation for this reaction is written as follows.

$$HCl(aq) + NaOH(aq) \longrightarrow NaCl(aq) + H_2O(l)$$

In an aqueous solution containing 1 mol of sodium hydroxide, NaOH dissociates as represented by the following equation.

$$NaOH(aq) \longrightarrow Na^+(aq) + OH^-(aq)$$

A solution containing 1 mol of hydrochloric acid ionizes as represented by the following equation.

$$HCl(aq) + H_2O(l) \longrightarrow H_3O^+(aq) + Cl^-(aq)$$

If the two solutions are mixed, as in Figure 15-14, a reaction occurs between the aqueous ions. Notice that sodium chloride, NaCl, and water are produced. The overall ionic equation is shown below.

$$H_3O^+(aq) + Cl^-(aq) + Na^+(aq) + OH^-(aq) \longrightarrow$$
$$Na^+(aq) + Cl^-(aq) + 2H_2O(l)$$

FIGURE 15-14 When aqueous hydrochloric acid, HCl, reacts with aqueous sodium hydroxide, NaOH, the reaction produces aqueous sodium chloride, NaCl. Ions that are present in each solution are represented by the models.

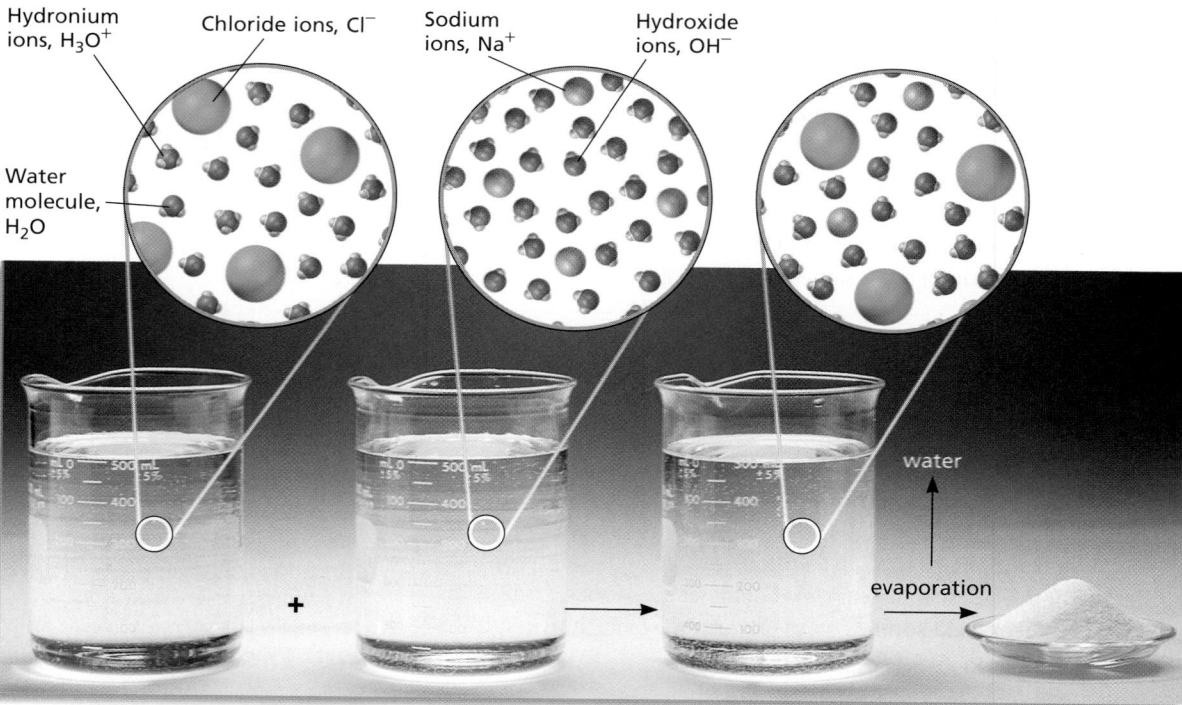

Hydronium ions, H_3O^+

Chloride ions, Cl^-

Sodium ions, Na^+

Hydroxide ions, OH^-

Water molecule, H_2O

water

evaporation

Because they appear on both sides of the overall ionic equation, Na^+ and Cl^- are spectator ions. The only participants in the reaction are the hydronium ion and the hydroxide ion, as shown in the following net ionic equation.

$$H_3O^+(aq) + OH^-(aq) \longrightarrow 2H_2O(l)$$

There are equal numbers of H_3O^+ and OH^- ions in this reaction, and they are fully converted to water. In aqueous solutions, **neutralization** *is the reaction of hydronium ions and hydroxide ions to form water molecules.*

Notice that water is not the only product of a neutralization. A salt is also produced. *A **salt** is an ionic compound composed of a cation from a base and an anion from an acid.*

Acid Rain

Many industrial processes produce gases such as NO, NO_2, CO_2, SO_2, and SO_3. These compounds can dissolve in atmospheric water to produce acidic solutions that fall to the ground in the form of rain or snow. The following reaction shows how sulfur trioxide, SO_3, dissolves in water to produce sulfuric acid.

$$SO_3(g) + H_2O(l) \longrightarrow H_2SO_4(aq)$$

Marble found in many buildings and statues is composed of calcium carbonate, $CaCO_3$. When acid snow or rain falls on these structures, the following reaction takes place.

$$CaCO_3(s) + 2H_3O^+(aq) \longrightarrow Ca^{2+}(aq) + CO_2(g) + 3H_2O(l)$$

The products of the reaction of an acid with any carbonate are a salt, water, and carbon dioxide. An example of the effects of acid rain can be seen in Figure 15-15; the marble in this statue has been eroded by the acidic precipitation. Even though the products themselves are harmless, the reaction has serious consequences.

FIGURE 15-15 Acid precipitation causes extensive damage to buildings and other structures.

SECTION REVIEW

1. Complete and balance the equations for the following acid-base reactions:
   a. $H_2CO_3 + Sr(OH)_2 \longrightarrow$
   b. $HClO_4 + NaOH \longrightarrow$
   c. $HBr + Ba(OH)_2 \longrightarrow$
   d. $NaHCO_3 + H_2SO_4 \longrightarrow$

2. Consider the equation for acetic acid plus water.

   $$HC_2H_3O_2 + H_2O \longrightarrow C_2H_3O_2^- + H_3O^+$$

   a. Refer to Table 15-6 to compare the strengths of the two acids in the equation. Do the same for the two bases.
   b. Determine which direction—forward or reverse—is favored in the reaction.

3. Explain how the presence of several oxygen atoms in a compound containing an –OH group can make the compound acidic.

SECTION REVIEW

1. a. $H_2CO_3 + Sr(OH)_2 \longrightarrow$
      $SrCO_3 + 2H_2O$

   b. $HClO_4 + NaOH \longrightarrow$
      $NaClO_4 + H_2O$

   c. $2HBr + Ba(OH)_2 \longrightarrow$
      $BaBr_2 + 2H_2O$

   d. $2NaHCO_3 + H_2SO_4 \longrightarrow$
      $Na_2SO_4 + 2H_2CO_3$

2. a. H_3O^+ is the stronger acid; $C_2H_3O_2^-$ is the stronger base.
   b. Reverse reaction is favored.

3. Oxygen atoms draw electron density away from the O–H bond, making it more polar (more easily broken).

CHAPTER SUMMARY

15-1
- Acids have a sour taste and react with active metals. They change the colors of acid-base indicators, and react with bases to produce salts and water. Some conduct electricity.
- Bases have a bitter taste, feel slippery to the skin in dilute aqueous solutions, change the colors of acid-base indicators, react with acids to produce salts and water, and conduct electricity.

- An Arrhenius acid contains hydrogen and ionizes in aqueous solution to form hydrogen ions. An Arrhenius base produces hydroxide ions in aqueous solution.
- The strength of an Arrhenius acid or base is determined by the extent to which it ionizes or dissociates in aqueous solutions.

Vocabulary

alkaline (461)	Arrhenius base (459)	oxyacid (455)	weak acids (460)
Arrhenius acid (459)	binary acid (454)	strong acid (460)	

15-2
- A Brønsted-Lowry acid is a proton donor. A Brønsted-Lowry base is a proton acceptor.
- A Lewis acid is an electron-pair acceptor. A Lewis base is an electron-pair donor.

- Acids are described as monoprotic, diprotic, or triprotic, depending on whether they can donate one, two, or three protons per molecule, respectively, in aqueous solutions.

Vocabulary

amphoteric (470)	Brønsted-Lowry base (465)	Lewis acid-base reaction (468)	monoprotic acid (465)
Brønsted-Lowry acid (464)	diprotic acid (466)	Lewis base (468)	polyprotic acid (465)
Brønsted-Lowry acid-base reaction (465)	Lewis acid (467)		triprotic acid (466)

15-3
- In every Brønsted-Lowry acid-base reaction, there are two conjugate acid-base pairs.
- A strong acid has a weak conjugate base; a strong base has a weak conjugate acid.
- Proton-transfer reactions favor the production of weaker acids and bases.
- The acidic or basic behavior of a molecule containing −OH groups may depend on the

electronegativity of other atoms in the molecule and the number of oxygen atoms bonded to the atom connected to the −OH group.
- A neutralization reaction produces water and an ionic compound called a salt.
- Acid rain neutralizes the calcium carbonate in marble structures, causing them to deteriorate.

Vocabulary

amphoteric (471)	conjugate base (469)	neutralization (475)	salt (475)
conjugate acid (469)			

REVIEWING CONCEPTS

1. Compare and contrast the general properties of acids and bases. (15-1)

2. a. Distinguish between binary acids and oxy-acids in terms of their component elements and the systems used in naming them.
b. Give three examples of each. (15-1)

3. Identify and describe the characteristic properties of five common acids used in industry. Give some examples of the typical uses of each. (15-1)

4. Although HCl(*aq*) exhibits Arrhenius acidic properties, pure HCl gas and HCl dissolved in a nonpolar solvent exhibit no acidic properties in the Arrhenius sense. Explain why. (15-1)

5. a. What distinguishes strong acids from weak acids?
b. Give two examples of each. (15-1)

6. H_3PO_4, which contains three hydrogen atoms per molecule, is a weak acid, whereas HCl, which contains only one hydrogen atom per molecule, is a strong acid. Explain why. (15-1)

7. a. What determines the strength of an Arrhenius base?
b. Give one example each of solutions that are strongly and weakly basic. (15-1)

8. Distinguish among a monoprotic, a diprotic, and a triprotic acid. Give an example of each. (15-2)

9. Which of the three acid definitions is the broadest? Explain. (15-2)

10. Define and give an equation to illustrate each of the following:
a. a conjugate base
b. a conjugate acid (15-3)

11. a. What is the relationship between the strength of an acid and that of its conjugate base?
b. What is the relationship between the strength of a base and its conjugate acid? (15-3)

12. a. What trend is there in the favored direction of proton-transfer reactions?
b. What determines the extent to which a proton-transfer reaction occurs? (15-3)

13. a. What is meant by the term *amphoteric*?
b. Give an example of a substance or ion with amphoteric characteristics. (15-3)

14. For each reaction listed, identify the proton donor or acid and the proton acceptor or base. Label each conjugate acid-base pair.
a. $CH_3COOH(aq) + H_2O(l) \rightleftharpoons$
$$H_3O^+(aq) + CH_3COO^-(aq)$$
b. $HCO_3^-(aq) + H_2O(l) \rightleftharpoons$
$$H_2CO_3(aq) + OH^-(aq)$$
c. $HNO_3 + SO_4^{2-} \longrightarrow HSO_4^- + NO_3^-$ (15-3)

15. Based on the information given in Table 15-6, determine the following relative to HF, H_2S, HNO_3, and CH_3COOH:
a. strongest acid
b. weakest acid
c. strongest conjugate base among the four produced by the acids listed
d. weakest conjugate base among the four produced (15-3)

16. Explain why the conjugate base of a strong acid is a weak base and the conjugate acid of a strong base is a weak acid. (15-3)

PROBLEMS

Acid Nomenclature

17. Name each of the following binary acids:
a. HCl
b. H_2S

18. Name each of the following oxyacids:
a. HNO_3
b. H_2SO_3
c. $HClO_3$
d. HNO_2

19. Write formulas for each of the following binary acids:
a. hydrofluoric acid
b. hydriodic acid

20. Write formulas for each of the following oxyacids:
a. perbromic acid
b. chlorous acid
c. phosphoric acid
d. hypochlorous acid

REVIEW ANSWERS

1. Both acids and bases change color of indicator and are electrolytes. Acids taste sour, react with active metals to release $H_2(g)$, and react with bases to form salt and water. Bases taste bitter, feel slippery, and react with acids to form salt and water.

2. **a.** Binary acids consist of hydrogen and a more electronegative element. They are named using the prefix *hydro-*, followed by the root name of the second element and the suffix *-ic*. Oxyacids consist of hydrogen, oxygen, and a third element (usually a nonmetal). Oxyacid names are based on the name of the anion.
b. examples of binary acids: HF, HCl, HBr; examples of oxyacids: $HClO_3$, HNO_3, H_2SO_4

3. H_2SO_4 is the most common acid, a dehydrating agent, used to make fertilizers, in petroleum refining, in metallurgy, and in automobile batteries. H_3PO_4 is used in making fertilizers, cleaners, and animal feed and as a flavoring agent. HNO_3 is a volatile, unstable liquid that stains proteins yellow. It is used to make fertilizers, explosives, rubber, plastics, dyes, and drugs. HCl, also called muriatic acid, is used as a cleaning agent, in food processing, to pickle iron, and in activating oil wells. Hydrochloric acid is also produced in the stomach to aid digestion. Acetic acid is an organic acid. It is a clear, colorless liquid produced by fermentation of malt, barley, and fruit juices, found in household vinegar, and used to make plastics, food supplements, and fungicides

4. HCl(*g*) consists of covalently bonded molecules that do not ionize. Nonpolar solvent molecules do not attract HCl molecules to cause them to be ionized.

5. a. Strong acids ionize completely in dilute aqueous solution; weak acids ionize much less.
b. examples of strong acids: HCl, HNO_3; examples of weak acids: HF, H_3PO_4

6. The strength of an acid depends on the degree of ionization, not on the amount of hydrogen in the molecule. HCl ionizes completely. H_3PO_4 ionizes only slightly.

7. a. concentration of OH^- ions in solution
b. Answers will vary. example: NaOH, strongly basic; $NH_3(aq)$, weakly basic

8. Monoprotic acids, such as HCl, can donate only one proton per molecule; diprotic acids, such as H_2SO_4, can donate two protons per molecule; and triprotic acids, such as H_3PO_4, can donate three protons per molecule.

9. The Lewis definition is the broadest. Any substance defined as an Arrhenius or Brønsted-Lowry acid is also an acid as defined by the Lewis theory. The reverse is not always true.

10. a. A conjugate base remains after an acid has given up a proton. example: HF + $H_2O \longrightarrow$ $H_3O^+ + F^-$
acid: HF; conjugate base: F^-
b. A conjugate acid is what forms when a proton is added to a base.
base: H_2O; conjugate acid: H_3O^+

11. a. The stronger an acid is, the weaker its conjugate base is.
b. The stronger a base is, the weaker its conjugate acid is.

Acid-Base Theory

21. a. Write the balanced equations that describe the two-stage ionization of sulfuric acid in a dilute aqueous solution.
b. How do the degrees of ionization in the two steps compare?

22. Dilute HCl(*aq*) and KOH(*aq*) are mixed in chemically equivalent quantities. Write the following:
a. formula equation for the reaction
b. overall ionic equation
c. net ionic equation

23. Repeat item 22 with $H_3PO_4(aq)$ and NaOH(*aq*).

24. Write the formula equation and net ionic equation for each of the following reactions:
a. $Zn(s) + HCl(aq) \longrightarrow$
b. $Al(s) + H_2SO_4(aq) \longrightarrow$

25. Write the formula equation and net ionic equation for the reaction between Ca(*s*) and HCl(*aq*).

Neutralization Reactions

26. Complete the following neutralization reactions. Balance each reaction, and then write the overall ionic and net ionic equation for each.
a. $HCl(aq) + NaOH(aq) \longrightarrow$
b. $HNO_3(aq) + KOH(aq) \longrightarrow$
c. $Ca(OH)_2(aq) + HNO_3(aq) \longrightarrow$
d. $Mg(OH)_2(aq) + HCl(aq) \longrightarrow$

27. Write the formula equation, the overall ionic equation, and the net ionic equation for the neutralization reaction involving aqueous solutions of H_3PO_4 and $Mg(OH)_2$. Assume that the solutions are sufficiently dilute so that no precipitates form.

28. Write the balanced chemical equation for each of the following reactions between an acid and a carbonate:
a. $BaCO_3(s) + HCl(aq) \longrightarrow$
b. $MgCO_3(s) + HNO_3(aq) \longrightarrow$
c. $Na_2CO_3(s) + H_2SO_4(aq) \longrightarrow$
d. $CaCO_3(s) + H_3PO_4(aq) \longrightarrow$

29. Write the formula equation, the overall ionic equation, and the net ionic equation for a neu-

tralization reaction that would form each of the following salts.
a. $RbClO_4$ **c.** $CaCl_2$
b. $BaSO_4$ **d.** K_2SO_4

Stoichiometry

30. Zinc reacts with 100. mL of 6.00 M cold, aqueous sulfuric acid through single replacement.
a. How many grams of zinc sulfate are produced?
b. How many liters of hydrogen gas would be released at STP?

31. A 211 g sample of barium carbonate, $BaCO_3$, is placed in a solution of nitric acid. Assuming that the acid is present in excess, what mass and volume of dry carbon dioxide gas at STP will be produced?

32. A seashell, composed largely of calcium carbonate, is placed in a solution of HCl. As a result, 1500 mL of dry CO_2 gas at STP is produced. The other products are $CaCl_2$ and H_2O.
a. Based on this information, how many grams of $CaCO_3$ are consumed in the reaction?
b. What volume of 2.00 M HCl solution is used in this reaction?

33. *Acid precipitation* is the term generally used to describe rain or snow that is more acidic than normal. One cause of acid precipitation is the formation of sulfuric and nitric acids from various sulfur and nitrogen oxides produced in volcanic eruptions, forest fires, and thunderstorms. In a typical volcanic eruption, for example, 3.50×10^8 kg of SO_2 may be produced. If this amount of SO_2 were converted to H_2SO_4 according to the two-step process given below, how many kilograms of H_2SO_4 would be produced from such an eruption?

$$SO_2 + \tfrac{1}{2}O_2 \longrightarrow SO_3$$
$$SO_3 + H_2O \longrightarrow H_2SO_4$$

MIXED REVIEW

34. Suppose that dilute $HNO_3(aq)$ and LiOH(*aq*) are mixed in chemically equivalent quantities. Write the following for the reaction:
a. formula equation
b. overall ionic equation
c. net ionic equation

35. Write the balanced chemical equation for the reaction between hydrochloric acid and magnesium metal.

36. Write equations for the three-step ionization of phosphoric acid, H_3PO_4. Compare the degree of ionization for the three steps.

37. Name or give the molecular formula for each of the following acids:
a. HF
b. acetic acid
c. phosphorous acid
d. $HClO_4$
e. H_3PO_4
f. hydrobromic acid
g. HClO
h. H_2CO_3
i. sulfuric acid

CRITICAL THINKING

38. Analyzing Conclusions In the eighteenth century, Antoine Lavoisier experimented with oxides such as CO_2 and SO_2. He observed that they formed acidic solutions. His observations led him to infer that for a substance to exhibit acidic behavior, it must contain oxygen. However, today that is known to be incorrect. Provide evidence to refute Lavoisier's conclusion.

HANDBOOK SEARCH

39. Group 16 of the *Elements Handbook* contains a section covering the acid-base chemistry of oxides. Review this material and answer the following:
a. What type of compounds form acidic oxides?
b. What is an acidic anhydride?
c. List three examples of compounds that are classified as acidic anhydrides.
d. What type of compounds form basic oxides? Why are they basic oxides?

40. a. Look at Table 7A in the *Elements Handbook*. What periodic trends do you notice regarding acid-base character of oxides?
b. How is the nature of the product affected by the concentration of NaOH in a reaction with CO_2?

RESEARCH & WRITING

41. Explain how sulfuric acid production serves as a measure of a country's economy. Write a report on your findings.

42. Performance Conduct library research to find out about the buffering of solutions. Include information on why buffering is typically carried out and on the kinds of materials used. Write a brief report on your findings.

43. Obtain some pH paper from your teacher. Determine whether the soil around your house is acidic or basic. Find one type of plant that would grow well in that type of soil and one that would not.

ALTERNATIVE ASSESSMENT

44. Antacids are designed to neutralize excess hydrochloric acid secreted by the stomach during digestion. Carbonates, bicarbonates, and hydroxides are the active ingredients in bringing about the neutralization reactions in the most widely used antacids. Examine the labels of several common antacids, and identify the active ingredients.

45. Performance Design an experiment that compares three brands of antacids in terms of reaction speed and amount of acid neutralized.

12. a. Production of the weaker acid and weaker base is favored.
b. It depends on the relative strengths of the acids and bases involved. For an acid-base reaction to approach completion, the reactants must be much stronger acids and bases than the products.

13. a. the term that describes a species that can react as either an acid or a base
b. example: $H_2PO_4^-$: the conjugate base of H_3PO_4, and can act as acid to further ionize to HPO_4^-

14. a. acid: CH_3COOH, conjugate base: CH_3COO^-; base: H_2O, conjugate acid: H_3O^+
b. acid: H_2O, conjugate base: OH^-; base: HCO_3^-, conjugate acid: H_2CO_3
c. acid: HNO_3, conjugate base: NO_3^-; base: SO_4^{2-}, conjugate acid: HSO_4^-

15. a. HNO_3
b. H_2S
c. HS^-
d. NO_3^-

16. Strong acids and bases are readily ionized in solution. For them to remain ionized, the corresponding conjugate base and acid, respectively, must be too weak to compete successfully with them.

17. a. hydrochloric acid
b. hydrosulfuric acid

18. a. nitric acid
b. sulfurous acid
c. chloric acid
d. nitrous acid

19. a. HF
b. HI

20. a. $HBrO_4$
b. $HClO_2$
c. H_3PO_4
d. HClO

21–44 *See page 479A.*

Continued from page 479

21. a. $H_2SO_4(aq) + H_2O(l) \longrightarrow H_3O^+(aq) + HSO_4^-(aq)$;
$HSO_4^-(aq) + H_2O(l) \rightleftarrows H_3O^+(aq) + SO_4^{2-}(aq)$

b. The degree of ionization in the first stage is much greater than that in the second.

22. a. $HCl(aq) + KOH(aq) \longrightarrow KCl(aq) + H_2O(l)$

b. $H_3O^+(aq) + Cl^-(aq) + K^+(aq) + OH^-(aq) \longrightarrow K^+(aq) + Cl^-(aq) + 2H_2O(l)$

c. $H_3O^+(aq) + OH^-(aq) \longrightarrow 2H_2O(l)$

23. a. $H_3PO_4(aq) + 3NaOH(aq) \longrightarrow Na_3PO_4(aq) + 3H_2O(l)$

b. $3H_3O^+(aq) + PO_4^{3-}(aq) + 3Na^+(aq) + 3OH^-(aq) \longrightarrow 3Na^+(aq) + PO_4^{3-}(aq) + 6H_2O(l)$

c. $H_3O^+(aq) + OH^-(aq) \longrightarrow 2H_2O(l)$

24. a. $Zn(s) + 2HCl(aq) \longrightarrow ZnCl_2(aq) + H_2(g)$
$Zn(s) + 2H_3O^+(aq) \longrightarrow Zn^{2+}(aq) + H_2(g) + 2H_2O(l)$

b. $2Al(s) + 3H_2SO_4(aq) \longrightarrow Al_2(SO_4)_3(aq) + 3H_2(g)$
$2Al(s) + 6H_2O^+(aq) \longrightarrow 2Al^{3+}(aq) + 3H_2(g) + 6H_2O(l)$

25. $Ca(s) + 2HCl(aq) \longrightarrow CaCl_2(aq) + H_2(g)$
$Ca(s) + 2H_3O^+(aq) \longrightarrow Ca^{2+}(aq) + H_2(g) + 2H_2O(l)$

26. a. $HCl(aq) + NaOH(aq) \longrightarrow NaCl(aq) + H_2O(l)$
$H_3O^+(aq) + Cl^-(aq) + Na^+(aq) + OH^-(aq) \longrightarrow Na^+(aq) + Cl^-(aq) + 2H_2O(l)$
$H_3O^+(aq) + OH^-(aq) \longrightarrow 2H_2O(l)$

b. $HNO_3(aq) + KOH(aq) \longrightarrow KNO_3(aq) + H_2O(l)$
$H_3O^+(aq) + NO_3^-(aq) + K^+(aq) + OH^-(aq) \longrightarrow K^+(aq) + NO_3^-(aq) + 2H_2O(l)$
$H_3O^+(aq) + OH^-(aq) \longrightarrow 2H_2O(l)$

c. $Ca(OH)_2(aq) + 2HNO_3(aq) \longrightarrow Ca(NO_3)_2(aq) + 2H_2O(l)$
$Ca^{2+}(aq) + 2OH^-(aq) + 2H_3O^+(aq) + 2NO_3^-(aq) \longrightarrow Ca^{2+}(aq) + 2NO_3^-(aq) + 4H_2O(l)$
$H_3O^+(aq) + OH^-(aq) \longrightarrow 2H_2O(l)$

d. $Mg(OH)_2(aq) + 2HCl(aq) \longrightarrow MgCl_2(aq) + 2H_2O(l)$
$Mg^{2+}(aq) + 2OH^-(aq) + 2H_3O^+(aq) + 2Cl^-(aq) \longrightarrow Mg^{2+}(aq) + 2Cl^-(aq) + 4H_2O(l)$
$H_3O^+(aq) + OH^-(aq) \longrightarrow 2H_2O(l)$

27. $2H_3PO_4(aq) + 3Mg(OH)_2(aq) \longrightarrow Mg_3(PO_4)_2(aq) + 6H_2O(l)$
$6H_3O^+(aq) + 2PO_4^{3-}(aq) + 3Mg^{2+}(aq) + 6OH^-(aq) \longrightarrow 3Mg^{2+}(aq) + 2PO_4^{3-}(aq) + 12H_2O(l)$
$H_3O^+(aq) + OH^-(aq) \longrightarrow 2H_2O(l)$

28. a. $BaCO_3(s) + 2HCl(aq) \longrightarrow BaCl_2(aq) + H_2O(l) + CO_2(g)$

b. $MgCO_3(s) + 2HNO_3(aq) \longrightarrow Mg(NO_3)_2(aq) + H_2O(l) + CO_2(g)$

c. $Na_2CO_3(s) + H_2SO_4(aq) \longrightarrow Na_2SO_4(aq) + H_2O(l) + CO_2(g)$

d. $3CaCO_3(s) + 2H_3PO_4(aq) \longrightarrow Ca_3(PO_4)_2(aq) + 3H_2O(l) + 3CO_2(g)$

29. a. $RbOH(aq) + HClO_4(aq) \longrightarrow RbClO_4(aq) + H_2O(l)$
$Rb^+(aq) + OH^-(aq) + H_3O^+(aq) + ClO_4^-(aq) \longrightarrow Rb^+(aq) + ClO_4^-(aq) + 2H_2O(l)$
$H_3O^+(aq) + OH^-(aq) \longrightarrow 2H_2O(l)$

b. $Ba(OH)_2(aq) + H_2SO_4(aq) \longrightarrow BaSO_4(s) + 2H_2O(l)$
$Ba^{2+}(aq) + 2OH^-(aq) + 2H_3O^+(aq) + SO_4^{2-}(aq) \longrightarrow BaSO_4(s) + 4H_2O(l)$
$Ba^{2+}(aq) + 2OH^-(aq) + 2H_3O^+(aq) + SO_4^{2-}(aq) \longrightarrow BaSO_4(s) + 4H_2O(l)$
(There are no spectator ions, so the net ionic equation is the same as the overall ionic equation.)

c. $Ca(OH)_2(aq) + 2HCl(aq) \longrightarrow CaCl_2(aq) + 2H_2O(l)$
$Ca^{2+}(aq) + 2OH^-(aq) + 2H_3O^+(aq) + 2Cl^-(aq) \longrightarrow Ca^{2+}(aq) + 2Cl^-(aq) + 4H_2O(l)$
$H_3O^+(aq) + OH^-(aq) \longrightarrow 2H_2O(l)$
(Cancellation of spectator ions gives $2H_3O^+(aq) + 2OH_2^-(aq) \longrightarrow 4H_2O(l)$; we then divide out the common factor of 2 to give the net ionic equation with smallest integers.)

d. $2KOH(aq) + H_2SO_4(aq) \longrightarrow K_2SO_4(aq) + 2H_2O(l)$
$2K^+(aq) + 2OH^-(aq) + 2H_3O^+(aq) + SO_4^{2-}(aq) \longrightarrow 2K^+(aq) + SO_4^{2-}(aq) + 4H_2O(l)$
$H_3O^+(aq) + OH^-(aq) \longrightarrow 2H_2O(l)$ (written with smallest integers)

30. a. 96.9 g $ZnSO_4$
  b. 13.4 L H_2

31. 47.1 g, 24.0 L CO_2

32. a. 6.7 g $CaCO_3$
  b. 0.067 L

33. 5.36×10^8 kg H_2SO_4

34. a. $HNO_3(aq) + LiOH(aq) \longrightarrow LiNO_3(aq) + H_2O(l)$
  b. $H_3O^+(aq) + NO_3^-(aq) + Li^+(aq) + OH^-(aq) \longrightarrow$
  $Li^+(aq) + NO_3^-(aq) + 2H_2O(l)$
  c. $H_3O^+(aq) + OH^-(aq) \longrightarrow 2H_2O(l)$

35. $Mg(s) + 2HCl(aq) \longrightarrow MgCl_2(aq) + H_2(g)$

36. $H_3PO_4(aq) + H_2O(l) \rightleftarrows H_3O^+(aq) + H_2PO_4^-(aq)$;
  greatest degree of ionization
  $H_2PO_4^-(aq) + H_2O(l) \rightleftarrows H_3O^+(aq) + HPO_4^{2-}(aq)$;
  less ionization
  $HPO_4^{2-}(aq) + H_2O(l) \rightleftarrows H_3O^+(aq) + PO_4^{3-}(aq)$;
  least ionization

37. a. hydrofluoric acid
  b. CH_3COOH
  c. H_3PO_3
  d. perchloric acid
  e. phosphoric acid
  f. HBr
  g. hypochlorous acid
  h. carbonic acid
  i. H_2SO_4

38. Answers will vary. Students should provide examples of acids that do not contain oxygen, such as HCl or HBr. They should discuss the different ways an acid can be defined that can either narrow or broaden the definition and that do not in any case require the presence of oxygen in the acid.

39. a. Oxides of nonmetals are acidic.
  b. Acidic anhydrides are oxide compounds that react with water to form acids.

c. The following are possible responses: B_2O_3, CO_2, N_2O_5, P_4O_{10}, SO_3, SeO_3, TeO_3, Cl_2O, I_2O_5.
d. Basic oxides are the dehydrated forms of the hydroxides of reactive metals (Groups 1 and 2). Basic oxides form metal hydroxides when reacted with water.

40. a. Basic oxides come from elements on the far left of the table. Elements in the metalloid region of the table form amphoteric oxides. Nonmetals form acidic oxides. Oxide character within a group is related to metallic character within a group.
  b. Reactions of CO_2 with excess NaOH will produce Na_2CO_3. Reactions of CO_2 with a limited amount of NaOH (less than the mole ratio) will result in the production of $NaHCO_3$.

41. Sulfuric acid is involved in many technical and manufacturing processes. Typically, the more highly industrialized a country is, the greater the level of sulfuric acid consumed by that country in the course of its everyday industrial activities. Thus, sulfuric acid production can serve as a measure of the degree of industrialization and economic activity of a country.

42. Refer to the *One-Stop Planner CD-ROM* for appropriate scoring rubrics. Answers should include an explanation of how buffers cause solutions to be resistant to changes in acidity or basicity.

43. Answers will vary.

44. Answers should include $CaCO_3$, $NaHCO_3$, $Mg(OH)_2$, and $Al(OH)_3$.

45. Check the design of students' experiments before they proceed.

Acid-Base Titration and pH

PACING CHART Compression Guide: (To shorten, eliminate items in italics.)	NSE Standards	CLASSROOM RESOURCES		
		Teaching Resources	Experiments	
16-1 **Aqueous Solutions and the Concept of pH** 2 45-minute periods 1 90-minute block *Calculations Involving pH, pp. 487–491*	PS 3c UCP 1–4 SAI 2 ST 2 SPSP 2, 5	**ATE Demo,** pp. 485, 486 **PE** Elements Handbook TM 70A, TM 71A	Quick Lab, p. 496	
16-2 **Determining pH and Titrations** 2 45-minute periods 1 90-minute block *Molarity and Titration, pp. 499–503*	PS 3c UCP 1–4 SAI 1–2	**ATE Demo,** pp. 495, 499, 500 T 89, T 90, T 91		

Review and Assessment 2 45-minute periods 1 90-minute block	REVIEW RESOURCES		
	Cumulative Review	Alternative Assessment	Traditional Assessment
	SR Chapter 16 Mixed Review PE Chapter 16 27–37, p. 506	PE 43–45, p. 507 ATE 503 AA Items for Chapter 16	Chapter 16 Text Test Generator items for Chapter 16

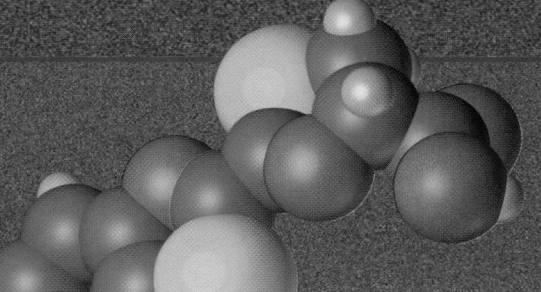

ASSIGNMENT RESOURCES

Section Homework Resources & Review	Problem-Solving Practice
HR Homework Worksheets 16-1, 16-2, 16-3 Graphic Org. Assignment 16-1 **PE** Section Review, 1–6, p. 491 Chapter Review, 1–7, 1–23, pp. 504–505 **SR** Section Review 16-1	**PE** Additional Samples 16-1, 16-2, 16-3, 16-4, 16-5 **ATE** Additional Samples, pp. 484, 487, 488, 489, 490 **PS** Chapter 17 pH
HR Homework Worksheets 16-4, 16-5, 16-6 Graphic Org. Assignment 16-5 **PE** Section Review, 1–4, p. 503 Chapter Review, 8–9, 24–26, pp. 504–505 **SR** Section Review 16-2	**PE** Additional Samples 16-6 **ATE** Additional Samples, p. 502 Additional Examples, p. 502 **PS** Chapter 18 Titrations

TECHNOLOGY RESOURCES

Technology & Internet Resources

 CTW 16 Segment 16 Acids in the Environment

 Holt Chemistry Videodiscs Teacher's Correlation Guide for Chapter 16

 Module 8: pH, Titrations

 On-line Student Resources:
GO TO: www.scilinks.org
The following SciLinks Internet resources can be found in the student text for this chapter.

TOPICS:
• pH, p. 481 (HC2161)
• Acid rain, p. 492 (HC2162)
• Titration/indicators, p. 499 (HC2163)

 On-line Teacher Resources:
GO TO: go.hrw.com
KEYWORD: HC2 HOME
Visit the HRW Web site for a variety of resources related to this chapter.

 Smithsonian Institution®
Internet Connections
Visit **www.si.edu/hrw** for additional on-line resources.

CNNfyi.com.
Visit **www.cnnfyi.com** for late-breaking news and current events stories selected just for you.

Resource Key

PE Pupil's Edition
ATE Teacher's Edition

One-Stop Planner CD-ROM Includes these resources and customizable daily lesson plans:

HR Homework Resources	**ChemFile**	**D** Consumer Experiments
SR Section Reviews	**A** Laboratory Experiments	**T** Transparencies
CTW Critical Thinking Worksheets	**B** Microscale Experiments	**TM** Transparency Masters
AA Alternative Assessments	**C** Technique Builders and Problem-Solving Experiments	**PS** Mini-Guide to Problem Solving
		SRW Supplemental Reading Worksheets

Scoring Rubrics for Labs, Alternative Assessments, Performance Tasks and Portfolio Projects are on the One-Stop Planner CD-ROM.

Acid-Base Titration and pH

CHAPTER 16

Acid-Base Titration and pH

Chapter Overview

16-1 covers the ionization of water and the equilibrium concentrations of H_3O^+ and OH^- in water and in aqueous solutions of acids and bases. The concept of pH is presented mathematically.

16-2 explains how acid-base indicators work and how indicators, pH meters, and titrations are used to determine the pH of a solution.

Concept Base

Students may need a review of the following concepts:

- stoichiometric calculations, Chapter 9
- the nature of solutions, Chapter 13
- ionization of solutes, Chapter 14
- acids, bases, and neutralization reactions, Chapter 15

 Reading Skill-Builder

K/W/L Write the term *pH* on the board. Have students list what they know or think they know about pH. Then have them list what they want to know about pH and its relation to acids and bases. After they have read Section 16-1, have them look at their lists and write down what they have learned about the pH of acids and bases. Also have them write down any new questions that they have after reading the section.

The pH of solutions is important to the chemistry of life.

Aqueous Solutions and the Concept of pH

OBJECTIVES

- Describe the self-ionization of water.

- Define *pH*, and give the pH of a neutral solution at 25°C.

- Explain and use the pH scale.

- Given [H_3O^+] or [OH^-], find pH.

- Given pH, find [H_3O^+] or [OH^-].

Lesson Starter

Have students view a model, chalkboard artwork, or overhead (with reaction not showing) representing the ionization of water, as shown in the figure on this page. Ask them to describe what they think is taking place in this reaction.

Visual Strategy

FIGURE 16-1 Ask students to compare their Lesson Starter responses with what they now know about this figure. Point out the charges on the ions.

✔ Teaching Tip

In 10 000 L of pure water, less than one drop would be ionized.

CHAPTER ⬌ CONNECTION

Students will use the concentration notation [X], meaning "the concentration of X in moles per liter," in their study of reaction rates in Chapter 17 and in their study of chemical equilibrium in Chapter 18.

Hydronium Ions and Hydroxide Ions

You have already seen that acids and bases form hydronium ions and hydroxide ions, respectively, in aqueous solutions. However, these ions formed from the solute are not the only such ions present in an aqueous solution. Hydronium ions and hydroxide ions are also provided by the solvent, water.

Self-Ionization of Water

Careful electrical-conductivity experiments have shown that pure water is an extremely weak electrolyte. Water undergoes self-ionization, as shown in the model in Figure 16-1. *In the* **self-ionization of water,** *two water molecules produce a hydronium ion and a hydroxide ion by transfer of a proton.* The following equilibrium takes place.

$$H_2O(l) + H_2O(l) \rightleftharpoons H_3O^+(aq) + OH^-(aq)$$

Conductivity measurements show that concentrations of H_3O^+ and OH^- in pure water are each only 1.0×10^{-7} mol/L of water at 25°C.

There is a standard notation to represent concentration in moles per liter. The formula of the particular ion or molecule is enclosed in brackets, [ ]. For example, the symbol [H_3O^+] means "hydronium ion concentration in moles per liter," or "molar hydronium ion concentration." In water at 25°C, [H_3O^+] = 1.0×10^{-7} M and [OH^-] = 1.0×10^{-7} M.

The mathematical product of [H_3O^+] and [OH^-] remains constant in water and dilute aqueous solutions at constant temperature. This

internet**connect**

SCI**LINKS**
NSTA

TOPIC: pH
GO TO: www.scilinks.org
*sci*LINKS CODE: HC2161

FIGURE 16-1 Water undergoes self-ionization to a slight extent. A proton is transferred from one water molecule to another. A hydronium ion, H_3O^+, and a hydroxide ion, OH^-, are produced.

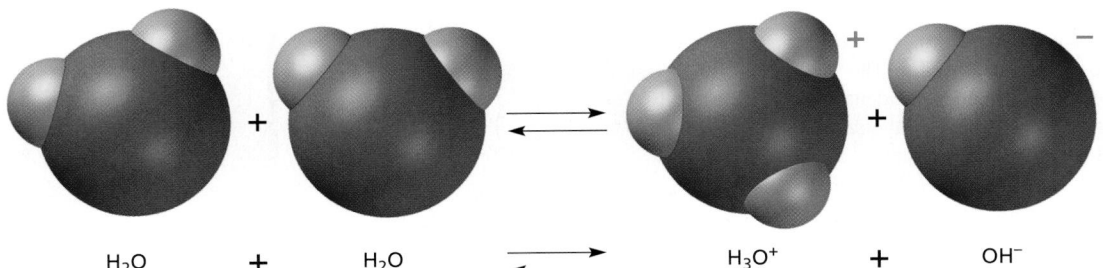

H_2O + H_2O H_3O^+ + OH^-

Table 16-1 This table once again emphasizes the importance of specifying conditions when stating a measured quantity. Students should note the variation of K_w in the range from 0°C to 50°C and realize the importance of citing temperature.

✔ Teaching Tip

Important relationships involving acidic, neutral, and basic solutions will be summarized in Table 16-4. It is suggested that you emphasize the most important of these now:

Acidic: $[H_3O^+] > [OH^-]$
Neutral: $[H_3O^+] = [OH^-]$
Basic: $[H_3O^+] < [OH^-]$

Visual Strategy

FIGURE 16-2 Write the equations for the reactions shown in the figure to emphasize that H_3O^+ is produced in the reaction in part (a) and OH^- is produced in the reaction in part (b).

$$CO_2(g) + H_2O(l) \longrightarrow H_2CO_3(aq)$$

$$H_2CO_3(aq) + H_2O(l) \rightleftharpoons$$
$$H_3O^+(aq) + HCO_3^-(aq)$$

$$Na_2O_2(s) + 2H_2O(l) \longrightarrow$$
$$2Na^+(aq) + 2OH^-(aq) + H_2O_2(g)$$

Ask students to speculate how $[OH^-]$ and $[H_3O^+]$ change as each reaction takes place.

TABLE 16-1 K_w at Selected Temperatures

Temperature (°C)	K_w (M²)
0	1.2×10^{-15}
10	3.0×10^{-15}
25	1.0×10^{-14}
50	5.3×10^{-14}

constant mathematical product is called the *ionization constant of water*, K_w, and is expressed by the following equation.

$$K_w = [H_3O^+][OH^-]$$

For example, in water and dilute aqueous solutions at 25°C, the following relationship is valid.

$$K_w = [H_3O^+][OH^-] = (1.0 \times 10^{-7} \text{ M})(1.0 \times 10^{-7} \text{ M}) = 1.0 \times 10^{-14} \text{ M}^2$$

The ionization of water increases as temperature increases. Therefore, the ion product, K_w, also increases as temperature increases, as shown in Table 16-1. However, at any given temperature K_w is always a constant value. The value 1.0×10^{-14} M² is assumed to be constant within the ordinary range of room temperatures. In this chapter, you can assume that these conditions are present unless otherwise stated.

Neutral, Acidic, and Basic Solutions

Because the hydronium ion and hydroxide ion concentrations are the same in pure water, it is *neutral*. Any solution in which $[H_3O^+] = [OH^-]$ is also neutral. Recall from Chapter 15 that acids increase the concentration of H_3O^+ in aqueous solutions, as shown in Figure 16-2(a). Solutions in which the $[H_3O^+]$ is greater than the $[OH^-]$ are *acidic*. Bases increase the concentration of OH^- in aqueous solutions, as shown in Figure 16-2(b). In *basic* solutions, the $[OH^-]$ is greater than the $[H_3O^+]$.

As stated earlier, the $[H_3O^+]$ and the $[OH^-]$ of a neutral solution at 25°C both equal 1.0×10^{-7} M. Therefore, if the $[H_3O^+]$ is increased to greater than 1.0×10^{-7} M, the solution is acidic. A solution containing 1.0×10^{-5} mol H_3O^+ ion/L at 25°C is acidic because 1.0×10^{-5} is greater than 1.0×10^{-7}. If the $[OH^-]$ is increased to greater than 1.0×10^{-7} M, the solution is basic. A solution containing 1.0×10^{-4} mol OH^- ions/L at 25°C is basic because 1.0×10^{-4} is greater than 1.0×10^{-7}.

FIGURE 16-2 (a) Addition of dry ice, carbon dioxide, to water increases the $[H_3O^+]$, which is shown by the color change of the indicator bromthymol blue to yellow. The white mist is formed by condensation of water droplets because the dry ice is cold. (b) Addition of sodium peroxide to water increases the $[OH^-]$, which is shown by the color change of the indicator phenolphthalein to pink.

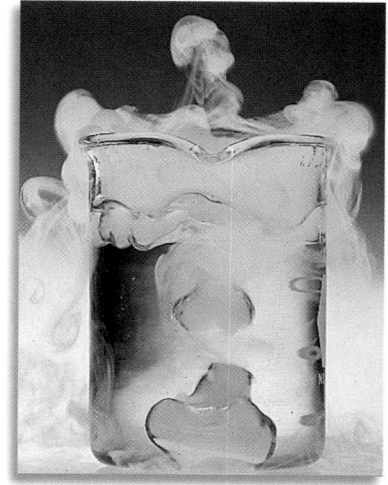

(a)

(b)

Calculating [H₃O⁺] and [OH⁻]

Recall that strong acids and bases are considered completely ionized or dissociated in weak aqueous solutions. A review of strong acids and bases is given in Table 16-2. Notice that 1 mol of NaOH will yield 1 mol of OH⁻ in an aqueous solution. Therefore, a 1.0×10^{-2} M NaOH solution has an [OH⁻] of 1.0×10^{-2} M, as shown by the following.

$$\text{NaOH}(s) \xrightarrow{\text{H}_2\text{O}} \text{Na}^+(aq) + \text{OH}^-(aq)$$
$$\text{1 mol} \qquad \text{1 mol} \qquad \text{1 mol}$$

$$\frac{1.0 \times 10^{-2} \text{ mol NaOH}}{\text{L solution}} \times \frac{1 \text{ mol OH}^-}{1 \text{ mol NaOH}} = \frac{1.0 \times 10^{-2} \text{ mol OH}^-}{\text{L solution}}$$

$$= 1.0 \times 10^{-2} \text{ M OH}^-$$

Notice that the [OH⁻] is greater than 1.0×10^{-7} M. This solution is basic.

Because the K_w of an aqueous solution is a relatively constant 1.0×10^{-14} M² at ordinary room temperatures, the concentration of either ion can be determined if the concentration of the other ion is known. The [H₃O⁺] of this solution is calculated as follows.

$$K_w = [\text{H}_3\text{O}^+][\text{OH}^-] = 1.0 \times 10^{-14} \text{ M}^2$$

$$[\text{H}_3\text{O}^+] = \frac{1.0 \times 10^{-14} \text{ M}^2}{[\text{OH}^-]} = \frac{1.0 \times 10^{-14} \text{ M}^2}{1.0 \times 10^{-2} \text{ M}} = 1.0 \times 10^{-12} \text{ M}$$

The [OH⁻], 1.0×10^{-2} M, is greater than the [H₃O⁺], 1.0×10^{-12} M, as is true for all basic solutions.

Now consider a 1.0×10^{-4} M H₂SO₄ solution. Because H₂SO₄ is a diprotic acid, the [H₃O⁺] is 2.0×10^{-4} M, as shown by the following.

$$\text{H}_2\text{SO}_4(l) + 2\text{H}_2\text{O}(l) \longrightarrow 2\text{H}_3\text{O}^+(aq) + \text{SO}_4^{2-}(aq)$$
$$\text{1 mol} \qquad \text{2 mol} \qquad\qquad \text{2 mol} \qquad \text{1 mol}$$

$$\frac{1.0 \times 10^{-4} \text{ mol H}_2\text{SO}_4}{\text{L solution}} \times \frac{2 \text{ mol H}_3\text{O}^+}{1 \text{ mol H}_2\text{SO}_4} = \frac{2.0 \times 10^{-4} \text{ mol H}_3\text{O}^+}{\text{L solution}}$$

$$= 2.0 \times 10^{-4} \text{ M H}_3\text{O}^+$$

Notice that the [H₃O⁺] is greater than 1.0×10^{-7} M. This solution is acidic. The [OH⁻] of this solution is calculated as follows.

$$K_w = [\text{H}_3\text{O}^+][\text{OH}^-] = 1.0 \times 10^{-14} \text{ M}^2$$

$$[\text{OH}^-] = \frac{1.0 \times 10^{-14} \text{ M}^2}{[\text{H}_3\text{O}^+]} = \frac{1.0 \times 10^{-14} \text{ M}^2}{2.0 \times 10^{-4} \text{ M}} = 5.0 \times 10^{-10} \text{ M}$$

As is true for all acidic solutions, the [H₃O⁺] is greater than the [OH⁻].

You may have realized that in order for K_w to remain constant, an increase in either the [H₃O⁺] or the [OH⁻] in an aqueous solution causes a decrease in the concentration of the other ion. Another example of the calculation of the [H₃O⁺] and [OH⁻] of an acidic solution is shown in Sample Problem 16-1.

TABLE 16-2 Common Strong Acids and Bases	
Strong Acids	**Strong Bases**
HCl	NaOH
HBr	KOH
HI	RbOH
HClO₄	CsOH
HNO₃	Ca(OH)₂
H₂SO₄	Sr(OH)₂
	Ba(OH)₂

✔ **Teaching Tip**

When an acid is added to a solution, the [H₃O⁺] increases. Because there is an excess of H₃O⁺ ions, some of the H₃O⁺ ions react with OH⁻ ions and reduce the [OH⁻]. At 25°C, this process continues until [H₃O⁺][OH⁻] = 1.0×10^{-14} M².

✔ **Teaching Tip**

It is helpful to correlate the common strong bases with the periodic table. These are the hydroxides of the Group 1 metals (formulas MOH) and of the heavier Group 2 metals (formulas M(OH)₂). Other metal hydroxides are not soluble enough to be strong bases.

16-1 Determine the $[H_3O^+]$ and $[OH^-]$ in a 0.01 M solution of $HClO_4$.

Ans. $[H_3O^+] = 1 \times 10^{-2}$ M; $[OH^-] = 1 \times 10^{-12}$ M

16-1 An aqueous solution of $Ba(OH)_2$ has a $[H_3O^+]$ of 1×10^{-11} M. What is the $[OH^-]$? What is the molarity of the solution?

Ans. $[OH^-] = 1 \times 10^{-3}$ M; 5×10^{-4} M $Ba(OH)_2$

SAMPLE PROBLEM 16-1

A 1.0×10^{-4} M solution of HNO_3 has been prepared for a laboratory experiment.
a. Calculate the $[H_3O^+]$ of this solution.   b. Calculate the $[OH^-]$.

SOLUTION

1 ANALYZE

Given: Concentration of the solution = 1.0×10^{-4} M HNO_3
Unknown: a. $[H_3O^+]$ **b.** $[OH^-]$

2 PLAN

HNO_3 is a strong acid, which means that it is essentially 100% ionized in dilute solutions. One molecule of acid produces one hydronium ion. The concentration of the hydronium ions thus equals the concentration of the acid. Because the ion product, $[H_3O^+] [OH^-]$, is a constant, $[OH^-]$ can easily be determined by using the value for $[H_3O^+]$.

a. $HNO_3(l) + H_2O(l) \longrightarrow H_3O^+(aq) + NO_3^-(aq)$ (assuming 100% ionization)
    1 mol   1 mol   1 mol   1 mol

$$\text{molarity of } HNO_3 = \frac{\text{mol } HNO_3}{\text{L solution}}$$

$$\frac{\text{mol } HNO_3}{\text{L solution}} \times \frac{1 \text{ mol } H_3O^+}{1 \text{ mol } HNO_3} = \frac{\text{mol } H_3O^+}{\text{L solution}} = \text{molarity of } H_3O^+$$

b. $[H_3O^+] [OH^-] = 1.0 \times 10^{-14}$ M^2

$$[OH^-] = \frac{1.0 \times 10^{-14} \text{ M}^2}{[H_3O^+]}$$

3 COMPUTE

a. $\dfrac{1.0 \times 10^{-4} \text{ mol } HNO_3}{\text{L solution}} \times \dfrac{1 \text{ mol } H_3O^+}{1 \text{ mol } HNO_3} = \dfrac{1.0 \times 10^{-4} \text{ mol } H_3O^+}{\text{L solution}} = 1.0 \times 10^{-4}$ M H_3O^+

b. $[OH^-] = \dfrac{1.0 \times 10^{-14} \text{ M}^2}{[H_3O^+]} = \dfrac{1.0 \times 10^{-14} \text{ M}^2}{1.0 \times 10^{-4} \text{ M}} = 1.0 \times 10^{-10}$ M

4 EVALUATE

Because the $[H_3O^+]$, 1.0×10^{-4}, is greater than 1.0×10^{-7}, the $[OH^-]$ must be less than 1.0×10^{-7}. The answers are correctly expressed to two significant digits.

PRACTICE

1. Determine the hydronium and hydroxide ion concentrations in a solution that is 1×10^{-4} M HCl.

   Answer
   $[H_3O^+] = 1 \times 10^{-4}$ M;
   $[OH^-] = 1 \times 10^{-10}$ M

2. Determine the hydronium and hydroxide ion concentrations in a solution that is 1.0×10^{-3} M HNO_3.

   Answer
   $[H_3O^+] = 1.0 \times 10^{-3}$ M;
   $[OH^-] = 1.0 \times 10^{-11}$ M

3. Determine the hydronium and hydroxide ion concentrations in a solution that is 3.0×10^{-2} M NaOH.

   Answer
   $[H_3O^+] = 3.3 \times 10^{-13}$ M;
   $[OH^-] = 3.0 \times 10^{-2}$ M

4. Determine the hydronium and hydroxide ion concentrations in a solution that is 1.0×10^{-4} M $Ca(OH)_2$.

   Answer
   $[H_3O^+] = 5.0 \times 10^{-11}$ M;
   $[OH^-] = 2.0 \times 10^{-4}$ M

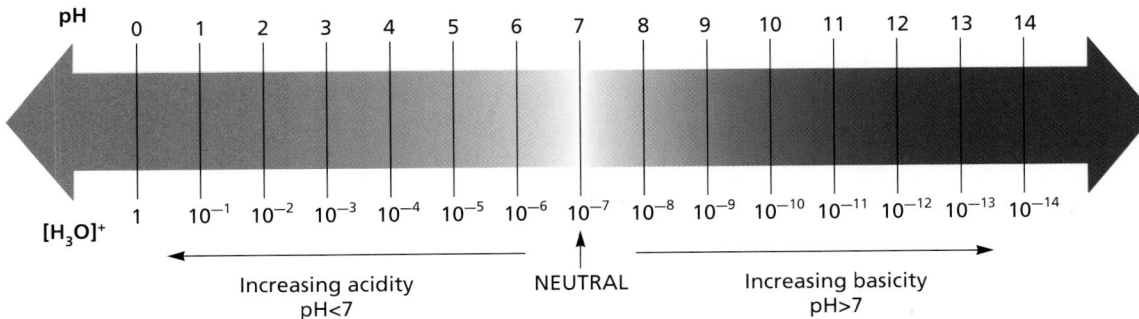

The pH Scale

Expressing acidity or basicity in terms of the concentration of H_3O^+ or OH^- can be cumbersome because the values tend to be very small. A more convenient quantity, called pH, also indicates the hydronium ion concentration of a solution. The letters *pH* stand for the French words *pouvoir hydrogène*, meaning "hydrogen power." *The* **pH** *of a solution is defined as the negative of the common logarithm of the hydronium ion concentration,* $[H_3O^+]$. The pH is expressed by the following equation.

$$pH = -\log [H_3O^+]$$

The common logarithm of a number is the power to which 10 must be raised to equal the number. A neutral solution at 25°C has a $[H_3O^+]$ of 1×10^{-7} M. The logarithm of 1×10^{-7} is −7.0. The pH is determined as follows.

$$pH = -\log [H_3O^+] = -\log (1 \times 10^{-7}) = -(-7.0) = 7.0$$

The relationship between the pH and $[H_3O^+]$ is shown on the scale in Figure 16-3.

Likewise, the **pOH** *of a solution is defined as the negative of the common logarithm of the hydroxide ion concentration,* $[OH^-]$.

$$pOH = -\log[OH^-]$$

A neutral solution at 25°C has a $[OH^-]$ of 1×10^{-7} M. Therefore, the pOH is 7.0.

Remember that the values of $[H_3O^+]$ and $[OH^-]$ are related by K_w. The negative logarithm of K_w at 25°C, 1×10^{-14}, is 14.0. You may have noticed that the sum of the pH and the pOH of a neutral solution at 25°C is also equal to 14.0. The following relationship is true at 25°C.

$$pH + pOH = 14.0$$

At 25°C the range of pH values of aqueous solutions generally falls between 0 and 14, as shown in Table 16-3.

FIGURE 16-3   As the concentration of hydronium ions increases, the solution becomes more acidic and the pH decreases. As the concentration of hydronium ions decreases, the solution becomes more basic and the pH increases.

Common Misconception
Some students have difficulty understanding that increasing $[H_3O^+]$ means decreasing pH. To emphasize the negative relationship between pH and $[H_3O^+]$, use an analogy in which an increase in one number has a negative effect on another number. For example, if a pizza is cut into 4 pieces, each piece is 1/4 of the pizza. If a pizza is cut into 8 pieces, then each piece is 1/8 of the pizza. The number 8 is bigger than 4, but 1/8 is smaller than 1/4.

DEMONSTRATION
Comparing Concentrations
You can reinforce the relationship between $[H_3O^+]$ and $[OH^-]$ in aqueous solution. Wrap a meterstick in white paper. Use a marker to divide each side into 14 equal intervals. Label one side $[H_3O^+]$, and number it from 10^0 M to 10^{-14} M. Starting at the same end, number the other side from 10^{-14} M to 10^0 M and label it $[OH^-]$. Have students pick concentrations of $[H_3O^+]$ on one side of the stick and read the corresponding concentration of $[OH^-]$ on the other side of the stick. The paper can be changed to show the same relationship between pH and pOH.

Reading Skill-Builder

READING ORGANIZER Have students read the selection on The pH Scale. Then have them combine the information presented in Table 16-3 on p. 486 with the diagram of the pH scale (Figure 16-3) into a graphic display showing the pH of common substances.

Table 16-4 Point out the connection between the relationships that are true under all conditions and those that are true at 25°C. For example, in acidic solutions at 25°C, the pH is less than 7.0 and the pOH is greater than 7.0. This follows the general condition that the pH is less than the pOH for acidic solutions. The text derives the relationships true for acidic solutions at 25°C. Go over the analogous calculations for basic solutions at 25°C.

DEMONSTRATION
The pH of Common Materials

Prepare small samples of the following: 1 M NaOH in a dropper bottle, household ammonia, milk of magnesia, sea water, lake water, baking-soda solution, distilled water, milk, rainwater, apple juice, orange juice, vinegar, lemon juice, and 1 M HCl in a dropper bottle. Test each with pH paper, and place the strips on a clean white plastic plate with labels for each material. Have students observe the colors and estimate the pH of each material.

Safety: Wear goggles and a lab apron. Students should remain at least 3 m from the demonstration.

Disposal: Keep HCl and NaOH solutions for later use. Combine all other waste liquids, adjust the mixture's pH to between 5 and 9, and pour it down the drain.

Module 8: Strong and Weakly Ionized Species, pH, and Titrations

Topic: pH Tutorial and Practice
Sections **e** and **f** of this engaging tutorial review and reinforce understanding of pH.

TABLE 16-3 Approximate pH Range of Some Common Materials (at 25°C)

Material	pH	Material	pH
Gastric juice	1.0–3.0	Bread	5.0–6.0
Lemons	2.2–2.4	Rainwater	5.4–5.8
Vinegar	2.4–3.4	Potatoes	5.6–6.0
Soft drinks	2.0–4.0	Milk	6.3–6.6
Apples	2.9–3.3	Saliva	6.5–7.5
Grapefruit	3.0–3.3	Pure water	7.0
Oranges	3.0–4.0	Blood	7.3–7.5
Cherries	3.2–4.0	Eggs	7.6–8.0
Tomatoes	4.0–4.4	Sea water	8.0–8.5
Bananas	4.5–5.7	Milk of magnesia	10.5

Suppose the $[H_3O^+]$ in a solution is greater than the $[OH^-]$, as is true for acidic solutions. For example, the pH of an acidic solution at 25°C with a $[H_3O^+]$ of 1×10^{-6} M is 6.0.

$$pH = -\log [H_3O^+] = -\log (1 \times 10^{-6}) = -(-6.0) = 6.0$$

The pH of this solution is less than 7. This is the case for all acidic solutions at 25°C. The following calculation shows that the pOH is greater than 7.0, as is true for all acidic solutions at 25°C.

$$pOH = 14.0 - pH = 14.0 - 6.0 = 8.0$$

Similar calculations show that the pH of a basic solution at 25°C is more than 7.0 and the pOH is less than 7.0. These and other relationships are listed in Table 16-4. Remember that as the temperature changes, the exact values will change because the value of K_w changes. However, the relationships between the values will remain the same.

Module 8: Strong and Weakly Ionized Species, pH, and Titrations

TABLE 16-4 [H₃O⁺], [OH⁻], pH, and pOH of Solutions

Solution	General condition	At 25°C
Neutral	$[H_3O^+] = [OH^-]$ pH = pOH	$[H_3O^+] = [OH^-] = 1 \times 10^{-7}$ M pH = pOH = 7.0
Acidic	$[H_3O^+] > [OH^-]$ pH < pOH	$[H_3O^+] > 1 \times 10^{-7}$ M $[OH^-] < 1 \times 10^{-7}$ M pH < 7.0 pOH > 7.0
Basic	$[H_3O^+] < [OH^-]$ pH > pOH	$[H_3O^+] < 1 \times 10^{-7}$ M $[OH^-] > 1 \times 10^{-7}$ M pH > 7.0 pOH < 7.0

Calculations Involving pH

If either the $[H_3O^+]$ or pH of a solution is known, the other can be calculated. Significant figures involving pH must be handled carefully. Because pH represents a logarithm, the number to the *left of the decimal* only locates the decimal point. It is not included when counting significant figures. So there must be as many significant figures to the *right of the decimal* as there are in the number whose logarithm was found. For example, a $[H_3O^+]$ value of 1×10^{-7} has *one* significant figure. Therefore, the pH, or –log, of this value must have one digit to the right of the decimal. Thus, pH = 7.0 has the correct number of significant figures.

Calculating pH from $[H_3O^+]$

You have already seen the simplest pH problems. In these problems, the $[H_3O^+]$ of the solution is an integral power of 10, such as 1 M or 0.01 M. The pH of this type of solution is the exponent of the hydronium ion concentration with the sign changed. For example, the pH of a solution in which $[H_3O^+]$ is 1×10^{-5} M is 5.0.

ADDITIONAL SAMPLE PROBLEMS

16-2 Determine the pH of a 1×10^{-4} M solution of HBr.

Ans. pH = 4.0

16-2 Determine the pH of a 5×10^{-4} M solution of $Ca(OH)_2$.

Ans. pH = 11.0

Problem-Solving Practice ChemFile

Chapter 17 of the Mini-Guide to Problem Solving (also found on the One-Stop Planner CD-ROM) includes more worked-out samples and additional practice problems involving pH.

SAMPLE PROBLEM 16-2

What is the pH of a 1.0×10^{-3} M NaOH solution?

SOLUTION

1 ANALYZE

Given: Identity and concentration of solution = 1.0×10^{-3} M NaOH
Unknown: pH of solution

2 PLAN

concentration of base $\longrightarrow$ concentration of $OH^- \longrightarrow$ concentration of $H_3O^+ \longrightarrow$ pH

NaOH is completely dissociated when it is dissolved in water. A 1.0×10^{-3} M NaOH solution therefore produces a $[OH^-]$ equal to 1.0×10^{-3} M. The ion product of $[H_3O^+]$ and $[OH^-]$ is a constant, 1.0×10^{-14} M^2. By substitution, the $[H_3O^+]$ can be determined. The pH can then be calculated.

3 COMPUTE

$$[H_3O^+][OH^-] = 1.0 \times 10^{-14} \ M^2$$

$$[H_3O^+] = \frac{1.0 \times 10^{-14} \ M^2}{[OH^-]} = \frac{1.0 \times 10^{-14} \ M^2}{1.0 \times 10^{-3} \ M} = 1.0 \times 10^{-11} \ M$$

$$pH = -\log [H_3O^+] = -\log (1.0 \times 10^{-11}) = 11.00$$

4 EVALUATE

The answer correctly indicates that NaOH forms a solution with pH > 7, which is basic.

PRACTICE

1. Determine the pH of the following solutions:
   a. 1×10^{-3} M HCl
   b. 1×10^{-5} M HNO_3
   c. 1×10^{-4} M NaOH
   d. 1.0×10^{-2} M KOH

Answer
a. pH = 3.0
b. pH = 5.0
c. pH = 10.0
d. pH = 12.00

Teaching Tip

Some calculators may have different keys for the same function. For example, some calculators may have a $(-)$ key instead of a $+/-$ key.

ADDITIONAL SAMPLE PROBLEMS

16-3 What is the pH of a solution whose $[H_3O^+] = 6.2 \times 10^{-9}$ M?

Ans. pH = 8.21

16-3 Determine the pH of a 0.00074 M solution of NaOH.

Ans. pH = 10.87

Using a Calculator to Calculate pH from $[H_3O^+]$

Some problems involve hydronium ion concentrations that are not equal to integral powers of 10. These problems require a calculator. Most scientific calculators have a "log" key. Consult the instructions for your particular calculator.

An estimate of pH can be used to check your calculations. For example, suppose the $[H_3O^+]$ of a solution is 3.4×10^{-5} M. Because 3.4×10^{-5} lies between 10^{-4} and 10^{-5}, the pH of the solution must be between 4 and 5. Sample Problem 16-3 continues the actual calculation of the pH value for a solution with $[H_3O^+] = 3.4 \times 10^{-5}$ M.

SAMPLE PROBLEM 16-3

What is the pH of a solution if the $[H_3O^+]$ is 3.4×10^{-5} M?

SOLUTION

1 ANALYZE

Given: $[H_3O^+] = 3.4 \times 10^{-5}$ M
Unknown: pH of solution

2 PLAN

$$[H_3O^+] \longrightarrow pH$$

The only difference between this problem and previous pH problems is that you will determine the logarithm of 3.4×10^{-5} using your calculator. You can convert numbers to logarithms on most calculators by using the "log" key.

3 COMPUTE

$$pH = -\log [H_3O^+]$$
$$= -\log (3.4 \times 10^{-5})$$
$$= 4.47$$

On most calculators, this problem is entered in the following steps.

4 EVALUATE

The pH of a 1×10^{-5} M H_3O^+ solution is 5.0. Therefore, it follows that a solution with a greater concentration of hydronium ions would be more acidic and have a pH less than 5.

PRACTICE

1. What is the pH of a solution if the $[H_3O^+]$ is 6.7×10^{-4} M?

   Answer
   pH = 3.17

2. What is the pH of a solution with a hydronium ion concentration of 2.5×10^{-2} M?

   Answer
   pH = 1.60

3. Determine the pH of a 2.5×10^{-6} M HNO_3 solution.

   Answer
   pH = 5.60

4. Determine the pH of a 2.0×10^{-2} M $Sr(OH)_2$ solution.

   Answer
   pH = 12.60

Calculating [H₃O⁺] and [OH⁻] from pH

You have now learned to calculate the pH of a solution, given its $[H_3O^+]$. Suppose that you are given the pH of a solution instead. How can you determine its hydronium ion concentration?

You already know the following equation.

$$pH = -\log [H_3O^+]$$

Remember that the base of common logarithms is 10. Therefore, the antilog of a common logarithm is 10 raised to that number.

$$\log [H_3O^+] = -pH$$
$$[H_3O^+] = antilog \; (-pH)$$
$$[H_3O^+] = 10^{-pH}$$

The simplest cases are those in which pH values are integers. The exponent of 10 that gives the $[H_3O^+]$ is the negative of the pH. For an aqueous solution that has a pH of 2, for example, the $[H_3O^+]$ is equal to 10^{-2} M. Likewise, when the pH is 0, the $[H_3O^+]$ is 1 M because $10^0 = 1$. Sample Problem 16-4 shows how to convert a pH value that is a positive integer. Sample Problem 16-5 shows how to use a calculator to convert a pH that is not an integral number.

SAMPLE PROBLEM 16-4

Determine the hydronium ion concentration of an aqueous solution that has a pH of 4.0.

SOLUTION

1 *ANALYZE*   **Given:** pH = 4.0
Unknown: $[H_3O^+]$

2 *PLAN*

$$pH \longrightarrow [H_3O^+]$$

This problem requires that you rearrange the pH equation and solve for the $[H_3O^+]$. Because 4.0 has one digit to the right of the decimal, the answer must have one significant figure.

$$pH = -\log [H_3O^+]$$
$$\log [H_3O^+] = -pH$$
$$[H_3O^+] = antilog \; (-pH)$$
$$[H_3O^+] = 1 \times 10^{-pH}$$

3 *COMPUTE*

$$[H_3O^+] = 1 \times 10^{-pH}$$
$$[H_3O^+] = 1 \times 10^{-4} \; M$$

4 *EVALUATE*   A solution with a pH of 4.0 is acidic. The answer, 1×10^{-4} M, is greater than 1.0×10^{-7} M, which is correct for an acidic solution.

16-5 The pH of a hydrochloric acid solution for cleaning tile is 0.45. What is the $[H_3O^+]$ in the solution?

Ans. $[H_3O^+] = 0.35$ M

16-5 A shampoo has a pH of 8.7. What are $[H_3O^+]$ and $[OH^-]$ in the shampoo?

Ans. $[H_3O^+] = 2 \times 10^{-9}$ M; $[OH^-] = 5 \times 10^{-6}$ M

SAMPLE PROBLEM 16-5

The pH of a solution is measured and determined to be 7.52.
a. What is the hydronium ion concentration?   **c. Is the solution acidic or basic?**
b. What is the hydroxide ion concentration?

SOLUTION

1   ANALYZE

Given: pH of the solution = 7.52
Unknown: **a.** $[H_3O^+]$ **b.** $[OH^-]$ **c.** Is the solution acidic or basic?

2   PLAN

$$pH \longrightarrow [H_3O^+] \longrightarrow [OH^-]$$

This problem is very similar to previous pH problems. You will need to substitute values into the pH = –log $[H_3O^+]$ equation and use a calculator. Once the $[H_3O^+]$ is determined, the ion-product constant $[H_3O^+] [OH^-] = 1.0 \times 10^{-14}$ may be used to calculate $[OH^-]$.

3   COMPUTE

a.
$$pH = -\log [H_3O^+]$$
$$\log [H_3O^+] = -pH$$
$$[H_3O^+] = antilog(-pH) = antilog(-7.52) = 1.0 \times 10^{-7.52} = 3.0 \times 10^{-8} \text{ M } H_3O^+$$

On most calculators, this is entered in one of the following two ways.

`7` `.` `5` `2` `+/-` `2nd` `10ˣ`   *or*   `7` `.` `5` `2` `+/-` `INV` `LOG`

b. $[H_3O^+] [OH^-] = 1.0 \times 10^{-14} \text{ M}^2$

$$[OH^-] = \frac{1.0 \times 10^{-14} \text{ M}^2}{[H_3O^+]}$$

$$= \frac{1.0 \times 10^{-14} \text{ M}^2}{3.0 \times 10^{-8} \text{ M}} = 3.3 \times 10^{-7} \text{ M } OH^-$$

c. A pH of 7.52 is slightly greater than a pH of 7. This means that the solution is slightly basic.

4   EVALUATE

Because the solution is slightly basic, a hydroxide ion concentration slightly larger than 10^{-7} M is predicted. A hydronium ion concentration slightly less than 10^{-7} M is also predicted. The answers agree with these predictions.

PRACTICE

1. The pH of a solution is determined to be 5.0. What is the hydronium ion concentration of this solution?

Answer
$[H_3O^+] = 1 \times 10^{-5}$ M

2. The pH of a solution is determined to be 12.0. What is the hydronium ion concentration of this solution?

Answer
$[H_3O^+] = 1 \times 10^{-12}$ M

3. The pH of an aqueous solution is measured as 1.50. Calculate the $[H_3O^+]$ and the $[OH^-]$.

Answer
$[H_3O^+] = 3.2 \times 10^{-2}$ M; $[OH^-] = 3.2 \times 10^{-13}$ M

4. The pH of an aqueous solution is 3.67. Determine $[H_3O^+]$.

Answer
$[H_3O^+] = 2.1 \times 10^{-4}$ M

TABLE 16-5 Relationship of $[H_3O^+]$ to $[OH^-]$ and pH (at 25°C)

Solution	$[H_3O^+]$	$[OH^-]$	pH
1.0×10^{-2} M KOH	1.0×10^{-12}	1.0×10^{-2}	12.00
1.0×10^{-2} M NH_3	2.4×10^{-11}	4.2×10^{-4}	10.62
Pure H_2O	1.0×10^{-7}	1.0×10^{-7}	7.00
1.0×10^{-3} M HCl	1.0×10^{-3}	1.0×10^{-11}	3.00
1.0×10^{-1} M CH_3COOH	1.3×10^{-3}	7.7×10^{-12}	2.88

pH Calculations and the Strength of Acids and Bases

So far, we have discussed the pH of solutions that contain only strong acids or strong bases. We must also consider weak acids and weak bases. Table 16-5 lists the $[H_3O^+]$, the $[OH^-]$, and the pH for several solutions.

KOH, the solute in the first solution listed, is a soluble ionic compound and a strong base. The molarity of a KOH solution directly indicates the $[OH^-]$, and the $[H_3O^+]$ can be calculated. Once the $[H_3O^+]$ is known, the pH can be calculated as in Sample Problem 16-3. If the pH of this solution is measured experimentally, it will be the same as this calculated value. Methods for experimentally determining the pH of solutions will be presented in Section 16-2. Hydrochloric acid, HCl, is a strong acid, and similar calculations can be made for solutions that contain HCl.

Solutions of weak acids, such as acetic acid, CH_3COOH, present a different problem. The $[H_3O^+]$ cannot be calculated directly from the molar concentration because not all of the acetic acid molecules are ionized. The same problem occurs for weak bases such as ammonia, NH_3. The pH of these solutions must be measured experimentally. The $[H_3O^+]$ and $[OH^-]$ can then be calculated from the measured pH values.

SECTION REVIEW

1. What is the concentration of hydronium and hydroxide ions in pure water at 25°C?

2. Why does the pH scale generally range from 0 to 14 in aqueous solutions?

3. Why does a pH of 7 represent a neutral solution at 25°C?

4. Identify each of the following as being true of acidic or basic solutions at 25°C:

   a. $[H_3O^+] = 1 \times 10^{-3}$ M   c. pH = 5.0
   b. $[OH^-] = 1 \times 10^{-4}$ M   d. pH = 8.0

5. A solution contains 4.5×10^{-3} HCl. Determine the following for the solution:
   a. $[H_3O^+]$ b. $[OH^-]$ c. pH

6. A $Ca(OH)_2$ solution has a pH of 8.0. Determine the following for the solution:
   a. $[H_3O^+]$ b. $[OH^-]$ c. $[Ca(OH)_2]$

CHAPTER ⟷ CONNECTION

Solution equilibria, including buffer solutions, will be covered in Chapter 18.

Class Discussion

Ask students why studies such as this one on liming must be carefully monitored. *(Responses may include that too much lime may change the pH too drastically for organisms living there. Also, the studies must be monitored to make sure that the factors other than the factor being tested remain constant.)*

✔ Teaching Tip

Rain is not neutral because carbon dioxide in the air reacts with water to form carbonic acid. The term acid rain refers to rain that is even more acidic than usual.

RESEARCH NOTES

Liming Streams

In 1987, Dr. Ken Simmons tested some rainbow trout in the waters of north-central Massachusetts' Whetstone Brook. He placed the trout in cages in the brook so that their behavior and survival could be monitored. Three days later, they were all dead. Acid rain had lowered the pH level of the water to a point at which the trout simply could not survive.

Acid rain begins with the fossil fuels we burn to power our cars and factories. The fumes released by those fuels contain sulfur dioxides and nitrous oxides that combine with the water vapor in the atmosphere and turn it acidic. While normal rainwater has a pH level around 5.7, acid rain's pH can be less than 4.2.

Usually soil has enough natural buffers in it to counteract acidic rain, but beneath streams like the Whetstone, the soil is very sandy and lacks the buffering agents that neutralize the acid. The rain lowers the pH level of the brook and significantly affects most of the organisms living in it. Some fish, like the rainbow trout, simply die. Other species refuse to spawn in acidic waters, as the Whetstone's brown trout did in 1987.

The year that the brown trout refused to spawn, the pH level of

Biologists studied trout to determine the effectiveness of liming Whetstone Brook to raise the pH.

Whetstone Brook averaged 5.97. The population of all the trout dropped dangerously low, and in 1989, Dr. Simmons and other researchers instituted an experiment to decrease the acidity of the stream. They created a system to constantly add calcium carbonate, or limestone, in measured amounts to part of the brook. The limestone, ground into a powder, dissolved instantly and acted as a buffer against the acid, raising the pH level of the water.

The experiment lasted three years and managed to raise the

average pH level of the stream from 5.97 to 6.54, meeting the scientists' goal. At the same time, the amount of toxic aluminum in the limed area decreased, while it increased in un-treated parts of the brook.

The success of the project was most convincingly demonstrated by the stream's residents. The population of brook trout increased, the mortality rate of brown trout decreased, and for the first time in years, fish actually began to move into the stream from its source, the Millers River. In 1991, Dr. Simmons again tested rainbow trout in the waters of the Whetstone. This time, they all survived.

"We clearly don't view it as a solution," says Dr. Simmons. "It's a band-aid approach, but we need data to make intelligent management decisions as to how useful or harmful liming could be. And I think that is the key thing this study has shown. It has provided us with information that we can use."

🌐 internet**connect**

SC*i*LINKS.
NSTA

TOPIC: Acid rain
GO TO: www.scilinks.org
***sci*LINKS CODE:** HC2162

Determining pH and Titrations

OBJECTIVES

- Describe how an acid-base indicator functions.

- Explain how to carry out an acid-base titration.

- Calculate the molarity of a solution from titration data.

Lesson Starter
The day before class, mix a few drops of phenolphthalein indicator with 20 mL of distilled water. Use this solution to write a message on a piece of white paper. Allow the paper to dry. To start the lesson, hang up the paper and spray the message with an ammonia-based window cleaner. Remind students that ammonia is a weak base. Ask them to speculate about the cause of the color change from colorless to pink.

Safety: Wear safety goggles and a lab apron. Students should remain at least 3 m from the demonstration. Spray the cleaner away from the students.

Disposal: Throw the sign into the trash.

✔ **Teaching Tip**

Acid-base indicators are organic compounds that act as very weak Brønsted acids and bases. They change color when they accept a proton from an acid or donate one to a base.

Indicators and pH Meters

An approximate value for the pH of a solution can be obtained using acid-base indicators. **Acid-base indicators** *are compounds whose colors are sensitive to pH.* In other words, the color of an indicator changes as the pH of a solution changes.

Indicators change colors because they are either weak acids or weak bases. In solution, the equilibrium of an indicator that is a weak acid can be represented by the equation below, which is modeled in Figure 16-4.

$$HIn \rightleftharpoons H^+ + In^-$$

(In^- is the symbol of the anion part of the indicator.) The colors that an indicator displays result from the fact that HIn and In^- are different colors.

In acidic solutions, any In^- ions that are present act as Brønsted bases and accept protons from the acid. The indicator is then present in largely nonionized form, HIn. The indicator has its acid-indicating color, as shown for litmus in Figure 16-4.

In basic solutions, the OH^- ions from the base combine with the H^+ ions produced by the indicator. The indicator molecules further ionize to offset the loss of H^+ ions. The indicator is thus present largely in the form of its anion, In^-. The solution now displays the base-indicating color, which for litmus is blue.

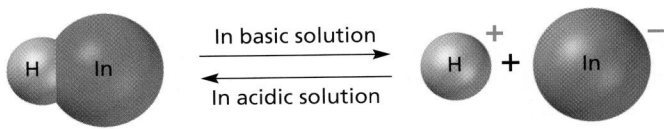

Nonionized form

Ionized form

FIGURE 16-4 Basic solutions shift the equilibrium of litmus to the right. The ionized form, In^-, then predominates, and the litmus turns blue. Acidic solutions shift the equilibrium of the indicator litmus to the left. The nonionized form, HIn, predominates, and the litmus turns red.

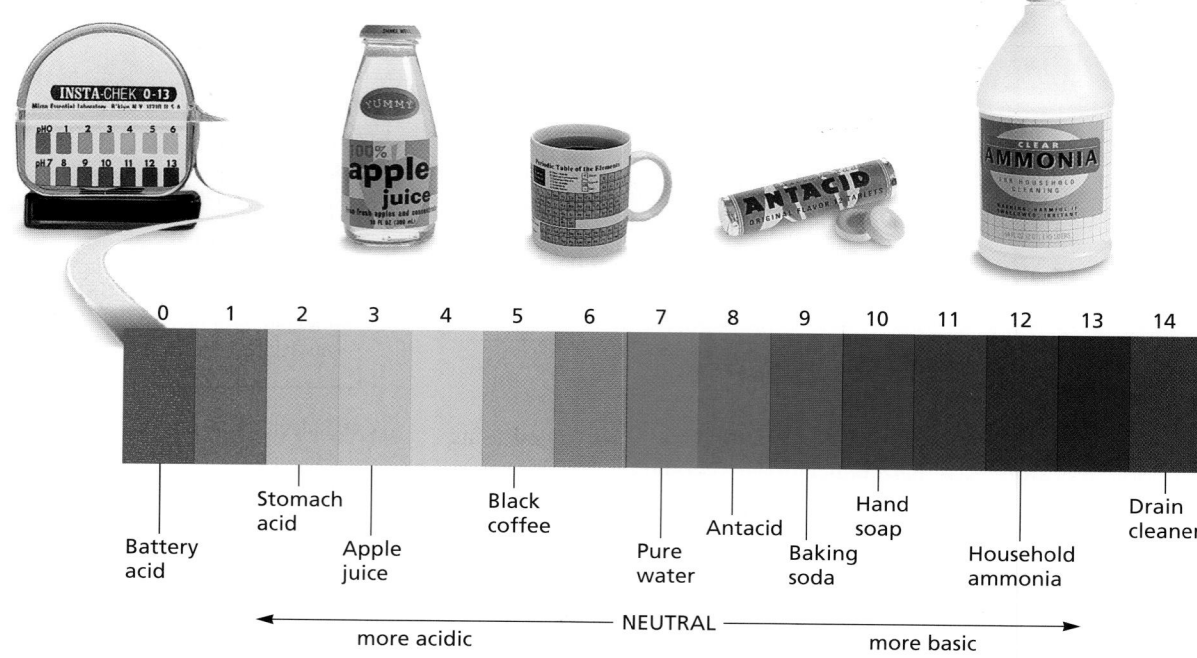

FIGURE 16-5 The pH of a solution can be determined by comparing the color it turns pH paper with the scale of the paper. The colors of pH paper at various pH values are shown, as are the pH values for some common materials.

FIGURE 16-6 A pH meter measures the exact pH of a solution.

Indicators come in many different colors. The exact pH range over which an indicator changes color also varies. *The pH range over which an indicator changes color is called its* **transition interval.** Table 16-6 gives the color changes and transition intervals for a number of common acid-base indicators.

Indicators that change color at pH lower than 7, such as methyl orange, are simply stronger acids than the other types of indicators. They tend to ionize more completely than the others. The In^- anions that these indicators produce are weaker Brønsted bases and have less tendency to accept protons from any acid being tested. These indicators therefore do not shift to their nonionized (HIn) form unless the concentration of H^+ is fairly high. The color transition of these indicators occurs at rather low pH. In contrast, indicators that undergo transition in the higher pH range, such as phenolphthalein, are weaker acids.

Universal indicators are made by mixing several different indicators. Paper soaked in universal indicator solution is called pH paper. This paper can turn almost any color of the rainbow and provides a fairly accurate way of distinguishing the pH of solutions, as shown in Figure 16-5.

If an exact value for the pH of a solution is needed, a pH meter, shown in Figure 16-6, should be used. *A* **pH meter** *determines the pH of a solution by measuring the voltage between the two electrodes that are placed in the solution.* The voltage changes as the hydronium ion concentration in the solution changes.

TABLE 16-6 *Color Ranges of Various Indicators Used in Titrations*

Titration type	Indicator	Acid color	Transition color	Base color
Strong-acid/ strong-base	methyl red (4.4–6.2)			
		3 4 5 6 7 8 9 10 11		
	bromthymol blue (6.2–7.6)			
Strong-acid/ weak-base	methyl orange (3.1–4.4)			
		0 1 2 3 4 5 6 7 8		
	bromphenol blue (3.0–4.6)			
Weak-acid/ strong-base	phenolphthalein (8.0–10.0)			
		4 5 6 7 8 9 10 11 12		
	phenol red (6.4–8.0)			

DEMONSTRATION

Natural Indicators

Tea and the juice from beets, carrots, and blueberries are natural indicators. Natural indicators can also be made by boiling rose petals and other vegetable sources in water until the liquid turns dark. Decant the liquid and discard the sediment.

Add a few drops of vinegar to a natural indicator and observe what happens. Then add some household ammonia solution.

Safety: Wear safety goggles and a lab apron. Students should remain at least 3 m from the demonstration.

Disposal: Combine all waste liquids, adjust the mixture's pH to between 5 and 9, and pour it down the drain.

Discussion

1. 7.0 ± 0.2

2. 5.4–5.8 (see Table 16-3); dissolved CO_2 and some pollutants, such as sulfur dioxide, lower pH, so the pH will vary slightly according to the amount of dissolved CO_2 or pollutants.

3. Answers could include optical distortion, the fact that submerging the ruler raises the water level, the formation of a meniscus when the ruler is too close to the side of the jar, and the fact that the bottom of the jar may not be flat. Use a calibrated rain gauge with markings on the glass to increase precision.

4. Answers will vary, depending on results.

5. Answers will vary. If the pH is below 5.6 consistently, you may have acid rain.

Quick LAB

Wear Safety Goggles and an Apron.

Testing the pH of Rainwater

Materials

- rainwater
- distilled water
- 500 mL jars
- thin, transparent metric ruler (± 0.1 cm)
- pH test paper: narrow range, ± 0.2–0.3, or pH meter

Question

Do you have acid precipitation in your area?

Procedure

Record all your results in a data table.

1. Each time it rains, set out five clean jars to collect the rainwater. If the rain continues for more than 24 hours, put out new containers at the end of each 24-hour period until the rain stops. (The same procedure can be used with snow if the snow is allowed to melt before measurements are taken. You may need to use larger containers if a heavy snowfall is expected.)

2. After the rain stops or at the end of each 24-hour period, measure the depth of the water to the nearest 0.1 cm with a thin plastic ruler. Test the water with the pH paper to determine its pH to the nearest 0.2–0.3.

3. Record the following information:
  a. the date and time the collection was started
  b. the date and time the collection was ended
  c. the location where the collection was made (town and state)
  d. the amount of rainfall in centimeters
  e. the pH of the rainwater

4. Find the average pH of each collection that you have made for each rainfall, and record it in the data table.

5. Collect samples on at least five different days. The more samples you collect, the more reliable your data will be.

6. For comparison, determine the pH of pure water by testing five samples of distilled water with pH paper. Record your results in a separate data table, and then calculate an average pH for distilled water.

Discussion

1. What is the pH of distilled water?

2. What is the pH of normal rainwater? How do you explain any differences between the pH readings?

3. What are the drawbacks of using a ruler to measure the depth of collected water? How could you increase the precision of your measurement?

4. Does the amount of rainfall or the time of day the sample is taken have an effect on its pH? Explain any variability among samples.

5. What conclusion can you draw from this investigation? Explain how your data support your conclusion.

Titration

As you know, neutralization reactions occur between acids and bases. The OH⁻ ion acquires a proton from the H_3O^+ ion, forming two molecules of water. The following equation summarizes this reaction.

$$H_3O^+(aq) + OH^-(aq) \longrightarrow 2H_2O(l)$$

This equation shows that one mol of hydronium ions, 19.0 g, and one mol of hydroxide ions, 17.0 g, are chemically equivalent masses. They combine in a one-to-one ratio. Neutralization occurs when hydronium ions and hydroxide ions are supplied in equal numbers by reactants, as shown in Figure 16-7.

One liter of a 0.10 M HCl solution contains 0.10 mol of hydronium ions. Now suppose that 0.10 mol of solid NaOH is added to 1 L of 0.10 M HCl solution. The NaOH dissolves and supplies 0.10 mol of hydroxide ions to the solution. HCl and NaOH are present in chemically equivalent amounts. Hydronium and hydroxide ions, which are present in equal numbers, combine until the product $[H_3O^+]\,[OH^-]$ returns to the value of 1×10^{-14} M². NaCl, the salt produced in the reaction, is the product of the neutralization of a strong acid and a strong base. The resulting solution is neutral.

Because acids and bases react, the progressive addition of an acid to a base (or a base to an acid) can be used to compare the concentrations of the acid and the base. **Titration** *is the controlled addition and measurement of the amount of a solution of known concentration required to react completely with a measured amount of a solution of unknown concentration.* Titration provides a sensitive means of determining the chemically equivalent volumes of acidic and basic solutions.

Module 8: Strong and Weakly Ionized Species, pH, and Titrations

FIGURE 16-7 The solution on the left turns pH paper red because it is acidic. The solution on the right turns pH paper blue because it is basic. When equal numbers of H_3O^+ and OH⁻ from the acidic and basic solutions react, the resulting solution is neutral. The neutral solution turns pH paper green.

✔ Teaching Tip

When a strong base, such as NaOH, is used to titrate a strong acid, such as HCl, or vice versa, the resulting solution is neutral at the point where the acid and base are stoichiometrically equivalent.

Did You Know?

In highly precise titrations, the quantity of acid or base needed to titrate the indicator itself must be taken into account.

📖 Reading Skill-Builder

READING HINT As students read through the section on Titration, have them use Figures 16-7, 16-8, and 16-9 to help them understand and explain equivalence points and end points.

Module 8: Strong and Weakly Ionized Species, pH, and Titrations

Topic: Titrations Tutorial and Practice
Sections **g** and **h** of this engaging tutorial review and reinforce understanding of titrations.

Problem-Solving Practice — HOLT ChemFile

Chapter 18 of the Mini-Guide to Problem Solving (also found on the One-Stop Planner CD-ROM) includes more worked-out samples and additional practice problems involving titrations.

Common Misconception

Students may think that all "neutralizations" occur at a pH of 7. At this point, students do not have the theoretical background to understand the reasons why neutralizations can occur at a pH above or below 7. A simplified explanation is that weak acids and bases are "more difficult" to titrate because they ionize so weakly. Students will learn why this occurs when they study hydrolysis of salts in Chapter 18.

✔ Teaching Tip

When weak acids or bases are titrated with strong acids or bases, the equivalence point occurs at a pH that differs from neutral in the direction of the strong component.

Equivalence Point

The point at which the two solutions used in a titration are present in chemically equivalent amounts is the **equivalence point.** Indicators and pH meters can be used to determine the equivalence point. A pH meter will show a large voltage change occurring at the equivalence point. If an indicator is used, it must change color over a range that includes the pH of the equivalence point, as shown in Figure 16-8. *The point in a titration at which an indicator changes color is called the* **end point** *of the indicator.*

Some indicators, such as litmus, change color at about pH 7. However, the color-change interval for litmus is broad, pH 5.5–8.0. This broad range makes it difficult to determine an accurate pH. Bromthymol blue is better because it has a limited transition interval, pH 6.0–7.6 (see Table 16-6). Indicators that undergo transition at about pH 7 are used to determine the equivalence point of strong-acid/strong-base titrations because the neutralization of strong acids with strong bases produces a salt solution with a pH of approximately 7.

Indicators that change color at pH lower than 7 are useful in determining the equivalence point of strong-acid/weak-base titrations. Methyl orange is an example of this type. The equivalence point of a strong-acid/weak-base titration is acidic because the salt formed is itself a weak acid. Thus the salt solution has a pH lower than 7.

Indicators that change color at pH higher than 7 are useful in determining the equivalence point of weak-acid/strong-base titrations. Phenolphthalein is an example. These reactions produce salt solutions whose pH is greater than 7. This occurs because the salt formed is a weak base.

You may be wondering what type of indicator is used to determine the equivalence point of weak-acid/weak-base titrations. The surprising answer is "none at all." The pH of the equivalence point of weak acids and weak bases may be almost any value, depending on the relative strengths of the reactants. The color transition of an indicator helps

FIGURE 16-8 Indicators change color at the end point of a titration. Phenolphthalein (a) turns pink and methyl red (b) turns red at the end point of these titrations.

(a)

(b)

Strong Acid Titrated with Strong Base

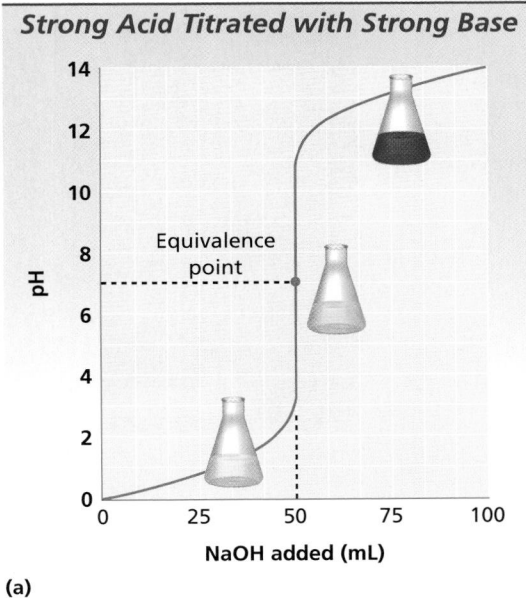

(a)

Weak Acid Titrated with Strong Base

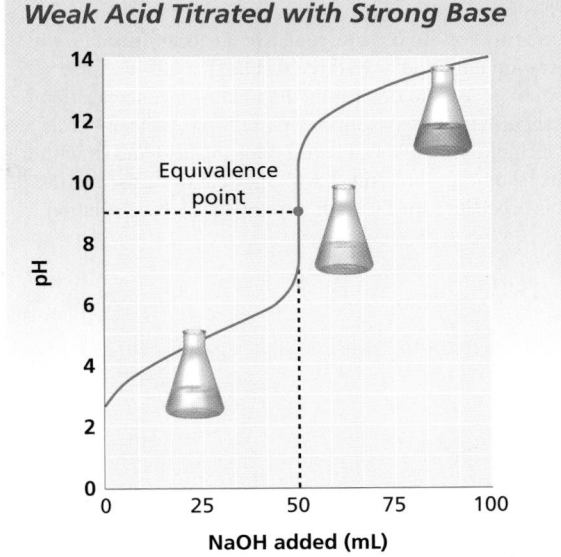

(b)

very little in determining whether reactions between such acids and bases are complete.

In a titration, successive additions of an aqueous base can be made to a measured volume of an aqueous acid. As base is added, the pH changes from a low numerical value to a high one. The change in pH occurs slowly at first, then rapidly through the equivalence point, then slowly again as the solution becomes more basic. Typical pH curves for strong-acid/strong-base and weak-acid/strong-base titrations are shown in Figure 16-9.

FIGURE 16-9 (a) When a strong acid, such as 50.0 mL of 1.00 M HCl, is titrated with a strong base, such as 1.00 M NaOH, the equivalence point occurs at about pH 7. (b) When a weak acid, such as 50 mL of 1.00 M CH_3COOH, is titrated with a strong base, such as 1.00 M NaOH, the equivalence point occurs at a pH above 7.

Molarity and Titration

Figure 16-10 on pages 500–501 shows the proper method of carrying out a titration. If the concentration of one solution is known precisely, the concentration of the other solution in a titration can be calculated from the chemically equivalent volumes. *The solution that contains the precisely known concentration of a solute is known as a* **standard solution.** It is often called simply the "known" solution.

To be certain of the concentration of the known solution, that solution must first be compared with a solution of a primary standard. *A* **primary standard** *is a highly purified solid compound used to check the concentration of the known solution in a titration.* The known solution is prepared first, and its volume is adjusted to give roughly the desired concentration. The concentration is then determined more precisely by titrating the solution with a carefully measured quantity of a solution of the primary standard.

internet **connect**

SCI LINKS

NSTA

TOPIC: Titration/indicators
GO TO: www.scilinks.org
*sci*LINKS **CODE:** HC2163

Visual Strategy

FIGURE 16-9 Emphasize that the equivalence point occurs at a pH that is halfway between the two break points. Also, the greater slope of the lower part of the curve in 16-9(b) is typical of a strong-weak titration.

DEMONSTRATION

pH Change in an Acid-Base Titration
Set up a buret on a buret stand, and fill it with a 0.1 M NaOH solution. Measure 25 mL of 0.1 M HCl into a beaker, and place the probe of a pH meter into the solution. Record the pH of the solution. Slowly add NaOH from the buret, and record the amount of NaOH added and the pH as you continue. Graph the resulting titration curve, and point out the very large change in pH that results when one drop of NaOH is added at the equivalence point.

Safety: Wear goggles and a lab apron. Make sure the meter is plugged into a grounded circuit. Be sure to follow the manufacturer's directions for using the pH meter.

Disposal: Combine all liquids, adjust the mixture's pH to between 5 and 9, and pour it down the drain.

FIGURE 16-10 Following is the proper method for carrying out an acid-base titration. To be sure you have an accurate value, you should repeat the titration until you have three results that agree within 0.05 mL. This procedure would be used to determine the unknown concentration of an acid using a standardized base solution. First set up two clean burets as shown. Decide which of the burets will be used for the acid and which for the base. Rinse the acid buret three times with the acid to be used in the titration. Repeat this procedure for the base buret with the base solution to be used.

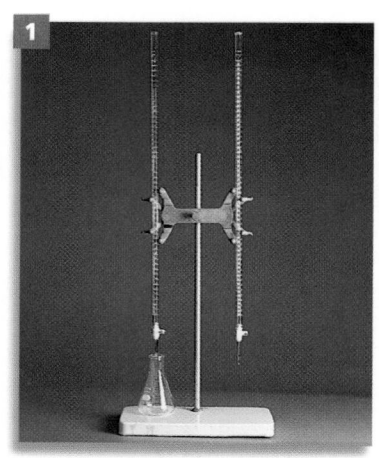

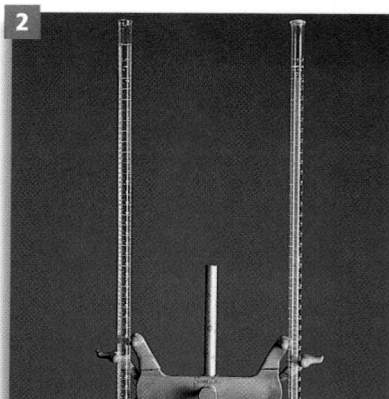

Fill the first buret to a point above the calibration mark with the acid of unknown concentration.

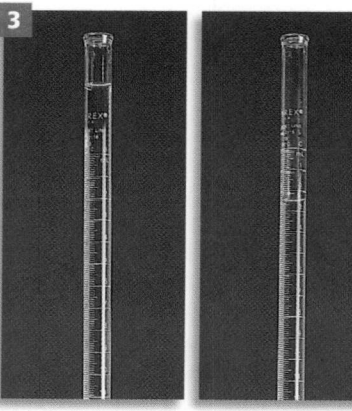

Release some acid from the buret to remove any air bubbles and to lower the volume to the calibrated portion of the buret.

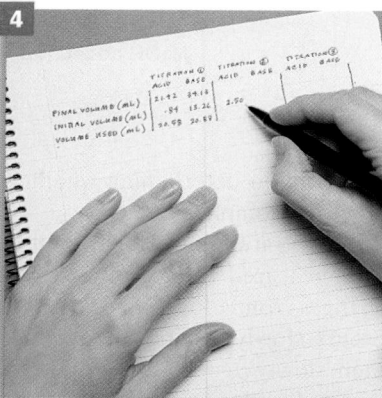

Record the reading at the top of the acid in the buret to the nearest 0.01 mL as your starting point.

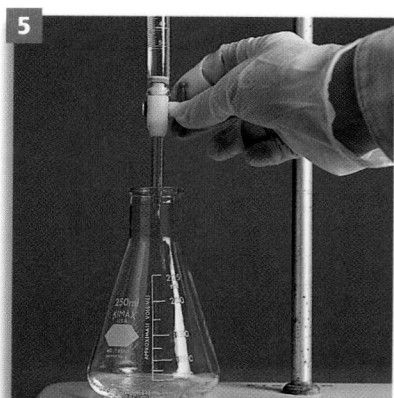

Release a predetermined volume of the acid (determined by your teacher or lab procedure) into a clean, dry Erlenmeyer flask.

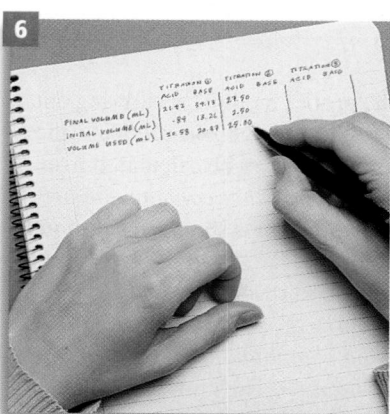

Subtract the current volume reading on the buret from the initial reading. This is the exact volume of the acid released into the flask. Record it to the nearest 0.01 mL.

Add three drops of the appropriate indicator (in this case phenolphthalein) to the flask.

Fill the other buret with the standard base solution to a point above the calibration mark. The concentration of the standard base is known to a certain degree of precision because it was previously titrated with an exact mass of solid acid.

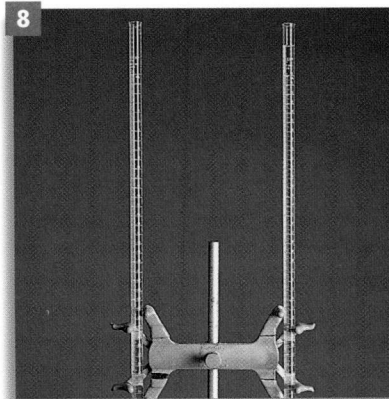

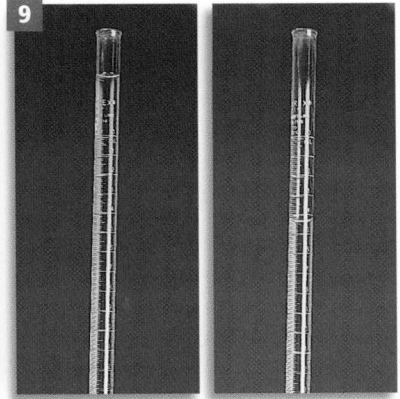

Release some base from the buret to remove any air bubbles and to lower the volume to the calibrated portion of the buret.

Record the reading at the top of the base to the nearest 0.01 mL as your starting point.

Place the Erlenmeyer flask under the base buret as shown. Notice that the tip of the buret extends into the mouth of the flask.

Slowly release base from the buret into the flask while constantly swirling the contents of the flask. The pink color of the indicator should fade with swirling.

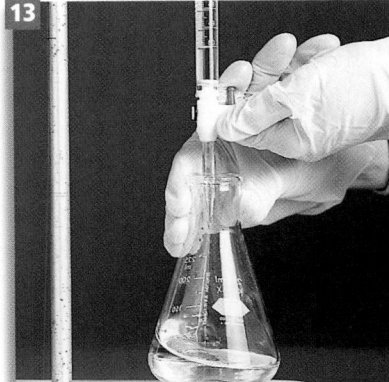

The titration is nearing the end point when the pink color stays for longer periods of time. At this point, add base drop by drop.

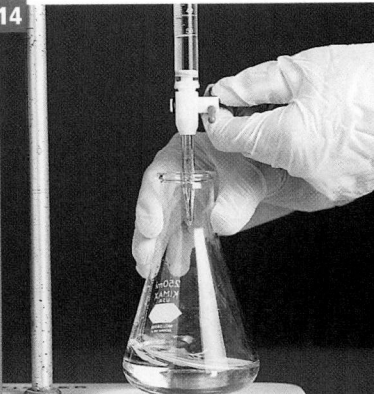

The equivalence point is reached when a very light pink color remains after 30 seconds of swirling.

Subtract the current volume reading on the buret from the initial reading. This is the exact volume of the base released into the flask. Record it to the nearest 0.01 mL.

It is common to run a quick, imprecise titration in order to determine approximately where the end point will fall. Thus, students must titrate slowly only near the end point.

Reading Skill-Builder

SEQUENCING/PATTERN PUZZLES Have students read pp. 500–501 silently. Then have student pairs list on a sheet of notebook paper the steps for carrying out an acid-base titration, one step per line without numbering the steps. Encourage students to write the steps in their own words, dividing longer steps into two or three shorter steps if necessary.

When students have finished, have them cut their sheets of paper into strips with only one step per strip. Direct students to shuffle the strips so they are out of order. Have students trade strips with their partners and place the strips in the proper sequence. Students can confirm the order of the process by checking with the text or their class notes.

Additional Example Problems

1. How many moles of HCl are in 31.15 mL of a 0.688 M solution?

Ans. 2.14×10^{-2} mol HCl

2. How many moles of NaOH would neutralize 20.0 mL of a 1.39 M solution of H_2SO_4?

Ans. 5.56×10^{-2} mol NaOH

3. How many milliliters of a 2.76 M KOH solution contain 0.0825 mol of KOH?

Ans. 29.9 mL

ADDITIONAL SAMPLE PROBLEMS

16-6 A 25.00 mL sample of a solution of RbOH is neutralized by 19.22 mL of a 1.017 M solution of HBr. What is the molarity of the RbOH solution?

Ans. 0.7819 M RbOH

16-6 If 29.96 mL of a solution of $Ba(OH)_2$ requires 16.08 mL of a 2.303 M solution of HNO_3 for complete titration, what is the molarity of the $Ba(OH)_2$ solution?

Ans. 0.6180 M $Ba(OH)_2$

16-6 You have a vinegar solution you believe to be 0.83 M. You are going to titrate 20.00 mL of it with a NaOH solution that you know to be 0.519 M. At what volume of added NaOH solution would you expect to see an end point?

Ans. 32 mL NaOH solution

The known solution can be used to determine the molarity of another solution by titration. Suppose 20.0 mL of 5.0×10^{-3} M NaOH is required to reach the end point in the titration of 10.0 mL of HCl of unknown concentration. How can these titration data be used to determine the molarity of the acidic solution?

Begin with the balanced neutralization reaction equation. From the equation, determine the chemically equivalent amounts of HCl and NaOH.

$$HCl(aq) + NaOH(aq) \longrightarrow NaCl(aq) + H_2O(l)$$
$$\text{1 mol} \qquad \text{1 mol} \qquad \text{1 mol} \qquad \text{1 mol}$$

Calculate the number of moles of NaOH used in the titration.

$$\frac{5.0 \times 10^{-3} \text{ mol NaOH}}{\cancel{L}} \times \frac{1 \cancel{L}}{1000 \text{ mL}} \times 20.0 \text{ mL} = 1.0 \times 10^{-4} \text{ mol NaOH used}$$

Because 1 mol of NaOH is needed to neutralize 1 mol of HCl, the amount of HCl in the titration must be 1.0×10^{-4} mol. This is confirmed by the following equation.

$$1.0 \times 10^{-4} \text{ mol NaOH} \times \frac{1 \text{ mol HCl}}{1 \text{ mol NaOH}} = 1.0 \times 10^{-4} \text{ mol HCl}$$

This amount of acid must be in the 10.0 mL of the HCl solution used for the titration. The molarity of the HCl solution can now be calculated.

$$\frac{1 \times 10^{-4} \text{ mol HCl}}{10.0 \text{ mL}} \times \frac{1000 \text{ mL}}{1 \text{ L}} = \frac{1.0 \times 10^{-2} \text{ mol HCl}}{L}$$

$$= 1.0 \times 10^{-2} \text{ M HCl}$$

Sample Problem 16-6 illustrates the following four steps.
1. Start with the balanced equation for the neutralization reaction, and determine the chemically equivalent amounts of the acid and base.
2. Determine the moles of acid (or base) from the known solution used during the titration.
3. Determine the moles of solute of the unknown solution used during the titration.
4. Determine the molarity of the unknown solution.

SAMPLE PROBLEM 16-6

In a titration, 27.4 mL of 0.0154 M $Ba(OH)_2$ is added to a 20.0 mL sample of HCl solution of unknown concentration. What is the molarity of the acid solution?

SOLUTION

1 **ANALYZE** **Given:** volume and concentration of known solution = 27.4 mL of 0.0154 M $Ba(OH)_2$
volume of unknown HCl solution = 20.0 mL
Unknown: molarity of acid solution

2 PLAN

1. balanced neutralization equation ⟶ chemically equivalent amounts

$$Ba(OH)_2 + 2HCl \longrightarrow BaCl_2 + 2H_2O$$
$$\text{1 mol} \quad \text{2 mol} \quad \text{1 mol} \quad \text{2 mol}$$

2. volume of known basic solution used (mL) ⟶ amount of base used (mol)

$$\frac{\text{mol } Ba(OH)_2}{L} \times \text{mL of } Ba(OH)_2 \text{ solution} \times \frac{1 \text{ L}}{1000 \text{ mL}} = \text{mol } Ba(OH)_2$$

3. mole ratio, moles of base used ⟶ moles of acid used from unknown solution

$$\frac{2 \text{ mol HCl}}{1 \text{ mol } Ba(OH)_2} \times \text{mol } Ba(OH)_2 \text{ in known solution} = \text{mol HCl in unknown solution}$$

4. volume of unknown, moles of solute in unknown ⟶ molarity of unknown

$$\frac{\text{amount of solute in unknown solution (mol)}}{\text{volume of unknown solution (mL)}} \times \frac{1000 \text{ mL}}{1 \text{ L}} = \text{molarity of unknown solution}$$

3 COMPUTE

1. The mole ratio from the equation is 1 mol $Ba(OH)_2$ for every 2 mol HCl.

2. $$\frac{0.0154 \text{ mol } Ba(OH)_2}{\cancel{L}} \times 27.4 \cancel{\text{ mL}} \times \frac{1 \cancel{L}}{1000 \cancel{\text{ mL}}} = 4.22 \times 10^{-4} \text{ mol } Ba(OH)_2$$

3. $$\frac{2 \text{ mol HCl}}{1 \cancel{\text{ mol } Ba(OH)_2}} \times 4.22 \times 10^{-4} \cancel{\text{ mol } Ba(OH)_2} = 8.44 \times 10^{-4} \text{ mol HCl}$$

4. $$\frac{8.44 \times 10^{-4} \text{ mol HCl}}{20.0 \cancel{\text{ mL}}} \times \frac{1000 \cancel{\text{ mL}}}{1 \text{ L}} = \frac{4.22 \times 10^{-2} \text{ mol HCl}}{L} = 4.22 \times 10^{-2} \text{ M HCl}$$

PRACTICE

1. A 15.5 mL sample of 0.215 M KOH solution required 21.2 mL of aqueous acetic acid solution in a titration experiment. Calculate the molarity of the acetic acid solution.

   Answer
   0.157 M CH_3COOH

2. By titration, 17.6 mL of aqueous H_2SO_4 neutralized 27.4 mL of 0.0165 M LiOH solution. What was the molarity of the aqueous acid solution?

   Answer
   0.0128 M H_2SO_4

SECTION REVIEW

1. Name an appropriate indicator for titrating the following:
   a. a strong acid and a weak base
   b. a strong base and a weak acid

2. Suppose you have an NaOH solution of unknown concentration. Name three possible substances that could be used in "known" solutions to titrate the NaOH solution.

3. If 20.0 mL of 0.0100 M aqueous HCl is required to neutralize 30.0 mL of an aqueous solution of NaOH, determine the molarity of the NaOH solution.

4. Suppose that 20.0 mL of 0.10 M $Ca(OH)_2$ is required to neutralize 12.0 mL of aqueous HCl solution. What is the molarity of the HCl solution?

Alternative Assessment
Have students write a balanced equation for the titration of H_2SO_3 with KOH. Ask them how they would prepare a 1.00 M standard solution of KOH and how many moles of KOH would react with each mole of H_2SO_3.

SECTION REVIEW

1. a. Methyl orange and bromphenol blue are possible answers.
b. Phenolphthalein and phenol red are possible answers.

2. Possible answers include standard solutions of most strong or weak acids, such as HCl, H_2SO_4, and CH_3COOH.

3. 6.67×10^{-3} M NaOH

4. 0.33 M HCl

REVIEW ANSWERS

1. Water undergoes self-ionization.

2. the concentration of the substance in moles per liter

3. **a.** 1.0×10^{-7} M
   b. no; $[H_3O^+]$ increases with increasing temperature because the ionization of water increases

4. **a.** The $[H_3O^+]$ is greater than the $[OH^-]$.
   b. The $[H_3O^+]$ is greater than 1.0×10^{-7} M.

5. **a.** the negative of the common logarithm of the hydronium ion concentration
   b. $pH = -\log [H_3O^+]$
   c. Answers may vary; the power to which 10 must be raised to give the number. For example, the log of 10^7 is 7.

6. **a.** neutral   **e.** neutral
   b. basic   **f.** acidic
   c. neutral   **g.** basic
   d. acidic

7. g, b, c, e, f, d, a, i, h

8. the pH range over which an indicator changes color

9. An acid-base indicator is a weak acid or a weak base. In solution, it is in equilibrium with an ionized form that has a different color. The addition of H_3O^+ pushes the equilibrium in one direction, toward one color. An increase in OH^- pushes the equilibrium toward the other color.

10. **a.** by using a pH meter
    b. A rapid change in pH occurs.

11. **a.** the point in a titration when an indicator changes color
    b. to change color when the equivalence point is reached
    c. Its transition interval must include the pH of the equivalence point.

CHAPTER SUMMARY

16-1
- Pure water undergoes self-ionization to give 1.0×10^{-7} M H_3O^+ and 1.0×10^{-7} M OH^- at 25°C.
- $pH = -\log[H_3O^+]$; $pOH = -\log[OH^-]$ At 25°C, $pH + pOH = 14.0$.
- At 25°C, acids have a pH of less than 7, bases have a pH of greater than 7, and neutral solutions have a pH of 7.
- If a solution contains a strong acid or a strong base, the $[H_3O^+]$, $[OH^-]$ and pH can be calculated from the molarity of the solution. If a solution contains a weak acid or a weak base, the $[H_3O^+]$ and the $[OH^-]$ must be calculated from an experimentally measured pH.

Vocabulary

pH (485)   pOH (485)   self-ionization of water (481)

16-2
- The pH of a solution can be determined using either a pH meter or acid-base indicators.
- Titration uses a solution of known concentration to determine the concentration of a solution of unknown concentration.
- To determine the end point of a titration, indicators are chosen that change color over ranges that include the pH of the equivalence point.
- When the molarity and volume of a known solution used in a titration are known, then the molarity of a given volume of an unknown solution can be found.

Vocabulary

end point (498)   acid-base indicators (493)   primary standard (499)   titration (497)
equivalence point (498)   pH meter (494)   standard solution (499)   transition interval (494)

REVIEWING CONCEPTS

1. Why does pure water weakly conduct an electric current?   (16-1)

2. What does it mean when the formula of a particular ion or molecule is enclosed in brackets?   (16-1)

3. **a.** What is the $[H_3O^+]$ of pure water at 25°C?
   b. Is this true at all temperatures? Why or why not?   (16-1)

4. **a.** What is always true about the $[H_3O^+]$ value of acidic solutions?
   b. What is true about the $[H_3O^+]$ value of acidic solutions at 25°C?   (16-1)

5. **a.** Describe what is meant by the pH of a solution.
   b. Write the equation for determining pH.
   c. Explain and illustrate what is meant by the common logarithm of a number.   (16-1)

6. Identify each of the following as being true of acidic, basic, or neutral solutions at 25°C:
   a. $[H_3O^+] = 1.0 \times 10^{-7}$ M
   b. $[H_3O^+] = 1.0 \times 10^{-10}$ M
   c. $[OH^-] = 1.0 \times 10^{-7}$ M
   d. $[OH^-] = 1.0 \times 10^{-11}$ M
   e. $[H_3O^+] = [OH^-]$
   f. pH = 3.0
   g. pH = 13.0   (16-1)

7. Arrange the following common substances in order of increasing pH:
   a. eggs   f. potatoes
   b. apples   g. lemons
   c. tomatoes   h. milk of magnesia
   d. milk   i. sea water
   e. bananas   (16-1)

8. What is meant by the transition interval of an indicator?   (16-2)

9. Explain how an indicator's equilibrium determines the color the indicator displays at a given pH.   (16-2)

10. a. Other than through indicators, how can the equivalence point of a titration experiment or the pH of a solution be determined?
    b. What can be observed about the rate of change in the pH of a solution near the end point of a titration? (16-2)

11. a. What is meant by the end point of a titration?
    b. What is the role of an indicator in the titration process?
    c. On what basis is an indicator selected for a particular titration experiment? (16-2)

12. For each of the four possible types of acid-base titration combinations, indicate the approximate pH at the end point. Also name a suitable indicator for detecting that end point. (16-2)

13. Based on Figures 14-9(a) and 14-9(b), draw a pH curve for a strong-acid/weak-base titration. (16-2)

14. An unknown solution is colorless when tested with phenolphthalein but causes the indicator phenol red to turn red. Based on this information, what is the approximate pH of this solution? (16-2)

PROBLEMS

pH Calculations

15. Calculate the $[H_3O^+]$ and $[OH^-]$ for each of the following. (Hint: See Sample Problem 16-1.)
    a. 0.03 M HCl
    b. 1×10^{-4} M NaOH
    c. 5×10^{-3} M H_2SO_4
    d. 0.01 M $Ca(OH)_2$

16. Determine the pH of each of the following solutions. (Hint: See Sample Problem 16-2.)
    a. 1.0×10^{-2} M HCl   c. 1.0×10^{-5} M HI
    b. 1.0×10^{-3} M HNO_3 d. 1.0×10^{-4} M HBr

17. Given the following $[OH^-]$ values, determine the pH of each solution.
    a. 1.0×10^{-6} M   c. 1.0×10^{-2} M
    b. 1.0×10^{-9} M   d. 1.0×10^{-7} M

18. Determine the pH of each solution.
    a. 1.0×10^{-2} M NaOH
    b. 1.0×10^{-3} M KOH
    c. 1.0×10^{-4} M LiOH

19. Determine the pH of solutions with each of the following $[H_3O^+]$. (Hint: See Sample Problem 16-3.)
    a. 2.0×10^{-5} M
    b. 4.7×10^{-7} M
    c. 3.8×10^{-3} M

20. Given the following pH values, determine the $[H_3O^+]$ for each solution. (Hint: See Sample Problem 16-4.)
    a. 3.0   c. 11.0
    b. 7.00   d. 5.0

21. Given the following pH values, determine the $[OH^-]$ for each solution.
    a. 7.00   c. 4.00
    b. 11.00   d. 6.00

22. Determine $[H_3O^+]$ for solutions with the following pH values. (Hint: See Sample Problem 16-5.)
    a. 4.23   b. 7.65   c. 9.48

23. A nitric acid solution is found to have a pH of 2.70. Determine each of the following:
    a. $[H_3O^+]$
    b. $[OH^-]$
    c. the number of moles of HNO_3 required to prepare 5.50 L of this solution
    d. the mass of the moles of HNO_3 in the solution in part (c)
    e. the milliliters of concentrated acid needed to prepare the solution in part (c) (Concentrated nitric acid is 69.5% HNO_3 by mass and has a density of 1.42 g/mL.)

Titrations

24. For each of the following acid-base titration combinations, determine the number of moles of the first substance listed that would be the chemically equivalent amount of the second substance.
    a. NaOH with 1.0 mol HCl
    b. HNO_3 with 0.75 mol KOH
    c. $Ba(OH)_2$ with 0.20 mol HF
    d. H_2SO_4 with 0.60 mol $Al(OH)_3$

25. Suppose that 15.0 mL of 2.50×10^{-2} M aqueous H_2SO_4 is required to neutralize 10.0 mL of an aqueous solution of KOH. What is the molarity of the KOH solution? (Hint: See Sample Problem 16-6.)

12. Answers may vary. Strong-acid/strong-base: pH about 7, litmus or bromthymol blue; strong-acid/weak-base: pH below 7, methyl orange or bromphenol blue; weak-acid/strong-base: pH above 7, phenolphthalein or phenol red; weak-acid/weak-base: pH may be either above or below 7, no indicator is satisfactory

13. Graph should be similar in shape to those found on p. 499, with the equivalence point below pH 7.

14. approximately 8

15. a. $[H_3O^+] = 3 \times 10^{-2}$ M; $[OH^-] = 3 \times 10^{-13}$ M
    b. $[H_3O^+] = 1 \times 10^{-10}$ M; $[OH^-] = 1 \times 10^{-4}$ M
    c. $[H_3O^+] = 1 \times 10^{-2}$ M; $[OH^-] = 1 \times 10^{-12}$ M
    d. $[H_3O^+] = 5 \times 10^{-13}$ M; $[OH^-] = 2 \times 10^{-2}$ M

16. a. 2.00   c. 5.00
    b. 3.00   d. 4.00

17. a. 8.00   c. 12.00
    b. 5.00   d. 7.00

18. a. 12.00   c. 10.00
    b. 11.00

19. a. 4.70   c. 2.42
    b. 6.33

20. a. 1×10^{-3} c. 1×10^{-11}
    b. 1.0×10^{-7} d. 1×10^{-5}

21. a. 1.0×10^{-7} c. 1.0×10^{-10}
    b. 1.0×10^{-3} d. 1.0×10^{-8}

22. a. 5.9×10^{-5} c. 3.3×10^{-10}
    b. 2.2×10^{-8}

23. a. 2.0×10^{-3}
    b. 5.0×10^{-12}
    c. 1.1×10^{-2} mol HNO_3
    d. 0.69 g HNO_3
    e. 0.70 mL concentrated acid

24. a. 1.0 mol NaOH
    b. 0.75 mol HNO_3
    c. 0.10 mol $Ba(OH)_2$
    d. 0.90 mol H_2SO_4

25. 7.50×10^{-2} M KOH

26. 3.02×10^{-2} M HNO$_3$

27. **a.** 8.0×10^{-4} M
    b. 1.3×10^{-11} M

28. **a.** 7.00
    b. 3.00
    c. 12.00
    d. 5.00

29. 1×10^{-6} M

30. 10.00

31. **a.** 10.08
    b. 3.2×10^{-3} M

32. **a.** 1.1×10^{-4} M
    b. 9.1×10^{-11} M

33. **a.** 1.3×10^{-9} M
    b. 7.7×10^{-6} M

34. 4.84

35. 1.1×10^{-2} M HCl

36. 9.0×10^{-4} M Ca(OH)$_2$

37. 3.0×10^{-2} M

38. The two sudden changes of pH at about 25 mL and 50 mL indicate a diprotic acid. The first change indicates the depletion of the first H$^+$ that dissociates, and the second change indicates the depletion of the second H$^+$. The pH ends near 13, which corresponds to that of a 0.1 M NaOH solution.

39. **a.** Accept an answer between 31 and 35 mL.
    b. Accept an answer between 0.7 and 0.9 pH.
    c. Accept an answer between 72 and 74 mL.

40. **a.** CO$_2$ and HCO$_3^-$
    b. acidosis
    c. Hyperventilation is rapid breathing for an extended period of time, which results in a reduction of CO$_2$ levels in the blood. To compensate, the equilibrium system of the blood shifts to favor the formation of CO$_2$, which reduces the H$_3$O$^+$ and causes the pH of the blood to rise.

26. In a titration experiment, a 12.5 mL sample of 1.75×10^{-2} M Ba(OH)$_2$ just neutralized 14.5 mL of HNO$_3$ solution. Calculate the molarity of the HNO$_3$ solution.

MIXED REVIEW

27. **a.** What is the [OH$^-$] of a 4.0×10^{-4} M solution of Ca(OH)$_2$?
    b. What is the [H$_3$O$^+$] of the solution?

28. Given the following [H$_3$O$^+$] values, determine the pH of each solution.
    a. 1.0×10^{-7} M   **c.** 1.0×10^{-12} M
    b. 1.0×10^{-3} M   **d.** 1.0×10^{-5} M

29. What is the [H$_3$O$^+$] for a solution that has a pH of 6.0?

30. Suppose that a 5.0×10^{-5} M solution of Ba(OH)$_2$ is prepared. What is the pH of the solution?

31. **a.** Calculate the pH of a solution that has an [H$_3$O$^+$] of 8.4×10^{-11} M.
    b. Calculate the [H$_3$O$^+$] of a solution that has a pH of 2.50.

32. **a.** What is the concentration of OH$^-$ in a 5.4×10^{-5} M solution of magnesium hydroxide, Mg(OH)$_2$?
    b. Calculate the concentration of H$_3$O$^+$ for this solution.

33. **a.** Calculate the molarity of H$_3$O$^+$ in a solution that has a pH of 8.90.
    b. Calculate the concentration of OH$^-$ in the solution.

34. What is the pH of a solution for which [OH$^-$] equals 6.9×10^{-10} M?

35. In a titration, 25.9 mL of 3.4×10^{-3} M Ba(OH)$_2$ neutralized 16.6 mL of HCl solution. What is the molarity of the HCl solution?

36. Find the molarity of a Ca(OH)$_2$ solution, given that 428 mL of it is neutralized in a titration by 115 mL of 6.7×10^{-3} M HNO$_3$.

37. Suppose that 10.1 mL of HNO$_3$ is neutralized by 71.4 mL of a 4.2×10^{-3} M solution of KOH in a titration. Calculate the concentration of the HNO$_3$ solution.

CRITICAL THINKING

38. **Interpreting Graphics**   The following titration curve resulted from the titration of an unknown acid with 0.10 M NaOH. Analyze the curve. Make inferences related to the type of acidic solution titrated.

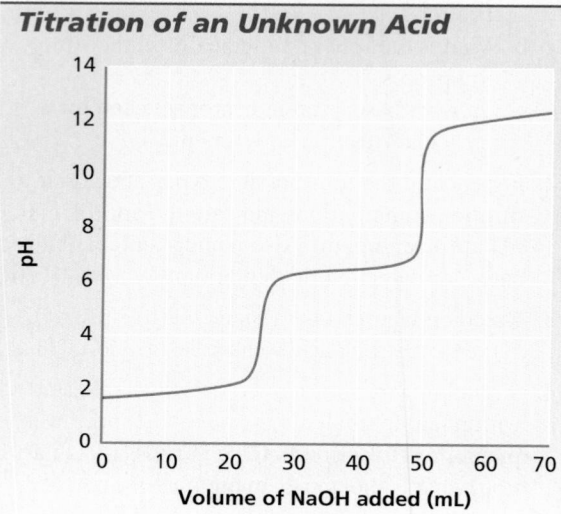

Titration of an Unknown Acid

TECHNOLOGY & LEARNING

39. **Graphing Calculator**   Graphing Titration Data

The graphing calculator can run a program that graphs data such as pH versus volume of base. Graphing the titration data will allow you to determine which combination of acid and base is represented by the shape of the graph. Begin by creating a table of data. Then program the calculator to plot the data.

Go to Appendix C. If you are using a TI 83 Plus, you can download the program and data and run the application as directed. If you are using another calculator, your teacher will provide you with keystrokes and data sets to use. Remember that after creating your lists, you will need to name the program and check the display, as explained in Appendix C. You will then be ready to run the program. After you have graphed the data, answer these questions.

a. At what approximate volume does the titration change from acidic to basic?

b. What would you expect the pH to be for a titration with a volume of 70 mL?

c. At what volume would you expect the titration to become purely acidic?

 HANDBOOK SEARCH

40. The normal pH of blood is about 7.4. When the pH shifts above or below that level, the results are acidosis or alkalosis. Review the section on blood pH in Group 14 of the *Elements Handbook*, then answer the following.

a. What chemical species keep H_3O^+ in blood at the appropriate pH?

b. What condition results when there is an excess of CO_2 in the blood?

c. What is hyperventilation and how does it affect blood pH?

RESEARCH & WRITING

41. Examine the labels of at least five brands of shampoo. Note what is written there, if anything, regarding the pH of the shampoo. Do library research to find out why such pH ranges are chosen and why other ranges might be harmful to hair or eyes.

42. Water quality depends on the ability of treatment facilities to reprocess waste water. Most waste-water treatment facilities use living organisms to break down wastes. Because of acid rain, the acidic nature of waste water can pose problems for a waste-treatment plant. Conduct library research on this topic and write a brief report. Include an inference to how pH affects waste-water treatment.

ALTERNATIVE ASSESSMENT

43. Performance Use pH paper to determine the approximate pH of various brands of orange juice, which contains citric acid.

44. Performance Design and conduct an experiment to extract possible acid-base indicators from sources such as red cabbage, berries, and flower petals. Use known acidic, basic, and neutral solutions to test the action of each indicator that you are able to isolate.

45. Performance Design and conduct an experiment to study the pH of rain for an extended period of time. Coordinate your data-collection activities with those of your classmates so that the pH readings are made in a variety of locations. Try to determine whether any patterns emerge in terms of location, season, time of day, degree of industrialization in the area, and so on.

41. The flexibility of healthy hair depends on the ability of the protein chains in the cuticle layer to shift. Scalp oils and a natural acid coating help protect it. A shampoo with a basic pH can neutralize the acidic protective coating of the hair and can also help eliminate scalp oils.

42. Answers will vary. The organic means used are microorganisms and bacteria, most of which cannot survive at a low pH.

Photo Descriptions

Center: silver bowls tarnished by oxidation

Lower left: copper reacting with nitric acid to form Cu^{2+}

Lower right: a Sistine chapel painting that has been restored by reversing the oxidation process

UNIT 6

Chemical Reactions

CHAPTERS

17 **Reaction Energy and Reaction Kinetics**

18 **Chemical Equilibrium**

19 **Oxidation-Reduction Reactions**

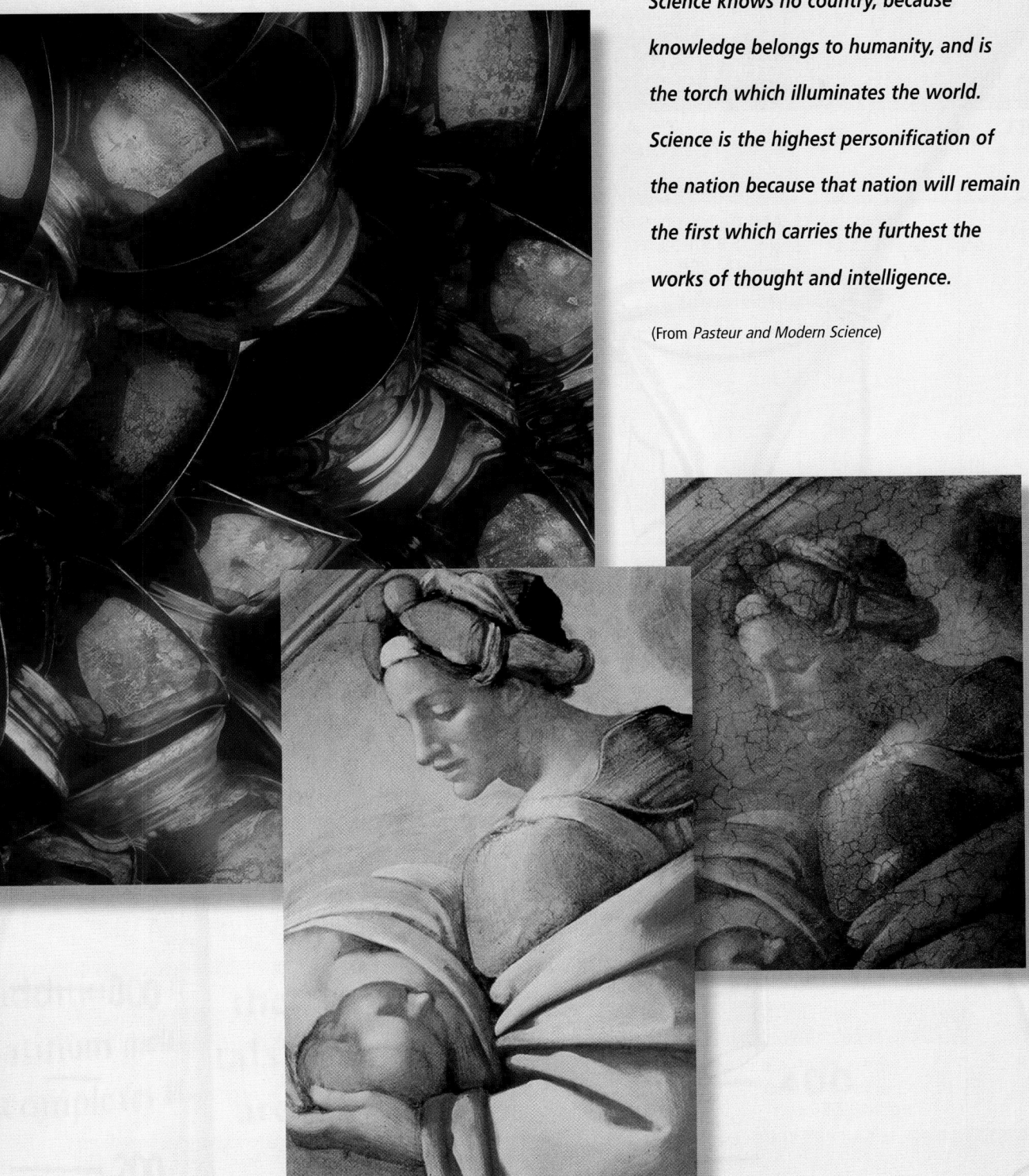

LOUIS PASTEUR, ON THE GLOBAL IMPORTANCE OF SCIENTIFIC PROGRESS

Science knows no country, because knowledge belongs to humanity, and is the torch which illuminates the world. Science is the highest personification of the nation because that nation will remain the first which carries the furthest the works of thought and intelligence.

(From *Pasteur and Modern Science*)

509

PACING CHART

Compression Guide: *(To shorten, eliminate items in italics.)*

CLASSROOM RESOURCES

	NSE Standards	Teaching Resources	Experiments
17-1 **Thermochemistry** 2 45-minute periods 1 90-minute block *Heat of Formation, pp. 517–518* *Stability and Heat of Formation, p. 518* *Heat of Combustion, pp. 518–519* *Calculating Heats of Reaction, pp. 519–522* *Determining Heat of Formation, pp. 522–524*	PS 3b UCP 1–3, 5 ST 1–2 SPSP 5	**ATE Demo,** pp. 512, 520 T 92, T 93, TM 92A, TM 93A, TM 94A	Calorimetry, p. 858 Measuring the Specific Heats of Metals, p. 860 Calorimetry and Hess's Law, p. 864 A16 Temperature of a Bunsen Burner Flame A18 Heat of Combustion C6 Specific Heat Capacity
17-2 **Driving Force of Reactions** 2 45-minute periods 1 90-minute block	PS 3b, 5e UCP 1–3	**ATE Demo,** p. 526 T 94, T 95, TM 96A	A14 Energy and Entropy C7 **EXP** Constructing a Heating/Cooling Curve
17-3 **The Reaction Process** 2 45-minute periods 1 90-minute block *Collision Theory, pp. 532–533*	PS 3b UCP 1–3	**ATE Demo,** p. 533 T 96, T 97, TM 95A	C7 **INV** Constructing a Cooling Curve—Melting Oils for Soap Production
17-4 **Reaction Rate** 2 45-minute periods 1 90-minute block *Rate Laws for Reactions, pp. 541–545*	PS 3b, 3e, 5c, 5e UCP 1–2 SAI 1–2	**ATE Demo,** pp. 538, 539, 541 T 98, TM 97A	Quick Lab, p. 545 Rate of a Chemical Reaction, p. 868 B18 Clock Reactions C20 Catalysts

REVIEW RESOURCES

Review and Assessment 2 45-minute periods 1 90-minute block	Cumulative Review	Alternative Assessment	Traditional Assessment
	SR Chapter 17 Mixed Review **PE** Chapter 17 31–39, pp. 549–550	**PE** 47, p. 551 **ATE** 518 **AA** Items for Chapter 17	Chapter 17 Text Test Generator items for Chapter 17

ASSIGNMENT RESOURCES

Section Homework Resources & Review	Problem-Solving Practice
HR Homework Worksheets 17-1, 17-2, 17-3, 17-4, 17-5 Graphic Org. Assignment 17-2, 17-5 **PE** Section Review, 1–6, p. 524 Chapter Review, 1–4, 16–23, p. 547 **SR** Section Review 17-1	**PE** Additional Samples 17-1, 17-2 **ATE** Additional Samples, pp. 514, 522 **PS** Chapter 19 Thermochemistry
HR Homework Worksheets 17-6, 17-7 Graphic Org. Assignment 17-7 **PE** Section Review, 1–8, p. 530 Chapter Review, 5–8, 24–25, pp. 547–548 **SR** Section Review 17-2	**PE** Additional Sample 17-4 **ATE** Additional Sample, p. 530 Additional Example, p. 529
HR Homework Worksheets 17-8, 17-9 Graphic Org. Assignment 17-9 **PE** Section Review, 1–5, p. 537 Chapter Review, 9–13, 26–27, pp. 547–548 **SR** Section Review 17-3	**PE** Additional Sample 17-5 **ATE** Additional Sample, p. 536
HR Homework Worksheets 17-10, 17-11, 17-12 Graphic Org. Assignment 17-10, 17-12 **PE** Section Review, 1–4, p. 545 Chapter Review, 14–15, 28–30, pp. 547–548 **SR** Section Review 17-4	**PE** Additional Sample 17-7 **ATE** Additional Sample, p. 544

TECHNOLOGY RESOURCES

Technology & Internet Resources

 CTW 20 Segment 20 What Is a Calorie?

 Holt Chemistry Videodiscs Teacher's Correlation Guide for Chapter 17

 Module 9: Heat, Enthalpy, Entropy, Spontaneity

internet connect

 On-line Student Resources:
www.scilinks.org
The following SciLinks Internet resources can be found in the student text for this chapter.

TOPICS:
- Heat/temperature, p. 511 (HC2171)
- Enthalpy, p. 516 (HC2172)
- Supercorrosion, p. 525 (HC2173)
- Entropy, p. 526 (HC2174)
- Factors affecting rates, p. 538 (HC2175)

On-line Teacher Resources:
 GO TO: go.hrw.com
KEYWORD: HC2 HOME
Visit the HRW Web site for a variety of resources related to this chapter.

Smithsonian Institution®
Internet Connections
Visit **www.si.edu/hrw** for additional on-line resources.

 CNN fyi.com
Visit **www.cnnfyi.com** for late-breaking news and current events stories selected just for you.

Resource Key

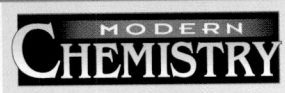
PE Pupil's Edition
ATE Teacher's Edition

One-Stop Planner CD-ROM Includes these resources and customizable daily lesson plans:

HR Homework Resources	**A** Laboratory Experiments	**D** Consumer Experiments	
SR Section Reviews	**B** Microscale Experiments	**T** Transparencies	
CTW Critical Thinking Worksheets	**C** Technique Builders and Problem-Solving Experiments	**TM** Transparency Masters	
AA Alternative Assessments		**PS** Mini-Guide to Problem Solving	
		SRW Supplemental Reading Worksheets	

Scoring Rubrics for Labs, Alternative Assessments, Performance Tasks and Portfolio Projects are on the One-Stop Planner CD-ROM.

CHAPTER 17

Chapter Overview

17-1 defines heat; temperature; heats of reaction, formation, and combustion; and enthalpy change.

17-2 explains how to use enthalpy, entropy, and free energy to predict whether a reaction will occur.

17-3 uses collision theory and activation energy to describe the mechanisms by which chemical reactions take place.

17-4 reviews the factors that influence the rate of a chemical reaction and shows how to calculate the reaction rate from experimental data.

Concept Base

Students may need a review of the following concepts:

• conservation of energy, Chapter 1

• bond energies, Chapter 6

• kinetic theory of matter, Chapter 10

• molar concentrations, Chapter 13

• heat of solution, Chapter 13

Reaction Energy and Reaction Kinetics

Many chemical reactions give off or take in energy as heat.

510

Thermochemistry

Virtually every chemical reaction is accompanied by a change in energy. Chemical reactions usually absorb or release energy as heat. You learned in Chapter 12 that heat is also absorbed or released in physical changes, such as melting a solid or condensing a vapor. **Thermochemistry** *is the study of the transfers of energy as heat that accompany chemical reactions and physical changes.*

Heat and Temperature

The energy absorbed or released as heat in a chemical or physical change is measured in a **calorimeter.** In one kind of calorimeter, known quantities of reactants are sealed in a reaction chamber, which is immersed in a known quantity of water in an insulated vessel. Therefore, the energy given off (or absorbed) during the reaction is equal to the energy absorbed (or given off) by the known quantity of water. The amount of energy is determined from the temperature change of the known mass of surrounding water. The data collected from calorimetry experiments are temperature changes because heat cannot be measured directly; but temperature, which is affected by the transfer of energy as heat, is directly measurable. To see why this is so, let us look at the definitions of heat and temperature and at how temperature is measured.

Temperature *is a measure of the average kinetic energy of the particles in a sample of matter.* The greater the kinetic energy of the particles in a sample, the higher the temperature and the hotter it feels. To assign a numerical value to temperature, it is necessary to define a temperature scale. For calculations in thermochemistry, we use the Celsius and Kelvin scales. A Celsius temperature can be converted to Kelvin temperature by adding 273.15, although in most calculations in this book, it is acceptable to add 273.

The ability to measure temperature is thus based on heat transfer. The amount of energy transferred as heat is usually measured in joules. *A* **joule** *is the SI unit of heat as well as all other forms of energy.* The joule, abbreviated J, is derived from the units for force and length.

$$N \times m = \frac{kg \times m^2}{s^2}$$

Because the joule is a rather small unit compared with other units for heat, the kilojoule, kJ, is also commonly used as a unit for heat.

OBJECTIVES

- Define *temperature* and state the units in which it is measured.

- Define *heat* and state its units.

- Perform specific-heat calculations.

- Explain heat of reaction, heat of formation, heat of combustion, and enthalpy change.

- Solve problems involving heats of reaction, heats of formation, and heats of combustion.

internet connect

SC*I*INKS
NSTA

TOPIC: Heat/temperature
GO TO: www.scilinks.org
*sci*LINKS **CODE:** HC2171

Lesson Starter

Fill a 250 mL beaker and a 10 mL graduated cylinder with hot water from the tap. Ask a student to confirm that the water in both containers has the same temperature. Ask students which container they think can potentially release more heat. Have them informally compare and contrast temperature and heat.

✔ Teaching Tip

Scientists have different understandings of what *heat* is. To some scientists, heat is the *process of energy transfer* between substances because of a difference in their temperatures. To other scientists, heat is the *energy that is transferred* between substances because of a difference in their temperatures. This textbook will use the latter understanding of heat. Explain to students that they may encounter the other understanding in a different science course.

📖 Reading Skill-Builder

L.I.N.K. Write the terms *heat* and *temperature* on the board. Have students brainstorm all the words, phrases, and ideas that they associate with these terms. Have a volunteer write students' contributions on the board. Lead students in a discussion about how the ideas on the board are related. As students read Section 17-1, have them add to the list and mark portions of the text that need clarification. After further class discussion, have students make notes of everything they remember about heat and temperature based on experience and the discussion.

Common Misconception

Students often misuse the terms *temperature* and *heat*. Be sure they understand that there is a difference. Temperature is a measure of the average kinetic energy of particles in a sample of matter. Heat is the energy that is transferred between samples of matter because of a difference in their temperatures.

Visual Strategy

FIGURE 17-1 Use the figures to emphasize that terms such as *hot* and *cold* are not scientific terms. They do not have absolute meanings and can be used only as comparisons.

Application

The kilocalorie (or Calorie) is used to measure the energy content of foods. The number of Calories supplied by a certain amount of a food is determined by reacting the food with oxygen in a calorimeter and measuring the amount of energy released as heat in the reaction.

DEMONSTRATION
Boiling Water in a Paper Cup

Place a small paper cup on wire gauze above a lit Bunsen burner, and watch the cup burn. Fill a second paper cup about half full of water and place it on the wire gauze above the Bunsen burner. The water will begin to boil in the cup, keeping the temperature of the cup below the combustion temperature of paper (233°C).

Safety: Wear safety goggles and a lab apron. Have students stand back at least 2 m from the demonstration.

Disposal: Pour any remaining water down the drain. Put used cups in the trash.

FIGURE 17-1 The direction of energy transfer is determined by the temperature differences between the objects within a system. The energy is transferred as heat from the hotter brass bar to the cooler water. This energy transfer will continue until the bar and the water reach the same temperature.

Heat *can be thought of as the energy transferred between samples of matter because of a difference in their temperatures.* Energy transferred as heat always moves spontaneously from matter at a higher temperature to matter at a lower temperature, as shown in Figure 17-1. The temperature of the cool water in the beaker increases as energy flows into it. Likewise, the temperature of the hot brass bar decreases as energy flows away from it. When the temperature of the water equals the temperature of the brass bar, energy is no longer transferred as heat within the system.

Heat Capacity and Specific Heat

The quantity of energy transferred as heat during a temperature change depends on the nature of the material changing temperature, the mass of the material changing temperature, and the size of the temperature change. One gram of iron heated to 100.0°C and cooled to 50.0°C in a calorimeter transfers 22.5 J of energy to the surrounding water. But one gram of silver transfers 11.8 J of energy under the same conditions. The difference results from the metals' differing capacities for absorbing this energy. A quantity called specific heat can be used to compare heat absorption capacities for different materials. **Specific heat** *is the amount of energy required to raise the temperature of one gram of substance by one Celsius degree (1°C) or one kelvin (1 K)*(because the sizes of the degree divisions on both scales are equal). Values of specific heat can be given in units of joules per gram per Celsius degree, $J/(g \cdot °C)$, joules per gram per kelvin, $J/(g \cdot K)$, or calories per gram per Celsius degree, $cal/(g \cdot °C)$. Table 17-1 gives the specific heats of some common substances. Notice the extremely high specific heat of water, one of the highest of most common substances.

Specific heat is usually measured under constant pressure conditions, so its symbol, c_p, contains a subscripted p as a reminder to the reader.

TABLE 17-1 Specific Heats of Some Common Substances at 298.15 K

Substance	Specific heat J/(g·K)
Water (*l*)	4.18
Water (*s*)	2.06
Water (*g*)	1.87
Ammonia (*g*)	2.09
Benzene (*l*)	1.74
Ethanol (*l*)	2.44
Ethanol (*g*)	1.42
Aluminum (*s*)	0.897
Calcium (*s*)	0.647
Carbon, graphite (*s*)	0.709
Copper (*s*)	0.385
Gold (*s*)	0.129
Iron (*s*)	0.449
Mercury (*l*)	0.140
Lead (*s*)	0.129

In the following mathematical equation, c_p is the specific heat at a given pressure, q is the energy lost or gained, m is the mass of the sample, and ΔT represents the difference between the initial and final temperatures.

$$c_p = \frac{q}{m \times \Delta T}$$

This equation can be rearranged to give an equation that can be used to find the quantity of energy gained or lost with a change in temperature.

$$q = c_p \times m \times \Delta T$$

SAMPLE PROBLEM 17-1

A 4.0 g sample of glass was heated from 274 K to 314 K, a temperature increase of 40 K, and was found to have absorbed 32 J of energy as heat.
a. What is the specific heat of this type of glass?
b. How much energy will the same glass sample gain when it is heated from 314 K to 344 K?

SOLUTION

1 ANALYZE   Given: $m = 4.0$ g
$\Delta T = 40$ K
$q = 32$ J
Unknown: c_p in J/(g·K)

17-1 A piece of copper alloy with a mass of 85.0 g is heated from 30.°C to 45°C. In the process, it absorbs 523 J of energy as heat.

a. What is the specific heat of this copper alloy?

b. How much energy will the same sample lose if it is cooled to 25°C?

Ans. **a.** 0.41 J/(g•K)
b. 697 J

17-1 The temperature of a 74 g sample of material increases from 15°C to 45°C when it absorbs 2.0 kJ of energy as heat. What is the specific heat of this material?

Ans. 0.90 J/(g•K)

17-1 How much energy is needed to raise the temperature of 5.0 g of gold by 25°C?

Ans. 16 J

17-1 Energy in the amount of 420 J is added to a 35 g sample of water at a temperature of 10.°C. What will be the final temperature of the water?

Ans. 13°C

17-1 What mass of liquid water at room temperature (25°C) can be raised to its boiling point with the addition of 24 kJ of energy?

Ans. 77 g

Problem-Solving Practice ChemFile

Chapter 19 of the Mini-Guide to Problem Solving (also found on the One-Stop Planner CD-ROM) includes more worked-out samples and additional practice problems involving thermochemistry.

---

2 PLAN

a. The specific heat, c_p, of the glass is calculated using the equation given for specific heat.

$$c_p = \frac{q}{m \times \Delta T}$$

b. The rearranged specific heat equation is used to find the energy gained when the glass was heated.

$$q = c_p \times m \times \Delta T$$

3 COMPUTE

a. $\dfrac{32 \text{ J}}{(4.0 \text{ g})(40 \text{ K})} = 0.20 \text{ J/(g•K)}$

b. $\dfrac{0.20 \text{ J}}{(g•K)} (4.0 \text{ g})(71 \text{ K} - 41 \text{ K})$

$\dfrac{0.20 \text{ J}}{(g•K)} (4.0 \text{ g})(30 \text{ K}) = 24 \text{ J}$

4 EVALUATE

The units combine or cancel correctly to give the specific heat in J/(g•K) and the energy in J. Both answers are correct given to two significant figures.

PRACTICE

1. Determine the specific heat of a material if a 35 g sample absorbed 48 J as it was heated from 293 K to 313 K.

Answer
0.069 J/(g•K)

2. If 980 kJ of energy are added to 6.2 L of water at 291 K, what will the final temperature of the water be?

Answer
329 K

Heat of Reaction

The **heat of reaction** *is the quantity of energy released or absorbed as heat during a chemical reaction.* You can think of heat of reaction as the difference between the stored energy of the reactants and the products.

If a mixture of hydrogen and oxygen is ignited, water will form and energy will be released explosively. The energy that is released comes from the reactants as they form products. Because energy is released, the reaction is exothermic, and the energy of the product, water, must be less than the energy of the reactants before ignition. The following chemical equation for this reaction indicates that when 2 mol of hydrogen gas at room temperature are burned, 1 mol of oxygen gas is consumed and 2 mol of water vapor are formed.

$$2H_2(g) + O_2(g) \longrightarrow 2H_2O(g)$$

The equation does not tell you that energy is evolved as heat during the reaction. Experiments have shown that 483.6 kJ of energy are evolved when 2 mol of gaseous water are formed at 298.15 K from its elements.

Modifying the chemical equation to show the amount of energy produced during the reaction gives the following expression.

$$2H_2(g) + O_2(g) \longrightarrow 2H_2O(g) + 483.6 \text{ kJ}$$

This expression is an example of a **thermochemical equation,** *an equation that includes the quantity of energy released or absorbed as heat during the reaction as written.* In any thermochemical equation, we must always interpret the coefficients as *numbers of moles* and never as *numbers of molecules.* The quantity of energy released as heat in this or any reaction depends on the amounts of reactants and products. The quantity of energy released during the formation of water from H_2 and O_2 is proportional to the quantity of water formed. Producing twice as much water vapor would require twice as many moles of reactants and would release 2×483.6 kJ of energy as heat, as shown in the following thermochemical equation.

$$4H_2(g) + 2O_2(g) \longrightarrow 4H_2O(g) + 967.2 \text{ kJ}$$

Producing one-half as much water would require one-half as many moles of reactants and would release only one-half as much energy, or $1/2 \times 483.6$ kJ. The thermochemical equation for this reaction follows.

$$H_2(g) + \frac{1}{2}O_2(g) \longrightarrow H_2O(g) + 241.8 \text{ kJ}$$

Fractional coefficients are sometimes used in thermochemical equations.

The situation is reversed in an endothermic reaction because products have a higher energy than reactants. The decomposition of water vapor is endothermic; it is the reverse of the reaction that forms water vapor. The amount of energy absorbed by water molecules to form hydrogen and oxygen equals the amount of energy released when the elements combine to form the water. This is to be expected because the difference between the energy of reactants and products is unchanged. Energy now appears on the reactant side of the thermochemical equation that follows, indicating that it was absorbed during the reaction.

$$2H_2O(g) + 483.6 \text{ kJ} \longrightarrow 2H_2(g) + O_2(g)$$

The physical states of reactants and products must always be included in thermochemical equations because they influence the overall amount of energy exchanged. For example, the energy needed for the decomposition of water would be greater than 483.6 kJ if we started with ice because extra energy would be needed to melt the ice and to change the liquid into a vapor.

The energy absorbed or released as heat during a chemical reaction at constant pressure is represented by ΔH. The H is the symbol for a quantity called *enthalpy.* Enthalpy has traditionally been defined as the heat content of a system at constant pressure. However, the term "heat content" is misleading. Also, it is not practical to talk just about enthalpy as a quantity, because we have no way to directly measure the enthalpy of a system. Only *changes* in enthalpy can be measured. The Greek

Module 9: Thermochemistry

Class Discussion
The discussion of thermochemical equations provides a good opportunity to review with students the alternative interpretations that can be given to coefficients in a chemical equation. Ask students why fractional coefficients can be used when the coefficients represent moles but not when they represent molecules.

✔ **Teaching Tip**
When chemical changes and changes of state occur at the same time, energy changes associated with both must be considered in determining total energy changes in the system.

Common Misconception
Phrases such as "at constant temperature" and "at constant pressure" are often misunderstood. Processes described using these phrases can involve changes in temperature or pressure. When such a process is complete, the products are brought back to the initial temperature and pressure. The change in enthalpy is the same as if the temperature and pressure had not changed during the process. So the phrase "at constant temperature and pressure" means only that the initial and final conditions are the same.

Module 9: Thermochemistry

Topic: Enthalpy Tutorial and Practice
Sections **a, b,** and **c** of this engaging tutorial review and reinforce understanding of heat and enthalpy.

Common Misconception

Emphasize that a negative value of ΔH does not indicate a negative energy value. No such condition exists because any substance contains at least some particle kinetic energy. Review with students the meaning of negative values of ΔH.

Visual Strategy

FIGURE 17-2 Demonstrate the relationship between the figure and the defining relationship for ΔH by replacing words in the figure with their mathematical equivalents wherever possible. For example, the label "Initial energy" can be replaced by $H_{reactants}$. Then the equation $\Delta H = H_{products} - H_{reactants}$ can be used to show how the sign of ΔH is obtained.

FIGURE 17-2 In an exothermic chemical reaction, energy is released from the system as heat, meaning the enthalpy change is negative.

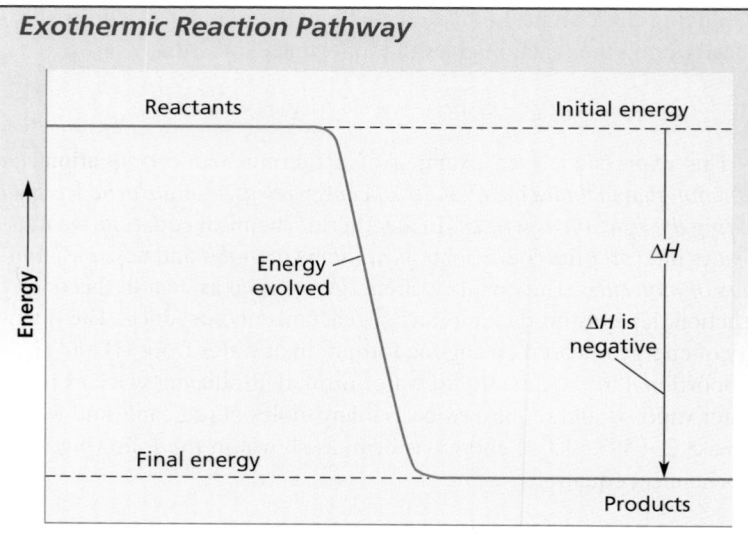

Exothermic Reaction Pathway

Reactants — Initial energy

Energy

Energy evolved

ΔH

ΔH is negative

Final energy

Products

Course of reaction ⟶

internet**connect**

SC*i*LINKS

NSTA

TOPIC: Enthalpy
GO TO: www.scilinks.org
*sci*LINKS **CODE:** HC2172

letter Δ (a capital "delta") stands for "change in." Therefore, ΔH is read as "change in enthalpy." *An* **enthalpy change** *is the amount of energy absorbed or lost by a system as heat during a process at constant pressure.* The enthalpy change is always the difference between the enthalpies of the products and the reactants. The following equation expresses an enthalpy change mathematically.

$$\Delta H = H_{products} - H_{reactants}$$

Thermochemical equations are usually written by designating the value of ΔH rather than writing the energy as a reactant or product. By convention, for an exothermic reaction, ΔH is always given a minus sign because the system loses energy. So the thermochemical equation for the exothermic formation of 2 mol of gaseous water from its elements now has the following form.

$$2H_2(g) + O_2(g) \longrightarrow 2H_2O(g) \quad \Delta H = -483.6 \text{ kJ/mol}$$

Figure 17-2 graphically shows the course of an exothermic reaction. The initial energy of the reactants is greater than the final energy of the products. This means energy is evolved, or given off, during the reaction; this is described as a negative enthalpy change.

For an endothermic reaction, ΔH is always given a positive value because the system gains energy. Thus, the endothermic decomposition of 2 mol of gaseous water has the following thermochemical equation.

$$2H_2O(g) \longrightarrow 2H_2(g) + O_2(g) \quad \Delta H = +483.6 \text{ kJ/mol}$$

The course of an endothermic reaction is illustrated in Figure 17-3.

Endothermic Reaction Pathway

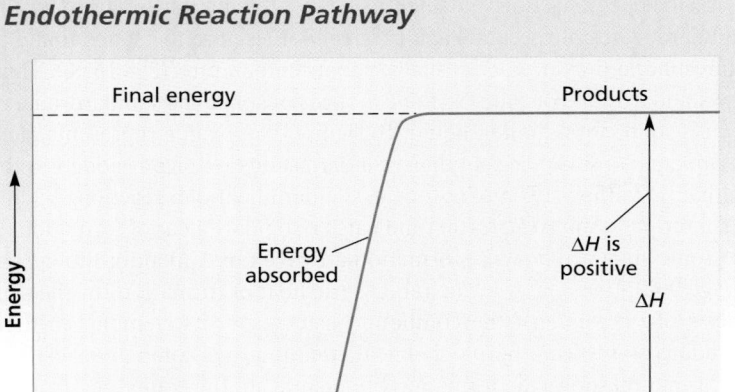

FIGURE 17-3 In an endothermic chemical reaction, the enthalpy change is positive because energy is absorbed into the system as heat.

Class Discussion
Ask students to use an analogy of an investor to explain the connection between the sign of ΔH and the gain or loss of energy in a reaction. If money is invested and a profit is made (taken in, as energy is in an endothermic reaction), the new amount of money the investor has is more (+) than the original amount. If money is lost (given out, as energy is in an exothermic reaction), the new amount of money is less (−) than the original amount.

Energy is absorbed in this reaction, meaning that the initial energy of the reactants is lower than the final energy of the products. In this case, ΔH is designated as positive.

Keep in mind the following concepts when using thermochemical equations.

1. The coefficients in a balanced thermochemical equation represent the numbers of *moles* of reactants and products and never the numbers of *molecules*. This allows us to write these coefficients as fractions rather than whole numbers when necessary.
2. The physical state of the product or reactant involved in a reaction is an important factor and therefore must be included in the thermochemical equation.
3. The change in energy represented by a thermochemical equation is directly proportional to the number of moles of substances undergoing a change. For example, if 2 mol of water are decomposed, twice as much energy, 483.6 kJ, is needed than for the decomposition of 1 mol of water.
4. The value of the energy change, ΔH, is usually not significantly influenced by changing temperature.

Heat of Formation

The formation of water from hydrogen and oxygen is a composition reaction—the formation of a compound from its elements. Thermochemical data are often recorded as the heats of such composition reactions. *The* **molar heat of formation** *is the energy released or absorbed as heat when one mole of a compound is formed by combination of its elements.*

Class Discussion
Present students with the following list of heats of formation and ask them to comment on the stability of each of the substances listed.

$Al_2O_3(s)$	−1676.0 kJ/mol
$CaCO_3(s)$	−1206.92 kJ/mol
$NO(g)$	90.29 kJ/mol
$O_3(g)$	142.7 kJ/mol

Alternative Assessment
Ask students to draw inferences from each of the pairs of heats of formation listed below. (All heats of formation are in kJ/mol.)

$C(s)$, diamond: 1.897
$C(s)$, graphite: 0.0

$I_2(s)$: 0.0
$I_2(g)$: 62.43

$P(s)$, white: 0.0
$P(s)$, red: −17.46

$SO_2(g)$: −296.84
$SO_3(g)$: −395.77

To make comparisons meaningful, heats of formation are given for the standard states of reactants and products—these are the states found at atmospheric pressure and, usually, room temperature (298.15 K). Thus, the standard state of water is liquid, not gas or solid. The standard state of iron is solid, not a molten liquid. To signify that a value represents measurements on substances in their standard states, a ^{0} sign is added to the enthalpy symbol, giving ΔH^0 for the standard heat of a reaction. Adding a subscript f, as in ΔH_f^0, further indicates a standard heat of formation.

Some standard heats of formation are given in Appendix Table A-14 (page 902). Each entry in the table is the heat of formation for the synthesis of *one mole* of the compound listed from its elements in their standard states. The thermochemical equation to accompany each heat of formation shows the formation of one mole of the compound from its elements in their standard states.

Stability and Heat of Formation

If a large amount of energy is released when a compound is formed, the compound has a high negative heat of formation. Such compounds are very stable. Once they start, the reactions forming them usually proceed vigorously and without outside assistance.

Elements in their standard states are *defined* as having $\Delta H_f^0 = 0$. The ΔH_f^0 of carbon dioxide is −393.5 kJ/mol of gas produced. Therefore, carbon dioxide is more stable than the elements from which it was formed. You can see in Appendix Table A-14 (page 902) that the majority of the heats of formation are negative.

Compounds with relatively positive values of heats of formation, or only slightly negative values, are relatively unstable and will spontaneously decompose into their elements if the conditions are appropriate. Hydrogen iodide, HI, is a colorless gas that decomposes somewhat when stored at room temperature. It has a relatively high positive heat of formation of +26.5 kJ/mol. As it decomposes, violet iodine vapor becomes visible throughout the container of the gas.

Compounds with a high positive heat of formation are sometimes very unstable and may react or decompose violently. For example, ethyne (acetylene), C_2H_2, ($\Delta H_f^0 = +226.7$ kJ/mol) reacts violently with oxygen and must be stored in cylinders as a solution in acetone. Mercury fulminate, $HgC_2N_2O_2$, has a very high heat of formation of +270 kJ/mol. Its instability makes it useful as a detonator for explosives.

Heat of Combustion

Combustion reactions produce a considerable amount of energy in the form of light and heat when a substance is combined with oxygen. *The energy released as heat by the complete combustion of one mole of a*

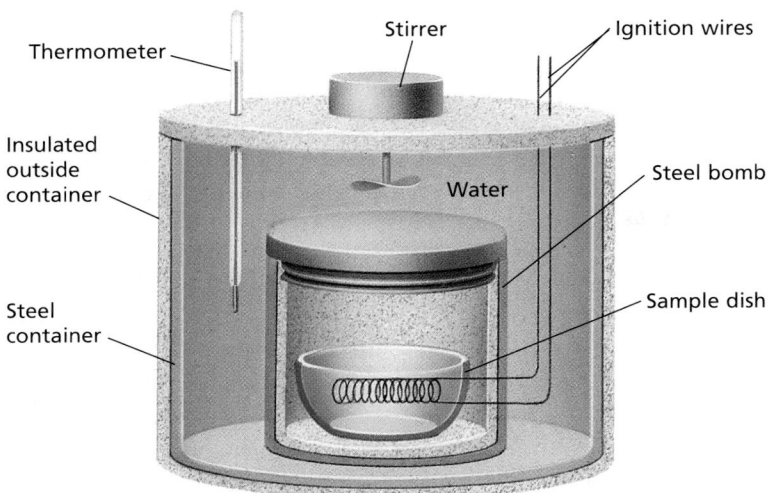

Thermometer

Stirrer

Ignition wires

Insulated outside container

Water

Steel bomb

Steel container

Sample dish

FIGURE 17-4 This is a diagram of a simple combustion calorimeter. A weighed sample is ignited by an electric spark and burned in the sample dish in an atmosphere of pure oxygen. The energy generated by the combustion reaction warms the steel bomb and the water surrounding it. The thermometer measures the initial and final temperatures of the water, and this temperature change is then used to calculate the energy evolved by the reaction as heat.

Visual Strategy

FIGURE 17-4 Ask students to clarify the function of each of the following parts of the calorimeter: ignition wires, insulated outer container, water, stirrer, and thermometer.

substance is called the **heat of combustion** of the substance. Heat of combustion is defined in terms of *one mole of reactant*, whereas the heat of formation is defined in terms of *one mole of product*. All substances are in their standard state. The general enthalpy notation, ΔH, applies to heats of reaction, but the addition of a subscripted c, ΔH_c, refers specifically to heat of combustion. A list of heats of combustion can be found in Appendix Table A-5 (page 896).

Carbon dioxide and water are the products of the complete combustion of organic compounds containing only carbon and hydrogen or carbon, hydrogen, and oxygen. Knowing this, we can write the thermochemical equation for the combustion of any organic compound listed by balancing the equation for the reaction of one mole of the compound. For example, propane is a major component of the fuel used for outdoor gas grills. Its reaction with oxygen in the air, forming carbon dioxide and water as products and releasing energy in the form of heat and light, is a common example of combustion. The complete combustion of one mole of propane, C_3H_8, is described by the following thermochemical equation.

$$C_3H_8(g) + 5O_2(g) \longrightarrow 3CO_2(g) + 4H_2O(l) \quad \Delta H_c^0 = -2219.2 \text{ kJ/mol}$$

Figure 17-4 shows a combustion calorimeter, one of the instruments used to determine heats of combustion.

Calculating Heats of Reaction

Thermochemical equations can be rearranged and added to give enthalpy changes for reactions not included in the data tables. The basis for calculating heats of reaction is known as **Hess's law:** *The overall enthalpy change in a reaction is equal to the sum of enthalpy changes for the individual steps in the process.* The energy difference between reactants and

520

DEMONSTRATION

Hess's Law

Write the following three equations on the chalkboard:

1. $NaOH + H_2O \longrightarrow$
$\qquad Na^+ + OH^- + H_2O + heat_1$

2. $Na^+ + OH^- + H_3O^+ + Cl^- \longrightarrow$
$\qquad 2H_2O + Na^+ + Cl^- + heat_2$

3. $NaOH + H_3O^+ + Cl^- \longrightarrow$
$\qquad 2H_2O + Na^+ + Cl^- + heat_3$

Have students show that equation 1 + equation 2 = equation 3. If equal numbers of moles are used, Hess's law applies, and $T_1 + T_2 = T_3$. For each of the following reactions, measure and record the temperature of the initial solution poured into a plastic-foam cup, then measure and record the temperature of the final system after the second reactant has been added and dissolved by stirring.

Reaction 1: 50 mL of distilled water; 1 g of NaOH pellets

Reaction 2: 25 mL of 1 M HCl; 25 mL of 1 M NaOH

Reaction 3: 50 mL of 1 M HCl; 1 g of NaOH pellets.

Compare $T_1 + T_2$ with T_3.

Safety: Wear safety goggles and a lab apron. Use a nonmercury thermometer. Follow first-aid instructions on the label if acid or base gets in the eyes or on skin or clothing.

Disposal: Rinse out the plastic-foam cups and put them in the trash. Combine all liquids, adjust the pH to between 5 and 9, and pour the mixture down the drain.

products is independent of the route taken to get from one to the other. In fact, measured heats of reaction can be combined to calculate heats of reaction that are difficult or impossible to actually measure.

To demonstrate how to apply Hess's law, we will work through the calculation of the heat of formation for the formation of methane gas, CH_4, from its elements, hydrogen gas and solid carbon (graphite), at 298.15 K (25°C).

$$C(s) + 2H_2(g) \longrightarrow CH_4(g) \quad \Delta H_f^0 = ?$$

In order to calculate the change in enthalpy for this reaction, we can use the combustion reactions of the elements, carbon and hydrogen, and of methane.

$$C(s) + O_2(g) \longrightarrow CO_2(g) \qquad \Delta H_c^0 = -393.5 \text{ kJ/mol}$$

$$H_2(g) + \tfrac{1}{2}O_2(g) \longrightarrow H_2O(l) \qquad \Delta H_c^0 = -285.8 \text{ kJ/mol}$$

$$CH_4(g) + 2O_2(g) \longrightarrow CO_2(g) + 2H_2O(l) \quad \Delta H_c^0 = -890.8 \text{ kJ/mol}$$

The general principles for combining thermochemical equations follow.

1. If a reaction is reversed, the sign of ΔH is also reversed.
2. Multiply the coefficients of the known equations so that when added together they give the desired thermochemical equation.

In this case, reverse the combustion equation for methane, and remember to change the sign of ΔH from negative to positive. This will change the exothermic reaction to an endothermic one.

$$CO_2(g) + 2H_2O(l) \longrightarrow CH_4(g) + 2O_2(g) \quad \Delta H^0 = +890.8 \text{ kJ/mol}$$

Now we notice that 2 formula units of water are used as a reactant; therefore, 2 formula units of water will be needed as a product. In the combustion reaction for hydrogen as it is written, it only produces one formula unit of water. We must multiply the coefficients of this combustion reaction and the value of ΔH by 2 in order to obtain the desired quantity of water.

$$2H_2(g) + O_2(g) \longrightarrow 2H_2O(l) \quad \Delta H_c^0 = 2(-285.8 \text{ kJ/mol})$$

We are now ready to add the three equations together using Hess's law to give the heat of formation for methane and the balanced equation.

$$C(s) + O_2(g) \longrightarrow CO_2(g) \qquad \Delta H_c^0 = -393.5 \text{ kJ/mol}$$

$$2H_2(g) + O_2(g) \longrightarrow 2H_2O(l) \qquad \Delta H_c^0 = 2(-285.8 \text{ kJ/mol})$$

$$CO_2(g) + 2H_2O(l) \longrightarrow CH_4(g) + 2O_2(g) \quad \Delta H^0 = +890.8 \text{ kJ/mol}$$

$$\overline{C(s) + 2H_2(g) \longrightarrow CH_4(g) \qquad \Delta H_f^0 = -74.3 \text{ kJ/mol}}$$

SAMPLE PROBLEM 17-2

Calculate the heat of reaction for the combustion of nitrogen monoxide gas, NO, to form nitrogen dioxide gas, NO_2, as given in the following thermochemical equation.

$$NO(g) + \frac{1}{2}O_2(g) \longrightarrow NO_2(g)$$

Use the heat-of-formation data in Appendix Table A-14 (page 902). Solve by combining the known thermochemical equations. Verify the result by using the general equation for finding heats of reaction from heats of formation.

SOLUTION

1 ANALYZE

Given: $\frac{1}{2}N_2(g) + \frac{1}{2}O_2(g) \longrightarrow NO(g)$ $\qquad \Delta H_f^0 = +90.29 \text{ kJ/mol}$

$\frac{1}{2}N_2(g) + O_2(g) \longrightarrow NO_2(g)$ $\qquad \Delta H_f^0 = +33.2 \text{ kJ/mol}$

Unknown: ΔH^0 for $NO(g) + \frac{1}{2}O_2(g) \longrightarrow NO_2(g)$

2 PLAN

The ΔH requested can be found by adding the ΔHs of the component reactions as specified in Hess's law. The desired equation has $NO(g)$ and $\frac{1}{2}O_2(g)$ as reactants and $NO_2(g)$ as the product.

$$NO(g) + \frac{1}{2}O_2(g) \longrightarrow NO_2(g)$$

We need an equation with NO as a reactant. Reversing the first reaction for the formation of NO from its elements and the sign of ΔH yields the following thermochemical equation.

$$NO(g) \longrightarrow \frac{1}{2}N_2(g) + \frac{1}{2}O_2(g) \quad \Delta H^0 = -90.29 \text{ kJ/mol}$$

The other equation should have NO_2 as a product, so we can retain the second equation for the formation of NO_2 from its elements as it stands.

$$\frac{1}{2}N_2(g) + O_2(g) \longrightarrow NO_2(g) \quad \Delta H_f^0 = +33.2 \text{ kJ/mol}$$

3 COMPUTE

$NO(g) \longrightarrow \frac{1}{2}N_2(g) + \frac{1}{2}O_2(g) \quad \Delta H^0 = -90.29 \text{ kJ/mol}$

$\frac{1}{2}N_2(g) + O_2(g) \longrightarrow NO_2(g) \quad \Delta H_f^0 = +33.2 \text{ kJ/mol}$

$NO(g) + \frac{1}{2}O_2(g) \longrightarrow NO_2(g) \quad \Delta H^0 = -57.1 \text{ kJ/mol}$

Note the cancellation of the $\frac{1}{2}N_2(g)$ and the partial cancellation of the $O_2(g)$.

4 EVALUATE

The unnecessary reactants and products cancel to give the desired equation. The general relationship between the heat of a reaction and the heats of formation of the reactants and products is described in the following word equation.

$$\Delta H^0 = \text{sum of } \Delta H_f^0 \text{ of products} - \text{sum of } \Delta H_f^0 \text{ of reactants}$$

Application

The equilibrium between nitrogen monoxide and nitrogen dioxide is of great interest to environmental chemists. The gases are involved in the production of photochemical smog. Nitrogen monoxide is formed during the combustion of gasoline in internal-combustion engines and is converted to nitrogen dioxide in the atmosphere. The exact mechanism by which this change takes place, however, is still unknown because the reaction $2NO + O_2 \longrightarrow 2NO_2$ takes place much too slowly to account for the change.

17-2 Calculate ΔH for the following reaction:

$$2N_2(g) + 5O_2(g) \longrightarrow 2N_2O_5(g)$$

Use the following data in your calculation:

$$H_2(g) + \tfrac{1}{2}O_2(g) \longrightarrow H_2O(l)$$
$$\Delta H_f^0 = -285.8 \text{ kJ/mol}$$

$$N_2O_5(g) + H_2O(l) \longrightarrow 2HNO_3(l)$$
$$\Delta H^0 = -76.6 \text{ kJ/mol}$$

$$\tfrac{1}{2}N_2(g) + \tfrac{3}{2}O_2(g) + \tfrac{1}{2}H_2(g) \longrightarrow$$
$$HNO_3(l)$$

$$\Delta H_f^0 = -174.1 \text{ kJ/mol}$$

Ans. 28.4 kJ/mol

To find the necessary sums, the ΔH_f^0 value for each reactant and each product must be multiplied by its respective coefficient in the desired equation. For the reaction of NO with O_2, applying this equation gives the following value for ΔH^0.

$$\Delta H^0 = \Delta H_f^0(NO_2) - [\Delta H_f^0(NO) + 0]$$
$$= +33.2 \text{ kJ/mol} - 90.29 \text{ kJ/mol} = -57.1 \text{ kJ/mol}$$

Note that zero is the assigned value for the heats of formation of elements in their standard states.

1. Calculate the heat of reaction for the combustion of methane gas, CH_4, to form $CO_2(g) + H_2O(l)$. Write all equations involved.

   Answer
   −890.36 kJ/mol

2. Carbon occurs in two distinct forms. It can be the soft, black material found in pencils and lock lubricants, called graphite, or it can be the hard, brilliant gem we know as diamond. Calculate ΔH^0 for the conversion of graphite to diamond for the following reaction.

   Answer
   2 kJ/mol

$$C_{graphite}(s) \longrightarrow C_{diamond}(s)$$

The combustion reactions you will need follow.

$$C_{graphite}(s) + O_2(g) \longrightarrow CO_2(g) \qquad \Delta H_c^0 = -394 \text{ kJ/mol}$$
$$C_{diamond}(s) + O_2(g) \longrightarrow CO_2(g) \qquad \Delta H_c^0 = -396 \text{ kJ/mol}$$

Determining Heat of Formation

When carbon is burned in a limited supply of oxygen, carbon monoxide is produced. In this reaction, carbon is probably first oxidized to carbon dioxide. Then part of the carbon dioxide is reduced with carbon to give some carbon monoxide. Because these two reactions occur simultaneously and we get a mixture of CO and CO_2, it is not possible to directly measure the heat of formation of $CO(g)$ from $C(s)$ and $O_2(g)$.

$$C(s) + \tfrac{1}{2}O_2(g) \longrightarrow CO(g) \quad \Delta H_f^0 = ?$$

However, we do know the heat of formation of carbon dioxide and the heat of combustion of carbon monoxide.

$$C(s) + O_2(g) \longrightarrow CO_2(g) \qquad \Delta H_f^0 = -393.5 \text{ kJ/mol}$$

$$CO(g) + \tfrac{1}{2}O_2(g) \longrightarrow CO_2(g) \quad \Delta H_c^0 = -283.0 \text{ kJ/mol}$$

We reverse the second equation because we need CO as a product. Adding gives the desired heat of formation of carbon monoxide.

Heats of Reaction

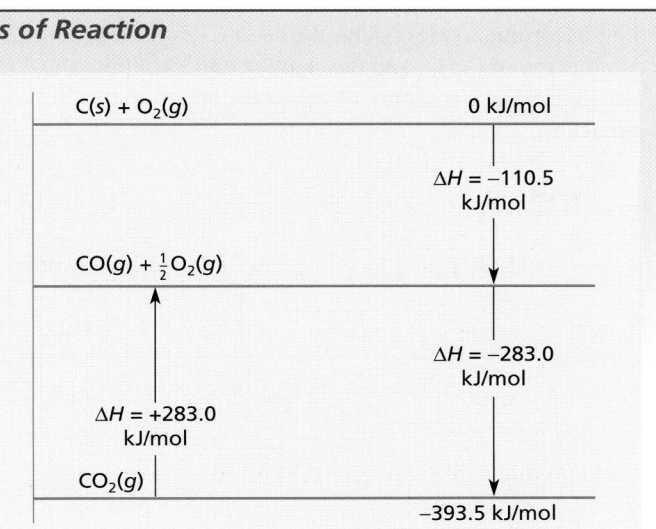

C(s) + O$_2$(g)   0 kJ/mol

$\Delta H = -110.5$ kJ/mol

CO(g) + $\frac{1}{2}$O$_2$(g)

$\Delta H = -283.0$ kJ/mol

$\Delta H = +283.0$ kJ/mol

CO$_2$(g)

-393.5 kJ/mol

FIGURE 17-5 This diagram shows the heat of reaction for carbon dioxide, CO$_2$, and carbon monoxide, CO.

Visual Strategy
FIGURE 17-5 Ask students to explain in words how the graph illustrates Hess's law.

Class Discussion
Ask students to explain why the heat of formation of carbon dioxide and the heat of combustion of carbon monoxide can be measured, but the heat of formation of carbon monoxide cannot be measured directly.

$$C(s) + O_2(g) \longrightarrow CO_2(g) \qquad \Delta H^0 = -393.5 \text{ kJ/mol}$$

$$CO_2(g) \longrightarrow CO(g) + \frac{1}{2}O_2(g) \qquad \Delta H^0 = +283.0 \text{ kJ/mol}$$

$$\overline{C(s) + \frac{1}{2}O_2(g) \longrightarrow CO(g) \qquad \Delta H^0 = -110.5 \text{ kJ/mol}}$$

Figure 17-5 is a model for the process described in this section. If we plot the reactions based on their relative energy, you can see the relationship among the values obtained for the heat of formation of carbon monoxide. The formation of CO$_2$ is plotted at a level corresponding to -393.5 kJ/mol. The diagram shows the reverse of the combustion reaction ($+283.0$ kJ/mol) is added to that level. From the diagram, you see the difference, which represents the formation of CO. This value is -110.5 kJ/mol.

SAMPLE PROBLEM 17-3

Calculate the heat of formation of pentane, C$_5$H$_{12}$, using the information on heats of formation in Appendix Table A-14 (page 902) and the information on heats of combustion in Appendix Table A-5 (page 896). Solve by combining the known thermochemical equations.

SOLUTION

1 ANALYZE

Given:
$$C(s) + O_2(g) \longrightarrow CO_2(g) \qquad\qquad \Delta H^0_f = -393.5 \text{ kJ/mol}$$

$$H_2(g) + \frac{1}{2}O_2(g) \longrightarrow H_2O(l) \qquad\qquad \Delta H^0_f = -285.8 \text{ kJ/mol}$$

$$C_5H_{12}(g) + 8O_2(g) \longrightarrow 5CO_2(g) + 6H_2O(l) \qquad \Delta H^0_c = -3535.6 \text{ kJ/mol}$$

Unknown: ΔH^0_f for $5C(s) + 6H_2(g) \longrightarrow C_5H_{12}(g)$

2 **PLAN** Combine the given equations according to Hess's law. We need C_5H_{12} as a product, so we reverse the equation for combustion of C_5H_{12} and the sign for ΔH_c^0. Multiply the equation for formation of CO_2 by 5 to give 5C as a reactant. Multiply the equation for formation of H_2O by 6 to give $6H_2$ as a reactant.

3 **COMPUTE**

$$5C(s) + 5O_2(g) \longrightarrow 5CO_2(g) \qquad\qquad \Delta H^0 = 5(-393.5 \text{ kJ/mol})$$

$$6H_2(g) + 3O_2(g) \longrightarrow 6H_2O(l) \qquad\qquad \Delta H^0 = 6(-285.8 \text{ kJ/mol})$$

$$\underline{5CO_2(g) + 6H_2O(l) \longrightarrow C_5H_{12}(g) + 8O_2(g) \quad \Delta H^0 = +3536.6 \text{ kJ/mol}}$$

$$5C(s) + 6H_2(g) \longrightarrow C_5H_{12}(g) \qquad\qquad \Delta H_f^0 = -145.7 \text{ kJ/mol}$$

4 **EVALUATE** The unnecessary reactants and products cancel to give the correct equation.

PRACTICE

1. Calculate the heat of formation of butane, C_4H_{10}, using the balanced chemical equation and information in Appendix Table A-5 (page 896) and Table A-14 (page 902). Write out the solution according to Hess's law.

   Answer
   −124.7 kJ/mol

2. Calculate the heat of combustion of 1 mol of nitrogen, N_2, to form NO_2 using the balanced chemical equation and Appendix Table A-14 (page 902). (Hint: The heat of combustion of N_2 will be equal to the sum of the heats of formation of the combustion products of N_2 minus the heat of formation of N_2.)

   Answer
   + 66.36 kJ/mol

3. Calculate the heat of formation for sulfur dioxide, SO_2, from its elements, sulfur and oxygen. Use the balanced chemical equation and the following information.

   Answer
   −296.1 kJ/mol

$$S(s) + \tfrac{3}{2}O_2(g) \longrightarrow SO_3(g) \qquad \Delta H_c^0 = -395.2 \text{ kJ/mol}$$

$$2SO_2(g) + O_2(g) \longrightarrow 2SO_3(g) \qquad \Delta H^0 = -198.2 \text{ kJ/mol}$$

SECTION REVIEW

1. What is meant by enthalpy change?

2. What is meant by heat of reaction?

3. Describe the relationship between a compound's stability and its heat of formation.

4. What is the importance of Hess's law to thermodynamic calculations?

5. How much energy would be absorbed as heat by 75 g of iron when heated from 295 K to 301 K?

6. When 1 mol of methane is burned at constant pressure, 890 kJ of energy is released as heat. If a 3.2 g sample of methane is burned at constant pressure, what will be the value of ΔH? (Hint: Convert the grams of methane to moles. Also make sure your answer has the correct sign for an exothermic process.)

SECTION REVIEW

1. Enthalpy change is the amount of energy absorbed or lost by a system as heat during a process at constant pressure.

2. The heat of reaction is the quantity of energy released or absorbed as heat during a reaction.

3. The more negative the heat of formation is, the more stable a compound is.

4. Hess's law provides a method of finding the value of ΔH for a given reaction by summing the discrete values of ΔH for other reactions that can be added to give that reaction.

5. 2.0×10^2 J

6. −180 kJ

Self-Heating Meals

W ho would have thought that corrosion could be useful? The HeaterMeals Company did. This company uses the properties of salt-water corrosion to heat TV-type dinners, and now it is taking packaged foods to a new level of convenience.

HeaterMeals' products, as their name implies, come with a self-contained heat source. Each meal contains a package of food, a tray that holds a porous pouch containing Mg and Fe alloy, and a 2 oz pouch filled with salt water. When the salt water is poured into the tray with the porous pouch, it begins to vigorously corrode the metals. The sealed, precooked food package is then placed on top of the tray and returned to its box, where the temperature of the food package is raised by 100°F, heating the meal in 14 min.

Corrosion, the process by which a metal reacts with air or water, is usually an undesirable event, such as when iron corrodes to form rust. With HeaterMeals, however, the corrosion process is speeded up to produce an exothermic reaction—with the excess heat as the desired result.

According to Drew McLandrich, of The HeaterMeals Company, the idea for using self-heating metallic

This product uses supercorrosion to give you a hot meal.

alloy powders has been around since the 1930s. "But," says McLandrich, "there really have been no significant uses of the product until the Desert Storm conflict, which led to the military's

taking this technology and adopting it for field use so that soldiers could heat a meal-ready-to-eat."

"We've made about 80 million heaters for the military in the last 10 years. Lately we've been successfully marketing them to long-distance truck drivers. The product is in about 800 truck stops in 48 states. Additional users include hunters, campers, fishermen, boaters ... football fans at half time ... , picnickers, and people at a music concert."

The company has plans to develop other products using the controlled use of "supercorrosion." "A beverage could be heated," says McLandrich, "and we do have prototypes for a baby-bottle warmer. We're also working on making a portable hot cup of coffee or a hot cup of tea or cocoa."

So the next time you need a hot meal and there are no kitchens or restaurants around, consider the possibilities of supercorrosion and exothermic reactions.

internet**connect**

SC*i*LINKS
NSTA

TOPIC: Supercorrosion
GO TO: www.scilinks.org
*sci*LINKS CODE: HC2173

✔ Teaching Tip

Many hot packs use heat of solution, not heat of reaction, to produce energy.

Class Discussion

Have students refer to earlier instruction concerning exothermic and endothermic reactions to think of possible ways in which the addition of water to a dry mixture could result in the release of energy as heat.

Ask students to name materials that they think are involved in the energy-producing reaction in the self-heating meals. Most of the energy is from the reaction of magnesium metal and water, producing magnesium hydroxide and hydrogen gas. Why are iron and sodium chloride added? *(Pure magnesium reacts with oxygen in the air, forming a coating of magnesium oxide, which prevents the metal from reacting with the water. Adding sodium chloride and iron prevents formation of the magnesium oxide coating.)*

Did You Know?

One mole of Mg (24.30 g), when mixed with water, produces enough energy to raise the temperature of 1 L of water from room temperature to 100°C.

Lesson Starter

Before class, make 9 M H_2SO_4 by slowly adding 100 mL of concentrated H_2SO_4 to 100 mL of H_2O with stirring. Cool to room temperature.

Caution: Be careful when handling the concentrated acid. Use H_2SO_4 only with proper ventilation. In case of spills, first dilute with water. Then mop the spill with wet cloths or a wet cloth mop designated for spill cleanup while wearing disposable gloves.

In class, place 100 g of liquid water at 0°C in a plastic foam cup, and record its temperature. Add 100 mL of 9 M H_2SO_4 to the cup, and stir. After 1 min, measure and record the temperature. Repeat these steps for 100 g of crushed ice at 0°C in a plastic foam cup.

Point out that the energy produced by dissolving H_2SO_4 in water causes the temperature in the first cup to increase but the temperature in the second cup to decrease. Ask students to try to explain these results. Student explanations may include that heat is used to break down the crystal structure of the ice in the second system. *(Entropy increases.)*

Safety: Wear goggles, lab apron, gloves, and a face shield. Be sure that an operating safety shower or eyewash station is nearby. Use a non-mercury thermometer. Have students stand 5 m away from the demonstration area.

Disposal: Adjust the pH of the solutions to between 5 and 9, and pour them down the drain.

CHEMISTRY

Module 9: Thermochemistry

Topic: Entropy Tutorial and Practice
Sections **e** and **f** of this engaging tutorial review and reinforce understanding of entropy.

SECTION 17-2

OBJECTIVES

- Explain the relationship between enthalpy change and the tendency of a reaction to occur.

- Explain the relationship between entropy change and the tendency of a reaction to occur.

- Discuss the concept of free energy, and explain how the value of this quantity is calculated and interpreted.

- Describe the use of free energy change to determine the tendency of a reaction to occur.

CHEMISTRY

Module 9: Thermochemistry

internet connect

SCLINKS
NSTA

TOPIC: Entropy
GO TO: www.scilinks.org
*sci***LINKS CODE:** HC2174

Driving Force of Reactions

The change in energy of a reaction system is one of two factors that allow chemists to predict whether a reaction will occur spontaneously and to explain how it occurs. The randomness of the particles in a system is the second factor affecting whether a reaction will occur spontaneously.

Enthalpy and Reaction Tendency

The great majority of chemical reactions in nature are exothermic. As these reactions proceed, energy is liberated and the products have less energy than the original reactants. The products are also more resistant to change, more stable, than the original reactants. The tendency throughout nature is for a reaction to proceed in a direction that leads to a lower energy state.

We might think that endothermic reactions, in which energy is absorbed, cannot occur spontaneously because the products are at higher potential energy and are less stable than the original reactants. They would be expected to proceed only with the assistance of an outside influence, such as continued heating. However, some endothermic reactions *do* occur spontaneously. We conclude that something other than enthalpy change must help determine whether a reaction will occur.

Entropy and Reaction Tendency

A naturally occurring endothermic process is melting. An ice cube melts spontaneously at room temperature as energy is transferred from the warm air to the ice. The well-ordered arrangement of water molecules in the ice crystal is lost, and the less-orderly liquid phase of higher energy content is formed. A system that can go from one state to another without an enthalpy change does so by becoming more disordered.

Look at the physical states of the reactants in the chemical equation for the decomposition of ammonium nitrate.

$$2NH_4NO_3(s) \longrightarrow 2N_2(g) + 4H_2O(l) + O_2(g)$$

On the left side are 2 mol of solid ammonium nitrate. The right-hand side of the equation shows 3 mol of gaseous molecules plus 4 mol of a liquid. The arrangement of particles on the right-hand side of the equation is more random than the arrangement on the left side of the equation and hence is less ordered. Figures 17-6(a) and (b) show the reactant and products of this decomposition reaction.

These examples illustrate that there is a tendency in nature to proceed in a direction that increases the disorder of a system. A disordered system is one that lacks a regular arrangement of its parts. This tendency toward disorder is called entropy. **Entropy, S,** can be defined in a simple qualitative way as *a measure of the degree of randomness of the particles, such as molecules, in a system.* In order to understand the concept of entropy, consider solids, liquids, and gases. In a solid, the particles are fixed in position in their small regions of space, but they are vibrating back and forth. Even so, we can determine with fair precision the location of the particles. The degree of randomness is low, so the entropy is low. When the solid melts, the particles are still very close together but they can move about somewhat. The system is more random, and it is more difficult to describe the location of the particles. The entropy is higher. When the liquid evaporates, the particles are moving rapidly and are also much farther apart. Locating an individual particle is much more difficult and the system is much more random. The entropy of the gas is still higher than that of the liquid. A general but not absolute rule is that the entropy of liquids is higher than that of solids, and the entropy of gases is higher than that of liquids. But this rule must be used with caution. For example, the entropy of liquid mercury is much lower than that of some solids.

At absolute zero, random motion ceases, so the entropy of a pure crystalline solid is by definition zero at absolute zero. As energy is added, the randomness of the molecular motion increases. Measurements of energy absorbed and calculations are used to determine the absolute entropy or standard molar entropy, and values are then recorded in tables. These molar values are reported as kJ/(mol·K). Entropy change, which can also be measured, is defined as the difference between the entropy of the products and the reactants. Therefore, an increase in entropy is represented by a positive value for ΔS, and a decrease in entropy is represented by a negative value for ΔS.

The process of forming a solution almost always involves an increase in entropy because there is an increase in randomness. This is true for mixing gases, dissolving a liquid in another liquid, and dissolving a solid in a liquid.

(a)

(b)

FIGURE 17-6 When ammonium nitrate, NH_4NO_3, decomposes, the entropy of the reaction system increases as (a) one solid reactant becomes (b) two gaseous products and one liquid product.

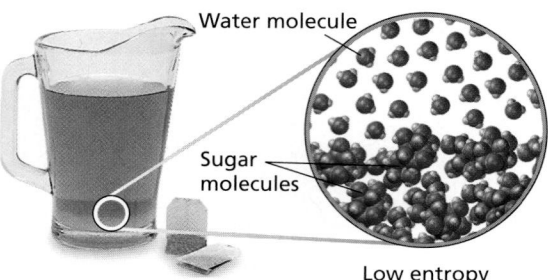

(a)

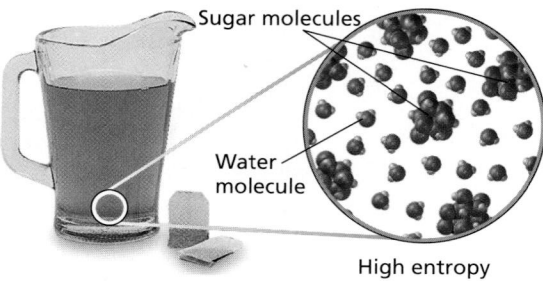

(b)

FIGURE 17-7 When a solid dissolves in a liquid, the entropy of the system increases.

Module 9: Thermochemistry

Figure 17-7 illustrates the entropy change that takes place when solid sugar is dissolved in liquid tea. In the sugar-water system shown in Figure 17-7(a), the solid sugar has just been added to the tea, but most of it has not yet dissolved. The entropy is low because the majority of the sugar molecules are in one region at the bottom of the pitcher and the majority of the water molecules can be found everywhere else in the pitcher. After the sugar dissolves in the tea, shown in Figure 17-7(b), the sugar molecules are thoroughly mixed throughout the tea solution. Sugar molecules and water molecules might be found anywhere in the solution, so the entropy, the randomness, of the system increases. This would give ΔS a positive value for this solid-liquid system. You can imagine the same series of events happening for a system of gases mixing with each other or a system of liquids mixing. In each case, ΔS would have a positive value once the solution was formed.

Free Energy

Processes in nature are driven in two directions: toward lowest enthalpy and toward highest entropy. When these two oppose each other, the dominant factor determines the direction of change. To predict which factor will dominate for a given system, a function has been defined to relate the enthalpy and entropy factors at a given temperature. *This combined enthalpy-entropy function is called the* **free energy,** *G, of the system.* This function simultaneously assesses both the enthalpy-change and entropy-change tendencies. Natural processes proceed in the direction that lowers the free energy of a system.

Only the *change* in free energy can be measured. The change in free energy can be defined in terms of the changes in enthalpy and entropy. *At a constant pressure and temperature, the* **free-energy change,** *ΔG, of a system is defined as the difference between the change in enthalpy, ΔH, and the product of the Kelvin temperature and the entropy change, which is defined as $T\Delta S$.*

$$\Delta G^0 = \Delta H^0 - T\Delta S^0$$

Note that this expression is for substances in their standard states. The product $T\Delta S$ and the quantities ΔG and ΔH have the same units, usually kJ/mol. The units of ΔS for use in this equation are usually kJ/(mol·K).

Each of the variables in the free-energy equation can have positive or negative values. This leads to four possible combinations of terms.

Table 17-2 (page 529) shows us that if ΔH is negative and ΔS is positive, then both terms on the right in the free energy equation are negative. Both factors contribute to the process being spontaneous.

Therefore, ΔG will always be negative, and the reaction is definitely spontaneous. On the other hand, if ΔH is positive (endothermic process) and ΔS is negative (decrease in randomness), then the reaction as written will definitely not occur. When the enthalpy and entropy changes are operating in different directions, sometimes one will predominate and sometimes the other will predominate. There are cases in which the enthalpy change is negative and the entropy change is negative. The enthalpy factor leads to a spontaneous process, but the negative entropy change opposes this. This is true in the following reaction. (The entropy decreases because there is a decrease in moles of gas.)

$$C_2H_4(g) + H_2(g) \longrightarrow C_2H_6(g)$$

There is a fairly large decrease in entropy, $\Delta S^0 = -0.1207$ kJ/(mol·K). However, the reaction is strongly exothermic, with a $\Delta H^0 = -136.9$ kJ/mol. The reaction proceeds because the enthalpy term predominates.

$$\Delta G^0 = \Delta H^0 - T\Delta S^0 = -136.9 \text{ kJ/mol} - 298 \text{ K}[-0.1207 \text{ kJ/(mol·K)}]$$
$$= -101.1 \text{ kJ/mol}$$

We can contrast this with the common commercial process for the manufacture of syngas, a mixture of CO and H_2. (This gas mixture is the starting point for the synthesis of a number of large-volume commercial chemicals, such as methanol, CH_3OH.)

$$CH_4(g) + H_2O(g) \longrightarrow CO(g) + 3H_2(g)$$

This reaction is endothermic, with $\Delta H^0 = +206.1$ kJ/mol and $\Delta S^0 = +0.215$ kJ/(mol·K), at standard conditions. The resulting ΔG is positive at room temperature. This tells us that the reaction will not occur at room temperature even though the entropy change is favorable.

$$\Delta G^0 = \Delta H^0 - T\Delta S^0 = +206.1 \text{ kJ/mol} - 298 \text{ K}[+0.215 \text{ kJ/(mol·K)}]$$
$$= +142.0 \text{ kJ/mol}$$

TABLE 17-2 Relating Enthalpy, Entropy, and Free Energy Changes to Reaction Occurrence

ΔH	ΔS	ΔG
− value (exothermic)	+ value (disordering)	always negative
− value (exothermic)	− value (ordering)	negative at *lower* temperatures
+ value (endothermic)	+ value (disordering)	negative at *higher* temperatures
+ value (endothermic)	− value (ordering)	never negative

Application

Scientists have long studied the use of syngas (or synthesis gas) as a substitute for petroleum and natural gas because it can be made from coal, which is far more abundant than is either crude oil or natural gas. The practical problem thus far is that syngas has only about a third of the heat value of either natural product.

TABLE STRATEGY

Table 17-2 Select simple values for ΔH, T, and ΔS to illustrate why ΔG is always negative, never negative, or either positive or negative, depending on the temperature.

Additional Example Problems

Predict whether the value of ΔS for each of the following reactions will be greater than, less than, or equal to zero.

1. $3H_2(g) + N_2(g) \longrightarrow 2NH_3(g)$

Ans. $\Delta S < 0$

2. $2Mg(s) + O_2(g) \longrightarrow 2MgO(s)$

Ans. $\Delta S < 0$

3. $C_6H_{12}O_6(s) + 6O_2(g) \longrightarrow 6CO_2(g) + 6H_2O(g)$

Ans. $\Delta S > 0$

4. $KNO_3(s) \longrightarrow K^+(aq) + NO_3^-(aq)$

Ans. $\Delta S > 0$

ADDITIONAL SAMPLE PROBLEM

17-4 Calculate the value of ΔG^0 for the reaction below, given the values of ΔH^0 and ΔS^0. Will the reaction be spontaneous at 298 K?

$$Cu_2S(s) + S(s) \longrightarrow 2CuS(s)$$

$\Delta H^0 = -26.7$ kJ/mol
$\Delta S^0 = -19.7$ J/(mol•K)

Ans. $\Delta G^0 = -20.8$ kJ/mol; yes

SECTION REVIEW

1. a large negative change

2. Entropy is a measure of disorder. An increase in entropy favors a spontaneous reaction.

3. Answers may include dissolving a solid, changing state from solid to liquid or gas or from liquid to gas, and increasing the number of particles during the course of a reaction.

4. Free energy is the function that assesses both the enthalpy-change and entropy-change tendencies. It equals the difference between the change in enthalpy and the product of the Kelvin temperature multiplied by the change in entropy.

5. To be spontaneous, the free energy of a reaction must decrease.

6. One mole of solid is converted into two moles of gas.

7. It will decrease.

8. a. +   **b.** −

SAMPLE PROBLEM 17-4

For the reaction $NH_4Cl(s) \longrightarrow NH_3(g) + HCl(g)$, at 298.15 K, $\Delta H^0 = 176$ kJ/mol and $\Delta S^0 = 0.285$ kJ/(mol•K). Calculate ΔG^0, and tell whether this reaction can proceed in the forward direction at 298.15 K.

SOLUTION

1 ANALYZE

Given: $\Delta H^0 = 176$ kJ/mol at 298.15 K
$\Delta S^0 = 0.285$ kJ/(mol•K) at 298.15 K
Unknown: ΔG^0 at 298.15 K

2 PLAN

$$\Delta S, \Delta H, T \rightarrow \Delta G$$

The value of ΔG can be calculated according to the following equation.

$$\Delta G^0 = \Delta H^0 - T\Delta S^0$$

3 COMPUTE

$$\Delta G^0 = 176 \text{ kJ/mol} - 298 \text{ K } [0.285 \text{ kJ/(mol•K)}]$$
$$= 176 \text{ kJ/mol} - 84.9 \text{ kJ/mol}$$
$$= 91 \text{ kJ/mol}$$

4 EVALUATE

The answer is reasonably close to an estimated value of 110, calculated as $200 - (300 \times 0.3)$. The positive value of ΔG shows that this reaction does not occur naturally at 298.15 K.

PRACTICE

1. For the vaporization reaction $Br_2(l) \longrightarrow Br_2(g)$, $\Delta H^0 = 31.0$ kJ/mol and $\Delta S^0 = 93.0$ J/(mol•K). At what temperature will this process be spontaneous?

Answer
above 333 K

SECTION REVIEW

1. What kind of enthalpy change favors a spontaneous reaction?

2. What is entropy, and how does it relate to spontaneity of reactions?

3. List several changes that result in an entropy increase.

4. Define *free energy*, and explain how its change is calculated.

5. Explain the relationship between free-energy change and spontaneity of reactions.

6. In the reaction in Sample Problem 17-4, why does the entropy increase?

7. How should increasing temperature affect the value of ΔG for the reaction in Sample Problem 17-4?

8. Predict the sign of ΔS^0 for each of the following reactions:
a. the thermal decomposition of solid calcium carbonate

$$CaCO_3(s) \longrightarrow CaO(s) + CO_2(g)$$

b. the oxidation of SO_2 in air

$$2SO_2(g) + O_2(g) \longrightarrow 2SO_3(g)$$

The Reaction Process

The enthalpy change, entropy change, and free energy of a chemical reaction are independent of the actual route by which a reaction occurs. What happens between the initial and final states of a reaction system is described by the energy pathway that a reaction follows and the changes that take place on the molecular level when substances interact.

Reaction Mechanisms

If you mix aqueous solutions of HCl and NaOH, an extremely rapid neutralization reaction occurs.

$$H_3O^+(aq) + Cl^-(aq) + Na^+(aq) + OH^-(aq) \longrightarrow 2H_2O(l) + Na^+(aq) + Cl^-(aq)$$

The reaction is practically instantaneous; the rate is limited only by the speed with which the H_3O^+ and OH^- ions can diffuse through the water to meet each other. On the other hand, reactions between ions of the same charge and between molecular substances are not instantaneous. Negative ions repel each other, and the electron clouds of molecules repel each other strongly at very short distances. Therefore, only ions or molecules with very high kinetic energy can overcome repulsive forces and get close enough to react. In this section we will limit our discussion to reactions between molecules.

Colorless hydrogen gas consists of pairs of hydrogen atoms bonded together as diatomic molecules, H_2. Violet-colored iodine vapor is also diatomic, consisting of pairs of iodine atoms bonded together as I_2 molecules. A chemical reaction between these two gases at elevated temperatures produces hydrogen iodide, HI, a colorless gas. Hydrogen iodide molecules, in turn, tend to decompose and re-form hydrogen and iodine molecules, producing the violet gas shown in Figure 17-8. The following chemical equations describe these two reactions.

$$H_2(g) + I_2(g) \longrightarrow 2HI(g)$$
$$2HI(g) \longrightarrow H_2(g) + I_2(g)$$

Such equations indicate only which molecular species disappear as a result of the reactions and which species are produced. They do not show the **reaction mechanism,** *the step-by-step sequence of reactions by which the overall chemical change occurs.*

FIGURE 17-8 Clear hydrogen iodide gas, HI, decomposes into clear hydrogen gas and violet iodine gas.

OBJECTIVES

- Explain the concept of reaction mechanism.

- Use the collision theory to interpret chemical reactions.

- Define *activated complex.*

- Relate activation energy to heat of reaction.

Lesson Starter

Use a molecular model kit or gumdrops and toothpicks to illustrate the reaction between H_2 and I_2. Point out that the reaction $H_2 + I_2 \longrightarrow 2HI$ need not occur in a single step. Have students list stepwise reactions that might be possible, such as
(1) $H_2 \longrightarrow 2H$, $2H + I_2 \longrightarrow 2HI$; or
(2) $I_2 \longrightarrow 2I$, $2I + H_2 \longrightarrow 2HI$; or
(3) $I_2 \longrightarrow 2I$, $H_2 + I \longrightarrow HI + H$, $H + I \longrightarrow HI$

✔ Teaching Tip

Some chemical reactions occur in one step. For example, the reaction between CO and NO_2 to form CO_2 and NO is thought to occur in a single collision between molecules.

Class Discussion

Ask students to identify intermediate species in the reaction between H_2 and I_2 illustrated in the Lesson Starter. Most chemical reactions involve two or more steps. Intermediate species are those that are formed in one step of a reaction mechanism and then used as reactants in a later step.

Application

Atmospheric chemists have unraveled the reaction mechanisms by which stratospheric ozone, O_3, is destroyed by chlorofluorocarbons (CFCs) released by human activities. The simplest of those mechanisms is:

(1) $Cl + O_3 \longrightarrow ClO + O_2$

(2) $ClO + O \longrightarrow Cl + O_2$

Notice that CFCs break down to release a free chlorine atom, Cl. The free chlorine atom then causes an ozone molecule to break down. Note that the original chlorine atom is regenerated each time the reaction mechanism occurs, making it available for the destruction of additional ozone molecules. Chemists have learned that even more complex reaction mechanisms may also be involved in the destruction of ozone by CFCs.

Although only the net chemical change is directly observable for most chemical reactions, experiments can often be designed that suggest the probable sequence of steps in a reaction mechanism. Each reaction step is usually a simple process. The equation for each step represents the *actual* atoms, ions, or molecules that participate in that step. Even a reaction that appears from its balanced equation to be a simple process may actually be the result of several simple steps.

For many years, the formation of hydrogen iodide was considered a simple one-step process. It was thought to involve the interaction of two molecules, H_2 and I_2, in the forward reaction and two HI molecules in the reverse reaction. Experiments eventually showed, however, that a direct reaction between H_2 and I_2 does not take place.

Alternative mechanisms for the reaction were proposed based on the experimental results. The steps in each reaction mechanism had to add together to give the overall equation. Note that two of the species in the mechanism steps—I and H_2I—do not appear in the net equation. *Species that appear in some steps but not in the net equation are known as* **intermediates.** (Notice that they cancel each other out in the following mechanisms.) The first possible mechanism has the following two-step pathway.

$$
\begin{aligned}
\textbf{Step 1:} \qquad & I_2 \rightleftharpoons 2\cancel{I} \\
\textbf{Step 2:} \qquad & \underline{2\cancel{I} + H_2 \rightleftharpoons 2HI} \\
& I_2 + H_2 \rightleftharpoons 2HI
\end{aligned}
$$

The second possible mechanism has a three-step pathway.

$$
\begin{aligned}
\textbf{Step 1:} \qquad & I_2 \rightleftharpoons 2\cancel{I} \\
\textbf{Step 2:} \qquad & \cancel{I} + H_2 \rightleftharpoons \cancel{H_2I} \\
\textbf{Step 3:} \qquad & \underline{\cancel{H_2I} + \cancel{I} \rightleftharpoons 2HI} \\
& I_2 + H_2 \rightleftharpoons 2HI
\end{aligned}
$$

The reaction between hydrogen gas and iodine vapor to produce hydrogen iodide gas is an example of a **homogeneous reaction,** *a reaction whose reactants and products exist in a single phase*—in this case, the gas phase. This reaction system is also an example of a homogeneous chemical system because all reactants and products in all intermediate steps are in the same phase.

Collision Theory

In order for reactions to occur between substances, their particles (molecules, atoms, or ions) must collide. Furthermore, these collisions must result in interactions. *The set of assumptions regarding collisions and reactions is known as* **collision theory.** Chemists use this theory to interpret many of their observations about chemical reactions.

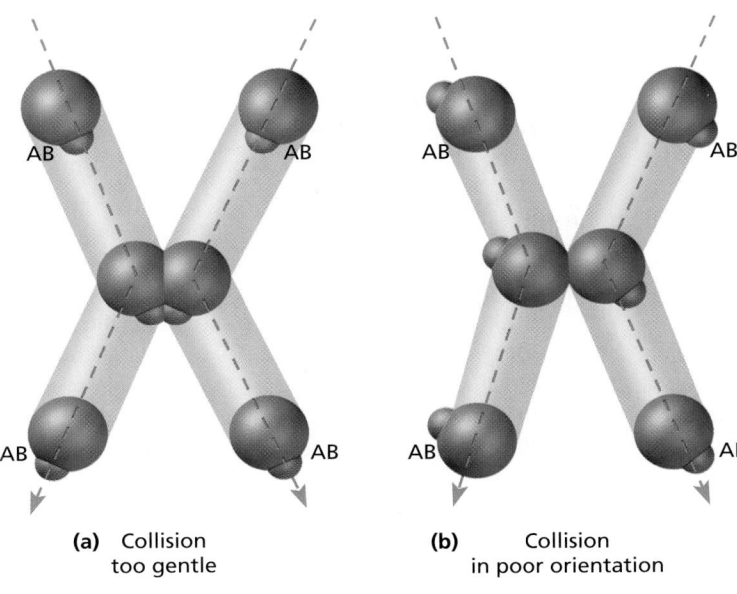

(a) Collision too gentle

(b) Collision in poor orientation

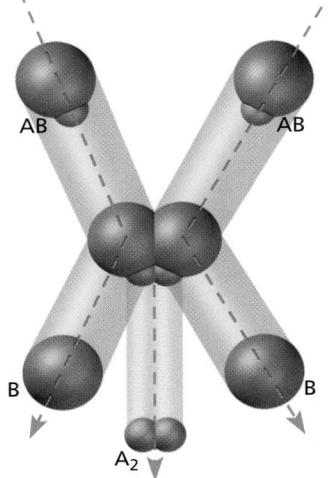

(c) Effective collision, correct orientation and energy

FIGURE 17-9 Three possible collision patterns for AB molecules are shown. Not every collision produces a chemical reaction.

Consider what might happen on a molecular scale in one step of a homogeneous reaction system. We will analyze a proposed first step in a hypothetical decomposition reaction.

$$AB + AB \rightleftharpoons A_2 + 2B$$

According to the collision theory, the two AB molecules must collide in order to react. Furthermore, they must collide while favorably oriented and with enough energy to merge the valence electrons and disrupt the bonds of the molecules. If they do so, a reshuffling of bonds leads to the formation of the products, one A_2 molecule and two B atoms. An effective collision is modeled in Figure 17-9(c).

If a collision is too gentle, the two molecules simply rebound from each other unchanged. This effect is illustrated in Figure 17-9(a). Similarly, a collision in which the reactant molecules are poorly oriented has little effect. The colliding molecules rebound without reacting. A poorly oriented collision is shown in Figure 17-9(b).

Thus, collision theory provides two reasons why a collision between reactant molecules may fail to produce a new chemical species: the collision is not energetic enough to supply the required energy, or the colliding molecules are not oriented in a way that enables them to react with each other.

Activation Energy

Consider the reaction for the formation of water from the diatomic gases oxygen and hydrogen according to the following equation.

$$2H_2(g) + O_2(g) \longrightarrow 2H_2O(l)$$

DEMONSTRATION
Using models from a molecular model kit or gumdrops and toothpicks, show students a variety of orientations in which two HI molecules could collide with each other. Have students predict and explain why some orientations would be effective and others would not.

✔ **Teaching Tip**

The kinetic energy of colliding particles can be converted into vibrational energy of the electrons that make up chemical bonds. The bonds can then rupture, making possible the formation of new bonds.

📖 **Reading Skill-Builder**

DISCUSSION Have students read pp. 533–535. Lead a discussion of the important features of the graphs shown in Figures 17-10 and 17-11. Highlight these features on an overhead transparency as you discuss them and students take notes. Then have student pairs work through the sample problem on p. 536, using the notes they took.

Reaction Pathways for Forward and Reverse Reactions

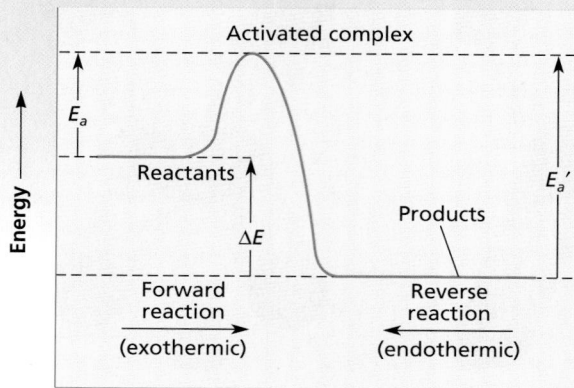

Course of reaction ⟶

FIGURE 17-10 The difference between the activation energies for the reverse and forward reactions of a reversible reaction equals the energy change in the reaction, ΔE. The quantity for ΔE is the same for both directions, but is negative for the exothermic direction and positive for the endothermic direction.

The heat of formation is quite high: $\Delta H_f^0 = -285.8$ kJ/mol at 298.15 K. The free-energy change is also large: $\Delta G^0 = -237.1$ kJ/mol. Why, then, don't oxygen and hydrogen combine spontaneously and immediately to form water when they are mixed at room temperature?

Hydrogen and oxygen gases exist as diatomic molecules. When the molecules approach each other, the electron clouds repel each other and the molecules bounce off and never actually meet. In order for a reaction to occur, the colliding molecules must have enough kinetic energy to actually intermingle the valence electrons. In other words, the bonds of these molecular species must be broken in order for new bonds to be formed between oxygen and hydrogen atoms. Bond breaking is an endothermic process, and bond forming is exothermic. Even though the net process for forming water is exothermic, an initial input of energy is needed to overcome the repulsion forces that occur between reactant molecules when they are brought very close together. This initial energy input activates the reaction.

Once an exothermic reaction is started, the energy released is enough to sustain the reaction by activating other molecules. Thus, the reaction rate keeps increasing. It is limited only by the time required for reactant particles to acquire the energy and make contact. Energy from a flame or a spark, or the energy associated with high temperatures or radiations, may start exothermic reactants along the pathway of reaction. A generalized reaction pathway for an exothermic reaction is shown as the forward reaction in Figure 17-10. The minimum amount of energy needed to activate this reaction is the activation energy represented by E_a. **Activation energy** *is the minimum energy required to transform the reactants into an activated complex.*

The reverse reaction, decomposition of water molecules, is endothermic because the water molecules lie at an energy level that is lower than that of the hydrogen and oxygen molecules. The water molecules require a larger activation energy before they can decompose to reform oxygen and hydrogen. The energy needed to activate an endothermic reaction is greater than that required for the original exothermic change and is represented by E_a' in Figure 17-10. The difference between E_a' and E_a is equal to the energy change in the reaction, ΔE. This energy change has the same numerical value for the forward reaction as it has for the reverse reaction but with the opposite sign.

The Activated Complex

When molecules collide, some of their high kinetic energy is converted into internal potential energy within the colliding molecules. If enough energy is converted, molecules with suitable orientation become activated. New bonds can then form. In this brief interval of bond breakage and bond formation, the collision complex is in a transition state. Some sort of partial bonding exists in this transitional structure. *A transitional structure that results from an effective collision and that persists while old bonds are breaking and new bonds are forming is called an* **activated complex.** The exact structure of this activated complex is not known.

Figure 17-11 graphically breaks down the reaction pathway of the formation of hydrogen iodide gas described on page 532 into three steps. Beginning with the reactants, H_2 and I_2, we see that a certain amount of activation energy, E_{a1}, is needed to form the activated complex that leads to the formation of the intermediates H_2 and $2I$. During the course of the reaction, more activation energy, E_{a2}, is needed to form the activated complex leading to the intermediates H_2I and I. In order to arrive at the final product, $2HI$, another increase in activation energy is necessary, as seen by the highest peak labeled E_{a3}.

An activated complex is formed when an effective collision raises the internal energies of the reactants to their minimum level for reaction, as shown in Figure 17-10. Both forward and reverse reactions go through the same activated complex. A bond that is broken in the activated complex for the forward reaction must be re-formed in the activated complex for the reverse reaction. Observe that an activated complex occurs at a high-energy position along the reaction pathway. In this sense, the activated complex defines the activation energy for the system.

From the kinetic-molecular theory presented in Chapter 10, you know that the speeds and therefore the kinetic energies of the molecules increase as the temperature increases. An increase in speed causes more collisions, which can cause an increase in reactions. However, the increase in reactions depends on more than simply the number of collisions, as Figure 17-9 illustrates. The collisions between molecules must possess sufficient energy to form an activated complex or a reaction will not take place. Raising the temperature of a reaction provides more molecules with this activation energy, causing an increase in reactions.

In its brief existence, the activated complex has partial bonding that is characteristic of both reactant and product. In this state, it may re-form the original bonds and separate back into the reactant particles, or it may form new bonds and separate into product particles. Usually, the formation of products is just as likely as the formation of reactants. Do not confuse the activated complex with the relatively stable intermediate products of different steps of a reaction mechanism. The activated complex, unlike intermediate products, is a very short-lived molecular complex in which bonds are in the process of being broken and formed.

Visual Strategy

FIGURE 17-11 Use models to explore with students possible structures for activated complexes represented in the figure. Show how energy is required to form each of the activated complexes hypothesized.

Class Discussion

Ask students why the exact structure of an activated complex cannot be determined. Have them suggest improvements in technology that might make it possible to make such a determination.

Ask students to compare and contrast the graphs shown in Figures 17-10 and 17-11.

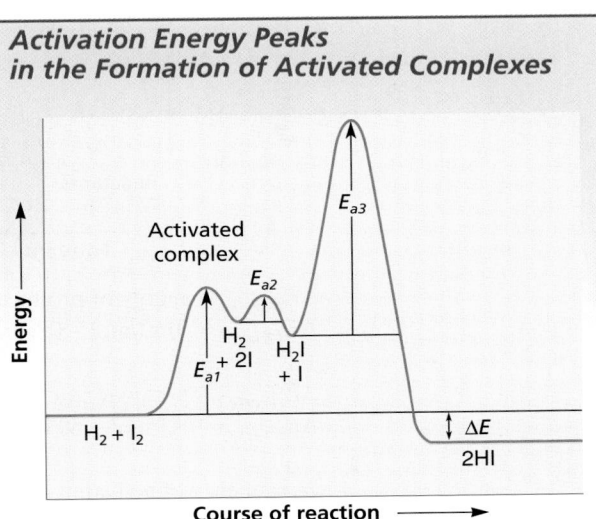

Activation Energy Peaks in the Formation of Activated Complexes

FIGURE 17-11 This energy profile graphically shows the formation of activated complexes during the gas-phase reaction $H_2 + I_2 \longrightarrow 2HI$.

Because a reaction can go in either direction, students may have trouble distinguishing reactants from products. Make sure that students are not confused by the labeling of the diagram in Sample Problem 17-5.

Class Discussion

Ask students to explain the meanings of the expressions E_a, E_a', and ΔE in the diagram for Sample Problem 17-5. Before solving the problem, have them predict whether the reaction shown is endothermic or exothermic.

ADDITIONAL
SAMPLE PROBLEM

17-5 Draw and label the energy diagram for a reaction in which $\Delta E = 30$ kJ/mol, and $E_a = 40$ kJ/mol. Place the reactants at energy level zero. Give values of $\Delta E_{forward}$, $\Delta E_{reverse}$, and E_a'.

Ans.

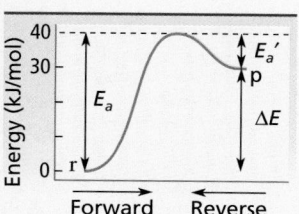

$\Delta E_{forward} = +30$ kJ/mol

$\Delta E_{reverse} = -30$ kJ/mol

$E_a' \quad = 10$ kJ/mol

SAMPLE PROBLEM 17-5

Copy the energy diagram below, and label the reactants, products, ΔE, E_a, and E_a'. Determine the value of $\Delta E_{forward}$, $\Delta E_{reverse}$, E_a, and E_a'.

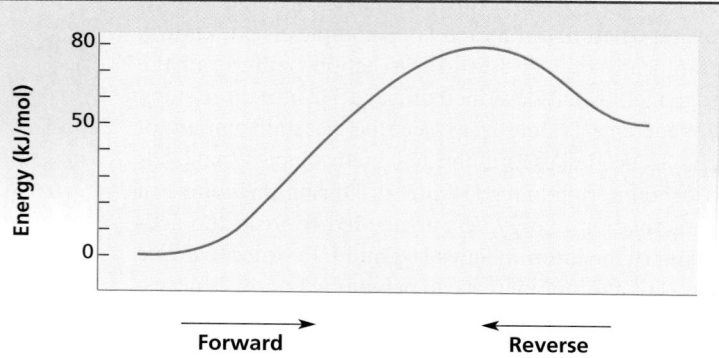

SOLUTION The energy level of reactants is always at the left-hand end of such a curve, and the energy level of products is always at the right-hand end. The energy change in the reaction, ΔE, is the difference between these two energy levels. The activation energy differs in the forward and reverse directions. As E_a, it is the difference between the reactant energy level and the peak in the curve. As E_a', it is the difference between the product energy level and the peak in the curve. It is the minimum energy needed to achieve effective reaction in either direction.

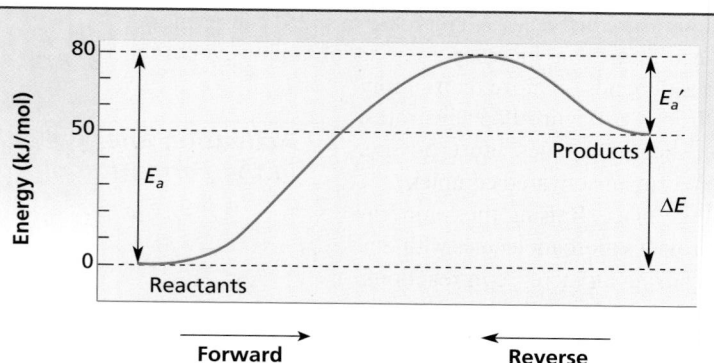

$\Delta E_{forward}$ = energy of products – energy of reactants
$\Delta E_{forward}$ = 50 kJ/mol – 0 kJ/mol = +50 kJ/mol

$\Delta E_{reverse}$ = energy of reactants – energy of products
$\Delta E_{reverse}$ = 0 kJ/mol – 50 kJ/mol = – 50 kJ/mol

E_a = energy of activated complex – energy of reactants
E_a = 80 kJ/mol – 0 kJ/mol = 80 kJ/mol

E_a' = energy of activated complex – energy of products
E_a' = 80 kJ/mol – 50 kJ/mol = 30 kJ/mol

PRACTICE

1. Use the method shown in the sample problem to redraw and label the following energy diagram. Determine the value of $\Delta E_{forward}$, $\Delta E_{reverse}$, E_a, and E_a'.

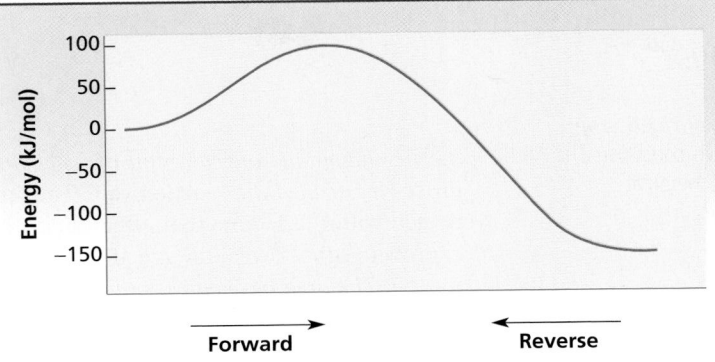

Answer

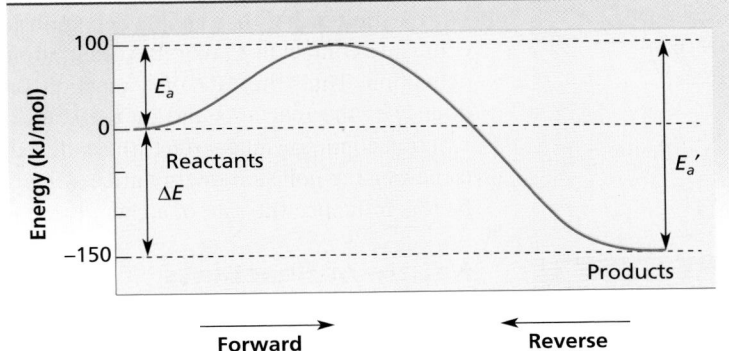

$\Delta E_{forward} = -150$ kJ/mol
$\Delta E_{reverse} = +150$ kJ/mol

$E_a = 100$ kJ/mol
$E_a' = 250$ kJ/mol

SECTION REVIEW

1. What is meant by reaction mechanism?

2. What factors determine whether a molecular collision produces a reaction?

3. What is activation energy?

4. What is an activated complex?

5. How is activation energy related to the energy of reaction?

SECTION REVIEW

1. a sequence of steps by which a reaction occurs

2. A reaction will occur if the species involved in a collision have sufficient energy and if they are oriented correctly toward each other.

3. Activation energy is the minimum energy required to transform reactants into an activated complex.

4. An activated complex is a transitional structure that results from an effective collision and that persists while old bonds are breaking and new bonds are forming.

5. The difference between the activation energies of the forward and reverse reactions is the energy of the reaction.

SECTION 17-4

Reaction Rate

OBJECTIVES

○ Define *chemical kinetics,* and explain the two conditions necessary for chemical reactions to occur.

○ Discuss the five factors that influence reaction rate.

○ Define *catalyst,* and discuss two different types.

○ Explain and write rate laws for chemical reactions.

internet connect

SCiLINKS
NSTA

TOPIC: Factors affecting rates
GO TO: www.scilinks.org
*sci*LINKS CODE: HC2175

The change in concentration of reactants per unit time as a reaction proceeds is called the **reaction rate.** The study of reaction rates is concerned with the factors that affect the rate and with the mathematical expressions that reveal the specific dependencies of the rate on concentration. *The area of chemistry that is concerned with reaction rates and reaction mechanisms is called* **chemical kinetics.**

Rate-Influencing Factors

For reactions other than simple decompositions to occur, particles must come into contact in a favorable orientation and with enough energy for activation. Thus, the rate of a reaction depends on the collision frequency of the reactants and on the collision efficiency. Any change in reaction conditions that affects the collision frequency, the collision efficiency, or the collision energy affects the reaction rate. Five important factors influence the rate of a chemical reaction.

Nature of Reactants

Substances vary greatly in their tendencies to react. For example, hydrogen combines vigorously with chlorine under certain conditions. Under the same conditions, it may react only feebly with nitrogen. Sodium and oxygen combine much more rapidly than iron and oxygen under similar conditions. Bonds are broken and other bonds are formed in reactions. The rate of reaction depends on the particular reactants and bonds involved.

Surface Area

Gaseous mixtures and dissolved particles can mix and collide freely; therefore, reactions involving them can occur rapidly. In heterogeneous reactions, the reaction rate depends on the area of contact of the reaction substances. **Heterogeneous reactions** *involve reactants in two different phases.* These reactions can occur only when the two phases are in contact. Thus, the surface area of a solid reactant is an important factor in determining rate. An increase in surface area increases the rate of heterogeneous reactions.

Solid zinc reacts with aqueous hydrochloric acid to produce zinc chloride and hydrogen gas according to the following equation.

$$Zn(s) + 2HCl(aq) \longrightarrow ZnCl_2(aq) + H_2(g)$$

This reaction occurs at the surface of the zinc solid. A cube of zinc measuring 1 cm on each edge presents only 6 cm² of contact area. The same amount of zinc in the form of a fine powder might provide a contact area thousands of times greater than the original area. Consequently, the reaction rate of the powdered solid is much higher.

A lump of coal burns slowly when kindled in air. The rate of burning can be increased by breaking the lump into smaller pieces, exposing more surface area. If the piece of coal is powdered and then ignited while suspended in air, it burns explosively. This is the cause of some explosions in coal mines.

Temperature

An increase in temperature increases the average kinetic energy of the particles in a substance; this can result in a greater number of effective collisions when the substance is allowed to react with another substance. If the number of effective collisions increases, the reaction rate will increase.

To be effective, the energy of the collisions must be equal to or greater than the activation energy. At higher temperatures, more particles possess enough energy to form the activated complex when collisions occur. Thus, a rise in temperature produces an increase in collision energy as well as in collision frequency.

Decreasing the temperature of a reaction system has the opposite effect. The average kinetic energy of the particles decreases, so they collide less frequently and with less energy, producing fewer effective collisions. Beginning near room temperature, the reaction rates of many common reactions roughly double with each 10 K (10°C) rise in temperature. This rule of thumb should be used with caution, however. The actual rate increase with a given rise in temperature must be determined experimentally.

Concentration

Pure oxygen has five times the concentration of oxygen molecules that air has at the same pressure; consequently, a substance that oxidizes in air oxidizes more vigorously in pure oxygen. For example, in Figure 17-12, the light produced when the lump of charcoal is burned in pure oxygen is much more intense than the light produced when the charcoal lump is heated in air until combustion begins. The oxidation of charcoal is a heterogeneous reaction system in which one reactant is a gas. The reaction rate depends not only on the amount of exposed charcoal surface but also on the concentration of the reacting species, O_2.

In homogeneous reaction systems, reaction rates depend on the concentration of the reactants. Predicting the mathematical relationship between rate and concentration is difficult because most chemical reactions occur in a series of steps, and only one of these steps determines the reaction rate. If the number of effective collisions increases, the rate

(a)

(b)

FIGURE 17-12 Carbon burns faster in pure oxygen (a) than in air (b) because the concentration of the reacting species, O_2, is greater.

DEMONSTRATION
Demonstrate the effect of temperature on the rate at which an effervescent tablet reacts with water. Place 150 mL of water in each of three 250 mL beakers. Use ice water in the first beaker, water at room temperature in the second beaker, and hot water in the third beaker. Record the temperature of the water in each beaker. Simultaneously add a tablet to each beaker and begin timing with a stopwatch. Record the amount of time needed for each tablet to dissolve completely. Construct a graph showing the relationship of temperature and reaction time.

Visual Strategy

FIGURE 17-12(b) Ask students to discuss the role of the nitrogen in air in determining the rate at which carbon burns in the reaction depicted in part (b) of the figure.

 Reading Skill-Builder

PREDICTION GUIDES Write the following factors on the board:
- type of reactants
- type of chemical bond
- surface area
- temperature
- concentration

Have students predict whether each of these factors has an effect on the rate at which a reaction occurs, and if so, how. Have a volunteer write students' predictions on the board. Return to these predictions when students finish the section. Have students cite passages to account for the change or reinforcement of their opinions about the effect of each factor on reaction rate.

540

Visual Strategy

FIGURE 17-13 Explain that the lines connecting the balls in the figure show each ball in the top row colliding with each ball in the bottom row. Thus, as the number of balls in one or both rows increases, the number of possible collisions also increases. If other factors remain constant, the ratio of effective collisions to total collisions remains the same. Therefore, if the total number of collisions increases, the number of effective collisions also increases.

Application

In reality, increasing concentration does not always produce an increase in the reaction rate of a desired reaction. Higher reactant concentrations may make side reactions or competing reactions more of a problem, which may slow down the primary reaction. This problem is one faced by chemical engineers when they scale up a chemical process from a flask in a laboratory to a vat in a chemical plant.

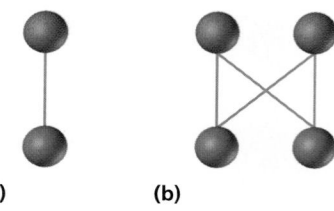 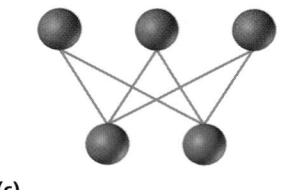 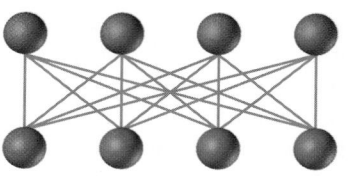

(a)   (b)   (c)   (d)

FIGURE 17-13 The concentration of reacting species affects the number of collisions and therefore the reaction rate.

FIGURE 17-14 The reaction rate of the decomposition of hydrogen peroxide, H_2O_2, can be increased by using a catalyst. The catalyst used here is manganese dioxide, MnO_2, a black solid. A 30% H_2O_2 solution is added dropwise onto the MnO_2 in the beaker and rapidly decomposes to O_2 and H_2O. Both the oxygen and water appear as gases because the high heat of reaction causes the water to vaporize.

increases as well. In general, an increase in rate is expected if the concentration of one or more of the reactants is increased, as depicted by the model in Figure 17-13. In the system with only two molecules, shown in Figure 17-13(a), only one collision can possibly occur. When there are four molecules in the system, as in Figure 17-13(b), there can be four possible collisions. Under constant conditions, as the number of molecules in the system increases, so does the total number of possible collisions between them. Figure 17-13(c) and (d) show a five- and eight-molecule system, allowing six and sixteen possible collisions, respectively. Lowering the concentration should have the opposite effect. The actual effect of concentration changes on reaction rate, however, must be determined experimentally.

Presence of Catalysts

Some chemical reactions proceed quite slowly. Sometimes their reaction rates can be increased dramatically by the presence of a catalyst. *A* **catalyst** *is a substance that changes the rate of a chemical reaction without itself being permanently consumed. The action of a catalyst is called* **catalysis.** The catalysis of the decomposition reaction of hydrogen peroxide by manganese dioxide is shown in Figure 17-14. A catalyst provides an alternative energy pathway or reaction mechanism in which the potential-energy barrier between reactants and products is lowered. The catalyst may be effective in forming an alternative activated complex that requires a lower activation energy—as suggested in the energy profiles of the decomposition of hydrogen peroxide, H_2O_2, shown in Figure 17-15—according to the following equation.

$$2H_2O_2(l) \longrightarrow O_2(g) + 2H_2O(l)$$

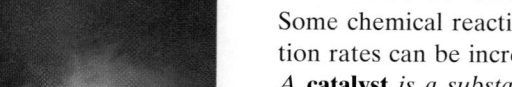

Catalysts do not appear among the final products of reactions they accelerate. They may participate in one step along a reaction pathway and be regenerated in a later step. In large-scale and cost-sensitive reaction systems, catalysts are recovered and reused. *A catalyst that is in the same phase as all the reactants and products in a reaction system is called a* **homogeneous catalyst.** *When its phase is different from that of the reactants, it is called a* **heterogeneous catalyst.** Metals are often used as heterogeneous catalysts. The catalysis of many reactions is promoted by adsorption of reactants on the metal surfaces, which has the effect of increasing the concentration of the reactants.

Comparison of Pathways for the Decomposition of H_2O_2 by Various Catalysts

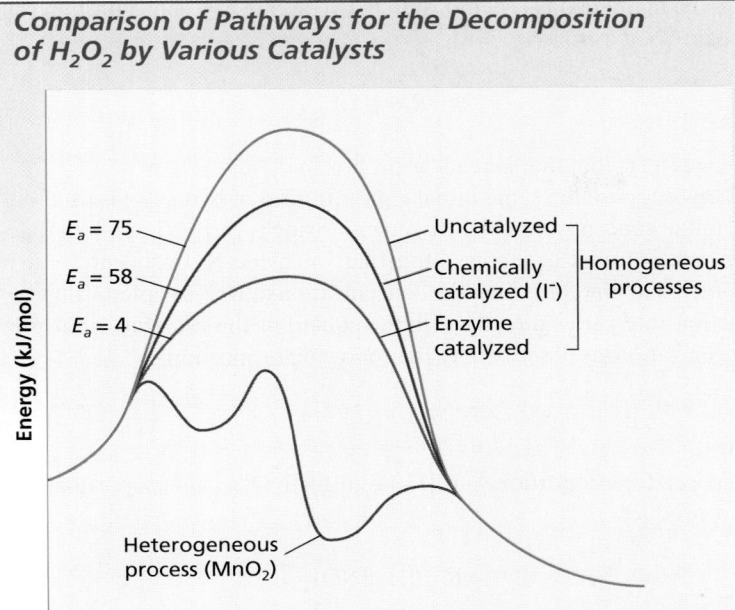

Course of reaction ⟶

Rate Laws for Reactions

The relationship between the rate of a reaction and the concentration of one reactant is determined experimentally by first keeping the concentrations of other reactants and the temperature of the system constant. Then the reaction rate is measured for various concentrations of the reactant in question. A series of such experiments reveals how the concentration of each reactant affects the reaction rate.

Hydrogen gas reacts with nitrogen monoxide gas at constant volume and at an elevated constant temperature, according to the following equation.

$$2H_2(g) + 2NO(g) \longrightarrow N_2(g) + 2H_2O(g)$$

Four moles of reactant gases produce three moles of product gases; thus, the pressure of the system diminishes as the reaction proceeds. The rate of the reaction can, therefore, be determined by measuring the change of pressure in the vessel with time.

Suppose a series of experiments is conducted using the same initial concentration of nitrogen monoxide but different initial concentrations of hydrogen. The initial reaction rate is found to vary directly with the hydrogen concentration: doubling the concentration of H_2 doubles the rate, and tripling the concentration of H_2 triples the rate. If R represents the reaction rate and $[H_2]$ is the concentration of hydrogen in moles per liter, the mathematical relationship between rate and concentration can be expressed as follows.

$$R \propto [H_2]$$

The $\propto$ is a symbol that is read "is proportional to."

Now suppose the same initial concentration of hydrogen is used but the initial concentration of nitrogen monoxide is varied. The initial reaction rate is found to increase fourfold when the NO concentration is doubled and ninefold when the concentration of NO is tripled. Thus, the reaction rate varies directly with the square of the nitrogen monoxide concentration, as described by the following proportion.

$$R \propto [NO]^2$$

Because R is proportional to $[H_2]$ and to $[NO]^2$, it is proportional to their product.

$$R \propto [H_2][NO]^2$$

By introduction of an appropriate proportionality constant, k, the expression becomes an equality.

$$R = k[H_2][NO]^2$$

An equation that relates reaction rate and concentrations of reactants is called the **rate law** *for the reaction.* It is applicable for a specific reaction at a given temperature. A rise in temperature increases the reaction rates of most reactions. The value of k usually increases as the temperature increases, but the relationship between reaction rate and concentration almost always remains unchanged.

Rate Laws and Reaction Pathway

The form of the rate law depends on the reaction mechanism. For a reaction that occurs in a *single step*, the reaction rate of that step is proportional to the product of the reactant concentrations, each of which is raised to its stoichiometric coefficient. For example, suppose one molecule of gas A collides with one molecule of gas B to form two molecules of substance C, according to the following equation.

$$A + B \longrightarrow 2C$$

One particle of each reactant is involved in each collision. Thus, doubling the concentration of either reactant will double the collision frequency. It will also double the reaction rate *for this step*. Therefore, the rate for this step is directly proportional to the concentration of A and B. The rate law for this one-step reaction follows.

$$R = k[A][B]$$

Now suppose the reaction is reversible. In the reverse step, two molecules of C must decompose to form one molecule of A and one of B.

$$2C \longrightarrow A + B$$

Thus, the reaction rate for this reverse step is directly proportional to $[C] \times [C]$. The rate law for the step is as follows.

$$R = k[C]^2$$

The power to which the molar concentration of each reactant is raised in the rate laws above corresponds to the coefficient for the reactant in the balanced chemical equation. Such a relationship holds *only* if the reaction follows a simple one-step path, that is, if the reaction occurs at the molecular level exactly as written in the chemical equation.

   If a chemical reaction proceeds in a sequence of steps, the rate law is determined from the slowest step because it has the lowest rate. *This slowest-rate step is called the* **rate-determining step** *for the chemical reaction.*

   Consider the reaction of nitrogen dioxide and carbon monoxide.

$$NO_2(g) + CO(g) \longrightarrow NO(g) + CO_2(g)$$

The reaction is believed to be a two-step process represented by the following mechanism.

Step 1: $NO_2 + NO_2 \longrightarrow NO_3 + NO$ slow
Step 2: $NO_3 + CO \longrightarrow NO_2 + CO_2$ fast

In the first step, two molecules of NO_2 collide, forming the intermediate species NO_3. This structure then collides with one molecule of CO and reacts quickly to produce one molecule each of NO_2 and CO_2. The first step is the slower of the two and is therefore the rate-determining step. We can write the rate law from this rate-determining step.

$$R = k[NO_2]^2$$

This tells us that two molecules of NO_2 are the reactants in the slower, rate-determining step. CO does not appear in the rate law because it reacts after the rate-determining step, so the reaction rate will not depend on [CO].

   The general form for the rate law is given by the following equation.

$$R = k[A]^n[B]^m \ldots$$

The reaction rate is represented by R, k is the rate constant, and [A] and [B]... represent the molar concentrations of reactants. The n and m are the respective powers to which the concentrations are raised. They must be determined from *experimental data*.

Class Discussion
Rate-determining steps are common in many everyday events. For example, suppose that a series of five individuals are involved in filling an order at a fast-food restaurant. The order can be filled no more quickly than the slowest-moving person in the sequence. Ask students to think of similar examples of rate-determining steps they may be familiar with.

✔ **Teaching Tip**

You cannot tell whether a reaction is a simple one-step reaction or a multi-step reaction simply by looking at the equation for that reaction. Additional information is necessary to make that determination.

Common Misconception
In many reaction mechanisms, the first step is not the slowest one. However, the prediction of an acceptable rate law for such mechanisms is somewhat more complex, and it will not be covered here.

17-7 The rate law of a reaction is found to be $R = k[X]^3$. By what factor does the rate increase if the concentration of X is tripled?

Ans. The rate will increase by a factor of 27.

17-7 The rate of reaction involving two reactants, X and Z, is found to double when the concentration of X is doubled and to quadruple when the concentration of Z is doubled. Write the rate law for this reaction.

Ans. $R = k[X][Z]^2$

17-7 The rate law for a single-step reaction that forms one product, C, is $R = k[A][B]^2$. Write the balanced reaction of A and B to form C.

Ans. $A + 2B \longrightarrow C$

QUICK LAB

Students should prepare a data table to record their observations. The table should reflect a rate-influencing factor for each step of the procedure.

Safety: Students must wear goggles and an apron during the investigation. Keep flammable and combustible materials away from the open flame of the Bunsen burner.

Disposal: Combine all liquids, adjust the pH to approximately 10, and pour them down the drain. Save all metal strips for reuse next time, but if they are too corroded, put them in the trash. Put all other solids in the trash.

SAMPLE PROBLEM 17-6

Nitrogen dioxide and fluorine react in the gas phase according to the following equation.

$$2NO_2(g) + F_2(g) \longrightarrow 2NO_2F(g)$$

A proposed mechanism for this reaction follows.

| Step 1: $NO_2 + F_2 \longrightarrow NO_2F + F$ | slow |
| Step 2: $F + NO_2 \longrightarrow NO_2F$ | fast |

Identify the rate-determining step and write an acceptable rate law.

SOLUTION   If we combine these two steps, the intermediate, F, cancels out and we are left with the original equation. The first step is the slower step, and is considered the rate-determining step. We can write the rate law from this rate-determining step.

$$R = k [NO_2][F_2]$$

SAMPLE PROBLEM 17-7

A reaction involving reactants X and Y was found to occur by a one-step mechanism: $X + 2Y \longrightarrow XY_2$. Write the rate law for this reaction, and then determine the effect of each of the following on the reaction rate:
a. doubling the concentration of X
b. doubling the concentration of Y
c. using one-third the concentration of Y

SOLUTION   Because the equation represents a single-step mechanism, the rate law can be written from the equation (otherwise, it could not be). The rate will vary directly with the concentration of X, which has an implied coefficient of 1 in the equation, and will vary directly with the square of the concentration of Y, which has the coefficient of 2: $R = k[X][Y]^2$.

a. Doubling the concentration of X will double the rate ($R = k[2X][Y]^2$).
b. Doubling the concentration of Y will increase the rate fourfold ($R = k[X][2Y]^2$).
c. Using one-third the concentration of Y will reduce the rate to one-ninth of its original value ($R = k[X][\frac{1}{3}Y]^2$).

PRACTICE

1. The rate of a reaction involving L, M, and N is found to double if the concentration of L is doubled, to increase eightfold if the concentration of M is doubled, and to double if the concentration of N is doubled. Write the rate law for this reaction.

   Answer
   $R = k[L][M]^3[N]$

2. At temperatures below 498 K, the following reaction takes place.

   $$NO_2(g) + CO(g) \longrightarrow CO_2(g) + NO(g)$$

   Doubling the concentration of NO_2 quadruples the rate of CO_2 being formed if the CO concentration is held constant. However, doubling the concentration of CO has no effect on the rate of CO_2 formation. Write a rate-law expression for this reaction.

   Answer
   $R = k[NO_2]^2$

Quick LAB

Wear Safety Goggles and an Apron.

Factors Influencing Reaction Rate

Materials

- Bunsen burner
- paper ash
- copper foil strip
- graduated cylinder, 10 mL
- magnesium ribbon
- matches
- paper clip
- sandpaper
- steel wool
- 2 sugar cubes
- white vinegar
- zinc strip
- 6 test tubes, 16 × 150 mm
- tongs

Question

How do the type of reactants, surface area of reactants, concentration of reactants, and catalysts affect the rates of chemical reactions?

Procedure

Remove all combustible material from the work area. Wear safety goggles and an apron. Record all your results in a data table.

1. Add 10 mL of vinegar to each of three test tubes. To one test tube, add a 3 cm piece of magnesium ribbon; to a second, add a 3 cm zinc strip; and to a third, add a 3 cm copper strip. (All metals should be the same width.) If necessary, sandpaper the metals until they are shiny.

2. Using tongs, hold a paper clip in the hottest part of the burner flame for 30 s. Repeat with a ball of steel wool 2 cm in diameter.

3. To one test tube, add 10 mL of vinegar; to a second, add 5 mL of vinegar plus 5 mL of water; and to a third, add 2.5 mL of vinegar plus 7.5 mL of water. To each of the three test tubes, add a 3 cm piece of magnesium ribbon.

4. Using tongs, hold a sugar cube and try to ignite it with a match. Then try to ignite it in a burner flame. Rub paper ash on a second cube, and try to ignite it with a match.

Discussion

1. What are the rate-influencing factors in each step of the procedure?

2. What were the results from each step of the procedure? How do you interpret each result?

Discussion

1. 1: the nature of the materials
   2: surface area of the metal
   3: concentration of the reactant
   4: the presence of a catalyst

2. 1: Mg reacts faster than Zn, which reacts faster than Cu; nature of reactants affects reaction rate
   2: steel wool reacts faster with oxygen than a paper clip does; increasing surface area increases rate of reaction
   3: Mg reacts faster with more concentrated vinegar; increased concentration increases reaction rate
   4: sugar reacts faster when covered with ash than without; catalysts increase rate of reaction

SECTION REVIEW

1. reaction rates and mechanisms

2. nature of reactants, surface area, concentration, temperature, presence of a catalyst

3. It increases the rate of a chemical reaction without itself being permanently consumed. It makes possible an alternative mechanism in which the activation energy is lower than it is without the catalyst.

4. It is an equation that relates reaction rate to concentrations of reactants. It can be written from a chemical equation if it is a single-step reaction. In a multistep reaction, the rate law must be obtained experimentally.

SECTION REVIEW

1. What is studied in the branch of chemistry that is known as chemical kinetics?

2. List the five important factors that influence the rate of chemical reactions.

3. What is a catalyst? Explain the effect of a catalyst on the rate of chemical reactions. How does a catalyst influence the activation energy required by a particular reaction?

4. What is meant by a rate law for a chemical reaction? Explain the conditions under which a rate law can be written from a chemical equation. When can a rate law not be written from a single step?

REVIEW ANSWERS

1. a. The energy is higher.
b. The energy is lower.

2. a. ΔH is the quantity of energy released or absorbed during a chemical reaction. ΔH_f is the energy released or absorbed when one mole of a compound is formed from its uncombined elements at room temperature. ΔH_c is the energy released by the complete combustion of one mole of a substance.
b. The heat of combustion is defined in terms of one mole of reactant. Heat of formation is defined in terms of one mole of product.

3. $\Delta H^0 =$ sum of ΔH_f^0 of products $-$ sum of ΔH_f^0 of reactants

4. the change in the number of bonds breaking and forming and the strengths of these bonds as the reactants form products

5. decrease; $-$

6. It causes an increase in entropy.

7. a negative ΔH and a positive ΔS

8. At low temperatures, $T\Delta S$ is generally small in comparison with ΔH, so the sign of ΔH determines the sign of ΔG. At high temperatures, the $T\Delta S$ factor may be large enough to exceed the ΔH value and thereby allow the sign and magnitude of ΔS to dictate the spontaneity of the reaction.

9. a. It is the set of assumptions regarding collisions and reactions between molecules.
b. It must be energetic enough to supply the necessary activation energy, and the colliding molecules must be oriented in a way that favors their efficient interaction.

10. a. The reactant particles must undergo an effective collision that raises the internal energies

CHAPTER SUMMARY

17-1
• Thermochemistry is the study of the changes in energy that accompany chemical reactions and physical changes.
• A thermochemical equation is an equation that includes the quantity of energy released or absorbed as heat during the reaction as written.
• The heat of reaction is the quantity of energy released or absorbed as heat during a chemical reaction.
• An enthalpy change is the amount of energy absorbed or lost as heat by a system in a process carried out at constant pressure.
• The heat of reaction is negative for exothermic reactions and positive for endothermic reactions.

• Compounds with highly negative heats of formation tend to be stable; compounds with highly positive or only slightly negative heats of formation tend to be unstable.
• The standard molar heat of formation is the energy absorbed or released as heat in the formation of one mole of a compound from its elements in their standard states at 25°C.
• The energy released as heat in a combustion reaction is called the heat of combustion.
• Heats of reaction can be calculated by using heats of formation of reactants and products.

Vocabulary

calorimeter (511)	heat of combustion (519)	joule (511)	temperature (511)
enthalpy change (516)	heat of reaction (514)	molar heat of formation (517)	thermochemical equation (515)
heat (512)	Hess's law (519)	specific heat (512)	thermochemistry (511)

17-2
• The tendency throughout nature is for a reaction to proceed in the direction that leads to a lower energy state.
• Entropy is a measure of the disorder of a system.
• Free-energy change combines the effects of entropy and enthalpy changes and temperature

of a system, and it is a measure of the overall tendency toward natural change.
• A reaction can occur spontaneously if it is accompanied by a decrease in free energy. It cannot occur spontaneously if there is an increase in free energy.

Vocabulary

entropy (527)	free energy (528)	free-energy change (528)

17-3
• The step-by-step process by which an overall chemical reaction occurs is called the reaction mechanism.
• In order for chemical reactions to occur, the particles of the reactants must collide.
• Activation energy is needed to merge valence electrons and loosen bonds sufficiently for molecules to react.

• An activated complex is formed when an effective collision between molecules of reactants raises the internal energy to the minimum level necessary for a reaction to occur.

Vocabulary

activated complex (535)	collision theory (532)	homogeneous reaction (532)	intermediates (532)
activation energy (534)			reaction mechanism (531)

CHAPTER SUMMARY (continued)

17-4 • The rate of reaction is influenced by the following factors: nature of reactants, surface area, temperature, concentration of reactants, and the presence of catalysts and inhibitors.

• The rates at which chemical reactions occur can sometimes be experimentally measured and expressed in terms of mathematical equations called rate laws.

Vocabulary

catalysis (540)
catalyst (540)
chemical kinetics (538)
heterogeneous catalyst (540)
heterogeneous reactions (538)
homogeneous catalyst (540)
rate-determining step (543)
rate law (542)
reaction rate (538)

REVIEWING CONCEPTS

1. How does the energy of the products of a reaction system compare with the energy of the reactants when the reaction is
   a. endothermic?
   b. exothermic? (17-1)

2. a. Distinguish between heats of reaction, formation, and combustion.
   b. On what basis are heats of formation and combustion defined? (17-1)

3. Write the equation that can be used to calculate the heat of reaction from heats of formation. (17-1)

4. What factors affect the value of ΔH in a reaction system? (17-1)

5. Would entropy increase or decrease for phase changes in which the reactant is a gas or liquid and the product is a solid? What sign would the entropy change have? (17-2)

6. How does an increase in temperature affect the entropy of a system? (17-2)

7. What combination of ΔH and ΔS values always produces a negative free-energy change? (17-2)

8. Explain the relationship between temperature and the tendency for reactions to occur spontaneously. (17-2)

9. a. What is the collision theory?
   b. According to this theory, what two conditions must be met in order for a collision between reactant molecules to be effective in producing new chemical species? (17-3)

10. a. What condition must be met in order for an activated complex to result from the collision of reactant particles?
    b. Where, in terms of energy, does the activated complex occur along a typical reaction pathway? (17-3)

11. In a reversible reaction, how does the activation energy required for the exothermic change compare with the activation energy required for the endothermic change? (17-3)

12. Would you expect the following equation to represent the mechanism by which ethane (C_2H_6) burns? Why or why not? (17-3)
    $$C_2H_6(g) + \tfrac{7}{2}O_2(g) \longrightarrow 2CO_2(g) + 3H_2O(g)$$

13. The decomposition of nitrogen dioxide $2NO_2 \longrightarrow 2NO + O_2$ occurs in a two-step sequence at elevated temperatures. The first step is $NO_2 \longrightarrow NO + O$. Predict a possible second step that, when combined with the first step, gives the complete reaction. (17-3)

14. What is meant by the rate-determining step for a chemical reaction? (17-4)

15. Write the general equation for the rate law, and label the various factors. (17-4)

of the reactants to their minimum level for reaction.
b. at the maximum-energy position

11. The activation energy required for the endothermic change is greater by the amount of heat of reaction of the system.

12. No; most reactions take place in a sequence of step-wise processes.

13. $NO_2 + O \longrightarrow NO + O_2$

14. It is the slowest step in a mechanism that determines the overall reaction rate.

15. $R = k[A]^n[B]^m \dots$, where R is the reaction rate; k is the rate constant; [A] and [B] ... are the molar concentrations of the reactants; and n and m are the respective powers to which the concentration is raised.

16. 3.6×10^3 J

17. 563 K

18. a. −393.51 kJ/mol; exothermic
    b. −890.31 kJ/mol; exothermic
    c. +176 kJ/mol; endothermic
    d. −44.02 kJ/mol; exothermic

19. a. $H_2(g) + \tfrac{1}{2}O_2(g) \longrightarrow H_2O(l) + 285.83$ kJ; exothermic
    b. $2Mg(s) + O_2(g) \longrightarrow 2MgO(s) + 1200$ kJ; exothermic
    c. $I_2(s) + 62.4$ kJ $\longrightarrow I_2(g)$; endothermic
    d. $3CO(g) + Fe_2O_3(s) \longrightarrow 2Fe(s) + 3CO_2(g) + 24.7$ kJ; exothermic

20. a. $Ca(s) + Cl_2(g) \longrightarrow CaCl_2(g) + 795.0$ kJ
    $\Delta H_{reverse} = +795.0$ kJ/mol
    b. $2C(s) + H_2(g) + 226.73$ kJ $\longrightarrow C_2H_2(g)$
    $\Delta H_{reverse} = -226.73$ kJ/mol
    c. $S(s) + O_2(g) \longrightarrow SO_2(g) + 296.83$ kJ
    $\Delta H_{reverse} = +296.83$ kJ/mol

21. a. +177.9 kJ/mol
    b. +109.3 kJ/mol
    c. −24.7 kJ/mol

22. a. −1559.83 kJ/mol
   b. −3267.05 kJ/mol

23. −1367.5 kJ/mol

24. a. 115 kJ/mol; not spontaneous
   b. −135 kJ/mol; spontaneous
   c. −623 kJ/mol; spontaneous

25. −394.40 kJ/mol; spontaneous

26. a.

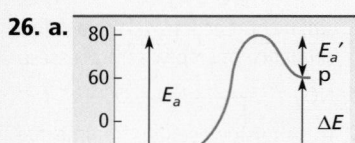

$\Delta E_{forward} = +80$ kJ/mol
$\Delta E_{reverse} = -80$ kJ/mol
$E_a = 100$ kJ/mol
$E_a' = 20$ kJ/mol

b.

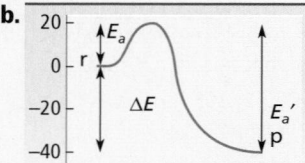

$\Delta E_{forward} = -40$ kJ/mol
$\Delta E_{reverse} = +40$ kJ/mol
$E_a = 20$ kJ/mol
$E_a' = 60$ kJ/mol

c.

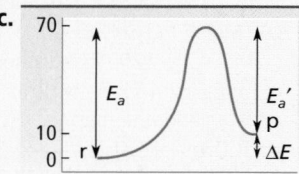

$\Delta E_{forward} = +10$ kJ/mol
$\Delta E_{reverse} = -10$ kJ/mol
$E_a = 70$ kJ/mol
$E_a' = 60$ kJ/mol

27 a.

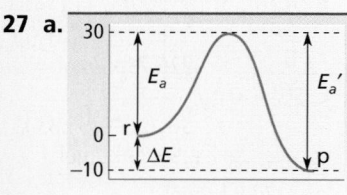

$\Delta E_{reverse} = 10$ kJ/mol
$E_a = 30$ kJ/mol

PROBLEMS

Specific Heat

16. How much heat energy is needed to raise the temperature of a 55 g sample of aluminum from 22.4°C to 94.6°C? Refer to Table 17-1 for the specific heat of aluminum. (Hint: See Sample Problem 17-1.)

17. 3.5 kJ of heat are added to a 28.2 g sample of iron at 20°C. What is the final temperature of the iron in kelvins? Refer to Table 17-1 for the specific heat of iron.

Reaction Heat

18. For each equation listed below, determine the ΔH and type of reaction (endothermic or exothermic).

  a. $C(s) + O_2(g) \longrightarrow CO_2(g) + 393.51$ kJ
  b. $CH_4(g) + 2O_2(g) \longrightarrow$
          $CO_2(g) + 2H_2O(l) + 890.31$ kJ
  c. $CaCO_3(s) + 176$ kJ $\longrightarrow CaO(s) + CO_2(g)$
  d. $H_2O(g) \longrightarrow H_2O(l) + 44.02$ kJ

19. Rewrite each equation below with the ΔH value included with either the reactants or the products, and identify the reaction as endothermic or exothermic.

  a. $H_2(g) + \frac{1}{2}O_2(g) \longrightarrow H_2O(l)$;
    $\Delta H^0 = -285.83$ kJ/mol
  b. $2Mg(s) + O_2(g) \longrightarrow 2MgO(s)$;
    $\Delta H^0 = -1200$ kJ/mol
  c. $I_2(s) \longrightarrow I_2(g)$; $\Delta H^0 = +62.4$ kJ/mol
  d. $3CO(g) + Fe_2O_3(s) \longrightarrow 2Fe(s) + 3CO_2(g)$;
    $\Delta H^0 = -24.7$ kJ/mol

20. Use Appendix Table A-14 to write the reaction illustrating the formation of each of the following compounds from its elements. Write the ΔH as part of each equation, and indicate the ΔH for the reverse reaction.

  a. $CaCl_2(s)$
  b. $C_2H_2(g)$ (ethyne or acetylene)
  c. $SO_2(g)$

21. Use heat-of-formation data given in Appendix Table A-14 (page 902) to calculate the heat of reaction for each of the following. Solve each by combining the known thermochemical equations. Verify each result by using the general equation for finding heats of reaction from heats of formation. (Hint: See Sample Problem 17-2.)

  a. $CaCO_3(s) \longrightarrow CaO(s) + CO_2(g)$
  b. $Ca(OH)_2(s) \longrightarrow CaO(s) + H_2O(g)$
  c. $Fe_2O_3(s) + 3CO(g) \longrightarrow 2Fe(s) + 3CO_2(g)$

22. Calculate the standard heats of reaction for combustion reactions in which ethane, C_2H_6, and benzene, C_6H_6, are the respective reactants and $CO_2(g)$ and $H_2O(l)$ are the products in each. Solve each by combining the known thermochemical equations using the ΔH_f^0 values in Appendix Table A-14 (page 902). Verify the result by using the general equation for finding heats of reaction from heats of formation.

  a. $C_2H_6(g) + O_2(g) \longrightarrow$
  b. $C_6H_6(l) + O_2(g) \longrightarrow$

23. The heat of formation of ethanol, C_2H_5OH, is −277.0 kJ/mol at 298.15 K. Calculate the heat of combustion of one mole of ethanol, assuming that the products are $CO_2(g)$ and $H_2O(l)$. (Hint: See Sample Problem 17-3.)

Entropy and Free Energy

24. Based on the following values, compute ΔG values for each reaction and predict whether the reaction will occur spontaneously. (Hint: See Sample Problem 17-4.)

  a. $\Delta H = +125 \dfrac{kJ}{mol}$, $T = 293$ K,
    $\Delta S = 0.0350 \dfrac{kJ}{(mol \cdot K)}$

  b. $\Delta H = -85.2 \dfrac{kJ}{mol}$, $T = 127°C$,
    $\Delta S = 0.125 \dfrac{kJ}{(mol \cdot K)}$

  c. $\Delta H = -275 \dfrac{kJ}{mol}$, $T = 773$ K,
    $\Delta S = 0.450 \dfrac{kJ}{(mol \cdot K)}$

25. The ΔS^0 for the reaction shown, at 298.15 K, is 0.003 00 kJ/(mol·K). Calculate the ΔG^0 for this reaction, and determine whether it will occur spontaneously at 298.15 K.

  $C(s) + O_2(g) \longrightarrow CO_2(g) + 393.51$ kJ

Reaction Diagrams

26. For each of the energy diagrams provided below, label the reactants, products, ΔE, E_a, and E_a'. Also determine the values of ΔE for the forward and reverse reactions, and the values of E_a and E_a'. (Hint: See Sample Problem 17-5.)

a.

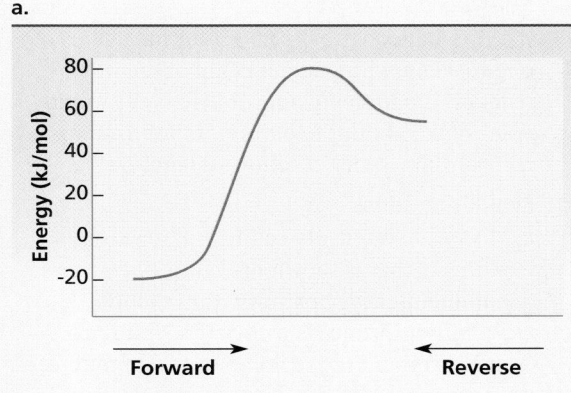

Forward   Reverse

b.

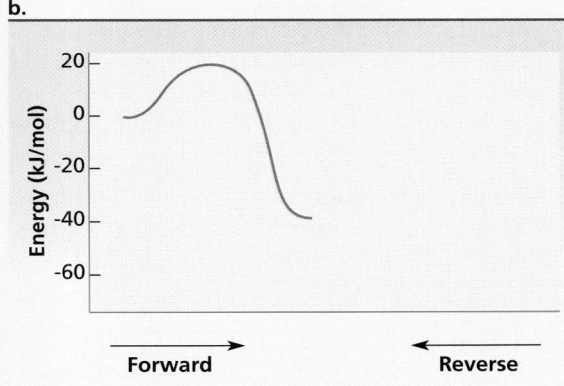

Forward   Reverse

c.

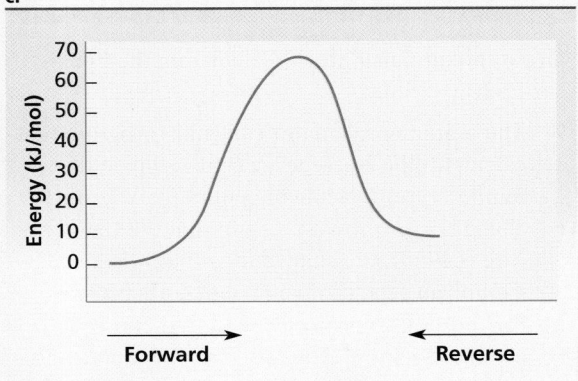

Forward   Reverse

27. Draw and label energy diagrams depicting the following reactions, and determine all remaining values. Place the reactants at energy level zero.
    a. $\Delta E_{forward} = -10$ kJ/mol $E_a' = 40$ kJ/mol
    b. $\Delta E_{forward} = -95$ kJ/mol $E_a = 20$ kJ/mol
    c. $\Delta E_{reverse} = -40$ kJ/mol $E_a' = 30$ kJ/mol

Rate Law

28. Determine the overall balanced equation for a reaction having the following proposed mechanism and write an acceptable rate law. (Hint: See Sample Problem 17-6.)
    Step 1: $B_2 + B_2 \longrightarrow E_3 + D$ slow
    Step 2: $E_3 + A \longrightarrow B_2 + C_2$ fast

29. A reaction involving reactants A and B is found to occur in the one-step mechanism: $2A + B \longrightarrow A_2B$. Write the rate law for this reaction, and predict the effect of doubling the concentration of either reactant on the overall reaction rate. (Hint: See Sample Problem 17-7.)

30. A chemical reaction is expressed by the balanced chemical equation $A + 2B \longrightarrow C$. Using the data below, answer the following:
    a. Determine the rate law for the reaction.
    b. Calculate the value of the specific rate constant.
    c. If the initial concentrations of both A and B are 0.30 M, at what initial rate is C formed?

Three reaction-rate experiments yield the following data.

Experiment number	Initial [A]	Initial [B]	Initial rate of formation of C
1	0.20 M	0.20 M	2.0×10^{-4} M/min
2	0.20 M	0.40 M	8.0×10^{-4} M/min
3	0.40 M	0.40 M	1.6×10^{-3} M/min

MIXED REVIEW

31. When graphite reacts with hydrogen at 300 K, ΔH is -74.8 kJ/mol and ΔS is -0.0809 kJ/(mol·K). Will this reaction occur spontaneously?

32. How might you change reaction conditions to induce an endothermic reaction that does not occur naturally?

b.

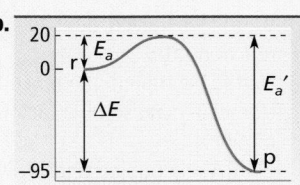

$\Delta E_{reverse} = 95$ kJ/mol
$E_a' = 115$ kJ/mol

c.

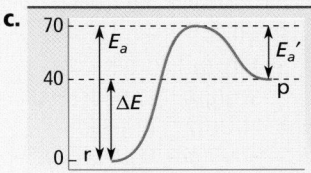

$\Delta E_{forward} = 40$ kJ/mol
$E_a = 70$ kJ/mol

28. $A + B_2 \longrightarrow C_2 + D$; $R = k\,[B_2]^2$

29. $R = k\,[A]^2[B]$; doubling [A] increases the rate by a factor of 4; doubling [B] doubles the rate of the reaction.

30. a. $R = k\,[A][B]^2$
    b. 2.5×10^{-2} min/M²
    c. 6.8×10^{-4} M/min

31. yes

32. Heat an endothermic reaction so that increasing entropy may play a larger role in making the reaction spontaneous.

33. 139 kJ

34. -868.7 kJ/mol

35. a.

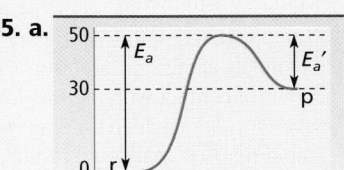

$E_a = 50$ kJ/mol

b.

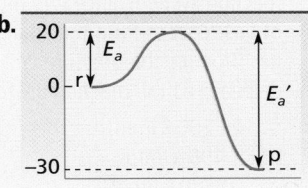

$E_a' = 50$ kJ/mol

36. a. If [A] is halved, so is the reaction rate.
b. If [B] is tripled, the reaction rate will increase by a factor of nine.
c. If [A] is doubled and [B] is halved, the rate of the reaction will be halved.
d. If the catalyst is specific for this reaction, the reaction will speed up.

37. a. $2SO_2(g) + O_2(g) \longrightarrow$
$2SO_3(g) + 197.8$ kJ; exothermic
b. $2NO_2(g) + 114.2$ kJ $\longrightarrow$
$2NO(g) + O_2(g)$; endothermic
c. $C_2H_4(g) + 3O_2(g) \longrightarrow$
$2CO_2(g) + 2H_2O(l)$
$+ 1411.0$ kJ; exothermic

38. a. powdered sugar
b. zinc in HCl at 410 K
c. thin platinum wire

39. -560.4 kJ/mol

40. As the formation of a single activated complex by the simultaneous collision of five molecules is highly improbable, the reaction mechanisms must involve some sequence of simple steps.

41. a. It is the one by which the potential energy of the reactants is raised to the minimum level needed for effective collisions.
b. The maximum energy region is reached when the activated complex is formed.

42. The powdered nature of the dry materials allows for large surface areas of contact with oxygen so even a spark could initiate a very rapid reaction that could result in an explosion.

43. Measure the pressure of the reaction system. Since two moles of gas react to form one mole of gas product, the pressure will decrease as the reaction proceeds.

44. a. 106.200 kJ/mol
b. 82.456 kJ/mol
c. 140.770 kJ/mol

33. The standard heat of formation for sulfur dioxide gas is -296.8 J/(mol•K). Calculate the amount of energy given off in kJ when 30.0 g of $SO_2(g)$ is formed from its elements.

34. The thermite reaction used in some welding applications has the following enthalpy and entropy changes at 298.15 K. Assuming ΔS and ΔH are constant, calculate ΔG at 448 K.
$Fe_2O_3 + 2Al(s) \longrightarrow 2Fe(s) + Al_2O_3(s)$
$\Delta H^o = -851.5$ kJ/mol $\Delta S^o = -38.5$ J/(mol•K)

35. Draw and label energy diagrams depicting the following reactions, and determine all remaining values. Place the reactants at energy level zero.
a. $\Delta E = +30$ kJ/mol $E_a{}' = 20$ kJ/mol
b. $\Delta E = -30$ kJ/mol $E_a = 20$ kJ/mol

36. A particular reaction is found to have the following rate law.

$$R = k[A][B]^2$$

How is the rate affected by each of the following changes?
a. the initial concentration of A is cut in half
b. the initial concentration of B is tripled
c. the concentration of A is doubled, but the concentration of B is cut in half
d. a catalyst is added

37. Rewrite each equation below with the ΔH value included in either the reactants or products, and identify the reaction as endothermic or exothermic.
a. $2SO_2(g) + O_2(g) \longrightarrow$
$2SO_3(g); \Delta H = -197.8$ kJ/mol
b. $2NO_2(g) \longrightarrow$
$2NO(g) + O_2(g); \Delta H = +114.2$ kJ/mol
c. $C_2H_4(g) + 3O_2(g) \longrightarrow$
$2CO_2(g) + 2H_2O(l); \Delta H = -1411.0$ kJ/mol

38. For each of the following pairs, choose the substance or process you would expect to react more rapidly.
a. granulated sugar or powdered sugar
b. zinc in HCl at 298.15 K or zinc in HCl at 410 K
c. 5 g of thick platinum wire or 5 g of thin platinum wire

39. Calculate the change in enthalpy for the following reaction.
$4FeO(s) + O_2(g) \longrightarrow 2Fe_2O_3(s)$

Use the heat-of-formation data listed in Appendix Table A-14.

CRITICAL THINKING

40. Predicting Outcomes The balanced equation for a rapid homogeneous reaction between two gases is as follows: $4A + B \longrightarrow 2C + 2D$. Since the simultaneous collision of four molecules of one reactant with one molecule of the other reactant is extremely improbable, what would you predict about the nature of the reaction mechanism for this reaction system?

41. Evaluating Ideas
a. How can you justify calling the reaction pathway that is shown in Figure 17-10 the minimum-energy pathway for reaction?
b. What significance is associated with the maximum-energy region of this minimum-energy pathway?

42. Applying Models Explain why there is a danger of explosion in places such as coal mines, saw mills, and grain elevators, where large amounts of dry, powdered combustible materials are present.

43. Evaluating Methods What property would you measure in order to determine the reaction rate for the following reaction? Justify your choice.
$$2NO_2(g) \longrightarrow N_2O_4(g)$$

TECHNOLOGY & LEARNING

44. Graphing Calculator Calculating the Free-Energy Change

The graphing calculator can run a program that calculates the free-energy change, given the temperature, T, change in enthalpy, ΔH, and change in entropy, ΔS. Given that the temperature is 298 K, the change in enthalpy is 131.3 kJ/mol, and the change in entropy is 0.134 kJ/(mol•K), you can calculate free-energy change in kJ/mol. Then use the program to make calculations.

Go to Appendix C. If you are using a TI 83 Plus, you can download the program and data and run the application as directed. If you are using another calculator, your teacher will provide you with keystrokes and data sets to use. Remember that you will need to name the program and check the display, as explained in Appendix C. You will then be ready to run the program. After you have graphed the data, answer these questions.

a. What is the free energy change given a temperature of 300 K, a change in enthalpy of 132 kJ/mol, and a change in entropy of 0.086 kJ/(mol·K)?

b. What is the free energy change given a temperature of 288 K, a change in enthalpy of 115 kJ/mol, and a change in entropy of 0.113 kJ/(mol·K)?

c. What is the free energy change given a temperature of 298 K, a change in enthalpy of 181 kJ/mol, and a change in entropy of 0.135 kJ/(mol·K)?

RESEARCH & WRITING

45. Obtain information on alternative units of measure used to express values of heat and other forms of energy. Also, find out how the quantities relate to SI metric units. Include information specifically on English units, such as the British Thermal Unit (BTU), and on typical BTU ratings of household appliances. Calculate how these ratings would be expressed in joules instead.

46. Look for situations around your house in which processes are speeded up by an increase in temperature or slowed down by a decrease in temperature. Make a list, and discuss the different processes.

ALTERNATIVE ASSESSMENT

47. Performance Design a simple calorimeter investigation to determine the molar heat of fusion of water. Use the following materials: a large plastic-foam cup with cover, a thermometer, a balance, water at room temperature, and an ice cube. Allow your teacher to review your design. Then carry out the investigation, and write a laboratory report including your calculations and a comparison of your quantitative results with known values. Try to account for any disagreements between the experimental and actual values.

45. In one joule, there are 9.488×10^{-4} British Thermal Units (BTU's), 0.2390 calories, and 1.0 Newton-meter.

46. Answers will vary considerably. Some possible responses might include: the metabolism of insects and reptiles, conductivity in the wires, and the functioning of air conditioning.

Chemical Equilibrium

PACING CHART	CLASSROOM RESOURCES		
Compression Guide: (To shorten, eliminate items in italics.)	NSE Standards	Teaching Resources	Experiments
18-1 **The Nature of Chemical Equilibrium** 2 45-minute periods 1 90-minute block *The Equilibrium Expression, pp. 555–559*	UCP 1–4 ST 2 HNS 1, 3 SPSP 2, 4, 5	T 99, TM 98A	Equilibrium Expression, p. 871
18-2 **Shifting Equilibrium** 2 45-minute periods 1 90-minute block *Common-Ion Effect, pp. 567–568*	UCP 1–2, 4	**ATE Demo,** p. 567 T 100	**B19** Equilibrium
18-3 **Equilibria of Acids, Bases, and Salts** 2 45-minute periods 1 90-minute block *Ionization Constant of a Weak Acid, pp. 569–570* *Ionization Constant of Water, p. 571*	PS 3c UCP 1–2, 4	T 101, T 102, TM 99A, TM 100A	Measuring K_a for Acetic Acid, p. 875 **A20** Buffering Capacity
18-4 **Solubility Equilibrium** 2 45-minute periods 1 90-minute block *Calculating Solubilities, pp. 581–582* *Precipitation Calculations, pp. 582–583* *Limitations on the Use of K_{sp}, p. 584*	UCP 1–2, 4	TM 101A	**A19** The Solubility Product Constant of NaCl **C15 EXP** Solubility Product Constant **C15 INV** Solubility Product Constant— Algae Blooms

Review and Assessment 2 45-minute periods 1 90-minute block	REVIEW RESOURCES		
	Cumulative Review	Alternative Assessment	Traditional Assessment
	SR Chapter 18 Mixed Review PE Chapter 18 38–45, p. 588	PE 52, p. 589 ATE 556, 565, 571, 581 AA Items for Chapter 18	Chapter 18 Text Test Generator items for Chapter 18

ASSIGNMENT RESOURCES

Section Homework Resources & Review	Problem-Solving Practice
HR Homework Worksheets 18-1, 18-2, 18-3 Graphic Org. Assignment 18-2 **PE** Section Review, 1–9, p. 559 Chapter Review, 1–3, 24–27, pp. 586–587 **SR** Section Review 18-1	**PE** Additional Sample 18-1 **ATE** Additional Sample, p. 558 **PS** Chapter 20 Equilibrium
HR Homework Worksheets 18-4, 18-5 Graphic Org. Assignment 18-5 **PE** Section Review, 1–6, p. 568 Chapter Review, 4–14, pp. 586–587 **SR** Section Review 18-2	
HR Homework Worksheets 18-6, 18-7 Graphic Org. Assignment 18-6 **PE** Section Review, 1–10, p. 576 Chapter Review, 15–19, pp. 586–587 **SR** Section Review 18-3	**PS** Chapter 21 Equilibrium of Acids and Bases, K_a and K_b
HR Homework Worksheets 18-8, 18-9 **PE** Section Review, 1–6, p. 584 Chapter Review, 20–23, 28–37, pp. 587–588 **SR** Section Review 18-4	**PE** Additional Samples 18-2, 18-3, 18-4 **ATE** Additional Samples, pp. 580, 582, 584 **PS** Chapter 22 Equilibrium of Salts, K_{sp}

TECHNOLOGY RESOURCES

Technology & Internet Resources

 CTW 17 Segment 17 Advances in Fuel Technology

 Holt Chemistry Videodiscs Teacher's Correlation Guide for Chapter 18

 Module 7: Equilibrium, Shifting Equilibrium Module 8: Buffers

internet **connect**

 On-line Student Resources:
www.scilinks.org
The following SciLinks Internet resources can be found in the student text for this chapter.

TOPICS:
• Nitrogen, p. 561 (HC2181)
• Haber process, p. 563 (HC2182)
• Buffers, p. 571 (HC2183)

On-line Teacher Resources:
 GO TO: go.hrw.com
KEYWORD: HC2 HOME
Visit the HRW Web site for a variety of resources related to this chapter.

 Smithsonian Institution®
Internet Connections
Visit **www.si.edu/hrw** for additional on-line resources.

CNN **fyi**.com.
Visit **www.cnnfyi.com** for late-breaking news and current events stories selected just for you.

Resource Key

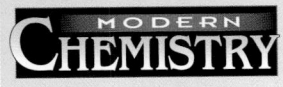
PE Pupil's Edition
ATE Teacher's Edition

One-Stop Planner CD-ROM Includes these resources and customizable daily lesson plans:

HR	Homework Resources	**A**	Laboratory Experiments	**D**	Consumer Experiments
SR	Section Reviews	**B**	Microscale Experiments	**T**	Transparencies
CTW	Critical Thinking Worksheets	**C**	Technique Builders and Problem-Solving Experiments	**TM**	Transparency Masters
AA	Alternative Assessments			**PS**	Mini-Guide to Problem Solving
				SRW	Supplemental Reading Worksheets

ChemFile

Scoring Rubrics for Labs, Alternative Assessments, Performance Tasks and Portfolio Projects are on the One-Stop Planner CD-ROM.

CHAPTER 18

Chemical Equilibrium

Chapter Overview
18-1 defines reversible reactions, the state of equilibrium, and *K*, the equilibrium constant.

18-2 describes how equilibria will shift in response to changes in concentration, pressure, and temperature and discusses the common-ion effect.

18-3 describes the equilibria of acids, bases, and salts; explains the acid-ionization constant, K_a; and discusses buffering and hydrolysis.

18-4 discusses solubility equilibria and explains calculations involving the solubility-product constant, K_{sp}, and precipitate formation.

Concept Base
Students may need a review of the following concepts:

- equilibrium, Chapter 12
- Le Châtelier's principle, Chapter 12
- Brønsted-Lowry acids and bases, Chapter 15
- pH and self-ionization of water, Chapter 16

Reading Skill-Builder

BRAINSTORMING Have students brainstorm a list of reactions that they think are reversible. Write students' contributions on the board. Have students suggest potential applications of reversible reactions in industry and in daily life.

CHAPTER 18

Chemical Equilibrium

*The creation of stalactites and stalagmites
is the result of a reversible chemical reaction.*

The Nature of Chemical Equilibrium

OBJECTIVES

○ Define *chemical equilibrium.*

○ Explain the nature of the equilibrium constant.

○ Write chemical equilibrium expressions and carry out calculations involving them.

In systems that are in equilibrium, opposing processes occur at the same time and at the same rate. For example, when an excess of sugar is placed in water, sugar molecules go into solution. At equilibrium, molecules of sugar are crystallizing at the same rate that molecules from the crystal are dissolving. The rate of evaporation of a liquid in a closed vessel can eventually be equaled by the rate of condensation of its vapor. The resulting equilibrium vapor pressure is a characteristic of the liquid at the prevailing temperature. Le Châtelier's principle, which you read about in Chapter 12, can help predict the outcome of changes made to these equilibrium systems. The preceding examples are physical equilibria. The concept of equilibrium and Le Châtelier's principle also apply to chemical processes.

Reversible Reactions

Theoretically, every reaction can proceed in two directions, forward and reverse. Thus, essentially all chemical reactions are considered to be reversible under suitable conditions. *A chemical reaction in which the products can react to re-form the reactants is called a* **reversible reaction.**

Mercury(II) oxide decomposes when heated.

$$2HgO(s) \xrightarrow{\Delta} 2Hg(l) + O_2(g)$$

Mercury and oxygen combine to form mercury(II) oxide when heated gently.

$$2Hg(l) + O_2(g) \xrightarrow{\Delta} 2HgO(s)$$

Figure 18-1 shows both of these reactions taking place. Suppose mercury(II) oxide is heated in a closed container from which neither the mercury nor the oxygen can escape. Once decomposition has begun, the mercury and oxygen released can recombine to form mercury(II) oxide again. Thus, both reactions can proceed at the same time. Under these conditions, the rate of the composition reaction will eventually equal that of the decomposition reaction. At equilibrium, mercury and oxygen will

FIGURE 18-1 When heated, mercury(II) oxide decomposes into the elements from which it was formed. Liquid mercury reacts with oxygen to re-form mercury(II) oxide. Together these reactions represent a reversible chemical process.

Module 7: Equilibrium

combine to form mercury(II) oxide at the same rate that mercury(II) oxide decomposes into mercury and oxygen. The amounts of mercury(II) oxide, mercury, and oxygen can then be expected to remain constant as long as these conditions persist. At this point, a state of dynamic equilibrium has been reached between the two chemical reactions. Both reactions continue, but there is no net change in the composition of the system. *A reversible chemical reaction is in* **chemical equilibrium** *when the rate of its forward reaction equals the rate of its reverse reaction and the concentrations of its products and reactants remain unchanged.* The chemical equation for the reaction at equilibrium is written using double arrows to indicate the overall reversibility of the reaction.

$$2HgO(s) \rightleftharpoons 2Hg(l) + O_2(g)$$

Equilibrium, a Dynamic State

Many chemical reactions are reversible under ordinary conditions of temperature and concentration. They will reach a state of equilibrium unless at least one of the substances involved escapes or is removed from the reaction system. In some cases, however, the forward reaction is nearly completed before the rate of the reverse reaction becomes high enough to establish equilibrium. Here, the products of the forward reaction are favored, meaning that at equilibrium there is a higher concentration of products than of reactants. The favored reaction that produces this situation is referred to as a reaction to the right because the convention for writing chemical reactions is that *left-to-right* is forward and *right-to-left* is reverse. An example of such a system is the dissociation of hydrobromic acid in aqueous solution.

$$HBr(aq) + H_2O(l) \rightleftharpoons H_3O^+(aq) + Br^-(aq)$$

Notice that the equation is written showing an inequality of the two arrow lengths. The forward reaction is represented by the longer arrow to imply that products are favored in this reaction.

In other cases, the forward reaction is barely under way when the rate of the reverse reaction becomes equal to that of the forward reaction, and equilibrium is established. In these cases, the products of the reverse reaction are favored and the original reactants are formed. That is, at equilibrium there is a higher concentration of reactants than of products. The favored reaction that produces this situation is referred to as a reaction to the left. An example of such a system is the acid-base reaction between carbonic acid and water.

$$H_2CO_3(aq) + H_2O(l) \rightleftharpoons H_3O^+(aq) + HCO_3^-(aq)$$

In still other cases, both forward and reverse reactions occur to nearly the same extent before chemical equilibrium is established. Neither reaction is favored, and considerable concentrations of both reactants and products are present at equilibrium. An example is the dissociation of sulfurous acid in water.

$$H_2SO_3(aq) + H_2O(l) \rightleftharpoons H_3O^+(aq) + HSO_3^-(aq)$$

Chemical reactions ordinarily are used to convert available reactants into more desirable products. Chemists try to convert as much of these reactants as possible into products. The extent to which reactants are converted to products can be determined from the numerical value of the equilibrium constant.

The Equilibrium Expression

Suppose two substances, A and B, react to form products C and D. In turn, C and D react to produce A and B. Under appropriate conditions, equilibrium occurs for this reversible reaction. This hypothetical equilibrium reaction is described by the following general equation.

$$nA + mB \rightleftharpoons xC + yD$$

Initially, the concentrations of C and D are zero and those of A and B are maximum. Figure 18-2 shows that over time the rate of the forward reaction decreases as A and B are used up. Meanwhile, the rate of the reverse reaction increases as C and D are formed. When these two reaction rates become equal, equilibrium is established. The individual concentrations of A, B, C, and D undergo no further change if conditions remain the same.

After equilibrium is attained, the concentrations of products and reactants remain constant, so a ratio of their concentrations should also

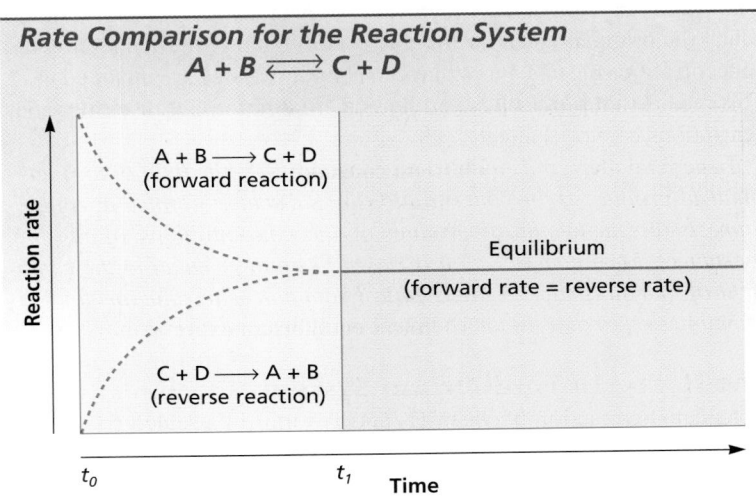

Rate Comparison for the Reaction System
$$A + B \rightleftharpoons C + D$$

Reaction rate

A + B $\longrightarrow$ C + D
(forward reaction)

Equilibrium
(forward rate = reverse rate)

C + D $\longrightarrow$ A + B
(reverse reaction)

t_0 t_1 **Time**

FIGURE 18-2   Shown are reaction rates for the hypothetical equilibrium reaction system A + B $\rightleftharpoons$ C + D. From the time A and B are mixed together at t_0, the rate of the forward reaction declines and the rate of the reverse reaction increases until both forward and reverse reaction rates are equal at t_1, when the equilibrium condition begins.

Alternative Assessment

On the chalkboard, write out several chemical equations representing equilibrium situations. Then have students work singly or in small groups to write the equilibrium expression for each. Have students compare their results with those of other students or groups.

✔ Teaching Tip

The higher the value of the equilibrium constant, the more the products are favored.

In Chapter 16, the ionization constant of water, K_w, was introduced. Its units were given as M^2. The equilibrium constant can be expressed in a number of different types of units or it can be unitless, depending on each specific reaction.

remain constant. The ratio of the mathematical product $[C]^x \times [D]^y$ to the mathematical product $[A]^n \times [B]^m$ for this reaction has a definite value at a given temperature. It is the equilibrium constant of the reaction and is designated by the letter K. The following equation describes the equilibrium constant for the hypothetical equilibrium system. [C] indicates the concentration of C in moles per liter. The concentrations of the other substances are indicated similarly.

$$K = \frac{[C]^x[D]^y}{[A]^n[B]^m}$$

The concentrations of substances on the right side of the chemical equation appear in the numerator of the equilibrium ratio, with each concentration raised to a power equal to the coefficient of that substance in the chemical equation. These substances are the products of the forward reaction. The concentrations of substances on the left side of the chemical equation are found in the denominator of the equilibrium ratio, with each concentration raised to a power equal to the coefficient of that substance in the chemical equation. These substances are the reactants of the forward reaction. The constant K is independent of the initial concentrations. It is, however, dependent on the temperature of the system.

The Equilibrium Constant

The numerical value of K for a particular equilibrium system is obtained experimentally. The chemist must analyze the equilibrium mixture and determine the concentrations of all substances. The value of K for a given equilibrium reaction at a given temperature shows the extent to which the reactants are converted into the products of the reaction. If K is equal to 1, the products of the concentrations raised to the appropriate power in the numerator and denominator have the same value. Therefore, at equilibrium, there are roughly equal concentrations of reactants and products. If the value of K is low, the forward reaction occurs only very slightly before equilibrium is established, and the reactants are favored. A high value of K indicates an equilibrium in which the original reactants are largely converted to products. Only the concentrations of substances that can actually change are included in K. This means that *pure* solids and liquids are omitted because their concentrations cannot change.

In general, then, *the **equilibrium constant**, K, is the ratio of the mathematical product of the concentrations of substances formed at equilibrium to the mathematical product of the concentrations of reacting substances. Each concentration is raised to a power equal to the coefficient of that substance in the chemical equation. The equation for K is sometimes referred to as the **chemical-equilibrium expression.**

The H$_2$, I$_2$, HI Equilibrium System

Consider the reaction between H_2 and I_2 vapor in a sealed flask at an elevated temperature. The rate of reaction can be followed by observing the rate at which the violet color of the iodine vapor diminishes, as shown in Figure 18-3. Suppose the hydrogen gas is present in excess and the reaction continues until all the iodine is used up. The color of the flask's contents, provided by the iodine gas, will gradually become less intense because the product, hydrogen iodide, HI, and the excess hydrogen are both colorless gases.

In actuality, the color fades to a constant intensity but does not disappear because the reaction is reversible. Hydrogen iodide decomposes to re-form hydrogen and iodine. The rate of this reverse reaction increases as the concentration of hydrogen iodide increases. The rate of the forward reaction decreases accordingly. The concentrations of hydrogen and iodine decrease as they are used up. As the rates of the opposing reactions become equal, an equilibrium is established. The constant color achieved indicates that equilibrium exists among hydrogen, iodine, and hydrogen iodide. The net chemical equation for the reaction system at equilibrium follows.

$$H_2(g) + I_2(g) \rightleftharpoons 2HI(g)$$

From this chemical equation, the following chemical-equilibrium expression can be written. The concentration of HI is raised to the power of 2 because the coefficient of HI in the balanced chemical equation is 2.

$$K = \frac{[HI]^2}{[H_2][I_2]}$$

Chemists have carefully measured the concentrations of H_2, I_2, and HI in equilibrium mixtures at various temperatures. In some experiments, the flasks were filled with hydrogen iodide at known pressure. The flasks were held at fixed temperatures until equilibrium was established. In other experiments, hydrogen and iodine were the original substances. Experimental data, together with the calculated values for K, are listed in Table 18-1. Experiments 1 and 2 began with hydrogen iodide. Experiments 3 and 4 began with hydrogen and iodine. Note the close agreement obtained for the numerical values of the equilibrium constant in all cases.

At 425°C, the equilibrium constant for this equilibrium reaction system has the average value of 54.34. This value for K should hold for any system of H_2, I_2, and HI at equilibrium at this temperature. If the

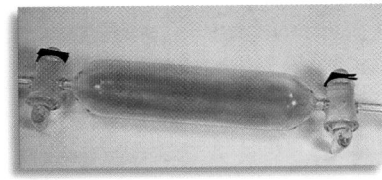

(a)

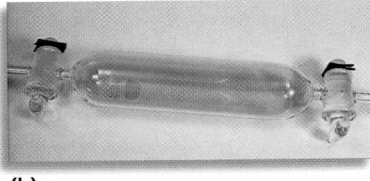

(b)

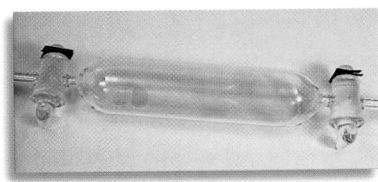

(c)

FIGURE 18-3 Hydrogen iodide gas is produced from gaseous hydrogen and iodine. The violet color of iodine gas (a) becomes fainter as the reaction consumes the iodine (b). The violet does not disappear but reaches a constant intensity when the reaction reaches equilibrium (c).

TABLE 18-1 *Typical Equilibrium Concentrations of H_2, I_2, and HI in mol/L at 425°C*

Experiment	[H_2]	[I_2]	[HI]	$K = \dfrac{[HI]^2}{[H_2][I_2]}$
1	0.4953×10^{-3}	0.4953×10^{-3}	3.655×10^{-3}	54.46
2	1.141×10^{-3}	1.141×10^{-3}	8.410×10^{-3}	54.33
3	3.560×10^{-3}	1.250×10^{-3}	15.59×10^{-3}	54.62
4	2.252×10^{-3}	2.336×10^{-3}	16.85×10^{-3}	53.97

ADDITIONAL SAMPLE PROBLEMS

18-1 At 25°C, an equilibrium mixture of gases contains 6.4×10^{-3} mol/L PCl_3, 2.5×10^{-2} mol/L Cl_2, and 4.0×10^{-3} mol/L PCl_5. What is the equilibrium constant for the following reaction?

$$PCl_5(g) \rightleftharpoons PCl_3(g) + Cl_2(g)$$

Ans. 4.0×10^{-2}

18-1 At equilibrium a 2.0 L vessel contains 0.36 mol of H_2, 0.11 mol of Br, and 37 mol of HBr. What is the equilibrium constant for the reaction

$$H_2(g) + Br_2(g) \rightleftharpoons 2HBr(g)$$

at this temperature?

Ans. 3.5×10^4

---

calculation for K yields a different result, there must be a reason. Either the H_2, I_2, and HI system has not reached equilibrium or the system is not at 425°C.

The balanced chemical equation for an equilibrium system helps establish the expression for the equilibrium constant. The data in Table 18-1 show that the validity of this expression is confirmed when the actual values of the equilibrium concentrations of reactants and products are determined experimentally. The values of K are calculated from these concentrations. No information concerning the kinetics of the reacting systems is required.

Once the value of the equilibrium constant is known, the equilibrium-constant expression can be used to calculate concentrations of reactants or products at equilibrium. Suppose an equilibrium system at 425°C is found to contain 0.015 mol/L each of H_2 and I_2. To find the concentration of HI in this system, the chemical equilibrium expression can be rearranged as shown in the two equations that follow.

$$K = \frac{[HI]^2}{[H_2][I_2]}$$

$$[HI] = \sqrt{K[H_2][I_2]}$$

Using the known K value and the given concentrations for H_2 and I_2, the equation can be solved for [HI].

$$[HI] = \sqrt{0.015 \times 0.015 \times 54.34}$$
$$= 0.11 \text{ mol/L}$$

SAMPLE PROBLEM 18-1

An equilibrium mixture of N_2, O_2, and NO gases at 1500 K is determined to consist of 6.4×10^{-3} mol/L of N_2, 1.7×10^{-3} mol/L of O_2, and 1.1×10^{-5} mol/L of NO. What is the equilibrium constant for the system at this temperature?

SOLUTION

1 ANALYZE   **Given:** $[N_2] = 6.4 \times 10^{-3}$ mol/L
$[O_2] = 1.7 \times 10^{-3}$ mol/L
$[NO] = 1.1 \times 10^{-5}$ mol/L
Unknown: K

2 PLAN   The balanced chemical equation is $N_2(g) + O_2(g) \rightleftharpoons 2NO(g)$.

The chemical equilibrium expression is $K = \dfrac{[NO]^2}{[N_2][O_2]}$.

3 COMPUTE   Substitute the given values for the concentrations into the equilibrium expression.

$$K = \frac{(1.1 \times 10^{-5} \text{ mol/L})^2}{(6.4 \times 10^{-3} \text{ mol/L})(1.7 \times 10^{-3} \text{ mol/L})} = 1.1 \times 10^{-5}$$

4 | **EVALUATE** | The answer has the correct number of significant figures and is close to an estimated value of

$$8 \times 10^{-6}, \text{ calculated as } \frac{1 \times 10^{-10}}{(6 \times 10^{-3})(2 \times 10^{-3})}.$$

PRACTICE	

1. At equilibrium a mixture of N_2, H_2, and NH_3 gas at 500°C is determined to consist of 0.602 mol/L of N_2, 0.420 mol/L of H_2, and 0.113 mol/L of NH_3. What is the equilibrium constant for the reaction $N_2(g) + 3H_2(g) \rightleftharpoons 2NH_3(g)$ at this temperature?

Answer
0.286

2. The reaction $AB_2C(g) \rightleftharpoons B_2(g) + AC(g)$ reached equilibrium at 900 K in a 5.00 L vessel. At equilibrium 0.084 mol of AB_2C, 0.035 mol of B_2, and 0.059 mol of AC were detected. What is the equilibrium constant at this temperature for this system?

Answer
4.9×10^{-3}

3. At equilibrium a 1.0 L vessel contains 20.0 mol of H_2, 18.0 mol of CO_2, 12.0 mol of H_2O, and 5.9 mol of CO at 427°C. What is the value of K at this temperature for the following reaction?
$$CO_2(g) + H_2(g) \rightleftharpoons CO(g) + H_2O(g)$$

Answer
0.20

4. A reaction between gaseous sulfur dioxide and oxygen gas to produce gaseous sulfur trioxide takes place at 600°C. At that temperature, the concentration of SO_2 is found to be 1.50 mol/L, the concentration of O_2 is 1.25 mol/L, and the concentration of SO_3 is 3.50 mol/L. Using the balanced chemical equation, calculate the equilibrium constant for this system.

Answer
4.36

SECTION REVIEW

1. What is meant by *chemical equilibrium*?

2. What is an equilibrium constant?

3. How does the value of an equilibrium constant relate to the relative quantities of reactants and products at equilibrium?

4. What is meant by a *chemical-equilibrium expression*?

5. Hydrochloric acid, HCl, is a strong acid that dissociates completely in water to form H_3O^+ and Cl^-. Would you expect the value of K for the reaction $HCl(aq) + H_2O(l) \rightleftharpoons H_3O^+(aq) + Cl^-(aq)$ to be 1×10^{-2}, 1×10^{-5}, or "very large"? Justify your answer.

6. Write the chemical-equilibrium expression for the reaction $4HCl(g) + O_2(g) \rightleftharpoons 2Cl_2(g) + 2H_2O(g)$.

7. At equilibrium at 2500 K, [HCl] = 0.0625 mol/L and $[H_2] = [Cl_2] = 0.0045$ mol/L for the reaction $H_2(g) + Cl_2(g) \rightleftharpoons 2HCl(g)$. Find the value of K.

8. An equilibrium mixture at 425°C is found to consist of 1.83×10^{-3} mol/L of H_2, 3.13×10^{-3} mol/L of I_2, and 1.77×10^{-2} mol/L of HI. Calculate the equilibrium constant, K, for the reaction $H_2(g) + I_2(g) \rightleftharpoons 2HI(g)$.

9. For the reaction $H_2(g) + I_2(g) \rightleftharpoons 2HI(g)$ at 425°C, calculate [HI], given $[H_2] = [I_2] = 4.79 \times 10^{-4}$ mol/L and $K = 54.3$.

SECTION REVIEW

1. The rates of forward and reverse chemical reactions are equal, and the concentrations of products and reactants remain unchanged.

2. the ratio of the mathematical product of concentrations of substances formed at equilibrium to the mathematical product of the reactant concentrations, each raised to a power equal to the corresponding coefficient in the balanced chemical equation

3. The larger the value of K is, the larger the relative amount of products.

4. the expression of product and reactant concentrations that equal an equilibrium constant, K

5. very large, because virtually all of the reactants have formed products

6. $K = \dfrac{[Cl_2]^2[H_2O]^2}{[HCl]^4[O_2]}$

7. 190

8. 54.7

9. 3.53×10^{-3} mol/L

GREAT DISCOVERIES

Fixing the Nitrogen Problem

HISTORICAL PERSPECTIVE

Each year, the chemical industry synthesizes tons of nitrogenous fertilizer, increasing agricultural production around the globe. But prior to 1915, humans had to rely solely on natural resources for fertilizer, and the dwindling supply of these materials caused widespread fear of world starvation. A crisis was averted, however, through the discovery of an answer to the "nitrogen problem," a term used at the time to describe the shortage of useful nitrogen despite its abundance in the atmosphere.

The Malthusian Threat

In 1798, Thomas Malthus published his famous "Essay on Population," a report predicting that the world's food supplies could not keep up with the growing human population and that famine, death, and misery were inevitable. Malthus's warning seemed to be echoed in the 1840s by the great Irish potato famine. In fact, the rest of Europe likely would have suffered serious food shortages as well had crop yields per acre not been increased through the use of fertilizers containing nitrogen.

Few living things can utilize the gas that forms 78 percent of the atmosphere; they need nitrogen that has been combined with other elements, or "fixed," to survive.

But soil often lacks sufficient amounts of the organisms that fix nitrogen for plants, so fertilizers containing usable nitrogen compounds are added. In 1898, two-thirds of the world's supply of these compounds came from Chile, where beds of sodium nitrate, or Chilean saltpeter, were abundant.

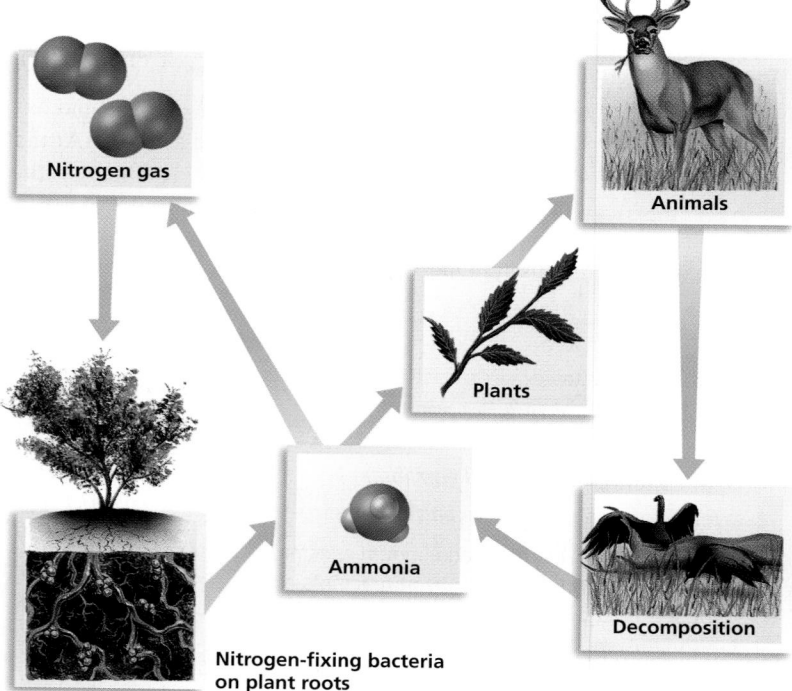

Nitrogen is released when living things die and also from animal wastes and plant material. A few kinds of bacteria are able to break the bond holding the nitrogen molecule together, freeing the nitrogen atoms to combine with hydrogen to form ammonia. Plants can absorb the nitrogen in this form from the soil. Animals then benefit from the nitrogen by eating the plants.

But, as the chemist William Crookes emphasized in his speech to the British Association that year, these reserves were limited; it was up to his colleagues to discover alternatives and prevent Malthus's dire forecast from coming true:

It is the chemist who must come to the rescue of the threatened communities.

The Haber-Nernst Controversy

As early as the 1890s, chemists had shown that ammonia, a practical source of fixed nitrogen, could be synthesized at high temperatures and at atmospheric pressure from elemental hydrogen and nitrogen. The problem was that the end-product was present in such minute amounts that the process was not industrially practical.

In 1904, the German chemist Fritz Haber seemed to confirm this assessment. He tried reacting hydrogen and nitrogen at temperatures of up to 1020°C using pure iron as well as other metals as a catalyst. He found that the amount of ammonia was a mere 0.005–0.012% at equilibrium. Thus, he concluded:

From dull red heat . . . no catalyst can produce more than traces of ammonia . . . and even at . . . increased pressures the position of the equilibrium must remain very unfavorable.

Haber had apparently closed the door on the synthesis of ammonia from its elements. But in 1906, Walther Nernst, using his new heat theorem, calculated the reaction's theoretical ammonia concentration at equilibria corresponding to several pressures. He found that his value at atmospheric pressure disagreed significantly with Haber's, and he publicly challenged Haber's values.

Haber was convinced that he was right. Applying Le Châtelier's principle, he ran the reaction at increased pressure to attain an amount of ammonia that could be measured more accurately.

Haber and his assistants confirmed their original findings, and Nernst later conceded a mathematical error. But more important, the new round of experiments indicated that a reasonable amount of ammonia might be attained at pressures of 200 atm (402 kPa) using a uranium or osmium catalyst.

Scaling Up

Large-scale equipment that could withstand such high pressures was unheard of at the time, and osmium and uranium were far too scarce to be cost-effective for industry. Nevertheless, in 1909, the German firm BASF bought the rights to Haber's findings and put its gifted chemical engineer Karl Bosch in charge of creating an industrial-scale system that would make the process profitable.

After nearly five years, Bosch and the company's chief chemist, Alwin Mittasch, succeeded in developing a suitable reactor that could handle the reaction's high pressures. They also discovered that a catalyst of iron containing small amounts of impurities was an effective replacement for the rare metals used by Haber. Haber was impressed:

It is remarkable how matter . . . reveals new facets. Iron . . . studied a hundred times in the

Today ammonia is produced on an industrial scale in plants like this one.

pure state, now works in the impure state.

An Eerie Epilogue

By September of 1913, BASF was producing 20 metric tons of ammonia a day using the Haber-Bosch process. Eventually, enough ammonia was produced by the chemical industry to free Germany and the world of dependence on Chilean saltpeter for fertilizer. Chemists had thwarted the Malthusian threat. Yet, the victory proved bittersweet; the new ammonia synthesis also became the basis of the production of nitric acid, used to make many of the explosives employed in the wars that rocked Europe and the rest of the globe in the first half of the twentieth century.

internet**connect**

SCI**LINKS** NSTA

TOPIC: Nitrogen
GO TO: www.scilinks.org
*sci***LINKS CODE:** HC2181

Application
To reduce the amount of chemical fertilizers needed, agriculturists usually rotate crops, alternating a nitrogen-fixing legume crop, such as clover, beans, peas, or peanuts, with other crops. Nodules in the roots of legumes contain nitrogen-fixing bacteria that convert atmospheric nitrogen to ammonia. Recently, researchers at the University of Sydney, in Australia, have succeeded in adding nitrogen-fixing bacteria to the roots of wheat plants. Similar research is ongoing with other crops, such as corn and rice.

✔ Teaching Tip
The Haber process for producing ammonia is dependent on the correct temperature, pressure, and catalyst.

SECTION 18-2

Shifting Equilibrium

OBJECTIVES

● Discuss the factors that disturb equilibrium.

● Discuss conditions under which reactions go to completion.

● Describe the common-ion effect.

Module 7: Equilibrium

In systems that have attained chemical equilibrium, the forward and reverse reactions are proceeding at equal rates. Any change that alters the rates of these reactions disturbs the original equilibrium. The system then seeks a new equilibrium state. By shifting an equilibrium in the desired direction, chemists can often improve the yield of the product they are seeking.

Predicting the Direction of Shift

Le Châtelier's principle provides a means of predicting the influence of stress factors on equilibrium systems. As you may recall from Chapter 12, Le Châtelier's principle states that *if a system at equilibrium is subjected to a stress, the equilibrium is shifted in the direction that tends to relieve the stress.* This principle is true for all dynamic equilibria, chemical as well as physical. Changes in pressure, concentration, and temperature illustrate the application of Le Châtelier's principle to chemical equilibrium.

Changes in Pressure
A change in pressure affects only equilibrium systems in which gases are involved. For changes in pressure to affect the system, the total number of moles of gas on the left side of the equation must be different from the total number of moles on the right side of the equation. For example, the balanced chemical equation for the decomposition of solid $CaCO_3$ given on page 564 indicates that 0 mol reactant gases produce 1 mol of product gases. The change in moles is 1. Therefore, a high pressure favors the reverse reaction because fewer CO_2 molecules are produced. A similar argument can explain the increased production of CO_2 that accompanies a low system pressure.

Next let us consider the Haber process for the synthesis of ammonia.

$$N_2(g) + 3H_2(g) \rightleftharpoons 2NH_3(g)$$

This situation is somewhat different. First consider an increase in pressure as the applied stress. Can the system shift in a way that reduces the stress? Yes. An increase in pressure causes increases in the concentrations of all species. The system can reduce the number of molecules, and hence the total pressure, by shifting the equilibrium to the right. For each four molecules of reactants there are two molecules of products. By producing more NH_3, and using up N_2 and H_2, the system can reduce the number of molecules. This leads to a decrease in pressure. However, the new equilibrium pressure is still higher than before, although not as high as the pressure caused by the initial stress.

An increase in pressure on confined gases causes an increase in the concentrations of these gases. So changes in pressure may shift the equilibrium position, but they do not affect the value of the equilibrium constant.

Ammonia produced in the Haber process is continuously removed by condensation to liquid. This condensation removes most of the product from the gas phase in which the reaction occurs. The resulting decrease in the partial pressure of NH_3 gas in the reaction vessel is the same as a decrease in product concentration and shifts the equilibrium to the right.

The introduction of an inert gas, such as helium, into the reaction vessel for the synthesis of ammonia increases the total pressure in the vessel. But it does not change the partial pressures of the reaction gases present. Therefore, increasing pressure by adding a gas that is not a reactant or a product *cannot* affect the equilibrium position of the reaction system.

Changes in Concentration

An increase in the concentration of a reactant is a stress on the equilibrium system. It causes an increase in collision frequency and, generally, an increase in reaction rate. Consider the following hypothetical reaction.

$$A + B \rightleftharpoons C + D$$

An increase in the concentration of A shifts the equilibrium to the right. Both A and B are used up faster, and more of C and D is formed. The equilibrium is reestablished with a lower concentration of B. The equilibrium has shifted to reduce the stress caused by the increase in concentration of A. Figure 18-4 illustrates the effect on a system in equilibrium produced by increasing the concentration of a reactant. Similarly, an increase in the concentration of B drives the reaction to the right. An increase in the concentration of either C or D increases the rate of the reverse reaction, and the equilibrium shifts to the left. A decrease in the concentration of C or D has the same effect on the position of the equilibrium as does an increase in the concentration of A or B; the equilibrium shifts to the right.

Changes in concentration have no effect on the value of the equilibrium constant. This is because such changes have an equal effect on the numerator and the denominator of the chemical equilibrium expression. Thus, all concentrations give the same value or numerical ratio for the equilibrium constant when equilibrium is reestablished.

Many chemical processes involve heterogeneous reactions in which the reactants and products are in different phases. The *concentrations* of pure substances in solid and liquid phases are not changed by adding or removing quantities of the substance. This is because concentration is density-dependent, and the density of these phases is constant, regardless of the total amounts present. *A pure substance in a condensed phase, solid or liquid, can be eliminated from the expression for the*

(a)

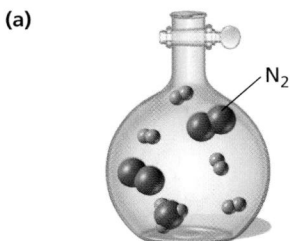

N₂

(b)

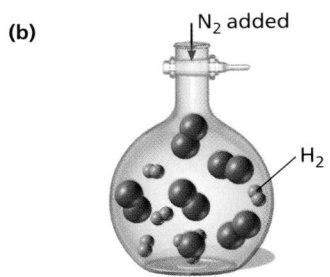

N₂ added

H₂

(c)

NH₃

$$N_2(g) + 3H_2(g) \rightleftharpoons 2NH_3(g)$$

FIGURE 18-4 (a) H_2, N_2, and NH_3 are in equilibrium within a closed system. (b) Addition of more N_2 causes a stress on the initial equilibrium. (c) The new equilibrium position for this system. There is now a higher concentration of N_2, a lower concentration of H_2, and a higher concentration of NH_3.

📶 internet**connect**

SC*i*LINKS
NSTA

TOPIC: Haber process
GO TO: www.scilinks.org
*sci*LINKS CODE: HC2182

Application

Le Châtelier's principle is applied in the bottling of carbonated soft drinks. Adding carbon dioxide to water produces carbonic acid in a reversible reaction:

$$H_2O + CO_2 \rightleftharpoons H_2CO_3$$

The beverages are bottled under increased pressure, placing stress on the equilibrium. The equilibrium shifts to the right to reduce the stress on the system. When the bottle is opened, the pressure is reduced. The reaction is forced to the left, and CO_2 forms and comes out of solution.

Common Misconception

Students generally master the concept that increases of pressure affect equilibrium, but they often misapply it to all pressure changes. In gaseous systems, the only situations affected by such imposed changes are those in which the total numbers of reactant molecules and product molecules differ. Also, only changes in the partial pressure of a gas taking part in the reaction cause a shift. The addition or removal of some other gas has no effect even though it changes the total pressure.

Common Misconception

Some students have difficulty remembering to exclude condensed phases in equilibrium expressions, partially because they do not understand why such phases should be excluded. Explain that the concentration of a pure condensed phase remains constant because it is fixed by the density of the substance, regardless of how much is present. The value remains the same despite imposed changes and thus can be eliminated from consideration.

equilibrium constant. The concentration of the pure solid or liquid is set equal to 1 in the equilibrium expression, signifying that the concentration is assumed to remain unchanged in the equilibrium system.

The following equation describes the equilibrium system established by the decomposition of solid calcium carbonate.

$$CaCO_3(s) \rightleftharpoons CaO(s) + CO_2(g)$$

The products are a solid and a gas, leading to the following expression for the equilibrium constant.

$$K = \frac{[CaO][CO_2]}{[CaCO_3]} = \frac{[1][CO_2]}{[1]} = [CO_2]$$

Carbon dioxide is the only substance in the system subject to changes in concentration. Because it is a gas, the system is affected by pressure changes.

Changes in Temperature

Reversible reactions are exothermic in one direction and endothermic in the other. The effect of changing the temperature of an equilibrium mixture depends on which of the opposing reactions is endothermic and which is exothermic.

According to Le Châtelier's principle, the addition of heat shifts the equilibrium so that heat is absorbed. This favors the endothermic reaction. The removal of heat favors the exothermic reaction. A rise in temperature increases the rate of any reaction. In an equilibrium system, however, the rates of the opposing reactions are raised unequally. Thus, the value of the equilibrium constant for a given system is affected by the temperature.

The synthesis of ammonia by the Haber process is exothermic, as indicated by the heat shown on the product side of the equation.

$$N_2(g) + 3H_2(g) \rightleftharpoons 2NH_3(g) + 92 \text{ kJ}$$

A high temperature is not desirable because it favors the decomposition of ammonia, the endothermic reaction. At low temperatures, however, the forward reaction is too slow to be commercially useful. The temperature used represents a compromise between kinetic and equilibrium requirements. It is high enough that equilibrium is established rapidly but low enough that the equilibrium concentration of ammonia is significant. Moderate temperature (about 500°C) and very high pressure (700–1000 atm) produce a satisfactory yield of ammonia.

The production of colorless dinitrogen tetroxide gas, N_2O_4, from dark brown NO_2 gas is also an exothermic reaction. Figure 18-5 shows how temperature affects the equilibrium of this system. In this figure, all three flasks contain the same total mass of gas, a mixture of NO_2 and N_2O_4. In Figure 18-5(a) the temperature of the system is lowered to 0°C. This causes the equilibrium of the system to shift to the right, allowing more of the colorless N_2O_4 gas to form, which produces a light brown color.

(a)   (b)   (c)

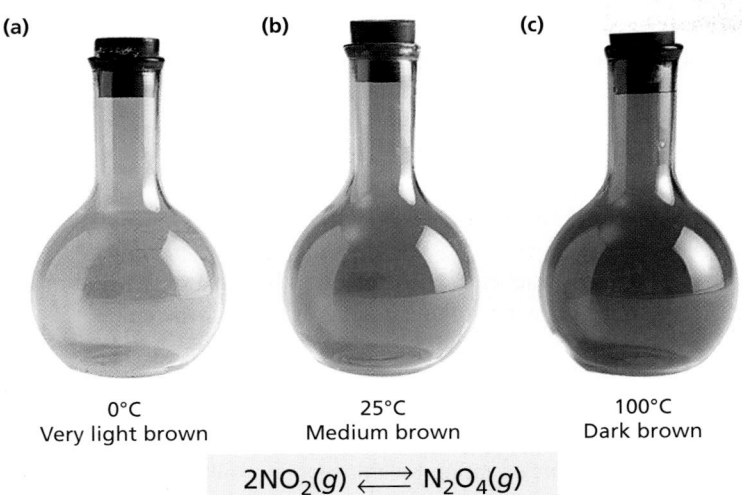

| 0°C | 25°C | 100°C |
| Very light brown | Medium brown | Dark brown |

$$2NO_2(g) \rightleftharpoons N_2O_4(g)$$

FIGURE 18-5   Different temperatures can cause an equilibrium system to shift and seek a new equilibrium position.

The system is at equilibrium at 25°C in Figure 18-5(b). The system contains an equilibrium mixture of NO_2 and N_2O_4, producing a medium brown color. As the temperature is raised to 100°C, as shown in Figure 18-5(c), the equilibrium shifts to the left, causing more of the dark brown NO_2 gas to form.

For an endothermic reaction, such as the decomposition of calcium carbonate, heat shows up on the reactant side of the equation.

$$556 \text{ kJ} + CaCO_3(s) \rightleftharpoons CaO(s) + CO_2(g)$$

An increase in temperature caused by adding heat to the system causes the value of K to increase and the equilibrium to shift to the right.

The reactions of the system are also accelerated by a suitable catalyst. However, catalysts have no effect on relative equilibrium amounts. They only affect the rates at which equilibrium is reached. This is because catalysts increase the rates of forward and reverse reactions in a system by equal factors. Therefore, they do not affect K.

Reactions That Go to Completion

Some reactions involving compounds formed by the chemical interaction of ions in solutions appear to go to completion in the sense that the ions are almost completely removed from solution. The extent to which reacting ions are removed from solution depends on the solubility of the compound formed and, if the compound is soluble, on the degree of ionization. Thus, a product that escapes as a gas, precipitates as a solid, or is only slightly ionized effectively removes from solution the bulk of the reacting ions that compose it. Consider some specific examples of situations in which such ionic reactions go to completion.

Visual Strategy
FIGURE 18-6 Have students note the various species shown in the dia-grams. Ask them to follow the precip-itation process that is occurring and to describe it in terms of equilibrium principles.

Formation of a Gas

Unstable substances formed as products of ionic reactions decompose spontaneously. An example is carbonic acid, H_2CO_3, the acid in carbon-ated water, such as club soda, which yields a gas as a decomposition product.

$$H_2CO_3(aq) \longrightarrow H_2O(l) + CO_2(g)$$

This reaction goes practically to completion because one of the prod-ucts, CO_2, escapes as a gas if the container is open to the air.

Formation of a Precipitate

When solutions of sodium chloride and silver nitrate are mixed, a white precipitate of silver chloride immediately forms, as shown in Figure 18-6. The overall ionic equation for this reaction follows.

$$Na^+(aq) + Cl^-(aq) + Ag^+(aq) + NO_3^-(aq) \longrightarrow Na^+(aq) + NO_3^-(aq) + AgCl(s)$$

If chemically equivalent amounts of the two solutes are used, only Na^+ ions and NO_3^- ions remain in solution in appreciable quantities. Almost all of the Ag^+ ions and Cl^- ions combine and separate from the solution as a precipitate of AgCl. This is because AgCl is only very sparingly soluble in water. It separates by precipitation from what turns out to be a saturated solution of its particles. The reaction thus effectively goes to completion because an essentially insoluble product is formed.

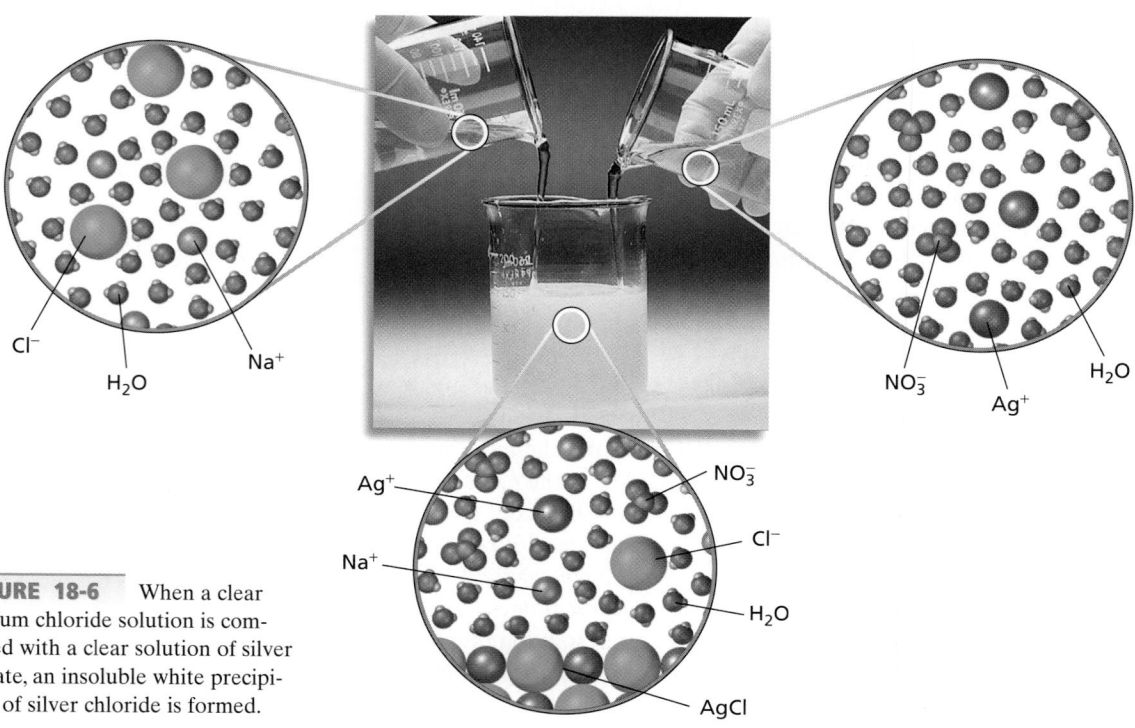

FIGURE 18-6 When a clear sodium chloride solution is com-bined with a clear solution of silver nitrate, an insoluble white precipi-tate of silver chloride is formed.

Formation of a Slightly Ionized Product

Neutralization reactions between H_3O^+ ions from aqueous acids and OH^- ions from aqueous bases result in the formation of water molecules, which are only slightly ionized. A reaction between HCl and NaOH illustrates this process. Aqueous HCl supplies H_3O^+ ions and Cl^- ions to the solution, and aqueous NaOH supplies Na^+ ions and OH^- ions, as shown in the following overall ionic equation.

$$H_3O^+(aq) + Cl^-(aq) + Na^+(aq) + OH^-(aq) \longrightarrow Na^+(aq) + Cl^-(aq) + 2H_2O(l)$$

Neglecting the spectator ions, the net ionic equation is as follows.

$$H_3O^+(aq) + OH^-(aq) \longrightarrow 2H_2O(l)$$

Because it is only slightly ionized, the water exists almost entirely as covalently bonded molecules. Thus, insofar as they are initially present in equal amounts, hydronium ions and hydroxide ions are almost entirely removed from the solution. The reaction effectively runs to completion because the product is only slightly ionized.

Common-Ion Effect

An equilibrium reaction may be driven in the desired direction by applying Le Châtelier's principle. Suppose hydrogen chloride gas is bubbled into a saturated solution of sodium chloride. Hydrogen chloride is extremely soluble in water, and it is almost completely ionized.

$$HCl(g) + H_2O(l) \longrightarrow H_3O^+(aq) + Cl^-(aq)$$

The equilibrium for a saturated solution of sodium chloride is described by the following equation.

$$NaCl(s) \rightleftharpoons Na^+(aq) + Cl^-(aq)$$

As the hydrogen chloride dissolves in sufficient quantity, it increases the concentration of Cl^- ions in the solution, which is a stress on the equilibrium system. The system can compensate, according to Le Châtelier's principle, by combining some of the added Cl^- ions with an equivalent amount of Na^+ ions. This causes some solid NaCl to precipitate out, relieving the stress of added chloride. The new equilibrium has a greater concentration of Cl^- ions but a decreased concentration of Na^+ ions. However, the product of $[Na^+]$ and $[Cl^-]$ still has the same value as before. *This phenomenon, in which the addition of an ion common to two solutes brings about precipitation or reduced ionization, is called the* **common-ion effect.**

The common-ion effect is also observed when one ion species of a weak electrolyte is added in excess to a solution. Acetic acid, CH_3COOH,

DEMONSTRATION
The Common-Ion Effect
Demonstrate the example of the common-ion effect shown on this page. In advance, prepare a saturated NaCl solution by placing 50 g of sodium chloride in a beaker containing 100 mL of water. Stir, and let stand overnight. To ensure that saturation is reached, stir again the next morning, then allow to settle. Some solid should remain in the bottom. In class, show students the beaker of solution, then carefully pour off some of the liquid into a large test tube. Add concentrated hydrochloric acid dropwise.

Caution: Be careful when handling the concentrated acid. In case of spills, first dilute with water. Then, while wearing disposable gloves, mop the spill with wet cloths or a wet cloth mop designated for spill cleanup.

Ask students to explain why solid NaCl precipitates. Student responses should mention the common-ion effect.

Safety: Wear goggles, gloves, and an apron, and do not allow students to stand too closely.

Disposal: Dilute with tap water and pour down the drain.

Visual Strategy

Visual Strategy

FIGURE 18-7 Use models to show students what is happening in the solutions. Have students explain what is happening in terms of the common-ion effect and Le Châtelier's principle.

is such an electrolyte. A 0.1 M CH_3COOH solution is only about 1.4% ionized to produce hydronium ions and acetate ions, CH_3COO^-. The ionic equilibrium is shown by the following equation.

$$CH_3COOH(aq) + H_2O(l) \rightleftharpoons H_3O^+(aq) + CH_3COO^-(aq)$$

FIGURE 18-7   The solution of CH_3COOH on the left is combined with the solution of $NaCH_3COO$ in the center. Both contain the common ion, CH_3COO^-. They produce the solution on the right, which is only slightly acidic due to the decreased ionization of the acid. The colors of the solutions are due to the addition of acid-base indicators.

Small additions of sodium acetate, $NaCH_3COO$ (an ionic salt that is completely dissociated in water), to a solution containing acetic acid greatly increase the acetate-ion concentration. The equilibrium shifts in the direction that uses up some of the acetate ions in accordance with Le Châtelier's principle. More molecules of acetic acid are formed and the concentration of hydronium ions is reduced. In general, the addition of a salt with an ion common to the solution of a weak electrolyte reduces the ionization of the electrolyte. Figure 18-7 shows a 0.25 M CH_3COOH solution on the left that has a pH of about 2.7. Mixing that with the 0.10 M $NaCH_3COO$ solution in the center produces the solution on the right, which has a pH of about 4.5, indicating lower $[H_3O^+]$ and thus lowered acetic acid ionization. (The universal indicator used turns red in acidic solutions, green in weakly basic solutions, and yellow in neutral solutions.)

SECTION REVIEW

1. change in concentration, pressure, or temperature

2. formation of gas, a precipitate, or a slightly ionized product

3. The addition of an ion common to two solutes brings about precipitation or reduced ionization.

4. **a.** Cl^-
   b. CH_3COO^-
   c. OH^-

5. **a.** no effect
   b. shift to the right
   c. shift to the right
   d. shift to the left

6. It will be more favorable because a product, heat, is being removed. The equilibrium will shift to produce more heat to counteract the imposed change.

SECTION REVIEW

1. Name three ways the chemical equilibrium can be disturbed.

2. Describe three situations in which ionic reactions go to completion.

3. Describe the common-ion effect.

4. Identify the common ion in each of the following situations.
   a. 5 g of NaCl is added to a 2.0 M solution of HCl
   b. 50 mL of 1.0 M $NaCH_3COO$ is added to 1.0 M CH_3COOH
   c. 10 pellets of NaOH are added to 100 mL of water

5. Predict the effect that decreasing pressure would have on each of the following reaction systems at equilibrium.
   a. $H_2(g) + Cl_2(g) \rightleftharpoons 2HCl(g)$
   b. $NH_4Cl(s) \rightleftharpoons NH_3(g) + HCl(g)$
   c. $2H_2O_2(aq) \rightleftharpoons 2H_2O(l) + O_2(g)$
   d. $3O_2(g) \rightleftharpoons 2O_3(g)$

6. When solid carbon reacts with oxygen gas to form carbon dioxide, 393.51 kJ of heat are released. Does this reaction become more favorable or less favorable as the temperature decreases? Explain.

Equilibria of Acids, Bases, and Salts

Ionization Constant of a Weak Acid

About 1.4% of the solute molecules in a 0.1 M acetic acid solution are ionized at room temperature. The remaining 98.6% of the acetic acid molecules, CH_3COOH, remain nonionized. Thus, the solution contains three species of particles in equilibrium: CH_3COOH molecules, H_3O^+ ions, and acetate ions, CH_3COO^-. The equilibrium constant for this system expresses the equilibrium ratio of ions to molecules. From the equilibrium equation for the ionization of acetic acid, the equilibrium constant equation can be written.

$$CH_3COOH + H_2O \rightleftharpoons H_3O^+ + CH_3COO^-$$

$$K = \frac{[H_3O^+][CH_3COO^-]}{[CH_3COOH][H_2O]}$$

At the 0.1 M concentration, water molecules greatly exceed the number of acetic acid molecules. Without introducing a measurable error, one can assume that the molar concentration of H_2O molecules remains constant in such a solution. Thus, because both K and $[H_2O]$ are constant, the product $K[H_2O]$ is constant.

$$K[H_2O] = \frac{[H_3O^+][CH_3COO^-]}{[CH_3COOH]}$$

The left side of the equation can be simplified by setting $K[H_2O] = K_a$.

$$K_a = \frac{[H_3O^+][CH_3COO^-]}{[CH_3COOH]}$$

The term K_a is called the **acid-ionization constant.** The acid ionization constant, K_a, like the equilibrium constant, K, is constant for a specified temperature but has a new value for each new temperature.

The acid-ionization constant for a weak acid represents a small value. To determine the numerical value of the ionization constant for acetic acid at a specific temperature, the equilibrium concentrations of H_3O^+ ions, CH_3COO^- ions, and CH_3COOH molecules must be known. The ionization of a molecule of CH_3COOH in water yields one H_3O^+ ion and one CH_3COO^- ion. These concentrations can, therefore, be found experimentally by measuring the pH of the solution.

OBJECTIVES

- Explain the concept of acid-ionization constants, and write acid-ionization equilibrium expressions.

- Review the ionization constant of water.

- Explain buffering.

- Compare cation and anion hydrolysis.

Lesson Starter
Measure the pH of 0.10 M HCl and the pH of 0.10 M CH_3COOH. Compare the results. Ask students to try to explain the difference in the pH. Repeat this exercise with 0.10 M NaOH and 0.10 M NH_3.

Did You Know?
The phrase *acetic acid* comes from the Latin word *acetum*, which means "vinegar." Acetic acid is the acid that gives vinegar its sour taste.

 Reading Skill-Builder

READING ORGANIZER Have students read the section and then organize the ideas presented in the section in the form of a concept map. Concept maps should include ionization constants and hydrolysis reactions.

Problem-Solving Practice  **ChemFile**

Chapter 21 of the Mini-Guide to Problem Solving (also found on the One-Stop Planner CD-ROM) includes more worked-out samples and additional practice problems involving equilibrium of acids and bases, K_a and K_b.

Low equilibrium constants indicate equilibria that favor the reactants. Therefore, K_a values for weak acids, which are only partially dissociated, are all much less than 1.0.

TABLE STRATEGY

Table 18-2 Draw attention to the near constancy of K_a values for acetic acid. Ask students to note that the concentrations of both the hydronium ion (and, logically, the acetate ion) and acetic acid decrease as molarity decreases. Because both the numerator and the denominator of the equilibrium expression decrease, the overall ratio, K_a, remains the same.

CHAPTER ⟺ CONNECTION

Carboxylic (organic) acids, such as acetic acid, will be discussed in more detail in Chapter 21.

CHEMISTRY INTERACTIVE TUTOR

Module 8: Strong and Weakly Ionized Species, pH, and Titrations

Topic: Buffer Tutorial
Section **i** of this engaging tutorial reviews and reinforces understanding of buffers.

CHEMISTRY INTERACTIVE TUTOR

Module 8: Strong and Weakly Ionized Species, pH, and Titrations

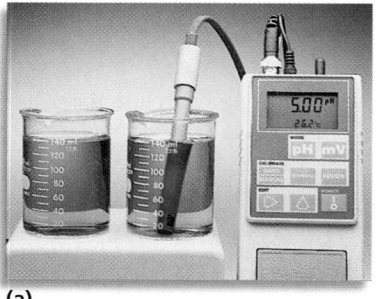

(a)

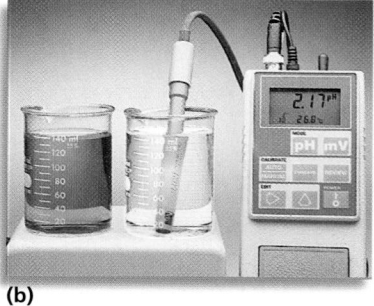

(b)

FIGURE 18-8 (a) The beaker on the left contains a buffered solution and an indicator with a pH of about 7. The beaker on the right contains mostly water with a trace amount of acid and an indicator. The pH meter shows a pH of 5.00 for this solution. (b) After 5 mL of 0.10 M HCl is added to both beakers, the beaker on the left does not change color, indicating no substantial change in its pH. However, the beaker on the right undergoes a definite color change, and the pH meter shows a pH of 2.17.

TABLE 18-2 *Ionization of Acetic Acid*				
Molarity	**% ionized**	**$[H_3O^+]$**	**$[CH_3COOH]$**	**K_a**
0.100	1.33	0.00133	0.0987	1.79×10^{-5}
0.0500	1.89	0.000945	0.0491	1.82×10^{-5}
0.0100	4.17	0.000417	0.00958	1.81×10^{-5}
0.00500	5.86	0.000293	0.00471	1.82×10^{-5}
0.00100	12.6	0.000126	0.000874	1.82×10^{-5}

Ionization data and constants for some dilute acetic acid solutions at 25°C are given in Table 18-2. Notice that the numerical value of K_a is almost identical for each solution molarity shown. The numerical value of K_a for CH_3COOH at 25°C can be determined by substituting numerical values for concentration into the equilibrium equation.

$$K_a = \frac{[H_3O^+][CH_3COO^-]}{[CH_3COOH]}$$

At constant temperature, an increase in the concentration of CH_3COO^- ions through the addition of sodium acetate, $NaCH_3COO$, disturbs the equilibrium. This disturbance causes a decrease in $[H_3O^+]$ and an increase in $[CH_3COOH]$. Eventually, the equilibrium is reestablished with the *same* value of K_a. But there is a higher concentration of nonionized acetic acid molecules and a lower concentration of H_3O^+ ions than before the extra CH_3COO^- was added. Changes in the hydronium-ion concentration affect pH. In this example, the reduction in $[H_3O^+]$ means an increase in the pH of the solution.

Buffers

The solution just described contains both a weak acid, CH_3COOH, and a salt of the weak acid, $NaCH_3COO$. The solution can react with either an acid or a base. When small amounts of acids or bases are added, the pH of the solution remains nearly constant. The weak acid and the common ion, CH_3COO^-, act as a "buffer" against significant changes in the pH of the solution. *Because it can resist changes in pH, this solution is a* **buffered solution.** Figure 18-8 shows how a buffered and a nonbuffered solution react to the addition of an acid.

Suppose a small amount of acid is added to the acetic acid–sodium acetate solution. Acetate ions react with most of the added hydronium ions to form nonionized acetic acid molecules.

$$CH_3COO^-(aq) + H_3O^+(aq) \longrightarrow CH_3COOH(aq) + H_2O(l)$$

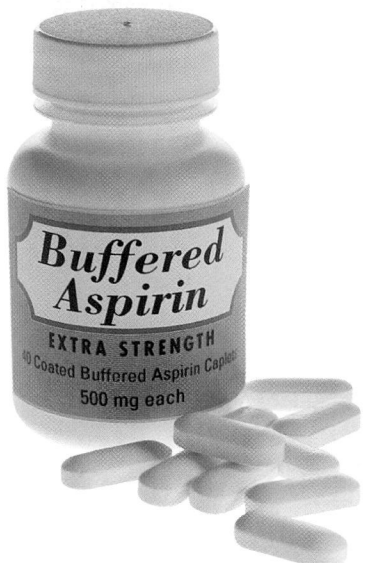

The hydronium ion concentration and the pH of the solution remain practically unchanged.

Suppose a small amount of a base is added to the original solution. The OH^- ions of the base react with and remove hydronium ions to form nonionized water molecules. Acetic acid molecules then ionize and restore the equilibrium concentration of hydronium ions.

$$CH_3COOH(aq) + H_2O(l) \longrightarrow H_3O^+(aq) + CH_3COO^-(aq)$$

The pH of the solution again remains practically unchanged.

A solution of a weak base containing a salt of the base behaves in a similar manner. The hydroxide ion concentration and the pH of the solution remain essentially constant with small additions of acids or bases. Suppose a base is added to an aqueous solution of ammonia that also contains ammonium chloride. Ammonium ions donate a proton to the added hydroxide ions to form nonionized water molecules.

$$NH_4^+(aq) + OH^-(aq) \longrightarrow NH_3(aq) + H_2O(l)$$

If a small amount of an acid is added to the solution instead, hydroxide ions from the solution accept protons from the added hydronium ions to form nonionized water molecules. Ammonia molecules in the solution then ionize and restore the equilibrium concentration of hydronium ions and the pH of the solution.

$$NH_3(aq) + H_2O(l) \longrightarrow NH_4^+(aq) + OH^-(aq)$$

Buffer action has many important applications in chemistry and physiology. Human blood is naturally buffered to maintain a pH of between 7.3 and 7.5. This is essential because large changes in pH would lead to serious disturbances of normal body functions. Figure 18-9 shows an example of one of the many medicines buffered to prevent large and potentially damaging changes in pH.

FIGURE 18-9 Many consumer products are buffered to protect the body from potentially harmful pH changes.

internet**connect**

SCILINKS

NSTA

TOPIC: Buffers
GO TO: www.scilinks.org
*sci*LINKS CODE: HC2183

Application

Aspirin, or acetylsalicylic acid, is often buffered because the acid it contains can irritate the stomach by lowering the pH of stomach secretions. Buffering involves the use of the salts of a weak acid whose anion can combine with the extra H^+ that is produced by the aspirin.

Alternative Assessment

Have students examine the equations on this page and identify the conjugate Brønsted acids and bases in each. They should explain their reasoning in each case.

☑ **Teaching Tip**

Remind students that $K_w =$ $[H_3O^+]$ $[OH^-]$ is the *ion product* constant for water, which was discussed in Chapter 16.

Ionization Constant of Water

Recall from Chapter 16 that the self-ionization of water is an equilibrium reaction.

$$H_2O(l) + H_2O(l) \rightleftharpoons H_3O^+(aq) + OH^-(aq)$$

Equilibrium is established with a very low concentration of H_3O^+ and OH^- ions. The following expression for the equilibrium constant is derived from the balanced chemical equation.

$$K_w = [H_3O^+][OH^-] = 1.0 \times 10^{-14}$$

Hydrolysis of Salts

Salts are formed during the neutralization reaction between a Brønsted acid and a Brønsted base. When a salt dissolves in water, it produces positive ions (cations) of the base from which it was formed and negative ions (anions) of the acid from which it was formed. Therefore, the solution might be expected to be neutral. The aqueous solutions of some salts, such as $NaCl$ and KNO_3, are neutral, having a pH of 7. However, when sodium carbonate dissolves in water, the resulting solution turns red litmus paper blue, indicating a pH greater than 7. Ammonium chloride produces an aqueous solution that turns blue litmus paper red, indicating a pH less than 7. Salts formed from the combination of strong or weak acids and bases are shown in Figure 18-10.

The variation in pH values can be accounted for by examining the ions formed when each of these salts dissociates. If the ions formed are from weak acids or bases, they react chemically with the water solvent, and the pH of the solution will have a value other than 7. *A reaction between water molecules and ions of a dissolved salt is* **hydrolysis.** If the anions react with water, the process is anion hydrolysis and results in a more basic solution. If the cations react with water molecules, the process is cation hydrolysis and results in a more acidic solution.

Anion Hydrolysis

In the Brønsted sense, the anion of the salt is the conjugate base of the acid from which it was formed. It is also a proton acceptor. If the acid is weak, its conjugate base (the anion) will be strong enough to remove protons from some water molecules, proton donors, to form OH^- ions. An

  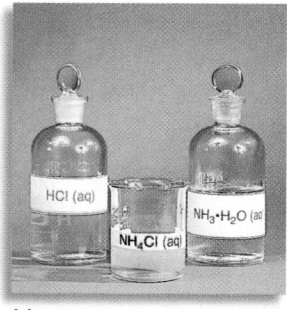 

(a)   (b)   (c)   (d)

FIGURE 18-10 The universal indicator shows that the pH of salt solutions varies, depending on the strength of the acid and the base that formed the salt. (a) NaCl is formed from a strong acid and a strong base; the color of the indicator shows the pH is neutral. (b) The indicator shows the pH of the sodium acetate solution is basic. This was formed from a strong base and a weak acid. (c) The strong acid and weak base combination in ammonium chloride produces an acidic solution, as shown by the color of the indicator. (d) The weak acid and weak base that form ammonium acetate are of comparable strength. A solution of ammonium acetate is essentially neutral.

equilibrium is established in which the net effect of the anion hydrolysis is an increase in the hydroxide-ion concentration, [OH⁻], of the solution.

The equilibrium equation for a typical weak acid in water, HA, forming hydronium ion and an anion, A⁻, is as follows.

$$HA(aq) + H_2O(l) \rightleftharpoons H_3O^+(aq) + A^-(aq)$$

From this equation, the generalized expression for K_a can be written. Recall that the concentration of water in dilute aqueous solutions is essentially constant, so it is included in the equilibrium constant instead of in the concentration ratio.

$$K_a = \frac{[H_3O^+][A^-]}{[HA]}$$

The hydrolysis reaction between water and the anion, A⁻, that is produced by the dissociation of the weak acid, HA, is represented by the general equilibrium equation that follows.

$$A^-(aq) + H_2O(l) \rightleftharpoons HA(aq) + OH^-(aq)$$

In the forward reaction, the anion, A⁻, acquires a proton from the water molecule to form the weak acid, HA, and hydroxide ion, OH⁻. The extent of OH⁻ ion formation and the position of the equilibrium depends on the relative strength of the anion, A⁻. The lower the K_a value of HA, the stronger the attraction for protons that A⁻ will have compared with OH⁻, and the greater the production of OH⁻ ion will be. Therefore, as the relative strength of A⁻ increases, the equilibrium position lies farther to the right.

Aqueous solutions of sodium carbonate are strongly basic. The sodium ions, Na⁺, in sodium carbonate do not undergo hydrolysis in aqueous solution, but the carbonate ions, CO_3^{2-}, react as a Brønsted base. A CO_3^{2-} anion acquires a proton from a water molecule to form the slightly ionized hydrogen carbonate ion, HCO_3^-, and the OH⁻ ion.

$$CO_3^{2-}(aq) + H_2O(l) \rightleftharpoons HCO_3^-(aq) + OH^-(aq)$$

The OH⁻ ion concentration increases until equilibrium is established. Consequently, the H_3O^+ ion concentration decreases so that the product $[H_3O^+][OH^-]$ remains equal to the ionization constant, K_w, of water at the temperature of the solution. Thus, the pH is *higher* than 7, and the solution is basic.

Cation Hydrolysis

In the Brønsted sense, the cation of the salt is the conjugate acid of the base from which it was formed. It is also a proton donor. If the base is weak, the cation is an acid strong enough to donate a proton to a water molecule, a proton acceptor, to form H_3O^+ ions. An equilibrium is established in which the net effect of the cation hydrolysis is an increase in the hydronium-ion concentration, $[H_3O^+]$, of the solution.

The following equilibrium equation for a typical weak base, B, is used to derive the generalized expression for K_b, the base dissociation constant.

$$B(aq) + H_2O(l) \rightleftharpoons BH^+(aq) + OH^-(aq)$$

$$K_b = \frac{[BH^+][OH^-]}{[B]}$$

The hydrolysis reaction between water and the cation, BH^+, produced by the dissociation of the weak base, B, is represented by the general equilibrium equation that follows.

$$BH^+(aq) + H_2O(l) \rightleftharpoons H_3O^+(aq) + B(aq)$$

In the forward reaction, the cation BH^+ donates a proton to the water molecule to form the hydronium ion and the weak base, B. The extent of H_3O^+ ion formation and the position of the equilibrium depend on the relative strength of the cation, BH^+. The lower the K_b value of B, the stronger the donation of protons that BH^+ will have compared with H_3O^+, and the greater the production of H_3O^+ ions will be. Therefore, as the relative strength of BH^+ increases, the equilibrium position lies farther to the right.

Ammonium chloride, NH_4Cl, dissociates in water to produce NH_4^+ ions, Cl^- ions, and an acidic solution. Chloride ions are the conjugate base of a strong acid, HCl, so they show no noticeable tendency to hydrolyze in aqueous solution. Ammonium ions, however, are the conjugate acid of a weak base, NH_3. Ammonium ions donate protons to water molecules. Equilibrium is established with an increased $[H_3O^+]$, so the pH is *lower* than 7.

FIGURE 18-11 At point *1* on the titration curve, only acetic acid is present. The pH depends on the weak acid alone. At *2* there is a mixture of CH_3COOH and CH_3COO^-. Adding NaOH changes the pH slowly. At point *3* all acid has been converted to CH_3COO^-. This hydrolyzes to produce a slightly basic solution. At *4* the pH is due to the excess OH^- that has been added.

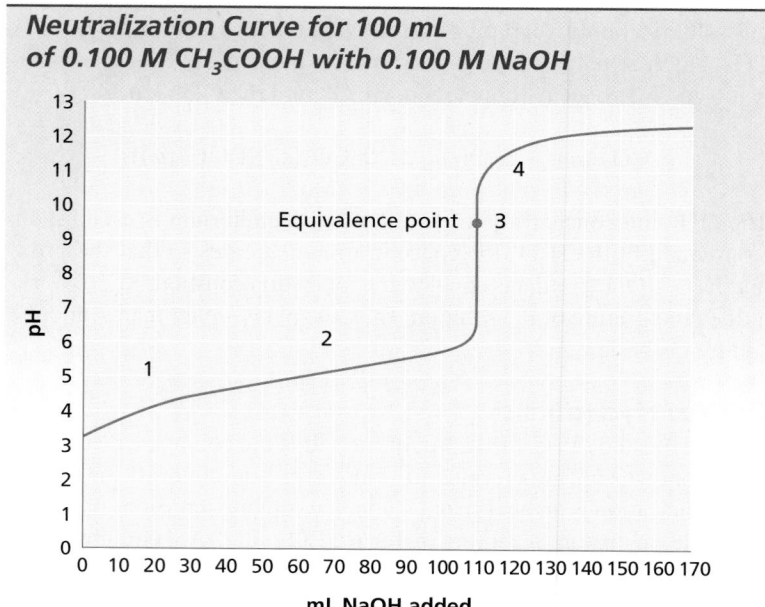

Neutralization Curve for 100 mL of 0.100 M CH₃COOH with 0.100 M NaOH

Equivalence point • 3

mL NaOH added

Hydrolysis in Acid-Base Reactions

Hydrolysis can help explain why the end point of a neutralization reaction can occur at a pH other than 7. The hydrolysis properties of salts are determined by the relative strengths of the acids and bases from which the salts were formed. Salts can be placed in four general categories, depending on their hydrolysis properties: strong acid–strong base, strong acid–weak base, weak acid–strong base, and weak acid–weak base.

Salts of strong acids and strong bases produce neutral solutions because neither the cation of a strong base nor the anion of a strong acid hydrolyze appreciably in aqueous solutions. HCl(aq) is a strong acid, and NaOH(aq) is a strong base. Neither the Na$^+$ cation of the strong base nor the Cl$^-$ anion of the strong acid undergoes hydrolysis in water solutions. Therefore, aqueous solutions of NaCl are neutral. Similarly, KNO$_3$ is the salt of the strong acid HNO$_3$ and the strong base KOH. Measurements show that the pH of an aqueous KNO$_3$ solution is always very close to 7.

The aqueous solutions of salts formed from reactions between weak acids and strong bases are basic, as Figure 18-11 shows. Anions of the dissolved salt are hydrolyzed in the water solvent, and the pH of the solution is raised, indicating that the hydroxide-ion concentration has increased. Aqueous solutions of sodium acetate, NaCH$_3$COO, are basic. The acetate ions, CH$_3$COO$^-$, undergo hydrolysis because they are the anions of the weak acid–acetic acid. The cations of the salt are the positive ions from a strong base, NaOH, and do not hydrolyze appreciably.

Figure 18-12 shows that salts of strong acids and weak bases produce acidic aqueous solutions. Cations of the dissolved salt are hydrolyzed in

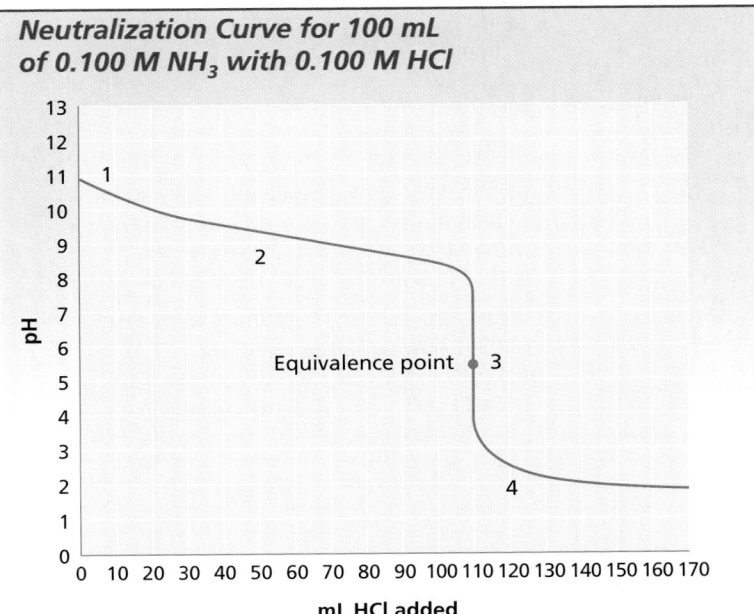

Neutralization Curve for 100 mL of 0.100 M NH₃ with 0.100 M HCl

(y-axis: pH, values 0–13; x-axis: mL HCl added, values 0 to 170)

1
2
Equipment point • 3
4

mL HCl added

Visual Strategy

FIGURE 18-12 Ask students to compare this graph with Figure 18-11. Have them explain why the pHs at the equivalence points differ.

Class Discussion

Have students compare the results of hydrolysis of different salts to a tug-of-war. Have them visualize the different sides as "acid" and "base." Have them explain the results of a tug-of-war for salts of strong bases and strong acids, strong bases and weak acids, weak bases and strong acids, and weak bases and weak acids.

✔ **Teaching Tip**

The results of hydrolysis of the salt of a weak acid and a weak base are more unpredictable than those for other types of salts.

FIGURE 18-12 At point *1* on the titration curve, only aqueous ammonia is present. The pH is determined by the base alone. At *2* there is a mixture of NH$_3$ and NH$_4^+$. Adding HCl changes the pH slowly. At point *3* all aqueous ammonia has been converted to NH$_4^+$. At *4* the pH is determined by the excess H$_3$O$^+$ that is being added.

SECTION REVIEW

1. the equilibrium constant, K_a, for the reaction that produces hydronium ions

2. K_a equals the product of the concentration of the ions formed by the acid divided by the concentration of the nonionized acid.

3. a solution that contains a weak acid or base and a salt of that acid or base and that can resist changes in pH

4. b

5. the equilibrium constant for the self-ionization of water, K_w, which equals $[H_3O^+][OH^-] = 10^{-14}$

6. a. H_2CO_3 and HCO_3^-; H_2O and H_3O^+
b. H_2O and OH^-; H_2O and H_3O^+
c. H_2S and HS^-; NH_3 and NH_4^+
d. $H_2PO_4^-$ and H_3PO_4; H_2O and OH^-

7. Hydrolysis is the reaction between water molecules and ions of a dissolved salt. Cation hydrolysis produces H_3O^+ and an acidic solution; anion hydrolysis produces OH^- and a basic solution.

8. b, c, e, g, h

9. a. neutral
b. basic
c. acidic
d. basic

10. a. H_2CrO_4, KOH
b. CH_3COOH, $Ca(OH)_2$
c. HF, $Ca(OH)_2$
d. H_2SO_4, NH_3

the water solvent, and the pH of the solution is lowered, indicating that the hydronium-ion concentration has increased. In this case, the cations of the salt undergo hydrolysis because they are the positive ions from a weak base. The anions of the salt are the negative ions from a strong acid and do not hydrolyze appreciably. Ammonium chloride, NH_4Cl, is a salt that produces an acidic solution.

Salts of weak acids and weak bases can produce either acidic, neutral, or basic aqueous solutions, depending on the salt dissolved. This is because both ions of the dissolved salt are hydrolyzed extensively. If both ions are hydrolyzed equally, the solution remains neutral. The ions in ammonium acetate, NH_4CH_3COO, hydrolyze equally, producing a neutral solution, as shown in Figure 18-10(d) on page 572.

In cases in which both the acid and the base are very weak, the salt may undergo essentially complete decomposition to the products of hydrolysis. For example, when aluminum sulfide is placed in water, both a precipitate and a gas are formed. The reaction is symbolized by the following chemical equation.

$$Al_2S_3(s) + 6H_2O(l) \longrightarrow 2Al(OH)_3(s) + 3H_2S(g)$$

Both products are sparingly soluble in water and are removed from solution.

SECTION REVIEW

1. What is meant by an *acid-ionization constant*?

2. How is an acid-ionization equilibrium expression written?

3. What is meant by the term *buffered solution*?

4. Which of the following combinations of solutions would form buffers when they are mixed?
a. 50 mL of 1.0 M HCl and 50 mL of 1.0 M NaCl
b. 25 mL of 0.5 M HNO_2 and 50 mL of 1.0 M $NaNO_2$
c. 25 mL of 1.0 M HNO_2 and 25 mL of 1.0 M NaCl

5. What is meant by the *ion-product constant* for water? What is the value of this constant?

6. For each of the following reactions, identify each conjugate acid-base pair.
a. $H_2CO_3 + H_2O \rightleftharpoons HCO_3^- + H_3O^+$
b. $H_2O + H_2O \rightleftharpoons H_3O^+ + OH^-$
c. $H_2S + NH_3 \rightleftharpoons HS^- + NH_4^+$
d. $H_2PO_4^- + H_2O \rightleftharpoons H_3PO_4 + OH^-$

7. What is hydrolysis? Compare cation and anion hydrolysis.

8. Which of the following ions hydrolyze in aqueous solution?
a. NO_3^- d. K^+ g. CO_3^{2-}
b. F^- e. CH_3COO^- h. PO_4^{3-}
c. NH_4^+ f. SO_4^{2-}

9. Identify the following solutions as acidic, basic, or neutral.
a. 0.5 M KI   c. 0.25 M NH_4NO_3
b. 0.10 M $Ba(OH)_2$ d. 0.05 M $BaCO_3$

10. Identify the acid and base from which each of the following salts was formed.
a. K_2CrO_4 c. CaF_2
b. $Ca(CH_3COO)_2$ d. $(NH_4)_2SO_4$

Solubility Equilibrium

OBJECTIVES

- Explain what is meant by *solubility-product constants*, and calculate their values.

- Calculate solubilities using solubility-product constants.

- Carry out calculations to predict whether precipitates will form when solutions are combined.

Ionic solids dissolve in water until they are in equilibrium with their ions. An equilibrium expression can be written from the balanced chemical equation of the solid's dissociation. Concentrations of the ions can be determined from the balanced chemical equation and solubility data. The ion concentrations can then be used to determine the value of the equilibrium constant. The numerical value for the equilibrium constant can be used to predict whether precipitation occurs when solutions of various concentrations are combined.

Solubility Product

A saturated solution contains the maximum amount of solute possible at a given temperature in equilibrium with an undissolved excess of the substance. A saturated solution is not necessarily a concentrated solution. The concentration may be high or low, depending on the solubility of the solute.

A general rule is often used to express solubilities qualitatively. By this rule, a substance is said to be *soluble* if the solubility is *greater than* 1 g per 100 g of water. It is said to be *insoluble* if the solubility is *less than* 0.1 g per 100 g of water. Substances whose solubilities fall between these limits are described as *slightly soluble.*

The equilibrium principles developed in this chapter apply to all saturated solutions of sparingly soluble salts. Silver chloride is so sparingly soluble in water that it is sometimes described as insoluble. Its solution reaches saturation at a very low concentration of its ions. All Ag^+ and Cl^- ions in excess of this concentration eventually precipitate as $AgCl$.

Consider the equilibrium system in a saturated solution of silver chloride containing an excess of the solid salt. This system is represented by the following equilibrium equation and equilibrium-constant expression.

$$AgCl(s) \rightleftharpoons Ag^+(aq) + Cl^-(aq)$$

$$K = \frac{[Ag^+][Cl^-]}{[AgCl]}$$

Because the concentration of a pure substance in the solid or liquid phase remains constant, adding more solid $AgCl$ to this equilibrium system does not change the concentration of the undissolved $AgCl$ present. Thus, $[AgCl]$ does not appear in the final expression. Rearranging

Lesson Starter
Show students unlabeled solutions of sodium hydroxide and copper(II) chloride. Ask them what they think each seems to contain. Then pour one into the other. A dark precipitate of $Cu(OH)_2$ will form. Ask students to think about what is occurring and how it is that ions are highly soluble in some combinations but only sparingly soluble in others.

Common Misconception
Use of the term *insoluble* leads some students to think that certain substances do not dissolve at all. Point out that there are no completely insoluble substances—that is, no substances for which K_{sp} is truly equal to zero. However, some substances can be considered insoluble for practical purposes.

Reading Skill-Builder

PAIRED SUMMARIZING
Assign pairs of students to read pp. 577–584. One member of the pair should concentrate on examples involving solubility calculations. The other member of the pair should do the same for precipitation calculations. Students should then explain to each other how to solve each kind of problem.

Problem-Solving Practice

Chapter 22 of the Mini-Guide to Problem Solving (also found on the One-Stop Planner CD-ROM) includes more worked-out samples and additional practice problems involving equilibrium of salts, K_{sp}.

Application

Although it might seem as if low solubility is a drawback in terms of usefulness of a substance, the extremely low solubility of a material may be the key to some of its uses. For example, the low solubility of glass makes it useful as a container.

Common Misconception

Students generally master the idea that the coefficients are to be used as exponents of concentration in the equilibrium expression. However, they often forget that the concentration values themselves must reflect the number of ions produced per formula unit. For example, if AB_2 produces a saturation concentration of 1×10^{-5} mol/L, the concentration of B^- will be twice that value, 2×10^{-5}, and that is the value that must be squared in the equilibrium expression.

✔ Teaching Tip

The very small K_{sp} of AgCl tells us that only about 6.2×10^{-6} mol of AgCl dissolves in 1 L of solution. The volume occupied by this minute amount of solute is very small compared to the total volume of solution. This allows us to make the assumption that the solubility of a sparingly soluble salt expressed in moles per liter of water is very nearly equal to moles per liter of solution.

the equilibrium expression so that both constants are on the same side of the equation gives the solubility-product constant K_{sp}. *The* **solubility-product constant** *of a substance is the product of the molar concentrations of its ions in a saturated solution, each raised to the power that is the coefficient of that ion in the chemical equation.*

$$K[AgCl] = [Ag^+][Cl^-]$$
$$K_{sp} = [Ag^+][Cl^-]$$

This equation is the solubility-equilibrium expression for the reaction. It expresses the fact that the solubility-product constant, K_{sp}, of AgCl is the product of the molar concentrations of its ions in a saturated solution.

Calcium fluoride is another sparingly soluble salt. The equilibrium in a saturated CaF_2 solution is described by the following equation.

$$CaF_2(s) \rightleftarrows Ca^{2+}(aq) + 2F^-(aq)$$

The solubility-product constant has the following form.

$$K_{sp} = [Ca^{2+}][F^-]^2$$

Notice that this constant is the product of the molar concentration of Ca^{2+} ions and the molar concentration of F^- ions squared, as required by the general chemical equilibrium expression.

The numerical value of K_{sp} can be determined from solubility data. Data listed in Appendix Table A-13 (page 901) indicate that a maximum of 8.9×10^{-5} g of AgCl can dissolve in 100. g of water at 10°C. One mole of AgCl has a mass of 143.32 g. The saturation concentration, or solubility, of AgCl can therefore be expressed in moles per liter of water, which is very nearly equal to moles per liter of solution.

$$\frac{8.9 \times 10^{-5} \text{ g AgCl}}{100. \text{ g H}_2\text{O}} \times \frac{1 \text{ g H}_2\text{O}}{\text{mL H}_2\text{O}} \times \frac{1000 \text{ mL}}{\text{L}} \times \frac{1 \text{ mol AgCl}}{143.32 \text{ g AgCl}}$$
$$= 6.2 \times 10^{-6} \text{ mol/L}$$

Silver chloride dissociates in solution, contributing equal numbers of Ag^+ and Cl^- ions. The ion concentrations in the saturated solution are therefore 6.2×10^{-6} mol/L.

$$[Ag^+] = 6.2 \times 10^{-6}$$
$$[Cl^-] = 6.2 \times 10^{-6}$$

and

$$K_{sp} = [Ag^+][Cl^-]$$
$$K_{sp} = (6.2 \times 10^{-6})(6.2 \times 10^{-6})$$
$$K_{sp} = (6.2 \times 10^{-6})^2$$
$$K_{sp} = 3.8 \times 10^{-11}$$

This result is the solubility-product constant of AgCl at 10°C.

From Appendix Table A-13, the solubility of CaF_2 is 1.7×10^{-3} g/100 g of water at 26°C. Expressed in moles per liter, as before, this concentration becomes 2.2×10^{-4} mol/L. CaF_2 dissociates in solution to yield twice as many F^- ions as Ca^{2+} ions. The ion concentrations in the saturated solution are 2.2×10^{-4} for the calcium ion and $2(2.2 \times 10^{-4})$, or 4.4×10^{-4}, for the fluoride ion. Note that at equilibrium at 26°C, $[Ca^{2+}]$ equals the solubility of 2.2×10^{-4} mol/L but $[F^-]$ equals twice the solubility, or 4.4×10^{-4} mol/L. The number of moles of positive and negative ions per mole of compound must always be accounted for when using K_{sp} and solubilities.

$$K_{sp} = [Ca^{2+}][F^-]^2$$
$$K_{sp} = (2.2 \times 10^{-4})(4.4 \times 10^{-4})^2$$
$$K_{sp} = 4.3 \times 10^{-11}$$

Thus, the solubility-product constant of CaF_2 is 4.3×10^{-11} at 26°C.

It is difficult to measure very small concentrations of a solute with precision. For this reason, solubility data from different sources may report different values of K_{sp} for a substance. Thus, calculations of K_{sp} ordinarily should be limited to two significant figures. Representative values of K_{sp} at 25°C for some sparingly soluble compounds are listed in Table 18-3. Assume that all data used in K_{sp} calculations have been taken at 25°C unless otherwise specified.

At this point, you should note the difference between the solubility of a given solid and its solubility-product constant. Remember that the

TABLE STRATEGY

Table 18-3 Have students compare the K_{sp} values shown. Direct their attention to the enormous ranges of solubility. Point out that exponents such as −50 indicate incredibly small numbers. Thus, some of the compounds, such as silver sulfide, are so nearly insoluble that if it were possible to put together an Earth-sized sample of the compound and place it in sufficient water, very few ions would break free into solution.

TABLE 18-3 Solubility-Product Constants, K_{sp}, at 25°C

Salt	Ion product	K_{sp}	Salt	Ion product	K_{sp}
$AgCH_3COO$	$[Ag^+][CH_3COO^-]$	1.9×10^{-3}	CuCl	$[Cu^+][Cl^-]$	1.2×10^{-6}
AgBr	$[Ag^+][Br^-]$	5.0×10^{-13}	CuS	$[Cu^{2+}][S^{2-}]$	6.3×10^{-36}
Ag_2CO_3	$[Ag^+]^2[CO_3^{2-}]$	8.1×10^{-12}	FeS	$[Fe^{2+}][S^{2-}]$	6.3×10^{-18}
AgCl	$[Ag^+][Cl^-]$	1.8×10^{-10}	$Fe(OH)_2$	$[Fe^{2+}][OH^-]^2$	8.0×10^{-16}
AgI	$[Ag^+][I^-]$	8.3×10^{-17}	$Fe(OH)_3$	$[Fe^{3+}][OH^-]^3$	4×10^{-38}
Ag_2S	$[Ag^+]^2[S^{2-}]$	6.3×10^{-50}	HgS	$[Hg^{2+}][S^{2-}]$	1.6×10^{-52}
$Al(OH)_3$	$[Al^{3+}][OH^-]^3$	1.3×10^{-33}	$MgCO_3$	$[Mg^{2+}][CO_3^{2-}]$	3.5×10^{-8}
$BaCO_3$	$[Ba^{2+}][CO_3^{2-}]$	5.1×10^{-9}	$Mg(OH)_2$	$[Mg^{2+}][OH^-]^2$	1.8×10^{-11}
$BaSO_4$	$[Ba^{2+}][SO_4^{2-}]$	1.1×10^{-10}	MnS	$[Mn^{2+}][S^{2-}]$	2.5×10^{-13}
CdS	$[Cd^{2+}][S^{2-}]$	8.0×10^{-27}	$PbCl_2$	$[Pb^{2+}][Cl^-]^2$	1.6×10^{-5}
$CaCO_3$	$[Ca^{2+}][CO_3^{2-}]$	2.8×10^{-9}	$PbCrO_4$	$[Pb^{2+}][CrO_4^{2-}]$	2.8×10^{-13}
CaF_2	$[Ca^{2+}][F^-]^2$	5.3×10^{-9}	$PbSO_4$	$[Pb^{2+}][SO_4^{2-}]$	1.6×10^{-8}
$Ca(OH)_2$	$[Ca^{2+}][OH^-]^2$	5.5×10^{-6}	PbS	$[Pb^{2+}][S^{2-}]$	8.0×10^{-28}
$CaSO_4$	$[Ca^{2+}][SO_4^{2-}]$	9.1×10^{-6}	SnS	$[Sn^{2+}][S^{2-}]$	1.0×10^{-25}
$CoCO_3$	$[Co^{2+}][CO_3^{2-}]$	1.4×10^{-13}	$SrSO_4$	$[Sr^{2+}][SO_4^{2-}]$	3.2×10^{-7}
CoS	$[Co^{2+}][S^{2-}]$	4.0×10^{-21}	ZnS	$[Zn^{2+}][S^{2-}]$	1.6×10^{-24}

ADDITIONAL

SAMPLE
PROBLEMS

18-2 What is the value of K_{sp} for tin(II) sulfide, given that its solubility is 5.2×10^{-12} g/100. g water?

Ans. 1.2×10^{-25}

18-2 Calculate the solubility product constant for calcium carbonate, given that it has a solubility of 5.3×10^{-5} g/L of water.

Ans. 2.8×10^{-9}

(Emphasize that these K_{sp} values can be calculated from the solubility, even though they are given in Table 18-3.)

solubility-product constant is an equilibrium constant representing the product of the molar concentrations of its ions in a saturated solution. It has only one value for a given solid at a given temperature. The *solubility* of a solid is an equilibrium position that represents the amount of the solid required to form a saturated solution with a specific amount of solvent. It has an infinite number of possible values at a given temperature and is dependent on other conditions, such as the presence of a common ion.

SAMPLE PROBLEM 18-2

Calculate the solubility-product constant, K_{sp}, for copper(I) chloride, CuCl, given that the solubility of this compound at 25°C is 1.08×10^{-2} g/100. g H_2O.

SOLUTION

1 **ANALYZE**   **Given:** solubility of CuCl = 1.08×10^{-2} g CuCl/100. g H_2O
Unknown: K_{sp}

2 **PLAN**   Start by converting the solubility of CuCl in g/100. g H_2O to mol/L. You will need the molar mass of CuCl to get moles CuCl from grams CuCl. Then use the solubility of the $[Cu^+]$ and $[Cl^-]$ ions in the K_{sp} expression and solve for K_{sp}.

$$\frac{\text{g CuCl}}{100. \text{ g } H_2O} \times \frac{1 \text{ g } H_2O}{1 \text{ mL } H_2O} \times \frac{1000 \text{ mL}}{1 \text{ L}} \times \frac{1 \text{ mol CuCl}}{\text{g CuCl}} = \text{solubility in mol/L}$$

$$CuCl(s) \rightleftharpoons Cu^+(aq) + Cl^-(aq)$$
$$K_{sp} = [Cu^+][Cl^-]$$
$$[Cu^+] = [Cl^-] = \text{solubility in mol/L}$$

3 **COMPUTE**   The molar mass of CuCl is 99.0 g/mol.

$$\text{solubility} = \frac{1.08 \times 10^{-2} \text{ g CuCl}}{100. \text{ g } H_2O} \times \frac{1 \text{ g } H_2O}{1 \text{ mL}} \times \frac{1000 \text{ mL}}{L} \times \frac{1 \text{ mol CuCl}}{99.0 \text{ g CuCl}} =$$

$$1.09 \times 10^{-3} \text{ mol/L CuCl}$$

$$[Cu^+] = [Cl^-] = 1.09 \times 10^{-3} \text{ mol/L}$$
$$K_{sp} = (1.09 \times 10^{-3})(1.09 \times 10^{-3}) = 1.19 \times 10^{-6}$$

4 **EVALUATE**   The answer contains the proper number of significant figures and is close to the K_{sp} value given in Table 18-3.

PRACTICE
1. Calculate the solubility-product constant, K_{sp}, of lead(II) chloride, $PbCl_2$, which has a solubility of 1.0 g/100. g H_2O at a temperature other than 25°C.

Answer
1.9×10^{-4}

2. Five grams of Ag_2SO_4 will dissolve in 1 L of water. Calculate the solubility product constant for this salt.

Answer
2×10^{-5}

Calculating Solubilities

Once known, the solubility-product constant can be used to determine the solubility of a sparingly soluble salt. Suppose you wish to know how much barium carbonate, $BaCO_3$, can be dissolved in 1 L of water at 25°C. From Table 18-3, K_{sp} for $BaCO_3$ has the numerical value 5.1×10^{-9}. The equilibrium equation is written as follows.

$$BaCO_3(s) \rightleftharpoons Ba^{2+}(aq) + CO_3^{2-}(aq)$$

Given the value for K_{sp}, we can write the solubility-equilibrium expression as follows.

$$K_{sp} = [Ba^{2+}][CO_3^{2-}] = 5.1 \times 10^{-9}$$

Therefore, $BaCO_3$ dissolves until the product of the molar concentrations of Ba^{2+} ions and CO_3^{2-} ions equals 5.1×10^{-9}. The solubility-equilibrium equation shows that Ba^{2+} ions and CO_3^{2-} ions enter the solution in equal numbers as the salt dissolves. Thus, they have the same concentration. Let $[Ba^{2+}] = x$. Then $[CO_3^{2-}] = x$ also.

$$[Ba^{2+}][CO_3^{2-}] = K_{sp} = 5.1 \times 10^{-9}$$
$$(x)(x) = 5.1 \times 10^{-9}$$
$$x = \sqrt{5.1 \times 10^{-9}}$$

The solubility of $BaCO_3$ is 7.14×10^{-5} mol/L.

Thus, the solution concentration is 7.14×10^{-5} M for Ba^{2+} ions and 7.14×10^{-5} M for CO_3^{2-} ions.

SAMPLE PROBLEM 18-3

Calculate the solubility of silver acetate, $AgCH_3COO$, in mol/L, given the K_{sp} value for this compound listed in Table 18-3.

SOLUTION

1 ANALYZE

Given: $K_{sp} = 1.9 \times 10^{-3}$
Unknown: solubility of $AgCH_3COO$

2 PLAN

$$AgCH_3COO \rightleftharpoons Ag^+(aq) + CH_3COO^-(aq)$$
$$K_{sp} = [Ag^+][CH_3COO^-]$$

$[Ag^+] = [CH_3COO^-]$, so let $[Ag^+] = x$ and $[CH_3COO^-] = x$

3 COMPUTE

$$K_{sp} = [Ag^+][CH_3COO^-]$$
$$K_{sp} = x^2$$
$$x^2 = 1.9 \times 10^{-3}$$
$$x = \sqrt{1.9 \times 10^{-3}}$$

Solubility of $AgCH_3COO = \sqrt{1.9 \times 10^{-3}} = 4.4 \times 10^{-2}$ mol/L

18-3 What is the solubility in mol/L of manganese(II) sulfide, MnS, given that its K_{sp} value is 2.5×10^{-13}?

Ans. 5.0×10^{-7} mol/L

18-3 Calculate the concentration of Zn^{2+} in a saturated solution of zinc sulfide, ZnS, given that K_{sp} of zinc sulfide equals 1.6×10^{-24}.

Ans. 1.3×10^{-12} mol/L

Visual Strategy

FIGURE 18-13 Point out to students that cloudiness of a mixture of solutions, as well as the appearance of a solid in the bottom, is evidence of formation of a precipitate. Have them look at each picture and decide whether a precipitate has formed *(precipitates form in (c), (d), and (e).)* Be sure students understand that a change of color does not indicate a precipitate if the solution remains clear (see photo at bottom right).

4 EVALUATE The answer has the proper number of significant figures and is close to an estimated value of 5.0×10^{-2} calculated as $\sqrt{2.5 \times 10^{-3}}$.

PRACTICE

1. Calculate the solubility of cadmium sulfide, CdS, in mol/L, given the K_{sp} value listed in Table 18-3.

   Answer
   8.9×10^{-14} mol/L

2. Determine the concentration of strontium ions in a saturated solution of strontium sulfate, $SrSO_4$, if the K_{sp} for $SrSO_4$ is 3.2×10^{-7}.

   Answer
   5.7×10^{-4} mol/L

Precipitation Calculations

In an earlier example, $BaCO_3$ served as the source of both Ba^{2+} and CO_3^{2-} ions. Because each mole of $BaCO_3$ yields one mole of Ba^{2+} ions and one mole of CO_3^{2-} ions, the concentrations of the two ions were equal. However, the equilibrium condition does not require that the two ion concentrations be equal. Equilibrium will still be established so that the ion product $[Ba^{2+}][CO_3^{2-}]$ does not exceed the value of K_{sp} for the system.

Similarly, if the ion product $[Ca^{2+}][F^-]^2$ is less than the value of K_{sp} at a particular temperature, the solution is unsaturated. If the ion product is greater than the value for K_{sp}, CaF_2 precipitates. This precipitation reduces the concentrations of Ca^{2+} and F^- ions until equilibrium is established.

Suppose that unequal quantities of $BaCl_2$ and Na_2CO_3 are dissolved in water and that the solutions are mixed. If the ion product $[Ba^{2+}][CO_3^{2-}]$ exceeds the K_{sp} of $BaCO_3$, a precipitate of $BaCO_3$ forms. Precipitation continues until the ion concentrations decrease to the point at which $[Ba^{2+}][CO_3^{2-}]$ equals the K_{sp}.

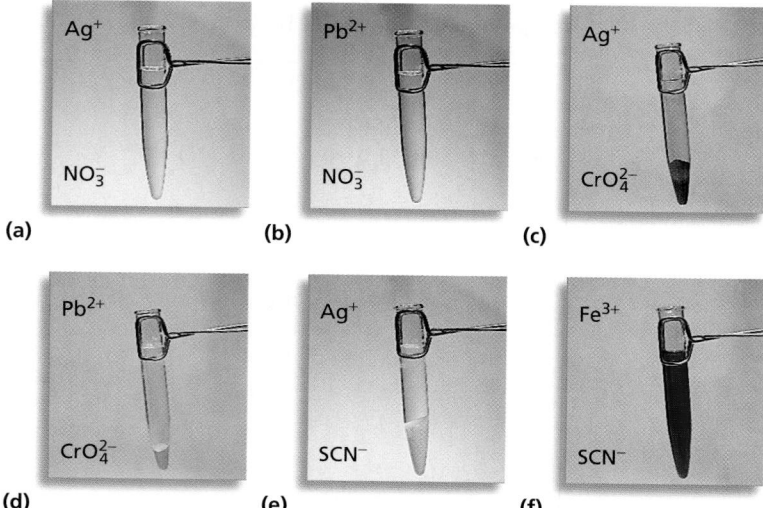

(a) (b) (c)

(d) (e) (f)

FIGURE 18-13 Nitrate salts of Ag^+ (a) and Pb^{2+} (b) are soluble. When chromate ions, CrO_4^{2-}, combine with Ag^+ (c) or Pb^{2+} (d), an insoluble salt forms. Thiocyanate ions, SCN^-, can form an insoluble salt with Ag^+ (e) or a soluble salt with Fe^{3+} (f).

Substances differ greatly in their tendencies to form precipitates when mixed in moderate concentrations. The photos in Figure 18-13 show the behavior of some negative ions in the presence of certain metallic ions. Note that some of the combinations have produced precipitates and some have not. The solubility product can be used to predict whether a precipitate forms when two solutions are mixed.

Most Na^+, K^+, NH_4^+, nitrate, acetate, sulfate, and halide salts are soluble. Most hydroxides, sulfides, carbonates, and phosphates are insoluble.

Common Misconception

Students often think simply in terms of solubility of a compound as a whole and assume that the ratio of ions present in solution is always the same as that in the compound. When different solutions are mixed, however, the initial ion concentrations in the mixture depend on the concentrations in the components and on the relative volumes mixed. Point out this concept to them as you go over the Sample Problem on this page.

SAMPLE PROBLEM 18-4

Will a precipitate form if 20.0 mL of 0.010 M $BaCl_2$ is mixed with 20.0 mL of 0.0050 M Na_2SO_4?

SOLUTION

1 ANALYZE

Given: concentration of $BaCl_2$ = 0.010 M
volume of $BaCl_2$ = 20.0 mL
concentration of Na_2SO_4 = 0.0050 M
volume of Na_2SO_4 = 20.0 mL
Unknown: whether a precipitate forms

2 PLAN

The two possible new pairings of ions are NaCl and $BaSO_4$. Of these, $BaSO_4$ is a sparingly soluble salt. It will precipitate if the ion product $[Ba^{2+}][SO_4^{2-}]$ in the combined solution exceeds K_{sp} for $BaSO_4$. From the list of solubility products in Table 18-3, the K_{sp} is found to be 1.1×10^{-10}. The solubility-equilibrium equation follows.

$$BaSO_4(s) \rightleftharpoons Ba^{2+}(aq) + SO_4^{2-}(aq)$$

The solubility-equilibrium expression is written as follows.

$$K_{sp} = [Ba^{2+}][SO_4^{2-}] = 1.1 \times 10^{-10}$$

First $[Ba^{2+}]$ and $[SO_4^{2-}]$ in the above solution must be found. Then the ion product is calculated and compared with the K_{sp}.

3 COMPUTE

Calculate the mole quantities of Ba^{2+} and SO_4^{2-} ions.

$$0.020 \; \cancel{L} \times \frac{0.010 \text{ mol } Ba^{2+}}{\cancel{L}} = 0.000 \; 20 \text{ mol } Ba^{2+}$$

$$0.020 \; \cancel{L} \times \frac{0.0050 \text{ mol } SO_4^{2-}}{\cancel{L}} = 0.000 \; 10 \text{ mol } SO_4^{2-}$$

Calculate the total volume of solution containing Ba^{2+} and SO_4^{2-} ions.

$$0.020 \text{ L} + 0.020 \text{ L} = 0.040 \text{ L}$$

Calculate the Ba^{2+} and SO_4^{2-} ion concentrations in the combined solution.

$$\frac{0.000 \; 20 \text{ mol } Ba^{2+}}{0.040 \text{ L}} = 5.0 \times 10^{-3} \text{ mol/L } Ba^{2+}$$

$$\frac{0.000 \; 10 \text{ mol } SO_4^{2-}}{0.040 \text{ L}} = 2.5 \times 10^{-3} \text{ mol/L } SO_4^{2-}$$

18-4 Will a precipitate form if 20. mL of 0.034 M NaCl and 15 mL of 0.083 M $CuNO_3$ are mixed?

Ans. Yes; CuCl precipitates.

18-4 Does a precipitate form if 100. mL of 0.0014 M $Ca(NO_3)_2$ and 200. mL of 0.000 20 M Na_2SO_4 are mixed?

Ans. No; $CaSO_4$ does not precipitate.

SECTION REVIEW

1. the product of the molar concentrations of the ions in a saturated solution, each raised to a power that is the coefficient of that ion in the chemical equation; from careful measurements of ion solubilities

2. by using the solubility equilibrium equation, solving for an ion concentration, and then relating ion concentration to moles of solute

3. the product of the ion concentrations present in solution, each raised to the appropriate power

4. The ion product is calculated; if it exceeds the K_{sp}, then a precipitate will form.

5. 2.07×10^{-5}

6. The ion product of silver and chloride ions in the sample solution is less than the solubility-product constant, so no precipitate will form.

Trial value of the ion product:

$$[Ba^{2+}][SO_4^{2-}] = (5.0 \times 10^{-3})(2.5 \times 10^{-3})$$
$$= 1.2 \times 10^{-5}$$

The ion product is much greater than the value of K_{sp}, so precipitation occurs.

4 EVALUATE   The answer contains the appropriate number of significant figures and is close to an estimated value of 1×10^{-5}, calculated as $(5 \times 10^{-3})(2 \times 10^{-3})$; because $10^{-5} > 10^{-10}$, precipitation should occur.

PRACTICE

1. Does a precipitate form when 100. mL of 0.0025 M $AgNO_3$ and 150. mL of 0.0020 M NaBr solutions are mixed?

   Answer
   AgBr precipitates.

2. Does a precipitate form when 20. mL of 0.038 M $Pb(NO_3)_2$ and 30. mL of 0.018 M KCl solutions are mixed?

   Answer
   $PbCl_2$ does *not* precipitate.

Limitations on the Use of K_{sp}

The solubility-product principle can be very useful when applied to solutions of sparingly soluble substances. It *cannot* be applied very successfully to solutions of moderately soluble or very soluble substances. This is because the positive and negative ions attract each other, and this attraction becomes appreciable when the ions are close together. Sometimes it is necessary to consider two equilibria simultaneously. For example, if either ion hydrolyzes, the salt will be more soluble than predicted when only the solubility-product constant is used. The solubility product is also sensitive to changes in solution temperature to the extent that the solubility of the dissolved substance is affected by such changes. All of these factors limit the conditions under which the solubility-product principle can be applied.

SECTION REVIEW

1. What is a solubility-product constant? How are such constants determined?

2. How are solubility-product constants used to calculate solubilities?

3. What is an ion product?

4. How are calculations to predict possible precipitation carried out?

5. What is the value of K_{sp} for Ag_2SO_4 if 5.40 g is soluble in 1.00 L of water?

6. Determine whether a precipitate will form if 20.0 mL of 1.00×10^{-7} M $AgNO_3$ is mixed with 20.0 mL of 2.00×10^{-9} M NaCl at 25°C.

CHAPTER 18 REVIEW

CHAPTER SUMMARY

18-1
- A reaction system in which the forward and reverse reactions occur simultaneously and at the same rate is said to be in *equilibrium*. Both reactions continue, but there is no net change in the composition of the system.
- At equilibrium, the ratio of the product of the mole concentrations of substances formed to the

product of the mole concentrations of reactants, each raised to the appropriate power, has a definite numerical value, K, which is the equilibrium constant at a given temperature. For values of K greater than 1, the products of the forward reaction are favored. For values of K less than 1, the products of the reverse reaction are favored.

Vocabulary

chemical equilibrium (554)   chemical-equilibrium expression (556)

equilibrium constant (556)   reversible reaction (553)

18-2
- Any change that alters the rate of either the forward or reverse reaction disturbs the equilibrium of the system. According to Le Châtelier's principle, the equilibrium is shifted in the direction that relieves the stress.
- Catalysts increase the rates of forward and reverse reactions equally, and they do not shift

an equilibrium or change the value of K.
- The common-ion effect is recognized when a solution containing ions like those of a reactant in an equilibrium system is added to the system. Le Châtelier's principle explains the response of the system to the stress.

Vocabulary

common-ion effect (567)

18-3
- The equilibrium expression for the ionization constant of the weak acid HA follows.

$$K_a = \frac{[H_3O^+][A^-]}{[HA]}$$

- Salts formed from strong bases and weak acids produce aqueous solutions that are basic because of *anion hydrolysis*.
- Salts formed from strong acids and weak bases

produce aqueous solutions that are acidic because of *cation hydrolysis*.
- Salts formed from strong acids and strong bases do not hydrolyze in water, and their solutions are neutral.
- Salts formed from weak acids and weak bases may produce neutral, acidic, or basic solutions, depending on the relative amounts of cation and anion hydrolysis. They may also hydrolyze completely in water solution.

Vocabulary

acid-ionization constant (569)   buffered solution (570)

hydrolysis (572)

18-4
- Ions of salts that are very sparingly soluble form saturated aqueous solutions at low concentrations. The solubility-equilibrium expression for such salts yields a useful constant—the solubility-product constant, K_{sp}. The value of K_{sp} equals

the product of the molar concentrations of solute ions in the saturated solution raised to a power equal to the coefficient in the balanced equation for the solution of one mole.

Vocabulary

solubility-product constant (578)

REVIEW ANSWERS

1. At the start, A and B are at their maximum concentrations and there is no C or D. As A and B react, their concentrations decrease and those of C and D increase. The rate at which C and D combine increases while the rate at which A and B combine decreases. Eventually, the two rates become equal and equilibrium is established. The concentrations of A, B, C, and D then remain constant as long as conditions remain the same.

2. **a.** $K = \dfrac{[C]^x[D]^y \cdots}{[A]^n[B]^m \cdots}$
   b. the extent to which reactants are converted into products

3. **a.** neither   **c.** forward
   b. reverse

4. **a.** forward   **b.** reverse

5. pure substances in the solid and liquid phases; because their concentrations are not changed by the addition or removal of quantities of these materials

6. It increases the rates of forward and reverse reactions equally, so the relative equilibrium amounts are not affected.

7. **a.** forward   **f.** neither
   b. forward   **g.** neither
   c. neither   **h.** reverse
   d. forward   **i.** neither
   e. reverse

8. [HCl] and K, respectively, would:
   a. increase, remain the same
   b. decrease, remain the same
   c. remain the same, remain the same
   d. increase, increase
   e. decrease, remain the same
   f. remain the same, remain the same
   g. remain the same, remain the same
   h. decrease, decrease

i. remain the same, remain the same

9. Such changes have an equal effect on the numerator and denominator, so K, the ratio, is not affected.

10. high pressure, because the forward reaction converts three molecules into two, relieving the stress imposed by the pressure increase

11. a. high reactant concentrations, high pressure, low temperature
b. high reactant concentrations, pressure not relevant, low temperature
c. high reactant concentrations, pressure not relevant, high temperature
d. high reactant concentrations, high pressure, low temperature
e. high reactant concentrations, low pressure, high temperature

12. a. an increase in rate
b. Air is only about one-fifth oxygen, which is a reactant. Use of pure oxygen would increase oxygen concentration.

13. solubility of the compound formed and degree of ionization

14. A gaseous product is formed:
$H_3O^+(aq) + HCO_3^-(aq) \longrightarrow$
$\qquad 2H_2O(l) + CO_2(g)$

A precipitate is formed:
$Ag^+(aq) + Cl^-(aq) \longrightarrow AgCl(s)$

A slightly ionized product is formed:
$H_3O^+(aq) + OH^-(aq) \longrightarrow$
$\qquad 2H_2O(l)$

15. a. $K_w = [H_3O^+][OH^-]$
b. $K_w = 10^{-14}$

16. *Salts of strong acids and strong bases:* neither the cations nor the anions hydrolyze appreciably. Neutral aqueous solutions with a pH of 7 result. NaCl is an example.

REVIEWING CONCEPTS

1. Describe and explain how the concentrations of A, B, C, and D change from the time when A and B are first combined to the point at which equilibrium is established for the reaction A + B $\rightleftarrows$ C + D. (18-1)

2. a. Write the general expression for an equilibrium constant based on the equation
$nA + mB + \ldots \rightleftarrows xC + yD + \ldots$
b. What information is provided by the value of K for a given equilibrium system at a specified temperature? (18-1)

3. In general, which reaction is favored (forward, reverse, or neither) if the value of K at a specified temperature is
a. equal to 1?
b. very small?
c. very large? (18-1)

4. Predict whether each of the following pressure changes would favor the forward or reverse reaction.
$2NO(g) + O_2(g) \rightleftarrows 2NO_2(g)$
a. increased pressure
b. decreased pressure (18-2)

5. In heterogeneous reaction systems, what types of substances do not appear in the equilibrium constant expression? Why? (18-2)

6. Explain the effect of a catalyst on an equilibrium system. (18-2)

7. Predict the effect of each of the following on the indicated equilibrium system in terms of which reaction will be favored (forward, reverse, or neither).
$H_2(g) + Cl_2(g) \rightleftarrows 2HCl(g) + 184 \text{ kJ}$
a. addition of Cl_2
b. removal of HCl
c. increased pressure
d. decreased temperature
e. removal of H_2
f. decreased pressure
g. addition of a catalyst
h. increased temperature
i. decreased system volume (18-2)

8. How would parts (a) through (i) of item 7 affect the new equilibrium concentration of HCl and the value of K at the new equilibrium? (18-2)

9. Changes in the concentrations of the reactants and products at equilibrium have no impact on the value of the equilibrium constant. Explain. (18-2)

10. What relative pressure (high or low) would result in the production of the maximum level of CO_2 according to the following? Explain. (18-2)
$2CO(g) + O_2(g) \rightleftarrows 2CO_2(g)$

11. What relative conditions (reactant concentrations, pressure, and temperature) would favor a high equilibrium concentration of the underlined substance in each of the following equilibrium systems?
a. $2CO(g) + O_2(g) \rightleftarrows \underline{2CO_2(g)} + 167 \text{ kJ}$
b. $Cu^{2+}(aq) + 4NH_3(aq) \rightleftarrows$
$\qquad \underline{Cu(NH_3)_4^{2+}(aq)} + 42 \text{ kJ}$
c. $2HI(g) + 12.6 \text{ kJ} \rightleftarrows H_2(g) + \underline{I_2(g)}$
d. $4HCl(g) + O_2(g) \rightleftarrows$
$\qquad 2H_2O(g) + \underline{2Cl_2(g)} + 113 \text{ kJ}$
e. $H_2O(l) + 42 \text{ kJ} \rightleftarrows \underline{H_2O(g)}$ (18-2)

12. A combustion reaction proceeding in air under standard pressure is transferred to an atmosphere of pure oxygen under the same pressure.
a. What effect would you observe?
b. How can you account for this effect? (18-2)

13. What two factors determine the extent to which reacting ions are removed from solution? (18-2)

14. Identify the three conditions under which ionic reactions can run to completion, and write an equation for each. (18-2)

15. a. Write the ion-product constant expression for water.
b. What is the value of this constant at 25°C? (18-3)

16. List and distinguish between the four general categories of salts, based on their hydrolysis properties, and give an example of each. (18-3)

17. The pH of a solution containing both acetic acid and sodium acetate is higher than that of a solution containing the same concentration of acetic acid alone. Explain. (18-3)

18. The ionization constant, K_a, for acetic acid is 1.8×10^{-5} at 25°C. Explain the significance of this value. (18-3)

19. a. From the development of K_a described in Section 18-3, show how you would express an ionization constant, K_b, for the weak base NH_3.
    b. In this case, $K_b = 1.8 \times 10^{-5}$. What is the significance of this numerical value to equilibrium? (18-3)

20. A saturated solution is not necessarily a concentrated solution. Explain. (18-4)

21. What rule of thumb is used to distinguish between soluble, insoluble, and slightly soluble substances? (18-4)

22. What is the major solubility characteristic of those types of substances typically involved in solubility-equilibrium systems? (18-4)

23. What is the relationship between K_{sp} and the product of the ion concentrations in terms of determining whether a solution of those ions is saturated? (18-4)

PROBLEMS

Equilibrium Constant

24. Determine the value of the equilibrium constant for each reaction given, assuming that the equilibrium concentrations are found to be those specified. (Concentrations are in mol/L.) (Hint: See Sample Problem 18-1.)
    a. $A + B \rightleftarrows C$; $[A] = 2.0$; $[B] = 3.0$; $[C] = 4.0$
    b. $D + 2E \rightleftarrows F + 3G$; $[D] = 1.5$; $[E] = 2.0$; $[F] = 1.8$; $[G] = 1.2$
    c. $N_2(g) + 3H_2(g) \rightleftarrows 2NH_3(g)$; $[N_2] = 0.45$; $[H_2] = 0.14$; $[NH_3] = 0.62$

25. An equilibrium mixture at a specific temperature is found to consist of 1.2×10^{-3} mol/L HCl, 3.8×10^{-4} mol/L O_2, 5.8×10^{-2} mol/L H_2O, and 5.8×10^{-2} mol/L Cl_2 according to the following: $4HCl(g) + O_2(g) \rightleftarrows 2H_2O(g) + 2Cl_2(g)$.

Determine the value of the equilibrium constant for this system.

26. At 450°C the value of the equilibrium constant for the following system is 6.59×10^{-3}. If $[NH_3] = 1.23 \times 10^{-4}$ M and $[H_2] = 2.75 \times 10^{-3}$ M at equilibrium, determine the concentration of N_2 at that point.
$$N_2(g) + 3H_2(g) \rightleftarrows 2NH_3(g)$$

27. The value of the equilibrium constant for the reaction below is 40.0 at a specified temperature. What would be the value of that constant for the reverse reaction under the same conditions? $H_2(g) + I_2(g) \rightleftarrows 2HI(g)$

Solubility-Product Constant

28. The ionic substance EJ dissociates to form E^{2+} and J^{2-} ions. The solubility of EJ is 8.45×10^{-6} mol/L. What is the value of the solubility-product constant? (Hint: See Sample Problem 18-2.)

29. Calculate the solubility-product constant K_{sp} for each of the following, based on the solubility information provided:
    a. $BaSO_4 = 2.4 \times 10^{-4}$ g/100. g H_2O at 20°C
    b. $Ca(OH)_2 = 0.173$ g/100. g H_2O at 20°C

30. Calculate the solubility of a substance MN that ionizes to form M^{2+} and N^{2-} ions, given that $K_{sp} = 8.1 \times 10^{-6}$. (Hint: See Sample Problem 18-3.)

31. Use the K_{sp} values given in Table 18-3 to evaluate the solubility of each of the following in moles per liter.
    a. AgBr
    b. CoS

32. Complete each of the following relative to the reaction that occurs when 25.0 mL of 0.0500 M $Pb(NO_3)_2$ is combined with 25.0 mL of 0.0400 M Na_2SO_4 if equilibrium is reached at 25°C.
    a. Write the solubility-equilibrium equation at 25°C.
    b. Write the solubility-equilibrium expression for the net reaction.

33. The ionic substance T_3U_2 ionizes to form T^{2+} and U^{3-} ions. The solubility of T_3U_2 is 3.77×10^{-20} mol/L. What is the value of the solubility-product constant?

Salts of weak acids and strong bases: the anions hydrolyze; the cations do not. Basic aqueous solutions result. $NaCH_3COO$ is an example.
Salts of strong acids and weak bases: the anions do not hydrolyze; the cations do. Acidic aqueous solutions result. NH_4Cl is an example.
Salts of weak acids and weak bases: both the cations and the anions hydrolyze. Aqueous solutions can be acidic, basic, or neutral. NH_4CH_3COO is an example.

17. Acetic acid is a weak electrolyte and slightly ionizes in water solution. Equilibrium is established between the acid molecules and the hydronium and acetate ions in the solution. Sodium acetate is an ionic salt that completely dissociates in water. When it is added to the acetic acid solution, the concentration of acetate ion is increased, driving the equilibrium to the left. This removes hydronium ions from the solution, making it higher in pH.

18. At equilibrium, the concentration of nonionized acetic acid is high and the concentrations of hydronium and acetate ions are low. Acetic acid is a weak acid.

19. a. $K_b = \dfrac{[NH_4^+][OH^-]}{[NH_3]}$

    b. K_b is small, so there are comparatively few ions at equilibrium. Ammonia is a weak base.

20. A saturated solution is at equilibrium and contains the maximum concentration of solute. But the actual concentration of dissolved solute may be high or low, depending on the solubility.

21. soluble: greater than 1 g/100 g water; insoluble: less than 0.1 g/100 g water; slightly soluble: between these limits

22. sparingly soluble in water

23. If the ion product is less than K_{sp}, the solution is unsaturated and precipitation will not occur. If the ion product is greater than K_{sp}, precipitation will occur until the ion concentrations decrease to equilibrium values.

24. **a.** 0.67   **c.** 310
     b. 0.52

25. 1.4×10^{10}

26. 110. M

27. 0.0250

28. 7.14×10^{-11}

29. **a.** 1.1×10^{-10} **b.** 5.09×10^{-5}

30. 2.8×10^{-3} mol/L

31. **a.** 7.1×10^{-7} mol/L
     b. 6.3×10^{-11} mol/L

32. **a.** $PbSO_4(s) \rightleftharpoons$
           $Pb^{2+}(aq) + SO_4^{2-}(aq)$
     b. $K_{sp} = [Pb^{2+}][SO_4^{2-}]$

33. 8.22×10^{-96}

34. 3.1×10^{-7} mol/L

35. No precipitate will form.

36. A precipitate of AgCl will form.

37. No precipitate will form.

38. **a.** $CaCO_3(s) \rightleftharpoons$
           $Ca^{2+}(aq) + CO_3^{2-}(aq)$
     b. $K = \dfrac{[Ca^{2+}][CO_3^{2-}]}{[CaCO_3]}$

        $K_{sp} = [Ca^{2+}][CO_3^{2-}]$

39. 1.3×10^{-26} mol/L; 1.3×10^2 L

40. 1.6

41. 5×10^{-7} mol/L

42. 5.6×10^{-9} mol/L

43. The solubility is 6.1×10^{-8} mol/L. The fluoridation produces a lowered solubility, which protects tooth enamel. Answers will vary as to the benefits of fluoridation.

44. A precipitate will form.

45. 2.0 g

---

34. A solution of AgI contains 2.7×10^{-10} mol/L Ag^+. What is the maximum I^- concentration that can exist in this solution?

35. Calculate whether a precipitate will form if 0.35 L of 0.0044 M $Ca(NO_3)_2$ and 0.17 L of 0.000 39 M NaOH are mixed at 25°C. (See Table 18-3 for K_{sp} values.) (Hint: See Sample Problem 18-4.)

36. Determine whether a precipitate will form if 1.70 g of solid $AgNO_3$ and 14.5 g of solid NaCl are dissolved in 200. mL of water to form a solution at 25°C.

37. If 2.50 g of solid $Fe(NO_3)_3$ is added to 100. mL of a 1.0×10^{-20} M NaOH solution, will a precipitate form?

MIXED REVIEW

38. Calcium carbonate is only slightly soluble in water.
     a. Write the equilibrium equation for calcium carbonate in solution.
     b. Write the equilibrium-constant expression, K, and the solubility-product constant expression, K_{sp}, for the equilibrium in a saturated solution of $CaCO_3$.

39. Calculate the concentration of Hg^{2+} ions in a saturated solution of HgS(s). What volume of solution contains one Hg^{2+} ion?

40. Calculate the equilibrium constant, K, for the following reaction at 900°C.

$$H_2(g) + CO_2(g) \rightleftharpoons H_2O(g) + CO(g)$$

The components were analyzed and it was found that $[H_2] = 0.61$ mol/L, $[CO_2] = 1.6$ mol/L, $[H_2O] = 1.1$ mol/L, and $[CO] = 1.4$ mol/L.

41. A solution in equilibrium with solid barium phosphate is found to have a barium ion concentration of 5×10^{-4} M and a K_{sp} of 3.4×10^{-23}. Calculate the concentration of phosphate ion.

42. At 25°C, the value of K is 1.7×10^{-13} for the following reaction.

$$N_2O(g) + \tfrac{1}{2}O_2(g) \rightleftharpoons 2NO(g)$$

It is determined that $[N_2O] = 0.0035$ mol/L and $[O_2] = 0.0027$ mol/L. Using this information, what is the concentration of NO(g) at equilibrium?

---

43. Tooth enamel is composed of the mineral hydroxyapatite, $Ca_5(PO_4)_3OH$, which has a K_{sp} of 6.8×10^{-37}. The molar solubility of hydroxyapatite is 2.7×10^{-5} mol/L. When hydroxyapatite is reacted with fluoride, the OH^- is replaced with the F^- ion on the mineral, forming fluorapatite, $Ca_5(PO_4)_3F$. (The latter is harder and less susceptible to caries.) The K_{sp} of fluorapatite is 1×10^{-60}. Calculate the solubility of fluorapatite in water. Given your calculations, can you support the fluoridation of drinking water?

44. Determine if a precipitate will form when 0.96 g Na_2CO_3 is combined with 0.20 g $BaBr_2$ in a 10 L solution ($K_{sp} = 2.8 \times 10^{-9}$).

45. For the formation of ammonia, the equilibrium constant is calculated to be 5.2×10^{-5} at 25°C. After analysis, it is determined that $[N_2] = 2.00$ M and $[H_2] = 0.80$ M. How many grams of ammonia are in the 10 L reaction vessel at equilibrium? Use the following equilibrium equation.

$$N_2(g) + 3H_2(g) \rightleftharpoons 2NH_3(g)$$

CRITICAL THINKING

46. **Predicting Outcomes** When gasoline burns in an automobile engine, nitric oxide is formed from oxygen and nitrogen. Nitric oxide is a major air pollutant. High temperatures like those found in a combustion engine are needed for the reaction. The reaction follows.

$$N_2(g) + O_2(g) \rightleftharpoons 2NO(g)$$

K for the reaction is 0.01 at 2000°C. If 4.0 mol of N_2, 0.1 mol of O_2, and 0.08 mol of NO are placed in a 1.0 L vessel at 2000°C, predict which reaction will be favored.

⊞ TECHNOLOGY & LEARNING

47. **Graphing Calculator** Calculating the Equilibrium Constant, K, for a System

The graphing calculator can run a program that calculates K for a system, given the concentrations of the products and the concentrations of the reactants.

Given the balanced chemical equation

$$H_2(g) + I_2(g) \longrightarrow 2HI(g)$$

and the equilibrium mixture at 425°C, you can calculate the equilibrium constant for the system. Then you can use the program to make calculations.

Go to Appendix C. If you are using a TI 83 Plus, you can download the program and data and run the application as directed. If you are using another calculator, your teacher will provide you with keystrokes and data sets to use. Remember that you will need to name the program and check the display, as explained in Appendix C. You will then be ready to run the program. After you have graphed the data, answer these questions.

a. What is the equilibrium constant given the following equilibrium concentrations? 0.012840 mol/L of H_2, 0.006437 mol/L of I_2, and 0.066807 mol/L of HI

b. What is the equilibrium constant given the following equilibrium concentrations? 0.000105 mol/L of H_2, 0.000107 mol/L of I_2, and 0.000779 mol/L of HI

c. What is the equilibrium constant given the following equilibrium concentrations? 0.000527 mol/L of H_2, 0.000496 mol/L of I_2, and 0.003757 mol/L of HI

HANDBOOK SEARCH

48. An equilibrium system helps maintain the pH of the blood. Review the material on the carbon dioxide–bicarbonate ion equilibrium system in Group 14 of the *Elements Handbook* and answer the following.
    a. Write the equation for the equilibrium system that responds to changes in H_3O^+ concentration.

b. Use Le Châtelier's principle to explain how hyperventilation affects this system.
c. How does this system maintain pH when acid is added?

49. The reactions used to confirm the presence of transition metal ions often involve the formation of precipitates. Review the analytical tests for the transition metals in the *Elements Handbook*. Use that information and Table 18-3 to determine the minimum concentration of Zn^{2+} needed to produce a precipitate that confirms the presence of Zn. Assume enough sulfide ion reagent is added to the unknown solution in the test tube to produce a sulfide ion concentration of 1.4×10^{-20} M.

RESEARCH & WRITING

50. Find photos of several examples of stalagmites and stalactites in various caves. Investigate the equilibrium processes involved in the formation of stalagmites and stalactites.

51. Carry out library research on the use of catalysts in industrial processes. Explain what types of catalysts are used for specific processes, such as the Haber process.

ALTERNATIVE ASSESSMENT

52. **Performance** Fill a drinking glass with water and add sugar by the teaspoonful, stirring after each addition. Continue adding the sugar until some of the sugar remains undissolved, even after vigorous stirring. Now heat the sugar-water solution. How are you using Le Châtelier's principle to shift the equilibrium of the system?

46. the reverse reaction
47. a. 54.000205
    b. 54.01344
    c. 53.99955
48. a. $CO_2(aq) + 2H_2O(l) \rightleftharpoons$ $H_3O^+(aq) + HCO_3^-(aq)$
    b. During hyperventilation, the CO_2 concentration of the system is reduced. The reverse reaction is favored to compensate for the reduced CO_2 concentration.
    c. The addition of acid favors the reverse reaction, which results in a decrease of H_3O^+ to compensate for the addition of acid.
49. The Zn^{2+} concentration must be greater than 1.1×10^{-4} M.

Oxidation-Reduction Reactions

PACING CHART

Compression Guide: (To shorten, eliminate items in italics.)

CLASSROOM RESOURCES

		NSE Standards	Teaching Resources	Experiments
19-1	**Oxidation and Reduction** 2 45-minute periods 1 90-minute block	PS 2c, 3c UCP 1–2 SAI 2 ST 1 HNS 1	**PE** Elements Handbook **ATE** Demo, p. 591 T 103, TM 102A	Blueprint Paper, p. 878 Reduction of Mn in MnO_4^-, p. 881 **A21, B20** Oxidation-Reduction Reactions
19-2	**Balancing Redox Equations** 2 45-minute periods 1 90-minute block	PS 3c UCP 1–2		
19-3	**Oxidizing and Reducing Agents** 2 45-minute periods 1 90-minute block *Autooxidation, pp. 604–605*	PS 3c UCP 1–2 SAI 1–2	**PE** Elements Handbook T 104	Quick Lab, p. 604
19-4	**Electrochemistry** 2 45-minute periods 1 90-minute block *Electrode Potentials, pp. 613–616*	PS 3b, 3c, 6d UCP 1–3, 5 ST 1 SPSP 5	**ATE** Demo, pp. 606, 608, 610 T 105, T 107, T 108, T 109, T 110, T 111, TM 103A	**A22, B21,** Cathodic Protection: Factors Affecting the Corrosion of Iron **C21 EXP** Electroplating for Corrosion Protection **C22 EXP** Voltaic Cells **C22 INV** Voltaic Cells—Designing Batteries

REVIEW RESOURCES

Review and Assessment 2 45-minute periods 1 90-minute block	Cumulative Review	Alternative Assessment	Traditional Assessment
	SR Chapter 19 Mixed Review **PE** Chapter 19 26–34, pp. 619–620	**PE** 43–45, p. 621 **ATE** 591, 598, 614 **AA** Items for Chapter 19	Chapter 19 Text Test Generator items for Chapter 19

ASSIGNMENT RESOURCES

Section Homework Resources & Review	Problem-Solving Practice
HR Homework Worksheets 19-1, 19-2 Graphic Org. Assignment 19-1 **PE** Section Review, 1–5, p. 595 Chapter Review, 1–3, 13–15, pp. 618–619 **SR** Section Review 19-1	
HR Homework Worksheet 19-3 Graphic Org. Assignment 19-3 **PE** Section Review, 1–3, p. 601 Chapter Review, 16–18, p. 619 **SR** Section Review 19-2	**PE** Additional Example 19-1 **ATE** Additional Example, p. 601 **PS** Chapter 23 Redox Equations
HR Homework Worksheet 19-4 **PE** Section Review, 1–15, p. 605 Chapter Review, 4–6, p. 618 **SR** Section Review 19-3	
HR Homework Worksheets 19-5, 19-6 Graphic Org. Assignment 19-5 **PE** Section Review, 1–6, p. 616 Chapter Review, 7–11, 19–25, pp. 618–619 **SR** Section Review 19-4	**PS** Chapter 24 Electrochemistry

TECHNOLOGY RESOURCES

Technology & Internet Resources

 CTW 29 Segment 29 Electric Car
CTW 30 Segment 30 Battery Technology

 Holt Chemistry Videodiscs Teacher's Correlation Guide for Chapter 19

 Module 10: Galvanic Cell, Electrolytic Cell

internet connect

 On-line Student Resources:
www.scilinks.org
The following SciLinks Internet resources can be found in the student text for this chapter.

TOPICS:
• Redox reactions, p. 593 (HC2191)
• Autooxidation, p. 604 (HC2192)
• Electrochemical cells, p. 606 (HC2193)
• Electroplating, p. 611 (HC2194)

On-line Teacher Resources:
GO TO: go.hrw.com
KEYWORD: HC2 HOME
Visit the HRW Web site for a variety of resources related to this chapter.

 Smithsonian Institution®
Internet Connections
Visit **www.si.edu/hrw** for additional on-line resources.

 CNNfyi.com
Visit **www.cnnfyi.com** for late-breaking news and current events stories selected just for you.

Resource Key

PE Pupil's Edition
ATE Teacher's Edition

☞ **One-Stop Planner CD-ROM** Includes these resources and customizable daily lesson plans:

HR Homework Resources	**ChemFile**	**D** Consumer Experiments	
SR Section Reviews	**A** Laboratory Experiments	**T** Transparencies	
CTW Critical Thinking Worksheets	**B** Microscale Experiments	**TM** Transparency Masters	
AA Alternative Assessments	**C** Technique Builders and Problem-Solving Experiments	**PS** Mini-Guide to Problem Solving	
		SRW Supplemental Reading Worksheets	

Scoring Rubrics for Labs, Alternative Assessments, Performance Tasks and Portfolio Projects are on the One-Stop Planner CD-ROM.

Oxidation-
Reduction
Reactions

Chapter Overview

19-1 defines oxidation and reduction reactions and provides rules for determining oxidation numbers.

19-2 presents guidelines for balancing redox equations by using the half-reaction method.

19-3 describes the roles of the oxidizing agent and the reducing agent in a redox reaction.

19-4 explains the operation of electrochemical cells and distinguishes between voltaic cells and electrolytic cells.

Concept Base

Students may need a review of the following concepts:

• oxidation numbers, Chapter 7

• balancing equations, Chapter 8

• electronegativity, Chapter 5

• the activity series, Chapter 8

Reading Skill-Builder

BRAINSTORMING Write the words *oxidation* and *reduction* on the board. In a class discussion, ask students to use prior knowledge to develop a definition for each term. Record the definitions so they can be referenced later when the specific chemical meaning of the terms are taught in the sections that follow.

Oxidation-Reduction Reactions

Oxidation-reduction reactions propel rockets into space.

Oxidation and Reduction

OBJECTIVES

- Assign oxidation numbers to reactant and product species.

- Define *oxidation* and *reduction*.

- Explain what an oxidation-reduction reaction (redox reaction) is.

Lesson Starter
Quickly review oxidation numbers in Chapter 7, and then go immediately to Table 19-1. Focus on each rule in turn, and ask students for additional examples. Emphasize that they should refer to Table 19-1 repeatedly until they know its contents.

DEMONSTRATION
A Spontaneous Redox Reaction
1. Add approximately 7 mL of 0.1 M KI to a 100 mm Petri dish, and place the dish on an overhead projector.

2. Add 7 mL of 0.01 M $KMnO_4$ to the Petri dish, and mix the solutions with a stirring rod.

3. Add a few drops of 1.0 M HCl to the mixture, stir, and observe. (The purple color of $KMnO_4$ fades. An orange-brown precipitate of MnO_2 forms, and the solution develops the red-brown color of dissolved I_2.)
   Make sure students recognize the significance of the changes they observe, and then proceed with the class discussion on page 592.

Disposal: Add 0.1 M KI to the $KMnO_4$ solution while stirring until all of the permanganate color is gone; then add sufficient 0.1 M $Na_2S_2O_3$ while stirring to reduce all of the iodine to iodide. Adjust the pH to between 5 and 9, and pour the solution down the drain.

O xidation-reduction reactions involve a transfer of electrons. Oxidation involves the loss of electrons, whereas reduction involves the gain of electrons. Reduction and oxidation half-reactions must occur simultaneously. These processes can be identified through the understanding and use of oxidation numbers (oxidation states).

Oxidation States

Oxidation states were defined in Chapter 7. The oxidation number assigned to an element in a molecule is based on the distribution of electrons in that molecule. The rules by which oxidation numbers are assigned were given in Chapter 7. These rules are summarized in Table 19-1.

TABLE 19-1 *Rules for Assigning Oxidation Numbers*

Rule	Example
1. The oxidation number of any uncombined element is 0.	The oxidation number of Na(s) is 0.
2. The oxidation number of a monatomic ion equals the charge on the ion.	The oxidation number of Cl^- is –1.
3. The more electronegative element in a binary compound is assigned the number equal to the charge it would have if it were an ion.	The oxidation number of O in NO is –2.
4. The oxidation number of fluorine in a compound is always –1.	The oxidation number of F in LiF is –1.
5. Oxygen has an oxidation number of –2 unless it is combined with F, when it is +2, or it is in a peroxide, such as H_2O_2, when it is –1.	The oxidation number of O in NO_2 is –2.
6. The oxidation state of hydrogen in most of its compounds is +1 unless it is combined with a metal, in which case it is –1.	The oxidation number of H in LiH is –1.
7. In compounds, Group 1 and 2 elements and aluminum have oxidation numbers of +1, +2, and +3, respectively.	The oxidation number of Ca in $CaCO_3$ is +2.
8. The sum of the oxidation numbers of all atoms in a neutral compound is 0.	The oxidation number of C in $CaCO_3$ is +4.
9. The sum of the oxidation numbers of all atoms in a polyatomic ion equals the charge of the ion.	The oxidation number of P in $H_2PO_4^-$ is +5.

Visual Strategy

FIGURE 19-1 illustrates how an element can exist in a number of different oxidation states. Reinforce this idea by asking students what oxidation numbers sulfur has in H_2S, S_8, SO_2, SO_4^{2-}, S_2O_3, and $S_2O_3^{2-}$ (−2, 0, +4, +6, +3, +2).

FIGURE 19-1 The color of solutions containing chromium compounds changes with the oxidation state of chromium.

Chromium provides a very visual example of different oxidation numbers. Different oxidation states of chromium have dramatically different colors, as can be seen in Figure 19-1. The chromium(II) chloride solution is blue, chromium(III) chloride solution is green, potassium chromate solution is yellow, and potassium dichromate solution is orange.

Oxidation

Reactions in which the atoms or ions of an element experience an increase in oxidation state are **oxidation** *processes.* The combustion of metallic sodium in an atmosphere of chlorine gas is shown in Figure 19-2. The sodium ions and chloride ions produced during this strongly exothermic reaction form a cubic crystal lattice in which sodium cations are ionically bonded to chloride anions. The chemical equation for this reaction is written as follows.

$$2Na(s) + Cl_2(g) \longrightarrow 2NaCl(s)$$

The formation of sodium ions illustrates an oxidation process because each sodium atom loses an electron to become a sodium ion. The oxidation state is represented by placing an oxidation number above the symbol of the atom and the ion.

$$\overset{0}{Na} \longrightarrow \overset{+1}{Na^+} + e^-$$

The oxidation state of sodium has changed from 0, its elemental state, to the +1 state of the ion (Rules 1 and 7, Table 19-1). *A species whose oxidation number increases is* **oxidized.** The sodium atom is *oxidized* to a sodium ion.

FIGURE 19-2 Sodium and chlorine react violently to form NaCl. The synthesis of NaCl from its elements illustrates the oxidation-reduction process.

Reduction

Reactions in which the oxidation state of an element decreases are **reduction** *processes.* Consider the behavior of chlorine in its reaction with sodium. Each chlorine atom accepts an electron and becomes a chloride ion. The oxidation state of chlorine decreases from 0 to –1 for the chloride ion (Rules 1 and 2, Table 19-1).

$$\overset{0}{Cl_2} + 2e^- \longrightarrow \overset{-1}{2Cl^-}$$

A species that undergoes a decrease in oxidation state is **reduced.** The chlorine atom is reduced to the chloride ion.

Oxidation and Reduction as a Process

Electrons are produced in oxidation and acquired in reduction. Therefore, for oxidation to occur during a chemical reaction, reduction must occur simultaneously. Furthermore, the number of electrons produced in oxidation must equal the number of electrons acquired in reduction. This makes sense when you recall that electrons are negatively charged and that for charge to be conserved, the number of electrons lost must equal the number of electrons gained. You learned in Chapter 8 that mass is conserved in any chemical reaction. Therefore, the masses of the elements that undergo oxidation and reduction and the electrons that are exchanged are conserved.

A transfer of electrons causes changes in the oxidation states of one or more elements. *Any chemical process in which elements undergo changes in oxidation number is an* **oxidation-reduction reaction.** This name is often shortened to **redox reaction.** An example of a redox reaction can be seen in Figure 19-3, in which copper is being oxidized and NO_3^- from nitric acid is being reduced. *The part of the reaction involving oxidation or reduction alone can be written as a* **half-reaction.** The overall equation for a redox reaction is the sum of two half-reactions. Because the number of electrons involved is the same for oxidation and reduction, they cancel each other out and do not appear in the overall chemical equation. Equations for the reaction between nitric acid and copper illustrate the relationship between half-reactions and the overall redox reaction.

$$\overset{0}{3Cu} \longrightarrow \overset{+2}{3Cu^{2+}} + 6e^- \qquad \text{(oxidation half-reaction)}$$

$$\overset{+5\ -2}{2NO_3^-} + 6e^- + \overset{+1}{8H^+} \longrightarrow \overset{+2\ -2}{2NO} + \overset{+1\ -2}{4H_2O} \qquad \text{(reduction half-reaction)}$$

$$\overset{0}{3Cu} + \overset{+5}{2NO_3^-} + 8H^+ \longrightarrow \overset{+2}{3Cu^{2+}} + \overset{+2}{2NO} + 4H_2O \qquad \text{(redox reaction)}$$

Notice that electrons lost in oxidation appear on the product side of the oxidation half-reaction. Electrons are gained in reduction and

FIGURE 19-3 Copper is oxidized and nitrogen monoxide is produced when this penny is placed in a nitric acid solution.

internet**connect**

SC*i*LINKS
NSTA

TOPIC: Redox reactions
GO TO: www.scilinks.org
*sci*LINKS CODE: HC2191

Application

Household bleach, sodium hypo-chlorite (NaOCl), removes stains from clothing through a redox reaction. The molecules that cause the stain are oxidized by OCl^-, and OCl^- is reduced to Cl^-.

Stain molecules(s) + OCl^-(aq) $\longrightarrow$ colorless molecules(s) + Cl^-(aq)

For further discussion, ask students to determine the oxidation numbers of oxygen and chlorine in OCl^-. *(Oxygen is more electronegative, so its oxidation number is –2, while that of chlorine is +1.)*

Class Discussion

Have students write the formulas of the reactants and products in the demonstration on page 591, and use Table 19-1 to determine the oxidation numbers of each atom. (It is not necessary to have done the demonstration.) Ask them to interpret the changes in oxidation number in terms of oxidation and reduction. Ask them how many electrons are lost by one mole of the oxidized reactant and how many electrons are gained by one mole of the reduced reactant. Emphasize that just as many electrons are gained in reduction as are lost in oxidation. Therefore, the equation for the reaction must be balanced. Students will later revisit this reaction and balance it.

appear as reactants in the reduction half-reaction. When metallic copper reacts in nitric acid, three copper atoms are oxidized to Cu^{2+} ions as two nitrogen atoms are reduced from a +5 oxidation state to a +2 oxidation state. Atoms are conserved. This is illustrated by the balanced chemical equation for the reaction between copper and nitric acid.

If none of the atoms in a reaction change oxidation state, the reaction is *not* a redox reaction. For example, sulfur dioxide gas, SO_2, dissolves in water to form an acidic solution containing a low concentration of sulf*ous* acid, H_2SO_3.

$$\overset{+4\ -2}{SO_2} + \overset{+1\ -2}{H_2O} \longrightarrow \overset{+1\ +4\ -2}{H_2SO_3}$$

The oxidation states of all elemental species remain unchanged in this composition reaction. Therefore, it is *not* a redox reaction.

When a solution of sodium chloride is added to a solution of silver nitrate, an ion-exchange reaction occurs and white silver chloride precipitates.

$$\overset{+1}{Na^+} + \overset{-1}{Cl^-} + \overset{+1}{Ag^+} + \overset{+5\ -2}{NO_3^-} \longrightarrow \overset{+1}{Na^+} + \overset{+5\ -2}{NO_3^-} + \overset{+1\ -1}{AgCl}$$

The oxidation state of each monatomic ion remains unchanged. Again, this reaction is not an oxidation-reduction reaction.

Redox Reactions and Covalent Bonds

Both the synthesis of NaCl from its elements and the reaction between copper and nitric acid involve ionic bonding. Substances with covalent bonds also undergo redox reactions. An oxidation number, unlike an ionic charge, has no physical meaning. That is, the oxidation number assigned to a particular atom is based on its electronegativity relative to the other atoms to which it is bonded in a given molecule; it is not based on any real charge on the atom. For example, an ionic charge of 1– results from the complete gain of one electron by an atom or other neutral species, whereas an oxidation state of –1 means an increased attraction for a bonding electron. A change in oxidation number does not require a change in actual charge.

When hydrogen burns in chlorine, a covalent bond forms from the sharing of two electrons. The two bonding electrons in the hydrogen chloride molecule are not shared equally. Rather, the pair of electrons is more strongly attracted to the chlorine atom because of its higher electronegativity.

$$\overset{0}{H_2} + \overset{0}{Cl_2} \longrightarrow \overset{+1\ -1}{2HCl}$$

As specified by Rule 3 in Table 19-1, chlorine in HCl is assigned an oxidation number of –1. Thus, the oxidation number for the chlorine atoms changes from 0, its oxidation number in the elemental state, to –1; chlorine atoms are reduced. As specified by Rule 1, the oxidation number of each hydrogen atom in the hydrogen molecule is 0. As specified by Rule 6, the oxidation state of the hydrogen atom in the HCl molecule is +1;

the hydrogen atom is oxidized. No electrons have been totally lost or gained by either atom. Hydrogen has donated a share of its bonding electron to the chlorine; it has not completely transferred that electron. The assignment of oxidation numbers allows the determination of the partial transfer of electrons in compounds that are not ionic. Thus, increases or decreases in oxidation number can be seen in terms of complete or partial loss or gain of electrons.

Reactants and products in redox reactions are not limited to monatomic ions and uncombined elements. Elements in molecular compounds or polyatomic ions can also be oxidized and reduced if they have more than one non-zero oxidation state. An example of this is provided in the reaction between the copper penny and nitric acid when the nitrate ion, NO_3^-, is converted to nitrogen monoxide, NO. Nitrogen is reduced in this reaction. Usually we refer to the oxidation or reduction of the entire molecule or ion. Instead of saying the nitrogen atom is reduced, we say the nitrate ion is reduced to nitrogen monoxide.

$$\cdots + \overset{+5}{NO_3^-} \longrightarrow \overset{+2}{NO} + \cdots$$

Alternative Assessment
Place a small piece of magnesium ribbon in a Petri dish on an overhead projector, and add enough 0.1 M HCl to cover the metal. Tell students the nature of the reactants. Allow students to observe the reaction, and then ask them to write the oxidation and reduction half-reactions and the complete redox equation.

SECTION REVIEW

1. How are oxidation numbers assigned?

2. Label each of the following half-reactions as either an oxidation or a reduction half-reaction:

   a. $\overset{0}{Br_2} + 2e^- \longrightarrow 2\overset{-1}{Br^-}$

   b. $\overset{0}{Na} \longrightarrow \overset{+1}{Na^+} + e^-$

   c. $2\overset{-1}{Cl^-} \longrightarrow \overset{0}{Cl_2} + 2e^-$

   d. $\overset{0}{Cl_2} + 2e^- \longrightarrow 2\overset{-1}{Cl^-}$

   e. $\overset{+1}{Na^+} + e^- \longrightarrow \overset{0}{Na}$

   f. $\overset{0}{Fe} \longrightarrow \overset{+2}{Fe^{2+}} + 2e^-$

   g. $\overset{+2}{Cu^{2+}} + 2e^- \longrightarrow \overset{0}{Cu}$

   h. $\overset{+3}{Fe^{3+}} + e^- \longrightarrow \overset{+2}{Fe^{2+}}$

3. Which of the following equations represent redox reactions?

   a. $2KNO_3(s) \longrightarrow 2KNO_2(s) + O_2(g)$
   b. $H_2(g) + CuO(s) \longrightarrow Cu(s) + H_2O(l)$

   c. $NaOH(aq) + HCl(aq) \longrightarrow NaCl(aq) + H_2O(l)$
   d. $H_2(g) + Cl_2(g) \longrightarrow 2HCl(g)$
   e. $SO_3(g) + H_2O(l) \longrightarrow H_2SO_4(aq)$

4. For each redox equation identified in the previous question, determine which element is oxidized and which is reduced.

5. Use the equations below for the redox reaction between aluminum metal and sodium metal to answer the following.

   $$\overset{0}{3Na} \longrightarrow 3\overset{+1}{Na^+} + 3e^- \qquad \text{(oxidation)}$$

   $$\overset{+3}{Al^{3+}} + 3e^- \longrightarrow \overset{0}{Al} \qquad \text{(reduction)}$$

   $$\overset{0}{3Na} + \overset{+3}{Al^{3+}} \longrightarrow 3\overset{+1}{Na^+} + \overset{0}{Al} \qquad \text{(redox reaction)}$$

   a. Explain how this reaction illustrates that charge is conserved in a redox reaction.
   b. Explain how this reaction illustrates that mass is conserved in a redox reaction.
   c. Explain why electrons do not appear as reactants or products in the combined equation.

SECTION REVIEW

1. See Table 19-1.

2. a. reduction   e. reduction
   b. oxidation   f. oxidation
   c. oxidation   g. reduction
   d. reduction   h. reduction

3. a. redox
   b. redox
   c. not redox
   d. redox
   e. not redox

4. a. $\overset{-2}{O}$ is oxidized to O_2,

   $\overset{+5}{N}$ is reduced to $\overset{+3}{N}$

   b. H_2 is oxidized to $\overset{+1}{H}$,

   Cu^{2+} is reduced to Cu

   d. H_2 is oxidized to $\overset{+1}{H}$,

   Cl_2 is reduced to $\overset{-1}{Cl}$

5. a. Three electrons are lost in the oxidation half-reaction; three electrons are gained in the reduction process. The balanced equation has a charge of 3+ on both sides.
   b. There are 3 mol of Na and 1 mol of Al on both sides of the equation.
   c. The number of electrons lost equals the number of electrons gained, so they cancel out in the overall equation.

The compounds in skunk spray that have a pervasive odor similar to that of hydrogen sulfide are mercaptans, organic compounds with the functional group —SH. Have students look up the structures of some other simple mercaptans in an organic chemistry textbook, and have them explain how these compounds relate to H_2S.

Class Discussion

1. The article states that receptors in the nose are sensitive to sulfur in its low oxidation state but not to sulfur in its high oxidation state. Ask students to give examples of sulfur in both a low and a high oxidation state. Have them specify the oxidation number of sulfur in H_2S.

2. Have students relate the effect of the reaction with H_2O_2 on the oxidation states discussed in item 1.

3. Ask students if another reactant for example, Na_2O_2, could have been used instead of H_2O_2. They may realize that the choice of H_2O_2 was based partly on its availability and its harmlessness to animals and humans.

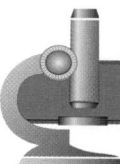

RESEARCH NOTES

Skunk-Spray Remedy

So that pretty black cat with the white stripe down its back wasn't a cat after all? Well, hold off on dumping Fido into a tomato-juice bath. Chemistry has a much better way of conquering skunk spray.

Paul Krebaum, the inventor of a new deskunking formula, says that while working as a materials engineer, he constantly had to deal with the less-than-pleasant smell of the hydrogen sulfide gas that was released from one of his experiments. Mr. Krebaum was losing popularity with his neighbors, and venting off the gas only partially solved the problem. A better solution, he decided, would be to find a way to eliminate the smell entirely.

Mr. Krebaum rifled through his old chemistry books and found that hydrogen peroxide could oxidize these sulfur-containing compounds to much less smelly components. And by decreasing the chemical's volatility, the reaction prevents the gas from reaching our noses quite so easily. He immediately whipped up a hydrogen peroxide mixture, and it worked like a charm.

The reaction by which the hydrogen sulfide was destroyed, producing sulfate compounds that do not have the unpleasant odor, can be seen in the following equation.

$$2NaOH + 4H_2O_2 + H_2S \longrightarrow Na_2SO_4 + 6H_2O$$

Skunk spray gets its odor from chemicals called mercaptans.

"The receptors that are in your nose are sensitive to sulfur in its low oxidation state," says Mr. Krebaum. "However, they are not sensitive to sulfur in its high oxidation state."

Some time later, a friend of Mr. Krebaum's complained to him that a skunk had sprayed his pet. Because the odor in a skunk's spray also comes from compounds containing sulfur in a low oxidation state, Mr. Krebaum thought his solution might also work on this age-old problem. He mixed up a milder version to try out on the pet: 1 quart 3% hydrogen peroxide solution, 1/4 cup baking soda, and 1 teaspoon liquid soap. His friend tried it out, and the result was one wet and unhappy—but much less smelly—pet.

Mr. Krebaum says that the hydrogen peroxide in the remedy actually oxidizes the compounds, while the baking soda reduces the acidity of the mixture and the soap helps to wash out the greasy skunk spray. The reaction that occurs can be seen in the following equation. The symbol R represents all the other elements in the sulfur-containing compound found in skunk spray.

$$RSH + 3H_2O_2 + NaHCO_3 \longrightarrow RSO_3Na + 4H_2O + CO_2$$

The pet should be washed thoroughly with the mixture, taking care to avoid its eyes. If the mixture is left on for a few minutes—long enough for the reaction to occur—and then rinsed away with tap water, the smell will disappear.

There's no reason to fear ending up with a platinum blond pet, Mr. Krebaum says. The formula does not bleach or have any other negative side effects. He does have one warning: mix the formula just before using it because the mixture breaks down quickly. The reaction releases oxygen, so the formula should not be put into a sealed container; it will build up pressure and could eventually blow the top. For these reasons, bottles of "Krebaum's Skunkinator" will not be appearing on drug-store shelves any time soon.

Balancing Redox Equations

OBJECTIVES

- Explain what must be conserved in redox equations.

- Balance redox equations by using the half-reaction method.

Equations for simple redox reactions can be balanced by inspection, which you learned to do in Chapter 8. Most redox equations, however, require more systematic methods. The equation-balancing process requires the use of oxidation numbers. In a balanced equation, both charge and mass are conserved. Although oxidation and reduction half-reactions occur together, their reaction equations are balanced separately, then combined to give the balanced redox-reaction equation.

Half-Reaction Method

The *half-reaction method*, or ion-electron method, for balancing redox equations consists of seven steps. Oxidation numbers are assigned to all atoms and polyatomic ions to determine which species are part of the redox process. The oxidation and reduction equations are balanced separately for mass and charge. They are then added together to produce a complete balanced equation. These seven steps are applied to balance the reaction of hydrogen sulfide and nitric acid. Sulfuric acid, nitrogen dioxide, and water are the products of the reaction.

1. *Write the formula equation if it is not given in the problem. Then write the ionic equation.*

   Formula equation: $H_2S + HNO_3 \longrightarrow H_2SO_4 + NO_2 + H_2O$

   Ionic equation: $H_2S + H^+ + NO_3^- \longrightarrow 2H^+ + SO_4^{2-} + NO_2 + H_2O$

2. *Assign oxidation numbers. Delete substances containing only elements that do not change oxidation state.*

$$\overset{+1\ -2}{H_2S} + \overset{+1}{H^+} + \overset{+5\ -2}{NO_3^-} \longrightarrow \overset{+1}{2H^+} + \overset{+6\ -2}{SO_4^{2-}} + \overset{+4\ -2}{NO_2} + \overset{+1\ -2}{H_2O}$$

The sulfur changes oxidation state from –2 to +6. The nitrogen changes oxidation state from +5 to +4. The other substances are deleted.

$$\overset{+1\ -2}{H_2S} + \overset{+5\ -2}{NO_3^-} \longrightarrow \overset{+6\ -2}{SO_4^{2-}} + \overset{+4\ -2}{NO_2}$$

The remaining species are used in step 3.

Lesson Starter

Students are already used to balancing equations by inspection and may resist the idea of following a procedure involving half-reactions. To make a point about the need for a systematic approach, write the equation for the reaction in the demonstration on page 591 on the board, and ask students to balance it.

$$MnO_4^- + I^- + H^+ \longrightarrow$$
$$MnO_2 + I_2 + H_2O$$

The likely result will be

$$MnO_4^- + 2I^- + 4H^+ \longrightarrow$$
$$MnO_2 + I_2 + 2H_2O$$

The equation is balanced as to mass but not balanced as to charge. Having made the point, use the half-reaction method to balance the equation. *(The two half-reactions are*
$$2MnO_4^- + 8H^+ + 6e^- \longrightarrow$$
$$2MnO_2 + 4H_2O$$
and $6I^- \longrightarrow 3I_2 + 6e^-$*)*

✔ Teaching Tip

Review how to convert formula equations into ionic equations (Sections 14-1 and 15-3). Strong acids, strong bases, and soluble ionic compounds are written in ionic form; weak acids, weak bases, and insoluble compounds are written in formula-unit form. In the ionic equations shown here, HNO_3 is written in ionic form because it is a strong acid; H_2S is written in formula-unit (molecular) form because it is a weak acid.

Problem-Solving Practice

Chapter 23 of the Mini-Guide to Problem Solving (also found on the One-Stop Planner CD-ROM) includes more worked-out samples and additional practice problems involving redox equations.

3. *Write the half-reaction for oxidation.* In this example, the sulfur is being oxidized.

$$\overset{-2}{H_2S} \longrightarrow \overset{+6}{SO_4^{2-}}$$

- *Balance the atoms.* To balance the oxygen in this half-reaction, H_2O must be added to the left side. This gives 10 extra hydrogen atoms on that side of the equation. Therefore, 10 hydrogen ions are added to the right side. In basic solution, OH^- ions and water may be used to balance atoms.

$$\overset{-2}{H_2S} + 4H_2O \longrightarrow \overset{+6}{SO_4^{2-}} + 10H^+$$

- *Balance the charge.* Electrons are added to the side having the greater positive net charge. The left side of the equation has no net charge; the right side has a net charge of 8+. For the charges to balance, each side must have the same net charge. Therefore, 8 electrons are added to the product side so that it has no charge and balances with the reactant side of the equation. Notice that the oxidation of sulfur from a state of −2 to +6 indicates a loss of 8 electrons.

$$\overset{-2}{H_2S} + 4H_2O \longrightarrow \overset{+6}{SO_4^{2-}} + 10H^+ + 8e^-$$

The oxidation half-reaction is now balanced.

4. *Write the half-reaction for reduction.* In this example, nitrogen is being reduced from a +5 state to a +4 state.

$$\overset{+5}{NO_3^-} \longrightarrow \overset{+4}{NO_2}$$

- *Balance the atoms.* H_2O must be added to the product side of the reaction to balance the oxygen atoms. Therefore, two hydrogen ions must be added to the reactant side to balance the hydrogen atoms.

$$\overset{+5}{NO_3^-} + 2H^+ \longrightarrow \overset{+4}{NO_2} + H_2O$$

- *Balance the charge.* Electrons are added to the side having the greater positive net charge. The left side of the equation has a net charge of 1+. Therefore, 1 electron must be added to this side to balance the charge.

$$\overset{+5}{NO_3^-} + 2H^+ + e^- \longrightarrow \overset{+4}{NO_2} + H_2O$$

The reduction half-reaction is now balanced.

5. *Conserve charge by adjusting the coefficients in front of the electrons so that the number lost in oxidation equals the number gained in reduction.* Write the ratio of the number of electrons lost to the number of electrons gained.

$$\frac{e^- \text{ lost in oxidation}}{e^- \text{ gained in reduction}} = \frac{8}{1}$$

This ratio is already in its lowest terms. If it were not, it would need to be reduced. Multiply the oxidation half-reaction by 1 (it remains unchanged) and the reduction half-reaction by 8. The number of electrons lost now equals the number of electrons gained.

$$1\left(\overset{-2}{H_2S} + 4H_2O \longrightarrow \overset{+6}{SO_4^{2-}} + 10H^+ + 8e^-\right)$$

$$8\left(\overset{+5}{NO_3^-} + 2H^+ + e^- \longrightarrow \overset{+4}{NO_2} + H_2O\right)$$

6. *Combine the half-reactions, and cancel out anything common to both sides of the equation.*

$$\overset{-2}{H_2S} + 4H_2O \longrightarrow \overset{+6}{SO_4^{2-}} + 10H^+ + 8e^-$$

$$\overset{+5}{8NO_3^-} + 16H^+ + 8e^- \longrightarrow \overset{+4}{8NO_2} + 8H_2O$$

$$\overset{+5}{8NO_3^-} + \overset{6}{\cancel{16}}H^+ + \cancel{8e^-} + \overset{-2}{H_2S} + \cancel{4H_2O} \longrightarrow$$
$$\overset{+4}{8NO_2} + \overset{4}{\cancel{8}}H_2O + \overset{+6}{SO_4^{2-}} + \cancel{10H^+} + \cancel{8e^-}$$

Each side of the above equation has $10H^+, 8e^-$, and $4H_2O$. These cancel each other out and do not appear in the balanced equation.

$$\overset{+5}{8NO_3^-} + \overset{-2}{H_2S} + 6H^+ \longrightarrow \overset{+4}{8NO_2} + 4H_2O + \overset{+6}{SO_4^{2-}}$$

7. *Combine ions to form the compounds shown in the original formula equation. Check to ensure that all other ions balance.* The NO_3^- ion appeared as nitric acid in the original equation. There are only 6 hydrogen ions to pair with the 8 nitrate ions. Therefore, 2 hydrogen ions must be added to complete this formula. If 2 hydrogen ions are added to the left side of the equation, 2 hydrogen ions must also be added to the right side of the equation.

$$8HNO_3 + H_2S \longrightarrow 8NO_2 + 4H_2O + SO_4^{2-} + 2H^+$$

The sulfate ion appeared as sulfuric acid in the original equation. The hydrogen ions added to the right side are used to complete the formula for sulfuric acid.

$$8HNO_3 + H_2S \longrightarrow 8NO_2 + 4H_2O + H_2SO_4$$

A final check must be made to ensure that all elements are correctly balanced.

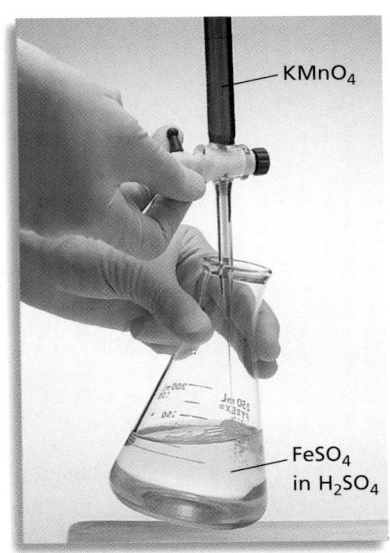

KMnO₄

FeSO₄
in H₂SO₄

FIGURE 19-4 As a KMnO₄ solution is titrated into an acidic solution of FeSO₄, deep purple MnO₄⁻ ions are reduced to colorless Mn²⁺ ions. When all Fe²⁺ ions are oxidized, MnO₄⁻ ions are no longer reduced to colorless Mn²⁺ ions. Thus, the first faint appearance of the MnO₄⁻ color indicates the end point of the titration.

SAMPLE PROBLEM 19-1

Write a balanced equation for the reaction shown in Figure 19-4. A deep purple solution of potassium permanganate is titrated into a colorless solution of iron(II) sulfate and sulfuric acid. The products are iron(III) sulfate, manganese(II) sulfate, potassium sulfate, and water—all of which are colorless.

Teaching Tip

For reactions that take place in basic solution, OH^- and H_2O are used to balance oxygen and hydrogen in redox half-reactions. Add OH^- to the side of the equation that needs oxygen atoms. Add twice the number of oxygen atoms needed, then add enough H_2O molecules to the other side of the equation to balance the hydrogen atoms. For example, ClO^- ions react with CrO_2^- ions in basic solution as follows.

ox: $2(CrO_2^- + 4OH^- \longrightarrow$
$\qquad CrO_4^- + 2H_2O + 3e^-)$

red: $3(ClO^- + H_2O + 2e^- \longrightarrow$
$\qquad Cl^- + 2OH^-)$

net: $2CrO_2^- + 3ClO^- + 2OH^- \longrightarrow$
$\qquad 2CrO_4^- + 3Cl^- + H_2O$

Alternative Assessment

Have students research the redox reactions that take place in the black-and-white photographic process and write equations for their half-reactions and complete redox reactions.

SOLUTION

1. *Write the formula equation if it is not given in the problem. Then write the ionic equation.*

$$KMnO_4 + FeSO_4 + H_2SO_4 \longrightarrow Fe_2(SO_4)_3 + MnSO_4 + K_2SO_4 + H_2O$$
$$K^+ + MnO_4^- + Fe^{2+} + SO_4^{2-} + 2H^+ + SO_4^{2-} \longrightarrow$$
$$2Fe^{3+} + 3SO_4^{2-} + Mn^{2+} + SO_4^{2-} + 2K^+ + SO_4^{2-} + H_2O$$

2. *Assign oxidation numbers to each element and ion. Delete substances containing an element that does not change oxidation state.*

$$\overset{+1}{K^+} + \overset{+7\ -2}{MnO_4^-} + \overset{+2}{Fe^{2+}} + \overset{+6\ -2}{SO_4^{2-}} + \overset{+1}{2H^+} + \overset{+6\ -2}{SO_4^{2-}} \longrightarrow$$

$$\overset{+3}{2Fe^{3+}} + \overset{+6\ -2}{3SO_4^{2-}} + \overset{+2}{Mn^{2+}} + \overset{+6\ -2}{SO_4^{2-}} + \overset{+1}{2K^+} + \overset{+6\ -2}{SO_4^{2-}} + \overset{+1\ -2}{H_2O}$$

Only ions or molecules whose oxidation numbers change are retained.

$$\overset{+7\ -2}{MnO_4^-} + \overset{+2}{Fe^{2+}} \longrightarrow \overset{+3}{Fe^{3+}} + \overset{+2}{Mn^{2+}}$$

3. *Write the half-reaction for oxidation.* The iron shows the increase in oxidation number. Therefore, it is oxidized.

$$\overset{+2}{Fe^{2+}} \longrightarrow \overset{+3}{Fe^{3+}}$$

- *Balance the mass.* The mass is already balanced.

- *Balance the charge.*

$$\overset{+2}{Fe^{2+}} \longrightarrow \overset{+3}{Fe^{3+}} + e^-$$

4. *Write the half-reaction for reduction.* Manganese shows a change in oxidation number from +7 to +2. It is reduced.

$$\overset{+7}{MnO_4^-} \longrightarrow \overset{+2}{Mn^{2+}}$$

- *Balance the mass.* Water and hydrogen ions must be added to balance the oxygen atoms in the permanganate ion.

$$\overset{+7}{MnO_4^-} + 8H^+ \longrightarrow \overset{+2}{Mn^{2+}} + 4H_2O$$

- *Balance the charge.*

$$\overset{+7}{MnO_4^-} + 8H^+ + 5e^- \longrightarrow \overset{+2}{Mn^{2+}} + 4H_2O$$

5. *Adjust the coefficients to conserve charge.*

$$\frac{e^- \text{ lost in oxidation}}{e^- \text{ gained in reduction}} = \frac{1}{5}$$

$$5(Fe^{2+} \longrightarrow Fe^{3+} + e^-)$$
$$1(MnO_4^- + 8H^+ + 5e^- \longrightarrow Mn^{2+} + 4H_2O)$$

6. *Combine the half-reactions and cancel.*

$$5Fe^{2+} \longrightarrow 5Fe^{3+} + 5e^-$$
$$MnO_4^- + 8H^+ + 5e^- \longrightarrow Mn^{2+} + 4H_2O$$
$$\overline{MnO_4^- + 5Fe^{2+} + 8H^+ + 5e^- \longrightarrow Mn^{2+} + 5Fe^{3+} + 4H_2O + 5e^-}$$

7. *Combine ions to form compounds from the original equation.* The iron(III) product appears in the original equation as $Fe_2(SO_4)_3$. Every iron(III) sulfate molecule requires two iron ions. Therefore, the entire equation must be multiplied by 2 to provide an even number of iron ions.

$$2(5Fe^{2+} + MnO_4^- + 8H^+ \longrightarrow 5Fe^{3+} + Mn^{2+} + 4H_2O)$$
$$10Fe^{2+} + 2MnO_4^- + 16H^+ \longrightarrow 10Fe^{3+} + 2Mn^{2+} + 8H_2O$$

The iron(II), iron(III), manganese(II), and 2 hydrogen ions in the original equation are paired with sulfate ions. Iron(II) sulfate requires 10 sulfate ions, and sulfuric acid requires 8 sulfate ions. To balance the equation, 18 sulfate ions must be added to each side. On the product side, 15 of these ions form iron(III) sulfate, and 2 of them form manganese(II) sulfate. That leaves 1 sulfate ion unaccounted for. The permanganate ion requires the addition of 2 potassium ions to each side. These 2 potassium ions form potassium sulfate on the product side of the reaction.

$$10FeSO_4 + 2KMnO_4 + 8H_2SO_4 \longrightarrow 5Fe_2(SO_4)_3 + 2MnSO_4 + K_2SO_4 + 8H_2O$$

Final inspection shows that atoms and charges are balanced.

PRACTICE

1. Copper reacts with hot, concentrated sulfuric acid to form copper(II) sulfate, sulfur dioxide, and water. Write and balance the equation for this reaction.

Answer
$$Cu + 2H_2SO_4 \longrightarrow$$
$$CuSO_4 + SO_2 + 2H_2O$$

2. Write and balance the equation for the reaction between nitric acid and potassium iodide. The products are potassium nitrate, iodine, nitrogen monoxide, and water.

Answer
$$8HNO_3 + 6KI \longrightarrow$$
$$6KNO_3 + 3I_2 + 2NO + 4H_2O$$

3. Rust occurs when iron reacts with oxygen and water to form iron(III) hydroxide. Write and balance the equation for this reaction.

Answer
$$4Fe + 3O_2 + 6H_2O \longrightarrow$$
$$4Fe(OH)_3$$

SECTION REVIEW

1. What two quantities are conserved in redox equations?

2. Why do we add H^+ and H_2O to some half-reactions and OH^- and H_2O to others?

3. Balance the following oxidation-reduction reaction:

$$Na_2SnO_2 + Bi(OH)_3 \longrightarrow Bi + Na_2SnO_3 + H_2O$$

19-1 The orange color of $K_2Cr_2O_7$ changes to the green color of a Cr^{3+} ion when an acid solution of potassium dichromate is used in a Breathalyzer to test for the presence of ethanol, C_2H_5OH. Write and balance the Breathalyzer equation. $K_2Cr_2O_7$, HCl, and C_2H_5OH are the reactants; $CrCl_3$, CO_2, KCl, and H_2O are the products.

Ans.

$$2K_2Cr_2O_7 + C_2H_5OH + 16HCl \longrightarrow$$
$$4CrCl_3 + 11H_2O + 2CO_2 + 4KCl$$

19-1 Write a balanced equation for the reaction in which sodium iodide reacts with xenon trioxide, XeO_3, in the presence of nitric acid. The products are xenon, sodium triiodide, NaI_3, water, and sodium nitrate.

Ans.

$$XeO_3 + 9NaI + 6HNO_3 \longrightarrow$$
$$3NaI_3 + Xe + 3H_2O + 6NaNO_3$$

SECTION REVIEW

1. charge and mass

2. Because these reactions take place in aqueous solution, there are always some H^+ and OH^- ions present. In acid solution, H^+ ions react with OH^- ions present in the water to form H_2O. In basic solution, OH^- ions react similarly with H^+ to form H_2O.

3. $3Na_2SnO_2 + 2Bi(OH)_3 \longrightarrow$
$$2Bi + 3Na_2SnO_3 + 3H_2O$$

SECTION 19-3

Lesson Starter

Introduce the definitions of *oxidizing agent* and *reducing agent* by labeling a small object (such as an empty box) "electrons." Ask a student to take the electrons from you. Point out that the student was the agent of your losing the electrons and that you were the agent of the student's gaining the electrons. Introduce the term *oxidizing agent* by telling the students that by causing you to lose your electrons, the student is the oxidizing agent. You are the *reducing agent* because you caused the student to gain electrons. The student is *reduced* by you, and you are *oxidized* by the student.

TABLE STRATEGY

Table 19-2 Encourage students to refer to this table repeatedly until they have thoroughly mastered the definitions and concepts of oxidation and reduction. Introduce them to the table by asking questions such as the following: Is the process oxidation or reduction when Br^- is converted to Br_2? Is Br^- an oxidizing or reducing agent? Does Fe^{2+} gain or lose electrons when it is converted to Fe^{3+}? When sodium reacts with chlorine, which is the oxidizing agent?

Reading Skill-Builder

PAIRED READING Pair each student with a partner. Have each read Section 19-3 silently. As they read, have them place self-adhesive notes with checkmarks next to passages they understand and with question marks next to passages they find confusing.

Both readers should work together to come to an understanding of all the passages. Have each paired group create a list of questions to pose to the class.

OBJECTIVES

- Relate chemical activity to oxidizing and reducing strength.

- Explain the concept of auto-oxidation.

Oxidizing and Reducing Agents

A **reducing agent** *is a substance that has the potential to cause another substance to be reduced.* Reducing agents lose electrons; they attain a more positive oxidation state during an oxidation-reduction reaction. Therefore, the reducing agent is the oxidized substance.

An **oxidizing agent** *is a substance that has the potential to cause another substance to be oxidized.* Oxidizing agents gain electrons and attain a more negative oxidation state during an oxidation-reduction reaction. The oxidizing agent is the reduced substance. Table 19-2 helps clarify the terms describing the oxidation-reduction process.

Strengths of Oxidizing and Reducing Agents

Different substances can be compared and rated on their relative potential as reducing and oxidizing agents. For example, the order of the elements in the activity series, found in Table 8-3 on page 266, is related to each element's tendency to lose electrons. Elements in this series lose electrons to the positively charged ions of any element below them in the series. The more active an element is, the greater its tendency to lose electrons and the better a reducing agent it is. The greater the distance is between two elements in the list, the more likely it is that a redox reaction will take place between them.

These elements and some other familiar substances are arranged in Table 19-3 according to their activity as oxidizing and reducing agents. The fluorine atom is the most highly electronegative atom. It is also the

TABLE 19-2 *Oxidation-Reduction Terminology*		
Term	**Change in oxidation number**	**Change in electron population**
Oxidation	in a positive direction	loss of electrons
Reduction	in a negative direction	gain of electrons
Oxidizing agent	in a negative direction	gains electrons
Reducing agent	in a positive direction	loses electrons

most active oxidizing agent. Because of its strong attraction for its own electrons, the fluoride ion is the weakest reducing agent. The negative ion of a strong oxidizing agent is a weak reducing agent.

The positive ion of a strong reducing agent is a weak oxidizing agent. As shown in Table 19-3, Li atoms are strong reducing agents because Li is a very active metal. When Li atoms oxidize, they produce Li^+ ions, which are unlikely to reacquire electrons, so Li^+ ions are weak oxidizing agents.

The left column of each pair also shows the relative abilities of metals listed in the table to displace other metals from their compounds. Zinc, for example, appears above copper. Thus, zinc is the more active reducing agent, and it displaces copper ions from solutions of copper compounds, as illustrated in Figure 19-5. The copper(II) ion, on the other hand, is a more active oxidizing agent than the zinc ion.

Nonmetals and some important ions also are included in the series in Table 19-3. Any reducing agent is oxidized by the oxidizing agents below it. Observe that F_2 displaces Cl^-, Br^-, and I^- ions from their solutions. Cl_2 displaces Br^- and I^- ions, and Br_2 displaces I^- ions. The equation for the displacement of Br^- by Cl_2 is as follows.

$$Cl_2 + 2Br^-(aq) \longrightarrow 2Cl^-(aq) + Br_2$$

$$2\overset{-1}{Br^-} \longrightarrow \overset{0}{Br_2} + 2e^- \qquad \text{(oxidation)}$$

$$\overset{0}{Cl_2} + 2e^- \longrightarrow 2\overset{-1}{Cl^-} \qquad \text{(reduction)}$$

In every redox reaction, there is one reducing agent and one oxidizing agent. In the preceding example, Br^- is the reducing agent and Cl_2 is the oxidizing agent.

FIGURE 19-5 Zinc displaces copper ions from a copper(II) sulfate solution. Metallic copper precipitates.

TABLE 19-3 *Relative Strength of Oxidizing and Reducing Agents*

Increasing strength →

Reducing agents	Oxidizing agents
Li	Li^+
K	K^+
Ca	Ca^{2+}
Na	Na^+
Mg	Mg^{2+}
Al	Al^{3+}
Zn	Zn^{2+}
Cr	Cr^{3+}
Fe	Fe^{2+}
Ni	Ni^{2+}
Sn	Sn^{2+}
Pb	Pb^{2+}
H_2	H_3O^+
H_2S	S
Cu	Cu^{2+}
I^-	I_2
MnO_4^{2-}	MnO_4^-
Fe^{2+}	Fe^{3+}
Hg	Hg_2^{2+}
Ag	Ag^+
NO_2^-	NO_3^-
Br^-	Br_2
Mn^{2+}	MnO_2
SO_2	H_2SO_4 (conc.)
Cr^{3+}	$Cr_2O_7^{2-}$
Cl^-	Cl_2
Mn^{2+}	MnO_4^-
F^-	F_2

Increasing strength ↓

TABLE STRATEGY

Table 19-3 Point out that the strong reducing agents are those that easily give up electrons. Lithium easily gives up an electron to form the 1+ ion. Relate this fact to the electron configuration of lithium. The lost electron is the $2s^1$ electron; by losing it, lithium achieves the stable noble-gas configuration of helium. Point out that other Group 1 and 2 elements are near the top of the first column in this table. This should not be a surprise because students have already learned that these groups have low ionization energies. F^- is at the bottom of the column of reducing agents, so it is not a strong reducing agent, which means it has little tendency to give up an electron and become oxidized. Students should recall that fluorine has the highest electron affinity of any element. A reducing agent can reduce any species in the right-hand column that is below it. So, lithium readily reduces F_2 to form LiF.

✔ Teaching Tip

The following polyatomic ions make excellent oxidizing agents because their central atoms have high oxidation numbers: IO_4^-, ClO_4^-, MnO_4^-, NO_3^-, CrO_4^{2-}, and $Cr_2O_7^{2-}$.

604

QUICK LAB

In the decomposition of H_2O_2, the MnO_2 acts as a catalyst to speed up the normally slow reaction.

Safety: Students should wear safety goggles and an apron. During the $CuCl_2$ experiment, the solution can get hot. Do not allow students to touch the beaker while the reaction is in progress.

Disposal: Solids should be removed from the solutions and thrown away. Add 1.0 M NaOH to the solution to precipitate any remaining copper as solid $Cu(OH)_2$; discard the solid. Adjust the pH so that it is between 5 and 9 and dilute with a tenfold excess of water. Then pour the diluted solutions down the drain, provided your school is connected to a sanitary sewer system and treatment plant.

Discussion

1. $2H_2O_2 \longrightarrow O_2 + 2H_2O$;
$3CuCl_2 + 2Al \longrightarrow 2AlCl_3 + 3Cu$

2. Hydrogen peroxide was oxidized to oxygen and reduced to water. Evidence for the formation of O_2 was seen when a glowing splint burst into flames when placed in the reaction test tube. Copper(II) ions were reduced to copper metal, and aluminum metal was oxidized to Al(III) ions.

Quick LAB

Redox Reactions

Wear Safety Goggles and an Apron.

Procedure

Record all your results in a data table.

1. Put 10 mL of hydrogen peroxide in a test tube, and add a small amount of manganese dioxide (equal to the size of about half a pea). What is the result?

2. Insert a glowing wooden splint into the test tube (see diagram). What is the result? If oxygen is produced, a glowing wooden splint inserted into the test tube will glow brighter.

3. Fill the 250 mL beaker halfway with the copper(II) chloride solution.

4. Cut foil into 2 cm × 12 cm strips.

5. Add the aluminum strips to the copper(II) chloride solution. Use a glass rod to stir the mixture, and observe for 12 to 15 minutes. What is the result?

Materials

- aluminum foil
- beaker, 250 mL
- 1 M copper(II) chloride solution, $CuCl_2$
- 3% hydrogen peroxide
- manganese dioxide
- metric ruler
- scissors
- test-tube clamp
- test tube, 16 × 150 mm
- wooden splint

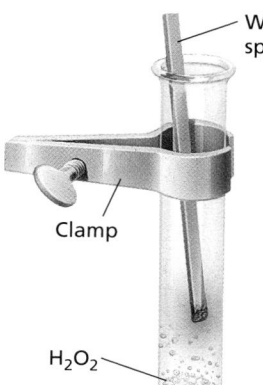

Wooden splint

Clamp

H_2O_2

Discussion

1. Write balanced equations showing what happened in each of the reactions.

2. Write a conclusion for the two experiments.

Autooxidation

Some substances can be both reduced and oxidized easily. For example, peroxide ions, O_2^{2-}, have a relatively unstable covalent bond between the two oxygen atoms. The electron-dot formula is written as follows.

$$\left[\ddot{\underset{..}{O}} : \ddot{\underset{..}{O}} \right]^{2-}$$

Each oxygen atom has an oxidation number of −1. The peroxide ion structure represents an intermediate oxidation state between O_2 and O^{2-}. Therefore, the peroxide ion is highly reactive.

Hydrogen peroxide, H_2O_2, contains the reactive peroxide ion. It decomposes into water and molecular oxygen, as shown in the equation below.

$$2H_2\overset{-1}{O}_2 \longrightarrow 2H_2\overset{-2}{O} + \overset{0}{O}_2$$

FIGURE 19-6 A bombardier beetle can repel large predators such as frogs with a chemical defense mechanism that uses the auto-oxidation of hydrogen peroxide.

Notice that in this reaction, hydrogen peroxide is both oxidized and reduced. Oxygen atoms that become part of gaseous oxygen molecules are oxidized. The oxidation number of theses oxygen atoms increases from −1 to 0. Oxygen atoms that become part of water are reduced. The oxidation number of these oxygen atoms decreases from −1 to −2. *A process in which a substance acts as both an oxidizing agent and a reducing agent is called* **autooxidation.** A substance that undergoes autooxidation is both *self-oxidizing* and *self-reducing*.

The bombardier beetle defends itself by spraying its enemies with an unpleasant hot chemical mixture as shown in Figure 19-6. The catalyzed autooxidation of hydrogen peroxide produces hot oxygen gas. This gas gives the insect an ability to eject irritating chemicals from its abdomen with explosive force.

SECTION REVIEW

1. Describe the chemical activity of the alkali metals and of the halogens on the basis of oxidizing and reducing strength.

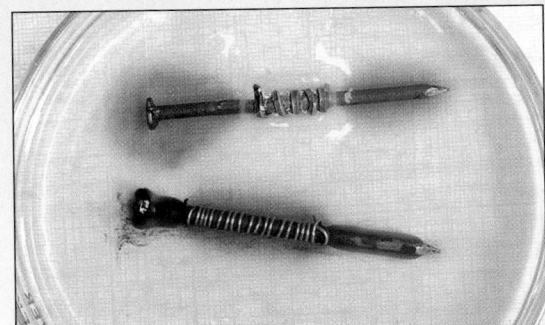

2. The photo on the left depicts two redox reactions. Use them to answer the following questions:
 a. When zinc is wrapped around an iron nail, is the iron reduced or oxidized?
 b. When copper is wrapped around an iron nail, is the iron reduced or oxidized?

3. Would Cl_2 be reduced by I^-? Explain.

4. Which is the stronger oxidizing agent in each of the following pairs?
 Cu^{2+} or Al^{3+}, H_2 or H_3O^+, Cr or Cu?

5. What is meant by *autooxidation*?

SECTION 19-4

Electrochemistry

DEMONSTRATION

Energy in an Electrochemical Cell

1. Fill a porous cup 3/4 full with 0.1 M $CuSO_4$ solution. Place the porous cup in a 250 mL beaker. Fill the beaker 3/4 full with 0.1 M $ZnSO_4$ solution.

2. Place a polished 4×150 mm copper strip in $CuSO_4$ solution and a polished 4×150 mm zinc strip in $ZnSO_4$ solution.

3. Connect leads from a voltmeter to the two electrodes, and note the voltage. Reverse the leads if you don't see a reading.

4. Relate the voltage reading to the chemical energy observed in Figure 19-7.

Disposal: Add sufficient 1 M NaOH to $ZnSO_4$ to precipitate $Zn(OH)_2$. Filter the solution, dry the precipitate, and put the solid in the trash. Adjust the pH of the filtrate to between 5 and 9, and pour the solution down drain. Scour six 6d iron nails with steel wool until they are shiny, and immerse them in the $CuSO_4$ solution overnight. Remove the nails and filter the solution. Heat the nails and any precipitate sufficiently to convert the copper to copper oxide. Let the nails cool, and put the copper oxide and nails in the trash. Pour the filtrate down the drain.

OBJECTIVES

- Explain what is required for an electrochemical cell.

- Describe the nature of voltaic cells.

- Describe the nature of electrolytic cells.

- Explain the process of electroplating.

- Describe the chemistry of a rechargeable cell.

- Calculate cell potentials from a table of standard electrode potentials.

internetconnect

SC*LINKS*
NSTA

TOPIC: Electrochemical cells
GO TO: www.scilinks.org
*sci***LINKS CODE:** HC2193

Oxidation-reduction reactions involve energy changes. Because these reactions involve electron transfer, the net *release* or net *absorption* of energy can occur in the form of electrical energy rather than as heat. This property allows for a great many practical applications of redox reactions. It also makes possible quantitative predictions and comparisons of the oxidizing and reducing abilities of different substances. *The branch of chemistry that deals with electricity-related applications of oxidation-reduction reactions is called* **electrochemistry.**

Electrochemical Cells

Oxidation-reduction reactions involve a transfer of electrons from the substance oxidized to the substance reduced. If the two substances are in contact with one another, a transfer of energy as heat accompanies the electron transfer. In Figure 19-7 a zinc strip is in contact with a copper(II) sulfate solution. The zinc strip loses electrons to the copper(II) ions in solution. Copper(II) ions accept the electrons and fall out of solution as copper atoms. As electrons are transferred between zinc atoms and copper(II) ions, energy is released as heat, as indicated by the rise in temperature.

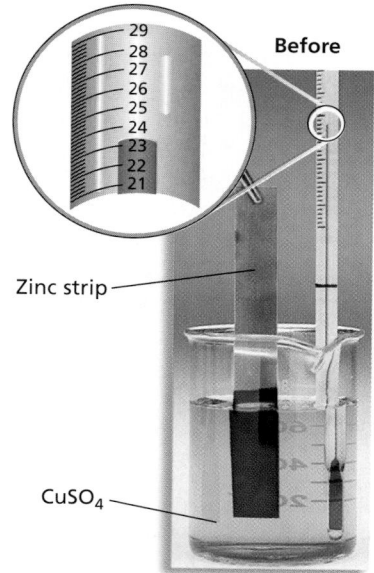
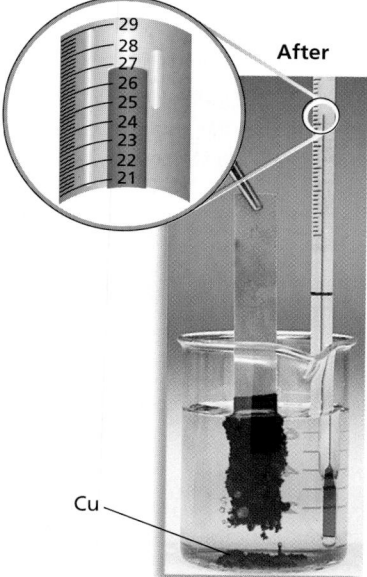

FIGURE 19-7 Heat energy given off when electrons are transferred directly from Zn atoms to Cu^{2+} ions causes the temperature of the aqueous $CuSO_4$ solution to rise.

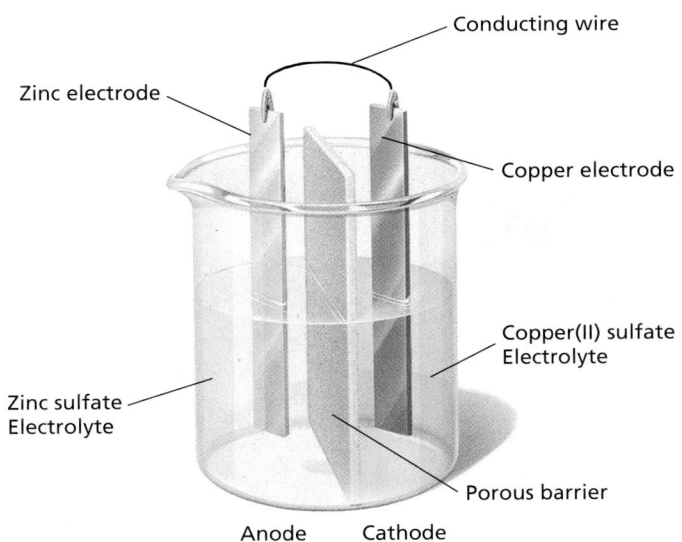

Conducting wire

Zinc electrode

Copper electrode

Copper(II) sulfate
Electrolyte

Zinc sulfate
Electrolyte

Porous barrier

Anode   Cathode

FIGURE 19-8 An electrochemical cell consists of two electrodes. Each electrode is in contact with an electrolyte; the electrode and the electrolyte make up a half-cell. The two electrodes are connected by a wire, and a porous barrier separates the two electrolytes.

If, however, we separate the substance that is oxidized during the reaction from the substance that is reduced during the reaction, the electron transfer is accompanied by a transfer of electrical energy instead of heat. One means of separating oxidation and reduction half-reactions is with a *porous barrier.* This barrier prevents the metal atoms of one half-reaction from mixing with the ions of the other half-reaction. Ions in the two solutions can move through the porous barrier. Electrons can be transferred from one side to the other through an external connecting wire. Electric current moves in a closed loop path, or *circuit,* so this movement of electrons through the wire is balanced by the movement of ions in solution.

Altering the system in Figure 19-7 so that electrical current is produced instead of heat would simply involve separating the copper and zinc, as shown in Figure 19-8. The Zn strip is in an aqueous solution of $ZnSO_4$. The Cu strip is in an aqueous solution of $CuSO_4$. Both solutions conduct electricity, so, as you learned in Chapter 14, they are classified as electrolytes. *An* **electrode** *is a conductor used to establish electrical contact with a nonmetallic part of a circuit, such as an electrolyte.* In Figure 19-8, the Zn and Cu strips are electrodes. *A single electrode immersed in a solution of its ions is a* **half-cell.** The Zn strip in aqueous $ZnSO_4$ is an **anode,** *the electrode where oxidation takes place.* The Cu strip in $CuSO_4$ is a **cathode,** *the electrode where reduction takes place.* The copper half-cell can be written as Cu^{2+}/Cu, and the zinc half-cell can be written as Zn^{2+}/Zn. The two half-cells together make an electrochemical cell. *An* **electrochemical cell** *is a system of electrodes and electrolytes in which either chemical reactions produce electrical energy or an electric current produces chemical change.* An electrochemical cell may be represented by the following notation: cathode | anode. For the example, the cell made up of zinc and copper could be written as Cu | Zn. There are two types of electrochemical cells: voltaic (also called galvanic) and electrolytic.

DEMONSTRATION

Fruit Battery

1. Obtain a lemon, grapefruit, or apple, and slice it into six sections.

2. Cut six Cu and six Zn strips, each 1 cm × 10 cm, and clean each strip with steel wool.

3. Insert one Cu strip and one Zn strip through the skin of each section of fruit. The strips should be separated by at least 1 cm.

4. Lay the fruit sections side by side. Using paper clips, attach the copper strip in the first fruit section to the zinc strip in the second section. Continue this process until all six sections are connected.

5. Connect the free copper strip to one end of a light-emitting diode, or LED, and the free zinc strip to the other end of the LED. The LED should glow brightly if the room lights are dimmed.

Safety: Do **not** eat the fruit. Wear goggles and a lab apron.

Disposal: Mark the fruit "Unfit for Food Use," and throw it in the trash. Save the metal strips for reuse.

CHEMISTRY INTERACTIVE TUTOR

Module 10: Electrochemical Cells

Topic: Galvanic Cell Tutorial
Section **c** of this engaging tutorial reviews and reinforces understanding of galvanic cells.

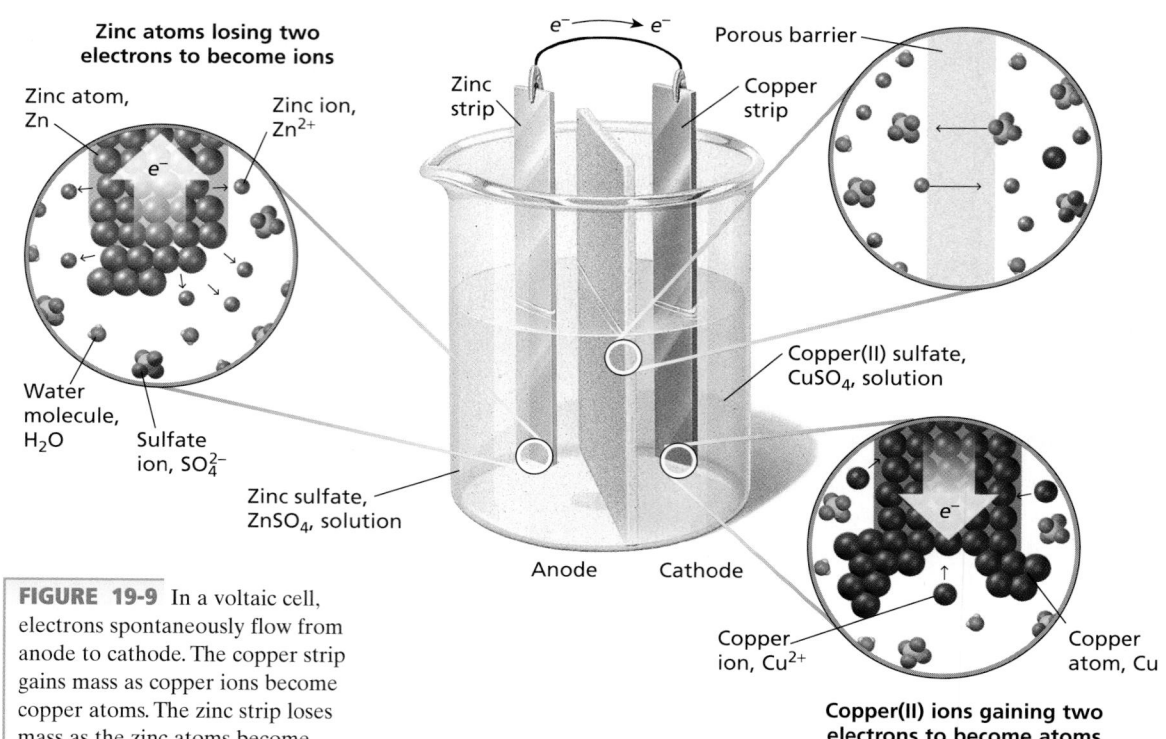

Zinc atoms losing two electrons to become ions

Zinc atom, Zn

Zinc ion, Zn^{2+}

Water molecule, H_2O

Sulfate ion, SO_4^{2-}

$e^- \longrightarrow e^-$

Porous barrier

Zinc strip

Copper strip

Copper(II) sulfate, $CuSO_4$, solution

Zinc sulfate, $ZnSO_4$, solution

Anode   Cathode

Copper ion, Cu^{2+}

Copper atom, Cu

Copper(II) ions gaining two electrons to become atoms

FIGURE 19-9 In a voltaic cell, electrons spontaneously flow from anode to cathode. The copper strip gains mass as copper ions become copper atoms. The zinc strip loses mass as the zinc atoms become zinc ions.

CHEMISTRY INTERACTIVE TUTOR

Module 10: Electrochemical Cells

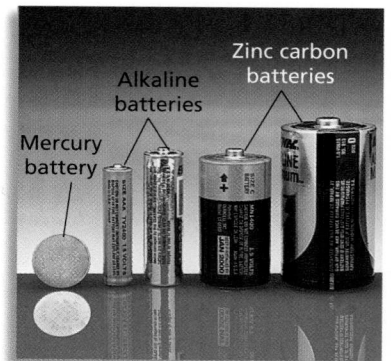

Mercury battery

Alkaline batteries

Zinc carbon batteries

FIGURE 19-10 Many common batteries are simple voltaic dry cells.

Voltaic Cells

If the redox reaction in an electrochemical cell occurs spontaneously and produces electrical energy, the cell is a **voltaic cell.** Cations in the solution are reduced when they gain electrons at the surface of the cathode to become metal atoms. This half-reaction for the voltaic cell shown in Figure 19-9 is as follows.

$$Cu^{2+}(aq) + 2e^- \longrightarrow Cu(s)$$

The half-reaction occurring at the anode is as follows.

$$Zn(s) \longrightarrow Zn^{2+}(aq) + 2e^-$$

Electrons given up at the anode pass along the external connecting wire to the cathode.

The movement of electrons through the wire must be balanced by a movement of ions in the solution. Anions move toward the anode to replace the negatively charged electrons that are moving away. Cations move toward the cathode as positive charge is lost through reduction. Thus, in Figure 19-9, sulfate ions in the $CuSO_4$ solution can move through the barrier into the $ZnSO_4$ solution. Likewise, the Zn^{2+} ions pass through the barrier into the $CuSO_4$ solution.

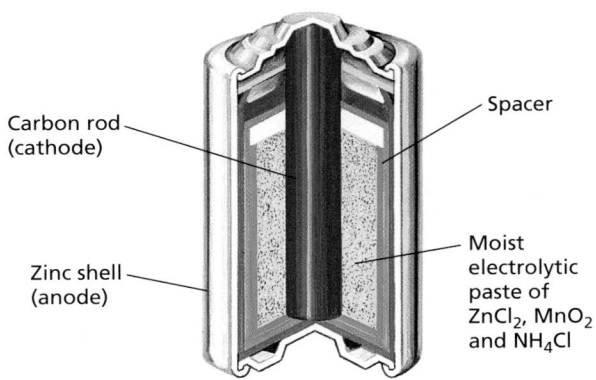

Carbon rod (cathode)

Spacer

Zinc shell (anode)

Moist electrolytic paste of $ZnCl_2$, MnO_2 and NH_4Cl

FIGURE 19-11 In a zinc dry cell, zinc is oxidized to Zn^{2+} at the anode, and manganese(IV) is reduced to manganese(III) at the cathode.

Visual Strategy

FIGURE 19-11 Students could be questioned about the role of the carbon rod. Point out that inert materials often act as electrodes. These materials do not react, but they provide a surface on which an oxidation or reduction half-reaction can take place.

Did You Know?

In 1800, Count Alessandro Volta (1745–1827) produced the first electric battery by stacking silver and zinc disks in a pile, separating them by cardboard pads soaked in salt water, and attaching a metal wire at each end. Ask students to think about the activity of Zn and Ag and to predict which metal is oxidized and which is reduced. Ask students to compare a Volta pile with the fruit battery made in the previous demonstration.

The terms *battery* and *cell* are often used interchangeably. However, a true battery is two or more cells connected together.

Reading Skill-Builder

DISCUSSION Have students read aloud or silently the selections on Electrochemical Cells, Voltaic Cells, and Electrolytic Cells. Start a class discussion about scenarios that involve the use of electrochemistry in industry or daily life. Be sure to emphasize that electrochemistry is another example of a redox reaction.

The dry cells pictured in Figure 19-10 are common sources of electrical energy. Like the wet cell previously described, dry cells are voltaic cells. The three most common types of dry cells are the zinc-carbon battery, the alkaline battery, and the mercury battery. They differ in the substances being oxidized and reduced.

Zinc-Carbon Dry Cells

Batteries such as those used in flashlights are zinc-carbon dry cells. These cells consist of a zinc container, which serves as the anode, filled with a moist paste of MnO_2, graphite, and NH_4Cl, as illustrated in Figure 19-11. When the external circuit is closed, zinc atoms are oxidized at the negative electrode, or anode.

$$\overset{0}{Zn}(s) \longrightarrow \overset{+2}{Zn^{2+}}(aq) + 2e^-$$

Electrons move across the circuit and reenter the cell through the carbon rod. The carbon rod is the cathode or positive electrode. Here MnO_2 is reduced in the presence of H_2O according to the following half-reaction.

$$2\overset{+4}{Mn}O_2(s) + H_2O(l) + 2e^- \longrightarrow \overset{+3}{Mn_2}O_3(s) + 2OH^-(aq)$$

Alkaline Batteries

The batteries found in a small, portable cassette player or other small electronic device are frequently alkaline dry cells. These cells do not have a carbon rod cathode, as in the zinc-carbon cell. The absence of the carbon rod allows them to be smaller. Figure 19-12 shows a model of an alkaline battery. This cell uses a paste of Zn metal and potassium hydroxide instead of a solid metal anode. The half-reaction at the anode is as follows.

$$\overset{0}{Zn}(s) + 2OH^-(aq) \longrightarrow \overset{+2}{Zn}(OH)_2(s) + 2e^-$$

The reduction half-reaction, the reaction at the cathode, is exactly the same as that for the zinc-carbon dry cell.

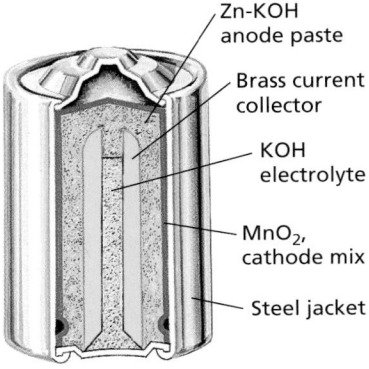

Zn-KOH anode paste

Brass current collector

KOH electrolyte

MnO_2, cathode mix

Steel jacket

FIGURE 19-12 KOH makes the electrolyte paste in this battery basic. Thus, it is called an alkaline dry cell.

1. Place a Petri dish on an overhead projector. Add 20 mL of 0.1 M KI solution.

2. Add a few drops of phenol-phthalein and a few drops of starch solution to the KI solution.

3. Using insulated leads, attach two electrodes to a 9 V transistor-radio battery.

4. Hold the electrodes in the KI solution.

I_2 can be detected at the anode by the characteristic blue-black color of starch in the presence of I_2. H_2 bubbles can be detected at the cathode. OH^- ions can be detected near the cathode by the appearance of the pink color of phenolphthalein.

5. Students can use the above evidence to write the half-reactions that took place.
Anode: $2I^-(aq) \longrightarrow I_2(aq) + 2e^-$
Cathode: $2e^- + 2H_2O(l) \longrightarrow$
$$H_2(g) + 2OH^-(aq)$$

6. Discuss the fact that the reaction did not proceed until the electrodes and battery were added. When students realize that this is a nonspontaneous reaction, have them trace the path of the electrons. Electrons are pumped from the anode, where I^- ions are oxidized, and forced through the external circuit to the cathode, where H^+ ions from the water are reduced to H_2.

Disposal: Add sufficient 1 M $Na_2S_2O_3$ to reduce I_2, and pour the solution down the drain.

CHEMISTRY INTERACTIVE TUTOR

Module 10: Electrochemical Cells

Topic: Electrolytic Cell Tutorial
Section **d** of this engaging tutorial reviews and reinforces understanding of electrolytic cells.

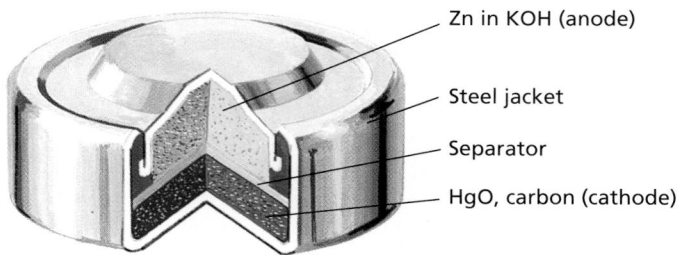

Zn in KOH (anode)
Steel jacket
Separator
HgO, carbon (cathode)

Mercury Batteries

The tiny batteries found in hearing aids, calculators, and camera flashes are mercury batteries, as shown in Figure 19-13. The anode half-reaction is identical to that found in the alkaline dry cell. However, the cathode, or reduction, half-reaction is different. The cathode half-reaction is described by the following equation.

$$\overset{+2}{Hg}O(s) + H_2O(l) + 2e^- \longrightarrow \overset{0}{Hg}(l) + 2OH^-(aq)$$

CHEMISTRY INTERACTIVE TUTOR

Module 10: Electrochemical Cells

Electrolytic Cells

Some oxidation-reduction reactions do not occur spontaneously, but can be driven by electrical energy. *The process in which an electric current is used to produce an oxidation-reduction reaction is* **electrolysis.** *If electrical energy is required to produce a redox reaction and bring about a chemical change in an electrochemical cell, it is an* **electrolytic cell.** Most commercial uses of redox reactions make use of electrolytic cells.

An electrolytic cell is depicted in Figure 19-14. The electrode of the cell connected to the negative terminal of the battery acquires an excess of electrons and becomes the cathode of the electrolytic cell. The electrode of the cell connected to the positive terminal of the battery loses electrons to the battery; it is the anode of the electrolytic cell. The battery can be thought of as an electron pump simultaneously supplying electrons to the cathode and recovering electrons from the anode. This energy input from the battery drives the electrode reactions in the electrolytic cell.

A comparison of electrolytic and voltaic cells can be seen in Figure 19-14. The voltaic cell shown in Figure 19-14 has a copper cathode and a zinc anode. If a battery is connected so that the positive terminal contacts the copper electrode and the negative terminal contacts the zinc electrode, the electrons flow in the opposite direction. The battery forces the cell to reverse its reaction; the zinc electrode becomes the cathode, and the copper electrode becomes the anode. The half-reaction at the anode, in which copper metal is oxidized, can be written as follows.

$$\overset{0}{Cu} \longrightarrow \overset{+2}{Cu^{2+}} + 2e^-$$

Voltaic Cell

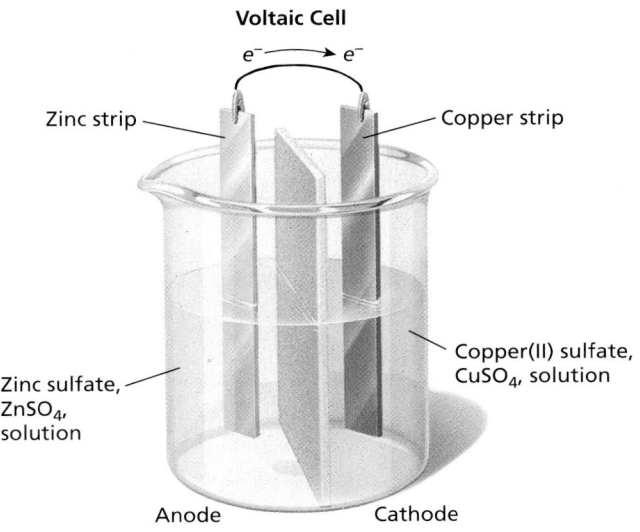

Zinc strip

Copper strip

Zinc sulfate, ZnSO₄, solution

Copper(II) sulfate, CuSO₄, solution

Anode   Cathode

Electrolytic Cell

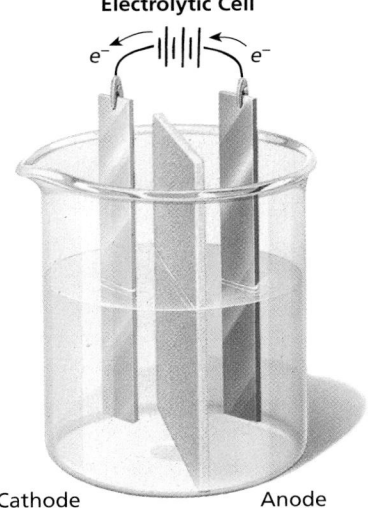

Cathode   Anode

The reduction half-reaction of zinc at the cathode is written as follows.

$$\overset{+2}{Zn^{2+}} + 2e^- \longrightarrow \overset{0}{Zn}$$

There are two important differences between the voltaic cell and the electrolytic cell.

1. The anode and cathode of an electrolytic cell are connected to a battery or other direct-current source, whereas a voltaic cell serves as a source of electrical energy.
2. Electrolytic cells are those in which electrical energy from an external source causes *nonspontaneous* redox reactions to occur. Voltaic cells are those in which *spontaneous* redox reactions produce electricity. In an electrolytic cell, electrical energy is converted to chemical energy; in a voltaic cell, chemical energy is converted to electrical energy.

Electroplating

Metals such as copper, silver, and gold are difficult to oxidize. In an electrolytic cell, these inactive metals form ions at an anode that are easily reduced at a cathode. This type of cell allows solid metal from one electrode to be deposited on the other electrode. *An electrolytic process in which a metal ion is reduced and a solid metal is deposited on a surface is called* **electroplating.**

An electroplating cell contains a solution of a salt of the plating metal. It has an object to be plated (the cathode) and a piece of the plating metal (the anode). A silver-plating cell contains a solution of a soluble silver salt and a silver anode. The cathode is the object to be plated. The silver anode is connected to the positive electrode of a battery or to some other source of direct current. The object to be plated is connected to the negative electrode.

FIGURE 19-14 The direction in which the electrons move reverses if a voltaic cell is connected to a direct current source to become an electrolytic cell.

internet**connect**

SCILINKS
NSTA

TOPIC: Electroplating
GO TO: www.scilinks.org
*sci*LINKS CODE: HC2194

Did You Know?

Pennies minted in the United States prior to 1982 are 95% copper and 5% zinc, but by 1982 the copper in a penny became more valuable than the buying power of a penny. To prevent the practice of melting down coins for the metal they contain, the composition of the penny was changed. Post–1982 pennies consist of a zinc core (97.5%) electroplated with a layer of copper.

FIGURE 19-15 Electroplating is often used to avoid corrosion (a redox reaction) at the object's surface by putting a layer of an inactive metal on a more-active metal.

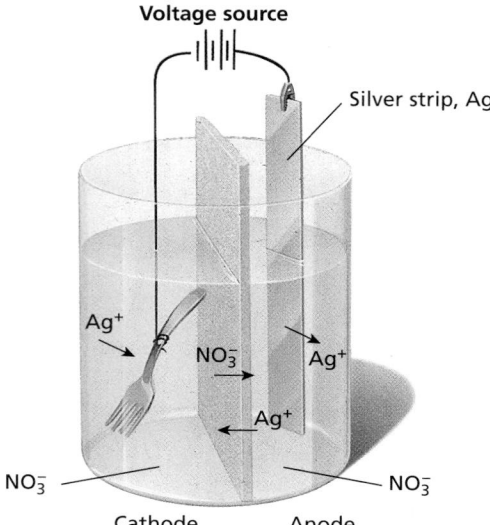

A cell in which silver is being electroplated onto a fork can be seen in Figure 19-15. Silver ions are reduced at the cathode according to the following equation and deposited as metallic silver when electrons flow through the circuit.

$$\overset{+1}{Ag^+} + e^- \longrightarrow \overset{0}{Ag}$$

Meanwhile, metallic silver is removed from the anode as ions. Silver atoms are oxidized at the anode according to the following half-reaction.

$$\overset{0}{Ag} \longrightarrow \overset{+1}{Ag^+} + e^-$$

This action maintains the Ag^+ ion concentration of the solution. Thus, in effect, silver is transferred from the anode to the cathode of the cell.

Rechargeable Cells

A rechargeable cell combines the oxidation-reduction chemistry of both voltaic cells and electrolytic cells. When a rechargeable cell converts chemical energy to electrical energy, it operates as a voltaic cell. But when the cell is recharged, it operates as an electrolytic cell, converting electrical energy to chemical energy.

The standard 12 V automobile battery, shown in Figure 19-16, is a set of six rechargeable cells. The anode in each cell is lead submerged in a solution of H_2SO_4. The anode half-reaction is described by the following equation.

$$Pb(s) + SO_4^{2-}(aq) \longrightarrow PbSO_4(s) + 2e^-$$

Electrons move through the circuit to the cathode, where PbO_2 is reduced according to the following equation.

$$PbO_2(s) + 4H^+(aq) + SO_4^{2-}(aq) + 2e^- \longrightarrow PbSO_4(s) + 2H_2O(l)$$

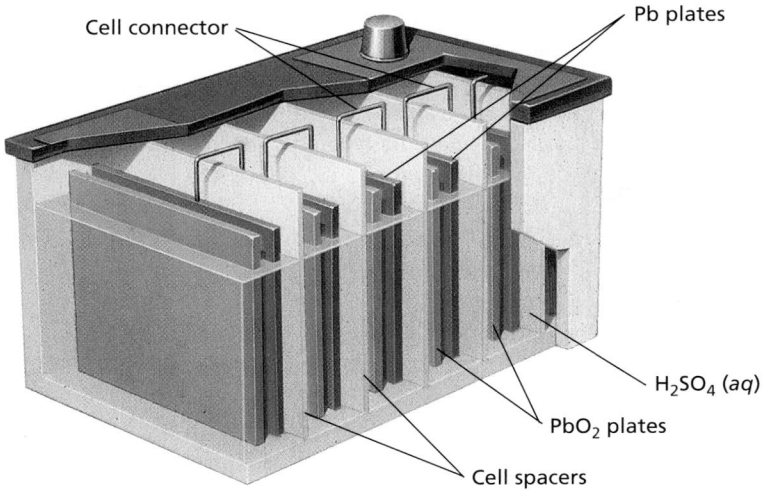

Cell connector

Pb plates

H_2SO_4 (aq)

PbO_2 plates

Cell spacers

Did You Know?
Although thermodynamic calculations show that the voltages of electrochemical cells sometimes decrease with decreasing temperature, this decrease for a lead storage battery is only about 0.05% per °C and cannot account for a battery going "dead" in cold weather. The cause can be attributed to an increase in viscosity of the electrolyte that becomes more pronounced as temperature decreases. Ions move more slowly in a viscous medium. Therefore, the ability of the electrolytic solution to conduct decreases and its resistance increases, leading to a decrease in the battery's ability to deliver current.

The net oxidation-reduction reaction for the discharge cycle is described by the following chemical equation.

$$Pb(s) + PbO_2(s) + 2H_2SO_4(aq) \longrightarrow 2PbSO_4(s) + 2H_2O(l)$$

A car's battery produces the electric energy needed to start its engine. Sulfuric acid, present as its ions, is consumed, and lead(II) sulfate accumulates as a white powder on the electrodes. Once the car is running, the half-reactions are reversed by a voltage produced by the alternator. The Pb, PbO_2, and H_2SO_4 are regenerated. A battery can be recharged as long as all reactants necessary for the electrolytic reaction are present, and all reactions are reversible.

Electrode Potentials

Reconsider the voltaic cell shown in Figure 19-9. There are two electrodes, Zn and Cu. According to Table 19-3, these two metals each have different tendencies for accepting electrons. *This tendency for the half-reaction of either copper or zinc to occur as a reduction half-reaction in an electrochemical cell can be quantified as a* **reduction potential.** There are two half-cells in Figure 19-9: a strip of zinc placed in a solution of $ZnSO_4$ and a strip of copper placed in a solution of $CuSO_4$. *The difference in potential between an electrode and its solution is known as its* **electrode potential.** When these two half-cells are connected and the reaction begins, a difference in potential is observed between the electrodes. This potential difference, or voltage, is a measure of the energy required to move a certain electric charge between the electrodes. Potential difference is measured in volts. A voltmeter connected across the Cu | Zn voltaic cell measures a potential difference of about 1.10 V when the solution concentrations of Zn^{2+} and Cu^{2+} ions are each 1 M.

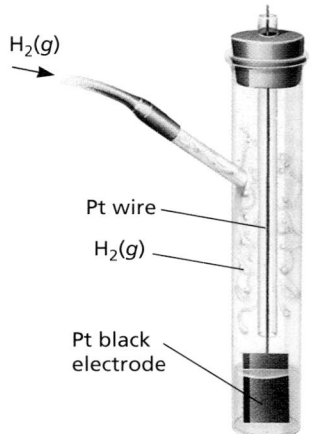

H₂(g)

Pt wire

H₂(g)

Pt black electrode

FIGURE 19-17 A hydrogen electrode is the standard reference electrode for measuring electrode potentials. The electrode surface in contact with the solution is actually a layer of hydrogen adsorbed onto the surface of the platinum.

The potential difference measured across the complete voltaic cell roughly equals the sum of the electrode potentials for the two half-reactions. But while the potential difference across a voltaic cell is easily measured, there is no way to measure an individual electrode potential directly. This is because there can be no transfer of electrons unless both the anode and the cathode are connected to form a complete circuit. A relative value for the potential of a half-reaction can be determined by connecting it to a standard half-cell as a reference. This standard half-cell, shown in Figure 19-17, is called a standard hydrogen electrode, or SHE. It consists of a platinum electrode dipped into a 1.00 M acid solution surrounded by hydrogen gas at 1 atm pressure and 25°C. Other electrodes are ranked according to their ability to reduce hydrogen under these conditions.

The anodic reaction for the standard hydrogen electrode is described by the forward half-reaction in the following equilibrium equation.

$$\overset{0}{H_2}(g) \rightleftharpoons 2\overset{+1}{H^+}(aq) + 2e^-$$

The cathodic half-reaction is the reverse. An arbitrary potential of 0.00 V is assigned to both of these half-reactions. Therefore, any voltage measurement obtained is attributed to the half-cell connected to the SHE. *A half-cell potential measured relative to a potential of zero for the standard hydrogen electrode is a* **standard electrode potential,** E^0. Electrode potentials are expressed as potentials for reduction. These reduction potentials provide a reliable indication of the tendency of a substance to be reduced. Half-reactions for some common electrodes and their standard electrode potentials are listed in Table 19-4.

Positive E^0 values indicate that hydrogen is more willing to give up its electrons than the other electrode. Half-reactions with positive reduction potentials are favored. Effective oxidizing agents, such as Cu and F_2, have positive E^0 values. Half-reactions with negative reduction potentials are not favored; these half-reactions prefer oxidation over reduction. Negative E^0 values indicate that the metal or other electrode is more willing to give up electrons than hydrogen. Effective reducing agents, such as Li and Zn, have negative E^0 values. When a half-reaction

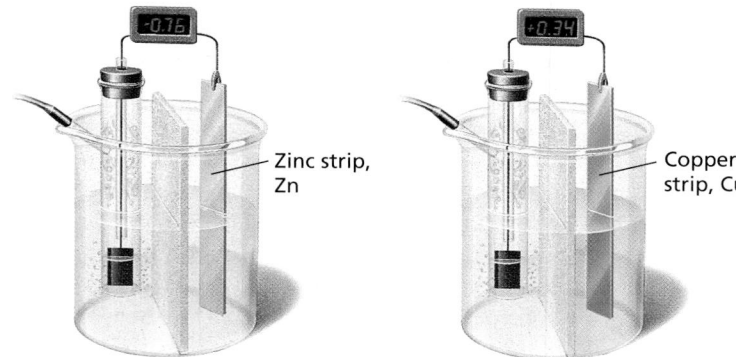

Zinc strip, Zn

Copper strip, Cu

FIGURE 19-18 The electrode potentials of zinc and copper half-cells are measured by coupling them with a standard hydrogen electrode.

TABLE 19-4 *Standard Reduction Potentials*

Half-cell reaction	Standard electrode potential, E^0 (in volts)	Half-cell reaction	Standard electrode potential, E^0 (in volts)
$F_2 + 2e^- \rightleftharpoons 2F^-$	+2.87	$Fe^{3+} + 3e^- \rightleftharpoons Fe$	−0.04
$MnO_4^- + 8H^+ + 5e^- \rightleftharpoons Mn^{2+} + 4H_2O$	+1.50	$Pb^{2+} + 2e^- \rightleftharpoons Pb$	−0.13
$Au^{3+} + 3e^- \rightleftharpoons Au$	+1.50	$Sn^{2+} + 2e^- \rightleftharpoons Sn$	−0.14
$Cl_2 + 2e^- \rightleftharpoons 2Cl^-$	+1.36	$Ni^{2+} + 2e^- \rightleftharpoons Ni$	−0.26
$Cr_2O_7^{2-} + 14H^+ + 6e^- \rightleftharpoons 2Cr^{3+} + 7H_2O$	+1.23	$Co^{2+} + 2e^- \rightleftharpoons Co$	−0.28
$MnO_2 + 4H^+ + 2e^- \rightleftharpoons Mn^{2+} + 2H_2O$	+1.22	$Cd^{2+} + 2e^- \rightleftharpoons Cd$	−0.40
$Br_2 + 2e^- \rightleftharpoons 2Br^-$	+1.07	$Fe^{2+} + 2e^- \rightleftharpoons Fe$	−0.45
$Hg^{2+} + 2e^- \rightleftharpoons Hg$	+0.85	$S + 2e^- \rightleftharpoons S^{2-}$	−0.48
$Ag^+ + e^- \rightleftharpoons Ag$	+0.80	$Cr^{3+} + 3e^- \rightleftharpoons Cr$	−0.74
$Hg_2^{2+} + 2e^- \rightleftharpoons 2Hg$	+0.80	$Zn^{2+} + 2e^- \rightleftharpoons Zn$	−0.76
$Fe^{3+} + e^- \rightleftharpoons Fe^{2+}$	+0.77	$Al^{3+} + 3e^- \rightleftharpoons Al$	−1.66
$MnO_4^- + e^- \rightleftharpoons MnO_4^{2-}$	+0.56	$Mg^{2+} + 2e^- \rightleftharpoons Mg$	−2.37
$I_2 + 2e^- \rightleftharpoons 2I^-$	+0.54	$Na^+ + e^- \rightleftharpoons Na$	−2.71
$Cu^{2+} + 2e^- \rightleftharpoons Cu$	+0.34	$Ca^{2+} + 2e^- \rightleftharpoons Ca$	−2.87
$Cu^{2+} + e^- \rightleftharpoons Cu^+$	+0.15	$Ba^{2+} + 2e^- \rightleftharpoons Ba$	−2.91
$S + 2H^+(aq) + 2e^- \rightleftharpoons H_2S(aq)$	+0.14	$K^+ + e^- \rightleftharpoons K$	−2.93
$2H^+(aq) + 2e^- \rightleftharpoons H_2$	0.00	$Li^+ + e^- \rightleftharpoons Li$	−3.04

TABLE STRATEGY

Table 19-4 Call attention to the change in the magnitude and sign of the E^0 values from the top to the bottom of the table. Ask students the significance of a high positive number for an E^0 value and the significance of a large negative number. Relate the table to electronegativity values, activities, electron affinities, and ionization energies. Ask students questions about the reducing strengths of various metals in the table, and then ask them about oxidizing strengths.

CHEMISTRY INTERACTIVE TUTOR

Module 10: Electrochemical Cells

Topic: Electrochemical Series Tutorial and Practice
Sections **e** and **f** of this engaging tutorial review and reinforce understanding of electrochemical series.

is written as an oxidation reaction, the sign of its electrode potential is changed as shown for the oxidation and reduction half-reactions for zinc.

$$Zn^{2+} + 2e^- \longrightarrow Zn \qquad E^0 = -0.76 \text{ V}$$
$$Zn \longrightarrow Zn^{2+} + 2e^- \qquad E^0 = +0.76 \text{ V}$$

To measure the reduction potential of a zinc half-cell, it is connected to a standard hydrogen electrode, as in Figure 19-18. The potential difference across the cell is −0.76 V. The negative number indicates that electrons flow through the external circuit from the zinc electrode, where zinc is oxidized, to the hydrogen electrode, where aqueous hydrogen ions are reduced.

A copper half-cell coupled with the standard hydrogen electrode gives a potential difference measurement of +0.34 V. This positive number indicates that $Cu^{2+}(aq)$ ions are more readily reduced than $H^+(aq)$ ions.

Standard electrode potentials can be used to predict if a redox reaction will occur naturally. A naturally occurring reaction will have a positive value for E^0_{cell}, which is calculated using the following equation.

$$E^0_{cell} = E^0_{cathode} - E^0_{anode}$$

CHEMISTRY INTERACTIVE TUTOR

Module 10: Electrochemical Cells

OXIDATION-REDUCTION REACTIONS **615**

This discussion involves only 1 M solutions. In order to discuss cell potentials for solutions at concentrations other than 1 M, the Nernst equation must be involved.

SECTION REVIEW

1. A voltaic cell is one in which a spontaneous redox reaction produces electricity.

2. An electrolytic cell is one in which electrical energy from an external source causes a nonspontaneous redox reaction to occur.

3. Electroplating is a process in which a metal ion is reduced and solid metal is deposited on a surface.

4. A rechargeable cell is one that operates both as a voltaic cell and as an electrolytic cell. It operates as a voltaic cell when it converts chemical energy to electrical energy; when the cell is recharging, it operates as an electrolytic cell, converting electrical energy to chemical energy.

5. Electrode potential is the potential difference between an electrode and its solution; its magnitude measures the tendency for reduction half-reactions to occur.

6. $K + Na^+ \longrightarrow K^+ + Na$
$E^0 = +0.22$ V

When evaluating the two half-reactions in a voltaic cell, the half-reaction with the lower standard reduction potential is the anode. Oxidation occurs at the anode, so the half-cell reaction is the reverse of the reduction reaction found in Table 19-4. When a reaction is reversed, the actual half-cell potential is the negative of the standard reduction potential. For this reason, the total potential of a cell is calculated by subtracting the standard reduction potential for the reaction at the anode (E^0_{anode}) from the standard reduction potential for the reaction at the cathode ($E^0_{cathode}$).

Consider cells made from Fe in a solution of $Fe(NO_3)_3$ and Ag in a solution of $AgNO_3$. Table 19-4 gives the following half-reactions and E^0 values for these half-cells.

$$Fe^{3+}(aq) + 3e^- \longrightarrow Fe(s) \qquad E^0 = -0.04 \text{ V}$$
$$3Ag^+(aq) + 3e^- \longrightarrow 3Ag(s) \qquad E^0 = +0.80 \text{ V}$$

Fe in $Fe(NO_3)_3$ is the anode because it has the lower reduction potential, and Ag in $AgNO_3$ is therefore the cathode. The overall cell reaction is

$$3Ag^+(aq) + Fe(s) \longrightarrow 3Ag^+(s) + Fe^{3+}(aq)$$

The reduction of silver ions is multiplied by 3 so that the number of electrons lost in that half-reaction equals the number of electrons gained in the oxidation of iron. The standard reduction potentials for the anode and cathode are as follows.

$$E^0_{anode} = -0.04 \text{ V}$$
$$E^0_{cathode} = +0.80 \text{ V}$$

Note that when a half-reaction is multiplied by a constant, the E^0 value is not multiplied but remains the same.

So the potential for this cell can be calculated as follows.

$$E^0_{cell} = E^0_{cathode} - E^0_{anode}$$
$$E^0_{cell} = +0.80 \text{ V} - (-0.04 \text{ V}) = 0.84 \text{ V}$$

If the calculated value for E^0_{cell} were negative, the reaction would not occur naturally in the direction written, so it would not occur in a voltaic cell. It could be made to occur in an electrolytic cell.

SECTION REVIEW

1. What is a voltaic cell?

2. Describe an electrolytic cell.

3. Explain the process of electroplating.

4. What is a rechargeable cell?

5. What is electrode potential, and how is it used to calculate information about an electrochemical reaction?

6. Given the Na^+/Na and K^+/K half-cells, determine the overall electrochemical reaction that proceeds spontaneously and the E^0 value.

CHAPTER SUMMARY

19-1
- Oxidation numbers are assigned by the set of rules listed in Table 19-1.
- Oxidation-reduction reactions consist of two half-reactions that must occur simultaneously.
- Oxidation-reduction reactions are identified by examining the reactants and products for changes in oxidation numbers of their constituent atoms.
- Oxidation involves the loss of electrons, and reduction involves the gain of electrons.

Vocabulary

half-reaction (593)	oxidation-reduction reaction (593)	oxidized (592)	reduced (593)
oxidation (592)		redox reaction (593)	reduction (593)

19-2
- Both charge and mass are conserved in a balanced redox equation.
- In the half-reaction method for balancing equations, oxidation and reduction equations are balanced separately for atoms and charge. Then they are combined to give a complete balanced equation.

19-3
- In redox reactions, the substance that is *reduced* acts as an *oxidizing agent* because it *acquires* electrons from the substance oxidized.
- The substance that is *oxidized* in a redox reaction is the *reducing agent* because it *supplies* the electrons to the substance reduced.

Vocabulary

autooxidation (605)	oxidizing agent (602)	reducing agent (602)

19-4
- Some oxidation-reduction reactions that occur naturally can be sources of electrical energy in voltaic cells. Other oxidation-reduction reactions that do not occur naturally can be driven by an external source of electrical energy in electrolytic cells; this process is called electrolysis.
- An electrode and its electrolyte in an electrochemical cell are called a half-cell.
- The potential difference between the electrode and its solution is called the electrode potential.
- The sum of the electrode potentials of the two half-reactions of an electrochemical cell is roughly equal to the potential difference across the cell.
- Standard electrode potentials are measured relative to a standard hydrogen electrode. They indicate the relative strengths of substances as oxidizing and reducing agents.

Vocabulary

anode (607)	electrode (607)	electroplating (611)	standard electrode potential (614)
cathode (607)	electrode potential (613)	half-cell (607)	
electrochemical cell (607)	electrolysis (610)	reduction potential (613)	voltaic cell (608)
electrochemistry (606)	electrolytic cell (610)		

REVIEW ANSWERS

1. a. Oxidation causes atoms or ions to attain a more positive oxidation state and lose e^-. Reduction causes atoms or ions to attain a more negative oxidation state and gain e^-.
b. oxidation: $Na \longrightarrow Na^+ + e^-$
reduction: $Cl_2 + 2e^- \longrightarrow 2Cl^-$

2. a, b, c, f, g, i

3.

Equation	Oxidized	Reduced
a	Na	Cl_2
b	C	O_2
c	$\overset{-2}{O}$	$\overset{+1}{H}$
f	$\overset{-2}{O}$	$\overset{+5}{Cl}$
g	H_2	Cl_2
i	Zn	Cu^{2+}

4. a. lithium
b. have weak attraction for their valence electrons and readily lose electrons to reduce other substances
c. fluorine

5. a. strongest: Ca, weakest: Cl^-
b. strongest: Al, weakest: Br^-
c. strongest: Na, weakest: F^-
d. strongest: K^+, weakest: NO_3^-
e. strongest: Zn^{2+}, weakest: Cl_2
f. strongest: Li^+, weakest: F_2

6. a. yes
b. yes
c. no
d. yes
e. no

7. spontaneous reaction in voltaic; nonspontaneous in electrolytic

8. a. an electrolytic process that deposits metal on a surface
b. object to be plated = cathode, plating metal = anode

9. a. a measure of the energy required to move a certain electric charge across the cell
b. measured in volts by a voltmeter connected across the two electrodes

REVIEWING CONCEPTS

1. a. Distinguish between the processes of oxidation and reduction.
b. Write an equation to illustrate each. (19-1)

2. Which of the following are redox reactions?
a. $2Na + Cl_2 \longrightarrow 2NaCl$
b. $C + O_2 \longrightarrow CO_2$
c. $2H_2O \longrightarrow 2H_2 + O_2$
d. $NaCl + AgNO_3 \longrightarrow AgCl + NaNO_3$
e. $NH_3 + HCl \longrightarrow NH_4^+ + Cl^-$
f. $2KClO_3 \longrightarrow 2KCl + 3O_2$
g. $H_2 + Cl_2 \longrightarrow 2HCl$
h. $H_2SO_4 + 2KOH \longrightarrow K_2SO_4 + 2H_2O$
i. $Zn + CuSO_4 \longrightarrow ZnSO_4 + Cu$ (19-1)

3. For each oxidation-reduction reaction in the previous question, identify what is oxidized and what is reduced. (19-1)

4. a. Identify the most active reducing agent among all common elements.
b. Why are all of the elements in its group in the periodic table very active reducing agents?
c. Identify the most active oxidizing agent among the common elements. (19-3)

5. Based on Table 19-3, identify the strongest and weakest reducing agents among the substances listed within each of the following groupings:
a. Ca, Ag, Sn, Cl^-
b. Fe, Hg, Al, Br^-
c. F^-, Pb, Mn^{2+}, Na
d. Cr^{3+}, Cu^{2+}, NO_3^-, K^+
e. Cl_2, S, Zn^{2+}, Ag^+
f. Li^+, F_2, Ni^{2+}, Fe^{3+} (19-3)

6. Use Table 19-3 to respond to each of the following:
a. Would Al be oxidized by Ni^{2+}?
b. Would Cu be oxidized by Ag^+?
c. Would Pb be oxidized by Na^+?
d. Would F_2 be reduced by Cl^-?
e. Would Br_2 be reduced by Cl^-? (19-3)

7. Distinguish between a voltaic cell and an electrolytic cell in terms of the nature of the reaction involved. (19-4)

8. a. What is electroplating?
b. Distinguish between the nature of the anode and cathode in such a process. (19-4)

9. a. Explain what is meant by the potential difference between the two electrodes in an electrochemical cell.
b. How, and in what units, is this potential difference measured? (19-4)

10. The standard hydrogen electrode is assigned an electrode potential of 0.00 V. Explain why this voltage is assigned. (19-4)

11. a. What information is provided by the electrode potential of a given half-cell?
b. What does the relative value of the potential of a given half-reaction indicate about its oxidation-reduction tendency? (19-4)

PROBLEMS

Redox Equations

12. Each of the following atom/ion pairs undergoes the oxidation number change indicated below. For each pair, determine whether oxidation or reduction has occurred, and then write the electronic equation indicating the corresponding number of electrons lost or gained.
a. $K \longrightarrow K^+$
e. $H_2 \longrightarrow H^+$
b. $S \longrightarrow S^{2-}$
f. $O_2 \longrightarrow O^{2-}$
c. $Mg \longrightarrow Mg^{2+}$
g. $Fe^{3+} \longrightarrow Fe^{2+}$
d. $F^- \longrightarrow F_2$
h. $Mn^{2+} \longrightarrow MnO_4^-$

13. Identify the following reactions as redox or nonredox:
a. $2NH_4Cl(aq) + Ca(OH)_2(aq) \longrightarrow$
$2NH_3(aq) + 2H_2O(l) + CaCl_2(aq)$
b. $2HNO_3(aq) + 3H_2S(g) \longrightarrow$
$2NO(g) + 4H_2O(l) + 3S(s)$
c. $[Be(H_2O)_4]^{2+}(aq) + H_2O(l) \longrightarrow$
$H_3O^+(aq) + [Be(H_2O)_3OH]^+(aq)$

14. Arrange the following in order of increasing oxidation number of the xenon atom: $CsXeF_8$, Xe, XeF_2, $XeOF_2$, XeO_3, XeF

15. Determine the oxidation number of each atom indicated in the following:
  a. H_2
  b. H_2O
  c. Al
  d. MgO
  e. Al_2S_3
  f. HNO_3
  g. H_2SO_4
  h. $Ca(OH)_2$
  i. $Fe(NO_3)_2$
  j. O_2

16. Balance the oxidation-reduction equation below by using the half-reaction method in response to each requested step. (Hint: See Sample Problem 19-1.)

$$K + H_2O \longrightarrow KOH + H_2$$

  a. Write the ionic equation, and assign oxidation numbers to all atoms to determine what is oxidized and what is reduced.
  b. Write the equation for the reduction, and balance it for both atoms and charge.
  c. Write the equation for the oxidation, and balance it for both atoms and charge.
  d. Adjust the oxidation and reduction equations by multiplying the coefficients as needed so that electrons lost equal electrons gained, and add the two resulting equations.
  e. Add species as necessary to balance the overall formula equation.

17. Use the method in the previous problem to balance each of the reactions below.
  a. $HI + HNO_2 \longrightarrow NO + I_2 + H_2O$
  b. $FeCl_3 + H_2S \longrightarrow FeCl_2 + HCl + S$

18. Balance the equation for the reaction in which hot, concentrated sulfuric acid reacts with zinc to form zinc sulfate, hydrogen sulfide, and water.

Voltaic and Electrolytic Cells

19. For each of the following pairs of half-cells, determine the overall electrochemical reaction that proceeds spontaneously:
  a. Cu^{2+}/Cu, Ag^+/Ag
  b. Cd^{2+}/Cd, Co^{2+}/Co
  c. Na^+/Na, Ni^{2+}/Ni
  d. I_2/I^-, Br_2/Br^-

20. Determine the values of E^0 for the cells in the previous problem.

21. Suppose chemists had chosen to make the $I_2 + 2e^- \rightleftharpoons 2I^-$ half-cell the standard electrode and had assigned it a potential of zero volts.
  a. What would be the E^0 value for the $Br_2 + 2e^- \rightleftharpoons 2Br^-$ half-cell?
  b. What would be the E^0 value for the $Al^{3+} + 3e^- \rightleftharpoons Al$ half-cell?
  c. How much change would be observed in the E^0 value for the reaction involving $Br_2 + I^-$ using the I_2 half-cell as the standard?

22. If a strip of Ni were dipped into a solution of $AgNO_3$, what would be expected to occur? Explain, using E^0 values and equations.

23. a. What would happen if an aluminum spoon were used to stir a solution of $Zn(NO_3)_2$?
  b. Could a strip of Zn be used to stir a solution of $Al(NO_3)_3$? Explain, using E^0 values.

24. How do the redox reactions for each of the following types of batteries differ?
  a. zinc-carbon
  b. alkaline
  c. mercury

25. a. Why are some standard reduction potentials positive and some negative?
  b. Compare the E^0 value for a metal with the reactivity of that metal.

MIXED REVIEW

26. Predict whether each of the following reactions will occur spontaneously as written by determining the E^0 value for potential reaction. Write and balance the overall equation for each reaction that does occur.
  a. $Mg + Sn^{2+} \longrightarrow$
  b. $K + Al^{3+} \longrightarrow$
  c. $Li^+ + Zn \longrightarrow$
  d. $Cu + Cl_2 \longrightarrow$

27. Why is it possible for alkaline batteries to be smaller than zinc-carbon dry cells?

28. Draw a diagram of a voltaic cell whose two half-reactions consist of Ag in $AgNO_3$ and Ni in $NiSO_4$. Identify the anode and cathode, and indicate the directions in which the electrons and ions are moving.

---

10. cannot directly measure an electrode potential; by assigning an arbitrary potential to the SHE, other electrode potentials can be measured against this reference

11. a. half-cell potential is an indication of the tendency of a substance to undergo reduction as compared with H^+
  b. Large reduction potential means greater tendency for reduction and less likely to undergo oxidation. Smaller potential means greater tendency for oxidation and less tendency for reduction.

12. a. oxidation: $K \longrightarrow K^+ + e^-$
  b. reduction: $S + 2e^- \longrightarrow S^{2-}$
  c. oxidation: $Mg \longrightarrow Mg^{2+} + 2e^-$
  d. oxidation: $2F^- \longrightarrow F_2 + 2e^-$
  e. oxidation: $H_2 \longrightarrow 2H^+ + 2e^-$
  f. reduction: $O_2 + 4e^- \longrightarrow 2O^{2-}$
  g. reduction: $Fe^{3+} + e^- \longrightarrow Fe^{2+}$
  h. oxidation: $Mn^{2+} \longrightarrow MnO_4^- + 5e^-$

13. a. nonredox   **b.** redox
  c. nonredox

14. Xe, XeF, XeF_2, $XeOF_2$, XeO_3, $CsXeF_8$

15. a. $\overset{0}{H_2}$
  b. $\overset{+1 \ -2}{H_2O}$
  c. $\overset{0}{Al}$
  d. $\overset{+2 \ -2}{MgO}$
  e. $\overset{+3 \ -2}{Al_2S_3}$
  f. $\overset{+1 \ +5 \ -2}{HNO_3}$
  g. $\overset{+1 \ +6 \ -2}{H_2SO_4}$
  h. $\overset{+2 \ -2 \ +1}{Ca(OH)_3}$
  i. $\overset{+2 \ +5 \ -2}{Fe(NO_3)_2}$
  j. $\overset{0}{O_2}$

16. *See page 621A*

17. *See page 621A*

18. *See page 621A*

19. a. $2Ag^+ + Cu \longrightarrow 2Ag + Cu^{2+}$
b. $Co^{2+} + Cd \longrightarrow Co + Cd^{2+}$
c. $2Na + Ni^{2+} \longrightarrow 2Na^+ + Ni$
d. $Br_2 + 2I^- \longrightarrow 2Br^- + I_2$

20. a. $+0.46$ V
b. $+0.12$ V
c. $+2.45$ V
d. $+0.53$ V

21. a. 0.53 V
b. -2.20 V
c. no change

22. $Ni + 2Ag^+ \longrightarrow Ni^{2+} + 2Ag$
$E^0 = 0.26$ V $+ 0.80$ V $= +1.06$ V
nickel dissolves, solid silver forms

23. a. $2Al + 3Zn^{2+} \longrightarrow 2Al^{3+} + 3Zn$
$E^0 = 1.66$ V $- 0.76$ V $= +0.90$ V
spoon disintegrates, solid Zn forms
b. $2Al^{3+} + 3Zn \longrightarrow 2Al + 3Zn^{2+}$
$E^0 = -1.66$ V $+ 0.76$ V $= -0.90$ V
Yes, no reaction would occur.

24. *See page 621A*

25. a. positive E^0 values for species
reduced more easily than H^+;
negative E^0 values for species
reduced less easily than H^+
b. smaller E^0 value = more
reactive

26. a. $E^0 = +2.23$ V; spontaneous
$Mg + Sn^{2+} \longrightarrow Mg^{2+} + Sn$
b. $E^0 = +1.27$ V; spontaneous
$3K + Al^{3+} \longrightarrow 3K^+ + Al$
c. $E^0 = -2.28$ V; nonspontaneous
d. $E^0 = +1.02$ V; spontaneous
$Cu + Cl_2 \longrightarrow Cu^{2+} + 2Cl^-$

27. Alkalines do not need carbon
rods, as zinc-carbon do. Thus,
alkaline batteries can be smaller.

28. *See page 621A*

29. a. redox
b. redox
c. nonredox
d. nonredox
e. nonredox
f. redox

29. Identify the following reactions as redox or
nonredox:
a. $Mg(s) + ZnCl_2(aq) \longrightarrow Zn(s) + MgCl_2(aq)$
b. $H_2(g) + OF_2(g) \longrightarrow H_2O(g) + HF(g)$
c. $2KI(aq) + Pb(NO_3)_2(aq) \longrightarrow$
$$PbI_2(s) + 2KNO_3(aq)$$
d. $CaO(s) + H_2O(l) \longrightarrow Ca(OH)_2(aq)$
e. $3CuCl_2(aq) + 2(NH_4)_3PO_4(aq) \longrightarrow$
$$6NH_4Cl(aq) + Cu_3(PO_4)_2(s)$$
f. $CH_4(g) + 2O_2(g) \longrightarrow CO_2(g) + 2H_2O(g)$

30. Can a solution of $Sn(NO_3)_2$ be stored in an
aluminum container? Explain, using E^0 values.

31. A voltaic cell is made up of a cadmium electrode
in a solution of $CdSO_4$ and a zinc electrode in
a solution of $ZnSO_4$. The two half-cells are
separated by a porous barrier.
a. Which is the cathode, and which is the
anode?
b. In which direction are the electrons flowing?
c. Write balanced equations for the two half-
reactions, and write a net equation for the
combined reaction.

32. Would the following pair of electrodes make
a good battery? Explain.
$$Cd \longrightarrow Cd^{2+} + 2e^-$$
$$Fe \longrightarrow Fe^{2+} + 2e^-$$

33. Arrange the following in order of decreasing
oxidation number of the nitrogen atom:
N_2, NH_3, N_2O_4, N_2O, N_2H_4, NO_3^-

34. Balance the following redox equations:
a. $SbCl_5 + KI \longrightarrow KCl + I_2 + SbCl_3$
b. $Ca(OH)_2 + NaOH + ClO_2 + C \longrightarrow$
$$NaClO_2 + CaCO_3 + H_2O$$

CRITICAL THINKING

35. Applying Models Explain how the oxidation-
reduction chemistry of both the voltaic cell and
the electrolytic cell are combined in the chemistry of rechargeable cells.

36. Applying Ideas In lead/acid batteries, such as
your car battery, the degree of discharge of the
battery can be determined by measuring the
density of the battery fluid. Explain how this is
possible.

37. Interpreting Graphics A voltaic cell is pictured below. Identify the species that is oxidized
if current is allowed to flow.

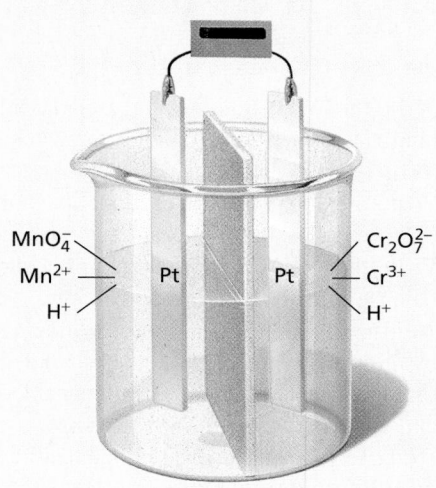

Digital voltmeter

MnO_4^- Mn^{2+} H^+ Pt Pt $Cr_2O_7^{2-}$ Cr^{3+} H^+

⊞ TECHNOLOGY & LEARNING

38. Graphing Calculator: Calculate the Equilibrium
Constant, Using the Standard Cell Voltage

The graphing calculator can run a program that
calculates the equilibrium constant for an electrochemical cell using an equation called the
Nernst equation, given the standard potential
and the number of electrons transferred. Given
that the standard potential is 2.041 V and that
two electrons are transferred, you will calculate
the equilibrium constant. The program will be
used to make the calculations.

Go to Appendix C. If you are using a TI 83
Plus, you can download the program and data
and run the application as directed. If you are
using another calculator, your teacher will provide you with keystrokes and data sets to use.

Remember that you will need to name the program and check the display, as explained in Appendix C. You will then be ready to run the program. After you have graphed the data, answer these questions.

a. What is the equilibrium constant when the standard potential is .099?

b. What is the equilibrium constant when the standard potential is 1.125?

c. What is the equilibrium constant when the standard potential is 2.500?

 HANDBOOK SEARCH

39. Several reactions of aluminum are shown in the common reactions section for Group 13 of the *Elements Handbook*. Use these reactions to answer the following.
   a. Which of the five reactions shown are oxidation-reduction reactions? How do you know?
   b. For the redox reactions you listed for item a, identify what is oxidized and what is reduced.
   c. Write half-reactions for each equation you listed in item a.

40. Aluminum is described in Group 13 of the *Elements Handbook* as a self-protecting metal. This property of aluminum results from a redox reaction.
   a. Write the redox equation for the oxidation of aluminum.
   b. Write the half-reactions for this reaction showing the number of electrons transferred.
   c. What problems are associated with the buildup of aluminum oxide on electrical wiring made of aluminum?

RESEARCH & WRITING

41. Go to the library and find out what you can about the electroplating industry in the United States. What are the top three metals used for plating, and how many metric tons of each are used in the United States each year for electroplating?

42. Investigate the types of batteries being considered for electric cars. Write a report on the advantages and disadvantages of these types of batteries.

ALTERNATIVE ASSESSMENT

43. Performance   Take an inventory of the types of batteries used in your home. Find out the voltage supplied by each battery and what electrochemical reaction each uses. Suggest why that electrochemical reaction is used in each case.

44. In our portable society, batteries have become a necessary power supply. As consumers, we want to purchase batteries that will last as long as possible. Advertisements tell us that some batteries last longer than others, but do they really? Design an investigation to answer the question. Is there a difference in longevity among the major brands of AA batteries? Add a cost-effectiveness component to your design.

45. When someone with a silver filling in a tooth bites down on an aluminum gum wrapper, saliva acts as an electrolyte. The system is an electrochemical cell which produces a small jolt of pain. Explain what occurs, using half-cell reactions and $E°$ values.

30. $E^0 = +1.52$ V; no, Al container dissolves and solid Sn forms

31. a. cathode = Cd; anode = Zn
   b. e^- flow from Zn to Cd
   c. $Zn \longrightarrow Zn^{2+} + 2e^-$
   $$\frac{Cd^{2+} + 2e^- \longrightarrow Cd}{Zn + Cd^{2+} \longrightarrow Zn^{2+} + Cd}$$

32. No; Fe and Cd are close in activity, cell voltage is +0.05 V.

33. NO_3^-, N_2O_4, N_2O, N_2, N_2H_4, NH_3

34. *See page 621A*

35. During the discharge cycle, spontaneous redox reactions typical of voltaic cells convert chemical energy to electrical energy. During the recharge cycle, electrical energy is converted to chemical energy through redox reactions characteristic of electrolytic cells.

36. *See page 621A*

37. Cr^{3+} is oxidized.

38. a. 2211.0298
   b. 1.0157×10^{38}
   c. 2.8804×10^{84}

39–45 *See pages 621A, 621B*

REVIEW ANSWERS

Answers from page 619

16. a. $\overset{0}{K} + \overset{+1\,-2}{H_2O} \longrightarrow \overset{+1}{K^+} + \overset{-2\,+1}{OH^-} + \overset{0}{H_2}$

b. $2H_2O + 2e^- \longrightarrow 2OH^- + H_2$

c. $K \longrightarrow K^+ + e^-$

d. $2H_2O + 2e^- \longrightarrow 2OH^- + H_2$

$\underline{2(K \longrightarrow K^+ + 2e^-)}$

$2H_2O + 2K \longrightarrow 2OH^- + H_2 + 2K^+$

e. $2H_2O + 2K \longrightarrow 2KOH + H_2$

17 a. $\overset{+1}{2H^+} + \overset{-1}{I^-} + \overset{+3\,-2}{NO_2^-} \longrightarrow \overset{+2\,-2}{NO} + \overset{0}{I_2} + \overset{+1\,-2}{H_2O}$

$2I^- \longrightarrow I_2 + 2e^-$

$\underline{2[NO_2^- + e^- + 2H^+ \longrightarrow NO + H_2O]}$

$2HI + 2HNO_2 \longrightarrow 2NO + I_2 + 2H_2O$

b.

$\overset{+3}{Fe^{3+}} + \overset{-1}{3Cl^-} + \overset{+1\,-2}{H_2S} \longrightarrow \overset{+2}{Fe^{2+}} + \overset{-1}{2Cl^-} + \overset{+1}{H^+} + \overset{-1}{Cl^-} + \overset{0}{S}$

$2[Fe^{3+} + e^- \longrightarrow Fe^{2+}]$

$\underline{H_2S \longrightarrow S + 2e^- + 2H^+}$

$2FeCl_3 + H_2S \longrightarrow 2FeCl_2 + 2HCl + S$

18. $\overset{+1\,+6\,-2}{H_2SO_4} + \overset{0}{Zn} \longrightarrow \overset{+2\,+6\,-2}{ZnSO_4} + \overset{+1\,-2}{H_2S} + \overset{+1\,-2}{H_2O}$

$SO_4^{2-} + 10H^+ + 8e^- \longrightarrow H_2S + 4H_2O$

$\underline{4[Zn \longrightarrow Zn^{2+} + 2e^-]}$

$4Zn + 5H_2SO_4 \longrightarrow 4ZnSO_4 + H_2S + 4H_2O$

24. Zinc-carbon and alkaline both have this cathode reaction:

$2MnO_2 + H_2O + 2e^- \longrightarrow Mn_2O_3 + 2OH^-$

zinc-carbon has anode in aqueous environment; alkaline has anode in alkaline environment; mercury anode is like alkaline, but cathode reaction is:

$HgO + H_2O + 2e^- \longrightarrow Hg + 2OH^-$

Answers from page 620

28.

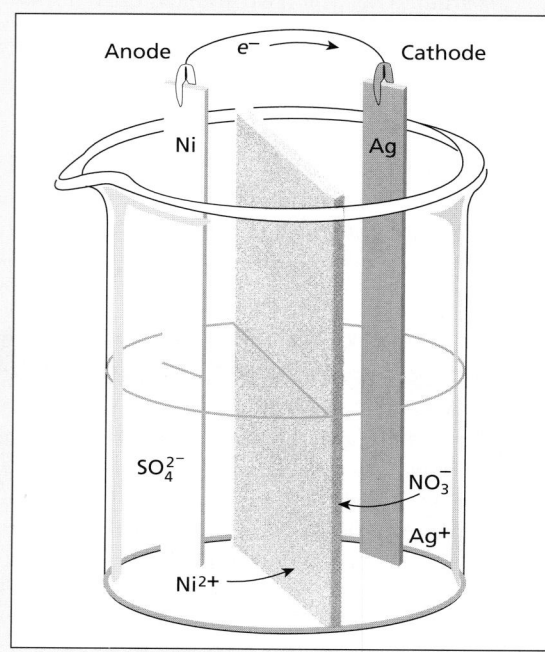

34. a. $SbCl_5 + 2KI \longrightarrow 2KCl + I_2 + SbCl_3$

b. $Ca(OH)_2 + 4NaOH + 4ClO_2 + C \longrightarrow$
$4NaClO_2 + CaCO_3 + 3H_2O$

36. Fully charged, a battery contains concentrated sulfuric acid. During discharge the acid is consumed as shown in this equation:

$Pb + PbO_2 + 2H_2SO_4 \longrightarrow 2PbSO_4 + H_2O$

Sulfuric acid is quite dense; as it is used up, the density of the fluid in the battery decreases. Therefore, a battery that is more fully charged will have fluid of a greater density than a battery that is less charged.

Answers from page 621

39. a. All of them are redox reactions. In each case aluminum metal is oxidized.

b.

	Oxidized	Reduced
reaction 1:	Al	H^+
reaction 2:	Al	H^+
reaction 3:	Al	N^{5+}
reaction 4:	Al	Cl_2
reaction 5:	Al	O_2

c. reaction 1: $2Al \longrightarrow 2Al^{3+} + 6e^-$

$6H^+ + 6e^- \longrightarrow 3H_2$

Half-reactions for the second reaction in the series are the same as those above.

reaction 3: $Al \longrightarrow Al^{3+} + 3e^-$

$NO_3^- + 3e^- + 4H^+ \longrightarrow NO + 2H_2O$

reaction 4: $2Al \longrightarrow 2Al^{3+} + 6e^-$

$3Cl_2 + 6e^- \longrightarrow 6Cl^-$

reaction 5: $4Al \longrightarrow 4Al^{3+} + 12e^-$

$3O_2 + 12e^- \longrightarrow 6O^{2-}$

40. a. $4Al(s) + 3O_2(g) \longrightarrow 2Al_2O_3(s)$

b. See reaction 5 for 39(c)

c. The buildup of Al_2O_3 increases the electrical resistance of the wire at contact points with switches and outlets. This increased resistance generates sufficient heat to start a fire within the walls of a home.

41. Refer to the *One-Stop Planner CD-ROM* for appropriate scoring rubrics. Students may not find information about the top three metals and production figures, but they should mention copper, silver, and gold as being important in electroplating.

42. Answers will vary. Be sure to examine the environmental costs of developing and disposing of the batteries.

43. Students can make a table displaying data. Tables can be posted for other students to learn from.

44. Check the design of student investigations before they begin.

45. The aluminum wrapper acts as the anode, and the filling acts as the cathode. The jolt of pain is from the voltage produced by the electrochemical cell.

$Al^{3+} + 3e^- \longrightarrow Al$

$Ag^+ + e^- \longrightarrow Ag$, $E^0_{cell} = +2.46$ V

Photo Descriptions

Center: tracks made by nuclear particles in a cloud chamber

Lower left: model for the start of a uranium fission chain reaction

Middle right: tetrahedral carbon structure of methane

Lower right: scanning electron micrograph of the polymer bristles of a special toothbrush

UNIT 7

Organic and Nuclear Chemistry

CHAPTERS

20 Carbon and Hydrocarbons

21 Other Organic Compounds

22 Nuclear Chemistry

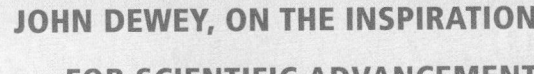

JOHN DEWEY, ON THE INSPIRATION FOR SCIENTIFIC ADVANCEMENT

Every great advance in science has issued from a new audacity of imagination.

(John Dewey, *The Quest for Certainty*)

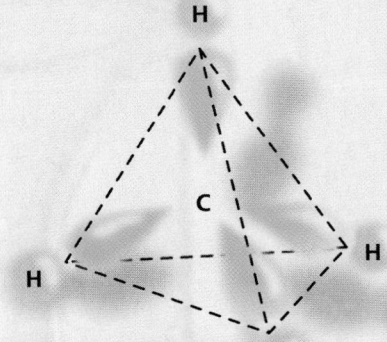

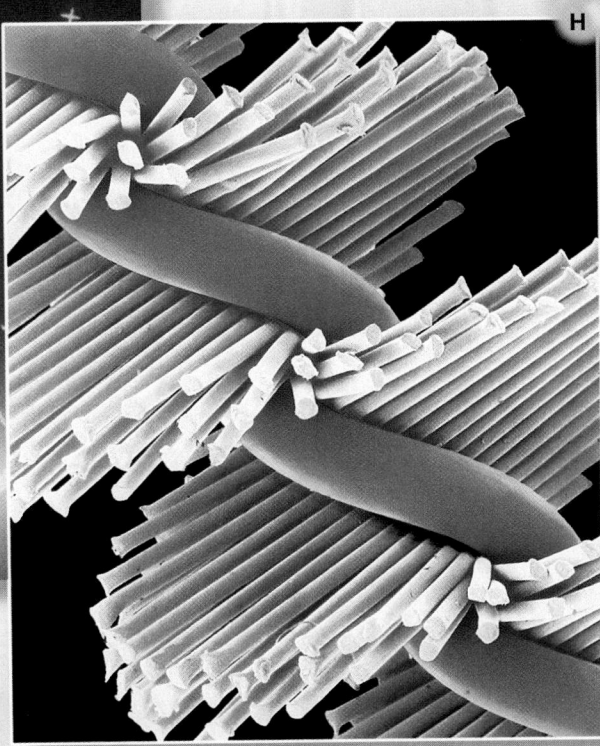

Carbon and Hydrocarbons

PACING CHART

Compression Guide: *(To shorten, eliminate items in italics.)*

CLASSROOM RESOURCES

	NSE Standards	Teaching Resources	Experiments
20-1 Abundance and Importance of Carbon 2 45-minute periods 1 90-minute block	PS 2c, 2f UCP 1–2, 5	**PE** Elements Handbook T 114, T 115, T 116, TM 114A	**A23** Carbon
20-2 Organic Compounds 2 45-minute periods 1 90-minute block	PS 2c, 2f UCP 1–2, 5	**ATE Demo,** pp. 631	
20-3 Saturated Hydrocarbons 2 45-minute periods 1 90-minute block *Properties and Uses of Alkanes, pp. 643–645*	PS 2c, 2f UCP 1–2, 5 ST 1–2 SPSP 5	**PE** Elements Handbook T 117, TM 115A, TM 116A, TM 117A	**A24** Oil-Degrading Microbes
20-4 Unsaturated Hydrocarbons 2 45-minute periods 1 90-minute block	PS 2c, 2f UCP 1–2, 5	T 118, T 119, TM 118A, TM 119A	

Review and Assessment
2 45-minute periods
1 90-minute block

REVIEW RESOURCES

Cumulative Review	Alternative Assessment	Traditional Assessment
SR Chapter 20 Mixed Review PE Chapter 20, 50–55, p. 660	PE 65, 66, p. 661 AA Items for Chapter 20	Chapter 20 Text Test Generator items for Chapter 20

Technology & Internet Resources

CTW 5	Segment 5 Making Fullerenees
CTW 6	Segment 6 Cleaner Gas
CTW 16	Segment 16 Carbon Nitride
CTW 16	Segment 22 Belching Cows

Holt Chemistry Videodiscs Teacher's Correlation Guide for Chapter 20

Module 4: Covalent/Ionic, Molecular Geometry

On-line Student Resources:
www.scilinks.org
The following SciLinks Internet resources can be found in the student text for this chapter.

TOPICS:
- Allotropes, p. 627 (HC2201)
- Diamond/graphite, p. 627 (HC2202)
- Buckminster Fuller, p. 628 (HC2203)
- Alkanes, p. 634 (HC2204)
- Alkenes, p. 647 (HC2205)
- Aromatic compounds, p. 653 (HC2206)

On-line Teacher Resources:
GO TO: go.hrw.com
KEYWORD: HC2 HOME
Visit the HRW Web site for a variety of resources related to this chapter.

Smithsonian Institution
Internet Connections
Visit **www.si.edu/hrw** for additional on-line resources.

Visit **www.cnnfyi.com** for late-breaking news and current events stories selected just for you.

ASSIGNMENT RESOURCES

Section Homework Resources & Review	Problem-Solving Practice
HR Homework Worksheet 20-1 PE Section Review, 1–4, p. 628 Chapter Review, 1–6, 45, pp. 657, 660 SR Section Review 20-1	

HR Homework Worksheets 20-2, 20-3
     Graphic Org. Assignment 20-2
PE Section Review, 1–4, p. 633
     Chapter Review, 7–11, 30–33, pp. 657–658
SR Section Review 20-2	

HR Homework Worksheets 20-4, 20-5, 20-6
     Graphic Org. Assignment 20-5
PE Section Review, 1–5, p. 645
     Chapter Review, 16–19, 34–37,
     48–49, pp. 657–660
SR Section Review 20-3
	PE Additional Samples 20-1, 20-2
	ATE Additional Samples, pp. 639, 640, 641
	     Additional Example, p. 642

HR Homework Worksheets 20-7, 20-8, 20-9
     Graphic Org. Assignments 20-8, 20-9
PE Section Review, 1–5, p. 655
     Chapter Review, 12–15, 20–29,
     38–44, pp. 657–660
SR Section Review 20-4
	PE Additional Samples 20-1, 20-4
	ATE Additional Samples, pp. 649, 654
	     Additional Examples, p. 652

Resource Key

PE Pupil's Edition
ATE Teacher's Edition

One-Stop Planner CD-ROM Includes these resources and customizable daily lesson plans:

HR	Homework Resources		D	Consumer Experiments
SR	Section Reviews	A Laboratory Experiments	T	Transparencies
CTW	Critical Thinking	B Microscale Experiments	TM	Transparency Masters
	Worksheets	C Technique Builders and	PS	Mini-Guide to Problem Solving
AA	Alternative Assessments	Problem-Solving Experiments	SRW	Supplemental Reading Worksheets

Scoring Rubrics for Labs, Alternative Assessments, Performance Tasks and Portfolio Projects are on the One-Stop Planner CD-ROM.

Carbon and Hydrocarbons

Chapter Overview

20-1 outlines the covalent bonding that occurs with carbon as well as carbon's major allotropes.

20-2 describes how to depict structural formulas and determine the difference between structural and geometric isomers.

20-3 describes how to name saturated hydrocarbons and explains the relationship between the structures of alkanes and some of their uses.

20-4 describes the naming and properties of unsaturated hydrocarbons.

Concept Base

Students may need a review of the following concepts:

- electron configurations, Chapter 4
- hybridization and covalent bonding, Chapter 6
- intermolecular attraction with liquids and solids, Chapter 12
- properties of solutes in solutions, Chapter 13

Reading Skill-Builder

K/W/L Have students list what they know or want to know about carbon and the importance of carbon compounds. After they have read the chapter, have them add to their lists what they have learned. If they still have questions, have them research these questions using other sources.

Carbon and Hydrocarbons

Three-dimensional models help us visualize the shape of carbon compounds.

Abundance and Importance of Carbon

Carbon is found in nature both as an element and in combined form. Although carbon ranks about 17th in abundance by mass among the elements in Earth's crust, it is exceedingly important because it is found in all living matter. Carbon is present in body tissues and in the foods you eat. It is also found in common fuels, such as coal, petroleum, natural gas, and wood.

Structure and Bonding of Carbon

Carbon, the first member of Group 14, has mostly nonmetallic properties. In its ground state, a carbon atom has an electronic configuration of $1s^2 2s^2 2p^2$. The two $1s$ electrons are tightly bound to the nucleus. The two $2s$ electrons and the two $2p$ electrons are the valence electrons. Carbon atoms show a very strong tendency to share electrons and form covalent bonds.

As was covered in Chapter 6, hybridization can be used to explain the bonding and geometry of most carbon compounds. Carbon atoms that form four single bonds have four sp^3 orbitals. These orbitals are directed toward the four corners of a regular tetrahedron, as shown in Figure 20-1. This results in the tetrahedral shape of methane, CH_4, and the zigzag pattern of molecules with multiple single-bonded carbon atoms, such as C_4H_{10}.

SECTION 20-1

OBJECTIVES

- Relate the ability of a carbon atom to form covalent bonds to its atomic structure and hybrid orbitals.

- Identify the different allotropes of carbon and their structural differences.

- Explain how the different structures of carbon allotropes affect their properties.

CHEMISTRY INTERACTIVE TUTOR

Module 4: Chemical Bonding

FIGURE 20-1 The orbital models show how the orientation of sp^3 hybrid orbitals relates to the geometry of CH_4 and C_4H_{10}.

Lesson Starter
Have students look around the room and identify all the items that contain carbon. Most of the items in view will in some manner involve carbon. This might lead to a discussion about our society's dependence on fossil fuels. For example, we depend on fossil fuels for electricity, fuel for automobiles, plastics, waxes, and fibers such as nylon, polyester, and spandex. Remind students that fossil fuels are, for all practical purposes, nonrenewable resources and are in limited supply.

Visual Strategy
FIGURE 20-1 Be sure students understand that a tetrahedron is the geometric shape that results when four corners of a three-dimensional structure are as far apart as possible. Ask students what the four objects are *(carbon's valence electrons)* and why they are as far apart as possible *(electron repulsion)*.

CHAPTER ⟷ CONNECTION

Students should review electron configurations in Chapter 3 and hybridization in Chapter 6 in order to better understand this section.

CHEMISTRY INTERACTIVE TUTOR

Module 4: Chemical Bonding

Topics: Covalent/Ionic Tutorial, Molecular Geometry Tutorials and Practice
Sections **d, e, f, g,** and **h** of this engaging tutorial review and reinforce understanding of chemical bonding.

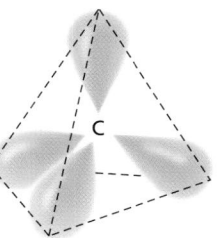

sp^3 hybrid orbitals

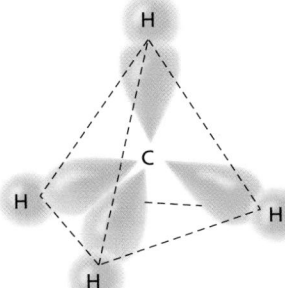

CH_4 orbital overlap

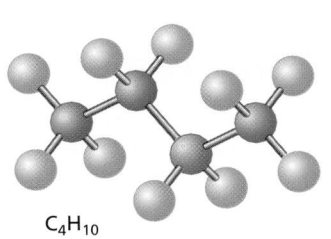

C_4H_{10}

CHAPTER ⟷ CONNECTION

In Chapter 6, students found out how single bonds are made from hybridized orbitals. Multiple bonds also involve some orbitals that are not hybridized. The overlap of unhybridized orbitals creates the additional bonding in double and triple bonds.

Visual Strategy

FIGURE 20-2 The geometry of hybridized orbitals is easily demonstrated with balloons. Obtain one balloon for each hybrid orbital, and hold the tied ends of the balloons together. Four balloons will form the shape of a tetrahedron, three balloons should show a triangular planar shape, and two balloons are linear. The balloons, like the electrons in hybrid orbitals, will be as far from each other as possible.

FIGURE 20-3 Be sure students recognize the tetrahedral arrangement of the carbon atoms in a diamond crystal. If the carbon atoms in diamond show a tetrahedral geometry, how are the orbitals in diamond hybridized?

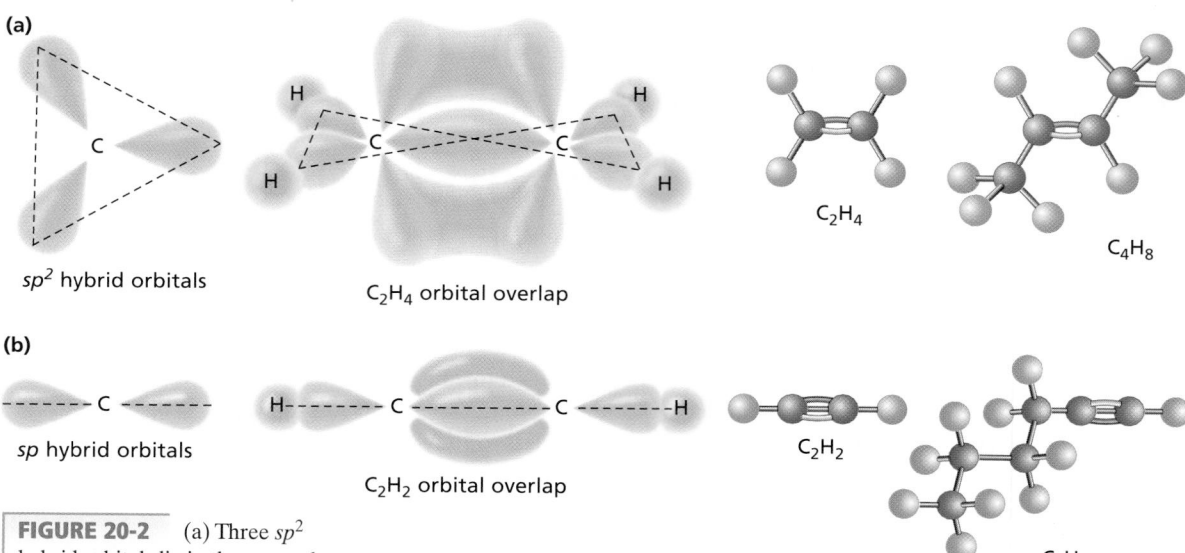

(a)

sp^2 hybrid orbitals

C_2H_4 orbital overlap

C_2H_4

C_4H_8

(b)

sp hybrid orbitals

C_2H_2 orbital overlap

C_2H_2

C_6H_{10}

FIGURE 20-2 (a) Three sp^2 hybrid orbitals lie in the same plane. The C_2H_4 orbital overlap model shows the orientation of sp^2 hybrid orbitals in molecules that contain a double bond, such as C_2H_4 and C_4H_8. (b) The C_2H_2 orbital overlap model shows the orientation of sp hybrid orbitals in molecules that contain a triple bond, such as C_2H_2 and C_6H_{10}.

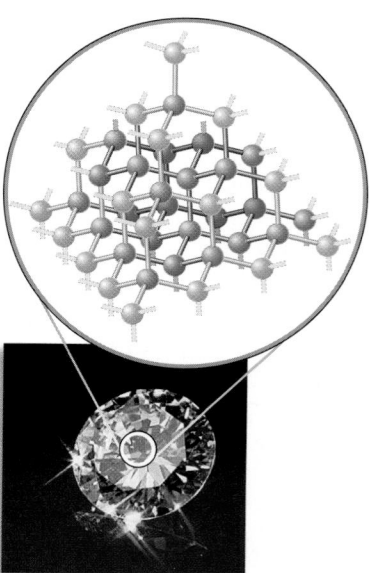

FIGURE 20-3 In diamond, the carbon atoms are densely packed because each carbon atom is bonded to four tetrahedrally oriented carbon atoms.

Carbon atoms form double bonds through sp^2 hybridization, as shown in Figure 20-2(a). When carbon atoms form double bonds, the sp^2 hybrid orbitals of both carbon atoms lie in the same plane, as shown in the orbital overlap model of ethene, C_2H_4. Because the hydrogen atoms of C_2H_4 also bond with carbon sp^2 orbitals, all six atoms lie in the same plane. The three-dimensional models of C_2H_4 and C_4H_8 show the geometry of molecules containing carbon-carbon double bonds.

Carbon triple bonds are linear due to the linear arrangement of two sp hybrid orbitals, as shown in Figure 20-2(b). This can be seen in the orbital overlap model for ethyne, C_2H_2. The three-dimensional models of C_2H_2 and C_6H_{10} show the geometry of molecules containing carbon-carbon triple bonds.

Allotropes of Carbon

Carbon occurs in several solid allotropic forms that have dramatically different properties. **Diamond** *is a colorless, crystalline, solid form of carbon.* **Graphite** *is a soft, black, crystalline form of carbon that is a fair conductor of electricity.* **Fullerenes** *are dark-colored solids made of spherically networked carbon-atom cages.*

Diamond

Diamond is the hardest material known. It is the most dense form of carbon—about 3.5 times more dense than water. It also has an extremely high melting point (greater than 3500°C). These properties of diamond can be explained by its structure. The model in Figure 20-3 shows carbon atoms in diamond bonded covalently in a network fashion. Each carbon atom is tetrahedrally oriented to its four nearest neighbors. The distance between the carbon-atom nuclei has been measured to be 154 pm. Because of diamond's extreme hardness and high melting point, its major industrial uses are for cutting, drilling, and grinding. Diamonds used in industry are not of gem quality.

Another property of diamond is its ability to conduct heat. A diamond crystal conducts heat more than five times more readily than silver or copper, which are the best metallic conductors. In diamond, heat is conducted by the transfer of energy of vibration from one carbon atom to the next. In a diamond crystal, this process is very efficient because the carbon atoms have a small mass. The forces holding the atoms together are strong and can easily transfer vibratory motion among the atoms. However, unlike metals, diamond does not conduct electricity. Because all the valence electrons are used in forming localized covalent bonds, none of the electrons can migrate.

Graphite

Graphite is nearly as remarkable for its softness as diamond is for its hardness. It feels greasy and crumbles easily, characteristics that are readily explained by its structure. The carbon atoms in graphite are arranged in layers that form thin hexagonal plates, as shown by the model in Figure 20-4.

The distance between the nuclei of adjacent carbon atoms within a layer has been measured to be 142 pm. This distance is less than the distance between adjacent carbon atom nuclei in diamond. However, the distance between the nuclei of atoms in adjacent layers measures 335 pm. Because the average distance between carbon atoms in graphite is greater than the average distance in diamond, graphite has a lower density.

The layers of carbon atoms in graphite are too far apart to be held together by covalent bonds. Only weak London dispersion forces hold the layers together. Because of the weak attraction, the layers can slide across one another. This property allows graphite to be used as a lubricant and in pencil "lead."

Within each layer, each carbon atom is bonded to only three other carbon atoms. These bonds are examples of resonance hybrid bonds, which were discussed in Chapter 6. The bonding electrons of resonance hybrid bonds can be thought of as delocalized. **Delocalized electrons** *are electrons shared by more than two atoms.*

Graphite is a fairly good conductor of electricity, even though it is a nonmetal, because the delocalized electrons move freely within each layer. Like diamond, graphite has a high melting point (3652°C). This is because the structure created by delocalized electrons results in a strongly bonded covalent network. Another use of graphite is in graphite fibers. Graphite fibers are stronger and stiffer than steel, but less dense. The strength of the bonds within a layer makes graphite difficult to pull apart in the direction parallel to the surface of the layers. The strength and light weight of graphite fiber have led to its use in products such as sporting goods and aircraft.

internet**connect**

SC*i*LINKS.
NSTA

TOPIC: Allotropes
GO TO: www.scilinks.org
*sci*LINKS CODE: HC2201

TOPIC: Diamond/graphite
GO TO: www.scilinks.org
*sci*LINKS CODE: HC2202

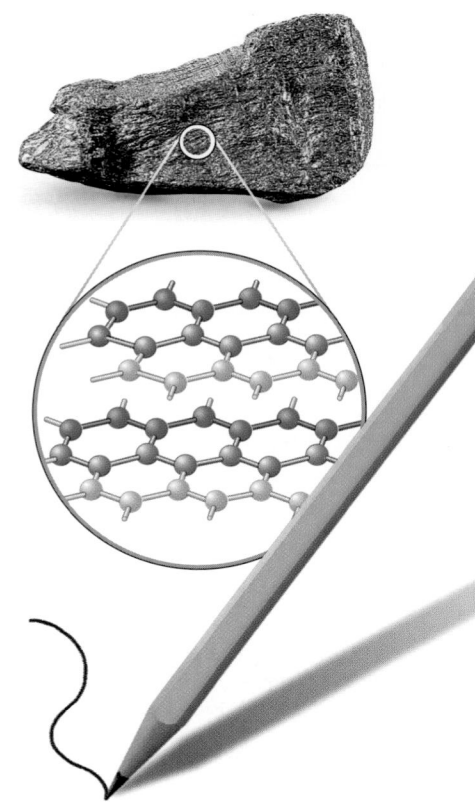

FIGURE 20-4 Notice the space between layers in the ball-and-stick model of graphite. Graphite pencils mark on paper because adjacent layers can slide past each other.

Did You Know?

- In 1772, Antoine Lavoisier heated a diamond with oxygen in a sealed container and produced carbon dioxide. From this, he concluded that diamonds are made entirely from carbon.

- The graphite found in pencil "lead" is actually mixed with clay. The number rating of the pencil increases as the percentage of clay mixed with graphite increases. Even though graphite occurs naturally, most of the graphite used to make pencils is produced in furnaces.

CHAPTER ⟷ CONNECTION

The delocalized electrons described on this page form the basis of *resonance structures,* studied in Chapter 6. A resonance structure is a theoretical combination of two or more structures, each showing bonding electrons in two or more different places. The electrons in the actual structure are *delocalized* over all the atoms involved. Delocalized electrons demonstrate one of the weaknesses of using Lewis dot structures to model covalent bonding: drawing an electron as a single dot assumes that the electron will remain between two atoms in the dot structure. As in the case of delocalized electrons, this assumption is not always valid.

HANDBOOK  **CONNECTION**

Physical properties of diamond and graphite are found in Group 14 of the *Elements Handbook.*

Did You Know?

- The structure of buckyballs makes them very stable—even harder than diamonds at high pressures.

- When one of the carbon atoms in a buckyball is replaced by silicon, the buckyball becomes a semiconductor. When a potassium atom is placed in the center of a buckyball, it becomes a superconductor at low temperatures. These and other traits make buckyballs attractive in the development of new plastics and medicines. Have students determine the hybridization of carbon atoms in buckminsterfullerene.

SECTION REVIEW

1. Carbon is present in all living matter.

2. sp^2, sp

3. The carbon atoms in graphite are arranged in layers of thin, hexagonal plates that are strong in the direction of the layers but slide across one another. The strength of graphite in the direction of the layers explains the strength of carbon fibers. The sliding of the layers explains the softness of graphite and why it is used as a lubricant.

4. a. All fullerenes have a near-spherical cagelike structure.
b. Fullerenes vary in the number of carbon atoms in the molecule.

(a)

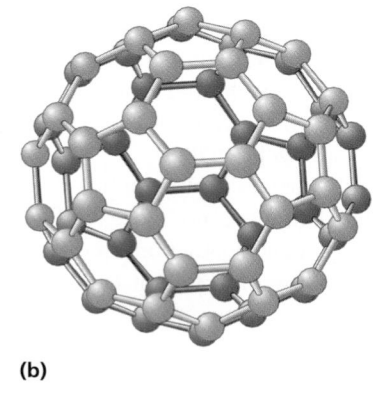
(b)

(c)

FIGURE 20-5 (a) Buckminsterfullerene was named after Buckminster Fuller, who invented geodesic domes like the one shown here. (b) The structure of buckminsterfullerene resembles the pattern of a soccer ball (c).

internet**connect**

SCi*LINKS*
NSTA

TOPIC: Buckminster Fuller
GO TO: www.scilinks.org
*sci***LINKS CODE:** HC2203

Fullerenes

In the mid-1980s a new allotropic form of carbon was discovered. The 1996 Nobel Prize in chemistry was awarded to Richard E. Smalley, Robert F. Curl, and Harold W. Kroto, leaders of the research teams that discovered this class of compounds, fullerenes.

Fullerenes are part of the soot that forms when carbon-containing materials are burned with limited oxygen. Their structures consist of near-spherical cages of carbon atoms. The most stable of these is C_{60}, shown in Figure 20-5. C_{60} is formed by 60 carbon atoms arranged in interconnected five- and six-membered rings.

Because of its structural resemblance to geodesic domes, Richard Smalley and his co-workers at Rice University named C_{60} "buckminsterfullerene" in honor of the geodesic-dome architect, Buckminster Fuller. The whole family of carbon-atom cages, which have a wide range in the number of carbon atoms, are therefore called fullerenes. Because the structure of C_{60} also resembles the design of a soccer ball, C_{60} is also known less formally as buckyball. Scientists are currently trying to find practical uses for these substances.

SECTION REVIEW

1. What makes carbon an important element in the study of chemistry?

2. What type of hybrid orbital is found in carbon double bonds? In carbon triple bonds?

3. How does the structure of graphite relate to its properties and uses?

4. a. How are the structures of different fullerenes similar?
   b. How do they differ?

Organic Compounds

SECTION 20-2

OBJECTIVES

- Explain how the structure and bonding of carbon lead to the diversity and number of organic compounds.
- Explain the importance and limitations of molecular and structural formulas.
- Compare structural and geometric isomers.

All organic compounds contain carbon atoms. However, not all carbon-containing compounds are classified as organic. There are a few exceptions, such as Na_2CO_3, CO, and CO_2, that are considered inorganic. **Organic compounds,** then, can be defined as *covalently bonded compounds containing carbon, excluding carbonates and oxides*. Figure 20-6 shows a few familiar items that contain organic compounds.

Carbon Bonding and the Diversity of Organic Compounds

The diversity of organic compounds results from the uniqueness of carbon's structure and bonding. Carbon's electronic structure allows it to bind to itself to form chains and rings, to bind covalently to other elements, and to bind to itself and other elements in different arrangements.

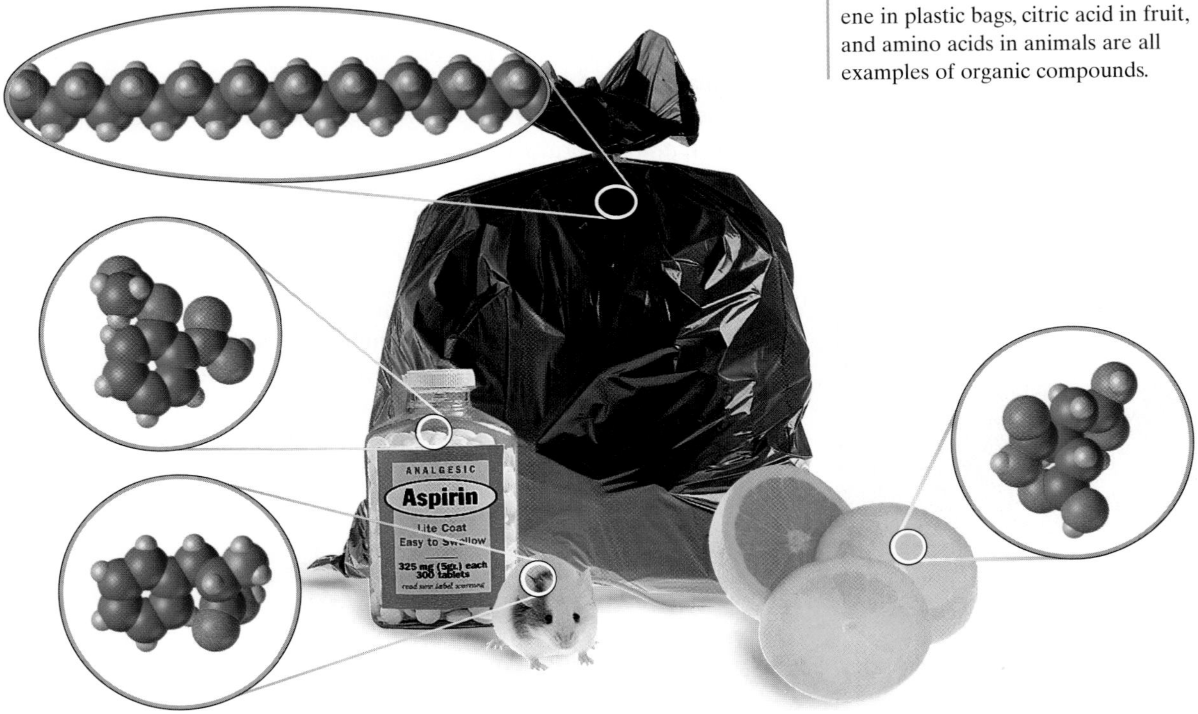

FIGURE 20-6 Aspirin, polyethylene in plastic bags, citric acid in fruit, and amino acids in animals are all examples of organic compounds.

Lesson Starter

Begin this lesson with a group-puzzle exercise. Before class, draw twenty 1.5×1.5 in. boxes on a sheet of paper. Draw a circle in each box. Write the letter *C* inside six of the circles, and add four lines from the circle to the sides of the square for four bonds. Write the letter *H* inside the remaining 14 circles, and add a single line from the circle to one side of the square for one bond.

Divide students into groups of three. Provide each group with a copy of the paper and a pair of scissors. Ask them to develop as many different molecules as possible in five minutes using all of the atoms and all of the bonds. Compare the findings. Ask the students how they could do this exercise three-dimensionally. Would anything change? How would it be different?

✔Teaching Tip

Using models will help students visualize the structures of the molecules covered in this chapter. Many commercial ball-and-stick and space-filling models are available. It is a good idea to have at least one of these for demonstration purposes. Models can also be made using gumdrops as atoms and toothpicks as bonds. Different colors and sizes of gumdrops can be used for different atoms. Start by having the students insert four toothpicks into one gumdrop so that they point to the four corners of a tetrahedron. This model, representing a carbon atom with sp^3 hybridized orbitals, can be used as a pattern to form chains and rings. Save these models to use throughout the chapter.

Safety: Discourage all eating in the lab because of possible contamination.

- The structural formula of ethanol:

$$\begin{array}{ccc} H & H & \\ | & | & \\ H-C-C-OH & \\ | & | & \\ H & H & \end{array}$$

- The structural formula of dimethyl ether:

$$\begin{array}{ccc} H & & H \\ | & & | \\ H-C-O-C-H \\ | & & | \\ H & & H \end{array}$$

- Be sure students recognize the difference between a two-dimensional representation and a three-dimensional representation. A two-dimensional representation of CH_4 appears to have 90° angles between hydrocarbon bonds. A three-dimensional representation shows the more realistic 109° angle. As students write and use structural formulas, constantly remind them that as they write a two-dimensional representation, they should be thinking in three dimensions.

Reading Skill-Builder

INTERPRETING VOCABULARY Explain that the word *catenation* comes from the Latin word *catena*, which means "chain." Tell students that carbon is one of just a few elements capable of forming chains and rings by bonding to other carbon atoms. Silicon, for example, also exhibits some catenation, but carbon exhibits catenation more than any other element does.

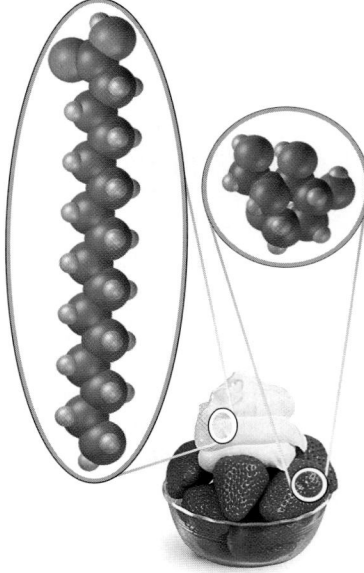

FIGURE 20-7 Compare the shape of a fatty acid found in cream with that of fructose, found in fruit. In the fatty acid, the carbon atoms are in chains. In fructose, carbon atoms form a ring.

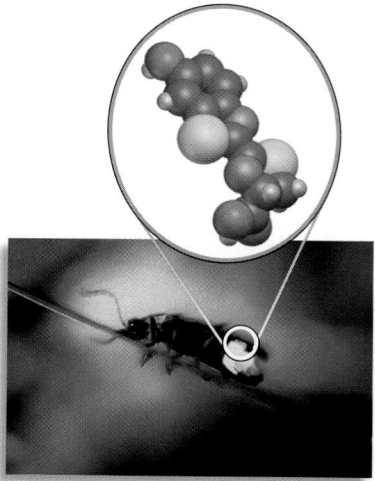

FIGURE 20-8 In firefly luciferin, carbon atoms bind to hydrogen, oxygen, nitrogen, and sulfur. Luciferin is responsible for the light emitted from the tail of a firefly.

Carbon-Carbon Bonding

Carbon atoms are unique in their ability to form long chains and rings of covalently bonded atoms. This type of bonding is known as **catenation,** *the covalent binding of an element to itself to form chains or rings.* This produces a multitude of chain, branched-chain, and ring structures. In addition, carbon atoms in these structures can be linked by single, double, or triple covalent bonds. Examples of molecules containing carbon-atom rings and chains are shown in Figure 20-7.

Carbon Bonding to Other Elements

Besides binding to other carbon atoms, carbon atoms bind readily to elements with similar electronegativities. Organic compounds consist of carbon and these other elements. **Hydrocarbons** *are composed of only carbon and hydrogen; they are the simplest organic compounds.* Other organic compounds contain hydrocarbon backbones to which other elements, primarily O, N, S, and the halogens, are attached. Figure 20-8 shows a molecule in which carbon atoms are bound to other elements.

Arrangement of Atoms

The bonding capabilities of carbon also allow for different arrangements of atoms. This means that some compounds may contain the same atoms but have different properties because the atoms are arranged differently. For example, the molecular formula C_2H_6O represents both ethanol and dimethyl ether. *Compounds that have the same molecular formula but different structures are called* **isomers.** As the number of carbon atoms in a molecular formula increases, the number of possible isomers increases rapidly. For example, there are 18 isomers with the molecular formula C_8H_{18}, 35 with the molecular formula C_9H_{20}, and 75 with the molecular formula $C_{10}H_{22}$. For the molecular formula of just 40 carbon atoms and 82 hydrogen atoms, $C_{40}H_{82}$, there are theoretically 69 491 178 805 831 isomers. To distinguish one from another, more information than just the molecular formula is needed.

Structural Formulas

For this reason, organic chemists use structural formulas to represent organic compounds. *A* **structural formula** *indicates the number and types of atoms present in a molecule and also shows the bonding arrangement of the atoms.* For example, one possible structural formula for an isomer of C_4H_{10} is the following.

$$\begin{array}{ccccc} H & & H & & H \\ | & & | & & | \\ H-C & \!\!\!\!\!\!- & C & \!\!\!\!\!\!- & C-H \\ | & & | & & | \\ H & & H-C-H & & H \\ & & | & & \\ & & H & & \end{array}$$

Structural formulas are sometimes condensed to make them easier to read. In one type of condensed structure, hydrogen single covalent bonds are not shown. The hydrogen atoms are understood to bind to the

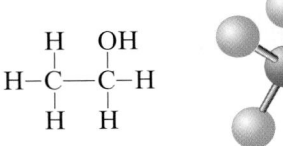

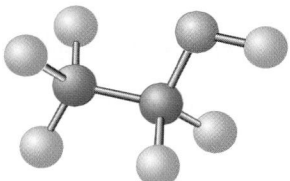

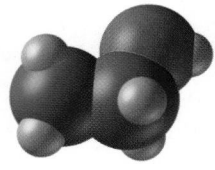

Ball-and-stick model   Space-filling model

FIGURE 20-9   The structure of ethanol can be represented in different ways. Ball-and-stick and space-filling models represent the three-dimensional shape of the molecule.

atom they are written beside. The following structural and condensed structural formulas represent the same molecule.

$$H-\overset{\overset{\displaystyle H}{|}}{\underset{\underset{\displaystyle H}{|}}{C}}-\overset{\overset{\displaystyle H}{|}}{\underset{\underset{\displaystyle H-\overset{\overset{\displaystyle H}{|}}{\underset{\underset{\displaystyle H}{|}}{C}}-H}{}}{C}}-\overset{\overset{\displaystyle H}{|}}{\underset{\underset{\displaystyle H}{|}}{C}}-H$$

is the same as

$$CH_3-\underset{\underset{\displaystyle CH_3}{|}}{CH}-CH_3$$

Remember that the structural formula does not accurately show the three-dimensional shape of the molecule. Three-dimensional shape is depicted with drawings or models, as shown for ethanol in Figure 20-9.

As you continue your study, you may find that the use of dashes can be eliminated by writing in a horizontal row the symbols and subscripts for the groups of carbon and hydrogen atoms that appear in a molecule. For example, ethane is written as CH_3CH_3 and propane as $CH_3CH_2CH_3$.

Isomers

You have learned that isomers are compounds that have the same molecular formula but different structural formulas. Isomers can be further classified by structure and geometry.

Structural Isomers

Structural isomers *are isomers in which the atoms are bonded together in different orders.* For example, the atoms of the molecular formula C_4H_{10} can be arranged in two different ways.

$$H-\overset{\overset{\displaystyle H}{|}}{\underset{\underset{\displaystyle H}{|}}{C}}-\overset{\overset{\displaystyle H}{|}}{\underset{\underset{\displaystyle H}{|}}{C}}-\overset{\overset{\displaystyle H}{|}}{\underset{\underset{\displaystyle H}{|}}{C}}-\overset{\overset{\displaystyle H}{|}}{\underset{\underset{\displaystyle H}{|}}{C}}-H$$

butane

$$H-\overset{\overset{\displaystyle H}{|}}{C}-\overset{\overset{\displaystyle H}{|}}{\underset{\underset{\displaystyle H-\overset{\overset{\displaystyle H}{|}}{\underset{\underset{\displaystyle H}{|}}{C}}-H}{}}{C}}-\overset{\overset{\displaystyle H}{|}}{C}-H$$

2-methylpropane

Notice that the formula for butane shows a continuous chain of four carbon atoms. The chain may be bent or twisted, but it is continuous. The formula of 2-methylpropane shows a continuous chain of three carbon atoms, with the fourth carbon atom attached to the second carbon atom of the chain.

Table 20-1 Point out the differences in melting and boiling points for the two butane isomers, and then explain the difference in terms of intermolecular attraction.

Common Misconception

It is easy for students to forget that there is free rotation around single bonds but not around double bonds. The different structural formulas available for a molecule as a result of bond rotation may appear to some students as different isomers. Draw 2,3-dimethylbutane on the board with three different bond rotations. For example:

$$\begin{array}{ccc} & H & H \\ & | & | \\ CH_3 & C & C \\ & | & | \\ & CH_3 & CH_3 \end{array} CH_3$$

Point out why the three different representations are really the same molecule. Demonstrate this with models.

TABLE 20-1	**Physical Properties of the Structural Isomers Butane and 2-Methylpropane**		
	Melting point (°C)	Boiling point (°C)	Density at 20°C (g/mL)
butane	−138.4	−0.5	0.5788
2-methylpropane	−159.4	−11.633	0.549

Structural isomers can have different physical or chemical properties. For example, butane and 2-methylpropane have different melting points, boiling points, and densities, as shown in Table 20-1.

Geometric Isomers

Geometric isomers *are isomers in which the order of atom bonding is the same but the arrangement of atoms in space is different.* Consider the molecule 1,2-dichloroethene, which contains a double bond. The double bond prevents free rotation and holds groups to either side of the molecule. This means there can be two different 1,2-dichloroethene geometric isomers as shown below.

cis   *trans*

Because the two chlorine atoms are on the same side of the molecule in the first structure, it is called *cis*. In the second molecule, the two chlorine atoms are on opposite sides of the molecule, and so the molecule is called *trans*. Notice that in both molecules the bonding order of the atoms is the same: each carbon atom in the double bond is also bound to one chlorine atom and one hydrogen atom.

Now consider the molecule 1,2-dichloroethane. Atoms attached to the carbon atoms can rotate freely around the single carbon-carbon bond, as shown in Figure 20-10. There are no geometric isomers of 1,2-dichloroethane. *In order for geometric isomers to exist, there must be a rigid structure in the molecule to prevent free rotation around a bond.*

Now consider two apparent structures for another molecule with a double bond, chloroethene.

Although these structures may appear different at first glance, they are actually the same. In *both* structures, two hydrogen atoms are on one side of the molecule, and one chlorine atom and one hydrogen atom are on the other. *A molecule can have a geometric isomer only if two carbon atoms in a rigid structure each have two different groups attached.*

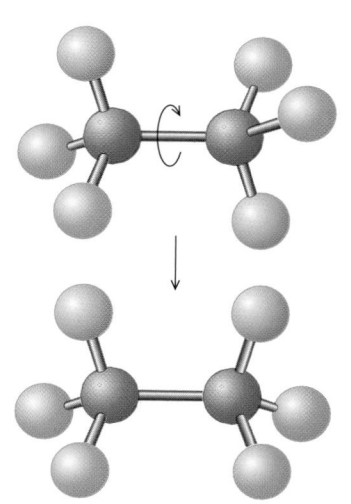

FIGURE 20-10 Unlike double bonds, single bonds allow free rotation within a molecule. Groups attached to the carbon atoms are not held to one side of the molecule, so there are no geometric isomers.

$$CH_3CH_2 \quad\quad (CH_2)_9CH_2OCCH_3$$

$$\overset{\displaystyle O}{\overset{\|}{}}$$

C=C

H   H

cis-11-tetradecenyl acetate

$$H \quad\quad (CH_2)_9CH_2OCCH_3$$

C=C

$$CH_3CH_2 \quad\quad H$$

trans-11-tetradecenyl acetate

FIGURE 20-11 Males of the Iowa strain of the European corn borer respond most strongly to mixtures of the female sex attractant pheromone that are 96% *cis* isomer. But males of the New York strain respond most strongly to mixtures containing 97% *trans* isomer.

Like structural isomers, geometric isomers differ in physical and chemical properties. Some geometric isomers are known to differ in physiological behavior as well. For example, insects can communicate by chemicals called pheromones and may distinguish between the geometric isomers of pheromones. One geometric isomer of a pheromone may be physiologically active, while the other will be only slightly active or not at all. The European corn borer, shown in Figure 20-11, distinguishes between isomers of its sex-attractant pheromone. Another example of differences between geometric isomers is found in fatty acids. Natural unsaturated fatty acids are primarily *cis*-fatty acids. Hydrogenation is used to convert vegetable oil, which contains unsaturated fatty acids, into a solid fat, such as margarine or vegetable shortening. During hydrogenation *trans*-fatty acids are produced. Research has shown that there may be health risks associated with diets high in *trans*-fatty acids.

SECTION REVIEW

1. What are three characteristics of carbon that contribute to the diversity of organic compounds?

2. Define the term *isomer,* and distinguish between structural and geometric isomers.

3. Which of the following types of molecular representations can be used to show differences between isomers? Explain why each can or cannot.
   a. molecular formula
   b. structural formula
   c. three-dimensional drawing or model

4. Write the formula for 2-methylpropane (shown at the right on page 631) in a horizontal row.

5. Which of the following can represent the same molecule?

   a.
   H H H H H
   H−C−C−C−C−C−H
   H H H H H

   b. $CH_3-CH_2-CH_2-CH_3$

   c. $CH_3-CH_2-CH_2$
                        CH_2
                        CH_3

   d. C_5H_{12}

SECTION REVIEW

1. its ability to bind to itself to form chains and rings, its ability to bind with other elements, and its ability to bind to itself and other elements in different arrangements

2. Compounds that have the same molecular formula but different structures are isomers. Structural isomers have atoms bonded together in a different order. Geometric isomers have atoms bonded in the same order, but the arrangement of atoms in space is different.

3. a. Molecular formulas cannot show the difference between isomers because they show only the ratio of atoms involved. They do not show how the atoms are arranged.
b. and **c.** A structural formula and a three-dimensional drawing, or model, can be used to show differences between isomers because they can show the order atoms are bonded together and arranged in space.

4. $CH_3CHCH_3CH_3$

5. a., c., and d.

SECTION 20-3

Saturated Hydrocarbons

Lesson Starter

Write the structural formulas of methane, ethane, propane, and butane on the board. Ask students to predict the formula for the next hydrocarbon in the series. Use these structures to introduce the alkane homologous series. Have students confirm that each formula follows the C_nH_{2n+2} rule for saturated alkanes. Have students predict the molecular formula for the alkane with 15 carbon atoms.

Reading Skill-Builder

READING ORGANIZER Have students read Section 20-3 and organize the information in a table titled "Organic Compounds." Students should include information on basic structural characteristics, rules for naming, properties, uses, and examples of saturated hydrocarbons. Students should also list any subcategories that exist, such as alkanes and cycloalkanes. Finally, students should draw a condensed structural formula for representative examples and correctly name them. Tell students to keep their tables so they can add to them as they learn more about organic compounds.

OBJECTIVES

- Recognize the important structural feature of saturated hydrocarbons, alkanes.

- Be able to name and write structural formulas for alkanes.

- Explain how structures of alkanes relate to their properties and how those properties affect the uses of specific alkanes.

internet**connect**

SC*LINKS*

NSTA

TOPIC: Alkanes
GO TO: www.scilinks.org
*sci***LINKS CODE:** HC2204

Hydrocarbons are grouped mainly by the type of bonding between carbon atoms. **Saturated hydrocarbons** *are hydrocarbons in which each carbon atom in the molecule forms four single covalent bonds with other atoms.*

Alkanes

Hydrocarbons that contain only single bonds are **alkanes.** In Table 20-2, the molecular formulas, structural formulas, and space-filling models are given for alkanes with one to four carbon atoms. If you examine the molecular formulas for successive alkanes in Table 20-2, you will see a clear pattern. Each member of the series differs from the preceding one by one carbon atom and two hydrogen atoms. For example, propane, C_3H_8, differs from ethane, C_2H_6, by one carbon atom and two hydrogen atoms, a $-CH_2-$ group.

$$
\begin{array}{ccc}
& \text{H} & \text{H} \\
& | & | \\
\text{H}- & \text{C}- & \text{C}-\text{H} \\
& | & | \\
& \text{H} & \text{H} \\
\end{array}
\qquad
\begin{array}{cccc}
& \text{H} & \text{H} & \text{H} \\
& | & | & | \\
\text{H}- & \text{C}- & \text{C}- & \text{C}-\text{H} \\
& | & | & | \\
& \text{H} & \text{H} & \text{H} \\
\end{array}
$$

ethane   propane

Compounds that differ in this fashion belong to a homologous series. A **homologous series** *is one in which adjacent members differ by a constant unit.* It is not necessary to remember the molecular formulas for all members of a homologous series. Instead, a general molecular formula can be used to determine the formulas. Look at the molecular formulas for ethane and propane, C_2H_6 and C_3H_8. They both fit the formula C_nH_{2n+2}. For ethane, $n = 2$, so there are two carbon atoms and $(2 \times 2) + 2 = 6$ hydrogen atoms. For propane, $n = 3$, so there are three carbon atoms and $(2 \times 3) + 2 = 8$ hydrogen atoms. Now consider a molecule for which we do not know the molecular formula. Suppose a member of this series has 30 carbon atoms in its molecules. Then $n = 30$, and there are $(2 \times 30) + 2 = 62$ hydrogen atoms. The formula is $C_{30}H_{62}$.

Notice that for alkanes with three or fewer carbon atoms, only one molecular structure is possible. However, in alkanes with more than three carbon atoms, the chains can be straight or branched. Thus,

TABLE 20-2 *Alkanes with One to Four Carbon Atoms*

Molecular formulas	Structural formulas	Space-filling models
CH_4	H | H–C–H | H **methane**	
C_2H_6	H H | | H–C–C–H | | H H **ethane**	
C_3H_8	H H H | | | H–C–C–C–H | | | H H H **propane**	

C_4H_{10}	H H H H
	| | | |
	H–C–C–C–C–H
	| | | |
	H H H H
	
	butane
	
	H H H
	| | |
	H–C———C———C–H
	| | |
	H H–C–H H
	      |
	      H
	
	2-methylpropane

alkanes with four or more carbon atoms have structural isomers. There are two possible structural isomers for alkanes with four carbon atoms, butane and 2-methylpropane.

Cycloalkanes

Cycloalkanes *are alkanes in which the carbon atoms are arranged in a ring, or cyclic, structure.* The structural formulas for cycloalkanes are often drawn in a simplified form. It is understood that there is a carbon

- If hydrocarbon molecules do not follow the C_nH_{2n+2} rule, then they must either be cyclic hydrocarbons or have multiple bonds. Hydrocarbons with double and triple bonds are called *unsaturated* because the carbon atoms are not saturated with hydrogen to the greatest extent possible.

- The IUPAC nomenclature used in this text is an international standard. However, older common names, such as ethylene for ethene, propylene for propene, acetylene for ethyne, and ethyl alcohol for ethanol (in Chapter 21), are still in use. These common names can also be found in *The Merck Index*.

TABLE STRATEGY

Table 20-3 Have students think of common terms that use the same prefixes as those in this table. Some examples include *pentagon, octopus,* and *decade.*

TABLE 20-3 *Carbon-Atom Chain Prefixes*

Number of carbon atoms	Prefix
1	meth-
2	eth-
3	prop-
4	but-
5	pent-
6	hex-
7	hept-
8	oct-
9	non-
10	dec-

atom at each corner and enough hydrogen atoms to complete the four bonds to each carbon atom.

cyclopentane   cyclopentane

Because there are no free ends where a carbon atom is attached to three hydrogen atoms, there are two fewer hydrogen atoms in cycloalkanes than in noncyclic alkanes.

butane   cyclobutane
C_4H_{10} C_4H_8

The general structure for cycloalkanes, C_nH_{2n}, shows that they have $2 \times n$ hydrogen atoms. This is two fewer hydrogen atoms than noncyclic alkanes, C_nH_{2n+2}, which have $(2 \times n) + 2$ hydrogen atoms.

Systematic Names of Alkanes

Historically, the names of many organic compounds were derived from the sources in which they were found. As more organic compounds were discovered, a systematic naming method became necessary. The systematic method used primarily in this book was developed by the International Union of Pure and Applied Chemistry, IUPAC.

The basic part of the systematic name of an organic compound is the name of the longest carbon chain, or parent hydrocarbon, in the molecule. Table 20-3 gives the names of the prefixes for carbon-atom chains up to 10 carbon atoms long. Beginning with *pent-*, the prefixes are Greek or Latin numerical prefixes.

Unbranched-Chain Alkane Nomenclature

To name an unbranched alkane, find the prefix in Table 20-3 that corresponds to the number of carbon atoms in the chain of the hydrocarbon. Then add the suffix *-ane* to the prefix. An example is shown below.

$$\overset{1}{C}H_3-\overset{2}{C}H_2-\overset{3}{C}H_2-\overset{4}{C}H_2-\overset{5}{C}H_2-\overset{6}{C}H_2-\overset{7}{C}H_3$$

heptane

The molecule has a chain seven carbon atoms long, so the prefix *hept-* is added to the suffix *-ane* to form *heptane.*

TABLE 20-4 *Some Straight-Chain Alkyl Groups*

Alkane	Name	Alkyl group	Name
CH_4	methane	$-CH_3$	methyl
CH_3-CH_3	ethane	$-CH_2-CH_3$	ethyl
$CH_3-CH_2-CH_3$	propane	$-CH_2-CH_2-CH_3$	propyl
$CH_3-CH_2-CH_2-CH_3$	butane	$-CH_2-CH_2-CH_2-CH_3$	butyl
$CH_3-CH_2-CH_2-CH_2-CH_3$	pentane	$-CH_2-CH_2-CH_2-CH_2-CH_3$	pentyl

Branched-Chain Alkane Nomenclature

The naming of branched-chain alkanes also follows a systematic method. The hydrocarbon branches of alkanes are alkyl groups. **Alkyl groups** *are groups of atoms that are formed when one hydrogen atom is removed from an alkane molecule.* Alkyl groups are named by replacing the suffix *-ane* of the parent alkane with the suffix *-yl*. Some examples are shown in Table 20-4. Alkyl group names are used when naming branched-chain alkanes. We will only present the method for naming simple branched-chain alkanes with only straight-chain alkyl groups. Consider the following molecule.

$$CH_3-CH_2-CH_2-\overset{\overset{\textstyle CH_3}{|}}{CH}-\overset{\overset{\textstyle CH_3}{|}}{CH}-\underset{\underset{\textstyle CH_3}{|}}{\underset{\underset{\textstyle CH-CH_3}{|}}{CH}}-CH_2-CH_3$$

To name this molecule, locate the parent hydrocarbon. The parent hydrocarbon is the longest continuous chain that contains the most straight-chain branches. In this molecule, there are two chains that are eight carbon atoms long. The parent hydrocarbon is the chain that contains the most straight-chain branches. Do not be tricked by the way the molecule is drawn. The longest chain may be shown bent.

$$CH_3-CH_2-CH_2-\overset{\overset{\textstyle CH_3}{|}}{CH}-\overset{\overset{\textstyle CH_3}{|}}{CH}-\underset{\underset{\textstyle CH_3}{|}}{\underset{\underset{\textstyle CH-CH_3}{|}}{CH}}-CH_2-CH_3$$

NOT

$$CH_3-CH_2-CH_2-\overset{\overset{\textstyle CH_3}{|}}{CH}-\overset{\overset{\textstyle CH_3}{|}}{CH}-\underset{\underset{\textstyle CH_3}{|}}{\underset{\underset{\textstyle CH-CH_3}{|}}{CH}}-CH_2-CH_3$$

Table 20-4 Write the structures of 3-ethyl-2,4,5-trimethyloctane and 5-butyl-2,2-dimethylnonane on the board. Have students identify all of the alkyl groups.

✔**Teaching Tip**

Point out that when drawing a structural formula, it is important to write the longest hydrocarbon sequence first. When given a structural formula, students should remember that the longest chain may not be represented in a straight line.

To name the parent hydrocarbon, add the suffix *-ane* to the prefix *oct-* (for a carbon-atom chain with eight carbon atoms) to form *octane.* Now identify and name the alkyl groups.

$$CH_3-CH_2-CH_2-\underset{\underset{\underset{CH_3}{|}}{\overset{}{CH-CH_3}}}{\overset{\overset{CH_3}{|}}{CH}}-\overset{\overset{CH_3}{|}}{CH}-CH-CH_2-CH_3$$

The three $-CH_3$ groups are methyl groups. The $-CH_2-CH_3$ group is an ethyl group. Arrange the names in alphabetical order in front of the name of the parent hydrocarbon.

ethyl methyloctane

To show that there are three methyl groups present, attach the prefix *tri-* to the name *methyl* to form *trimethyl.*

ethyl **tri**methyloctane

Now we need to show the locations of the alkyl groups on the parent hydrocarbon. Number the octane chain so that the alkyl groups have the lowest numbers possible.

$$\overset{8}{C}H_3-\overset{7}{C}H_2-\overset{6}{C}H_2-\overset{5}{C}H-\overset{4}{C}H-\underset{\underset{\underset{1CH_3}{|}}{\overset{}{2CH-CH_3}}}{\overset{\overset{CH_3\ CH_3}{|\ \ |}}{C}}H-\overset{3}{C}H-CH_2-CH_3$$

NOT

$$\overset{1}{C}H_3-\overset{2}{C}H_2-\overset{3}{C}H_2-\overset{4}{C}H-\overset{5}{C}H_2-\underset{\underset{\underset{8CH_3}{|}}{\overset{}{7CH-CH_3}}}{\overset{\overset{CH_3\ CH_3}{|\ \ |}}{\overset{6}{C}}}H-CH_2-CH_3$$

Place the location numbers of *each* of the alkyl groups in front of its name. Separate the numbers from the names of the alkyl groups with hyphens. The ethyl group is on carbon *3.*

3-ethyl trimethyloctane

Because there are three methyl groups, there will be three numbers, separated by commas, in front of *trimethyl.*

3-ethyl-**2,4,5-**trimethyloctane

The full name is 3-ethyl-2,4,5-trimethyloctane.

The procedure for naming simple branched-chain alkanes can be summarized as follows.

Alkane Nomenclature

1. **Name the parent hydrocarbon.** Find the longest continuous chain of carbon atoms with straight-chain branches. Add the suffix *-ane* to the prefix corresponding to the number of carbon atoms in the chain.

2. **Add the names of the alkyl groups.** Add the names of the alkyl groups in front of the name of the parent hydrocarbon in alphabetical order. When there is more than one branch of the same alkyl group present, attach the appropriate numerical prefix to the name, *di* = 2, *tri* = 3, *tetra* = 4, and so on. Do this after the names have been put in alphabetical order.

3. **Number the carbon atoms in the parent hydrocarbon.** If one or more alkyl groups are present, number the carbon atoms in the continuous chain so that the alkyl groups have the lowest position numbers possible. If there are two equivalent lowest positions with two different alkyl groups, give the lowest number to the alkyl group that comes first in the name. (This will be the alkyl group that is first in alphabetical order, *before* any prefixes are attached.)

4. **Insert position numbers.** Put the position numbers of each alkyl group in front of the name of that alkyl group.

5. **Punctuate the name.** Separate the position numbers from the names with hyphens. If there are more than one number in front of a name, separate the numbers by commas.

ADDITIONAL SAMPLE PROBLEM

Additional Sample Problem is found on page 661A.

SAMPLE PROBLEM 20-1

Name the following simple branched-chain alkane:

$$CH_3-CH-CH_2-CH-CH-CH_3$$
$$\qquad\ |\qquad\qquad\ |\quad\ |$$
$$\qquad CH_3\qquad\quad CH_3\ CH_3$$

SOLUTION

1. Identify and name the parent hydrocarbon.

$$CH_3-CH-CH_2-CH-CH-CH_3$$
$$\qquad\ |\qquad\qquad\ |\quad\ |$$
$$\qquad CH_3\qquad\quad CH_3\ CH_3$$

Because the longest continuous chain contains six carbon atoms, the parent hydrocarbon is *hexane*.

2. Identify and name the alkyl groups attached to the chain.

$$CH_3-CH-CH_2-CH-CH-CH_3$$
$$\qquad\ |\qquad\qquad\ |\quad\ |$$
$$\qquad CH_3\qquad\quad CH_3\ CH_3$$

There is only one type of alkyl group, with one carbon atom. Alkyl groups with one carbon atom are methyl groups. Add the name *methyl* in front of the name of the continuous chain. Add the prefix *tri-* to show that there are three methyl groups present.

trimethylhexane

20-2 Draw the condensed structural formula of each of the following molecules:

a. 2,4-dimethylpentane

b. 4-ethyl-3-methylheptane

c. 2-methylpropane

See page 661A for answers.

3. Number the carbon atoms in the continuous chain so that the alkyl groups have the lowest numbers possible.

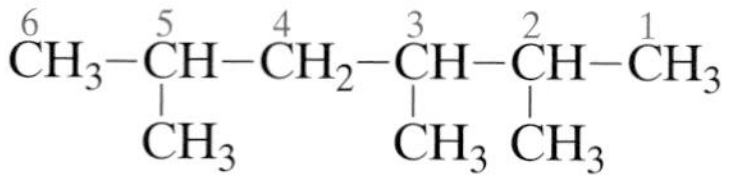

$$\overset{6}{C}H_3-\overset{5}{C}H-\overset{4}{C}H_2-\overset{3}{C}H-\overset{2}{C}H-\overset{1}{C}H_3$$
$$\qquad\quad | \qquad\qquad\quad | \quad\ |$$
$$\qquad\ CH_3 \qquad\quad CH_3\ CH_3$$

4. The methyl groups are on the carbon atoms numbered *2, 3*, and *5*. Put the numbers of the positions of the alkyl groups, separated by commas, in front of the name of the alkyl group. Separate the numbers from the name with a hyphen.

2,3,5-trimethylhexane

The complete name is 2,3,5-trimethylhexane.

SAMPLE PROBLEM 20-2

Draw the condensed structural formula of 3-ethyl-4-methylhexane.

SOLUTION

1. Identify the name of the parent hydrocarbon.

3-ethyl-4-methyl**hexane**

The parent hydrocarbon is hexane, so there are six carbon atoms in the chain. Draw and number the carbon atoms in the chain.

$$\overset{1}{C}\text{———}\overset{2}{C}\text{———}\overset{3}{C}\text{———}\overset{4}{C}\text{———}\overset{5}{C}\text{———}\overset{6}{C}$$

2. Identify the alkyl groups, and determine the number of carbon atoms in the alkyl groups.

3-**ethyl**-4-**methyl**hexane

Methyl groups have one carbon atom and ethyl groups have two carbon atoms.

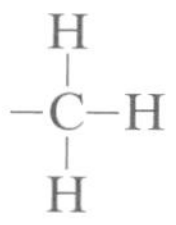

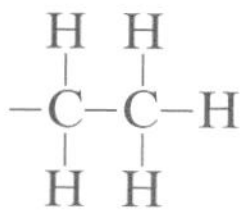

3. Locate the position numbers for the ethyl and methyl groups.

3-ethyl-**4**-methylhexane

Draw the alkyl groups on the parent hydrocarbon in the correct positions.

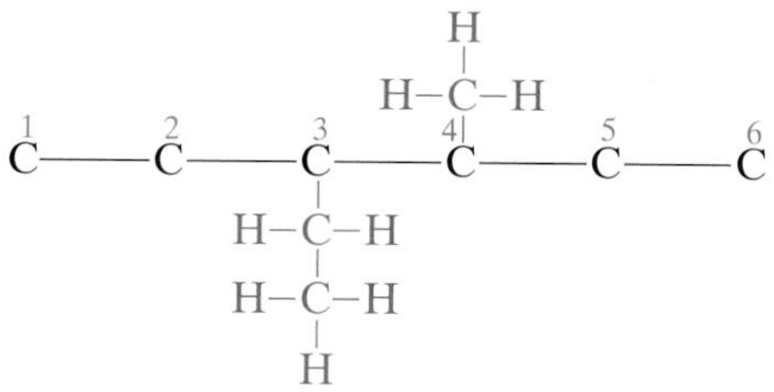

Notice that in this molecule the methyl group and the ethyl group were in equivalent positions from the end of the chain. They are both on third carbons from the end. In such a case, the alkyl group that comes first in the name is given the lower number.

4. Add the correct number of hydrogen atoms so that each carbon atom has four single bonds. This is the complete, uncondensed, structural formula.

$$
\begin{array}{c}
\overset{\displaystyle H}{\underset{}{|}}\\
\overset{\displaystyle H}{\underset{\displaystyle H}{H-\overset{|}{\underset{|}{C}}}}
-\overset{\displaystyle H}{\underset{\displaystyle H}{\overset{|}{\underset{|}{C}}}}
-\overset{\displaystyle H}{\underset{\displaystyle H-\overset{|}{\underset{|}{C}}-H}{\overset{|}{\underset{|}{C}}}}
-\overset{\displaystyle H-\overset{|}{\underset{|}{C}}-H}{\underset{\displaystyle H-\overset{|}{\underset{|}{C}}-H}{\overset{|}{\underset{|}{C}}}}
-\overset{\displaystyle H}{\underset{\displaystyle H}{\overset{|}{\underset{|}{C}}}}
-\overset{\displaystyle H}{\underset{\displaystyle H}{\overset{|}{\underset{|}{C}}-H}}
\end{array}
$$

5. To draw the condensed structural formula, show only the bonds between carbon atoms.

$$
\begin{array}{c}
CH_3\\
|\\
CH_3-CH_2-CH-CH-CH_2-CH_3\\
|\\
CH_2\\
|\\
CH_3
\end{array}
$$

PRACTICE

1. Name the following molecule:

$$
\begin{array}{c}
CH_3-CH-CH_2-CH_3\\
|\\
CH_3
\end{array}
$$

Answer
2-methylbutane

2. Draw the condensed structural formula for 3,3-diethyl-2,5-dimethylnonane.

Answer

$$
\begin{array}{c}
CH_3\\
|\\
CH_2\\
|\\
CH_3-CH-C-CH_2-CH-CH_2-CH_2-CH_2-CH_3\\
|||\\
CH_3CH_2CH_3\\
|\\
CH_3
\end{array}
$$

3. Draw the condensed structural formulas for the two structural isomers of methylpentane and name the isomers.

Answer

$$
\begin{array}{c}
CH_3-CH-CH_2-CH_2-CH_3\\
|\\
CH_3
\end{array}
$$

2-methylpentane

$$
\begin{array}{c}
CH_3-CH_2-CH-CH_2-CH_3\\
|\\
CH_3
\end{array}
$$

3-methylpentane

Cycloalkane Nomenclature

When naming simple cycloalkanes, the cycloalkane is the parent hydrocarbon. Cycloalkanes are named by adding the prefix *cyclo-* to the name of the straight-chain alkane with the same number of hydrocarbons.

$CH_3-CH_2-CH_3$

propane

cyclopropane

When there is only one alkyl group attached to the ring, no position number is necessary. When there is more than one alkyl group attached to the ring, the carbon atoms in the ring are numbered to give the lowest numbers possible to the alkyl groups. This means that one of the alkyl groups will always be in position 1.

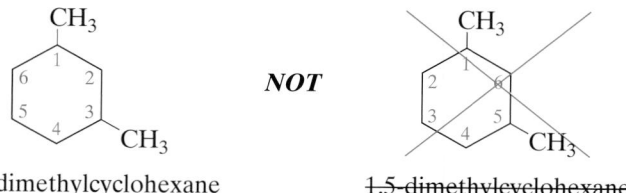

1,3-dimethylcyclohexane   *NOT*   1,5-dimethylcyclohexane

The rules for naming cycloalkanes can be summarized as follows.

Cycloalkane Nomenclature

> **Use the rules for alkane nomenclature on page 639, with the following exceptions.**
> **1. Name the parent hydrocarbon.** Count the number of carbon atoms in the ring. Add the prefix *cyclo-* to the name of the corresponding straight-chain alkane.
> **2. Add the names of the alkyl groups.**
> **3. Number the carbon atoms in the parent hydrocarbon.** If there are two or more alkyl groups attached to the ring, number the carbon atoms in the ring. Assign position number one to the alkyl group that comes first in alphabetical order. Then, number in the direction that gives the rest of the alkyl groups the lowest numbers possible.
> **4. Insert position numbers.**
> **5. Punctuate the name.**

Two examples of correctly named cycloalkanes are given below.

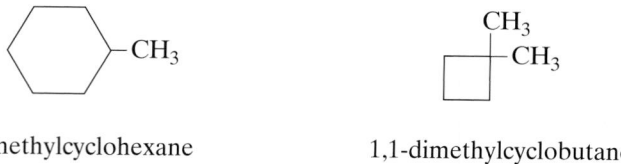

methylcyclohexane   1,1-dimethylcyclobutane

TABLE 20-5 *Properties of Straight-Chain Alkanes*			
Molecular formula	IUPAC name	Boiling point (°C)	State at room temperature
CH_4	methane	–164	gas
C_2H_6	ethane	–88.6	
C_3H_8	propane	–42.1	
C_4H_{10}	butane	–0.5	
C_5H_{12}	pentane	36.1	liquid
C_8H_{18}	octane	125.7	
$C_{10}H_{22}$	decane	174.1	
$C_{17}H_{36}$	heptadecane	301.8	solid
$C_{20}H_{42}$	eicosane	343	

Properties and Uses of Alkanes

Properties for some straight-chain alkanes are listed in Table 20-5. The trends in these properties can be explained by examining the structure of alkanes. The carbon-hydrogen bonds of alkanes are nonpolar. The only forces of attraction between nonpolar molecules are weak intermolecular forces, or London dispersion forces. The strength of London dispersion forces increases as the mass of a molecule increases.

Physical States
The physical states at which some alkanes exist at room temperature and atmospheric pressure are found in Table 20-5. Alkanes with the lowest molecular mass, those with one to four carbon atoms, are gases. **Natural gas** *is a fossil fuel composed primarily of alkanes containing one to four carbon atoms.* The existence of these alkanes as gases agrees with the idea that very small molecules have weak London dispersion forces between them and are not held together tightly. Larger alkanes are liquids. Gasoline and kerosene consist mostly of liquid alkanes. Stronger London dispersion forces hold these molecules close enough together to form liquids. Alkanes with a very high molecular mass are solids, corresponding to a greater increase in London dispersion forces. Paraffin wax contains solid alkanes. It can be used in candles, as shown in Figure 20-12.

Boiling Points
The boiling points of alkanes, also shown in Table 20-5, increase with increasing molecular mass. As London dispersion forces increase, more energy, or heat, is required to pull the molecules apart. This property is used in the separation of petroleum, a major source of alkanes. **Petroleum** *is a complex mixture of different hydrocarbons that varies greatly in composition.* The hydrocarbon molecules in petroleum contain from one to more than fifty carbon atoms. This range allows the separation of

FIGURE 20-12 Paraffin wax, used in candles, contains solid alkanes. Molecules of paraffin wax contain 26 to 30 carbon atoms.

TABLE STRATEGY

Table 20-5 Be sure students recognize that the boiling point of the alkane increases as the number of carbon atoms increases. This is also reflected in the state of the alkane at room temperature. Refer students back to the demonstration involving Velcro. The longer the strip of Velcro, the more difficult it was to separate it from another strip. Similarly, the longer the straight-chain alkane is, the greater its attraction to other alkanes and the higher its boiling point.

CHAPTER ⟷ CONNECTION

Students may need to review intermolecular attraction in Chapter 6.

Table 20-6 Ask students why the hydrocarbons with only one, two, and three carbon atoms are not on this table. *(The smaller hydrocarbons are volatile and are not in the gasoline fraction.)* Once again, be sure students recognize the relationship between the number of carbon atoms and the boiling point. The larger hydrocarbons have higher boiling points because they experience stronger intermolecular attractions.

Common Misconception

Many students might think that oil was formed from decayed dinosaurs. Although some of the organic material that makes up existing oil reserves may have come from dinosaur tissue, the vast majority has come from plants and bacteria.

Crude oil is a solution of different hydrocarbons. Have students review Chapter 13 to determine which properties of solutions are mentioned in this section.

Visual Strategy

FIGURE 20-13 Separate students into groups of three or four. Have each group of students use the table on this page to determine the temperature at different heights of the distillation column shown in this figure. Have them brainstorm about how a series of distillation columns can help produce a very pure product.

TABLE 20-6 *Petroleum Fractions*

Fraction	Size range of molecules	Boiling-point range (°C)
Gasoline	C_4–C_{12}	up to 200
Kerosene	C_{10}–C_{14}	180–290
Middle distillate, such as heating oil, gas-turbine fuel, diesel	C_{12}–C_{20}	185–345
Wide-cut gas oil, such as lubricating oil, waxes	C_{20}–C_{36}	345–540
Asphalt	above C_{36}	residues

FIGURE 20-13 (a) Fractional distillation takes place in petroleum refinery towers. (b) This is a model of a fractional distillation tower. Because fractions contain hydrocarbons of different masses, they condense and are drawn off at different levels.

petroleum into different portions with different boiling point ranges, as shown in Table 20-6. In **fractional distillation,** shown in Figure 20-13, *components of a mixture are separated on the basis of boiling point, by condensation of vapor in a fractionating column.* During its fractional distillation, petroleum is heated to about 370°C. Nearly all the components of the petroleum are vaporized at this temperature. As the vapors rise in the fractionating column, or tower, they are gradually cooled.

(a)

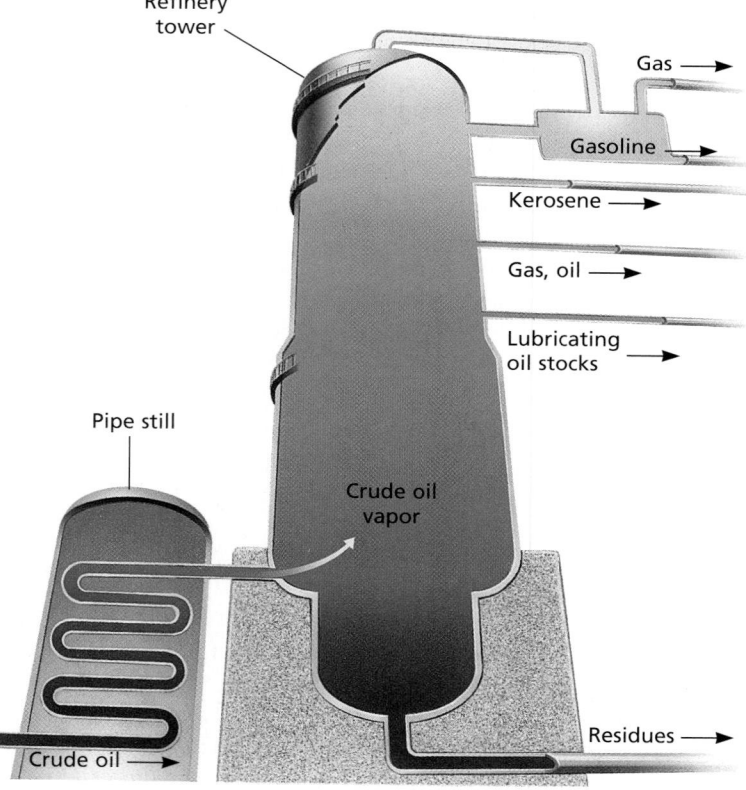

(b)

Alkanes with higher boiling points have higher condensation temperatures and condense for collection lower in the tower. For example, lubricating oils, which have higher condensation temperatures than gasoline has, are collected lower in the fractionating tower.

Combustion

Alkanes are less reactive than other hydrocarbons because of the stability of their single covalent bonds. One reaction alkanes do undergo is combustion. Because alkanes make up a large proportion of gaseous and liquid fossil fuels, combustion is their most important reaction. Complete combustion of hydrocarbons produces energy, CO_2, and H_2O. The reaction for the combustion of methane produces 890 kJ/mol.

$$CH_4 + 2O_2 \longrightarrow CO_2 + 2H_2O$$

One concern about the combustion of fossil fuels is their possible contribution to the greenhouse effect. CO_2 is one of the atmospheric molecules that absorbs infrared radiation. Increased levels of CO_2 through the combustion of fossil fuels may increase the amount of infrared energy absorbed by the atmosphere to a level that can increase the average temperature of Earth.

Engines can be powered by gasoline combustion. When fuel ignites spontaneously before it is reached by the flame front, there is a decrease in the amount of power gained, and engine knocking results. Straight-chain hydrocarbons are more likely to ignite spontaneously than branched-chain hydrocarbons. This tendency is the basis for the octane rating scale. *The **octane rating** of a fuel is a measure of its burning efficiency and its antiknock properties.* The octane rating scale is based on mixtures of 2,2,4-trimethylpentane, a highly branched alkane, and heptane, a straight-chain alkane. The term *octane* comes from the common name of 2,2,4-trimethylpentane, *isooctane.* Pure 2,2,4-trimethylpentane is very resistant to knocking and is assigned an octane number of 100. Pure heptane has an octane number of 0 and burns with a lot of knocking. Increasing the percentage of branched-chain alkanes in gasoline is one way to increase octane rating. The octane rating on gasoline pumps is shown in Figure 20-14.

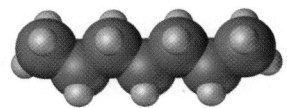

heptane

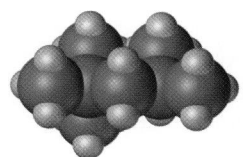

2,2,4-trimethylpentane

FIGURE 20-14 The octane rating scale is based on a rating of 100 for 2,2,4-trimethylpentane and 0 for heptane. Compare their molecular shapes.

SECTION REVIEW

1. What is the basic structural characteristic of alkanes?

2. Draw all of the condensed structural formulas that can represent C_5H_{12}.

3. Give the systematic name for each of the compounds whose formulas appear in item 2.

4. Relate the properties of some alkanes to their uses.

5. Draw the condensed structural formulas of 2-ethyl-3-methylpentane and 1-methyl-3-propylcyclopentane.

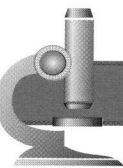
RESEARCH NOTES

Class Discussion

Prompt students through the reading by asking the following questions:

1. What properties of diamond are useful to industry? *(hardness, heat conductivity)*

2. What are two methods used to make artificial diamonds? *(Chemical Vapor Deposition and laser formation of plasma)*

3. How are the two methods for producing artificial diamonds similar? *(Both methods separate carbon atoms from carbon compounds and recombine the carbon atoms alone.)*

Synthetic Diamonds

Diamonds made to order? Almost. A thin coating of diamond film may not be pretty to look at, but it does offer many useful properties to industry. A number of methods are being developed to produce diamond coatings cheaply and efficiently. If successful, the processes will affect the way tools, containers, computer chips, and a host of other items are manufactured.

James Adair is an associate professor of material science and engineering at the University of Florida. "Natural diamonds are made at very, very high pressures and heat," Adair says. "Basically, it's a naturally occurring process that literally took millennia to form the diamond. We make diamonds in a couple of minutes." The process involves sticking very fine diamond particles on all kinds of different surfaces. Chemical Vapor Deposition is then used to grow more diamond from these diamond "seeds."

In Chemical Vapor Deposition, the objects to be coated—in this case, the diamond seeds—are placed inside a chamber filled with methane and other gases. The gases are subjected to microwave radiation, which breaks them down into hydrogen, carbon, and its mixtures (carbon-hydrogen radicals). Diamond crystals grow when these carbon atoms coat the diamond-seed crystals.

Another method of coating with diamond, invented by metallurgist Pravin Mistry, uses lasers to scan the object to be coated. The energy of the lasers breaks down CO_2 (supplied by a gas delivery system) into carbon and oxygen

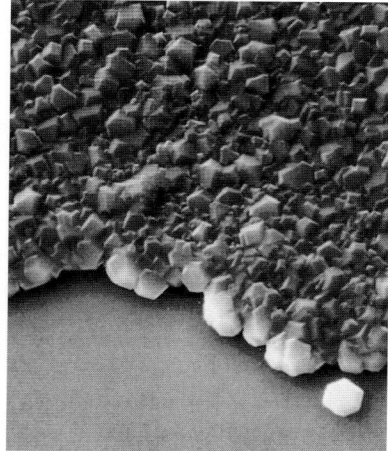

This picture, taken with an electron microscope, shows synthetic diamond formed by Chemical Vapor Deposition.

atoms and vaporizes the surface of the object, forming a superheated plasma. The plasma serves as an environment for bonding the carbon atoms into a coating of crystalline diamond.

One of the biggest challenges in making synthetic diamond coatings is making sure that the carbon crystallizes correctly to form diamond and not graphite. Graphite is useful for making lubricants and pencil leads, but it is not as strong and durable as diamond. In the crystalline molecular structure of graphite, the spaces between carbon atoms are relatively far apart. The process must compress the spaces to form a compact octagonal diamond crystal.

Diamond is one of the hardest materials known to man, so diamond coatings would be particularly useful for making machine tools, work surfaces, and other applications where a durable protective covering is needed. Diamond also has the highest thermoconductivity of any material, which means that it transports heat very effectively. You wouldn't want to drink from a diamond coffee cup because the cup would warm up rapidly and you'd burn your lips. But diamond's ability to conduct heat makes it very useful as a coating on silicon computer chips.

"For microelectronics," says Adair, "dealing with the heat generated by the circuit is one of the biggest problems. If the heat builds up too much within a silicon circuit, it can literally melt the silicon. And it's not going to act as a very good computer brain for you. Diamond can pull that heat out of the silicon chip, so the circuit can run a little bit cooler."

If a computer chip is prevented from getting too hot, it can perform faster. And a faster chip can lead to a new breed of computers with enhanced capabilities.

Unsaturated Hydrocarbons

OBJECTIVES

- Distinguish between the structures of alkenes, alkynes, and aromatic hydrocarbons.

- Be able to name and write structural formulas for unsaturated hydrocarbons.

- Explain how structures of unsaturated hydrocarbons relate to their properties and how those properties affect the uses of specific hydrocarbons.

Lesson Starter

During an earlier lesson, students examined the homologous series of alkanes—molecules in which carbon atoms are saturated with hydrogen atoms. Alkanes were described as hydrocarbons with the formulas that fit the relationship C_nH_{2n+2}. Alkenes are hydrocarbons that contain double bonds. Have students think of dot structures that would accommodate the formula C_3H_6.

CHAPTER ⟺ CONNECTION

Double bonds are stronger than single bonds, but not twice as strong. The initial single bond is much stronger and therefore has a higher bond energy than each additional bond. Confirm this by reviewing bond energies in Chapter 17.

Reading Skill-Builder

COMPARING AND CONTRASTING Have students complete another section of their table for unsaturated hydrocarbons, including basic structural characteristics, rules for naming, properties, uses, formulas for, and examples of alkenes, alkynes, and aromatic hydrocarbons. Then have them use their tables to compare and contrast saturated and unsaturated hydrocarbons.

Hydrocarbons that do not contain the maximum amount of hydrogen are referred to as unsaturated. **Unsaturated hydrocarbons** *are hydrocarbons in which not all carbon atoms have four single covalent bonds.*

Alkenes

Alkenes *are hydrocarbons that contain double covalent bonds.* Some examples of alkenes are given in Table 20-7. Notice that because alkenes have a double bond, the simplest alkene, ethene, has two carbon atoms.

Carbon atoms linked by double bonds cannot bind as many atoms as those that are linked by only single bonds. An alkene with one double bond has two fewer hydrogen atoms than the corresponding alkane.

$$
\begin{array}{c}
\text{H} \quad \text{H} \quad \text{H} \\
| \quad\ | \quad\ | \\
\text{H}-\text{C}-\text{C}-\text{C}-\text{H} \\
| \quad\ | \quad\ | \\
\text{H} \quad \text{H} \quad \text{H} \\
C_3H_8
\end{array}
\qquad
\begin{array}{c}
\quad\quad\quad \text{H} \\
\quad\quad\quad | \\
\text{H}-\text{C}=\text{C}-\text{C}-\text{H} \\
\quad\quad\quad | \\
\text{H} \quad \text{H} \quad \text{H} \\
C_3H_6
\end{array}
$$

Thus, the general formula for noncyclic alkenes with one double bond is C_nH_{2n}.

internet connect

SCLINKS
NSTA

TOPIC: Alkenes
GO TO: www.scilinks.org
*sci*LINKS CODE: HC2205

TABLE 20-7 Structures of Alkenes

	ethene	propene	*trans*-2-butene	*cis*-2-butene
Structural formula	$\begin{array}{c}\text{H}\quad\quad\text{H}\\ \diagdown\quad\diagup\\ \text{C}=\text{C}\\ \diagup\quad\diagdown\\ \text{H}\quad\quad\text{H}\end{array}$	$\begin{array}{c}\text{H}\quad\quad\text{H}\\ \diagdown\quad\diagup\\ \text{C}=\text{C}\\ \diagup\quad\diagdown\\ \text{CH}_3\quad\text{H}\end{array}$	$\begin{array}{c}\text{H}\quad\quad\text{CH}_3\\ \diagdown\quad\diagup\\ \text{C}=\text{C}\\ \diagup\quad\diagdown\\ \text{CH}_3\quad\text{H}\end{array}$	$\begin{array}{c}\text{H}\quad\quad\text{H}\\ \diagdown\quad\diagup\\ \text{C}=\text{C}\\ \diagup\quad\diagdown\\ \text{CH}_3\quad\text{CH}_3\end{array}$
Ball-and-stick model				

✔ Teaching Tip

- Many students will have trouble determining whether an alkene has geometric isomers. Have them draw and examine the structural formulas of each molecule in geometric isomer form.

- An alkene is numbered so that the double bonds are closest to carbon atoms with the lowest numbers. Have students compare the structures of 2-pentene and 3-pentene. *(They are both the same molecule.)* Which is the correct name? *(2-pentene; the name that has the double bond closest to the lowest-numbered carbon)*

Because alkenes have a double bond, they can have geometric isomers, as shown in the examples below.

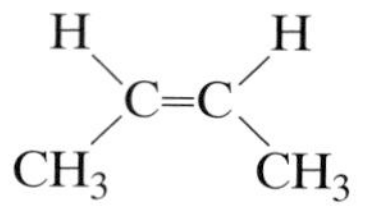

cis-2-butene 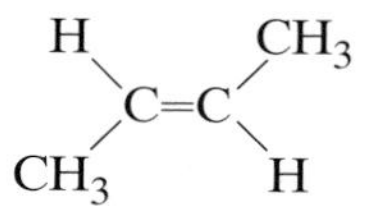   *trans*-2-butene

Systematic Names of Alkenes

The rules for naming a simple alkene are similar to those for naming an alkane. The parent hydrocarbon is the longest continuous chain of carbon atoms *that contains the double bond.* If there is only one double bond, the suffix *-ene* is added to the carbon-chain prefix. Here, the longest chain that contains the double bond has five carbon atoms and one double bond, so the parent hydrocarbon is pentene.

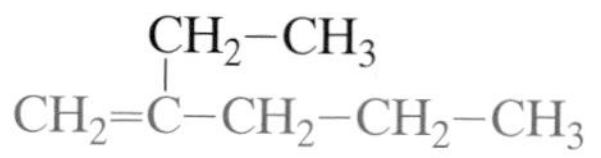

The carbon atoms in the chain are numbered so that the first carbon atom in the double bond has the lowest number. The number indicating the position of the double bond is placed before the name of the hydrocarbon chain and separated by a hyphen.

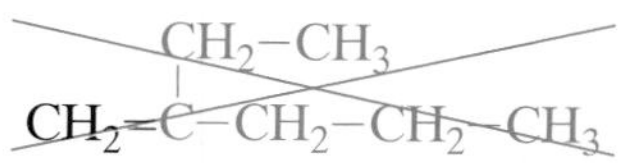

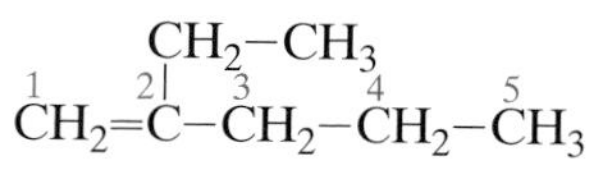

1-pentene

The position number and name of the alkyl group are placed in front of the double-bond position number. This alkyl group has two carbon atoms, an ethyl group. It is on the second carbon atom of the parent hydrocarbon.

2-ethyl-1-pentene

The molecule is 2-ethyl-1-pentene.

If there is more than one double bond, the suffix is modified to indicate the number of double bonds: 2 = *-adiene*, 3 = *-atriene*, and so on.

$$CH_2=CH-CH_2-CH=CH_2$$

1,4-pentadiene

If numbering from both ends gives equivalent positions for the double bonds in an alkene with two double bonds, then the chain is numbered from the end nearest the first alkyl group.

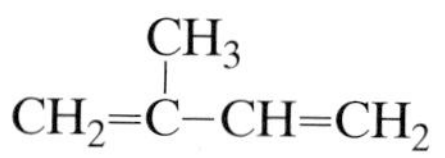

2-methyl-1,3-butadiene

The procedure for naming alkenes can be summarized as follows.

Alkene Nomenclature

Use the rules for alkane nomenclature on page 639, with the following exceptions.

1. Name the parent hydrocarbon. Locate the longest continuous chain that *contains the double bond(s)*. If there is only one double bond, add the suffix *-ene* to the prefix corresponding to the number of carbon atoms in this chain. If there is more than one double bond, modify the suffix to indicate the number of double bonds. For example, 2 = *-adiene*, 3 = *-atriene*, and so on.

2. Add the names of the alkyl groups.

3. Number the carbon atoms in the parent hydrocarbon. Number the carbon atoms in the chain so that the first carbon atom in the double bond nearest the end of the chain has the lowest number. If numbering from both ends gives equivalent positions for two double bonds, then number from the end nearest the first alkyl group.

4. Insert position numbers. Place double-bond position numbers immediately before the name of the parent hydrocarbon alkene. Place alkyl group position numbers immediately before the name of the corresponding alkyl group.

5. Punctuate the name.

ADDITIONAL SAMPLE PROBLEM

Additional Sample Problem is found on page 661A.

SAMPLE PROBLEM 20-3

Name the following alkene.

$$\begin{array}{c} \text{CH}_3 \\ | \\ \text{CH}_3-\text{CH}-\text{C}=\text{CH}_2 \\ | \\ \text{CH}_2-\text{CH}_3 \end{array}$$

SOLUTION

1. Identify and name the parent hydrocarbon.

$$\begin{array}{c} \text{CH}_3 \\ | \\ \text{CH}_3-\text{CH}-\text{C}=\text{CH}_2 \\ | \\ \text{CH}_2-\text{CH}_3 \end{array}$$

The parent hydrocarbon has four carbon atoms and one double bond, so it is named *butene*.

2. Identify and name the alkyl groups.

$$\begin{array}{c} \text{CH}_3 \\ | \\ \text{CH}_3-\text{CH}-\text{C}=\text{CH}_2 \\ | \\ \text{CH}_3-\text{CH}_3 \end{array}$$

The alkyl groups are *ethyl* and *methyl*.
Place their names in front of the name of the parent hydrocarbon in alphabetical order.

ethyl methyl butene

✔ Teaching Tip

Ask students to interchange the methyl and ethyl groups in 2-ethyl-3-methyl-1-butene and then name the resulting alkene. *(The longest chain contains five carbon atoms and the name is 2,3-dimethyl-1-pentene.)*

✔ Teaching Tip

Ask students to interchange the methyl and ethyl groups in 2-ethyl-3-methyl-1-butene and then name the resulting alkene. *(The longest chain contains five carbon atoms and the name is 2,3-dimethyl-1-pentene.)*

Common Misconception

People often read the names of chemicals in their food and cosmetics and wince because they are intimidated by the IUPAC names that are sometimes used. Some are afraid to buy products that list ingredients using IUPAC names. They do not understand that any organic compound, no matter how "natural," can be expressed using an IUPAC name.

Visual Strategy

FIGURE 20-15 The IUPAC name of α-farnesene is 3,7,11-trimethyl-1,3,6,10-dodecatetraene.

3. Number the carbon chain to give the double bond the lowest position.

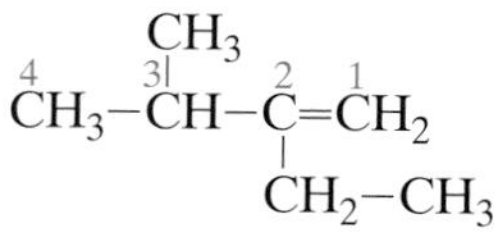

$$\overset{4}{C}H_3-\overset{3}{C}H-\overset{2}{C}=\overset{1}{C}H_2$$
with CH_3 on carbon 3 and CH_2-CH_3 below carbon 2.

4. Place the position number of the double bond in front of butene. Place the position numbers of the alkyl groups in front of each alkyl group. Separate the numbers from the name with hyphens.

The first carbon in the double bond is in position *1*.
The ethyl group is on carbon *2*.
The methyl group is on carbon *3*.

2-ethyl-**3**-methyl-**1**-butene

The full name is 2-ethyl-3-methyl-1-butene.

PRACTICE

1. Name the following alkene:

$$CH_3-CH_2-CH_2-CH=CH-CH_3$$

Answer
2-hexene

2. Draw the condensed structural formula for 4-methyl-1,3-pentadiene.

Answer
$$CH_2=CH-CH=C-CH_3$$
with CH_3 below the C.

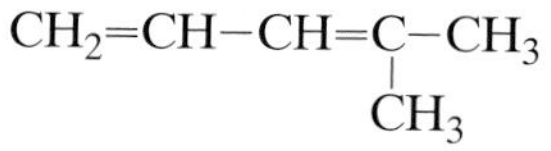

3. Name the following alkenes:

a.
$$CH_3-CH=CH-CH_3$$
with CH_3 above the third carbon.

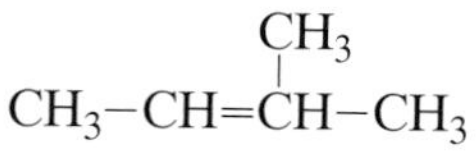

b.
$$CH_3-CH-CH=CH-CH_2-CH_3$$
with CH_3 above the second carbon.

Answer
a. 2-methyl-2-butene
b. 2-methyl-3-hexene

FIGURE 20-15 α-farnesene is a solid alkene found in the natural wax covering of apples. Can you determine the IUPAC name for this large alkene?

Properties and Uses of Alkenes

Alkenes are nonpolar and show trends in properties similar to those of alkanes in boiling points and physical states. For example, α-farnesene has 15 carbon atoms and 4 double bonds, as shown in Figure 20-15. This large alkene is a solid at room temperature and atmospheric pressure. It is found in the natural wax covering of apples. Ethene, the smallest alkene, is a gas.

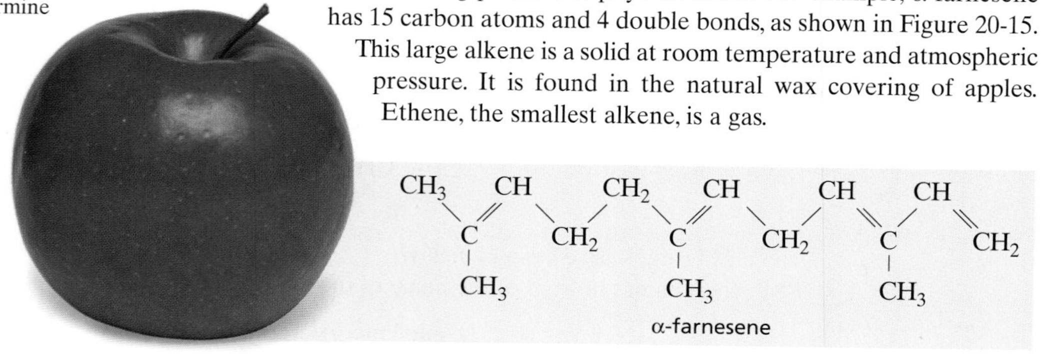

α-farnesene

Ethene is the hydrocarbon commercially produced in the greatest quantity in the United States. It is used in the synthesis of many plastics and commercially important alcohols. Ethene is also an important plant hormone. Induction of flowering and fruit ripening, as shown in Figure 20-16, are effects of ethene hormone action that can be manipulated by commercial growers.

Alkynes

Hydrocarbons with triple covalent bonds are **alkynes.** Like the double bond of alkenes, the triple bond of alkynes requires that the simplest alkyne has two carbon atoms.

$$H-C{\equiv}C-H$$

ethyne

The general formula for the alkynes is C_nH_{2n-2}. Alkynes have four fewer hydrogen atoms than the corresponding alkanes and two fewer than the corresponding alkenes.

C_2H_6 C_2H_4 C_2H_2

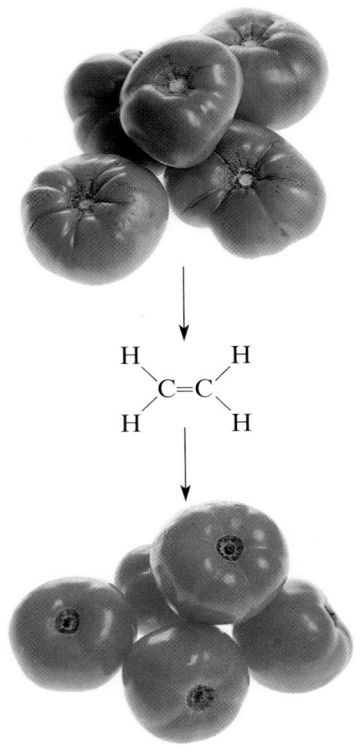

FIGURE 20-16 Ethene is a plant hormone that triggers fruit ripening. Its small size allows it to travel as a gas.

Systematic Naming of Alkynes
Alkyne nomenclature is almost the same as alkene nomenclature. The only difference is that the *-ene* suffix of the corresponding alkene is replaced with *-yne*. A complete list of rules follows.

Alkyne nomenclature

Use the rules for alkane nomenclature on page 639, with the following exceptions.
1. **Name the parent hydrocarbon.** Locate the longest continuous chain that *contains the triple bond(s)*. If there is only one triple bond, add the suffix *-yne* to the prefix corresponding to the number of carbon atoms in the chain. If there is more than one triple bond, modify the suffix to indicate the number of triple bonds. For example, 2 = *-adiyne*, 3 = *-atriyne*, and so on.
2. **Add the names of the alkyl groups.**
3. **Number the carbon atoms in the parent hydrocarbon.** Number the carbon atoms in the chain so that the first carbon atom in the triple bond nearest the end of the chain has the lowest number. If numbering from both ends gives the same positions for two triple bonds, then number from the end nearest the first alkyl group.

Additional Example Problems

1. Name each of the following:

a. $CH_3-CH_2-C\equiv CH$

b.
$$CH_3-C\equiv C-CH_2-\underset{\underset{CH_3}{|}}{CH}-CH_3$$

c.
$$CH\equiv C-\underset{\underset{CH_3}{|}}{\overset{\overset{CH_3}{|}}{C}}-CH_3$$

Ans. **a.** 1-butyne
b. 5-methyl-2-hexyne
c. 3,3-dimethyl-1-butyne

2. Draw structural formulas for each of the following:

a. 2-butyne

b. 3-methyl-1-pentyne

Ans. **a.** $CH_3-C\equiv C-CH_3$

b.
$$CH\equiv C-\underset{\underset{CH_3}{|}}{CH}-CH_2-CH_3$$

FIGURE 20-17 Ethyne is the fuel used in oxyacetylene torches. Oxyacetylene torches can reach temperatures of over 3000°C.

4. Insert position numbers. Place the position numbers of the triple bonds immediately before the name of the parent hydrocarbon alkyne. Place alkyl group position numbers immediately before the name of the corresponding alkyl group.

5. Punctuate the name.

Two examples of correctly named alkynes are given below.

$$CH_3-CH_2-CH_2-C\equiv CH$$

1-pentyne

$$CH\equiv C-\underset{\underset{CH_3}{|}}{CH}-CH_3$$

3-methyl-1-butyne

Properties and Uses of Alkynes

Alkynes are nonpolar and exhibit the same trends in boiling points and physical state as other hydrocarbons. The smallest alkyne, ethyne, is a gas. The combustion of ethyne when it is mixed with pure oxygen produces the intense heat of welding torches, as shown in Figure 20-17. The common name of ethyne is *acetylene,* and these welding torches are commonly called oxyacetylene torches.

Aromatic Hydrocarbons

Aromatic hydrocarbons *are hydrocarbons with six-membered carbon rings and delocalized electrons.* **Benzene** *is the primary aromatic hydrocarbon.* The molecular formula of benzene is C_6H_6. One possible structural formula is a six-carbon atom ring with three double bonds.

However, benzene does not behave chemically like an alkene. All of the carbon–carbon bonds in the molecule are the same. Like graphite, benzene contains resonance hybrid bonds. The structure of the benzene ring allows the delocalized electrons to be spread over the ring. The entire molecule lies in the same plane, as shown in Figure 20-18. The following structural formulas are often used to show this spreading of electrons. In the condensed form, the hydrogen atom at each corner is understood.

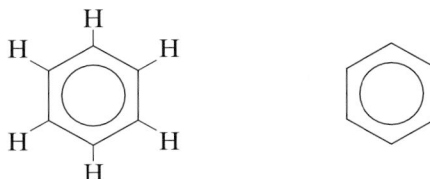

Aromatic hydrocarbons can be thought of as derivatives of benzene. The simplest have one benzene ring, as shown in the following example.

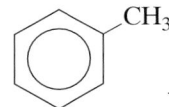

methylbenzene

Systematic Names of Aromatic Hydrocarbons

The simplest aromatic hydrocarbons are named as alkyl-substituted benzenes. The names of the alkyl groups are added in front of the word *benzene* according to the rules for other hydrocarbons. As with cycloalkanes, the carbon atoms in the ring do not need to be numbered if there is only one alkyl group. If there is more than one alkyl group, the carbons are numbered in order to give all of the alkyl groups the lowest possible numbers. Following are some examples.

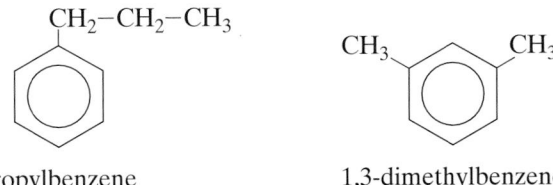

propylbenzene   1,3-dimethylbenzene

The rules for naming simple aromatic hydrocarbons can be summarized as follows.

Simple Aromatic Hydrocarbon Nomenclature

Use the rules for alkane nomenclature on page 639, with the following exceptions.

1. Name the parent hydrocarbon. The parent hydrocarbon is the benzene ring, *benzene*.

2. Add the names of the alkyl groups.

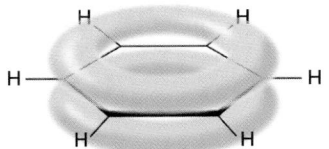

FIGURE 20-18   Electron orbitals in benzene overlap to form continuous orbitals that allow the delocalized electrons to spread uniformly over the entire ring.

Did You Know?

Friedrich August Kekulé claimed that his structure of benzene came from a dream. In his dream, he saw six snakes holding on to each other head to tail. When he woke up, Kekulé realized that the only way the structure would work is to have the carbon atoms line up in the same manner as the snakes in his dream. Whether he truly solved the structure of benzene from a dream or invented the story to advance his theory ahead of others is debated.

CHAPTER ⟷ CONNECTION

Each carbon atom in benzene is sp^2 hybridized. To draw an accurate Lewis dot structure, one must show two resonance structures, with each showing alternating double bonds. To find out more about hybridization and Lewis dot structures, see Chapter 6.

internet connect

SC/LINKS

NSTA

TOPIC: Aromatic compounds
GO TO: www.scilinks.org
*sci*LINKS CODE: HC2206

20-4 Draw structures for each of the following:

a. 1,3-dimethylbenzene

b. 1-ethyl-2-methylbenzene

c. butylbenzene

Ans. **a.**

CH₃

CH₃

b.

CH₂—CH₃

CH₃

c.

CH₂—CH₂—CH₂—CH₃

20-4 Each of the following names represents an incorrect name for an aromatic hydrocarbon. Replace each name with the correct IUPAC name.

a. 2-methylbenzene

b. 1-ethyl-5-methylbenzene

c. 1-methyl-2-butylbenzene

Ans. **a.** 1-methylbenzene
b. 1-ethyl-3-methylbenzene
c. 1-butyl-2-methylbenzene

---

3. **Number the carbon atoms in the parent hydrocarbon.** If there are two or more alkyl groups attached to the benzene ring, number the carbon atoms in the ring. Assign position number one to the alkyl group that comes first in alphabetical order. Then number in the direction that gives the rest of the alkyl groups the lowest numbers possible.

4. **Insert position numbers.**

5. **Punctuate the name.**

SAMPLE PROBLEM 20-4

Draw the condensed structural formula for 1,2-dimethylbenzene.

SOLUTION

1. Identify the parent hydrocarbon in the name.

1,2-dimethyl**benzene**

2. Draw the benzene ring.

3. Number the carbon atoms in the benzene ring.

4. Identify any alkyl groups.

1,2-di**methyl**benzene

There are only methyl groups in this molecule. The prefix *di-* is attached to the word *methyl*, so there are two methyl groups.

5. Locate the position numbers for the methyl groups.

1,2-dimethylbenzene

6. Attach the methyl groups to the carbon atoms numbered *1* and *2*.

CH₃

CH₃

7. The complete structural formula for 1,2-dimethylbenzene is as follows.

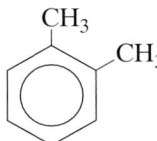

Application
Both crude oil and gasoline contain benzene, which is toxic and can be absorbed through the skin. This is why people should always protect themselves when exposed to either crude oil or gasoline.

PRACTICE

1. Name the following compound:

CH₂–CH₃ (on benzene ring)

Answer
ethylbenzene

2. Draw the condensed structural formula for 1-ethyl-4-methylbenzene.

Answer

CH₃–CH₂–⟨benzene⟩–CH₃

Properties and Uses of Aromatic Hydrocarbons

Benzene rings are chemically very stable, a property that can be explained by the concept of delocalized electrons. Therefore, aromatic hydrocarbons are less reactive than alkenes and alkynes are. In the past, benzene was used as a nonpolar solvent because of this stability. However, benzene is both a poison and a carcinogen. Like other hydrocarbons, benzene is nonpolar and has limited solubility in water. It appears that oxidation of the benzene ring, in an attempt to solubilize it for elimination from the body, produces toxic molecules. This has led to the replacement of benzene as a solvent with methylbenzene, which is less toxic. Another aromatic hydrocarbon, 3,4-benzpyrene, is found in coal tar, tar from cigarette smoke, and soot in heavily polluted urban areas. Studies have shown this compound can cause cancer.

SECTION REVIEW

1. List the basic structural features that characterize each of the following:
a. alkenes
b. alkynes
c. aromatic hydrocarbons

2. Draw three condensed structural formulas that can represent C_4H_8.

3. Give the systematic name for each compound in your answer to item 2.

4. Give examples of a property or use of three unsaturated hydrocarbons.

5. Draw the condensed structural formula for each of the following:
a. 1,3-butadiene
b. 2-pentyne
c. 1,2-diethylbenzene

SECTION REVIEW

1. a. double bonds
b. triple bonds
c. benzene rings

2. $CH_2=CH-CH_2-CH_3$

$CH_3-CH=CH-CH_3$

$CH_3-C=CH_2$
      |
     CH_3

Other answers are also possible, such as: □ ▷–CH₃

3. 1-butene, 2-butene, 2-methyl-1-propene; some students may also think of cyclobutane and methyl-cyclopropane.

4. Answers will vary. Possible responses include the following: the delocalized electrons of benzene make it very stable, large alkenes are solid at room temperature, and ethyne is used as fuel for welding torches.

5. a. $CH_2=CH-CH=CH_2$
b. $CH_3-C\equiv C-CH_2-CH_3$
c. ⟨benzene⟩ with CH₂–CH₃ and CH₂–CH₃

CHAPTER 20 REVIEW

CHAPTER 20 REVIEW

REVIEW ANSWERS

1. They are oriented toward the four corners of a regular tetrahedron.

2. diamond, graphite, fullerenes; in diamond, each carbon atom is tetrahedrally oriented to its four nearest neighbors; in graphite, carbon atoms are arranged in thin hexagonal plates; in fullerenes, carbon atoms compose near-spherical cages.

3. hardness and high melting point

4. Graphite has delocalized electrons, while diamond does not. The delocalized electrons move in an electric field, allowing graphite to conduct electricity.

5. Graphite's structure consists of layers that can slide across one another.

6. spherical, soccer-ball shape

7. **a.** Catenation is the covalent binding of an element to itself to form chains or rings.
   b. Catenation contributes to organic diversity by allowing carbon atoms to bond together in many possible shapes.

8. Hydrocarbons are molecules composed of hydrogen and carbon. They are important because they are the backbones of other organic compounds.

9. **a.** the exact number and types of atoms in a molecule and the order in which they are bonded together
   b. to show the structure of a molecule and distinguish one isomer from another

10. No. They have different formulas.

11. No. They do not have rigid structures.

12. **a.** A *saturated* hydrocarbon has as many hydrogen atoms as possible bonded with single

CHAPTER SUMMARY

20-1
- Carbon is important because all living matter contains carbon.
- Hybridized orbitals allow carbon atoms to form single, double, and triple covalent bonds.
- Carbon occurs in several solid allotropic forms, such as diamond, graphite, and fullerenes, all of which have different structures and properties.

Vocabulary

delocalized electrons (627)   diamond (626)   fullerenes (626)   graphite (626)

20-2
- All organic compounds contain carbon, but not all carbon-containing compounds are classified as organic.
- The number of possible organic compounds is virtually unlimited because of the bonding properties of carbon. The unique catenation ability of carbon allows it to link together to form long chains and rings. The ability of carbon to bind other elements and to allow different arrangements of atoms adds to the diversity of carbon compounds.
- Isomers are compounds with the same molecular formula but different structures. Structural formulas are needed to show the bonding order and arrangement of atoms in an organic molecule to distinguish between isomers.
- Structural isomers are isomers in which the atoms are bonded together in different orders. Geometric isomers are isomers in which the order of atom bonding is the same but the atoms are arranged differently in space.

Vocabulary

catenation (630)   hydrocarbons (630)   organic compounds (629)   structural isomers (631)
geometric isomers (632)   isomers (630)   structural formula (630)

20-3
- In saturated hydrocarbons, each carbon atom has four single covalent bonds. Alkanes are saturated hydrocarbons.
- Organic compounds are named according to a systematic method developed by IUPAC.
- Alkanes contain only single bonds. Because alkanes consist of saturated single covalent bonds, these compounds are not very reactive. One important reaction they do undergo is combustion.
- Trends in physical states, boiling points, and combustion properties correspond to trends in alkane size and amount of branching.

Vocabulary

alkanes (634)   fractional distillation (644)   natural gas (643)   petroleum (643)
alkyl groups (637)   homologous series (634)   octane rating (645)   saturated hydrocarbons (634)
cycloalkanes (635)

20-4
- Carbon atoms in unsaturated hydrocarbons do not all have four single covalent bonds. Alkenes, alkynes, and aromatic hydrocarbons are unsaturated hydrocarbons.
- Alkenes contain carbon-carbon double bonds and can have geometric isomers. The smallest alkene, ethene, is an important industrial and agricultural chemical.
- Alkynes contain carbon-carbon triple bonds.
- Benzene and derivatives of benzene are aromatic hydrocarbons. The concept of delocalized electrons helps explain the stability of the benzene ring.

Vocabulary

alkenes (647)   aromatic hydrocarbons (652)   benzene (652)   unsaturated hydrocarbons (647)
alkynes (651)

REVIEWING CONCEPTS

1. What is the orientation of the four covalent bonds and the sp^3 orbitals of a carbon atom? (20-1)

2. Name and describe the structures of three allotropic forms of carbon. (20-1)

3. What properties of diamond determine most of its industrial uses? (20-1)

4. Why does graphite conduct electricity while diamond does not? (20-1)

5. Explain why the structure of graphite makes it useful as a lubricant. (20-1)

6. Describe the structure of buckminster-fullerene. (20-1)

7. a. What is catenation?
   b. How does catenation contribute to the diversity of organic compounds? (20-2)

8. What are hydrocarbons, and what is their importance? (20-2)

9. a. What information about a compound is provided by a structural formula?
   b. How are structural formulas used in organic chemistry? (20-2)

10. Can molecules with the molecular formulas C_4H_{10} and $C_4H_{10}O$ be structural isomers of one another? Why or why not? (20-2)

11. Can molecules with only single bonds (and no rings) have geometric isomers? Why or why not? (20-2)

12. a. What do the terms *saturated* and *unsaturated* mean when applied to hydrocarbons?
    b. What other meanings do these terms have in chemistry?
    c. Classify alkenes, alkanes, alkynes, and aromatic hydrocarbons as either saturated or unsaturated. (20-3 and 20-4)

13. Classify each of the following as an alkane, alkene, alkyne, or aromatic hydrocarbon.

    a.
    CH_2-CH_3
    CH_2-CH_3

    b. $CH_3-CH=CH_2$

    c.
    $$CH \equiv C - \underset{\underset{CH_3}{|}}{CH} - CH_2 - CH_3$$

    d. $CH_3 - \underset{\underset{CH_3}{|}}{CH} - CH_2 - CH_2 - CH_2 - CH_2 - CH_3$
    (20-3 and 20-4)

14. Give the general formula for the members of the following:
    a. alkane series
    b. alkene series
    c. alkyne series (20-3 and 20-4)

15. Give the molecular formula for each type of hydrocarbon if it contains seven carbon atoms.
    a. an alkane
    b. an alkene
    c. an alkyne (20-3 and 20-4)

16. a. What is a homologous series?
    b. By what method are straight-chain hydrocarbons named?
    c. Name the straight-chain alkane with the molecular formula $C_{10}H_{22}$. (20-3)

17. What are cycloalkanes? (20-3)

18. a. What trend occurs in the boiling points of alkanes?
    b. How would you explain this trend?
    c. How is the trend in alkane boiling points used in petroleum fractional distillation? (20-3)

19. How does the structure of alkanes affect the octane rating of gasoline? (20-3)

20. Write a balanced equation for the complete combustion of each of the following:
    a. methane
    b. ethyne (20-3 and 20-4)

21. Which types of isomers are possible for alkanes (with no rings), alkenes, and alkynes? Why? (20-3 and 20-4)

22. Give examples of ethene's commercial uses. (20-4)

23. a. Alkyne nomenclature is very similar to the nomenclature of what other group of hydrocarbons?
    b. How do these nomenclatures differ? (20-4)

covalent bonds to every carbon atom. An *unsaturated* hydrocarbon does not have as many hydrogen atoms because not all carbon atoms have four single covalent bonds.
   b. whether or not a solution contains the maximum amount of dissolved solute possible
   c. Alkanes are saturated. Alkenes, alkynes, and aromatic hydrocarbons are unsaturated.

13. a. aromatic hydrocarbon
    b. alkene
    c. alkyne
    d. alkane

14. a. C_nH_{2n+2}
    b. C_nH_{2n}
    c. C_nH_{2n-2}

15. a. C_7H_{16}
    b. C_7H_{14}
    c. C_7H_{12}

16. a. a series in which adjacent members differ by a constant unit
    b. Add the suffix *-ane* to the prefix that corresponds to the number of carbon atoms in the chain.
    c. decane

17. saturated hydrocarbons that contain ring structures

18. a. As the number of carbon atoms in alkanes increases, so does their boiling point.
    b. The increased boiling point in larger alkanes is due to greater intermolecular attraction (dispersion forces).
    c. Petroleum products are distilled in various fractions divided by similar boiling points. In a distillation tower, the products with lower boiling points condense at the top, where it is cooler. The larger fractions with higher boiling points condense and are removed near the bottom.

19. A higher percentage of branched-chain alkanes increases the octane rating.

20. a. $CH_4 + 2O_2 \longrightarrow 2H_2O + CO_2$
b. $2C_2H_2 + 5O_2 \longrightarrow 2H_2O + 4CO_2$

21. All can have structural isomers because of the bonding capability of carbon atoms. Alkanes (with no rings) cannot have geometric isomers because they have no rigid structures. Alkenes can have geometric isomers because they have double bonds—rigid structures. Alkynes cannot have geometric isomers because they cannot have two different groups attached to each carbon atom in a triple bond.

22. to ripen fruit, to induce flowering, and to make plastics and commercially important alcohols

23. a. alkenes
b. The names of alkenes end with -ene. The names of alkynes end with -yne.

24. combustion in welding torches

25. a. electrons that are shared between more than two atoms
b. Delocalized electrons contribute to the stability of aromatic hydrocarbons.

26. benzene

27. When the human body oxidizes benzene in an attempt to solubilize it for elimination, toxic products are formed.

28. See page 661A for structure.

29. a. same   **c.** different
b. different   **d.** same

30. a. same
b. structural isomers
c. structural isomers

31. See page 661A for structure.

32. See page 661A for structure.

33. See page 661A for structure.

24. Give one use for ethyne.   (20-4)

25. a. What are delocalized electrons?
b. What is their effect on the reactivity of aromatic hydrocarbons?   (20-4)

26. What is the name of the parent hydrocarbon of simple aromatic hydrocarbons?   (20-4)

27. Describe a possible cause of benzene toxicity.   (20-4)

PROBLEMS

Structural Formulas

28. Draw the condensed structural formula for the following:

$$H-\underset{\underset{H}{|}}{C}=\underset{\underset{H-\underset{\underset{H}{|}}{C}-H}{|}}{C}\underset{}{---}\underset{\underset{H}{|}}{\overset{\overset{H}{|}}{C}}-H$$

29. Identify each of the following pairs of formulas as representing the same or different molecules:

a. C_5H_{12} AND

$$H-\underset{\underset{H}{|}}{\overset{\overset{H}{|}}{C}}-\underset{\underset{H}{|}}{\overset{\overset{H}{|}}{C}}\underset{}{----}\underset{\underset{H-\underset{\underset{H}{|}}{C}-H}{|}}{C}\underset{}{----}\underset{\underset{H}{|}}{\overset{\overset{H}{|}}{C}}-H$$

b. $CH_3-CH_2-CH_3$

AND

$$H-\underset{\underset{H}{|}}{\overset{\overset{H}{|}}{C}}-\underset{\underset{H}{|}}{\overset{\overset{H}{|}}{C}}-\underset{\underset{H}{|}}{\overset{\overset{H}{|}}{C}}-\underset{\underset{H}{|}}{\overset{\overset{H}{|}}{C}}-H$$

c. C_6H_{10} AND $CH_3-CH=\underset{\underset{CH_3}{|}}{C}-CH_3$

d.

$$H-\underset{\underset{H}{|}}{\overset{\overset{H}{|}}{C}}\underset{}{----}\underset{\underset{H-\underset{\underset{H}{|}}{C}-H}{|}}{C}\underset{}{----}\underset{\underset{H-\underset{\underset{H}{|}}{C}-H}{|}}{C}\underset{}{----}\underset{\underset{H}{|}}{\overset{\overset{H}{|}}{C}}-\underset{\underset{H}{|}}{\overset{\overset{H}{|}}{C}}-H$$

AND

$$CH_3-\underset{\underset{CH_3}{|}}{CH}-\underset{\underset{CH_3}{|}}{CH}-CH_2-CH_3$$

Isomers

30. Identify whether each pair represents the same molecule or structural isomers.

a. $CH_3-CH_2-CH_2-CH_3$ $\underset{\underset{CH_2-CH_2-CH_3}{|}}{CH_3}$

b. $\underset{\underset{\underset{\underset{CH_3}{|}}{CH_2}}{|}}{CH_3-CH-CH_2-CH_2}$

$\underset{\underset{CH_3}{|}}{CH_3-CH-CH_2-\overset{\overset{CH_3}{|}}{CH}-CH_3}$

c. $CH_3-CH_2-\overset{\overset{O}{\|}}{C}-OH$ $CH_3-O-CH_2-\overset{\overset{O}{\|}}{CH}$

31. Draw structural formulas for the five isomers of C_6H_{14}.

32. Draw the geometric isomers of the following molecule. Label each isomer as cis or trans.

$CH_3-CH=CH-CH_2-CH_3$

33. a. Which of the following can have geometric isomers?

$CH_3-CH=CH-Cl$ $CH_3-CH=\overset{\overset{CH_3}{|}}{C}-CH_3$

$CH_3-CH_2-CH=CH-CH_2-CH_3$

b. Draw the geometric isomers for those that can have geometric isomers.
c. Label each geometric isomer as cis or trans.

Alkane Nomenclature

34. Name the following molecules. (Hint: See Sample Problem 20-1.)

a. $CH_3-CH_2-CH_2-CH_2-CH_2-CH_2-CH_3$

b.

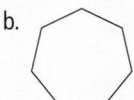

c. $\underset{\underset{CH_3}{|}}{CH_3-\overset{\overset{CH_3}{|}}{C}-CH_2-CH-CH-CH_3}$ $\underset{CH_3}{}$

d.
$$CH_3-\underset{\underset{CH_3}{|}}{\overset{\overset{CH_3}{|}}{C}}-CH_2-CH_2-\underset{\underset{}{|}}{\overset{\overset{CH_2-CH_2-CH_2-CH_3}{|}}{CH}}-CH_2-CH_2-CH_2-CH_3$$

35. Give the complete, uncondensed, structural formula for each of the following alkanes. (Hint: See Sample Problem 20-2.)
a. decane
b. 3,3-dimethylpentane

36. Give the condensed structural formula for each of the following alkanes:
a. 1,1-dimethylcyclopropane
b. 2,2,4,4-tetramethylpentane

37. For each of the following, determine whether the alkane is named correctly. If it is not, give the correct name.

a.
$$CH_3-CH_2-\underset{\underset{CH_3}{|}}{CH_2}$$
1-methylpropane

b.
$$CH_3-CH_2-CH_2-CH_2-CH_2-CH_2-\underset{\underset{\underset{CH_3}{|}}{\overset{\overset{}{|}}{CH_2}}}{CH_2}$$
nonane

c.
$$CH_3-CH_2-CH_2-\underset{\underset{}{|}}{\overset{\overset{CH_3}{|}}{CH}}-CH_2-CH_3$$
4-methylhexane

d.
$$CH_3-CH_2-\underset{\underset{CH_2-CH_3}{|}}{CH}-CH_2-\overset{\overset{CH_3}{|}}{CH}-CH_3$$
4-ethyl-2-methylhexane

Alkene Nomenclature
38. Name the following alkenes. (Hint: See Sample Problem 20-3.)
a. $CH_2{=}CH-CH_2-CH_2-CH_3$

b.
$$\underset{CH_3}{\overset{CH_3}{\diagdown}}C{=}C\underset{CH_3}{\overset{H}{\diagup}}$$

c.
$$CH_2{=}CH-\underset{\underset{\underset{CH_3}{|}}{\overset{\overset{}{|}}{CH_2}}}{\overset{\overset{CH_3}{|}}{C}}-CH_2-CH_3$$

d.
$$CH{\equiv}C-\underset{\underset{CH_3}{|}}{CH}-CH_2-CH{=}CH_2$$

39. Draw the condensed structural formula for each of the following alkenes:
a. 2-methyl-2-hexene
b. 3-ethyl-2,2-dimethyl-3-heptene

40. Draw structural formulas for geometric isomers of each of the following:
a. $CH_3-CH_2-CH_2-CH{=}CH-CH_3$
b. 3-methyl-2-pentene

Alkyne Nomenclature
41. Name the following alkynes:
a. $CH{\equiv}C-CH_3$

b.
$$CH_3-C{\equiv}C-\underset{\underset{CH_3}{|}}{CH}-CH_3$$

c.
$$CH_3-\underset{\underset{CH_3}{|}}{CH}-C{\equiv}C-\underset{\underset{CH_3}{|}}{CH}-CH_3$$

d. $CH{\equiv}C-CH_2-CH_2-CH_2-C{\equiv}CH$

42. Draw the condensed structural formula for each of the following alkynes:
a. 1-decyne
b. 6,6-dimethyl-3-heptyne

Aromatic Hydrocarbon Nomenclature
43. Name the following aromatic hydrocarbons. (Hint: See Sample Problem 20-4.)

a.
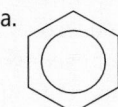

b.
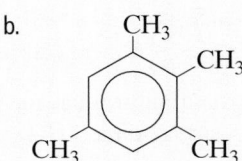

34. a. heptane
b. cycloheptane
c. 2,2,4-trimethylhexane
d. 5-butyl-2,2-dimethylnonane

35. *See page 661A for structure.*

36. *See page 661A for structure.*

37. a. butane
b. correct
c. 3-methylhexane
d. correct

38. a. 1-pentene
b. 2-methyl-2-butene
c. 3-ethyl-3-methyl-1-pentene
d. 2-methyl-1,5-hexadiene

39. *See page 661B for structure.*

40. *See page 661B for structure.*

41. a. propyne
b. 4-methyl-2-pentyne
c. 2,5-dimethyl-3-hexyne
d. 1,6-heptadiyne

42. *See page 661B for structure.*

43. a. benzene
b. 1,2,3,5-tetramethylbenzene

44. *See page 661B for structure.*

45. 0.0570 cm^3

46. a. 1.85 mol
b. 1.11×10^{24} molecules

47. C = 85.6%; H = 14.4%

48. 45.0 L

49. 31.4 kg

50. a-b. *See page 661B for structure.*
c. from the structural formula: C_9H_{20}; from the general formula: $C_nH_{2n+2} = C_9H_{2\times9+2} = C_9H_{20}$; they are the same.

51. *See page 661B for structure.*

52. *See page 661B for structure.*

53. *See page 661B for structure.*

54. a. no geometric isomers
b. *See page 661B for structure.*
c. no geometric isomers
d. no geometric isomers

55. a. same compound
b. different compounds, not isomers
c. same compound
d. isomers

56. Ionic bonds are usually stronger than covalent bonds; more energy is needed to break ionic bonds.

57. Almost all carbon compounds contain hydrogen. In addition, hydrogen is contained in acids, hydroxides, ammonium compounds, and many other inorganic compounds.

58. The percentage of hydrogen decreases as the number of carbon atoms in an alkane increases.

59. a. ethylene and propylene
b. $CH_2=CH_2$ $CH_2=CH-CH_3$
   ethylene   propylene
c. They are both alkenes.

60. a. the amount of oxygen present
b. CO is a deadly poison that binds more readily than O_2 with heme in the blood. Cells die from a lack of O_2.

61. a. Silicon bonds to oxygen rather than to other silicon atoms. Carbon bonds directly to other carbon atoms.
b. SiO_4, tetrahedral

62. a. See page 661B for structure.
b. dimethyl mercury

63. The actual list of compounds published will vary year to year.

64. Student lists will vary. Be sure students are considering petroleum products, such as clothes and food, that may not be immediately obvious.

65. Try not to model large molecules with this method; it becomes very difficult for the models to keep their shape.

44. Draw the condensed structural formula for each of the following molecules:
a. 1,3,5-trimethylbenzene
b. 1,3-dimethylbenzene

Calculations with Carbon Compounds

45. The jewelers' mass unit for diamond is the carat. By definition, 1 carat equals exactly 200 mg. What is the volume of a 1.00 carat diamond? The density of diamond is 3.51 g/cm^3.

46. For 100.0 g of butadiene, C_4H_6, calculate the following:
a. number of moles   b. number of molecules

47. An alkene has the molecular formula $C_{12}H_{24}$. Determine its percent composition.

48. Assuming that the volumes of carbon dioxide and of propane are measured under the same experimental conditions, what volume of carbon dioxide is produced by the complete combustion of 15.0 L of propane?

49. Assume a gasoline is isooctane, which has a density of 0.692 g/mL. What is the mass in kilograms of 12.0 gal of the gasoline (1 gal = 3.78 L)?

MIXED REVIEW

50. a. Draw the complete, uncondensed structural formula for 4-methyloctane.
b. Convert it into the condensed structural formula.
c. Determine the molecular formula for the molecule from both the structure you drew and the general molecular formula for alkanes. Compare the two. Are they the same?

51. Draw and name two different condensed structural formulas for molecules of each of the following types of hydrocarbons containing eight carbon atoms:
a. alkane   c. alkyne
b. alkene   d. aromatic hydrocarbon

52. Draw the condensed structural formulas for 4,4-dimethyl-2-pentyne and 2,2-dimethyl-4-propyloctane.

53. Draw the three structural isomers for an alkyne containing five carbon atoms and one triple bond. Name the molecules you draw.

54. Which of the following molecules have geometric isomers? Draw all possible geometric isomers. Label the molecules you draw as either *cis* or *trans*.
a. butane
b. 2-pentene
c. 2-hexyne
d. 2-methyl-1-butene

55. Identify the following pairs as the same compound, isomers, or different compounds that are not isomers:

a.

AND

$CH_3-CH-CH_2-CH_2-CH_3$
         $|$
         CH_3

b. C_4H_8

AND

c.

AND

CH_3
$|$
$CH_3-C-CH_2-CH_2-CH_3$
$|$
CH_3

d. $CH_3-C=CH-CH_2-CH_3$
          $|$
          CH_3

AND

$CH_3-CH_2-CH-CH=CH_2$
            $|$
            CH_3

CRITICAL THINKING

56. Inferring Conclusions   Why are organic compounds with covalent bonds usually less stable when heated than inorganic compounds with ionic bonds?

57. Inferring Relationships   The element that appears in the greatest number of compounds is hydrogen. The element found in the second greatest number of compounds is carbon. Why are there more hydrogen compounds than carbon compounds?

58. Relating Ideas   As the number of carbon atoms in an alkane molecule increases, does the percentage of hydrogen increase, decrease, or remain the same?

 HANDBOOK SEARCH

59. The top 10 chemicals produced in the United States are listed in Table 7B of the *Elements Handbook.* Review this material, and answer the following:
   a. Which of the top ten compounds are organic?
   b. Write structural formulas for the compounds you listed in item (a).
   c. To what homologous series do each of these compounds belong?

60. The reaction of methane with oxygen produces two different oxides of carbon. Review this material in the *Elements Handbook,* and answer the following:
   a. What conditions determine whether the product of the methane reaction is CO_2 or CO?
   b. If a home heating system is fueled by natural gas, what difference does it make if the combustion produces CO_2 or CO?

61. Silicon is similar to carbon in forming long-chain compounds. Review the material on silicon in the *Elements Handbook* and answer the following.
   a. How does a long-chain silicon compound differ in composition from a long-chain carbon compound?
   b. The simplest alkane is methane. Methyl groups are found in all alkanes. What is a common subunit of a silicate? What is the geometry of that subunit?

62. Mercury in the environment poses a hazard to living things. Review the section on mercury poisoning in the *Elements Handbook.*
   a. Draw a structure formula for the organic mercury compound described in that section.
   b. What is the IUPAC name for this compound?

RESEARCH & WRITING

63. *Chemical and Engineering News* publishes a list once a year of the top 50 chemicals. Find out which chemicals on the current year's list are hydrocarbons, and report your findings to the class.

64. Consult reference materials at the library, and read about products made from hydrocarbons. Keep a list of the number of petroleum-related products you use in a single day.

ALTERNATIVE ASSESSMENT

65. Performance   Models are often used to visualize the three-dimensional shape of molecules. Using gumdrops as atoms and toothpicks to bond them together, construct models of different hydrocarbons. Use large gumdrops for carbon and smaller gumdrops for hydrogen. Refer to Figures 20-1 and 20-2 for guidelines on the three-dimensional shapes of hydrocarbons.

66. Performance   Using your gumdrop models, demonstrate why alkenes can have geometric isomers, while alkanes cannot.

66. This activity will focus on the different groups on both sides of the double bond. The gumdrop models will easily show how there can be free rotation around a single bond. When two toothpicks are used to make the double bond, they will prevent rotation.

ADDITIONAL SAMPLE PROBLEMS

Additional Sample Problem from page 639

20-1 Name the following simple branched-chain alkanes:

a. $CH_3-CH_2-CH_2-CH-CH-CH_3$
  $\quad\quad\quad\quad\quad\quad\quad | \quad\; |$
  $\quad\quad\quad\quad\quad\quad\; CH_3 \; CH_3$

b. $CH_3-CH_2-CH_2-CH-CH-CH_2-CH_2-CH_3$
  $\quad\quad\quad\quad\quad\quad\quad\quad | \quad\; |$
  $\quad\quad\quad\quad\quad\quad\quad\; CH_3 \; CH_3$

c. $CH_2-CH_2-CH-CH_3$
  $\quad\quad\quad\quad\quad |$
  $\quad\quad\quad\quad\; CH_3$

d. $CH_3-CH_2-CH-CH-CH_2$
  $\quad\quad\quad\quad\quad | \quad\; | \quad\; |$
  $\quad\quad\quad\quad CH_3 \; CH_3 \; CH_2-CH_2-CH_2-CH_3$

e. $CH_3-CH_2-CH-CH_2-CH_2-CH_2-CH_3$
  $\quad\quad\quad\quad\quad\quad |$
  $\quad\quad\quad\quad\quad CH_3$

Ans. **a.** 2,3-dimethylhexane
  b. 4,5-dimethyloctane
  c. 2-methylbutane
  d. 3,4-dimethylnonane
  e. 3-methylheptane

Answers from page 640

20-2 a. 2,4-dimethylpentane

$CH_3-CH-CH_2-CH-CH_3$
$\quad\quad\; | \quad\quad\quad\quad |$
$\quad\quad CH_3 \quad\quad\quad CH_3$

b. 4-ethyl-3-methylheptane

$CH_3-CH_2-CH-CH-CH_2-CH_2-CH_3$
$\quad\quad\quad\quad\quad | \quad\; |$
$\quad\quad\quad\quad CH_3 \; CH_2-CH_3$

c. 2-methylpropane

$CH_3-CH-CH_3$
$\quad\quad\; |$
$\quad\quad CH_3$

Answers from page 641

20-2

$\quad\quad\quad CH_3-CH_2 \; CH_2-CH_3$
$\quad\quad\quad\quad\quad | \quad\quad\; |$
$CH_3-CH_2-C----C-CH_2-CH_3$
$\quad\quad\quad\quad\quad | \quad\quad\; |$
$\quad\quad\; CH_3-CH_2 \; CH_3$

3,3,4-triethyl-4-methylhexane

20-2 $CH_3-CH_2-CH-CH_2-CH_2-CH_3$
  $\quad\quad\quad\quad\quad\quad |$
  $\quad\quad\quad\quad\quad CH_3$

$CH_3-CH_2-CH_2-CH_2-CH_2-CH_3-CH_3$
(Other structures are also possible.)

20-2 $\quad\quad\; CH_3 \; CH_2-CH_3$
  $\quad\quad\quad | \quad\quad |$
  $CH_3-C----CH-CH_2-CH_3$
  $\quad\quad\quad |$
  $\quad\quad CH_3$

3-ethyl-2,2-dimethylpentane

Additional Sample Problem from page 649

20-3 Name the following alkenes:
a. $CH_3-CH_2-CH-CH_2-CH_2-CH=CH_2$
  $\quad\quad\quad\quad\quad | $
  $\quad\quad\quad\quad CH_3$

b. $CH_3-CH=CH-CH=CH-CH_3$

c. $CH_3-CH-CH=CH-CH_2-CH_2-CH_3$
  $\quad\quad\quad |$
  $\quad\quad CH_3$

Ans. **a.** 5-methyl-1-heptene
  b. 2,4-hexadiene
  c. 2-methyl-3-heptene

REVIEW ANSWERS

Answers from page 658

28. $CH_2=CH-CH-CH_3$
  $\quad\quad\quad\quad\quad |$
  $\quad\quad\quad\quad CH_3$

31. $CH_3-CH_2-CH_2-CH_2-CH_2-CH_3$

$CH_3-CH_2-CH-CH_2-CH_3$
$\quad\quad\quad\quad\quad |$
$\quad\quad\quad\quad CH_3$

$CH_3-CH-CH_2-CH_2-CH_3$
$\quad\quad\; |$
$\quad\quad CH_3$

$\quad\quad\quad\quad CH_3$
$\quad\quad\quad\quad |$
$CH_3-CH-CH-CH_3$
$\quad\quad\quad\quad |$
$\quad\quad\quad\quad CH_3$

$\quad\quad\quad CH_3$
$\quad\quad\quad |$
$CH_3-C-CH_2-CH_3$
$\quad\quad\quad |$
$\quad\quad\quad CH_3$

---

32. cis

trans

33. a. $CH_3-CH=CH-Cl$

$CH_3-CH_2-CH=CH-CH_2-CH_3$

b-c cis

trans

cis

trans

Answers from page 659

35. a.

b.

36. a.

b. $CH_3-C----CH_2----C-CH_3$
  $\quad\quad\quad | \quad\quad\quad\quad\quad |$
  with CH_3 groups above and below each quaternary carbon

661A

39. a.

$$CH_3-\overset{\overset{\displaystyle CH_3}{|}}{C}=CH-CH_2-CH_2-CH_3$$

b.

$$CH_3-\overset{\overset{\displaystyle CH_3}{|}}{\underset{\underset{\displaystyle CH_3}{|}}{C}}-C=CH-CH_2-CH_2-CH_3$$
$$CH_2-CH_3$$

40. a.

$$CH_3-CH_2-CH_2\diagdown\diagup CH_3$$
$$C=C$$
$$H\diagup\diagdown H$$

$$CH_3-CH_2-CH_2\diagdown\diagup H$$
$$C=C$$
$$H\diagup\diagdown CH_3$$

b.

$$CH_3\diagdown\diagup CH_2-CH_3$$
$$C=C$$
$$H\diagup\diagdown CH_3$$

$$H\diagdown\diagup CH_2-CH_3$$
$$C=C$$
$$CH_3\diagup\diagdown CH_3$$

42. a.

$$CH\equiv C-CH_2-CH_2-CH_2-CH_2$$
$$CH_3-CH_2-CH_2-CH_2$$

b.

$$CH_3-CH_2-C\equiv C-CH_2-\overset{\overset{\displaystyle CH_3}{|}}{\underset{\underset{\displaystyle CH_3}{|}}{C}}-CH_3$$

44. a.

b.

50. a.

b.

$$CH_3-CH_2-CH_2-\overset{\overset{\displaystyle CH_3}{|}}{CH}-CH_2-CH_2-CH_2-CH_3$$

51. Answers will vary.

a.

$$CH_3-\overset{\overset{\displaystyle CH_3}{|}}{\underset{\underset{\displaystyle CH_3}{|}}{C}}-CH_2-CH_2-CH_2-CH_3$$

2,2-dimethylhexane

$$CH_3-CH_2-CH_2-\overset{\overset{\displaystyle CH_3}{|}}{CH}-CH_2-CH_2-CH_3$$

4-methylheptane

b.

$$CH_3-CH_2-CH=CH-\overset{\overset{\displaystyle CH_3}{|}}{\underset{\underset{\displaystyle CH_3}{|}}{C}}-CH_3$$

2,2-dimethyl-3-hexene

$$CH_3-\overset{\overset{\displaystyle CH_3}{|}}{CH}-\overset{\overset{\displaystyle CH_3}{|}}{C}=\overset{\overset{\displaystyle CH_3}{|}}{C}-CH_3$$

2,3,4-trimethyl-2-pentene

c.

$$CH_3-C\equiv C-\overset{\overset{\displaystyle CH_3}{|}}{CH}-\overset{\overset{\displaystyle CH_3}{|}}{CH}-CH_3$$

4,5-dimethyl-2-hexyne

$$CH\equiv C-CH_2-\overset{\overset{\displaystyle CH_3}{|}}{CH}-CH_2-CH_3$$
$$CH_2-CH_3$$

4-ethyl-1-hexyne

d.

1,2-dimethylbenzene

ethylbenzene

52.

$$CH_3-C\equiv C-\overset{\overset{\displaystyle CH_3}{|}}{\underset{\underset{\displaystyle CH_3}{|}}{C}}-CH_3$$

4,4-dimethyl-2-pentyne

$$CH_3-\overset{\overset{\displaystyle CH_3}{|}}{\underset{\underset{\displaystyle CH_3}{|}}{C}}-CH_2-\overset{\overset{\displaystyle CH_2-CH_2-CH_3}{|}}{CH}-CH_2-CH_2-CH_2-CH_3$$

2,2-dimethyl-4-propyloctane

53. a.

$$CH\equiv C-CH_2-CH_2-CH_3$$

1-pentyne

$$CH_3-C\equiv C-CH_2-CH_3$$

2-pentyne

$$CH\equiv C-\overset{\overset{\displaystyle CH_3}{|}}{CH}-CH_3$$

3-methyl-1-butyne

54. b.

$$CH_3\diagdown\diagup CH_2-CH_3$$
$$C=Ccis$$
$$H\diagup\diagdown H$$

$$CH_3\diagdown\diagup H$$
$$C=Ctrans$$
$$H\diagup\diagdown CH_2-CH_3$$

Answer from page 661

62. a.

$$H-\overset{\overset{\displaystyle H}{|}}{\underset{\underset{\displaystyle H}{|}}{C}}-Hg-\overset{\overset{\displaystyle H}{|}}{\underset{\underset{\displaystyle H}{|}}{C}}-H$$

Other Organic Compounds

PACING CHART

Compression Guide: *(To shorten, eliminate items in italics.)*

CLASSROOM RESOURCES

		NSE Standards	Teaching Resources	Experiments
21-1	**Functional Groups and Classes of Organic Compounds** 2 45-minute periods 1 90-minute block *Alkyl Halides, pp. 666–669*	PS 2c, 2f UCP 1–2, 5	**PE** Elements Handbook T 120, T 121	
21-2	**More Classes of Organic Compounds** 2 45-minute periods 1 90-minute block	PS 2c, 2f LS 2a UCP 1–2, 5 HNS 1–3	**PE** Elements Handbook **ATE Demo,** pp. 676–677, 681 T 122, T 123, T 124, T 125, T 126, TM 120A, TM 121A, TM 123A	**B22** Determination of Vitamin C in Fruit Juices
21-3	**Organic Reactions** 2 45-minute periods 1 90-minute block	PS 2f UCP 1–2, 5	**ATE Demo,** p. 682 T 127, TM 122A	Acid Catalyzed Iodination of Acetone, p. 884 Casein Glue, p. 888
21-4	**Polymers** 2 45-minute periods 1 90-minute block *Polymer Thermal Properties and Structure, p. 685*	PS 2c, 2f UCP 1–2, 5 ST 1–2 SPSP 5	**ATE Demo,** p. 692 **PE** Elements Handbook T 129, TM 124A	Polymers for Toy Balls, p. 891 **A25** Polymers

REVIEW RESOURCES

Review and Assessment
2 45-minute periods
1 90-minute block

Cumulative Review	Alternative Assessment	Traditional Assessment
SR Chapter 21 Mixed Review **PE** Chapter 21 62–67, pp. 697–698	**PE** 74–77, p. 699 **ATE** 663, 690 **AA** Items for Chapter 21	Chapter 21 Text Test Generator items for Chapter 21

ASSIGNMENT RESOURCES

Section Homework Resources & Review	Problem-Solving Practice
HR Homework Worksheets 21-1, 21-2, 21-3 Graphic Org. Assignment 21-1, 21-3 **PE** Section Review, 1-4, p. 671 Chapter Review, 1–7, 37–42, 57, 60–61, pp. 694–697 **SR** Section Review 21-1	**PE** Additional Samples 21-1, 21-2 **ATE** Additional Samples, pp. 667, 670 Additional Example, p. 664
HR Homework Worksheets 21-4, 21-5 Graphic Org. Assignment 21-5 **PE** Section Review, 1-6, p. 679 Chapter Review, 8–18, 43–52, 58–59, pp. 694–697 **SR** Section Review 21-2	**ATE** Additional Examples, pp. 672, 673, 674, 675, 677
HR Homework Worksheet 21-6 **PE** Section Review, 1–4, p. 684 Chapter Review, 19–24, 53–56, pp. 695–697 **SR** Section Review 21-3	
HR Homework Worksheets 21-7, 21-8, 21-9 Graphic Org. Assignment 21-8, 21-9 **PE** Section Review, 1–4, p. 691 Chapter Review, 25–36, p. 695 **SR** Section Review, 21-4	

TECHNOLOGY RESOURCES

Technology & Internet Resources

 CTW 18 Segment 18 Chemical Separation Techniques

 Holt Chemistry Videodiscs Teacher's Correlation Guide for Chapter 21

 Module 7: Shifting Equilibrium

internet connect

 On-line Student Resources:
www.scilinks.org
The following SciLinks Internet resources can be found in the student text for this chapter.

TOPICS:
• Alcohols, p. 663 (HC2211)
• Alkyl halides, p. 666 (HC2212)
• Ethers, p. 671 (HC2213)
• Aldehydes/ketones, p. 672 (HC2214)
• DNA, p. 681 (HC2215)
• Polymers, p. 685 (HC2216)

On-line Teacher Resources:
GO TO: go.hrw.com
KEYWORD: HC2 HOME
Visit the HRW Web site for a variety of resources related to this chapter.

 Smithsonian Institution®
Internet Connections
Visit **www.si.edu/hrw** for additional on-line resources.

 CNNfyi.com
Visit **www.cnnfyi.com** for late-breaking news and current events stories selected just for you.

Resource Key

PE Pupil's Edition
ATE Teacher's Edition

One-Stop Planner CD-ROM Includes these resources and customizable daily lesson plans:

HR Homework Resources	**ChemFile**	**D** Consumer Experiments	
SR Section Reviews	**A** Laboratory Experiments	**T** Transparencies	
CTW Critical Thinking Worksheets	**B** Microscale Experiments	**TM** Transparency Masters	
AA Alternative Assessments	**C** Technique Builders and Problem-Solving Experiments	**PS** Mini-Guide to Problem Solving	
		SRW Supplemental Reading Worksheets	

Scoring Rubrics for Labs, Alternative Assessments, Performance Tasks and Portfolio Projects are on the One-Stop Planner CD-ROM.

Chapter Overview

21-1 defines functional groups and certain classes of organic compounds, including alcohols, alkyl halides, and ethers.

21-2 discusses properties and uses of aldehydes, ketones, carboxylic acids, esters, and amines.

21-3 describes four major types of organic reactions: substitution, addition, elimination, and condensation.

21-4 defines different types of polymers and describes their structures and properties.

Concept Base

Students may need a review of the following concepts:

• electron configuration, Chapter 4

• covalent bonding and the structure of molecules, Chapter 6

• types of chemical reactions, Chapter 8

• structural formulas, hydrocarbons, and nomenclature of organic molecules, Chapter 20

Reading Skill-Builder

SUMMARIZING As students read Sections 21-1 and 21-2, ask for volunteers to summarize each subsection for the class. After the summary is completed, have members of the class ask for clarification. All students may consult the text during the clarification process.

CHAPTER 21

Other Organic Compounds

Organic compounds are used to make many of the products we use every day.

Functional Groups and Classes of Organic Compounds

A **functional group** *is an atom or group of atoms that is responsible for the specific properties of an organic compound;* the bonds within functional groups are often the site of chemical reactivity. A given functional group undergoes the same types of chemical reactions in every molecule in which it is found. Therefore, all compounds that contain the same functional group have similar properties and can be classified together.

Alcohols

Alcohols *are organic compounds that contain one or more hydroxyl groups.* The general formula for a class of organic compounds consists of the functional group and the letter R, which stands for the rest of the molecule. The general formula for alcohols is $R-OH$. Systematic names of organic compounds indicate which functional groups are present in a molecule. The rules for naming simple alcohols are as follows.

Alcohol Nomenclature

1. **Name the parent compound.** Locate the longest continuous chain of carbon atoms *that contains the hydroxyl group*. If there is only one hydroxyl group, change the final *-e* in the name of the corresponding alkane to *-ol*. If there is more than one hydroxyl group, use the full name of the corresponding alkane and add the suffix modified to indicate the number of hydroxyl groups. For example, *-diol* = 2, *-triol* = 3, and so on.
2. **Number the carbon atoms in the parent chain.** Number the carbon atoms in the chain so that the hydroxyl groups have the lowest numbers possible.
3. **Insert position numbers.** Place the hydroxyl position number or numbers immediately before the name of the parent alcohol.
4. **Punctuate the name.** Separate the position numbers from the name with a hyphen. If there is more than one position number, separate the position numbers with commas.

OBJECTIVES

- Define *functional group*, and explain why functional groups are important.

- Identify alcohols, alkyl halides, and ethers based on the functional group present in each.

- Classify alcohols, alkyl halides, and ethers from names and structural formulas.

- Relate properties of alcohols, alkyl halides, and ethers to their structures. Describe how these properties influence the uses of specific organic compounds.

internet **connect**

SC*i*LINKS
NSTA

TOPIC: Alcohols
GO TO: www.scilinks.org
*sci*LINKS CODE: HC2211

Lesson Starter
Provide groups of students with toothpicks and two different colors of gumdrops. Ask them to make as many different molecules as they can using only four carbon atoms and ten hydrogen atoms. Remind students that carbon atoms can have single bonds, double bonds, and triple bonds. Hydrogen atoms can each have one single bond. Repeat this activity after adding two gumdrops of a third color to represent two oxygen atoms, which can have two single bonds or one double bond. Have students compare their results.

Safety: Do not allow students to eat materials used in the laboratory.

Alternative Assessment
Have students identify items at home or in a store that contain alcohol. Tell them to read product labels and look for the *-ol* ending, found in IUPAC names and some common names, and the word *alcohol*, found in some common names. Examples include windshield-cleaning fluid (methanol or methyl alcohol), liquid medicines (ethanol or ethyl alcohol), and hand lotion (1,2,3-propanetriol or glycerol).

✔ **Teaching Tip**

Though they have similar symbols, be sure that students understand that the hydroxyl group, $-OH$, and hydroxide ion, OH^-, are not the same.

1. Draw the condensed structural formula for the following:
a. 2,3-pentanediol
b. 1,2,3-butanetriol

Ans.

a. $CH_3-CH-CH-CH_2-CH_3$
             | |
             OH OH

b. $CH_2-CH_2-CH_2-CH_3$
          | | |
          OH OH OH

TABLE STRATEGY

Table 21-1 Have students make a line graph of molar mass versus boiling point for the alkanes listed in the table. On the same grid, have them use a different color to graph molar mass versus boiling point for the alcohols listed. Have them use these graphs to estimate the boiling points of the following compounds: 1-butanol (molecular mass, 74; boiling point, 117.2°C) and *n*-pentane (molecular mass, 72; boiling point, 36.1°C).

TABLE 21-1 Boiling Points of Some Alcohols and Alkanes

Compound	Molecular formula	Molar mass (g/mol)	Boiling point (°C)
methanol	CH_3OH	32	64.7
ethane	C_2H_6	30	−88
ethanol	C_2H_5OH	46	78.3
propane	C_3H_8	44	−42.1
1-propanol	C_3H_7OH	60	97.2
butane	C_4H_{10}	58	−0.50

Following are three examples of correctly named alcohols.

$$CH_3-CH_2-\overset{\displaystyle OH}{\overset{|}{CH_2}} \qquad CH_3-CH_2-\overset{\displaystyle OH}{\overset{|}{CH}}-CH_3 \qquad CH_3-\overset{\displaystyle OH}{\underset{\underset{\displaystyle OH}{|}}{\overset{|}{C}}}-CH_2-CH_3$$

    1-propanol   2-butanol   2,2-butanediol

Properties and Uses of Alcohols

As shown in Table 21-1, the boiling points of alcohols tend to be higher than those of alkanes of comparable molar mass. For example, the molar mass of ethanol, 46 g/mol, is close to that of propane, 44 g/mol. However, their boiling points are very different. The boiling point of ethanol is 78.3°C, while the boiling point of propane is −42.1°C. In addition, boiling points increase as the number of hydroxyl groups in the molecule increases. This trend can be seen in Table 21-2, which shows the boiling points for alcohols with one, two, and three hydroxyl groups.

The boiling point trends shown in Tables 21-1 and 21-2 can be explained by hydrogen bonding, which was discussed in Chapter 6. Compared to alkanes, extra energy is required to break hydrogen bonds between alcohol molecules before conversion from a liquid to a gas. When more than one hydroxyl group is present, an alcohol molecule may form multiple hydrogen bonds. In this case, even more energy is required to break the hydrogen bonds before the liquid is converted to a gas.

TABLE 21-2 Multiple Hydroxyl Groups and Boiling Points

Alcohol	Number of hydroxyl groups	Boiling point (°C)
ethanol	1	78.3
1,2-ethanediol	2	197.3
1-propanol	1	97.2
1,2-propanediol	2	188
1,2,3-propanetriol	3	258–260

TABLE 21-3 *Solubility of Some Alcohols in Water*

Alcohol	Molecular formula	Solubility (g/100. g of water)
methanol	CH_3OH	∞ (completely soluble)
1-butanol	C_4H_9OH	7.4
1-pentanol	$C_5H_{11}OH$	2.7
1-octanol	$C_8H_{17}OH$	0.06

As explained in Chapter 13, alcohols are soluble in water because of hydrogen bonding. However, the solubility of alcohols in water tends to decrease with an increase in the size of the molecule. The longer the hydrocarbon chain in an alcohol, the larger the nonpolar, insoluble portion of the molecule. Table 21-3 illustrates this trend.

Hydrogen bonding in alcohols can also explain other properties and uses of alcohols. Cold creams, lipsticks, body lotions, and similar products generally include 1,2,3-propanetriol, commonly called glycerol, to keep them moist. A model for glycerol is shown in Figure 21-1. Multiple hydroxyl groups allow glycerol to form many hydrogen bonds with water molecules in the air or in the surrounding material.

Alcohols are sometimes used today as alternative fuels and as octane enhancers in fuel for automobiles. Ethanol is combined with gasoline, for example, in a one-to-nine ratio to produce gasohol. Some experts have promoted the use of gasohol as a fuel for automobiles because it burns more cleanly, helps save valuable petroleum reserves, and reduces our nation's dependence on foreign imports of petroleum. However, there are also disadvantages. The combustion of ethanol produces only 60% as much energy per gram as does the combustion of gasoline. The presence of ethanol also causes increased water absorption in the fuel.

FIGURE 21-1 Glycerol contains three hydroxyl groups. This structure allows it to form multiple hydrogen bonds with water. Glycerol is added as a moisturizer to skin products.

Application

1,2-ethanediol, commonly known as ethylene glycol, is used as an automobile antifreeze and is highly toxic. About 100 mL is a lethal dose. It is converted in the liver to oxalic acid, which kills kidney cells and depresses the nervous system. Ethylene glycol tastes sweet, and pets have been known to die from drinking ethylene glycol.

All simple alcohols are poisonous to some extent. When ethanol is consumed, it is broken down by the enzyme alcohol dehydrogenase. This enzyme rapidly converts ethanol to an oxidized form known as acetaldehyde, which is then converted to acetic acid. Acetic acid, a component of household vinegar, is relatively harmless to the human body. However, consuming large amounts of ethanol can be fatal. The lethal dose varies for different individuals. The amount of ethanol found in a liter of hard liquor, 400 mL, is usually fatal.

Other simple alcohols are attacked by alcohol dehydrogenase more slowly, making these alcohols more toxic than ethanol. For example, methanol, or wood alcohol, is converted to formaldehyde and formic acid, both of which are toxic. A great deal of damage can be done to cells before these chemicals are completely metabolized by the body. Methanol is about 10 times more toxic than is ethanol. Toxic effects of methanol include damage to the optic nerve, coma, and death.

internet connect

SCI**LINKS**

NSTA

TOPIC: Alkyl halides
GO TO: www.scilinks.org
sciLINKS CODE: HC2212

Alkyl Halides

Alkyl halides *are organic compounds in which one or more halogen atoms—fluorine, chlorine, bromine, or iodine—are substituted for one or more hydrogen atoms in a hydrocarbon.* Because $-X$ is often used to represent any halogen, an alkyl halide may be represented by the general formula $R-X$. The rules for naming simple alkyl halides in the IUPAC system are as follows.

Alkyl Halide Nomenclature

1. **Name the parent compound.** Locate the longest continuous chain of carbon atoms *that contains the halogen.* Add the prefixes for the attached halogen atoms to the name of the alkane corresponding to the number of carbon atoms in this chain. The prefixes to use are *fluoro-* for fluorine, *chloro-* for chlorine, *bromo-* for bromine, and *iodo-* for iodine. If more than one kind of halogen atom is present, add the halogen prefixes in alphabetical order. If there is more than one atom of the same halogen, add the appropriate prefix (*di-, tri-,* and so on) after the prefixes are arranged in alphabetical order.
2. **Number the carbon atoms in the parent chain.** Number the carbon-atom chain so that the sum of the halogen numbers is as low as possible. If there are different halogen atoms in equivalent positions, give the lower number to the one that comes first in alphabetical order.
3. **Insert position numbers.** Place the halogen position number or numbers immediately before the halogen prefixes.
4. **Punctuate the name.** Separate the position numbers from the name with hyphens. If there is more than one position number, separate the position numbers with commas.

SAMPLE PROBLEM 21-1

Name the alkyl halide shown.

$$
\begin{array}{ccc}
& \text{H} \quad \text{H} \quad \text{H} & \\
\text{H} & -\text{C} - \text{C} - \text{C} - & \text{H} \\
& \text{Br} \ \ \text{Br} \ \ \text{H} &
\end{array}
$$

SOLUTION

1. Locate the longest continuous chain of carbon atoms that contains the halogen.

$$
\begin{array}{ccc}
& \text{H} \quad \text{H} \quad \text{H} & \\
\text{H} & -\text{C} - \text{C} - \text{C} - & \text{H} \\
& \text{Br} \ \ \text{Br} \ \ \text{H} &
\end{array}
$$

The chain has three carbon atoms, so the name of the chain is *propane*.

2. Identify and name the halogen atoms attached to the chain.

$$
\begin{array}{ccc}
& \text{H} \quad \text{H} \quad \text{H} & \\
\text{H} & -\text{C} - \text{C} - \text{C} - & \text{H} \\
& \text{Br} \ \ \text{Br} \ \ \text{H} &
\end{array}
$$

Bromine atoms are attached to the chain. Add the prefix *bromo-* in front of *propane*. Add the prefix *di-* to show that there are two bromine atoms present.

dibromopropane

3. Number the carbon-atom chain so that the sum of the halogen numbers is as low as possible.

$$
\begin{array}{ccc}
& \text{H} \quad \text{H} \quad \text{H} & \\
\text{H} & -\text{C}^1 - \text{C}^2 - \text{C}^3 - & \text{H} \\
& \text{Br} \ \ \text{Br} \ \ \text{H} &
\end{array}
$$

4. The bromine atoms are on carbons numbered *1* and *2*. Place these numbers immediately before the halogen prefix. Separate the numbers from the prefix with a hyphen. Separate the numbers with a comma.

1,2-dibromopropane

The complete name is 1,2-dibromopropane.

PRACTICE

1. Name each of the following alkyl halides:

a.
$$
\begin{array}{c}
\text{Br} \\
| \\
\text{CH}_3 - \text{CH} - \text{CH}_3
\end{array}
$$

b.
$$
\begin{array}{c}
\text{F} \quad \text{F} \quad \text{F} \\
| \quad\ | \quad\ | \\
\text{CH}_3 - \text{CH} - \text{CH} - \text{CH}_2
\end{array}
$$

2. Draw condensed structures for each of the following alkyl halides:

a. 2-iodopropane

b. 1,1,1,2-tetrabromobutane

Answer

1. a. 2-bromopropane
   b. 1,2,3-trifluorobutane

2. a.
$$
\begin{array}{c}
\text{I} \\
| \\
\text{CH}_3 - \text{CH} - \text{CH}_3
\end{array}
$$

b.
$$
\begin{array}{c}
\text{Br} \ \ \text{Br} \\
| \quad\ | \\
\text{Br} - \text{C} - \text{CH} - \text{CH}_2 - \text{CH}_3 \\
| \\
\text{Br}
\end{array}
$$

ADDITIONAL SAMPLE PROBLEMS

21-1 Name the following alkyl halides.

a.
$$
\begin{array}{ccc}
\text{Cl} & \text{Cl} & \text{Cl} \\
| & | & | \\
\text{CH}_2 - \text{CH}_2 - \text{CH} - \text{CH}_2 - \text{CH} \\
& & | \\
& & \text{Br}
\end{array}
$$

b.
$$
\begin{array}{cc}
\text{Cl} & \text{F} \\
| & | \\
\text{Cl} - \text{C} - \text{CH}_2 - \text{C} - \text{CH}_3 \\
| & | \\
\text{Cl} & \text{F}
\end{array}
$$

Ans.
a. 1-bromo-1,3,5-trichloropentane
b. 1,1,1-trichloro-3,3-difluorobutane

21-1 Draw the structural formulas for the following alkyl halides:

a. 1-bromo-1,1,3,3,3-pentaiodo-propane

b. 6-bromo-3,4-dichloro-2,2-difluoro-hexane

Ans.

a.
$$
\begin{array}{cc}
\text{I} & \text{I} \\
| & | \\
\text{I} - \text{C} - \text{CH}_2 - \text{C} - \text{I} \\
| & | \\
\text{Br} & \text{I}
\end{array}
$$

b.
$$
\begin{array}{cccc}
\text{F} & \text{Cl} & \text{Cl} & \text{Br} \\
| & | & | & | \\
\text{CH}_3 - \text{C} - \text{CH} - \text{CH} - \text{CH}_2 - \text{CH}_2 \\
| & & & \\
\text{F} & & &
\end{array}
$$

Properties and Uses of Alkyl Halides

Alkyl halides are some of the most widely used organic chemicals. A family of alkyl halides that has received widespread attention in recent years is the chlorofluorocarbons, or CFCs. *CFCs* are alkyl halides that contain both chlorine and fluorine. The formulas for two widely used CFCs, Freon-11 and Freon-12, are shown below.

$$F-\underset{\underset{Cl}{|}}{\overset{\overset{Cl}{|}}{C}}-Cl \qquad\qquad Cl-\underset{\underset{Cl}{|}}{\overset{\overset{F}{|}}{C}}-F$$

trichlorofluoromethane (Freon-11)   dichlorodifluoromethane (Freon-12)

CFC-11 and CFC-12 are odorless, nontoxic, nonflammable, and very stable. They also easily change physical states. These properties make them useful in a number of commercial operations. They have been used in the manufacture of plastic foam and as liquid refrigerants in commercial refrigerators. At the height of their production, in 1985, more than 700 million kilograms of CFC-11 and CFC-12 were manufactured worldwide.

However, CFCs contribute to the destruction of ozone in the upper atmosphere, as shown in Figure 21-2. When released into the atmosphere, CFCs can break down and release free chlorine atoms.

$$CCl_2F_2 \xrightarrow{\text{solar radiation}} Cl + CClF_2$$

The released chlorine atoms attack molecules of ozone (O_3) found in the upper atmosphere. The ozone is converted to diatomic oxygen.

$$Cl + O_3 \longrightarrow ClO + O_2$$

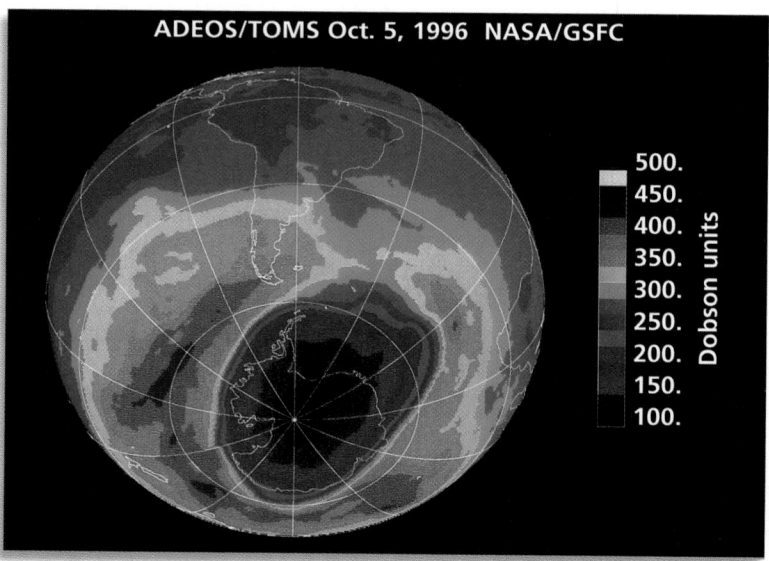

ADEOS/TOMS Oct. 5, 1996 NASA/GSFC

FIGURE 21-2 The depletion of ozone in the upper atmosphere above Antarctica has produced an area of very low ozone concentration, called the ozone hole. The black region over Antarctica shows the area of greatest ozone depletion.

FIGURE 21-3 The nonstick coating on this pan is made of Teflon, an alkyl halide.

Chlorine atoms are eventually regenerated.

$$\text{ClO} + \text{O} \longrightarrow \text{Cl} + \text{O}_2$$

This makes it possible for a single chlorine atom to destroy thousands of ozone molecules.

The depletion of ozone in the upper atmosphere has produced an area of very low concentration, called an ozone hole, over Antarctica. Ozone molecules absorb ultraviolet radiation from sunlight, preventing most of that radiation from reaching Earth. Ultraviolet radiation is known to cause skin cancer in humans, to kill some forms of microscopic life, to damage plant tissue, and to cause other harmful effects in plants and animals. Because CFCs are a major cause of ozone depletion, more than 100 nations signed an agreement in 1987 to reduce the amount of CFCs produced.

Another alkyl halide is tetrafluoroethene, C_2F_4. It is joined in long chains to make a material with the trade name Teflon. Because of the unreactive carbon-fluorine bond, Teflon is inactive and stable to about 325°C. It also has a low coefficient of friction, which means that other objects slide smoothly over its surface. These properties enable Teflon to be used in heat-resistant machine parts that cannot be lubricated. It is also used in making utensils with "nonstick" surfaces, such as the frying pan in Figure 21-3.

Ethers

Ethers *are organic compounds in which two hydrocarbon groups are bonded to the same atom of oxygen.* They can be represented by the general formula $R-O-R'$. In this formula, R' may be the same hydrocarbon group as R or a different one. The IUPAC rules for naming simple ethers are as follows.

Application

Because of ozone depletion, CFCs are being replaced as refrigerants by hydrochlorofluorocarbons (HCFCs) and hydrofluorocarbons (HFCs). HCFCs and HFCs contain at least one hydrogen atom, whereas CFCs contain no hydrogen atoms. HCFCs and HFCs break down in the atmosphere, just as CFCs do, but they are much less stable and remain in the atmosphere a much shorter period of time.

Common Misconceptions

Students may think that ozone exists in large amounts in the stratosphere. Actually, if all the ozone in the atmosphere could be transported to Earth's surface, it would form a layer no more than 3 mm thick at atmospheric pressure.

More information on O_3 can be found with Group 16 of the *Elements Handbook*.

ADDITIONAL
SAMPLE
PROBLEMS

21-2 Name the following ethers:

a. CH_3-O-CH_3

b. $CH_3-O-CH_2CH_3$

Ans. **a.** dimethyl ether
b. ethyl methyl ether

21-2 Draw the structural formulas for the following ethers:

a. dipropyl ether
b. cyclopentyl methyl ether

See page 699A for answers.

Ether Nomenclature

1. **Name the parent compound.** The word *ether* will come at the end of the name.
2. **Add the names of the alkyl groups.** If there are two different alkyl groups, arrange the names in alphabetical order in front of the word *ether.* If both alkyl groups are the same, the prefix *di-* is added to the name of the alkyl group in front of the word *ether.*
3. **Leave appropriate spaces in the name.** There should be spaces between the names of the alkyl groups and between the alkyl groups and the word *ether.*

SAMPLE PROBLEM 21-2

Name the ether shown below.

$$CH_3-CH_2-O-CH_2-CH_3$$

SOLUTION

1. The word *ether* will come at the end of the name.

ether

2. Identify and name the two alkyl groups joined to the oxygen atom.

$$CH_3-CH_2-O-CH_2-CH_3$$

They are both ethyl groups. Add the prefix *di-* to show that there are two ethyl groups present. Place *diethyl* in front of *ether,* separated by a space.

diethyl ether

The full name is diethyl ether. Diethyl ether is the most common ether and is also known as ethyl ether, or just ether.

PRACTICE

1. Name each of the following ethers:
   a. $CH_3-CH_2-CH_2-O-CH_3$
   b.

   ⬠—O—⬠

   c. $CH_3-O-CH_2-CH_2-CH_2-CH_2-CH_3$

Answer

1. a. methyl propyl ether
   b. dicyclopentyl ether
   c. methyl pentyl ether

2. Draw condensed structures for the following ethers:
   a. ethyl propyl ether
   b. dicyclohexyl ether
   c. butyl methyl ether

2. a. $CH_3-CH_2-O-CH_2-CH_2-CH_3$
   b.

   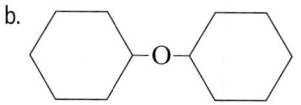

   c. $CH_3-CH_2-CH_2-CH_2-O-CH_3$

TABLE 21-4 *Comparison of the Boiling Points of an Ether, Alkane, and Alcohol*

Compound	Molar mass	Boiling point (°C)
diethyl ether	74	34.6
pentane	72	36.1
1-butanol	74	117.7

internet**connect**

SC*LINKS*
NSTA

TOPIC: Ethers
GO TO: www.scilinks.org
*sci***LINKS CODE:** HC2213

TABLE STRATEGY

Table 21-4 Ask students to predict an ether that would have a boiling point similar to that of hexane. *(Ethyl propyl ether has a boiling point of 63.6°C, compared with 69°C for hexane.)*

Properties and Uses of Ethers

The solubilities of ethers and alcohols in water are similar. For example, diethyl ether and 1-butanol have the same molar mass. They also have approximately the same solubility, 6 g/100 g of water for diethyl ether and 7.4 g/100 g of water for 1-butanol. This similarity can be explained by the fact that ethers, like alcohols, can form hydrogen bonds with water molecules.

In comparison, the boiling points of ethers are much lower than those of alcohols of similar molar mass. But, they are about the same as those of alkanes of similar molar mass. This trend is clear from the comparison in Table 21-4. This trend can also be explained by hydrogen bonding. Unlike alcohols, ethers cannot form hydrogen bonds with each other because they do not have a hydrogen atom bonded to a highly electronegative atom. Therefore, no extra energy is needed to break hydrogen bonds for ethers to boil.

Like alkanes, ethers are not very reactive compounds. This property explains their most common uses as solvents. In many organic reactions in which water cannot be used as a solvent, an ether is used instead.

Methyl-*tertiary*-butyl ether (MTBE) is the most widely used ether. It is another gasoline octane enhancer. At one time, tetraethyl lead, $(C_2H_5)_4Pb$, was widely used for this purpose. However, concerns about the release of lead into the environment have increased, so tetraethyl lead has been replaced by MTBE and other octane enhancers.

SECTION REVIEW

1. Give the general formula and class of organic compounds for each of the following:
   a. CH_3-OH
   b. CH_3-O-CH_3
   c. $Br-CH_2-CH_2-CH_3$

2. Give the name of each of the following:
   a.
$$CH_3-\overset{\overset{\displaystyle OH}{|}}{CH}-CH_3$$
   b. CH_3-O-CH_3

   c.
$$CH_3-CH_2-\overset{\overset{\displaystyle F}{|}}{\underset{\underset{\displaystyle F}{|}}{CH}}$$

3. Compare the boiling points of alcohols, ethers, and alkanes, and explain one reason for the differences.

4. Draw condensed structures for each of the following:
   a. 1,2-propanediol
   b. ethyl methyl ether
   c. dichloromethane

SECTION REVIEW

1. a. *R*-OH; alcohol
b. *R*-O-*R'*; ether
c. *R*-*X*; alkyl halide

2. a. 2-propanol
b. dimethyl ether
c. 1,1-difluoropropane

3. The boiling points of alcohols are higher than those of alkanes and ethers of the same molar mass because hydrogen bonds must be broken in alcohols before they are able to boil.

4. a.
$$\overset{\overset{\displaystyle OH}{|}}{CH_2}-\overset{\overset{\displaystyle OH}{|}}{CH}-CH_3$$
b. $CH_3-O-CH_2-CH_3$

c.
$$\overset{\overset{\displaystyle Cl}{|}}{\underset{\underset{\displaystyle Cl}{|}}{CH_2}}$$

Lesson Starter

Write expanded structural formulas for the following compounds on the board: propanal, propanone, and propanoic acid. Ask students to identify ways in which the three structures are similar to each other. Answers may include that all contain six hydrogen atoms, three carbon atoms, and one oxygen atom that is double bonded to a carbon atom. Ask students to identify three ways in which the structures differ from each other. Differences will probably focus on what is bonded to the carbon atom that is double-bonded to the oxygen atom.

Common Misconception

Students often have trouble distinguishing between names of alcohols and aldehydes because of the similarities of the endings for alcohols (-ol) and aldehydes (-al). Emphasize the necessity of writing neatly so that the difference is clear.

Additional Example Problems

Additional Example Problems are found on page 699A.

 **Reading Skill-Builder**

BRAINSTORMING Ask students to name examples of everyday products that they think are made from organic compounds. List as many examples as possible on the board. Then ask students if they can sort the items into categories based on functional groups. Keep students' ideas on the board for reference as they complete the chapter. When students have finished reading this section, have them expand the list and sort the items by class of organic compound.

OBJECTIVES

- Identify aldehydes, ketones, carboxylic acids, esters, and amines based on the functional group present in each.

- Classify aldehydes, ketones, carboxylic acids, esters, and amines from names and structural formulas.

- Relate properties of aldehydes, ketones, carboxylic acids, esters, and amines to their structures. Describe how these properties influence the uses of specific organic compounds.

 internet**connect**

SC*i*LINKS.
NSTA

TOPIC: Aldehydes/ketones
GO TO: www.scilinks.org
*sci*LINKS CODE: HC2214

More Classes of Organic Compounds

Aldehydes and Ketones

Aldehydes and ketones contain the *carbonyl group*, shown below.

The difference between aldehydes and ketones is the location of the carbonyl group. **Aldehydes** *are organic compounds in which the carbonyl group is attached to a carbon atom at the end of a carbon-atom chain.* **Ketones** *are organic compounds in which the carbonyl group is attached to carbon atoms within the chain.* These differences can be seen in their general formulas, shown below.

$$R-\overset{\overset{\textstyle O}{\|}}{C}-H$$
aldehyde

$$R-\overset{\overset{\textstyle O}{\|}}{C}-R'$$
ketone

The IUPAC rules for naming simple aldehydes and ketones are as follows.

Aldehyde Nomenclature

Name the parent compound. Locate the longest continuous chain *that contains the carbonyl group*. Change the final *-e* in the name of the corresponding alkane to *-al*.

Following are three examples of correctly named aldehydes.

$$H-\overset{\overset{\textstyle O}{\|}}{C}-H$$
methanal

$$CH_3-\overset{\overset{\textstyle O}{\|}}{C}-H$$
ethanal

$$CH_3-CH_2-\overset{\overset{\textstyle O}{\|}}{C}-H$$
propanal

Ketone Nomenclature

1. **Name the parent compound.** Locate the longest continuous chain *that contains the carbonyl group*. Change the final *-e* in the name of the corresponding alkane to *-one*.

2. **Number the carbon atoms in the parent chain.** Number the carbon atoms in the chain so that the carbon atom in the carbonyl group has the lowest possible number.

3. **Insert position numbers.** Place the carbonyl position number in front of the name.

4. **Punctuate the name.** Separate the position number from the name with a hyphen.

Following are three examples of correctly named ketones.

$$CH_3{-}\overset{\overset{\displaystyle O}{\|}}{C}{-}CH_3 \qquad CH_3{-}\overset{\overset{\displaystyle O}{\|}}{C}{-}CH_2{-}CH_3 \qquad CH_3{-}CH_2{-}\overset{\overset{\displaystyle O}{\|}}{C}{-}CH_2{-}CH_3$$

2-propanone   2-butanone   3-pentanone

Properties and Uses of Aldehydes and Ketones

The simplest aldehyde is methanal, also known as formaldehyde. It was once commonly used in biology laboratories as a preservative for dead animals. Its most important commercial use, however, is in the production of plastics. One of the first commercial plastics, bakelite, was made by combining phenol and formaldehyde in a long chain.

The simplest ketone is 2-propanone, whose common name is acetone. Acetone is found in some nail-polish removers because it dissolves the organic substances in nail polish. However, artificial fingernails are made of plastics that are also dissolved by acetone. Today other solvents are being used more frequently as nail-polish removers.

Aldehydes and ketones are often responsible for odors and flavors. For example, cinnamaldehyde contributes to the odor and flavor of cinnamon. Figure 21-4 gives some examples of odors and flavors that come from aldehydes and ketones.

FIGURE 21-4 Many common odors and flavors come from aldehydes and ketones.

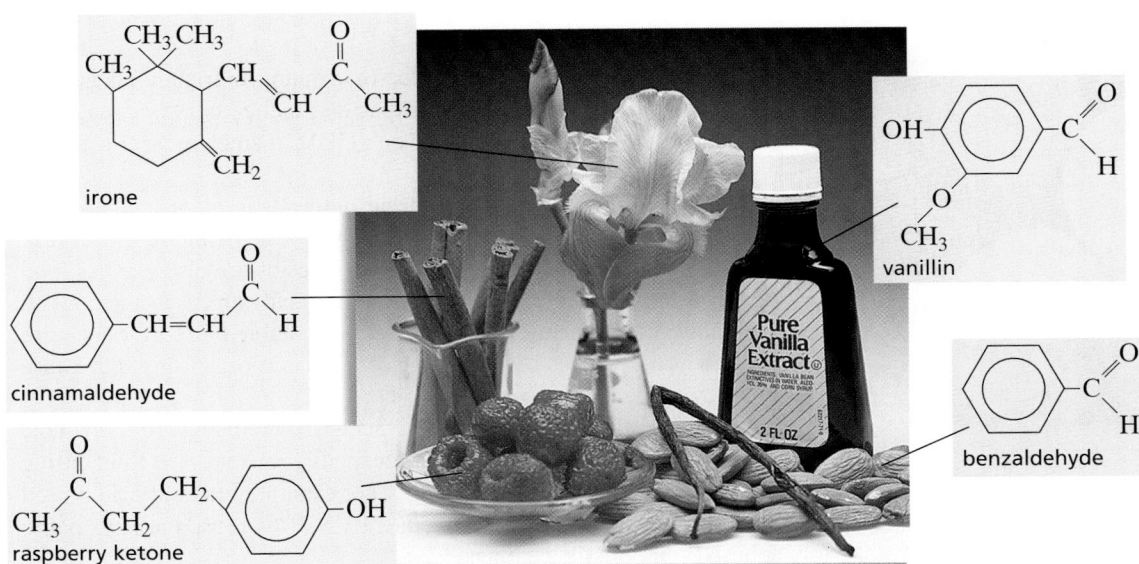

irone

cinnamaldehyde

raspberry ketone

vanillin

benzaldehyde

Additional Example Problem

4. Name the following compounds.

a.
$$CH_3-\overset{\displaystyle O}{\overset{\|}{C}}-OH$$

b.
$$HO-\overset{\displaystyle O}{\overset{\|}{C}}-CH_2-\overset{\displaystyle O}{\overset{\|}{C}}-OH$$

Ans. **a.** ethanoic acid
b. propanedioic acid

CHAPTER ⟷ CONNECTION

Acids were discussed in Chapter 15. Because they are often explained separately, students may think that the properties of carboxylic acids differ from the properties of inorganic acids, such as hydrochloric and nitric acid. Write ionization equations that illustrate how a carboxylic acid, such as acetic acid, takes part in the same kinds of chemical reactions as does hydrochloric acid.

$$HO-\overset{O}{\overset{\|}{C}}-CH_2-\overset{OH}{\underset{\underset{OH}{\overset{\|}{C=O}}}{C}}-CH_2-\overset{O}{\overset{\|}{C}}-OH$$

citric acid

FIGURE 21-5 Citric acid, found in citrus fruits, contains three carboxylic acid groups shown in red on the structural formula.

Carboxylic Acids

Carboxylic acids *are organic compounds that contain the carboxyl functional group.* The carboxyl group always comes at the end of a carbon-atom chain. A member of this class of organic compounds can be represented by the general formula shown below.

$$R-\overset{\displaystyle O}{\overset{\|}{C}}-OH$$

The rules for naming simple carboxylic acids are as follows.

Carboxylic Acid Nomenclature

Name the parent compound. Locate the longest continuous chain *that contains the carboxyl group.* If there is only one carboxyl group, change the final *-e* in the name of the corresponding alkane to *-oic acid.* If there is more than one carboxyl group, use the full name of the corresponding alkane, and add the suffix modified to indicate the number of carboxyl groups. For example, *-dioic acid* = 2, *-trioic acid* = 3, and so on.

Following are three examples of correctly named carboxylic acids.

$$H-\overset{\displaystyle O}{\overset{\|}{C}}-OH \qquad CH_3-CH_2-CH_2-\overset{\displaystyle O}{\overset{\|}{C}}-OH \qquad HO-\overset{\displaystyle O}{\overset{\|}{C}}-\overset{\displaystyle O}{\overset{\|}{C}}-OH$$

methanoic acid   butanoic acid   ethanedioic acid

Properties and Uses of Carboxylic Acids

Carboxylic acids, like inorganic acids, react to lose a hydrogen ion and become a negatively charged ion in water.

$$R-\overset{\displaystyle O}{\overset{\|}{C}}-OH \underset{}{\overset{H_2O}{\rightleftharpoons}} R-\overset{\displaystyle O}{\overset{\|}{C}}-O^- + H^+$$

Carboxylic acids are much weaker than many inorganic acids, such as hydrochloric, sulfuric, and nitric acids. Acetic acid, the weak acid in vinegar, is a carboxylic acid. The IUPAC name for acetic acid is ethanoic acid.

A number of carboxylic acids occur naturally in plants and animals. For example, citrus fruits, shown in Figure 21-5, contain citric acid. Table 21-5 lists more examples. Carboxylic acids are also used as food additives. For example, ethanoic and citric acids are used in foods to give them a tart or acidic flavor. Benzoic, propanoic, and sorbic acids are used as preservatives. All three acids kill microorganisms that cause foods to spoil.

The most widely used carboxylic acids are methanoic and ethanoic acids. Because they can be made inexpensively, they are the starting material for many chemical processes. For example, ethanoic acid is used in the production of polyvinyl acetate, PVA. PVA is used in latex paint, adhesives, and textile coatings.

TABLE 21-5 *Some Carboxylic Acids and Their Natural Sources*

Carboxylic acid	Structural formula	Source
methanoic acid	$$\overset{\displaystyle O}{\underset{\displaystyle \parallel}{}}$$ H–C–OH	ants
butanoic acid	$CH_3-CH_2-CH_2-\overset{O}{\overset{\parallel}{C}}-OH$	rancid butter
hexanoic acid	$CH_3-CH_2-CH_2-CH_2-CH_2-\overset{O}{\overset{\parallel}{C}}-OH$	milk fats, coconut oil, palm oil
lactic acid	$CH_3-\overset{OH}{\overset{\mid}{C}}H-\overset{O}{\overset{\parallel}{C}}-OH$	sour milk, blood, and muscle fluid
malic acid	$HO-\overset{O}{\overset{\parallel}{C}}-CH_2-\overset{OH}{\overset{\mid}{C}}H-\overset{O}{\overset{\parallel}{C}}-OH$	apples
oxalic acid	$HO-\overset{O}{\overset{\parallel}{C}}-\overset{O}{\overset{\parallel}{C}}-OH$	rhubarb

TABLE STRATEGY

Table 21-5 Point out the presence of two different functional groups— the hydroxyl group and the carboxyl group—in the lactic acid and malic acid molecules. Explain to students that complex molecules often have more than one functional group.

✔Teaching Tip

A common name for ethyl ethanoate is ethyl acetate.

Additional Example Problems

Additional Example problems are found on page 699A.

Esters

Esters *are organic compounds with carboxylic acid groups in which the hydrogen of the hydroxyl group has been replaced by an alkyl group.* The general formula for an ester is given below.

$$R-\overset{O}{\overset{\parallel}{C}}-O-R'$$

The IUPAC system for naming simple esters is as follows.

Ester Nomenclature

1. **Name the parent compound.** Name the carboxylic acid from which the ester was formed (see page 674). Change the *-oic acid* ending in the name of this acid to *-oate*. This gives the second half of the ester's name.
2. **Add the name of the alkyl group.** Identify and name the alkyl group that has replaced the hydrogen of the hydroxyl group. Add the name of the alkyl group to the front of the name.
3. **Leave appropriate spaces in the name.** There should be a space between the name of the alkyl group and the name of the parent compound.

Following are two examples of correctly named esters.

$$CH_3-\overset{O}{\overset{\parallel}{C}}-O-CH_2-CH_3 \qquad CH_3-CH_2-CH_2-\overset{O}{\overset{\parallel}{C}}-O-CH_2-CH_3$$

ethyl ethanoate   ethyl butanoate

676

DEMONSTRATION

Odors from Esters

Safety: Teacher should wear safety goggles, a face shield, gloves, and a lab apron. Students should wear safety goggles. A safety shower and an eyewash fountain must be in working condition and within 30 seconds walking distance. Make sure there are no sources of ignition in the room. Use a nonsparking hot plate.

Procedure: Fill a 400 mL beaker half full of water, and heat it to boiling on a hot plate. Number seven medium-sized test tubes. Using the reagents chart, add 2 mL of each alcohol and 2 mL of each liquid acid to each test tube. If the acid is a solid, add 1 g. Add 1 mL of concentrated sulfuric acid to each test tube. To mix, tap the bottom of each tube with your finger. Place the test tubes in the boiling-water bath for a few minutes.

REAGENTS		
Tube	Acid	Alcohol
1	butyric	pentyl
2	butyric	ethyl
3	acetic	isopentyl
4	acetic	ethyl
5	acetic	octyl
6	salicylic	methyl
7	decanoic	ethyl

Cut pieces of filter paper into seven circles and fit them into the bottom of seven 50 mL beakers. Dip a clean stirring rod into each test tube, and wet each filter paper with a different ester by touching the stirring rod to the paper. Line up the beakers on a table and have the students cautiously smell the odors by wafting the air above each beaker with their hands.

TABLE 21-6 *Common Flavors and Odors Produced by Esters*

Ester	Structural formula	Flavor or odor
ethyl butanoate	$CH_3-CH_2-CH_2-\overset{\displaystyle O}{\overset{\displaystyle \|}{C}}-O-CH_2-CH_3$	pineapple
methyl salicylate	OH, $\overset{\displaystyle O}{\overset{\displaystyle \|}{C}}-O-CH_3$ (benzene ring)	wintergreen oil
geraniol formate	$H-\overset{\displaystyle O}{\overset{\displaystyle \|}{C}}-O-CH_2-CH=\overset{\displaystyle CH_3}{\overset{\displaystyle \|}{C}}-CH_2-CH_2-CH=\overset{\displaystyle CH_3}{\overset{\displaystyle \|}{C}}-CH_3$	rose
methyl anthranilate	NH_2, $\overset{\displaystyle O}{\overset{\displaystyle \|}{C}}-O-CH_3$ (benzene ring)	grape juice and jasmine
linalyl acetate	$CH_3-\overset{\displaystyle O}{\overset{\displaystyle \|}{C}}-O-\overset{\displaystyle CH_3}{\underset{\displaystyle CH=CH_2}{C}}-CH_2-CH_2-CH=\overset{\displaystyle CH_3}{\overset{\displaystyle \|}{C}}-CH_3$	lavender

Properties and Uses of Esters

Esters are common in plants and are responsible for some distinctive flavors and odors. Table 21-6 lists some of these esters and the flavors and odors with which they are associated. At one time, compounds such as those listed in the table were obtained only from natural materials. But chemists have learned how to synthesize these and many other naturally occurring compounds for use as food additives. Figure 21-6 shows the structure of isoamyl acetate, which is found in bananas and is also used as an artificial flavoring.

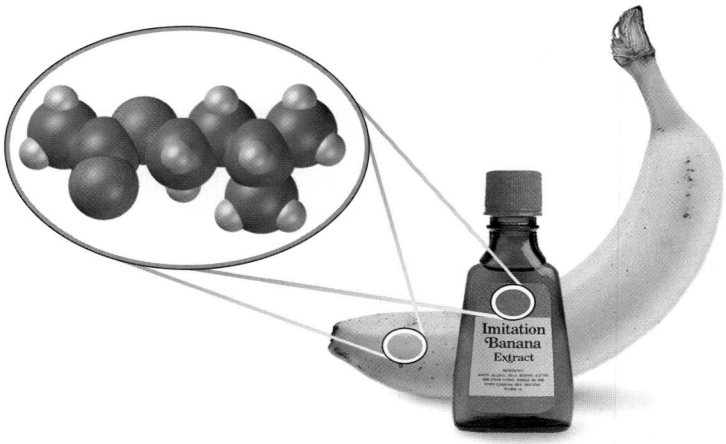

FIGURE 21-6 The ester in bananas can be synthesized and used as a flavoring.

Amines

Amines *are organic compounds that can be considered to be derivatives of ammonia, NH₃.* They can be represented by the following general formula. Note that the functional group does *not* contain oxygen.

$$R-\underset{\underset{R'}{|}}{N}-R''$$

Amines are often named by a common system rather than the IUPAC system. The steps in naming a simple amine by the common system are as follows.

Amine Nomenclature

1. **Name the parent compound.** The end of the name will be *-amine*.
2. **Add the names of the alkyl groups.** Arrange the names of the alkyl groups attached to the nitrogen atom in alphabetical order. Add the prefixes *di-* or *tri-* in front of the group name if two or three, respectively, of the same kind are included in the amine. Combine these names in front of *-amine* to form one word.

Following are three examples of correctly named amines.

$$CH_3-\underset{\underset{H}{|}}{N}-H \qquad CH_3-\underset{\underset{CH_2-CH_3}{|}}{N}-H \qquad CH_3-\underset{\underset{CH_3}{|}}{N}-CH_3$$

methylamine   ethylmethylamine   trimethylamine
(primary amine)   (secondary amine)   (tertiary amine)

Amines are categorized as primary, secondary, or tertiary, depending on the number of hydrogen atoms of the ammonia molecule that have been replaced. As shown in the structures above, *in a* **primary amine,** *one hydrogen atom of an ammonia molecule has been replaced by an alkyl group. In a* **secondary amine,** *two hydrogen atoms of an ammonia molecule have been replaced by alkyl groups. In a* **tertiary amine,** *all three hydrogen atoms of an ammonia molecule have been replaced by alkyl groups.*

Properties and Uses of Amines

The chemical properties of the amines depend largely on the electronic structure of the nitrogen atom, which has an unshared pair of electrons. This region of negative charge makes amines weak bases in aqueous solutions. The unshared pair of electrons on the amine molecule attracts a positive hydrogen atom in a water molecule. The hydrogen atom bonds with the amine, forming a positively charged ion and leaving the hydroxide ion behind.

$$R-\underset{\underset{R'}{|}}{\overset{..}{N}}-R'' + H-O-H \rightleftharpoons R-\underset{\underset{R'}{|}}{\overset{\overset{H^+}{|}}{N}}-R'' + OH^-$$

OTHER ORGANIC COMPOUNDS **677**

RESULTS

Tube	Odor	Ester
1	apricot	*n*-amyl butyrate
2	pineapple	ethyl butanoate
3	banana	isoamyl acetate
4	apple	ethyl acetate
5	orange	octyl acetate
6	wintergreen	methyl salicylate
7	grape	ethyl decanoate

Disposal: Combine test tubes 3 and 4. While stirring, slowly add 1 M NaOH to bring the pH to between 10 and 11. Pour the mixture down the drain. Make sure that test tube 6 is completely esterified with no unreacted methyl alcohol present. Then combine it with test tubes 1, 2, 5, and 7. Adjust the pH of the mixture to between 5 and 9 with 1 M NaOH. Dilute the mixture tenfold with water, and pour it down the drain.

✔ Teaching Tip

Amines are named in the IUPAC system as amino derivatives of the alkanes. For example, the IUPAC name for methylamine is amino methane.

Additional Example Problems

Additional Example Problems are found on page 699A.

Visual Strategy

FIGURE 21-7 Ask students to explain how they know that batrachotoxinin A is an amine and how they know what class of amine it is. *(It is a tertiary amine because all three hydrogen atoms in ammonia have been replaced.)*

✔ **Teaching Tip**

Putrescine and cadaverine are, respectively, 1,4-butanediamine and 1,5-pentanediamine.

Application

Many alkaloids act as neurotoxins because they compete with acetylcholine at receptor sites on nerve cells. Examples of such alkaloids are atrophine, curare, nicotine, caffeine, morphine, and codeine. Such compounds are used as muscle relaxants, painkillers, and pesticides.

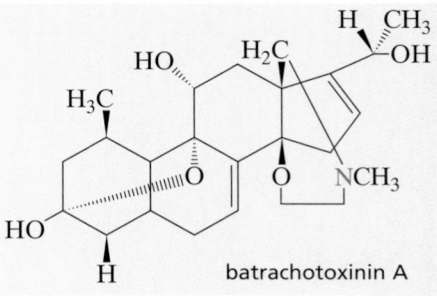

batrachotoxinin A

FIGURE 21-7 The poison dart frog produces toxic amines, one of which is batrachotoxinin A, that kill nerve cells. The nitrogen atom of the amine is shown in red.

An interesting example of this reaction involves two naturally occurring and toxic amines known as batrachotoxin and batrachotoxinin A. These compounds are produced by the poison dart frog, shown in Figure 21-7, which lives in the rain forests of Colombia. In water solution, both of these amines gain protons and become positively charged ions. Because these two amines carry the same charge as sodium ions found in the nervous system, they behave in much the same way. Both batrachotoxin ions can move through the openings in nerve cells, called sodium channels. These ions are much larger than sodium ions, however. They force the sodium channels to remain in the "open" position, and sodium ions are allowed to flood a nerve cell. This causes the nerve cell to continuously transmit nerve impulses, resulting in rapid death of the cell.

Amines are common in nature. They are often formed during the breakdown of proteins in animal cells. Two such amines are putrescine and cadaverine. Their names reflect their foul odors and presence in decaying bodies. Another amine, methylamine, has the unpleasant odor associated with dead fish. Yet a fourth amine, skatole, is found in feces and contributes to their odor.

The class of organic compounds known as alkaloids also consists of amines. *Alkaloids* are naturally occurring amine products of plants that have physiological effects on animals. Examples of alkaloids include caffeine, nicotine, morphine, and coniine (found in poisonous hemlock). Alkaloids tend to have complex chemical structures, as illustrated by the structure for morphine.

morphine (a tertiary amine)

Table 21-7 summarizes the functional groups and the general formulas of the classes of organic compounds discussed in Sections 21-1 and 21-2.

TABLE 21-7 Classes of Organic Compounds

Class	Functional group	General formula
alcohol	$-OH$	$R-OH$
alkyl halide	$-X$ (X = F, Cl, Br, I)	$R-X$
ether	$-O-$	$R-O-R'$
aldehyde	$\overset{\displaystyle O}{\overset{\|}{-C-H}}$	$\overset{\displaystyle O}{\overset{\|}{R-C-H}}$
ketone	$\overset{\displaystyle O}{\overset{\|}{-C-}}$	$\overset{\displaystyle O}{\overset{\|}{R-C-R'}}$
carboxylic acid	$\overset{\displaystyle O}{\overset{\|}{-C-OH}}$	$\overset{\displaystyle O}{\overset{\|}{R-C-OH}}$
ester	$\overset{\displaystyle O}{\overset{\|}{-C-O-}}$	$\overset{\displaystyle O}{\overset{\|}{R-C-O-R'}}$
amine	$\overset{\displaystyle }{\underset{\|}{-N-}}$	$\underset{\underset{R'}{\|}}{R-N-R''}$

SECTION REVIEW

1. Give the general formula and class of organic compounds for each of the following:
   a. $CH_3-CH_2-\overset{\overset{\displaystyle O}{\|}}{C}-OH$
   b. $CH_3-\overset{\overset{\displaystyle O}{\|}}{C}-H$
   c. $CH_3-CH_2-NH_2$
   d. $CH_3-\overset{\overset{\displaystyle O}{\|}}{C}-O-CH_2-CH_3$
   e. $CH_3-\overset{\overset{\displaystyle O}{\|}}{C}-CH_3$

2. Give the name of each of the following:
   a. $CH_3-\overset{\overset{\displaystyle O}{\|}}{C}-CH_2-CH_2-CH_3$
   b. $CH_3-CH_2-CH_2-\overset{\overset{\displaystyle O}{\|}}{C}-OH$
   c. $CH_3-NH-CH_3$

3. Draw condensed structures for each of the following:
   a. ethyl ethanoate
   b. triethylamine
   c. butanal

4. How are aldehydes and ketones alike? How do they differ from each other?

5. How do the strengths of organic acids compare with the strengths of most inorganic acids?

6. Show the reaction that occurs when amines are dissolved in water.

SECTION REVIEW

1. a. $\overset{\overset{\displaystyle O}{\|}}{R-C}-OH$; carboxylic acid

   b. $\overset{\overset{\displaystyle O}{\|}}{R-C}-H$; aldehyde

   c. $R-NH_2$; amine

   d. $\overset{\overset{\displaystyle O}{\|}}{R-C}-O-R'$; ester

   e. $\overset{\overset{\displaystyle O}{\|}}{R-C}-R'$; ketone

2. a. 2-pentanone
   b. butanoic acid
   c. dimethylamine.

3. a. $CH_3-\overset{\overset{\displaystyle O}{\|}}{C}-O-CH_2-CH_3$

   b. $CH_3-CH_2-\underset{\underset{CH_2-CH_3}{\|}}{N}-CH_2-CH_3$

   c. $CH_3-CH_2-CH_2-\overset{\overset{\displaystyle O}{\|}}{C}-H$

4. Both contain the carbonyl group. The carbonyl group is at the end of a carbon chain in an aldehyde and within a carbon chain in a ketone.

5. Organic acids are weaker.

6. See page 699A for answer.

✔ **Teaching Tip**

DNA (deoxyribonucleic acid) and RNA (ribonucleic acid) are the two kinds of nucleic acids found in cells.

Class Discussion

Ask students to list several genetic diseases, such as Down syndrome, sickle cell anemia, muscular dystrophy, or hemophilia. These and other genetic diseases are encoded into DNA. Discuss the ethical issues of whether genetic engineers should be allowed to change the DNA in organisms to eliminate genetic diseases. How might this process be abused?

Unraveling the Mystery of DNA

HISTORICAL PERSPECTIVE

Today genetic engineers can identify, modify, and even transplant genes, but virtually nothing was known about the chemical mechanism of heredity at the beginning of the twentieth century. The term **gene** *was coined in 1909 to describe a molecule that existed only in theory at the time. By the century's midpoint, however, scientists were poised to discover the molecular structure of the gene and explain the biochemical process that is the foundation of modern genetics.*

The Chemical Nature of the Gene

By the early part of the twentieth century, scientists knew that genes were one of two types of organic macromolecules: proteins or nucleic acids. Most researchers believed genes to be the former until 1944, when it was shown that hereditary information could be transmitted from one bacterial cell to another by DNA alone.

An Important New Technique

One problem early researchers encountered was the inability to directly observe the minuscule genes. The development of a relatively new crystallographic technique proved vital to the elucidation of the structures of DNA and other biological macromolecules.

The technique was called X-ray diffraction and involved shining X rays onto crystallized molecular samples to take "snapshots" of their structure. Until the 1950s, most X-ray crystallography was focused on proteins. But in 1951, James D. Watson realized the

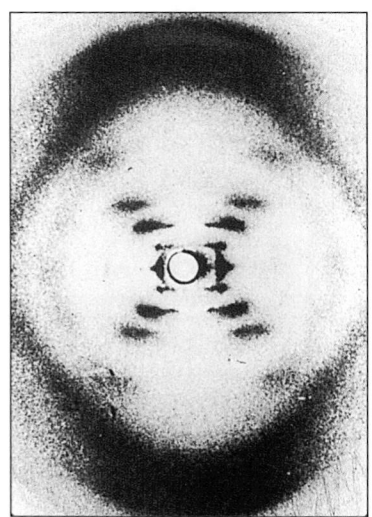

X-ray diffraction patterns of DNA taken by Rosalind Franklin were used to determine the structure of DNA.

potential value of X-ray diffraction in determining a model for DNA. That year, he accepted a position at Cambridge University's Cavendish Laboratory to learn more about the procedure.

A Fateful Union

At Cavendish, Watson befriended Francis Crick, a theoretical

biophysicist. Crick did not know how to perform X-ray diffraction either, but he was adept at analyzing the images that resulted from it. Fortunately, Cavendish was also home to two experts on X-ray crystallography of DNA: Maurice Wilkins and Rosalind Franklin. With the help of these two experimentalists, Watson and Crick set out to solve the riddle of DNA.

A Big Leap

One of the team's biggest clues was the result of an investigation into proteins by Linus Pauling, the eminent chemist at the California Institute of Technology. Pauling determined the basic shape of a polypeptide chain, or protein strand, to be an α-helix, a large molecule of repeating units that twist around a central axis.

This discovery inspired Watson and Crick to look for a similar but more complex structure in DNA. Watson wrote:

In the α-helix, a single polypeptide . . . chain folds up into a helical arrangement held

DEMONSTRATION
Making a Helix
To help students visualize a helix, wrap colored wire around the threads of a large screw. Carefully remove the screw from the coil of wire and let the students observe the wire helix.

together by hydrogen bonds between groups on the same chain. Maurice told Francis, however, that the diameter of the DNA molecule was thicker than would be the case if only one polynucleotide (DNA strand) were present. This made him think that the DNA molecule was a compound helix composed of several polynucleotide chains twisted about each other.

Watson and Crick began contemplating DNA configurations with two, three, and four helices. They correctly hypothesized that the sugar and phosphate groups of DNA's basic repeating units, or nucleotides, alternated to form the molecular backbone of each helix in the molecule. However, they mistakenly situated the sugar-phosphate backbones in the center of the molecule, with the bases of the nucleotides jutting outward.

The DNA Solution

Redirected by new X-ray diffraction data obtained by Franklin, Watson began considering models with the sugar-phosphate chains on the outside of the DNA molecule and the bases pointing inward. After reviewing a titration study of DNA indicating that many, if not all, of the molecule's bases formed hydrogen bonds with each other, he speculated:

Conceivably the crux of the matter was a rule governing

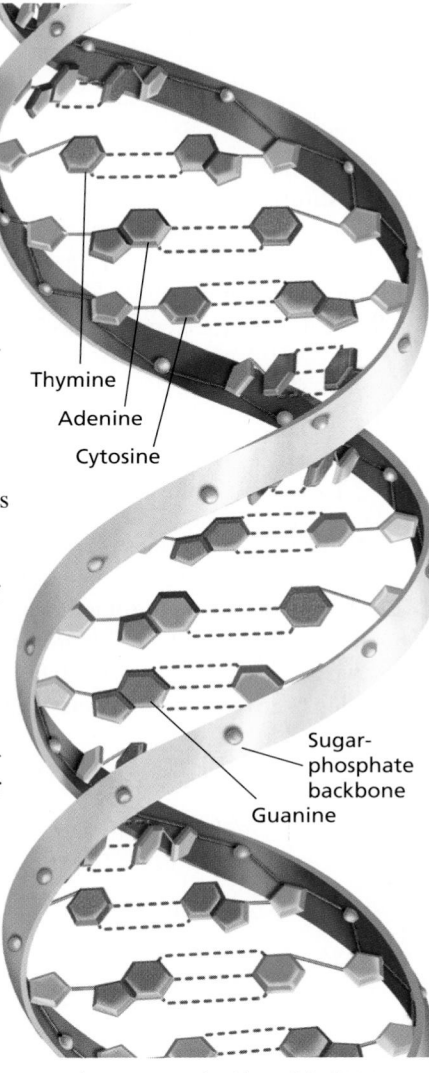

Thymine
Adenine
Cytosine

Sugar-phosphate backbone
Guanine

The Watson-and-Crick model of DNA contains opposing adenine-thymine and guanine-cytosine bases on a double-helical sugar-phosphate backbone.

hydrogen bonding between bases. . . . I thus started wondering whether each DNA molecule consisted of two chains with identical base sequences held together by

hydrogen bonds between pairs of identical bases.

Crick immediately observed that this like-with-like double-stranded model did not satisfy the symmetry requirements of the X-ray data. When Watson began exploring models pairing different bases, he uncovered the final clue to the DNA mystery:

. . . an adenine-thymine pair held together by two hydrogen bonds was identical in shape to a guanine-cytosine pair held together by at least two hydrogen bonds.

Fitting the opposing adenine-thymine and guanine-cytosine bases inside the double-helical sugar-phosphate backbones resulted in the first correct molecular model of DNA, for which they were awarded a Nobel Prize in 1962.

A Long-Standing Theory

The model of DNA discovered by James Watson and Francis Crick has continued to be the basis of biochemical genetics. The model has enabled scientists to explain genetic mutations, to predict or correct certain genetic disorders, and to genetically engineer organisms to have desirable traits.

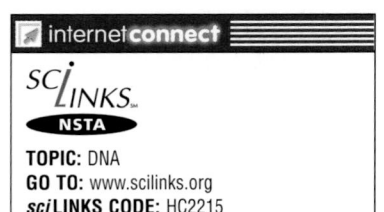

internetconnect

SCiLINKS
NSTA

TOPIC: DNA
GO TO: www.scilinks.org
sciLINKS CODE: HC2215

Organic Reactions

Lesson Starter

This is a demonstration of an addition reaction that tests for double bonds in oils. Using a fume hood, prepare an iodine solution by dissolving 1.5 g of iodine in 50 mL of mineral oil. Pour 10 mL of cooking oil into a 50 mL beaker. Put the beaker on an overhead projector, and project the image onto a screen. Add 3 mL of the iodine solution to the oil, and stir thoroughly. The color will disappear, indicating the addition of the iodine to the double bonds of the oil. This shows that cooking oil has double bonds and thus is an unsaturated fat. See page 699A for such a reaction.

Safety: Teacher should wear safety goggles, gloves, and a lab coat.

Disposal: Add sufficient unsaturated cooking oil to the saturated cooking oil and iodine mixture to react with the iodine. Combine all liquids, and store them in a labeled container for disposal by the school waste contractor.

Reading Skill-Builder

READING ORGANIZER Have students read the section and then organize what they have learned in a concept map. Concept maps should start with *Types of Organic Reactions*. Students should list each type of reaction, describe it, and provide examples.

Module 7: Equilibrium

Topic: Shifting Equilibrium Tutorial and Practice
Sections **b**, **c**, and **d** of this engaging tutorial review and reinforce understanding of equilibrium.

OBJECTIVES

- Describe and distinguish between the organic reactions: substitution, addition, condensation, and elimination.

- Relate some functional groups to some characteristic reactions.

Module 7: Equilibrium

Substitution Reactions

A **substitution reaction** *is one in which one or more atoms replace another atom or group of atoms in a molecule.* The reaction between an alkane, such as methane, and a halogen, such as chlorine, to form an alkyl halide is an example of a substitution reaction. Notice that in this reaction, a chlorine atom replaces a hydrogen atom on the methane molecule.

$$
\begin{array}{c}
\quad\quad H \\
| \\
H-C-H \\
| \\
H
\end{array}
+ Cl-Cl \longrightarrow
\begin{array}{c}
\quad\quad H \\
| \\
H-C-Cl \\
| \\
H
\end{array}
+ \quad H-Cl
$$

methane   chlorine   chloromethane   hydrogen chloride

Additional compounds can be formed by replacing the other hydrogen atoms remaining in the methane molecule. The products are dichloromethane, trichloromethane, and tetrachloromethane. Trichloromethane is also known as chloroform, and tetrachloromethane is also known as carbon tetrachloride. CFCs are formed by further substitution reactions between chloroalkanes and HF.

$$
\begin{array}{c}
Cl \\
| \\
Cl-C-Cl \\
| \\
Cl
\end{array}
+ H-F \xrightarrow{SbF_5}
\begin{array}{c}
Cl \\
| \\
Cl-C-F \\
| \\
Cl
\end{array}
+ H-Cl
$$

$$
\begin{array}{c}
Cl \\
| \\
Cl-C-F \\
| \\
Cl
\end{array}
+ H-F \xrightarrow{SbF_5}
\begin{array}{c}
F \\
| \\
Cl-C-F \\
| \\
Cl
\end{array}
+ H-Cl
$$

Addition Reactions

An **addition reaction** *is one in which an atom or molecule is added to an unsaturated molecule and increases the saturation of the molecule.* A common type of addition reaction is hydrogenation. In *hydrogenation*, one or more hydrogen atoms are added to an unsaturated molecule. Vegetable oils contain unsaturated fatty acids, long chains of carbon atoms with many double bonds. The following equation shows just one portion of an oil molecule. When hydrogen gas is blown through an oil, hydrogen atoms may add to the double bonds in the oil molecule.

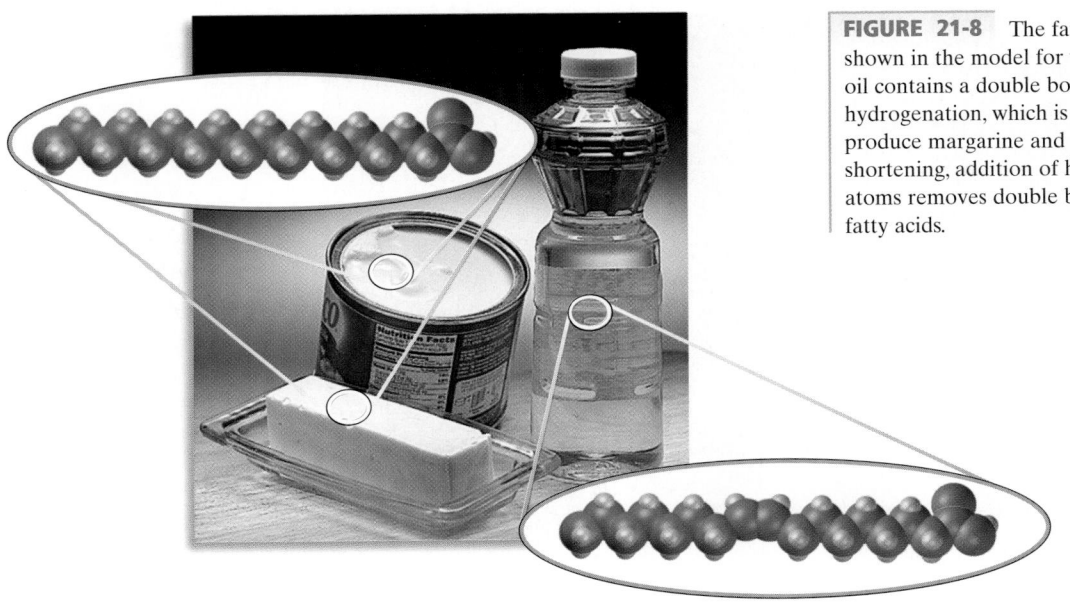

FIGURE 21-8 The fatty acid shown in the model for vegetable oil contains a double bond. During hydrogenation, which is used to produce margarine and vegetable shortening, addition of hydrogen atoms removes double bonds from fatty acids.

Application

Hydrogenation can be carefully controlled to produce a product of almost any consistency, from a liquid to a brittle solid. Hydrogenation of vegetable oils produces products such as margarine and cooking fats, which are easy to package and store. Research indicates, however, that there are health problems associated with diets high in saturated fats.

✔ Teaching Tip

Elimination reactions can occur with groups other than the hydroxyl group. For example, the elimination of a hydrogen halide from an alkyl halide is a common and important industrial reaction.

$$\begin{pmatrix} H & H & H & H & H & H & H \\ | & | & | & | & | & | & | \\ \!\!-C\!-\!C\!=\!C\!-\!C\!=\!C\!-\!C\!- \\ | & & | & & | \\ H & & H & & H \end{pmatrix} + H_2 \xrightarrow{\text{catalyst}} \begin{pmatrix} H & H & H & H & H & H & H \\ | & | & | & | & | & | & | \\ \!\!-C\!-\!C\!=\!C\!-\!C\!-\!C\!-\!C\!-\!C\!- \\ | & & | & | & | & | \\ H & & H & H & H & H \end{pmatrix}$$

The molecule still consists of long chains of carbon atoms, but it contains far fewer double bonds. The conversion of these double bonds to single bonds changes the material from an oil, which is a liquid, into a fat, which is a solid. When you see the word *hydrogenated* on a food product, you know that an oil has been converted to a fat by this process. Examples of an oil and hydrogenated fats are shown in Figure 21-8.

Condensation Reactions

A **condensation reaction** *is one in which two molecules or parts of the same molecule combine.* A small molecule, such as water, is usually removed during the reaction. An example is the reaction between two amino acids, which contain both amine and carboxyl groups. One hydrogen from the amine group of one amino acid combines with the hydroxyl from the carboxyl group of the other amino acid to form a molecule of water. When repeated many times, this reaction forms a protein molecule.

$$\underset{\text{amino acid}}{\text{H}-\text{N}-\overset{\text{H}}{\underset{R}{\text{C}}}-\overset{\text{O}}{\text{C}}-\text{OH}} + \underset{\text{amino acid}}{\text{H}-\text{N}-\overset{\text{H}}{\underset{R'}{\text{C}}}-\overset{\text{O}}{\text{C}}-\text{OH}} \longrightarrow \underset{\text{dipeptide}}{\text{H}-\text{N}-\overset{\text{H}}{\underset{R}{\text{C}}}-\overset{\text{O}}{\text{C}}-\text{N}-\overset{\text{H}}{\underset{R'}{\text{C}}}-\overset{\text{O}}{\text{C}}-\text{OH}} + \underset{\text{water}}{\text{H}_2\text{O}}$$

HANDBOOK  CONNECTION

The uses of H_2SO_4 as a dehydrating agent are also discussed with Group 16 of the *Elements Handbook*.

FIGURE 21-9 Sucrose is dehydrated when it reacts with concentrated sulfuric acid. Elimination of water produces a compound that is mostly carbon.

Elimination Reactions

*An **elimination reaction** is one in which a simple molecule, such as water or ammonia, is removed from adjacent carbon atoms of a larger molecule.* A simple example of an elimination reaction is the heating of ethanol in the presence of concentrated sulfuric acid. Under these conditions, a hydrogen atom bonded to one carbon atom and a hydroxyl group bonded to the second carbon atom are removed from the ethanol molecule. The hydrogen atom and hydroxyl group combine to form a molecule of water.

$$H-\underset{\underset{H}{|}}{\overset{\overset{H}{|}}{C}}-\underset{\underset{H}{|}}{\overset{\overset{OH}{|}}{C}}-H \xrightarrow[\triangle]{H_2SO_4} H-\underset{\underset{H}{|}}{C}=\underset{\underset{H}{|}}{C}-H + H_2O$$

ethanol   ethene   water

Another example of an elimination reaction is the dehydration of sucrose with concentrated sulfuric acid, shown in Figure 21-9.

SECTION REVIEW

1. No; addition can occur only on a double or triple bond. Ethane is a saturated hydrocarbon with neither.

2. increase

3. The water molecule comes from a hydrogen atom on the amine group and a hydroxyl group on the carboxyl group of the acid.

4. An elimination reaction results in the formation of double bonds (a decrease in saturation), while an addition reaction results in the loss of double bonds (an increase in saturation).

SECTION REVIEW

1. Can an addition reaction occur between chlorine and ethane? Why or why not?

2. Does an addition reaction increase or decrease the saturation of a molecule?

3. What functional groups does the molecule of water come from in the condensation reaction between two amino acids?

4. Explain how elimination reactions could be considered the opposite of addition reactions.

Polymers

Polymers *are large molecules made of many small units joined to each other through organic reactions. The small units are* **monomers.** *A polymer can be made from identical or different monomers. A polymer made from two or more different monomers is a* **copolymer.**

Polymers are all around us. The foods we eat and clothes we wear are made of polymers. Some of the most common natural polymers include starch, cellulose, and proteins. Some synthetic polymers may be familiar to you as plastics and synthetic fibers.

Polymer Thermal Properties and Structure

Polymers can be classified by the way they behave when heated. *A* **thermoplastic polymer** *melts when heated and can be reshaped many times. A* **thermosetting polymer** *does not melt when heated but keeps its original shape.* The thermal properties of polymers can be explained by whether their structure is linear, branched, or cross-linked, as shown in Figure 21-10.

The molecules of a *linear polymer* are free to move. They slide back and forth against each other easily when heated. So, linear polymers are thermoplastic. The molecules of a *branched polymer* contain side chains that prevent the molecules from sliding across each other easily. However, branched polymers are still likely to be thermoplastic. In *cross-linked polymers,* adjacent molecules in the polymer have formed bonds with each other. Individual molecules are not able to slide past each other when heated. Cross-linked polymers retain their shape when heated and are thermosetting polymers.

OBJECTIVES

- Explain the relationship between monomers and polymers.

- Describe how the differences in the general structures of linear, branched, and cross-linked polymers contribute to their properties.

- Identify the two main types of polymers and the basic reaction mechanisms by which they are made.

- Relate the structures of specific polymers to their properties and uses.

internetconnect

SC**I**INKS
NSTA

TOPIC: Polymers
GO TO: www.scilinks.org
sciLINKS CODE: HC2216

FIGURE 21-10 Compare structures of the three types of polymers. Linear polymers are free to slide. Branched and cross-linked polymers are inhibited.

Lesson Starter
Illustrate the formation of a polymer from monomers by using paper clips. Show how linear, branched, and cross-linked polymers can all be made by combining monomers (paper clips) with each other in different ways. Use different sizes and colors of paper clips to demonstrate copolymers.

Reading Skill-Builder

DISCUSSION Have students refer to the list of products from organic compounds. Discuss which products are examples of polymers. Students may be surprised to learn that polymers include plastics, rubbers, fabrics, and paints.

Linear   Side chain   **Branched**   **Cross-linked**

Ask students to identify the critical feature of the ethene molecule *(the double bond)* that makes addition polymerization possible. Point out that in this polymerization reaction, ethene molecules are added to the double bond of other ethene molecules. It might help to show a hypothetical polymerization-reaction equation with only two molecules. (The actual reaction involves radicals.)

$$CH_2=CH_2 + CH_2=CH_2 \longrightarrow$$
$$\{CH_2-CH_2-CH_2-CH_2\}$$

Visual Strategy

FIGURE 21-11 Show students a juice bottle like the one shown in the figure. Have them look on the bottom to note the recycling symbol with the number 2 in it and the letters "HDPE" below it. Type-2 plastics are commonly recycled. Have students hypothesize as to why this type of polymer is more easily recyclable than other types, such as cross-linked polyethylene (cPE).

Addition Polymers

An **addition polymer** *is a polymer formed by chain addition reactions between monomers that contain a double bond.* For example, molecules of ethene can polymerize with each other to form polyethene, commonly called polyethylene.

$$n\ CH_2=CH_2 \xrightarrow{\text{catalyst}} \{CH_2-CH_2\}_n$$

ethene   polyethylene

The letter n shows that the addition reaction can be repeated multiple times to form a polymer n monomers long. In fact, this reaction can be repeated hundreds or thousands of times.

Forms of Polyethylene and Related Polymers

Various forms of polyethylene, shown in Figure 21-11, have different molecular structures. High-density polyethylene (HDPE) is a linear polymer. It has a high density because linear molecules can pack together closely. One use of HDPE is in plastic containers such as milk and juice bottles because HDPE tends to remain stiff and rigid.

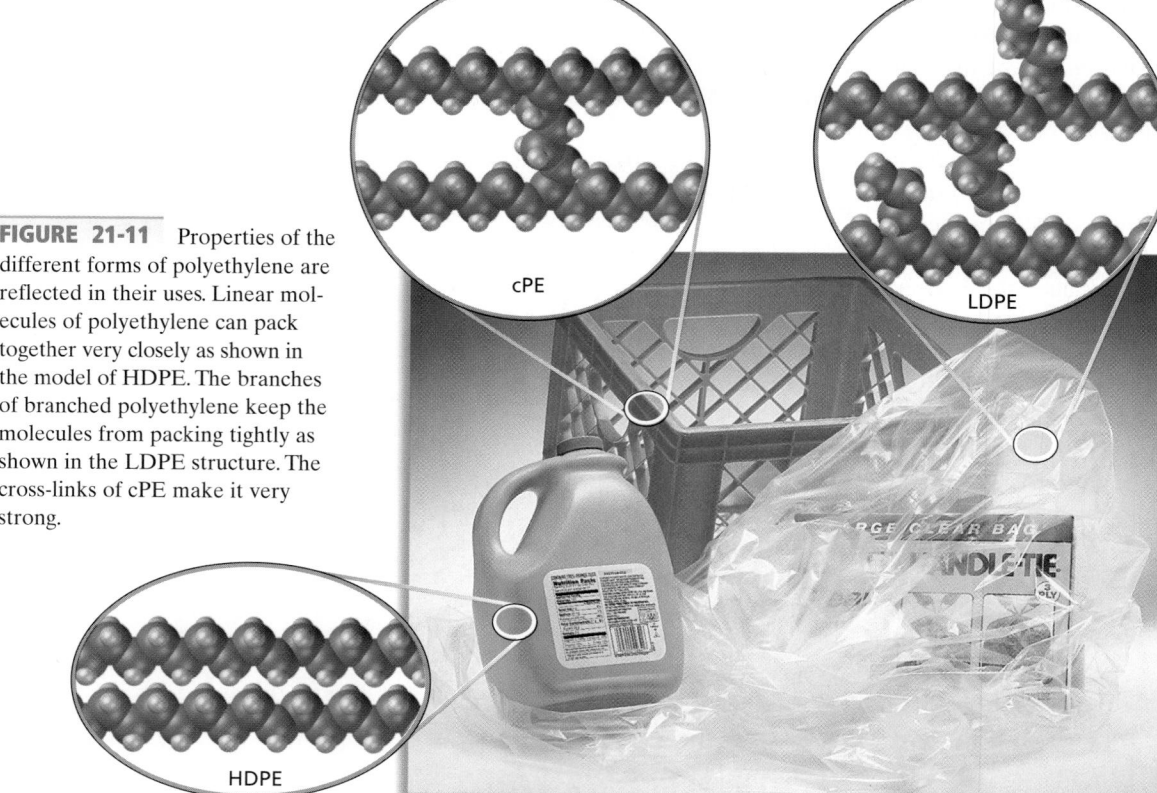

FIGURE 21-11 Properties of the different forms of polyethylene are reflected in their uses. Linear molecules of polyethylene can pack together very closely as shown in the model of HDPE. The branches of branched polyethylene keep the molecules from packing tightly as shown in the LDPE structure. The cross-links of cPE make it very strong.

TABLE 21-8 *Some Addition Polymers*

Monomer structure	Monomer name	Polymer name	Typical use
$CH_2=CH-CH_3$	propylene	polypropylene	plastic bottles
$CH_2=CH-Cl$	vinyl chloride	polyvinyl chloride (PVC)	piping
$CH_2=CH-CN$	acrylonitrile	polyacrylonitrile	fabrics
$CH_2=CH-\bigcirc$	styrene	polystyrene	insulation
$CH_2=CH-O-\overset{\displaystyle O}{\overset{\displaystyle \|}{C}}-CH_3$	vinyl acetate	polyvinyl acetate	adhesives, paints

If ethylene is heated to about 200°C at pressures above 200 atmospheres, random branching of the molecule chains may occur during polymerization. Branches form when hydrogen atoms are removed from the molecule and ethylene molecules add at these locations. Branched-chain molecules are not able to cluster as closely together as are linear molecules. Thus, the density of branched-chain polyethylene is less than that of linear polyethylene. The branched-chain form of polyethylene is known as low-density polyethylene (LDPE). LDPE tends to be less rigid than HDPE and is used, for example, in plastic bags.

When hydrogen atoms are removed from polyethylene molecules, two adjacent molecule chains may bond with each other. This forms a cross-link between the two molecules. Cross-linked polyethylene (sometimes called cPE) is even tougher and more rigid than HDPE. It is used for objects that need to be very strong.

Addition polymers similar to polyethylene can be made by substituting an atom or group of atoms for a hydrogen atom in ethene to form the monomer. Table 21-8 lists examples of these addition polymers.

Polystyrene, a polymer found in this table, is another example of a polymer whose properties can be altered. Pure polystyrene can be melted and molded for use in clear plastic cold-drink cups. Or it can be formed into tiny beads and then soaked in a low-boiling-point liquid, such as pentane. When this mixture is heated, the liquid vaporizes, expands, and forms tiny bubbles within the polystyrene. The product of this reaction is an opaque white material used to make hot-drink cups. Figure 21-12 shows the two types of polystyrene cups.

FIGURE 21-12 Both of these cups are made of polystyrene. Depending on how it is processed, polystyrene can be either flexible or rigid and brittle.

Did You Know?

The orientation of side groups on linear polymers affects their melting points. In the case of vinyl polymers, for example, a molecule in which all side groups are on the same side of the chain (the isotactic form) has the highest melting point; one in which the side groups alternate regularly from side to side (the syndiotactic form) has an intermediate melting point; and one in which the side groups alternate irregularly from side to side (the atactic form) has the lowest melting point.

TABLE STRATEGY

Table 21-8 Assume that any monomer with the structure $CH_2=CH-X$ can polymerize. Have students write the chemical formula for X in each of the monomers shown in the table.

Common Misconception

Cups for hot drinks are often incorrectly referred to as Styrofoam cups. The correct term is molded expanded polystyrene. STYROFOAM is a trademark of The Dow Chemical Company.

FIGURE 21-13 A rubber tree secretes latex, which is a suspension of rubber particles in water. When the rubber particles are precipitated, a gooey, sticky mass forms. An idealized model of natural rubber is shown in this figure.

Natural and Synthetic Rubber

Natural rubber is produced by the rubber tree, *Hevea brasiliensis*, shown in Figure 21-13. It is formed as the result of an addition reaction. The monomer in this reaction is 2-methyl-1,3-butadiene, commonly called isoprene.

$$2n \quad \begin{array}{c} H \\ \\ H \end{array}\!\!\!\!\!\!\!\!\!\!\!\! \begin{array}{c} CH_3 \\ C{=}C \\ \quad C{=}C \\ H \quad\quad H \end{array}\!\!\!\!\!\!\!\!\!\! \begin{array}{c} H \\ \\ \end{array} \xrightarrow[\text{polymerization}]{\text{addition}} \left(\!\!\!\begin{array}{c} CH_2 \quad\quad CH_2{-}CH_2 \quad\quad CH_2 \\ C{=}C \quad\quad\quad\quad C{=}C \\ CH_3 \quad H \quad CH_3 \quad H \end{array}\!\!\!\right)_{\!n}$$

isoprene   polyisoprene

Natural rubber has relatively few practical applications. When warmed, individual molecules of polyisoprene slide easily back and forth past each other. The rubber gets soft and gooey, making it useless for many purposes.

A process for converting natural rubber into a useful commercial product was accidentally discovered by Charles Goodyear in 1839. Goodyear found that the addition of sulfur to molten rubber produces a material that remains very hard and tough when cooled. He called this process vulcanization. **Vulcanization** *is a cross-linking process between adjacent polyisoprene molecules that occurs when the molecules are heated with sulfur atoms.* Sulfur atoms bond to a carbon atom in one molecule and a second carbon atom in a second molecule, forming a cross-link between the two molecules. This is shown in the model in Figure 21-14. Vulcanization enabled rubber to be used in a wide variety of products, such as hoses, rainwear, and tires.

In the first year of World War II, Japan controlled large portions of Southeast Asia, where most of the world's natural rubber is obtained. The United States and other Allied nations were forced to develop

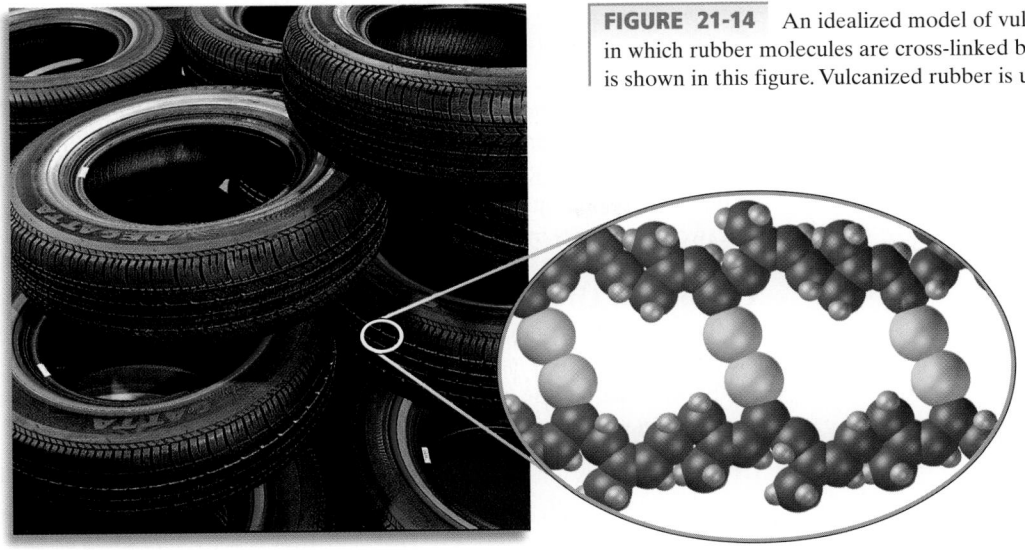

FIGURE 21-14 An idealized model of vulcanized rubber, in which rubber molecules are cross-linked by sulfur atoms, is shown in this figure. Vulcanized rubber is used in tires.

FIGURE 21-14 An idealized model of vulcanized rubber, in which rubber molecules are cross-linked by sulfur atoms, is shown in this figure. Vulcanized rubber is used in tires.

✔**Teaching Tip**

• Have students locate the three 1,3-butadiene monomers in the SBR structural formula. Ask them to compare the placement of double bonds of both SBR monomers before and after polymerization.

• The presence of chlorine in neoprene makes the product more resistant to oils, greases, and other hydrocarbon solvents.

Application

After World War II, the demand for natural rubber went into sharp decline as synthetic rubbers with superior properties were invented. That pattern changed in the early 1970s because of reduced availability of petroleum, from which synthetic rubbers are made; a large increase in the amount of land planted with rubber trees; and changes in tire technology that called for natural rather than synthetic rubbers. Today, SBR rubber makes up about 26% of the rubber market of the United States, and natural rubber makes up about 30%.

synthetic substitutes for natural rubber. Some synthetic rubbers have superior properties to natural rubber. Styrene-butadiene rubber, SBR, is a copolymer made in the reaction between styrene and butadiene, as shown below. SBR is used primarily in tires.

1,3-butadiene   styrene

styrene-butadiene rubber (SBR)

Another substitute, neoprene, is formed during the polymerization of 2-chlorobutadiene. Notice that 2-chlorobutadiene is identical to isoprene, the monomer of natural rubber, except for the presence of a chlorine atom in place of a methyl group on the number 2 carbon atom.

2-chlorobutadiene   isoprene

Condensation Polymers

A **condensation polymer** *is a polymer formed by condensation reactions.* Monomers of condensation polymers must contain two functional groups. This allows each monomer to link with two other monomers by condensation reactions. Condensation polymers are usually copolymers with two monomers in an alternating order.

Nylon and the Polyamides

One example of a condensation polymer is shown below. A carboxylic acid with two carboxyl groups, adipic acid, and an amine with two amine groups, hexanediamine, react with each other through the elimination of a molecule of water.

$$n \text{ H}-\overset{\overset{\displaystyle \text{H}}{|}}{\text{N}}-\text{CH}_2-\text{CH}_2-\text{CH}_2-\text{CH}_2-\text{CH}_2-\text{CH}_2-\overset{\overset{\displaystyle \text{H}}{|}}{\text{N}}-\text{H} + n \text{ HO}-\overset{\overset{\displaystyle \text{O}}{\|}}{\text{C}}-\text{CH}_2-\text{CH}_2-\text{CH}_2-\text{CH}_2-\overset{\overset{\displaystyle \text{O}}{\|}}{\text{C}}-\text{OH} \longrightarrow$$

hexanediamine　　　　　　　　　　　　　　　　　　　　　adipic acid

$$\left(-\overset{\overset{\displaystyle \text{H}}{|}}{\text{N}}-\text{CH}_2-\text{CH}_2-\text{CH}_2-\text{CH}_2-\text{CH}_2-\text{CH}_2-\overset{\overset{\displaystyle \text{H}}{|}}{\text{N}}-\overset{\overset{\displaystyle \text{O}}{\|}}{\text{C}}-\text{CH}_2-\text{CH}_2-\text{CH}_2-\text{CH}_2-\overset{\overset{\displaystyle \text{O}}{\|}}{\text{C}}-\right)_n + n \text{ H}_2\text{O}$$

nylon 66　　　　　　　　　　　　　　　　　　　　　water

This reaction is shown in Figure 21-15. The product contains two kinds of monomers, the adipic acid monomer and the hexanediamine monomer. This copolymer is known as nylon 66 because each of the monomers contains six carbon atoms. Nylon 66 was invented by Dr. Wallace Carothers in 1935 and is one of the most widely used of all synthetic polymers.

FIGURE 21-15 Nylon 66, shown here being wound onto a stirring rod, is produced from the polymerization of adipic acid (the top layer) and hexanediamine (the bottom layer).

Nylon 66 is an example of a polyamide polymer. The word *polyamide* comes from the presence of the amide group in the polymer. The structure of the amide group is shown below.

Polyamides have become commercial successes because they can be fabricated into so many different forms. For example, they can be knitted and woven, like natural fibers, to make stockings and other types of clothing. When polyamides are treated with radiation, extensive cross-linking occurs and the final product becomes very rigid and strong. One product made in this way, Kevlar, is so strong that it is used in the manufacture of bullet-proof vests used by police officers.

Polyester

Polyesters are another common type of condensation polymer. Polyethylene terephthalate, PET, is a polyester formed when terephthalic acid reacts with ethylene glycol.

$n\,OH-CH_2-CH_2-OH \;+\; n\,HO-\overset{\displaystyle O}{\overset{\|}{C}}-\!\!\left\langle\text{benzene ring}\right\rangle\!\!-\overset{\displaystyle O}{\overset{\|}{C}}-OH \longrightarrow$

ethylene glycol   terephthalic acid

$\left(\!-O-CH_2-CH_2-O-\overset{\displaystyle O}{\overset{\|}{C}}-\!\!\left\langle\text{benzene ring}\right\rangle\!\!-\overset{\displaystyle O}{\overset{\|}{C}}-\!\right)_{\!n} \;+\; n\,H_2O$

PET   water

PET has a vast range of uses, such as in tires, photographic film, food packaging, and bottles. Its best known use may be as a fiber called polyester, which is widely used in permanent-press clothing. Polyester fabric is made wrinkle resistant by the cross-linking of its polymer strands. Polyester thread is shown in Figure 21-16.

FIGURE 21-16 This thread is made from polyester.

SECTION REVIEW

1. Would the handles of cookware more likely be made of a thermosetting polymer or a thermoplastic polymer? Why?

2. Would it be possible to have an addition polymer synthesized from a monomer that has only single bonds? Why or why not?

3. Make a simple diagram showing how the structure of a soft, pliable polyethylene differs from the structure of the form that is the most rigid and stiff.

4. Why can a molecule with only one functional group *not* undergo a condensation reaction to form a polymer?

Alternative Assessment
- Ask students to locate the structure of 1,4-benzenedicarboxylic acid. *(It is the IUPAC name for terephthalic acid, a reactant in the polyester reaction.)*

- Have students locate the ester functional group in the portion of the polyester molecule, PET, shown on this page.

SECTION REVIEW

1. These handles are likely to be made of thermosetting plastics because heat from a stove might soften or even melt a thermoplastic polymer.

2. No; double bonds are required for addition reactions.

3. Diagrams should be similar to those of branched and cross-linked polymers in Figure 21-10.

4. When a molecule with a single functional group takes part in the first step of a condensation reaction, no functional groups remain in the product to continue the reaction.

Class Discussion

Ask students to name other composites that have properties more desirable than the properties of each of their components. Responses might include reinforced steel, fiberglass, or one of the many new materials used in sports equipment such as tennis rackets and ice-skate blades.

DEMONSTRATION

How Many Holes?

Blow up a mylar balloon and a regular balloon. If possible, use helium. Tie each balloon securely so that gas does not escape from the neck. Observe the balloons for several days, and have students explain why the mylar balloon stays inflated longer than the regular balloon does.

✔ Teaching Tip

When liquid crystals melt, they lose their structure in only one or two dimensions, not in all three dimensions as a regular solid would.

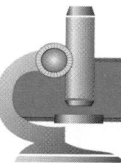

High-Barrier Plastics

Flat-tasting soda? Technology comes to the rescue. No matter how tightly the cap is sealed on a bottle, soda loses fizz over time. Because of the nature of plastic, the carbon dioxide gas actually escapes through the bottle. Benny Freeman, an associate professor of chemical engineering at North Carolina State University, has discovered how to stop this problem with a special kind of plastic called a liquid crystalline polymer.

According to Freeman, the long molecules that make up plastics do not fit together tightly. Instead, the plastic molecules are constantly moving and opening gaps between them similar to the spaces between noodles in a bowl of cooked spaghetti. Gas molecules can pass through these gaps. In a soda bottle, the carbon dioxide in the soft drink dissolves into the plastic and escapes into the air outside the bottle. Conversely, plastic containers also allow oxygen to seep inside them, which can spoil the food they hold.

Liquid crystal polymers, or LCPs, are made up of long molecules, like other plastics are. But, says Freeman, the molecules in an LCP are much straighter, and they all point in the same general direction. Instead of looking like a bowl of cooked pasta, LCP molecules more closely resemble a box of uncooked spaghetti packed tightly together. Because

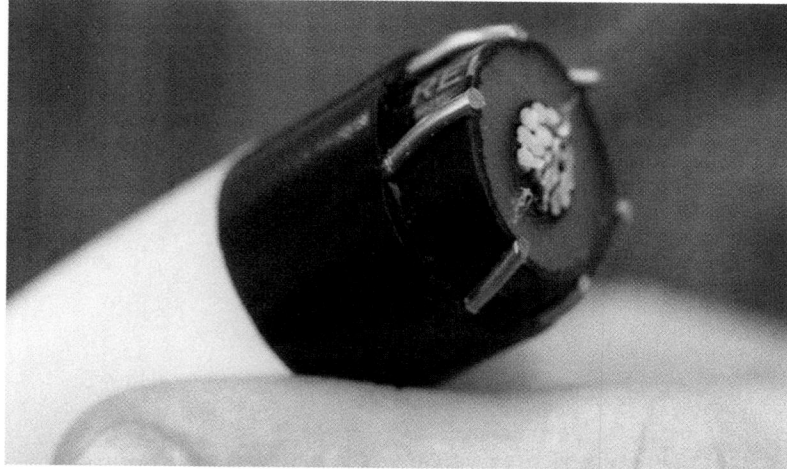

The LCP layer (white) of this power cable makes the cable waterproof.

it is much more difficult for gas molecules to squeeze through them, LCPs make an ideal material for manufacturing containers.

Aside from keeping soft drinks fresh, these high-barrier plastics could also replace glass packaging for foods that easily become stale or spoiled from contact with oxygen. That would result in much lighter, unbreakable containers. Gas tanks made from LCPs would better prevent harmful fumes from leaking out and polluting the environment. The liquid crystal polymer could also be used as a protectant to line underground electrical cables, making them virtually waterproof and corrosion-free. LCPs are currently used to line the breathing system of NASA's new spacesuits.

Liquid crystal polymers have not yet made it into the packaging of everyday products because they are several times more expensive than regular plastics. Freeman thinks that this problem could be solved by creating what he calls a composite structure: a combination of regular plastic and the liquid crystal polymer. By sandwiching a thin LCP layer between two pieces of regular plastic, manufacturers could keep their costs down and still keep your soda fizzy.

"We are," says Freeman, "at the beginning of really understanding where you can start to manipulate structure and actually control properties in these materials. There's still a lot of uncharted territory in the science of these materials."

CHAPTER 21 REVIEW

CHAPTER SUMMARY

21-1
- A functional group is an atom or group of atoms responsible for the properties of the organic compound which contains the functional group.
- Systematic names of organic compounds indicate the type and position of functional groups present.
- Alcohols contain the hydroxyl functional group. Their tendency to form hydrogen bonds affects their properties and uses.
- In alkyl halides, one or more hydrogen atoms of an alkane have been replaced by one or more halogen atoms. One class of alkyl halides, the CFCs, has many important industrial uses but may cause serious environmental problems.
- Two alkyl groups are joined to an oxygen atom in ethers. Generally unreactive, they are widely used as solvents.
- The physical and chemical properties of organic classes often reflect the ability or inability of molecules in each class to form hydrogen bonds.

Vocabulary

alcohols (663)	alkyl halides (666)	ethers (669)	functional group (663)

21-2
- Aldehydes and ketones both contain the carbonyl group and are responsible for some odors and flavors. In aldehydes, the carbonyl group is attached to the first carbon atom of a carbon-atom chain. In ketones, it is in the middle of a carbon-atom chain.
- Carboxylic acids contain carboxyl groups. They act as weak acids in aqueous solutions.
- In esters, the hydrogen atom of a carboxylic acid group has been replaced with an alkyl group. Natural and synthetic esters give many foods their flavors and odors.
- Amines are derivatives of ammonia in which one or more hydrogen atoms are replaced by one or more alkyl groups. They behave as weak bases in aqueous solutions.

Vocabulary

aldehydes (672)	carboxylic acids (674)	ketones (672)	secondary amine (677)
amines (677)	esters (675)	primary amine (677)	tertiary amine (677)

21-3
- Both addition and substitution reactions add atoms to a molecule. In substitution reactions, an atom or group of atoms is replaced. In addition reactions, an atom or group of atoms is added to a double or triple bond.
- A small molecule is usually removed during both condensation reactions and elimination reactions. In a condensation reaction, two molecules or parts of the same molecule combine. In an elimination reaction, a large molecule eliminates a small molecule.

Vocabulary

addition reaction (682)	condensation reaction (683)	elimination reaction (684)	substitution reaction (682)

REVIEW ANSWERS

1. **a.** $R-OH$
   b. $R-O-R'$
   c. $R-X$

2. Water; the higher boiling point indicates that it has more hydrogen bonds that must be broken for the liquid to boil.

3. **a.** It tends to absorb water.
   b. It has three hydroxyl groups that can each form a hydrogen bond with water.

4. Answers will vary. Possible answers include: gasohol reduces use of petroleum and burns more cleanly, but it is a less efficient fuel than gasoline.

5. Chlorine atoms formed by the breakdown of CFCs in the atmosphere attack ozone molecules and reduce them to normal oxygen. Ozone protects Earth from harmful UV radiation.

6. In alcohols, an oxygen atom is bonded to one carbon atom and one hydrogen atom. In ethers, an oxygen atom is bonded to two carbon atoms.

7. Ethers are used as solvents because they tend to be unreactive.

8. **a.**
$$R-\overset{\overset{\displaystyle O}{\|}}{C}-OH$$
   b.
$$R-\overset{\overset{\displaystyle O}{\|}}{C}-R'$$
   c.
$$R-\overset{\overset{\displaystyle O}{\|}}{C}-OH$$
   d.
$$R-\overset{\overset{\displaystyle O}{\|}}{C}-O-R'$$
   e. $R-\underset{\underset{\displaystyle R'}{|}}{N}-R''$

9. In aldehydes, the carbonyl group is at the end of a carbon-atom chain. In ketones, it occurs on a carbon atom within the chain.

10. a. cinnamon
 b. aldehydes

11. Three of the four bonds on the carboxyl carbon are used in forming the functional group, leaving only a single bond with which to bond to other carbon atoms.

12. *See page 699A.*

13. Esters contain carboxylic acid groups in which the hydrogen of the hydroxyl group has been replaced by an alkyl group.

14. nitrogen

15. The unshared pair of electrons on the nitrogen atom in an amine attracts protons from water molecules, leaving OH^- ions in solution.

16. *See page 699B.*

17. aldehydes, ketones, carboxylic acids, esters, and amines

18. alcohols, ethers, aldehydes, ketones, carboxylic acids, and esters

19. addition

20. one; two

21. In a substitution reaction, an atom or group of atoms replaces a hydrogen atom in a molecule. In an addition reaction, an atom or group of atoms adds to a double or triple bond, forming single bonds.

22. Hexane is already fully saturated and cannot accept additional hydrogen atoms.

23. condensation

24. decrease

25. Answers will vary. Answers may include starch, cellulose, and natural rubber; polyethylene, SBR, and nylon.

26. They are thermosetting plastics, so they will not melt when the engine gets hot.

CHAPTER SUMMARY continued

21-4 • Polymers are large molecules made of many repeating units called monomers. A copolymer consists of two or more different monomers.
 • Thermosetting polymers cannot be melted once they are formed. Thermoplastic polymers can be melted more than once.
 • The physical properties of polymers are strongly influenced by the presence or absence of branching and cross-linking among polymer chains.

• Addition reactions require that the monomers contain a double bond. Polyethylene and related polymers as well as natural and synthetic rubbers involve addition polymerization.
• Monomers of condensation polymers must contain two functional groups. Nylon 66, other polyamides, and polyesters are condensation polymers.

Vocabulary

addition polymer (686)	copolymer (685)
condensation polymer (690)	monomers (685)

polymers (685)	thermosetting polymer (685)
thermoplastic polymer (685)	vulcanization (688)

REVIEWING CONCEPTS

1. Write the general formula for each of the following:
 a. alcohol
 b. ether
 c. alkyl halide (21-1)

2. Based on the boiling points of water and methanol, in which would you expect to observe a greater degree of hydrogen bonding? Explain your answer. (21-1)

3. a. Why is glycerol used in moisturizing skin lotions?
 b. How does this relate to the chemical structure of glycerol? (21-1)

4. State two advantages and one disadvantage of using gasohol as an automotive fuel. (21-1)

5. Why are CFCs regarded as an environmental hazard? (21-1)

6. Alcohols and ethers are both organic compounds that contain oxygen. Explain how their chemical structures differ. (22-1)

7. What is the important chemical property of ethers that leads to their most common use? (21-1)

8. Write the general formula for each of the following:
 a. aldehyde **d.** ester
 b. ketone **e.** amine
 c. carboxylic acid (21-2)

9. Aldehydes and ketones both contain the same functional group. Why are they classified as separate classes of organic compounds? (21-2)

10. a. Cinnamaldehyde is responsible for what odor?
 b. The IUPAC name for cinnamaldehyde is 3-phenyl-2-propenal. Based on its names, to which class of compounds does it belong? (21-2)

11. Why can a carboxyl group not be in the middle of a carbon-atom chain? (21-2)

12. a. Show the reaction that occurs when carboxylic acids are dissolved in water.
 b. What property of carboxylic acids does this reaction illustrate? (21-2)

13. How are esters related to carboxylic acids? (21-2)

14. What element do amines contain besides carbon and hydrogen? (21-2)

15. Explain why an amine acts as a base. (21-2)

16. Show the reaction that occurs when aqueous solutions of carboxylic acids and amines are mixed. (21-2)

17. Name five classes of organic compounds that are often responsible for odors and flavors. (21-2)

18. What classes of organic compounds contain oxygen? (21-1 and 21-2)

19. What type of chemical reaction would you expect to occur between 2-octene and hydrogen bromide, HBr? (21-3)

20. How many molecules of chlorine, Cl_2, can be added to a molecule of 1-propene? a molecule of 1-propyne? (21-3)

21. Compare substitution and addition reactions. (21-3)

22. What problems would you expect to encounter in trying to hydrogenate hexane, C_6H_{14}? (21-3)

23. In a chemical reaction, two small molecules are joined and a water molecule is produced. What type of reaction took place? (21-3)

24. Do elimination reactions increase or decrease the saturation of a molecule? (21-3)

25. Name three common natural products and three synthetic products made of polymers. (21-4)

26. Some automobile engine parts are made of polymers. Do you think these polymers are thermosetting or thermoplastic? Explain your answer. (21-4)

27. Classify each of the following as thermosetting or thermoplastic:
a. linear polymer
b. branched polymer
c. cross-linked polymer (21-4)

28. What are two reactions by which polymers can be formed? (21-4)

29. What is the structural requirement for a molecule to be a monomer in an addition polymer? (21-4)

30. Explain the structural molecular differences between the following three types of polyethylene: HDPE, LDPE, and cPE. (21-4)

31. What is the primary structural difference between polyethylene and polystyrene? (21-4)

32. Give a molecular explanation for the fact that natural rubber melts when it is heated but vulcanized rubber does not. (21-4)

33. How is the molecular structure of neoprene different from that of natural rubber? (21-4)

34. Could ethanoic acid be used as a monomer in a condensation polymer? Why or why not? (21-4)

35. Draw the structural formula for the amide group. (21-4)

36. Why is polyester wrinkle resistant? (21-4)

PROBLEMS

Organic Compound Nomenclature

37. Name the following alcohols:
a. CH_3-OH

b.
$$CH_3-\overset{\overset{\displaystyle OH}{|}}{C}H-CH_2-OH$$

c.
$$CH_3-\overset{\overset{\displaystyle OH}{|}}{C}H-CH_2-CH_3$$

d.
$$CH_3-CH_2-CH_2-CH_2-\overset{\overset{\displaystyle OH}{|}}{C}H-CH_3$$

38. Draw condensed structures for each of the following alcohols:
a. 2,3-pentanediol   c. 1,2,3-propanetriol
b. 1-pentanol   d. ethanol

39. Name the following alkyl halides. (Hint: See Sample Problem 21-1.)
a. CH_3-I

b. $Cl-CH_2-CH_2-Cl$

c.
$$CH_3-\overset{\overset{\displaystyle I}{|}}{\underset{\underset{\displaystyle I}{|}}{C}}-\overset{\overset{\displaystyle Br}{|}}{\underset{\underset{\displaystyle Br}{|}}{C}}-CH_3$$

d.
$$CH_3-CH_2-\overset{\overset{\displaystyle Br}{|}}{\underset{\underset{\displaystyle Br}{|}}{C}}-Br$$

40. Draw condensed structures for each of the following alkyl halides:
a. 2,3,4-trichloropentane
b. 1,1-diiodopropane
c. 1-fluorohexane
d. 2,2-dichloro-1,1-difluoropropane

41. Name the following ethers. (Hint: See Sample Problem 21-2.)
a. $CH_3-CH_2-CH_2-O-CH_2-CH_2-CH_3$

27. a. thermoplastic
b. probably thermoplastic, but possibly thermosetting
c. thermosetting

28. addition and condensation

29. It must contain a double or a triple bond.

30. HDPE consists of close-packed, linear molecules; LDPE, less densely packed, branched molecules; and cPE, cross-linked molecules.

31. Polystyrene contains a benzene ring in place of one of the hydrogen atoms in polyethylene.

32. Few cross-links occur between adjacent molecules in natural rubber, allowing the molecules to flow smoothly past each other. Vulcanized rubber contains many sulfur-bonded cross-links that prevent the flow of these molecules.

33. The monomer of neoprene contains a chlorine atom in place of the methyl group in isoprene.

34. No; because it contains only one functional group

35.
$$\overset{\overset{\displaystyle O}{\|}}{-C}-NH-$$

36. Its molecules are cross-linked.

37. a. methanol
b. 1,2-propanediol
c. 2-butanol
d. 2-hexanol

38. See page 699B.

39. a. iodomethane
b. 1,2-dichloroethane
c. 2,2-dibromo-3,3-diiodobutane
d. 1,1,1-tribromopropane

40. See page 699B.

41. a. dipropyl ether
b. ethyl methyl ether
c. dibutyl ether
d. butyl ethyl ether

42. *See page 699B.*

43. a. ethanal
   b. pentanal
   c. propanal
   d. butanal

44. *See page 699B.*

45. a. 2-propanone (or propanone)
   b. 2-butanone
   c. 2-pentanone
   d. 3-pentanone

46. *See page 699B.*

47. a. propanoic acid
   b. pentanoic acid
   c. methanoic acid
   d. 1,4-butanedioic acid

48. *See page 699B.*

49. a. methyl ethanoate
   b. methyl methanoate
   c. ethyl propanoate
   d. ethyl pentanoate

50. *See page 699B.*

51. a. methylamine
   b. diethylamine
   c. ethylmethylamine
   d. trimethylamine

52. *See page 699B.*

53. b

54. a

55. c

56. b

57. 137.36 amu

58. a. C_2H_4O
   b. $C_4H_8O_2$

59. pH = 3.03

60. 21.9 mL of ethanol

61. a. −42.9°C
   b. Freezing-point-depression calculations are based on a relationship that holds experimentally only for dilute solutions.

62. a. elimination
   b. elimination
   c. condensation
   d. condensation

696

---

b. $CH_3-O-CH_2-CH_3$

c. $CH_3-CH_2-CH_2-CH_2-O-CH_2-CH_2-CH_2-CH_3$

d. $CH_3-CH_2-O-CH_2-CH_2-CH_2-CH_3$

42. Draw condensed structures for each of the following ethers:
   a. dimethyl ether   **c.** butyl propyl ether
   b. methyl propyl ether   **d.** ethyl heptyl ether

43. Name the following aldehydes:
   a.
$$CH_3-\overset{\overset{\displaystyle O}{\|}}{C}-H$$

   b.
$$CH_3-CH_2-CH_2-CH_2-\overset{\overset{\displaystyle O}{\|}}{C}-H$$

   c.
$$CH_3-CH_2-\overset{\overset{\displaystyle O}{\|}}{C}-H$$

   d.
$$CH_3-CH_2-CH_2-\overset{\overset{\displaystyle O}{\|}}{C}-H$$

44. Draw condensed structures for each of the following aldehydes:
   a. methanal   **c.** octanal
   b. hexanal   **d.** ethanal

45. Name the following ketones:
   a.
$$CH_3-\overset{\overset{\displaystyle O}{\|}}{C}-CH_3$$

   b.
$$CH_3-CH_2-\overset{\overset{\displaystyle O}{\|}}{C}-CH_3$$

   c.
$$CH_3-CH_2-CH_2-\overset{\overset{\displaystyle O}{\|}}{C}-CH_3$$

   d.
$$CH_3-CH_2-\overset{\overset{\displaystyle O}{\|}}{C}-CH_2-CH_3$$

46. Draw condensed structures for each of the following ketones:
   a. 3-hexanone   **c.** 2-octanone
   b. 2-pentanone   **d.** 2-hexanone

47. Name the following carboxylic acids:
   a.
$$CH_3-CH_2-\overset{\overset{\displaystyle O}{\|}}{C}-OH$$

   b.
$$CH_3-CH_2-CH_2-CH_2-\overset{\overset{\displaystyle O}{\|}}{C}-OH$$

---

   c.
$$H-\overset{\overset{\displaystyle O}{\|}}{C}-OH$$

   d.
$$HO-\overset{\overset{\displaystyle O}{\|}}{C}-CH_2-CH_2-\overset{\overset{\displaystyle O}{\|}}{C}-OH$$

48. Draw condensed structures for each of the following carboxylic acids:
   a. butanoic acid   **c.** hexanedioic acid
   b. hexanoic acid   **d.** heptanoic acid

49. Name the following esters:
   a.
$$CH_3-\overset{\overset{\displaystyle O}{\|}}{C}-O-CH_3$$

   b.
$$H-\overset{\overset{\displaystyle O}{\|}}{C}-O-CH_3$$

   c.
$$CH_3-CH_2-\overset{\overset{\displaystyle O}{\|}}{C}-O-CH_2-CH_3$$

   d.
$$CH_3-CH_2-CH_2-CH_2-\overset{\overset{\displaystyle O}{\|}}{C}-O-CH_2-CH_3$$

50. Draw condensed structures for each of the following esters:
   a. butyl ethanoate   **c.** propyl propanoate
   b. ethyl methanoate   **d.** methyl butanoate

51. Name the following amines:
   a. CH_3-NH_2
   b. $CH_3-CH_2-NH-CH_2-CH_3$
   c. $CH_3-CH_2-NH-CH_3$
   d. $CH_3-\underset{\underset{\displaystyle CH_3}{|}}{N}-CH_3$

52. Draw condensed structures for each of the following amines:
   a. butylmethylamine   **c.** diethylmethylamine
   b. ethylamine   **d.** ethylpropylamine

Organic Reactions

53. Which of the following reactions is a substitution reaction?
   a. $CH_2{=}CH_2 + Cl_2 \longrightarrow Cl-CH_2-CH_2-Cl$
   b. $CH_3-CH_2-CH_2-CH_3 + Cl_2 \longrightarrow$
           $Cl-CH_2-CH_2-CH_2-CH_3 + HCl$

c.

$$CH_3-OH + CH_3-\overset{\overset{\displaystyle O}{\|}}{C}-OH \longrightarrow$$

$$CH_3-\overset{\overset{\displaystyle O}{\|}}{C}-O-CH_3 + H_2O$$

54. Which of the following reactions is an addition reaction?

a. $CH_3-CH_2-CH=CH_2 + Br_2 \longrightarrow$
$$CH_3-CH_2-\underset{\underset{\displaystyle Br}{|}}{CH}-CH_2-Br$$

b.
$\xrightarrow[\text{heat}]{85\% \text{ H}_3\text{PO}_4}$ ... $+ H_2O$

c.

$$CH_3-\overset{\overset{\displaystyle O}{\|}}{C}-OH + CH_3-OH \longrightarrow$$

$$CH_3-\overset{\overset{\displaystyle O}{\|}}{C}-O-CH_3 + H_2O$$

55. Which of the following reactions is a condensation reaction?

a.
$$CH_3C\equiv CH + HBr \xrightarrow{\text{ether}} CH_3-\underset{\underset{\displaystyle Br}{|}}{\overset{\overset{\displaystyle Br}{|}}{C}}=CH_2$$

b.
$+ Br_2 \xrightarrow{\text{CCl}_4}$

c.
$$CH_3-CH_2-OH + CH_3-CH_2-OH \xrightarrow{\text{H}_2\text{SO}_4}$$
$$CH_3-CH_2-O-CH_2-CH_3 + H_2O$$

56. Which of the following reactions is an elimination reaction?

a. $CH_2=CH-CH_2-CH_3 + Cl_2 \longrightarrow$
$$Cl-CH_2-\underset{\underset{\displaystyle Cl}{|}}{CH}-CH_2-CH_3$$

b.
$$CH_3-\underset{\underset{\displaystyle OH}{|}}{CH}-CH_3 \xrightarrow{\text{H}_3\text{O}^+}$$
$$CH_3-CH=CH_2 + H_2O$$

c. $CH_3CH_3 + Cl_2 \xrightarrow[\text{heat}]{\text{light or}} CH_3CH_2Cl + HCl$

Calculations with Organic Compounds

57. Calculate the molecular mass of trichloro-fluoromethane.

58. A compound is found to contain 54.5% carbon, 9.1% hydrogen, and 36.4% oxygen.
a. Determine the simplest formula.
b. The molecular mass of this compound is 88.1 g. What is the molecular formula?

59. The hydronium ion concentration in 0.05 M acetic acid is 9.4×10^{-4} mol/L. What is the pH of the solution?

60. What volume of ethanol must be diluted with water to prepare 500. mL of 0.750 M solution? The density of ethanol is given as 0.789 g/mL.

61. 1,2-ethanediol, also called ethylene glycol, is commonly used as an antifreeze. The density of ethylene glycol is 1.432 g/mL.
a. Calculate the theoretical freezing point of the water in a 50% (by volume) solution of ethylene glycol.
b. The actual freezing point of such a solution is about $-37°C$. Account for any difference between this and the value you calculated.

MIXED REVIEW

62. Classify each of the following reactions as an elimination reaction or a condensation reaction:

a.
$$CH_3-\underset{\underset{\displaystyle Br}{|}}{\overset{\overset{\displaystyle Br}{|}}{C}}=CH_2 + NaNH_2 \longrightarrow$$
$$CH_3C\equiv CH + NaBr + NH_3$$

b.
$$CH_3-CH_2-\underset{\underset{\displaystyle OH}{|}}{CH}-CH_3 \xrightarrow[\text{heat}]{85\% \text{ H}_3\text{PO}_4}$$
$$CH_3-CH=CH-CH_3 + H_2O$$

c.
$$CH_3-CH_2-OH + CH_3-\overset{\overset{\displaystyle O}{\|}}{C}-OH \longrightarrow$$
$$CH_3-CH_2-O-\overset{\overset{\displaystyle O}{\|}}{C}-CH_3 + H_2O$$

d.

63. a. 3-hexanone
   b. propyl ethanoate
   c. nonanoic acid
   d. ethyldimethylamine
   e. hexanal
   f. ethyl propyl ether
   g. 3-bromo-1,1-dichlorobutane
   h. cyclohexanol

64. a. substitution
   b. addition
   c. addition
   d. addition

65. *See page 699B.*

66. a. correct
   b. 2,2-dibromopentane
   c. pentyl ethanoate
   d. correct

67. a. condensation
   b. addition
   c. substitution
   d. elimination

68. The presence of ethylene glycol raises the boiling point and lowers the freezing point of the water in the radiator.

69. Yes, because it has twice as many hydroxyl groups.

70. a. $-9.3°C$
   b. $-18.6°C$
   c. $-24.2°C$

Additional answers are found on pages 699A and 699B.

63. Name the following compounds:

a.

$$CH_3-CH_2-CH_2-\overset{\overset{\displaystyle O}{\|}}{C}-CH_2-CH_3$$

b.

$$CH_3-\overset{\overset{\displaystyle O}{\|}}{C}-O-CH_2-CH_2-CH_3$$

c.

$$\begin{array}{c} CH_3 \\ | \\ CH_2 \\ | \\ CH_2-CH_2-CH_2-CH_2-CH_2-CH_2-\overset{\overset{\displaystyle O}{\|}}{C}-OH \end{array}$$

d.

$$\begin{array}{c} CH_3 \\ | \\ CH_3-N-CH_2-CH_3 \end{array}$$

e.

$$CH_3-CH_2-CH_2-CH_2-CH_2-\overset{\overset{\displaystyle O}{\|}}{C}-H$$

f. $CH_3-CH_2-O-CH_2-CH_2-CH_3$

g.

$$\begin{array}{c} \qquad\qquad Cl \\ \qquad\qquad | \\ CH_3-CH-CH_2-CH \\ \quad\;\; | \qquad\qquad | \\ \quad\;\; Br \qquad\qquad Cl \end{array}$$

h.

[cyclohexane ring]—OH

64. Classify each of the following reactions as a substitution reaction or an addition reaction:

a.
$$CH_3-CH_2-CH_2-CH_2-OH + HCl \xrightarrow[\text{heat}]{\text{ZnCl}_2}$$
$$CH_3-CH_2-CH_2-CH_2-Cl + H_2O$$

b. $CH_2{=}CH_2 + HBr \xrightarrow[25°C]{\text{Ether}} CH_3-CH_2-Br$

c. $CH{\equiv}CH + HCl \xrightarrow{\text{HgCl}_2} CH_2{=}CH-Cl$

d.
[cyclohexene with CH₃] + HBr $\xrightarrow{\text{Ether}}$ [cyclohexane with CH₃ and Br]

65. Draw structural formulas for each of the following compounds:
a. 1,2,3-trichloropropane d. propanoic acid
b. 1-butanol e. methyl propanoate
c. ethyl methyl ether f. triethylamine

66. For each of the following, determine if the compound is named correctly. If it is not, give the correct name.

a.
$$\begin{array}{c} \qquad\qquad OH \\ \qquad\qquad | \\ CH_3-CH_2-CH-CH_3 \end{array}$$
2-butanol

b.
$$\begin{array}{c} \qquad\qquad Br \\ \qquad\qquad | \\ CH_3-CH_2-CH_2-C-CH_3 \\ \qquad\qquad | \\ \qquad\qquad Br \end{array}$$
4-dibromopentane

c.
$$CH_3-\overset{\overset{\displaystyle O}{\|}}{C}-O-CH_2-CH_2-CH_2-CH_2-CH_3$$
ethyl pentanoate

d. $CH_3-NH-CH_2-CH_2-CH_3$
methylpropylamine

67. Identify each of the following reactions as an addition, substitution, elimination, or condensation reaction:

a.
$$CH_3-\overset{\overset{\displaystyle O}{\|}}{C}-OH + CH_3-\overset{\overset{\displaystyle OH}{|}}{CH}-CH_3 \longrightarrow$$
$$CH_3-\overset{\overset{\displaystyle O}{\|}}{C}-O-\overset{\overset{\displaystyle CH_3}{|}}{CH}-CH_3 + H_2O$$

b. $CH_2{=}CH-CH_3 + Cl_2 \longrightarrow$
$$\begin{array}{c} Cl-CH_2-CH-CH_3 \\ | \\ Cl \end{array}$$

c.
[cyclohexane] + Cl_2 $\xrightarrow[\text{heat}]{\text{light or}}$ [cyclohexane with Cl] + HCl

d.
$$\begin{array}{c} CH_3 \;\; OH \end{array}$$
[cyclohexane with CH₃ and OH] $\xrightarrow[50°C]{\text{H}_3\text{O}^+,\text{ THF}}$ [cyclohexene with CH₃] + H_2O

CRITICAL THINKING

68. Applying Ideas How does ethylene glycol protect radiator fluid in an automobile from both freezing in the winter and boiling over in the summer?

69. Predicting Outcomes Would a collection of 1,2-ethanediol molecules be likely to form twice as many hydrogen bonds as an equal number of ethanol molecules? Why or why not?

TECHNOLOGY & LEARNING

70. Graphing Calculator   Predict the Freezing Point

The graphing calculator can run a program that predicts the freezing point of ethylene glycol solutions, given the concentration. Begin by creating a table of data. Use the program to carry out the predictions.

Go to Appendix C. If you are using a TI 83 Plus, you can download the program and data and run the application as directed. If you are using another calculator, your teacher will provide you with keystrokes and data sets to use. Remember that after creating your lists, you will need to name the program and check the display, as explained in Appendix C. You will then be ready to run the program. After you have graphed the data, answer these questions.

a. What is the approximate freezing point of the solution with a molality of 5.00m?
b. What is the approximate freezing point of the solution with a molality of 10.00m?
c. What is the approximate freezing point of the solution with a molality of 13.00m?

RESEARCH & WRITING

71. A class of CFCs known as hydrochlorofluoro-carbons (HCFCs) has been suggested as a substitute for CFCs in many applications. How does the chemical structure of an HCFC differ from that of a CFC? Why are the HCFCs more acceptable environmentally than other CFCs?

72. At one time, a group of compounds known as the PCBs were very popular for a number of industrial applications. Find out the general structural formula for these compounds and the properties that made them so popular. Also find out why the PCBs were eventually banned for most industrial uses.

73. The widespread use of synthetic polymers in modern society has created a number of new environmental problems. Find out what some of these problems are and what can be done to reduce them.

ALTERNATIVE ASSESSMENT

74. Performance   Devise a set of experiments to study how well biodegradable plastics break down. If your teacher approves your plan, conduct a class experiment to test the procedure on products labeled "biodegradable."

75. Performance   Your teacher will make available unlabeled samples of benzoic acid, ethyl alcohol, and hexanediamine. Develop an experiment to identify each. If your teacher approves your plan, identify the unknown substances.

76. Keep a list of the food you consume in a single day. Compare the content labels from those foods, and then list the most commonly used chemicals in them. With the aid of your teacher and some reference books, try to classify the organic chemicals by their functional groups.

77. As a class or small group, research the preservatives used in various foods. Examine their chemical structure. Determine a way to test for organic functional groups of possibly hazardous preservatives.

Answers from page 670

21-2

a. $CH_3-CH_2-CH_2-O-CH_2-CH_2-CH_3$

b.

CH_3-O-

Additional Example Problems from page 672

1. Name the following compound:

$$CH_3-CH_2-CH_2-CH_2-CH_2-CH_2-CH_2-\overset{\overset{\displaystyle O}{\|}}{CH}$$

Ans. octanal

2. Draw the structural formula for pentanal.

Ans.

$$CH_3-CH_2-CH_2-CH_2-\overset{\overset{\displaystyle O}{\|}}{CH}$$

Answers from page 673

3. *Ans.*

a.

b.

$$CH_3-CH_2-\overset{\overset{\displaystyle O}{\|}}{C}-CH_2-CH_2-CH_2-CH_3$$

Additional Example Problems from page 675

5. Name the following esters:

a.

$$CH_3-CH_2-\overset{\overset{\displaystyle O}{\|}}{C}-O-CH_2-CH_3$$

b.

$$CH_3-CH_2-CH_2-\overset{\overset{\displaystyle O}{\|}}{C}-O-CH_2-CH_2-CH_2-CH_3$$

Ans. **a.** ethyl butanoate
b. butyl butanoate

6. Write structural formulas for the following:
a. propyl ethanoate
b. ethyl methanoate

Ans.

a.

$$CH_3-\overset{\overset{\displaystyle O}{\|}}{C}-O-CH_2-CH_2-CH_3$$

b.

$$H-\overset{\overset{\displaystyle O}{\|}}{C}-O-CH_2-CH_3$$

Additional Example Problems from page 677

7. Name the following amines:

a.

$$CH_3-CH_2-CH_2-\underset{\underset{\displaystyle CH_3}{|}}{N}-CH_3$$

b.

$$CH_3-CH_2-\underset{\underset{\displaystyle CH_2-CH_2-CH_2-CH_3}{|}}{N}-CH_2-CH_2-CH_2-CH_3$$

Ans. **a.** dimethylpropylamine
b. dibutylethylamine

8. Write the structural formula for butylamine.

Ans. $CH_3-CH_2-CH_2-CH_2-NH_2$

Answers to Section Review from page 679

6. $R-\overset{\displaystyle ..}{N}H_2 + H_2O \rightleftharpoons R-NH_3^+ + OH^-$

Reactions from Lesson Starter, page 682

$$CH_2-O-\overset{\overset{\displaystyle O}{\|}}{C}-(CH_2)_7CH=CH(CH_2)_7CH_3$$

$$CH-O-\overset{\overset{\displaystyle O}{\|}}{C}-(CH_2)_7CH=CH(CH_2)_5CH_3 + 3I_2 \longrightarrow$$

$$CH_2-O-\overset{\overset{\displaystyle O}{\|}}{C}-(CH_2)_7CH=CH(CH_2)_7CH_3$$

$$CH_2-O-\overset{\overset{\displaystyle O}{\|}}{C}-(CH_2)_7-\overset{\overset{\displaystyle I}{|}}{CH}-\overset{\overset{\displaystyle I}{|}}{CH}-(CH_2)_7CH_3$$

$$CH-O-\overset{\overset{\displaystyle O}{\|}}{C}-(CH_2)_7-\overset{\overset{\displaystyle I}{|}}{CH}-\overset{\overset{\displaystyle I}{|}}{CH}-(CH_2)_5CH_3$$

$$CH_2-O-\overset{\overset{\displaystyle O}{\|}}{C}-(CH_2)_7-\overset{\overset{\displaystyle I}{|}}{CH}-\overset{\overset{\displaystyle I}{|}}{CH}-(CH_2)_7CH_3$$

Answers from page 694

12. a.

$$R-\overset{\overset{\displaystyle O}{\|}}{C}-OH \xrightarrow{H_2O} R-\overset{\overset{\displaystyle O}{\|}}{C}-O^- + H^+$$

b. Carboxylic acids are weak acids.

16.

$$R-\overset{\displaystyle O}{\overset{\|}{C}}-OH + R-NH_2 \longrightarrow R-\overset{\displaystyle O}{\overset{\|}{C}}-\overset{\displaystyle H}{\overset{|}{N}}-R + H_2O$$

38. a. $CH_3-\underset{\underset{\displaystyle OH}{|}}{CH}-\underset{\underset{\displaystyle OH}{|}}{CH}-CH_2-CH_3$

   b. $CH_3-CH_2-CH_2-CH_2-CH_2-OH$

   c. $\underset{\underset{\displaystyle OH}{|}}{CH_2}-\underset{\underset{\displaystyle OH}{|}}{CH}-\underset{\underset{\displaystyle OH}{|}}{CH_2}$

   d. CH_3-CH_2-OH

40. a. $CH_3-\underset{\underset{\displaystyle Cl}{|}}{CH}-\underset{\underset{\displaystyle Cl}{|}}{CH}-\underset{\underset{\displaystyle Cl}{|}}{CH}-CH_3$

   b. $I-\underset{\underset{\displaystyle I}{|}}{CH}-CH_2-CH_3$

   c. $CH_3-CH_2-CH_2-CH_2-CH_2-CH_2-F$

   d. $F-CH-\underset{\underset{\displaystyle Cl}{|}}{\overset{\overset{\displaystyle Cl}{|}}{C}}-CH_3$ with F below first CH

42. a. CH_3-O-CH_3

   b. $CH_3-O-CH_2-CH_2-CH_3$

   c. $CH_3-CH_2-CH_2-CH_2-O-CH_2-CH_2-CH_3$

   d. $CH_3-CH_2-O-CH_2-CH_2-CH_2-\underset{\underset{\displaystyle CH_3-CH_2-CH_2}{|}}{CH_2}$

44. a. $H-\overset{\displaystyle O}{\overset{\|}{C}}-H$

   b. $CH_3-CH_2-CH_2-CH_2-CH_2-\overset{\displaystyle O}{\overset{\|}{C}}-H$

   c. $\underset{}{\overset{\overset{\displaystyle CH_3}{|}}{CH_2}}-CH_2-CH_2-CH_2-CH_2-CH_2-\overset{\displaystyle O}{\overset{\|}{C}}-H$

   d. $CH_3-\overset{\displaystyle O}{\overset{\|}{C}}-H$

46. a. $CH_3-CH_2-\overset{\displaystyle O}{\overset{\|}{C}}-CH_2-CH_2-CH_3$

   b. $CH_3-\overset{\displaystyle O}{\overset{\|}{C}}-CH_2-CH_2-CH_3$

   c. $CH_3-\overset{\displaystyle O}{\overset{\|}{C}}-CH_2-CH_2-CH_2-CH_2-CH_2-CH_3$

   d. $CH_3-\overset{\displaystyle O}{\overset{\|}{C}}-CH_2-CH_2-CH_2-CH_3$

48. a. $CH_3-CH_2-CH_2-\overset{\displaystyle O}{\overset{\|}{C}}-OH$

   b. $CH_3-CH_2-CH_2-CH_2-CH_2-\overset{\displaystyle O}{\overset{\|}{C}}-OH$

   c. $OH-\overset{\displaystyle O}{\overset{\|}{C}}-CH_2-CH_2-CH_2-CH_2-\overset{\displaystyle O}{\overset{\|}{C}}-OH$

   d. $CH_3-CH_2-CH_2-CH_2-CH_2-CH_2-\overset{\displaystyle O}{\overset{\|}{C}}-OH$

50. a. $CH_3-\overset{\displaystyle O}{\overset{\|}{C}}-O-CH_2-CH_2-CH_2-CH_3$

   b. $H-\overset{\displaystyle O}{\overset{\|}{C}}-O-CH_2-CH_3$

   c. $CH_3-CH_2-\overset{\displaystyle O}{\overset{\|}{C}}-O-CH_2-CH_2-CH_3$

   d. $CH_3-CH_2-CH_2-\overset{\displaystyle O}{\overset{\|}{C}}-O-CH_3$

52. a. $CH_3-CH_2-CH_2-CH_2-NH-CH_3$

   b. $CH_3-CH_2-NH_2$

   c. $CH_3-CH_2-\underset{\underset{\displaystyle CH_3}{|}}{N}-CH_2-CH_3$

   d. $CH_3-CH_2-NH-CH_2-CH_2-CH_3$

65. a. $\underset{\underset{\displaystyle Cl}{|}}{CH_2}-\underset{\underset{\displaystyle Cl}{|}}{CH}-\underset{\underset{\displaystyle Cl}{|}}{CH_2}$

   b. $\underset{\underset{\displaystyle OH}{|}}{CH_2}-CH_2-CH_2-CH_3$

   c. $CH_3-CH_2-O-CH_3$

   d. $CH_3-CH_2-\overset{\displaystyle O}{\overset{\|}{C}}-OH$

   e. $CH_3-CH_2-\overset{\displaystyle O}{\overset{\|}{C}}-O-CH_3$

   f. $CH_3-\underset{\underset{\displaystyle CH_3}{|}}{N}-CH_3$

PACING CHART Compression Guide: *(To shorten, eliminate items in italics.)*	NSE Standards	CLASSROOM RESOURCES	
		Teaching Resources	Experiments
22-1 **The Nucleus** 2 45-minute periods 1 90-minute block *Nucleons and Nuclear Stability, pp. 702–703*	PS 1b, 1c UCP 1–3	T 130, T 131	
22-2 **Radioactive Decay** 2 45-minute periods 1 90-minute block *Decay Series, pp. 710–711*	PS 1b, 1d UCP 1–3, 5	T 132, T 133, TM 125A, TM 126A	A26 Radioactivity
22-3 **Nuclear Radiation** 2 45-minute periods 1 90-minute block *Radiation Detection, p. 714*	PS 1d UCP 2 SPSP 1, 4, 5	ATE Demo, pp. 713, 714	A27 Detecting Radioactivity
22-4 **Nuclear Fission and Nuclear Fusion** 2 45-minute periods 1 90-minute block	PS 1c UCP 1–2 ST 1–2 HNS 1, 3 SPSP 5	ATE Demo, p. 717 T 134, T 135, T 136	

Review and Assessment 2 45-minute periods 1 90-minute block	REVIEW RESOURCES		
	Cumulative Review	Alternative Assessment	Traditional Assessment
	SR Chapter 22 Mixed Review PE Chapter 22 40–47, p. 724	PE 54, p. 725 ATE 707 AA Items for Chapter 22	Chapter 22 Text Test Generator items for Chapter 22

ASSIGNMENT RESOURCES

Section Homework Resources & Review	Problem-Solving Practice
HR Homework Worksheets 22-1, 22-2 **PE** Section Review, 1–4, p. 704 Chapter Review, 1–2, 25–32, pp. 723–724 **SR** Section Review 22-1	**PE** Additional Sample 22-1 **ATE** Additional Sample, p. 704 Additional Examples, p. 702
HR Homework Worksheets 22-3, 22-4 Graphic Org. Assignment 22-3 **PE** Section Review, 1–5, p. 712 Chapter Review, 3–14, 33–40, pp. 723–724 **SR** Section Review 22-2	**PE** Additional Sample 22-2 **ATE** Additional Sample, p. 709
HR Homework Worksheet 22-5 **PE** Section Review, 1–4, p. 716 Chapter Review, 15–19, p. 723 **SR** Section Review 22-3	
HR Homework Worksheet 22-6 Graphic Org. Assignment 22-6 **PE** Section Review, 1–4, p. 719 Chapter Review, 20–24, p. 723 **SR** Section Review 22-4	

TECHNOLOGY RESOURCES

Technology & Internet Resources

 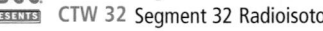 CTW 31 Segment 31 Nuclear Waste
CTW 32 Segment 32 Radioisotopes in Medicine

 Holt Chemistry Videodiscs Teacher's Correlation Guide for Chapter 22

 Module 2: Atomic Structure

 internet**connect**

On-line Student Resources:
www.scilinks.org
The following SciLinks Internet resources can be found in the student text for this chapter.

TOPICS:
• Radioactive decay, p. 705 (HC2221)
• Half-life, p. 708 (HC2222)
• Radioisotopes, p. 715 (HC2223)
• Fission, p. 718 (HC2224)
• Fusion, p. 718 (HC2225)
• Enrico Fermi, p. 721 (HC2226)

On-line Teacher Resources:
 GO TO: go.hrw.com
KEYWORD: HC2 HOME
Visit the HRW Web site for a variety of resources related to this chapter.

 Smithsonian Institution®
Internet Connections
Visit **www.si.edu/hrw** for additional on-line resources.

CNN**fyi**.com
Visit **www.cnnfyi.com** for late-breaking news and current events stories selected just for you.

Resource Key

PE Pupil's Edition
ATE Teacher's Edition

One-Stop Planner CD-ROM Includes these resources and customizable daily lesson plans:

HR Homework Resources
SR Section Reviews
CTW Critical Thinking Worksheets
AA Alternative Assessments

ChemFile
A Laboratory Experiments
B Microscale Experiments
C Technique Builders and Problem-Solving Experiments

D Consumer Experiments
T Transparencies
TM Transparency Masters
PS Mini-Guide to Problem Solving
SRW Supplemental Reading Worksheets

Scoring Rubrics for Labs, Alternative Assessments, Performance Tasks and Portfolio Projects are on the One-Stop Planner CD-ROM.

CHAPTER 22

Nuclear Chemistry

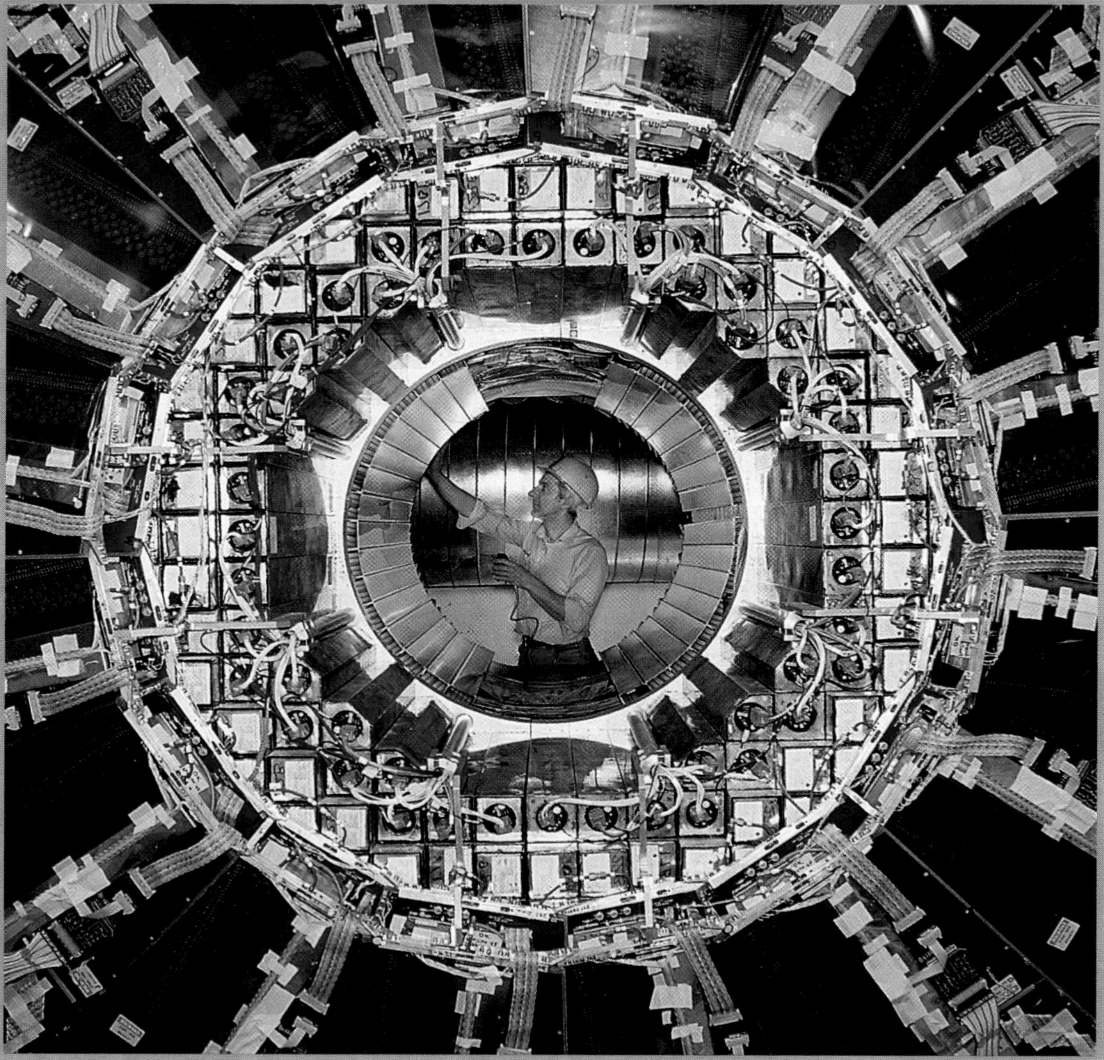

Chapter Overview

22-1 identifies the forces that affect the stability of the nucleus. This section also shows how to write balanced nuclear equations.

22-2 outlines the different types of radioactive decay and demonstrates calculations involving the half-life of an isotope.

22-3 surveys the penetrating ability of nuclear radiation and methods for detecting radiation. This section also describes some common applications of nuclear radiation.

22-4 explains the difference between fission and fusion and discusses their uses and potential uses as energy sources.

Concept Base

Students may need a review of the following concepts:

• conservation of mass and energy, Chapter 3

• atomic structure, Chapters 3–4

• units of energy, Chapter 17

 Reading Skill-Builder

BRAINSTORMING Ask students to come up with words and phrases that relate to the concept and definition of *nuclear chemistry*. Have a student record the class's responses on the board. Encourage students to devise a hypothesis about the definition of the phrase based on their combined thoughts.

Nuclear Chemistry

Particle detectors are important tools in the study of nuclear chemistry.

The Nucleus

A tomic nuclei are made of *protons and neutrons, which are collectively called* **nucleons.** In nuclear chemistry, *an atom is referred to as a* **nuclide** *and is identified by the number of protons and neutrons in its nucleus.* Nuclides can be represented in two ways: when a symbol such as $^{228}_{88}$Ra is used, the superscript is the mass number and the subscript is the atomic number; the same nuclide can also be written as radium-228.

Mass Defect and Nuclear Stability

Because an atom is made of protons, neutrons, and electrons, you might expect the mass of an atom to be the same as the mass of an equal number of isolated protons, neutrons, and electrons. However, this is not the case. Let's consider a $^{4}_{2}$He atom as an example. The combined mass of two protons, two neutrons, and two electrons is calculated below.

$$2 \text{ protons:} \quad (2 \times 1.007\ 276\ \text{amu}) = 2.014\ 552\ \text{amu}$$
$$2 \text{ neutrons:} \quad (2 \times 1.008\ 665\ \text{amu}) = 2.017\ 330\ \text{amu}$$
$$2 \text{ electrons:} \quad (2 \times 0.000\ 5486\ \text{amu}) = \underline{0.001\ 097\ \text{amu}}$$
$$\text{total combined mass: } 4.032\ 979\ \text{amu}$$

However, the atomic mass of a $^{4}_{2}$He atom has been measured to be 4.002 60 amu. The measured mass, 4.002 60 amu, is 0.030 38 amu *less* than the calculated mass, 4.032 98 amu. *The difference between the mass of an atom and the sum of the masses of its protons, neutrons, and electrons is called the* **mass defect.**

Nuclear Binding Energy

What causes the loss in mass? According to Albert Einstein's equation $E = mc^2$, mass can be converted to energy, and energy to mass. The mass defect is caused by the conversion of mass to energy upon formation of the nucleus. The mass units of the mass defect can be converted to energy units by using Einstein's equation. First, convert 0.030 38 amu to kilograms to match the units for energy, kg·m^2/s^2.

$$0.030\ 38 \text{ amu} \times \frac{1.6605 \times 10^{-27} \text{ kg}}{1 \text{ amu}} = 5.0446 \times 10^{-29} \text{ kg}$$

OBJECTIVES

- Explain what a nuclide is, and describe the different ways nuclides can be represented.

- Define and relate the terms *mass defect* and *nuclear binding energy.*

- Explain the relationship between nucleon number and stability of nuclei.

- Explain why nuclear reactions occur, and know how to balance a nuclear equation.

CHEMISTRY INTERACTIVE TUTOR

Module 2: Models of the Atom

Lesson Starter
Begin the lesson by discussing the stability of the atom. Remind students that electrons exist in certain energy levels and are paired in orbitals. Atoms undergo chemical reactions that result in a loss or gain of energy to increase their stability. Likewise, nucleons exist in energy levels, and most stable nuclei contain paired nucleons. Nuclear reactions result in much larger energy changes and increase the stability of the nucleus.

✔ Teaching Tip

Be sure students use isotopic atomic masses (not average atomic masses) when calculating the mass defect.

CHEMISTRY INTERACTIVE TUTOR

Module 2: Models of the Atom

Topic: Atomic Structure Tutorial and Practice
Sections **a** and **b** of this engaging tutorial review and reinforce understanding of atomic structure.

Visual Strategy

FIGURE 22-1 Turn this graph upside down and ask students where a marble would rest if you were to let it roll along on the top of this graph. That resting point represents the greatest amount of binding energy per nucleon and thus the most stable nucleus.

Did You Know?

The figure on this page identifies iron as the most stable nucleus. The elements between hydrogen and iron are made during the lifetime of a star in a process called fusion, which is discussed later in this chapter. After most of the nuclear fuel has been used up, the star "dies." Many stars undergo a tremendous explosion called a nova. At the instant a nova occurs, the energy from the massive explosion produces the elements that are heavier than iron. So in a sense, we and all that surrounds us are forged in the furnaces of the stars.

Additional Example Problems

1. Calculate the nuclear binding energy of a $^{32}_{16}$S atom. The measured atomic mass of $^{32}_{16}$S is 31.972 070 amu.

Ans. 4.36×10^{-11} J

2. Calculate the nuclear binding energy for a mole of $^{16}_{8}$O atoms. The measured atomic mass of $^{16}_{8}$O is 15.994 915 amu.

Ans. 1.23×10^{13} J/mol

3. Calculate the binding energy per nucleon of a $^{55}_{25}$Mn atom. The measured atomic mass of $^{55}_{25}$Mn is 54.938 047 amu.

Ans. 1.41×10^{-12} J/nucleon

FIGURE 22-1 This graph shows the relationship between binding energy per nucleon and mass number. The binding energy per nucleon is a measure of the stability of a nucleus.

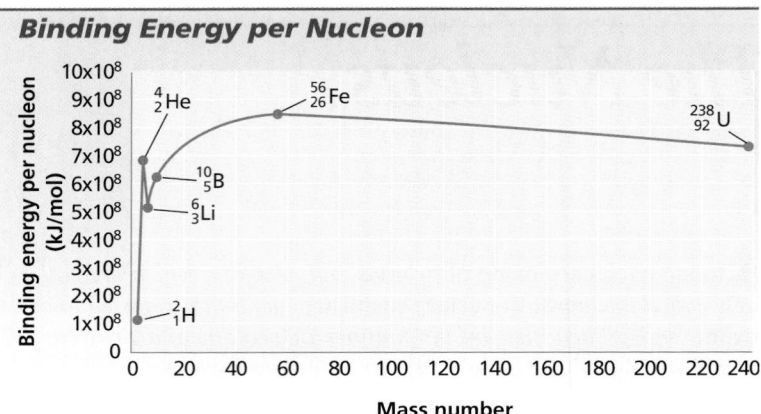

Binding Energy per Nucleon

The energy equivalent can now be calculated.

$$E = mc^2$$
$$E = (5.0446 \times 10^{-29} \text{ kg})(3.00 \times 10^8 \text{ m/s})^2$$
$$= 4.54 \times 10^{-12} \text{ kg}\cdot\text{m}^2/\text{s}^2 = 4.54 \times 10^{-12} \text{ J}$$

This is the **nuclear binding energy,** *the energy released when a nucleus is formed from nucleons.* This energy can also be thought of as the amount of energy required to break apart the nucleus. Therefore, the nuclear binding energy is also a measure of the stability of a nucleus.

Binding Energy per Nucleon

The binding energy per nucleon is used to compare the stability of different nuclides, as shown in Figure 22-1. *The* **binding energy per nucleon** *is the binding energy of the nucleus divided by the number of nucleons it contains.* The higher the binding energy per nucleon, the more tightly the nucleons are held together. Elements with intermediate atomic masses have the greatest binding energies per nucleon and are therefore the most stable.

Nucleons and Nuclear Stability

Stable nuclides have certain characteristics. When the number of protons in stable nuclei is plotted against the number of neutrons, as shown in Figure 22-2, a beltlike graph is obtained. *This stable nuclei cluster over a range of neutron-proton ratios is referred to as the* **band of stability.** Among atoms having low atomic numbers, the most stable nuclei are those with a neutron-proton ratio of approximately 1:1. For example, $^4_2$He, a stable isotope of helium with two neutrons and two protons, has a neutron-proton ratio of 1:1. As the atomic number increases, the stable neutron-proton ratio increases to about 1.5:1. For example, $^{206}_{82}$Pb, with 124 neutrons and 82 protons, has a neutron-proton ratio of 1.51:1.

This trend can be explained by the relationship between the nuclear force and the electrostatic forces between protons. Protons in a nucleus repel all other protons through electrostatic repulsion, but the short

The Band of Stability

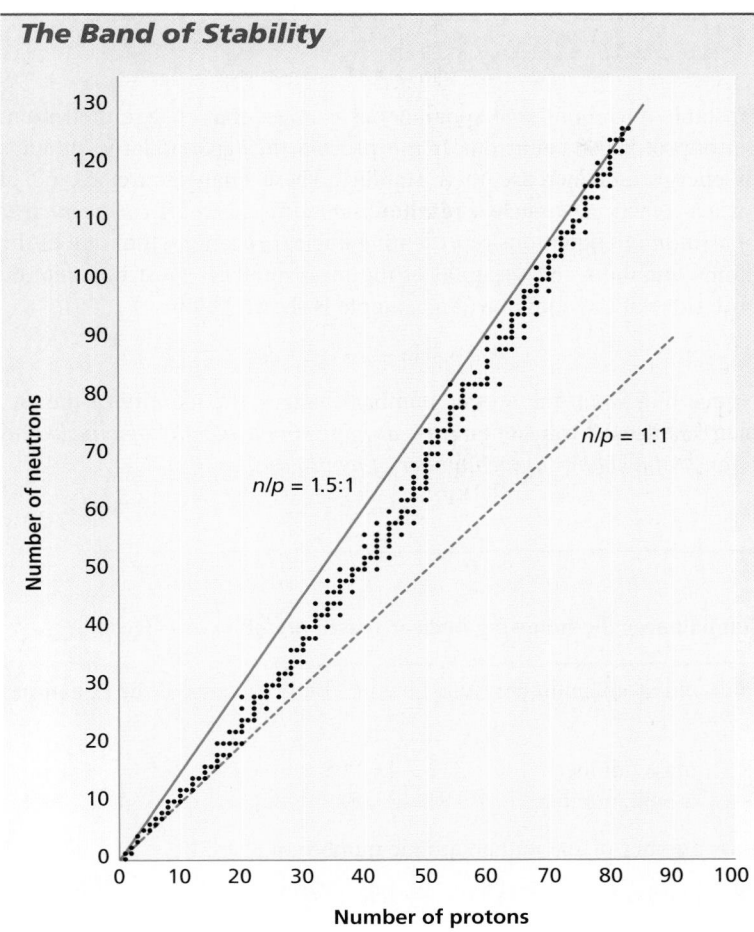

FIGURE 22-2 The neutron-proton ratios of stable nuclides cluster together in a region known as the band of stability. As the number of protons increases, the ratio increases from 1:1 to about 1.5:1.

range of the nuclear force allows them to attract only protons very close to them, as shown in Figure 22-3. So as the number of protons in a nucleus increases, the electrostatic force between protons increases faster than the nuclear force. More neutrons are required to increase the nuclear force and stabilize the nucleus. Beyond the atomic number 83, bismuth, the repulsive force of the protons is so great that no stable nuclides exist.

Stable nuclei tend to have even numbers of nucleons. Out of 265 stable nuclides, 159 have even numbers of both protons and neutrons. Only four nuclides have odd numbers of both. This indicates that stability of a nucleus is greatest when the nucleons—like electrons—are paired.

The most stable nuclides are those having 2, 8, 20, 28, 50, 82, or 126 protons, neutrons, or total nucleons. This extra stability at certain numbers supports a theory that nucleons—like electrons—exist at certain energy levels. According to the **nuclear shell model,** *nucleons exist in different energy levels, or shells, in the nucleus. The numbers of nucleons that represent completed nuclear energy levels—2, 8, 20, 28, 50, 82, and 126—are called* **magic numbers.**

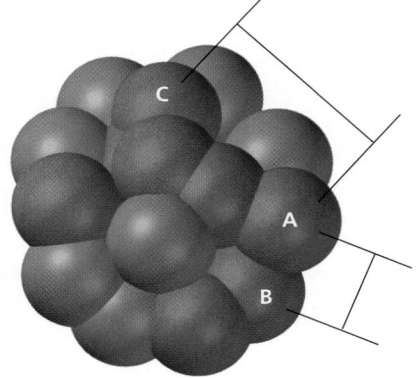

FIGURE 22-3 Proton A attracts proton B through the nuclear force but repels it through the electrostatic force. Proton A mainly repels proton C through the electrostatic force because the nuclear force reaches only a few nucleon diameters.

ADDITIONAL SAMPLE PROBLEMS

Complete the following equations:

22-1 $^{238}_{92}U \longrightarrow$? $+ ^{234}_{90}Th$

Ans. $^{4}_{2}He$

22-1 $^{37}_{18}Ar +$? $\longrightarrow ^{37}_{17}Cl$

Ans. $^{0}_{-1}e$

SECTION REVIEW

1. a. an atom with a specified number of protons and neutrons
b. proton or neutron in a nucleus
c. the difference between the mass of an atom and the sum of the masses of its protons, neutrons, and electrons
d. the energy released when a nucleus is formed from protons and neutrons

2. A certain number of neutrons are needed to increase the nuclear force enough to hold a nucleus together. For small atoms, a stable neutron/proton ratio is 1:1; for large atoms, 1.5:1.

3. to increase their ultimate stability

4. a. $^{2}_{1}H$ **b.** $^{12}_{6}C$ **c.** $^{0}_{-1}e$

Nuclear Reactions

Unstable nuclei undergo spontaneous changes that change their number of protons and neutrons. In this process, they give off large amounts of energy and increase their stability. These changes are a type of nuclear reaction. *A **nuclear reaction** is a reaction that affects the nucleus of an atom.* In equations representing nuclear reactions, the total of the atomic numbers and the total of the mass numbers must be equal on both sides of the equation. An example is shown below.

$$^{9}_{4}Be + ^{4}_{2}He \longrightarrow ^{12}_{6}C + ^{1}_{0}n$$

Notice that when the atomic number changes, the identity of the element changes. *A **transmutation** is a change in the identity of a nucleus as a result of a change in the number of its protons.*

SAMPLE PROBLEM 22-1

Identify the product that balances the following nuclear reaction: $^{212}_{84}Po \longrightarrow ^{4}_{2}He +$?

SOLUTION

1. The total mass number and atomic number must be equal on both sides of the equation.

$$^{212}_{84}Po \longrightarrow ^{4}_{2}He +$$?

mass number: $212 - 4 = 208$
atomic number: $84 - 2 = 82$

2. The nuclide has a mass number of 208 and an atomic number of 82, $^{208}_{82}Pb$.

3. The balanced nuclear equation is $^{212}_{84}Po \longrightarrow ^{4}_{2}He + ^{208}_{82}Pb$

PRACTICE

Complete the following nuclear equations:

1. $^{218}_{84}Po \longrightarrow ^{4}_{2}He +$?   *Answer* $^{218}_{84}Po \longrightarrow ^{4}_{2}He + ^{214}_{82}Pb$

2. $^{253}_{99}Es + ^{4}_{2}He \longrightarrow ^{1}_{0}n +$?   *Answer* $^{253}_{99}Es + ^{4}_{2}He \longrightarrow ^{1}_{0}n + ^{256}_{101}Md$

3. $^{142}_{61}Pm +$? $\longrightarrow ^{142}_{60}Nd$ *Answer* $^{142}_{61}Pm + ^{0}_{-1}e \longrightarrow ^{142}_{60}Nd$

SECTION REVIEW

1. Define the following terms:
   a. nuclide   c. mass defect
   b. nucleon   d. nuclear binding energy
2. How is nuclear stability related to the neutron-proton ratio?
3. Why do unstable nuclides undergo nuclear reactions?

4. Complete and balance the following nuclear equations:
   a. $^{187}_{75}Re +$? $\longrightarrow ^{188}_{75}Re + ^{1}_{1}H$
   b. $^{9}_{4}Be + ^{4}_{2}He \longrightarrow$? $+ ^{1}_{0}n$
   c. $^{22}_{11}Na +$? $\longrightarrow ^{22}_{10}Ne$

Radioactive Decay

In 1896, Henri Becquerel was studying the possible connection between light emission of some uranium compounds after exposure to sunlight and X-ray emission. He wrapped a photographic plate in a lightproof covering and placed a uranium compound on top of it. He then placed them in sunlight. The photographic plate was exposed even though it was protected from visible light, suggesting exposure by X rays. When he tried to repeat his experiment, cloudy weather prevented him from placing the experiment in sunlight. To his surprise, the plate was still exposed. This meant that sunlight was not needed to produce the rays that exposed the plate. The rays were produced by radioactive decay. **Radioactive decay** *is the spontaneous disintegration of a nucleus into a slightly lighter nucleus, accompanied by emission of particles, electromagnetic radiation, or both.* The radiation that exposed the plate was **nuclear radiation,** *particles or electromagnetic radiation emitted from the nucleus during radioactive decay.*

Uranium is a **radioactive nuclide,** *an unstable nucleus that undergoes radioactive decay.* Studies by Marie Curie and Pierre Curie found that of the elements known in 1896, only uranium and thorium were radioactive. In 1898, the Curies discovered two new radioactive metallic elements, polonium and radium. Since that time, many other radioactive nuclides have been identified. In fact, all of the nuclides beyond atomic number 83 are unstable and thus radioactive.

Types of Radioactive Decay

A nuclide's type and rate of decay depend on the nucleon content and energy level of the nucleus. Some common types of radioactive nuclide emissions are summarized in Table 22-1.

OBJECTIVES

- Define and relate the terms *radioactive decay* and *nuclear radiation*.

- Describe the different types of radioactive decay and their effects on the nucleus.

- Define the term *half-life*, and explain how it relates to the stability of a nucleus.

- Define and relate the terms *decay series, parent nuclide,* and *daughter nuclide*.

- Explain how artificial radioactive nuclides are made, and discuss their significance.

internet**connect**

SC**LINKS**

NSTA

TOPIC: Radioactive decay
GO TO: www.scilinks.org
*sci***LINKS CODE:** HC2221

TABLE 22-1 *Radioactive Nuclide Emissions*			
Type	**Symbol**	**Charge**	**Mass (amu)**
Alpha particle	$_2^4\text{He}$	2+	4.002 60
Beta particle	$_{-1}^0\beta$	1−	0.000 5486
Positron	$_{+1}^0\beta$	1+	0.000 5486
Gamma ray	γ	0	0

Lesson Starter
Place a transparency of the band of stability on the overhead projector. Ask the students to propose different ways for an unstable nucleus to get into the band of stability. *(An atom can gain or lose protons, gain or lose neutrons, or gain or lose protons and neutrons.)* Use this transparency when discussing the different types of radioactive decay. On the projected figure, show how each of these types of emission can lead to a more stable nucleus. This will show that radioactive decay is a process by which unstable nuclei become stable.

TABLE STRATEGY

Table 22-1 Point out that a beta particle, an electron, and a positron all have the same mass. A beta particle is another name for an electron emitted from the nucleus.

 **Reading Skill-Builder**

READING HINT Have students read silently about the different types of radioactive decay on pp. 706–707. Then group the students in pairs and have them use Table 22-1 to explain and summarize the characteristics of each. Encourage students to use the text they read as a resource to find additional characteristics of the types of nuclear radiation.

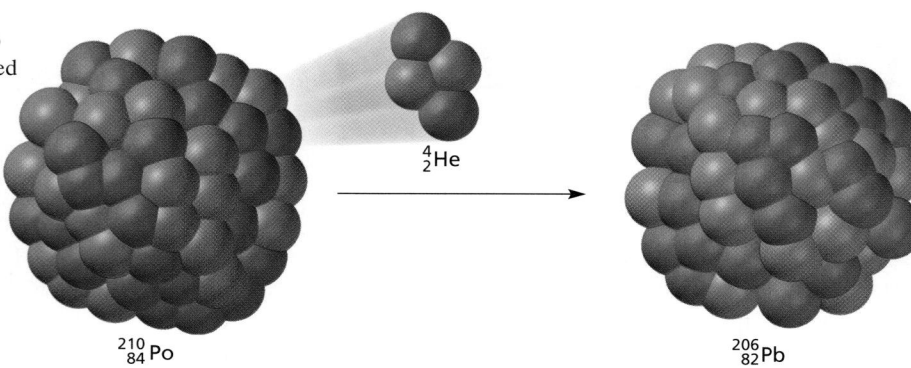

FIGURE 22-4 An alpha particle, identical to a helium nucleus, is emitted during the radioactive decay of some very heavy nuclei.

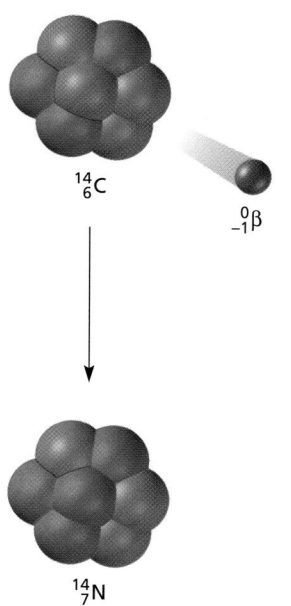

FIGURE 22-5 Beta emission causes the transmutation of $^{14}_{6}C$ into $^{14}_{7}N$. Beta emission is a type of radioactive decay in which a proton is converted to a neutron with the emission of a beta particle.

Alpha Emission

*An **alpha particle** (α) is two protons and two neutrons bound together and is emitted from the nucleus during some kinds of radioactive decay.* Alpha particles are helium nuclei and have a charge of 2+. They are often represented with the symbol $^{4}_{2}He$. Alpha emission is restricted almost entirely to very heavy nuclei. In these nuclei, both the number of neutrons and the number of protons need to be reduced in order to increase the stability of the nucleus. An example of alpha emission is the decay of $^{210}_{84}Po$ into $^{206}_{82}Pb$, shown in Figure 22-4. The atomic number decreases by two, and the mass number decreases by four.

$$^{210}_{84}Po \longrightarrow {}^{206}_{82}Pb + {}^{4}_{2}He$$

Beta Emission

Elements above the band of stability are unstable because they have too many neutrons. To decrease the number of neutrons, a neutron can be converted into a proton and an electron. The electron is emitted from the nucleus as a beta particle. *A **beta particle** (β) is an electron emitted from the nucleus during some kinds of radioactive decay.*

$$^{1}_{0}n \longrightarrow {}^{1}_{1}p + {}^{0}_{-1}\beta$$

An example of beta emission, shown in Figure 22-5, is the decay of $^{14}_{6}C$ into $^{14}_{7}N$. Notice that the atomic number increases by one and the mass number stays the same.

$$^{14}_{6}C \longrightarrow {}^{14}_{7}N + {}^{0}_{-1}\beta$$

Positron Emission

Elements below the band of stability have too many protons to be stable. To decrease the number of protons, a proton can be converted into a neutron by emitting a positron. *A **positron** is a particle that has the same mass as an electron, but has a positive charge, and is emitted from the nucleus during some kinds of radioactive decay.*

$$_1^1p \longrightarrow _0^1n + _{+1}^0\beta$$

An example of positron emission is the decay of $_{19}^{38}$K into $_{18}^{38}$Ar. Notice that the atomic number decreases by one but the mass number stays the same.

$$_{19}^{38}\text{K} \longrightarrow _{18}^{38}\text{Ar} + _{+1}^0\beta$$

Electron Capture

Another type of decay for nuclides with too many protons is electron capture. *In electron capture, an inner orbital electron is captured by the nucleus of its own atom.* The inner orbital electron combines with a proton, and a neutron is formed.

$$_{-1}^0e + _1^1p \longrightarrow _0^1n$$

An example of electron capture is the radioactive decay of $_{47}^{106}$Ag into $_{46}^{106}$Pd. Just as in positron emission, the atomic number decreases by one but the mass number stays the same.

$$_{47}^{106}\text{Ag} + _{-1}^0e \longrightarrow _{46}^{106}\text{Pd}$$

Gamma Emission

Gamma rays (γ) *are high-energy electromagnetic waves emitted from a nucleus as it changes from an excited state to a ground energy state.* The position of gamma rays in the electromagnetic spectrum is shown in Figure 22-6. The emission of gamma rays is another piece of evidence supporting the nuclear shell model. According to the nuclear shell model, gamma rays are produced when nuclear particles undergo transitions in nuclear-energy levels. This is similar to the emission of light when an electron drops to a lower-energy level, which was covered in Chapter 4. Gamma emission usually occurs immediately following other types of decay, when other types of decay leave the nucleus in an excited state.

FIGURE 22-6   Gamma rays, like visible light, are a form of electromagnetic radiation, but they have a much shorter wavelength and are much higher in energy than visible light.

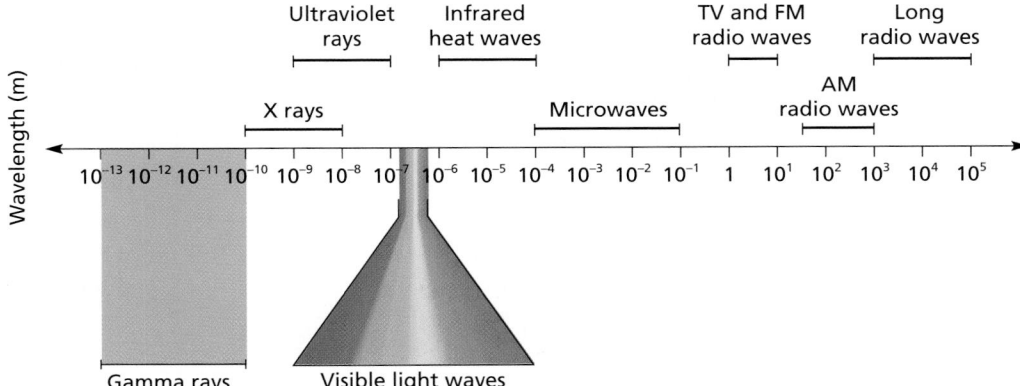

CHAPTER ⟷ CONNECTION

The relationship between the frequency of electromagnetic radiation and its energy is discussed in Chapter 4. The energy of electromagnetic radiation is directly proportional to its frequency. Gamma radiation carries the greatest amount of energy.

✔ **Teaching Tip**

Because a beta particle has the same atomic number and mass number as an electron, students may be confused as to which symbol to use when solving for an unknown in a nuclear equation. Point out to them that if the unknown is a reactant, the nuclear reaction is electron capture and the symbol *e* should be used. If the unknown is a product, then the reaction is beta emission and the symbol β should be used.

Alternative Assessment

Determine whether each of the following nuclear reactions involves alpha decay, beta decay, positron emission, or electron capture.

1. $_{90}^{234}\text{Th} \longrightarrow _{-1}^0\beta + _{91}^{234}\text{Pa}$
(beta decay)

2. $_{92}^{238}\text{U} \longrightarrow _2^4\text{He} + _{90}^{234}\text{Th}$
(alpha decay)

3. $_8^{15}\text{O} \longrightarrow _{+1}^0\beta + _7^{15}\text{N}$
(positron emission)

4. $_{11}^{22}\text{Na} + _{-1}^0e \longrightarrow _{10}^{22}\text{Ne}$
(electron capture)

Teaching Tip

The following is one way to help students understand half-life: put all the students on one side of the room. Have half the students move to the other side of the room, and then have half the remaining students go to the other side of the room. Do this process three or four times; each time represents one half-life. The number of students represents the number of atoms of a particular isotope. Notice that the students do not—or should not—disappear. Greater meaning can be given to the figure on this page if you graph the number of students remaining after each "half-life."

TABLE STRATEGY

Table 22-2 Have students compare half-lives of the nuclei listed on this table. How many times faster does the polonium-214 nuclide decompose than potassium-40? (The polonium nuclide decomposes almost instantaneously. The potassium nuclide decomposes in 1.3×10^9 years.) Which nuclides are the most unstable? *(those with the shortest half-lives)*

FIGURE 22-7 The half-life of radium-226 is 1599 years. Half of the remaining radium-226 decays by the end of each additional half-life.

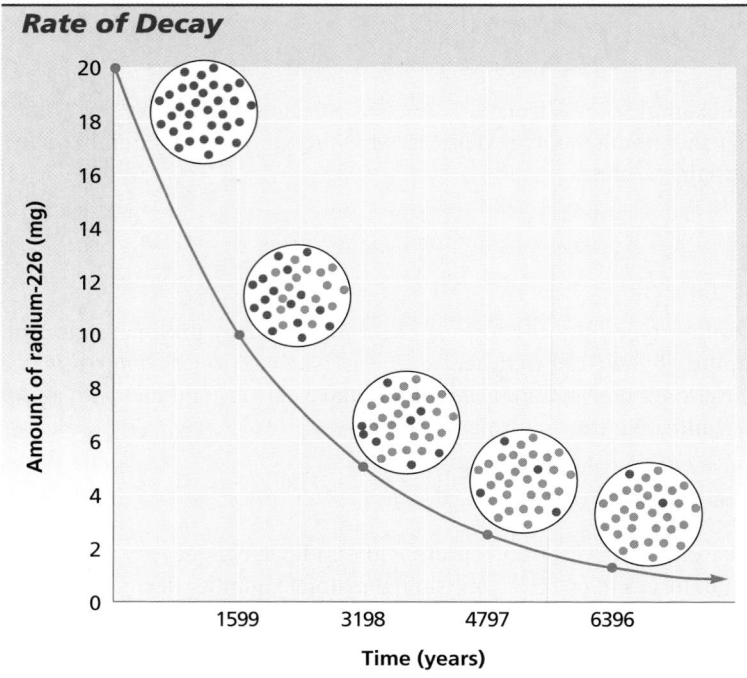

internet**connect**

SC*i*LINKS.
NSTA

TOPIC: Half-life
GO TO: www.scilinks.org
*sci***LINKS CODE:** HC2222

Half-Life

No two radioactive isotopes decay at the same rate. **Half-life,** $t_{1/2}$, *is the time required for half the atoms of a radioactive nuclide to decay.* Look at the graph of the decay of radium-226 in Figure 22-7. Radium-226 has a half-life of 1599 years. Half of a given amount of radium-226 decays in 1599 years. In another 1599 years, half of the remaining radium-226 decays. This process continues until there is a negligible amount of radium-226. Each radioactive nuclide has its own half-life. More-stable nuclides decay slowly and have longer half-lives. Less-stable nuclides decay very quickly and have shorter half-lives, sometimes just a fraction of a second. Some representative radioactive nuclides, along with their half-lives and types of decay, are given in Table 22-2.

TABLE 22-2 *Representative Radioactive Nuclides and Their Half-Lives*			
Nuclide	**Half-life**	**Nuclide**	**Half-life**
$^{3}_{1}H$	12.32 years	$^{214}_{84}Po$	163.7 μs
$^{14}_{6}C$	5715 years	$^{218}_{84}Po$	3.0 min
$^{32}_{15}P$	14.28 days	$^{218}_{85}At$	1.6 s
$^{40}_{19}K$	1.3×10^9 years	$^{238}_{92}U$	4.46×10^9 years
$^{60}_{27}Co$	10.47 min	$^{239}_{94}Pu$	2.41×10^4 years

SAMPLE PROBLEM 22-2

Phosphorus-32 has a half-life of 14.3 days. How many milligrams of phosphorus-32 remain after 57.2 days if you start with 4.0 mg of the isotope?

SOLUTION

1 ANALYZE

Given: original mass of phosphorus-32 = 4.0 mg
half-life of phosphorus-32 = 14.3 days
time elapsed = 57.2 days
Unknown: mass of phosphorus-32 remaining after 57.2 days

2 PLAN

To determine the number of milligrams of phosphorus-32 remaining, we must first find the number of half-lives that have passed in the time elapsed. Then the amount of phosphorus-32 is determined by reducing the original amount by half for every half-life that has passed.

$$\text{number of half-lives} = \text{time elapsed (days)} \times \frac{1 \text{ half-life}}{14.3 \text{ days}}$$

amount of phosphorus-32 remaining =
$$\text{original amount of phosphorus-32} \times \tfrac{1}{2} \text{ for each half-life}$$

3 COMPUTE

$$\text{number of half-lives} = 57.2 \text{ days} \times \frac{1 \text{ half-life}}{14.3 \text{ days}} = 4 \text{ half-lives}$$

$$\text{amount of phosphorus-32 remaining} = 4.0 \text{ mg} \times \tfrac{1}{2} \times \tfrac{1}{2} \times \tfrac{1}{2} \times \tfrac{1}{2} = 0.25 \text{ mg}$$

4 EVALUATE

A period of 57.2 years is four half-lives for phosphorus-32. At the end of one half-life, 2.0 mg of phosphorus-32 remains; 1.0 mg remains at the end of two half-lives; 0.50 mg remains at the end of three half-lives; and 0.25 mg remains at the end of four half-lives.

PRACTICE

1. The half-life of polonium-210 is 138.4 days. How many milligrams of polonium-210 remain after 415.2 days if you start with 2.0 mg of the isotope? — *Answer* 0.25 mg

2. Assuming a half-life of 1599 years, how many years will be needed for the decay of $\frac{15}{16}$ of a given amount of radium-226? — *Answer* 6396 years

3. The half-life of radon-222 is 3.824 days. After what time will one-fourth of a given amount of radon remain? — *Answer* 7.648 days

4. The half-life of cobalt-60 is 10.47 min. How many milligrams of cobalt-60 remain after 104.7 min if you start with 10.0 mg? — *Answer* 0.00977 mg

5. The half-life of uranium-238 is 4.46×10^9 years. If 4.46×10^9 years ago a sample contained 4.0 mg of uranium-238, how many milligrams of uranium-238 does the sample contain today? — *Answer* 2.0 mg

6. The half-life of polonium-218 is 3.0 min. If you start with 16 mg, how long will it be before only 1.0 mg remains? — *Answer* 12 min

✔ Teaching Tip

This method works only for an integer number of half-lives.

ADDITIONAL SAMPLE PROBLEMS

22-2 The Environmental Protection Agency and health officials nationwide are concerned about the levels of radon gas in homes. The half-life of the radon-222 isotope is 3.8 days. If a sample of gas taken from a basement contains 4.38 μg of radon-222, how much radon will remain in the sample after 15.2 days?

Ans. 0.274 mg

22-2 Uranium-238 decays through alpha decay with a half-life of 4.46×10^9 years. How long would it take for 7/8 of a sample of uranium-238 to decay?

Ans. three half-lives, or 1.34×10^{10} years

22-2 The half-life of carbon-14 is 5715 years. How long will it be until only half of the carbon-14 in a sample remains?

Ans. 5715 years

22-2 The half-life of iodine-131 is 8.040 days. What percentage of an iodine-131 sample will remain after 40.2 days?

Ans. 3.13%

Visual Strategy

FIGURE 22-8 Be sure students understand the type of radioactive decay that converts one isotope to another in this decay series. Have them write the nuclear equations for the different decays represented on this chart.

Did You Know?

• Have students locate radon in the U-238 decay series. Because it is a gas, radon formed by uranium decay inside the Earth rises to the surface and into the atmosphere. This is the source of radon that can accumulate in buildings, as is discussed in the next section.

• The Curies discovered polonium and radium when the uranium ore they were studying was found to be more radioactive than would have been expected on the basis of its uranium content alone. Have the students locate polonium and radium in the U-238 decay series. Polonium and radium are present in some uranium ores because they are daughter nuclides of U-238.

Decay Series

One nuclear reaction is not always enough to produce a stable nuclide. *A* **decay series** *is a series of radioactive nuclides produced by successive radioactive decay until a stable nuclide is reached. The heaviest nuclide of each decay series is called the* **parent nuclide.** *The nuclides produced by the decay of the parent nuclides are called* **daughter nuclides.** All naturally occurring nuclides with atomic numbers greater than 83 are radioactive and belong to one of three natural decay series. The parent nuclides are uranium-238, uranium-235, and thorium-232. The transmutations of the uranium-238 decay series are charted in Figure 22-8.

Locate the parent nuclide, uranium-238, on the chart. As the nucleus of uranium-238 decays, it emits an alpha particle. The mass number of the nuclide, and thus the vertical position on the graph, decreases by four. The atomic number, and thus the horizontal position, decreases by two. The daughter nuclide is an isotope of thorium.

$$^{238}_{92}\text{U} \longrightarrow ^{234}_{90}\text{Th} + ^{4}_{2}\text{He}$$

FIGURE 22-8 This chart shows the transmutations that occur as $^{238}_{92}\text{U}$ decays to the final, stable nuclide, $^{206}_{82}\text{Pb}$. Decay usually follows the solid arrows. The dotted arrows represent alternative routes of decay.

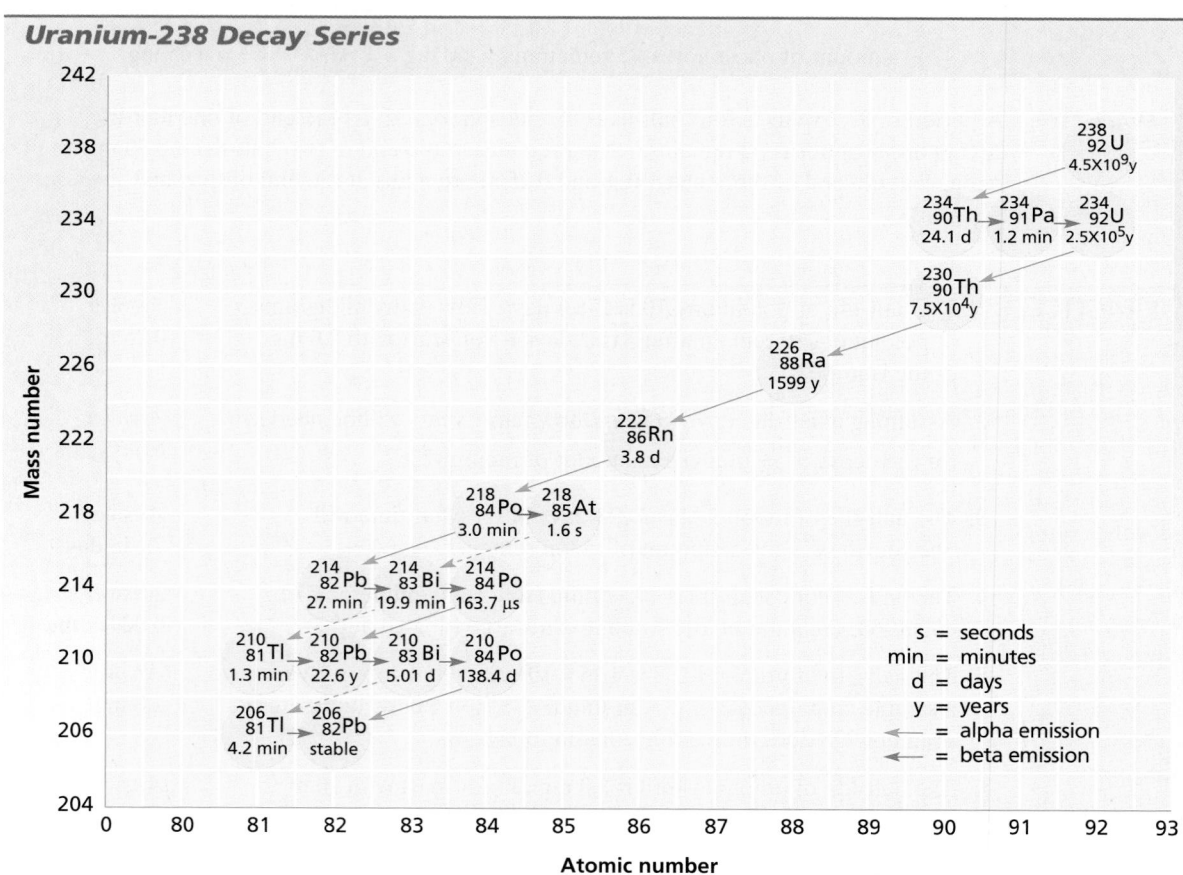

Uranium-238 Decay Series

The half-life of $^{234}_{90}\text{Th}$, about 24 days, is indicated on the chart. It decays by giving off beta particles. This increases its atomic number, and thus its horizontal position, by one. The mass number, and thus its vertical position, remains the same.

$$^{234}_{90}\text{Th} \longrightarrow ^{234}_{91}\text{Pa} + ^{0}_{-1}\beta$$

The remaining atomic number and mass number changes shown on the decay chart are also explained in terms of the particles given off. In the final step, $^{210}_{84}\text{Po}$ loses an alpha particle to form $^{206}_{82}\text{Pb}$. This is a stable, nonradioactive isotope of lead. Notice that $^{206}_{82}\text{Pb}$ contains 82 protons, a magic number. It contains the extra-stable nuclear configuration of a completed nuclear shell.

Artificial Transmutations

Artificial radioactive nuclides are radioactive nuclides not found naturally on Earth. They are made by **artificial transmutations,** *bombardment of stable nuclei with charged and uncharged particles.* Because neutrons have no charge, they can easily penetrate the nucleus of an atom. However, positively charged alpha particles, protons, and other ions are repelled by the nucleus. Because of this repulsion, great quantities of energy are required to bombard nuclei with these particles. The necessary energy may be supplied by accelerating these particles in the magnetic or electrical field of a particle accelerator. An example of an accelerator is shown in Figure 22-9.

FIGURE 22-9   This is an aerial view of the Fermi International Accelerator Laboratory (Fermilab), in Illinois. The particle accelerators are underground. The Tevatron ring, the larger particle accelerator, has a circumference of 4 mi. The smaller ring in the background is a new accelerator, the Main Injector.

Did You Know?
Particle accelerators can be linear or circular. The linear accelerator at Stanford Linear Accelerator Center (SLAC), in Palo Alto, California, is 2 mi long.

SECTION REVIEW

1. the spontaneous disintegration of a nucleus into a lighter, more stable nucleus, accompanied by the emission of particles, radiation, or both

2. a. alpha emission, beta emission, positron emission, gamma emission, and electron capture
b. beta emission, positron emission, electron capture

3. 1/16

4. when a stable nuclide has been produced

5. Natural radioactive nuclides are found naturally on Earth, and artificial nuclides are not. They are made by bombarding stable nuclides with particles.

TABLE 22-3 Reactions for the First Preparation of Several Transuranium Elements

Atomic number	Name	Symbol	Nuclear reaction
93	neptunium	Np	$^{238}_{92}U + ^{1}_{0}n \longrightarrow ^{239}_{92}U$
			$^{239}_{92}U \longrightarrow ^{239}_{93}Np + ^{0}_{-1}\beta$
94	plutonium	Pu	$^{238}_{93}Np \longrightarrow ^{238}_{94}Pu + ^{0}_{-1}\beta$
95	americium	Am	$^{239}_{94}Pu + 2^{1}_{0}n \longrightarrow ^{241}_{95}Am + ^{0}_{-1}\beta$
96	curium	Cm	$^{239}_{94}Pu + ^{4}_{2}He \longrightarrow ^{242}_{96}Cm + ^{1}_{0}n$
97	berkelium	Bk	$^{241}_{95}Am + ^{4}_{2}He \longrightarrow ^{243}_{97}Bk + 2^{1}_{0}n$
98	californium	Cf	$^{242}_{96}Cm + ^{4}_{2}He \longrightarrow ^{245}_{98}Cf + ^{1}_{0}n$
99	einsteinium	Es	$^{238}_{92}U + 15^{1}_{0}n \longrightarrow ^{253}_{99}Es + 7^{0}_{-1}\beta$
100	fermium	Fm	$^{238}_{92}U + 17^{1}_{0}n \longrightarrow ^{255}_{100}Fm + 8^{0}_{-1}\beta$
101	mendelevium	Md	$^{253}_{99}Es + ^{4}_{2}He \longrightarrow ^{256}_{101}Md + ^{1}_{0}n$
102	nobelium	No	$^{246}_{96}Cm + ^{12}_{6}C \longrightarrow ^{254}_{102}No + 4^{1}_{0}n$
103	lawrencium	Lr	$^{252}_{98}Cf + ^{10}_{5}B \longrightarrow ^{258}_{103}Lr + 4^{1}_{0}n$

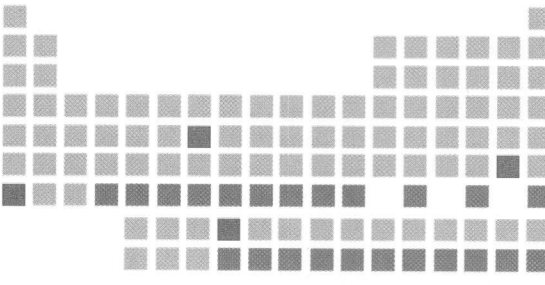

FIGURE 22-10 Artificial transmutations filled the gaps in the periodic table, shown in red, and extended the periodic table with the transuranium elements, shown in blue.

Artificial Radioactive Nuclides

Radioactive isotopes of all the natural elements have been produced by artificial transmutation. In addition, production of technetium, astatine, francium, and promethium by artificial transmutation has filled gaps in the periodic table. Their positions are shown in Figure 22-10.

Artificial transmutations are also used to produce the transuranium elements. **Transuranium elements** *are elements with more than 92 protons in their nuclei.* All of these elements are radioactive. The nuclear reactions for the synthesis of several transuranium elements are shown in Table 22-3. Currently, 17 artificially prepared transuranium elements have been reported. The positions of the transuranium elements in the periodic table are also shown in Figure 22-10.

SECTION REVIEW

1. Define *radioactive decay.*

2. a. What are the different types of radioactive decay?
b. List the types of radioactive decay that involve conversion of particles.

3. What fraction of a given sample of a radioactive nuclide remains after four half-lives?

4. When does a decay series end?

5. Distinguish between natural and artificial radioactive nuclides.

Nuclear Radiation

In Becquerel's experiment, nuclear radiation from the uranium compound penetrated the lightproof covering and exposed the film. Different types of nuclear radiation have different penetrating abilities. Nuclear radiation includes alpha particles, beta particles, and gamma rays.

Alpha particles have a range of only a few centimeters in air and have a low penetrating ability due to their large mass and charge. They cannot penetrate skin. However, they can cause damage if ingested or inhaled. Beta particles travel at speeds close to the speed of light and have a penetrating ability about 100 times greater than that of alpha particles. They have a range of a few meters in air. Gamma rays have the greatest penetrating ability. The penetrating abilities and shielding requirements of different types of nuclear radiation are shown in Figure 22-11.

Radiation Exposure

Nuclear radiation can transfer its energy to the electrons of atoms or molecules and cause ionization. *The* **roentgen** *is a unit used to measure nuclear radiation; it is equal to the amount of radiation that produces* 2×10^9 *ion pairs when it passes through 1 cm^3 of dry air.* Ionization can damage living tissue. Radiation damage to human tissue is measured in rems (<u>r</u>oentgen <u>e</u>quivalent, <u>man</u>). *One* **rem** *is the quantity of ionizing radiation that does as much damage to human tissue as is done by 1 roentgen of high-voltage X rays.* Cancer and genetic effects caused by DNA mutations are long-term radiation damage to living tissue. DNA

OBJECTIVES

- Compare the penetrating ability and shielding requirements of alpha particles, beta particles, and gamma rays.

- Define the terms *roentgen* and *rem*, and distinguish between them.

- Describe three devices used in radiation detection.

- Discuss applications of radioactive nuclides.

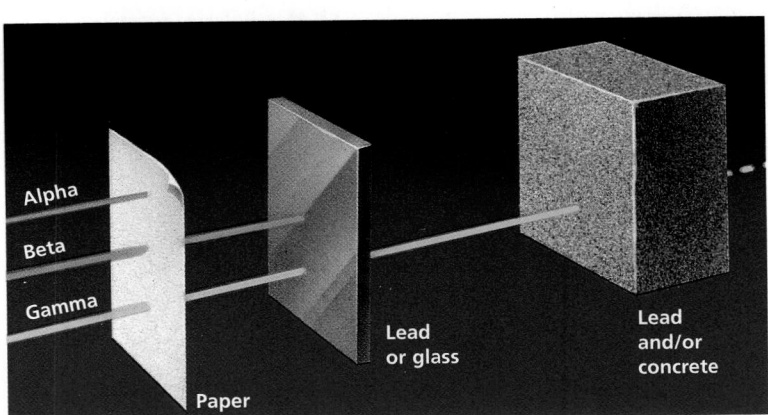

FIGURE 22-11 The different penetrating abilities of alpha particles, beta particles, and gamma rays require different levels of shielding. Alpha particles can be shielded with just a sheet of paper. Lead or glass is often used to shield beta particles. Gamma rays are the most penetrating and require shielding with thick layers of lead or concrete, or both.

Lesson Starter
DEMONSTRATION
Detecting and Measuring Beta Radiation

This demonstration should give students a sense of how distance and different types of shielding affect beta radiation.

1. Obtain a beta source in a sealed container from a scientific supply house.

2. With the radiation source 10 ft away from the students and the counter, take a reading of background radiation with a Geiger-Müller counter.

3. Measure the radiation by placing the Geiger-Müller tube 5 cm away from the beta source.

4. Repeat step 3 at distances of 10 cm, 30 cm, and 1 m away from the beta source.

5. Repeat step 3, but place a piece of paper between the source and the Geiger-Müller tube.

6. Repeat step 3 using a plywood board 1 cm thick and then using a piece of aluminum 1 cm thick. Other types of shielding, for example plexiglass, may also be used.

Safety Safety glasses, a lab apron, and gloves must be worn. Students must be 10 ft or more from the demonstration. Obtain isotopes from scientific supply houses in quantities that do not require licensing. Use only sources in sealed containers. Do not allow students to handle the sources or the Geiger-Müller counter. Be sure to follow the manufacturer's directions for using the Geiger-Müller counter.

No Disposal Save all materials for future use.

Did You Know?
Exposure to radiation increases when humans are at high altitude. What does that say about one of the useful functions of our atmosphere?

DEMONSTRATION
Radon detection kits for mail-in laboratory analysis can be found at some hardware stores. You can use these to test the radon level in your classroom.

 Reading Skill-Builder

READING RESPONSE LOGS
Have students draw a vertical line down the middle of a sheet of paper. In the left-hand column, have them write passages from Section 22-3 about which they have reactions, thoughts, feelings, questions, or associations. In the right-hand column, have them write those reactions, thoughts, feelings, questions, or associations. Ask volunteers to read some of those passages and responses to the class.

can be mutated directly by interaction with radiation or indirectly by interaction with previously ionized molecules.

Everyone is exposed to environmental background radiation. Average exposure for people living in the United States is estimated to be about 0.1 rem per year. However, actual exposure varies. The maximum permissible dose of radiation exposure for a person in the general population is 0.5 rem per year. Airline crews and people who live at high altitudes have increased exposure levels because of increased cosmic-ray levels at high altitudes. Radon-222 trapped inside homes may also cause increased exposure. Because it is a gas, radon can move up from the soil into homes through cracks and holes in the foundation. Radon trapped in homes increases the risk of lung cancer among smokers.

Radiation Detection

Film badges, Geiger-Müller counters, and scintillation counters are three devices commonly used to detect and measure nuclear radiation. A film badge and a Geiger-Müller counter are shown in Figure 22-12. As previously mentioned, nuclear radiation exposes film just as visible light does. This property is used in film badges. **Film badges** *use exposure of film to measure the approximate radiation exposure of people working with radiation*. **Geiger-Müller counters** *are instruments that detect radiation by counting electric pulses carried by gas ionized by radiation*. Geiger-Müller counters are typically used to detect beta-particle radiation. Radiation can also be detected when it transfers its energy to substances that *scintillate*, or absorb ionizing radiation and emit visible light. **Scintillation counters** *are instruments that convert scintillating light to an electric signal for detecting radiation*.

FIGURE 22-12 Film badges (a) and Geiger-Müller counters (b) are both used to detect nuclear radiation.

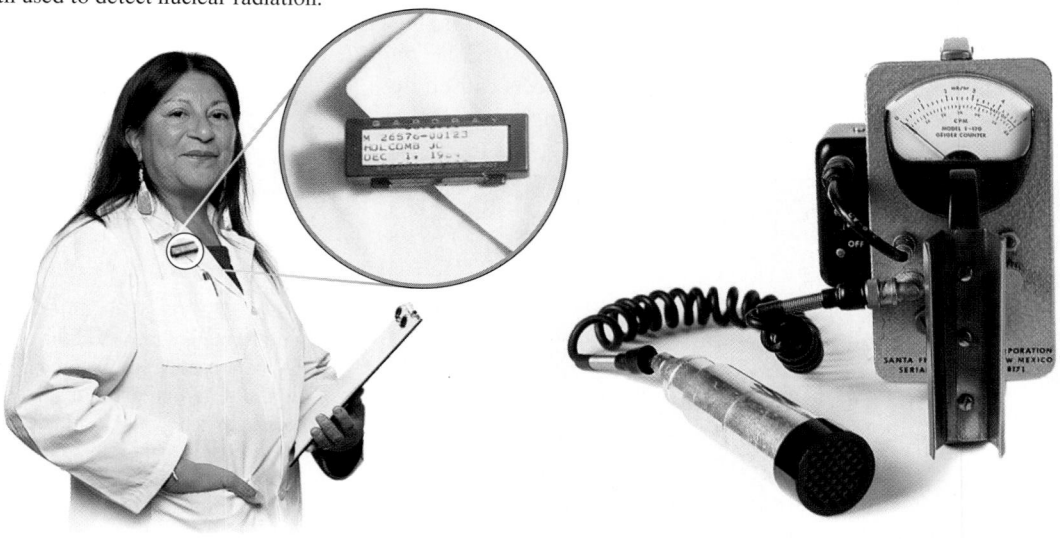

(a)

(b)

Applications of Nuclear Radiation

Many applications are based on the fact that the physical and chemical properties of stable isotopes are essentially the same as those of radioactive isotopes of the same element. A few uses of radioactive nuclides are discussed below.

Radioactive Dating

Radioactive dating *is the process by which the approximate age of an object is determined based on the amount of certain radioactive nuclides present.* Such an estimate is based on the fact that radioactive substances decay with known half-lives. Age is estimated by measuring either the accumulation of a daughter nuclide or the disappearance of the parent nuclide.

Carbon-14 is radioactive and has a half-life of approximately 5715 years. It can be used to estimate the age of organic material up to about 50 000 years old. Nuclides with longer half-lives are used to estimate the age of older objects; methods using nuclides with long half-lives have been used to date minerals and lunar rocks more than 4 billion years old.

Radioactive Nuclides in Medicine

In medicine, radioactive nuclides, such as the artificial radioactive nuclide cobalt-60, are used to destroy certain types of cancer cells. Many radioactive nuclides are also used as **radioactive tracers,** *which are radioactive atoms that are incorporated into substances so that movement of the substances can be followed by radiation detectors.* Detection of radiation from radioactive tracers can be used to diagnose cancer and other diseases. See Figure 22-13.

Radioactive Nuclides in Agriculture

In agriculture, radioactive tracers in fertilizers are used to determine the effectiveness of the fertilizer. The amount of radioactive tracer absorbed by a plant indicates the amount of fertilizer absorbed. Nuclear radiation is also used to prolong the shelf life of food. For example, gamma rays from cobalt-60 can be used to kill bacteria and insects that spoil and infest food.

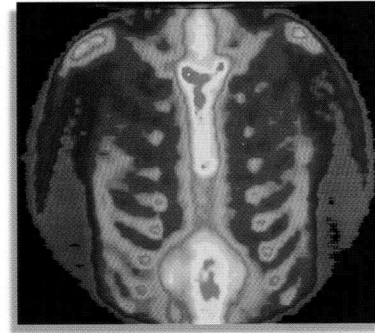

FIGURE 22-13 Radioactive nuclides, such as technetium-99, can be used to detect bone cancer. In this procedure, technetium-99 accumulates in areas of abnormal bone metabolism. Detection of the nuclear radiation then shows the location of bone cancer.

internet**connect**

SC*L*INKS.
NSTA

TOPIC: Radioisotopes
GO TO: www.scilinks.org
*sci*LINKS CODE: HC2223

Nuclear Waste

Nuclear Fission and Nuclear Fusion

In nuclear fission, the nucleus of a very heavy atom, such as uranium, is split into two or more nuclei. The products of the fission include the nuclei as well as the nuclides formed from the fragments' radioactive decay. Fission is the primary system powering nuclear reactors, nuclear missiles, and nuclear-powered submarines and aircraft carriers. Fusion is the opposite process of fission. In fusion, very high temperatures and pressures are used to combine light atoms, such as hydrogen, to make heavier atoms, such as helium. Fusion is the primary process that fuels

Did You Know?
Smoke detectors contain small radioactive samples. Americium-241 is often used for this purpose. The radiation ionizes air molecules, and the ions conduct a small electric current. When this current is reduced by the presence of smoke particles, an alarm sounds.

Class Discussion
Never before has there been a discovery in science that offered such potential for both destruction and progress as the discovery of radioactivity. Discuss both the benefits and hazards of using radioactivity. To prepare for the discussion, have the students bring to class newspaper and magazine articles that refer to topics such as CAT scanners, PET scanners, radiation therapy, tracer studies, radioactive dating, particle accelerators, nuclear power plants, disposal of nuclear wastes, nuclear armaments, and the lasting effects of nuclear disasters.

CHAPTER ⬌ CONNECTION

The next section, 22-4, gives much more detailed information about fission and fusion. Let students know that this is just a brief introduction while focusing their attention on the issue of containment.

Class Discussion

Have students discuss why the issue of dealing with nuclear waste is such an emotionally charged topic. You might ask students how they would react if they lived near the Yucca Mountain site. Would they want the facility close to their homes? Why or why not?

✔ **Teaching Tip**

To strengthen their understanding of the issues involved in the containment and disposal of nuclear waste, students may want to check out the following websites. Some of these sites have information that pertains to Yucca Mountain.

Nuclear Regulatory Commision
http://www.nrc.gov

NRC/Sandia Labs Modal Study Page
http://ttd.sandia.gov/nrc/modal.htm

Environmental Protection Agency
http://www.epa.gov/radiation/yucca/

Department of Energy
http://www.ymp.gov

Nuclear Information and Resource Service   http://www.nirs.org

SECTION REVIEW

1. Very little material is required as a shield to alpha particles because the particles have large mass and charge.

2. a. about 0.1 rem per year
b. The average exposure is about one-fifth of the maximum permissible dose.

3. film badges

4. Radiation kills bacteria and insects that can spoil and infest food.

5. Contained in on-site storage and off-site disposal; fuel rods are stored in storage pools and casks; disposed of in 77 special sites. Nuclear waste is radioactive and can take hundreds of thousands of years to decay. People disagree on the best way to dispose of nuclear waste.

our sun and the stars. Creating and maintaining a fusion reaction is more complex and expensive than performing fission. Both fission and fusion release enormous amounts of energy that can be converted into heat and electricity, and both produce **nuclear waste.** Fission produces more waste than fusion. As new processes are developed to use energy from fission and fusion, a more vexing question arises: how to contain, store, and dispose of nuclear waste.

Containment of Nuclear Waste

Every radioactive substance has a half-life, which is the amount of time needed for half of a given material to decay into a stable nuclear form and lose its radioactivity. Radioactive waste from medical research, for example, has a half-life of a few months. Waste that is produced in a nuclear reactor will take hundreds of thousands of years to decay, and it needs to be contained so that living organisms can be shielded from radioactivity. There are two main types of containment: on-site storage and off-site disposal.

Storage of Nuclear Waste

The most common form of nuclear waste is spent fuel rods from nuclear power plants. These fuel rods can be contained above the ground by placing them in water pools or in dry casks. Each nuclear reactor in the United States has large pools of water where spent rods can be stored, and some of the radioactive materials will decay. When these pools are full, the rods are moved to dry casks, which are usually made of concrete and steel. Both storage pools and casks are meant for only temporary storage before the waste is moved to permanent underground storage facilities.

Disposal of Nuclear Waste

Disposal of nuclear waste is done with the intention of never retrieving the materials. Because of this, building disposal sites takes careful planning. Currently, there are 77 disposal sites around the United States. The U. S. Department of Energy is considering a new site near Las Vegas, Nevada, called Yucca Mountain, for the permanent disposal of much of this waste. This plan, however, is controversial—some organizations oppose the idea of the disposal site, and others have alternate plans. If the Yucca Mountain site is approved, nuclear waste will be transported there by truck and train beginning in 2010.

SECTION REVIEW

1. What is required to shield alpha particles? Why are these materials effective?

2. a. What is the average exposure of people living in the United States to environmental background radiation?
b. How does this relate to the maximum permissible dose?

3. What device is used to measure the radiation exposure of people working with radiation?

4. Explain why nuclear radiation can be used to preserve food.

5. Explain how nuclear waste is contained, stored, and disposed of, and how each method affects the environment.

Nuclear Fission and Nuclear Fusion

OBJECTIVES

- Define *nuclear fission, chain reaction,* and *nuclear fusion,* and distinguish between them.

- Explain how a fission reaction is used to generate power.

- Discuss the possible benefits and the current difficulty of controlling fusion reactions.

Lesson Starter

- Fission and fusion can be explained by looking at the graph of the binding energy per nucleon for different elements in Section 22-1. For all of the elements below iron, fusion of two smaller elements into a larger element emits energy. For elements larger than iron, fission of a larger element into two smaller elements emits energy.

- Compare the relative energy changes in a physical change, chemical reaction, and nuclear reaction.

DEMONSTRATION

A fission chain reaction can be modeled in the following way: set out a series of mousetraps with a Ping-Pong ball on each one, and throw another Ping-Pong ball into the group of traps. The first ball will spring one trap, then those two balls will spring two traps, then those four balls will spring four traps, and so on. The effect is more dramatic with a large number of traps.

Visual Strategy

FIGURE 22-14 Make sure students realize that this figure has been simplified for easier study. The escaping neutrons will bombard more atoms unless absorbed by neutron-absorbing materials such as the control rods of nuclear reactors.

Nuclear Fission

Review Figure 22-1 on page 702, which shows that nuclei of intermediate mass are the most stable. *In* **nuclear fission,** *a very heavy nucleus splits into more-stable nuclei of intermediate mass.* This process releases enormous amounts of energy. Nuclear fission can occur spontaneously or when nuclei are bombarded by particles. When uranium-235 is bombarded with slow neutrons, a uranium nucleus may capture one of the neutrons, making it very unstable. The nucleus splits into medium-mass parts with the emission of more neutrons. The mass of the products is less than the mass of the reactants. The missing mass is converted to energy.

Nuclear Chain Reaction

When fission of an atom bombarded by neutrons produces more neutrons, a chain reaction can occur. *A* **chain reaction** *is a reaction in which the material that starts the reaction is also one of the products and can start another reaction.* As shown in Figure 22-14, two or three neutrons can be given off when uranium-235 fission occurs. These neutrons can cause the fission of other uranium-235 nuclei. Again neutrons are emitted, which

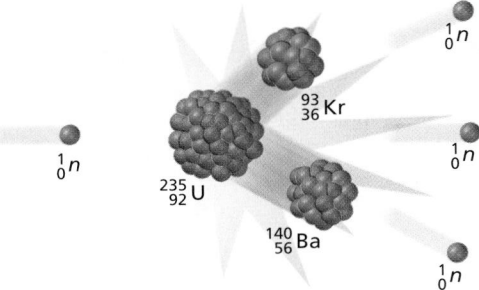

FIGURE 22-14 Fission induction of uranium-235 by bombardment with neutrons can lead to a chain reaction when a critical mass of uranium-235 is present.

Did You Know?

- Nuclear power provides about 20% of the electrical power in the United States.

- The Chernobyl accident occurred shortly after technicians briefly removed most of the control rods—which act as neutron absorbers—during a test.

- Canada has an abundant supply of natural uranium but no facilities for enriching it. Canada has specialized in heavy water, or D_2O, reactors. The heavy water is used both as a coolant and as a moderator.

Reading Skill-Builder

K/W/L Students probably have preconceptions about nuclear reactions and the energy they release. Have students list what they know about nuclear fission and fusion. Then have them list what they want to know about these reactions. After reading Section 22-4, students should determine whether their questions have been answered, noting any unanswered questions as well as new questions they may have.

internetconnect

SC*LINKS*

NSTA

TOPIC: Fission
GO TO: www.scilinks.org
*sci*LINKS CODE: HC2224

TOPIC: Fusion
GO TO: www.scilinks.org
*sci*LINKS CODE: HC2225

FIGURE 22-15 In this model of a nuclear power plant, pressurized water is heated by fission of uranium-235. This water is circulated to a steam generator. The steam drives a turbine to produce electricity. Cool water from a lake or river is then used to condense the steam into water. The warm water from the condenser may be cooled in cooling towers before being reused or returned to the lake or river.

can cause the fission of still other uranium-235 nuclei. This chain reaction continues until all of the uranium-235 atoms have split or until the neutrons fail to strike uranium-235 nuclei. If the mass of uranium-235 is below a certain minimum, too many neutrons will escape without striking other nuclei, and the chain reaction will stop. *The minimum amount of nuclide that provides the number of neutrons needed to sustain a chain reaction is called the* **critical mass.** Uncontrolled chain reactions provide the explosive energy of atomic bombs. **Nuclear reactors** *use controlled-fission chain reactions to produce energy or radioactive nuclides.*

Nuclear Power Plants

Nuclear power plants *use heat from nuclear reactors to produce electrical energy.* They have five main components: shielding, fuel, control rods, moderator, and coolant. The components, shown in Figure 22-15, are surrounded by shielding. **Shielding** *is radiation-absorbing material that is used to decrease exposure to radiation, especially gamma rays, from nuclear reactors.* Uranium-235 is typically used as the fissionable fuel to produce heat, which is absorbed by the coolant. **Control rods** *are neutron-absorbing rods that help control the reaction by limiting the number of free neutrons.* Because fission of uranium-235 is more efficiently induced by slow neutrons, a **moderator** *is used to slow down the fast neutrons produced by fission.* Current problems with nuclear power plant development include environmental requirements, safety of operation, plant construction costs, and storage and disposal of spent fuel and radioactive wastes.

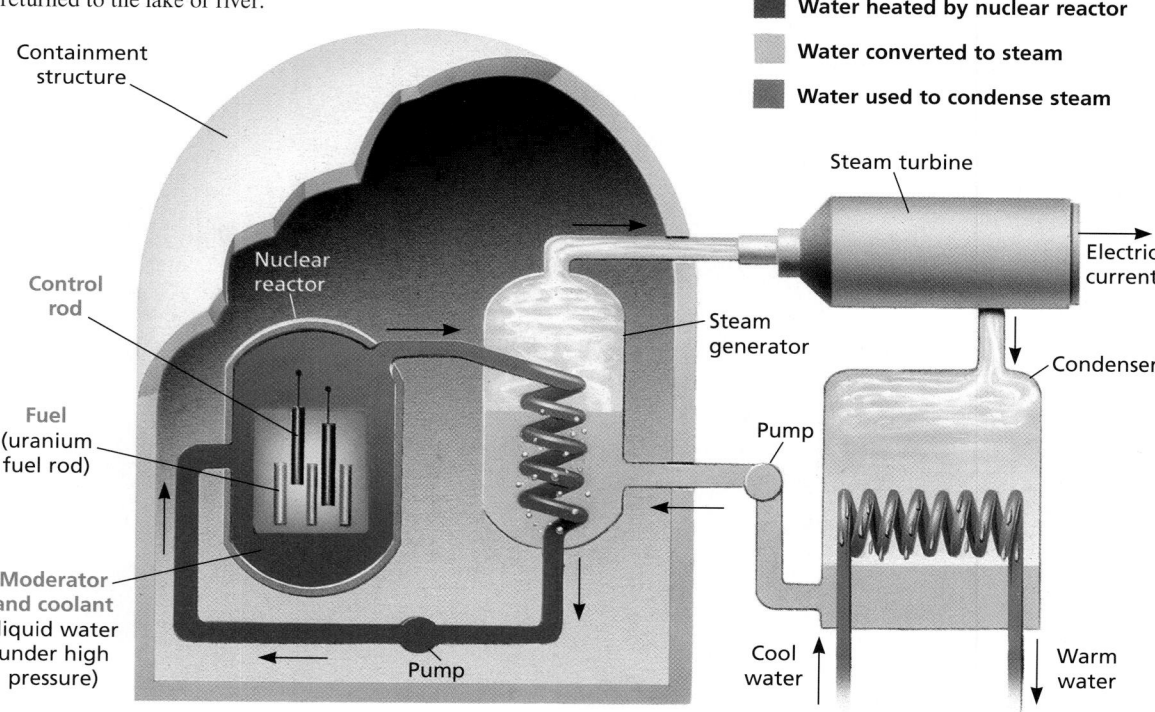

Containment structure

Control rod

Fuel (uranium fuel rod)

Moderator and coolant (liquid water under high pressure)

Nuclear reactor

Pump

Steam generator

Steam turbine

Electric current

Condenser

Pump

Cool water

Warm water

■ Water heated by nuclear reactor
■ Water converted to steam
■ Water used to condense steam

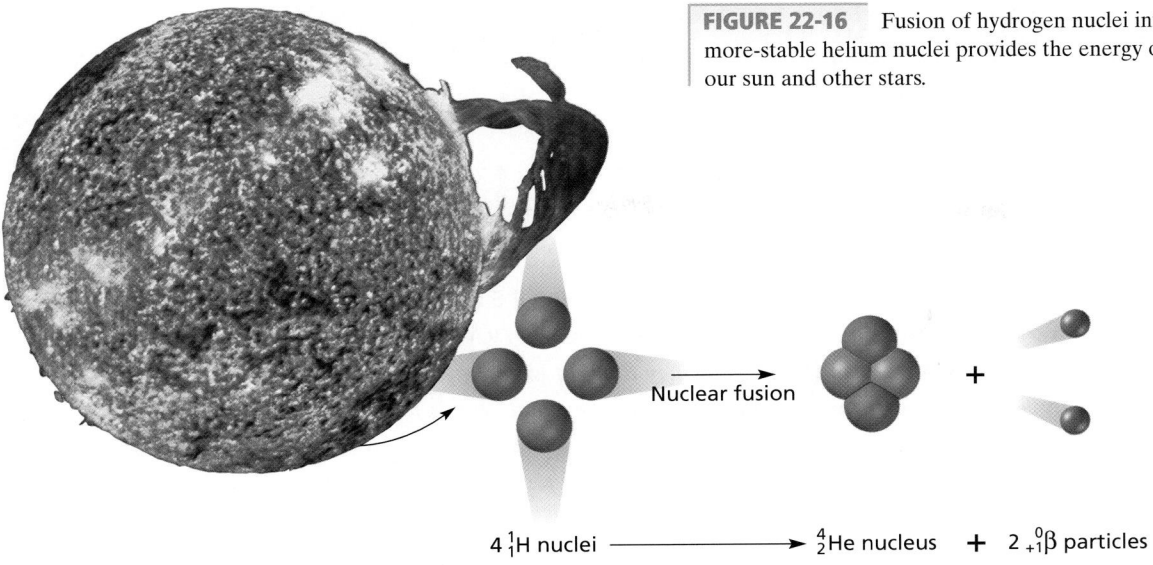

FIGURE 22-16 Fusion of hydrogen nuclei into more-stable helium nuclei provides the energy of our sun and other stars.

Nuclear fusion

$4 \,^1_1\text{H}$ nuclei $\longrightarrow$ ^4_2He nucleus $+$ $2 \,^0_{+1}\beta$ particles

Nuclear Fusion

The high stability of nuclei with intermediate masses can also be used to explain nuclear fusion. *In* **nuclear fusion,** *light-mass nuclei combine to form a heavier, more stable nucleus.* Nuclear fusion releases even more energy per gram of fuel than nuclear fission. In our sun and other stars, four hydrogen nuclei combine at extremely high temperature and pressure to form a helium nucleus with a loss of mass and release of energy. This reaction is illustrated in Figure 22-16.

Uncontrolled fusion reactions of hydrogen are the source of energy for the hydrogen bomb, as shown in Figure 22-17. A fission reaction is used to provide the heat and pressure necessary to trigger the fusion of nuclei. Current research indicates that fusion reactions may be controllable if some major problems can be overcome. One of the problems is that no known material can withstand the initial temperatures, about 10^8 K, required to induce fusion at high temperatures. Methods that contain the fusion reactions within a magnetic field or induce fusion at lower temperatures are being investigated.

FIGURE 22-17 The enormous amount of energy released by fusion reactions is illustrated by this explosion of a hydrogen bomb.

SECTION REVIEW

1. Nuclear fission releases energy when large nuclei are broken up; nuclear fusion releases energy when small nuclei are fused together.

2. A chain reaction is a reaction in which the material that starts the reaction is also one of the products. The products of one reaction can then begin other reactions.

3. shielding, control rods, moderator, fuel, and coolant

4. Fusion is the energy source of the sun.

SECTION REVIEW

1. Distinguish between nuclear fission and nuclear fusion.

2. Define *chain reaction.*

3. List the five main components of a nuclear power plant.

4. Explain how fusion is one of our sources of energy.

An Unexpected Finding

HISTORICAL PERSPECTIVE

The discovery of the artificial transmutation of uranium in 1934 triggered great excitement in science. Chemists preoccupied with identifying what they thought were the final missing elements of the periodic table suddenly had to consider the existence of elements beyond atomic number 92, while physicists began to probe the stability of the nucleus more deeply. By 1939, nuclear investigators in both fields had collaborated to provide a stunning explanation for the mysterious results of uranium's forced transformation.

Neutrons in Italy

In 1934, uranium had the most protons of any known element, 92. But that year, Italian physicist Enrico Fermi believed he had synthesized elements with even higher atomic numbers. After bombarding a sample of uranium with neutrons, Fermi and co-workers recorded measurements that seemed to indicate that some uranium nuclei had absorbed neutrons and then undergone beta decay:

$$^{238}_{92}U + ^{1}_{0}n \longrightarrow ^{239}_{92}U \longrightarrow$$
$$^{239}_{93}? + ^{0}_{-1}\beta$$

This apparatus from Otto Hahn's lab was used to produce fission reactions.

His report noted further, subsequent beta decays, by which he hypothesized the existence of a whole new series of "transuranic" elements:

$$^{238}_{92}U \longrightarrow ^{238}_{93}? + ^{0}_{-1}\beta \longrightarrow$$
$$^{238}_{94}?? + ^{0}_{-1}\beta \longrightarrow ^{238}_{95}??? + ^{0}_{-1}\beta$$

Unfortunately, the Italian group could not verify the existence of the transuranes because, as Fermi put it, "We did not know enough chemistry to separate the products of uranium disintegration from one another."

Curiosity in Berlin

Fermi's experiments caught the attention of a physicist in Berlin, Lise Meitner. Knowing that she could not perform the difficult task of chemically separating radionuclides either, Meitner persuaded a colleague, radiochemist Otto Hahn, to help her explain Fermi's results. Joined by expert chemical analyst Fritz Strassman, the team began investigating neutron-induced uranium decay at the end of 1934.

From the onset, the Berlin team, along with all other scientists at the time, operated under two false assumptions. The first involved the makeup of the bombarded nuclei. In every nuclear reaction observed previously, the resulting nucleus had never differed from the original by more than a few protons or neutrons. Thus, it was assumed that the products of neutron bombardment were radioisotopes of elements at most a few places in the periodic table before or beyond the atoms being bombarded (as Fermi had presumed in hypothesizing the transuranes).

The second assumption concerned the periodicity of the transuranes. Because the elements Ac, Th, Pa, and U chemically resembled the third-row transition elements, La, Hf, Ta, and W, it was believed that elements beyond U would correspondingly resemble those following W. Thus, the transuranes were thought to be homologues of Re, Os, Ir, Pt, and so on. This belief was generally unquestioned and seemed to be confirmed. In fact, by 1937 Hahn was sure of the chemical evidence of transuranes:

> . . . the chemical behavior of the transuranes . . . is such that their position in the periodic system is no longer in doubt. . . . their chemical distinction from all previously known elements needs no further discussion.

Meitner's Exile

By 1938, the political situation in Germany had become dangerous for Meitner. Because she was of Jewish descent, she was being targeted by the Nazis and fled to Sweden to escape persecution. Meanwhile in Berlin, the anti-Nazi Hahn and Strassman had to be careful of every move they made under the watchful eyes of the fascists around them.

Despite censorship, the Berlin team continued to communicate through letters. Meitner could not come up with a satisfying physical explanation for the chemical results of Hahn and Strassman,

and she insisted that her partners re-examine their findings. As Strassman later recalled, Meitner

> . . . requested that [the] experiments be scrutinized . . . one more time. . . . Fortunately L. Meitner's opinion and judgment carried so much weight . . . the necessary control experiments were immediately undertaken.

The politics of World War II prevented Lise Meitner from receiving the Nobel Prize in physics for explaining nuclear fission.

A Shocking Discovery

Prompted by Meitner, Hahn and Strassman realized they had been looking in the wrong place to find the cause of their results. In analyzing a fraction of a solution assay that they had previously ignored, they found the critical evidence they had been seeking.

The analysis indicated that barium appeared to be a result of

neutron bombardment of uranium. Suspecting the spectacular truth but lacking confidence, Hahn wrote to Meitner for an explanation. After consultation with her nephew, Otto Frisch, Meitner proposed that the uranium nuclei had been broken apart into elemental fragments, one of which was Ba. On January 3, 1939, she wrote to Hahn:

> . . . the two of you really do have a splitting to Ba . . . a truly beautiful result, for which I most heartily congratulate you and Strassman.

Thus, the transuranes turned out to be merely radioisotopes of known elements—atomic fragments of uranium atoms that had burst apart on being struck by neutrons.

For the discovery of this unexpected phenomenon, which Meitner named nuclear fission, the talented Hahn was awarded the 1944 Nobel Prize in chemistry. Due to wartime politics, however, Lise Meitner did not receive the corresponding award in physics, and she was not popularly recognized until well after her death in 1968 for her role in clarifying the process that she first explained and named.

internet**connect**

SC*i*LINKS

NSTA

TOPIC: Enrico Fermi
GO TO: www.scilinks.org
*sci*LINKS CODE: HC2226

REVIEW ANSWERS

1. a. Mass defect is the mass equivalent of binding energy in the equation $E = mc^2$.
b. Binding energy per nucleon increases with increased mass number until it reaches a maximum for intermediate mass nuclei; then it decreases with increased mass number.
c. The higher the binding energy per nucleon, the more tightly the nucleons are held together.

2. Certain ratios of neutrons to protons, nucleons of even numbers, and magic numbers of nucleons are the most stable.

3. beyond atomic number 83

4. a. decreases the mass number by four and the atomic number by two
b. increases the atomic number by one but does not change the mass number
c. decreases the atomic number by one but does not change the mass number
d. decreases the atomic number by one but does not change the mass number

5. alpha decay, beta decay, positron emission, and electron capture

6. Beta emission decreases the neutron-proton ratio. Positron emission and electron capture both increase the neutron-proton ratio.

7. a. $^1_0n \longrightarrow {}^1_1p + {}^0_{-1}\beta$

b. $^1_1p \longrightarrow {}^1_0n + {}^0_{+1}\beta$

c. $^0_{-1}e + {}^1_1p \longrightarrow {}^1_0n$

8. Beta particles are electrons that originate in the nucleus. Positrons have masses similar to those of electrons, but they are positively charged.

CHAPTER SUMMARY

22-1
• The difference between the sum of the masses of the nucleons and electrons in an atom and the actual mass of an atom is the mass defect, or nuclear binding energy.
• Nuclear stability tends to be greatest when nucleons are paired, when there are magic numbers of nucleons, and when there are certain neutron-proton ratios.
• Nuclear reactions, represented by nuclear equations, can involve the transmutation of nuclides.

Vocabulary

band of stability (702)	mass defect (701)	nuclear shell model (703)	nuclide (701)
binding energy per nucleon (702)	nuclear binding energy (702)	nucleons (701)	transmutation (704)
magic numbers (703)	nuclear reaction (704)		

22-2
• Radioactive nuclides become more stable by radioactive decay, a type of nuclear reaction.
• Alpha, beta, positron, and gamma emission, and electron capture are all types of radioactive decay. A nuclide's type of decay is related to its nucleon content and the energy level of the nucleus.
• The half-life of a radioactive nuclide is the length of time that it takes for half of a given number of atoms of the nuclide to decay.
• A decay series starts with a parent nuclide and ends with a stable daughter nuclide.
• Artificial transmutations are used to produce artificial radioactive nuclides, including the transuranium elements.

Vocabulary

alpha particle (706)	decay series (710)	nuclear radiation (705)	radioactive nuclide (705)
artificial transmutations (711)	electron capture (707)	parent nuclide (710)	transuranium elements (712)
beta particle (706)	gamma ray (707)	positron (706)	
daughter nuclides (710)	half-life (708)	radioactive decay (705)	

22-3
• Alpha particles, beta particles, and gamma rays have different penetrating abilities and therefore different shielding requirements.
• Film badges, Geiger-Müller counters, and scintillation detectors are used to detect radiation.
• Everyone is exposed to environmental back-ground radiation. Exposure levels vary.
• Radioactive nuclides have many uses, including radioactive dating and cancer detection.
• Nuclear waste must be contained, stored, and disposed of in a way that does not harm people or the environment.

Vocabulary

film badges (714)	nuclear waste (716)	radioactive tracers (715)	roentgen (713)
Geiger-Müller counters (714)	radioactive dating (715)	rem (713)	scintillation counters (714)

22-4
• Nuclear fission and nuclear fusion are nuclear reactions in which the splitting and fusing of nuclei produce more stable nuclei and release enormous amounts of energy.
• Controlled fission reactions are used to produce energy and radioactive nuclides.
• Fusion reactions produce the sun's heat and light. If fusion reactions could be controlled, they would produce more usable energy per gram of fuel than fission reactions.

Vocabulary

chain reaction (717)	moderator (718)	nuclear fusion (719)	nuclear reactors (718)
control rods (718)	nuclear fission (717)	nuclear power plant (718)	shielding (718)
critical mass (718)			

REVIEWING CONCEPTS

1. **a.** How does mass defect relate to nuclear binding energy?
   b. How does binding energy per nucleon vary with mass number?
   c. How does binding energy per nucleon affect the stability of a nucleus?   (22-1)

2. Describe three ways in which the number of protons and the number of neutrons in a nucleus affect its stability.   (22-1)

3. Where on the periodic table are most of the natural radioactive nuclides located?   (22-2)

4. What changes in atomic number and mass number occur in each of the following types of radioactive decay?
   a. alpha emission
   b. beta emission
   c. positron emission
   d. electron capture   (22-2)

5. Which types of radioactive decay cause the transmutation of a nuclide? (Hint: Review the definition of *transmutation*.)   (22-2)

6. Explain how beta emission, positron emission, and electron capture affect the neutron-proton ratio.   (22-2)

7. Write out the nuclear reactions that show particle conversion for the following types of radioactive decay:
   a. beta emission
   b. positron emission
   c. electron capture   (22-2)

8. Compare and contrast electrons, beta particles, and positrons.   (22-2)

9. **a.** What are gamma rays?
   b. How do scientists think they are produced?   (22-2)

10. How does the half-life of a nuclide relate to its stability?   (22-2)

11. List the three parent nuclides of the natural decay series.   (22-2)

12. How are artificial radioactive isotopes produced?   (22-2)

13. Neutrons are more effective than protons or alpha particles for bombarding atomic nuclei. Why?   (22-2)

14. Why are all of the transuranium elements radioactive? (Hint: See Section 22-1.)   (22-2)

15. Why can a radioactive material affect photographic film even though the film is well wrapped in black paper?   (22-3)

16. How does the penetrating ability of gamma rays compare with that of alpha particles and beta particles?   (22-3)

17. How does nuclear radiation damage biological tissue?   (22-3)

18. Explain how film badges, Geiger-Müller counters, and scintillation detectors are used to detect radiation and measure radiation exposure.   (22-3)

19. How is the age of an object containing a radioactive nuclide estimated?   (22-3)

20. How is the fission of a uranium-235 nucleus induced?   (22-4)

21. How does the fission of uranium-235 produce a chain reaction?   (22-4)

22. Describe the purposes of the five major components of a nuclear power plant.   (22-4)

23. Describe the reaction that produces the sun's energy.   (22-4)

24. What is one problem that must be overcome before energy-producing controlled fusion reactions are a reality?   (22-4)

PROBLEMS

Mass Defect

25. The mass of a $^{20}_{10}\text{Ne}$ atom is 19.992 44 amu. Calculate its mass defect.

26. The mass of a $^{7}_{3}\text{Li}$ atom is 7.016 00 amu. Calculate its mass defect.

Nuclear Binding Energy

27. Calculate the nuclear binding energy of one lithium-6 atom. The measured atomic mass of lithium-6 is 6.015 amu.

28. Calculate the binding energies of the following two nuclei, and indicate which releases more

9. **a.** high-energy electromagnetic radiation
   b. Scientists believe that gamma rays are produced when nuclear particles undergo transition in nuclear energy levels.

10. The longer the half-life, the greater the stability.

11. U-238, U-235, Th-232

12. by bombarding stable nuclei with charged and uncharged particles

13. They do not carry any charge.

14. They are beyond atomic number 83, so the repulsive force of the protons is too great for a stable nuclide to exist.

15. Radiation can penetrate paper.

16. Gamma rays have much more penetrating ability.

17. It can ionize the atoms and molecules in the tissue.

18. Film badges use the exposure of film; Geiger-Müller counters count electric pulses carried by gas ionized by the radiation; scintillation counters convert scintillating light, from substances that absorb ionizing energy and then emit visible light, to an electric signal for detection.

19. by measuring the accumulation of a daughter nuclide or the disappearance of a parent nuclide, correlating this information with the half-life of the parent nuclide

20. by bombarding it with slow neutrons

21. When slow neutrons are absorbed by uranium-235, the atom splits and emits more neutrons, which in turn bombard more uranium atoms, and so on.

22. The fuel contains the fissioning material. The coolant absorbs heat created in the reaction. The moderator slows down fast neutrons produced by fission. Shielding protects the surroundings from radiation. Control rods limit the number of free neutrons by absorbing them.

23. Four hydrogen nuclei combine at an extremely high temperature and pressure to form a helium nucleus with loss of mass and release of energy.

24. Fusion reactions require so much heat that nothing can contain them.

25. 0.172 46 amu per atom

26. 0.042 13 amu per atom

27. 5.2×10^{-12} J

28. a. 4.47×10^{-11} J
b. 2.99×10^{-11} J
The nucleus in (a) releases more energy.

29. a. K-39: 1.28×10^{-12} J/nucleon
Na-23: 1.30×10^{-12} J/nucleon
b. Na-23

30. 9.00×10^{-13} J/nucleon

31. a. 1:1   **c.** 1.51:1
b. 2:1   **d.** 1.68:1

32. a. a, c
b. (a) is close to the 1:1 ratio; (c) is close to the 1.5:1 ratio

33. a. $_{-1}^{0}\beta$ **c.** $_{-1}^{0}e$
b. $_{2}^{4}He$ **d.** $_{6}^{13}C$

34. $_{84}^{210}Po \longrightarrow _{2}^{4}He + _{82}^{206}Pb$

35. $_{82}^{210}Pb \longrightarrow _{-1}^{0}\beta + _{83}^{210}Bi$

36. 6.25 g

37. 37.44 days

38. 1/16

39. 0.938 mg

40. a. $_{94}^{239}Pu$ **c.** $_{0}^{1}n$
b. $_{6}^{13}C$ **d.** $_{56}^{139}Ba$

41. 0.0313 g

---

energy when formed. You will need information from the periodic table and the text.
a. atomic mass 34.988011 amu, $_{19}^{35}K$
b. atomic mass 22.989767 amu, $_{11}^{23}Na$

29. a. What is the binding energy per nucleon for each nucleus in the previous problem?
b. Which nucleus is more stable?

30. The mass of $_{3}^{7}Li$ is 7.016 00 amu. Calculate the binding energy per nucleon for $_{3}^{7}Li$. Convert the mass in amu to binding energy in joules.

Neutron-Proton Ratio

31. Calculate the neutron-proton ratios for the following nuclides:
a. $_{6}^{12}C$ c. $_{82}^{206}Pb$
b. $_{1}^{3}H$ d. $_{50}^{134}Sn$

32. a. Locate the nuclides in problem 31 on the graph in Figure 22-2. Which ones lie on the band of stability?
b. For the stable nuclides, determine whether their neutron-proton ratio tends toward 1:1 or 1.5:1.

Nuclear Equations

33. Balance the following nuclear equations. (Hint: See Sample Problem 22-1.)
a. $_{19}^{43}K \longrightarrow _{20}^{43}Ca + \underline{\ ?\ }$
b. $_{92}^{233}U \longrightarrow _{90}^{229}Th + \underline{\ ?\ }$
c. $_{6}^{11}C + \underline{\ ?\ } \longrightarrow _{5}^{11}B$
d. $_{7}^{13}N \longrightarrow _{+1}^{0}\beta + \underline{\ ?\ }$

34. Write the nuclear equation for the release of an alpha particle by $_{84}^{210}Po$.

35. Write the nuclear equation for the release of a beta particle by $_{82}^{210}Pb$.

Half-Life

36. The half-life of plutonium-239 is 24 110 years. Of an original mass of 100.g, how much remains after 96 440 years? (Hint: See Sample Problem 22-2.)

37. The half-life of thorium-227 is 18.72 days. How many days are required for three-fourths of a given amount to decay?

38. The half-life of protactinium-234 is 6.69 hours. What fraction of a given amount remains after 26.76 hours?

---

39. How many milligrams remain of a 15.0 mg sample of radium-226 after 6396 years? The half-life of radium-226 is 1599 years.

MIXED REVIEW

40. Balance the following nuclear reactions;
a. $_{93}^{239}Np \longrightarrow _{-1}^{0}\beta + \underline{\ ?\ }$
b. $_{4}^{9}Be + _{2}^{4}He \longrightarrow \underline{\ ?\ }$
c. $_{15}^{32}P + \underline{\ ?\ } \longrightarrow _{15}^{33}P$
d. $_{92}^{236}U \longrightarrow _{36}^{94}Kr + \underline{\ ?\ } + 3_{0}^{1}n$

41. After 4797 years, how much of an original 0.250 g of radium-226 remains? Its half-life is 1599 years.

42. The parent nuclide of the thorium decay series is $_{90}^{232}Th$. The first four decays are as follows: alpha emission, beta emission, beta emission, and alpha emission. Write the nuclear equations for this series of emissions.

43. The half-life of radium-224 is 3.66 days. What was the original mass of radium-224 if 0.0500 g remains after 7.32 days?

44. Calculate the neutron-proton ratios for the following nuclides, and determine where they lie in relation to the band of stability.
a. $_{92}^{235}U$ c. $_{26}^{56}Fe$
b. $_{8}^{16}O$ d. $_{60}^{156}Nd$

45. Calculate the binding energy per nucleon of $_{92}^{238}U$ in joules. The atomic mass of a $_{92}^{238}U$ nucleus is 238.050 784 amu.

46. The energy released by the formation of a nucleus of $_{26}^{56}Fe$ is 7.89×10^{-11} J. Use Einstein's equation, $E = mc^2$, to determine how much mass is lost (in kilograms) in this process.

47. Calculate the binding energy for one mole of deuterium atoms. The measured mass of deuterium is 2.0140 amu.

CRITICAL THINKING

48. Why do we compare binding energy per nuclear particle of different nuclides instead of the total binding energy per nucleus?

49. Why is the constant rate of decay of radioactive nuclei so important in radioactive dating?

⊞ TECHNOLOGY & LEARNING

50. Graphing Calculator Calculating the Amount of Radioactive Material

The graphing calculator can run a program that graphs the relationship between the amount of radioactive material and elapsed time. Given the half-life of the radioactive material and the initial amount of the material in grams, you will graph the relationship between the amount of radioactive material and the elapsed time. Then, with an elapsed time, you will trace the graph to calculate the amount of radioactive material. The program will prompt the half-life and initial amount of material, and then can be used to create a graph. Trace the curve to make the calculation.

Go to Appendix C. If you are using a TI 83 Plus, you can download the program and data and run the application as directed. If you are using another calculator, your teacher will provide you with keystrokes and data sets to use. Remember that you will need to name the program and check the display, as explained in Appendix C. You will then be ready to run the program. After you have graphed the data, answer these questions.

a. Deteine the amount of neptunium-235 left after 2.0 years, given the half-life of neptunium-235 is 1.08 years and the initial amount was 8.00 g.

b. Determine the amount of neptunium-235 left after 5.0 years, given the half-life of neptunium-235 is 1.08 years and the initial amount was 8.00 g.

c. Determine the amount of uranium-232 left after 100 years, given the half-life of uranium-232 is 69 years and the initial amount was 10.0 g.

RESEARCH & WRITING

51. Investigate the history of the Manhattan Project.

52. Research the 1986 nuclear reactor accident at Chernobyl, Ukraine. What factors combined to cause the accident?

53. Find out about the various fusion-energy research projects that are being conducted in the United States and other parts of the world. How close are the researchers to finding an economical method of producing energy? What obstacles must still be overcome?

ALTERNATIVE ASSESSMENT

54. Your local grocery store may sell irradiated foods. Find out what stores in your area sell irradiated foods and determine whether you have any of these foods at home. What are the shelf lives of these foods before and after irradiation? Report your findings to the class.

42. $^{232}_{90}\text{Th} \longrightarrow {}^{4}_{2}\text{He} + {}^{228}_{88}\text{Ra}$
$^{228}_{88}\text{Ra} \longrightarrow {}^{0}_{-1}\beta + {}^{228}_{89}\text{Ac}$
$^{228}_{89}\text{Ac} \longrightarrow {}^{0}_{-1}\beta + {}^{228}_{90}\text{Th}$
$^{228}_{90}\text{Th} \longrightarrow {}^{4}_{2}\text{He} + {}^{224}_{88}\text{Ra}$

43. 0.200 g

44. a. 1.55:1; outside
b. 1:1; within
c. 1.15:1; within
d. 1.6:1; outside

45. 1.21×10^{-12} J/nucleon

46. 8.77×10^{-28} kg

47. 2.24×10^{11} J/mol

48. Binding energy per nuclear particle is a more accurate measure of stability than total binding energy. A large nucleus would have a greater total binding energy but not necessarily a greater binding energy per nucleon.

49. If the rate of decay varied, the length of time could not be determined from the amount of decay.

50. a. 2.22 g
b. 0.32 g
c. 3.7 g

51. The Manhattan Project took place at the University of Chicago and other locations during WW II and resulted in the development of the atomic bomb.

52. The Chernobyl accident was caused partly by an unsafe test on a reactor that had an old design with few safeguards.

53. Various fusion energy projects involve the use of lasers or electromagnetic "bottles" to contain the extremely hot fusion material. Containing this material long enough to produce a net gain in energy is still the major obstacle.

54. Answers will vary widely. Students can compare shelf lives of irradiated food with those of non-irradiated food for their report.

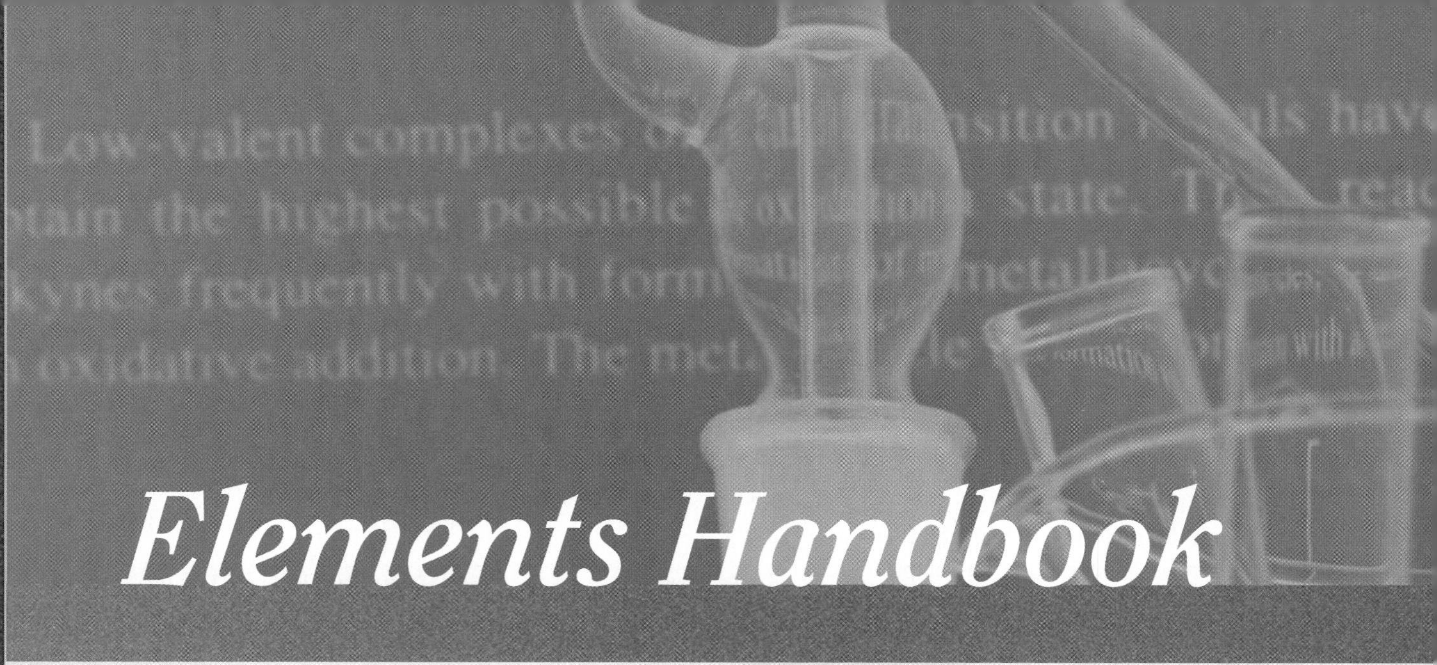

Elements Handbook

GROUP 1	ALKALI METALS	728

APPLICATION: *Technology*
Sodium Vapor Lighting — 730

APPLICATION: *Health*
Electrolyte Balance in the Body — 731

GROUP 2	ALKALINE EARTH METALS	734

APPLICATION: *Technology*
Fireworks — 736

APPLICATION: *Health*
Calcium: An Essential
Mineral in the Diet — 738

Magnesium: An Essential
Mineral in the Diet — 738

GROUPS 3–12	TRANSITION METALS	740

APPLICATION: *Geology*
Gemstones and Color — 743

APPLICATION: *Technology*
Alloys — 744

APPLICATION: *The Environment*
Mercury Poisoning — 747

APPLICATION: *Health*
Elements in the Body — 748
Role of Iron — 749

GROUP 13	BORON FAMILY	750

APPLICATION: *Technology*
Aluminum — 752
Aluminum Alloys — 753

| GROUP 14 | CARBON FAMILY | 754 |

APPLICATION: *Chemical Industry*
Carbon and the Reduction
of Iron Ore — 756
Carbon Dioxide — 757
Carbon Monoxide — 757

APPLICATION: *Biochemistry*
Carbon Dioxide and Respiration — 758
Macromolecules — 761

APPLICATION: *The Environment*
Carbon Monoxide Poisoning — 760

APPLICATION: *Chemical Industry*
Silicon and Silicates — 767
Silicones — 767

APPLICATION: *Technology*
Semiconductors — 768

| GROUP 15 | NITROGEN FAMILY | 770 |

APPLICATION: *Biology*
Plants and Nitrogen — 772

APPLICATION: *Chemical Industry*
Fertilizers — 773

| GROUP 16 | OXYGEN FAMILY | 774 |

APPLICATION: *Chemical Industry*
Oxides — 776

APPLICATION: *The Environment*
Ozone — 778

APPLICATION: *Chemical Industry*
Sulfuric Acid — 779

| GROUP 17 | HALOGEN FAMILY | 780 |

APPLICATION: *The Environment*
Chlorine in Water Treatment — 782
Fluoride and Tooth Decay — 783

GROUP 1
ALKALI METALS

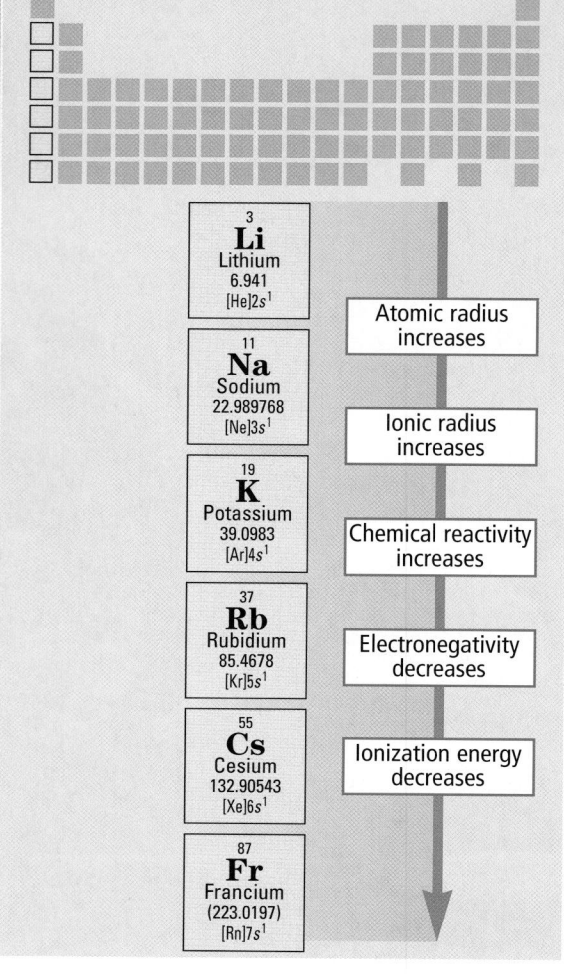

CHARACTERISTICS

- do not occur in nature as elements
- are reactive metals obtained by reducing the 1+ ions in their natural compounds
- are stored under kerosene or other hydrocarbon solvent because they react with water vapor or oxygen in air
- consist of atoms with one electron in the outermost energy level
- form colorless ions, each with a 1+ charge
- form ionic compounds
- form water-soluble bases
- are strong reducing agents
- consist of atoms that have low ionization energies
- are good conductors of electricity and heat
- are ductile, malleable, and soft enough to be cut with a knife
- have a silvery luster, low density, and low melting point

| 3 |
| **Li** |
| Lithium |
| 6.941 |
| [He]2s^1 |

| 11 |
| **Na** |
| Sodium |
| 22.989768 |
| [Ne]3s^1 |

| 19 |
| **K** |
| Potassium |
| 39.0983 |
| [Ar]4s^1 |

| 37 |
| **Rb** |
| Rubidium |
| 85.4678 |
| [Kr]5s^1 |

| 55 |
| **Cs** |
| Cesium |
| 132.90543 |
| [Xe]6s^1 |

| 87 |
| **Fr** |
| Francium |
| (223.0197) |
| [Rn]7s^1 |

Atomic radius increases

Ionic radius increases

Chemical reactivity increases

Electronegativity decreases

Ionization energy decreases

Lithium was discovered in 1817. It is found in most igneous rocks and is used in batteries as an anode because it has a very low reduction potential. Lithium is soft and is stored in oil or kerosene to prevent it from reacting with the air.

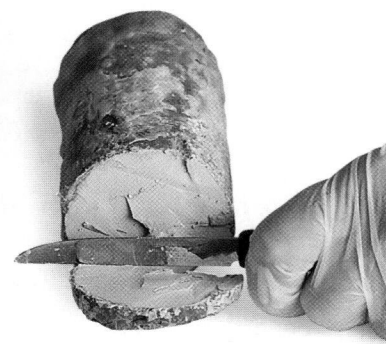

Sodium derives its name from the word soda. It was first isolated in 1807 from the electrolysis of caustic soda, NaOH. Sodium is soft enough to be cut with a knife. It is shiny until it reacts with oxygen, which causes the surface to lose its luster.

Potassium was first isolated in 1807 from the electrolysis of caustic potash, KOH.

COMMON REACTIONS

With Water and Acids to Form Bases and Hydrogen Gas

Example: $2Na(s) + 2H_2O(l) \longrightarrow 2NaOH(aq) + H_2(g)$
Li, K, Rb, and Cs also follow this pattern.

Example: $2Na(s) + 2HCl(aq) \longrightarrow 2NaCl(aq) + H_2(g)$
Li, K, Rb, and Cs also follow this pattern.

With Halogens to Form Salts

Example: $2Na(s) + F_2(g) \longrightarrow 2NaF(s)$
Li, K, Rb, and Cs also follow this pattern in reacting
    with F_2, Cl_2, Br_2, and I_2.

With Oxygen to Form Oxides, Peroxides, or Superoxides

Lithium forms an oxide.
$4Li(s) + O_2(g) \longrightarrow 2Li_2O(s)$

Sodium forms a peroxide.
$2Na(s) + O_2(g) \longrightarrow Na_2O_2(s)$

*Alkali metals with higher molecular masses can
form superoxides.*
$K(s) + O_2(g) \longrightarrow KO_2(s)$
Rb and Cs also follow this pattern.

Alkali-Metal Oxides with Water to Form Bases

Oxides of Na, K, Rb, and Cs can be prepared indirectly.
These basic anhydrides form hydroxides in water.

Example: $K_2O(s) + H_2O(l) \longrightarrow 2KOH(aq)$
Li, Na, Rb, and Cs also follow this pattern.

*A small piece of potassium dropped into water will
react explosively, releasing H_2 to form a strongly
basic hydroxide solution. The heat of the reaction
ignites the hydrogen gas that is produced.*

*Sodium reacts vigorously with chlorine to produce
NaCl. Most salts of Group 1 metals are white
crystalline compounds.*

ANALYTICAL TEST

Alkali metals are easily detected by flame tests
because each metal imparts a characteristic
color to a flame.

When sodium and potassium are both present
in a sample, the yellow color of the sodium masks
the violet color of the potassium. The violet color
can be seen only when the combined sodium-
potassium flame is viewed through a
cobalt-blue glass. The glass blocks the yellow
flame of sodium and makes it possible to see
the violet flame of potassium.

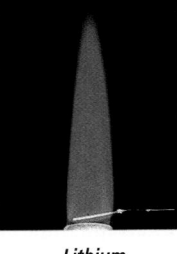

Lithium   *Sodium*

 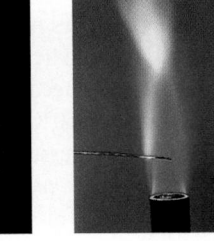

Potassium   *Rubidium*   *Cesium*

PROPERTIES OF THE GROUP 1 ELEMENTS

	Li	Na	K	Rb	Cs	Fr
Melting point (°C)	180.5	97.8	63.25	38.89	28.5	27
Boiling point (°C)	1342	882.9	760	691	668	—
Density (g/cm³)	0.534	0.971	0.862	1.53	1.87	—
Ionization energy (kJ/mol)	520	496	419	403	376	—
Atomic radius (pm)	152	186	227	248	265	270
Ionic radius (pm)	76	102	138	152	167	180
Common oxidation number in compounds	+1	+1	+1	+1	+1	—
Crystal structure	bcc*	bcc	bcc	bcc	bcc	—
Hardness (Mohs' scale)	0.6	0.4	0.5	0.3	0.2	—

*body-centered cubic

APPLICATION *Technology*

Sodium Vapor Lighting

The flame test for sodium shows a bright line between 589.0 and 589.5 nm, which is the yellow range of the emission spectrum. Sodium can be vaporized at high temperatures in a sealed tube and made to give off light using two electrodes connected to a power source. Sodium vapor lighting is often used along highways and in parking lots because it provides good illumination while using less energy than other types of lighting.

Sodium vapor lighting comes in both low-pressure and high-pressure bulbs. Low-pressure lamps reach an internal temperature of 270°C to vaporize the sodium under a pressure of about 1 Pa. High-pressure lamps contain mercury and xenon in addition to sodium. These substances reach an internal temperature of 1100°C under a pressure of about 100 000 Pa. The high-pressure lamp provides a higher light intensity. The design of both types of lamps must take into account the high reactivity of sodium, which increases at high temperatures. Because ordinary glass will react with sodium at 250°C, a special sodium-resistant glass is used for low-pressure lamps. High-pressure lamps use an aluminum oxide material for the column containing the sodium, mercury, and xenon. Both types of lamps contain tungsten electrodes.

The light intensity per watt for sodium vapor lamps far exceeds that of fluorescent lamps, high-pressure mercury vapor lamps, tungsten halogen lamps, and incandescent bulbs.

APPLICATION *Health*

Electrolyte Balance in the Body

The elements of Group 1 are important to a person's diet and body maintenance because they form ionic compounds, that are present in the body as solutions of the ions. All ions carry an electric charge, so they are electrolyte solutes. Two of the most important electrolyte solutes found in the body are K^+ and Na^+ ions. Both ions facilitate the transmission of nerve impulses and control the amount of water retained by cells.

During situations where the body is losing water rapidly through intense sweating or diarrhea for a prolonged period (more than 5 hours), a sports drink can hydrate the body and restore electrolyte balance.

TABLE 1A Sodium-Potassium Composition of Body Fluids

Cation	Inside cells (mmol/L)	Outside cells or in plasma (mmol/L)
Na^+	12	145
K^+	140	4

The sodium and potassium ion concentrations of body fluids are shown in Table 1A. Sodium ions are found primarily in the fluid outside cells, while potassium ions are largely found in the fluid inside cells. Anions are present in the fluids to balance the electrical charge of the Na^+ and K^+ cations.

Abnormal electrolyte concentrations in blood serum can indicate the presence of disease. The ion concentrations that vary as a result of disease are Na^+, K^+, Cl^-, and HCO_3^-. Sodium ion concentration is a good indicator of the water balance between blood and tissue cells. Unusual potassium ion levels can indicate kidney or gastrointestinal problems. Chloride ion is the anion that balances the positive charge of the sodium ion in the fluid outside the cells. It also diffuses into a cell to maintain normal electrolyte balance when hydrogen carbonate ions diffuse out of the cell into the blood. Table 1B shows medical conditions associated with electrolyte imbalances.

TABLE 1B Electrolyte Imbalances

Electrolyte	Normal range (mmol/L)	Causes of imbalance	
		Excess	Deficiency
Sodium, Na^+	135–145	hypernatremia (increased urine excretion; excess water loss)	hyponatremia (dehydration; diabetes-related low blood pH; vomiting; diarrhea)
Potassium, K^+	3.5–5.0	hyperkalemia (renal failure; low blood pH)	hypokalemia (gastrointestinal conditions)
Hydrogen carbonate, HCO_3^-	24–30	hypercapnia (high blood pH; hypoventilation)	hypocapnia (low blood pH; hyperventilation; dehydration)
Chloride, Cl^-	100–106	hyperchloremia (anemia; heart conditions; dehydration)	hypochloremia (acute infection; burns; hypoventilation)

Sodium-Potassium Pump in the Cell Membrane

The process of active transport allows a cell to maintain its proper electrolyte balance. To keep the ion concentrations at the proper levels shown in Table 1B, a sodium-potassium pump embedded in the cell membrane shuttles sodium ions out of the cell across the cell membrane. A model for the action of the sodium-potassium pump is shown below.

Nerve Impulses and Ion Concentration

An uneven distribution of Na^+ and K^+ ions across nerve cell membranes is essential for the normal operation of the nervous system. This uneven distribution of ions creates a voltage across nerve cell membranes. When a nerve cell is stimulated, sodium ions diffuse into the cell from the surrounding fluid, raising voltage across the nerve cell membrane from −70 mV to nearly +60 mV. Potassium ions then diffuse out of the cell into the surrounding fluid, restoring the voltage across the nerve cell membrane to −70 mV. This voltage fluctuation initiates the transmission of a nerve impulse. The amount of Na^+ inside the cell has increased slightly, and the amount of K^+ outside the cell has decreased. But the sodium-potassium pump will restore these ions to their proper concentrations.

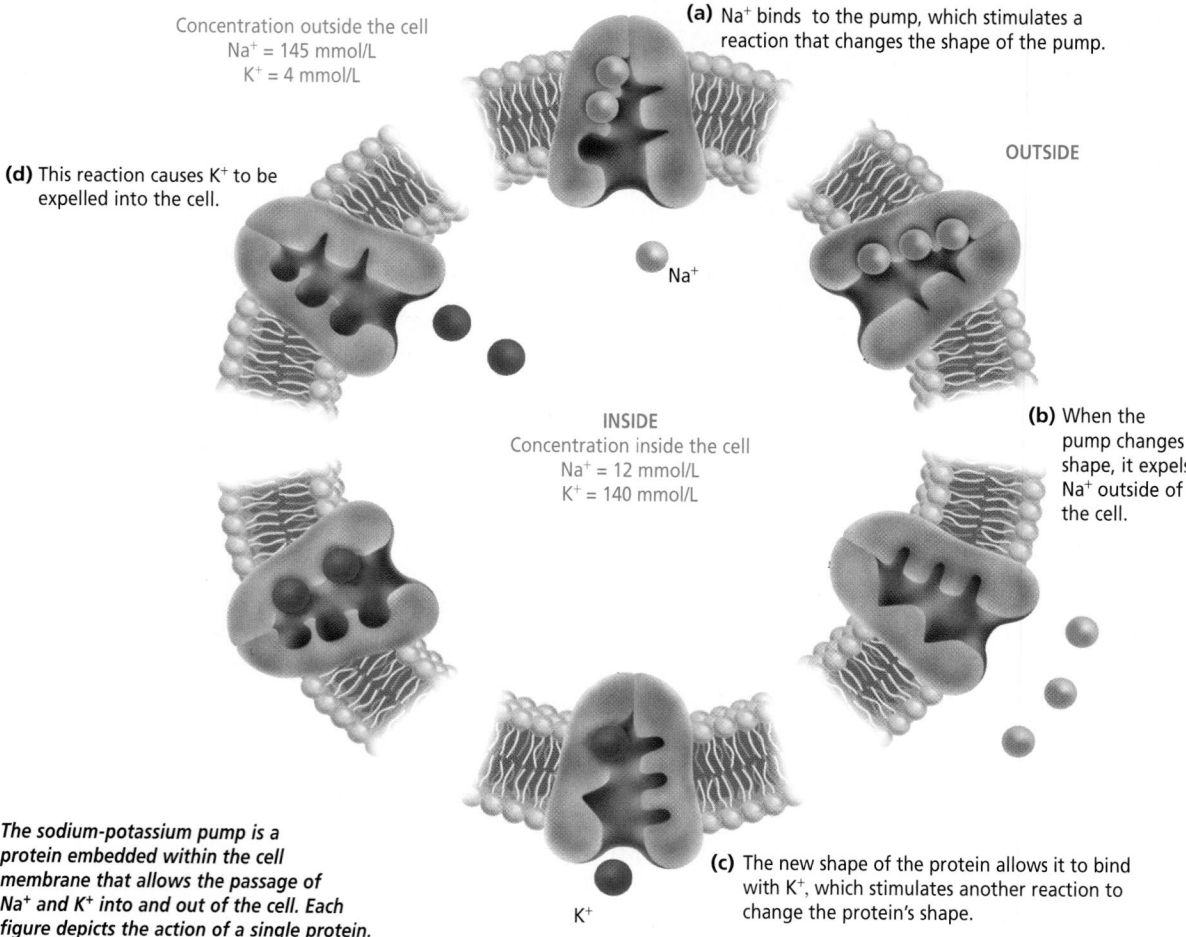

Concentration outside the cell
Na^+ = 145 mmol/L
K^+ = 4 mmol/L

(a) Na^+ binds to the pump, which stimulates a reaction that changes the shape of the pump.

OUTSIDE

(d) This reaction causes K^+ to be expelled into the cell.

Na^+

INSIDE
Concentration inside the cell
Na^+ = 12 mmol/L
K^+ = 140 mmol/L

(b) When the pump changes shape, it expels Na^+ outside of the cell.

(c) The new shape of the protein allows it to bind with K^+, which stimulates another reaction to change the protein's shape.

K^+

The sodium-potassium pump is a protein embedded within the cell membrane that allows the passage of Na^+ and K^+ into and out of the cell. Each figure depicts the action of a single protein.

What's your sodium IQ?

Though sodium is an important mineral in your body, a diet that is high in sodium is one of several factors linked to high blood pressure, also know as hypertension. High Na^+ levels cause water retention, which results in increased blood pressure. Sodium is not the direct cause of all hypertension, but reducing sodium levels in the diet can affect individuals with a condition known as salt-sensitive hypertension. Therefore, the Dietary Guidelines for Americans recommend consuming salt and sodium in moderation. Test your knowledge about sodium in foods with the questions below.

1. Which of the following condiments do you think has the lowest salt content?
a. mustard   c. catsup   e. vinegar
b. steak sauce d. pickles

2. One-fourth of a teaspoon of salt contains about _____ of sodium.
a. 10 mg   c. 500 mg   e. 1 kg
b. 100 g   d. 500 g

3. According to FDA regulations for food product labels, a food labeled *salt-free* must contain less than _____ mg of sodium ion per serving.
a. 100   c. 0.001   e. 0.00005
b. 5   d. 0.005

4. The Nutrition Facts label for a particular food reads "Sodium 15 mg." This is the amount of sodium ion per _____.
a. package   c. serving   e. RDA
b. teaspoon   d. ounce

5. The recommended average daily intake of sodium ion for adults is 2400 mg. For a low-sodium diet the intake should be _____.
a. 200 mg   c. 750 mg   e. 150 mg
b. 2000 mg   d. 500 mg

6. Each of the following ingredients can be found in the ingredients lists for some common food products. Which ones indicate that the product contains sodium?
a. trisodium phosphate d. sodium sulfate
b. sodium bicarbonate   e. MSG
c. sodium benzoate   f. baking soda

7. Which of the following spices is NOT a salt substitute?
a. caraway seeds   d. ginger
b. dill   e. onion salt
c. mace

8. Most salt in the diet comes from salting foods too heavily at the dinner table.
a. true   b. false

9. Which of the following foods are high in sodium?
a. potato chips   c. doughnuts   e. figs
b. pizza   d. banana

10. Your body requires about 200 mg of sodium ion, or 500 mg of salt, per day. Why do these numbers differ?

Answers 1. e; 2. c; 3. b; 4. c; 5. c; 6. all of them; 7. e; 8. b; processed foods can contain very high levels of sodium; 9. a, b, c; 10. Salt is not pure sodium.

GROUP 2
ALKALINE EARTH METALS

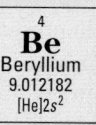

CHARACTERISTICS

- do not occur naturally in their elemental state
- occur most commonly as the carbonates, phosphates, silicates, and sulfates
- occur naturally as compounds that are either insoluble or only slightly soluble in water
- consist of atoms that contain two electrons in their outermost energy level
- consist of atoms that tend to lose two electrons per atom, forming ions with a 2+ charge
- are less reactive than alkali metals
- form ionic compounds primarily
- react with water to form bases and hydrogen gas
- are good conductors of heat and electricity
- are ductile and malleable
- have a silvery luster
- include the naturally radioactive element radium

| 4 |
| **Be** |
| Beryllium |
| 9.012182 |
| [He]$2s^2$ |

| 12 |
| **Mg** |
| Magnesium |
| 24.3050 |
| [Ne]$3s^2$ |

| 20 |
| **Ca** |
| Calcium |
| 40.078 |
| [Ar]$4s^2$ |

| 38 |
| **Sr** |
| Strontium |
| 87.62 |
| [Kr]$5s^2$ |

| 56 |
| **Ba** |
| Barium |
| 137.327 |
| [Xe]$6s^2$ |

| 88 |
| **Ra** |
| Radium |
| (226.0254) |
| [Rn]$7s^2$ |

Atomic radius increases

Ionic radius increases

Chemical reactivity increases

Electronegativity decreases

Ionization energy decreases

Calcium carbonate is a major component of marble.

Beryllium is found in the mineral compound beryl. Beryl crystals include the dark green emerald and the blue-green aquamarine. The colors of these gems come from other metal impurities.

The mineral dolomite, $CaCO_3 \cdot MgCO_3$, is a natural source of both calcium and magnesium.

COMMON REACTIONS

With Water to Form Bases and Hydrogen Gas
Example: $Mg(s) + 2H_2O(l) \longrightarrow Mg(OH)_2(aq) + H_2(g)$
Ca, Sr, and Ba also follow this pattern.

With Acids to Form Salts and Hydrogen Gas
Example: $Mg(s) + 2HCl(aq) \longrightarrow MgCl_2(aq) + H_2(g)$
Be, Ca, Sr, and Ba also follow this pattern.

With Halogens to Form Salts
Example: $Mg(s) + F_2(g) \longrightarrow MgF_2(s)$
Ca, Sr, and Ba also follow this pattern in reacting
with F_2, Cl_2, Br_2, and I_2.

With Oxygen to Form Oxides or Peroxides
Magnesium forms an oxide.
$2Mg(s) + O_2(g) \longrightarrow 2MgO(s)$
Be and Ca also follow this
pattern.

Strontium forms a peroxide.
$Sr(s) + O_2(g) \longrightarrow SrO_2(s)$
Ba also reacts in this way.

With Hydrogen to Form Hydrides
Example: $Mg(s) + H_2(g) \longrightarrow MgH_2(s)$
Ca, Sr, and Ba also follow this pattern.

With Nitrogen to Form Nitrides
Example: $3Mg(s) + N_2(g) \longrightarrow$
$Mg_3N_2(s)$
Be and Ca also follow this
pattern.

Calcium reacts with water to form hydrogen gas.

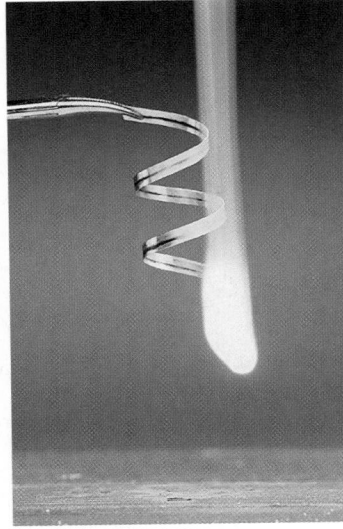

Magnesium burns in air to form MgO and Mg₃N₂.

Magnesium reacts with HCl to produce MgCl₂(aq).

ANALYTICAL TEST

Flame tests can be used to identify three of the alkaline earth elements. The colors of both calcium and
strontium can be masked by the presence of barium,
which produces a green flame.

 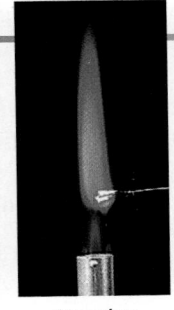 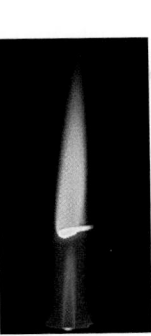

Calcium   *Strontium*   *Barium*

ALKALINE EARTH METALS **735**

PROPERTIES OF THE GROUP 2 ELEMENTS

	Be	Mg	Ca	Sr	Ba	Ra
Melting point (°C)	1287 ± 5	649	839 ± 2	769	725	700
Boiling point (°C)	2467	1107	1484	1384	1640	1737
Density (g/cm^3)	1.85	1.74	1.54	2.6	3.51	—
Ionization energy (kJ/mol)	900	738	590	550	503	509
Atomic radius (pm)	112	160	197	215	222	220
Ionic radius (pm)	45	72	100	118	136	148
Common oxidation number in compounds	+2	+2	+2	+2	+2	+2
Crystal structure	hcp*	hcp	fcc**	fcc	bcc	bcc
Hardness (Mohs' scale)	4.0	2.0	1.5	1.8	1.5	—

*hexagonal close-packed   **face-centered cubic

APPLICATION *Technology*

Fireworks

Fireworks are made from pyrotechnics—chemical substances that produce light and smoke when they are ignited. Pyrotechnics are also used in flares, smoke bombs, explosives, and matches. An aerial fireworks device is a rocket made of a cylinder, chemicals inside the cylinder, and fuses attached to the cylinder. The illustration on the right shows how the device works. The lift charge at the bottom of the cylinder consists of a small amount of black gunpowder. When the side fuse ignites the gunpowder, it explodes like a small bomb. The gunpowder consists of potassium nitrate, charcoal, and sulfur. When these three chemicals react with one another, they produce gases. In this case, the gases produced are carbon monoxide, carbon dioxide, sulfur dioxide, and nitrogen monoxide. These hot gases expand very rapidly, providing the thrust that lifts the rocket into the sky.

About the time the shell reaches its maximum altitude and minimum speed, the time fuse ignites the chemicals contained in the cylinder. The chemicals inside the cylinder determine the color of the burst.

Time-delay fuses activate the reactions in the other chambers

Ignition fuse activates the reaction in the bottom chamber

Red star bursts

Blue star bursts

Flash and sound mixture

Black powder propellant

The cylinder of a multiple-burst rocket contains separate reaction chambers connected by fuses. A common fuse ignites the propellant and the time-delay fuse in the first reaction chamber.

Chemical Composition and Color

One of the characteristics of fireworks that we enjoy most is their variety of rich colors. These colors are created in much the same way as the colors produced during a flame test. In a fireworks device, the chloride salt is heated to a high temperature, causing the excited atoms to give off a burst of light. The color of light produced depends on the metal used. The decomposition of barium chloride, $BaCl_2$, for example, produces a burst of green light, whereas strontium chloride, $SrCl_2$, releases red light.

People who design fireworks combine artistry with a technical knowledge of chemical properties. They have found ways to combine different colors within a single cylinder and to make parts of the cylinder explode at different times. Fireworks designers have a technical knowledge of projectile motion that is used to determine the height, direction, and angle at which a fireworks device will explode to produce a fan, fountain, flower, stream, comet, spider, star, or other shape.

Strontium and the Visible Spectrum

When heated, some metallic elements and their compounds emit light at specific wavelengths that are characteristic of the element or compound. Visible light includes wavelengths between about 400 and 700 nanometers. The figure below shows the emission spectrum for strontium. When heated, strontium gives off the maximum amount of visible light at about 700 nanometers, which falls in the red-light region of the visible spectrum.

The emission spectrum for strontium shows strong bands in the red region of the visible light spectrum.

Flares

Flares operate on a chemical principle that is different from that of fireworks. A typical flare consists of finely divided magnesium metal and an oxidizing agent. When the flare is ignited, the oxidizing agent reacts with the magnesium metal to produce magnesium oxide. This reaction releases so much energy that it produces a glow like that of the filaments in a light bulb. The brilliant white light produced by the flare is caused by billions of tiny particles of magnesium that glow when they react. If slightly larger particles of magnesium metal are used in the flare, the system glows for a longer period of time because the particles' reaction with the oxidizing agent is slower.

A colored flare can be thought of as a combination of a white flare and a chemical that produces colored light when burned. For example, a red flare can be made from magnesium metal, an oxidizing agent, and a compound of strontium. When the flare is ignited, the oxidizing agent and magnesium metal react, heating the magnesium to white-hot temperatures. The heat from this reaction causes the strontium compound to give off its characteristic red color.

A flare is made up of billions of reacting magnesium particles.

For safety reasons, some fireworks manufacturers store their products in metal sheds separated by sand banks. Also, people who work with fireworks are advised to wear cotton clothing because cotton is less likely than other fabrics to develop a static charge, which can cause a spark and accidentally ignite fireworks.

4000	4500	5000	5500	6000	6500	7000	7500

Health

Calcium: An Essential Mineral in the Diet

Calcium is the most abundant mineral in the body. It is the mineral that makes up a good portion of the teeth and the bone mass of the body. A small percentage of calcium in the body is used in the reactions by which cells communicate and in the regulation of certain body processes. Calcium is so important to normal body functioning that if the calcium level of the blood falls far below normal, hormones signal the release of calcium from bone and signal the gastrointestinal tract to absorb more calcium during the digestion process.

A prolonged diet that is low in calcium is linked to a disease characterized by a decrease in bone mass, a condition called osteoporosis. Reduced bone mass results in brittle bones that fracture easily. Osteoporosis generally occurs later in life and is more prevalent in females. However, because you achieve peak bone mass during the late teens or early twenties, it is critical that your diet meet the recommended requirements to increase your peak bone mass. The recommended dietary intake for calcium is 1000 mg per day. Maintaining that level in the diet along with regular exercise through adulthood are thought to reduce the rate of bone loss later in life. Excess calcium in the diet (consuming more than 2500 mg daily) can interfere with the absorption of other minerals.

Dairy products are generally good sources of calcium.

Magnesium: An Essential Mineral in the Diet

Though magnesium has several functions in the body, one of the more important functions is its role in the absorption of calcium by cells. Magnesium, like sodium and potassium, is involved in the transmission of nerve impulses. Like calcium, magnesium is a component of bone.

A major source of magnesium in the diet is plants. Magnesium is the central atom in the green plant pigment chlorophyll. The structure of chlorophyll in plants is somewhat similar to the structure of heme—the oxygen-carrying molecule in animals. (See page 758 for the heme structure.)

TABLE 2A   Good Sources of Calcium in the Diet

Food	Serving size	Calcium present (mg)
Broccoli	6.3 oz	82
Cheddar cheese	1 oz	204
Cheese pizza, frozen	pizza for one	375
Milk, low-fat 1%	8 oz	300
Tofu, regular	4 oz	130
Vegetable pizza, frozen	pizza for one	500
Yogurt, low-fat	8 oz	415
Yogurt, plain whole milk	8 oz	274

The recommended dietary intake of magnesium is 400 mg per day. This is equivalent to just 4 oz of bran cereal. Because magnesium levels are easily maintained by a normal diet, it is unusual for anyone to have a magnesium deficiency. Most magnesium deficiencies are the result of factors that decrease magnesium absorption. People with gastrointestinal disorders, alcohol abusers, and the critically ill are most likely to have these types of absorption problems.

Excess magnesium in the diet is excreted by the kidneys, so there are no cumulative toxic effects.

Spinach is a good source of magnesium. Magnesium is the central atom in the green plant pigment chlorophyll. The chlorophyll structure is shown on the right.

TABLE 2B	Good Sources of Magnesium in the Diet	
Food	**Serving size**	**Magnesium present (mg)**
Barley, raw	1 cup	244
Beef, broiled sirloin	4 oz	36
Cabbage, raw	1 med. head	134
Cashews, dry-roasted	1 oz	74
Chicken, roasted breast	4 oz	31
Lima beans, boiled	1/2 cup	63
Oatmeal	1 oz	39
Potato, baked	7.1 oz	115
Prunes, dried	4 oz	51
Rice bran	8 oz	648
Salmon, canned	4 oz	39
Spinach, raw	10 oz	161

GROUPS 3–12
TRANSITION METALS

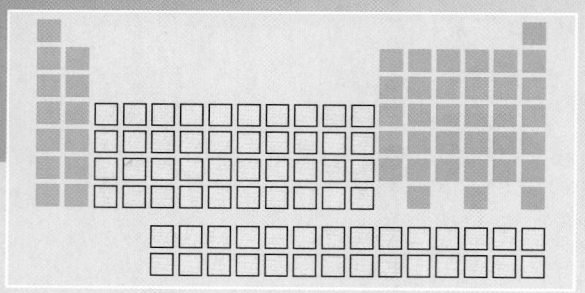

CHARACTERISTICS

- consist of metals in Groups 3 through 12
- contain one or two electrons in their outermost energy level
- are usually harder and more brittle than metals in Groups 1 and 2
- have higher melting and boiling points than metals in Groups 1 and 2
- are good conductors of heat and electricity
- are malleable and ductile
- have a silvery luster, except copper and gold
- include radioactive elements with numbers 89 through 112
- include mercury, the only liquid metal at room temperature
- have chemical properties that differ from each other
- tend to have two or more common oxidation states
- often form colored compounds
- may form complex ions

Iron ore is obtained from surface mines. Hematite, Fe_2O_3, is the most common iron ore.

Copper ores are also obtained from surface mines. Copper ore is shown here.

Gold, silver, platinum, palladium, iridium, rhodium, ruthenium, and osmium are sometimes referred to as the noble metals because they are not very reactive. These inert metals are found in coins, jewelry, and metal sculptures.

COMMON REACTIONS

Because this region of the periodic table is so large, you would expect great variety in the types of reaction characteristics of transition metals. For example, copper oxidizes in air to form the green patina you see on the Statue of Liberty. Copper reacts with concentrated HNO_3 but not with dilute HNO_3. Zinc, on the other hand, reacts readily with dilute HCl. Iron oxidizes in air to form rust, but chromium is generally unreactive in air. Some common reactions for transition elements are shown by the following.

May form two or more different ions

Example: $Fe(s) \longrightarrow Fe^{2+}(aq) + 2e^-$

Example: $Fe(s) \longrightarrow Fe^{3+}(aq) + 3e^-$

May react with oxygen to form oxides

Example: $4Cr(s) + 3O_2(g) \longrightarrow 2Cr_2O_3(s)$

Example: $2Cu(s) + O_2(g) \longrightarrow 2CuO(s)$

May react with halogens to form halides

Example: $Ni(s) + Cl_2(g) \longrightarrow NiCl_2(s)$

May form complex ions

See examples in the lower right.

Copper reacts with oxygen in air.

Copper reacts with concentrated nitric acid.

Zinc reacts with dilute hydrochloric acid.

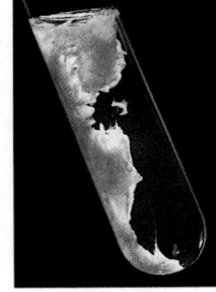

Soluble iron(III) salts form insoluble $Fe(OH)_3$ when they are reacted with a hydroxide base.

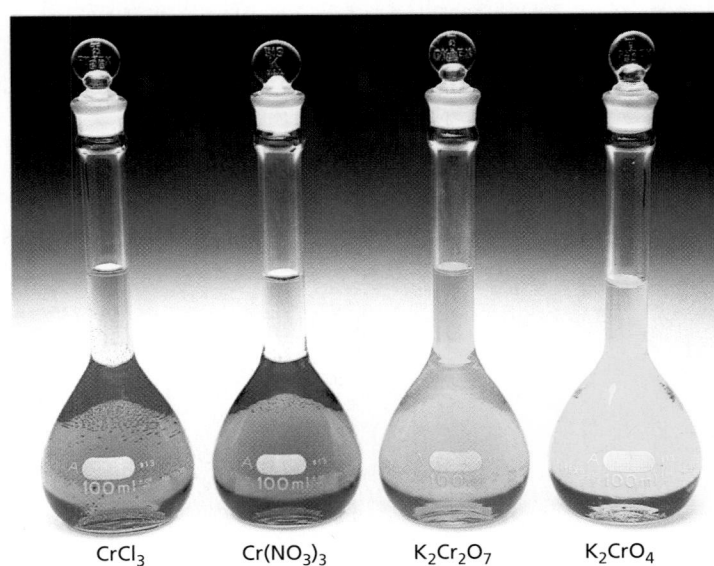

CrCl₃   Cr(NO₃)₃   K₂Cr₂O₇   K₂CrO₄

Chromium has several common oxidation states, represented here by aqueous solutions of its compounds. The violet and green solutions contain chromium in the +3 state, and the yellow and orange solutions contain chromium in the +6 oxidation state.

$Cu[(CH_3)_2SO]_2Cl_2$ $Cu(NH_3)_4SO_4 \cdot H_2O$

$[Co(NH_3)_4CO_3]NO_3$

$[Co(NH_3)_5(NO_2)]Cl_2$ $K_3[Fe(C_2O_4)_3]$

Complex ions belong to a class of compounds called coordination compounds. Coordination compounds show great variety in colors. Several transition-metal coordination compounds are shown.

ANALYTICAL TEST

Flame tests are not commonly used to identify transition metals. The presence of a certain transition-metal ion in a solution is sometimes obvious from the solution's color. Some transition-metal ions can be more accurately identified using a procedure called qualitative analysis. **Qualitative analysis** *is the identification of ions by their characteristic reactions.* The transition-metal ions most often identified through qualitative analysis include copper, nickel, zinc, chromium, iron cobalt, cadmium, manganese, and tin. Most tests to identify the presence of an ion in a mixture involve causing the ion to precipitate out of solution. Some of the more dramatic precipitation reactions for transition metals are shown.

KMnO$_4$ NiCl$_2$ CoCl$_2$ CuSO$_4$

Some transition metal ions can be identified by characteristic colors of their salt solutions.

Copper (formation of [Cu(NH$_3$)$_4$](OH)$_2$)

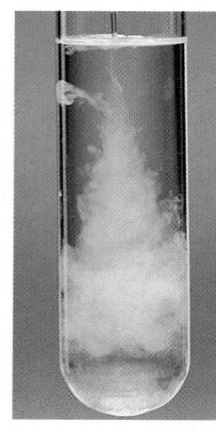

Cadmium (formation of CdS)

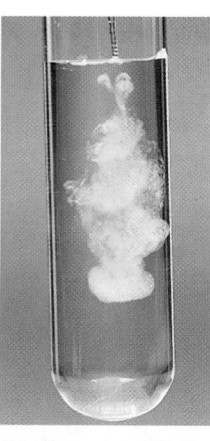

Zinc (formation of ZnS)

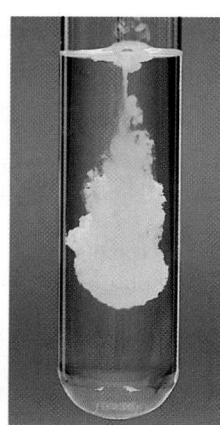

Chromium (formation of PbCrO$_4$)

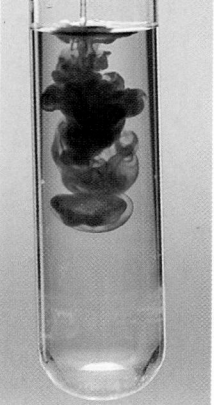

Iron (formation of [Fe(SCN)]$^{2+}$)

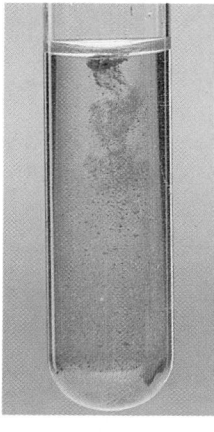

Manganese (formation of MnO$_4^-$)

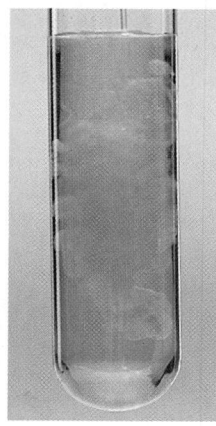

Nickel (formation of a nickel dimethylglyoxime complex)

PROPERTIES OF SOME TRANSITION METALS

	Cr	Fe	Co	Ni	Cu	Zn	Ag	Au	Hg
Melting point (°C)	1857 ± 20	1535	1495	1455	1083	420	962	1064	−38.8
Boiling point (°C)	2672	2750	2870	2732	2567	907	2212	2808 ± 2	356.6
Density (g/cm³)	7.20	7.86	8.9	8.92	8.96	7.14	10.5	19.3	13.5
Ionization energy (kJ/mol)	653	762	760	737	46	906	731	890	1007
Atomic radius (pm)	128	126	125	124	128	134	144	144	151
Common oxidation numbers	+2, +3, +6	+2, +3	+2, +3	+2	+1, +2	+2	+1	+1, +3	+1, +2

APPLICATION   *Geology*

Gemstones and Color

A gemstone is a mineral that can be cut and polished to make gems for an ornament or piece of jewelry. At one time, all gemstones were naturally occurring minerals mined from the Earth's crust. Today, however, chemists can duplicate natural processes to produce artificial gemstones. Amethyst, emerald, jade, opal, ruby, sapphire, and topaz occur naturally and can also be produced synthetically.

The color of a gemstone is determined by the presence of small amounts of one or more transition metals. For example, aluminum oxide, Al_2O_3, often occurs naturally as corundum—a clear, colorless mineral. However, if as few as 1 to 2% of the aluminum ions, Al^{3+}, are replaced by chromium ions, Cr^{3+}, the corundum takes on a reddish color and is known as ruby. If a small fraction of aluminum ions in corundum are replaced by Fe^{3+} and Ti^{3+}, the corundum has a greenish color and is known as emerald. In another variation, if vanadium ions, V^{3+}, replace a few Al^{3+} ions in corundum, the result is a gemstone known as alexandrite. This gemstone appears green in reflected natural light and red in transmitted or artificial light.

Table 3A lists transition metals that are responsible for the colors of various gemstones. The table provides only a general overview, however, as most naturally occurring gemstones occur in a range of hues, depending on the exact composition of the stone.

Artificial Gemstones

In 1902, the French chemist Auguste Verneuil found a way to melt a mixture of aluminum oxide and chromium salts and then cool the mixture very slowly to produce large crystals of reddish aluminum oxide—rubies.

Sapphire

Ruby

Peridot

Garnet

TABLE 3A   Transition Metals and Gemstone Colors

Gemstone	Color	Element
Amethyst	purple	iron
Aquamarine	blue	iron
Emerald	green	iron/titanium
Garnet	red	iron
Peridot	yellow-green	iron
Ruby	red	chromium
Sapphire	blue	iron/titanium
Spinel	colorless to red to black	varies
Turquoise	blue	copper

Verneuil's method, although somewhat modified, is still the one most widely used today for the manufacture of colored gemstones. When magnesium oxide is substituted for aluminum oxide, a colorless spinel-like product is formed. The addition of various transition metals then adds a tint to the spinel that results in the formation of synthetic emerald, aquamarine, tourmaline, or other gemstones. Synthetic gems look very much like their natural counterparts.

Synthetic sapphire

Synthetic ruby

APPLICATION *Technology*

Alloys

An alloy is a mixture of a metal and one or more other elements. In most cases, the second component of the mixture is also a metal.

Alloys are desirable because mixtures of elements usually have properties different from and often superior to the properties of individual metals. For example, many alloys that contain iron are harder, stronger, and more resistant to oxidation than iron itself.

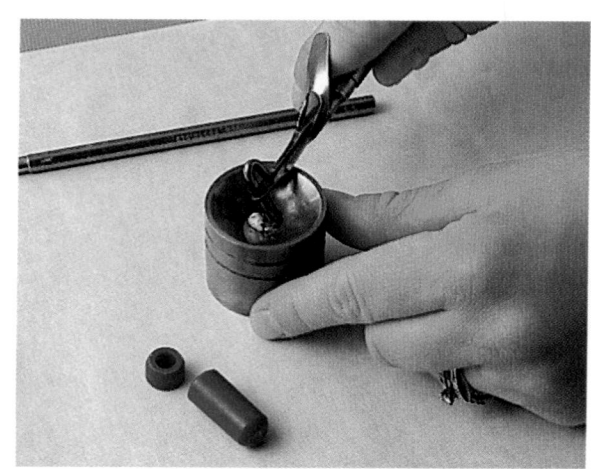

Amalgams are alloys that contain mercury. They are soft and pliable when first produced, but later become solid and hard. Dental fillings were once made of an amalgam of mercury and silver. Concerns about the possible toxicity of mercury led to the development of other filling materials.

Cast Iron and Steel

The term *steel* applies to any alloy consisting of iron and less than 1.5% carbon, and often other elements. When iron ore is treated with carbon in the form of coke to extract pure iron metal, some of the carbon also reacts with the iron to produce a form of iron carbide known as cementite. The reaction can be represented by the following equation.

$$3Fe + C \longrightarrow Fe_3C$$

Cast iron is a mixture that consists of some pure iron, known as ferrite, some cementite, and some carbon atoms trapped within the crystalline structure of the iron and cementite. The rate at which cast iron is cooled changes the proportion of these three components. If the cast iron is cooled slowly, the ferrite and cementite tend to separate from each other, forming a banded product that is tough but not very hard. However, if the cast iron is cooled quickly, the components of the original mixture cannot separate from each other, forming a product that is both tough and hard.

Stainless steel, which is hard and resists corrosion, is made of iron and chromium (12–30%). The properties of stainless steel make it a suitable alloy for making cutlery and utensils.

TABLE 3B   Composition and Uses of Some Alloys

Name of alloy	Composition	Uses
Brass	copper with up to 50% zinc	inexpensive jewelry; hose nozzles and couplings; piping; stamping dies
Bronze	copper with up to 12% tin	coins and medals; heavy gears; tools; electrical hardware
Coin metal	copper: 75% nickel: 25%	United States coins
Duralumin	aluminum: 95% copper: 4% magnesium: 0.5% manganese: <1%	aircraft, boats, railroad cars, and machinery because of its high strength and resistance to corrosion
Nichrome	nickel: 80–85% chromium: 15–20%	heating elements in toasters, electric heaters, etc.
Phosphor bronze	bronze with a small amount of phosphorus	springs, electrical springs, boat propellers
Solder	lead: 50%, tin: 50% or tin: 98%, silver: 2%	joining two metals to each other joining copper pipes
Sterling silver	silver: 92.5% copper: 7.5%	jewelry, art objects, flatware
Type metal	lead: 75–95% antimony: 2–18% tin: trace	used to make type for printing because it expands as it cools

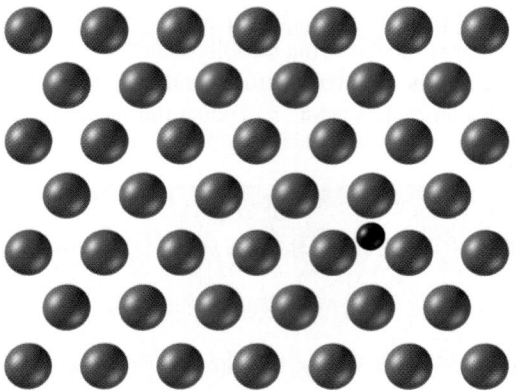

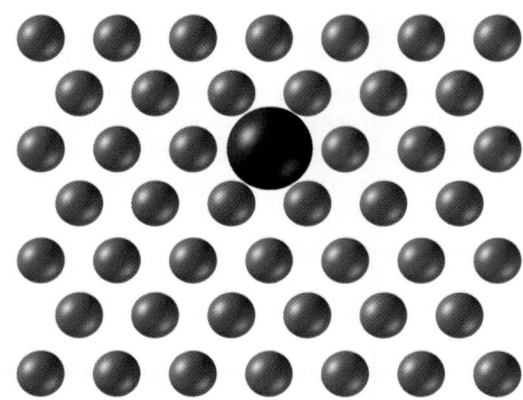

Interstitial crystal
A smaller atom or ion fits into a small space between particles in the array.

Substitutional crystal
A larger atom or ion is substituted for a particle in the array.

Structures and Preparation of Alloys

Alloys generally crystallize in one of two ways, depending on relative sizes of atoms. If the atoms of one of the metals present are small enough to fit into the spaces between the atoms of the second metal, they form an alloy with an interstitial structure (*inter* means "between," and *stitial* means "spaces"). If atoms of the two metals are of similar size or if one is larger, the atoms of one metal can substitute for the atoms of the second metal in its crystalline structure. Such alloys are substitutional alloys. Models for both types of crystals are shown above.

Techniques for making alloys depend on the metals used in the mixture. In some cases, the two metals can simply be melted together to form a mixture. The composition of the mixture often varies within a range, evidence that the final product is indeed a mixture and not a compound. In other cases, one metal may be melted first and the second dissolved in it. Brass is prepared in this way. If copper and zinc were heated together to a high temperature, zinc (bp 907°C) would evaporate before copper (mp 1084°C) melted. Therefore, the copper is melted first, and the zinc is added to it.

Brass has a high luster and resembles gold when cleaned and polished. A brass object can be coated with a varnish to prevent reactions of the alloy with air and water.

Sterling silver is more widely used than pure silver because it is stronger and more durable.

APPLICATION *The Environment*

Mercury Poisoning

Mercury is the only metal that is liquid at room temperature. It has a very high density compared with most other common transition metals and has a very high surface tension and high vapor pressure. Mercury and many of its compounds must be handled with extreme care because they are highly toxic. Mercury spills are especially hazardous because the droplets scatter easily and are often undetected during cleanup. These droplets release toxic vapors into the air.

Overexposure to mercury vapor or its compounds can occur by absorption through the skin, respiratory tract, or digestive tract. Mercury is a cumulative poison, which means that its concentration in the body increases as exposure increases.

Mercury that enters the body damages the kidneys, heart, and brain. The action of mercury on the brain affects the nervous system. Symptoms of mercury poisoning include numbness, tunnel vision, garbled speech, bleeding and inflammation of the gums, muscle spasms, anemia, and emotional disorders, such as depression, irritability, and personality changes. The saying "mad as a hatter" probably came about because of mercury poisoning. Mercury salts were once routinely used to process the felt used in hats.

Hatters often displayed the nerve and mental impairments associated with overexposure to mercury.

Methylmercury in Freshwater Ecosystems

Mercury, Hg, can be found in our environment and in our food supply. Fortunately, the body has some protective mechanisms to deal with trace amounts of mercury. However, levels of mercury and of an organic mercury compound, methylmercury $(CH_3)_2Hg$, are increasing in the environment due to mercury mining operations and runoff from the application of pesticides and fungicides.

Mercury is easily converted to methylmercury by bacteria. Methylmercury is more readily absorbed by cells than mercury itself. As a result, methylmercury accumulates in the food chain as shown in the diagram below. A serious incident of methylmercury poisoning occurred in Japan in the 1950s. People living in Minamata, Japan, were exposed to high levels of methylmercury from eating shellfish.

In the United States there is concern about mercury levels in fish from some freshwater lakes. Though environmental regulations have reduced the level of lake pollutants, it takes time to see a reduction in the concentration of an accumulated poison.

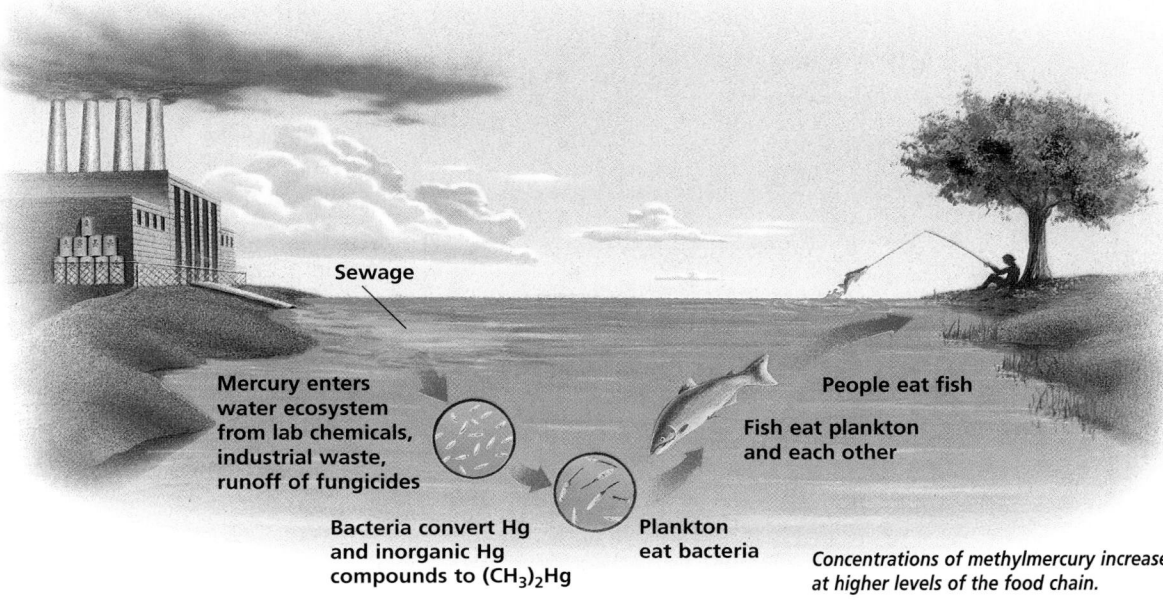

Sewage

Mercury enters water ecosystem from lab chemicals, industrial waste, runoff of fungicides

Bacteria convert Hg and inorganic Hg compounds to $(CH_3)_2Hg$

Plankton eat bacteria

Fish eat plankton and each other

People eat fish

Concentrations of methylmercury increase at higher levels of the food chain.

Elements in the Body

The four most abundant elements in the body (oxygen, carbon, hydrogen, and nitrogen) are the major components of organic biomolecules, such as carbohydrates, proteins, fats, and nucleic acids. Other elements compose a dietary category of compounds called minerals. Minerals are considered the inorganic elements of the body. Minerals fall into two categories— the major minerals and the trace minerals, or trace elements, as they are sometimes called. Notice in the periodic table below that most elements in the trace elements category of minerals are transition metals.

Trace elements are minerals with dietary daily requirements of 100 mg or less. They are found in foods derived from both plants and animals. Though these elements are present in very small quantities, they perform a variety of essential functions in the body, as shown in Table 3C on the next page.

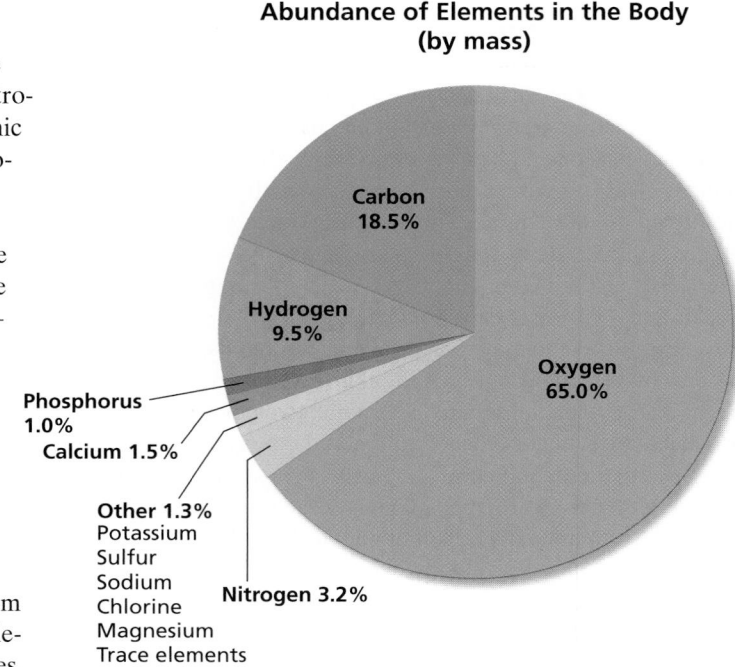

Abundance of Elements in the Body (by mass)

- Carbon 18.5%
- Hydrogen 9.5%
- Oxygen 65.0%
- Phosphorus 1.0%
- Calcium 1.5%
- Other 1.3%
  Potassium
  Sulfur
  Sodium
  Chlorine
  Magnesium
  Trace elements
- Nitrogen 3.2%

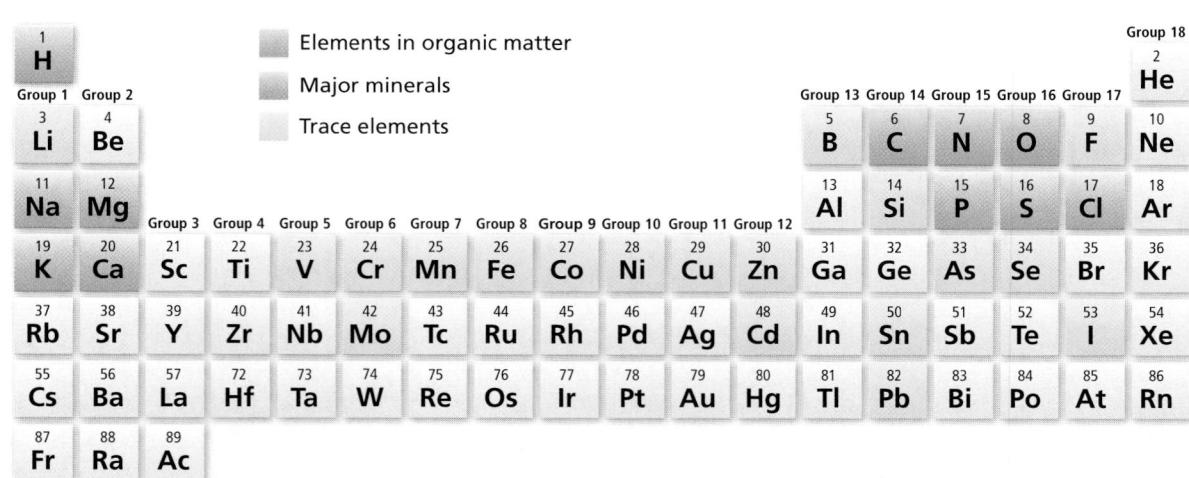

- Elements in organic matter
- Major minerals
- Trace elements

TABLE 3C   Transition Metal Trace Elements

Transition metal	Function
Vanadium, Cadmium	function not fully determined, but linked to a reduced growth rate and impaired reproduction
Chromium	needed for glucose transport to cells
Manganese	used in the enzyme reactions that synthesize cholesterol and metabolize carbohydrates
Iron	central atom in the heme molecule—a component of hemoglobin, which binds oxygen in the blood for transport to cells
Cobalt	a component of vitamin B_{12}
Nickel	enzyme cofactor in the metabolism of fatty acids and amino acids
Copper	a major component of an enzyme that functions to protect cells from damage
Zinc	needed for tissue growth and repair and as an enzyme cofactor
Molybdenum	enzyme cofactor in the production of uric acid

Role of Iron

Most iron in the body is in hemoglobin. Fe^{3+} is the central ion in the heme molecule, which is a component of the proteins hemoglobin and myoglobin. Hemoglobin in red blood cells transports oxygen to cells and picks up carbon dioxide as waste. Myoglobin is a protein that stores oxygen to be used in muscle contraction. Iron is also in the proteins of the electron transport system and the immune system.

Mechanisms of the body control the rate of iron absorption from food in the diet. When iron reserves are low, chemical signals stimulate cells of the intestines to absorb more iron during digestion. If the diet is low in iron, causing a deficiency, hemoglobin production stops and a condition called iron-deficiency anemia results. The blood cells produced during this state are stunted and unable to deliver adequate oxygen to cells. As a result, a person with iron-deficiency anemia feels tired and weak and has difficulty maintaining normal body temperature. The recommended daily intake of iron is 15 mg. The recommended level doubles for pregnant women. Iron supplements are for people who do not get enough iron in their daily diets. Table 3D lists some foods that are good sources of iron in the diet. Too much iron can be toxic because the body stores iron once it is absorbed. Abusing iron supplements can cause severe liver and heart damage.

TABLE 3D   Sources of Iron in Foods

Food	Serving size	Iron present (mg)
Beef roast (lean cut)	4 oz	3.55
Beef, T-bone steak (lean cut)	4 oz	3.40
Beef, ground (hamburger)	4 oz	2.78
Broccoli	6.3 oz	1.50
Chicken, breast	4 oz	1.35
Chicken, giblets	4 oz	7.30
Oatmeal, instant enriched	1 pkg	8.35
Pita bread, white enriched	6 1/2 in. diameter	1.40
Pork roast	4 oz	1.15
Prunes	4 oz	2.00
Raisins	4 oz	1.88

GROUP 13
BORON FAMILY

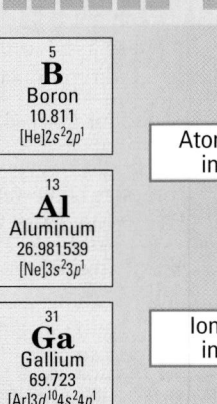
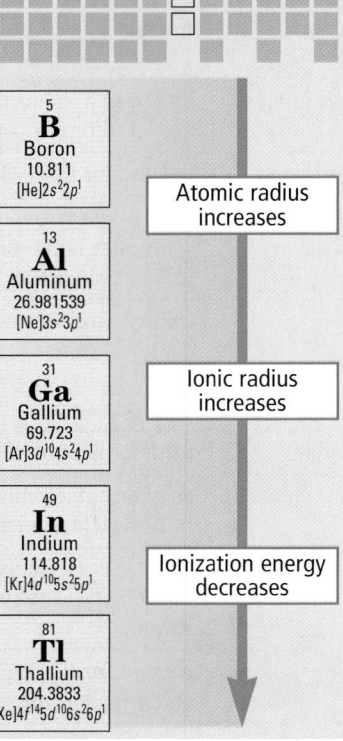

CHARACTERISTICS

- do not occur naturally in element form

- are scarce in nature (except aluminum, which is the most abundant metallic element)

- consist of atoms that have three electrons in their outer energy level

- are metallic solids (except boron, which is a solid metalloid)

- are soft and have low melting points (except boron, which is hard and has a high melting point)

- are chemically reactive at moderate temperatures (except boron)

5 **B** Boron 10.811 [He]$2s^2 2p^1$	Atomic radius increases
13 **Al** Aluminum 26.981539 [Ne]$3s^2 3p^1$	
31 **Ga** Gallium 69.723 [Ar]$3d^{10} 4s^2 4p^1$	Ionic radius increases
49 **In** Indium 114.818 [Kr]$4d^{10} 5s^2 5p^1$	
81 **Tl** Thallium 204.3833 [Xe]$4f^{14} 5d^{10} 6s^2 6p^1$	Ionization energy decreases

Boron is a covalent solid. Other members of the family are metallic solids.

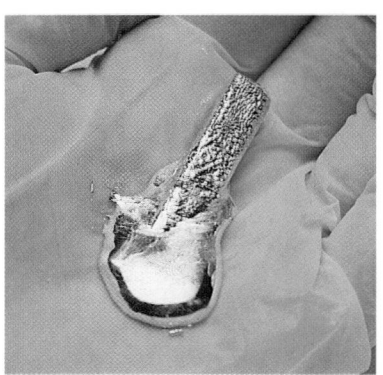

The warmth of a person's hand will melt gallium. Gallium metal has the lowest melting point (29.77°C) of any metal except mercury.

Aluminum is the most abundant metal in Earth's crust. It exists in nature as an ore called bauxite.

COMMON REACTIONS

The reaction chemistry of boron differs greatly from that of the other members of this family. Pure boron is a covalent network solid, whereas the other members of the family are metallic crystals in pure form. Boron resembles silicon more closely than it resembles the other members of its family.

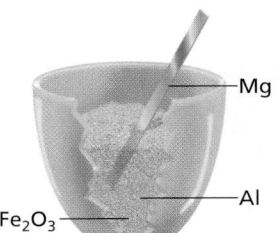

Mg

Al

Fe$_2$O$_3$

With Strong Bases to Form Hydrogen Gas and a Salt
Example: $2Al(s) + 2NaOH(aq) + 2H_2O(l) \longrightarrow$
$\quad 2NaAlO_2(aq) + 3H_2(g)$
Ga also follows this pattern.

With Dilute Acids to Form Hydrogen Gas and a Salt
Example: $2Al(s) + 6HCl(aq) \longrightarrow 2AlCl_3(aq) + 3H_2(g)$
Ga, In, and Tl follow this pattern in reacting
   with dilute HF, HCl, HBr, and HI.
Example: $Al(s) + 4HNO_3(aq) \longrightarrow Al(NO_3)_3(aq) +$
$\quad NO(g) + 2H_2O(l)$

With Halogens to Form Halides
Example: $2Al(s) + 3Cl_2(g) \longrightarrow 2AlCl_3(s)$
B, Al, Ga, In, and Tl also follow this pattern in reacting
   with F$_2$, Cl$_2$, Br$_2$, and I$_2$ (except BF$_3$).

With Oxygen to Form Oxides
Example: $4Al(s) + 3O_2(g) \longrightarrow 2Al_2O_3(s)$
Ga, In, and Tl also follow this pattern.

A mixture of powdered aluminum and iron(III) oxide is called thermite. Al reacts with Fe$_2$O$_3$ using Mg ribbon as a fuse to provide activation energy. The energy produced by the thermite reaction is sufficient to produce molten iron as a product.

ANALYTICAL TEST

Other than atomic absorption spectroscopy, there is no simple analytical test for all the members of the boron family.

The confirmatory test for the presence of aluminum in qualitative analysis is the formation of Al(OH)$_3$, which may be hard to detect in solution. The precipitate is made visible by the addition of a red dye called aluminum reagent.

Aluminum forms a thin layer of Al$_2$O$_3$, which protects the metal from oxidation and makes it suitable for outdoor use.

PROPERTIES OF THE GROUP 13 ELEMENTS

	B	Al	Ga	In	Tl
Melting point (°C)	2300	660.37	29.77	156.61	303.5
Boiling point (°C)	2550	2467	2203	2080	1457
Density (g/cm³)	2.34	2.702	5.904	7.31	11.85
Ionization energy (kJ/mol)	801	578	579	558	589
Atomic radius (pm)	85	143	135	167	170
Ionic radius (pm)	—	54	62	80	89
Common oxidation number in compounds	+3	+3	+1, +3	+1, +3	+1, +3
Crystal structure	monoclinic	fcc	orthorhombic	fcc	hcp
Hardness (Mohs' scale)	9.3	2.75	1.5	1.2	1.2

APPLICATION *Technology*

Aluminum

Chemically, aluminum is much more active than copper, and it belongs to the category of *self-protecting metals*. These metals are oxidized when exposed to oxygen in the air and form a hard, protective metal oxide on the surface. The oxidation of aluminum is shown by the following reaction.

$$4Al(s) + 3O_2(g) \longrightarrow 2Al_2O_3(s)$$

This oxide coating protects the underlying metal from further reaction with oxygen or other substances. Self-protecting metals are valuable in themselves or when used to coat iron and steel to keep them from corroding.

Aluminum is a very good conductor of electric current. Many years ago, most high-voltage electric power lines were made of copper. Although copper is a better conductor of electricity than aluminum, copper is heavier and more expensive. Today more than 90% of high-voltage transmission lines are made of relatively pure aluminum. The aluminum wire does not have to be self-supporting because steel cable is incorporated to bear the weight of the wire in the long spans between towers.

In the 1960s, aluminum electric wiring was used in many houses and other buildings. Over time, however,

These high-voltage transmission lines are made of aluminum supported with steel cables.

because the aluminum oxidized, Al_2O_3 built up and increased electric resistance at points where wires connected to outlets, switches, and other metals. As current flowed through the extra resistance, enough heat was generated to cause a fire. Though some homes have been rewired, aluminum wiring is still prevalent in many homes.

Aluminum Alloys

Because aluminum has a low density and is inexpensive, it is used to construct aircraft, boats, sports equipment, and other lightweight, high-strength objects. The pure metal is not strong, so it is mixed with small quantities of other metals—usually manganese, copper, magnesium, zinc, or silicon—to produce strong low-density alloys. Typically, 80% of a modern aircraft frame consists of aluminum alloy.

Aluminum and its alloys are good conductors of heat. An alloy of aluminum and manganese is used to make cookware. High-quality pots and pans made of stainless steel may have a plate of aluminum on the bottom to help conduct heat quickly to the interior.

Automobile radiators made of aluminum conduct heat as hot coolant from the engine enters the bottom of the radiator. The coolant is deflected into several channels. These channels are covered by thin vanes of aluminum, which conduct heat away from the coolant and transfer it to the cooler air rushing past. By the time the coolant reaches the top of the radiator, its temperature has dropped so that when it flows back into the engine it can absorb more heat. To keep the process efficient, the outside of a radiator should be kept unobstructed and free of dirt buildup.

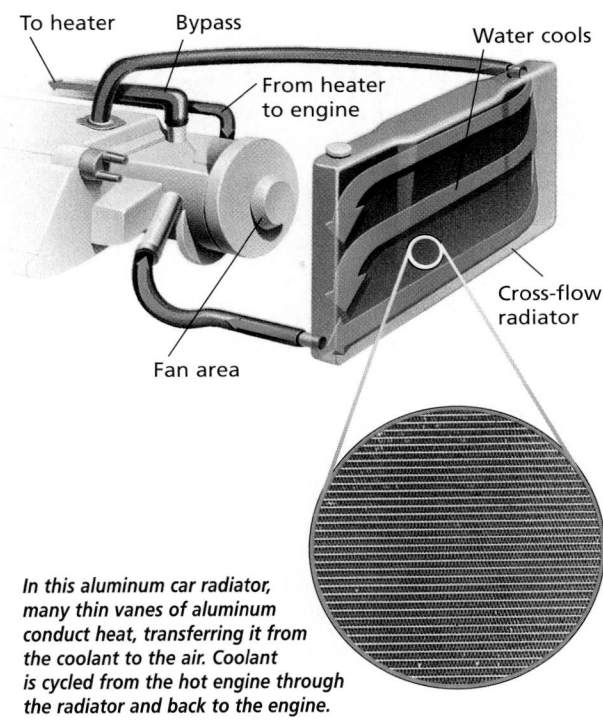

In this aluminum car radiator, many thin vanes of aluminum conduct heat, transferring it from the coolant to the air. Coolant is cycled from the hot engine through the radiator and back to the engine.

TABLE 4A   Alloys of Aluminum and Their Uses

Principal alloying element(s)*	Characteristics	Application examples
Manganese	moderately strong, easily worked	cookware, roofing, storage tanks, lawn furniture
Copper	strong, easily formed	aircraft structural parts; large, thin structural panels
Magnesium	strong, resists corrosion, easy to weld	parts for boats and ships, outdoor decorative objects, tall poles
Zinc and magnesium	very strong, resists corrosion	aircraft structural parts, vehicle parts, anything that needs high strength and low weight
Silicon	expands little on heating and cooling	aluminum castings
Magnesium and silicon	resists corrosion, easily formed	exposed parts of buildings, bridges

* All these alloys have small amounts of other elements.

GROUP 14
CARBON FAMILY

CHARACTERISTICS

- include a nonmetal (carbon), two metalloids (silicon and germanium), and two metals (tin and lead)

- vary greatly in both physical and chemical properties

- occur in nature in both combined and elemental forms

- consist of atoms that contain four electrons in the outermost energy level

- are relatively unreactive

- tend to form covalent compounds (tin and lead also form ionic compounds)

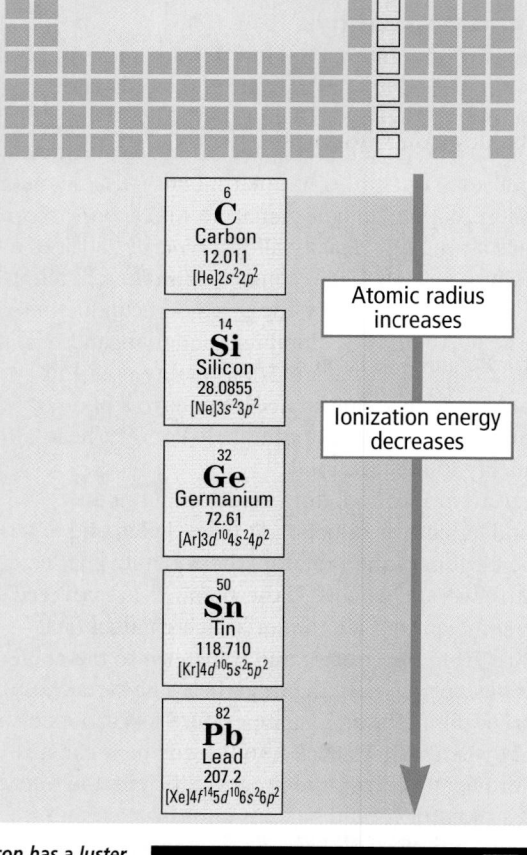

6	
C	
Carbon	
12.011	
[He]$2s^2 2p^2$	Atomic radius increases
14	
Si	
Silicon	
28.0855	
[Ne]$3s^2 3p^2$	Ionization energy decreases
32	
Ge	
Germanium	
72.61	
[Ar]$3d^{10} 4s^2 4p^2$	
50	
Sn	
Tin	
118.710	
[Kr]$4d^{10} 5s^2 5p^2$	
82	
Pb	
Lead	
207.2	
[Xe]$4f^{14} 5d^{10} 6s^2 6p^2$	

Lead has a low reactivity and is resistant to corrosion. It is very soft, highly ductile, and malleable. Lead is toxic and, like mercury, it is a cumulative poison.

Silicon has a luster but does not exhibit metallic properties. Most silicon in nature is a silicon oxide, which occurs in sand and quartz, which is shown here.

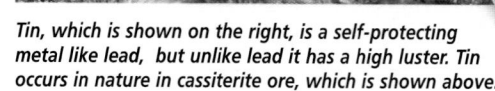

Tin, which is shown on the right, is a self-protecting metal like lead, but unlike lead it has a high luster. Tin occurs in nature in cassiterite ore, which is shown above.

COMMON REACTIONS

With Oxygen to Form Oxides

Example: $Sn(s) + O_2(g) \longrightarrow SnO_2(s)$

Pb follows this pattern, as do C, Si, and Ge at high temperatures.

With Acids to Form Salts and Hydrogen Gas

Only the metallic elements of this group react slowly with aqueous acids.

Example: $Sn(s) + 2HCl(aq) \longrightarrow SnCl_2(aq) + H_2(g)$

Both Sn and Pb can also react to form tin(IV) and lead(IV) salts, respectively.

With Halogens to Form Halides

Example: $Sn(s) + 2Cl_2(g) \longrightarrow SnCl_4(s)$

Si, Ge, and Pb follow this pattern, reacting with F_2, Cl_2, Br_2, and I_2.

ANALYTICAL TEST

The only way to identify all the elements of this group is by atomic absorption spectroscopy. Ionic compounds of tin and lead can be identified in aqueous solutions by adding a solution containing sulfide ions. The formation of a yellow precipitate indicates the presence of Sn^{4+}, and the formation of a black precipitate indicates the presence of Pb^{2+}.

$$Sn^{4+}(aq) + 2S^{2-}(aq) \longrightarrow SnS_2(s)$$
$$Pb^{2+}(aq) + S^{2-}(aq) \longrightarrow PbS(s)$$

PbS   *SnS₂*

PROPERTIES OF THE GROUP 14 ELEMENTS

	C	Si	Ge	Sn	Pb
Melting point (°C)	3500/3652*	1410	937.4	231.88	327.502
Boiling point (°C)	3930	2355	2830	2260	1740
Density (g/cm³)	3.51/2.25*	2.33 ± 0.01	5.323	7.28	11.343
Ionization energy (kJ/mol)	1086	787	762	709	716
Atomic radius (pm)	77	118	122	140	175
Ionic radius (pm)	260 (C^{4-} ion)	—	—	118 (Sn^{2+} ion)	119 (Pb^{2+} ion)
Common oxidation number in compounds	+4, −4	+4	+2, +4	+2, +4	+2, +4
Crystal structure	cubic/hexagonal*	cubic	cubic	tetragonal	fcc
Hardness (Mohs' scale)	10/0.5*	6.5	6.0	1.5	1.5

* The data are for two allotropic forms: diamond/graphite.

Carbon and the Reduction of Iron Ore

Some metals, especially iron, are separated from their ores through reduction reactions in a blast furnace. The blast furnace gets its name from the fact that air or pure oxygen is blown into the furnace, where it oxidizes carbon to form carbon monoxide, CO. Carbon and its compounds are important reactants in this process.

What happens inside the blast furnace to recover the iron from its ore? The actual chemical changes that occur are complex. A simplified explanation begins with the reaction of oxygen in hot air with coke, a form of carbon. Some of the coke burns to form carbon dioxide.

$$C(s) + O_2(g) \longrightarrow CO_2(g)$$

As the concentration of oxygen is increased, the carbon dioxide comes in contact with pieces of hot coke and is reduced to carbon monoxide.

$$CO_2(g) + C(s) \longrightarrow 2CO(g)$$

The carbon monoxide now acts as a reducing agent to reduce the iron oxides in the ore to metallic iron.

$$Fe_2O_3(s) + 3CO(g) \longrightarrow 2Fe(l) + 3CO_2(g)$$

The reduction is thought to occur in steps as the temperature in the furnace increases. The following are some of the possible steps.

$$Fe_2O_3 \longrightarrow Fe_3O_4 \longrightarrow FeO \longrightarrow Fe$$

The white-hot liquid iron collects in the bottom of the furnace and is removed every four or five hours. The iron may be cast in molds or converted to steel in another process.

Limestone, present in the center of the furnace, decomposes to form calcium oxide and carbon dioxide.

$$CaCO_3(s) \longrightarrow CaO(s) + CO_2(g)$$

The calcium oxide then combines with silica, a silicon compound, to form calcium silicate slag.

The relatively high carbon content of iron produced in a blast furnace makes the metal hard but brittle. It also has other impurities, like sulfur and phosphorus, that cause the recovered iron to be brittle. The conversion of iron to steel is essentially a purification process in which impurities are removed by oxidation. This purification process is carried out in another kind of furnace at very high temperatures. All steel contains 0.02 to 1.5% carbon. In fact, steels are graded by their carbon content. Low-carbon steels typically contain 0.02 to 0.3% carbon. Medium-carbon steels typically contain 0.03 to 0.7% carbon. High-carbon steels contain 0.7 to 1.5% carbon.

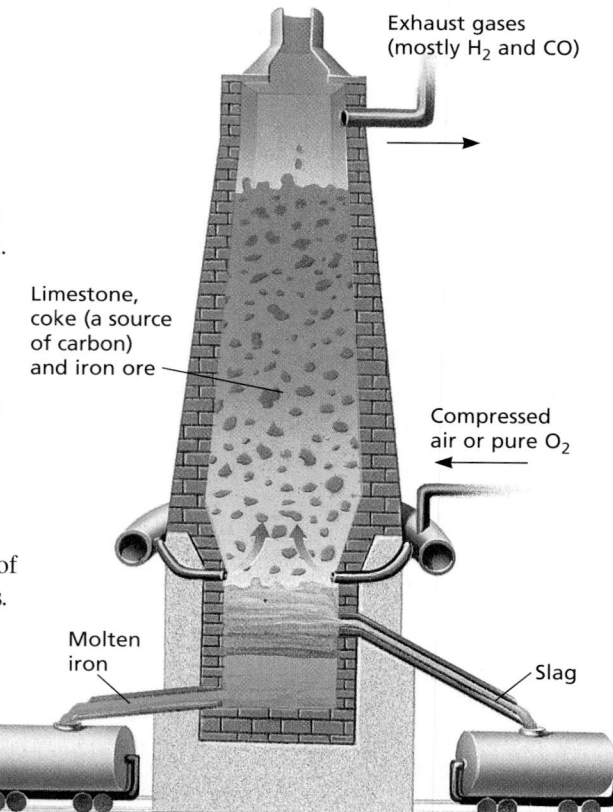

Molten iron flowing from the bottom of a blast furnace has been reduced from its ore through a series of reactions at high temperatures in different regions of the furnace.

Carbon Dioxide

Carbon dioxide is a colorless gas with a faintly irritating odor and a slightly sour taste. The sour taste is the result of the formation of carbonic acid when CO_2 dissolves in the water in saliva. It is a stable gas that does not burn or support combustion. At temperatures lower than 31°C and at pressures higher than 72.9 atm, CO_2 condenses to the liquid form. A phase diagram for CO_2 is found in the chapter review section of Chapter 12. At normal atmospheric pressure, solid CO_2 (dry ice) sublimes at –78.5°C. The linear arrangement of carbon dioxide molecules makes them nonpolar.

CO_2 is produced by the burning of organic fuels and from respiration processes in most living things. Most CO_2 released into the atmosphere is used by plants during photosynthesis. Recall that photosynthesis is the process by which green plants and some forms of algae and bacteria make food. During photosynthesis, CO_2 reacts with H_2O, using the energy from sunlight. The relationships among the various processes on Earth that convert carbon to carbon dioxide are summarized in the diagram of the carbon cycle, which is pictured below.

Carbon Monoxide

Carbon monoxide is a poisonous gas produced naturally by decaying plants, certain types of algae, volcanic eruptions, and the oxidation of methane in the atmosphere.

Because CO is colorless, odorless, and tasteless, it is difficult to detect. It is slightly less dense than air and slightly soluble in water. Its main chemical uses are in the reduction of iron, described on page 756, and the production of organic compounds, such as ethanol.

$$CO(g) + 2H_2(g) \longrightarrow CH_3OH(l)$$

Carbon monoxide is also produced during the incomplete combustion of organic fuels. Incomplete combustion of methane occurs when the supply of oxygen is limited.

$$2CH_4(g) + 3O_2(g) \longrightarrow 2CO(g) + 4H_2O(g)$$

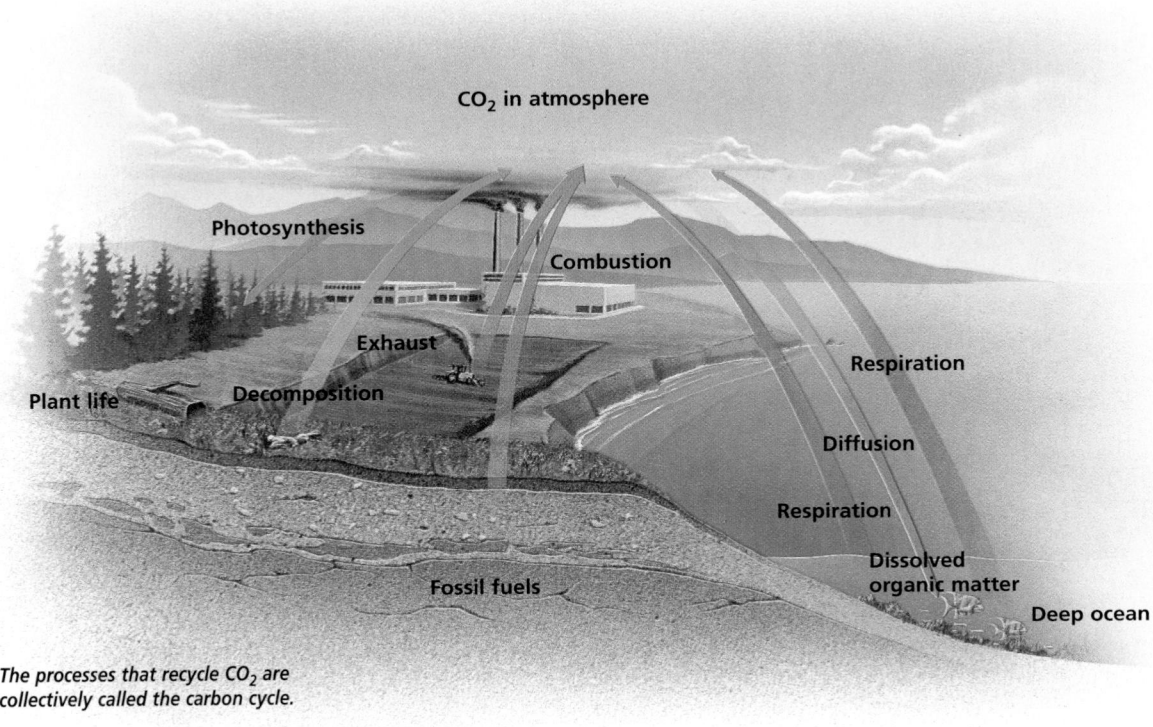

The processes that recycle CO_2 are collectively called the carbon cycle.

Biochemistry

Carbon Dioxide and Respiration

Many organisms, including humans, carry out cellular respiration. In this process, cells break down food molecules and release the energy used to build those molecules during photosynthesis. Glucose, $C_6H_{12}O_6$, is a common substance broken down in respiration. The following chemical equation expresses this process.

$$C_6H_{12}O_6 + 6O_2 \longrightarrow 6CO_2 + 6H_2O + energy$$

In humans and most other vertebrate animals, the oxygen needed for this reaction is delivered to cells by hemoglobin found in red blood cells. Oxygen binds with hemoglobin as blood passes through capillaries in the lungs, as represented by the following reaction.

$$Hb + O_2 \longrightarrow HbO_2$$

Hb represents the hemoglobin molecule, and HbO_2 represents oxyhemoglobin, which is hemoglobin with bound oxygen. When the red blood cells pass through capillaries near cells that have depleted their oxygen supply through respiration, the reaction reverses and oxyhemoglobin gives up its oxygen.

$$HbO_2 \longrightarrow Hb + O_2$$

Carbon dioxide produced during respiration is a waste product that must be expelled from an organism. Various things happen when CO_2 enters the blood. Seven percent dissolves in the plasma, about 23% binds loosely to hemoglobin, and the remaining 70% reacts reversibly with water in plasma to form hydrogen carbonate, HCO_3^- ions. To form HCO_3^- ions, CO_2 first combines with H_2O to form carbonic acid, H_2CO_3, in a reversible reaction.

$$CO_2(aq) + H_2O(l) \rightleftharpoons H_2CO_3(aq)$$

The dissolved carbonic acid ionizes to HCO_3^- ions and aqueous H^+ ions in the form of H_3O^+.

$$H_2CO_3(aq) + H_2O \rightleftharpoons H_3O^+(aq) + HCO_3^-(aq)$$

The combined equilibrium reaction follows.

$$CO_2(aq) + 2H_2O(l) \rightleftharpoons H_3O^+(aq) + HCO_3^-(aq)$$

When the blood reaches the lungs, the reaction reverses and the blood releases CO_2, which is then exhaled to the surroundings.

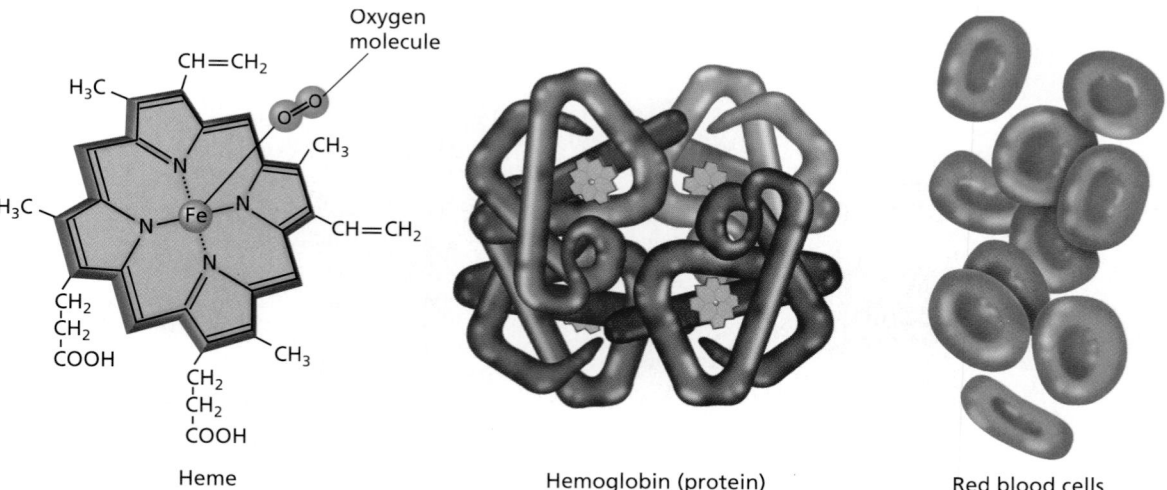

Oxygen molecule

Heme

Hemoglobin (protein)

Red blood cells

The oxygen carrier molecule, heme, is a component of the more-complex protein hemoglobin. Note that each hemoglobin molecule has four heme subunits. Hemoglobin is a component of red blood cells.

Exchange of CO₂ and O₂ in the Lungs

Why does CO_2 leave the blood as it passes through the lung's capillaries, and why does O_2 enter the blood? The exchange is caused by the difference in concentrations of CO_2 and O_2 in the blood and in the atmosphere. Oxygen is 21% of the atmosphere. Although the amount of CO_2 varies from place to place, it averages about 0.033% of the atmosphere. Thus, O_2 is about 640 times more concentrated in the atmosphere than is CO_2.

Substances tend to diffuse from regions of higher concentration toward regions of lower concentration. Thus, when blood reaches the capillaries of the lung, O_2 from the air diffuses into the blood, where its pressure is only 40 mm Hg, while CO_2 diffuses out of the blood, where its pressure is 45 mm Hg, and into the air. The diagram below summarizes the process.

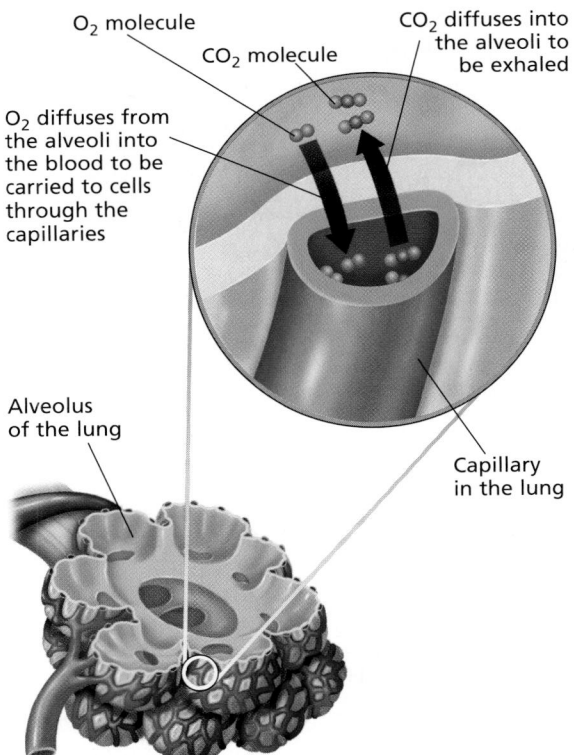

O₂ molecule

CO₂ molecule

CO₂ diffuses into the alveoli to be exhaled

O₂ diffuses from the alveoli into the blood to be carried to cells through the capillaries

Alveolus of the lung

Capillary in the lung

The pressure of O₂ in the blood entering the lung is much lower than it is in the atmosphere. As a result, O₂ diffuses into the blood. The opposite situation exists for CO₂, so it diffuses from the blood into the air. Note that blood leaving the lung still contains a significant concentration of CO₂.

Acidosis and Alkalosis

In humans, blood is maintained between pH 7.3 and 7.5. The pH of blood is dependent on the concentration of CO_2 in the blood. Look again at this equilibrium system.

$$CO_2(aq) + 2H_2O(l) \rightleftharpoons H_3O^+(aq) + HCO_3^-(aq)$$

Notice that the right side of the equation contains the H_3O^+ ion, which determines the pH of the blood. If excess H_3O^+ enters the blood from tissues, the reverse reaction is favored. Excess H_3O^+ combines with HCO_3^- to produce more CO_2 and H_2O. If the H_3O^+ concentration begins to fall, the forward reaction is favored, producing additional H_3O^+ and HCO_3^-. To keep H_3O^+ in balance, adequate amounts of both CO_2 and HCO_3^- must be present. If something occurs that changes these conditions, a person can become very ill and can even die.

Hyperventilation occurs when a person breathes too rapidly for an extended time. Too much CO_2 is eliminated, causing the reverse reaction to be favored, and H_3O^+ and HCO_3^- are used up. As a result, the person develops a condition known as alkalosis because the pH of the blood rises to an abnormal alkaline level. The person begins to feel lightheaded and faint, and, unless treatment is provided, he or she may fall into a coma. Alkalosis is treated by having the victim breathe air that is rich in CO_2. One way to accomplish this is to have the person breathe with a bag held tightly over the nose and mouth. Alkalosis is also caused by fever, infection, intoxication, hysteria, and prolonged vomiting.

The reverse of alkalosis is a condition known as acidosis. This condition is often caused by a depletion of HCO_3^- ions from the blood, which can occur as a result of kidney dysfunction. The kidney controls the excretion of HCO_3^- ions. If there are too few HCO_3^- ions in solution, the forward reaction is favored and H_3O^+ ions accumulate, which lowers the blood's pH. Acidosis can also result from the body's inability to expel CO_2, which can occur during pneumonia, emphysema, and other respiratory disorders. Perhaps the single most common cause of acidosis is uncontrolled diabetes, in which acids normally excreted in the urinary system are instead retained by the body.

APPLICATION   *The Environment*

Carbon Monoxide Poisoning

Standing on a street corner in any major city exposes a person to above-normal concentrations of carbon monoxide from automobile exhaust. Carbon monoxide also reacts with hemoglobin. The following reaction takes place in the capillaries of the lung.

$$Hb + CO \longrightarrow HbCO$$

Unlike CO_2 or O_2, CO binds strongly to hemoglobin. Carboxyhemoglobin, HbCO, is 200 times more stable than oxyhemoglobin, HbO_2. So as blood circulates, more and more CO molecules bind to hemoglobin, reducing the amount of O_2 bond sites available for transport. Eventually, CO occupies so many hemoglobin binding sites that cells die from lack of oxygen. Symptoms of carbon monoxide poisoning include headache, mental confusion, dizziness, weakness, nausea, loss of muscular control, and decreased heart rate and respiratory rate. The victim loses consciousness and will die without treatment.

If the condition is caught in time, a victim of carbon monoxide poisoning can be revived by breathing pure oxygen. This treatment causes carboxyhemoglobin to be converted slowly to oxyhemoglobin according to the following chemical equation.

$$O_2 + HbCO \longrightarrow CO + HbO_2$$

Mild carbon monoxide poisoning usually does not have long-term effects. In severe cases, cells are destroyed. Damage to brain cells is irreversible.

The level of danger posed by carbon monoxide depends on two factors: the concentration of the gas in the air and the amount of time that a person is exposed to the gas. Table 5A shows the effects of increasing levels of carbon monoxide in the bloodstream. These effects vary considerably depending on a person's activity level and metabolic rate.

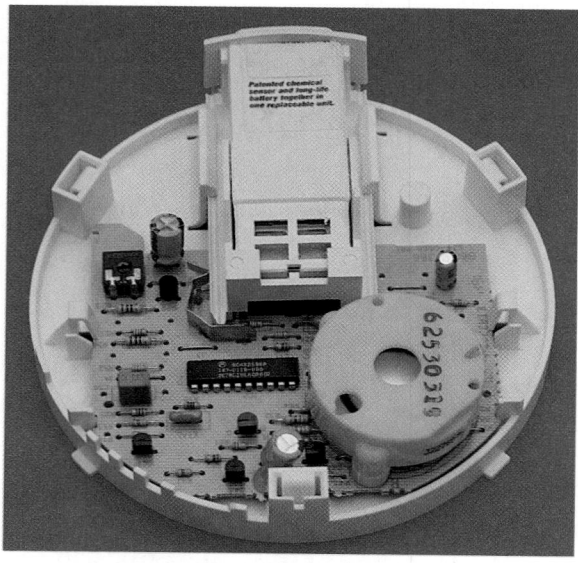

Carbon monoxide detectors are now available to reduce the risk of poisoning from defective home heating systems. The Consumer Products Safety Commission recommends that all homes have a CO detector with a UL label.

TABLE 5A   Symptoms of CO Poisoning at Increasing Levels of CO Exposure and Concentration

Concentration of CO in air (ppm)*	Hemoglobin molecules as HbCO	Visible effects
100 for 1 hour or less	10% or less	no visible symptoms
500 for 1 hour or less	20%	mild to throbbing headache, some dizziness, impaired perception
500 for an extended period of time	30–50%	headache, confusion, nausea, dizziness, muscular weakness, fainting
1000 for 1 hour or less	50–80%	coma, convulsions, respiratory failure, death

* ppm is parts per million

APPLICATION   *Biochemistry*

Macromolecules

Large organic polymers are called macromolecules (the prefix *macro* means "large"). Macromolecules play important roles in living systems. Most macromolecules essential to life belong to four main classes, three of which we know as nutrients in food:

1. **Proteins** Hair, tendons, ligaments, and silk are made of protein. Other proteins act as hormones, transport substances throughout the body, and fight infections. Enzymes are proteins that control the body's chemical reactions. Proteins provide energy, yielding 17 kJ/g.

2. **Carbohydrates** Sugars, starches, and cellulose are carbohydrates. Carbohydrates are sources of energy, yielding 17 kJ/g.

3. **Lipids** Fats, oils, waxes, and steroids are lipids, nonpolar substances that do not dissolve in water. Fats are sources of energy, yielding 38 kJ/g.

4. **Nucleic acids** The nucleic acids are DNA and RNA. In most organisms, DNA is used to store hereditary information and RNA helps to assemble proteins.

Proteins

Proteins are macromolecules formed by condensation reactions between amino acid monomers. Proteins contain carbon, oxygen, hydrogen, nitrogen, and usually some sulfur.

All amino acids have a carboxyl group, —COOH, and an amino group, —NH_2, attached to a central carbon atom, which is also attached to hydrogen, —H. Amino acids differ from one another at the fourth bond site of the central carbon, which is attached to a functional group (called an *R* group). *R* groups differ from one amino acid to another, as shown in the structures for several amino acids below. The proteins of all organisms contain a set of 20 common amino acids. The reaction that links amino acids is a condensation reaction, which is described in Chapter 21.

Each protein has its own unique sequence of amino acids. A complex organism has at least several thousand different proteins, each with a special structure and function. For instance, *insulin,* a hormone that helps the body regulate the level of sugar in the blood, is made up of two linked chains.

Amino acids have the same general structure. These examples show some of the variations within this class of compounds.

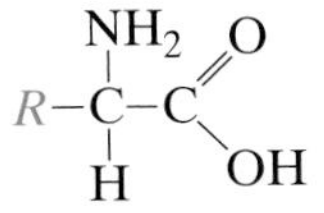

General structure

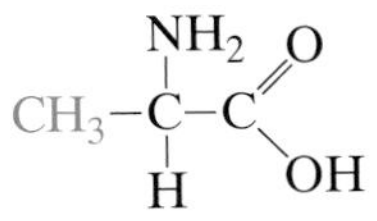

Alanine

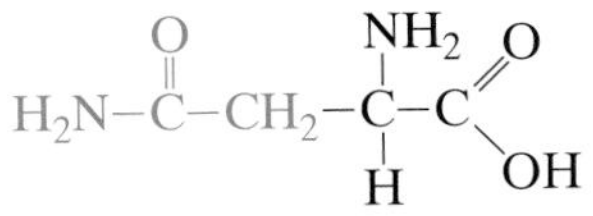

Asparagine

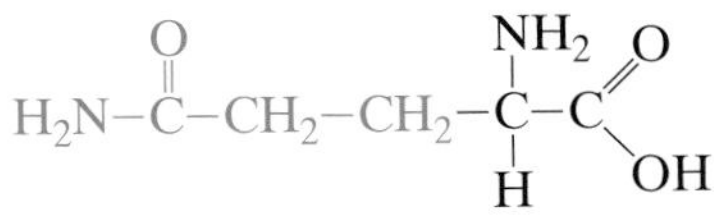

Glutamine

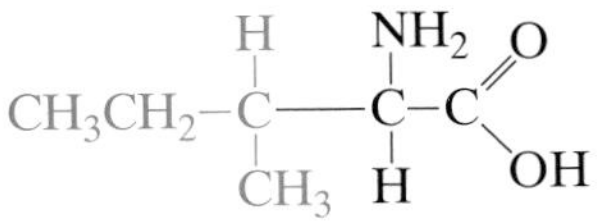

Isoleucine

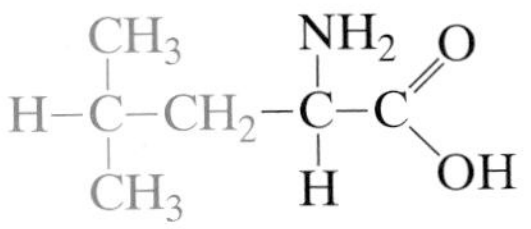

Leucine

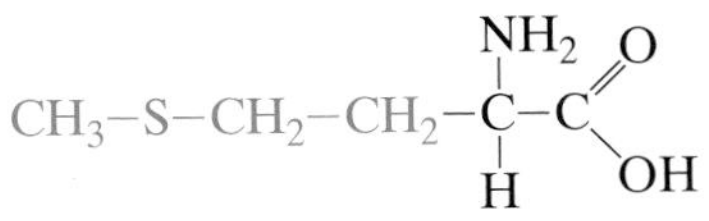

Methionine

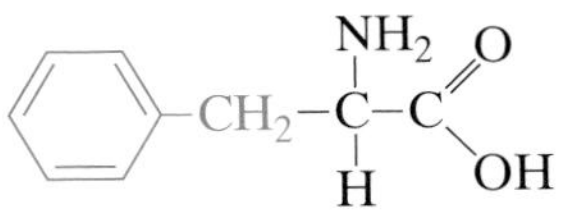

Phenylalanine

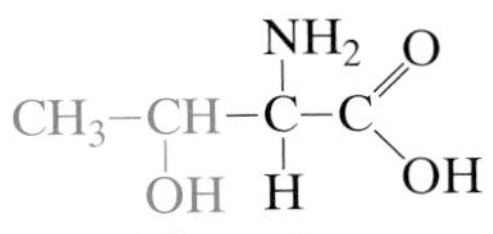

Threonine

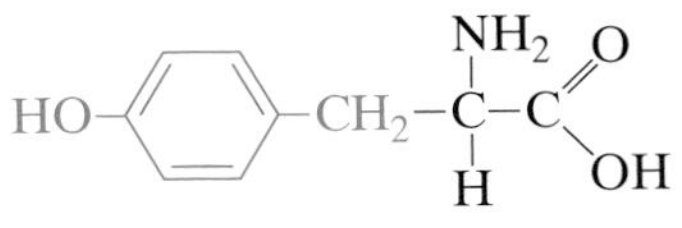

Tyrosine

Hemoglobin is a complex protein made of hundreds of amino acids. Its 3-dimensional shape is called a tertiary structure. Tertiary structures break down when a protein is denatured.

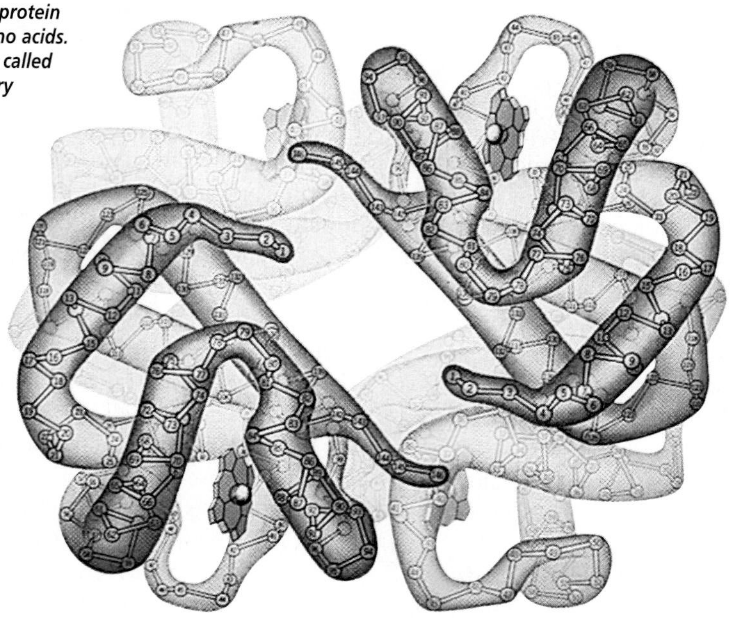

The chains are held together by S—S bonds between sulfur atoms in two cysteine amino acids. Insulin is one of the smaller proteins, containing only 51 amino acids. In contrast, hemoglobin, which carries oxygen in the blood, is a large protein consisting of four long chains with the complicated three-dimensional structures shown above. Proteins can lose their shape with increases in temperature or changes in the chemical composition of their environment. When they are returned to normal surroundings, they may fold or coil up again and re-form their original structure.

Changing even one amino acid can change a protein's structure and function. For example, the difference between normal hemoglobin and the hemoglobin that causes sickle cell anemia is just two amino acids.

Enzymes

You learned how enzymes alter reaction rates in Chapter 17. Some enzymes cannot bind to their substrates without the help of additional molecules. These may be *minerals,* such as calcium or iron ions, or helper molecules called *coenzymes* that play accessory roles in enzyme-catalyzed reactions. Many vitamins are coenzymes or parts of coenzymes.

Vitamins are organic molecules that we cannot manufacture and hence need to eat in small amounts.

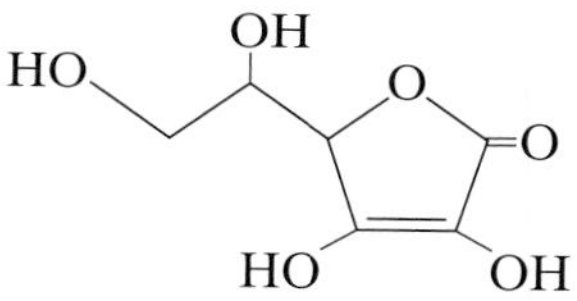

Vitamin C, $C_6H_8O_6$
Water-soluble

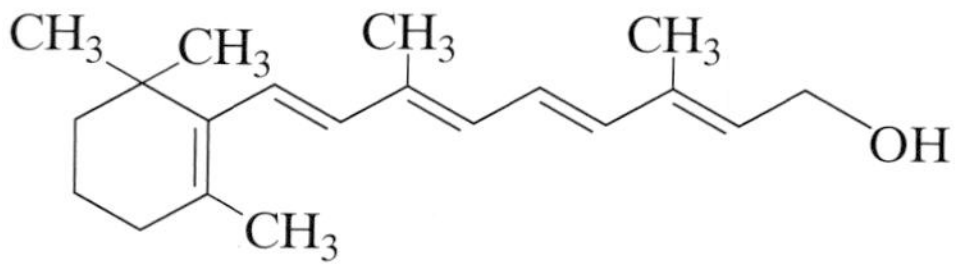

Vitamin A, $C_{20}H_{30}O$
Fat-soluble

You can see why we need vitamins and minerals in our diet—to enable our enzymes to work. You can also see why we need only small amounts of them. Minerals and coenzymes are not destroyed in biochemical reactions. Like enzymes, coenzymes and minerals can be used over and over again.

Temperature and pH have the most significant effects on the rates of reactions catalyzed by enzymes. Most enzymes work best in a solution of approximately neutral pH. Most body cells have a pH of 7.4. However, some enzymes function only in acidic or basic environments. For example, pepsin, the collective

The protein in fish is denatured by the low pH of lime juice. Notice that the flesh shown with the limes has turned white compared with the flesh at normal pH.

term for the digestive enzymes found in the human stomach, works best at a very acidic pH of about 1.5. Cells that line the stomach secrete hydrochloric acid to produce this low pH environment. When food travels down the digestive tract, it carries these enzymes out of the stomach into the intestine. In the intestine, stomach enzymes stop working because sodium bicarbonate in the intestine raises the pH to about 8. Digestive enzymes in the intestine are formed by the pancreas and work best at pH 8.

Most chemical reactions, including enzyme reactions, speed up with increases in temperature. However, high temperatures (above about 60°C) destroy, or denature, protein by breaking up the three-dimensional structure. For example, the protein in an egg or a piece of meat denatures when the egg or meat is cooked. Proteins in the egg white become opaque when denatured. Heating can preserve food by denaturing the enzymes of organisms that cause decay. In milk pasteurization, the milk is heated to denature enzymes that would turn it sour. Refrigeration and freezing also help preserve food by slowing the enzyme reactions that cause decay.

Carbohydrates

Carbohydrates are sugars, starches, and related compounds. The monomers of carbohydrates are monosaccharides, or simple sugars, such as fructose and glucose. A monosaccharide contains carbon, hydrogen, and oxygen in about a 1:2:1 ratio, which is an empirical formula of CH_2O.

$$
\begin{array}{cc}
\text{D-Glucose} & \text{D-Fructose} \\
\text{D-Ribose} & \text{2-Deoxy-D-ribose}
\end{array}
$$

Monosaccharides chain representation

Two monosaccharides may be joined together to form a disaccharide. Sucrose, shown below, is a disaccharide. A disaccharide can be hydrolyzed to produce the monosaccharides that formed it. By a series of condensation reactions, many monosaccharides can be joined to form a polymer called a polysaccharide (commonly known as a complex carbohydrate).

Lactose—made from glucose and galactose

Sucrose—made from glucose and fructose

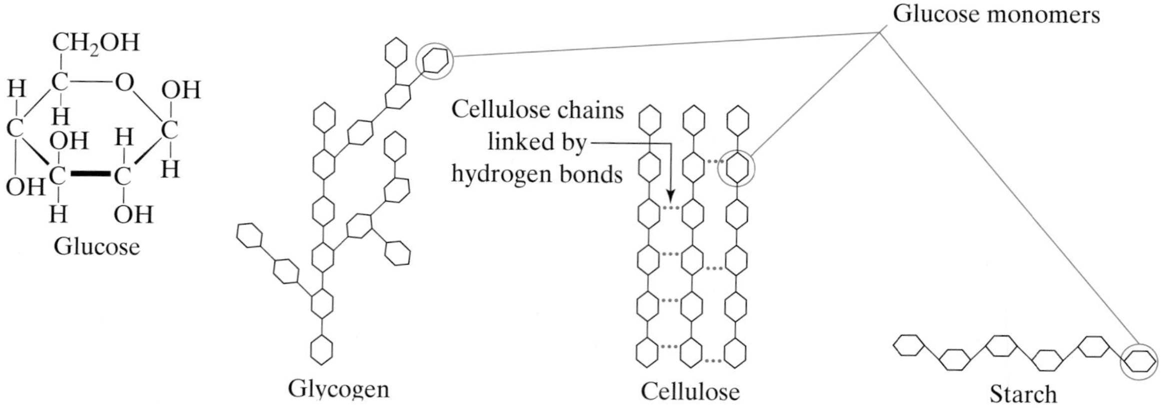

Glucose is the structural unit for glycogen, cellulose, and starch. Notice that these three polymers differ in the arrangement of glucose monomers.

Three important polysaccharides made of glucose monomers are glycogen, starch, and cellulose. Animals store energy in glycogen. The liver and muscles remove glucose from the blood and condense it into glycogen, which can later be hydrolyzed back into glucose and used to supply energy as needed.

Starch consists of two kinds of glucose polymers. It is hydrolyzed in plants to form glucose for energy and for building material to produce more cells. The structural polysaccharide cellulose is probably the most common organic compound on Earth. Glucose monomers link cellulose chains together at the hydroxyl groups to form cellulose fibers. Cotton fibers consist almost entirely of cellulose.

Lipids

Lipids are a varied group of organic compounds that share one property: they are not very soluble in water. Lipids contain a high proportion of C—H bonds, and they dissolve in nonpolar organic solvents, such as ether, chloroform, and benzene.

Fatty acids are the simplest lipids. A fatty acid consists of an unbranched chain of carbon and hydrogen atoms with a carboxyl group at one end. Bonding within the carbon chain gives both saturated and unsaturated fatty acids, just as the simple hydrocarbons (see Chapter 20) can be saturated or unsaturated.

The bonds in a carboxyl group are polar, and so the carboxyl end of a fatty acid attracts water

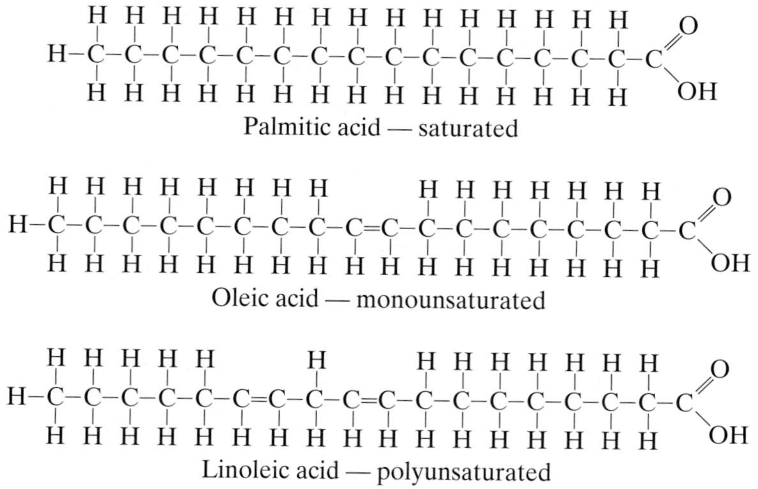

Palmitic acid — saturated

Oleic acid — monounsaturated

Linoleic acid — polyunsaturated

These examples of common fatty acids show the differences in saturation level.

This phospholipid molecule contains two fatty-acid chains.

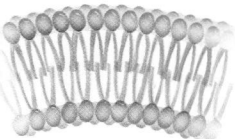

The lipid bilayer is the framework of the cell membrane.

The fatty acids are oriented toward the interior of the bilayer because they have a low attraction for water.

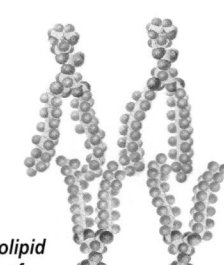

This phospholipid chain is part of the lipid bilayer.

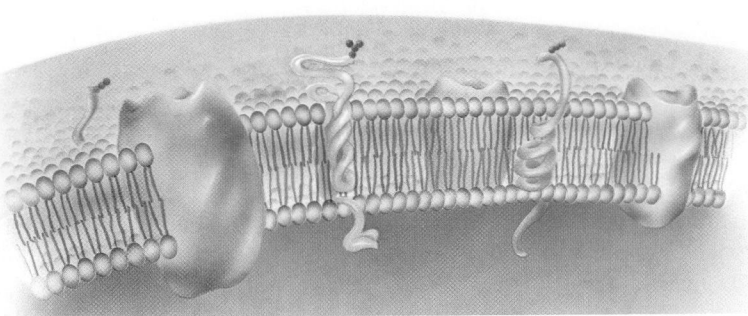

molecules. The carbon-hydrogen bonds of a lipid's hydrocarbon chain are nonpolar, however. The polar end will dissolve in water, and the other end will dissolve in nonpolar organic compounds. This behavior enables fatty acids to form membranes when they are dropped into water. It also gives soaps and detergents their cleaning power.

Lipids are the main compounds in biological membranes, such as the cell membrane. Because lipids are insoluble, the lipid bilayer of a cell membrane is adapted to keep the contents of the cell inside separated from the outer environment of the cell.

The structural component of a cell membrane is a phospholipid. The "head" of the phospholipid is polar, and the fatty acid tails are nonpolar, as shown in the model above.

Most fatty acids found in foods and soaps belong to a class of compounds called triglycerides. The fat content shown on a nutrition label for packaged food represents a mixture of the triglycerides in the food. Triglycerides have the general structure shown below.

Fatty acids are usually combined with other molecules to form classes of biomolecules called glycolipids (made from a carbohydrate and a lipid) or lipoproteins (made from a lipid and a protein). These compounds are also parts of more-complex lipids found in the body.

$$
\begin{array}{c}
\text{Saturated fatty acids} + \text{Glycerol} \longrightarrow \text{Triglyceride}
\end{array}
$$

Triglycerides are made from three long-chain fatty acids bonded to a glycerol backbone.

Nucleic Acids

Nucleic acids are macromolecules that transmit genetic information. Deoxyribonucleic acid (DNA) is the material that contains the genetic information that all organisms pass on to their offspring during reproduction. This information includes instructions for making proteins as well as for making the other nucleic acid, ribonucleic acid (RNA). Ribonucleic acid (RNA) assists in protein synthesis by helping to coordinate the process of protein assembly.

Nucleotides are the monomers of nucleic acids. A nucleotide has three parts: one or more phosphate groups, a sugar containing five carbon atoms, and a ring-shaped nitrogen base, as shown below. RNA nucleotides contain the simple sugar ribose. DNA nucleotides contain deoxyribose (ribose stripped of one oxygen atom). Structures for both of these sugars are shown on page 763. Cells contain nucleotides with one, two, or three phosphate groups attached. Besides being the monomers of nucleic acids, several nucleotides play other roles. For example, adenosine triphosphate (ATP) is the

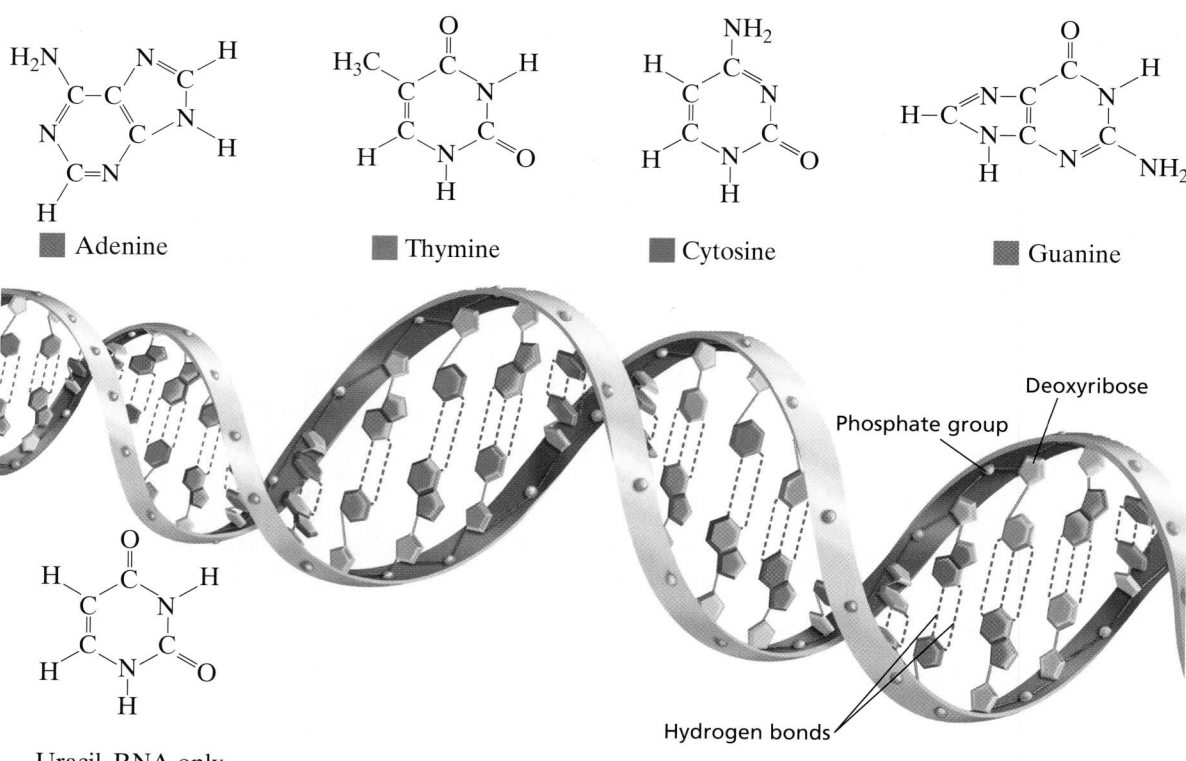

ATP structure

nucleotide that supplies the energy for many metabolic reactions.

The bases in nucleic acids attract each other in pairs, a phenomenon known as base-pairing. DNA is made of four different nucleotides—those containing the bases adenine (A), thymine (T), guanine (G), and cytosine (C). The attraction between base pairs is hydrogen bonding. Adenine forms hydrogen bonds with thymine. Similarly, cytosine bonds to guanine. This base-pairing holds strands of DNA together.

■ Adenine   ■ Thymine   ■ Cytosine   ■ Guanine

Uracil, RNA only

APPLICATION *Chemical Industry*

Silicon and Silicates

Silicon is as important in the mineral world as carbon is in living systems. Silicon dioxide and silicates make up about 87% of the Earth's crust. Silicates are a class of compounds containing silicon, oxygen, one or more metals, and possibly hydrogen. Many mineral compounds are silicates. Sand is probably the most familiar silicate.

Glasses consist of 75% silicate. Borosilicate glass is the special heat-resistant glass used in making laboratory beakers and flasks. The addition of 5% boron oxide to the glass increases the softening temperature of the glass. Because boron and silicon atoms have roughly similar radii, these atoms can be substituted for one another to make borosilicate glass.

Asbestos is the name given to a class of fibrous magnesium silicate minerals. Asbestos is very strong and flexible, and it does not burn, so it was widely used as a heat-insulating material.

It is now known that asbestos is a carcinogen. When handled, asbestos releases dust particles that are easily inhaled and can cause lung cancer. Asbestos materials found in older homes and buildings should be removed by firms licensed by the Environmental Protection Agency (EPA).

Silicones

Silicones are a class of organic silicon polymers composed of silicon, carbon, oxygen, and hydrogen. The silicon chain is held together by bonding with the oxygen atoms. Each silicon atom is also bonded to different hydrocarbon groups to create a variety of silicone structures.

Silicones are widely used for their adhesive and protective properties. They have good electric insulating properties and are water-repellent. Some silicones have the character of oils or greases, so they are used as lubricants. Silicones are also used in automobile and furniture polishes as protective agents.

Silicon has the ability to form long chain compounds by bonding with oxygen. The SiO_4 subunit in this silicate is tetrahedral.

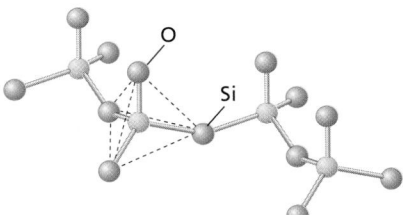

Silicones also have a tetrahedral structure. How does this structure differ from that of a silicate?

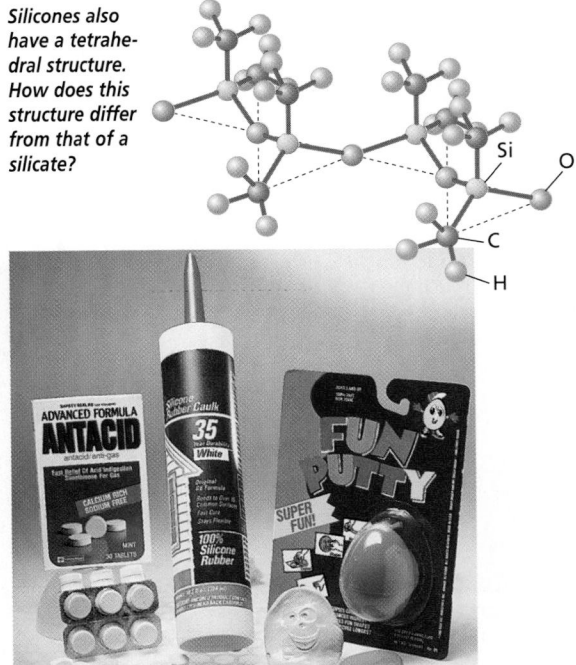

Silicates exist in a variety of mineral forms, including mica.

Because of their protective properties, silicones are used in a number of consumer products, from cosmetics to caulkings.

APPLICATION *Technology*

Semiconductors

When electrons can move freely through a material, the material is a conductor. The electrons in metals are loosely held and require little additional energy to move from one vacant orbital to the next. A set of overlapping orbitals is called a *conduction band.* Because electrons can easily jump to the conduction band, metals conduct electricity when only a very small voltage is applied.

Semiconductors conduct a current if the voltage applied is large enough to excite the outer-level electrons of their atoms into the higher energy levels. With semiconductors, more energy, and thus a higher voltage, is required to cause conduction. By contrast, nonmetals are insulators because they do not conduct at ordinary voltages. Too much energy is needed to raise their outer electrons into conduction bands.

Semiconductor devices include transistors; diodes, including light-emitting diodes (LEDs); some lasers;

and photovoltaic cells ("solar" cells). Though silicon is the basis of most semiconductor devices in the computer industry, pure silicon has little use as a semiconductor. Instead, small amounts of impurities are added to increase its conductive properties. Adding impurities to silicon is called *doping,* and the substances added are *dopants.* The dopant is usually incorporated into just the surface layer of a silicon chip. Typical dopants include the Group 15 elements phosphorus and arsenic and the Group 13 elements boron, aluminum, gallium, and indium.

A silicon atom has four electrons in its outer energy level whereas Group 13 atoms have three and Group 15 atoms have five. Adding boron to silicon creates a mix of atoms having four valence electrons and atoms having three valence electrons. Boron atoms form only three bonds with silicon, whereas silicon forms four bonds with other silicon atoms. The unbonded spot between a silicon atom

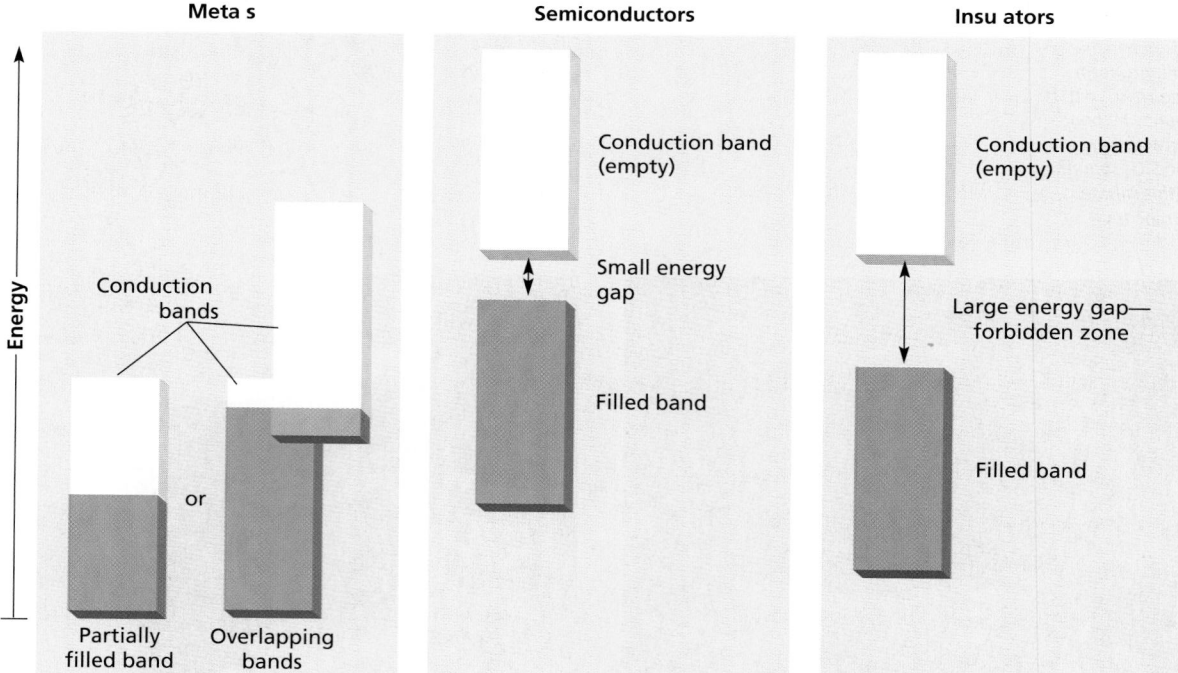

This model shows the difference in the levels of energy required to excite electrons into the conduction band in metals, semiconductors, and insulators. The forbidden zone is too great an energy gap in insulators for these elements to function as conductors. The energy gap for semiconductors is small enough that it can be crossed under certain conditions.

1 H																	Group 18 2 He

Group 1 Group 2

☐ Dopants
▨ Semiconductor elements
▨ Forms semiconductor compounds

Group 13 Group 14 Group 15 Group 16 Group 17

| 3 Li | 4 Be | | | | | | | | | | | | 5 B | 6 C | 7 N | 8 O | 9 F | 10 Ne |

| 11 Na | 12 Mg | | | | | | | | | | | | 13 Al | 14 Si | 15 P | 16 S | 17 Cl | 18 Ar |

Group 3 Group 4 Group 5 Group 6 Group 7 Group 8 Group 9 Group 10 Group 11 Group 12

| 19 K | 20 Ca | 21 Sc | 22 Ti | 23 V | 24 Cr | 25 Mn | 26 Fe | 27 Co | 28 Ni | 29 Cu | 30 Zn | 31 Ga | 32 Ge | 33 As | 34 Se | 35 Br | 36 Kr |

| 37 Rb | 38 Sr | 39 Y | 40 Zr | 41 Nb | 42 Mo | 43 Tc | 44 Ru | 45 Rh | 46 Pd | 47 Ag | 48 Cd | 49 In | 50 Sn | 51 Sb | 52 Te | 53 I | 54 Xe |

| 55 Cs | 56 Ba | 57 La | 72 Hf | 73 Ta | 74 W | 75 Re | 76 Os | 77 Ir | 78 Pt | 79 Au | 80 Hg | 81 Tl | 82 Pb | 83 Bi | 84 Po | 85 At | 86 Rn |

| 87 Fr | 88 Ra | 89 Ac |

*Semiconductor elements and dopants fall in the metalloid region of the periodic table.
Semiconductor compounds often contain metals.*

and a boron atom is a hole that a free electron can occupy. Because this hole "attracts" an electron, it is viewed as if it were positively charged. Semiconductors that are doped with boron, aluminum, or gallium are *p-type semiconductors*, the *p* standing for "positive." P-type semiconductors conduct electricity better than pure silicon because they provide spaces that moving electrons can occupy as they flow through the material.

Doping silicon with phosphorus or arsenic produces the opposite effect. When phosphorus is added to silicon, it forms four bonds to silicon atoms and has a nonbonding electron left over. This extra electron is free to move through the material when a voltage is applied, thus increasing its conductivity compared with pure silicon. These extra electrons have a negative charge. Therefore, the material is an *n-type semiconductor*. Compare these two types of semiconductors in the models below.

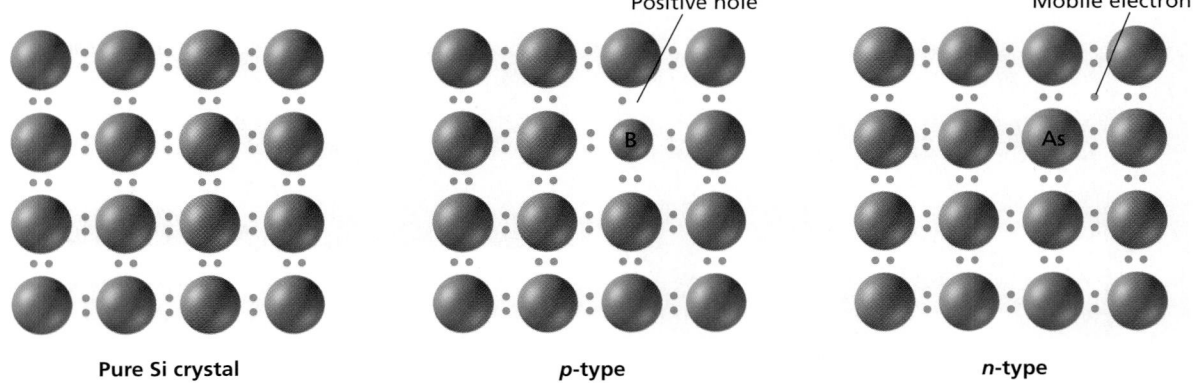

Pure Si crystal   ***p*-type**   ***n*-type**

Each silicon atom in the pure crystal is surrounded by four pairs of electrons. The p-type semiconductor model contains an atom of boron with a hole that an electron can occupy. The n-type semiconductor model contains an atom of arsenic, which provides the extra electron that can move through the crystal.

GROUP 15
NITROGEN FAMILY

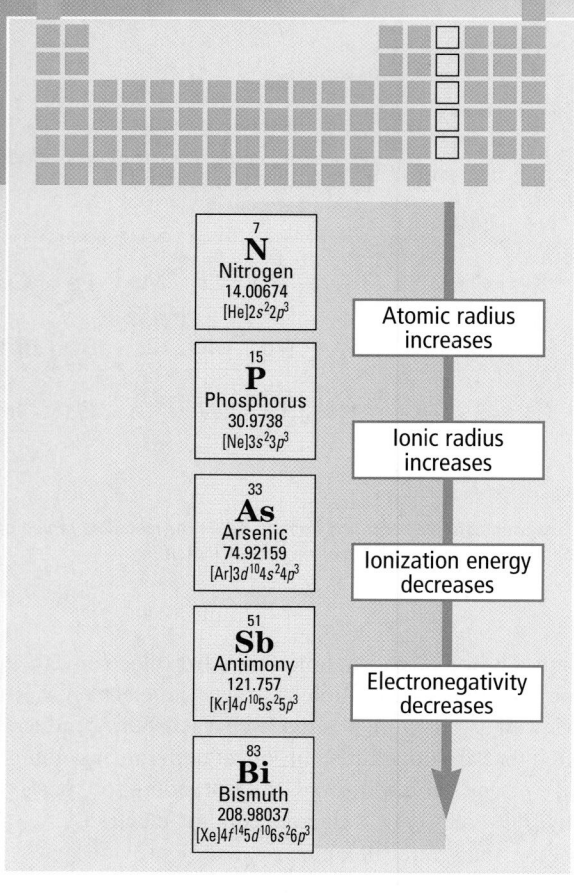

7 **N** Nitrogen 14.00674 [He]$2s^2 2p^3$	
15 **P** Phosphorus 30.9738 [Ne]$3s^2 3p^3$	Atomic radius increases
33 **As** Arsenic 74.92159 [Ar]$3d^{10}4s^2 4p^3$	Ionic radius increases
51 **Sb** Antimony 121.757 [Kr]$4d^{10}5s^2 5p^3$	Ionization energy decreases
83 **Bi** Bismuth 208.98037 [Xe]$4f^{14}5d^{10}6s^2 6p^3$	Electronegativity decreases

CHARACTERISTICS

- consist of two nonmetals (nitrogen and phosphorus), two metalloids (arsenic and antimony), and one metal (bismuth)

- Nitrogen is most commonly found as atmospheric N_2; phosphorus as phosphate rock; and arsenic, antimony, and bismuth as sulfides or oxides. Antimony and bismuth are also found as elements.

- range from very abundant elements (nitrogen and phosphorus) to relatively rare elements (arsenic, antimony, and bismuth)

- consist of atoms that contain five electrons in their outermost energy level

- tend to form covalent compounds, most commonly with oxidation numbers of +3 or +5

- exist in two or more allotropic forms, except nitrogen and bismuth

- are solids at room temperature, except nitrogen

You can see the contrast in physical properties among the elements of this family. Arsenic, antimony, and bismuth are shown.

Some matches contain phosphorus compounds in the match head. Safety matches contain phosphorus in the striking strip on the matchbox.

Phosphorus exists in three allotropic forms. White phosphorus must be kept underwater because it catches on fire when exposed to air. The red and black forms are stable in air.

COMMON REACTIONS

With Oxygen to Form Oxides
Example: $P_4(s) + 5O_2(g) \longrightarrow P_4O_{10}(s)$
As, Sb, and Bi follow this reaction pattern, but as
monatomic elements. N reacts as N_2 to form N_2O_3
and N_2O_5.

With Metals to Form Binary Compounds
Example: $3Mg(s) + N_2(g) \longrightarrow Mg_3N_2(s)$

ANALYTICAL TEST

Other than atomic absorption spectroscopy, there
are no simple analytical tests for the presence of
nitrogen or phosphorus compounds in a sample.
Antimony produces a pale green color in a flame
test, and arsenic produces a light blue color. Arsenic,
antimony, and bismuth are recognized in qualitative
analyses by their characteristic sulfide colors.

Formation of sulfides is the confirmatory qualitative analysis
test for the presence of bismuth, antimony, and arsenic.

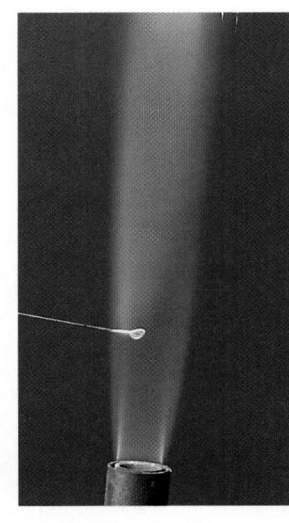

Arsenic flame test

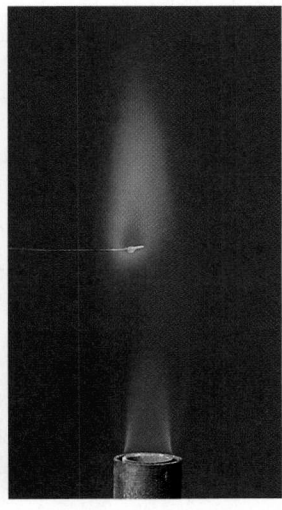

Antimony flame test

PROPERTIES OF THE GROUP 15 ELEMENTS

	N	P*	As	Sb	Bi
Melting point (°C)	−209.86	44.1	817 (28 atm)	630.5	271.3
Boiling point (°C)	−195.8	280	613 (sublimes)	1750	1560 ± 5
Density (g/cm³)	1.25×10^{-3}	1.82	5.727	6.684	9.80
Ionization energy (kJ/mol)	1402	1012	947	834	703
Atomic radius (pm)	75	110	122	143	151
Ionic radius (pm)	146 (N^{3-})	212 (P^{3-})	—	76 (Sb^{3+})	103 (Bi^{3+})
Common oxidation number in compounds	−3, +3, +5	−3, +3, +5	+3, +5	+3, +5	+3
Crystal structure†	cubic (as a solid)	cubic	rhombohedral	hcp	rhombohedral
Hardness (Mohs' scale)	none (gas)	—	3.5	3.0	2.25

* Data given apply to white phosphorus.
† Crystal structures are for the most common allotropes.

Plants and Nitrogen

All organisms, including plants, require certain elements to survive and grow. These elements include carbon, hydrogen, oxygen, nitrogen, phosphorus, potassium, sulfur, and several other elements needed in small amounts. An organism needs nitrogen to synthesize structural proteins, enzymes, and the nucleic acids DNA and RNA.

Carbon, hydrogen, and oxygen are available to plants from carbon dioxide in the air and from water in both the air and the soil. Nitrogen is necessary for plants' survival. Although nitrogen gas, N_2, makes up 78% of air, plants cannot take nitrogen out of the air and incorporate it into their cells, because the strong triple covalent bond in N_2 is not easily broken. Plants need nitrogen in the form of a compound that they can take in and use. The process of using atmospheric N_2 to make NH_3 is called *nitrogen fixation*. Several kinds of nitrogen-fixing bacteria live in the soil and in the root nodules of plants called legumes. Legumes obtain the nitrogen they need through a symbiotic relationship with nitrogen-fixing bacteria. Legumes include peas, beans, clover, alfalfa, and locust trees. The bacteria convert nitrogen into ammonia, NH_3, which is then absorbed by the host plants.

Because wheat, rice, corn, and potatoes cannot perform the same feat as legumes, these plants depend on nitrogen-fixing bacteria in the soil. Soil bacteria convert NH_3 into nitrate ions, NO_3^-, the form of nitrogen that can be absorbed and used by plants. These plants also often need nitrogen fertilizers to supplement the work of the bacteria. Besides supplying nitrogen, fertilizers are manufactured to contain phosphorus, potassium, and trace minerals.

Nitrogen-fixing bacteria, Rhizobium, *live in these small nodules that grow on the roots of soybeans.*

Soybeans are legumes that live in a symbiotic relationship with nitrogen-fixing bacteria.

APPLICATION *Chemical Industry*

Fertilizers

Fertilizers can supply nitrogen to plants in the form of ammonium sulfate, ammonium nitrate, and urea, all of which are made from NH_3. Now you know why there is such a demand for ammonia. Though some soils contain sufficient concentrations of phosphorus and potassium, most soils need additional nitrogen for adequate plant growth. Ammonia, ammonium nitrate, or urea can fill that need.

Most fertilizers contain all three major plant nutrients N, P, and K, and are called *complete fertilizers*. A typical complete fertilizer might contain ammonium nitrate or sodium nitrate to provide nitrogen. Calcium dihydrogen phosphate, $Ca(H_2PO_4)_2$, or the anhydrous form of phosphoric acid, P_2O_5, can provide phosphorus. Potassium chloride, KCl, contains sufficient K_2O impurities to provide potassium.

The proportion of each major nutrient in a fertilizer is indicated by a set of three numbers printed on the container. These numbers are the N-P-K formula of the fertilizer and indicate the percentage of N, P, and K, respectively. A fertilizer graded as 6-12-6, for example, contains 6% nitrogen, 12% phosphorus, and 6% potassium by weight and all in the form of compounds.

Nitrogen stimulates overall plant growth. Phosphorus promotes root growth and flowering. Potassium regulates the structures in leaves that allow CO_2 to enter the leaf and O_2 and H_2O to exit. Fertilizers are available in N-P-K formulas best suited for their intended use. For example, plants that produce large amounts of carbohydrates (sugars) need more potassium than most other types of plants. Grain crops need higher concentrations of phosphorus. Lawn fertilizers applied in the spring are generally high in nitrogen to stimulate shoot growth in grasses. Lawn fertilizers applied in the fall of the year should have a higher phosphorus content to stimulate root growth during the winter.

TABLE 6A   Some Commercial Fertilizers and Uses

Fertilizer composition (N-P-K)	Uses
1-2-1 ratio 10-20-10 15-30-15	early-spring application for trees and shrubs with flowers and fruit; general-purpose feedings of the following: cucumbers, peppers, tomatoes
3-1-2 ratio 12-4-8 15-5-10 21-7-4 16-4-8 20-5-10	lawns and general-purpose feedings of the following: trees, shrubs, most berries, apple trees, grapes, vines, walnut trees, broccoli, cabbage, carrots, onions
High nitrogen 33-0-0 21-0-0 40-4-4 36-6-6	pecan trees, lawns, early feedings of corn
Balanced 13-13-13	general purpose feeding of the following: broccoli, cabbage, melons, potatoes
Special purpose: acid-loving flowering shrubs 12-10-4	azaleas, rhododendrons, camellias, gardenias
Special purpose 18-24-16	roses
Special purpose: flowering 12-55-6	flowering plants and shrubs (annuals and perennials)
Special purpose: root growth 5-20-10	starter fertilizer for transplants

GROUP 16
OXYGEN FAMILY

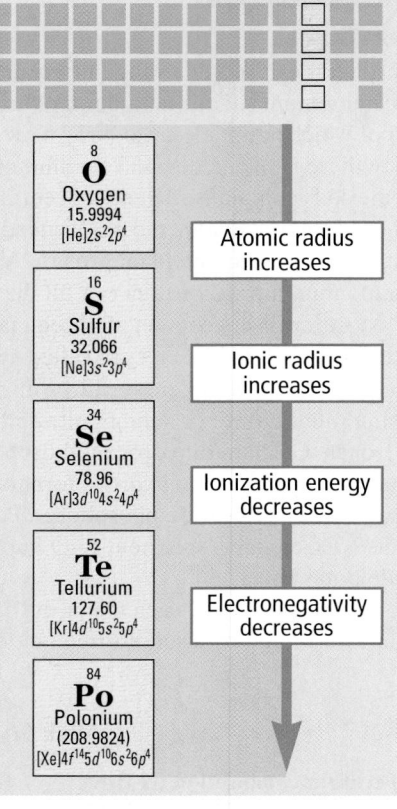

CHARACTERISTICS

- occur naturally as elements and in combined states
- consist of three nonmetals (oxygen, sulfur, and selenium), one metalloid (tellurium), and one metal (polonium)
- consist of atoms that have six electrons in their outermost energy level
- tend to form covalent compounds with other elements
- exist in several allotropic forms
- tend to exist as diatomic and polyatomic molecules, such as O_2, O_3, S_6, S_8, and Se_8
- commonly exist in compounds with the −2 oxidation state but often exhibit other oxidation states

8 **O** Oxygen 15.9994 [He]$2s^2 2p^4$	
16 **S** Sulfur 32.066 [Ne]$3s^2 3p^4$	Atomic radius increases
34 **Se** Selenium 78.96 [Ar]$3d^{10}4s^2 4p^4$	Ionic radius increases
52 **Te** Tellurium 127.60 [Kr]$4d^{10}5s^2 5p^4$	Ionization energy decreases
84 **Po** Polonium (208.9824) [Xe]$4f^{14}5d^{10}6s^2 6p^4$	Electronegativity decreases

Sulfur is found naturally in underground deposits and in the steam vents near volcanoes.

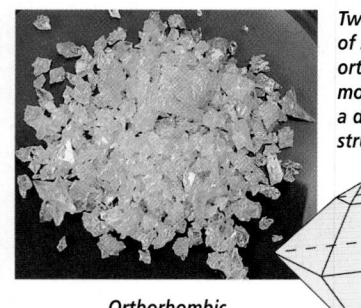

Sulfur exists in combined forms in many minerals. Iron pyrite, FeS_2, black galena, PbS, and yellow orpiment, As_2S_3, are shown.

Two allotropic forms of sulfur are orthorhombic and monoclinic. Each has a different crystal structure.

Orthorhombic

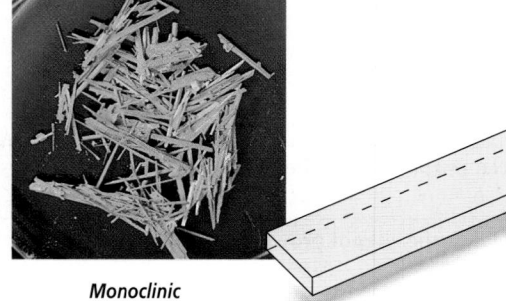

Monoclinic

COMMON REACTIONS

With Metals to Form Binary Compounds

Example: $8Mg(s) + S_8(l) \longrightarrow 8MgS(s)$

O_2, Se, and Te follow this pattern in reacting with Na, K, Ca, Mg, and Al.

With Oxygen to Form Oxides

Example: $Se(s) + O_2(g) \longrightarrow SeO_2(s)$

S, Te, and Po follow this pattern. S, Se, and Te can form SO_3, SeO_3, and TeO_3.

With Halogens to Form Binary Compounds

Example: $S_8(l) + 8Cl_2(g) \longrightarrow 8SCl_2(l)$

O, Se, Te, and Po follow this pattern in reacting with F_2, Cl_2, Br_2, and I_2.

With Hydrogen to Form Binary Compounds

$2H_2(g) + O_2(g) \longrightarrow 2H_2O(l)$

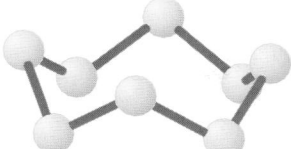
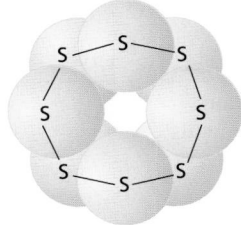

Sulfur exists as S_8 molecules in which the atoms are bonded in a ring, as shown by the ball-and-stick and space-filling models.

ANALYTICAL TEST

Other than atomic absorption spectroscopy, there is no simple analytical test to identify all elements of this family. Selenium and tellurium can be identified by flame tests. A light blue flame is characteristic of selenium, and a green flame is characteristic of tellurium. Oxygen can be identified by the splint test, in which a glowing splint bursts into flame when thrust into oxygen. Elemental sulfur is typically identified by its physical characteristics, especially its color and its properties when heated. It melts to form a viscous brown liquid and burns with a blue flame.

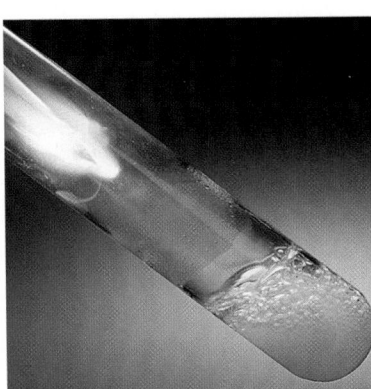

A glowing splint thrust into oxygen bursts into a bright flame.

Sulfur burns with a characteristically deep blue flame.

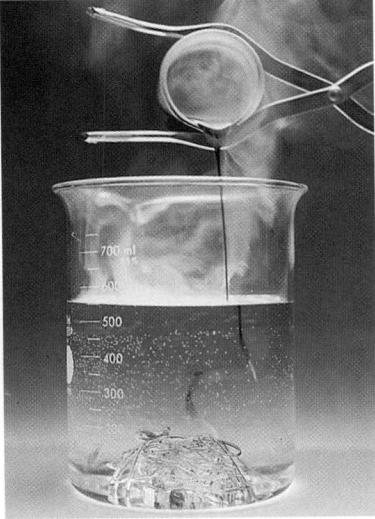

Molten sulfur returns to its orthorhombic form upon cooling.

PROPERTIES OF THE GROUP 16 ELEMENTS

	O	S	Se	Te	Po
Melting point (°C)	−218.4	119.0	217	449.8	254
Boiling point (°C)	−182.962	444.674	685	989.9	962
Density (g/cm^3)	1.429×10^{-3}	1.96	4.82	6.24	9.4
Ionization energy (kJ/mol)	1314	1000	941	869	812
Atomic radius (pm)	73	103	119	142	168
Ionic radius (pm)	140	184	198	221	—
Common oxidation number in compounds	−2	−2, +4, +6	−2, +2, +4, +6	−2, +2, +4, +6	−2, +2, +4, +6
Crystal structure*	orthorhombic, rhombohedral, cubic (when solid)	orthorhombic, monoclinic	hexagonal	hexagonal	cubic, rhombohedral
Hardness (Mohs' scale)	none (gas)	2.0	2.0	2.3	—

* Most elements of this family can have more than one crystal structure.

APPLICATION   *Chemical Industry*

Oxides

Oxides of the reactive metals are ionic compounds. The oxide ion from any soluble oxide reacts immediately with water to form hydroxide ions as represented by the following equation.

$$O^{2-}(aq) + H_2O(l) \longrightarrow 2OH^-(aq)$$

The reactive metal oxides of Groups 1 and 2 react vigorously with water and release a large amount of heat. The product of the reaction is a metal hydroxide. The following equation is an example of this reaction.

$$Na_2O(s) + H_2O(l) \longrightarrow 2NaOH(aq)$$

A basic oxide can be thought of as the dehydrated form of a hydroxide base. Oxides of the less reactive metals, such as magnesium, can be prepared by using thermal decomposition to drive off the water.

$$Mg(OH)_2(s) \xrightarrow{\text{heat}} MgO(s) + H_2O(g)$$

Hydroxides of the reactive metals of Group 1 are too stable to decompose in this manner.

If a hydroxide formed by a metal oxide is water-soluble, it dissolves to form a basic solution. An oxide that reacts with water to form a basic solution is called a basic oxide or a basic anhydride. Table 7A on the next page lists oxides that form basic solutions with water.

Molecular Oxides

Nonmetals, located on the right side of the periodic table, form molecular oxides. For example, sulfur forms two gaseous oxides: sulfur dioxide, SO_2, and sulfur trioxide, SO_3. In reactions typical of nonmetal oxides, each of the sulfur oxides reacts with water to form an oxyacid.

An oxide that reacts with water to form an acid is called an acidic oxide or an acid anhydride. As with the basic anhydrides, each acid anhydride can be thought of as the dehydrated form of the appropriate oxyacid. For example, when sulfuric acid decomposes, the loss of H_2O leaves the oxide SO_3, which is an anhydride.

$$H_2SO_4(aq) \xrightarrow{\text{heat}} H_2O(g) + SO_3(g)$$

Amphoteric Oxides

Table 7A lists some common oxides of main-group elements. You can see that the active metal oxides are basic and that the nonmetal oxides are acidic. Between these lies a group of oxides, the *amphoteric oxides*. The bonding in amphoteric oxides is intermediate between ionic and covalent bonding. As a result, oxides of this type show behavior intermediate between that of acidic oxides and basic oxides, and react as both acids and bases.

Aluminum oxide, Al_2O_3, is a typical amphoteric oxide. With hydrochloric acid, aluminum oxide acts as a base. The reaction produces a salt and water.

$$Al_2O_3(s) + 6HCl(aq) \longrightarrow 2AlCl_3(aq) + 3H_2O(l)$$

With aqueous sodium hydroxide, aluminum oxide acts as an acid. The reaction forms a soluble ionic compound and water. That compound contains aluminate ions, AlO_2^-. (The AlO_2^- formula is used here rather than the more precise hydrated aluminate formula, $Al(OH)_4^-$.)

$$Al_2O_3(s) + 2NaOH(aq) \longrightarrow 2NaAlO_2(aq) + H_2O(l)$$

Reactions of Oxides

In the reaction between an acid and a metal oxide, the products are a salt and water—the same as the products in a neutralization reaction. For example, when magnesium oxide reacts with dilute sulfuric acid, magnesium sulfate and water are produced.

$$MgO(s) + H_2SO_4(dil.\ aq) \longrightarrow MgSO_4(aq) + H_2O(l)$$

The reaction between a basic metal oxide, such as MgO, and an acidic nonmetal oxide, such as CO_2, tends to produce an oxygen-containing salt. The dry oxides are mixed and heated without water. Salts such as metal carbonates, phosphates, and sulfates can be made by this synthesis reaction.

$$MgO(s) + CO_2(g) \longrightarrow MgCO_3(s)$$

$$6CaO(s) + P_4O_{10}(s) \longrightarrow 2Ca_3(PO_4)_2(s)$$

$$CaO(s) + SO_3(g) \longrightarrow CaSO_4(s)$$

Reactions of Hydroxides with Nonmetal Oxides

Nonmetal oxides tend to be acid anhydrides. The reaction of a hydroxide base with a nonmetal oxide is an acid-base reaction. The product is either a salt or a salt and water, depending on the identities and relative quantities of reactants. For example, 2 mol of the hydroxide base sodium hydroxide and 1 mol of the nonmetal oxide carbon dioxide form sodium carbonate, which is a salt, and water.

$$CO_2(g) + 2NaOH(aq) \longrightarrow Na_2CO_3(aq) + H_2O(l)$$

However, if sodium hydroxide is limited, only sodium hydrogen carbonate is produced.

$$CO_2(g) + NaOH(aq) \longrightarrow NaHCO_3(aq)$$

TABLE 7A Periodicity of Acidic and Basic Oxides of Main-Group Elements

Group Number						
1	2	13	14	15	16	17
Li_2O basic	BeO amphoteric	B_2O_3 acidic	CO_2 acidic	N_2O_5 acidic		
Na_2O basic	MgO basic	Al_2O_3 amphoteric	SiO_2 acidic	P_4O_{10} acidic	SO_3 acidic	Cl_2O acidic
K_2O basic	CaO basic	Ga_2O_3 amphoteric	GeO_2 amphoteric	As_4O_6 amphoteric	SeO_3 acidic	
Rb_2O basic	SrO basic	In_2O_3 basic	SnO_2 amphoteric	Sb_4O_6 amphoteric	TeO_3 acidic	I_2O_5 acidic
Cs_2O basic	BaO basic	Tl_2O_3 basic	PbO_2 amphoteric	Bi_2O_3 basic		

APPLICATION *The Environment*

Ozone

Ozone, O_3, is an allotrope of oxygen that is important for life on Earth. Like O_2, O_3 is a gas at room temperature. However, unlike O_2, O_3 is a poisonous bluish gas with an irritating odor at high concentrations. The triatomic ozone molecule is angular (bent) with a bond angle of about 116.5°. The O—O bonds in ozone are shorter and stronger than a single bond, but longer and weaker than a double bond. The ozone molecule is best represented by two resonance hybrid structures.

Ozone forms naturally in Earth's atmosphere more than 24 km above the Earth's surface in a layer called the stratosphere. There, O_2 molecules absorb energy from ultraviolet light and split into free oxygen atoms.

$$O_2(g) \xrightarrow{\text{ultraviolet light}} 2O$$

A free oxygen atom has an unpaired electron and is highly reactive. A chemical species that has one or more unpaired or unshared electrons is referred to as a *free radical*. A free radical is a short-lived fragment of a molecule. The oxygen free radical can react with a molecule of O_2 to produce an ozone molecule.

$$O + O_2(g) \longrightarrow O_3(g)$$

A molecule of O_3 can then absorb ultraviolet light and split to produce O_2 and a free oxygen atom.

$$O_3(g) \xrightarrow{\text{ultraviolet light}} O_2(g) + O$$

The production and breakdown of ozone in the stratosphere are examples of *photochemical* processes, in which light causes a chemical reaction.

In this way, O_3 is constantly formed and destroyed in the stratosphere, and its concentration is determined by the balance among these reactions. The breakdown of ozone absorbs the sun's intense ultraviolet light in the range of wavelengths between 290 nm and 320 nm. Light of these wavelengths damages and kills living cells, so if these wavelengths were

to reach Earth's surface in large amounts, life would be impossible. Even now, the normal amount of ultraviolet light reaching Earth's surface is a major cause of skin cancer and the damage to DNA molecules that causes mutations. One life-form that is very sensitive to ultraviolet radiation is the phytoplankton in the oceans. These organisms carry out photosynthesis and are the first level of oceanic food webs.

Ozone and Air Pollution

Ozone in the lower atmosphere is a harmful pollutant. Ozone is highly reactive and can oxidize organic compounds. The products of these reactions are harmful substances that, when mixed with air, water vapor, and dust, make up *photochemical smog*. This mixture is the smog typically found in cities.

Typically, ozone is produced in a complex series of reactions involving unburned hydrocarbons and nitrogen oxides given off from engines in the form of exhaust and from fuel-burning power plants. When fuel burns explosively in the cylinder of an internal-combustion engine, some of the nitrogen in the cylinder also combines with oxygen to form NO, a very reactive nitrogen-oxide free radical.

$$N_2(g) + O_2(g) \longrightarrow 2NO$$

When the free radical reaches the air, it reacts with oxygen to produce NO_2 radicals, which react with water in the air to produce HNO_3.

$$2NO + O_2(g) \longrightarrow 2NO_2$$
$$3NO_2 + H_2O(l) \longrightarrow NO + 2HNO_3(aq)$$

In sunlight, nitrogen dioxide decomposes to give nitric oxide and an atom of oxygen. Note that the NO produced is free to undergo the previous reaction once more.

$$NO_2 \xrightarrow{\text{sunlight}} NO + O$$

Just as it is in the stratosphere, a free oxygen atom in the lower atmosphere is highly reactive and reacts with a molecule of diatomic oxygen to form ozone.

$$O + O_2(g) \longrightarrow O_3(g)$$

APPLICATION *Chemical Industry*

Sulfuric Acid

Sulfuric acid is the so-called "king of chemicals" because it is produced in the largest volume in the United States. It is produced by the contact process. This process starts with the production of SO_2 by burning sulfur or roasting iron pyrite, FeS_2. The purified sulfur dioxide is mixed with air and passed through hot iron pipes containing a catalyst. The contact between the catalyst, SO_2, and O_2 produces sulfur trioxide, SO_3, and gives the contact process its name. SO_3 is dissolved in concentrated H_2SO_4 to produce pyrosulfuric acid, $H_2S_2O_7$.

$$SO_3(g) + H_2SO_4(aq) \longrightarrow H_2S_2O_7(aq)$$

The pyrosulfuric acid is then diluted with water to produce sulfuric acid.

$$H_2S_2O_7(aq) + H_2O(l) \longrightarrow 2H_2SO_4(aq)$$

Properties and Uses of Sulfuric Acid

Concentrated sulfuric acid is a good oxidizing agent. During the oxidation process, sulfur is reduced from +6 to +4 or −2. The change in oxidation state for a reaction depends on the concentration of the acid and on the nature of the reducing agent used in the reaction.

Sulfuric acid is also an important dehydrating agent. Gases that do not react with H_2SO_4 can be dried by being bubbled through concentrated sulfuric acid. Organic compounds, like sucrose, are dehydrated to leave carbon, as shown by the following reaction.

$$C_{12}H_{22}O_{11}(s) + 11H_2SO_4(aq) \longrightarrow$$
$$12C(s) + 11H_2SO_4 \cdot H_2O(l)$$

The decomposition of sucrose proceeds rapidly, as shown in Figure 21-9 on page 684.

About 60% of the sulfuric acid produced in this country is used to make superphosphate, which is a mixture of phosphate compounds used in fertilizers.

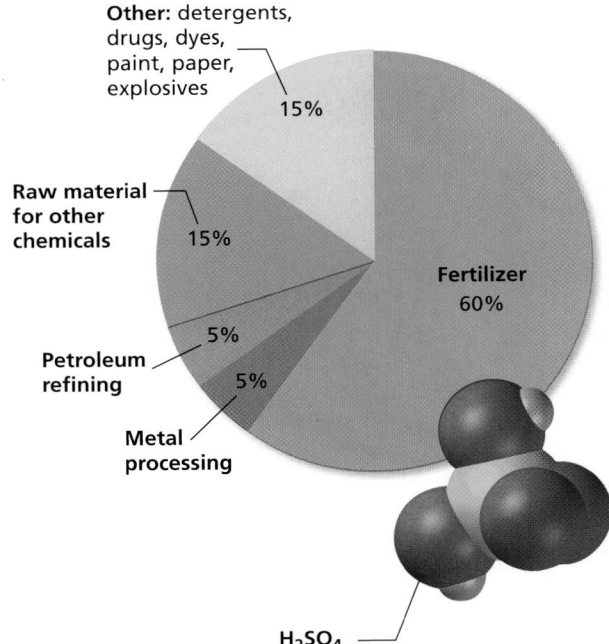

Other: detergents, drugs, dyes, paint, paper, explosives
15%

Raw material for other chemicals
15%

Petroleum refining
5%

Metal processing
5%

Fertilizer
60%

H_2SO_4

Important uses of the U.S. supply of sulfuric acid

	TABLE 7B	Top Ten Chemicals Produced in the U.S.	
Rank	**Chemical**	**Physical state**	**Formula**
1	sulfuric acid	*l*	H_2SO_4
2	nitrogen	*g*	N_2
3	oxygen	*g*	O_2
4	ethylene	*g*	C_2H_4
5	calcium oxide (lime)	*s*	CaO
6	ammonia	*g*	NH_3
7	phosphoric acid	*l*	H_3PO_4
8	sodium hydroxide	*s*	$NaOH$
9	propylene	*g*	C_3H_6
10	chlorine	*g*	Cl_2

GROUP 17
HALOGEN FAMILY

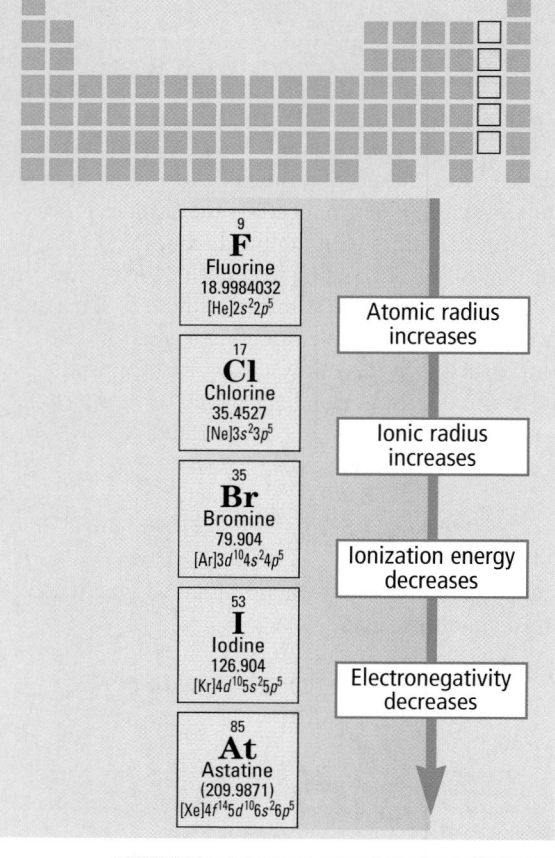

CHARACTERISTICS

- are all nonmetals and occur in combined form in nature, mainly as metal halides

- are found in the rocks of Earth's crust and dissolved in sea water

- range from fluorine, the 13th most abundant element, to astatine, which is one of the rarest elements

- exist at room temperature as a gas (F_2 and Cl_2), a liquid (Br_2), and a solid (I_2 and At)

- consist of atoms that have seven electrons in their outermost energy level

- tend to gain one electron to form a halide, X^- ion, but also share electrons and have positive oxidation states

- are reactive, with fluorine being the most reactive of all nonmetals

9	
F	
Fluorine	
18.9984032	
[He]$2s^2 2p^5$	

Atomic radius increases

17	
Cl	
Chlorine	
35.4527	
[Ne]$3s^2 3p^5$	

Ionic radius increases

35	
Br	
Bromine	
79.904	
[Ar]$3d^{10} 4s^2 4p^5$	

Ionization energy decreases

53	
I	
Iodine	
126.904	
[Kr]$4d^{10} 5s^2 5p^5$	

Electronegativity decreases

85	
At	
Astatine	
(209.9871)	
[Xe]$4f^{14} 5d^{10} 6s^2 6p^5$	

Halogens are the only family that contains elements representing all three states of matter at room temperature. Chlorine is a yellowish green gas; bromine is a reddish brown liquid; and iodine is a purple-black solid.

Iodine sublimes to produce a violet vapor that recrystallizes on the bottom of the evaporating dish filled with ice.

COMMON REACTIONS*

With Metals to Form Halides

Example: $Mg(s) + Cl_2(g) \longrightarrow MgCl_2(s)$

Example: $Sn(s) + 2F_2(g) \longrightarrow SnF_4(s)$

The halide formula depends on the oxidation state of the metal.

With Hydrogen to Form Hydrogen Halides

Example: $H_2(g) + F_2(g) \rightarrow 2HF(g)$

Cl_2, Br_2, and I_2 also follow this pattern.

With Nonmetals and Metalloids to Form Halides

Example: $Si(s) + 2Cl_2(g) \longrightarrow SiCl_4(s)$

Example: $N_2(g) + 3F_2(g) \longrightarrow 2NF_3(g)$

Example: $P_4(s) + 6Br_2(l) \longrightarrow 4PBr_3(s)$

The formula of the halide depends on the oxidation state of the metalloid or nonmetal.

With Other Halogens to Form Interhalogen Compounds

Example: $Br_2(l) + 3F_2(g) \longrightarrow 2BrF_3(l)$

* Chemists assume that astatine undergoes similar reactions, but few chemical tests have been made.

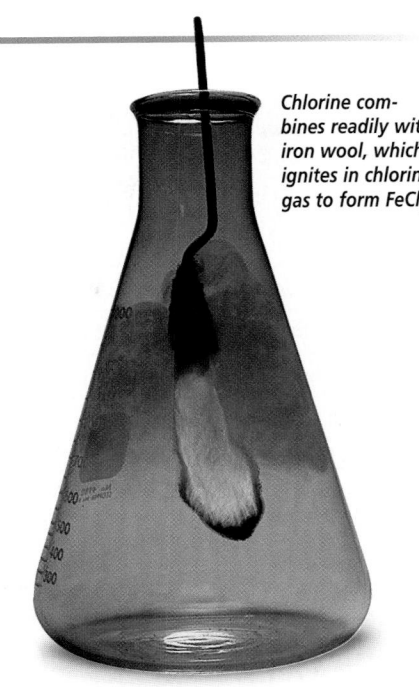

Chlorine combines readily with iron wool, which ignites in chlorine gas to form $FeCl_3$.

Hydrofluoric acid is used to etch patterns into glass.

Shown here from left to right are precipitates of AgCl, AgBr, and AgI.

ANALYTICAL TEST

As with most elements, the presence of each of the halogens can be determined by atomic absorption spectroscopy. Fluorides react with concentrated sulfuric acid, H_2SO_4, to release hydrogen fluoride gas. Three of the halide ions can be identified in solution by their reactions with silver nitrate.

$$Cl^-(aq) + Ag^+(aq) \longrightarrow AgCl(s)$$
$$Br^-(aq) + Ag^+(aq) \longrightarrow AgBr(s)$$
$$I^-(aq) + Ag^+(aq) \longrightarrow AgI(s)$$

PROPERTIES OF THE GROUP 17 ELEMENTS

	F	Cl	Br	I	At
Melting point (°C)	−219.62	−100.98	−7.2	113.5	575.2
Boiling point (°C)	−188.14	−34.6	58.78	184.35	610
Density (g/cm^3)	1.69×10^{-3}	3.214×10^{-3}	3.119	4.93	not known
Ionization energy (kJ/mol)	1681	1251	1140	1008	—
Atomic radius (pm)	72	100	114	133	140
Ionic radius (pm)	133	181	196	220	—
Common oxidation number in compounds	−1	−1, +1, +3, +5, +7	−1, +1, +3, +5, +7	−1, +1, +3, +5, +7	−1, +5
Crystal structure	cubic	orthorhombic	orthorhombic	orthorhombic	not known

APPLICATION   *The Environment*

Chlorine in Water Treatment

For more than a century, communities have treated their water to reduce the amount of toxic substances in the water and to prevent disease. A treatment process widely used in the United States is chlorination. All halogens kill bacteria and other microorganisms. Chlorine, however, is the only halogen acceptable for large-scale treatment of public water supplies.

When chlorine is added to water, the following reaction produces HCl and hypochlorous acid, HOCl.

$$Cl_2(g) + H_2O(l) \longrightarrow HCl(aq) + HOCl(aq)$$

Hypochlorous acid is a weak acid that ionizes to give hydrogen ions and hypochlorite ions, OCl$^-$.

$$HOCl(aq) + H_2O(l) \longrightarrow H_3O^+(aq) + OCl^-(aq)$$

NaHClO

CaCl$_2$O$_2$

Swimming pools are routinely tested to be sure the chlorine level is safe.

The "chlorine" used in swimming pools is really the compounds shown above and not chlorine at all.

The OCl$^-$ ions are strong oxidizing agents that can destroy microorganisms.

In some water-treatment plants, calcium hypochlorite, $Ca(ClO)_2$, a salt of hypochlorous acid, is added to water to provide OCl$^-$ ions. Similar treatments are used in swimming pools.

Nearly a hundred cities in the United States and thousands of communities in Europe use chlorine in the form of chlorine dioxide, ClO_2, as their primary means of disinfecting water. The main drawback to the use of ClO_2 is that it is unstable and cannot be stored. Instead, ClO_2 must be prepared on location by one of the following reactions involving sodium chlorite, $NaClO_2$.

$$10NaClO_2(aq) + 5H_2SO_4(aq) \longrightarrow$$
$$8ClO_2(g) + 5Na_2SO_4(aq) + 2HCl(aq) + 4H_2O(l)$$

$$2NaClO_2(aq) + Cl_2(g) \longrightarrow 2ClO_2(g) + 2NaCl(aq)$$

The expense of using ClO_2 makes it less desirable than Cl_2 in water-treatment systems unless there are other considerations. For example, the use of ClO_2 is likely to result in purified water with less of the aftertaste and odor associated with water purified by Cl_2.

Fluoride and Tooth Decay

In the 1940s, scientists noticed that people living in communities that have natural water supplies with high concentrations of fluoride ions, F$^-$, have significantly lower rates of dental caries (tooth decay) than most of the population.

In June 1944, a study on the effects of water fluoridation began in two Michigan cities, Muskegon and Grand Rapids, where the natural level of fluoride in drinking water was low (about 0.05 ppm). In Grand Rapids, sodium fluoride, NaF, was added to the drinking water to raise levels to 1.0 ppm. In Muskegon, no fluoride was added. Also included in the study was Aurora, Illinois, a city that was similar to Grand Rapids and Muskegon, except that it had a natural F$^-$ concentration of 1.2 ppm in the water supply. After 10 years, the rate of tooth decay in Grand Rapids had dropped far below that in Muskegon and was about the same as it was in Aurora.

Tooth enamel is made of a strong, rocklike material consisting mostly of calcium hydroxyphosphate, $Ca_5(PO_4)_3(OH)$, also known as apatite. Apatite is an insoluble and very hard compound—ideal for tooth enamel. Sometimes, however, saliva becomes more acidic, particularly after a person eats a high-sugar meal. Acids ionize to produce hydronium ions, which react with the hydroxide ion, OH$^-$, in the apatite to form water. The loss of OH$^-$ causes the apatite to dissolve.

$$Ca_5(PO_4)_3(OH)(s) + H_3O^+(aq) \longrightarrow$$
$$5Ca^{2+}(aq) + 3PO_4^{3-}(aq) + 2H_2O(l)$$

Saliva supplies more OH$^-$ ions, and new apatite is formed, but slowly.

If fluoride ions are present in saliva, some fluorapatite, $Ca_5(PO_4)_3F$, also forms.

$$5Ca^{2+}(aq) + 3PO_4^{3-}(aq) + F^-(aq) \longrightarrow Ca_5(PO_4)_3F(s)$$

Fluorapatite resists attack by acids, so the tooth enamel resists decay better than enamel containing no fluoride.

When the beneficial effect of fluoride had been established, public health authorities proposed that fluoride compounds be added to water supplies in low-fluoride communities. Fluoridation started in the 1950s, and by 1965, nearly every medical and dental association in the United States had endorsed fluoridation of water supplies. In the past decade, however, that trend slowed as opposition to fluoridation grew.

Laboratory Program

SAFETY IN THE CHEMISTRY LABORATORY   786

Pre-Lab Extraction and Filtration   790

   1-1 Mixture Separation   792

   1-2 Water Purification   794

   3-1 Conservation of Mass   798

   4-1 Flame Tests   801

Pre-Lab Gravimetric Analysis   804

   7-1 Separation of Salts by
       Fractional Crystallization   806

   7-2 Naming Ionic Compounds   810

   7-3 Determining the Empirical
       Formula of Magnesium Oxide   813

   9-1 Mass and Mole Relationships
       in a Chemical Reaction   816

   9-2 Stoichiometry and
       Gravimetric Analysis   819

  12-1 "Wet" Dry Ice   822

  12-2 Measuring the Triple Point
       Pressure of CO_2 824

Pre-Lab Paper Chromatography   828

  13-1 Separation of Pen Inks by Paper
       Chromatography   830

  13-2 Colorimetry and Molarity   834

  14-1 Testing Water   838

Pre-Lab Volumetric Analysis   842

    16-1 How Much Calcium Carbonate
           Is in an Eggshell?   844

    16-2 Investigating Overwrite
           Marking Pens   848

    16-3 Is It an Acid or a Base?   851

    16-4 Percentage of Acetic Acid
           in Vinegar   854

Pre-Lab Calorimetry   858

    17-1 Measuring the Specific
           Heats of Metals   860

    17-2 Calorimetry and Hess's Law   864

    17-3 Rate of a Chemical Reaction   868

    18-1 Equilibrium Expressions   871

    18-2 Measuring K_a for Acetic Acid   875

    19-1 Blueprint Paper   878

    19-2 Reduction of Manganese
           in Permanganate Ion   881

    21-1 Acid Catalyzed Iodination
           of Acetone   884

    21-2 Casein Glue   888

    21-3 Polymers and Toy Balls   891

Safety in the Chemistry Laboratory

Any chemical can be dangerous if it is misused. Always follow the instructions for the experiment. Pay close attention to the safety notes. Do not do anything differently unless told to do so by your teacher.

Chemicals, even water, can cause harm. The challenge is to know how to use chemicals correctly. If you follow the rules stated below, pay attention to your teacher's directions, follow cautions on chemical labels and in the experiments, then you will be using chemicals correctly.

THESE SAFETY RULES ALWAYS APPLY IN THE LAB

1. **Always wear a lab apron and safety goggles.** Even if you aren't working on an experiment at the time, laboratories contain chemicals that can damage your clothing. Keep the apron strings tied.

   Some chemicals can cause eye damage, and even blindness. If your safety goggles are uncomfortable or cloud up, ask your teacher for help. Try lengthening the strap, washing the goggles with soap and warm water, or using an anti-fog spray.

2. **No contact lenses in the lab.** Even while wearing safety goggles, chemicals can get between contact lenses and your eyes and cause irreparable eye damage. If your doctor requires that you wear contact lenses instead of glasses, then you should wear eye-cup safety goggles in the lab. Ask your doctor or your teacher how to use this very important and special eye protection.

3. **NEVER work alone in the laboratory.** You should do lab work only under the supervision of your teacher.

4. **Wear the right clothing for lab work.** Necklaces, neckties, dangling jewelry, long hair. and loose clothing can knock things over or catch on fire. Tuck in neckties or take them off. Do not wear a necklace or other dangling jewelry, including hanging earrings. It might also be a good idea to remove your wristwatch so that it is not damaged by a chemical splash.

   Pull back long hair, and tie it in place. Nylon and polyester fabrics burn and melt more readily than cotton, so wear cotton clothing if you can. It's best to wear fitted garments, but if your clothing is loose or baggy, tuck it in or tie it back so that it does not get in the way or catch on fire.

   Wear shoes that will protect your feet from chemical spills—no open-toed shoes or sandals, and no shoes with woven leather straps. Shoes made of solid leather or polymer are much better than shoes made of cloth. It is also important to wear pants, not shorts or skirts.

5. **Only books and notebooks needed for the experiment should be in the lab.** Do not bring textbooks, purses, bookbags, backpacks, or other items into the lab; keep these things in your desk or locker.

6. **Read the entire experiment before entering the lab.** Memorize the safety precautions. Be familiar with the instructions for the experiment. Only materials and equipment authorized by your teacher should be used. When you do your lab work, follow the instructions and safety precautions described in the directions for the experiment.

7. **Read chemical labels.** Follow the instructions and safety precautions stated on the labels.

8. **Walk with care in the lab.** Sometimes you will have to carry chemicals *from* the supply station to your lab station. Avoid bumping into other students and spilling the chemicals. Stay at your lab station at other times.

9. **Food, beverages, chewing gum, cosmetics, and smoking are NEVER allowed in the lab.** (You should already know this.)

10. **NEVER taste chemicals or touch them with your bare hands.** Keep your hands away from your face and mouth while working, even if you are wearing gloves.

11. **Use a sparker to light a Bunsen burner.** Do not use matches. Be sure that all gas valves are turned off and that all hot plates are turned off and unplugged when you leave the lab.

12. **Be careful with hot plates, Bunsen burners, and other heat sources.** Keep your body and clothing away from flames. Do not touch a hot plate after it has just been turned off because it is probably hotter than you think. The same is true of glassware, crucibles, and other things after removing them from the flame of a Bunsen burner or from a drying oven.

13. **Do not use electrical equipment with frayed or twisted wires.**

14. **Be sure your hands are dry before using electrical equipment.** Before plugging an electrical cord into a socket, be sure the electrical equipment is turned off. When you are finished with it, turn it off. Before you leave the lab, unplug it, but be sure to turn it off FIRST.

15. **Do not let electrical cords dangle from work stations, dangling cords can cause tripping or electrical shocks.** The area under and around electrical equipment should be dry; cords should not lie in puddles of spilled liquid.

16. **Know fire drill procedures and the locations of exits.**

17. **Know the location and operation of safety showers and eyewash stations.**

18. **If your clothes catch on fire, walk to the safety shower, stand under it, and turn it on.**

19. **If you get a chemical in your eyes, walk immediately to the eyewash station, turn it on, and lower your head so your eyes are in the running water.** Hold your eyelids open with your thumbs and fingers, and roll your eyeballs around. You have to flush your eyes continuously for at least 15 minutes. Call your teacher while you are doing this.

20. **If you have a spill on the floor or lab bench, call your teacher rather than trying to clean it up by yourself.** Your teacher will tell you if it is OK for you to do the cleanup; if not, your teacher will know how the spill should be cleaned up safely.

21. **If you spill a chemical on your skin, wash it off using the sink faucet, and call your teacher.** If you spill a solid chemical on your clothing brush it off carefully without scattering it on somebody else, and call your teacher. If you get liquid on your clothing, wash it off right away using the sink faucet, and call your teacher. If the spill is on your pants or somewhere else that will not fit under the sink faucet, use the safety shower. Remove the pants or other affected clothing while under the shower, and call your teacher. (It may be temporarily embarrassing to remove pants or other clothing in front of your class, but failing to flush that chemical off your skin could cause permanent damage.)

22. **The best way to prevent an accident is to stop it before it happens.** If you have a close call, tell your teacher so that you and your teacher can find a way to prevent it from happening again. Otherwise, the next time, it could be a harmful accident instead of just a close call.

23. **All accidents should be reported to your teacher, no matter how minor.** Also, if you get a headache, feel sick to your stomach, or feel dizzy, tell your teacher immediately.

24. **For all chemicals, take only what you need.** However, if you do happen to take too much and have some left over, DO NOT put it back in the bottle. If somebody accidentally puts a chemical into the wrong bottle, the next person to use it will have a contaminated sample. Ask your teacher what to do with any leftover chemicals.

25. **NEVER take any chemicals out of the lab.** (This is another one that you should already know. You probably know the remaining rules also, but read them anyway.)

26. **Horseplay and fooling around in the lab are very dangerous.** NEVER be a clown in the laboratory

27. **Keep your work area clean and tidy.** After your work is done, clean your work area and all equipment.

28. **Always wash your hands with soap and water before you leave the lab.**

29. **Whether or not the lab instructions remind you, all of these rules apply all of the time.**

SAFETY SYMBOLS

To highlight specific types of precautions, the following symbols are used throughout the lab program. Remember that no matter what safety symbols you see in the lab instructions, all 29 of the safety rules previously described should be followed at all times.

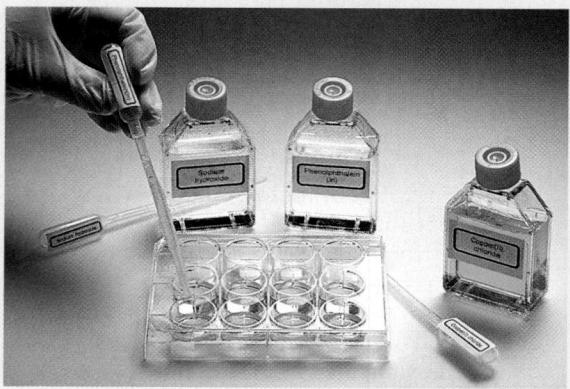

CLOTHING PROTECTION

◆ Wear laboratory aprons in the laboratory. Keep the apron strings tied so that they do not dangle.

EYE SAFETY

◆ Wear safety goggles in the laboratory at all times. Know how to use the eyewash station.

HAND SAFETY

◆ If a chemical gets on your skin or clothing or in your eyes, rinse it immediately, and alert your teacher.

GLASSWARE SAFETY

◆ Never place glassware, containers of chemicals, or anything else near the edges of a lab bench or table.

CHEMICAL SAFETY

◆ Never return unused chemicals to the original container.

◆ It helps to label the beakers and test tubes containing chemicals. (This is not a new rule, just a good idea.)

◆ Never transfer substances by sucking on a pipet or straw; use a suction bulb.

CAUSTIC SAFTEY

◆ If a chemical is spilled on the floor or lab bench, tell your teacher, but do not clean it up yourself unless your teacher says it is OK to do so.

HEATING SAFETY

◆ When heating a chemical in a test tube, always point the open end of the test tube away from yourself and other people.

CLEAN UP

◆ Never taste, eat, or swallow any chemicals in the laboratory. Do not eat or drink any food from laboratory containers. Beakers are not cups, and evaporating dishes are not bowls.

WASTE DISPOSAL

◆ Some chemicals are harmful to our environment. You can help protect the environment by following the instructions for proper disposal.

Look at the list of rules and identify whether a specific rule applies, or if the rule presented is a new rule.

1. Tie back long hair, and confine loose clothing. (Rule ? applies.)

2. Never reach across an open flame. (Rule ? applies.)

3. Use proper procedures when lighting Bunsen burners. Turn off hot plates, Bunsen burners, and other heat sources when not in use. (Rule ? applies.)

4. Heat flasks or beakers on a ringstand with wire gauze between the glass and the flame. (Rule ? applies.)

5. Use tongs when heating containers. Never hold or touch containers while heating them. Always allow heated materials to cool before handling them. (Rule ? applies.)

6. Turn off gas valves when not in use. (Rule ? applies.)

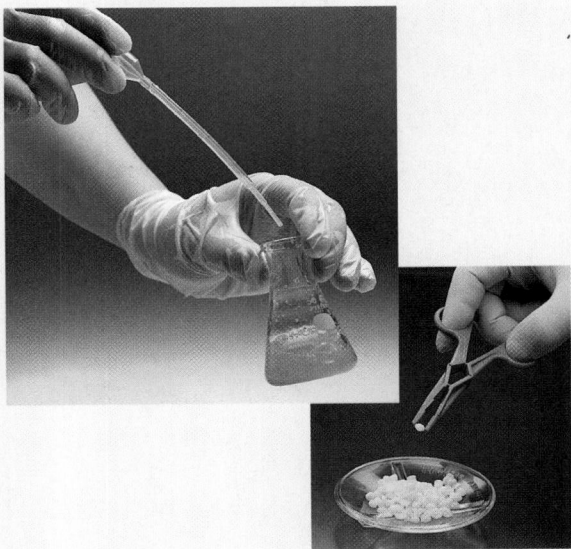

7. Use flammable liquids only in small amounts. (Rule ? applies.)

8. When working with flammable liquids, be sure that no one else is using a lit Bunsen burner or plans to use one. (Rule ? applies.)

9. Check the condition of glassware before and after using it. Inform your teacher of any broken, chipped, or cracked glassware because it should not be used. (Rule ? applies.)

10. Do not pick up broken glass with your bare hands. Place broken glass in a specially designated disposal container. (Rule ? applies.)

11. Never force glass tubing into rubber tubing, rubber stoppers, or wooden corks. To protect your hands, wear heavy cloth gloves or wrap toweling around the glass and the tubing, stopper, or cork, and gently push in the glass. (Rule ? applies.)

12. Do not inhale fumes directly. When instructed to smell a substance, use your hand to wave the fumes toward your nose, and inhale gently. (Rule ? applies.)

13. Keep your hands away from your face and mouth. (Rule ? applies.)

14. Always wash your hands before leaving the laboratory. (Rule ? applies.)

Finally, if you are wondering how to answer the questions that asked what additional rules apply to the safety symbols, here is the correct answer.

Any time you see any of the safety symbols, you should remember that all 29 of the numbered laboratory rules always apply.

Extraction and Filtration

Extraction, the separation of substances in a mixture by using a solvent, depends on solubility. For example, sand can be separated from salt by adding water to the mixture. The salt dissolves in the water, and the sand settles to the bottom of the container. The sand can be recovered by decanting the water. The salt can then be recovered by evaporating the water.

Filtration separates substances based on differences in their physical states or in the size of their particles. For example, a liquid can be separated from a solid by pouring the mixture through a paper-lined funnel or, if the solid is more dense than the liquid, the solid will settle to the bottom of the container, leaving the liquid on top. The liquid can then be decanted, leaving the solid.

SETTLING AND DECANTING

1. Fill an appropriate-sized beaker with the solid-liquid mixture provided by your teacher. Allow the beaker to sit until the bottom is covered with solid particles and the liquid is clear.

2. Grasp the beaker with one hand. With the other hand, pick up a stirring rod and hold it along the lip of the beaker. Tilt the beaker slightly so that liquid begins to pour out in a slow, steady stream, as shown in Figure A.

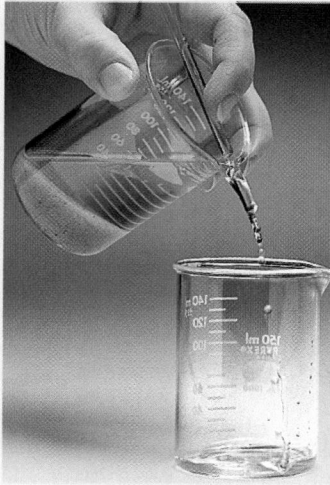

FIGURE A
Settling and decanting

GRAVITY FILTRATION

1. Prepare a piece of filter paper as shown in Figure B. Fold it in half and then in half again. Tear the corner of the filter paper, and open the filter paper into a cone. Place it in the funnel.

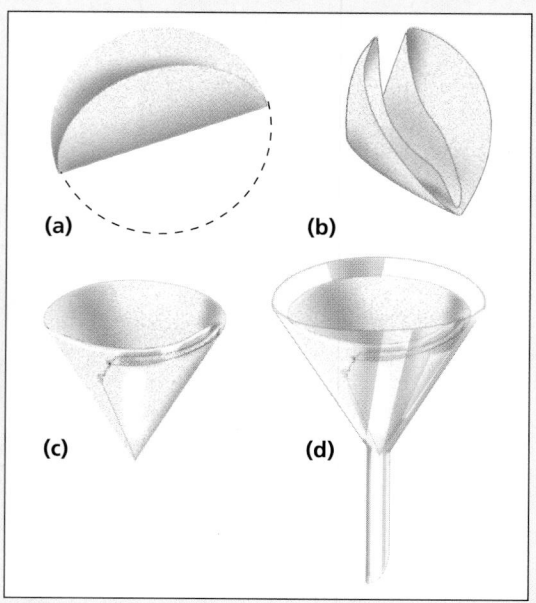

(a)   (b)

(c)   (d)

FIGURE B

FIGURE C   Gravity filtration

2. Put the funnel, stem first, into a filtration flask, or suspend it over a beaker using an iron ring, as shown in Figure C.

3. Wet the filter paper with distilled water from a wash bottle. The paper should adhere to the sides of the funnel, and the torn corner should prevent air pockets from forming between the paper and the funnel.

4. Pour the mixture to be filtered down a stirring rod into the filter. The stirring rod directs the mixture into the funnel and reduces splashing.

5. Do not let the level of the mixture in the funnel rise above the edge of the filter paper.

6. Use a wash bottle to rinse all of the mixture from the beaker into the funnel.

VACUUM FILTRATION

1. Check the T attachment to the faucet. Turn on the water. Water should run without overflowing the sink or spitting while creating a vacuum. To test for a vacuum, cover the opening of the horizontal arm of the T with your thumb or index finger. If you feel your thumb being pulled inward, you have a vacuum. Note the number of turns of the knob that are needed to produce the flow of water that creates a vacuum.

2. Turn the water off. Attach the pressurized rubber tubing to the *horizontal* arm of the T. (You do not want water to run through the tubing.)

3. Attach the free end of the rubber tubing to the side arm of a filter flask. Check for a vacuum. Turn on the water so that it rushes out of the faucet (refer to step 1). Place the palm of your hand over the opening of the Erlenmeyer flask. You should feel the vacuum pull your hand inward. If you do not feel any pull or if the pull is weak, increase the flow of water. If increasing the flow of water fails to work, shut off the water and make sure your tubing connections are tight.

4. Insert the neck of a Büchner funnel into a one-hole rubber stopper until the stopper is about two-thirds to three-fourths up the neck of the funnel. Place the funnel stem into the Erlenmeyer flask so that the stopper rests in the mouth of the flask, as shown in Figure D.

5. Obtain a piece of round filter paper. Place it inside the Büchner funnel over the holes. Turn on the water as in step 1. Hold the filter flask with one hand, place the palm of your hand over the mouth of the funnel, and check for a vacuum.

6. Pour the mixture to be filtered into the funnel. Use a wash bottle to rinse all of the mixture from the beaker into the funnel.

FIGURE D   Vacuum filtration

EXPERIMENT 1-1

OBJECTIVES
Students will

- design a step-by-step procedure for separating a four-component mixture.
- evaluate their success in separating and recovering the components.
- justify their evaluation by referring to their observations.
- relate the techniques they used to the physical properties of the components.

RECOMMENDED TIME
1 hour

MATERIALS
(for each lab group)

- 20 g samples of salt, sand, iron filings, poppy seeds, and the mixture of these four materials
- Petri dish
- tape dispenser with transparent tape

ADDITIONAL EQUIPMENT
(shared by the class)

- 500 mL distilled water
- cotton balls, 15
- filter funnels, 15
- filter papers, 50
- forceps, 10
- magnets, 15
- paper clips, 10
- pipets, 30
- plastic forks, 10
- plastic spoons, 10
- plastic straws, 10
- roll of aluminum foil
- roll of paper towels
- roll of tissue paper
- rubber stoppers, 15
- test tubes, 50 (13 × 100)
- test-tube rack
- wooden splints, 10

Mixture Separation

OBJECTIVES

- *Observe* the chemical and physical properties of a mixture.
- *Relate* knowledge of chemical and physical properties to the task of purifying the mixture.
- *Analyze* the success of methods of purifying the mixture.

MATERIALS

- **aluminum foil**
- **cotton balls**
- **distilled water**
- **filter funnels**
- **filter paper**
- **forceps**
- **magnet**
- **paper clips**
- **paper towels**
- **Petri dish**
- **pipets**

- **plastic forks**
- **plastic spoons**
- **plastic straws**
- **rubber stoppers**
- **sample of mixture and components (sand, iron filings, salt, poppy seeds)**
- **test tubes and rack**
- **tissue paper**
- **transparent tape**
- **wooden splints**

BACKGROUND

The ability to separate and recover pure substances from mixtures is extremely important in scientific research and industry. Chemists need to work with pure substances, but naturally occurring materials are seldom pure. Often, differences in the physical properties of the components in a mixture provide the means for separating them. In this experiment, you will have an opportunity to design, develop, and implement your own procedure for separating a mixture. The mixture you will work with contains salt, sand, iron filings, and poppy seeds. All four substances are in dry, granular form.

SAFETY

 Always wear safety goggles and a lab apron to protect your eyes and clothing. If you get a chemical in your eyes, immediately flush the chemical out at the eyewash station while calling to your teacher. Know the location of the emergency lab shower and eyewash station and the procedures for using them.

 Call your teacher in the event of a spill. Spills should be cleaned up promptly according to your teacher's directions.

PREPARATION

1. Your task will be to plan and carry out the separation of a mixture. Before you can plan your experiment, you will need to investigate the properties of each component in the mixture. The properties will be used to design your mixture separation. Copy the data table on the following page in your lab notebook, and use it to record your observations.

DATA TABLE

Properties	Sand	Iron filings	Salt	Poppy seeds
Dissolves				
Floats				
Magnetic				
Other				

PROCEDURE

1. Obtain separate samples of each of the four mixture components from your teacher. Use the equipment you have available to make observations of the components and determine their properties. You will need to run several tests with each substance, so don't use all of your sample on the first test. Look for things like whether the substance is magnetic, whether it dissolves, or whether it floats. Record your observations in your data table.

2. Make a plan for what you will do to separate a mixture that includes the four components from step 1. Review your plan with your teacher.

3. Obtain a sample of the mixture from your teacher. Using the equipment you have available, run the procedure you have developed.

CLEANUP AND DISPOSAL

4. Clean your lab station. Clean all equipment, and return it to its proper place. Dispose of chemicals and solutions in the containers designated by your teacher. Do not pour any chemicals down the drain or throw anything in the trash unless your teacher directs you to do so. Wash your hands thoroughly after all work is finished and before you leave the lab.

ANALYSIS AND INTERPRETATION

1. **Evaluating Methods:** On a scale of 1 to 10, how successful were you in separating and recovering each of the four components: sand, salt, iron filings, and poppy seeds? Consider 1 to be the best and 10 to be the worst. Justify your ratings based on your observations.

CONCLUSIONS

1. **Evaluating Methods:** How did you decide on the order of your procedural steps? Would any order have worked?

2. **Designing Experiments:** If you could do the lab over again, what would you do differently? Be specific.

3. **Designing Experiments:** Name two materials or tools that weren't available that might have made your separation easier.

4. **Applying Ideas:** For each of the four components, describe a specific physical property that enabled you to separate the component from the rest of the mixture.

EXTENSIONS

1. **Evaluating Methods:** What methods could be used to determine the purity of each of your recovered components?

2. **Designing Experiments:** How could you separate each of the following two-part mixtures?
   a. lead filings and iron filings
   b. sand and gravel
   c. sand and finely ground polystyrene foam
   d. salt and sugar
   e. alcohol and water
   f. nitrogen and oxygen

SOLUTION/MATERIALS PREPARATION

1. Mix about 5 g of each of the four components in a large resealable (zippered) plastic bag for each lab group. Give 20 g samples of each of the four components to each lab group for step 1 of the procedure. They may be dispensed in stoppered test tubes to the students.

2. You may wish to modify the list of additional equipment, but the list should remain extensive enough to provide students with a wide range of choices.

REQUIRED PRECAUTIONS

- Safety goggles and a lab apron must be worn at all times.
- Read all safety precautions, and discuss them with your students.
- In case of a spill, use a damp cloth or paper towels to mop up the spill. Then rinse the cloth in running water at the sink, wring it out thoroughly, and put it in the trash.

PRE-LAB DISCUSSION

This experiment is intended to be an open-ended, self-designed activity in which students are presented only with the problem and a list of equipment available to them. They are required to develop and test their own procedures. To shorten the time necessary, allow 15–20 min of class or lab time for students to plan their experiments, or assign the development of a written plan as homework prior to the lab. Some of the separation procedures (especially those involving evaporation of a solvent) may require equipment such as Petri dishes to stand overnight.

It is best to avoid giving direct answers to any student's questions. Encourage members of each lab team to work cooperatively as they develop their procedural plan.

Continued on page 893A

EXPERIMENT 1-2

OBJECTIVES
Students will

• demonstrate appropriate technique in using micropipets, separatory bulbs, and funnels.

• describe changes in the chemical and physical properties of a mixture.

• classify mixtures as solutions, colloids, or suspensions.

• explain how the height of a liquid in a test tube can be a measure of volume.

RECOMMENDED TIME
50 min, including disposal

MATERIALS
(for each lab group)
• 3 mL foul water
• 3–4 g activated charcoal
• 6–7 g sand
• 12 cm wire, (10 or 12 gauge)
• flashlight or slide projector and screen
• calibrated wooden splint
• long-stemmed microfunnels, 2
• microtip pipet
• plastic spoon
• separatory bulb
• strainer
• test-tube rack
• test tubes, 4, (13 mm × 100 mm or 10 mm × 80 mm)
• thin-stemmed pipet
• tissue paper
• tray
• wash basins, 2 (recovery bins for sand and charcoal)

SOLUTIONS/MATERIALS PREPARATION
1. To make 75 mL of foul water, mix 60 mL of tap water with 0.25 tsp of sifted coffee grounds and 0.25 tsp of sifted garlic powder in a 125 mL Erlenmeyer flask. Add 15 mL of mineral oil, then stopper and shake the

Water Purification

OBJECTIVES

• *Observe* the chemical and physical properties of a mixture.

• *Relate* knowledge of these properties to the task of purifying a mixture.

• *Compare* different techniques of purifying a mixture.

MATERIALS

• **activated charcoal**

• **flashlight or slide projector and screen**

• **foul-water sample**

• **calibrated wooden splint**

• **long-stemmed microfunnels**

• **microtip pipet**

• **plastic spoon**

• **sand**

• **separatory bulb**

• **strainer**

• **test-tube rack**

• **test tubes**

• **thin-stemmed pipet**

• **tissue paper**

• **tray**

• **wire**

BACKGROUND

Few substances are found naturally in a pure state, so separating mixtures such as metal ore, petroleum, and impure water to create pure substances is frequently necessary. A series of steps is often required to remove the different impurities in a mixture. Knowledge of the chemical and physical properties of the impurities is important in creating a workable plan for separating them.

In this experiment, a sample of foul water will be purified using the following steps: oil-water-sediment separation, sand filtration, and charcoal adsorption and filtration. These three approaches are similar to approaches used in everyday life. For example, in some homes water is passed through charcoal filters to remove impurities that cause a bad odor or taste. Your objective is to purify a sample of water containing several impurities and to recover as much pure water as possible from the sample.

SAFETY

 Always wear safety goggles and a lab apron to protect your eyes and clothing. If you get a chemical in your eyes, immediately flush the chemical out at the eyewash station while calling to your teacher. Know the location of the emergency lab shower and eyewash station and the procedure for using them.

 Do not touch any chemicals. If you get a chemical on your skin or clothing, wash the chemical off at the sink while calling to your teacher. Make sure you carefully read the labels and follow the precautions on all containers of chemicals that you use. If no precautions are stated on the label, ask your teacher what precautions to follow. Do not taste any chemicals or items used in the laboratory. Never return leftover chemicals

DATA TABLE

	Before treatment	After oil-water-sediment separation	After sand filtration	After charcoal adsorption-filtration
Color				
Clarity				
Odor				
Volume				
Oil present				
Solids present				

to their original containers; take only small amounts to avoid wasting supplies.

 Call your teacher in the event of a spill. Spills should be cleaned up promptly according to your teacher's directions.

PREPARATION

1. Make a data table like the one above and provide space for six observations at each of the four stages of purification: before treatment, after oil-water-sediment separation, after sand filtration, and after charcoal adsorption/filtration. The six observations are color, clarity, odor, volume, whether oil is present, and whether solids are present.

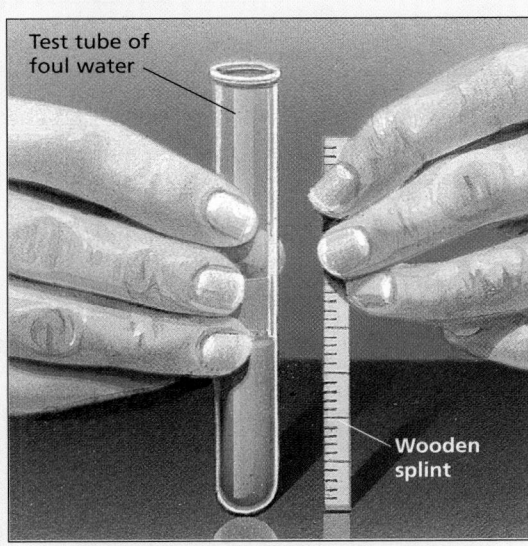

FIGURE A The height of the water in the test tube is a measure of the relative volume of the water.

PROCEDURE

1. Use a test tube to obtain a sample of foul water from your teacher. Record your observations of the foul-water sample in your data table. Obtain a calibrated wooden splint from your teacher. Position the test tube vertically on the lab table with the calibrated wooden splint alongside it, and estimate the volume to the nearest tenth of a milliliter, as shown in Figure A.

2. Place four clean, dry test tubes in a test-tube rack. Use the thin-stemmed pipet to draw up the entire foul-water sample and deliver it into the separatory bulb. Turn the separatory bulb mouth-side down, and set it back on top of the first test tube, as shown in Figure B. Surface

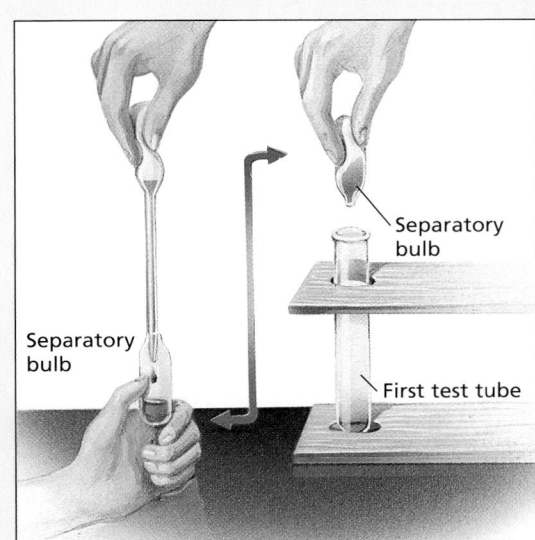

FIGURE B Use a thin-stemmed pipet to deliver the foul-water sample to the separatory bulb. Then squeeze out the layer of sediment into the first test tube.

flask. To make a convenient dispenser, slide a graduated beral pipet through a 1-hole rubber stopper that fits the flask mouth. Put the stopper on the flask, as shown in Figure 1, and shake vigorously. To draw up a sample the instant you stop shaking the flask, squeeze and release the bulb, and then dispense the sample. This can help provide a consistent mixture of ingredients and deliver a reproducible 3.0 mL of foul water.

FIGURE 1

2. To calibrate the wooden splints, add 1.0 mL of water to one of the test tubes, place the tube upright on the table, and place the wooden splint alongside it. Draw a line level with the bottom of the meniscus. Add another 1.0 mL, and draw another graduate mark. Repeat for the entire length of the test tube. Use this wooden splint as a template for marking the remaining splints.

3. Separatory bulbs may be made by cutting all but 4–5 mm of the stem from a graduated or thinned-stemmed pipet, as shown in Figure 2.

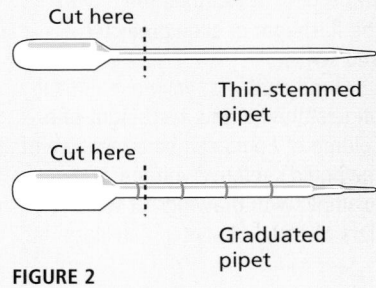

FIGURE 2

4. Microfunnels may be made by cutting the top section off the bulb of a jumbo pipet, as shown in Figure 3.

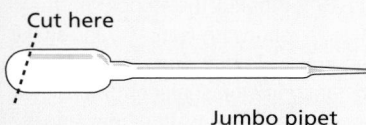

Cut here

Jumbo pipet

FIGURE 3

5. Sand should be rinsed and dried.

6. Use aquarium-grade activated charcoal, crushed by a mortar and pestle to granular consistency.

7. Use a flashlight or slide projector and screen when testing mixtures for the Tyndall effect to determine if the mixtures are colloids.

8. Students may share trays, plastic spoons, wires, and strainers.

REQUIRED PRECAUTIONS

- Safety goggles and a lab apron must be worn at all times.
- Read all safety precautions, and discuss them with your students.
- In case of a spill, use a damp cloth or paper towel to mop up the spill. Then rinse the cloth in running water at the sink, wring it out thoroughly, and put it in the trash.

SAMPLE DATA
Student data will vary.

PRE-LAB DISCUSSION
Review with students the properties of solutions, colloids, and suspensions and the ways that the three types of mixtures can be distinguished. Have samples of a solution, a colloid, and a suspension available, and demon-strate how to examine them with the flashlight or slide projector and screen.

Some students may have difficulty understanding how the height of a column of liquid can be a measure of the liquid's relative volume. Show an example with drawings of two cylin-ders of equal diameter. Calculate the

tension should keep the liquid from spilling out. Let it stand undisturbed until two liquid layers form and some sediment particles settle into a layer on the bottom.

3. While keeping the separatory bulb mouth-side down, carefully squeeze out the first drop or two of sediment into the first test tube. Then deliver the water layer to the second test tube, but be careful to keep the oily top layer from dripping out. Finally, squeeze out the remaining oil layer into the first test tube.

4. Observe the properties and measure the volume of the water in the second test tube after the oil-water-sediment separation. Record this information in your data table. Set aside the water sample in the second test tube.

5. Place a spoonful of sand in a strainer and sift it for about 15 s over a plastic tray.

6. Place the coarse sand (the sand left inside the strainer) and the fine sand (the sand in the tray) in layers in the bottom half of a long-stemmed microfunnel, as shown in Figure C.

7. Place the microfunnel over the third test tube, and carefully pour the water sample from step 4 into it. When filtration is complete, remove the funnel. Be sure to retrieve as much water as possible.

8. Observe the properties and measure the volume of the water sample after the sand filtration. Record this information in your data table. Set aside the filtered water sample in the third test tube.

9. Tear off a piece of tissue paper about the size of a quarter, wad it up, and place it in a second long-stemmed microfunnel. Use a piece of wire to pack the tissue down gently but securely into the tapered tip. Then add enough charcoal to fill the lower half of the stem, as shown in Figure D. Place the funnel over the fourth test tube.

10. Carefully pour the water from the third test tube into the funnel and allow the water to filter through. (Hint: To help speed up this process, increase the pressure on the water by placing a finger or thumb securely over the top rim of the funnel and gently squeezing inward on the sides of the cut-off bulb, as shown in Figure D. This should help push the liquid through the charcoal and tissue paper.)

Fine sand

Coarse sand

FIGURE C Prepare a microfunnel for sand filtration by placing a layer of fine sand between layers of coarse sand.

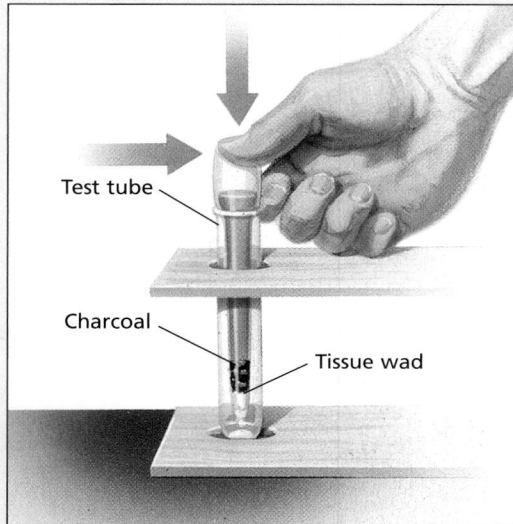

Test tube

Charcoal

Tissue wad

FIGURE D Close off the top of the microfunnel with your thumb or finger and gently squeeze the sides. This will speed up the adsorption/filtration process.

11. When the charcoal filtration is complete, observe the properties of your sample, and measure its final volume. Record this information in your data table. Show your purified water sample to your teacher.

CLEANUP AND DISPOSAL

12. To recover the sand, hold the sand-filter funnel upside down over the sand disposal container, squeeze the tip, and roll the tip between your fingers. Use a microtip pipet to squirt water through the opening and flush the sand into the container.

13. To recover the charcoal, pinch and roll the tip of the pipet and use a small piece of wire to push any remaining charcoal into the charcoal-disposal container.

14. Oily residue on equipment should be absorbed onto paper towels, which may be placed in the trash. Then wash and scrub the equipment with soap and water.

15. Any foul water, oil, or other liquids should be absorbed onto paper towels and placed in the trash.

16. Purified water may be poured down the sink. Clean your lab station. Clean all equipment and return it to its proper place. Dispose of chemicals and solutions in containers designated by your teacher. Do not pour any chemicals down the drain or throw anything in the trash unless your teacher directs you to do so. Wash your hands thoroughly after all work is finished and before you leave the lab.

ANALYSIS AND INTERPRETATION

1. **Analyzing Methods:** By using the calibrated wooden splint to measure the volume of liquid in all of the test tubes, what assumption are you making about the test tubes?

2. **Analyzing Methods:** What is the purpose of the coarse sand at the bottom of the funnel? What is the purpose of the fine sand in the middle of the funnel? What is the purpose of the coarse sand at the top of the funnel?

3. **Analyzing Methods:** Since charcoal does the best job of removing smaller impurities from the water, why don't you just use charcoal from the start and skip all of the other steps?

4. **Analyzing Methods:** Why were clean test tubes used to hold the sample after each purification?

CONCLUSIONS

1. **Inferring Relationships:** Rank the following in order from lowest density to highest density: water, sediment particles, oil. How do you know from this investigation what the order should be?

2. **Inferring Conclusions:** Which are larger, the particles that make the water appear cloudy (instead of transparent) or the particles that make the water appear colored (but transparent)? Explain your reasoning.

3. **Evaluating Methods:** Calculate the percentage of water recovered by using the following equation:

$$\frac{\text{percentage}}{\text{recovered}} = \frac{\text{volume of purified water}}{\text{volume of initial sample}} \times 100$$

4. **Evaluating Methods:** Compare your results with those of other lab groups. How should each group's success with the techniques be judged?

EXTENSIONS

1. **Designing Experiments:** How can you improve the percentage of water recovered or the purity of the water recovered? If your teacher approves your suggestions, test your ideas on another sample of foul water.

2. **Applying Ideas:** Find out how water is purified where you live. What are the most common impurities present, and what steps are taken to separate them from the water? Prepare a report describing the system.

3. **Analyzing Ideas:** In the sedimentation step, a solid and a liquid were separated because one was more dense than the other. In the process called distillation, a mixture is gradually heated until one of the substances in the mixture reaches its boiling point and becomes a gas. Explain how you would use distillation to separate a mixture of two miscible liquids with different boiling points.

volumes, and show that the ratio of the two volumes is the same as the ratio of the two heights.

DISPOSAL
Put out two wash basins to serve as recovery bins for the sand and charcoal. Fill the basins halfway with water and allow students to follow the Cleanup and Disposal steps outlined in the lab. Discard the tissue wad used in the second long-stemmed microfunnel. Wash the charcoal, and dry it for several hours in the oven. (This also helps to reactivate it.) The sand may be washed, dried, and used again.

The test tubes can be washed and scrubbed well with soap and water. The oily residue in the first test tube should be absorbed onto paper towels, which then may be placed in the trash. Remember that oily paper towels can create a fire hazard, so be sure they are disposed of promptly.

ANALYSIS AND INTERPRETATION—ANSWERS

1. The assumption being made is that the test tubes have the same thickness in the bottom and the same cross-sectional area so that the length along the splint is directly proportional to the volume of the liquid.

2. The coarse sand at the bottom of the funnel holds the fine sand in the funnel. The fine sand in the middle filters out small particles. The coarse sand in the top filters out larger particles.

3. Charcoal filtration was the slowest step, and with a variety of very large particles, it could take even longer. If the mixture was very impure, the charcoal could become so full of impurities that it would be unable to adsorb all of them.

Continued on page 893A

EXPERIMENT 3-1

MICRO-**LAB**

OBJECTIVES
Students will
- use a balance to measure initial and final mass.
- infer from data that the given lab procedure is flawed.
- design a procedure that adequately tests the law of conservation of mass.
- relate the results of their new procedure to the law of conservation of mass.

RECOMMENDED TIME
30 min

MATERIALS
(for each lab group)
- 2 L plastic soda bottle
- 17 g baking soda (sodium hydrogen carbonate)
- 100 mL graduated cylinder
- 270 mL vinegar (5% acetic acid solution)
- balance, triple beam or electronic
- clear plastic cups, 2
- hook-insert cap for bottle
- microplunger
- resealable (zippered) plastic bags (for Extension 2)

SOLUTIONS/MATERIALS PREPARATION
1. Use vinegar and baking soda instead of diluted glacial acetic acid. The suggested amounts of vinegar and baking soda are sufficient to do the Extensions.

2. Provide medium-sized (1 qt) plastic bags.

3. To make the hook-insert caps for the bottles, use hot-melt glue to attach a wire hook to the inside center of the bottle cap, as shown in Figure 1. The hook may be handmade or purchased from a hardware store.

Conservation of Mass

OBJECTIVES

- *Observe* the signs of a chemical reaction.
- *Infer* that a reaction has occurred.
- *Compare* masses of reactants and products.
- *Resolve* chemical discrepancies.
- *Design* experiments.
- *Relate* observations to the law of conservation of mass.

MATERIALS

- **2 L plastic soda bottle**
- **5% acetic acid solution (vinegar)**
- **balance**
- **clear plastic cups, 2**
- **graduated cylinder**
- **hook-insert cap for bottle**
- **microplunger**
- **sodium hydrogen carbonate (baking soda)**

BACKGROUND

The law of conservation of mass states that matter is neither created nor destroyed during a chemical reaction. Therefore, the mass of a system should remain constant during any chemical process. In this experiment, you will determine whether mass is conserved by examining a simple chemical reaction and comparing the mass of the system before the reaction with its mass after the reaction.

SAFETY

Always wear safety goggles and a lab apron to protect your eyes and clothing. If you get a chemical in your eyes, immediately flush the chemical out at the eyewash station while calling to your teacher. Know the location of the emergency lab shower and eyewash station and the procedure for using them.

Do not touch any chemicals. If you get a chemical on your skin or clothing, wash the chemical off at the sink while calling to your teacher. Make sure you carefully read the labels and follow the precautions on all containers of chemicals that you use. If no precautions are stated on the label, ask your teacher what precautions to follow. Do not taste any chemicals or items used in the laboratory. Never return leftover chemicals to their original containers; take only small amounts to avoid wasting supplies.

Call your teacher in the event of a spill. Spills should be cleaned up promptly according to your teacher's directions.

PREPARATION

1. Make two data tables in your lab notebook, one for Part I and another for Part II. In each table, create three columns labeled *Initial mass (g)*,

Final mass (g), and *Change in mass (g)*. Each table should also have space for observations of the reaction.

PROCEDURE—PART I

1. Obtain a microplunger and tap it down into a sample of baking soda until the bulb end is packed with a plug of the powder (4–5 mL of baking soda should be enough to pack the bulb).

2. Hold the microplunger over a plastic cup, and squeeze the sides of the microplunger to loosen the plug of baking soda so that it falls into the cup.

3. Use a graduated cylinder to measure 100 mL of vinegar, and pour it into a second plastic cup.

4. Place the two cups side by side on the balance pan and measure the total mass of the system (before reaction) to the nearest 0.01 g. Record the mass in your data table.

5. Add the vinegar to the baking soda a little at a time to prevent the reaction from getting out of control, as shown in Figure A. Allow the vinegar to slowly run down the inside of the cup. Observe and record your observations about the reaction.

FIGURE A   Slowly add the vinegar to prevent the reaction from getting out of control.

6. When the reaction is complete, place both cups on the balance and determine the total final mass of the system to the nearest 0.01 g. Calculate any change in mass. Record both the final mass and any change in mass in your data table.

7. Examine the plastic bottle and the hook-insert cap. Try to develop a modified procedure that will test the law of conservation of mass more accurately than the procedure in Part I.

8. In your notebook, write the answers to items 1 through 3 in Analysis and Interpretation—Part I.

PROCEDURE—PART II

9. Your teacher should approve the procedure you designed in Procedure—Part 1, step 7. Implement your procedure with the same chemicals and quantities you used in Part I, but use the bottle and hook-insert cap in place of the two cups. Record your data in the data table.

10. If you were successful in step 9 and your results reflect the conservation of mass, proceed to complete the experiment. If not, find a lab group that was successful, and discuss with them what they did and why they did it. Your group should then test the other group's procedure to determine whether their results are reproducible.

CLEANUP AND DISPOSAL

11. Clean your lab station. Clean all equipment and return it to its proper place. Dispose of chemicals and solutions in the containers designated by your teacher. Do not pour any chemicals down the drain or throw anything in the trash unless your teacher directs you to do so. Wash your hands thoroughly after all work is finished and before you leave the lab.

ANALYSIS AND INTERPRETATION— PART I

1. **Inferring Conclusions:** What evidence was there that a chemical reaction occurred?

2. **Organizing Data:** How did the final mass of the system compare with the initial mass of the system?

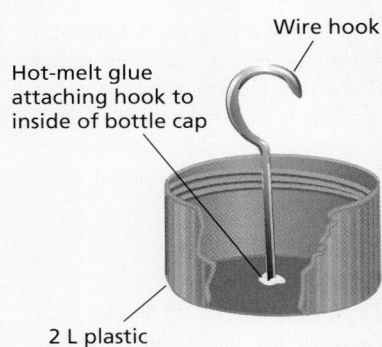

Wire hook

Hot-melt glue attaching hook to inside of bottle cap

2 L plastic soda bottle cap

FIGURE 1

4. To make the microplungers, cut graduated pipets and thread a loop of string or thread through the tip as shown in Figure 2.

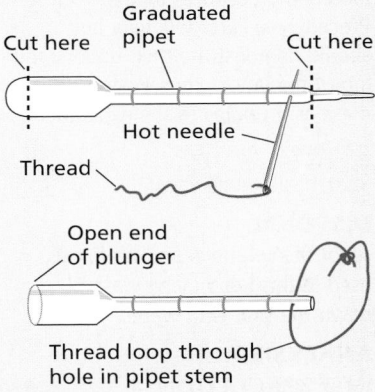

Cut here

Graduated pipet

Cut here

Hot needle

Thread

Open end of plunger

Thread loop through hole in pipet stem

FIGURE 2

REQUIRED PRECAUTIONS

- Safety goggles and a lab apron must be worn at all times.

- Read all safety precautions, and discuss them with your students.

- If, instead of using vinegar, glacial acetic acid is used to prepare a 5% acetic acid solution, wear safety goggles, a face shield, impermeable gloves, and a lab apron while preparing the solution. Work in a fume hood that is known to be in good working order, and have another person stand by to call for help in case of an emergency.

• In case of a spill, use a dampened cloth or paper towel (or more than one towel if necessary) to mop up the spill. Then rinse the cloth in running water at the sink, wring it out thoroughly, and put it in the trash.

TECHNIQUES TO DEMONSTRATE

Show students how to fill the microplunger with a plug of baking soda and how to manipulate the plunger to deliver the baking soda in the plastic cup. Demonstrate how to control the rapid fizzing of the baking soda by the slow addition of vinegar down the inside of the cup. Students' modified procedures to step 7 in Procedure—Part I will vary but should demonstrate their understanding of the law of conservation of mass as it relates to the experiment.

SAMPLE DATA

Student data will vary.

DISPOSAL

All of the solutions and chemicals used in this lab may be washed down the sink with water.

ANALYSIS AND INTERPRETATION— PART I—ANSWERS

1. The reactants bubbled and fizzed with the formation of a new gaseous substance. The baking soda seemed to disappear eventually.

2. Students' answers will vary, but typical results show a mass loss of 1.0–1.5 g for Part I.

3. Students' answers should indicate that although the mass loss appears to violate the law of conservation of mass, the law probably still holds. This is because not all of the products were present for the second measurement of mass. The bubbles that formed and popped were a gaseous product that escaped into the air.

Continued on page 893A

800

3. Resolving Discrepancies: Does your answer to the previous question show that the law of conservation of mass was violated? (Hint: Another way to express the law of conservation of mass is to say that the mass of all of the products equals the mass of all of the reactants.) What do you think might cause the mass difference?

ANALYSIS AND INTERPRETATION— PART II

1. Inferring Conclusions: Was there any new evidence in Part II indicating that a chemical reaction occurred?

2. Organizing Ideas: Identify the state of matter for each reactant in Part II. Identify the state of matter for each product.

CONCLUSIONS

1. Relating Ideas: What is the difference between the system in Part I and the system in Part II? What change led to the improved results in Part II?

2. Evaluating Methods: Why did the procedure for Part II work better than the procedure for Part I?

EXTENSIONS

1. Designing Experiments: How would you verify the law of conservation of mass if you were given a resealable (zippered) plastic bag, as shown in Figure B, and a twist tie instead of the bottle and hook-cap? Write your proposed procedure, step by step.

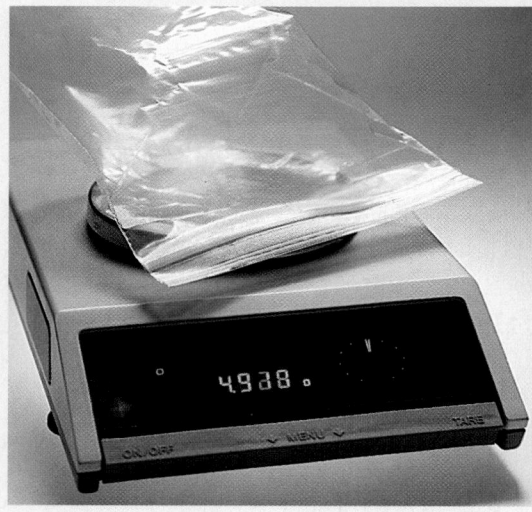

FIGURE B

2. Predicting Outcomes: Would you have been as successful with the resealable plastic bag and twist tie? Why or why not? If time allows, try the procedure you wrote in Extension item 1 and test your prediction. Report your results, and try to explain any discrepancies you find. (Hint: What are the differences between what happened with the bag and what happened with the bottle?)

3. Apply Models: When a log burns, the resulting ash obviously has less mass than the unburned log did. Explain whether this loss of mass violates the law of conservation of mass.

4. Designing Experiments: Design a procedure that would test the law of conservation of mass for the burning log described in Extension item 3.

EXPERIMENT 4-1

MICRO-LAB

Flame Tests

OBJECTIVES

- *Identify* a set of flame-test color standards for selected metal ions.

- *Relate* the colors of a flame test to the behavior of excited electrons in a metal ion.

- *Identify* an unknown metal ion by using a flame test.

- *Demonstrate* proficiency in performing a flame test and in using a spectroscope.

MATERIALS

- 1.0 M HCl solution

- 250 mL beaker

- Bunsen burner and related equipment

- $CaCl_2$ solution

- cobalt glass plates

- crucible tongs

- distilled water

- flame-test wire

- glass test plate (or a microchemistry plate with wells)

- K_2SO_4 solution

- Li_2SO_4 solution

- Na_2SO_4 solution

- NaCl crystals

- NaCl solution

- $SrCl_2$ solution

- spectroscope

- unknown solution

OPTIONAL EQUIPMENT

- wooden splints

BACKGROUND

The characteristic light emitted by each individual atom is the basis for the chemical test known as a flame test.

To identify an unknown atom, you must first determine the characteristic colors produced by different atoms. You will do this by performing a flame test on a variety of standard solutions of metal compounds. Then you will perform a flame test with an unknown sample to see if it matches any of the standard solutions. The presence of even a speck of another substance can interfere with the identification of the true color of a particular type of atom, so be sure to keep your equipment very clean and perform multiple trials to check your work.

SAFETY

Always wear safety goggles and a lab apron to protect your eyes and clothing. If you get a chemical in your eyes, immediately flush the chemical out at the eyewash station while calling to your teacher. Know the locations of the emergency lab shower and eyewash station and the procedures for using them.

Do not touch any chemicals. If you get a chemical on your skin or clothing, wash the chemical off at the sink while calling to your teacher. Make sure you carefully read the labels and follow the precautions on all containers of chemicals that you use. If no precautions are stated on the label, ask your teacher what precautions to follow. Do not taste any chemicals or items used in the laboratory. Never return leftover chemicals to their original containers; take only small amounts to avoid wasting supplies.

OBJECTIVES
Students will
- use a Bunsen burner.
- perform flame tests on a variety of metal compounds.
- identify an unknown based on the results of a flame test.

RECOMMENDED TIME
1–2 lab periods

MATERIALS
(for each lab group)
- 3 g NaCl crystals
- 5 cm flame-test wire
- 5 mL 1.0 M HCl solution
- 250 mL beaker
- Bunsen burner, gas tubing, striker
- $CaCl_2$ solution
- cobalt glass plate
- crucible tongs
- distilled water
- glass test plate (either a 7 cm × 15 cm plate, or a microchemistry plate with wells)
- K_2SO_4 solution
- Li_2SO_4 solution
- NaCl solution
- Na_2SO_4 solution
- $SrCl_2$ solution
- spectroscope
- unknown solution

OPTIONAL EQUIPMENT
wooden splints

SOLUTION/MATERIALS PREPARATION
1. To prepare 1.0 M HCl, observe the required precautions. Add 83 mL of concentrated HCl to enough distilled water to make 1.00 L of solution. Add the acid slowly, and stir to avoid overheating.

2. To prepare 0.5 M $CaCl_2$, add 55 g of $CaCl_2$ to enough water to make 1.00 L of solution.

3. To prepare 0.5 M K_2SO_4, add 87 g

of K_2SO_4 to enough water to make 1.00 L of solution.

4. To prepare 0.5 M Li_2SO_4, add 65 g of $Li_2SO_4 \cdot H_2O$ to enough water to make 1.00 L of solution.

5. To prepare 0.5 M Na_2SO_4, add 71 g of Na_2SO_4 to enough water to make 1.00 L of solution.

6. To prepare 0.5 M NaCl, add 29 g of NaCl to enough water to make 1.00 L of solution.

7. To prepare 0.5 M $SrCl_2$, add 133.3 g of $SrCl_2 \cdot 6H_2O$ to enough water to make 1.00 L of solution.

8. For the unknown solution, use any of the above solutions.

9. For flame-test wire, use either No. 24 platinum wire or nichrome wire. Some teachers prefer to use wooden splints for the flame tests. If the splints are soaked in the appropriate solutions overnight, they provide a colored flame that is long-lasting and easy to view with the spectroscope. If this is done, however, each splint should be extinguished in the waste beaker. Be sure to label the splints with the compound they were soaked in so that they can be reused. The sodium content of the splint may interfere with some flame tests.

REQUIRED PRECAUTIONS

- Safety goggles and a lab apron must be worn at all times.
- Tie back long hair and loose clothing when you are working in the lab.
- Read all safety precautions, and discuss them with your students.
- Students should not handle concentrated acid solutions.
- Wear safety goggles, a face shield, impermeable gloves, and a lab apron when you prepare the HCl solution. Work in a hood known to be in good working order, and have another person stand by to call for help in case of an emergency. Work within a 30 s walk from a safety shower and eyewash station.

 When using a Bunsen burner, confine long hair and loose clothing. Do not heat glassware that is broken, chipped, or cracked. Use tongs or a hot mitt to handle heated glassware and other equipment; heated glassware does not always look hot. If your clothing catches fire, WALK to the emergency lab shower and use it to put out the fire.

 Call your teacher in the event of an acid or base spill. Acid or base spills should be cleaned up promptly according to your teacher's instructions.

PREPARATION

1. Prepare a data table in your lab notebook. Include rows for each of the solutions of metal compounds listed in the materials list as well as for NaCl crystals and an unknown solution. The table should have three wide columns for the three trials you will perform with each substance. Each column should have room to record the colors and wavelengths of light. Be sure you have plenty of room to write your observations about each test.

DATA TABLE			
Substance	Trial 1	Trial 2	Trial 3
1.0 M HCl			
$CaCl_2$			
K_2SO_4			
Li_2SO_4			
Na_2SO_4			
NaCl crystals			
NaCl			
$SrCl_2$			
Unknown			

2. Label a beaker *Waste*. Thoroughly clean and dry a well strip. Fill the first well one-fourth full with 1.0 M HCl on the plate. Clean the test wire by first dipping it in the HCl and then holding it in the colorless flame of the Bunsen burner. Repeat this procedure until the flame is not colored by the wire. When the wire is ready, rinse the well with distilled water and collect the rinse water in the waste beaker.

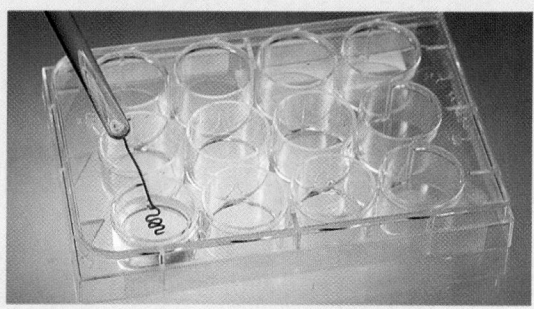

FIGURE A   Be sure that you record the positions of the various metal ion solutions in each well of the well strip.

3. Put 10 drops of each metal ion solution listed in the materials list, except NaCl, in a row in each well of the well strip. Put a row of 1.0 M HCl drops on a glass plate across from the metal ion solutions. Record the positions of all of the chemicals placed in the wells. The wire will need to be cleaned thoroughly between each test solution with HCl to avoid contamination from the previous test, as shown in Figure A.

PROCEDURE

1. Dip the wire into the $CaCl_2$ solution, and then hold it in the Bunsen burner flame. Observe the color of the flame, and record it in the data table. Repeat the procedure again, but this time look through the spectroscope to view the results. Record the wavelengths you see from the flame. Repeat each test three times. Clean the wire with the HCl as you did in Preparation step 2.

2. Repeat step 1 with the K_2SO_4 and with each of the remaining solutions in the well strip. For each solution that you test, record the color of each flame and the wavelength observed with the spectroscope. After the solutions are tested, clean the wire thoroughly, rinse the plate with distilled water, and collect the rinse water in the waste beaker.

3. Test another drop of Na_2SO_4, but this time view the flame through two pieces of cobalt glass. Clean the wire, and repeat the test. Record in your data table the colors and wavelengths of the flames as they appear when viewed through the cobalt glass. Clean the wire and the well strip, and rinse the well strip with distilled water. Pour the rinse water into the waste beaker.

4. Put a drop of K_2SO_4 in a clean well. Add a drop of Na_2SO_4. Flame-test the mixture. Observe the flame without the cobalt glass. Repeat the test again, this time observing the flame through the cobalt glass. Record the colors and wavelengths of the flames in the data table. Clean the wire, and rinse the well strip with distilled water. Pour the rinse water into the waste beaker.

5. Test a drop of the NaCl solution in the flame, and then view it through the spectroscope. (Do not use the cobalt glass.) Record your observations. Clean the wire, and rinse the well strip with distilled water. Pour the rinse water into the waste beaker. Place a few crystals of NaCl on the plate, dip the wire in the crystals, and do the flame test once more. Record the color of the flame test. Clean the wire, and rinse the well strip with distilled water. Pour the rinse into the waste beaker.

6. Obtain a sample of the unknown solution. Perform flame tests for it, with and without the cobalt glass. Record your observations. Clean the wire, and rinse the well strip with distilled water. Pour the rinse water into the waste beaker.

CLEANUP AND DISPOSAL

7. Dispose of the contents of the waste beaker in the container designated by your teacher. Wash your hands thoroughly after cleaning up the area and equipment.

ANALYSIS AND INTERPRETATION

1. **Organizing Data:** Examine your data table, and create a summary of the flame test for each metal ion.

2. **Analyzing Data:** Account for any differences in the individual trials for the flame tests for the metals ions.

3. **Organizing Ideas:** Explain how viewing the flame through cobalt glass can make it easier to analyze the ions being tested.

4. **Relating Ideas:** For three of the metal ions tested, explain how the flame color you saw relates to the lines of color you saw when you looked through the spectroscope.

CONCLUSIONS

1. **Inferring Conclusions:** What metal ions are in the unknown solution?

2. **Evaluating Methods:** How would you characterize the flame test with respect to its sensitivity? What difficulties could there be when identifying ions by the flame test?

3. **Evaluating Methods:** Explain how you can use a spectroscope to identify the components of solutions containing several different metal ions.

EXTENSIONS

1. **Inferring Conclusions:** A student performed flame tests on several unknowns and observed that they all were shades of red. What should the student do to correctly identify these substances? Explain your answer.

2. **Applying Ideas:** During a flood, the labels from three bottles of chemicals were lost. The three unlabeled bottles of white solids were known to contain the following: strontium nitrate, ammonium carbonate, and potassium sulfate. Explain how you could easily test the substances and relabel the three bottles. (Hint: Ammonium ions do not provide a distinctive flame color.)

3. **Applying Ideas:** Some stores sell "fireplace crystals." When sprinkled on a log, these crystals make the flames blue, red, green, and violet. Explain how these crystals can change the flame's color. What ingredients do you expect them to contain?

- In case of an acid spill, dilute the spill with water. Then mop up the spill with wet cloths or a wet cloth mop designated for spill cleanup. Wear disposable plastic gloves while cleaning spills.

TECHNIQUES TO DEMONSTRATE
Demonstrate the flame-test technique, including the procedure for cleaning the flame-test wire. Point out that because the color lasts only a short time, several trials may be necessary. If you have spectroscopes, demonstrate how to use them. Your students can use the spectroscope to identify the specific lines in the spectra of the light emitted in the flame tests (see page 893B for Sample Data Table). NOTE: Student data tables should show three trials for each compound.

PRE-LAB DISCUSSION
This identification technique can be used to introduce concepts related to the behavior and arrangement of electrons in atoms. To emphasize this point, you might apply high voltage to a gas-discharge tube containing helium or neon, or place a few crystals of sodium chloride on the grating of a lit Fisher burner. Explain that the colored lights are actually a combination of several specific wavelengths of light. Each wavelength of light corresponds to excited electrons moving from a different energy level to their ground state, emitting light in the process.

DISPOSAL
Set out a disposal container for the students. After all of the waste beakers have been emptied into it, neutralize the resulting solution with 0.1 M NaOH. When the solution's pH is between 5 and 9, pour the solution down the drain.

Continued on page 893B

Gravimetric Analysis

Gravimetric analytical methods are based on accurate and precise mass measurements. They are used to determine the amount or percentage of a compound or element in a sample material. For example, if we want to determine the percentage of iron in an ore or the percentage of chloride ion in drinking water, gravimetric analysis would be used.

A gravimetric procedure generally involves reacting the sample to produce a reaction product that can be used to calculate the mass of the element or compound in the original sample. For example, to calculate the percentage of iron in a sample of iron ore, the mass of the ore is determined. The ore is then dissolved in hydrochloric acid to produce $FeCl_3$. The $FeCl_3$ precipitate is converted to a hydrated form of Fe_2O_3 by adding water and ammonia to the system. The mixture is then filtered to separate the hydrated Fe_2O_3 from the mixture. The hydrated Fe_2O_3 is heated in a crucible to drive the water from the hydrate, producing anhydrous Fe_2O_3. The mass of the crucible and its contents is determined after successive heating steps to ensure that the product has reached constant mass and that all of the water has been driven off. The mass of Fe_2O_3 produced can be used to calculate the mass and percentage of iron in the original ore sample.

Gravimetric procedures require accurate and precise techniques and measurements to obtain suitable results. Possible sources of error are the following:

1. The product (precipitate) that is formed is contaminated.
2. Some product is lost when transferring the product from a filter to a crucible.
3. The empty crucible is not clean or is not at constant mass for the initial mass measurement.
4. The system is not heated sufficiently to obtain an anhydrous product.

GENERAL SAFETY

Always wear safety goggles and a lab apron to protect your eyes and clothing. If you get a chemical in your eyes, immediately flush the chemical out at the eyewash station while calling to your teacher. Know the location of the emergency lab shower and eyewash station and the procedure for using them.

When using a Bunsen burner, confine long hair and loose clothing. Do not heat glassware that is broken, chipped, or cracked. Use tongs or a hot mitt to handle heated glassware and other equipment; heated glassware does not always look hot. If your clothing catches fire, WALK to the emergency lab shower and use it to put out the fire.

 Never put broken glass or ceramics in a regular waste container. Broken glass and ceramics should be disposed of in a separate container designated by your teacher.

SETTING UP THE EQUIPMENT

1. The general setup for heating a sample in a crucible is shown in Figure A. Attach a metal ring clamp to a ring stand, and lay a clay triangle on the ring.

CLEANING THE CRUCIBLE

2. Wash and dry a metal or ceramic crucible and lid. Cover the crucible with its lid, and use a balance to obtain its mass. If the balance is located far from your working station, use crucible tongs to place the crucible and lid on a piece of wire gauze. Carry the crucible to the balance, using the wire gauze as a tray.

HEATING THE CRUCIBLE TO OBTAIN A CONSTANT MASS

3. After recording the mass of the crucible and lid, suspend the crucible over a Bunsen burner by placing it on the clay triangle as shown in Figure B. Then place the lid on the crucible so that the entire contents are covered.

4. Light the Bunsen burner. Heat the crucible for 5 minutes with a gentle flame, and then adjust the burner to produce a strong flame. Heat for 5 minutes more. Shut off the gas to the burner. Allow the crucible and lid to cool. Using crucible tongs, carry the crucible and lid to the balance, as shown in Figure C. Measure and record the mass. If the mass differs from the mass before heating, repeat the process until mass data from heating trials are within 1% of each other. This assumes that the crucible has a constant mass. The crucible is now ready to be used in a gravimetric analysis procedure. Details will be found in the following experiments.

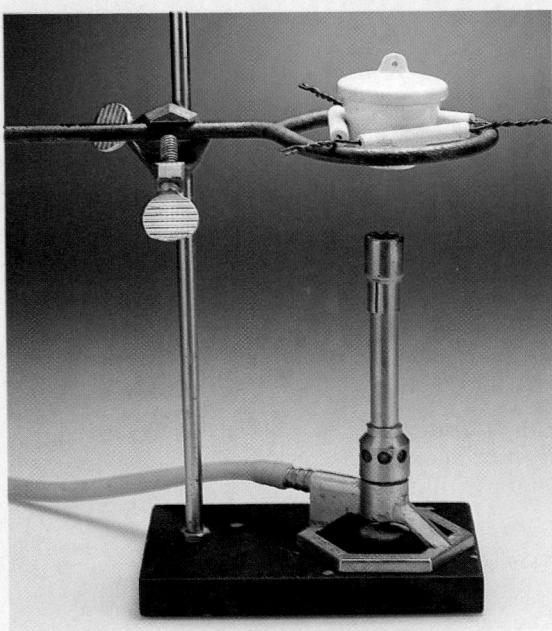
FIGURE A

FIGURE B

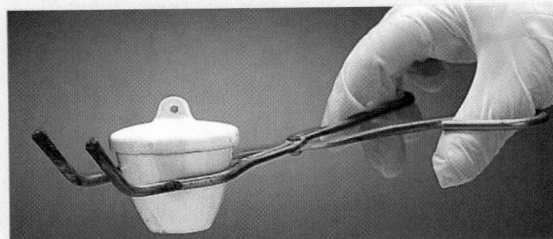
FIGURE C

Gravimetric methods are used in Experiment 7-3 to synthesize magnesium oxide, and to separate $SrCO_3$ from a solution in Experiment 9-2.

EXPERIMENT 7-1

OBJECTIVES
Students will

• use appropriate lab safety procedures.

• interpret a temperature-solubility graph.

• measure temperature.

• use a Bunsen burner and an ice bath to control temperature.

• use a laboratory balance to measure mass.

• demonstrate appropriate technique in transferring liquids and filtering.

RECOMMENDED TIME
2 lab periods

MATERIALS
(For each lab group)

• 1.5 L ice

• 20 g rock salt

• 50 mL NaCl-KNO₃ solution

• 100 mL graduated cylinder

• 150 mL beakers, 4

• balance, centigram

• Celsius thermometer, nonmercury type, range from −10°C to 120°C

• filter paper

• hot plate or Bunsen burner with gas tubing and striker

• ring stand, ring, and wire gauze (non-asbestos)

• rubber policeman and glass stirring rod

• spatula

• tray, tub, or pneumatic trough for ice bath

GRAVITY FILTRATION OPTION
• glass funnel

VACUUM FILTRATION OPTION
• aspirator for spigot

• Büchner funnel (either ceramic or plastic)

Separation of Salts by Fractional Crystallization

OBJECTIVES

• *Recognize* how the solubility of a salt varies with temperature.

• *Demonstrate* proficiency in fractional crystallization and in vacuum filtration or gravity filtration.

• *Determine* the percentage of two salts recovered by fractional crystallization.

MATERIALS

• **50 mL NaCl-KNO₃ solution**

• **100 mL graduated cylinder**

• **150 mL beakers, 4**

• **balance, centigram**

• **Büchner funnel, one-hole rubber stopper, vacuum filtration setup with filter flask and tubing, or glass funnel**

• **Bunsen burner and related equipment or hot plate**

• **filter paper**

• **glass stirring rod**

• **ice**

• **nonmercury thermometer**

• **ring and wire gauze**

• **ring stand**

• **rock salt**

• **rubber policeman**

• **spatula**

• **tray, tub, or pneumatic trough**

BACKGROUND

In this experiment, you will separate a mixture of sodium chloride, NaCl, and potassium nitrate, KNO₃. Both of these substances dissolve in water, so filtering alone cannot separate them. Figure A shows that temperature does not greatly affect the amount of sodium chloride that dissolves in water, but the amount of KNO₃ that dissolves in water does vary with temperature. This difference will enable you to separate them by a technique known as fractional crystallization.

If a water solution of NaCl and KNO₃ is cooled from room temperature to a temperature near 0°C, some KNO₃ will crystallize. This KNO₃ residue can then be separated from the NaCl solution by filtration. The NaCl can be isolated from the filtrate by evaporation of the water. After drying the KNO₃ residue and the NaCl, you can measure the mass of each of the recovered substances.

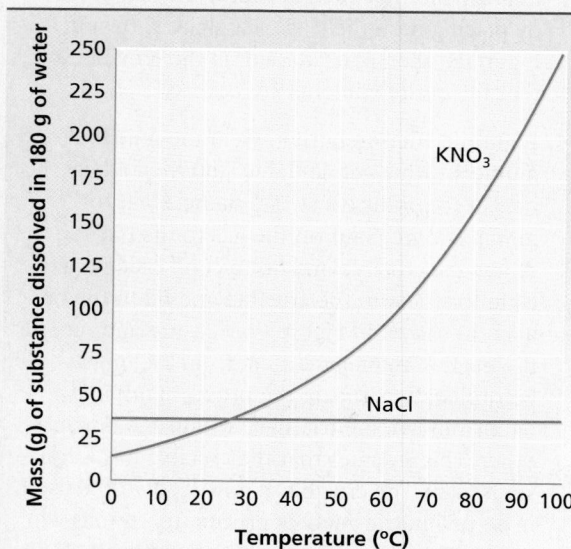

FIGURE A This graph shows the relationship between temperature and the solubility of NaCl and the solubility of KNO₃.

SAFETY

Always wear safety goggles and a lab apron to protect your eyes and clothing. If you get a chemical in your eyes, immediately flush the chemical out at the eyewash station while calling to your teacher. Know the locations of the emergency lab shower and eyewash station and the procedures for using them.

Do not touch chemicals. If you get a chemical on your skin or clothing, wash the chemical off at the sink while calling to your teacher. Make sure you carefully read the labels and follow the precautions on all containers of chemicals that you use. If no precautions are stated on the label, ask your teacher what precautions to follow. Do not taste any chemicals or items used in the laboratory. Never return leftover chemicals to their original containers; take only small amounts to avoid wasting supplies.

When using a Bunsen burner, confine long hair and loose clothing. Do not heat glassware that is broken, chipped, or cracked. Use tongs or a hot mitt to handle heated glassware and other equipment; heated glassware does not always look hot. If your clothing catches fire, WALK to the emergency lab shower and use it to put out the fire.

PREPARATION

1. Prepare a data table in your lab notebook. It should contain spaces for *Volume of salt solution added to beaker 1*, *Mass of beaker 1*, *Mass of filter paper*, *Mass of beaker 1 with filter paper and KNO₃*, *Mass of beaker 4*, and *Mass of beaker 4 with NaCl*. You will also need room to record the temperature of the mixture before and after cooling.

2. Obtain four clean, dry 150 mL beakers, and label them *1, 2, 3,* and *4*.

PROCEDURE

1. Measure the mass of beaker 1 to the nearest 0.01 g and record its mass in your data table.

2. Measure about 50 mL of the NaCl-KNO₃ solution into a graduated cylinder. Record the exact volume in your data table. Pour this mixture into beaker 1.

3. Using a thermometer, measure the temperature of the mixture. Record this temperature in your data table.

4. Measure the mass of a piece of filter paper to the nearest 0.01 g and record the mass in your data table.

5. Set up your filtering apparatus as described in the Pre-Laboratory Procedure on pages 790–791.

6. Make an ice bath by filling a tray, tub, or trough half full with ice. Add a handful of rock salt. The salt lowers the freezing point of water so that the ice bath can reach a lower temperature. Fill the ice bath with water until the container is three-quarters full.

7. Using a fresh supply of ice and distilled water, fill beaker 2 half full with ice and add water. Do not add rock salt to this ice-water mixture. You will use this water to wash your purified salt.

8. Put beaker 1, containing your NaCl-KNO₃ solution, into the ice bath. Place a thermometer into the solution to monitor the temperature. Stir the solution with a stirring rod while it cools. The lower the temperature of the mixture is, the more KNO₃ will crystallize out of the solution. When the temperature nears 4°C, follow step 8a if you are using the Büchner funnel and step 8b if you are using a glass funnel.

Never stir a solution with a thermometer; the bulb is very fragile.

a. Vacuum filtration

Refer to page 791 for instructions on how to set up this system. Turn on the water at the faucet that has the aspirator nozzle attached

- one-hole rubber stopper or sleeve
- vacuum flask (sidearm flask) and tubing

SOLUTION/MATERIALS PREPARATION

1. For every liter of solution, add about 140 g of NaCl and 320 g of KNO₃. It is necessary to stir and gently heat the solution to completely dissolve the salts. A hot-plate stirrer is an invaluable tool.

2. Students should use only nonmercury thermometers. If a mercury thermometer breaks, the droplets that are not cleaned up will quickly evaporate, creating toxic mercury vapors.

3. Centigram balances will give the best results, but less precise balances are acceptable.

REQUIRED PRECAUTIONS

- Safety goggles and a lab apron must be worn at all times.
- Read all safety precautions and discuss them with your students.
- Remind students that when equipment has been heated, it should be handled with tongs or a hot mitt. Hot glassware does not look hot.
- If a hot plate is used, the hot plate should be equipped with a three-wire cord and a three-prong plug. Each electrical socket in the laboratory must have three holes, with a GFI (ground-fault interrupter) circuit. Check the polarity of the circuit with a polarity tester from an electronics supply store. Repair any incorrectly wired sockets.

  Be sure electrical equipment is turned off before plugging it in. Turn it off again before unplugging it. Wiring hookups should be made or altered only when the apparatus is disconnected from the power source and the power switch is in the off position.

  Do not let electrical cords dangle from work stations; dangling cords are a tripping and shock hazard.

Do not use electrical equipment with frayed or kinked cords.

The area under and around electrical equipment should be dry.

Cords should not lie in puddles of spilled liquid. Students should have dry hands when they are using electrical equipment.

Turn off and unplug all electrical equipment before leaving the laboratory.

TECHNIQUES TO DEMONSTRATE

Review the procedures you will be using for filtration. If using gravity filtration, show students how to fold the filter paper. Be sure to review the vocabulary associated with filtering, especially the difference between the *filtrate* and the *residue*. Show students how to use a rubber policeman to collect crystals. Remind students to heat the water gradually to avoid violent bubbling and loss of product.

SAMPLE DATA

volume of solution added to beaker 1	46.5 mL
mass of beaker 1	65.40 g
mass of filter paper	0.40 g
mass of beaker 1 with filter paper and KNO_3 (day 2)	78.22 g
mass of beaker 4	66.25 g
mass of beaker 4 with NaCl	72.37 g
temperature before cooling	25°C
temperature after cooling	−2°C

PRE-LAB DISCUSSION

Thoroughly discuss the procedure used in this lab. The students need to work quickly and efficiently if they are to complete this lab in a little over one lab period. Students tend to work on the lab in a step-by-step process, which can take too long. Instead, encourage them to perform multiple

to it. Prepare the filtering apparatus by pouring approximately 50 mL of ice-cold distilled water from beaker 2 through the filter paper. After the water has gone through the funnel, empty the filter flask into the sink. Reconnect the filter flask, and pour the mixture in beaker 1 into the funnel. Use the rubber policeman to transfer all of the cooled mixture into the funnel, especially any crystals that are visible. It may be helpful to add small amounts of the ice-cold water from beaker 2 to beaker 1 to wash any crystals onto the filter paper. After all of the solution has passed through the funnel, wash the KNO_3 residue by pouring a very small amount of ice-cold water over it. When this water has passed through the filter paper, turn off the faucet and carefully remove the tubing from the aspirator. Empty the filtrate, which has passed through the filter paper and is now in the filter flask, into beaker 3. When finished, continue with Procedure step 9.

b. Gravity filtration

Refer to page 790 for instructions on how to set up this system. Place beaker 3 under the glass funnel. Prepare the filtering apparatus by pouring approximately 50 mL of ice-cold water from beaker 2 through the filter paper. The water will pass through the filter paper and drip into beaker 3. When the dripping stops, empty beaker 3 into the sink. Place beaker 3 under the glass funnel so that it can collect the filtrate from the funnel. Pour the mixture in beaker 1 into the funnel. Use the rubber policeman to transfer all of the cooled mixture into the funnel, especially any crystals that are visible. It may be helpful to add small amounts of ice-cold water from beaker 2 to beaker 1 to wash any crystals onto the filter paper. After all of the solution has passed through the funnel, wash the KNO_3 by pouring a very small amount of ice-cold water from beaker 2 over it.

9. After you have finished filtering, use either a hot plate or a Bunsen burner, ring stand, ring, and wire gauze to heat beaker 3. When the liquid in

beaker 3 begins to boil, continue heating gently until the volume is approximately 25–30 mL.

 Be sure to use beaker tongs. Remember that hot glassware does not always look hot.

10. Allow the solution in beaker 3 to cool, and then set it in the ice-bath. Stir until the temperature is approximately 4°C.

11. Measure the mass of beaker 4. Record the mass in your data table.

12. Repeat Procedure step 8a or step 8b, pouring the solution from beaker 3 onto the filter paper and using beaker 4 to collect the filtrate that passes through the filter.

13. Wash and dry beaker 1. Carefully remove the filter paper with the KNO_3 from the funnel and put it in the beaker. Be certain to avoid spilling the crystals. Place the beaker in a drying oven overnight.

14. Heat beaker 4 with a hot plate or Bunsen burner until it begins to boil. Continue to heat gently until all of the water has vaporized and the salt appears dry. Turn off the hot plate or burner, and allow the beaker to cool. Use beaker tongs to move the beaker, as shown in Figure B. Measure the mass of beaker 4 with the NaCl to the nearest 0.01 g and record this mass in your data table.

FIGURE B   Use beaker tongs to move a beaker that has been heated, even if you believe that the beaker is cool.

15. The next day, use beaker tongs to remove beaker 1 with the filter paper and KNO_3 from the drying oven. Allow the beaker to cool. Measure the mass, with the same balance you used when you measured the mass of the empty beaker. Record the new mass in your data table.

CLEANUP AND DISPOSAL

16. Once the mass of the NaCl has been determined, add water to dissolve the NaCl and rinse the solution down the drain. Dispose of the KNO_3 in the waste container designated by your teacher. Clean up the lab and all equipment after use. Wash your hands thoroughly after all lab work is finished and before you leave the lab.

ANALYSIS AND INTERPRETATION

1. Organizing Data: Find the mass of NaCl in your 50 mL sample by subtracting the mass of beaker 4 from the mass of beaker 4 with NaCl.

2. Organizing Data: Find the mass of KNO_3 in your 50 mL sample by subtracting the mass of beaker 1 and the mass of the filter paper from the mass of beaker 1 with the filter paper and KNO_3.

3. Organizing Data: Determine the total mass of the two salts by addition.

CONCLUSIONS

1. Inferring Conclusions: Calculate the percentage by mass of NaCl in the salt mixture. Calculate the percentage by mass of KNO_3 in the salt mixture. Assume that the density of your 50-mL solution is 1.0 g/mL.

2. Evaluating Methods: Use the graph shown at the beginning of this experiment to estimate how much KNO_3 could still be contaminating the NaCl you recovered.

3. Relating Ideas: Use the graph shown at the beginning of this experiment to explain why it is impossible to separate the two compounds completely by fractional crystallization.

4. Evaluating Methods: Why was it important that you use ice-cold water to wash the KNO_3 after filtration?

5. Evaluating Methods: If it was important to use very cold water to wash the KNO_3, why wasn't the salt and ice-water mixture from the bath used? After all, it had a lower temperature than the ice and distilled water from beaker 2.

6. Evaluating Methods: Why was it important to keep the amount of cold water used to wash the KNO_3 as small as possible?

7. Relating Ideas: Your lab partner tries to dissolve 95 g of KNO_3 in 100 g of water, but no matter how well the mixture is stirred, some KNO_3 remains undissolved. Using the graph, explain what your lab partner must do to make the KNO_3 dissolve in this amount of water.

EXTENSIONS

1. Designing Experiments: Describe how you could use the properties of the compounds to test the purity of your recovered samples. If your teacher approves your plan, use it to check your separation of the mixtures.

2. Designing Experiments: How could you improve the yield or the purity of the compounds you recovered? If you can think of ways to modify the procedure, ask your teacher to approve your plan, and run the experiment again.

tasks simultaneously through teamwork. While one partner is cooling the solution, the other lab partner could be cleaning, drying, and measuring the mass of the other beakers.

Students may have difficulty reading the solubility graph at first. It is not necessary for students to understand all aspects of solutions and solubility, but an understanding of this graph is important to understanding the concept of fractional crystallization. Practice taking several readings from the graph by asking students how many grams of each salt would dissolve in 180 g of water at a given temperature. Relate the results to the cycles of cooling and heating in the procedure.

Results are greatly improved if a second filtration step is performed after some water has been evaporated, but this takes more time.

Students get very frustrated when their results do not match calculated ideal values. Students should realize when they answer Conclusions item 4 that it is impossible to achieve a perfect separation with this technique.

This experiment provides an opportunity for discussion on the uncertain nature of science and the constant need to improve on lab techniques at all levels of science.

DISPOSAL

Potassium nitrate, KNO_3, cannot be disposed of because it is a strong oxidizer, but it can be reused the next time you do this lab. Allow the crystals to dry in the disposal container you designated for the students. Store the dried crystals in a sealed, labeled glass bottle completely away from bottles of reducing substances, especially those that can burn. Reuse the crystals the following

Continued on page 893B

EXPERIMENT 7-2

EXPERIMENT 7-2

OBJECTIVES
Students will
- use appropriate safety procedures.
- demonstrate appropriate techniques for using micro equipment.
- relate the experimental data to the chemical equation.
- infer the formulas of the unknowns from experimental data.
- predict the outcome if more concentrated solutions were to be used.

RECOMMENDED TIME
45–60 min

MATERIALS
(for each lab group)
- 1 mL phenolphthalein solution
- 2 mL 0.1 M CuCl$_2$ solution
- 2 mL 0.1 M CuCl$_2$ solution (for Extensions item 3)
- 2 mL 0.1 M FeCl$_3$ solution,
- 2 mL 0.5 M FeCl$_3$ solution (for Extensions item 3)
- 2 mL unknown solution of CuCl$_2$ (for Extensions item 4)
- 2 mL unknown solution of FeCl$_3$, (for Extensions item 4)
- 10 mL 0.1 M NaOH solution
- 8-well strips, 2
- fine-tipped dropper bulbs, 4
- marking pencil
- toothpicks, 10

SOLUTIONS/MATERIALS PREPARATION
1. To prepare 30 mL of 0.1 M copper(II) chloride solution only, dissolve 0.43 g of CuCl$_2$•2H$_2$O in 30 mL of solution. To prepare both 0.1 M and 0.5 M solutions, first dissolve 4.27 g of CuCl$_2$•2H$_2$O in 60 mL of solution to provide a concentration of 0.5 M. Then take 6 mL of 0.5 M solution and dilute it with water to make 30 mL of 0.1 M solution. Reserve at least 30 mL of the 0.5 M solution for Extensions item 3. Dilute part of what remains to make the mystery solution for

Naming Ionic Compounds

OBJECTIVES

- *Observe* chemical replacement reactions.
- *Use* reagent measurements to determine the formula of a chemical substance.
- *Infer* a conclusion from experimental data.
- *Apply* reaction stoichiometry concepts.

MATERIALS

- **0.1 M copper chloride**
- **0.1 M iron chloride**
- **0.1 M sodium hydroxide**
- **8-well flat-bottom strips, 2**
- **fine-tipped dropper bulbs, 4**
- **marking pencil**
- **phenolphthalein indicator**
- **toothpicks, 10**

BACKGROUND

Chemists often identify unknown substances by observing how they react with known substances. A common method involves a replacement reaction, in which a measured amount of a known substance is reacted with the unknown substance.

In this investigation, you will determine the formulas of two metallic salts. One salt is copper chloride, but you will need to find out if it is copper(I) chloride or copper(II) chloride. The other salt is iron chloride, but is it iron(II) chloride or iron(III) chloride?

The reaction to be used is a double-replacement reaction with sodium hydroxide, NaOH. Aqueous solutions of both copper and iron ions form precipitates when they are combined with a solution containing aqueous hydroxide ions.

Phenolphthalein is an indicator that turns bright pink or red in the presence of unreacted aqueous OH$^-$ ions. It will be used to indicate when the reaction is complete. When there is no more metal left to react with the OH$^-$ ions being added, the OH$^-$ ions will trigger this color change.

SAFETY

Always wear safety goggles and a lab apron to protect your eyes and clothing. If you get a chemical in your eyes, immediately flush the chemical out at the eyewash station while calling to your teacher. Know the location of the emergency lab shower and eyewash station and the procedures for using them.

Do not touch chemicals. If you get a chemical on your skin or clothing, wash the chemical off at the sink while calling to your teacher. Make sure you carefully read the labels and follow the precautions on all containers of chemicals that you use. If no precautions are stated on the label, ask your teacher what precautions to follow. Do not taste any chemicals or items used in the laboratory. Never return leftover chemicals to their original containers; take only small amounts to avoid wasting supplies.

 Call your teacher in the event of a spill. Spills should be cleaned up promptly according to your teacher's directions.

PREPARATION

1. Prepare a data table like the one below for the copper chloride solution. Record the number of drops of NaOH added to wells 1, 2, 3, 4, and 5 of your well strip. Prepare a similar data table for the iron chloride solution.

DATA TABLE

Copper chloride					
	1	2	3	4	5
Drops of NaOH					

Iron chloride					
	1	2	3	4	5
Drops of NaOH					

2. Obtain four dropper bulbs. Label them *Cu*, *Fe*, *NaOH*, and *In*.

PROCEDURE

1. Fill the bulb labeled *Cu* with the copper chloride solution. Fill the bulb labeled *NaOH* with the sodium hydroxide solution.

2. Using one 8-well strip, place five drops of the copper chloride solution in each of the first five wells. For best results, try to make all the drops in this experiment about the same size.

3. Using the bulb labeled *In*, put one drop of the phenolphthalein indicator in each of the five wells, as shown in Figure A.

4. Add the sodium hydroxide solution one drop at a time to the first well, mixing the solution in the well with a toothpick before adding each drop, as shown in Figure B. Continue adding NaOH until the pink or red color of the phenolphthalein just begins to show clearly. The change in color indicates that the copper chloride has reacted completely. Record the number of drops of NaOH added in your copper chloride data table. Add drops of NaOH to the other four wells in turn, and record the results. Use a different toothpick to stir the solution for each well.

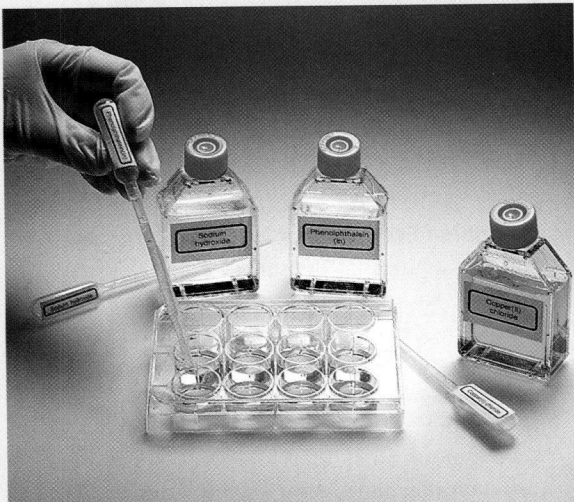

FIGURE A   Add one drop of phenolphthalein to each well containing copper chloride. The size of the drops should be as uniform as possible.

FIGURE B   Add NaOH one drop at a time, stirring after each addition. A change in color to pink tells you that all the copper chloride has reacted.

Extensions item 4. (Remember to keep track of the dilution so that you can tell students how close their concentration estimates are.)

2. To prepare 30 mL of 0.1 M iron(III) chloride solution only, dissolve 0.82 g of $FeCl_3 \cdot 6H_2O$ in 30 mL of solution. To prepare both 0.1 M and 0.5 M solutions, first dissolve 8.17 g of $FeCl_3 \cdot 6H_2O$ in 60 mL of solution to provide a concentration of 0.5 M. Then take 6 mL of 0.5 M solution and dilute it with water to make 30 mL of 0.1 M solution. Reserve at least 30 mL of the 0.5 M solution for Extensions item 3. Dilute part of what remains to make the mystery solution for Extensions item 4. (Remember to keep track of the dilution so that you can tell students how close their concentration estimates are.)

3. To prepare 150 mL of 0.1 M sodium hydroxide solution, dissolve 0.60 g of NaOH in 150 mL of solution.

4. To prepare phenolphthalein solution, dissolve 0.13 g of phenolphthalein in 6 mL of denatured alcohol and add 7 mL of water.

5. Fine-tipped dropper bulbs may be reused from class to class and year to year. They are available commercially or may be made out of thin-stem pipets. Stretch the pipets by hand, and then cut them off. For more accurate drop sizes, place the dropper bulb in a tubing screw-clamp. Each turn of the screw will force out a reproducible drop.

REQUIRED PRECAUTIONS

- Safety goggles and a lab apron must be worn at all times.
- Read all safety precautions, and discuss them with your students.
- In case of a spill, use a dampened cloth or paper towel (or more than one towel if necessary) to mop up the spill. Then rinse the cloth in running water at the sink, wring it out thoroughly, and put it in the trash.

TECHNIQUES TO DEMONSTRATE

Demonstrate the best technique for obtaining reproducible drops with a fine-tipped dropper bulb.

If a tubing screw-clamp is to be used to help produce uniform drops, show how it works.

If students are unfamiliar with phenolphthalein, titrate a sample to show the expected color change.

SAMPLE DATA

Data will vary.

PRE-LAB DISCUSSION

Review double replacement reactions. Write equations for some examples in which the reactants and products are in different ratios. Discuss the ratios revealed in the equations.

DISPOSAL

Combine all solutions and precipitates. While stirring, add enough 0.1 M NaOH to raise the pH to approximately 10. Then, while stirring, slowly add 0.1 M HCl to reduce the pH to 8, but do not allow the pH to become less than 8. Allow the mixture to dry; then wrap it in newspaper and put it into the trash.

ANALYSIS AND INTERPRETATION—ANSWERS

1. a. $CuCl(aq) + NaOH(aq) \longrightarrow$
   $CuOH(s) + NaCl(aq)$
   b. $CuCl_2(aq) + 2NaOH(aq) \longrightarrow$
   $Cu(OH)_2(s) + 2NaCl(aq)$
   c. $FeCl_2(aq) + 2NaOH(aq) \longrightarrow$
   $Fe(OH)_2(s) + 2NaCl(aq)$
   d. $FeCl_3(aq) + 3NaOH(aq) \longrightarrow$
   $Fe(OH)_3(s) + 3NaCl(aq)$

2. Drops of equal size will have an equal number of formula units of the compounds in them.

3. Students' answers will vary, but if the drop sizes were equal, the copper chloride should require about 10 drops on average and the iron chloride should require about 15 drops on average.

Continued on page 893C

812

5. Fill the bulb labeled *Fe* with the iron chloride solution, and repeat Procedure steps 1–4 in the second 8-well strip, using the iron chloride solution instead of the copper chloride solution. In your iron chloride data table, record the number of drops of the sodium hydroxide solution that were added to each of the five wells to cause a change in color.

CLEANUP AND DISPOSAL

1. Clean your lab station. Clean all equipment and return it to its proper place. Dispose of chemicals and solutions in the containers designated by your teacher. Do not pour any chemicals down the drain or throw anything in the trash unless your teacher directs you to do so. Wash your hands thoroughly after all work is finished and before you leave the lab.

ANALYSIS AND INTERPRETATION

1. **Organizing Ideas:** Write the balanced chemical equation for a double replacement reaction between sodium hydroxide and
   a. copper(I) chloride.
   b. copper(II) chloride.
   c. iron(II) chloride.
   d. iron(III) chloride.

2. **Organizing Ideas:** You may already have noticed that each of the solutions used has 0.1 mol of formula units for every liter of solution. Assuming that all of the drops were the same size, how do the numbers of formula units in a drop of each solution compare?

3. **Organizing Data:** On average, how many drops of NaOH were needed to react with the copper chloride? On average, how many drops of NaOH were needed to react with the iron chloride?

CONCLUSIONS

1. **Relating Ideas:** Using your answers from Analysis and Interpretation questions 2 and 3, determine how many NaOH formula units

were needed to react with each copper chloride formula unit in your experiment. How many NaOH formula units were needed to react with each iron chloride formula unit?

2. **Inferring Conclusions:** Compare your answers to the previous question with the balanced chemical equations from the Analysis and Interpretations section. Which chlorides of copper and iron were in the solutions you used?

EXTENSIONS

1. **Evaluating Methods:** Share your data with other lab groups. Calculate a class average for the ratio of NaOH formula units to copper chloride formula units. Calculate a class average for the ratio of NaOH formula units to iron chloride formula units. Compare these averages with your results. Using the class average ratios as the accepted values, calculate your percent error.

2. **Designing Experiments:** What are some likely areas of imprecision in this experiment? If you can think of ways to eliminate them, ask your teacher to approve your suggestions, and run more trials.

3. **Predicting Outcomes:** How many drops of NaOH would it take to react with a solution of copper chloride (the type used in this experiment) that contains 0.5 mol/L of solution? How many drops of NaOH would it take to react with a solution of iron chloride (the type used in this experiment) that contains 0.5 mol/L of solution? If the solutions are available and your teacher approves, test your predictions.

4. **Designing Experiments:** What if your teacher made a solution of the same kind of copper chloride (or iron chloride) used in this experiment but forgot what the mol/L concentration is? Can you think of a way to use samples of this solution and your 0.1 mol/L solution of NaOH to find out what the concentration of the mystery solution is? If a mystery solution is available, ask your teacher to approve your suggestion, and try to determine the concentration.

EXPERIMENT 7-3

Determining the Empirical Formula of Magnesium Oxide

OBJECTIVES

- *Measure* the mass of magnesium oxide.

- *Perform* a synthesis reaction by using gravimetric techniques.

- *Determine* the empirical formula of magnesium oxide.

- *Calculate* the class average and standard deviation for moles of oxygen used.

MATERIALS

- **10 mL graduated cylinder**

- **15 cm magnesium ribbon, 2**

- **Bunsen burner assembly**

- **clay triangle**

- **crucible and lid, metal or ceramic**

- **crucible tongs**

- **distilled water**

- **eyedropper or micropipet**

- **ring stand**

BACKGROUND

This gravimetric analysis involves the combustion of magnesium metal in air to synthesize magnesium oxide. The mass of the product is greater than the mass of magnesium used because oxygen bonds to the magnesium metal. Like all gravimetric analyses, success depends on attaining a product yield near 100%. Therefore, the product will be heated, cooled, and measured until two mass readings are within 0.02% of one another. When the masses of the reactant and product have been carefully measured, then the amount of oxygen used in the reaction can be calculated. The ratio of oxygen to magnesium can then be established and the empirical formula of magnesium oxide can be determined.

SAFETY

Always wear safety goggles and a lab apron to protect your eyes and clothing. If you get a chemical in your eyes, immediately flush the chemical out at the eyewash station while calling to your teacher. Know the location of the emergency lab shower and eyewash station and the procedure for using them.

Do not touch or taste any chemicals. If you get a chemical on your skin or clothing, wash the chemical off at the sink while calling to your teacher. Make sure you carefully read the labels and follow the precautions on all containers of chemicals that you use. If no precautions are stated on the label, ask your teacher what precautions you should follow. Do not taste any chemicals or items used in the laboratory. Never return leftovers to their original containers; take only small amounts to avoid wasting supplies.

EXPERIMENT 7-3

OBJECTIVES
Students will
- use appropriate lab safety procedures.
- use a laboratory balance to measure mass.
- perform a quantitative combustion reaction.
- determine the empirical formula of magnesium oxide.

RECOMMENDED TIME
45–60 min

MATERIALS
(for each lab group)
- 10 mL graduated cylinder
- 15 cm magnesium ribbon, 2
- Bunsen burner assembly
- clay triangle
- crucible and lid, metal or ceramic
- crucible tongs
- distilled water
- eye dropper or micropipet
- ring stand

SOLUTION/MATERIALS PREPARATION
1. Cut two 15 cm lengths of magnesium ribbon for each lab group.
2. Provide an assortment of steel wool pads for cleaning the magnesium ribbon.

REQUIRED PRECAUTIONS
- Safety goggles and a lab apron must be worn at all times.
- Read all safety precautions, and discuss them with your students.
- Remind students that heated objects can be hot enough to burn even though they look cool. Students should always use crucible tongs when handling the crucible and lid.

TECHNIQUES TO DEMONSTRATE

Review Pre-Laboratory Procedure: Gravimetric Analysis with your students. Show them the proper way of holding crucible tongs.

PRE-LAB DISCUSSION

Discuss synthesis reactions and how empirical formulas are obtained. Make sure students understand how to calculate averages. Remind students about how these values can help them assess the quality of their lab technique.

SAMPLE DATA

1. Mass of crucible, lid, and metal (g)	6.218
2. Mass of crucible, lid, and product (g)	6.336
3. Mass of crucible and lid (g)	6.000

CLEANUP AND DISPOSAL

You will need two disposal containers: one for the solid magnesium oxide waste and one for the unused magnesium ribbon. Put the solid magnesium oxide in a large beaker, add water, and neutralize the solution with 1 M HCl. Pour the neutralized solution down the drain. Put the unused magnesium ribbon in a labeled brown glass jar with a tightly fitting lid, and store until the next time you perform this lab.

ANALYSIS AND INTERPRETATION—ANSWERS

1. magnesium = 0.218 g

2. oxygen = 0.118 g

3. moles of oxygen = 0.00738
moles of magnesium = 0.00897

CONCLUSIONS—ANSWERS

1. The mole ratio of Mg to O is 0.00897:0.00738 or 1:0.82. The empirical formula is probably MgO.

When using a Bunsen burner, confine long hair and loose clothing. Do not heat glassware that is broken, chipped, or cracked. Use tongs or a hot mitt to handle heated glassware and other equipment; heated glassware does not always look hot. If your clothing catches fire, WALK to the emergency lab shower and use it to put out the fire.

Never put broken glass or ceramics in a regular waste container. Broken glass and ceramics should be disposed of in a separate container designated by your teacher.

PREPARATION

1. Copy the following data table in your lab notebook.

DATA TABLE

	Trial 1	Trial 2
1. Mass of crucible, lid, and metal (g)		
2. Mass of crucible, lid, and product (g)		
3. Mass of crucible and lid (g)		

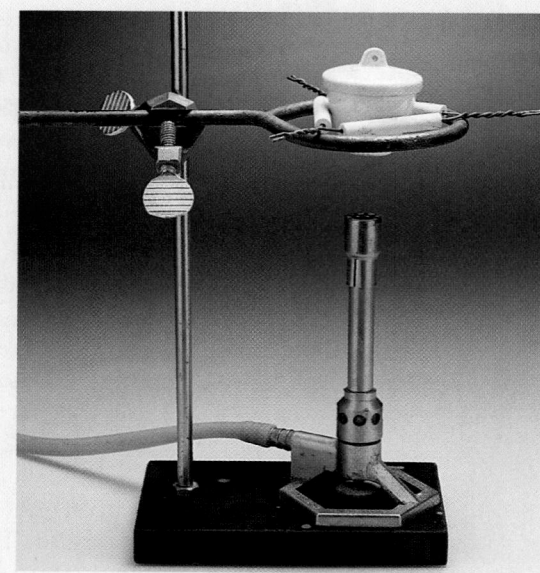

FIGURE A

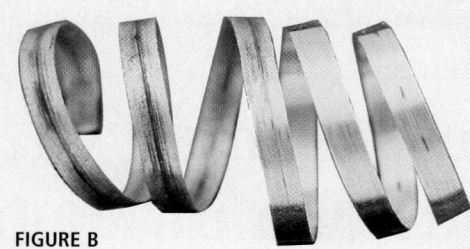

FIGURE B

PROCEDURE

1. Construct a setup for heating a crucible as shown in Figure A and as demonstrated in the Pre-Laboratory Procedure on page 805.

2. Strongly heat the crucible and lid for 5 min to burn off any impurities.

3. Cool the crucible and lid to room temperature. Measure their combined mass, and record the measurement on line 3 of your data table.

NOTE: Handle the crucible and lid with crucible tongs. This prevents burns and the transfer of dirt and oil from your hands to the crucible and lid.

4. Polish a 15 cm strip of magnesium with steel wool. The magnesium should be shiny, as shown in Figure B. Cut the strip into small pieces to make the reaction proceed faster, and place the pieces in the crucible.

5. Cover the crucible with the lid, and measure the mass of the crucible, lid, and metal. Record the measurement on line 1 of your data table.

6. Use tongs to replace the crucible on the clay triangle. Heat the covered crucible gently. Lift the lid occasionally to allow air in, as shown in Figure C.

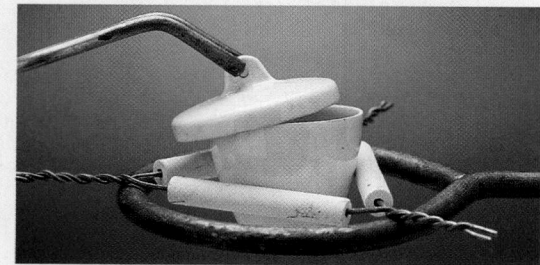

FIGURE C

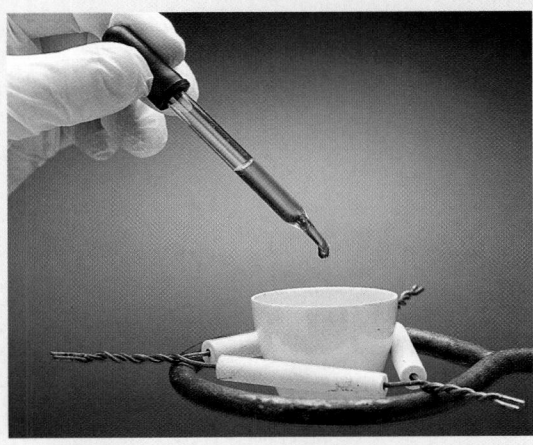

FIGURE D

CAUTION: Do not look directly at the burning magnesium metal. The brightness of the light can blind you.

7. When the magnesium appears to be fully re-acted, partially remove the crucible lid and continue heating for 1 min.

8. Remove the burner from under the crucible. After the crucible has cooled, use an eyedropper to carefully add a few drops of water, as shown in Figure D, to decompose any nitrides that may have formed.

CAUTION: Use care when adding water. Too much water can cause the crucible to crack.

9. Cover the crucible completely. Replace the burner under the crucible and continue heating for about 30–60 s.

10. Turn off the burner. Cool the crucible, lid, and contents to room temperature. Measure the mass of the crucible, lid, and product. Record the measurement in the margin of your data table.

11. Replace the crucible, lid, and contents on the clay triangle and reheat for another 2 min. Cool to room temperature and remeasure the mass of the crucible, lid, and contents. Compare this mass measurement with the measurement obtained in step 10. If the new mass is ±0.02% of the mass in step 10, record the new mass on line 2 of your data table. If not, your reaction is still incomplete. Repeat this step.

12. Clean the crucible, and repeat steps 2–11 with a second strip of magnesium ribbon. Record your measurements under Trial 2 in your data table.

CLEANUP AND DISPOSAL

1. Put the solid magnesium oxide in the designated waste container. Return any unused magnesium ribbon to your teacher. Clean your equipment and lab station. Thoroughly wash your hands after completing the lab session and cleanup.

ANALYSIS AND INTERPRETATION

1. **Applying Ideas:** Calculate the mass of the magnesium metal and the mass of the product.

2. **Evaluating Data:** Determine the mass of the oxygen consumed.

3. **Applying Ideas:** Calculate the number of moles of magnesium and the number of moles of oxygen in the product.

CONCLUSIONS

1. **Inferring Relationships:** Determine the empirical formula for magnesium oxide, Mg_xO_y. (Divide your mole ratio by the moles of magnesium since this value is derived from a measured quantity instead of a calculated quantity.)

EXPERIMENT 9-1

OBJECTIVES
Students will
- use appropriate lab safety procedures.
- observe the double-displacement reaction between CH_3COOH and $NaHCO_3$ and the subsequent decomposition of H_2CO_3.
- use a laboratory balance to measure mass.
- determine the mole ratio of the reactants and products.
- calculate the number of moles of the reactants and products.

RECOMMENDED TIME:
45–60 min

MATERIALS
(for each lab group)
- 3 g $NaHCO_3$
- 50 mL 1.0 M acetic acid
- balance, centigram
- beaker tongs
- dropper or pipet
- evaporating dish
- graduated cylinder
- spatula
- watch glass

HOT PLATE OPTION
- hot plate

BUNSEN BURNER OPTION
- Bunsen burner with gas tubing and striker
- ring stand and ring
- wire gauze with ceramic center

SOLUTION/MATERIAL PREPARATION
1. To prepare 1.0 M CH_3COOH, observe the required precautions. Add 87 mL of glacial CH_3COOH to water. Dilute to make 1 L of solution.
2. Better results are obtained with hot plates instead of Bunsen burners.

REQUIRED PRECAUTIONS
- Safety goggles and a lab apron must be worn at all times.

Mass and Mole Relationships in a Chemical Reaction

OBJECTIVES

- *Demonstrate* proficiency in measuring masses.

- *Determine* the number of moles of reactants and products in a reaction experimentally.

- *Use* the mass and mole relationships of a chemical reaction in calculations.

- *Perform* calculations that involve density and stoichiometry.

MATERIALS

- 1.0 M CH_3COOH

- 2–3 g $NaHCO_3$

- balance

- beaker tongs

- Bunsen burner and related equipment or hot plate

- dropper or pipet

- evaporating dish

- graduated cylinder

- ring stand and ring (for use with Bunsen burner)

- spatula

- watch glass

- wire gauze with ceramic center (for use with Bunsen burner)

CH₃COOH
Acetic Acid

BACKGROUND

In this experiment, you will determine the amounts of sodium hydrogen carbonate and acetic acid needed to produce a specific amount of carbon dioxide by reacting a carefully measured mass of reactant, $NaHCO_3$, with vinegar and then measuring the mass of the product, CH_3COONa. You can then determine the number of moles of acetic acid reacted and the number of moles of CO_2 produced. Using mole relationships between reactants and products, you can calculate the mass and the number of moles of each reactant needed to produce any given volume of CO_2. To obtain the volume of CO_2 from its mass, you will need to know that the density of CO_2 is 1.25 g/L at baking temperature.

SAFETY

 Always wear safety goggles and a lab apron to protect your eyes and clothing. If you get a chemical in your eyes, immediately flush the chemical out at the eyewash station while calling to your teacher. Know the locations of the emergency lab shower and eyewash station and the procedures for using them.

 Do not touch any chemicals. If you get a chemical on your skin or clothing, wash the chemical off at the sink while calling to your teacher. Make sure you carefully read the labels and follow the directions on all containers of chemicals that you use. If no precautions are stated on the label, ask your teacher what precautions to follow. Do not taste any chemicals or items used in the laboratory. Never return leftover chemicals to their original containers; take only small amounts to avoid wasting supplies.

When using a Bunsen burner, confine long hair and loose clothing. Do not heat glassware that is broken, chipped, or cracked. Use tongs or a hot mitt to handle heated glassware and other equipment; heated glassware does not always look hot. If your clothing catches fire, WALK to the emergency lab shower and use it to put out the fire.

 Never put broken glass or ceramics in a regular waste container. Broken glass and ceramics should be disposed of in a separate container designated by your teacher.

 Call your teacher in the event of an acid or base spill. Acid or base spills should be cleaned up promptly according to your teacher's instructions.

PREPARATION

1. Prepare a data table in your lab notebook. It should contain space to record the mass of the empty evaporating dish and watch glass, the mass of the evaporating dish with the watch glass and $NaHCO_3$, and the mass of the evaporating dish with the watch glass and CH_3COONa after heating.

PROCEDURE

1. Measure the mass of a clean, dry evaporating dish and watch glass to the nearest 0.01 g. Record this mass in your data table.

2. Add 2–3 g $NaHCO_3$ to your evaporating dish. Measure the exact mass of the $NaHCO_3$ with the watch glass, to the nearest 0.01 g. Record this mass in your data table.

3. Slowly add 30 mL of the acetic acid solution to the $NaHCO_3$ in the evaporating dish. Add more acetic acid with a dropper or pipet until the bubbling stops.

4. If you are using a Bunsen burner, place the evaporating dish and its contents on a ceramic-centered wire gauze placed on an iron ring attached to the ring stand, as shown in Figure A.

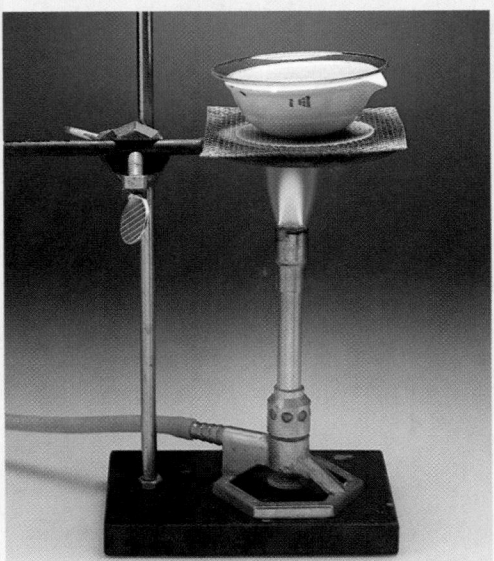

FIGURE A The watch glass is placed concave side up on the evaporating dish, which is centered on a ceramic-centered wire gauze.

Place the watch glass, concave side up, on top of the dish, making sure that there is a slight opening for steam to escape. If you are using a hot plate, position the watch glass the same way, but place the evaporating dish directly on the hot plate.

5. Gently heat the evaporating dish until only a dry solid remains. Make sure that no water droplets remain on the underside of the watch glass. *Do not heat too rapidly or the material will boil and the product will spatter out of the evaporating dish.*

6. Turn off the gas burner or hot plate. Allow the apparatus to cool for at least 15 min. Determine the mass of the cooled equipment to the nearest 0.01 g. Record the mass of the dish, residue, and watch glass in your data table.

7. If time permits, reheat the evaporating dish and contents for 2 min. Let it cool, and measure its mass again. You can be certain the sample is dry when you obtain two successive measurements within 0.02 g of each other.

- Tie back long hair and loose clothing when working in the lab.
- Read all safety precautions, and discuss them with your students.
- Students should not handle glacial acetic acid.
- Wear safety goggles, a face shield, impermeable gloves, and a lab apron while preparing the acetic acid. Work in a hood known to be in good working order, and have another person stand by to call for help in case of an emergency. Work within a 30 s walk from a safety shower and eyewash station.
- In case of an acid spill, dilute the spill with water. Then mop up the spill with wet cloths or a wet cloth mop designated for spill cleanup. Wear disposable plastic gloves while cleaning spills.

TECHNIQUES TO DEMONSTRATE

Remind students to add the acetic acid very slowly; otherwise, the reaction will be so vigorous that some of the product will be lost. Also make sure that they heat the solution gently to avoid losing the product.

Demonstrate how to hold an evaporating dish with beaker tongs. Students should wait 15 minutes for the evaporating dish to cool before measuring its mass. Even then, they should continue to use beaker tongs to hold the evaporating dish.

SAMPLE DATA	
mass of dish and glass	71.17 g
mass of dish, glass, and $NaHCO_3$	73.27 g
mass of dish, glass, and residue (CH_3COONa) after 1st heating	73.22 g
mass of dish, glass, and residue (CH_3COONa) after 2nd heating	73.20 g

PRE-LAB DISCUSSION

This lab involves stoichiometry calculations with mass, moles, volume, and density. You may want to work through similar calculations with sample data with the class. Encourage students to use teamwork so that they will have time to dry their products twice.

DISPOSAL

The products may be poured down the drain.

ANALYSIS AND INTERPRETATION—ANSWERS

1. $NaHCO_3(s) + CH_3COOH(aq) \longrightarrow$
$CO_2(g) + H_2O(l) + CH_3COOH(aq)$

2. $NaHCO_3$ molar mass: 84.01 g/mol
CH_3COOH molar mass: 60.06 g/mol
CO_2 molar mass: 44.01 g/mol
H_2O molar mass: 18.02 g/mol
CH_3COONa molar mass: 82.04 g/mol

3. The bubbling was caused by the formation of carbon dioxide gas.

4. The residue is entirely CH_3COONa because CH_3COOH was added in excess to be certain that the reaction went to completion.

Continued on page 893C

CLEANUP AND DISPOSAL

8. Clean up the lab and all equipment after use. Dispose of any unused chemicals in the containers designated by your teacher. Wash your hands thoroughly before you leave the lab after all lab work is finished. Make sure to turn off all gas valves.

ANALYSIS AND INTERPRETATION

1. Analyzing Results: Write a balanced equation for the reaction of baking soda and acetic acid. Be sure to include the physical states of matter for all of the reactants and products.

2. Organizing Data: Use a periodic table to calculate the molar mass for each of the reactants and products.

3. Analyzing Results: Explain what caused the bubbling when the reaction took place.

4. Analyzing Methods: How do you know that all the residue is actually sodium acetate rather than a mixture of sodium bicarbonate and sodium acetate?

5. Organizing Data: Calculate the mass of $NaHCO_3$, the number of moles of $NaHCO_3$, the mass of CH_3COONa, and the number of moles of CH_3COONa.

6. Evaluating Data: Using the balanced equation and the amount of $NaHCO_3$, determine the theoretical yield of CH_3COONa in moles and grams.

CONCLUSIONS

1. Analyzing Conclusions: What is the percent yield for your reaction?

2. Inferring Conclusions: What is the theoretical yield of CO_2? Using the density value given, 1.25 g/L, calculate the volume of CO_2 produced in the reaction. Show your calculations.

3. Applying Conclusions: How many moles of $NaHCO_3$ and CH_3COONa are necessary to produce 425 mL of CO_2? Show your calculations.

(Hint: Be sure to include your percent yield for this reaction in your calculations.)

EXTENSIONS

1. Designing Experiments: If your percent yield is less than 100%, explain why. If you can think of ways to eliminate sources of error, ask your teacher to approve your plans, and run the procedure again.

2. Research and Communications: Many recipes for breads use yeast, instead of baking soda, as a source of CO_2. A cake of yeast is shown in Figure B. Research the use of yeast, and explain what ingredients are necessary for the yeast to produce carbon dioxide. What is the balanced chemical equation for the reaction that yeast uses to produce CO_2?

FIGURE B　Yeast can be compressed into cakes and used in baking as a source of carbon dioxide.

EXPERIMENT 9-2

Stoichiometry and Gravimetric Analysis

OBJECTIVES

- *Observe* the double-displacement reaction between solutions of strontium chloride and sodium carbonate.

- *Demonstrate* proficiency with gravimetric methods.

- *Measure* the mass of the precipitate formed.

- *Relate* the mass of the precipitate formed to the mass of the reactants before the reaction.

- *Calculate* the mass of sodium carbonate in a solution of unknown concentration.

MATERIALS

- **15 mL Na₂CO₃ solution of unknown concentration**

- **50 mL 0.30 M SrCl₂ solution**

- **250 mL beakers, 2**

- **balance**

- **beaker tongs**

- **distilled water**

- **drying oven**

- **filter paper**

- **glass funnel or Büchner funnel with related equipment**

- **graduated cylinder**

- **glass stirring rod**

- **paper towels**

- **ring and ring stand**

- **rubber policeman**

- **spatula**

- **water bottle**

BACKGROUND

This gravimetric analysis involves a double-displacement reaction between strontium chloride, $SrCl_2$, and sodium carbonate, Na_2CO_3. In general, this type of reaction can be used to determine the amount of any carbonate compound in a solution. For accurate results, essentially all of the reactant of unknown amount must be converted into product. If the mass of the product is carefully measured, you can use stoichiometry calculations to determine how much of the reactant of unknown amount was involved in the reaction. Accurate results depend on precise mass measurements, so keep all glassware very clean, and minimize the loss of any reactants or products during your lab work.

SAFETY

Always wear safety goggles and a lab apron to protect your eyes and clothing. If you get a chemical in your eyes, immediately flush the chemical out at the eyewash station while calling to your teacher. Know the locations of the emergency lab shower and eyewash station and the procedure for using them.

Do not touch any chemicals. If you get a chemical on your skin or clothing, wash the chemical off at the sink while calling to your teacher. Make sure you carefully read the labels and follow the precautions on all containers of chemicals that you use. If no precautions are stated on the labels, ask your teacher what precautions to follow. Do not taste any items used in the laboratory. Never return leftover chemicals to their original containers; take only small amounts to avoid wasting supplies.

OBJECTIVES
Students will

- use appropriate lab safety procedures.

- observe the double-displacement reaction between solutions of strontium chloride and sodium carbonate.

- use a laboratory balance to measure mass.

- demonstrate appropriate technique in transferring liquids.

- demonstrate appropriate technique in filtering.

- perform stoichiometric calculations to determine the mass of the sodium carbonate present in the solution.

RECOMMENDED TIME
2 lab periods

MATERIALS
(for each lab group)

- 15 mL Na₂CO₃ solution (unknown concentration)
- 50 mL 0.30 M SrCl₂ solution
- 250 mL beakers, 2
- balance
- beaker tongs
- distilled water
- drying oven
- filter paper
- glass stirring rod
- graduated cylinder
- paper towels
- pipe-stem triangle
- ring and ring stand
- rubber policeman
- spatula
- water bottle

GRAVITY FILTRATION OPTION

- glass funnel

VACUUM FILTRATION OPTION

- aspirator for spigot
- Büchner funnel (either ceramic or plastic)
- one-hole rubber stopper or sleeve
- vacuum flask (sidearm flask) and tubing

SOLUTION/MATERIALS PREPARATION

1. To prepare 0.30 M $SrCl_2$, dissolve 80.0 g of $SrCl_2 \cdot 6H_2O$ in enough water to make 1.00 L of solution.
2. For the unknown, 0.50 M Na_2CO_3 is recommended. To prepare 0.50 M Na_2CO_3, dissolve 53.0 g of Na_2CO_3 in enough water to make 1.00 L of solution.

REQUIRED PRECAUTIONS

- Safety goggles and a lab apron must be worn at all times.
- Read all safety precautions, and discuss them with your students.
- Remind students that heated objects can be hot enough to burn even if they look cool. Students should always use beaker tongs to place samples in a drying oven.

TECHNIQUES TO DEMONSTRATE

Review the procedures for the filtration method your students will use.
  Remind students of the importance of using clean glassware and avoiding loss of product.

SAMPLE DATA

Volume of 0.30 M $SrCl_2$	35.0 mL
Volume of Na_2CO_3	15.0 mL
Mass of filter paper	0.30 g
Mass of filter paper + $SrCO_3$	1.36 g

PRE-LAB DISCUSSION

Thoroughly discuss mass-mass stoichiometry and its application in the laboratory. It would be useful to work through a set of calculations

 Never put broken glass or ceramics in a regular waste container. Broken glass and ceramics should be disposed of in a separate container designated by your teacher.

PREPARATION

1. Copy the data table below in your lab notebook.

DATA TABLE

Volume of Na_2CO_3 solution added	
Volume of $SrCl_2$ solution added	
Mass of dry filter paper	
Mass of beaker with paper towel	
Mass of beaker with paper towel, filter paper, and precipitate	

2. Clean all of the necessary lab equipment with soap and water, even if it has already been cleaned once. Rinse each piece of equipment with distilled water.

3. Measure the mass of a piece of filter paper to the nearest 0.01 g, and record this value in your data table.

4. Set up a filtering apparatus, either a vacuum filtration or a gravity filtration, depending on the equipment that is available. Use the Pre-Laboratory Procedure described on page 790.

5. Label a paper towel with your name, your class, and the date. Place the paper towel in a clean, dry 250 mL beaker, and measure and record the mass of the paper towel and beaker to the nearest 0.01 g.

PROCEDURE

1. Measure about 15 mL of the Na_2CO_3 solution into the graduated cylinder. Record this volume to the nearest 0.5 mL in your data table. Pour the Na_2CO_3 solution into a clean, empty 250 mL beaker. Carefully wash the graduated cylinder, and rinse it with distilled water.

2. Measure about 25 mL of the 0.30 M $SrCl_2$ solution in the graduated cylinder. Record this volume to the nearest 0.5 mL in your data table.

FIGURE A   The precipitate is a product of the reaction between Na_2CO_3 and $SrCl_2$. Add enough $SrCl_2$ to react with all of the Na_2CO_3 present.

Pour the $SrCl_2$ solution into the beaker with the Na_2CO_3 solution, as shown in Figure A. Gently stir the solution and precipitate with a glass stirring rod.

3. Carefully measure another 10 mL of the $SrCl_2$ solution into the graduated cylinder. Record the volume to the nearest 0.5 mL in your data table. Slowly add it to the beaker. Repeat this step until no more precipitate forms.

4. Once the precipitate has settled, slowly pour the mixture into the funnel. Be careful not to overfill the funnel because some of the precipitate could be lost between the filter paper and the funnel. Use the rubber policeman to transfer as much of the precipitate into the funnel as possible.

5. Rinse the rubber policeman over the beaker with a small amount of distilled water, and pour this solution into the funnel. Rinse the beaker several more times with small amounts of distilled water, as shown in Figure B. Pour the rinse water into the funnel each time.

FIGURE B   Rinse with small amounts of water, directed at all sides of the beaker, to wash all the precipitate into the funnel.

6. After all of the solution and rinses have drained through the funnel, slowly rinse the precipitate on the filter paper in the funnel with distilled water to remove any soluble impurities.

7. Carefully remove the filter paper from the funnel, and place it on the paper towel that you labeled with your name. Unfold the filter paper, and place the paper towel, filter paper, and precipitate in the rinsed beaker. Then place the beaker in the drying oven. For best results, allow the precipitate to dry overnight.

8. Using beaker tongs, remove your sample from the drying oven, and allow it to cool. Measure and record the mass of the beaker with paper towel, filter paper, and precipitate to the nearest 0.01 g.

CLEANUP AND DISPOSAL

9. Dispose of the precipitate in a designated waste container. Pour the filtrate in the other 250 mL beaker into the designated waste container. Clean up the lab and all equipment after use, and dispose of substances according to your teacher's instructions. Wash your hands thoroughly after all lab work is finished and before you leave the lab.

ANALYSIS AND INTERPRETATION

1. **Organizing Ideas:** Write a balanced equation for the reaction. What is the precipitate? Write its empirical formula.

2. **Applying Ideas:** Calculate the mass of the dry precipitate. Calculate the number of moles of precipitate produced in the reaction. (Hint: Use the results from Procedure item 8.)

3. **Applying Ideas:** How many moles of Na_2CO_3 were present in the 15 mL sample?

4. **Evaluating Methods:** There were 0.30 mol of $SrCl_2$ in every liter of solution. Calculate the number of moles of $SrCl_2$ that were added. Determine whether $SrCl_2$ or Na_2CO_3 was the limiting reactant. Would this lab have worked if the other reactant had been chosen as the limiting reactant? Explain why or why not.

5. **Evaluating Methods:** Why was the precipitate rinsed in Procedure step 6? What soluble impurities could have been on the filter paper along with the precipitate? How would the calculated results vary if the precipitate had not been completely dry? Explain your answer.

CONCLUSIONS

1. **Inferring Conclusions:** How many grams of Na_2CO_3 were present in the 15 mL sample?

2. **Applying Conclusions:** How many grams of Na_2CO_3 are present in 575 L of the Na_2CO_3 solution? (Hint: Create a conversion factor to convert from the sample with a volume of 15 mL to a solution with a volume of 575 L.)

EXTENSIONS

1. **Evaluating Methods:** From your teacher, find out the theoretical mass of Na_2CO_3 in the sample, and calculate your percent error.

2. **Designing Experiments:** What possible sources of error can you identify in your procedure? If you can think of ways to eliminate them, ask your teacher to approve your plans, and run the procedure again.

with sample data before performing the lab.

DISPOSAL
You will need two disposal containers: one for solids and another for liquids. The solids may be disposed of in the trash. The liquids can be washed down the drain with an excess of water.

ANALYSIS AND INTERPRETATION—ANSWERS
1. $SrCl_2(aq) + Na_2CO_3(aq) \longrightarrow$
$\qquad 2NaCl(aq) + SrCO_3(s)$
The precipitate is strontium carbonate, $SrCO_3$.

Continued on page 893C

EXPERIMENT 12-1

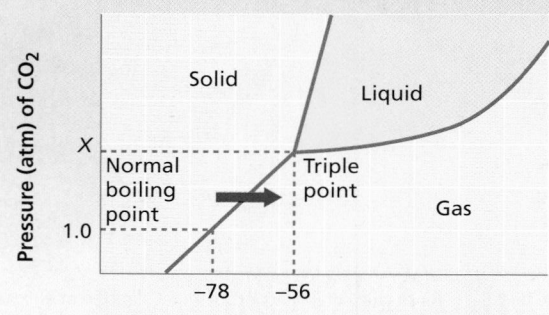

MICRO-LAB

OBJECTIVES
Students will

- use appropriate lab safety techniques.
- describe what happens when the pressure on a sample of CO_2 is varied above ambient pressure.
- relate observations to the phase diagram of CO_2.
- predict the results of using smaller and larger samples of CO_2.

RECOMMENDED TIME
30 min; allow more time for Extensions

MATERIALS
(for each lab group)
- 4–5 g CO_2 as dry ice, in rice-sized pieces
- forceps
- graduated pipet
- metric ruler
- pliers
- scissors
- transparent plastic cup

SOLUTION/MATERIALS PREPARATION
1. Dry ice often may be ordered from ice-cream stores or from businesses that make and sell regular ice cubes. Keep the dry ice wrapped in many layers of newspaper or other insulating material in an ice chest.

2. C-clamps can be used instead of pliers. If neither are available, your students may be able to bring pliers or clamps from home. Some students may suggest using their fingers to hold the pipet shut, but it may be difficult to achieve enough of a seal to build up the pressure required for melting the dry ice.

REQUIRED PRECAUTIONS
- Safety goggles and a lab apron must be worn at all times.

"Wet" Dry Ice

OBJECTIVES

- *Interpret* a phase diagram.
- *Observe* the melting of CO_2 while varying pressure.
- *Relate* observations of CO_2 to its phase diagram.

MATERIALS

- **4–5 g CO_2 as dry ice, broken into rice-sized pieces**
- **forceps**
- **graduated pipet**
- **metric ruler**
- **pliers**
- **scissors**
- **transparent plastic cup**

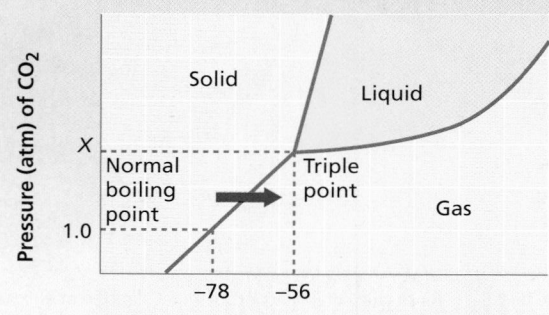

FIGURE A   The phase diagram for CO_2 shows the temperatures and pressures at which CO_2 can undergo phase changes.

BACKGROUND

The phase diagram for carbon dioxide in Figure A shows that CO_2 can exist only as a gas at ordinary room temperature and pressure. To observe the transition of solid CO_2 to liquid CO_2, it will be necessary for you to increase the pressure until it is at or above the triple point pressure, labeled X in the diagram.

SAFETY

 Always wear safety goggles and a lab apron to protect your eyes and clothing. If you get a chemical in your eyes, immediately flush the chemical out at the eyewash station while calling to your teacher. Know the location of the emergency lab shower and eyewash station and the procedure for using them.

 Call your teacher in the event of a spill. Spills should be cleaned up promptly according to your teacher's directions.

 Dry ice is cold enough to cause frostbite, so heat- and cold-resistant gloves should be used if you handle it.

PREPARATION

1. Organize a place in your lab notebook for recording your observations.

PROCEDURE

1. Place 2–3 very small pieces of dry ice on the table, and observe them until they have completely sublimed.

2. Fill a plastic cup with tap water to a depth of 4–5 cm.

3. Cut the tapered end (tip) off the graduated pipet.

4. Use forceps to carefully slide 8–10 pieces of dry ice down the stem and into the bulb of the pipet.

5. Using a pair of pliers, clamp the opening of the pipet stem securely shut so that no gas can escape. Hold the tube by the pliers, and lower the pipet into the cup just until the bulb is submerged as shown in Figure B. From the side of the cup, observe the behavior of the dry ice.

6. As soon as the dry ice has begun to melt, quickly loosen the pliers while still holding the bulb in the water. Observe the CO_2.

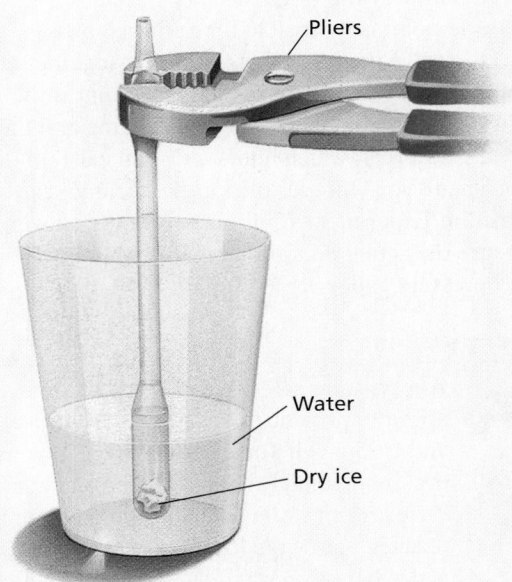

FIGURE B   Clamp the end of the pipet shut with the pliers. Submerge the bulb in water in a transparent cup.

(Pliers)

(Water)

(Dry ice)

7. Tighten the pliers again, and observe.

8. Repeat Procedure steps 6 and 7 as many times as possible.

CLEANUP AND DISPOSAL

9. Clean all apparatus and your lab station. Return equipment to its proper place. Dispose of chemicals and solutions in the containers designated by your teacher. Do not pour any chemicals down the drain or in the trash unless your teacher directs you to do so. Wash your hands thoroughly before you leave the lab and after all work is finished.

ANALYSIS AND INTERPRETATION

1. **Analyzing Results:** What differences did you observe between the subliming and the melting of CO_2?

2. **Analyzing Methods:** As you melted the CO_2 sample over and over, why did it eventually disappear? What could you have done to make the sample last longer?

3. **Analyzing Methods:** What purpose(s) do you suppose the water in the cup served?

EXTENSIONS

1. **Predicting Outcomes:** What would have happened if fewer pieces of dry ice (only 1 or 2) had been placed inside the pipet bulb? If time permits, test your prediction.

2. **Predicting Outcomes:** What might have happened if more pieces of dry ice (20 or 30, for example) had been placed inside the pipet bulb? How quickly would the process have occurred? If time permits, test your prediction.

3. **Predicting Outcomes:** What would have happened if the pliers had not been released once the dry ice melted? If time permits, test your prediction.

- Read all safety precautions, and discuss them with your students.

- In case of a spill, use a dampened cloth or paper towel (or more than one towel, if necessary) to mop up the spill. Then rinse the cloth in running water at the sink, wring it out thoroughly, and put it in the trash.

- To crush dry ice into small pieces, wrap one or two chunks in a cloth towel. Then, wearing safety goggles, pulverize the chunks inside the towel with a hammer.

- If students do not loosen the pliers as instructed, the pipet will burst, and the water will splash, possibly startling other students.

TECHNIQUES TO DEMONSTRATE

Show students how to cut the tip from the pipet and how to use the pliers or C-clamp to seal the pipet.

SAMPLE DATA

No numerical data

PRE-LAB DISCUSSION

Have students examine the partial phase diagram for CO_2, and ask them what phase change CO_2 can undergo at a pressure of 1 atm, or 101.3 kPa. Ask if there is any temperature at which CO_2 will change to a liquid at 1 atm. When students recognize that CO_2 will melt only at elevated pressures, regardless of the temperature, they will understand why it is a rare experience to observe liquid carbon dioxide. Encourage students to record their observations in detail.

DISPOSAL

Any remaining dry ice that does not need to be saved for later can be left to sublime. Be sure the room is well ventilated so that the CO_2 gas does not build up above tolerable levels. Water may be poured down the drain.

Continued on page 893D

EXPERIMENT 12-2

OBJECTIVES
Students will

- use appropriate lab safety procedures.

- construct a micropressure gauge.

- use the micropressure gauge to measure the triple-point pressure of CO_2.

- relate observations to the phase diagram for CO_2.

RECOMMENDED TIME
45 min; less if micropressure gauges are prepared in advance, more for Extensions activities

MATERIALS
(for each lab group)

- 4–5 g CO_2 as dry ice, broken into rice-sized pieces

- 7 cm tube cut from a thin-stemmed pipet

- 15–20 cm of thread

- dark-colored water

- forceps

- graduated pipet

- micropressure gauge

- fine-tipped dropper bulb

- fine-tipped permanent marker

- hot-glue gun

- metric ruler

- pliers

- scissors

- transparent plastic cup

SOLUTION/MATERIALS PREPARATION

1. Dry ice often may be ordered from ice-cream stores or from businesses that make and sell regular ice cubes. Keep the dry ice wrapped in many layers of newspaper or other insulating material in an ice chest.

2. Fine-tipped dropper bulbs are available commercially, or they may be made out of thin-stemmed pipets. Stretch the pipets by hand, and then cut off the dropper bulbs. One dropper

Measuring the Triple-Point Pressure of CO_2

OBJECTIVES

- *Interpret* a phase diagram.

- *Observe* changes in pressure during a phase change.

- *Relate* pressure values to observations of air-column length.

- *Determine* the triple-point pressure of CO_2.

- *Infer* a conclusion from experimental data.

MATERIALS

- **4–5 g CO_2 as dry ice, broken into rice-sized pieces**

- **7 cm tube, cut from a thin-stemmed pipet**

- **15–20 cm of thread**

- **dark-colored water**

- **fine-tipped dropper bulb**

- **fine-tipped permanent marker**

- **forceps**

- **graduated pipet**

- **hot-glue gun**

- **metric ruler**

- **micropressure gauge**

- **pliers**

- **scissors**

- **transparent plastic cup**

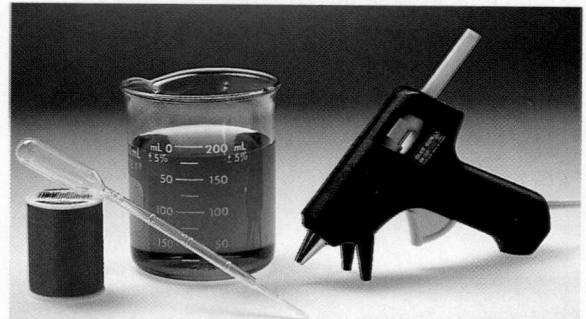

FIGURE A   The phase diagram for CO_2 shows the temperatures and pressures at which CO_2 can undergo phase changes.

BACKGROUND

In the phase diagram shown in Figure A, the triple-point pressure of CO_2 is labeled X. Only at the triple-point is it possible for the three phases of CO_2—solid, liquid, and gas—to exist together at equilibrium. The pressure at the triple-point is the highest pressure at which CO_2 will sublime and the lowest pressure at which liquid CO_2 can exist. In this experiment, you will use some of the techniques you learned in Experiment 12–1, but this time you will measure the actual pressure at the triple point with a micropressure gauge.

SAFETY

Always wear safety goggles and a lab apron to provide protection for your eyes and clothing. If you get a chemical in your eyes, immediately flush the chemical out at the eyewash station while calling to your teacher. Know the location of the emergency lab shower and eyewash station and the procedure for using them.

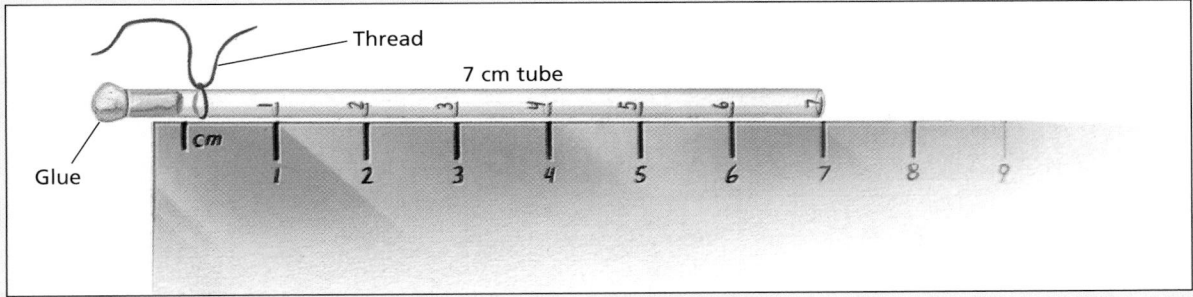

FIGURE B   The sealed 7 cm tube, with thread attached, is calibrated by marking the tube at 1 cm intervals from the inside edge of the glue plug.

 Do not touch any chemicals. If you get a chemical on your skin or clothing, wash the chemical off at the sink while calling to your teacher. Make sure you carefully read the labels and follow the precautions on all containers of chemicals that you use. If there are no precautions stated on the label, ask your teacher what precautions to follow. Do not taste any chemicals or items used in the laboratory. Never return leftovers to their original containers; take only small amounts to avoid wasting supplies.

 Call your teacher in the event of a spill. Spills should be cleaned up promptly according to your teacher's directions.

 Dry ice is cold enough to cause frostbite, so heat- and cold-resistant gloves should be used if you handle it.

 The tip of the hot-glue gun is very hot, as is the glue.

PREPARATION

1. Copy the data table shown below in your lab notebook.

2. Fill a plastic cup with tap water to a depth of about 4–5 cm. Cut the tapered tip off a graduated pipet. If the micropressure gauges are already prepared, go to Procedure step 1. If not, Preparation steps 3–5 will explain how to make a micropressure gauge.

3. Take the 7 cm tube cut from a thin-stemmed pipet, and place a small drop of hot glue on one end to seal it. When the glue has cooled, tie the thread around the tube below the glue, as shown in Figure B. Trim away any excess glue so that the tube will easily pass through the end of the graduated pipet you prepared in Preparation step 2.

4. Using the metric ruler to measure from the inside edge of the glue, mark off every centimeter along the length of the tube with the fine-tipped permanent marker. Number the centimeter marks as shown in Figure B.

5. Using the fine-tipped dropper bulb, place a small drop of dark-colored water inside the open end of the tube. Record the position of the drop on the scale from the inside edge of the drop to the inside edge of the glue plug. This is a measurement of the length of the air column trapped inside the tube, as shown in Figure C. Note this measurement in your data table.

bulb will be sufficient if students share. They are reusable.

3. Students can share the scissors, metric rulers, fine-tipped markers, and hot-glue gun.

4. You may want to prepare the gauges beforehand to save time or if students do not have the dexterity needed to make them. Once prepared, the micropressure gauges can be reused for other lab sections and from year to year. However, a new drop of colored water will probably be needed each time.

5. One beaker containing about 15 mL of water and several drops of food coloring may be shared by all students.

REQUIRED PRECAUTIONS
- Safety goggles and a lab apron must be worn at all times.
- Read all safety precautions, and discuss them with your students.
- In case of a spill, use a dampened cloth or paper towel (or more than one towel, if necessary) to mop up the spill. Then rinse the cloth in running water at the sink, wring it out thoroughly, and put it in the trash.
- To crush dry ice into small pieces, wrap one or two chunks in a cloth towel. Then, wearing safety goggles, pulverize the chunks inside the towel with a hammer.
- If students do not loosen the pliers as instructed, the pipet will burst, and the water will splash, possibly startling other students.

TECHNIQUES TO DEMONSTRATE
If students make their own micropressure gauges, demonstrate the techniques needed for Preparation steps 3–5. If students have not done Experiment 12-1, show them how to use the pliers to close off the end of the pipet.

DATA TABLE					
	Trial 1	Trial 2	Trial 3	Trial 4	Trial 5
Initial reading (cm)					
CO_2 melting-point reading (cm)					

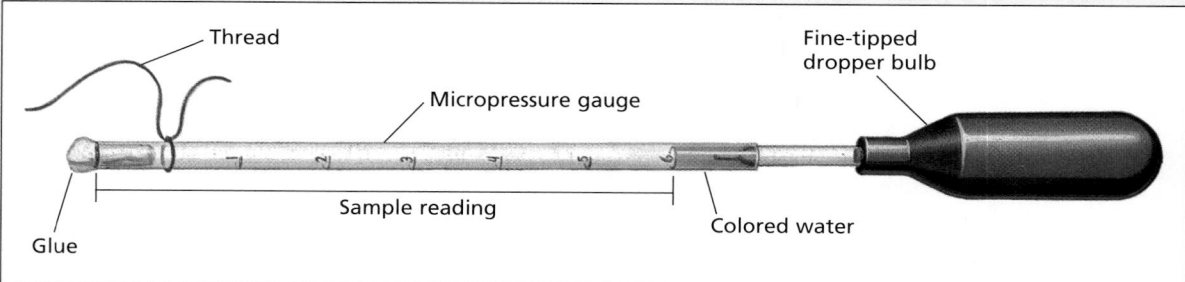

FIGURE C   The pressure is equivalent to the length of the column of air measured from the inside edge of the glue plug to the inside edge of the water drop.

SAMPLE DATA

Initial reading (cm): 6.2 cm

CO_2 melting-point reading: 1.2 cm

PRE-LAB DISCUSSION

Review students' understanding of the phase diagram for CO_2 in Experiment 12-1 by asking them what phase changes are possible along the various line segments in the diagram. Ask about the significance of the triple point. The experiment may also be useful for helping students understand the relationship between the pressure and temperature of gases.

DISPOSAL

Any remaining dry ice that does not need to be saved for later can be left to sublime. Be sure the room is well ventilated so that the CO_2 gas does not build up to intolerable levels. Water may be poured down the drain.

ANALYSIS AND INTERPRETATION—ANSWERS

1. Before the dry ice melted, the pressure inside the bulb steadily increased as the dry ice sublimed. During the melting, the pressure remained the same. After melting, when the pliers were loosened, the pressure dropped.

2. Students' answers will vary. If their work was fairly accurate, the measurement of the length of the air column when the dry ice began melting should be about one-fifth of the initial measurement. The initial pressure inside the tube was about 1 atm, or the pressure inside the room.

CONCLUSIONS—ANSWERS

1. Students' answers will vary. The accepted value for the triple-point pressure of CO_2 is 5.11 atm. Sample calculations follow.

$$P_1 \times V_1 = P_2 \times V_2 \; ; \; P_2 = \frac{P_1 \times V_1}{V_2}$$

PROCEDURE

1. As in Experiment 12-1, carefully slide 8–10 pieces of dry ice down the stem and into the graduated pipet bulb from Preparation step 2. However, instead of clamping the graduated pipet shut, insert the micropressure gauge, open-end downward, so that the gauge hangs in the stem and NOT in the bulb of the graduated pipet, as shown in Figure D. The thread of the micropressure gauge should be hanging out of the end of the pipet. Use the pliers to clamp the

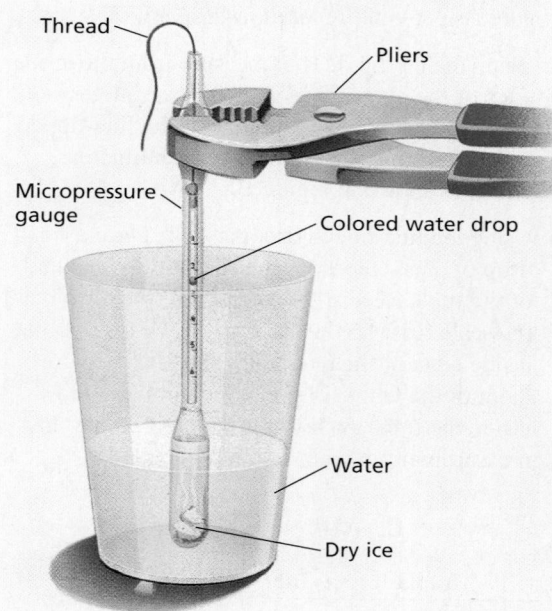

FIGURE D   The micropressure gauge hangs in the stem of the pipet. The thread extends from its open end. The bulb containing the dry ice is submerged in water.

pipet shut around the thread so that no gas can escape and the micropressure gauge remains suspended in the stem of the pipet.

2. Holding the pipet with the pliers, lower the bulb, NOT the stem of the pipet, until it is submerged in the cup of water, as shown in Figure D.

3. From the side of the cup, observe the movement of the drop of colored water in the micropressure gauge before and while the CO_2 melts. Note the position in centimeters, as marked on the micropressure gauge, of the top of the colored-water drop the instant the dry ice begins to melt. Quickly loosen the grip on the pliers. Record the position of the drop (melting point reading) in your data table.

4. With the pliers loosened, observe the CO_2 and the drop of colored water in the micropressure gauge.

5. Tighten the grip on the pliers again and observe as before.

6. Repeat Procedure steps 3–5 as many times as possible.

CLEANUP AND DISPOSAL

1. Clean all apparatus and your lab station. Return equipment to its proper place. Dispose of chemicals and solutions in the containers designated by your teacher. Do not pour any chemicals down the drain or in the trash unless your teacher directs you to do so. Wash your hands thoroughly before you leave the lab and after all work is finished.

ANALYSIS AND INTERPRETATION

1. **Analyzing Information:** What happened to the pressure inside the bulb before, while, and after the dry ice melted?

2. **Organizing Data:** What was the initial length of the air column inside the tube? What was the length of the air column at the instant the dry ice started to melt? What was the initial pressure in atm inside the tube when you placed the drop of liquid in it?

CONCLUSIONS

1. **Inferring Relationships:** For micropressure gauges, the length of the gauge is proportional to volume. Therefore, the final pressure of the system can be calculated as follows.

$$P_2 = \frac{P_1 \times \text{length}_1}{\text{length}_2}$$

Using your answers to item 2 in Analysis and Interpretation, calculate the pressure in atm inside the pipet, P_2, when liquid CO_2 first appeared. Show your work.

2. **Relating Ideas:** How does your answer to Conclusions item 1 relate to the triple-point pressure X? Justify your explanation with evidence from the phase diagram for CO_2.

3. **Evaluating Methods:** The accepted value for the triple point of CO_2 is 5.11 atm. Compare this value with your experimental value, and calculate your percent error.

EXTENSIONS

1. **Evaluating Methods:** When you used the micropressure gauge, you measured the **length** of a trapped air column, with a glue plug at one end and a drop of water at the other. However, the calculations for gases are for a relationship between pressure and **volume**, not length. What assumptions are being made in using the length of the trapped air column in place of volume?

2. **Evaluating Methods and Designing Experiments:** What possible sources of error can you identify in this procedure? If you can think of a way to eliminate errors, ask your teacher to approve your suggestion. Then run the procedure again, and calculate the percent error.

3. **Inferring Relationships:** Determine the volume of the pipet bulb. Assuming that the pressure measured on the micropressure gauge is correct and that the temperature at the triple point for CO_2 is −56°C, calculate the number of moles of CO_2 gas that were present. Calculate the number of grams that this would be. What is the density of CO_2 gas under these conditions?

For micropressure gauges, length is proportional to volume. Therefore, the final pressure of the system can be calculated as follows.

$$P_2 = \frac{P_1 \times \text{length}_1}{\text{length}_2}$$

$P_1 = 1$ atm; length$_1$ = 6.2 cm; length$_2$ = 1.2 cm

$$P_2 = \frac{1 \text{ atm} \times 6.2 \text{ cm}}{1.2 \text{ cm}} = 5.2 \text{ atm}$$

2. The pressure found experimentally should be the triple-point pressure of CO_2, if the observation were made exactly at the point where melting began. As the phase diagram shows, as the temperature increases, there is a minimum pressure at which CO_2 can form a liquid, and this minimum corresponds to the triple point.

3. Students' answers will vary.

EXTENSIONS—ANSWERS

1. The assumptions are that the width and shape of the trapped air column are constant and that volume is directly proportional to length.

2. Students' answers will vary but may include difficulty in precisely measuring the length of the air column and calculation errors added by assuming pressure to be equal to exactly 1 atm. Suggested changes may include adding smaller calibration marks to the micropressure gauge and reading the barometric pressure in the lab.

3. Students' answers will vary, but they should be based on the ideal gas law relationship:

$$n = \frac{P \cdot V}{R \cdot T},$$

where m = $n \times$ molar mass,

and $D = \frac{m}{V}$

Continued on page 893D

Paper Chromatography

Chromatography is a technique used to separate substances dissolved in a mixture. The Latin roots of the word are *chromato,* which means "color," and *graphy,* which means "to write." Paper is one medium used to separate the components of a solution.

Paper is made of cellulose fibers that are pressed together. As a solution passes over the fibers and through the pores, the paper acts as a filter and separates the mixture's components. Particles of the same component group together, producing a colored band. Properties such as particle size, molecular mass, and charge of the different solute particles in the mixture affect the distance the components will travel on the paper. The components of the mixture that are the most soluble in the solvent and the least attracted to the paper will travel the farthest. Their band of color will be closest to the edge of the paper.

GENERAL SAFETY

Always wear safety goggles and a lab apron to protect your eyes and clothing. If you get a chemical in your eyes, immediately flush the chemical out at the eyewash station while calling to your teacher. Know the location of the emergency lab shower and eyewash station and the procedure for using them.

PROCEDURE

1. Use a lead pencil to sketch a circle about the size of a quarter in the center of a piece of circular filter paper that is 12 cm in diameter.

2. Write one numeral for each substance, including any unknowns, around the inside of this circle. In this experiment, 6 mixtures are to be separated, so the circle is labeled 1 through 6, as shown in Figure A.

3. Use a micropipet to place a spot of each substance to be separated next to a number. Make one spot per number. If the spot is too large,

you will get a broad, tailing trace with little or no detectable separation.

4. Use the pencil to poke a small hole in the center of the spotted filter paper. Insert a wick through the hole. A wick can be made by rolling a triangular piece of filter paper into a cylinder: start

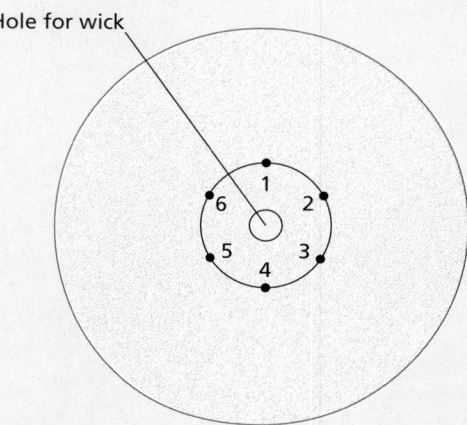

FIGURE A Filter paper used in paper chromatography is spotted with the mixtures to be separated. Each spot is labeled with a numeral or a name that identifies the mixture to be separated. A hole punched in the center of the paper will attach to a wick that delivers the solvent to the paper.

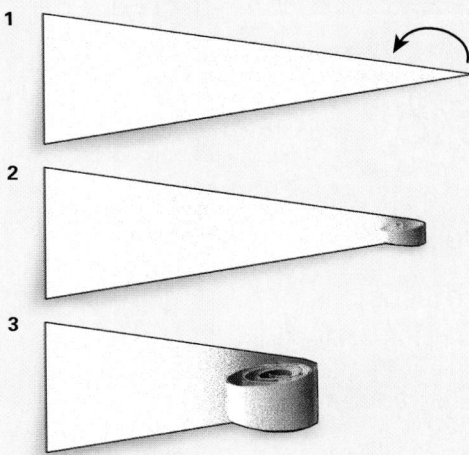

1

2

3

FIGURE B Cut the triangle from filter paper. Roll the paper into a cylinder starting at the narrow end.

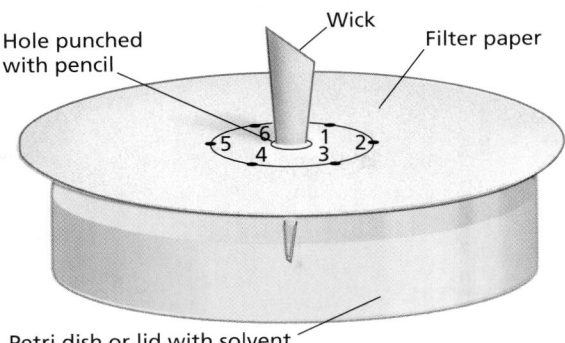

Wick

Hole punched with pencil

Filter paper

5 6 1 2
4 3

Petri dish or lid with solvent

FIGURE C The wick is inserted through the hole of the spotted filter paper. The filter paper with the wick is then placed on top of a petri dish or lid filled two-thirds full of water or another solvent.

at the point of the triangle, and roll toward its base. See Figure B.

5. Fill a petri dish or lid two-thirds full of solvent (usually water or alcohol).

6. Set the bottom of the wick in the solvent so that the filter paper rests on the top of the petri dish. See Figure C.

7. When the solvent is 1 cm from the outside edge of the paper, remove the paper from the petri dish, and allow the chromatogram to dry. Sample chromatograms are shown in Figures D and E.

Most writing or drawing inks are mixtures of various components that give them specific properties. Therefore, paper chromatography can be used to study the composition of an ink. Experiments 13-1 and 16-2 investigate the composition of ball-point-pen ink and marker ink, respectively.

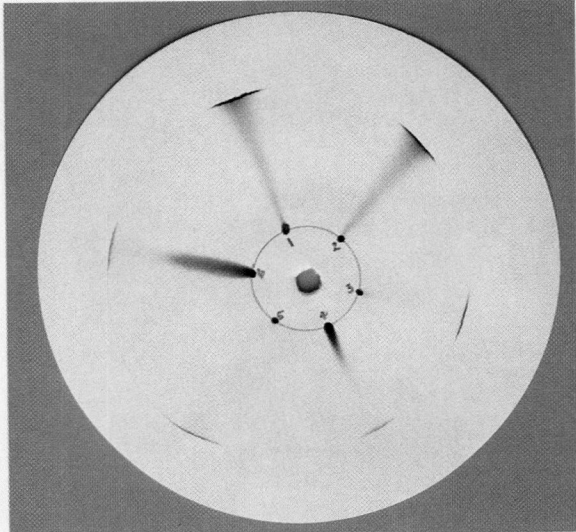

FIGURE D Each of the original spots has migrated along with the solvent toward the outer edge of the filter paper. For each substance that was a mixture, you should see more than one distinct spot of color in its trace.

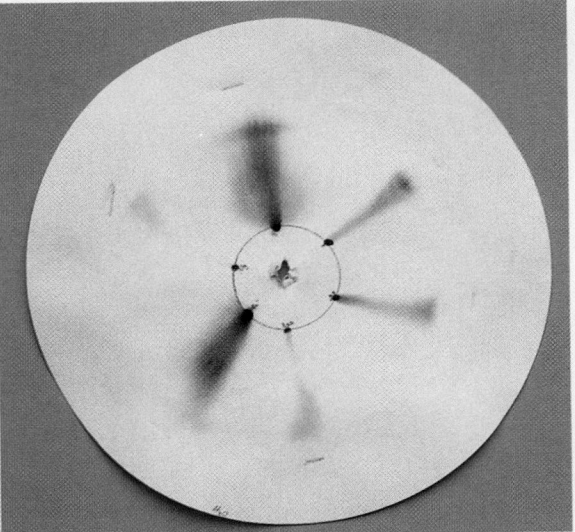

FIGURE E This chromatogram is unacceptable due to bleeding or spread of the pigment front. Too much ink was used in the spot, or the ink was too soluble in the solvent.

EXPERIMENT 13-1

Separation of Pen Inks by Paper Chromatography

EXPERIMENT 13-1

OBJECTIVES
Students will

- demonstrate proficiency in qualitatively separating mixtures using paper chromatography.
- calculate the R_f factor for each color in the separated inks.
- relate the results of a chromatogram to the solubility properties of the components of a mixture.

RECOMMENDED TIME
1 lab period

MATERIALS
(for each lab group)
- 12 cm circular chromatography papers or filter papers, 2
- 25 mL isopropanol
- ballpoint pens, black ink, 4 different types
- distilled water
- filter paper wicks, 2 cm equilateral triangles, 2
- pencil
- petri dish with lid
- ruler
- scissors
- tape or stapler with staples

SOLUTION/MATERIALS PREPARATION
1. Label the pens *1, 2, 3* and *4*.

REQUIRED PRECAUTIONS
- Wear safety goggles and a lab apron at all times.
- Read all safety cautions, and discuss them with your students.
- The isopropanol is extremely flammable. It should be kept in a closed bottle in an operating fume hood. Place only 300 mL at a time in the bottle. Students should replace the lid when they are finished.
- No burners, flames, hot plates, or other heat sources should be in use

OBJECTIVES

- *Demonstrate* proficiency in qualitatively separating mixtures using paper chromatography.
- *Determine* the R_f factor(s) for each component of each tested ink.
- *Explain* how the inks are separated by paper chromatography.
- *Observe* the separation of a mixture by the method of paper chromatography.

MATERIALS

- **12 cm circular chromatography paper or filter paper**
- **distilled water**
- **filter paper wick, 2 cm equilateral triangle**
- **isopropanol**
- **numbered pens, each with a different black ink, 4**
- **pencil**
- **petri dish with lid**
- **scissors**

BACKGROUND

Paper Chromatography
Details on this technique can be found in the Pre-Laboratory Procedure on pages 828–829.

Writing Inks
In general, writing inks are of two types—water soluble and oil based. Inks can be pure substances or mixtures. Most ballpoint pen inks are complex mixtures, containing pigments or dyes that can be separated by paper chromatography, as shown in Figure A. Although there are thousands of different formulations for inks, the chemicals used to make them can be broadly classed into three categories: color, solvents, and resins.

An ink's color is due to dyes or pigments, which account for about 25% of the ink's mass. Black inks can contain three or more colors; the number of colors depends on the manufacturer. Each ink

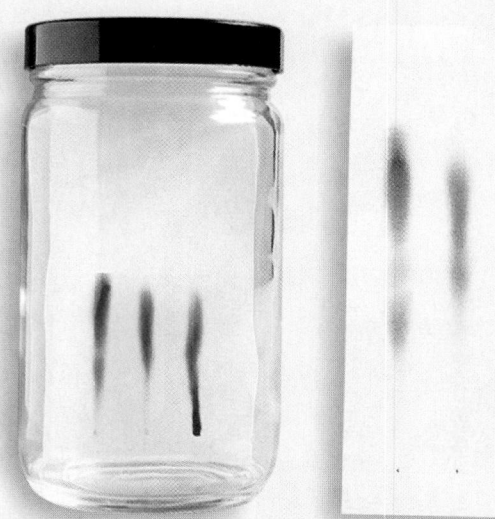

FIGURE A   Paper chromatography reveals the different colored dyes that black ink contains.

formulation has a characteristic pattern that uniquely identifies it.

The pigments or dyes of ink are dissolved or suspended in solvents, which comprise approximately 50% of the mass of the ink. Solvents are also responsible for the smooth flow of the ink over the roller ball in the tip of a ballpoint pen. Inks manufactured prior to 1950 have an oily base. They are usually soluble in alcohol but not in water. Inks manufactured after 1950 have a mixture of glycols as their solvent, so they are soluble in water.

The remaining 25% of the ink's mass is composed of resins. Resins control the creep, or flow, of the ink after it is applied to the surface of the paper.

In this experiment you will develop radial paper chromatograms for four black ballpoint pen inks, using water as solvent. You will then repeat this process using isopropanol as the solvent. You will then measure the distance traveled by each of the individual ink components and the distance traveled by the solvent front. Finally, you will use these measurements to calculate the R_f factor for each component.

SAFETY

Always wear safety goggles and a lab apron to protect your eyes and clothing. If you get a chemical in your eyes, immediately flush the chemical out with water at the eyewash station while calling to your teacher. Know the locations of the emergency lab shower and eyewash station and the procedure for using them.

Do not touch any chemicals. If you get a chemical on your skin or clothing, wash the chemical off at the sink while calling to your teacher. Make sure you carefully read the labels and follow the precautions on all containers of chemicals that you use. If there are no precautions stated on the label, ask your teacher what precautions to follow. Do not taste any chemicals or items in the laboratory. Never return leftovers to their original containers; take only small amounts to avoid wasting supplies.

Because the isopropanol is volatile and flammable, no Bunsen burners, hot plates, or other sources of heat should be in use in the room during this lab. Carry out all work with isopropanol in the hood.

PREPARATION

1. Determine the formula, structure, polarity, density and volatility at room temperature for water and isopropanol. The following titles are sources that provide general information on specific elements and compounds: *CRC Handbook of Chemistry and Physics, McGraw-Hill Dictionary of Chemical Terms*, and *Merck Index*.

2. Draw two data tables, one for the chromatogram made with water and one for the chromatogram made with isopropanol. Use the column headings shown below.

3. Leave room below each data table to record the distance that the solvent reaches.

in the lab when isopropanol is being used.

TECHNIQUES TO DEMONSTRATE

The general setup for paper chromatography is discussed on pages 828–829 of the text, but students may need to see an actual chromatography setup before they understand what they will be trying to achieve. Students may need help finding the center of an ink component's color band when marking distances for R_f calculations.

PRE-LAB DISCUSSION

The solubility properties discussed in Chapter 13 can explain in part why this technique works. Make certain students understand this link. Students should also understand that measuring distances traveled by the inks' components and calculating their R_f factors allows for quantitative comparisons.

DISPOSAL

Set out a disposal container for any isopropanol left over at the end of the procedure. Dilute it with 10 times its volume of water and pour it down the drain. Students are instructed to pour the water down the drain. The chromatograms may be discarded in the trash can.

ANALYSIS AND INTERPRETATION—ANSWERS

1. The black inks are made with multiple dyes because the inks separate into more than one color. NOTE: Some inks might not separate when water is the solvent but should separate when isopropanol is the solvent. Some inks may separate well with water but may be too soluble in the isopropanol to separate cleanly.

2. Water is a polar molecule that will dissolve polar and charged substances. Ethanol is a better solvent for nonpolar substances because the molecule has a nonpolar region.

DATA TABLE: Chromatogram Formed with Water									
Pen no.	Dot no.	Color 1		Color 2		Color 3		Color 4	
		Distance	R_f value	Distance	R_f value	Distance	R_f value	Distance	R_f value

DATA TABLE: Chromatogram Formed with Isopropanol									
Pen no.	Dot no.	Color 1		Color 2		Color 3		Color 4	
		Distance	R_f value	Distance	R_f value	Distance	R_f value	Distance	R_f value

Yes, isopropanol and ethanol would behave similarly because they are both alcohols.

H :ÖH H
| | |
H − C − C − C − H
| | |
H   H   H

Isopropanol

H − Ö − H

Water

3. Larger molecules are likely to move more slowly through the filter paper and to travel a shorter distance than smaller molecules. Large molecules would be expected to have small R_f values.

4. Components that are minimally attracted to the filter paper and are very soluble in the solvent would be very close to the solvent front during chromatography.

5. The component is soluble in the solvent but is more attracted to the filter paper than to the solvent because it moved only half as far.

6. Student answers will vary depending on the pens used.

7. If the process continued overnight, the solvent would reach the edge of the filter paper and begin to evaporate. The slower components would catch up with the faster ones, and they all would end up near the edge of the filter paper.

8. The isopropanol gave a better separation. When the ink was dipped into the water solvent, most of it dissolved in the dish instead of being pulled across the filter paper with the solvent.

9. The solvent evaporates when it reaches the edge of the filter paper, so the distance traveled by the solvent could not be accurately determined.

PROCEDURE

Part A: Prepare a chromatogram using water as the solvent

1. Record your observations in the appropriate data table when you are instructed to do so in the procedures.

2. Construct an apparatus for paper chromatography as described in the Pre-Laboratory Procedure on page 828. You will make only four dots. You will use ballpoint pens rather than micropipets to spot your paper.

3. After 15 min or when the water is about 1 cm from the outside edge of the paper, remove the paper from the Petri dish and allow the chromatogram to dry. Record in the data table the colors that have separated from each of the four different black inks. You may want to use colored pencils to record this information.

Part B: Prepare a chromatogram using isopropanol as the solvent

4. Repeat Procedure steps 1 through 3, replacing the water in the petri dish with isopropanol.

Part C: Determine R_f values for each component

5. After the chromatogram is dry, use a pencil to mark the point where the solvent front stopped.

6. With a ruler, measure the distance from the initial ink spot to your mark, and record this distance on your data table.

7. Make a small dot with your pencil in the center of each color band.

8. With a ruler, measure the distance from the initial ink spot to each dot separately, and record each distance on your data table.

9. Divide each value recorded in Procedure step 8 by the value recorded in Procedure step 6. The result is the R_f value for that component. Record the R_f values in your data table. Tape or staple the chromatogram to your data table.

CLEANUP AND DISPOSAL

10. The water may be poured down the sink. Chromatograms and other pieces of filter paper may be discarded in the trash. The isopropanol solution should be placed in the waste disposal container designated by your teacher. Clean up your equipment and lab station. Thoroughly wash your hands after completing the lab session and cleanup.

ANALYSIS AND INTERPRETATION

1. Evaluating Conclusions: Is the color in each pen the result of a single dye or multiple dyes? Justify your answer.

2. Building Models: The polarity of water and ethanol is discussed in Chapter 13. What types of substances are most likely to dissolve in each one? Would you expect isopropanol to behave similarly to ethanol?

3. Relating Ideas: The diffusion of a solute in a solvent is somewhat similar to the diffusion of gases discussed in Chapter 10. Where on the filter paper would you expect the larger molecules to be located in the final chromatogram? Would these molecules have large or small R_f values?

4. Applying Ideas: Some components of ink are minimally attracted to the filter paper and are very soluble in the solvent. Where are these components found on the chromatogram?

5. Relating Ideas: What can be said about the properties of a component ink that has an R_f value of 0.50?

6. Analyzing Methods: Suggest a reason for stopping the process when the solvent front is 1 cm from the edge of the filter paper rather than when it is even with the edge of the paper.

7. Predicting Outcomes: Predict the results of forgetting to remove the chromatogram from the water in the petri dish until the next day.

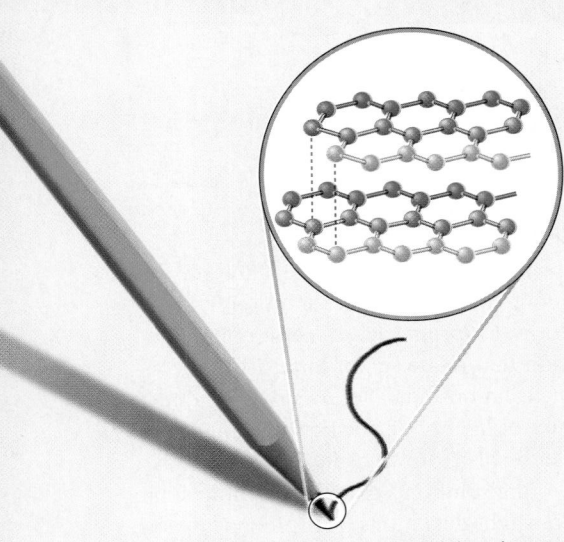

FIGURE B   What type of bond does the graphite found in this pencil have?

8. **Analyzing Results:** Was there a difference in the appearance of the separations obtained with water and the separations obtained with isopropanol? If so, explain the difference.

9. **Analyzing Methods:** At Bryan High School, Armando was performing a chromatography experiment. He thought it was going too slowly and decided to work without a wick. He dipped the sample into the solvent so that the ink dot was even with the top of the water. But when he finished, the chromatogram was too faint to be seen. Explain why Armando's experiment failed.

10. **Evaluating Methods:** Explain why the labels numbering the pen spots were written in pencil. (Hint: Think about the nature of the bonds and structure of the graphite that is found in pencils. See Figure B.)

CONCLUSIONS

1. **Analyzing Results:** Compare the R_f values for the colors from pen number 2 when water was the solvent and the R_f values obtained when isopropanol was the solvent. Explain why they differ.

2. **Evaluating Methods:** Would you consider isopropanol a better choice for the solvent than water? Why or why not?

3. **Analyzing Conclusions:** Are the properties of the component that traveled the farthest in the water chromatogram likely to be similar to the properties of the component that traveled the farthest in the isopropanol chromatogram? Explain your reasoning.

4. **Inferring Conclusions:** What can you conclude about the composition of the inks in ballpoint pens from your chromatogram?

5. **Building Models:** If ethylene glycol were used for a solvent, would you expect the R_f factors to increase or decrease relative to isopropanol?

$$H-\overset{\displaystyle H}{\underset{\displaystyle OH}{C}}-\overset{\displaystyle H}{\underset{\displaystyle OH}{C}}-H$$

ethylene glycol

6. **Relating Ideas:** Consider the length of time that each chromatogram took to prepare and the polarity of each solvent. Can you suggest a relationship between solvent polarity and the time needed to develop a chromatogram?

7. **Analyzing Conclusions:** Support or refute the following statement: R_f values indicate the solubility of a substance.

8. **Evaluating Methods:** Why would increasing the size of the filter paper improve the efficiency of the separation?

9. **Designing Experiments:** Investigators at the scene of a crime strongly suspect that a handwritten promissory note for $10,000.00 has been altered to read $40,000.00. How might this theory be proven?

10. The graphite in pencil lead is composed of sheets of covalently bonded carbon molecules that are nonpolar and are insoluble in water or isopropanol. Thus, these molecules will not dissolve and contaminate the chromatogram.

CONCLUSIONS—ANSWERS

1. Student answers will vary but should attribute any differences in the R_f values to differences in the solvents and their interaction with solutes.

2. Student answers should be based on the quality of the separations. Usually, isopropanol gives better separation.

3. The component that travels the farthest in the water chromatogram is likely to be either small and ionic or polar. The component that travels the farthest in the isopropanol chromatogram is also likely to be small, but probably nonpolar.

4. Student answers will vary, but they should indicate that black inks are made with more than one color of dye and that the number and colors of the dyes vary. Answers may also include statements about the oily base of the inks if one or more inks separated in alcohol but not in water or about the glycol base of the inks if one or more inks separated in water but followed the solvent front in the isopropanol.

5. increase

6. In this case, less time was needed for chromatogram development with the less-polar isopropanol. This fact might suggest that the less polar the solvent, the less time is needed to run a chromatogram. However, there are too many factors for this evidence to be conclusive or to extend it to chromatography in general.

7. R_f values are indicators of solubility in a particular solvent because the distance that each component moves relative to the solvent front is unique.

Continued on page 893D

MICRO LAB

EXPERIMENT 13-2

OBJECTIVES
Students will
- prepare a stock solution of a specified concentration.
- perform dilutions to create a series of solutions of different molar concentrations.
- make colorimetric observations or measurements and relate them to molar concentration.
- plot a standard curve for absorbance.
- determine the molar concentration of an unknown solution based on absorbance measurements and the standard curve.

RECOMMENDED TIME
1 lab period

MATERIALS
(for each lab group)
- 1.0 M HCl, 25 mL
- 10 mL graduated cylinder
- 10.0 mL unknown solution (0.25 M $FeCl_3$)
- 250 mL beaker
- 250 mL volumetric flask
- distilled water
- 35 g $FeCl_3 \cdot 6H_2O$
- glass stirring rod
- test-tube rack
- test tubes, 7

OPTIONAL
- cuvettes
- lint-free wipes for cuvettes
- spectrophotometer

SOLUTION/MATERIALS PREPARATION
1. To prepare 1.0 M HCl, observe the required precautions. Add 83 mL of concentrated HCl to enough distilled water to make 1.00 L of solution. Add the acid slowly, and stir it occasionally to avoid overheating.

Colorimetry and Molarity

OBJECTIVES

- *Demonstrate* proficiency in preparing a solution and performing colorimetric measurements or observations.

- *Relate* colorimetric measurements or observations to concentration.

- *Determine* the molarity of a solution of unknown concentration.

MATERIALS

- **1.0 M HCl**
- **10 mL graduated cylinder**
- **250 mL beaker**
- **250 mL volumetric flask**
- **distilled water**
- **$FeCl_3 \cdot 6H_2O$ crystals**
- **glass stirring rod**
- **test-tube rack**
- **test tubes, 7**
- **unknown solution**

OPTIONAL EQUIPMENT

- **cuvettes**
- **lint-free wipes for cuvettes**
- **spectrophotometer**

0.5M $FeCl_3$

BACKGROUND

An aqueous solution of $FeCl_3$ is colored, and in general, the more concentrated the solution is, the darker its color is. *Colorimetry* is a measurement of concentration that relates color intensity and concentration. The relationship called Beer's law states that the amount of light of a specific wavelength that a solution absorbs, also known as its absorbance, is proportional to the solution's concentration. In some cases, there are slight deviations from Beer's law, so the graph of the relationship between absorbance and molarity is a curve instead of a straight line.

You will use colorimetry to determine the concentration of an $FeCl_3$ solution. First, you will make several standard solutions of $FeCl_3$ of known concentrations and measure their absorbance. You can then compare the absorbance of the solutions of known concentration with that of the solution of unknown concentration to determine the unknown molarity. If a spectrophotometer is available, you will make a graph of absorbance versus concentration.

SAFETY

Always wear safety goggles and a lab apron to protect your eyes and clothing. If you get a chemical in your eyes, immediately flush the chemical out at the eyewash station while calling to your teacher. Know the locations of the emergency lab shower and eyewash station and the procedure for using them.

Do not touch any chemicals. If you get a chemical on your skin or clothing, wash the chemical off at the sink while calling to your teacher. Make sure you carefully read the labels and follow the precautions on all containers of chemicals that you use. If there are no precautions stated on the label, ask your teacher what precautions to follow. Do not taste any chemicals or items

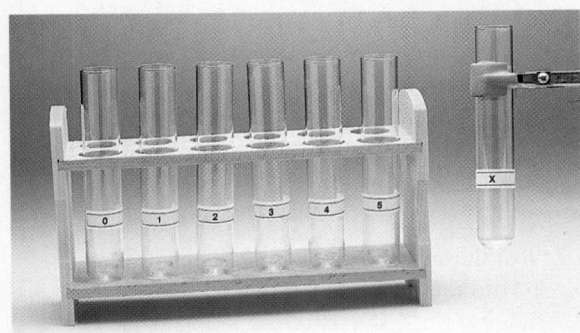

FIGURE A

used in the laboratory. Never return left-overs to their original containers; take only small amounts to avoid wasting supplies.

PREPARATION

1. Prepare a data table in your lab notebook like the one shown below. If you are using a spectrophotometer, add a fifth row to your table and label the first box in the fifth row *Measurements*. You will also need space for calculations.

2. Label seven test tubes *0, 1, 2, 3, 4, 5,* and *Unknown*, as shown in Figure A. Label the beaker *Waste*.

3. If you will be using a spectrophotometer, turn it on now because it must warm up for approximately 10 min.

4. Using a periodic table, determine the molar mass of $FeCl_3 \cdot 6H_2O$. Record the mass in your lab notebook.

5. Perform the necessary calculations to determine the number of grams of $FeCl_3 \cdot 6H_2O$ needed to make 250 mL of a 0.50 M solution. Record this mass in your lab notebook.

DATA TABLE

Test tube	0	1	2	3	4	5	Unknown
mL 0.50 M $FeCl_3$							
mL H_2O							
Estimates							
Measurements							

PROCEDURE

Solution preparation

1. Measure the appropriate mass of $FeCl_3 \cdot 6H_2O$, using a balance. Be sure to measure the mass to the nearest 0.01 g. Record the mass used in your lab notebook. Add 25 mL of 1.0 M HCl to the $FeCl_3 \cdot 6H_2O$. Dilute this mixture to 250 mL with distilled water.

2. Set the test tubes in a test-tube rack. Using a graduated cylinder, fill each test tube with the appropriate solutions listed in Table 1.

TABLE 1

Test tube	0	1	2	3	4	5
Water (mL)	10	8	6	4	2	0
$FeCl_3$ (mL)	0	2	4	6	8	10

Colorimetric estimation and measurement

3. Estimate the intensity of the color of your solutions on a scale from 0 (distilled water in test tube 0) to 1.0 (undiluted solution in test tube 5). To make comparisons easier, hold a piece of white paper behind the test tubes you are comparing. Record these values in your data table under *Estimates*. Comparing the unknown and known solutions, estimate the unknown solution's concentration. If you are not using a spectrophotometer, proceed to step 8.

4. Check with your teacher about whether you should evaluate your sample by using measures of absorbance or percent transmittance. If you are using a spectrophotometer, set it up and calibrate it.

Spectrophotometer—Percent transmittance or absorbance

a. Check to be certain that the spectrophotometer has warmed up for about 10 min.

b. With the sample compartment empty and the lid closed, adjust the %T dial to 0%, as shown in Figure B on the next page.

c. Turn the right knob clockwise until you meet resistance.

d. Insert a clean and dry cuvette.

2. To prepare the unknown solution (0.25 M $FeCl_3$), add 67.58 g of $FeCl_3 \cdot 6H_2O$ to 500 mL of distilled water. Add a few drops of 1.0 M HCl until the cloudiness disappears. Add distilled water gradually, stopping to add HCl at the sign of any cloudiness, until the solution is diluted to 1.00 L of solution.

3. For improved results, students can use 10 mL volumetric pipets instead of graduated cylinders in the dilution steps. Be sure to use pipets with bulbs. Never let students pipet with their mouth.

REQUIRED PRECAUTIONS

- Safety goggles and a lab apron must be worn at all times.
- Read all safety precautions, and discuss them with your students.
- Students should not handle concentrated acid solutions.
- Wear safety goggles, a face shield, impermeable gloves, and a lab apron when you prepare the HCl. Work in a fume hood known to be in good operating condition and with another person standing nearby to call for help in case of an emergency. Be sure you are within a 30 s walk from a safety shower and eyewash station known to be in good operating condition.
- In case of an acid spill, dilute the spill with water. Then mop up the spill with wet cloths or a wet cloth mop designated for spill cleanup. Wear disposable plastic gloves while cleaning spills.

TECHNIQUES TO DEMONSTRATE

Show students how to operate the spectrophotometer if one is being used. Emphasize the need to check the calibration of the instrument after each measurement and to wipe the cuvettes with lint-free wipes. Students should prepare all of their dilutions before using the instrument.

Make sure students add the proper amount of $FeCl_3 \cdot 6H_2O$, 33.79 g, to make their 0.5 M stock solution. If students try other amounts, it could be a sign that they have forgotten to factor in the mass of water in the hydrated compound.

PRE-LAB DISCUSSION

Discuss the concept of molarity, with an emphasis on how to calculate the concentration of a solution that is made through dilution. Relate the use of spectrophotometry and colorimetry to the discussion of atomic structure and electron excitation in Chapter 4. Be certain students understand how to make and use a standard curve.

DISPOSAL

Set out a disposal container for the solutions. When all of the solutions and rinses have been added to the container, add an excess of 1.0 M NaOH to precipitate the iron as insoluble $Fe(OH)_3$. Filter and put the precipitate in the trash. Neutralize the filtrate with 1.0 M acid until its pH is between 5 and 9, and pour it down the drain.

ANALYSIS AND INTERPRETATION—ANSWERS

NOTE: Omit Analysis and Interpretation item 4 unless percent transmittance was measured.
1. Test tube 0: 0.0 M
Test tube 1: 0.1 M
Test tube 2: 0.2 M
Test tube 3: 0.3 M
Test tube 4: 0.4 M
Test tube 5: 0.5 M

2. The estimated concentration is 0.25 M because the solution seems darker than the contents of test tube 2 but lighter than the contents of test tube 3.

3. The results might be better because the volumes and amounts of solution would be measured more precisely with a pipet than with a graduated cylinder.

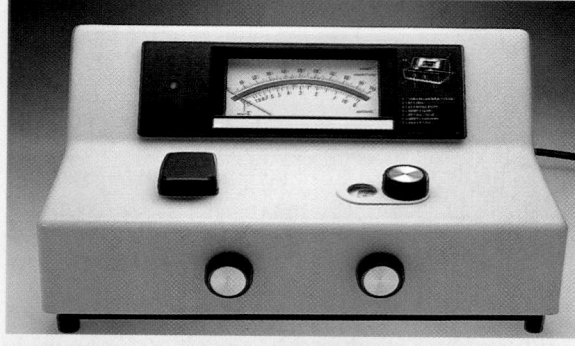
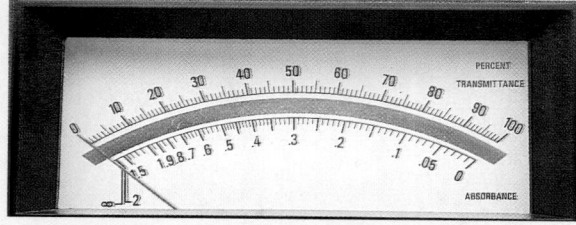

FIGURE B

e. Turn the wavelength knob to 625 nm (yellow light), and then turn the right front knob until the %T dial reads 100%.
Never wipe cuvettes with paper towels or scrub them with a test-tube brush. Use only lint-free tissues, which will not scratch the cuvette's surface. The outside of the cuvette must be completely dry, as shown in Figure C, before it is placed inside the instrument, or you will get an invalid reading.

5. Remove the cuvette and rinse it several times with distilled water, discarding the rinses in the waste beaker. Fill the cuvette approximately three-quarters full with the solution from test tube 1. Be sure the outside of the cuvette is dry by wiping it clean with a lint-free tissue. Place the cuvette in the sample compartment and place the cover over the cuvette.

6. Remove the cuvette and pour sample 1 back into the test tube. Rinse the cuvette several times with distilled water, discarding the rinses in the waste beaker. Repeat the procedure for samples from test tubes 2–5. Be sure to dry the outside of the cuvette with a lint-free tissue after each transfer. Between samples 3 and 4 check the calibration of the meter as follows: If you

are measuring percent transmittance, retest the distilled water to be certain the reading is 100%; if you are measuring absorbance, retest the solution from test tube 5 to be sure the reading is 1. If the calibration test does not give the appropriate reading, start over with Procedure step 4. Otherwise, continue with Procedure step 7.

7. Test the sample of unknown concentration, and record the results in your data table.

CLEANUP AND DISPOSAL

8. Dispose of the solutions in the container designated by your teacher. Rinse the cuvettes several times with distilled water before putting them away. Clean up the lab station and all equipment after use. Wash your hands thoroughly after all work is finished and before you leave the lab.

ANALYSIS AND INTERPRETATION

1. Analyzing Ideas: What are the concentrations of $FeCl_3$ in test tubes 0, 1, 2, 3, 4, and 5?

2. Analyzing Results: What is your estimate for the concentration of the unknown? Explain your answer.

3. Analyzing Methods: Would you have obtained better results if, during the dilution steps, you had used a volumetric pipet that measures exactly 2.00 mL instead of using the graduated cylinder? Explain your answer.

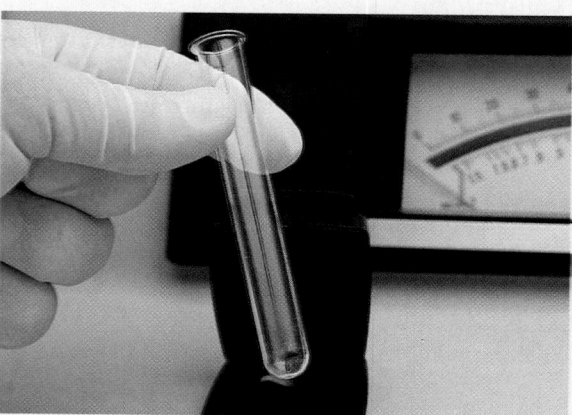

FIGURE C

4. **Organizing Data:** If you used a spectrophoto-meter and measured percent transmittance instead of absorbance, convert to absorbance by using the following equation. Otherwise, go on to Analysis and Interpretation item 5.

$$\text{absorbance} = \log\left(\frac{100}{\text{percent transmittance}}\right)$$

5. **Analyzing Data:** Make a graph of your data with concentration of $FeCl_3$ on the x-axis and absorbance on the y-axis. (If you did not use the spectrophotometer to make your measure-ments, use your values from the *Estimates* part of your data table as absorbance values.)

6. **Analyzing Data:** If your graph is a straight line, write an equation for the line in the following form:

$$y = mx + b$$

If it is not a straight line, explain why, and draw the straight line that comes closest to including all of your data points. Give the equation of this line. (Hint: If you have a graphing calculator, use the [STAT] mode to enter your data, and make a linear regression equation using the LinReg function from the STAT menu.)

7. **Interpreting Graphics:** Using the graph from Analysis and Interpretation item 5 or the equa-tion from Analysis and Interpretation item 6, determine the concentration of the unknown to give the measured absorbance value.

Phenylalanine

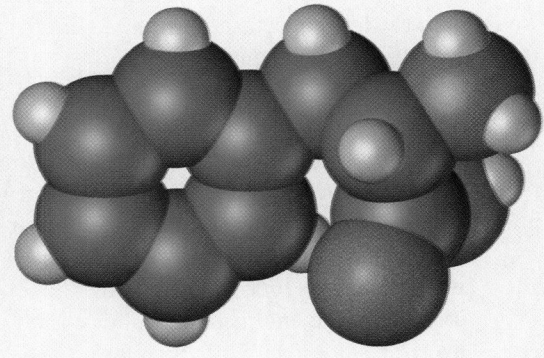

CONCLUSIONS

1. **Applying Conclusions:** A pharmaceutical company produces a 0.30 M solution of $FeCl_3$ for use in a test for the disease phenylketonuria in infants. People who have this disease are unable to break down the amino acid phenylala-nine. The structure of a phenylanine molecule is shown below. The analytical department of the company found that one batch of its product had a concentration of 0.25 M rather than 0.30 M. Which of the following could have caused the problem: too much $FeCl_3$ added to the solution, too little $FeCl_3$ added to the solution, too much water added to the solution, or too little water added to the solution?

EXTENSIONS

1. **Evaluating Methods:** What are some advantages or disadvantages of colorimetry compared with other methods, such as gravimetric analysis?

2. **Relating Ideas:** Absorbance describes how much light is blocked by a sample. Transmittance describes how much light passes through a sample. As absorbance values go up, how do transmittance values change?

3. **Designing Experiments:** What possible sources of error can you identify with the procedure used in this lab? If you can think of ways to eliminate the errors, ask your teacher to approve your plan, and run the procedure again.

4. **Predicting Outcomes:** How would your absorbance or percent transmittance values for the unknown solution change if someone added an additional yellow-colored compound along with the $FeCl_3$?

5. **Evaluating Methods:** If you used a spectropho-tometer, calculate the percent error for each of your estimates of absorbance compared with the values given by the equipment. (Hint: Divide each absorbance measurement by the largest measurement so that they will be on a scale of 0 to 1.00, just as your estimates are.)

4. The following is a representative sample calculation of absorbance for a solution with a 75% transmittance:

$$\text{absorbance} = \log\left(\frac{100}{75}\right) = 0.125$$

5.

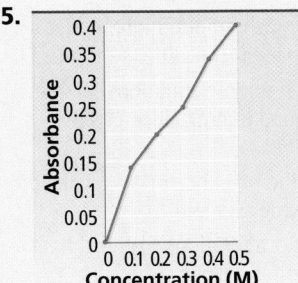

6. Answers will vary slightly. For the sample data, the graphing calculator gives the following regression equa-tion, rounded for significant figures.

$$\text{absorbance} = 0.74(\text{concentration}) + 0.03$$

7. unknown concentration =
$$\frac{0.222 - 0.03}{0.74} = 0.26 \text{ M}$$

CONCLUSIONS—ANSWERS

1. The problem is that the solution is too dilute. This could be due to too little $FeCl_3$ or too much water.

EXTENSIONS—ANSWERS

NOTE: Omit item 6 if spectropho-tometers and colorimeters are unavailable.

1. There is less room for human error in colorimetry because volumes and masses aren't measured and because a precipitate does not have to be purified. Colorimetry also leaves the sample intact.

2. Transmittance values decrease.

3. Students' suggestions for improv-ing the procedure will vary. Be sure answers are safe and include care-fully planned procedures.

Continued on page 893D

EXPERIMENT 14-1

MICRO
L A B

OBJECTIVES
Students will

- identify and describe positive tests for Fe^{3+}, Ca^{2+}, Cl^-, and SO_4^{2-} ions.
- distinguish among high, moderate, and low concentrations of ions.
- write net ionic equations for the reactions that produce positive tests.
- infer the presence of a specific ion in a water sample.
- relate observations to the chemical properties of ions.

RECOMMENDED TIME
1 lab period

MATERIALS
(for each lab group)
- 24-well microplate lid
- fine-tipped dropper bulbs, labeled, with solutions, 10
- paper towels
- solution 1: reference, 1 mL
- solution 2: distilled water, 1 mL
- solution 3: tap water, 1 mL
- solution 4: bottled spring water, 1 mL
- solution 5: local river or lake water, 1 mL
- solution 6: solution X, 1 mL
- solution A: NaSCN solution, 1–2 mL
- solution B: $Na_2C_2O_4$ solution, 1–2 mL
- solution C: $AgNO_3$ solution, 1–2 mL
- solution D: $Sr(NO_3)_2$ solution, 1–2 mL
- white paper, 1 sheet

OPTIONAL
- overhead projector

ADDITIONAL MATERIALS FOR EXTENSIONS
(may be requested by students)
- fine-tipped dropper bulbs for acquiring additional samples, 6 or 7 (for Extension 1)

Testing Water

OBJECTIVES

- *Observe* chemical reactions involving aqueous solutions of ions.
- *Relate* observations of chemical properties to the presence of ions.
- *Infer* whether an ion is present in a water sample.
- *Apply* concepts concerning aqueous solutions of ions.

MATERIALS

- **24-well microplate lid**
- **fine-tipped dropper bulbs, labeled, with solutions, 10**
- **overhead projector (optional)**
- **paper towels**
- **solution 1: reference (all ions)**
- **solution 2: distilled water (no ions)**
- **solution 3: tap water (may have ions)**
- **solution 4: bottled spring water (may have ions)**
- **solution 5: local river or lake water (may have ions)**
- **solution 6: solution X, prepared by your teacher (may have ions)**
- **solution A: NaSCN solution (Fe^{3+} test)**
- **solution B: $Na_2C_2O_4$ solution (Ca^{2+} test)**
- **solution C: $AgNO_3$ solution (Cl^- test)**
- **solution D: $Sr(NO_3)_2$ solution (SO_4^{2-} test)**
- **white paper**

BACKGROUND

The presence of ions in an aqueous solution, even when the ions are present in small amounts, changes the physical and chemical properties of that solution so that it is no longer the same as pure water. For example, if a sample of water contains enough Mg^{2+} or Ca^{2+} ions, something unusual happens when you use soap to wash something in it. Instead of forming lots of bubbles and lather, the soap forms an insoluble white substance that floats on top of the water. This problem, created by hard water, is common in places where the water supply contains many minerals.

Aqueous solutions of other ions, such as Pb^{2+} and Co^{2+}, can be poisonous because these ions tend to accumulate in body tissues. Lead plumbing pipes in some older houses may introduce Pb^{2+} into water used for drinking and cooking because the lead metal in the pipes slowly ionizes and dissolves. The plumbing systems of such houses should be converted to another type of pipe, such as copper or polyvinyl chloride.

Because many sources of water contain harmful or unwanted substances, it is important to be able to find out what dissolved substances are present. In this experiment, you will test a variety of water samples for the presence of four ions: Fe^{3+}, Ca^{2+}, Cl^-, and SO_4^{2-}. Some of the water samples may contain these ions at very low concentrations, so be sure to make very careful observations.

SAFETY

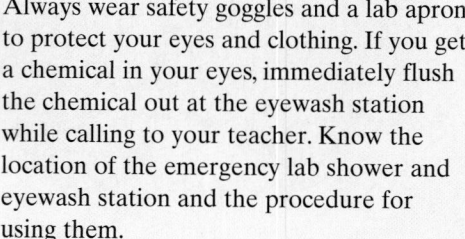

Always wear safety goggles and a lab apron to protect your eyes and clothing. If you get a chemical in your eyes, immediately flush the chemical out at the eyewash station while calling to your teacher. Know the location of the emergency lab shower and eyewash station and the procedure for using them.

Do not touch any chemicals. If you get a chemical on your skin or clothing, wash the chemical off at the sink while calling to your teacher. Make sure you carefully read the labels and follow the precautions on all containers of chemicals that you use. If there are no precautions stated on the label, ask your teacher what precautions to follow. Do not taste any chemicals or items used in the laboratory. Never return leftovers to their original containers; take only small amounts to avoid wasting supplies.

Call your teacher in the event of a spill. Spills should be cleaned up promptly according to your teacher's directions.

PREPARATION

1. Copy the data table below into your lab notebook, and record all your observations in it.

2. Place the 24-well plate lid in front of you on a piece of white paper or other white background, and align it as shown in Figure A. Label the columns and rows as shown in Figure A. The coordinates shown will be used to designate the individual circles. For example, the circle in the top right corner would be designated 1-D, and the circle in the lower left corner would be designated 6-A.

PROCEDURE

1. Obtain labeled dropper bulbs containing the 6 different solutions from your teacher.

FIGURE A
Label the sheet of paper that is underneath the 24-well plate to keep track of where each solution is placed.

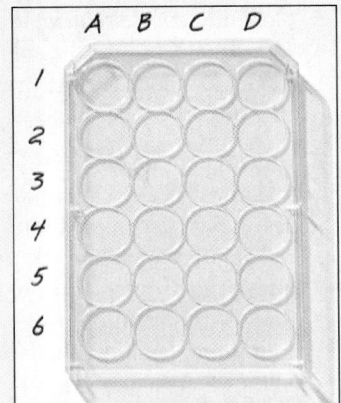

2. Place a drop of the solution from bulb 1 in circles 1-A, 1-B, 1-C, and 1-D (the top row). Solution 1 contains all four of the dissolved ions, so these drops will show what a **positive** test for each of the ions looks like. **Be careful to keep the solutions in the appropriate circles. Any spills will cause poor results.**

3. Place a drop of the solution from bulb 2 in circles 2-A, 2-B, 2-C, and 2-D (the second row). Solution 2 is distilled water and should contain none of the ions, so it will be used to show what a **negative** test for each of the ions looks like.

4. Place a drop from bulb 3 in each of the circles in row 3, a drop from bulb 4 in each of the circles in row 4, and so on with bulbs 5 and 6. These solutions may or may not contain ions. Bulb 3 contains ordinary tap water. Bulb 4 contains bottled spring water. Bulb 5 contains local river or lake water. Bulb 6 contains solution X, which was prepared by your teacher.

- conductivity tester (for Extension 5)
- filter paper, 4 pieces (for Extension 5)
- freezer (for Extension 5)
- funnel (for Extension 5)
- thermometer, alcohol-filled (for Extension 5)

SOLUTION/MATERIALS PREPARATION

1. Fill the 10 fine-tipped dropper bulbs with 1 mL of each of the 10 solutions and label them as listed above. Fewer bulbs are needed if students share.

2. To make 15 mL of solution 1 (reference), dissolve 0.1 g $CaSO_4$ (plaster of paris) and 2.0 g of $FeCl_3 \cdot 6H_2O$ in 15 mL of solution. NOTE: This will make a saturated calcium sulfate solution. If there is some undissolved $CaSO_4$ in the bottom of the solution, filter it out before putting the solution in the dropper bulbs.

3. To make solution 6 (solution X), you can use any of the four ions in whatever amounts you choose. Remember that calcium together with sulfate is only slightly soluble, so if you include both of these ions in your solution X, you will need to filter it before giving it to students. Be sure to keep track of which ions you add so that you can evaluate students' results.

4. To make 25 mL of solution A (0.5 M NaSCN solution), dissolve 1.01 g NaSCN in 25 mL of solution.

5. To make 25 mL of solution B (0.5 M $Na_2C_2O_4$ solution), dissolve 1.68 g $Na_2C_2O_4$ in 25 mL of solution.

6. To make 25 mL of solution C (0.1 M $AgNO_3$ solution), dissolve 0.43 g $AgNO_3$ in 25 mL of solution.

7. To make 25 mL of solution D (0.5 M $Sr(NO_3)_2$ solution), dissolve 2.64 g $Sr(NO_3)_2$ in 25 mL of solution.

8. To make conductivity testers, see the instructions on page 876,

DATA TABLE

Test for:	Fe^{3+}	Ca^{2+}	Cl^-	SO_4^{2-}
Reacting with:	SCN^-	$C_2O_4^{2-}$	Ag^+	Sr^{2+}
Reference (all 4 ions)				
Distilled H_2O (control—no ions)				
Tap water				
Bottled spring water				
River or lake water				
Solution X				

immediately following the equipment and chemical lists.

9. For Extension 5, students may ask for materials other than those listed above.

REQUIRED PRECAUTIONS
- Safety goggles and a lab apron must be worn at all times.
- Read all safety precautions and discuss them with your students.
- In case of a spill, use a dampened cloth or paper towel (or more than one towel if necessary) to mop up the spill. Then rinse the cloth in running water at the sink, wring it out thoroughly, and put it in the trash.

TECHNIQUES TO DEMONSTRATE
Make sure that students understand how to set up the grid for testing solutions 1–6 and how the grid relates to the data table they copied into their notebooks.

PRE-LAB DISCUSSION
Review double-displacement reactions, solubility, precipitates, and equilibria.

DISPOSAL
Save leftover $AgNO_3$ solution for reuse or treat with an excess of 1 M NaOH to precipitate the silver as the hydrated oxide. Filter. Neutralize the filtrate with 0.5 M acid and pour it down the drain. After the Ag_2O has dried, wrap it in newspaper and put it in the trash.

Combine all other solutions and precipitates, and filter them. Pour the filtrate down the drain. After the combined precipitates dry, wrap them in newspaper and put them in the trash.

ANALYSIS AND INTERPRETATION—ANSWERS
1. Test A:
$Fe^{3+}(aq) + NaSCN(aq) \longrightarrow$
$\quad Na^+(aq) + Fe(SCN)^{2+}(aq)$, red color

Test B:
$Ca^{2+}(aq) + Na_2C_2O_4(aq) \longrightarrow$
$\quad 2Na^+(aq) + CaC_2O_4(s)$, precipitate

5. Now that each circle contains a drop of solution to be analyzed, use the solutions in bulbs A, B, C, and D to test for the presence or absence of the ions.

6. Bulb A contains NaSCN, sodium thiocyanate, which will react with any Fe^{3+} present to form $Fe(SCN)^{2+}$, a complex ion that forms a deep red solution. **Holding the tip of the bulb 1–2 cm above the drop of water to be tested,** add one drop of this solution to the drop of reference solution in circle 1-A and one drop to the distilled water in circle 2-A below it. Circle 1-A should show a positive test, and circle 2-A should show a negative test. Record in your data table your observations about what the positive and negative tests look like.

7. Use the NaSCN solution in bulb A to test the rest of the water drops in column A (the far left column) of the plate to determine whether any of them contains the Fe^{3+} ion. Record your observations in your data table. For each of the tests in which the ion was found to be present, specify whether it seemed to be present at a high, moderate, or low concentration. (If the evidence was quite visible, assume the ion was at a high concentration. If it was somewhat visible, assume the ion was at a moderate concentration. If the evidence was barely visible, assume a low concentration of the ion.)

8. Bulb B contains $Na_2C_2O_4$, sodium oxalate, which will undergo a displacement reaction with the Ca^{2+} ion to form an insoluble precipitate. **Holding the tip of the bulb 1–2 cm above the drop of water to be tested,** add one drop of this solution to the solutions in column B.

9. In your data table, record your observations about what the positive and negative $Na_2C_2O_4$ tests looked like and about whether any of the solutions contained the Ca^{2+} ion. For each of the positive tests, specify whether the Ca^{2+} ion seemed to be present at a high, moderate, or low concentration. A black background may be useful for this test and for the following tests.

10. Bulb C contains $AgNO_3$, silver nitrate, which will undergo a displacement reaction with the Cl^- ion to form an insoluble precipitate. **Holding the tip of the bulb 1–2 cm above the drop of water to be tested,** add one drop of this solution to the solutions in column C.

11. In your data table, record your observations about what the positive and negative $AgNO_3$ tests looked like and about whether any of the solutions contained the Cl^- ion. For each of the tests in which the ion was found to be present, specify whether it seemed to be present at a high, moderate, or low concentration.

12. Bulb D contains $Sr(NO_3)_2$, strontium nitrate, which will undergo a displacement reaction with the SO_4^{2-} ion to form an insoluble precipitate. **Holding the tip of the bulb 1–2 cm above the drop of water to be tested,** add one drop of this solution to the solutions in column D.

13. In your notebook, record your observations about what the positive and negative $Sr(NO_3)_2$ tests looked like and about whether any of the solutions contained the SO_4^{2-} ion. For each of the tests in which the ion was found to be present, specify whether it seemed to be present at a high, moderate, or low concentration.

14. If some of the tests are difficult to discern, place your plate on an overhead projector, if one is available. Examine the drops carefully for any signs of cloudiness. Be sure your line of vision is 10–15° above the plane of the lid, as shown in Figure B, so that you are looking at the drops from the side. Compare each drop tested with the control drops (the distilled water) in row 2. If any signs of cloudiness are detected in a tested sample, it is due to the Tyndall effect and should be considered a positive test result. Record your results in your lab notebook.

CLEANUP AND DISPOSAL

15. Clean all apparatus and your lab station. Return equipment to its proper place. Dispose of chemicals and solutions in

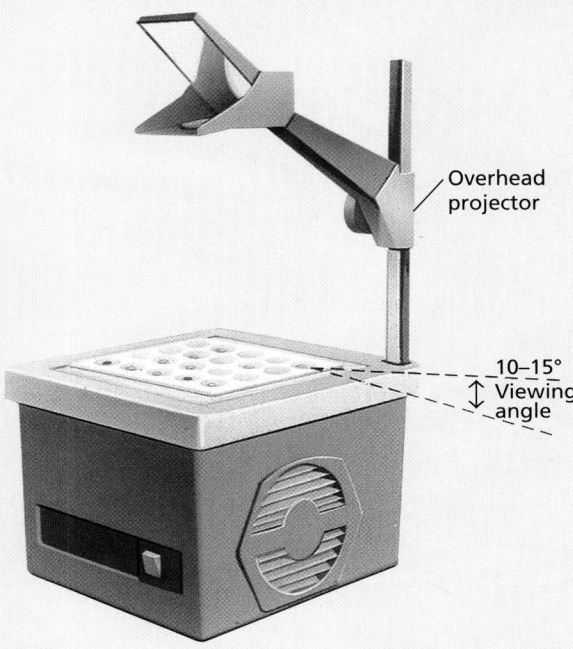

FIGURE B Look at the drops from the side of the well lid when you determine whether the drops test positive for an ion.

the containers designated by your teacher. Do not pour any chemicals down the drain or in the trash unless your teacher directs you to do so. Wash your hands thoroughly before you leave the lab and after all work is finished.

ANALYSIS AND INTERPRETATION

1. **Organizing Ideas:** Write the balanced chemical equations for each of the positive tests. Describe what each positive test looked like.

2. **Organizing Ideas:** Write the net ionic equation for each of the positive tests. (Hint: Net ionic equations are discussed in Chapter 14.)

3. **Analyzing Methods:** Why was it important to hold the dropper containing the testing solution 1–2 cm above each of the drops of water samples? Why was it important to be sure that the water samples were not spilled and accidentally mixed?

4. **Analyzing Methods:** Why was it important to use a control in the experiment? Why was distilled water used as the control?

CONCLUSIONS

1. **Organizing Conclusions:** List the solutions tested and the ions you found in each. Include notes on whether the concentration of each ion was high, moderate, or low, depending on the color or the amount of precipitate formed.

2. **Applying Conclusions and Predicting Outcomes:** Using your test results, predict which water sample would be the "hardest." Explain your reasoning.

EXTENSIONS

1. **Applying Conclusions and Predicting Outcomes:** Try to collect water samples from a variety of sources. Also collect rainwater, melted snow, swimming pool water, running water from creeks and streams, well water, and, if you're near the coast, some salt water from the ocean. Before testing the water, make a chart and try to predict which ions you will find in each sample.

2. **Relating Ideas:** Consider the substances used in the tests for this experiment and your results. What can you say about the solubilities of most sodium compounds and most nitrate compounds? Explain your reasoning without referring to a chart of solubility rules.

3. **Predicting Outcomes and Resolving Discrepancies:** Suppose you decided to determine the amount of chloride ion present in the reference solution by evaporating the water and measuring the mass of the residue left behind. If you were left with 0.37 g of white powder, could you safely assume that it was all chloride ions? Explain your reasoning.

4. **Predicting Outcomes and Resolving Discrepancies:** If you were given a sample of a solution that tested positive for sulfate ions but negative for the other three ions in this investigation and you evaporated the water and were left with 0.21 g of white powder, could you safely assume that it was all sulfate ions? Explain your reasoning.

Test C:
$$Cl^-(aq) + AgNO_3(aq) \longrightarrow NO_3^-(aq) + AgCl(s), \text{ precipitate}$$
Test D:
$$SO_4^{2-}(aq) + Sr(NO_3)_2(aq) \longrightarrow 2NO_3^-(aq) + SrSO_4(s), \text{ precipitate}$$

2. Test A:
$$Fe^{3+}(aq) + SCN^-(aq) \longrightarrow Fe(SCN)^{2+}(aq)$$

Test B:
$$Ca^{2+}(aq) + C_2O_4^{2-}(aq) \longrightarrow CaC_2O_4(s)$$
Test C:
$$Cl^-(aq) + Ag^+(aq) \longrightarrow AgCl(s)$$
Test D:
$$SO_4^{2-}(aq) + Sr^{2+}(aq) \longrightarrow SrSO_4(s)$$

3. Holding the dropper 1–2 cm above the wells prevents accidental contamination. If any of the sample solutions were accidentally mixed, you could not be sure whether positive tests were due to one solution, the other, or both.

4. A control was necessary to show what the solutions look like when there is no reaction. Distilled water was chosen as a control because it should have had none of the ions tested present in it.

CONCLUSIONS—ANSWERS

1. Students' answers will vary, depending on the source of the water samples. All students should indicate that the reference solution had all the ions present and the distilled water had none of the ions present.

2. Students' answers will vary, depending on the sources of the water samples. The solution that showed the strongest test for calcium ions is likely to be "harder" than the other samples because calcium ions are one cause of hardness in water. Some students may suggest that unless the solutions are tested for the presence of magnesium ions, you cannot be certain which is the hardest.

Continued on page 893E

Volumetric Analysis

Volumetric analysis, the quantitative determination of the concentration of a solution, is achieved by adding a substance of known concentration to a substance of unknown concentration until the reaction between them is complete. The most common application of volumetric analysis is titration.

A buret is used in titrations. The solution with the known concentration is usually in the buret. The solution with the unknown concentration is usually in the Erlenmeyer flask. A few drops of a visual indicator also are added to the flask. The solution in the buret is then added to the flask until the indicator changes color, signaling that the reaction between the two solutions is complete. Then, using the volumetric data obtained and the balanced chemical equation for the reaction, the unknown concentration is calculated.

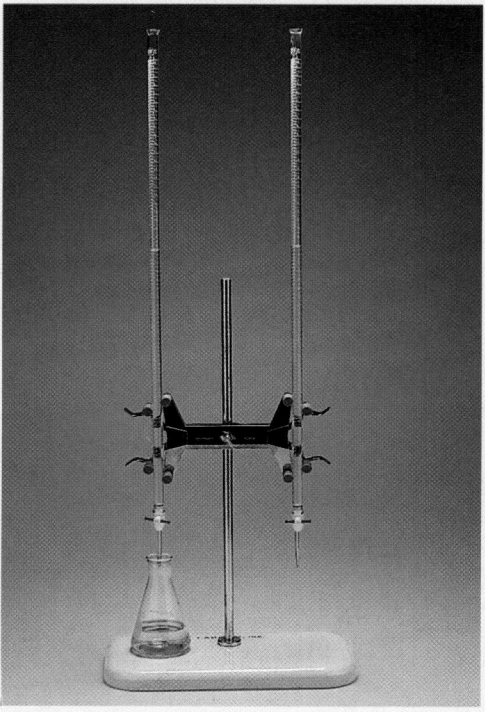

FIGURE A

GENERAL SAFETY

Always wear safety goggles and a lab apron to protect your eyes and clothing. If you get a chemical in your eyes, immediately flush the chemical out at the eyewash station while calling to your teacher. Know the location of the emergency lab shower and eyewash station and the procedure for using them.

The general setup for a titration is shown in Figure A. The steps for setting up this technique follow.

ASSEMBLING THE APPARATUS

1. Attach a buret clamp to a ring stand.

2. Thoroughly wash and rinse a buret. If water droplets cling to the walls of the buret, wash it again and gently scrub the inside walls with a buret brush.

3. Attach the buret to one side of the buret clamp.

4. Place a Erlenmeyer flask for waste solutions under the buret tip as shown in Figure A.

FIGURE B

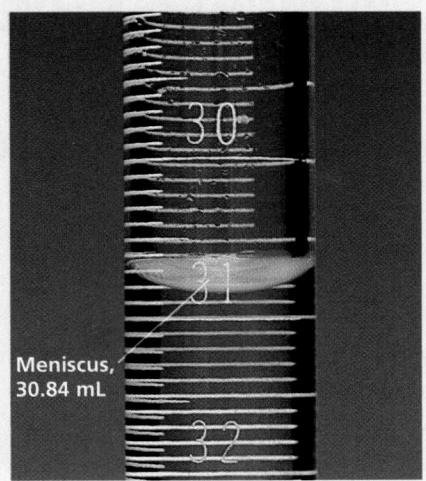

Meniscus,
30.84 mL

FIGURE C

OPERATING THE STOPCOCK

1. The stopcock should be operated with the left hand. This method gives better control but may prove awkward at first for right-handed students. The handle should be moved with the thumb and first two fingers of the left hand, as shown in Figure B.

2. Rotate the stopcock back and forth. It should move freely and easily. If it sticks or will not move, ask your teacher for assistance. Turn the stopcock to the closed position. Use a wash bottle to add 10 mL of distilled water to the buret. Rotate the stopcock to the open position. The water should come out in a steady stream. If no water comes out or if the stream of water is blocked, ask your teacher to check the stopcock for clogs.

FILLING THE BURET

1. To fill the buret, place a funnel in the top of the buret. Slowly and carefully pour the solution of known concentration from a beaker into the funnel. Open the stopcock, and allow some of the solution to drain into the waste beaker. Then add enough solution to the buret to raise the level above the zero mark, but do not allow the solution to overflow.

READING THE BURET

1. Drain the buret until the bottom of the meniscus is on the zero mark or within the calibrated portion of the buret. If the solution level is not at zero, record the exact reading. If you start from the zero mark, your final buret reading will equal the amount of solution added. Remember, burets can be read to the second decimal place. Burets are designed to read the volume of liquid delivered to the flask, so numbers increase as you read downward from the top. For example, the meniscus in Figure C is at 30.84 mL, not 31.16 mL.

2. Replace the waste beaker with an Erlenmeyer flask containing a measured amount of the solution of unknown concentration.

An acid-base titration is used in Experiment 16-4 to determine the concentration of acetic acid in vinegar. Experiment 16-1 is an example of a back-titration applied to an acid-base reaction; it can be performed on a larger scale if micropipets are replaced with burets. Experiment 19-1 combines a redox reaction with the titration technique to determine the concentration of Fe^{3+}.

EXPERIMENT 16-1

OBJECTIVES
Students will
- use appropriate lab safety procedures.
- measure volume by using graduated cylinders.
- measure volume with a buret or by calibrating a dropper to measure the number of drops per milliliter.
- measure mass by using a laboratory balance.
- observe the reaction of $CaCO_3$ with a carefully measured excess of acid.
- perform a back-titration (titrating the excess acid with a base).
- apply stoichiometry concepts to determine the amounts of each reactant for the neutralization reaction and $CaCO_3$ reaction.

RECOMMENDED TIME
1–2 lab periods (shorter if eggshells are prepared in advance)

MATERIALS
(for each lab group)
- 1 mL phenolphthalein solution
- 15 mL 1.00 M NaOH
- 15 mL 1.00 M HCl
- 10 mL graduated cylinder
- 100 mL beaker
- 50 mL bottle, or small Erlenmeyer flask
- distilled water
- eggshell
- balance
- desiccator (optional)
- drying oven
- forceps
- microscale pipets or medicine droppers, 3
- mortar and pestle
- weighing paper
- white paper for background

How Much Calcium Carbonate Is in an Eggshell?

OBJECTIVES

- *Determine* the amount of calcium carbonate present in an eggshell.

- *Relate* experimental titration measurements to a balanced chemical equation.

- *Infer* a conclusion from experimental data.

- *Apply* reaction-stoichiometry concepts.

MATERIALS

- **1.00 M HCl**
- **1.00 M NaOH**
- **10 mL graduated cylinder**
- **50 mL micro solution bottle, or small Erlenmeyer flask**
- **100 mL beaker**
- **balance**
- **dessicator (optional)**
- **distilled water**

- **drying oven**
- **eggshell**
- **forceps**
- **mortar and pestle**
- **phenolphthalein solution**
- **thin-stemmed pipets or medicine droppers, 3**
- **weighing paper**

BACKGROUND

The calcium carbonate content of eggshells can be easily determined by means of an acid/base back-titration, using some of the techniques and calculations described in Chapter 16. In this back-titration, a carefully measured excess of a strong acid will react with the calcium carbonate. The resulting solution will be titrated with a strong base to determine how much acid remains unreacted. From this measurement, the amount of acid that reacted with the eggshell and the amount of calcium carbonate it reacted with can be determined. Phenolphthalein will be used as an indicator to signal the endpoint of the titration.

SAFETY

Always wear safety goggles and a lab apron to protect your eyes and clothing. If you get a chemical in your eyes, immediately flush the chemical out at the eyewash station while calling to your teacher. Know the location of the emergency lab shower and eyewash station and the procedure for using them.

Do not touch any chemicals. If you get a chemical on your skin or clothing, wash the chemical off at the sink while calling to your teacher. Make sure you carefully read the labels and follow the precautions on all containers of chemicals that you use. If there are no precautions stated on the label, ask your teacher what precautions to follow. Do not taste any chemicals or items used in the laboratory. Never return leftovers to their original containers; take only small amounts to avoid wasting supplies.

The oven used in this experiment is hot; use tongs to remove beakers from the oven because heated glassware does not always look hot.

 Call your teacher in the event of an acid or base spill. Acid or base spills should be cleaned up promptly, according to your teacher's instructions.

PREPARATION

1. Remove the white and the yolk from an egg as shown in Figure A and dispose of them according to your teacher's directions. Wash the shell with distilled water and carefully peel all the membranes from the inside of the shell. Place *all* of the shell in a premassed beaker and dry the shell in the drying oven at 110°C for about 15 min. Continue with Preparation steps 2–5 while the eggshell is drying.

2. Make data and calculations tables like the ones below in your lab notebook.

3. Put exactly 5.0 mL of water in the 10.0 mL graduated cylinder. Record this volume in the data table in your lab notebook. Fill the first thin-stemmed pipet with water. This pipet should be labeled *acid*. **Do not use this pipet for the base solution.** Holding the pipet vertically, add 20 drops of water to the cylinder. **For the best results, keep the sizes of the drops as even as possible throughout this investigation.** Record the new volume of water in the graduated cylinder in the first data table under Trial 1.

FIGURE A

4. Without emptying the graduated cylinder, add an additional 20 drops from the pipet as before, and record the new volume for Trial 2. Repeat this procedure once more for Trial 3.

5. Repeat Preparation steps 3 and 4 for the second thin-stemmed pipet. Label this pipet *base*. **Do not use this pipet for the acid solution.**

6. Make sure that the three trials produce data that are similar to each other. If one is greatly different from the others, perform Preparation steps 3–5 again. If you're still waiting for the eggshell in the drying oven, calculate and record the total volume of the drops and the average volume per drop.

Graduated Cylinder Readings (Pipet Calibration: Steps 3–5)

Trial	Initial—acid pipet	Final—acid pipet	Initial—base pipet	Final—base pipet
1				
2				
3				

Total volume of drops—acid pipet _____
Average volume of each drop _____
Total volume of drops—base pipet _____
Average volume of each drop _____

Titration: Steps

Mass of entire eggshell	
Mass of ground eggshell sample	
Number of drops of 1.00 M HCl added	150 drops
Volume of 1.00 M HCl added	
Number of drops of 1.00 M NaOH added	
Volume of 1.00 M NaOH added	
Volume of 1.00 M HCl reacting with NaOH	
Volume of 1.00 M HCl reacting with eggshell	
Number of mol of HCl reacting with eggshell	
Number of mol of $CaCO_3$ reacting with HCl	
Mass of $CaCO_3$ in eggshell sample	
% of $CaCO_3$ in eggshell sample	

MACRO-SCALE OPTION
- 100 mL 1.00 M NaOH
- 100 mL 1.00 M HCl
- burets

MICRO-SCALE OPTION
- 15 mL 1.00 M NaOH
- 15 mL 1.00 M HCl
- medicine droppers or thin-stemmed pipets, 3

SOLUTION/MATERIAL PREPARATION

1. Desiccators are optional. Fewer balances, mortars, pestles, and graduated cylinders will be required if students share.

2. If droppers or pipets are labeled as *acid, base,* and *indicator,* these can be re-used from class to class. For more reproducible drop sizes, place the pipet or dropper bulb in a tubing screw-clamp. Each turn of the screw will force out a reproducible drop.

3. To prepare 1.00 M HCl, add 82.6 mL of concentrated HCl to enough distilled water to make 1.00 L of solution. Add the acid slowly, and stop to stir it in order to avoid overheating.

4. To prepare 1.00 M NaOH, add 40.0 g of NaOH pellets to enough distilled water to make 1.00 L of solution. Add a few pellets at a time, and stop to stir it in order to avoid overheating.

5. To prepare phenolphthalein solution, dissolve 1.00 g phenolphthalein in 50.0 mL of denatured alcohol, and add 50.0 mL of distilled water.

6. Provide miscellaneous shells, such as clam, oyster, and snail shells, for Extension item 4. Provide students with chalk for Extension item 6.

REQUIRED PRECAUTIONS
- Safety goggles and a lab apron must be worn at all times.
- Tie back long hair and loose clothing when working in the lab.

- Read all safety cautions, and discuss them with your students.
- Students should not handle concentrated acid solutions.
- Wear safety goggles, a face shield, impermeable gloves, and a lab apron when you prepare the HCl and NaOH. Work in a hood known to be in operating condition and have another person stand by to call for help in case of an emergency. Be sure you are within a 30 second walk from a safety shower and eyewash station known to be in operating condition.
- In case of an acid or base spill, dilute the spill with water. Then mop up the spill with wet cloths or a wet cloth mop designated for spill cleanup. Wear disposable plastic gloves while cleaning spills. Designate separate cloths or mops for acid and base spills. For liability reasons, it may be best to avoid having students handle spills themselves.
- As always, it is very important for students to keep the chemicals in this lab off their skin and to keep their hands and fingers away from their faces and mouths at all times.
- Remind students that beakers in the oven will be hot and that they should use tongs to remove them. Broken glass should be disposed of in a separate container, away from regular waste.
- As always, students should wash their hands thoroughly when finished.

PRE-LAB DISCUSSION
Be sure to explain the nature of a back-titration. Students may not realize that the amount of $CaCO_3$ is being measured indirectly.

PROCEDURAL CHANGES
- To run this experiment as a *macro* experiment using burets instead of pipets, note the following changes.

FIGURE B
Use a mortar and pestle to grind the eggshell

7. Remove the eggshell and beaker from the oven. Cool them in a dessicator. Record the mass of the entire eggshell in the second table. Place half of the shell into the clean mortar and grind it to a very fine powder as shown in Figure B. This will save time when you are dissolving the eggshell. (If time permits, dry the powder again and cool it in the dessicator.)

PROCEDURE

1. Measure the mass of a piece of weighing paper. Transfer about 0.1 g of ground eggshell to a piece of weighing paper, and measure the eggshell's mass as accurately as possible. Record the mass in the second data table. Place this eggshell sample into a clean 50 mL micro solution bottle (or Erlenmeyer flask).

2. Fill the acid pipet with 1.00 M HCl acid solution, and then empty the pipet into an extra 100 mL beaker. Label the beaker *waste*. Fill the base pipet with the 1.00 M NaOH base solution, and then empty the pipet into the waste beaker.

3. Fill the acid pipet once more with 1.00 M HCl. Holding the acid pipet vertically, add exactly 150 drops of 1.00 M HCl to the bottle or flask containing the eggshell, as shown in Figure C. Swirl gently for 3 to 4 min. Observe the reaction taking place. Wash down the sides of the flask with about 10 mL of distilled water. Using a third pipet, add two drops of phenolphthalein solution.

Acid pipet

Ground eggshell

FIGURE C

4. Fill the base pipet with the 1.00 M NaOH. Slowly add NaOH from the base pipet into the bottle or flask containing the eggshell reaction mixture, as shown in Figure D, until a faint pink color persists in the mixture, even after it is swirled gently. **Be sure to add the base drop by drop, and be certain the drops end up in the reaction mixture and not on the walls of the bottle or flask. Keep careful count of the number of drops used.** Record the number of drops of base used in the second data table.

CLEANUP AND DISPOSAL

5. Clean all apparatus and your lab station. Return the equipment to its proper place. Dispose of chemicals and solutions in the containers designated by your teacher. Do not pour any chemicals down the drain or in the trash unless your teacher directs you to do so. Wash your hands thoroughly before you leave the lab and after all work is finished.

ANALYSIS AND INTERPRETATION

1. **Organizing Ideas:** The calcium carbonate in the eggshell sample undergoes a double-replacement

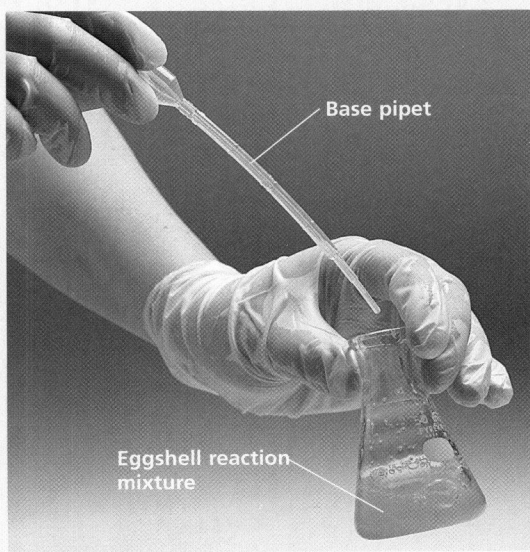

Base pipet

Eggshell reaction mixture

FIGURE D

reaction with the hydrochloric acid in Procedure step 3. Write a balanced chemical equation for this reaction. (Hint: The gas observed was carbon dioxide.)

2. **Organizing Ideas:** Write the balanced chemical equation for the acid/base neutralization of the excess unreacted HCl with the NaOH.

3. **Organizing Data:** Make the necessary calculations from the first data table to find the volume of each drop in milliliters. Using this mL/drop ratio, convert the number of drops of each solution in the second data table to volume in mL of each solution used.

4. **Organizing Data:** Using the relationship between the molarity and volume of acid and the molarity and volume of base needed to neutralize it, calculate the volume of the HCl solution that was neutralized by the NaOH, and record it in your table. (Hint: This relationship was discussed in Section 16-2.)

5. **Analyzing Results:** If the volume of HCl originally added is known and the volume of excess acid is determined by the titration, then the difference will be the amount of HCl that reacted

with the $CaCO_3$. Calculate the volume and the number of moles of HCl that reacted with the $CaCO_3$ and record both in your table.

CONCLUSIONS

1. **Organizing Data:** Use the stoichiometry of the reaction in Analysis and Interpretation item 1 to calculate the number of moles of calcium carbonate that reacted with the HCl, and record this number in your table.

2. **Organizing Data:** Use the periodic table to calculate the molar mass of calcium carbonate. In your data table, record the mass of calcium carbonate present in your eggshell sample by using the number of moles of $CaCO_3$ you calculated in Conclusions item 1.

3. **Organizing Data:** Using your answer to Conclusions item 2, calculate the percentage of calcium carbonate in your eggshell sample, and record it in your table.

4. **Evaluating Methods:** The percentage of calcium carbonate in a normal eggshell ranges from 95% to 99%. Calculate the percent error for your measurement of the $CaCO_3$ content, using 97% $CaCO_3$ as the accepted value.

EXTENSIONS

1. **Inferring Conclusions:** Calculate an estimate of the mass of $CaCO_3$ present in the entire eggshell, based on your results for the sample of eggshell. (Hint: Apply the percent composition of your sample to the mass of the entire eggshell.)

2. **Designing Experiments:** What possible sources of error can you identify in this procedure? If you can think of ways to eliminate the errors, ask your teacher to approve your suggestion, and run the procedure again.

Detailed instructions on preparing burets for titrations are given in the Pre-Laboratory Procedure for Volumetric Analysis.

- Step 2: Delete the first data table and "number of drops" entries in the second data table.
- Steps 3–6: Omit for calibration of the droppers.
- Step 8: Use a sample size near 1.00 g instead of 0.10 g.
- Step 9: Rinse burets in the same way that droppers are rinsed.
- Step 10: Instead of 100 drops, use 50.0 mL of HCl from the acid buret to react with the $CaCO_3$.
- Step 11: Titrate the mixture with NaOH from the base buret until the phenolphthalein changes color.
- Omit item 3 in the Analysis and Interpretation section.

TECHNIQUES TO DEMONSTRATE

Demonstrate titration procedures, showing the proper way to add drops from burets and droppers and to swirl the flask after adding each drop. Show the end point of the titration. Remind the students that the pink color that first appears often disappears when the flask is swirled.

DISPOSAL

Set out three disposal containers: one for unused acid solutions, one for unused base solutions, and one for partially neutralized substances and the contents of the waste beaker. One at a time, slowly combine the solutions while stirring. Adjust the pH of the final waste liquid with 1.0 M acid or base until the pH is between 5 and 9. Pour the neutralized liquid down the drain. (See page 893E for Data Table.)

Continued on page 893E

MICRO-LAB

EXPERIMENT 16-2

OBJECTIVES
Students will
• use appropriate lab safety procedures.
• demonstrate proficiency in qualitatively separating mixtures by using paper chromatography.
• relate the results of a chromatogram to the acidic or basic nature of the marking fluids.
• construct an overwrite pen set using acid-base indicator solutions.
• apply the theory of acid-base indicators and the results of chromatograms to the development of a pen set.
• design and implement their own procedure.

RECOMMENDED TIME
1–2 lab periods

MATERIALS
(for each lab group)
• 1 M HCl
• 1 M NaOH (or household ammonia)
• 12 cm circular chromatography paper or filter paper, 24
• alizarin red
• aniline blue
• brilliant green
• bromcresol green
• bromcresol purple
• bromphenol blue
• crystal violet
• distilled water
• gloves
• isopropanol
• litmus
• methyl red
• petri dish
• phenolphthalein
• pH paper
• scissors
• set of overwrite marker pens
• tape or stapler with staples

Investigating Overwrite Marking Pens

OBJECTIVES

• *Demonstrate* proficiency in qualitatively separating marker pen inks, using paper chromatography.

• *Determine* the pH of colorless marking pens with pH paper.

• *Determine* which of the commercial pens tested are acid-bases indicators and which are not, using chromatograms.

• *Explain* the operation of overwrite marking pens in terms of acids, bases, visual indicators, and the pH scale. Suggest a method for reversing the color-change process.

• *Develop* a set of overwrite marking pens by using your knowledge of acid-base-indicator behavior in solutions with a range of pH values.

MATERIALS

• **1 M HCl**
• **1 M NaOH (or household ammonia)**
• **alizarin red**
• **aniline blue**
• **brilliant green**
• **bromcresol green**
• **bromcresol purple**
• **bromphenol blue**
• **circular chromatography paper (or filter paper)**
• **crystal violet**
• **distilled water**
• **isopropanol**

• **gloves**
• **litmus**
• **methyl red**
• **petri dish**
• **phenolphthalein**
• **pH paper**
• **scissors**
• **set of overwrite marking pens**
• **tape or stapler with staples**
• **thymolphthalein**
• **universal indicator**

BACKGROUND

Paper Chromatography
Details on this technique can be found in the Pre-Laboratory Procedure on page 828.

Color-Change Markers
Color-change markers have been on the market for some time. The cap of each colored pen is one color, and its plug is a second color. Marks made by the pen are the same color as the cap. When these marks are overwritten by the colorless pens, they become the same color as that of the plug. The color-change properties of these markers depend on the pH values of the dyes.

Visual pH Indicators
Chapter 16 discusses the function of an acid-base indicator and the relationship between pH and H_3O^+ concentration.

Assignment
In Part A of this experiment, you will separate the inks found in marking pens by using water, isopropanol, and an acid or a base as solvents. The resulting chromatograms will help you formulate an opinion about how color changes

occur in commercial overwrite marking pens. Keep a record of your data and conclusions in your lab notebook.

In Part B, you will apply your knowledge of how these pens work to develop your own set of overwrite marking pens. The colors for your ink will be derived from the acid-base indicators listed in the materials section. Record your methods, findings, and reasoning in your lab notebook.

SAFETY

Always wear safety goggles and a lab apron to protect your eyes and clothing. If you get a chemical in your eyes, immediately flush the chemical out with water at the eyewash station while calling to your teacher. Know the locations of the emergency lab shower and eyewash station and the procedure for using them.

Because the isopropanol is volatile and flammable, no Bunsen burners, hot plates, or other heat sources should be in use in the room during this lab. Carry out all work with isopropanol in an operating fume hood.

Do not touch any chemicals. If you get a chemical on your skin or clothing, wash the chemical off at the sink while calling to your teacher. Make sure you carefully read the labels and follow the precautions on all containers of chemicals that you use. Never return leftovers to their original containers; take only small amounts to avoid wasting supplies.

PREPARATION

1. Determine the formula, color changes over a pH range, and special handling requirements for each acid-base indicator in the materials list. The following handbooks, manuals, and dictionaries provide general information on specific elements and compounds: *CRC Handbook of Chemistry and Physics, McGraw-Hill Dictionary of Chemical Terms,* and the *Merck Index.*

2. Before preparing your pen set, you may wish to read about the subtractive color process in an encyclopedia or introductory physics text.

3. You will need data tables, like those in Experiment 13-1, that describe the ink separation and any color changes for the chromatograms of the commercial pens. You will need separate spaces for recording the pH of the colorless pen, for identifying the color change as acid-to-base or base-to-acid, and for identifying each pen that is an acid-base indicator.

PROCEDURE

Part A: Examining commercial pens for function and operation

1. Set up a paper chromatography apparatus, using water as the solvent to separate all of the pen dyes in your set of markers. Tape or staple the dry chromatogram to a page of your laboratory notebook. Record the composition of each ink in your data table.

2. Repeat Procedure step 1 with isopropanol as the solvent to separate all of the pen dyes. Tape or staple the dry chromatogram to a page of your laboratory notebook.

3. Determine the pH of the two colorless overwrite markers with a piece of pH paper. Record the value (or values) on your data sheet.

4. Use your result from Procedure step 3 to determine whether an acid or a base should be used as the solvent for separating the pen dyes, and repeat Procedure step 1. You should now be able to identify which dyes are acid-base indicators.

5. Evaluate your results from Procedure steps 1 through 4 by answering questions 1 through 4 under Analysis and Interpretation.

Part B: Developing a new product

6. Use the results of your evaluation to sketch out a plan in your lab notebook for making your own set of overwrite marker pens from the pH indicators in the materials list.

- thymolphthalein
- universal indicator

SOLUTION/MATERIALS PREPARATION

1. Label and set out small bottles of indicator powders. You may wish to provide the indicators as solutions and dispense them in small dropper bottles rather than providing them in the powdered form for students to dilute as they see fit. Suggested indicators are thymolphthalein, crystal violet, bromphenol blue, aniline blue, bromcresol green, congo red, universal indicator, brilliant green, neutral red, phenolphthalein, methyl red, and litmus.

2. Set out marker pen sets—one for each lab group. The orange marker is hard to clean out, so you may not want to use it.

REQUIRED PRECAUTIONS

- Safety goggles and a lab apron must be worn at all times.
- Read all safety cautions, and discuss them with your students.
- The isopropanol is extremely flammable. It should be kept in closed bottles, with no more than 100 mL in a single bottle and no more than 3 such bottles in the laboratory at any time. Students should replace the cap when they are finished. If household ammonia is used, work in a hood known to be in operating condition.
- No burners, flames, hot plates, or other heat sources should be in use in the lab when isopropanol is being used.

TECHNIQUES TO DEMONSTRATE

The general setup for paper chromatography is discussed on pages 828–829. Students may still need to see an actual chromatography setup before they understand exactly what they will be trying to do. Students may also need to see an overwrite pen dismantled and re-assembled.

PRE-LAB DISCUSSION

Students must understand how an acid-base indicator is affected by excess acid or excess base. Make certain students understand this link. Students should understand that the color of an acid-base indicator may vary over its pH range and that colors can be combined to form new colors. Point out the applicable parts of the subtractive color process.

DISPOSAL

1. Set out a disposal container for any isopropanol left over at the end of the procedure. Dilute it with 10 times as much water, and pour it down the drain. Students are instructed to pour the water down the drain.

2. Set out a disposal container for any used indicator solutions that are left over at the end of the procedure.

Continued on page 893F

---

7. Implement your plan, making modifications as necessary. Then suggest a plan for a pen that would reverse the color change process, to restore the original color. Keep a detailed, accurate account of your work.

8. To clean a marker for making your pen ink (indicator solution), use needle-nose pliers to remove the plug from one of the commercial pens, as shown in Figure A. Make sure you are wearing disposable gloves. Remove the cotton insert from the marker. Remove the dye by holding the cotton insert under running water for 2–3 min, until all dye is removed. Then run water over the tip of the pen and through the pen itself to remove all dye from the tip. Squeeze, but do not wring, water from the cotton insert with your fingers. Then place the insert between paper towels and press down on it to blot water from the insert. The drier the insert, the better your pen will work.

9. To fill the pen with your indicator solution, dip the hollowed-out end of the cotton insert into the solution. Capillary action will fill the insert about three-fourths full. Put the insert back into the pen (hollowed-out end toward tip), and, while holding the pen over a sink, use a beral pipet to

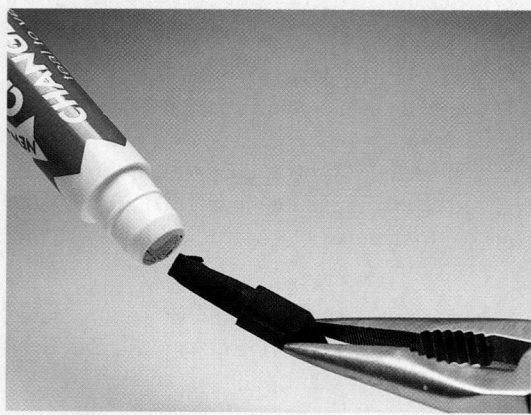

FIGURE A

---

drip the indicator solution on the insert until the cotton is saturated with dye. Soak the pen tip in the dye solution, and replace the cap.

CLEANUP AND DISPOSAL

10. Clean all apparatus and your lab station. Return equipment to its proper place. Dispose of chemicals and solutions in the containers designated by your teacher. Do not pour any chemicals down the drain or in the trash unless your teacher directs you to do so. Wash your hands thoroughly before you leave the lab and after all work is finished.

ANALYSIS AND INTERPRETATION

1. Evaluating Results: Is the fluid in the colorless pens acidic or basic? How does knowing the pH assist you in choosing an acidic or basic solution for the solvent in your third chromatogram?

2. Analyzing Methods: Why might it be advantageous to decide on the pH of your overwrite marking pen *before* developing your colored pens?

3. Applying Ideas: What determines the color of the ink when it is first applied to a sheet of paper? What causes the color to change?

4. Building Models: What are the properties of the compound in a pen that reverses the changeable process, restoring the original color?

CONCLUSIONS

1. Predicting Outcomes: Why were the inks separated with isopropanol as well as with water?

2. Inferring Conclusions: From your chromatograms, what can you conclude about the solubility of the inks?

3. Relating Ideas: Why is the pH of the colorless pen important?

EXPERIMENT 16-3

MICRO-LAB

Is It an Acid or a Base?

OBJECTIVES

- *Design* an experiment to solve a chemical problem.
- *Relate* observations of chemical properties to identify unknowns.
- *Infer* a conclusion from experimental data.
- *Apply* acid-base concepts.

MATERIALS

- 24-well microplate or 24 small test tubes
- labeled pipets containing solutions numbered *1–8*
- toothpicks

For other supplies, check with your teacher

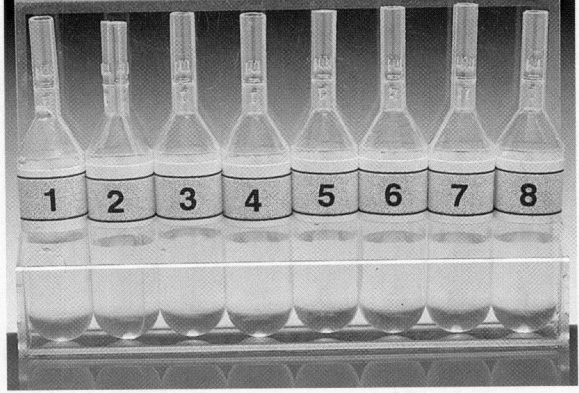

BACKGROUND

When scientists uncover a problem they need to solve, they think carefully about the problem and then use their knowledge and experience to develop a plan for solving it. In this experiment, you will be given a set of eight colorless solutions. Four of them are acidic solutions (dilute hydrochloric acid) and four are basic solutions (dilute sodium hydroxide). The concentrations of both the acidic and the basic solutions are 0.1 M, 0.2 M, 0.4 M, and 0.8 M. Phenolphthalein has been added to the acidic solutions. (Phenolphthalein is an indicator that is colorless in acidic solution but red or pink in basic solution. For more information about phenolphthalein, see Section 16-2.)

You will first write a procedure to determine which solutions are acidic and which are basic and then carry out your procedure. You will then develop and carry out another procedure that will allow you to rank the concentrations of both the acidic and basic solutions from weakest to strongest. As you plan your procedures, consider the properties of acids and bases that are discussed in Chapter 15. Predict what will happen to a solution of each type and concentration when you do each test. Then compare your predictions with what actually happens. You will have limited amounts of the unknown solutions to work with, so use them carefully. Ask your teacher what additional supplies (if any) will be available to you.

SAFETY

Always wear safety goggles and a lab apron to protect your eyes and clothing. If you get a chemical in your eyes, immediately flush the chemical out at the eyewash station while calling to your teacher. Know the location of the emergency lab shower and eyewash station and the procedure for using them.

OBJECTIVES

Students will
- use appropriate lab safety procedures.
- plan procedures to distinguish an acid from a base and to determine the concentrations of acidic and basic solutions.
- predict the results of the planned procedures.
- infer conclusions from experimental data.
- apply acid-base concepts.

RECOMMENDED TIME
45–60 min

MATERIALS
(for each lab group)
- 24-well microplate or 24 small test tubes
- labeled thin-stemmed pipets containing solutions numbered *1–8*
- toothpicks, 10

OPTIONAL MATERIALS
(Note: The level of difficulty of this experiment can be controlled by whether or not you allow students to use optional materials. All of the optional materials listed need not be available for students. Additional materials should be ready, but out of sight, so that they may be provided only as students ask for them and at your discretion. Students may also ask for other items not included here.)

- 0.1 M standard NaOH solution, 5 mL
- 0.1 M standard HCl solution, 5 mL
- $CaCO_3$, 6–7 g
- $FeCl_3 \cdot 6H_2O$, 6–7 g
- conductivity tester
- iron filings, 6–7 g
- methyl orange indicator solution
- phenolphthalein solution
- pH or litmus paper
- thin-stemmed pipets, extra, 2

SOLUTION/MATERIALS PREPARATION

1. An empty cassette box is a convenient container for storing each set of thin-stemmed pipets containing the eight solutions. Assemble the pipets, bulb side down, with part of the long stems cut off to fit. (See photo on page 851.) Label the bulbs with a fine-tipped permanent marker. Keep a master list of which concentrations correspond to which numbered solutions. You may want to mix up solutions, so that solution 1 is not the same for all students.

NOTE: Remember to add about 1 mL of phenolphthalein solution to each acid solution before preparing individual sets of unknown solutions.

2. Observe the required safety precautions when preparing 150 mL of 0.8 M HCl. Add 10 mL of concentrated HCl to enough distilled water to make 150 mL of solution. 75 mL of this will be used for unknowns, and 75 mL for the next solution.

3. To prepare 150 mL of 0.4 M HCl, add 75 mL of 0.8 M HCl (see previous step) to enough distilled water to make 150 mL of solution (75 mL for unknowns and 75 mL for the next solution).

4. To prepare 150 mL of 0.2 M HCl, add 75 mL of 0.4 M HCl (see previous step) to enough distilled water to make 150 mL of solution (75 mL for unknowns and 75 mL for the next solution).

5. To prepare 150 mL of 0.1 M HCl, add 75 mL of 0.2 M HCl (see previous step) to enough distilled water to make 150 mL of solution (75 mL for unknowns and 75 mL as a possible standard solution for students).

6. Observe the required safety precautions when preparing 150 mL of 0.8 M NaOH. Add 16 g of NaOH, while stirring, to enough distilled water to make 150 mL of solution

 Do not touch any chemicals. If you get a chemical on your skin or clothing, wash the chemical off at the sink while calling to your teacher. Make sure you carefully read the labels and follow the precautions on all containers of chemicals that you use. If there are no precautions stated on the label, ask your teacher what precautions you should follow. Do not taste any chemicals or items used in the laboratory. Never return leftovers to their original containers; take only small amounts to avoid wasting supplies.

 Call your teacher in the event of a spill. Spills should be cleaned up promptly according to your teacher's directions.

PREPARATION

1. Make two data tables in your lab notebook similar to those shown below. In the columns of Data Table 1, you will list the numbers of the unknown solutions as you identify them.

Data Table 1

Acids	Bases

Data Table 2

Concentration	HCl	NaOH
0.1 M		
0.2 M		
0.4 M		
0.8 M		

2. In you lab notebook write the steps you will use to determine which solutions are acids and which solutions are bases. Figure A shows one test you can use to make this determination.

FIGURE A   After adding phenolphthalein indicator, it becomes easier to determine which solution is acidic and which solution is basic.

3. Ask your teacher to approve your plan and give you any additional supplies you will need.

PROCEDURE

1. Carry out your plan for determining which solutions are acids and which are bases. As you perform your tests, avoid letting the tips of the storage pipets come into contact with other chemicals. Squeeze drops out of the pipets onto the 24-well plate and then use these drops for your tests. Record all observations in your lab notebook, and then record your results in your first data table.

2. In your lab notebook, write your procedure for determining the concentrations of the solutions. Ask your teacher to approve your plan, and request any additional supplies you will need.

3. Carry out your procedure for determining the concentrations of the solutions. Record all observations in your lab notebook, and record your results in the second data table.

CLEANUP AND DISPOSAL

4. Clean all apparatus and your lab station. Return equipment to its proper place. Dispose of chemicals and solutions in the containers designated by your teacher. Do not pour any chemicals down the drain or in the trash unless your teacher directs you to do so. Wash your hands thoroughly before you leave the lab and after all work is finished.

CONCLUSIONS

1. **Analyzing Conclusions:** List the numbers of the solutions and their concentrations.

2. **Analyzing Conclusions:** Describe the test results that led you to identify some solutions as acids and others as bases. Explain how you determined the concentrations of the unknown solutions.

EXTENSIONS

1. **Evaluating Methods:** Compare your results with those of another lab group. Do you think that your teacher gave both groups the same set of solutions? (Is your solution 1 the same as their solution 1, and so on?) Explain your reasoning.

2. **Designing Experiments:** Although your teacher may have allowed you to use a variety of materials and methods to figure out the classes (acid or base) and concentrations of the solutions, there is a way you could do this with just the pipets of unknown solutions and the 24-well plate. Write out a procedure that would identify the solutions by using only these materials. If time permits, test your procedure and compare the results you get with your first results.

3. **Applying Conclusions:** Imagine that you are helping to clean out the school's chemical storeroom. You find a spill coming from a large unlabeled reagent bottle filled with a clear liquid. What tests would you do to quickly determine if the substance is acidic or basic?

(75 mL for unknowns and 75 mL for the next solution).

7. To prepare 150 mL of 0.4 M NaOH, add 75 mL of 0.8 M NaOH solution (see previous step) to enough distilled water to make 150 mL of solution (75 mL for unknowns and 75 mL for the next solution).

8. To prepare 150 mL of 0.2 M NaOH, add 75 mL of 0.4 M NaOH solution (see previous step) to enough distilled water to make 150 mL of solution (75 mL for unknowns and 75 mL for the next solution).

9. To prepare 150 mL of 0.1 M NaOH, add 75 mL of 0.2 M NaOH solution (see previous step) to enough distilled water to make 150 mL of solution (75 mL for unknowns and 75 as possible standard solution for students).

10. To make 15 mL of phenolphthalein solution, dissolve 0.15 g of phenolphthalein in 7 mL of denatured alcohol and add 8 mL of distilled water.

11. To prepare 100 mL of *optional* methyl orange indicator solution, dissolve 0.1 g of the powdered iodine in 50 mL denatured alcohol and add 50 mL of distilled water.

12. To build optional conductivity testers, see instructions on page 876.

REQUIRED PRECAUTIONS

- Safety goggles and a lab apron must be worn at all times.
- Read all safety precautions, and discuss them with your students.
- In case of a spill, use a dampened cloth or paper towel (or more than one towel if necessary) to mop up the spill. Then rinse the cloth in running water at the sink, wring it out thoroughly, and put it in the trash.
- Wear safety goggles, a face shield, impermeable gloves, and a lab apron when you prepare the HCl and NaOH. Work in a hood known to be in operating condition and

Continued on page 893F

EXPERIMENT 16-4

OBJECTIVES
Students will
- use appropriate lab safety procedures.
- use burets in a titration.
- identify the end point in an acid-base titration.
- derive the mole ratio for an acid and base from the chemical equation.
- determine the molarity and mass percentage of acetic acid in vinegar.

RECOMMENDED TIME
45–60 min

MATERIALS
(for each lab group)
- 1 mL phenolphthalein indicator
- 80 mL white vinegar
- 80 mL 0.6 M NaOH solution, standardized
- 100 mL beakers, 3
- 125 mL Erlenmeyer flask
- 250 mL beaker
- burets, 2
- buret clamp
- ring stand
- wash bottle

SOLUTION/MATERIALS PREPARATION
1. The NaOH solution that students use should be less than 1.0 M. Directions are given for preparing approximately 0.6 M sodium hydroxide solution for standardization. Observe the required precautions. Add 24 g of NaOH, while stirring, to enough distilled water to make 1.00 L of solution. Use reagent grade NaOH.

2. If you or your students are to standardize the NaOH solution, prepare 0.100 M HCl, using a fresh bottle of concentrated HCl, preferably one that shows the actual assay of HCl rather than an average assay. Observe the required precautions. Assuming that

Percentage of Acetic Acid in Vinegar

OBJECTIVES

- *Determine* the endpoint of an acid-base titration.
- *Use* burets for accurately measuring quantities of solution.
- *Calculate* the molarity of vinegar from experimental data.
- *Calculate* the percentage of acetic acid in vinegar.

MATERIALS

- **125 mL Erlenmeyer flask**
- **100 mL beakers, 3**
- **250 mL beaker (for waste solutions)**
- **burets, 2**
- **buret clamp**
- **NaOH solution, standardized**
- **phenolphthalein indicator**
- **ring stand**
- **wash bottle**
- **white vinegar**

BACKGROUND

When sweet apple cider is fermented, the product is either an alcohol called apple jack or an acid called vinegar. If fermentation takes place without oxygen, alcohol and carbon dioxide are produced. But if oxygen is present in the fermentation process, acetic acid and carbon dioxide are produced. Most commercial vinegars have a mass percentage of acetic acid between 4.0% and 5.5%. The white vinegar you will use in this experiment is not produced by fermentation; it is obtained by the dilution of 100% acetic acid.

The percentage of acetic acid in a sample of vinegar may be found by titrating the sample against a standard basic solution. By determining the volume of sodium hydroxide solution of known molarity necessary to neutralize a measured quantity of vinegar, the molarity of the vinegar can be calculated. The molarity can be converted to the percentage CH_3COOH in vinegar.

SAFETY

Always wear safety goggles and a lab apron to protect your eyes and clothing. If you get a chemical in your eyes, immediately flush the chemical out at the eyewash station while calling to your teacher. Know the location of the emergency lab shower and eyewash station and the procedure for using them.

Do not touch any chemicals. If you get a chemical on your skin or clothing, wash the chemical off at the sink while calling to your teacher. Make sure you carefully read the labels and follow the precautions on all containers of chemicals that you use. If there are no precautions stated on the label, ask your teacher what precautions you should follow. Do not taste any chemicals or items used in the laboratory. Never return leftovers to their original containers; take only small amounts to avoid wasting supplies.

FIGURE A

 Call your teacher in the event of a spill. Spills should be cleaned up promptly, according to your teacher's directions.

 Never put broken glass in a regular waste container. Broken glass should be disposed of in the broken glass waste container.

PREPARATION

1. Copy the data table below in your lab notebook. Leave a space for the molarity of the standardized NaOH solution.

2. Label one clean, dry 100 mL beaker *Vinegar* and the other *NaOH*, as shown in Figure A. Label one buret *Vinegar* and the other *NaOH*.

PROCEDURE

1. Transfer approximately 80 mL of vinegar and approximately 80 mL of NaOH to the appropriately labeled beakers.

2. Pour approximately 5 mL of vinegar from the beaker into the appropriately labeled buret. Rinse the walls of the buret thoroughly with the vinegar. Allow the vinegar to drain through the stopcock into the 250 mL beaker for waste. Rinse the buret two more times in this way,

using a new 5 mL portion of vinegar each time. Collect all rinses in the waste beaker.

3. Fill the buret with vinegar above the zero mark. Withdraw enough vinegar to remove the air from the tip of the buret and bring the liquid level into the graduated region of the buret.

4. Repeat Procedure steps 2 and 3 with the sodium hydroxide solution and the appropriately labeled buret.

5. Record the initial readings of both burets, estimating the volumes to the nearest 0.01 mL.

6. Allow about 10 mL of vinegar to flow into a clean Erlenmeyer flask. Add about 10 mL of distilled water to the flask to increase the volume. This procedure will make it easier to determine the color change when the end point is reached. Add one or two drops of phenolphthalein solution to serve as an indicator.

7. Titrate the vinegar with the standard solution of sodium hydroxide. Continually swirl the flask as shown in Figure B. Stop frequently to wash down the sides of the flask with distilled water from

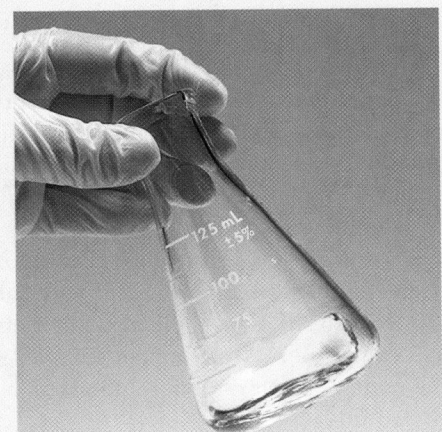

FIGURE B

the concentrated HCl is 12 M, slowly add 8.33 mL concentrated HCl, while stirring, to enough water to make 1.00 L of solution. Adjust the exact volume of concentrated HCl you use, depending on the assay of the acid you are using.

3. To prepare 100 mL of phenolphthalein indictor, dissolve 1.0 g of phenolphthalein in 50 mL of denatured alcohol and add 50 mL of water.

4. Use white vinegar rather than diluted acetic acid. Avoid cider vinegar because the color will make the recognition of the end point more difficult.

REQUIRED PRECAUTIONS

• Safety goggles and a lab apron must be worn at all times.

• Read all safety cautions, and discuss them with your students.

• Students should not handle concentrated acid or base solutions.

• Use commercially available distilled white vinegar instead of diluting glacial acetic acid.

• In case of an acid or base spill, dilute the spill with water. Then mop up the spill with wet cloths or a wet cloth mop designated for spill cleanup. Wear disposable plastic gloves while cleaning spills.

• Wear safety goggles, a face shield, impermeable gloves, and a lab apron if you prepare HCl for standardizing NaOH. Work in a hood known to be in good working order and have another person stand by to call for help in case of an emergency. Be sure you are within a 30 second walk from a safety shower and eyewash station known to be in good operating condition.

TECHNIQUES TO DEMONSTRATE

If students have never used burets, caution them that burets can be broken easily and need to be treated with care. Show them how to rinse

Data Table 1

Trial number	Initial NaOH reading (mL)	Final NaOH reading (mL)	Initial vinegar reading (mL)	Final vinegar reading (mL)
1				
2				
3				

PERCENTAGE OF ACETIC ACID IN VINEGAR   **855**

the buret by turning it upside down several times to coat the inside surfaces with the rinse liquid. Tell them that after filling the buret and before reading the volume, they should allow the liquid to drain down the inside walls of the buret and should be sure that the buret tip is full of titrant. Demonstrate how buret readings should be made with the eye at the level of the meniscus, and explain that the volume of the liquid is read at the bottom of the curved surface of the meniscus. Some students have difficulty in deciding whether to read the scale up or down. A classroom exercise using a chalkboard drawing of a buret scale with a meniscus can help prevent problems.

SAMPLE DATA

(See page 893G)
Molarity of standardized NaOH:
0.605 M

PRELAB DISCUSSION

Review the stoichiometry of acid-base reactions and relate it to the endpoint of the titration. Review the definition of molarity.

DISPOSAL

Set out three disposal containers labeled for the disposal of acidic liquid wastes, neutral liquid wastes, and basic liquid wastes. While stirring, slowly combine the contents of the three liquid-waste containers. Neutralize the resulting solution with 1.0 M acid or base until the pH is between 5 and 9, and then pour it down the drain.

ANALYSIS AND INTERPRETATION—ANSWERS

1. Volume of NaOH
Trial 1:
11.57 mL − 1.38 mL = 10.19 mL
Trial 2:
23.69 mL − 11.57 mL = 12.12 mL
Trial 3:
32.33 mL − 23.69 mL = 8.64 mL

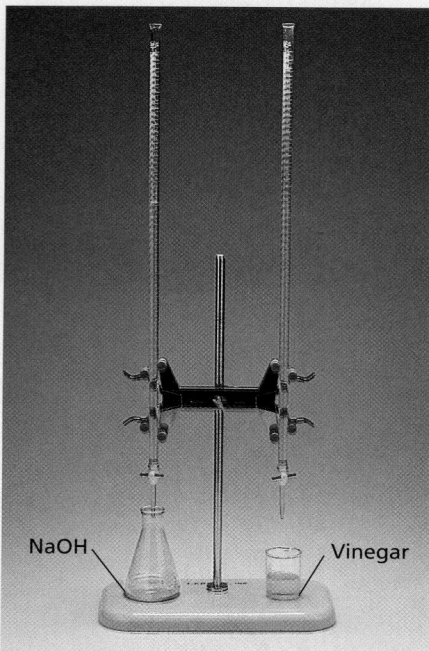

FIGURE C

your wash bottle. Add the sodium hydroxide drop by drop near the end of the titration until the last drop keeps the solution a pink color that remains after swirling.

8. Add successive quantities of both solutions, drop by drop, going back and forth from pink to colorless until the end point is clearly established. This point is indicated by the slightest suggestion of pink coloration in the flask, as shown in Figure C. You will be able to see the pink color more clearly if the flask is resting on a sheet of white paper with a beaker of distilled water next to it for comparison. Record in your data table the final buret readings of both solutions to the nearest 0.01 mL.

9. Discard the liquid in the Erlenmeyer flask in the disposal container provided by your teacher. Rinse the flask thoroughly with distilled water, and repeat the titration two more times, following Procedure steps 5–8.

CLEANUP AND DISPOSAL

10. Clean all apparatus and your lab station. Return equipment to its proper place. Dispose of chemicals and solutions in the containers designated by your teacher. Do not pour any chemicals down the drain or in the trash unless your teacher directs you to do so. Wash your hands thoroughly before you leave the lab and after all work is finished.

ANALYSIS AND INTERPRETATION

1. Organizing Data: Calculate the volumes of vinegar and NaOH used for each of the three trials.

2. Organizing Data: In your data table write the molarity of the standardized NaOH solution you used. Determine the moles of NaOH used in each of the three trials.
Hint: By definition,

$$\text{molarity} = \frac{\text{moles of solute}}{\text{1 L solution}}$$

moles of solute = molarity × liters of solution

3. Organizing Ideas: Write the balanced equation for the reaction between vinegar and sodium hydroxide. (Hint: The formula for acetic acid is CH_3COOH.)

4. Organizing Data: Use the results of your calculations in Analysis and Interpretation item 2 and the mole ratio from the equation in Analysis and Interpretation item 3 to determine the moles of base used to neutralize the vinegar (acid) in each trial.

5. Organizing Data: Use the moles of base calculated in Analysis and Interpretation item 4 and the volumes of the acid used for each trial to calculate the molarities of the vinegar for the three trials.

6. Organizing Data: Calculate the average molarity of the vinegar.

Rice Vinegar   Red Wine Vinegar   Cider Vinegar

7. Organizing Ideas: Use the periodic table to calculate the molar mass of acetic acid, CH_3COOH.

8. Organizing Data: Use the average molarity for your vinegar sample to determine the mass of CH_3COOH in 1 L of vinegar.

CONCLUSIONS

1. Organizing Conclusions: Assume that the density of vinegar is very close to 1.00 g/mL so that the mass of 1 L of vinegar is 1000 g. Calculate the percentage of acetic acid in your vinegar sample. (Hint: The mass of acetic acid in 1 L of vinegar was calculated in Analysis and Interpretation item 8. Divide the mass of CH_3COOH in 1 L by the total mass of vinegar in a liter, then multiply by 100 to get the percentage of acetic acid in vinegar.)

2. Applying Conclusions: Why is it important for a company manufacturing vinegar to regularly check the molarity of its product?

3. Analyzing Methods: What was the purpose of using the phenolphthalein? Could you have titrated the vinegar sample without the phenolphthalein?

4. Analyzing Methods: At the beginning of each titration, 10 mL of vinegar was run into the Erlenmeyer flask and the vinegar was diluted with distilled water. Why was the calculated molarity of the acetic acid not affected by the water?

EXTENSIONS

1. Evaluating Data: Share your data with other lab groups, and calculate a class average for the molarity of the vinegar.

2. Designing Experiments: What possible sources of error can you identify in this procedure? If you can think of ways to eliminate the errors, ask your teacher to approve your plan, and run the procedure again.

3. Relating Ideas: Explain the difference between the equivalence point and the end point. Can they be the same?

4. Resolving Discrepancies: An industrial chemist measured the following values when titrating 10.0 mL samples from a single vat of vinegar: 15.04 mL, 16.03 mL, and 14.98 mL. What could be the source error in these titrations?

Volume of vinegar
Trial 1:
9.21 mL − 0.55 mL = 8.66 mL
Trial 2:
19.43 mL − 9.21 mL = 10.22 mL
Trial 3:
26.67 mL − 19.43 mL = 7.24 mL

2. Moles of NaOH
Trial 1:
0.605 M × 0.01019 L = 0.00617 mol
Trial 2:
0.605 M × 0.01212 L = 0.00733 mol
Trial 3:
0.605 M × 0.00864 L = 0.00523 mol

3. $CH_3COOH(aq) + NaOH(aq) \longrightarrow$
$H_2O(l) + CH_3COONa(aq)$

4. Trial 1:
$0.00617 \text{ mol NaOH} \times \dfrac{1 \text{ mol vinegar}}{1 \text{ mol NaOH}}$

$= 0.00617$ mol vinegar

Trial 2:
$0.00733 \text{ mol NaOH} \times \dfrac{1 \text{ mol vinegar}}{1 \text{ mol NaOH}}$

$= 0.00733$ mol vinegar

Trial 3:
$0.00523 \text{ mol NaOH} \times \dfrac{1 \text{ mol vinegar}}{1 \text{ mol NaOH}}$

$= 0.00523$ mol vinegar

5. Trial 1: $\dfrac{0.00617 \text{ mol}}{0.00866 \text{ L}} = 0.712$ M

Trial 2: $\dfrac{0.00733 \text{ mol}}{0.01022 \text{ L}} = 0.717$ M

Trial 3: $\dfrac{0.00523 \text{ mol}}{0.00724 \text{ L}} = 0.722$ M

6. Average molarity of vinegar =
$\dfrac{0.712M + 0.717M + 0.722M}{3} =$

0.717 M

7. H = 1.01 g × 4 =   4.00 g
C = 12.0 g × 2 = 24.0 g
O = 16.0 g × 2 = 32.0 g
60.0 g

Continued on page 893G

Calorimetry

Calorimetry, the measurement of heat transfer, allows chemists to determine thermal constants, such as the specific heat of metals and the heat of solution.

When two substances at different temperatures touch one another, heat flows from the warmer substance to the cooler substance until the two substances are at the same temperature. The amount of heat transferred is measured in joules. (One joule equals 4.184 calories.)

A device used to measure heat transfer is a calorimeter. Calorimeters vary in construction depending on the purpose and the accuracy of the heat measurement required. No calorimeter is a perfect insulator; some heat is always lost to the surroundings. Therefore, every calorimeter must be calibrated to obtain its calorimeter constant.

GENERAL SAFETY

Always wear safety goggles and a lab apron to protect your eyes and clothing. If you get a chemical in your eyes, immediately flush the chemical out at the eyewash station while calling to your teacher. Know the location of the emergency lab shower and eyewash station and the procedure for using them.

Turn off hot plates and other heat sources when not in use. Do not touch a hot plate after it has just been turned off; it is probably hotter than you think. Use tongs when handling heated containers. Never hold or touch containers with your hands while heating them.

The general setup for a calorimeter made from plastic foam cups is shown in Figure A. The steps for constructing this setup follow.

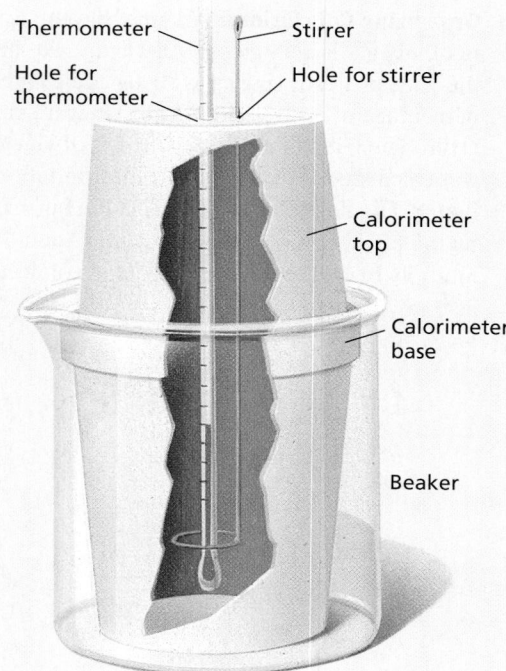

FIGURE A   Position the hole for the stirrer so that the thermometer is in the center of the wire ring.

CONSTRUCTING THE CALORIMETER

1. Trim the lip of one plastic foam cup, and use that cup as the top of your calorimeter. The other cup will be used as the base.

2. Use the pointed end of a pencil to gently make a hole in the center of the calorimeter top. The hole should be large enough to insert a thermometer. Make a hole for the wire stirrer. As you can see in Figure A, this hole should be positioned so that the wire stirrer can be raised and lowered without interfering with the thermometer.

3. Place the calorimeter in a beaker to prevent it from tipping over.

CALIBRATING A PLASTIC FOAM CUP CALORIMETER

1. Measure 50 mL of distilled water in a graduated cylinder. Pour it into the calorimeter. Measure and record the temperature of the water in the polystyrene cup.

2. Pour another 50 mL of distilled water into a beaker. Set the beaker on a hot plate, and warm the water to about 60°C, as shown in Figure B. Measure and record the temperature of the water.

3. Immediately pour the warm water into the cup, as shown in Figure C. Cover the cup, and move

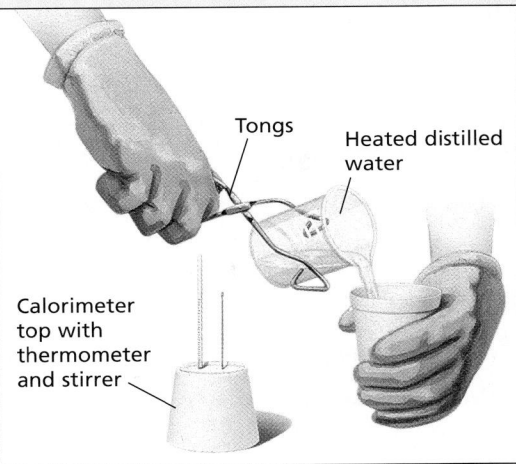

FIGURE C When transferring warm water from the beaker to the calorimeter, hold the bottom of the calorimeter steady so it does not tip over.

the stirrer gently up and down to mix the contents thoroughly. **Take care not to break the thermometer.**

4. Watch the thermometer and record the highest temperature attained (usually after about 30 s).

5. Empty the calorimeter.

6. The derivation of the equation to find the calorimeter constant starts with the following relationship.
Heat lost by the warm water = Heat gained by the cool water + Heat gained by the calorimeter

$$q_{warm\ H_2O} = q_{cool\ H_2O} + q_{calorimeter}$$
The heat lost by the warm water is calculated by

$$q_{warm\ H_2O} = mass_{warm\ H_2O} \times 4.184\ J/g \cdot °C \times \Delta t$$
The heat gained by the calorimeter system equals the heat lost by the warm water. You can use the following equation to calculate the calorimeter constant C′ for your calorimeter.

$$q_{calorimeter} = q_{\ warm\ H_2O}$$
$$= (mass_{cool\ H_2O})\ (4.184\ J/g \cdot °C)\ (\Delta t_{cool\ H_2O}) +$$
$$C'(\Delta t_{cool\ H_2O})$$

Substitute the data from your calibration and solve for C′.

60°C

FIGURE B Heat the distilled water to approximately 60°C.

EXPERIMENT 17-1

EXPERIMENT 17-1

OBJECTIVES

Students will

• use appropriate lab safety procedures.

• calibrate a simple calorimeter.

• relate changes in temperature to heat content.

• calculate the specific heats of known metals from experimental data.

• determine the identity of an unknown metal from its measured specific heat.

RECOMMENDED TIME

45–60 min

MATERIALS

(for each lab group)

• 400 mL beakers

• 75 g metal samples

• 75 g unknown metal sample

• balance

• beaker tongs

• boiling chips

• Bunsen burner, gas tubing, and striker, or hot plate

• glass stirring rod

• graduated cylinder, 100 mL

• plastic-foam cups for calorimeter, 2

• ring stand and ring

• scissors or tools to trim cups

• test-tube clamp

• test tube, large

• thermometer, alcohol filled

• tongs for handling metal

• wire gauze with ceramic center

• wire stirrer

OPTIONAL MATERIALS FOR EXTENSIONS

• 75 g glass beads for Extension 4

• materials for improved calorimeter for Extension 3

Measuring the Specific Heats of Metals

OBJECTIVES

• *Calibrate* a simple calorimeter.

• *Relate* measurements of temperature to changes in heat content.

• *Calculate* the specific heats of several metals.

• *Determine* the identity of an unknown metal.

MATERIALS

• **100 mL graduated cylinder**

• **400 mL beakers, 2**

• **balance**

• **beaker tongs**

• **boiling chips**

• **Bunsen burner, gas tubing, striker, or hot plate**

• **glass stirring rod**

• **metal samples**

• **plastic-foam cups for calorimeter, 2**

• **ring stand and ring**

• **scissors or tools to trim cups**

• **test tube, large**

• **test-tube clamp**

• **thermometer**

• **tongs for handling metal**

• **unknown metal sample**

• **wire gauze with ceramic center**

• **wire stirrer**

BACKGROUND

Changes in heat can be determined by measuring changes in temperature. When a substance is heated, the heat gained, q, depends on three factors: the mass of the substance, m, in grams; the specific heat of the substance, c_p; and the change in temperature of the substance, Δt. The following equation is used to calculate the amount of heat absorbed or lost by a substance.

$$q = m \times c_p \times \Delta t$$

In this experiment, you will measure the specific heats of several metals, but first you will need to make and calibrate a calorimeter. You will start with a known mass of water in your calorimeter. When the heated metal is added to the water, you can measure the change in temperature for the water. Using the specific heat of water (4.184 J/g•°C) and your calorimeter's calibration constant, you will be able to calculate the amount of heat gained by the water and the calorimeter. This amount is equal to the amount of heat lost by the metal. If the temperature change and mass of the metal are known, its specific heat can be determined.

$$q_{\text{metal}} = q_{\text{calorimeter}}$$
$$m_{\text{metal}} \times \Delta t_{\text{metal}} \times c_{p,\,\text{metal}} =$$
$$[(m_{\text{H}_2\text{O}} \times c_{p,\,\text{H}_2\text{O}} \times \Delta t_{\text{H}_2\text{O}}) + (C' \times \Delta t_{\text{H}_2\text{O}})]$$

SAFETY

Always wear safety goggles and a lab apron to protect your eyes and clothing. If you get a chemical in your eyes, immediately flush the chemical out at the eyewash station while calling to your teacher. Know the location of the emergency lab shower and eyewash station and the procedure for using them.

Do not touch any chemicals. If you get a chemical on your skin or clothing, wash the chemical off at the sink while calling to your teacher. Make sure you carefully read the labels and follow the precautions on all containers of chemicals that you use. If there are no precautions stated on the label, ask your teacher what precautions to follow. Do not taste any chemicals or items used in the laboratory. Never return left-overs to their original containers; take only small amounts to avoid wasting supplies.

 Call your teacher in the event of a spill. Spills should be cleaned up promptly, according to your teacher's directions.

 When you use a Bunsen burner, confine long hair and loose clothing. Do not heat glassware that is broken, chipped, or cracked. Use tongs or a hot mitt to handle heated glassware and other equipment because heated glassware does not always look hot. If your clothing catches fire, WALK to the emergency lab shower, and use it to put out the fire.

 Never put broken glass in a regular waste container. Broken glass should be disposed of in a separate container designated by your teacher. Use a wire stirrer; do not use a thermometer to stir because it is fragile and can break easily.

 Scissors are sharp; use with care to avoid cutting yourself or others.

PREPARATION

1. In your lab notebook, you will need one data table for the calibration of your calorimeter and one table for specific heat test data for each metal you will be testing, including the unknown metal. Copy the table below in your lab notebook. You will not use the spaces for volume and mass in the *Calorimeter* column and the spaces for *Calorimeter heat capacity* in the *Cool H_2O* and *Hot H_2O* columns. For the specific heat tests, make as many data tables as you will need for the known and unknown metals you will be testing. Each table should have three columns and five rows. Label the second and third columns of the first row H_2O and *Metal*. In the first column, label rows 2 through 5 *Initial temp.*, *Final temp.*, *Change in temp.*, and *Mass*.

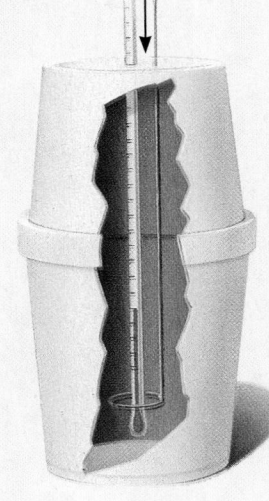

FIGURE A

2. Construct a calorimeter as in Pre-Laboratory Procedure: Calorimetery on page 858.

PROCEDURE

1. Calibrate the calorimeter as demonstrated in the Pre-Laboratory Procedure on page 858. Use the calorimeter constant in each of your calculations.

SOLUTION/MATERIALS PREPARATION

1. Smaller amounts of metals can be used if less precision is acceptable. Rather than purchasing reagent grade metals, try to locate inexpensive materials such as iron nails, discarded copper wire, and aluminum pellets. For unknown metals, choose a metal from those in Table 17-1—aluminum, iron, copper, or lead.

2. Depending on the size of the plastic–foam cups used, you may need to adjust the amounts of water used in the calibration step.

If time allows, encourage students to repeat the calibration process and to calculate an average value for the specific heat of the calorimeter, C′. If time is short, consider omitting the calibration of the calorimeter: part of step 1 (making the calibration data table), step 3, Analysis and Interpretation items 3–5, and calculations of the heat capacity of the calorimeter in other items.

3. To make the wire stirrers, cut 15 cm lengths of wire. (Any gauge will do, provided it is easily bent.) At one end, make a loop with a diameter of at least 1 cm. Bend the wire at the loop so that the loop is perpendicular to the length of the wire. Make a smaller loop at the other end of the wire. Use this as a handle for stirring.

REQUIRED PRECAUTIONS
- Safety goggles and a lab apron must be worn at all times.
- Tie back long hair and loose clothing.
- Read all safety precautions, and discuss them with your students.
- Remind students to use beaker tongs when handling the beaker containing hot water because it can burn or scald.

DATA TABLE			
	Cool H_2O	**Hot H_2O**	**Calorimeter**
Initial temp.			
Final temp.			
Change in temp.			
Volume			
Mass			
Calorimeter heat capacity			

- In case of a spill, use a dampened cloth or paper towel (or more than one towel if necessary) to mop up the spill. Then rinse the cloth in running water at the sink, wring it out thoroughly, and put it in the trash.

TECHNIQUES TO DEMONSTRATE

Show students how to set up the equipment for heating the metal samples. Emphasize that they should use as much metal as can be submerged in the boiling water without having the bottom of the test tube touch the bottom of the beaker. Show students how to use beaker tongs, and insist that students use tongs or oven mitts when moving the beaker containing hot water.

Demonstrate how to trim the lid of the calorimeter and how to position and make the holes for the thermometer and wire stirrer. Show students how to stir gently up and down so that the thermometer will not be broken.

SAMPLE DATA

Student data will vary. See page 893G for Data Tables.

PRE-LAB DISCUSSION

Students may have difficulty understanding the equations presented in the Background section. It may help if you discuss the equations before the lab and work through them with a set of actual data. Make a point of doing a unit analysis.

DISPOSAL

All of the metals used can be disposed of in a landfill that is approved for the disposal of chemical and hazardous wastes. But because they undergo no reactions in this lab, the metals can be saved and used year after year if students are instructed to dry them well after each use.

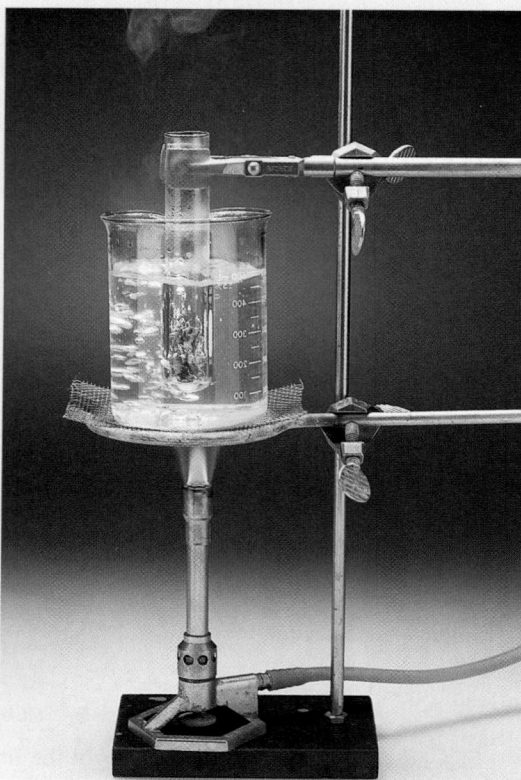

FIGURE B　The metal pieces are heated to the temperature of boiling water either by a Bunsen burner or a hot plate.

2. Measure 75.0 mL of water and pour it into the calorimeter. Allow the water to come to room temperature. Record the mass and temperature of the water in one of the specific heat data tables along with the identity of the metal you will use for this trial.

3. Fill a 400 mL beaker with water and add some boiling chips. Place pieces of the metal you will test in the large test tube. Use as much metal as possible, but be sure that when the test tube is placed in the beaker of water, all the metal is below the surface of the water. **Measure the mass of the metal as precisely as possible before placing it in the test tube.** Record the mass of the metal in your data table.

4. Clamp the test tube to the ring stand, as shown in Figure B. Set the beaker on the wire gauze, and lower the test-tube clamp so that all the

metal in the test tube is below the surface of the water. Heat the water until it boils. Allow the water to boil for 10 min. You can now assume that the metal is at the temperature of boiling water. Record this temperature in the data table.

5. Holding the test tube with the clamp, transfer the metal to the calorimeter without splashing out any water. **Be careful not to burn your skin with the hot water or the metal.** Put the top on the calorimeter. Stir gently for 30 s while observing the temperature. Record the highest temperature reached by the water.

6. Repeat Procedure steps 2–5 for other metals, including the unknown metal.

CLEANUP AND DISPOSAL

7. Turn off the heat source and allow the boiling water to cool. Then pour the cooled water down the drain. Place the metal samples on paper towels to dry. Place the dried metals in separate disposal containers designated by your teacher. Make sure to completely shut off the gas valve before leaving the laboratory. Clean all apparatus and your lab station. Return equipment to its proper place. Wash your hands thoroughly before you leave the lab.

ANALYSIS AND INTERPRETATION

1. **Organizing Ideas:** State the scientific law that is the basis for the assumption that the heat energy lost by the metal as it cools is equal to the heat energy gained by the water and the calorimeter.

2. **Organizing Data:** Using the density value given for water in Table 2-4 of the textbook, calculate the masses of water used in the calibration step, and record your results in the calibration data table.

3. **Organizing Data:** Finish filling out the calibration data table by calculating the changes in temperature that occurred. Using the value of 4.184 J/g·°C for the specific heat of water, determine how much heat was lost by the hot water in the calibration portion of the experiment. How much heat was gained by the cool water?

4. **Inferring Conclusions:** Based on your answer to Analysis and Interpretation item 3, how much heat was gained by the calorimeter?

5. **Organizing Data:** Calculate the calorimeter constant, C', of the calorimeter by using the relationship shown in the Pre-Laboratory Procedure on page 859. Record your answer in the calibration data table.

6. **Inferring Relationships:** For the second part of the experiment, write a word equation for the relationship between the heat lost by a metal, the heat gained by the water, and the heat gained by the calorimeter. Solve for the specific heat of the metal by substituting the mathematical equation for specific heat ($q = m \times c_p \times \Delta t$) into the first equation. Show all your work for each metal. (Hint: Be sure to include the calorimeter constant of the calorimeter, C', in the substituted equation.)

CONCLUSIONS

1. **Inferring Conclusions:** Finish filling in the specific heat data tables for each metal. Use the relationship from Analysis and Interpretation item 6 to calculate the specific heat of each metal tested.

2. **Evaluating Conclusions:** Compare your value for the unknown metal with the values given in Table 17-1 in the text. What metal do you think your unknown is?

3. **Analyzing Conclusions:** How do the specific heats of the metals compare with the specific heat of water? What does that comparison imply about the amount of heat needed to bring equal masses of metal and water to the same temperature? Which one would absorb heat better?

4. **Organizing Ideas:** Are higher values or lower values better for the specific heat of a calorimeter? Why?

EXTENSIONS

1. **Evaluating Methods:** Share your data with other lab groups, and calculate a class average for each of the specific heats of the metals you tested. Compare the averages to the figures in a chemical handbook, and calculate the percent error for the class averages.

2. **Designing Experiments:** What are some likely sources of imprecision in this experiment? If you can think of ways to eliminate the imprecision, ask your teacher to approve your suggestion, and run more trials.

3. **Designing Experiments:** Design a different calorimeter. If your teacher approves the design, construct it, and compare its performance with that of the plastic-foam cups.

4. **Applying Ideas:** The specific heat of a material is often a determining property in its practical use. What practical applications can you think of that are based on the specific heat of the materials involved?

5. **Applying Ideas:** Explain how the large specific heat of water is responsible for the moderating effects that the oceans have on weather.

ANALYSIS AND INTERPRETATION—ANSWERS

1. The law of conservation of energy.

2. Students should recognize that because the density of water is given as 1.00 g/mL, the mass of the water in grams is equal to the volume of water in milliliters. If directions were followed as written, the masses would be 50.0 g of cool water and 50.0 g of hot water.

Continued on page 893G

EXPERIMENT 17-2

OBJECTIVES

Students will

- use appropriate lab safety procedures.
- use a thermometer to measure temperature.
- use a calorimeter to determine heat of reaction for various combinations of an acid and a base.
- determine the change in temperature between reactants and products.
- use measured heats of reaction in energy-stoichiometry calculations.

RECOMMENDED TIME

45–60 min

MATERIALS

(for each lab group)

- 4 g NaOH pellets
- 50 mL 1.0 M HCl
- 50 mL 1.0 M NaOH
- 100 mL 0.50 M HCl
- 100 mL graduated cylinder
- balance, centigram
- Celsius thermometer, nonmercury type, with a range from −10°C to 120°C
- distilled water
- forceps
- glass stirring rod
- gloves
- plastic-foam cups or calorimeters
- spatula
- watch glass

SOLUTION/MATERIAL PREPARATION

1. To prepare 0.50 M HCl, observe the required precautions. Add 42 mL of concentrated HCl to enough distilled water to make 1.00 L of solution. Add the acid slowly, and stop to stir it in order to avoid overheating.

2. To prepare 1.0 M HCl, add 83 mL of concentrated HCl to enough distilled water to make 1.00 L of solution.

Calorimetry and Hess's Law

OBJECTIVES

- *Demonstrate* proficiency in the use of calorimeters and related equipment.
- *Relate* temperature changes to enthalpy changes.
- *Determine* heats of reaction for several reactions.
- *Demonstrate* that heats of reactions can be additive.

MATERIALS

- **4 g NaOH pellets**
- **50 mL 1.0 M HCl acid solution**
- **50 mL 1.0 M NaOH solution**
- **100 mL 0.50 M HCl solution**
- **100 mL graduated cylinder**
- **balance**
- **distilled water**
- **forceps**
- **glass stirring rod**
- **gloves**
- **plastic-foam cups (or calorimeter)**
- **spatula**
- **thermometer**
- **watch glass**

BACKGROUND

Hess's law states that the overall enthalpy change in a reaction is equal to the sum of the enthalpy changes in the individual steps in the process. You can infer from this statement that no matter how many steps it might take to convert reactants to products, the energy released or absorbed is the same as if the reaction had taken place in one step.

In this experiment, you will use a calorimeter to carefully measure the amount of heat released in three chemical reactions. From your experimental data, you will calculate the enthalpies of the three reactions in kilojoules per mole, and you will use the equations for the reactions and the enthalpies to verify Hess's law.

SAFETY

Always wear safety goggles and a lab apron to protect your eyes and clothing. Do not touch any chemicals. If you get a chemical in your eyes, immediately flush the chemical out at the eyewash station while calling to your teacher. Know the locations of the emergency lab shower and eyewash station and the procedure for using them.

Do not touch any chemicals. If you get a chemical on your skin or clothing, wash the chemical off at the sink while calling to your teacher. Make sure you carefully read the labels and follow the precautions on all containers of chemicals that you use. If there are no precautions stated on the label, ask your teacher what precautions to follow. Do not taste any chemicals or items used in the laboratory. Never return leftovers to their original containers; take only small amounts to avoid wasting supplies.

Never put broken glass in a regular waste container. Broken glass should be disposed of separately in a container designated by your teacher.

Call your teacher in the event of an acid or base spill. Acid or base spills should be cleaned up promptly, according to your teacher's instructions.

PREPARATION

1. Prepare a data table in your notebook like the one shown below. Reactions 1 and 3 will each require two additional spaces to record the mass of the empty watch glass and the mass of the watch glass and NaOH.

2. If you are not using a plastic-foam cup as a calorimeter, ask your teacher for instructions on using the calorimeter. At various points in steps 1 through 11, you will need to measure the temperature of the solution within the calorimeter. If you are using a thermometer, measure the temperature by gently inserting the thermometer into the hole in the calorimeter lid, as shown in

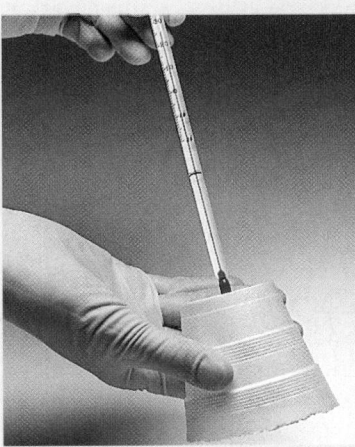
FIGURE A

Figure A. The thermometer takes time to reach the same temperature as the solution inside the calorimeter, so wait to be sure you have an accurate reading. **Thermometers break easily, so be careful with them, and do not use them to stir a solution.**

PROCEDURE

Reaction 1: Dissolving NaOH

1. Pour about 100 mL of distilled water into a graduated cylinder. Measure and record the volume of the water to the nearest 0.1 mL. Pour the water into your calorimeter. Record the water temperature to the nearest 0.1°C.

2. Determine and record the mass of a clean and dry watch glass to the nearest 0.01 g. Remove the watch glass from the balance. Wear gloves and obtain about 2 g of NaOH pellets, and put them on the watch glass. Use forceps when handling NaOH pellets, as shown in Figure B. Measure and record the mass of the watch glass and the pellets to the nearest 0.01 g. **It is important that this step be done quickly because NaOH is hygroscopic. It absorbs moisture from the air, increasing its mass as long as it remains exposed to the air.**

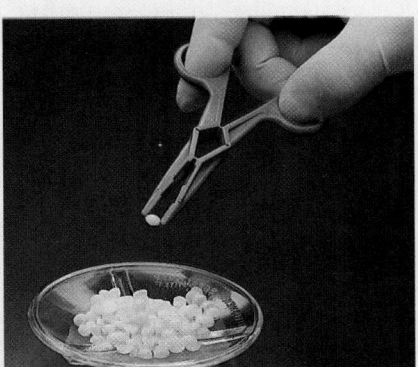
FIGURE B

Add the acid slowly, and stop to stir it in order to avoid overheating.
3. To prepare 1.0 M NaOH, add 40.0 g of NaOH to enough distilled water to make 1.00 L of solution.
4. To prevent the hygroscopic NaOH pellets from absorbing too much water, keep them in a reagent bottle with a stopper, and instruct students to replace the stopper after they have obtained what they need.

REQUIRED PRECAUTIONS
- Safety goggles and a lab apron must be worn at all times.
- Read all safety cautions, and discuss them with your students.
- Students should not handle concentrated acid solutions.
- Wear safety goggles, a face shield, impermeable gloves, and a lab apron when you prepare the HCl. Work in a hood known to be in good working order and have another person stand by to call for help in case of an emergency. Be sure you are within a 30 second walk from a safety shower and eyewash station known to be in good operating condition.
- In case of an acid spill or base spill, dilute the spill with water. Then mop up the spill with wet cloths or a wet cloth mop designated for spill cleanup. Wear disposable plastic gloves while cleaning spills.

TECHNIQUES TO DEMONSTRATE
Make certain that students use forceps to handle NaOH pellets. The pellets should not be picked up with fingers. The mass measurements must be made quickly before the pellets absorb too much moisture from the air. Make sure students use a watch glass instead of weighing paper when measuring the mass of the NaOH.

DATA TABLE	Reaction 1	Reaction 2	Reaction 3
Total volumes of liquid(s)			
Initial temp.			
Final temp.			

SAMPLE DATA

See page 893H for Data Tables.

PRE-LAB DISCUSSION

Thoroughly discuss the calorimetry equation, with reference to page 859. Consider working through some sample data with the class. At first, students may have difficulty understanding that together reactions 1 and 2 are the equivalent of reaction 3. A thorough discussion of Hess's law, as described on pages 519–520, should alleviate this problem.

DISPOSAL

Set out four disposal containers. Designate one for acidic liquids, one for basic liquids, one for neutral liquids, and one for excess NaOH pellets. When students are finished, slowly combine the liquid contents of the containers, one at a time. If there are any excess NaOH pellets, add them a few at a time to the mixture, stirring constantly to be sure the pellets dissolve. Then check the pH. Add 1.0 M acid or base until the pH is within 5 to 9, and then pour down the drain.

ANALYSIS AND INTERPRETATION—ANSWERS

1. $NaOH(s) \longrightarrow NaOH(aq)$
$NaOH(aq) + HCl(aq) \longrightarrow$
$$H_2O(l) + NaCl(aq)$$
$NaOH(s) + HCl(aq) \longrightarrow$
$$H_2O(l) + NaCl(aq)$$

2. equation 1 + equation 2 = equation 3

3. A good calorimeter must insulate so that any heat created by the reaction is absorbed by the water instead of the surroundings. Plastic-foam cups insulate better than paper ones, so they make better calorimeters.

4. $\Delta t_1 = 26.5°C - 21.5°C = 5.0°C$
$\Delta t_2 = 28.1°C - 22.0°C = 6.1°C$
$\Delta t_3 = 33.0°C - 22.0°C = 11.0°C$

5. $m = 100.0 \text{ mL } H_2O \times \dfrac{1.00 \text{ g}}{1 \text{ mL } H_2O} =$

100.0 g H_2O for all three reactions

3. Immediately place the NaOH pellets in the calorimeter cup, and gently stir the solution with a stirring rod. **Do not stir with a thermometer.** Place the lid on the calorimeter. Watch the thermometer and record the highest temperature in the data table. When finished with this reaction, pour the solution into the container designated by your teacher for disposal of basic solutions.

4. Be sure to clean all equipment and rinse it with distilled water before continuing with the next procedure.

Reaction 2: NaOH and HCl in solution

5. Pour about 50 mL of 1.0 M HCl into a graduated cylinder. Measure and record the volume of the HCl solution to the nearest 0.1 mL. Pour the HCl solution into your calorimeter. Record the temperature of the HCl solution to the nearest 0.1°C.

6. Pour about 50 mL of 1.0 M NaOH into a graduated cylinder. Measure and record the volume of the NaOH solution to the nearest 0.1 mL. **For this step only, rinse the thermometer, and measure the temperature of the NaOH solution in the graduated cylinder to the nearest 0.1°C. Record the temperature in your data table and then replace the thermometer in the calorimeter.**

7. Pour the NaOH solution into the calorimeter cup, and stir gently. Place the lid on the calorimeter. Watch the thermometer and record the highest temperature in the data table. When finished with this reaction, pour the solution into the container designated by your teacher for disposal of mostly neutral solutions.

8. Clean and rinse all equipment before continuing with the procedure.

Reaction 3: Solid NaOH and HCl in solution

9. Pour about 100 mL of 0.50 M HCl into a graduated cylinder. Measure and record the volume to the nearest 0.1 mL. Pour the HCl solution into your calorimeter. Record the temperature of the HCl solution to the nearest 0.1°C.

10. Measure the mass of a clean and dry watch glass, and record the mass in your data table. Wear gloves, and using forceps, obtain approximately 2 g of NaOH pellets. Place them on the watch glass, and record the total mass to the nearest 0.01 g. **It is important that this step be done quickly because NaOH is hygroscopic. It absorbs moisture from the air, increasing its mass as long as it remains exposed to the air.**

11. Immediately place the NaOH pellets in the calorimeter, and gently stir the solution. Place the lid on the calorimeter. Watch the thermometer and record the highest temperature in the data table. When finished with this reaction, pour the solution into the container designated by your teacher for disposal of mostly neutral solutions.

CLEANUP AND DISPOSAL

12. Check with your teacher for the proper disposal procedures. Any excess NaOH pellets should be disposed of in the designated container. Always wash your hands thoroughly after cleaning up the lab area and equipment.

ANALYSIS AND INTERPRETATION

1. **Organizing Ideas:** Write a balanced chemical equation for each of the three reactions that you performed. (Hint: Be sure to include the physical states of matter for all substances in each equation.)

2. **Organizing Ideas:** Write the equation for the total reaction by adding two of the equations from item 1 and then canceling out substances that appear in the same form on both sides of the new equation. (Hint: Start with the equation that has a product which is a reactant in the second equation. Add those two equations together.)

3. **Analyzing Methods:** Explain why a plastic-foam cup makes a better calorimeter than a paper cup does.

4. **Organizing Data:** Calculate the change in temperature for each of the reactions.

5. **Organizing Data:** Assuming that the density of the water and the solutions is 1.00 g/mL, calculate the mass of liquid present for each of the reactions.

6. **Analyzing Results:** Using the calorimeter equation, calculate the heat released by each reaction. Hint: Use the specific heat capacity of water in your calculations.

$$c_{p, H_2O} = 4.180 \text{ J/g} \cdot °C$$

$$\text{Heat} = m \times \Delta t \times c_{p, H_2O}$$

7. **Organizing Data:** Calculate the moles of NaOH used in each of the reactions.

8. **Analyzing Results:** Calculate the ΔH value in kJ/mol of NaOH for each of the three reactions.

9. **Organizing Ideas:** Using your answer to Analysis and Interpretation item 2 and your knowledge of Hess's law from Chapter 17, explain how the enthalpies for the three reactions should be mathematically related.

10. **Organizing Ideas:** Which of the following types of heats of reaction apply to the enthalpies calculated in Analysis and Interpretation item 8: heat of combustion, heat of solution, heat of reaction, heat of fusion, heat of vaporization, and heat of formation?

CONCLUSIONS

1. **Evaluating Methods:** Use your answers to items 8 and 9 in Analysis and Interpretation to determine the ΔH value for the reaction of solid NaOH with HCl solution by direct measurement and by indirect calculation.

2. **Inferring Conclusions:** Third-degree burns can occur if skin comes into contact for more than 4 s with water that is hotter than 60°C (140°F). Suppose someone accidentally poured hydrochloric acid into a glass disposal container that already contained a drain cleaner, NaOH.

The container shattered. Investigators estimated that the drain cleaner was about 55 g NaOH and the 450 mL of HCl contained 1.35 mol of HCl (a 3.0 M HCl solution). If the initial temperature of each solution was 25°C, could the mixture have been hot enough to cause burns?

3. **Applying Conclusions:** For the reaction between drain cleaner and HCl described in Conclusions item 2, which chemical is the limiting reactant? How many moles of the other reactant remained unreacted?

EXTENSIONS

1. **Applying Ideas:** When chemists make a solution from NaOH pellets, they often keep the solution in an ice bath. Explain why.

2. **Applying Ideas:** When a strongly acidic or basic solution is spilled on a person, the first treatment step is to dilute the solution by washing the area of the spill with a lot of water. Explain why adding an acid or base to neutralize the solution immediately is not a good idea.

3. **Evaluating Methods:** You have worked with heats of solution for exothermic reactions. Could the same type of procedure be used to determine the temperature changes for endothermic reactions? What parts of the procedure would stay the same?

4. **Applying Ideas:** A chemical supply company is going to ship NaOH pellets to a very humid place, and the company has asked for your advice on packaging. Design a package for the NaOH pellets. Explain the advantages of your package's design and materials. (Hint: Remember that the reaction in which NaOH absorbs moisture from the air is an exothermic one and that NaOH reacts exothermically with other compounds as well.)

5. **Inferring Conclusions:** Which is more stable, solid NaOH or a solution of NaOH? Explain.

6. Heat for reaction 1:

$$100.0 \text{ g } H_2O \times 5.0°C \times \frac{4.184 \text{ J}}{1 \text{ g} \cdot °C} = 2100 \text{ J} = 2.1 \text{ kJ}$$

Heat for reaction 2:

$$100.0 \text{ g } H_2O \times 6.1°C \times \frac{4.184 \text{ J}}{1 \text{ g} \cdot °C} = 2500 \text{ J} = 2.5 \text{ kJ}$$

Heat for reaction 3:

$$100.0 \text{ g } H_2O \times 11.0°C \times \frac{4.184 \text{ J}}{1 \text{ g} \cdot °C} = 4600 \text{ J} = 4.6 \text{ kJ}$$

7. Moles NaOH for reaction 1:

$$2.00 \text{ g} \times \frac{1 \text{ mol NaOH}}{40.00 \text{ g}} = 5.00 \times 10^{-2} \text{ mol}$$

Moles NaOH for reaction 2:

$$50 \text{ mL} \times \frac{1 \text{ L}}{1000 \text{ mL}} \times \frac{1.00 \text{ mol NaOH}}{1 \text{ L}} = 5.00 \times 10^{-2} \text{ mol}$$

Moles NaOH for reaction 3:

$$2.01 \text{ g} \times \frac{1 \text{ mol NaOH}}{40.00 \text{ g}} = 5.02 \times 10^{-2} \text{ mol}$$

8. Enthalpy changes should be negative because the reactions are exothermic.

$$\Delta H_1 = \frac{-2.1 \text{ kJ}}{5.00 \times 10^{-2} \text{ mol NaOH}} = -42 \text{ kJ/mol NaOH}$$

$$\Delta H_2 = \frac{-2.5 \text{ kJ}}{5.00 \times 10^{-2} \text{ mol NaOH}} = -50 \text{ kJ/mol NaOH}$$

$$\Delta H_3 = \frac{-4.6 \text{ kJ}}{5.02 \times 10^{-2} \text{ mol NaOH}} = -92 \text{ kJ/mol NaOH}$$

9. The sum of heats for the first two reactions should equal the heat for the third reaction.

10. Reaction 1 involved heat of solution. Reaction 2 involved heat of reaction. Reaction 3 involved heat of solution and heat of reaction.

Continued on page 893H

EXPERIMENT 17-3

OBJECTIVES
Students will
- use appropriate lab safety procedures.
- prepare reaction mixtures of several different concentrations.
- observe chemical processes and interactions.
- measure time elapsed before the color change of an indicator.
- graph data to determine the relationship between concentration and reaction rate.
- describe the relationship in terms of a rate law.

RECOMMENDED TIME
45–60 min

MATERIALS
(for each lab group)
- solution A, 5 mL (1.0 M H_2SO_4, $Na_2S_2O_5$, and soluble starch)
- solution B, 5 mL (KIO_3)
- distilled or deionized water
- 8-well microscale reaction strips, 2
- fine-tipped dropper bulbs or small microtip pipets, 3
- stopwatch or clock with second hand

SOLUTION/MATERIAL PREPARATION
1. To prepare solution A, make a paste of 1 g of water-soluble starch and about 10 mL of water. Add 225 mL of boiling distilled water. Reheat and boil for a few minutes. After the solution has cooled, add 0.05 g of $Na_2S_2O_5$ (sodium metabisulfate) and 1.3 mL of 1.0 M H_2SO_4. Dilute with enough distilled water to make 250 mL of solution. (Note: This solution should be prepared within two months of use.)
2. To prepare 10 mL of 1.0 M H_2SO_4, observe the required precautions.

EXPERIMENT 17-3

Rate of a Chemical Reaction

OBJECTIVES

- *Prepare* and *observe* several different reaction mixtures.
- *Demonstrate* proficiency in measuring reaction rates.
- *Relate* experimental results to a rate law that can be used to predict the results of various combinations of reactants.

MATERIALS

- **8-well microscale reaction strips, 2**
- **distilled or deionized water**
- **fine-tipped dropper bulbs or small microtip pipets, 3**
- **solution A**
- **solution B**
- **stopwatch or clock with second hand**

BACKGROUND

In this experiment, you will determine the rate of an *oxidation-reduction*, or *redox*, reaction. Reactions of this type involve a special kind of electron transfer and will be discussed in Chapter 19. The net equation for the reaction you will study is written as follows:

$$3Na_2S_2O_5(aq) + 2KIO_3(aq) + 3H_2O(l) \xrightarrow{H^+} 2KI(aq) + 6NaHSO_4(aq)$$

One way to study the rate of this reaction is to observe how fast $Na_2S_2O_5$ is used up. After all the $Na_2S_2O_5$ solution has reacted, the concentration of iodine, I_2, an intermediate in the reaction, builds up. A starch indicator solution, added to the reaction mixture, will signal when this happens. The colorless starch will change to a blue-black color in the presence of I_2.

In the procedure, the concentrations of the reactants are given in terms of drops of solution A and drops of solution B. Solution A contains $Na_2S_2O_5$, the starch indicator solution, and dilute sulfuric acid to supply the hydrogen ions needed to catalyze the reaction. Solution B contains KIO_3. You will run the reaction with several different concentrations of the reactants and record the time it takes for the blue-black color to appear.

SAFETY

Always wear safety goggles and a lab apron to protect your eyes and clothing. If you get a chemical in your eyes, immediately flush the chemical out at the eyewash station while calling to your teacher. Know the locations of the emergency lab shower and eyewash station and the procedure for using them.

Do not touch any chemicals. If you get a chemical on your skin or clothing, wash the chemical off at the sink while calling to your teacher. Make sure you carefully read the labels and follow the precautions on all containers of chemicals that you use. Never return leftovers to their original containers; take only small amounts to avoid wasting supplies.

PREPARATION

1. Prepare a data table in your lab notebook. The table should have six rows and six columns. Label the boxes in the first row of the second through sixth columns *Well 1*, *Well 2*, *Well 3*, *Well 4*, and *Well 5*. In the first column, label the boxes in the second through sixth rows *Time reaction began*, *Time reaction stopped*, *Drops of solution A*, *Drops of solution B*, and *Drops of H_2O*.

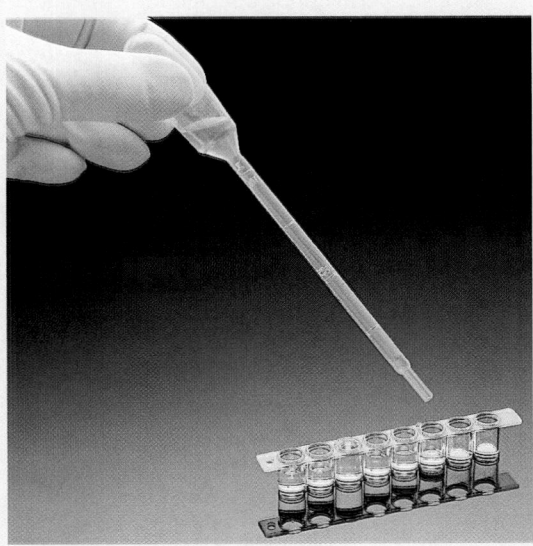

FIGURE A

2. Obtain three dropper bulbs or small microtip pipets, and label them *A*, *B*, and *H_2O*.

3. Fill the bulb or pipet A with solution A, the bulb or pipet B with solution B, and the bulb or pipet for H_2O with distilled water.

PROCEDURE

1. Using the first 8-well strip, place five drops of solution A into each of the first five wells, as shown in Figure A. (Disregard the remaining three wells.) Record the number of drops in the appropriate places in your data table. **For best results, try to make all drops about the same size.**

2. In the second 8-well reaction strip, place one drop of solution B in the first well, two drops in the second well, three drops in the third well, four drops in the fourth well, and five drops in the fifth well. Record the number of drops in the appropriate places in your data table.

3. In the second 8-well strip that contains drops of solution B, add four drops of water to the first well, three drops to the second well, two drops to the third well, and one drop to the fourth well. Do not add any water to the fifth well.

4. Carefully invert the second strip. The surface tension should keep the solutions from falling out of the wells. Place the strip well-to-well on top of the first strip, as shown in Figure B.

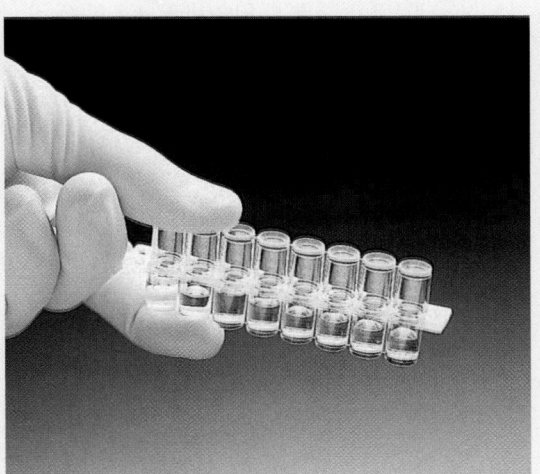

FIGURE B

Add 0.6 mL of concentrated H_2SO_4 to 9.4 mL of distilled water. Add the acid slowly, and stop to stir it in order to avoid overheating.

3. To prepare solution B, dissolve 1.07 g KIO_3 in enough distilled water to make 250 mL of solution.

4. If the reaction suggested here is too slow, add a few milligrams of $Na_2S_2O_5$ to solution A. If it is too fast, add some distilled water to solution B to lower the concentration of KIO_3.

5. Other clock reactions may be used, but they should give distinctive end points. Be sure to test the reaction you use beforehand. Make certain you are familiar with proper disposal methods for the reactants and products.

6. Fine-tipped dropper bulbs are available commercially or may be made out of thin-stemmed pipets. Stretch the pipets by hand, narrowing the tube near the bulb, and then cut off the excess.

REQUIRED PRECAUTIONS
- Safety goggles and a lab apron must be worn at all times.
- Read all safety cautions, and discuss them with your students.
- Students should not handle concentrated acid solutions.
- Wear safety goggles, a face shield, impermeable gloves, and a lab apron when you prepare the H_2SO_4. Work in a hood known to be in good working order and have another person stand by to call for help in case of an emergency. Work within a 30 second walk from a safety shower and eyewash station known to be in good operating condition.
- In case of an acid spill, dilute the spill with water. Then mop up the spill with wet cloths or a mop designated for spill cleanup. Wear disposable plastic gloves while cleaning spills.

TECHNIQUES TO DEMONSTRATE
Point out that holding the dropper bulbs vertically will help ensure that drops are consistent in size.

SAMPLE DATA
See page 893H for Data Table.

PRE-LAB DISCUSSION
Thoroughly discuss the concept of reaction rate. Work through a calculation with sample data, relating time elapsed to rate and the resulting rate data to a rate expression that involves concentration.

DISPOSAL
Set out one container for disposal. Treat the waste with 1.0 M $Na_2S_2O_3$ solution to be certain all iodine is reduced to iodide. Neutralize the solution with 1.0 M acid or base, and pour it down the drain.

ANALYSIS AND INTERPRETATION—ANSWERS
1. Students will need to convert from minutes and seconds to seconds alone.

Well 1: 143 s   Well 4: 35 s
Well 2: 67 s   Well 5: 26 s
Well 3: 43 s

2.

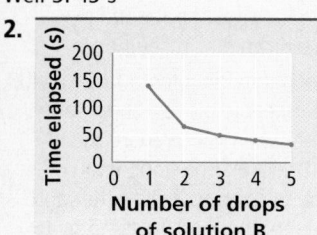

Number of drops of solution B

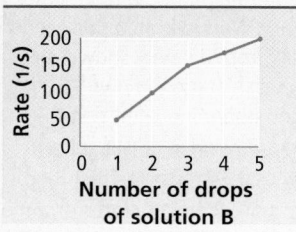

Number of drops of solution B

Continued on page 893H

5. Holding the strips tightly together as shown in Figure B, record the exact time, or set the stopwatch, as you shake the strips once, using a vigorous motion. This procedure should effectively mix the upper solutions with each of the corresponding lower ones.

6. Observe the lower wells. Note the sequence in which the solutions react, and record the number of seconds it takes for each solution to turn a blue-black color.

CLEANUP AND DISPOSAL
7. Dispose of the solutions in the container designated by your teacher. Wash your hands thoroughly after cleaning up the area and equipment.

ANALYSIS AND INTERPRETATION
1. Organizing Data: Calculate the time elapsed for the complete reaction of each combination of solution A and B.

2. Evaluating Data: Make a graph of your results. Label the x-axis *Number of drops of solution B*. Label the y-axis *Time elapsed*. Make a similar graph for drops of solution B versus rate (1/time elapsed).

3. Analyzing Information: Which mixture reacted the fastest? Which mixture reacted the slowest?

4. Evaluating Methods: Why was it important to add the drops of water to the wells that contained fewer than five drops of solution B? (Hint: Figure out the total number of drops in each of the reaction wells.)

CONCLUSIONS
1. Analyzing Methods: How can you be sure that each of the chemical reactions began at about the same time?

2. Evaluating Conclusions: Which of the following variables that can affect the rate of a reaction is tested in this experiment: temperature, catalyst, concentration, surface area, or nature of reactants? Explain your answer.

3. Applying Ideas: Use your data and graphs to determine the relationship between the concentration of solution B and the rate of the reaction. Describe this relationship in terms of a rate law.

EXTENSIONS
1. Analyzing Methods: What are some possible sources of error in this procedure? If you can think of ways to eliminate them, ask your teacher to approve your plan and run your procedure again.

2. Predicting Outcomes: What combination of drops of solutions A and B would you use if you wanted the reaction to last exactly 2.5 min?

3. Predicting Outcomes: How would your data differ if the experiment was repeated but solution A was diluted with one part solution for every seven parts distilled water?

4. Designing Experiments: How would you determine the smallest interval of time during which you could distinguish a reaction? Design an experiment to find out. If your teacher approves your plan, perform your experiment.

5. Designing Experiments: How would the results of this experiment be affected if the reaction took place in a cold environment?

6. Designing Experiments: Devise a plan to determine the effect of solution A on the rate law. If your teacher approves your plan, perform your experiment, and determine the rate law for this reaction.

7. Relating Ideas: If solution B contains 0.02 M KIO_3, calculate the value for the constant, k, in the expression below. (Hint: Remember that solution B is diluted when it is added to solution A.)

$$Rate = k[KIO_3]$$

EXPERIMENT 18-1

Equilibrium Expressions

OBJECTIVES

- *Demonstrate* proficiency in preparing serial dilutions from a standard solution and in comparing solutions visually or by spectrophotometer.

- *Relate* spectrophotometric determinations to solution concentration.

- *Determine* experimentally the equilibrium expression of a chemical reaction.

MATERIALS

- **10 mL 0.200 M Fe(NO₃)₃**
- **10 mL graduated cylinder**
- **25 mL 0.002 00 M KSCN**
- **25 mL 0.6 M HNO₃**
- **glass stirring rod**
- **test-tube rack**
- **test tubes, 6**

OPTIONAL EQUIPMENT

- **cuvettes**
- **lint-free wipes for cuvettes**
- **spectrophotometer**

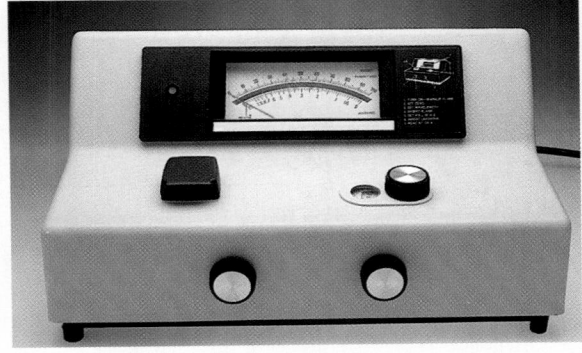

BACKGROUND

The reaction of iron(III) nitrate, $Fe(NO_3)_3$, and potassium thiocyanate, KSCN, is one that usually reaches equilibrium. The following is the net ionic equation for the reaction.

$$Fe^{3+}(aq) + SCN^-(aq) \longrightarrow FeSCN^{2+}(aq)$$
$$\text{(yellow)} \quad \text{(colorless)} \qquad \text{(red)}$$

At equilibrium, $FeSCN^{2+}$ is produced at a rate equal to the rate at which $FeSCN^{2+}$ is breaking up into Fe^{3+} and SCN^-. If the concentration of Fe^{3+} ions is increased, the equilibrium will be disturbed and a new equilibrium will be reached with different concentrations of the reactants and product. The reaction can be studied by colorimetry because the product, $FeSCN^{2+}$, is red. The greater the concentration of $FeSCN^{2+}$, the more intense the red color.

You will prepare several solutions of $Fe(NO_3)_3$, each with a different concentration, and mix them with a 0.002 00 M solution of KSCN. You can compare the intensity of the red color for each solution to the colors of known concentrations of $FeSCN^{2+}$. You can then calculate the concentrations of Fe^{3+} and SCN^- at equilibrium.

The molar concentration of reactants and products at equilibrium can be arranged in a mathematical expression called the *equilibrium expression*. At any given temperature, the equilibrium expression has a constant value called the *equilibrium constant, K_{eq}*.

Using your data, you can calculate the equilibrium constant and then use the equilibrium expression to evaluate your determinations of $FeSCN^{2+}$ concentrations.

SAFETY

Always wear safety goggles and a lab apron to protect your eyes and clothing. If you get a chemical in your eyes, immediately flush the chemical out at the eyewash station

OBJECTIVES
Students will
- use appropriate safety procedures.
- perform serial dilutions to create solutions of different concentrations.
- combine two different solutions to create an equilibrium system.
- relate colorimetric observations or measurements to the concentration of one substance in an equilibrium system.
- graph data to create a standard curve for absorbance.
- determine the equilibrium expression of a chemical reaction.

RECOMMENDED TIME
45–60 min (depends on availability of equipment)

MATERIALS
(for each lab group)
- 10 mL 0.002 00 M KSCN
- 10 mL graduated cylinder
- 25 mL 0.200 M Fe(NO₃)₃
- 25 mL 0.6 M HNO₃
- glass stirring rod
- test-tube rack
- test tubes, 6

OPTIONAL EQUIPMENT
- cuvettes
- lint-free wipes
- spectrophotometer

SOLUTION/MATERIALS PREPARATION
1. Do not prepare the solutions too far in advance because they will oxidize and change color. The students running tests at the end of the period may have different results from those performing the same tests earlier.
2. To prepare 0.200 M Fe(NO₃)₃, add 80.80 g Fe(NO₃)₃·9H₂O to enough distilled water to make 1.00 L of solution.

3. To prepare 0.6 M HNO_3, observe the required precautions. Add 38 mL of concentrated HNO_3 to enough distilled water to make 1.00 L of solution. Add the acid slowly, and stop to stir it in order to avoid overheating.

4. To prepare 0.002 00 M KSCN, add 0.194 g KSCN to enough distilled water to make 1 L of solution.

5. Use test tubes that are 18 mm × 150 mm or larger.

REQUIRED PRECAUTIONS

- Read all safety precautions, and discuss them with your students.
- Safety goggles and a lab apron must be worn at all times.
- Students should not handle concentrated acid solutions.
- In case of an acid spill, dilute the spill with water. Then mop up the spill with wet cloths or a mop designated for spill cleanup. Wear disposable plastic gloves while cleaning spills.
- Wear safety goggles, a face shield, impermeable gloves, and a lab apron when you prepare the HNO_3. Work in a hood known to be in good working order and have another person stand by to call for help in case of an emergency. Work within a 30 second walk from a safety shower and eyewash station.

TECHNIQUES TO DEMONSTRATE

Show students how to operate the spectrophotometer if it is to be used. Emphasize the need to check the calibration of the instrument repeatedly and to wipe the cuvettes with lint-free wipes. Students should prepare all of their dilutions before using the instrument. Discuss the preparation of the standard absorbance curve.

 while calling to your teacher. Know the locations of the emergency lab shower and eyewash station and the procedure for using them.

 Do not touch any chemicals. If you get a chemical on your skin or clothing, wash the chemical off at the sink while calling to your teacher. Make sure you carefully read the labels and follow the precautions on all containers of chemicals that you use. Do not taste any chemicals or items used in the laboratory. Never return leftover chemicals to their original containers; take only small amounts to avoid wasting supplies.

PREPARATION

1. Copy the data table below into your lab notebook.

2. If you will be using a spectrophotometer, turn it on now, as it must warm up for approximately 10 min.

3. Label six test tubes *1*, *2*, *3*, *4*, *5*, and *6*.

PROCEDURE

1. Carefully measure 5.0 mL of 0.200 M $Fe(NO_3)_3$ using a 10 mL graduated cylinder. Pour this solution into test tube 1, as shown in Figure A. Record this volume and concentration in the data table.

2. Carefully measure another 5.0 mL of 0.200 M $Fe(NO_3)_3$ using the 10 mL graduated cylinder. Add 5.0 mL of 0.6 M HNO_3 to the $Fe(NO_3)_3$ solution in the graduated cylinder. Mix well with a glass stirring rod. Pour 5.0 mL of this mixture

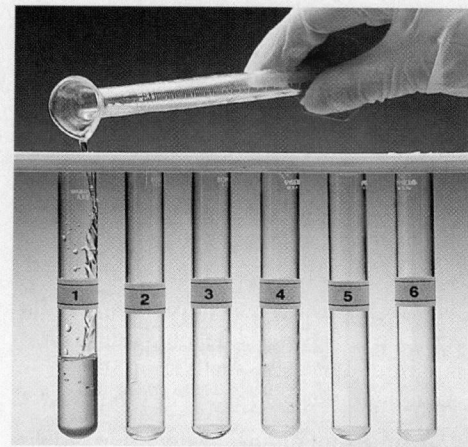

FIGURE A

into the test tube 2. Record 5 mL as the volume in the test tube 2 and record the Fe^{3+} concentration in the data table. (Hint: The concentration of Fe^{3+} is half of what it was for test tube 1 because the $Fe(NO_3)_3$ has been diluted by an equal volume of HNO_3.)

3. Add 5.0 mL of 0.6 M HNO_3 to the remaining 5.0 mL of the mixture in the graduated cylinder. Mix well with a glass stirring rod. Pour 5.0 mL of this mixture into test tube 3. Record 5.0 mL as the volume for test tube 3 and record the Fe^{3+} concentration in the data table.

4. Repeat Procedure step 3 until you have filled all six test tubes.

5. Discard the contents of test tube 2, pouring it into the waste container designated by your teacher. (This dilution does not provide a measurable difference in light absorption.)

DATA TABLE

Test tube no.	Fe^{3+} conc.	mL of Fe^{3+}	mL of KSCN	Absorbance value
1				
2				
3				
4				
5				
6				
Observations				

6. Add 5.0 mL of 0.002 00 M KSCN to test tubes 1, 3, 4, 5, and 6. Mix each solution thoroughly with a stirring rod. Record the volume of KSCN used in the data table.

7. Compare the solutions while holding a piece of white paper behind the test tubes. If you are not using a spectrophotometer, estimate the intensity of the red color on a scale from 0 (clear) to 1.0 (test tube 1), and enter your estimate in the *Absorbance value* column of the data table.

8. If you are not using a spectrophotometer, go on to step 11. If you are using a spectrophotometer, allow it to warm up for 10 minutes.

Spectrophotometer
Set the wavelength to 590 nm. **Note that you should be measuring absorbance, NOT percent transmittance.** Calibrate the spectrophotometer by turning the left front knob to 0 percent transmittance while using an empty sample compartment with the lid closed. Then pour some solution from test tube 1 into the cuvette and adjust the absorbance value with the right front knob to read as close to 1.00 as possible. **Never wipe cuvettes with paper towels or scrub them with a test-tube brush. Use only lint-free tissues that will not scratch the cuvette's surface. The outside of the cuvette must be completely dry before it is placed inside an instrument, or you will get an invalid reading.**

9. With your instrument adjusted accordingly, record the absorbance value for the solution from test tube 1. If you have only one cuvette, rinse it several times with distilled water, and then make absorbance measurements for test tube 3. Record this value in your data table. Rinse the cuvette several times with distilled water, and measure and record absorbance values for test tubes 4, 5, and 6 in your data table.

10. To check your measurements, retest the solution from test tube 1 after you have finished the other measurements. Its absorbance value should still be the same, close to 1.00. If not, repeat the procedure for all solutions.

CLEANUP AND DISPOSAL

11. Dispose of all solutions in the container designated by your teacher. Wash your hands thoroughly after cleaning up the area and equipment.

ANALYSIS AND INTERPRETATION

1. **Analyzing Data:** Determine how each of the absorbance values relates to the absorbance value for test tube 1 by dividing each value by the value obtained for test tube 1. (Hint: After this calculation, the new value for test tube 1 should be 1.00, and the values for the other test tubes should be less than 1.00 because they were less concentrated than test tube 1. If you were using estimates instead of colorimetry measurements, this step can be skipped.)

2. **Analyzing Data:** Calculate the initial concentrations of SCN^- for test tubes *1, 3, 4, 5,* and *6.* Remember that each 5.0 mL of 0.002 00 M KSCN was mixed with 5.0 mL of $Fe(NO_3)_3$ solution to give a total volume of 10.0 mL. (Hint: The value will be the same for all the test tubes.)

3. **Analyzing Data:** Calculate the actual initial concentration of Fe^{3+} in the test tubes in a similar way. (Hint: The values recorded in the data table show the concentration of Fe^{3+} before it was diluted by 5.0 mL of 0.002 00 M KSCN.)

4. **Applying Ideas:** Determine the equilibrium concentrations for test tube 1. Because the initial concentration of Fe^{3+} was 0.100 M—much larger than the initial concentration of SCN^-, 0.001 M—assume that practically all of the SCN^- ions are consumed in the reaction. (Even though this is not necessarily true, the deviation from the true SCN^- concentration is so much smaller than the other factors in this equation that it can be disregarded in this case.)

5. **Analyzing Data:** Calculate the $FeSCN^{2+}$ equilibrium concentration for test tubes *3, 4, 5,* and *6* based on the absorbance data and the equilibrium concentration for test tube 1 determined in Analysis and Interpretation item 4.

See page 893I for Data Table.

PRE-LAB DISCUSSION
This experiment gives students a practical example of the concept of an equilibrium expression for a chemical reaction and provides some practice in performing equilibrium calculations. Students may be confused by the calculations and lose sight of what they are measuring and why. Remind students that if they keep track of what all of the numbers mean, it will help them avoid common errors. Because these calculations are so complicated, it is important to work through a set of sample data before the lab.

DISPOSAL
Set out one disposal container for the solutions from this lab. Neutralize the waste with 1.0 M base until the pH is between 5 and 9, and store it.

ANALYSIS AND INTERPRETATION—ANSWERS
1. Student answers will vary. If the instrument was calibrated to give a reading of 1.00 for test tube 1, this step is unnecessary and the values in the data table will suffice.

Continued on page 893I

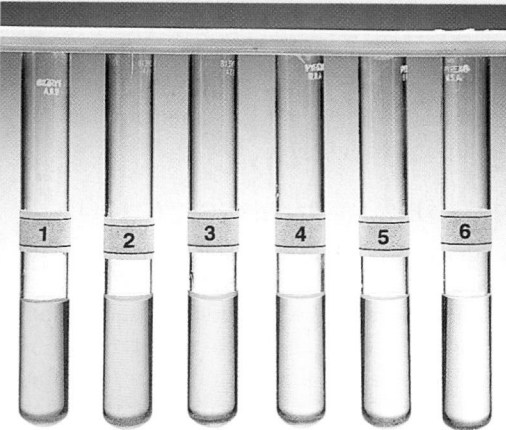

FIGURE B

(Hint: Multiply the concentration for test tube 1 by the factors calculated in Analysis and Interpretation item 1.)

6. **Analyzing Data:** Calculate the SCN^- concentration for test tubes 3–6 at equilibrium. (Hint: You know the initial SCN^- concentration from Analysis and Interpretation item 2, and you know the amount of SCN^- that has formed $FeSCN^{2+}$ from item 5.)

7. **Analyzing Data:** For test tubes 3–6, calculate the Fe^{3+} concentration at equilibrium. (Hint: You know the initial Fe^{3+} concentration from Analysis and Interpretation item 3, and you know the amount of Fe^{3+} that has formed $FeSCN^{2+}$ from Analysis and Interpretation item 5.)

8. **Analyzing Data:** Graph the adjusted absorbance values from Analysis and Interpretation item 1 against the initial concentration values for Fe^{3+}.

CONCLUSIONS

1. **Evaluating Data:** For test tubes 3–6, determine the value of the equilibrium constant, K_{eq}, for this reaction by using the equation given below. (Hint: Use the equilibrium concentrations determined in Analysis and Interpretation items 5, 6, and 7.)

$$K_{eq} = \frac{[FeSCN^{2+}]}{[Fe^{3+}][SCN^-]}$$

2. **Evaluating Methods:** Although the values for K_{eq} should be equal, describe the conditions that could cause these values to differ.

3. **Interpreting Graphics:** What general statement can you make about the absorbance values compared with the concentrations of Fe^{3+} and $FeSCN^{2+}$?

EXTENSIONS

1. **Designing Experiments:** How would you revise this procedure to determine the value of the equilibrium constant at different temperatures? Would you be able to maintain accurate data analysis for high or low temperature ranges? Explain your answers.

2. **Designing Experiments:** What possible sources of error can you identify with this procedure? If you can think of ways to eliminate them, ask your teacher to approve your plans, and run the procedure again.

3. **Applying Ideas:** Hundreds of different equilibrium reactions are taking place constantly in your body. One very important equilibrium reaction involves oxygen, O_2, and hemoglobin, a complex protein abbreviated as Hb, to form oxyhemoglobin, HbO_2.

$$Hb + O_2 \rightleftharpoons HbO_2$$

In your lungs, where oxygen is abundant, the forward reaction is favored. The oxyhemoglobin then travels in your bloodstream to your oxygen-starved cells. In the cells, the reverse reaction is favored, releasing the oxygen. In this way, equilibrium is maintained as you continue to live and breathe. Write the equilibrium expression for the reaction above involving oxygen, hemoglobin, and oxyhemoglobin.

4. **Predicting Outcomes:** At the elevation of Mexico City, 2300 m (7500 ft), the concentration of oxygen is 75% of that at sea level. Yet the same amount of oxygen needs to be delivered to the muscle cells. To compensate, does the body produce more or less hemoglobin? Explain your answer. How is your breathing rate affected at high elevations?

Measuring K_a for Acetic Acid

OBJECTIVES

- *Compare* the conductivities of solutions of known and unknown hydronium ion concentrations.

- *Relate* conductivity to the concentration of ions in solution.

- *Explain* the validity of the procedure on the basis of the definitions of strong and weak acids.

- *Compute* the numerical value of K_a for acetic acid.

MATERIALS

- **1.0 M acetic acid, CH₃COOH**
- **1.0 M hydrochloric acid, HCl**
- **24-well plate**
- **distilled or deionized water**
- **LED conductivity testers**
- **paper towels**
- **thin-stemmed pipets**

BACKGROUND

The acid-dissociation constant, K_a, is a measure of the strength of an acid. Strong acids, which are almost completely ionized in water, have much larger K_a values than weak acids because weak acids are only partly ionized. Properties that depend on the ability of a substance to ionize, such as conductivity and colligative properties, can be used to measure K_a. In this experiment, you will compare the conductivity of a 1.0 M solution of acetic acid, CH_3COOH, a weak acid, with the conductivities of solutions of varying concentrations of hydrochloric acid, HCl, a strong acid. From the comparisons you make, you will be able to estimate the concentration of hydronium ions in the acetic acid solution and calculate its K_a.

SAFETY

Always wear safety goggles and a lab apron to protect your eyes and clothing. If you get a chemical in your eyes, immediately flush the chemical out at the eyewash station while calling to your teacher. Know the location of the emergency lab shower and eyewash station and the procedures for using them.

Do not touch any chemicals. If you get a chemical on your skin or clothing, wash the chemical off at the sink while calling to your teacher. Read labels carefully and follow the precautions on all containers of chemicals that you use. If no precautions are stated on the label, ask your teacher what precautions to follow. Do not taste any chemicals or items used in the laboratory. Never return leftover chemicals to their original containers; take only small amounts to avoid wasting supplies.

OBJECTIVES
Students will
- use appropriate safety procedures.
- use microscale techniques effectively.
- compare the conductivities of acid solutions.
- infer the concentration of hydronium ions from observations.
- predict outcomes when this procedure is applied to concentrations of different acids.

RECOMMENDED TIME
45–60 min, including Extensions

MATERIALS
(for each lab group)
- 3 mL 1.0 M CH₃COOH
- 3 mL 0.10 M CH₃COOH, for Extension 3
- 3 mL 1.0 M HCl
- 3 mL 0.50 M lactic acid, for Extension 4
- distilled or deionized water
- 24-well plate
- LED conductivity tester
- paper towels
- thin-stemmed pipets, 2

SOLUTION/MATERIALS PREPARATION

1. To prepare 50 mL of 1.0 M hydrochloric acid, observe the safety precautions. Add 4.3 mL of concentrated HCl to enough water to make 50 mL of solution.

2. To prepare 50 mL of 1.0 M acetic acid, observe the safety precautions. Add 2.3 mL of glacial acetic acid to enough water to make 50 mL of solution. To prepare 50 mL of 0.10 M acetic acid for Extension 3, dilute 5 mL of 1.0 M acetic acid to 50 mL.

3. To prepare 50 mL of 0.50 M lactic acid for Extension 4, add 2.2 mL of 85% lab grade lactic acid to enough water to make 50 mL of solution.

4. LED conductivity testers may be assembled from parts or bought from Lab Aids. Lab Aids also sells a conductivity tester that emits a tone rather than light. Students may find that distinguishing small differences in tone is easier than distinguishing small differences in light intensity.

    If you want to make conductivity testers, you will need the following materials for each tester:

• 1 kΩ resistor (1/4 W)
• LED (light-emitting diode)
• 9 V battery with battery clips
• film canister with lid
• 10 cm and 20 cm lengths of hook-up wire (22 GA, solid)
• 3.5 cm length of straw or tubing
• electrician's tape
• glue gun (optional)

CONDUCTIVITY TESTER ASSEMBLY

See the diagrams in the margin, on the next page.

1. Strip 1.5 cm of insulation from the ends of the hook-up wires and from the battery clip leads. Cut the resistor leads down to half of their length.

2. Poke two holes near the edge of the canister cap about as far apart as the two LED leads are. Insert the leads through the holes, and spread them apart slightly.

3. Connect the circuit as shown in the diagram. **Be sure the *red* battery clip lead is connected to the *longer* LED lead.** The black battery clip lead should connect to the resistor, and the other end of the resistor should connect to the 10 cm wire. The shorter LED lead should be connected to the 20 cm wire. Bend the leads up and tape them against the inside of the lid so that they are not touching each other and there are no exposed wires.

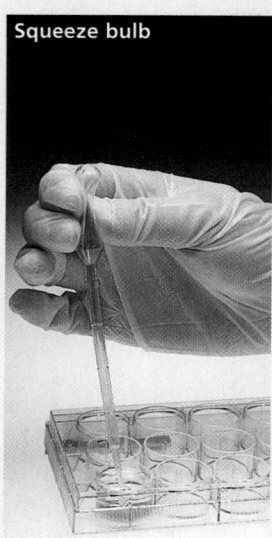 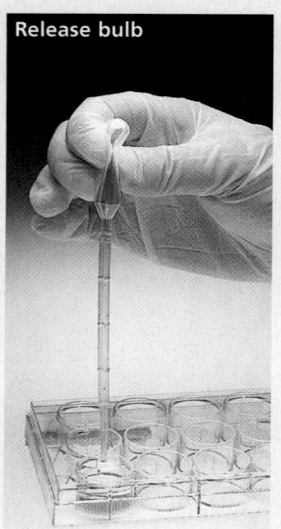 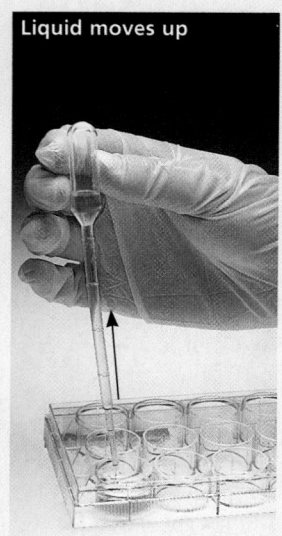 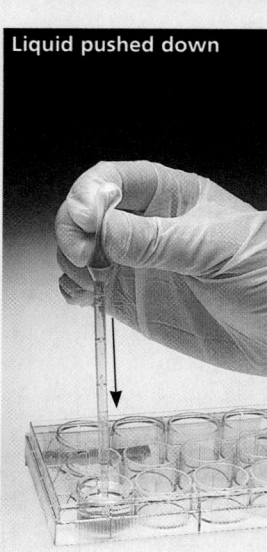

Squeeze bulb   Release bulb   Liquid moves up   Liquid pushed down

FIGURE A   Use this technique for mixing the contents of a well. The pipet used for mixing can also be used to transfer a sample of the mixture to the next well, but use a clean pipet for mixing each new solution.

 Call your teacher in the event of a spill. Spills should be cleaned up promptly according to your teacher's directions.

PREPARATION

1. Create a table with two columns for recording your observations. Head the first column *HCl concentration*. A wide second column can be headed *Observations and comparisons*.

PROCEDURE

1. Obtain samples of 1.0 M HCl solution and 1.0 M CH_3COOH solution.

2. Place 20 drops of HCl in one well of a 24-well plate. Place 20 drops of CH_3COOH in an adjacent well. Label the location of each sample.

3. Test the HCl and CH_3COOH with the conductivity tester. Your teacher may have prepared a conductivity tester like the one shown in Figure B. Note the relative intensity of the tester light for each solution. After testing, rinse the tester probes with distilled water. Remove any excess moisture with a paper towel.

4. Place 18 drops of distilled water in each of six wells in your 24-well plate. Add two drops of 1.0 M HCl to the first well to make a total of 20 drops of solution. Mix the contents of this well thoroughly by picking the contents up in a pipet and returning them to the well, as shown in Figure A.

5. Repeat this procedure by taking two drops of the previous dilution and placing it in the next well containing 18 drops of water. Return any unused solution in the pipet to the well from which it was taken. Mix the new solution with a new pipet. (You now have 1.0 M HCl in the well from Procedure step 2, 0.10 M HCl in the first dilution well, and 0.010 M HCl in the second dilution.)

 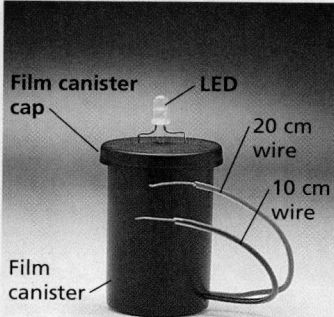

Film canister cap   LED   20 cm wire   10 cm wire   Film canister

FIGURE B
Teacher-made LED conductivity tester

6. Continue diluting in this manner until you have six successive dilutions. The $[H_3O^+]$ should now range from 1.0 M to 1.0×10^{-6} M. Write the concentrations in the first column of your data table.

7. Using the conductivity tester shown in Figure B, test the cells containing HCl in order from most concentrated to least concentrated. Note the brightness of the tester bulb and compare it with the brightness of the bulb when it was placed in the acetic acid solution. (Retest the acetic acid well any time for comparison.) After each test, rinse the tester probes with distilled water, and use a paper towel to remove any excess moisture. When the brightness produced by one of the HCl solutions is about the same as that produced by the acetic acid, you can infer that the two solutions have the same hydronium ion concentration and that the pH of the HCl solution is equal to the pH of the acetic acid. If the glow from the bulb is too faint to see, turn off the lights or build a light shield around your conductivity tester bulb.

8. Record the results of your observations by noting which HCl concentration causes the intensity of the bulb to most closely match that of the bulb when it is in acetic acid. (Hint: If the conductivity of no single HCl concentration matches that of the acetic acid, then estimate the value between the two concentrations that match the best.)

CLEANUP AND DISPOSAL

9. Clean your lab station. Clean all equipment and return it to its proper place. Dispose of chemicals and solutions in containers designated by your teacher. Do not pour any chemicals down the drain or throw anything in the trash unless your teacher directs you to do so. Wash your hands thoroughly after all work is finished and before you leave the lab.

ANALYSIS AND INTERPRETATION

1. **Resolving Discrepancies:** How did the conductivity of the 1.0 M HCl solution compare with that of the 1.0 M CH_3COOH solution? Why do you think this was so?

2. **Organizing Data:** What is the H_3O^+ concentration of the HCl solution that most closely matched the conductivity of the acetic acid?

3. **Inferring Conclusions:** What was the H_3O^+ concentration of the 1.0 M CH_3COOH solution? Why?

CONCLUSIONS

1. **Applying Models:** The acid-ionization expression for CH_3COOH is the following:

$$K_a = \frac{[H_3O^+][CH_3COO^-]}{[CH_3COOH]}$$

Use your answer to Analysis and Interpretation item 3 to calculate K_a for the acetic acid solution.

2. **Applying Models:** Explain how it is possible for solutions HCl and CH_3COOH to show the same conductivity but have different concentrations.

EXTENSIONS

1. **Evaluating Methods:** Compare the K_a value that you calculated with the value found on page 570 of your text. Calculate the percent error for this experiment.

2. **Predicting Outcomes:** How would your results be affected if you tested the conductivity of a 0.10 M acetic acid solution instead of a 1.0 M acetic acid solution? What effect would it have on the value of the K_a that you calculated? If your teacher approves, try the experiment again with a different concentration of acetic acid solution.

3. **Predicting Outcomes:** Lactic acid ($HOOCCHOHCH_3$) has a K_a of 1.4×10^{-4}. Predict whether a solution of lactic acid would cause the conductivity tester to glow brighter or dimmer than a solution of acetic acid with the same concentration. How noticeable would the difference be?

4. Wrap tape around the resistor and its exposed wires.

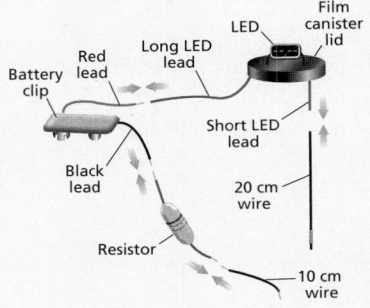

5. Poke two holes, about 1 cm apart, in the side of a film canister near the bottom. Insert the hook-up wires through these holes.

6. Connect the battery and resistor, and place them in the canister, snapping the lid shut. Adjust the protruding hook-up wires so they extend out about 5 cm. (Optional: place drops of hot-melt glue around the LED and the hook-up wires so that the canister is waterproof.)

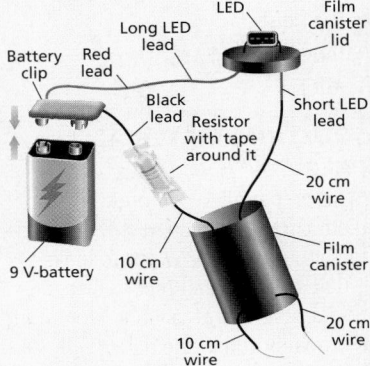

7. Wrap electrician's tape around the straw, and place it over the LED to provide a "dark tunnel" through which the LED may be viewed when testing weak electrolytes.

REQUIRED PRECAUTIONS

- Safety goggles and a lab apron must be worn at all times.

- Read all safety precautions, and discuss them with your students.

Continued on page 893J

EXPERIMENT 19-1

EXPERIMENT 19-1

OBJECTIVES
Students will

- use appropriate lab safety procedures.
- prepare blueprint paper and create a blueprint.
- infer the role of oxidation-reduction reactions in the preparation.

RECOMMENDED TIME
45–60 min

MATERIALS
(for each lab group)

- 8 cm × 15 cm white paper, 1 piece
- 15 mL 10% iron(III) ammonium citrate
- 15 mL 10% potassium hexacyano-ferrate(III) solution (potassium ferricyanide)
- 25 mL graduated cylinders, 2
- corrugated cardboard, 2 pieces, 20 cm × 30 cm
- glass stirring rod
- Petri dish
- thumbtacks, 4
- tongs

SOLUTION/MATERIALS PREPARATION

1. To prepare a 10% iron(III) ammonium citrate solution, dissolve 100 g in enough distilled water to make 1.00 L of solution. Prepare the solution on the day of use and store it in a brown bottle in the dark.

2. To prepare 10% potassium hexacyanoferrate(III), dissolve 100 g of $K_3Fe(CN)_6$ in enough distilled water to make 1.00 L of solution. Prepare the solution on the day of the lab and store it in a brown bottle in the dark.

3. When preparing solutions, be sure that solid iron(III) ammonium citrate and potassium hexacyanoferrate(III) are not heated and do not come into contact with concentrated acids.

Blueprint Paper

OBJECTIVES

- *Prepare* blueprint paper and create a blueprint.
- *Infer* the role of oxidation-reduction reactions in the preparation.

MATERIALS

- **10% iron(III) ammonium citrate solution**
- **10% potassium hexacyanoferrate(III) solution**
- **25 mL graduated cylinders, 2**
- **2 pieces corrugated cardboard, 20 cm × 30 cm**
- **glass stirring rod**
- **Petri dish**
- **thumbtacks, 4**
- **tongs**
- **white paper, 8 cm × 15 cm, 1**

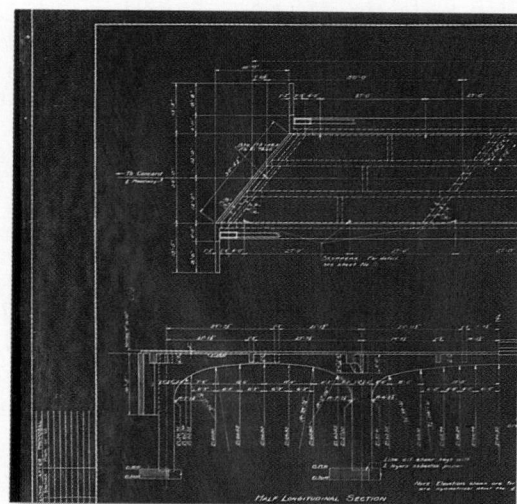

BACKGROUND

Blueprint paper is prepared by coating paper with a solution of two soluble iron(III) salts—potassium hexacyanoferrate(III), commonly called potassium ferricyanide, and iron(III) ammonium citrate. These two salts do not react with each other in the dark. However, when exposed to UV light, the iron(III) ammonium citrate is converted to an iron(II) salt. Potassium hexacyanoferrate(III), $K_3Fe(CN)_6$, reacts with iron(II) ion, Fe^{2+}, to produce an insoluble blue compound, $KFeFe(CN)_6 \cdot H_2O$. In this compound, iron appears to exist in both the +2 and +3 oxidation states.

A blueprint is made by using black ink to make a sketch on a piece of tracing paper or clear, colorless plastic. This sketch is placed on top of a piece of blueprint paper and exposed to ultraviolet light. Wherever the light strikes the paper, the paper turns blue. The paper is then washed to remove the soluble unexposed chemical and is allowed to dry. The result is a blueprint—a blue sheet of paper with white lines. Blueprints produce negative images; the part exposed to light becomes dark.

SAFETY

Always wear safety goggles and a lab apron to protect your eyes and clothing. If you get a chemical in your eyes, immediately flush the chemical out at the eyewash station while calling to your teacher. Know the location of the emergency lab shower and eyewash station and the procedure for using them.

Do not touch any chemicals. If you get a chemical on your skin or clothing, wash the chemical off at the sink while calling to your teacher. Make sure you carefully read the labels and follow the precautions on all containers of chemicals that you use. If there are no precautions stated on the label,

FIGURE A

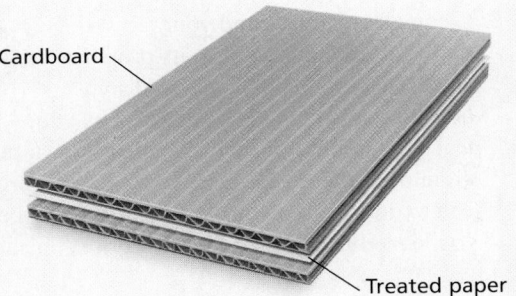

Cardboard

Treated paper

FIGURE B

ask your teacher what precautions to follow. Do not taste any chemicals or items used in the laboratory. Never return leftovers to their original containers; take only small amounts to avoid wasting supplies.

 Call your teacher in the event of a spill. Spills should be cleaned up promptly according to your teacher's directions.

PROCEDURE

1. Pour 15 mL of a 10% solution of potassium hexacyanoferrate(III) solution into a petri dish. With most of the classroom lights off or dimmed, add 15 mL of 10% iron(III) ammonium citrate solution. Stir the mixture.

2. Write your name on an 8 cm × 15 cm piece of white paper. Carefully coat one side of the 8 cm × 15 cm piece of paper by using tongs to drag it over the top of the solution in the petri dish, as shown in Figure A.

3. With the coated side up, tack your wet paper to a piece of corrugated cardboard, and cover the paper with another piece of cardboard, as shown in Figure B. **Wash your hands before proceeding to step 4.**

4. Take your paper and cardboard assembly outside into the direct sunlight. Remove the top piece of cardboard so that the paper is exposed. Quickly place an object such as a fern, a leaf, or a key on the paper. If it is windy, you may need to put small weights, such as coins, on the object to keep it in place, as shown in Figure C.

5. After about 20 min, remove the object and again cover the paper with the cardboard. Return to the lab, remove the tacks, and *thoroughly* rinse the blueprint paper under cold running water. Allow the paper to dry. In your notebook, record the amount of time the paper was exposed to sunlight.

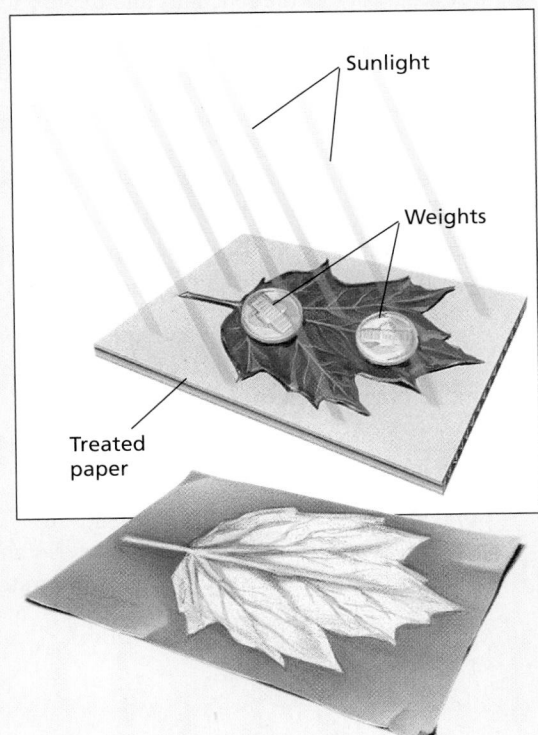

Sunlight

Weights

Treated paper

FIGURE C   To produce a sharp image, the object must be flat, with its edges on the blueprint paper, and it must not move.

4. Some teachers prefer using unbleached muslin cloth instead of paper although the cloth is more expensive.

REQUIRED PRECAUTIONS
- Safety goggles and a lab apron must be worn at all times.
- Read all safety cautions and discuss them with your students.
- During the preparation of the blueprint paper, the lab must be lighted well enough for students to be able to exit safely in the event of an emergency.
- Students should wash their hands thoroughly when finished.

SAMPLE DATA
No numerical data

PRE-LAB DISCUSSION
Emphasize that to prevent their hands from turning blue, students must wash after preparing the paper and before going out into the sunlight. Explain to students that even if the day is not sunny, this experiment works well because the iron(III) ammonium citrate is activated by the sun's ultraviolet radiation, which penetrates the clouds. Classroom lighting emits so little ultraviolet light that it is not necessary to prepare the blueprint paper in complete darkness.

DISPOSAL
Let the treated paper dry if it is wet. Then put it into the trash. Combine all solutions and pour them down the drain.

ANALYSIS AND INTERPRETATION—ANSWERS

1. Iron(III) ammonium citrate solution is light-sensitive. The brown bottle filters out the ultraviolet light.

2. The new oxidation state is +2.

3. $Fe^{2+}(aq) + Fe(CN)_6^{3-}(aq) \longrightarrow$ $FeFe(CN)_6^{1-}(s)$

4. The two compounds that were mixed and spread on the paper—iron(III) ammonium citrate and potassium hexacyanoferrate(III)—were washed away. They are soluble and did not react because the iron(III) ammonium citrate was not activated by UV radiation.

5. Ultraviolet radiation penetrates the clouds.

6. If the mixture of iron(III) ammonium citrate and potassium hexacyanoferrate(III) had been left on the hands, they could have turned blue in the sunlight.

CONCLUSIONS—ANSWERS

1. If some unreacted chemicals are left on the blueprint, exposure to light over a period of time can slowly cause a reaction that will adversely affect the original image.

2. The wavelength of red light is longer than the wavelength of ultraviolet light. The less energetic red light does not activate the light sensitive chemicals on photographic paper. The same is true for blueprint paper.

EXTENSIONS—ANSWERS

1. Students' answers will vary. One possible procedure is to spread a thin layer of sunscreen lotion on half of a piece of transparent acetate and place it over the blueprint paper before exposing it to sunlight. After developing the blueprint, compare the two areas.

2. Students' answers will vary. Be sure that student procedures are safe.

3. Students' answers will vary.

CLEANUP AND DISPOSAL

6. Clean all apparatus and your lab station. Return equipment to its proper place. Dispose of chemicals and solutions in the containers designated by your teacher. Do not pour any chemicals down the drain or in the trash unless your teacher directs you to do so. Wash your hands thoroughly before you leave the lab and after all work is finished.

ANALYSIS AND INTERPRETATION

1. Relating Ideas: Why is the iron(III) ammonium citrate solution in a brown bottle?

2. Organizing Ideas: When iron(III) ammonium citrate is exposed to light, the oxidation state of the iron changes. What is the new oxidation state of the iron?

3. Organizing Ideas: Write a chemical equation showing the reaction of the hexacyanoferrate ion, $Fe(CN)_6^{3-}$, with the iron(II) ion. Include the physical states of the reactants and the product.

4. Analyzing Methods: What substances were washed away when you rinsed the blueprint in water after it had been exposed to sunlight? (Hint: Compare the solubilities of the two ammonium salts you used to coat the paper and of the blue product that formed.)

5. Analyzing Ideas: The blueprint seems to develop as well on a cloudy day as on a clear day. Explain.

6. Analyzing Methods: Why was it important that you wash your hands after coating your paper and before going outside into the sunlight?

CONCLUSIONS

1. Applying Ideas: Insufficient washing of the exposed blueprints results in a slow deterioration of images. Suggest a reason for this deterioration.

FIGURE D

2. Relating Ideas: Photographic paper shown in Figure D can be safely exposed to red light in a darkroom. Do you think the same would be true of blueprint paper? Explain your answer.

EXTENSIONS

1. Applying Ideas: How could you use this blueprint paper to test the effectiveness of a brand of sunscreen lotion?

2. Designing Experiments: Can you think of ways to improve this procedure? If so, ask your teacher to approve your plan, and create a new blueprint. Evaluate both the efficiency of the procedure and the quality of blueprint.

3. Research and Communications: The common name for the compound $KFeFe(CN)_6 \cdot H_2O$ is Prussian blue. This compound has been used for many years as a pigment because of its intense color. Write a report about how Prussian blue is manufactured and the ways in which it is used.

EXPERIMENT 19-2

Reduction of Manganese in Permanganate Ion

OBJECTIVES

- *Demonstrate* proficiency in performing redox titrations and recognizing end points of a redox reaction.

- *Write* a balanced oxidation-reduction equation for a redox reaction.

- *Determine* the concentration of a solution by using stoichiometry and volume data from a titration.

MATERIALS

- 0.0200 M $KMnO_4$

- 1.0 M H_2SO_4

- 100 mL graduated cylinder

- 125 mL Erlenmeyer flasks, 4

- 250 mL beakers, 2

- 400 mL beaker

- burets, 2

- distilled water

- double buret clamp

- $FeSO_4$ solution

- ring stand

- wash bottle

BACKGROUND

In Chapter 13, you studied acid-base titrations in which an unknown amount of acid is titrated with a carefully measured amount of base. In this procedure a similar approach called a *redox titration* is used. In a redox titration, the reducing agent, Fe^{2+}, is oxidized to Fe^{3+} by the oxidizing agent, MnO_4^-. When this process occurs, the Mn in MnO_4^- changes from a +7 to a +2 oxidation state and has a noticeably different color. You can use this color change in the same way that you used the color change of phenolphthalein in acid-base titrations to signify a redox reaction "end point." When the reaction is complete, any excess MnO_4^- added to the reaction mixture will give the solution a pink or purple color. The volume data from the titration, the known molarity of the $KMnO_4$ solution, and the mole ratio from the balanced redox equation will give you the information you need to calculate the molarity of the $FeSO_4$ solution.

SAFETY

Always wear safety goggles and a lab apron to protect your eyes and clothing. If you get a chemical in your eyes, immediately flush the chemical out at the eyewash station while calling to your teacher. Know the locations of the emergency lab shower and eyewash station and the procedure for using them.

Do not touch any chemicals. If you get a chemical on your skin or clothing, wash the chemical off at the sink while calling to your teacher. Make sure you carefully read the labels and follow the precautions on all containers of chemicals that you use. Do not taste any chemicals or items used in the laboratory. Never return leftovers to their original containers; take only small amounts to avoid wasting supplies.

EXPERIMENT 19-2

OBJECTIVES
Students will
- use appropriate lab safety procedures.
- measure volume by using burets.
- perform a redox titration.
- recognize the end point of a redox reaction.
- write a balanced oxidation-reduction equation.
- determine the concentration of a solution by using stoichiometry and titration data.

RECOMMENDED TIME
45–60 min

MATERIALS
(for each lab group)
- 5 mL 1.0 M H_2SO_4
- 50 mL 0.0200 M $KMnO_4$
- 50 mL unknown $FeSO_4$ solution (0.15 M)
- 100 mL graduated cylinder
- 125 mL Erlenmeyer flasks, 4
- 250 mL beakers, 2
- 400 mL beaker
- burets, 2
- distilled water
- double buret clamp
- ring stand
- wash bottle

SOLUTION/MATERIALS PREPARATION
1. To prepare 0.0200 M $KMnO_4$, add 3.16 g of $KMnO_4$ to enough distilled water to make 1.00 L of solution. For best results, this solution must be freshly prepared shortly before the experiment.

2. To prepare 0.15 M $FeSO_4$, dissolve 41.70 g of $FeSO_4 \cdot 7H_2O$ in enough distilled water to make 1.00 L of solution.

3. To prepare 1.00 liter of 1.0 M H_2SO_4, observe the required

precautions. Slowly add 56 mL of concentrated H_2SO_4 to enough distilled water to make 1.00 L of solution. Add the acid slowly, and stop to stir it in order to avoid overheating.

REQUIRED PRECAUTIONS

- Safety goggles and a lab apron must be worn at all times.
- Read all safety cautions and discuss them with your students.
- Students should not handle concentrated acid solutions.
- Wear safety goggles, a face shield, impermeable gloves, and a lab apron when you prepare the H_2SO_4. Work in a hood known to be in good operating condition and have another person stand by to call for help in case of an emergency. Be sure you are within a 30 second walk from a safety shower and eyewash station known to be in good operating condition.
- In case of an acid spill, dilute the spill with water. Then mop up the spill with wet cloths or a cloth mop designated for spill cleanup. Wear disposable plastic gloves while cleaning spills.

TECHNIQUES TO DEMONSTRATE

At this point, students should have had plenty of practice in using burets for acid-base titrations. Remind students to create the end point standard in step 8.

SAMPLE DATA

See page 893K for Data Table.

Never put broken glass in a regular waste container. Broken glass should be disposed of separately according to your teacher's instructions.

Call your teacher in the event of an acid, base, or potassium permanganate spill. Such spills should be cleaned up promptly. Acids and bases are corrosive; avoid breathing fumes. $KMnO_4$ is a strong oxidizer. If any of the oxidizer spills on you, immediately flush the area with water and notify your teacher.

PREPARATION

1. Prepare a data table in your lab notebook like the one shown below.

2. Clean two 50 mL burets with a buret brush and distilled water. Rinse each buret at least three times with distilled water to remove any contaminants.

3. Label two 250 mL beakers *0.0200 M KMnO₄*, and *FeSO₄ solution.* Label three of the flasks *1, 2,* and *3.* Label the 400 mL beaker *Waste.* Label one buret *KMnO₄* and the other *FeSO₄.*

4. Measure approximately 75 mL of 0.0200 M $KMnO_4$ and pour it into the appropriately labeled beaker. Obtain approximately 75 mL of $FeSO_4$ solution and pour it into the appropriately labeled beaker.

5. Rinse one buret three times with a few milliliters of 0.0200 M $KMnO_4$ from the appropriately labeled beaker. Collect these rinses in the waste beaker. Rinse the other buret three times with small amounts of $FeSO_4$ solution from the appropriately labeled beaker. Collect these rinses in the waste beaker.

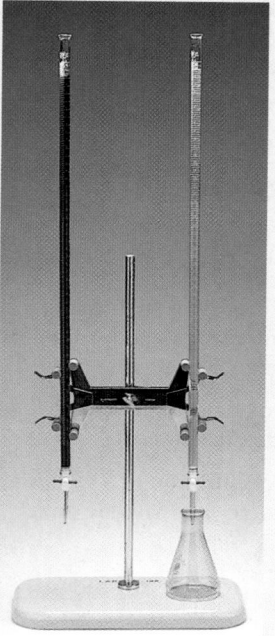

FIGURE A

6. Set up the burets as shown in Figure A. Fill one buret with approximately 50 mL of the 0.0200 M $KMnO_4$ from the beaker and the other buret with approximately 50 mL of the $FeSO_4$ solution from the other beaker.

7. With the waste beaker underneath its tip, open the $KMnO_4$ buret long enough to be sure the buret tip is filled. Repeat the process for the $FeSO_4$ buret.

8. Add 50 mL of distilled water to one of the 125 mL Erlenmeyer flasks, and add one drop of the 0.0200 M $KMnO_4$ to the flask. Set this flask aside to use as a color standard, as shown in Figure B, for comparison with the titration mixture to determine the end point.

DATA TABLE				
Trial	Initial KMnO₄ volume	Final KMnO₄ volume	Initial FeSO₄ volume	Final FeSO₄ volume
1				
2				
3				

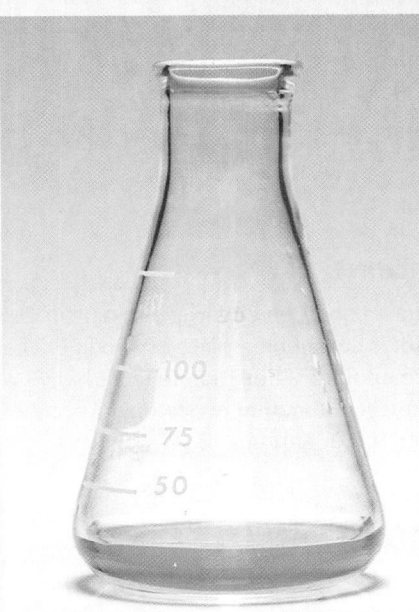

FIGURE B

PROCEDURE

1. Record the initial buret readings for both solutions in your data table. Add 10 mL of the hydrated iron(II) sulfate solution, $FeSO_4 \cdot 7H_2O$, to flask 1. Add 5 mL of 1 M H_2SO_4 to the $FeSO_4$ solution in this flask. The acid will help keep the Fe^{2+} ions in the reduced state, allowing you time to titrate.

2. Slowly add $KMnO_4$ from the buret to the $FeSO_4$ in the flask while swirling the flask. When the color of the solution matches the color standard you prepared in Preparation step 8, record the final readings of the burets in your data table.

3. Empty the titration flask into the waste beaker. Repeat the titration procedure in steps 1 and 2 with flasks 2 and 3.

CLEANUP AND DISPOSAL

4. Dispose of the contents of the waste beaker in the container designated by your teacher. Also pour the color-standard flask into this container. Wash your hands thoroughly after cleaning up the area and equipment.

ANALYSIS AND INTERPRETATION

1. **Organizing Ideas:** Write the balanced equation for the redox reaction of $FeSO_4$ and $KMnO_4$.

2. **Evaluating Data:** Calculate the number of moles of MnO_4^- reduced in each trial.

3. **Analyzing Information:** Calculate the number of moles of Fe^{2+} oxidized in each trial.

4. **Applying Conclusions:** Calculate the average concentration (molarity) of the iron(II) sulfate solution.

5. **Analyzing Methods:** Explain why it was important to rinse the burets with $KMnO_4$ or $FeSO_4$ before adding the solutions. (Hint: Consider what would happen to the concentration of each solution if it were added to a buret that had been rinsed only with distilled water.)

EXTENSIONS

1. **Designing Experiments:** What possible sources of error can you identify with this procedure? If you can think of ways to eliminate them, ask your teacher to approve your plan, and run the procedure again.

2. **Applying Ideas:** Hydrogen peroxide, H_2O_2, was once widely used as an antiseptic. It decomposes by the oxidation and reduction of its oxygen atoms. The products are water and molecular oxygen. Write the balanced redox equation for this reaction.

3. **Applying Ideas:** When gaseous hydrogen sulfide burns in air to form sulfur dioxide and water, the oxidation number of hydrogen does not change but that of sulfur changes from −2 to +4 and that of oxygen changes from 0 to −2. Which substance is oxidized and which is reduced? Write the balanced chemical equation for the combustion reaction.

PRE-LAB DISCUSSION
Thoroughly discuss the concept of oxidation-reduction and how this type of reaction can result in a color change. Review the concept of molar ratios and balancing redox equations.

DISPOSAL
Set out one container for disposal. The mixture that results should be acidic. If the mixture is purple, add $FeSO_4$ solution slowly while stirring until the color is gone. Precipitate the iron by adding 1.0 M NaOH. Filter and put the precipitate in the trash. Neutralize the filtrate with 1.0 M acid or base until its pH is between 5 and 9, and pour it down the drain.

Continued on page 893K

EXPERIMENT 21-1

OBJECTIVES
Students will

- use appropriate lab safety procedures.
- prepare and observe four iodination reactions.
- determine the elapsed time for each reaction.
- calculate reactant concentrations and rates.
- determine the rate law.

RECOMMENDED TIME
One lab period

MATERIALS
(for each lab group)

- 8–9 mL 0.0012 M iodine solution
- 8–9 mL 1.0 M HCl solution
- 8–9 mL 1% starch solution
- 8–9 mL 4.0 M acetone,
- 24-well microplate
- distilled water
- clock with second hand or stopwatch
- thin-stemmed pipets, 5
- toothpicks, 5
- white paper, 1 sheet

SOLUTION/MATERIALS PREPARATION

1. To prepare 125 mL of 4.0 M acetone, add 36.9 mL of acetone to enough distilled water to make 125 mL of solution.

2. To prepare 125 mL of 1.0 M HCl, observe safety precautions. While stirring, slowly add 10.3 mL of concentrated HCl to enough distilled water to make 125 mL of solution.

3. To prepare 125 mL of 0.0012 M iodine solution, add 0.10 g of I_2 to enough water to make 125 mL of solution. Iodine dissolves slowly, so make the solution a week in advance or dissolve the iodine in 5 mL of methanol before adding the water.

Acid-Catalyzed Iodination of Acetone

OBJECTIVES

- *Observe* chemical processes in the iodination of acetone.
- *Measure* and *compare* rates of chemical reactions.
- *Relate* reaction rate concepts to observations.
- *Infer* a conclusion from experimental data.
- *Evaluate* methods.

MATERIALS

- **0.0012 M iodine solution**
- **1.0 M HCl solution**
- **1% starch solution**
- **4.0 M acetone**
- **24-well microplate**
- **distilled water**
- **stopwatch or clock with second hand**
- **thin-stemmed pipets, 5**
- **toothpicks**
- **white paper, 1 sheet**

BACKGROUND

Under certain conditions, hydrogen atoms in an acetone molecule can be replaced by iodine. The resulting compound is both a ketone and a halocarbon. The iodination of acetone proceeds according to this equation.

$$CH_3-\overset{\displaystyle O}{\overset{\|}{C}}-CH_3(aq) + I_2(aq) \xrightarrow{HCl}$$

$$CH_3-\overset{\displaystyle O}{\overset{\|}{C}}-CH_2I(aq) + HI(aq)$$

Note that the placement of HCl above the arrow indicates that the reaction solution is acidic. In this experiment, HCl(*aq*) is used to provide hydronium ions. The hydronium ions act as catalysts, so the acid concentration appears in the rate equation along with the concentrations of acetone and iodine. The general rate equation for the reaction follows.

$$R = k[\text{acetone}]^x[\text{HCl}]^y[I_2]^z$$

In this experiment, you will measure the rate of the iodination reaction by using a starch indicator solution to signal the disappearance of I_2. The reaction is complete when the blue-black color disappears. By measuring the rate experimentally with differing concentrations of reactants, you can determine the values of exponents *x*, *y*, and *z*. These values can be determined only through experimentation.

SAFETY

Always wear safety goggles and a lab apron to protect your eyes and clothing. If you get a chemical in your eyes, immediately flush the chemical out at the eyewash station while calling to your teacher. Know the location of the emergency lab shower and eyewash station and the procedure for using them.

Do not touch any chemicals. If you get a chemical on your skin or clothing, wash the chemical off at the sink while calling to your teacher. Make sure you carefully read the labels and follow the precautions on all containers of chemicals that you use. If there are no precautions stated on the label, ask your teacher what precautions to follow. Do not taste any chemicals or items used in the laboratory. Never return leftovers to their original containers; take only small amounts to avoid wasting supplies.

 Call your teacher in the event of a spill. Spills should be cleaned up promptly according to your teacher's directions.

 Acetone solutions are flammable and the vapors can explode when mixed with air. Make sure that there are no flames or sources of sparks in the room when you are using acetone. Acetone can react violently with pure iodine and with concentrated solutions of iodine. Use only the dilute 0.0012 M solution that your teacher has provided for your use.

PREPARATION

1. Copy the data table below into your lab notebook, including the blank columns.

2. Label the five thin-stemmed pipets *Acetone*, *HCl*, *Iodine*, *Starch*, and *Water*. Label four wells on the 24-well plate *1, 2, 3*, and *4*.

3. Place the piece of white paper underneath the 24-well plate.

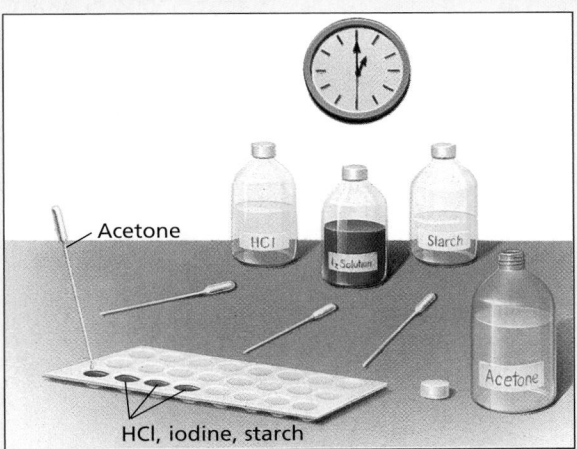

FIGURE A HCl, iodine, and starch are mixed before acetone is added. Start timing as you add the acetone

PROCEDURE

1. Using the four labeled wells of the 24-well plate, mix the starch, water, iodine, and HCl solutions in the proportions and order indicated in the data table in your notebook. **Use the appropriately labeled pipet for each solution.**

2. For reaction 1, note the time or start the stopwatch as you add 10 drops of acetone solution to well 1, as shown in Figure A. **The acetone must be added last, and you must keep track of the time elapsed.** Stir with a toothpick to thoroughly mix the reagents.

3. Continue stirring until the blue-black color disappears, as shown in Figure B on the next page. Record in your data table the time it took for the color to disappear. Also record the number of drops of acetone solution you added.

4. Reagent-grade starch is not necessary for this reaction. To make 125 mL of approximately 1% starch, bring 125 mL of distilled water to a boil and spray laundry starch into the water until a faint translucence is visible (about 6 seconds). Do not let the solution get cloudy. Some brands of laundry starch work better than others.

5. Students can share pipets as long the same pipet is not used for more than one reagent.

REQUIRED PRECAUTIONS

- Wear safety goggles and a lab apron at all times.
- Read all safety precautions, and discuss them with your students.
- In case of a spill, use a dampened cloth or paper towel (or more than one towel if necessary) to mop up the spill. Then rinse the cloth in running water at the sink, wring it out thoroughly, and put it in the trash.
- Acetone is a hazardous, volatile, and extremely flammable chemical. When it is mixed with air, the vapors are explosive. Liquid acetone is an active reducing agent when in contact with oxidizing agents such as pure iodine. The reaction can be violent. The 4.0 M aqueous solution of acetone is less hazardous, but the vapors can explode when mixed with air. Ensure that all flames are extinguished and that there are no other sources of ignition, such as sparks, when students are using the 4.0 M solution and when you handle pure acetone. The 0.0012 M iodine solution is a weak oxidizing agent; ensure that no student uses a more concentrated form of iodine.

TECHNIQUES TO DEMONSTRATE

Mixing the solutions and measuring elapsed time requires cooperation.

DATA TABLE					
Reaction no.	Starch + H_2O (drops)	0.0012 M I_2 (drops)	1.0 M HCl (drops)	4.0 M acetone (drops)	Time (s)
1	10 + 10 H_2O	10	10	10	
2	10	10	10	20	
3	10	10	20	10	
4	10	20	10	10	

A demonstration of how a pair of students might share the tasks could help improve the accuracy of the data. It may also be appropriate to have students work in larger groups.

SAMPLE DATA
See page 893K for Data Table.

PRE-LAB DISCUSSION
Students should be aware that the iodination of acetone is an example of an organic replacement reaction that produces a product with two different functional groups. Some students may need to have the functional groups identified. You may need to guide students through the calculations in Conclusions item 1 and review logarithms. Discuss reaction mechanisms, and explain how the rate law can help identify the rate-determining step.

DISPOSAL
Combine all liquids and decolorize, if necessary, by slowly adding 1.0 M $Na_2S_2O_3$ while stirring until the dark color has disappeared. Dilute the mixture with at least 10 times its volume of water. Then pour it down the drain.

ANALYSIS AND INTERPRETATION—ANSWERS
1. See Sample Data on page 893K.

2. Answers will vary.

3. If students are accurate, the rate for reaction 2 will be double that for reaction 1; the rate for reaction 3 will be double that for reaction 1; and the rate for reaction 4 will be the same as that for reaction 1. In other words, the rates for reactions 2 and 3 should be about the same and should be double the rates for reactions 1 and 4.

CONCLUSIONS—ANSWERS
1. Students' answers may vary slightly but should be close to the following solutions.
$Rate = k[acetone]^1[HCl]^1$

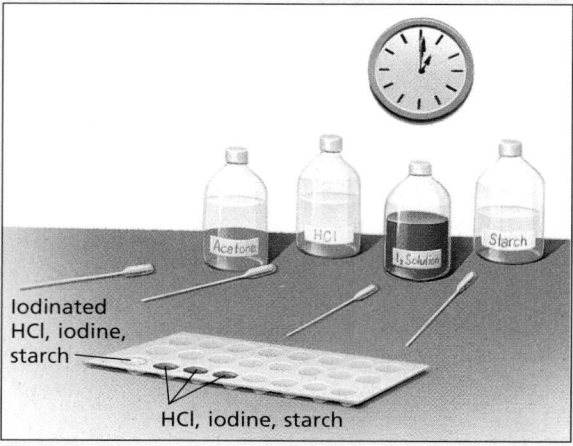

FIGURE B
When the blue-black color disappears, note and record the time.

4. Repeat Procedure steps 2 and 3 for reactions 2, 3, and 4, using 20 drops of acetone solution for reaction 2, 10 drops of acetone solution for reaction 3, and 10 drops of acetone solution for reaction 4. Record these amounts of acetone in your data table.

CLEANUP AND DISPOSAL

5. Clean all apparatus and your lab station. Return equipment to its proper place. Dispose of chemicals and solutions in the containers designated by your teacher. Do not pour any chemicals down the drain or in the trash unless your teacher directs you to do so. Wash your hands thoroughly before you leave the lab and after all work is finished.

ANALYSIS AND INTERPRETATION

1. Organizing Data: Make a data table similar to the one below. In your table, fill in the concentrations of the reactants in the reaction mixture. For example, in the first mixture, 10 drops of

DATA TABLE

Reaction no.	[HCl]	[I₂]	[Acetone]	Rate
1				
2				
3				
4				

1.0 M HCl were diluted to a solution having a total of 50 drops, so the new HCl concentration is $\frac{10}{50}$ of the original, or 0.20 M.

Determine the concentrations of all the reactants in the four reactions in this way.

2. Organizing Data: Determine the rates for the four reactions and add them to your table. The rate of a reaction is equal to the amount of a reactant consumed divided by the time elapsed. Because the iodine concentration can be assumed to be zero at the end of this reaction, the average rate for the reaction can be determined as follows.

$$\text{Average rate} = \frac{[I_2]_{final} - [I_2]_{initial}}{time} \approx \frac{0 - [I_2]_{initial}}{time}$$

3. Analyzing Information: Compare pairs of reaction data in your calculations table: reactions 1 and 2, reactions 1 and 3, and reactions 1 and 4. Notice that in each pair, the concentration of one substance changed while the concentrations of the others remained the same. Use this information to determine how the reaction rate was affected when the concentration of one reactant was doubled and the concentrations of all the other reactants remained constant. Summarize your conclusions.

CONCLUSIONS

1. Inferring Conclusions: Write the rate law for the reaction in this experiment. What are the values of x, y, and z as determined by your data? Hint: Remember that the rate of a reaction should be related to the concentration of the reactants as follows.

$$R = k[acetone]^x[HCl]^y[I_2]^z$$

If trials were run in which the concentrations of I_2 and HCl stayed the same but the concentration of acetone differed in one trial, the following relationships would be true.

$$R_1 = k[acetone_1]^x[HCl]^y[I_2]^z \text{ and}$$
$$R_2 = k[acetone_2]^x[HCl]^y[I_2]^z$$

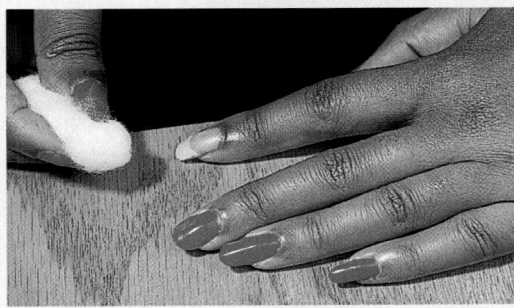

FIGURE C
Acetone is an active ingredient in nail-polish remover.

Because k, [HCl], and [I_2] are the same for both reactions, you can solve for x as follows.

$$\frac{R_1}{R_2} = \frac{k[\text{acetone}_1]^x[\text{HCl}]^y[I_2]^z}{k[\text{acetone}_2]^x[\text{HCl}]^y[I_2]^z}$$

$$\frac{R_1}{R_2} = \frac{[\text{acetone}_1]^x}{[\text{acetone}_2]^x}$$

Taking the logarithm of both sides yields the following equations.

$$\log\frac{R_1}{R_2} = x\log\frac{[\text{acetone}_1]}{[\text{acetone}_2]}$$

$$x = \frac{\log\dfrac{R_1}{R_2}}{\log\dfrac{[\text{acetone}_1]}{[\text{acetone}_2]}}$$

A similar calculation can be used to determine the values of the other exponents in the rate equation.

2. **Inferring Conclusions:** Using your data, calculate the value of k for this reaction.

3. **Resolving Discrepancies and Relating Ideas:** Is it possible for the concentration of one reactant to have no effect on the rate? Explain your answer.

EXTENSIONS

1. **Inferring Conclusions and Relating Ideas:** Look at the values you have determined for x, y, and z in the reaction rate equation. What can you infer about the slowest step in the mechanism for this reaction?

2. **Predicting Outcomes:** What would be the rate for the reaction if the amounts of reactants shown in the data table below were used? How much time would elapse before the reaction was complete? If time allows, perform this experiment and check your prediction. **Remember to add the acetone last, only after the other reagents are mixed.** Calculate the percent error for your prediction; consider your experimental results to be the accepted values.

Data Table				
Reaction no.	Starch (drops)	0.0012 M I_2 (drops)	1.0 M HCl (drops)	4.0 M acetone (drops)
5	5	15	15	15

3. **Evaluating Methods and Designing Experiments:** You may not have come up with whole numbers for x, y, and z. Can you think of possible sources of error or imprecision in this procedure? If you can think of ways to eliminate the errors, ask your teacher to approve your plan, and run more trials.

4. **Evaluating Viewpoints:** Share your data with the rest of the class. Calculate class averages for x, y, and z, and determine your percent error, using the class averages for the exponents as the accepted values.

or $R = k[\text{acetone}]^1[\text{HCl}]^1[I_2]^0$, $x = 1$, $y = 1$, $z = 0$

2. Values for k will vary depending on lab conditions but should probably be near 10^{-5}.

3. Some reactants, such as I_2 in this reaction, have no effect on the rate. This means that the reactant does not play a part in the slowest, or rate-determining, step of the reaction mechanism.

EXTENSIONS—ANSWERS

1. The slowest step of the reaction mechanism must include only acetone and the HCl catalyst. Iodine does not play a role in this step.

2. Students' answers will vary, but the predicted times elapsed should be between one-half and one-third of the times elapsed for reactions 1 and 4.

3. Students' answers will vary but may include difficulty in making drops the same size, difficulty in determining precise end points, and imprecision of time measurements. Students may suggest minimizing these errors by repeated trials, by using the same dropper (washed out between uses) for the different solutions, or by using indicator standards for comparison.

4. Students' answers will vary. Check to see that calculations have been properly carried out. Students should recognize that large values for standard deviation mean poor class technique and poor precision, while small values for standard deviation imply good class technique and good precision.

EXPERIMENT 21-2

OBJECTIVES

Students will

- prepare and test a casein glue.
- describe the charge distribution in proteins as determined by pH.
- use a chemical equation to show the formation of a peptide bond.
- relate the precipitation of casein to digestion and milk spoilage.

RECOMMENDED TIME

30 min

MATERIALS

(for each lab group)
- 1.2 g $NaHCO_3$
- 20 mL white vinegar
- 100 mL graduated cylinder
- 125 mL nonfat milk
- 250 mL beaker
- 250 mL Erlenmeyer flask
- funnel
- glass stirring rod
- hot plate
- medicine dropper
- paper
- paper towel
- thermometer
- wooden splints, 2

SOLUTION/MATERIALS PREPARATION

1. If students design and build a strength-testing device as suggested in Extension item 3, provide them with uniform pieces of wood.

2. Any kind of milk works, but nonfat milk seems to make a stronger glue.

REQUIRED PRECAUTIONS

- Safety goggles and a lab apron must be worn at all times.
- Read all safety cautions, and discuss them with your students.
- In case of an acid or base spill, dilute the spill with water. Then mop up the spill with wet cloths or a wet cloth mop designated for

Casein Glue

OBJECTIVES

- *Recognize* the structure of a protein.
- *Predict* and *observe* the result of acidifying milk.
- *Prepare* and *test* a casein glue.
- *Deduce* the charge distribution in proteins as determined by pH.

MATERIALS

- **100 mL graduated cylinder**
- **250 mL beaker**
- **250 mL Erlenmeyer flask**
- **funnel**
- **glass stirring rod**
- **hot plate**
- **medicine dropper**
- **baking soda, $NaHCO_3$**
- **nonfat milk**
- **paper**
- **paper towel**
- **thermometer**
- **white vinegar**
- **wooden splints, 2**

BACKGROUND

Cow's milk contains 4.4% fat, 3.8% protein, and 4.9% lactose. At the normal pH of milk, 6.3 to 6.6, the protein remains dispersed because it has a net negative charge due to the dissociation of the carboxylic acid group, as shown in Figure A below. As the pH is lowered by the addition of an acid, the protein acquires a net charge of zero, as shown in Figure B. After the protein loses its negative charge, it can no longer remain in solution, and it coagulates into an insoluble mass. The precipitated protein is known as casein and has a molecular mass between 75 000 and 375 000 amu. The pH at which the net charge on a protein becomes zero is called the isoelectric pH. For casein, the isoelectric pH is 4.6.

$$H_2N - \boxed{protein} - COO^- \qquad {}^+H_3N - \boxed{protein} - COO^-$$

FIGURE A　　　　　　　**FIGURE B**

In this experiment, you will coagulate the protein in milk by adding acetic acid. The casein can then be separated from the remaining solution by filtration. This process is known as separating the curds from the whey. The excess acid in the curds can be neutralized by the addition of sodium hydrogen carbonate, $NaHCO_3$. The product of this reaction is casein glue.

SAFETY

Always wear safety goggles and a lab apron to protect your eyes and clothing. If you get a chemical in your eyes, immediately flush the chemical out at the eyewash station while calling to your teacher. Know the location of the emergency lab shower and eyewash station and the procedure for using them.

Do not touch any chemicals. If you get a chemical on your skin or clothing, wash the chemical off at the sink while calling to your teacher. Make sure you carefully read the labels and follow the precautions on all containers of chemicals that you use. If there are no precautions stated on the label, ask your teacher what precautions you should follow. Do not taste any chemicals or items used in the laboratory. Never return leftovers to their original containers; take only small amounts to avoid wasting supplies.

Call your teacher in the event of a spill. Spills should be cleaned up promptly according to your teacher's directions.

Never put broken glass in a regular waste container. Broken glass should be disposed of separately according to your teacher's instructions.

PREPARATION

1. Prepare your notebook for recording observations at each step of the procedure.

2. Predict the characteristics of the product that will be formed when the acetic acid is added to the milk. Record your predictions in your notebook.

PROCEDURE

1. Pour 125 mL of nonfat milk into a 250 mL beaker. Add 20 mL of 4% acetic acid (white vinegar).

2. Place the mixture on a hot plate and heat it to 60°C. Record your observations in your lab notebook, and compare them with the predictions you made in Preparation step 2.

3. Filter the mixture through a folded piece of paper towel into an Erlenmeyer flask, as shown in Figure C.

4. Discard the filtrate which contains the whey. Scrape the curds from the filter paper back into the 250 mL beaker.

FIGURE C
Use a folded paper towel in the funnel to separate the curds.

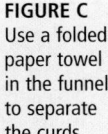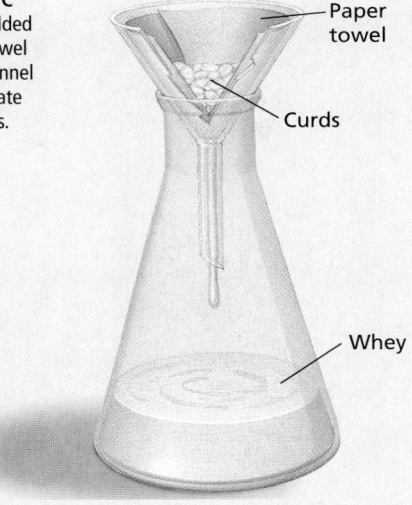

Paper towel

Curds

Whey

5. Add 1.2 g of $NaHCO_3$ to the beaker and stir. Slowly add drops of water, stirring intermittently, until the consistency of white glue is obtained.

6. Use your glue to fasten together two pieces of paper. Also fasten together two wooden splints. Allow the splints to dry overnight, and then test the joint for strength.

CLEANUP AND DISPOSAL

1. Clean all apparatus and your lab station. Return equipment to its proper place. Dispose of chemicals and solutions in the containers designated by your teacher. Do not pour any chemicals down the drain or in the trash unless your teacher directs you to do so. Wash your hands thoroughly before you leave the lab and after all work is finished.

ANALYSIS AND INTERPRETATION

1. **Organizing Ideas:** Write the net ionic equation for the reaction between the excess acetic acid and the sodium hydrogen carbonate. Include the physical states of the reactants and products.

2. **Evaluating Methods:** In this experiment, what happened to the lactose and fat portions of the milk?

TECHNIQUES TO DEMONSTRATE
In the filtration step, a paper towel is used instead of filter paper because filter paper is too slow. Show students how to fold the paper towel and fit it into the funnel.

SAMPLE DATA
None

PRE-LAB DISCUSSION
Explain to students that the glue they will make is similar to a commercial product, but because it has no preservatives, it will soon develop mold. Discuss the formation of a protein polymer from amino acid monomers by means of the peptide bond. Review acid-base concepts by discussing what happens to the amine and carboxyl groups as the pH of the protein changes.

DISPOSAL
Combine all liquids and pour down the drain. Allow the curds to dry and put into the trash.

ANALYSIS AND INTERPRETATION—ANSWERS
1. $CH_3COOH(aq) + HCO_3^-(aq) \longrightarrow$
   $H_2O(l) + CH_3COO^-(aq) + CO_2(g)$
2. They are contained in the filtrate (whey) that is discarded.

CONCLUSIONS—ANSWERS

1. The charge is positive below the isoelectric pH.

$$^+H_3N - \boxed{protein} - COOH$$

EXTENSIONS—ANSWERS

1. Students' answers will vary.

2. $H_2N - \boxed{protein} - COOH$

3. Students' suggestions will vary. If students are to test their devices, make sure that the procedures they propose are safe.

FIGURE D
This painting was created using paints containing casein.

CONCLUSIONS

1. Inferring Conclusions: Figure A shows that the net charge on a protein is negative at pH values higher than its isoelectric pH because the carboxyl group is ionized. Figure B shows that at the isoelectric pH, the net charge is zero. Predict the net charge on a protein at pH values lower than the isoelectric point, and draw a diagram to represent the protein.

EXTENSIONS

1. Research and Communications: In addition to its use as an adhesive, casein has been used for centuries in artists' paints such as used on the painting in Figure D. Investigate the use of casein in paint—how and when it is used, its advantages and disadvantages, and its special qualities. Present your findings in a written or oral report.

2. Relating Ideas: Figure B represents a protein as a dipolar ion, or zwitterion. The charges in a zwitterion suggest that the carboxyl group donates a hydrogen ion to the amine group. Is there any other way to represent the protein in Figure B so that it still has a net charge of zero?

3. Designing Experiments: Design a strength-testing device for the glue joint between the two wooden splints. If your teacher approves your design, create the device and use it to test the strength of the glue.

EXPERIMENT 21-3

Polymers and Toy Balls

OBJECTIVES

- *Synthesize* two different polymers.

- *Prepare* a small toy ball from each polymer.

- *Observe* the similarities and differences of the two types of balls.

- *Measure* the density of each polymer.

- *Compare* the bounce height of the two balls.

MATERIALS

- 2 L beaker, or plastic bucket or tub

- 3 mL 50% ethanol solution

- 5 oz paper cups, 2

- 10 mL 5% acetic acid solution (vinegar)

- 25 mL graduated cylinder

- 10 mL graduated cylinder

- 10 mL liquid latex

- 12 mL sodium silicate solution

- distilled water

- gloves

- meterstick

- paper towels

- wooden stick

BACKGROUND

What polymers make the best toy balls? Two possibilities are latex rubber and a polymer produced from ethanol and sodium silicate. Latex rubber is a polymer of covalently bonded atoms.

The polymer formed from ethanol, C_2H_5OH, and a solution of sodium silicate, $Na_2Si_3O_7$, also has covalent bonds. It is known as water glass because it dissolves in water.

In this experiment you will synthesize rubber and the ethanol sodium silicate polymer and test their properties.

SAFETY

Always wear safety goggles and a lab apron to protect your eyes and clothing. If you get a chemical in your eyes, immediately flush the chemical out at the eyewash station while calling to your teacher. Know the locations of the emergency lab shower and eyewash station and the procedure for using them.

Do not touch any chemicals. If you get a chemical on your skin or clothing, wash the chemical off at the sink while calling to your teacher. Make sure you carefully read the labels and follow the directions on all containers of chemicals that you use. Do not taste any chemicals or items used in the laboratory. Never return leftovers to their original containers; take only small amounts to avoid wasting supplies.

Wear disposable plastic gloves; the sodium silicate solution and the alcohol silicate polymer are irritating to your skin.

EXPERIMENT 21-3

OBJECTIVES
Students will
- use appropriate lab safety procedures.
- use polymers to make a latex rubber ball and an ethanol-silicate polymer ball ("super ball").
- observe similarities and differences in the properties of the two balls.
- measure the bounce height of the two types of polymer balls.
- calculate volume from measurements of ball diameter.
- calculate the density of each type of ball.

RECOMMENDED TIME
45–60 min

MATERIALS
(for each lab group)
- 2 L beaker, or plastic bucket or tub
- 3 mL 50% ethanol solution
- 5 oz paper cups, 2
- 10 mL 5% acetic acid solution (vinegar)
- 10 mL graduated cylinder
- 10 mL liquid latex
- 12 mL sodium silicate solution
- 25 mL graduated cylinder
- distilled water
- gloves
- meterstick
- paper towels
- wooden stick

SOLUTION/MATERIAL PREPARATION
1. For 5% acetic acid, use white vinegar. Do not dilute glacial acetic acid.
2. Liquid latex may be purchased from Flinn Scientific, Inc., Batavia, IL. The following catalog numbers can be used: L0004—500 mL; L0110—1.00 L; L0222—4.00 L.
3. Sodium silicate solution, also known as water glass, can be

purchased ready to use from many scientific supply firms.

4. Keep the bottles of latex and acetic acid solution in an operating fume hood because the vapors are irritating. Keep the bottle of ethanol in an operating hood because the vapors are flammable. For all three, remind students to keep the containers closed when not in use.

5. If balls need to be kept overnight, place them in plastic bags. If the ethanol-silicate polymer ball crumbles, add a few drops of water to it.

REQUIRED PRECAUTIONS

- Wear safety goggles and lab apron during the lab.
- Read all safety cautions, and discuss them with your students.
- Promptly clean up all spills with paper towels.
- Ethanol is flammable. Ensure that there are no flames anywhere in the room when an alcohol is present. Keep the alcohol in a hood, use a container with a lid, and restrict the amount kept in the hood to the minimum needed by the students.
- Do not allow students to take any ethanol-silicate polymer from the laboratory.

TECHNIQUES TO DEMONSTRATE

Show students how to roll the latex and the ethanol-silicate polymer into a ball. Students will have difficulty making a perfect sphere, but they should try to make it as regular as possible. The more irregular the shape, the more difficulty they will have in calculating volume and determining the bounce height (the ball will not bounce straight up).

Students should use mathematical calculations and measurements of the diameters, not water displacement, to determine the volume of the balls. The ethanol-silicate polymer will dissolve in water.

 Ethanol is flammable. Make sure there are no flames anywhere in the laboratory when you are using it. Also, keep it away from other sources of heat.

PREPARATION

1. Organizing Data: Copy the data table below in your lab notebook. Prepare one for each polymer. Leave space to record observations about the balls.

DATA TABLE			
Trial	Height (cm)	Mass (g)	Diameter (cm)
1			
2			
3			

PROCEDURE

1. Fill the 2 L beaker, bucket, or tub about half-full with distilled water.

2. Using a clean 25 mL graduated cylinder, measure 10 mL of liquid latex and pour it into one of the paper cups.

3. Thoroughly clean the 25 mL graduated cylinder with soap and water and then rinse it with distilled water.

4. Measure 10 mL of distilled water. Pour it into the paper cup with the latex.

5. Measure 10 mL of the 5% acetic acid solution, and pour it into the paper cup with the latex and water.

6. Immediately stir the mixture with the wooden stick.

7. As you continue stirring, a polymer lump will form around the wooden stick. Pull the stick with the polymer lump from the paper cup and immerse the lump in the 2 L beaker, bucket, or tub.

8. While wearing gloves, gently pull the lump from the wooden stick. Be sure to keep the lump immersed under the water, as shown in Figure A.

9. Keep the latex rubber underwater and use your gloved hands to mold the lump into a ball, as shown in Figure B, and then squeeze the lump several times to remove any unused chemicals. You may remove the latex rubber from the water as you roll it in your hands to smooth the ball.

10. Set aside the latex-rubber ball to dry. While it is drying, proceed to step 11.

11. In a clean 25 mL graduated cylinder, measure 12 mL of sodium silicate solution, and pour it into the other paper cup.

12. In a clean 10 mL graduated cylinder, measure 3 mL of 50% ethanol. Pour the ethanol into

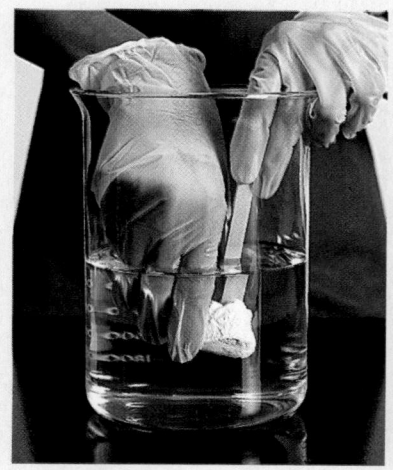
FIGURE A

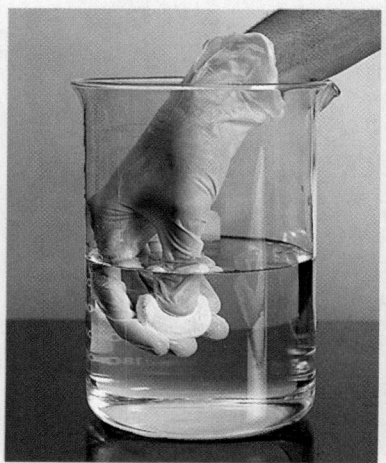
FIGURE B

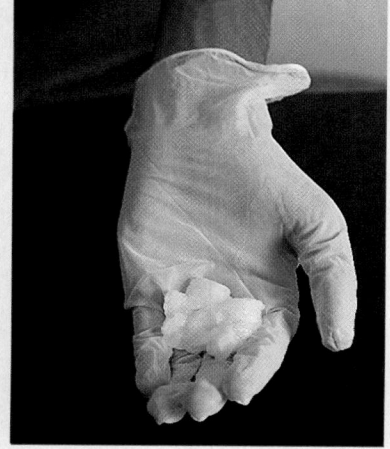
FIGURE C

the paper cup with the sodium silicate, and mix with the wooden stick until a solid substance is formed.

13. While wearing gloves, remove the polymer that forms and place it in the palm of one hand, as shown in Figure C. Gently press it with the palms of both your hands until a ball that does not crumble is formed. This takes a little time and patience. The liquid that comes out of the ball is a combination of ethanol and water. Occasionally moisten the ball by letting a small amount of water from a faucet run over it. When the ball no longer crumbles, you are ready to go on to the next step.

14. Observe as many physical properties of the balls as possible, and record your observations in your lab notebook.

15. Drop each ball several times, and record your observations.

16. Drop one ball from a height of 1 m, and measure its bounce. Perform three trials for each ball.

17. Measure the diameter and the mass of each ball.

CLEANUP AND DISPOSAL

18. Dispose of any extra solutions in the containers indicated by your teacher. Clean up your lab area. Remember to wash your hands thoroughly when your lab work is finished.

ANALYSIS AND INTERPRETATION

1. **Analyzing Information:** List at least three observations you made of the properties of the two different balls.

2. **Organizing Data:** Calculate the average height of the bounce for each type of ball.

3. **Organizing Data:** Calculate the volume for each ball. Even though the balls may not be perfectly spherical, assume that they are. (Hint: The volume of a sphere is equal to $\frac{4}{3} \times \pi \times r^3$, where r is the radius of the sphere, which is one-half of the diameter.)

4. **Organizing Data:** Using your measurements for the mass and the volumes from Analysis and Interpretation item 3, calculate the density of each ball.

CONCLUSIONS

1. **Inferring Conclusions:** Which polymer would you recommend to a toy company for making new toy balls? Explain your reasoning.

2. **Evaluating Viewpoints:** Using the table shown below, calculate the unit cost, that is, the amount of money it costs to make a single ball. (Hint: Calculate how much of each reagent is needed to make a single ball.)

Data Table

Reagent	Price (dollars per liter)
Acetic acid solution	1.50
Ethanol solution	9.00
Latex solution	20.00
Sodium silicate solution	10.00

3. **Evaluating Viewpoints:** What are some other possible practical applications for each of the polymers you made?

EXTENSIONS—ANSWERS

1. **Predicting Outcomes:** When a ball bounces up, kinetic energy of motion is converted into potential energy. With this in mind, explain which will bounce higher, a perfectly symmetrical, round sphere or an oblong shape that vibrates after it bounces.

2. **Predicting Outcomes:** Explain why you didn't measure the volume of the balls by submerging them in water.

Remind students to be patient with the ethanol-silicate polymer, which tends to crumble. If it crumbles too much, a few drops of water will rehydrate it and allow it to be shaped into a ball.

SAMPLE DATA
See page 893L for Data Table.

PRE-LAB DISCUSSION
Review the material on polymers in Chapter 2. Be certain students understand the differences between a monomer and a polymer. Be sure to relate the properties of these polymers, such as strength, flexibility, and elasticity, to the nature of the covalent bonds holding them together.

DISPOSAL
Paper cups, paper towels, disposable gloves, latex, and ethanol-silicate polymer balls and fragments should be disposed of in the trash can. Waste liquids from this lab can be poured down the drain.

ANALYSIS AND INTERPRETATION—ANSWERS
1. Answers will vary but could include the following: The latex ball is more opaque, less smooth, and less crumbly than the ethanol-silicate polymer ball. The ethanol-silicate polymer ball breaks down after a period of time. Both balls bounce. The ethanol-silicate ball bounces higher than the latex rubber ball.

2. Average bounce height for latex ball: $\frac{50 + 50 + 55}{3} = 52$ cm

Average bounce height for ethanol-silicate polymer ball:

$\frac{58 + 60 + 50}{3} = 56$ cm

Continued on page 893L

EXPERIMENT 1-1

Continued from page 793

If you wish, the experiment can be made more quantitative by emphasizing concepts such as percent composition of a mixture and percent recovery. Students can measure the mass of the original sample (after the representative sample has been set aside) and the mass of each of the recovered components (before the representative sample has been placed in the appropriate well). These data will allow the class to compare the effectiveness of different techniques in providing high yields of recovered substances.

DISPOSAL

Put out five disposal containers, one each for the iron, poppy seeds, sand, salt, and unseparated mixture. Even if students have not done a good job of separation, the materials may be reused the next time the lab is performed because you will be mixing the same substances again.

ANALYSIS AND INTERPRETATION—ANSWERS

1. Students' answers will vary. They may justify their estimations of success by the presence (or lack) of impurities in the separated components and by the amount recovered.

CONCLUSIONS—ANSWERS

1. Students' answers will vary.

2. Students' answers will vary but should be logical and demonstrate students' understanding of the physical properties of each substance.

3. Students' answers will vary. Note the suggestions students make and consider making those items available the next time you use this experiment.

4. Students' answers will vary but may include magnetism, density, and solubility: iron is attracted by a magnet, salt dissolves in water, poppy seeds float on water, and sand sinks in water.

EXTENSIONS—ANSWERS

1. Students' answers will vary but may include comparing the densities of their samples with the densities of standard samples of the pure components and picking through small samples from within their samples to check for visible impurities.

2. Students' answers will vary but may include the following:
a. using a magnet
b. pouring the mixture through a screen or sifter
c. adding water and checking for flotation
d. dissolving the mixture in a solvent that dissolves one component but not the other
e. distillation
f. distillation

EXPERIMENT 1-2

Continued from page 797

4. If clean test tubes weren't used, the purified water would be put back into test tubes that could contain residues from the impure water, thus contaminating the sample.

CONCLUSIONS—ANSWERS

1. The correct arrangement of densities is: oil, water, and sediment particles. In the separation step, the denser substances formed layers near the bottom of the bulb. In this case, the sediment particles were on the bottom, with a layer of water (and impurities) above them. The oily material formed a layer on the top, indicating that it is the least dense of the substances.

2. The particles that make the water cloudy are larger than the particles that make the water colored. Particles that color the water are likely to be in solution and by definition are very small, but particles that cause cloudiness are likely to be parts of colloids or suspensions and are larger than those in solution. The cloudiness was eliminated in a step of the purification before the color was eliminated.

3. Students' answers should be far less than 80 percent if the recipe for making the foul water was followed.

4. Students' answers will vary, but students should note that there is a trade-off between the purity of the water and the percentage recovered. The purer the recovered water is, the smaller the volume that is likely to be recovered.

EXTENSIONS—ANSWERS

1. Students' answers will vary but may include suggestions to perform the filtration steps twice in a row or to repeat the experiment with the discarded materials to try to get more pure water from it.

2. Students' answers will vary.

3. Students' answers will vary, but students should note that if one of the liquids is boiled and becomes a gas, it will be considerably less dense than the other liquid. Then, if the gas and liquid components are separated, the purity of each should improve. Some students may also suggest that by cooling the separated gas, it could be condensed and returned to its original liquid state.

EXPERIMENT 3-1

Continued from page 800

ANALYSIS AND INTERPRETATION—PART II—ANSWERS

1. Again, there was vigorous bubbling for the first few seconds. However, the fizzing noise was not very audible. The sides of the bottle became tight and hard to push in, and when the cap was removed, the hissing noise of gas escaping under high pressure could be heard.

2. The reactants were a liquid (vinegar) and a solid (baking soda). The products of the reaction were a gas (the carbon dioxide seen forming the bubbles) and a liquid (a solution of excess vinegar and sodium acetate).

CONCLUSIONS—ANSWERS

1. In Part I the system was left open, but it was closed in Part II so that not even gas could escape.

2. Part II worked better because one of the products was a gas and the bottle-and-cap system kept the gas trapped so that its mass could be measured with the other products. In Part I, the gas escaped.

EXTENSIONS—ANSWERS

1. Students' answers will vary but should demonstrate students' understanding of the law of conservation of mass. The following is a possible response:
• Place the baking soda in one corner of the bag. Use a twist tie to close off the corner and isolate the baking soda from the rest of the bag.
• Add the vinegar to the rest of the bag.
• Seal the bag.
• Measure the mass of the bag.
• Undo the twist tie and mix the reactants.
• Measure the mass of the bag and its contents at the end of the reaction. Include the twist tie in the mass measurement.

2. Students' answers will vary. Some students may think that the bag will be just as successful because it is a closed system. Other students might argue that the bag is more likely to leak than the bottle, so a mass loss is possible.

If the procedure is tested, a mass loss of 0.5–0.7 g will be found, even if the bag is perfectly sealed and does not leak. Students may be able to recognize that, unlike the bottle, the bag inflates during the reaction. They may suggest that the CO_2 escaped (effused) through the sides of the bag, but actually this loss is negligible.

The real reason the mass appears to change is that a balance actually measures weight, not mass. Because the bag occupies more space after the reaction, it will displace more air, and according to Archimedes' principle, it will appear to weigh slightly less, even though it has the same mass. (In other words, the bag will have a greater buoyant force.) Thus, to verify the law of conservation of mass by using a balance to measure mass, the system must be closed and must be rigid enough to have a fixed volume, such as that of the soda bottle.

3. Just as the reaction studied in this experiment produced a product that escaped into the environment, the burning of a log produces many products, not just ashes. The smoke, CO_2, and water vapor escape as the log burns. Presumably, if one had a way to measure the total mass of the products, it would be the same as the mass total of the reactants.

4. Students' answers will vary, but they should describe a way to burn a log in a closed, rigid container that could withstand heat and flames without reacting. Students may also recognize that the amount of oxygen needed to burn the log would require a very large container unless the oxygen were purified from the air or kept under high pressure. You may want to point out to students that this experiment would be very difficult and potentially dangerous because of the pressures that would build up as a result of the carbon in the log being converted to carbon dioxide gas.

EXPERIMENT 4-1

Continued from page 803

SAMPLE DATA

Metal compound	Color of flame	Wavelengths detected (nm)
$CaCl_2$	yellowish red (orange)	420, 445, 460, 485, 610, 645, 650
K_2SO_4	violet (purple)	405, 408, 695, 700
Li_2SO_4	red (carmine)	462, 498, 612, 670
Na_2SO_4	yellow	590, 595
$SrCl_2$	scarlet	405, 420, 460, 485, 490, 500, 665, 685, 710
NaCl solution	yellow	590, 595
NaCl crystals	yellow	590, 595
Na only (cobalt glass)	only blue of the glass is visible	
K only (cobalt glass)	violet (purple)	
Na and K	yellow	
Na and K (cobalt glass)	violet	
Unknown	Answers will vary.	

ANALYSIS AND INTERPRETATION—ANSWERS

NOTE: Assign only Analysis and Interpretation items 1–3 if spectroscopes are unavailable.

1. See sample data table.

2. Student answers will vary. Some students may have had difficulty properly cleaning the wire, so the first test of a new compound may have traces of the previous one.

3. The flame color of potassium is purple, but it is so weak that it can be overpowered by the yellow sodium light if a mixture is tested. The cobalt glass screens out the yellow sodium light.

4. Answers will vary, but students should realize that the colors seen by the eye were the result of combining the colors of light seen in the line spectra.

CONCLUSIONS—ANSWERS

NOTE: Assign only Conclusion items 1 and 2 if spectroscopes are unavailable.

1. Answers will vary. Students should be able to identify the unknown by comparing its results with the results for the other metal compounds tested.

2. The flame test is fairly specific because it can show an easily detectable signal with a very small amount of material. Possible difficulties include problems with contamination and the fact that some metals have similar colors when flame tested.

3. You can compare the lines in the spectrum of the mixture with the lines in the spectra of individual known metals. The pattern of spectral lines for each metal in the unknown can be sorted out to identify the individual metal components of the mixture.

EXTENSIONS—ANSWERS

1. The student should compare the shades of red with the colors of the known samples. If information about spectral lines is available, that would also help determine which metal is the unknown.

2. Strontium nitrate will change the color of the flame to red, potassium sulfate will change the flame color to purple, and ammonium will not change the flame color.

3. The crystals contain a mixture of metal salts. When sprinkled on a fire, they color the flame, just as if several flame tests were being performed.

EXPERIMENT 7-1

Continued from page 809

year instead of ordering more. Because this is a separation exercise, it does not matter if impurities are present.

ANALYSIS AND INTERPRETATION—ANSWERS

1. 72.37 g − 66.25 g = 6.12 g NaCl

2. 78.22 g − 65.40 g − 0.40 g = 12.42 g KNO_3

3. 12.42 g + 6.12 g = 18.54 g total

CONCLUSIONS—ANSWERS

1. $\frac{6.12 \text{ g NaCl}}{18.54 \text{ g total}} \times 100 = 33.0\%$ NaCl

$\frac{12.42 \text{ g KCl}}{18.54 \text{ g total}} \times 100 = 66.9\%$ KNO_3

2. As much as 7 g of KNO_3 could still be contaminating the NaCl if the solution was filtered only once.

3. Because the solubility of KNO_3 is never actually 0.0 g, it is always possible that some of the KNO_3 is dissolved in the solution after filtration.

4. Because the water was ice cold, the KNO_3 did not dissolve very well in it, but if there was any NaCl mixed with the KNO_3 crystals, the NaCl would have dissolved in the ice-cold water and passed through the filter paper.

5. Although the rock salt and ice mixture was cooler, it contained NaCl and would have contaminated the KNO_3 crystals if used in the rinsing step.

6. By keeping the amount of water used to wash the crystals small, the amount of KNO_3 that redissolved in the water was also kept to a minimum.

7. According to the graph, the temperature must be raised to at least 60°C for that much KNO_3 to dissolve in 100 g of water.

EXTENSIONS—ANSWERS

1. Students' suggestions for determining purity will vary but could include measuring the density or determining the melting point. The latter would require special equipment.

2. Students' suggestions for improving purity will vary. Be sure answers are safe and include carefully planned procedures.

EXPERIMENT 7-2

Continued from page 812

CONCLUSIONS—ANSWERS

1. For every formula unit of copper chloride, two formula units of sodium hydroxide were needed. For every formula unit of iron chloride, three formula units of sodium hydroxide were needed.

2. Students should choose copper(II) chloride, $CuCl_2$, and iron(III) chloride, $FeCl_3$.

EXTENSIONS—ANSWERS

1. Students' answers will vary.

2. Students' answers will vary but may include the following: difficulty in making drops the same size, unfamiliarity with the end point of the reaction, and a large margin of error with such small samples. Students may suggest minimizing these errors by conducting repeated trials, using the same dropper for all solutions and washing it out well between uses, and calibrating drop sizes with a graduated cylinder. Comparison with a standard to identify the end point may also be suggested. Students familiar with pH paper may suggest using it instead of phenolphthalein. Another few trials may be run using test tubes and larger quantities, for example, 25 drops instead of 5 drops.

3. Students' answers will vary, but the 0.5 M copper chloride should take about 50 drops of 0.1 M NaOH, and the 0.5 M iron chloride should take about 75 drops of 0.1 M NaOH.

4. Students' answers will vary, but students should suggest that they could compare the amount of NaOH needed to react with the solution of known concentration in the main procedure with the amount of NaOH needed to react with the same number of drops of the mystery solution. The concentrations will be in the same proportion as the amounts of NaOH needed.

EXPERIMENT 9-1

Continued from page 818

5. $NaHCO_3$ mass = 2.10 g

$$2.10 \text{ g} \times \frac{1 \text{ mol}}{84.01 \text{ g}} = 2.50 \times 10^{-2} \text{ mol NaHCO}_3$$

CH_3COONa mass = 2.03 g

$$2.03 \text{ g} \times \frac{1 \text{ mol}}{82.04 \text{ g}} = 2.47 \times 10^{-2} \text{ mol CH}_3\text{COONa}$$

6. Theoretical yield of CH_3COONa:

$$2.50 \times 10^{-2} \text{ mol NaHCO}_3 \times \frac{1 \text{ mol CH}_3\text{COONa}}{1 \text{ mol NaHCO}_3} =$$

$$2.50 \times 10^{-2} \text{ mol CH}_3\text{COONa}$$

$$2.50 \times 10^{-2} \text{ mol CH}_3\text{COONa} \times \frac{82.04 \text{ g}}{1 \text{ mol CH}_3\text{COONa}}$$

$$= 2.05 \text{ g CH}_3\text{COONa theoretical yield}$$

CONCLUSIONS—ANSWERS

1. Percent yield:

$$\frac{2.03 \text{ g actual}}{2.05 \text{ g theoretical}} \times 100 = 99.0\%$$

2. Theoretical yield of CO_2:

$$2.50 \times 10^{-2} \text{ mol NaHCO}_3 \times \frac{1 \text{ mol CO}_2}{1 \text{ mol NaHCO}_3} \times \frac{44.01 \text{ g}}{1 \text{ mol CO}_2}$$

$$= 1.10 \text{ g CO}_2$$

$$1.10 \text{ g CO}_2 \times \frac{1 \text{ L}}{1.25 \text{ g CO}_2} = 0.880 \text{ L CO}_2$$

3. $425 \text{ mL CO}_2 \times \frac{2.50 \times 10^{-2} \text{ mol reactants}}{880 \text{ mL CO}_2} =$

$$1.21 \times 10^{-2} \text{ mol reactants}$$

EXTENSIONS—ANSWERS

1. Students' suggestions for sources of error and plans for improving the procedure will vary. Possible suggestions could include improving technique, using larger quantities, and performing multiple trials. Be sure student suggestions for improvements are safe and include carefully planned procedures.

2. Yeasts use the cellular respiration reaction to produce CO_2. This process requires oxygen and sugar, usually in the form of glucose.

$$C_6H_{12}O_6 + 6O_2 \longrightarrow 6CO_2 + 6H_2O$$

EXPERIMENT 9-2

Continued from page 821

2. mass of dry $SrCO_3$ = 1.36 g − 0.30 g = 1.06 g

$$\text{mol of SrCO}_3 = 1.06 \text{ g} \times \frac{1 \text{ mol SrCO}_3}{147.63 \text{ g}} =$$

$$7.18 \times 10^{-3} \text{ mol SrCO}_3$$

3. moles of Na_2CO_3 =

$$7.18 \times 10^{-3} \text{ mol SrCO}_3 \times \frac{1 \text{ mol NaCO}_3}{1 \text{ mol SrCO}_3} =$$

$$7.18 \times 10^{-3} \text{ mol Na}_2\text{CO}_3$$

4. $35.0 \text{ mL SrCl}_2 \times \frac{1 \text{ L}}{1000 \text{ mL}} \times \frac{0.30 \text{ mol}}{1 \text{ L}} =$

$$1.05 \times 10^{-2} \text{ mol SrCl}_2$$

Sodium carbonate is the limiting reactant. If strontium chloride were chosen as the limiting reactant, some of the sodium carbonate would not have reacted. A smaller mass of strontium carbonate would have been formed, leading to a final calculated mass of sodium carbonate that was lower than its actual value.

5. The precipitate was rinsed to remove any NaCl impurities that may have remained on the $SrCO_3$.

CONCLUSIONS—ANSWERS

1. mass of Na_2CO_3 in 15 mL sample =

$$7.18 \times 10^{-3} \text{ mol Na}_2\text{CO}_3 \times \frac{105.99 \text{ g}}{1 \text{ mol NaCO}_3} =$$

$$0.761 \text{ g Na}_2\text{CO}_3/15 \text{ mL}$$

2. mass of Na_2CO_3 in 575 L sample =

$$\frac{0.761 \text{ g Na}_2\text{CO}_3}{15 \text{ mL}} \times \frac{1000 \text{ mL}}{1 \text{ L}} \times 575 \text{ L} =$$

$$2.92 \times 10^4 \text{ g Na}_2\text{CO}_3$$

EXTENSIONS—ANSWERS

1. correct mass of Na_2CO_3: 0.795 g for every 15.0 mL (if students were given a 0.50 M solution)

$$\text{percent error} = \frac{0.795 - 0.761}{0.795} \times 100 = 4.3\%$$

2. Students' suggestions for improving the procedure will vary. Students may suggest using larger amounts of each reactant or running multiple trials. Be sure answers are safe and include carefully planned procedures.

EXPERIMENT 12-1

Continued from page 823

ANALYSIS AND INTERPRETATION—ANSWERS

1. Students' answers may vary. At first, the dry ice sublimes, but then it should gradually begin to melt.

2. The sample was used up because every time the pliers were loosened, some gaseous CO_2 escaped.

3. Students' answers will vary but may include one or more of the following: The water in the cup provided the heat that the dry ice needed to absorb in order to sublime and melt. The water also absorbed the heat when the dry ice froze again, so the temperature of the system did not fluctuate much. This was important because plastic materials like the pipet bulb tend to get brittle when cold. If the experiment had been performed outside the water, condensation would have formed on the outside of the pipet bulb, obscuring the view. Since the cup is curved, the water slightly magnified the view of the dry ice in the pipet bulb. Finally, if the bulb had burst due to the pressure of CO_2, the water would have caught the dry ice and the pieces of the bulb and muffled the sound of the small explosion.

EXTENSIONS—ANSWERS

1. If fewer pieces of dry ice were used, it would take longer to reach a pressure high enough for the dry ice to melt, if it melted at all.

2. If more dry ice were used, the conditions for melting would be achieved very quickly, but the rapid increase in the pressure in the bulb might cause it to stretch or explode. A large amount of dry ice could also absorb enough heat from the water as it sublimed and melted to turn the water into ice.

3. The pressure will continue to build as the dry ice melts and vaporizes until the bulb stretches out or blows apart, releasing the CO_2 gas.

EXPERIMENT 12-2

Continued from page 827

$V = 4.1$ mL (measured by filling the spent pipet with water and then emptying the water into a graduated cylinder)

$$V = 4.1 \text{ mL} \times \frac{1 \text{ L}}{10^3 \text{ mL}}$$

$$= 4.1 \times 10^{-3} \text{ L}$$

$P = 5.11$ atm

$T = -56°C = 217$ K

$R = 0.0821$ L · atm/mol · K

$$n = \frac{5.11 \text{ atm} \cdot 4.1 \times 10^{-3} \text{ L}}{217 \text{ K} \cdot 0.0821 \text{ L} \cdot \text{atm/mol} \cdot \text{K}} = 1.2 \times 10^{-3} \text{ mol}$$

$$m = 1.2 \times 10^{-3} \text{ mol} \cdot 44 \text{ g/mol} = 5.3 \times 10^{-2} \text{ g}$$

$$d = \frac{5.3 \times 10^{-2} \text{ g}}{4.1 \times 10^{-3} \text{ L}} = 13 \text{ g/L at 5.11 atm and } -56°C$$

EXPERIMENT 13-2

Continued from page 836

Test tube	0	1	2	3	4	5	Unknown
				DATA TABLE			
mL 0.5 M $FeCl_3$	0	2.0	4.0	6.0	8.0	10.0	n/a
mL H_2O	10.0	8.0	6.0	4.0	2.0	0.0	n/a
Estimates	0	0.2	0.4	0.6	0.8	1.0	0.6
Measurements (absorbance)	0.008	0.125	0.190	0.261	0.330	0.390	0.222
Measurements (transmittance)	100%	75%	65%	55%	47%	41%	60%

Continued from page 837

4. If an additional yellow compound is added, it would absorb even more light. The absorbance would increase, and the percent transmittance would decrease.

5. $\dfrac{0.320 - 0.2}{0.320} \times 100 = 38\%$ error

$\dfrac{0.487 - 0.4}{0.487} \times 100 = 18\%$ error

$\dfrac{0.669 - 0.6}{0.669} \times 100 = 10\%$ error

$\dfrac{0.846 - 0.8}{0.846} \times 100 = 5\%$ error

EXPERIMENT 13-1

Continued from page 833

Movement through the filter paper depends on the attraction for both the paper and for the solvent. The more soluble the component is, the less attracted it is to the paper.

8. The solvent travels a longer distance, so components that move slowly through the filter paper have more time to separate.

9. Students answers will vary but should indicate that microdot samples of the ink in the lines of the unaltered letters and of the possibly altered letters could be tested for compositional differences with chromatography. Some inks fluoresce under ultraviolet light. Placing the promissory note under a UV lamp might reveal the alteration if one ink fluoresced and the other did not.

EXPERIMENT 14-1

Continued from page 841

EXTENSIONS—ANSWERS

1. Students' answers will vary, although students may guess that well water and salt water from an ocean are likely to contain many ions, while rainwater and running water will probably contain fewer ions.

2. Most sodium compounds and nitrate compounds are soluble. The two test solutions for the cations (Fe^{3+} and Ca^{2+}) contained different sodium salts, but each of the salts was soluble. However, the calcium salt of oxalate precipitated and was not soluble. Similarly, the two test solutions for the anions (Cl^- and SO_4^{2-}) contained nitrate salts, but each of these salts was soluble. However, other compounds of silver and strontium, such as silver chloride and strontium sulfate, formed precipitates and were not soluble.

3. Students' answers will vary, but students should recognize that, by definition, the reference solution contained chloride ions, sulfate ions, iron(III) ions, and calcium ions. Any precipitate left after evaporation would be a combination of salts containing all of these substances (and possibly others as well).

4. Students' answers will vary, but students should recognize that sulfate ions cannot exist alone. There must be an equal amount of positive charge provided by some unidentified cation(s) in this solution. Thus, the white powder left after evaporation is probably an ionic compound consisting of the cation(s) and the sulfate ions.

EXPERIMENT 16-1

Continued from page 847

SAMPLE DATA	
Mass of entire eggshell	5.27 g
Mass of ground eggshell sample	0.11 g
Number of drops of 1.00 M HCl added	150 drops
Volume of 1.00 M HCl added	6.00 mL
Number of drops of 1.00 M NaOH added	99 drops
Volume of 1.00 M NaOH added	4.06 mL
Volume of 1.0 M HCl reacted with eggshell	1.94 mL
Number of moles of HCl reacted with eggshell	1.94×10^{-3}
Number of moles of $CaCO_3$ reacted with HCl	9.70×10^{-4}
Mass of $CaCO_3$ in eggshell sample	0.097 g
% of $CaCO_3$ in eggshell sample	88

Student calibration of mL/drop will vary depending on equipment.

ANALYSIS AND INTERPRETATION—ANSWERS

1. $CaCO_3(s) + 2HCl(aq) \longrightarrow$
$\quad\quad CO_2(g) + H_2O(l) + CaCl_2(aq)$

2. $HCl(aq) + NaOH(aq) \longrightarrow$
$\quad\quad NaCl(aq) + H_2O(l)$

3. Sample calculation for acid pipet: 60 drops is equivalent to 2.40 mL;

$$\frac{2.40 \text{ mL}}{60 \text{ drops}} = 0.040 \text{ mL/drop}$$

Sample calculation for base pipet:

60 drops is equivalent to 2.46 mL;

$$\frac{2.46 \text{ mL}}{60 \text{ drops}} = 0.041 \text{ mL/drop}$$

150 drops of acid used × 0.040 mL/drop = 6.00 mL of acid used

99 drops of base used × 0.041 mL/drop = 4.06 mL of base used

4. Students' answers will vary. The following is a sample calculation. From item 2, there is a one-to-one mole ratio between acid and base in the neutralization reaction, so the following equation may be used.

$M_{acid} \times V_{acid} = M_{base} \times V_{base}$
$(1.0 \text{ M}) (X \text{ mL}) = (1.0 \text{ M}) (4.06 \text{ mL})$
$X \text{ mL} = 4.06 \text{ mL}$

5. The eggshell was dissolved in 6.0 mL of acid. The base neutralized 4.06 mL of acid. Therefore, 1.94 mL of acid reacted with the eggshell.

$$1.94 \text{ mL acid} \times \frac{1 \text{ L}}{1000 \text{ mL}} \times \frac{1.0 \text{ mol}}{1 \text{ L}} =$$

1.94×10^{-3} mol HCl

CONCLUSIONS—ANSWERS

1. 1.94×10^{-3} mol HCl $\times \dfrac{1 \text{ mol CaCO}_3}{2 \text{ mol HCl}} =$

$\quad\quad 9.70 \times 10^{-4}$ mol $CaCO_3$

2. 9.70×10^{-4} mol $CaCO_3 \times \dfrac{100.09 \text{ g}}{1 \text{ mol}} =$

$\quad\quad 0.0971$ g $CaCO_3$

3. $\dfrac{0.0971 \text{ g CaCO}_3}{0.11 \text{ g eggshell}} \times 100 = 88\%$ $CaCO_3$

4. $\dfrac{97\% \text{ accepted value} - 88\% \text{ experimental value}}{97\% \text{ accepted value}} =$

$\quad\quad 9.3\%$ error

EXTENSIONS—ANSWERS

1. 5.27 g total eggshell $\times \dfrac{88\% \text{ CaCO}_3}{100\% \text{ total eggshell}} =$

$\quad\quad 4.6$ g $CaCO_3$

2. Sources of error include end point recognition, control of buret spigot, inadequate cleaning of the eggshell, angle at which the pipet is held when drops are added, and too small or too large of a sample size. Students' suggestions for improving the procedure will vary. Possible suggestions include running several trials to improve buret technique and precision of data, drying the eggshell until its mass is constant for several trials, using a microtip pipet for greater accuracy, or using larger or smaller samples of eggshells. Be sure the proposed experiments are safe and include carefully planned procedures.

EXPERIMENT 16-2

Continued from page 850

Titrate the mixture with 0.1 M HCl or 0.1 M NaOH, as required, until the pH is between 6 and 8, and pour it down the drain. Unused indicators should be tightly covered and returned to the storage shelf.

3. The chromatograms may be discarded in the trash can.

4. Pens can be rinsed thoroughly and placed in the trash can or sealed in a plastic storage bag and reused from year to year.

ANALYSIS AND INTERPRETATIONS—ANSWERS

1. The fluid in the colorless pens causes the pen colors to change. This fluid is basic, so the solvent in the third chromatogram should be basic to observe color changes and determine which pens are acid-base indicators.

2. If one pen is to change the colors of all the dyes, it is best to decide on the pH of the colorless pen before developing the pen sets because some dyes are pH sensitive and some dyes vary their colors over small pH ranges.

3. The pH of the solution in the pen determines the color of the pen when it is first drawn on a sheet of paper. The solvent in the third chromatogram has a higher pH than the fluid in the pen, therefore, when it mixes with the color in the pen, the dyes that are acid-base indicators reflect the increase in pH by changing color.

4. The compound(s) in a pen that reverses the "changeable process" should have a pH very near that of the original solution.

CONCLUSIONS—ANSWERS

1. Isopropanol is less polar than water, so the dyes dissolve less readily, move more slowly through the filter paper, and better separation is attained.

2. The inks are much more soluble in water than in isopropanol, suggesting that they are polar molecules or ionic compounds.

3. The pH of the colorless pen indicates whether acid or base was used to prepare the colors in the changeable pens. This knowledge provides a basis for the designs of the overwrite pen set and for a pen set in which both overwrite and underwrite pens that write with colored "ink" produce a third color when mixed.

EXPERIMENT 16-3

Continued from page 853

have another person stand by to call for help in case of an emergency. Be sure that you are within a 30 second walk from a safety shower and eyewash station known to be in good operating condition.

TECHNIQUES TO DEMONSTRATE

Show students how to hold the pipet 1–2 cm above the well plate and squeeze out the drops. Caution students that their results may be faulty if solutions become contaminated by touching the tip of the pipet to drops of other solutions or chemicals.

SAMPLE DATA

Student results will vary.

PRE-LAB DISCUSSION

Have students develop a plan before coming to lab. If you have extra time, dedicate one lab period to planning and another lab period to executing the plan. Encourage brainstorming and cooperative work, even among different lab groups. To help those who are having trouble developing a plan, you may want to give clues every 15 minutes about the techniques that can be used. Give students time to process your clues, be more specific each time.

Caution students that refills of the solutions will not be available, so they should use them carefully.

DISPOSAL

Combine all solutions and precipitates containing iron. Add 0.4 M NaOH slowly while stirring until all of the iron has been precipitated as the hydroxide. If the pH of the resulting solution is greater than 10, slowly, while stirring, add sufficient 0.4 M acid to reduce the pH to approximately 8. Filter. Pour the filtrate down the drain. Allow the iron hydroxide to dry, wrap it in newspaper, and put in the trash.

Combine all other solutions and precipitates (if any). Neutralize the supernatant liquid with 0.4 M acid or base, as necessary. If there are no precipitates, pour the neutralized liquid down the drain. If there are precipitates, filter the mixture and pour the filtrate down the drain. Allow the mixed precipitates (if any) to dry, wrap in newspaper, and put in the trash.

CONCLUSIONS—ANSWERS

1. Students' answers depend on the numbers assigned to the unknown solutions.

2. Students' answers may vary. Students may have tried to measure the volumes of the standard solutions needed to neutralize the unknown solutions in order to determine their concentrations, or they may have gauged concentration by comparing reaction rates.

EXTENSIONS—ANSWERS

1. Students' answers will vary, but if the order of the acids and bases, determined by one group and recorded in the second data table, is different from that of the other group, students should infer that the two groups do not have the same set of solutions.

2. One possible method of figuring out the solutions' identities by using only the solutions and the well plate would be to take several 8-drop samples of each of the solutions and count how many (if any) drops of each of the other solutions are required to turn the phenolphthalein in the sample red and how many (if any) are required to neutralize it again. The strongest base will be the solution that is able to turn the greatest number of solutions red with the same number of drops. The strongest acid will be the solution that requires the most drops of the strongest base to neutralize. The other solutions should be easy to identify after the strongest of each type are determined. (Note: Caution students to record the results carefully because the plate would have to be cleaned off several times to perform as many as 56 tests.)

3. Students' answers will vary but should involve some characteristic property, such as the use of acid-base indicators or paper, or a reaction such as that of acids and $CaCO_3$ or that of bases and $FeCl_3$.

EXPERIMENT 16-4

Continued from page 857

8. $\dfrac{\text{mass CH}_3\text{COOH}}{1 \text{ L vinegar}} =$

$\dfrac{0.717 \text{ mol CH}_3\text{COOH}}{1 \text{ L vinegar}} \times \dfrac{60 \text{ g CH}_3\text{COOH}}{1 \text{ mol CH}_3\text{COOH}} =$

$\dfrac{43.0 \text{ g CH}_3\text{COOH}}{1 \text{ L vinegar}}$

CONCLUSIONS—ANSWERS

1. Percent $CH_3COOH = \dfrac{43.0 \text{ g CH}_3\text{COOH}}{1000 \text{ g vinegar}} \times 100 = 4.30\%$

SAMPLE DATA

Trial	NaOH Initial V (mL)	NaOH Final V (mL)	Vinegar Initial V (mL)	Vinegar Final V (mL)
1	1.38	11.57	0.55	9.21
2	11.57	23.69	9.21	19.43
3	23.69	32.33	19.43	26.67

2. Consumers expect a certain degree of sourness (acidity) in the vinegar they buy. They would not be satisfied if the acidity varied from one bottle to the next.

3. The change in the color of phenolphthalein showed when the titration was complete. Without that signal, it would not have been possible to know when enough NaOH had been added to neutralize the acetic acid.

4. Although the distilled water changed the molarity of the acetic acid in the titration flask, the flask still contained the same number of moles of acid as it did before dilution. Enough moles of NaOH were added in the titration to neutralize the number of moles that were contained in 10 mL of the original solution.

EXTENSIONS—ANSWERS

1. Students' answers will vary.

2. Students' answers will vary. Be sure that any procedures are safe.

3. The end point is the point at which the indicator used in a titration changes color. The equivalence point is the point at which the number of moles of acid (H^+) equals the number of moles of base (OH^-). If the indicator is chosen properly, its color change will occur near the equivalence point. The equivalence point and end point can be the same.

4. The first and third volumes are very close, but the second differs by approximately one milliliter. It is possible that the chemist incorrectly read 16 rather than 15 on the buret.

EXPERIMENT 17-1

Continued from page 862

SAMPLE DATA—CALIBRATION

	Cool H_2O	Hot H_2O	Calorimeter
Initial temp.	25.0°C	75.0°C	25.0°C
Final temp.	49.5°C	49.5°C	49.5°C
Change in temp.	24.5°C	−25.5°C	24.5°C
Volume	50.0 mL	50.0 mL	(not needed)
Mass	50.0 g	50.0 g	(not needed)
Calorimeter heat capacity	(not needed)	(not needed)	8.2 J/°C

SAMPLE DATA

Aluminum Specific Heat Test

	H_2O	Metal
Initial temp.	21.0°C	99.0°C
Final temp.	28.2°C	28.2°C
Change in temp.	7.2°C	−70.8°C
Mass	75.0 g	35.2 g

Iron Specific Heat Test

	H_2O	Metal
Initial temp.	21.0°C	99.0°C
Final temp.	28.1°C	28.1°C
Change in temp.	7.1°C	−70.9°C
Mass	75.0 g	69.2 g

Continued from page 863

3. Students' answers will vary. A sample calculation follows.
Hot water:
$50.0 \text{ g H}_2\text{O} \times 25.5°C \times 4.184 \text{ J/g H}_2\text{O}•°C = 5330 \text{ J} = 5.33 \text{ kJ lost}$
Cool water:
$50.0 \text{ g H}_2\text{O} \times 24.5°C \times 4.184 \text{ J/g H}_2\text{O}•°C = 5130 \text{ J} = 5.13 \text{ kJ gained}$

4. Students' answers will vary. A sample calculation follows.
5.33 kJ lost by hot H_2O − 5.13 kJ gained by cool H_2O = 0.20 kJ gained by calorimeter

5. Students' answers will vary. A sample calculation follows.

$q_{\text{calorimeter}} = C' \times \Delta t; C' = \dfrac{q_{\text{calorimeter}}}{\Delta t}$

$C' = \dfrac{0.20 \text{ kJ}}{24.5 \text{ °C}} = 8.2 \text{ J/°C}$

6. The appropriate equations are in boldface type below.
$\boldsymbol{q_{\text{metal}} = q_{\text{water}} + q_{\text{calorimeter}}};$
$q = m \times c_p \times \Delta t$

$m_{\text{metal}} \times c_{p, \text{metal}} \times \Delta t_{\text{metal}} = (m_{\text{water}} \times c_{p, \text{water}} \times \Delta t_{\text{water}}) + (C' \times \Delta t_{\text{calorimeter}})$
Because $\Delta t_{\text{calorimeter}} = \Delta t_{\text{water}}$

$$c_{p,\text{metal}} = \dfrac{\Delta t_{H_2O} \, [(m_{H_2O} \times c_{p,H_2O}) + C']}{m_{\text{metal}} \times \Delta t_{\text{metal}}}$$

CONCLUSIONS—ANSWERS

1. See Sample Data section for specific heat data for aluminum and iron. Sample calculations follow.

$$c_{p,\text{metal}} = \dfrac{\Delta t_{\text{water}} \, [(m_{\text{water}} \times c_{p, \text{water}}) + C']}{m_{\text{metal}} \times \Delta t_{\text{metal}}}$$

Specific heat of Al = $c_{p,\text{Al}} =$

$\dfrac{7.2°C \, [(75.0 \text{ g} \times 4.184 \text{ J/g•°C}) + 8.2 \text{ J/°C}]}{(35.2 \text{ g})(70.8°C)} = 0.93 \text{ J/g•°C}$

Specific heat of Fe = $c_{p,\text{Fe}} =$

$\dfrac{7.1°C \, [(75.0 \text{ g} \times 4.184 \text{ J/g•°C}) + 8.2 \text{ J/°C}]}{(69.2 \text{ g})(70.9°C)} = 0.47 \text{ J/g•°C}$

2. Students' answers will vary, depending on their unknown metal.

3. Metals have lower specific heats than water. As a result, they are better conductors of heat than water. The same amount of heat will raise the temperature of a certain mass of metal higher than it would raise the temperature of the same mass of water. Water absorbs heat better.

4. The lower the heat capacity of the calorimeter, the more accurate the measurement of any change in heat content will be because little heat will be lost to the environment. (Some students will note that even though calorimeter heat capacity can be used to adjust results, the change in heat of the calorimeter itself in different situations will vary more than the change in heat of the water.)

EXTENSIONS—ANSWERS

1. Students' answers will vary depending on the accuracy of the class measurements.

2. Students' answers will vary but may include inaccuracies in mass or volume measurements, the escape of heat through the holes in the calorimeter for insertion of the thermometer and stirrer, cooling of the metal while it is transferred to the calorimeter, and error introduced by the assumption that the density of liquid water is 1.0 g/mL (true only at 4°C).

3. Students' designs will vary, but improvements may include adjusting the water content of the calorimeter so that it is nearly all water with little air remaining, insulating the thermometer and stirrer holes in some way, and insulating the entire calorimeter more.

4. There are many possible answers. Tiles on the space shuttle must have high specific heats to withstand the heat of reentry to the Earth's atmosphere. Pots, pans, and baking sheets must be made of materials that have low specific heats and will conduct heat well. Energy-efficient homes should be made of materials with high specific heats that will help insulate against changes in temperature. Automobile coolants must also have high specific heats to absorb the maximum amount of heat from an engine with a given amount of coolant.

5. In winter, the oceans cool more slowly than the land, so air moving onto land after passing over the oceans is not as cold as air traveling over the colder land masses. In summer, the air moving over the oceans is not as warm as the air over the land because the oceans warm more slowly than the land. A small-scale version of this effect can be observed when night and day temperatures are compared.

EXPERIMENT 17-2

Continued from page 866

SAMPLE DATA

Reaction	1	2	3
Volume of liquid(s), mL	100.0	100.0	100.0
Initial temperature, °C	21.5	22.0	22.0
Highest temperature, °C	26.5	28.1	33.0
Mass of empty watch glass, g	30.15		30.15
Mass of watch glass + NaOH, g	32.15		32.15

Continued from page 867
CONCLUSIONS—ANSWERS

1. By direct measurement, ΔH should be −92 kJ/mol. By indirect calculation, it is also

$$-92 \text{ kJ/mol} = [-50 \text{ kJ/mol} + (-42 \text{ kJ/mol})].$$

2. amount of NaOH:

$$55 \text{ g} \times \frac{1 \text{ mol NaOH}}{40.00 \text{ g}} = 1.4 \text{ mol}$$

amount of HCl: 1.35 mol

Heat of dissolving: $1.4 \text{ mol NaOH} \times \dfrac{-42 \text{ kJ}}{1 \text{ mol NaOH}} = -59 \text{ kJ}$

Heat of reaction: $1.35 \text{ mol HCl} \times \dfrac{-50 \text{ kJ}}{1 \text{ mol HCl}} =$

$$-67.5 \text{ kJ}$$

(The remaining NaOH is an excess reactant that remains unreacted.)

Total heat of reaction: −59 kJ + (−67.5 kJ) = −126 kJ

Δt_{H_2O}: $126\,000 \text{ J} \times \dfrac{1 \text{ g} \cdot °C}{4.184 \text{ J}} \times \dfrac{1}{450 \text{ g } H_2O} = 67°C$

Final temperature = 25°C + 67°C = 92°C
The mixture is likely to cause burns because the temperature is much higher than 60°C.

3. HCl is the limiting reactant. There was 0.05 mol of NaOH left unreacted.

EXTENSIONS—ANSWERS

1. Chemists use an ice bath because the heat of solution for NaOH pellets is high enough to make the solution dangerously hot.

2. If acid or base spills are neutralized instead of diluted, the heat of reaction for the neutralization could cause a heat burn, along with any chemical burns caused by the acid or base.

3. The same procedure could be used for endothermic reactions. However, the temperature of the water will decrease, and the enthalpy change for the reaction will have a positive value.

4. Students' suggestions for package design will vary. Be sure each design addresses the dangers of moisture, breakage, and spills.

5. NaOH in solution is more stable than solid NaOH. The products of an exothermic reaction are comparatively more stable than the reactants.

EXPERIMENT 17-3

Continued from page 870

SAMPLE DATA

Well	1	2	3	4	5
Time rxn. began	00:00	00:00	00:00	00:00	00:00
Time rxn. stopped	02:23	01:07	00:43	00:35	00:26
Drops of A	5	5	5	5	5
Drops of B	1	2	3	4	5
Drops of H_2O	4	3	2	1	0

3. The most concentrated solution (5 drops of solution B) had the fastest reaction time. The least concentrated solution (1 drop of solution B and 4 drops of water) had the slowest reaction time.

4. The total number of drops for each well should be the same to make valid comparisons of different concentrations.

CONCLUSIONS—ANSWERS

1. The reactions began at the same time because the shaking mixes all of the solutions at once. Therefore, the reactions all started simultaneously and under the same conditions.

2. The effect of reactant concentration (solution B) on reaction rate is being measured.

3. The rate of the reaction is directly proportional to the concentration of solution B.

EXTENSIONS—ANSWERS

1. Students' suggestions for improving the procedure will vary. Possibilities may include minimizing errors by performing multiple trials or keeping drop size standard. Be sure answers are safe and include carefully planned procedures.

2. Students' answers will vary, depending on the conditions in your lab. For the sample data, it would require a mixture close to 4 drops A: 25 drops B: 21 drops H_2O. Students may need to use a different reaction vessel if this is too much for the microwell strips. Be sure answers are safe and include carefully planned procedures.

3. Students' suggestions will vary. Be sure answers are safe and include carefully planned procedures. Students should find that the rate is seven times slower.

4. Student answers may vary, but the key is to determine how much of a difference in time is involved for the smallest different amounts of the reactants. Be sure answers are safe and include carefully planned procedures.

5. Students' suggestions will vary. Be sure answers are safe and include carefully planned procedures. The rate is slower at lower temperatures.

6. Students may suggest using drops of water and solution A and keeping the amount of solution B constant. Another linear relationship is involved. $R = k[A][B]$.

7. Well 1: $k = \dfrac{6.99 \times 10^{-3}}{0.0020 \text{ M}} = 3.5$

Well 2: $k = \dfrac{0.015}{0.0040 \text{ M}} = 3.8$

Well 3: $k = \dfrac{0.023}{0.0060 \text{ M}} = 3.8$

Well 4: $k = \dfrac{0.029}{0.0080 \text{ M}} = 3.6$

Well 5: $k = \dfrac{0.038}{0.010 \text{ M}} = 3.8$

Average value for k = 3.7

EXPERIMENT 18-1

Continued from page 873

SAMPLE DATA

Test tube no.	Fe^{3+} conc.	mL of Fe^{3+}	mL of KSCN	Absorbance value
1	0.200 M	5.0	5.0	1.00
2	0.100 M	5.0	n/a	n/a
3	0.0500 M	5.0	5.0	0.94
4	0.0250 M	5.0	5.0	0.89
5	0.0125 M	5.0	5.0	0.80
6	0.00625 M	5.0	5.0	0.72

2. Each 5.0 mL of 0.002 00 M KSCN was mixed with 5.0 mL of $Fe(NO_3)_3$ solution to make a total of 10.0 mL.

$\dfrac{5.0 \text{ mL } SCN^-}{10.0 \text{ mL total}} \times 0.002\ 00 \text{ M } SCN^- =$

$0.001\ 00 \text{ M } SCN^-$ for all test tubes

3. Each 5.0 mL of $Fe(NO_3)_3$ was mixed with 5.0 mL of 0.002 00 M KSCN solution to make a total of 10.0 mL.

$\dfrac{5.0 \text{ mL } Fe(NO_3)_3}{10.0 \text{ mL total}} \times 0.200 \text{ M } Fe(NO_3)_3 =$

$0.100 \text{ M } Fe(NO_3)_3$ in test tube 1

$\dfrac{5.0 \text{ mL } Fe(NO_3)_3}{10.0 \text{ mL total}} \times 0.0500 \text{ M } Fe(NO_3)_3 =$

$0.0250 \text{ M } Fe(NO_3)_3$ in test tube 3

$\dfrac{5.0 \text{ mL } Fe(NO_3)_3}{10.0 \text{ mL total}} \times 0.0250 \text{ M } Fe(NO_3)_3 =$

$0.0125 \text{ M } Fe(NO_3)_3$ in test tube 4

$\dfrac{5.0 \text{ mL } Fe(NO_3)_3}{10.0 \text{ mL total}} \times 0.0125 \text{ M } Fe(NO_3)_3 =$

$0.0063 \text{ M } Fe(NO_3)_3$ in test tube 5

$\dfrac{5.0 \text{ mL } Fe(NO_3)_3}{10.0 \text{ mL total}} \times 0.006\,25 \text{ M } Fe(NO_3)_3 =$

$0.00313 \text{ M } Fe(NO_3)_3$ in test tube 6

4. Assuming that all of the SCN^- in test tube 1 is converted to $FeSCN^{2+}$, the concentration of $FeSCN^{2+}$ in test tube 1 must be 0.001 00 M, the same as the initial SCN^- concentration. This amount must be subtracted from the initial Fe^{3+} concentration to give the final Fe^{3+} concentration:

0.100 M initial − 0.001 M used = 0.099 M final.

5. At equilibrium:

Test tube 3:

$0.001\ 00 \text{ M} \times 0.94 = 0.000\ 94 \text{ M } FeSCN^{2+}$

Test tube 4:

$0.001\ 00 \text{ M} \times 0.89 = 0.000\ 89 \text{ M } FeSCN^{2+}$

Test tube 5:

$0.001\ 00 \text{ M} \times 0.80 = 0.000\ 80 \text{ M } FeSCN^{2+}$

Test tube 6:

$0.001\ 00 \text{ M} \times 0.72 = 0.000\ 72 \text{ M } FeSCN^{2+}$

6. At equilibrium:

Test tube 3:

$0.001\ 00 \text{ M} - 0.000\ 94 \text{ M} = 0.000\ 06 \text{ M } SCN^-$

Test tube 4:

$0.001\ 00 \text{ M} - 0.000\ 89 \text{ M} = 0.000\ 11 \text{ M } SCN^-$

Test tube 5:

$0.001\ 00 \text{ M} - 0.000\ 80 \text{ M} = 0.000\ 20 \text{ M } SCN^-$

Test tube 6:

$0.001\ 00 \text{ M} - 0.000\ 72 \text{ M} = 0.000\ 28 \text{ M } SCN^-$

7. At equilibrium:

Test tube 3:

$0.025\ 00 \text{ M} - 0.000\ 94 \text{ M} = 0.0241 \text{ M } Fe^{3+}$

Test tube 4:

$0.012\ 50 \text{ M} - 0.000\ 89 \text{ M} = 0.0116 \text{ M } Fe^{3+}$

Test tube 5:

$0.006\ 25 \text{ M} - 0.000\ 80 \text{ M} = 0.005\ 45 \text{ M } Fe^{3+}$

Test tube 6:

$0.003\ 12 \text{ M} - 0.000\ 72 \text{ M} = 0.002\ 40 \text{ M } Fe^{3+}$

8.

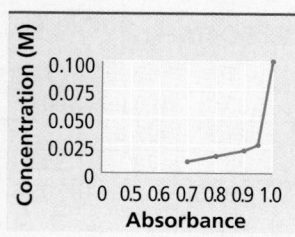

CONCLUSIONS

1. K_{eq} for test tube 3: $\dfrac{[0.000\,94]}{[0.0241]\,[0.000\,06]} = 700$

(rounded to 1 significant figure)

K_{eq} for test tube 4: $\dfrac{[0.000\,89]}{[0.0116]\,[0.000\,11]} = 700$

K_{eq} for test tube 5: $\dfrac{[0.000\,80]}{[0.005\,45]\,[0.000\,20]} = 730$

K_{eq} for test tube 6: $\dfrac{[0.000\,72]}{[0.002\,40]\,[0.000\,28]} = 1100$

2. Student answers will vary. Some possible causes for different values could be that the system did not reach equilibrium, the systems were not at equal temperatures, the measurements were inaccurate (either volume or instrument readings), or the dilutions were not exact.

3. As the concentration increased, so did the absorbance. For Fe^{3+}, this was not a linear relationship.

EXTENSIONS

1. Student answers will vary. Be certain students are very explicit in their procedures.

2. Students' suggestions for improving the procedure will vary. One possible suggestion is to use pipets to measure the volumes of the solutions more accurately in the dilution steps. Be sure answers include safe and carefully planned procedures.

3. $K_{eq} = \dfrac{[HbO_2]}{[O_2]\,[Hb]}$

4. Although there is less oxygen at high altitudes, the muscle cells still need the same amount of oxygen. The only way for the equilibrium constant to be maintained is for the body to produce more hemoglobin.

EXPERIMENT 18-2

Continued from page 877

- Wear safety goggles, a face shield, impermeable gloves, and a lab apron while preparing the acetic and hydrochloric acid solutions. Work in a hood known to be in good operating condition and have another person stand by to call for help in case of an emergency. Work within a 30 second walk from a safety shower and eyewash station.

- In case of an acid spill, dilute the spill with water. Then mop up the spill with wet cloths or a mop designated for spill cleanup. Wear disposable plastic gloves while cleaning spills.

TECHNIQUES TO DEMONSTRATE

Show students how to use the conductivity tester, and demonstrate ways in which they can shield the LED to provide maximum visibility when conductivity is weak.

Have students test the conductivity testers before each investigation. You may want to have them test various conductors, such as the metal faucets in the lab.

SAMPLE DATA

Students should find that either the 10^{-2} M solution or the 10^{-3} M solution is the best match for the 1.0 M acetic acid solution. K_a, calculated using $[H_3O^+] = 10^{-3}$ M, is 1×10^{-6}.

PRE-LAB DISCUSSION

You may want to review acid-ionization constants as a category of equilibrium constants. Make sure students recognize that K_a applies to weak acids because weak acids are not fully ionized like strong acids are. Students should be aware that because a strong acid is almost completely ionized, $[H_3O^+]$ is the same as the molar concentration of the solution. However, for weak acids, which are only partly ionized, this is not the case. Other methods must be employed to find $[H_3O^+]$ for weak acids. In this experiment, the conductivity of a weak acid is compared with the conductivity of a strong acid at various concentrations, and $[H_3O^+]$ of the weak acid is inferred from the results.

DISPOSAL

All solutions can be neutralized with 1 M Na_2CO_3 solution and poured down the drain.

ANALYSIS AND INTERPRETATION— ANSWERS

1. The conductivity of the 1.0 M CH_3COOH solution was much less than that of the 1.0 M HCl solution. Hydrochloric acid is a strong acid and ionizes completely

in water, but acetic acid is a weak acid and ionizes only partly in water. The greater number of ions in the HCl solution accounts for its greater conductivity.

2. Students should find that either the 10^{-2} M or the 10^{-3} M HCl solution is the best match for the acetic acid solution. Some students will estimate that the $[H_3O^+]$ falls between these values.

3. The estimates for $[H_3O^+]$ should range between 10^{-2} M and 10^{-3} M because these values match the values of the respective HCl solutions with the same conductivity and thus have the same number of ions and the same $[H_3O^+]$ as the HCl solutions.

CONCLUSIONS—ANSWERS

1. Student values for K_a will vary depending on student estimates of $[H_3O^+]$. Those who estimate it as being close to 10^{-2} M should calculate a K_a value of 10^{-4}. Those who estimate $[H_3O^+]$ as closer to 10^{-3} M should calculate a value of 10^{-6}.

$$K_a = \frac{[H_3O^+]\,[CH_3COO^-]}{[CH_3COOH]} = \frac{(10^{-3})\,(10^{-3})}{(1.0 - 10^{-3})} = \frac{(10^{-3})^2}{1.0} = 1 \times 10^{-6}$$

2. The conductivity of a solution is a function of the number of ions in the solution. Both HCl and CH_3COOH ionize to form an anion and the hydronium ion. When the conductivites of two solutions match, they each contain the same total number of ions and the same number of hydronium ions even though their concentrations differ. This occurs because HCl is a strong acid and therefore ionizes completely. CH_3COOH is a weak acid and does not ionize completely.

EXTENSIONS—ANSWERS

1. Students' answers will vary.

2. If an acetic acid solution of a different concentration is used, it will have a different conductivity but the calculated value of the K_a will be the same (for the same temperature).

3. Lactic acid has a larger K_a than acetic acid, so it will produce a more intense light in a conductivity tester. However, the glow produced by lactic acid should only be about as bright as that of the 0.01 M HCl solution because $[H_3O^+]$ in a 1.0 M solution of lactic acid is approximately 0.01. Because the conductivity of the acetic acid solution was between that of the 0.01 M HCl and that of the 0.001 M HCl, the difference will not be very great.

EXPERIMENT 19-2

Continued from page 882

SAMPLE DATA

Trial	Initial KMnO$_4$ volume (mL)	Final KMnO$_4$ volume (mL)	Initial FeSO$_4$ volume (mL)	Final FeSO$_4$ volume (mL)
1	50.0	35.0	50.0	40.0
2	35.0	20.5	40.0	30.0
3	20.5	5.0	30.0	20.0

Continued from page 883

ANALYSIS AND INTERPRETATION— ANSWERS

1. $MnO_4^-(aq) + 8H^+(aq) + 5Fe^{2+}(aq) \longrightarrow$
$$5Fe^{3+}(aq) + Mn^{2+}(aq) + 4H_2O(l)$$

2. Trial 1:

$$15.0 \text{ mL KMnO}_4 \times \frac{1 \text{ L}}{1000 \text{ mL}} \times \frac{0.020 \text{ mol KMnO}_4}{1 \text{ L}} =$$
$$3.0 \times 10^{-4} \text{ mol KMnO}_4$$

Trial 2:

$$14.5 \text{ mL KMnO}_4 \times \frac{1 \text{ L}}{1000 \text{ mL}} \times \frac{0.020 \text{ mol KMnO}_4}{1 \text{ L}} =$$
$$2.9 \times 10^{-4} \text{ mol KMnO}_4$$

Trial 3:

$$15.5 \text{ mL KMnO}_4 \times \frac{1 \text{ L}}{1000 \text{ mL}} \times \frac{0.020 \text{ mol KMnO}_4}{1 \text{ L}} =$$
$$3.1 \times 10^{-4} \text{ mol KMnO}_4$$

3. The ratio of Fe^{2+} to MnO_4^- is 5:1.
Trial 1:

$$3.0 \times 10^{-4} \text{ mol MnO}_4^- \times \frac{5 \text{ mol Fe}^{2+}}{1 \text{ mol MnO}_4^-} =$$
$$1.5 \times 10^{-3} \text{ mol Fe}^{2+}$$

Trial 2:

$$2.9 \times 10^{-4} \text{ mol MnO}_4^- \times \frac{5 \text{ mol Fe}^{2+}}{1 \text{ mol MnO}_4^-} =$$
$$1.4 \times 10^{-3} \text{ mol Fe}^{2+}$$

Trial 3:

$$3.1 \times 10^{-4} \text{ mol MnO}_4^- \times \frac{5 \text{ mol Fe}^{2+}}{1 \text{ mol MnO}_4^-} =$$
$$1.6 \times 10^{-3} \text{ mol Fe}^{2+}$$

4. Average molarity =
$$\frac{1.5 \times 10^{-3} + 1.4 \times 10^{-3} + 1.6 \times 10^{-3}}{3} =$$
$$1.5 \times 10^{-3} \text{ M Fe}^{2+}$$

5. The concentration of each solution is very important. If you rinse the buret with only distilled water, the solutions might be diluted by any water left in the buret. By using the solution being measured to rinse the buret, you can be sure any solution left behind will not dilute the solution added.

EXTENSIONS—ANSWERS

1. Students' suggestions for improving the procedure will vary. Possible suggestions include performing repeated trials or using larger volumes. Be sure answers are safe and include carefully planned procedures.

2. $2H_2O_2(l) \longrightarrow 2H_2O(l) + O_2(g)$

3. $\overset{+1\,-2}{H_2S}(g) + \overset{0}{O_2}(g) \longrightarrow \overset{+4\,-2}{SO_2}(g) + \overset{+1\,-2}{H_2O}(g)$
Oxidized: sulfur (loss of electrons)
Reduced: oxygen (gain of electrons)

EXPERIMENT 21-1

Continued from page 886

SAMPLE DATA

Reaction no.	[HCl]	[I$_2$]	[Acetone]	Rate
1	0.2 M	0.00024 M	0.8 M	(will vary)*
2	0.2 M	0.00024 M	1.6 M	(will vary)*
3	0.4 M	0.00024 M	0.8 M	(will vary)*
4	0.2 M	0.00048 M	0.8 M	(will vary)*

*See Analysis and Interpretation item 2.

EXPERIMENT 21-3

Continued from page 893

SAMPLE DATA

Latex rubber

Bounce height—trial 1	50 cm
Bounce height—trial 2	50 cm
Bounce height—trial 3	55 cm
Mass	45.20 g
Diameter	6.0 cm
Other observations	Does not crumble very easily. Seems more opaque.

SAMPLE DATA

Ethanol-silicate polymer

Bounce height—trial 1	58 cm
Bounce height—trial 2	60 cm
Bounce height—trial 3	50 cm
Mass	84.03 g
Diameter	7.0 cm
Other observations	Tends to bounce higher than other balls. Crumbles easily. Seems translucent.

3. Volume for latex ball:

$\frac{4}{3} (3.14)(3.0 \text{ cm})^3 = 110 \text{ cm}^3$

Volume for ethanol-silicate polymer ball:

$\frac{4}{3} (3.14)(3.5 \text{ cm})^3 = 180 \text{ cm}^3$

4. Density for latex ball: $\frac{45.20 \text{ g}}{110 \text{ cm}^3} = 0.41 \text{ g/cm}^3$

Density for ethanol-silicate polymer ball: $\frac{84.03 \text{ g}}{180 \text{ cm}^3} =$

0.47 g/cm^3

CONCLUSIONS—ANSWERS

1. Student answers will vary but should be based on the properties of the ball. Some students may argue that because the ethanol-silicate polymer ball crumbles in time, it would be a poor candidate for a toy.

2. Unit cost for latex ball: $0.215
Unit cost for ethanol-silicate polymer ball: $0.147

3. Student answers will vary but should be based on the properties of each substance.

EXTENSIONS—ANSWERS

1. A ball with an oblong shape will not bounce as high because some of the kinetic energy will be transferred into the energy of vibration, leaving less to be transformed into gravitational potential energy. A sphere that bounces will transfer nearly all of its kinetic energy into gravitational potential energy.

2. The ethanol-silicate polymer ball would break down in the water, so density must be calculated from measurements of mass and diameter.

TABLE A-1 SI MEASUREMENT

Metric Prefixes

Prefix	Symbol	Factor of Base Unit
giga	G	1 000 000 000
mega	M	1 000 000
kilo	k	1 000
hecto	h	100
deka	da	10
deci	d	0.1
centi	c	0.01
milli	m	0.001
micro	μ	0.000 001
nano	n	0.000 000 001
pico	p	0.000 000 000 001

Mass

1 kilogram (kg)	= SI base unit of mass
1 gram (g)	= 0.001 kg
1 milligram (mg)	= 0.000 001 kg
1 microgram (μg)	= 0.000 000 001 kg

Length

1 kilometer (km)	= 1 000 m
1 meter (m)	= SI base unit of length
1 centimeter (cm)	= 0.01 m
1 millimeter (mm)	= 0.001 m
1 micrometer (μm)	= 0.000 001 m
1 nanometer (nm)	= 0.000 000 001 m
1 picometer (pm)	= 0.000 000 000 001 m

Area

1 square kilometer (km^2)	= 100 hectares (ha)
1 hectare (ha)	= 10 000 square meters (m^2)
1 square meter (m^2)	= 10 000 square centimeters (cm^2)
1 square centimeter (cm^2)	= 100 square millimeters (mm^2)

Volume

1 liter (L)	= common unit for liquid volume (not SI)
1 cubic meter (m^3)	= 1000 L
1 kiloliter (kL)	= 1000 L
1 milliliter (mL)	= 0.001 L
1 milliliter (mL)	= 1 cubic centimeter (cm^3)

TABLE A-2 ABBREVIATIONS

amu	=	atomic mass unit (mass)	mol	=	mole (quantity)
atm	=	atmosphere (pressure, non-SI)	M	=	molarity (concentration)
Bq	=	becquerel (nuclear activity)	N	=	newton (force)
°C	=	degree Celsius (temperature)	Pa	=	pascal (pressure)
J	=	joule (energy)	s	=	second (time)
K	=	kelvin (temperature, thermodynamic)	V	=	volt (electric potential difference)

TABLE A-3 SYMBOLS

Symbol	Meaning
α	= helium nucleus (also $^4_2$He) emission from radioactive materials
β	= electron (also $^0_{-1}e$) emission from radioactive materials
γ	= high-energy photon emission from radioactive materials
Δ	= change in a given quantity (e.g., ΔH for change in enthalpy)
c	= speed of light in vacuum
c_p	= specific heat capacity (at constant pressure)
D	= density
E_a	= activation energy
E^0	= standard electrode potential
E^0 cell	= standard potential of an electro-chemical cell
G	= Gibbs free energy
ΔG^0	= standard free energy of reaction
ΔG^0_f	= standard molar free energy of formation
H	= enthalpy

Symbol	Meaning
ΔH^0	= standard enthalpy of reaction
ΔH^0_f	= standard molar enthalpy of formation
K_a	= ionization constant (acid)
K_b	= dissociation constant (base)
K_{eq}	= equilibrium constant
K_{sp}	= solubility-product constant
KE	= kinetic energy
m	= mass
N_A	= Avogadro's number
n	= number of moles
P	= pressure
pH	= measure of acidity ($-\log[H_3O^+]$)
R	= ideal gas law constant
S	= entropy
S^0	= standard molar entropy
T	= temperature (thermodynamic, in kelvins)
t	= temperature ($\pm$ degrees Celsius)
V	= volume
v	= velocity

TABLE A-4 PHYSICAL CONSTANTS

Quantity	Symbol	Value
Atomic mass unit	amu	$1.660\ 5402 \times 10^{-27}$ kg
Avogadro's number	N_A	$6.022\ 137 \times 10^{23}$/mol
Electron rest mass	m_e	$9.109\ 3897 \times 10^{-31}$ kg 5.4858×10^{-4} amu
Ideal gas law constant	R	8.314 L • kPa/mol • K 0.0821 L • atm/mol • K
Molar volume of ideal gas at STP	V_M	$22.414\ 10$ L/mol
Neutron rest mass	m_n	$1.674\ 9286 \times 10^{-27}$ kg $1.008\ 665$ amu
Normal boiling point of water	T_b	373.15 K $= 100.0°$C
Normal freezing point of water	T_f	273.15 K $= 0.00°$C
Planck's constant	h	$6.626\ 076 \times 10^{-34}$ J • s
Proton rest mass	m_p	$1.672\ 6231 \times 10^{-27}$ kg $1.007\ 276$ amu
Speed of light in a vacuum	c	$2.997\ 924\ 58 \times 10^8$ m/s
Temperature of triple point of water		273.16 K $= 0.01°$C

TABLE A-5 HEAT OF COMBUSTION

Substance	Formula	State	ΔH_c	Substance	Formula	State	ΔH_c
hydrogen	H_2	g	−285.8	benzene	C_6H_6	l	−3267.6
graphite	C	s	−393.5	toluene	C_7H_8	l	−3910.3
carbon monoxide	CO	g	−283.0	naphthalene	$C_{10}H_8$	s	−5156.3
methane	CH_4	g	−890.8	anthracene	$C_{14}H_{10}$	s	−7076.5
ethane	C_2H_6	g	−1560.7	methanol	CH_3OH	l	−726.1
propane	C_3H_8	g	−2219.2	ethanol	C_2H_5OH	l	−1366.8
butane	C_4H_{10}	g	−2877.6	ether	$(C_2H_5)_2O$	l	−2751.1
pentane	C_5H_{12}	g	−3535.6	formaldehyde	CH_2O	g	−570.7
hexane	C_6H_{14}	l	−4163.2	glucose	$C_6H_{12}O_6$	s	−2803.0
heptane	C_7H_{16}	l	−4817.0	sucrose	$C_{12}H_{22}O_{11}$	s	−5640.9
octane	C_8H_{18}	l	−5470.5				
ethene (ethylene)	C_2H_4	g	−1411.2				
propene (propylene)	C_3H_6	g	−2058.0				
ethyne (acetylene)	C_2H_2	g	−1301.1				

ΔH_c = heat of combustion of the given substance. All values of ΔH_c are expressed as kJ/mol of substance oxidized to $H_2O(l)$ and/or $CO_2(g)$ at constant pressure and 25°C.
s = solid, l = liquid, g = gas

TABLE A-6 THE ELEMENTS—SYMBOLS, ATOMIC NUMBERS, AND ATOMIC MASSES

Name of element	Symbol	Atomic number	Atomic mass	Name of element	Symbol	Atomic number	Atomic mass
actinium	Ac	89	[227.0278]	copper	Cu	29	63.546
aluminum	Al	13	26.981539	curium	Cm	96	[247.0703]
americium	Am	95	[243.0614]	dubnium	Db	105	[262.114]
antimony	Sb	51	121.757	dysprosium	Dy	66	162.50
argon	Ar	18	39.948	einsteinium	Es	99	[252.083]
arsenic	As	33	74.92159	erbium	Er	68	167.26
astatine	At	85	[209.9871]	europium	Eu	63	151.966
barium	Ba	56	137.327	fermium	Fm	100	[257.0951]
berkelium	Bk	97	[247.0703]	fluorine	F	9	18.9984032
beryllium	Be	4	9.012182	francium	Fr	87	[223.0197]
bismuth	Bi	83	208.98037	gadolinium	Gd	64	157.25
bohrium	Bh	107	[262.12]	gallium	Ga	31	69.723
boron	B	5	10.811	germanium	Ge	32	72.61
bromine	Br	35	79.904	gold	Au	79	196.96654
cadmium	Cd	48	112.411	hafnium	Hf	72	178.49
calcium	Ca	20	40.078	hassium	Hs	108	[265]
californium	Cf	98	[251.0796]	helium	He	2	4.002602
carbon	C	6	12.011	holmium	Ho	67	164.930
cerium	Ce	58	140.115	hydrogen	H	1	1.00794
cesium	Cs	55	132.90543	indium	In	49	114.818
chlorine	Cl	17	35.4527	iodine	I	53	126.904
chromium	Cr	24	51.9961	iridium	Ir	77	192.22
cobalt	Co	27	58.93320	iron	Fe	26	55.847

TABLE A-6   CONTINUED

Name of element	Symbol	Atomic number	Atomic mass	Name of element	Symbol	Atomic number	Atomic mass
krypton	Kr	36	83.80	rhodium	Rh	45	102.906
lanthanum	La	57	138.9055	rubidium	Rb	37	85.4678
lawrencium	Lr	103	[262.11]	ruthenium	Ru	44	101.07
lead	Pb	82	207.2	rutherfordium	Rf	104	[261.11]
lithium	Li	3	6.941	samarium	Sm	62	150.36
lutetium	Lu	71	174.967	scandium	Sc	21	44.955910
magnesium	Mg	12	24.3050	seaborgium	Sg	106	[263.118]
manganese	Mn	25	54.93805	selenium	Se	34	78.96
meitnerium	Mt	109	[266]	silicon	Si	14	28.0855
mendelevium	Md	101	[258.10]	silver	Ag	47	107.8682
mercury	Hg	80	200.59	sodium	Na	11	22.989768
molybdenum	Mo	42	95.94	strontium	Sr	38	87.62
neodymium	Nd	60	144.24	sulfur	S	16	32.066
neon	Ne	10	20.1797	tantalum	Ta	73	180.9479
neptunium	Np	93	[237.0482]	technetium	Tc	43	[97.9072]
nickel	Ni	28	58.6934	tellurium	Te	52	127.60
niobium	Nb	41	92.90638	terbium	Tb	65	158.92534
nitrogen	N	7	14.00674	thallium	Tl	81	204.3833
nobelium	No	102	[259.1009]	thorium	Th	90	232.0381
osmium	Os	76	190.23	thulium	Tm	69	168.93421
oxygen	O	8	15.9994	tin	Sn	50	118.710
palladium	Pd	46	106.42	titanium	Ti	22	47.88
phosphorus	P	15	30.9738	tungsten	W	74	183.84
platinum	Pt	78	195.08	uranium	U	92	238.0289
plutonium	Pu	94	[244.0642]	vanadium	V	23	50.9415
polonium	Po	84	[208.9824]	xenon	Xe	54	131.29
potassium	K	19	39.0983	ytterbium	Yb	70	173.04
praseodymium	Pr	59	140.908	yttrium	Y	39	88.90585
promethium	Pm	61	[144.9127]	zinc	Zn	30	65.39
protactinium	Pa	91	231.03588	zirconium	Zr	40	91.224
radium	Ra	88	[226.0254]				
radon	Rn	86	[222.0176]				
rhenium	Re	75	186.207				

A value given in brackets denotes the mass number of the most stable or most common isotope. The atomic masses of most of these elements are believed to have an error no greater than ±1 in the last digit given.

TABLE A-7 COMMON IONS

Cation	Symbol	Anion	Symbol
aluminum	Al^{3+}	acetate	CH_3COO^-
ammonium	NH_4^+	bromide	Br^-
arsenic(III)	As^{3+}	carbonate	CO_3^{2-}
barium	Ba^{2+}	chlorate	ClO_3^-
calcium	Ca^{2+}	chloride	Cl^-
chromium(II)	Cr^{2+}	chlorite	ClO_2^-
chromium(III)	Cr^{3+}	chromate	CrO_4^{2-}
cobalt(II)	Co^{2+}	cyanide	CN^-
cobalt(III)	Co^{3+}	dichromate	$Cr_2O_7^{2-}$
copper(I)	Cu^+	fluoride	F^-
copper(II)	Cu^{2+}	hexacyanoferrate(II)	$Fe(CN)_6^{4-}$
hydronium	H_3O^+	hexacyanoferrate(III)	$Fe(CN)_6^{3-}$
iron(II)	Fe^{2+}	hydride	H^-
iron(III)	Fe^{3+}	hydrogen carbonate	HCO_3^-
lead(II)	Pb^{2+}	hydrogen sulfate	HSO_4^-
magnesium	Mg^{2+}	hydroxide	OH^-
mercury(I)	Hg_2^{2+}	hypochlorite	ClO^-
mercury(II)	Hg^{2+}	iodide	I^-
nickel(II)	Ni^{2+}	nitrate	NO_3^-
potassium	K^+	nitrite	NO_2^-
silver	Ag^+	oxide	O^{2-}
sodium	Na^+	perchlorate	ClO_4^-
strontium	Sr^{2+}	permanganate	MnO_4^-
tin(II)	Sn^{2+}	peroxide	O_2^{2-}
tin(IV)	Sn^{4+}	phosphate	PO_4^{3-}
titanium(III)	Ti^{3+}	sulfate	SO_4^{2-}
titanium(IV)	Ti^{4+}	sulfide	S^{2-}
zinc	Zn^{2+}	sulfite	SO_3^{2-}

TABLE A-8   WATER-VAPOR PRESSURE

Temperature (°C)	Pressure (mm Hg)	Pressure (kPa)	Temperature (°C)	Pressure (mm Hg)	Pressure (kPa)
0.0	4.6	0.61	23.0	21.1	2.81
5.0	6.5	0.87	23.5	21.7	2.90
10.0	9.2	1.23	24.0	22.4	2.98
15.0	12.8	1.71	24.5	23.1	3.10
15.5	13.2	1.76	25.0	23.8	3.17
16.0	13.6	1.82	26.0	25.2	3.36
16.5	14.1	1.88	27.0	26.7	3.57
17.0	14.5	1.94	28.0	28.3	3.78
17.5	15.0	2.00	29.0	30.0	4.01
18.0	15.5	2.06	30.0	31.8	4.25
18.5	16.0	2.13	35.0	42.2	5.63
19.0	16.5	2.19	40.0	55.3	7.38
19.5	17.0	2.27	50.0	92.5	12.34
20.0	17.5	2.34	60.0	149.4	19.93
20.5	18.1	2.41	70.0	233.7	31.18
21.0	18.6	2.49	80.0	355.1	47.37
21.5	19.2	2.57	90.0	525.8	70.12
22.0	19.8	2.64	95.0	633.9	84.53
22.5	20.4	2.72	100.0	760.0	101.32

TABLE A-9   DENSITIES OF GASES AT STP

Gas	Density (g/L)
air, dry	1.293
ammonia	0.771
carbon dioxide	1.997
carbon monoxide	1.250
chlorine	3.214
dinitrogen monoxide	1.977
ethyne (acetylene)	1.165
helium	0.1785
hydrogen	0.0899
hydrogen chloride	1.639
hydrogen sulfide	1.539
methane	0.7168
nitrogen	1.2506
nitrogen monoxide (at 10°C)	1.340
oxygen	1.429
sulfur dioxide	2.927

TABLE A-10   DENSITY OF WATER

Temperature (°C)	Density (g/cm³)
0	0.999 84
2	0.999 94
3.98 (maximum)	0.999 973
4	0.999 97
6	0.999 94
8	0.999 85
10	0.999 70
14	0.999 24
16	0.998 94
20	0.998 20
25	0.997 05
30	0.995 65
40	0.992 22
50	0.988 04
60	0.983 20
70	0.977 77
80	0.971 79
90	0.965 31
100	0.958 36

TABLE A-11 SOLUBILITIES OF GASES IN WATER

Volume of gas (in liters) at STP that can be dissolved in 1 L of water at the temperature (°C) indicated.

Gas	0°C	10°C	20°C	60°C
air	0.029 18	0.022 84	0.018 68	0.012 16
ammonia	1130	870	680	200
carbon dioxide	1.713	1.194	0.878	0.359
carbon monoxide	0.035 37	0.028 16	0.023 19	0.014 88
chlorine	—	3.148	2.299	1.023
hydrogen	0.021 48	0.019 55	0.018 19	0.016 00
hydrogen chloride	512	475	442	339
hydrogen sulfide	4.670	3.399	2.582	1.190
methane	0.055 63	0.041 77	0.033 08	0.019 54
nitrogen*	0.023 54	0.018 61	0.015 45	0.010 23
nitrogen monoxide	0.073 81	0.057 09	0.047 06	0.029 54
oxygen	0.048 89	0.038 02	0.031 02	0.019 46
sulfur dioxide	79.789	56.647	39.374	—

*Atmospheric nitrogen–98.815% N_2, 1.185% inert gases

TABLE A-12 SOLUBILITY CHART

	acetate	bromide	carbonate	chlorate	chloride	chromate	hydroxide	iodine	nitrate	oxide	phosphate	silicate	sulfate	sulfide
aluminum	S	S	—	S	S	—	A	S	S	a	A	I	S	d
ammonium	S	S	S	S	S	S	S	S	S	—	S	—	S	S
barium	S	S	P	S	S	A	S	S	S	S	A	S	a	d
calcium	S	S	P	S	S	S	S	S	S	P	P	P	S	S
copper(II)	S	S	—	S	S	—	A	—	S	A	A	A	S	A
hydrogen	S	S	—	S	S	—	—	S	S	S	S	I	S	S
iron(II)	—	S	P	S	S	—	A	S	S	A	A	—	S	A
iron(III)	—	S	—	S	S	A	A	S	S	A	P	—	P	d
lead(II)	S	S	A	S	S	A	P	P	S	P	A	A	P	A
magnesium	S	S	P	S	S	S	A	S	S	A	P	A	S	d
manganese(II)	S	S	P	S	S	—	A	S	S	A	P	I	S	A
mercury(I)	P	A	A	S	a	P	—	A	S	A	A	—	P	I
mercury(II)	S	S	—	S	S	P	A	P	S	P	A	—	d	I
potassium	S	S	S	S	S	S	S	S	S	S	S	S	S	S
silver	P	a	A	S	a	P	—	I	S	P	A	—	P	A
sodium	S	S	S	S	S	S	S	S	S	d	S	S	S	S
strontium	S	S	P	S	S	P	S	S	S	S	A	A	P	S
tin(II)	d	S	—	S	S	A	A	S	d	A	A	—	S	A
tin(IV)	S	S	—	—	S	S	P	d	—	A	—	—	S	A
zinc	S	S	P	S	S	P	A	S	S	P	A	A	S	A

S = soluble in water. A = soluble in acids, insoluble in water. P = partially soluble in water, soluble in dilute acids.
I = insoluble in dilute acids and in water. a = slightly soluble in acids, insoluble in water. d = decomposes in water.

TABLE A-13   SOLUBILITY OF COMPOUNDS

Solubilities are given in grams of solute that can be dissolved in 100 g of water at the temperature (°C) indicated.

Compound	Formula	0°C	20°C	60°C	100°C
aluminum sulfate	$Al_2(SO_4)_3$	31.2	36.4	59.2	89.0
ammonium chloride	NH_4Cl	29.4	37.2	55.3	77.3
ammonium nitrate	NH_4NO_3	118	192	421	871
ammonium sulfate	$(NH_4)_2SO_4$	70.6	75.4	88	103
barium carbonate	$BaCO_3$	—*	$0.0022^{18°}$	—*	0.0065
barium chloride dihydrate	$BaCl_2 \cdot 2H_2O$	31.2	35.8	46.2	59.4
barium hydroxide	$Ba(OH)_2$	1.67	3.89	20.94	$101.40^{80°}$
barium nitrate	$Ba(NO_3)_2$	4.95	9.02	20.4	34.4
barium sulfate	$BaSO_4$	—*	$0.000\ 246^{25°}$	—*	0.000 413
calcium carbonate	$CaCO_3$	—*	$0.0014^{25°}$	—*	$0.0018^{75°}$
calcium fluoride	CaF_2	$0.0016^{18°}$	$0.0017^{26°}$	—*	—*
calcium hydrogen carbonate	$Ca(HCO_3)_2$	16.15	16.60	17.50	18.40
calcium hydroxide	$Ca(OH)_2$	0.189	0.173	0.121	0.076
calcium sulfate	$CaSO_4$	—*	$0.209^{30°}$	—*	0.1619
copper(II) chloride	$CuCl_2$	68.6	73.0	96.5	120
copper(II) sulfate pentahydrate	$CuSO_4 \cdot 5H_2O$	23.1	32.0	61.8	114
lead(II) chloride	$PbCl_2$	0.67	1.00	1.94	3.20
lead(II) nitrate	$Pb(NO_3)_2$	37.5	54.3	91.6	133
lithium chloride	$LiCl$	69.2	83.5	98.4	128
lithium sulfate	Li_2SO_4	36.1	34.8	32.6	$30.9^{90°}$
magnesium hydroxide	$Mg(OH)_2$	—*	$0.0009^{18°}$	—*	0.004
magnesium sulfate	$MgSO_4$	22.0	33.7	54.6	68.3
mercury(I) chloride	Hg_2Cl_2	—*	$0.000\ 20^{25°}$	$0.001^{43°}$	—*
mercury(II) chloride	$HgCl_2$	3.63	6.57	16.3	61.3
potassium bromide	KBr	53.6	65.3	85.5	104
potassium chlorate	$KClO_3$	3.3	7.3	23.8	56.3
potassium chloride	KCl	28.0	34.2	45.8	56.3
potassium chromate	K_2CrO_4	56.3	63.7	70.1	$74.5^{90°}$
potassium iodide	KI	128	144	176	206
potassium nitrate	KNO_3	13.9	31.6	106	245
potassium permanganate	$KMnO_4$	2.83	6.34	22.1	—*
potassium sulfate	K_2SO_4	7.4	11.1	18.2	24.1
silver acetate	$AgC_2H_3O_2$	0.73	1.05	1.93	$2.59^{80°}$
silver chloride	$AgCl$	$0.000\ 089^{10°}$	—*	—*	0.0021
silver nitrate	$AgNO_3$	122	216	440	733
sodium acetate	$NaC_2H_3O_2$	36.2	46.4	139	170
sodium chlorate	$NaClO_3$	79.6	95.9	137	204
sodium chloride	$NaCl$	35.7	35.9	37.1	39.2
sodium nitrate	$NaNO_3$	73.0	87.6	122	180
sucrose	$C_{12}H_{22}O_{11}$	179.2	203.9	287.3	487.2

*Dashes indicate that values are not available.

TABLE A-14   HEAT OF FORMATION

Substance	State	ΔH_f	Substance	State	ΔH_f
ammonia	g	−45.9	lead(IV) oxide	s	−274.5
ammonium chloride	s	−314.4	lead(II) nitrate	s	−451.9
ammonium sulfate	s	−1180.9	lead(I) sulfate	s	−919.94
barium chloride	s	−858.6	lithium chloride	s	−408.6
barium nitrate	s	−992.1	lithium nitrate	s	−483.1
barium sulfate	s	−1473.2	magnesium chloride	s	−641.5
benzene	g	+82.88	magnesium oxide	s	−601.6
benzene	l	+49.080	magnesium sulfate	s	−1284.9
calcium carbonate	s	−1207.6	manganese(IV) oxide	s	−520.0
calcium chloride	s	−795.4	manganese(II) sulfate	s	−1065.3
calcium hydroxide	s	−983.2	mercury(I) chloride	s	−264.2
calcium nitrate	s	−938.2	mercury(II) chloride	s	−230.0
calcium oxide	s	−634.9	mercury(II) oxide (red)	s	−90.8
calcium sulfate	s	−1434.5	methane	g	−74.9
carbon (diamond)	s	+1.9	nitrogen dioxide	g	+33.2
carbon (graphite)	s	0.00	nitrogen monoxide	g	+90.29
carbon dioxide	g	−393.5	dinitrogen monoxide	g	+82.1
carbon monoxide	g	−110.5	dinitrogen tetroxide	g	+9.2
copper(II) nitrate	s	−302.9	oxygen (O_2)	g	0.00
copper(II) oxide	s	−157.3	ozone (O_3)	g	+142.7
copper(II) sulfate	s	−771.4	diphosphorus pentoxide	s	−3009.9
ethane	g	−83.8	potassium bromide	s	−393.8
ethyne (acetylene)	g	+228.2	potassium chloride	s	−436.49
hydrogen (H_2)	g	0.00	potassium hydroxide	s	−424.58
hydrogen bromide	g	−36.29	potassium nitrate	s	−494.6
hydrogen chloride	g	−92.3	potassium sulfate	s	−1437.8
hydrogen fluoride	g	−273.3	silicon dioxide (quartz)	s	−910.7
hydrogen iodide	g	+26.5	silver chloride	s	−127.01 ± 0.5
hydrogen oxide (water)	g	−241.8	silver nitrate	s	−120.5
hydrogen oxide (water)	l	−285.8	silver sulfide	s	−32.59
hydrogen peroxide	g	−136.3	sodium bromide	s	−361.8
hydrogen peroxide	l	−187.8	sodium chloride	s	−385.9
hydrogen sulfide	g	−23.9	sodium hydroxide	s	−425.9
iodine (I_2)	s	0.00	sodium nitrate	s	−467.9
iodine (I_2)	g	+62.4	sodium sulfate	l	−1387.1
iron(II) chloride	s	−399.4	sulfur dioxide	g	−296.8
iron(II) oxide	s	−825.5	sulfur trioxide	g	−395.7
iron(II, III) oxide	s	−1118.4	tin(IV) chloride	l	−511.3
iron(II) sulfate	s	−928.4	zinc nitrate	s	−483.7
iron(II) sulfide	s	−100.0	zinc oxide	s	−350.5
lead(II) oxide	s	−217.3	zinc sulfate	s	−980.14

ΔH_f is heat of formation of the given substance from its elements. All values of ΔH_f are expressed as kJ/mol at 25°C. Negative values of ΔH_f indicate exothermic reactions. s = solid, l = liquid, g = gas

TABLE A-15 PROPERTIES OF COMMON ELEMENTS

Name	Form/color at room temperature	Density (g/cm³)†	Melting point (°C)	Boiling point (°C)	Common oxidation states
aluminum	silver metal	2.702	660.37	2467	3+
arsenic	gray metalloid	5.727^{14}	817 (28 atm)	613 (sublimes)	3−,3+,5+
barium	bluish white metal	3.51	725	1640	2+
bromine	red-brown liquid	3.119	−7.2	58.78	1−,1+,3+,5+,7+
calcium	silver metal	1.54	839 ± 2	1484	2+
carbon	diamond	3.51	3500 (63.5 atm)	3930	2+,4+
	graphite	2.25	3652 (sublimes)	—	
chlorine	green-yellow gas	3.214*	−100.98	−34.6	1−,1+,3+,5+,7+
chromium	gray metal	7.2028	1857 ± 20	2672	2+,3+,6+
cobalt	gray metal	8.9	1495	2870	2+,3+
copper	red metal	8.92	1083.4 ± 0.2	2567	1+,2+
fluorine	yellow gas	1.69‡	−219.62	−188.14	1−
germanium	gray metalloid	5.323^{25}	937.4	2830	4+
gold	yellow metal	19.31	1064.43	2808 ± 2	1+,3+
helium	colorless gas	0.1785*	−272.2 (26 atm)	−268.9	0
hydrogen	colorless gas	0.0899*	−259.34	−252.8	1−,1+
iodine	blue-black solid	4.93	113.5	184.35	1−,1+,3+,5+,7+
iron	silver metal	7.86	1535	2750	2+,3+
lead	bluish white metal	11.343716	327.502	1740	2+,4+
lithium	silver metal	0.534	180.54	1342	1+
magnesium	silver metal	1.745	648.8	1107	2+
manganese	gray-white metal	7.20	1244 ± 3	1962	2+,3+,4+,6+,7+
mercury	silver liquid metal	13.5462	−38.87	356.58	1+,2+
neon	colorless gas	0.9002*	−248.67	−245.9	0
nickel	silver metal	8.90	1455	2730	2+,3+
nitrogen	colorless gas	1.2506*	−209.86	−195.8	3−,3+,5+
oxygen	colorless gas	1.429*	−218.4	−182.962	2−
phosphorus	yellow solid	1.82	44.1	280	3−,3+,5+
platinum	silver metal	21.45	1772	3827 ± 100	2+,4+
potassium	silver metal	0.86	63.25	760	1+
silicon	gray metalloid	2.33 ± 0.01	1410	2355	2+,4+
silver	white metal	10.5	961.93	2212	1+
sodium	silver metal	0.97	97.8	882.9	1+
strontium	silver metal	2.6	769	1384	2+
sulfur	yellow solid	1.96	119.0	444.674	2−,4+,6+
tin	white metal	7.28	231.88	2260	2+,4+
titanium	white metal	4.5	1660 ± 10	3287	2+,3+,4+
uranium	silver metal	19.05 ± 0.02^{25}	1132.3 ± 0.8	3818	3+,4+,6+
zinc	blue-white metal	7.14	419.58	907	2+

† Densities obtained at 20°C unless otherwise noted (superscript)

‡ Density of fluorine given in g/L at 1 atm and 15°C

* Densities of gases given in g/L at STP

Study Skills for Chemistry
Table of Contents

Succeeding in Your Chemistry Class 905

Making Concept Maps 908

Making Power Notes 911

Making Two-Column Notes 913

Using the K/W/L Strategy 914

Using Sequencing/Pattern Puzzles 915

Other Reading Strategies 916

Other Studying Strategies 917

Cooperative Learning Techniques 918

Study Skills for Chemistry

Succeeding in Your Chemistry Class

Your success in this course will depend on your ability to apply some basic study skills to learning the material. Studying chemistry can be difficult, but you can make it easier using simple strategies for dealing with the concepts and problems. Becoming skilled in using these strategies will be your keys to success in this and many other courses.

▶ Reading the Text

- **Read the assigned material before class** so that the class lecture makes sense. Use a dictionary to help you build and interpret vocabulary. Remember that, while reading, one of your tasks is to figure out what information is important.

  Working together with others using Paired Reading and Discussion strategies can help you decide what is important and clarify the material. (For more discussion, see Other Reading Strategies on page 916.)

- **Select a quiet setting** away from distractions so that you can concentrate on what you are reading.

- **Have a pencil and paper nearby to jot down notes and questions** you may have. Be sure to get these questions answered in class. Power Notes (see page 911) can help you organize the notes you take and prepare you for class.

- **Use the Objectives in the beginning of each section as a list of what you need to know from the section.** Teachers generally make their tests based on the text objectives or their own objectives. Using the objectives to focus your reading can make your learning more efficient.

Using the K/W/L strategy (see page 914) can help you relate new material to what you already know and what you need to learn.

▶ Taking Notes in Class

- **Be prepared to take notes during class.** Have your materials organized in a notebook. Separate sheets of paper can be easily lost.

- **Don't write down everything your teacher says.** Try to tell which parts of the lecture are important and which are not. Reading the text before class will help in this. You will not be able to write down everything, so you must try to write down only the important things.

- **Recopying notes later is a waste of time** and does not help you learn material for a test. Do

it right the first time. Organize your notes as you are writing them down so that you can make sense of your notes when you review them without needing to recopy them.

► Reviewing Class Notes

• **Review your notes as soon as possible after class.** Write down any questions you may have about the material covered that day. Be sure to get these questions answered during the next class. You can work with friends to use strategies such as Paired Summarizing and L.I.N.K. (See page 918.)

• **Do not wait until the test to review.** By then you will have forgotten a good portion of the material.

• **Be selective about what you memorize.** You cannot memorize everything in a chapter. First of all, it is too time consuming. Second, memorizing and understanding are not the same thing. Memorizing topics as they appear in your notes or text does not guarantee that you will be able to correctly answer questions that require understanding of those topics. You should only memorize material that you understand. Concept Maps and other Reading Organizers, Sequencing/Pattern Puzzles, and Prediction Guides can help you understand key ideas and major concepts. (See pages 908, 915, and 917.)

► Working Problems

In addition to understanding the concepts, the ability to solve problems will be a key to your success in chemistry. You will probably spend a lot of time working problems in class and at home. The ability to solve chemistry problems is a skill, and like any skill, it requires practice.

• **Always review the Sample Problems in the chapter.** The Sample Problems in the text provide road maps for solving certain types of problems. Cover the solution while trying to work the problem yourself.

• **The problems in the Chapter Review are similar to the Sample Problems.** If you can relate an assigned problem to one of the Sample Problems in the chapter, it shows that you understand the material.

• **The four steps: Analyze, Plan, Compute, and Evaluate should be the steps you go through when working assigned problems.** These steps will allow you to organize your thoughts and help you develop your problem-solving skills.

• **Never spend more than 15 minutes trying to solve a problem.** If you have not been able to come up with a plan for the solution after 15 minutes, additional time spent will only cause you to become frustrated. What do you do? Get help! See your teacher or a classmate. Find out what it is that you do not understand.

• **Do not try to memorize the Sample Problems; spend your time trying to understand how the solution develops.** Memorizing a particular sample problem will not ensure that you understand it well enough to solve a similar problem.

• **Always look at your answer and ask yourself if it is reasonable and makes sense.** Check to be sure you have the correct units and numbers of significant figures.

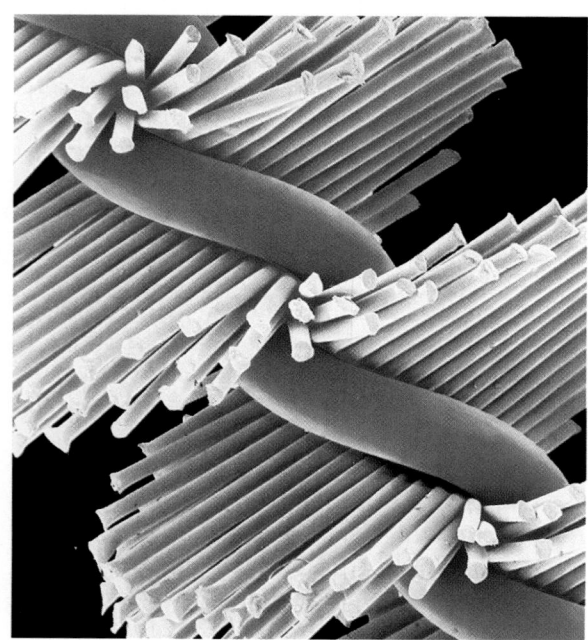

► **Completing Homework**

Your teacher will probably assign questions and problems from the Section Reviews and Chapter Reviews or assign *Modern Chemistry* Daily Homework. The purpose of these assignments is to review what you have covered in class and to see if you can use the information to answer questions or solve problems. As in reviewing class notes, do your homework as soon after class as possible while the topics are still fresh in your mind. Do not wait until late at night, when you are more likely to be tired and to become frustrated.

► **Preparing for and Taking Exams**

Reviewing for an exam

• **Don't panic and don't cram! It takes longer to learn if you are under pressure.** If you have followed the strategies listed here and reviewed along the way, studying for the exam should be less stressful.

• **When looking over your notes and concept maps, recite ideas out loud.** There are two reasons for reciting:

1. You are hearing the information, which is effective in helping you learn.

2. If you cannot recite the ideas, it should be a clue that you do not understand the material, and you should begin rereading or reviewing the material again.

• **Studying with a friend provides a good opportunity for recitation.** If you can explain ideas to your study partner, you know the material.

Taking an exam

• **Get plenty of rest before the exam so that you can think clearly.** If you have been awake all night studying, you are less likely to succeed than if you had gotten a full night of rest.

• **Start with the questions you know.** If you get stuck on a question, save it for later. As time passes and you work through the exam, you may recall the information you need to answer a difficult question or solve a difficult problem.

Good luck!

Making Concept Maps

Making concept maps can help you decide what material in a chapter is important and how to efficiently learn that material. A concept map presents key ideas, meanings, and relationships for the concepts being studied. It can be thought of as a visual road map of the chapter. Learning happens efficiently when you use concept maps because you work with only the key ideas and how they fit together.

The concept map shown as **Map A** was made from vocabulary terms in Chapter 1. Vocabulary terms are generally labels for concepts, and concepts are generally nouns. In a concept map, linking words are used to form propositions that connect concepts and give them meaning in context. For example, on the map below, "matter is described by physical properties" is a proposition.

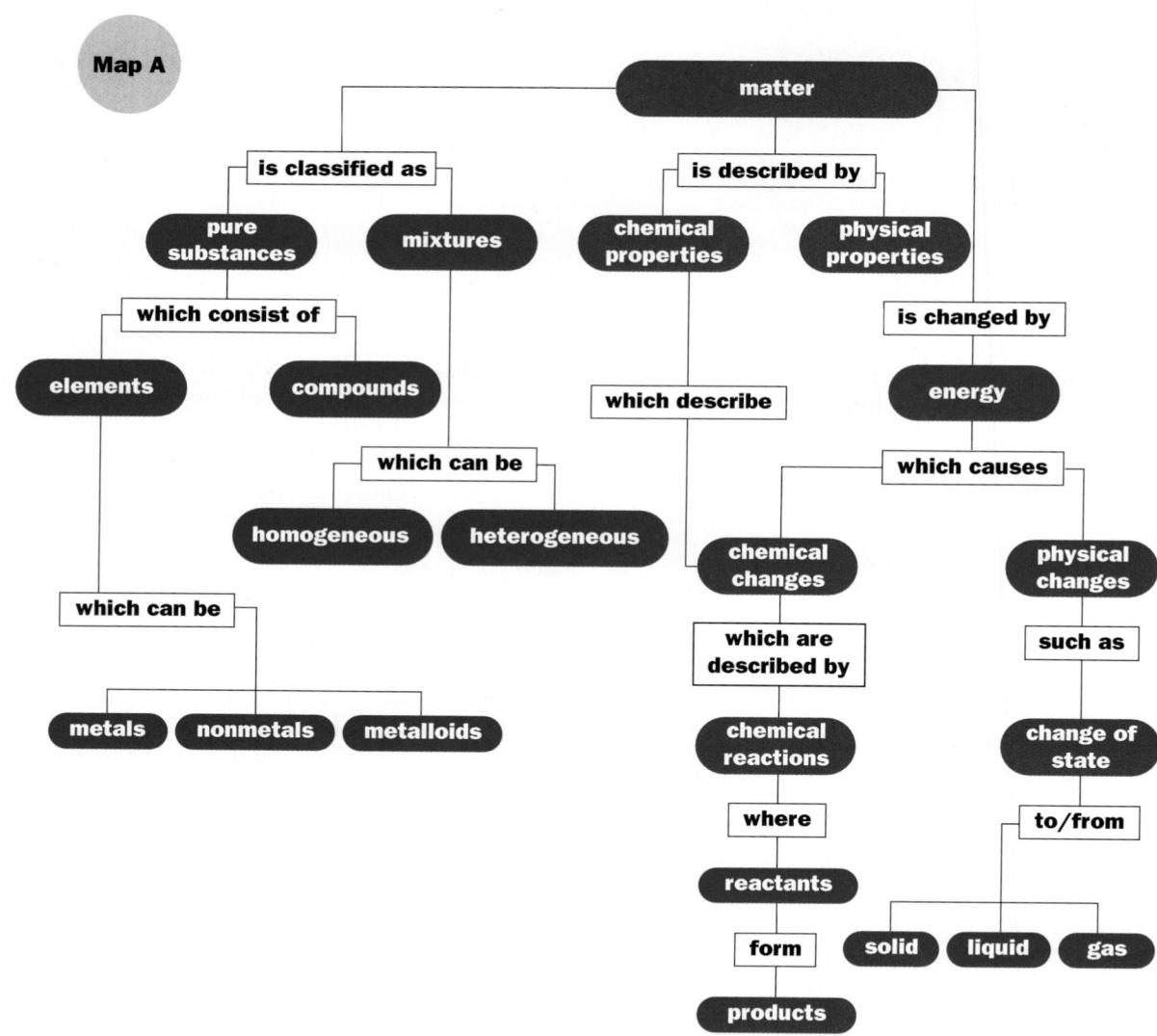

Studies show that people are better able to remember materials presented visually. A concept map is better than an outline because you can see the relationships among many ideas. Because outlines are linear, there is no way of linking the ideas from various sections of the outline. Read through the map to become familiar with the information presented. Then look at the map in relation to all of the text pages in Chapter 1; which gives a better picture of the important concepts—the map or the full chapter?

▶ **To Make a Concept Map**

1. List all the important concepts.
We'll use some of the boldfaced and italicized terms from Section 1-2.

matter	mixture
compound	pure substance
element	
homogenous mixture	
heterogeneous mixture	

• From this list, group similar concepts together. For example, one way to group these concepts would be into two groups—one that is related to mixtures and one that is related to pure substances.

mixture	*pure substance*
heterogeneous mixture	compound
homogeneous mixture	element

2. Select a main concept for the map.
We will use *matter* as the main concept for this map.

3. Build the map by placing the concepts according to their importance under the main concept, *matter*.
One way of arranging the concepts is shown in **Map B.**

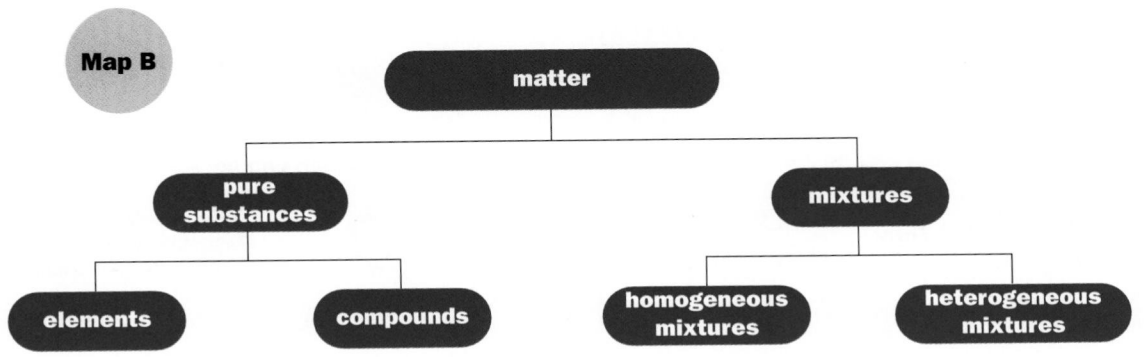

4. Add linking words to give meaning to the arrangement of concepts.

When adding the links, be sure that each proposition makes sense. To distinguish concepts from links, place your concepts in circles, ovals, or rectangles, as shown in the maps. Then make cross-links. Cross-links are made of propositions and lines connecting concepts across the map. Links that apply in only one direction are indicated with an arrowhead. **Map C** is a finished map covering the main ideas listed in Step 1.

Making maps might seem difficult at first, but the process forces you to think about the meanings and relationships among the concepts. If you do not understand those relationships, you can get help early on.

Practice mapping by making concept maps about topics you know. For example, if you know a lot about a particular sport, such as basketball, or if you have a particular hobby, such as playing a musical instrument, you can use that topic to make a practice map. By perfecting your skills with information that you know very well, you will begin to feel more confident about making maps from the information in a chapter.

Remember, the time you devote to mapping will pay off when it is time to review for an exam.

Practice

1. Classify each of the following as either a concept or linking word(s).

a. classification _____

b. is classified as _____

c. forms _____

d. is described by _____

e. reaction _____

f. reacts with _____

g. metal _____

h. defines _____

2. Write three propositions from the information in **Map A.** _____

_____

_____

_____

3. List two cross-links shown on **Map C.**

_____

_____

_____

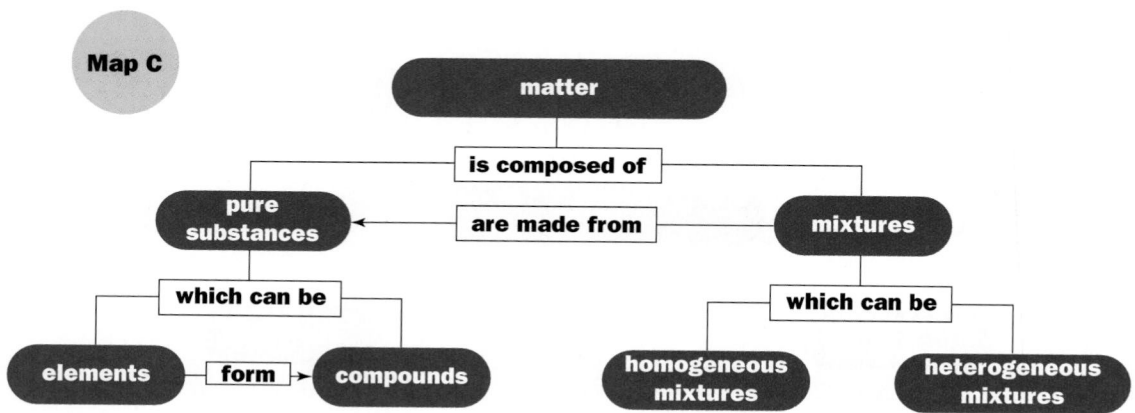

Map C

Making Power Notes

Power notes help you organize the chemical concepts you are studying by distinguishing main ideas from details. Similar to outlines, power notes are linear in form and provide you with a framework of important concepts. Power notes are easier to use than outlines because their structure is simpler. Using the power notes numbering system you assign a *1* to each main idea and a *2, 3,* or *4* to each detail.

Power notes are an invaluable asset to the learning process, and they can be used frequently throughout your chemistry course. You can use power notes to organize ideas while reading your text or to restructure your class notes for studying purposes.

To learn to make power notes, practice first by using single-word concepts and a subject you are especially interested in, such as animals, sports, or movies. As you become comfortable with structuring power notes, integrate their use into your study of chemistry. For an easier transition, start with a few boldfaced or italicized terms. Later you can strengthen your notes by expanding these single-word concepts into more-detailed phrases and sentences. Use the following general format to help you structure your power notes.

Power 1: Main idea
  Power 2: Detail or support for power 1
    Power 3: Detail or support for power 2
      Power 4: Detail or support for power 3

1. Pick a Power 1 word from the text.
The text you choose does not have to come straight from your chemistry textbook. You may be making power notes from your lecture notes or from an outside source. We'll use the term *atom* found in Section 3-2 of your textbook.

Power 1: Atom

2. Using the text, select some Power 2 words to support your Power 1 word.
We'll use the terms *nucleus* and *electrons,* which are two parts of an atom.

Power 1: Atom
  Power 2: Nucleus
  Power 2: Electrons

3. Select some Power 3 words to support your Power 2 words.
We'll use the terms *positively charged* and *negatively charged,* two terms that describe the Power 2 words.

Power 1: Atom
  Power 2: Nucleus
    Power 3: Positively charged
  Power 2: Electrons
    Power 3: Negatively charged

4. Continue to add powers to support and detail the main idea as necessary.

There are no restrictions on how many power numbers you can use in your notes. If you have a main idea that requires a lot of support, add more powers to help you extend and organize your ideas. Be sure that words having the same power number have a similar relationship to the power above. Power 1 terms do not have to be related to each other. You can use power notes to organize the material in an entire section or chapter of your text. Doing so will provide you with an invaluable study guide for your classroom quizzes and tests.

Power 1: Atom
  Power 2: Nucleus
    Power 3: Positively charged
    Power 3: Protons
      Power 4: Positively charged
    Power 3: Neutrons
      Power 4: No charge
  Power 2: Electrons
    Power 3: Negatively charged

Practice

1. Use a periodic table and the power notes structure below to organize the following terms: *alkaline-earth metals, nonmetals, calcium, sodium, halogens, metals, alkali metals, chlorine, barium,* and *iodine.*

1 _____

  2 _____

    3 _____

  2 _____

    3 _____

    3 _____

1 _____

  2 _____

    3 _____

    3 _____

Making Two-Column Notes

Two-column notes can be used to learn and review definitions of vocabulary terms, examples of multiple-step processes, or details of specific concepts. The two-column-note strategy is simple: write the term, main idea, step-by-step process, or concept in the left-hand column, and the definition, example, or detail on the right.

One strategy for using two-column notes is to organize main ideas and their details. The main ideas from your reading are written in the left-hand column of your paper and can be written as questions, key words, or a combination of both. Details describing these main ideas are then written in the right-hand column of your paper.

1. **Identify the main ideas.** The main ideas for a chapter are listed in the section objectives. However, you decide which ideas to include in your notes. For example, here are some main ideas from the objectives in Section 5-2.
   - Describe the locations in the periodic table and the general properties of the alkali metals, alkaline-earth metals, the halogens, and the noble gases.

2. **Divide a blank sheet of paper into two columns and write the main ideas in the left-hand column.** Summarize your ideas using quick phrases that are easy for you to understand and remember. Decide how many details you need for each main idea, and write that number in parentheses under the main idea.

3. **Write the detail notes in the right-hand column.** Be sure you list as many details as you designated in the main-idea column. Here are some main ideas and details from the objective in Section 5-2.

The two-column method of review is perfect whether you use it to study for a short quiz or for a test on the material in an entire chapter. Just cover the information in the right-hand column with a sheet of paper, and after reciting what you know, uncover the notes to check your answers. Then ask yourself what else you know about that topic. Linking ideas in this way will help you to gain a more complete picture of chemistry.

Main Idea	Detail Notes
• Alkali metals (4 properties)	• Group 1 • highly reactive • ns^1 electron configuration • soft, silvery
• Alkaline-earth metals (4 properties)	• Group 2 • reactive • ns^2 electron configuration • harder than alkali metals
• Halogens (3 properties)	• Group 17 • reactive • nonmetallic
• Noble gases	• Group 18 • low reactivity • stable ns^2np^6 configuration

Using the K/W/L/ Strategy

The K/W/L strategy stands for "what I Know—what I Want to know—what I Learned." You start by brainstorming about the subject matter before reading the assigned material. Relating new ideas and concepts to those you have learned previously will help you better understand and apply the new knowledge you obtain. The section objectives throughout your textbook are ideal for using the K/W/L strategy.

1. **Read the section objectives.** You may also want to scan headings, boldfaced terms, and illustrations before reading. Here are two of the objectives from Section 1-2 to use as an example.
   - Explain the gas, liquid, and solid states in terms of particles.
   - Distinguish between a mixture and a pure substance.
2. **Divide a sheet of paper into three columns, and label the columns "What I Know," "What I Want to Know," and "What I Learned."**
3. **Brainstorm about what you know about the information in the objectives, and write these ideas in the first column.** Because this chart is designed primarily to help you integrate your own knowledge with new information, it is not necessary to write complete sentences.
4. **Think about what you want to know about the information in the objectives, and write these ideas in the second column.** Include information from both the section objectives and any other objectives your teacher has given you.
5. **While reading the section or afterwards, use the third column to write down the information you learned.** While reading, pay close attention to any information about the topics you wrote in the "What I Want to Know" column. If you do not find all of the answers you are looking for, you may need to reread the section or reference a second source. Be sure to ask your teacher if you still cannot find the information after reading the section a second time.

   It is also important to review your brainstormed ideas when you have completed reading the section. Compare your ideas in the first column with the information you wrote down in the third column. If you find that some of your brainstormed ideas are incorrect, cross them out. It is extremely important to identify and correct any misconceptions you had prior to reading before you begin studying for your test.

What I Know	What I Want to Know	What I Learned
• gas has no definite shape or volume	• how gas, liquid, and solid states are related to particles	• molecules in solid and liquid states are close together, but are far apart in gas state
• liquid has no definite shape, but has definite volume	• how mixtures and pure substances are different	• molecules in solid state have fixed positions, but molecules in liquid and gas states can flow
• solid has definite shape and volume		
• mixture is combination of substances		• mixtures are combinations of pure substances
• pure substance has only one component		• pure substances have fixed compositions and definite properties

Using Sequencing/Pattern Puzzles

You can use pattern puzzles to help you remember sequential information. Pattern puzzles are not just a tool for memorization. They also promote a greater understanding of a variety of chemical processes, from the steps in solving a mass-mass stoichiometry problem to the procedure for making a solution of specified molarity.

1. **Write down the steps of a process in your own words.** For an example, we will use the process for converting the amount of a substance in moles to mass in grams. (See Sample Problem 3-2 on page 82.) On a sheet of notebook paper, write down one step per line, and do not number the steps. Also, do not copy the process straight from your textbook.

   Writing the steps in your own words promotes a more thorough understanding of the process. You may want to divide longer steps into two or three shorter steps.

   - List the given and unknown information.
   - Look at the periodic table to determine the molar mass of the substance.
   - Write the correct conversion factor to convert moles to grams.
   - Multiply the amount of substance by the conversion factor.
   - Solve the equation and check your answer.

2. **Cut the sheet of paper into strips with only one step per strip of paper.** Shuffle the strips of paper so that they are out of sequence.

   - Look at the periodic table to determine the molar mass of the substance.
   - Solve the equation and check your answer.
   - List the given and unknown information.
   - Multiply the amount of substance by the conversion factor.
   - Write the correct conversion factor to convert moles to grams.

3. **Place the strips in their proper sequence.** Confirm the order of the process by checking your text or your class notes.

   - List the given and unknown information.
   - Look at the periodic table to determine the molar mass of the substance.
   - Write the correct conversion factor to convert moles to grams.
   - Multiply the amount of substance by the conversion factor.
   - Solve the equation and check your answer.

Pattern puzzles are especially helpful when you are studying for your chemistry tests. Before tests, use your puzzles to practice sequencing and to review the steps of chemistry processes. You and a classmate can also take turns creating your own pattern puzzles of different chemical processes and putting each other's puzzles in the correct sequence. Studying with a classmate in this manner will help make studying fun and will enable you to help each other.

Other Reading Strategies

► Brainstorming

Brainstorming is a strategy that helps you recognize and evaluate the knowledge you already have before you start reading. It works well individually or in groups. When you brainstorm, you start with a central term or idea, then quickly list all the words, phrases, and other ideas that you think are related to it.

Because there are no "right" or "wrong" answers, you can use the list as a basis for classifying terms, developing a general explanation, or speculating about new relationships. For example, you might brainstorm a list of terms related to the word *element* before you read Section 1-2. The list might include gold, metals, chemicals, silver, carbon, oxygen, and water. As you read the textbook, you might decide that some of the terms you listed are *not* elements. Later, you might use that information to help you distinguish between elements and compounds.

► Building/Interpreting Vocabulary

Using a dictionary to look up the meanings of prefixes and suffixes as well as word origins and meanings helps you build your vocabulary and interpret what you read. If you know the meaning of prefixes like *kilo-* (one thousand) and *milli-* (one thousandth), you have a good idea what kilograms, kilometers, milligrams, and millimeters are and how they are different. (See page 35 for a list of SI Prefixes.)

Knowledge of prefixes, suffixes, and word origins can help you understand the meaning of new words. For example, if you know the suffix *-protic* comes from the same word as *proton,* it will help you understand what monoprotic and polyprotic acids are (see page 465).

► Reading Hints

Reading hints help you identify and bookmark important charts, tables, and illustrations for easy reference. For example, you may want to use a self-adhesive note to bookmark the periodic table on pages 130–131 or on the inside back cover of your book so you can easily locate it and use it for reference as you study different aspects of chemistry and solve problems involving elements and compounds.

► Interpreting Graphic Sources of Information

Charts, tables, photographs, diagrams, and other illustrations are graphic, or visual, sources of information. The labels and captions, together with the illustrations help you make connections between the words and the ideas presented in the text.

► Reading Response Logs

Keeping a reading response log helps you interpret what you read and gives you a chance to express your reactions and opinions about what you have read. Draw a vertical line down the center of a piece of paper. In the left-hand column, write down or make notes about passages you read to which you have reactions, thoughts, feelings, questions, or associations. In the right-hand column, write what those reactions, thoughts, feelings, questions, or associations are. For example, you might keep a reading response log when studying about Nuclear Energy in Chapter 22.

Other Studying Strategies

▶ Comparing and Contrasting

Comparing and contrasting is a strategy that helps you note similarities and differences between two or more objects or events. When you determine similarities, you are comparing. When you determine differences, you are contrasting.

You can use comparing and contrasting to help you classify objects or properties, differentiate between similar concepts, and speculate about new relationships. For example, as you read Chapter 1 you might begin to make a table in which you compare and contrast metals, non-metals, and metalloids. As you continue to learn about these substances in Chapters 4 and 5, you can add to your table, giving you a better understanding of the similarities and differences among elements.

▶ Identifying Cause and Effect

Identifying causes and effects as you read helps you understand the material and builds logical reasoning skills. An effect is an event or the result of some action. A cause is the reason the event or action occurred. Signal words, such as *because, so, since, therefore, as a result,* and *depends on,* indicate a cause-and-effect relationship.

You can use arrows to show cause and effect. For example, you might write this cause-and-effect relationship as you read Section 10-3: At constant pressure, increase in temperature (cause) → increase in gas volume (effect).

▶ Making a Prediction Guide

A prediction guide is a list of statements about which you express and try to justify your opinions based on your current knowledge. After reading the material, you re-evaluate your opinion in light of what you learned. Using prediction guides helps you evaluate your knowledge, identify assumptions you may have that could lead to mistaken conclusions, and form an idea of expected results.

1. **Read the statements your teacher writes on the board.** For example, look at the five statements from Dalton's theory listed on page 66 of your textbook.
2. **Decide whether you think each statement is true or false and discuss reasons why you think so.**
3. **After reading the section, re-evaluate your opinion of each statement. Discuss why your opinion changed or remained the same. Find passages in the text that account for the change of reinforcement of your opinions.** For example, you might have agreed with all five statements from Dalton's theory before reading the text. Then, after reading about atoms and subatomic particles, you might have changed your opinion about the first statement.

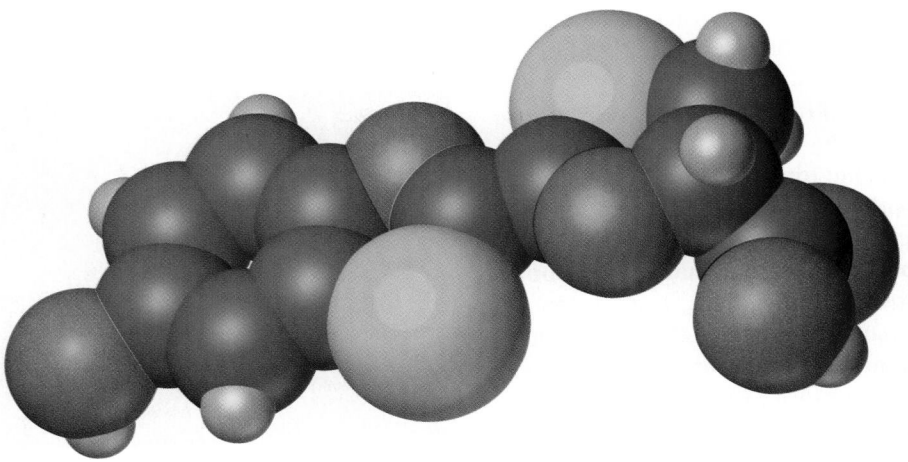

Cooperative Learning Techniques

▶ Reading with a Partner

Reading with a partner is a strategy that can help you understand what you read and point out where more explanation is needed.

1. **First read the text silently by yourself. Use self-adhesive notes to mark those parts of the text that you do not understand.** For example, you might have difficulty with some of the material about quantum numbers in Section 4-2, while another student understands quantum numbers but has trouble with electron configurations in Section 4-3.

2. **Work with a partner to discuss the passages each of you marked.** Take turns listening and trying to clarify the difficult passages for each other. Together, study the related tables and illustrations and explain to each other how they relate to the text.

3. **For concepts that need further explanation, work together to formulate questions for class discussion or for your teacher to answer.**

▶ Using L.I.N.K.

The L.I.N.K. strategy stands for **L**ist, **I**nquire, **N**otes, **K**now. It is similar to the K/W/L strategy, but you work as a class or in groups.

1. **Brainstorm all the words, phrases, and ideas associated with the term your teacher provides.** Volunteers can keep track of contributions on the board or on a separate sheet of paper.

2. **Your teacher will direct you in a class or group discussion about the words and ideas listed.** Now is the time to inquire, or ask your teacher and other students for clarification of the listed ideas.

3. **At the end of the discussion, make notes about everything you can remember.** Look over your notes to see if you have left anything out.

4. **See what you now know about the given concept based on your own experience and the discussion.**

▶ Summarizing/Paired Summarizing

A summary is a brief statement of main ideas or important concepts. Making a summary of what you have read provides you with a way to review what you have learned, see what information needs further clarification, and helps you make connections to previously studied material.

Paired summarizing helps strengthen your ability to read, listen, and understand. It is especially useful when a section of text has several subdivisions, each dealing with different concepts, such as Section 2-3 in your textbook.

1. **First read the material silently by yourself.**

2. **Then you and your partner take turns being the "listener" and the "reteller."** The reteller summarizes the material for the listener, who does not interrupt until the reteller has finished. If necessary, the reteller may consult the text, and the listener may ask for clarification. The listener then states any inaccuracies or omissions made by the reteller.

3. **Work together to refine the summary.** Make sure the summary states the important ideas in a clear and concise manner.

▶ Discussing Ideas

Discussing ideas with a partner or in a group before you read is a strategy that can help you broaden your knowledge base and decide what concepts to focus on as you are reading. Discussing ideas after you have read a section or chapter can help you check your understanding, clarify difficult concepts, and lead you to speculate about new ideas.

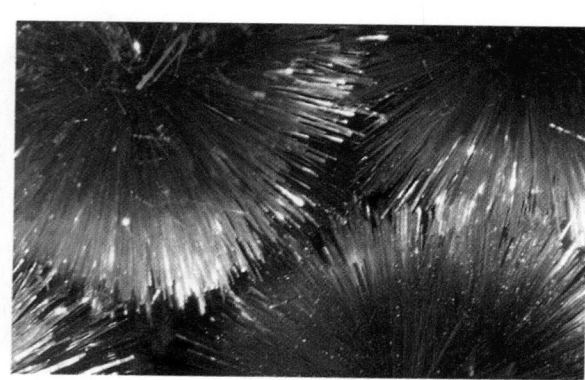

Graphing Calculator Technology

Downloading

To solve the Graphing Calculator problems in Technology & Learning sections of the Chapter Reviews, you will need to download the programs and the datasets. The application for this text, called "MODCHEM," can be found go.hrw.com.

internetconnect

GO TO: go.hrw.com
KEYWORD: HC2 TI83

This Web site contains links for downloading programs and applications you will need for Technology and Learning exercises.

Note: *In order to transfer programs and applications from a computer to your calculator, you will need a TI-Graph Link cable. Programs can also be transferred directly between calculators using a unit-to-unit cable. Refer to the TI Web site or to your calculator's user's manual for instructions.*

▶ **If your computer does not already have TI-Graph Link software installed, click** Step 1: TI-Graph Link Software and follow the links for downloading and installing TI-Graph Link from the TI Web site.

▶ **Click** Step 2: ChemProg. This will load the file CHEMPROG.ZIP onto your computer. Once the file is downloaded, double-click the icon and the file will be extracted into a file called chemprog.8xg.

▶ **Click** Step 3: Getting Started and follow the instructions for your TI-Graph Link to load chemprog.8xg onto your TI calculator. When the file is sent to the calculator, it should expand into 17 programs. These programs should appear in the PRGM menu.

▶ **Download** the "MODCHEM" application from go.hrw.com.

Using the Data Sets

Once you have loaded the application, you can use it via the "apps" function on the calculator. Press the blue [APPS] button in the upper left portion of the keypad. A menu will be displayed of the applications in your calculator's memory. Look for an application titled "MODCHEM." Select it either by using the arrow keys and pressing ENTER or by using the number keys. Do this each time you choose to open the application. A title screen will appear for a few seconds, and then a menu will be displayed, listing all of the available data sets. The sets are listed by chapter and can be selected with either the arrow keys and [ENTER] or with the number keys.

The instructions are essentially the same for every chapter. You can select the lists to be loaded by placing the cursor beside them and pressing the [ENTER] key or, if you would like to load all of the lists from that chapter at one time, you can use the arrow keys to go to the **All** menu and choose the first option **All+** and then press [ENTER]. When you have chosen all of the data sets that you need, use the arrow keys to go to the **Load** menu. The **SetUpEditor** allows you to decide where you would like the lists to be stored. **1: Add to Editor** adds the lists to the end of the List editor. By choosing [STAT] and **1: Edit…,** you can see these lists behind L_6. **2: Exchange Lists** replaces the data values in those with the sets from the application. They will be replaced in order, so if you have only one list, L_1 will be replaced, and so on. **3: No change** will not add the list to the List editor; however, by going to the List menu via [2nd] [LIST], you will see the names of the data sets listed under L_6. After you have finished, choose **Load,** and the sets will be loaded into the desired location.

Graphing Data Sets

The sets for all graphing programs are listed in the order that they should be loaded—the x-axis data is listed before the y-axis data, as all the graphing programs are designed to put x-coordinates into L_1 and y-coordinates into L_2. If there are three sets, as is the case with Chapter 1, it is because one of the lists can be used with either of the others. If there are four sets, the two pairs are distinguished with the letters A and B. For example, in Chapter 10, the pressure values A are to be used with volume values A, and pressure values B are to be used with volume values B.

Before you load the sets, use the **SetUpEditor** and choose the second option, **Exchange Lists**, as L_1 and L_2 are expressly used in the graphing programs.

Calculations, Classifications (Chapter 6) and Extrapolations (Chapter 13)

These data sets must be entered somewhat manually. The programs are not designed to gain input from lists, but once you have the data in the lists, it is only a matter of referring to them.

When you run a program, the calculator will prompt you for information. When it does, press [2nd] [LIST]. This will show you the names of all of the lists that you have in your list editor. Select the list with the arrow keys and press [ENTER] or with the numbers or letters associated with the list. By choosing a list, you will be taken back to the prompting screen with the list name in the place of your input. You must also include an index number. Type this number in parentheses behind the list name and press [ENTER]. If more data are needed, the calculator will prompt you. All corresponding data are listed with the same index number.

If the data are in one of the six main lists (L_1 through L_6), you can simply select the list from the keypad using the [2nd] key and choosing the corresponding number. You must still add the index number in parentheses behind the name of the list.

If you do not know the index number of the datum/data you would like to use, press [STAT] and choose option **1: Edit…** Every list will be shown with all of its values. By scrolling down the list, you can find out what the index number is. At the bottom of the screen is the list name followed by a number in parentheses, an equal sign, and the value of that location in the list. The number in parentheses is the index number.

Troubleshooting

▶ Calculator instructions in the *Modern Chemistry* program are written for the TI-83 Plus. You may use other graphing calculators, but some of the programs and instructions may not work exactly as described.

▶ If you have problems loading programs or applications onto your calculator, you may need to clear programs or other data from your calculator's memory.

▶ Always make sure that you are downloading correct versions of the software. TI-Graph Link has different versions for Windows and for Macintosh as well as different versions for different calculators.

▶ If you need additional help, Texas Instruments can provide technical support at 1-800 TI-CARES.

Problem Bank

Conversions, Section 2-2

Converting Simple SI Units

1. State the following measured quantities in the units indicated.
   a. 5.2 cm of magnesium ribbon in millimeters
   b. 0.049 kg of sulfur in grams
   c. 1.60 mL of ethanol in microliters
   d. 0.0025 g of vitamin A in micrograms
   e. 0.020 kg of tin in milligrams
   f. 3 kL of saline solution in liters

2. State the following measured quantities in the units indicated.
   a. 150 mg of aspirin in grams
   b. 2500 mL of hydrochloric acid in liters
   c. 0.5 g of sodium in kilograms
   d. 55 L of carbon dioxide gas in kiloliters
   e. 35 mm in centimeters
   f. 8740 m in kilometers
   g. 209 nm in millimeters
   h. 500 000 μg in kilograms

3. The greatest distance between Earth and the sun during Earth's revolution is 152 million kilometers. What is this distance in megameters?

4. How many milliliters of water will it take to fill a 2.00 L bottle that already contains 1.87 L of water?

5. A piece of copper wire is 150 cm long. How long is the wire in millimeters? How many 50 mm segments of wire can be cut from the length?

6. The ladle at an iron foundry can hold 8500 kg of molten iron; 646 metric tons of iron are needed to make rails. How many ladlefuls of iron will it take to make 646 metric tons of iron? (1 metric ton = 1000 kg)

Converting Derived SI Units

7. State the following measured quantities in the units indicated.
   a. 310 000 cm^3 of concrete in cubic meters
   b. 6.5 m^2 of steel sheet in square centimeters
   c. 0.035 m^3 of chlorine gas in cubic centimeters
   d. 0.49 cm^2 of copper in square millimeters
   e. 1200 dm^3 of acetic acid solution in cubic meters
   f. 87.5 mm^3 of actinium in cubic centimeters
   g. 250 000 cm^2 of polyethylene sheet in square meters

8. How many palisade cells from plant leaves would fit in a volume of 1.0 cm^3 of cells if the average volume of a palisade cell is 0.0147 mm^3?

Mixed Review

9. Convert each of the following quantities to the required unit.
   a. 12.75 Mm to kilometers
   b. 277 cm to meters
   c. 30 560 m^2 to hectares (1 ha = 10 000 m^2)
   d. 81.9 cm^2 to square meters
   e. 300 000 km to megameters

10. Convert each of the following quantities to the required unit.
    a. 0.62 km to meters
    b. 3857 g to milligrams
    c. 0.0036 mL to microliters
    d. 0.342 metric tons to kg (1 metric ton = 1000 kg)
    e. 68.71 kL to liters

11. Convert each of the following quantities to the required unit.
    a. 856 mg to kilograms
    b. 1 210 000 μg to kilograms
    c. 6598 μL to cubic centimeters (1 mL = 1 cm^3)
    d. 80 600 nm to millimeters
    e. 10.74 cm^3 to liters

12. Convert each of the following quantities to the required unit.
    a. 7.93 L to cubic centimeters
    b. 0.0059 km to centimeters
    c. 4.19 L to cubic decimeters
    d. 7.48 m^2 to square centimeters
    e. 0.197 m^3 to liters

13. An automobile uses 0.05 mL of oil for each kilometer it is driven. How much oil in liters is consumed if the automobile is driven 20 000 km?

14. How many microliters are there in a volume of 370 mm^3 of cobra venom?

15. A baker uses 1.5 tsp of vanilla extract in each cake. How much vanilla extract in liters should the baker order to make 800 cakes? (1 tsp = 5 mL)

16. A person drinks eight glasses of water each day, and each glass contains 300 mL. How many liters of water will that person consume in a year? What is the mass of this volume of water in kilograms? (Assume one year has 365 days and the density of water is 1.00 kg/L.)

17. At the equator Earth rotates with a velocity of about 465 m/s.

SECTION REVIEW

1. a. 52 mm   b. 49 g
   c. 1600 μL   d. 2500 μg
   e. 20 000 mg   f. 3000 L

2. a. 0.15 g   b. 2.5 L
   c. 0.0005 kg   d. 0.055 kL
   e. 3.5 cm   f. 8.74 km
   g. 0.000 209 mm
   h. 0.0005 kg

3. 152 000 Mm

4. 130 mL

5. 1500 mm; 30 pieces

6. 76 ladlefuls

7. a. 0.31 m^3
   b. 65 000 cm^2
   c. 35 000 cm^3 d. 49 mm^2
   e. 1.2 m^3
   f. 0.0875 cm^3
   g. 25 m^2

8. 68 027 cells

9. a. 12 750 m   b. 2.77 m
   c. 3.056 hectares
   d. 0.008 19 m^2
   e. 300 Mm

10. a. 620 m
    b. 3 875 000 mg
    c. 3.6 μL   d. 342 kg
    e. 68 710 L

11. a. 0.000 856 kg
    b. 0.001 21 kg
    c. 6.598 cm^3
    d. 0.0806 mm
    e. 0.010 74 L

12. a. 7930 cm^3 b. 590 cm
    c. 4.19 dm^3
    d. 74 800 cm^2
    e. 197 L

13. 1 L

14. 370 μL

15. 6 L

16. 0.876 L of water per year; 876 kg of water

17. a. 1674 km/h
    b. 40 176 km/day

18. 7.8 kg of sodium hydroxide

19. 45 m of plastic tubing

20. a. 13.2 mL/day **b.** 150 kg/min
  c. 62 cm³/min   **d.** 1.7 m/s

21. a. 2.97 g/cm³
  b. 0.041 28 kg/cm²
  c. 5.27 kg/dm³
  d. 0.006 91 mg/mm³

22. a. 750 mL   **b.** 5.56 kg

23. 1250 kg

24. a. 2.80 L   **b.** 1.05 g/cm³
  c. 0.056 m²

25. a. 0.04 mL per drop
  b. 1.48 mL
  c. 17 000 drops

26. a. 0.5047 kg; 504.7 g
  b. 0.0092 kg; 9.2 g
  c. 0.000 122 kg; 0.122 g
  d. 0.071 95 kg; 71.95 g

27. a. 0.582 L; 582 mL
  b. 2.5 L; 2500 mL
  c. 1.18 L; 1180 mL
  d. 0.0329 L; 32.9 mL

28. a. 1370 g/L; 1370 kg/m³
  b. 692 g/L; 692 kg/m³
  c. 5200 g/L; 5200 kg/m³
  d. 38 g/L; 38 kg/m³
  e. 5790 g/L; 5790 kg/m³
  f. 0.0011 g/L; 0.0011 kg/m³

29. a. 360 g/min
  b. 518.4 kg/day
  c. 6 mg/ms

30. 27.8 m/s

31. 4732 kcal/h

32. 620 kg

33. $34.164 \text{ L/year} = \dfrac{3.9 \text{ mL}}{h} \times$
$\dfrac{1 \text{ L}}{1000 \text{ mL}} \times \dfrac{24 \text{ h}}{1 \text{ day}} \times \dfrac{365 \text{ days}}{1 \text{ year}}$

34. 40 doses

35. a. 2   **b.** 4
  c. 4   **d.** 4
  e. 1   **f.** 5
  g. 2   **h.** 4
  i. 6   **j.** 6

a. What is this velocity in kilometers per hour?
b. What is this velocity in kilometers per day?

18. A chemistry teacher needs to determine what quantity of sodium hydroxide to order. If each student will use 130 g and there are 60 students, how many kilograms of sodium hydroxide should the teacher order?

19. The teacher in item 18 also needs to order plastic tubing. If each of the 60 students needs 750 mm of tubing, what length of tubing in meters should the teacher order?

20. Convert the following to the required units.
  a. 550 μL/h to milliliters per day
  b. 9.00 metric tons/h to kilograms per minute
  c. 3.72 L/h to cubic centimeters per minute
  d. 6.12 km/h to meters per second

21. Express the following in the units indicated.
  a. 2.97 kg/L as grams per cubic centimeter
  b. 4128 g/dm² as kilograms per square centimeter
  c. 5.27 g/cm³ as kilograms per cubic decimeter
  d. 6.91 kg/m³ as milligrams per cubic millimeter

22. A gas has a density of 5.56 g/L.
  a. What volume in milliliters would 4.17 g of this gas occupy?
  b. What would be the mass in kilograms of 1 m³ of this gas?

23. The average density of living matter on Earth's land areas is 0.10 g/cm². What mass of living matter in kilograms would occupy an area of 0.125 ha?

24. A textbook measures 250. mm long, 224 mm wide, and 50.0 mm thick. It has a mass of 2.94 kg.
  a. What is the volume of the book in cubic meters?
  b. What is the density of the book in grams per cubic centimeter?
  c. What is the area of one cover in square meters?

25. A glass dropper delivers liquid so that 25 drops equal 1.00 mL.
  a. What is the volume of one drop in milliliters?
  b. How many milliliters are in 37 drops?
  c. How many drops would be required to get 0.68 L?

26. Express each of the following in kilograms and grams.
  a. 504 700 mg   **c.** 122 mg
  b. 9 200 000 μg **d.** 7195 cg

27. Express each of the following in liters and milliliters.
  a. 582 cm³   **c.** 1.18 dm³
  b. 0.0025 m³ **d.** 32 900 μL

28. Express each of the following in grams per liter and kilograms per cubic meter.
  a. 1.37 g/cm³   **d.** 38 000 g/m³
  b. 0.692 kg/dm³ **e.** 5.79 mg/mm³
  c. 5.2 kg/L   **f.** 1.1 μg/mL

29. An industrial chemical reaction is run for 30.0 h and produces 648.0 kg of product. What is the average rate of product production in the stated units?
  a. grams per minute
  b. kilograms per day
  c. milligrams per millisecond

30. What is the speed of a car in meters per second when it is moving at 100. km/h?

31. A heater gives off heat at a rate of 330 kJ/min. What is the rate of heat output in kilocalories per hour? (1 cal = 4.184 J)

32. The instructions on a package of fertilizer tell you to apply it at the rate of 62 g/m². How much fertilizer in kilograms would you need to apply to 1.0 ha? (1 ha = 10 000 m²)

33. A water tank leaks water at the rate of 3.9 mL/h. If the tank is not repaired, what volume of water in liters will it leak in a year? Show your setup for solving this. Hint: Use one conversion factor to convert hours to days and another to convert days to years, and assume that one year has 365 days.

34. A nurse plans to give flu injections of 50 μL each from a bottle containing 2.0 mL of vaccine. How many doses are in the bottle?

Significant Figures, Section 2-3

35. Determine the number of significant figures in the following measurements.
  a. 640 cm³   **f.** 20.900 cm
  b. 200.0 mL   **g.** 0.000 000 56 g/L
  c. 0.5200 g   **h.** 0.040 02 kg/m³
  d. 1.005 kg   **i.** 790 001 cm²
  e. 10 000 L   **j.** 665.000 kg•m/s²

36. Perform the following calculations, and express the result in the correct units and number of significant figures.
  a. 47.0 m ÷ 2.2 s
  b. 140 cm × 35 cm
  c. 5.88 kg ÷ 200 m³
  d. 0.00 50 m² × 0.042 m
  e. 300.3 L ÷ 180. s
  f. 33.00 cm² × 2.70 cm
  g. 35 000 kJ ÷ 0.250 min

37. Perform the following calculations and express the results in the correct units and number of significant figures.
  a. 22.0 m + 5.28 m + 15.5 m
  b. 0.042 kg + 1.229 kg + 0.502 kg
  c. 170 cm² + 3.5 cm² − 28 cm²
  d. 0.003 L + 0.0048 L + 0.100 L
  e. 24.50 dL + 4.30 dL + 10.2 dL
  f. 3200 mg + 325 mg − 688 mg
  g. 14 000 kg + 8000 kg + 590 kg

Mixed Review

38. Determine the number of significant figures in the following measurements.
  a. 0.0120 m   **f.** 1000 kg
  b. 100.5 mL   **g.** 180. mm
  c. 101 g   **h.** 0.4936 L
  d. 350 cm²   **i.** 0.020 700 s
  e. 0.97 km

39. Round the following quantities to the specified number of significant figures.
  a. 5 487 129 m to three significant figures
  b. 0.013 479 265 mL to six significant figures

c. 31 947.972 cm² to four significant figures
d. 192.6739 m² to five significant figures
e. 786.9164 cm to two significant figures
f. 389 277 600 J to six significant figures
g. 225 834.762 cm³ to seven significant figures

40. Perform the following calculations, and express the answer in the correct units and number of significant figures.
    a. 651 cm × 75 cm
    b. 7.835 kg ÷ 2.5 L
    c. 14.75 L ÷ 1.20 s
    d. 360 cm × 51 cm × 9.07 cm
    e. 5.18 m × 0.77 m × 10.22 m
    f. 34.95 g ÷ 11.169 cm³

41. Perform the following calculations, and express the answer in the correct units and number of significant figures.
    a. 7.945 J + 82.3 J − 0.02 J
    b. 0.0012 m − 0.000 45 m − 0.000 11 m
    c. 500 g + 432 g + 2 g
    d. 31.2 kPa + 0.0035 kPa − 0.147 kPa
    e. 312 dL − 31.2 dL − 3.12 dL
    f. 1701 kg + 50 kg + 43 kg

42. A rectangle measures 87.59 cm by 35.1 mm. Express its area with the proper number of significant figures in the specified unit.
    a. in cm²   c. in m²
    b. in mm²

43. A box measures 900. mm by 31.5 mm by 6.3 cm. State its volume with the proper number of significant figures in the specified unit.
    a. in cm³   c. in mm³
    b. in m³

44. A 125 mL sample of liquid has a mass of 0.16 kg. What is the density of the liquid in the following measurements?
    a. kg/m³   c. kg/dm³
    b. g/mL

45. Perform the following calculations, and express the results in the correct units and with the proper number of significant figures.
    a. 13.75 mm × 10.1 mm × 0.91 mm
    b. 89.4 cm² × 4.8 cm
    c. 14.9 m³ ÷ 3.0 m²
    d. 6.975 m × 30 m × 21.5 m

46. What is the volume of a region of space that measures 752 m × 319 m × 110 m? Give your answer in the correct unit and with the proper number of significant figures.

47. Perform the following calculations, and express the results in the correct units and with the proper number of significant figures.
    a. 7.382 g + 1.21 g + 4.7923 g
    b. 51.3 mg + 83 mg − 34.2 mg
    c. 0.007 L − 0.0037 L + 0.012 L
    d. 253.05 cm² + 33.9 cm² + 28 cm²
    e. 14.77 kg + 0.086 kg − 0.391 kg
    f. 319 mL + 13.75 mL + 20. mL

48. A container measures 30.5 mm × 202 mm × 153 mm. When it is full of a liquid, it has a mass of 1.33 kg. When it is empty, it has a mass of 0.30 kg. What is the density of the liquid in kilograms per liter?

49. If 7.76 km of wire has a mass of 3.3 kg, what is the mass of the wire in g/m? What length in meters would have a mass of 1.0 g?

50. A container of plant food recommends an application rate of 52 kg/ha. If the container holds 10 kg of plant food, how many square meters will it cover? (1 ha = 10 000 m²)

51. A chemical process produces 974 550 kJ of heat in 37.0 min. What is the rate in kilojoules per minute? What is the rate in kilojoules per second?

52. A water pipe fills a container that measures 189 cm × 307 cm × 272 cm in 97 s.
    a. What is the volume of the container in cubic meters?
    b. What is the rate of flow in the pipe in liters per minute?
    c. What is the rate of flow in cubic meters per hour?

53. Perform the following calculations, and express the results in the correct units and with the proper number of significant figures. Note, in problems with multiple steps, it is better to perform the entire calculation and then round to significant figures.
    a. $(0.054 \text{ kg} + 1.33 \text{ kg}) \times 5.4 \text{ m}^2$
    b. $67.35 \text{ cm}^2 \div (1.401 \text{ cm} - 0.399 \text{ cm})$
    c. $4.198 \text{ kg} \times (1019 \text{ m}^2 - 40 \text{ m}^2) \div (54.2 \text{ s} \times 31.3 \text{ s})$
    d. $3.14159 \text{ m} \times (4.17 \text{ m} + 2.150 \text{ m})$
    e. $690\,000 \text{ m} \div (5.022 \text{ h} - 4.31 \text{ h})$
    f. $(6.23 \text{ cm} + 3.111 \text{ cm} - 0.05 \text{ cm}) \times 14.99 \text{ cm}$

Scientific Notation, Section 2-3

Converting Quantities to Scientific Notation

54. Express the following quantities in scientific notation.
    a. 8 800 000 000 m
    b. 0.0015 kg
    c. 0.000 000 000 06 kg/m³
    d. 8 002 000 Hz
    e. 0.009 003 A
    f. 70 000 000 000 000 000 km
    g. 6028 L
    h. 0.2105 g
    i. 600 005 000 kJ/h
    j. 33.8 m²

Calculating with Quantities in Scientific Notation

55. Carry out the following calculations. Express the results in scientific notation and with the correct number of significant figures.
    a. $4.74 \times 10^4 \text{ km} + 7.71 \times 10^3 \text{ km} + 1.05 \times 10^3 \text{ km}$
    b. $2.75 \times 10^{-4} \text{ m} + 8.03 \times 10^{-5} \text{ m} + 2.122 \times 10^{-3} \text{ m}$
    c. $4.0 \times 10^{-5} \text{ m}^3 + 6.85 \times 10^{-6} \text{ m}^3 - 1.05 \times 10^{-5} \text{ m}^3$
    d. $3.15 \times 10^2 \text{ mg} + 3.15 \times 10^3 \text{ mg} + 3.15 \times 10^4 \text{ mg}$
    e. $3.01 \times 10^{22} \text{ atoms} + 1.19 \times 10^{23} \text{ atoms} + 9.80 \times 10^{21} \text{ atoms}$
    f. $6.85 \times 10^7 \text{ nm} + 4.0229 \times 10^8 \text{ nm} - 8.38 \times 10^6 \text{ nm}$

36. a. 21 m/s   b. 4900 cm²
    c. 0.03 kg/m³
    d. 0.000 21 m³
    e. 1.67 L/s   f. 89.1 cm³
    g. 140 000 kJ/min

37. a. 42.8 m   b. 1.773 kg
    c. 150 cm²   d. 0.108 L
    e. 39.0 dL   f. 2800 mg
    g. 23 000 kg

38. a. 3   b. 4
    c. 3   d. 2
    e. 2   f. 1
    g. 3   h. 4
    i. 5

39. a. 5 490 000 m
    b. 0.013 479 3 mL
    c. 31 950 cm²
    d. 192.67 m²
    e. 790 cm
    f. 389 278 000 J
    g. 225 834.8 cm³

40. a. 49 000 cm²   b. 3.1 kg/L
    c. 12.3 L/s
    d. 170 000 cm³
    e. 41 m³
    f. 3.129 g/cm³

41. a. 90.2 J   b. 0.0006 m
    c. 900 g   d. 31.1 kPa
    e. 278 dL   f. 1790 kg

42. a. 307 cm²
    b. 30 700 mm²
    c. 0.0307 m²

43. a. 1800 cm³   b. 0.0018 m³
    c. 1 800 000 mm³

44. a. 1300 kg/m³   b. 1.3 g/mL
    c. 1.3 kg/dm³

45. a. 130 mm³   b. 430 cm³
    c. 5.0 m   d. 4000 m³

46. 26 000 000 m³

47. a. 13.38 g   b. 100. mg
    c. 0.015 L   d. 315 cm²
    e. 14.47 kg   f. 353 mL

48. 1.09 kg/L

49. 0.43 g/m; 2.3 m

50. 2000 m²

51. 26 300 kJ/min; 439 kJ/s

52. a. 15.8 m³
   b. 9800 L/min
   c. 590 m³/h

53. a. 7.5 kg•m²   **b.** 67.22 cm
   c. 2.4 kg•m²/s² **d.** 19.9 m²
   e. 970 000 m/h   **f.** 139 cm²

54. a. 8.8×10^9 m
   b. 1.5×10^{-3} kg
   c. 6×10^{-11} kg/m³
   d. 8.002×10^6 Hz
   e. 9.003×10^{-3} A
   f. 7×10^{16} km
   g. 6.028×10^3 L
   h. 2.105×10^{-1} g
   i. $6.000\ 05 \times 10^8$ kJ/h
   j. 3.38×10^1 m²

55. a. 5.62×10^4 km
   b. 2.477×10^{-3} m
   c. 3.6×10^{-5} m³
   d. 3.50×10^4 mg
   e. 1.59×10^{23} atoms
   f. 4.624×10^8 nm

56. a. 5.82×10^7 cm²
   b. 2.4×10^{13} mm³
   c. 6.2×10^{-4} m³
   d. 1.89×10^{-26} kg•m²
   e. 2.08×10^{20} dm³

57. a. 5.29×10^3 cm/s
   b. 2.514×10^{-3} L/m²
   c. 9.13 L/km
   d. 2.22×10^{-2} km/min
   e. 4.06×10^2 g/km²

58. a. 1.58×10^5 km
   b. 9.782×10^{-6} L
   c. 8.371×10^8 cm³
   d. 6.5×10^9 mm²
   e. 5.93×10^{-3} g
   f. 6.13×10^{-9} m
   g. 1.2552×10^7 J
   h. 8.004×10^{-6} g/L
   i. 1.0995×10^{-2} kg
   j. 1.05×10^9 Hz

59. a. 9.49×10^3 kg
   b. 7.1×10^{-2} mg
   c. 9.8×10^3 m³
   d. 1.56×10^{-7} m
   e. 3.18×10^6 J
   f. 9.63×10^{27} molecules
   g. 7.47×10^6 cm

56. Carry out the following computations, and express the result in scientific notation.
   a. 7.20×10^3 cm $\times 8.08 \times 10^3$ cm
   b. 3.7×10^4 mm $\times 6.6 \times 10^4$ mm $\times 9.89 \times 10^3$ mm
   c. 8.27×10^2 m $\times 2.5 \times 10^{-3}$ m $\times 3.00 \times 10^{-4}$ m
   d. 4.44×10^{-35} m $\times 5.55 \times 10^{19}$ m $\times 7.69 \times 10^{-12}$ kg
   e. 6.55×10^4 dm $\times 7.89 \times 10^9$ dm $\times 4.01893 \times 10^5$ dm

57. Carry out the following computations, and express the result in scientific notation.
   a. 2.290×10^7 cm $\div 4.33 \times 10^3$ s
   b. 1.788×10^{-5} L $\div 7.111 \times 10^{-3}$ m²
   c. 5.515×10^4 L $\div 6.04 \times 10^3$ km
   d. 3.29×10^{-4} km $\div 1.48 \times 10^{-2}$ min
   e. 4.73×10^{-4} g $\div (2.08 \times 10^{-3}$ km $\times 5.60 \times 10^{-4}$ km)

Mixed Review

58. Express the following quantities in scientific notation.
   a. 158 000 km
   b. 0.000 009 782 L
   c. 837 100 000 cm³
   d. 6 500 000 000 mm²
   e. 0.005 93 g
   f. 0.000 000 006 13 m
   g. 12 552 000 J
   h. 0.000 008 004 g/L
   i. 0.010 995 kg
   j. 1 050 000 000 Hz

59. Perform the following calculations, and express the result in scientific notation with the correct number of significant figures.
   a. 2.48×10^2 kg $+ 9.17 \times 10^3$ kg $+ 7.2 \times 10^1$ kg
   b. 4.07×10^{-5} mg $+ 3.966 \times 10^{-4}$ mg $+ 7.1 \times 10^{-2}$ mg
   c. 1.39×10^4 m³ $+ 6.52 \times 10^2$ m³ $- 4.8 \times 10^3$ m³
   d. 7.70×10^{-9} m $- 3.95 \times 10^{-8}$ m $+ 1.88 \times 10^{-7}$ m
   e. 1.111×10^5 J $+ 5.82 \times 10^4$ J $+ 3.01 \times 10^6$ J
   f. 9.81×10^{27} molecules $+ 3.18 \times 10^{25}$ molecules $- 2.09 \times 10^{26}$ molecules
   g. 1.36×10^7 cm $+ 3.456 \times 10^6$ cm $- 1.01 \times 10^7$ cm $+ 5.122 \times 10^5$ cm

60. Perform the following computations, and express the result in scientific notation with the correct number of significant figures.
   a. 1.54×10^{-1} L $\div 2.36 \times 10^{-4}$ s
   b. 3.890×10^4 mm $\times 4.71 \times 10^2$ mm²
   c. 9.571×10^3 kg $\div 3.82 \times 10^{-1}$ m²
   d. 8.33×10^3 km $\div 1.97 \times 10^2$ s
   e. 9.36×10^2 m $\times 3.82 \times 10^3$ m $\times 9.01 \times 10^{-1}$ m
   f. 6.377×10^4 J $\div 7.35 \times 10^{-3}$ s

61. Your electric company charges you for the electric energy you use, measured in kilowatt-hours (kWh). One kWh is equivalent to 3 600 000 J. Express this quantity in scientific notation.

62. The pressure in the deepest part of the ocean is 11 200 000 Pa. Express this pressure in scientific notation.

63. Convert 1.5 km to millimeters, and express the result in scientific notation.

64. Light travels at a speed of about 300 000 km/s.
   a. Express this value in scientific notation.
   b. Convert this value to meters per hour.
   c. What distance in centimeters does light travel in 1 μs?

65. There are 7.11×10^{24} molecules in 100.0 cm³ of a certain substance.
   a. What is the number of molecules in 1.09 cm³ of the substance?
   b. What would be the number of molecules in 2.24×10^4 cm³ of the substance?
   c. What number of molecules are in 9.01×10^{-6} cm³ of the substance?

66. The number of transistors on a particular integrated circuit is 3 578 000, and the integrated circuit measures 9.5 mm $\times$ 8.2 mm.
   a. What is the area occupied by each transistor?
   b. Using your answer from (a), how many transistors could be formed on a silicon sheet that measures 353 mm $\times$ 265 mm?

67. A solution has 0.0501 g of a substance in 1.00 L. Express this concentration in grams per microliter.

68. Cesium atoms are the largest of the naturally occurring elements. They have a diameter of 5.30×10^{-10} m. Calculate the number of cesium atoms that would have to be lined up to give a row of cesium atoms 2.54 cm (1 in.) long.

69. The neutron has a volume of approximately 1.4×10^{-44} m³ and a mass of 1.675×10^{-24} g. Calculate the density of the neutron in g/m³. What is the mass of 1.0 cm³ of neutrons in kilograms?

70. The pits in a compact disc are some of the smallest things ever mass-produced mechanically by humans. These pits represent the 1s and 0s of digital information on a compact disc. These pits are only 1.6×10^{-8} m deep (1/4 the wavelength of red laser light). How many of these pits would have to be stacked on top of each other to make a hole 0.305 m deep?

71. 22 400 mL of oxygen gas contains 6.022×10^{23} oxygen molecules at 0°C and standard atmospheric pressure.
   a. How many oxygen molecules are in 0.100 mL of gas?
   b. How many oxygen molecules are in 1.00 L of gas?
   c. What is the average space in milliliters occupied by one oxygen molecule?

72. The mass of the atmosphere is calculated to be 5.136×10^{18} kg, and there are 6 500 000 000 people living on Earth. Calculate the following values.
   a. The mass of atmosphere in kilograms per person.
   b. The mass of atmosphere in metric tons per person.
   c. If the number of people increases to 9 500 000 000, what is the mass in kilograms per person?

73. The mass of the sun is 1.989×10^{30} kg, and the mass of Earth is 5.974×10^{24} kilograms. How many Earths would be needed to equal the mass of the sun?

74. A new landfill has dimensions of 2.3 km $\times$ 1.4 km $\times$ 0.15 km.

a. What is the volume in cubic kilometer?
b. What is the volume in cubic meters?
c. If 250 000 000 objects averaging 0.060 m³ each are placed into the landfill each year, how many years will it take to fill the landfill?

75. A dietary calorie (C) is exactly equal to 1000 cal. If your daily intake of food gives you 2400 C, what is your intake in joules per day? (1 cal = 4.184 J)

Four Steps for Solving Quantitative Problems, Section 2-3

76. Gasoline has a density of 0.73 g/cm³. How many liters of gasoline would be required to increase the mass of an automobile from 1271 kg to 1305 kg?

77. A swimming pool measures 9.0 m long by 3.5 m wide by 1.75 m deep. What mass of water in metric tons (1 metric ton = 1000 kg) does the pool contain when filled? The density of the water in the pool is 0.997 g/cm³.

78. A tightly packed box of crackers contains 250 g of crackers and measures 7.0 cm × 17.0 cm × 19.0 cm. What is the average density in kilograms per liter of the crackers in the package? Assume that the unused volume is negligible.

Mixed Review

Solve these problems by using the Four Steps for Solving Quantitative Problems.

79. The aluminum foil on a certain roll has a total area of 18.5 m² and a mass of 1275 g. Using a density of 2.7 g per cubic centimeter for aluminum, determine the thickness in millimeters of the aluminum foil.

80. If a liquid has a density of 1.17 g/cm³, how many liters of the liquid have a mass of 3.75 kg?

81. A stack of 500 sheets of paper measuring 28 cm × 21 cm is 44.5 mm high and has a mass of 2090 g. What is the density of the paper in grams per cubic centimeter?

82. A triangular-shaped piece of a metal has a mass of 6.58 g. The triangle is 0.560 mm thick and measures 36.4 mm on the base and 30.1 mm in height. What is the density of the metal in grams per cubic centimeter?

83. A packing crate measures 0.40 m × 0.40 m × 0.25 m. You must fill the crate with boxes of cookies that each measure 22.0 cm × 12.0 cm × 5.0 cm. How many boxes of cookies can fit into the crate?

84. Calculate the unknown quantities in the following table. Use the following relationships for volumes of the various shapes.

Volume of a cube = $l \times l \times l$
Volume of a rectangle = $l \times w \times h$
Volume of a sphere = $4/3 \pi r^3$
Volume of a cylinder = $\pi r^2 \times h$

	D	m	V	Shape	Dimensions
a.	2.27 g/cm³	3.93 kg	? L	cube	? m × ? m × ? m
b.	1.85 g/cm³	? g	? cm³	rectangle	33 mm × 21 mm × 7.2 mm
c.	3.21 g/L	? kg	? dm³	sphere	3.30 m diameter
d.	? g/cm³	497 g	? m³	cylinder	7.5 cm diameter × 12 cm
e.	0.92 g/cm³	? kg	? cm³	rectangle	3.5 m × 1.2 m × 0.65 m

85. When a sample of a metal alloy that has a mass of 9.65 g is placed into a graduated cylinder containing water, the volume reading in the cylinder increases from 16.0 mL to 19.5 mL. What is the density of the alloy sample in grams per cubic centimeter?

86. Pure gold can be made into extremely thin sheets called gold leaf. Suppose that 50. kg of gold is made into gold leaf having an area of 3620 m². The density of gold is 19.3 g/cm³.
a. How thick in micrometers is the gold leaf?
b. A gold atom has a radius of 1.44×10^{-10} m. How many atoms thick is the gold leaf?

87. A chemical plant process requires that a cylindrical reaction tank be filled with a certain liquid in 238 s. The tank is 1.2 m in diameter and 4.6 m high. What flow rate in liters per minute is required to fill the reaction tank in the specified time?

88. The radioactive decay of 2.8 g of plutonium-238 generates 1.0 joule of heat every second. Plutonium has a density of 19.86 g/cm³. How many calories (1 cal = 4.184 J) of heat will a rectangular piece of plutonium that is 4.5 cm × 3.05 cm × 15 cm generate per hour?

89. The mass of Earth is 5.974×10^{24} kg. Assume that Earth is a sphere of diameter 1.28×10^4 km and calculate the average density of Earth in grams per cubic centimeter.

90. What volume of magnesium in cubic centimeters would have the same mass as 1.82 dm³ of platinum? The density of magnesium is 1.74 g/cm³, and the density of platinum is 21.45 g/cm³.

91. A roll of transparent tape has 66 m of tape on it. If an average of 5.0 cm of tape is needed each time the tape is used, how many uses can you get from a case of tape containing 24 rolls?

92. An automobile can travel 38 km on 4.0 L of gasoline. If the automobile is driven 75% of the days in a year and the average distance traveled each day is 86 km, how many liters of gasoline will be consumed in one year (assume the year has 365 days)?

93. A hose delivers water to a swimming pool that measures 9.0 m long by 3.5 m wide by 1.75 m deep. It requires 97 h to fill the pool. At what rate in liters per minute will the hose fill the pool?

94. Automobile batteries are filled with a solution of sulfuric acid, which has a density of 1.285 g/cm³. The solution used to fill the battery is 38% (by mass) sulfuric

60. a. 6.53×10^2 L/s
b. 1.83×10^7 mm³
c. 2.51×10^4 kg/m²
d. 4.23×10^1 km/s
e. 3.22×10^6 m³
f. 8.68×10^6 J/s

61. 3.6×10^6 J

62. 1.12×10^7 Pa

63. 1.5×10^6 mm

64. a. 3×10^5 km/s
b. 1×10^{12} m/h
c. 3×10^4 cm

65. a. 7.75×10^{22} molecules
b. 1.59×10^{27} molecules
c. 6.41×10^{17} molecules

66. a. 2.2×10^{-5} mm²/transistor
b. 4.3×10^9 transistors

67. 5.01×10^{-8} g/μL

68. 4.79×10^7 cesium atoms

69. 1.2×10^{20} g/m³; 1.2×10^{14} kg

70. 1.9×10^7 pits

71. a. 2.69×10^{18} molecules of oxygen
b. 2.69×10^{22} molecules of oxygen
c. 3.72×10^{-20} mL/molecule

72. a. 7.9×10^8 kg/person
b. 7.9×10^5 metric ton/person
c. 5.4×10^8 kg/person

73. 3.329×10^5 Earths

74. a. 4.8×10^{-1} km³
b. 4.8×10^8 m³
c. 32 years

75. 1.0×10^7 J/day

76. 47 L

77. 55 metric tons

78. 0.11 kg/L

79. 0.026 mm

80. 3.21 L

81. 0.80 g/cm³

82. 21.4 g/cm³

83. 30 boxes

84. a. 1.73 L
   0.120 m × 0.120 m ×
   0.120 m
   b. 9.2 g; 5.0 cm^3
   c. 60.4 kg; 1.88 × 10^4 dm^3
   d. 0.94 g/cm^3; 5.3 × 10^{-4} m^3
   e. 2.5 × 10^3 kg;
   2.7 × 10^6 cm^3

85. 2.8 g/cm^3

86. a. 0.72 μm
   b. 2.5 × 10^3 atoms

87. 1300 L/min

88. 1.3 × 10^6 cal/h

89. 5.44 g/cm^3

90. 2.24 × 10^4 cm^3

91. 32 000 uses

92. 2500 L

93. 9.5 L/min

94. 244.15 g H$_2$SO$_4$

95. a. 2.38 mol Al
   b. 1.00 mol Si
   c. 7.95 × 10^{-3} mol S
   d. 13.01 mol Zn

96. a. 28.0 g Na   **b.** 921 g Cu
   c. 55.2 g Hg   **d.** 0.228 Mg

97. a. 0.500 mol Rb
   b. 0.134 mol Kr
   c. 9.5 × 10^{-15} mol Pb
   d. 49.77 mol V

98. a. 6.046 × 10^{23} atoms Bi
   b. 1.5 × 10^{24} atoms Mg
   c. 1 × 10^{17} atoms He
   d. 1.96 × 10^{25} atoms Sr

99. a. 1.21 × 10^{24} atoms Al
   b. 3.011 × 10^{23} atoms La
   c. 6.02 × 10^{21} atoms Ga
   d. 1.3 × 10^{15} atoms Be

100. a. 1810. g Ta
   b. 0.295 g Co
   c. 99.91 g Ar
   d. 79.7 g He

101. a. 0.0120 mol BBr$_3$
   b. 0.0112 mol NaF
   c. 23.4 mol CH$_3$OH
   d. 0.242 mol Ca(ClO$_3$)$_2$

---

acid. How many grams of sulfuric acid are present in 500 mL of battery acid?

Mole Concept, Sections 3-3; 7-3

Problems Involving Atoms and Elements

95. Calculate the number of moles in each of the following masses.
   a. 64.1 g of aluminum
   b. 28.1 g of silicon
   c. 0.255 g of sulfur
   d. 850.5 g of zinc

96. Calculate the mass of each of the following amounts.
   a. 1.22 mol sodium
   b. 14.5 mol copper
   c. 0.275 mol mercury
   d. 9.37 × 10^{-3} mol magnesium

97. Calculate the amount in moles in each of the following quantities.
   a. 3.01 × 10^{23} atoms of rubidium
   b. 8.08 × 10^{22} atoms of krypton
   c. 5 700 000 000 atoms of lead
   d. 2.997 × 10^{25} atoms of vanadium

98. Calculate the number of atoms in each of the following amounts.
   a. 1.004 mol bismuth
   b. 2.5 mol manganese
   c. 0.000 0002 mol helium
   d. 32.6 mol strontium

99. Calculate the number of atoms in each of the following masses.
   a. 54.0 g of aluminum
   b. 69.45 g of lanthanum
   c. 0.697 g of gallium
   d. 0.000 000 020 g beryllium

100. Calculate the mass of the following numbers of atoms.
   a. 6.022 × 10^{24} atoms of tantalum
   b. 3.01 × 10^{21} atoms of cobalt
   c. 1.506 × 10^{24} atoms of argon
   d. 1.20 × 10^{25} atoms of helium

Problems Involving Molecules, Formula Units, and Ions

101. Calculate the number of moles in each of the following masses.
   a. 3.00 g of boron tribromide, BBr$_3$
   b. 0.472 g of sodium fluoride, NaF
   c. 7.50 × 10^2 g of methanol, CH$_3$OH
   d. 50.0 g of calcium chlorate, Ca(ClO$_3$)$_2$

102. Determine the mass of each of the following amounts.
   a. 1.366 mol of NH$_3$
   b. 0.120 mol of glucose, C$_6$H$_{12}$O$_6$
   c. 6.94 mol barium chloride, BaCl$_2$
   d. 0.005 mol of propane, C$_3$H$_8$

103. Calculate the number of molecules in each of the following amounts.
   a. 4.99 mol of methane, CH$_4$
   b. 0.005 20 mol of nitrogen gas, N$_2$

---

   c. 1.05 mol of phosphorus trichloride, PCl$_3$
   d. 3.5 × 10^{-5} mol of vitamin C, ascorbic acid, C$_6$H$_8$O$_6$

104. Calculate the number of formula units in the following amounts.
   a. 1.25 mol of potassium bromide, KBr
   b. 5.00 mol of magnesium chloride, MgCl$_2$
   c. 0.025 mol of sodium carbonate, Na$_2$CO$_3$
   d. 6.82 × 10^{-6} mol of lead(II) nitrate, Pb(NO$_3$)$_2$

105. Calculate the amount in moles of the following numbers of molecules or formula units.
   a. 3.34 × 10^{34} formula units of Cu(OH)$_2$
   b. 1.17 × 10^{16} molecules of H$_2$S
   c. 5.47 × 10^{21} formula units of nickel(II) sulfate, NiSO$_4$
   d. 7.66 × 10^{19} molecules of hydrogen peroxide, H$_2$O$_2$

106. Calculate the mass of each of the following quantities.
   a. 2.41 × 10^{24} molecules of hydrogen, H$_2$
   b. 5.00 × 10^{21} formula units of aluminum hydroxide, Al(OH)$_3$
   c. 8.25 × 10^{22} molecules of bromine pentafluoride, BrF$_5$
   d. 1.20 × 10^{23} formula units of sodium oxalate, Na$_2$C$_2$O$_4$

107. Calculate the number of molecules or formula units in each of the following masses.
   a. 22.9 g of sodium sulfide, Na$_2$S
   b. 0.272 g of nickel(II) nitrate, Ni(NO$_3$)$_2$
   c. 260 mg of acrylonitrile, CH$_2$CHCN

Mixed Review

108. Calculate the number of moles in each of the following masses.
   a. 0.039 g of palladium
   b. 8200 g of iron
   c. 0.0073 kg of tantalum
   d. 0.006 55 g of antimony
   e. 5.64 kg of barium
   f. 3.37 × 10^{-6} g of molybdenum

109. Calculate the mass in grams of each of the following amounts.
   a. 1.002 mol of chromium
   b. 550 mol of aluminum
   c. 4.08 × 10^{-8} mol of neon
   d. 7 mol of titanium
   e. 0.0086 mol of xenon
   f. 3.29 × 10^4 mol of lithium

110. Calculate the number of atoms in each of the following amounts.
   a. 17.0 mol of germanium
   b. 0.6144 mol of copper
   c. 3.02 mol of tin
   d. 2.0 × 10^6 mol of carbon
   e. 0.0019 mol of zirconium
   f. 3.227 × 10^{-10} mol of potassium

111. Calculate the number of moles in each of the following quantities.
   a. 6.022 × 10^{24} atoms of cobalt
   b. 1.06 × 10^{23} atoms of tungsten
   c. 3.008 × 10^{19} atoms of silver

d. 950 000 000 atoms of plutonium
e. 4.61×10^{17} atoms of radon
f. 8 trillion atoms of cerium

112. Calculate the number of atoms in each of the following masses.
 a. 0.0082 g of gold
 b. 812 g of molybdenum
 c. 2.00×10^2 mg of americium
 d. 10.09 kg of neon
 e. 0.705 mg of bismuth
 f. 37 μg of uranium

113. Calculate the mass of each of the following.
 a. 8.22×10^{23} atoms of rubidium
 b. 4.05 Avogadro's constants of manganese atoms
 c. 9.96×10^{26} atoms of tellurium
 d. 0.000 025 Avogadro's constants of rhodium atoms
 e. 88 300 000 000 000 atoms of radium
 f. 2.94×10^{17} atoms of hafnium

114. Calculate the number of moles in each of the following masses.
 a. 45.0 g of acetic acid, CH_3COOH
 b. 7.04 g of lead(II) nitrate, $Pb(NO_3)_2$
 c. 5000 kg of iron(III) oxide, Fe_2O_3
 d. 12.0 mg of ethylamine, $C_2H_5NH_2$
 e. 0.003 22 g of stearic acid, $C_{17}H_{35}COOH$
 f. 50.0 kg of ammonium sulfate, $(NH_4)_2SO_4$

115. Calculate the mass of each of the following amounts.
 a. 3.00 mol of selenium oxybromide, $SeOBr_2$
 b. 488 mol of calcium carbonate, $CaCO_3$
 c. 0.0091 mol of retinoic acid, $C_{20}H_{28}O_2$
 d. 6.00×10^{-8} mol of nicotine, $C_{10}H_{14}N_2$
 e. 2.50 mol of strontium nitrate, $Sr(NO_3)_2$
 f. 3.50×10^{-6} mol of uranium hexafluoride, UF_6

116. Calculate the number of molecules or formula units in each of the following amounts.
 a. 4.27 mol of tungsten(VI) oxide, WO_3
 b. 0.003 00 mol of strontium nitrate, $Sr(NO_3)_2$
 c. 72.5 mol of toluene, $C_6H_5CH_3$
 d. 5.11×10^{-7} mol of α-tocopherol (vitamin E), $C_{29}H_{50}O_2$
 e. 1500 mol of hydrazine, N_2H_4
 f. 0.989 mol of nitrobenzene $C_6H_5NO_2$

117. Calculate the number of molecules or formula units in each of the following masses.
 a. 285 g of iron(III) phosphate, $FePO_4$
 b. 0.0084 g of C_5H_5N
 c. 85 mg of 2-methyl-1-propanol, $(CH_3)_2CHCH_2OH$
 d. 4.6×10^{-4} g of mercury(II) acetate, $Hg(C_2H_3O_2)_2$
 e. 0.0067 g of lithium carbonate, Li_2CO_3

118. Calculate the mass of each of the following quantities.
 a. 8.39×10^{23} molecules of fluorine, F_2
 b. 6.82×10^{24} formula units of beryllium sulfate, $BeSO_4$
 c. 7.004×10^{26} molecules of chloroform, $CHCl_3$
 d. 31 billion formula units of chromium(III) formate, $Cr(CHO_2)_3$
 e. 6.3×10^{18} molecules of nitric acid, HNO_3
 f. 8.37×10^{25} molecules of freon 114, $C_2Cl_2F_4$

119. Precious metals are commonly measured in troy ounces. A troy ounce is equivalent to 31.1 g. How many moles are in a troy ounce of gold? How many moles are in a troy ounce of platinum? of silver?

120. A chemist needs 22.0 g of phenol, C_6H_5OH, for an experiment. How many moles of phenol is this?

121. A student needs 0.015 mol of iodine crystals, I_2, for an experiment. What mass of iodine crystals should the student obtain?

122. The weight of a diamond is given in carats. One carat is equivalent to 200. mg. A pure diamond is made up entirely of carbon atoms. How many carbon atoms make up a 1.00 carat diamond?

123. 8.00 g of calcium chloride, $CaCl_2$, is dissolved in 1.000 kg of water.
 a. How many moles of $CaCl_2$ are in solution? How many moles of water are present?
 b. Assume that the ionic compound, $CaCl_2$, separates completely into Ca^{2+} and Cl^- ions when it dissolves in water. How many moles of each ion are present in the solution?

124. How many moles are in each of the following masses?
 a. 453.6 g (1.000 pound) of sucrose (table sugar), $C_{12}H_{22}O_{11}$
 b. 1.000 pound of table salt, NaCl

125. When the ionic compound NH_4Cl dissolves in water, it breaks into one ammonium ion, NH_4^+, and one chloride ion, Cl^-. If you dissolved 10.7 g of NH_4Cl in water, how many moles of ions would be in solution?

126. What is the total amount in moles of atoms in a jar that contains 2.41×10^{24} atoms of chromium, 1.51×10^{23} atoms of nickel, and 3.01×10^{23} atoms of copper?

127. The density of liquid water is 0.997 g/mL at 25°C.
 a. Calculate the mass of 250.0 mL (about a cupful) of water.
 b. How many moles of water are in 250.0 mL of water? Hint: Use the result of (a).
 c. Calculate the volume that would be occupied by 2.000 mol of water at 25°C.
 d. What mass of water is 2.000 mol of water?

128. An Avogadro's constant (1 mol) of sugar molecules has a mass of 342 g, but an Avogadro's constant (1 mol) of water molecules has a mass of only 18 g. Explain why there is such a difference between the mass of 1 mol of sugar and the mass of 1 mol of water.

129. Calculate the mass of aluminum that would have the same number of atoms as 6.35 g of cadmium.

130. A chemist weighs a steel cylinder of compressed oxygen, O_2, and finds that it has a mass of 1027.8 g. After some of the oxygen is used in an experiment, the cylinder has a mass of 1023.2 g. How many moles of oxygen gas are used in the experiment?

131. Suppose that you could decompose 0.250 mol of Ag_2S into its elements.
 a. How many moles of silver would you have? How many moles of sulfur would you have?
 b. How many moles of Ag_2S are there in 38.8 g of Ag_2S? How many moles of silver and sulfur would be produced from this amount of Ag_2S?
 c. Calculate the masses of silver and sulfur produced in (b).

102. a. 23.28 g NH_3
 b. 21.6 g $C_6H_{12}O_6$
 c. 1.45×10^3 g or 1.45 kg $BaCl_2$
 d. 0.2 g C_3H_8

103. a. 3.00×10^{24} molecules CH_4
 b. 3.13×10^{21} molecules N_2
 c. 6.32×10^{23} molecules PCl_3
 d. 2.1×10^{19} molecules $C_6H_8O_6$

104. a. 7.53×10^{23} formula units KBr
 b. 3.01×10^{24} formula units $MgCl_2$
 c. 1.5×10^{22} formula units Na_2CO_3
 d. 4.11×10^{18} formula units $Pb(NO_3)_2$

105. a. 5.55×10^{10} mol $Cu(OH)_2$
 b. 1.94×10^{-8} mol H_2S
 c. 9.08×10^{-3} mol $NiSO_4$
 d. 1.27×10^{-4} mol H_2O_2

106. a. 8.08 g H_2
 b. 0.648 g $Al(OH)_3$
 c. 24.0 g BrF_5
 d. 26.7 g $Na_2C_2O_4$

107. a. 1.77×10^{23} formula units Na_2S
 b. 8.96×10^{20} formula units $Ni(NO_3)_2$
 c. 3.0×10^{21} molecules CH_2CHCN

108. a. 3.7×10^{-4} mol Pd
 b. 150 mol Fe
 c. 0.040 mol Ta
 d. 5.38×10^{-5} mol Sb
 e. 41.1 mol Ba
 f. 3.51×10^{-8} mol Mo

109. a. 52.10 g Cr
 b. 1.5×10^4 g or 15 kg Al
 c. 8.23×10^{-7} g Ne
 d. 3×10^2 g or 0.3 kg Ti
 e. 1.1 g Xe
 f. 2.28×10^5 g or 228 kg Li

110. a. 1.02×10^{25} atoms Ge
b. 3.700×10^{23} atoms Cu
c. 1.82×10^{24} atoms Sn
d. 1.2×10^{30} atoms C
e. 1.1×10^{21} atoms Zr
f. 1.943×10^{14} atoms K

111. a. 10.00 mol Co
b. 0.176 mol W
c. 4.995×10^{-5} mol Ag
d. 1.6×10^{-15} mol Pu
e. 7.66×10^{-7} mol Rn
f. 1×10^{-11} mol Ce

112. a. 2.5×10^{19} atoms Au
b. 5.10×10^{24} atoms Mo
c. 4.96×10^{20} atoms Am
d. 3.011×10^{26} atoms Ne
e. 2.03×10^{18} atoms Bi
f. 9.4×10^{16} atoms U

113. a. 117 g Rb
b. 223 g Mn
c. 2.11×10^5 g Te
d. 2.6×10^{-3} g Rh
e. 3.31×10^{-8} g Ra
f. 8.71×10^{-5} g Hf

114. a. 0.749 mol CH_3COOH
b. 0.0213 mol $Pb(NO_3)_2$
c. 3×10^4 mol Fe_2O_3
d. 2.66×10^{-4} mol $C_2H_5NH_2$
e. 1.13×10^{-5} mol $C_{17}H_{35}COOH$
f. 378 mol $(NH_4)_2SO_4$

115. a. 764 g $SeOBr_2$
b. 4.88×10^4 g $CaCO_3$
c. 2.7 g $C_{20}H_{28}O_2$
d. 9.74×10^{-6} g $C_{10}H_{14}N_2$
e. 529 g $Sr(NO_3)_2$
f. 1.23×10^{-3} g UF_6

116. a. 2.57×10^{24} formula units WO_3
b. 1.81×10^{21} formula units $Sr(NO_3)_2$
c. 4.37×10^{25} molecules $C_6H_5CH_3$
d. 3.08×10^{17} molecules $C_{29}H_{50}O_2$
e. 9.0×10^{26} molecules N_2H_4
f. 5.96×10^{23} molecules $C_6H_5NO_2$

Percentage Composition, Section 7-3

132. Determine the percentage composition of each of the following compounds.
a. sodium oxalate, $Na_2C_2O_4$
b. ethanol, C_2H_5OH
c. aluminum oxide, Al_2O_3
d. potassium sulfate, K_2SO_4

133. Suppose that a laboratory analysis of white powder showed 42.59% Na, 12.02% C, and 44.99% oxygen. Would you report that the compound is sodium oxalate or sodium carbonate? (Use 43.38% Na, 11.33% C, and 45.29% O for sodium carbonate, and 34.31% Na, 17.93% C, and 47.76% O for sodium oxalate.)

134. Calculate the mass of the given element in each of the following compounds.
a. bromine in 50.0 g potassium bromide, KBr
b. chromium in 1.00 kg sodium dichromate, $Na_2Cr_2O_7$
c. nitrogen in 85.0 mg of the amino acid lysine, $C_6H_{14}N_2O_2$
d. cobalt in 2.84 g cobalt(II) acetate, $Co(C_2H_3O_2)_2$

Hydrates
135. Calculate the percentage of water in each of the following hydrates.
a. sodium carbonate decahydrate, $Na_2CO_3 \cdot 10H_2O$
b. nickel(II) iodide hexahydrate, $NiI_2 \cdot 6H_2O$
c. ammonium hexacyanoferrate(III) trihydrate (commonly called ammonium ferricyanide), $(NH_4)_2Fe(CN)_6 \cdot 3H_2O$
d. aluminum bromide hexahydrate

Mixed Review
136. Write formulas for the following compounds and determine the percentage composition of each.
a. nitric acid
b. ammonia
c. mercury(II) sulfate
d. antimony(V) fluoride

137. Calculate the percentage composition of the following compounds.
a. lithium bromide, LiBr
b. anthracene, $C_{14}H_{10}$
c. ammonium nitrate, NH_4NO_3
d. nitrous acid, HNO_2
e. silver sulfide, Ag_2S
f. iron(II) thiocyanate, $Fe(SCN)_2$
g. lithium acetate
h. nickel(II) formate

138. Calculate the percentage of the given element in each of the following compounds.
a. nitrogen in urea, NH_2CONH_2
b. sulfur in sulfuryl chloride, SO_2Cl_2
c. thallium in thallium(III) oxide, Tl_2O_3
d. oxygen in potassium chlorate, $KClO_3$
e. bromine in calcium bromide, $CaBr_2$
f. tin in tin(IV) oxide, SnO_2

139. Calculate the mass of the given element in each of the following quantities.

a. oxygen in 4.00 g of manganese dioxide, MnO_2
b. aluminum in 50.0 metric tons of aluminum oxide, Al_2O_3
c. silver in 325 g silver cyanide, AgCN
d. gold in 0.780 g of gold(III) selenide, Au_2Se_3
e. selenium in 683 g sodium selenite, Na_2SeO_3
f. chlorine in 5.0×10^4 g of 1,1-dichloropropane, $CHCl_2CH_2CH_3$

140. Calculate the percentage of water in each of the following hydrates.
a. strontium chloride hexahydrate, $SrCl_2 \cdot 6H_2O$
b. zinc sulfate heptahydrate, $ZnSO_4 \cdot 7H_2O$
c. calcium fluorophosphate dihydrate, $CaFPO_3 \cdot 2H_2O$
d. beryllium nitrate trihydrate, $Be(NO_3)_2 \cdot 3H_2O$

141. Calculate the percentage of the given element in each of the following hydrates. You must first determine the formulas of the hydrates.
a. nickel in nickel(II) acetate tetrahydrate
b. chromium in sodium chromate tetrahydrate
c. cerium in cerium(IV) sulfate tetrahydrate

142. Cinnabar is a mineral that is mined in order to produce mercury. Cinnabar is mercury(II) sulfide, HgS. What mass of mercury can be obtained from 50.0 kg of cinnabar?

143. The minerals malachite, $Cu_2(OH)_2CO_3$, and chalcopyrite, $CuFeS_2$, can be mined to obtain copper metal. How much copper could be obtained from 1.00×10^3 kg of each? Which of the two has the greater copper content?

144. Calculate the percentage of the given element in each of the following hydrates.
a. vanadium in vanadium oxysulfate dihydrate, $VOSO_4 \cdot 2H_2O$
b. tin in potassium stannate trihydrate, $K_2SnO_3 \cdot 3H_2O$
c. chlorine in calcium chlorate dihydrate, $CaClO_3 \cdot 2H_2O$

145. Heating copper sulfate pentahydrate will evaporate the water from the crystals, leaving anhydrous copper sulfate, a white powder. *Anhydrous* means "without water." What mass of anhydrous $CuSO_4$ would be produced by heating 500.0 g of $CuSO_4 \cdot 5H_2O$?

146. Silver metal may be precipitated from a solution of silver nitrate by placing a copper strip into the solution. What mass of $AgNO_3$ would you dissolve in water in order to get 1.00 g of silver?

147. A sample of Ag_2S has a mass of 62.4 g. What mass of each element could be obtained by decomposing this sample?

148. A quantity of epsom salts, magnesium sulfate heptahydrate, $MgSO_4 \cdot 7H_2O$, is heated until all the water is driven off. The sample loses 11.8 g in the process. What was the mass of the original sample?

149. The process of manufacturing sulfuric acid begins with the burning of sulfur. What mass of sulfur would have to be burned in order to produce 1.00 kg of H_2SO_4? Assume that all of the sulfur ends up in the sulfuric acid.

Empirical Formulas, Section 7-4

150. Determine the empirical formula for compounds that have the following analyses.
  a. 28.4% copper, 71.6% bromine
  b. 39.0% potassium, 12.0% carbon, 1.01% hydrogen, and 47.9% oxygen
  c. 77.3% silver, 7.4% phosphorus, 15.3% oxygen
  d. 0.57% hydrogen, 72.1% iodine, 27.3% oxygen

151. Determine the simplest formula for compounds that have the following analyses. The data may not be exact.
  a. 36.2% aluminum and 63.8% sulfur
  b. 93.5% niobium and 6.50% oxygen
  c. 57.6% strontium, 13.8% phosphorus, and 28.6% oxygen
  d. 28.5% iron, 48.6% oxygen, and 22.9% sulfur

152. Determine the molecular formula of each of the following unknown substances.
  a. empirical formula CH_2
    experimental molar mass 28 g/mol
  b. empirical formula B_2H_5
    experimental molar mass 54 g/mol
  c. empirical formula C_2HCl
    experimental molar mass 179 g/mol
  d. empirical formula C_6H_8O
    experimental molar mass 290 g/mol
  e. empirical formula C_3H_2O
    experimental molar mass 216 g/mol

Mixed Review

153. Determine the empirical formula for compounds that have the following analyses.
  a. 66.0% barium and 34.0% chlorine
  b. 80.38% bismuth, 18.46% oxygen, and 1.16% hydrogen
  c. 12.67% aluminum, 19.73% nitrogen, and 67.60% oxygen
  d. 35.64% zinc, 26.18% carbon, 34.88% oxygen, and 3.30% hydrogen
  e. 2.8% hydrogen, 9.8% nitrogen, 20.5% nickel, 44.5% oxygen, and 22.4% sulfur
  f. 8.09% carbon, 0.34% hydrogen, 10.78% oxygen, and 80.78% bromine

154. Sometimes, instead of percentage composition, you will have the composition of a sample by mass. Using the actual mass of the sample, determine the empirical formula for compounds that have the following analyses.
  a. a 0.858 g sample of an unknown substance is composed of 0.537 g of copper and 0.321 g of fluorine
  b. a 13.07 g sample of an unknown substance is composed of 9.48 g of barium, 1.66 g of carbon, and 1.93 g of nitrogen
  c. a 0.025 g sample of an unknown substance is composed of 0.0091 g manganese, 0.0106 g oxygen, and 0.0053 g sulfur

155. Determine the empirical formula for compounds that have the following analyses.
  a. a 0.0082 g sample contains 0.0015 g of nickel and 0.0067 g of iodine
  b. a 0.470 g sample contains 0.144 g of manganese, 0.074 g of nitrogen, and 0.252 g of oxygen
  c. a 3.880 g sample contains 0.691 g of magnesium, 1.824 g of sulfur, and 1.365 g of oxygen
  d. a 46.25 g sample contains 14.77 g of potassium, 9.06 g of oxygen, and 22.42 g of tin

156. Determine the empirical formula for compounds that have the following analyses:
  a. 60.9% As and 39.1% S
  b. 76.89% Re and 23.12% O
  c. 5.04% H, 35.00% N, and 59.96% O
  d. 24.3% Fe, 33.9% Cr, and 41.8% O
  e. 54.03% C, 37.81% N, and 8.16% H
  f. 55.81% C, 3.90% H, 29.43% F, and 10.85% N

157. Determine the molecular formulas for compounds having the following empirical formulas and molar masses.
  a. C_2H_4S; experimental molar mass 179
  b. C_2H_4O; experimental molar mass 176
  c. $C_2H_3O_2$; experimental molar mass 119
  d. C_2H_2O, experimental molar mass 254

158. Use the experimental molar mass to determine the molecular formula for compounds having the following analyses.
  a. 41.39% carbon, 3.47% hydrogen, and 55.14% oxygen; experimental molar mass 116.07
  b. 54.53% carbon, 9.15% hydrogen, and 36.32% oxygen; experimental molar mass 88
  c. 64.27% carbon, 7.19% hydrogen, and 28.54% oxygen; experimental molar mass 168.19

159. A 0.400 g sample of a white powder contains 0.141 g of potassium, 0.115 g of sulfur, and 0.144 g of oxygen. What is the empirical formula for the compound?

160. A 10.64 g sample of a lead compound is analyzed and found to be made up of 9.65 g of lead and 0.99 g of oxygen. Determine the empirical formula for this compound.

161. A 2.65 g sample of a salmon-colored powder contains 0.70 g of chromium, 0.65 g of sulfur, and 1.30 g of oxygen. The molar mass is 392.2. What is the formula of the compound?

162. Ninhydrin is a compound that reacts with amino acids and proteins to produce a dark-colored complex. It is used by forensic chemists and detectives to see fingerprints that might otherwise be invisible. Ninhydrin's composition is 60.68% carbon, 3.40% hydrogen, and 35.92% oxygen. What is the empirical formula for ninhydrin?

163. Histamine is a substance that is released by cells in response to injury, infection, stings, and materials that cause allergic responses, such as pollen. Histamine causes dilation of blood vessels and swelling due to accumulation of fluid in the tissues. People sometimes take *anti*histamine drugs to counteract the effects of histamine. A sample of histamine having a mass of 385 mg is composed of 208 mg of carbon, 31 mg of hydrogen, and 146 mg of nitrogen. The molar mass of histamine is 111 g/mol. What is the molecular formula for histamine?

117. a. 1.14×10^{24} formula units $FePO_4$
  b. 6.4×10^{19} molecules C_5H_5N
  c. 6.9×10^{20} molecules $(CH_3)_2CHCH_2OH$
  d. 8.7×10^{17} formula units $Hg(C_2H_3O_2)_2$
  e. 5.5×10^{19} formula units Li_2CO_3

118. a. 52.9 g F_2
  b. 1.19×10^3 g or 1.19 kg $BeSO_4$
  c. 1.388×10^5 g or 138.8 kg $CHCl_3$
  d. 9.6×10^{-12} g $Cr(CHO_2)_3$
  e. 6.6×10^{-4} g HNO_3
  f. 2.38×10^4 g or 23.8 kg $C_2Cl_2F_4$

119. 0.158 mol Au
  0.159 mol Pt
  0.288 mol Ag

120. 0.234 mol C_6H_5OH

121. 3.8 g I_2

122. 1.00×10^{22} atoms C

123. a. 0.0721 mol $CaCl_2$
  55.49 mol H_2O
  b. 0.0721 mol Ca^{2+}
  0.144 mol Cl^-

124. a. 1.325 mol $C_{12}H_{22}O_{11}$
  b. 7.762 mol NaCl

125. 0.400 mol ions

126. 4.75 mol atoms

127. a. 249 g H_2O
  b. 13.8 mol H_2O
  c. 36.1 mL H_2O
  d. 36.0 g H_2O

128. The mass of a sugar molecule is much greater than the mass of a water molecule. Therefore, the mass of 1 mol of sugar molecules is much greater than the mass of 1 mol of water molecules.

129. 1.52 g Al

130. 0.14 mol O_2

131. a. 0.500 mol Ag
  0.250 mol S

b. 0.157 mol Ag_2S
0.313 mol Ag
0.157 mol S
c. 33.8 g Ag
5.03 g S

132. a. 34.31% Na,
17.93% C, 47.76% O
b. 52.13% C, 13.15% H,
34.72% O
c. 52.92% Al, 47.08% O
d. 44.87% K, 18.40% S,
36.72% O

133. sodium carbonate

134. a. 33.6 g Br
b. 397 g Cr
c. 16.3 mg N
d. 0.945 g Co

135. a. 62.97% H_2O in
$Na_2CO_3 \cdot 10H_2O$
b. 25.71% H_2O in $NiI_2 \cdot 6H_2O$
c. 17.89% H_2O in
$(NH_4)_2Fe(CN)_6 \cdot 3H_2O$
d. 28.85% H_2O in $AlBr_3 \cdot 6H_2O$

136. a. HNO_3
1.60% H
22.23% N
76.17% O
b. NH_3
82.22% N
17.78% H
c. $HgSO_4$
67.616% Hg
10.81% S
21.57% O
d. SbF_5
56.173% Sb
43.83% F

137. a. 7.99% Li
92.01% Br
b. 94.33% C
5.67% H
c. 35.00% N
5.05% H
59.96% O
d. 2.15% H
29.80% N
68.06% O
e. 87.059% Ag
12.94% S

164. You analyze two substances in the laboratory and discover that each has the empirical formula CH_2O. You can easily see that they are different substances because one is a liquid with a sharp, biting odor and the other is an odorless, crystalline solid. How can you account for the fact that both have the same empirical formula?

Stoichiometry, Sections 9-1; 9-2

165. How many moles of sodium will react with water to produce 4.0 mol of hydrogen in the following reaction?

$$2Na(s) + 2H_2O(l) \rightarrow 2NaOH(aq) + H_2(g)$$

166. How many moles of lithium chloride will be formed by the reaction of chlorine with 0.046 mol of lithium bromide in the following reaction?

$$2LiBr(aq) + Cl_2(g) \rightarrow 2LiCl(aq) + Br_2(l)$$

167. Aluminum will react with sulfuric acid in the following reaction.

$$2Al(s) + 3H_2SO_4(l) \rightarrow Al_2(SO_4)_3(aq) + 3H_2(g)$$

a. How many moles of H_2SO_4 will react with 18 mol Al?
b. How many moles of each product will be produced?

168. Propane burns in excess oxygen according to the following reaction.

$$C_3H_8 + 5O_2 \rightarrow 3CO_2 + 4H_2O$$

a. How many moles each of CO_2 and H_2O are formed from 3.85 mol of propane?
b. If 0.647 mol of oxygen are used in the burning of propane, how many moles each of CO_2 and H_2O are produced? How many moles of C_3H_8 are consumed?

169. Phosphorus burns in air to produce a phosphorus oxide in the following reaction:

$$4P(s) + 5O_2(g) \rightarrow P_4O_{10}(s)$$

a. What mass of phosphorus will be needed to produce 3.25 mol of P_4O_{10}?
b. If 0.489 mol of phosphorus burns, what mass of oxygen is used? What mass of P_4O_{10} is produced?

170. Hydrogen peroxide breaks down, releasing oxygen, in the following reaction.

$$2H_2O_2(aq) \rightarrow 2H_2O(l) + O_2(g)$$

a. What mass of oxygen is produced when 1.840 mol of H_2O_2 decompose?
b. What mass of water is produced when 5.0 mol O_2 is produced by this reaction?

171. Sodium carbonate reacts with nitric acid according to the following equation:

$$Na_2CO_3(s) + 2HNO_3 \rightarrow 2NaNO_3 + CO_2 + H_2O$$

a. How many moles of Na_2CO_3 are required to produce 100.0 g of $NaNO_3$?
b. If 7.50 g of Na_2CO_3 reacts, how many moles of CO_2 are produced?

172. Hydrogen is generated by passing hot steam over iron, which oxidizes to form Fe_3O_4, in the following equation:

$$3Fe(s) + 4H_2O(g) \rightarrow 4H_2(g) + Fe_3O_4(s)$$

a. If 625 g of Fe_3O_4 is produced in the reaction, how many moles of hydrogen are produced at the same time?
b. How many moles of iron would be needed to generate 27 g of hydrogen?

173. Calculate the mass of silver bromide produced from 22.5 g of silver nitrate in the following reaction:

$$2AgNO_3(aq) + MgBr_2(aq) \rightarrow$$
$$2AgBr(s) + Mg(NO_3)_2(aq)$$

174. What mass of acetylene, C_2H_2, will be produced from the reaction of 90. g of calcium carbide, CaC_2, with water in the following reaction?

$$CaC_2(s) + 2H_2O(l) \rightarrow C_2H_2(g) + Ca(OH)_2(s)$$

175. Chlorine gas can be produced in the laboratory by adding concentrated hydrochloric acid to manganese(IV) oxide in the following reaction:

$$MnO_2(s) + 4HCl(aq) \rightarrow$$
$$MnCl_2(aq) + 2H_2O(l) + Cl_2(g)$$

a. Calculate the mass of MnO_2 needed to produce 25.0 g of Cl_2.
b. What mass of $MnCl_2$ is produced when 0.091 g of Cl_2 is generated?

Mixed Review

176. How many moles of ammonium sulfate can be made from the reaction of 30.0 mol of NH_3 with H_2SO_4 according to the following equation:

$$2NH_3 + H_2SO_4 \rightarrow (NH_4)_2SO_4$$

177. In a very violent reaction called a thermite reaction, aluminum metal reacts with iron(III) oxide to form iron metal and aluminum oxide according to the following equation:

$$Fe_2O_3 + 2Al \rightarrow 2Fe + Al_2O_3$$

a. What mass of Al will react with 150 g of Fe_2O_3?
b. If 0.905 mol Al_2O_3 is produced in the reaction, what mass of Fe is produced?
c. How many moles of Fe_2O_3 will react with 99.0 g of Al?

178. The reaction $N_2(g) + 3H_2(g) \rightarrow 2NH_3(g)$ is used to produce ammonia commercially. If 1.40 g of N_2 are used in the reaction, how many grams of H_2 will be needed?

179. What mass of sulfuric acid, H_2SO_4, is required to react with 1.27 g of potassium hydroxide, KOH? The products of this reaction are potassium sulfate and water.

180. Ammonium hydrogen phosphate, $(NH_4)_2HPO_4$, a common fertilizer; is made from reacting phosphoric acid, H_3PO_4, with ammonia.
a. Write the equation for this reaction.
b. If 10.00 g of ammonia react, how many moles of fertilizer will be produced?

c. What mass of ammonia will react with 2800 kg of H_3PO_4?

181. The following reaction shows the synthesis of zinc citrate, a ingredient in toothpaste, from zinc carbonate and citric acid:

$$3ZnCO_3(s) + 2C_6H_8O_7(aq) \rightarrow$$
$$Zn_3(C_6H_5O_7)_2(aq) + 3H_2O(l) + 3CO_2(g)$$

a. How many moles of $ZnCO_3$ and $C_6H_8O_7$ are required to produce 30.0 mol of $Zn_3(C_6H_5O_7)_2$?
b. What quantities, in kilograms, of H_2O and CO_2 are produced by the reaction of 500. mol of citric acid?

182. Methyl butanoate, an oily substance with a strong fruity fragrance can be made by reacting butanoic acid with methanol according to the following equation:

$$C_3H_7COOH + CH_3OH \rightarrow C_3H_7COOCH_3 + H_2O$$

a. What mass of methyl butanoate is produced from the reaction of 52.5 g of butanoic acid?
b. In order to purify methyl butanoate, water must be removed. What mass of water is produced from the reaction of 5800. g of methanol?

183. Ammonium nitrate decomposes to yield nitrogen gas, water, and oxygen gas in the following reaction:

$$2NH_4NO_3 \rightarrow 2N_2 + O_2 + 4H_2O$$

a. How many moles of nitrogen gas are produced when 36.0 g of NH_4NO_3 reacts?
b. If 7.35 mol of H_2O are produced in this reaction, what mass of NH_4NO_3 reacted?

184. Lead(II) nitrate reacts with potassium iodide to produce lead(II) iodide and potassium nitrate. If 1.23 mg of lead nitrate are consumed, what is the mass of the potassium nitrate produced?

185. A car battery produces electrical energy with the following chemical reaction:

$$Pb(s) + PbO_2(s) + 2H_2SO_4(aq) \rightarrow$$
$$2PbSO_4(s) + 2H_2O(l)$$

If the battery loses 0.34 kg of lead in this reaction, how many moles of lead(II) sulfate are produced?

186. In a space shuttle, the CO_2 that the crew exhales is removed from the air by a reaction within canisters of lithium hydroxide. On average, each astronaut exhales about 20.0 mol of CO_2 daily. What mass of water will be produced when this amount reacts with LiOH? The other product of the reaction is Li_2CO_3.

187. Water is sometimes removed from the products of a reaction by placing them in a closed container with excess P_4O_{10}. Water is absorbed by the following reaction:

$$P_4O_{10} + 6H_2O \rightarrow 4H_3PO_4$$

a. What mass of water can be absorbed by 1.00×10^2 g of P_4O_{10}?
b. If the P_4O_{10} in the container absorbs 0.614 mol of water, what mass of H_3PO_4 is produced?
c. If the mass of the container of P_4O_{10} increases from 56.64 g to 63.70 g, how many moles of water are absorbed?

188. Ethanol, C_2H_5OH, is considered a clean fuel because it burns in oxygen to produce carbon dioxide and water with few trace pollutants. If 95.0 g of H_2O are produced during the combustion of ethanol, how many grams of ethanol were present at the beginning of the reaction?

189. Sulfur dioxide is one of the major contributors to acid rain. Sulfur dioxide can react with oxygen and water in the atmosphere to form sulfuric acid, as shown in the following equation:

$$2H_2O(l) + O_2(g) + 2SO_2(g) \rightarrow 2H_2SO_4(aq)$$

If 50.0 g of sulfur dioxide from pollutants reacts with water and oxygen found in the air, how many grams of sulfuric acid can be produced? How many grams of oxygen are used in the process?

190. When heated, sodium bicarbonate, $NaHCO_3$, decomposes into sodium carbonate, Na_2CO_3, water, and carbon dioxide. If 5.00 g of $NaHCO_3$ decomposes, what is the mass of the carbon dioxide produced?

191. A reaction between hydrazine, N_2H_4, and dinitrogen tetroxide, N_2O_4, has been used to launch rockets into space. The reaction produces nitrogen gas and water vapor.
a. Write a balanced chemical equation for this reaction.
b. What is the mole ratio of N_2O_4 to N_2?
c. How many moles of N_2 will be produced if 20 000 mol of N_2H_4 are used by a rocket?
d. How many grams of H_2O are made when 450. kg of N_2O_4 are consumed?

192. Joseph Priestley is credited with the discovery of oxygen. He produced O_2 by heating mercury(II) oxide, HgO, to decompose it into its elements. How many moles of oxygen could Priestley have produced if he had decomposed 517.84 g of mercury oxide?

193. Iron(III) chloride, $FeCl_3$, can be made by the reaction of iron with chlorine gas. How much iron, in grams, will be needed to completely react with 58.0 g of Cl_2?

194. Sodium sulfide and cadmium nitrate undergo a double-replacement reaction as shown by the following equation:

$$Na_2S + Cd(NO_3)_2 \rightarrow 2NaNO_3 + CdS$$

What is the mass, in milligrams, of cadmium sulfide that can be made from 5.00 mg of sodium sulfide?

195. Potassium permanganate and glycerin react explosively according to the following equation:

$$14KMnO_4 + 4C_3H_5(OH)_3 \rightarrow$$
$$7K_2CO_3 + 7Mn_2O_3 + 5CO_2 + 16H_2O$$

a. How many moles of carbon dioxide can be produced from 4.44 mol of $KMnO_4$?
b. If 5.21 g of H_2O are produced, how many moles of glycerin, $C_3H_5(OH)_3$, were used?
c. If 3.39 mol of potassium carbonate are made, how many grams of manganese(III) oxide are also made?
d. How many grams of glycerin will be needed to react with 50.0 g of $KMnO_4$? How many grams of CO_2 will be produced in the same reaction?

196. Calcium carbonate found in limestone and marble reacts with hydrochloric acid to form calcium chloride,

f. 32.47% Fe
13.96% C
16.29% N
37.28% S
g. $LiC_2H_3O_2$
10.52% Li
36.40% C
4.59% H
48.49% O
h. $Ni(CHO_2)_2$
39.46% Ni
16.15% C
1.36% H
43.03% O

138. a. 46.65% N
b. 23.76% S
c. 89.491% Tl
d. 39.17% O
e. 79.95% Br in $CaBr_2$
f. 78.767% Sn in SnO_2

139. a. 1.47 g O
b. 26.5 metric tons Al
c. 262 g Ag
d. 0.487 g Au
e. 312 g Se
f. 3.1×10^4 g Cl

140. a. 40.55% H_2O
b. 43.86% H_2O
c. 20.70% H_2O
d. 28.90% H_2O

141. a. $Ni(C_2H_3O_2)_2 \cdot 4H_2O$
23.58% Ni
b. $Na_2CrO_4 \cdot 4H_2O$
22.22% Cr
c. $Ce(SO_4)_2 \cdot 4H_2O$
34.65% Ce

142. 43.1 kg Hg

143. malachite: 5.75×10^2 kg Cu
chalcopyrite: 3.46×10^2 kg Cu
malachite has a greater Cu content

144. a. 25.59% V
b. 39.71% Sn
c. 22.22% Cl

145. 319.6 g anhydrous $CuSO_4$

146. 1.57 g $AgNO_3$

147. 54.3 g Ag
8.08 g S

148. 23.1 g $MgSO_4 \cdot 7H_2O$

149. 3.27×10^2 g S

150. a. $CuBr_2$ **b.** $KHCO_3$
c. Ag_3PO_4 **d.** HIO_3

151. a. Al_2S_3 **b.** Nb_5O_2
c. $Sr_3P_2O_8$ or $Sr_3(PO_4)_2$
d. $Fe_2S_3O_{12}$ or $Fe_2(SO_4)_3$

152. a. C_2H_4 **b.** B_4H_{10}
c. $C_6H_3Cl_3$ **d.** $C_{18}H_{24}O_3$
e. $C_{12}H_8O_4$

153. a. $BaCl_2$
b. BiO_3H_3 or $Bi(OH)_3$
c. AlN_3O_9 or $Al(NO_3)_3$
d. $ZnC_4H_6O_4$ or $Zn(CH_3COO)_2$
e. $NiN_2S_2H_8O_8$ or $Ni(NH_4)_2SO_4$
f. $C_2HBr_3O_2$ or CBr_3COOH

154. a. CuF_2 **b.** $Ba(CN)_2$
c. $MnSO_4$

155. a. NiI_2
b. MgN_2O_6 or $Mg(NO_3)_2$
c. MgS_2O_3, magnesium thiosulfate
d. K_2SnO_3, potassium stannate

156. a. As_2S_3 **b.** Re_2O_7
c. $N_2H_4O_3$ or NH_4NO_3
d. $Fe_2Cr_3O_{12}$ or $Fe_2(CrO_4)_3$
e. $C_5H_9N_3$
f. $C_6H_5F_2N$ or $C_6H_3F_2NH_2$

157. a. $C_6H_{12}S_3$ **b.** $C_8H_{16}O_4$
c. $C_4H_6O_4$ **d.** $C_{12}H_{12}O_6$

158. a. $C_4H_4O_4$ **b.** $C_4H_8O_2$
c. $C_9H_{12}O_3$

159. $K_2S_2O_5$, potassium metabisulfite

160. Pb_3O_4

161. $Cr_2S_3O_{12}$ or $Cr_2(SO_4)_3$, chromium(III) sulfate

162. $C_9H_6O_4$

163. $C_5H_9N_3$, the empirical formula and the molecular formula are the same

164. The molecular formulas of the compounds are different multiples of the same empirical formula. (FYI: The first could be acetic acid, $C_2H_4O_2$, and the

carbon dioxide, and water according to the following equation:

$$CaCO_3(s) + 2HCl(aq) \rightarrow CaCl_2(aq) + CO_2(g) + H_2O(l)$$

a. What mass of HCl will be needed to produce 5.00×10^3 kg of $CaCl_2$?
b. What mass of CO_2 could be produced from the reaction of 750 g of $CaCO_3$?

197. The fuel used to power the booster rockets on the space shuttle is a mixture of aluminum metal and ammonium perchlorate. The following balanced equation represents the reaction of these two ingredients:

$$3Al(s) + 3NH_4ClO_4(s) \rightarrow Al_2O_3(s) + AlCl_3(g) + 3NO(g) + 6H_2O(g)$$

a. If 1.50×10^5 g of Al react, what mass of NH_4ClO_4, in grams, is required?
b. If aluminum reacts with 620 kg of NH_4ClO_4, what mass of nitrogen monoxide is produced?

198. Phosphoric acid is typically produced by the action of sulfuric acid on rock that has a high content of calcium phosphate according to the following equation:

$$3H_2SO_4 + Ca_3(PO_4)_2 + 6H_2O \rightarrow 3[CaSO_4 \cdot 2H_2O] + 2H_3PO_4$$

a. If 2.50×10^5 kg of H_2SO_4 react, how many moles of H_3PO_4 can be made?
b. What mass of calcium sulfate dihydrate is produced by the reaction of 400. kg of calcium phosphate?
c. If the rock being used contains 78.8% $Ca_3(PO_4)_2$, how many metric tons of H_3PO_4 can be produced from 68 metric tons of rock?

199. Rusting of iron occurs in the presence of moisture according to the following equation:

$$4Fe(s) + 3O_2(g) \rightarrow 2Fe_2O_3(s)$$

Suppose that 3.19% of a heap of steel scrap with a mass of 1650 kg rusts in a year. What mass will the heap have after one year of rusting?

Limiting Reactants, Section 9-3

200. Aluminum oxidizes according to the following equation:

$$4Al + 3O_2 \rightarrow 2Al_2O_3$$

Powdered Al (0.048 mol) is placed into a container containing 0.030 mol O_2. What is the limiting reactant?

201. A process by which zirconium metal can be produced from the mineral zirconium(IV) orthosilicate, $ZrSiO_4$, starts by reacting it with chlorine gas to form zirconium(IV) chloride:

$$ZrSiO_4 + 2Cl_2 \rightarrow ZrCl_4 + SiO_2 + O_2$$

What mass of $ZrCl_4$ can be produced if 862 g of $ZrSiO_4$ and 950. g of Cl_2 are available? You must first determine the limiting reactant.

Mixed Review

202. Heating zinc sulfide in the presence of oxygen yields the following:

$$ZnS + O_2 \rightarrow ZnO + SO_2$$

If 1.72 mol of ZnS is heated in the presence of 3.04 mol of O_2, which reactant will be used up? Balance the equation first.

203. Use the following equation for the oxidation of aluminum in the following problems:

$$4Al + 3O_2 \rightarrow 2Al_2O_3$$

a. Which reactant is limiting if 0.32 mol Al and 0.26 mol O_2 are available?
b. How many moles of Al_2O_3 are formed from the reaction of 6.38×10^{-3} mol of O_2 and 9.15×10^{-3} mol of Al?
c. If 3.17 g of Al and 2.55 g of O_2 are available, which reactant is limiting?

204. In the production of copper from ore containing copper(II) sulfide, the ore is first roasted to change it to the oxide according to the following equation:

$$2CuS + 3O_2 \rightarrow 2CuO + 2SO_2$$

a. If 100 g of CuS and 56 g of O_2 are available, which reactant is limiting?
b. What mass of CuO can be formed from the reaction of 18.7 g of CuS and 12.0 g of O_2?

205. A reaction such as the one shown here is often used to demonstrate a single replacement reaction:

$$3CuSO_4(aq) + 2Fe(s) \rightarrow 3Cu(s) + Fe_2(SO_4)_3(aq)$$

If you place 0.092 mol of iron filings in a solution containing 0.158 mol of $CuSO_4$, what is the limiting reactant? How many moles of Cu will be formed?

206. In the reaction $BaCO_3 + 2HNO_3 \rightarrow Ba(NO_3)_2 + CO_2 + H_2O$, what mass of $Ba(NO_3)_2$ can be formed by combining 55 g $BaCO_3$ and 26 g HNO_3?

207. Bromine replaces iodine in magnesium iodide by the following process:

$$MgI_2 + Br_2 \rightarrow MgBr_2 + I_2$$

a. Which is the excess reactant when 560 g of MgI_2 and 360 g of Br_2 react, and what mass remains?
b. What mass of I_2 is formed in the same process?

208. Nickel replaces silver from silver nitrate in solution according to the following equation:

$$2AgNO_3 + Ni \rightarrow 2Ag + Ni(NO_3)_2$$

a. If you have 22.9 g of Ni and 112 g of $AgNO_3$, which reactant is in excess?
b. What mass of nickel(II) nitrate would be produced given the quantities above?

209. Carbon disulfide, CS_2, is an important industrial substance. Its fumes can burn explosively in air to form sulfur dioxide and carbon dioxide:

$$CS_2(g) + O_2(g) \rightarrow SO_2(g) + CO_2(g)$$

If 1.60 mol of CS_2 burns with 5.60 mol of O_2, how many moles of the excess reactant will still be present when the reaction is over?

210. Although poisonous, mercury compounds were once used to kill bacteria in wounds and on the skin. One was called "ammoniated mercury" and is made from mercury(II) chloride according to the following equation:

$$HgCl_2(aq) + 2NH_3(aq) \rightarrow Hg(NH_2)Cl(s) + NH_4Cl(aq)$$

a. What mass of $Hg(NH_2)Cl$ could be produced from 0.91 g of $HgCl_2$ assuming plenty of ammonia is available?

b. What mass of $Hg(NH_2)Cl$ could be produced from 0.91 g of $HgCl_2$ and 0.15 g of NH_3 in solution?

211. Aluminum chips are sometimes added to sodium hydroxide-based drain cleaners because they react to generate hydrogen gas which bubbles and helps loosen material in the drain. The equation follows:

$$Al(s) + NaOH(aq) + H_2O(l) \rightarrow NaAlO_2(aq) + H_2(g)$$

a. Balance the equation.

b. How many moles of H_2 can be generated from 0.57 mol Al and 0.37 mol NaOH in excess water?

c. Which reactant should be limiting in order for the mixture to be most effective as a drain cleaner? Explain your choice.

212. Copper is changed to copper(II) ions by nitric acid according to the following equation:

$$4HNO_3 + Cu \rightarrow Cu(NO_3)_2 + 2NO_2 + 2H_2O$$

a. How many moles each of HNO_3 and Cu must react in order to produce 0.0845 mol of NO_2?

b. If 5.94 g of Cu and 23.23 g of HNO_3 are combined, which reactant is in excess?

213. One industrial process for producing nitric acid begins with the following reaction:

$$4NH_3 + 5O_2 \rightarrow 4NO + 6H_2O$$

a. If 2.90 mol NH_3 and 3.75 mol O_2 are available, how many moles of each product are formed?

b. Which reactant is limiting if 4.20×10^4 g of NH_3 and 1.31×10^5 g of O_2 are available?

c. What mass of NO is formed in the reaction of 869 kg of NH_3 and 2480 kg O_2?

214. Acetaldehyde, CH_3CHO, is manufactured by the reaction of ethanol with copper(II) oxide according to the following equation:

$$CH_3CH_2OH + CuO \rightarrow CH_3CHO + H_2O + Cu$$

What mass of acetaldehyde can be produced by the reaction between 620 g of ethanol and 1020 g of CuO? What mass of which reactant will be left over?

215. Hydrogen bromide can be produced by a reaction among bromine, sulfur dioxide, and water as follows:

$$SO_2 + Br_2 + H_2O \rightarrow 2HBr + H_2SO_4$$

If 250 g of SO_2 and 650 g of Br_2 react in the presence of excess water, what mass of HBr will be formed?

216. Sulfur dioxide can be produced in the laboratory by the reaction of hydrochloric acid and a sulfite salt such as sodium sulfite:

$$Na_2SO_3 + 2HCl \rightarrow 2NaCl + SO_2 + H_2O$$

What mass of SO_2 can be made from 25.0 g of Na_2SO_3 and 22.0 g of HCl?

217. The rare-earth metal terbium is produced from terbium(III) fluoride and calcium metal by the following single replacement reaction:

$$2TbF_3 + 3Ca \rightarrow 3CaF_2 + 2Tb$$

a. Given 27.5 g of TbF_3 and 6.96 g of Ca, how many grams of terbium could be produced?

b. How many grams of the excess reactant is left over?

Percent Yield, Section 9-3

218. Calculate the percent yield in each of the following cases.

a. theoretical yield is 50.0 g of product; actual yield is 41.9 g

b. theoretical yield is 290 kg of product; actual yield is 270 kg

c. theoretical yield is 6.05×10^4 kg of product; actual yield is 4.18×10^4 kg

d. theoretical yield is 0.00192 g of product; actual yield is 0.00089 g

219. In the commercial production of the element arsenic, arsenic(III) oxide is heated with carbon, which reduces the oxide to the metal according to the following equation:

$$2As_2O_3 + 3C \rightarrow 3CO_2 + 4As$$

a. If 8.87 g of As_2O_3 is used in the reaction and 5.33 g of As is produced, what is the percent yield?

b. If 67 g of carbon is used up in a different reaction and 425 g of As is produced, calculate the percent yield of this reaction.

Mixed Review

220. Ethyl acetate is a sweet-smelling solvent used in varnishes and fingernail-polish remover. It is produced industrially by heating acetic acid and ethanol together in the presence of sulfuric acid, which is added to speed up the reaction. The ethyl acetate is distilled off as it is formed. The equation for the process is as follows:

$$\underset{acetic\ acid}{CH_3COOH} + \underset{ethanol}{CH_3CH_2OH} \xrightarrow{H_2SO_4}$$
$$\underset{ethyl\ acetate}{CH_3COOCH_2CH_3} + H_2O$$

Determine the percent yield in the following cases.

a. 68.3 g of ethyl acetate should be produced but only 43.9 g is recovered.

b. 0.0419 mol of ethyl acetate is produced but 0.0722 mol is expected. (Hint: Percent yield can also be calculated by dividing the actual yield in moles by the theoretical yield in moles.)

c. 4.29 mol of ethanol is reacted with excess acetic acid, but only 2.98 mol of ethyl acetate is produced.

d. A mixture of 0.58 mol ethanol and 0.82 mol acetic acid is reacted and 0.46 mol ethyl acetate is produced. (Hint: What is the limiting reactant?)

221. Assume the following hypothetical reaction takes place:

$$2A + 7B \rightarrow 4C + 3D$$

Calculate the percent yield in each of the following cases.

a. The reaction of 0.0251 mol of A produces 0.0349 mol of C.

second could be glucose, $C_6H_{12}O_6$, or some other simple sugar.)

165. 8.0 mol Na

166. 0.046 mol LiCl

167. a. 27 mol H_2SO_4
b. 27 mol H_2, 9 mol $Al_2(SO_4)_3$

168. a. 11.6 mol CO_2, 15.4 mol H_2O
b. 0.388 mol CO_2
0.518 mol H_2O
0.129 mol C_3H_8

169. a. 403 g P
b. 19.6 g O_2, 15.4 g P_2O_4

170. a. 29.44 g O_2
b. 180 g H_2O

171. a. 0.5882 mol Na_2CO_3
b. 0.0708 mol CO_2

172. a. 10.8 mol H_2
b. 10. mol Fe

173. 24.9 g AgBr

174. 37 g C_2H_2

175. a. 30.7 g MnO_2
b. 0.16 g $MnCl_2$

176. 15 mol $(NH_4)_2SO_4$

177. a. 51 g Al
b. 101 g Fe
c. 1.83 mol Fe_2O_3

178. 0.303 g H_2

179. $H_2SO_4 + 2KOH \rightarrow K_2SO_4 + 2H_2O$; 1.11 g H_2SO_4

180. a. $H_3PO_4 + 2NH_3 \rightarrow (NH_4)_2HPO_4$
b. 0.293 mol $(NH_4)_2HPO_4$
c. 970 kg NH_3

181. a. 90.0 mol $ZnCO_3$; 60.0 mol $C_6H_8O_7$
b. 13.5 kg H_2O; 33.0 kg CO_2

182. a. 60.9 g methyl butanoate
b. 3261 g H_2O

183. a. 0.450 mol N_2
b. 294 g NH_4NO_3

184. $Pb(NO_3)_2 + 2KI \rightarrow PbI_2 + 2KNO_3$; 0.751 mg KNO_3

185. 3.3 mol $PbSO_4$

186. $2LiOH + CO_2 \rightarrow H_2O + Li_2CO_3$; 360 g H_2O

187. a. 38.1 g H_2O
b. 40.1 g H_3PO_4
c. 0.392 mol H_2O

188. $C_2H_5OH + 3O_2 \rightarrow 2CO_2 + 3H_2O$; 81.0 g C_2H_5OH

189. 76.5 g H_2SO_4; 12.5 g O_2

190. $2NaHCO_3 \rightarrow Na_2CO_3 + H_2O + CO_2$; 1.31 g CO_2

191. a. $2N_2H_4 + N_2O_4 \rightarrow 3N_2 + 4H_2O$
b. 1 mol N_2O_4 to 3 mol N_2
c. 30 000 mol N_2
d. 3.52×10^5 g H_2O

192. $2HgO(s) \rightarrow 2Hg(l) + O_2(g)$; 1.1954 mol O_2

193. $2Fe + 3Cl_2 \rightarrow 2FeCl_3$; 30.5 g Fe

194. 9.26 mg CdS

195. a. 1.59 mol CO_2
b. 0.0723 mol $C_3H_5(OH)_3$
c. 535 g Mn_2O_3
d. 8.33 g $C_3H_5(OH)_3$; 4.97 g CO_2

196. a. 3.29×10^3 kg of HCl
b. 330 g CO_2 (s)

197. a. 6.53×10^5 g NH_4ClO_4
b. 160 kg NO(g)

198. a. 1.70×10^6 mol H_3PO_4
b. 666 kg of $CaSO_4 \cdot 2H_2O$
c. 34 metric tons of H_3PO_4

199. 1670 kg

200. O_2

201. $ZrSiO_4$, 1.10×10^3 g $ZrCl_4$

202. $2ZnS + 3O_2 \rightarrow 2ZnO + 2SO_2$; Zn is limiting

203. a. Al is limiting
b. 4.25×10^{-3} mol Al_2O_3
c. O_2 is limiting

204. a. CuS is limiting
b. 15.6 g CuO

205. Fe is limiting; 0.158 mol Cu

206. 54 g $Ba(NO_3)_2$

---

b. The reaction of 1.19 mol of A produces 1.41 mol of D.
c. The reaction of 189 mol of B produces 39 mol of D.
d. The reaction of 3500 mol of B produces 1700 mol of C.

222. Elemental phosphorus can be produced by heating calcium phosphate from rocks with silica sand (SiO_2) and carbon in the form of coke. The following reaction takes place:

$$Ca_3(PO_4)_2 + 3SiO_2 + 5C \rightarrow 3CaSiO_3 + 2P + 5CO$$

a. If 57 mol of $Ca_3(PO_4)_2$ is used and 101 mol of $CaSiO_3$ is obtained, what is the percent yield?
b. Determine the percent yield obtained if 1280 mol of carbon is consumed and 622 mol of $CaSiO_3$ is produced.
c. The engineer in charge of this process expects a yield of 81.5%. If 1.4×10^5 mol of $Ca_3(PO_4)_2$ is used, how many moles of phosphorus will be produced?

223. Tungsten (W) can be produced from its oxide by reacting the oxide with hydrogen at a high temperature according to the following equation:

$$WO_3 + 3H_2 \rightarrow W + 3H_2O$$

a. What is the percent yield if 56.9 g of WO_3 yields 41.4 g of tungsten?
b. How many moles of tungsten will be produced from 3.72 g of WO_3 if the yield is 92.0%?
c. A chemist carries out this reaction and obtains 11.4 g of tungsten. If the percent yield is 89.4%, what mass of WO_3 was used?

224. Carbon tetrachloride, CCl_4, is a solvent that was once used in large quantities in dry cleaning. Because it is a dense liquid that does not burn, it was also used in fire extinguishers. Unfortunately, its use was discontinued because it was found to be a carcinogen. It was manufactured by the following reaction:

$$CS_2 + 3Cl_2 \rightarrow CCl_4 + S_2Cl_2$$

The reaction was economical because the byproduct disulfur dichloride, S_2Cl_2, could be used by industry in the manufacture of rubber products and other materials.

a. What is the percent yield of CCl_4 if 719 kg is produced from the reaction of 410. kg of CS_2?
b. If 67.5 g of Cl_2 are used in the reaction and 39.5 g of S_2Cl_2 is produced, what is the percent yield?
c. If the percent yield of the industrial process is 83.3%, how many kilograms of CS_2 should be reacted to obtain 5.00×10^4 kg of CCl_4? How many kilograms of S_2Cl_2 will be produced, assuming the same yield for that product?

225. Nitrogen dioxide, NO_2, can be converted to dinitrogen pentoxide, N_2O_5, by reacting it with ozone, O_3. The reaction of NO_2 takes place according to the following equation:

$$2NO_2(g) + O_3(g) \rightarrow N_2O_5(s \text{ or } g) + O_2(g)$$

a. Calculate the percent yield for a reaction in which 0.38 g of NO_2 reacts and 0.36 g of N_2O_5 is recovered.
b. What mass of N_2O_5 will result from the reaction of 6.0 mol of NO_2 if there is a 61.1% yield in the reaction?

---

226. In the past, hydrogen chloride, HCl, was made using the *salt-cake* method as shown in the following equation:

$$2NaCl(s) + H_2SO_4(aq) \rightarrow Na_2SO_4(s) + 2HCl(g)$$

If 30.0 g of NaCl and 0.250 mol of H_2SO_4 are available, and 14.6 g of HCl is made, what is the percent yield?

227. Cyanide compounds such as sodium cyanide, NaCN, are especially useful in gold refining because they will react with gold to form a stable compound that can then be separated and broken down to retrieve the gold. Ore containing only small quantities of gold can be used in this form of "chemical mining." The equation for the reaction follows:

$$4Au + 8NaCN + 2H_2O + O_2 \rightarrow \\ 4NaAu(CN)_2 + 4NaOH$$

a. What percent yield is obtained if 410 g of gold produces 540 g of $NaAu(CN)_2$?
b. Assuming a 79.6% yield in the conversion of gold to $NaAu(CN)_2$, what mass of gold would produce 1.00 kg of $NaAu(CN)_2$?
c. Given the conditions in (b), what mass of gold ore that is 0.001% gold would be needed to produce 1.00 kg of $NaAu(CN)_2$?

228. Diiodine pentoxide is useful in devices such as respirators because it reacts with the dangerous gas carbon monoxide, CO, to produce relatively harmless CO_2 according to the following equation:

$$I_2O_5 + 5CO \rightarrow I_2 + 5CO_2$$

a. In testing a respirator, 2.00 g of carbon monoxide gas is passed through diiodine pentoxide. Upon analyzing the results, it is found that 3.17 g of I_2 was produced. Calculate the percent yield of the reaction.
b. Assuming that the yield in (a) resulted because some of the CO did not react, calculate the mass of CO that passed through.

229. Sodium hypochlorite, NaClO, the main ingredient in household bleach, is produced by bubbling chlorine gas through a strong lye (sodium hydroxide, NaOH) solution. The following equation shows the reaction that occurs:

$$2NaOH(aq) + Cl_2(g) \rightarrow \\ NaCl(aq) + NaClO(aq) + H_2O(l)$$

a. What is the percent yield of the reaction if 1.2 kg of Cl_2 reacts to form 0.90 kg of NaClO?
b. If a plant operator wants to make 25 metric tons of NaClO per day at a yield of 91.8%, how many metric tons of chlorine gas must be on hand each day?
c. What mass of NaCl is formed per mole of chlorine gas at a yield of 81.8%?
d. At what rate in kg per hour must NaOH be replenished if the reaction produces 370 kg/h of NaClO at a yield of 79.5%? Assume that all of the NaOH reacts to produce this yield.

230. Magnesium burns in oxygen to form magnesium oxide. However, when magnesium burns in air, which is only about one-fifth oxygen, side reactions form other products, such as magnesium nitride, Mg_3N_2.

934

a. Write a balanced equation for the burning of magnesium in oxygen.

b. If enough magnesium burns in air to produce 2.04 g of magnesium oxide but only 1.79 g is obtained, what is the percent yield?

c. Magnesium will react with pure nitrogen to form the nitride, Mg_3N_2. Write a balanced equation for this reaction.

d. If 0.097 mol of Mg react with nitrogen and 0.027 mol of Mg_3N_2 is produced, what is the percent yield of the reaction?

231. Some alcohols can be converted to organic acids by using sodium dichromate and sulfuric acid. The following equation shows the reaction of 1-propanol to propanoic acid:

$3CH_3CH_2CH_2OH + 2Na_2Cr_2O_7 + 8H_2SO_4 \rightarrow$
$3CH_3CH_2COOH + 2Cr_2(SO_4)_3 + 2Na_2SO_4 + 11H_2O$

a. If 0.89 g of 1-propanol reacts and 0.88 g of propanoic acid is produced, what is the percent yield?

b. A chemist uses this reaction to obtain 1.50 mol of propanoic acid. The reaction consumes 136 g of propanol. Calculate the percent yield.

c. Some 1-propanol of uncertain purity is used in the reaction. If 116 g of $Na_2Cr_2O_7$ are consumed in the reaction and 28.1 g of propanoic acid are produced, what is the percent yield?

232. Acrylonitrile, $C_3H_3N(g)$, is an important ingredient in the production of various fibers and plastics. Acrylonitrile is produced from the following reaction:

$C_3H_6(g) + NH_3(g) + O_2(g) \rightarrow C_3H_3N(g) + H_2O(g)$

If 850. g of C_3H_6 is mixed with 300. g of NH_3 and unlimited O_2, to produce 850. g of acrylonitrile, what is the percent yield? You must first balance the equation.

233. Methanol, CH_3OH, is frequently used in race cars as fuel. It is produced as the sole product of the combination of carbon monoxide gas and hydrogen gas.

a. If 430. kg of hydrogen react, what mass of methanol could be produced?

b. If 3.12×10^3 kg of methanol are actually produced, what is the percent yield?

234. The compound, $C_6H_{16}N_2$, is one of the starting materials in the production of nylon. It can be prepared from the following reaction involving adipic acid, $C_6H_{10}O_4$:

$C_6H_{10}O_4(l) + 2NH_3(g) + 4H_2(g) \rightarrow$
$C_6H_{16}N_2(l) + 4H_2O$

What is the percent yield if 750. g of adipic acid results in the production of 578 g of $C_6H_{16}N_2$?

235. Plants convert carbon dioxide to oxygen during photosynthesis according to the following equation:

$CO_2 + H_2O \rightarrow C_6H_{12}O_6 + O_2$

Balance this equation, and calculate how much oxygen would be produced if 1.37×10^4 g of carbon dioxide reacts with a percent yield of 63.4%.

236. Lime, CaO, is frequently added to streams and lakes which have been polluted by acid rain. The calcium

oxide reacts with the water to form a base that can neutralize the acid as shown in the following reaction:

$$CaO(s) + H_2O(l) \rightarrow Ca(OH)_2(s)$$

If 2.67×10^2 mol of base are needed to neutralize the acid in a lake, and the above reaction has a percent yield of 54.3%, what is the mass, in kilograms, of lime that must be added to the lake?

Gas Laws, Section 10-3

Boyle's Law

In each of the following problems, assume that the temperature and molar quantity of gas do not change.

237. Calculate the unknown quantity in each of the following measurements of gases.

P_1	V_1	P_2	V_2
a. 3.0 atm	25 mL	6.0 atm	? mL
b. 99.97 kPa	550. mL	? kPa	275 mL
c. 0.89 atm	? L	3.56 atm	20.0 L
d. ? kPa	800. mL	500. kPa	160. mL
e. 0.040 atm	? L	250 atm	1.0×10^{-2} L

238. A sample of neon gas occupies a volume of 2.8 L at 1.8 atm. What will its volume be at 1.2 atm?

239. To what pressure would you have to compress 48.0 L of oxygen gas at 99.3 kPa in order to reduce its volume to 16.0 L?

240. A chemist collects 59.0 mL of sulfur dioxide gas on a day when the atmospheric pressure is 0.989 atm. On the next day, the pressure has changed to 0.967 atm. What will the volume of the SO_2 gas be on the second day?

241. 2.2 L of hydrogen at 6.5 atm pressure is used to fill a balloon at a final pressure of 1.15 atm. What is its final volume?

Charles's Law

In each of the following problems, assume that the pressure and molar quantity of gas do not change.

242. Calculate the unknown quantity in each of the following measurements of gases:

V_1	T_1	V_2	T_2
a. 40.0 mL	280. K	? mL	350. K
b. 0.606 L	300. K	0.404 L	? K
c. ? mL	292 K	250. mL	365 K
d. 100. mL	? K	125 mL	305 K
e. 0.0024 L	22°C	? L	−14°C

207. a. 38 g Br_2
b. 510 g I_2

208. a. Ni is in excess
b. 60.2 g $Ni(NO_3)_2$

209. $CS_2(g) + 3O_2(g) \rightarrow 2SO_4(g) + CO_2(g)$
0.80 mol O_2 remain

210. a. 0.84 g $Hg(NH_2)Cl$
b. 0.84 g

211. a. $2Al(s) + 2NaOH(aq) + 2H_2O(l) \rightarrow 2NaAlO_2(aq) + 3H_2(g)$
b. NaOH is limiting; 0.56 mol H_2
c. Al should be limiting because you would not want aluminum metal remaining in the drain.

212. a. 0.0422 mol Cu; 0.169 mol HNO_3
b. Cu is in excess
c. 3.32 g H_2O

213. a. 2.90 mol NO; 4.35 mol H_2O
b. NH_3 is limiting
c. NH_3 is limiting; 1.53×10^3 kg NO

214. 565 g CH_3CHO; 29 g CH_3CH_2OH remains

215. 630 g HBr

216. 11.3 g SO_2

217. a. 18.4 g Tb
b. 2.4 g TbF_3

218. a. 83.8% yield
b. 93% yield
c. 69.1% yield
d. 46% yield

219. a. 79.3% yield
b. 76% yield

220. a. 64.3% yield
b. 58.0% yield
c. 69.5% yield
d. CH_3CH_2OH is limiting; 79% yield

221. a. 69.5% yield
b. 79.0% yield

c. 48% yield
d. 85% yield

222. a. 59% yield
b. 81.0% yield
c. 2.3×10^5 mol P

223. a. 91.8% yield
b. 0.0148 mol W
c. 16.1 g WO_3

224. a. 86.8% yield
b. 92.2% yield
c. 2.97×10^4 kg CS_2;
4.39×10^4 kg S_2Cl_2

225. a. 81% yield
b. 2.0×10^2 g N_2O_5

226. 80.1% yield

227. a. 95% yield
b. 9.10×10^2 g Au
c. 9×10^4 kg ore

228. a. 87.5% yield
b. 0.25 g CO

229. a. 71% yield
b. 26 metric tons
c. 47.8 g NaCl
d. 500 kg per hour NaOH

230. a. $2Mg + O_2 \rightarrow 2MgO$
b. 87.7% yield
c. $3Mg + N_2 \rightarrow Mg_3N_2$
d. 56% yield

231. a. 80.% yield
b. 66.2% yield
c. 57.1% yield

232. $2C_3H_6(g) + 2NH_3(g) + 3O_2(g) \rightarrow 2C_3H_3N(g) + 6H_2O(g)$
91.0% yield

233. a. $CO + 2H_2 \rightarrow CH_3OH$
3.41×10^3 kg
b. 91.5% yield

234. 96.9% yield

235. $6CO_2 + 6H_2O \rightarrow C_6H_{12}O_6 + 6O_2$
6.32×10^3 g O_2

236. 27.6 kg CaO

237. a. 13 mL
b. 200. kPa
c. 80. L

243. A balloon full of air has a volume of 2.75 L at a temperature of 18°C. What is the balloon's volume at 45°C?

244. A sample of argon has a volume of 0.43 mL at 24°C. At what temperature in degrees Celsius will it have a volume of 0.57 mL?

Gay-Lussac's Law

In each of the following problems, assume that the volume and molar quantity of gas do not change.

245. Calculate the unknown quantity in each of the following measurements of gases.

	P_1	T_1	P_2	T_2
a.	1.50 atm	273 K	? atm	410 K
b.	0.208 atm	300. K	0.156 atm	? K
c.	? kPa	52°C	99.7 kPa	77°C
d.	5.20 atm	?°C	4.16 atm	−13°C
e.	8.33×10^{-4} atm	−84°C	3.92×10^{-3} atm	? °C

246. A cylinder of compressed gas has a pressure of 4.882 atm on one day. The next day, the same cylinder of gas has a pressure of 4.690 atm, and its temperature is 8°C. What was the temperature on the previous day in °C?

247. A mylar balloon is filled with helium gas to a pressure of 107 kPa when the temperature is 22°C. If the temperature changes to 45°C, what will be the pressure of the helium in the balloon?

The Combined Gas Law

In each of the following problems, it is assumed that the molar quantity of gas does not change.

248. Calculate the unknown quantity in each of the following measurements of gases.

	P_1	V_1	T_1	P_2	V_2	T_2
a.	99.3 kPa	225 mL	15°C	102.8 kPa	? mL	24°C
b.	0.959 atm	3.50 L	45°C	? atm	3.70 L	37°C
c.	0.0036 atm	62 mL	373 K	0.0029 atm	64 mL	? K
d.	100. kPa	43.2 mL	19°C	101.3 kPa	? mL	0°C

249. A student collects 450. mL of HCl(g) hydrogen chloride gas at a pressure of 100. kPa and a temperature of 17°C. What is the volume of the HCl at 0°C and 101.3 kPa?

Dalton's Law of Partial Pressures

250. A chemist collects a sample of $H_2S(g)$ over water at a temperature of 27°C. The total pressure of the gas that

has displaced a volume of 15 mL of water is 207.33 kPa. What is the pressure of the H_2S gas collected?

In each of the following problems, assume that the molar quantity of gas does not change.

251. Some hydrogen is collected over water at 10°C and 105.5 kPa pressure. The total volume of the sample was 1.93 L. Calculate the volume of the hydrogen corrected to STP.

252. One student carries out a reaction that gives off methane gas and obtains a total volume by water displacement of 338 mL at a temperature of 19°C and a pressure of 0.9566 atm. Another student does the identical experiment on another day at a temperature of 26°C and a pressure of 0.989 atm. Which student collected more CH_4?

Mixed Review

In each of the following problems, assume that the molar quantity of gas does not change.

253. Calculate the unknown quantity in each of the following measurements of gases.

	P_1	V_1	P_2	V_2
a.	127.3 kPa	796 cm³	? kPa	965 cm³
b.	7.1×10^2 atm	? mL	9.6×10^{-1} atm	3.7×10^3 mL
c.	? kPa	1.77 L	30.79 kPa	2.44 L
d.	114 kPa	2.93 dm³	4.93×10^4 kPa	? dm³
e.	1.00 atm	120. mL	? atm	97.0 mL
f.	0.77 atm	3.6 m³	1.90 atm	? m³

254. A gas cylinder contains 0.722 m³ of hydrogen gas at a pressure of 10.6 atm. If the gas is used to fill a balloon at a pressure of 0.96 atm, what is the volume in m³ of the filled balloon?

255. A weather balloon has a maximum volume of 7.50×10^3 L. The balloon contains 195 L of helium gas at a pressure of 0.993 atm. What will be the pressure when the balloon is at maximum volume?

256. A rubber ball contains 5.70×10^{-1} dm³ of gas at a pressure of 1.05 atm. What volume will the gas occupy at 7.47 atm?

257. Calculate the unknown quantity in each of the following measurements of gases.

	V_1	T_1	V_2	T_2
a.	26.5 mL	? K	32.9 mL	290. K
b.	? dm³	100.°C	0.83 dm³	29°C
c.	7.44×10^4 mm³	870.°C	2.59×10^2 mm³	? °C
d.	5.63×10^{-2} L	132 K	? L	190. K
e.	? cm³	243 K	819 cm³	409 K
f.	679 m³	−3°C	? m³	−246°C

258. A bubble of carbon dioxide gas in some unbaked bread dough has a volume of 1.15 cm^3 at a temperature of 22°C. What volume will the bubble have when the bread is baked and the bubble reaches a temperature of 99°C?

259. A perfectly elastic balloon contains 6.75 dm^3 of air at a temperature of 40.°C. What is the temperature if the balloon has a volume of 5.03 dm^3?

260. Calculate the unknown quantity in each of the following measurements of gases.

	P_1	T_1	P_2	T_2
a.	0.777 atm	?°C	5.6 atm	192°C
b.	152 kPa	302 K	? kPa	11 K
c.	? atm	−76°C	3.97 atm	27°C
d.	395 atm	46°C	706 atm	?°C
e.	? atm	−37°C	350. atm	2050°C
f.	0.39 atm	263 K	0.058 atm	? K

261. A 2 L bottle containing only air is sealed at a temperature of 22°C and a pressure of 0.982 atm. The bottle is placed in a freezer and allowed to cool to −3°C. What is the pressure in the bottle?

262. The pressure in a car tire is 2.50 atm at a temperature of 33°C . What would the pressure be if the tire were allowed to cool to 0°C? Assume that the tire does not change volume.

263. A container filled with helium gas has a pressure of 127.5 kPa at a temperature of 290. K. What is the temperature when the pressure is 3.51 kPa?

264. Calculate the unknown quantity in each of the following measurements of gases.

	P_1	V_1	T_1	P_2	V_2	T_2
a.	1.03 atm	1.65 L	19°C	0.920 atm	? L	46°C
b.	107.0 kPa	3.79 dm^3	73°C	? kPa	7.58 dm^3	217°C
c.	0.029 atm	249 mL	? K	0.098 atm	197 mL	293 K
d.	113 kPa	? mm^3	12°C	149 kPa	3.18 × 10^3 mm^3	−18°C
e.	1.15 atm	0.93 m^3	−22°C	1.01 atm	0.85 m^3	?°C
f.	? atm	156 cm^3	195 K	2.25 atm	468 cm^3	

265. A scientist has a sample of gas that was collected several days earlier. The sample has a volume of 392 cm^3 at a pressure of 0.987 atm and a temperature of 21°C. On the day the gas was collected, the temperature was 13°C and the pressure was 0.992 atm. What volume did the gas have on the day it was collected?

266. Hydrogen gas is collected by water displacement. Total volume collected is 0.461 L at a temperature of 17°C and a pressure of 0.989 atm. What is the pressure of dry hydrogen gas collected?

267. One container with a volume of 1.00 L contains argon at a pressure of 1.77 atm, and a second container of 1.50 L volume contains argon at a pressure of 0.487 atm. They are then connected to each other so that the pressure can become equal in both containers. What is the equalized pressure? Hint: Each sample of gas now occupies the total space. Dalton's law of partial pressures applies here.

268. Oxygen gas is collected over water at a temperature of 10.°C and a pressure of 1.02 atm. The volume of gas plus water vapor collected is 293 mL. What volume of oxygen at STP was collected?

269. A 500 mL bottle is partially filled with water so that the total volume of gases (water vapor and air) remaining in the bottle is 325 cm^3, measured at 20.°C and 101.3 kPa. The bottle is sealed and taken to a mountaintop where the pressure is 76.24 kPa and the temperature is 10.°C. If the bottle is upside down and the seal leaks, how much water will leak out? The key to this problem is to determine the pressure in the 325 cm^3 space when the bottle is at the top of the mountain.

270. An air thermometer can be constructed by using a glass bubble attached to a piece of small-diameter glass tubing. The tubing contains a small amount of colored water that rises when the temperature increases and the trapped air expands. You want a 0.20 cm^3 change in volume to equal a 1°C change in temperature. What total volume of air at 20.°C should be trapped in the apparatus below the liquid?

271. A sample of nitrogen gas is collected over water, yielding a total volume of 62.25 mL at a temperature of 22°C and a total pressure of 97.7 kPa. At what pressure will the nitrogen alone occupy a volume of 50.00 mL at the same temperature?

272. The theoretical yield of a reaction that gives off nitrogen trifluoride gas is 844 mL at STP. What total volume of NF_3 plus water vapor will be collected over water at 25°C and a total pressure of 1.017 atm?

273. A weather balloon is inflated with 2.94 kL of helium at a location where the pressure is 1.06 atm and the temperature is 32°C. What will be the volume of the balloon at an altitude where the pressure is 0.092 atm and the temperature is −35°C?

274. The safety limit for a certain can of aerosol spray is 95°C. If the pressure of the gas in the can is 2.96 atm when it is 17°C, what will the pressure be at the safety limit?

275. A chemistry student collects a sample of ammonia gas at a temperature of 39°C. Later, the student measures the volume of the ammonia as 108 mL, but its temperature is now 21°C. What was the volume of the ammonia when it was collected?

276. A quantity of CO_2 gas occupies a volume of 624 L at a pressure of 1.40 atm. If this CO_2 is pumped into a gas

d. 100. kPa
e. 63 L

238. 4.2 L

239. 298 kPa

240. 60.3 mL

241. 12 L

242.
  a. 50.0 mL
  b. 200. K
  c. 200. mL
  d. 244 K
  e. 0.0021 L

243. 3.01 L

244. 121°C

245.
  a. 2.25 atm
  b. 225 K
  c. 92.6 kPa
  d. 52°C
  e. 616°C

246. 20.°C

247. 115 kPa

248.
  a. 224 mL
  b. 0.884 atm
  c. 310 K
  d. 39.9 mL

249. 418 mL

250. 203.76 kPa

251. 1.92 L

252. The second student collected more CH_4.

253.
  a. 105 kPa
  b. 5.0 mL
  c. 42.4 kPa
  d. 6.78 × 10^{-3} dm^3
  e. 1.24 atm
  f. 1.5 m^3

254. 8.0 m^3

255. 0.0258 atm

256. 8.01 × 10^{-2} dm^3

257.
  a. 234 K
  b. 1.2 dm^3
  c. −269.17°C
  d. 8.10 × 10^{-2} L
  e. 487 cm^3
  f. 67.9 m^3

258. 1.45 cm³

259. −40.°C

260. a. −208.6°C
b. 5.5 kPa
c. 2.61 atm
d. 297°C
e. 35.6 atm
f. 39 K

261. 0.899 atm

262. 2.23 atm

263. 7.98 K

264. a. 2.02 L
b. 75.8 kPa
c. 110 K
d. 4.69 × 10³ mm³
e. −72°C
f. 2.25 atm

265. 379 cm³

266. 98 kPa

267. 1.00 atm; use Boyle's law to find the pressure of each gas in the whole space; add the partial pressures of both gases when they occupy the whole space.

268. 285 mL

269. 89 cm³ The pressure in the bottle on top of the mountain is the sum of $P_{O_2 \text{ dry}}$ at the temperature of the mountaintop and $P_{H_2O \text{ vapor}}$ at the temperature on top of the mountain.

270. 59 cm³
Solve the equation:
$V_{total}/293 \text{ K} =$
$(V_{total} + 0.20 \text{ cm}^3)/294 \text{ K}$

271. 118 kPa

272. 935 mL

273. 26.4 kL

274. 3.76 atm

275. 115 mL

276. 10.9 atm

277. a. 2.00 L
b. 1.22 × 10⁻³ mol
c. 109 kPa

---

cylinder that has a volume of 80.0 L, what pressure will the CO_2 exert on the cylinder?

The Ideal Gas Law, Section 11-2

277. Use the ideal-gas-law equation to calculate the unknown quantity in each of the following sets of measurements. You will need to convert Celsius temperatures to Kelvin temperatures and volume units to liters.

P	V	n	T
a. 1.09 atm	? L	0.0881 mol	302 K
b. 94.9 kPa	0.0350 L	? mol	55°C
c. ? kPa	15.7 L	0.815 mol	−20.°C
d. 0.500 atm	629 mL	0.0337 mol	? K
e. 0.950 atm	? L	0.0818 mol	19°C
f. 107 kPa	39.0 mL	? mol	27°C

278. A student collects 425 mL of oxygen at a temperature of 24°C and a pressure of 0.899 atm. How many moles of oxygen did the student collect?

Applications of the Ideal Gas Law

279. A sample of an unknown gas has a mass of 0.116 g. It occupies a volume of 25.0 mL at a temperature of 127°C and has a pressure of 155.3 kPa. Calculate the molar mass of the gas.

280. Determine the mass of CO_2 gas that has a volume of 7.10 L at a pressure of 1.11 atm and a temperature of 31°C. Hint: Solve the equation for m, and calculate the molar mass using the chemical formula and the periodic table.

281. What is the density of silicon tetrafluoride gas at 72°C and a pressure of 144.5 kPa?

282. At what temperature will nitrogen gas have a density of 1.13 g/L at a pressure of 1.09 atm?

Mixed Review

283. Use the ideal-gas-law equation to calculate the unknown quantity in each of the following sets of measurements.

P	V	n	t
a. 0.0477 atm	15 200 L	? mol	−15°C
b. ? kPa	0.119 mL	0.000 350 mol	0°C
c. 500.0 kPa	250. mL	0.120 mol	?°C
d. 19.5 atm	?	4.7 × 10⁴ mol	300.°C

---

284. Use the ideal-gas-law equation to calculate the unknown quantity in each of the following sets of measurements.

P	V	m	M	t
a. 0.955 atm	3.77 L	8.23 g	? g/mol	25°C
b. 105.0 kPa	50.0 mL	? g	48.02 g/mol	0°C
c. 0.782 atm	? L	3.20 × 10⁻³ g	2.02 g/mol	−5°C
d. ? atm	2.00 L	7.19 g	159.8 g/mol	185°C
e. 107.2 kPa	26.1 mL	0.414 g	? g/mol	45°C

285. Determine the volume of one mole of an ideal gas at 25°C and 0.915 kPa.

286. Calculate the unknown quantity in each of the following sets of measurements.

P	Molar Mass	Density	t
a. 1.12 atm	? g/mol	2.40 g/L	2°C
b. 7.50 atm	30.07 g/mol	? g/L	20.°C
c. 97.4 kPa	104.09 g/mol	4.37 g/L	? °C
d. ? atm	77.95 g/mol	6.27 g/L	66°C

287. What pressure in atmospheres will 1.36 kg of N_2O gas exert when it is compressed in a 25.0 L cylinder and is stored in an outdoor shed where the temperature can reach 59°C during the summer?

288. Aluminum chloride sublimes at high temperatures. What density will the vapor have at 225°C and 0.939 atm pressure?

289. An unknown gas has a density of 0.0262 g/mL at a pressure of 0.918 atm and a temperature of 10.°C. What is the molar mass of the gas?

290. A large balloon contains 11.7 g of helium. What volume will the helium occupy at an altitude of 10 000 m, where the atmospheric pressure is 0.262 atm and the temperature is −50.°C?

291. A student collects ethane by water displacement at a temperature of 15°C (vapor pressure of water is 1.5988 kPa) and a total pressure of 100.0 kPa. The volume of the collection bottle is 245 mL. How many moles of ethane are in the bottle?

292. A reaction yields 3.75 L of nitrogen monoxide. The volume is measured at 19°C and at a pressure of 1.10 atm. What mass of NO was produced by the reaction?

293. A reaction has a theoretical yield of 8.83 g of ammonia. The reaction gives off 10.24 L of ammonia measured at 52°C and 105.3 kPa. What was the percent yield of the reaction?

294. An unknown gas has a density of 0.405 g/L at a pressure of 0.889 atm and a temperature of 7°C. Calculate its molar mass.

295. A paper label has been lost from an old tank of compressed gas. To help identify the unknown gas, you must calculate its molar mass. It is known that the tank has a capacity of 90.0 L and weighs 39.2 kg when empty. You find its current mass to be 50.5 kg. The gauge shows a pressure of 1780 kPa when the temperature is 18°C. What is the molar mass of the gas in the cylinder?

296. What is the pressure inside a tank that has a volume of 1.20×10^3 L and contains 12.0 kg of HCl gas at a temperature of 18°C?

297. What pressure in kPa is exerted at a temperature of 20.°C by compressed neon gas that has a density of 2.70 g/L?

298. A tank with a volume of 658 mL contains 1.50 g of neon gas. The maximum safe pressure that the tank can withstand is 4.50×10^2 kPa. At what temperature will the tank have that pressure?

299. The atmospheric pressure on Mars is about 6.75 millibars (1 bar = 100 kPa = 0.9869 atm), and the nighttime temperature can be about −75°C on the same day that the daytime temperature goes up to −8°C. What volume would a bag containing 1.00 g of H_2 gas have at both the daytime and nighttime temperatures?

300. What is the pressure in kPa of 3.95 mol of Cl_2 gas if it is compressed in a cylinder with a volume of 850. mL at a temperature of 15°C?

301. What volume in mL will 0.00660 mol of hydrogen gas occupy at a pressure of 0.907 atm and a temperature of 9°C?

302. What volume will 8.47 kg of sulfur dioxide gas occupy at a pressure of 89.4 kPa and a temperature of 40.°C?

303. A cylinder contains 908 g of compressed helium. It is to be used to inflate a balloon to a final pressure of 128.3 kPa at a temperature of 2°C. What will the volume of the balloon be under these conditions?

304. The density of dry air at 27°C and 100.0 kPa is 1.162 g/L. Use this information to calculate the molar mass of air (calculate as if air were a pure substance).

Stoichiometry of Gases, Section 11-3

305. In one method of manufacturing nitric acid, ammonia is oxidized to nitrogen monoxide and water:

$$4NH_3(g) + 5O_2(g) \rightarrow 4NO(g) + 6H_2O(l)$$

What volume of oxygen will be used in a reaction of 2800 L of NH_3? What volume of NO will be produced? All volumes are measured under the same conditions.

306. Fluorine gas reacts violently with water to produce hydrogen fluoride and ozone according to the following equation:

$$3F_2(g) + 3H_2O(l) \rightarrow 6HF(g) + O_3(g)$$

What volumes of O_3 and HF gas would be produced by the complete reaction of 3.60×10^4 mL of fluorine gas? All gases are measured under the same conditions.

307. A sample of ethanol burns in O_2 to form CO_2 and H_2O according to the following equation:

$$C_2H_5OH + 3O_2 \rightarrow 2CO_2 + 3H_2O$$

If the combustion uses 55.8 mL of oxygen measured at 2.26 atm and 40.°C, what volume of CO_2 is produced when measured at STP?

308. Dinitrogen pentoxide decomposes into nitrogen dioxide and oxygen. If 5.00 L of N_2O_5 reacts at STP, what volume of NO_2 is produced when measured at 64.5°C and 1.76 atm?

309. Complete the table below using the following equation, which represents a reaction that produces aluminum chloride:

$$2Al(s) + 3Cl_2(g) \rightarrow 2AlCl_3(s)$$

	Mass Al	Volume Cl_2	Conditions	Mass $AlCl_3$
a.	excess	? L	STP	7.15 g
b.	19.4 g	? L	STP	NA
c.	1.559 kg	? L	20.°C and 0.945 atm	NA
d.	excess	920. L	STP	? g
e.	? g	1.049 mL	37°C and 5.00 atm	NA
f.	500.00 kg	? m^3	15°C and 83.0 kPa	NA

Mixed Review

310. The industrial production of ammonia proceeds according to the following equation:

$$N_2(g) + 3H_2(g) \rightarrow 2NH_3(g)$$

  a. What volume of nitrogen at STP is needed to react with 57.0 mL of hydrogen measured at STP?

  b. What volume of NH_3 at STP can be produced from the complete reaction of 6.39×10^4 L of hydrogen?

  c. If 20.0 mol of nitrogen is available, what volume of NH_3 at STP can be produced?

  d. What volume of H_2 at STP will be needed to produce 800. L of ammonia, measured at 55°C and 0.900 atm?

311. Propane burns according to the following equation:

$$C_3H_8(g) + 5O_2(g) \rightarrow 3CO_2(g) + 4H_2O(g)$$

  a. What volume of water vapor measured at 250.°C and 1.00 atm is produced when 3.0 L of propane at STP is burned?

  b. What volume of oxygen at 20.°C and 102.6 kPa is used if 640. L of CO_2 is produced? The CO_2 is also measured at 20.°C and 102.6 kPa.

  c. If 465 mL of oxygen at STP is used in the reaction, what volume of CO_2, measured at 37°C and 0.973 atm, is produced?

  d. When 2.50 L of C_3H_8 at STP burns, what total volume of gaseous products is formed? The volume of the products is measured at 175°C and 1.14 atm.

d. 114 K
e. 2.06 L
f. 1.67×10^{-3} mol

278. 1.57×10^{-2} mol O_2

279. 99.4 g/mol

280. 13.9 g

281. 5.24 g/L

282. 329 K or 56°C

283. **a.** 34.2 mol
b. 6.68×10^3 kPa
c. −148°C
d. 1.1×10^5 L

284. **a.** 55.9 g/mol   **b.** 0.111 g
c. 4.46×10^{-2} L
d. 0.846 atm
e. 391 g/mol

285. 2.71×10^3 L

286. **a.** 48.4 g/mol
b. 9.38 g/L
c. 6°C
d. 2.24 atm or 227 kPa

287. 33.7 atm

288. 3.06 g/L

289. 663 g/mol

290. 204 L

291. 0.0101 mol ethane

292. 5.16 g NO

293. 77.0% yield

294. 10.5 g/mol

295. 171 g/mol

296. 6.55 atm

297. 326 kPa

298. 479 K or 206°C

299. 1210 L at −75°C; 1620 L at −8°C

300. 1.11×10^4 kPa

301. 168 mL

302. 3.85×10^3 L

303. 4.05×10^3 L

304. 29.0 g/mol

305. 3500 L O_2
2800 L NO

306. 1.20×10^4 mL O_3
7.20×10^4 mL HF

307. 73.3 mL CO_2

308. 7.02 atm

309. a. 1.80 L Cl_2
b. 24.2 L Cl_2
c. 2.21×10^3 L Cl_2
d. 3.65×10^3 g $AlCl_3$
e. 3.71×10^{-3} g Al
f. 8.02×10^2 m^3 Cl_2

310. a. 19.0 mL N_2
b. 4.26×10^4 L NH_3
c. 896 L NH_3
d. 899 L H_2

311. a. 23 L H_2O
b. 1070 L O_2
c. 326 mL CO_2
d. 25.2 L total products

312. 1550 L O_2 at STP

313. 0.894 L SiF_4

314. a. 3.36 L H_2
b. 488 g Fe
c. 112 L H_2

315. 0.013 L H_2 or 13 mL H_2

316. 7.50 L O_2 at STP;
4.14 g diethyl ether

317. a. 3.36 L N_2; 6.72 L CO_2;
5.60 L H_2O; 0.560 L O_2
b. 15.0 L total volume all gases

318. 0.894 g NH_4NO_3

319. 2.19 L PH_3

320. 1.2×10^3 kg Al;
7.4×10^5 L HCl

321. 7.08×10^7 L NH_3

322. 3.77 g BaO_2

323. 5.85 L Cl_2

324. 28.0 kL NH_3; 28.0 kL NO_2; overall reaction is: $4NH_3 + 7O_2 \rightarrow 4NO_2 + 6H_2O$

325. 18.2 g $KClO_3$

326. a. 38 000 L NH_3
b. 1.30×10^5 g $NaHCO_3$
c. 12.3 L NH_3
d. 5.60×10^3 L

312. Carbon monoxide will burn in air to produce CO_2 according to the following equation:
$$2CO(g) + O_2(g) \rightarrow 2CO_2(g)$$
What volume of oxygen at STP will be needed to react with 3500. L of CO measured at 20.°C and a pressure of 0.953 atm?

313. Silicon tetrafluoride gas can be produced by the action of HF on silica according to the following equation:
$$SiO_2(s) + 4HF(g) \rightarrow SiF_4(g) + 2H_2O(l)$$
1.00 L of HF gas under pressure at 3.48 atm and a temperature of 25°C reacts completely with SiO_2 to form SiF_4. What volume of SiF_4, measured at 15°C and 0.940 atm, is produced by this reaction?

314. One method used in the eighteenth century to generate hydrogen was to pass steam through red-hot steel tubes. The following reaction takes place:
$$3Fe(s) + 4H_2O(g) \rightarrow Fe_3O_4(s) + 4H_2(g)$$
a. What volume of hydrogen at STP can be produced by the reaction of 6.28 g of iron?
b. What mass of iron will react with 500. L of steam at 250.°C and 1.00 atm pressure?
c. If 285 g of Fe_3O_4 are formed, what volume of hydrogen, measured at 20.°C and 1.06 atm, is produced?

315. Sodium reacts vigorously with water to produce hydrogen and sodium hydroxide according to the following equation:
$$2Na(s) + 2H_2O(l) \rightarrow 2NaOH(aq) + H_2(g)$$
If 0.027 g of sodium reacts with excess water, what volume of hydrogen at STP is formed?

316. Diethyl ether burns in air according to the following equation:
$$C_4H_{10}O(l) + 6O_2(g) \rightarrow 4CO_2(g) + 5H_2O(l)$$
If 7.15 L of CO_2 is produced at a temperature of 125°C and a pressure of 1.02 atm, what volume of oxygen, measured at STP, was consumed and what mass of diethyl ether was burned?

317. When nitroglycerin detonates, it produces large volumes of hot gases almost instantly according to the following equation:
$$4C_3H_5N_3O_9(l) \rightarrow$$
$$6N_2(g) + 12CO_2(g) + 10H_2O(g) + O_2(g)$$
a. When 0.100 mol of nitroglycerin explodes, what volume of each gas measured at STP is produced?
b. What total volume of gases is produced at 300.°C and 1.00 atm when 10.0 g of nitroglycerin explodes?

318. Dinitrogen monoxide can be prepared by heating ammonium nitrate, which decomposes according to the following equation:
$$NH_4NO_3(s) \rightarrow N_2O(g) + 2H_2O(l)$$
What mass of ammonium nitrate should be decomposed in order to produce 250. mL of N_2O, measured at STP?

319. Phosphine, PH_3, is the phosphorus analogue to ammonia, NH_3. It can be produced by the reaction between

calcium phosphide and water according to the following equation:
$$Ca_3P_2(s) + 6H_2O(l) \rightarrow$$
$$3Ca(OH)_2(s \text{ and } aq) + 2PH_3(g)$$
What volume of phosphine, measured at 18°C and 102.4 kPa, is produced by the reaction of 8.46 g of Ca_3P_2?

320. In one method of producing aluminum chloride, HCl gas is passed over aluminum and the following reaction takes place:
$$2Al(s) + 6HCl(g) \rightarrow 2AlCl_3(g) + 3H_2(g)$$
What mass of Al should be on hand in order to produce 6.0×10^3 kg of $AlCl_3$? What volume of compressed HCl at 4.71 atm and a temperature of 43°C should be on hand at the same time?

321. Urea, $(NH_2)_2CO$, is an important fertilizer that is manufactured by the following reaction:
$$2NH_3(g) + CO_2(g) \rightarrow (NH_2)_2CO(s) + H_2O(g)$$
What volume of NH_3 at STP will be needed to produce 8.50×10^4 kg of urea if there is an 89.5% yield in the process?

322. An obsolete method of generating oxygen in the laboratory involves the decomposition of barium peroxide by the following equation:
$$2BaO_2(s) \rightarrow 2BaO(s) + O_2(g)$$
What mass of BaO_2 reacted if 265 mL of O_2 is collected by water displacement at 0.975 atm and 10.°C?

323. It is possible to generate chlorine gas by dripping concentrated HCl solution onto solid potassium permanganate according to the following equation:
$$2KMnO_4(aq) + 16HCl(aq) \rightarrow$$
$$2KCl(aq) + 2MnCl_2(aq) + 8H_2O(l) + 5Cl_2(g)$$
If excess HCl is dripped onto 15.0 g of $KMnO_4$, what volume of Cl_2 will be produced? The Cl_2 is measured at 15°C and 0.959 atm.

324. Ammonia can be oxidized in the presence of a platinum catalyst according to the following equation:
$$4NH_3(g) + 5O_2(g) \rightarrow 4NO(g) + 6H_2O(l)$$
The NO that is produced reacts almost immediately with additional oxygen according to the following equation:
$$2NO(g) + O_2(g) \rightarrow 2NO_2(g)$$
If 35.0 kL of oxygen at STP react in the first reaction, what volume of NH_3 at STP reacts with it? What volume of NO_2 at STP will be formed in the second reaction, assuming there is excess oxygen that was not used up in the first reaction?

325. Oxygen can be generated in the laboratory by heating potassium chlorate. The reaction is represented by the following equation:
$$2KClO_3(s) \rightarrow 2KCl(s) + 3O_2(g)$$
What mass of $KClO_3$ must be used in order to generate 5.00 L of O_2, measured at STP?

326. One of the reactions in the Solvay process is used to make sodium hydrogen carbonate. It occurs when carbon dioxide and ammonia are passed through concentrated salt brine. The following equation represents the reaction:

$$NaCl(aq) + H_2O(l) + CO_2(g) + NH_3(g) \rightarrow NaHCO_3(s) + NH_4Cl(aq)$$

a. What volume of NH_3 at 25°C and 1.00 atm pressure will be required if 38 000 L of CO_2, measured under the same conditions, react to form $NaHCO_3$?

b. What mass of $NaHCO_3$ can be formed when the gases in (a) react with NaCl?

c. If this reaction forms 46.0 kg of $NaHCO_3$, what volume of NH_3, measured at STP, reacted?

d. What volume of CO_2, compressed in a tank at 5.50 atm and a temperature of 42°C, will be needed to produce 100.00 kg of $NaHCO_3$?

327. The combustion of butane is represented in the following equation:

$$2C_4H_{10}(g) + 13O_2(g) \rightarrow 8CO_2(g) + 10H_2O(l)$$

a. If 4.74 g of butane react with excess oxygen, what volume of CO_2, measured at 150.°C and 1.14 atm, will be formed?

b. What volume of oxygen, measured at 0.980 atm and 75°C, will be consumed by the complete combustion of 0.500 g of butane?

c. A butane-fueled torch has a mass of 876.2 g. After burning for some time, the torch has a mass of 859.3 g. What volume of CO_2, at STP, was formed while the torch burned?

d. What mass of H_2O is produced when butane burns and produces 3720 L of CO_2, measured at 35°C and 0.993 atm pressure?

Concentration of Solutions, Section 13-3

Percentage Concentration

328. What is the percentage concentration of 75.0 g of ethanol dissolved in 500.0 g of water?

329. A chemist dissolves 3.50 g of potassium iodate and 6.23 g of potassium hydroxide in 805.05 g of water. What is the percentage concentration of each solute in the solution?

330. A student wants to make a 5.00% solution of rubidium chloride using 0.377 g of the substance. What mass of water will be needed to make the solution?

331. What mass of lithium nitrate would have to be dissolved in 30.0 g of water in order to make an 18.0% solution?

Molarity

332. Determine the molarity of a solution prepared by dissolving 141.6 g of citric acid, $C_3H_5O(COOH)_3$, in water and then diluting the resulting solution to 3500.0 mL.

333. What is the molarity of a salt solution made by dissolving 280.0 mg of NaCl in 2.00 mL of water? Assume the final volume is the same as the volume of the water.

334. What is the molarity of a solution that contains 390.0 g of acetic acid, CH_3COOH, dissolved in enough acetone to make 1000.0 mL of solution?

335. What mass of glucose, $C_6H_{12}O_6$, would be required to prepare 5.000×10^3 L of a 0.215 M solution?

336. What mass of magnesium bromide would be required to prepare 720. mL of a 0.0939 M aqueous solution?

337. What mass of ammonium chloride is dissolved in 300. mL of a 0.875 M solution?

Molality

338. Determine the molality of a solution of 560 g of acetone, CH_3COCH_3, in 620 g of water.

339. What is the molality of a solution of 12.9 g of fructose, $C_6H_{12}O_6$, in 31.0 g of water?

340. How many moles of 2-butanol, $CH_3CHOHCH_2CH_3$, must be dissolved in 125 g of ethanol in order to produce a 12.0 m 2-butanol solution? What mass of 2-butanol is this?

Mixed Review

341. Complete the table below by determining the missing quantity in each example. All solutions are aqueous. Any quantity that is not applicable to a given solution is marked NA.

Solution Made	Mass of Solute Used	Quantity of Solution Made	Quantity of Solvent Used
a. 12.0% KMnO₄	? g KMnO₄	500.0 g	? g H₂O
b. 0.60 M BaCl₂	? g BaCl₂	1.750 L	NA
c. 6.20 m glycerol, HOCH₂CHOHCH₂OH	? g glycerol	NA	800.0 g H₂O
d. ? M K₂Cr₂O₇	12.27 g K₂Cr₂O₇	650. mL	NA
e. ? m CaCl₂	288 g CaCl₂	NA	2.04 kg H₂O
f. 0.160 M NaCl	? g NaCl	25.0 mL	NA
g. 2.00 m glucose, C₆H₁₂O₆	? g glucose	? g solution	1.50 kg H₂O

342. How many moles of H_2SO_4 are in 2.50 L of a 4.25 M aqueous solution?

343. Determine the molal concentration of 71.5 g of linoleic acid, $C_{18}H_{32}O_2$, in 525 g of hexane, C_6H_{14}.

344. You have a solution that is 16.2% sodium thiosulfate, $Na_2S_2O_3$, by mass.

a. What mass of sodium thiosulfate is in 80.0 g of solution?

b. How many moles of sodium thiosulfate are in 80.0 g of solution?

c. If 80.0 g of the sodium thiosulfate solution is diluted to 250.0 mL with water, what is the molarity of the resulting solution?

327. a. 9.93 L CO_2 b. 1.63 L O_2
c. 26.0 L CO_2
d. 3.29×10^3 g H_2O

328. 13.0% ethanol

329. 0.430% KIO_3
0.765% KOH

330. 7.16 g H_2O

331. 6.59 g $LiNO_3$

332. 0.2106 M

333. 2.40 M

334. 6.494 M

335. 1.94×10^5 g

336. 12.4 g

337. 14.0 g

338. 16 m

339. 2.31 m

340. 1.50 mol 2-butanol
111 g 2-butanol

341. a. 60.0 g $KMnO_4$; 440.0 g H_2O
b. 220 g $BaCl_2$
c. 457 g glycerol
d. 0.0642 M $K_2Cr_2O_7$
e. 1.27 m $CaCl_2$
f. 0.234 g NaCl
g. 541 g glucose; 2040 g total

342. 10.6 mol H_2SO_4

343. 0.486 m linoleic acid

344. a. 13.0 g $Na_2S_2O_3$
b. 0.0820 mol
c. 0. 328 M

345. 338 g $CoCl_2$

346. 0.442 L

347. 203 g urea

348. 18.8 g $Ba(NO_3)_2$

349. add 3.5 g $(NH_4)_2SO_4$ to 96.5 g H_2O

350. 54 g $CaCl_2$

351. 1.25 mol; 1.25 M

352. 93.6 g/mol

353. 49.6 kg water; 0.5 kg NaCl

354. 8.06%

355. 1.4 L ethyl acetate

356. $CdCl_2(aq) + Na_2S(aq) \rightarrow$ $CdS(s) + 2\,NaCl(aq)$

   a. 0.196 mol $CdCl_2$
   b. 0.196 mol CdS
   c. 28.3 g CdS

357. 34.4 g H_2SO_4

358. 1.54×10^5 mol HCl

359. 85.7 mL $BaCl_2$ solution

360. a. Measure out 9.39 g $CuSO_4 \cdot 5H_2O$ and add 90.61 g H_2O to make 100. g of solution. The 9.39 g of $CuSO_4 \cdot 5H_2O$ contributes the 6.00 g of $CuSO_4$ needed.

   b. Measure out 200. g $CuSO_4 \cdot 5H_2O$, dissolve in water, then add water to make 1.00 L. Water of hydration does not have to be considered here as long as the molar mass of the hydrate is used in determining the mass to weigh out.

   c. Measure out 870 g $CuSO_4 \cdot 5H_2O$ and add 685 g H_2O. The hydrate contributes 315 g of H_2O, so only 685 g H_2O must be added.

361. 383 g $CaCl_2 \cdot 6H_2O$

362. 0.446 g arginine

363. 3254 g H_2O; the hydrate contributes 987.9 g H_2O

364. 9.646 g $KAl(SO_4)_2 \cdot 12H_2O$; 25.35 g H_2O

365. a. 0.100 M
   b. 38 mL
   c. 0.986 M
   d. 1.7 L
   e. 50. mL

366. 50.6 mL H_2O

367. 0.0948 M

368. 0.44 mL

369. a. 3.0 M
   b. 0.83 L
   c. 1.5×10^3 g

345. What mass of anhydrous cobalt(II) chloride would be needed in order to make 650.00 mL of a 4.00 M cobalt(II) chloride solution?

346. A student wants to make a 0.150 M aqueous solution of silver nitrate, $AgNO_3$, and has a bottle containing 11.27 g of silver nitrate. What should be the final volume of the solution?

347. What mass of urea, NH_2CONH_2, must be dissolved in 2250 g of water in order to prepare a 1.50 m solution?

348. What mass of barium nitrate is dissolved in 21.29 mL of a 3.38 M solution?

349. Describe what you would do to prepare 100.0 g of a 3.5% solution of ammonium sulfate in water.

350. What mass of anhydrous calcium chloride should be dissolved in 590.0 g of water in order to produce a 0.82 m solution?

351. How many moles of ammonia are in 0.250 L of a 5.00 M aqueous ammonia solution? If this solution were diluted to 1.000 L, what would be the molarity of the resulting solution?

352. What is the molar mass of a solute if 62.0 g of the solute in 125 g of water produce a 5.3 m solution?

353. A saline solution is 0.9% NaCl. What masses of NaCl and water would be required to prepare 50. L of this saline solution? Assume that the density of water is 1.000 g/mL and that the NaCl does not add to the volume of the solution.

354. A student weighs an empty beaker on a balance and finds its mass to be 68.60 g. The student weighs the beaker again after adding water and finds the new mass to be 115.12 g. A mass of 4.08 g of glucose is then dissolved in the water. What is the percentage concentration of glucose in the solution?

355. The density of ethyl acetate at 20°C is 0.902 g/mL. What volume of ethyl acetate at 20°C would be required to prepare a 2.0% solution of cellulose nitrate using 25 g of cellulose nitrate?

356. Aqueous cadmium chloride reacts with sodium sulfide to produce bright-yellow cadmium sulfide. Write the balanced equation for this reaction and answer the following questions.
   a. How many moles of $CdCl_2$ are in 50.00 mL of a 3.91 M solution?
   b. If the solution in (a) reacted with excess sodium sulfide, how many moles of CdS would be formed?
   c. What mass of CdS would be formed?

357. What mass of H_2SO_4 is contained in 60.00 mL of a 5.85 M solution of sulfuric acid?

358. A truck carrying 22.5 kL of 6.83 M aqueous hydrochloric acid used to clean brick and masonry has overturned. The authorities plan to neutralize the acid with sodium carbonate. How many moles of HCl will have to be neutralized?

359. A chemist wants to produce 12.00 g of barium sulfate by reacting a 0.600 M $BaCl_2$ solution with excess H_2SO_4, as shown in the reaction below. What volume of the $BaCl_2$ solution should be used?

$$BaCl_2 + H_2SO_4 \rightarrow BaSO_4 + 2HCl$$

360. Many substances are hydrates. Whenever you make a solution, it is important to know whether or not the solute you are using is a hydrate and, if it is a hydrate, how many molecules of water are present per formula unit of the substance. This water must be taken into account when weighing out the solute. Something else to remember when making aqueous solutions from hydrates is that once the hydrate is dissolved, the water of hydration is considered to be part of the solvent. A common hydrate used in the chemistry laboratory is copper sulfate pentahydrate, $CuSO_4 \cdot 5H_2O$. Describe how you would make each of the following solutions using $CuSO_4 \cdot 5H_2O$. Specify masses and volumes as needed.
   a. 100. g of a 6.00% solution of $CuSO_4$
   b. 1.00 L of a 0.800 M solution of $CuSO_4$
   c. a 3.5 m solution of $CuSO_4$ in 1.0 kg of water

361. What mass of calcium chloride hexahydrate is required in order to make 700.0 mL of a 2.50 M solution?

362. What mass of the amino acid arginine, $C_6H_{14}N_4O_2$, would be required to make 1.250 L of a 0.00205 M solution?

363. How much water would you have to add to 2.402 kg of nickel(II) sulfate hexahydrate in order to prepare a 25.00% solution?

364. What mass of potassium aluminum sulfate dodecahydrate, $KAl(SO_4)_2 \cdot 12H_2O$, would be needed to prepare 35.00 g of a 15.00% $KAl(SO_4)_2$ solution? What mass of water would be added to make this solution?

Dilutions, Section 13-3

365. Complete the table below by calculating the missing value in each row.

Molarity of Stock Solution	Volume of Stock Solution	Molarity of Dilute Solution	Volume of Dilute Solution
a. 0.500 M KBr	20.00 mL	? M KBr	100.00 mL
b. 1.00 M LiOH	? mL	0.075 M LiOH	500.00 mL
c. ? M HI	5.00 mL	0.0493 M HI	100.00 mL
d. 12.0 M HCl	0.250 L	1.8 M HCl	? L
e. 7.44 M NH_3	? mL	0.093 M NH_3	4.00 L

366. What volume of water would be added to 16.5 mL of a 0.0813 M solution of sodium borate in order to get a 0.0200 M solution?

Mixed Review

367. What is the molarity of a solution of ammonium chloride prepared by diluting 50.00 mL of a 3.79 M NH_4Cl solution to 2.00 L?

368. A student takes a sample of KOH solution and dilutes it with 100.00 mL of water. The student determines that the diluted solution is 0.046 M KOH, but has forgotten to record the volume of the original sample. The concentration of the original solution is 2.09 M. What was the volume of the original sample?

369. A chemist wants to prepare a stock solution of H_2SO_4 so that samples of 20.00 mL will produce a solution with a concentration of 0.50 M when added to 100.0 mL of water.
  a. What should the molarity of the stock solution be?
  b. If the chemist wants to prepare 5.00 L of the stock solution from concentrated H_2SO_4, which is 18.0 M, what volume of concentrated acid should be used?
  c. The density of 18.0 M H_2SO_4 is 1.84 g/mL. What mass of concentrated H_2SO_4 should be used to make the stock solution in (b)?

370. To what volume should 1.19 mL of an 8.00 M acetic acid solution be diluted in order to obtain a final solution that is 1.50 M?

371. What volume of a 5.75 M formic acid solution should be used to prepare 2.00 L of a 1.00 M formic acid solution?

372. A 25.00 mL sample of ammonium nitrate solution produces a 0.186 M solution when diluted with 50.00 mL of water. What is the molarity of the stock solution?

373. Given a solution of known percentage concentration by mass, a laboratory worker can often measure out a calculated mass of the solution in order to obtain a certain mass of solute. Sometimes, though, it is impractical to use the mass of a solution, especially with fuming solutions, such as concentrated HCl and concentrated HNO_3. Measuring these solutions by volume is much more practical. In order to determine the volume that should be measured, a worker would need to know the density of the solution. This information usually appears on the label of the solution bottle.
  a. Concentrated hydrochloric acid is 36% HCl by mass and has a density of 1.18 g/mL. What is the volume of 1.0 kg of this HCl solution? What volume contains 1.0 g of HCl? What volume contains 1.0 mol of HCl?
  b. The density of concentrated nitric acid is 1.42 g/mL, and its concentration is 71% HNO_3 by mass. What volume of concentrated HNO_3 would be needed to prepare 10.0 L of a 2.00 M solution of HNO_3?
  c. What volume of concentrated HCl solution would be needed to prepare 4.50 L of 3.0 M HCl? See (a) for data.

374. A 3.8 M solution of $FeSO_4$ solution is diluted to eight times its original volume. What is the molarity of the diluted solution?

375. A chemist prepares 480. mL of a 2.50 M solution of $K_2Cr_2O_7$ in water. A week later, the chemist wants to use the solution, but the stopper has been left off the flask and 39 mL of water has evaporated. What is the new molarity of the solution?

376. You must write out procedures for a group of lab technicians. One test they will perform requires 25.00 mL of a 1.22 M solution of acetic acid. You decide to use a 6.45 M acetic acid solution that you have on hand. What procedure should the technicians use in order to get the solution they need?

377. A chemical test has determined the concentration of a solution of an unknown substance to be 2.41 M. A 100.0 mL volume of the solution is evaporated to dryness, leaving 9.56 g of crystals of the unknown solute. Calculate the molar mass of the unknown substance.

378. Tincture of iodine can be prepared by dissolving 34 g of I_2 and 25 g of KI in 25 mL of distilled water and diluting the solution to 500. mL with ethanol. What is the molarity of I_2 in the solution?

379. Phosphoric acid is commonly supplied as an 85% solution. What mass of this solution would be required to prepare 600.0 mL of a 2.80 M phosphoric acid solution?

380. Commercially available concentrated sulfuric acid is 18.0 M H_2SO_4. What volume of concentrated H_2SO_4 would you use in order to make 3.00 L of a 4.0 M stock solution?

381. Describe how to prepare 1.00 L of a 0.495 M solution of urea, NH_2CONH_2, starting with a 3.07 M stock solution.

382. Honey is a solution consisting almost entirely of a mixture of the hexose sugars fructose and glucose; both sugars have the formula $C_6H_{12}O_6$, but they differ in molecular structure.
  a. A sample of honey is found to be 76.2% $C_6H_{12}O_6$ by mass. What is the molality of the hexose sugars in honey? Consider the sugars to be equivalent.
  b. The density of the honey sample is 1.42 g/mL. What mass of hexose sugars are in 1.00 L of honey? What is the molarity of the mixed hexose sugars in honey?

383. Industrial chemicals used in manufacturing are almost never pure, and the content of the material may vary from one batch to the next. For these reasons, a sample is taken from each shipment and sent to a laboratory, where its makeup is determined. This procedure is called assaying. Once the content of a material is known, engineers adjust the manufacturing process to account for the degree of purity of the starting chemicals.

 Suppose you have just received a shipment of sodium carbonate, Na_2CO_3. You weigh out 50.00 g of the material, dissolve it in water, and dilute the solution to 1.000 L. You remove 10.00 mL from the solution and dilute it to 50.00 mL. By measuring the amount of a second substance that reacts with Na_2CO_3, you determine that the concentration of sodium carbonate in the diluted solution is 0.0890 M. Calculate the percentage of Na_2CO_3 in the original batch of material. The molar mass of Na_2CO_3 is 105.99 g. (Hint: Determine the number of moles in the original solution and convert to mass of Na_2CO_3.)

384. A student wants to prepare 0.600 L of a stock solution of copper(II) chloride so that 20.0 mL of the stock solution diluted by adding 130.0 mL of water will yield

370. 6.35 mL

371. 348 mL

372. 0.558 M

373. **a.** 850 mL; 2.4 mL; 86 mL
  b. 1.3 L concentrated HNO_3
  c. 1.16 L concentrated HCl

374. 0.48 M

375. 2.72 M

376. Dilute 4.73 mL of the 6.45 M acetic acid to 25 mL. This means adding 20.27 mL of water.

377. 39.7 g/mol

378. 0.27 M

379. 1.9×10^2 g

380. 0.667 L

381. For 1.00 L of 0.495 M urea solution, take 161 mL of 3.07 M stock solution of urea and dilute with water (839 mL of water) to make 1.00 L.

382. **a.** 17.8 *m*
  b. 1080 g, 6.01 M

383. 47.17 g Na_2CO_3 per 50.00 g sample = 94.3% Na_2CO_3

384. 151 g $CuCl_2$

385. Add 2.3 volumes of H_2O per volume of stock solution.

386. **a.** 14.9 g
  b. 7.02×10^{-2} mol
  c. 0.167 M

387. $-7.74°C$

388. $-20.4°C$

389. 102.6°C

390. 104.3°C

391. 60.4 g/mol

392. 82.1 g/mol

393. $-9.88°C$; 102.7°C

394. 103.3°C

395. 201.6°C

396. 50. g ethanol

397. 82 g/mol

398. −18.2°C

399. 15.5 g/mol

400. 66.8 g/mol

401. 183.3°C

402. a. −15.0°C
b. 104.1°C

403. 292 g/mol

404. −47.0°C

405. 190 g/mol

406. 107.2°C

407. −27.9°C

408. 204.4 g/mol; $C_{16}H_{10}$

409. 9.9 g $CaCl_2$; 49 g glucose

410. $C_3H_6O_3$

411. −29.2°C

412. 2.71 kg; 104.9°C

413. a. 2.2 m
b. 1.7 m

414. 92.0 g H_2O

415. 150 g/mol; $C_5H_{10}O_5$

416. 124 g/mol; $C_6H_6O_3$

417. 1.6×10^{-10} M

418. $[H_3O^+] = 7.50 \times 10^{-4}$ M
$[OH^-] = 1.33 \times 10^{-11}$ M

419. 2.928

420. a. 0.00
b. − 0.30
c. − 1.00

421. a. 9.0
b. 6.7
c. 3.46

422. pOH = 5.08
$[OH^-] = 8.3 \times 10^{-6}$ M

423. a. 1.40
b. 11.6
c. 8.96
d. 12.8

424. $[OH^-] = 0.0350$ M
$[H_3O^+] = 2.86 \times 10^{-13}$ M

425. 13.20

a 0.250 M solution. What mass of $CuCl_2$ should be used to make the stock solution?

385. You have a bottle containing a 2.15 M $BaCl_2$ solution. You must tell other students how to dilute this solution to get various volumes of a 0.65 M $BaCl_2$ solution. By what factor will you tell them to dilute the stock solution? In other words, when a student removes any volume, V, of the stock solution, how many times V of water should be added to dilute to 0.65 M?

386. You have a bottle containing an 18.2% solution of strontium nitrate (density = 1.02 g/mL).
a. What mass of strontium nitrate is dissolved in 80.0 mL of this solution?
b. How many moles of strontium nitrate are dissolved in 80.0 mL of the solution?
c. If 80.0 mL of this solution is diluted with 420.0 mL of water, what is the molarity of the solution?

Colligative Properties, Section 14-2

387. Determine the freezing point of a solution of 60.0 g of glucose, $C_6H_{12}O_6$, dissolved in 80.0 g of water.

388. What is the freezing point of a solution of 645 g of urea, H_2NCONH_2, dissolved in 980. g of water?

389. What is the expected boiling point of a brine solution containing 30.00 g of KBr dissolved in 100.00 g of water?

390. What is the expected boiling point of a $CaCl_2$ solution containing 385 g of $CaCl_2$ dissolved in 1.230×10^3 g of water?

391. A solution of 0.827 g of an unknown non-electrolyte compound in 2.500 g of water has a freezing point of −10.18°C. Calculate the molar mass of the compound.

392. A 0.171 g sample of an unknown organic compound is dissolved in ether. The solution has a total mass of 2.470 g. The boiling point of the solution is found to be 36.43°C. What is the molar mass of the organic compound?

Mixed Review

In each of the following problems, assume that the solute is a nonelectrolyte unless otherwise stated.

393. Calculate the freezing point and boiling point of a solution of 383 g of glucose dissolved in 400. g of water.

394. Determine the boiling point of a solution of 72.4 g of glycerol dissolved in 122.5 g of water.

395. What is the boiling point of a solution of 30.20 g of ethylene glycol, $HOCH_2CH_2OH$, in 88.40 g of phenol?

396. What mass of ethanol, CH_3CH_2OH, should be dissolved in 450. g of water to obtain a freezing point of − 4.5°C?

397. Calculate the molar mass of a nonelectrolyte that lowers the freezing point of 25.00 g of water to − 3.9°C when 4.27 g of the substance is dissolved in the water.

398. What is the freezing point of a solution of 1.17 g of 1-naphthol, $C_{10}H_8O$, dissolved in 2.00 mL of benzene at 20°C? The density of benzene at 20°C is 0.876 g/mL. K_f for benzene is − 5.12°C/m, and benzene's normal freezing point is 5.53°C.

399. The boiling point of a solution containing 10.44 g of an unknown nonelectrolyte in 50.00 g of acetic acid is 159.2°C. What is the molar mass of the solute?

400. A 0.0355 g sample of an unknown molecular compound is dissolved in 1.000 g of liquid camphor at 200.0°C. Upon cooling, the camphor freezes at 157.7°C. Calculate the molar mass of the unknown compound.

401. Determine the boiling point of a solution of 22.5 g of fructose, $C_6H_{12}O_6$, in 294 g of phenol.

402. Ethylene glycol, $HOCH_2CH_2OH$, is effective as an antifreeze, but it also raises the boiling temperature of automobile coolant, which helps prevent loss of coolant when the weather is hot.
a. What is the freezing point of a 50.0% solution of ethylene glycol in water?
b. What is the boiling point of the same 50.0% solution?

403. The value of K_f for cyclohexane is − 20.0°C/m, and its normal freezing point is 6.6°C. A mass of 1.604 g of a waxy solid dissolved in 10.000 g of cyclohexane results in a freezing point of − 4.4°C. Calculate the molar mass of the solid.

404. What is the expected freezing point of an aqueous solution of 2.62 kg of nitric acid, HNO_3, in a solution with a total mass of 5.91 kg? Assume that the nitric acid is completely ionized.

405. An unknown organic compound is mixed with 0.5190 g of naphthalene crystals to give a mixture having a total mass of 0.5959 g. The mixture is heated until the naphthalene melts and the unknown substance dissolves. Upon cooling, the solution freezes at a temperature of 74.8°C. What is the molar mass of the unknown compound?

406. What is the boiling point of a solution of 8.69 g of the electrolyte sodium acetate, $NaCH_3COO$, dissolved in 15.00 g of water?

407. What is the expected freezing point of a solution of 110.5 g of H_2SO_4 in 225 g of water? Assume sulfuric acid completely dissociates in water.

408. A compound called pyrene has the empirical formula C_8H_5. When 4.04 g of pyrene is dissolved in 10.00 g of benzene, the boiling point of the solution is 85.1°C. Calculate the molar mass of pyrene and determine its molecular formula. The molal boiling-point constant for benzene is 2.53°C/m. Its normal boiling point is 80.1°C.

409. What mass of $CaCl_2$, when dissolved in 100.00 g of water, gives an expected freezing point of − 5.0°C; $CaCl_2$ is ionic? What mass of glucose would give the same result?

410. A compound has the empirical formula CH_2O. When 0.0866 g is dissolved in 1.000 g of ether, the solution's boiling point is 36.5°C. Determine the molecular formula of this substance.

411. What is the freezing point of a 28.6% (by mass) aqueous solution of HCl? Assume the HCl is 100% ionized.

412. What mass of ethylene glycol, $HOCH_2CH_2OH$, must be dissolved in 4.510 kg of water to result in a freezing point of $-18.0°C$? What is the boiling point of the same solution?

413. A water solution containing 2.00 g of an unknown molecular substance dissolved in 10.00 g of water has a freezing point of $-4.0°C$.
   a. Calculate the molality of the solution.
   b. When 2.00 g of the substance is dissolved in acetone instead of in water, the boiling point of the solution is 58.9°C. The normal boiling point of acetone is 56.00°C, and its K_b is 1.71°C/m. Calculate the molality of the solution from this data.

414. A chemist wants to prepare a solution with a freezing point of $-22.0°C$ and has 100.00 g of glycerol on hand. What mass of water should the chemist mix with the glycerol?

415. An unknown carbohydrate compound has the empirical formula CH_2O. A solution consisting of 0.515 g of the carbohydrate dissolved in 1.717 g of acetic acid freezes at 8.8°C. What is the molar mass of the carbohydrate? What is its molecular formula?

416. An unknown organic compound has the empirical formula C_2H_2O. A solution of 3.775 g of the unknown compound dissolved in 12.00 g of water is cooled until it freezes at a temperature of $-4.72°C$. Determine the molar mass and the molecular formula of the compound.

pH, Section 16-1

417. The hydroxide ion concentration of an aqueous solution is 6.4×10^{-5} M. What is the hydronium ion concentration?

418. Calculate the H_3O^+ and OH^- concentrations in a 7.50×10^{-4} M solution of HNO_3, a strong acid.

419. Determine the pH of a 0.001 18 M solution of HBr.

420. a. What is the pH of a solution that has a hydronium ion concentration of 1.0 M?
   b. What is the pH of a 2.0 M solution of HCl, assuming the acid remains 100% ionized?
   c. What is the theoretical pH of a 10. M solution of HCl?

421. What is the pH of a solution with the following hydroxide ion concentrations?
   a. 1×10^{-5} M
   b. 5×10^{-8} M
   c. 2.90×10^{-11} M

422. What are the pOH and hydroxide ion concentration of a solution with a pH of 8.92?

423. What are the pOH values of solutions with the following hydronium ion concentrations?
   a. 2.51×10^{-13} M
   b. 4.3×10^{-3} M
   c. 9.1×10^{-6} M
   d. 0.070 M

424. A solution is prepared by dissolving 3.50 g of sodium hydroxide in water and adding water until the total volume of the solution is 2.50 L. What are the OH^- and H_3O^+ concentrations?

425. If 1.00 L of a potassium hydroxide solution with a pH of 12.90 is diluted to 2.00 L, what is the pH of the resulting solution?

Mixed Review

426. Calculate the H_3O^+ and OH^- concentrations in the following solutions. Each is either a strong acid or a strong base.
   a. 0.05 M sodium hydroxide
   b. 0.0025 M sulfuric acid
   c. 0.013 M lithium hydroxide
   d. 0.150 M nitric acid
   e. 0.0200 M calcium hydroxide
   f. 0.390 M perchloric acid

427. What is the pH of each solution in item 426?

428. Calculate $[H_3O^+]$ and $[OH^-]$ in a 0.160 M solution of potassium hydroxide. Assume that the solute is 100% dissociated at this concentration.

429. The pH of an aqueous solution of NaOH is 12.9. What is the molarity of the solution?

430. What is the pH of a 0.001 25 M HBr solution? If 175 mL of this solution is diluted to a total volume of 3.00 L, what is the pH of the diluted solution?

431. What is the pH of a 0.0001 M solution of NaOH? What is the pH of a 0.0005 M solution of NaOH?

432. A solution is prepared using 15.0 mL of 1.0 M HCl and 20.0 mL of 0.50 M HNO_3. The final volume of the solution is 1.25 L. Answer the following questions:
   a. What are the $[H_3O^+]$ and $[OH^-]$ in the final solution?
   b. What is the pH of the final solution?

433. A container is labeled 500.0 mL of 0.001 57 M nitric acid solution. A chemist finds that the container was not sealed and that some evaporation has taken place. The volume of solution is now 447.0 mL.
   a. What was the original pH of the solution?
   b. What is the pH of the solution now?

434. Calculate the hydroxide ion concentration in an aqueous solution that has a 0.000 35 M hydronium ion concentration.

435. A solution of sodium hydroxide has a pH of 12.14. If 50.00 mL of the solution is diluted to 2.000 L with water, what is the pH of the diluted solution?

436. An acetic acid solution has a pH of 4.0. What are the $[H_3O^+]$ and $[OH^-]$ in this solution?

437. What is the pH of a 0.000 460 M solution of $Ca(OH)_2$?

426. a. $[OH^-] = 0.05$ M, $[H_3O^+] = 2 \times 10^{-13}$ M
   b. $[OH^-] = 2.0 \times 10^{-12}$ M, $[H_3O^+] = 5.0 \times 10^{-3}$ M
   c. $[OH^-] = 0.013$ M, $[H_3O^+] = 7.7 \times 10^{-13}$ M
   d. $[OH^-] = 6.67 \times 10^{-14}$ M, $[H_3O^+] = 0.150$ M
   e. $[OH^-] = 0.0400$ M, $[H_3O^+] = 2.50 \times 10^{-13}$ M
   f. $[OH^-] = 2.56 \times 10^{-14}$ M, $[H_3O^+] = 0.390$ M

427. a. 10   **b.** 2.3
   c. 12.11   **d.** 0.824
   e. 12.602   **f.** 0.409

428. $[OH^-] = 0.160$ M $[H_3O^+] = 6.25 \times 10^{-14}$ M

429. 0.08 M

430. 2.903; 4.137

431. 10.0; 10.7

432. a. $[H_3O^+] = 0.020$ M, $[OH^-] = 5.0 \times 10^{-13}$ M
   b. 1.7

433. a. 2.804   **b.** 2.755

434. 2.9×10^{-11} M

435. 10.54

436. $[H_3O^+] = 1 \times 10^{-4}$ M $[OH^-] = 1 \times 10^{-10}$ M

437. 10.96

438. 0.2 g

439. $[H_3O^+] = 1.0 \times 10^{-3}$ M $[OH^-] = 1.0 \times 10^{-4}$ M

440. a. 0.40%   **b.** 1.3%
   c. 4.0%

441. 1.402

442. a. 4.50   **b.** 2.40
   c. 3.83   **d.** 5.63

443. $[H_3O^+] = 1 \times 10^{-9}$ M $[OH^-] = 1 \times 10^{-5}$ M

444. 11.70

445. $[H_3O^+] = 0.020$ M $[HCl] = 0.020$ M

446. 3.2×10^{-4} M

447. pH = 0.000
10. kL
1.0×10^2 L
10. kL

448. 0.052 mol NaOH
2.1 g NaOH

449. 7.9×10^{-3} mol

450. $[H_3O^+] = 7.1 \times 10^{-4}$ M
$[OH^-] = 1.4 \times 10^{-11}$ M

451. 0.1824 M HBr

452. 0.832 M

453. 0.1247 M $Sr(OH)_2$

454. 1.26 M NH_3

455. 92.5% acetic acid

456. 94.28% Na_2CO_3

457. 0.4563 M KOH

458. 2.262 M CH_3COOH

459. 2.433 M NH_3

460. a. 20.00 mL base
b. 10.00 mL acid
c. 80.00 mL acid

461. 5.066 M HF

462. 0.2216 M oxalic acid

463. 1.022 M H_2SO_4

464. 0.1705 M KOH

465. 0.5748 M citric acid

466. 0.3437 M KOH

467. 43.2 mL NaOH

468. 23.56 mL H_2SO_4

469. 0.06996 mol KOH; 3.926 g
KOH; 98.02% KOH

470. 51.7 g $Mg(OH)_2$

471. 0.514 M NH_3

472. 20.85 mL oxalic acid

473. a. 0.5056 M HCl
b. 0.9118 M RbOH

474. 570 kg $Ca(OH)_2$

475. 16.9 M HNO_3

476. 33.58 mL

477. 2024 kJ

478. 179.2 kJ/mol

438. A solution of strontium hydroxide with a pH of 11.4 is to be prepared. What mass of strontium hydroxide would be required to make 1.00 L of this solution?

439. A solution of NH_3 has a pH of 11.00. What are the concentrations of hydronium and hydroxide ions in this solution?

440. Acetic acid does not completely ionize in solution. Percent ionization of a substance dissolved in water is equal to the moles of ions produced as a percentage of the moles of ions that would be produced if the substance were completely ionized. Calculate the percent ionization of acetic acid in the following solutions.
a. 1.0 M acetic acid solution with a pH of 2.40
b. 0.10 M acetic acid solution with a pH of 2.90
c. 0.010 M acetic acid solution with a pH of 3.40

441. Calculate the pH of a solution that contains 5.00 g of HNO_3 in 2.00 L of solution.

442. A solution of HCl has a pH of 1.50. Determine the pH of the solutions made in each of the following ways.
a. 1.00 mL of the solution is diluted to 1000. mL with water.
b. 25.00 mL is diluted to 200. mL with distilled water.
c. 18.83 mL of the solution is diluted to 4.000 L with distilled water.
d. 1.50 L is diluted to 20.0 kL with distilled water.

443. An aqueous solution contains 10 000 times more hydronium ions than hydroxide ions. What is the concentration of each ion?

444. A potassium hydroxide solution has a pH of 12.90. Enough acid is added to react with half of the OH^- ions present. What is the pH of the resulting solution? Assume that the products of the neutralization have no effect on pH and that the amount of additional water produced is negligible.

445. A hydrochloric acid solution has a pH of 1.70. What is the $[H_3O^+]$ in this solution? Considering that HCl is a strong acid, what is the HCl concentration of the solution?

446. What is the molarity of a solution of the strong base $Ca(OH)_2$ in a solution that has a pH of 10.80?

447. You have a 1.00 M solution of the strong acid, HCl. What is the pH of this solution? You need a solution of pH 4.00. To what volume would you dilute 1.00 L of the HCl solution to get this pH? To what volume would you dilute 1.00 L of the pH 4.00 solution to get a solution of pH 6.00? To what volume would you dilute 1.00 L of the pH 4.00 solution to get a solution of pH 8.00?

448. A solution of perchloric acid, $HClO_3$, a strong acid, has a pH of 1.28. How many moles of NaOH would be required to react completely with the $HClO_3$ in 1.00 L of the solution? What mass of NaOH is required?

449. A solution of the weak base NH_3 has a pH of 11.90. How many moles of HCl would have to be added to 1.00 L of the ammonia to react with all of the OH^- ions present at pH 11.90?

450. The pH of a citric acid solution is 3.15. What are the $[H_3O^+]$ and $[OH^-]$ in this solution?

Titrations, Section 16-2

In each of the following problems, the acids and bases react in a mole ratio of 1 mol base : 1 mol acid.

451. A student titrates a 20.00 mL sample of a solution of HBr with unknown molarity. The titration requires 20.05 mL of a 0.1819 M solution of NaOH. What is the molarity of the HBr solution?

452. Vinegar can be assayed to determine its acetic acid content. Determine the molarity of acetic acid in a 15.00 mL sample of vinegar that requires 22.70 mL of a 0.550 M solution of NaOH to reach the equivalence point.

453. A 20.00 mL sample of a solution of $Sr(OH)_2$ is titrated to the equivalence point with 43.03 mL of 0.1159 M HCl. What is the molarity of the $Sr(OH)_2$ solution?

454. A 35.00 mL sample of ammonia solution is titrated to the equivalence point with 54.95 mL of a 0.400 M sulfuric acid solution. What is the molarity of the ammonia solution?

In the problems below, assume that impurities are not acidic or basic and that they do not react in an acid-base titration.

455. A supply of glacial acetic acid has absorbed water from the air. It must be assayed to determine the actual percentage of acetic acid. 2.000 g of the acid is diluted to 100.00 mL, and 20.00 mL is titrated with a solution of sodium hydroxide. The base solution has a concentration of 0.218 M, and 28.25 mL is used in the titration. Calculate the percentage of acetic acid in the original sample. Write the titration equation to get the mole ratio.

456. A shipment of crude sodium carbonate must be assayed for its Na_2CO_3 content. You receive a small jar containing a sample from the shipment and weigh out 9.709 g into a flask, where it is dissolved in water and diluted to 1.0000 L with distilled water. A 10.00 mL sample is taken from the flask and titrated to the equivalence point with 16.90 mL of a 0.1022 M HCl solution. Determine the percentage of Na_2CO_3 in the sample. Write the titration equation to get the mole ratio.

Mixed Review

457. A 50.00 mL sample of a potassium hydroxide is titrated with a 0.8186 M HCl solution. The titration requires 27.87 mL of the HCl solution to reach the equivalence point. What is the molarity of the KOH solution?

458. A 15.00 mL sample of acetic acid is titrated with 34.13 mL of 0.9940 M NaOH. Determine the molarity of the acetic acid.

459. A 12.00 mL sample of an ammonia solution is titrated with 1.499 M HNO_3 solution. A total of 19.48 mL of acid is required to reach the equivalence point. What is the molarity of the ammonia solution?

460. A certain acid and base react in a 1:1 ratio.
  a. If the acid and base solutions are of equal concentration, what volume of acid will titrate a 20.00 mL sample of the base?
  b. If the acid is twice as concentrated as the base, what volume of acid will be required to titrate 20.00 mL of the base?
  c. How much acid will be required if the base is four times as concentrated as the acid, and 20.00 mL of base is used?

461. A 10.00 mL sample of a solution of hydrofluoric acid, HF, is diluted to 500.00 mL. A 20.00 mL sample of the diluted solution requires 13.51 mL of a 0.1500 M NaOH solution to be titrated to the equivalence point. What is the molarity of the original HF solution?

462. A solution of oxalic acid, a diprotic acid, is used to titrate a 16.22 mL sample of a 0.5030 M KOH solution. If the titration requires 18.41 mL of the oxalic acid solution, what is its molarity?

463. A H_2SO_4 solution of unknown molarity is titrated with a 1.209 M NaOH solution. The titration requires 42.27 mL of the NaOH solution to reach the equivalent point with 25.00 mL of the H_2SO_4 solution. What is the molarity of the acid solution?

464. Potassium hydrogen phthalate, $KHC_8H_4O_4$, is a solid acidic substance that reacts in a 1:1 mole ratio with bases that have one hydroxide ion. Suppose that 0.7025 g of potassium hydrogen phthalate is titrated to the equivalence point by 20.18 mL of a KOH solution. What is the molarity of the KOH solution?

465. A solution of citric acid, a triprotic acid, is titrated with a sodium hydroxide solution. A 20.00 mL sample of the citric acid solution requires 17.03 mL of a 2.025 M solution of NaOH to reach the equivalence point. What is the molarity of the acid solution?

466. A flask contains 41.04 mL of a solution of potassium hydroxide. The solution is titrated and reaches an equivalence point when 21.65 mL of a 0.6515 M solution of HNO_3 is added. Calculate the molarity of the base solution.

467. A bottle is labeled 2.00 M H_2SO_4. You decide to titrate a 20.00 mL sample with a 1.85 M NaOH solution. What volume of NaOH solution would you expect to use if the label is correct?

468. What volume of a 0.5200 M solution of H_2SO_4 would be needed to titrate 100.00 mL of a 0.1225 M solution of $Sr(OH)_2$?

469. A sample of a crude grade of KOH is sent to the lab to be tested for KOH content. A 4.005 g sample is dissolved and diluted to 200.00 mL with water. A 25.00 mL sample of the solution is titrated with a 0.4388 M HCl solution and requires 19.93 mL to reach the equivalence point. How many moles of KOH were in the 4.005 g sample? What mass of KOH is this? What is the percent of KOH in the crude material?

470. What mass of magnesium hydroxide would be required for the magnesium hydroxide to react to the equivalence point with 558 mL of 3.18 M hydrochloric acid?

471. An ammonia solution of unknown concentration is titrated with a solution of hydrochloric acid. The HCl solution is 1.25 M, and 5.19 mL are required to titrate 12.61 mL of the ammonia solution. What is the molarity of the ammonia solution?

472. What volume of 2.811 M oxalic acid solution is needed to react to the equivalence point with a 5.090 g sample of material that is 92.10% NaOH? Oxalic acid is a diprotic acid.

473. Standard solutions of accurately known concentration are available in most laboratories. These solutions are used to titrate other solutions to determine their concentrations. Once the concentration of the other solutions are accurately known, they may be used to titrate solutions of unknowns.
  The molarity of a solution of HCl is determined by titrating the solution with an accurately known solution of $Ba(OH)_2$, which has a molar concentration of 0.1529 M. A volume of 43.09 mL of the $Ba(OH)_2$ solution titrates 26.06 mL of the acid solution. The acid solution is in turn used to titrate 15.00 mL of a solution of rubidium hydroxide. The titration requires 27.05 mL of the acid.
  a. What is the molarity of the HCl solution?
  b. What is the molarity of the RbOH solution?

474. A truck containing 2800 kg of a 6.0 M hydrochloric acid has been in an accident and is in danger of spilling its load. What mass of $Ca(OH)_2$ should be sent to the scene in order to neutralize all of the acid in case the tank bursts? The density of the 6.0 M HCl solution is 1.10 g/mL.

475. A 1.00 mL sample of a fairly concentrated nitric acid solution is diluted to 200.00 mL. A 10.00 mL sample of the diluted solution requires 23.94 mL of a 0.0177 M solution of $Ba(OH)_2$ to be titrated to the equivalence point. Determine the molarity of the original nitric acid solution.

476. What volume of 4.494 M H_2SO_4 solution would be required to react to the equivalence point with 7.2280 g of $LiOH(s)$?

Thermochemistry, Sections 17-1; 17-2

477. Calculate the reaction enthalpy for the following reaction:
$$5CO_2(g) + Si_3N_4(s) \rightarrow 3SiO(s) + 2N_2O(g) + 5CO(g)$$
Use the following equations and data:
(1) $CO(g) + SiO_2(s) \rightarrow SiO(g) + CO_2(g)$
(2) $8CO_2(g) + Si_3N_4(s) \rightarrow$
$$3SiO_2(s) + 2N_2O(g) + 8CO(g)$$

$\Delta H_{\text{reaction 1}} = +520.9$ kJ

$\Delta H_{\text{reaction 2}} = +461.05$ kJ

479. 533 kJ/mol
480. 194 kJ/mol
481. -534.5 kJ/mol
482. -71.8 kJ/mol
483. -1683 kJ/mol
484. -260.8 kJ/mol
485. -385.9 kJ/mol
486. $-390.$ kJ/mol
487. -492.3 kJ/mol
488. -107.6 kJ/mol
489. -121.8 kJ/mol
490. -384.9 kJ/mol
491. 74.2 kJ/mol
492. -169.0 kJ/mol
493. a. $CH_4(g) + 2O_2(g) \rightarrow$
$$CO_2(g) + 2H_2O(g)$$
$C_3H_8(g) + 5O_2(g) \rightarrow$
$$3CO_2(g) + 4H_2O(g)$$
  b. for methane: $\Delta H =$
$$-802.2 \text{ kJ/mol}$$
  for propane: $\Delta H =$
$$-2043 \text{ kJ/mol}$$
  c. $\text{output}_{\text{methane}} = -4.998 \times$
$$10^4 \text{ kJ/kg}$$
  $\text{output}_{\text{propane}} = -4.632 \times$
$$10^4 \text{ kJ/kg}$$
  Methane yields more heat per mass.
494. -132.7 kJ/mol
495. -7171.4 kJ/mol
496. -141.1 kJ/mol
497. 20.2 kJ/mol
498. -285 kJ/mol•K
499. a. 786.8 kJ/mol
  b. -36 kJ/mol
  c. 2154 kJ/mol
  d. -496 kJ/mol
  e. 1346.4 kJ/mol
500. a. $K = 1.83 \times 10^{-3}$
  b. $K = 1.55 \times 10^5$
  c. $K = 9.47$
  d. $K = 7.71 \times 10^{-2}$
  e. $K = 5.88 \times 10^{-3}$
  f. $K = 1.53 \times 10^3$

501. 0.197 M

502. 5.39×10^{-3} M

503. 1.98×10^{-7}

504. 2.446×10^{-12}

505. 3.97×10^{-5}

506. a. 8.13×10^{-4} M
b. 0.0126 M

507. a. The concentrations are equal.
b. K will increase.

508. 0.09198 M

509. a. 0.7304 M
b. 6.479×10^{-4} M

510. a. $[A] = [B] = [C] = 1/2[A]_{initial}$
b. [A], [B], and [C] will increase equally. K remains the same.

511. a. $K = \dfrac{[HBr]^2}{[H_2][Br_2]}$
b. 2.11×10^{-10} M
c. Br_2 and H_2 will still have the same concentration. HBr will have a much higher concentration than the two reactants; at equilibrium, essentially only HBr will be present.

512. 1.281×10^{-6}

513. 4.61×10^{-3}

514. a. $K = \dfrac{[HCN]}{[HCl]}$
b. 3.725×10^{-7} M

515. a. The reaction yields essentially no products at 25°C; as a result, the equilibrium constant is very small. At 1100 K, the reaction proceeds to some extent.
b. 2.51 M

516. 0.0424

517. 0.0390

518. $K_a = 1.8 \times 10^{-4}$

519. $K_a = 0.167$

520. $K_a = 5.2 \times 10^{-9}$

Determine ΔH for each of the following three reactions.

478. The following reaction is used to make CaO from limestone:
$$CaCO_3(s) \rightarrow CaO(s) + CO_2(g)$$

479. The following reaction represents the oxidation of FeO to Fe_2O_3:
$$2FeO(s) + O_2(g) \rightarrow Fe_2O_3(s)$$

480. The following reaction of ammonia and hydrogen fluoride produces ammonium fluoride:
$$NH_3(g) + HF(g) \rightarrow NH_4F(s)$$

481. Calculate the free energy change, ΔG, for the combustion of hydrogen sulfide according to the following chemical equation. Assume reactants and products are at 25°C:
$$H_2S(g) + O_2(g) \rightarrow H_2O(l) + SO_2(g)$$
$\Delta H_{reaction} = -562.1$ kJ/mol
$\Delta S_{reaction} = -0.09278$ kJ/mol•K

482. Calculate the free energy change for the decomposition of sodium chlorate. Assume reactants and products are at 25°C:
$$NaClO_3(s) \rightarrow NaCl(s) + O_2(g)$$
$\Delta H_{reaction} = -19.1$ kJ/mol
$\Delta S_{reaction} = -0.1768$ kJ/mol•K

483. Calculate the free energy change for the combustion of 1 mol of ethane. Assume reactants and products are at 25°C:
$$C_2H_6(g) + O_2(g) \rightarrow 2CO_2(g) + 3H_2O(l)$$
$\Delta H_{reaction} = -1561$ kJ/mol
$\Delta S_{reaction} = -0.4084$ kJ/mol•K

Mixed Review

484. Calculate ΔH for the reaction of fluorine with water:
$$F_2(g) + H_2O(l) \rightarrow 2HF(g) + O_2(g)$$

485. Calculate ΔH for the reaction of calcium oxide and sulfur trioxide:
$$CaO(s) + SO_3(g) \rightarrow CaSO_4(s)$$
Use the following equations and data:
$$H_2O(l) + SO_3(g) \rightarrow H_2SO_4(l)$$
$\Delta H = -132.5$ kJ/mol
$$H_2SO_4(l) + Ca(s) \rightarrow CaSO_4(s) + H_2(g)$$
$\Delta H = -602.5$ kJ/mol
$$Ca(s) + O_2(g) \rightarrow CaO(s)$$
$\Delta H = -634.9$ kJ/mol
$$H_2(g) + O_2(g) \rightarrow H_2O(l)$$
$\Delta H = -285.8$ kJ/mol

486. Calculate ΔH for the reaction of sodium oxide with sulfur dioxide:
$$Na_2O(s) + SO_2(g) \rightarrow Na_2SO_3(s)$$

487. Use enthalpies of combustion to calculate ΔH for the oxidation of 1-butanol to make butanoic acid:
$$C_4H_9OH(l) + O_2(g) \rightarrow C_3H_7COOH(l) + H_2O(l)$$

Combustion of butanol:
$$C_4H_9OH(l) + 6O_2(g) \rightarrow 4CO_2(g) + 5H_2O(l)$$
$\Delta H_c = -2675.9$ kJ/mol
Combustion of butanoic acid:
$$C_3H_7COOH(l) + 5O_2(g) \rightarrow 4CO_2(g) + 4H_2O(l)$$
$\Delta H_c = -2183.6$ kJ/mol

488. Determine the free energy change for the reduction of CuO with hydrogen. Products and reactants are at 25°C.
$$CuO(s) + H_2(g) \rightarrow Cu(s) + H_2O(l)$$
$\Delta H = -128.5$ kJ/mol
$\Delta S = -70.1$ J/mol•K

489. Calculate the enthalpy change at 25°C for the reaction of sodium iodide and chlorine. Use only the data given.
$$NaI(s) + Cl_2(g) \rightarrow NaCl(s) + I_2(l)$$
$\Delta S = -79.9$ J/mol•K
$\Delta G = -98.0$ kJ/mol

490. The element bromine can be produced by the reaction of hydrogen bromide and manganese(IV) oxide:
$$4HBr(g) + MnO_2(s) \rightarrow MnBr_2(s) + 2H_2O(l) + Br_2(l)$$
ΔH for the reaction is -291.3 kJ/mol at 25°C. Use this value and the following values of ΔH_f^0 to calculate ΔH_f^0 of $MnBr_2(s)$.
$\Delta H_{fHBr}^0 = -36.29$ kJ/mol
$\Delta H_{fMnO_2}^0 = -520.0$ kJ/mol
$\Delta H_{fH_2O}^0 = -285.8$ kJ/mol
$\Delta H_{fBr_2}^0 = 0.00$ kJ/mol

491. Calculate the change in entropy, ΔS, at 25°C for the reaction of calcium carbide with water to produce acetylene gas:
$$CaC_2(s) + 2H_2O(l) \rightarrow C_2H_2(g) + Ca(OH)_2(s)$$
$\Delta G = -147.7$ kJ/mol
$\Delta H = -125.6$ kJ/mol

492. Calculate the free energy change for the explosive decomposition of ammonium nitrate at 25°C. Note that H_2O is a gas in this reaction:
$$NH_4NO_3(s) \rightarrow N_2O(g) + 2H_2O(g)$$
$\Delta S = 446.4$ J/mol•K

493. In locations where natural gas, which is mostly methane, is not available, many people burn propane, which is delivered by truck and stored in a tank under pressure.
a. Write the chemical equations for the complete combustion of 1 mol of methane, CH_4, and 1 mol of propane, C_3H_8.
b. Calculate the enthalpy change for each reaction to determine the amount of heat evolved off by burning 1 mol of each fuel.
c. Using the molar heats of combustion you calculated, determine the heat output per kilogram of each fuel. Which fuel yields more heat per unit mass?

494. The hydration of acetylene to form acetaldehyde is shown in the following equation:
$$C_2H_2(g) + H_2O(l) \rightarrow CH_3CHO(l)$$

Use heats of combustion for acetylene and acetaldehyde to compute the enthalpy of the above reaction.

$$C_2H_2(g) + 2O_2(g) \rightarrow 2CO_2(g) + H_2O(l)$$

$\Delta H = -1299.6$ kJ/mol

$$CH_3CHO(l) + 2O_2(g) \rightarrow 2CO_2(g) + 2H_2O(l)$$

$\Delta H = -1166.9$ kJ/mol

495. Calculate the enthalpy for the combustion of decane. ΔH_f^0 for liquid decane is -300.9 kJ/mol.

$$C_{10}H_{22}(l) + 15O_2(g) \rightarrow 10CO_2(g) + 11H_2O(l)$$

496. Find the enthalpy of the reaction of magnesium oxide with hydrogen chloride:

$$MgO(s) + 2HCl(g) \rightarrow MgCl_2(s) + H_2O(l)$$

Use the following equations and data.

$$Mg(s) + 2HCl(g) \rightarrow MgCl_2(s) + H_2(g)$$

$\Delta H = -456.9$ kJ/mol

$$Mg(s) + O_2(g) \rightarrow MgO(s)$$

$\Delta H = -601.6$ kJ/mol

$$H_2O(l) \rightarrow H_2(g) + O_2(g)$$

$\Delta H = +285.8$ kJ/mol

497. What is the free energy change for the following reaction at 25°C?

$$2NaOH(s) + 2Na(s) \xrightarrow{\Delta} 2\,Na_2O(s) + H_2(g)$$

$\Delta S = 10.6$ J/mol•K
$\Delta H_{f\,NaOH}^0 = -425.9$ kJ/mol

498. The following equation represents the reaction between gaseous HCl and gaseous ammonia to form solid ammonium chloride:

$$NH_3(g) + HCl(g) \rightarrow NH_4Cl(s)$$

Calculate the entropy change in J/mol•K for the reaction of hydrogen chloride and ammonia at 25°C using the following data and the table following item 500.

$\Delta G = -91.2$ kJ/mol

499. The production of steel from iron involves the removal of many impurities in the iron ore. The following equations show some of the purifying reactions. Calculate the enthalpy for each reaction. Use the table following item 500 and the data given.

a. $3C(s) + Fe_2O_3(s) \rightarrow 3CO(g) + 2Fe(s)$
$\Delta H_{f\,CO(g)}^0 = -110.53$ kJ/mol

b. $3Mn(s) + Fe_2O_3(s) \rightarrow 3MnO(s) + 2Fe(s)$
$\Delta H_{f\,MnO(s)}^0 = -384.9$ kJ/mol

c. $12P(s) + 10Fe_2O_3(s) \rightarrow 3P_4O_{10}(s) + 20Fe(s)$
$\Delta H_{f\,P_4O_{10}(s)}^0 = -3009.9$ kJ/mol

d. $3Si(s) + 2Fe_2O_3(s) \rightarrow 3SiO_2(s) + 4Fe(s)$
$\Delta H_{f\,SiO_2(s)}^0 = -910.9$ kJ/mol

e. $3S(s) + 2Fe_2O_3(s) \rightarrow 3SO_2(g) + 4Fe(s)$

Equilibrium, Section 18-1

500. Calculate the equilibrium constants for the following hypothetical reactions. Assume that all components of the reactions are gaseous.

a. $A \rightleftarrows C + D$

For problems 498–499

Substance	ΔH_f^0 (kJ/mol)	Substance	ΔH_f^0 (kJ/mol)
$NH_3(g)$	-45.9	$HF(g)$	-273.3
$NH_4Cl(s)$	-314.4	$H_2O(g)$	-241.82
$NH_4F(s)$	-125	$H_2O(l)$	-285.8
$NH_4NO_3(s)$	-365.56	$H_2O_2(l)$	-187.8
$Br_2(l)$	0.00	$H_2SO_4(l)$	-813.989
$CaCO_3(s)$	-1207.6	$FeO(s)$	-825.5
$CaO(s)$	-634.9	$Fe_2O_3(s)$	-1118.4
$CH_4(g)$	-74.9	$MnO_2(s)$	-520.0
$C_3H_8(g)$	-104.7	$N_2O(g)$	$+82.1$
$CO_2(g)$	-393.5	$O_2(g)$	0.00
$F_2(g)$	0.00	$Na_2O(s)$	-414.2
$H_2(g)$	0.00	$Na_2SO_3(s)$	-1101
$HBr(g)$	-36.29	$SO_2(g)$	-296.8
$HCl(g)$	-92.3	$SO_3(g)$	-395.7

At equilibrium, the concentration of A is 2.24×10^{-2} M and the concentrations of both C and D are 6.41×10^{-3} M.

b. $A + B \rightleftarrows C + D$

At equilibrium, the concentrations of both A and B are 3.23×10^{-5} M and the concentrations of both C and D are 1.27×10^{-2} M.

c. $A + B \rightleftarrows 2C$

At equilibrium, the concentrations of both A and B are 7.02×10^{-3} M and the concentration of C is 2.16×10^{-2} M.

d. $2A \rightleftarrows 2C + D$

At equilibrium, the concentration of A is 6.59×10^{-4} M. The concentration of C is 4.06×10^{-3} M, and the concentration of D is 2.03×10^{-3} M.

e. $A + B \rightleftarrows C + D + E$

At equilibrium, the concentrations of both A and B are 3.73×10^{-4} M and the concentrations of C, D, and E are 9.35×10^{-4} M.

f. $2A + B \rightleftarrows 2C$

At equilibrium, the concentration of A is 5.50×10^{-3} M, the concentration of B is 2.25×10^{-3}, and the concentration of C is 1.02×10^{-2} M.

501. Calculate the concentration of product D in the following hypothetical reaction:

$$2A(g) \rightleftarrows 2C(g) + D(g)$$

At equilibrium, the concentration of A is 1.88×10^{-1} M, the concentration of C is 6.56 M, and the equilibrium constant is 2.403×10^2.

502. At a temperature of 700 K, the equilibrium constant is 3.164×10^3 for the following reaction system for the hydrogenation of ethene, C_2H_4, to ethane, C_2H_6:

$$C_2H_4(g) + H_2(g) \rightleftarrows C_2H_6(g)$$

521. pH = 11.573
$K_b = 4.0 \times 10^{-4}$

522. 4.4×10^{-3} M

523. pH = 2.857
$K_a = 1.92 \times 10^{-5}$

524. pH = 1.717
$K_a = 2.04 \times 10^{-3}$

525. a. $[H_3O^+] = 3.70 \times 10^{-11}$ M
pH = 10.431
$K_b = 1.82 \times 10^{-7}$
b. $[B] = 4.66 \times 10^{-3}$ M
$K_b = 1.53 \times 10^{-4}$
pH = 10.93
c. $[OH^-] = 1.9 \times 10^{-3}$ M
$[H_3O^+] = 5.3 \times 10^{-12}$ M
$[B] = 0.0331$ M
$K_b = 1.1 \times 10^{-4}$
d. $[B]_{initial} = 7.20 \times 10^{-3}$ M
$K_b = 1.35 \times 10^{-4}$
pH = 10.96

526. 6.4×10^{-5}

527. $K_b = 3.1 \times 10^{-5}$
$[H_2NCH_2CH_2OH] = 6.06 \times 10^{-3}$ M

528. 1.3×10^{-4}

529. $[OH^-] = 1.58 \times 10^{-5}$ M
pH = 9.20

530. $K_a = 2.2 \times 10^{-3}$
$[HB]_{initial} = 0.0276$ M

531. 4.63×10^{-3}

532. 2.62×10^{-4}

533. $[H_3O^+] = 0.0124$ M
pH = 1.907

534. $[H_3O^+] = 0.0888$ M
pH = 1.05

535. $K_a = 3.50 \times 10^{-4}$
pH = 2.241

536. a. 3.16×10^{-6} M
b. 5.500
c. 0.025 M
d. 4.0×10^{-10}
e. HCN is a fairly weak acid.
f. 5.8×10^{-6} M

537. a. 0.740
b. 0.0325
c. 1.02 M
d. It is moderately weak.

538. 2.80×10^{-11}

539. a. 0.200 M
b. 0.233

540. pH $= 11.37$
$K_b = 7.41 \times 10^{-5}$

541. 7.36×10^{-4}
dimethylamine is the stronger base

542. a. 8.3×10^{-7}
b. 1.3×10^{-4} M
c. 10.11

543. $K_{sp} = 6.09 \times 10^{-5}$

544. $K_{sp} = 4.20 \times 10^{-11}$

545. 3.0×10^{-3} M

546. a. $[X_2Y] = 4.74 \times 10^{-3}$ M
b. $[AZ] = 6.52 \times 10^{-4}$ M

547. ion product $= 1.9 \times 10^{-5}$
precipitation occurs

548. ion product $= 8.1 \times 10^{-4}$
no precipitate

549. ion product $= 1.5 \times 10^{-5}$
no precipitate

550. ion product $= 1.1 \times 10^{-13}$
no precipitate

551. 1.0×10^{-4}

552. 1.51×10^{-7}

553. a. 1.6×10^{-11}
b. 0.49 g

554. 2.000×10^{-7}

555. a. 8.9×10^{-4} M
b. 0.097 g

556. 0.036 M

557. a. 1.1×10^{-4} M
b. 4.6 L

558. a. 5.7×10^{-4} M
b. 2.1 g

559. 0.83 g remains

560. 2.8×10^{-3} M

561. a. 1.2×10^{-5}
b. Yes

562. a. 1.1×10^{-8}
b. No

What will be the equilibrium concentration of ethene if the concentration of H_2 is 0.0619 M and the concentration of C_2H_6 is 1.055 M?

Mixed Review

503. Using the reaction $A + 2B \rightleftarrows C + 2D$, determine the equilibrium constant if the following equilibrium concentrations are found. All components are gases.

$[A] = 0.0567$ M
$[B] = 0.1171$ M
$[C] = 0.000\ 3378$ M
$[D] = 0.000\ 6756$ M

504. In the reaction $2A \rightleftarrows 2C + 2D$, determine the equilibrium constant when the following equilibrium concentrations are found. All components are gases.

$[A] = 0.1077$ M
$[C] = 0.000\ 4104$ M
$[D] = 0.000\ 4104$ M

505. Calculate the equilibrium constant for the following reaction. Note the phases of the components.

$$2A(g) + B(s) \rightleftarrows C(g) + D(g)$$

The equilibrium concentrations of the components are

$[A] = 0.0922$ M
$[C] = 4.11 \times 10^{-4}$ M
$[D] = 8.22 \times 10^{-4}$ M

506. The equilibrium constant of the following reaction for the decomposition of phosgene at 25°C is 4.282×10^{-2}.

$$COCl_2(g) \rightleftarrows CO(g) + Cl_2(g)$$

a. What is the concentration of $COCl_2$ when the concentrations of both CO and Cl_2 are 5.90×10^{-3} M?
b. When the equilibrium concentration of $COCl_2$ is 0.003 70 M, what are the concentrations of CO and Cl_2? Assume the concentrations are equal.

507. Consider the following hypothetical reaction.

$$A(g) + B(s) \rightleftarrows C(g) + D(s)$$

a. If $K = 1$ for this reaction at 500 K, what can you say about the concentrations of A and C at equilibrium?
b. If raising the temperature of the reaction results in an equilibrium with a higher concentration of C than A, how will the value of K change?

508. The following reaction occurs when steam is passed over hot carbon. The mixture of gases it generates is called *water gas* and is useful as an industrial fuel and as a source of hydrogen for the production of ammonia.

$$C(s) + H_2O(g) \rightleftarrows CO(g) + H_2(g)$$

The equilibrium constant for this reaction is 4.251×10^{-2} at 800 K. If the equilibrium concentration of $H_2O(g)$ is 0.1990 M, what concentrations of CO and H_2 would you expect to find?

509. When nitrogen monoxide gas comes in contact with air, it oxidizes to the brown gas nitrogen dioxide according to the following equation:

$$2NO(g) + O_2(g) \rightleftarrows 2NO_2(g)$$

a. The equilibrium constant for this reaction at 500 K is 1.671×10^4. What concentration of NO_2 is present at equilibrium if $[NO] = 6.200 \times 10^{-2}$ M and $[O_2] = 8.305 \times 10^{-3}$ M?
b. At 1000 K, the equilibrium constant, K, for the same reaction is 1.315×10^{-2}. What will be the concentration of NO_2 at 1000 K given the same concentrations of NO and O_2 as were in (a)?

510. Consider the following hypothetical reaction, for which $K = 1$ at 300 K:

$$A(g) + B(g) \rightleftarrows 2C(g)$$

a. If the reaction begins with equal concentrations of A and B and a zero concentration of C, what can you say about the relative concentrations of the components at equilibrium?
b. Additional C is introduced at equilibrium, and the temperature remains constant. When equilibrium is restored, how will the concentrations of all components have changed? How will K have changed?

511. The equilibrium constant for the following reaction of hydrogen gas and bromine gas at 25°C is 5.628×10^{18}:

$$H_2(g) + Br_2(g) \rightleftarrows 2HBr(g)$$

a. Write the equilibrium expression for this reaction.
b. Assume that equimolar amounts of H_2 and Br_2 were present at the beginning. Calculate the equilibrium concentration of H_2 if the concentration of HBr is 0.500 M.
c. If equal amounts of H_2 and Br_2 react, which reaction component will be present in the greatest concentration at equilibrium? Explain your reasoning.

512. The following reaction reaches an equilibrium state:

$$N_2F_4(g) \rightleftarrows 2NF_2(g)$$

At equilibrium at 25°C the concentration of N_2F_4 is found to be 0.9989 M and the concentration of NF_2 is 1.131×10^{-3} M. Calculate the equilibrium constant of the reaction.

513. The equilibrium between dinitrogen tetroxide and nitrogen dioxide is represented by the following equation:

$$N_2O_4(g) \rightleftarrows 2NO_2(g)$$

A student places a mixture of the two gases into a closed gas tube and allows the reaction to reach equilibrium at 25°C. At equilibrium, the concentration of N_2O_4 is found to be 5.95×10^{-1} M and the concentration of NO_2 is found to be 5.24×10^{-2} M. What is the equilibrium constant of the reaction?

514. Consider the following equilibrium system:

$$NaCN(s) + HCl(g) \rightleftarrows HCN(g) + NaCl(s)$$

a. Write a complete expression for the equilibrium constant of this system.
b. The equilibrium constant for this reaction is 2.405×10^6. What is the concentration of HCl remaining when the concentration of HCN is 0.8959 M?

515. The following reaction is used in the industrial production of hydrogen gas:

$$CH_4(g) + H_2O(g) \rightleftarrows CO(g) + 3H_2(g)$$

The equilibrium constant of this reaction at 298 K (25°C) is 3.896×10^{-27}, but at 1100 K the constant is 3.112×10^{2}.

a. What do these equilibrium constants tell you about the progress of the reaction at the two temperatures?

b. Suppose the reaction mixture is sampled at 1100 K and found to contain 1.56 M of hydrogen, 3.70×10^{-2} M of methane, and 8.27×10^{-1} M of gaseous H_2O. What concentration of carbon monoxide would you expect to find?

516. Dinitrogen tetroxide, N_2O_4, is soluble in cyclohexane, a common nonpolar solvent. While in solution, N_2O_4 can break down into NO_2 according to the following equation:

$$N_2O_4(cyclohexane) \rightleftarrows NO_2(cyclohexane)$$

At 20°C, the following concentrations were observed for this equilibrium reaction:

$[N_2O_4] = 2.55 \times 10^{-3}$ M

$[NO_2] = 10.4 \times 10^{-3}$ M

What is the value of the equilibrium constant for this reaction? Note: the chemical equation must be balanced first.

517. The reaction given in item 516 also occurs when the dinitrogen tetroxide and nitrogen dioxide are dissolved in carbon tetrachloride, CCl_4, another nonpolar solvent.

$$N_2O_4(CCl_4) \rightleftarrows NO_2(CCl_4)$$

The following experimental data were obtained at 20°C:

$[N_2O_4] = 2.67 \times 10^{-3}$ M

$[NO_2] = 10.2 \times 10^{-3}$ M

Calculate the value of the equilibrium constant for this reaction occurring in carbon tetrachloride.

Equilibrium of Acids and Bases, K_a and K_b, Section 18-3

518. At 25°C, a 0.025 M solution of formic acid, HCOOH, is found to have a hydronium ion concentration of 2.03×10^{-3} M. Calculate the ionization constant of formic acid.

519. The pH of a 0.400 M solution of iodic acid, HIO_3, is 0.726 at 25°C. What is the K_a at this temperature?

520. The pH of a 0.150 M solution of hypochlorous acid, HClO, is found to be 4.55 at 25°C. Calculate the K_a for HClO at this temperature.

521. The compound propylamine, $CH_3CH_2CH_2NH_2$, is a weak base. At equilibrium, a 0.039 M solution of propylamine has an OH^- concentration of 3.74×10^{-3} M. Calculate the pH of this solution and K_b for propylamine.

522. The K_a of nitrous acid is 4.6×10^{-4} at 25°C. Calculate the $[H_3O^+]$ of a 0.0450 M nitrous acid solution.

Mixed Review

523. Hydrazoic acid, HN_3, is a weak acid. The $[H_3O^+]$ of a 0.102 M solution of hydrazoic acid is 1.39×10^{-3} M. Determine the pH of this solution, and calculate K_a at 25°C for HN_3.

524. Bromoacetic acid, $BrCH_2COOH$, is a moderately weak acid. A 0.200 M solution of bromoacetic acid has a H_3O^+ concentration of 0.0192 M. Determine the pH of this solution and the K_a of bromoacetic acid at 25°C.

525. A base, B, dissociates in water according to the following equation:

$$B + H_2O \rightleftarrows BH^+ + OH^-$$

Complete the following table for base solutions with the characteristics given.

Initial [B]	[B] at Equilibrium	[OH⁻]	K_b	[H₃O⁺]	pH
a. 0.400 M	NA	2.70×10^{-4} M	?	? M	?
b. 0.005 50 M	? M	8.45×10^{-4} M	?	NA	?
c. 0.0350 M	? M	? M	?	? M	11.29
d. ? M	0.006 28 M	0.000 92 M	?	NA	?

526. The solubility of benzoic acid, C_6H_5COOH, in water at 25°C is 2.9 g/L. The pH of this saturated solution is 2.92. Determine K_a at 25°C for benzoic acid. (Hint: first calculate the initial concentration of benzoic acid.)

527. A 0.006 50 M solution of ethanolamine, $H_2NCH_2CH_2OH$, has a pH of 10.64 at 25°C. Calculate the K_b of ethanolamine. What concentration of undissociated ethanolamine remains at equilibrium?

528. The weak acid hydrogen selenide, H_2Se, has two hydrogen atoms that can form hydronium ions. The second ionization is so small that the concentration of the resulting H_3O^+ is insignificant. If the $[H_3O^+]$ of a 0.060 M solution of H_2Se is 2.72×10^{-3} M at 25°C, what is the K_a of the first ionization?

529. Pyridine, C_5H_5N, is a very weak base. Its K_b at 25°C is 1.78×10^{-9}. Calculate the $[OH^-]$ and pH of a 0.140 M solution. Assume that the concentration of pyridine at equilibrium is equal to its initial concentration because so little pyridine is dissociated.

530. A solution of a monoprotic acid, HA, at equilibrium is found to have a 0.0208 M concentration of nonionized acid. The pH of the acid solution is 2.17. Calculate the initial acid concentration and K_a for this acid.

531. Pyruvic acid, $CH_3COCOOH$, is an important intermediate in the metabolism of carbohydrates in the cells of the body. A solution made by dissolving 438 mg of pyruvic acid in 10.00 mL of water is found to have a pH of 1.34 at 25°C. Calculate K_a for pyruvic acid.

563. a. $Mg(OH)_2 \rightleftarrows Mg^{2+} + 2OH^-$
b. 11 L
c. A suspension contains undissolved $Mg(OH)_2$ suspended in a saturated solution of $Mg(OH)_2$. As hydroxide ions are depleted by titration, the dissociation equilibrium continues to replenish them until all of the $Mg(OH)_2$ is used up.

564. a. 0.184 M
b. 46.8 g

565. 5.040×10^{-3}

566. a. 1.0   **b.** 0.25
c. 0.01   **d.** 1×10^{-6}

567. 4×10^{-4}; 3×10^{-5}; 3×10^{-5}; 1×10^{-6}; 3×10^{-7}

568. 7.1×10^{-7} M; 1.3×10^{-3} g

569. a. 0.011 M   **b.** 0.022 M
c. 12.35

570. 0.063 g

571. $2Fe + 3SnCl_4 \rightarrow 2FeCl_3 + 3SnCl_2$

572. $H_2O_2 + 2FeSO_4 + H_2SO_4 \rightarrow Fe_2(SO_4)_3 + 2H_2O$

573. $3CuS + 8HNO_3 \rightarrow 3Cu(NO_3)_2 + 2NO + 3S + 4H_2O$

574. $K_2Cr_2O_7 + 14 HI \rightarrow 2CrI_3 + 2KI + 3I_2 + 7H_2O$

575. $CO_2 + 2NH_2OH \rightarrow CO + N_2 + 3H_2O$

576. $2Bi(OH)_3 + 3K_2SnO_2 \rightarrow 2Bi + 3K_2SnO_3 + 3H_2O$

577. $3Mg + N_2 \rightarrow Mg_3N_2$

578. $SO_2 + Br_2 + 2H_2O \rightarrow 2HBr + H_2SO_4$

579. $H_2S + Cl_2 \rightarrow S + 2HCl$

580. $PbO_2 + 4HBr \rightarrow PbBr_2 + Br_2 + 2H_2O$

581. $S + 6HNO_3 \rightarrow 6NO_2 + H_2SO_4 + 2H_2O$

582. $NaIO_3 + N_2H_4 + 2HCl \rightarrow N_2 + NaICl_2 + 3H_2O$

583. $MnO_2 + H_2O_2 + 2HCl \rightarrow$
$MnCl_2 + O_2 + 2H_2O$

584. $3AsH_3 + 4NaClO_3 \rightarrow$
$3H_3AsO_4 + 4NaCl$

585. $K_2Cr_2O_7 + 3H_2C_2O_4 + 8HCl \rightarrow$
$2CrCl_3 + 6CO_2 + 2KCl + 7H_2O$

586. $2Hg(NO_3)_2 \rightarrow$
$2HgO + 4NO_2 + O_2$

587. $4HAuCl_4 + 3N_2H_4 \rightarrow$
$4Au + 3N_2 + 16HCl$

588. $5Sb_2(SO_4)_3 + 4KMnO_4 +$
$24H_2O \rightarrow 10H_3SbO_4 + 2K_2SO_4 +$
$4MnSO_4 + 9H_2SO_4$

589. $3Mn(NO_3)_2 + 5NaBiO_3 +$
$9HNO_3 \rightarrow 5Bi(NO_3)_2 +$
$3HMnO_4 + 5NaNO_3 + 3H_2O$

590. $H_3AsO_4 + 4Zn + 8HCl \rightarrow$
$AsH_3 + 4ZnCl_2 + 4H_2O$

591. $KClO_3 + 6HCl \rightarrow$
$3Cl_2 + 3H_2O + KCl$

592. $2KClO_3 + 4HCl \rightarrow$
$Cl_2 + 2ClO_2 + 2H_2O + 2KCl$

593. $2MnCl_3 + 2H_2O \rightarrow$
$MnCl_2 + MnO_2 + 4HCl$

594. $2NaOH + 6H_2O + 2Al \rightarrow$
$2NaAl(OH)_4 + 3H_2$

595. $6Br_2 + 6Ca(OH)_2 \rightarrow$
$5CaBr_2 + Ca(BrO_3)_2 + 6H_2O$

596. $N_2O + 2NaClO + 2NaOH \rightarrow$
$2NaCl + 2NaNO_2 + H_2O$

597. $4HBr + MnO_2 \rightarrow$
$MnBr_2 + 2H_2O + Br_2$

598. $Au + 4HCl + HNO_3 \rightarrow$
$HAuCl_4 + NO + 2H_2O$

599. $+0.79$ V; spontaneous

600. -0.90 V; nonspontaneous

601. -1.64 V; nonspontaneous

602. $+0.80$ V; spontaneous

603. $+0.24$ V; spontaneous

604. -2.91 V; nonspontaneous

605. -0.29 V; nonspontaneous

606. -1.02 V; nonspontaneous

532. The $[H_3O^+]$ of a solution of acetoacetic acid, CH_3COCH_2COOH, is 4.38×10^{-3} M at 25°C. The concentration of nonionized acid is 0.0731 M at equilibrium. Calculate K_a for acetoacetic acid at 25°C.

533. The K_a of 2-chloropropanoic acid, $CH_3CHClCOOH$, is 1.48×10^{-3}. Calculate the $[H_3O^+]$ and the pH of a 0.116 M solution of 2-chloropropionic acid. Let $x = [H_3O^+]$. The degree of ionization of the acid is too large to ignore. If your set up is correct, you will have a quadratic equation to solve.

534. Sulfuric acid ionizes in two steps in water solution. For the first ionization shown in the following equation, the K_a is so large that in moderately dilute solution the ionization can be considered 100%.

$$H_2SO_4 + H_2O \rightarrow H_3O^+ + HSO_4^-$$

The second ionization is fairly strong, and $K_a = 1.3 \times 10^{-2}$:

$$HSO_4^- + H_2O \rightleftarrows H_3O^+ + SO_4^{2-}$$

Calculate the total $[H_3O^+]$ and pH of a 0.0788 M H_2SO_4 solution. Hint: If the first ionization is 100%, what will $[HSO_4^-]$ and $[H_3O^+]$ be? Remember to account for the already existing concentration of H_3O^+ in the second ionization. Let $x = [SO_4^{2-}]$.

535. The hydronium ion concentration of a 0.100 M solution of cyanic acid, HOCN, is found to be 5.74×10^{-3} M at 25°C. Calculate the ionization constant of cyanic acid. What is the pH of this solution?

536. A solution of hydrogen cyanide, HCN, has a 0.025 M concentration. The cyanide ion concentration is found to be 3.16×10^{-6} M.
a. What is the hydronium ion concentration of this solution?
b. What is the pH of this solution?
c. What is the concentration of nonionized HCN in the solution? Be sure to use the correct number of significant figures.
d. Calculate the ionization constant of HCN.
e. How would you characterize the strength of HCN as an acid?
f. Determine the $[H_3O^+]$ for a 0.085 M solution of HCN.

537. A 1.20 M solution of dichloroacetic acid, CCl_2HCOOH, at 25°C has a hydronium ion concentration of 0.182 M.
a. What is the pH of this solution?
b. What is the K_a of dichloroacetic acid at 25°C?
c. What is the concentration of nonionized dichloroacetic acid in this solution?
d. What can you say about the strength of dichloroacetic acid?

538. Phenol, C_6H_5OH, is a very weak acid. The pH of a 0.215 M solution of phenol at 25°C is found to be 5.61. Calculate the K_a for phenol.

539. A solution of the simplest amino acid, glycine (NH_2CH_2COOH), is prepared by dissolving 3.75 g in 250.0 mL of water at 25°C. The pH of this solution is found to be 0.890.
a. Calculate the molarity of the glycine solution.
b. Calculate the K_a for glycine.

540. Trimethylamine, $(CH_3)_3N$, dissociates in water the same way that NH_3 does—by accepting a proton from a water molecule. The $[OH^-]$ of a 0.0750 M solution of trimethylamine at 25°C is 2.32×10^{-3} M. Calculate the pH of this solution and the K_b of trimethylamine.

541. Dimethylamine, $(CH_3)_2NH$, is a weak base similar to the trimethylamine in item 540. A 5.00×10^{-3} M solution of dimethylamine has a pH of 11.20 at 25°C. Calculate the K_b of dimethylamine. Compare this K_b with the K_b for trimethylamine that you calculated in item 540. Which substance is the stronger base?

542. Hydrazine dissociates in water solution according to the following equations:

$$H_2NNH_2 + H_2O(l) \rightleftarrows H_2NNH_3^+(aq) + OH^-(aq)$$
$$H_2NNH_3^+(aq) + H_2O(l) \rightleftarrows H_3NNH_3^{2+}(aq) + OH^-(aq)$$

The K_b of this second dissociation is 8.9×10^{-16}, so it contributes almost no hydroxide ions in solution and can be ignored here.
a. The pH of a 0.120 M solution of hydrazine at 25°C is 10.50. Calculate K_b for the first ionization of hydrazine. Assume that the original concentration of H_2NNH_2 does not change.
b. Make the same assumption as you did in (a) and calculate the $[OH^-]$ of a 0.020 M solution.
c. Calculate the pH of the solution in (b).

Equilibrium of Salts, K_{sp}, Section 18-4

543. Silver bromate, $AgBrO_3$, is slightly soluble in water. A saturated solution is found to contain 0.276 g $AgBrO_3$ dissolved in 150.0 mL of water. Calculate K_{sp} for silver bromate.

544. 2.50 L of a saturated solution of calcium fluoride leaves a residue of 0.0427 g of CaF_2 when evaporated to dryness. Calculate the K_{sp} of CaF_2.

545. The K_{sp} of calcium sulfate, $CaSO_4$, is 9.1×10^{-6}. What is the molar concentration of $CaSO_4$ in a saturated solution?

546. A salt has the formula X_2Y, and its K_{sp} is 4.25×10^{-7}.
a. What is the molarity of a saturated solution of the salt?
b. What is the molarity of a solution of AZ if its K_{sp} is the same value?

In each of the following problems, include the calculated ion product with your answer.

547. Will a precipitate of $Ca(OH)_2$ form when 320. mL of a 0.046 M solution of NaOH mixes with 400. mL of a 0.085 M $CaCl_2$ solution? K_{sp} of $Ca(OH)_2$ is 5.5×10^{-6}.

548. 20.00 mL of a 0.077 M solution of silver nitrate, $AgNO_3$, is mixed with 30.00 mL of a 0.043 M solution of sodium acetate, $NaC_2H_3O_2$. Does a precipitate form? The K_{sp} of $AgC_2H_3O_2$ is 2.5×10^{-3}.

549. If you mix 100. mL of 0.036 M $Pb(C_2H_3O_2)_2$ with 50. mL of 0.074 M NaCl, will a precipitate of $PbCl_2$ form? The K_{sp} of $PbCl_2$ is 1.9×10^{-4}.

550. If 20.00 mL of a 0.0090 M solution of $(NH_4)_2S$ is mixed with 120.00 mL of a 0.0082 M solution of $Al(NO_3)_3$, does a precipitate form? The K_{sp} of Al_2S_3 is 2.00×10^{-7}.

Mixed Review

551. The molar concentration of a saturated calcium chromate, $CaCrO_4$, solution is 0.010 M at 25°C. What is the K_{sp} of calcium chromate?

552. A 10.00 mL sample of a saturated lead selenate solution is found to contain 0.00136 g of dissolved $PbSeO_4$ at 25°C. Determine the K_{sp} of lead selenate.

553. A 22.50 mL sample of a saturated copper(I) thiocyanate, CuSCN, solution at 25°C is found to have a 4.0×10^{-6} M concentration.
   a. Determine the K_{sp} of CuSCN.
   b. What mass of CuSCN would be dissolved in 1.0×10^3 L of solution?

554. A saturated solution of silver dichromate, $Ag_2Cr_2O_7$, has a concentration of 3.684×10^{-3} M. Calculate the K_{sp} of silver dichromate.

555. The K_{sp} of barium sulfite, $BaSO_3$, at 25°C is 8.0×10^{-7}.
   a. What is the molar concentration of a saturated solution of $BaSO_3$?
   b. What mass of $BaSO_3$ would dissolve in 500. mL of water?

556. The K_{sp} of lead(II) chloride at 25°C is 1.9×10^{-4}. What is the molar concentration of a saturated solution at 25°C?

557. The K_{sp} of barium carbonate at 25°C is 1.2×10^{-8}.
   a. What is the molar concentration of a saturated solution of $BaCO_3$ at 25°C?
   b. What volume of water would be needed to dissolve 0.10 g of barium carbonate?

558. The K_{sp} of $SrSO_4$ is 3.2×10^{-7} at 25°C.
   a. What is the molar concentration of a saturated $SrSO_4$ solution?
   b. If 20.0 L of a saturated solution of $SrSO_4$ were evaporated to dryness, what mass of $SrSO_4$ would remain?

559. The K_{sp} of strontium sulfite, $SrSO_3$, is 4.0×10^{-8} at 25°C. If 1.0000 g of $SrSO_3$ is stirred in 5.0 L of water until the solution is saturated and then filtered, what mass of $SrSO_3$ would remain?

560. The K_{sp} of manganese(II) arsenate is 1.9×10^{-11} at 25°C. What is the molar concentration of $Mn_3(AsO_4)_2$ in a saturated solution? Note that five ions are produced from the dissociation of $Mn_3(AsO_4)_2$.

561. Suppose that 30.0 mL of a 0.0050 M solution of $Sr(NO_3)_2$ is mixed with 20.0 mL of a 0.010 M solution of K_2SO_4 at 25°C. The K_{sp} of $SrSO_4$ is 3.2×10^{-7}.
   a. What is the ion product of the ions that can potentially form a precipitate?
   b. Does a precipitate form?

562. Lead(II) bromide, $PbBr_2$, is slightly soluble in water. Its K_{sp} is 6.3×10^{-6} at 25°C. Suppose that 120. mL of a 0.0035 M solution of $MgBr_2$ is mixed with 180. mL of a 0.0024 M $Pb(C_2H_3O_2)_2$ solution at 25°C.
   a. What is the ion product of Br^- and Pb^{2+} in the mixed solution?
   b. Does a precipitate form?

563. The K_{sp} of $Mg(OH)_2$ at 25°C is 1.5×10^{-11}.
   a. Write the equilibrium equation for the dissociation of $Mg(OH)_2$.
   b. What volume of water would be required to dissolve 0.10 g of $Mg(OH)_2$?
   c. Considering that magnesium hydroxide is essentially insoluble, why is it possible to titrate a suspension of $Mg(OH)_2$ to an equivalence point with a strong acid such as HCl?

564. Lithium carbonate is somewhat soluble in water; its K_{sp} at 25°C is 2.51×10^{-2}.
   a. What is the molar concentration of a saturated Li_2CO_3 solution?
   b. What mass of Li_2CO_3 would you dissolve in order to make 3440 mL of saturated solution?

565. A 50.00 mL sample of a saturated solution of barium hydroxide, $Ba(OH)_2$, is titrated to the equivalence point by 31.61 mL of a 0.3417 M solution of HCl. Determine the K_{sp} of $Ba(OH)_2$.

566. Calculate the K_{sp} for salts represented by QR that dissociate into two ions, Q^+ and R^-, in each of the following solutions:
   a. saturated solution of QR is 1.0 M
   b. saturated solution of QR is 0.50 M
   c. saturated solution of QR is 0.1 M
   d. saturated solution of QR is 0.001 M

567. Suppose that salts QR, X_2Y, KL_2, A_3Z, and D_2E_3 form saturated solutions that are 0.02 M in concentration. Calculate K_{sp} for each of these salts.

568. The K_{sp} at 25°C of silver bromide is 5.0×10^{-13}. What is the molar concentration of a saturated AgBr solution? What mass of silver bromide would dissolve in 10.0 L of saturated solution at 25°C?

569. The K_{sp} at 25°C for calcium hydroxide is 5.5×10^{-6}.
   a. Calculate the molarity of a saturated $Ca(OH)_2$ solution.
   b. What is the OH^- concentration of this solution?
   c. What is the pH of the saturated solution?

570. The K_{sp} of magnesium carbonate is 3.5×10^{-8} at 25°C. What mass of $MgCO_3$ would dissolve in 4.00 L of water at 25°C?

Redox Equations, Section 19-2

Reactions in Acidic Solution

Balance the following redox equations. Assume that all reactions take place in an acid environment where H^+ and H_2O are readily available.

571. $Fe + SnCl_4 \rightarrow FeCl_3 + SnCl_2$

572. $H_2O_2 + FeSO_4 + H_2SO_4 \rightarrow Fe_2(SO_4)_3 + H_2O$

573. $CuS + HNO_3 \rightarrow Cu(NO_3)_2 + NO + S + H_2O$

574. $K_2Cr_2O_7 + HI \rightarrow CrI_3 + KI + I_2 + H_2O$

607. cathode: $Fe^{3+} + 3e^- \rightarrow Fe$
   anode: $Ca \rightarrow Ca^{2+} + 2e$
   $E^0_{cell} = +2.83$ V

608. cathode: $Ag^+ + e^- \rightarrow Ag$
   anode: $H_2S \rightarrow S + 2H^+ + 2e^-$
   $E^0_{cell} = +0.66$ V

609. cathode: $Fe^{3+} + e^- \rightarrow Fe^{2+}$
   anode: $Sn \rightarrow Sn^{2+} + 2e^-$
   $E^0_{cell} = +0.91$ V

610. cathode: $Au^{3+} + 3e^- \rightarrow Au$
   anode: $Cu \rightarrow Cu^{2+} + 2e^-$
   $E^0_{cell} = +1.16$ V

611. $E^0 = +2.77$ V; spontaneous

612. $E^0 = +1.11$ V; spontaneous

613. $E^0 = -0.46$ V; not spontaneous

614. $E^0 = +1.50$ V; spontaneous

615. $E^0 = +2.46$ V; spontaneous

616. $E^0 = +1.28$ V; spontaneous

617. $E^0 = +3.71$ V; spontaneous

618. $E^0 = -3.41$ V; not spontaneous

619. $E^0 = +1.32$ V; spontaneous

620. $E^0 = -3.60$ V; not spontaneous

621. Overall reaction:
   $Cl_2 + Ni \rightarrow Ni^{2+} + 2Cl^-$
   Cathode reaction:
   $Cl_2 + 2e^- \rightarrow 2Cl^-$
   Anode reaction:
   $Ni \rightarrow Ni^{2+} + 2e^-$
   Cell voltage: $+1.62$ V

622. Overall reaction:
   $3Hg^{2+} + 2Fe \rightarrow 3Hg + 2Fe^{3+}$
   Cathode reaction:
   $Hg^{2+} + 2e^- \rightarrow Hg$
   Anode reaction:
   $Fe \rightarrow Fe^{3+} + 3e^-$
   Cell voltage: $+0.89$ V

623. Overall reaction:
$$3MnO_4^- + Al \to 3MnO_4^{2-} + Al^{3+}$$
Cathode reaction:
$$MnO_4^- + e^- \to MnO_4^{2-}$$
Anode reaction:
$$Al \to Al^{3+} + 3e^-$$
Cell voltage: +2.22 V

624. Overall reaction:
$$2MnO_4^- + 6H^+ + 5H_2S \to$$
$$2Mn^{2+} + 8H_2O + 5S$$
Cathode reaction:
$$MnO_4^- + 8H^+ + 5e^- \to$$
$$Mn^{2+} + 4H_2O$$
Anode reaction:
$$H_2S \to S + 2H^+ + 2e^-$$
Cell voltage: +1.36 V

625. Overall reaction:
$$Ca^{2+} + 2Li \to Ca + 2Li^+$$
Cathode reaction:
$$Ca^{2+} + 2e^- \to Ca$$
Anode reaction: $Li \to Li^+ + e^-$
Cell voltage: +0.17 V

626. Overall reaction:
$$2MnO_4^- + 16H^+ + 10Br^- \to$$
$$2Mn^{2+} + 8H_2O + 5Br_2$$
Cathode reaction:
$$MnO_4^- + 8H^+ + 5e^- \to$$
$$Mn^{2+} + 4H_2O$$
Anode reaction:
$$2Br^- \to Br_2 + 2e^-$$
Cell voltage: +0.43 V

627. Overall reaction:
$$2Fe^{3+} + Sn \to 2Fe^{2+} + Sn^{2+}$$
Cathode reaction:
$$Fe^{3+} + e^- \to Fe^{2+}$$
Anode reaction:
$$Sn \to Sn^{2+} + 2e^-$$
Cell voltage: +0.91 V

628. Overall reaction:
$$Cr_2O_7^{2-} + 14H^+ + 3Zn \to$$
$$2Cr^{3+} + 7H_2O + 3Zn^{2+}$$
Cathode reaction:
$$Cr_2O_7^{2-} + 14H^+ + 6e^- \to$$
$$2Cr^{3+} + 7H_2O$$
Anode reaction:
$$Zn \to Zn^{2+} + 2e^-$$
Cell voltage: +1.99 V

Reactions in Basic Solution

Balance the following redox equations. Assume that all reactions take place in a basic environment where OH^- and H_2O are readily available.

575. $CO_2 + NH_2OH \to CO + N_2 + H_2O$

576. $Bi(OH)_3 + K_2SnO_2 \to Bi + K_2SnO_3$
(Both of the potassium-tin-oxygen compounds dissociate into potassium ions and tin-oxygen ions.)

Mixed Review

Balance each of the following redox equations. Unless stated otherwise, assume that the reaction occurs in acidic solution.

577. $Mg + N_2 \to Mg_3N_2$

578. $SO_2 + Br_2 + H_2O \to HBr + H_2SO_4$

579. $H_2S + Cl_2 \to S + HCl$

580. $PbO_2 + HBr \to PbBr_2 + Br_2 + H_2O$

581. $S + HNO_3 \to NO_2 + H_2SO_4 + H_2O$

582. $NaIO_3 + N_2H_4 + HCl \to N_2 + NaICl_2 + H_2O$ (N_2H_4 is hydrazine; do not separate it into ions.)

583. $MnO_2 + H_2O_2 + HCl \to MnCl_2 + O_2 + H_2O$

584. $AsH_3 + NaClO_3 \to H_3AsO_4 + NaCl$ (AsH_3 is arsine, the arsenic analogue of ammonia, NH_3.)

585. $K_2Cr_2O_7 + H_2C_2O_4 + HCl \to CrCl_3 + CO_2 + KCl + H_2O$ ($H_2C_2O_4$ is oxalic acid; it can be treated as $2H^+ + C_2O_4^{2-}$.)

586. $Hg(NO_3)_2 \xrightarrow{heat} HgO + NO_2 + O_2$ (The reaction is not in solution.)

587. $HAuCl_4 + N_2H_4 \to Au + N_2 + HCl$ ($HAuCl_4$ can be considered as $H^+ + AuCl_4^-$.)

588. $Sb_2(SO_4)_3 + KMnO_4 + H_2O \to$
$$H_3SbO_4 + K_2SO_4 + MnSO_4 + H_2SO_4$$

589. $Mn(NO_3)_2 + NaBiO_3 + HNO_3 \to$
$$Bi(NO_3)_2 + HMnO_4 + NaNO_3 + H_2O$$

590. $H_3AsO_4 + Zn + HCl \to AsH_3 + ZnCl_2 + H_2O$

591. $KClO_3 + HCl \to Cl_2 + H_2O + KCl$

592. The same reactants as in item 591 can combine in the following way when more $KClO_3$ is present. Balance the equation.
$$KClO_3 + HCl \to Cl_2 + ClO_2 + H_2O + KCl$$

593. $MnCl_3 + H_2O \to MnCl_2 + MnO_2 + HCl$

594. $NaOH + H_2O + Al \to NaAl(OH)_4 + H_2$ in basic solution

595. $Br_2 + Ca(OH)_2 \to CaBr_2 + Ca(BrO_3)_2 + H_2O$ in basic solution

596. $N_2O + NaClO + NaOH \to NaCl + NaNO_2 + H_2O$ in basic solution

597. Balance the following reaction, which can be used to prepare bromine in the laboratory:
$$HBr + MnO_2 \to MnBr_2 + H_2O + Br_2$$

598. The following reaction occurs when gold is dissolved in *aqua regia*. Balance the equation.
$$Au + HCl + HNO_3 \to HAuCl_4 + NO + H_2O$$

Electrochemistry, Section 19-4

Use the reduction potentials in the table on page 955 to determine whether the following reactions are spontaneous as written. Report the E^0_{cell} for the reactions.

599. $Cu^{2+} + Fe \to Fe^{2+} + Cu$

600. $Pb^{2+} + Fe^{2+} \to Fe^{3+} + Pb$

601. $Mn^{2+} + 4H_2O + Sn^{2+} \to MnO_4^- + 8H^+ + Sn$

602. $MnO_4^{2-} + Cl_2 \to MnO_4^- + 2Cl^-$

603. $Hg_2^{2+} + 2MnO_4^{2-} \to 2Hg + 2MnO_4^-$

604. $2Li^+ + Pb \to 2Li + Pb^{2+}$

605. $Br_2 + 2Cl^- \to 2Br^- + Cl_2$

606. $S + 2I^- \to S^{2-} + I_2$

If a cell is constructed in which the following pairs of reactions are possible, what would be the cathode reaction, the anode reaction, and the overall cell voltage?

607. $Ca^{2+} + 2e^- \rightleftarrows Ca$
$Fe^{3+} + 3e^- \rightleftarrows Fe$

608. $Ag^+ + e^- \rightleftarrows Ag$
$S + 2H^+ + 2e^- \rightleftarrows H_2S$

609. $Fe^{3+} + e^- \rightleftarrows Fe^{2+}$
$Sn^{2+} + 2e^- \rightleftarrows Sn$

610. $Cu^{2+} + 2e^- \rightleftarrows Cu$
$Au^{3+} + 3e^- \rightleftarrows Au$

Mixed Review

Use reduction potentials to determine whether the reactions in the following 10 problems are spontaneous.

611. $Ba + Sn^{2+} \to Ba^{2+} + Sn$

612. $Ni + Hg^{2+} \to Ni^{2+} + Hg$

613. $2Cr^{3+} + 7H_2O + 6Fe^{3+} \to Cr_2O_7^{2-} + 14H^+ + 6Fe^{2+}$

614. $Cl_2 + Sn \to 2Cl^- + Sn^{2+}$

615. $Al + 3Ag^+ \to Al^{3+} + 3Ag$

616. $Hg_2^{2+} + S^{2-} \to 2Hg + S$

617. $Ba + 2Ag^+ \to Ba^{2+} + 2Ag$

618. $2I^- + Ca^{2+} \to I_2 + Ca$

619. $Zn + 2MnO_4^- \to Zn^{2+} + 2MnO_4^{2-}$

620. $2Cr^{3+} + 3Mg^{2+} + 7H_2O \to Cr_2O_7^{2-} + 14H^+ + 3Mg$

In the following problems, you are given a pair of reduction half-reactions. If a cell were constructed in which the pairs of half-reactions were possible, what would be the balanced equation for the overall cell reaction that would occur? Write the half-reactions that occur at the cathode and anode, and calculate the cell voltage.

621. $Cl_2 + 2e^- \rightleftarrows 2Cl^-$
$Ni^{2+} + 2e^- \rightleftarrows Ni$

622. $Fe^{3+} + 3e^- \rightleftarrows Fe$
$Hg^{2+} + 2e^- \rightleftarrows Hg$

623. $MnO_4^- + e^- \rightleftarrows MnO_4^{2-}$
$Al^{3+} + 3e^- \rightleftarrows Al$

624. $MnO_4^- + 8H^+ + 5e^- \rightleftarrows Mn^{2+} + 4H_2O$
$S + 2H^+ + 2e^- \rightleftarrows H_2S$

625. $Ca^{2+} + 2e^- \rightleftarrows Ca$
$Li^+ + e^- \rightleftarrows Li$

626. $Br_2 + 2e^- \rightleftarrows 2Br^-$
$MnO_4^- + 8H^+ + 5e^- \rightleftarrows Mn^{2+} + 4H_2O$

627. $Sn^{2+} + 2e^- \rightleftarrows Sn$
$Fe^{3+} + e^- \rightleftarrows Fe^{2+}$

628. $Zn^{2+} + 2e^- \rightleftarrows Zn$
$Cr_2O_7^{2-} + 14H^+ + 6e^- \rightleftarrows 2Cr^{3+} + 7H_2O$

629. $Ba^{2+} + 2e^- \rightleftarrows Ba$
$Ca^{2+} + 2e^- \rightleftarrows Ca$

630. $Hg_2^{2+} + 2e^- \rightleftarrows 2Hg$
$Cd^{2+} + 2e^- \rightleftarrows Cd$

629. Overall reaction:
$Ba + Ca^{2+} \rightarrow Ba^{2+} + Ca$
Cathode reaction:
$Ca^{2+} + 2e^- \rightarrow Ca$
Anode reaction:
$Ba \rightarrow Ba^{2+} + 2e^-$
Cell voltage: $+0.04$ V

630. Overall reaction:
$Cd + Hg_2^{2+} \rightarrow Cd^{2+} + 2Hg$
Cathode reaction:
$Hg_2^{2+} + 2e^- \rightarrow 2Hg$
Anode reaction:
$Cd \rightarrow Cd^{2+} + 2e^-$
Cell voltage: $+1.25$ V

For problems 599–606

Reduction Half-reaction	Standard Electrode Potential, E^0 (in volts)	Reduction Half-reaction	Standard Electrode Potential, E^0 (in volts)
$MnO_4^- + 8H^+ + 5e^- \rightleftarrows$ $Mn^{2+} + 4H_2O$	+1.50	$Fe^{3+} + 3e^- \rightleftarrows Fe$	−0.04
$Au^{3+} + 3e^- \rightleftarrows Au$	+1.50	$Pb^{2+} + 2e^- \rightleftarrows Pb$	−0.13
$Cl_2 + 2e^- \rightleftarrows 2Cl^-$	+1.36	$Sn^{2+} + 2e^- \rightleftarrows Sn$	−0.14
$Cr_2O_7^{2-} + 14H^+ + 6e^- \rightleftarrows$ $2Cr^{3+} + 7H_2O$	+1.23	$Ni^{2+} + 2e^- \rightleftarrows Ni$	−0.26
$MnO_2 + 4H^+ + 2e^- \rightleftarrows$ $Mn^{2+} + 2H_2O$	+1.22	$Cd^{2+} + 2e^- \rightleftarrows Cd$	−0.40
$Br_2 + 2e^- \rightleftarrows 2Br^-$	+1.07	$Fe^{2+} + 2e^- \rightleftarrows Fe$	−0.45
$Hg^{2+} + 2e^- \rightleftarrows Hg$	+0.85	$S + 2e^- \rightleftarrows S^{2-}$	−0.48
$Ag^+ + e^- \rightleftarrows Ag$	+0.80	$Zn^{2+} + 2e^- \rightleftarrows Zn$	−0.76
$Hg_2^{2+} + 2e^- \rightleftarrows 2Hg$	+0.80	$Al^{3+} + 3e^- \rightleftarrows Al$	−1.66
$Fe^{3+} + e^- \rightleftarrows Fe^{2+}$	+0.77	$Mg^{2+} + 2e^- \rightleftarrows Mg$	−2.37
$MnO_4^- + e^- \rightleftarrows MnO_4^{2-}$	+0.56	$Na^+ + e^- \rightleftarrows Na$	−2.71
$I_2 + 2e^- \rightleftarrows 2I^-$	+0.54	$Ca^{2+} + 2e^- \rightleftarrows Ca$	−2.87
$Cu^{2+} + 2e^- \rightleftarrows Cu$	+0.34	$Ba^{2+} + 2e^- \rightleftarrows Ba$	−2.91
$S + 2H^+(aq) + 2e^- \rightleftarrows$ $H_2S(aq)$	+0.14	$K^+ + e^- \rightleftarrows K$	−2.93
$2H^+(aq) + 2e^- \rightleftarrows H_2$	0.00	$Li^+ + e^- \rightleftarrows Li$	−3.04

A

absolute zero the temperature −273.15°C, given a value of zero in the Kelvin scale (317)

accuracy the closeness of measurements to the correct or accepted value of the quantity measured (44)

acid-base indicator a compound whose color is sensitive to pH (493)

acid-ionization constant the term K_a (569)

actinide one of the 14 elements with atomic numbers from 90 (thorium, Th) through 103 (lawrencium, Lr) (126)

activated complex a transitional structure that results from an effective collision and that persists while old bonds are breaking and new bonds are forming (535)

activation energy the minimum energy required to transform the reactants into an activated complex (534)

activity series a list of elements organized according to the ease with which the elements undergo certain chemical reactions (265)

actual yield the measured amount of a product obtained from a reaction (293)

addition polymer a polymer formed by chain addition reactions between monomers that contain a double bond (686)

addition reaction a reaction in which an atom or molecule is added to an unsaturated molecule and increases the saturation of the molecule (682)

alcohol an organic compound that contains one or more hydroxyl groups (663)

aldehyde an organic compound in which a carbonyl group is attached to a carbon atom at the end of a carbon-atom chain (672)

alkali metal one of the elements of Group 1 of the periodic table (lithium, sodium, potassium, rubidium, cesium, and francium) (132)

alkaline a solution in which a base has completely dissociated in water to yield aqueous OH⁻ ions (461)

alkaline-earth metal one of the elements of Group 2 of the periodic table (beryllium, magnesium, calcium, strontium, barium, and radium) (132)

alkane a hydrocarbon that contains only single bonds (634)

alkene a hydrocarbon that contains double covalent bonds (647)

alkyl group a group of atoms that is formed when one hydrogen atom is removed from an alkane molecule (637)

alkyl halide an organic compound in which one or more halogen atoms —fluorine, chlorine, bromine, or iodine—are substituted for one or more hydrogen atoms in a hydrocarbon (666)

alkyne a hydrocarbon with triple covalent bonds (651)

alpha particle two protons and two neutrons bound together and emitted from the nucleus during some kinds of radioactive decay (706)

amine an organic compound that can be considered to be a derivative of ammonia, NH_3 (677)

amorphous solid a solid in which the particles are arranged randomly (368)

amphoteric any species that can react as either an acid or a base (471)

angular momentum quantum number the quantum number that indicates the shape of the orbital (101)

anion a negative ion (149)

anode the electrode where oxidation takes place (607)

aromatic hydrocarbon a hydrocarbon with six-membered carbon rings and delocalized electrons (652)

Arrhenius acid a chemical compound that increases the concentration of hydrogen ions, H⁺, in aqueous solution (459)

Arrhenius base a substance that increases the concentration of hydroxide ions, OH⁻, in aqueous solution (459)

artificial transmutation bombardment of stable nuclei with charged and uncharged particles (711)

atmosphere of pressure exactly equivalent to 760 mm Hg (311)

atom the smallest unit of an element that maintains the properties of that element (10)

atomic mass unit a unit of mass that is exactly 1/12 the mass of a carbon-12 atom, or $1.660\ 540 \times 10^{-27}$ kg (78)

atomic number the number of protons in the nucleus of each atom of an element (75)

atomic radius one-half the distance between the nuclei of identical atoms that are bonded together (140)

Aufbau principle an electron occupies the lowest-energy orbital that can receive it (105)

autooxidation a process in which a substance acts as both an oxidizing agent and a reducing agent (605)

average atomic mass the weighted average of the atomic masses of the naturally occurring isotopes of an element (79)

Avogadro's law equal volumes of gases at the same temperature and pressure contain equal numbers of molecules (334)

Avogadro's number $6.022\ 1367 \times 10^{23}$; the number of particles in exactly one mole of a pure substance (81)

B

band of stability the stable nuclei cluster over a range of neutron-proton ratios (702)

barometer a device used to measure atmospheric pressure (310)

benzene the primary aromatic hydrocarbon (652)

beta particle an electron emitted from the nucleus during some kinds of radioactive decay (706)

binary acid an acid that contains only two different elements: hydrogen and one of the more-electronegative elements (454)

binary compound a compound composed of two different elements (206)

binding energy per nucleon the binding energy of the nucleus divided by the number of nucleons it contains (702)

boiling the conversion of a liquid to a vapor within the liquid as well as at its surface; occurs when the equilibrium vapor pressure of the liquid equals the atmospheric pressure (378)

boiling point the temperature at which the equilibrium vapor pressure of a liquid equals the atmospheric pressure (378)

boiling-point elevation the difference between the boiling point of a pure solvent and a nonelectrolyte of that solvent, directly proportional to the molal concentration of the solution (440)

bond energy the energy required to break a chemical bond and form neutral isolated atoms (167)

bond length the distance between two bonded atoms at their minimum potential energy, that is, the average distance between two bonded atoms (167)

Boyle's law the volume of a fixed mass of gas varies inversely with pressure at constant temperature (314)

Brønsted-Lowry acid a molecule or ion that is a proton donor (464)

Brønsted-Lowry acid-base reaction the transfer of protons from one reactant (the acid) to another (the base) (465)

Brønsted-Lowry base a molecule or ion that is a proton acceptor (465)

buffered solution a solution that can resist changes in pH (570)

calorimeter a device used to measure the heat absorbed or released in a chemical or physical change (511)

capillary action the attraction of the surface of a liquid to the surface of a solid (365)

carboxylic acid an organic compound that contains the carboxyl functional group (674)

catalysis the action of a catalyst (540)

catalyst a substance that changes the rate of a chemical reaction without itself being permanently consumed (540)

catenation the covalent binding of an element to itself to form chains or rings (630)

cathode the electrode where reduction takes place (607)

cation a positive ion (149)

chain reaction a reaction in which the material that starts the reaction is also one of the products and can start another reaction (717)

change of state a physical change of a substance from one state to another (12)

Charles's law the volume of a fixed mass of gas at constant pressure varies directly with the Kelvin temperature (317)

chemical any substance that has a definite composition (6)

chemical bond a mutual electrical attraction between the nuclei and valence electrons of different atoms that binds the atoms together(161)

chemical change a change in which one or more substances are converted into different substances (13)

chemical equation a representation, with symbols and formulas, of the identities and relative amounts of the reactants and products in a chemical reaction (241)

chemical equilibrium a state of balance in which the rate of a forward reaction equals the rate of its reverse reaction and the concentrations of its products and reactants remain unchanged (554)

chemical-equilibrium expression the equation for the equilibrium constant, K (556)

chemical formula a formula that indicates the relative numbers of atoms of each kind in a chemical compound by using atomic symbols and numerical subscripts (164)

chemical kinetics the area of chemistry that is concerned with reaction rates and reaction mechanisms (538)

chemical property the ability of a substance to undergo a change that transforms it into a different substance (12)

chemical reaction a reaction in which one or more substances are converted into different substances (13)

chemistry the study of the composition, structure, and properties of matter and the changes it undergoes (5)

coefficient a small whole number that appears in front of a formula in a chemical equation (243)

colligative properties properties that depend on the concentration of solute particles but not on their identity (436)

collision theory the set of assumptions regarding collisions and reactions (532)

colloid a mixture consisting of particles that are intermediate in size between those in solutions and suspensions forming mixtures known as colloid dispersions (397)

combined gas law the relationship between the pressure, volume, and temperature of a fixed amount of gas (321)

combustion reaction a reaction in which a substance combines with oxygen, releasing a large amount of energy in the form of light and heat (263)

common ion effect the phenomenon in which the addition of an ion common to two solutes brings about precipitation or reduced ionization (567)

composition reaction a reaction in which two or more substances combine to form a new compound (256)

composition stoichiometry calculations involving the mass relationships of elements in compounds (275)

compound a substance that is made from the atoms of two or more elements that are chemically bonded (11)

concentration a measure of the amount of solute in a given amount of solvent or solution (412)

condensation the process by which a gas changes to a liquid (373)

condensation polymer a polymer formed by condensation reactions (690)

condensation reaction a reaction in which two molecules or parts of the same molecule combine (683)

conjugate acid the species that is formed when a Brønsted-Lowry base gains a proton (469)

conjugate base the species that remains after a Brønsted-Lowry acid has given up a proton (469)

continuous spectrum the emission of a continuous range of frequencies of electromagnetic radiation (94)

control rod a neutron-absorbing rod that helps control a nuclear reaction by limiting the number of free neutrons (718)

conversion factor a ratio derived from the equality between two different units that can be used to convert from one unit to the other (40)

copolymer a polymer made from two different monomers (685)

covalent bonding a chemical bond resulting from the sharing of an electron pair between two atoms (161)

critical mass the minimum amount of nuclide that provides the number of neutrons needed to sustain a chain reaction (718)

critical point indicates the critical temperature and critical pressure of a substance (381)

critical pressure the lowest pressure at which a substance can exist as a liquid at the critical temperature (382)

critical temperature the temperature above which a substance cannot exist in the liquid state (381)

crystal a substance in which the particles are arranged in an orderly, geometric, repeating pattern (368)

crystal structure the total three-dimensional arrangement of particles of a crystal (369)

crystalline solid a solid consisting of crystals (368)

cycloalkane an alkane in which the carbon atoms are arranged in a ring, or cyclic, structure (635)

Dalton's law of partial pressures the total pressure of a mixture of gases is equal to the sum of the partial pressures of the component gases (322)

daughter nuclide a nuclide produced by the decay of a parent nuclide (710)

decay series a series of radioactive nuclides produced by successive radioactive decay until a stable nuclide is reached (710)

decomposition reaction a reaction in which a single compound produces two or more simpler substances (259)

delocalized electron an electron shared by more than two atoms (627)

density the ratio of mass to volume or mass divided by volume (38)

deposition the change of state from a gas directly to a solid (380)

derived unit a unit that is a combination of SI base units (36)

diamond a colorless, crystalline, solid form of carbon (626)

diatomic molecule a molecule containing only two atoms (164)

diffusion spontaneous mixing of the particles of two substances caused by their random motion (305)

dipole equal but opposite charges that are separated by a short distance (190)

dipole-dipole force a force of attraction between polar molecules (190)

diprotic acid an acid that can donate two protons per molecule (466)

direct proportion two quantities that give a constant value when one is divided by the other (55)

displacement reaction a reaction in which one element replaces a similar element in a compound (261)

dissociation the separation of ions that occurs when an ionic compound dissolves (425)

double bond a covalent bond produced by the sharing of two pairs of electrons between two atoms (172)

double-replacement reaction a reaction in which the ions of two compounds exchange places in an aqueous solution to form two new compounds (262)

ductility the ability of a substance to be drawn, pulled, or extruded through a small opening to produce a wire (182)

effervescence the rapid escape of a gas from the liquid in which it is dissolved (407)

effusion a process by which gas particles pass through a tiny opening (306)

elastic collision a collision between gas particles and between gas particles and container walls in which there is no net loss of kinetic energy (303)

electrochemical cell a system of electrodes and electrolytes in which either chemical reactions produce electrical energy or an electric current produces chemical change (607)

electrochemistry the branch of chemistry that deals with electricity-related applications of oxidation-reduction reactions (606)

electrode a conductor used to establish electrical contact with a non-metallic part of a circuit, such as an electrolyte (607)

electrode potential the difference in potential between an electrode and its solution (613)

electrolysis the process in which an electric current is used to produce an oxidation-reduction reaction (610); also the decomposition of a substance by an electric current (259)

electrolyte a substance that dissolves in water to give a solution that conducts electric current (399)

electrolytic cell an electrochemical cell in which electrical energy is required to produce a redox reaction and bring about a chemical change (610)

electromagnetic radiation a form of energy that exhibits wavelike behavior as it travels through space (91)

electromagnetic spectrum all the forms of electromagnetic radiation (91)

electron affinity the energy change that occurs when an electron is acquired by a neutral atom (147)

electron capture the process in which an inner orbital electron is captured by the nucleus of its own atom (707)

electron configuration the arrangement of electrons in an atom (105)

electron-dot notation an electron-configuration notation in which only the valence electrons of an atom of a particular element are shown, indicated by dots placed around the element's symbol (170)

electronegativity a measure of the ability of an atom in a chemical compound to attract electrons (151)

electroplating an electrolytic process in which a metal ion is reduced and solid metal is deposited on a surface (611)

element a pure substance made of only one kind of atom (10)

elimination reaction a reaction in which a simple molecule, such as water or ammonia, is removed from adjacent carbon atoms of a larger molecule (684)

empirical formula the symbols for the elements combined in a compound with subscripts showing the smallest whole-number mole ratio of the different atoms in the compound (229)

end point the point in a titration at which an indicator changes color (498)

enthalpy change the amount of energy absorbed or lost by a system during a process at constant pressure (516)

entropy a measure of the degree of randomness of the particles, such as molecules, in a system (527)

equilibrium a dynamic condition in which two opposing changes occur at equal rates in a closed system (372)

equilibrium constant the ratio of the mathematical product of the concentrations of substances formed at equilibrium to the mathematical product of the concentrations of the reacting substances. Each concentration is raised to a power equal to the coefficient of that substance in the chemical equation (556)

equilibrium vapor pressure the pressure exerted by a vapor in equilibrium with its corresponding liquid at a given temperature (376)

equivalence point the point at which the two solutions used in a titration are present in chemically equivalent amounts (498)

ester an organic compound with a carboxylic acid group in which the hydrogen of the hydroxyl group has been replaced by an alkyl group (675)

ether an organic compound in which two hydrocarbon groups are bonded to the same atom of oxygen (669)

evaporation the process by which particles escape from the surface of a nonboiling liquid and enter the gas state (365)

excess reactant the substance that is not used up completely in a reaction (288)

excited state a state in which an atom has a higher potential energy than it has in its ground state (94)

extensive property a property that depends on the amount of matter that is present (11)

family a vertical column of the periodic table (21)

film badge a device that uses exposure of film to measure the approximate radiation exposure of people working with radiation (714)

fluid a substance that can flow and therefore take the shape of its container; a liquid or a gas (305)

formula equation a representation of the reactants and products of a chemical reaction by their symbols or formulas (244)

formula mass the sum of the average atomic masses of all the atoms represented in the formula of any molecule, formula unit, or ion (221)

formula unit the simplest collection of atoms from which an ionic compound's formula can be established (176)

fractional distillation distillation in which components of a mixture are separated, on the basis of boiling point, by condensation of vapor in a fractionating column (644)

free energy the combined enthalpy-entropy function of a system (528)

free-energy change the difference between the change in enthalpy, ΔH, and the product of the Kelvin temperature and the entropy change, which is defined as $T\Delta S$, at a constant pressure and temperature (528)

freezing the physical change of a liquid to a solid by the removal of heat (366)

freezing point the temperature at which a solid and liquid are in equilibrium at 1 atm (101.3 kPa) pressure (379)

freezing-point depression the difference between the freezing points of a pure solvent and a solution of a nonelectrolyte in that solvent; is directly proportional to the molal concentration of the solution (438)

frequency the number of waves that pass a given point in a specific time, usually one second (91)

fullerene a dark-colored solid made of spherically networked carbon-atom cages (626)

functional group an atom or group of atoms that is responsible for the specific properties of an organic compound (663)

gamma ray a high-energy electromagnetic wave emitted from a nucleus as it changes from an excited state to a ground energy state (707)

gas the state of matter in which a substance has neither definite volume nor definite shape (12)

gas laws simple mathematical relationships between the volume, temperature, pressure, and quantity of a gas (313)

Gay-Lussac's law the pressure of a fixed mass of gas at constant volume varies directly with the Kelvin temperature (319)

Gay-Lussac's law of combining volumes of gases at constant temperature and pressure, the volumes of gaseous reactants and products can be expressed as ratios of small whole numbers (333)

Geiger-Müller counter an instrument that detects radiation by counting electric pulses carried by gas ionized by radiation (714)

geometric isomers isomers in which the order of atom bonding is the same but the arrangement of atoms in space is different (632)

Graham's law of effusion the rates of effusion of gases at the same temperature and pressure are inversely proportional to the square roots of their molar masses (352)

graphite a soft, black, crystalline form of carbon that is a fair conductor of electricity (626)

ground state the lowest energy state of an atom (94)

group a vertical column of the periodic table (21)

half-cell a single electrode immersed in a solution of its ions (607)

half-life the time required for half the atoms of a radioactive nuclide to decay (708)

half-reaction the part of a reaction involving oxidation or reduction alone (593)

halogen one of the elements of Group 17 (fluorine, chlorine, bromine, iodine, and astatine) (137)

heat the energy transferred between samples of matter because of a difference in their temperature (512)

heat of combustion energy released as heat by the complete combustion of one mole of a substance (519)

heat of reaction the quantity of energy released or absorbed as heat during a chemical reaction (514)

heat of solution the net amount of energy absorbed or released as heat when a specific amount of solute dissolves in a solvent (410)

Heisenberg uncertainty principle it is impossible to determine simultaneously both the position and velocity of an electron or any other particle (99)

Henry's law the solubility of a gas in a liquid is directly proportional to the partial pressure of that gas on the surface of the liquid (407)

Hess's law the overall enthalpy change in a reaction is equal to the sum of the enthalpy changes for the individual steps in the process (519)

heterogeneous not having a uniform composition throughout (16)

heterogeneous catalyst a catalyst whose phase is different from that of the reactants (540)

heterogeneous reaction a reaction involving reactants in two different phases (538)

highest occupied energy level the electron-containing main energy level with the highest principal quantum number (110)

homogeneous having a uniform composition throughout (16)

homogeneous catalyst a catalyst that is in the same phase as all the reactants and products in a reaction system (540)

homogeneous reaction a reaction whose reactants and products exist in a single phase (532)

homologous series a series in which adjacent members differ by a constant unit (634)

Hund's rule orbitals of equal energy are each occupied by one electron before any orbital is occupied by a second electron, and all electrons in singly occupied orbitals must have the same spin (106)

hybrid orbitals orbitals of equal energy produced by the combination of two or more orbitals on the same atom (188)

hybridization the mixing of two or more atomic orbitals of similar energies on the same atom to produce new orbitals of equal energies (187)

hydration a solution process with water as the solvent (405)

hydrocarbon the simplest organic compound, composed of only carbon and hydrogen (630)

hydrogen bonding the intermolecular force in which a hydrogen atom that is bonded to a highly electronegative atom is attracted to an unshared pair of electrons of an electronegative atom in a nearby molecule (192)

hydrolysis a reaction between water molecules and ions of a dissolved salt (572)

hydronium ion the H_3O^+ ion (431)

hypothesis a testable statement (30)

ideal gas an imaginary gas that perfectly fits all the assumptions of the kinetic-molecular theory (303)

ideal gas constant the constant R, 0.082 057 84 L·atm/mol·K (342)

ideal gas law the mathematical relationship of pressure, volume, temperature, and the number of moles of a gas (340)

immiscible liquid solutes and solvents that are not soluble in each other (406)

inner-shell electron an electron that is not in the highest occupied energy level (110)

intensive property a property that does not depend on the amount of matter present (11)

intermediate a species that appears in some steps of a reaction but not in the net equation (532)

intermolecular force the force of attraction between molecules (189)

inverse proportion two quantities that have a constant mathematical product (56)

ion an atom or group of bonded atoms that has a positive or negative charge (143)

ionic bonding the chemical bond resulting from electrical attraction between large numbers of cations and anions (161)

ionic compound a compound composed of positive and negative ions that are combined so that the numbers of positive and negative charges are equal (176)

ionization the formation of ions from solute molecules by the action of the solvent (431); any process that results in the formation of an ion (143)

ionization energy the energy required to remove one electron from a neutral atom of an element (143)

isomers compounds that have the same molecular formula but different structures (630)

isotopes atoms of the same element that have different masses (76)

J

joule the SI unit of heat energy as well as all other forms of energy (511)

K

ketone an organic compound in which a carbonyl group is attached to a carbon atom within the chain (672)

kinetic-molecular theory a theory based on the idea that particles of matter are always in motion (303)

L

lanthanide one of the 14 elements with atomic numbers from 58 (cerium, Ce) to 71 (lutetium, Lu) (126)

lattice energy the energy released when one mole of an ionic crystalline compound is formed from gaseous ions (178)

law of conservation of mass mass is neither created nor destroyed during ordinary chemical or physical reactions (66)

law of definite proportions a chemical compound contains the same elements in exactly the same proportions by mass regardless of the size of the sample or the source of the compound (66)

law of multiple proportions if two or more different compounds are composed of the same two elements, then the ratio of the masses of the second element combined with a certain mass of the first element is always a ratio of small whole numbers (66)

Le Châtelier's principle when a system at equilibrium is disturbed by application of a stress, it attains a new equilibrium position that minimizes the stress (374)

Lewis acid an atom, ion, or molecule that accepts an electron pair to form a covalent bond (467)

Lewis acid-base reaction the formation of one or more covalent bonds between an electron-pair donor and an electron-pair acceptor (468)

Lewis base an atom, ion, or molecule that donates an electron pair to form a covalent bond (468)

Lewis structure a formula in which atomic symbols represent nuclei and inner-shell electrons, dot-pairs or dashes between two atomic symbols represent electron pairs in covalent bonds, and dots adjacent to only one atomic symbol represent unshared electrons (171)

limiting reactant the reactant that limits the amounts of the other reactants that can combine—and the amount of product that can form—in a chemical reaction (288)

line-emission spectrum a series of specific wavelengths of emitted light created when the visible portion of light from excited atoms is shined through a prism (94)

liquid the state of matter in which the substance has a definite volume but an indefinite shape (12)

London dispersion force an intermolecular attraction resulting from the constant motion of electrons and the creation of instantaneous dipoles (193)

lone pair a pair of electrons that is not involved in bonding and that belongs exclusively to one atom (171)

M

magic numbers the numbers of nucleons that represent completed nuclear energy levels—2, 8, 20, 28, 50, 82, and 126 (703)

magnetic quantum number the quantum number that indicates the orientation of an orbital around the nucleus (102)

main-group element an element in the s-block or p-block (136)

malleability the ability of a substance to be hammered or beaten into thin sheets (182)

mass a measure of the amount of matter (10)

mass defect the difference between the mass of an atom and the sum of the masses of its protons, neutrons, and electrons (701)

mass number the total number of protons and neutrons in the nucleus of an isotope (76)

matter anything that has mass and takes up space (10)

melting the physical change of a solid to a liquid by the addition of heat (368)

melting point the temperature at which a solid becomes a liquid (368)

metal an element that is a good conductor of heat and electricity (22)

metallic bonding chemical bonding that results from the attraction between metal atoms and the surrounding sea of electrons (181)

metalloid an element that has some characteristics of metals and some characteristics of nonmetals (24)

millimeters of mercury a common unit of pressure (311)

miscible liquid solutes and solvents that are able to dissolve freely in one another in any proportion (406)

mixture a blend of two or more kinds of matter, each of which retains its own identity and properties (15)

model an explanation of how phenomena occur and how data or events are related (31)

moderator a material used to slow down the fast neutrons produced by fission (718)

molal boiling-point constant the boiling-point elevation of a solvent in a 1-molal solution of a nonvolatile, nonelectrolyte solute (440)

molal freezing-point constant the freezing-point depression of the solvent in a 1-molal solution of a nonvolatile, nonelectrolyte solute (438)

molality the concentration of a solution expressed in moles of solute per kilogram of solvent (416)

molar heat of formation the heat released or absorbed when one mole of a compound is formed by the combination of its elements (517)

molar heat of fusion the amount of heat energy required to melt one mole of solid at its melting point (380)

molar heat of vaporization the amount of heat energy needed to vaporize one mole of liquid at its boiling point (379)

molar mass the mass of one mole of a pure substance (81)

molarity the number of moles of solute in one liter of solution (412)

mole the amount of a substance that contains as many particles as there are atoms in exactly 12 g of carbon-12 (81)

mole ratio a conversion factor that relates the amounts in moles of any two substances involved in a chemical reaction (276)

molecular compound a chemical compound whose simplest units are molecules (164)

molecular formula a formula showing the types and numbers of atoms combined in a single molecule of a molecular compound (164)

molecular polarity the uneven distribution of molecular charge (183)

molecule a neutral group of atoms that are held together by covalent bonds (164)

monatomic ion an ion formed from a single atom (204)

monomer a small unit that joins with others to make a polymer (685)

monoprotic acid an acid that can donate only one proton (hydrogen ion) per molecule (465)

multiple bond a double or triple bond (173)

natural gas a fossil fuel composed primarily of alkanes containing one to four carbon atoms (643)

net ionic equation an equation that includes only those compounds and ions that undergo a chemical change in a reaction in an aqueous solution (429)

neutralization the reaction of hydronium ions and hydroxide ions to form water molecules (475)

newton the SI unit for force; the force that will increase the speed of a one kilogram mass by one meter per second each second it is applied (309)

noble gas a Group 18 element (helium, neon, argon, krypton, xenon, and radon) (111)

noble-gas configuration an outer main energy level fully occupied, in most cases, by eight electrons (112)

nomenclature a naming system (206)

nonelectrolyte a substance that dissolves in water to give a solution that does not conduct an electric current (400)

nonmetal an element that is a poor conductor of heat and electricity (23)

nonpolar-covalent bond a covalent bond in which the bonding electrons are shared equally by the bonded atoms, resulting in a balanced distribution of electrical charge (162)

nonvolatile substance a substance that has little tendency to become a gas under existing conditions (436)

nuclear binding energy the energy released when a nucleus is formed from nucleons (702)

nuclear fission a process in which a very heavy nucleus splits into more-stable nuclei of intermediate mass (717)

nuclear force a short-range proton-neutron, proton-proton, or neutron-neutron force that holds the nuclear particles together (74)

nuclear fusion the combining of light-mass nuclei to form a heavier, more stable nucleus (719)

nuclear power plant a facility that uses heat from nuclear reactors to produce electrical energy (718)

nuclear radiation the particles or electromagnetic radiation emitted from the nucleus during radioactive decay (705)

nuclear reaction a reaction that affects the nucleus of an atom (704)

nuclear reactor a device that uses controlled-fission chain reactions to produce energy or radioactive nuclides (718)

nuclear shell model nucleons exist in different energy levels, or shells, in the nucleus (703)

nuclear waste radioactive products of fission and fusion reactions (716)

nucleon a proton or neutron (701)

nuclide the general term for any isotope of any element (77); another term for an atom that is identified by the number of protons and neutrons in its nucleus (701)

octane rating a measure of a fuel's burning efficiency and its antiknock properties (645)

octet rule chemical compounds tend to form so that each atom, by gaining, losing, or sharing electrons, has an octet of electrons in its highest occupied energy level (169)

orbital a three-dimensional region around the nucleus that indicates the probable location of an electron (100)

organic compound a covalently bonded compound containing carbon, excluding carbonates and oxides (629)

osmosis the movement of solvent through a semipermeable membrane from the side of lower solute concentration to the side of higher solute concentration (442)

osmotic pressure the external pressure that must be applied to stop osmosis (442)

oxidation a reaction in which the atoms or ions of an element experience an increase in oxidation state (592)

oxidation number a number assigned to an atom in a molecular compound or molecular ion that indicates the general distribution of electrons among the bonded atoms (216)

oxidation-reduction reaction any chemical process in which elements undergo changes in oxidation number (593)

oxidation state a number assigned to an atom in a molecular compound or ion that indicates the general distribution of electrons among the bonded atoms (216)

oxidized having experienced an increase in oxidation number (592)

oxidizing agent a substance that has the potential to cause another substance to be oxidized (602)

oxyacid an acid that is a compound of hydrogen, oxygen, and a third element, usually a non-metal (455)

oxyanion a polyatomic ion that contains oxygen (209)

pH the negative of the common logarithm of the hydronium ion concentration of a solution (485)

pH meter a device used to determine the pH of a solution by measuring the voltage between the two electrodes that are placed in the solution (494)

pOH the negative of the common logarithm of the hydroxide ion concentration of a solution (485)

parent nuclide the heaviest nuclide of each decay series (710)

partial pressure the pressure of each gas in a mixture (322)

pascal the pressure exerted by a force of one newton acting on an area of one square meter (311)

Pauli exclusion principle no two electrons in the same atom can have the same set of four quantum numbers (106)

percent error a value calculated by subtracting the experimental value from the accepted value, dividing the difference by the accepted value, and then multiplying by 100 (45)

percent yield the ratio of the actual yield to the theoretical yield, multiplied by 100 (293)

percentage composition the percentage by mass of each element in a compound (227)

period a horizontal row of elements in the periodic table (21)

periodic law the physical and chemical properties of the elements are periodic functions of their atomic numbers (125)

periodic table an arrangement of the elements in order of their atomic numbers so that elements with similar properties fall in the same column, or group (125)

petroleum a complex mixture of different hydrocarbons that varies greatly in composition (643)

phase any part of a system that has uniform composition and properties (373)

phase diagram a graph of pressure versus temperature that shows the conditions under which the phases of a substance exist (381)

photoelectric effect the emission of electrons from a metal when light shines on the metal (93)

photon a particle of electromagnetic radiation that has zero rest mass and carries a quantum of energy (94)

physical change a change in a substance that does not involve a change in the identity of the substance (12)

physical property a characteristic that can be observed or measured without changing the identity of the substance (11)

plasma a high-temperature physical state of matter in which atoms lose their electrons (12)

polar having an uneven distribution of charge (162)

polar-covalent bond a covalent bond in which the bonded atoms have an unequal attraction for the shared electrons (162)

polyatomic ion a charged group of covalently bonded atoms (180)

polymer a large molecule made of many small units joined to each other through organic reactions (685)

polyprotic acid an acid that can donate more than one proton per molecule (465)

positron a particle that has the same mass as an electron but that has a positive charge, and is emitted from the nucleus during some kinds of radioactive decay (706)

precipitate a solid that is produced as a result of a chemical reaction in solution and that separates from the solution (242)

precision the closeness of a set of measurements of the same quantity made in the same way (44)

pressure the force per unit area on a surface (308)

primary amine an organic compound in which one hydrogen atom in an ammonia molecule has been replaced by an alkyl group (677)

primary standard a highly purified solid compound used to check the concentration of a known solution in a titration (499)

principal quantum number the quantum number that indicates the main energy level occupied by the electron (101)

product a substance that is formed by a chemical change (13)

pure substance a substance that has a fixed composition and differs from a mixture in that every sample of a given pure substance has exactly the same characteristic properties and composition (17)

quantity something that has magnitude, size, or amount (33)

quantum the minimum quantity of energy that can be gained or lost by an atom (93)

quantum number a number that specifies the properties of atomic orbitals and the properties of electrons in orbitals (101)

quantum theory a mathematical description of the wave properties of electrons and other very small particles (99)

radioactive dating the process by which the approximate age of an object is determined based on the amount of certain radioactive nuclides present (715)

radioactive decay the spontaneous disintegration of a nucleus into a slightly lighter and more stable nucleus, accompanied by emission of particles, electromagnetic radiation, or both (705)

radioactive nuclide an unstable nucleus that undergoes radioactive decay (705)

radioactive tracer a radioactive atom that is incorporated into a substance so that movement of the substance can be followed by a radiation detector (715)

rate-determining step the slowest-rate step for a chemical reaction (543)

rate law an equation that relates the reaction rate and concentrations of reactants (542)

reactant a substance that reacts in a chemical change (13)

reaction mechanism the step-by-step sequence of reactions by which the overall chemical change occurs (531)

reaction rate the change in concentration of reactants per unit time as a reaction proceeds (538)

reaction stoichiometry calculations involving the mass relationships between reactants and products in a chemical reaction (275)

real gas a gas that does not behave completely according to the assumptions of the kinetic-molecular theory (306)

redox reaction any chemical process in which elements undergo changes in oxidation number (593)

reduced having experienced a decrease in oxidation state (593)

reducing agent a substance that has the potential to cause another substance to be reduced (602)

reduction a reaction in which the oxidation state of an element decreases (593)

reduction potential the measurement of the tendency for a half-reaction to occur as a reduction half-reaction in an electrochemical cell (613)

rem the quantity of ionizing radiation that does as much damage to human tissue as is done by 1 roentgen of high-voltage X rays (713)

resonance the bonding in molecules or ions that cannot be correctly represented by a single Lewis structure (175)

reversible reaction a chemical reaction in which the products re-form the original reactants (246)

roentgen a unit used to measure nuclear radiation; equal to the amount of radiation that produces 2×10^9 ion pairs when it passes through 1 cm^3 of dry air (713)

salt an ionic compound composed of a cation and the anion from an acid (215); an ionic compound composed of a cation from a base and an anion from an acid (473)

saturated hydrocarbon a hydrocarbon in which each carbon atom in the molecule forms four single covalent bonds with other atoms (634)

saturated solution a solution that contains the maximum amount of dissolved solute (403)

scientific method a logical approach to solving problems by observing and collecting data, formulating hypotheses, testing hypotheses, and formulating theories that are supported by data (29)

scientific notation numbers written in the form $M \times 10^n$ where the factor M is a number greater than or equal to 1 but less than 10 and n is a whole number (50)

scintillation counter an instrument that converts scintillating light to an electric signal for detecting radiation (714)

secondary amine an organic compound in which two hydrogen atoms of an ammonia molecule have been replaced by alkyl groups (677)

self-ionization of water a process in which two water molecules produce a hydronium ion and a hydroxide ion by transfer of a proton (481)

semipermeable membrane a membrane that allows the movement of some particles while blocking the movement of others (442)

shielding radiation-absorbing material that is used to decrease radiation exposure from nuclear reactors, especially gamma rays (718)

SI (*Le Système International d'Unités*) the measurement system accepted worldwide (33)

significant figure any digit in a measurement that is known with certainty plus one final digit, which is somewhat uncertain or is estimated (46)

single bond a covalent bond produced by the sharing of one pair of electrons between two atoms (171)

single-replacement reaction a reaction in which one element replaces a similar element in a compound (261)

solid the state of matter in which the substance has definite volume and definite shape (12)

solubility the amount of a substance required to form a saturated solution with a specific amount of solvent at a specified temperature (404)

solubility product constant the product of the molar concentrations of ions of a substance in a saturated solution, each raised to the power that is the coefficient of that ion in the chemical equation (578)

soluble capable of being dissolved (395)

solute the substance dissolved in a solution (396)

solution a homogeneous mixture of two or more substances in a single phase (396)

solution equilibrium the physical state in which the opposing processes of dissolution and crystallization of a solute occur at equal rates (402)

solvated a solute particle that is surrounded by solvent molecules (409)

solvent the dissolving medium in a solution (396)

specific heat the amount of heat energy required to raise the temperature of one gram of substance by one Celsius degree (1°C) or one kelvin (1 K) (512)

spectator ion an ion that does not take part in a chemical reaction and is found in solution both before and after the reaction (429)

spin quantum number the quantum number that has only two possible values, +1/2 and –1/2, which indicate the two fundamental spin states of an electron in an orbital (104)

standard electrode potential a half-cell potential measured relative to a potential of zero for the standard hydrogen electrode (614)

standard molar volume of a gas the volume occupied by one mole of a gas at STP, 22.414 10 L (335)

standard solution a solution that contains a precisely known concentration of a solute (499)

standard temperature and pressure the agreed-upon standard conditions of exactly 1 atm pressure and 0°C (312)

strong acid an acid that ionizes completely in aqueous solution (460)

strong electrolyte any compound of which all or almost all of the dissolved compound exists as ions in aqueous solution (432)

structural formula a formula that indicates the number and types of atoms present in a molecule and also shows the bonding arrangement of the atoms (630); a formula that indicates the kind, number, arrangement, and bonds but not the unshared electron pairs of the atoms in a molecule (171)

structural isomers isomers in which the atoms are bonded together in different orders (631)

sublimation the change of state from a solid directly to a gas (380)

substitution reaction a reaction in which one or more atoms replace another atom or group of atoms in a molecule (682)

supercooled liquid a substance that retains certain liquid properties even at temperatures at which it appears to be solid (368)

supersaturated solution a solution that contains more dissolved solute than a saturated solution contains under the same conditions (403)

surface tension a force that tends to pull adjacent parts of a liquid's surface together, thereby decreasing surface area to the smallest possible size (365)

suspension a mixture in which the particles in the solvent are so large that they settle out unless the mixture is constantly stirred or agitated (397)

synthesis reaction a reaction in which two or more substances combine to form a new compound (256)

system a specific portion of matter in a given region of space that has been selected for study during an experiment or observation (29)

temperature a measure of the average kinetic energy of the particles in a sample of matter (511)

tertiary amine an organic compound in which all three hydrogen atoms of an ammonia molecule have been replaced by alkyl groups (677)

theoretical yield the maximum amount of product that can be produced from a given amount of reactant (293)

theory a broad generalization that explains a body of facts or phenomena (31)

thermochemical equation an equation that includes the quantity of heat released or absorbed during the reaction as written (515)

thermochemistry the study of the changes in heat energy that accompany chemical reactions and physical changes (511)

thermoplastic polymer a polymer that melts when heated and can be reshaped many times (685)

thermosetting polymer a polymer that does not melt when heated but keeps its original shape (685)

titration the controlled addition and measurement of the amount of a solution of known concentration required to react completely with a measured amount of a solution of unknown concentration (497)

transition element one of the *d*-block elements that is a metal, with typical metallic properties (134)

transition interval the pH range over which an indicator changes color (494)

transmutation a change in the identity of a nucleus as a result of a change in the number of its protons (704)

transuranium element an element with more than 92 protons in its nucleus (712)

triple bond a covalent bond produced by the sharing of three pairs of electrons between two atoms (173)

triple point the temperature and pressure conditions at which the solid, liquid, and vapor of a substance can coexist at equilibrium (381)

triprotic acid an acid able to donate three protons per molecule (466)

unit cell the smallest portion of a crystal lattice that shows the three-dimensional pattern of the entire lattice (369)

unsaturated hydrocarbon a hydrocarbon in which not all carbons have four single covalent bonds (647)

unsaturated solution a solution that contains less solute than a saturated solution under the existing conditions (403)

unshared pair a pair of electrons that is not involved in bonding and that belongs exclusively to one atom (171)

valence electron an electron that is available to be lost, gained, or shared in the formation of chemical compounds (150)

vaporization the process by which a liquid or solid changes to a gas (365)

volatile liquid a liquid that evaporates readily (377)

voltaic cell an electrochemical cell in which the redox reaction occurs naturally and produces electrical energy (608)

volume the amount of space occupied by an object (37)

VSEPR theory repulsion between the sets of valence-level electrons surrounding an atom causes these sets to be oriented as far apart as possible (183)

vulcanization a cross-linking process between adjacent polyisoprene molecules that occurs when the molecules are heated with sulfur atoms (688)

W

wavelength the distance between corresponding points on adjacent waves (91)

weak acid an acid that is a weak electrolyte (460)

weak electrolyte a compound of which a relatively small amount of the dissolved compound exists as ions in an aqueous solution (433)

weight a measure of the gravitational pull on matter (35)

word equation an equation in which the reactants and products in a chemical reaction are represented by words (243)

Boldfaced page references denote illustrations; *t* references denote information in tables.

absolute zero, 317
accuracy, **44**–46, 58
acetaldehyde, 666
acetic acid: as buffer, 570–571; equilibrium of, 460, *t* 460, 470, 567–570, **568,** *t* 570; formula of, *t* 214, *t* 455; pH of, 491, **574;** properties of, *t* 410, 457; strength of, 470, *t* 471, **473;** in vinegar, 453, 457, 486; as weak electrolyte, 433
acetone, 673
acetylene, 287, 518, **652**
acid-base theories, 464–471
acid-ionization constant(s), 569–570, *t* 570, 573, 585
acidosis, 759
acid rain, 259, **475,** 478, 492, 496
acid(s): Arrhenius, 459, *t* 468, 476; binary, *t* 214, *t* 454, 454–455; Brønsted-Lowry, 464–471, *t* 468, 476, 572–573; conjugate, 469–471, *t* 471, 476; decomposition of, 260, 454; dilution of, 463; diprotic, 466, 476; as electrolytes, 432–433; ionization constants of, 569–570, *t* 570, 573, 585; Lewis, 467–468, *t* 468; neutralization of, 473–475. *See also* neutralization reaction(s); nomenclature of, *t* 454, 454–455, *t* 455; organic, 460; overview of, 214–215, 454–455, 476; oxyacids, *t* 214, 455, *t* 455, 470; strong/weak, 460–461, *t* 483, 491, 498, **499,** 504
ACS (American Chemical Society), 18
actinide series of elements, **21,** 126, 138, *t* 147
activation energy, 533–537, 540–541, 546
activity series of the elements, 265–267, *t* 266, 269, 272–273. *See also* chemical reaction(s)
Adair, James, 646
addition polymer(s), 686–689
addition reaction(s), 682–683, 693–694

adenosine triphosphate (ATP), **766**
adipic acid, 690
aerosol(s), 398
air, discovery of, 338–339
air pollution, 43, *t* 398, 778
alchemy, **8**
alcohol, ethyl. *See* ethanol
alcohol dehydrogenase, 666
alcohol(s), 663–666, *t* 671, *t* 679, 693. *See also individual alcohols*
aldehyde(s), 672–673, *t* 679, 693
alexandrite, 743
alkali metal(s), **132,** 728–733
alkaline batteries, **609**
alkaline earth metal(s), **132,** 734–739
alkalinity, 461
alkaloid(s), 678
alkalosis, 759
alkane(s): branched-chain, *t* 637, 637–641; cycloalkane(s), 635–636, 642; nomenclature of, *t* 636, 636–642, 656; overview of, 634–636; properties of, *t* 643, 643–645, *t* 671
alkene(s), 647–651, 656
alkyl group(s), nomenclature and, *t* 637, 637–642
alkyl halide(s), 666–669, *t* 679, 682, 693
alkyne(s), 651–652, 656
allotrope(s), **626**–628
alloy(s), **396,** 397, **740,** *t* 745, 746, *t* 753
alpha particle(s): discovery of the nucleus and, **72, 73;** exposure to, **713;** overview of, **72, 73,** *t* 705, 706, **710;** radioactive decay and, **710,** 722
aluminum: activity series and, 265, *t* 266; in alloys, *t* 745, 753, *t* 753; analysis of, **751;** electron configuration of, *t* 111; in gemstones, 743; heat of vaporization of, *t* 182; molar mass of, 83–84; properties of, **22,** 39, **55,** *t* 55, **750,** *t* 752; reactions of, 751; in redox reactions, *t* 591, *t* 603, *t* 615; in semiconductors, 768–769; specific heat of, *t* 513; uses of, **752**–753
aluminum carbide, 253
aluminum hydroxide, 253, 453
aluminum oxide, 206–207, 276–277, **751,** 752, 777

aluminum sulfate, 426
aluminum sulfide, 576
aluminum trichloride, 184
amalgam(s), dental, **396, 744**
American Chemical Society (ACS), 18
amine(s), 677–679, *t* 679, 693
amino acid(s), **761**
ammonia: acid/base strength of, *t* 471, 472; in aqueous solution, 461–462; configuration of, 172, **185,** *t* 186, **188;** fertilizers and, 560–561, 773; formation of, 282, 561, 562–564, **563,** *t* 779; household, **453, 494;** oxidation of, 284–285; pH of, 461, **494,** 571, **575;** properties of, *t* 190, **191**–192, *t* 410, *t* 513
ammonium acetate, **572,** 576
ammonium chloride, **408,** *t* 410, 426, 530, **572,** 574–576
ammonium dichromate, **241**
ammonium ion, 180, *t* 471, 571
ammonium nitrate, *t* 410, 429, 526–**527**
amorphous solid(s), 368, 371
ampere, *t* 34, 58
amphoteric compound(s), 471–473, 777
anemia, 749, 762
angular momentum quantum number(s), 101–102, *t* 102
anhydride(s), 776–777
aniline, 462
anion(s): in electrochemical cells, 608; hydrolysis of, 572–573, 585; nomenclature for, 209–210, *t* 210, 234; oxyanions, 209–211, 214; radii of, **149**–150
anode(s), **70**–71, **607,** 610–614, 616
antacid(s), 453, 473, 479, **494**
antimony: in alloys, *t* 745; analysis of, **771;** electron configuration of, *t* 114; origin of symbol for, *t* 20; properties of, 24, **770,** *t* 771; reactions of, *t* 266, 771
apatite, 783
aqueous solution(s), 425–433, 461, 481–491
aragonite, **369**
argon: discovery of, 108–109, 125; electron configuration of, *t* 111, 112, 139; light from, **24**

Aristotle, 8, 65, 338
aromatic hydrocarbon(s), 652–656, **653**
Arrhenius, Svante, 435, 459
Arrhenius acids and bases, 459–462, 464, *t* 468, 476
arsenic: analysis of, **771;** electron configuration of, 129; properties of, **770,** *t* 771; reactions of, 771; in semiconductors, 768–**769**
ascorbic acid, **453**
aspirin, 296–297, **571**
astatine, 137, *t* 708, **780,** *t* 782
atmosphere, unit of, 311, *t* 311
atmospheric pressure, **309**–312, **310,** 326
atomic absorption spectroscopy, 751, 755, 775, 781
atomic mass(es), 78–80, *t* 80, 86
atomic mass unit(s), 78
atomic number(s), 75, 77–78, 86, 155
atomic radii: of alkali metals, *t* 730; of alkaline earth metals, *t* 736; of boron family elements, *t* 752; of carbon family elements, *t* 755; of *d*- and *f*-block elements, 153; of nitrogen family elements, *t* 771; overview of, 74, 140–**141, 142;** of oxygen family elements, *t* 776; of transition metals, *t* 743
atomic theory, 8, 65–67, 96–97, 98–104
atom(s), 70–82, 94, 160–199
ATP (adenosine triphosphate), **766**
Aufbau principle, 105, 110, 113, 117
automobile batteries, 612, **613**
autooxidation, 604–605
Avogadro, Amedeo, 81, 334, 339
Avogadro's law, **334**–335, 341, 356
Avogadro's number, 81, 84–86, 225, 335
azurite, **369**

bakelite, 673
baking powder, 297–298, 473
baking soda (sodium hydrogen carbonate), **453, 494**
Balmer series, 95, **97**

band of stability, 702, **703**

barium: activity series and, *t* 266; electron configuration of, 115, 116; flame test for, **735**; properties of, **734**, 735, *t* 736; in redox reactions, 257, *t* 615; uranium decay and, 721

barium carbonate, *t* 579, 581–582

barium chloride, *t* 445, 583–584, 737

barium chromate, **16**

barium nitrate, 223, 426, 430, 444–445

barium sulfate, 430, *t* 579, 583–584

barometer(s), 310, 326, 338–339

base(s): aqueous solutions of, 461; Arrhenius, 459, *t* 468, 476; Brønsted-Lowry, 464–467, *t* 468, 476, 493–494, 572–573; conjugate, 469–471, *t* 471, 476; dissociation constants of, 574; Lewis, 467–468, *t* 468; neutralization of, 473–475. *See also* neutralization reaction(s); in nucleic acids, **766**; properties of, 457–458, 476; strong/weak, 461–462, *t* 483, 491, 498, **499**, 504

batrachotoxinin A, **678**

batteries, 434, 608–**613**, **609**

battery acid, **494**. *See also* sulfuric acid

bauxite, **750**

Becquerel, Henri, 8, 705, 713

benzaldehyde, **673**

benzene, *t* 190, 406, *t* 513, 652–656

benzoic acid, **453**, 674

3,4-benzpyrene, 655

beryl, **734**

beryllium: electron configuration of, 110, *t* 110, 183–184; ionization energies of, 145, *t* 145; properties of, **734**, 735, *t* 736

beryllium fluoride(s), **184**, *t* 186

Berzelius, Jöns Jacob, 435

beta particle(s), *t* 705, 706, **710**, **713**

binary acid(s), *t* 214, *t* 454, 454–455

binary compound(s), 206–213, *t* 214, 259, *t* 454, 454–455

binding force(s), in crystals, 369–371

biochemistry, 6, 761–766

bismuth: analysis of, **771**; nuclear stability of, 703;

properties of, 22, **770**, *t* 771; reactions of, *t* 266, 771

blast furnace(s), **756**

blood, **16**, 17, 411, 486, 571, 758–759. *See also* hemoglobin

Böhr, Niels, **95**, 96–97

Böhr's model of the atom, 96–97, 98

boiling, 366, 378–379

boiling point(s): of alcohols and alkanes, *t* 664, *t* 671; of alkali metals, *t* 730; of alkaline earth metals, *t* 736; of boron family elements, *t* 752; of carbon family elements, *t* 755; of ethers, *t* 671; of liquids, **377**, 378–379; molal boiling-point constants, *t* 438, 441, 447; molecular forces and, 179, 189, *t* 190; of nitrogen family elements, *t* 771; of organic compounds, *t* 632, *t* 643, 643–645, *t* 644; overview of, 11–**12**, 378; of oxygen-family elements, *t* 776; of solids, *t* 370; of solutions, 436–438, 440–441, 443; of transition metals, *t* 743

boiling point elevation, 440–441, 447

bombardier beetle(s), **605**

bond energy, 167, *t* 168, *t* 173

bonding, chemical, 160–199

bond length, 167, *t* 168, *t* 173, 194

bond strength, 182

boron: covalent bonds of, 169; electron configuration of, 107, *t* 110, *t* 170; ionization energies of, 145, *t* 145; properties of, **750**, *t* 752; reactions of, 751; uses of, 767–**769**

boron family elements, 750–753

boron trifluoride, 468

Bosch, Karl, 561

Boyle, Robert, 313, 338–339

Boyle's law: calculations using, 330; development of, 313–315, 321, 326, 338–339; ideal gas law and, 341, 356

branched-chain alkane(s), *t* 637, 637–641

brass, 396, *t* 745, **746**

bromide, *t* 471, **781**

bromine: boiling point of, *t* 190, 530; covalent bonds of, *t* 168; electron configuration of, 136; properties of, 137, 152, **366**, **780**, *t* 782; reactions of, **781**; in redox reactions, *t* 219, *t* 603, *t* 615

bromine fluoride, 190–**191**

bromphenol blue, **495**

bromthymol blue, **482**, **495**, 498

Brown, Robert, 398

Brownian motion, 398

Brønsted, J. N., 464

Brønsted-Lowry acids and bases, 464–467, *t* 468, 476

buckyball(s) (fullerenes), 626, **628**

buffer(s), 570–571. *See also* pH

butane: boiling point of, *t* 643, *t* 664; properties of, *t* 632; structure of, **625**, 631, **635**, 636; 2,2-butanediol, 664

butanoic acid, 674, *t* 675

butanol, 664, *t* 671

2-butanone, 673

butyl methyl ether, 670

C

cadaverine, 678

cadmium, *t* 114, *t* 266, 266–267, *t* 615, **742**, 749

cadmium sulfide, 429, *t* 579

caffeine, 678

calcite, **369**

calcium: activity series and, *t* 266; in the body, 738, *t* 738; electron configuration of, 112, *t* 112; flame test for, **735**; properties of, 83, *t* 513, **734**, **735**, *t* 736; in redox reactions, *t* 603, *t* 615

calcium carbonate: acid rain and, **475**; decomposition of, 260, 349, 564–565; liming streams with, 492; solubility of, *t* 579

calcium chloride, 426

calcium fluoride, 177–**178**, *t* 179, 578–579, *t* 579, 582

calcium hydroxide, 260, *t* 404, *t* 461, *t* 579

calcium hypochlorite, 783

calcium oxide, *t* 179, 258, 294, *t* 779

calcium phosphate, 428

calculator(s), **52**

calorimeter(s), 511, **519**, 551

candela, *t* 34, 58

Cannizzaro, Stanislao, 123

carbohydrate(s), 763–764

carbon: cycling of, 68; electron configuration of, *t* 110, 138, **188**; ionization energies of, 145, *t* 145; iron ore reduction and, 756; isotopes of, 78, *t* 80, *t* 708, 715; oxidation num-

bers for, *t* 219; properties of, **23**, **81**, *t* 513, **754**, *t* 755; reactions of, 755; structure and bonding of, *t* 170, *t* 173, 625–626, 629–630

carbon-12, 78, 81, 86

carbon cycle, **757**

carbon dioxide: dry ice, 380; formation of, 13–14, 68, 281, 757; polarity of, **191**; properties of, 757; respiration and, 68, 758–759; solubility of, *t* 404, **407**, **408**; structure of, 187, 757

carbon disulfide, 294

carbon family elements, 754–769

carbonic acid: decomposition of, 260; dissociation of, *t* 460, *t* 471, 554; formula of, *t* 214, *t* 455; respiration and, 758 uses of, **453**

carbon monoxide: in car exhaust, 43, 307; catalysts for, 307; heat of formation of, 522–523; poisoning by, 307, 760, *t* 760; production of, 291, 757; structure of, 66–**67**

carbon tetrachloride: formation of, 270, 682; properties of, *t* 190, **191**; as solvent, 405–406, 418

carboxylic acid(s), 674–675, *t* 679, 693

Carothers, Wallace, 690

casein, 395

catalyst(s): carbon monoxide, 307; in chemical equations, *t* 246, 246–247; equilibrium and, 565, 585; reaction rate and, 540, **541**, 546

catalytic converter(s), 307

catenation, 630, 656

cathode ray(s), **70**, 71, 86

cathode(s), **70**–71, **607**, 610–614, 616

cation(s), **149**–150, 234, 573–574, 585, 608

cavitation, 166

cell membrane(s), 443, 765

cellulose, **764**

cementite, 745

centimeter, 35–**36**

centrifuge(s), **16**, 17

cerium, 115

cerium sulfate, *t* 404, 409

cesium: analysis of, **729**; electron configuration of, 115; isotopes of, *t* 80; properties of, 163, **728**, 729, *t* 730

cesium chloride, **408**

CFC(s) (chlorofluorocarbons), 668–669, 682, 693, 699
chalcopyrite, 22, **369**
change(s) of state, 12–13, 25, 247, *t* 372, 372–382
Charles, Jacques, 316, 339
Charles's law, 316–319, 321, 326, 341, 356
chemical bonding, 160–199
chemical equation(s): balancing, 244–**245**, 247, 250–254, 264, 597–600; calculations from, 280–287; for dissociation reactions, 426–429; equilibrium and, 374, 555–559, 585; formula, 244–245, 250–252, 430; net ionic, 429–430, 447; for neutralization reactions, 474–475; overview of, 241–250; for redox reactions, 597–601; symbols used in, 245–248, *t* 246; thermochemical, 515–524; word, 243–244, 247–248, 250–252
chemical equilibrium. *See also* equilibrium constant(s); of acids, bases, and salts, 569–576; changes of state and, 372–375; effect of pressure on, 407; equations of, 374, 555–559, 585; reversibility of, 553–555, 585; shifting, 562–568, 585; in solution, **402**
chemical formula(s): in chemical equations, 242–245, 250–252, 430; determination of, 229–233; empirical, 229–233, 234; experimental, 232–233; formula masses, 221–223; molecular, 164, 232–233; overview of, 164, 203–204, 234; oxidation numbers and, 218–219; structural, 171, 630–631, 635, 640–641, 656
chemical kinetics, 538–545, 547, 555–557
chemical reaction(s): activity series, 265–267, *t* 266, 269, 272–273; atomic theory and, 65–66; completion of, 565–567; discussion of, 13; double-replacement, 262–263, 269, 428–430; elimination, 684, 693; endothermic, **409**, 515–**517**, *t* 529, 546, 564–565; exothermic. *See* exothermic reaction(s); heats of, **513**, 514–523, 546; homogeneous, 532; indications of, 241–242, 269; intermediates in, 532, 535;

mechanisms of, 526–537, 542–544, 546; neutralization, 473–475, 497, 502–503, 567, 574–575; organic, 682–684; oxidation-reduction, 591–617; pathways of, 542–543; rates of, 538–545, 547, 555–557; reactants and products in, 13; reversible, 246–247, 249–250, 553–555; substitution, 682, 693; synthesis, 256–259, 269; types of, 256–264
chemical(s), description of, 6, 25
chemistry: biochemistry, 6, 761–766; electrochemistry, 606–616; inorganic, 6; organic. *See* organic chemistry; overview of, 5, 6, 32; physical, 6; theoretical, 6; thermochemistry, 511–524, 546
Chilean saltpeter (sodium nitrate), *t* 404, **408**, *t* 410, 560
chlorate, 187, *t* 471
chloric acid, *t* 471, **472**
chloride, *t* 190, *t* 471, 731, *t* 731, **781**
chlorine: chlorine-37, 77–78; covalent bonds of, *t* 168, **169;** electron configuration of, *t* 111, 139, 149; oxidation numbers of, *t* 219; production of, *t* 779; properties of, 23, 137, **140,** 163, **780,** *t* 782; reactions of, **781;** in redox reactions, 593, *t* 603, *t* 615
chlorine dioxide, 783
chlorobenzene, 293
chloroethene, 632
chlorofluorocarbon(s) (CFCs), 668–669, 682, 693, 699
chloroform (trichloromethane), 255, 682
chlorophyll, 738, **739**
chlorous acid, *t* 214, *t* 455, *t* 471, **472**
chromic acid, 473
chromium: activity series and, *t* 266; in alloys, **745,** *t* 745; analysis of, **742;** in the body, 749; electron configuration of, *t* 112, 113; in gemstones, 743; properties of, 22, *t* 743; in redox reactions, 592, *t* 603, *t* 615, **741**
chromium fluoride, 209
chromium hydroxide, 473
cinnamaldehyde, **673**
cis isomer(s), 632–633, 648
citric acid, **453, 674**
cPE (cross-linked polyethylene), 686–687

coal gasification, 298
cobalt: analysis of, **742;** in the body, 749; electron configuration of, *t* 112, 113; properties of, *t* 743; radioactive nuclides, *t* 708, 715; reactions of, 258, 265, *t* 266, *t* 615
coefficient(s) in chemical equations, 243–245, 248–254, 515, 517
coenzyme(s), 762
colligative properties of solutions, 436–447
collision theory, 532–535, **533,** 538–540, 542–543, 546, 563
colloid(s), 397–399, *t* 398, 419
combustion, 263, 278–279, 645
common-ion effect, 567–568, 585
composition reaction(s), 256–259, 269
composition stoichiometry, 275
compound(s): amphoteric, 471–473, 777; in aqueous solution, 425–433; binary, 206–213, *t* 214, 259, *t* 454, 454–455; coordination, **741;** covalent bonding in, 164–175; description of, **15,** 25; ionic. *See* ionic compound(s), molecular; molecular compound(s)
compressibility, 305, 364, 368
concentration: equilibrium and, 375, 556–558, 563–564; reaction rate and, **539**–544; of solution(s), 412–418; units of, *t* 36, 412–418
condensation, 373–377
condensation polymer(s), 690–691, 694
condensation reaction(s), 683, 693
conduction band(s), **768**
coniine, 678
conservation of energy, 15
conservation of mass, 66, 86, 241, 243–244, 251, 279
contact theory of electrolysis, 435
control rod(s), 718
conversion factor(s): molar, 224–226, 234, 276–277, 280–286, 299; overview of, 40–42, 58; significant digits and, 50, 58
coordination compound(s), **741**
copolymer(s), 685, 694
copper: activity series and, *t* 266, 266–267; in alloys and ores, **740,** *t* 745, *t* 753; analysis of, **742;** in the body, 749;

density of, **38,** *t* 38, 39, 57; in drinking water, 268; in electrochemical cells, **606–608,** 610–611, 613–615; electron configuration of, *t* 112, 113; isotopes of, 80, *t* 80; origin of symbol for, *t* 20; properties of, **22**–23, 25, **81,** 82, 84–85, *t* 743; redox reactions of, **593, 603,** *t* 603, **741;** reduction potential of, *t* 615; specific heat of, *t* 513
copper(I) chloride, *t* 579, 580
copper(II) hydroxide, 462
copper(II) sulfate, 405, **413, 416,** 601
copper(II) sulfide, 227, *t* 579
corn borer(s), 633
corundum, 743
cotton, 764
covalent bonding: boiling points and, *t* 190; in crystals, 370–371; double, 172, 186, 626, 632, 648; ionization and, 431; Lewis acids and, 467–468; molecular compounds and, 164–175, *t* 168, *t* 173, 194; multiple, 172–174, 194; nonpolar, **162, 163;** overview of, 161–163, **162;** polar, **162, 163;** in polyatomic ions, 180, 186; redox reactions and, 594–595; single, 171, 194; triple, 173, 186, 626, 651
covalent-network bonding, 175, 214
covalent network crystal(s), **370, 371**
Crick, Francis, 680–681
critical mass, 718
critical point(s), 381
critical pressure(s), 382
critical temperature(s), 381
Crookes, William, 560
cross-linked polyethylene (cPE), 686–687
crystal lattice(s): hydration and, **405;** ionic bonding and, **177, 178, 179;** metallic bonding and, **181;** types of, **369**
crystalline solid(s), 368–371, 387
crystal structure(s): of alkali metals, *t* 730; of alkaline earth metals, *t* 736; of alloys, 746; of boron family elements, *t* 752; of carbon family elements, *t* 755; of nitrogen family elements, *t* 771; of oxygen family elements, *t* 776
cuprum, *t* 20. *See also* copper

Curie(s), Marie and Pierre, 8–9, 705
Curl, Robert F., 628
cyanide, hydrogen, 166, *t* 460
cycloalkane(s), 635–636, 642

Dalton, John, 8, 66, 67, 70, 86, 322
Dalton's atomic theory, 8, 66–67
Dalton's law of partial pressures, 322–326, 334
daughter nuclide(s), 710
Davy, Humphry, 434–435
de Broglie, Louis, 98
Debye, Peter, 446
decay series, 710–711, 722
decomposition reaction(s), 259–260, 269
definite proportions, law of, 66, 86
Democritus, 65, 67
density: of alkali metals, *t* 730; of alkaline earth metals, *t* 736; of boron family elements, *t* 752; of carbon family elements, *t* 755; determination of, 39; of gases, 305, 345–346, 353; of liquids, 364; of nitrogen family elements, *t* 771; of oxygen family elements, *t* 776; of solids, 368; of transition metals, *t* 743; units of, *t* 36, **38**, *t* 38
2-deoxy-D-ribose, **763**
deoxyribonucleic acid (DNA), 680–681, 713, **766**
deposition, 380–381
deuterium (hydrogen-2), 76–77, *t* 80
diabetes, 759
diamond(s): density of, *t* 38, 40; structure of, **10**, 370, **626**–627; synthetic, 646
diatomic molecule(s), 164, 168–169, **183**, *t* 243, 334
diborane, 229–230
1,2-dibromopropane, 667
dichlorodifluoromethane (Freon-12), 668
1,2-dichloroethene, 632
dicyclohexyl ether, 670
diethyl ether, **377**, 670, *t* 671
diffraction patterns, 98, **99**
diffusion, **305**, 351–355, 364, 369
1,2-dimethylbenzene, 654
dinitrogen tetroxide, 564–**565**
dioxins, 166

dipole-dipole force(s), 190–192, 195, 371
diprotic acid(s), 466, 476
direct proportion(s), *t* 55, 55–56, 58
disaccharide(s), **763**
dispersion(s), 397. *See also* colloid(s)
displacement reaction(s), 261–262, 265, 269
dissociation, 425–430, 447, 574
dissolution. *See also* solubility; in aqueous solution, 425–430; entropy and, **528**; rate of, 401–402, 404, 419; temperature and, 401–403, *t* 404, **408**–409
DNA (deoxyribonucleic acid), 680–681, 713, **766**
dolomite, **734**
dopant(s), 768, *t* 769
Dorn, Friedrich Ernst, 109, 126
double bond(s), 172, 626, 632, 648
double-replacement reaction(s), 262–263, 269, 428–430
drinking water, 258, 268, 782–783
dry cell(s), **608, 609**
ductility, 22, 182, 194

effervescence, **407**
effusion of gases, 306, 351–356
Einstein, Albert, 93–94
Einstein's equation, 701
electrical conductivity: acids and bases and, 454, 458; bonding and, 179, 181; in electrochemical cells, 607; electrolytes and, 399–400, 419; in metals, metalloids, and nonmetals, 22–24, 134, 194; in semiconductors, 24, 137, **768**–769; through gases, 70; wiring for, 752
electric current, units of, *t* 34, 58
electrochemical cell(s), 606–613, 617
electrochemistry, 606–616
electrode potential(s), 613–614, 617
electrode(s), **607**, 613–616
electrolysis: electrolytic cells for, 610, 617; history of, 434–435; of water, **17, 250**, 259
electrolyte(s), 399–400, 419, 432–433, 443–447, *t* 731, 731–732

electrolytic cell(s), 607, 610–613, **611**, 617
electrolytic theory, 434–435
electromagnetic radiation, 91–94, **92**
electron capture, 707
electron density, 162, **163**, 167, 473
electron-dot notation, **170**–171, 174, 176–177, 464
electronegativity, **151**–154, **152**, 161–163, **162**, 473
electron pair(s), 161–162, 171, 183–187, 195
electron(s): affinity, *t* 147, 147–149, **148**; charge and mass of, 71, 73, *t* 74; configurations, 105–116, 128–139, 140–154; delocalized, 627, 653, 655–656; discovery of, 70–71; dual wave-particle nature of, 98–99, 117; in electrochemical cells, 608–612; lone pairs, 171, 185–187; orbitals of, 96, 100–104, **102, 103**, *t* 104, **105**; in oxidation-reduction reactions, 593–595, 598–599; valence, *t* 150, 150–151, 155
electron-sea model of metallic bonding, 181–182, 194
electroplating, 611–**612**
element(s): activity series of the, 265–267; description of, 8, **15**; electron configuration of, 110–115; Group 1, 22, 132, 728–733, *t* 777; Group 2, 132, 734–739, *t* 777; Group 3–12, 740–749; Group 13, 750–753, *t* 777; Group 14, 754–769, *t* 777; Group 15, 770–773, *t* 777; Group 16, 774–779, *t* 777; Group 17, 23, 265, 432, *t* 777, 780–783; Group 18, 24, 111; periodic table of. *See* periodic table of the elements; periods of, 21, 110–115, 128–139; symbols of, *t* 20; types of, 22–25
elimination reaction(s), 684, 693
emerald, **369**, 743–744, *t* 744
empirical formula(s), 229–233, 234
emulsion(s), 397, *t* 398
endothermic reaction(s), **409**, 515–**517**, *t* 529, 546, 564–565
end point(s) of titration, 498, **501**, 504
energy, changes in, 14–15; in chemical reactions, 513–23; units of, *t* 36

enthalpy, 515–521, 526, 529, 546
entropy, 526–529, 546
enzyme(s), 762–763
equation(s). *See* chemical equation(s)
equilibrium. *See* chemical equilibrium
equilibrium constant(s). *See also* chemical equilibrium; in acid and base reactions, 569–571, 573–574, 585; calculation of, 588–589; concentration and, 375, 556–558, 563–564; Nernst equation and, 620–621; overview of, 556–559; solubility-product constants, 578–580
equilibrium vapor pressure. *See* vapor pressure
equivalence point(s), 498–499, 504, **574, 575**
error(s) in measurement, 45–46, 58
ester(s), 675–676, *t* 679, 693
ethane, 296, 634, **635**, *t* 643, *t* 664
ethanedioic acid, 674
1,2-ethanediol, 664
ethanol: as fuel, 665–666; ingestion of, 666; properties of, *t* 38, 366, **376, 377**, *t* 513, *t* 664; as solvent, **406**; structure of, **473, 631**
ethene: configuration of, 172, **626**; formation of, 683; properties and uses of, 650–**651**, 656
ether(s), 669–671, *t* 679, 693
ethyl alcohol. *See* ethanol
ethyl butanoate, 675, *t* 676
ethylene glycol, 699
ethyl ethanoate, 675
ethylmethylamine, 677
2-ethyl-3-methyl-1-butene, 649–650
3-ethyl-4-methylhexane, 640–641
ethyl propyl ether, 670
ethyne (acetylene), 287, 518, **652**
evaporation, 365–366, **373**–379
exhaust emission(s), 43
exothermic reaction(s): activation energy and, 534; equilibria and, 564; heat of reaction in, 514–**516**, *t* 529; heat of solution in, **409**; overview of, **241**, 546; redox and, **606**; self-heating meals and, 525
expansion of gases, 304

F

Faraday, Michael, 434–435
fatty acid(s), 630, 633, 764–**765**
Fermi, Enrico, 720–721
Fermi International Accelerator Laboratory (Fermilab), **711**
fertilizer(s), 560–561, 715, 773, *t* 773, 779
film badge(s), **714**, 722
filtration, **16**
fire extinguisher(s), 296
fireflies, 630
fireworks, **736**–737
flame test(s), 729–730 **735**, 737, 771, 775
flare(s), 737
flashlight batteries, 609
flavoring(s), 676
fluidity of gases, 304–305
fluid(s), 363
fluorapatite, 783
fluoridation of drinking water, 258, 783
fluoride, *t* 471, 781, 783
fluorine: covalent bonds of, *t* 168, **169**–171, *t* 170; electron configuration of, 107, *t* 110, 111; ionization energy of, *t* 145; metal compounds with, 258; oxidation number of, 216–217, *t* 591; properties of, 23, 137, **780,** *t* 782; reactions of, 781; in redox reactions, *t* 603, *t* 615
fluorite, **369**
fluorosis, 783
foam, 397, *t* 398
food additive(s), 676
Food Chemical Code (FCC) purity specifications, *t* 18
food preservative(s), 674
foods, self-heating, 525
force, pressure and, 308–312
formaldehyde, 174, 307, 666, 673
formic acid, 666
formula(s). *See* chemical formula(s)
formula unit(s), 176
fractional distillation, **644**
francium, **728,** *t* 730
Franklin, Rosalind, 680–681
free energy, 528–530, 546, 550–551
Freeman, Benny, 692
free radical(s), 778
freezing, 366, 379
freezing point(s), 379, 436–441, *t* 438, 443–447, 699

freezing point depression, *t* 438, 438–440, *t* 445, 447
Freon(s), 668
frequency, 91–94, **92**
Frisch, Otto, 721
fructose, 630, **763**
fruit, pH of, 486, **494**
Fuller, Buckminster, **628**
fullerene(s), 626, **628**
functional group(s), 663–679, *t* 679, 693

G

galactose, **763**
galena, **774**
gallium, **124, 750,** 751, *t* 752, 768–769
galvanic cell(s) (voltaic cells), 607–614, **608, 611,** 616–617, 620
gamma ray(s), 9, *t* 705, 707, **713**
garnet, **743,** *t* 744
gas(es): Avogadro's law of, **334**–335, 341, 356; Boyle's law of. *See* Boyle's law; Charles's law of, 316–319, 321, 326, 341, 356; in chemical equations, 245; from chemical reactions, 242, 262–263, 269, 566; combined gas law, 321–322, 326; effusion of, 306, 351–356; elastic collisions of, 303; Gay-Lussac's law of, 319–321, 326, 333–334, 341, 356; ideal behavior of, 303, 306, 326; ideal gas law, 339–341, 340–346, 356, 360; kinetic energy of, 351; kinetic-molecular theory of, 303–306, 313, 323, 326; pressure and, 308–315, 319–321, 340, 562–563; properties of, 12; real, 306; solubility of, **407–408,** 410, 419; stoichiometry of, 347–350; velocity of, 351–352; volume of. *See* gas volume; water displacement by, 324
gasohol, 665–666
gasoline, *t* 38, 406, 643, *t* 644
gastric juice(s), 457, 486, **494,** *t* 731
gas volume: Avogadro's law and, 334–335; Boyle's law and, **313,** 338–339; Charles's law and, *t* 317, **318,** *t* 318; combined gas law and, 321; ideal gas law and, 340–344; measuring, 333; molar vol-

umes, 335–337; overview of, 313–319; volume-mass relationships, 333–337, 348–350, 356; volume-volume relationships, 347–348, 356
Gay-Lussac's law, 319–321, 326, 333–334, 341, 356
Geiger, Hans, 72
Geiger-Müller counter(s), **714,** 722
gel(s), 398
gemstone(s), 743–744
gene(s), 680
geometric isomer(s), 632–633, 656
germanium, **124, 754,** 755, *t* 755
glass, 368, 371, 513–514, 767
glucose, 282, 758, **763, 764**
glycerol (1,2,3-propanetriol), 664–**665, 765**
glycogen, **764**
glycolipid(s), 765
gold: activity series and, 266, *t* 266; in alloys, **397;** electron configuration of, 116; molar mass of, 83, 85; origin of symbol for, *t* 20; properties of, **22,** 57, *t* 513, *t* 743; in redox reactions, *t* 615; transmutation into, 9
Goodyear, Charles, 688
Graham, Thomas, 352
Graham's law of effusion, 351–356
graphite, 81, *t* 513, 626–**627,** 646
gravity, 35
ground-state, 105, 117
gunpowder, 736

H

Haber, Fritz, 561
Haber process for ammonia synthesis, 561, 562–564
hafnium, 138
Hahn, Otto, 720–721
half-cell(s), 607, 614–615, 617
half-life, *t* 708, 708–709, 716, 722, 725
half-reaction(s), 593–594, 597–601, 608–617, *t* 615
halogen(s), 137, 261–262, *t* 266, 666, 780–783
hardness scale, *t* 730, *t* 736, *t* 752, *t* 755, *t* 771, *t* 776
HDPE (high-density polyethylene), 686
heat. *See also* exothermic reaction(s), temperature; in chemical equations, *t* 246,

246–247; from chemical reactions, 241, 263, 269, **513,** 514–523, 546; Le Châtelier's principle and, 380; from redox reactions, 606; specific, 512–514, *t* 513
heat capacity, 512–514
heat energy, 512
heat of combustion, 518–519, 546
heat of formation, 517–518, 522–524, 546
heat of fusion, 380, 387
heat of reaction, **513,** 514–523, 546
heat of solution, 409–410, *t* 410, 419
heat of vaporization, 182, 379, 387
Heisenberg, Werner, 99
Heisenberg uncertainty principle, 99–100, 117
helium: discovery of, 109, 126; electron configuration of, **106,** 110, 132–133; ionization energy of, *t* 145; isotopes of, 77; nuclear fusion and, **719;** properties and uses of, 24, 54, 81–82, **193**
hematite, **740**
heme, 738, 749, **758**
hemoglobin: artificial blood and, 411; iron and, 749; respiration and, **758,** 760, *t* 760; structure of, **762**
Henry's law, 407
heptane, **645**
hertz, unit of, 92
Hess's law, 463, 519–520, 524
hexanediamine, 690
2-hexene, 650
high blood pressure, 733
high-density polyethylene (HDPE), 686
HIV (human immunodeficiency virus), 411
Hoffmann, Michael, 166
Hoffmann, Roald, 32
Holmes, Sherlock, 255
homogeneous mixture(s). *See* solution(s)
homologous series, 634
Hooke, Robert, 338
Hückel, Erich, 446
human immunodeficiency virus (HIV), 411
Hund's rule, 106, **107,** 110, 113, 117
hybridization of orbitals, 187–189, **188,** *t* 189, 195, 625–626, 656

hydrate(s), 227, 405
hydration, **405,** 431
hydrazine, 289
hydride(s), 470–**472,** t 471, 735
hydriodic acid, t 214, t 454, t 460, t 471. *See also* hydrogen iodide
hydrobromic acid, t 454, t 460, t 471, 554
hydrocarbon(s), 630, 634–645, 647–656
hydrochloric acid. *See also* hydrogen chloride; formula of, 2, t 454; ionization and, 431, t 460, 465, 470; neutralization of, **474;** pH of, 491, 575; properties of, 457, 459, t 471
hydrocyanic acid, 460, t 460
hydrofluoric acid, 214, t 454, t 460, t 471, **781.** *See also* hydrogen fluoride
hydrogen: activity series and, t 266, 266–267; Böhr model of, 96–97, 98; displacement reactions of, 261; electrodes, **614**–615, 617; electron configuration of, 110, 132–133, **183;** electronegativity of, 163; formation of, 287, **324,** 454, 729, 735, 751; ionization energy of, t 145; isotopes of, 75–78, **76,** t 80, t 708; line-emission spectra of, 94–97, **95;** nuclear fusion and, **719;** properties of, t 190, 305, 368, t 471; in redox reactions, 216–218, t 591, t 603, t 615
hydrogenation, 633, 682–**683**
hydrogen bonding: boiling point and, 664, 671; bond energy of, t 168; in cosmetics, 665; in crystals, 371; formation of, **165,** 167–169; in liquids, 365, 379; in nucleic acids, 681, 766; overview of, 192, 195; in water, 384–**385, 406**
hydrogen carbonate, t 471, 731, t 731
hydrogen chloride. *See also* hydrochloric acid; in ammonia, 464; boiling point of, t 190; configuration of, **183;** as electrolyte, 399, **400;** formation of, 594; ionization of, 431; molarity of, 414–415; properties of, t 190, t 410
hydrogen cyanide, 166, t 460
hydrogen fluoride, t 190, 192, 289, 433. *See also* hydrofluoric acid

hydrogen iodide. *See also* hydriodic acid; decomposition of, **531**–532; formation of, **535,** 556–558, **557,** t 557; heat of formation of, 518; heat of solution of, t 410
hydrogen peroxide, **540,** 596, 604–605
hydrogen sulfide, 172, t 190, 258–259, **408,** t 471, t 603
hydrolysis of salt(s), 572–576
hydronium ion(s), 431, 447, 460–461, 469–471, t 471, 481–491
hydrosulfuric acid, t 454, t 460, t 471
hydroxide(s), 258–259, t 471, 481–482, 776–777. *See also* individual compounds
hydroxyl group(s), 473, 476, 664
hygrothermograph(s), 220
hyperchloremia, t 731
hypernatremia, t 731
hypertension, 733
hyperventilation, 759
hypochlorite, t 471
hypochlorous acid, t 214, t 455, t 471, **472,** 782
hypotheses, formulating and testing, 30–**31,** 58

ibuprofen, 225–226
ice, t 38, **385**–386
ideal gas constant, 342, t 342
ideal gas law, 339–346, 356, 360
indicator(s), acid-base, 454, **457,** 458, 493–498, **500–501,** 504
indium, t 114, **750,** 751, t 752, 768
infrared light, 91, **707**
inorganic chemistry, 6
insulator(s), **768**
insulin, 761
interference of waves, 98, 100
intermolecular force(s), 189–193
International Union of Pure and Applied Chemistry (IUPAC), 636, t 643, 666, 669–670, 672–675, 677. *See also* nomenclature
inverse proportion(s), 56–58
iodide, t 471, **781**
iodine: covalent bonds of, t 168; electron configuration of, t 114, 115; Mendeleev and, 124; properties of, **23,** 137,

780, t 782; reactions of, 781; in redox reactions, t 219, t 603, t 615; solutions of, 418; sublimation of, 380
iodomethane, 171–172
ion-electron method, 597–601
ionic bonding, 161–163, **162,** 176–180, t 190
ionic compound(s): binary, 206–211, 234; chemical equations of, 253–254; dissociation of, 425–430, 447; ionic bonding and, 176–180, 194; metal halogen, 258; nomenclature of, 210–211; properties of, 203; solubility of, 405, **427,** 577–584
ionic crystal(s), **370**
ionic liquid(s), 377
ionic radii: of alkali metals, t 730; of alkaline earth metals, t 736; of boron family elements, t 752; of carbon family elements, t 755; of nitrogen family elements, t 771; overview of, **149**–150, 154; of oxygen family elements, t 776
ionization constant(s), 482, t 482, 569–571, t 570, 573
ionization energy: of alkali metals, t 730; of alkaline earth metals, t 736; of boron family elements, t 752; of carbon family elements, t 755; of d-block elements, 154; first and second, 143–144, t 145; of nitrogen family elements, t 771; of oxygen family elements, t 776; of transition metals, t 743; trends in, **143**–146, **144,** t 730
ionization in solution, 431, 447, 481–484
ion(s): electron transfer and, 145, 148–149; interactions in solution, 446–447; monatomic, 204–205, 217, 234; nomenclature of, 204–205, t 205; overview of, 143, 155, 204–205, 234; oxidation numbers of, 216–217; polyatomic, 180, 186, 204, 209–211
iron: activity series and, t 266; analysis of, **742;** in the body, 749; in cast iron and steel, **745,** 756; dietary sources of, 749; electron configuration of, t 112, 113, 114, 154; formation of, 296; in gemstones, 743; origin of symbol for, t 20; oxides of, **257, 740;**

properties of, 22, 81, 83, t 190, t 513, t 743; in redox reactions, t 603, t 615
irone, **673**
iron oxide(s), 601
iron sulfate(s), **599**–601
iron(III) thiocyanate, **582**
isoamyl acetate, 676
isomer(s), 630–633, 648, 656
isoprene, 688–689
isotope(s), 75–80, t 80. *See also* radioactive nuclide(s)

joule, t 36, 511–512

Keipert, Peter, 411
Kelvin temperature scale, t 34, 58, 317–320, 512
kerosene, t 38, 643, t 644
ketone(s), 672–673, t 679, 693
Kevlar, 691
kidney(s), 759
kinetic energy, 303–304, 326, 378, **379,** 511–512
kinetic-molecular theory: of gases, 303–306, 313, 323, 326; of liquids, 363–367; of matter, 303–306, 313–323, 326, 535; of solids, 367–369; vapor pressure and, 376–377
kinetics of reactions, 538–545, 547, 555–557
Krebaum, Paul, 596
Kroto, Harold W., 628
krypton, **24,** 109, 126

lactic acid, 453, t 675
lactose, **763**
lanthanide series of elements, **21,** 126, 138–139, t 147
lanthanum, 115, 138
laser(s), 7, 307
latex, 688
lattice energy, 178, t 179, 196
laughing gas (nitrous oxide), 287, 558–559
Lavoisier, Antoine-Laurent, 278–279, 479
LCPs (liquid crystal polymers), 692
LDPE (low-density polyethylene), 686–687

lead: in alloys, *t* 745; analysis of, 755; in batteries, 612, **613;** crystal, **754;** decay series and, 711; origin of symbol for, *t* 20; poisoning by, 268; properties of, 38, *t* 38, 84, *t* 513, **754,** *t* 755; reactions of, *t* 266, 266–267, *t* 603, *t* 615, 755
lead(II) chromate, 248, *t* 579
lead(II) iodide, 262
lead(II) oxide(s), 208, 219
Le Châtelier, Henri Louis, 374
Le Châtelier's principle: heat and, 380; overview of, 374–375, 387; pressure and, 407; shifting equilibrium and, 562, 564, 567–568, 585
length, units of, *t* 34, 35–36, 58
Lewis acids and bases, 467–468, *t* 468, 476
Lewis structure(s), 170–175, 180, 184–185, 187
light: absorption of, 181; from chemical reactions, 241, 263, 269; dual wave/particle nature of, 93–94, 100, 117; infrared, 91, **707;** properties of, 91–93; scattering, 398, *t* 398, 419; sodium vapor, 730; speed of, 91, 93; ultraviolet, 91, 669, **707;** visible, 707
limestone, 68, 492
linoleic acid, **764**
lipid(s), 764–765
lipoprotein(s), 765
liquid crystal polymer(s) (LCPs), 692
liquid(s): in chemical equations, *t* 246; equilibria and, 563; kinetic-molecular theory of, 363–367; properties of, 12, 363–366, 377–379, 387; supercooled, 368
lithium: activity series and, *t* 266; analysis of, **729;** electron configuration of, 110, *t* 110, 132; ionization energies of, 145, *t* 145; properties of, 81, 132, **728,** *t* 730; in redox reactions, *t* 615; as reducing agent, *t* 603, 614
lithium carbonate, *t* 404, **408**
lithium chloride, *t* 179, *t* 404, **405,** 409, *t* 410
lithium sulfate, **408**
litmus, **493, 495,** 498. *See also* indicator(s), acid-base
logarithm(s), 487–491
London dispersion forces, 193, 195, 371, 406, 627, 643
low-density polyethylene (LDPE), 686–687

Lowry, T. M., 464
luciferin, 630
luminous intensity, *t* 34, 58
lungs, respiration and, 759–760
Lyman, Balmer, and Paschen series, 94, **95, 97**
lysine, 457

macromolecule(s), 761–766
magic number(s), 703, 722
magnesium: activity series and, *t* 266, 267; in alloys, *t* 745, *t* 753; in the body, 738–739; electron configuration of, *t* 111, *t* 170; in flares, 737; properties of, 78, **734, 735,** *t* 736; in redox reactions, **257,** 284, *t* 603, *t* 615
magnesium bromide, 206
magnesium chloride, 252
magnesium hydroxide, 453, *t* 579
magnesium nitrate, 252
magnesium sulfate, *t* 410, *t* 445
magnetic quantum number(s), 102–104
magnetite, 290
main-group element(s), 136–138, 144, *t* 150, 154
malachite, 22
malic acid, 453, *t* 675
malleability, 22, 182, 194
Malthus, Thomas, 560–561
manganese: activity series and, *t* 266, 267; in alloys, *t* 745, *t* 753; analysis of, **742;** in the body, 749; electron configuration of, *t* 112, 113, 115; properties of, 22; in redox reactions, *t* 603, *t* 615
manganese(IV) oxide, **540**
manometer(s), 311, 326
marble, 40, **475,** 476, **734**
Marsden, Ernest, 72
mass: atomic, 78–80, *t* 80, 86; critical, 718; molar. *See* molar mass; moles and, 275–277, 282–285, 290–291; percentage, 226–228; as property of matter, 10; relationship to volume, **55,** *t* 55, 348–350; relative, 249; units of, *t* 34, 34–35, 58
mass defect, 701–702, 722
mass number, 76–78, *t* 80, 86
matter: classification of, **15**–18; properties of, 10–11; states of, 12, 25, 247; theories of, 9, 65, 303–306, 313–323, 326, 535

mayonnaise, 397–398
McLandrich, Drew, 525
medicine, radionuclides in, 715
Meitner, Lise, 720–721
melting point(s): of alkali metals, *t* 730; of alkaline earth metals, *t* 736; of boron family elements, *t* 752; of carbon compounds, *t* 632; of carbon family elements, *t* 755; of crystalline solids, *t* 370; of nitrogen family elements, *t* 771; overview of, 11–12, 368, 380, 387; of oxygen family elements, *t* 776; of transition metals, *t* 743
Mendeleev, Dmitri, 123–125, **124**
meniscus, 365
mercaptan(s), 596
mercury: activity series and, *t* 266; amalgam, **396, 744;** batteries, **610;** columns of, 310, **311,** *t* 311, 338–339; density of, **38,** *t* 38, 40; electron configuration of, 134; formation of, **14;** origin of symbol for, 20; poisoning from, 747; properties of, 22, 81, *t* 513, *t* 743, 747; in redox reactions, *t* 603, *t* 615
mercury fulminate, 518
mercury oxide, **14,** 285, **553**–554
metal(s): alkali, **132,** 728–733; alkaline earth, **132,** 734–739; bonding of, 181–182, *t* 190, 194; displacement reactions of, 261–262, 265; ductility of, 182, 194; hydroxides of, 258–259; ionization energy of, 144; noble, **740;** properties of, 11, 22, 25, 132–134, 137, 181–182; reactions with halogens, 258; transition, 134, 740–749
metal carbonate(s), 260
metal chlorate(s), 260
metal hydroxide(s), 260
metallic crystal(s), 370–371
metalloids, 23–25, 137
meter, *t* 34, **36,** 58
methanal (formaldehyde), 174, 307, 666, 673
methane: boiling point of, *t* 190, *t* 643; formation of, 298; heat of formation of, 520; structure of, **184,** *t* 186, 187, **188, 625, 635;** substitutions on, 682
methanoic acid, 674, *t* 675
methanol, 294, 296, 359, *t* 664, 666

methionine, **761**
methylamine, 677–678
methylbenzene, 655
methylmercury, **747**
methyl orange, 494, **495,** 498
methyl pentyl ether, 670
2-methylpropane, 630–631, *t* 632, **635**
methyl propyl ether, 670
methyl red, **498**
methyl-*tertiary*-butyl ether (MTBE), 671
mica, **767**
microwave(s), 91, **707**
milk, *t* 38, **395,** 486, 763
milk of magnesia, 486. *See also* magnesium hydroxide
Millikan, Robert A., 71
miscibility, 406
Mistry, Pravin, 646
Mittasch, Alwin, 561
mixture(s), **15**–16, 25, 395–400, 419
model(s): for balancing equations, 264; Böhr's, 96–97, 98; construction of, 69; description of, 31; electron-sea, 181–182, 194; molecular compounds, **183, 631, 635, 647;** nuclear shell, 703, 707
moderator(s), fission and, 718
Mohs' scale of hardness, *t* 730, *t* 736, *t* 752, *t* 755, *t* 771, *t* 776
molal boiling-point constant(s), *t* 438, 441, 447
molal freezing-point constant(s), *t* 438, 438–441, 447
molality, 416–419
molar heat of formation, 517–518, 522–524, 546
molar heat of fusion, 380, 387
molar heat of vaporization, 379, 387
molarity, 412–415, 419, 499–504
molar mass: calculations and, 82–83, 238, 277, 282–287, 291; of compounds, 222–223, **224;** as conversion factor, 224–226, 234, 276–277, 280–286, 299; Graham's law of effusion and, 351–355; ideal gas law and, 345–346; overview of, 81–82, 86; units of, *t* 36
molar volume, *t* 36, 335–337
molecular compound(s): binary, 211–213, 234; models of, **183, 631, 635, 647;** polarity in, 183, 190–192; properties of, 179, 203; VSEPR theory and, 183–187

molecular formula(s), 164,
232–233
molecular mass(es), 221
molecule(s), 164, 170–172,
183–193
mole(s). *See also* molar mass;
calculations involving, **82,**
275–277, 280–287; ideal gas
law and, 340–344; ratios,
276–277, 282–287, 295
units of, *t* 34, 58, 81
molybdenum, *t* 114, 749
Monel alloy, **396**
monomer(s), 685, 694
monoprotic acid(s), 465, 476
monosaccharide(s), **763, 764**
morphine, **678**
Moseley, Henry, 125
MTBE (methyl-*tertiary*-butyl
ether), 671
multiple proportions, law of,
66, 86
myoglobin, 749

Nagyvary, Joseph, **19**
National Aeronautics and Space
Administration (NASA), 307
natural gas, 643
neon: discovery of, 109; electron configuration of, *t* 110,
111, *t* 170; ionization energy
of, *t* 145; light from, **94;**
properties of, **24,** 75
neoprene, 689
neptunium, 138, *t* 712
Nernst, Walther, 561
Nernst equation, 620–621
net ionic equation(s), 429–430,
447
network bonding, 175, 214
neutralization reaction(s),
473–475, 497, 502–503, 567,
574–575
neutron(s), 70, 73, *t* 74, 703
newton, unit of, 309
nickel: activity series and, 266,
t 266; in alloys, *t* 745; analysis
of, **742;** in the body, 749;
electron configuration of,
t 112, 113, 134; properties of,
t 743; in redox reactions,
t 603, *t* 615
nickel(II) sulfide, 430
nicotine, 678
nitrate, 180, *t* 471, *t* 603
nitric acid: formula of, *t* 214,
t 455; manufacture of, 284–
285, 297, 561; mercury and,

14; properties of, **456**–457,
459, *t* 460, *t* 471
nitride(s), 735
nitrogen: compounds with oxygen, *t* 213, 521; covalent
bonding of, *t* 170, **173,** *t* 173;
electron configuration of,
107, *t* 110; fixation, 560; ionization energy of, *t* 145; noble
gases and, 108–109; oxidation
numbers for, *t* 219; plant
growth and, 560–561, **772**–
773, *t* 773; production of,
t 779; properties of, 23, *t* 56,
57, 770, *t* 771; reactions of, 771
nitrogen dioxide, 521, 564–**565**
nitrogen family element(s),
770–773
nitrogen fixation, **772**
nitrous acid, *t* 214, *t* 455
nitrous oxide, 287, 558–559
Nobel Prize winner(s), 8, 109,
628, 681, 721
noble gas(es): configuration of,
168; discovery of, 108–109;
ideality of, 306; ionization
energies of, 144; London
forces and, 193; in the periodic table, **125**–126, 155;
properties of, **24**–25, 128, 152
noble gas notation, 111, 112,
114
nomenclature: for acids, *t* 454,
454–455, *t* 455; for alkanes,
t 636, 636–642, 656; for
alkenes, 647–650; for
alkynes, 651–652; for aromatic hydrocarbons, 653–655; for
binary compounds, 206–213;
for ions, 204–205, *t* 205, 209–
210, *t* 210, 234; prefix system
of, *t* 212, 219, 234; in redox
reactions, *t* 602; Stock system
of, 205, 208–209, 219, 234
nonelectrolyte(s), **432**
nonmetal(s), 23, 25, 136
nonpolar covalent bonding,
162, 163
nuclear binding energy, 701–
702, 722
nuclear chain reaction(s), 717–
718
nuclear fission, 715–719, 721–
722
nuclear force(s), 74, 86
nuclear fusion, 715–716, 719,
722
nuclear power plant(s), 718
nuclear radiation, 705, 713–
715
nuclear reaction(s), 704

nuclear shell model, 703, 707
nuclear waste, 715–716, 722
nucleic acid(s), 680–681, 766
nucleon(s), 701–703, 722
nucleus, 70, 72–74, 86, 701–
704, 722
nuclide(s), 77, 701–702. *See
also* radioactive nuclide(s)
nylon, **690**–691, 694

octane rating(s), **645**
octet rule, 168–169, 184, 194
oleic acid, **764**
orbital notation, *t* 102, 102–
104, *t* 104, 106, 187–188
orbital quantum number(s),
101–104
orbital(s): in carbon compounds, 625–626; covalent
bonds and, 168; hybridization of, 187–189, **188,** *t* 189,
195, 625–626, 656
organic chemistry: description
of, 6, 656; nomenclature in,
663–664, 666, 670, 672–675,
677, 679; organic com-
pounds, 460, 629–633
osmium, 368, 561
osmosis, 442–443
osmotic pressure, 442–443
osteoporosis, 738
Ostwald process, 297
oxidation and reduction,
591–617
oxidation number(s): of alkali
metals, *t* 730; of alkaline
earth metals, *t* 736; in balancing equations, 247, *t* 591,
597–600; of boron family
elements, *t* 752; of carbon
family elements, *t* 755; of
nitrogen family elements,
t 771; of oxygen family elements, *t* 776; of transition
metals, *t* 743; using, 216–219,
234, *t* 591, 591–592, 617
oxide(s), 256–259, 729, 776–
777, *t* 777
oxidizing agent(s), 602–605,
t 603, 614, 617
oxyacetylene, **652**
oxyacid(s), *t* 214, 455, *t* 455,
472
oxyanion(s), 209–211, 214
oxygen: compounds with nitrogen, *t* 213; covalent bonding
of, *t* 170, *t* 173; discovery of,
259, **260,** 279; electron con-

figuration of, *t* 110, 111;
flame test for, **775;** ionization energy of, *t* 145; isotopes of, *t* 80; oxidation
number of, 216–218, *t* 591;
polarity of, 191–**192;** production of, 324, *t* 779; properties
of, 23, 78, *t* 190, 224–225,
774, *t* 776; reactions of, 14,
279, 775; respiration and,
758–759; solubility of, *t* 404,
408; structure of, **164**
oxygen family element(s),
774–779
Oxygent, 411
oxyhemoglobin, 758
ozone, 7, 175, **668**–669, 778

palladium, *t* 114, 134
palmitic acid, **764**
paper chromatography, **16, 365**
paraffin wax, 383, **643**
partial pressure(s), 322–326,
334, 563
particle accelerator(s), **711**
Pascal, Blaise, 311
pascal, unit of, 36–37, 311, *t* 311
Paschen series, 95, **97**
Pauli exclusion principle, **106,**
108, 117
Pauling, Linus, 151, 680
Pauling scale of electronegativity, **151**
pectinase, 19
pennies, density of, 39
pentane, 523–524, *t* 643, *t* 671
3-pentanone, 673
pepsin, 763
percentage composition, 226–
228, 234
percent error, 45, 58
percent yield, 293–295
perchloric acid, *t* 214, *t* 455,
t 460, 470–471, *t* 471, **472**
perfluorocarbon(s), 411
peridot, **743,** *t* 744
periodicity, 126
periodic law, 125
periodic table of atomic radii,
141
periodic table of the electronegativities, **151**
periodic table of the elements,
123–159; blocks in, **129,** 132–
134, 153–155; chart of, **21,**
130–131; design of, 127, 158–
159; electron configurations
and, 128–139, 140–154; histo-

ry of, 123–127; of Mendeleev, **124**; modern, 125–127; overview of, 20–21, 25, 155

pesticide(s), 166

PET (polyethylene terephthalate), 691

petroleum, 643–645, **644**

pH: of blood, 759; buffers, 570–571; calculation of, 487–491; of common materials, 268, *t* 486, **572**; concept of, 481–491; enzymes and, 763; indicators, acid-base, 454, **457**, 458, 493–498, **500–501**, 504; measurement of, 493–503, **494, 500–501**; neutralization curves, **574, 575**; scale, 485–486

phase-change material(s), 383

phase diagram(s), **381**–382

phenolphthalein, **482**, 494, **495**, 498, **500–501**

phenol red, **495**

phenylalanine, **761**

phenylisocyanide, 255

pheromone(s), 633

phlogiston, 278–279

phosphate ion, 180, *t* 471

phosphine, 192

phospholipid(s), **765**

phosphoric acid: formula for, *t* 214, **455**; ionization and strength of, *t* 460, 466–467, *t* 471; production of, *t* 779; properties and uses of, **453**, 457; structure of, **455**

phosphorus: compounds with oxygen, 231–232; electron configuration of, *t* 111; isotopes of, 78, *t* 708; oxidation numbers for, *t* 219; plant growth and, **30**, 773, *t* 773, 779; properties of, **23, 770**, *t* 771; reactions of, 771; in semiconductors, 768–769; white, **770**

phosphorus pentachloride, *t* 186, 219

phosphorus trichloride, *t* 190, 219

photochemical reaction(s), 220

photoelectric effect, **93**–94

photon(s), **95**, 96, 117

photosynthesis, 282–283, 757

physical chemistry, 6

physical properties, 11–12, 25

picometer, 74

pitchblende, 8

Planck, Max, 93

Planck's constant, 93

plastic(s), 50, 220, 457, 685–692, **686**, 694

platinum, 134, 139, *t* 266

Plexiglas UF-3, 220

poison dart frog(s), **678**

polar covalent bonding, **162, 163**

polarity: acid strength and, **473**; dipole-dipole forces, 190–192, 195, 371; ideal gases and, 306; in molecular compounds, 183, 190–192; solvent properties and, 404–406; of water, **191–192**

pollution detector(s), 43

polonium: discovery of, 8, 705; half-life of, *t* 708; properties of, **774**, *t* 776; reactions of, 704, 775

polyamide polymer(s), 691, 694

polyatomic ion(s), 180, 194, 204, 209–210, 251, *t* 591

polyester(s), 691, 694

polyethylene (polyethene), **686**–687, 691, 694

polyethylene terephthalate (PET), 691

polymer(s), 685–691, 694

polyprotic acid(s), 465–467, 476

polysaccharide(s), 763–764

polystyrene, 687, *t* 687

polyvinyl acetate (PVA), 674, *t* 687

porous barrier(s) in electrochemical cells, 607

positron(s), *t* 705, 706–707

potassium: analysis of, **729**; in the body, *t* 731, 731–**732**; electron configuration of, 112, *t* 112; origin of symbol for, *t* 20; plant growth and, 773, *t* 773; properties of, **728**, 729, *t* 730; radioactive nuclides of, *t* 708; reactivity of, **132**, 265, *t* 266, 729; in redox reactions, *t* 603, *t* 615

potassium carbonate, 268

potassium chlorate, 222, 260, 282, 324, *t* 410

potassium chloride: freezing-point depression and, *t* 445, 446; heat of solution of, *t* 410; lattice energy of, *t* 179, 196; solubility of, *t* 404, **408**

potassium hydroxide, *t* 410, *t* 461, 491

potassium iodide, *t* 404, 409, *t* 410, 601

potassium nitrate, *t* 404, **408**, 409, *t* 410, 601

potassium permanganate, **599**–601

potential energy in bonds, **165**, 167, **177**, 194

precipitate(s): in chemical equations, 245, *t* 246, 248, 430; from chemical reactions, **242, 262**, 269, 447; equilibrium and, 566; solubility and, 427–429, 582–584

precision, **44**–46, 58

pressure: in chemical equations, *t* 246; chemical equilibrium and, 562–563; critical, 382; force and, 308–312; gases and, 308–315, 319–321, 340–344, 360, 562–563; measurement of, 310–311; partial, 322–326, 334, 563; relationship to volume, *t* 56, **57, 313**–315, *t* 314; solubility and, 407; standard, 312; units of, 36–37, 311

Priestley, Joseph, 259, 279, 285

principal quantum number(s), **101**–102, *t* 104

products in chemical equations, 13, 241–250

propane, 347–348, 634, **635**, *t* 643, *t* 664

1,2-propanediol, 664

1,2,3-propanetriol, 664–**665, 765**

propanoic acid, 674

propanone, 673

properties, physical, 10–12, 25, 367–371, 387, 399, 443–447

proportional relationship(s), *t* 55, 55–58

protein(s), 684, **761**–763

protium (hydrogen-1), 76–77, *t* 80

proton(s), 70, 73, *t* 74, 464–471, 702–**703**

pure substance(s), 17–18

putrescine, 678

pyrite, **774**

pyrotechnics, **736**–737

qualitative analysis, 742, 771

quantitative data, 29, 33

quantum number(s), 101–104, *t* 102, 117, 121

quantum theory, 94, 98–104, 117

quartz, 289, 370, **371, 754**

quicklime (calcium oxide), *t* 179, 258, 294, *t* 779

radioactive dating, 715

radioactive decay, 705–712, 722, 725

radioactive nuclide(s), 705–712, **708**, 715, 720, 722, 740

radioactive tracer(s), 715

radioactive waste, 716

radioactivity, discovery of, 8–9

radio wave(s), 91, **707**

radium, 8, 705, **708, 734**, *t* 736

radon, 109, 126, 714

rain water, 259, 486, 492, 496

Ramsay, William, **108**–109, 125–126

raspberry ketone, **673**

rate-determining step, 543–544

rate law(s), 541–546

Rayleigh, Lord, **108**–109, 125

reactant(s): in chemical equations, 13, 241–250; excess, 288, 290–291, 294; limiting, 288–295; purity of, **18**

reaction(s). *See* chemical reaction(s)

reaction stoichiometry, 275–299

reactor(s), nuclear, 715–716

reagent(s), purity standard for, **18**, description of, 11

rechargeable cell(s), 612–613

redox reaction(s), 591–617

reducing agent(s), 602–605, *t* 603, 614, 617

reduction potential(s), 613–615, *t* 615

reduction processes, 593–595

reference electrode(s), **614**

relative atomic mass(es), 78–79

rem (roentgen equivalent, man), 713

resonance structure(s), 175, 194

respiration, 328, 758–759

rhodonite, **369**

ribonucleic acid (RNA), 766

rocket propellant, 289

roentgen(s), 713

rounding, 48, *t* 48, 58

rubber, natural and synthetic, 688–689, 694

rubidium: activity series and, *t* 266; analysis of, **729**; electron configuration of, *t* 114, 116; oxidation of, 257; properties of, **728**, 729, *t* 730

ruby, **743**–744, *t* 744
rust, 601
Rutherford, Daniel, 278–279
Rutherford, Ernest, 9, 72–**73**, 86, 91, 97, 125

saliva, 486
salt(s): chemical equilibrium of, 569–576; formation of, 454, 458, 474–475, 476, 729, 735; hydrolysis of, 572–576; overview of, 215; qualitative analysis of, 742
salt water, **395**. *See also* sea water
Salyer, Ival, 383
samarium, 139
sample problems, how to solve, 52–54
sapphire, **743**, *t* 744
saturated hydrocarbon(s), 634–645, 656
saturation of solutions, **403**
SBR (styrene-butadiene rubber), 689
scandium, *t* 112, 113, **124, 134,** *t* 182
scanning electron micrography, **5, 368**
Schrödinger, Erwin, 99
Schrödinger wave equation, 99–101, 117
Schryer, David, 307
scientific method, 29–31, 58
scientific notation, 50–52, 58
scientific theories, 58, 67, 86
scintillation counter(s), 714, 722
Seaborg, Glenn, 159
sea water, *t* 38, 315, 486
second(s), *t* 34, 58
selenium, **23, 774,** 775, *t* 776
semiconductor(s), 24, 137, **768**–769
semipermeable membrane(s), 442
SHE (standard hydrogen electrode), **614**–615, 617
shielding of radiation, 718, 722
sickle-cell anemia, 762
significant figure(s), 46–54, *t* 47, 58, 487
silicate mineral(s), **767**
silicon: in alloys, *t* 753; compounds of, 214, **754;** electron configuration of, *t* 111; properties of, **754,** *t* 755; reactions of, 755

silicon carbide, 370
silicone(s), **767**
silver: activity series and, *t* 266, 267; in alloys, 396, *t* 745, **746;** electron configuration of, *t* 114; electroplating of, **612;** origin of symbol for, *t* 20, 84; properties of, *t* 743; in redox reactions, *t* 603, *t* 615
silver acetate, *t* 579, 581–582
silver chloride, 432–433, **566,** 577–578, *t* 579
silver chromate, 415
silver nitrate, *t* 404, *t* 410, 420–421, 781
silver thiocyanate, **582**
Simmons, Ken, 492
single bond(s), 171, 194
single-replacement reaction(s), 261–262, 265, 269
SI units *(Le Système International d'Unités),* 33–38, *t* 34, *t* 35, 58
skatole, 678
skunk spray, 596
Smalley, Richard E., 628
smog, *t* 398, 778
Soddy, Frederick, 9
sodium: analysis of, **729,** 730; in the body, *t* 731, 731–733, **732;** compounds, 427; crystal lattice of, **181;** electron configuration of, 111, *t* 111, 132, *t* 170; origin of symbol for, *t* 20; properties of, **728,** 729, *t* 730; reactivity of, 265, *t* 266, 729; in redox reactions, *t* 603, *t* 615
sodium acetate, **572,** 575
sodium bicarbonate (sodium hydrogen carbonate), **453**
sodium carbonate, 427, 573, 582
sodium carbonate decahydrate, 227–228
sodium chloride: formation of, **474, 592;** ionic bonding in, 176–**178, 177;** lattice energy of, *t* 179, 196; pH of, **572;** properties of, *t* 190, *t* 404, **408,** 409, *t* 410; in solution, 399, **400,** 403, 414, **425**–426
sodium chromate, 248
sodium hydrogen carbonate (baking soda), **453, 494**
sodium hydroxide: decomposition of, *t* 461; dissociation of, 461; formation of, 247, 272, *t* 779; heat of solution of, *t* 410; neutralization of, **474;** pH of, 574–575; uses of, **453;** sodium nitrate, *t* 404, **408,** *t* 410, 560

sodium sulfate, 583–584
sodium sulfide, 252, 426
sodium vapor lighting, 730
solid(s), 12, 366, 367–371, 387, 396, 563
sol(s), 398
solubility: of alcohols, 665, *t* 665; calculation of, 581–582; equilibrium, 577–584; of gases, **407**–**408,** 410, 419; guidelines, 404, *t* 404, *t* 427; overview of, 395, 402–404, 419; pressure and, 407; product, 577–585, *t* 579; temperature and, **408**–409, 419
solubility-product constant(s), 578–585, *t* 579
solute(s): electrolytes, 399–400; interactions with solvent, 404–409; overview of, **396,** 419; surface area of, 401; temperature and, **408;** vapor-pressure and, 436–437
solution(s), 394–423: in chemical equations, *t* 246, 247; concentration of, 412–418; description of, 16; dissolution process, 401–410. *See also* dissolution; equilibrium in, **402;** overview of, 395–397; pH of, 481–491; properties of, *t* 398, 399, 409–410, 436–437, **442**–443; saturation in, **403;** solid, 396; standard, 499–503
solvation, 409
solvent(s): overview of, **396,** 419; polarity of, 404–**406,** 671; solute interactions with, 404–409; temperature of, 401–403; vapor pressure of, **436**
sorbic acid, **453,** 674
specific heat, 512–514, *t* 513
spectator ion(s), 429, 447, 475
spinel, 744, *t* 744
spin quantum number(s), 104
stalactite(s), **552**
standard electrode potential(s), 614–615, *t* 615, 617
standard hydrogen electrode(s) (SHE), **614**–615, 617
standard molar entropy, 527
standard molar volume, 335, 356. *See also* molar volume
standard reduction potential(s), *t* 615, 616
standard solution(s) for titrations, 499–503
standard state(s), 518–519, 528, 546

standard temperature and pressure (STP), 312, 326
stannous fluoride, 286
starch, **764**
state(s) of matter, 12, 25, 247
Stedman, Donald, 43
steel, 745, 756
sterling silver, 396, *t* 745, **746**
Stock system of nomenclature, 205, 208–209
stoichiometry, 274–299, 347–350
STP (standard temperature and pressure), 312, 326
Stradivari, Antonio, 19
Strassman, Fritz, 720–721
stream(s), liming, 492
strontium: activity series and, *t* 266; electron configuration of, *t* 114; flame test for, **735,** 737; properties of, **734,** 735, *t* 736
strontium chloride, 737
structural formula(s), 171, 630–631, 635, 640–641, 656
structural isomer(s), 631–632, 656
Strutt, John William (Lord Rayleigh), **108**–109, 125
styrene-butadiene rubber (SBR), 689
subatomic particle(s), 70
sublimation, 380–381
substitution reaction(s), 682, 693
sucrose: boiling points and, 441, 443; breakdown of, **17,** 18; dehydration of, **684;** density of, *t* 38; freezing points and, 439, 443; osmotic pressure and, **442;** solubility of, *t* 404; in solution, 417; structure of, **10, 164, 763;** vapor-pressure and, 437
sugar(s). *See also* sucrose; classification of, 11; properties of, **400,** 404; structure of, **763, 764;** in urine, **11**
sulfate ion, 180, *t* 471
sulfur: electron configuration of, *t* 111; flame test for, **775;** mercury and, 14; molar mass of, 85; oxidation numbers for, *t* 219; properties of, **23,** 163, **774, 775,** *t* 776; reactions of, 256–257, *t* 615, 775; structure of, **775**
sulfur dioxide, 219, **408**
sulfuric acid: in batteries, 612–**613;** decomposition of, 260; formula of, *t* 214, **455;** ioniza-

tion of, *t* 460, 465–466, 471–472; production of, 779, *t* 779; in redox reactions, *t* 603; strength of, *t* 471; structure of, **455;** uses of, 456, **779**
sulfurous acid, *t* 214, *t* 455, *t* 460, 555
sulfur trioxide, 219, 475
supercooled liquid(s), 368
supercorrosion, 525
superoxide(s), 729
supersaturation, 403
surface area, 401, 538–539, 546
surface tension, **365**
suspension(s), 397, *t* 398, 399, 419
syngas, 529
synthesis reaction(s), 256–259, 269
system(s), 29–30

tartaric acid, 453
technetium, *t* 114, 715
Teflon, 6–7, **669**
tellurium, *t* 114, 124, **774,** 775, *t* 776
temperature: activation energy and, 535; in chemical equations, *t* 246; critical, 381; effect on dissolution, 401–403, *t* 404, **408**–409, 584; equilibrium and, 374–375, 564–565; of gases, 304, 316–321, *t* 317, *t* 318, 340–344; ionization of water and, 482, *t* 482; measurement of, 511–512; reaction rate and, 539; standard, 312; units of, *t* 34, 58
tensile strength, 22
tetraethyl lead, 671
tetrafluoroethene (Teflon), **669**
thallium, **750,** 751, *t* 752
theoretical chemistry, 6
theorizing, **31,** 58
theory of matter, 9, 303–306, 313–323, 326, 535
thermal conductivity, 22, 194, 627, 646, 753
thermite, **751**
thermochemistry, 511–524, 546
thermoplastic polymer(s), 685, 694
Thomson, Joseph John, 71
thorium, 9, 138, 705, 710–711
time, units of, *t* 34, 58

tin: in alloys, *t* 745; analysis of, 755; electron configuration of, *t* 114, 115; isotopes of, 76; origin of symbol for, *t* 20; properties of, **754,** *t* 755; reactions of, *t* 266, 267, *t* 603, *t* 615, 755
tin(II) fluoride, 286
tin(IV) sulfate, 211
titanium, *t* 112, 113, 135, 743
titration(s), 497–503, **500–501,** 506–507, **574, 575**
TNT, 166
toluene, 405, **406**
tooth decay and fluoridation, 783
Torricelli, Evangelista, 310, **311,** 338
tourmaline, 744
trans isomer(s), 632–633, 648
transition interval of pH indicators, 494
transition metal(s), 134, 740–749
transmutation(s), 8–9, 704, 706, 711–712, 720, 722
transuranium element(s), 712, *t* 712, 720, 722
Travers, Morris, 109
trichlorofluoromethane (Freon-11), 668
trichloromethane (chloroform), 255, 682
triglyceride(s), **765**
trimethylamine, 677
2,2,4-trimethylpentane, **645**
triple bond(s), 173, 626, 651
triple point of water, *t* 34, **381**
triprotic acid(s), 466–467, 476
tritium, 76–77, *t* 708
tungsten, *t* 20, 22, 113, 134, *t* 190, 349–350
Tyndall effect, 398

ultrasound, 166
ultraviolet light, 91, 669, **707**
unit cell(s) of crystals, 369
United States Department of Energy, 716
United States Pharmacopoeia (USP), 18
unit(s) of measurement, 33–43; conversion of, 40–42, 58; prefixes, *t* 35; SI, 33–38, *t* 34, *t* 35, 58
unsaturated hydrocarbon(s), 647–656

unshared pair(s), 171, 185–187
uranium: as catalyst, 561; decay of, **9, 710,** 720–721; discovery of, 705; isotopes of, 77, *t* 80, 354, *t* 708; nuclear fission and, 258, **717**–718; oxidation number of, 217–218; radiation from, 8–9

vacuum evaporator(s), 378
valence electron(s), 169–170, *t* 170, 172, 174
valence-shell, electron-pair repulsion (VSEPR) theory, 183–187, 195
vanadium, *t* 112, 113, 134, 743, 749
van der Waals, Johannes, 306
van Guericke, Otto, 338
vanillin, **673**
vaporization, 182, *t* 182, 365–366, 379, 385–387
vapor pressure: boiling points and, 378, 387, 440; calculation of, 390; kinetic-molecular theory and, 376–377; lowering of, 436–**437,** 447; of water, 324
Verneuil, Auguste, 743–744
vinegar, 453, 457, 486
violin(s), 19
vitamin(s), **762**
volatility, 377, 436–**437**
volcanic eruption(s), 478
Volta, Alessandro, 434
voltaic cell(s), 607–614, **608, 611,** 616–617, 620
voltaic pile(s), 434
volt(s), 613
volume: of gases. *See* gas volume; molar, *t* 36, 335–337; of a sphere, 61; units of, *t* 36, 36–**37,** 54
VSEPR theory, 183–187, 195
vulcanization, 688, **689**

water: acid/base properties of, 464, *t* 471, 472, 486; boiling point of, 11, **12,** *t* 190; chlorination of, **782**–783; composition of, 17; compressibility of, 364; critical temperature of, 381; decomposition of, **17,**

250, 259; density of, **38,** *t* 38, 385; diffusion of, **364;** drinking, 258, 268, 782–783; fluoridation of, 783; formation of, **263,** 534; ionization constant of, 482, *t* 482, 571; molar heat of fusion of, 385–386; molar heat of vaporization of, 385–386; phase diagram for, **381;** polarity of, **191–192;** purification of, 253; replacement reactions and, 265–266; self-ionization of, 481–482, 504; specific heat of, *t* 513; structure of, **164, 185,** *t* 186, **188,** 384–385, 388; sublimation of, 380–381; triple point of, *t* 34, **381;** vapor pressure of, **377**
Watson, James D., 680–681
wave function(s), 100
wavelength, 91–93, **92**
wave properties, 91–93, 98–100
weight, 35, 58
Whetstone Brook, 492
Wilkins, Maurice, 680–681
wolfram, *t* 20. *See also* tungsten

xenon, **24,** 109, *t* 114, 126
X-ray diffraction, 6, 680
X ray(s), 5, 91, **707**

yield, theoretical, 293–295
Yucca Mountain, 716

zero, as significant figure, *t* 47
zinc: in alloys, *t* 745, *t* 753; analysis of, **742;** in batteries, 609; in the body, 749; electron configuration of, *t* 112, 113; properties of, *t* 743; reactions of, 265–267, *t* 266, **741;** redox reactions of, **603,** *t* 603, **606–611, 608,** 613–615; reduction potential of, *t* 615
zinc chloride, 251–252, 538–539
zinc iodide, 207
zinc sulfide, 207, 291, *t* 579

Periodic Table of the Elements

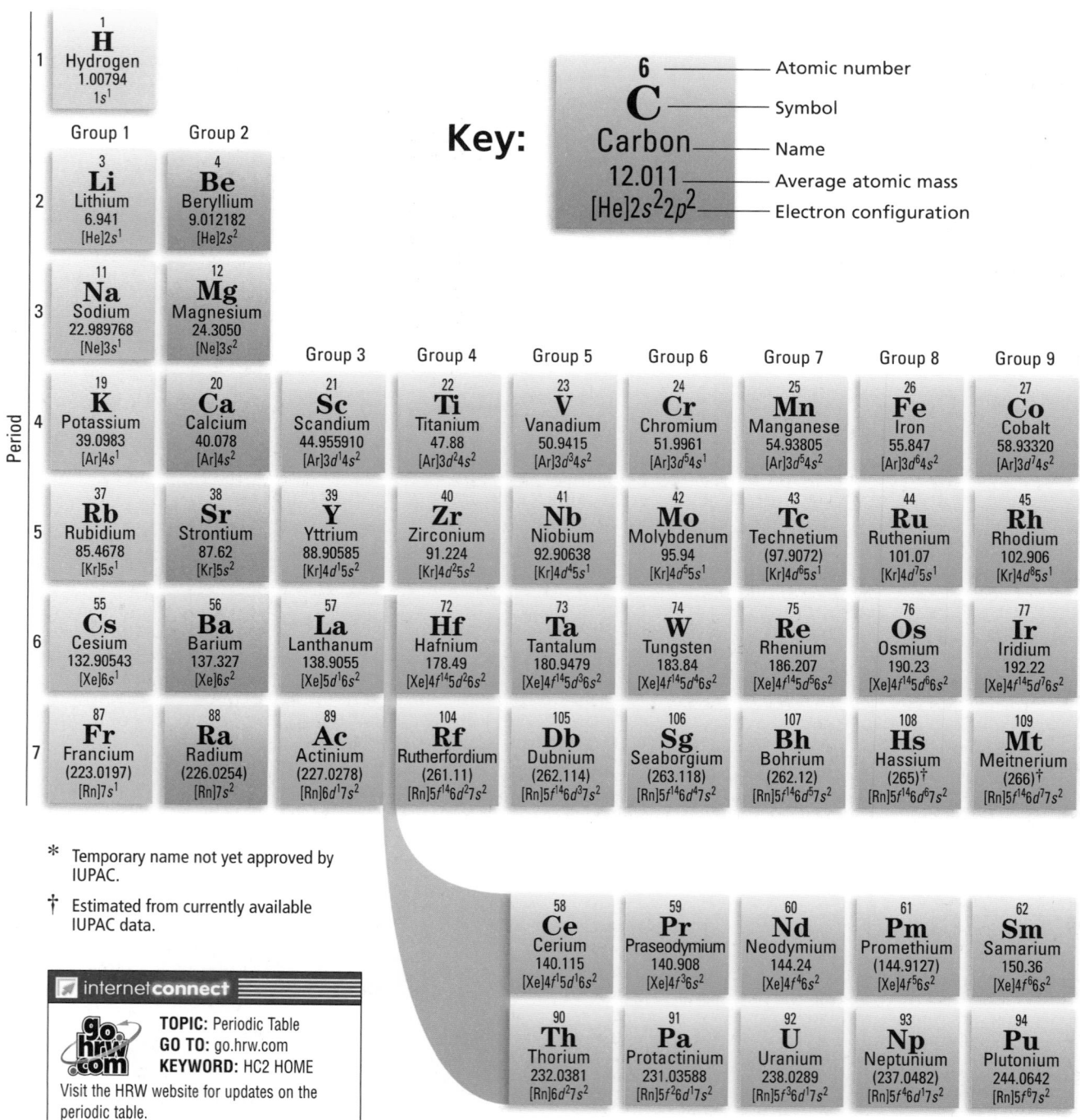

Key:

6	— Atomic number
C	— Symbol
Carbon	— Name
12.011	— Average atomic mass
$[He]2s^22p^2$	— Electron configuration

Period

Group 1	Group 2

1

1
H
Hydrogen
1.00794
$1s^1$

2

3
Li
Lithium
6.941
$[He]2s^1$

4
Be
Beryllium
9.012182
$[He]2s^2$

3

11
Na
Sodium
22.989768
$[Ne]3s^1$

12
Mg
Magnesium
24.3050
$[Ne]3s^2$

Group 3	Group 4	Group 5	Group 6	Group 7	Group 8	Group 9

4

19
K
Potassium
39.0983
$[Ar]4s^1$

20
Ca
Calcium
40.078
$[Ar]4s^2$

21
Sc
Scandium
44.955910
$[Ar]3d^14s^2$

22
Ti
Titanium
47.88
$[Ar]3d^24s^2$

23
V
Vanadium
50.9415
$[Ar]3d^34s^2$

24
Cr
Chromium
51.9961
$[Ar]3d^54s^1$

25
Mn
Manganese
54.93805
$[Ar]3d^54s^2$

26
Fe
Iron
55.847
$[Ar]3d^64s^2$

27
Co
Cobalt
58.93320
$[Ar]3d^74s^2$

5

37
Rb
Rubidium
85.4678
$[Kr]5s^1$

38
Sr
Strontium
87.62
$[Kr]5s^2$

39
Y
Yttrium
88.90585
$[Kr]4d^15s^2$

40
Zr
Zirconium
91.224
$[Kr]4d^25s^2$

41
Nb
Niobium
92.90638
$[Kr]4d^45s^1$

42
Mo
Molybdenum
95.94
$[Kr]4d^55s^1$

43
Tc
Technetium
(97.9072)
$[Kr]4d^65s^1$

44
Ru
Ruthenium
101.07
$[Kr]4d^75s^1$

45
Rh
Rhodium
102.906
$[Kr]4d^85s^1$

6

55
Cs
Cesium
132.90543
$[Xe]6s^1$

56
Ba
Barium
137.327
$[Xe]6s^2$

57
La
Lanthanum
138.9055
$[Xe]5d^16s^2$

72
Hf
Hafnium
178.49
$[Xe]4f^{14}5d^26s^2$

73
Ta
Tantalum
180.9479
$[Xe]4f^{14}5d^36s^2$

74
W
Tungsten
183.84
$[Xe]4f^{14}5d^46s^2$

75
Re
Rhenium
186.207
$[Xe]4f^{14}5d^56s^2$

76
Os
Osmium
190.23
$[Xe]4f^{14}5d^66s^2$

77
Ir
Iridium
192.22
$[Xe]4f^{14}5d^76s^2$

7

87
Fr
Francium
(223.0197)
$[Rn]7s^1$

88
Ra
Radium
(226.0254)
$[Rn]7s^2$

89
Ac
Actinium
(227.0278)
$[Rn]6d^17s^2$

104
Rf
Rutherfordium
(261.11)
$[Rn]5f^{14}6d^27s^2$

105
Db
Dubnium
(262.114)
$[Rn]5f^{14}6d^37s^2$

106
Sg
Seaborgium
(263.118)
$[Rn]5f^{14}6d^47s^2$

107
Bh
Bohrium
(262.12)
$[Rn]5f^{14}6d^57s^2$

108
Hs
Hassium
(265)†
$[Rn]5f^{14}6d^67s^2$

109
Mt
Meitnerium
(266)†
$[Rn]5f^{14}6d^77s^2$

* Temporary name not yet approved by IUPAC.

† Estimated from currently available IUPAC data.

58
Ce
Cerium
140.115
$[Xe]4f^15d^16s^2$

59
Pr
Praseodymium
140.908
$[Xe]4f^36s^2$

60
Nd
Neodymium
144.24
$[Xe]4f^46s^2$

61
Pm
Promethium
(144.9127)
$[Xe]4f^56s^2$

62
Sm
Samarium
150.36
$[Xe]4f^66s^2$

90
Th
Thorium
232.0381
$[Rn]6d^27s^2$

91
Pa
Protactinium
231.03588
$[Rn]5f^26d^17s^2$

92
U
Uranium
238.0289
$[Rn]5f^36d^17s^2$

93
Np
Neptunium
(237.0482)
$[Rn]5f^46d^17s^2$

94
Pu
Plutonium
244.0642
$[Rn]5f^67s^2$